International Directory of

COMPANY HISTORIES

International Directory of

COMPANY HISTORIES

VOLUME 23

Editor
Tina Grant

ST. JAMES PRESS

AN IMPRINT OF GALE

DETROIT • NEW YORK

STAFF

Tina N. Grant, *Editor*

Miranda H. Ferrara, *Project Manager*

Joann Cerrito, David J. Collins, Nicolet V. Elert, Kristin Hart,
Margaret Mazurkiewicz, Michael J. Tyrkus, *Contributing Editors*

Peter M. Gareffa, *Managing Editor, St. James Press*

Library of Congress Catalog Number: 89-190943

British Library Cataloguing in Publication Data

International directory of company histories. Vol. 23
I. Tina N. Grant
338.7409

ISBN 1-55862-364-7

Printed in the United States of America
Published simultaneously in the United Kingdom

St. James Press is an imprint of Gale

Cover photograph: The Johannesburg Stock Exchange, South Africa
(courtesy Johannesburg Stock Exchange)

10 9 8 7 6 5 4 3 2 1

CONTENTS _____

Preface . . . . page vii
List of Abbreviations ix

Company Histories

Abigail Adams National Bancorp, Inc. 3
Abrams Industries Inc. 6
Air Canada 9
Analogic Corporation 13
Anam Group 17
AR Accessories Group, Inc. 20
Atari Corporation 23
Atlanta Gas Light Company 27
The Atlantic Group 31
Azcon Corporation 34
Bank Austria AG 37
Battle Mountain Gold Company 40
Bayernwerk AG 43
Beckett Papers 48
Best Buy Co., Inc. 51
BIC Corporation 54
The Bon Marché, Inc. 58
Bowne & Co., Inc. 61
Brazos Sportswear, Inc. 65
Brenntag AG 68
Bristol Hotel Company 71
Broadcast Music Inc. 74
Brown & Haley 78
Brown & Sharpe Manufacturing Co. 81
Burda Holding GmbH. & Co. 85
The Bureau of National Affairs, Inc. 90
Burelle S.A. 94
Butterick Co., Inc. 97
Cadmus Communications Corporation 100
Carolina Power & Light Company 104
Central Garden & Pet Company 108
Central Independent Television 111
Chick-fil-A Inc. 115
The Chronicle Publishing Company, Inc. . . . 119

Cineplex Odeon Corporation 123
Cinnabon Inc. 127
Clear Channel Communications, Inc. 130
Comsat Corporation 133
Comshare Inc. 137
Continental General Tire Corp. 140
Cooper Tire & Rubber Company 143
Copart Inc. 147
The Copley Press, Inc. 150
Corrections Corporation of America 153
Cowles Media Company 156
Cunard Line Ltd. 159
Del Monte Foods Company 163
DeMoulas / Market Basket Inc. 167
Desc, S.A. de C.V. 170
The Dial Corp. 173
Dollar Tree Stores, Inc. 176
Eagle-Picher Industries, Inc. 179
El Al Israel Airlines Ltd. 184
Ethicon, Inc. 188
Fieldale Farms Corporation 191
Fisons plc 194
Florida Progress Corporation 198
FoodBrands America, Inc. 201
Foster Wheeler Corporation 205
Franklin Electronic Publishers, Inc. 209
Fred's, Inc. 214
Fromageries Bel 217
Galeries Lafayette S.A. 220
Giant Cement Holding, Inc. 224
Grand Hotel Krasnapolsky N.V. 227
Groupe Castorama-Dubois Investissements . . 230
Groupe Legris Industries 233
Groupe Yves Saint Laurent 236

Guerlain 240
The Gunlocke Company 243
Guyenne et Gascogne 246
Handy & Harman 249
Hankyu Corporation 253
Hanna-Barbera Cartoons Inc. 257
Harris Teeter Inc. 260
Harry's Farmers Market Inc. 263
Hitchiner Manufacturing Co., Inc. 267
N.V. Holdingmaatschappij De Telegraaf . . . 271
Home Box Office Inc. 274
Hongkong Electric Holdings Ltd. 278
IDEXX Laboratories, Inc. 282
Insurance Auto Auctions, Inc. 285
Isuzu Motors, Ltd. 288
Jacor Communications, Inc. 292
Jacuzzi Inc. 296
Jason Incorporated 299
The Jim Henson Company 302
Johnstown America Industries, Inc. 305
Jordache Enterprises, Inc. 308
Kaufhof Warenhaus AG 311
King & Spalding 315
Lamb Weston, Inc. 319
LeaRonal, Inc. 322
Lehigh Portland Cement Company 325
LensCrafters Inc. 328
L'Entreprise Jean Lefebvre 331
Margarete Steiff GmbH 334
Mazda Motor Corporation 338
McClatchy Newspapers, Inc. 342
Meier & Frank Co. 345
Mirror Group Newspapers plc 348
Mitsubishi Motors Corporation 352
Nash Finch Company 356
Novell, Inc. 359
Office Depot Incorporated 363
Papeteries de Lancey 366
Pathmark Stores, Inc. 369
P.C. Richard & Son Corp. 372
Perdue Farms Inc. 375

Philippine Airlines, Inc. 379
Pilgrim's Pride Corporation 383
Playmates Toys 386
PolyGram N.V. 389
Publishers Clearing House 393
Putt-Putt Golf Courses of America, Inc. 396
R. Griggs Group Limited 399
Rainier Brewing Company 403
Red Apple Group, Inc. 406
Reno Air Inc. 409
Rhodes Inc. 412
Rodale Press, Inc. 415
Royal Crown Company, Inc. 418
S&K Famous Brands, Inc. 421
Seita 424
ServiceMaster Inc. 428
Sheldahl Inc. 432
Shoney's, Inc. 436
SilverPlatter Information Inc. 440
Southwire Company, Inc. 444
Sport Supply Group, Inc. 448
Stinnes AG 451
SunTrust Banks Inc. 455
Suzuki Motor Corporation 459
Swisher International Group Inc. 463
Taco Cabana, Inc. 466
Tatung Co. 469
Taylor Made Golf Co. 472
Télévision Française 1 475
True North Communications Inc. 478
Trump Organization 481
The Turner Corporation 485
Tyler Corporation 489
Valeo 492
Varta AG 495
Viacom Inc. 500
Wendy's International, Inc. 504
Westwood One, Inc. 508
William Morris Agency, Inc. 512
Wolverine Tube Inc. 515
Wood-Mode, Inc. 518

Index to Companies 521
Index to Industries 667
Notes on Contributors 689

PREFACE

The St. James Press series *The International Directory of Company Histories (IDCH)* is intended for reference use by students, business people, librarians, historians, economists, investors, job candidates, and others who seek to learn more about the historical development of the world's most important companies. To date, *IDCH* has covered over 3,300 companies in 23 volumes.

Inclusion Criteria

Most companies chosen for inclusion in *IDCH* have achieved a minimum of US$100 million in annual sales and are leading influences in their industries or geographical locations. Companies may be publicly held, private, or non-profit. State-owned companies that are important in their industries and that may operate much like public or private companies also are included. Wholly owned subsidiaries and divisions are profiled if they meet the requirements for inclusion. Entries on companies that have had major changes since they were last profiled may be selected for updating.

The *IDCH* series highlights 10% private and non-profit companies, and features updated entries on approximately 35 companies per volume.

Entry Format

Each entry begins with the company's legal name, the address of its headquarters, its telephone and fax numbers, and its web site. A statement of public, private, state, or parent ownership follows. A company with a legal name in both English and the language of its headquarters country is listed by the English name, with the native-language name in parentheses.

The company's founding or earliest incorporation date, the number of employees, and the most recent sales figures available follow. Sales figures are given in local currencies with equivalents in U.S. dollars. For some private companies, sales figures are estimates. The entry lists the exchanges on which a company's stock is traded, as well as the company's principal Standard Industrial Classification codes.

Entries generally contain a *Company Perspectives* box which provides a short summary of the company's mission, goals, and ideals, a list of *Principal Subsidiaries*, *Principal Divisions*, *Principal Operating Units*, and articles for *Further Reading*.

American spelling is used throughout *IDCH*, and the word "billion" is used in its U.S. sense of one thousand million.

Sources

Entries have been compiled from publicly accessible sources both in print and on the Internet such as general and academic periodicals, books, annual reports, and material supplied by the companies themselves.

Cumulative Indexes

IDCH contains two indexes: the **Index to Companies**, which provides an alphabetical index to companies discussed in the text as well as companies profiled, and the **Index to Industries**, which allows researchers to locate companies by their principal industry. Both indexes are cumulative and specific instructions for using them are found immediately preceding each index.

Suggestions Welcome

Comments and suggestions from users of *IDCH* on any aspect of the product as well as suggestions for companies to be included or updated are cordially invited. Please write:

The Editor
International Directory of Company Histories
St. James Press
835 Penobscot Building
Detroit, Michigan 48226-4094

ABBREVIATIONS FOR FORMS OF COMPANY INCORPORATION

A.B.	Aktiebolaget (Sweden)
A.G.	Aktiengesellschaft (Germany, Switzerland)
A.S.	Atieselskab (Denmark)
A.S.	Aksjeselskap (Denmark, Norway)
A.Ş.	Anomin Şirket (Turkey)
B.V.	Besloten Vennootschap met beperkte, Aansprakelijkheid (The Netherlands)
Co.	Company (United Kingdom, United States)
Corp.	Corporation (United States)
G.I.E.	Groupement d'Intérêt Economique (France)
GmbH	Gesellschaft mit beschränkter Haftung (Germany)
H.B.	Handelsbolaget (Sweden)
Inc.	Incorporated (United States)
KGaA	Kommanditgesellschaft auf Aktien (Germany)
K.K.	Kabushiki Kaisha (Japan)
LLC	Limited Liability Company (Middle East)
Ltd.	Limited (Canada, Japan, United Kingdom, United States)
N.V.	Naamloze Vennootschap (The Netherlands)
OY	Osakeyhtiöt (Finland)
PLC	Public Limited Company (United Kingdom)
PTY.	Proprietary (Australia, Hong Kong, South Africa)
S.A.	Société Anonyme (Belgium, France, Switzerland)
SpA	Società per Azioni (Italy)

ABBREVIATIONS FOR CURRENCY

DA	Algerian dinar		Dfl	Netherlands florin
A$	Australian dollar		Nfl	Netherlands florin
Sch	Austrian schilling		NZ$	New Zealand dollar
BFr	Belgian franc		N	Nigerian naira
Cr	Brazilian cruzado		NKr	Norwegian krone
C$	Canadian dollar		RO	Omani rial
RMB	Chinese renminbi		P	Philippine peso
DKr	Danish krone		Esc	Portuguese escudo
E£	Egyptian pound		SRls	Saudi Arabian riyal
Fmk	Finnish markka		S$	Singapore dollar
FFr	French franc		R	South African rand
DM	German mark		W	South Korean won
HK$	Hong Kong dollar		Pta	Spanish peseta
Rs	Indian rupee		SKr	Swedish krona
Rp	Indonesian rupiah		SFr	Swiss franc
IR£	Irish pound		NT$	Taiwanese dollar
L	Italian lira		B	Thai baht
¥	Japanese yen		£	United Kingdom pound
W	Korean won		$	United States dollar
KD	Kuwaiti dinar		B	Venezuelan bolivar
LuxFr	Luxembourgian franc		K	Zambian kwacha
M$	Malaysian ringgit			

International Directory of
COMPANY
HISTORIES

Abigail Adams National Bancorp, Inc.

1627 K Street N.W.
Washington, District of Columbia 20006
U.S.A.
(202) 466-4090
Web site: http://www.adamsbank.com

Public Company
Incorporated: 1977 as The Women's National Bank of
Washington
Employees: 45
Total Assets: $112.16 million (1996)
Stock Exchanges: NASDAQ
SICs: 6022 State Commercial Banks

Abigail Adams National Bancorp, Inc. is a bank holding company overseeing its sole wholly owned subsidiary, The Adams National Bank. The Bank provides banking and other financial services to individuals, small to medium-sized businesses and nonprofit and other organizations. Adams National Bank was the first federally chartered bank in the United States to be owned and managed by women. Originally named The Women's National Bank, the bank changed its name in 1986 to The Adams National Bank. The bank serves the nation's capital through three full-service offices in Washington, D.C.

The Adams National Bank is the largest U.S. bank owned predominantly by women, and the first such federally-chartered bank. As it enters its third decade, the bank continues to grow by paying attention to traditionally underserved niches. In the mid-1990s Adams completed a successful stock offering, which retained the female character of its ownership while supplying capital to expand beyond downtown Washington, D.C.

The Women's Movement Spawns a New Bank in the 1970s

Banking is the most conservative of businesses, and in spite of the growth of the feminist movement, credit and respect remained more difficult for women to come by even to the end of the century. Banks traditionally insisted on dealing with the head of the household—the male head of the household, i.e.—when approving loans. In 1977 the Women's National Bank was chartered in Washington, D.C.; its purpose was to incorporate more women on both sides of the operation: as owners and as customers. Offices were established at 1627 K Street N.W. The bank was not alone in its mission—the First Women's Bank of Maryland, the Women's Bank of Richmond, and the First Women's Bank of New York were similar enterprises launched in the mid-1970s.

Emily Womach, a respected Delaware banker, served as the first president and led the board of directors—assuming the title of "chair" rather than the traditional "chairman." Womach had been elected treasurer of Delaware in 1970 and fielded an unsuccessful campaign for governor two years later. Although unimpressed by the methods employed by another feminist financial institution, the First Women's Bank of New York, she agreed to lead Women's National due to what she perceived as its more responsible grounding.

In April 1978 the company completed a $2-million initial stock offering, which had begun six months earlier. Although 1,000 investors subscribed at $20 per share, a partnership of two Washington-area developers and their wives became the largest shareholders. However, this auspicious event would ultimately threaten the company's sovereignty. A decade later, significant losses in the local real estate market would force the partners to default on a $4.5 million loan and relinquish controlling ownership (71 percent) to Citibank.

The Women's National Bank opened for business in May 1978. The bank posted a first year loss of $76,000—quite respectable compared to the $400,000 the First Women's Bank of New York lost during its first half year. In addition, the Women's National Bank had already begun to operate profitably on a monthly basis, well ahead of the two years it took most start-up banks to achieve that status. By this time assets had grown to $7 million; deposits of $4.6 million indicated it was still the smallest bank in Washington. However, as results improved year after year, it became fifth most profitable by 1981, when it earned $240,345 after taxes. Nevertheless, its small size made compliance with inflexible and cumbersome banking regulations seem an inordinate burden.

Approximately two-thirds of the bank's 5,000 customers were women, as were most of the officers and directors. Women were granted about 60 percent of all loans. The bank geared its personalized service and educational efforts towards making women feel comfortable and confident in the world of finance. The bank's interior design, complete with plants and local pieces of art, reflected a feminine touch as well.

Significant practical benefits accompanied the bank's pioneering status at a time when the Equal Credit Opportunity Act gave women more assertiveness in dealing with banks. The federal government encouraged businesses owned by minorities and women, and the bank received preferential treatment from the federal government's Minority Bank Deposit Program, both through direct grants and by requiring its various agencies and contractors to utilize these businesses. Unfortunately, some of these funds were placed in special accounts in the Federal Reserve, out of the bank's control.

Lagging behind in the 1980s

Although its phenomenal initial growth could not be sustained, the Women's National Bank remained strong. The initial momentum was gone by the mid-1980s, as men shied away from the feminist institution. Other threats included a very serious national inflation rate and disproportionate taxes from the local District of Columbia government.

Women's National hired Barbara Davis Blum as CEO in 1983. Blum was formerly a senior executive at the Environmental Protection Agency. In 1986, the bank's name was changed to The Adams National Bank in honor of Abigail Adams, wife of President John Adams. The financially-savvy, pioneering feminist seemed an ideal symbol. However, the name change emphasized that the expanding bank was interested in serving not only women. Still, its feminist agenda would remain relevant into the 1990s. Although women carried more leverage as consumers, there still remained a perceivable gap when it came to women as independent entrepreneurs seeking bank loans—at least without a male co-signer.

Citibank assumed control of the Adams National Bank in 1988 when a group of its investors defaulted on a real estate loan. In 1989 the bank had three branches and had assets worth $63.1 million. While the rest of the country was celebrating a revived economy, Adams National was missing many opportunities as it stood neglected under Citibank's indifferent yoke. However, in the mid-1990s the bank did successfully bid for the assets of some failed financial institutions in the Washington area. In 1994 it began issuing its own Visa credit cards, enhancing its consumer offerings.

New Investors, New Hope in the 1990s

Women and minorities are classified together for the purposes of government entitlement programs. Using this logic, Citibank agreed to the sale of Adams in 1994 to National Bancshares, an African-American veterans group. However, Adams management, offended at the assault on the bank's identity, vigorously defended the feminine character of its ownership. National Bancshares abandoned its pursuit, and a series of lawsuits were initiated between company management and Citibank.

A search for new capital produced West Virginian Marshall T. Reynolds, whose group of eight investors included five women. Besides being more in tune with the bank's tradition, the Reynolds group offered to pay substantially more per share—$17—than National Bancshares, with an additional $4-per-share premium to minority shareholders (though most kept their shares). Reynolds, chairman and CEO of printing and office product supplier Champion Industries Inc., also invested in other community banks in the South.

In the spring of 1996, Adams National initiated a public stock offering to fund new expansion plans. The offering was made in the bank's holding company, Abigail Adams National Bancorp (known until 1986 as First WNB Corp.), through NASDAQ. In order to maintain the bank's minority status, the bank's broker, Ferris Baker Watts Inc., pitched the investment specifically to women. Men were encouraged to buy shares jointly or as gifts for female relatives. The unprecedented offering was wildly successful, raising nearly $7 million. Women retained a narrow majority of ownership, and the bank retained such privileges as the right to keep its three ATMs in Union Station (owned by the Department of Transportation), and the other business the federal government steered its way—at the time, seven percent of deposits and four percent of loans. However, the bank would have to tabulate its female ownership annually in order to remain eligible.

The newly-liberated bank, with assets valued at $89 million, embarked on an energetic search for acquisitions in Washington's neighboring suburbs, where the bank reported making 55 percent of its loans. Several likely candidates emerged in Virginia and Maryland, two states that allowed interstate branching. The bank also opened its fifth office in the District of Columbia, at the MCI Center in Chinatown, in fall 1997, and scouted locations for its own branches in the neighboring states.

In spring 1997, Abigail Adams National Bancorp agreed to buy Ballston Bancorp, Inc., the holding company of the Bank of Northern Virginia, in a deal worth $14 million. In November 1997, Marshall Reynolds, the bank's largest shareholder, withdrew his support for the merger, claiming its financial liabilities would overshadow its strategic advantages. Blum had already designated her son Devin to head the acquisition's lending operations.

Adams National invested heavily in technology—an approach that had been initiated when it introduced the first dual-language, English/Spanish ATM in the capital. CEO Barbara Blum told *American Banker,* "We want to move ahead of the curve of community banks in this area and offer the same technological services that you can find at the big banks." However, she pointed out in *Inc.* magazine that most small business customers were not vitally interested in such innovations as PC-based banking, although Adams did market this service, under the "ExecuBanc" label. Twenty-four–hour telephone banking was also available. The company launched a web site in July 1996 that enabled on-line credit applications

CONTENTS _____

Preface . . . . page vii
List of Abbreviations ix

Company Histories

Abigail Adams National Bancorp, Inc. 3	Cineplex Odeon Corporation 123
Abrams Industries Inc. 6	Cinnabon Inc. 127
Air Canada 9	Clear Channel Communications, Inc. 130
Analogic Corporation 13	Comsat Corporation 133
Anam Group 17	Comshare Inc. 137
AR Accessories Group, Inc. 20	Continental General Tire Corp. 140
Atari Corporation 23	Cooper Tire & Rubber Company 143
Atlanta Gas Light Company 27	Copart Inc. 147
The Atlantic Group 31	The Copley Press, Inc. 150
Azcon Corporation 34	Corrections Corporation of America 153
Bank Austria AG 37	Cowles Media Company 156
Battle Mountain Gold Company 40	Cunard Line Ltd. 159
Bayernwerk AG 43	Del Monte Foods Company 163
Beckett Papers 48	DeMoulas / Market Basket Inc. 167
Best Buy Co., Inc. 51	Desc, S.A. de C.V. 170
BIC Corporation 54	The Dial Corp. 173
The Bon Marché, Inc. 58	Dollar Tree Stores, Inc. 176
Bowne & Co., Inc. 61	Eagle-Picher Industries, Inc. 179
Brazos Sportswear, Inc. 65	El Al Israel Airlines Ltd. 184
Brenntag AG 68	Ethicon, Inc. 188
Bristol Hotel Company 71	Fieldale Farms Corporation 191
Broadcast Music Inc. 74	Fisons plc 194
Brown & Haley 78	Florida Progress Corporation 198
Brown & Sharpe Manufacturing Co. 81	FoodBrands America, Inc. 201
Burda Holding GmbH. & Co. 85	Foster Wheeler Corporation 205
The Bureau of National Affairs, Inc. 90	Franklin Electronic Publishers, Inc. 209
Burelle S.A. 94	Fred's, Inc. 214
Butterick Co., Inc. 97	Fromageries Bel 217
Cadmus Communications Corporation 100	Galeries Lafayette S.A. 220
Carolina Power & Light Company 104	Giant Cement Holding, Inc. 224
Central Garden & Pet Company 108	Grand Hotel Krasnapolsky N.V. 227
Central Independent Television 111	Groupe Castorama-Dubois Investissements . . 230
Chick-fil-A Inc. 115	Groupe Legris Industries 233
The Chronicle Publishing Company, Inc. . . . 119	Groupe Yves Saint Laurent 236

Guerlain 240
The Gunlocke Company 243
Guyenne et Gascogne 246
Handy & Harman 249
Hankyu Corporation 253
Hanna-Barbera Cartoons Inc. 257
Harris Teeter Inc. 260
Harry's Farmers Market Inc. 263
Hitchiner Manufacturing Co., Inc. 267
N.V. Holdingmaatschappij De Telegraaf . . . 271
Home Box Office Inc. 274
Hongkong Electric Holdings Ltd. 278
IDEXX Laboratories, Inc. 282
Insurance Auto Auctions, Inc. 285
Isuzu Motors, Ltd. 288
Jacor Communications, Inc. 292
Jacuzzi Inc. 296
Jason Incorporated 299
The Jim Henson Company 302
Johnstown America Industries, Inc. 305
Jordache Enterprises, Inc. 308
Kaufhof Warenhaus AG 311
King & Spalding 315
Lamb Weston, Inc. 319
LeaRonal, Inc. 322
Lehigh Portland Cement Company 325
LensCrafters Inc. 328
L'Entreprise Jean Lefebvre 331
Margarete Steiff GmbH 334
Mazda Motor Corporation 338
McClatchy Newspapers, Inc. 342
Meier & Frank Co. 345
Mirror Group Newspapers plc 348
Mitsubishi Motors Corporation 352
Nash Finch Company 356
Novell, Inc. 359
Office Depot Incorporated 363
Papeteries de Lancey 366
Pathmark Stores, Inc. 369
P.C. Richard & Son Corp. 372
Perdue Farms Inc. 375

Philippine Airlines, Inc. 379
Pilgrim's Pride Corporation 383
Playmates Toys 386
PolyGram N.V. 389
Publishers Clearing House 393
Putt-Putt Golf Courses of America, Inc. . . . 396
R. Griggs Group Limited 399
Rainier Brewing Company 403
Red Apple Group, Inc. 406
Reno Air Inc. 409
Rhodes Inc. 412
Rodale Press, Inc. 415
Royal Crown Company, Inc. 418
S&K Famous Brands, Inc. 421
Seita 424
ServiceMaster Inc. 428
Sheldahl Inc. 432
Shoney's, Inc. 436
SilverPlatter Information Inc. 440
Southwire Company, Inc. 444
Sport Supply Group, Inc. 448
Stinnes AG 451
SunTrust Banks Inc. 455
Suzuki Motor Corporation 459
Swisher International Group Inc. 463
Taco Cabana, Inc. 466
Tatung Co. 469
Taylor Made Golf Co. 472
Télévision Française 1 475
True North Communications Inc. 478
Trump Organization 481
The Turner Corporation 485
Tyler Corporation 489
Valeo 492
Varta AG 495
Viacom Inc. 500
Wendy's International, Inc. 504
Westwood One, Inc. 508
William Morris Agency, Inc. 512
Wolverine Tube Inc. 515
Wood-Mode, Inc. 518

Index to Companies 521
Index to Industries 667
Notes on Contributors 689

and bill payment. The bank's physical branches were linked via a PC-based network. Adams subcontracted its data processing and back room operations.

In 1997 federal set-asides accounted for five percent of the bank's deposits. It made three percent of its loans through preferential federal programs. The bank concentrated on small businesses, professional organizations, and the nonprofit organizations that clustered in and around the nation's capital, which accounted for $1.5 million of the bank's commercial and real estate loan portfolio in 1996. Labor unions owned some of the bank's largest accounts; however, the company's own employees were not represented by a union. Some Fortune 500 corporations also banked at Adams National.

As part of its focus on local small businesses, the bank participated in the financing program run by the Small Business Administration (SBA), which offered loans at favorable, flexible terms in order to spur development of the small business sector. Most of the money lent was guaranteed by the SBA; therefore, the bank expected to cultivate some long term relationships with these growing businesses while exposed to little risk. The bank's commercial and real estate SBA loans were worth $3 million at the end of 1996.

Net income for 1996, the bank's most successful year to date, was $1.13 million, up nearly 20 percent from the previous year, and assets totaled $112.2 million. Commercial loans were worth $39.4 million in 1996. Construction loans totaled $4.1 million. Commercial real estate loans accounted for $24.8 million and residential, $2.6 million. Loans to consumers were worth $2.2 million. In the late 1990s Adams National seemed poised for a promising new century, and women for a new era in financial empowerment.

Principal Subsidiaries

The Adams National Bank.

Further Reading

Andrejczak, Matt, "Adams National Eyes Merger Partners in Suburbs," *Washington Business Journal,* April 7, 1997.

——, "Adams Shareholder Opposes Bank Merger," *Washington Business Journal,* November 24, 1997.

Cannon, Carl M., "The Adams Chronicle," *Working Woman,* October 1997, pp. 24–27, 88.

Fraser, Jill Andresky, "Will Banking Go Virtual?" *Inc. Technology #3,* 1996, p. 49.

Gaiter, Dorothy J., "Energy Agency Moves on Aiding Minority Businesses; Deposits at Certain Banks to Be Increased Tenfold to $250 Million," *Wall Street Journal,* May 26, 1992, p. B2.

McDermott, John P., "Adams National Tries to Calm Depositors, Fight off Buy out," *Washington Business Journal,* April 22, 1994, p. 6.

Peabody, Alvin, "Disability Discrimination Suit Resolved with Adams Bank," *Washington Informer,* June 29, 1994.

Rhoads, Christopher, "Freed from Hobbles, Adams National Looks to Run," *American Banker,* July 22, 1996, p. 12.

Seaberry, Jane, "A New Generation of Women's Banks," *Washington Post,* June 27, 1979, pp. D8, D13.

——, "New Women's National Bank Now Part of Establishment," *Washington Post,* March 29, 1979, pp. C1, C3.

——, "Women's National Bank Still Optimistic," *Washington Post,* March 27, 1980, p. B3.

"US Banks: Hitting the Big Time," *The Banker,* April 1982, pp. 80–81.

Williams, Fred O., "Adams Hits Bull's Eye in Woman-Targeted Offering," *Washington Business Journal,* July 22, 1996.

Young, Wayne A., "Disabled Workers Sue Adams National Bank," *Washington Afro-American,* June 4, 1994.

—Frederick C. Ingram

Abrams Industries Inc.

Suite 202
5775-A Glenridge Drive NE
Atlanta, Georgia 30328
U.S.A.
(770) 953-0304
Fax: (770) 953-0302

Public Company
Incorporated: 1925 as A.R. Abrams Inc.
Employees: 244
Sales: $136.1 million (1997)
SICs: 1542 Nonresidential Construction, Not Elsewhere
Classified; 1541 Industrial Buildings and Warehouses;
1731 Electrical Work; 2541 Wood Partitions and
Fixtures; 2542 Partitions and Fixtures Except Wood;
6519 Real Property Lessors, Not Elsewhere Classified;
6719 Holding Companies, Not Elsewhere Classified

Atlanta-based Abrams Industries Inc. is a construction and development company focusing on the thriving Sun Belt markets of Georgia and Florida and consisting of three business segments. Of these, Abrams Construction Inc.—which builds, remodels or expands large commercial properties such as shopping centers, stores, banks, and warehouses—performed well during the 1980s and 1990s. The real estate segment, represented by Abrams Properties Inc., had begun to recover in the mid-1990s from what some observers saw as an overdependance on a single client. To a larger extent, recovery was the name of the game at the company's third subsidiary, Abrams Fixture Corporation, which creates displays for retail stores. In spite of sometimes troublesome circumstances in recent decades, Abrams' leadership—several of whom were sons or grandsons of the company's founder—remained unshaken in their optimism for the company's future.

Alfred Abrams and His Sons

In 1925, World War I veteran Alfred R. Abrams, then 26 years old, started a construction business in West Palm Beach,

Florida. It was a pioneering effort in more ways than one, because Florida's boom years still lay ahead. Air conditioning was still relatively new and far from universal, meaning that people were not yet flocking to Miami and Fort Lauderdale, as they would in coming decades. Abrams himself would move his business north 15 years later, to Atlanta.

Not long after Abrams relocated in 1940, America entered another world war, and when it was over in 1946, his company began producing in-store fixtures for retailers. This was the origin of Abrams Industries' manufacturing segment, which became Abrams Fixture Corporation. At that time, however, the overall company was simply A. R. Abrams Inc., a sole proprietorship. In 1960, Albert Abrams incorporated Abrams Industries under Delaware law. That year also saw the beginnings of the company's third segment, real estate.

Alfred Abrams had two sons: Bernard, born in 1925, the year Alfred began his business, and Edward, born in 1927. Like his father, Bernard Abrams entered the military and considered a career in the army, but suffered wounds during the Korean War, in which he served as a captain, that forced him to return to civilian life. Younger son Edward Abrams would later describe his father as "a real martinet" as a corporate leader. The statement, in an *Atlanta Journal and Constitution* article about family-run public companies, referred not to the elder Abrams' policies with his work force in general, but rather to his treatment of his sons. Clearly Alfred Abrams did not want his boys to grow up thinking that just because they were the boss's sons, they should have it easy.

When Alfred Abrams died in 1979, at the age of 80, his sons had long since taken charge of the company; within just a few years, their sons as well would come on board. Thus Abrams Industries, whose stock is traded on NASDAQ, would become both a public and a family-run enterprise.

Ups and Downs in the 1980s

In the mid-1980s, Bernard Abrams served as chairman and chief executive officer of the company, while Edward Abrams served as president. The company had several things going for it, but it faced potential challenges as well. At that time Abrams Industries consisted of seven subsidiaries, including a division

Company Perspectives:

The company's six principles: make a profit so that the company will remain financially sound; help to develop the people in our organization to achieve their maximum potential in a climate that creates good working conditions, mutual trust and happiness; encourage our people to practice thrift, to take an active interest in their church or synagogue, community projects and government, and to be good citizens; manufacture products and provide services of the highest quality, so that we may merit the respect, confidence and loyalty of our customers; be a source of strength to our customers and suppliers, conducting all of our transactions with them with fairness; plan and carry out all of our activities so that the company can expand its leadership and be regarded as a model in industry.

specializing in electrical and fire protection contracting. A 1986 profile of the company in the *Atlanta Journal and Constitution* lauded the development of what had grown from a small construction company into a $61.5 million-a-year corporation, but also regarded the firm as on the defensive in the face of declining market share.

At the time a single client, discount retailer Kmart, accounted for more than one-third of Abrams Industries' revenue, and this company's share of Abrams' total business had declined from 44 percent in 1983 to 35 percent in 1985. With such a heavy reliance on a single client, the company's fortunes were bound to rise and fall with the retailer's, and the *Journal and Constitution* reported that "Kmart and other retailers aren't adding stores and fixtures as they used to."

Moreover, Bernard Abrams's outside responsibilities created another challenge, because they placed a strain on his time and diverted his attention as chairman of the company. Though he had long since left the army, he remained committed to acting on behalf of the military, becoming involved in public work to improve communication between U.S. citizens and their armed forces by working as an aide to the Secretary of the Army. These activities, along with his other civic commitments, often divided his attentions, and in 1986 he admitted, "I feel as though I must give more time to the business."

The *Journal and Constitution* article noted that Abrams Industries had "the kind of strategic defense any soldier would write home about," and the military-minded Bernard Abrams spoke of how his experience in the army had taught him to handle "moments of tension." His defensive strategy involved relying on the most successful parts of the company to make up for those that lagged behind, and also required that management stay calm: "If a wall falls down," Bernard said, "we don't panic. We'll just fix the wall."

In fact, while Abrams Industries had experienced slowing in some areas, other segments helped offset losses with larger profits. The electrical and fire protection segment was small, and would eventually be discontinued altogether; production of store fixtures, however, while not being the largest area of the

company in terms of dollar volume, was nonetheless highly profitable. Contracting and engineering had suffered losses, though, partly because of overbuilding in the multi-family housing market, and real estate had likewise posted losses.

The Third Generation of Abramses

In the 1980s, a third generation of the Abrams family began to move into management positions. Edward's sons Alan and J. Andrew (Andy), and Bernard's son David, all joined the family business. Edward told the *Journal and Constitution* in 1989 that he had wanted his sons to join the company for several years: "I thought, wouldn't it be a shame not to give these kids an opportunity to continue?" Bernard said proudly of his son and nephews, "These men know that my brother and I have worked very hard for this business."

All three of Alfred Abrams's grandsons had extensive educations. Alan R. Abrams, who had studied history at Columbia University and earned an MBA from Atlanta's Emory University, had first gone into investment banking before joining Abrams Industries. Andy Abrams graduated from Notre Dame University with a double major in English and electrical engineering, and he too found himself being invited into the family firm. "Dad had never asked me for anything," he told Susan Harte of the *Journal and Constitution,* adding that "so when he did, I listened." His first job with the company was hardly one that put all his education to work: "I can still shape a very nice ditch," he recalled of his early employment at an Abrams construction site in Florida. By 1989, he was working as construction coordinator for Abrams Properties. As for David Abrams, he was the only one of the Abrams cousins who had "an underlying assumption that the family business would be a part of my life." Hence his education most closely mirrored the needs of the company: a chemical engineering degree from Princeton and MBA training from Harvard.

By 1996, the company's annual report would show that Alan Abrams and Andy Abrams, who had grown up less prepared for a career with Abrams, remained with the company. Alan Abrams was serving as president of Abrams Properties Inc. while Andy Abrams was named vice-president of Abrams Fixture Corporation. As for the older generation, they had changed roles: Edward Abrams was now chairman of the board and CEO of Abrams Industries Inc., and Bernard Abrams was chairman of the executive committee for Abrams Industries Inc. Seven years had brought a great deal of change, not only in the company's leadership, but throughout Abrams Industries.

The Uneven 1990s

In the quarter ended July 31, 1990, the company reported net losses of around $300,000 for the company, attributed mainly to Abrams Fixture, the segment that created merchandise displays. According to Bernard Abrams, this disappointing showing owed chiefly to the fact that two large retailers had postponed orders until later in the year.

The poor performance of the manufacturing segment portended future results in that area of the company. Once a highly profitable part of Abrams' operations, by the time of the 1996 annual report, the subsidiary had definitely fallen on hard times. In response, management decided to "build our business to our customers,'' rather than ''build our customers to our business,'' by re-engineering the manufacturing segment. Toward that end, according to the Abrams annual report, leadership decided to redesign Abrams Fixture Corporation from the ground up: ''Our people were told that nothing was sacred,'' the report relayed. Abrams instituted a three-part renovation of the company which would last into the summer of 1997. As for revenues and profits from the manufacturing segment during this time, profits had dipped in 1993, risen slightly in 1994, and then plummeted in 1995. By 1996, the losses were smaller, and the company anticipated gains from the closing of some facilities.

Real estate was in better shape, partly because the company had redeveloped a Kmart location in Jackson, Michigan, that it had owned since the early 1970s, creating a 105,000-square-foot shopping center with Kroger and Big Lots as its ''anchor stores.'' Abrams properties also had activities at a North Fort Myers, Florida, shopping center in which, by adding a large portion in 1996, it held 240,000 square feet of leasable area. It also had properties in Oakwood and Tifton, Georgia; Englewood, Florida; and other locations. Revenues from real estate were down from a 1994 high, and losses exceeded $1 million on receipts of almost $11.5 million. The company attributed the shortfall to two factors: the loss of rental income during the renovation of the Michigan site and costs of maintaining and retenanting that and other locations. Again, the company was optimistic about future returns from present activities, in this case its addition of new leasable space.

In contrast to the corporate picture a decade earlier, construction was the brightest spot for Abrams. In 1996, the company completed more than 130 projects in some 22 states, mostly for major retailers. Revenues in this area exceeded $108 million, and earnings were nearly $3 million. The company attributed the success of its construction segment to ''the untiring effort and dedication of all our people to produce the customer's product in the most efficient manner and in the shortest possible time.''

While dramatic changes had taken place in corporate structure and performance, some aspects of Abrams were much the same as before. Uneven performance of the different subsidiaries remained, though the underperformers had shifted. And a high degree of reliance on a few customers still existed, though now the emphasis had shifted away from Kmart. In 1996, the company did 48 percent of its business with Atlanta-based Home Depot Inc. and some 18 percent in building and development for Baby Superstore.

Alan Abrams, as Abrams Properties president, told the *Atlanta Business Chronicle* in 1997 that the company had sold off two Kmart properties besides the one in Michigan, the others being in Georgia and Oklahoma. More importantly, the company was adopting a new diversified strategy in its real estate operations. To that end, Alan Abrams and executive vice-president Gerald T. Anderson II had spent a great deal of time on the road, drumming up new business.

For the fourth quarter of its 1997 fiscal year, which ended on April 30, the company had posted profits in all three of its segments. Alan Abrams told the *Business Chronicle:* ''It's important for people who follow us to know that we're using the proceeds to invest in a more diversified mix.'' He added, ''We had 22 properties where Kmart was either the lead tenant or single tenant in all but one. We've now sold several of those Kmart properties, and we're trying to broaden the base of our tenants.'' Among the significant elements in the invigorated real estate strategy, he said, were a new involvement with office and industrial properties as well as a focus on ''second-tier'' cities such as Chattanooga, Tennessee, and Macon, Georgia.

Gerald Anderson told the *Business Chronicle* that he and Alan Abrams had ''lived on airplanes for quite a while'' as they went around the country to grow the business and ''turn our portfolio.'' Alan Abrams was cautiously upbeat: ''We had a couple of tough years,'' he said, ''but the companies, especially the manufacturing subsidiary, have done a remarkable turnaround.''

Principal Subsidiaries

Abrams Construction Inc.; Abrams Fixture Corporation; Abrams Properties Inc.

Further Reading

Burritt, Chris, ''Abrams Industries to Report Net Loss for Quarter,'' *Atlanta Journal and Constitution,* August 22, 1990, p. B8.

Garrett, Montgomery, ''Abrams Shakes Up Portfolio, Seeks New Markets,'' *Atlanta Business Chronicle,* August 4, 1997.

Harte, Susan, ''A Relative Question: Nepotism in a Publicly Traded Firm Frowned On, But Could Be Beneficial,'' *Atlanta Journal and Constitution,* July 17, 1989, p. C1.

Lawrence, Calvin, ''Company Profile: Abrams Industries Inc. Undoubtedly Has Battle Plan for Total Victory,'' *Atlanta Journal and Constitution,* February 3, 1986, p. C2.

Mallard, W. Morgan, ''Abrams Wants Its House a Bit More Orderly,'' *Atlanta Journal and Constitution,* November 17, 1986, p. E6.

Wilbert, Tony, ''Unhappy Investor Tells Abrams to Improve,'' *Atlanta Business Chronicle,* April 25, 1997, p. A10.

—Judson Knight

AIR CANADA

Air Canada

Air Canada Centre
P.O. Box 14000
Saint-Laurent, Quebec
Canada H4Y 1H4
(514) 422-5000
Fax: (514) 422-5789
Web site: http://www.aircanada.ca

Public Company
Incorporated: 1937 as Trans-Canada Air Lines
Employees: 21,300
Sales: C$5.57 billion (1997)
Stock Exchanges: Montreal Toronto Winnipeg Alberta
   Vancouver NASDAQ
SICs: 4516 Air Transportation, Scheduled; 4522 Air
   Transportation, Nonscheduled

Canada's largest airline, Air Canada's wide-ranging network has extended even farther with the advent of an open skies agreement with the United States and aggressive plans for transcontinental expansion. Thanks to its partnership with the Star Alliance, the carrier can offer passengers more than 650 destinations in more than 100 countries. Air Canada has weathered privatization, the threat of scandal, and the industry's usual crises to emerge as one of North America's most respected airlines.

Interwar Origins

The Canadian government created Trans-Canada Air Lines (TCA) as a Crown corporation in 1937 to provide transcontinental airline service within Canada's borders. From its founding through 1959, the government-owned company had a complete monopoly on all of Canada's domestic air routes; it also had a monopoly on all trans-border routes (routes that crossed the Canadian border with the United States) until 1967. The federal Cabinet of Canada approved all of the airline's routes and fares, and government regulators issued licenses approved by the Cabinet for the airline.

In 1959 the Canadian government allowed CP Air of Vancouver, British Columbia to provide one flight each day in each direction between Vancouver and Montreal, Quebec. From that small bit of business, CP Air grew through 1965 to acquire an average of 12.7 percent—the total it was allowed by federal regulations—of the domestic intercontinental traffic formerly held by Air Canada. In 1967 the Canadian government further relaxed its regulations and allowed CP Air two flights per day and, by 1970, CP Air was permitted to gain 25 percent of the intercontinental traffic in Canada. Also in 1967 the Canadian government allowed CP Air, which was given the right to establish international air routes across the Pacific Ocean in 1948, to establish a route from Vancouver to San Francisco, California—the first trans-border route not flown by TCA. Despite the encroaching competition from CP Air and that airline's dominance in international routes across the Pacific Ocean, TCA held, by government fiat, a monopoly on all other international routes and intercontinental domestic air travel.

Changes in the 1960s and 1970s

TCA adopted the name Air Canada in 1965. Government regulations set forth the next year prevented regional air carriers to compete with both Air Canada and CP Air, which were directed to work with the regional carriers to establish joint fare and commission arrangements and to cooperate on technical and servicing matters, including service to specific areas that required special equipment. Later, in 1969, the Canadian government established specific regions in which each of the five regional Canadian airlines could operate; those regulations lasted through the early 1980s.

Throughout the 1970s several pressures (many of which arose or were centered in the United States) challenged the Canadian government and the Air Canada monopoly. Larger jets for airline service provided air carriers with roomier vehicles, but high air fares, which were regulated in both the United States and Canada by federal agencies, prevented the efficient use of those vehicles. The power of consumers increased during the decade, and customers used that power to demand lower air fares from more competitive airlines. Information on how deregulated industries would perform was convincing many regula-

---

Company Perspectives:

There are two sides to every ledger: revenues and expenditures. Expenditures can be predicted and controlled, revenues less so. Revenues are a measure of the esteem in which customers hold our product. To win for shareholders, Air Canada also must win for customers. That means improving the Air Canada travel experience by implementing a revenue growth strategy which is both creative and cost effective and which respects four values key to customer satisfaction: customer recognition, convenience, comfort, reliability.

---

tors, airline executives, and consumers that a regulated airline industry was not in the best interest of anyone. In the late 1970s these forces combined to gain the support of leading politicians in the United States. The deregulation process of the U.S. airline industry began, with Canadian politicians watching closely, especially as Canadian passengers increasingly chose U.S. airlines for their international and transcontinental flights to take advantage of lower fares and improved services.

When Parliament passed the Air Canada Act of 1978, the Crown corporation was finally subjected to the same regulations and regulatory agencies that other Canadian airlines faced, bringing it more fully into competition with CP Air and the other regional airlines that were then operating. That act ended the government's unique regulatory control over Air Canada's routes, fare structures, and services—control the government wielded over the company throughout its first 41 years of business. On March 23, 1979, the minister of transport removed all capacity restraints on CP Air's share of transcontinental traffic, and it was given a license to provide domestic transcontinental flights. CP Air established transcontinental service in May of 1980 to compete directly with Air Canada. While these changes were occurring in its domestic competition, Air Canada was also facing increasing competition in international routes from American Airlines, British Airways, SwissAir, and Lufthansa.

The Competitive 1980s

By 1984 Air Canada hinted in its annual report that, to continue to compete with other international airlines, it would require a tremendous amount of new capital to replace its aging fleet of airliners with state-of-the-art jets. To upgrade its fleet, Air Canada was considering buying, between the years 1984 and 1993, more than 40 new airliners at a cost of more than $135 million each; the company also stated that it did not believe it could finance such purchases from retained earnings. At that time, six airline companies were operating in Canada, and Air Canada, which had more than a 50 percent share of the market, owned and operated the country's only computer reservations system. This provided them with access to all of the major travel agents in Canada and enabled them to collect a fee from other airlines when their tickets were sold on the computerized system. CP Air, which became Canadian Airlines International Ltd. in the mid-1980s, established its own computerized reservation system, but in 1987 the two airlines' systems were merged into a single network called the Gemini Group Limited Partnership.

In 1985, then Transport Minister Donald Mazankowski said that the Canadian government was planning to allow Air Canada and the Canadian National Railways the freedom to operate as private companies. The Canadian public appeared to support that move. In its annual report for the year 1985, Air Canada said it was determined to resolve the challenges it faced from its competition by managing its own destiny and achieving "a standard of financial credibility that will ultimately enable the shareholder to pursue a course of private and employee equity participation." This statement pointed toward the direction the company intended to move and coincided with further relaxation of regulations that encouraged its domestic and international competitors.

The complete deregulation of Canada's airline industry was first proposed in a policy paper from Mazankowski to Parliament in July of 1985. That policy was not enacted until Parliament passed the National Transportation Act of 1987, which became effective January 1, 1988. On April 12, 1988, Mazankowski, who was then the minister responsible for privatization, announced that Air Canada would be sold to the public as "market conditions permit" with an initial treasury issue of up to 45 percent of its shares. When it was announced, the sale was seen as the most ambitious act of privatization that the Canadian government had attempted thus far; Air Canada had assets of $3.18 billion and revenues of $3.13 billion in 1987. The sale was subjected to several conditions that were placed into the enabling legislation, which Parliament approved in August of 1988.

The legislation stipulated several things: the company's headquarters would remain in Montreal, Quebec; the airline, for the indefinite future, would maintain major operational and overhaul centers at Winnipeg, Manitoba, and in Montreal and Toronto; no more than 45 percent of the company's shares would be sold and the proceeds would go to the airline, not to the government; employees would be given the first chance to buy shares in the company, small shareholders the second opportunity, followed by institutional investors and, finally, foreign investors; no individual shareholder would be allowed to hold more than ten percent of the company's shares and foreign ownership was limited to 25 percent of the initial offering; and the government's 55 percent holding in the company would be voted in accordance with the private sector shareholders to give the company an arm's length relationship to the government.

On September 26, 1988, Air Canada filed the prospectus on its stock, stating that its net income after taxes was $101 million for the year ended March 31, 1988. The next day the price of the stock was set at $8 per share, and the company issued 30.8 million shares—42.8 percent of the company's total—with an option offered to brokers to buy an additional 3.5 percent of the total shares of the company at $8 per share. The company netted $225.8 million on the $246.2 million sale, with underwriting fees taking $12.3 million and with the airline absorbing $8 million in discounts to its employees. By the end of March of 1989 the company's shares were trading at $11.75 per share, and the stock hit a high of $14.83 in August that same year.

Air Canada's efficacious move to becoming a private company was seen as a result of a successful public relations program directed by the company's chairman, Claude I. Taylor, and its president and chief executive officer, Pierre J. Jeanniot. The executives focused the public relations program on the company's employees, the media, communities, customers, and potential shareholders; this was done in two carefully structured parts—pre-announcement and post-announcement—that were designed to ensure the success of the move to privatization by emphasizing the company's strengths and competitive position as it worked to improve its service and operations.

In July of 1989 the company completed its move to privatization with the filing of a prospectus for its second issue of stock. The company sold 41.1 million shares—for a total of 57 percent of its equity in the filing—at $12 per share. Proceeds from that sale went to the government. As an indication of the issue's success, by the end of the first week after the shares were issued the company's stock was trading at $12.75 per share. The company subsequently updated its fleet by ordering almost three dozen Airbus A320s jets. (The Canadian government later accused Brian Mulroney, prime minister at the time, of taking ''kick-backs'' in the deal, a charge that was eventually retracted.)

Finding Its Wings in the 1990s

The company's operating results, however, did not reflect the enthusiastic welcome that its stock had met in the market. Air Canada reported losses of $74 million in 1990 and $218 million in 1991, and it reported that it had nearly two million fewer passengers in 1991 than in the previous year. The company blamed its losses and decreased passenger load on the combined effects of the economic recession and the falloff in travel that resulted from the war in the Persian Gulf. It also, however, was seen as being hurt extensively by the pressures of competition with other international carriers.

In July of 1990 Jeanniot surprised his colleagues at Air Canada by announcing his retirement. Jeanniot, who spent 35 years with the company, told *Traffic World* magazine that he believed the time was right for him to retire: ''I have done my time. A chief executive should not hang around forever.'' Jeanniot was replaced in early 1992 by Hollis L. Harris, a former top executive at Delta Airlines and Continental Airlines; he was named vice-chairman, president, and chief executive officer.

The year that Harris joined Air Canada was a difficult one for his company and for the airline industry in general. Air Canada restructured its operations, eliminating five senior management positions, including four senior vice-presidents and the position of executive vice-president and chief operating officer; it also cut 250 other management positions and 100 administrative and technical support positions, all in an effort to save $20 million a year. The restructuring was part of the move to cut operating expenses by ten percent—$300 million a year—by 1993 and was expected to be accompanied by a reduction of nonmanagement union employees later in 1992. The restructuring enhanced Harris's position in day-to-day operations and gave him direct responsibility for the six divisions that were formed in the restructuring. The Harris regimen would make Air Canada more competitive and, beginning in 1994, profitable once again.

The restructuring also resulted in the sale of Air Canada's ''En Route'' credit card operations to Diners Club of America,

the selling of its Montreal headquarters building, and the relocating of its headquarters staff from downtown Montreal to Dorval Airport; in addition, the company enacted a plan to sell and lease back three of the Boeing 747-400s in its fleet. The restructuring was seen as a move to make Air Canada more efficient.

To gain further efficiencies, Air Canada proposed a merger in early 1992 with Canadian Airlines International Ltd., its primary Canadian competitor; the merger would have made Air Canada once again Canada's only international carrier. Canadian Airlines International Ltd. rebuffed Air Canada's merger proposal, however, and the idea was viewed as politically unpopular in Canada where it would have likely eliminated more than 10,000 jobs.

Air Canada took to warmer climes with relish after the signing of an ''open skies'' agreement between Canada and the United States in early 1995. Beginning with Atlanta, the carrier opened almost 30 new U.S. routes, mostly nonstop, within the year. They proved enduringly popular and profitable. The airline renovated its fleet of smaller aircraft with Canadair regional transports to provide flexibility on its shorter routes. Montreal and Vancouver airports were opened to U.S. carriers in 1997; Toronto followed in 1998.

Air Canada initiated code sharing agreements with U.S. carriers after gaining access to that market. Its networking took on a much larger scale with the creation of the Star Alliance in 1997, through which Air Canada, Lufthansa, SAS, THAI International, and United Airlines (later joined by VARIG Brazilian Airlines) linked their routes. Each carrier also agreed to honor each other's frequent flyer miles. International fares accounted for more than half of passenger revenue, and the company continued to expand its services in this area while leveling off domestic growth.

A Happy Sixtieth Anniversary in 1997

Air Canada had record profits as well as a sixtieth anniversary to celebrate in 1997. As the company wooed patrons with refinements and innovations such as the Xerox Business Centres located in Maple Leaf Lounges and the Skyriders frequent flyer program for children, it reaped a net income of C $427 million on total revenues of more than C $5 billion. The positive performance was tempered somewhat by a labor disruption among pilots for its regional subsidiaries. Air Canada divested itself of Northwest Territorial Airways Ltd. in June 1997 and the next month sold most of its interest in Galileo Canada Distribution Systems Inc.

Harris was succeeded by Lamar Durrett as president and CEO in May 1996. John Fraser succeeded him as chairman in August. The airline's young fleet of 157 planes boasted one of the continent's best on-time records, carrying 40,000 passengers a day.

Principal Subsidiaries

Touram Inc. (conducts business as Air Canada Vacations); Air Nova Inc.; AirBC Ltd.; Air Ontario Inc.; Air Alliance Inc.

Further Reading

Came, Barry, " 'Straight Out of Kafka': Mulroney Lashes Out at the Federal Government's Allegations," *Maclean's,* April 29, 1996.

Dawson, Phil, "Air Canada: Sixty Years of Innovation and Progress," *Airways,* January/February 1998, pp. 19–27.

Flint, Perry, "The Business Is Actually Fun Again!," *Air Transport World,* June 1995.

Foster, Cecil, "Air Canada Searching for a New CEO After Jeanniot's Surprise Retirement," *Traffic World,* August 13, 1990.

——, "Tough Guys Don't Cuss," *Canadian Business,* February 1995.

McKenna, Edward, "Air Canada Restructures," *Aviation Week and Space Technology,* May 4, 1992.

Ouellet, Francine Vallee, "The Privatization of Air Canada," *Canadian Business Review,* Winter 1989.

Oum, Tae Hoon, Stanbury, W. T., and Tretheway, Michael W., "Airline Deregulation in Canada and Its Economic Effects," *Transportation Journal,* Summer 1991.

Shiffrin, Carole A., "Aggressive Start for Canadian Carriers in Open Skies Pact," *Aviation Week and Space Technology,* March 25, 1996.

Tower, Courtney, "Air Canada Charting Its Own Unique Flight Path(s)," *Journal of Commerce and Commercial,* August 13, 1997, p. 14A.

Turner, Craig, "Air Canada's Aboot-Face," *Los Angeles Times,* August 8, 1996.

Van Velzen, Andrew and Turner, Craig, "Canada Settles Suit, Apologizes to Ex-Premier; Courts," *Los Angeles Times,* January 1, 1997.

—Bruce Vernyi
—updated by Frederick C. Ingram

ANALOGIC.■

Analogic Corporation

8 Centennial Drive
Peabody, Massachusetts 01960
U.S.A.
(978) 977-3000
Fax: (978) 977-6811
Web site: http://www.analogic.com

Public Company
Incorporated: 1964 as Gordon Engineering
Employees: 1,500
Sales: $256.7 million (1997)
Stock Exchanges: NASDAQ
SICs: 3823 Process Control Instruments; 3825
Instruments to Measure Electricity; 3829 Measuring
and Controlling Devices, Not Elsewhere Classified;
3845 Electromedical Equipment

Analogic Corporation is a leading custom designer, manufacturer, and seller of sophisticated precision instruments for data acquisition conversion and signal processing. At the heart of Analogic's technology is the conversion of biomedical and industrial signals into computer-readable language. The company's products have a wide market among OEMs (Original Equipment Manufacturers) in the medical, scientific, industrial, and telecommunications fields. The company's chief products include medical equipment for magnetic resonance imaging (MRI) tests, ultrasounds, and patient monitoring. It also designs and manufactures digital image processing and computer telephony products.

During the early 1990s Analogic expanded its focus from producing instruments for the medical and industrial segments exclusively, to also developing and manufacturing complex systems for a private customer base. Thus, even though Analogic's products are found in many hospitals and laboratories, they are often designed confidentially for specific customers and so do not bear Analogic's name. The shift in focus proved successful, but as a result the Analogic name is not well known to the general public, despite the company's growing presence within the public medical equipment and electronics fields.

Foundings

In the early 1950s, Bernard M. Gordon was a young engineer helping to develop UNIVAC, the world's first commercial digital computer. From there Gordon went on to develop air traffic control and radar systems, and at the age of 26, he invented a system for converting analog signals to digital signals, a technology that became the core of many future products in the medical, industrial, and telecommunications fields.

By 1964, Gordon had founded his own development company, Gordon Engineering, whose products included the first solid-state X-ray generator. Five years later, Gordon Engineering was ready to branch out into the actual manufacture of innovative products, and Analogic Corporation was founded. Gordon's work at Analogic eventually led to almost 200 patented products and numerous awards, including the U.S. National Medal of Technology (1986) and the Benjamin Franklin Award for Innovation in Engineering and Technology (1992). Gordon still played an ongoing leadership role within the company in the late 1990s; as of 1997 he served as chairman of the board and chief executive officer at Analogic.

The 1970s–80s: Developing Medical Subsystems

In the 1970s and 1980s Analogic was a key company in the development of many tools for medical diagnosis, patient care, and industrial controls and measurement. The cornerstone of its products was founder Gordon's invention, the high-speed, analog/digital converter. Many of Analogic's products were subsystems manufactured under contract to OEMs, often large companies who did not want it generally known that they had farmed out product development to a small newcomer in the field. As a result, much of Analogic's early work went into final products that bore another company's name.

Even under this cloak of confidentiality, Analogic quickly gained a reputation in the electronics and medical equipment

13

Company Perspectives:

Since its inception, the Company's mission has evolved from the design and manufacture of high precision measurement, data acquisition and signal processing components to the conception, design, and manufacture of proprietary complete, complex medical and industrial imaging and measurement systems and subsystems. Central to our success is our resourceful engineering team of more than 400 engineers and scientists, including design engineers, physicists, mathematicians, materials scientists, and support personnel who further the state of the art as they innovatively apply advanced and proven technology to solve our customers' problems.

industries, as a leading developer and supplier of high quality signal processing components and subsystems. In 1975 an Analogic research team, led by founder Gordon, invented the first instant imaging Computed Tomography (CT, or popularly known as CAT-Scan) scanning equipment, for an OEM customer. Analogic built on this invention in the following two decades, to become a major supplier of medical imaging machines.

Analogic also began to develop Magnetic Resonance Imaging (MRI) products in these early years; via this sideline the company gradually grew into the leading such supplier internationally, supplying almost half of the world's systems by 1997. Development and manufacturing of patient monitoring instruments, produced in early years for an OEM customer, eventually were discontinued until the mid-1990s when Analogic would decide to re-enter this field.

Change of Direction in the Early 1990s

By the early 1990s, Analogic had built a solid business by designing subsystems and system components for its customers, many of which were larger and more established companies. However, its management wisely perceived that there was much greater potential for growth if the company branched out into the design and manufacture of complete systems, particularly state-of-the-art medical imaging systems. In its 1992 annual report, Analogic announced its changing approach, in which the company became a provider of complete systems as well as complex subsystems.

The development and bringing to market of a relatively inexpensive and mobile Computed Tomography (CT) medical scanning system was the first major product step undertaken with this new approach. Conventional systems had high power requirements and were extremely expensive. Analogic decided to attempt making a smaller, more rugged unit that could be marketed outside of major hospitals. Development and marketing of this unit became a major task through the 1990s.

Along with its change in focus, Analogic also made several acquisitions and created new subsidiaries. A subsidiary, Camtronics Ltd., was formed in 1992 by three Analogic employees

to design and manufacture digital video medical imaging systems and networks. As of 1996, Analogic had acquired 68 percent of Camtronic's stock and retained an option to purchase further amounts. Camtronics, located in Wisconsin, had independently developed the Archium digital cardiac network, which allowed viewing of cardiac X-rays at multiple locations simultaneously.

In 1992 Analogic also acquired all of the stock of SKY Computers, Inc. From its origins in providing off-the-shelf commercial products, SKY's operations were expanded into the design of systems for the detection of explosives and development of other systems for large OEM customers. This subsidiary became a leading provider of embedded multicomputers and parallel processing hardware and software. Its products had numerous applications, including medical imaging, radar, and sonar.

The 1990s also found Analogic more involved in international operations. As of January 1, 1993, Analogic acquired a 57 percent interest in a new company, B&K Medical A/S (later renamed B&K Ultrasound Systems A/S), a Danish corporation that concentrated on the design and manufacture of ultrasound imaging devices used in sonographic techniques and urology. In 1996, Analogic purchased the remainder of B&K's stock. Also during the mid-1990s, Analogic entered into a joint venture with Kejian Corporation in the People's Republic of China, in which each corporation owned half of Analogic Scientific, Inc. However, this joint venture had not proven profitable as of 1997. In 1996 and 1997 revenues from Analogic's international operations accounted for about ten percent of the company's total revenues.

To accompany its change of direction to complete system design, Analogic spent large amounts of money on research and development. For instance, in 1995 the company's research and development costs increased almost $4 million over 1994, with these funds earmarked for design and development costs as well as additional investment in research staff and equipment.

1992 Refocusing

In fiscal 1992 (before Analogic's management consciously shifted to development of complete systems for the medical and industrial technology markets, and greatly increased its research and development spending), Analogic's total revenues stood at $149.2 million. Over the next five fiscal years, revenues jumped steadily ($177.8 million in 1993; $193.7 million in 1994; $208.8 million in 1995; $230.5 million in 1996; and $256.7 million in 1997). During that time, net income more than doubled, from $9.9 million in 1992 to $20.1 million in 1997.

While a large amount of the increased revenues came from increased sales of medical technology products, sales of signal processing products also grew. Analogic also took in $11.6 million in revenues as of 1997 from a hotel adjoining its headquarters, purchased in the early 1990s. Expenses associated with operating this hotel generally consumed only about half of the revenues it took in. At the same time, Analogic maintained a low level of corporate long-term debt, falling from $16.5 million in 1992 to only $8.6 million in 1997.

During the late 1990s, some of Analogic's customers, who previously had requested confidentiality in their dealings, realized that Analogic's reputation in the field was growing and became more open about publicizing the fact that their products had been developed by Analogic. By 1997, Analogic could list among its largest customers Philips Electronics (17.1 percent of sales); General Electric (8.4 percent) and Siemens AG (7.8 percent). Its ten largest customers in 1997 accounted for about 57 percent of its product, service, engineering, and licensing revenue.

One of the few questionable Analogic management moves during the late 1990s concerned its investment in a Canadian corporation, Park Meditech, Inc. Park Meditech developed and manufactured nuclear medicine imaging equipment, as well as computer systems and software to operate this equipment. In 1994, Analogic had received Park Meditech stock in exchange for cancelling a debt owed by another company. The following year, Analogic loaned Park Meditech $1.5 million; then, in February 1996, it purchased another 1.7 million shares, bringing its total holdings to 5.7 million shares, 14 percent of Park Meditech's total shares. In December 1996 and February 1997, Analogic loaned Park Meditech an additional $515,000. Unfortunately, pumping in these resources did not prevent one of Park Meditech's subsidiaries, Park Medical Systems, from filing for bankruptcy in July 1997. At the end of 1997, Analogic was forced to write off $1.7 million of its investment as a loss.

Because of its rapid growth and overall performance in the late 1990s, Analogic was ranked as number 43 in the *Boston Globe* list of 1997's top 100 Massachusetts publicly held companies. It had not even appeared on the list in the previous year, but its 23 percent jump in revenues between 1995 and 1996 definitely caught the eye of local business analysts. Analogic's stock value also rose about 75 percent in value during 1996. As *Research* magazine noted in early 1997, several fund managers regarded the company's future as bright, adding, "in fact, many regard the company's shares as undervalued at recent price levels, offering an attractive opportunity for investors seeking long-term growth." *Research* further pointed out the vast market potential for Analogic's mobile and less costly diagnostic and medical equipment in both developed and developing nations.

Analogic's management was acutely aware of the need to add to its existing group of top level managers even as its success grew steadily. Beginning in the mid-1990s, the company began to recruit a new generation of technical and manufacturing managers to assure a smooth transition. As president and CEO Bruce R. Rusch and chairman/founder Bernard M. Gordon noted in the 1997 annual report, "We are well aware of the fact that several of the senior managers of the Company, including its founder, are, to put it politely, getting on in years." At the time, founder Gordon was 70 and had spent 28 years at the company's highest levels.

Promising New Products for the 1990s

During the late 1990s Analogic put great effort into marketing its lightweight, low-power Computed Tomography (CT) diagnostic imaging system. This product promised to become popular in hospital intensive care units. Rather than having to move critically ill patients to a testing unit, the mobile CT instead could be brought to the patient's bedside. Because the mobile CT also could operate from almost any electrical outlet, Analogic opened new markets for itself in the developing countries in Africa, Asia, and South America, where even small hospitals and clinics in outlying areas could utilize this technology.

Another promising product being developed in the late 1990s was the Explosive Assessment Computed Tomography (EXACT) system. EXACT was an explosives detection system for scanning baggage being checked at airports. This system employed a CT scanner which, through the use of high and low-energy X-rays, took several hundred images of each piece of baggage passing through the scanner on a conveyor belt. The images then were fed into a data system that would compare the images to profiles of known explosives and sound an alarm if a match was found. This elaborate process could be completed within five seconds. As of late 1997, the EXACT system had been delivered to Analogic's anonymous customer and was scheduled to be submitted to the Federal Aviation Administration for testing.

One of the key products of Analogic's Danish subsidiary B&K was the Leopard 2001 ultrasound scanning system. By the late 1990s this product had become a key tool for physicians who were treating prostate cancer. Instead of performing traditional radical surgery in which the prostate gland was removed, physicians using the Leopard 2001 could implant tiny radioactive seeds in the tumor and hopefully destroy it. This procedure, which did not require an incision, was less expensive and involved less risk and pain for the patient.

Other products under development in the late 1990s included digital imaging technology for use in hospital and radiology laboratories, and advanced Magnetic Resonance Imaging (MRI) systems and fetal monitoring instruments. Like the mobile CT, the fetal monitoring equipment was designed to be tough, durable, and portable, for use in small hospitals and outpatient clinics. Analogic had developed and produced patient monitoring equipment for an OEM customer in the 1970s and 1980s, but this activity had been dormant for several years. In the late 1990s, Analogic decided to produce a new breed of portable fetal monitors independently, and soon a new OEM with operations in the United States and Europe entered into an agreement with Analogic, under which the OEM would market the monitoring equipment.

According to *Research* magazine, technology under development at Analogic would be key in making internet-based "telemedicine" (connecting physicians and patients in distant areas through an online network) possible. Scanned images and patient information could be archived and accessed as needed via the internet.

As articulated in its 1997 annual report, Analogic planned to continue designing and producing complete systems, in cooperation with its major OEM customers, affiliates, and strategic partners: "We are confident that by continuing to pursue this course, Analogic will remain *The World Resource for Precision Signal Technology*."

Principal Subsidiaries

Analogic Foreign Sales Corporation (U.S. Virgin Islands); Analogic Limited (U.K.); B&K Ultrasound Systems A/S (Denmark); Camtronics Ltd. (68%); Camtronics Foreign Sales Corporation (U.S. Virgin Islands); SKY Computers; SKY Limited (U.K.).

Principal Divisions

Computed Tomography Engineering Group; Computer Design and Applications Division; Data Conversion Products Division; Medical Imaging Division; Measurement & Control Division.

Further Reading

"Corporate Profile: Analogic Corporation," *Research: Ideas for Today's Investors,* March 1997.
Crum, Rex, "Massachusetts High-Techs Report Strong Sales, Profits," *Boston Business Journal,* October 27, 1997.
"The Globe 100," *Boston Globe,* May 20, 1997.

—Gerry Azzata

Anam Group

Anam Industrial Co., Ltd.
280-8 Songsu 2-ga
Sungdong-gu
Seoul
Korea
+82 2-460-5114
Fax: +82 2-460-5780
Web Site: http://www.anamic.co.kr

Amkor Electronics, Inc.
1345 Enterprise Drive
West Chester, Pennsylvania 19380
U.S.A.
(610) 431-9600
Fax: (610) 431-5881
Web Site: http://www.amkor.com

Public Company
Incorporated: 1956
Employees: 8,169
Sales: KW 1.3 trillion (1997 est. for Anam Industrial
only)
SICs: 3663 Radio & TV Communications Equipment;
3674 Semiconductors & Related Devices; 3822
Environmental Controls; 3823 Process Control
Instruments; 3651 Household Audio & Video
Equipment; 3824 Fluid Meters & Counting Devices;
3543 Current-Carrying Wiring Devices; 3873
Watches, Clocks, Watchcases & Parts; 3651
Household Audio & Video Equipment; 5064
Electrical Appliances, TV & Radios

With an estimated one-third of the global semiconductor assembly market, the Anam Group ranks among South Korea's largest companies. A family affair, this billion-dollar business comprises two companies, both led by members of the Kim family. The larger company, Anam, handles semiconductor testing and packaging, while its U.S.-based sibling Amkor is in charge of global marketing. Though the companies are for tax purposes legally separate, they operate as exclusive associates and are often considered a group. Amkor (at this writing privately held, but in the process of going public) holds about ten percent of Anam's publicly traded stock. Anam's revenues more than doubled from 1993 to 1997 as the company and its affiliates added semiconductor manufacturing to their core testing and packaging services. By that time, both companies were chaired by Kim Joo-Jin (also known as James "Jim" Kim), the son of the founder.

Founded in Late 1960s

Anam was created in the late 1960s by South Korean Kim Hyang-Soo, a self-made bicycle magnate who was looking for a second career. His first had started in 1921, when he left home at the age of 17. Equipped only with an elementary education and a bookkeeping course, Kim proved adept at selecting growth industries in which to participate. According to a 1985 article in *Electronic Business,* Kim's first company "dominated 90 percent of the Korean bicycle market in the 1950s."

Perhaps regretting his own limited education, Kim sent his seven children to some of the world's best institutions of higher learning. Eldest son Kim Joo-Jin traveled to the University of Pennsylvania in 1955 to pursue a degree in economics at the prestigious Wharton School. Joo-Jin, who later Anglicized his name to James Kim and became a U.S. citizen in 1971, received a bachelor's degree in 1959 and earned a Ph.D. from Villanova University in 1963. He was teaching at the latter institution when his father came to the United States for a visit in 1967.

It was not just a social call. The elder Kim, who had been operating a labor pool since the early 1960s, was looking for a new business interest. Over his son's objections, Kim decided to move into semiconductors.

Jim Kim must have been pleasantly surprised when, in 1968, he made his first trip home in well over a decade. He found that instead of entering the cyclical semiconductor manufacturing segment, his father had created South Korea's first semiconductor packaging and testing operation. Clients sent integrated

Company Perspectives:

Since our early days, we have recognized the need to remain at the forefront of industry technology. We devoted an entire division to technology enhancing activities, and as consumer technology continues to advance at a rapid pace, we are dedicated to providing the latest technology to meet and exceed the market's rapidly changing requirements. At Anam, we focus on intimately understanding each customer's market challenges so that we can discover workable, cost effective solutions. Acting more as a business partner than a supplier, we develop close relationships with every customer, providing each one with dedicated service and top quality products.

circuit components to Anam, where they were tested for quality control, packaged into protective housings, retested, and sent back to the manufacturer for installation. The company charged by the second for its services: the average test took four to five seconds and cost 20 cents. Demand for such services was on the rise, for as integrated circuitry (IC) became increasingly complex, the expensive equipment required to test semiconductors faced briefer periods of usefulness before obsolescence. By serving multiple manufacturers, Anam was able to attain efficiencies of scale that OEMs could not achieve in-house.

Anam earned the top spot in the packaging and testing industry through two key strategies: it kept pace with its customers' technological developments, and it created a marketing operation that promoted its services to the leaders of the IC industry. Anam embraced automation, established high quality control standards, and developed leading-edge technology. An early affiliation with VLSI Technology won Anam the contract to test that company's application-specific integrated circuits (ASICs) when they came out in the early 1980s. The company developed tape automated bonding (TAB)—a time- and money-saving manufacturing process—in the early 1990s. Anam also devised housings for ever-shrinking cell phones and laptop computers.

Jim Kim returned to the United States and founded Amkor (a contraction of ''America'' and ''Korea'') in 1968 to market his father's products and services. In pursuit of lower corporate taxes, the younger Kim set up his business as a fee-for-service contractor—albeit with only one client, Anam. Based in Valley Forge, Pennsylvania, Amkor quickly became a key factor in its predecessor's success, establishing offices in Dallas, Hong Kong, and Tokyo. As Anam president Hwang In-Kil told *Electronic Business Today* in 1997, ''The strength of Anam is Amkor. Because we have Amkor, which has a worldwide sales organization with sales offices everywhere, we can concentrate on developing manufacturing technology. And Amkor can't exist without Anam, so we depend on each other.''

Group Diversification in the 1970s and 1980s

In 1973 the Kim family created Korea National Electric Co., Ltd., a joint venture with Songha Electric Industry Inc., to manufacture consumer electronics like televisions, VCRs, and audio equipment. This subsidiary took over Songha Electric in 1980 and went public four years later as Anam Electronics. Led by Jim Kim's sibling, Kim Joo-Chai (also known as Jay Kim), this business brought big-screen TVs to Korean consumers in the mid-1980s, and had diversified into computers, fax machines, and VCRs by the mid-1990s. By that time, Anam Electronics was generating sales of KW 264.5 trillion.

Amkor's retail subsidiary, Electronics Boutique, Inc., evolved from a sideline launched by Jim Kim's wife, Agnes, in 1977. That year, she set up a cart in a Pennsylvania mall to sell digital watches manufactured by Anam. When the digital watch fad faded, the U.S. Kims rented mall stores and began selling high-end computer software, PCs, and video games. The chain grew from 55 stores in 1986 to 400 stores in the United States and Canada and was generating about $300 million in annual revenues by the mid-1990s.

Growth through Acquisition in the 1990s

Though Korea's semiconductor manufacturing industry was hit especially hard by the global price declines of the early and mid-1990s, the Anam Group's niche in packaging and testing continued to enjoy profitable growth. As president Hwang In-Kil noted in a January 1997 interview with *Business Korea,* 'Anam has gained world renown for its technology and quality of products. That's the secret of our continued high growth.'' The group boosted its capacity with the $30 million acquisition of Manila-based Advanced Micro Device Inc.'s Philippine plant in 1990. Subsequent capital investments were expected to increase this subsidiary's assembly capacity to 220 million chips per month, or an annual export volume of nearly $2 billion, by the end of 1998. The group acquired a second Philippine plant, this time from American Microelectronics, Inc., in 1990 as well, and built a third factory there in 1996. Amkor oversaw (and held majority interests in) these operations.

While others entrenched, Anam diversified into a new growth niche mid-decade. In 1996 the group licensed processing technology from Texas Instruments and invested $1.2 billion in a new industrial park in Kwangju, Korea, near Seoul. The new plant was set up to custom-manufacture (or fabricate, in industry parlance) non-memory or digital signal processor (DSP) chips used in electronic devices like stereos and camcorders. Anam executives forecast that this segment would enjoy a 30 percent annual growth rate through the turn of the century, and it planned to build massive wafer fabrication facilities to accommodate this demand. Its first facility was the size of two football fields. Texas Instruments agreed to purchase 40 percent of the new plant's total output of 25,000 8-inch DSPs per month. Amkor/Anam forecast that, when complete in 2001, the Kwangju campus would employ 6,000 people and have the capacity to fabricate 120,000 chips or ten million semiconductor packages each month. Jim Kim told *Electronic News* that the addition of manufacturing capabilities made Amkor/Anam ''one of the first to provide fully integrated manufacturing services under a single umbrella.'' In keeping with its time-tested organizational formula, the group set up a separate subsidiary, Amkor Wafer Fabrication Services in Chandler, Arizona, to market its expanded capabilities.

Amkor Technologies was reorganized as a holding company in 1997 in anticipation of a 1998 initial public offering. In 1996 the U.S. arm of the Anam Group had revenues of $1.2 billion and net income of $31.3 million.

In a 1997 interview with Lewis Young of *Electronic Business Today,* Jim Kim forecast that the global semiconductor packaging market would grow 30 percent to $5.7 billion in 1997. Though he expected his company's share of that pie to decline from an industry-leading high of 50 percent in 1990 to 15 percent as newcomers entered the fray and integrated circuit manufacturers brought testing and packaging functions in-house, he predicted that Amkor/Anam would continue to enjoy a 25 percent annual sales growth rate.

Principal Subsidiaries

Anam Industrial Co., Ltd.; Anam Electronics Co., Ltd.; Anam Instruments (67.2%); Anam Engineering & Construction Co., Ltd. (49.1%); Anam Semiconductor & Technology Co., Ltd.; Anam Environmental Industry Co., Ltd.; Korea National Electric Co., Ltd.; Amkor/Anam Pilipino (40%).

Further Reading

Abelson, Reed, "Native Korean Plugged in to U.S. Electronics Market," *Philadelphia Business Journal,* November 17, 1986, pp. 10–11.

"Anam Promises Quality," *Business Korea,* July 1996, pp. 27–28.

Card, David, and Y.D. Lee, "Amkor-Anam: Building for a Better Tomorrow?" *Electronic Business,* January 1, 1985, pp. 58, 61.

Eisenstodt, Gale, "A Shrimp among Whales," *Forbes,* December 19, 1994, pp. 92–94.

Kim, Nak-Hieon, "Anam to Boost Investment in the Philippines," *Electronics,* September 26, 1994, p. 10.

Lee, Charles S., "Risky High-Tech Leap," *Far Eastern Economic Review,* October 31, 1996, p. 60.

Levine, Bernard, "Korea's Anam Starts DSP Production," *Electronic News,* November 10, 1997, p. 6.

Sohn Young-Ju, "A Shining Star," *Business Korea,* January 1997, p. 34.

Young, Lewis H., "An American-Korean One-Two Punch," *Electronic Business Today,* October 1997, pp. 55–56.

—April D. Gasbarre

AR Accessories Group, Inc.

4300 W. Brown Deer Road
Milwaukee, Wisconsin 53223
U.S.A.
(414) 371-6600
Fax: (414) 371-6300

Private Company
Incorporated: 1915 as Amity Leather Products Company
Employees: 1,100
Sales: $64 million (1996 est.)
SICs: 3172 Personal Leather Goods

AR Accessories Group, Inc. is best known as the maker of the Amity and Rolfs lines of personal leather goods. Amity and Rolfs billfolds for men and checkbook clutch purses for women are fixtures in department and specialty stores ranging from discount outlets to fashionable high-end shops. In recent years the company has made a big splash with its Macro Bag, a miniature purse that found a huge market among the fashion-conscious crowd that had previously looked to other brands. AR Accessories, known until 1996 as Amity Leather Products Company, is privately owned. It is based in the Milwaukee, Wisconsin area.

AR Accessories was formed as Amity Leather Products Company in 1915, by Robert H. Rolfs. Convinced that he could improve upon the personal leather goods that were being sold at the time, Rolfs rented a room upstairs from Peters' Store on Main Street in West Bend, Wisconsin, and using his entire life savings of a few dollars, he began designing, manufacturing, marketing, and selling his line of leather accessories. With the idea that fine leather goods made excellent gifts, he wanted to give his company a name that reflected the friendliness of gift giving. He eventually found just the right word to communicate that idea: Amity.

Early Expansion

Rolfs incorporated the Amity Leather Products Company in February of 1916, with initial capital stock of $25,000. Within a year the company had outgrown its one-room headquarters.

Rolfs moved the operation in 1917 to another West Bend location, the third floor of the Hangartner Building. By that time Rolfs had 15 employees. Later that year he established a sales office in New York, from where the company's sales force could better service East Coast accounts. By the following year Amity was again bursting at the seams. The company expanded into the first and second floors of the Hangartner Building, which provided enough space for a work force that had grown to 50 people.

With the entrance of the United States into World War I, Amity shifted its operations to wartime production. Under government contract, the company began making leather jackets for military use. Returning to civilian production at the end of the war, Amity found demand for its goods higher than ever. Business continued to boom, and the company's sales force grew to 20 people, covering the entire United States from coast to coast. In 1924 Amity built and moved into an entirely new building of its own, on South Main St. in West Bend, outfitted with state-of-the-art leather goods manufacturing equipment. The new plant was staffed by 165 production workers, plus another 13 employees to handle clerical duties.

At about the same time Amity was moving into its new home, the company also began advertising its wares in magazines with nationwide circulation. These early ads used a line that would become the company's slogan for decades to come: "If stamped Amity it's leather." The ads helped shift company sales, already brisk, into even higher gear. Another expansion of company headquarters took place in 1930.

Revolutionized Wallets During Depression

While the Depression emptied out a lot of wallets, it had no apparent effect on the demand for the wallets themselves. Amity continued to grow steadily during the 1930s, emerging during that decade as the largest personal leather goods manufacturer in the country. In 1932 the company introduced a new line of high quality billfolds named for its founder. The Rolfs line was an instant success, and within a few short years merchandise labeled "Rolfs" was being sold by more than 5,000 dealers nationwide. Two years later Amity acquired the LaGarde Handbag Company and moved it to West Bend, where it operated as The LaGarde Division. The handbag operation was later renamed the Rolfs Handbag Division.

In 1937 Amity introduced a product that changed the wallet industry forever. Called the "Director," this new billfold was the first to include a number of features that have since become standard. Among the new wrinkles that the "Director" brought to the wallet market were the secret pocket, spare key pockets, and the "Findex" for cards and photos. As the first billfold designed to hold anything other than cash, the "Director" can be largely credited with turning the wallet into the multipurpose container it is for most men today. The "Director" quickly became the best-selling billfold the world had ever seen and the design against which all subsequent billfolds would be compared.

Amity added another new product, the travel kit, to its line in 1940. This addition took place through the company's purchase of the Eiseman-Kaye Company, which was known primarily for making a kit called the "Fitall." The Fitall soon became one of Amity's anchor products. Two years later the government again asked the company to retool its operation for wartime production. As a leather goods manufacturer, there was plenty the company could produce for military use without making too many adjustments. Among the products Amity manufactured during World War II were leather handbags for WAVES, WACS, and Army Nurses. Meanwhile, company founder Rolfs turned his attention to hawking War Bonds for the U.S. Treasury Department, a task for which he was officially thanked by the president.

Postwar Boom Brings New Products, Big Sales

In the hope of capitalizing on the sense of prosperity felt by many Americans after the end of World War II, Amity announced, to great media fanfare, the introduction of the world's first $100 billfold. The billfold was made of a special leather and embellished with a solid gold bar suitable for engraving the owner's signature. By 1946 the company was ready to expand yet again. A new plant was purchased in the Wisconsin city of Sturgeon Bay. A year later another plant went into operation in that town. Amity's handbag and travel kit manufacturing operations were moved to Sturgeon Bay.

Amity's expansion continued into the 1950s, as the company added space and manufacturing capacity to its West Bend and Sturgeon Bay facilities. In 1959 the company built a new administrative office building in West Bend, adjacent to its South Main St. manufacturing and office compound. Robert Rolfs died in 1965, exactly half a century after launching his company. Although shares of the company were available to the public for much of its history, and employees were able to acquire additional stock though a retirement plan, the Rolfs family, including longtime chairman Tom Rolfs, remained in control of Amity into the 1990s.

Although Amity continued to dominate the market for mid-priced personal leather goods into the 1970s, competition from European and Japanese manufactures began to heat up by this time. In response, Amity set out to explore new markets overseas. In 1976 the company established an international division to market its products outside of the United States. Meanwhile, Amity continued to advertise regularly in general interest magazines like *Look* and *Life,* emphasizing the expert craftsmanship

that went into the making of their products. Growth remained steady, and in 1980 the company again found it necessary to enlarge its West Bend administrative building.

The 1980s: A Time for Image-Polishing

By the 1980s the market for mid-priced leather accessories was worth about $450 million, and Amity remained firmly in command of it. In addition to competition from foreign firms, however, Amity was beginning to face pressure from the trend among domestic competitors, such as Prince Gardner and Buxton, toward moving production operations overseas to take advantage of cheaper manufacturing costs. Rather than follow suit, Amity chose to focus on promoting its quality rather than competing strictly on price. "We built our business on quality products," Chairman Tom Rolfs was quoted as saying in *Adweek's Marketing Week,* "and we don't think we can maintain that quality by going overseas."

Instead, the company launched its most aggressive advertising campaign ever. In 1988 Amity produced a series of full-page color magazine ads that focused heavily on craftsmanship, using the tagline "Good Things Last." The following year Amity switched gears in its advertising and, instead, began to point more toward their products' prestige and fashion values. Focusing on style rather than quality, the company hoped the ads would appeal to women, who made up 85 percent of the customers for Rolfs products, despite the fact that nearly half of the company's sales were of products used by men.

Since personal leather goods are notorious for being bought mainly on impulse—very few shoppers make a special trip to buy a wallet or purse—Amity also concentrated on the way its products were displayed in stores. It was Tom Rolfs who pioneered the vertical billfold stand that is now the standard way to display a billfold in a department store or general merchandise outlet. By the end of the 1980s goods bearing the Rolfs brand name could be found across the entire spectrum of dealers, from Sears to Lord & Taylor. The price range for Rolfs' women's products—the chief item among them being the Rolfs retriever checkbook clutch bag—was $12 to $51, while men's leather accessories—mainly billfolds—sold for between $10 and $38. To support sales, Amity provided these stores with detailed sales guides that contained merchandising suggestions as well as comprehensive product information covering materials and construction.

New Ownership and a Hot Bag in the 1990s

Amity eventually did move part of its manufacturing operation to the Far East, but much of it also remained in Wisconsin. In 1990 the company finished work on a design center—an extension of its West Bend complex—that housed not only Amity's design staff but an employee fitness center as well. Two years later the Rolfs family, led by Chairman Tom Rolfs and President Robert Rolfs, sold their interest in the company to a management group led by John Rozek, who became Amity's president and chief executive officer. It did not take long for the new owners to strike gold. In 1993 the company came out with its "Macro Bag," a sort of mini-purse small enough to wear under a coat, yet big enough to carry a checkbook, glasses, and other essential handbag items. At four-and-a-half by seven inches, it was described in promotional material as "a wallet on a string."

The Macro Bag became an instant fashion sensation, quickly outselling the clutch bag that had been Amity's anchor women's product for years. The company originally planned to make just 30,000 of the bags, but immediately after they were introduced high-end department stores all over the country were clamoring for more. Amity, previously known more for sturdiness than style, was suddenly trendy. The company ended up selling about 400,000 Macro Bags by the end of 1993, at $25 to $45 a pop. The *Milwaukee Journal* quoted Cathy Loid, a buyer for major department store company P. A. Bergner, as saying, "This (the Macro Bag) is the hottest thing to hit this industry in 10 years."

By the mid-1990s Amity was producing a wide range of accessories under the brand names Amity, Rolfs, LaGarde, and Vangarde. In 1994 the company purchased the Connecticut-based New England Accessories, acquiring in the process the license to make the Duck Head Apparel line of personal leather goods. New England Accessories also produced a line of belts and suspenders.

In 1995 Rozek was promoted to the new position of vice-chairman. He was succeeded as president and chief executive officer of Amity by Lawrence Slowik, who previously worked as an independent management consultant. The year 1996 was one of transition for Amity under Slowik. In June, Amity officials announced that the company would leave West Bend, the only home it had ever known, for a location closer to Milwaukee. It was hoped that moving to a new site closer to Milwaukee's Mitchell International Airport would make it easier to serve the company's far-flung customers on the coasts and in other remote markets.

In August of 1996 the company announced that it had adopted a new corporate name, AR Accessories Group, Inc., marking the first name change in its history. Of the change, Slowik was quoted by *Business Wire* as saying, "We're very proud of the Amity name, but it is closely identified with only one of our product lines. Our new name . . . better reflects both the current scope of the company's products and opportunities

for future growth." By this time AR had 1,200 employees scattered among its Wisconsin production and distribution facilities, manufacturing plants in Puerto Rico and Ireland, and a national sales office in New York. The company also owned 75 Wallet Works factory outlet stores located across the United States.

Meanwhile, AR Accessories found a new location that suited its needs. The company sold its West Bend building to the West Bend School District and moved its corporate headquarters into a facility in Brown Deer, Wisconsin, a northern suburb of Milwaukee. From its new base of operations, AR hopes to continue to dominate the personal leather goods niche that it virtually created and has led for most of the 20th century.

Principal Divisions

Amity; Rolfs.

Further Reading

"Amity Leather Products Company Changes Name to AR Accessories Group, Inc.," *Business Wire*, August 29, 1996.

"Amity Leather To Leave Its Roots," *Wisconsin State Journal*, June 22, 1996.

Bednarek, David I., "Amity Leather Bags a Best-Seller," *Milwaukee Journal*, October 31, 1993.

Davis, Anne, "Amity Runs in the Family for West Bend's Conrads," *Milwaukee Journal Sentinel*, September 5, 1997.

Duggleby, John, "Challenged by Foreign Competitors, Rolfs Fights Back With Force," *Adweek's Marketing Week*, December 11, 1989, p. 28.

Gray, Jacquelyn, "Amity Makes a Big Splash With the Macro Bag," *Milwaukee Journal*, July 17, 1994, p. G8.

"The History of the Amity Leather Products Company," *40th Anniversary, Amity Leather Products Company*, West Bend, Wis.: Amity Leather Products Co., 1955.

McKinney, Melonee, "New Halston Small Leather Goods for Fall '98," *Daily News Record*, November 7, 1997, p. 18.

Schuldt, Gretchen, "Wisconsin's AR Accessories Sues Former Shareholders Over Tax Payments," *Milwaukee Journal Sentinel*, August 29, 1997.

—Robert R. Jacobson

Atari Corporation

**455 South Mathilda Avenue
Sunnyvale, California 94086
U.S.A.**

*Formerly a Wholly Owned Subsidiary of JTS
   Corporation*
Incorporated: 1972
SICs: 3571 Electronic Computers; 3944 Games, Toys &
   Children's Vehicles; 7372 Prepackaged Software

Before its merger with disk drive maker JTS Corporation in 1996 the Atari Corporation was a prominent manufacturer of video games and home computers that pioneered the industry of video entertainment. Its history was beset by a series of successes and defeats: it made money from arcade games, then nearly went bankrupt; it took on new life and astronomical profits in the early 1980s, only to see its industry crash once again, leaving the company to rebuild slowly under different management and then finally succumb to the rise of the PC-based CD-ROM as the preferred medium for computer games.

Nolan Bushnell's Game: 1972–75

Atari was founded by Nolan Bushnell in 1972. Bushnell had first become interested in computer games as an engineering student at the University of Utah. After graduation, he worked as a researcher in a Silicon Valley firm, and there he developed his first electronic game, called Computer Space, in 1971. Although this game, like all the other fledgling products before it, was not a commercial success, Bushnell used $500 to start a company with a friend anyway, naming it Atari, a term from the Japanese game of "go" used to politely alert opponents that they are about to be overrun.

Bushnell's second game was a revolutionary development, in that it was far simpler than other games had been. Called "Pong," it was an electronic version of ping pong, played on a screen with a vertical line down the middle and two sliding paddles that batted a blip back and forth. The company first marketed a coin-operated version of this game in 1972 for use in arcades. Since the game could be played by two people in direct competition with each other, Pong was a dramatic departure from the solitary skills of pinball, and it changed the nature of arcade games.

Unfortunately, Atari was unable to reap the rewards of this advance, since dozens of competitors quickly duplicated the game and grabbed a large portion of the market. Within two years of Pong's introduction, its inventors had sold only ten percent of the machines in existence.

Atari channeled the profits it had made into ventures that turned out to be shortsighted and nonproductive. The company wasted half a million dollars on an abortive attempt to market its products in Japan. In addition, it sunk resources into an attempt to open game arcades in Hawaii. Although Atari introduced a series of new games to follow Pong, formulated in the company's informal, unstructured atmosphere, none caught on as its first offering had.

Video games for use in the home had first been introduced by Magnavox in 1972, and Atari decided that a logical next step would be to introduce a home version of Pong, to be played on a television screen. Short of funds, the company worked out an arrangement with Sears, Roebuck & Company for the retailer to buy all 100,000 of the devices that Atari manufactured, as well as helping out with funding for Atari's inventories, to guarantee delivery. In the fall of 1975, the home version of Pong was introduced.

Enter Warner Communications: 1976–80

Clearly, Atari needed further funds to expand. Rather than sell stock to the public, the company decided to look for a buyer. In 1976, after four months of legal wrangling complicated by a lawsuit filed against Bushnell by his first wife, Atari was sold to Warner Communications Inc. for $28 million. Of this, Pong's inventor collected about $15 million.

By the next year, however, Atari's problems had moved beyond funding. The company's products at the time could be used to play only one game, and consumers were beginning to feel that the novelty of playing that one game had worn off. In late 1977, however, Atari's researchers introduced the Video Computer System, or VCS 2600, which used a semiconductor chip in a programmable device. With this product, the customer gained versatility. Any number of games could be played on cartridges, which were inserted into the set like cassette tapes.

Introduced shortly before the big Christmas selling season, the new games initially failed to conclusively dislodge the old, single-purpose products. In addition, the company had come up against steep competition from several of its competitors, who had also introduced multipurpose video game equipment. Throughout 1978, Atari saw its new product languish on the shelves.

This disappointing news was compounded by administrative confusion at company headquarters. Original Atari employees felt no loyalty toward their new bosses, and top administrators also disagreed with some of Warner's key decisions. After a chaotic budget meeting in New York, Bushnell was ousted from his position as chair of the company.

In his place, executives with backgrounds at large companies were installed, and procedures and practices at Atari became much more businesslike. In an effort to sell off some of the backlogged inventory of slow-moving games that the company had built up, Atari launched a $6 million advertising campaign in the last seven weeks of 1978, designed to clear out inventory and make way for new products.

The strategy worked. At the important, industry-wide Consumer Electronics Show in January 1979, store owners demanded more products to sell. Over the next 12 months, Atari was able to sell all of the game devices it manufactured.

In addition to its game operations, Atari ambitiously branched out into the hotly competitive personal computer field, introducing two models, dubbed the Atari 400 and the Atari 800. These were intended for the home rather than office market. In the company's second year of operation in this field, it lost about $10 million on sales of twice that amount.

With the start of the 1980s, however, Atari's successes in the video game field more than made up for its losses in other areas, as its growth and profits shot up. In January 1980, Atari began an effort to shift the emphasis of the video game industry away from holiday-generated sales, to prove that people were willing to buy video games all year round. To do this, Atari introduced four new video game cartridges late in the first month of the year. The tactic was successful, and demand for the company's product continued to build. By the end of the year, Atari had sold all of the video game machines that it had manufactured. Among its biggest selling cartridges was Space Invaders, an adaptation of a coin-operated arcade game originally designed in Japan.

New Games, New Markets, New Competition: 1980–83

Atari's arcade operations were also going strong. In 1980, the company introduced Asteroids to compete with the Space Invaders arcade game, which was produced by another company. Atari's version proved to be a popular alternative. By the end of the year, 70,000 of the units had been shipped. Overall, revenues from coin-operated games reached $170 million, up from $52 million the year before. In addition to its arcade business, in 1980 Atari also began to explore the market for its products overseas. The company's overall revenues had more than doubled in just one year, topping $415 million, and its operating income had increased by five times.

Because the sale of video cartridges was extremely profitable, Atari introduced new games at a steady pace, releasing titles at the rate of one per month. In 1981, with demand running at feverish pitch, the company decided to ration its product. More than one million cartridges of Space Invaders had been sold. All in all, with its competitors falling by the wayside, Atari was the world's largest producer of video games, holding 80 percent of the American market. At the end of 1981, the company had sold more than $740 million worth of video game equipment and cartridges. In addition, its home computer operations had become profitable, and Atari products dominated the sales of low-priced machines.

To protect its strong market position in the video game field, Atari also began an aggressive effort to shut down video game pirates by taking legal action against them. In November 1981, the company won an important case against a company that was selling a copycat "Centipede" game.

Although Atari was aggressive in introducing lucrative new software, it lagged behind in marketing new hardware. Essentially, the company had not followed its introduction of the Video Computer System with a second, more sophisticated generation, except to produce a remote-control model, known as Touch Me, that cost $100 more than the basic set.

The introduction of a Pac-Man cartridge in the spring of 1982, however, helped to stave off these concerns, as the company estimated that it would sell nine million of the games, to reap over $200 million in that year alone. Pac-Man was a breakthrough game, attracting many women and families to the video game market for the first time, and thereby expanding the industry's consumer base. In the fall of that year, Atari also took steps to update its game equipment, introducing a more elaborate version of its game machine, which sold for $350. It also quadrupled its sales of personal computers. In general, Atari poured tens of millions of dollars into research and development, in an effort to stay out in front of the competitive industry.

Despite these efforts, however, by the end of 1982, Atari's rise in the industry, which many had believed would continue indefinitely, had been checked. Competition in the video games industry had expanded dramatically, as new companies rushed into the lucrative field. Now, Atari faced more than 30 other game makers, some of which had lured away the company's top game designers, a damaging loss in a field where innovation was suddenly as important as distribution. On December 8, 1982, Atari's corporate parent, Warner Communications, announced that previous sales estimates would not be met because of "unexpected cancellations and disappointing sales during the first week of December," as the *New York Times* reported at the time. In the wake of this sudden news, the company's stock value dropped precipitously, and several Atari executives were later investigated for insider stock trading, since they had sold off large blocks of stock just before the announcement.

Following this setback, Atari announced in February 1983, that it would fire 1,700 U.S. workers in order to move manufacturing facilities to Hong Kong and Taiwan. This move set off a wave of protest. In the financial community, it was taken as the sign of a company adrift, since Atari had hired 2,500 new U.S. workers just the year before in a campaign to build up its domestic production capacity, only to undo itself a short time later.

In addition, Atari found itself being challenged by competitors in its home computer business. In May 1983, the company reduced the price of its outmoded 400 computer by two-thirds, from $299 to $100. By the end of its first quarter, losses overall had reached $46 million. In an effort to restore some of the original creative luster to Atari, the company announced an agreement with ousted founder Nolan Bushnell to sell consumer versions of the coin-operated games he was developing in his new business.

By September 1983, quarterly losses had reached $180.3 million, and its nine-month losses reached $536.4 million. The company ended the year with overall losses of $538.6 million on sales of $1.12 billion, half its previous year sales of $2 billion.

Turnaround under Jack Tramiel: 1984–87

To stem Atari's losses, Warner brought in a new head executive who fired more than half the company's 10,000 employees. Nevertheless, costs could not be brought in line with revenues, and the company needed an infusion of further funds to pay for research on new products. Unable to support this continuing drain on its resources, Warner Communications began to look for a buyer for its failing subsidiary. In July 1984, the company announced that it had agreed to sell all Atari operations, with the exception of the small coin-operated arcade video game business and a new telecommunications venture, called Ataritel, to Jack Tramiel, a businessperson who had made his reputation as the head of Commodore International, Ltd., a computer company. The price for Atari was $240 million.

Three days after purchasing the company, Tramiel began his own aggressive effort to cut costs, laying off hundreds more employees and taking steps to collect outstanding funds owed to the company. Unable to sell unwanted video game cartridges, Atari dumped truckloads of them into a landfill in New Mexico. Tramiel installed three of his sons in top management positions, brought in former associates to fill other key spots, and made plans to raise funds through the sale of stock to the public. To Tramiel, Atari was poised to become a computer manufacturer to rival his previous company, despite the fact that its extant computer offering, the 800XL, was outmoded and less powerful than its competitors.

In January 1985, Atari unveiled two new lines of home computers, the XE series—an improved version of the old 800XL made cheaper by a reduction in the number of components and renegotiated contracts with suppliers—and the ST line, a cut-rate imitation of the Apple Macintosh, that used a color screen, fancy graphics, and a mouse, in an effort to move

in on the market for Apple computers in the home. By July, the 520-ST had started to make its way into stores. The computer arrived past schedule, with no advertising to announce its presence, and no software to demonstrate its capabilities. Many machines in the first shipment did not work at all because microchips inside had been shaken loose in transit. Nevertheless, with a price of $799, the product initially seemed to have found a receptive public, with a large percentage of sales taking place in Europe.

Despite this good news, Tramiel continued to run Atari in crisis mode. The company's U.S. staff had shrunk to 150, and in May 1985, executives agreed to have one-third of their salaries withheld indefinitely. The company finished out 1985 posting a loss of $26.7 million.

By 1986, the industry in which Atari originally made its mark, video games, was beginning to show signs of life once again. This time, however, product lines were led by sophisticated, expensive Japanese equipment, sold by companies such as Nintendo and Sega. Atari re-entered the field with its old machine, the VCS 2600, which sold for only $40, and also introduced the 7800, a more advanced unit, which sold for twice as much. The company also began a modest advertising campaign for these products for the first time in two years. By the end of the year, these efforts, combined with Atari's home computer sales, had resulted in profits of $45 million, on sales of $258 million. With these strong results, the company was able to offer stock to the public for the first time in November 1986.

With these funds, Atari increased its advertising budget in support of new products it introduced. In 1987, the company began to market a clone of IBM's PC, priced at under $500, as well as a more sophisticated video game console, in addition to introducing products for the desktop publishing field. In October 1987, Atari purchased the Federated Group, a chain of 62 electronics stores based in California and the Southwest, for $67 million. Tramiel hoped that the stores could provide a good distribution outlet for Atari products, and he put his youngest son in charge of the chain. Operating in a depressed area of the country, however, Federated continued to lose money, and the company was forced to shut the stores after just one year.

At the end of 1987, Atari held 20 percent of the U.S. video game market and relied on foreign sales of its home computers, which remained unpopular in the United States, for a significant portion of its income. Overall, the company earned $57 million, on sales that neared $500 million.

Slipping Sales: 1988–93

The following year, Atari once again allied itself with its founder, Nolan Bushnell, agreeing to market video games that he had developed. Furthermore, the company announced another big advertising push, in an effort to ensure that the video game crash that had threatened Atari in the early 1980s would not recur. Atari also turned to the courts in December 1988, charging that Nintendo's licensing policies monopolized the market. These moves reflected the continuing lack of demand for Atari's home computer products in the United States, as the company, hampered by its image as a toymaker rather than a high-tech powerhouse, fought for part of this highly competitive market.

In January 1989, Nintendo followed up Atari's suit with a countersuit charging copyright infringement, and by the end of the year, the dispute had reached the U.S. House of Representatives, whose subcommittee on anti-trust echoed Atari's charges. In November 1989, Atari continued its push into the game market by introducing a portable video game player called Lynx, which sold for $200, to compete with Nintendo's popular Game Boy. The company finished out the year with earnings of $4.02 million.

In the spring of 1990, Atari introduced its Portfolio palmtop personal computer. Early the following year, the company came out with a revamped, color Lynx product, and several months later it introduced new notebook computers. Despite these advances, however, Atari was in trouble. Sales of its home computers in Europe began to flag as the company faced increased competition, and in 1991 foreign sales collapsed. In the video games field, Atari's efforts to challenge Nintendo through legal means had been rebuffed, and the company was unable to regain significant market share from its Japanese competitors. By the first quarter of 1992, losses over a three-month period had reached $14 million.

In September 1992, Atari took steps to stem its losses by cutting its research and development expenditures in half and closing branch offices in three states. The company hoped that the introduction of new products, such as the Falcon030 multimedia home entertainment computer would help to revive its fortunes. In addition, the company was working on a more sophisticated video game machine, called the "Jaguar." Nevertheless, 1992 ended with a loss of $73 million.

As Atari began to ship its Falcon030 system to stores in small numbers in early 1993, the company's fate was unclear. Decidedly, it was experiencing another severe downturn, which by the summer had snowballed into what the *San Jose Mercury News* called a full-fledged financial meltdown: between the second quarters of 1992 and 1993 Atari's sales plummeted 76 percent to only $5.7 million. Sales of its hand-held Lynx games were poor and its Falcon systems were barely visible in the PC marketplace. Atari's hopes now rested on the vaunted 64-bit technology of its soon-to-be-unveiled Jaguar game system, which promised to unseat Sega and Nintendo with the next generation of "high-performance interactive multimedia."

Atari Unravels: 1993–96

In June 1993, IBM signed a $500 million deal with Atari to manufacture Jaguar's hardware, and the first sets hit stores in November. As Jaguar tested the marketplace in 1994, Atari settled a licensing dispute with Nintendo by way of an agreement with former parent Time Warner to raise its stake in Atari to 27 percent. Atari also licensed Jaguar to Sigma Design of California, whose full-motion video technology promised to enable Atari to make the jump from dedicated video game players to the home PC. In September 1994, arch rival Sega also agreed to pay Atari $90 million for the rights to Atari's 70 U.S. game patents. Finally, a partnership with Britain's Virtuality

Group seemed to promise a new cutting-edge application for the Jaguar platform: Atari and Virtuality would design a 3-D virtual reality home gaming system to debut in 1995. Within a year of Jaguar's introduction Atari boasted 30 titles for the system, and in mid-1995 Atari announced a CD accessory that would allow CD-ROM games to be played on the Jaguar platform.

All Atari's partnerships and cross-platform efforts, however, could not convince consumers to abandon Sega's Saturn and Nintendo's Playstation for Jaguar, and in October 1995 Atari announced that third quarter revenues had fallen a brutal 40 percent from the previous year. Atari responded by slashing Jaguar's retail price and announcing "Atari Interactive," a new division to make CD-ROM video games for PCs. But the writing was on the wall, and in January 1996 Jaguar was pulled from the U.S. market.

A month later Atari announced that JTS Corporation, a San Jose-based disk drive maker whose 1994 startup Jack Tramiel had helped fund, would merge with Atari in June. Although Atari publicly maintained that it would continue to market video game consoles and software as a JTS's Atari Division, it soon became clear that Atari's attraction for JTS was not its game technology but its still sizable cash reserves, which JTS would tap to battle disk drive competitors like Seagate and Quantum.

When the JTS merger was finalized in mid-1996 Atari's staff was gutted by 80 percent and its assets liquidated. Some Atari titles lived on through its licensing agreement with Sega, but by the end of 1996 Atari's quarter-century history as an early video entertainment pioneer had come to an end.

Further Reading

Bernstein, Peter W., "Atari and the Video-Game Explosion," *Fortune,* July 27, 1981.

Biggs, Brooke Shelby, "Success Killed Pac-Man Creator Atari," *Business Journal Serving San Jose and Silicon Valley,* July 22, 1996, p. 1A.

Chronis, George, "The Game's Over for Goldstar, Atari in Next-Gen War," *Video Store Magazine,* January 28, 1996, p. 1.

"Game Maker to Merge: Pong Pioneer to Unite with JTS Corp.," *San Jose Mercury News,* February 14, 1996.

Hector, Gary, "The Big Shrink Is On at Atari," *Fortune,* July 9, 1984.

Machan, Dyan, "Cheap Didn't Sell," *Forbes,* August 3, 1992.

Petre, Peter, "Jack Tramiel Is Back on the Warpath," *Fortune,* March 4, 1985.

Shao, Maria, "Jack Tramiel Has Atari Turned Around—Halfway," *Business Week,* June 20, 1988.

——, "There's a Rumble in the Video Arcade," *Business Week,* February 20, 1989.

"U.S. Video Game Firm Gets Back in the Action," *Miami Herald,* November 7, 1993.

"Video Games Are Suddenly a $2 Billion Industry," *Business Week,* May 24, 1982.

"What Sent Atari Overseas," *Business Week,* March 14, 1983.

—Elizabeth Rourke
—updated by Paul S. Bodine

Atlanta Gas Light Company

303 Peachtree Street, N.E.
Atlanta, Georgia 30308-3251
U.S.A.
(404) 584-4000
Fax: (404) 584-3709
Web site: http://www.aglr.com

Wholly Owned Subsidiary of AGL Resources Inc.
Incorporated: 1856
Employees: 2,986
Sales: $1.28 billion (1997; combined for AGL Resources
    Inc.)
SICs: 4924 Natural Gas Distribution

Atlanta Gas Light Company is the southeastern United States' largest natural gas distribution company. It serves more than 1.3 million customers in 229 Georgia communities and more than 51,000 customers in Chattanooga and Cleveland, Tennessee. Its predominant business is gas distribution, but the company also has several diversified operations. In 1996, the company was restructured such that it became the principal subsidiary of a new holding company, AGL Resources Services Company, which also oversaw the operations of the newly formed AGL Investments, Inc., The Energy Spring, Inc., and AGL Energy Services, Inc.

Mid-19th-Century Origins

Atlanta Gas Light got its start in 1855 when William Helme, an enterprising Philadelphian who had already built several gas retorts, persuaded the Atlanta City Council and several influential Atlanta citizens to invest in a private corporation to build a street-lighting system for the city. Helme built his gas plant and laid three miles of main, and by the end of 1855 gas lamps could be seen on the city's streets. Julius Hayden became the company's first president, and gas lights rapidly became popular in Atlanta homes and businesses. City officials were happy with their investment, because stock dividends were paying the city's entire street lighting bill. Five years later, when the Civil War broke out, stock held by northern investors, including Helme, was declared "alien" and sold to the highest bidder. As the war progressed, coal, and therefore gas, grew short. When General Sherman took the city, the gasworks was burned to the ground.

After the war, the company reconstituted and elected former *Atlanta Intelligencer* editor John W. Duncan president. Duncan issued bonds and completed massive repairs that culminated on September 15, 1866, when the gas plant went back into service.

In the late 1860s, Atlanta was rebuilt. Northerners flowed south and the city began to grow. By the early 1870s Hayden, who had returned to the presidency after Duncan's death in 1869, was expanding service and adding to gas-producing capacity. Hayden's relationship with the city council, populated by members of the company's board, was at times antagonistic. The council even threatened to grant another company a franchise.

In 1873 a panic hit the stock market. During the depression that followed, Hayden was forced to repeatedly lower residential and street-lighting rates. Meanwhile, the city council turned off street lights to cut costs and asked the gas company rather than the police department to light and extinguish lamps. The former action caused a public outcry, while the latter did not result in expected savings.

The Healey Years, 1877–97

In 1877 brick manufacturer and construction executive Thomas G. Healey became gas company president. His term was marked by several momentous changes. In 1884 the Gate City Company erected the Gate City Gas Works and began advertising for customers, claiming its "water gas" was better than Atlanta Gas Light's "coal gas." Healey in turn slashed rates and appealed to Atlantans' loyalty. Within a year the price of a thousand cubic feet of gas fell from $2.40 to $1.00.

In 1887 Atlanta, which had profited greatly from its one-third ownership of the company, sold its shares to raise funds for the Georgia Institute of Technology. The following year the city council resolved to replace gas and gasoline lights with incandescent electric lights. Healey, who was doing a far greater business with private individuals and firms, responded to the incursion of the electric light by introducing the recently invented Welsbach Mantle, a cone of incombustible minerals that considerably brightened the relatively dim gas light.

On April 13, 1889, the United Gas Improvement Company (UGI), which months previously had bought the Gate City Gas Works, announced it had gained control of Atlanta Gas Light. Healey remained as president, and Atlanta Gas Light continued to grow and prosper.

Healey and John H. Mecaslin, who replaced him as president in 1897, surmised that electric light would eventually replace the gas light, so throughout the 1890s they worked to introduce the gas stove. But Atlantans stuck to their coal stoves despite offers of completely installed gas stoves for as little as ten dollars. Not until the anthracite coal strike of 1902, when coal could not be bought at any price, did large numbers of customers switch to gas cookstoves, which eventually became a bigger business than gas lighting had ever been. In mid-1903, after the great switch-over, the company had 122 miles of mains, 11,000 customers, and an average daily send-out of 1.6 million cubic feet.

Decades of Changes, 1900s–20s

In July of that year Georgia Railway and Electric Company (GR&E), a trust that had already consolidated Atlanta's steam, street railway, and electric light and power operations, gained control of Atlanta Gas Light. GR&E president Preston Arkwright became the de facto head of Atlanta Gas Light and in 1904, W. L. Cosgrove was named company president. This new company was extremely unpopular because of its "foreign" ownership. The Hearst-owned newspaper, the *Georgian,* and politicians such as James L. Key, soon began calling for municipal ownership.

The rhetoric of Key and others did little to modify the behavior of Arkwright, who appointed customer-oriented R. C. Congdon manager but continued to manipulate Atlanta Gas Light. In 1912, he and his associates reorganized their Georgia holdings to better exploit their capital-raising potential. They consolidated various hydroelectric projects under a new company called Georgia Railway and Power (GR&P) which in turn guaranteed itself the Atlanta market, and therefore access to capital, by leasing the properties of GR&E.

When, during World War I, coal quality diminished and the government demanded that gas companies extract Tulol from gas for TNT manufacture, Arkwright claimed he could do nothing about the high-priced, low-BTU product that resulted. Nevertheless, when the Railroad Commission ordered the company to buy better gas, quality increased.

After the war Arkwright asked for, and got, three rate increases between 1918 and 1920. This incited protests from the *Georgian* and from Key, who by then was mayor. This situation reversed itself in the deflationary early 1920s, when the commission ordered two rate reductions, the second of which Arkwright fought all the way to the Supreme Court.

Ownership of Atlanta Gas Light changed hands several times in the second half of the 1920s. In April 1926 GR&P became the property of Southeastern Power and Light Company. In a series of mergers, Southeastern combined its extensive Georgia utility holdings into a new company called Georgia Power. Finally, in May 1929, Georgia Power sold Atlanta Gas Light to Central Public Service Corporation of Chicago.

Central Public Service Corporation President A. E. Pierce became the president of Atlanta Gas Light. M. L. Kane, who formerly managed Georgia Power's "gas department," became Atlanta Gas Light's manager.

Other changes followed. In 1928 Southern Natural Gas of Birmingham announced plans to build a natural gas pipeline from Louisiana to Atlanta and offer higher BTU natural gas at lower prices than Atlanta Gas Light. Southern's plan might have bankrupted Atlanta Gas Light; however, Pierce went to Atlanta and successfully gained the natural gas franchise on March 29, 1929.

In the months that followed, the company renovated its old gas lines and built new ones to the Southern Natural lines on the outskirts of the city. R. C. Hoffman, Central Public Service's on-site representative, hired a new gas manager and a professional sales manager. His capital budget for 1930 alone was approximately $2 million.

The excitement and activity which went along with the changeover stimulated business. In 1929 the company sent out a total of 200 million cubic feet of 550 BTU manufactured gas. In 1930 it sent out 274 million cubic feet of 1000 BTU natural gas. In equivalent BTUs, the 1930 send-out doubled that of 1929.

In the midst of this huge expansion, the Depression hit. At first the slowdown seemed to have little effect. In 1930 the customer count rose 15 percent to 49,238, but then customer rolls fell to 47,583 and 46,089 in 1931 and 1932, respectively. The Depression had a larger effect on Central Public Service, which to shore up its finances sold worthless stock and for accounting purposes shifted Atlanta Gas Light first to its United States Electric and Gas Company subsidiary and then to its New York-based Consolidated Electric and Gas subsidiary.

In January 1935, W. W. Winter, a Central Public Service vice-president, became president of Atlanta Gas Light. Winter supervised several mid-1930s gains in business. He formed crews of "House Warmers" who went door-to-door selling gas radiators, and he convinced factories that higher-BTU natural gas was a good source of energy. While Winter struggled to keep Atlanta Gas Light growing, Congress was passing the Public Utilities Holding Company Act of 1935 (PUHCA), which prohibited holding companies from owning more than one integrated utility system. PUHCA ultimately gave Atlanta Gas Light its independence and initially led Consolidated Electric & Gas to merge its diverse Georgia holdings in preparation for divestiture.

The Era of Mergers, 1930s–40s

On July 1, 1937, H. Carl Wolf, who became president in August 1938, supervised a merger with the Georgia Natural Gas Corporation. Then, on March 1, 1941, Consolidated Electric and Gas merged its remaining Georgia gas companies— Georgia Public Utilities Company and Macon Gas Company— into Atlanta Gas Light. After this transaction, Atlanta Gas Light served 102,859 customers and 28 cities and towns, including two in South Carolina.

Final divestiture was delayed by World War II, which also caused labor shortages at the company. After the war, Central Public Service attempted to satisfy the Act's requirements by selling Atlanta Gas Light to Southern Natural Gas. This transaction was canceled when Georgia regulators informed the Securities and Exchange Commission (SEC) that Southern Natural might be controlled by the same people who controlled Central Public Service.

Finally, on November 1, 1947, after 58 years of holding company control, Atlanta Gas Light once again became an independent, investor-owned utility. Under the SEC-approved plan, Atlanta Gas Light was spun off to Consolidated Electric & Gas's preferred shareholders. At its independence Atlanta Gas Light served 33 incorporated cities, and had net earnings of $1.5 million and $14 million in revenues.

In the postwar period, the Georgia economy boomed and gas-powered appliances sold briskly. Atlanta Gas Light extended service, adding towns and signing up more than 35,000 new customers in 1949 and 1950. Rock Granite Tabor, who became company president in 1945, responded to increased demand by converting the remaining coal gas facilities to higher BTU water gas; building peak-shaving facilities to add propane to the gas flow when supplies grew short; signing contracts to increase the amount of gas the company obtained from Southern Natural Gas; and bringing a second pipeline supplier, Transcontinental Gas Pipeline Corporation, to Georgia.

The new pipelines allowed the company to offer natural gas in areas previously served by manufactured gas. Demand continued to increase, and in 1957 Tabor built a new peak-shaving facility in rural Riverdale. He soon added other peak-shaving facilities, and by the end of 1957 the customer count reached 322,000.

Expansion and Industry Shortages, the Lee Tenure: 1960–76

In February 1960 Tabor was succeeded by Duncan A. Crawford, a longtime Atlanta Gas Light vice-president and former employee of Stone & Webster, a consulting firm which the company often relied on for management expertise. Crawford served for less than a year before retiring; he was replaced by Wallace L. Lee, a trained engineer and the first native Georgian ever to head Atlanta Gas Light.

Lee was a dynamo of an executive. He soon reorganized and energized the sales department, wrote new, customer-friendly main and service line extension rules, began selling gas lights, retained an advertising agency, and announced plans to build a 150-mile pipeline that ultimately brought natural gas to 37 previously unserved southeast Georgia communities. Lee's aggressive style was suited to a time when the electric industry was using hardball tactics to promote the all-electric home. He sold new gas-powered appliances such as air conditioners, and through a builder consultant sales force he persuaded builders to outfit new homes with gas. He successfully fought a Southern Natural rate increase and cut residential rates. Finally, in a controversial move, he sought to sidestep rural Georgia's anti-Atlanta bias by establishing the Georgia Natural Gas trade name for gas sold outside Atlanta.

Throughout the 1960s Lee continued to expand service, in 1964 acquiring the Mid-Georgia and Georgia Natural Gas Companies. With more than 460,000 customers by 1965, Lee further broadened Atlanta Gas Light's base in 1966 by merging with Savannah Gas Company, the oldest gas system in the state. Between 1965 and 1970 the company gained more than 100,000 new customers.

The company's growth was interrupted by the gas shortage of the 1970s, which drove up prices and squeezed company finances. The public utility commission allowed the company to pass along wholesale prices but not the cost of inflation. As a result, earnings fell from $1.61 per share in 1969 to $1.01 in 1970, and were continually pressured, even though the company was granted rate relief four times over the decade.

Lee cut costs and charged for service calls. He expanded and built peak-shaving facilities, constructed a liquefied natural gas facility in Riverdale, called for new exploration, and encouraged consumers to conserve gas. Despite these measures, the supply situation was far from remedied in February 1976, when Joe T. LaBoon succeeded Lee as president. The winter of 1976–77, one of the coldest on record, put extraordinary demands on the company. Reserves grew short, and the company had to cut off industrial users in order not to interrupt residential service.

The Rise and Decline of Prices, Late 1970s–80s

In the late 1970s, supply problems began to ease, and Atlanta Gas Light again began to grow. Unfortunately, skyrocketing prices were one of the side effects of the Natural Gas Policy Act of 1978, which began the deregulation of gas prices at the wellhead and led to a glut in the market. In the five years following the Act's passage, prices increased 159 percent. For the first time gas, long the cheapest fuel, faced price competition from No. 6 fuel oil in industrial markets. Even so, by the end of the decade Atlanta Gas Light had 800,000 customers in more than 200 cities and towns. Following the complete deregulation of natural gas prices at the wellhead in 1985, the company's customers enjoyed a lengthy decline in gas prices. Prices were lower in 1992 than in 1984—even with no adjustment for inflation.

LaBoon, who became CEO in 1980 and chairman in 1985, emphasized service and friendliness. He also initiated an energy assistance program for low-income customers. Still, because the low cost of gas was no longer its biggest selling point, financial pressures continued. The recession of 1982–83 increased the company's difficulties and, despite successive rate increases, brought into question its ability to pay its dividends.

In 1984 the company's financial situation improved along with the Atlanta economy. Prices settled and LaBoon reorganized the company to better supervise its burgeoning nonutility operations. By 1986, David R. Jones—who succeeded LaBoon as president in 1985—could count one million customers on Atlanta Gas Light's rolls.

In the late 1980s, Atlanta Gas Light worked to keep up with Georgia's rapidly expanding economy and population. It came to a regulatory agreement that took into account how changes in weather patterns could affect the company's bottom line. In 1988 it acquired the Chattanooga Gas Light Company, expanding its services into southern Tennessee. Jones, like other natural gas distributors, in the early 1990s promoted natural gas as an environmentally sound source of clean energy for homes and for such new uses as natural gas vehicles.

Despite the regulatory agreement, which helped to even out receipts in unseasonably warm winters such as that of 1988–89, profits at Atlanta Gas Light lagged. Wall Street analysts predicted losses of 35 to 40 cents a share by the end of the 1980s, at a time when the company projected $565 million in capital expenditures over the next five years. Most of that money would be spent on improvements, especially new pipes, along with innovations such as a computerized system for reading meters which would increase meter-reading capacity from 300 a day for a human meter-reader to 3,000 an hour for a computer. The company made such efforts in preparation for the phenomenon of deregulation, soon to hit the gas industry in Georgia.

Opportunity in the Face of Challenge: The 1990s

By 1995, the *Atlanta Journal and Constitution* was asking its readers, "Now that you've chosen a long-distance telephone carrier, are you ready for dinner-hour calls from natural gas companies trying to sell you cheaper home-heating service? That's not as far-fetched as it may sound." Atlanta Gas Light, as the article reported, was not passively facing the transition "from regulated monopoly to a competitive market." In opposition to a group of large industrial customers called Fair Access to Competition Today (FACT), who demanded across-the-board deregulation, Atlanta Gas Light proposed a "competitive pricing" plan in which it would separately negotiate contracts with each of its large industrial clients. Atlanta Gas Light had already experienced a $4 million loss after its largest customer, Arcadia Corporation, took advantage of deregulation in 1993 to connect its Augusta, Georgia, fertilizer plant to an interstate pipeline, thus bypassing the utility. Hence the company had powerful incentive to face deregulation head-on: among the measures it took was downsizing, reducing some 700 jobs and closing down staffed payment offices.

And yet there was opportunity in the face of challenge, symbolized by the fact that in February 1996, Atlanta Gas Light had a record day of sales, when it used 2.043 billion cubic feet of natural gas during a single 24-hour period. Of more significance was the creation, on March 6, of a new parent corporation, AGL Resources Inc. The latter would operate not only Atlanta Gas Light—which remained regulated for the time being—but also nonregulated, nonutility subsidiaries that in-

cluded AGL Investments Inc. and AGL Energy Services Inc. Thus the company would be involved in the distribution and delivery of gas through Atlanta Gas Light, as well as the sales and marketing of it through other subsidiaries.

Atlanta Gas Light had a number of public relations opportunities associated with the 1996 Olympic Games in Atlanta. The company supplied two natural gas-powered press trucks to lead the men's and women's marathon races, which were internationally televised to an audience in the billions. It also built and maintained compressed natural gas (CNG) buses for Atlanta's rapid transit system, MARTA, and these too made their debut during the Olympics. AGL predicted that by the year 2000, the city would have some 200 CNG buses in operation. Atlanta Gas Light engineers, working with a team from Georgia Tech, designed the Olympic torch used to light the Olympic Cauldron, which was also designed by company engineers. Later in the year, the company sent its own public relations ambassador, the mascot "Burnie Blue," on a home safety tour throughout the state.

In October 1996, Atlanta Gas Light encountered a minor difficulty due to a Teamsters' strike, but maintained service levels through the use of management and trained employees in the field as replacements for the striking Teamsters. In April 1997, with the enactment of deregulation by the Georgia General Assembly, the company faced competition from some 55 other marketing companies. But as company leadership told the *Atlanta Journal and Constitution,* deregulation offered plenty of potential. The AGL annual report for 1997 stated that the company expected to see six to seven percent annual growth during the next five years. Expansion would come in areas such as propane distribution, an area in which Jones stated "We'd like to be in the top 10."

Further Reading

Luke, Robert, "Planning a Growth Future: Despite Problems, Utility Believes Good Days Ahead," *Atlanta Journal and Constitution,* September 24, 1989, p. R1.

Quinn, Matthew C., "AGL Sees Potential After Gas Deregulation," *Atlanta Journal and Constitution,* September 25, 1997, p. F3.

——, "Natural Gas Firms to Compete," *Atlanta Journal and Constitution,* September 14, 1997, p. G2.

——, "Tremors in the Gas Industry: Different Rules: As Deregulation Comes Down the Pipe, Atlanta Gas and a Group of Industrial Customers Vie to Shape a New System," *Atlanta Journal and Constitution,* December 9, 1995, p. D1.

Tate, James H., *Keeper of the Flame: The Story of Atlanta Gas Light Company,* Atlanta: Atlanta Gas Light Company, 1985.

—Jordan Wankoff
—updated by Judson Knight

The Atlantic Group

1290 Sixth Avenue
New York, New York 10104
U.S.A.
(212) 707-2000
Web site: http://www.atlantic-records.com

Wholly Owned Subsidiary of Time-Warner Inc.
Incorporated: 1947 as Atlantic Records
Employees: 400
Sales: $750 million (1997)
SICs: 7812 Services-Motion Picture & Video Tape
    Production; 3652 Phonograph Records & Prerecorded
    Audio Tapes & Disks; 7389 Services-Business
    Services, Not Elsewhere Classified

The Atlantic Group consistently ranks among the most successful recording companies in the United States. Atlantic has helped shape popular culture for more than 50 years and has recorded hundreds of legendary popular songs. Although its size and profits have grown and ebbed over the years, it belongs in a rare category of music industry survivors. After several years of expansion, Atlantic has shifted its emphasis to working harder to promote a smaller number of releases.

Jazz and Blues in the 1940s

As the child of a Turkish diplomat, Ahmet Ertegun, born in 1923, was raised in some of the world's most cosmopolitan cities. Part of his education included experiencing the birth of jazz at the hands of some of the great swing orchestras as they toured the world. Ertegun made his first homemade record at the age of 11. By this time the family had been transferred to Washington, DC, and when a visiting friend offered to take him to New York, he took this chance to visit his unlikely mecca: Harlem. After staying out all night, he was promptly escorted back to Washington.

Ahmet Ertegun continued to love jazz and the blues. He and his older brother Nesuhi eventually collected thousands of records, landing them a mention in a 1938 *Esquire* article while Ahmet was still a schoolboy. In spite of their youthful enthusiasm, the brothers were deeply dismayed by Washington's segregation. The two defiantly staged decidedly desegregated, mixed race concerts.

After Ertegun's father died in 1944, Nesuhi moved to Los Angeles while Ahmet remained in Washington, ostensibly to study philosophy at Georgetown University. His extracurricular observations of record distributors, who seemed totally ignorant of the music they were moving, convinced him that he could do better.

Ertegun also convinced his family's dentist, Dr. Vahdi Sabit, who invested $10,000 in the fledgling enterprise. Ertegun offered a partnership to the debonair jazz lover from New York City, Herb Abramson, also a dentist by training, who invested $2,500. Abramson had been a talent scout for National Records, the growth of which had not matched his ambitions. Like Ertegun, he believed there was a large vein of black music that merited greater exposure.

Atlantic Records was conceived in October 1947. Abramson was president and Ertegun was vice-president. Although initially housed in Manhattan's Ritz Hotel, limited finances forced the pair to a cramped room in the Hotel Jefferson, which was later condemned. Ertegun and Abramson had their attention focused outside the office, however, hunting for talent across the country. There was also a desperate need for new material, which led to hasty compositions by Ertegun (transcribed by hired musicians) under the pen name "A. Nugetre."

Raw, southern blues performed by sophisticated jazz players became the label's trademark, although Abramson pushed the company to record a variety of more literary offerings. Atlantic's strenuous efforts produced little income until they recorded "Drinking Wine, Spo-Dee-O-Dee" with Stick McGhee in 1949. This eventually sold 400,000 copies.

Rockin' 'n' Rollin' in the 1950s

In the 1950s the rock music industry had little respectability and performers were accorded none of the rights of other creative artists. The American Society of Composers, Authors, and Publishers (ASCAP), which for years had collected songwriter

Company Perspectives:

Initially conceived as a rhythm & blues and jazz label, the Atlantic label has been home to such groundbreaking artists as Ray Charles, John Coltrane, Aretha Franklin and Led Zeppelin. By the mid-1950s, Atlantic had become the premier R&B label, with artists like Ruth Brown, LaVern Baker, Charles Mingus and The Modern Jazz Quartet. In the '60s Atlantic moved into the pop marketplace with top sellers by Bobby Darin and soul singers Otis Redding and Wilson Pickett. In the late '60s and early '70s, Atlantic tapped the British talent pool. Atlantic had the leading label market share for the first six months of 1997. Also, Atlantic's soundtrack to the Warner Bros. hit film Space Jam was the top-selling album for the first half of the year. Atlantic's Rhino Records label signed an agreement with Ray Charles for exclusive North American rights to Charles's ABC-Paramount, Tangerine and Crossover label master records from 1959 to the present. LeeAnn Rimes (Curb label) won two 1997 Grammy Awards—New Artist and Female Country Vocal Performance—and Riverdance on Celtic Heartbeat/ Atlantic was best Musical Show Album.

royalties for other types of popular music, would not even license rock and roll songs, a situation that did not change until the creation of Broadcast Music International. The stewards of the blues were particularly mistreated. Many, such as Muddy Waters and Little Richard, profited little from their creations, even after their songs were embraced by mainstream audiences.

Atlantic paid artists royalties, then an unprecedented practice. It took care of its artists in other ways, and Ertegun became known for his generosity—as well as a fair measure of self-indulgence. Acts such as Ruth Brown and the Drifters began to top the rhythm-and-blues (R&B) charts (which simply were not tracked in other charts, however great their sales). The Drifters caused a sensation in the south, where their records were banned because of their lascivious overtones.

The U.S. Army drafted Abramson in 1953 and he served two years as a dentist in Germany. Ertegun brought Jerry Wexler, a music journalist and fellow jazz lover, into the operation (the two can be heard singing backup on Big Joe Turner's version of "Shake, Rattle and Roll"). Tom Dowd had been with the team as an engineer and was elevated to "producer." Together the team began producing covers of the label's black material by white artists for the "pop" market. The hits began to add up, as disc jockeys began to play more R&B music.

When Abramson returned in 1955, Ertegun and Wexler were caught up in the momentum of their success (although they could not raise the $45,000 needed to sign Elvis Presley to their label). Soon Ertegun convinced his brother to join the partnership. As Abramson's wife was also a partner and worked in the office, and he had returned from Germany with a pregnant girlfriend, tensions were high. Abramson ran the newly created Atco subsidiary for a few months before selling out his share of the company in frustration. After a fallow year, 1957, Atlantic went on to score several top 10 hits by the end of the decade.

Bobby Darin earned two Grammy awards for one of these songs, "Mack the Knife."

The New Sounds of the 1960s

Unfortunately, both Darin and blues singer Ray Charles soon left the label. But in 1959 the label's salvation arrived on their doorstep in the form of Phil Spector, an aspiring Los Angeles songwriter who would become known for his distinctive "wall of sound" productions. He apprenticed with the songwriting and production team of Jerry Leiber and Mike Stoller, the talents behind many of Atlantic's early successes, and supplanted them when they left Atlantic in 1961 after a disagreement over a royalty audit. In the same year Ertegun married his second wife, an aristocratic Romanian model named Mica Banu. Their subsequent social life distanced Ertegun from his business associates such as Wexler and Spector, who quit Atlantic on Ertegun's wedding day.

After leaving Atlantic Leiber and Stoller spawned a string of hits recorded by girl groups on their newly formed Red Bird label. A proposed merger with Atlantic in 1964 failed. With the Beatles arriving for the first time in America that February, it was a dismal year for most competing record companies. The black R&B artists in whom Atlantic specialized would never again have the same hold on the masses. Atco did manage a number one single in 1965, the folky ballad "I Got You Babe" recorded by Sonny and Cher. Atlantic also distributed the music of Stax Records, a small label in Memphis, or "Soulsville, USA," and teamed with Fame Studios of Muscle Shoals, Alabama to produce Aretha Franklin's first hits. The sound of Atlantic's future, however, was not R&B, or folk, or pop, but the amalgamation of all types of American music that became known as simply "rock." The group Buffalo Springfield, as well as its successor Crosby, Stills, and Nash, heralded the beginning of this new sound in the late 1960s. Atlantic also caught the British wave with the signing of Eric Clapton's band, Cream, followed by the Bee Gees, Yes, and Led Zeppelin.

Wexler was anxious about losing the financial ground the company had made and persuaded the rest of the partners to sell the company in October 1967. Ahmet was particularly reticent about selling and, in hindsight, the price of $17.5 million seemed ridiculously low to observers, given the company's 1968 sales of $45 million. Wexler and Ertegun were subsequently unable to buy the company back from the new owners.

Warner Seven-Arts was formed when a small film distributor bought the remains of the declining Warner Brothers film and music empire. Unlike Atlantic's founders, Warner Seven-Arts management was interested more in profits and share value than in its artists. Nevertheless, Ertegun was able to leverage a better deal by threatening to quit. Seven-Arts CEO Elliot Hyman resigned first, however, before 1968 was over.

Warner Seven-Arts was itself bought by a diversified New York company known as the Kinney Corporation. The firm was originally built from family businesses and had acquired interests in real estate, parking lot, publishing, and office cleaning. Kinney's CEO, Steve Ross, was able to persuade a reluctant Ertegun to remain at Atlantic Records.

Wexler, somewhat perplexed by his loss of control under the new corporate umbrella and despondent over the displacement of his beloved R&B acts by the new wave of "rockoids," moved to Florida in an to attempt to enjoy the spoils of the sale he had urged. With Wexler out of sight, Ertegun took over the day-to-day administration of the company.

Rolling through the 1970s and 1980s

In 1971 Ertegun signed the Rolling Stones, billed as "the greatest rock and roll band in the world." As part of the terms of their deal a new subsidiary, Rolling Stones Records, was created for the group.

David Geffen, a manager at Atlantic's corporate sibling the Ashley-Famous talent agency, founded Asylum Records in 1970 with financing from Ertegun. This label recorded a new generation of legendary west coast songwriters such as Jackson Browne and the Eagles. The hugely successful Asylum became a subsidiary of Atlantic in 1973. Eventually Elektra Records, which Warner had bought in 1970, was merged with Asylum in the hope that the wunderkind Geffen would improve its fortunes. He slashed Elektra's roster and subsequently turned it into the world's most profitable label.

Ertegun and Geffen had planned to merge Elektra/Asylum with Atlantic Records itself in 1974, becoming co-chairmen while at the same time demoting Wexler to vice-president. After the plan was canceled, Geffen took a position on the board of Warner Brothers Pictures, which he resigned after a year. After leading a relatively low-profile existence for five years, he formed the highly successful Geffen Records, also in cooperation with Warner, in 1980.

Wexler had returned to New York upon separating from his wife in 1973; his influence, however, had diminished in his five-year absence. He perceived a lack of support for his efforts to promote country music, such as the signing of Willie Nelson for his unsuccessful first album. Wexler parted company with Atlantic in 1975. He continued his career producing and consulting.

Atlantic signed Foreigner, one of the most commercially successful acts of the decade, in 1977. Genesis, Yes, and Pete Townsend of The Who also sold their share of records for Atlantic.

A global recession fostered an atmosphere of caution at the beginning of the 1980s, but 1981 proved to be one of Atlantic's best years. Although Atlantic released Peter Gabriel, former lead singer for Genesis, just before he reached international solo success, it scored more than its share of success with his old band and its new singer, Phil Collins, who would also become an international superstar on his own. Another of the decade's great acts, the Australian rock band INXS, also recorded on Atlantic. It lost the Rolling Stones, however, to CBS Records, which agreed to pay the stellar fee of $24 million for the next four Stones albums. At the end of the decade Atlantic began to languish. Further misfortune arrived when Ahmet Ertegun's brother, Nesuhi, died in 1989.

A Rising Tide in the 1990s and Beyond

Doug Morris, a veteran songwriter turned executive, began sharing the position of chairman with Ertegun in 1990, when revenues were $400 million. Like his predecessor, his closeness to music lent him credibility with artists. Before he left Atlantic and joined the Universal Music Group, Morris increased sales by creating or acquiring smaller record companies and en-

couraging their staff to take risks in signing new talent. The female R&B group En Vogue, the grunge band Stone Temple Pilots, rapper Snoop Doggy Dogg, and the confessional songwriter Tori Amos reestablished Atlantic's position as market leader in the mid-1990s, in spite of its losses in 1992. One of the decade's biggest sales sensations, the suburban rock band Hootie and the Blowfish, sold a staggering 14 million copies of its major label debut album. The subsequent launch of Jewel proved Atlantic had a reliable formula for creating superstars.

In spite of his track record, Morris was dismissed in 1995, prompting suits and countersuits. Val Azzoli, former manager for the Canadian rock band Rush, became co-chair and CEO of the Atlantic Group (with Ertegun) in January 1996.

Industrywide sales lagged in the mid-1990s, however, and even Atlantic was not immune. As a result, the Atlantic Group began to eliminate or consolidate several of its imprints in 1997 as well as trim its roster and staff. The debt assumed with Time Warner's merger with Turner Broadcasting Inc. applied further pressure to cut costs. The number of new songs it released was scaled back by nearly two-thirds. Its market share hovered around eight percent, making it the leading label for most of the year.

Under the command of Azzoli and Ertegun, Atlantic continued to redefine itself. Unlike in its earlier days, when it had a relatively narrow focus, the 50-year-old company embraced a variety of styles of music and discovered a new appreciation for country performers such as LeeAnn Rimes. With its aggressive determination in breaking new artists, Atlantic seemed likely to keep making waves.

Principal Labels

Atlantic Records; Lava Records; Rhino Records; Curb Records; Atlantic Classics (Erato, Finlandia, Nonesuch, Teldec); Atlantic Jazz; Atlantic Nashville; Atlantic Theatre; Big Beat; Blackground; Breaking Records; Igloo; Mesa/Bluemoon; Modern.

Further Reading

Bennetts, Leslie, "Devil in a Bespoke Suit," *Vanity Fair,* December 1997, pp. 96–103, 130–33.

Borzillo, Carrie, "Mammoth Makes a Big Splash at Atlantic," *Billboard,* July 13, 1996, pp. 3, 115.

Gillet, Charlie, *Atlantic Records: Making Tracks: Atlantic Records and the Growth of a Multi Billion Dollar Industry,* New York: E.P. Dutton & Co., 1974.

Newman, Melinda, "Goldberg To Head East for Atlantic Presidency," *Billboard,* January 22, 1994, pp. 11, 85.

Reilly, Patrick M., "Rich Marketing Alliances Let Musicians Maintain Their Glow," *The Wall Street Journal,* January 22, 1998.

——, "Time Warner's Atlantic Looks Likely To Top Charts as No. 1 Record Label," *The Wall Street Journal,* December 1, 1997.

Ruppli, Michael, *Atlantic Records: A Discography (Discographies, No. 1),* Greenwood, 1979.

Stodghill, Ron, II, and Grover, Ronald, "Atlantic's Sweet Listenin' Guy," *Business Week,* June 20, 1994.

Verna, Paul, "Atlantic Group To Streamline Structure," *Billboard,* October 12, 1996, pp. 12, 109.

Wade, Dorothy, and Picardie, Justine, *Music Man: Ahmet Ertegun, Atlantic Records, and the Triumph of Rock'n'Roll,* New York: W.W. Norton, 1990.

—Frederick C. Ingram

Azcon Corporation

---

224 South Michigan Avenue
Chicago, Illinois 60604
U.S.A.
(312) 362-0066
Fax: (312) 362-0094

Wholly Owned Division of Blue Tee Corporation
Incorporated: 1911 as Hyman-Michaels Company
Employees: 235
Sales: $180 million (1997 est.)
SICs: 5093 Scrap & Waste Materials; 5051 Metals
  Service Centers & Offices; 5088 Transportation
  Equipment & Supplies

Azcon Corporation, one of Chicago's most successful and oldest firms, is widely recognized as part of the top-ten American leaders in the processing and brokering of ferrous scrap metal. In addition, Azcon Corporation purchases, collects, warehouses, and distributes a wide variety of rail and track accessories for the railroad industry throughout North America, including an extensive network of suppliers situated in Canada. Purchasing and selling railroad cars and their component parts is also one of the core activities of the company. Finally, at its facility in Gary, Indiana, the firm warehouses and distributes prime bar steel. With operating plants and facilities in Alton, Pennsylvania; Duluth, Minnesota; Sharpsburg, Pennsylvania; and New York City, the company is the largest of parent Blue Tee Corporation's operating divisions.

Early History

The earliest incarnation of Azcon can be traced back to the year 1863, when an ambitious and enterprising young man named Joseph Block came up with the idea to purchase and sell surplus rail. At the time, the United States was in the midst of civil war that had split the country into North and South. Both sides used the extensive railroad systems to transport troops and materials to strategic locations and battlefields. The northern Union forces benefitted through their control of the major routes of railroad track. The Confederate forces, although controlling less track, were also heavily dependent on the supply of food and war material provided by the railroad system.

Establishing his company in Cincinnati, Ohio, Block began to buy and sell surplus rail that had been manufactured by northern steel companies to replace track that had been destroyed during the course of the war. Cincinnati was the perfect location for such an enterprise since it was one of the rail system's crossroads between the northern and southern sections of the country. As the Union forces drove deeper into southern territory, and as the Confederacy and its troops began to falter, there was even more of a need for the Union to send larger amounts of supplies to its troops engaged in battle. Thus after the Union troops had destroyed railroad track that had been used by the Confederacy, they immediately laid new track for their own transportation needs. Block's business boomed, and by the end of the war in 1865 he saw the need for additional investment to maintain the growth of his company.

Block combined his assets with Emil Pollack and the two men established the Block and Pollack Iron Company, which focused on buying and selling the enormous quantities of surplus rail manufactured for the war effort. Block and Pollack had entered the marketplace at precisely the most opportune time, since the United States government was in the process of settling the expansive regions of the great plains to the Pacific Coast. In order to make this an easier task, the government encouraged railroad companies to lay as much track as possible through the plains and over the Rocky Mountains. Block and Pollack soon became rich selling rail track to the firms laying train routes across the country.

When Block and Pollack decided to relocate their company from Cincinnati to Chicago, they also changed its name to the Block, Pollack Company. The most important reason for the change in location had to do with the city of Chicago and its burgeoning reputation as the fastest growing city in the Midwest, and the center of the railroad system in the middle of the country. As the firm continued to grow two men, Joseph Hyman, who initially worked as rail purchaser, and Joseph Michaels, who started work as a night watchman, joined the Block, Pollack Company. These two individuals, both extremely ambitious and talented, would eventually become the owners of the firm.

By the early 1890s, the company and its revenues were growing so rapidly that Block decided to build a mill to reroll used rail track and make different kinds of steel products. Established and incorporated as Inland Steel Corporation, the firm was to develop into one of the largest and most successful steel mills in the history of the United States. This related venture was the forerunner of the company's involvement in the development of the steel industry, especially in the midwestern part of the nation.

The New Century

As the company continued to grow, Block and Pollack, who were still managing the firm during the early years of the new century, entered their first international business transaction by purchasing all of the scrap metal in Cuba that was a result of the fighting during the Spanish-American War. The collected scrap metal was soon reworked into other products, and before long the company had formed a new venture for itself. By 1911, however, Block and Pollack were no longer managing the company, and the former rail purchaser and night watchman, who had climbed the managerial ladder within the firm, decided to dissolve the Block, Pollack Company and rename it the Hyman-Michaels Company, in honor of themselves. Although members of the Block family retained their association with the company, they finally decided to withdraw their participation and focus on the management and development of Inland Steel.

In 1915, the Hyman-Michaels Company opened a scrap processing yard and facility in St. Louis. The opening of this facility, which involved the decision to expand the company's geographical base, was a major development. Years later, the plant was relocated across the Mississippi River to the city of Madison, Illinois, and still later to the facility's present location in Alton, Illinois. However, this was the first time the company had established a permanent facility or plant outside of its traditional headquarters in Chicago.

With antiquated manufacturing plants from the latter part of the 19th century eclipsed by modern technology, the automobile companies introducing new models each year to take the place of what would soon be relegated to the junk heap, and the railroads starting their long but slow period of decline, the company concentrated more and more on its scrap processing operations, and rapidly developed into one of the most prominent and successful firms within the scrap industry. By the time America entered World War I in 1917, the company was one of the leaders in scrap processing, and it was thought appropriate by many people within the industry that Joseph Michaels was chosen by the United States federal government to head the Scrap Division of America's War Industry Board.

The wartime economy was good to the Hyman-Michaels Company, and its scrap processing operations benefitted significantly by the ever-growing needs of the American Expeditionary Forces. As the war continued, more and more scrap metal was needed for armaments, thus company management decided to enter the rail dismantling business to meet this growing need. Automobiles were becoming a part of everyday life for Americans throughout the country, and roads were built to connect cities and towns that were previously served only by an extensive interurban railroad system. The electrified streetcar-like rail systems, with thousands of miles of track throughout the country, was obsolete almost overnight.

The company negotiated its first rail track dismantling contract in 1918 with the Woodstock and Sycamore Traction Company working out of Genoa, Illinois. Continuing its rail dismantling operations after World War I ended in 1919, and during the entire decade of the 1920s, the company ultimately removed approximately 20,000 miles of obsolete and abandoned rail track across the country. Much of this dismantled rail was, of course, processed in the company's own scrap yards. The Hymen-Michaels Company received a good deal of press when the firm's workmen removed the "golden spike" located at Promontory, Utah, and dismantled the track at the famous site of the first transcontinental railroad connection in the United States.

The Great Depression and World War II

The company's fortunes took a turn for the worse when the stock market crashed in the autumn of 1929. As the economy worsened, management was forced to lay off many of its employees in order to cut costs and maintain financial viability. When Franklin Delano Roosevelt was elected president in 1932, and then closed the nation's banks to reorganize them, the state of affairs for the company seemed to go from bad to worse. But one year later, a stroke of good luck turned the financial condition of the company around. Management had been working hard to organize a syndicate to keep its dismantling business afloat, and the syndicate was able to combine its resources and purchase approximately 16,000 old freight cars from the Southern Railway line for dismantling. This was the single largest transaction of its type ever made in the United States, and coming when it did saved not only the railroad from bankruptcy but also provided the money for the Hyman-Michaels Company to continue operations.

With America's entry into World War II on December 7, 1941, the company was assured of better days since its scrap metal processing business was in high demand. Once again, the company was at the forefront of the war effort and figured prominently in the U.S. government's strategy to turn scrap metal into usable material for the supply of its soldiers overseas. As the company grew, so did its revenues, and consequently more employees were hired to staff plant operations around the clock. By the end of the war, the company was one of the largest scrap metal processing firms within the United States. At the same time, the company's dismantling operations were also growing at a fast pace, and when the federal government looked for help to dismantle railroad or get rid of unused rail track left over from the war, it turned to the Hyman-Michaels Company.

The Postwar Era

With the cessation of hostilities in the European theatre in April 1945, company management was encouraged by the American occupation forces to establish a depot and later a facility in Belgium. Located in Brussels, the depot was used to liquidate the tons of railroad track that had been stockpiled by the United States and their European Allies for the invasion of the continent. This depot was the first company operation established outside the United States and brought an enormous amount of income to the firm. By the time the entire stockpile of unused rail had been relegated to scrap metal, the 1940s were drawing to an end, and the Hyman-Michaels Company had become one of the most financially successful scrap metal operations in the industry.

As Hyman-Michaels continued expanding its scrap metal processing and dismantling operations into the 1950s, a new company dedicated to dismantling steam locomotives was being established in Sharpsburg, Pennsylvania. In a small, former repair plant for trains and boxcars just outside of Pittsburgh, A. Leon Deitch opened the doors of The Deitch Company for business. Soon after its incorporation, The Deitch Company was asked to use its dismantling crews to tear down abandoned or antiquated steel mills throughout New Jersey and Pennsylvania. In 1952, the company garnered a reputation for innovation within the industry when it created an iron breaking operation under crane runways, the first time this kind of hoisting power had been used in scrap processing operations.

The Deitch Company's growing reputation was enhanced when management decided to install a hydraulic machine weighing 2,200 tons that was used as a scrap shear. The largest of its kind in the world, the new machine was located at the company's Sharpsburg plant. Within a few years, management invested more of its capital in two additional shears similar to the first machine in its capacity. Modern balers were also installed at the same facility to augment the large scrap shears. Since these machines were installed during the late 1950s and early 1960s, the company's plant has remained the largest scrap shearing operation in the United States.

Expansion and Consolidation: 1970s–80s

In 1962, as The Deitch Company was making its mark in the scrap metal processing industry, the Hyman-Michaels Company acquired the Duluth Iron and Metal Company located in Duluth, Minnesota. Management at Hyman-Michaels was correct in its strategy to purchase the operation in order to take advantage of a brand new scrap export opportunity, namely, the recently constructed St. Lawrence Seaway which connected the Great Lakes and the surrounding region to the Atlantic Ocean. The first major exporter of scrap metal from the Great Lakes region, Hyman-Michaels bought and operated a fleet of ships to transport the material. Throughout the remainder of the 1960s, the company's revenues steadily increased due to the scrap exports by way of the St. Lawrence Seaway.

Unfortunately, with the arrival of the 1970s, the Hyman-Michaels Company experienced hard times. The price for scrap metal dropped precipitously, and the company was forced to sell all of its ships traversing the Great Lakes and St. Lawrence Seaway. As a result of its financial difficulties, the company was acquired by Consolidated Gold Fields, the forerunner to Blue Tee Corporation, in 1976. To increase its market share, Consolidated Gold also purchased The Deitch Company in 1979. Although the two firms operated as separate businesses for a short while, in 1982 management at the Blue Tee Corporation merged Hyman-Michaels Company and The Deitch Company to create Azcon Corporation. As a division of Blue Tee Corporation, the merged companies streamlined their operations and forged ahead throughout the 1980s as one of the premier scrap metal firms in the country.

The 1990s and Beyond

By the early 1990s, Azcon Corporation had developed into one of the largest scrap metal processing firms in the nation. The company had operations in Alton, Chicago, Sharpsburg, Duluth, and New York, and also acted as a broker of ferrous scrap metal. At the same time, the company continued its history of dismantling operations by purchasing and selling railroad cars and their component parts. Rail and track accessories also became a significant business of the company in the United States and Canada.

By maintaining a strong position within the scrap metal processing industry, Azcon Corporation has been able to weather the price fluctuations of the market rather easily. Its leadership role as one of the nation's most prominent processors and brokers of ferrous scrap metal will not be challenged in the near future, and Blue Tee Corporation, its parent firm, is able to make capital investments for Azcon's improvement when necessary.

Further Reading

"A Brief History of Azcon," *Tee Times* (company newsletter), Vol. III, No. 1, Spring 1995.

Burgert, Philip, and Michael Marley, "BIR Scrap Forecasts Upbeat, but Not Carefree," *American Metal Market,* October 22, 1997, p. 1.

Marley, Michael, "Demand Fuels Scrap," *American Metal Market,* November 11, 1997, p. 1.

——, "U.S. Ferrous Scrap Exports Slow," *American Metal Market,* November 25, 1997. p. 1.

Munzer, Michael, "Metal Service Centers Sensitive to Markets," *American Metal Market,* October 7, 1997, p. 14.

Petry, Corinna C., "Service Centers Set Torrid Shipping Pace; Statistics Indicate Record Year Brewing," *American Metal Market,* July 25, 1997, p. 1.

——, "Steel Center Shipments Hot," *American Metal Market,* December 1, 1997, p. 16.

—Thomas Derdak

Bank Austria

Bank Austria AG

Vordere Zollamtsstrasse 13
A-1030 Vienna
Austria
+43 1 711 91-0
Fax: +43 1 711 91-6155
Web Site: http://www.bankaustria.com

Public Company
Incorporated: 1991
Employees: 18,000
Total Assets: AS 1.4 trillion (US$109 billion) (1997)
Stock Exchanges: Brussels Paris Vienna
SICs: 6021 National Commercial Banks; 6035 Federal
     Savings Institutions; 6099 Functions Related to
     Deposit Banking; 6211 Security Brokers and Dealers;
     6282 Investment Advice

With over one-fifth of the nation's banking business, Bank Austria AG is Austria's largest and most profitable banking group. Formed through the October 1991 union of Zentralsparkasse und Kommerzialbank Wien (Z-Bank) and Österreichische Länderbank (ÖLB or Länderbank), the financial institution boasts nearly 300 offices nationwide and an additional 40 outlets around the world. Bank Austria leads all the nation's financial segments, including retail, commercial, private, asset management, investment banking, trade finance, and insurance. In late 1997 its assets totaled AS 1.4 trillion (US$109 billion). Due to its substantial investments over the decades, it also ranked as Austria's largest private holding company, but was divesting non-bank interests in the mid- to late 1990s.

The institution has more than just size in its favor; due in part to a deposit guarantee by the City of Vienna, it enjoys a stellar credit rating. Moody's Global Finance placed it among the world's twenty safest banks, and it earned the titles of ''Best Bank in Austria'' and ''Best Security Firm in Austria'' from trade magazine *Euromoney* every year from 1993 through 1996. While it has operations throughout the world, Austria remains its key market.

Bank Austria's equity is controlled by a group of governmental and institutional investors including the Anteilsverwaltung Zentralsparkasse (AV-Z), a foundation owned by the City of Vienna, with a 45 percent share; the federal government of Austria, which holds a 19 percent stake; Germany's Westdeutsche Landesbank Girozentrale (WestLB), with ten percent; Italy's Cariplo (the world's largest savings bank), with 5.6 percent; and the Wiener Städtische Austrian insurance group, with about ten percent.

Foundations and Development

Bank Austria was created in 1991, when Zentralsparkasse und Kommerzialbank Wien (Z-Bank) absorbed Österreichische Länderbank (ÖLB or Länderbank). ÖLB was the older of the two banking groups. It was founded in November 1880 as k.k. privilegierte Österreichische Länderbank, a subsidiary of France's Société de L'Union Genérale. Länderbank was spun off from the parent company in 1882, and opened its first branch bank in Paris in 1882. The Austrian bank later established branch locations in Prague, London, Bolzano, and Pilsen.

Over the course of its development, Länderbank came to emphasize commercial and retail banking as well as securities trading. The establishment came under state control in 1946, and although privatization began in 1956, the federal government still owned a controlling stake in Länderbank through 1990. By that time, ÖLB was the nation's fourth-largest financial institution, with 4,200 employees, 1.1 million accounts, 140 domestic offices, and 24 foreign offices.

Though younger, Z-Bank had grown to become the larger of the two merged banks. It had been founded in 1905 by a resolution of the Vienna City Council and opened its headquarters branch there in 1907. Over the course of its first quarter-century in business, the institution built 23 offices throughout Vienna and captured one-fifth of the capital city's savings accounts. Z-Bank was transformed into a joint stock company in 1990, with 90 percent of its shares held by the City of Vienna's AV-Z trust and the remaining ten percent in the hands of institutional investors. Its liabilities continued to be guaranteed by the City of Vienna even after the merger with Länderbank.

By the time of the merger, Z-Bank was Austria's largest savings bank, and Europe's seventh-largest financial institution overall. In addition to its nearly 1,300 offices in Austria, the bank had branches in Milan, London, Tokyo, Frankfurt, Moscow, Paris, and Prague.

1991 Banking Consolidation in Austria

The 1991 union of these two massive banks was perceived as a first step to relieving what *Euromoney* called an "over-banked, over-branched, and over-staffed" Austrian banking industry. Under the chairmanship of Rene Alfons Haiden, it took five difficult years to consolidate and rationalize the two banks' operations. Dozens of branches were shuttered, and group employment was reduced by nearly 11 percent, from 9,929 in 1991 to 8,867 by the end of 1996. Productivity (in terms of pre-tax net per employee) doubled during the period, from AS 292,000 to AS 586,000. Assets increased 44 percent to AS 742 billion, and operating profit jumped 80 percent to AS 5.2 billion. During that time, however, Bank Austria's return on equity fluctuated between four percent and seven percent, and its share price reflected that vacillation. Nevertheless, the merger was, according to the *Economist,* "widely seen as a success."

Having advanced through Zentralsparkasse and served as deputy chairman of Bank Austria from 1991, Gerhard Randa became chairman of the group in 1995. Nicknamed "Rambo" by his colleagues in the Viennese banking community, the Harley-Davidson aficionado was known as an "aggressive deal maker" whose zeal sometimes got him in trouble. Such was the case with Bank Austria's 1994 acquisition of third-ranking GiroCredit Bank Aktiengesellschaft der Sparkassen. Although the two institutions were considered a logical fit, Bank Austria divested its holdings in GiroCredit in 1997. Though acquisitions took center stage during Randa's tenure, he continued to emphasize efficiency, telling *Euromoney* that "The key element to our strategy is productivity," in a June 1996 interview.

1997 Union with Creditanstalt

The ongoing restructuring of Austria's banking industry also entailed privatization of long-held government positions in key banks. In 1997 Bank Austria beat Italian, German, American, and domestic rivals with an AS 17.2 billion (US$1.5 billion) bid to acquire the federal government's 70 percent stake in the Creditanstalt-Bankverein. Known as Austria's most worldly bank, Creditanstalt was founded by the wealthy Rothschild family and later ranked among Europe's largest banks. It was at one time so influential that some historians assert that its 1931 crash triggered the Great Depression.

The merger agreement kept the venerable bank in Austrian hands, but came with some strings attached. For example, the government-brokered deal required that Creditanstalt "remain a separate legal operating entity for five years and that no targeted staff reductions may be undertaken by Bank Austria." This factor seemed to preclude many potential cost savings and economies. As the *Economist* pointed out in May 1997, "Instead of weeding out wasteful duplication, the two banks will continue to compete, even where they have branches side by side." *Institutional Investor's* Giles Peel noted that the deal, which was supposed to have privatized Creditanstalt, "effec-

tively postponed the long-awaited privatization" by merely transferring ownership of Austria's best-known bank from the federal government to the municipal government of Vienna, which still indirectly owned 45 percent of Bank Austria. (In fact, the federal government continued to own 19 percent of Bank Austria through the end of 1997.)

Early in 1997, Austria's coalition government outlined a privatization program through which the City of Vienna's Anteilsverwaltung Zentralsparkasse (AV-Z) foundation would reduce its 45 percent stake in Bank Austria to less than 25 percent within five years. Progress toward that goal was hindered that June, when the bank revealed that minority stakeholder Westdeutsche Landesbank Girozentrale (WestLB) of Germany, which already owned just over ten percent of Bank Austria, enjoyed right of first refusal over any shares divested by AV-Z before the end of 2001. Analysts observed that this factor would likely prevent AV-Z from selling any equity in order to preclude the German bank from becoming the majority owner of Austria's flagship bank.

Randa also quickly sidestepped the government's requirement that Creditanstalt remain independent by integrating international operations as well as the two institutions' investment banking subsidiaries. He also expected to achieve some economies by unifying back office operations, a process that was forecast for completion by the end of 1999. Thus, while the Creditanstalt name and legal entity persisted, many operations were merged.

The Late 1990s and Beyond

Chairman Randa's strategy for the future targeted expansion into eastern and central Europe and Asia. Hoping to apply Bank Austria's extensive privatization and initial public offering experience (the institution had participated in the launches of British Petroleum, British Telecom, Wellcome, Adidas, and many Austrian firms) in former communist countries, Randa established operations in Slovenia, the Czech Republic, Hungary, Poland, Russia, and Croatia. By mid-1997, Bank Austria was the leading foreign bank throughout eastern and central Europe.

Principal Subsidiaries

Bank: BA Treuhand AG f. Immob. & Bet. Fonds; VISA-Service Kreditkarten AG; BA-Handelsbank AG; BA Wohnbaubank AG; Investmentbank Austria AG; EB und HYPO-Bank Bergenland AG; BANKINVEST Austria GmbH; ÖCI-GZB BeteiligungsgmbH; ÖKB-HoldinggmbH; Investkredit Holding GmbH; Europay Austria Zahlungsverkehrssysteme GmbH; BA Leasing GmbH; BA Leasing Holding 2 GmbH; BA Finanzservice GmbH; BA Teleservice GmbH; BA AG-Immobilien u. Mobilien-vermietungs OHG; DATASERVICE Invormatik GmbH; DATASERVICE Org. u. Datenverarb. GmbH; Garage AM Hof GmbH; GANYMED Immob. GmbH; HYPERION Immob. GmbH; Lassallestr. Bau-, Planungs-, Errichtungs-und VerwertungsgmbH; GELDSERVICE Logistik für Wertgestionierung und Transport-koordination GmbH.; BA & GrECo Versicherungs-management GmbH; UNION Versicherungs-AG; Vereinigte Pensions-kasse AG Wiener Städtische Allgemeine Versicherung AG; BA (CR) a.s. (Czech Republic); BA

(SR) a.s. (Slovakia); BA d.d. (Slovenia); EURÓPAI KERESKEDELMI BANK RT (Hungary); BA (Switzerland) Ltd.; BA Croatia d.d.; BA Cayman Islands Ltd.; LB Fonds BeratungsgmbH (United States); BA Property Investment Ltd. (United Kingdom). Non-Bank: BA Industrieholding GmbH; UNITECH AG; Wiener Betriebs- und Baugesmbh; Allgemeine Baugesellschaft-A. Porr AG; BA Handelsholding AG; USEA Umweltservice Austria GmbH; Colpack-Kolkoks-Wihoko Brennstoff-handel GmbH; Wiener Kühlhaus Frigoscandia GmbH; Center Nachrichtentechnische Anlagen GmbH; TSG EDV Terminal Service GmbH; Gewista WerbegmbH; Wiener Hafen und Lager Ausbau- und Vermögensverwaltungs-gmbH (WHV); Wiener Messen und Congress GmbH; Hotel & Touristik Holding AG; Heilbad Sauerbrunn BetriebsgmbH & CoKG; Palais am Stadtpark Hotel Betriebs GmbH & CoKG; Immobilien Holding GmbH; Wohnbauerrichtungs-und Verwertungs AG; ARWAG Holding-AG; Erste Wiener Hotel AG; Wiener BauträgergmbH; BA Wohnbau AG; Ekazent RealitätengmbH; Klea Terrain-und Bau-GmbH; Interring GmbH; IMMOTRUST Anlagen AG;

Further Reading

"A Long Way from America: Creditanstalt's Flawed Renaissance," *Economist*, May 17, 1997, pp. 84–85.
"Bank Austria," *Banker*, May 1995, pp. 4–5.
"Bank Austria: A Bank for Europe," *Euromoney*, July 1997, pp. 88–91.
"Bank Austria: A Wealth of Experience in Privatization," *Euromoney*, June 1996, p. 27.
"Bank Austria: Number One in the Domestic Market," *Euromoney*, June 1996, p. 24–25.
"Bank Austria Takes the Stage," *Banker*, November 1991, pp. 8–9.
"Best Firm in Austria," *Euromoney*, September 1994, pp. 46–47.
"Deals in the Balance," *Euromoney*, September 1997, pp. 409–10.
Hall, William, "The Waltz Stops Here," *Banker*, February 1997, pp. 37–39.
King, Paul, "Take Your Partners," *Euromoney*, January 1992, pp. 29–33.
——, "Banking Tangles Begin to Unravel," *Euromoney*, January 1993, pp. 56–58.
Peel, Giles, "Banking; Can Randa Make It Work?" *Institutional Investor*, September 1997, p. 29.
"A Powerhouse in Austria," *Euromoney*, September 1994, pp. 44–45.
"Red Faces in Vienna," *Banker*, June 1993, p. 4.
Shirreff, David and John McGrath, "Death of a Bank," *Euromoney*, March 1997, pp. 44–50.
"Strategic Alliances: An Interview with Gerhard Randa, Chairman," *Euromoney*, June 1996, pp. 25–26.

—April Dougal Gasbarre

Battle Mountain Gold

Battle Mountain Gold Company

333 Clay Street
Houston, Texas 7702
U.S.A.
(713) 650-6400
Fax: (713) 650-3636
Web site: http://www.bmgold.com

Public Company
Incorporated: 1985
Employees: 2,100
Sales: $365.6 million (1996)
Stock Exchanges: New York Chicago Australian
    Frankfurt Swiss
SICs: 1081 Metal Mining Services; 1041 Gold Ores;
    1044 Silver Ores

One of the largest gold miners in the United States, Battle Mountain Gold Company mines and processes gold, silver, and copper ore at seven mines on three continents. Formerly a unit of The Pennzoil Company, Battle Mountain was spun off from Pennzoil in 1985, emerging on its own with its mainstay Fortitude mine in Battle Mountain, Nevada. To increase its reserves and develop a replacement for Fortitude, the company entered a number of joint ventures with other partners to explore and develop mines, focusing its efforts on international projects. Battle Mountain established operations in Chile, Bolivia, Papua New Guinea, and Australia, recording its greatest success in Bolivia with its 88 percent-owned Kori Kollo mine. In 1996 the company merged with Hemlo Gold Mines, Inc., a union that created North America's fifth largest, and the world's fifteenth largest, pure gold producer. The most significant gains for Battle Mountain from the deal were two mines in Canada, the Golden Giant and the Holloway, both of which were located in the province of Ontario.

1985 Separation from Pennzoil

As an independent company, Battle Mountain got a head start in its corporate life, springing from the starting block as a spin-off of The Pennzoil Company in 1985. At the time of the spin-off, when Battle Mountain was let loose from the protective care of its parent company and given the opportunity either to succeed or fail on its own, a countrywide trend was changing the face of the gold industry. High gold prices early in the decade had attracted a number of new competitors who registered startling success by making what *Financial World* called "craftily financed acquisitions" and developing revolutionary methods to reduce mining costs. These upstart mining companies were able to capture market share from long-established competitors, entrenched in their old ways of turning bodies of ore into corporate profits. As in any industry, success gave birth to heightened competition, and a series of mining company spin-offs occurred, beginning with the 1983 spin-off of Echo Bay Mines, a subsidiary of conglomerate IU International. In the wake of Echo Bay's spin-off followed a spate of mining company spin-offs from larger, diversified parent companies, including Freeport-McMoran Gold, Newmont Gold, St. Joe Gold, Sherr-Gold, and Battle Mountain Gold. Consequently, the head start Battle Mountain enjoyed when the company emerged from under the corporate umbrella of Pennzoil was an advantage enjoyed by many of its equally sized competitors. Together, these "new" mining concerns took their first independent steps in what was regarded as one of North America's hottest growth industries, each attempting to forge a successful future with the inherited assets of its past.

From Pennzoil, Battle Mountain took its management, led by Douglas J. Bourne, group vice-president of mining at Pennzoil, and its original and flagship mine, Fortitude, located in the Battle Mountain area of Nevada. With Bourne serving as chairman and chief executive officer, Battle Mountain set out on its own, debt free and in pursuit of additional reserves. The search for new reserves figured as Bourne's chief objective as he directed the company's course following the spin-off. Although the Fortitude mine provided for Battle Mountain's existence, accounting for virtually all of the company's revenues and profits, it could not be expected to serve such a role forever. Its deposits were shrinking and its usefulness as a primary source for the company's gold would not last much longer. Accordingly, there was a pressing need for new reserves, which the company recorded considerable success in fulfilling. During its first five years as an independent mining concern Battle Mountain increased its reserves five-fold,

Company Perspectives:

Battle Mountain Gold Company is an international gold mining company. Using our skills and technologies, we will seek to enhance shareholder value through growth and industry leadership. We will succeed by exploring for and acquiring reserves, constructing and operating profitable mines, and providing challenging opportunities for our employees. We will apply our resources to the fundamental obligations that we have to our shareholders, employees, communities and the environment, while capitalizing upon opportunities worldwide.

demonstrating the aggressiveness and astuteness that had distinguished the cadre of smaller and ''smarter'' mining firms midway through the 1980s.

Although Battle Mountain's foundation rested on the Fortitude mine, the bulk of the new reserves secured during the latter half of the 1980s was located not only outside the borders of Nevada but beyond the shores of the United States. In foreign countries, gold was typically more inexpensive to mine than it was domestically and the number of potential exploration sites overseas was greater than in the United States, which provided sufficient inducement for Bourne to direct the company's exploration efforts abroad. Battle Mountain worked mines in Australia, Indonesia, Papua New Guinea, and Chile, building up its reserves to create a replacement for Fortitude. Thanks to these developments and the company's debt-free status once cut loose from Pennzoil, Battle Mountain remained profitable throughout its first half-decade of existence. Annual revenues increased from $93 million in 1986 to $294 million in 1989, and the company's net income surged forward during the same period from $27 million to $54 million. Battle Mountain's peak financial year during the 1980s was 1988, when sales eclipsed $300 million and net income topped $95 million.

Profitable and growing, Battle Mountain stood in good shape as it entered the 1990s, with the only nagging concern stemming from the inevitable obsolescence of its Fortitude mine. The push overseas had assuaged some of the fears of the flagship mine's imminent demise, but the company had yet to locate a mine that could replace the production output of Fortitude. As the 1990s began, company officials were projecting that Fortitude could not be expected to survive ''at full speed'' for more than five years, which intensified the need to find a sizable body of ore that could inherit the role of Battle Mountain's premier gold mine. In October 1990 Battle Mountain officials revealed that the company might have found such a mine. Located in Bolivia, the exploration site would be developed into Battle Mountain's signature gold mine for the 1990s.

A New Mine for the 1990s

Battle Mountain had entered into the exploration of the Bolivian mine in a joint venture with other partners. Holding a majority interest in the project, Battle Mountain controlled a 51 percent stake in the South American mine, with Westworld Resources Inc., another Houston-based mining company, holding a 24.5 percent stake in the project and Zealand Mines S.A., a Bolivian partner, controlling a 24.5 percent interest. Westworld Resources had originally staked itself with a 50 percent interest in the speculative venture in 1982, enlisting the financial help of Bolivian investors. Battle Mountain was brought into the joint venture in 1989 as operating partner with one-third interest. Roughly a year later, the years of explorative efforts paid off with a significant discovery that augured well for Battle Mountain's future. The mine, known as Kori Kollo, was expected to yield 4.1 million ounces of gold and 26.8 ounces of silver, a sufficient amount to increase Battle Mountain's reserves 40 percent.

By the end of 1990 Battle Mountain was ready to go ahead with the Bolivian project, laying out $100 million in December 1990 to begin development of Kori Kollo. The production facility at Kori Kollo was scheduled to be completed in 1992, and as that opening date approached Battle Mountain significantly increased its interest in the venture. In mid-1991 Battle Mountain acquired Westworld Resources, thereby gaining the company's chief asset, its 24.5 interest in Kori Kollo. Following the acquisition, Westworld Resources was organized as a Battle Mountain subsidiary named Kori Kollo Corp. In addition to acquiring Westworld Resources, Battle Mountain also purchased 9.5 percent of Zealand Mines' interest in Kori Kollo, giving the company an 85 percent interest in the promising Bolivian mine.

As Battle Mountain upped its ante in Kori Kollo, important changes were taking place back in Houston, where new management took control of the company. Karl E. Elers, a former Pennzoil employee who joined Battle Mountain in 1987 as executive vice-president, was named chairman and chief executive officer in April 1990, shortly before the company announced its discovery in Bolivia. Elers assumed leadership over a company that increasingly was looking to expand abroad, as were many U.S.-based mining firms. Diminishing reserves, stiff environmental regulations, and escalating taxes conspired to make mining in the United States what one analyst characterized as a ''nightmare.'' For evidence of these domestic difficulties, Battle Mountain executives had to look no further than at their own operations. In Colorado, where the company had been attempting to develop a mine since 1988, progress had been delayed for two years as the company completed an environmental study and worked to resolve concerns of the local community. Meanwhile, as progress was stalled in Colorado, the company was able to gain considerable ground on foreign soil, acquiring a mine in Australia and moving forward with Kori Kollo. Although Battle Mountain's operations in Bolivia, Chile, Papua New Guinea, and Australia were subject to taxes and environmental regulations, the measures imposed by foreign governments were neither as costly nor as time-consuming as they were in the United States.

Despite Battle Mountain's emphasis on exploration and development overseas, the Fortitude mine continued to rank as the company's largest mine through the early 1990s, but once Kori Kollo began producing the company looked to Bolivia for its most important supply of gold. During its first year the Kori Kollo mine produced in excess of 300,000 ounces of gold, a benchmark it would eclipse during its first three years of production.

Mid-1990s

With the production facilities at Kori Kollo up and running, Battle Mountain next moved to solidify its position in several of its other mining projects, which were typically owned and operated through a joint venture with another mining company. In Australia, where the company allied itself with Normandy Mining Ltd. in a development project named Vera-Nancy, Battle Mountain began developing an open pit mine in mid-1996. Earmarking $40 million to develop the mine, its infrastructure, and renovate processing facilities, Battle Mountain expected its Vera-Nancy mine eventually to produce 100,000 ounces of gold annually.

At roughly the same time the capital development program at Vera-Nancy was beginning, Battle Mountain began exercising its majority control in a joint venture project with a Sydney, Australia company named Niugini Mining Ltd. Battle Mountain owned 50.4 percent of Niugini, which controlled a 17 percent interest in the Lihir gold project in Papua New Guinea and interests in two other gold properties, the San Cristobal Mine in Chile and the Red Dome Mine in Australia. Battle Mountain officials were unhappy with the progress of Niugini, and their majority interest gave them the power to voice their concerns. The relationship between the two companies had been strained for several years, with no resolution to the situation in sight. In August 1996 Battle Mountain proposed acquiring the 49.6 percent of Niugini it did not already own, but Niugini's directors refused the price put on the table by Battle Mountain. Battle Mountain had the last say in the matter, however, by replacing Niugini's chairman and founding director with Dennis O'Connell, Battle Mountain's chief financial officer. Other members of Niugini's executive management were replaced with Battle Mountain executives in November 1996, providing the company with greater control over the management of its mines in Papua New Guinea, Australia, and Chile.

Prior to the flare-up between Battle Mountain and Niugini, Battle Mountain completed the most significant deal in its history. In July 1996 the company merged with Hemlo Gold Mines Inc., a Canadian gold mining firm based in Toronto. The union created the fifth largest pure-play gold producer in North America and the twelfth largest in the world, with operating mines in five countries, spread across three continents. Much of the far-ranging geographic scope of the new company was attributable to Battle Mountain's international operations; Hemlo Gold's strength was located in Canada, particularly its Golden Giant mine in Ontario. Thanks to the assets brought by Hemlo Gold into the new, larger Battle Mountain, two-thirds of the reserves owned by the merged companies was located in North America and another flagship mine was brought into Battle Mountain's fold, the Golden Giant, which yielded more than 350,000 ounces of gold annually. With Kori Kollo and Golden Giant underpinning the "new" Battle Mountain of the late 1990s, the company prepared for the beginning of the 21st century, intent on building its reserves across the globe. "Our goals," a Battle Mountain official explained, "include increasing reserves and production by 10 percent per year through exploration programs focused on deposits in North America and South America, the Western Pacific and West Africa, as well as through value-added acquisitions."

Principal Subsidiaries

Empressa Minera Inti Raymi, SA (88%); Battle Mountain Complex.

Further Reading

Brubaker, Laura, "The New Gold Bug," *Houston Business Journal,* January 19, 1987, p. 1.

Caney, Derek J., "Battle Proposes Crown Merger," *American Metal Market,* April 19, 1995, p. 2.

Carey, David, "Panning Out," *Financial World,* September 2, 1986, p. 16.

Darwin, Jennifer, "Losing Luster," *Houston Business Journal,* February 14, 1997, p. 14A.

Dennis, Darienne L., "Gold: Still the Safest Commodity," *Fortune,* Fall 1987, p. 28.

Fineberg, Seth, "Battle Mt.-Hemlo Link Called Good Fit," *American Metal Market,* March 14, 1996, p. 12.

LaRue, Gloria T., "Battle Mountain Takes Niugini Controls," *American Metal Market,* November 12, 1996, p. 2.

McNamara, Victoria, "Hollywood Saga Ends with Acquisition," *Houston Business Journal,* July 1, 1991, p. 1.

Schiff, Frank, "Battle Mountain Wraps Up Acquisition of Hemlo Gold," *American Metal Market,* July 23, 1996, p. 2.

"Vera-Nancy Development Begins," *American Metal Market,* August 30, 1996, p. 5.

—Jeffrey L. Covell

Bayernwerk AG

Nymphenburger Strasse 39
D-8000 Munich 2
Federal Republic of Germany
(49) 89-1254-3428
Fax: (49) 89-1254-3081
Web site: http://www.bayernwerk.de

Public Company
Incorporated: 1921
Employees: 12,739
Sales: DM 9.54 billion (US $6.87 billion) (1996)
Stock Exchanges: Munich
SICs: 4911 Electric Services; 4931 Electric & Other
  Services Combined

Bayernwerk AG is the largest electricity supplier in Bavaria and one of the largest in Germany. It provides about two-thirds of the electricity requirement for the Free State of Bavaria. Bayernwerk's purpose is to guarantee electricity supply through electricity generation, electricity distribution, and cooperative business ventures at home and abroad. As a national electricity supplier Bayernwerk builds and runs power stations that use nuclear and conventional sources of energy. In 1995 the company's power station capacity stood at approximately 8,570 megawatts (MW). The most important concerns serviced by the company are the regional energy supply companies within the greater Bayernwerk group, the German state-owned railway company, Deutsche Bundesbahn (DB), and large chemical companies. In 1997 the company supplied more than 50 billion kilowatt hours (kwh) of electricity. Up to 1994, some 60 percent of Bayernwerk was owned by the state of Bavaria and its governing regions, and some 40 percent by Vereinigte Industrie-Unternehmungen AG (VIAG); in that year, VIAG took over the majority of Bayernwerk stock as part of an ongoing process of privatization.

Bringing Electric Power to Bavaria

Since the beginning of the industrial age, which in Germany dated from 1795, every German state endeavoured to build up a good energy supply of its own. Bavaria was handicapped in this respect, no possessing large deposits of fossil fuels such as coal. Moreover, it did not have cheap transport facilities, and because it was not densely populated, the transport routes were long and transport costs high. Bavaria was well provided, however, with rapid mountain streams and powerful rivers. The development of energy supply in Bavaria therefore began with "white coal": hydroelectric power.

Visitors to the International Electricity Exhibition in Munich in 1882 were offered an unusual attraction—an artificial waterfall powered by electricity. The electrical current had been carried over 57 kilometers from Miesbach to Munich, the royal seat and capital. With this demonstration, the organizer of the exhibition company, the Bavarian pioneer in electrical engineering Oskar von Miller, proved that with the help of electric current, the production and application of energy could be divided from each other by large distances. Oskar von Miller had recognized the possibilities offered by the use of the great hydroelectric power on hand in Bavaria, especially the Alpine rivers. As technical director of the Frankfurt Electricity Exhibition in 1891, he succeeded in carrying an appreciably greater capacity over a distance of 175 kilometers. This achievement created the breakthrough for the first high-tension transmission lines; electric power stations could be constructed in locations where energy sources could be supplied cheaply. In 1894 Isarwerke GmbH, the first German long-distance supply station, began to operate. It ran a large hydroelectric power plant near Höllriegelskreuth, south of Munich on the Isar River. Oskar von Miller contributed to the design for the mechanical and electrical installation.

Early 20th Century: von Miller Founds Bayernwerk

Oskar von Miller, son of the brass founder Ferdinand von Miller, was a civil engineer by training. When he visited the Paris Electricity Exhibition in 1881, he was so impressed by what he saw that he began to study the relatively new subject of electrical engineering. In 1884 von Miller went to Berlin with Emil Rathenau to set up the Deutsche Edison-Gesellschaft, later to become the Allgemeine ElektrizitätsGesellschaft (AEG). In 1890 he opened an office in Munich and soon made a name for

---

Company Perspectives:

Bayernwerk is committed on a variety of levels to keeping open every conceivable option for the energy supply of the future.

---

himself as a power transmission expert. Together with his achievements in the field of electrical engineering, his name is inseparably associated with the Deutsches Museum in Munich. Oskar von Miller was always in search of new sources of money for this collection, which consisted of masterpieces of science and technology.

In the early 20th century, public electricity supply made huge strides forward. Power stations and overhead power works were established all over Bavaria, but there was no comprehensive, unified plan for supplying the whole state. In 1911 von Miller proposed devising a general plan for the conversion of Bavaria's hydroelectric power. A thorough estimate of requirements was projected, as was the registration of existing power stations and the building of additional installations. Furthermore, a unified electricity grid was to be created to deliver energy from large state-owned hydroelectric power stations to overhead electricity works. Oskar von Miller was also responsible for naming this project: Bayernwerk.

He was unable initially to put his ideas into practice, since it was not settled as to whether and under which form the Walchensee power station should be established. The particular geographical location of the Walchensee and the Kochelsee, separated from each other by a height of 200 meters, had already been thought of in 1897 for use in producing energy. There were lengthy discussions, but it was ten years before a design could be drawn up, after it became clear that the Bavarian state railroad's electrification would depend upon the energy produced by the Walchensee power station. When it was revealed how high the costs would be for construction and electrification, the Bavarian transport ministry shied away from the project. A motion was even proposed in the Bavarian state parliament that the Bavarian state should give up completely its plans for constructing the Walchensee power station. However, Oskar von Miller's proposal to use the huge volume of energy from the Walchensee power station for his planned Bayernwerk finally won the day.

Before the planning could begin, World War I started. In September 1914 Oskar von Miller declared himself willing to take on the preparatory work for the building of the Walchensee power station and the planning for Bayernwerk at his own expense. Hindered by the war, Oskar von Miller was only able to table his plans as state government commissioner. On June 21, 1918, the founding of Bayernwerk as well as that of the Walchensee power station was voted through.

The socialist revolution of November 1918 in Bavaria and the attendant radical political changes posed new problems for Oskar von Miller. He succeeded, however, in winning the approval he needed from the socialist government for his plans by drawing attention to the jobs that would be created for the soldiers demobilized after World War I. The construction work advanced rapidly despite the difficulties caused by Germany's losing the war. However, the project's financing became increasingly difficult to guarantee due to rising inflation, and both companies had to be changed into public limited companies. On April 5, 1921, Oskar von Miller went to the offices of a Munich solicitor, accompanied by several representatives of the Finance Ministry and Ministry of the Interior, to register Bayernwerk AG. The company was capitalized at Papiermarks 100 million. Forty-nine percent of the shares were intended to be distributed among the future electricity purchasers—cities and long-distance electricity companies—but the Bavarian state took up all the shares. The board of directors of the new company was also nominated: Rudolf Decker, assistant head of the Ministry of Trade and Industry, and Ernst Obpacher, chief planning officer in the Bavarian Ministry of the Interior. The founding of Walchenseewerk AG, with capital of Papiermarks 50 million, had taken place a few months earlier on January 5, 1921. The Bavarian state had taken up eight-ninths of the shares, and the Deutsche Reichsbahn took the other ninth. Oskar von Miller acted as chairman of both companies until the end of June 1921, when he stepped down to turn to other tasks.

Alongside Walchenseewerk AG, another large hydroelectric power company, the Mittlere Isar AG, fed into Bayernwerk's network. A private consortium had created the Mittlere Isar GmbH toward the end of World War I to exploit the Munich-Landshut stretch of the Isar. Dr. Theodor Rümelin, a hydraulic engineer, was commissioned to draw up a design. When the Bavarian government was faced with the problem of finding jobs for soldiers returning from military service after the war, the conversion of the Isar's water power became part of its emergency program. The Bavarian parliament had approved the project on March 25, 1919, and took over the shares of the company as well as the incomplete plans. The assistant secretary to the government, Franz Krieger, was appointed state commissioner, and the senior civil servant, Dr. Siegfried Kurzmann, his deputy. The construction work close to Munich began immediately, and the founding of the Mittlere Isar AG followed on January 5, 1921, with a capital of Papiermarks 75 million. The Bavarian state took eight-ninths of the shares and the Deutsche Reichsbahn one-ninth. Like Walchenseewerk AG, Mittlere Isar AG was to contribute to the electrification of the railway lines in southern Germany.

In the statutes of the three companies, which were adapted to work in close cooperation, the responsibilities of a public utility were brought to the fore. They were to be run according to commercial principles, but the interest return to the shareholders was limited. In accordance with the general plan drawn up, Bayernwerk gave up the right to supply the end user with electricity, in contrast to other big supply companies in other German states. Its role, rather, was to supply the electricity distribution companies with energy if they could not meet their electricity needs through their own power stations. The first 25-year contracts to deliver electricity, which Bayernwerk concluded between June 23 and June 30, 1923 with nine large electricity distributors in Bavaria, were based on this principle. Contracts with firms outside Bavaria were also concluded in the same year, the first being a contract to deliver electricity to the electricity supply company of the town of Stuttgart. Despite rising inflation, the two power stations on the Walchensee and the Middle Isar were able to start providing electricity as early as 1924. The growing demand for electricity and a water level which was at the mercy of the seasons led the company to look for new sources of energy.

In 1928 Bayernwerk acquired the Wackersdorf mine from the Bayerische Braunkohlenindustrie AG and built its own steam power station in Schwandorf, which began operating in 1930. Although Bayernwerk had not escaped the effects of the worldwide Depression, there was a considerable upturn in business with the general armaments boom. For example, the Vereinigte Aluminiumwerke AG (VAW) agreed on a contract with Bayernwerk for the supply of steam, electricity, and briquettes to its aluminum oxide factory in Schwandorf. In view of the strong demand for electricity that came with the economic revival, Bayernwerk was once again forced to develop additional sources of potential energy. The brown coal power stations in central Germany presented an obvious choice, situated close to the coal supplies. A contract with AG Sächsische Werke and Elektrowerke AG, the latter owned by the Reich, to deliver electricity followed in 1939.

Furthermore, Bayernwerk set about extending the electricity grid to guarantee the electricity supply for the chemical works situated in Innviertel, to the southeast of Bavaria, which were important in the arms build-up before World War II. In the course of the National Socialists' implementation of a policy of forcibly placing enterprises under state control, the Reich also strove to ensure its influence over energy supplies. Bayernwerk's share capital was taken over by the Reich's Vereinigte Industrie-Unternehmungen AG (VIAG) on April 1, 1939. Since 1933, Bayernwerk had carried out the business for the Walchenseewerk AG and Mittlere Isar power stations, but in 1942 the latter companies were formally merged with Bayernwerk. The Reichsbahn, which had held one-ninth of Bayernwerk's shares up until then, relinquished its holdings. Sixty percent of the capital went to the Bavarian state, and 40 percent was taken over by VIAG. In the business year 1943–44, Bayernwerk's electricity sales peaked, only to decline considerably in fiscal year 1944 to 1945. In the air attacks by the Allied Forces, industrial works, railway installations, and towns were increasingly bombarded. When the Americans marched into Bavaria in April 1945, there was virtually no electricity supply remaining.

Postwar Rebuilding

Like many other Bavarian companies, at the end of the war, Bayernwerk found itself in extreme difficulties. Its own electricity plants had remained intact to a large degree, but division of Germany into zones, and the dismantling of both the brown coal power stations in central Germany and the electricity grids linked with power and distribution stations in Bavaria, meant that Bayernwerk lost its most important suppliers of thermal energy. As building materials were in short supply in Bavaria after the war, it was not possible to redevelop the electricity grid. In addition, the Allied Control Council had forbidden the building of new power station plants. Bayernwerk was therefore obliged to extend its already existing sources of power. Thanks to a seven-kilometer-long tunnel, the fast-flowing Rissbach river on the Tyrolean border was diverted into the Walchensee. Furthermore, Bayernwerk made efforts to link up with the West

German thermal power station network, building a 220 kilovolt (kv) grid from Ludersheim near Nuremberg to its own transformer station in Aschaffenburg. In 1949 Bayernwerk concluded a contract with RheinischWestfälisches Elektrizitätswerk AG (RWE), Essen.

Once the Allied ban on building had been lifted in 1947, Bayernwerk embarked with increased vigor on the construction of power stations on the Alpine rivers and on the great rivers of the Danube and the Main in Bavaria. The company was aware, however, that there were natural limits to the further expansion of hydroelectric power, and that the reserves of brown coal in the Upper Palatinate would one day be exhausted. It decided to supplement the energy supply from hydroelectric power and brown coal with hard coal from the Ruhr area. In 1952 the first engines of a thermal energy power station built on the Main near Aschaffenburg went into operation. Both DB and the Prussische Elektrizitäts-AG had shareholdings in this power station. As Bayernwerk's oldest coal-fired power station, it has been equipped with the most up-to-date flue-gas treating installations, and is drawn on at times of peak demand.

For Bayernwerk, the 1950s brought economic and political challenges in the field of energy. Bavaria's position, both politically and geographically on the edge of the western European economic sphere, brought high energy prices and hampered its economic growth. At the same time, Bavarian industry was dependent upon a dynamically growing energy supply. The state had to find new and cheaper sources of energy. The ''Bavarian economic miracle'' took place with the introduction of atomic energy and the use of petroleum, and Bayernwerk bore this development in mind from an early stage. As early as 1957 an internal nuclear energy department had been created, and employees were being sent to train in England, Sweden, and the United States. Bayernwerk took part in the research into a new type of reactor using heavy water and carbon dioxide cooling via the Gesellschaft für die Entwicklung der Atomkraft in Bayern mbH.

New Forms of Energy: 1960–90

The atomic age for Bavaria's electricity supply industry dawned on June 17, 1961, when the 15MW experimental nuclear power station of Kahl am Main fed the first nuclear-generated electricity into the grid system integrated with the Bavarian network. Bayernwerk had a 20 percent holding in the operating company, the Versuchsatomkraftwerk Kahl GmbH (VAK). In 1966 the first large German nuclear power station, in Gundremmingen on the Danube, was connected to the grid. Bayernwerk took a 25 percent share in the construction of this 250MW nuclear power station.

Bavaria owed its efficient oil industry of the 1990s to the initiative of the Bavarian economic minister Dr. Otto Schedl. His plan to lay oil lines to the Mediterranean ports of Genoa and Trieste was initially viewed with skepticism. At the end of 1963, however, work began on this project with the construction of the first two refineries located at Ingolstadt. Bayernwerk constructed a power station in the heart of the new refinery center of Ingolstadt, which came into operation in 1965 with a 150MW engine. Further down the Danube, near Pleinting, another 300MW oil-fired power station was built in 1968. By the end of the 1960s, thermal energy had overtaken hydroelectric power, the former supplying more than 60 percent of Bavaria's electricity requirement. Therefore Bayernwerk concluded a long-term contract with Tiroler Wasserkraftwerke AG and RWE for the financing of the Kaunertal power station in the Tyrol, and for the supply of electricity from the Prutz power station to the upper Inntal.

Oil became the driving force behind Bavaria's economic development in the 1960s. It was possible to reduce substantially the oil prices between the port of Hamburg and the Bavarian city of Munich. However, the massive use of oil also meant that Bavaria was particularly affected by the oil crises of 1973–74 and 1979. Bayernwerk learned its lesson from the oil shocks of the 1970s, with the enormous increases in the price of oil. A secure and inexpensive electricity supply meant that the company had to free itself from dependence on unstable imports, and Bayernwerk's decision to expand its activities in nuclear energy proved crucial for the future.

As early as 1977, the 907MW nuclear power station Isar I, close to Landshut, came into operation, and Bayernwerk had a 50 percent share in the enterprise. The first electricity generation from the nuclear power station of Grafenrheinfeld followed in 1981. With a capacity of 1,300MW, it was Bayernwerk's biggest power station to date. In 1984 Bayernwerk took a share in the addition to the network of two new blocks at the Gundremmingen nuclear power station. Each block has a capacity of 1,300MW. Growing energy demand made it necessary to build a new installation, the 1,400MW nuclear power station Isar II, 50 percent owned by the Bayernwerk group. From a technical point of view this power station counted among the most modern in the world. With an electricity production of 10.3 billion kwh each, the nuclear power stations Grafenrheinfeld and Isar II were among the leaders in the 21 nuclear power stations in operation in Germany.

The 1990s and Beyond

By the early 1990s, more than half of Bavaria's electricity needs were generated by nuclear power stations. While the price of electricity in Bavaria was clearly above the German average in the 1960s and 1970s, Bayernwerk's expansion into nuclear power contributed to the fact that Bavaria, although poor in raw materials, had cheap electricity at its disposal by the beginning of the 1990s. Furthermore, the preservation of the environment played an important part in Bayernwerk's policies: with electricity generated by nuclear and hydroelectric power, harmful substances such as carbon dioxide were not released. In 1991 almost one-quarter of the electricity Bayernwerk generated came from coal-fired power stations, while oil and gas power stations only served as reserve generators, thus conserving precious fossil fuel reserves. Moreover, as part of Bayernwerk's environment program, the removal of nitrogen and desulfurization of the coal and oil in modern flue-gas treating installations reduced to a minimum emissions of harmful substances.

Along with good-value electricity and care for the environment, the reliability of supply was one of Bayernwerk's stated aims. As a national electricity supply company, Bayernwerk was running a network of high voltage and maximum voltage lines totaling 5,500 kilometers in length, and is linked to the Western European grid system. Bayernwerk regulated the provision to this grid, as well as the use of the power stations, from its distribution center in Karlsfeld near Munich, whose high-technology computer installations ensured that the balance between electricity demand and electricity production was maintained.

The constantly growing demand for energy and the limited quantity of natural resources made the development of new technologies and research into possible energy sources for the future indispensable. In the early 1990s, Bayernwerk had a 60 percent share in the Solar-Wasserkraft-Bayern GmbH in Neunburg vorm Wald in the Upper Palatinate. Hydrogen—perhaps *the* energy source of the future—was derived from the fission of water in electrolysis plants in this research center, and the electricity for this process came from solar cells. The hydrogen produced in this manner could be stored and employed according to requirements. Furthermore, Bayernwerk put into operation a trial model for providing solar energy in Flanitzhütte, a remote area in the natural park of the Bayerischer Wald. The aim was to supply five estates there, totally independently from the public network, with electricity derived from solar power from a photovoltaic plant.

The reunification of Germany in the early 1990s provided Bayernwerk with another task for the future, and it undertook the construction of a highly efficient and environmentally friendly energy supply in the former German Democratic Republic. Three new subsidiary companies—Energieversorgung Nordthüringen AG, Ostthüringer Energieversorgung AG, and Südthüringer Engergieversorgung AG—were founded at the beginning of 1991, Bayernwerk holding a 51 percent majority share in them. These subsidiaries, provided with a great deal of investment and specialist technical support, would bring about the reorganization of the supply of electricity and long-distance heating in the eastern German state of Thuringia. In 1991 Bayernwerk had already built a 380-kilovolt grid from Redwitz in Bavaria to Remptendorf in Thuringia.

The opening of the Iron Curtain also enabled closer cooperation with the states of eastern Europe. Thanks to the direct current network coupling in the border region near Etzenricht in the Upper Palatinate, the company planned to make possible exchange of current between the two maximum voltage networks in Bavaria and the Czech Republic. This would make mutual help possible in the case of power station breakdowns, or if power stations had to be closed down temporarily owing to a danger of smog.

In the mid- to late 1990s, Bayernwerk placed an emphasis on many of the issues on which it had focused in the earlier part of the decade: continued reunification of Germany, and exploration of joint-venture opportunities with businesses in other parts of the newly unified European continent; and development of alternative energy sources and other methods for preserving the environment. Added to these concerns were new ones, in the form of expanded business ventures, particularly in the realm of telecommunications; privatization of utilities; and the concomitant downsizing and streamlining of the vast enterprise that is Bayernwerk and the Bayernwerk Group.

A principal area of activity for the company in eastern Germany was in the state of Thuringia, where it operated through a number of subsidiaries including Vereinigte Energiewerke AG (VEAG). Outside of Germany, Bayernwerk explored joint ventures both to the west—with EdF, a French utility—and to the east. Together with EdF and Germany's own RWE, Bayernwerk belonged to a consortium devoted to increasing the interface between eastern and western Europe. It built a gas line connecting Bavaria and Austria, completed at the end of 1996, and became heavily involved in supplying energy to the Czech Republic, Slovakia and most notably Hungary. In the latter country it acquired interests in an electrical utility, DÉDÀSZ Rt., and a gas company, KÖGÀZ.

Of the electric power Bayernwerk produced in 1996, more than 70 percent came from power stations under its ownership. Power was generated by hydroelectric and nuclear plants, but the company also looked to new sources of energy. It continued to operate its acclaimed Solar-Wasserstoff-Bayern GmbH (SWB) in Neunburg vorm Wald for the production and application of hydrogen. It also held slightly less than half of Siemens Solar GmbH (SSG), the world's largest producer of photovoltaic modules for solar power. Also, the company backed public relations campaigns such as ''Citizens for Solar Energy'' and ''Sun in Schools,'' which assisted classrooms throughout Bavaria in developing their own photovoltaic construction kits. (The Germany Ministry of Economics took over the latter program at the end of 1996.) In addition, the company devoted considerable resources toward Energy Future in Bavaria, a program designed to promote conservation of resources. It also held a heavy interest in waste management activities through several subsidiaries.

Besides its gas and electric businesses, Bayernwerk in the mid- to late 1990s expanded into the area of telecommunications. On February 15, 1996, it established Bayernwerk Netkom GmbH out of the merger of its communications engineering departments in Bavaria and Thuringia. Though the venture into telecommunications may seem an unusual one, in fact energy companies had been allowed to operate their own telecommunications networks since 1922, the year after Bayernwerk was founded. Bayernwerk Netkom had two aims: first, to provide member companies of the Bayernwerk Group with efficient telecommunications services; and second, to develop a communications network that would serve consumers around the country. In so doing, it would enter into joint ventures, through VIAG, with companies including British Telecom and MCI.

On the first day of 1996, Germany ceased subsidization of coal, another move in a nationwide trend to take the government out of the realm of business enterprises. Bayernwerk continued to change with the successive movements toward privatization. In 1996, the company reduced its numbers of employees,

chiefly by the concentration of hydropower and telecommunications activities. But for the slimmed-down work force, new opportunities presented themselves. For instance, the company implemented flexible work hours to increase efficiency and give workers a greater sense of personal freedom. It also increased its vocational training programs, in part as a response to high unemployment in reunified Germany. As its contribution to the ''Employment in Bavaria Pact,'' a statewide jobs program, the Bayernwerk Group in 1996 undertook the vocational training of almost 650 young people. As Bayernwerk enters the 21st century, privatization would likely continue to have far-reaching effects on the company, the group, and all subsidiaries.

Principal Subsidiaries

Energieversorgung Oberfranken AG (26.3%); CONTIGAS Deutsche Energie AG (Contigas) (88.8%); Energieversorgung Ostbayern AG (95.7%); Uberlandwerk Unterfranken AG (55.4%); Grosskraftwerk Franken AG (98.3%); Fränkische Gas-Lieferungs-Gesellschaft mbH (65%); Untere Iller AG (60%); Solar-Wasserstoff-Bayern GmbH (70%); WBG—Wohnen, Bauen, Grund, Gesellschaft für Wohn—u. Gewerbeimmobilien GmbH (99.9%); Thüringer Energie AG (53%); Isar-Amperwerke AG (80.8%); ILSE-Bayernwerk Energieanlagen GmbH; Gasversorgung Thüringen GmbH (89.8%); Thyssengas GmbH (50%); Gerresheimer Glas AG (51%); Klöckner & Co. AG; VIAG-Bayernwerk Beteiligungsges. mbH (50%); Gesellschaft der Energiewirtschaft für Daten- and Organisationsservice mbH (51%); Telekommunikation Gesellschaft für Betrieb und Dienstleistungen mbH (50%); Bayernwerk Netkom; Bayerische Wasserkraftwerke AG; Rhein-Main-Donau AG (77.5%); Bayernwerk Wasserkraft AG (69%); ReCon Projektentwicklungs- und Beteiligungsges. mbH (90%).

Further Reading

25 Jahre Bayernwerk, Munich: Bayernwerk AG, 1946.
30 Jahre Bayernwerk AG Bayerische Landeselektrizitätsversorgung, 1921–1951, Munich: Bayernwerk AG, 1952.
''Fünfzig Jahre Bayernwerk 1921–1971,'' in *Bayerischer Braunkohlen Bergbau,* No. 81, June 1971.
Kristl, Wilhelm Lukas, *Der weißblaue Despot. Oskar von Miller in seiner Zeit,* Munich: Richard Pflaum Verlag, 1965.
Responsibility and Vision. Munich: Bayernwerk AG, 1996.
von Miller, Walther, *Oskar von Miller,* Munich: Bruckmann Verlag, 1932, 2nd edition, Munich, 1955.
Zorn, Wolfgang, ''Bayerns Gewerbe, Handel und Verkehr (1806–1970)'', in Max Spindler, *Handbuch der bayerischen Geschichte,* vol. IV, Das neue Bayern 1800–1970, verbesserter Nachdruck, Munich, 1979.

—updated by Judson Knight

Beckett Papers

Two Gateway Boulevard
East Granby, Connecticut 06026
U.S.A.
(860) 844-2400
Fax: (860) 844-2552

Wholly Owned Division of Hammermill Paper Co.
Incorporated: 1887 as The Beckett Paper Company
Employees: 500 (1994)
Sales: $70 million (1994 est.)
SICs: 2621 Paper Mills

With sales of less than $100 million, Beckett Papers is a rather small, yet distinctive, segment of the Fine Papers Division of Hammermill Paper Co., itself a subsidiary of $20 billion International Paper Co. Nevertheless, Beckett enjoys a long and distinguished heritage in the paper industry, stretching back 50 years earlier, in fact, than that of International Paper. Established in 1848, Beckett was controlled and managed by descendants of founder William Beckett until 1959, when it became a subsidiary of Hammermill Paper Co. Hammermill was in turn acquired by International Paper in 1984.

A well-established brand presence in the fine papers, stationery, and uncoated recycled stock segments enabled Beckett to retain its own identity and logo through the mid-1990s. But while its goods continued to be milled at the company's birthplace in Hamilton County, Ohio, its headquarters was moved to East Granby, New Jersey, along with the rest of International Papers' Fine Papers Group.

Mid-19th-Century Foundations

Beckett Papers was founded and eventually named for William Beckett. Born in 1821 and educated at southern Ohio's Miami University, Beckett, along with a couple of partners, bought into an abandoned paper mill in the town of Hamilton in 1848. At first, the mill churned out newsprint made of rags for sale to newspaper publishers in nearby Cincinnati. Though the mill struggled to stay in the black during its first two years, efficiencies achieved through the addition of a second paper making machine led to a decade-long period of profitability. The Civil War helped to lengthen this prosperous period, as newspaper sales skyrocketed, fueled by public hunger for news from the battlefields. These high times subsided during the late 19th century, when panics and recessions hurt the company's results.

Partners came and went over the course of the company's first four decades in operation, and the business endured several name changes before its incorporation as The Beckett Paper Company in 1887. By this time Thomas Beckett, son of the founder, had joined the company. The second-generation leader brought new production methods to the company, including modern paper making machines that used wood pulp. Though his changes were vehemently resisted by some managers, modernizations kept the company's costs competitive and eventually brought it out of the red. Thomas launched the Buckeye Cover brand of colored paper in 1894, a stock that soon gained a reputation for high quality. The buckeye, Ohio's state tree, would serve as Beckett's corporate logo for some 100 years, until the launch of a new logo in mid-1998.

Difficulties in Early 20th Century

The early years of the 20th century proved difficult for the company, due to economic fluctuations and natural disasters. The Panic of 1907 ushered in a multi-year economic depression. Just as the nation and the mill were emerging from that crisis, cities along the Great Miami River, including Dayton and Hamilton, were struck by the Great Flood of 1913. Though the Beckett mill was lost, it was rebuilt within six months—just in time for another recession.

World War I brought high demand and a period of profitability for the company, which carried it through the 1910s, such that the mill was even expanded in 1918. Before his death in 1928, Thomas Beckett shared his good fortune via the creation of an employee stock option plan, likely one of the first in the paper industry. He was succeeded as president by his eldest son, Minor, who had earned a degree from the Massachusetts Institute of Technology before joining the family business in 1921. Tragedy forced a second transfer of power before the end of 1928, however. That year, Minor Beckett died unexpectedly. His mother, Thomas's wife Mary, assumed the presidency, an honorary post she held until 1947. Minor's cousin, Guy Beckett, son of Thomas's brother William, was also brought into the business at this time.

The mill operated under the general management of vice-president W. Verne Williams for two years. When Williams resigned in 1930, Guy Beckett advanced to the lead administrative post. Like the vast majority of businesses, Beckett encountered severe difficulties during the Great Depression. Though the company lost a customer constituting about 20 percent of sales during this period, it replaced that business and more with the production of Beckett Offset lithography paper. Upgrades of the physical plant brought efficiencies and productivity enhancements that were put to good use as the nation emerged from the financial crisis.

Beckett also diversified into greeting card and announcement stock during the 1930s. By the end of the decade, the company had expanded its branded lines to include text, offset, opaque, and cover stocks. The company supported these products with innovative marketing tools, including the Beckett Color Guide and the Beckett Color Finder. Perhaps most powerful was *The Buckeye Book of Advertising and Printing,* a reference compiled by Beckett advertising director Carl Richard Greer. According to a 1978 company history, this tome was "widely distributed throughout the graphic arts industry [and] it was considered a definitive textbook on the subject."

Postwar Era

Guy Beckett succeeded his aunt as president of Beckett Paper in 1947 and continued to hold that office through 1958. The company increased its production capacity by half in the immediate postwar era to accommodate a number of new product developments. Although Beckett was a relatively small player in the national paper making industry (it ranked 36th in the mid-1960s), it laid claim to a number of industry firsts, among them the 1954 launch of Beckett Hi-White, the first fluorescent white printing paper. Beckett also made several advances in the area of packaging and shipping, introducing

corrugated and polyethylene-lined cartons as well as polyethylene wrap on skids. Improvements in products, production methods, and distribution helped increase Beckett's sales by some 160 percent during the postwar era.

Guy's cousin William advanced to the presidency in 1958. Born in 1909 of Thomas and Mary Beckett and named for the founder of the family business, William Beckett attended Tufts University and the Massachusetts Institute of Technology before joining the family business in 1933. One of his first actions as president was to effect a merger with the Hammermill Paper Company through an equity exchange in 1959. The marriage provided Beckett with the financial backing necessary to launch a major capacity increase as well as more than a dozen new colored papers.

The printing industry's transition from letterpress or typographic printing to offset lithography in the late 1950s and early 1960s brought with it increased demand for Beckett's high-quality papers. As it had in the 1930s, trade advertising played an important role in the company's success during this period. Beckett targeted artists and designers, tailoring new papers with new finishes, textures, and colors to their demanding needs. From 1951 to 1966, sales nearly tripled.

Upon William Beckett's 1974 retirement, David L. Belew became the first non-family member to lead Beckett Paper. A former advertising agency executive, Belew had joined the company in 1960 and advanced through the advertising department. By the time Belew took the helm, Beckett was producing more than a dozen exclusive grades of paper in 120 different colors, including 13 whites. The company continued to introduce new lines during the 1970s and 1980s, including Cambric brand linen printing and writing papers as well as the Ridge and Enhance! lines. These papers were often used for embossed personal and business stationery.

Acquisition by International Paper in 1986

In 1986, Hammermill came under a hostile takeover attempt by a group of investors led by Paul Bilzerian. International Paper Co. entered the fray as a white knight, paying $1.1 billion to acquire the Pennsylvania-based company and its subsidiaries, including Beckett Paper. In fact, Alison Leigh Cowan of *Business Week* asserted that Beckett's high-quality, high-priced, and high-margin papers were among the key factors in the sale. The agreement came with several strings attached, among them the requirement that Hammermill endure as a separate business. This provision, in turn, helped sustain Beckett as a business entity.

David Belew advanced to the chairmanship of Beckett Paper in 1990 and was succeeded as president and general manager by John L. Throckmorton, Jr. In the years since becoming a part of the massive International Paper group, Beckett has become more of a brand than an operating entity. In 1997, it was subsumed into IP's Fine Papers Division, and Beckett's headquarters were moved to East Granby, Connecticut. By that time, Beckett encompassed seven grades of writing, text, and cover papers, including a variety of finishes from linen to "ultrasmooth" and matching envelopes in a broad range of colors. Having had a waste reclamation program in place since the

1970s, Beckett incorporated recycled fiber into all its products beginning in 1991, and all but the brightest whites in its lines were recycled by 1998.

With a heritage of more than 150 years of paper making behind its products, Beckett Papers has carved out a relatively small, yet profitable and vital niche in its corporate family as well as the paper industry. Backed by a new logo and a strong reputation, Beckett appeared poised to endure and celebrate its bicentennial.

Further Reading

The Beckett Paper Company, 1843–1978: 125 Years of Fine Paper Making, Hamilton, Ohio: Beckett Paper Co., 1973.

Cowan, Alison Leigh, ''International Paper Pays a Fancy Price for a Fancy Papermaker,'' *Business Week,* September 1, 1986, p. 69.

Greer, Carl Richard, *What a Buckeye Cover Man Saw in Europe and at Home,* Hamilton, Ohio: Beckett Paper Co., 1923.

—April D. Gasbarre

Best Buy Co., Inc.

7075 Flying Cloud Drive
Eden Prairie, Minnesota 55344
U.S.A.
(612) 947-2200
Fax: (612) 947-2422
Web site: http://www.bestbuy.com

Public Company
Incorporated: 1966 as Sound of Music Inc.
Employees: 36,300
Sales: $7.7 billion (1997)
Stock Exchanges: New York
SICs: 5722 Household Appliance Stores; 5731 Radio,
  Television & Electronics Stores; 5734 Computer &
  Software Stores; 5735 Record & Prerecorded Tape
  Stores; 5946 Camera & Photographic Supply Stores

One of two powerhouses among consumer electronics retailers, Minnesota-based Best Buy Co., Inc., dominates the central U.S. market through a network of more than 280 stores in 32 states. In addition to personal computers and consumer video and audio products, the company offered large and small appliances, ranging from refrigerators to coffeemakers, and entertainment software, including compact discs, audio and video cassettes, and computer software. Although the company had overtaken archrival Circuit City in the late 1990s to become the largest consumer electronics retailer in the United States, its victory was marginal and the price reductions needed to capture market share had hurt Best Buy's profit margins.

Early History

Best Buy is the brainchild of the company's founder, chairman, and CEO, Richard M. Schulze. In 1966 Schulze and a partner opened Sound of Music Inc. in an attempt to capture a share of the Twin Cities' home and car stereo retail market. First year sales reached $173,000. Four years later Schulze bought out his partner and proceeded to expand his retail chain; his

product line, however, was limited to audio components until the early 1980s. Then, according to an Executive of the Year cover story for *Corporate Report Minnesota,* Schulze said, "The lights began to turn on." Writer S. C. Biemesderfer explained: "Schulze had come to realize that there wasn't much of a future in a market glutted with vendors, serving a shrinking audience of 15- to 18-year-olds with limited resources." His ability to alter the course of his company was enhanced by a week-long management seminar he attended in 1981. Departing the seminar as a "reformed controller," Schulze saw the dynamic possibilities that lay ahead and turned them into reality.

His first step was to expand Sound of Music's offerings to include appliances and VCRs. Schulze saw sales quickly climb. In 1982 revenues reached $9.3 million; the following year the company renamed itself Best Buy and firmly oriented itself toward an older, broader, and more affluent customer base. Then, in 1984, Schulze took another major step by introducing the superstore format and quickly capturing 42 percent of the local market. At the time the company operated just eight stores in the Midwest, but by 1987 this number had tripled, while sales and earnings had spiraled upward to $239 million and $7.7 million, respectively. In addition to greatly expanded warehouse size and product offerings, the superstore format meant significantly smaller margins to maintain its good service, low prices image.

Price Wars in the Late 1980s

Of course Best Buy was not alone among upstart chains during the 1980s in capitalizing on the superstore format and such hot-ticket consumer items as VCRs. "But after a raft of these chains went public," wrote Mary J. Pitzer in 1987, "they expanded rapidly and began colliding head-on. As a result, many companies took a beating on profit margins and are now gravely wounded." It was, in a very real sense, the best of times and the worst of times for Best Buy. Although sales had practically doubled to $439 million in fiscal 1988, net earnings had declined by 64 percent. Price wars were the chief culprit, and they were still escalating to a frenzied pitch in Best Buy's core Twin Cities market, which Highland Superstores had boldly entered in early 1987.

For a while, both companies benefited from market share increases, if not profit gains, by the battle. Then, finally, a saturation point was reached, with too many stores in the same area competing for the same dollars. According to Biemesderfer, ''Rumor had it that, as Best Buy limped into the fall of 1988 Schulze tried to sell his company to Sears and failed because of his demands for certain perks.'' Biemesderfer went on to write, ''Schulze denies the allegation, but to this day, even his backers question his version of the story.'' Schulze's own explanation was as follows: ''At no point in time were there ever any concerns or fears about the future of the company. . . . Our discussion with Sears Roebuck was simply an attempt to understand the interest they would have in supplying capital necessary to grow the company independently.''

Despite the earnings downturn in fiscal 1989 (net profits for the year ending March 31 slumped 26 percent, to just $2 million) and the looming presence of Highland, revenues were still climbing, albeit more slowly. In Schulze's mind, the key to regaining the momentum of the mid-1980s was to stand out from the competition, for the average customer recognized little difference among superstores, with their discount prices, multiple-step purchase processes, commissioned salespeople, and ubiquitous service plan and extended warranty packages. Schulze's answer? Concept II stores.

The unveiling of Best Buy's first Concept II stores in 1989 was the culmination of a daring new advance by Schulze. The idea behind Concept II was that the traditional superstore format was out of sync, in large part, with the needs or preferences of most shoppers. Shoppers were entering electronics discount stores with only a limited need for sales help and a desire for hassle-free buying (no service plan contracts, no waiting for merchandise from the back room, no switching from counter to counter). Thus the revamped Best Buy stores would feature well-stocked showrooms averaging around 36,000 square feet, fewer salespeople, more self-help product information, Answer Centers for those requiring personal assistance, and one-stop purchasing. As a veteran Best Buy analyst, quoted by Biemesderfer, proclaimed: ''Concept II is the most innovative thing to happen in this industry—ever.'' The revenue Best Buy sacrificed in de-emphasizing service plans was compensated for by lowered employee costs. Stores without commissioned sales help now were able to operate at two-thirds of the work force required in the past.

Continued Expansion in the Early 1990s

In April 1991, even before Best Buy had gotten around to converting its ten Twin Cities stores, loss-ravaged Highland exited the metropolitan area, conceding defeat and closing all six of its stores there. Best Buy itself reported a loss of $9.4 million for fiscal 1991, but this was due to a $14 million change in its method of accounting for extended service plans. From fiscal 1992 to fiscal 1993, Best Buy reported ''the best financial performance in the company's 27-year history.'' In addition to its stunning increases in revenues and earnings, the fast-growing retailer opened 38 new stores and saw comparable store sales (sales from stores open at least 14 months) increase by 19.4 percent.

During the calendar year 1993, Best Buy opened nine more stores in Chicago, for a total of 23, to solidify its leadership position in the Midwest, and entered the key Circuit City markets of Atlanta and Phoenix with an additional 13 stores. Numerous other openings, including a small number of megastores (40,000- to 50,000-square-foot self-service warehouses emphasizing the emerging growth lines of prerecorded music and computers), brought Best Buy's tally to 151 stores by year-end 1993. At that point the only internal factor seriously saddling the company was a hefty 43 percent debt-to-capital ratio. Best Buy's ''push'' distribution system, however, in which products are automatically shipped to outlets based on computer analysis of past sales trends, along with its rapid turnover time and its expectation of rising sales per store, indicated that the company could hold its costs while continuing to expand.

Its greatest concern for the future was the bottom line impact of Circuit City's latest moves. Just as Best Buy had looked to the outer corridors of the country, Circuit City had looked inward. It, too, had embraced Chicago, where price wars began anew. The Virginia company also had plans to enter Kansas City, Missouri and the Twin Cities in 1994. Whether the two would be able to operate side by side for long was unknown. Whatever the case, the stakes were high, not only for the companies but for related retailers and manufacturers. Such high-image manufacturers as Mitsubishi already had retreated from both store chains, complaining of poor price and sales support. And, wrote Berss, ''The last thing retailers need this Christmas—the biggest selling period of the year—is a price war. But that's what they're getting.''

By 1993 both superstore titans had virtually vanquished the remaining competition, which included such former number two retailers as Highland Superstores (forced to liquidate) and Dixons Group's Silo Holdings (forced to downsize and sell to Fretter Inc.). Best Buy's growth had been nothing short of spectacular. From 1989 to 1992 corporate sales rose annually by 23 percent, while the industry as a whole expanded by a yearly average of just three percent. From 1992 to 1993 revenues catapulted for the first time beyond the $1 billion mark, from $929 million to $1.6 billion, for an increase of 74 percent. During this same period net earnings soared 107 percent to just less than $20 million. Although Circuit City was a significantly larger and more stable company in the eyes of investors, with a history of wider profit margins and negligible debt, it was Best Buy that generated the most excitement on Wall Street. For the first half of 1991, Best Buy outshone all other New York Stock Exchange stocks in percentage appreciation. With excitement, however, came volatility: in 1993 the stock nearly doubled within a three-month period but then dropped by ten percent in a single day in mid-November. Part of this roller coaster pattern was due to Best Buy's increasingly heated battle with Circuit City, which had many analysts wary.

The roller coaster ride continued into 1994, with Best Buy's stock hitting a high of $37 a share in April, then falling almost 40 percent in the next five months to $22. It rose again to $45 only to drop by December to $34. Competition with Circuit City remained fierce, with Best Buy challenging its archrival by entering its traditional strongholds in California, Washington, D.C., and Ohio. The head-on clash prompted renewed price wars, which Best Buy was positioned to withstand because of its low cost structure. Lowered prices, however, meant lower earnings for Best Buy.

The company's strategy of cutting service to help offer lower prices continued to cost the company suppliers. By 1995 the electronics manufacturer Hitachi had stopped supplying Best Buy, as had the appliance maker Kenwood. In addition, Whirlpool pulled its top-line Whirlpool brand from the store, although it continued to supply its lower-priced Roper brand. President of Mitsubishi Consumer Electronics America Jack Osborn explained to *Forbes* in 1995 that his company chose to sell through smaller retailers because they offer better service and cannot use their size to pressure Mitsubishi into offering lower wholesale prices. Osborn said at the time, "We will not be in a national chain."

In an effort to reverse this trend, Best Buy announced in 1995 that it would revamp its merchandising format for high-quality audio products. Brad Anderson, the president of Best Buy, told *Forbes* that the move was needed because, "We could not land some of the products we wanted."

Expanding Territory and Market Share in the Late 1990s

Despite these problems, Best Buy continued to expand its territory and to take over market share. In 1995 the company added 47 new stores and moved into new areas, including Miami and Cincinnati. By late 1995 Best Buy was breathing down the neck of Circuit City in terms of market share. With 8.7 percent of the consumer electronics market, Best Buy stood only a tenth of a percent behind Circuit City.

The company added almost 50 new stores in its fiscal year 1996 and moved into additional new territories, including Philadelphia. Revenues rose to more than $7 billion in fiscal year 1996 from 1995 revenues of $3 billion. Earnings, however, actually dropped, from about $58 million in 1995 to $48 million in 1996. The downward earnings spiral continued in 1997. Although revenues rose slightly in fiscal 1997 to 7.7 billion, earnings had plummeted to $1.7 million. The company cited falling computer prices and a soft consumer electronics market as reasons for its poor performance.

The drastic cut in profit margins forced Best Buy to rethink its product offerings. For instance, the company began offering cut-rate compact discs in 1988 as a loss leader and pushed the idea in the mid-1990s. Although people bought the low-priced discs, they did not stay to purchase the big-ticket, high-margin items. In 1997 the company cut back its CD selection and raised the remaining titles' prices slightly. It also added an assortment of books and magazines to its entertainment section. In addition, it decided to concentrate on higher margin items, such as computer peripherals, high-end appliances, and service plans.

By 1997 Best Buy had achieved its goal of becoming the industry leader, but it paid the price in profits, which had fallen to a dismal 0.02 percent of sales. With computer prices continuing to fall, 1998 would test the efficacy of Best Buy's adjustments to its product offerings. The first three quarters of fiscal 1998 did indeed show improvement: net earnings had passed $30 million, compared with a net loss of almost $11 million for the same nine months in fiscal 1997.

Further Reading

Apgar, Sally, "Best Buy Planning To Spend $5 Million To Upgrade Stores in Twin Cities Area," *Star Tribune*, March 31, 1993, p. 1D.
"Best Buy Files for New Stock Offering," *Star Tribune*, April 21, 1993, p. 1D.
Bernstein, Elizabeth, "Best Buy Breaks into Book Market," *Publishers Weekly*, September 1, 1997, p. 9.
Berss, Marcia, "High Noon," *Forbes*, December 20, 1993, pp. 44–45.
——, "We Will Not Be in a National Chain," *Forbes*, March 27, 1995, p. 50.
"Best Buy Co.," *Wall Street Journal*, January 9, 1992, p. B8.
"Best Buy Earnings Soar 114 Percent for Quarter," *Star Tribune*, December 17, 1993, p. 4D.
"Best Buy Inc.," *Chain Store Age Executive with Shopping Center Age*, December 1992, pp. 64, 66.
Biemesderfer, S. C., "Laughing Last (Executive of the Year: Richard M. Schulze)," *Corporate Report Minnesota*, January 1992, pp. 33–42.
Carvell, Tim, "The Crazy Record Business: These Prices Really Are Insane," *Fortune*, August 4, 1997, pp. 108–115.
Haran, Leah, "Best Buy, Circuit City Raising the Stakes in Electronics Warfare," *Advertising Age*, September 27, 1995, p. 4.
Kennedy, Tony, "Best Buy Predicting Flat Earnings for First Half," *Star Tribune*, June 17, 1993, p. 3D.
Marcotty, Josephine, "Best Buy Co. Stock Takes a Beating as Possible Price War with Circuit City Looms," *Star Tribune*, November 12, 1993, pp. 1–2D.
Pitzer, Mary J., "Electronics 'Superstores' May Have Blown a Fuse," *Business Week*, June 8, 1987, pp. 90, 94.
"Sales at Best Buy Coincide with Rally of Its Stock," *Star Tribune*, July 9, 1993, pp. 1D, 7D.
Sullivan, R. Lee, "Appealing to the Technophiles," *Forbes*, April 27, 1992, pp. 52, 54.
Voskoboynik, Henry, "Best Buy: A Best Buy Indeed," *Financial World*, September 1, 1994, p. 12.

—Jay P. Pederson
—updated by Susan Windisch Brown

BIC Corporation

500 BIC Drive
Milford, Connecticut 06460
U.S.A.
(203) 783-2000
Fax: (203) 783-2081

86% Owned Subsidiary of Société BIC, S.A.
Incorporated: 1958 as Waterman-BIC Pen Corporation
Employees: 2,700
Sales: $1.2 billion (1996)
SICs: 3951 Pens & Mechanical Pencils; 3999
  Manufacturing Industries, Not Elsewhere Classified;
  3421 Cutlery

BIC Corporation is the country's leading manufacturer of disposable ballpoint pens and cigarette lighters. It is also an industry leader in the production of disposable shavers. BIC has extensive manufacturing facilities in North and South America, including in Toronto, Canada; Milford, Connecticut; Clearwater and St. Petersburg, Florida; Guatemala City, Guatemala; and Cuautitlan, Mexico. BIC's products are primarily low-cost plastic items. Its pens, lighters, and shavers are typically the most affordable in their category, retailing for less than other brands. Pens comprise about half of the company's production, as well as half of its sales and earnings. One of BIC's most prominent products is its clear plastic ballpoint. BIC's lighter is the top-selling lighter in North America, first popularized in the 1970s with the slogan "Flick my BIC." BIC also makes correction fluid and correction pens and has acquired a premium pen manufacturer, Sheaffer.

Early History

The company was founded by Marcel Bich, who left his job as production manager for an ink company in 1945 to set up his own business outside of Paris, manufacturing parts for fountain pens and mechanical pencils. During this time ballpoint pens, although still very expensive, were becoming popular in Europe, and the first ballpoint pens were introduced in the United States, selling for $12.50 each at New York's Gimbel's Department Store.

First Bich expanded his business to include the manufacture of plastic barrels for ballpoint pen companies, and then, in 1949, he introduced his own line of ballpoint pens. Called BICs—using the phonetic spelling of Bich's name—the pens were of a simple design, nonretractable with clear plastic barrels, and sold for around 19 cents each. Whereas early ballpoint pens were known to clog and leak, Bich's pens proved reliable and achieved immediate success in Europe with annual sales exceeding $5 million by 1955. Bich then turned his attention to marketing his products in the United States.

The Waterman Pen Company in Seymour, Connecticut was founded by Lewis E. Waterman, a U.S. insurance salesperson and part-time inventor, who developed the first practical fountain pen in 1884. At one time Waterman Pen was the world's leading maker of fountain pens. In the 1950s, however, with the growing popularity of ballpoint pens, the company had begun to falter. In 1958 Bich agreed to purchase 60 percent of the company for $1 million. When the true financial condition of the company became known, Bich was able to acquire the remaining 40 percent for nothing. The company was renamed the Waterman-BIC Pen Corporation, and its headquarters was moved to Milford, Connecticut.

The inexpensive BIC pens did not catch on as quickly in the United States as they had in Europe, probably because the U.S. market had been flooded with shoddy pens by other companies. The leading brand in the "over-a-dollar" pen market was made by the PaperMate pen company, purchased in 1955 by The Gillette Company. Bich's U.S. managers urged him to make a more expensive ballpoint to compete with PaperMate, but Bich resisted. He reportedly told his advisers, "Waterman is 100 percent mine. You are going to do what you are told."

Expansion in the 1960s

In the early 1960s Waterman-BIC launched an aggressive television advertising campaign that boasted that BIC pens would write "First Time, Every Time." To prove that a 29 cent BIC pen would perform as well as pens costing several times

Company Perspectives:

Bic's core activities are the manufacture and sale of stationery products, lighters and shavers. Bic monitors the entire manufacturing process, giving constant attention to the development and improvement of its products. Bic's aim is to provide consumers with top quality products for their day-to-day lives at the minimum fair price.

more, the commercials showed BIC pens still working after being drilled through wallboard, shot from guns, fire-blasted, and strapped to the feet of ice skaters. In another effort to establish a market in the United States, Waterman-BIC distributed its pens for sale in grocery stores and small shops near schools where students congregated, rather than in the department stores that carried more expensive pens.

After a rocky start, Waterman-BIC established itself as the largest maker of ballpoint pens in the United States. By 1967 the company was turning out nearly 500 million pens annually, accounting for nearly 60 percent of the U.S. market. In 1972 *Time* reported, "Baron Bich has done for ballpoints what Henry Ford did for cars: he has produced a cheap but serviceable model." In 1974 a reporter for *Forbes* wrote, "From the start, Bich concentrated on the cheap end of the market—but with a difference. Where his competitors were turning out junk, Bich made a reliable pen that could command a premium, but still cheap price. ... By the time his competitors figured out how to build an equally good pen for the price, Bich had a lock on the market."

In 1971 Waterman-BIC became the BIC Pen Corporation, more accurately reflecting its business. That name soon became outdated, however, as the company embarked on its first diversification.

Expanding Its Product Line in the 1970s

In 1970 Gillette purchased the S. T. Dupont Company, a prestigious French manufacturer whose principal product was luxury cigarette lighters that sold for hundreds of dollars. During this time Dupont explored the possibilities of marketing a disposable lighter, developing an inexpensive disposable lighter called Cricket, which it introduced in the United States in 1972. Later that year *Time* reported that BIC was test marketing a disposable lighter that could provide 3,000 lights before wearing out. BIC introduced this lighter in 1973.

To compete with Gillette, which was solidly entrenched as the market leader, BIC again turned to creative television advertising. A series of commercials soon showed sensuous women urging cigarette smokers to "Flick my BIC," a phrase perceived as having sexual connotations, that soon became a part of the national lexicon. Writing about network censors in *The Best Thing on TV: Commercials,* Jonathan Price remarked, "They absolutely do not see sex in advertising if it's blatant. ... They can find sex in a garage mechanic talking about shock absorbers. But let somebody say, 'Flick my BIC,'—this is beautifully obscene—everyone nods their heads and lets that

go, because ... well, we know you can't possibly mean that, that would be obscene."

BIC also slashed the wholesale price of its lighters so they sold at retail for less than one dollar. This action set off a fierce price war with Gillette. But, by the end of 1978, BIC had surpassed Cricket and, in 1984, Gillette acknowledged defeat. It pulled Cricket from the market and later sold the brand to Swedish Match Corporation, which licensed the lighter for distribution in the United States. At the time BIC controlled about 65 percent of the market for disposable lighters.

During the time that BIC and Gillette were battling over disposable lighters, the companies were also going head-to-head for a new segment of Gillette's traditional business, disposable shavers. King C. Gillette had invented the safety razor in 1903, and the company he founded dominated the market for the next 70 years. Then in 1975, BIC's parent corporation, the French Société BIC, S.A., introduced a disposable plastic shaver in Europe. Anticipating that BIC next would bring out the shaver in the United States, Gillette quickly introduced its own disposable razor dubbed "Good News!" in 1976, a full year before the BIC shaver made its U.S. debut. Gillette seriously underestimated the demand for disposable razors, however. Furthermore, it was not eager to see customers switch from its reusable razor systems to its disposables, since Good News! cost more to make and sold for less than the company's replacement blades. Therefore, Gillette spent very little on advertising.

BIC, however, advertised heavily, again relying on catchy television commercials. In one series of commercials, people were blindfolded and shaved by professional barbers, using either the BIC Shaver or Gillette's nondisposable Trac II razor. According to the ads, 58 percent of the participants claimed that there was no difference between the BIC shave and the Gillette shave. Gillette leaders were incensed by the ads and asked the three major television networks not to run the commercials unless BIC could document its claims.

By the end of 1979 Gillette and BIC each controlled about 50 percent of the market for disposables, which had grown to represent 20 percent of the total market for wet-shave razors. Disposables were especially popular among teenagers, and women appreciated the BIC Lady Shaver, the first razor specially designed and marketed with them in mind. Within ten years, Gillette would stop advertising its disposables to concentrate on its razor systems and replacement blades.

Challenges in the 1980s

In 1982, with revenues approaching $220 million, BIC acknowledged its expanding status as a leading maker of lighters and shavers by dropping "pen" from its name to become, officially, BIC Corporation. By then BIC had also taken a tentative step into sports equipment. In 1982 the company introduced the BIC Sailboard, which quickly became the North American market leader. In 1985, however, the company was forced to stop selling the sailboard in the United States when a U.S. District Court ruled that BIC had infringed on a patent owned by Windsurfing International. BIC reintroduced the sailboard to the U.S. market when the patent expired in 1987.

Having weathered fierce competitive battles for three decades, BIC faced perhaps its most serious threat in April 1987 when the *New York Times* reported that at least three people had died because BIC lighters had malfunctioned. The newspaper also reported that the company agreed to pay $3.2 million in damages to a Pennsylvania woman who claimed her lighter ignited in a pocket while she was on a camping trip.

The Pennsylvania case was the first involving BIC to go to trial, and the *Times* reported that although "claims began to trickle in soon after Bic introduced its throwaway lighters in 1972 . . . the company has until recently been able to keep the cases quiet by settling them out of court." The newspaper stated that BIC had settled more than 20 cases for amounts ranging from $5,000 to almost $500,000. During the trial, design engineers testified that BIC lighters occasionally leaked, and debris could cause the shut-off valve to fail. There were also reports of BIC lighters flaring up while they were being used or accidentally igniting while lying on overheated automobile dashboards.

At the time lighters accounted for about 40 percent of BIC's revenues, and the day the story appeared, BIC stock fell 25 percent, from $32 to $24 per share. For a week the company stonewalled, refusing to provide information or answer questions about the allegations amid rumors that thousands of lawsuits had been brought against the company and that a New Jersey congressman was threatening to hold hearings on the safety of BIC lighters. Eventually, the company changed its tactics and revealed that there were 42 lawsuits then pending. BIC maintained that most of the incidents were caused by user negligence. Also acknowledging that a woman had died in an accident involving one of its lighters, BIC reassured the public that it had discontinued the model that was involved in the accident.

As a result of BIC management's candor, the company's stock began to regain value. Although it stumbled again briefly in September following the airing of the ABC television program "20/20," which featured a story on lighter safety, the stock was back to $31 per share by October. Bruno Bich, Marcel's son, who became president of the U.S. subsidiary in 1982, later told *Investor Relations*, "With hindsight we should have given out more information and done it faster to avoid the inaccuracies and exaggerations that appeared in the press."

Safety Issues in the Early 1990s

According to BIC, the company defended itself in more than 50 lawsuits involving lighters between 1988 and 1993, losing only three. In one of those, however, a jury in Creek County, Oklahoma found BIC responsible for injuries to three children severely burned while playing with a lighter, awarding $22 million in actual and punitive damages. The lighter allegedly exploded when it was dropped while lit. Attorneys for the children argued that the lighter should have been more child resistant; BIC argued that the children should have been better supervised.

In its 1992 annual report, the company said it was "vigorously appealing the verdict." The annual report went on to say, "The legal expenses of defending product liability claims involving lighters continue to be heavy. However, as a result of our longstanding philosophy to vigorously defend these claims, and our success in doing so, the number of lawsuits continues to

decline." The first adverse decision resulted in a $1,000 verdict, and the second verdict that went against BIC was reversed and remanded for a new trial following BIC's successful appeal.

Also that year, BIC introduced a lighter with a "child resistant" catch, reportedly the result of a seven-year, $21 million development program. The patented Child Guard lighter required that a safety latch be moved to the side and up before it would light. The latch slid back into place automatically after each use. The Consumer Product Safety Commission also adopted a child-resistant standard for disposable lighters that became effective in July 1994.

The issue of safety became even more convoluted in 1992, however, when a U.S. Court of Appeals in Philadelphia ruled that manufacturers of products completely safe when used as intended may also have an obligation to make the product safe in unconventional circumstances. The ruling involved a case in which a three-year-old child took a BIC lighter from his father's pants pocket and set fire to an infant's bedclothes. The case, *Griggs v. BIC Corp.,* was remanded to a lower court that had originally dismissed the case.

Other Developments in the 1990s

During this time BIC attempted a further diversification by launching a line of inexpensive, pocket-sized perfume "spritzers" in 1989. Marketed under the name Parfum BIC, the fragrances were first introduced by Société BIC, S.A. in Europe, where they were sold alongside other BIC products. Analysts were skeptical whether U.S. consumers would accept an inexpensive French perfume since part of the appeal of French perfumes lay in their image as luxurious and expensive. Despite an ad campaign that *Advertising Age* estimated as costing $22 million, touting the fragrances as "Paris in your pocket," Parfum BIC lasted less than a year in the United States. Sales of the fragrances lasted longer in Europe, but were eventually dropped overseas as well in 1991.

In 1992 BIC purchased Wite-Out Products, Inc., the second largest maker of correction fluids for office use in the United States. The correction fluid subsequently was reintroduced as BIC Wite-Out. The company also changed the name of its Writing Instruments division to Stationery Products, indicating an intention to market an expanded line of stationery-related products, while continuing to expand its successful lines of pens, lighters, and shavers. The company reported its highest ever sales and earnings in 1992 and moved its trading from the American Stock Exchange to the New York Stock Exchange.

The company's share price climbed astronomically in the early 1990s, rising from $8 a share in November 1990 to peak at $41 by March 1993. Though BIC still trailed Gillette's pens in terms of pens sold to offices, the firm led the market for pens sold to individuals and had enhanced its line with many attractive new models. BIC marketed a line of "fashion" pens, featuring bright colors and graphics wrapped around the barrel, to appeal to children and teenagers. This so-called Wavelengths line soon led the market in the fashion pen category. BIC also broke out a new shaver, a twin-blade model. BIC's lighters also continued to sell well, enhanced with the new child-resistant features. By the mid-1990s lighters accounted for 24 percent of the company's sales. Lighters continued to be profitable for BIC in spite of increasing competition from China and Thailand. In 1994 BIC filed a petition with the Department of Commerce and the U.S. International Trade Commission asking to impose antidumping duties against disposable lighters from these two countries. BIC alleged that imports from China and Thailand were being sold at below market value, with lighters going for as little as six cents each wholesale, and the numbers of such cheap lighters were increasing yearly. Nevertheless, BIC, with its massive name recognition, did not appear to be struggling.

The company's great profitability seemed due to its efficient, low-cost manufacturing. Double-digit growth in sales and net income was steady and, sometimes, spectacular. For the fourth quarter of 1995, BIC announced a 22 percent increase in profits and a 17 percent increase in sales. The company was a Wall Street favorite. Even when the stocks of many name-brand consumer product manufacturers hit a bump in the summer of 1993, analysts predicted more rosy growth for BIC. In 1995, with exchange rates very favorable to the French franc, BIC's parent, Société BIC, S.A., offered to buy up a large chunk of BIC Corporation's stock and take the company private. The offer came at a time when there was some speculation that rising plastic prices might cut into BIC Corporation's profit margins. Société BIC was anxious to take advantage of the weak dollar and quickly made a sweet deal with stockholders to secure the merger. In December 1995 BIC Corporation ceased trading as a public company on the New York Stock Exchange. Société BIC now owned 86 percent of its U.S. subsidiary.

After the merger, business did not change substantially at BIC Corporation. The company had for the most part operated independently of its European parent, and the relationship did not alter after BIC Corporation went private. The company brought out a correction pen in 1996, using technology gained from its earlier acquisition of Wite-Out. This strengthened BIC's position in the correction products market. Another significant development in the late 1990s was BIC's acquisition of Sheaffer Group in 1997. The privately held Fort Madison, Iowa company manufactured high-end fountain pens, ballpoints, roller pens, and pencils. Sheaffer pens retailed from $25 to as much as $5,000 each, in stark contrast to BIC's line, all of which sold for less than a couple of dollars. BIC planned to continue to market the Sheaffer pens under the Sheaffer name. The acquisition of Sheaffer put BIC in a better position against its long-time competitor Gillette, which had acquired two high-end pen companies several years earlier.

Principal Subsidiaries

BIC Sport, Inc.; Guy Laroche NA; Bic Inc. (Canada); No Sabe Fallar SA (Mexico); Bic de Guatemala; Bic Puerto Rico.

Further Reading

"Are the Talents Transferable?," *Forbes,* April 1, 1974, p. 62.

Armstrong, Jeffrey D., "BIC Corp.: The Stock Will Strengthen as the Issue of Lighter Safety Fades," *Barron's,* October 12, 1987, p. 69.

"Bich the Ballpoint King," *Fortune,* August 15, 1969, p. 122.

Byrnes, Nanette, "Bic Corp.: Write on the Money," *Financial World,* June 8, 1993, p. 14.

Cooper, Wendy, "The Case of the Exploding Lighters," *Institutional Investor,* December 1987, p. 209.

"Discovering the Potential in BIC," *Business Week,* July 30, 1979, p. 65.

"Extinguished: Gillette Puts Out Its Cricket," *Time,* October 15, 1984, p. 93.

Flax, Steven, "Why Bic Got Flicked," *Forbes,* September 27, 1982, p. 38.

Fox, Harriot Lane, "Bic Launch Sets Off Razor Wars," *Marketing,* February 3, 1994, p. 2.

"Gillette Challenges Bic To Verify Its Ad Claims," *Business Week,* March 19, 1979, p. 32.

"Going Bananas Over Bic," *Time,* December 18, 1972, p. 93.

Hayes, Linda Snyder, "Gillette Takes the Wraps Off," *Fortune,* February 25, 1980, p. 148.

"An Igniting Controversy," *Time,* April 20, 1987, p. 56.

Ingrassia, Lawrence, "Gillette Holds Its Edge by Endlessly Searching for a Better Shave," *Wall Street Journal,* December 10, 1992, p. A1.

Kalita, S. Mitra, "Bic Agrees To Acquire Sheaffer in Bid," *Wall Street Journal,* August 1, 1997, p. A9B.

King, Resa W., "Will $4 Perfume Do the Trick for Bic?," *Business Week,* June 20, 1988, p. 89.

Langway, Lynn, "Razor Fighting," *Newsweek,* November 22, 1976, p. 103.

Moskowitz, Daniel, "Courts Tackle Safety Liability in Product Design," *Washington Post,* February 8, 1993, p. WB11.

"Scents and Sensibility," *Time,* May 20, 1991, p. 47.

Sloan, Pat, "Bic Pulls Fragrances After Flickering Sales," *Advertising Age,* March 12, 1990, p. 77.

Somasundaram, Meera, "Bic Stock Surges on Hopes of Higher Offer from Parent," *Dow Jones News Service,* May 19, 1995, DJ513919207.

———, "$22M Campaign Urges: Spritz Your Bic," *Advertising Age,* February 20, 1989, p. 3.

"Starting To Click; Mainstay Products Help BIC Mark Profit Gains," *Barron's,* June 23, 1986, p. 52.

Warner, Liz, "Bic Scents a Quick Killing," *Marketing,* June 30, 1988, p. 1.

"Waterman-Bic Pen Corp.: On the Ball with the Ball-point," *Nation's Business,* December 1970, p. 72.

Welles, Chris, "The War of the Razors," *Esquire,* February 1980, p. 29.

—Dean Boyer
—updated by A. Woodward

$\mathcal{T}he$ BON MARCHÉ

The Bon Marché, Inc.

1601 3rd Avenue
Seattle, Washington 98181
U.S.A.
(206) 344-2121
Fax: (206) 344-6251

Wholly Owned Subsidiary of Federated Stores, Inc.
Incorporated: 1890
Employees: 6,200
Sales: $892 million (1996)
SICs: 5311 Department Stores

A venerable department store operator for more than a century, The Bon Marché, Inc. operates 42 stores in the northwestern United States. Tailoring itself as a moderately priced retailer, Bon Marché held sway as the dominant department store operator in the Pacific Northwest during the late 1990s. The company's greatest concentration of stores was in Washington State, where the company was founded in 1890.

19th Century Origins

In 1875 Edward Ludwig Nordhoff left his native Germany on a journey that ended 15 years later in Seattle, Washington, where he founded The Bon Marché. Nordhoff left Germany at age 17 and made his first stop in Paris, where he gained his first experience in retail business. Nordhoff worked at the Louvre department store while he lived in Paris, displaying a keen interest in the way department stores were operated during his five-year stay there. He was most impressed with an innovative store on the Left Bank called the Maison à Boucicault au Bon Marché, reportedly the first store to arrange like goods by department and thus earn the distinction as the first department store. Nordhoff was impressed with the service at the Maison à Boucicault, and he vowed that if presented with the opportunity to own his own store he would operate it like the famed store on the Left Bank.

Next, Nordhoff was off to Buffalo, New York, where he joined his brother Rudolph in 1881. Nordhoff worked briefly at his brother's dry goods store in upstate New York, then re-newed his westward travels before the end of the year, relocating to Chicago. In Chicago Nordhoff worked at a well-known department store called Willoughby and Robey, eventually earning a promotion to manager by 1887, the same year he became a U.S. citizen. One year after his promotion, Nordhoff married a Willoughby and Robey saleswoman named Josephine Patricia Brennan. The newlyweds had a child the following year. Just when it seemed Nordhoff was putting down roots in Chicago, however, he moved again. Health problems convinced Nordhoff that he needed to move to a milder climate, and he chose Seattle, arriving there in 1889 with his wife and their one-year-old baby girl.

One year after their arrival, Edward and Josephine Nordhoff invested their life savings of $1,200 to start their own department store, which they christened "The Bon Marché," in homage to Edward's inspiration in Paris. A brick veneer building, located north of Seattle's business district, was rented for $25 per month. Still in her teenage years, Josephine took an active role in running the store, helping stock shelves, keep books, clean, mop, and wait on customers. She was frequently seen measuring dry goods with her baby girl on her hip, as she attended to customers while Edward was away on trips to buy merchandise for the store. When Edward returned from his first buying trip to the East Coast in the early 1890s, he brought back a sack of pennies, introducing the coins into Seattle's economy. Until that time all change had been given to the nearest nickel, but with his sack of pennies, Edward was able to advertise merchandise for prices such as 19 cents, 29 cents, and 49 cents. Seattlites made the additional effort to walk the several blocks north from the city's business district to take advantage of the savings, and for those customers who took a streetcar to the Nordhoffs' store, their fare was refunded.

The Nordhoffs kept their store open 14 hours a day during the week and 15½ hours on Saturdays, working day and night to ensure their fledgling store stayed in business. Josephine learned to speak the Chinook language to better serve the store's Native American customers, while Edward labored to make The Bon Marché a worthy replication of the esteemed department store he had frequented in Paris as a youth. The Nordhoffs' industriousness paid off. By 1896 their store was doing well enough to necessitate a move to larger quarters, this time to a

Company Perspectives:

Service to the community, support of human and social needs, and seeing our efforts help others, are the cornerstones of The Bon Marché's community service mission. Together we build the future.

location closer to Seattle's expanding business district. Although the store's business was growing each year, the 1890s would be the last decade the couple worked together. The health problems that had prompted Edward's move to Seattle finally took their ultimate toll. Edward died in 1899 of tuberculosis, leaving Josephine solely in charge of running The Bon Marché.

Josephine was not alone for long, however. Just before he had died, Edward had written to his brother Rudolph for help in running the store. Rudolph was en route when his brother died. When he arrived in Seattle, Rudolph helped his sister-in-law run the store, but by no means did Josephine fade into the background. She was as active as ever in running the store, spearheading its expansion once again in 1901. That year she married a merchant tailor named Frank McDermott, who, along with Rudolph and Josephine, helped run the store. Under the stewardship of this triumvirate, The Bon Marché flourished. The store underwent numerous expansions, as annual sales swelled from $340,000 at the beginning of the century to $8 million by the early 1920s. Death marked another transition in management in 1920, when Josephine died of cancer. Her death, mourned by thousands of Seattlites, left McDermott, Rudolph Nordhoff, and a long-time employee, Frank Radford, in charge of the company's fortunes.

Excavation for a new, four-story building began in 1927, as McDermott, Nordhoff, and Radford sought to end the nearly annual store expansions by constructing a store with what were then massive proportions. As work was under way to construct a Bon Marché that would occupy an entire city block, Nordhoff and McDermott arrived at an important conclusion. Their health was failing, so they decided to sell the company and selected Radford, who had joined the Bon Marché in 1898 as a package wrapper for $6 a week, to represent the company at its sale in New York. In 1928 the sale was completed, with New York-based Hahn Department Stores gaining control of the nearly 40-year-old, Seattle department store. The relationship between the Bon Marché and its parent company was an important one, an affiliation that gave the Bon Marché financial support that proved instrumental in the company's expansion outside of Seattle. At the time of the sale to Hahn, however, the years of geographic expansion were decades away; what occupied the minds of Bon Marché management at the time of the sale was the completion of its new store.

One year after the sale, the new store opened, a $5 million structure with 12 acres of retail space, the grand opening ceremonies of which were attended by 135,000 onlookers. The store, which was located in the heart of Seattle's business district, proved to be a remarkable success and stood as the signature property of Bon Marché, the company, for decades to follow. Radford, back from New York after representing Bon

Marché's sale to Hahn, returned as president of the company to oversee the grand opening and remained as president of the company for the ensuing 16 years. During Radford's tenure, Hahn evolved into Allied Stores Corp., becoming the new parent company of the Bon Marché in 1933. For the remainder of the decade, as Bon Marché fought to withstand the effects of the Great Depression, the company drew its business exclusively from the sprawling store on Fourth Avenue. The next significant milestone in Bon Marché's history occurred following the conclusion of World War II.

Post-World War II Expansion

Radford moved up to chairman of the company in 1945, making room for the promotion of Rex Allison to the position of president. Under Allison's direction, the company began considering the establishment of branch stores in outlying areas of Seattle to take advantage of the migration of urbanites into the suburbs. Allison studied aerial photographs of the Seattle area to determine the best location for a store, convinced Radford and other executives that branching out represented a prudent move, and in 1949 announced plans of what was referred to as the "Northgate project." That same year the company took the more expeditious path to expansion by acquiring a department store in Everett (north of Seattle) and converting it into a Bon Marché, but the scope of the Northgate project overshadowed the significance of expanding through acquisition. The Northgate project was to be the first of several ventures that would combine the deep financial pockets of Allied Stores and the popularity of Bon Marché. Allied Stores agreed to finance the construction of a mall, and Bon Marché enjoyed the lucrative position of being the flagship retailer of the mall. This concerted approach to expansion would be used on several occasions, but the first was the mall slated to be built in Northgate, which would have a Bon Marché as its focal point.

The Northgate mall and its attendant Bon Marché opened in 1950 amid great fanfare and snaking lines of patrons. It was the first shopping center in the United States that was surrounded by a parking lot with a walking mall in the center, positioned in a location that Allison had determined was within a 12-minute drive of 275,000 people. As was true with the opening of the downtown store in 1929, the opening of the Northgate Bon Marché in 1950 proved to be a remarkable success. A week after the store opened, gross sales figures were double the projections of Bon Marché executives, a welcomed surprise that ushered in the era of Bon Marché's branch expansion.

Having registered considerable success with its first branch store, Bon Marché was quick to follow with the establishment of additional stores beyond the boundaries of Seattle's city limits. The 1950s and 1960s witnessed the transformation of a 60-year-old, one-store business into a chain of retail units spreading steadily throughout Washington State. During the 1950s the company expanded south, east, and north of Seattle, acquiring stores in Tacoma, Yakima, and Bellingham. Midway through the decade the downtown Seattle store was expanded, a $3-million project that made the flagship store the largest department store west of Chicago. In 1963 the company opened its seventh branch store, a Bon Marché in Spokane, that established the retailer's presence across the width of the state.

As in the 1950s, the 1960s saw Bon Marché couple geographic expansion with the renovation of existing units. The same year the company opened the doors of its Spokane store, it nearly doubled the original size of its Northgate store. The Northgate project, first envisioned in the late 1940s, provided a model for the company's expansion during the 1960s. Developing malls around Bon Marché units represented the preferred method of expansion, and it was a method made viable by the financial support offered by Allied Stores. Such was the case with the development of the Tacoma Mall during the mid-1960s. Allied Stores developed the regional shopping center—situated to serve southwest Washington—and Bon Marché established its retail anchor, opening the new Bon Marché unit one year before the Tacoma Mall was completed in 1965. Over the course of the next three years, three existing Allied stores were converted into Bon Marché stores, fleshing out the company's presence in Washington with stores in Longview and Walla Walla and extending its presence beyond Washington's borders for the first time with a store in Eugene, Oregon. Before the decade ended two more malls featuring Bon Marché stores were developed, Southcenter Mall and Columbia Center, giving Bon Marché a total of 12 stores as it entered the 1970s.

Recessive economic conditions during the early 1970s put a freeze on expansion for much of the decade, but once the company resumed expansion in the late 1970s, it did so in earnest. Two new stores were opened in 1977 and the following year eight existing Allied stores in Idaho, Montana, and Utah were added to Bon Marché's fold. By the end of the 1970s three decades of expansion had produced a 27-store chain operating in a five-state region comprising Washington, Oregon, Idaho, Montana, and Utah. Annual sales eclipsed $300 million.

1980s and 1990s

The three decades of steady expansion touched off by the completion of the Northgate Mall in 1950 was followed by a decade of more animated growth, growth orchestrated by an individual who had witnessed all of the company's postwar expansion. Wilbur J. Fix joined Bon Marché when the Northgate Bon Marché made its debut, and he rose through the company's ranks for the next 30 years, becoming president in 1978 and chief executive officer in 1980. Under Fix's stewardship, Bon Marché recorded prodigious growth, more than doubling its revenues during the 1980s and nearly tripling yearly profits. Three smaller stores were closed during the decade, but their departure was more than compensated for by the addition of 18 new stores. As expansion was under way, new ownership took control when Allied Stores Corp. and Campeau Corp., led by Canadian developer Robert Campeau, merged in 1986. Fix was named chairman in 1987. The following year Campeau completed additional retail acquisitions that made him one of the largest retail operators in the United States and Bon Marché one of nine retail divisions within his empire. In the hierarchy of Campeau's businesses, Bon Marché was positioned as a subsidiary of Federated Stores, Inc., a component of the massive Campeau Corp.

Bon Marché celebrated its centennial as a thriving enterprise, bolstered significantly by the expansion of the 1980s and holding sway as the jewel of the Campeau empire as the 1990s began. In 1990 Bon Marché comprised 42 stores, 23 of which were located in Washington, that generated roughly $700 million in sales a year. Its parent company, however, was experiencing profound difficulties. In 1990 Federated filed for bankruptcy, lingering in Chapter 11 for two years before reorganizing and regaining its feet. During Federated's bankruptcy Bon Marché was heralded as a robust money earner and glorified as a model for other businesses higher up Campeau's organizational ladder to emulate. The company registered its greatest progress with its "Home Store" concept: retail units that sold home furnishings, accessories, and electronics. By the time Federated emerged from bankruptcy, there were five Home Stores within Bon Marché's fold and plans for the establishment of additional units.

A series of management changes at Bon Marché occurred during the mid-1990s, beginning with the retirement of Fix in 1993 after 43 years as a Bon Marché employee. Robert J. DiNicola succeeded Fix as chairman and chief executive officer, but his tenure was brief. DiNicola left Bon Marché in April 1994 to become chairman and chief executive officer of Zale Corp., a large jewelry retailer. To fill the posts vacated by DiNicola's sudden departure, Thomas P. Harville, a company employee since 1977, was selected. Three years later Harville was gone as well, opting to retire and make room for Ira Pickell, named chairman and chief executive officer in 1997. The spate of senior executive departures during the mid-1990s represented an anomaly for Bon Marché, which for decades had been known as a company that underwent little managerial change. When Fix assumed control of Bon Marché, he was only the fifth person to control the company since Nordhoff and McDermott had decided to sell the company in 1927. After Fix retired in 1993 the company fell under the leadership of three different senior executives during a four-year span.

Despite the managerial flux of the mid-1990s, Bon Marché entered the late 1990s as a formidable regional player. With 42 stores in operation in 1997, the company's 107-year legacy as a department store operator pointed to a future as profitable as its past, although there was speculation that Federated might convert Bon Marché units into Macy's stores, another Federated subsidiary. Rumors about the conversion to Macy's had been circulating since 1995, but were flatly denied by both Federated and Bon Marché spokespeople. Whether or not the Bon Marché name would endure for a second century was a question to be answered by the events of the future.

Further Reading

The Bon Marché, *1890–1990: A Century of Success,* Seattle: The Bon Marché, Inc., 1990, p. 23.

"Pickell To Get Helm of the Bon," *WWD,* February 20, 1997, p. 2.

Prinzing, Debra, "Bon Marché Plans a Push into Portland," *Puget Sound Business Journal,* November 5, 1990, p. 1.

——, "Bon's Wilbur Fix Gears for 'Next 101 Years,' " *Puget Sound Business Journal,* November 25, 1991, p. 1.

Spector, Robert, "Good News at Bon Marché, One of Top Federated Allied Performers, Chain Repositions Adding to Mid and Upper Levels," *HFD—The Weekly Home Furnishings Newspaper,* January 4, 1993, p. 10.

Szymanski, Jim, "Seattle's The Bon Marché Rumored To Face Merger with Macy's," *Knight-Ridder/Tribune Business News,* June 20, 1995, p. 6.

—Jeffrey L. Covell

BOWNE

Bowne & Co., Inc.

---

345 Hudson Street
New York, New York 10014
U.S.A.
(212) 924-5500
Fax: (212) 229-3420
Web site: http://www.bowne.com

Public Company
Incorporated: 1909
Employees: 2,800
Sales: $716.6 million (1997)
Stock Exchanges: American
SICs: 2759 Commercial Printing, Not Elsewhere
   Classified; 7373 Computer Integrated Systems Design;
   7372 Prepackaged Software; 7374 Data Processing &
   Preparation

The world's largest financial printer and one of the oldest companies in the United States, Bowne & Co., Inc. operates corporate printing operations that print prospectuses, offering circulars, annual reports, stock certificates, and other legal documents. Bowne also ranked as the leading provider of EDGAR electronic filing services to clients. The company's clients include corporations, law firms, investment banks, and mutual fund groups. In addition to its core business, which traces its roots back to the 18th century, Bowne & Co. provides document-building solutions, Internet, and print on-demand services to its financial and legal clients, concentrating specifically on the reformatting of documents for online viewing. With offices throughout the United States and in strategic locations across the globe, Bowne recorded the most prolific growth in its more than two centuries of business during the 1990s. Annual sales swelled from $205 million in 1990 to more than $700 million in 1997.

18th Century Origins

A year and a half before the Declaration of Independence was signed, Bowne opened for business. On a February morning in 1775, Robert Bowne and his two business associates began carrying crates and boxes of merchandise through the door of Number 39 Queen Street, in New York City. Above the threshold of the door hung a placard that read, "Bowne & Co. Merchants." The name would endure for more than two centuries, earning its distinction as the oldest business operating under the same name in the history of New York commerce. The Bowne family, beginning with its patriarch, Robert Bowne, owned and operated the company for more than a century, developing a small street-side store into one of the nation's most venerable commercial institutions. The Bownes arrived on the shores of their future homeland in 1649, when Thomas Bowne left England and sailed to Boston. Four generations later, Thomas Bowne's great-great-grandson, Robert Bowne, was preparing to open the doors to his new general merchandise store, christening an enterprise whose formation predated the birth of the United States.

Robert Bowne was 31 years old when he opened his store on Queen Street, having left his family home in Flushing, New York, to start a mercantile business in the city. Inside the store, the shelves were stocked with writing paper, account books, quills and pens, binding and printing materials, powder, furs, nails, glass, dry goods, and, among a list of other items, "a few casks of low-priced Cutlery," as announced in a 1775 newspaper advertisement. Business at Bowne & Co. was underway in February 1775, but before long the company fell victim to the first of many historic events that would occur during its long corporate life. When British troops led by General Howe defeated General George Washington's outnumbered forces at Brooklyn Heights in August 1776, the American Army retreated into Manhattan, prompting thousands of New Yorkers, Robert Bowne included, to flee from the battle front.

Bowne left New York with his wife and infant daughter, leaving the doors of Bowne & Co. closed behind him until it was safe to return. When New Yorkers were able to return, considerable rebuilding work awaited them. Many found their homes destroyed, lying in ruins from years of fire and battle. Bowne returned as well, and reestablished himself as a general merchant. During the post-Revolutionary War period, Bowne & Co. began doing printing work, making its foray into the type of work that would later become the company's mainstay business. More important to Bowne at the time, however, was the brisk sale of stationery supplies. It was during the post-Revolutionary War years that Bowne & Co. etched its identity as a stationery supply store. Although the company continued to sell a diverse range of merchandise, the increasing sales derived from stationery supplies were fueling the store's prosperity. Stationery figured as an essential facet of the company's business until it was abandoned in the early 20th century.

As Bowne built his store into a solid and reputable enterprise, he also spent considerable time building a reputation for himself as one of New York's prominent citizens. He was a prodigious organizer of philanthropic organizations and spent many evenings gathered around a table with some of the country's early luminaries organizing the basic institutions a fledgling nation required. Bowne helped organize New York's first bank, he fought against slavery, he served as governor of the New York Hospital for 34 years, he helped organize the first fire insurance company, and he promoted the development of the Erie Canal. His tireless efforts away from his store paid large dividends for Bowne & Co., because in many respects the company reflected the individual at its helm. Like its creator, Bowne & Co. blossomed during the early 19th century, securing itself as a fixture of the burgeoning city it served. Although stationery supplies figured large in Bowne & Co.'s business, the company was involved in a number of business activities, as wide-ranging as the extracurricular activities performed by its founder. Straying far beyond the sale of stationery and printing services, Bowne & Co. served as agents for other merchants, it speculated in land, bought and sold commodities such as wheat, flour, wine, and brandy, and provided banking services.

Bowne died in 1818, leaving behind him a solid foundation upon which succeeding generations could build. He also left an ample number of heirs to inherit his business to begin building on the business foundation he created. Bowne, who came from a family comprising 14 brothers and sisters, had nine children of his own. After his death, Robert Bowne's genealogical legacy proliferated exponentially, giving him 50 grandchildren and 112 great-grandchildren. From this vast pool of direct descendants, Bowne & Co. would draw its leadership for the ensuing century.

Bowne & Co. in the 19th Century

Control of Bowne & Co. after Bowne's death in 1818 fell to two of his sons, Robert H. Bowne and John L. Bowne. Their first great test arrived in 1835, when Bowne & Co. was destroyed by fire, as was most of New York, which lost 17 city blocks and nearly 600 buildings to a fire that started in a dry goods store. The mayor of New York referred to the "Great

Fire" as "the most awful calamity which has ever visited the United States," a disaster that forced the Bowne brothers to rebuild Bowne & Co. on a new site at the corner of Wall, Pearl (formerly Queen), and Beaver streets. In its new quarters, the company gained a reputation as a manufacturer of leatherbound account books, one of the several special talents the company developed during its long record of business.

By the 1850s, Bowne & Co. was headed by three of the founder's grandchildren, Robert, William, and John, the last generation of Bownes to manage the firm. During their tenure, which began in 1843 and ended in 1898, Bowne & Co. supplemented its thriving account book business with a variety of general printing work. Of the three Bownes who headed the company during the latter half of the 19th century, Robert Bowne's length of service was most enduring, encompassing a half-century. His retirement in 1898 signaled the end of Bowne family management and set the stage for the first non-family member to head the company, Stanley M. Dewey, who joined Bowne & Co. at age 16.

Dewey had been with Bowne & Co. for 30 years by the time he was appointed the company's fifth president in 1909, the year the business was incorporated for the first time. Much of the company's business at this juncture in its history was realized from the sale of stationery supplies. Dewey himself visited banks and insurance companies during his years as a senior partner, noting whether or not customers were in need of ink, quills, sealing wax, account books, and other related items. This line of business, which had been a mainstay for the company since its inception, became less important after the 1909 incorporation. Eventually, the stationery business was abandoned altogether, as the company concentrated its efforts on developing its printing business.

A 20th-Century Financial Printer

Dewey retired as president in 1922, but stayed on as chairman of the board until his death in 1941. Upon his retirement in 1922, Dewey sold his interest in the company to a young Bowne & Co. associate named Edmund A. Stanley, who had joined the firm in 1908. Stanley took over as Bowne & Co. was in transition, gradually becoming less of a stationery supplier and more of a printing enterprise. To supplement the company's traditional work for banking and insurance companies, Bowne & Co. responded to the printing needs of the surrounding financial district, printing a substantial portion of the securities offering circulars of New York underwriters. Its printing operations received a major boost in business when the Securities and Exchange Commission (SEC) was formed in 1933. The SEC required, by law, stock issue prospectuses and instituted annual reporting requirements for publicly-held corporations, creating a wealth of business for companies like Bowne & Co. In the years after the SEC's formation, Bowne & Co. began specializing in meeting the precise printing demands of underwriters, attorneys, publicly-traded corporations, and any party responsible for complying with SEC requirements.

The formation of the SEC established the framework for Bowne & Co.'s most important business during the 20th century, but the timing of the federal organization's debut could have been better from Bowne & Co.'s perspective. When the

SEC was formed, the nation was in the midst of its most severe economic depression, a time when the fabric of the country's financial community was unraveling with alarming speed. Those companies able to stay in business during the Great Depression cut costs dramatically, reducing their advertising and promotional budgets to an absolute minimum. Bowne & Co. felt the sting of the harsh economic times and suffered along with nearly every other business in the country. Annual sales remained static during the decade-long crisis, hovering around $300,000. Annual financial losses occurred too frequently for any Bowne & Co. official to take lightly.

Bowne & Co. did not enjoy the full rewards of the SEC's presence until the 1940s, but once the economic climate improved, the company enjoyed an encouraging and much-needed surge of growth. Sales exceeded the $1-million-mark for the first time in 1946 and remained at that level until the beginning of the 1950s.

By the 1950s, the next generation of Bowne & Co.'s executive management had joined the firm. Stanley was joined by his son, Edmund A. Stanley, Jr., in 1949. The younger Stanley rose swiftly through the company's executive management ranks, becoming vice-president in 1953 and president of the company in 1956 when his father died. Victor Simonte, Jr., who succeeded Stanley in the 1970s, experienced a lengthier climb to the presidential post than Stanley, working the full gamut of jobs at Bowne before taking charge. Simonte joined the company in 1950 as a helper in the composing room when he was 17 years old. He subsequently held a variety of positions before being named president, laboring as an apprentice, journeyman, foreman, and plant superintendent. Together, Stanley, Jr., and Simonte would lead the company into the 1980s.

With Stanley, Jr., in charge, Bowne & Co. headed into the 1960s after a decade of measured financial growth. The $1 million in sales generated in 1950 rose to $3 million by 1961, the year the company moved to larger quarters on Hudson Street, where it would be located for the remainder of the century. Along with the move came the addition of new, modern printing equipment and new communications systems. With the aid of this new equipment and several important acquisitions, Bowne & Co. rose to the top of the financial printing industry in terms of annual sales, climbing from third to first during the 1960s. In 1966, the company acquired Garber-Pollack Co., a trade bindery, and two years later, when Bowne & Co. converted to public ownership, The La Salle Street Press, Inc. was purchased, giving the company the largest financial printer in Chicago. Following its debut as a publicly-traded company, Bowne & Co. either started or acquired financial printing companies in Boston, Houston, Los Angeles, and San Francisco.

By 1974, as Bowne & Co.'s bicentennial approached and Simonte took over as president, annual sales stood at $38 million, far above the $3 million recorded in 1961. Under Simonte's watch, the company registered another decade of energetic financial growth and was generating more than $100 million in sales by the beginning of the 1980s. Although the sales growth recorded during Simonte's first decade of leadership kept Bowne & Co. ahead of all other rivals in the United States, its lead was diminishing as it headed into the 1980s. Pandick Press Inc., Bowne & Co.'s closest rival, was gaining

ground during the 1980s, recording 20 percent annual gains in sales while Bowne & Co.'s sales volume shrank. Critics charged that Simonte had failed to make the transition into the computer age, and in late 1982 Bowne & Co.'s directors acknowledged this failure by announcing Simonte's retirement. Simonte left the company he had joined as a teenager at age 49 and was replaced by Franz von Ziegesar, ten years Simonte's senior. On the heels of this change in management, the benefits of embracing the computer age were made manifest by the SEC.

New Technology of the 1980s and 1990s

In 1984, the SEC introduced a voluntary electronic filing program for corporations called EDGAR. Bowne & Co. was the first corporation to join the program and lent its assistance to the prime contractor in the development of the program. Although corporations were not obliged to file electronically at EDGAR's outset, participation eventually became mandatory. Bowne & Co., involved with the program from its start, found itself closely involved in what would prove to be a highly lucrative market, and one that underscored the importance of adopting to the changes engendered by the pervasive influence of computers in the business world.

By the 1990s, the ubiquity of computers had significantly altered the thinking of Bowne & Co.'s management. The company, after more than two centuries of business, was tailoring itself to be an information management company, a provider not only of the printing services to disseminate data and text but also a company capable of assisting its corporate clients in managing their endless flows of information through the latest technologies. The push to become this new type of company helped insulate Bowne & Co. from the cyclicality of its mainstay business. Historically, the financial printing business had been dependent on the economic cycles that influenced stock issues, mergers, and acquisitions, but by branching into providing corporate services for the Internet and helping clients manage information through computer-based technologies, Bowne & Co. could depend on business free from the economic fluctuations that affected financial printing.

With the movement toward becoming this new type of company underway as the 1990s began, Bowne & Co. started to record animated growth in earnings and sales, in proportions that never had been achieved before. The bulk of the financial growth was realized midway through the decade, after Bowne & Co. had established two subsidiary companies that represented its commitment to its new role as an information management company. Bowne Business Services, formed in fiscal 1996, was created to lead Bowne & Co.'s diversification into non-financial printing businesses. The company's intent was to manage customers' desktop publishing, word processing, and multimedia operations and also to offer services facilitating the creation and management of Internet and intranet sites. Bowne & Co. officials projected a potential $250 million in revenues in this area of business by the year 2000. The other subsidiary, Bowne Digital Services, was formed to take advantage of the emerging business created by the convergence of database processing and digital print technologies. Through Bowne Digital Services, Bowne & Co. positioned itself as a service provider for database management, on-demand printing, and digital print technologies.

With the addition of these new businesses, Bowne & Co.'s financial might was strengthened significantly. From $205 million in sales in 1990, the company's revenue total leaped to $501 million in 1996 and soared to $716 million in 1997. Bowne & Co.'s net income during the decade increased from 1990's $8.4 million to the record-setting $54 million registered in 1997. Buoyed by this remarkable surge of financial growth, the world's largest financial printer headed toward the 21st century, the fourth century in which the Bowne & Co. name would be a fixture of the U.S. business world.

Principal Subsidiaries

Bowne Business Services, Inc.; Bowne Business Communications, Inc.; Bowne Information Services, Inc.; Bowne International, Inc.; Bowne of Atlanta, Inc.; Bowne of Boston, Inc.; Bowne of Chicago, Inc.; Bowne of Cleveland, Inc.; Bowne of Dallas, Inc.; Bowne of Los Angeles, Inc.; Bowne of New York City, Inc.; Bowne of Phoenix, Inc.; Bowne of Canada, Ltd.; Bowne of Montreal, Inc. (Canada); IDOC, Inc. (80%)

Further Reading

Jaffe, Thomas, "Survivor," *Forbes,* September 4, 1989, p. 317.
Power, Christopher, "The Wrong Type?," *Forbes,* February 28, 1983, p. 2.
Stanley, Edmund A., Jr., *Of Men and Dreams,* New York: Bowne & Co., Inc., 1975, 83 p.

—Jeffrey L. Covell

Brazos Sportswear, Inc.

4101 Founders Boulevard
Batavia, Ohio 45103-2553
U.S.A.
(513) 753-3400
Fax: (513) 752-8508
Web site: http://www.brzs.com

Public Company
Incorporated: 1981 as Sun Sportswear, Inc.
Employees: 1,900
Sales: $284.5 million (1997)
Stock Exchanges: NASDAQ
SICs: 2329 Mens & Boys Clothing, Not Elsewhere
   Classified; 2339 Womens Misses & Jr. Outerwear,
   Not Elsewhere Classified; 2369 Outerwear Girls, Not
   Elsewhere Classified

With the capacity to decorate more than 20 million garments per year, Brazos Sportswear, Inc. ranks among the largest clothing screen printers in the United States. Its network of six manufacturing plants, 11 distribution centers, and three sales offices extends from the United States to Japan, China, and Israel. The company designs T-shirts, shorts, outerwear, tank tops, jerseys, and fleecewear featuring both licensed and proprietary cartoon characters, film properties, professional sports trademarks, and collegiate logos. Its stable of character licenses includes Disney's Mickey Mouse and Winnie the Pooh; Warner Bros.' Bugs Bunny and Tazmanian Devil; Betty Boop, and many others. The company also holds licenses from the International Hockey League and Major League Baseball. Brazos also sells private label apparel. A broad array of decorating techniques are used, including screen printing, embroidery, and appliqué. The company sells its goods to such mass merchandisers as Wal-Mart, Target, and Kmart, and to department stores, including J.C. Penney Co.

Privately held until its 1997 reverse merger with the publicly traded Sun Sportswear, Inc., Brazos calls itself "a family of companies" in reference to the many acquisitions that transformed it from a distributor of blank T-shirts into one of the fastest-growing firms in the apparel industry.

Roots Reaching Back to 1970s

A total of nine acquisitions fueled Brazos' rapid growth in the 1990s. Due to its reverse takeover with Sun Sportswear in 1997, Sun is the company's legal predecessor. This profile, however, will trace Brazos' history to Gulf Coast Sportswear Inc., a firm that can most accurately be called Brazos' historical forebear.

Founded in 1974 by Tom McKnight and George Warney, this company had its first headquarters in Clute, Texas. According to a 1997 report prepared by Jack Henry of the Dillon, Read & Co. Inc. investment firm, Gulf Coast started out wholesaling "blank goods"—T-shirts and sweatshirts sold to college bookstores, screen printing firms, and other businesses that put their own logos on the clothing. Driven in part by the nascent jogging craze, high demand and limited supply allowed McKnight and Warney to mine a profitable niche of the apparel industry for about 15 years. But when T-shirt manufacturers began boosting output and bypassing distributors to sell directly to screen printers, Gulf Coast saw its profit margins shrivel rapidly and inexorably. The partners quickly realized that they had to adapt to the new imperatives of their chosen business or face failure.

The agent of change came from outside the company. In 1989, Equus Capital Corp., a Texas venture capital firm, acquired a 55 percent controlling interest in Gulf Coast Sportswear Inc. Equus had been founded five years earlier by Sam P. Douglass to engineer leveraged buyouts. The new parent renamed its acquisition after the nearby Brazos River, injected capital, and formulated a growth plan that pushed the company into the heretofore highly fragmented screen printing industry.

Acquisitions Drive Rapid Growth in 1990s

Realizing that building its own network of manufacturing plants, license agreements, and customers would be a prohibitively expensive and time-consuming process, Brazos sought growth through acquisition. Friendly takeovers would increase

Company Perspectives:

Throughout its history, Brazos Sportswear has remained true to its business objectives: delivering superior quality clothing and adhering to meaningful customer service standards. This combination of products and service, balanced with diversification and ongoing improvements, has formed the company's building blocks for success in the past, present, and future.

the company's revenues more than tenfold, from $29 million in 1990 to an estimated $310 million in 1997. As chief financial officer Clayton Chambers told *The Press* in 1997, "Each company has typically brought to us (something) . . . that we did not have before." In 1992, Brazos gobbled up CC Creations, thereby gaining a vital connection to Wal-Mart, a mass marketer with a voracious appetite for T-shirts. CC Creations' Red Oak brand held licenses for numerous colleges around the nation. Capital Industries, maker of custom athletic uniforms under the Red Fox and Lady Fox brands, was acquired in 1991.

Brazos made what one analyst deemed its "most significant" acquisition in 1994, when it brought Cincinnati-based Velva-Sheen Manufacturing Co. into the fold. Founded in the late 1930s, Velva-Sheen held licenses with the Walt Disney Company for such timeless characters as Mickey Mouse and Winnie the Pooh, as well as Warner Bros.' Looney Tunes characters. Velva-Sheen became a cornerstone of the Brazos organization, so much so that the parent company moved its headquarters to greater Cincinnati soon after the acquisition. A 1995 restructuring pared administrative personnel, reduced inventories, and focused Velva-Sheen squarely on products featuring licensed characters. The company's roster of over 7,500 customers gave Brazos a broader distribution through which to sell its CC Creations products, thereby reducing somewhat its dependence on Wal-Mart.

The 1995 acquisition of Needleworks, Inc. gave Brazos expertise in machine embroidery, a growing segment of the decorated sportswear market. In August 1996, Brazos acquired Plymouth Mills Inc., a New York manufacturer whose valuable licensing agreements with Chic by H.I.S. and Cherokee added about $40 million to Brazos' top line. At that time, J. Ford Taylor advanced from president of the decorated sportswear division to president and CEO, succeeding Randall Hale, who continued to serve as chairman of the board.

Merger with Sun Sportswear in 1997

In the spring of 1997, Brazos and its parent companies performed an intricate reverse stock swap with Sun Sportswear, Inc. Founded in 1981 by David A. Sabey, Sun grew over the course of the decade to become a major player in the casual sportswear segment. Its proprietary "Rude Dog" character, launched in 1986, sold three million T-shirts and sweatshirts in 1989 and at one time had his own Saturday morning animated series. The company also garnered licenses for U.S. and overseas college logos. By 1989 Sun was netting $6.6 million on

sales of $59 million per year. That October, Sabey decided to sell 20 percent of his company to the public. The IPO marked a turn for the worse.

By the late 1980s, Sun had become dependent on faddish licenses with short-lived popularity and was locked into a cycle of boom and bust. Its California Raisins license, for example, sold $8.4 million worth of T-shirts and sweatshirts in the first half of 1988, but brought in less than $500,000 in the first half of 1989. Sales of Sun's line of shirts printed with heat-sensitive ink declined from $5.8 million in 1991 to nil in 1992. Company-wide sales had declined from $73.3 million in 1989 to $70.6 million in 1992, and net income slid from a $4.1 million profit to a $517,000 loss over that period. The proverbial "other shoe" dropped in 1992, when another of David Sabey's business ventures, the Frederick & Nelson chain of department stores, went bankrupt. Sabey's banker, Seafirst Corp., called in the collateral on his loans: his 68 percent stake in Sun Sportswear. Sabey resigned as chairman and CEO of Sun in 1993 and was succeeded by Larry Mounger.

Mounger executed a quick turnaround focused on expanding Sun's customer base from a heavy dependence on mass merchandisers into higher-margin lines for department stores, investing $4 million into new design and manufacturing technology in the process. Sun's sales jumped from $70.6 million in 1992 to $104.8 million in 1993 on the strength of Disney film character licenses, including *The Little Mermaid* and *101 Dalmatians*. Net income amounted to $2.7 million in the latter year. But when Sun's net income slid to $2.4 million on sales of $113.2 million in 1995, Mounger resigned. Under his successor, William Wiley, Sun sunk into a deep well of red ink, losing $3.7 million on sales of just $94 million in 1996. The reverse takeover offer from Brazos came in 1997.

By purchasing all but eight percent of Seafirst Bank's stake and converting all of Brazos' equity into Sun shares, Brazos ended up with 88 percent of Sun and went public in the process. Though Sun was legally the surviving business entity, it was quickly renamed Brazos Sportswear, Inc. Equus II Inc. continued to hold a controlling 56.3 percent interest in Brazos after the merger.

Reorganization to Unite Profitability with Growth

Although bedeviled by numerous difficulties, Sun had several strengths, including licenses to Warner Bros. and Disney characters (both cartoon and film); an award-winning staff of in-house artists backed by cutting-edge design technology; and shiny new manufacturing machinery. Brazos quickly exorcised Sun's demons: 150 redundant employees, loss-making licenses, excess manufacturing capacity, and surplus inventory.

But Brazos was not finished with 1997's corporate machinations. That June, it acquired Morning Sun, Inc., a Seattle-based apparel company, for $31.9 million. Barely a month passed before the T-shirt maker added its third acquisition of the year, paying $7.6 million for Boulder, Colorado's Premier Sport Group Inc. In September, Brazos paid $13.5 million for CS Crable Sportswear Inc., also of Colorado. With their focus on middle-aged women, international sourcing strengths, and catalog divisions, these acquisitions gave Brazos new methods by which to purchase blank goods and sell finished garments.

Brazos' series of acquisitions built a company with many strengths. It boasted a vital licensing program; strong proprietary characters and the means to create and market new ones; state-of-the-art plants; and a nationwide distribution network reaching more than 12,000 customers. From 1994 through 1996, the company won design and vendor awards from J.C. Penney, Disney, Chic by H.I.S., Warner Bros., and Target.

Because of the reverse merger, Brazos carried with it Sun's poor financial record, with sales declining from a high of $113.2 million in 1994 to $65.6 million in 1996 and a net loss of $5.8 million. Through the first three quarters of 1997, Brazos had sales of $196.3 million and $3.6 million in net income. By the end of the year, the company reported sales of over $284 million, representing an impressive increase over the previous year of 68 percent.

Principal Subsidiaries

Brazos Embroidery Inc.; Brazos Inc.

Further Reading

"Brazos Acquires Plymouth," *Daily News Record,* October 9, 1996, p. 12.

"Brazos in Deal to Buy Premier," *Daily News Record,* June 13, 1997, p. 2.

De Lombaerde, Geert, "Brazos Goes on Buying Binge After Going Public," *Cincinnati Business Courier,* October 3, 1997, p. 28.

Farnsworth, Steve, "Sun Sportswear Ends Up with New Majority Owner," *WWD,* January 7, 1993, p. 13.

Fasig, Lisa Biank, "Brazos to Expand Again," *Cincinnati Enquirer,* April 16, 1997, p. B10.

Gold, Howard, "The Poor Man's LBO," *Forbes,* August 13, 1984, p. 123.

Henry, Jack C., "Brazos Sportswear, Inc.," *Dillon Read High Yield Research,* New York: Dillon, Read & Co., Inc. August 12, 1997.

Klempin, Raymond, "Equus Buys Wholesale Sportswear Company," *Houston Business Journal,* March 6, 1989, p. 15.

Marlow, Michael, "Sun Shines," *Daily News Record,* June 4, 1996, p. 20.

Prinzing, Debra, "Hot Flash: Clothes That Change Color," *Puget Sound Business Journal,* July 15, 1991, pp. 1–2.

——, "Mounger Shining Up Sun Sportswear's Strategy," *Puget Sound Business Journal,* February 12, 1993, p. 11.

——, "Sabey Slates an IPO for Sun Sportswear," *Puget Sound Business Journal,* October 30, 1989, pp. 1–2.

Rodriguez, Robert A., "It's a Small World for the Brazos Sportswear Empire," *The Press,* November 1997, pp. 34–36.

Spector, Robert, "Larry Mounger Finds His Place in the Sun," *Daily News Record,* May 2, 1994, p. 20.

——, "Licensing Finds a Place in the Sun," *Daily News Record,* June 4, 1990, pp. 14–15.

——, "Sun: Expecting to Shine Again," *WWD,* July 18, 1990, p. 9.

——, "Sun Sportswear Pouring Millions into Technology," *WWD,* September 22, 1994, p. S13.

"Sun to Merge with Brazos Unit," *WWD,* December 4, 1996, p. 18.

"Velva Sheen Celebrates 200M T-Shirts," *Daily News Record,* November 7, 1986, p. 11.

—April D. Gasbarre

Brenntag AG

Humboldtring 15
Postfach 10 03 52
D-45472 Muelheim an der Ruhr
Germany
49-208-494-7228
Fax: 49-208-494-7282
Web site: http://wwwbrenntag.de

Wholly Owned Subsidiary of Stinnes AG
Incorporated: 1874 as the Philipp Muehsam Company
Employees: 3,500
Sales: DM 4.5 billion
SICs: 5169 Chemicals & Allied Products, Not Elsewhere
  Classified; 8640 Chemical Industry; 8999 Services,
  Not Elsewhere Classified; 6120 Wholesale
  Distribution of Fuels, Ores, Metals & Industrial
  Materials

Brenntag AG is Europe's largest distributor of industrial chemicals. A multibillion dollar company and affiliate of Germany's largest transportation and distribution firm, Stinnes AG, Brenntag is headquartered in the small city of Muelheim on the Ruhr River, the country's most industrialized corridor. Also a global leader in the distribution of chemicals, the company has more than 80 distribution centers in Europe and 50 in the United States, its most important non-European market.

19th-Century Roots

Brenntag has been in continuous operation since it was founded in 1874. The early 1870s were a propitious time for establishing new businesses in Germany, which had recently been unified after a series of bloody wars. Germany's nationalistic government was anxious to put an end to centuries of economic stagnation and to assert the country's primacy in Europe.

In this favorable climate, Philipp Muehsam, a young German entrepreneur, founded a small business dealing in the transportation and sale of raw materials on the river Spree, the chief artery of Germany's new capital, Berlin. Named after its founder, the Philipp Muehsam Company did a flourishing business. As the capital city of the largest European country, Berlin was rapidly becoming the showplace of everything modern in the late 19th century, and also the center of the country's new chemical industry. In fact, the modern German chemical industry was by the turn of the century the most advanced in the world and the first to employ academically trained researchers.

Contributing to Germany's emerging chemical industry became the chief role of the Philipp Muehsam company. By the turn of the century, its core businesses focused on petroleum as well as on the purchase and distribution of industrial chemicals. Such activities necessitated an international transportation network, which would be upset temporarily during the upheavals of World War I and the subsequent civil unrest. Back on its feet during the 1920s, the company expanded its network under the leadership of Muehsam's successors, and despite the worldwide economic depression of the 1930s, the firm remained the largest distributor of petroleum and industrial chemicals in Germany.

Wartime Shift in Production

During this time, one of Germany's largest industrial concerns, the Hugo Stinnes corporation, had been eyeing the Philipp Muehsam company. In 1938, it made a bid for the company and acquired it. The name of the firm was changed to Brennstoff-Chemikalien-Transport AG, and while its traditional operations in petroleum and industrial chemical distribution remained, a new and important branch was added—the allocation of mineral oil byproducts of petroleum—which would be indispensable to the manufacture of cosmetics during the postwar era.

Wartime, however, generated other needs. While raw materials such as petroleum could still be obtained in the vast Nazi-held territories of eastern Europe during World War II, daily allied bombing took its toll on Brennstoff's business, which during this time consisted wholly of distribution and transportation. By the end of the war, Brennstoff-Chemikalien-Transport AG lay in utter ruin. The parent company, the vast Hugo Stinnes corporation, was confiscated by the occupation authorities, with only a small branch of the company left in the hands of the Stinnes family. Brennstoff, renamed Brenntag AG after the war (in order to disassociate itself with its prewar past), belonged to this branch. Meanwhile that part of the Stinnes firm that had been confiscated by the Allies was reconstituted by the able Dr. Heinz P. Kemper, who was chosen by the U.S. occupation authority in West Berlin because of his lack of party affiliation. In 1964, the Hugo Stinnes firm bought the Brenntag company for what was considered the immense sum of DM 13 million.

Postwar Recovery

Brenntag had been slowly recovering from the turmoil of the war years. Headquarters were moved in 1948 from Berlin in Germany's eastern zone to the more secure town of Muelheim on the Ruhr, in western Germany. With only 20 employees, the company slowly recaptured its former lead in the chemical transportation industry.

Recovery would not have been possible without major currency reform in the western zones in 1948; the unification of the three occupation zones into the Federal Republic of Germany in 1949; and the onset of the Marshall Plan for European economic recovery which followed unification. Brenntag became decidedly more attuned to the market, especially in the international arena. Management divested the company of its former shares in various manufacturing enterprises, as well as of its shipping business, and concentrated instead on broadening its product lines and increasing its focus on chemical distribution and transportation.

Of great urgency in the postwar years was expansion into international markets. Aggressive inroads, most particularly in the biggest and richest market of all—the United States—were made in the 1950s, in the company's first venture on the North American continent. During this time, thousands of tons of industrial chemicals landed in the ports of the low countries for transshipment throughout Europe by Brenntag AG. Inroads were also made into Eastern Europe, an area to which Brenntag had had commercial ties for decades. In the following three decades, the Communist countries of the East would constitute a stable but limited market for Brenntag's chemical products. This market would explode in significance and range with the fall of Communism in the late 1980s.

New product lines were developed in the prosperous 1950s, including aromatic petrochemicals for the cosmetics industry, synthetic materials and resins, and chemical solvents, all of which would be purchased and distributed to the major European chemical manufacturers from sources in Europe and overseas.

New Parentage in the 1960s

The largest transportation and distribution company in West Germany, Hugo Stinnes AG, purchased Brenntag from the Bank für Gemeinwirtschaft in 1964. With one stroke, Stinnes had plunged into the lucrative industrial chemical distribution market, which complemented its other businesses in the distribution and transportation of raw materials and petroleum, as well as overseas shipping. The transaction represented a major step towards diversifying Stinnes (which altered its name in 1976 to Stinnes AG) as well as towards greatly broadening Brenntag's customer base. By then Brenntag's sales revenues were in the hundreds of millions of dollars; 20 years later, they would exceed a billion. Another advantage of Brenntag's acquisition by Stinnes was the greater financial resources of the parent company, which continues to endow Brenntag with a secure economic base. In 1965, Stinnes AG and Brenntag were acquired by Germany's largest firm, the energy company VEBA AG. Stinnes remained a wholly owned subsidiary of VEBA.

After becoming a member of the Stinnes Group of companies, Brenntag's growth was dramatic. Branch offices were established throughout Germany and the rest of Europe. Out of necessity the company became involved in more than just the buying and selling of a wide array of products, including industrial chemicals, agricultural chemicals or made-to-order specialty chemicals. Large investments were also made in fleets of trucks, storage facilities, and tanks that remain indispensable in the distribution of Brenntag's products. Sales offices expanding in key geographical areas rapidly transmitted and facilitated customer orders.

Great Changes in the 1990s

In the late 1980s, Brenntag underwent tremendous expansion. The fall of Communism in Eastern Europe and the demise of the Soviet Union enabled Brenntag to expand its bases in the East and open new branches in Warsaw, Prague, and even Moscow. With the fall of the Berlin Wall, Brenntag was one of the first West German companies to expand into eastern Germany, opening up fifteen branches in a year, and establishing Brenntag affiliates in Erfurt, Chemnitz, and the former East Berlin.

In the early 1990s, chemical firms and their suppliers came under increasing scrutiny for their possible roles in polluting and diminishing the world's natural resources. In addition, stringent new environmental laws forced many of these companies out of business, and burdened the remaining ones with enormous cleanup and safety costs. This was just one of many economic factors influencing a shift toward consolidation as a means of rationalization—that is, greater efficiency in use of financial and other resources.

As *Chemical Week* reported in 1995, the German chemical distribution industry was the largest in Europe, and at its pinnacle was Brenntag, which according to board member Ernst-Hermann Luttmann had experienced two percent growth in the preceding fiscal year—its first increase since 1991. The company's more efficient use of resources received much of the credit for this improvement. In Berlin, for instance, Brenntag jointly operated a warehousing venture with Biesterfeld, the second-largest chemical distributor in the country. In Nuremberg, Brenntag subsidiary Staub & Co. similarly cooperated with Biesterfeld in its logistical operations. Such cooperation might have seemed strange a few years before, but the new business climate would be characterized by fewer companies possessing more resources and applying more efficient methods—even joining forces with a competitor.

In line with moves toward consolidation, Brenntag shut down several smaller warehouses and brought together a number of its operations. When in 1994 it acquired F & A Wulfing of Gevelsberg, Brenntag closed down two other warehouses in Solingen and Wuppertal. From 1990 to 1995, according to *Chemical Week,* the company had gone from 22 distribution centers in Germany to just 12, six of them operated with partners. In fact, its cooperation with Biesterfeld had caused some in Germany to speculate that the companies might merge, though as of early 1998 this had not materialized.

Consolidation of resources did not stop the company from continuing to acquire subsidiaries, and indeed its acquisitions in the 1990s were consistent with the industry-wide trend toward larger companies. Just as Stinnes AG consisted of many companies, Brenntag also came to represent a group of firms specializing in different chemicals and services. For instance, in the same city on the Ruhr where the parent company was located, Brenntag Eurochem GmbH provided made-to-order specialty chemicals.

Among Brenntag's acquisitions in 1997 were Spanish, American, Franco-Belgian, and Swiss companies. With yearly receipts of DM 145 million, Productos Quimicos Sevillanos, S.A. of Seville was Spain's second-largest chemical distributor; by putting it with its other holdings, Brenntag became the leader in the Spanish market. In 1997 Brenntag also acquired the Franco-Belgian company Bonnave, with cumulative annual sales of DM 165 million in the two countries. This acquisition solidified Brenntag's leadership in the French market, and put it in first place in Belgium as well. Also, Brenntag acquired Christ Chemie AG of Switzerland.

Outside of Europe, Brenntag was most heavily represented in the United States, where SOCO Chemical Inc. in Pennsylvania coordinated all U.S. activities, involving seven American distribution firms with branches in more than 50 locations throughout the country. Even during the recession of the early 1990s, Brenntag's U.S. business fared well, although cost-cutting and streamlining accounted for much of the gain in profitability. In 1997 SOCO acquired Burris Chemical Inc. of Charleston, South Carolina, the largest independent distributor of industrial chemicals in the Southeastern United States. Burris also maintained operations in North Carolina and Alabama.

As it approached the end of the century, Brenntag offered an increasingly sophisticated and detailed list of chemical products and services to chemical processors. In the increasingly vital environmental area and related fields, a host of Brenntag companies provided recycling services, packaging materials, drying and cleaning assistance, waste hauling, consulting and marketing. A visit to its web site offered an A-to-Z sampling of the company's wide array of products, from absorbent, acetic acid, and acetone to zinc oxides, zinc stearates, and zinc sulphate. Among the services Brenntag offered in the late 1990s was online tank sensor equipment. When supplies of a chemical fell to a certain point, this registers on the sensor, and it transmitted the information online to the company. This alerted the latter to dispatch a resupply delivery.

As the largest chemical provider and transporter in Europe, Brenntag has survived the onslaught of environmental legislation and public criticism and has managed to adapt to and even profit from these challenges. Recycling and waste disposal loom as strategic business segments in the future. In any case, with its widespread global distribution and transportation network in an era of increasingly free trade, Brenntag's future seems promising. Even if the world market for chemical raw materials contracts, the possibilities for recycling and efficient waste disposal are numerous.

Principal Subsidiaries

Brenntag Chemiepartner GmbH; Brenntag Eurochem GmbH; Brenntag International Chemicals GmbH; Chemische Fabrik Lehrte Dr. Andreas Kossel GmbH; CVH Chemie-Vertrieb GmbH & Co.; Industik GmbH; Staub & Co. Chemiehandelsges, mbH; Brenntag (U.K.) Ltd.; Brenntag Guzmán Ibérica S.A. (Spain); Brenntag Nederland B.V. (Netherlands); Brenntag Portugal Productos Quimicos Lda.; Brenntag Eurochem Sp.z.o.o. (Poland); Brenntag International Chemicals (Russia); Brenntag International Chemicals spol.s.r.o. (Czech Republic); Brenntag International Chemicals Sp.z.o.o. (Poland); Brenntag S.A. (France); Brenntag SpA (Italy); Brenntag Spezialchemikalien GmbH (Austria); Brenntag Volkers Benelux S.A.; Brenntag Volkers Loosdrecht B.V. (Loosdrecht); Bonnave-Dubar S.A. (France-Belgium); Chemproha B.V. (Netherlands); Christ Chemie AG (Switzerland); E. Brunner S.A. (France); N.V. Boucquillon S.A. (Netherlands); PQS Productos Quimicos Sevillanos, S.A. (Spain); Brenntag International Chemicals Inc. (U.S.); Delta Distributors (U.S.); Eastech Inc. (U.S.); PB&S Chemical Company (U.S.); SOCO Chemicals Inc. (U.S.); SOCO-Lynch Corporation (U.S.); SOCO-LYnch Corporation Division Crown Chemical Corp. (U.S.); SOUTHCHEM Inc. (U.S.); Textile Chemical Company Inc. (U.S.); Brenntag (Taiwan) Co. Ltd.; Brenntag AG (Singapore).

Further Reading

Brenntag, Your Partner in the Market, Düsseldorf: Econ Verlag, 1974.
Making Sure the Chemistry Is Right, Muelheim an der Ruhr, Germany: Brenntag AG, 1991.
Young, Ian, "Consolidation Benefits Leading Distributors," *Chemical Week,* May 24, 1994, p. 30.
——, "On the Road to Quality in Europe's Competitive Market," *Chemical Week,* July 22, 1992, pp. 30–32.
——, "Stinnes Agrarchemie Builds Five Centers," *Chemical Week,* February 3, 1993, p. 13.

—Sina Dubovoj
—updated by Judson Knight

Bristol Hotel Company

14285 Midway Road, Suite 300
Dallas, Texas 75244
U.S.A.
(972) 391-3910
Fax: (972) 391-3799
Web site: http://www.businesspr.com/bristol

Public Company
Incorporated: 1981 as Harvey Hotel Company
Employees: 4,500
Sales: $504.5 million (1997)
Stock Exchanges: New York
SICs: 7011 Hotels & Motels

One of the largest owners and operators of full-service hotels in North America, Bristol Hotel Company operates in 19 of the top 25 lodging markets in the United States, with more than 120 hotels clustered in 25 states and in Canada. Bristol, the largest Holiday Inn franchisee in the world, recorded animated growth during the mid- and late 1990s, as it developed from primarily a southern U.S. chain into a national chain with extensive coverage in the mid-priced to upscale segments of the hotel industry. Through acquisition deals that brought more than 80 Holiday Inn hotels under its control during the late 1990s, Bristol ranked as one of the fastest growing operators in its industry as the 21st century neared.

Origins and 1980s Expansion

Founded in 1981, Bristol began business as Harvey Hotel Company, the owner and operator of The Harvey Hotel, located in Dallas, Texas. The Harvey Hotel was the first of many hotel properties the company would control during its first two decades of existence. During this first chapter in the company's history, Bristol grew from one hotel in Dallas to more than 120 hotels clustered in 25 states, achieving its growth through aggressive acquisitions completed in the 1980s and, at a more accelerated pace, in the 1990s. Although the ambitious acquisition campaign waged by Bristol engendered constant change at

the company's headquarters in Dallas, there was one key element during Bristol's swift rise within the hotel industry that never changed: the senior management at Bristol remained the same. Two senior executives orchestrated Bristol's resolute growth; the first was the company's first employee, J. Peter Kline, who joined Bristol in January 1981.

Prior to joining Harvey Hotel Company (the company changed its name to Bristol Hotel Company in 1995), Kline worked for Laventhol & Horwath, a prestigious consulting firm. Like the growth of the company he would later lead, Kline's rise within Laventhol & Horwath was swift. He was named partner of the firm in record time, assuming control over Laventhol & Horwath's entire consulting practice in Texas and surrounding states. Between 1976 and 1980, Kline and his staff conducted market studies for virtually every hotel project proposed for development in Texas, experience that greatly assisted his development of Harvey Hotel Company in Texas, where the greatest concentration of the company's hotels would be located. A graduate of Cornell University, where he earned bachelor of science and master of science degrees, Kline was joined by another Cornell graduate, John A. Beckert, during Harvey Hotel Company's inaugural year. Prior to joining Harvey Hotel Company, Beckert operated his own restaurant and catering business in Dallas and spent three years working at the hotel and theme park divisions of Marriott Corporation. Together, these two Cornell alumni helped direct the growth of the one-hotel Harvey Hotel Company into the Bristol hotel chain.

With Kline in charge and Beckert serving as the general manager of The Harvey Hotel in Dallas, Bristol operated its lone hotel for two years before another property was added. In 1983, the company opened the first of five new hotels it developed during the 1980s, The Harvey Hotel in Plano, Texas. When the hotel in Plano opened, Beckert vacated his general manager post at the Dallas hotel, making room for his brother and future senior vice-president of administration for the company to take over as general manager of the Dallas hotel. Beckert then served as the general manager of the new Plano hotel for the property's first two years before being promoted to vice-president of operations. When Beckert moved into Harvey Hotel Company's executive offices in 1985, the company

---

opened its third hotel, The Harvey Hotel in Addison, Texas, followed by the development of another Harvey Hotel in 1987 at the Dallas-Fort Worth Airport. Subsequent hotel developments during the remainder of the 1980s were opened under two new proprietary brands, Bristol Suites and Harvey Suites. The first was a Bristol Suites in Dallas that opened in 1988, followed by a Harvey Suites at the Dallas-Fort Worth Airport, which opened in 1989. Late in 1989, the company acquired The Sheraton Hotel in Houston and renovated it, converting it to Harvey Suites.

By the end of the 1980s, steady expansion had created an eight-unit chain operating under three proprietary brands. Although the pace of expansion during the decade represented the rise of a growing contender in the Texas hotel market, the methodical physical growth of the company was not enough to turn heads, at least in comparison to the aggressive expansion of the company during the 1990s, as it spread its presence throughout the southern half of the United States, up the Atlantic Coast to Boston, and into the Canadian province of Ontario. At its briskest, expansion during the 1980s occurred at yearly intervals. Expansion during the 1990s, however, was a monthly event, occurring at a dizzying pace that greatly increased the physical and geographic scope of the company.

Behind the frenzied acquisitive activity at the company's corporate offices in Dallas there was a carefully thought-out strategy. Kline and Beckert were not simply trying to make their company the largest hotel operator in the industry, they were clustering their new hotels in concentrated groups, thereby realizing significant efficiencies for the marketing, management, and logistical coordination of their burgeoning enterprise. Further, they were shaping Harvey Hotel Company to compete in a specific market category, tailoring their hotels through renovations to compete in upper mid-priced and upscale segments of the hotel industry. As the number of hotels operating under Harvey Hotel Company's corporate umbrella increased, general characteristics of the chain emerged. All the hotels were primarily larger, full-service facilities offering state-of-the-art banquet and meeting facilities, with a variety of dining options. Sales were promoted locally, by on-site marketing teams that addressed the specific needs and desires of the area.

Mid-1990s Acquisitions

Although the company's physical growth during the 1990s would dwarf the accomplishments of the 1980s, expansion did not get underway until mid-way through the decade. In August 1994, the company made its first move since the establishment of the Harvey Suites at the Dallas-Fort Worth Airport in 1989, acquiring a Holiday Inn in Houston and converting it into a Harvey Suites. Next, the company made its boldest move to date when it acquired 26 hotels owned by Memphis-based United Inns, Inc. Overnight, the deal lifted Harvey Hotel Company's hotel count to 36 and extended the company's geographic presence into seven states. The purchase of the United Inns hotels also ushered in an exhaustive, $130-million renovation program aimed at redeveloping the hotels, most of which were in disrepair, to bring them up to Harvey Hotel Company standards, which represented part of the company's general strategy to purchase distressed hotels and transform them into vibrant money-earners once again. Phase one of the United Inns redevelopment program began in March 1995, when renovations on seven of the properties started. As this program was underway, the company picked up another Sheraton Hotel, located at the Atlanta Airport, in June and converted it to a Harvey Hotel. In September, the company changed its name to Bristol Hotel Company.

Phase one of the United Inns renovation program was completed in October 1995. Phase two began the following month, when work started on renovating five more of the former United Inns properties. The company also purchased another hotel in the Dallas area in November 1995, acquiring the downtown Dallas Holiday Inn/Howard Johnson, to which Bristol added its restorative touch and converted it to a Hampton Inn. In December, after a year of frenetic activity that increased the company's hotel count from ten to 38 and included extensive renovation work, Bristol converted to public ownership. In the company's December initial public offering, 4.89 million shares were sold to investors at $20.50 per share, and Bristol made its debut on the New York Stock Exchange.

Phase two of Bristol's redevelopment program, which began in November 1995, was finished in June 1996, but before the second phase ended phase three began. In March 1996, the last of the $130 million earmarked for the renovation of United Inns was invested in the redevelopment of eight more United Inns properties. This final stage of the redevelopment project lasted a year, during which time the company continued to acquire hotels, selecting mismanaged or deteriorating properties near a cluster of Bristol-operated hotels. In May 1996, the company acquired a Holiday Inn in Plano, Texas, and in January 1997 the company purchased the historic Allerton Hotel in Chicago. Located on Chicago's North Michigan Avenue, where the most heavily concentrated area of upscale retail stores in the country flanked a famous section of the city known as the "Magnificent Mile," the Allerton Hotel stood as a landmark, comprising 383 rooms divided among 25 floors. Bristol paid $35 million for the hotel, but intended to spend more on the property to finance its conversion to a more than 400-unit Crowne Plaza hotel.

1997: A National Contender Emerges

Although Bristol's pace of acquisitions slowed significantly from the ambitious rate of expansion in 1995, the company's accomplishments in 1997 more than made up for the temporary lull. Phase three of the redevelopment program concluded in April 1997, the same month Bristol completed a mammoth deal that more than doubled its size and made it the largest franchisee of Holiday Inn properties in the world. At a price of $665 million, the company acquired 60 full-service Holiday Inn hotels located in the United States and Canada from U.K.-based Bass Plc, a deal that raised Bristol's number of hotels to 98. As it had throughout its history, Bristol intended to renovate the acquired properties and set aside $200 million to fund capital improvements on the 60 hotels. When Kline announced the completion of the deal, his words underscored the significance of the acquisition to Bristol's stature within the U.S. hotel industry. "This transaction," he told reporters, "marks a new era for Bristol, taking our regional presence to a national level. The deal," he added, "also signals a new strategic alliance between Bristol and Holiday Inn Worldwide, and firmly establishes Holiday Inn as a leader in the competitive corporate business category."

After a decade and a half of converting money-losing hotels in disrepair into well-appointed, profitable properties, Bristol had proven its capabilities as one of the most successful hotel owners and operators in the country. The April 1997 deal with Bass Plc was testament to this esteemed record of accomplishment, and its successful completion promised further acquisitions of Holiday Inn hotels. Bristol, having completed the evolutionary step from regional hotel operator to national hotel operator, had no intention of slowing its acquisitive pace.

Three more Holiday Inns were acquired in separate transactions before the end of 1997, a 318-room hotel in St. Louis in October, a 364-room hotel in Philadelphia in December, and a 305-room hotel in San Jose, California, also in December. In February 1998, the company increased the number of hotel rooms under its control 14 percent in a $100 million transaction that included 20 midwestern Holiday Inns.

As Bristol prepared for the future, with co-founder Kline at the helm, the company was one of the fastest-growing hotel companies in North America. Its remarkable physical expansion during the late 1990s had pushed its financial total upward, making Bristol a company to watch as the 21st century approached. From $70 million in revenues generated in 1994, the company's sales volume swelled to more than $500 million three years later, while the company's earnings rose strongly, jumping 163 percent in Bristol's fourth quarter in 1997 alone. Additional acquisitions in the years ahead appeared assured, as the company narrowed its sights on the $15 to $20 billion of acquisition targets it had identified by the end of 1997. With this vast selection of hotels that met the company's buying criteria, Bristol's expansion throughout North America was highly likely, provided its enviable record of profitability and astute management continued into the future.

Principal Subsidiaries

Airport Utilities, Inc.; Austin Innkeepers, Inc.; Bristol Dallas Downtown, Inc.; Bristol-Harvey Partners, Ltd.; Bristol HHCL Company; Bristol Hotel Asset Company; Bristol Hotel Beverage Company; Bristol Hotel Management Corporation; Bristol HTS Company; Bristol IP Company; Bristol Plano Company; Endlease, Inc.; Glenjon, Inc.; Harvey BHP, Inc.; Harvey Hotel Company, Ltd.; Harvey Hotel Corporation; Harvey Hotel DFW, Inc.; Harvey Hotel Management Corporation; Harvey Hotel Purchasing Company; Harvey Hotels Financing I, Inc.; Harvey Hotels Financing II, Inc.; Harvey Hotels Gen Par, Inc.; Harvey Hotels Investments I, Ltd.; Harvey Hotels Investments II, Ltd.; Harvey Hotels Limpar, Ltd.; HHH Hotel Corporation; HHHC GenPar, L. P.; Houston Inns Service Company; Lammons Hotel Courts, Inc.; Limited Service Inns, Inc. of Mississippi; Mid-Atlanta Investment Company; Penrod Club; Rier Properties, Inc.; Rodgers Hotel Courts, Inc.; United Inns, Inc. of Tennessee; Wichita Harvey Partners, Ltd.

Further Reading

"Bristol Hotel Company Reports 162% Increase in Fourth Quarter Earnings Completing a Year Record," *PR Newswire*, February 18, 1998, p. 2.

—Jeffrey L. Covell

Broadcast Music Inc.

320 West 57th Street
New York, New York 10019
U.S.A.
(212) 586-2000
Fax: (212) 830-8329
Web site: http://www.bmi.com

Not-for-Profit Organization
Founded: 1940
Employees: not available
Sales: $421 million (1997 est.)
SICs: 7389 Business Services, Not Elsewhere Classified

Broadcast Music Inc. (BMI), a performance rights organization, makes sure that the people who write, compose, and publish music receive payment whenever a piece is performed publicly. Copyrighted music cannot be performed in public without the permission of the copyright holder, so BMI contractually acquires performing rights from copyright holders, signs agreements with and collects fees from music users, and distributes license fees to the copyright holders. More than 200,000 music artists have contracts with BMI, protecting over three million musical works in all genres. The second largest such organization in the United States, BMI controls 45 percent of the performance rights copyright market and has offices in New York, Nashville, London, Puerto Rico, Atlanta, and Miami. Its artists include 70 percent of Academy Award–winning songwriters and 75 percent of Rock & Roll Hall of Fame inductees.

Some Industry Background

The copyright laws of the United States recognize that all creative works, including musical compositions, have a property right known as a copyright, and that the makers of those works are entitled to receive payment when their works are used in public. Generally, when a musical composition is written, copyright vests either in the writer, who licenses it to a music publishing company, or in the publishing company. Similarly, when a recording is made, copyright vests in the artist and is licensed to a recording company, or in the record company itself.

A piece of music can generate five types of income: 1) performance royalties for public or live performance; 2) print royalties for the sale of printed music; 3) mechanical income for the right to make sound recordings (CDs, tapes); 4) commercial royalties for using the piece in background music; and 5) synchronization fees for use in movies, television programs, commercials, or videos.

In the field of music, it was impossible for individuals to keep track of the when and where their music was played, so in 1941 the American Society of Composers, Authors and Publishers (ASCAP) was founded to license radio stations, clubs, restaurants, and others in their use of copyrighted musical works. The users paid fees (primarily performance and print royalties) to ASCAP, and ASCAP made payments to its affiliated copyright holders. Music publishing companies were expected to share a portion of the fees with the songwriters and composers. To belong to ASCAP, a songwriter had to have five published hit songs. There were similar standards for music publishers, with the result that, by the late 1930s, according to BMI's organizational history, about 15 well-known publishers controlled 90 percent of the most-played songs on network radio.

Three radio networks—National Broadcasting Company (NBC), Columbia Broadcasting System (CBS), and Mutual Broadcasting System—dominated the airwaves, and the music publishing business was increasingly controlled by movie studios, which needed music for their films. During the 1930s radio stations paid licensing fees based on a percentage of advertising time. This meant that ASCAP was collecting fees for any music being played but only paid those artists with whom it had agreements. The men and women who wrote or performed blues, ragtime, or jazz, and who did not belong to ASCAP, received no royalties even when their work was performed. In 1933 the broadcasters began pushing for a system that would pay copyright holders on a per-program basis and allow non-ASCAP songwriters and composers to supply royalty-free music for radio. By 1939 radio stations paid $4.3 million in licensing payments, based on advertising sales.

1939–50: The Early Years

In the fall of 1939, with the most recent ASCAP licensing agreement about to expire, leaders in the radio industry met in

Chicago to discuss establishing a new licensing body for their music as a less expensive alternative to ASCAP.

BMI was chartered as a nonprofit organization in October 1939 and began operating in New York City the following February. Under the charter, radio organizations paid for the new entity's operating and capital expenses, pledging amounts equal to half their 1937 payments to ASCAP. When ASCAP proposed increasing radio's fees 100 percent, many broadcasters quickly shifted to BMI. By the end of 1940, some 650 had signed licensing agreements with BMI. In addition to broadcasters, several of the major music publishers signed with BMI.

From the very beginning BMI operated an open-door policy for musical artists, particularly those without a track record of hits. Now, people who were writing blues, country, and rhythm and blues (R&B) would get their music played more often and more widely on the radio and get paid when it was performed. To provide more opportunities for writers and composers, BMI created its own publishing company, sending thousands of arrangements to radio stations that used live music, and also provided advances and guarantees to aspiring publishers to enable them to start their own companies. Among those taking advantage of BMI's support were band leaders Jimmie Lunceford (New Era Music) and Lionel Hampton (Swing and Tempo Music).

Among the catalogs of music BMI offered broadcasters were those of E. B. Marks and Peer International, with thousands of tunes from Latin America. The company's connection with music from Central and South America continued and strengthened during the following decades and provided a foundation for relationships with musicians in other countries.

In late 1940 BMI began negotiating with the American Composers Alliance (ACA) and its publisher arm, Arrow Press, for licensing rights to serious or symphonic music. That agreement, and one for broadcast rights to the music of leading European serious-music houses, increased BMI's repertory and helped its reputation as an organization for all types of music. In 1941 BMI formed BMI Canada as a subsidiary. That organization quickly developed a catalog of 5,000 works, one-third of which had French lyrics.

While it was important, of course, for the new entity to sign contracts with writers and publishers and licensing agreements with broadcasters, the key to its operations was establishing a system of licensing fees. Where ASCAP had based their fees on advertising sales, BMI focused on paying for what actually was performed. To do this, BMI had Paul Lazerfield of the Office of Radio Research at Columbia University design a process that enabled BMI to document the air play of a scientific sample of non-network programs as well as of network broadcasts from New York, Chicago, and other major cities. The system, known

as "logging," incorporated a daily census, i.e., a program log, from the radio networks and from a sampling of local radio stations. The sample was then multiplied to reflect the national picture.

According to BMI the process involved examining 60,000 hours of logs a year, and while most of the music was broadcast live at the beginning, using sheet music, the process also identified performances of recorded music. That ability became very important when the radio networks later shifted to recordings. In 1942 the basic payment for local-station performances was four cents, and six cents per station for network performances.

The record industry grew significantly during the 1940s, with record sales reaching $224 million in 1947. Added to the pent-up demand following World War II were better equipment such as high fidelity and then stereo, and better products—the 45 rpm disc and the long-playing 33⅓ rpm disc—which caused sales to keep growing.

The types of music being recorded expanded as well. In 1942 *Billboard* began tracking releases of "folk" records. By 1949 that label had been changed to "country and western." BMI helped new publishing companies get going, including Acuff-Rose Publications and Range Songs, both leaders in country music. Between 1944 and 1954, 77 percent of all the songs on the Top 10 of *Billboard*'s country charts were licensed by BMI, including "Tennessee Waltz" and "Your Cheatin' Heart."

The postwar period also saw the rise of black musicians and rhythm and blues music, and new independent record labels, including Atlantic Records, Specialty Records, and Chess Records, to record R&B artists. BMI licensed more than 90 percent of R&B radio hits on a weekly basis.

On the management side of the organization, Carl Haverlin became BMI's first full-time, paid president in 1947. Haverlin pushed BMI to become more active in the publishing side of the business, and concluded negotiations which gave the organization all publishing and performing rights for a group of 15 European music houses.

The major radio networks agreed to extend their contracts with BMI until 1959, and over 1,000 independent broadcasters soon agreed to the same time period. This made it possible for BMI to enter contracts with publishers and songwriters for longer than 24 months, the limit under the existing licensing agreements. However, the radio networks used little of BMI's music, and the organization's income was only one-third of that taken in by ASCAP.

Other important actions taken by Haverlin were the development of a songwriter payment plan, which BMI put into effect in 1949, and payment for recorded performances. This brought in unaffiliated publishers and record companies, whose records were generally played on independent radio stations. For the first time since the organization was founded, BMI-licensed music was prominent on all the charts.

1950–60: Shifts in the Industry

The 1950s were a period of great change in the music industry. Not only did records displace most sheet music, television was a growing medium, and the public's view of "popular" music shifted dramatically, with the development of rock and roll.

BMI was deeply involved in the growing popularity of country, rhythm and blues, and rock and roll, but it also supported "serious" music. In 1951 BMI president Carl Haverlin instituted the Student Composer Awards for promising young composers. In 1954 the organization created a new Concert Music Department and began sponsoring such events as the ten-concert festival on Music Mountain in the Connecticut Berkshire foothills.

During this period BMI arranged its first annual awards presentation specifically for writers and publishers of country music. When the Country Music Association was founded in 1958, BMI vice-president Bob Burton served on its first board of trustees, and that year, BMI opened a branch office in Nashville. The office was run out of the home of Frances Williams, who, as Frances Preston, became president of BMI in 1986. In the late 1950s BMI also opened an office in London to help negotiate reciprocal licenses with the major performing rights societies in Western Europe. The company went on to establish similar agreements with societies in Scandinavia, Japan, and Latin America.

BMI also helped establish publishing houses specializing in jazz. A large number of jazz composers who were also recording artists signed up with BMI, so that by the early 1960s the company's roster included such names as Dave Brubeck, Charles Mingus, Charlie Parker, and Miles Davis. BMI's vice-president of public relations, Russell Sanjek, helped promote jazz by organizing major jazz festivals and publishing a series of brochures, which were distributed around the world by the U.S. Information Agency.

The changes in the industry, particularly the development of rock and roll, were not popular with the people who wrote and composed "traditional" popular songs. In November 1953 a group of 33 composers claimed a conspiracy of broadcasters and producers was keeping "good music" from being recorded or aired. They brought a $150 million antitrust suit against BMI, the three national broadcast networks (who owned 20 percent of BMI), RCA Victor Records, Columbia Records, and 27 individuals. The composers, all members of ASCAP, included such well known songwriters as Alan Jay Lerner, Ira Gershwin, and Oscar Hammerstein. The suit was supported by other ASCAP members, who pledged five percent of their ASCAP royalties to help pay for the legal costs. As the case was brought, more than 9,000 writers were members of BMI, receiving royalties.

In 1956 the plaintiffs, who called themselves "The Songwriters of America," took their case to Congress, where hearings were held to look into the involvement of radio and television networks in music publishing and promotion. More hearings were held in 1958 in the Senate. While the networks and their recording business were the subject of the hearings, the music available through BMI also came under attack. Witnesses as diverse as the Governor of Tennessee and the head of Paramount Pictures testified against the charges and the proposed legislation, which died in committee. However, the networks did divest themselves of BMI stock. Congress continued to investigate BMI for unlawful practices, including "payola,"

paying disc jockeys to play certain records. Neither those investigations nor the suit proved successful, although The Songwriters of America fought for 15 years before the suit was dismissed with prejudice in 1968.

In the mid-1950s the Senate ratified the Universal Copyright Convention, making the United States a participant in an international copyright agreement for the first time. While U.S. copyright law exempted jukeboxes from any music licensing fee, owners of jukeboxes or other coin machines in most of the other nations had to pay a royalty on the music. Congress began proposing legislation to eliminate the jukebox exemption.

On the West Coast, BMI concentrated on the new medium of television, because most of the movie studios owned their own ASCAP publishing companies. Many TV producers used "canned music" in scoring their programs, and by the end of the decade BMI had signed 85 percent of the track libraries that provided the music. As television producers began wanting original theme and background music, the company aggressively sought and signed television composers, many of whom came from jazz and the big bands. By November 1963 viewers were hearing BMI music on 112 of the 163 regularly scheduled network shows.

While focusing on television, the company did not ignore music for films, with works such as "Song from Moulin Rouge," "Never on Sunday," (which won an Academy Award), and "More," the score from *Mondo Cane,* becoming popular hits. A large part of BMI's attraction to screen composers was that it made payments when films were shown in foreign countries.

Meanwhile, back in New York, BMI established a musical theater department in 1957, and in 1961, created the Musical Theatre Workshop to support composers interested in that genre. Eventually, BMI's Broadway repertoire ranged from *Fiorello!* to *Cabaret* to *Little Shop of Horrors* to *Cats.*

1960–90

Robert Burton became BMI's second paid president in 1963. Burton helped get licensing payments from new sources, most particularly, one percent of gross admissions at live and closed-circuit concerts. That policy went into effect at the Beatles' 1964 closed-circuit television show. The Beatles had released their first U.S. single, "I Want to Hold Your Hand," that year, and it topped *Billboard*'s charts within three weeks. Dick James, the Fab Four's publisher in England, quickly sewed up all publishing rights for the Beatles in North America through his own BMI-affiliated company, Maclen Music.

BMI also instituted a new distribution policy for writers, which tripled their payments, and resulted in the buildup of BMI's collection of scores from movies and musical theater. That same year, BMI moved into its own office building in Nashville. By 1965 the organization claimed 9,000 songwriters and 7,000 publishing affiliates.

In 1965 a federal court ordered BMI to get out of the business of recording, printing, or distributing music, and limited its contracts to no more than five years. The same year, the Federal Communications Commission (FCC) prohibited stations from broadcasting the same AM programming on FM stations in markets of over 100,000 listeners. FM stations began programming album cuts, playing all sorts of music, from jazz and classical to blues, rock and roll, and folk. BMI began in-depth logging of FM stations, and the company's income from local radio alone grew from $3 million in 1963 to $15.5 million in 1971.

During the 1970s disco dancing was the rage, the quality of tape cassettes improved and their sales soared, superstar songbooks led to a jump in printed music, and the revised U.S. copyright law included the licensing of jukeboxes. BMI Canada became an independent, Canadian-owned and operated company, Performing Rights Organization-Canada (PRO-Canada). BMI began offering various insurance packages, including medial and life insurance, to its affiliates living in the United States. In 1977 BMI introduced a new payment plan, emphasizing performances. With material available from *TV Guide,* the organization was able to include local syndicated television shows in its sampling system.

In the 1980s new musical technologies began emerging: music videos and compact disks. Music video cable channels such as VH-1 and MTV found avid audiences, particularly among teenagers, for the sound (and sights) of heavy metal bands. BMI took the lead in licensing the new cable television industry. College radio stations were also becoming an increasingly important source of new music, as young bands such as REM and the B-52s made a name for themselves on college radio before moving to commercial stations. BMI was the first performing rights organization to comprehensively log college stations, adding more than 1,000 to its logging system in 1989.

In 1985 BMI Foundation Inc., a separate tax exempt, non-profit organization, was established. Through endowed funds, it offered grants, scholarships, awards, and prizes to young composers. It also supported groups around the country involved in education about or performance of music.

The 1990s: New Technologies/New Challenges

As BMI celebrated its 50th anniversary, there were over 10,000 broadcasting stations (TV and radio) in the United States. The company estimated it analyzed over six million broadcast hours a year using its census and sampling system, 100 times the number of hours examined back in 1940.

The 1990s saw BMI's licensing departments expand their reach beyond bars and restaurants to new users of BMI music, including health clubs, banks, shopping malls, and amusement parks. The organization remained active on the legislative front, lobbying on various bills pertaining to copyrights and musical licensing. BMI also increased the services available to its affiliates, adding musical instrument coverage to its insurance offerings and expanding the types of options available for life, dental, and medical coverage.

Yet much of BMI's activity related to new technologies. In 1995 BMI negotiated the first agreement licensing music performed on the Internet, and in 1997, announced the creation of "MusicBot™"—a web robot that will comb the World Wide Web, tracking the use of BMI music. That same year, a new agreement with local television stations included language that enabled stations to use BMI music on world wide web promotional sites as well as on future high-definition TV signals.

Most far-reaching, perhaps, was BMI's involvement in the creation of an international, digital song registry, the "Works Information Database." Under the plan, each musical composition would have a digital identification number, and, with regional and national databases linked through the Internet, make it possible for a copyright organization to accurately identify the ownership of a musical piece, no matter if it shared a title with 30 other pieces. BMI President Frances Preston saw the registry as a logical continuation of BMI's goals. "We must, at the beginning of the next century, be able to identify the performance of a creative work by its digital identifier anywhere in the world, transmit the information rapidly and efficiently across linguistic, cultural and national borders, and compensate the creator and owner quickly and accurately."

Further Reading

BMI, "BMI 50th Anniversary History Book, The Explosion of American Music: 1940–1990," http://www.bmi.com/reading/archives/historyo1.html.

Sanjek, Russell, and David Sanjek, *American Popular Music Business in the 20th Century,* New York: Oxford University Press, 1991.

—Ellen D. Wernick

Brown & Haley

P.O. Box 1596
Tacoma, Washington 98401
U.S.A.
(800) 426-8400
Fax: (206) 272-6742

Private Company
Incorporated: 1914 as Oriole Candy Company
Employees: 300
Sales: $50 million (1997 est.)
SICs: 2064 Candy & Other Confectionery Products

The third-largest manufacturer of boxed chocolates in the United States, Brown & Haley makes a variety of confection products but is most widely known for its Mountain Bars and Almond Roca candies. During the late 1990s, Almond Roca ranked as the largest exported gift candy in the United States, having been introduced in foreign countries during World War II. In addition to the company's three flavors of Mountain Bars and its flagship Almond Roca brand, Brown & Haley sold cream-filled chocolates under the Belgium Cremes brand name and an assortment of chocolate, nut, and cream-filled confections. Based in Tacoma, Washington, the company was owned and managed by the Haley family.

Turn of the Century Origins

The foundation for Brown & Haley rested on the business and personal relationship forged by the company's founders, Henry L. Brown and Jonathan Clifford Haley. The two co-founders met in 1908 in Tacoma, Washington, where Brown owned a small confectionery store. Haley was a newcomer to Tacoma, having left Ohio for the Pacific Northwest to start a new life where opportunities abounded and, according to infectious gossip, quick fortunes could be made. After Haley and Brown crossed paths for the first time, the two men struck a friendship that manifested itself in the business arena, where each could apply their individual talents. Of the two, Haley was the businessman, adept at sales and marketing. Brown's inter-

ests ran in a different direction. He envisioned himself as a candymaker and spent his time experimenting with different recipes for making chocolate and sugar candies. Brown and Haley began working together to develop a business venture in 1912, the year observed by Brown & Haley as the founding date for the company. Two years later, the complementary business relationship between Henry Brown and J. C. Haley was made official with the incorporation of their business, the Oriole Candy Company, the predecessor to Brown & Haley.

Two years after their 1914 incorporation, Brown and Haley had created a full line of candy products and had already created one of the two signature products that would drive sales for the remainder of the century. Originally marketed as "Mt. Tacoma," the company's signal product was a chocolate and nut confection with a vanilla-cream center that debuted perhaps as early as 1915, but was definitely an integral part of the company's product line by 1916. Quickly, Brown and Haley had developed a product that, by itself, could support their company and, perhaps more important, its introduction had occurred at a propitious time.

Not far from the company's production site, a military base named Camp Lewis was swelling at its fences with new inductees ready to join the war in Europe. The soldiers in training at Camp Lewis represented a burgeoning pool of customers for the candies produced by Brown and Haley, particularly their recently introduced Mt. Tacoma bar. Company sales quickly shot upward, fueled by the presence of a captive audience that eagerly satiated its collective sweet tooth. Brown and Haley supplied the soldiers with taffy chews, butterscotch balls, Mt. Tacoma bars, and a full list of other confections, collecting enough money to finance the relocation of their manufacturing facility to an abandoned shoe factory at the end of the war.

In the history of Brown & Haley, military conflicts proved to be a boon to the company's business. The United States' decision to enter World War I provided the company with an initial surge in sales that helped it make the frequently difficult transition from start-up business venture to established company. World War II would be equally, if not more, beneficial to Brown & Haley's financial well-being, and to a lesser extent the United States' involvement in Korea, Vietnam, and the Persian

Gulf would provide welcomed boosts in sales, but the company's benefits from the country's entrance into World War I turned out to be short-lived. The end of World War I reverted nearly all U.S. soldiers back to civilian life, and, accordingly, the number of soldiers residing at Camp Lewis quickly dwindled, dipping to prewar population levels. Sales at Brown & Haley dipped as well, dropping as quickly as they had risen during the war. Henry Brown and J. C. Haley, with their recently acquired manufacturing facility at their disposal, were at a loss for what to do next.

Forced to rethink their approach, Brown and Haley decided that the key to survival in the competitive candy market was to be innovative: to distinguish their company from competitors by developing one great product that could win the hearts of consumers. It was time for Brown to retreat to the kitchen to create such a confection. For several years, various recipes were developed, as Brown struggled to find the solution to the company's financial ills. As the search was on, however, the company already had a product that was performing admirably. The company's flagship Mt. Tacoma bar was a hit, selling well in the region encompassing the company's offices in Tacoma and winning over customers in neighboring regions as well. By 1923, the sale of Mt. Tacoma bars had spread geographically far enough to justify a name change of the brand. Mt. Tacoma became the less geographically specific "Mountain," the brand name under which the company's cream-filled candy bars would become famous. The same year Brown & Haley rechristened its flagship product, the years of experimenting to develop another flagship product came to an end. The result would constitute the essence of Brown & Haley during the 20th century.

Almond Roca Created in 1923

From Brown & Haley's kitchen emerged a crunchy, log-shaped candy with butter inside and a coating of chocolate and diced almonds on the outside. Unique, the creation fulfilled the company's objective of developing an innovative product to distinguish itself from competitors. For a name for the small, log-shaped candies, Brown & Haley took the suggestion of a local librarian, who proposed "Roca," which meant "rock" in Spanish. Considering that almonds came primarily from Spain during the 1920s, the name was a logical selection and its sound had a catchy ring to it, giving birth to the Almond Roca brand name that would flourish during the ensuing decades.

Almond Roca candies proved to be an immediate success, but fundamental refinements had to be made before the candy's full potential could be unlocked. Although consumers in the region surrounding Tacoma were eagerly grabbing Almond Roca candies off store shelves, it quickly became clear that the product's short shelf life was limiting sales and barring widespread distribution. An alarming percentage of the candies were turning rancid, which forced the company to devise a packaging solution. Haley found one, drawing inspiration from the way in which coffee was packaged. In 1927, Brown & Haley began packaging Almond Rocas in airtight tin cans, thereby extending the candy's shelf life three-fold. Owing to its distinction as the first candy in the world to be packaged in a sealed tin can, Almond Roca's suitability for distribution was greatly enhanced by the packaging change. In the decades to follow, the importance of the packaging innovation became manifestly clear, as Almond Roca candies were distributed across the globe and developed into the largest exported gift candy in the United States.

World War II Fuels Growth

Before Almond Roca developed into a globally distributed product, it enjoyed popularity as a regional favorite in the Pacific Northwest, remaining a local secret throughout the Great Depression. This, however, would soon change. The end of the 1930s witnessed the start of another war in Europe, and like the Great War 20 years earlier, World War II would shower a wealth of business on the small, Pacific Northwest candymaker, Brown & Haley. When the United States entered the war in 1941, the prospects for candy manufacturers looked bleak, Brown & Haley included. Sugar was among the numerous items that fell under rationing restrictions at the beginning of the United States' involvement in the war, which promised to severely damage the business of candymakers throughout the country. Brown & Haley was making as many as 25 different candy products when World War II started, but once sugar rationing was announced the company decided to substantially trim its product line and concentrate on producing its greatest money winners, Mountain Bars and Almond Roca. As it had 20 years earlier, the population at nearby Camp Lewis mushroomed as the country braced itself for another protracted military struggle. This time, however, Brown & Haley was not dependent on the burgeoning number of recruits pouring into Camp Lewis. Packed in air-tight tin cans, Almond Rocas could be shipped to troops wherever they went, and Brown & Haley was quick to take advantage of this ability by signing a contract with the U.S. War Department to supply Almond Rocas to military personnel stationed overseas. What followed made Almond Rocas a national treasure and an international delight.

During the war, Almond Rocas were shipped to troops in Europe, the Middle East, and the Pacific, popping up wherever U.S. soldiers were camped. A coveted treat, the hard, crunchy candies took on a legendary stature during the war, their presence so pervasive that the almond-covered candies were the subject of an entire chapter in a government historical study of World War II. At one point during the war, U.S. generals refused to hand over responsibility for an occupied country to other Allied forces until they were guaranteed that three railroad cars of Almond Rocas could be taken with them, a stipulation that pointed to the widespread popularity of the candies. The armada of Almond Rocas sent overseas during the war, which would not have been possible without the 1927 introduction of tin packaging, did much to strengthen Brown & Haley's business. Not only did it give the company a thriving business during the years of sugar rationing, it also transformed the candies from a local favorite to a national favorite. When U.S. soldiers returned from overseas after the war and resumed their civilian lives throughout the country, many yearned for the candies made in Tacoma. As a result, the postwar years would see Brown & Haley's customer base broaden from the Pacific Northwest region until it embraced the entire country.

Before the war ended, the legacy of the Brown family's involvement in the candy business came to an end. In 1944 the Brown family sold their interest in the company to the Haley family, which was led by Fred Haley, the second generation of Haleys to guide the fortunes of the company. Under Fred Haley's tutelage, the company reaped the rewards of its World War II activities, gaining a national presence as demand for Almond Rocas spread throughout the country. Business grew steadily during the 1950s, 1960s, and into the 1970s, driven by the popularity of the company's two signature products, Mountain Bars, and the considerably more successful, Almond Roca candies. Although the company marketed other candies, nothing matched the sales strength of its two leading brands.

With nearly all of its growth underpinned by the success of Mountain Bars and Almond Roca candies, Brown & Haley concentrated its marketing and distribution efforts on those two brands for decades. Essentially a two-product company, the company was content to rely on its leading brands for its sales growth. During the 1970s, Brown & Haley made two moves that boosted the sales derived from Mountain Bars and Almond Roca candies. Originally, Mountain Bars had a vanilla-flavored center, the only flavor available until the end of World War II when Brown & Haley's Cherry Bounce brand was rechristened Cherry Mountain Bar. In 1974 a third flavor was added, the Peanut Butter Mountain Bar. Its debut marked an increase in the sales derived from Mountain Bar production. The company's second major achievement during the 1970s provided a considerably more powerful boost to sales, making the Almond Roca brand an internationally recognized name.

Export Business Begins in 1974

During the early 1970s, Fred Haley began looking seriously at building overseas business, and Almond Roca, which had traveled the world during World War II, represented the logical choice for extending the company's presence into foreign markets. The push overseas was given life with the first substantial order in 1974, when a Japanese wholesaler agreed to buy $250,000 worth of Almond Roca candies. From there, Brown & Haley's export business grew steadily, developing into a significant arm of the company's business and accounting for a substantial portion of total annual sales.

A decade after Fred Haley began developing Brown & Haley's export business, the next generation of the Haley family

assumed control over the company. In 1984, Mark Haley, Fred Haley's son, took over as president, inheriting a business that still drew much of its strength from its two leading brands. By this point, Brown & Haley was producing up to 400,000 pounds of Almond Roca each day and exporting an estimated 20 percent of its production total to 40 countries on six continents, having achieved remarkable progress on the international front. Once settled into his new position, Mark Haley began making subtle changes, endeavoring to make Brown & Haley known as something other than "the Almond Roca company." His efforts bore fruit in 1990, when the company introduced Belgium Cremes, a line of molded chocolates with 12 varieties of cream fillings. Belgium Cremes proved to be highly popular, with orders quadrupling during the product's second year of availability.

Encouraged by the success of Belgium Cremes, Haley furthered his efforts toward broadening Brown & Haley's image as the 1990s progressed. Part of his strategy included a thorough redesign of the packaging and labeling of the company's staple products to emphasize the Brown & Haley name. Additionally, the company was stepping up its marketing efforts to highlight the other candies in its product line. Although more attention was being paid to other products manufactured under the Brown & Haley banner, the company by no means abandoned sales support for its two signature products. Almond Roca candies and Mountain Bars had fueled Brown & Haley's growth since their development, and they figured to do so in the future.

By the late 1990s, Almond Roca was sold in 63 countries, reigning as the market leader in several foreign nations. The brand was a market leader for imported gift confections in Hong Kong, China, Singapore, the United Arab Emirates, Bahrain, the Philippines, and Taiwan. Much of the company's future success hinged on continued worldwide demand for Almond Roca, which did not appear to be diminishing. Accordingly, as Brown & Haley prepared to enter the 21st century, its future growth seemed as secure as the time-tested demand for its most popular product. Seventy-five years after the company made its first batch of Almond Roca, Brown & Haley was churning out 800,000 pieces of the candy each day, still occupying the converted shoe factory purchased by Harry Brown and J. C. Haley in 1919.

Further Reading

Brown & Haley, *The Brown & Haley Story,* Tacoma: Brown & Haley, 1997.
"Brown and Haley Celebrates Eight Decades of Candymaking," *Candy Industry,* August 1994, p. 58.
"Candy Firm Not Sweet on Tacoma, Wash., Region," *Knight-Ridder/ Tribune Business News,* October 18, 1993, p. 10.
Haley, Mark, "When Quality Is the Bottom Line," *Candy Industry,* June 1994, p. 77.
Liebman, Larry, "Brown & Haley Aiming for Upscale Market," *Puget Sound Business Journal,* December 18, 1992, p. 16.
"Product Parade," *Candy Industry,* June 1996, p. 10.

—Jeffrey L. Covell

brown & sharpe

Brown & Sharpe Manufacturing Co.

200 Frenchtown Road
North Kingston, Rhode Island 02852-2937
U.S.A.
(401) 886-2000
Fax: (401) 886-2214
Web site: http://www.bwnshp.com

Public Company
Incorporated: 1868
Employees: 2,383
Sales: $344.9 million (1996)
Stock Exchanges: New York
SICs: 3545 Cutting Tools, Machine Tool Accessories &
    Machinists' Precision Measuring Devices; 3823
    Industrial Instruments for Measurement, Display &
    Control of Process Variables & Related Products

Brown & Sharpe Manufacturing Co. is a manufacturer and marketer of metrology products, measuring everything from car bodies to electronic chips to accuracies of 20-millionth of an inch. Its products in the mid-1990s ranged from hand-held micrometers to $1.5 million car-inspection coordinate measuring machines for the accurate measurement, gauging, and inspection of parts to meet quality control objectives. About one-fifth of its revenue was coming from selling software used by its products and providing aftermarket services such as training, retrofits, and parts.

The First Century, 1833–1933

David Brown and his son Joseph formed a partnership in 1833, opening a shop in Providence under the name David Brown & Son for the making and repair of clocks and watches and to perform other light mechanical work of precision. They made many church clocks in New England. The partnership broke up in the 1840s, however, with the father settling in Illinois and the son remaining to run a retail and jobbing business. In 1850 Joseph R. Brown started out again on new lines.

Intent on raising the standard of accuracy in machine shop operations, he built an automatic linear dividing engine that year so fundamentally correct in design and workmanship that it remained in continuous service. His pocket vernier caliper of 1851 has been called "the first practical tool for exact measurement which could be sold in any country at a price within the reach of the ordinary machinist."

Lucien Sharpe joined the business as an apprentice in 1848 and became a full partner in the newly created enterprise of J.R. Brown & Sharpe in 1853. While Brown concentrated on mechanical problems, Sharpe provided the business acumen. Brown & Sharpe made a regular line of watchmen's clocks and certain textile manufacturing appliances. Brown built a precision gear cutting and dividing engine in 1855 that led to an expanding business in gear cutting, circular graduating, and index drilling. Another of the firm's activities begun in that decade was the production of accurate gauges. Soon after the company also began building sewing machines for special purposes.

In 1861 Brown invented the modern universal milling machine for cutting spirals. This machine has been called an important step in advancing the modern lines of manufacture of which the automobile and airplane are examples. Also important were his micrometer caliper of 1868—the world's first to be mass-produced—and universal grinding machine, first exhibited in 1876, to fabricate accurate cylindrical work. After Brown's death in 1876, Oscar J. Beale became the company's genius in the field of mechanical design. As a tool for Brown & Sharpe's gauges, he developed a measuring machine enabling the company to make and sell its gauges within a guarantee of accuracy to within one ten-thousandth of an inch. He also invented an automatic screw machine in 1880.

In 1866 the company merged with a competitor, forming a partnership under the name Darling, Brown & Sharpe that lasted until Darling's interest was bought out in 1892. Brown & Sharpe proper was incorporated in 1868, with Brown's wife and daughter remaining as stockholders following his death. A new plant on Promenade Street in Providence was constructed in 1872. After Sharpe died in 1899, his son Henry Dexter Sharpe became chief executive officer.

Company Perspectives:

We provide superior services, knowledge and products. We contribute to our customers' success by enabling them to dominate their design and manufacturing processes. We provide our customers: complete line of measurement products; global service and distribution; world class product support; long term partnerships; in-process solutions; optimized capital equipment use; common CAD integrated processes; reduced product development cycle time.

Brown & Sharpe's plant grew from 6.5 acres of floor space in 1896 to holdings occupying nearly 32 acres in 1925. The property was something of a curiosity in that it was not located on a railroad siding or boat slip, making it necessary to transport all incoming raw materials and outgoing finished products first by horse and wagon, later by motor truck. Moreover, the property was intersected by three public streets, frequently leading to delays. The company was employing some 6,000 men in 1930.

Changing Times, 1933–1980

The Great Depression hit Brown & Sharpe hard, its sales reaching only $2.9 million in 1933, when the company recorded a loss of $933,427. It returned to profitability the following year, however, and began paying dividends again. With the outbreak of World War II the United States began to rearm, and in 1940 the company almost doubled its net sales to $29.1 million. Net income reached almost $5 million. Sales volume attained a peak of $60.6 million in 1943, although high costs and taxes reduced profits. In 1942 Brown & Sharpe's open-shop policy, perhaps the oldest in U.S. industry, was swept aside when the National War Labor Board awarded the International Association of Machinists a contract in the wake of an election in which a substantial majority of the firm's 10,000 employees chose this union to represent them.

Even before the war ended, Brown & Sharpe's revenues were falling. In 1949 they sank to $15.3 million, and the firm lost $315,562. Better times returned with the Korean War, and although the company lost $1.4 million in 1951, it more than doubled its sales the following year, earning $3.2 million on revenue of $59.4 million. With the end of the war in 1953, sales plummeted again, but the company remained in the black, in part because the work force was cut from nearly 9,000 during the war to 3,500 in 1955.

Under Henry D. Sharpe, Jr., who succeeded his father as president of the firm in 1951, Brown & Sharpe became a very different company. He got rid of machines of somewhat outmoded design and took the firm out of the business of making sewing machines, hair clippers, and low-volume plain-cylindrical grinding machines. Instead he invested in the mass production of automatic screw machines, capable of performing about a dozen different cutting operations on a long bar of metal. A three-year, $4 million refitting program for the Providence plant was completed in 1957. In addition, Brown & Sharpe was reorganized into divisions, with each one responsible for its own profit and loss.

Brown & Sharpe also began expanding by acquisition. A British subsidiary was established in 1955, with a plant in Plymouth, England. In 1957 the company purchased Double A Products Co. of Manchester, Michigan, and in 1958 it acquired the power-unit portion of Rosaen Co. of Hazel Park, Michigan. The following year it acquired Howe & Fant, Inc. of East Norwalk, Connecticut, and American Twist Drill Co. of Detroit. In 1964 the company, which had been Providence's second biggest taxpayer, moved its main operations to a modern plant and headquarters in the suburb of North Kingston. Only the foundry was left at the old Promenade Street site, which became an industrial park.

Machine-tool products, all of the cutting type and used by manufacturers to shape metal parts, were accounting for 55 to 60 percent of Brown & Sharpe's annual sales in 1965, with the greatest volume in single-spindle automatic screw machines and in grinding machines. The company also was making milling machines, turret drills, machinists' precision measuring instruments, and products allied to machine tools, such as cutting tools and hydraulic valves and pumps. In 1963 it introduced a computer-controlled coordinate measuring machine. Almost all of the company's components were being manufactured internally, starting with castings from its own foundry.

With the advent of the Vietnam War, Brown & Sharpe's sales rose rapidly again, reaching a high of $75.9 million in 1967, when it had net income of $5.3 million. In 1968 the company developed a unique new steel tool it named Sharpaloy and acquired certain assets of Cleveland Grinding Machine Co. and Cleve-Co Jig Boring Co., which were merged into a new subsidiary, Cleveland Precision Instruments, Inc. That year Brown & Sharpe also acquired Tesa, S.A., a Swiss manufacturer of precision measuring instruments. Such instruments, also called metrology products, were being used in the quality testing of manufacturing products.

Brown & Sharpe's acquisition spree continued in 1969, when the company purchased a controlling interest in Anocout Engineering Co. of Elk Grove Village, Illinois; acquired Olmstead Products Co. of Ann Arbor, Michigan, producer of high-flow-capacity hydraulic valves; and purchased 20 percent of Chamberlain Group, Ltd. of London, manufacturer of the Staffa hydraulic motor. In 1979 it purchased the remainder of Chamberlain Group. Brown & Sharpe established a German subsidiary in 1970 and a French subsidiary in 1971.

Brown & Sharpe's prosperity came to a sudden halt in 1970, when a recession cut its sales by $15 million and resulted in a $5.6 million loss for the year. The company lost money again in 1971 and, after three improved years, fell into the red again in 1975. One reason was the demise of the single-spindle automatic screw machine, whose prime markets had been auto, appliance, and office-equipment manufacturers. During this period the first two switched small parts to plastic and the latter became electronic rather than electromechanical. Beginning in 1977, Brown & Sharpe developed an electronically controlled version of the screw machine. During the decade's second half, sales and income improved each year, and in 1980 the company had net income of $14.5 million on net sales of $227.5 million.

Metrology Displaces Machine Tools, 1980–1996

Measuring instruments became Brown & Sharpe's chief source of business in the 1980s. The company's principal metrology product was Validator, a high-technology, computer-controlled coordinate-measurement robotic system first produced in 1968. A securities analyst described it in 1980 as far superior to anything competitors could offer in the automation field. Brown & Sharpe's specialized hydraulic devices included small gear-type pumps for metal-cutting coolants and lubricants, Double A and Olmstead valves, British-made motors, and components for high-water-base fluids. Besides automatic screw machines, the company's machine-tool output included a line of surface grinders, among them computer-controlled vertical machining centers. In 1981 Brown & Sharpe acquired Roch, S.A., a Swiss precision tool manufacturer, and Melbourne Engineering Co., a British machinery firm.

Although Brown & Sharpe had adopted a no-layoffs policy in the mid-1970s, it demanded in return the right to shift machinists wherever needed, often cutting across traditional seniority lines. In response, 1,600 machinists walked off the job in October 1981. The company broke the strike by hiring nonunion replacements. Cutting costs was vital, because the company was facing competition from Japanese machine tools during a severe national recession. In 1982 it sold its Greystone, Rhode Island cutting-tool plant, and in 1984 it phased out its line of vertical computer numerically controlled machine tools, a field now dominated by Japanese models. Brown & Sharpe lost $11.2 million in 1982 but made a profit the next three years.

Brown & Sharpe sold its hydraulic operations in 1985 to Vickers, Inc., a subsidiary of Libbey-Owens Ford Co. The sale included the company's Double A Products subsidiary and its fluid-power operations in Britain, France, and Germany. These businesses had sales of about $36 million in 1983. Metrology equipment accounted for 70 percent of Brown & Sharpe's net sales in 1988, the first profitable year since 1985. The firm acquired three gaugemaking companies between 1986 and 1988.

The year 1989 was another profitable year, but in 1990 Brown & Sharpe lost $14.6 million, an outcome the company blamed chiefly on investment writedowns and restructuring costs. The following year it omitted its dividend for the first time since 1933 and announced that it would discontinue making machine tools entirely. This phase of its business had accounted for 29 percent of its 1990 sales. The last piece of the machine-tool business was sold in 1993. By that year employment at the North Kingston plant had fallen to 700, compared with 2,000 in 1982.

Repositioned Brown & Sharpe now was focusing all its energy on its metrology business, especially coordinate measuring machines (CMMs). It acquired a number of companies in France, Germany, and Switzerland, the most important of which was, in 1990, the purchase of a division of the German firm Wild Leitz G.m.b.H., makers of the first digital computer-controlled coordinate measuring machine (1974) and CMM with full 3-D scanning probe (1978). With the acquisition of

this business, Brown & Sharpe gained $40 million in annual sales and boosted its proportion of sales made abroad to 61 percent in 1991.

In 1994 Brown & Sharpe surrendered more than 40 percent of its Class A common stock to acquire Italy's Finmeccanica S.p.A, whose DEA Group was its closest competitor in the metrology business. DEA had manufactured the first CMM (1963) and shop-floor measuring robot (1981). Brown & Sharpe also had formed a manufacturing joint venture with a Lithuanian-based manufacturer. It had 12 overseas manufacturing locations in 1996, each managed by local nationals.

After five consecutive years of losing money, Brown & Sharpe earned $1.9 million on revenues of $328 million in 1995, of which automotive companies and suppliers accounted for 46 percent. The following year it had net income of $7.8 million on net sales of $344.9 million, with international sales accounting for 61 percent. Finmeccanica sold all but 2.6 percent of the 42 percent of the company's Class A common stock that it held in October 1996 for about $37 million. Its shares had been worth about $21 million when it acquired them in 1994. The sale took place as part of a public offering of nearly 7.3 million Brown & Sharpe shares, priced at $11.75 a share. Brown & Sharpe, which sold four million shares and received $48.9 million, said it planned to use the net proceeds mainly to pay off debt. The long-term debt was $33.7 million in June 1997.

The Firm in 1996

Brown & Sharpe's products in 1996 were dominated by CMMs and high-speed process-control systems, which accounted for about 69 percent of its sales that year. About 18,000 CMMs had been installed worldwide, mostly for installation in the automotive, aerospace, earth-moving, and industrial-manufacturing industries. This stock consisted of a wide range of manual and computer-controlled high-precision contact and optical CMMs and shop-floor measuring robots under the Brown & Sharpe, DEA, and Leitz names.

Precision measuring instruments accounted for about 28 percent of the company's 1996 net sales. They consisted of a wide range of mechanical and electronic measuring and inspection tools, including height gauges, calipers, dial indicators, micrometers, and gauge blocks. Brown & Sharpe also was manufacturing a wide variety of specialty products and systems under the Tesa brand name.

Largest of Brown & Sharpe's three units, the Measuring Systems Group had its headquarters in North Kingston, Rhode Island, where it was manufacturing CMMs under the Brown & Sharpe name. Group products sold under the DEA name were being made in Turin, Italy, and those under the Leitz name were being made in Wetzler, Germany. The Precision Measuring Instruments Division had its headquarters in Renens, Switzerland and had manufacturing plants there and in Rolls, Switzerland; Poughkeepsie, New York; Leicester, Plymouth, and St. Albans, England; and Luneville, France. Ranging in price from $100 to about $13,000, its products included micrometers, dial indicators, calipers, electronic height gauges, and gauge blocks. The Custom Metrology Division, with headquarters in Telford, England, was engaged in engineering and in manufacturing laser interferometers, measuring sensors, and contact and optical measuring machines and fixtures aimed at specific niche markets.

Principal Subsidiaries

Borel & Dunner, Inc.; Brown & Sharpe Group Ltd. and its subsidiaries (Great Britain); Brown & Sharpe International Capital Corp. and its subsidiaries; DEA-Brown & Sharpe S.p.A. and its subsidiaries (Italy); Mauser Prazisions Messmittel GmbH (Germany); Roch-Brown & Sharpe S.A. (France); Technicomp Inc.

Principal Divisions

Custom Metrology Division; Measuring Systems Group; Precision Measuring Instruments Division.

Further Reading

Braig, L. Michael, "Brown & Sharpe Manufacturing Company," *Wall Street Transcript,* July 13, 1981, pp. 62,316–62,317.

"Brown & Sharpe Selling Overseas Hydraulics Unit," *Boston Globe,* January 31, 1985, p. 32.

DeMaio, Don, "B & S Abandons Machine Tools for Metrology," *Providence Business News,* July 18, 1994, p. 1.

Downing, Neil, "Italian Firm Sells Brown & Sharpe Stock," *Providence Journal-Bulletin,* October 12, 1996, pp. B10–B11.

Glicker, Barbara, "Brown & Sharpe Says It Will Close Machine Tool Line," *Wall Street Journal,* March 28, 1991, p. A9.

Gordon, Mitchell, "Tooling Down," *Barron's,* October 23, 1985, pp. 43–44.

"Handling Under Difficulties," *Industrial Management,* August 1925, pp. 67–72.

McLaughlin, Mark, "The Stormy Decade," *New England Business,* September 1987, pp. 12, 16, 18, 23–24.

"Mass Production Comes Home," *Business Week,* December 3, 1955, pp. 140, 144.

The Metrology Company, North Kingston, R.I.: Brown & Sharpe, 1995.

Prosnitz, Franklin S., "CEO Returns Brown & Sharpe to Profitability," *Providence Business News,* June 2, 1997, p. 2 and continuation.

"Risk of Cyclical Dip in Brown & Sharpe," *United States Investor,* March 14, 1966, p. 44.

Salpukas, Agis, "Immunity from Tool Slump," *New York Times,* July 9, 1981, pp. D1, D6.

Sharpe, Henry Dexter, *Measure of Perfection: The History of Brown & Sharpe,* North Kingston, R.I.: Brown & Sharpe, no date. (Also available on the company's Web site.)

"Software Will Dominate the World of Metrology," *Tooling & Production,* September 1996, p. 11 and continuation.

—Robert Halasz

Burda ◈ Medien

Burda Holding GmbH. & Co.

Arabellastrasse 23
81925 Munich
Germany
(49) (89) 9250-3422
Fax: (49) (89) 9250-2745
Web site: http://www.burda.de

Private Company
Employees: 4,342 (1996)
Sales: DM 1.72 million (US$1.1 billion) (1996)
SICs: 2711 Newspapers, Publishing or Publishing and
   Printing; 2721 Periodicals; 2752 Commercial
   Printing—Lithographic; 7379 Computer Related
   Services

Burda Holding GmbH. & Co. is a conglomerate, wholly owned by the Burda family, comprised of companies involved in magazine and newspaper publishing, television, and radio broadcasting, online computer services, and commercial printing. Publishing is the heart of Burda's business. In Germany it publishes over 20 magazines and newspapers, read by an audience of 24.85 million annually. Burda has the third largest circulation among German periodical publishers, behind Gruner & Jahr and Bauer; its 19.2 percent share of advertising revenues in Germany ranks second in Germany. In addition, the company publishes numerous foreign titles in eastern and western Europe and Asia. The company has started an online travel service, and despite disappointments in the computer field, remains committed to the medium. In 1996, Burda invested DM 325 million in a modernization program in its printing companies.

Early 20th-Century Founding

Burda got its start in 1908 when Franz Burda I, the grandfather of the present owner, opened his own print shop in the Bavarian town of Offenburg where he and his family lived. It was a small business with only three employees. In 1925 Burda's son, Franz, then working on his Ph.D. in economics,

started working at the shop. Radio was just beginning to boom as an entertainment medium at that time, and in 1927 the junior Burda conceived of printing a radio program guide for southwestern Germany. The magazine *S rag* was the Burdas' first venture into publishing with an initial circulation of 3,000.

In 1929 the elder Burda died, and the business was taken over by his son, then only 26 years of age. It still had only three employees, but the company began to grow in the 1930s. Thanks to the popularity of radio, *S rag*'s circulation had reached 60,000 by 1933. In 1935, Burda recognized the importance of the rotogravure process for the printing of mass circulation publications, and built a new printing plant in Offenburg equipped with state-of-the-art machinery. After that, the business expanded rapidly. By the end of the decade, Burda had acquired a printing facility in Mannheim where he employed 350 workers. 250 were employed workers in Offenburg by then. *S rag*'s circulation had nearly tripled to 179,000. Everything turned around rapidly during World War II. Nazi censorship of radio caused *S rag*'s circulation to drop so sharply that in 1941 Burda terminated publication of the magazine. For the remainder of the war the company was limited to printing maps for the German General Staff. The company's multicolored aerial maps were among the first ever produced in Germany.

Postwar Activities

After the war German printing and publishing, because of its potential for disseminating Nazi propaganda, was tightly controlled by the Allies, and would-be publishers had to have untainted pasts. Franz Burda went to work under the occupation. From 1945 to 1947, he was limited to printing stamps and school books for the French occupation forces. But in 1948, with the creation of the Federal Republic of Germany, Burda dove back into publishing. In 1948 he launched *Das Ufer,* a weekly illustrated magazine that specialized in photo stories on the rich and famous and was aimed primarily at female readers. In 1954 its name was changed to *Bunte,* which became the flagship of the Burda publishing company until *Focus* was introduced in 1993. Another Burda publication, *Das Haus,* launched in 1949, capitalized on the desire of many Germans

---

Company Perspectives:

Burda is a company focused on publishing, printing and new media. The evolution of the classic Burda publications, together with the development of successful new magazines and novel means of communication have made Burda one of the most innovative companies in German media.

---

for a beautiful and comfortable home at a time when much of the country still lay in rubble. *S rag* resumed publication the same year.

In 1949 Franz Burda's wife Aenne started her own publishing house, the Modenverlag A. Burda, known in the 1990s as Verlag Aenne Burda. "Modenverlag" means fashion publisher, but its first magazine, *burda MODEN (Burda Fashion)*, released in 1950, not only presented pictures of the latest fashions but included tips and patterns for making them at home. *Burda MODEN* became one of the most successful of the Burda family of publications. By the mid-1990s, together with its sister publication—*BURDA International* begun in 1953—it was sold in about 100 countries where it had more than one million readers every month. In fact, in 1987, after Aenne Burda met with Raissa Gorbachev in Moscow, *burda MODEN* became the first western magazine to be published in the Soviet Union. And so powerful was the force of A. Burda's personality that in 1989 her publishing house, together with Burda GmbH, took over the sale of advertising for *Isvestia*, the newspaper of the Communist Party of the Soviet Union.

By 1950, Burda GmbH had 13 production sites in the Federal Republic, and more were planned. Circulation of Burda magazines was climbing gradually: *S rag* and its new Bavarian edition *Bild + Funk* were selling a quarter of a million copies every month and *Das Haus* 136,000 copies. At the same time, Franz Burda cultivated the role of a caring employer. In 1952 he introduced a comprehensive health care package for his workers that included coverage of preventative examinations for cancer; in 1955 he provided employees with paid sick leave. Both plans were instituted years before they were required by German law.

By 1957 the staff of Burda's printing and publishing companies had grown to 1,400; its annual turnover passed DM 50 million. Its three best-selling magazines, *Bunte, Das Haus,* and *S rag* (the latter retitled *Bild + Funk*), were each selling about a half million copies every month. At the start of the 1960s Burda geared for growth, and Franz Burda increased the capital invested in the company from DM 450,000 to DM 8 million. Expansion was necessary in part to handle the explosive growth of *Bunte,* whose circulation had doubled in three years time, reaching one million in 1960.

Expansion in the 1960s–70s

Burda made a series of acquisitions, in both publishing and printing, during the 1960s as well. It bought the Klebe Printing Company in Darmstadt in 1960 and built a new facility in that

city in 1967. It constructed a new printing facility in its home city of Offenburg in 1968. Between 1958 and 1963, Burda obtained a number of local and regional magazines, *Deutsche Illustrierte* (1958), *Munchner Illustrierte* (1960), *Frankfurter Illustrierte* (1962), and *Osterreich Illustrierte* (1963). In 1960 Burda bought Neue Verlagsgesellschaft, a publishing house that published *freundin,* a magazine that would become one of the leading women's magazines in Germany in the following decades.

In 1965 Burda, then employing nearly 3,000 workers, moved into new headquarters in Munich. In 1966 a new era was in the making. That year Franz Burda's third son, Hubert, joined the company, 26 years old and fresh out of graduate school with a Ph.D. in art history. Hubert Burda, who would oversee Burda's rapid growth in the 1990s, got his start in the family company as the head of publishing and advertising at *Bild + Funk,* Burda's national TV guide publication. Hubert moved through a variety of jobs acquiring experience: in 1969 he took over product management, and in 1972 he became head of sales and advertising for all of Burda GmbH. In 1973 Franz Burda made his three sons managing partners of Burda GmbH, and each was given his own area of responsibility: Franz III was put in charge of the printing operation, Frieder headed up administration, and Hubert was given the publishing arm. In addition to overseeing all Burda publishing, Hubert edited *Bunte* from 1975 until 1985.

The 1970s were a time of continued growth for Burda. Three magazines were founded that went on to become established in the German publishing world. *Freizeit Revue* (1970) was another gossipy illustrated weekly with slightly less edge than *Bunte. Mein schoner Garten* (1972) was a magazine for home gardeners, who in Germany numbered in the millions. *Meine Familie und ich* (1974) was aimed at homemakers, with a heavy concentration on cooking. All three magazines quickly established themselves with German readers.

Burda Druck, the printing company, made the big jump across the Atlantic Ocean in 1971, when it signed a joint venture deal with Meredith Corporation. The two companies opened a rotogravure plant in Lynchburg, Virginia. Between 1976 and 1978, Burda Druck, initiated a modernization program in its German facilities, investing DM 100 million in new printing equipment.

Legal Challenges in the 1980s

By 1979 Burda had quietly become one of the largest German publishing houses. That same year it was involved in a minor controversy when the German Cartel Office, the German antitrust agency, fined three of the country's three leading publishers a total of $14.2 million. The office charged Burda Verlag, Axel Springer Verlag and Heinrich Bauer Verlag with price fixing, after they simultaneously raised the prices of their TV guides. The $7 million fine levied against Springer was, at the time, the second largest in Cartel Office history. Burda, whose *Bild + Funk* had about ten percent of the market, was fined $1.4 million. Executives at the three publishers were fined $54,300 each as well.

In June 1981, Axel Springer and Franz Burda began negotiating the sale of a portion of Springer Verlag stock. Company founder Axel Springer, the sole owner of the company, was then 69 years of age and was said to be arranging business so that his company would survive his death. His only son had died the year before, and he felt he did not have any heirs who could take over the company. Burda, whose turnover had surpassed DM 750 million the year before, was anxious to expand into the national newspaper market, and Springer's *Bild Zeitung* was the largest-selling daily newspaper in the entire Federal Republic. Under the plan Burda and Springer worked out, Burda GmbH would purchase an initial 26 percent of Springer stock and would later acquire a total of 51 percent. The Cartel Office blocked the sale, however, maintaining it would ''create excessive market dominance in the publishing field by both companies,'' as the *Wall Street Journal* reported at the time.

Burda appealed the ruling to the West German Monopoly Commission, which in February 1982 upheld the Cartel Office's decision. The publishers even considered selling the Springer or the Burda TV guide to a third party to encourage a positive decision. After the appeal, it was reported that the two companies intended to use their combined resources to break into the German cable TV market, which was considered underdeveloped then. The Springer controversy extended into the political realm as well. The final ruling had to be made by the Economics Minister, Otto Lambsdorff, a member of the Free Democratic Party. It was alleged, particularly by his Social Democratic opponents, that Lambsdorff had made a deal with the two publishers; he would approve the merger in exchange for favorable press coverage in the upcoming federal election. Finally, in January 1983, the Cartel Office approved a revised plan, in which Burda would acquire only 25 percent of Springer stock, not enough, the Cartel Board said, for a blocking minority on the Springer board of directors.

The Springer stock deal made news again in 1988. Axel Springer had finally divided the shares between his family, the Burda family, and Leo Kirch. After Springer's death, a three-way struggle for control of his publishing empire erupted. After the Burdas and Kirch were unable to reach an agreement that would have let them share control of Springer Verlag, the Springer heirs continued the battle with Kirch alone. The Burda sons, Franz III and Frieder, eventually agree to sell their 25.6 percent of Springer stock to the Springer heirs, an amount that would give the heirs a majority interest in the company.

New Leadership and New Markets in the 1980s

In 1985, Franz Burda II divided the remaining shares of Burda stock among his three sons, and in October 1986 he died. In 1987 Hubert Burda became the sole owner and chairman of the board of Burda GmbH. The ascendancy of Hubert Burda changed the course of the Burda company. He diversified the company, becoming involved in television broadcasting; he expanded the palette of magazines; he started online computer services; he used the opening of East Germany in 1989 to establish Burda as a force to be reckoned with in German publishing; and, he challenged—and won—against the most ''unchallengeable'' magazine in Germany, a popularity battle.

To provide the basis for the empire he envisioned, the Burda Holding GmbH. & Co. KG was founded in 1990.

Under Franz Burda II, Burda magazines had had a plebeian feel. Their appearance and content were aimed at readers, primarily housewives, without intellectual pretensions; readers of *Bunte* and *Freizeit Revue* were likely to be the same people who read the sensationalist *Bild Zeitung* tabloid. Hubert Burda, however, began to alter the company profile. One of his first moves, in 1988, was to sign a deal with France Editions et Publications, the French publisher of the haute couture fashion magazine *Elle.* Burda obtained the rights to develop a German *Elle,* a magazine that afterwards proved hugely successful for Burda. By the mid-1990s the magazine had a circulation of 220,000 a month and had spun off three other publications, *Elle Decoration, Elle TopModel,* and *Elle Bistro* with a combined circulation of over 550,000 in 1996.

Forbes von Burda was a less successful venture. In 1990 Burda received the license to publish a German edition of *Forbes,* the American business magazine. Burda planned a business magazine that would be livelier and more colorful than the rest of the German business press. After five years, however, *Forbes von Burda* was discontinued, having lost most of its credibility, the result of questionable business advice it had offered its readers, dubious rankings of executive salaries it published, and interviews and editorials that had left the German business community shaking their heads. The *Forbes* U.S. parent withdrew Burda's license, complaining that Burda had failed to maintain *Forbes* quality. ''Burda is primarily a mass-market publisher,'' a *Forbes* spokesperson explained to the *Wall Street Journal,* ''while *Forbes* has a highly focused, upscale approach.'' In its five years of publication Burda's Forbes never once turned a profit; in fact, the company was suffering monthly losses in the DM 1 million range. Afterwards Burda announced that it planned to withdraw from business publishing completely to concentrate on the online market.

Hubert Burda's successes outweighed his failures however. He was quick to grasp the significance of the fall of the Berlin Wall in 1989 for Burda. He used the new German markets in East Germany to move Burda ''from provincial obscurity to be taken seriously at last,'' as Frederick Studemann wrote in *International Management* in 1991. Burda had failed once in his bid to enter newspaper publishing, when the Burda takeover of Axel Springer Verlag was prohibited by the German Cartel Office. The East provided a second chance, and he jumped at it. He quickly acquired two regional papers, the *Schweriner Volkszeitung* in Schwerin and the *Norddeutsche Neueste Nachrichten* in Rostock. While other publishers accused Hubert Burda of exploiting his political connections to influence the Treuhandanstalt, the federal agency that was charged with privatizing and selling off assets of the old East German state, Burda countered that his company had simply showed more initiative.

With Rupert Murdoch, Burda started *Super! Zeitung (SZ),* a paper modeled on Murdoch's sensationalist *Daily Sun* tabloid and meant to compete with Springer's *Bild Zeitung.* What made *SZ* different was that it was produced specifically for East German readers; the paper was not even sold in West Germany.

After six months, the paper was selling 465,000 copies daily and soundly beating *Bild Zeitung.*

Unfortunately *SZ* lacked the proper advertising support. Western German companies with money knew neither the paper nor its readership; companies in eastern Germany were in the grip of a deep recession. Despite its promising beginnings, the paper lasted less than one year. In 1990 Burda developed a new magazine for the eastern market, called *Super Illu,* which was similar to *Bunte,* only for East Germany. Its coveres and articles featured the stars they had known and followed in the German Democratic Republic. The magazine was an overwhelming success. After a year, it had a circulation of one million. Sales declined somewhat after that, but leveled off around 600,000 per month, making it the best-selling magazine in the five eastern states by the late 1990s. Burda also introduced a TV guide for eastern Germany, *Super TV,* with similarly high sales.

On the topic of publishers making the most of the opening of the east, a spokesman for rival publisher Bauer Verlag told Frederick Studemann of *International Management,* "There's no question that Hubert [Burda] has come out of this best." Burda developed editions of many of its magazines—*Mein schoner Garten, Lisa, Meine Familie und ich,* for example, as well as *Burda Moden*—for Russia, Poland, and other nations in Eastern Europe.

Success with Focus in the Early 1990s

Perhaps the most notable of all Burda's achievements during this time, however, took place on January 18, 1993, when the first issue of *Focus* was published. *Focus,* a newsmagazine, was going up against *Der Spiegel,* a German institution that for years had not had any competition. Most critics predicted that *Focus* would fail, but the magazine, conceived by Burda and editor Helmut Markwort, made a special appeal to the adult children of the television generation. Eschewing the long, often densely written articles presented in *Der Spiegel, Focus* offered short pieces, punctuated with color photographs and graphs. Its audience was waiting for it. By 1994 circulation had reached the break-even point at 300,000 a week, and by 1996 circulation was at 800,000, a serious challenge to *Der Spiegel*'s readership of 1.1 million.

Interestingly, *Focus* seemed to attract readers who were not generally newsmagazine readers at all, and 1993 circulation of *Der Spiegel* fell by only 100. However, *Focus* advertising revenues jumped from number four, after *Der Spiegel, Stern,* and *Wirtschaftswoche,* to number two behind *Der Spiegel* in April 1994. Some analysts speculated that this success reflected a protest from advertisers in such industries as banking and pharmaceuticals, who had long been dissatisfied with *Der Spiegel*'s liberal politics. By 1997 some 5.76 million Germans were reading *Focus* every week, about nine percent of the country's population.

Burda moved with varying success into the computer online services market in the 1990s. The company entered a partnership with AT&T and the British Pearson Group to start Europe Online (EOL) in 1994. EOL was to have been a multilingual service marketed for PC users throughout Europe. As planned, it would have been accessible in English, German, and French from the onset, but problems plagued the enterprise early on. Development fell 18 months behind its start-up schedule, and then, once the service was made available, the estimated number of subscribers to the service fell well below expectations, attracting only 20,000 customers, rather than the 70,000 that had been confidently predicted. In 1996, with its other partners pulling out and no others on the horizon, Burda withdrew from the project. A similar fate befell Health Online, a project planned as a free online research and information service exclusively for physicians and hospitals expected to pay for itself through advertising and sponsorship. Burda pulled out of that service abruptly at the end of 1997. Nevertheless, the company continued to maintain web sites for its most popular magazines, *Focus, Bunte, Meine Familie und ich, Lisa,* and *Freundin,* as well as overseeing a popular online travel service known as TRAXXX.

In 1995, Burda signed an agreement of cooperation with Rizzoli, Italy's second largest publisher. Under its terms, the two companies agreed to work jointly in developing magazines for the international market. As part of the agreement, Burda obtained an interest in Verlagsgruppe Milchstrasse in Hamburg, a company with about DM 250 million in annual sales that published the trendy *Fit For Fun.* At the same time, Rizzoli received a 20 percent stake in Burda's Eastern European activities (excluding *Burda MODEN*). A 50–50 joint venture for magazines in Asia was formed as well, and the agreement as a whole was expected to increase Burda's annual sales from DM 1.54 billion to DM 1.8 billion.

Burda made an unsuccessful move to break into the video rental market in 1995 when it signed a joint agreement with Blockbuster Video to open a chain of Blockbuster stores in Germany. Blockbuster predicted the chain would grow to between 250 and 300 stores by the year 2000. The first store was opened in Berlin in mid-1996, and was followed by 19 more in Berlin and Munich over the next year and a half. Blockbuster failed to reckon with the nature of the video business in Germany, however, in which one-fifth of all video rentals were X-rated films, or "adult movies," which Blockbuster had a policy of not stocking. By the summer of 1997 the implications of that missed calculation were clear, and in December of that year Burda announced that retroactive to April 1997, it was ending its participation in the venture. The *Berliner Kurier* reported that only one store out of the entire chain had made a profit. As a result of the closings, 90 full-time and 160 part-time employees lost their jobs. Still, as it approached a new century, Burda's role as a major player in German media was secure. In fact, despite the intensely competitive climate in the 1990s, many wondered whether Burda might be in a position to overtake rivals for the top spot in German publishing.

Principal Subsidiaries

Burda GmbH; Aenna Burda Verlag GmbH; Bunte Verlag GmbH; Burda Druck, GmbH; Imprimerie et Editions Braun S.A.; Burda Online Service BOS GmbH; Focus Magazin Verlag GmbH; Burda Moden Inc. (U.S.); Burda Moden-Riga GmbH (Latvia).

Further Reading

"Blockbuster-Video schliesst alle LÓden in Deutschland," *Berliner Morgenpost,* January 2, 1998.

"Burda expandiert ins Ausland," *Berliner Morgenpost,* October 13, 1997.

"Burda-Konzern kooperiert mit Rizzoli," *Die Welt,* September 28, 1995.

Dickenson, Nicole, "A Clash of the Titles," *Campaign,* April 22, 1994.

"German Forbes Falls Victim to Differences Over its Direction," *Wall Street Journal,* May 5, 1995.

Goodacre, Clive, "Burda Puts Health on the Web," *Seybold Report on Publishing Systems,* January 29, 1996.

Knofel, Ulrike, "Ohne Europe Online will Burda schneller ans Ziel," *Die Welt,* July 10, 1996.

Schulenburg, Wolf. "Rivals Eye Focus Success," *The European,* December 24, 1993.

"Springer Heirs Gain Control in Power Fight," *Wall Street Journal,* April 21, 1988.

"Springer of Germany May Sell Interest to Other Publisher," *Wall Street Journal,* June 30, 1981.

Studemann, Frederick, "Germany's Paper Tigers," *International Management,* November 1991.

"Taking Europe Off Line," *The Economist,* August 10, 1996.

"West Germans Debate Big Press Merger Weighing Politics and Antitrust Rules," *Wall Street Journal,* November 22, 1982.

"West Germany Fines 3 Publishing Houses in Price-Fixing Case," *Wall Street Journal,* February 7, 1979.

—Gerald E. Brennan

The Bureau of National Affairs, Inc.

1231 25th Street N.W.
Washington, District of Columbia 20037
U.S.A.
(202) 452-4200
Fax: (202) 452-4610
Web site: http://www.bna.com

Private Company
Founded: 1929
Employees: 1,800
Sales: $232.6 million (1996)
SICs: 2731 Books: Publishing or Publishing & Printing;
   7372 Prepackaged Software

The Bureau of National Affairs, Inc. is a leading publisher of print and electronic information and is the oldest privately held, wholly employee-owned company in the United States. Its products include more than 200 news and information services, specializing in reporting on public policy and regulatory developments in business, labor relations, law, health care, economics, taxation, environmental protection, and health and safety.

Early History: 1929–46

Journalist David Lawrence started the Bureau of National Affairs (BNA) in 1929 as a subsidiary of his U.S. News Publishing Company. At that point, BNA focused on patents, trademarks, and copyrights, publishing a series of bound volumes containing the text of court and regulatory decisions on these matters.

In March 1933 Lawrence ended publication of his newspaper, the *United States Daily,* and relaunched it as a weekly newspaper that he called *USNews.* At the same time he reorganized and expanded the products of BNA. That year, BNA began publishing two weekly information services. The first, *Patent, Trademark and Copyright Reports,* provided the text of decisions on a weekly basis. That information was bound into volumes quarterly, which led to the service being known as

Patents Quarterly. The second weekly service, *U.S. Law Week,* gave clients the complete text of all opinions, and a journal of the proceedings, of the U.S. Supreme Court along with digests of major decisions from lower federal courts, state supreme courts, and federal regulatory agencies.

The news services brought money into the publishing company, as clients paid in advance for a year's information. However, Lawrence had a lot of printing equipment sitting idle, so in 1937, after the Supreme Court decreed that the Wagner Act (which recognized the right of unions to organize and bargain collectively) was constitutional, he introduced *Labor Relations Reporter* (*LRR*), covering developments in the growing field of labor law. John Stewart, who would become president of BNA and write its history, joined the editorial staff of *Labor Relations Reporter* in 1939.

The same year he started *LRR,* Lawrence also made a proposal to Congress's Temporary National Economic Committee to deliver *free* copies of the complete transcript of the previous day's proceedings to Committee members and staff. For anyone else interested in the Committee's actions (major corporations, banks, and investment companies), BNA provided overnight delivery of the printed transcript for $25 a week. The service quickly had 2,000 subscribers, bringing in $50,000 each week.

With that cash flow Lawrence made *USNews* into a weekly news magazine in 1940, to compete against *Time* and *Newsweek.* He also introduced a series of daily reports from BNA aimed at the business community to provide in-depth coverage of activities in Washington. The first of these, launched in November 1941, was *Daily Labor Report.* This was quickly followed with reports on industrial commodities, agricultural commodities, oil, and taxation and finance.

BNA's most popular service during the war years was *Price and Production Controls,* providing full coverage, in a looseleaf, indexed format, of, to quote Stewart, "every official document relating to price controls and controls on industrial production." The service was so important that the government gave it an unlimited paper quota, and its publication made BNA the largest private user of air mail and special delivery during

Company Perspectives:

BNA is an employee-owned company that provides professionals in business and government with timely, accurate, and objective information enhanced by intellectual effort, application of technology, and superior service to the customer.

World War II. By the end of the war its contents filled 129 loose-leaf binders.

During 1945 Lawrence consolidated all of BNA's daily reports except *Daily Labor Report* into a single publication, *Daily Report for Executives,* hoping there would continue to be a peacetime market for the information. *Price and Production Controls* ceased publishing when the unionized printers refused to work overtime. Lawrence incorporated the printing operation as a corporate subsidiary and began looking for a buyer. His publishing company also introduced a new magazine, *World Report,* to cover world affairs as *USNews* did at home.

In October 1946 Lawrence invited five editors from BNA to buy the operation for $600,000 with $10,000 down and the balance to be paid over eight years. BNA's tangible assets, according to John Stewart, consisted of "its inventory of books, mainly reference volumes for *PQ* and *Labor Relations Reporter,* binders and pages in stock to fill new orders for loose-leaf services, and some pretty beat-up office equipment and furniture. We would get all accounts receivable on the date of sale, but none of the cash. We would be liable for fulfilling all subscriptions on the books." Returning from the meeting, the five men agreed that the ownership of the new company should be open to everyone at BNA, though as Stewart recalls, "no one can tell you whether we agreed to that idea because we were idealists or because we were chicken, looking to spread the risk."

In setting up the plan for employee ownership the organizing committee found in their research that most employee-owned publishing companies kept the decision-making power in the hands of top management. The folks at BNA wanted something different. The result: any employee, but only an employee, could buy stock (the original price was $10 per share). Stock could be purchased only with cash, there were no special stock options or bonus plans for executives and managers, and the officers and directors of the company would receive no payment for their official services.

A New Company: 1947–64

The Bureau of National Affairs, Inc. began operations on January 1, 1947. Dean Dinwoodey had been elected president of the company, which had 279 full-time employees and 49 who worked part-time. The Newspaper Guild was certified to represent the editorial employees. Money was tight that first year, with the business grossing less that $2.5 million. By the end of the year, however, the company had substantially more money than it had started with, although on paper, BNA showed a loss. By 1949, the company showed a net gain of $6,302.

With the onset of the Korean conflict in 1950, BNA responded to the demand for information about wage and price controls and production restrictions by incorporating coverage of them in the company's existing services. When the truce was signed BNA had increased the circulation of several of its services, and unlike its competitors, which started new publications to cover the emergency measures, kept most of those clients, since the services were not dependent on the Korean-related information. With the boost in business BNA opened the Guild contract in midterm as it had promised it would do should the company start making money, and agreed to the first pay increase.

One service that benefited from the strategy for covering the emergency measures was *Labor Policy and Practice.* Introduced in 1950, the service was actually a revamping of one begun during World War II to provide new supervisors with information about what they could do under the labor laws. The new service was broader, covering employer-employee relations in general, and it was a huge success. During the Korean conflict it expanded to include information about wage and salary controls. In 1969 BNA changed the service's name to *BNA's Policy and Practice Series.*

In 1951 the company declared its first dividend, $2 per share. As Stewart explained the size of the dividend, "It's probable the Board of Directors, nearly all of whom were substantial stockholders and none of whom had had a raise in pay in the past five years, figured they were entitled to some reward, and it's hard to blame them."

That year BNA tried its hand at producing a four-page, weekly newsletter. The company bought the newsletter, which had a circulation of a little over 11,000, from David Lawrence and renamed it *Report for the Business Executive.* BNA produced the newsletter for ten years, by which time the circulation had dropped to 7,500, and then sold it to another publisher.

During 1951 the company also made its first acquisition, buying the Pickley Corporation, which sold motivational posters to improve employee morale. The new subsidiary was renamed BNA Inc. and, after some false starts with posters the field reps were not able to sell, began making money by producing informational pamphlets for employees. Early topics ranged from why it is important to vote, to how to write to your congressional representative, to "The Social Security Fact Sheet."

Broadening its approach to employee communication, BNA Inc. began producing a series of pamphlets aimed at the front-line supervisor. The series, which dealt with such topics as discipline and giving instructions, began with one entitled "How to Listen." That led to the production of a ten-minute film, "Listen Please," and added a new field to BNA's operations, the making of management training films. Training activities eventually were placed in BNA Communications Inc., a subsidiary that produced and published multimedia training programs for corporations and government agencies, specializing in equal employment opportunity and health and safety.

Another new venture was launched in 1959, to publish *Tax Management.* The new service published a series of portfolios, each written by a tax expert and explaining a narrow segment of corporate taxation. The undertaking proved very expensive. Production costs were high and the fragmentary nature of the service was different from BNA's other offerings, making sales difficult. In 1962 the company reported its first loss since 1947, due largely to the nearly $1 million investment in *Tax Management.* Nevertheless, BNA stuck with the service, and by 1995, Tax Management, Inc. was a wholly owned subsidiary grossing $45 million a year and paying an annual dividend of almost $4 million to BNA. In 1964 John Stewart was elected president of BNA. He was one of the five editors asked by David Lawrence to buy BNA and served as president until 1980.

Expanding Services: 1965–80

BNA was interested in getting more involved with computers and electronic data processing. To that end, in 1965 BNA bought Fisher-Stevens, Inc., a New Jersey–based company that handled mass mailings for pharmaceutical companies to doctors, and had its own computer school. That relationship lasted for 20 years, when BNA sold Fisher-Stevens to IMS.

In 1970 BNA moved into the developing field of environmental and safety regulation. The new service, *Environmental Reporter,* covered current developments and provided the full text of court opinions and federal and state laws and regulations. As regulatory activities in these areas increased, the service was pumping out one or two binders a year. Librarians began complaining that they had no more space for the binders on their shelves, and secretaries were not happy about the amount of time they were spending filing the service's loose-leaf supplements. Health and safety in the work place also was receiving attention in Congress, which passed the Occupational Safety and Health Act (OSHA), creating the Occupational Safety and Health Administration within the U.S. Department of Labor. Keeping with its tradition of quick response to governmental action, BNA had a new service, *Occupational Safety and Health Reporter,* up and running the day OSHA went into effect.

On the organizational side of things, BNA shareholders amended the bylaws in 1971 to increase the size of the board of directors by one seat and to allow the election of one ''outside'' director, someone who was neither an employee nor a stockholder. In 1990 the board was increased to 15 members, with three seats reserved for outside directors. By the mid-1970s BNA was publishing some 40 services.

The 1980s: New Divisions, New Subsidiaries

William Beltz was elected president of BNA in 1980. The company was doing very well financially by the early 1980s, with its stock price at $16. In 1982 the privately held International Thomson Organization Ltd., one of the world's largest communications companies, offered $45 a share in a takeover bid for BNA. After 12 months of internal debate, shareholders voted to continue BNA's ''commitment to employee ownership of the Corporation.'' That decision did not deter Thomson, however, which made another offering, this time for $65 a share. In 1984 that second bid was also rejected by the shareholders.

Even as the Thomson offer was being discussed, BNA was putting its cash to use. In 1983 Tax Management, Inc. established a new division, BNA Software, to publish software for accountants, lawyers, financial planners, and other tax professionals. Clients could now purchase software in the areas of income tax planning, estate tax planning and compliance, corporate tax and corporate foreign tax credit planning, sales tax compliance, and fixed asset depreciation reporting and management.

BNA also grew through acquisitions. Within a 12-month period beginning in March 1984, BNA bought four companies. Two of these had ties with BNA and went on to become important contributors to the company. Pike & Fisher, a small legal publisher, had been in business for nearly 50 years, and its president was BNA's first outside director. Its major revenues came from several information services covering radio law and from editing, on a contract basis, a news service on the Uniform Commercial Code. As a BNA subsidiary, Pike & Fisher continued and enlarged these services, particularly those dealing with communications law, and developed new offerings, including legal reference services in administrative law, criminal law, and ocean shipping regulations. It also published newsletters on the chemical fertilizer industry, a weekly trade and commodity report, and a newsletter for North American agrichemical distributors and dealers.

McArdle Printing Company had once been David Lawrence's Business Printing Company. The McArdle brothers bought it and began operating it as their own company in 1947. About 60 percent of their total business came from BNA in 1984. With both of these purchases, BNA kept the new subsidiaries intact, only naming someone from BNA as president.

The other two acquisitions did not prove as successful for BNA. The main product of Executive Telecom System, Inc. (ETSI) was an on-line information service for human resource executives. Although that seemed a logical fit with BNA's other databases in this field, after several years it was evident that there were not enough customers willing to pay for the service. BNA sold ETSI in 1992.

What excited BNA about its fourth purchase, Information Consultants, Inc. (ICI), was the full-text litigation support service for the legal profession it was in the process of developing. However, that service never met expectations, and after substantial losses, BNA liquidated ICI in 1987.

The 1990s

BNA continued to use new technologies to improve their services. For a company producing thousands of pages of information, CD-ROM was an obvious resource, and BNA took advantage of it. Among the BNA products published on CD-ROM were all the state laws and regulations regarding the environment, and a comprehensive reference service on intellectual property. The company was also marketing its products through such various on-line database vendors as LEXIS/NEXIS, Dialog, and Legislate. In 1996 BNA began offering electronic delivery of many of its services via Lotus Notes and the Internet.

However, technologies were not the only changes occurring. As health care became a major topic of national debate, BNA launched a variety of new services including *Health Law Reporter, Health Care Policy Report, Managed Care Reporter,* and *Medicare Report.*

In 1995 Paul Wojcik took over from William Beltz, becoming BNA's fourth president. In 1997 as BNA celebrated 50 years of employee ownership, Wojcik was named CEO, while keeping the title of president. That same year BNA acquired the Institute of Management and Administration, Inc. (IOMA). A privately held company based in New York City, IOMA published 32 newsletters with practical information aimed at lawyers, accountants, and human resource professionals.

As BNA moved into its second half-century, BNA employees and retirees still owned 100 percent of the company' stock. With all other major legal publishers having been acquired by multinational corporations, BNA remained the largest independent, U.S.-owned company in its field and the oldest private, wholly employee-owned company in the country.

Principal Subsidiaries

Pike & Fisher, Inc.; BNA Communications Inc.; BNA International Inc.; Tax Management, Inc.; McArdle Printing Co.; Institute of Management and Administration, Inc. (IOMA).

Principal Divisions

BNA Books; BNA Software.

Further Reading

''About BNA and Subsidiaries,'' http://www.bna.com/corp/about.html.
''BNA Acquires N.Y. City–Based IOMA,'' Washington, D.C.: BNA, October 24, 1997.
''New CEO Takes Over as Company Marks 50 Years of Employee Ownership,'' Washington, D.C.: BNA, January 6, 1997.
Stewart, John D., *Making Employee Ownership Work,* Washington, D.C.: Bureau of National Affairs, Inc., 1997.

—Ellen D. Wernick

Burelle S.A.

19, avenue Jules-Carteret
69007 Lyon
France
(33) 04.78.72.54.07
Fax: (33) 04.72.73.46.92

Public Company
Incorporated: 1957
Employees: 10,000
Sales: FFr 8 billion (1996)
Stock Exchanges: Paris
SICs: 3089 Plastics Products, Not Elsewhere Classified;
3714 Motor Vehicle Parts & Accessories; 3993 Signs
& Advertising Displays; 6719 Holding Companies,
Not Elsewhere Classified

Burelle S.A., based in Lyons, France, is a holding company for two principal businesses: Compagnie Plastic Omnium and Compagnie Signature. By far, Plastic Omnium—Burelle's original business—represents the company's most important holding, accounting for more than FFr 7.2 billion of Burelle's 1996 sales. The group is also distinctly international, with more than 50 factories in 20 countries, and with more than half of the company's consolidated revenues generated outside of France.

Plastic Omnium is one of Europe's leading plastics groups and the oldest member of Burelle's holdings. A publicly traded subsidiary, Plastic Omnium is active in four primary markets: Automotive; Municipal Environment and Leisure; Medical and Pharmaceutical; and High Performance Plastics. In the automotive market, Plastic Omnium is one of Europe's leading suppliers of interior and exterior plastics components. The company's interior products focus on door panels, capturing ten percent of the European market, side panels, with 20 percent of the European market, and dashboards and other interior fittings. Plastic Omnium's exterior automobile products concentrate on its bumper systems, which have gained 25 percent of the European market. The company is also a leading maker of fuel and exhaust components and turnkey systems. In the mid-1990s Plastic Omnium extended its product lines to include components for automobile bodies, including trunks, and blow-molded and extruded products. Plastic Omnium has long been a privileged supplier to the three major French automotive manufacturers, Peugeot, Renault, and Citroen, and supplies many foreign brands, including BMW, Volvo, Volkswagen, Ford, General Motors–Opel, Seat, and Toyota.

While the automobile market accounts for more than 55 percent of Plastic Omnium's and Burelle's annual sales, Plastic Omnium's Environment and Leisure division has gained a leading share of the French market for municipal waste and recycling container systems, and is a prominent player throughout the European market. The company has also pioneered and captured the French lead in outdoor plastics-based playground designs. Plastic Omnium's Medical division has also played a leading role in bringing specialized sterile plastic products into the medical and pharmaceutical laboratory. In the high performance category, Plastic Omnium's 3P subsidiary (Produits Plastiques Performants) has captured worldwide leadership of the fabrication of high performance polymer-based products for the chemical, pharmaceutical, automobile, aerospace, petrochemical, and other industries.

Burelle's youngest holding is its Compagnie Signature subsidiary, created in 1991 to group Burelle's interests in the production and placement of road sign, signaling, and security strategies for the urban, highway, and freeway markets. Primarily active in Europe, with a focus on France, Germany, Spain, Sweden, and the United Kingdom, Signature's subsidiaries are leaders in their respective markets, providing directional signs and supports, signaling equipment, traffic detection and other traffic management systems, as well as fixtures such as bus stop shelters, and subway lighting fixtures and encasements. Signature's contribution to Burelle's annual sales reached FFr 1 billion in 1996.

Burelle continues to be led by founder and CEO Pierre Burelle. The company's principal subsidiaries are led by Pierre Burelle's sons: Jean Burelle is CEO of Plastic Omnium, and Laurent Burelle is CEO of Signature.

Plastics Pioneer in the 1940s

While most of the major types of plastics had been invented by the 1940s, the new material found little acceptance within the automobile industry. Indeed, plastics in general would long be held in disdain as inferior rivals to traditional wood and metal designs. Yet Pierre Burelle, who had been working as an engineer for the French conglomerate Saint Gobain, wagered that plastics could indeed find a place in the automobile. In 1946, Burelle, seeking to make his own fortune, left Saint Gobain and set up shop in a small Parisian cellar.

The French passion for automobiles—once again liberated after four years of German occupation during the Second World War—made the prospect of accepting the ''vulgar'' plastic as an automobile component decidedly dim. Burelle took the risk, however. Approaching Renault, which had just been nationalized, Burelle offered to fabricate from plastic a small piece of the steering column for the 4 CV—France's answer to the German Volkswagen. To Burelle's own surprise, Renault agreed, and Burelle entered the privileged ranks of the French auto giant's official providers.

Burelle's company—Plastic Omnium—soon added the other French car makers to its customer list, and could begin looking for customers among Europe's leading brands. Burelle's wager was paying off: where an automobile of the 1950s might contain just a few hundred grams of plastic, the material would soon establish itself among the important components of the average automobile. Weight concerns of both the automaker and car consumer—and particularly the effect of an automobile's weight on its fuel consumption—helped boost plastic's attractiveness. By the 1970s the average automobile contained some 38 kilos of plastic; by the 1980s a typical car would contain as much as 60 kilos of plastic, while a decade later, more than 100 kilos of plastic, representing more than ten percent of the total weight of many automobiles, were being used—and forecasts estimated that the automobiles of the year 2000 would contain up to 200 kilos or more of plastic components.

By the mid-1960s Burelle's revenues had reached FFr 17 million. Automobile components would remain the company's principal revenue generator. Yet Burelle looked to extend its range—and buffer its sales during downswings in the automotive market—with other plastics applications. For this, Burelle could remain in the family, buying up the assets of Pierre Burelle's grandfather's company, the Union Mutelle des Propriértaires Lyonnais, which supplied street-cleaning and other municipal refuse disposal services. Burelle introduced a new wrinkle to the market: the trash can on wheels. Once again wagering on an idea, Burelle offered the new product for free to the municipality, providing cleaning, maintenance, and replacement services as well, in exchange for a per-household rental fee. The plan caught on, slowly but surely—by the 1990s Plastic Omnium waste container services—which expanded to include central and household-based recycling bins—were featured in more than ten percent of France's 36,000 municipalities, giving the company a wide lead in that market.

In the mid-1970s Burelle turned to a new material to enhance Plastic Omnium's range of products. Developed in the mid-1960s by Du Pont in the United States, PTFE's (polytetrafluorethylene) best-known application was Teflon, used for coating cookware and other products. Burelle, however, recognized the new plastic form's potential for the high technology industry. Instead of developing its own product line, however, Burelle acquired a small French company, SIREM, the only French company working with PTFE at the time. Once again, Burelle captured a French market, now for high performance plastics components for high technology and other products, in industries ranging from aerospace to household appliances.

The final piece of the Burelle puzzle came at the beginning of the 1980s. With its municipal trash collection and management services flourishing, Burelle identified a new market: providing equipment to its municipal customers' public playgrounds. Once again, Burelle entered a market in which plastic had traditionally remained absent. Designing and producing a range of plastic-based, modular play sets and furnishings, Burelle set out to conquer this market as well, again offering a rental and servicing agreement. In addition, despite the project's initial failure, Burelle succeeded in transforming the French and international playground. By the late 1980s the popularity of Burelle's playground fixtures had grown to such an extent that demand outstripped supply. Burelle's playground fixtures found eager municipal customers not only in such major French cities as Paris and Lyons, but in cities including Athens, Houston, Oslo, Dortmund, Lisbon, Albuquerque, and Seoul.

Acquiring Growth in the 1980s and 1990s

By 1985 Burelle's revenues had reached FFr 800 million. Five years later, the company's annual sales topped FFr 3.75 billion, and by 1996 Burelle's consolidated revenues swelled to FFr 10 billion, making the company one of the world's leading plastics companies.

Pierre Burelle, joined by sons Jean and Laurent, had again wagered on an idea: growing the company through acquisitions. Indeed, between 1986 and 1996, the company acquired more than 30 companies, including rival automobile supplier Reydel in 1996. The first of these acquisitions was made in 1986, with the purchases of Landry Plastiques and Techni-Plaste Industrie. The following year—after taking the company public with a listing on the Lyons over-the-counter market—the Burelles acquired Doré, giving the company a foothold not only in the Netherlands, but in the United States as well. Furthering the company's Dutch position, the company acquired Raka in 1988, while at the same time moving into Spain with the acquisition of that country's Uldesa.

While sales of the company's stock helped fuel its acquisition drive, many of the company's purchases remained autofinanced, investing from FFr 300 million to FFr 450 million or more each year on acquisitions. Burelle was not shy about going into debt to drive its growth—by 1996 the company's debt extended to FFr 3 billion. Nevertheless, the company remained consistently profitable, with the exception of 1995, the sole year of net losses in Burelle's history. This profitability came in the face of the economic crisis that gripped France and much of Europe during the first half of the decade.

In 1989 Burelle began preparing the way for the creation of its Signature subsidiary, with the acquisition of 35 percent of

France's Neuhaus, a position boosted to 80 percent the following year, and shortly thereafter to full ownership. In 1990 Burelle acquired another French road sign maker, Sodilor; the following year, that division was enhanced by the acquisition of Webs in Switzerland and Segor in Germany. In 1991 Burelle reorganized the company, creating the Signature subsidiary for its growing holdings in directional and other roadside services. Through 1996 Burelle would continue adding to its Signature portfolio, expanding into the subsidiary's five principal European markets with the acquisitions of companies including Sermo Electronique and TNS of France, Pathfinder and Road Signs Franco of Great Britain, Gerecke + Lauer of Germany, and Signal of Switzerland. By 1996 the Signature division had grown from FFr 337 million to nearly FFr 1 billion in sales.

Burelle's largest growth remained, however, with its Plastic Omnium subsidiary. Between 1990 and 1996 the company acquired more than 12 plastics producers throughout the world. Janssens, S 3E, Scotra, Profutex, and Reydel Industries would consolidate Burelle's French leadership. In the United States the company added Zarn, Epsco, and EGC, while adding Janssens in Belgium, Lander in Italy, B. PO in Turkey, Vasam in Spain, and Fransaf Ltd. in South Africa. The addition—by hostile takeover—of Reydel Industries in 1995 and 1996 not only brought Reydel's complementary product line of automobile interiors, but also introduced Plastic Omnium to Reydel's customers, including Fiat and Nissan.

By the mid-1990s, however, Burelle seemed to be ready to take a pause. For one, the recession had finally caught up with the company, causing a net loss of FFr 150 million in 1995, the first loss in the company's history. However, the loss proved short-lived: by 1996, with its sales rising to FFr 10 billion, the company was back in profitability. Additionally, with France—and most of Europe—recovering from the long recession of the first half of the 1990s, Burelle could begin making plans to continue its growth towards the next century.

Principal Subsidiaries

Plastic Omnium; Compagnie Signature; Sofiparc.

Further Reading

"Fabricant mondial d'équipements plastiques et numéro un français de la poubelle," *Le Monde,* June 28, 1991.

—M. L. Cohen

Butterick Co., Inc.

161 Avenue of the Americas
New York, New York 10013
U.S.A.
(212) 620-2500
Fax: (212) 620-2746
Web site: http://www.butterick.com

Private Company
Incorporated: 1902
Employees: 1,000
Sales: $110 million (1996 est.)
SICs. 2721 Periodicals. Publishing, or Publishing &
   Printing; 2741 Miscellaneous Publishing; 2771
   Greeting Cards

Butterick Co., Inc. produces and sells patterns for the home sewing of women's and girls' clothing and publishes magazines in which these patterns appear. These patterns and periodicals are found in sewing centers and department, variety, and piece-goods stores. Butterick also prepares and publishes greeting cards.

Butterick to the Great Depression

Ebenezer Butterick, a tailor in Sterling, Massachusetts, was the father of a baby boy in 1863, when his wife, fashioning a dress for the infant at her sewing table, remarked how much easier it would be if she had a pattern to go by that was the same size as her son. There were patterns that served as a guide, but they came in one size only, and the sewer had to grade (enlarge or reduce) the pattern to the size needed. Ebenezer experimented with the idea of graded patterns and discovered that tissue paper was ideal to work with and much easier to package than the heavy cardboard templates he first created.

The first graded sewing patterns were cut and folded by members of the Butterick family and sold from their home. In no time they needed extra space and expanded, first into an adjoining house and then to a larger house in Fitchburg, Massa-

chusetts. In the next year they established quarters in New York City. Butterick first specialized in men's and boys' clothing but in 1866 began to manufacture dress patterns. Soon the women's line included dresses, jackets, and capes in 13 sizes and skirts in five sizes. By 1873 Butterick was selling some six million patterns a year, at 25 cents each.

By 1876 the firm (then called E. Butterick & Co.) had 100 branch offices and 1,000 agencies throughout the United States and Canada. Butterick patterns also had made their debuts in London, Vienna, Berlin, and even Paris, the international center of fashion, where more patterns were sold from the Butterick Shop than anywhere else in the world. Corporate headquarters were moved in 1903 to the new 16-story Butterick Building in what is now known as Manhattan's Soho district. Butterick was now one of the largest manufacturing concerns in the industry, and the building, constructed expressly for the firm and featuring interiors designed by Louis Tiffany, housed the largest printing plant in the world except for the Government Printing Office in Washington, D.C.

Inside the Butterick Building, which employed some 2,000 workers, merchandisers brought ideas fresh from the latest European designer showings. New styles were made up in muslins, scrutinized for line silhouettes and fashion, and also for practicality and suitability to the company's customers. After the season's styles had been chosen, patterns were created, graded into sizes, printed on tissue papers, and cut, folded, and inserted into envelopes, complete with instruction sheets. These patterns sold for ten or 15 cents each. For use in magazine articles and advertisements, garments were constructed, sketched with pen and ink, and engraved for colored fashion plates.

Butterick entered the magazine business in 1867 in order to showcase its patterns and induce women to order patterns by mail. The *Delineator,* founded in 1873, evolved into a service magazine with general topics of interest to women as well as fashion news. This magazine, which included articles by Edith Wharton and Rudyard Kipling, and two other Butterick periodicals had a combined circulation of about 1.3 million in 1907, when novelist Theodore Dreiser became editor of all three. Among Dreiser's innovations was a column on baby care; when the doctor assigned to contribute the pieces proved inadequate, Dreiser hired bachelor H. L. Mencken to ghostwrite them. The Butterick stable expanded in 1909, when the firm acquired Ridgway Co. and its thriving *Everybody's Magazine,* whose contributors included Lincoln Steffens and Walter Lippmann.

A public company, Butterick had net income of $516,593 in 1913 but soon began to exhibit signs of malaise. It paid out its last dividend on common stock in 1916, except for a single dividend in 1926 that was mostly in stock rather than cash. Sales peaked at $15.9 million in 1922 and net income at $729,162 the following year. Sales volume had dropped to $10.9 million in 1929, just before the onset of the Great Depression. The company lost money in 1932, 1933, and 1936, and probably also in 1934 and 1935, years concerning which no figures were released.

Gradual Resurgence, 1936–67

Effectively bankrupt, Butterick was reorganized in 1936. Many of its publications, including the *Delineator,* which was accounting for one-third of company sales, were sold in 1937. The company also sold its building, where it continued to lease space, for $3 million. With its expenses reduced, Butterick was in the black, although barely, in 1937, 1938, and 1939, but in 1940 it lost $123,729 on sales of only $2.1 million. The number of company employees had dropped to fewer than 500. Butterick still published a few fashion magazines and *Progressive Grocer,* a trade magazine. Its presence remained strong, with branches in principal cities of the United States and in Toronto, Canada, and publishing subsidiaries in Great Britain and Australia.

Butterick's sales volume fell as low as $1.7 million in 1942, when it lost money for the third consecutive year. However, despite the shortage of cloth for civilians due to World War II, the war years proved good for the company. The diminished stock of ready-to-wear goods resulted in a boom in home sewing and, consequently, a sharp increase in demand for patterns. Butterick focused on classic styles and, in the interest of conserving cloth, patterns with fewer pieces. Shorter lengths were adopted for both jackets and skirts, and details such as buttons, trims, and appliques were kept to a minimum.

Butterick's sales reached $3.1 million in 1948. By then the company had decided it needed new quarters for manufacturing, stock, and shipping. It purchased advanced printing equipment, including full-color presses, for a new manufacturing plant in Altoona, Pennsylvania. The first full-color photograph appeared on the cover of the company catalog in 1950. Another factory was located in Toronto. The 1950s was a decade of steady sales growth although only modest profit for Butterick. During this decade subsidiaries were established in Italy, New Zealand, and South Africa. Sales reached a new high of $8.3 million in 1960, but net profit was only $121,856.

In 1961 Butterick purchased the patterns division of Condé Nast Publications, Inc., and licensed the name and trademark "Vogue Patterns" from Condé Nast. This purchase for stock made Condé Nast a substantial stockholder in Butterick. Vogue Patterns dated from 1905. In the early days *Vogue* magazine readers purchased a pattern by clipping a coupon and mailing it in along with 50 cents. By 1913, when the name was changed to "Vogue Pattern Service," it comprised a major segment of the

publication, and by 1917 the patterns were selling in major department stores. By 1920 the Vogue Patterns business had become so extensive that the patterns no longer appeared in *Vogue* but were featured instead in their own publication, *Vogue Pattern Book.* In 1949 Vogue Patterns became the only pattern company licensed to produce designs from the world's leading couturiers, establishing a precedent that continued into the late 1990s.

The acquisition of Vogue Patterns, which maintained its own staff of merchandisers, designers, artists, and editors, swelled Butterick's sales by about $5 million a year, moving it into second place in the patternmaking industry, behind Simplicity Pattern Co. The Butterick and Vogue services were not competitive, because Vogue's patterns were high-style and relatively high-priced—75 cents to $3.50 apiece—while Butterick patterns were being produced for the mass market and ranged in price from 40 to 75 cents. However, after the merger management eliminated duplicate manufacturing in the United States, Canada, England, and Australia, and it closed Vogue distribution branches in San Francisco, Toronto, and Memphis. The servicing of customers was now handled entirely through Butterick's main plant in Altoona and the six branches in the United States and Canada.

Butterick also was establishing thousands of sewing centers selling the firm's patterns, needles, thread, buttons, zippers, and other sewing "notions" in supermarkets. More than 3,000 such units had been established by May 1962. All told, the company now was distributing 1,400 pattern styles, in five sizes, through some 10,000 outlets. About 20 percent of its business was being conducted overseas, notably in the four countries where it had subsidiaries.

Butterick's dealings at this time with retailers such as department stores normally rested on a five-year contract stipulating that the dealer would purchase an initial stock of patterns and also an average, fixed-dollar amount of new ones each month. As the products were sold, the dealer ordered replacements from the company. Since styles changed, at periodic intervals Butterick would classify certain patterns as discards, allowing dealers to return its stock of discards at 90 percent of the wholesale price. About one-third of gross pattern sales involved such discards.

Further Changes, 1967–92

By 1967 Butterick's patterns, under its own or the Vogue name, were being sold in about 12,000 stores. In 1966, its last full year as an independent public company, Butterick had net profit of $1.1 million on sales of $20 million. It was purchased in 1967 by American Can Co. and became a subsidiary renamed Butterick Fashion Marketing Co. Butterick's two pattern magazines had a combined circulation of four million in 1969. *Progressive Grocer* was sold to Maclean Hunter Media Inc. in 1981.

The 1960s were widely regarded as a boom period for home sewing. The market was said to comprise more than 40 million of the nation's female population in 1967, with these self-styled seamstresses turning out an average of 27 garments apiece each year. Four out of five teenage girls were sewing, making almost 70 million pieces of clothing a year, according to a *Barron's* report. In 1971 a *Forbes* article claimed that of the 82 million

U.S. females between ages 12 and 65, an estimated 44 million now sewed, and that the proportion was rising each year. Home sewing was said to be a $2.3 billion market in 1970. But this revival of home sewing seems to have been overblown, for a 1992 *Forbes* article declared, ''In the 1970s schools stopped teaching sewing and women began joining the work force in large numbers, leaving their sewing machines to gather dust.''

In the early 1980s makers of home sewing machines, patterns, and fabrics were again speaking of a revival of the craft. Enormous catalogs with patterns for 700 styles or more and frighteningly complex instructions were said to have intimidated potential customers, so to make things easier Butterick in 1980 introduced a See & Sew line of only 96 styles, with fewer pattern pieces, only one view of a finished dress to consult, and instructions that allowed for a graded fit. The price was only $1.19 each, compared to the $2.75 pattern average. By late 1982 See & Sew was accounting for about seven percent of the more than 100 million patterns sold annually in the United States. Vogue revived publication of an earlier knitting magazine in 1982.

Butterick's management purchased the company from American Can in 1983 in one of the first leveraged buyouts of the decade, paying, according to *Forbes*, $12.5 million, of which all but $500,000 was borrowed. The company, which had annual sales of somewhere between $55 million and $70 million at the time, assumed a high level of debt. Its response was to cut costs, firing employees, reducing inventory, and eliminating all of the six printing and distribution plants except the main one in Altoona, where all these operations were consolidated. The new owners paid off their acquisition loan within two years and in 1988 sold about 60 percent of the company to Robert Bass's Acadia Investors for about $90 million.

Butterick also took out new loans to invest in computerized design systems and thereby reduce by more than half the time it took to market a new pattern. Speed was important because popular high-fashion styles were being appropriated and falling out of fashion so quickly. After Butterick shored up its Vogue line with quick release of high-fashion style patterns it raised its profile at the lower end of the market. Between 1988 and early 1992 the company nearly doubled the total number of less-expensive patterns it was introducing. Butterick supplemented its two sewing magazines, *Butterick Home Catalog* and *Vogue Patterns,* plus *Vogue Knitting International,* by adding four new titles, including *Weddings* and *Fine Sewing,* to enhance its efforts in niche markets.

Searching for ways to offset a decline in pattern sales, the company chose greeting cards, because like patterns, they were paper-based consumer products aimed at women. Butterick purchased four companies between 1986 and 1992 for a total of $7 million to $8 million. Some of Butterick's cards were beautifully crafted, retailing for as much as $7 each, and sales from greeting cards grew from $11 million in 1985 to about $24 million in 1992. However, this sector of business failed to produce the profits and cash flow that the company had hoped for, so to reduce costs it consolidated three Chicago plants in 1992 and began farming out printing to outside vendors.

Patterns remained Butterick's main business in 1992, accounting for $95 million of the company's $120 million in annual sales. Profit figures were not released. According to a *Crain's New York Business* article, the company was still saddled with about $50 million in senior debt. Nevertheless, it was better off than its rivals, Simplicity and McCall Pattern Co., which each held, along with Butterick, about a third of the domestic patterns market. Simplicity had changed hands four times in about a decade and had defaulted on notes, while McCall had been bought and sold twice before falling for a time into bankruptcy in 1988 after also defaulting on notes.

William P. Wilson was the first chief executive officer of privatized Butterick. He was succeeded in 1988 by John Lehmann, previously the company's head of international divisions. Lehmann, who held ten percent of Butterick in 1992, was still its president in 1996.

Further Reading

Chatzky, Jean Sherman, ''Reaping from Sewing,'' *Forbes,* May 25, 1992, pp. 154, 156.

''Dirndls, Sheaths and Shifts,'' *Barron's,* July 23, 1962, pp. 11–12.

Greene, Joan, ''Affluent Sew-ciety,'' *Barron's,* August 21, 1967, pp. 11, 19.

Hobby, Edward K., ''Simplicity Itself,'' *Barron's,* December 7, 1964, pp. 9–10.

''I Made It Myself!'' *Forbes,* April 15, 1971, pp. 43–44.

Jaffe, Thomas, ''A Stitch in Time,'' *Forbes,* September 13, 1982, p. 203.

Swanberg, W. A., *Dreiser,* New York: Scribner's, 1965, pp. 119–35.

Temes, Judy, ''CFO Prints Pattern for Greeting Cards,'' *Crain's New York Business,* March 16, 1992, p. 13.

—Robert Halasz

Cadmus Communications Corporation

6620 W. Broad St., Ste. 240
Richmond, Virginia 23230
U.S.A.
(804) 287-5680
Fax: (804) 287-6267
Web site: http://www.cadmus.com

Public Company
Incorporated: 1984
Employees: 3,000
Sales: $385 million (1997)
Stock Exchanges: NASDAQ
SICs: 2721 Periodicals: Publishing & Printing; 2731
   Books: Publishing & Printing; 2752 Commercial
   Printing, Lithographic; 2759 Commercial Printing,
   Not Elsewhere Classified; 2796 Platemaking &
   Related Services; 7311 Advertising Agencies; 7331
   Direct Mail Advertising Services

Cadmus Communications Corporation was named after the Greek mythological figure who founded Thebes and introduced the alphabet to Greece. Through a series of acquisitions in the 1980s and 1990s, the company became the world's number one publisher of scientific, technical, medical, and scholarly journals. This sector, Professional Communications, also provides its clients with a full range of production and distribution services, including composition, editing, printing, electronic services, and worldwide distribution. The Marketing Communications sector provides services including preparing financial documents; designing and marketing promotional materials, directories, and catalogs; providing production services to other periodical publishers; and designing and producing cartons, mailers, and other promotional packaging; direct-response marketing; marketing strategy development and execution; and interactive and electronic services.

Beginning in 1995, the company transformed itself from a holding company managing 15 independent companies to an inte-grated operating company focused on two broad market sectors: professional communications and marketing communications.

Formed by Merger in 1984

In 1984, with the merger of The William Byrd Press Inc. of Richmond, Virginia, and Washburn Graphics Inc. of Charlotte, North Carolina, Cadmus Communications was formed as a holding company. The William Byrd Press was founded in Richmond, Virginia, in 1913. It began with 18 employees and was a commercial printer that printed periodicals and other commercial jobs. At the time of the merger it was an established printer of scholarly journals employing web offset printing technology. Washburn was primarily a financial printer. After the merger, William Byrd and Washburn continued to operate under separate management.

Cadmus went through a period of external expansion and diversification in the late 1980s. At this time Cadmus operated under a decentralized management policy, allowing the companies it acquired to operate independently, with little interference. In 1986 Cadmus acquired American Graphics of Atlanta, Georgia, which specialized in printing point-of-purchase advertising materials. In 1987 it acquired Three Score, a catalog design and photography production firm, also based in Atlanta. Other acquisitions around this time included Dataset Communications Inc. of New York, a composition operation, Garamond Press of Baltimore, Maryland, and Vaughan Printers Inc. of Orlando, Florida.

In the early 1990s, the printing industry continued to change dramatically. One of the changes was a trend by print purchasers toward vendor consolidation and "one-stop shopping." To respond to this trend, Cadmus began to integrate and package its services for its clients. The result, according to the *Richmond Times-Dispatch,* was that "instead of just printing Hardee's signs touting a new product, Cadmus now creates the promotional campaign, prints the material, distributes it to restaurants and takes orders for the signs from the stores." The goal was to make Cadmus "the one-stop shop in the communications world." Company officials referred to it as "end-to-end" service or "seamless integration."

Company Perspectives:

The Cadmus mission is to provide customers with integrated 21st century information and communications solutions. To achieve this mission, Cadmus is organized around two broad market sectors: Professional Communications which serves those who create and convey information, and Marketing Communications which serves those who create and convey marketing messages. Within these groups, the company offers end-to-end services including message creation, production, distribution, and fulfillment for well-defined niches. Our goal is to maximize the impact and effectiveness of our clients' communications while reducing the cost, time, and complexity of creating them.

28th Largest Graphic Communications Firm in North America, 1991

Industry data for 1991 indicated that Cadmus was the 28th largest graphic communications firm in North America. It was the 12th largest publicly held company in the United States in the field of graphic communications. As a result of its acquisitions, company sales had grown from $93 million in 1986 to $170.4 million in 1990. A similar pattern of growth would occur over the next five years.

At the beginning of the 1990s, Cadmus was focused on three market segments: periodical production services, promotional and financial printing, and direct marketing. It considered itself an integrator and innovator of new graphic communication technologies. From 1991 to 1995, Cadmus invested nearly $60 million in technology to improve productivity and quality and to develop new products and markets. Some of the funds were invested in new printing equipment, including two double-round web presses at The William Byrd Press, one in 1991 and another in 1992. In the early 1990s, the most significant sources of printing business for Cadmus were scientific journals, magazines, retail catalogs, and promotional materials. Financial printing revenues came from registration statements, documents that accompanied securities sales, and annual reports.

Became Magazine Publisher in 1992

Two acquisitions in 1992 marked Cadmus's entry into publishing. First Cadmus acquired Tuff Stuff Publications, based in Richmond, which published a line of consumer specialty magazines. Later that year, Cadmus acquired Marblehead Communications, Inc., a Boston, Massachusetts-based publisher of newsletters and magazines. Marblehead's clients included Continental Airlines, Johnson & Johnson, the League of American Theatres & Producers, the Massachusetts Office of Travel & Tourism, New England Telephone, and others.

Also that year Cadmus established the Cadmus Color Center to provide pre-press and color separation services for customers. The primary purpose of the Color Center was to provide those services to Cadmus's two printing subsidiaries, Expert/Brown and William Byrd Press.

Waverly Press Acquisition Propels Cadmus to the Top, 1993

It was in 1993 that the William Byrd Press, Cadmus's periodical printing operation, decided to focus on printing journals. Previously, it had built its reputation on two major products, journals and magazines. In October 1993 Cadmus paid $20 million for Waverly Press, one of its biggest competitors. Waverly Press was the printing subsidiary of Waverly Inc., a publicly traded research journal publishing company. Based in Baltimore, Waverly Press had about $50 million in annual revenues. For fiscal 1993, Cadmus posted $198.1 million in revenues. Adding the Waverly Press operation more than doubled the company's journal business and increased its revenues by 25 percent. It also made Cadmus the number one producer of scientific, medical, and technical journals in the world. For the fiscal year ending June 30, 1994, Cadmus's sales jumped to $247.7 million as a result of the acquisition.

Cadmus combined Waverly with the research journal portion of its William Byrd Press subsidiary to form Cadmus Journal Services. Following the acquisition, Waverly Inc. (Waverly Press's former parent company) became Cadmus Journal Services's largest customer, accounting for some $12 million in annual sales. Other customers of the new subsidiary included The Lancet (a British medical journal) and the American Academy of Pediatrics.

In another development that year, Cadmus announced in March 1993 that it would merge its Orlando, Florida, printing subsidiary, Vaughan Printers, with Central Florida Press, owned by Washington, D.C.-based Lanman Companies, Inc., to form Central Florida Press L.C.

Entry into Multimedia Interactive Market, 1994

In the fall of 1994 Cadmus acquired ModelMation, Inc., an Atlanta-based multimedia company. With 1994 revenues of approximately $1 million, ModelMation provided high-quality interactive services to technology companies, including AT&T, Siemens, Sprint, and Scientific Atlanta. At the same time Cadmus established Cadmus Interactive, a new subsidiary focused on the development and marketing of multimedia and new media products and services. Based in Atlanta, Cadmus Interactive joined ModelMation with the executive leadership of Christian Holljes, a former multimedia engineer with Apple Computer Inc., and Dan Backus, a noted interactive media developer.

According to Cadmus's Chairman, President, and CEO C. Stephenson Gillispie, Jr., "Cadmus is responding to the burgeoning demand by our customers for digital communication media products such as CD-ROM and on-line information services." Jim Hernandez, the newly named president of Cadmus Interactive, added, "Cadmus Interactive is prepared to create digital communications products today and our sights are squarely set on prospects for digital delivery on the network of tomorrow."

Subsequent acquisitions in this area included PeachWeb, an Atlanta-based Internet applications firm that developed web sites, and The Software Factory, an Atlanta-based provider of software packaging and media duplication services. Cadmus also acquired the Atlanta division of Encryption Technology Corporation, a provider of software packaging, media duplication, and documentation services.

Cadmus Direct, the company's direct marketing subsidiary based in Charlotte, North Carolina, made two acquisitions in 1995: Ronald James Direct, a Los Angeles-based direct-response agency with $12 million in billings, and The Mowry Co., a Long Beach, California, direct marketing agency with nearly $16 million in annual billings. These acquisitions opened new markets on the West Coast and in Denver, Colorado.

Began Major Restructuring, 1995

Prior to its 1995 reorganization (the first of three reorganizations) Cadmus was a collection of 15 independent companies. These companies were active in direct marketing, interactive publishing, promotional printing, packaging, software duplication, financial communications, and journal and magazine printing. In July 1995 the name Cadmus was attached to all of its divisions, and Cadmus changed from a holding company to an operating company. Rather than letting its subsidiaries stand alone, the company would attempt to integrate them. All of the subsidiaries were organized under three business units: printing, marketing, and publishing.

The purpose of the reorganization, said Chairman C. Stephenson Gillispie, was to shift the company's focus from companies to products. He was quoted as saying, "Our intent is to leverage the knowledge and experience of our associates across the entire corporation, rather than segmenting our expertise by company or geographic location."

At the time of the 1995 reorganization, Cadmus was the 22nd largest graphic communications company in North America, but it was facing increased competition in a rapidly changing industry. Gillispie outlined the challenge facing the company, "Our industry is changing as much as any industry in the nation. Today customers are looking for a company to do all its communications needs. We must get better on how we market and promote." He also noted that Cadmus was facing "challenges from companies we never heard of or weren't in existence two or three years ago. Who would have thought we'd be in competition with BellSouth?," he told the *Richmond Times-Dispatch.* "We have to be aware of what we're up against."

That fall Cadmus made a public offering of 1.7 million shares of stock that raised $39 million in capital. It was the company's first offering since it went public in 1984. Some of the proceeds would be used to fund Cadmus's acquisitions strategy.

More Acquisitions, Divestitures, Restructuring, 1996

In 1996 Cadmus acquired Lancaster Press, based in Lancaster, Pennsylvania, which printed about 400 journals. Cadmus acquired it for approximately $58.7 million and further solidified its position as the industry leader. Overall, company sales jumped from $279.6 million in fiscal 1995 to $336.7 million in fiscal 1996.

In May 1996 Cadmus restructured for the second time by splitting its printing unit into a graphic communications group and a periodicals group. In September it sold Tuff Stuff, its consumer publishing division, for $6.5 million. The publishing group ceased to exist, and the company's custom publishing was realigned into the marketing group.

In September 1996 Cadmus acquired O'Keefe Marketing, a Richmond-based ad agency. Kelly O'Keefe, the agency's founder, would remain as its president. The name was changed to Cadmus/O'Keefe Marketing, Inc. O'Keefe Marketing was recognized as one of the first advertising agencies to have a division devoted to interactive work, such as creating World Wide Web pages and CD-ROMs for its clients. The acquisition was initiated by Steve Isaac, president of the Cadmus Marketing Group. At the time it was acquired, O'Keefe Marketing had 21 employees and annual billings of $22 million.

The O'Keefe acquisition signaled a move into marketing services. While some ad agencies perceived Cadmus as becoming a competitor, David Martin, founder of the Richmond ad agency The Martin Agency and head of Cadmus Identity Marketing, which was established in June 1997, told the *Richmond Times-Dispatch,* that he saw the company as a partner for advertising agencies rather than as a competitor. "This is a different kind of business: integrated marketing," he told the newspaper. "We are not trying to replace the ad agency. We are building an orchestra by assembling the musicians. This is not just the strings or the percussion."

Still, Cadmus Identity Marketing was creating advertising and marketing campaigns for its clients. Its goal was to help clients find their core identity, then develop communications for them. Another Cadmus unit, CadmusCom, produced advertising, direct-response marketing, publication development, catalog design and production, interactive production, trade show booths, package design, point-of-sale materials, billboards, custom publications, logos, and public relations. The unit was headed by Kelly O'Keefe. He told the *Richmond Times-Dispatch,* "Ad agencies are single solution providers." These business units were part of Cadmus Marketing Communications, which was, in effect, a $180 million marketing agency. It was headed by Steve Isaac, who joined the company in 1996.

Third Major Reorganization, 1997

Cadmus Marketing Communications was formed as a result of the company's third major restructuring, which took place in April 1997. At that time the company's three business units were combined into two. Cadmus's periodicals division became Cadmus Professional Communications, and its graphic communications and marketing units were combined into Cadmus Marketing Communications. Some 70 local jobs were cut and operations were closed in Long Beach, California (direct marketing), and Baltimore, Maryland (printing). The Atlanta and Richmond interactive divisions were consolidated.

Cadmus Professional Communications included the company's journal and magazine services for scientific, technical, and medical publishers, trade associations, and commercial publishers. Cadmus Marketing Communications included financial services, packaging, and promotional printing, point of purchase, direct marketing, catalogs, custom publishing, and interactive product lines. Gillispie noted in late 1997, "Since

July 1995 we have been working to make this a new company with a new structure.''

Cadmus Professional Communications and its sub-unit, Cadmus Journal Services, was headed by David G. Wilson, whose grandfather founded the William Byrd Press in 1913. In 1997 the division had six locations and 1,900 employees. It accounted for about $210 million of Cadmus's $385 million in sales in fiscal 1997. About $175 million of the journal revenues came from sales of scientific, technical, and medical journals. Magazines accounted for the other $35 million in revenue.

In addition to printing journals, Cadmus Journal Services helped design and edit them. It also was able to put them online or publish them on CD-ROM. It stored files and handled orders for back issues as well. Wilson described the outlook of the journal publishing operation to the *Richmond Times-Dispatch* in 1997, ''Maybe through strategic partnerships and responsible acquisitions we'll have more of a presence in Europe. Already more than 30 percent of everything we produce is distributed outside the U.S.''

The company's restructuring did not come without cost. Although Cadmus reported record sales of $385 million in fiscal 1997, it showed a net loss of $5 million for the year. That was largely the result of a one-time $19.7 million restructuring charge. Management expected all actions related to the restructuring to be completed by the end of fiscal 1998.

Recognizing that its strengths lay in marketing and professional communications, Cadmus was poised to better compete in those areas with its streamlined organizational structure. It has added several talented individuals with advertising and marketing expertise to its marketing communications team— notably Steve Isaac, David Martin, and Kelly O'Keefe. On the professional communications side, it has strengthened its leadership position by acquiring some of its major competitors and selling off its consumer publishing division.

Principal Operating Units

Cadmus Journal Services; Cadmus Identity Marketing; Cadmus Financial Communications; Cadmus Specialty Packaging and Promotional Printing; Cadmus Point of Purchase Services; Cadmus Print Outsourcing Services; Cadmus Tactical Marketing Communications (includes Cadmus Custom Publishing, Cadmus Direct Marketing, Cadmus O'Keefe Marketing, Cadmus Interactive, and Cadmus Catalogs).

Further Reading

Bosher, David E., ''Cadmus Communications Announces Formation of Cadmus Interactive and Acquisition of Atlanta-based Multimedia Company,'' *Business Wire,* September 14, 1994.
——, ''Cadmus Communications Corp. Acquires Marblehead Communications Inc.,'' *Business Wire,* January 4, 1993.
——, ''Cadmus Communications Corp. Announces CEO of the William Byrd Press Inc.,'' *Business Wire,* May 15, 1992.
Gore, Mollie, ''Cadmus Buys Assets of Rival,'' *Richmond Times-Dispatch,* October 1, 1993.
——, ''Washington-Based Company, Cadmus Plan Joint Venture,'' *Richmond Times-Dispatch,* March 23, 1993.
Middleton, Otesa, ''Cadmus Buys O'Keefe Marketing,'' *Richmond Times-Dispatch,* September 21, 1996, p. C1.
——, ''Cadmus Integration Proceeds, Chief Says at Annual Meeting,'' *Richmond Times-Dispatch,* November 11, 1997, p. B15.
——, ''A New Type Cadmus Communications Transforms the Role of Printers,'' *Richmond Times-Dispatch,* November 24, 1997, p. E16.
Row, Steve, ''Cadmus Communications Establishes Color Center,'' *Richmond News-Leader,* March 9, 1992.
Royall, Roderick, ''Cadmus Inks Out a Deal with Garamond,'' *Baltimore Business Journal,* September 28, 1987.
Shean, Tom, ''The Black Ink Flows Freely at Cadmus,'' *Virginian-Pilot,* April 13, 1992.
Stanley, Bonnie Newman, ''At Long Last, Cadmus Melded into One Firm,'' *Richmond Times-Dispatch,* July 20, 1995, p. 7.
Suiter, Sarah, ''Cadmus Stock Offering to Help Fund Acquisitions,'' *Business Journal-Charlotte,* October 9, 1995, p. 5.

—David Bianco

Carolina Power & Light Company

411 Fayetteville Street
Raleigh, North Carolina 27602
U.S.A.
(919) 546-6111
Fax: (919) 546-7678
Web site: http://www.CP&LC.com

Public Company
Incorporated: 1926
Employees: 6,700
Sales: $3 billion
Stock Exchanges: New York Pacific
SICs: 4911 Electric Services

Carolina Power & Light Company (CP&L) supplies electricity to over a million customers in eastern and western North Carolina and central South Carolina, using an array of coal-fired steam, nuclear, and hydroelectric plants. Having planned in the 1970s to increase greatly the proportion of its nuclear generators, CP&L, like many other utilities, ran into severe regulatory and cost problems and abandoned many of its nuclear projects. CP&L continued to use nuclear and coal-fired plants for the bulk of its electricity in the 1990s. As of 1997, the company operated 16 power plants, with a total generating capacity of 9,613 megawatts.

Company Origins

Carolina Power & Light was one of the many utilities created and nurtured by General Electric (GE). The latter was formed in 1889 by a group of investors led by J.P. Morgan, with the purpose of amalgamating a number of the manufacturing facilities associated with Thomas Edison's early work in light and power transmission. GE supplied the nation's new power industry with much of its equipment and technical leadership, often receiving as payment shares of stock in the young, under-capitalized utilities.

Some of GE's client companies grew into thriving businesses, but many others—most of them small utilities in rural areas—had trouble attracting the vast amounts of capital needed to build a system of electrical distribution. In order to help these smaller utilities raise capital—and in turn become good customers for GE equipment as well as increase the value of GE's equity holdings—GE created in 1905 a wholly owned subsidiary called Electric Bond & Share Company (EBS). EBS was given GE's stock portfolio and told to arrange financing, provide technical aid, and advise the management of these struggling utilities, including a number of companies in England and France. EBS generally owned but a small percentage of stock in each of its client firms. It was not a holding company, but the recommendations of EBS were followed by its much-smaller partners.

Among the many U.S. cities in which EBS became active was Raleigh, North Carolina, where electric lights were first provided in 1886 by the Thomson-Houston Electric Light Company. In 1892 Thomson-Houston was merged with GE, which thereby acquired a position in a number of the small power plants then beginning to harness the hydroelectric potential of the Appalachian river systems. When GE had formed EBS in 1905, it transferred its interest in these local plants to EBS, which quickly arranged for a merger of three of them in 1908. In that year, Carolina Power & Light Company was established in Raleigh by the merger of Raleigh Electric Company, Central Carolina Power Company, and Consumer Light and Power Company. Unlike many of EBS's ventures, CP&L was controlled directly by EBS and its president, S.Z. Mitchell, who for many years was a leader of the electrical industry in the United States. As EBS was wholly owned by GE, Carolina Power was controlled indirectly by the company from which it bought all of its equipment, a situation that was common in the electrical industry and that later would prompt charges of conflict of interest leading to the dissolution of the great U.S. electrical holding companies.

Early Expansion

The chief obstacle faced by Mitchell was the fragmentation of power generation in the Raleigh area, compounded by the difficulty of raising enough capital to consolidate and expand CP&L's system. The early electric power companies generally did not foresee the enormous growth in demand for electricity; they operated generators of limited capacity and charged customers a relatively high price for power. Mitchell and other early leaders of the electrical business believed that electricity was unlike any other commodity: it was destined to become universally and intensively utilized; it was a fungible product; and its generation and distribution required so much capital that competing firms could not survive in the same geographical area. It was thought that electric power was a natural monopoly, with a large central power station serving many square miles of customers. It was the chief goal of men like Mitchell to develop the electrical industry according to these principles: Mitchell encouraged mergers and expansion among EBS's many affiliates, and arranged the funding for same; he stressed the advantages of large central power stations; and he urged his colleagues to sell more electricity at a lower rate rather than less at a higher rate. That all of these rationalizations of the industry would benefit GE was, of course, understood from the beginning, but they were also to a large degree dictated by the nature of electric power.

CP&L accordingly set about expanding its facilities, which originally consisted of two hydroelectric plants and one steam plant generating a total of 3,900 kilowatts of power. In 1911 the company acquired the assets of two struggling power companies in nearby Henderson and Oxford, North Carolina, and the following year opened a western branch with the purchase of Asheville Power & Light Company. To help finance the construction of main transmission lines between CP&L's growing network of stations, EBS in 1911 created a second subsidiary to handle construction projects. North State Hydro Electric Company built and maintained power lines that it then leased to CP&L, obviating the need for CP&L to raise the cash needed for such large undertakings.

After battling the local gas company for several years, CP&L bought out its rival in 1911, becoming the sole supplier of both gas and electricity for the city of Raleigh. Its next milestone was a 1913 agreement to sell electricity wholesale to the city of Smithfield, North Carolina, which would handle its distribution to the customer. Such rapid expansion on the part of power companies raised the concerns of local legislators, who saw the threat of onerous rates by utilities given such monopolies. In 1913 North Carolina accordingly placed all power companies under the jurisdiction of its Corporation Commission, which would eventually be granted power to regulate all utility business, including rate schedules. A similar commission had already been formed in South Carolina, where another EBS subsidiary, Yadkin River Power Company, was operated by CP&L management. CP&L thus became a regulated monopoly, one of a great many around the country affiliated with EBS and ultimately with General Electric.

As the economies of North Carolina and South Carolina grew following World War I, an increasing number of manufac-

turing plants and residential customers alike switched to electricity for a growing number of applications. Most important among industrial users were the textile and tobacco manufacturers. Residential customers were encouraged to use electricity for a plethora of new gadgets and tools, often sold directly by CP&L's representatives. As with many technical evolutions, electrical customers often had to be shown the possibilities of electric power, and CP&L was eager to push the sale of GE appliances. It was the dawn of a new era for rural Carolinians, and electricity was soon in great demand.

However, as always, there remained a shortage of capital required to meet such demands. Through its wide experience in the industry, EBS had learned that the best method for smaller utilities such as CP&L to raise large amounts of capital was to form a holding company in charge of many such small firms. The holding company's larger asset base would attract investors more readily than could the individual utilities. One such holding company was National Power and Light, formed by EBS in 1921. Carolina Power & Light was made a part of National in 1927, and for the next 20 years would satisfy its capital requirements via its new parent company.

The Great Depression

On April 6, 1926, CP&L was itself reconstituted into a new and larger corporation. Along with the former CP&L, the new company included Yadkin River Power Company, Asheville Power and Light, Pigeon River Power Company, and Carolina Power Company. Together, the utilities served 130 communities throughout the central parts of North Carolina and South Carolina, providing up to 59,000 kilowatts of power to about 20,000 customers. It was not long before the Great Depression slowed CP&L's growth, however, as the region's big textile mills reduced operations and the economy generally crumbled. To replace the lost industrial revenue, new CP&L president Louis V. Sutton initiated a sales program designed once again to increase the amount of electricity used in the home. CP&L published an "electric cookbook" and encouraged the adoption of the latest home conveniences, cut its rates, and halted all new construction until the economy showed signs of reviving.

In the meantime, the electrical industry's highly concentrated organization continued to attract criticism. The power trust, as its opponents labeled the GE-based network of utilities, responded by pointing out that the cost of electricity per kilowatt hour had fallen steadily since the industry's beginning, but the persistent allegations of monopoly caused GE to distribute its EBS stock to GE's shareholders in 1924. Of equal concern, however, was the number of electrical holding companies across the country whose often-precarious financing was underscored in 1932 by the collapse of Samuel Insull's midwestern power conglomerate. In response, Congress passed the Public Utility Holding Company Act in 1935, setting restrictions on such organizations and placing them under the jurisdiction of the Securities and Exchange Commission (SEC).

Becoming a Public Company

As part of a general campaign, the SEC began dissolution proceedings against National Power and Light in 1940, and the holding company's stock was finally given over in 1946 to its parent, EBS. Two years later, EBS in turn sold most of its stock in CP&L to the public, at which time CP&L became a wholly independent, investor-owned utility with its stock traded on the New York Stock Exchange.

The robust postwar economy of the 1950s was accompanied by a huge increase in the demand for electricity among both residential and industrial consumers. To provide the needed power, CP&L began constructing a series of new plants of unprecedented size. Major plants were added at a rate of about one every two years during the 1950s, the majority of them using coal-fired steam generators in place of the earlier hydro-electric units. In 1956 CP&L began experimenting with the third great source of electric power, nuclear reaction. It formed the Carolinas-Virginia Nuclear Power Association with three other regional utilities to study the details of nuclear power generation. The group built a prototype reactor at Parr Shoals, South Carolina, where electricity was first obtained from nuclear fission in 1963. Encouraged by the results, CP&L applied for and received approval from the Atomic Energy Commission to build its own full-scale nuclear plant, upon which it began work at Hartsville, South Carolina, in 1966. When it came on-line several years later, the Robinson Number 2 Reactor was the first commercial nuclear reactor in the Carolinas, and, with energy sales tripling during the hectic 1960s, CP&L planned a second unit at Southport, North Carolina. Along with its growing confidence in nuclear power, CP&L increased its electrical capacity by joining a power pool formed by utilities in the Carolinas-Virginia area. This 1964 agreement, and its 1970 revision, provided for a flexible sale and purchase of power among the participating utilities as needed.

Problems in the 1970s

With the death of Sutton in 1970, CP&L entered a new era, in several ways. Shearon Harris became the company's chief executive, but more fundamental were the changes wrought by the 1973–74 oil crisis and subsequent, prolonged "stagflation." CP&L was hit by a double blow of rocketing fuel costs and a contracting economy, at a time when its ambitious construction projects were well under way and soaking up great amounts of cash. When Consolidated Edison of New York, the nation's largest public utility, failed to pay a dividend in the first quarter of 1974, Wall Street's faith in utilities was shaken, and CP&L found that it could not obtain financing at reasonable rates. Thus, although the company escaped immediate damage during the energy crunch by passing along to the customer its higher fuel costs, CP&L was forced in 1975 to postpone plans for two steam and three nuclear generators, the first in a series of delays and cancellations that would continue to trouble CP&L.

To cope with the company's difficult conditions, CP&L shook up its management. Harris remained chairman but handed the presidency to Sherwood H. Smith, Jr., who remained the company's chief executive in 1991. Under Smith, CP&L abandoned uncontrolled growth for a more conservative strategy. With the financial, construction, and fuel costs of new plants rising faster than consumers would agree to higher rates, most utilities began to advocate energy conservation in the 1970s to relieve themselves of the need to raise ever more capital. In the aftermath of the Three Mile Island, Pennsylvania, nuclear accident of 1979, nuclear construction came to a virtual standstill for the next decade. CP&L canceled the nuclear units it had postponed in 1975, and, during the 1980s, slowly gave up hope of completing more than one of the four nuclear units originally planned for its Shearon Harris Plant in New Hill, North Carolina. In the atmosphere of tighter inspections following Three Mile Island, CP&L had not won for itself a particularly distinguished reputation. The Nuclear Regulatory Commission levied a number of fines against the company for poor performance, including a 1983 levy of $600,000 that was then the largest civil penalty ever assessed for nuclear mismanagement.

CP&L planned no new coal or nuclear construction projects through the end of the century. With electrical demand slowing and the company's problems with nuclear plants still fresh in the minds of management, CP&L decided to supply its next 2,000 megawatts of capacity by means of smaller, combustion turbine generators. These provided, in the words of CP&L chairman and president Smith, "reasonably short construction schedules, relatively low cost, and quick start-up when needed"—three qualities lacking in the average coal- or nuclear-fired steam plant. The company also planned to continue purchasing significant amounts of electricity from its sister utilities in the region, and had even resorted to selling four of its units to a state agency and then buying back electricity as needed.

Transition to Deregulation in the 1990s

The company was forced to rethink its long-term plans, however, when Congress passed the Federal Energy Policy Act of 1992. Although many utilities welcomed the coming deregulation, the transition from monopoly to competitive marketplace would be challenging. CP&L in particular was threatened by the prospect of competition. Having relied on set rates to recover the costs of its nuclear power plants, CP&L would have a difficult time if low-cost utilities forced electric prices down. The depreciation on such an expensive capital investment would create a large burden for CP&L in a competitive market.

CP&L approached the coming deregulation by cutting costs and attempting to make its nuclear plants more efficient. The company hired new managers for its nuclear plants in 1993, and the Brunswick nuclear plant, which had been plagued with problems, began to show improvement. Two years later, the company announced plans to lower the operating costs of its nuclear plants by $80 million by the end of the century.

An expanding economy in 1995 increased demand for electricity and helped raise CP&L's systemwide sales by almost ten percent. The company's bulk-power sales more than tripled that year, and the company responded by raising its shareholder's dividends. The following year Sherwood Smith retired as chief executive officer, although he continued on as chair of the company's board. William Cavanaugh, who took over as CEO, oversaw further cost cutting and sales expansion. Systemwide sales were up 2.9 percent, and bulk-power sales were up approximately 50 percent. In 1996 operating costs were reduced by $8 million, and the company lowered its fuel costs by renegotiating a coal-supply contract. According to CP&L, this new contract and another renegotiated the previous year would save the company more than $275 million.

The realization of the company's ambitious cost-cutting goals was postponed by the extensive damage caused by Hurricane Fran, which swept through in September 1996 and left 70 percent of CP&L's customers without electricity. The Federal Emergency Management Agency calculated that the power outage caused by Fran was the largest caused by any hurricane in U.S. history. Still, CP&L managed to restore power to almost all customers within ten days. The cost, however, totaled $95 million, $40 million of which was attributed to operations and maintenance and would be amortized over a 40-month period.

In 1997 cost cutting at the company's nuclear plants continued, with CP&L planning to eliminate 150 positions at the Brunswick plant by the end of the year. CP&L also announced plans to make a major acquisition as part of the company's goal to double its annual revenues and net income by 2001. Industry analysts speculated that a natural gas distribution company was the most likely target. CP&L would face fewer regulatory constraints with the acquisition of a natural gas company, although the purchase of one or more electric utilities in territories not adjoining CP&L's current territory remained a possibility.

Although CP&L was preparing for its inevitable entrance into a more competitive arena, the company urged regulators to move slowly in changing the existing system. Pointing to a booming local economy and the Carolinas' relatively low electric rates, CP&L advocated a wait-and-see approach, claiming this strategy would let them learn from other states' mistakes. With deregulation imminent, Cavanaugh remarked in the company's 1996 annual report, "The urgency I feel is for preparing this company to grow and succeed no matter what the rules of the game are. I'm confident we will not only be a successful competitor, we will be a leader. As for the issue of restructuring the industry, it's more important to do it right than do it fast."

Principal Subsidiaries

CaroNet, LLC; CaroHome, LLC; CaroCapital, Inc.; Nuclear Power Associates, Inc.

Further Reading

A *Brief History of Carolina Power & Light Company,* Raleigh, N.C.: Carolina Power & Light Company, 1984.
"Carolina Power Plans to Cut 150 Positions," *Greensboro News and Record,* November 26, 1997, p. B6.
Marshall, Kyle, "CP&L May Be in Buying Mood," *The News and Observer,* November 1, 1997, p. D1.
Mitchell, Sidney A., *S.Z. Mitchell and the Electrical Industry,* New York: Farrar Strauss & Cudahy, 1960.

—Jonathan Martin
—updated by Susan Windisch Brown

Central Garden & Pet Company

3697 Mt. Diablo Boulevard
Lafayette, California 94549
U.S.A.
(510) 283-4573
Fax: (510) 283-6165

Public Company
Incorporated: 1992
Employees: 2,700
Sales: $841 million (1997)
Stock Exchanges: NASDAQ
SICs: 5191 Farm Supplies; 5169 Chemicals & Allied
   Products, Not Elsewhere Classified; 5199 Nondurable
   Goods, Not Elsewhere Classified; 3524 Lawn &
   Garden Equipment; 5083 Farm & Garden Machinery

The largest distributor of lawn and garden and pet supplies in the United States, Central Garden & Pet Company stocks approximately 45,000 products made by 1,000 manufacturers and distributes the merchandise to high-volume retailers such as Kmart, Wal-Mart, and Costco. Central Garden recorded explosive growth during the 1990s as it took advantage of consolidation in its industry by acquiring competitors. From $25 million in sales in 1987, the company's sales volume mushroomed to $841 million a decade later. During the late 1990s, the company operated 41 distribution centers, using these facilities as warehouses to service much of the United States. In addition to its distribution centers, Central Garden also operated eight manufacturing facilities. These production sites were used to manufacture the company's line of lawn and garden and pet supply products, which were sold under the Four Paws, Zodiac, and Grant's brand names.

Background

Central Garden was originally incorporated in 1955, beginning as a small distributor of lawn and garden supplies based in California. Regional in scope, the company recorded measured growth for more than three decades. It was not until the late 1980s that Central Garden began its meteoric rise.

During the late 1980s, distributors in the lawn and garden industry were entering a consolidation phase. As aggressive distributors swallowed up competing firms to increase their stature, a form of corporate Darwinism decided survival: it was either jump on the acquisition bandwagon or be acquired by a competitor. As this industry trend became pervasive, Central Garden sat poised as a $25-million-in-sales company, respectably sized, to be sure, but not nearly large enough to effectively compete once consolidation had progressed to the point where companies of its stature would be dwarfed by industry giants. Accordingly, Central Garden began acquiring competitors to insure its long-term survival.

Given its financial limitations, Central Garden could not become too ambitious in its acquisition campaign. The company concentrated on purchasing small, "mom-and-pop" distributors and gradually added retail customers to its fold. This incremental strategy worked well, as the company inherited the strong client relationships developed by its local and regional acquisitions. At the beginning of the 1990s, however, the company made one enormous acquisition that proved instrumental in its transformation.

1990 Acquisition of Weyerhaeuser Garden Supply

In the late 1980s, one of the nation's largest companies was implementing a corporate strategy that would provide Central Garden with the opportunity to realize phenomenal growth in one bold move. Late in the decade, forest-products behemoth Weyerhaeuser Company was reeling from the weight and sprawl of its multifarious operations. Diversification into a host of businesses had carried the corporation into insurance, home building, mortgage banking, and as far afield as disposable diaper production, creating an incongruous whole capable of generating more than $10 billion in annual revenue but hindered by depressingly low profits. New management put into place in 1988 was determined to arrest the downward slide of profits and decided to divest all businesses that did not fit with the corporation's core forest products business. One subsidiary after an-

Company Perspectives:

Central—which supplies more than 45,000 products to over 10,000 retail stores each week—continues to demonstrate its unique capabilities which go beyond the scope of traditional distribution services. In addition to providing order taking, shipping, and billing services, Central also offers customers a wide array of value-added services designed to increase the sales and profitability of manufacturers and retailers alike. For example, Central offers just-in-time inventory management, in-store shelf design and display building support, advertising and promotional programs, weekly store sales calls, training, merchandising, and Electronic Data Interchange (EDI) for paperless, cost-saving transactions with our customers.

other was put on the auction block as the 1980s concluded, including Weyerhaeuser's lawn and garden supplies business, Weyerhaeuser Garden Supply Co.

Central Garden acquired Weyerhaeuser Garden Supply in 1990, paying $32 million for the distributor. "It's definitely a case of the shark swallowing the whale," a Central Garden executive noted in reference to the deal that, overnight, made the company a major, national player. By the end of 1991, the first full year that Central Garden and Weyerhaeuser Garden Supply operated as one entity, sales reached $280 million, with the former Weyerhaeuser operations accounting for $190 million, or nearly 70 percent, of the total. Bolstered by the network of clients inherited through the deal, Central Garden entered the early 1990s with 25 distribution centers that enabled it to serve retail clients in 37 states.

In the wake of the acquisition, Central Garden derived roughly half its revenue volume from ten customers, the high-volume retailers that included mass merchants, warehouse clubs, regional and national chains of drug and grocery stores, and large nurseries. These customers relied on Central Garden as the source for selected merchandise because of the efficiency of dealing with one supplier rather than numerous manufacturers. For their part, manufacturers turned to Central Garden for distribution help because many, either purposely or because of financial constraints, eschewed the heavy costs associated with operating their own direct-sales distribution operations. Central Garden helped retailers organize and schedule inventories, provided quick, reliable delivery of a broad assortment of merchandise unavailable from one manufacturer, and made the process of obtaining merchandise more cost-effective.

Early 1990s Expansion

Poised as one of the nation's largest distributors in an industry whose annual volume exceeded $20 billion, Central Garden sought to make itself the distributor of choice for all manufacturers and high-volume retailers of lawn and garden supplies. To accomplish this goal, the company focused on further expansion through acquisition.

Intent not only on expanding its lawn and garden distributing network, Central Garden also was looking to diversify its business and thereby reduce its dependence on the seasonal lawn and garden business. In 1991 the company acquired a pet supplies distributor, and pet supplies soon became Central Garden's fastest-growing business segment. With this promising venture beginning to develop, Central Garden next moved to consolidate its acquisitions and pay off mounting debt by selling shares in the company in a mid-1992 public offering. The investing public considered Central Garden an attractive opportunity, wooed by its position as the principal distributor to major retail chains Kmart, Costco, Home Base, and Payless Cashways. The company by this point also ranked as a major supplier to Wal-Mart, Home Depot, and Price Club, and figured to strengthen and increase its portfolio of clientele given the expansion-oriented mindset of the company's management. The public offering raised roughly $13 million, and from there the company resumed its acquisitive activities, building its distributor network thread by thread.

Between January 1993 and January 1994, Central Garden acquired six small garden and pet distributors, purchases that added $70 million to the company's sales volume. By the end of 1993, sales had swelled to $330 million, and the company showed no signs of slowing its growth. With more than 18,000 gardening, pet, and pool supplies in its 30 distribution warehouses, the company's influence in manufacturing and retailing sectors was increasing with each acquisition. Sales rose to $421 million in 1994 and to $437 million in 1995. By the time 1995's financial totals were tallied, Central Garden held sway in the lawn and garden supplies industry, ranking as the largest distributor in the country. In terms of the pet supplies industry, Central Garden was rapidly gaining ground on its competition. The company figured as the dominant distributor on the West Coast and its national presence was building steadily. Acquisitions—12 had been completed during the previous three years—had catapulted the company to the top. Industry consolidation, which had been invigorated by the concurrent consolidation of sales in the retail sector, had forced distributors to consolidate their operations. In this endeavor, Central Garden came out as the winner, drawing praise from industry observers and gaining significant business from large national retailers. "Central Garden," one analyst remarked, "has been able to lead the pet supply and lawn and garden product industry consolidation and has emerged as the preeminent distributor." Although much had been achieved, with annual sales increasing more than 15-fold in a seven-year span, the company exited the mid-1990s prepared to increase its stature further.

One important development that greatly increased Central Garden's revenue-generating capabilities was an agreement signed with The Solaris Group in 1995. Solaris manufactured lawn and garden products sold under the Ortho, Round-Up, and Green Sweep brand names, which historically had been major contributors to Central Garden's sales volume. Before 1995, Central Garden had served as the non-exclusive distributor for Solaris, but during the mid-1990s Solaris increasingly pursued direct sales to retailers and, consequently, took substantial business away from Central Garden. The agreement signed in 1995 named Central Garden as the exclusive distributor for Solaris. The benefits of the agreement were substantial in both the long and the short term, adding nearly $100 million to Central Garden's sales volume in 1996.

Late 1990s Growth

Acquisitions continued to be the prevailing theme describing Central Garden's development in 1996. Two pet supply distributors, Kenlin Pet Supply and Longhorn Pet Supply, were purchased in 1996, extending the company's national distributorship coverage. Following these two acquisitions, Central Garden ranked as the leading distributor of pet supplies in the country, having parlayed its dominant position in the West to secure many of the nation's markets. In December 1996, the company further strengthened its pet-supply business by acquiring Sandoz Agro for $41 million. The addition of Sandoz Agro added $43 million in sales, gave Central Garden ownership of products marketed to pet and veterinary industries, and ceded production rights to Methoprene, an insect growth regulator that served as the active ingredient in flea and pest control sprays, shampoos, collars, powders, foggers, and aerosols.

By the end of the company's 1996 fiscal year, sales rose to $619.6 million, which represented a more than 40 percent increase over the previous year's total. The increase recorded in 1997 was nearly as large, as the acquisitions completed after 1995 began to deliver their full influence on the company's financial stature.

In 1997 several key acquisitions promised to boost sales for the remainder of the decade. Early in the year, before the Sandoz Agro transaction was finalized, Central Garden acquired Four Paws Products, Ltd., Inc., a manufacturer of branded pet supply products. One of the nation's largest manufacturers of dog, cat, reptile, and small animal products, Four Paws sold its products under the Magic Coat and Four Paws brand names and distributed them throughout the United States, Canada, Europe, and Asia. On the heels of this deal, Central Garden acquired the pet supply business of Country Pet Supply, a distributor of pet supply and pet food products in the southeastern United States. Next, Central Garden strengthened its lawn and garden holdings, acquiring southern California-based Ezell Nursery Supply, Inc., a distributor of lawn and garden, barbecue, and patio products. At roughly the same time the Ezell Nursery deal was completed, Central Garden acquired a one-third equity interest in Commerce LLC, the leading distributor of lawn and garden products on the East Coast.

The bustling activity in 1997 lifted Central Garden's total sales by more than 35 percent. Ten years after recording $25 million in sales, Central Garden comprised operations that generated $841 million in sales. Although the company entered the late 1990s as an enterprise nearing its 50th anniversary, nearly all that constituted the company had been developed during the previous decade. Viewed from this perspective, Central Garden's management hoped the company's second decade of existence as a national distributor would be as successful as the first.

Principal Subsidiaries

Grant Laboratories, Inc.; Matthews Redwood and Nursery Supply Co.; Wellmark International; Four Paws Products, Ltd.; Ezell Nursery Supply, Inc.

Principal Divisions

Lawn & Garden Group; Pet Group; Proprietary Brands Group.

Further Reading

Carlsen, Clifford, "Garden Products Firm to Harvest $30M in Offering," *San Francisco Business Times,* November 3, 1995, p. 3.
"Central Garden & Pet," *Fortune,* February 7, 1994, p. 137.
"Central Garden, Kenlin Hit Acquisition Trail," *Pet Product News,* March 1997, p. 4.
Chadwell, John, "Central Garden Makes Move on Industry," *Pet Product News,* February 1994, p. 9.
Dustman, Karen Dale, "Survival of the Fittest?," *Pet Product News,* January 1997, p. 1.
Hunt-Stewart, Linnea, "Central Flea & Tick," *Pet Product News,* January 1997, p. 1.
Sweet, Jack, "Central Garden & Pet Acquires Sandoz Flea Business," *Pet Product News,* December 1996, p. 27.

—Jeffrey L. Covell

Central Independent Television

Central House
Broad Street
Birmingham B1 2JP
England
44 171-634-4000
Fax: 44 171-615-1794
Web site: http://www.centraltv.co.uk

Wholly Owned Subsidiary of Carlton Communications plc
Incorporated: 1982
Sales: £400 million (1994 est.)
Employees: 830
SICs: 4833 Television Broadcasting Stations

Since 1993, Central Independent Television has been an operating unit of one of Great Britain's largest broadcast television and video companies, Carlton Communications plc. Central was ranked third among the nation's independent television (ITV) broadcasters when it received a £760 million (US$1.1 billion) takeover bid from number-two Carlton. The combination of these two companies' operations formed Britain's largest independent broadcaster, with the ability to reach more than one-third of the nation's population and a 30 percent share of the ITV segment's annual advertising income.

Even before the merger, Central boasted ITV's largest geographic reach and its biggest audience, encompassing nine million homes in the British Midlands region. The company's award-winning resumé of programs has included *Spitting Image*, the 1980s series that used puppets to parody international politicians and celebrities; the *Viewpoint* series of documentaries; and some of ITV's longest-airing drama series, including *Boon, Inspector Morse,* and *Soldier, Soldier.*

Postwar Roots

Central's roots as a broadcaster date back to 1954 when independent commercial television was introduced in England to break the monopoly of the BBC, the country's state-run television network. In February 1956, Independent Television (ITV) arrived in the Midlands with weekend broadcasts, which were replaced by daily programming by the end of the year. During the weekdays, programming was handled by Associated Television (ATV), a subsidiary of Associated Communications Corporation, and by ABC on the weekends.

ATV was granted the franchise for the Midlands broadcasting operation in 1968 and held it until January 1982, when the Independent Broadcasting Authority (IBA), Britain's television regulatory body at the time, announced the franchise would not be automatically re-awarded. What was more, the IBA stipulated that ACC could hold no more than a 51 percent interest in Central and had to build and operate studios in regions served by the broadcaster with the latest in equipment.

A new company named Central Independent Television was formed to take control of the new Midlands franchise in January 1982. Major stockholders included ACC (51 percent), leisure group Ladbrokes (ten percent), publishing group DC Thomson (15 percent) and Pergamon (nine percent), led by the late Robert Maxwell. Central's boundaries at the time ranged from the borders of Wales in the west to Lincolnshire in the east, and from Cheshire in the north to the Home Counties in the south. Covering an estimated 14,000 square miles and serving more than nine million people, Central had the largest audience of Britain's 12 independent ITV broadcasters.

In May 1982, ACC was taken over by TVW Enterprises, led by Australian media magnate, Robert Holmes à Court. The IBA ruled that ACC's 51 percent stake in Central be put in trust, thus freezing its voting right until ACC had reduced its shareholding in the broadcaster. Therefore, in May 1983, ACC sold off its stake in Central. Sears Holdings purchased a 20 percent shareholding, Ladbrokes and DC Thomson increased their stakes to 20 percent each, and Pergamon took its ownership to 12.5 percent.

In line with IBA requirements, renovation of Central's four Birmingham studios at Broad Street was completed in 1982. A new broadcast center was opened a year later. In addition, Nottingham saw the opening of the $42.5 million, four-studio East Midlands Television Center in late 1983. The formal ribbon-cutting ceremony in March 1984 was attended by the Duke of Edinburgh.

IPO in 1986

In October 1986, Central issued public shares to be listed on the London International Stock Exchange. Institutional investors in London were among the broadcaster's leading stockholders.

From its beginnings, Central had a mandate to operate a local news service broadcast to each of the company's three main markets: Central West, East, and South. The broadcaster eventually had the most morning and evening local news viewers of any ITV news program. For its news broadcasts, Central was supplied with national and international programs by Independent Television News (ITN), the national news bureau owned and operated by all ITV regional broadcasters.

Central also continued to produce strong drama and entertainment programs for broadcast in its own market and throughout Britain and internationally. The broadcaster's most popular programs included the satirical weekly *Spitting Image,* the investigative current affairs program *The Cook Report,* and such drama series as *Inspector Morse* and *Soldier Soldier.*

Much, though certainly not all, of Central's drama output, tended towards high-brow content for sale abroad. The popular *Legacy of Civilization* series, a six-part documentary exploring the effects of ancient history on modern life, was an early example. British television has always emphasized cultural programming. Central and other ITV franchises still broadcast a large amount of ballet and opera to complement their lighter drama and entertainment content. Broadcasts of the established arts, though top sellers in foreign markets for Central, are in part defensive. Because quality of programming is a key factor in the granting of franchises to broadcasting companies, a tendency for high culture is often observed in ITV programming when franchises are up for renewal.

International Alliances, New Technologies in the Late 1980s

In 1986, Central established Television Sales and Marketing Services Ltd. (TSMS), a joint venture between itself and Anglia Television, another ITV broadcaster. The role of TSMS was to secure airtime sales and program sponsorships, in part to recover production costs. In addition, TSMS acted as consultant to international broadcasters like BBC Select, Nederland 1 in The Netherlands, and Westcountry.

In 1989, Central spent $10 million to build a high-tech regional news center at Abingdon, near Oxford. This gave the broadcasters three main regional centers: Abingdon, Nottingham, and Birmingham. In addition, Central operated offices in London, New York, Sydney, and Hamburg. Besides functioning as news-gathering centers, these international bureaus also facilitated international sales and sponsorship of Central's programs.

International cooperation between program makers had become the buzzword in the increasingly global television market during the late 1980s. Broadcasters found they could spread out the cost—and the risk—of producing programs, if they could bring in overseas partners. The key was recognizing, and taking advantage of, the demands of the television industry beyond their own home markets. British English-language programming—Central's included—had long secured wide audiences around the world, a legacy of the British Empire. Central looked to tap into this growing international system of coproduction, cofinancing, sales, pre-sales, and sponsor-packaging to reduce the cost of its own program production by pooling resources with others and securing yet more markets for its output.

Central also had to keep pace with rapid changes in the technology of the television industry. In the mid- to late 1980s, the number of terrestrial, cable, and satellite television channels worldwide was escalating. In addition, a revolution was taking place in high-definition television. Program production and distribution was entering the world of digital compression, which would multiply the available frequency spectrum and transform home television viewing.

The regional broadcaster was also looking to counter the growing influence of U.S. programs being sold to Europe and worldwide. As Leslie Hill, Central's managing director, said in 1990: "American culture seems to be in danger of overwhelming that of some other countries, including Britain. I believe we should guard against that." Hill felt that cooperation between foreign broadcasters, especially between those in Canada, Europe, and Australia, could not only reduce production costs but counter a U.S. programming offensive. "This international activity may appear to boost the ego and self-importance of an industry notoriously aware of its image, but it is this international cooperation that lies behind some of our more ambitious program projects," Hill commented. By the late 1980s, Central was the United Kingdom's top commercial exporter of programming to the United States.

International Coproductions Central completed the 1988 *Legacy of Civilization* documentary series, made in conjunction with Maryland Public Television. Another series, *Nuclear Age,* was produced along with WGBH, a Boston-based public television station, and NHK, a Japanese broadcaster.

Early 1990s Brings Deregulation

Deregulation of the British television industry, first introduced by then Prime Minister Margaret Thatcher in 1988, had a profound effect on Central Television's future. The British government sought to shake up the country's television market by ending the monopoly that existing ITV franchise broadcasters, including Central, seemingly enjoyed. The 1989 Broadcasting Bill, introduced by the government and leading to the 1990 Broadcasting Act, called for 16 ITV contractors to bid in May 1991 to retain their franchises against rival tenders.

With no anticipated rivals for its franchise, Central was expected to emerge strongly from the 1991 auction, since it could bid low and win. Prior to the sale, the broadcasting company had focused on its core strength: quality program production and distribution. For the East, West, and South Midlands television regions, Central bid a mere £2,000 ($3,400) per year. That figure paled in comparison to those of other ITV franchise bidders, who offered many millions as part of annual bids to the British treasury. But without a challenger, Central's low-ball bid won. In addition to this flat fee, Central agreed to pay the British Treasury 11 percent of each year's advertising, subscription, and sponsorship income. In October 1991, the company was granted the seven-day-a-week broadcast license extending from January 1, 1993 through the year 2002. This low cost structure would make Central what *Variety* magazine's Steve Clarke called "the best financial bet in British television."

Central profited yet again from the ITV auction after Meridian, a consortium in which Central held a 20 percent stake, was successful in securing the license to broadcast in South and South East England. Meridian was led by MAI, a financial services group whose businesses included brokerage and market research, and had a 65 percent stake in the bidding consortium.

In September 1991, just prior to the announcement of license awards, David Justham, Central's chairperson, died. He was replaced as company chair by Leslie Hill, who had joined Central as managing director in 1987. An accountant with no previous experience in broadcast television, Hill's ability to guide the company was viewed with skepticism. Over the next five years, however, the new leader of Central would earn the respect of both his broadcasting peers and his company's shareholders.

In November 1991, Central purchased its rented headquarters in Birmingham and renamed it West Midlands Television Center. Also that year, Television Sales and Marketing Services acquired the airtime sales operation of Ulster Television in Northern Ireland. Continued cost-cutting measures at this time included the sale in 1991 of Film Fair, the film animation company owned by Central. The broadcaster also disposed of its 25 percent stake in Starstream, the British children's channel, and Central Communications Network, once Central's in-house public relations department before becoming a consultancy. Central also refocused its business by severing ties with Chris Bearde Entertainment, a game show production house that had lost an estimated US$5 million, and Wordstar, a company providing newspapers and magazines with entertainment news worldwide. An internal reorganization split Central into three profit centers: Birmingham-based Central Broadcasting, charged with operation of the ITV license; Nottingham-based Central Productions, the programming arm; and London-based Central Television Enterprises, responsible for international operations. During this same period, employment at the company was slashed by more than half, from over 2,000 to 850.

Central's repositioning after the ITV auction was reflected in its bottom line. Although advertising revenues had fallen throughout the British broadcast market owing to the harsh recession of the early 1990s, Central still posted pre-tax profits up nearly 25 percent at £24.4 million for fiscal 1991, compared with a figure of £19.2 million a year earlier. This profit rise came as company sales continued falling. Revenues of £306.6 million in 1991 were down 2.7 percent from a year earlier, or £315.1 million in 1990. This performance was accomplished on pretax profits of £27 million posted in fiscal 1989, prior to the recession. The broadcaster's stock price multiplied from £3.40 (US$5.84) in 1987 to £12.53 (US$21.55) by the spring of 1992.

That year Zodiac, Central's USA program production subsidiary, unveiled its second animated program, *Mr. Bogus.* Its first series, *Widget,* began re-runs in the all-important U.S. television market. Also that year, Central Music was formed as a separate company within Central Productions to produce music-based programs largely funded by music companies and video distribution. Among its first programs was *Bedrock 11,* a late night music series, and *Lafter Hours,* featuring popular British comedians. *Lafter Hours* triggered a video distribution deal with Virgin Music, a leading British record producer and retailer.

Union With Carlton Communications in 1994

Central appeared in an enviable position among ITV broadcasters in holding the largest franchise, and yet paying the lowest Exchequer levy of a mere £2,000 annually. At the same time, its high profitability made Central a favorable takeover target. In fact, the number-three ITV broadcaster received its first takeover proposal in November 1993, just over one month before legislation permitting the purchase of ITV licensees went into effect. Central accepted the £26 per share, £624 million (US$925 million) bid from Carlton Communications plc during the first week of 1994. (Carlton had owned about 20 percent of Central's equity since 1987, and offered to purchase the remaining shares it did not already own. The bid valued Central at £758 million or US$1.12 billion.) Central's quick acquiescence prompted *The Economist* to frame the deal as "a defensive ploy by two companies frightened of being taken over themselves in 1994, when firms in the rest of Europe will be allowed to buy British commercial-TV stations."

Under the direction of Michael Green, Central's new parent had grown from a US$15 million enterprise in 1983 into a film processing and broadcast media giant. The addition of Central ITV vaulted Carlton Communications' commercial television broadcasting division from a mere seven percent of annual revenues to the company's biggest and most profitable business interest, and made Carlton the UK's second-largest ITV broadcaster. Central's estimated £400 million in revenues boosted Carlton's total turnover to a debt-free £1.4 billion in 1994. But as *The Economist* noted, Carlton was still "a pipsqueak" among global media firms like Rupert Murdoch's News Corp. Ltd., Time Warner Inc., Germany's Bertlsmann, and Walt Disney Company. Carlton executives countered that "size for size's sake is not important."

In 1997 analysts with Morgan Stanley, Dean Whitter asserted that "the glory days of ITV broadcasting are over," forecasting that the annual growth of advertising revenues would amount to about two to three percent over inflation. However, Central and Carlton's other ITV properties would continue to serve a valuable function at the media company by providing programming fodder for its growing third-party business. Carlton planned to parlay Central's string of critically- and popularly-acclaimed hits into high-profit international blockbusters.

Principal Divisions

World International Network; Zodiac; Television Sales and Marketing Services; Central Television Enterprises.

Further Reading

"Bidders Facing Becher's Brook of Quality TV," *Observer* (London), May 19, 1991.

"Big Two Face Toughest TV Franchise Fight," *Guardian,* May 16, 1991.

"CIT Optimistic Despite Profit Dip," *Variety,* October 7, 1991, p. 216.

Clarke, Steve, "Central Slowly Climbs to Top With Hill," *Variety,* October 18, 1993, pp. 41–42.

——, "Showtime for Carlton," *Management Today,* February 1996, pp. 34–38.

Coopman, Jeremy, "Corporate Report: Central TV at 10," *Variety,* April 6, 1992, pp. 149–54.

"The Darling Bids of May," *Observer,* May 19, 1991.

Dawtry, Adam, "Carlton's Central Takeover Done Deal," *Variety,* January 10, 1994, p.56.

——, "It's Buyout Hour on ITV," *Variety,* December 13, 1993, pp. 33–34.

"Greenland: British Television," *Economist,* December 4, 1993, pp. 68–69.

"Programming Free-For-All," *Financial Weekly,* March 23–29, 1990.

Root, Jane, *Open the Box: About Television,* London: Comedia Publishing Group, 1986.

—Etan Vlessing
—updated by April Dougal Gasbarre

Chick-fil-A Inc.

5200 Buffington Road
Atlanta, Georgia 30349
U.S.A.
(404) 765-8000
Fax: (404) 765-8140
Web site: http://www.chick-fil-a.com

Private Company
Incorporated: 1964
Employees: 200
Sales: $569.9 million (1996)
SICs: 5812 Eating Places

With some 722 units in 35 states, Chick-fil-A Inc. is, after KFC and Popeye's/Church's, the United States' third largest fast-food chain specializing in chicken. In addition to the Chick-fil-A restaurants, which are run according to a unique "Operator Agreement," the company in 1985 launched the Dwarf House line of sit-down establishments, and in 1996 opened Truett's Grill as a nostalgic 1950s-style diner. Whatever the type of restaurant, the focus remains chicken, and by far Chick-fil-A's most famous product is its chicken fillet sandwich, created by founder Truett Cathy in the early 1960s. From small beginnings in a restaurant outside Atlanta, Cathy has built Chick-fil-A into a firm worth an estimated $1 billion, but as of the late 1990s he had no plans to take it public. To sell shares to stockholders would, he suggested, change the very core of Chick-fil-A as a family-run business with a focus on people.

The First Dwarf House

On May 23, 1946, 25-year-old Truett Cathy and his younger brother Ben opened a restaurant called the Dwarf House at 461 South Central Avenue in Hapeville, Georgia, a small town south of Atlanta. The Cathy brothers had begun the enterprise with $4,000 they were able to raise, partly by selling Truett's car, combined with $6,600 on loan from a bank, and for their money they had a restaurant only 50 feet wide and 150 feet deep—including the kitchen. To further enhance the difficulties

facing them, the recent shift from a wartime to a peacetime economy had created supply problems that affected companies much bigger than their own. At least larger firms established before the end of World War II had been able to adapt to an environment of scarcity; the Cathy brothers, on the other hand, had to educate themselves quickly in the procurement of scarce resources, even using discarded building materials to finish off their restaurant in time for opening day.

The Cathys' father, an insurance salesman, had lost heavily in the stock market crash of 1929, and had never recovered emotionally from his loss. Eventually the father died, and their mother had to take in boarders. In addition to offering a room, she served meals, and Truett Cathy later recalled watching her cook for her guests one of the South's most distinctive contributions to American cuisine: fried chicken. But her boy Truett was already a young food-service entrepreneur in his own right, having figured out that he could purchase six-packs of Coca-Cola in Atlanta, then sell them to neighbors in Hapeville for a nickel apiece, thus making five cents profit on every six bottles sold.

Eventually he would make more money selling magazine subscriptions, but at about the time he came of age, war broke out. Ben went to fight in Europe, but Truett had relatively easy duty as a clerk, and never went further from home than Fort Lewis, Washington. Truett was discharged in 1944, and once Ben came home, the two brothers began to plan their future. They decided they would start a restaurant, and after spending some time as employees of a woman who promised to set them up in business but never did, they opened the Dwarf House.

Besides problems with supply, the Cathys had to deal with bureaucracy and other foibles, and they ended their first day with sales of $58.20—a modest beginning, but a beginning still. Most of their patronage came from employees of the nearby Ford plant, as well as the emerging Atlanta airport next to Hapeville, and many of these seemed to be repeat customers. The fact of this steady repeat clientele engendered in Truett an awareness of what would become a key element of Chick-fil-A's success: as he stated it in his 1989 book *It's Easier to Succeed Than to Fail,* "Word of mouth in the food business is more important than any other source of advertising. It's better

---

Company Perspectives:

The mission of Chick-fil-A is "to glorify God by being a faithful steward of all that is entrusted to us; and to have a positive influence on all who come in contact with Chick-fil-A."

---

to maintain your present customers than to spend a lot of time and expense replacing them with new ones.''

Another key element of the Chick-fil-A corporate identity was forged in those early days: the policy of operating six days a week, but "never on Sunday." The Dwarf House, in fact, was open 24 hours a day, but closed from midnight on Saturday night to midnight on Sunday night; and in more than five decades, the policy has not changed. In the beginning, Cathy said in a 1997 speech to the Newcomen Society, "it wasn't that we were holy—we were just tired!" But in fact Cathy's religious beliefs as a devout Christian informed not only this aspect of his business, which is based on the fourth of the Ten Commandments from the Bible, but many others. Yet Cathy did not set out to proselytize so much as to set an example: "I never intended to make a big issue out of being closed on Sunday," he told the Newcomen Society. "In fact, it always amazes me that other people bring up the subject so often." On a professional level, he has said, the policy helps him and his employees to stay fresh in body and soul, and thus it ultimately redounds to the company's benefit.

In 1949, Ben Cathy was killed in a plane crash along with a third brother, Horace. Now Truett had to run Dwarf House on his own, and in 1951 he opened a second restaurant in the nearby town of Forest Park. For the next nine years, Cathy prospered as he and his wife Jeannette raised their family; then in 1960, another tragedy came when fire destroyed the Forest Park restaurant. "Without adequate insurance to rebuild the restaurant," Cathy said in his 1997 speech, "I faced some tough questions. Do I take a giant step back to just one restaurant, which would mean having to lay off employees? Do I incur more debt and rebuild the restaurant as it was? Or is it time for something new? I was convinced it was time for something new."

The Birth of Chick-fil-A

Cathy had become aware of the idea of fast-food restaurants, which he judged to be the coming wave in food service. So with $90,000 in borrowed capital, he opened a new restaurant in Forest Park based on the concept of Li'l Abner restaurants in Chicago. It seemed like the right idea, but he soon discovered that customers preferred the Dwarf House to his new idea. (In *It's Easier to Succeed,* Cathy would later write "Customers are very sensitive to change.") So, he recalled in 1997, "I settled back into the original Hapeville restaurant, [but] I started getting restless." Inspired by a comment from a friend and colleague, Ted Davis, he started experimenting with ways to make chicken a viable fast-food item.

In the kitchen, Cathy began experimenting with different ways to cook and serve poultry quickly and economically. He started with a breast fillet, and began serving it fried on a bun, which eliminated the problem of customers getting grease on their fingers. This was the prototypical Chick-fil-A sandwich, and Cathy began to perfect it with different cooking methods (eventually he settled on a pressure cooker with peanut oil), and different spices and seasonings—including the addition of a pickle to the sandwich, which would become a lasting part of the Chick-fil-A formula.

But they were not yet called Chick-fil-A sandwiches; they were just chicken sandwiches, which rapidly began to outsell hamburgers on the Dwarf House menu. In 1963 Cathy decided to give them a name in order to market the product. A patent attorney had advised him that he could use ordinary words for his product name, as long as he misspelled or in some way altered the terms from their dictionary usage. Working with the words "chicken" and "fillet," Cathy came up with Chick-fil-A, making use of the "A" to convey the concept of being the first or best. He hired the Richard Heiman Company to create the logo that Chick-fil-A still used more than three decades later, and in 1964 he incorporated the company.

At first Chick-fil-A sold its product to other restaurants during the mid-1960s, but Cathy—wary that a large chain would take his idea, change it slightly, and make it their own—decided to move from selling licensed products to operating Chick-fil-A restaurants. In 1967 the first of these opened in Greenbriar Mall south of Atlanta, the first indoor mall in the Southeast.

Growing with the Malls

The next 15 years would see extraordinary growth, both for Chick-fil-A and for its hometown of Atlanta. The latter's airport, now named Hartsfield, would become one of the busiest in the world. Hapeville and Forest Park, once just small towns down the road from Atlanta, would become suburbs, absorbed in the urban sprawl of one of the nation's fastest growing cities. Atlanta's leading homegrown businesses would come to include not just Coca-Cola, but Delta Airlines, the Turner communications empire, and Chick-fil-A.

In 1967 Cathy had hit on a stroke of brilliance, one which would come to seem as basic as sliced bread, but like sliced bread was once revolutionary: "At the time," he told the Newcomen Society 30 years later, "there were precious few restaurants—fast-food or otherwise—in malls. People would come to the malls to shop and go elsewhere to eat. We saw this as an opportunity to reach customers where they shopped and before they went elsewhere." As malls grew, so did Chick-fil-A. By 1971, it had seven restaurants in Georgia and the Carolinas, and within three years, it would triple that number.

But before the explosive growth of 1971–74, several key aspects of Chick-fil-A's corporate philosophy would develop. Cathy articulated four basic tenets: (1) the company would grow not by selling franchises, but by forming joint ventures with independent operators; (2) they would operate exclusively out of shopping malls; (3) financing would come not through debt, but primarily from the company's own profits;

and (4) *people* would be the primary focus of Chick-fil-A. With the exception of (2), which had to be adjusted as shopping malls became saturated with restaurants in the 1980s—a hallmark of Cathy's foresight—these tenets have remained in effect ever since.

Chick-fil-A's operator agreement, and its emphasis on people, are both highly unusual. As the company plans a new location, instead of looking for franchisees, Chick-fil-A conducts a search for a highly responsible person—often from within the organization—to become an operator. That person invests only $5,000 (a token sum compared to the typical investment of a franchisee, which can easily be a quarter of a million dollars) to sublease the restaurant. After six weeks of paid training, the operator is in business with a guaranteed salary of $30,000 a year, plus half of net profits after 15 percent of gross sales goes to Chick-fil-A, Inc. An operator can earn a six-figure income, and operators are motivated to make their restaurants profitable; for this reason, other companies, most notably Outback Steakhouse, have begun to emulate the Chick-fil-A operator agreement.

There are a number of other bonuses for operators, including an annual business meeting for which the company pays all expenses to fly its operators and their spouses to a given location—one year it was Bermuda—for five days of fellowship and training. As for hourly employees, referred to as team members, among their incentives is the "Team Member Scholarship Award" of $1,000, offered to any high school graduate who has worked with the chain for two years at an average of 20 or more hours a week, and has been recommended by their operator. Through these and many other means, Chick-fil-A has managed to have a turnover rate of just 50 percent for hourly employees—compared to a fast-food industry average of 150 percent.

With its strong personnel and its distinctive product, Chick-fil-A grew rapidly in the 1970s alongside the shopping malls in which its restaurants were located. But in 1982, as Cathy recalled in his Newcomen speech, the company "fell victim to its own success." Other restaurant chains, impressed by Chick-fil-A, began marketing their own chicken fillet sandwiches. To counter their competition, Chick-fil-A put coupons in newspapers throughout the country, and the response rate turned out to be twice as much as expected, thus leading to heavy losses. Added to these problems were difficulties created by construction delays and inflation. Cathy, who chose not to receive a salary in 1982 in order not to force a pay cut on employees, called a special meeting of the chain's executive committee. It was to be, in his words, the company's "defining moment."

Cathy's son Dan, by then a leading company executive, asked the committee members three questions: "Why are we in business? Why are we here? Why are we alive?" Because all of the board members were Christians, Cathy recalled in 1997, it was not long before the discussion came to focus on matters of faith. "We all agreed," he recalled, "in the important role Jesus Christ played in our own lives, but none of us liked the idea of parading around our religious faith. We sought, then, to create a statement of our corporate purpose—not to press our beliefs onto others, but rather to influence others in our organization by the example we set in our lifestyle and by the way we treat people." As a result of these discussions, they came up with the company's twofold purpose, which would remain in effect from then on: "To glorify God by being a faithful steward of all that is entrusted to us; To have a positive influence on all who come in contact with Chick-fil-A." Armed with a renewed sense of purpose, Cathy and his leadership began to fight the competition.

Growing Profits, Growing People

Previously reliant mostly on word of mouth, Chick-fil-A in 1982 began to put more focus on advertising, first with the abortive coupon campaign, and then with a successful slogan aimed at reminding the public who created the first chicken fillet sandwich: "First 'n' Best." The company began to impress on its operators three key principles embodied in the abbreviation "QSC": Quality, Service, and Cleanliness. Within six months, sales by the reinvigorated chain had increased by more than 40 percent, and "From that point on," Cathy recalled in 1997, "Chick-fil-A seemed to enjoy one success after another."

In 1982, the company pioneered a new product, chicken nuggets, that would eventually make its way onto the menus of large competitors such as McDonald's. During that year, Chick-fil-A also built a five-story corporate headquarters building on 72 acres of woodland near Hartsfield International Airport. Three years later, in 1985, Chick-fil-A introduced its Dwarf House line, named after the original restaurant, which offered customers a choice of sit-down family dining or carryout. In 1986, Chick-fil-A first ventured outside of the malls, and as the number of free-standing restaurants grew, the company in 1997 predicted that by 2002, these would outnumber mall units.

Menus continued to diversify, though the focus remained on chicken—whether chargrilled, in a salad, cooked as a low-calorie item, or in strips. (The latter, introduced as Chick-n-Strips in 1995, became the company's most successful new addition to its menu.) The company opened new types of restaurants in new types of locations: on a college campus (1992); in a medical facility (1993); in a supermarket (1993); in a business/industrial location at Alabama Power in Birmingham (1994); in a foreign country (at the University of Alberta in Edmonton, Canada, 1994); overseas (in South Africa, 1995); and in an airport (1996).

In 1993, Chick-fil-A opened its 500th restaurant, and in 1996—to celebrate the 50th anniversary of the original Dwarf House—it introduced Truett's Grill as a 1950s-style diner. The "Eat Mor Chickin" advertising campaign, launched in 1997, became enormously successful. Using a style reminiscent of Gary Larson's *Far Side* cartoons, these billboards (the company also introduced radio ads with witty scripts) featured cows painting crudely lettered signs encouraging customers to eat chicken—rather than beef.

The company experienced its 30th consecutive year of increased sales in 1997, and though it was far behind KFC and the Popeye's/Church's chains in sales, it was the third largest company in the chicken segment of the fast-food market. Wall Street analysts estimated the company's worth at $1 billion, but Cathy had no plans to take it public, in part because Chick-fil-A was his creation and he liked the independence offered by a private company, and partly because stockholders would not approve of one of his favorite activities: giving away money.

Cathy remained heavily involved with charities, especially one that he created called WinShape, through which he was able to give educational opportunities to disadvantaged children. The program began in 1983, when he learned that Berry College in Rome, Georgia, would have to close down part of its campus that housed Berry Academy, for children in grades five through 12. Cathy had long been inspired by the story of Martha Berry, who had started the college with little more than a dream, and he was also concerned with having a positive effect on a rising generation of youth. "Every child they build," he told the Newcomen Society, "will be one less adult to mend."

For several decades, Cathy has taught a Sunday school class for 13-year-old boys, and whenever he speaks before a public gathering, he is an ardent booster for WinShape. Starting with a 1996 LPGA golf tournament, the company has sponsored a number of sports activities, most notably the Peach Bowl football game, for which it signed a multiyear contract in 1996. These, too, Cathy sees as opportunities to promote WinShape, and he is just as apt to speak about giving money away as he is about making money. "The purpose of life is giving," he told *Executive Excellence* in 1995. "Contrary to what you may have been taught in business school, your net worth is not the sum of all you have managed to accumulate in your lifetime. When you die, those who survive you will measure your net worth by what you have given." As for the money he has made, as he said in *It's Easier to Succeed Than to Fail,* "Profits should be the score, not the name of the game."

Further Reading

Cathy, Truett, *It's Easier to Succeed Than Fail,* Nashville, Tenn.: Oliver Nelson, 1989.

——, "Speech to Newcomen Society," 1997.

Englander, Todd, "Chick-fil-A: Not Just Chicken Feed," *Incentive,* January 1989, pp. 24, 26.

Gindin, Rona, "Market Segment Report: Chicken," *Restaurant Business,* October 10, 1992, pp. 165–88.

Girardot, Gina, "S. Truett Cathy," *Restaurant Hospitality,* July 1996, p. 34.

Halamandaris, Bill, "The Bottom Line," *Executive Excellence,* August 1995, pp. 11–12.

Hayes, Jack, "Chick-fil-A Launches Retro-Themed Truett's Grill Prototype," *Nation's Restaurant News,* June 3, 1996, p. 71.

——, "Truett Cathy," *Nation's Restaurant News,* February 1996 special issue, p. 52.

Howard, Theresa, "Chick-fil-A Milks Campaign Cows Till They Come Home," *Nation's Restaurant News,* August 26, 1996, p. 14.

McCarthy, Joseph L., "Through the Needle's Eye: The Spiritual CEO," *Chief Executive,* January/February 1996, pp. 48–51.

McNerny, Donald J., "Creating a Motivated Workforce," *HR Focus,* August 1996, pp. 1, 4.

Papiernick, Richard L., "Chick-fil-A System Has 1996 Sales of $569.9M," *Nation's Restaurant Sales,* February 17, 1997, p. 12.

Wolson, Shelly, "RB Leadership Awards: S. Truett Cathy—Never on Sunday."

—Judson Knight

The Chronicle Publishing Company, Inc.

901 Mission Street
San Francisco, California 94103
U.S.A.
(415) 777-1111
Fax: (415) 777-7131
Web site: http://www.sfgate.com

Private Company
Incorporated: 1865
Employees: 2,500
Sales: $534 million (1995)
SICs: 2711 Newspapers; 2731 Book Publishing; 4833
Television Broadcasting Stations; 4822 Telegraph &
Other Communications

Publisher of *The San Francisco Chronicle,* The Chronicle Publishing Company, Inc. is a family owned business with holdings in television broadcasting, book publishing, and newspaper publishing. In addition to *The Chronicle,* Chronicle Publishing owns the Massachusetts-based *Worcester Telegram and Gazette* and the Bloomington, Illinois, *Pantagraph.* The company's book division comprises San Francisco-based Chronicle Books and Osceola, Wisconsin-based Motorbooks International. The company's broadcasting holdings include two television stations in Kansas—KAKE-TV in Wichita and KLBY-TV in Colby—as well as KRON-TV in San Francisco, and WOWT-TV in Omaha, Nebraska.

19th-Century Origins

Exactly 130 years before a publicly-contested family feud erupted over the control of Chronicle Publishing, the two patriarchs of the family, Michael and Charles de Young, were spending their days in a print shop on San Francisco's Clay Street, embarking upon their entrepreneurial career in publishing. Their descendants would wage a bitter war against one another in 1995 for control over a half-billion-dollar enterprise that got its start in that Clay Street print shop, but in 1865, brothers Michael and Charles de Young had to focus on financial matters

of a far lesser magnitude. They had to recoup their initial investment in the business, an outlay of $20. Michael and Charles de Young were teenagers when they resolved to enter the publishing business, but to do so the ambitious brothers needed start-up money. They borrowed a $20 gold piece from their landlord, used the money to buy an old desk, several fonts of used type, some newsprint, and then tucked themselves away in the corner of their landlord's Clay Street print shop. From there began a publishing business that would enrich generations of their descendants and evolve into the venerable media empire known as Chronicle Publishing.

The de Young brothers started with a free theater program sheet they called *The Daily Dramatic Chronicle,* which debuted on January 16, 1865. The four-page *Daily Dramatic* purported itself to be "a daily record of affairs--local, critical, and theatrical," but represented little more than a gossip sheet. The two teenagers handed out the *Daily Dramatic* at hotels, theaters, restaurants, and saloons, and by the end of their first week were able to pay their landlord back. By the end of their first month, the de Young's had increased the circulation of their fledgling effort to 2,000. It was an encouraging start, to be sure, but that successful first month would be soon forgotten when the de Youngs broke free from their role as upstarts and scored an even more remarkable coup. In April—three months after the inexperienced brothers had printed the first copy of the *Daily Dramatic*—Abraham Lincoln was assassinated, and the first newspaper to report the news to San Franciscans was the *Daily Dramatic.* Word of the president's death appeared in the de Youngs' first "extra" edition, hitting the streets several hours before the city's other daily journals reported on the national tragedy. The scoop represented a significant coup for the de Youngs and quickly legitimized their position as news reporters, marking the first pivotal step in their bid to become aggressive, competitive journalists.

Having made a name for themselves with their first great achievement, the de Youngs continued publishing the *Daily Dramatic* for another three years, building their readership base until they believed they had the necessary support to launch what they referred to as a "real newspaper." In 1868, their aspiration materialized with the first issue of *The Daily Morning*

Chronicle, which debuted along with the de Youngs' emphatic proposal ''to publish a bold, bright, fearless and truly independent newspaper, independent in all things, neutral in nothing.'' With this resolute mission statement guiding its course, *The Chronicle* thrived under the stewardship of the de Youngs. Promising talents in San Francisco's literary scene were brought into the fold, including Mark Twain and Bret Harte, who wrote short articles for *The Chronicle* in exchange for desk space. Before long, *The Chronicle* had eclipsed all its rivals in San Francisco and eventually secured the largest circulation west of the Mississippi River.

Although the newspaper's maturation occurred swiftly and strongly, the first few decades of *The Chronicle's* history were not without incident. Readers in San Francisco became keenly aware of the conviction behind the de Youngs' mission statement for *The Chronicle,* particularly the adjectives ''bold'' and ''fearless.'' In 1879, *The Chronicle* published a headline comparing a mayoral candidate named Isaac Kalloch to an ''unclean leper.'' Kalloch, who was a preacher, was not flattered by the comparison and used the pulpit at his church as a soapbox. During a sermon, Kalloch referred to the de Young family as ''bastards of progeny of a whore born in the slums and nursed in the lap of prostitution,'' a description that brought Charles de Young to his feet. Charles countered Kalloch's disparaging remark with his own salvo, but his riposte elevated the feud to a decidedly higher level. Charles shot the preacher in the chest, took aim, and shot him again in the thigh. Kalloch survived the assault, but de Young was not as fortunate. In 1880, Kalloch's son assumed the mantle of revenge, got drunk, and shot Charles de Young in the neck, killing him instantly.

Michael de Young, who managed to avoid the flurry of bullets touched off by his newspaper's ''bold'' and ''fearless'' reporting, stood solely in charge of *The Chronicle* after his brother's demise and, thanks to his early start in the business, enjoyed a remarkably long reign of command. Michael de Young led the family business for 60 years, holding sway until his death in 1925. Shortly before his death, de Young selected his replacement and initiated what would turn out to be a legacy of de Young family control over *The Chronicle* and the businesses that would later be acquired from the profits gleaned from the newspaper. De Young was intent on keeping *The Chronicle* a family business, but he had no son to pass the reins of command to. His only son had died in 1913, leaving him with four daughters at the time of his death. Social customs of the 1920s did not look highly on according women powerful business positions, but de Young was able to keep *The Chronicle* within the family by naming his son-in-law, George Cameron, as his successor. In the decades to come, three branches of the de Young family would take turns controlling *The Chronicle* and its subsidiary businesses. Although none of the company's future leaders bore the de Young name, all were related either through blood or marriage to Michael de Young.

Great Depression and Postwar Period

Not long after Michael de Young's death, *The Chronicle* began to suffer financially, as advertising dropped off during the 1930s. It was the first meaningful setback in what would turn out to be a roller-coaster ride for *The Chronicle* during the 20th century, as the company's fortunes dipped and rose with the passing of every decade. The turnaround from declining advertising during the first half of the 1930s was begun in 1936 when Paul Smith took over as editor. Under Smith's watch, the newspaper was rejuvenated, thanks in large part to the increased attention paid to covering international news. Giving a priority to international news would be *The Chronicle's* saving grace following the conclusion of World War II, when the newspaper's readership began to wane during the late 1940s and early 1950s. Sunday editor Scott Newhall emerged as the hero during this postwar era after being promoted to editor-in-chief in 1952. Newhall recaptured the readers lost during the late 1940s by orchestrating a series of promotions and giveaways. Perhaps more importantly, Newhall increased the coverage allotted to foreign news, building on the work achieved under the leadership of Paul Smith. Newhall established a network of correspondents that stretched around the globe, increasing *The Chronicle's* stature among the leading metropolitan daily newspapers.

While Newhall busied himself at *The Chronicle,* a de Young descendent was managing a new facet of the family business. In 1949, *The Chronicle* had branched out into broadcasting by starting a television station in San Francisco known by its call letters, KRON. An affiliate of the National Broadcasting Company, Inc. (NBC), KRON-TV was headed by a grandson of Michael de Young named Charles de Young Thieriot. Thieriot's rise through the ranks of Chronicle Publishing brought him to the position of assistant publisher at the company by 1952, and it was he who selected Newhall as a replacement for Smith. Thieriot was named editor and publisher in 1955—titles he would hold for more than two decades—and oversaw several of the most definitive changes in the company's history.

Together, Newhall and Thieriot shaped *The Chronicle* into a popular favorite among San Francisco readers. Comics were added, gossip-oriented articles were emphasized, and, perhaps most importantly, columnists were added. By 1960, *The Chronicle* had fully recovered from its postwar problems and slipped past its archrival, *The San Francisco Examiner,* to hold the largest circulation in northern California. As the newspaper flourished, Thieriot continued to expand the reach of his family's business into other areas, furthering the diversification begun with the establishment of KRON. In 1962, Chronicle Features Syndicate was formed to market the work of *The Chronicle's* star columnists, and in 1968 a San Francisco-based book division was formed and named Chronicle Books.

The Chronicle celebrated its 100th anniversary in 1965, a century after the de Young brothers began printing their free theater and gossip sheet on Clay Street. The historic milestone was marked by a historic development that was forward-looking rather than retrospective: in 1965, *The Chronicle* joined forces with its long-time nemesis, the Hearst-controlled *Examiner.* The two newspapers entered into a joint operating agreement (JOA) by forming an agency to handle the operations of the two newspapers jointly, with the exception of the newspapers' editorial departments.

New management took control of Chronicle Publishing and its flagship property *The Chronicle* during the 1970s. Although the transition from one generation of the de Young family to another generation was a peaceful one, the individuals who entered the spotlight in the 1970s became the chief protagonists of the family spat that would capture headlines during the 1990s. Nan Tucker McEvoy, a granddaughter of Michael de Young, began serving as board chairman of the family owned company in 1974, three years before Thieriot's death paved the way for the succession of his son and Michael de Young's great-grandson, Richard Tobin Thieriot, as editor and publisher. Although McEvoy did not take an active role in running Chronicle Publishing until nearly two decades after being named board chairman, her influence would be strongly felt once she became more involved in running the family enterprise. As the leadership issue stood by the late 1970s, however, there were no outward signs of intra-familial dissent. This would change by the mid-1990s. During the interim, Chronicle Publishing diversified its interests.

In the 1980s, Chronicle Publishing began acquiring other newspapers. *The Pantagraph,* published in Bloomington, Illinois, was purchased, as were *The Worcester Telegram and Gazette* and *Sunday Telegram,* which served the second-largest market in New England. Eventually, Chronicle Publishing increased the scope of its newspaper division to include four daily newspapers, three Sunday newspapers, and four weekly publications. By the end of the 1980s, the company had also solidified its position in broadcasting, adding television stations WOWT-TV, an NBC affiliate in Omaha, Nebraska, and three stations in Kansas—KAKE-TV in Wichita, an independent station in Copeland, and KLBY-TV, a satellite station in Colby. In addition to these television stations, Chronicle Publishing also added half a dozen cable television companies. It was these additions to Chronicle Publishing's operations— particularly the broadcasting acquisitions—that were partly responsible for igniting the family feud between McEvoy and her cousins.

Turbulent 1990s

By the early 1990s, Nan McEvoy was the single largest shareholder in the family business and closely involved in running the company's affairs. Her presence alone was probably enough to irk other family members because McEvoy was decidedly more liberal than other de Young descendants who sat on the company's board. Her political leanings were expressed in *The Chronicle's* editorial page, which became far less conservative under her control. Philosophically, McEvoy and her cousins were at odds, creating fundamental differences that were exacerbated by the anemic profitability of the Chronicle Publishing empire. With the exception of the company's book division, each facet of Chronicle Publishing's operations was performing miserably during the early 1990s, and much of the blame was cast on Richard Thieriot, who reportedly rarely entered *The Chronicle's* newsroom and, according to insiders, read the newspaper just as infrequently. The charges of mismanagement were rife, prompting McEvoy to suggest what other family members regarded as unthinkable. McEvoy wanted to bring in outside professional help, an experienced executive from outside the de Young family, something that had never been done in the company's 127-year history.

Under McEvoy's direction, room was made among Chronicle Publishing's nepotistic upper management for the arrival of new blood. Among the notable de Young family members given the axe in 1992 were Richard Thieriot, who had served as editor and publisher since 1977, and Frances "Rannie" Martin III, who headed the company's television operations. Thieriot was replaced in 1993 with John Sias, a retired executive vice-president of Capital Cities/ABC who became the first non-family member to preside as chief executive officer in Chronicle Publishing's existence.

Sias immediately began cutting costs wherever he could and struggled to cure the ills brought about by years of mismanagement, but the ongoing feud within the de Young family took center stage. The excommunication of Thieriot and the arrival of an outsider had added fuel to the contentious struggle between McEvoy and roughly 20 of her cousins. The conflict intensified in 1994 when McEvoy rejected a $900 million offer by Tele-Communications Inc. (TCI) and Rupert Murdoch's News Corp. for KRON and several of Chronicle Publishing's cable systems. A faction of de Young family members wanted to sell some of Chronicle Publishing's assets, but McEvoy, holding sway as the largest shareholder, adamantly refused to do so. As one media analyst noted, "The dispute stems largely from a philosophical division on the board about raising cash versus holding onto assets like KRON and the newspaper. Nan (McEvoy) was a staunch defender of holding onto assets. Others were interested in selling."

The "others" often referred to in newspaper accounts were the de Young family members pitted against McEvoy, a group of cousins reportedly led by the disgruntled and usurped Thieriot and Frances Martin III. Thwarted by McEvoy's refusal to sell any of the company's assets, this warring faction took aim at McEvoy in 1995 by passing a corporate bylaw that barred anyone over the age of 73 from sitting on Chronicle Publishing's board of directors. McEvoy, 75 years old at the time, was ousted from the company's board, but she fought back by filing a lawsuit, which put the long-running family squabble into the public spotlight. McEvoy eventually dropped the lawsuit in exchange for a director emeritus title, but the resolution of the de Young family fight did nothing to resolve the problems Chronicle Publishing faced as it entered the late 1990s.

In 1996, Chronicle Publishing's cable systems in California, Hawaii, and New Mexico were sold to TCI for $580 million in stock. The divestiture of the company's cable systems, however, was not a panacea. As Chronicle Publishing entered the late 1990s, its future was unclear. Some pundits speculated that *The Chronicle* would be sold, while others pointed to a future merger with *The Examiner.* Whatever the fate of the company's flagship property, Chronicle Publishing was in need of wholesale changes as the 21st century neared. The responsibility for orchestrating such changes and perpetuating a more than 130-year family dynasty fell to John Sias, Chronicle Publishing's chairman and president.

Principal Divisions

Newspaper Division; Chronicle Book Division; Chronicle Broadcasting Company; Chronicle Features Syndicate; City-Line.

Further Reading

DeBare, Ilana, "San Francisco Chronicle Boardroom Brawl the Talk of the Town," *Knight-Ridder/Tribune Business News,* May 28, 1995, p. 5.

Ewell, Miranda, "San Francisco Examiner May Go Out of Business," *Knight-Ridder/Tribune Business News,* September 24, 1995, p. 9.

Freeman, Michael, "Chronicle to Quit Cable," *Mediaweek,* August 8, 1994, p. 5.

Liedtke, Michael, "Judge Upholds Coup in San Francisco Chronicle's Family Feud," *Knight-Ridder/ Tribune Business News,* May 28, 1995, p. 52.

Machan, Dyan, "New Blood," *Forbes,* April 25, 1994, p. 74.

Sharkey, Betsy, "A Giant Quakes in S.F.; Fox-TCI Offer for TV Properties Set Chronicle's Problems in Motion," *Mediaweek,* May 8, 1995, p. 6.

Stein, M.L., "How and Why the Leadership Changed," *Editor & Publisher,* December 4, 1993, p. 13.

——, "Shutdown in San Francisco?," *Editor & Publisher,* May 4, 1996, p. 23.

——, "The New Regime at the Chronicle," *Editor & Publisher,* December 4, 1993, p. 11.

—Jeffrey L. Covell

CINÉMAS
CINEPLEX ODEON

Cineplex Odeon Corporation

1303 Yonge Street
Toronto, Ontario M4T 2Y9
Canada
(416) 323-6600
Fax: (416) 323-6677

Public Company
Incorporated: 1977 as Cineplex Corporation
Employees: 7,662
Sales: US$509.69 million (1996)
Stock Exchanges: Toronto New York
SICs: 7830 Services—Motion Picture Theaters

Cineplex Odeon Corporation, with headquarters in Toronto, is one of the largest motion picture theater circuits in North America. The company operates high-quality theaters in most metropolitan areas in the United States and all of the primary urban markets in Canada. In 1997, Cineplex had 1,543 screens in 315 locations in North America.

Modest Beginnings

Cineplex Odeon commenced operations in 1979 when Garth Drabinsky, an energetic young Toronto entertainment lawyer, persuaded Nathan A. Taylor, a veteran of the motion picture exhibition business, to provide C$1 million (US$840,000) to purchase space in the basement of Toronto's Eaton Centre shopping complex. Drabinsky had first impressed Taylor several years earlier when, as a law student, he had asked the theater circuit manager to invest in a free film magazine he was distributing. Taylor refused, but he offered Drabinsky a position as editor of his own film industry paper *Canadian Film Digest,* a job Drabinsky accepted. Although Taylor had pioneered the idea of multi-theater locations as early as 1948, the new site, with 18 screening rooms, was much more ambitious than anything he had previously built. In order to distinguish the Eaton Centre location, Taylor coined the name Cineplex, an abbreviation of "cinema complex," and the company was born.

From the beginning, Drabinsky was the driving force behind Cineplex's development into the second-largest theater chain in North America. He adopted a two-pronged approach that involved both the restoration of dignified old theaters and the introduction of small theaters in such locations as shopping malls. This combination of luxury and variety changed the movie-going experience and halted the decline in movie attendance that had become pronounced in the 1970s.

Nevertheless, the operation had modest beginnings. When the Eaton Centre multiplex first opened its doors, major distribution circuits controlled access to most of the expensive first-run films. Small, independent distributors, such as Cineplex, were left with less popular first-runs and second-run films that had already been playing for some time. Cineplex was also committed to showing foreign-language and independent art films with a small but loyal audience. For this reason, competitors failed to take the operation seriously at first. The consensus in the industry was that Drabinsky and Taylor would be lucky to last six months.

Cineplex confounded the experts by earning C$50,000 (US$42,000) a week during its first three years of operation. During this period, the multiplex gradually began to attract the attention of outside investors who wanted to duplicate the formula in other locations. However, in spite of its impressive performance, Cineplex was encumbered with substantial loans from the Toronto Dominion Bank and the Claridge Corporation, a Montreal development company headed by Charles Bronfman. In 1982, attendance at the Cineplex theaters dropped dramatically, and creditors threatened to call in their high-interest loans. In a bold move to avoid bankruptcy, Drabinsky flew to Montreal and persuaded The Bronfman Group to buy a large stake in the company. Cineplex went public on the Toronto Stock Exchange in October 1982, and began trading on the New York Stock Exchange in 1987.

Meanwhile, Drabinsky was tackling the problem of first-run distribution malpractice in a typically forthright way. He went to the Combines Investigation Branch, a Canadian federal investigative body, with documents proving that competitors such as Canadian Odeon Theatres and Famous Players had enjoyed preferential distribution agreements with the major U.S. film companies for several decades. The Canadian government threatened to take the exhibitors and the film companies to court, but a settlement was reached allowing Cineplex and other small chains to bid for first-run films on an individual basis. The settlement was widely viewed as a victory for Cineplex. Shortly afterward, using capital generated by The Bronfman Group collaboration, Taylor and Drabinsky bought the 297 screens of Canadian Odeon Theatres for a modest C$16 million (US$13.4 million) and in June 1985 changed the company name to the Cineplex Odeon Corporation.

Expansion in the 1980s

From the beginning, Cineplex pursued a strategy of expansion into key markets, notably the United States, where the Los Angeles Beverly Center 14-screen multiplex opened on July 15, 1982. The Beverly 14, a collection of small theaters in the middle of a shopping complex that offered free parking, generated revenues of US$4 million in the first year, almost twice the initial projections. This set the stage for a systematic penetration of the U.S. market, as Cineplex began to buy up both individual movie houses and theater chains. Los Angeles remained an important focus, and the company made a number of acquisitions throughout the city in the 1980s, culminating in the June 1987 opening of the 18-screen Cineplex Odeon Cinemas at Universal City.

In November 1985 Drabinsky purchased the debt-ridden Plitt Theatres, which increased his holdings by 574 screens in 21 states in the United States. The acquisition left Cineplex in a vulnerable financial position, forcing Drabinsky and vice-chairman Myron Gottlieb to look for a major financial backer. In December 1985, Drabinsky met with Lew Wasserman and Sidney Sheinberg, chair and president respectively of MCA, Inc. In January 1986, MCA announced that it had agreed to buy 49.7 percent of Cineplex for US$239 million. This injection of much-needed cash heralded a series of acquisitions of American theaters negotiated through the company's U.S. subsidiary, Plitt Theatres. Between April and December 1986 Cineplex purchased five movie theater chains, adding a total of 372 screens in 128 locations. In addition to these acquisitions, the company constructed 31 theaters with 163 screens in the United States and Canada during 1987. An additional 229 screens were opened in 1988. By 1989, Cineplex Odeon controlled 1,825 screens in 499 locations in North America. In order to offset the costs of the rapid expansion program, Drabinsky encouraged landlords of the new premises to invest in the company. He also adopted a practice of selling off individual properties if their real estate value increased dramatically. By constantly juggling

his assets, and by the force of his confident and persuasive personality, Drabinsky managed to keep enough credit on hand to continue his policy of rapid growth, even as share prices fell in the wake of the October 1987 stock market crash. In 1988, the company moved into the United Kingdom, with the stated intention of "developing and operating" over 100 screens in the British Isles by the end of 1991. To do so, he increased the company's debt-load to over US$500 million, a level considered unacceptably high by many shareholders.

Drabinsky's ambitions went beyond operating a large number of screens. Determined to make theater-going a clean, civilized, and exciting experience, he established quality service and attractive locations as priorities in any operation that he took over. To this end, he spent millions of dollars refurbishing run-down theater complexes and in some cases painstakingly restoring historical landmarks to their former glory. Throughout the 1980s, every new acquisition was evaluated and refurbished by a 100-person design and construction team under the direction of Cineplex head architect David Mesbur. Cineplex undertook the restoration of cinemas on Vancouver's Granville Street, and the new complex quickly became one of the most profitable venues in Canada. According to company reports, the Gordon Theater in Los Angeles brought in a weekly revenue of US$6,000 before a US$650,000 facelift by the Cineplex design team. Renamed the Showcase, the refurbished cinema averaged US$30,000 a week. Art Deco motifs, plush seating, state-of-the-art sound equipment, and cappuccino bars revolutionized the way Americans thought of the cinema experience. Even Drabinsky's rivals admit that he forced the standard of service and appearance in the industry to rise. The luxurious surroundings, however, came at a high price: in May 1989 *Forbes* estimated that Cineplex spent approximately US$1,400 per leased seat compared to an industry average of US$500 a seat.

The cost of entertainment in a Cineplex theater was also high. In 1988, the average ticket price in the industry was US$4, compared with US$7 at Cineplex. The elevated prices occurred at a time when the number of movies going into production each year was dropping, and multiplexes were being forced to show first-releases on more than one screen in order to fill their playbills. Nevertheless, Drabinsky remained convinced that patrons would pay more for the opportunity to view in comfort.

They were also paying for the opportunity to snack in comfort. Concession stands in Cineplex theaters were among the most innovative in the industry, and included upscale cafes in selected locations that served cappuccino, herbal tea, and croissants. Even the more mundane establishments offered real butter on their popcorn, an executive decision that cost Cineplex a great deal of money over the years. Since concession revenues accounted for approximately one-third of overall box office revenue at Cineplex locations in 1989, the effort was judged worthwhile. Cineplex also invested considerable sums in its supervisors, most of whom participated in a six-week in-house management training program.

In view of Drabinsky's celebrated attempts to restore glamour to the movie-going experience, competitors were surprised when he introduced on-screen advertising to his Canadian venues in 1985. At a time when theaters were losing audiences to video and cable television, commercial-free screening seemed one of the movie industry's most important attractions. Drabinsky defended his decision in pragmatic terms, pointing out that the timeliness of a movie's release surpassed in importance the presence of advertising. Disgruntled patrons publicly took issue with this viewpoint, in some cases throwing objects at the screen when a commercial aired. Drabinsky refused to withdraw advertising from all but 26 art-house venues in Canada, but the experience may have influenced his decision to introduce advertising to his United States screens on a more limited basis.

Diversification in the Late 1980s

Not content with celluloid success, Drabinsky soon turned his attention to live theater. In 1986, Cineplex acquired the lease to half of the Imperial Theatre in downtown Toronto. The building had an illustrious history dating back to 1920 when it opened with a combination of vaudeville and silent movies. For many years, the other half of the building had been leased by Famous Players, one of Cineplex's biggest rivals on the Canadian circuit. Cineplex acquired the lease to the second half of the building in 1986 but due to legal wrangles was not able to begin restoration of the theater until 1989, when it purchased half of the building outright. Renamed the Pantages, the property was gutted in a make-over that restored the theater to the original design of architect Thomas Lamb at the cost of US$18 million. Drabinsky then bought exclusive Canadian rights to Andrew Lloyd Webber's musical *Phantom of the Opera*, which premiered to record box office advance sales in late 1989. The production was the most expensive ever staged in Canada. The company became involved in other theatrical projects during this period, including a North American tour of songs and music by Lloyd Webber. The program of diversification was completed with the purchase of the Film House group, a post-production facility, in 1986, and the financing of films by Oliver Stone and John Schlesinger in the United States.

Meanwhile, MCA and The Bronfman Group, Cineplex's major shareholders, were becoming increasingly concerned about the level of debt that the company had accumulated. By 1988, properties were being sold to raise money. In 1989, Cineplex's 50 percent interest in Universal Studios Florida was sold to the Rank Organisation in the United Kingdom. In early 1989, the Bronfmans indicated that they wanted to sell their 30 percent voting interest in Cineplex. Drabinsky and chief administrative officer Gottlieb recognized an opportunity to gain control of the company by acquiring The Bronfman Group's 30 percent interest. Although MCA owned 49.7 percent of the company, Canadian law allowed it only 33 percent of the voting rights. MCA president Sidney Sheinberg responded by asking that an investigation be made into Cineplex's irregular accounting practices, long a source of concern to investors. Financial improprieties were uncovered, and by the end of 1989 Cineplex's apparently healthy profit had been recalculated as a US$78.6 million loss. Drabinsky and Gottlieb were unable to secure sufficient financing to close their deal, and in December 1989 the era of Cineplex's wild leveraged expansion came to an end when both men were forced out of the company. They later purchased the Pantages theater and rights to *The Phantom of the Opera*. Cineplex, meanwhile, was left with a US$600 million debt.

Cost-Cutting in the 1990s

In a letter to shareholders dated April 1991, Leo Kolber and Allen Karp, Cineplex's new chairman and chief executive officer respectively, stated that whereas before 1989 the company had attempted to create "an entertainment conglomerate with a presence in many aspects of the industry," the focus in the 1990s would be "the business we know best—motion picture exhibition." In keeping with this philosophy, the company entered the 1990s by selling most of its peripheral assets, including the live entertainment division, a residual interest in Universal Studio Florida, the Film House post-production facility, the theaters in the United Kingdom, and a number of unprofitable United States screens. Plans to buy new theaters proceeded at a modest pace, and the full-time design team was reduced from 100 people to fewer than ten. The new management recognized that it would be several years before their cost-cutting efforts would be rewarded, but already in 1991 they could claim that their "fire-fighting" phase was over.

The company continued to focus on motion picture exhibition and pursued only modest expansion for the next few years. This strategy, combined with the company's cost cutting, brought Cineplex back to profitability in 1993. MCA, the company's major stockholder, also helped boost revenues that year. It's studio, Universal Pictures, was Cineplex's major supplier, and its 1993 blockbuster *Jurassic Park* made money for the movie exhibitor.

Although the relationship was beneficial in 1993, the next year Universal Pictures' lack of hits dragged Cineplex down. With hits from Disney and Paramount, the industry enjoyed box office revenue growth of 4.7 percent, but Cineplex was restricted by its ties to Universal and saw revenues drop 1.3 percent.

In 1995 Cineplex Odeon announced a merger in the works with Cinemark USA, which would have created the largest motion picture exhibitor in the world. The proposed $445 million deal never materialized, however, and Cineplex pursued expansion with limited new screen openings. The company's ownership structure did change slightly in 1995, however. That year Seagram Co. bought 80 percent of MCA from Matsushita Electric Industrial Co. Seagram's majority shareholders, the Bronfman family, also owned 24 percent of Cineplex. With Seagram's acquisition of MCA, the Bronfmans gained a controlling interest in Cineplex.

Multiplexing in the Late 1990s

The following year MCA and the Bronfmans invested US$50 million into Cineplex. The much-needed capital helped Cineplex construct more multiscreen theaters. Multiplexing, or constructing many screens in one theater, became a popular strategy in the mid-1990s for creating economies of scale for movie exhibitors. With one ticket taker and one concessionaire, a theater could serve patrons for a dozen or more screens. Multiplexes also tended to offer a wider range of concessions, such as espresso and pizza. Cineplex began a $145 million expansion plan that called for 200 new screens in Canada; the scheduled completion date was the end of 1998.

Multiplexing made way for megaplexing in the late 1990s. Hoping to attract more customers and keep them on-site and spending their money longer, exhibitors were not only raising the number of screens, they were also adding entertainment centers with such features as interactive video game rooms. Cineplex rival AMC Entertainment was building 24- to 30-screen theaters and surrounding them with bars, restaurants, book and music stores, and video game centers. AMC directly challenged Cineplex by building several of these megaplexes in major Canadian markets. Howard Lichtman, Cineplex Odeon's executive vice-president told *Maclean's,* "We're not afraid of competition."

Cineplex took a cautious approach with constructing megaplexes. It did build some, including sites at Universal Studios, Florida, and in the Latin Quarter of Quebec. However, it was wary of the effect a studio drought could have on a 30-screen complex and proceeded slowly. Still, the company moved forward with its expansion plans, adding 111 new screens in 1996 and then also closed or sold 84 old or unprofitable screens that year. Also during this time, the company expanded for the first time outside North America, opening six screens in Hungary in 1996.

Despite the optimism indicated by its expansion program, Cineplex Odeon saw net losses in 1995 and 1996 of $32 million and $31 million, respectively. Once again, Cineplex seemed to be hurt by the relatively poor performance of the movies from its suppliers. Industry-wide box office revenues rose 7.6 percent in 1996, to $5.9 billion, and Cineplex apparently did not reap the rewards of the industry's spectacular performance. The company attributed some of the poor showing to a six percent industry-wide increase in screens, which they regarded as watering down their returns, especially since most of Cineplex's new screens did not open until late in 1996.

In late 1997 Cineplex Odeon announced plans to merge with Sony's Loews Theatre Group. The proposed merger would create the largest motion picture exhibitor in North America, with $1 billion in sales and 2,600 screens in the United States alone. Early details of the deal indicated Sony would own 51 percent of the new company, Loews Cineplex Entertainment,

and Cineplex's shareholders would hold the rest as follows: Seagram, 26 percent; the Bronfman family, 9.7 percent; all other Cineplex shareholders, 13.3 percent. Both Cineplex and Sony hoped their combined forces would help them expand overseas and compete with other rapidly consolidating exhibitors. Cineplex planned to complete the merger by mid-1998, despite opposition from consumer groups, who claimed the new company would violate anti-trust laws.

Principal Subsidiaries

Plitt Theatres, Inc.

Principal Divisions

Cineplex Odeon Theatres; RKO Century Warner Theatres; Walter Reade Theatres; Neighborhood Theatres; Washington Circle Theatres.

Further Reading

"Cineplex at the Altar," *Maclean's,* October 13, 1997, p. 41.
"Cineplex Odeon Tenth Anniversary Salute," *Variety,* April 26–May 2, 1989.
Galarza, Pablo, "Cineplex Odeon: Hollywood Stepchild," *Financial World,* March 11, 1996, p. 14.
Halbfinger, David M., "Seagram Agrees to Buy 80 Percent of MCA," *New York Newsday,* April 10, 1995, p. A8.
Lathan, K. J., and Suzane Ayscough, "The Last Emperor," *Film Comment,* January–February 1990.
Lieberman, David, "Merger to Create Biggest Movie Chain," *USA Today,* March 3, 1995, p. B1.
Murray, Karen, "Exhibber Back from the Brink: Once Troubled Theater Chain on Track for Modest Growth," *Variety,* July 25, 1994, pp. 31–32.
Posner, Michael, "A Really Big Show," *Maclean's,* August 11, 1997, pp. 38–39.
Simon, Cecilia Capuzzi, "The Fall of Garth Drabinsky," *Premiere,* March 1991.
Wechsler, Dana, "Every Trick in the Books," *Forbes,* May 29, 1989.

—Moya Verzhbinsky
—updated by Susan Windisch Brown

CINNABON®

Cinnabon Inc.

936 North 34th Avenue
Seattle, Washington 98103
U.S.A.
(206) 634-2355
Fax: (206) 634-2355
Web site: http://www.cinnabon.com

Private Company
Incorporated: 1985
Employees: 1,500
Sales: $135 million (1996 est.)
SICs: 5461 Retail Bakeries

One of the fastest-growing companies in the United States, Cinnabon Inc. is the operator of Cinnabon World Famous Cinnamon Rolls, a chain of specialty cinnamon roll outlets scattered throughout North America. Originally a division of Seattle, Washington–based Restaurants Unlimited, Inc., Cinnabon outgrew its parent company and became a separate business in 1996. During the late 1990s the company operated approximately 400 Cinnabon units in the United States, Canada, and Mexico.

Thriving Restaurant Chain Launches Cinnabon

In 1985 Richard Komen and a handful of Restaurants Unlimited executives gathered around a table to discuss the possibilities of entering a sideline business. Their decision gave birth to the Cinnabon chain of specialty cinnamon roll bakeries. Komen, who presided at the table during the pivotal meeting, was midway through a decade that would establish him as one of the most successful restaurateurs in the United States. His company, Restaurants Unlimited, operated a collection of variously named dining establishments that were performing admirably, attracting crowds of patrons, and growing in number with each passing year. It was a particularly gratifying achievement for Komen, who five years earlier was at a loss for what to do with Restaurants Unlimited. His company, founded in 1969, grew vigorously throughout much of the 1970s by opening a series of theme

restaurants featuring prime rib, lobster and a dark, wood-paneled decor reminiscent of Edwardian English pubs. However, by the end of the 1970s the concept had grown stale, and his company was struggling. Komen needed a new approach for the 1980s, and found one in 1981 when he replaced the dark wood paneling and rich, butter-based sauces of Restaurants Unlimited's Clinkerdagger restaurants with a new breed of dining establishments featuring lightly colored, weathered wood, large glass windows, and an eclectic, multinational menu offering pasta, chicken, seafood, salads, and vegetables. The transformation saved the company and rekindled optimism at Restaurants Unlimited's corporate offices in Seattle, Washington, setting the stage for the genesis of the Cinnabon concept.

Seated at the table with Komen and other executives in 1985 was Dennis Waldron, a Restaurants Unlimited officer and investor who had experienced the roller-coaster ride during the 1970s and 1980s. Although Komen, who was ultimately in charge of Restaurants Unlimited, was responsible for creating the Cinnabon chain, it was Waldron who was chiefly responsible for developing the concept into the resounding success that it became. Waldron initially set out to be a doctor, graduating from Seattle University with a bachelor of science degree in the pre-medical curriculum, but his years spent working in restaurants to pay for his education ultimately prevailed as the inspiration for his professional career. Waldron began working in restaurants during his high school years in the 1960s and continued during his years at Seattle University. When he was a senior preparing to enter the next level of his medical education, he was offered a job managing a 250-seat cafeteria. "I ran it for about four years," Waldron remembered, "and I was hooked." From there, Waldron went on to manage a Seattle waterfront restaurant named Windjammer for several years, then, at age 27, he set out on his own and opened an Irish-themed restaurant featuring singing waiters. His restaurant did well but exhibited little potential for expansion, so he sold it. It was at this juncture in his career that he met Komen and became part of Restaurants Unlimited.

Waldron joined Restaurants Unlimited in 1974 when expansion was underway with the company's signature Clinkerdagger concept. A decade later, after the chain of Clinkerdaggers had been replaced with a collection of restaurants operating vari-

---

Company Perspectives:

The Cinnabon experience includes World Famous Cinnamon Rolls which delight guests with swirls of light, moist dough, filled with lots of thick brown sugar and Makara cinnamon, then topped with freshly made cream cheese frosting. The rolls are served within 30 minutes of the oven. Cinnabon's "guest-first" culture, born out of the company's roots in the restaurant industry, make attentive and cheerful service a standard at each bakery. In fact, the company credits its success to the uniqueness of its products and dedication to guest service.

---

ously as Cutter's Bayhouse, Ryan's, Skates on the Bay, and Stepps on the Court, Waldron, Komen, and several other executives were plotting their next move. Expansion of the company's multimillion-dollar restaurants was in full swing; 16 restaurants, with more to come, were generating roughly $40 million a year in revenue. With this primary objective achieved, the executives turned to secondary goals. "We were looking for something simpler to operate with a limited menu that would give us a small niche segment for a low capital investment," Waldron recalled. The executives settled on a specialty cinnamon roll concept, drawing their inspiration from several cinnamon roll chains that were emerging at the time.

Komen liked the idea because of the low start-up costs involved and because of the high profit margins recorded by successful cinnamon roll chains in operation in 1985, both of which matched the criteria established for Restaurants Unlimited's sideline venture. Moreover, the creation of a cinnamon roll chain would accomplish two strategic objectives for Restaurants Unlimited, giving the company a presence in shopping malls, where the first Cinnabon units were to be located, and adding a division that could grow through franchising. Aside from achieving these goals, Komen, Waldron, and the other executives had modest expectations for the new venture. "We first thought the entire system might grow to 40 or 50 units over time," Waldron confided. "And that looked like a really big number for the concept, which we didn't think could get much larger than that." To their surprise, the Cinnabon concept proved to be an enormous hit, creating a division that in a decade's time would eclipse the stature of its parent company.

First Cinnabon Established in 1985

The first Cinnabon opened in December 1985 in a shopping mall near the Seattle-Tacoma International Airport, followed by another unit in a Las Vegas mall and a third in a Chicago mall. Each of the units, decorated with Italian marble and cobalt-blue and white tile, featured a bakery in open view that allowed customers to watch the rolls being made by hand. Initially, Restaurants Unlimited planned on opening these three units and gradually expanding, but the concept demonstrated surprising strength, prompting accelerated expansion plans. By the end of its first year, the Cinnabon concept had quickly developed into a chain comprising 15 units, despite being treated as a sideline venture. It was at this point that Restaurants Unlimited began to take the Cinnabon concept more seriously. "It became clear," Waldron noted, "that if we were really going to pursue the growth of Cinnabon, we needed our own culture, separate from the full-service restaurant group, and we went into our own offices." Selected by Komen to head Cinnabon's corporate offices was Waldron, who would guide the chain toward exponential growth.

After its first year of existence, the Cinnabon chain stretched from Hawaii to Illinois, its expansion progressing with huge geographic leaps that mirrored the company's initial deployment of Cinnabon units in Seattle, Las Vegas, and Chicago. "That was one of our early mistakes," Waldron recalled. "We had no geographic focus." Skipping over regions to establish a Cinnabon in isolated markets, however, did not check the unbridled success of the chain. The burgeoning chain was registering growing sales and high profits, and additional bakeries established during the late 1980s fleshed out the scattered Cinnabon units into a blanket that quickly covered much of the nation. During the division's second year of business in 1987, 16 more units were opened that filled in some of the geographic gaps. By the beginning of the 1990s, the number of Cinnabon units, all located in shopping malls, had grown to 72, well above the highest figure Waldron had expected the chain to reach when plans were first discussed five years earlier. By this point, what had started as a sideline business for Restaurants Unlimited had matured into a powerful revenue-generating engine for the full-service restaurant operator. In 1990 Restaurants Unlimited collected $100 million in sales; Cinnabon generated 25 percent of that total.

Early 1990s Expansion

Cinnabon entered the 1990s growing by leaps and bounds, thriving as a simple concept that offered one product to customers: cinnamon rolls. Demand for that one product was rabid, fueling the expansion of additional Cinnabon units. By 1992 there were over 180 Cinnabon units in the United States and Canada, more than twice the number in operation two years earlier, which translated into an average of more than one store opening each week. Much of the expansion had been achieved through franchising, which made Cinnabon's contribution to Restaurants Unlimited's revenue volume only a portion of the concept's total might. All told, the Cinnabon chain by 1992 was an estimated $65 million enterprise, although the division only accounted for 25 percent of Restaurants Unlimited's 1992 sales of $105 million. Two years later, the Cinnabon chain totaled more than 260 units and had developed into a $100 million enterprise itself, far exceeding the growth rate recorded by its parent company. Individual Cinnabon locations by this point were averaging $250,000 in annual sales.

Cinnabon, organized as a wholly owned subsidiary named "Cinnabon World Famous Cinnamon Rolls," began breaking new ground during the mid-1990s, implementing the first significant changes to the concept since its creation in 1985. For years, all Cinnabon bakeries were established in malls, but by 1994 there were 40 units established in test locations that included variety stores, supermarkets, airports, and one unit located in Seattle's Woodland Park Zoo. Supermarkets and airports would turn out to be the most successful of these initial test locations, but Waldron was by no means abandoning future expansion in shopping malls, where the vast majority of Cinnabon outlets were located and where the concept had risen to its illustrious heights. In 1994 Waldron envisioned great opportunities for growth, stating there were another 200 viable sites in shopping malls that he had identified. Coupled with this figure, Waldron's statement that there were more than 20 airports slated as potential sites for Cinnabon units and an even greater number of supermarket locations augured extremely well for the division. The division, even after a decade of fast-paced expansion, appeared to be on the brink of explosive growth. Provoked by the optimism created by this realization, Cinnabon officials predicted there were would be 700 Cinnabon locations in operation by the end of the 1990s. The road ahead looked more promising than it ever had before.

Mid-1990s: Independence and Expansion

By 1995 more than 300 Cinnabons were in operation, with expansion extending the company's geographic presence from the United States and Canada into Mexico. Waldron, who had been asked to superintend the development of a promising division less than a decade earlier, was presiding over a facet of Restaurants Unlimited's business that physically and financially was greater than his parent company's full-service restaurant business, itself a rising star in the food service industry. In 1995 Restaurants Unlimited collected $196 million in sales, nearly five times the total generated a decade earlier, but Cinnabon accounted for $120 million of the company's 1995 total, having developed into Restaurants Unlimited's primary revenue-generating business. Cinnabon's increasingly integral role within the Restaurants Unlimited enterprise appeared to be destined for an even greater importance. As Waldron scanned the horizon in 1995, he was planning to open at least one new Cinnabon per week in malls, airports, supermarkets, and other urban locations throughout North America by tapping into Cinnabons' virtually boundless potential. In the midst of this heady optimism, Cinnabon officials began declaring enormous projections for the concept's future growth, with some announcements targeting the number of Cinnabons at 1,500 by the end of the 1990s, or more than twice the number projected in 1994.

Considering that Cinnabon accounted for the bulk of Restaurants Unlimited's annual sales total, maintained a far greater geographic presence, and appeared destined for continued explosive growth, the officials of Restaurants Unlimited could have more appropriately named their company "Cinnabon Inc." by the mid-1990s. Restaurants Unlimited officials recognized as much, but instead of swapping names for their enterprise, they decided to spin off Cinnabon into a separate company to be independently owned and operated. The separation was made in April 1996, when Cinnabon was generating $77 million in sales through roughly 225 company-owned units, franchise fees, and royalties. Systemwide, annual sales stood at $136 million. The spin-off was made in anticipation of an initial public offering (IPO) of stock in Cinnabon, slated to occur later in the year. Piper Jaffray was hired as the investment banker to prepare for the IPO, but the conversion to public ownership did not take place as scheduled. Although the IPO would have raised substantial capital for expansion, Cinnabon's vitality did not appear to suffer much from the shelved IPO. Ray Lindstrom, Restaurants Unlimited's chief executive officer and long-time company executive moved over from Restaurants Unlimited's offices to help lead the company with Waldron, who, along with the Thomas H. Lee Company and Union Bank of Switzerland retained ownership in the chain he had nurtured nearly from its inception.

In the wake of its separation from its parent company, Cinnabon continued to display remarkable progress, with individual stores averaging $425,000 in annual sales and the best performers generating between $2 million and $3 million each year. By the beginning of 1997, when there were 350 Cinnabons operating in North America, the company was collecting roughly $140 million in sales, having secured an entrenched position in many major markets. With plans to add 60 more units in 1997, the company was also experimenting with expanding its menu for the first time in its history. New baked goods, including bagels, muffins, and croissants, were added to the familiar refrain of over-sized cinnamon rolls, and some units began offering cream cheese.

As Cinnabon headed into the late 1990s and prepared for the future, expectations for future growth and profitability were as strong as ever. Although projections for expansion by the end of the 1990s had been reduced to 500 units, the reduction was perhaps attributable to the common occurrence of wild-eyed optimism settling into reality. The late 1990s and the beginning of the 21st century promised to see a different type of Cinnabon as plans were being developed in late 1997. In June 1997 the company began testing a much larger baking and coffeehouse concept, experimenting with two units in New York City that served as the proving ground for the company's attempt to develop into a more complex retail operation. In addition to the transformation into a broader concept, Waldron ordered the renovation of some units, touching off the gradual process of changing Cinnabon's decor. Warm-colored wood and copper were slated to replace the familiar blue and white tile, while a new logo, new graphics, and new packaging were in the offing. With these changes set to be implemented as the 1990s drew to a close, Cinnabon embarked on its second decade of existence, firmly situated as a market leader in its industry.

Further Reading

Baker, M. Sharon, "Roll-ing Out a New Look and Expanded Menu," *Puget Sound Business Journal*, June 27, 1997, p. 59.
Buck, Richard, "Cinnabon to be Spun Off," *Seattle Times*, April 5, 1996, p. B1.
Harper, Roseanne, "Cinnamon Roll Outlet Added to Genuardi's Food Court," *Supermarket News*, February 1, 1993, p. 46.
Liddle, Alan, "Not Just Coffee: Operators Are Brewing Up Diverse Opportunities," *Nation's Restaurant News*, October 28, 1996, p. 24.
——, "Richard Komen: 'Visionary' on the Move," *Nation's Restaurant News*, September 21, 1992, p. 96.
McDowell, Bill, "Cinnabon," *Restaurants & Institutions*, August 1, 1994, p. 64.
Papiernik, Richard L., "Dennis Waldron," *Nation's Restaurant News*, January 1997, p. 22.
Raffio, Ralph, "Restaurants Unlimited: Marketing to an Urban Niche," *Restaurant Business*, February 10, 1985, p. 159.
"Restaurants Unlimited," *Restaurants & Institutions*, May 29, 1989, p. 64.

—Jeffrey L. Covell

CLEAR CHANNEL COMMUNICATIONS, INC.

Clear Channel Communications, Inc.

200 Concord Plaza, Suite 600
San Antonio, Texas 78216
U.S.A.
(210) 822-2828
Fax: (210) 822-2299
Web Site: http://www.clearchannel.com

Public Company
Incorporated: 1974
Employees: 3,219
Sales: $351.7 million (1997)
Stock Exchanges: New York
SICs: 4832 Radio Broadcasting Stations; 4833 Television
Broadcasting Stations; 7312 Outdoor Advertising
Services

A fast-growing, diversified media company, Clear Channel Communications, Inc., operates nearly 200 radio stations and roughly 20 television stations in 39 markets in the United States. The company acquired the bulk of its broadcasting properties following the Telecommunications Act of 1996, which lifted restrictions on national radio station ownership. During the late 1990s, the company was diversifying beyond the broadcasting business by acquiring billboards in major metropolitan markets. By 1997, the company ranked as the second-largest outdoor advertiser in the United States. In addition to its domestic radio and television stations, Clear Channel also operated broadcasting properties in New Zealand and Australia.

Early 1970s Origins

For L. Lowry Mays, everything changed in 1972. A graduate of Texas A&M University, Mays left Texas with a degree in petroleum engineering and entered Harvard University, where he earned a graduate degree in business. From there, it was back to Texas, where Mays settled in as an investment banker. It was a natural progression from his years at Harvard, but when two businessmen walked into his office at the small investment

banking concern he was running in San Antonio, Mays' life took a defining turn. The two men, both San Antonio professionals, asked the 36-year-old Mays for help in raising $175,000 to buy a struggling FM radio station named KEEZ. Mays agreed, and delved into researching the details of the radio business, demonstrating a thoroughness that would become one of his trademarks in later years. As preparations for the project were underway, the two businessmen backed out of the deal, leaving Mays with a headful of information about the radio industry. Mays pursued the investment opportunity on his own, enlisting the help of a local car dealer named B. J. (Red) McCombs, borrowing $175,000 from a bank, and purchasing KEEZ strictly as an investment. "I had no intention of getting into the broadcast business," Mays recalled years later.

Nevertheless, he soon began to demonstrate the assiduous, hands-on type of management that would become another one of his defining trademarks. He and McCombs (whose later business achievements included acquiring the San Antonio Spurs professional basketball team) poured more cash into the station and changed its format to country music. At the same time, the partners expanded the station's sales force and increased its promotion budget, with a focus on maximizing advertising revenue. Making money in broadcasting, Mays reasoned, required forging a close and profitable relationship with the advertisers whose dollars drove a radio station's financial growth. Music format changes and programming adjustments were made, to be sure, but increasing cash flow by attracting advertisers was the chief concern. "Our whole philosophy, whether it's radio or television," Mays later remarked, "is that our business is selling automobiles, or tamales, or toothpaste. That's our business: helping people sell Fords."

Under Mays's scrutiny, the floundering KEEZ was transformed into a profitable business within a year, and this success encouraged May to delve deeper into the broadcasting business. With the cash flow generated by KEEZ, Mays and McCombs purchased two radio stations located in Tulsa, Oklahoma, over the next two years. By this point, in 1974, Mays had already established the blueprint for Clear Channel's future expansion. In the years to follow, he would acquire distressed stations in such mid-sized, second-tier markets as El Paso, Memphis, Louisville, and New Orleans, and bring them to profitability. Each acquisition candidate had to meet strict criteria before joining the Clear Channel fold, and, once added to the company's portfolio of broadcasting properties, each acquisition was transformed by the same principles: the company's sales force was doubled, its marketing activities were increased, and an emphasis was placed on attracting new advertisers. Mays rarely tinkered with a station's programming format. Instead, all efforts were directed at the acquisition's financial performance. "We want to be able to have both an immediate impact on the revenues," Mays explained, "and an immediate impact on the expenses."

1984 Public Offering Spawns Little Growth

Moving cautiously in the decade that followed the acquisition of the two Tulsa stations, Mays gradually added to his stable of radio stations as he learned the business. Developments in 1984, however, promised to usher in a new era of animated growth. In that year, the Federal Communications Commission (FCC) loosened ownership restrictions for radio and television properties, decreeing that companies could own up to 12 AM stations, 12 FM stations, and 12 television stations. Prior to 1984, the FCC barred companies from owning more than seven properties in each category. Mays and the rest of the broadcasting industry celebrated the news. "We knew this was going to be a trend, that these laws would continue to change," remembered Mays. Preparing for period of energetic expansion, he took Clear Channel public in 1984, raising $7.5 million in an initial public offering. As expected, companies began acquiring broadcasting properties in earnest, swallowing up one after another to take advantage of the relaxed ownership restrictions; Clear Channel, however, stood by. Conspicuous by his absence from the acquisition frenzy, Mays was criticized by industry observers as a former investment banker who analyzed deals and then decided not to get involved. Mays later explained that Clear Channel's inactivity was not due to a lack of effort or interest. "We looked at radio properties every day," he said. "They just didn't meet the investment criteria we set up. If you stick by your targets for return on investment, it will take you out of the market."

In the wake of the 1984 FCC ruling, Mays made several acquisitions, but by 1987 his company was effectively out of the radio acquisition market. In 1988, when all radio acquisitions had been put on hold, Mays jumped into the television market, acquiring a station in Mobile, Alabama, that was an affiliate of the Fox TV network, which was just beginning its bid to become the fourth major network in the country. After acquiring the station in Mobile, Mays went on to purchase television stations in Tucson, Jacksonville, Tulsa, Wichita, and Memphis, each a Fox affiliate except for the Tucson property.

The foray into television broadcasting proved to be a financial boon for Clear Channel, particularly because of the success enjoyed by the Fox TV network as it developed into the country's fourth major television network. Clear Channel issued a second stock offering in mid-1991, raising $25 million to pay for debt incurred in its late 1980s acquisition campaign, which had significantly strengthened the company's financial stature. By end of 1991, the company's 18 radio stations and six television stations generated revenues of $74 million and earnings of more than $1 million.

Early 1990s Expansion

Beginning in mid-1992, Mays changed course and began to acquire radio stations at a voracious rate, motivated by changing conditions in the radio industry. Companies that had acquired radio stations during the 1980s had paid high prices, and during the economic recession of the early 1990s many of those companies were saddled with debt and forced to sell. Consequently, the price of radio properties dropped dramatically, creating numerous opportunities for Mays. For the financial resources to wage an acquisition campaign, Mays relied on the guarantees of nine major banks, which totaled a hefty $150 million. By mid-1993, $110 million of the total had been used to acquire 31 radio stations and seven television stations in mid-sized Sunbelt markets, and Clear Channel had catapulted to the top of its industry.

In 1994 Clear Channel merged with a Tampa, Florida, competitor named Metroplex Communications. In 1995 the company leaped well beyond its established operating territory when it acquired a 50 percent interest in the Australian Radio Network. By the end of that year, Clear Channel owned 36 radio stations and 10 television stations, which represented a modest increase over the total number of properties it owned in 1993. The figures were deceiving, however, because they did not accurately convey the financial progress the company had made during the two-year period. Annual revenues between 1993 and 1995 exploded from $135 million to $244 million, while the company's net income swelled from $9 million to $32 million.

Because of the strategy employed by Mays, Clear Channel exited 1995 in enviable financial shape and ready to take advantage of a momentous announcement by the FCC. The Telecommunications Act of 1996 lifted national radio ownership restrictions and eased local limitations, touching off a spate of acquisitions for those with the financial wherewithal to acquire broadcasting properties. Clear Channel was one of those companies in a financial position that permitted aggressive expansion and, in fact, was leading the pack. The Telecommunications Act of 1996 took effect in February 1996; by June, Clear Channel had acquired or was in the process of acquiring $581 million worth of radio and television stations. "They're very savvy and they're very focused," one analyst remarked as Clear Channel grew rapidly during the first half of 1996. "All their acquisitions are great, and they have yet to trip up." With 70 radio stations (43 FM, 27 AM) and 16 television stations under its control by June 1996 and 34 more acquisitions pending, the company had ample opportunities to make a mistake, but under the guiding eye of Mays, Clear Channel had moved resolutely forward and emerged from the mid-1990s stronger than ever. The company's history of robust cash-flow growth and its discipline in acquiring stations for bargain prices had investors clamoring for more. Between 1990 and 1996, the company's stock soared from $2.72 a share to a remarkable $73 a share, piquing Wall Street's interest in what the company would do during the late 1990s.

By October 1996, clear Channel owned 121 radio stations and 11 television stations, making it the second-largest radio group in the country behind Westinghouse/CBS. As the company prepared plans for the late 1990s and the beginning of the 21st century, more acquisitions were in the offing. At the beginning of 1997, Mays had more than $1 billion at his disposal for future acquisitions and expressed no desire to slow down in the years ahead. ''We're the fastest-growing media company in the country,'' Mays boasted to *Fortune* magazine. ''We're going to be the acquirer, not the acquiree,'' he promised.

Clear Channel's progress in 1997 set the tone for the company's course of development in the future. In April, the company acquired Eller Media Company, the oldest and largest billboard operator in the United States with more than 50,000 outdoor display faces in 15 major metropolitan markets. In June, the company acquired a 32 percent interest in Spanish-language broadcaster Heftel Broadcasting Corp., which carried Clear Channel into major metropolitan markets for the first time. ''We're trying to consolidate the Spanish broadcasting industry itself,'' Mays explained, as he formulated plans for developing clusters of Spanish-language stations. In October, the company made its next definitive move, signing an agreement to purchase Universal Outdoor Inc., which added 88,000 outdoor display faces to Clear Channel's billboard holdings and made the company the second-largest outdoor advertiser in the country. On the heels of these forays into Spanish-language broadcasting and into billboards, Mays and the rest of Clear Channel's management scanned the horizon for future acquisition targets, intent on building their company into a formidable giant.

Principal Subsidiaries

Clear Channel Communications of Memphis, Inc.; Clear Channel Television, Inc.; Clear Channel Radio, Inc.; Clear Channel Television Licenses, Inc.; Clear Channel Radio Licenses, Inc.; Clear Channel Management, Inc.; Clear Channel Metroplex, Inc.; Clear Channel Metroplex Licenses, Inc.; Clear Channel Holdings, Inc.; Clear Channel Productions, Inc.; CCC-Houston AM Ltd.; CCR Houston-Nevada, Inc.; Clear Channel Real Estate, Inc.

Further Reading

Brockinton, Langdon, ''Clear Channel Tunes in Billboard Business,'' *MEDIAWEEK,* October 27, 1997, p. 20.

Poole, Claire, ''The Accidental Broadcaster,'' *Forbes,* June 8, 1992, p. 58.

Rathbun, Elizabeth, ''Texas Size: Clear Channel Builds a Broadcast Dynasty,'' *Broadcasting & Cable,* October 7, 1996, p. 56.

——, ''Offering Follows Clear Channel Buying Spree,'' *Broadcasting & Cable,* June 3, 1996, p. 44.

Roman, Leigh Ann, ''Clear Channel's Presence in Memphis Mirrors Nationwide Trend of Station Consolidation,'' *Memphis Business Journal,* March 24, 1997, p. 49.

Serwer, Andrew E., ''The Best Li'l Broadcaster in Texas,'' *Fortune,* August 19, 1996, p. 26.

Viles, Peter, ''Clear Channel: Sunbelt Success Story,'' *Broadcasting & Cable,* July 5, 1993, p. 19.

—Jeffrey L. Covell

Comsat Corporation

6560 Rock Spring Drive
Bethesda, Maryland 20817
U.S.A.
(301) 214-3000
Fax: (301) 214-7100
Web site: http://www.comsat.com

Public Company
Incorporated: 1963 as Communications Satellite
Corporation
Employees: 3,766
Sales: $1.01 billion (1996)
Stock Exchanges: New York Chicago Pacific
SICs: 4899 Communication Services, Not Elsewhere
Classified

The first commercial satellite operator, Comsat Corporation has ownership in two global satellite systems, Intelsat and Inmarsat, and a strong presence in personal and business satellite communications services. Comsat was responsible for launching the first commercial communications satellite, Early Bird, in 1965 and from that historic achievement went on to launch numerous satellites in the decades to follow. Based in Bethesda, Maryland, the company was formed by the U.S. Congress to spearhead the country's interests in commercial satellite communications.

The First Ten Years

Comsat's unique position in the business world was carved out by the passage of the Communications Satellite Act of 1962, completed by the U.S. Congress on August 27, 1962. Signed by President John F. Kennedy four days later, the Communications Satellite Act established a national policy for the creation of a commercial communications satellite system in cooperation with other nations. Additionally, the act authorized the formation of a new, private company to represent the United States in the development and operation of the planned global satellite system. That company was Communications Satellite Corporation, or Comsat, a start-up company unlike any other business venture in the world. Its origins were singular, predicated on the decision by political leaders during the early 1960s to establish a commercial satellite network rather than spearheading such an undertaking through government agencies. Comsat, as the company was envisioned in August 1962, would be the first commercial satellite operator, a company operating in the private sector that would propel the United States into the commercial satellite arena and promote the commercial interests of the nation's businesses and population in satellite communications. Although unfettered in many respects from government control, Comsat would operate under the supervision of the Federal Communications Commission (FCC) as it endeavored, in the words of the Communications Satellite Act, "to provide global coverage at the earliest practicable date." Those words represented the marching orders for what *Newsweek* heralded as "the biggest new company ever created."

The incorporators of Comsat were nominated by Kennedy and confirmed by the U.S. Senate in October 1962. Responsible for forming the company and selecting its management, the group of individuals tapped by Kennedy included top executives from across the country, partners of prestigious law firms, bank presidents, newspaper publishers, and labor leaders—12 individuals in all. On February 1, 1963, the distinguished board of incorporators accomplished their first major task when they incorporated Comsat. Later in the month, they secured a $5 million line of credit with commercial banks for the company's start-up costs. Next, in March 1963, the company's incorporators filled Comsat's top two executive posts. After trimming down a list of 50 candidates to eight finalists, the incorporators selected Leo D. Welch, the soon-to-retire chairman of Standard Oil Company, as chairman and chief executive officer, and Dr. Joseph V. Charyk, Under Secretary of the Air Force for the previous three years, as president and chief operating officer. Each had specific roles to play for the company. Welch, with an extensive background in banking and international business, would be responsible for finances and negotiating international agreements, while Charyk, an aeronautical engineer with aerospace experience at Lockheed Aircraft and Ford Motor Co., would spend much of his time with technical studies, including the pressing decision of what type of satellite to use. After being informed of his appointment, Charyk referred to Comsat as ''a pioneering enterprise [that] will be judged as a demonstration of the free-enterprise system.'' Welch sounded nonplussed, calling the business venture ''rather a unique project,'' before adding, ''it's rather far out.''

With management in place, there was a sense of urgency to press forward and carry out the mission set forth in the Communications Satellite Act, which stipulated that the global commercial communications satellite system be established ''as expeditiously as practicable.'' In accordance with the spirit of the law, a steady stream of historic milestones punctuated Comsat's first decade of existence, beginning in April 1964 when the company awarded its first hardware contract to Hughes Aircraft Company for the production of the first commercial communications satellites. Comsat ordered the creation of an experimental-operational satellite to test the feasibility of placing a satellite in geosynchronous orbit, that is, a satellite able to mirror the rotation of the earth and thus remain in a fixed position over a particular point on the earth's surface. As work got underway, the groundbreaking satellite became known as ''Early Bird,'' gaining its official designation later as ''Intelsat I.''

While Hughes Aircraft worked toward making Early Bird a reality, Welch and Charyk concerned themselves with tasks familiar to all executives operating in the private sector. Comsat was a private corporation operating independently from the U.S. Government, and, consequently, did not receive any money from federal coffers. Like any other company aspiring to succeed, Comsat needed money. To raise the cash for the capital expenditures to complete their prodigious task, Welch and Charyk sold shares in the company in an initial public offering (IPO) in June 1964, netting proceeds of $196 million. The IPO was a resounding success, as investors scrambled to pick up shares in the company, paying $20 a share to own a piece of history and invest in what promised to be a lucrative market worth billions of dollars.

In August 1964, The International Telecommunications Satellite Consortium (Intelsat) was formed, a multi-national organization representing the interests of member countries in a global commercial communications satellite system. Comprising 15 countries at its outset, Intelsat became a chief source of revenue for Comsat in the decades to follow. Comsat, the U.S. member of Intelsat, was selected as manager of Intelsat on behalf of the 15 countries involved.

A year after Hughes Aircraft began work on Early Bird, the satellite was ready to be launched. In April 1965, Early Bird took to the skies, soared 22,300 miles above the earth, and was successfully emplaced in geosynchronous orbit over the coast of Brazil, becoming the world's first commercial communications satellite. The benefits for commercial use were meaningful, enabling live, transatlantic television broadcast and increasing by nearly two-thirds the telephone capacity across the Atlantic Ocean. The success of Early Bird, or Intelsat I, paved the way for successive generations of Intelsat satellites and filled in one piece of the puzzle that Welch and Charyk were charged with completing. Having secured satellite coverage between the United States and Europe, the two Comsat leaders next moved to provide satellite coverage for the rest of the world.

One month after the successful launch of Intelsat I, the FCC awarded Comsat the sole responsibility for the design, construction, and operation of three initial U.S. earth stations for international communications. The three earth stations, with their giant satellite antennas, were the first of 65 earth stations constructed during Comsat's first decade of business. In November 1965, work began on the second generation of Intelsat satellites. Comsat awarded a contract to Hughes Aircraft for the Intelsat II satellites, which were expected to provide early communications support for NASA's Apollo moon-landing program. Before the first Intelsat II was launched, construction of the next generation of satellites began when Comsat contracted TRW Systems, Inc. to build six Intelsat III satellites. With five times the capacity of Intelsat IIs, the Intelsat III satellites were slated to provide the final link connecting global satellite coverage.

Comsat's first major setback occurred in October 1966 when the first of the Intelsat II satellites failed to reach geosynchronous orbit. The second launch in January 1967 was successful, however, providing the first full-time satellite coverage over the Pacific Ocean. Construction of Intelsat IV satellites, which had five times the capacity of Intelsat IIIs, began in October 1968 under the auspices of Hughes Aircraft, but the most important event of the late 1960s occurred in July 1969 when an Intelsat III satellite was successfully emplaced in geosynchronous orbit over the Indian Ocean, providing full global satellite coverage for the first time.

Search for Identity in the 1970s and 1980s

In less than seven years, Comsat had achieved the major thrust of the Communications Satellite Act of 1962, compiling a laudable list of pioneering feats that ranked high in the history of the communications industry. From nothing, a new breed of competitor had been created and a new, potentially massive industry had been born, but the question facing Comsat as it prepared to enter its second decade of existence was: What to do next? Comsat Laboratories, located in Clarksburg, Maryland, was completed and occupied by a staff of 300—half of which where professional scientists and engineers—in September 1969, giving the company a research and development facility to advance the technology of satellite communications, but what direction would that advancement take the company? To Charyk, who took control of the company following Welch's departure and presided over its fortunes until the mid-1980s, fell the responsibility of running Comsat like a publicly-held corporation rather than a research and development entity focused wholly on advancing science and technology. Consistent profits would have to be made to please shareholders and new businesses would have to be developed to complement the company's satellite communications business, as attention shifted from historic achievements in the sky to the more mundane objective of achieving solid financial growth. As it turned out, operating Comsat as a profitable, diversified business proved harder to accomplish than establishing a global satellite communications system.

Comsat's entire business revolved around its global satellite network, Intelsat, until the mid-1970s, when unwelcomed news arrived that intensified the need to establish other business ventures. In late 1975, after deliberating over the issue for nearly a decade, the FCC decided that Comsat was nothing more than a utility, subject to the same rate regulations as other, more conventional utilities. The FCC's decision dealt a considerable blow to Comsat, barring the company from using high rates to recover development costs and start-up expenses on new projects and strictly regulating the company's rate of return. In the wake of the ruling, Comsat's net income dropped steadily, slipping from $4.62 per share in 1975 to $3.83 in 1976 and down to $3.12 in 1977.

Fortunately for Comsat, the company had begun to take its first measured steps into new business ventures just prior to the FCC's announcement. In 1975, through a subsidiary named Comsat General, the company formed Satellite Business Systems in a joint venture with IBM and Aetna Life & Casualty. Satellite Business Systems was created to provide extensive private communications networks to customers with widely dispersed facilities, enabling corporate clientele to transmit messages via satellite and bypass entirely the Bell telephone system. The problem for Comsat was that Satellite Business Systems would not be operational for a number of years and its start-up costs were hefty, leaving the company with no response to its dwindling profits. The company did find an answer in 1976, however, by starting its Marisat system, which provided maritime communications for the U.S. Navy, shipping companies, and offshore drilling operators. Also in 1976, Comsat established itself as a competitor in the domestic market with its Comstar system, which provided satellite services to AT&T. The revenues generated from Comstar and Marisat were sorely needed, bringing in roughly $69 million in sales of the company's $185 million total sales volume and lifted earnings to $4.28 per share, or $34 million.

Satellite Business Systems was hindered from the start by escalating start-up costs, and remained inoperative for years, dragging Comsat's revenues and profits downward. During the early 1980s, as work plodded forward with the joint venture, Comsat looked elsewhere for business opportunities and in 1982 found one that presented considerable potential for growth. In June 1982, the FCC dramatically extended the boundaries restricting satellite operators by approving direct broadcasting from satellites to homeowners' rooftops, ushering in the age of direct broadcast systems and opening up the consumer market to operators such as Comsat. In October 1982, Comsat formed Satellite Television Corporation to enter what was projected to be a $6 billion-a-year market. Headed, by Irving Goldstein, who joined Comsat in 1966, Satellite Television Corporation also was slated to market Comsat's own programming to the more than 20 million customers that the satellite television services were expected to attract. The foray into satellite television services was expected to ultimately be a $1 billion undertaking for Comsat.

By the mid-1980s, Comsat's record of diversification could be characterized as representing considerable potential, but delivering little in the way of positive, financial growth. In 1984, the company pulled out of its partnership with IBM Aetna Life in Satellite Business Systems after losing $50 million during the previous decade. In 1985, Comsat sold a company, Environmental Research and Technology, Inc., it had acquired in 1979 for less than the original purchase price, and, more devastating, plans were scrubbed for its direct pay-television venture, resulting in an after-tax write-off of $13.5 million. Long criticized for moving slowly and inexpertly, Comsat stood as a 22-year-old company that was still groping for the right answers. The company had ploughed millions of dollars into ventures, yet rarely garnered any appreciable return for its investments. As a reporter from *Forbes* noted, Comsat had "spent regulated profits on diversified losses."

Charyk's 22-year tenure of control ended in 1985, making room for the promotion of Goldstein, the former head of the satellite pay-television business, from president to chairman and chief executive officer. Goldstein promised wholesale changes, vowing to reverse Comsat's historical trend of diversifying imprudently. "We're going to see a new corporate ethic," he declared to reporters, "that stresses competitive markets and making money." To support his claim, Goldstein pointed to a contract with NBC to distribute programming to affiliate stations that was expected to generate up to $400 million in revenues during the ensuing decade. For further evidence, he pointed to a contract with Holiday Inns to provide hotel-room entertainment via a nationwide satellite that had the potential to bring in $200 million in revenues during the ensuing decade.

1990s and the Road Ahead

Industry pundits sat back and waited to see if Comsat could deliver on its promises, expectations, and potential. During the late 1980s, the company moved heavily into the entertainment business, seeking the sizeable profits that eluded it for nearly all of its existence. The leap into the entertainment business was precipitated in part by the burgeoning growth during the late 1980s of fiber-optic networks, which threatened Comsat's primary business. Consequently, the need to diversify became more intense as the 1980s drew to a close, leading to the company's acquisition of 62 percent of the Denver Nuggets, a National Basketball Association franchise in 1989. The remainder of the Denver of Nuggets was purchased in 1992. In 1991, Comsat acquired a partial stake in On Command Video Corp., a California-based company that developed and marketed a proprietary video entertainment system to hotels, and grouped the acquisition with its Denver Nuggets property in what would eventually be a subsidiary named Ascent Entertainment Group, Inc. In 1994, the scope of this subsidiary was widened with the acquisition of Beacon Communications Group, a film and television production company based in Los Angeles, and strengthened further with the acquisition in 1995 of the Quebec Nordiques, a National Hockey League franchise. The

Nordiques were subsequently moved to Denver, Colorado and renamed the Avalanche, winning the Stanley Cup during their inaugural year.

Comsat entered the mid-1990s supported by three primary business segments: international communications, technology services, and entertainment. The composition of the company's operations soon changed, however, when new management, led by president and chief executive officer Betty C. Alewine and chairman C.J. Silas, took over in mid-1996. Financially, the company was exhibiting the same symptoms that had dogged it for decades. Revenues were climbing steadily, but profitability continued to be a problem. Money managers believed the company's stock should have been trading at $55 per share, but Comsat's share price hovered below $30. Further, the company's bottom line provided clear signs that something was wrong. Between 1995 and 1996, revenues rose 18 percent to eclipse the $1 billion mark for the first time, but the company's net income plummeted 77 percent, dropping from $37.8 million to $8.6 million. The lackluster financial totals prompted Alewine and Silas to restructure the company, leading to the divestiture of its entertainment segment (Ascent Entertainment Group) and its manufacturing subsidiary, Comsat RSI, from the company's fold.

Refocused on international satellite services and digital networking services, Comsat entered the late 1990s facing the same fundamental challenge it had been struggling to overcome for decades. Sputtering profitability and a depressed stock value haunted the company. As the company prepared for the beginning of the 21st century, there were two promising avenues of growth that fueled hope for a brighter, more profitable future. In 1996, the company introduced Planet 1, a personal portable satellite telephone that served as a satellite terminal enabling data and voice transmissions via Comsat's network of earth stations and satellites. On another front, Comsat was enjoying encouraging success with its digital communications networks for multinational and national corporations. Between 1992 and 1996, Comsat established 14 operating companies in 12 markets stretching around the globe that provided its business customers with communications services in areas where communi-

cations needs outpaced the capabilities of existing public telecommunications networks. Revenues generated from these international companies increased nearly tenfold in three years, reaching $58 million in 1996. With Planet 1 and international digital communications networks providing hope for the future, Comsat headed into the late 1990s, confident that its new, promising business opportunities would at last deliver robust financial growth.

Principal Subsidiaries

Comsat Argentina, S.A.; Comsat Brasil, Ltda.; Comsat Capital I, L.P.; Comsat de Bolivia, S.R.L.; Comsat Columbia, S.A.; Comsat Guatemala, S.A.; Comsat Dijital Hizmetleri Ticaret Anonim Sirketi (Turkey); Comsat do Brasil Equipamentos de Telecommunicacoes Ltda. (Brazil); Comsat Enhanced Services, inc.; Comsat General Corporation; Comsat General Telematics, Inc.; Comsat Iletisim Hizmetleri Ticaret Anonim Sirketi (Turkey); Comsat Investments, Inc.; Comsat Mobile India, Inc.; Comsat Mobile Investments, Inc.; Comsat Overseas, Inc.; Comsat Personal Communications, Inc.; Comsat Peru S.A.; Comsat Technology, Inc.

Principal Divisions

Satellite Services; Network Services and Technology.

Further Reading

"Abble Telecom Announces Signing of Definitive Agreement with Comsat Corporation to Purchase Assets of Its Wholly Owned Subsidiary Comsat RSI JEFA Wireless Systems," *PR Newswire,* December 4, 1997, p. 12.
"Comsat: Gambling $1 Billion on its Entry into Home Satellite Services," *Business Week,* July 19, 1982, p. 124.
Fix, Janet L., "Comsat's Midlife Renewal," *Forbes,* October 21, 1985.
Kulkosky, Edward, "Comsat: Still Groping for a Higher Orbit," *Financial World,* August 1, 1979, p. 16.
Sparks, Debra, "Dear Betty," *Financial World,* March 18, 1997, p. 34.
"Two in Orbit," *Newsweek,* March 11, 1963, p. 78.

—Jeffrey L. Covell

COMSHARE®

Comshare Inc.

555 Briarwood Circle
Ann Arbor, Michigan 48108
U.S.A.
(800) 922-7979
Fax: (734) 769-6943
Web site: http://www.comshare.com

Public Company
Incorporated: 1966 as Com-Share Inc.
Employees: 600
Sales: $92.83 million (1997)
Stock Exchanges: NASDAQ
SICs: 7372 Prepackaged Software

Comshare Inc. is a developer and marketer of client/server and Web-based software designed specifically for analytic applications for business. Comshare's market-leading software includes applications that can perform budgeting, financial analysis and reporting, performance measurement, and retail strategic merchandise management tasks. The second-largest computer company in Michigan, Comshare began in 1966 as a spin-off of a University of Michigan project that provided computer timesharing to engineers. Through time the company's products have mirrored the evolution of the computer industry, moving from timesharing to mainframe applications, PCs, local area networks and Web-based software.

Company Origins in 1966

Comshare, originally spelled Com-Share, was founded in 1966 by six employees of the University of Michigan computer center. The young entrepreneurs had combined experience in engineering, computer science, management, and finance and together hoped to establish the first computer utility in the Midwest. With microcomputers only a distant dream, technological visionaries of the 1960s foresaw a world driven by giant mainframe computers in central locations which users would tap into through remote keyboards, as well as a telecommunications network which people could use to run their homes and businesses. The founders of Comshare shared this vision and were determined to be at the heart of this new computerized world. With original funding from the Weyerhauser lumber family, Comshare developed a proprietary system to facilitate timesharing functions and manage the huge amount of data that was handled by the company's mainframes.

Comshare went public in 1968 when optimism about the future of computer technology saw the company's stock price doubling in only two weeks to $50 a share. Despite the company's conviction that timesharing on mainframes would become a staple of life in the last quarter of the century, Comshare's early customer base consisted mostly of computer literate engineers who needed the data management and analytic computation functions of the company's computers. After only four years in business, however, this customer base collapsed as the recession of the early 1970s hit particularly hard in the technological industries that employed Comshare's clients. With engineers flipping burgers instead of equations, Comshare's losses began to match their total revenues and share price plummeted to the $2 range. The company had to find a new market for their computer services.

Into the Business Market in the 1970s

Although mainframe computers had been purchased and used by large companies since the 1960s, it was in the 1970s that smaller companies began to look for computer solutions to their data management problems. Comshare realized that the company's mainframe database technology could be applied to decision-making for business analysts and managers and that timesharing could provide an inexpensive solution for smaller companies. In the early 1970s Comshare began to target their product to business executives who needed graphic and statistical analysis of complex data. The company's Commander II timesharing software system was developed during this period with the business market in mind. The company also expanded its computer capacity with the use of newer, more powerful computers and company engineered telecommunications systems hardware.

By the mid-1970s the company had returned to profitability, earning about $1 million on sales of $13 million in 1976. By the

Company Perspectives:

Comshare's approach goes well beyond just providing world-class application software. We are a full-service vendor and have developed a comprehensive service infrastructure to help customers maximize their information technology investment. Customer Helpline Services, implementation services, and training programs are provided through Comshare's worldwide network of offices and appointed agents. Two hundred consultants each with product and industry expertise, work closely with customers to ensure smooth implementation and optimal business results. These are all elements of what we refer to as our "whole product" approach—our commitment to deliver value to our customers.

end of the 1970s sales had climbed to $78 million although net income failed to keep pace, hovering at about $4 million for most of the last half of the decade. With its new success in marketing timesharing to the business world, Comshare began to reach out to an international business market. A system of agents, joint ventures, and licensing created offices or affiliated companies in Canada, Europe, and Japan. The company also made its first acquisition during this period with the 1979 purchase of the Chicago-based Computer Research Company, one of the leading suppliers of large scale computer services.

Transition to Software in the 1980s

Despite the relative success of Comshare's timesharing business, by 1980 it became clear to company executives that with the drastic lowering in hardware prices for mainframes and the advent of affordable personal computers, timesharing was destined to become obsolete. The company, under the direction of CEO Richard Crandall, made the decision to convert the expertise they had developed with timesharing software into the creation of data analysis software for mainframes and PCs. "We needed to make sure that we were there when the software market coalesced," Wallace Wrathall, Comshare's chief financial officer through the 1980s, said in a 1995 interview with *Management Accounting*. "We put together a five-year plan basically and said, 'We're going to make a transition. It's going to take us five years to do that'," he noted.

The transition was a difficult one. In the early 1980s Comshare derived 98 percent of its revenues from timesharing and only two percent from packaged software. To turn that ratio around would require a complete revamping of the company's operations, including a significant downsizing of its employee base. In 1980 the company employed 1,400 workers, a figure that would drop to 780 some six years later. Comshare's first step in the reorganization process was to look to expand the company's range of services to a variety of potential markets. To that end the company was divided into five specialty groups each targeted to a specific market and each with the mission of designing, developing, marketing, and supporting specific services for that market. The groups included: Profiles—for human resource management; Parsec—for corporate money

management; 4.1.1.—for telephone companies; Compass—for certified public accountants; and Trust Services—for banks.

The costs of Comshare's restructuring began to be reflected on the balance sheet in the mid-1980s as revenues couldn't keep up with the expenses involved in new product development. By 1985, sales had dropped to $62 million, the company recorded a net loss of almost $5 million and share price plummeted from $20 to $3. "We had to take the long-term view and let earnings suffer short-term. We were betting the company," Wrathall told *Corporate Detroit Magazine*.

Comshare's emergence from this transitional period was achieved primarily by the development of the company's decision support system software, System W, and its promotion through an alliance with IBM. System W offered multidimensional modelling, consolidation, data manipulation, forecasting, what-if analysis, ad hoc inquiry, and reporting. It became the primary engine behind the company's Commander EIS (Executive Information System). Commander EIS, was designed to help executives extract information from the abundant data that most companies stored in their computer systems. The System W/Commander EIS software provided a collection of applications that sought to mimic the daily information activities of the executive. By the late 1980s five modules had been developed: Briefing Book, a collection of reports from sources throughout the organization; Newswire, a news tracking program tied to the Dow Jones News/Retrieval service; Execu-View, a nontechnical way of windowing through corporate information; Redi-Mail, a front-end to IBM's electronic mail system; and Reminder, an electronic tickler file.

The System W/Commander EIS system, which used the IBM operating system for mainframe computers, became the center of a marketing agreement whereby IBM would recommend Comshare's System W and Micro W decision support system software for use in IBM information centers and would include Comshare's EIS product in the computing package that IBM offered to business customers. Of all of the services that Comshare sought to develop in the early 1980s, System W and its Commander EIS applications were the only products to achieve a major success, and Comshare was quick to make this system the center of their software development plans. By the end of the decade the company had become the leader in the estimated $89 million Executive Information Systems market. Sales which had declined in the mid-1980s, began to rise once again, and by 1990 the company had record net income of almost $7 million on sales of $103 million. It appeared that Comshare had successfully made the transition from timesharing, which now made up only a small percentage of sales and would be discontinued entirely in 1992, to software development.

Up and Down in the 1990s

Although Comshare entered the 1990s with analysts predicting further growth for the Michigan company, by 1991 net income had dropped to $4.4 million and then plummeted to a net loss of $11 million the following year. Share price, which had climbed back to $20 since its nadir in the mid-1980s, collapsed by 75 percent almost overnight. Ironically, it was Comshare's close relationship with IBM, an alliance that had brought rich rewards in the 1980s, that was partly responsible for the company's problems in the 1990s. The battle between IBM and Microsoft for control of the world's computer operating systems which had begun in the late 1980s, was decided in Microsoft's favour in the early 1990s as Microsoft Windows became the operating system of choice for most PC users. "Comshare bet on IBM at that time," Wallace Wrathall, who was appointed CEO of the company in 1994, told *Management Accounting*. He continued, "In hindsight we wish we hadn't, but we were one of the many that bet on IBM. . . . Windows became the force for the GUI [graphical user interface], and we didn't have it."

To make matters worse for the struggling company, the demise of mainframe-based computing in favor of Local Area Networks (LAN) and client-server technology, which had been predicted by analysts for years but had failed to materialize, suddenly hit in the early 1990s, catching Comshare without a viable LAN product. "You never thought it wasn't going to happen. You thought it was going to be a slow transition," Wrathall said of the networking explosion of 1991 in an interview in *Corporate Detroit Magazine*, adding "the market changed so fast, we were behind. We were doing marketing. Focus groups told us we were doing the right thing. Six months later we weren't."

Comshare scrambled to revamp their software to accommodate client-server and LAN technology, but the transition was not an easy one. Applications needed to be completely redesigned for distributed operation, and the company's in-house development team had difficulty responding to the new market demands quickly. Sales continued to fall, dropping to $96 million in fiscal 1994. Wallace Wrathall, who had been the company's chief financial officer since the 1970s, was named CEO in 1994. Wrathall immediately undertook a reorganization program that would see the number of employees cut from 862 in 1993 to 640 by the end of the year. Even more significantly, for the first time Comshare began looking to outside sources for their software development needs. In early 1994, Comshare signed an agreement whereby California-based Arbor Software's Esspace on-line analytical processor would become the engine behind Comshare's new software vehicle, Commander EIS 4.0. Wrathall felt that this outsourcing would enable Comshare to respond more quickly to the dynamic computer software market.

Commander EIS 4.0, was a Microsoft Windows compatible application designed to work on desktop and client/server platforms. In addition to improvements in the services previously provided by the company's EIS products, the new software offered a robot-like function called Detect and Alert which, based on a set of rules provided by the client, could circle a company's databases and automatically report inconsistencies or problems in the form of a daily electronic newspaper.

By 1995 Comshare's sales had climbed back up to $108 million and it appeared that Wrathall's reorganization was a success. By mid-1996, the company's stock price was at an all-time high of $32 and sales had neared $120 million. But Comshare's roller-coaster performance wasn't over. In July 1996 a routine audit of the company's U.K. sales office revealed what management would call a "revenue-recognition problem." It appeared that the U.K. sales force, without the knowledge of the home office, were signing licensing agreements for software so they could get the sales on the books in one quarter and then allowing the client to return the product in the following quarter. Following the news of the scandal, stock price was cut in half overnight, and some stockholders initiated a class-action lawsuit claiming that the company should have known about the problem. Wrathall moved quickly to fire the U.K. management team, but stockholder confidence remained shaky.

To make matters worse, Arbor Software, the provider of the primary engine behind Comshare's EIS system, sued the company, alleging underpayment of software royalties. Comshare countersued, but while the case was in mediation clients could obtain the software from either company, creating a chaotic market. In fiscal 1996 Comshare recorded a net loss of almost $10 million, to be followed by a devastating loss of $17 million the following year.

Under pressure from the board Wallace Wrathall announced his retirement in August 1997 and the vice-president of product development, Dennis Ganster, was appointed to replace him. Ganster moved to restore shareholder confidence by solving cash-flow problems and improving sales force productivity. Comshare's EIS analytic applications including Comshare BudgetPLUS, Comshare FDC, and Comshare Decision were joined by Arthur Enterprise Suite, a merchandise planning, allocation, and analysis application for the retail industry. As the company reached the end of the 1990s, the computer industry was once again undergoing a major shift in direction with the explosion of the internet. This time Comshare appeared prepared for the transition with the development of Web-enabled decision support software. Given the extremely dynamic nature of the computer industry, it remained to be seen whether Comshare could retain its leading position in the analytic applications market.

Further Reading

Henderson, Tom, "Comshare Hopes End of Turmoil Is at Hand," *Detroit News*, September 28, 1997, p. C1.

——, "What Next?: Comshare," *Corporate Detroit Magazine*, October, 1994, p. 10.

Hodges, Judith, and Deborah Melewski, "Comshare Inc.," *Software Magazine*, July, 1993, p. 102.

Knight, Robert, "At Helm of Comshare, Crandall Executes Plan," *Software Magazine*, July, 1989, p. 90.

Williams, Kathy, and James Hart, "Comshare, Expanding the Third Dimension," *Management Accounting*, September, 1995, p. 59.

—Hilary Gopnik

Continental General Tire Corp.

1800 Continental Boulevard
Charlotte, North Carolina 28273-6311
U.S.A.
(704) 588-5895
Fax: (704) 583-8540
Web sites http://www.contigentire.com

Wholly Owned Subsidiary of Continental
Aktiengesellschaft
Incorporated: 1915 as The General Tire & Rubber
Company
Employees: 8,500
Sales: $1.4 billion (1996)
SICs: 3011 Tires & Inner Tubes

Continental General Tire Corp. is a leader in the manufacture, marketing, and export of tires. The company manufactures tires used as original equipment on vehicles from Ford, Chevrolet, General Motors, Mercedes-Benz, Nissan, and Toyota. Replacement tires are sold under the Continental, General, and Hoosier brand names. The company also manufactures private-label tires for mass marketers and independent dealers across the United States. A subsidiary of Continental Aktiengesellschaft A.G. (the world's fourth-largest tire maker) since 1987, the manufacturer struggled to maintain profitability in the late 1980s and early 1990s. Under the leadership of Bernd Frangenberg from 1994 through 1997, the company regained its focus and improved its bottom line, netting two percent on sales in 1996, its first year in the black since 1992. That same year General Tire added "Continental" to its name and moved its headquarters from Akron, Ohio, to Charlotte, North Carolina, near an existing tire plant.

Early 19th-Century Foundation

On the eve of the 21st century, the worldwide tire and rubber industry was in the hands of three major producers: Goodyear Tire and Rubber Co., Bridgestone/Firestone Inc., and Michelin Tire Corp. Continental General ranked among what *Modern Tire Dealer* called "The 'Other' Guys." But in the 19th century, long before the invention of synthetic rubber and only a few decades after the discovery of vulcanization, hundreds of rubber and tire companies vied with one another. A very unlikely city, Akron, Ohio, was dubbed the "rubber capital of the world," and it was in Akron that the General Tire and Rubber Company was established in 1915. It is one of the few original American tire companies to have survived to the present day.

The founder of the company, William F. O'Neil, was a native of the city, although he and his partner, Winfred E. Fouse, had first entered the rubber tire business in Kansas City, Missouri. In early 1909 O'Neil and Fouse pooled their capital and established the Western Rubber & Supply Company (renamed the Western Tire & Rubber Company in 1911), which sold tires. Both partners, however, had bigger dreams: where O'Neil's father, a wealthy merchant, agreed to give the two young entrepreneurs a loan to open a manufacturing business in their native Akron. In 1915 the General Tire & Rubber Company was launched. While O'Neil's father was president of the new company, William O'Neil, in the role of general manager, wielded most of the authority, and delegated little of it until his death in 1960.

Although there were hundreds of tire companies in the United States at the time, it was a propitious era for tires: in 1915 the number of passenger cars in the United States had surpassed two million, with one million produced in 1915 alone. In addition, World War I boosted the U.S. economy in almost all respects. Even the lower middle class by then could afford Model Ts. Because of more frequent blowouts, the vast majority of cars in those days came equipped with two spare tires, and the more expensive models even came with four spares. Hence business was ample for tire companies, and the General Tire & Rubber Company even turned a profit in its first year of operation.

One year later, the company manufactured its first tire bearing the General name. It was the first oversized tire on the market, especially fitted for passenger cars. No stranger to advertising, O'Neil paid $5,000 in 1917 to the prestigious *Saturday Evening Post* for a full-page ad introducing his new tire. While large-scale national advertising was common, it was highly uncommon—for a tire company at least—to appeal to individual car owners rather than to the car manufacturers in

Detroit. O'Neil's was an innovative marketing approach, and it worked. Franchised tire dealerships became crucial to the success of the General Tire & Rubber Company. The company also initiated the concept of trading in used tires for a complete set of ''Generals,'' as the tires were dubbed.

Emphasis on R&D: 1920–40

The growing importance of trucks and their particular tire needs did not escape the company's notice. Almost from the outset of its existence, truck tires became a specialty. The General Tire & Rubber Company pioneered the recapping of truck tires and in the 1930s came out with a series of low-pressure truck tires. By 1934 the company's research and development specialists had experimented with a revolutionary new ''drum method'' for producing truck tires that dramatically slashed the cost of manufacturing them and at the same time accelerated the speed at which they were manufactured by 50 percent. Without the ''drum method'' of truck tire production, the tremendous wartime demand for tires would not have been met. In 1940 the General Tire & Rubber Company produced the largest truck tire in the world.

In 1923, only eight years after the establishment of General Tire, the company had earned its first $1 million in sales after taxes (forty years later, the company would achieve its first $1 billion in sales). Its product innovations continued apace. The company had already come out in 1920 with its ''General Jumbo'' low pressure tire, which became a great success with car owners because of its superior mileage and maneuverability. In the late 1920s and throughout the financially difficult years of the Great Depression, General Tire not only pioneered in the development of truck tires, but entered the airplane tire business and continued to churn out new automobile tires, such as the Dual 8, the Dual 10, and the Squeegee. The company had acquired its first subsidiary in Mexico, and was exporting its tires throughout the world. Despite these signs of vigor and the fact that the 1930s witnessed the biggest vehicle registration in history—surpassing the 100 million mark by the mid-1930s—the company made no profit throughout most of the decade. Its survival alone had to stand as testimony to its vitality.

The survival years of the Depression gave way to prosperity during World War II. The dearth of natural rubber and the initial poor quality of synthetic rubber, however, hindered General Tire's profit potential. There was virtually a halt to all civilian automobile tire production, and many smaller tire companies were closed by the government or turned into munitions plants. While the General Tire & Rubber Company continued to operate, the company built a munitions plant in Mississippi and

operated it for the duration of the war. It also fulfilled other wartime requests, including building intricate pontoon bridges and improved gas masks.

Post-World War II Diversification

At the beginning of the war, with founder O'Neil still at the helm, the company had ventured outside the tire business by purchasing a 50 percent interest in the Pasadena, California-based Aerojet Engineering Corporation, which would become Aerojet General in the near future. This purchase marked the onset of an explosion of growth and diversification at the end of the war, which, among other distinctions, would make General Tire the country's biggest private radio and television owner by 1960.

The postwar years heralded great prosperity for General Tire. As for the tire business, the company began to supply General Motors, hence entering the new car or ''original equipment'' market in a significant way (it had already entered the original equipment market for trucks in the 1930s, as a supplier for International Harvester). Plant expansion was initiated: in 1959 the world's largest tire test track was completed in Uvalde, Texas; in 1967 the company's fourth tire plant was completed, in Bryan, Ohio; and in 1973 a radial tire manufacturing facility was constructed in Mt. Vernon, Illinois. William O'Neil did not live to see the company reap its first $1 billion in annual revenues in 1963. By then, however, he had witnessed radical changes in his company.

In the postwar years, the General Tire & Rubber Company gradually ceased to be exclusively a tire manufacturer and marketer. It entered the entertainment business, followed by tennis ball, wrought iron, and soft drink production, as well as chemicals and plastics manufacturing. In the early 1980s General Tire even began motion picture and video production. The identity of the company had altered so drastically that by 1984, the shareholders agreed to change the name and transform the company into a holding company consisting of four major subsidiaries. GenCorp, Inc., would be the name of the new parent company. General Tire, Inc., emerged as the tire manufacturing entity, a separate corporation operated independently.

The formation of General Tire, Inc., signaled a return to the original identity and purpose of the General Tire and Rubber Company. With subsidiaries in Canada (closed in 1991) and Mexico (sold in 1993), it was the fifth major tire company in North America, consisting of six manufacturing facilities, a tire fabric processing plant, and the giant Uvalde, Texas, tire test center, which was the largest in the world.

Continental A.G.'s Acquires General Tire, 1987

In 1987 GenCorp underwent large-scale restructuring, in part to ward off a hostile takeover attempt by General Acquisition, Inc. When one of Europe's largest tire manufacturers, Continental Aktiengesellschaft of Hanover, Germany, became interested in the possibility of purchasing General Tire, the shareholders of GenCorp were more than willing to sell.

Continental was one of Europe's oldest tire manufacturing companies, and the first tire company in the world to develop—in 1904—tires with treads. Flush with capital from one of its most successful years, Continental was determined to broaden its market base, which was largely domestic. Taking the U.S. tiremaker's "Sooner or later you'll own General" slogan to heart, Continental acquired the Akron-based company for $628 million in June 1987. General became Continental's largest subsidiary and transformed its parent into the fourth-largest tire company in the world. Gone, possibly forever, were the days when hundreds of tire companies could profit by serving the same domestic market. In the 1990s more than 80 percent of the tires sold worldwide were produced by five major tire companies, only one of which, Goodyear, was American-owned.

The parent company applied a "clean sweep" strategy to its newest and largest subsidiary. Gil Neal, General's well-liked president and CEO, left the company in 1989 and was succeeded by German Wilhelm Borgmann for the next 15 months. In 1991 Continental recruited Alan L. Ockene from Goodyear to serve as president and CEO. Ockene guided General Tire through its most difficult period since the Great Depression, a painful era of retrenchment experienced by all of the world's major tire companies. General was downsized—its Canadian plant was closed, a retail chain was sold, and the number of employees was reduced by 20 percent—and restructured into three major business units. Unfortunately, the huge cost of restructuring was barely recouped when the recession of the early 1990s took a severe toll on the company. Deepening losses and ongoing layoffs eroded employee morale.

The competitive environment remained intense, marked by escalating labor costs and tougher environmental demands. Recycling of the mountains of used tires generated by tire manufacturers in an environmentally acceptable manner, installing expensive emission controls in factories, and developing "energy saving" tires were some of the concerns of General Tire in the early 1990s.

Despite its problems the company continued to introduce innovative new tire products, including the Hydro 2000, a premium, all-weather tire designed to provide optimum performance on wet roads, and the Genseal tire, which self-sealed minor punctures. Both new products were ultra-premium tires for affluent customers, to whom General Tire's new products were increasingly marketed. In 1991 Ford Motor Company distinguished General Tire with its TQE (or top quality) Award, which only twelve of Ford's 4,000 tire suppliers received that year.

Since acquiring General in 1987, Continental had invested more than $300 million in the subsidiary and had little more than red ink to show for it. The parent company drew the line when 1993 ended with a nearly $23 million loss. Alan Ockene retired late in 1994, just after making two sad announcements: General had just registered another losing year, and the company's headquarters would be moved from its Akron home to Charlotte, North Carolina, near an existing tire manufacturing plant. Ockene was replaced as president by Bernd Frangenberg, former head of Continental's European Uniroyal tire operations.

Frangenberg's arrival confirmed Akron employees' fears that nothing less than a complete transformation of General Tire's corporate culture would satisfy its overseas parent. In fact, Frangenberg told *Modern Tire Dealer* that the transfer of General Tire's headquarters from Akron to Charlotte was more for cultural than logistical reasons, noting a need to do away with "old boy networks and politics." Though General—which tacked the Continental designation onto its name in 1996—struggled with difficult labor negotiations, lost a significant amount of business with Sam's Club, and relocated to a new headquarters, Frangenberg managed to eke out a break-even bottom line in 1995. Better yet, the company achieved a two percent profit on sales of $1.4 billion in 1996. Perhaps more importantly, Continental General (CGT) boosted its share of the original equipment (OEM) market from 11 percent to 15 percent and hiked its stake in commercial tire sales from 6.5 to 7.5 percent. Frangenberg was rewarded for his turnaround skills with the title of CEO (a position that had remained unfilled since Ockene's departure) and a clear leadership role.

"Take Charge" Attitude for the Late 1990s and Beyond

Under the slogan "Take Charge of the Road," Continental General faced the turn of the 21st century with a three-pronged strategy for profitable growth. CEO Frangenberg noted these "three pillars" in a special section of *Modern Tire Dealer* published in June 1997. "Transatlantic Synergy" coordinated the design, manufacturing, and technological strengths of both the parent and its subsidiary. The second pillar shifted Continental General's corporate emphasis from manufacturing to marketing and distribution, while pillar three stressed competitiveness. The company expected to adopt an innovative new manufacturing system in 1998. At a cost of $100 million, this process promised to "deliver remarkable improvements in quality, productivity, and flexibility."

Further Reading

"At Continental General: Moving toward 'A New Culture,'" *Modern Tire Dealer,* August 1995, pp. 35–37.

Birkland, Carol, "Tires: The Evolution Continues," *Fleet Equipment,* May 1991, pp. 18–25.

Bowman, Robert, "Warehousing: General Tire," *Distribution,* March 1989, p. 119.

"Continental General Tire Rebounds; Sets Strategy of Growth," *Modern Tire Dealer,* June 1997, pp. S6–S8.

Crovitz, L. Gordon, "Continental Divide: Blowout of Tire Merger Bid Underscores Europe's Unfinished Business," *Barron's,* December 16, 1991, p. 12.

"General Tire," *Rubber World,* January 1995, p. 6.

Kalail, Edward G., "General Tire Reorganizes Company into Three Major Business Units," *Business Wire,* April 3, 1992, p. 1.

——, "General Tire Announces Price Increase on All Private Brand Products Sold to Replacement Customers in U.S.," *Business Wire,* April 10, 1992, p. 1.

O'Neill, Dennis John, *A Whale of a Story: The Story of Bill O'Neil,* New York, N.Y.: McGraw-Hill, 1966.

Soffen, S. L., "Global Tire Review—Industry Report," Shearson Lehman Brothers, Inc., November 16, 1992.

Stoyer, Lloyd, "Conti General Faces Reality," *Modern Tire Dealer,* February 1996, pp. 49–51.

Ulrich, Bob, "The 'Other' Guys," *Modern Tire Dealer,* October 1994, pp. 19–22.

—Sina Dubovoj
—updated by April D. Gasbarre

Cooper Tire & Rubber Company

Lima & Western Avenues
Findlay, Ohio 45839-0550
U.S.A.
(419) 423-1321
Fax: (419) 424-4108
Web site: http://www.coopertire.com/

Public Company
Incorporated: 1960
Employees: 10,000
Sales: $1.6 billion (1996)
Stock Exchanges: Chicago New York Pittsburgh
SICs: 3011 Tires & Inner Tubes; 3069 Fabricated Rubber
Products, Not Elsewhere Classified; 3052 Rubber
Plastics Hose & Belting; 3714 Motor Vehicle Parts &
Accessories; 3061 Mechanical Rubber Goods

America's fourth largest tire manufacturer, Cooper Tire & Rubber Company ranks among the world's top ten tiremakers and is one of only two independent tire manufacturers in the United States. The company has developed a niche market within a huge commodity by concentrating on the manufacture of replacement tires. Its products are marketed through independent dealers and distributors under four brands, Cooper, Mastercraft, Starfire, and, since March 1997, Cooper-Avon. The company also makes tires for several private label marketers.

Cooper surpassed $1 billion annual sales for the first time in 1991, and although it is one of the smaller major tire companies, its earnings have led the industry: the company has paid dividends every year since 1950 and has increased the dividend annually since 1980. Although passenger car and truck tires constitute the majority of Cooper's production, the company is also involved in the manufacture of such engineered automotive products as vibration control devices, window and door sealing systems, hoses, and adjustable seating devices that provide lumbar support for passenger cars. Cooper is also one of the world's largest inner tube producers. Twelve plants in Ohio, Mississippi, Arkansas, Georgia, Indiana, the United Kingdom, and Mexico churned out more than 100,000 passenger tires per day in the mid-1990s.

Early 20th-Century Origins

In 1914 brothers-in-law John F. Schaefer and Claude E. Hart bought the M and M Manufacturing Company in Akron, Ohio. Schaefer and Hart entered the industry in the midst of a period of vigorous growth; between 1910 and 1916, tire production doubled every two years. As real incomes increased over the decade and the Ford Motor Company introduced its more affordable Model T, the demand for tires increased. Tire manufacturers increased capacity, designed new machinery, and promoted their new products.

At that time Ohio was a hub of tire manufacturing: one-third of the 134 tire companies in the United States were located in the state, and in the early decades of the 20th century Akron alone supplied one-third of the country's rubber goods. In this "rubber capital of the world," M and M Manufacturing produced tire patches, cement, and repair kits. These products were in high demand during the early years of the automotive tire industry because the first pneumatic tires were easily punctured. Poor tire quality also prompted consumers to seek rebuilt tires, and in 1915 Schaefer and Hart purchased a tire rebuilding business, The Giant Tire & Rubber Company, also in Akron.

In 1917 the Giant Tire & Rubber operations, including its staff of 29, were moved to Findlay, Ohio, into buildings abandoned by the failed Toledo Findlay Tire Company. Also that year Ira J. Cooper, whose name would later come to represent the company, joined Giant's board of directors. Fire destroyed the main building of the Giant plant in 1919, but reconstruction of a new, single story plant began immediately. As Giant rebuilt and continued to grow, Cooper became involved in forming his own company to manufacture new tires, The Cooper Corporation, which began operations in 1920. As founder, Cooper emphasized dedication to three principles: good merchandise, fair play, and a square deal. This "Cooper Creed" would serve as a corporate doctrine for many years to come.

Company Perspectives:

Cooper's greatest strength is its wide customer and market base. In tires, we maintain a healthy balance between house brands, which we market to a loyal 1,300 member independent dealer network, and private label customers such as Sears Roebuck and Co., Pep Boys and Winston Tires. In engineered rubber products, we serve virtually every light vehicle manufacturer in North America. In fact, our products were found on all of the top ten selling vehicles in the U.S. We're also expanding internationally, where we see significant opportunity to capitalize on the growing demand for American-made tires and engineered parts. Another key strength is our dedicated, high-caliber employee team. They are continually working to expand our production capabilities, improve productivity and increase manufacturing efficiencies. These are the bases for our position as a competitive, low-cost producer. Finally, Cooper has a proven long-term track record, strong operating cash flows, an enviable balance sheet and a rigorously followed capital investment policy. When you put it all together, that's what has—and will—continue to drive our success.

Industry Consolidation in the 1920s

The tire industry underwent several changes during the 1920s. New tire and rim designs made it easier for consumers to replace worn or punctured tires, and improved durability meant they would have to do so less often. Lower pressure tires developed during the decade improved comfort and road handling. Technological advances in the manufacturing process helped larger companies gain economies of scale that made them more competitive and promoted a consolidation of the industry in the 1920s and 1930s.

In 1930 The Giant Tire Company and The Cooper Corporation merged with the Falls Rubber Company of Cuyahoga Falls, Ohio, to form the Master Tire & Rubber Company. Falls had been a minor tire manufacturer established in the 1910s. Within one year, production at the three plants totaled 2,850 tires per day. At that time the company marketed tires under several brand names, including Falls, Giant, Sterchi, Hoover, Savage, Linco, Williams, Swinehart, Tigerfoot, and Englert. Downsizing in the 1930s brought all tire operations to Findlay by 1936.

Ira J. Cooper died in 1941, the first year the Cooper oval trademark was registered and used. In those early years of the brand's identification, the logo also included a banner proclaiming the tires' "armored-cord" construction. The company's red, white, and blue logo would become one of the most easily recognized emblems in the tire industry.

During World War II the company manufactured pontoons, landing boats, waterproof bags and camouflage items, inflatable barges, life jackets and tank decoys, and, of course, tires, to benefit the Allied effort. The company's contribution to the war effort was acknowledged in 1945 by the armed forces in a special ceremony bestowing the Army-Navy "E" Award. Soon after the war the company name was officially changed to Cooper Tire & Rubber Company, in recognition of Cooper's contribution to Master Tire & Rubber.

Post-World War II Expansion

The postwar era heralded expansion at Cooper and in the industry as a whole. Many factors contributed to the growth of the business. Increasing disposable income facilitated extensive car ownership. The expansion of the interstate highway system and suburbanization in the postwar era meant more wear and tear on tires, which in turn increased demand for replacement tires. Furthermore, rail transportation was supplanted by buses, taxis, and trucks for local and long-distance needs. In 1956 Cooper purchased a plant from the Dismuke Tire and Rubber Company in Clarksdale, Mississippi. The refurbished factory helped Cooper meet demand for tubes and tread rubber.

Between 1947 and 1964, Cooper Tire developed its own national wholesaling system. The company strengthened its ability to supply private brand customers and earned retailer loyalty by pledging not to open its own sales outlets. This marketing scheme simultaneously enabled Cooper to avoid the vagaries of the retail market.

Cooper went public in 1960. The distribution of shares facilitated another decade of growth for the company. Also that year a plant at Auburn, Indiana, where all automotive and custom engineered rubber parts were produced, was acquired. In 1964 an industrial rubber products division was established as a separate corporation known as Cooper Industrial Products, Inc. A second industrial products plant near El Dorado, Arkansas was acquired to expand those operations.

Capital improvements at the corporate headquarters during the 1960s included a new warehouse, which made operations at the Findlay plant more efficient. A research and engineering building was added to the location in 1964 to accommodate testing, laboratories, tire design, engineering, and sales training operations. Also that year the company completed the first phase of construction on its new tire plant in Texarkana, Arkansas.

One year later production facilities at the Texarkana, El Dorado, Auburn, and Clarksdale plants were expanded. Original outlets in Los Angeles and Atlanta were replaced with new and enlarged Cooper factory branches. Before the decade was ended, the Texarkana plant was expanded and a modernization plan was completed. The modernization included installation of one of the first cold feed tread tire tubers in the industry and inauguration of one of the largest 27 Banburys in the tire business.

Conversion to Radials in 1970s

In the 1970s Cooper strove to convert from bias-ply to radial tire manufacture. Bias tires had been produced by placing cords in rubberized fabric at an angle of 25 to 40 degrees to the direction traveled. Radial tires were first conceived in 1913, but the first practical application of the idea was not achieved until 1948. Radial assembly called for cords or belts that were arranged at a 90 degree angle to the direction traveled. Advantages of radial construction included improved wear (from an average of 23,000 to 40,000 miles), improved handling, and lower fuel consumption. The disadvantages, however, prohibited many companies from making the conversion until the 1970s. They included more complex and time-consuming production requirements, incompatibility with bias tires on the same vehicle, and diminished cushioning. For a brief period, many manufacturers in the industry compromised by introducing a bias-belted tire, but steel-belted radials became the norm in the late 1970s. Once the core of the tire industry, the bias-ply market had shrunk almost 75 percent by 1977.

Cooper completed research and development of its own radial tire manufacturing equipment and in-house product testing in 1973 and began full-scale production of steel-belted radial passenger tires at the Findlay and Texarkana plants the following year. During this time Cooper purchased a plant in Bowling Green, Ohio, for the manufacture of reinforced hose and extruded rubber products. Within three years, the plant was upgraded to produce rubber trunk, car door, window, and sunroof seals.

Near the end of the decade the U.S. government imposed the Uniform Tire Quality Grading System (UTQGS) to regulate the manufacture and labeling of bias and belted tires to help consumers in comparative shopping for tires. A voluntary system of tire grading had been proposed by the National Highway Traffic Safety Administration and accepted by the Rubber Manufacturers Association in 1966, but the guidelines were expensive and hard to enforce. The federal government advanced regulations several times during the 1970s, but grading did not begin until 1979 for bias-belted tires and 1980 for radial tires.

Counter Cyclical Strategies for the 1980s

The 1980s were years of significant change for Cooper Tire and the tire industry overall. Many American manufacturers scrambled to lower production capacity as the domestic market became saturated. From 1979 to 1987 a total of 23 U.S. plants were closed in the rush to downsize. Ironically, some of the industry's contraction could be attributed to successful technological advances that produced radial tires that withstood three times more mileage than previous models.

But while many of the world's original equipment tire manufacturers strove to consolidate in the face of steadily falling automobile sales, Cooper executives calmly delineated strategies for continued growth and even expansion of production. Cooper based its plans on several consistent factors that President and Chief Operating Officer Ivan Gorr described in a 1987 study. First, Cooper executives observed that there was as yet no other form of personal transportation that could provide the speed and convenience of the automobile and, therefore, no alternatives for the pneumatic tire. Planners at Cooper also noticed that, as auto manufacturing in the United States improved in the 1970s, consumers kept their cars longer. Demand for replacement tires grew in proportion to the average age of cars.

So as its competitors deserted plants, Cooper bought them and upgraded them. By overhauling older facilities, Cooper added capacity for one-third the cost of building new ones. In 1981 the Texarkana plant reached a production record of more than five million tires. The following year a three-phase expansion project at Texarkana was undertaken and three building additions at the Findlay plant were completed. Production capacity continued to increase with the purchase of a radial tire plant at Tupelo, Mississippi, and even more expansion at the Findlay plant.

By 1983 Cooper was ranked among the "Fortune 500" register of America's largest industrial companies, and a year later net sales exceeded $500 million. Over the next two years, Cooper made its first foreign acquisition, that of Rio Grande Servaas, S.A. de C.V., in Piedras Negras, Mexico, a manufacturer of inner tubes. The Cooper sales force was honored in the 1980s with the designation "best in the rubber industry" by *Sales & Marketing Management Magazine's* annual survey of industry executives. And in 1985, Cooper Tire & Rubber Company was enumerated among The 101 Best Performing Companies in America.

Research and development at Cooper were enhanced by several capital investments during the decade. A technical center for design, research and development, and testing was completed in 1984 at the Auburn, Indiana engineered products plant. The following year saw the completion of an addition to Findlay's Research and Engineering complex. The expansion facilitated increased in-house tire testing. A third addition enhanced the Findlay facility in 1988.

Distribution was also improved during the 1980s, with centers opening or expanding in Moraine, Ohio; Atlanta, Georgia; and Tacoma, Washington. Cooper warehousing capacity totaled 3.2 million tires by mid-decade. By the end of the 1980s distribution centers at Findlay and Moraine were granted foreign trade subzone status from the U.S. Department of Commerce. The designation diminished and suspended Cooper's payment of duty on imported raw materials.

As the company celebrated its 75th anniversary, Cooper's emphasis on the replacement tire market was vindicated. Statistics showed that the replacement tire market was three times larger than the original equipment market and had grown much faster over the decade. Investors appreciated the company's performance as well; Cooper's stock rose 6,800 percent during the 1980s. And with a per share price that amounted to 14 times earnings, Cooper was insulated from takeover threats.

During the 1980s foreign competitors took over six of the United States' largest tiremakers. By early 1990 six companies controlled 80 percent of the free world's capacity for tire production after the scramble for market share. The acquiring corporations reasoned that their size would provide bargaining power with American automakers as well as economies of scale. Domestic tire prices remained stuck, however, at 1985 levels.

The 1990s and Beyond

Cooper's capital investments and focus on the replacement market paid off in the 1990s. The company's efficient means of production propelled it to the highest gross profit margins in the industry at 33 percent. When larger competitors turned to the replacement market and tried to undercut Cooper's prices, those high margins gave the company leeway to join in the price wars.

Despite a lingering U.S. recession, Cooper's net sales topped the $1 billion mark in 1991 and the company added almost a quarter of a billion more the following year. Capital investments continued to grow in the 1990s: the company purchased a 1.8 million-square-foot tire manufacturing plant in Albany, Georgia, in 1990, then expanded its Findlay and Bowling Green locations in 1993. Construction of a new plant at Mt. Sterling, Kentucky, got under way in 1995, and a $10.5 million upgrade of the Clarksdale, Mississippi, facility began in 1994. Ongoing cost-cutting efforts almost doubled Cooper's operating margin from the late 1980s to the early 1990s.

In the meantime, Cooper's annual revenues increased from $1.2 billion in 1992 to $1.4 billion in 1994, while net income climbed to $128.5 million. Ivan Gorr retired that year, leaving behind a sterling record: sales had increased threefold and profits almost sextupled during his last decade at the helm. Gorr was succeeded as chairman and CEO by Pat Rooney, a 40-year company veteran who had joined the company right out of college in 1956. Sales continued to grow under Rooney's leadership, totaling $1.6 billion by 1996. But high raw material costs that, because of competitive pressures, could not be passed on to customers in the form of price increases, cut into Cooper's net in the intervening years. Profits declined to $112.8 million in 1995 and slid to 107.9 million in 1996. Cooper's usually high-flying stock suffered as well, dropping from a high of more than $39.50 per share in 1993 to less than $18 in 1996.

Though Cooper-made tires are sold in dozens of countries worldwide, overseas sales totaled less than ten percent of the company's total revenues that year. The Ohio firm boosted its foreign operations with the March 1997 acquisition of Great Britain's Avon Rubber plc for $110.4 million. The purchase gave Cooper a plant in England, distribution throughout France, Germany, and Switzerland, and footholds in several emerging markets in Asia. It also added $169 million to Cooper's sales column and $6.5 million to the bottom line.

By that time the Cooper Tire & Rubber Company no longer ranked among *Fortune*'s elite. Nevertheless, it remained a widely admired firm, both for its labor/management relations and its long-term stock performance. In 1993 authors Levering and Moskowitz named it one of America's best employers, giving particular note to Cooper's high pay, employee longevity, and workplace pride. And even after the rocky ride its shares took in the mid-1990s, author Gene Walden singled out Cooper's equity among *The 100 Best Stocks to Own in America.*

Principal Divisions

Tire Products, Engineered Products.

Further Reading

Abelson, Reed, "Companies To Watch: Cooper Tire & Rubber," *Fortune,* October 9, 1989, p. 82.

"At Cooper Tire: New Man's Old Hand," *Modern Tire Dealer,* August 1995, pp. 40–42.

"At Cooper Tire: Playing a Pat hand," *Modern Tire Dealer,* August 1996, pp. 38–40.

Blado, Anthony, "Cooper Tire: Under Some Pressure," *Financial World,* July 10, 1990, p. 18.

Bremner, Brian, and Schiller, Zachary, "Three Who Bucked the Urge to Merge—and Prospered," *Business Week,* October 14, 1991, p. 94.

Byrne, Harlan S., "Cooper Tire & Rubber: Ohio Company Sets the Pace in the Replacement Market," *Barron's,* November 26, 1990, p. 39.

——, "Ready To Accelerate," *Barron's,* March 21, 1994, p. 19.

"Cooper Tire Company," *Modern Tire Dealer,* September 1994, p. 72.

Driscoll, Mary, "Cooper Tire & Rubber: A Short Course in Value Pricing," *CFO, The Magazine for Senior Financial Executives,* January 1994, p. 24.

Dubashi, Jagannath, "Cooper Tire: Retreading Growth," *Financial World,* August 3, 1993, p. 17.

Gorr, Ivan, "Cooper Tire: Successful Adaptation in a Changing Industry," *Journal of Business Strategy,* Winter 1987, pp. 83–86.

Holzinger, Albert G., "A Successful Competitor," *Nation's Business,* April 1993, pp. 59–60.

"Our History," Findlay, Ohio: Cooper Tire & Rubber Company, company document, 1993.

Marcial, Gene G., "How Cooper May Make Tracks," *Business Week,* December 26, 1994, p. 128.

Schiller, Zachary, "Why Tiremakers Are Still Spinning Their Wheels," *Business Week,* February 26, 1990, pp. 62–63.

Stoyer, Lloyd, "Avon Purchase a Global Boost for Cooper: Agreement Enhances European Presence," *Modern Tire Dealer,* March 1997, pp. 38–39.

Taylor, Alex III, "Now Hear This, Jack Welch!," *Fortune,* April 6, 1992, pp. 94–95.

"The Tire Industry's Costly Obsession with Size," *Economist,* June 8, 1991, pp. 65–66.

—April D. Gasbarre

Copart Inc.

5500 East Second Street, 2nd Floor
Benicia, California 94510
U.S.A.
(707) 748-5003
Fax: (707) 748-5099
Web site: http://www.copart.com

Public Company
Incorporated: 1982
Employees: 1,050
Sales: $126.3 million (1997)
Stock Exchanges: NASDAQ
SICs: 7389 Business Services, Not Elsewhere Classified

With 50 locations across the nation, Copart Inc. is one of America's biggest chains of junkyards, or more accurately, salvage vehicle auction services. The fast-growing company was among the first to consolidate this industry, expanding from four California auction yards in 1990 to 53 locations in 26 states by October 1997. By that time it was processing more than 410,000 units—in excess of half-a-billion dollars worth of autos—each year, accounting for over 16 percent of the $3 billion vehicle salvage industry's volume. Acquisitions have driven an astounding average annual growth rate of more than 100 percent in the early 1990s, with sales multiplying from $6 million in 1992 to over $126 million by 1997. Net income grew even faster as the company spearheaded the consolidation of a highly fragmented industry, from less than $500,000 to almost $12 million. This rapid expansion ranked Copart 21st among *Fortune* magazine's roster of 1997's 100 Fastest-Growing Companies. Cofounder and CEO Willis Johnson took the company public in 1994, retaining a 31 percent stake.

The Auto Salvage Industry

Copart was founded in 1982 by Willis Johnson, a 34-year-old with ten years of experience in the auto salvage business. (Johnson had a partner for four years but bought him out in 1986.) The word "junkyard" generally conjures up thoughts of rusting hulks of twisted, useless metal surrounded by corrugated metal fence. However, while auto salvage yards (also known in industry parlance as "pools") are obviously a key element of Copart's business, they are just the visible tip of the auto salvage iceberg. In fact, the business is essentially an intermediary service between insurance companies and others with undriveable vehicles to sell and used parts dealers looking for inventory. About 80 percent of the time, the chain of events starts with a totaled car, but Copart also processes stolen vehicles that have been recovered and those damaged in natural disasters. Insurance companies (the industry's core "suppliers") bring these seemingly useless vehicles to salvagers hoping either to recoup some costs or at least minimize disposal expenses. The salvager first determines whether a vehicle can be economically repaired and sold on the used car market or should be dismantled. If the car is truly totaled, it is up to the salvage company to sell it to a dismantler, usually via auction. Whether the car is fixed, "parted out," or scrapped, the insurer gets the proceeds.

So how does a salvager like Copart make a profit? It charges auto suppliers for its towing, assessment, processing, and storage services. These fees are customarily realized in one of two ways: by consignment, charging a flat unit rate, or by outright purchase, wherein the salvager buys the vehicle from the insurer and auctions it at a profit. At the other end of the transaction, the auto rebuilders and dismantlers who bought the vehicles also paid fees for storage and towing.

Origins in Mid-1980s

Until the 1980s, the salvage industry was composed of many small, local facilities. Seeking to trim underwriting costs by outsourcing peripheral activities, insurance companies began to demand more efficient service from salvagers. Copart was one of the few companies in the industry to answer the challenge with a comprehensive plan of action. It pursued operating efficiencies via two general strategies: consolidation and innovation.

Copart president Willis Johnson started out in 1982 with one salvage yard near Oakland, California. Over the course of the

---

Company Perspectives:

Now that the company has reached the position of having broad market coverage for its services throughout the country and has become a leading provider to the major vehicle suppliers, the challenge for Copart is threefold: to continue to expand selectively through acquisitions and new openings where market conditions are positive; to continue to integrate all operations and facilities for maximum efficiency and profitability, and to continue to innovate by providing new services supporting the salvage vehicle disposition process.

---

decade, he used Copart's cash flow to acquire four more salvage/auction operations in the state. Yet Johnson was not satisfied with growth by brute force. He sought to enhance service to his two client groups—car suppliers and buyers—and simultaneously to maximize his own profits by implementing a multifaceted expansion plan. Over the course of the ensuing 15 years, he introduced innovative purchase programs, developed advanced management information systems, cultivated a loyal customer base, and expanded geographically.

A key to Johnson's strategy was the development of the Percentage Incentive Program, or "PIP." Under PIP, Copart pockets a fixed percentage (usually 15 percent) of the return on each vehicle it processes. In contrast to the traditional consignment method, which promised a set return to the yard no matter how much a given vehicle actually brought at auction, this arrangement gave Copart a vested interest in squeezing every dime from the resale process. Just as used car dealers clean and repair autos they purchase, Copart would wash and in some cases repair incoming vehicles in order to enhance resale value. Cars with broken windows but intact interiors might warrant special storage considerations ranging from tape and plastic to shrink-wrapping. Finally, Copart made efforts to promote its auctions in order to encourage higher attendance and thereby to ensure higher bidding. According to a 1994 report on Copart by the Oppenheimer investment group, per-car proceeds from PIP exceeded normal consignment fees by about $50 while adding negligible amounts to the auctioneer's expenses. Though Copart clearly preferred and promoted the PIP program, it offered suppliers the option of choosing the fixed-fee consignment and purchase options as well. Many of the chain's customers agreed that PIP was a good concept; by 1990, about 70 percent of Copart's vehicle transactions were made through the program.

Johnson also pioneered innovations in information management, compiling and publishing what Oppenheimer called "the industry's definitive salvage estimating guide." An automated version of this manual was dubbed the Copart Asset Manager. Insurance adjusters could enter a vehicle's make, model, options, mileage and damage, and the software would calculate a value based on past returns on comparable vehicles. The software gave insurance companies easy access to information that helped adjusters decide whether to repair a vehicle or write it off as a total loss. Copart inspired confidence in the accuracy of the system by promising to purchase vehicles at the quoted value.

However, the service did not stop there. Copart's exclusive Salvage Lynk tracking software enabled vehicle suppliers to obtain information on their property throughout the transaction period, which averaged one to three months. Copart provided dedicated network terminals to insurers who took advantage of this system. The company also compiled monthly transaction and status reports, developed training programs to familiarize insurance adjusters with state vehicle registration regulations and procedures, and let some of its biggest customers set up inspection areas at Copart yards. A database of over 18,000 potential buyers enabled Copart to target marketing efforts through direct mail. The company even offered "frequent buyer" incentives.

Nationwide Expansion in 1990s

Johnson tapped private loans and bonds to finance his growth strategy in the early 1990s. Acquisitions in Oregon, Washington, and Texas nearly tripled Copart's yearly volume, from 17,200 autos in 1990 to over 45,000 by July 1993. Johnson's acquisition push proved well timed. Many operators of the nation's independent salvage yards were nearing retirement age, and few of these local operators had successors lined up. Johnson's stellar professional reputation made him an ideal acquirer. Copart made an initial public stock offering in March 1994, raising $26 million to finance a flurry of acquisitions. By that July, the chain had increased its annual unit volume to over 100,000 at 15 locations.

The company's largest purchase to date came in May 1995, when it bought NER Auction Group for $43.6 million. NER's network of 20 auto salvage facilities in 11 midwestern states doubled Copart's total auto processing volume to more than 220,000 units per year by July. However, NER proved a difficult fit with Copart's previous operations due to the fact that it relied almost exclusively on the fixed-fee consignment method in contrast with Copart's emphasis on the PIP program. This factor skewed Copart's financial results for fiscal 1996. Furthermore, the ratio of vehicles processed through PIP declined to just 25 percent in fiscal 1996. Copart's profit margin as a percentage of sales suffered a corresponding decline, sliding from 11.9 percent in fiscal 1995 to 9.5 percent in fiscal 1996 and 1997. The new parent quickly set to work converting the former NER operations to its preferred program. By the end of fiscal 1997, about one-third of Copart's total sales were through PIP, and 61 percent remained on fixed-fee consignment.

Competition between Copart and its chief rival, Insurance Auto Auctions, Inc., to purchase the biggest and best salvage yards in key markets drove up acquisition prices, making the establishment of "greenfield" operations more attractive in some cases. Although acquisitions continued to be the company's primary growth vehicle, it also founded six new locations from July 1995 to July 1996.

While Copart's operations spanned coast-to-coast by the mid-1990s, many areas remained in which the firm did not have a presence. In order to provide nationwide service to the country's biggest insurance companies, the company established The Copart Network, a confederation of independent vehicle auction houses. Having built a nationwide chain of facilities supported by sophisticated information systems, Copart CEO

Willis Johnson was poised to proceed with the next step in his master plan: to procure regional and national contracts with the nation's leading insurance companies. Johnson's fiscal 1996 letter to shareholders boasted that "Vehicle suppliers can make one phone call to Copart to assign a vehicle for salvage anywhere in the country as well as monitor and track each vehicle in the disposition process."

Though some industry observers predicted that the decline in collisions that started in 1980 would continue indefinitely, Copart's strategy of consolidation and professional management seemed to assure it of profitable growth through the remainder of the 20th century.

Further Reading

"Anatomy of a Deal: Mezzanine Financing as IPO Foundation," *Inc.,* September 1995, p. 113.

Croghan, Lore, "Copart: Crash Cow," *Financial World,* March 11, 1996, p. 16.

McLean, Bethany, "An Urge to Merge," *Fortune,* January 13, 1997, p. 159.

Murphy, H. Lee, "At the Top of the Junk Heap of Cars," *Crain's Chicago Business,* July 8, 1996, pp. 4, 23.

Oppenheimer & Co., Inc., "Copart Inc.—Company Report," *The Investext Group,* May 27, 1994.

—April D. Gasbarre

The Copley Press, Inc.

7776 Ivanhoe Avenue
La Jolla, California 92037
U.S.A.
(619) 454-0411
Fax: (619) 454-5014
Web site: http://www.uniontrib.com

Private Company
Incorporated: 1928
Employees: 3,500
Sales: $398 million (1995 est.)
SICs: 2711 Newspapers: Publishing, or Publishing and
    Printing; 7375 Information Retrieval Services

Owned and operated by the namesake Copley family, The Copley Press, Inc. encompasses over 40 mostly suburban newspapers in and around Chicago and Los Angeles. The company's flagship, the *San Diego Union-Tribune,* is one of America's largest privately-owned dailies. Other operations include a San Diego County joint venture in fiber-optics, a California resort, and a newsprint mill. For a quarter of a century, the company has operated under publisher and CEO Helen Copley, widow of second-generation chairman James Copley.

Turn-of-the-Century Roots

The roots of this publishing company reach back to 1905, when patriarch Ira Clifton Copley acquired his first newspaper, the *Aurora (Illinois) Daily Beacon.* A graduate of Yale, at 25 years old Copley had assumed management of his father's floundering gas company in 1889. In the intervening years, he had built a network of utilities in northeast Illinois, served as a lieutenant colonel in the Illinois National Guard (earning the lifelong designation "Colonel Copley"), and was elected to the U.S. Congress. In fact, political ambition provided the motivation for his earliest newspaper acquisitions.

Established in 1846, the *Beacon* had changed hands several times before Copley came along and was losing an estimated

$12,000 per year by the turn of the century. Within just six years, Copley had not only turned the periodical around, but had also merged it with three other local papers. His budding publishing empire expanded to Elgin, Illinois, in 1910 with the acquisition of the *Elgin Daily Courier* (later *The Courier-News*). He added the *Joliet Herald-News* in 1913.

At this time, the newspaperman established three key ideals later related by Walter S. J. Swanson in *The Thin Gold Watch*: "that the reader comes first, so news must be told without bias; that what an advertiser properly can ask of a newspaper is good results; and that a local newspaper is 'in partnership' with its area and its people, and must be as locally run as possible." As the Copley publishing group grew over the decades, these hallmarks—especially local editorial autonomy—continued to be honored.

Copley sold his utilities group, Western United Gas & Electric Co., in 1926 and devoted his attention to the publishing business. He used the proceeds of the utility sale to fund a flurry of acquisitions, including the *Illinois State Journal*, the state's oldest daily newspaper. Copley purchased the *San Diego Union/Evening Tribune,* one of California's oldest business, from the Spreckles family in 1928. That same year he acquired Kellogg Newspapers, Inc., a group of nine Los Angeles-area papers and three commercial printing plants, from Frederick W. Kellogg and renamed them the Southern California Associated Newspapers. The unlikely geographic arrangement of his properties—a cluster in Illinois and another group in distant California—arose in part out of family considerations, for both Copley's parents and his in-laws lived in Los Angeles County. The Copley Press, Inc., with headquarters in Illinois, was organized in 1928. The California papers operated as two separate subsidiaries of The Copley Press.

The Great Depression proved challenging but not devastating to Copley. Advertising revenues were halved from 1929 to 1933, but circulation actually rose during some years of the fiscal crisis. In 1932, the company disposed of two ailing California papers. By the late 1930s, Colonel Copley was amassing broadcast properties, acquiring radio stations in communities already served by his newspapers.

150

Company Perspectives:

The Copley Creed: The newspaper is a bulwark against regimented thinking. One of its duties is to enhance the integrity of the individual, which is the core of American greatness. Each city in which we publish is a city of distinctive personality. Each newspaper must be a distinctive newspaper reflecting the life of each hometown. No one can think for the American people. We believe it is our responsibility to ring out the truth loud and clear, and to stimulate thought at the close personal level of the individual and the community.

New Leadership Faces Postwar Difficulties

In 1942, Colonel Copley made himself chairman of the company and named Audus W. Shipton, a career newspaperman, to succeed him as president. When the patriarch died five years later, his adopted sons, James and William, shared ownership of the family empire. William's stake was held in trust until his 40th birthday in 1959, and while he continued as a "reporter" in Paris, elder brother James was given the corporate chairmanship in addition to his responsibilities as executor of Colonel Copley's will. At the same time, the Copley Press was struggling with a newsprint shortage and subsequent high printing costs. Unlike other businesses that prospered during this period, Copley and the newspaper industry struggled to achieve profitability in the immediate postwar era.

It took James three nerve-racking years to settle his father's will before he assumed the more direct management role of president and publisher of the *San Diego Union* and *San Diego Tribune.* Over the course of the next five years, James invested virtually all the Copley Press's profits in four new production plants and two small California newspapers. He also acquired Los Angeles television station KCOP in 1953 for $1.37 million, and founded the Copley News Service, which by the late 1990s had offices in Washington D.C., Mexico City, Sacramento, Los Angeles, and Springfield, Illinois.

Perhaps impatient to collect his inheritance, Parisian William Copley sued to liquidate the company in 1955, accusing James of mismanaging their father's estate and its assets. James sold the Los Angeles TV station for $4 million (a handsome profit) in 1957 and bought out William's stake in 1959 for a total consideration of $11.8 million. The price valued the entire estate at over $26 million, more than five times the sum of Colonel Copley's estate in 1947. It was a powerful vindication of James' management skill, expertise that he would wield for another 24 years as head of the family empire.

Over the course of his newspaper career, James Copley increased chainwide circulation from 390,000 to 768,000. He started a film production company, a small book publisher, a scholarly journalism review, and acquired a resort hotel. During this period, he also moved the Copley Press headquarters from Illinois to California and inaugurated the "Ring of Truth" corporate logo. He died in 1973 after a lengthy illness, and his wife, Helen Kinney Copley, surprised many by assuming the presidency of the Copley Press.

Helen Takes the Helm in the 1970s

Described by *Newsweek* in 1975 as "a business novice who had been shielded from corporate life," Helen Kinney Copley had started her career at Copley Press as secretary to James. She held that position for 13 years before being "promoted" to spouse. After James' death, Helen quickly succeeded Robert Letts Jones, who had served as president since 1965. She would not only prove herself up to the task of running a cross-country newspaper empire, but would go on to become one of San Diego's most influential women.

It was not an easy career transition. Several of the company's operations were in the red, the widow owed millions in inheritance taxes, and her late husband had authorized a $40 million program of capital improvements. Within two years Helen Copley had decisively divested five dailies—including the *Sacramento Union,* which later went under—and nine weeklies, cut loose five percent of the work force, and sold off the corporate jet and Illinois real estate. Helen also revised the papers' famously conservative editorial stance, embracing investigative reporting and increasing coverage of women's and minorities' issues and the arts.

Mergers Mark 1990s

Ever since their induction into the Copley family of newspapers, *The San Diego Union,* a morning paper, and the *San Diego Tribune,* which came out in the afternoon, had shared a headquarters and several back-office functions such as advertising and distribution. Although the *Tribune* had two Pulitzer prizes to its credit, circulation declined from 133,000 in 1979 to 116,700 in 1991. That year, Helen Copley announced her intent to combine the two dailies as *The San Diego Union-Tribune,* a paper with both a morning and an afternoon edition, as of January 1992.

Copley Press acquired five more suburban Chicago newspapers in 1991 and took part in the development of a fiber-optic network in San Diego County in 1994. In 1996, Copley Press acquired two more Illinois newspapers, the *Peoria Journal Star* and the *(Galesburg) Register-Mail,* for a total of $174.5 million. Their combined daily circulation of over 100,000 increased the total daily circulation of Copley's eight Illinois newspapers to more than 300,000.

David, Helen's son by a first marriage who was later adopted by James Copley, became company president in 1988. By the time he celebrated his tenth anniversary in that position, his mother had made it clear that he would inherit the family business, as the 75-year-old chairman had "no plans to sell the company."

Principal Divisions

The San Diego Union-Tribune; *The Daily Breeze* (Torrance, Calif.); *The Outlook* (Santa Monica, Calif.); *Borrego Sun* (Borrego Springs, Calif.); *The News-Pilot* (San Pedro, Calif.); *The Beacon News* (Aurora, Ill.); *The Herald News* (Joliet, Ill.);

The Register-Mail (Galesburg, Ill.); *The Courier* (Lincoln, Ill.); *The News Sun* (Waukegan, Ill.); *The State Journal-Register* (Springfield, Ill.); *The Courier News* (Elgin, Ill.); *The Peoria Journal Star* (Peoria, Ill.); SUN Publications (Naperville, Ill.).

Further Reading

Bonfante, Jordan, "Lady Power in the Sunbelt," *Time,* March 19, 1990, pp. 21–22.

The Copley Press, Aurora, IL, Aurora: Copley Press, Inc., 1953.

Dower, Rick, "Bright New Paper, Same Old Bosses," *San Diego Business Journal,* December 16, 1991, p. 11.

——, "U-T Merger Causes Staffers to Brace for Possible Layoffs," *San Diego Business Journal,* September 16, 1991, pp. 3–4.

Leavitt, Judith A., *American Women Managers and Administrators,* Westport, Conn.: Greenwood Press, 1985.

McDowell, Barbare, and Hana Umlauf, eds., *Good Housekeeping Woman's Almanac,* New York: Newspaper Enterprise Association, 1977.

Peer, Elizabeth, and Peter S. Greenberg, "Coping at Copley," *Newsweek,* December 29, 1975.

"San Diego Daily Fades as Market Outgrows It," *The New York Times,* September 23, 1991, p. D14.

Swanson, Walter S.J. *The Thin Gold Watch: A Personal History of the Newspaper Copleys,* New York: Macmillan, 1970.

—April D. Gasbarre

Corrections Corporation of America

10 Burton Hills Boulevard
Nashville, Tennessee 37215
U.S.A.
(615) 263-3000
Fax: (615) 269-8635

Public Company
Incorporated: 1983
Employees: 7,410
Sales: $462.2 million (1997)
Stock Exchanges: New York
SICs: 8744 Facilities Support Services

Celebrating its 15th anniversary in 1998, Corrections Corporation of America (CCA) is the leader of the private prison management industry with more than 50 percent of the market. CCA designs, constructs, owns, and manages prisons for governments at the local, state, and federal level. In February 1998, it operated 67 facilities in Nevada, Arizona, New Mexico, Colorado, Texas, Oklahoma, Kansas, Minnesota, Louisiana, Mississippi, Tennessee, Indiana, Georgia, Florida, South Carolina, Virginia, Maryland, New York, and Ohio as well as Australia, Puerto Rico, and the United Kingdom. With a capacity to hold nearly 53,000 prisoners, its facilities range from minimum to maximum security and include men's, women's, and juvenile institutions.

Founded 1983

CCA was founded in 1983, but its roots can be traced to the late 1970s. Tom Beasley, chairman of the Tennessee Republican Party, was at that time serving on a committee charged with choosing a new state corrections officer. Beasley's research revealed a system plagued by high turnover, tight budgets, and overcrowding. The experience made him begin to wonder if there might not be a private sector solution to this growing public sector problem.

By 1983, Beasley was convinced that the application of a few simple business practices could transform the corrections system from an inefficient bureaucracy into a profitable enterprise. He recruited his former West Point roommate, Doctor ("Doc") Crants, as well as Terrell Don Hutto to help bring the concept into being. The troika's talents and experience melded excellently. Beasley had vital political connections. Crants brought an M.B.A. and a law degree, both earned at Harvard, to the table. Hutto possessed sterling corrections credentials, having not only directed two state prison systems, but also served as president of the American Correctional Association.

The threesome presented their prison privatization concept to Massey Burch Investment Group, a venture capital firm, on February 14, 1983. The investment company (which had also backed Kentucky Fried Chicken and Hospital Corp. of America) floated the partners $500,000 after a mere 15-minute presentation. The founders and their financial sponsors envisioned a "market" ripe for growth: though the crime rate had actually been declining, the U.S. inmate population doubled from 1975 to 1984 and tough new sentencing laws promised ever-greater volume. "We're on the ground floor of a multibillion-dollar industry," Beasley gushed to *Financial World* in 1985.

Faced with overcrowding, skyrocketing costs, crumbling infrastructure, and lawsuits and court injunctions to bring facilities up to code, bureaucrats soon began to warm to the idea of privatization. At the same time, government officials found themselves under increasing pressure to economize and shrink their budgets. CCA promised to design and build or refurbish state-of-the-art facilities, to manage the institutions and their inmates, and to do it all for a low inmate-per-day charge.

Within six months the startup had its first client, a 350-bed Immigration & Naturalization Service facility in Houston. CCA hoped to glean profits through efficiency, starting with construction and maintenance expenses. According to Beasley, CCA's construction costs were about 25 percent less than comparable public institutions. Eliminating bureaucratic red tape helped speed up the decision-making and supply procurement processes, thereby gaining lost time and money. CCA also reduced staffing through the use of high-tech surveillance and security devices. It gave employees a vested interest in the success of the venture through an employee stock ownership plan. Although it avoided highly unionized regions, its employees earned somewhat higher wages than their counterparts in organized labor. In

---

Company Perspectives:

*CCA is quality, meeting the highest standards of perform-
ance as established by the American Correctional Association. CCA is value, providing more programs and services
for its price. CCA is innovation, looking at every project on
its own merits to determine the solution that is best for
government and the company. CCA is strength, handling the
toughest assignments with dignity and professionalism. CCA
is commitment, protecting its partnerships with government
despite political pressure and controversy.*

1988, Doc Crants said that the company's profit-making formula was "so simple, it's shocking."

CCA also established numerous inmate activities in an effort
to maintain order among its prison populations. Prisoners participated in a rigorous schedule of drug rehabilitation, recreational, vocational, and educational courses. Programs such as
these gave inmates the chance to leave prison with skills that
would help them avoid a return trip. But rehabilitation was not
CCA's primary goal. Crants talked about the motivation behind
his company's inmate programs in a 1997 *Newsweek* article,
saying, "We don't do it because we're good guys. We do it
because an inmate who is busy and filled with hope is easier to
manage than an inmate who is filled with rage."

Florida's Bay County Jail has been held up as an example of
CCA's success at privatization. Before the Tennessee company
took charge of this facility, it was described as a violation-prone
"shambles," rated one of the state's worst institutions by the
Department of Corrections. CCA won a contract to manage
the prison in 1985, and not only earned accreditation from the
American Correctional Association in 1988, but also saved the
county half a million dollars by 1990.

Not everyone was keen on prison privatization, however.
Critics and opponents included civil rights advocates like the
American Civil Liberties Union, organized labor and civil service groups. In 1986, the American Bar Association passed a
resolution calling for a moratorium on privatization until the
satisfactory resolution of "complex constitutional, statutory,
and contractual issues." In 1987, the National Sheriffs' Association announced its opposition to privatization. Some opposed
the concept on philosophical grounds, decrying the very idea of
profiting from criminals. One privatization advocate countered
that argument by noting that "You could say that hospitals
profit at the expense of sick people, or that private schools profit
from ignorant school children." Others argued that the company's prisons—which often featured color televisions, educational programs, and hot food—were "too nice."

There were obvious hazards inherent to running prisons,
including the potential liabilities arising from escapees who
committed crimes outside the facilities as well as liabilities for
inmate welfare within the prison walls. As *Inc.* magazine's Erik
Larson noted in a 1988 profile of CCA, "Clearly, every new
venture risks failure. But CCA risks riot, murder, mayhem. At
any one moment, its inmate population includes kids who stole

cars, adults who took lives. If its product fails, dangerous people
escape." Indeed, CCA was not immune to these hazards. Over
the course of its first decade-and-a-half in business, the company encountered escapes, quelled riots, and defended itself and
its employees against prisoner litigation.

IPO in 1986

By August 1986, CCA was managing eight detention centers in Tennessee, Texas, New Mexico, and Florida with an
average capacity of about 275 inmates. These included facilities
for men, women, and juveniles at the municipal, county, and
federal levels. Although CCA appeared to be doing a good job
of saving tax dollars, it was not making money for its investors.
While revenues grew from less than $10 million in 1984 to
$24.8 million in 1988, the company ran annual deficits through-
out these years. CCA finally logged its first $1.6 million profit
on sales of $36.8 million in 1989. Crants called the milestone
"a watershed year for CCA," adding, "Frankly, I believe our
industry has come of age."

Notwithstanding its struggle for profitability, CCA went
public on the NASDAQ exchange in 1986 at $9 per share,
raising $18 million to fund continued growth. The stock de-
clined from its 1986 issue price of $9 to $3 the following year.
The company experienced its first major management transition
one year later, when Doc Crants succeeded Tom Beasley as
chief executive officer. Beasley continued as chairman. Under
Crants's leadership, CCA began to target larger facilities that
held out the possibility for increased economization. CCA won
its first state-level contract in October 1987. The agreement
called for the construction of two Texas prisons with a combined capacity of 1,000 inmates. The average size of its institutions increased from about 275 beds in the mid-1980s to 460
beds by the end of 1990. At that time, CCA had 16 institutions
in five states and a joint-venture institution in Australia for a
total capacity of over 7,800 inmates. Chairman Beasley boasted
to the *Memphis Business Journal* that his company was "bigger
than 24 state Departments of Corrections."

The 1990s Bring Financial Success, Rapid Growth

In mid-1992, CCA opened the industry's first privately
managed maximum-security facility, a 256-bed federal detention center, in Leavenworth, Kansas. That December, CCA took
the privatization concept to the United Kingdom through a joint
venture known as U.K. Detention Services, Ltd. The 649-bed
HM Blakenhurst Prison became Great Britain's first privately
managed prison. In an effort to accelerate international expansion, CCA contracted with Paris-based Sodexho Group in 1994.
The company opened two prisons in Puerto Rico in 1995.

CCA also grew through acquisitions during this period,
purchasing TransCor America, Inc., a company that provided
interstate prisoner transport, in January 1995. Later that same
year, CCA added more than 7,250 beds to its capacity through
the acquisitions of Concept, Inc. and Corrections Partners, Inc.

The focus on larger, more efficient facilities drove CCA's
revenues and net income to new heights in the early 1990s.
Sales multiplied eightfold from $55.5 million in 1990 to $462.2
million in 1997 while profits soared from a meager $198,000 to
a whopping $54 million. Wall Streeters sat up and took notice,

and after wallowing at the single-digit level for nearly a decade, CCA's stock took off in the mid-1990s. Taking into account two-for-one splits in 1995 and 1996, the shares shot from about $8 at the beginning of 1995 to nearly $30 in March 1997.

Opportunities for Growth Proliferate in Late 1990s and Beyond

In 1997, three jurisdictions—Tennessee, Florida, and the District of Columbia—announced that they were investigating the possibility of privatizing all or a significant portion of their entire corrections systems. That January, CCA paid the city of Washington, D.C., $52 million for an 866-bed, medium-security jail, marking the first-ever sale of a prison. CCA leased the facility back to the city for $2.8 million per year and retained management. CEO Crants' 1997 letter to shareholders asserted that "the possibility of assuming management of an entire state system" was "the next milestone for our industry, and one that we intend for CCA to be the first to reach." CCA had in fact floated a $250 million proposal to take over the entire Tennessee state corrections system in 1985, but was turned down. Whether the plan would yet come to fruition remained to be seen.

That same year saw the creation of the first prison real estate investment trust, CCA Prison Realty Trust. Over the course of 1997, CCA sold a dozen of its facilities to the new venture, which was owned and operated by Doc Crants and his son, 28-year-old D. Robert Crants III.

As the company entered its 15th year in the private prison business, its future still held out the promise of growth. In 1998, only about five percent of America's prison beds were privately operated. That figure was expected to double by 2001, fueled in part by "three strikes and you're out" provisions, lengthy sentences, and ongoing attempts to reduce government bureaucracies and budgets at all levels. In a 1997 article for *The Commercial Appeal*, CEO Crants asserted that "The fundamental driving principles for CCA are even more true today than they were in 1983: government needs to figure out ways to become more cost-effective in areas like corrections, so it can refocus its resources on things more important, like education and job training."

CCA targeted California with the creation of a West Coast territory in early 1998. By that time, the company had garnered contracts to build and manage three projects with a total of 4,500 beds in the state. In addition to these facilities, CCA had forged agreements to open six prisons in five states with total capacity of more than 5,600 inmates. Clearly, CCA planned to retain its position of leadership in the private prison industry.

Principal Facilities

Bartlett State Jail; Bay Correctional Facility; Bay County Jail; Bay County Jail Annex; Bent County Correctional Facility; HM Prison Blakenhurst (United Kingdom); Borallon Correctional Centre (Australia); Bridgeport Pre-Parole Transfer Facility; Brownfield Intermediate Sanction Facility; Central Arizona Detention Center; Cimarron Correctional Facility; Citrus County Detention Facility; Cleveland Pre-Release Center; Columbia Training Center; Correctional Treatment Facility; Davidson County Juvenile Detention Center; Davis Correctional Facility; Jesse R. Dawson State Jail; Delta Correctional Facility; Eden Detention Center; Elizabeth Detention Center; Florida Maximum Risk Juvenile Facility; Great Plains Correctional Facility; Centro Correccional de Guayama (Puerto Rico); Hardeman County Correctional Center; Hernando County Jail; Houston Processing Center; T. Don Hutton Correctional Center; Huerfano County Correctional Facility; Lake City Correctional Facility; Laredo Processing Center; Lawrenceville Correctional Center; Leavenworth Detention Center; Liberty County Jail and Juvenile Center; Marion County Jail Annex; Metro-Davidson County Detention Facility; Metropolitan Women's Correctional Centre (Australia); Mineral Wells Pre-Parole Transfer Facility; B.M. Moore Pre-Release Center; Nevada Women's Prison; New Mexico Women's Correctional Facility; North Fork Correctional Center; Northeast Ohio Correctional Center; Polk County jail Annex; Centro Correccional de Ponce (Puerto Rico); Prairie Correctional Facility; Sante Fe Detention Center; Shelby Training Center; Silverdale Facilities; South Central Correctional Facility; Southwest Indiana regional Youth Village; Tall Trees; Torrance County Detention Facility; Venus Pre-Release Center; West Tennessee Detention Facility; Wilkinson County Correctional Facility; Winn Correctional Center.

Further Reading

Bai, Matt, "On the Block: Can a Private Company Run a Tough Urban Jail—and Turn a Profit?" *Newsweek,* August 4, 1997, pp. 60–61.

Behar, Richard, "Partners in Crime," *Forbes,* February 11, 1985, pp. 112–13.

Button, Graham, "Will Crime Finally Pay?" *Forbes,* October 26, 1992, p. 14.

"Dividends of Crime," *Money,* November 1985, p. 14.

Epstein, Joseph, "Wackenhut and CCA: Convicts R Us," *Financial World,* March 25, 1996, pp. 24–25.

Giese, William, "Unappetizing Suggestions for Tasty Stock Profits," *Kiplinger's Personal Finance Magazine,* October 1991, p. 73.

Kaberline, Brian, "Investing in Inmates: Area Gets For-Profit Jail," *Kansas City Business Journal,* June 26, 1992, pp. 1–2.

Knowlton, Christopher, "Companies to Watch: Corrections Corp. of America," *Fortune,* January 18, 1988, p. 64.

Larson, Erik, "Captive Company," *Inc.,* June 1988, pp. 86–90.

Mahtesian, Charles, "Dungeons for Dollars," *Florida Trend,* October 1996.

McBrien, P. Clare, "Criminal Justice—Your Prison or Mine?" *National Catholic Reporter,* March 31, 1995, pp. 28–29.

McCarthy, Abigail, "Your Money or Your Lifestyle: Privatizing the Prison System," *Commonweal,* September 23, 1994, pp. 8–9.

Nielsen, John, and H. John Steinbreder, "Second Thoughts on Private Slammers," *Fortune,* March 17, 1986, p. 10.

"No Prison Break," *Forbes,* February 24, 1986, p. 12.

Oliver, Valeri, "Investment Experts Say Private-Jail Operator Is Beyond the 'Testing' Phase," *Memphis Business Journal,* October 26, 1992, p. 32.

Reeves, Scott, "They Want Out; Do You Want In?" *Barron's,* October 13, 1997, p. 44.

Scott, Jonathan, "Corrections Corp. of America Paving the Way for Private Management of Prisons," *Memphis Business Journal,* July 15, 1991, p. 10.

Stevens, Catherine, "Are We Ready for This Growth Industry?" *Financial World,* October 30, 1985, p. 26.

Vinocur, Barry, "Investors Rush into a Prison REIT, Though Some View It As Pricey," *Barron's,* July 14, 1997, p. 31.

—April D. Gasbarre

Cowles Media Company

329 Portland Avenue
Minneapolis, Minnesota 55415-1112
U.S.A.
(612) 673-7100
Fax: (612) 673-7020
Web site: http://www.cowles.com

Wholly Owned Subsidiary of McClatchy Newspapers Inc.
Established: 1935
Employees: 3,274
Revenues: $517 million (1997)
SICs: 2711 Newspapers: Publishing, or Publishing &
    Printing; 7375 Information Retrieval Services

Until the late 1990s, Cowles Media Company stood as one of the nation's leading independent newspaper publishers. That status ended in November 1997, when the Cowles family, which owned more than half of the firm's voting equity through a trust, surprised many observers by agreeing to sell the company to Sacramento, California-based McClatchy Newspapers Inc. for $1.4 billion. In an effort to recoup some of the purchase price, McClatchy planned to divest the Cowles Enthusiast Media Inc. and Cowles Business Media Inc. subsidiaries to Primedia Inc. for $200 million in January 1998. Another subsidiary, Cowles Creative Publishing, included affinity books and magazines for do-it-yourselfers and outdoor enthusiasts. McClatchy hoped to divest this division as well.

The spin-offs would leave McClatchy with Cowles's "crown jewel," the Minneapolis *Star Tribune*. Ranked among America's top 20 metropolitan dailies, the "Strib's" 387,300 daily and 678,000 Sunday circulation had generated an estimated 66 percent of Cowles's total revenues. In addition to being Minnesota's largest newspaper, the *Star Tribune's* trophy case included a Pulitzer Prize and three Robert F. Kennedy awards. The acquisition, which McClatchy expected to close by the end of March 1998, made the California firm one of America's top ten newspaper companies, with a daily circulation of 1.4 million.

Early 20th-Century Foundations

For most of its history the family enterprise had existed as two separate companies that shared board members and heritage. A banker by trade, founder and namesake Gardner Cowles formed the Register & Tribune Co. in 1903 to acquire Iowa's *Des Moines Register* for $300,000. Sons Gardner "Mike" Cowles, Jr., and John struck out on their own in the 1930s. John's business, the Minneapolis Star & Tribune Co., came to dominate that city's newspaper market through the purchase of three publications: the *Minneapolis Star,* an afternoon daily; the *Minneapolis Journal;* and the morning *Minneapolis Tribune.* Mike spearheaded the creation of *Look,* a photojournalistic magazine along the lines of *Life,* in 1937. The family also added radio stations to its growing media conglomerate during the Depression. Over the ensuing decades the family added a number of less significant and less successful media holdings, including community newspapers, magazines, and broadcasters throughout the Midwest.

John Cowles's 1968 retirement proved a watershed in the history of the family business, for as *Time* magazine noted in a brief obituary of the media magnate, "The Minneapolis Star & Tribune Co. [then] began a long decline." When he ended his career, the Cowles companies—Iowa's Register & Tribune Co. as well as the Star & Tribune Co.—were ranked among America's ten best. But by the early 1980s the family media empire was on the verge of oblivion.

Decline of Star & Tribune Co. in the 1970s

Son John Cowles Jr. captained the Minneapolis firm's plunge. The Harvard-educated heir soon earned a reputation for having more intellect and ambition than business acumen. Over the course of the 1970s, John, Jr., guided the Star & Tribune's acquisition of one-third of book publisher Harper & Row, 50 percent of *Harper's* magazine, and perhaps most disastrously, the morning *Buffalo Courier-Express* (New York) in 1979. Harper & Row struggled to break even throughout the decade, *Harper's* lost $3 million in the late 1970s, and the *Courier-Express* bled $25 million in red ink before John Jr. shuttered the paper in 1982.

Company Perspectives:

The Cowles Media Company Charter: We are a trusted source of information and ideas that help people pursue their interests and enrich their lives. We are a family of independent companies responsible for their own success and corporate citizenship. The skill and dedication of our people working individually and together are essential to our success. We produce high-quality products and act with integrity while achieving competitive financial returns to create superior long-term value. Customer satisfaction is a fundamental responsibility for each of us. We aim high, accepting the risks and rewarding performance and results. We believe in an open and fair environment, one that values diversity of backgrounds and ideas, and encourages personal growth.

Turning his attention to the two Minneapolis newspapers he had inherited, Cowles found them chronically overstaffed. Profits were squeezed by the twin demons of inflation and recession. Though revenues increased from $159.7 million in 1979 to $237.7 million in 1982, the Minneapolis company's net income declined from $12.2 million to a measly $747,000 during the period. John Jr. plowed millions into the struggling afternoon *Star,* then opted instead to cut costs. An early retirement program softened the impact of massive staff reductions at both the *Star* and the *Tribune.* In desperation, John Jr. merged the two Minneapolis papers in 1982 and renamed the company Cowles Media. The marriage eliminated more than 100 employees, but even that move was not enough to stop the earnings slide. That October, the company slashed another 75 people from the payroll, prompting Strib editor Charles Bailey's resignation. A month later, John Jr. canned publisher Donald Dwight and installed himself in that capacity.

Amid all this upheaval, members of the Cowles family (who through a trust and board membership controlled a majority of the privately held companies' voting shares) flirted with the idea of merging the Minneapolis and Iowa publishing entities (which already had cross-shareholdings). Instead the family-dominated board voted unanimously to oust John Jr. and elect his cousin, David Kruidenier, chairman of the Register & Tribune Co. (R&T), to Cowles Media's chief executive office in January 1983.

Decline of Register & Tribune in the 1970s

Kruidenier's record at R&T was not much better than that of his Minneapolis cousin. In 1971 he, too, had inherited a profitable, cash-rich newspaper company. An acquisition spree included the *Jackson (Tennessee) Sun,* an Illinois television station, and two Madison, Wisconsin radio stations. While these purchases proved successful, the 1978 acquisition of McCoy Broadcasting, a broadcaster with a television station in Honolulu and two stateside radio stations, pushed Register's debt over the $40 million mark. This heavy debt load, coupled with rising interest rates, shrunk the Iowa company's net income from $8.6 million in 1978 to $423,000 in 1981. The decline

culminated in a pretax loss of $1.6 million in 1982, the company's first in its eight decades under the Cowles family.

Having gained control of both of the Cowles family enterprises, Kruidenier began to retreat from his earlier diversification strategy, divesting $17 million in broadcasting and publishing properties and merging the two flagship Iowa newspapers in 1982. Kruidenier managed to squeeze a meager profit from R&T in 1983 before coming under a hostile takeover organized by two of his own lieutenants, Register president Michael Gartner and publisher Gary Gerlach. In cooperation with Dow Jones & Co. (publisher of *The Wall Street Journal*), these two board members brought a $112 million bid for the Des Moines newspaper and its assets. The proposal placed the entire Cowles family empire in jeopardy, for a sale would put 14 percent of Cowles Media under Dow Jones's control. At the same time, dissident shareholder Kingsley Murphy Jr. put his 17 percent stake in Cowles Media up for sale.

The threat was diffused early in 1985, when Gannett Co. brought a $200 million offer for the *Des Moines Register,* the Tennessee newspaper, and two Iowa weeklies. That March, Murphy sold his stake in Cowles Media to The Washington Post Co. for an estimated $5 million. Acting as an investor, not an acquirer, The Post increased its Cowles holding to more than 28 percent by the mid-1990s, while Gannett retained its 14 percent interest.

Successful Rediversification: Late 1980s and Early 1990s

Strib publisher Roger Parkinson, who had been promoted to that position in 1983, oversaw the mid-decade construction of the paper's Heritage Center printing plant at a cost of $110 million. The publisher also positioned the *Star Tribune* as the "Newspaper of the Twin Cities," expanding its editorial, advertising, and circulation reach into St. Paul. Expanded business, suburban, and sports coverage widened the paper's "news hole" and special telephone and fax services diversified the paper's access points and brand equity. Over the course of the decade, Parkinson reduced employment by about 250 through early retirement packages. Parkinson resigned in 1992 and was succeeded by *Star Tribune* editor Joel Kramer.

In 1985 Kruidenier was succeeded as president and CEO of Cowles Media by David Cox. Over the course of his more than a decade at the helm, Cox was able not only to return the company to a pattern of growth and profitability, but also to rebuild its peripheral interests. After divesting Montana and South Dakota newspapers, the parent company formed Cowles Business Media Inc. in 1990. With an emphasis on publishing, direct marketing, travel, information technology, and telecommunications, the CBM roster would grow to include *Cable World, Folio, Catalog Age,* and *American Demographics.* By the mid-1990s CBM boasted more than one dozen magazines, on-line services, newsletters, and related conferences and organizations. Cowles Magazines Inc. (later Cowles Enthusiast Media) focused on niche and special interest publications like *Southwest Are, Fly Fisherman, Vegetarian Times, American History,* and *Doll Reader.* By 1997 this subsidiary would include more than two dozen magazines with a combined circulation of three million. Cowles also formed a video division in

1993 to produce programs based on its special interest magazines for cable television. Concepts included the Wild West, Military History, and American History in general.

Cowles Creative Publishing was spun off from Cowles Enthusiast Media in 1997 to publish affinity books and series for the do-it-yourself, recreation, and "home arts" markets. These publications were often produced in cooperation with companies like Singer, the sewing machine manufacturer, and the Black & Decker tool company.

1997 Acquisition by McClatchy

The 1997 fiscal year (ended March 31) saw Cowles surpass the half-billion revenue mark and achieve record earnings of nearly $30 million. Perhaps sensing a high water mark for newspaper company valuations, the Cowles family put its Midwest media empire up for sale that September. Rivals for the paper reportedly included The Washington Post Co., which already owned a 28 percent stake in Cowles, Gannett Co., with another 14 percent share, the Chicago Tribune Co., the New York Times Co., and McClatchy Newspapers Inc. McClatchy surprised many observers by bringing a $1.4 billion winning offer, a bid 50 percent higher than financial analysts had predicted. The megadeal ranked third among newspaper purchases up to that time.

Controlled for five generations by the McClatchy and Maloney families, the company had gone public in 1988 but continued to be majority owned by the clans. By 1997 McClatchy was a decentralized group of ten daily newspapers and 13 community papers in California, Alaska, the Pacific Northwest, and the Carolinas.

The widely publicized deal came with several strings. McClatchy agreed to honor the Cowles family's philanthropic obligations to the tune of $3 million per year through 2007 and took on CMC's $90 million debt obligations. In total, the acquiring company shouldered $1.3 billion in long-term debt. Though the Cowles family required that McClatchy purchase the entire media group, the latter company quickly arranged to spin off virtually everything but the *Star Tribune*. Early in 1998 McClatchy announced its plan to sell Cowles Enthusiast Media and Cowles Business Media to Primedia Inc. for $200 million.

Investors showed their disapproval of the deal by sending McClatchy's stock down 14 percent on the day after the agreement was made public. A few of the negative influences on the newspaper industry included declining readership, especially among the young, correspondingly decreasing circulation rates, and the escalating price of newsprint, which rose by nearly one-third in 1995 alone. Nonetheless the acquiring company's CEO, Gary Pruitt, hailed the purchase as "a rare opportunity for McClatchy to obtain a quality newspaper while adding geographic diversity in a premiere growth market." Moreover, *Folio* (a Cowles publication) noted, "McClatchy has made its

reputation by paying a premium for quality newspaper properties and improving profitability to get the number to make sense." One way to improve profitability was to cut labor costs, and the new parent company expected to eliminate about 40 executives during the merger.

McClatchy expected to close the Cowles acquisition by the end of March 1998. The addition of the *Star Tribune* to its roster of newspaper properties would increase the California firm's revenues to nearly $1 billion, making it one of America's top ten newspaper companies with a daily circulation of 1.4 million. After the divestments, McClatchy expected to rename the subsidiary as the Star Tribune Co.

Further Reading

"Bitter Ending: An Editor Walks Out," *Time,* October 18, 1982, p. 101.

Cassidy, Neil, "Newspaper Chain Buys Cowles," *Folio: The Magazine for Magazine Management,* December 1, 1997, p. 12.

Cowles, Gardner, *Mike Looks Back: The Memoirs of Gardner Cowles, Founder of Look Magazine,* New York: G. Cowles, 1985.

"Cowles Magazine Buys Hobby Titles," *Folio: The Magazine for Magazine Management,* February 1, 1992, p. 15.

"The Family Feud at Cowles," *Business Week,* February 14, 1983, p. 48.

Fitzgerald, Mark, and Neuwirth, Robert, "Twin City Slickers," *Editor & Publisher,* November 22, 1997, pp. 8–10.

Gardner Cowles, 1861–1946: Publisher of the Des Moines Register and Tribune, 1903–1946, Des Moines, Iowa: [Board of Directors of the Des Moines Register and Tribune Co.], 1946.

Gibson, Richard, "Minneapolis Publisher Awaits Suitors, Looks in Mirror," *The Wall Street Journal,* September 12, 1997, p. B4(E).

Gilyard, Burl, "Cowles' Comfort Farm," *Corporate Report Minnesota,* July 1997, p. 22.

——, "The Strib's Ad-vantage," *Corporate Report Minnesota,* October 1997, p. 22.

Kasler, Dale, "McClatchy Newspapers Takes the Long View on Its Big Buy," *The Sacramento Bee,* via Knight Ridder/Tribune Business News, November 17, 1997.

Lewis, Matthew, "Getting a Newspaper Back on Track," *ADWEEK,* May 6, 1985, n.p.

Levin, Gary, "Cowles Cloaked in Anti-Takeover Garb," *Advertising Age,* April 8, 1985, p. 14.

Moore, Thomas, "Trouble and Strife in the Cowles Empire," *Fortune,* April 4, 1983, pp. 156–161.

Nicholson, Tom, McCormick, John, and Leslie, Connie, "The Cash in the Register," *Newsweek,* November 26, 1984, p. 74.

125 Years: Star Tribune, 125 Years of History in the Making, [Minnesota]: Star Tribune, 1992.

"Primedia Pays $200M for Cowles Units," *MEDIAWEEK,* January 12, 1998, p. 4.

Souder, William, "Welcome to the Fun House: Strange Days at the Star Tribune," *MPLS-St. Paul Magazine,* June 1996, pp. 54–67.

Sullivan, John, "$1 Billion Jewel in Play," *Editor & Publisher,* September 13, 1997, p. 23.

Welch, Michael, "Pressing On: Record Results Are Not Enough for Star Tribune Publisher Joel R. Kramer," *Corporate Report Minnesota,* December 1992, p. 30.

—April D. Gasbarre

CUNARD

Cunard Line Ltd.

6100 Blue Lagoon Drive, Suite 400
Miami, Florida 33126
U.S.A.
(305) 463-3000
Fax: (305) 463-3010
Web site: http://www.cunardline.com

Wholly Owned Subsidiary of Kvaerner A/S
Incorporated: 1878 as The Cunard Steam Ship Co. Ltd.
Employees: 427
Sales: $440 million (1995)
SICs: 4481 Deep Sea Transportation of Passengers,
    Except by Ferry

Cunard Line Ltd. has been in the forefront of passenger shipping since Samuel Cunard began the first regularly scheduled transatlantic steamship service in 1840. The company's recent history has been one of growth through refurbishment and the implementation of strategic marketing agreements.

In June 1994, Cunard purchased the world's most highly rated cruise ship, *Royal Viking Sun,* for $170 million. As a result, Cunard operates the largest fleet of luxury ships in the world. From November to December 1994, *QE2* underwent a $45 million refurbishment, which included a major modification to the layout and style of most public areas that resulted in the natural flow and cohesion of the passenger experience and the creation of a distinctive lifestyle reflecting the vessel's heritage and tradition. And during November–December 1996, an additional $18 million was invested in further enhancements to Cunard's flagship.

Cunard's place as the world's superlative cruise line seems assured due to the consistently high ratings of its five luxury liners, a concept defined by legendary Cunarders such as the *Queen Mary,* the *Queen Elizabeth,* and the *Queen Elizabeth 2.* Besides providing a high standard of leisure accommodations, the company has often been called upon to lend its ships for wartime use. According to Winston Churchill, the troop-carrying work of the first two Queens shortened World War II in Europe by at least a year.

19th-Century Beginnings

Samuel Cunard, the son of a prosperous carpenter, was born in Halifax, Nova Scotia, in 1787. His parents, both Loyalists, had fled the United States after the Revolutionary War. His father, Abraham, had worked his way up, establishing a thriving business at the dockyard. After a stint in the civil service, Samuel Cunard traveled to Boston where he apprenticed in shipbroking. He began shipping to the United States during the War of 1812 and in 1815 won a crown contract to establish mail service linking Nova Scotia, Newfoundland, Boston, and Bermuda.

After the dockyard operations at Halifax were moved to Bermuda in 1819, Cunard and his brothers developed a lumbering and fishing business which eventually collapsed in 1848. Before then, Cunard's prominence grew as he became involved in a variety of enterprises.

Excited by the possibilities of the new steamships, Cunard sailed for England in 1839 to bid on a contract transatlantic mail service. Before approaching the Admiralty, Cunard ordered three wooden paddle steamships from Glasgow shipbuilder Robert Napier. In May 1839, Cunard had signed a seven-year contract to deliver mail from Liverpool to Halifax to Boston and, part of the year, to Quebec. Originally worth £55,000 per year, the value was increased to £80,000 after further requirements, such as the use of four ships instead of three, were added. (The ships also carried at least one cat on board to keep rats from eating through the mail bags.)

Contracts in hand, Cunard turned again to Napier for help in raising sufficient capital to launch the venture. James Donaldson and managing partners George Burns and David MacIver joined the two men in their investment, and in 1840 the British and North American Royal Mail Steam Packet Company was born. Nearly 20 other Glasgow merchants had also bought shares. While Burns remained in Glasgow, overseeing the building of the new ships, MacIver and Cunard, respectively, oversaw the Liverpool and Halifax and Boston terminals.

Company Perspectives:

Cunard, the world's leading luxury cruise line, maintains a fleet of five elegant ships: Cunard's flagship Queen Elizabeth 2, Royal Viking Sun, Vistafjord, *and super yachts* Sea Goddess I *and* Sea Goddess II. *The ships call at more than 300 ports throughout the world.*

The first of the company's steamships, the *Britannia,* sailed from Liverpool to Boston on July 4, 1840. The mail operation followed closely to schedule. However, the *Columbia,* one of the original mail vessels, wrecked in 1843. No mail was lost and most of the ship's value was insured. The company continued to slowly expand its network.

The size and power of steamships grew rapidly. Although both company management and the Admiralty were rather conservative in applying new technology, an iron-hulled, screw-driven steamship was delivered in 1851. However, this vessel and several others were soon pressed into service in the Crimean War. In 1856, Napier built the company the largest ship in the world. Called the *Persia,* it was still rather old-fashioned in being powered by paddles rather than a screw (propeller).

The company lost some business to the faster vessels of the short-lived Collins line (the United States Mail Steamship Co.), although the Cunard service proved more reliable. The two companies entered into a price-fixing and revenue-pooling agreement to ease the sting of competition; several others also joined in regulating rates before falling demand induced a series of rate wars at the end of the century.

In the 1850s, the Cunard, Burns, and MacIver families had begun a separate line, the British and Foreign Steam Navigation Company, to operate between Britain and the Mediterranean. However, the Burns family came to hard times and George Burns retired from both these partnerships by 1859, passing most of his interests to family members.

The 1860s Bring New Challenges

In 1866, the British government canceled the subsidy arrangement it had with the Cunard line and opened the mail contract to competition. The new carrier would be compensated based on the weight of mail carried. Cunard, however, was able to retain smaller regular payments in exchange for a scaled down service.

Sir Samuel Cunard died in 1865. Two sons, Edward and William, continued to play a role in the company. By this time, Mediterranean trading had proven itself quite profitable, as had the transport of emigrants across the Atlantic from England. The two distinct lines were merged by 1867, with control of the company divided between the Cunard, MacIver, and Burns families. Sir Edward Cunard died in 1869. These interests were incorporated in 1878, under the title The Cunard Steam Ship Co. Ltd. William Cunard, John and James Cleland Burns, and Charles MacIver were the sole partners.

The *Servia,* built in 1881, carried the line into an age of new materials and power. The 392-ton vessel, the company's first steel ship, was the first in the world to use electric lights. At the time, the company's gross annual income had reached £1,000,000.

In the last half of the century, the line paid more attention to the steerage trade, although the company never became as dependent on it as other lines. The treatment of immigrants from Britain and the Mediterranean was no frills to the extreme, while first class passengers were pampered, according to ship dinner menus. At the time, immigrants and cabin class passengers accounted for nearly 75 percent of company income.

Beginning in 1901, the legendary American financier J. P. Morgan assembled a combine of shipping interests that sent shivers through the rest of the industry. The group attempted to buy an interest in the Cunard line and, after that failed, engaged them in a fierce round of price competition.

Between 1912 and 1916, Cunard acquired an interest in several shipping firms that extended its routes to Canada, India, Australia, and New Zealand. In March 1912, Cunard acquired an interest in a longtime rival, the Anchor Line, which itself became associated with the Donaldson Line in 1916. Cunard bought the Commonwealth and Dominion Line, which specialized in shipping between the United Kingdom and Australia and New Zealand; this division became known as the Port Line Ltd. Cunard merged with the venerable firm of T. and J. Brocklebank Ltd. soon thereafter.

The Great War and Great Depression

The *Carmania* introduced the company to steam turbine propulsion in 1905. Cunard bought two other historic vessels in the next two years. The *Lusitania* and its sister ship, the *Mauretania,* built in 1907, both garnered the "Blue Riband" trophy for fastest Atlantic crossing. The *Mauretania* held the record from 1909 until usurped by the *Queen Mary* in 1936.

Most Cunard ships were converted to military use as armed cruisers or troop transports during World War I. One exception was the luxury liner *Lusitania,* which remained in normal commercial service until torpedoed on May 7, 1915. The war claimed many of Cunard's fastest ships, which handicapped the company after the war in spite of replacements provided.

In 1921, Congress restricted immigration to the United States, scalping third-class passenger traffic. (The situation was entirely different in Canada. The Canadian government pressured Cunard to keep fares low in order to encourage immigration.) There was excess capacity in the cargo market as well. Cunard responded by diversifying its financial interests, creating subsidiaries in Germany, Hungary, and Romania and buying a London ship-repair firm and the remaining shares of Brocklebank. In addition, the company promoted tourist business, adding some amenities to third-class service and upgrading deluxe accommodations. The fleet was converted to burn oil rather than coal.

Cunard began losing money in the 1930s due to the Great Depression. The company merged with its financially strapped rival, the Oceanic Steam Navigation Co., commonly known as the White Star Line, in 1934. The White Star Line had been founded in the height of the booming emigrant business in 1869. A new company was created, Cunard White Star Ltd., which would coexist with the Cunard Steam Ship Co. until the latter bought its remaining shares in 1947. In 1935, Cunard disposed of the last of its investment in the over-extended Anchor Line.

The *Queen Mary,* delivered in 1936, helped right the company's fortunes. Its large scale and lavish outfitting were products of pre-Depression planning. Designed to replace the *Mauretania,* it too became the fastest liner in the water and, at 81,000 tons, the largest by far. Construction had idled for more than two years due to difficulties in financing the vessel, which ultimately proved very profitable. An even larger ship, the *Queen Elizabeth,* followed in 1938.

World War II and Postwar Planning

Unfortunately, the outbreak of World War II scuttled the company's plans for a twice weekly transatlantic service, as well as other offerings designed to increase revenue. Instead, these new ships were used to ferry more than a million troops. One of the war's worst naval disasters came when the *Lancastria* was bombed while anchored at a French port, killing 5,000. In October 1942, the *Queen Mary* collided with an escort vessel, the H.M.S. *Curaçao,* sinking it.

More than £30 million was needed to replace and restore ships after World War II. The cost of making ships had risen four times during the war. Facilities on new ships were improved to satisfy American tourists, who became the prime market due to Europe's postwar austerity. Cunard emphasized flexibility in its planning, running scheduled service during spring and summer, offering cruises during the winter. The company generally allocated more resources towards freight operations, however.

It became apparent before the war that air travel would amount to serious competition both for passengers and mail. Although government officials discussed Cunard's support in a new airline, in the end Cunard was not among the sponsors of the newly created British Airways and was later, as a matter of national policy, not allowed to invest in the amalgamated national carrier BOAC.

Dog Days After 1955

Besides rising costs and high taxes, labor strife and the threat of war in the Middle East also plagued shipping companies from the mid-1950s through the 1960s. In 1957, revolution in Hungary contributed to Cunard's losses of £1 million. After the first transatlantic jet crossing in 1959, air traffic would take away more and more business from cruise ships. In 1958, after years of increase, the amount of passenger traffic traveling by sea began to decline. By 1965, six times as many passengers crossed the Atlantic by plane as by ship.

In 1959, Cunard bought Eagle Airways Ltd., which connected Europe with much of the Western hemisphere. However, gaining access to U.S. markets was difficult, and complicated by BOAC's intervention. In 1962, Cunard took a 30 percent interest in a new joint venture with the British national carrier called BOAC-Cunard Ltd. So much capital would be needed to update the fleet with jumbo jets that Cunard sold its share of the investment in 1966.

The 1960s: Launch of a New Industry

With shipping on the ropes as a form of transport, Cunard took on a whole new strategy for survival. It aligned itself with the leisure industry, seeing its ships as floating resorts—a destination in themselves. A grand new ship/hotel, known then as the *Q.4,* would be the centerpiece of this vision.

In 1962, a management company, Cunard Line Ltd., was formed. To become more self-sufficient, in the next two years Cunard formed its own insurance company and created a handling company, Cunard Stevedoring Ltd. In 1964, Cunard bought the H.E. Moss and Company Tankers Ltd., entering it in the tanker trade. The company also began trimming its fleet and workforce while selling several of its historic office buildings.

Cargo operations responded well, buoying the company towards profitability. The company began shipping containerized packages in 1966, which required a significant investment in facilities and new ships. It subsequently became a partner in the multinational consortiums Atlantic Container Lines Ltd. and, through the Port Line, Associated Container Transportation.

The share of revenues derived from passenger traffic declined from 50 percent in 1965 to 20 percent by 1968, and the company managed to control losses in this category. Since they were no longer profitable, the *Queen Mary* and the *Queen Elizabeth* were sold in the late 1960s. The *Queen Elizabeth,* on its way to becoming a floating university in Hong Kong, was destroyed by fire in 1972.

The ship identified in early plans as the *Q.4*—the *Queen Elizabeth 2*—was launched in 1969. Although immense, its dimensions were compact enough to allow it into exotic new ports and through the Panama Canal. It also boasted unprecedented efficiency and flexibility. As Cunard only operated two other passenger ships at the time (besides 60 freighters), it proved enormously important to the company. Its financing, including a £25 million loan from the Crown, achieved a similar scale of complexity.

A New House in the 1970s and 1980s

Trafalgar House Investments Ltd., whose diversified portfolio included 260 companies, bought Cunard in August 1971. Trafalgar's luxury hotel interests were combined with the company, hoping to derive benefits from Cunard's superior sales network. This paved the way for integrated holiday packages. The company bought the renowned Ritz Hotel in London in 1976. Trafalgar House poured money into the Cunard Line, financing two new cruise ships, the *Cunard Adventurer* and the *Cunard Countess.* In the late 1970s Cunard also engaged in several aviation ventures, including Heavy Lift Cargo Airlines, which used giant RAF-surplus Belfast jets to carry uniquely large loads.

Four Cunarders were used in the 1982 Falklands Island campaign. The *Atlantic Conveyor* was sunk by missile while ferrying aircraft from Britain to the South Atlantic. The *QE2* underwent an extensive conversion in order to deliver 3,500 troops.

In 1983, Cunard's cruise fleet increased to five with the addition of two more luxury vessels from Norwegian American Cruises. Cunard joined British Airways to offer an unusual round-trip package in 1984: one way across the Atlantic on the *QE2*, the other via Concorde.

The *QE2*'s amenities grew to include television and delivery of a daily newspaper (the *International Herald Tribune*). It was retrofitted with diesel electric engines and variable pitch propellers. Cunard Line added two new cruise ships in 1986, the *Sea Goddess I* and the *Sea Goddess II*.

Navigating the 1990s

Like so many of its predecessors, the *Cunard Princess* carried troops for Operation Desert Storm. After divesting its cargo interests, Cunard refurbished several of its cruisers in the mid-1990s, including the *QE2*, which received $45 million of improvements. Cunard bought additional ships, including the award-winning *Royal Viking Sun* in 1994.

Kvaerner A/S, Europe's largest shipbuilding concern, acquired Trafalgar House in April 1996 for £904 million. Cunard was losing money at the time, £16.4 million in 1995. In the autumn of 1996, Cunard launched a massive advertising campaign. The *QE2* completed yet another multimillion-dollar refurbishment in December 1996. In 1997, the company headquarters was relocated from New York to Miami and Captain Paris G. Katsoufis was named president and chief operating officer. Antti Pankakoski was the company's chairman and chief executive. His predecessor, Peter Ward, had resigned after a year.

Berlitz guides rated all of Cunard's cruise ships at five stars and *Business Traveler International* readers voted Cunard "Best Cruise Line in the World." Although the company only operated five ships, they still comprised the largest fleet of luxury ships in the world. Approximately 200 Cunarders have carried passengers over more than a century and a half, and this prestigious tradition formed a valuable part of Kvaerner A/S's NOK 60 billion empire.

Further Reading

Blum, Ernest, "Cunard: Sailing the World in Style," *Travel Weekly,* February 4, 1993.

Carroll, Cathy, "Cunard Readies Marketing Campaign to Present Clear Image," *Travel Weekly,* July 29, 1996, p. 26.

Hyde, Francis E., *Cunard and the North Atlantic, 1840–1973: A History of Shipping and Financial Management,* London: Macmillan, 1975.

Johnson, Howard, *The Cunard Story,* London: Whittet Books, 1987.

"Pick-Up Lines: Cruising," *Economist,* May 4, 1996, p. 70.

Pitt, William, "Rush on to Repair QE2," *Business Insurance,* August 17, 1992.

Saporito, Bill, "The QE2 Goes on the Block: Britain's Cunard Is Cruising for a New Owner," *Time,* April 8, 1996, p. 46.

University of Liverpool, "Cunard Archives: General Booklist," http://www.liv.ac.uk/ archives/cunard/genbks.htm#Histories.

Woolley, Peter W., and Terry Moore, *The Cunard Line: A Pictorial History, 1840–1990,* Norfolk, Va.: Ship Pictorial Publications, 1990.

—Frederick C. Ingram

Del Monte Foods Company

One Market Plaza
P.O. Box 193575
San Francisco, California 94119-3575
U.S.A.
(415) 442-4000
Fax: (415) 442-4894
Web site: http://www.delmonte.com

Private Company
Incorporated: 1916 as California Packing Corporation
Employees: 12,500
Sales: $1.55 billion (1996 est.)
SICs: 2033 Canned Fruits & Vegetables; 2034
   Dehydrated Fruits, Vegetables & Soups; 2086 Bottled
   and Canned Soft Drinks; 2032 Canned Specialties

Among the largest canners of fruits and vegetables in the United States, the Del Monte Foods Company is less than half the size it was at the beginning of the 1980s as a subsidiary of R. J. Reynolds Industries. R. J. Reynolds became RJR Nabisco, which in 1988 was consumed by Kohlberg Kravis Roberts & Co. (KKR). KKR quickly divested itself of a number of RJR Nabisco properties, including Del Monte's fresh fruits operations (purchased by British-based Polly Peck International) and its processed foods and Japanese rights (purchased by Kikkoman). Although Del Monte management and an investor group led by Merrill Lynch & Co. bought the company's remaining businesses in early 1990, they were also forced to divest various branches of the company, including the Hawaiian Punch division, the European canned food divisions, the dried fruit operations, and the pudding division. Despite the loss of so many of its products, San Francisco-based Del Monte Foods remained intact and tied to its heritage, that of a quality marketer of canned fruit and vegetables under an internationally recognized—albeit increasingly confusing—brand name. In 1997, Fort Worth entrepreneur David Bonderman and his $2.5 billion Texas Pacific Group investment company approached Del Monte with an investment offer intended to help Del Monte get back on its feet following a period of declining sales and increasing debt.

Early History

Del Monte traces its origins to the pioneering 19th-century figures in West Coast canning, Daniel Provost and Francis Cutting. Along with the influx of settlers from the California gold rush came a need for new regional food manufacturers, and these men led the way. While Provost holds the distinction of forming the first foodpacking operation there, Cutting became the first of a long line of entrepreneurs to manufacture metal and glass containers—rather than having them shipped from the East—and the first to export California-processed fruit back to the East Coast as well as Europe. As the California orchard industry grew, so did the canning industry; a virtual boom in agriculture came to the region during the 1800s, following construction of the first railroad networks, and dozens of canneries were established.

One such business, the Oakland Preserving Company, was launched in 1891. At this time, uniformity in labeling and product quality, under the auspices of the recently established California Canned Goods Association, was becoming a foremost marketing concern. The intent of this service organization was to ensure that the label "California grown" stood for an uncommonly high standard; its efforts ultimately led to effective legislation governing the canning industry. Oakland's own efforts in this area generated the Del Monte brand, a name that would soon become synonymous with exceptional value.

During this time the need arose for sustaining high consumer demand within an industry that now seemed to be rapidly outgrowing its economic limits. Talks of consolidation among canners eventually produced the California Fruit Canners Association (CFCA) in 1899. CFCA represented a historical merger of 18 separate canneries, including the Oakland Preserving Company. Upon consolidation, CFCA was so vast that it comprised approximately half of the entire California canning industry and ranked, in effect, as the largest canner of fruits and vegetables in the world. There were several key promoters of the CFCA consolidation, including Frederick Tillman, Jr., of

Oakland Preserving; Sydney Smith of Cutting Fruit Packing Company; Robert and Charles Bentley of Sacramento Packing; and Mark Fontana and William Fries of Fontana & Co. By popular assent, Fries became the company's president.

Given CFCA's wide area of operations and the strong wills of its various principals, true integration of the canneries never materialized. Furthermore, the retention of a large number of name brands prevented CFCA from developing a strong, cohesive marketing presence during its early years. Nonetheless, the multidimensional cannery prospered, spreading beyond the borders of California with the acquisitions of the Oregon Packing Company and the Hawaii Preserving Company. Like the other canneries already within the fold, these continued to operate fairly autonomously. However, as William Braznell pointed out in his *History of the Del Monte Corporation,* "One notable concession made to corporate solidarity was the adoption of the *Del Monte* label as the association's premier brand." The brand name, courtesy of Tillman and the Oakland Preserving Company, derived from a coffee blend prepared by Tillman and a partner for the Hotel Del Monte in Monterey as early as 1886. Now the Del Monte label graced over 50 products, including squash, sweet potatoes, peppers, berries, jams, jellies, cranberry sauce, and olives.

Del Monte Precursor Formed in 1916

CFCA's reliance upon commission agents to sell most of its produce led to a curious chain of events and, ultimately, the formation of the California Packing Corporation (Calpak), the immediate ancestor of the Del Monte Corporation. For some time, CFCA employed San Francisco-based J. K. Armsby Co., the West Coast's largest wholesaler, as its exclusive agent. After CFCA terminated the arrangement, Armsby sought out the region's second-largest manufacturer, Central California Canneries (CCC). This new arrangement soured when the Armsby brothers, J. K. and George, began rapidly accumulating stock in CCC. George, the more aggressive and visionary-minded of the two, had begun to conceive of a single, dominant food concern that would, at the very least, include the Armsby Co., CCC, and CFCA. Although CCC president William Hotchkiss managed to repel the takeover attempt, he eventually proved amenable to the idea of such a merger.

On November 19, 1916, after numerous meetings, disagreements, and compromises, George Armsby's dream was realized and the monolithic Calpak was formed. Joining the three major companies in the merger were Alaska Packers Association and Griffin & Skelley. Save for Alaska Packers, all of the consolidated companies were headquartered in San Francisco within a short distance of each other. By 1917, a new headquarters had been established and a committee system of management adopted. J. K. Armsby and Fries were elected to serve as president and chairperson, respectively. Like the CFCA merger, the Calpak merger presented a host of organizational problems for the new management, not the least of which was establishing production consistency within the 71 plants in California, Washington, Oregon, and Idaho, as well as the territories of Alaska and Hawaii. According to Braznell, what held everything together was the understanding by the owners that "California Packing Corporation would present a solid front in the market place. There would be only one premium Calpak label—Del Monte. It would stand for products of uniformly high quality, and it would be promoted for all it was worth."

A year after the merger, Calpak made promotional history by placing its first Del Monte advertisement in the *Saturday Evening Post.* Mass advertising was a new medium, and Calpak's intent was to use it to create a national market for its Del Monte label. What the company hoped to overcome was the prevailing image among consumers that canned goods were "rainy day" items, adequate though not preferable replacements for fresh produce. The concept of brand loyalty was another potential stumbling block for the company, for most grocers at the time were "full service," filling customers orders themselves and paying little attention to manufacturers or labels. Piggly Wiggly was among the first grocery chains to alter this practice. By the 1920s the evolution toward self-service supermarkets in the grocery industry was well underway, and the success of the Del Monte marketing plan was ensured.

However, Calpak entered the 1920s in a precarious situation. Although earnings were some $7 million on revenues of $85 million following record-high commodity prices, an agricultural depression loomed, made worse by the plight of many farmers who had heavily mortgaged their land to sink new capital into their operations. The company weathered the crisis better than many of its growers, strengthening itself through the establishment of a national sales network and the initiation of mass production, quality assurance, and other internal systems that both improved efficiency and enhanced the Del Monte brand. A major development came in 1925, when Calpak acquired Rochelle Canneries of Rochelle, Illinois. The purchase of this Midwest company signified Calpak's expansion into corn and pea packing, then the two most lucrative segments of the vegetable canning industry. Related acquisitions included plants in Wisconsin and Minnesota. Several overseas ventures, in such countries as the Philippines and Haiti, also highlighted the decade.

Losses During the Great Depression

With the onset of the Great Depression, Calpak's earnings crumbled. From 1930 to 1931 they fell from $6.16 per share to just 9¢ per share. In 1932, the company posted the worst losses in its history. Yet, within two years, earnings began to rebound and, after one more unfavorable year, the company was firmly back in the black. In addition to the poor economy and fierce competition from other major canners, Calpak also faced pressure at the time from a flurry of new canneries. Enormous changes within the industry also came about as a result of the agricultural labor movement. The International Longshoremen and Warehousemen's Union (ILWU), after demonstrating its clout through well-planned strikes, eventually won the right to represent cannery workers in wage, plant safety, and benefit negotiations.

Having aided the Allied effort during World War II, while sustaining profit losses and the temporary closing of operations in the Philippines, Calpak emerged a much stronger company during the late 1940s due to the postwar expansion and rising per capita consumption of canned products. In 1948 the company acquired East Coast producer Edgar H. Hurff Co. Two years later Calpak moved into new headquarters, and in 1951 the company named its seventh president, Roy Lucks. Braznell characterized him as: "coolly logical, an avid student of management sciences . . . a leader who recognized no jurisdictional boundaries and no allegiances other than those owed to the corporation and its shareholders." Under Lucks, wrote Braznell, "Calpak/Del Monte moved into the modern era."

By 1951, Calpak had an estimated worth of $158 million and annual revenues of $223 million. Yet it remained an unwieldy business whose potential for growth had barely been tapped. Until the end of his presidency in 1963, Lucks drove the company forward not so much by acquisition as by a devotion to, marketing research, field sales, new promotions, new product introductions (including fruit drinks), and a consolidation of its operating units. Of course one merger did prove singularly beneficial to Calpak. This was the purchase of a two-thirds interest in Canadian Canners Limited in 1956. The $14-million-dollar deal attracted considerable attention from industry analysts, for it not only gave Calpak a controlling voice in the operations of the world's second-largest fruit and vegetable canner, but it also ensured a dominant position for the company in the prized British trade bloc.

When Jack Countryman succeeded Lucks, he fortified Del Monte's competitive advantages by establishing a highly efficient warehouse distribution system. In 1967, in an attempt to heighten the company's profile and attract new management talent, he gave Calpak the name it had come to prize above all others, Del Monte. After streamlining its now famous shield logo, the Del Monte Corporation launched boldly into the new territory of soft drinks (which was abandoned after four years) as well as an entire line of canned fruit drinks (which survived until 1974). Other forays included potato chips, frozen french fries, fruit turnovers, frozen prepared entrees, and real estate. Only the last two held any real promise for the company. Strong earnings growth typified the period not because of these attempts at diversification but because of Countryman's parallel commitment to international expansion. The president also proved astute in thwarting a potential takeover from United Fruit (now Chiquita Brands) by acquiring a Miami-based banana importer which, under a U.S. District Court antitrust ruling, nullified any such attempt. United would later sell its Guatemalan operations to Del Monte for $20 million, thus conferring status on the canner as a potentially major player in the fresh fruit market. Alfred W. Eames, Jr., assumed the reins from Countryman in 1968, just prior to a "canner's recession." Accordingly, profits during 1969 and 1970 dropped substantially.

Acquisition by RJR Nabisco in 1979

Profit Improvement Project, or PIP, teams dominated Del Monte corporate culture during the 1970s. U.S. Grocery Products, U.S. Subsidiaries, International Grocery Products, and Seafood were named as the company's major divisions and decentralization became the guiding management philosophy. By 1978, Del Monte had weathered several economic crises— the devaluation of the dollar, rising manufacturing costs, and price freezes—to emerge with record sales of $1.56 billion. Through conservative management of its assets, it was positioning itself for a pivotal acquisition of large proportions that might render it less vulnerable to downswings in its core industry. However, the company's balance sheets were beginning to look so attractive that its privately issued stock, which was once

closely held but now freely traded among a widening circle of private investors, began unexpectedly ratcheting upward. In August 1978, J. Paul Sticht and Joseph Abely, Jr. of R. J. Reynolds Industries arranged a meeting with the new Del Monte president, Dick Landis. In a little over a month an agreement to merge, worth $618 million, was reached and then officially ratified in early 1979, with Del Monte becoming the acquired rather than the acquirer.

For the next ten years, Del Monte benefited from the added RJR Foods labels (Hawaiian Punch, Chun King, Patio, etc.) but also suffered from RJR managerial impulses. The company underwent at least four reorganizations, as well as a succession of managers, and saw its longtime San Francisco headquarters moved to Miami. All of this came to an abrupt end in 1988, when Kohlberg, Kravis, Roberts & Co. effected the biggest leveraged buyout in U.S. history, purchasing RJR for more than $24 billion. In order to reduce debt incurred by the transaction, substantial portions of Del Monte were auctioned off to overseas buyers.

A new Del Monte management team, led by Ewan Macdonald, who had served as marketing vice-president since 1985, salvaged the remainder of the business via another leveraged buyout in 1990. The cost of this acquisition was $1.48 billion, 80 percent of which was financed with outside capital. According to Fara Warner in *Adweek's Marketing Week:* "Del Monte is one of the success stories to come out of the RJR leveraged buyout, despite the heavy debt load the current owners incurred in buying Del Monte from RJR; sales have grown annually by 9 percent during Macdonald's tenure." Most attribute the success to Macdonald's strategy of advertising only in magazines. Yet, a $50 million dollar campaign to introduce the failed Del Monte Vegetable Classics, a considerable portion of which was earmarked for television ads, belied this strategy.

Struggling with Debt in the 1990s

Throughout all the turmoil, Del Monte maintained its good reputation. In 1992, it still ranked number one in brand preference in several categories and controlled 16 percent of the $3.5 billion canned vegetable market. However, heavy debt load gave the company little flexibility. Necessary computer upgrades had to be done on the cheap and advertising expenditures remained relatively low. To lighten the debt burden, the company sold off further divisions in the mid-1990s; its dried fruit division went to Yorkshire Food Group in 1993 and its pudding division went to Kraft in 1995.

Moreover, demand for canned foods had been declining throughout the 1980s and 1990s, as Americans sought to increase their consumption of fresh fruits and vegetables. To combat this trend, Del Monte initiated an advertising campaign aimed at 18 to 34 year olds. Using new print advertising, new packaging, and new products, the company appealed to young adult consumers, such as single parents and unmarried couples, who might not have time for preparing fresh fruits and vegetables.

Also during this time, the Federal Trade Commission ruled that a supply agreement Del Monte had with Pacific Coast Producers substantially reduced competition in the processed fruit market. The decision led Del Monte to pay out $4 million to settle an antitrust suit brought against them by Pacific Coast.

To offset this large debt, Del Monte's owners sought a purchaser for the company, coming close to closing a deal in the mid-1990s. Del Monte had agreed to a $1 billion takeover by Grupo Cabal, a group of investors led by Carlos Cabal, in 1994. The deal would have reunited some of the Del Monte brands, since Cabal had already purchased Fresh Del Monte Produce from the liquidators of Polly Peck International in 1992. However, the deal fell through at the last minute when Cabal disappeared after being charged with illegally transferring money from a trade finance firm to his personal accounts.

As the canned foods market continued to decline and as debts continued to burden the company, Del Monte sought another buyer. In the meantime, it announced in 1996 that it would reduce its work force by 20 percent. The following year, another suitor appeared. Texas Pacific Group, a private investment partnership, had begun a food business shopping spree in 1995, and became known for buying up companies that most analysts regarded as trouble. Beginning with the purchase of Kraft Foods' marshmallow and confections operations, Texas Pacific was soon the fourth largest U.S. candy and confections company. The Group also invested in Continental Airlines, Ducati motorcycles, and the ailing Oxford Health Plans Inc. Rumors placed their offer for Del Monte at $800 million but neither company would confirm the price when they announced their agreement in early 1997. As part of the transition, Richard Wolford, previously the president of Dole Foods, would take over the company as chief executive officer. While Del Monte's success under the Texas Pacific corporate umbrella remained uncertain, the Del Monte name remained a familiar brand with a proud history on supermarket shelves.

Further Reading

Anders, George, "Italian Financier Begins Talks Aimed at Buying Del Monte for $300 Million," *Wall Street Journal*, May 28, 1992.

Braznell, William, *California's Finest: The History of the Del Monte Corporation*, San Francisco: Del Monte Corporation, 1982.

"Del Monte Names Macdonald CEO," *Advertising Age*, October 22, 1990.

DeNitto, Emily, "Del Monte Sets Its Sights Younger," *Advertising Age*, October 4, 1993, p. 8.

Elliott, Dorinda, "Dole and Del Monte Are Staying Put—No Matter What," *Business Week*, November 18, 1985.

Fuquay, Jim, "Fort Worth Group to Buy Del Monte," *Fort Worth Star-Telegram*, March 1, 1997, p. 1.

Johnson, Bradley, "Vexed over Vegetables: Churlish Children Hawk Del Monte's New Line," *Advertising Age*, January 14, 1991.

Kindel, Sharen, "Bringing Mother Nature On Line," *Financial World*, December 8, 1992, pp. 78–79.

Loeffelholz, Suzanne, "Thrice Shy: Del Monte and Sansui Are the Jewels in Polly Peck's Crown," *Financial World*, May 29, 1990.

Maremont, Mark, "Meet Asil Nadir, the Billion-Dollar Fruit King," *Business Week*, September 18, 1989.

Paris, Ellen, "Swimming Through Syrup," *Forbes*, November 21, 1983.

"A Peach or a Raspberry from Mexico?" *The Economist*, July 2, 1994, p. 63.

"Refinancing of Debt Related to Buy-Out Is Completed," *Wall Street Journal*, September 13, 1991.

"A Time to Grow," *Brand News: A Quarterly Publication for the Employees of Del Monte Foods*, March 1991.

Waldman, Peter, "RJR Completes Del Monte Sale for $1.48 Billion," *Wall Street Journal*, January 11, 1990.

Warner, Fara, "Del Monte Has a Rendezvous with an Italian Suitor," *Adweek's Marketing Week*, June 1, 1992.

——, "What's Happening at Del Monte Foods?," *Adweek's Marketing Week*, November 18, 1991.

—Jay P. Pederson
—updated by Susan Windisch Brown

DeMoulas / Market Basket Inc.

875 East Street
Tewksbury, Massachusetts 01876
U.S.A.
(978) 851-8000
Fax: (978) 640-8390

Private Company
Incorporated: 1954
Employees: 11,900
Sales: $1.76 billion (1996)
SICs: 5411 Grocery Stores

DeMoulas / Market Basket Inc. oversees the operation of two chains of supermarkets and superstores in the Northeast, with warehouse facilities and headquarters in the Massachusetts towns of Lawrence and Tewksbury, respectively. In 1997 there were 57 DeMoulas Super Market and Market Basket stores throughout Massachusetts and New Hampshire. The chain's holdings also included shopping malls in which its stores were located, a hotel, and a golf course. The company is perhaps best known, however, for the family feud that sprang up in the 1980s between the sons of the founder over control of the supermarkets and resdistribution of its assets. Despite the ongoing internal turmoil, which has garnered significant media attention, the chain continued to be profitable; its 1996 revenues were approximately $1.76 billion.

Humble Beginnings

In 1917 Greek-American Athansios "Arthur" Demoulas and his wife Efrosine left their factory jobs and opened a "mom and pop" grocery store in Lowell, a working-class city in northeastern Massachusetts. Their specialty was fresh lamb, processed at a slaughterhouse behind their home. The DeMoulas Market (featuring the upper-case "M" not present in the family name) managed to survive through the Great Depression, despite having allowed customers to buy on credit during the rough times. This community generosity almost cost the couple their store; in 1938 their bank threatened to foreclose on the family home if a $100 payment was not made. At this point son Telemachus (later known as "Mike") left school to work at the store. The family raised the $100 payment, and their business stayed afloat. After World War II, the oldest son in the family, George, returned from serving in the Army and also joined the store.

Arthur and Efrosine Demoulas continued to operate the same store for over 40 years, until it was finally replaced with a new building in 1950, which was then bought by their sons, Mike and George, in 1954. The brothers expanded the store in 1956 and the business began to blossom; between 1950 and 1956 annual sales rose from $2,000 to $900,000. Members of the local Greek community were brought into key company positions.

Brothers Divide the Business in the 1960s

Mike and George Demoulas and their families were extremely close. Both brothers married local Greek women and had four children; both also named a son Arthur after their father. In 1964, the two brothers and their wives met at the office to sign the brothers' wills, in which each was named executor of the other's estate. At that meeting, Mike and George reportedly made a verbal agreement to the effect that whichever of the brothers lived longer would care for the other's family, and that the business would be divided evenly between the two sides of the family. This agreement would later become the basis for a decade of lawsuits.

By the end of the 1960s, the single store had been expanded into a 15-store chain. After George Demoulas died unexpectedly of a heart attack while vacationing in Greece in 1971, his widow Evanthea and their children acquired half of the shares of the business. Mike Demoulas continued to operate it, with Evanthea and George's son Evan sitting on the board of directors. Various members of the family were given bonuses and even homes, paid for from the company's rapidly growing profits.

Over the next two decades, Mike Demoulas oversaw the operation of the DeMoulas Super Market stores, and also opened a new chain of Market Basket stores. The new chain was created, according to Mike Demoulas, in order to circumvent a Massachusetts law limiting the number of liquor licenses that could be held by one supermarket chain. During this time, Evanthea and her children routinely let Mike Demoulas handle all of their paperwork, trusting him as patriarch of the family.

A Family Feud Begins in the 1980s

The first sign of real trouble brewing came in 1980, when Mike Demoulas had Evanthea removed from the board of directors. According to a statement filed in one of the later lawsuits, Mike Demoulas had apparently discovered that his sister-in-law was carrying on an affair with a married man and thus found her unsuitable for sitting on the board of the family business.

In 1990, Evanthea and her children received a tax notice concerning their sale of stock in the company, an event of which they claimed in later lawsuits to be totally unaware. An investigation disclosed that Evanthea and her children now owned not half, but only eight percent of the entire group of stores. As also was revealed in later lawsuits, Mike Demoulas had begun to shift company assets into his own name, beginning six weeks after George Demoulas' death. Many of the assets had been transferred from the jointly-owned DeMoulas chain to the Market Basket chain, which turned out to be controlled by Mike Demoulas and his side of the family. George Demoulas' family now alleged that they had been unknowingly signing away their share of the company for almost 20 years. This discovery paved the way for a series of lawsuits that spanned the next decade and threatened to extend into the next century.

During the 1990s, the Demoulas family feud would become the most expensive and most drawn-out lawsuit in Massachusetts history, with no sign of ending as the decade closed. Nine of Boston's most prestigious law firms became involved in the various proceedings, with one of them having earned $13 million in fees by the end of 1996. At one of the trials, a *Boston Globe* reporter observed a total of 19 lawyers seated with Mike Demoulas. Such legal overkill led one observer of the trials, quoted anonymously in the *Boston Globe*'s in-depth profile, "Demoulas v. Demoulas," to refer to the case as "the legal Full Employment Act." The trials also involved events of tabloid proportions: a stripper being paid by one side to obtain wiretapping evidence from her ex-boyfriend; lawyers being investigated by the FBI; jurors soliciting bribes; and fistfights in the courtroom. There were even elaborate masquerades in which the judge's law clerk was invited to "job interviews" in other cities, which were allegedly held by Mike Demoulas' investigators in hopes of obtaining evidence of the judge's bias against Mike Demoulas.

The first of six lawsuits, heard in court from 1990 through 1997, was filed by George Demoulas' heirs in 1990. These lawsuits overlapped with each other in time, but involved distinct issues: a trial challenging Mike Demoulas' transfer of stock owned by George Demoulas' heirs into his own name, plus an appeal by Mike Demoulas after he lost the case; a contempt trial against Mike Demoulas, for transferring $68 million more assets of the firm into his own family's name after a court had ordered them frozen; a case in which Mike Demoulas was accused of shifting company assets into the Market Basket chain which he owned; another suit by George

Demoulas' heirs, claiming that Mike Demoulas had improperly handled the company's pension plan fund; and two trials in which Mike Demoulas accused George Demoulas' heirs of wiretapping company headquarters.

In the cases brought by George Demoulas' heirs, the issues were fairly uncomplicated. They argued that they had not been aware that they were signing away their share of the business. When George Demoulas died, the children were very young; in later years, after they became adults, the children, along with their mother, still relied totally on Mike and developed little business sense of their own. In these cases, some handwriting experts suggested that their signatures on some documents had been forged, while appraisers of the stock testified that the amount paid by Mike Demoulas for the stock, even if George's heirs had been aware of what they were signing, gave them only a tiny fraction of the stock's value. The 1964 oral agreement between the two brothers to split the business evenly was repeatedly relied upon as a binding agreement that both brothers upheld till the day that George Demoulas died.

In the most important of the cases (deciding whether Mike Demoulas had illegally diverted stock belonging to his brother's heirs), Massachusetts judge Nancy Lopez ruled in 1994 that Mike Demoulas had to return stock valued at perhaps half a billion dollars to his brother's family. She also ordered 51 percent of the company to be placed under control of George's branch of the family. The state's highest court upheld these orders after Mike Demoulas appealed them. The stock diversion cases were also notable for a bizarre situation in which a juror phoned a Demoulas family member and offered to change his vote in the case if he was paid $220,000. Following a meeting with an undercover FBI agent to discuss payment of the bribe, the juror was arrested. In the other case against Mike Demoulas, claiming that he had improperly invested the company's pension fund, he likewise found himself losing the decision.

In the midst of these cases, Mike Demoulas filed two separate suits alleging that George's family had planted electronic bugs in the corporate offices, in an attempt to find out how he planned to challenge their lawsuits. At one point, Mike Demoulas' lawyers allegedly paid a former stripper and acknowledged drug addict $500,000 (for "protection and housing"), so that she would meet with her former boyfriend and tape his admission that he had bugged the headquarters. However, in both trials the jury remained unconvinced that any illegal wiretapping had occurred.

The legal scramble did not end with these cases. Throughout the proceedings, Mike Demoulas suspected that the judge, Nancy Lopez, was biased against him, claiming that she had even discussed the case in a restaurant with an attorney for his brother's heirs. His challenges went the whole way to the state's highest court, but were repeatedly rejected.

In 1997, according to some critics, Mike Demoulas' legal team perhaps crossed the line in zealously representing their client. The law clerk for Judge Lopez, Paul Walsh, made public another bizarre development in the case. He had been invited for job interviews in New York and Canada, supposedly with representatives of an international insurance firm. During the interviews he was repeatedly asked about his involvement in writing the opinions in the Demoulas case, as well as whether he thought the judge had made up her mind before the trial began.

Walsh, after returning home, called the U.S. Justice Department and claimed that two of the interviewers actually had been renowned Boston attorneys who were representing Mike Demoulas. The attorneys—Gary Crossen, a former assistant U.S. attorney, and Richard K. Donahue, once an advisor to John F. Kennedy—said that private investigators for Mike Demoulas had actually created the scheme, but justified the scheme because they felt that they had a duty to investigate possible judicial corruption. Almost immediately an FBI investigation of the attorneys was launched, and Crossen resigned as chair of the state panel responsible for nominating judges.

Despite having endured eight years of litigation already, in 1998 the two branches of the family seemed prepared to continue their legal and personal animosity indefinitely. From a tightly knit family in which business and personal matters overlapped broadly, relationships deteriorated to the point that the courts were forced to post Massachusetts State Police officers in the courtrooms during hearings. Mike Demoulas' branch portrayed George's children as worthless spendthrifts. George's branch in return was so angry that, according to the *Boston Globe,* when George's son Evan was killed in a car accident in 1993, Mike's family was informed by the attorneys for George's heirs—and told not to attend the funeral. Another of Mike and George's brothers, John, came to the wake and was refused entrance.

Business Outlook in the Late 1990s

Despite these legal nightmares, DeMoulas and Market Basket stores continued to be successful during the late 1990s. 1996 sales were estimated at $1.76 billion, representing an increase of almost seven percent over 1995. The stores were repeatedly listed by *Forbes* magazine among the top 500 U.S. private companies, ranking 103rd in 1995, 90th in 1996, and 91st in 1997. The Demoulas family itself was included by *Forbes* in its ''400 Richest People in America'' list for 1997. The company also developed a reputation for community involvement in the economically struggling area where it was founded, continuing to operate in towns that other chains had abandoned and contributing heavily to local charities.

Still, the company had two reasons for concern about its future. First, its management continued to be constantly embroiled in legal battles. In addition to appeals of decisions dividing the assets, Mike Demoulas also faced new allegations of fraud by real estate partners in 1997. Moreover, the next Demoulas generation, Mike's son Arthur T. Demoulas and George's son Arthur S. Demoulas, had become engaged in its

own legal argument involving wiretapping at the company headquarters, in addition to the ongoing family battle over assets. These ongoing battles left analysts wondering how effective management could be in the face of such disparity.

Equally important, competition among grocery stores in the Massachusetts—New Hampshire area intensified. Chief competitors (among them Star Markets Company, Inc.; Big Y Foods, Inc.; Shaw's Supermarkets, Inc.; and Stop and Shop Companies, Inc.) brought in larger profits by developing ''superstores,'' stores devoted to natural and organic products, wholesale operations, gourmet food departments, and pet departments. Other growing competitors included warehouse stores and wholesale clubs. The DeMoulas chain did begin to address this trend by enhancing its offerings. For instance, the company entered into an exclusive retail relationship with the Alden Merrell Corporation, to sell that company's highly popular gourmet cheesecakes in Market Basket stores. However, as it approached a new century DeMoulas / Market Basket Inc. would clearly have to take time out from the courtroom to keep abreast of food retailing trends in order to stay competitive.

Principal Subsidiaries

DeMoulas Super Markets Inc.; Market Basket Inc.

Further Reading

Auerbach, Jon, ''Patriarch Loses Reins of Demoulas Fortune,'' *Boston Globe,* August 21, 1996, p. F1.

Hyten, Todd, ''Cheesecake Maker to Expand Newburyport Plant,'' *Boston Business Journal,* November 18, 1996.

Kennedy, John H., ''Bitter Legal Feud Tears Asunder One of State's Wealthiest Families,'' *Boston Globe,* February 26, 1993, p. 37.

——, ''Demoulas Pension Plan Suit Is Settled,'' *Boston Globe,* June 1, 1994, p. 29.

——, ''Demoulas' Widow Wins Suit,'' *Boston Globe,* May 27, 1994, p. B1.

Nealon, Patricia, ''Federal Court Jury Clears Demoulas; Second Acquittal in Bugging Case,'' *Boston Globe,* August 5, 1997, p. B2.

——, ''Wiretap Claims Are Key to Demoulas Fight in Fourth Trial,'' *Boston Globe,* July 16, 1997, p. B1.

Rakowsky, Judy, ''Demoulas Lawyer Quits State Panel,'' *Boston Globe,* September 19, 1997, p. B1.

——, ''Former Juror Pleads Guilty to Bribery,'' *Boston Globe,* March 14, 1995, p. 39.

Reidy, Chris, ''Pension Trustees Cleared; Judge Says Demoulas Violated Guidelines,'' *Boston Globe,* April 14, 1995, p. 21.

——, ''SJC Upholds Decision in Demoulas Feud,'' *Boston Globe,* March 14, 1997, p. D2.

Zernicke, Kate, ''Demoulas v. Demoulas,'' *Boston Globe Magazine,* January 11, 1998, pp. 16–30.

—Gerry Azzata

Desc, S.A. de C.V.

Paseo de los Tamarindos 400-B
05230 Mexico City, D.F.
Mexico
(525) 261-8000
Fax: (525) 261-8098

Public Company
Incorporated: 1973
Employees: 18,880
Sales: 11.98 billion pesos ($1.53 billion) (1996)
Stock Exchanges: Mexico City New York
SICs: 0213 Hogs; Broiler, Fryer & Roaster Chickens;
0273 Animal Aquaculture; 2011 Meat Packing Plants;
2048 Prepared Feeds & Feed Ingredients for Animals
& Fowls, Except Dogs & Cats; 2492 Particle Board;
2821 Plastics Materials, Synthetic Resins &
Nonvulcanizable Elastomers; 2822 Synthetic Rubber
(Vulcanizable Elastomers); 2865 Cyclic Organic
Crudes & Intermediates, & Organic Dyes &
Pigments; 2891 Adhesives & Sealants; 2895 Carbon
Black; 3713 Truck & Bus Bodies; 3714 Motor
Vehicle Parts & Accessories; 6552 Land Developers
& Subdividers, Except Cemeteries; 6719 Offices of
Holding Companies, Not Elsewhere Classified

Desc, S.A. de C.V. is one of Mexico's largest industrial conglomerates. Through subsidiaries, it was engaged in 1997 in five business sectors: auto parts; chemicals; consumer uses of such chemical products as adhesives, glues, and sealings; agribusiness; and real estate. Through Unik, a wholly owned subsidiary, it was believed to be the largest independent manufacturer of automotive parts in Mexico. Through its Girsa subsidiary, Desc was the only Mexican manufacturer of phenol and carbon black. Through its Dine subsidiary, Desc believed itself to be the largest real estate developer in Mexico.

1970s Formation

Desc was founded under the name Desc (for Descuento), Sociedad de Fomento Industrial, in 1973, by a group of 42 Mexican investors. Among them was Manuel Senderos Irigoyen, who had acquired a good part of the big brewery Cerveceria Moctezuma from the Bailleres family and had founded the auto parts firm Spicer as a joint venture with Dana Corp. of the United States in 1951. Another was Eneko de Belausteguigoitia Arocena, who held interests in cornmeal, sugar, chemicals, and steel. Still another was Antonio Ruiz Galindo, whose family-owned enterprise, D.M. Nacional, began to make metal products and wooden office furniture in 1929.

Desc was established with initial paid-up capital of 617 million pesos ($49.4 million). The following year it had a 35 percent interest in Industrias Resistol, whose annual sales came to 1.25 billion pesos, or $100 million. This firm was also known as Irsa, or Girsa, acronyms for (Grupo) Industrias Resistol S.A., which had 16 plants in 1976 and was involved in petrochemicals, refrigerators, radio and television sets, and typewriters as well as chemicals. Founded by Rodolfo Patron Tenorio in 1925 to produce starch from tapioca, the enterprise took the Resistol name in 1951. The Mexican subsidiary of Monsanto Corp. took a 40 percent share in 1971.

In addition to its stake in Resistol, Desc in 1974 purchased 40 percent of Spicer, which had sales of 674 million pesos, or $54 million, and 35 percent of Industrias Negromex, a manufacturer of chemicals and plastics with sales of 403 million pesos, or $32.2 million. In all, the new conglomerate had taken an average of 32 percent in eight industrial firms with total sales in 1974 of 2.88 billion pesos ($230.6 million).

Desc began selling shares to the public in 1975. The largest shareholder in 1982 was Fomento de Valores, S.A. de C.V., with 48 percent, followed by Banamex, with 11 percent. The largest individual shareholders were Ruiz and Senderos. Desc was the 11th-ranking company in Mexico in 1977 in terms of sales volume. Resistol ranked 33rd among Mexican companies with 3.21 billion pesos ($140.4 million), and Spicer ranked 79th, with 1.15 billion pesos ($50.2 million). By 1979 Desc held an average of 35 percent of the shares of more than 30 enterprises. Among these was Compania Hulera Euzkadi, a manufacturer of automobile tires in which B.F. Goodrich Co.'s Mexican affiliate held a 35 percent stake.

Ruiz Galindo was president of Negromex in 1984. Among its directors were Senderos Irigoyen and his son Fernando Senderos Mestre. Adolfo Patron Lujan was president of Resistol. Members of Resistol's board of directors that year included Antonio Ruiz Galindo Gomez, Jr., Senderos Irigoyen, Senderos Mestre, Belausteguigoitia, and Roger Patron Lujan. Both firms continued to be profitable despite the debt crisis and peso devaluation of 1982. In 1983 Negromex had net income of 1.53 billion pesos (about $11.4 million) on net sales of 12.67 billion pesos (about $93.9 million). Resistol had net income of 5.21 billion pesos (about $38.6 million) on net sales of 34.33 billion pesos (about $254.3 million). During 1985–1986 Desc sold about six companies that did not contribute to its objectives of obtaining leading-edge technology and developing a strong export base. It also acquired four firms.

Desc: 1987–96

After an impressive reduction in its foreign debt burden, Desc was estimated to be worth $300 million in 1987. In February of that year Novum was formed as the holding company for Negromex. The various operating divisions of Novum were manufacturing and selling synthetic rubber, carbon black, fatty acids, rubber chemicals, other chemicals, and pharmaceutical specialties. The international division included Housmex Inc., a Houston-based North American sales and trading company. Novum was doing business in 27 countries. In 1990 Novum acquired majority control of Hules Mexicanos, a rival firm, thereby increasing its carbon black capacity from 65,000 to 161,000 metric tons a year and its synthetic rubber capacity from 80,000 to 155,000 metric tons a year.

Desc, with Antonio Ruiz Galindo, Jr., now at the head of the enterprise, had sales of 2,839 billion pesos (about $1.15 billion) in 1989. Spicer and Irsa remained the main units, contributing 40 and 34 percent to sales, respectively. Univasa, an enterprise founded in 1982 to breed poultry, contributed nearly 12 percent. Irsa was 40 percent foreign-owned, Spicer was one-third foreign-owned, and Univasa was 36 percent foreign-owned. Desc as a whole was 29 percent foreign-owned. In 1992 Grupo Irsa closed its least efficient chemicals plants and divested certain products lines. That year, however, Desc bought Monsanto's stake in the group for about $50 million. In 1994 Desc acquired Politos, S.A. de C.V., Grupo Irsa's only domestic competitor in phosphate production. The company shortened its name simply to Desc in that year.

Desc continued to do fairly well in the early 1990s, although its profit margin dropped. In 1992 the company had net income of 354.09 billion pesos ($114.4 million) on net sales of 5,158 billion pesos ($1.67 billion). The long-term debt was $125 million at the end of the year. Senderos Mestre was now the chief executive officer.

One company in Desc's hands was Dine, a real estate firm that, starting in the late 1960s, developed Bosques de las Lomas, a five-million-square-meter upper income residential and commercial area at the western end of Mexico City, where Desc itself located its main offices. Dine resumed activities in the 1990s after being inactive for most of the previous decade because of the economic crisis that gripped Mexico following the 1982 peso devaluation. Spicer purchased Transmisiones y Equipos Mecanicos, S.A. de C.V. (Tremec), a Mexican manufacturer of light-duty transmissions, in 1994.

The currency crisis and peso devaluation of late 1994 resulted in a net loss of 1.44 billion pesos ($411.4 million), primarily because of heavy losses in noncash foreign exchange. During 1995 an outstanding performance by the chemicals sector, largely because exports doubled, enabled Desc to record a modest net profit of 329 million pesos ($48.4 million) on net sales of 11.46 billion pesos ($1.69 billion). The company had invested heavily in Grupo Irsa, raising its output to 100 percent of capacity and capitalizing on cheap raw materials and low labor costs to flood the United States and Europe with its products. High interest rates and continuing recession took a heavy toll on Desc's auto parts and real estate sectors.

Sparked by the North American Free Trade Agreement, the Unik auto parts division did very well in 1996. Exports accounted for almost half of its sales as the division became a premier supplier to Detroit's Big Three. In October 1996 Spicer agreed to purchase Borg-Warner Automotive Inc.'s unprofitable North American manual transmission business for about $40 million. This business was expected to have sales of about $105 million for the year. Spicer, in July 1997, purchased Dana Corp.'s transmission division. Desc was planning to move the purchased Borg-Warner and Dana plants to its automotive center in Queretaro.

Desc added to its agribusiness holdings in August 1987 by purchasing Corfuerte S.A. de C.V., a Mexican producer of canned vegetables, tomato puree, corn oil, coffee, and other food products. The company had six production plants in Mexico and one in California. Desc paid $89 million for a 95 percent share in Corfuerte, which had sales of $84.6 million in 1996.

Desc recorded net sales in 1996 of 11.98 billion pesos ($1.53 billion) and net income of 1.90 billion pesos ($241.7 million). Chemicals accounted for 44 percent of net sales; automotive parts for 36.8 percent; agribusiness for 13.6 percent; consumer products for four percent; and real estate for 1.8 percent. Exports accounted for 31 percent. The company's long-term debt was 3.34 billion pesos (about $428 million) in March 1997. The Senderos family held 51 percent of the Class A shares, 40 percent of the Class B shares, and 18 percent of the Class C shares. (Class A shareholders had the right to elect a majority of directors to the company board.)

DESC in 1996

In 1996 Unik was conducting Desc's automotive parts business, manufacturing 43 different types of automotive products at 28 plants in Mexico. These included everything from pick-up truck bodies and transmissions to pistons, gaskets, seals, ignition coils, and spark plugs. Spicer accounted for about 51 percent of Unik's revenue in 1995.

Girsa (Grupo Irsa) was managing all of Desc's businesses in the chemical sector, manufacturing 31 chemical products at 21 plants. Synthetic rubber, manufactured by Negromex, was its chief chemicals product, followed by phosphates and polystyrene. The phosphates business produced chemicals for use in household detergents, soft drinks, and water treatment. Following, in descending order of 1995 sales, came carbon black, acrylics, natural pigments/animal-food supplements, phenol, emulsions (specialty lattices), and pharmaceuticals. (The pharmaceuticals business was sold in 1997.) Girsa also administered the consumer products division, which consisted chiefly of glues and adhesives under the Resistol name and waterproofing sealants under the Fester name. In addition, there were Revoplas and Actriton products, consisting mainly of acrylic coatings.

The Agrobios subsidiary was conducting Desc's agribusiness activities at 156 farms, installations, and plants through two subsidiaries: Univas and Holding Aquanova. Univasa was engaged in the production and sale of poultry, pork, and animal feed. Aquanova was engaged in the production and sale of shrimp. Desc believed it was the largest producer of broiler chickens in southeastern Mexico. Its market share of animal feed was also largest in this area, where most of its feed mills were located. Most of the feed was for the company's own chickens and hogs. Shrimp production facilities were situated in the states of Sinaloa and Nayarit, but the business was still in the developmental stage.

Dine, the real estate subsidiary, was believed to own the largest land reserves for residential development in the Mexico City metropolitan area. Focusing on the upper income segments of the market, it also owned properties for tourism development along the Caribbean and Pacific coasts of Mexico. Its biggest holdings in size were in Punta Mita, Nayarit, and (with others, including Senderos family members) Ranchos La Estadia, an area in a high-income residential suburb of Mexico City. During 1996 Dine completed Arcos Torre I of the Arcos Bosques Corporativo complex in Mexico City, making it the largest business center in Latin America. Reaching a height of 160 meters (525 feet), Arcos Torre I was Mexico's second tallest building.

Principal Subsidiaries

Agrobios S.A.; Dine S.A.; Girsa, S.A.; Unik, S.A.

Further Reading

Concheira, Elvira, et. al, *El poder de la gran burgesia,* Mexico City: Ediciones de Cultura Popular, 1979, pp. 156–169.

"DESC: Un nuevo concepto corporativo," *Expansion,* September 17, 1975, pp. 32–36.

Dignan, Larry, "Signs of Gold in Latin America's Blue Chips," *New York Times,* May 25, 1997, Sec. 3, p. 5.

Dombey, Daniel, "Mexicans Buy into the US," *Financial Times,* July 18, 1997, p. 4.

Friedman, Alan, "Monsanto Sells Stake in Mexican Venture," *Financial Times,* December 16, 1992, p. 27.

Hernandez Moron, Leticia, "Desc, sobre ruedas; crecen 4.4% las ventas en 96," *El Financiero,* February 7, 1997, p. 13.

"How a Major Mexican Firm Forged a Winning Strategy for Exporting to the US," *Business Latin America,* June 1, 1987, p. 171.

"Mexico's Industrial Groups," *Business Latin America,* April 27, 1987, p. 133.

Millman, Joel, "Big Latin Firms Resist Slimming Trend," *Wall Street Journal,* August 19, 1997, p. A12.

"Negromex Moves into Europe," *European Rubber Journal,* June 1988, p. 14.

—Robert Halasz

The Dial Corp.

15501 North Dial Boulevard
Scottsdale, Arizona 85260-1619
U.S.A.
(602) 754-3425
Fax: (602) 754-1098
Web site: http://www.dialcorp.com

Public Company
Incorporated: 1926, as Armour & Company
Employees: 2,812
Sales: $1.4 billion (1996)
Stock Exchanges: New York
SICs: 2841 Soap & Other Detergents

The Dial Corp. is a leading manufacturer of consumer products in the United States, with four core brands: Dial soaps, Purex detergents, Renuzit air fresheners, and Armour Star canned meats. Dial led the U.S. antibacterial soap market in 1997 and was the third largest seller of detergents. Its canned meats were second in sales only to Hormel. Having grown to an unwieldy conglomerate in the 1960s and 1970s, the corporation underwent several episodes of restructuring and name changes. In 1987 it sold its Greyhound bus lines; in 1992, it spun off its financial services division to form Finova; and in 1996, it spun off its other service businesses to form Viad Corp.

Early History

The Dial brand name was first given to a unique deodorant soap developed by researchers at the Chicago-based meat processing business of Armour & Company. Introduced in 1948, Dial featured a newly developed germicide, known as AT-7, that was believed to reduce up to 80 percent more of the bacteria found on the skin than other soaps. Said to provide " 'Round the Clock Protection," Dial was first advertised in the *Chicago Tribune,* on paper printed with scented ink. The innovative advertisement attracted a great deal of attention, and the soap achieved high sales from the onset. One Chicago store reportedly sold more than 4,000 bars in one day.

Dial soon became the leading deodorant soap in the country. In 1953 the company adopted a slogan—"Aren't you glad you use Dial? Don't you wish everybody did?"—that would continue to be used into the 1990s. In 1966 Armour announced that it would begin marketing aerosol can and roll-on deodorant products as well as shaving creams under the Dial brand name. Over the next five years, the new Dial products achieved record sales, and a shampoo was added to the Dial line.

Acquired by Greyhound

In 1970 Armour was acquired by the Greyhound Corporation. The country's leader in the motorcoach industry since 1930, Greyhound, under chairperson and CEO Gerald H. Trautman, had begun to diversify its operations in the 1960s in response to declining bus ticket sales. As automobiles and airline tickets became less expensive and bus line profits dwindled, Greyhound acquired small companies in the fields of automobile leasing, money orders, insurance, and catering. Greyhound board members were approached by Armour in the late 1960s when General Host threatened Armour with a hostile takeover, and Greyhound was persuaded to add Armour to its subsidiaries. The 1970 $400 million purchase was Greyhound's first major acquisition. To reduce its investment, Greyhound immediately sold $225 million of Armour assets, retaining only the meat-packing and consumer products subsidiaries. The meat-packing operation was renamed Armour Foods, while the consumer products operation was renamed Armour-Dial.

In 1971 construction was completed on a new plant for manufacturing Dial soap in Aurora, Illinois. However, while Armour-Dial was now better equipped to meet consumer demands for the soap, the company was also faced with the possibility of having to alter the soap's ingredients. Although Dial had an excellent record of consumer satisfaction and the company had neither received any complaints during the soap's 23-year history nor been given any reason to consider the product unsafe, the U.S. Food and Drug Administration (FDA) found during this time that one of the soap's germicidal ingredients, hexachlorophene, was dangerous if misused or ingested. When the FDA banned the use of the chemical in cosmetics and restricted its use in soaps, Armour management planned, in

---

Company Perspectives:

Value Leader. These words tell who we are and how we manage our Company. Providing good value is our goal in every area of operation. This goal has guided us in restructuring the work force, in deciding the cost structure of our products and in focusing on building our four core brands. By offering good value to our consumers, these brands will strengthen the value of Dial stock for our shareholders. Our goal of providing value also has placed Dial among the front runners in motivating employees. We reward outstanding employee performance with stock options and bonuses and tie everyone's compensation squarely to the Company's performance. Taken together, every facet of the way we do business signals Value Leader.

---

conjunction with the FDA, to continue to market Dial with a label on the packaging warning users that the soap was for external use only and should be thoroughly rinsed off the skin after each use. Eventually, however, researchers at the company were able to develop an alternative ingredient that proved to be as successful as hexachlorophene had been as a germicide. Although the formula of Dial changed, it continued to rank as one of the nation's most popular soaps. In 1971 Armour-Dial's headquarters were moved to Phoenix, Arizona, where operations were reorganized under two primary headings: the Toiletries & Household Products Division and the Administrative Division.

Although Trautman had taken Greyhound from bus line to successful conglomerate, the company was still known on Wall Street as "the dog," due to the unpredictable swings in profits and losses it incurred from year to year. Problems were attributed to the rapid expansion of Greyhound's holdings to include such a vast and unrelated array of products and services. Furthermore, while Armour Foods and Armour-Dial accounted for over 50 percent of the company's revenues, their earnings proved extremely erratic, ranging from nine percent growth one year to 21 percent the next. The Armour Foods subsidiary in particular had also been troubled by frequent restructuring and changes in management. In general, analysts found that Greyhound was suffering from a lack of focus.

Refocusing the Conglomerate

An overhaul of the company began in 1982 when John W. Teets was named chairperson and CEO. Teets began working for Greyhound in 1964 when he took a job managing the company's restaurants at the New York World's Fair. Recently devastated by a series of personal tragedies, including the deaths of both his wife and his brother as well as a fire that destroyed a restaurant of which he had been part owner, Teets threw himself into his new job at Greyhound, working long hours and exhibiting a determination and enthusiastic management style that was soon noticed by Greyhound executives. He was promoted to president of Post Houses, a Greyhound subsidiary that ran bus terminal restaurants, where he remained until 1968, when he accepted an offer from a Chicago-based restau-

rant chain. Teets returned to Greyhound in 1976 to head the company's Food Service Group subsidiary. By this time he had become known for his ability to help struggling companies return to profitability, and he was soon credited with turning around the entire food service division. By 1980 Teets held the executive office of vice-chairperson and was a contender for the presidency when Trautman retired.

Upon his appointment as president and CEO, Teets acted immediately to restructure the company, quickly establishing his reputation as a tough and demanding leader through his implementation of a new standard of 15 percent return on equity, a level of performance that he expected of each subsidiary. Reexamining Greyhound's holdings, he was quoted in *Forbes* as concluding that the company needed to "lean down, be tougher in the marketplace," through a long term agenda that included selling off several subsidiaries and cutting costs. In 1983, in one of his first major decisions, Teets cut the wages of union food and commercial workers at Armour Foods. When the workers refused to accept the cut, Teets shut down the 29 plants and sold the operations to Conagra Inc., which offered Greyhound a 15-percent stake in its company, a deal equaling around $150 million.

Also that year the company was faced with a widely publicized strike by Greyhound bus drivers strike. The bus line had experienced dramatic losses in ridership and nearly $35 million in operating losses in 1981 and 1982. Finding that Greyhound drivers were earning as much as 50 percent more than drivers at competing companies, Teets threatened to replace them with nonunion employees if they did not accept a cut in wages. A violent 47-day strike ensued, during which buses were kept running by nonunion labor. Eventually Teets prevailed, and union drivers returned to work at a lower wage. Although Teets was able to cut its operating costs, Greyhound never recovered financially, and early in 1987, he sold the Greyhound bus company to a group of investors from Dallas.

Having restructured the company's interests, Teets began a plan of selective acquisitions that would better fit the company's portfolio. Relying on the unmitigated success of the Armour-Dial division to provide expert management in the field, Greyhound acquired Purex Industries Inc., makers of laundry soap, for $264 million in 1985. The purchase doubled Greyhound's consumer product sales, and after a brief period of losses, the company recaptured its market share. Two years later, the company restructured the consumer products subsidiary along product lines, creating a personal care division that handled the marketing of bath and deodorant soaps, as well as the new and profitable Liquid Dial soap; a household and laundry division responsible for such items as detergents, air fresheners, and cleansers; and a food division that during this time introduced Lunch Bucket single-serving microwaveable meals.

By the late 1980s Greyhound had completed its plans for restructuring. With profits high from the sales of the popular Dial, Purex, and newly acquired Brillo steel wool soap pads, and stock prices low at around $27 per share, the streamlined company was ripe for a takeover, and rumors spread on Wall Street. In order to discourage raiders, Teets was faced with the challenge of raising the stock prices. By 1991, however, the company's debts had shrunk, its earnings improved dramatically, and stock prices had risen to $44 per share.

To minimize confusion for its investors and consumers by distinguishing the company from the Greyhound bus line it had sold off three years before, the company changed its name to Greyhound Dial in March 1990. At the time Teets decided to retain "Greyhound" as part of the company's new name in order to reflect the ten subsidiaries the company still owned that carried the Greyhound name, such as Greyhound Exhibit group. Within the year, however, when Greyhound Dial switchboard operators were still receiving numerous calls regarding bus routes and fares, management decided to make the message clearer still by renaming the company The Dial Corp.

In 1991 The Dial Corp. reported a loss of $57.6 million due to its restructuring and the costs involved in spinning off some of its subsidiaries. Revenues were up from $3.5 to $3.6 billion, however, and management estimated that without the onetime charges against earnings in 1991, The Dial Corp. would have reported a net income of $122.4 million.

Divestiture of Service Businesses

To further streamline the company, Dial spun off its financial services company in 1992. Finova, the former Greyhound Financial Co., saw dramatic growth in the first few years after its divestiture from Dial. By 1996 its earnings doubled, to $97 million, and its sales more than doubled, to $781 million. More important to shareholders, its stock more than doubled, to $55. Such success left shareholders clamoring for further spinoffs. However, the company did not follow such a clear-cut plan in 1993. Although it did sell off its bus-making division that year, it expanded its airline services division by acquiring United Air Lines' kitchens. CEO Teets also instituted some cost cutting measures, which helped the company achieve a rise in income from continuing operations from 1992's $74 million to $110 million in 1993. Growth continued in 1994, but it was mostly spurred by further acquisitions.

The idea of further divestiture simmered for the next couple of years, coming to a boil in 1996. That year Dial split into two publicly held companies: Viad Corp., which took the $2.2 billion services businesses, and The Dial Corp., which took the $1.4 billion consumer products businesses. The new services company comprised the former Dial's airline catering and services, including Aircraft Services Inc. and Dobbs International; convention services, including GES Exposition Services and Exhibitgroup/Giltspur, Inc.; leisure and payment services, including Travelers Express, the food service company Restaura, and Premier Cruise Lines; and the company's majority stake in Greyhound Lines of Canada.

The plan for the newly slimmed Dial Corp. called for a focus on its four core brands: Dial soaps, Purex detergents, Renuzit air fresheners, and Armour Star canned meats. These four product lines accounted for 90 percent of Dial's revenues in 1996. The company intended to raise that proportion even higher by selling or discontinuing underperforming brands. In July 1997 it followed through on that plan by selling Brillo soap pads, Parsons ammonia, Bo Peep ammonia, Sno Bol toilet bowl cleaner, Cameo metal cleaner, and Rain Drops water softener. Church & Dwight, manufacturer of Arm & Hammer products, bought the brands and Dial's London, Ohio, Brillo plant. The same year Dial also sold its Bruce floor care brand to Triangle Pacific Corp. Dial received about $30 million for these sales, and the company used the proceeds to pay down its heavy debt load.

With stiff competition in the domestic soap and detergent market, particularly from giants Procter & Gamble, Colgate-Palmolive, and Unilever, Dial needed further measures to improve their returns. In an effort to cut costs, the company moved its headquarters from Phoenix, Arizona, to suburban Scottsdale in 1997. It also eliminated approximately 250 jobs, mostly in management and administration.

"Working together, we have taken the tough steps to make Dial more competitive," Mal Jozoff, Dial chair and chief executive officer, said in a company release in mid-1997. "We've gotten our costs under control with actions such as moving our headquarters to a lower-cost facility. . . . In addition, we have trimmed our product line and are focusing on our highly successful core brands." There was some indication that these steps, in combination with the 1996 restructuring, were bearing fruit. The company's 1997 third quarter earnings rose to $22.4 million, compared to 1996's net income before restructuring charges of $7.4 million.

Further Reading

Byrne, Harlan S., "Investment News & Views: Dial Corp.," *Barron's,* August 26, 1991, pp. 378.

"Dial Corp. Restructures along Product Lines," *Arizona Business Gazette,* January 5, 1987.

"Dial Enjoys Its Liquid Assets," *Packaging Digest,* July 1989, pp. 74, 79.

"Dial: More Spin Required," *Financial World,* November 22, 1994, p. 22.

Forbes, Steve, "All-Around Successful CEO," *Forbes,* November 21, 1994, p. 26.

Galaraza, Pablo, "Dialing Up the Next Spin-Off," *Financial World,* September 16, 1996, pp. 42–5.

Gillespie, Phyllis, "Turning the Dial," *Arizona Republic,* December 22, 1991.

Kiley, David, "Greyhound Dials Up a Name Change More or Less," *Adweek's Marketing Week,* March 5, 1990, p. 5.

Sivy, Michael, "Pump Up Your Fund Profits with Four Choice Stocks," *Money,* July 1997, p. 180.

Stuart, Alexander, "Greyhound Gets Ready for a New Leader," *Fortune,* December 15, 1980, pp. 58–64.

"Will More Soap Help Greyhound Shine?" *Business Week,* March 11, 1985.

—Tina Grant
—updated by Susan Windisch Brown

Dollar Tree Stores, Inc.

500 Volvo Parkway
Chesapeake, Virginia 23320
U.S.A.
(757) 321-5000
Fax: (757) 321-5292

Public Company
Incorporated: 1986 as Only One Dollar, Inc.
Employees: 11,000
Sales: $635.5 million (1997)
Stock Exchanges: NASDAQ
SICs: 5331 Variety Stores

Dollar Tree Stores, Inc. is the largest operator of discount variety stores in the United States selling merchandise priced at $1.00. With stores designed to update the traditional variety store concept, the company offers a wide assortment of general merchandise, including food, toys, housewares, health and beauty aids, hardware, books, stationery, and other consumer items. As of December 31, 1997, Dollar Tree operated 887 stores in 26 states in the South, Southeast, Mid-Atlantic, Northeast, and Midwest regions of the United States. The company estimated that in 1996, 85 to 90 million people shopped in its stores, which operated under the names of Dollar Tree, Dollar Bills, and Only $1.00.

1986–90: From Toys to a Dollar Store

The founders of Dollar Tree, Inc. first worked together managing K&K Toys, Inc., building that company from one toy store to a 136-store toy retailer. In 1986, the three men, J. Douglas Perry, Macon F. Brock, Jr., and H. Ray Compton decided to diversify and established a new company, incorporating it in Virginia as Only One Dollar, Inc. "We had all started out in the variety store business, so it seemed a natural transition for us," Brock told *Chain Store Executive.* The company opened with five stores in Virginia, Georgia, and Tennessee, and, typical of the dollar format, offered primarily closeout

merchandise. Perry became chairman of the new company, Brock served as president, and Compton was executive vice-president and chief financial officer.

Over the next five years, the company grew to 171 stores, while the three men continued also to manage K&K Toys. In October 1991, they sold the toy chain, then one of the largest mall-based toy retailers in the country, to a subsidiary of Melville Corporation, and turned their full attention to their discount operation.

1991–92: Changing Inventory and Locations

They began by implementing two major strategic shifts in their efforts to expand. First, rather than continue to be a purveyor of closeout merchandise, they moved to make their stores the modern equivalent of traditional variety stores, with a wide assortment of basic goods priced at no more than $1.00.

To do this, they had to change their purchasing strategies, which had emphasized deals and novelties. They started buying directly from foreign manufacturers and worked with manufacturers in the United States to offer customized packaging, a broader selection, and products that were larger or held more than normal. Management's aim was to "exceed its customers' expectations of the range and quality of products that can be purchased for $1.00," and to offer at that price items that other stores usually sold for more.

To underscore that value, they also changed where they located stores. Until then most of the stores were in enclosed malls, since that was what management knew from K&K Toys. Now they concentrated on opening stores in strip centers anchored by a large grocery store or a mass merchandiser such as Kmart, Target, or Wal-Mart that it could undersell. That strategy not only helped customers compare prices, it also saved the company money, because strip centers generally charged less rent and tended to generate higher operating margins than mall locations. By the end of 1992, the company had 256 stores. Net sales for the year grew by over 70 percent from $71.1 million to $120.5 million with net income of $10.8 million.

Company Perspectives:

Dollar Tree Stores, Inc. is a customer-oriented, value-driven variety store, operating at the one dollar price point. We serve our customers by providing the best value for their dollar.

1993–95: A New Name

During 1993, Macon Brock, Jr., was named CEO, the company changed its name to Dollar Tree Stores, Inc., and Dollar Tree continued its expansion, gaining a net 72 new stores, all of which were located in strip shopping centers. Because management believed their stores had a relatively small shopping radius, they were able to open several locations in a single market without having the outlets compete with each other for customers. Most of the stores were located in mid-sized cities and small towns; the rest operated in major metropolitan areas. New stores historically were profitable within their first year of operation, and that fact reinforced the company's expansion plans of opening new stores rather than growing through acquisition or merger.

The typical store was approximately 3,200 square feet, with 85 to 90 percent of that area devoted to selling space. Unlike many of its dollar competitors, Dollar Tree paid a lot of attention to the design of its stores and the physical presentation of its merchandise. The chain used the same layout plan in each of its stores, with merchandise organized by category and displayed in densely stocked bins and shelves. Carpeting, bright lighting, background music, and the use of vibrant colors such as red checkout stands, made the stores attractive and comfortable. With an average purchase of $6.50 per customer, the chain did not accept credit cards, nor did it scan purchases at checkout. "We locate our stores where people are already shopping, hoping they will be curious enough to check us out," Brock explained to *Chain Store Executive with Shopping Center Age.* "And then we try and make the outlets as easy as possible for customers to get in and out of."

By the end of 1993, the chain had 328 locations, sales of $167.8 million, and net income of $9.5 million. The drop in income was due to $4 million in costs associated with a recapitalization. As part of the recapitalization, the founders and their spouses sold 50 percent of the outstanding stock to The SK Equity Fund, L.P. and four associates for a total of $23.6 million.

The company continued its successful formula in 1994, expanding to 409 stores, with sales topping the $200 million mark for the first time to reach $231.6 million. One of the key factors in the company's operations was its distribution system. Sharing space (186,000 square feet) at the Norfolk headquarters was one of the company's two distribution centers; the other, with 244,000 square feet, was located in Memphis, Tennessee. This capacity allowed the company to buy large quantities at good prices and to receive early shipment discounts, thus keeping prices within its $1 range. Given the relatively small size of most of the stores, backup inventories were kept at the distribution

centers, with stores receiving weekly shipments of merchandise from the centers. During the busy Christmas season, the company could make two weekly deliveries to high-volume stores.

The company began 1995 with the creation of two subsidiaries, Dollar Tree Management, Inc. and Dollar Tree Distribution, Inc. In March management took Dollar Tree public, and during the year the company opened its 500th store. Sales topped $300 million, with per share earnings of 76 cents.

1996: Acquired Dollar Bills, Inc.

In January 1996, the company bought Dollar Bills, Inc. for approximately $52.6 million in cash and $2 million in inventory. The purchase moved the company into three new states (Iowa, Minnesota, and Wisconsin) and added 136 stores, increasing Dollar Tree's store base by 27 percent. A modern 250,000-square-foot distribution center and a wholesale division in the Chicago area completed the acquisition.

Most of the Dollar Bills stores were concentrated in urban areas, a different retail market than the existing Dollar Tree stores. The new additions were also typically larger (4,000 to 4,500 square feet), had higher average sales, and carried less inventory per square foot. They also had a higher proportion of low-margin items such as food, health and beauty aids, and household supplies. According to the company's 1996 annual report, the acquisition "taught us about urban marketing, intensified our commitment to variety merchandise, and showed us new ideas in warehousing and distribution." By the end of the year, the new acquisitions had been successfully integrated into the company. To help make sure that all locations followed the same operational procedures, the company instituted a new training program, "Dollar Tree University," at corporate headquarters.

In April, the company initiated a stock dividend, with the effect of a 3-for-2 stock split, and in June, made a second stock offering to the public. While Asia continued to be the company's largest source of imported goods, the company added sources from Italy, Brazil, Argentina, and Mexico to its list of vendors. Imports made up over one-third of Dollar Tree's merchandise, and around 40 percent of its sales. Closeout merchandise, which had been the company's initial concept, now made up less than 15 percent of its offerings.

In evaluating the overall merchandise mix, the company added more higher-margin inventory such as toys and gifts to the items available at the Dollar Bills locations and more consumable products on the shelves of the Dollar Tree stores. The integration was accomplished with little disruption to either the company's opening of 104 new Dollar Tree stores nor the operations of the individual stores. Over 90 percent of the Dollar Tree stores that were opened the entire year had operating income profits of more than 15 percent, as did over 85 percent of the Dollar Bills stores. The company ended 1996 with 737 stores and sales up more than 64 percent, to $493 million. About half the increase was attributable to the Dollar Bills operations.

The mid-1990s were a tough period for many of Dollar Tree's competitors. Several, including Jamesway Corp., Ben Franklin Retail Stores, 50-Off Stores, and Solo Serve Corp.

were no longer publicly traded by the end of 1996. Others closed many of their stores or abandoned the $1 concept.

1997 and Beyond

In January 1997, Dollar Tree began construction, at an estimated cost of $34 million, of a Store Support Center in Chesapeake, Virginia, 10 miles from its Norfolk location. In April, Dollar Tree issued $30 million of unsecured notes to pay off some of its existing revolving credit facility so that the credit could be used to fund capital expenditures for the Store Support Center. In June, the founders, SK Equity Fund, and other shareholders offered 4 million shares of Dollar Tree stock for sale. The company itself did not receive any of the proceeds of that sale, but in July, issued a three-for-two stock split.

During the year, the company continued to grow according to its expansion play, opening a net 150 new stores, and reaching 887 locations. Many of the new locations fit the company's larger prototype for future Dollar Tree stores, which increased store space to between 3,500 and 4,000 square feet. The company hoped that by creating larger aisles, with more space for recently added shopping carts, customers would buy more. Net sales for the year rose nearly 29 percent to $635.5 million, with sales at stores open for a year up more than seven percent. Net earnings increased from $33.8 million in 1996 to $48.6 million. This performance occurred as one of the company's variety store competitors, Woolworth's, closed its stores in the United States.

Staff moved into the new corporate headquarters at the Store Support Center before the year ended, and the new, automated distribution center began operating in January 1998. With an automated conveyor and sorting system, the new facility had the capacity to support up to 800 stores. Dollar Tree president and CEO Macon Brock, Jr., announced that the company was in the process of buying land in Olive Branch, Mississippi, for another distribution center to replace the nearby Memphis facility. The Olive Branch center, some 425,000 square feet in size, was expected to be in operation in early 1999.

In March 1998, certain shareholders, including Brock and the other founders, along with SK Equity Fund, filed to sell 4.5 million shares of Dollar Tree stock. "There's nothing wrong with the dollar-store concept," Brock told *Chain Store Executive with Shopping Center Age*. "But the way you execute it can mean the difference between success and failure." By concentrating on finding a wide variety of merchandise it could sell for $1, by making its stores exciting and attractive, by closely watching costs, and by locating its stores in centers where their customers were already shopping, Dollar Tree obviously had found its niche. As Brock summed it up, "The failure of the traditional variety store, as seen in the recent closing of Woolworth's, and the dominance of the big-box retailers have left a huge gap that we can fill."

Principal Subsidiaries

Dollar Bills, Inc.; Dollar Tree Management, Inc.; Dollar Tree Distribution, Inc.

Further Reading

"Dollar Tree Launches Operations at New Distribution Center," *Business Wire*, January 15, 1998.
"Dollar Tree Stores, Inc. Reports Earnings Per Share of $1.13 for 1997," *Business Wire*, January 22, 1998.
"Racking Up Profit At Dollar Tree Stores," *Chain Store Age Executive with Shopping Center Age*, November 1997, p. 54.

—Ellen D. Wernick

Eagle-Picher Industries, Inc.

Suite 500
250 East Fifth Street
Cincinnati, Ohio 45202
U.S.A.
(513) 721-7010
Fax: (513) 721-2341
Web site: http://www.epcorp.com

Wholly Owned Subsidiary of Granaria Holdings B.V.
Incorporated: 1916 as Eagle-Picher Lead Company
Employees: 6,700
Sales: $906 million (1997)
SICs: 3295 Minerals—Ground or Treated; 3625 Relays
& Industrial Controls; 3613 Switchgear &
Switchboard Apparatus; 3812 Search & Navigation
Equipment

With over 150 years of manufacturing experience, Eagle-Picher Industries, Inc., dominates numerous niche markets with its industrial products. Primarily supplying machinery and parts to companies around the world, Eagle-Picher manufactures hundreds of different products for the automotive, aerospace, defense, construction, and other industries. The company survived the demise of several of the industries it operated in, managing to diversify without bringing on disaster, as many other conglomerates have done in similar circumstances. Following a deluge of lawsuits related to asbestos in its insulation products, Eagle-Picher managed to withstand bankruptcy proceedings begun in 1991 and was reorganized and acquired by the Dutch conglomerate Granaria Holdings in 1998.

Company Antecedents

The earliest predecessor of Eagle Picher was established as a partnership in Cincinnati in 1842. Two brothers, Edgar and Stephen Conkling, set up a small operation to produce white lead, a by-product of corrosion that was especially useful as a durable paint when mixed with linseed oil. In 1847, the Conkl-ing brothers went into partnership with William Wood, who later took over the company when Edgar Conkling joined the Texas West Railroad Company. With new partners, Wood moved the company to a new location in 1858 and changed the name of the firm to the Eagle White Lead Works.

Great instability came to the metals market after the Civil War. Overcapacity, a lack of commodity price controls, and strong competition from the ready-mix paint industry pushed Eagle and several other white lead manufacturers to the brink of bankruptcy. By 1887, a consortium of eastern lead companies formed a powerful association called the Lead Trust. The Trust tried and failed on numerous occasions to include Eagle in its collaborations. William Christie Wood, who succeeded his father as president of Eagle in 1883, led the fight to keep Eagle independent. He initiated strong financial controls and attempted to branch the company into related businesses. Wood left in 1887, and was replaced by G. W. Boyce, who stayed for six months and was then succeeded by Benjamin H. Cox.

Unable to sustain the company in light of the actions of the powerful 31 Lead Trust firms (which merged to form the National Lead Company in 1891), Cox hired three managers away from his Cincinnati rival, the Eckstein White Lead Company. These managers, led by John B. Swift, reorganized Eagle in an effort to fend off National Lead. The company had a strong customer base and a solid reputation for quality.

Certain that he could not succeed indefinitely, Swift attempted to vertically integrate the company, as Rockefeller's Standard Oil Co. had done. Several years passed when, finally, in 1903, Eagle and several other independents secured a stake in the American Metal Company, a mining and smelting house. Meanwhile, Eagle diversified the product line to include lead pipe and plumbing supplies.

In December 1905, after receiving an invitation to join National Lead, Eagle received an inquiry from the Picher Lead Company, a mining outfit in Joplin, Missouri, proposing a buyout. With a steady supply of lead from Picher, Eagle would be free of National Lead's ability to influence market prices. The transaction was completed on April 5, 1906.

Company Perspectives:

Eagle-Picher is an industrial products company. As such, the company is subject to the volatility of the markets it serves. To help protect itself from market fluctuations and business cycle pressures, the strategy of Eagle-Picher has been to diversify its product lines. This strategy has served the company well in the past, and all indications suggest it will serve the company well in the future.

Eagle, which had expanded its operations, provided Picher with capital to expand its facilities and fund further exploration in the mineral-rich tri-state region of Missouri, Oklahoma, and Kansas. Picher tried unsuccessfully for several years to locate new mineral deposits on the Quapaw Indian lands of the tri-state area. Fearing that the region had been depleted, Picher began wildcat drilling, again without success.

Late in 1913 a Picher drill rig became stuck in five feet of mud while being shipped during a thunderstorm. Picher suggested drilling in place before ordering the rig dismantled. To everyone's surprise, the chance drilling yielded an extremely rich lead-zinc ore concentrate that led to 20 more strikes by 1915 and the establishment of a huge zinc smelter at Henryetta, Oklahoma. The following year, Eagle and Picher formally merged into a single company.

However, management failed to address the problem of merging separate business cultures, an issue that engendered considerable internal turmoil for many years. Many Picher employees held a strong grudge against Eagle, which they felt didn't fully appreciate the work they did in the tri-state. Oliver S. Picher, who became president of the new company, chose Chicago as the neutral site on which to establish a new headquarters. In 1919 he ordered the decentralization enterprise, forming an organization similar to General Electric, General Motors, and DuPont, in which specific divisions enjoyed operating autonomy.

Zinc Operations Successful in Early 20th Century

Under Oliver Picher, Eagle-Picher became the nation's leading zinc manufacturer, as well as one of its largest lead producers. Growth in the zinc market was augmented by World War I, in which demand for zinc in brass artillery and other weapons increased dramatically. Seeking to enter the finished zinc products markets, Picher acquired a zinc oxide plant at Hillsboro, Illinois.

Clearly set on a strong path, Eagle-Picher lost some momentum the following year when Oliver Picher died suddenly. The board appointed Swift to succeed Picher as president. Swift continued Picher's diversification strategy by purchasing the Midland Chemical Company's lithopone plant at Argo, Illinois. From its origins in lead, Eagle-Picher had become one of the nation's only integrated mine-to-market zinc companies.

Swift ordered the company's research department, established in 1915 by Picher, to develop new uses for zinc. This led

to several partnerships with battery companies in 1922 and the development of highly efficient lead batteries. Thus, with the advent of automobiles, a promising new market was created as demand for white lead pigment had begun to trail off.

Buoyed by the newly founded productivity of the tri-state deposits, Eagle-Picher began buying large tracts of land in the region adjacent to its existing mines, organizing them under a new subsidiary, the Consolidated Lead and Zinc Company. Eagle-Picher expanded its production capacity in 1925 by taking control of the Ontario Smelting Company of Hockerville, Oklahoma. This enabled the company to squeeze additional ores out of mines that were thought to have been depleted.

Declines in the Late 1920s

Now listed on the Cincinnati Stock Exchange, Eagle-Picher entered a difficult period in 1927 when yields from the tri-state mines began to decline. Arthur Bendelari succeeded Swift as president of the company in February 1928 and eventually moved the company's headquarters back to Cincinnati.

Serious economic declines occurred in the months following the stock market crash in 1929. To improve managerial efficiency, Bendelari reorganized all the company's production interests into a new subsidiary, Eagle-Picher Mining and Smelting. The subsidiary also shielded the parent company from potential liabilities in its field operations. As the Great Depression set in, lead and zinc prices continued to plummet. Eagle-Picher remained solvent mainly from the use of cash reserves accumulated during the boom years of the 1920s.

During this time, George Washington Potter, a veteran of the tri-state mines, recommended the establishment of a central smelting facility to replace the more than 200 smaller smelters located in the area. Potter won government permission to centralize production, as well as the right to operate Eagle-Picher locomotives on railroads in the region. The Central mill opened in October 1932. During this time, the company also began producing slag wool, an insulation product made from smelter wastes. This stable, fire-proof material proved highly successful, bolstering the company's product line.

Union Busting in the 1930s

In 1933, Eagle-Picher faced a serious threat from the International Union of Mine, Mill and Smelter Workers, which had begun to organize workers in the tri-state region. Eagle-Picher and the Ore Producers Association to which it belonged refused to recognize the union, which called a strike for representation in May 1935. Subsequently, Eagle-Picher helped to establish a rival company-sponsored union called the Blue Card Union. Using gangs of thugs, the local sheriff, and even the National Guard, the Blue Card succeeded in breaking the strike and seriously disrupting the union's activity in the area.

The union filed suits against Eagle-Picher and other companies with the National Labor Relations Board, charging interference in the administration of a labor union. The union prevailed, and Eagle-Picher gained a proven reputation for opposing union activity and being uncompromising and difficult in negotiations. Despite its legal victory, however, the union had little success in the tri-state.

Fearing that Eagle-Picher was losing control of its operations, the company's board asked Joel M. Bowlby, a Chicago accountant, to perform an analysis of the company. In January 1937, Bowlby recommended further decentralization of the enterprise, creating fully autonomous divisions. Bendelari resigned shortly thereafter due to ill health and was replaced by Joseph Hummel, Jr. During this time, Potter approached management with a plan to acquire the Commerce Mining and Royalty Company, which held extensive ore reserves and several mills in the tri-state area, in addition to the Northeast Oklahoma Railroad. The $10 million deal was finalized in 1938, and Commerce was added to Eagle-Picher as a separate division, following Bowlby's recommendations.

Wartime Production

The Commerce acquisition did little more than extend the life of a dying industry in the tri-state region. However, during this time, the Germans invaded Poland and war began in Europe, creating a huge demand for war industry minerals, including Eagle-Picher's lead and zinc. Production capacity was expanded to meet the new demand, and in late 1941 the company even took over a zinc operation in Taxco, Mexico. To cope with the new demand, Eagle-Picher enlisted the Robert Heller consulting firm to present its own set of recommendations. Heller advised elevating Bowlby to the presidency and shuffling Hummel off to head the board.

Bowlby's ascension to the presidency was well timed. As a bookish accountant who possessed tremendous knowledge of the company, Bowlby was perfectly suited for the job. A fact that became evident after Pearl Harbor, when the company came under the direction of the War Production Board.

Eagle-Picher held several advantages over other wartime industries. Unlike Singer, which converted from sewing machines to machine guns, and Ford, which went from automobiles to bombers, Eagle-Picher already produced what the war effort needed: slab zinc, paint pigments, lead and zinc oxides, bearing metals, antimonial leads, solders, and insulation products.

The war brought a production boom back to the tri-state area. But even so, Eagle-Picher had difficulty operating its mines at capacity with a work force depleted by conscription, despite increased mechanization and the addition of another mine near Tucson. Furthermore, the company's profits from war production were strictly controlled by the government. Meanwhile, Potter, who had given so much to the company, became seriously disillusioned with Eagle-Picher under Bowlby, who used wartime profits to move Eagle-Picher out of mining and into manufacturing. Potter resigned in protest in 1944.

The war brought Eagle-Picher into several new markets, particularly production of germanium, the first semiconducting material, essential to the invention of the transistor in 1947 as well as to the development of solid state electronics. The company also emerged from the war with highly-advanced battery systems which held tremendous commercial potential. Commercialization of these products required no conversion back to the civilian economy.

Postwar Diversification

Having dropped the name "Lead" from its name in 1945, Eagle-Picher purchased smelters and fabricating plants in Dallas and East Chicago in 1946, and the Alston-Lucas paint company two years later. Hoping to build on the postwar housing boom, the company also purchased the Orange Screen Company, a manufacturer of screen doors and windows.

In the attempt to diversify, Eagle-Picher purchased a diatomaceous earth plant, which produced filtration products, in Clark, Nevada. Abandoning an effort to exit the metallic products business, Eagle-Picher later purchased the Kansas City Smelting and Refining Company, the Cleveland Lead Works, and parts of the Southern Lead Company.

Bowlby resigned in 1948 due to a family illness and was replaced by T. Spencer Shore, a company director and partner with Goldman-Sachs. Shore set new, more meaningful corporate performance goals based on earnings per share. He also limited Eagle-Picher's acquisitions to closely held companies serving specialized industrial markets. Shore understood that Eagle-Picher could not run these companies as well as their original management. He added the condition that acquisitions require the management of these companies to remain after being taken over by Eagle-Picher. Other emerging conglomerates of the day, including Textron, Ling Electronics (later LTV), and ITT, did not understand the importance of this and succeeded in destroying many of the companies they took over.

Eagle-Picher saw a second defense-related increase in demand during the Korean War, when American forces again became engaged in combat and the military began massive stockpiling efforts in the event of a wider war with communist countries. Still, with the decline of the tri-state area, the need for the Mining and Smelting subsidiary disappeared. These operations were converted back into an operating division of Eagle-Picher. Back on the acquisition trail in 1952, Eagle-Picher took over the Ohio Rubber Company of Willoughby, Ohio, making it a division of the company.

In 1954, Shore liquidated Eagle-Picher's Paint and Varnish and Metallic Product divisions, which were only marginally profitable, and used the proceeds to acquire the Fabricon Products division of Fisher Body for $9.9 million. Fabricon manufactured plastic products for the automotive, food, and packaging industries. Eagle-Picher later acquired another plastics company, Wilson and Hoppe, which it merged with Fabricon.

After divesting its Mexican operations for $1.4 million in 1956, Eagle-Picher purchased the Chicago Vitreous Corporation, a porcelain enameling company, and the Gora-Lee Corporation, a Connecticut-based rubber molds manufacturer. The company's divisional structure made these acquisitions all the easier to metabolize.

During the early 1950s, Bell Labs, RCA, Texas Instruments, Raytheon, Sylvania, and General Electric provided strong markets for Eagle-Picher germanium, which was used to develop even more advanced transistor products. By 1955, Eagle-Picher held 95 percent of the market. This market dried up quickly, however, after Texas Instruments developed a silicon transistor made essentially from sand. Eagle-Picher failed to develop its own silicon business winding up that operation in 1960.

Continued Expansion in the 1960s

Nevertheless, Eagle-Picher continued to benefit from its leading research in silver-zinc battery technologies, which gained new importance with the development of rocket and missile programs during the 1950s. The "couples" battery, named for its dual chamber construction, led Eagle-Picher's product line in a zero defects quality program. The battery program ultimately drew Eagle-Picher into the prestigious and profitable aerospace and defense business, as well as into space exploration. Eventually, Shore combined the germanium and battery operations into a new electronics division.

During the early 1960s, Eagle-Picher continued to diversify by taking over several other companies, including the Akron-based Standard Mold tire products company, Davis Wire, a steel fence and net manufacturer in Los Angeles, and the Premier Rubber Manufacturing Company in Dayton. In 1966, to emphasize its increasingly diverse nature, the company changed its name from the Eagle-Picher Company to Eagle-Picher Industries. Shore maintained his strict acquisition policy and, because Eagle-Picher remained in closely related markets, came to hate the description of the company as a "conglomerate."

Under Shore, who retired in favor of William D. Atterbury in 1967, Eagle-Picher fell short of establishing dominant horizontal or vertical monopolies yet remained too closely tied to specific industrial markets to be considered typically diversified. Acquisitions continued that year, with the Detroit-based gasket maker, Wolverine Fabricating and Manufacturing, and the Markey Bronze Corporation. The following year Eagle-Picher took over Cincinnati Cleaning and Finishing, a manufacturer of cleaning solvents, and Union Steel, which produced welded wire and sheet metal. In 1969, Eagle-Picher acquired the Ross Pattern and Foundry company, a manufacturer of aluminum castings for the automotive, electronics, and aerospace industries.

With lowered growth from divestitures and operating profit, Atterbury attempted to raise investment capital by emphasizing the synergy of Eagle-Picher's various divisions. The profit-center approach to these divisions served the cause well. The company raised sufficient capital to purchase the A. D. Weiss Lithograph Company and the Hillsdale Tool company. Meanwhile, in March 1972, Eagle-Picher spun off Davis Wire to a group led by the division's management for $23.5 million.

In 1973, Eagle-Picher acquired the Johnson Manufacturing Company, Faulkner Concrete Pipe, and Plas Chem, an anti-corrosion chemical company. These were followed in 1976 with the purchase of Elmac, a mining supply company, and Pritchett Engineering, a precision machining company serving the petroleum industry.

Legal Challenges in the 1980s and 1990s

Many of Eagle-Picher's industrial markets were adversely affected by a serious recession in 1979 that bottomed out in 1982. This caused numerous operational reverses at Eagle-Picher and placed the company on shaky ground for its next challenge, a spate of lawsuits related to the use of asbestos in Eagle-Picher's insulation products.

Thomas Petry, appointed president in March 1981 to ensure an orderly transition as Atterbury approached retirement age, was forced to take action in 1984 when more than 19,000 asbestos injury claims had been filed. The wave of litigation meant easy money for lawyers, whose actions led several other manufacturers, including Johns-Manville, into bankruptcy.

Petry, however, elected to ride out the litigation by funding settlements with money from a special reserve that was replenished with operating income. To lessen the effect of the suits, Eagle-Picher concentrated on expansion from its other operations. This strategy succeeded in keeping the company out of bankruptcy but still seriously damaged earnings. Petry succeeded Atterbury as chairperson in 1989 and was replaced as president by John W. Painter.

As the volume of settlements increased, Eagle-Picher was forced to divest several operations, including the Akron Standard and flight operations divisions, to maintain the fund. By 1991, however, the company could not keep up and was forced to file for reorganization under bankruptcy laws. Ironically, this had the positive effect of halting all injury settlements.

In March 1992, Painter retired, and his duties were assumed again by Thomas Petry. The company remained under court protection, as the number of property damage claims reached 1,000, and personal injury claims escalated to more than 160,000. Thus, while operations remained strong, the asbestos litigation continued to vex the company.

Although it remained diversified within related industrial markets, Eagle-Picher began to move toward greater centralized control, made necessary by the asbestos litigation. The company remained organized in three main divisions: an industrial group, a machinery group, and an automotive group.

Bankruptcy Reorganization Successful

As bankruptcy proceedings dragged on, the company attempted to continue operations undisturbed. As a testament to its success, almost no customers, suppliers, or vendors abandoned the company during this time. In fact, sales rose substantially during the reorganization, from $599 million in 1991 to $891 million in 1996, the last full year before the reorganization was complete. Earnings rose even more dramatically, from $19 million in 1991 to $62 million in 1996.

Eagle-Picher also continued to develop its new markets during that time. In 1995 the company created a new technologies division by combining its electronics division with its specialty materials division. By combining the former divisions' expertise in making batteries for space satellites and silicon wafers for solar cells, the new division directed its attention to creating power systems for space satellites.

Eagle-Picher emerged from court protection in early 1997, having achieved its primary objective in filing for bankruptcy: protecting itself from being destroyed by injury claims. The reorganization settlement included a permanent court injunction against current or future asbestos or lead-related injury claims against the company. In return for this protection, Eagle-Picher financed the Eagle-Picher Industries Personal Injury Settlement Trust with ten million shares of newly issued stock, $250 million in ten-year debentures, $69 million in notes for tax refunds, $50 million in cash, and $18 million in three-year notes. The trust was to use these funds to settle all the asbestos and lead-related injury claims. Claims from injury claimants and trade creditors would be paid approximately 37 cents on the dollar. Shareholders, however, were left with nothing, having been given no stake in the newly reorganized company.

Once out of bankruptcy reorganization, Eagle-Picher had optimistic plans for the future. Andries Ruijssenaars, president of Eagle-Picher since 1994 and slated to become chief executive officer, said in 1996 that he thought a rise in revenues to $3 billion in the next five to ten years was possible. The company planned to focus on expanding international business, aiming for an even split of $1 billion in revenues in each of the company's three main territories: the United States, Europe, and the Pacific Rim.

In early 1998 Eagle-Picher was acquired by Granaria Holdings B.V., a Dutch investment firm, for more than $700 million. Joel P. Wyler, chair of the privately held Dutch company, became chair of Eagle-Picher when the transaction was completed. As part of the deal, the management of Eagle-Picher became part owners of the company.

Principal Subsidiaries

Michigan Automotive Research Corporation; Eagle-Picher-Boge L.L.C.; Eagle-Picher Fluid Systems, Inc.; Eagle-Picher Minerals, Inc.; Transicoil Inc.; Eagle-Picher Industries Europe GmbH (Netherlands); Eagle-Picher Far East, Inc. (Japan).

Principal Divisions

Hillsdale Tool and Manufacturing; Ross Aluminum Foundries; Rubber Molding; Wolverine Gasket; Trim; Cincinnati Industrial Machinery; Construction Equipment; Technologies; Fabricon Products; Plastics; Suspension Systems.

Further Reading

Boyer, Mike, "Dark Clouds Pass for Eagle-Picher," *The Cincinnati Enquirer,* March 16, 1997, p. I1.
Frazier, Lynne McKenna, "Cambridge Industries Aims to Dominate Slice of Auto Supply Industry," *The News Sentinel* (Fort Wayne, Ind.), July 21, 1997.
Knerr, Douglas, *Eagle-Picher Industries, Strategies for Survival in the Industrial Marketplace, 1840–1980,* Columbus: Ohio State University Press, 1992.

—John Simley
—updated by Susan Windisch Brown

El Al Israel Airlines Ltd.

Ben-Gurion Airport
P.O. Box 41
IL-70100 Lod
Israel
3 9716111
Fax: 3 9721442
Web site: http://www.elal.com

State-Owned Company
Incorporated: 1949 as El Al Israel Airlines Ltd.
Employees: 3,500
Sales: $1.20 billion (1996)
SICs: 4512 Air Transportation, Scheduled; 4522 Air
   Transportation, Nonscheduled

In its 50-year history El Al Israel Airlines Ltd. has often had to maneuver around terrorists and hostile airspace. El Al flies in the face of danger like no other airline, but with plans to privatize the company underway in 1998, the most serious threats to its survival were financial. As part of its unique character, El Al offers kosher in-flight meals and does not fly passengers on the Jewish Sabbath or certain religious holidays.

To the Skies in 1948

El Al was created as a symbol of national independence. Immediately after its founding on May 14, 1948, Israel found itself embroiled in a battle for survival with neighboring Arab states. The United States and most European countries subsequently imposed an embargo on all combatants. Although Israel's provisional government had already made establishing a civil airline a priority, President Chaim Weizmann's trip to Geneva gave the project impetus. The Israeli government wanted to fly him home in one of its own planes, but its military craft could not make the trip due to the embargo.

A four-engine C-54 military transport was repainted in civilian colors, and outfitted with extra fuel tanks to make the ten-hour flight nonstop—the meandering flight path was also neces-

sitated by the embargo. With a cabin full of fine furnishings, the first plane marked ''El Al Ltd./Israel National Aviation Company'' departed Israel's Ekron Air Base on September 28, 1948. After returning from Switzerland the next day, the plane was stripped of its civilian luxuries and returned to military service.

Although the flight and its accompanying documentation were hastily arranged, the crew was adorned in tradition. Uniform insignia featured a flying camel, the mascot of early Jewish aviators, and the airline's name itself harkened back even further. Taken from the book of Hosea (11:7), ''el al'' means ''to the skies.'' The Star of David was also incorporated into the airline's livery. Despite these trappings the airline had existed on paper only a couple of days and would not be formally incorporated until November 15.

Aryeh Pincus, a lawyer originally from South Africa, was chosen to lead the company, which faced impressive challenges from the beginning. Airlifting imperiled Jewish refugees from Yemen and Iraq were among its earliest priorities. El Al borrowed military aircraft until February 1949, when it bought a couple of Douglas DC-4 aircraft (converted military C-54s) from American Airlines. After the necessary clearances were negotiated, the two planes flew to their home base, Lod Airport in Israel. Its first scheduled flights, between Tel Aviv and Paris (refueling in Rome), started in July 1949. By the end of the year, the airline had flown passengers to London and Johannesburg as well. In the fall of 1950, El Al acquired Universal Airways, founded by South African Zionists. A state-run domestic airline, Arkia, was also founded, with El Al half owner.

The Challenging 1950s

The company began shipping freight to Europe using military surplus C-46 transports in 1950. It also initiated its first charter service to the United States; scheduled service soon followed. Disaster struck in February 1950, however, when one of El Al's DC-4s was destroyed attempting at take off in Tel Aviv. There were no casualties. Another DC-4 carrying cargo crashed into a Swiss hillside the next year, killing several crew members. In July 1955 an El Al Constellation returning to Tel Aviv from Vienna was downed in flight by Bulgarian MiG-15 interceptors.

Company Perspectives:

Established in 1949 as the national airline of Israel, El Al has grown into a prestigious international carrier, ranked by IATA as one of the world's three most efficient air carriers, boasting a consecutive ten-year profitability record. Productivity. Punctuality. Polished professionalism. In-flight services and indulgences, pampering the passenger with exciting Kosher culinary delights—from Indian tandoori to Japanese teriyaki—and a myriad of audio and video entertainment programs. Uncompromising security. Expanded global coverage. And, incomparable Israeli hospitality. The friendliness and personalized touch that make time fly make El Al more than just a convenient mode of travel. A unique combination of amenities and advantages. . . earning international appeal, and making El Al a preferred global gateway to every corner of the world.

The newly acquired Constellations were superior aircraft with pressurized cabins that could fly above bad weather. However, they were noisy and unreliable, and challenged El Al's ambitious timetables. In 1955 the airline placed a controversial order for two Bristol Britannia turboprops—a bold leap in both technology and cost for the fledgling carrier. El Al became only the second airline to fly the Britannia after the British Overseas Airways Corporation.

In spite of the hopeful purchase, times were hard for the airline, as yet unprofitable, as well as the Israeli government. Both were pressed for qualified professionals, compounded by the challenges of taking on thousands of dispossessed immigrants amid hostile surroundings. During the Sinai War, Egypt blocked Israel's shipping lanes. After Israeli forces invaded the Sinai Peninsula, no foreign airlines would fly into the country. Having an independent civil airline remained an important government priority, and El Al endured.

El Al ended the decade with a capable new leader, Efraim Ben-Arzi, and the capacity to compete in the London–New York route with its swift, and popular, new Britannias—the fastest scheduled Atlantic crossing at the time. The company's bookings increased to impressive levels; the $18 million gamble on the new planes seemed to have paid off. Trans-Atlantic fares increased from 8,000 in 1957, before the turboprop service was introduced, to 32,000 in 1960. However, the de Havilland Comet 4, Boeing 707, and Douglas DC-8 jets, all introduced by 1959, soon eliminated the Britannia's speed advantage. The jet age had arrived.

Reaching New Heights in the Jet Age

El Al posted its first profit in 1960. However, in order to remain competitive, El Al began flying the new Boeing 707 jet. The airline promptly set records in June 1961 for longest nonstop commercial flight (New York to Tel Aviv) and speed (in 9.5 hours). A jet similar to the 707, the Boeing 720B, provided the power and endurance needed to carry the *Star of David* to Johannesburg via Teheran. Due to airspace restrictions, El Al had previously been forced to lease jets from other airlines to complete the passage, which lasted 16 hours even with the 720B.

The speed and comfort offered by the Boeing 707 helped El Al land more than half of all passengers flying into Israel. (The company subsequently became the country's chief promoter of tourism; only a fraction of its passengers were business travelers.) In spite of the high cost, jet service would boost company profits for years to come. News of these first profits precipitated a series of walk-outs among dissatisfied pilots and mechanics.

Egypt laid siege to Israel's Red Sea port of Eliat in May 1967, prompting El Al to evacuate tourists there. Its planes flew military support missions, and many of its staff were conscripted. In a month, actual hostilities were underway. Though they lasted only a week, the airline lost four of its pilots in battle. Not surprisingly, the only carrier serving Israel was El Al, though it did modify its schedule to mostly night flights.

After the Six-Day War, Israel controlled several new territories, including all of Jerusalem. After an intense public relations effort, tourism returned to Israel in unrelenting waves. Control of the Sinai gave the airline a direct route to Johannesburg, cutting flying time from Tel Aviv by nearly one half.

In order to promote tourism, the Israeli government proposed lifting the five-year-old ban on incoming charter flights. Although El Al was for the most part successful in fighting the charters, chairman Ben-Arzi and president Col. Shlomo Lahat resigned in the wake of this vigorous political contest. Mordechai Ben-Ari, previously the airline's commercial manager, was designated company president.

El Al began flying behind the Iron Curtain with scheduled visits to Bucharest commencing in 1968. Increased demand soon led to dedicated cargo flights to Europe and America. A catering subsidiary, Teshet Tourism and Aviation Services Ltd., was also formed in this year. El Al posted annual profits of approximately $2 million in 1968 and 1969.

New Challenges in the 1970s

During this time the airline was forced to reckon with an alarming new development which would remain a grave concern for commercial aviation: terrorism. An El Al flight from Rome to Tel Aviv was hijacked to Algeria in July 1968; during the next two years attacks by Arab terrorists increased in violence. El Al quickly began developing the tough (and expensive) security measures that would become its trademark, including manning every flight with undercover armed guards and sealing the cockpit area. They proved effective on September 6, 1970, when operatives of the Popular Front for the Liberation of Palestine attacked four airliners in one day. While Pan Am, TWA, and Swissair saw their planes destroyed, El Al's survived: the pilot plunged the aircraft 14,000 feet to help the crew gain the upper hand on the terrorists.

The stakes increased even more when El Al began operating the colossal 400-seat Boeing 747 "jumbo jet." New facilities were needed to house and service the aircraft, which was twice as large as any of its predecessors. Although the first two jets sold for more than $30 million each, the accompanying preparations required another three times the investment. El Al's first 747, resplendent in a new paint scheme, was delivered in May 1971.

As with its previous investments in new aircraft such as the Constellation and the 707, this purchase did not escape controversy. Critics believed it was simply too risky, given the enormous cost and the already serious threat of terrorism. However, traffic soared with the two 747s, and El Al's relatively small operation (totaling just 12 jets) became one to emulate world wide. A third 747 was delivered in 1973. The airline used it to introduce nonstop service from Tel Aviv to New York. At 13 hours against the prevailing winds, it was the longest scheduled flight in the world. The success of the 747 service inspired plans for expansion, but they were truncated by the surprise attacks of October 1973 that launched the Yom Kippur War. Again El Al aircraft and personnel were mobilized for the country's defense, and again all foreign airlines canceled flights to Israel. Although hostilities lasted only three weeks, El Al was forced to contend with the effects for some time to come. All operations in Ethiopia were halted due to Arab political pressure there. The Arab oil embargo greatly increased the price of jet fuel.

Fighting between Cyprus and Turkey scared all other airlines out of the eastern Mediterranean again in July 1974, adding to El Al's workload. In addition, El Al was plagued with labor unrest. Although a tentative settlement was reached in February 1975, workers walked out for almost three weeks in October. This was repeated in April 1978, further damaging the company's reputation. The company averaged ten work stoppages a year.

In 1977 El Al created a subsidiary to offer nonscheduled flights, El Al Charter Services Ltd., later renamed Sun d'Or International Airlines Ltd. A global recession kept tourists home and in 1975, El Al failed to post a profit for the first time in a dozen years. Delays in replacing the Boeing 707 and 720 jetliners, relatively inefficient and too noisy for some European airports, did not help the bottom line.

Miserable financial results and continuing labor strife prompted the Israeli government to install new management. Mordechai Hod, an air force commander, became president in 1977 but resigned less than two years later. Avraham Shavit, a manufacturing executive, was appointed board chairman, and eventually El Al veteran Itzhak Shander was named president.

In Iran the situation progressively deteriorated in 1978 with the rise of the Ayatollah Khomeini. Despite unstable local fuel supplies and little control tower support, El Al dispatched additional 747s to fly thousands of emigrants out of the country. The company's facilities in Teheran were eventually either burned or confiscated. El Al also scaled back certain operations elsewhere in the world. It canceled a money-losing route to Mexico City in 1979. Some progress was made, however. A historically significant and popular new route to Cairo, El Al's only Arab destination, opened in 1980.

A New El Al for a New Decade

New management succeeded in both negotiating pay cuts and deflating the bloated work force, which had reached 6,000 employees. Some poorly-performing sales offices were closed. The Israeli government privatized the domestic carrier Arkia, in which El Al had a 50 percent share. Morale was also turned around, and the airline's on-time record and customer service again earned world class status. However, after an independent audit recommended further layoffs, labor troubles erupted again.

The government grounded El Al after a flight steward strike in September 1982, canceling all but a handful of flight operations. The government appointed Amram Blum receiver, with ultimate authority for running the company. Rafi Harlev was named president. Employee and management representatives were able to produce an agreement under the glare of bankruptcy court. An end to strikes was negotiated, although a thousand more workers were to be furloughed.

The Israeli government provided El Al with two new Boeing 737 mid-size airliners and also agreed to purchase four state-of-the-art Boeing 767 long-range jets worth $200 million. El Al could begin flying again in January 1983, but the damage seemed grave indeed. For the fiscal year ending in April, the airline lost $123.3 million. Fortunately, its customers proved loyal and eager to return to the skies. Within a couple of years the airline was again the model of productivity. Profitability returned in 1987, in spite of increased terrorism in Europe. The route system of the revived carrier expanded quickly. In May 1988 El Al surpassed its old record by flying 7,000 miles from Tel Aviv to Los Angeles nonstop. Due to *glasnost,* flights to Poland and Yugoslavia were able to commence in 1989.

At the end of the decade, the airline seemed likely to recover from receivership, although increased terrorism again dampened tourism. In 1988 the carrier eked out a small $19 million profit on total revenues of $665 million. The government planned to sell about half of the company to employees and investors. El Al operated 20 aircraft in 1990, including nine 747 jumbo jets, and had begun replacing its aging Boeing 707s with the state-of-the-art 757 model.

New Partnerships for a New Century

El Al continued to operate profitably throughout the Gulf War by concentrating on cargo flights. Cargo operations experienced one of the company's worst disasters in October 1992 when a 747 freighter crashed into a Dutch apartment building.

In cooperation with Aeroflot, El Al conducted another airlift of Jewish refugees in January 1990. The airline transported more than 400,000 Soviet Jews from Moscow within three years. In May 1991 more than a thousand Ethiopian immigrants were airlifted on a single Boeing 747. In contrast, El Al usually seated only ten passengers in the first class section of these planes.

El Al's wings stretched next to Asia, first with charter flights. Harlev boasted of the airline's exclusive "wall to wall" service: i.e., from the Wailing Wall to the Great Wall of China. The company also increased efficiency, investing in a 24.9 percent share of North American Airlines to give it flexibility in carrying passengers within the United States. In November 1995 El Al entered its first code-sharing agreement, with American Airlines.

The Israeli government began adopting "open skies" policies in the mid-1990s, exposing the airline to severe competition at home. Approximately 40 scheduled airlines and 40 charter airlines served the market at the time. In 1996 Arkia and Royal Jordanian Airlines began connecting Tel Aviv with Amman. Nevertheless, after nearly ten consecutive years of profits, the airline emerged from receivership status in 1995. Unfortunately, the next year El Al posted the considerable loss of $83.1 million, due in part to a new wave of terrorism.

In order to keep all its planes in the sky, El Al introduced flights ''to nowhere'': passengers would enjoy various in-flight entertainments while circling the Mediterranean. It also promoted day trips for shopping in London or visiting newly accessible sites of religious importance in eastern Europe. With routes connecting East and West and decades of experience flying the longest routes, El Al hoped to develop Ben-Gurion Airport into a hub for intercontinental travel. The North American market remained responsible for nearly one-third of the carrier's revenues.

Harlev resigned in March 1996, frustrated by government privatization plans that had dragged on over a decade. Joel Feldschuh took over as president in October. El Al carried nearly three million passengers per year and more than 270,000 tons of cargo on 27 jets, including three state of the art Boeing 747-400s. The Israeli government planned to sell all shares of the company, not just 50 percent as previously planned, in a public offering in 1998.

Principal Subsidiaries

Teshet Tourism and Aviation Services Ltd.; Larrome Hotels (Int.) Company; Borenstein Caterers; Sun D'Or International Airlines Ltd.; Near East Tours (Holland); Tammam (77%); Air Consolidators (50%); Maman (26%); Israel Tours (Denmark; 76%); Fox Travel (Switzerland; 26%); T.C.D. Travel Bureau (Hungary; 50%); North American Airlines, Inc. (USA; 24.9%).

Further Reading

Goldman, Marvin G., *El Al: Star in the Sky,* Miami: World Transport Press, 1990.

Hill, Leonard, ''Never on Shabbat,'' *Air Transport World,* June 1996, pp. 29–31.

Hornblower, Margot, ''Disasters: Who Was to Blame?'' *Time International,* October 19, 1992, p. 24.

Hughes, David, ''Design, Checks Cited in Crash,'' *Aviation Week and Space Technology,* November 1, 1993, pp. 39–41.

Kestin, Hesh, ''Buy Me, I'm El Al,'' *Forbes,* November 27, 1989, pp. 42–43.

Morrocco, John D., ''El Al Plots Recovery Path to Privatization,'' *Aviation Week and Space Technology,* May 26, 1997, pp. 48–49.

Reichel, Arie, and John F. Preble, ''The El Al Strike in New York,'' *Journal of Management Case Studies,* Fall 1987, pp. 270–76.

Reingold, Lester, ''El Al: Instrument of National Purpose,'' *Air Transport World,* June 1992, pp. 200–03.

Sandler, Neal, and Andrea Rothman, ''And You Thought US Airlines Had It Tough,'' *Business Week,* October 12, 1992.

Selwitz, Robert, ''The Secret to El Al's Success,'' *Global Trade and Transportation,* March 1994, pp. 23, 26.

Shapiro, Haim, ''El Al Offers 'Spiritual' Day Trips to Eastern Europe,'' *Jerusalem Post,* January 2, 1998, p. 1.

Sherman, Arnold, *To the Skies: The El Al Story,* Bantam, 1972.

—Frederick C. Ingram

Ethicon, Inc.

P.O. Box 151
Somerville, New Jersey 08876
U.S.A.
(908) 218-0707
Fax: (908) 218-3373
Web site: http://www.ethiconinc.com

Wholly Owned Subsidiary of Johnson & Johnson Co.
Incorporated: 1921 as Johnson Suture Corp.
Employees: 4,000
Sales: $1.3 billion (1996 est.)
SICs: 3841 Surgical and Medical Instruments and
    Apparatus

Ethicon, Inc. is the subsidiary of the giant healthcare products firm Johnson & Johnson Co. that principally develops, manufactures, and markets sutures, ligatures, staplers, and other wound-closing products. Hospitals are its chief clients. The company's clinical and business services offer seminars, programs, and educational materials for the professional education of healthcare personnel and the financial concerns of management personnel.

The First Half-Century: 1921–71

The company was founded in 1921 as Johnson Suture Corp. The line of sutures called Ethicon grew out of this subsidiary. Commonly used "catgut" sutures were actually made from the muscular tissue of sheep intestines. They were first soaked in alkaline solutions that "plumped" them to several times normal thickness, then split into half-inch-thick ribbons that were next scraped to remove all tissue except the innermost layer. When the ribbons were as thin as tissue paper, several were twisted into a single strand. The strands were then strung under tension on poles 20 feet apart and dried, the natural glue of the ribbons binding them together in the strand. The next step was polishing and smoothing by hand. The strands were then tested for tensile strength and other desired properties.

With the advent of World War II, Johnson and other suture makers were asked to produce scores of millions more sutures than they had ever done before. Women made up the swelling number of production workers, because the operations of manufacture were 90 percent handwork and called for great dexterity and accuracy—qualities that women had been found to possess to a far greater degree than men.

Johnson Suture was renamed Ethicon in 1949. In collaboration with High Voltage Engineering Corp. of Cambridge, Massachusetts, Ethicon conducted research on sterilizing its sutures, and it purchased a linear electron accelerator for its own research in 1953. In 1956 Ethicon began what it believed to be the first major commercial application of radiation, bombarding packaged sutures with electronics from an accelerator. The electrons killed any bacteria or other microorganisms lingering in the sutures. Since no heating was involved in the process, the sutures remained more pliable and 10 to 15 percent stronger than those sterilized by heat.

By the end of 1958 almost all Ethicon's output of sutures was passing under this atom smasher—not only the ones made from animal intestine but also those made of silk. Bursts of electrons were fired into a powerful radar-wave beam and then hurled into the target area at nearly the speed of light, with these bursts fired at the rate of 800 per second. Each suture was in a tray traveling under the electron gun and was sprayed for around two seconds.

Ethicon was accounting for perhaps 75 percent of the total U.S. suture production in 1964. It also was sterilizing by radiation some other Johnson & Johnson products and from time to time doing such jobs for other clients, such as 125 mink pelts infected with anthrax, an especially tough and virulent germ. By this time Ethicon was thinking of converting to new machines employing gamma rays from cobalt-60. Unlike the accelerators, cobalt machines were said to have greater capacity with less likelihood of breakdown. Moreover, they could irradiate large boxes, even shipping cartons, while accelerators required the products to be run through in relatively thin layers because of the limited penetrating power of electrons.

Progress in the 1970s and 1980s

Ethicon was the world's leading producer of ligatures and sutures in 1971 and was also making other wound-closing surgical instruments. In that year an estimated seven percent of Johnson & Johnson's income was coming from sutures and an estimated 11 percent from surgical products. Ethicon had three U.S. manufacturing plants in 1972, covering 800,000 square feet of space. In 1978 Ethicon's revenues were estimated at $120 million. Its gross profits—the profits on its goods sold without deducting selling and general administrative expenses and taxes—were estimated at $85 million, indicating that its gross profit margin was an astonishing 70 percent—higher than any other Johnson & Johnson division or subsidiary in what was a high-profit-margin industry.

By 1980 Ethicon's sutures were being used in more than 7,500 U.S. hospitals. Its product list included more than 2,500 suture-needle combinations. They ranged from suture needles for microsurgery or ophthalmic surgery that could barely be seen by the naked eye to extremely large steel-wire suture needles for orthopedic surgery. The 11 basic suture materials included gut, silk, cotton, steel, and various plastics in 11 diameters, with lengths ranging from three to 60 inches. That year Ethicon introduced a newly redesigned suture packaging system for efficient use in the operating room. When the outer pouch was peeled back, an inner, color-coded pouch made of foil laminate was exposed. This pouch was then torn open, exposing a paper folder that held the suture. The suture's needle was then placed in a needle holder and presented to the surgeon.

Ethicon's products in 1986 for precise wound closures included mechanical instruments as well as sutures and ligatures. The company had plants in Albuquerque; Cincinnati; Chicago; Cornelia, Georgia; and San Angelo, Texas, with more than 1.3 million square feet of manufacturing space. Somerville, New Jersey, remained the site of its corporate headquarters. Foreign subsidiaries were located in Edinburgh; Rome; Norderstedt, Germany; and Peterborough, Ontario.

In 1989 Ethicon held about 60 percent of the worldwide wound-closure market, whose revenues were rated at $1.28 billion a year. Ethicon's suture products included natural and synthetic and absorbable and nonabsorbable sutures for use by the various surgical specialties. Its mechanical disposable wound-closure products included surgical stapling instruments for skin and internal closures, and absorbable and nonabsorbable clip products for ligation. Its principal trademarks were Ethicon, Vicryl, PDS, Prolene, Ligaclip, and Proximate. The company's products were being sold principally through distributors to hospitals.

Ethicon in the 1990s

By 1991 Ethicon had entered the rapidly growing field of laparascopic surgery. This procedure was revolutionizing traditional surgery by its ability to conduct procedures like gallbladder removal with tiny disposable devices. United States Surgical Corp. originally dominated the market, but Ethicon introduced its own disposable cutting and grasping tools early in 1991. It followed with a blunt-tipped trocar (a surgical instru-

ment intended to avoid accidental cuts) and a device to fire single staples. By the end of the year Ethicon had introduced no less than 45 products for endoscopic procedures involving gall bladders, hernia repairs, bowel resections, and thoracic and gynecological surgery. Ethicon's sales came to about $1.2 billion in 1991.

Ethicon established a plant in Blue Ash, Ohio, for manufacturing its endoscopic-surgery products and invested more than $40 million during 1990–91 in endoscopic-product development and marketing, tripling its engineering staff to 500 people. The Blue Ash plant was employing about 1,400 people in early 1992, including 560 hourly production workers.

For its manufacture of surgical fasteners at Blue Ash, Ethicon was replacing old computers with a computer-integrated manufacturing system. It also was installing a business-information computer system to help manage processes such as inventory control, accounts payable and procurement, document management, and computer networking, and was upgrading its computer-aided engineering and design system. In all, Ethicon had eight plants in 1991, with the largest in San Angelo, where 1,750 workers were employed. The company was engaged in efforts to make all its workers computer literate and had also instituted a diversity-training program intended to create an environment where ethnic minorities and women could succeed.

This program was in effect not only in the United States but also at Ethicon's facilities in and near Edinburgh, Scotland. In 1996 this subsidiary had increased its direct labor force by some 25 percent since 1992 in response to increasing demand for its products and the transfer of some activities from Johnson & Johnson plants elsewhere in Europe. A great deal of recruiting and training also had become necessary in order to enable a reduced support staff to take on extra responsibilities. The training process there encouraged workers to teach their skills to others, focusing on achieving targets and goals and reinforcing the relationship between behavior and reward.

By this time, however, the Blue Ash plant was no longer part of Ethicon, Inc. Johnson & Johnson announced in February 1992 that the development and marketing of endoscopic products would be spun off into a new subsidiary, Ethicon Endo-Surgery, Inc. Ethicon, Inc. continued in the business of sutures and other wound-closing surgical supplies and held an 80 percent market share in sutures for traditional surgeries.

Ethicon continued to lead the wound-closure sutures market in 1995, accounting for an estimated 75 percent of the U.S. market. Johnson & Johnson's worldwide sutures sales were estimated at nearly $1.3 billion in 1996. A strong marketing effort, including group purchasing contracts, was said to have created a virtual barrier to entry into the sutures market by other firms. Other reasons for Ethicon's continued success included, of course, the high quality of its products and the breadth of its product line. The company provided a 100 percent guarantee on the quality and integrity of every product it sold and claimed a 99.5 percent error-free delivery rate.

The sutures market was accounting for only a little more than half of the total market for wound-closure products in 1997. A chief explanation for the slow growth in sutures could be attributed partly to minimally invasive surgical procedures such as endoscopic surgery and partly to skin-stapling products. U.S. suture shipments peaked in 1992 at 25.5 million units. Several studies in the late 1990s showed that certain wounds closed with glue—sterilized and modified for medical purposes—healed just as well as those closed with stitches, and that the cosmetic results up to a year later were comparable. In one of these studies, doctors predicted that medical glue could replace stitches for about one-third of the 11 million wounds treated in hospital emergency rooms in the United States each year.

Johnson & Johnson announced in August 1997 that it was purchasing Gynecare Inc., a developer of devices to treat uterine bleeding, for about $79 million. Gynecare was scheduled to become part of Ethicon.

Further Reading

Boehm, George A. W., "What Radiation Can Do for the Production Line," *Fortune,* December 1964, pp. 140–141, 152.

Cebulski, Cathy, "Ethicon Preparing Aggressive Training Program," *Greater Cincinnati Business Record,* July 29, 1991, p. 11.

"Electron Bullets Now Utilized Commercially to Sterilize Sutures," *Wall Street Journal,* January 17, 1958, p. 7.

Foster, Lawrence G., *A Company That Cares,* New Brunswick, N.J.: Johnson & Johnson, 1986, pp. 100–01, 166, 171–72.

Freudenheim, Milt, "The Tiniest, Kindest Cut of All," *New York Times,* July 10, 1991, pp. D1, D7.

Friend, Janin, "Diversity at Work," *Dallas Times Herald,* August 4, 1991, pp. 1+.

Gilbert, Susan, "Using Glue Instead of Stitches," *New York Times,* May 21, 1997, p. C11.

Hewlett, John, "Weaving the Loom of Life," *Travel,* June 1945, pp. 22–26, 32.

"Johnson & Johnson's Fat City," *Forbes,* June 26, 1978, p. 98.

LaBell, Frances, "Suture Packaging System Redesign Improves Function," *Food & Drug Packaging,* August 21, 1980, pp. 3–4.

Mezzacappa, Katherine, "Trading HR Skills for Mutual Benefit," *People Management,* August 29, 1996, pp. 28–30.

Werner, Curt, "Sutures Market Still Dominated by Johnson & Johnson," *Health Industry Today,* February 1997, pp. 1, 10–11.

—Robert Halasz

fieldale farms corporation

Fieldale Farms Corporation

P.O. Box 558
Baldwin, Georgia 30511
U.S.A.
(706) 778-5100
Fax: (706) 778-3767

Private Company
Incorporated: 1972
Employees: 4,010
Sales: $360 million (1996 est.)
SICs: 2015 Poultry Slaughtering & Processing

In 1995, the *Atlanta Journal and Constitution* reported that Fieldale Farms Corporation was the sixth largest privately owned company in the state of Georgia. The company, which is a "fully integrated" facility for processing of broilers—that is, whole chickens smaller than 2.5 pounds dressed weight—oversees its product at every stage. Chickens are bred at 700 different Fieldale breeder farms, hatched at one of four Fieldale hatcheries, fed with the product of Fieldale field mills, and—once slaughtered—are processed and packed at one of Fieldale's three processing plants in north Georgia. The information appeared in a special report on Georgia companies, and it seems to be one of the few times in the 1990s that the *Journal and Constitution* offered a positive report on northeast Georgia's largest privately owned company. Much of the other coverage on Fieldale related to environmental complaints and a state ethics imbroglio; but unquestionably Fieldale was a business with a significant dollar volume, which provided a number of jobs to people in its areas of operations.

Hatfield and the Arrendale Brothers

Long before I-985 was built in the 1980s, making the northeastern corner of Georgia a popular recreation spot and a way-point for vacationers headed to the Smoky Mountains of Tennessee and North Carolina, the Arrendale brothers began the business that would become Fieldale. Tom and Lee Arrendale were born in Rabun County, in the tip of the state near the joint border with North and South Carolina, in the 1920s. Tom

attended Lakemont Consolidated High School, later studying at Georgia Tech, and during World War II, he served in the Army Air Corps. After he returned to north Georgia, he began a career in the poultry business as Lee's partner. In January 1946, the Arrendale brothers went into business together growing live broilers, and eventually they would become involved in chicken processing as well.

The Arrendales had their operation in Clarkesville, county seat of Habersham County; further south lay Gainesville, a much larger town which served as the county seat of Hall. In the early 1950s, Joe Hatfield moved to Gainesville, and also became involved in the poultry industry, working first in the processing and then the marketing areas. He and several partners established a processing company that they called Gainesville Fryers.

Throughout the 1950s, Hatfield with Gainesville Fryers, and the Arrendale brothers with their farms and processing facilities, continued to prosper. But by the end of the decade, the poultry industry entered a slump, and both the Arrendales and Gainesville Fryers were hit by potentially hard times. By the beginning of the 1960s, all three men faced difficult choices.

Ralston Purina and the Founding of Fieldale

In 1961, Tom and Lee Arrendale made what must have been a difficult decision, opting to sell their business to Ralston Purina. The latter, a large and well-known company with interests in many geographic and commercial areas, had begun to move into the northeast Georgia poultry processing business, and in September 1961, the Arrendales sold all their interests to Ralston Purina. At around the same time, Hatfield and his associates reached a similar decision, and they too sold their company to Ralston Purina. Not only that, but all three men went to work for their former companies' new owner.

Thus Tom Arrendale became the general manager for Ralston Purina's Clarkesville operations, while Lee took the general manager's position for their Gainesville facilities. Hatfield, on the other hand, was assigned the job of general manager of southeastern poultry operations. During the 1960s, Ralston Purina's poultry enterprises in the area expanded, and partly on the strength of its lucrative north Georgia business, by the latter part of the decade it became the world's largest producer of broilers.

Yet the company's leadership decided in 1971 to sell off all its poultry operations in the United States. Learning of this, Hatfield and the Arrendale brothers, along with other associates, decided to take advantage of the opportunity to gain a sizable share in the broiler operation, and purchased the entire northeast Georgia operations of Ralston Purina. The three entrepreneurs had been forced to sell their companies and go to work for a large corporation; now, almost exactly a decade later, they were about to take control once again, this time of a larger company. Combining parts of both last names, they dubbed their corporation "Fieldale," and began operations under that name in February 1972.

Growth and Jobs

The three businessmen, already leaders in their communities, became some of the wealthiest men in the northeast region of Georgia. They were recognized for their contributions: Tom Arrendale, for instance, won numerous awards from local organizations, and became a member of the board of directors of a prominent local bank. Fieldale had emerged as the largest of the homegrown local businesses, and its economic impact was enormous.

Poultry, always more viable than traditional farming in a mountainous area that did not have particularly rich soil for growing crops, provided numerous jobs in the surrounding counties. First there were the farmers, who grew chickens in large chicken houses; then there were also the employees in the processing plants. Thus poultry could be said to span a variety of businesses from agricultural to industrial, and from the viewpoint of owners, it was an extremely lucrative enterprise. From the perspective of potential employees, some in white-collar positions and many more in blue-collar processing jobs, it meant employment; and there were far more people outside the company, including the affiliated chicken farms, who benefited from their relationship with Fieldale.

Circumstances in the 1980s seemed to coalesce to Fieldale's benefit. A trend toward health-consciousness had made chicken an increasingly more popular source of protein, as opposed to beef and pork. Waves of immigration, a result of the spread of Communism in Southeast Asia, and later an economic crisis in the Texas oil industry, respectively brought large numbers of Laotians and Mexicans to the region. In many cases, these people were willing to work at jobs unpopular among the area's mostly white population of American citizens, either because these jobs paid poorly, or because they involved unpleasant activities, or both. Hence in 1996, the *Atlanta Journal and Constitution* reported that chicken-processing jobs, which seldom paid more than $6.50 an hour, were mostly filled by Mexican and South American immigrants. "I don't think anyone says, 'After graduation, I want to get a job in the blood room at Fieldale,' " a Hall County Chamber of Commerce spokeswoman told the *Atlanta Constitution*.

But to high school students and unskilled workers, jobs in the processing plants such as the one in Cornelia, near company headquarters in Baldwin, represented an opportunity that might not have existed elsewhere. Clearly Fieldale was having a strong economic impact on the community; in the 1990s, how-

ever, the region's growing prosperity ironically helped to raise concerns about the environmental impact Fieldale was having on northeast Georgia.

Troubles in 1990

The company suffered two blows in 1990, the first of which came early in the year, when Lee Arrendale was killed in a plane crash. Later a nearby school, as well as a road, were named in his honor; and in 1994 the local rotary club would award Tom Arrendale its "W. Lee Arrendale Award for Vocational Excellence."

The other blow of 1990 came later in the year. On December 1, 1990, the *Journal and Constitution* ran an exposé on alleged dumping of wastewater by a Fieldale facility in the tiny community of Murrayville, in Hall County. In October, the State of Georgia had fined the company $100,000 for illegal discharge of "thousands of gallons of sewage" into streams that ultimately fed into Lake Lanier, one of the north Georgia region's largest lakes, and a popular recreation spot.

Chicken processing is messy work, and the paper reported that for every chicken processed by the plant, "three gallons of clay-colored water—dyed by blood, guts and millions of feathers" was produced as well. This wastewater was supposedly treated, then sprayed onto pasture land for fertilizer. But according to several former employees, the water was actually being dumped, sometimes under cover of night, into Lake Lanier.

Fieldale executives responded that it was true that their plant, which was processing a million chickens a week, had reached its legal waste disposal limit. Because of high production rates, they said, they were nearly at capacity in their 115-acre disposal field; but, they claimed, they had not exceeded capacity. After being fined in October 1990, the company had cut production levels. "We have these [production] lines up there because they make us money," the plant's wastewater manager told the paper. "When they're sitting idle, they lose us money. I'd say that's a gesture of good faith right there."

The charges of illegal waste disposal activities, according to Fieldale executives, came from disgruntled ex-workers with ulterior motives. And in fact one of the two former employees making the charges had been fired for fighting. But scientists and state officials had confirmed signs of heavy environmental impact. Biologists who studied the lake—which among other things is a source of drinking water for metropolitan Atlanta— reported that the area near the plant was "aging" faster than any other section along the shores of Lake Lanier.

After complaints by neighbors, an official with the Georgia Department of Natural Resources (DNR) had conducted an inspection, and found the company guilty of violations, which had resulted in the $100,000 fine. Fieldale, which had invested $2 million in a new treatment system in 1989, had applied for permits from the county and state to expand its disposal fields. Neighbors, officials, scientists, and certainly the company's leadership hoped the problem would be alleviated.

Continuing Controversy in the Mid-1990s

In 1993, Fieldale ran into another problem, but this time the accusation was dirty politics rather than dirty water. Tom Arrendale, whose company had contributed $10,000 to the election campaign of Governor Zell Miller in 1990, had paid to fly two state legislators, along with Georgia Agricultural Commissioner Tommy Irvin, to Daytona, Florida, for the Daytona 500 auto race. When the media learned of this, they raised an uproar at the apparent attempt to buy influence; but according to a loophole in the state law, the three officials were not legally required to report that they had been the beneficiaries of Arrendale's hospitality.

The "loophole" had been left in the law because, as the newspaper stated, members of the Georgia General Assembly had held that "People such as bank presidents and hardware-store owners. . . ought to be able to take their local legislators to lunch without having to register as lobbyists and file disclosure forms." But according to the Atlanta paper's editorial, Arrendale had taken advantage of the law to woo the legislators, one of whom was the head of the state's Environmental Protection Division. And since he was technically not a lobbyist, neither Arrendale nor the public officials were required to report the Daytona junket.

The editorial at least judged as true the claim by Arrendale and the officials that they discussed no politics on the trip: "Talking politics on such trips is considered impolite, because it shatters the fragile illusion that it's an outing among friends. It is only later that friends begin to help each other, as friends are wont to do." In December 1993, another editorial called on the state's general assembly to "Close the Fieldale Farms Loophole," and said that doing so had become legislators' "top ethics-reform priority" in 1994.

Nor was this the end of Fieldale's troubles in the 1990s. Years before, Arrendale and Hatfield might never have imagined that their company would get attention from the *New York Times,* but when it happened, it was not pleasant. Under the heading "Chicken Farm's Food Is Banned," the paper reported that certain school districts had banned use of food provided by Fieldale Farms after one of its shipments was found to contain bone and cartilage.

In 1996, the company made headlines in another prominent national paper, the *Wall Street Journal,* but again the reasons were not good. This time the cause was a lawsuit filed by the company against Franklin County, Georgia, because the latter had established an environmental ordinance—more stringent than existing state law—to keep a Fieldale plant out. Throughout Georgia and beyond, businesspeople, government officials, and citizens' groups took notice of the lawsuit, which would determine much about the relative powers of businesses, local governments, and state governments. Economic growth in the region, it turned out, had created a prosperous local economy in which people could afford to have concerns for the environment, and not merely their pocketbooks: "Franklin County officials say that 10 years ago they never would have considered passing an environmental ordinance." But now, thanks to growing prosperity in north Georgia—prosperity for which, ironically, Fieldale could claim some share of the credit—Franklin County was keeping Fieldale out in favor of the cleaner, better-paying jobs being offered by auto-plant supply manufacturers, including makers of windshield wipers and exhaust systems.

Coming of Age with Its Community

Around the same time as the *Wall Street Journal* article, in April 1996, the *Journal and Constitution*'s "Southern Economic Survey" reported what appeared to be a telling fact. The town of Gainesville, in preparation for hosting visitors to Olympic rowing events on Lake Lanier that summer, was painting over the water tower in the center of town, thus obscuring the slogan it had carried for a quarter of a century: "Poultry Capital of the World." Gainesville still had a strong interest in poultry, its mayor told the paper, "but we're so much more than that."

Clearly the news from Gainesville and Franklin County indicated that north Georgia was coming of age, and was more resistant to the influence of Fieldale and other firms involved in the region's large chicken processing industry. Just as Fieldale had benefited from social changes in the 1980s, now it seemed to be suffering from changes in the 1990s, particularly a growing concern for the environment, worries over the health hazards posed by chicken, and the growth of north Georgia from an out-of-the-way mountain region to an adjunct of metro Atlanta.

But reports of the eclipse of the poultry industry were highly exaggerated. In its economic survey, the *Journal and Constitution* went on to report that in Hall County, the poultry industry alone—of which Fieldale was a part, along with ConAgra and other companies—put $145 million into the county's economy. And "This one-county poultry farm income," according to Abit Massey, executive director of the Georgia Poultry Federation, "is larger than the combined statewide income for peaches, pecans, apples, blueberries, grapes, and onions." This claim is impressive, particularly considering that the first of the fruits named is the one most commonly associated with Georgia.

Further proof of Fieldale's stability was offered by its continued growth. In 1994, the trade journal *Feedstuffs* reported that Fieldale and another company were spurring a "building boom" in the Southeast, and that Fieldale planned to build 110 broiler houses in Georgia and South Carolina within a short period of time. In 1995, in its survey of Georgia's leading private companies, the *Journal and Constitution* reported that sixth-place Fieldale Farms had contracts with 700 chicken growers in two states, and that it operated three processing plants, four hatcheries, and a feed mill.

Further Reading

Brown, Robert H., "Broiler House Construction Up in Southeast," *Feedstuffs,* March 28, 1994, p. 19.

"Close the Fieldale Farms Loophole," *Atlanta Journal and Constitution,* February 22, 1993, p. A18.

Higginbotham, Mickey, "Southern Economic Survey: Poultry and Pluto: 1996; Gainesville No Longer Puts All Its Eggs in One Basket," *Atlanta Journal and Constitution,* April 14, 1996, p. H12.

Jaffe, Greg, "Southeast Journal: Suit Targets Local Laws on Pollution," *Wall Street Journal,* June 12, 1996, p. S1.

"Running A-Fowl of the Ethics Law," *Atlanta Journal and Constitution,* February 18, 1993, p. A14.

Stock, Robert W., "Chicken Farm's Food Is Banned," *New York Times,* May 11, 1995, p. B1.

Teegardin, Carrie, "Workers: Poultry Plant Often Dumped Sewage," *Atlanta Journal and Constitution,* December 1, 1990, p. A1.

—Judson Knight

Fisons plc

Fison House, Princes Street
Ipswich, Suffolk
United Kingdom

Subsumed by Rhone-Poulenc Rorer, Inc.
Incorporated: 1843 as James Fison and Sons
SICs: 2834 Pharmaceutical Preparations; 3820 Measuring
   and Controlling Devices; 2870 Agricultural Chemicals

In 1995 Fisons plc was acquired by Pennsylvania-based Rhone-Poulenc Rorer, Inc., in turn wholly owned by France's chemical giant Rhone-Poulenc S.A. Though its status among the world's pharmaceutical companies was subsequently subsumed in layers of corporate ownership, Fisons had boasted a history of more than 300 years in business before its dismantling. Founded as a flour mill in the late 18th century, it quickly developed into one of the world's largest fertilizer producers. As the fertilizer market matured into a low-profit commodity over the course of the 20th century, the company diversified into horticultural products, pharmaceuticals, and scientific instruments. In the mid-1980s, Fisons divested its fertilizer interests to focus on the highly profitable medical side of the business. By 1993 the company was the world's third-largest manufacturer of scientific instruments and ranked among the world's 60 largest pharmaceutical concerns. Fisons' weak research and development efforts and inadequate marketing efforts, however, led to annual losses and a steep decline in its stock price mid-decade. The British company tried to fight off the advances of its Franco-American competitor, but relinquished ownership in the fall of 1995.

Late 18th-Century Origins

Fisons plc began as a flour mill and bakery founded by James Fisons in Barningham, England, in the late 18th century. In 1789 a son, also named James, started a maltings business that expanded into Stowmarket and Thetford, two river towns that helped the family businesses expand.

James Fison and Sons was formed in 1808, and by 1840 the firm was recording £100,000 in annual sales. Later that decade, the family entered the developing field of fertilizers and moved the business's headquarters to Ipswich. Within a few years, Fisons had built a manure works and was producing its own sulfuric acid. As fertilizers became the company's primary business, pesticides based on sulphur were added to the product mix.

In 1895 the company was split into two parts: James Fison and Sons and Joseph Fison and Co. During World War I, Fisons helped make explosives, but the company returned to fertilizer by the end of the war to buoy dwindling food production. When fertilizer prices plunged after the war, the two Fison companies, along with two others with which they had recently merged, were reunited to form Fison, Packard, Prentice and Co. (Fisons) in 1929.

Diversification through Acquisition: Mid-20th Century

During the 1930s, Fisons began to expand through acquisitions. The company's most significant addition was the Anglo-Continental Guano Works Ltd., which doubled the size of Fisons. Anglo-Continental was a budding conglomerate with a pharmaceutical subsidiary, Genatosan; Fisons was thus brought into that lucrative market. Fisons' acquisitions continued throughout the 1930s, and by 1939, with 39 subsidiaries, it was the largest fertilizer company in Great Britain.

During World War II Fisons felt the pressure of both a manpower shortage and increased demand for fertilizers. Some of the company's manufacturing plants were bombed as well. The company name was shortened to Fisons Ltd. for marketing clarity in 1942, and it emerged from the war with nearly two-thirds of Great Britain's fertilizer market.

Fisons made more acquisitions after the war's end, first purchasing Wiffen and Son, a fine chemicals manufacturer. The new subsidiary became part of Fisons's chemicals and biologicals division, headed by Genatosan. The Wiffen acquisition included the Loughborough Glass Company, which would later develop into Fisons's Scientific Equipment division. The purchase of Pest Control Limited during the 1950s brought Fisons into agrochemicals, a market that was closely related to the fertilizer business. Fisons hoped to capitalize on the two fields' common research, development, and distribution methods.

In 1968 researchers at Genatosan discovered disodium cromoglycate (DSCG), which was developed as the branded anti-allergenic Intal. The drug differed from its competitors because it was a prophylactic, whereas others were taken after the onset of allergic symptoms. Intal sales boosted the pharmaceutical division's profits from £1.14 million in 1968 to £2.43 million in 1970 and £5.6 million in 1973.

Unsuccessful Reorganizations in 1970s

By 1971 Fisons had organized its many subsidiaries into four divisions: Fertilizers, Agrochemicals, Pharmaceuticals, and Scientific Equipment. The company developed these primary businesses through acquisitions as well as product and market expansion. Acquisitions were focused geographically in Europe, Australia, and the United States.

Fertilizers contributed 50 percent of the conglomerate's annual sales at that time, and Fisons fought to maintain a competitive edge in Great Britain's fertilizer market: 80 percent of the division's sales were in its home country. However, the supply side of this division was hamstrung, since its primary ammonia supplier was also its primary competitor, Imperial Chemical Industries plc. During the first half of the 1970s, Fisons tried to remedy this situation by increasing its bulk buying in global markets, especially patronizing Morocco. Morocco increased its prices six-fold in 1973, though, and other suppliers quickly followed suit. At the same time, U.K. price controls held fertilizer prices below the world market price for ammonia, effectively eliminating Fisons's fertilizer profits.

Fisons's Agrochemicals group also ran into trouble during the 1970s, when it lost a valuable customer, Ciba-Geigy Ltd. Fisons tried to support this group by increasing capital investments, especially in the United States. The company also boosted research and development funds, but since most of this division's efforts focused on creating substitutes for products that were already on the market, Fisons lacked a strong selling suit.

During the 1970s, anti-allergens comprised between 60 and 70 percent of the Pharmaceutical division's sales, but Intal had only captured 6.1 percent of the anti-allergy market, which was led by Glaxo's Ventolin. After a decade of research, the division was dealt a serious blow when Fisons decided not to market its new drug, Proxicromil, a successor to Intal, because it was found to cause cancer in animals. With Intal's nonrenewable patents set to run out in 1982, the Pharmaceutical division's prospects were not good.

In 1972 the Scientific Equipment Division was spun off from the Pharmaceutical division, and acquisitions in Germany and Australia, as well as the purchase of Britain's Gallenkamp, helped Fisons become Great Britain's top scientific equipment manufacturer. Many of Gallenkamp's contracts were with the government, universities, and hospitals, however, many of which cut their expenditures in the recessionary 1970s.

Fisons's Horticulture division was separated from the Agrochemical division in 1977. It produced and marketed amateur and professional gardening products, and its strengths were in peat-based products, especially the popular and well-established Fisons Gro-Bags—self-contained, nutritionally balanced soil sacks. The peat operations were extended with a new plant in Yorkshire and the acquisition of Howlett's, a company with peat reserves in Cumbria and Scotland. Although it was a new focus for Fisons, horticulture was actually one of the company's most secure businesses by the end of the 1970s. It was vertically integrated and held commanding shares of the markets in which it operated: 50 percent of the lawn fertilizer market; 20 percent of the solid fertilizer market; 30 percent of the peat market; and 12 percent of Great Britain's weed and pest control business.

Throughout the 1970s, Fisons had gone into debt to make a nebulous reorganization and prop up its historical focus—fertilizers—just as competition and global consolidation in this market eroded profits. At the same time, high interest rates and inflation dug into the profits Fisons managed to earn through its other operations. By 1980 Fisons's prospects looked dim. The Fertilizers division was operating at a loss; Agrochemicals could not hope to compete with the research and development outlays of bigger competitors; the Scientific Equipment division was suffering from government cutbacks; horticulture was a small, underdeveloped business; and the Pharmaceuticals division, a primary profit-maker, had suddenly lost its only long-term growth product. Fisons was on the verge of bankruptcy.

Shift to Focus on Pharmaceuticals in 1980s

John Kerridge was promoted to chief executive officer (CEO) from executive director in mid-1980 and given the task of reversing Fisons' downward spiral. He began the reformation by cutting costs, closing down four production units and three farms in the Fertilizer division, then eliminating more than 1,000 positions in the group. Fisons's corporate headquarters were moved from high-rent London back to Ipswich, and economizations were made in the Scientific Equipment division as well. Kerridge's most fundamental change was the sale of the Fertilizer division to Norsk Hydro a.s. in 1982 for £59 million. The divestment was a radical change for Fisons and involved the disposal of what had been the foundation of the company for more than a century, as well as the division with the most sales. The troublesome Agrochemicals division was sold the following year to Schering A.G. for £60 million.

These divestments left Fisons with three primary businesses: Pharmaceuticals, Horticulture, and Scientific Equipment. The pharmaceutical group was expanded with the 1980 purchase of Great Britain's Charnwood Pharmaceuticals, Australia's Orbit Chemical Pty. Ltd. in 1982, and Italy's Intersint in 1983. Great Britain's Weddel Pharmaceutical was acquired in 1983 and merged with Charnwood, which would specialize in generic drugs.

Fisons's Horticultural operations grew geographically through a joint venture with Canada's Western Peat Moss in 1980, and the acquisition of Langley Peat North Ltd. of Alberta in 1983. These purchases gave Fisons access to large peat supplies and the North American market. The British operations were supplanted with the acquisition of Webb and Bees seed operations from Shell Holdings (U.K.) Ltd. in the early 1980s.

The Scientific Equipment division grew through the addition of Watson Victor, a New Zealand distributor of laboratory equipment, in 1982. Haake-Butler Instruments, of which Fisons owned 67 percent, was subsequently founded in the United States. Overall, Kerridge's fundamental changes improved Fisons's balance sheet dramatically; the corporation went from making annual interest payments of £13 million in 1980 to having no net borrowings in 1983. Fisons was even secure enough to make a successful stock offer of £28 million that year.

The Pharmaceutical division's continued heavy research and development expenditures resulted in two new drugs: DSCG-based Opticrom, released in 1984, and Tilade, a new asthma treatment, introduced in 1986. This division acquired Laboratorios Caesen, of Spain, in 1984, and Bracco de Mexico in 1986.

Kerridge was made chairman in 1984, and he clarified the strategy he had been using to turn Fisons around: "We wish to operate in industries of inherent attractiveness, which have potential for growth and a record of profitability of successful participants, [and] we wish to be in clearly defined business segments where Fisons can reasonably aspire to being an effective competitor by virtue of its size and its financial and managerial resources." The company would no longer operate on the fringes of its chosen markets, as it had in the 1970s. For example, Fisons concentrated on the horticulture and scientific equipment markets, which were not yet consolidated or dominated by a single powerful company. Fisons hoped to be that company.

Fisons burst onto the U.S. market for scientific equipment, which was home to 40 percent of the world's research activity, with the acquisition of Curtin Matheson Scientific Inc. (CMS) in 1984. CMS was the second-largest distributor of scientific equipment in the United States. Fisons also purchased United Diagnostics Inc. and Pacific Hemostasis Laboratories Inc., which were combined with CMS to give the latter manufacturing capacity. By the beginning of 1985, Fisons' Scientific division was the third-largest organization of its type in the world and the largest outside the United States.

Fisons continued to grow, acquiring in 1985 Murphy Chemical, which helped widen the Horticulture division's portfolio of products, extend marketing in Europe and North America, and shore up Fisons's peat supplies. Later in the decade, the Horticulture division would sell its 50 percent share of Asef-Fison B.V. to its joint-venture partner, DSM Agro Specialties B.V. In 1986 Fisons bought Applied Research Laboratories, a leading manufacturer of scientific equipment with global marketing capacity, and two years later it purchased Union Scientific Limited, a Hong Kong company.

Several important acquisitions were also made by the Pharmaceutical division in the late 1980s. Italchimici SpA, an Italian firm, and Pennwalt Corporation's pharmaceutical division, a U.S. manufacturer of ethical and over-the-counter drugs, were purchased in 1988. A French company, Gerbitol S.A., brought expertise in cardiovascular medicine, antibiotics, and dietary supplements to the division in 1989. In all, with the help of its significant 1980s acquisitions, Fisons's pre-tax profits increased

by an average of 56 percent per year to £230 million (US$410 million). The corporation's market capitalization rose from £40 million in 1980 to £3 billion in 1990.

Declining Profits Lead To Divestments in 1990s

The 1990 purchase of VG Instruments, a manufacturer of mass spectrometers and surface analysis instruments, more than doubled Fisons' output of analytical instruments and catapulted the Scientific Equipment division to the number three spot in the global marketplace. It looked as if Fisons had launched its second consecutive decade of growth and prosperity. By the end of 1991, however, it was clear that problems in the Pharmaceutical division had dragged the entire company down. Late that year, Fisons revealed that two of its important new drugs, Opticrom for hay fever and Imferon for anemia, had been recalled from the U.S. market after the Food and Drug Administration (FDA) denied approval of the company's British factories. According to a 1992 *Economist* article, the FDA's routine check of Fisons' U.K. factory revealed warehouses with holes in their outside walls; poor record keeping; and "the possibility of rodent, insect or avian activity in the [transport] containers." Fisons's pre-tax profits for 1991 dropped 17 percent to £190 million, and the company faced required investments of more than £25 million to bring its British factory up to U.S. standards.

John Kerridge resigned "on health grounds" in mid-January 1992 and was temporarily replaced by Patrick Egan. In April of that year, Egan became chairman, while Cedric Scroggs was selected as chief executive officer. The new leaders decided to sharpen Fisons' focus on pharmaceuticals and scientific equipment by divesting its OTC drug and horticultural businesses.

In November 1992, Fisons agreed to sell its North American OTC drug operations to Swiss drug concern Ciba-Geigy Ltd. for £92 million (US$60.3 million). This segment represented approximately 50 percent of Fisons's global consumer health division sales and 40 percent of that group's profits. Egan and Scroggs recognized that the British company lacked the resources and marketing influence necessary to compete in the American consumer drug market.

Fisons's new management forged a joint development and marketing agreement with Allergan Inc., a U.S. opthalmic company, early in 1993. The arrangement called for Fisons' 400 U.S. salespeople to co-market Allergan's opthalmic drug Acular. The U.S. company's sales force, in turn, would help market Fisons' opthalmic treatment Opticrom. The arrangement presumed that Opticrom would be re-registered by the FDA. By early 1993, Fisons had made significant improvements in its Opticrom factory, but new FDA inspections had still not resulted in approval late in the year.

Fisons suffered yet another setback when it suspended development of an asthma medicine, tipredane. The company had been banking on the new drug to bolster its core respiratory business in the late 1990s. Tipredane had been licensed by Fisons from Bristol-Myers Squibb Co. and was in the midst of unsuccessful clinical trials in more than a dozen countries. The failure of tipredane left Fisons with only one new drug, remacemide—an epilepsy treatment—in development.

In May 1993 Fisons sold its North American horticulture business to a consortium led by Macluan Capital Corp. of Vancouver for US$60 million in cash and used the proceeds to reduce its debt. Fisons also planned to sell the remainder of its Horticulture division as soon as an opportunity arose. In July the company sold its consumer health products business in Australia and New Zealand to Warner-Lambert for about US$23 million. The sale included the Rosken line of therapeutic skin-care products.

Acquisition By Rhone-Poulenc Rorer in 1995

Despite Fisons's early 1990s efforts to bolster its pharmaceutical business, some analysts insisted that the company had neither the research and development strength nor the marketing clout necessary to compete in an ethical pharmaceutical business that demanded frequent discovery of innovative medicines. Industry observers anticipated an imminent merger or takeover for Fisons.

Those expectations intensified as Fisons' share price declined from £2.45 in mid-1992 to £1.13 by the end of 1993. Over the course of the latter year, the company's scientific instruments division went £16 million into the red. CEO Cedric Scroggs was fired that December, Finance Director Roy Thomas took early (and presumably involuntary) retirement, and Stuart Wallis took the helm of the battered firm.

Throughout the 18 months, Wallis made a valiant and reasonably successful effort to bolster Fisons' stock price. Though the company suffered a loss on 1994, a major reorganization and divestment program eliminated at least 1,000 jobs, cut costs, and helped the firm's stock price rebound nearly 75 percent to £1.93 by mid-August 1995.

That gain was not enough to prevent Franco-American rival Rhone-Poulenc Rorer, Inc. (R-PR) from making a hostile £1.7 billion (US$2.6 billion) bid for control of Fisons on August 18th. Though some analysts thought the offering price, at 16.7 times expected net revenues, was too high, CEO Wallis complained to *Chemical Marketing Reporter* that the price "significantly undervalues Fisons." The British company backed up that assertion when it reported a 40 percent increase in net income, to £48.6 million, for the first half of 1995. That happy news helped advance the firm's stock to £2.60 by the end of September.

In October, R-PR upped its bid of £2.65 per share, or US$2.9 billion. Unable to find a more amicable suitor, Fisons accepted the takeover that month. Though the British firm and its many subsidiaries around the world continued to be listed among R-PR's operations through 1996, it soon became clear that the tri-centenarian entity would eventually cease to exist. Over the course of 1996 and 1997, R-PR slashed almost 3,000 redundant jobs in the United States and Great Britain, divested several Fisons divisions (including the scientific instruments business), and discontinued many of the subsumed company's pharmaceutical research and development programs.

For its nearly US$3 billion, Rhone-Poulenc Rorer got an entree into the US$15 billion and growing respiratory drug market, or more specifically, the respiratory drug delivery segment. At the time of its purchase, Fisons had two promising delivery media in the development pipeline: a non-CFC aerosol and a dry-powder inhaler. Indeed, Fisons likely played a role in an increase in sales and net at R-PR from 1995 to 1996. Year-over-year revenues increased six percent, to US$5.4 billion, and net grew by almost one-third, to US$473.5 million.

In November 1997, when Rhone-Poulenc acquired the remaining one-third of R-PR that it did not already own, Fisons' fate appeared sealed. Officials at the company's U.S. and U.K. headquarters early in 1998 asserted that Fisons no longer existed, either as a group of subsidiaries or a division.

Further Reading

Finlay, Paul N., "How Fisons Managed its Turnaround," *European Journal of Marketing*, Vol. 22, pp. 103–17.

"Firm's Horticulture Business to Be Sold for $60 Million," *Wall Street Journal*, May 19, 1993, p. A11.

"Fisons' Shares Plunge as Scroggs is Sacked," *ECN-European Chemical News*, December 20, 1993, p. 8.

"Fisons Stock Tumbles as Drug Maker Halts New Medicine's Trials," *Wall Street Journal*, April 7, 1993, p. A10.

"Fisons' Strong Profit Gain is Ammo in Takeover Fight," *Chemical Marketing Reporter*, September 18, 1995, p. 20.

"Fisons to Cut 1,000 Jobs in Continuing Reorganization," *Chemical & Engineering News*, January 31, 1994, p. 12.

"Fisons to Sell Some Operations in Canada, U.S. to Ciba-Geigy," *Wall Street Journal*, November 27, 1992, p. A6.

From a Corner of Suffolk to the Four Corners of the Earth, Ipswich, England: Fisons plc, 1984.

"Full Circle," *The Economist*, January 18, 1992, p. 69.

Leblond, Doris, "Reaping a Home Harvest," *ECN-European Chemical News*, February 17, 1997, p. 22.

"A Lot of Hot Air: Fisons," *The Economist*, September 23, 1995, p. 55.

Moore, Stephen D., "U.K.'s Fisons and Allergan Link up to Develop, Sell Opthalmic Products, *Wall Street Journal*, February 5, 1993, p. B3A.

"R-PR To Slash Jobs as Fisons Comes on Board," *ECN-European Chemical News*, February 5, 1996, p. 19.

Thayer, Ann, "Fison Gives in to Rhone-Poulenc Rorer," *Chemical & Engineering News*, October 16, 1995, p. 6.

—April Dougal Gasbarre

Florida Progress Corporation

Barnett Tower
One Progress Plaza
Suite 2600
St. Petersburg, Florida 33701
U.S.A.
(813) 824-6400
Fax: (813) 824-6751
Web site: http://www.fpc.com

Public Company
Incorporated: 1899 as St. Petersburg Electric Light &
    Power Company
Employees: 7,291
Total Assets: $6.1 billion (1997)
Stock Exchanges: New York Pacific
SICs: 4911 Electric Services; 1222 Bituminous Coal—
    Underground; 4449 Water Transportation of Freight,
    Not Elsewhere Classified; 6719 Holding Companies,
    Not Elsewhere Classified

Florida Progress Corporation is a diversified holding company whose primary businesses are fuel supply and power. Its primary subsidiary, Florida Power Corporation, the state's second largest utility, was supplying electricity to 1.3 million customers in 1997. Its service area was primarily in northern and central Florida, including the cities of Clearwater, St. Petersburg, and Winter Park. The electric utility accounted for 90 percent of Florida Progress's earnings; the remaining ten percent was contributed by the subsidiary Electric Fuels, a fuel supply and transportation company. Florida Progress had recently divested itself of its real estate and financial services subsidiaries and was expected to get rid of its failing life insurance company in the late 1990s.

Early History

Florida Progress was formed in 1982 as a holding company for Florida Power, for the purpose of diversifying beyond utility operations. Florida Power itself originated in 1899 as St. Petersburg Electric Light & Power Company. Its name was changed to St. Petersburg Lighting Company in 1915, to Pinellas County Power Company in 1923, and to Florida Power Corporation in 1927. Florida Power's parent company was General Gas & Electric Corporation, part of the Associated Gas & Electric System, one of the large utility holding companies prominent in the early 20th century.

In the 1920s and the 1930s the utility expanded through acquisitions of both investor-owned electric companies and municipal systems in Florida. Among the former purchases were Clearwater Lighting Company in 1923 and both Oklawaha Power Company and West Florida Power Company in 1935. Florida Power acquired several municipal electric systems in 1930, in New Port Richey, Dunnellon, and Branford, and in 1934 added the operations of four other small Florida communities.

The Public Utility Holding Company Act of 1935 eventually broke up the Associated Gas & Electric System, which included utilities in Georgia, New Jersey, New York, and Pennsylvania, as well as Florida. The act limited each holding company's operations to a single contiguous system, rather than the far-flung empires that many such companies had. The Securities and Exchange Commission, which administered the holding companies' divestiture, organized Associated Gas & Electric's Florida and Georgia operations into a single system. Florida Power became an independent, publicly-held company in 1945, with Georgia Power & Light Company as a subsidiary.

Growth in the 1950s and 1960s

In 1951 Florida Power acquired electrical operations in Madison, Monticello, and Perry, Florida, from Florida Power & Light Company. In 1957 it sold Georgia Power & Light to Georgia Power Company for about $11.8 million.

Florida Power's sales and earnings grew steadily during the 1960s, and the company gained a reputation for good management. *Electric Light & Power,* a trade magazine, named the company electric utility of the year in 1970. The utility, however, had a potential problem in its heavy dependence on imported oil to run its generating plants. Florida Power had researched nuclear energy for several years during the 1960s, and in 1968 it began construction of a nuclear unit at its Crystal River plant, which already had two fossil-fuel units.

Energy Problems in the 1970s

The nuclear unit was scheduled for completion in 1972 but cost far more than expected and also had construction problems that delayed its completion. Meanwhile, the soaring cost of oil after the Middle East oil embargo of the early 1970s plunged Florida Power into financial difficulties, as imported oil accounted for about 80 percent of its fuel consumption. In 1974, when Florida Power's earnings fell 35 percent from the previous year, it temporarily suspended construction of the nuclear unit to conserve cash.

During this period, to reduce its use of foreign oil, Florida Power looked to coal as well as nuclear power. It began converting two oil-burning plants to coal in 1975. In 1976 it formed Electric Fuels Corporation, a company involved in coal mining and the transportation of coal and other commodities via rail and barge, with customers including Florida Power and other utility and industrial companies.

The nuclear unit finally went into operation in March 1977, and saved the utility $46.7 million in fuel costs during the remainder of the year. Florida Power's 1977 earnings were up 38 percent from their 1976 level.

However, problems soon developed. In March 1978, the utility was forced to shut down the nuclear unit after a coolant leakage was detected. Company officials subsequently discovered that a latch had given way, shattering a reactor assembly and flushing pieces through the coolant system. Broken tubes then caused the leaks. The unit was shut down for repairs for seven months in 1978. Florida Power wanted Babcock & Wilcox Company, the firm that had built the unit, to perform the repairs at its own expense, but Babcock & Wilcox refused, citing a limited warranty clause in its contract. It then did the repairs for an additional fee.

In 1981 Florida Power sued Babcock & Wilcox in an effort in recover its costs. The utility contended that the unit's design and construction had been inadequate in the first place; therefore, Babcock & Wilcox was responsible for the accident. In 1984 Florida Power reached a settlement with Babcock & Wilcox, in which the utility received $11.8 million—about $7.2 million from insurers and $4.6 million directly from the construction firm. The latter was mainly in the form of credits against future bills for equipment and services.

Diversification in the 1980s

During this period, diversification became a priority for Florida Power. Taking advantage of Florida's rapid population growth, in 1981 it formed Talquin Corporation, a real estate developer and building-products manufacturer. Stepping up its move beyond utility operations, it formed Florida Progress Corporation in 1982, and Florida Power became its principal subsidiary. Florida Power's stockholders received one Florida Progress common share for each common share of Florida Power they held. Florida Power's subsidiaries, Electric Fuels and Talquin Corporation, became subsidiaries of Florida Progress.

In 1983 Florida Progress formed Progress Credit Corporation, an equipment-leasing and -financing business concentrating on aircraft. In 1985 the holding company formed Progress Technologies Corporation to develop and market technology-based products and processes for use in a variety of industries. The following year Florida Progress bought Mid-Continent Life Insurance Company, which specialized in low-premium life insurance marketed through independent agents, was based in Oklahoma City, and dated back to 1909. These diversifications, along with the diversification of Florida Power's fuel sources, produced improvements in Florida Progress's sales, earnings, and stock price. Florida's population growth was a factor as well; in 1987 the company's utility customer base increased 4.4 percent, double the U.S. average.

In 1988 Florida Progress formed Progress Capital Holdings, Inc. to handle financing for its nonutility operations. Progress Capital subsequently became the parent of all the nonutility subsidiaries except Electric Fuels. Also formed that year was Progress Energy Corporation, whose purpose was to invest in cogeneration projects and small power plants outside Florida, but Florida Progress discontinued this business just two years later.

Another venture begun in 1988 was Talquin Corp.'s formation of partnerships to construct luxury apartment buildings in Florida cities, including Tampa, Orlando, and Fort Myers. The real estate company was seeking projects that would provide a quick return on investment, but the recession in Florida's real estate market and the national economy hurt results in 1989 and 1990. In 1990 Florida Progress decided to sell Talquin's building-products operations, because they did not fit in with the company's future direction. The establishment of a $14 million reserve to cover the expected loss on sales of these businesses was the principal reason for a 12.5 percent drop in Florida Progress's earnings in 1990.

In 1990 Talquin sold 3,200 acres of south Florida citrus groves it had acquired as an investment six years earlier, for an after-tax profit of about $10 million. That same year Talquin completed and sold its first luxury apartment complex, in Orlando, and finished other projects including Barnett Tower, a 26-story building in downtown St. Petersburg that became the new headquarters for Florida Progress, with portions occupied by several other companies.

Florida Progress's insurance and coal operations both grew in the late 1980s and early 1990s. From 1986, when it was acquired, through 1990, Mid-Continent had a 19 percent annual increase in its insurance in force, topping $8.5 billion in 1990. Its earnings increased an average of 26.5 percent annually during those five years. It added more than 4,000 agents, putting the total at more than 6,000, and doubled its number of regional offices, to 26. Electric Fuels bought a rail-car repair company, Kustom Karr, in 1990. It also added to its coal reserves that year, buying Kentucky mines with a capacity of producing about two million tons of coal annually. During 1990 it sold five million tons of coal to companies other than Florida Power. Its operations also reduced the cost of coal used by Florida Power by 14 percent from 1985 to 1990.

New Directions and Leadership in the 1990s

By 1990 Florida Power had greatly decreased its use of foreign-produced oil. In fact, its fuel mix was 54 percent coal, 22 percent oil, 13 percent nuclear energy, ten percent purchased power, and one percent natural gas. In 1990 Florida Power signed a 20-year contract to purchase power from The Southern Company and made plans to build a transmission line to connect it with Southern's operations in south Georgia. The nuclear unit at Crystal River, despite experiencing a variety of outages in 1988 and 1989, received its highest performance rating ever from the Nuclear Regulatory Commission in 1990. The nuclear unit was one of five electricity-generating units at the Crystal River site, the others being fossil-fueled; Florida Power explored sites for another complex of a similar size.

As it entered the 1990s, Florida Power was a relatively energy-efficient utility, able to offer its customers low rates. About 90 percent of its customers were residential, leaving the company less vulnerable to the vagaries of the economy than utilities that depend more on industrial and commercial customers. Its customer base had grown 3.8 percent annually from 1985 to 1990, almost twice the national average, thanks to the influx of people into Florida.

Florida Progress's efforts at diversification, however, showed mixed results in the early 1990s. Electric Fuels was maintaining a constant level of coal sales to Florida Power, while increasing sales to other companies, and was contributing 4.5 percent of Florida Progress's earnings. Mid-Continent Life Insurance Co. and Progress Credit Corp., contributing four and five percent respectively to the parent company's earnings, were faring respectably. Talquin, however, was facing a weak real estate market, reporting losses in 1991 that represented four percent of Florida Progress's earnings. Other investments in businesses unrelated to the company's core industries, such as its 80 percent interest in the chemicals research company Advanced Separation Technologies Inc., were making dubious contributions to the company's health.

In 1991 Jack B. Critchfield took over the reins from chairman Andrew Hines. With the change in leadership came a change in direction for Florida Progress. Critchfield narrowed the company's focus to electricity generation, fuel supply, and financial services. Unrelated investments or wholly owned subsidiaries were sold off. Critchfield also began a gradual process of divesting its real estate and financial services holdings, starting in 1991 with the sale of Talquin's building products operations and certain assets of Progress Credit.

Problems with the Crystal River nuclear plant also plagued Florida Power in the mid-1990s. Although the plant achieved a capacity factor of 100 percent in 1995, it was shut down for much of 1996 and perhaps all of 1997 because of a scheduled refueling, repairs, and concerns about the design of the backup safety system. The plant was expected to return to service near the end of 1997. The problems cost the company not only financially but also in customer goodwill. Florida Power at-tempted to regain some of its repair costs by raising rates, but customer outrage led the company to rescind the rate hike.

Florida Progress continued its process of divesting its real estate and financial services holdings in the mid-1990s. In 1996 the company spun off the remaining assets of Talquin and Progress Credit, creating the independent company Echelon International Corporation. In May 1997 Mid-Continent Life Insurance Co. was placed in receivership by the insurance commissioner of Oklahoma. Florida Progress was expected to lose some or all of its 85.6 million investment in the company.

Deregulation in the Late 1990s

Nuclear plant problems and diversification woes were not Florida Progress's only concerns in the late 1990s. Looming deregulation demanded a transition plan. Florida Power enjoyed certain advantages over other utilities in the nation as deregulation neared. Rapid population growth in Florida and slow movement by state legislators to institute competition gave Florida Power a stable customer base for the near future. In addition, as a peninsula, Florida was relatively isolated from power lines stretching across state lines. However, Florida Power suffered from a poor public image, caused by high rates, frequent outages, and the lengthy shutdown of its nuclear plant. As a medium-sized utility, it could not compete with the largest utilities in the nation, which were already positioning themselves to cherry pick the choicest commercial customers when deregulation took effect.

Growth was seen as the surest route to success in a competitive environment. To that end, in September 1997 Florida Progress announced a joint venture with Cinergy and New Century Energies to market energy services to large commercial customers. The alliance, called Cadence, had a two-step plan: first, offer advice on lowering energy costs and help consolidate customer's energy bills, and second, provide electricity to these customers once deregulation took effect. Late in 1997 the joint venture had attracted one major customer, Service Merchandise. Analysts speculated that a merger could result from this alliance.

Principal Subsidiaries

Florida Power Corporation; Electric Fuels Corporation; Mid-Continent Life Insurance Co.

Further Reading

"Florida Progress Then and Now," *St. Petersburg Times,* November 10, 1997, p. 10.
Hannon, Kerry, "Lights, Action, Prudence," *Forbes,* September 19, 1988.
Sachdev, Ameet, "Florida Progress: Not Just for Power Anymore," *St. Petersburg Times,* November 10, 1997, p. 10.
"Today A Hero. But Tomorrow?," *Forbes,* December 15, 1974.

—Donald R. Stabile and Trudy Ring
—updated by Susan Windisch Brown

FoodBrands America, Inc.

1601 N.W. Expressway
Suite 1700
Oklahoma City, Oklahoma 73118
U.S.A.
(405) 879-4100
Fax: (405) 879-4173
Web site: http://www.foodbrands.com

Independent Subsidiary of IBP, inc.
Incorporated: 1964 as Doskocil Companies, Inc.
Employees: 3,400
Sales: $835.1 million (1996)
SICs: 2013 Sausages & Other Prepared Meats; 2051
Bread, Cake & Related Products; 2011 Meat Packing
Plants; 2038 Frozen Specialties, Not Elsewhere
Classified

A market leader in the foodservice industry, FoodBrands America, Inc. produces and sells branded and processed perishable foods for foodservice, delicatessen, and retail customers. FoodBrands America formerly operated as Doskocil Companies, Inc., a company that reigned as the largest supplier of pizza toppings to national pizza chains before filing for bankruptcy in 1990. After reorganizing and then changing its name in 1995, the company emerged as FoodBrands America, with more than 1,600 products comprising its product line. During the late 1990s, the company maintained a presence in numerous niche markets through four operating divisions. Its foodservice division ranked as the largest supplier of pepperoni and pizza toppings in the United States. Its specialty brands division produced ethnic frozen food under the Rotanelli's and Little Juan brand names. The company's deli division marketed more than 100 products under brand names such as Fresh Cuts and American Favorite. The retail division marketed approximately 300 products under the Wilson Foods and Corn King labels. In 1997, FoodBrands America became a subsidiary of IBP, inc., a global meatpacking conglomerate based in Nebraska that ranked as the world's largest producer of fresh beef and pork.

Early 1960s Origins

Larry Doskocil decided what he wanted to become in life while working at the meat department in a Safeway supermarket, earning money for his tuition at Bethany Nazarene College in Bethany, Oklahoma. He decided he wanted to become the sausage king of Kansas. While working behind the counter at Safeway's meat department, Doskocil handled all types of meat and became familiar with a variety of leading brand names, but he was impressed most with Oklahoma's greatest selling brand of sausage, J.C. Potter. During the 1950s, Oklahomans must have been voracious fans of J.C. Potter sausage because Doskocil viewed the product as if it were a pot of gold. ''I decided that I was going to become the J.C. Potter of Kansas,'' Doskocil later related, recalling the defining moment that sent him headlong into the sausage business. The fruits of his efforts, which were arduous and fortuitously exerted at a time of opportunity, led to the formation of Doskocil Companies, Incorporated, the predecessor to the nearly $1 billion FoodBrands America that was flourishing during the 1990s.

Having picked the direction his life would take, Doskocil moved toward his objective of becoming the sausage king of Kansas with an extraordinary display of determination. In 1961, he leased an abandoned chicken hatchery in Hutchinson, Kansas, and began his bid to develop a powerful brand name of sausage in the Kansas market. His efforts were tireless and his conviction was unwavering. Doskocil started his day with seven hours of sausage making, beginning at five a.m., and working until noon. After cleaning up, he climbed into his truck to sell the sausage he had made and drove around the outlying areas surrounding Wichita, Kansas until dark. Once night settled in, Doskocil returned to his modest headquarters and slaughtered hogs until midnight, ending his workday 19 hours after it had begun. Doskocil followed this schedule religiously. During the entire first year of his business, Doskocil slept on a cot in his makeshift plant.

When he started out, Doskocil figured it would take him at least 10 years to come close to achieving his objective. Building his brand, which he named ''Country Cousin,'' into the Kansas equivalent of the J.C. Potter brand in Oklahoma would be a lengthy process no matter how many hours a day he worked.

Company Perspectives:

How do we retain our diverse customer base? FoodBrands America exceeds expectations by providing products that are formulated, cooked, handled, flavored and delivered exactly as ordered, on schedule. That dedication pays off for everyone. It allows our customers to expand their market share and enables FoodBrands America to grow sales. FoodBrands America is not only recognized as one of the nation's top foodservice providers, but we're earning a solid reputation for being a growth catalyst, too.

Doskocil's realization of this fact made his early efforts that much more remarkable, but the fledgling entrepreneur did not have to struggle for a decade before success came his way. In 1963, a serendipitous visit to a start-up pizza chain proved to be Doskocil's big break. One night in 1963, Doskocil stopped at a new restaurant in Wichita named Pizza Hut and ordered a pizza. At the time, Pizza Hut was a small Wichita chain just getting started. Doskocil watched the owner make toppings from fresh meat and listened to his complaints about the time it took to make meat toppings from scratch. The Pizza Hut owner remarked that the laborious efforts were keeping him off the softball field, so Doskocil posed a solution. He offered to cook a batch of sausage for the owner and the owner immediately agreed. Doskocil then called other pizza franchises and offered the same service. The response was overwhelming, and Doskocil, unexpectedly, had found his niche in the Kansas meat market.

Doskocil's timing was perfect. He approached pizza chain operators just as their enterprises were beginning to develop into regional and national chains. As the chains expanded, so did Doskocil's business, its growth driven by the prolific growth recorded by Pizza Hut, Godfather's, Domino's, and other operators during the 1960s and 1970s. More business meant hiring more workers, freeing Doskocil from having to do everything by himself, but a steadily increasing workforce did not mean Doskocil sat behind a desk while his employees labored. Doskocil directed his tireless efforts in another direction, and the result had as much to do with his company's success as his chance entry into the pizza topping business.

One of the chief reasons Doskocil enjoyed enviable success during the 1960s and 1970s was his emphasis on vertical integration. His company, Doskocil Companies, Incorporated, did not expand because of exhaustive marketing efforts; the company, in fact, did not have a marketing department. Doskocil sold exclusively to just a few huge chains and never attempted to develop any business with smaller buyers and independent food service operators. Instead, Doskocil made every effort to make his operations as efficient as possible and as self-reliant as possible. The characteristics of his personality that displayed themselves during the early years of his career, when he performed every task himself during a 19-hour workday, were demonstrated in a different way once his company became successful. Doskocil looked at every aspect of his business and made his own changes, tailoring Doskocil Companies into a force in the pizza topping business that no competitor could rival.

Doskocil studied every detail of his business. He determined precast concrete walls would cost less in the long run, saving money on maintenance and cleaning costs at his production facility. Doskocil could not get precast concrete locally, so he manufactured his own walls. When he made a survey of the insulation material available on the market, Doskocil was unimpressed and decided he could make a better, more efficient kind on his own, so he did. When Doskocil purchased automated production equipment, he immediately began tinkering with his new purchase, making improvements that fit his needs. When no manufacturer offered what he needed in production automation, Doskocil manufactured his own equipment. For the fuel required to cook his meat, Doskocil did not turn to a supplier for his needs, he purchased his own natural gas wells and his own natural gas transmission company. Doskocil owned or made nearly everything his company needed, restricting his vertical integration efforts only in the business of raising hogs and cattle. The result was a low-cost producer that held sway in the pizza topping market. No other competitor could match the efficiency of the Doskocil-designed production processes. Said a spokesperson for Hormel, which briefly tried to challenge Doskocil Companies but failed: "They make an excellent product and they're doing it a lot cheaper than we could."

1980s: Preeminence and Failure

By the beginning of the 1980s, Doskocil could not only rightly refer to himself as the sausage king of Kansas but also as the budding pizza-topping king of the United States. His company made 70 percent of the precooked processed beef and pork used by national pizza restaurant chains, a dominating percentage that generated more than $110 million in annual sales by the mid-1980s. "We have a neat little niche here," Doskocil remarked at the time to reporters. "We're very happy." The company took advantage of its success by taking on the role of an acquirer, purchasing Stoppenbauch Inc., a pepperoni, smoked meat, and cheese maker based in Wisconsin and a crab meat processor in South Carolina. With these added plumes to Doskocil Companies' already thriving operations, the company stood poised as a formidable force, holding sway as the national leader in its business. By this point, Doskocil had far eclipsed his ambitious dreams of the early 1960s and had begun to search for a new chief executive for his company. "We're past the entrepreneurial stage," he remarked to reporters in 1984, understating the maturity of his enterprise. "And I don't want to run a $1 billion company." As it turned out, Doskocil may have regretted not finding a replacement in 1984 because his company began to stumble during the mid-1980s. By the end of the decade, Doskocil Companies was mired in profound financial problems and bankruptcy was imminent.

The sudden turn for the worse began to manifest itself during the mid-1980s when the telltale financial signs appeared. The root of the financial ills stretched back to a reverse merger Doskocil completed with the billionaire Bass brothers in 1983. The transaction enabled Doskocil to acquire Stoppenbauch Inc. and the South Carolina crabmeat processor, and it gave his company some of the corporate trappings it had previously lacked. After the reverse merger, Doskocil Companies had sophisticated financing capabilities, a new marketing organization, and a more ambitious long-term goal. Doskocil remarked that the financial deal with the Bass brothers "blossomed us out . . . it showed us what we can do, which is more than just make sausage," but the sudden transformation also diverted attention away from one of the company's primary strengths: its low-cost productivity methods. The company's profit margins began to shrink and its net income began to slip in 1985, as competitors made up lost ground and began to approximate Doskocil Companies' processing technology and productivity. In 1986, gross margins and net income slid downward again, causing company officials to grow anxious. "We're no longer five years ahead," Doskocil confided to reporters in reference to the wide lead the company had had over competitors in terms of cost advantage. "Not even three years," he mused.

To mend the problems, Doskocil went back to where he started and returned to the production floor. Labor costs were subsequently trimmed by 12 percent and the company made strides toward recovery. Heading into the late 1980s, the company was generating roughly $225 million a years in annual sales and reigned as the greatest purveyor of pizza toppings to pizza chains in the United States. Although the company's profitability problems were not completely eliminated, management felt confident enough about the company's position to entertain an enormous acquisition in 1988. The acquisition candidate was Wilson Foods, a meatpacker whose annual sales towered at $1.3 billion, or five times the total collected by Doskocil Companies. The company went ahead with the purchase, paying $238 million for Wilson Foods line of retail pork products, which included hot dogs, ham, sausage, and sliced bacon.

For a while, the acquisition of Wilson Foods appeared to be a smart move, at least one that investors liked. The company's stock value swelled to $14 in 1989, but a year later it plummeted to $1.37. The cause for the stock's collapse was the collapse of Doskocil Companies itself. The purchase of Wilson Foods had left the company overextended, and when the credit market tightened as a national economic recession set in, Doskocil Companies had nowhere to turn except for the protective shelter of Chapter 11. Doskocil Companies filed for bankruptcy in 1990 after flourishing for nearly three decades. It was a dark period in the company's history, marking the fall of the sausage king and the end of the type of Doskocil Companies that had been in operation for 26 years. Bankruptcy was not the end for the company, however. Instead, it gave the company time to rethink its strategy and emerge with an entirely different operating philosophy. The merits of this new approach were borne out during the 1990s.

1990s Resurgence

Roughly a year after filing for Chapter 11, Doskocil Companies emerged from bankruptcy restructured and reorganized. Looking toward the future, management envisioned a company involved in a variety of specialty foods niche markets, ranging from sauces to meats and crusts. What emerged was a company without a core business, a company entirely unlike the old Doskocil Companies that relied heavily on the sales of pork and beef toppings to pizza chains. Instead of catering to one type of customer, the post-bankruptcy Doskocil Companies would market its products to a wide spectrum of customers, ranging from the company's original customer, Pizza Hut, to numerous other customers, including grocery store delis, wholesale distributors,

casual dining chains, hospitals, and schools. Further, the new version of the company would market hundreds and hundreds of specialty foods products instead of the handful that had sustained it prior to bankruptcy. Hewing to this new course of development, management began reshaping the company in earnest in 1994.

That year, the company acquired the Frozen Specialty Foods Division of International Multifoods Corp. for approximately $135 million. The acquisition gave Doskocil Companies roughly $185 million in annual sales to add to its revenue volume and a product line that included appetizers, entrees, portion meats, and ethnic specialties. Brands acquired with the purchase of the division included Fred's, Rotanelli's, Posada, and Little Juan's. After its acquisition, Frozen Specialty was organized as Doskocil Specialty Brands Co. Next, the company moved in the opposite direction by divesting one of its businesses, but before the sale, the company changed its name from Doskocil Companies to FoodBrands America, Inc. After this name change, which reflected the increasingly variegated nature of the company's product line, it sold a substantial facet of its business. In May 1995, the company sold the retail pork division it had acquired seven years earlier in the Wilson Foods deal. Although the division accounted for roughly $220 million of FoodBrands America's revenue volume, the business was regarded as a low-profit-margin business and industry observers applauded its exit from the company's fold. The division was sold to Thorn Apple Valley Inc. for $76 million.

Before the end of 1995, the company resumed its acquisitive activities, purchasing KPR Holdings Inc. in December. A manufacturer of sauces, soups, pizza toppings, and side dishes, KPR sold its product line to clients such as TGI Friday's and Brinker International. Aside from diversifying FoodBrands America' product line and adding $99 million in annual sales to its revenue volume, the acquisition of KPR provided FoodBrands America with access to international markets. Through a partnership with The Quelly Group of Ireland, KPR Holdings was involved in a joint venture to produce pizza toppings for food service operators in Europe, the Middle East, Africa, and the Pacific Rim. One week after the KPR deal was finalized, FoodBrands America completed another acquisition, purchasing TNT Crust, Inc., a producer of partially baked and frozen self-rising crusts for use by pizza chains, restaurants, and frozen pizza manufacturers.

With these deals behind it, FoodBrands America entered 1996 as a thoroughly reshaped company with a product line that included more than 1,600 products. The company's strength was its diversity. With no core business, FoodBrands America was involved in numerous, profitable niche markets that generated $835 million in sales in 1996. The company ranked as the largest supplier of pepperoni and precooked pork and beef to the pizza industry and held the leading market share in partially baked and self-rising pizza crusts, deli ham, and food-service frozen burritos. As management plotted the company's future course, more acquisitions were in the offing. The strategy of targeting the foodservice industry as a whole by penetrating into niche markets had revived the moribund Doskocil Companies and created a powerful company able to grow through acquisitions during the late 1990s and into the 21st century.

In 1997, FoodBrands America joined forces with meat-packing conglomerate IBP inc. In April, IBP acquired Food-Brands America for $640 million as part of its strategy to diversify beyond its core fresh-meats business. Following the completion of the transaction, FoodBrands America was organized as an independent subsidiary of IBP, retaining its senior management and remaining in Oklahoma City. From the deal, FoodBrands America gained IBP's operating expertise, a financial supporter with the resources to finance future acquisitions, and greater access to foreign markets. On the heels of its alliance with IBP, FoodBrands America prepared for the new century ahead, intending to acquire companies with strong niche market positions and cash flow margins of at least ten percent.

Principal Subsidiaries

Continental Deli Foods, Inc.; Doskocil Food Service Company, L.L.C.; Specialty Brands, Inc.; KPR Holdings, L.P.

Principal Divisions

Food Service Division; Specialty Brands Division; Deli Division; KPR Foods Division.

Further Reading

Bork, Robert H., Jr., "On Top of the Pizza," *Forbes,* October 22, 1984, p. 115.

Colodny, Mark M., "The Bass Brothers Lose One," *Fortune,* July 30, 1990, p. 243.

"Doskocil Buys Multifoods' Frozen Specialty Division," *Nation's Restaurant News,* April 4, 1994, p. 74.

Fondiller, David S., "The Pizza Connection: Foodbrands America Has a Niche Strategy that Flouts Conventional Practices," *Forbes,* October 21, 1996, p. 202.

"Foodbrands America Buys TNT Crust in Acquisition," *Nation's Restaurant News,* December 11, 1995, p. 50.

Froman, Brett Duval, "Doskocil Cos.," *Fortune,* May 25, 1987, p. 62.

"IBP inc. to Buy Foodbrands for $640M in Cash," *Nation's Restaurant News,* April 14, 1997, p. 66.

Richman, Tom, "Ordinary Business," *Inc.,* May 1987, p. 73.

—Jeffrey L. Covell

Foster Wheeler Corporation

Perryville Corporate Park
Clinton, New Jersey 08809-4000
U.S.A.
(908) 730-4000
Fax: (908) 730-4404
Web site: http://www.fwc.com

Public Company
Incorporated: 1927
Employees: 12,085
Sales: $4.04 billion (1996)
Stock Exchanges: New York
SICs: 8711 Engineering Services; 1629 Heavy
    Construction, Not Elsewhere Classified

Foster Wheeler Corporation is an international company overseeing a wide range of engineering and construction enterprises. The company is organized into three business groups: an engineering and construction group, an energy equipment group, and a power systems group. The engineering and construction (E&C) group designs, engineers, and manages the construction of process plants for oil refiners, chemical and pharmaceutical producers, and a wide range of other industries. The E&C group also provides a broad range of services, including recruiting and training plant staff, maintenance and operating services, and environmental remediation services. The energy equipment group designs and fabricates steam generating equipment, condensers, and related equipment, and conducts research in such areas as fluid dynamics, combustion and fuel technology, and materials engineering. The power systems group develops, operates, and in some cases owns plants that produce electricity, thermal energy, and hydrogen.

Company Origins

Although Foster Wheeler was incorporated in 1927, the origins of the enterprise date several decades earlier to the founding of two manufacturing companies: Wheeler Condenser & Engineering Company and Power Specialty Company. In 1891, Wheeler Condenser and Engineering Company was created with offices in New York City and a plant in Carteret, New Jersey. Its steam condensers, pumps, and heat exchangers were bought primarily by the power and marine industries. During the Spanish-American War the U.S. Navy contracted with the company for condensers for a number of vessels, beginning what would later be a long and important relationship for Foster Wheeler with the armed forces. In the ensuing years, the Wheeler Condenser & Engineering Company became a primary equipment supplier to the growing electrical utility industry.

Power Specialty Company, founded in New York City in 1900, followed a pattern of growth similar to that of Wheeler Condenser & Engineering. The company began by marketing waterworks equipment but was soon designing and manufacturing boiler components in its Dansville, New York, plant. Primarily building superheaters, Power Specialty also expanded to serve the new electrical power industry.

Like Wheeler Condenser & Engineering, Power Specialty developed an affiliation with the armed forces early in the company's history. During World War I, the company used its engineering expertise to design an advanced marine boiler for the U.S. Merchant Marines. In the 1920s Power Specialty diversified its operations by entering the industry of petroleum refinery equipment—designing and manufacturing—including crude oil distillation units and fired heaters.

In 1927 the two companies merged, forming the Foster Wheeler Corporation, and established their headquarters in New York City. The same year, a former Power Specialty office in London was incorporated as a Foster Wheeler subsidiary. In 1928, Foster Wheeler Limited (Canada), another former Power Specialty office, was incorporated, with a manufacturing plant and offices in Ontario, Canada. Two years after the merger, the New York Stock Exchange offered Foster Wheeler common and preferred stock.

Early Expansion

The new corporation's first goal was expanding its product line, which was initiated through the production of feedwater heaters, evaporators, and cooling towers. The company also

Company Perspectives:

Whether it's fueling transportation, lighting cities, warming homes, or protecting the environment, Foster Wheeler is at the forefront: helping developing nations utilize their natural resources to improve their standard of living; helping to produce cleaner fuels for transportation and home heating; providing the energy to light up cities around the world; helping to protect the environment and the world's natural resources. This is Foster Wheeler—engineering to help the world run better.

acquired the D. Connelly Boiler Company in 1931, enabling them to design and produce all steam generator system components. Foster Wheeler had another burst of expansion during World War II, when engineering expertise and manufacturing were in demand from the armed forces.

The establishment of Foster Wheeler France, S.A. in 1949 opened an era of international expansion for Foster Wheeler. Operations were begun in Milan in 1957 with the organization of Foster Wheeler Italiana, S.p.A., Foster Wheeler Iberia was established in Madrid in 1965, and Foster Wheeler Australia Pty. Ltd. was established in Victoria, Australia, in 1967. The company also created a subsidiary to handle international construction.

Challenges in the Late 1950s

Although the company was expanding internationally, several engineering crises hurt Foster Wheeler's reputation and bottom line in the late 1950s and early 1960s. Former corporation president Frank A. Lee told *Forbes* writer Geoffrey Smith, "When you're talking about a 600-megawatt boiler that looks like a 14-story apartment house, and some tubes begin to rupture, you're talking about a tremendous amount of money. A couple of those a year and you're going to be in a loss position. And that's what happened. We had quite a few engineering problems in our boiler business—and an image problem in the market." Foster Wheeler's revenues dropped, and the company even operated at a loss in 1957 and 1963.

Over the next several years, the company gradually regained a good reputation in the boiler manufacturing business. However, those earlier setbacks caused Foster Wheeler to adopt a conservative attitude toward growth. Rather than expand into new business areas where the company lacked expertise, such as the growing field of nuclear energy, Foster Wheeler expanded geographically, selling products and services in regions where it could confidently establish a foothold.

Although Foster Wheeler was more cautious in buying out companies in the late 1960s and 1970s than many competitors, the corporation did acquire several subsidiaries that eventually composed the core of its industrial and environmental group. The first, Fritz W. Glitsch and Sons, Inc. (renamed Glitsch International, Inc.), manufactures fractionating equipment and pressure vessels and was obtained in 1967. In 1973, the company acquired Ullrich Copper, Inc. This subsidiary produced bus bar and copper extrusions used in electrical switch gear and motor-control centers, and specialty copper components used in rapid-transit systems and computers. In 1976, another major subsidiary was obtained: Thermacote Welco Company, a distributor of welding supplies, including welding rod and wire, connectors, electrode holders, safety goggles, and brazing materials.

Reorganization and Profitability in the 1970s

Beginning in 1974, the company embarked on a significant reorganization plan. Foster Wheeler Corporation became a holding company, and Foster Wheeler Energy Corporation became the major operating company in the United States. Its responsibilities were later divided, with Foster Wheeler USA Corporation handling the process plants and project direction duties, and Foster Wheeler Energy Corporation the energy equipment operations. Other subsidiaries were created to improve the operating efficiency of the company's engineering and construction group, including Foster Wheeler Constructors, Inc., which handled project construction; FW Management Operations, Ltd., which provided management and plant operating services and trained staff for industry; Foster Wheeler Development Corporation, which provided contract research and development services; and Foster Wheeler Petroleum Development Ltd., which provided storage and shipping terminals, equipment for offshore gas and oil drilling, wellhead recovery and piping systems, and field development services.

Foster Wheeler's conservative strategy apparently paid off. Despite the drop in refinery construction after the oil embargo of 1974, the company's share price quadrupled from 1974 to 1979 and the return on equity steadily increased; while other companies were hard pressed to keep up with rampant inflation, Foster Wheeler was earning 19.3 percent.

Foster Wheeler's large backlogs and substantial cash reserves made the corporation a prime target for takeover. In 1979, McDonnell Douglas seemed poised to attempt a takeover, having bought 4.9 percent of Foster Wheeler's common stock. However, corporation president Frank Lee was adamant in his refusal to consider a takeover.

Foster Wheeler developed several technological advances that contributed to the company's high standing in the industry. For example, in 1980 the energy equipment group designed and constructed the first private industry fluidized bed steam generator fired by coal in the United States. They also created a unique cyclone design for their circulating fluidized bed boiler, a design which increased heat transfer, enabled a quicker start-up, reduced space requirements, and lowered maintenance costs.

Slowdown in the 1980s

In the late 1970s and early 1980s, Foster Wheeler benefited greatly from the boom in oil and utility power industries, achieving excellent profit margins in their contracts. However, the industry's heavy overbuilding resulted in a substantial reversal in the 1980s. Foster Wheeler's profits slumped, as indicated by a period of several years when dividends on common stock were held at 11 cents per share. The company's backlog, generally a reliable predictor of future revenues, lingered at approximately $1 billion through the mid-1980s.

To lessen its reliance on the sagging oil and power utility industries, Foster Wheeler developed subsidiaries in new industries, including Foster Wheeler Power Systems, Inc., and Foster Wheeler Environmental Services, Inc. Foster Wheeler Power Systems built, owned, and operated waste-to-energy plants, recycling and composting plants, and cogeneration facilities. The company had some experience to draw on in this area, having built the first waterfall mass-burning refuse boiler in the United States. Foster Wheeler Environmental Services handled hazardous waste management and later became the holding company of the subsidiaries Foster Wheeler Enviresponse, Inc., which offered environmentally related regulatory, technical, design, and remediation services, and Barsotti's, Inc., which offered asbestos abatement services.

Foster Wheeler also reacted to the economic downturn of the early 1980s by selling real estate properties and underperforming subsidiaries. In 1988 Conergics Corporation was sold to Phillips Industries, Inc., for $43.2 million, and in 1989 TANCO Corporation bought Forney Engineering Company for an undisclosed sum. The proceeds were used to strengthen Foster Wheeler's ventures into waste-to-energy and hazardous waste management.

In 1987 Foster Wheeler moved headquarters to Clinton, New Jersey, after nearly 25 years in Livingston, New Jersey; the same year, Foster Wheeler became the object of another takeover attempt. Asher B. Edelman seemed determined to have the company, stating that if the board of directors would not consider his offer, he would appeal directly to the stockholders. Although he garnered stock holdings of nearly 12 percent, the company rejected his offer. Edelman backed down, reducing his holdings over several months until they reached 4.9 percent.

Steady Growth in the 1990s

The company's traditional businesses, particularly its engineering and construction enterprises, were revitalized in the early 1990s. The company's backlog grew from the steady $1 billion mark of the 1980s to $3.47 billion by 1992. Foster Wheeler received several international contracts for oil refinery construction or modernization, including an upgrading project at three Saudi Arabian oil refineries with an estimated final cost of $4 billion, refinery work in France worth approximately $50 million, and an $80 million joint venture in the Soviet Union for materials and engineering for a new refining unit. In addition, the reconstruction in Kuwait after the Gulf War provided some refinery work for Foster Wheeler.

Although most of the company's new business had come from international contracts, particularly in Europe and Asia, Foster Wheeler anticipated a surge of refinery work in the United States due to new federal clean-air legislation that required many refineries to upgrade their facilities by 1995. Other business areas also seemed to be improving in the early 1990s, as indicated by Foster Wheeler's first order for a large central station steam generator in several years. The general outlook for Foster Wheeler in the early 1990s seemed good. The company's book value per share had been rising steadily—from $12.79 in

1988 to $15.13 in 1991. Despite a recession, Foster Wheeler's revenues increased 20 percent in 1991, and the growing backlog of business suggested a continued rise in revenues.

Along with increased oil refinery renovation, the company expected to see demand for utility construction to rise with the economic recovery in the United States in the mid-1990s. However, domestic business for Foster Wheeler grew more slowly than many analysts had predicted. With pressure from energy companies, legislators pushed back compliance dates mandated by the Clean Air Act. Therefore, the massive improvements to oil refineries Foster Wheeler was anticipating were delayed. Utility construction also did not materialize with the economic recovery. Apparently, supply had so outstripped demand in the United States in the late 1980s that even the warming economy did not require new plant construction.

Nevertheless, Foster Wheeler's international presence benefited the company in the mid-1990s. With environmental concerns growing in Europe, the demand for improvements to refineries and coal-burning plants increased, offering opportunities to Foster Wheeler's engineering and construction group. With offices in Singapore and Thailand, the company was well positioned to take advantage of the Asian economic boom. In 1993 the company signed new contracts with China to build two 600-megawatt boilers, and in 1996 it signed a $200 million contract with the Philippines to build a polyethylene plant.

Foster Wheeler reorganized in 1993, incorporating its environmental group into its engineering and construction group. The following year the company acquired Enserch Environmental Corporation. By merging it with its Environmental Services Division to form Foster Wheeler Environmental Corporation, Foster Wheeler created the largest full-service environmental services company in the world. The acquisition of Optimized Process Designs in 1994 provided Foster Wheeler with the means to provide engineering and construction to the hydrocarbon processing industry.

In 1995 the company expanded further both internationally and domestically. It acquired the power-generating company Pyropower from the A. Ahlstrom Corporation, bringing Foster Wheeler operations into Finland, Poland, and Japan. The $207.5 million deal also expanded Foster Wheeler's operations in the former Soviet Union. The same year the company bought a Texas-based supplier of sulfur-recovery equipment, TPA, Inc.

The analysts' predictions of booming contracts for Foster Wheeler came to fruition in the mid-1990s. The company's backlog of unfilled orders rose from 2.5 billion in 1992 to $5.1 billion in 1994. By 1996, that number stood at a record $7.1 billion. Much of the increase came from Foster Wheeler's international business, which accounted for approximately 70 percent of new bookings in 1996. Revenues and net earnings had grown commensurably throughout the mid-1990s. The company's revenues of $2.3 billion in 1994 had almost doubled to $4.0 billion in 1996, and net earnings had risen from $65 million in 1994 to $82 million in 1996.

In 1997 Foster Wheeler reorganized its pharmaceutical and fine chemicals unit. As part of the engineering and construction group, the unit accounted for 42 percent of that group's operating revenue in 1996. Later in 1997, the company sold Glitch

International, Inc., a supplier of mass transfer systems and chemical separations equipment. The company received $250 million cash for Glitch, which had revenues of $300 million in 1996.

The outlook for Foster Wheeler in the late 1990s seemed bright. Its strong international presence stood to gain from the rising energy needs of developing nations in Latin America and Asia, particularly in China. The company also anticipated new projects for its energy equipment group from the increasingly privatized power generating industry in Europe.

Principal Subsidiaries

Foster Wheeler International Corporation; Foster Wheeler USA Corporation; Foster Wheeler Constructors, Inc.; Foster Wheeler Environmental Corporation; Foster Wheeler Energy Limited (United Kingdom); Foster Wheeler Energy International, Inc.; Foster Wheeler Energy Corporation; Foster Wheeler Power Systems, Inc.

Further Reading

"A Comeback for Foster Wheeler?," *Business Week,* August 8, 1988.
"Foster Wheeler Reorganizes Drug Unit," *The Record,* March 28, 1997, p. B3.
"Foster Wheeler Sells Unit for $250M Cash," *The Report,* June 28, 1997, p. A9.
Halpern, Steve, "Investors Eye China," *Knight Ridder/Tribune News Service,* November 19, 1993.
Hardman, Adrienne, "All Pumped Up," *Financial World,* May 11, 1993, p. 30.
Kuhn, Susan E., "The Best Capital Goods Stocks to Buy Now," *Fortune,* April 4, 1994, pp. 33–34.
Smith, Geoffrey, "No Hiding Place," *Forbes,* September 3, 1979.
"Swelling Backlog Sets Stage for a Surge in Earnings," *Barrons,* August 19, 1991.

—Susan Windisch Brown

Franklin Electronic Publishers, Inc.

One Franklin Plaza
Burlington, New Jersey 08016-4907
U.S.A.
(609) 386-2500
Fax: (609) 239-5950
Web site: http://www.franklin.com

Public Company
Incorporated: 1983
Employees: 358
Sales: $88.7 million (1997)
Stock Exchanges: New York
SICs: 2741 Miscellaneous Publishing; 3571 Electronic
Computers; 3579 Office Machines, Not Elsewhere
Classified; 7372 Prepackaged Software

Franklin Electronic Publishers, Inc. is the worldwide market leader in handheld electronic books. Using microcomputer technology, electronic books retrieve information from a database for display on a liquid crystal display. Franklin created the first handheld electronic book in 1986 when it introduced the Spelling Ace, an electronic spelling corrector that allowed users to type in a word phonetically, then read the correct spelling. Licensing content from Merriam-Webster, Inc. and other publishers, Franklin succeeded in publishing an extensive electronic library of dictionaries, thesauri, medical reference works, encyclopedias, and a variety of entertainment, educational, and tutorial electronic publications. In October 1996 Franklin entered the personal productivity market by acquiring Rolodex Electronics and becoming the exclusive producer of Rolodex Electronics personal information management (PIM) and telephone products. By 1998 Franklin had sold more than 15 million electronic books through some 45,000 worldwide retail outlets and through catalogs. It had published more than 200 titles.

Founding as a Computer Manufacturer

Founded as Franklin Computer Corporation in 1981, the company made general purpose personal computers. Its first products were Apple clones, but it later produced IBM-compatible machines as well. The company was founded by three Philadelphia-area computer professionals: Joel Shusterman, who had started one of the largest Apple dealerships in the Philadelphia area, and Russell Bower and R. Barry Borden, who were experienced in computer manufacturing and engineering.

When Franklin released its first line of Apple-compatible computers, Apple sued Franklin for patent and copyright infringement on its hardware and software. Franklin eventually agreed to pay Apple $2.5 million. Further disputes with Apple persisted through 1985, when the issues between the two companies were finally resolved. Although Franklin experienced huge growth in the early 1980s and became one of the top ten personal computer makers, it posted big losses in the face of intense competition and a slumping market. When both Apple and IBM lowered their prices, Franklin lost its competitive advantage, which it had obtained by selling its computers through mass retail outlets. Sales peaked at $71.4 million in fiscal 1984 (ending March 31), but the company posted a $10.3 million loss that year.

New CEO and New Directions in the Mid-1980s

Morton David joined the company in May 1984 as chairman of the board and CEO, replacing Borden, who had recently resigned. In 1985 he also became president, replacing Shusterman, who had left Franklin to start a software company but had returned as temporary president. Prior to joining Franklin, David was chairman and CEO of Mura Corporation, a manufacturer of portable audio products. David was a Harvard Law School graduate and a Phi Beta Kappa at the City College of New York. Under his leadership the business moved into electronic publishing.

In June 1984 Franklin filed for protection from its creditors under Chapter 11 of the U.S. Bankruptcy Act. David's assignment, clearly, was to turn the company around. It emerged from Chapter 11 in early 1985 following the settlement of Apple's copyright infringement suit. As part of the settlement, Apple agreed not to challenge Franklin's programs on the basis of copyright.

Company Perspectives:

Franklin Electronic Publishers, Inc. created the handheld electronic book category in 1986 with the introduction of the Spelling Ace electronic spelling corrector. Electronic books instantly retrieve information for viewing on a liquid crystal display. Users can access this data anywhere—at home, at the office, or while traveling. The Company offers an extensive electronic library including dictionaries and bilingual dictionaries; Bibles; medical reference works; encyclopedias; and entertainment, educational and tutorial publications. Franklin leads the field in areas vital to handheld electronic publishing: publisher relations; manufacturing; hardware and software technology; and market position in North America, Europe, The Middle East and Africa.

It was in 1985 that the company changed direction, leading to the introduction in late 1986 of its first electronic book, the Spelling Ace. Instead of trying to get a computer into every home, Franklin decided to try to get five computers in every home. The company decided to develop a new product, one that was small and inexpensive and had a limited set of functions.

In May 1986 Franklin acquired Proximity Technology, which was the nation's largest supplier of linguistic software. Proximity licensed more than one million spell-check and related products to typewriter and computer producers annually. Its CEO, Peter Yianilos, became Franklin's chief scientist and remained head of the Proximity subsidiary. While with Proximity, he had developed a prototype of a pocket-sized spell-check product with Jim Simons, who was now Franklin's largest stockholder with a 45.7 percent interest in the company. When Yianilos approached David about the product, David gave him an immediate go-ahead. The result was Spelling Ace, the world's first electronic speller.

1986: First Electronic Book Released

Spelling Ace debuted at around $90 retail. The price was later reduced to $70, attracting the interest of retailers such as K Mart and Sears. The response was sensational, and Franklin sold more than 800,000 Spelling Aces in the first two years. The new product triggered Franklin's first profitable quarter since 1984, and for fiscal 1998 Franklin turned a profit of $2.8 million. The Spelling Ace and other new electronic books accounted for about half of the company's sales. The rest of its revenues still came from selling and supporting Apple- and IBM-compatible computers.

Soon after, Franklin introduced an electronic dictionary and thesaurus, followed by a speller for children. Word Wiz, designed for children who spell poorly, combined Spelling Ace with the capability to play word games. Spellmaster was the adult version of Word Wiz. Other new products included Word Master, an electronic thesaurus with 470,000 synonyms for 35,000 words, and Language Master, which included a dictionary, thesaurus, and spell-checker.

Commenting on the company's change of direction, CEO David told the *Philadelphia Business Journal,* "We're really becoming a publishing company." One of the company's new strengths was its exclusive agreement with Merriam-Webster, Inc., which allowed it to use the dictionary-maker's words and definitions.

Expanding to International Markets in 1987

In 1987 Franklin developed and produced British English versions of its American English electronic books for the U.K. and Australian markets, beginning with a British version of Spelling Ace. Some of the first British English products were an electronic spelling book based on a list of 70,000 words licensed from HarperCollins and a children's dictionary incorporating a database from the *Oxford Children's Dictionary.* Monolingual books were subsequently developed for other international markets such as France, Germany, and Spain and South America.

For the 1987 Christmas season Franklin only had four products for sale. By the end of 1988 it had introduced ten new products, including new and more sophisticated versions of its thesauri and dictionaries. Franklin claimed 80 percent of the electronic book market. It faced growing competition from companies such as Smith Corona Inc., Seiko Instruments USA Inc., Selectronics Inc., and Texas Instruments Inc., but by 1991 Smith Corona had exited the electronic reference book business after its spell-checkers and thesauri failed to sell well. Following the success of Spelling Ace, the Minneapolis-based Selectronics introduced Wordfinder, which contained 100,000 words in its spelling bank and 220,000 synonyms.

During 1988 Franklin moved into larger headquarters, from its 27,000-square-foot offices in Pennsauken, New Jersey to a 40,000-square-foot facility in Mount Holly, New Jersey. Its products were manufactured in Asian factories, although the company was considering manufacturing some of its more expensive products at its Mount Holly facility. Sales in fiscal 1989 (ending March 31) were $67.3 million, more than the total domestic sales of paper dictionaries, which were estimated to be in the range of $55 to $65 million. With prices ranging from $49 to $350 for its products, Franklin claimed that one or more of its products was carried in some 13,000 retail outlets ranging from K Mart and Sears to Bloomingdales and The Sharper Image.

In January 1989 Franklin introduced several new products targeted at the school market, including a spelling dictionary packaged with a Merriam-Webster Elementary School Dictionary. Students could type in what they thought a word sounded like and then see the correct spelling. Franklin marketed directly to schools through its Franklin Learning Division. By 1992 the company claimed its products were in use in 9,000 schools.

Name Change in 1990

Franklin changed its name to Franklin Electronic Publishers, Inc. in 1990. The company reported losses for fiscal 1990 and 1991, but with the quarter ending September 30, 1991, Franklin returned to profitability. It earned $1.47 million on sales of $17.73 million that quarter. During the next quarter, typically the company's strongest because of Christmas retail sales, it reported the second highest Christmas quarter earnings in its history: $1.9 million on declining sales of $16.74 million. The profitable quarters were a result of cost cutting and improved profit margins. The company was able to reduce the price of its new electronic dictionary to around $100, compared with $300 for its first electronic dictionary.

Profitability in Fiscal 1992

After two years of losses, Franklin was on solid footing with net income of $3.1 million on sales of $53.8 million for the fiscal year 1992 ending March 31. It was the first of several years of growing profitability, as the company was able to cut costs and expenses, introduce new products, and expand into international markets.

Research and development on new products and technologies would be an important part of Franklin's growth over the next several years. In November 1991 the company named Edgar T. "Ned" Irons as chief scientist. Irons had achieved national recognition for his invention of the Syntax Directed Compiler, a technique for parsing sentences according to a formal description of grammar. The former chairman and co-founder of the Computer Science Department at Yale University, Irons was hired to lead Franklin's research and development team. According to the *Burlington (N.J.) County Times,* "The company hopes to develop machines that can comprehend the nuances of a language, such as the difference between 'threw' and 'through.' Presently, computers can tell if the word is spelled correctly, but not if it's being used correctly."

In January 1992 Franklin unveiled its Language Master at the Las Vegas consumer electronics show. The company described it as "the world's first talking hand-held dictionary, spell checker, and grammar guide," according to the *Burlington (N.J.) County Times.* At the same show Franklin introduced Big League Baseball, an electronic baseball encyclopedia with data supplied by Total Baseball. Franklin's Big League Baseball contained key statistics for every player in the history of the National and American Leagues.

In 1992 Franklin began to market its products directly in selected international markets by establishing wholly owned, local subsidiaries. The first, Franklin Electronic Publishers (U.K.) Ltd., was established in the United Kingdom in mid-1992 to market and distribute British English versions of Franklin's books. Franklin hoped that its presence in England would help it forge closer ties with Oxford University Press, with whom it was developing new electronic titles. French and Canadian subsidiaries were established in 1994, and German and Australian subsidiaries were established in 1995.

Franklin's line of electronic books included more than 30 titles in 1992, prior to the introduction of the Digital Book System (DBS) in October. Each title was self-contained within a dedicated playing unit. With the introduction of the Digital Book System, however, users would have a single playing unit that would take interchangeable electronic book cartridges. This would result in lower costs to consumers purchasing multiple titles.

The first DBS retail package included two digital books and sold for approximately $200. One was Merriam-Webster's Dictionary Plus dictionary and thesaurus, which contained more than 274,000 definitions and 496,000 synonyms. The second was Word Games, a package of ten challenging word games. Also available was the Video Companion, a guide to 10,000 movies available on videotape, and The Medical Letter Handbook of Adverse Drug Interactions.

The Digital Book System won several awards, including "Best of What's New" from *Popular Science,* the first Technical Achievement/Innovation award presented at the third annual LMP Awards, and the Innovations '93 Design & Engineering Honors presented at the 1993 Summer Consumer Electronics Show.

By this time Franklin claimed to have sold more than five million handheld electronic dictionaries, spelling correctors, puzzle solvers, Bibles, and sports encyclopedias.

Franklin established Medical Digital Book Systems and introduced the Digital Book System for the medical market in 1992. One of its first medical titles was called Med-Spell, which contained some 250,000 medical terms, drug names, and words of general usage. Franklin's Digital Book library grew to include several medical titles, including *Physicians Desk Reference (PDR), Handbook of Adverse Drug Interactions, The Merck Manual, Harrison's Principles of Internal Medicine Companion Handbook,* and other titles.

By negotiating with key medical publishers to produce electronic versions of their products, Franklin was able to capture a large vertical market for its electronic books. In the course of just a few months Franklin sold more than 20,000 Digital Book Systems to doctors. In some cases, the medical publishers themselves would distribute both the print and electronic versions of their titles. For example, Medical Economics Data, the publisher of the *Physicians Desk Reference,* distributed both the printed and electronic book versions of that title.

Sales for fiscal 1993 increased to $65.4 million, and net income more than doubled to $7.1 million, due in large part to the popularity of the baseball encyclopedia and other new products. By mid-1993 the company offered approximately 15 electronic books for use with its Digital Book System, including *Parker's Wine Guide, The Concise Columbia Encyclopedia,* a baseball encyclopedia, several medical reference works, and dictionaries and thesauri.

In fall 1993 Franklin released DBS-2, the second generation of its Digital Book System. The DBS-2 could access 200 megabytes of data, substantially more than the DBS-1. It was also cheaper, retailing for approximately $130. The new model had audio capabilities and serial connectivity.

Franklin also established a Custom Book Division to develop custom electronic books for commercial applications. The first such custom electronic book that Franklin produced was an electronic catalog for Allen-Bradley, a $1.5 billion manufacturer of sensors and components, that could be used by the company's sales force. Although the Allen-Bradley deal was not "significant to Franklin's revenues," according to Executive Vice-President Michael Strange, it was expected to be the first of many such deals. Franklin boasted that it could convert a prototype of a company database or other intellectual property in a single day, and once the customized electronic book was refined, it could be sold to the company for less than $100 per unit.

In other ventures Franklin partnered with SkyTel Corporation to produce an electronic paging system for use with Franklin's Digital Book System. SkyTel, a leading provider of nationwide messaging services, and Franklin would produce a matchbook-size electronic pager card to work with Franklin's Digital Book System. Users would then be able to receive wireless messaging services directly on their handheld Digital Book System unit. The product was aimed at mobile professionals who rely on portable electronic databases when traveling and working in the field.

Launching New Product Lines in the Mid-1990s

In 1995 Franklin launched its Bookman product line, which came with an installed database and included a slot for plugging in a second electronic book. Prices varied depending on the title. Previously, the DBS product was a player only, with two slots for electronic book cards. With the advent of the Bookman product line, the Digital Book System eventually was limited to medical titles. The company planned to phase out the DBS in March 1998 and replace it with a product that better served the medical marketplace.

Meanwhile, the company's international business was exploding. During fiscal 1995, international sales accounted for 28 percent of Franklin's $83.2 million in sales, up from 14 percent in fiscal 1994. In November 1995 the company announced it would open a subsidiary in Mexico in 1996 as a way to enter the Latin American market, which it did. It also established a subsidiary in Colombia in 1996 and, in early 1997, Franklin Italy opened in Milan. In April 1997 Franklin further expanded into Europe by acquiring Advanced Data Management Group S.A., a Belgian-based distributor of electronic products that served the Benelux countries (Belgium, Netherlands, and Luxembourg).

In other ventures, Franklin licensed its Bookman technology to the electronic firm Brother International, which would begin including built-in Bookman slots in selected word processors in 1996. Until now, Bookman cartridges could only be accessed through Franklin's handheld Bookman hardware, which retailed for between $50 and $130. Now, Bookman cartridge owners could use the product in a word processor with a larger screen. Approximately 30 different Bookman cartridges were available at this time.

In 1996 Franklin completed construction of its new 90,000-square-foot corporate headquarters in Burlington, New Jersey.

Franklin's first personal information management (PIM) product, the Bookman Sidekick Palmtop Organizer, was introduced in 1996. In 1997 the company began selling this line of personal organizers under the Rolodex Electronics trademark, which it acquired from Insilco Corporation for approximately $16 million in cash in October 1996.

Following the Rolodex Electronics acquisition, Franklin released its first entry into the telephone business, a high-quality Rolodex Electronics conference telephone, and planned to in-

troduce a line of full-feature Caller ID products. Using the Rolodex Electronics brand name, Franklin planned to enter much larger markets than those served by its content-driven products. Franklin hoped to use the Rolodex Electronics brand name to achieve the same dominance in the PIM market as it had in the electronic book market.

In spite of weakness in the domestic consumer electronic market during fiscal 1996 and 1997, Franklin continued to introduce new content-rich products and expand into international markets. During fiscal 1997 it introduced Homework Wiz for kids, a low price-point dictionary for six- to seven-year-olds. During the 1996–97 school year the company introduced the Speak English! Language Tutor as part of its Bookman line. The product helps people learn how to speak English by recording the user's speech and playing it back and comparing it to Franklin's compressed speech. Several new Bookman products for nurses were also introduced, including *Nursing Diagnoses and Classifications* and Springhouse's *Nursing97 Drug Handbook*.

In February 1997 Franklin entered into an agreement with Liris to develop, publish, and distribute French titles in handheld electronic platforms and ROM cards. Liris is a publisher of dictionaries, thesauri, and encyclopedias under several well-known French trademarks, including Larousse, Le Robert, Nathan, Dalloz, Masson, and Bouquins.

In May 1997 Franklin formed a joint venture called Pacrim with Kinpo Electronic, a Taiwan-based manufacturer of electronic products, to develop a range of handheld electronic products for China, Taiwan, Hong Kong, and other international markets. The company quickly established a new wholly owned subsidiary in Singapore to service markets in southeast Asia.

Franklin was also interested in incorporating voice recognition technology into some of its products, and in May 1997 it acquired certain existing product lines and technology from Voice Powered Technology International, Inc. It planned to develop a line of voice-controlled electronic organizers as part of the Rolodex Electronics line.

In October 1997 Franklin began shipping the Rex PC Companion, which enabled users to download organizer data from their personal computers to the portable device. The credit card-size PC-Card was developed in partnership with Starfish Software and the Citizen Watch Company of Japan. Since the original files reside on the PC, users can ''download and go'' without worrying about losing organizer data. Two available models were priced at around $130 and $150.

In October 1997 CEO and President David announced he would be leaving the company in February 1998, after 14 years there. After steering Franklin out of bankruptcy in the 1980s, David redefined the company and changed it from a computer maker to an electronic publisher. Under his leadership, Franklin refined its electronic books, steadily lowering their prices to make them more affordable to a wide range of consumers. He built upon the success of Franklin's electronic books to expand the company's product lines into personal information management and related areas. At the time of his departure, he had set Franklin on a course to grow in several directions.

Principal Subsidiaries

Franklin France, Franklin Australia, Franklin Colombia, Franklin Mexico, Franklin Italy, Franklin Germany, Franklin Canada, Franklin Europe.

Further Reading

Abbazia, Len, "Franklin Announces First in Series of Electronic Books for Nurses," *PR Newswire,* November 13, 1995.

——, "Franklin To Acquire Distributor of Electronic Products for the Netherlands, Belgium and Luxembourg," *PR Newswire,* April 14, 1997.

Abelson, Reed, "Franklin Won't Fold Its Hand in Competitive PC Industry," *Philadelphia Business Journal,* September 8, 1986.

——, "If at First . . . Franklin Tries, Tries Again with New Computer, Capital," *Philadelphia Business Journal,* September 2, 1985.

Aregood, Chris, "Franklin, Brother Form Alliance in Technology," *Philadelphia Business Journal,* October 20, 1995.

Armstrong, Michael W., "Franklin Computer Scores by Assisting Poor Spellers," *Philadelphia Business Journal,* December 28, 1987.

——, "Franklin Steps in with Stats Junkies," *Philadelphia Business Journal,* January 27, 1992.

——, "Still Spelling Success at Franklin Computer," *Philadelphia Business Journal,* August 22, 1988.

——, "Surviving Competition, Franklin Looks To Expand," *Philadelphia Business Journal,* July 30, 1990.

David, Morton E., "Franklin Electronic Publishers Establishes Subsidiary for Sale of Electronic Books in the United Kingdom," *Business Wire,* May 28, 1995.

Davis, Jessica, "New Division for Franklin Electronic," *Philadelphia Business Journal,* October 8, 1993.

Elser, Christopher, "He Dreams Up Programs for Computer Firm," *Burlington County Times,* January 6, 1992.

Fendrick, Mindy, "Franklin and SkyTel Join Forces To Create Pager System That Will Offer Wireless Messaging Plus Data Updates," *Business Wire,* January 6, 1994.

——, "Franklin Ships World's First PDA—$199 Digital Book System," *Business Wire,* October 26, 1992.

——, "Franklin To Publish Hoover's Handbook of American Business," *Business Wire,* July 28, 1993.

Fendrick, Mindy, and Goldman, Jill, "Franklin Names Edgar T. Irons as Chief Scientist," *Business Wire,* November 11, 1991.

Gill, David, "Franklin's Find," *Business Journal of New Jersey,* September 1988.

Stoltzfus, Duane, "Merck Manual Goes Digital," *Record* (Hackensack, New Jersey), June 1, 1994.

Van Horn, James, "Franklin Computer Corp.: Trying To Turn Reorganization Plan into Profits," *Business Journal of New Jersey,* May 23, 1985.

Walters, Laurel Shaper, "At Hand: Palm Size Computer Helpers," *Christian Science Monitor,* August 26, 1991.

Wilen, John, "Franklin Electronic Takes a Byte Out of the Mexican Market," *Philadelphia Business Journal,* November 24, 1995.

Winsky, Gregory J., "Simon & Schuster and Franklin Sign Electronic Book Distribution Agreement," *Business Wire,* July 23, 1992.

—David Bianco

Fred's, Inc.

4300 New Getwell Road
Memphis, Tennessee 38118
U.S.A.
(901) 365-8880
Fax: (901) 365-8865

Public Company
Incorporated: 1947 as Baddour, Inc.
Employees: 4,800
Sales: $492.2 million (1997)
Stock Exchanges: NASDAQ
SICs: 5331 Variety Stores

Fred's, Inc. is a discount retailer with stores in ten states in the southeastern United States. Serving small and medium sized towns, Fred's stores offer housewares, pharmaceuticals, clothing and linens, health and beauty aids, paper and cleaning supplies, food, and tobacco products, including more than 300 items with the proprietary Fred's label. According to demographic studies, the company's typical customer is a woman over age 25 who lives in a rural location and has a household income of $25,000. As of February 1998, Fred's operated 261 discount general merchandise stores, over a dozen stand-alone Fred's Xpress pharmacies, and a mail order pharmacy facility. More than 110 of the stores have full-service pharmacies and some 90 locations have lawn and garden centers. The company also markets goods and services to 31 franchised Fred's stores.

1947–88: Founding as Baddour, Inc.

The history of Fred's, Inc. may be traced to the mid-1940s founding of Baddour, Inc. Paul Baddour and his two brothers, sons of Lebanese immigrants, started the family-owned retail business in 1947, with one "Good Luck" store in Coldwater, Mississippi. Paul incorporated the company as Baddour, Inc., but as he expanded the chain throughout the Southeast, he began naming the individual stores after one of his brothers, Fred.

Fred's stores were located in such small towns as Stamps, Arkansas, and Iuka, Mississippi, and offered mostly closeout items that could be sold at discounted prices. The company grew in its niche market, opening franchised units as well as its own new stores for nearly 20 years, until a major upheaval occurred on the discount store scene with the arrival of Sam Walton and his Wal-Mart stores.

Beginning in 1962, Walton moved into rural areas, first in Arkansas and Missouri, and then across the South, opening stores that were much larger than those already serving a town and stocking a much wider variety of discount priced merchandise.

Paul M. Baddour took over the presidency of Baddour Inc. from his father in the early 1970s, determined to compete head-on with Wal-Mart. He built bigger stores, increasing the size of the average Fred's from 5,000 square-feet to 30,000 square-feet, and ordered a broader inventory of merchandise, including products with the "Fred's" label. In 1980, he created a subsidiary, Retail Consulting Services, Inc., to provide advice and services to other retailers. One of its first projects, developed originally for the rapidly growing Fred's, was an integrated inventory management system called SWORD (Store, Warehouse, Ordering, Replenishment and Distribution). Among the customers for at least certain aspects of the program were G.C. Murphy Co. and Grand Central in Salt Lake City.

By the mid-1980s, Fred's company had over 200 locations, but the expansion had left Baddour $56 million in debt, and its banks wanted their money. At this time, the Memphis Retail Investors Limited Partnership (MRILP) entered the scene, lending Baddour Inc. $15.3 million at an interest rate of 8.95 percent in 1986. This allowed the company to pay back its more expensive debt. In return, MRILP got the right to convert its note into 51 percent of the company's equity.

One of the major players in MRILP was Michael Hayes, who had just left Wall Street's Oppenheimer & Co., where he had been head of corporate finance. According to William Stern's article in *Forbes,* Hayes thought that with an infusion of money, Paul M. Baddour would be able to get the company back on track, and then MRILP would convert the note into shares, take the company public, and sell its equity at a big profit. Hayes, along with his partner, David Gardner, were elected to the board of directors in January 1987.

But things did not work out as Hayes hoped. Instead, the company lost $27 million over the next three years. MRILP went to court in Tennessee and, in the autumn of 1989, received 51 percent of the company under a court settlement. Paul M. Baddour resigned immediately, and Hayes and Gardner took over as managing directors in October, with Hayes also serving as chief executive.

1989–91: New Management and a New Name

Hayes and Gardner quickly moved to improve profitability, adopting five goals: 1) recapture traditional Fred's customers; 2) focus management, store managers, buyers, and pharmacists on profitability; 3) reduce employee turnover; 4) reduce corporate operating expenses; and 5) increase pharmacy and related products sales.

To accomplish these, Hayes revised the merchandise mix, eliminating expensive items such as microwaves and color TVs and concentrating on inexpensive household goods. He standardized store size and layout around a 13,000 square-foot model and closed several unprofitable locations. He also put into place a bonus incentive plan for all salaried employees and started a management training program. Finally, Hayes also changed the company's advertising strategy, eliminating direct mail circulars, adding coupon books, and using television and radio advertising, with an actor playing the role of "Fred" in the television ads.

Hayes' strategy was to make the smaller size of his stores a strength by appealing to customers who wanted to buy between five and ten specific items at a competitive price, in a friendly, familiar environment. He targeted customers who were not interested in roaming a huge superstore to find things they might need, and the company made the differentiation between "buying" at Fred's and "shopping" at larger, less conveniently located stores.

The changes quickly improved Fred's financial picture. In 1990, comparable store sales rose by six percent, and for the first time in four years, the company earned a profit. In 1991, net income tripled to $3.8 million on sales of $291 million. Moreover, the bonus incentive and training programs helped reduce the turnover among store management personnel, from 75 percent in 1988 to less than 25 percent in 1991. For store managers alone, turnover dropped from 55 percent to less than 20 percent in the same period.

Fred's stores were typically located in a shopping center or "strip mall" (anchored by a high-traffic grocery store) in small-to-medium sized towns. According to the 1993 *Forbes* article, Fred's could be profitable in a town with only 1,500 citizens, compared to Wal-Mart, which targeted towns with a population of 10,000 or more. Customers were generally low, middle, and fixed income families.

Fred's stores offered some 12,000 items, primarily merchandise that people purchased frequently. Stores with pharmacies stocked an additional 600 items. By 1991, the 45 in-store pharmacies accounted for 12.1 percent of store sales, up from 7.2 percent in 1988.

Fred's discount prices were typically lower than those at drug or smaller variety/dollar stores. In 1991, household goods made up just over a quarter of store sales, followed by health and beauty aids (17.5 percent), apparel and linens (17 percent), paper and cleaning supplies (15.2 percent), pharmaceuticals (12.1 percent), and food and tobacco products (11.4 percent). The company's private label products included pet foods, disposable diapers, paper products, beverages, household cleaning supplies, and health and beauty aids. In 1991, these products constituted about four percent of total sales.

In May 1991, Hayes was named company president, and the shareholders voted to change the company name from Baddour Inc. to Fred's Inc. The change, according to the company prospectus, reflected the company's focus on its store operations and away from the family name of the founders and former management.

1992–95: Emphasizing Pharmacies

In 1992, Hayes took the company public, selling 39 percent of the shares for $52 million and using proceeds to pay off most of the bank debt. At the time, Fred's operated in eight states and had 144 company-owned stores and 43 franchise stores.

During the year, Hayes opened 12 new stores, reaching 156 company-owned locations, while the number of franchised stores dropped to 39. As a result, in both 1991 and 1992, wholesale sales to franchisees and others declined as a percentage of total sales. Hayes also added pharmacies in 15 stores, bringing the total to 60. At end of the fiscal year, the company, which was now operating in nine states, paid its first quarterly cash dividend, $.04 per share.

In 1993, Hayes began exploring the possibilities of significantly increasing the company's size. In March, the company announced plans to buy Bill's Dollar Stores. Bill's, a privately held discount retailer based in Jackson, Mississippi, had 530 stores in 13 southern states. If the two chains had joined, they would have had total sales of over $540, but the merger did not happen. Three years later, on March 1, 1996, the company announced it had reached an agreement in principal to a merger with Rose's Stores, Inc. But the acquisition of Rose's, which had 105 retail stores in ten southeastern states, was also canceled later that year.

While Fred's management had concluded that merging with these other discount store chains would not be as beneficial as originally anticipated, the company did acquire a drug store chain. In 1995, Fred's paid Southern Wholesale Co. $3 million in cash for 18 Super D stores in Alabama, Georgia, North Carolina, and Tennessee. The company also acquired one independent pharmacy that year. Five of the purchases were established as stand-alone Fred's Xpress pharmacies. That concept, with locations ranging in size from 1,000 to 6,000 square feet and selling pharmaceuticals and other health and beauty items, allowed Fred's to enter a new market less expensively than if it were to open a new store. The company's plan was to expand these locations into a full-size Fred's when business warranted. At the end of 1995, in addition to the five Fred's Xpress units, the company had 87 stores with full service pharmacies.

Prescriptions and other pharmacy products were an increasingly important part of Fred's merchandise mix. In 1995, pharmaceuticals accounted for nearly 18 percent of sales, the second largest sales category, behind household goods. This performance occurred amid the growth in alternative sources for prescriptions resulting from the managed care movement. Third-party firms, such as health maintenance organizations, hospitals, and mail-order houses, paid 70 percent of all prescription drug bills in 1995, up from four percent in 1960.

As more employers shifted their employees' health coverage to managed care or health maintenance organizations, pharmacies and drug store chains were under great pressure. That pressure led to consolidation in the drugstore business and helped Fred's strategy of expanding its pharmacy activities by acquiring established independent pharmacies. The company either employed the pharmacists whose operation the company bought or purchased customer lists from retiring independent pharmacists.

The Mid-1990s and Beyond

Fred's continued to increase the number of pharmacies in its stores, reaching 101 by the end of 1996, more than double the number of pharmacies there had been five years before. The importance of this segment of products to the company was reflected in its portion of sales, which reached nearly 20 percent in 1996. The company also implemented a new pharmacy management system that provided centralized control of its chain of pharmacies.

Still, the company was not ignoring its other merchandise categories. It expanded its selection of garden supplies and established lawn and garden centers. By 1996, 89 of the stores had such centers, and 26 were full-line centers complete with green houses, a wide selection of garden equipment and tools, and live plants. During the year, Fred's also introduced moderately priced videos and pre-paid telephone calling cards as well as new items with the Fred's label.

During this period, the company restructured its management ranks and revised its pricing strategy, introducing everyday low prices in 1994. The process involved reducing prices for many key items and eliminating four sale events in 1995 and two in 1996. Initially, this resulted in a significant drop in net income in 1995. But by 1996, customers began to shop at Fred's more regularly, not just during sales events. Although the average customer in 1996 spent 10 cents less each time she shopped at Fred's ($11.15), there were one million more customer transactions (34 million) than there were in 1995.

1997 proved to be a very good year for the company, with record sales and growth. Sales for the year increased 17.7 percent to $492.2 million, up from $418.3 in 1996. Sales in stores that had been operating for a least 12 months rose 8.3 percent from the prior year. In November, Fred's bought 17 drug stores from CVS Corporation, expanding the company's presence in Georgia, Mississippi, and Tennessee and continuing its growing presence in the pharmacy business. That presence was further enhanced when Hayes announced in February 1998 that Fred's had opened a mail order pharmacy facility and had signed its first national contract with participants in all 50 states. Fred's moved into its sixth decade of operations secure in its own niche. And through its pharmacy segment, with its increased buying power and systems capabilities, the company was moving to become the preeminent pharmacy in its markets.

Principal Subsidiaries

Fred's Stores of Tennessee, Inc.; Fred's Capital Management Company; Fred's Real Estate and Equipment Management Corporation.

Further Reading

"At Baddour: How Fred's Is Flourishing with Its SWORD," *Stores,* March 1983, p. 56.

"Fred's Completes Acquisition of 17 Stores," *Business Wire,* November 24, 1997.

"Fred's Reports Record January and Full-Year Sales," *Business Wire,* February 5, 1998.

Stern, William, "From Wall Street to Nowhere Street," *Forbes,* November 8, 1993, p. 116.

—Ellen D. Wernick

Fromageries Bel

16, boulevard Malesherbes
75008 Paris
France
(33) 1.40.07.75.69
Fax: (33) 1.40.07.72.30

Public Company
Incorporated: 1922 as S.A. Fromageries Bel, La Vache
   Qui Rit
Employees: 7,807
Sales: FFr 8.62 billion (US $1.5 billion) (1996)
Stock Exchanges: Paris
SICs: 5143 Dairy Products Except Dried or Canned

Fromageries Bel is France's third largest cheese producer, after Besnier and Bongrain. Together these three companies produce more than half of the total cheese sales in the country with the highest per capita cheese consumption in the world. Whereas Besnier and Bongrain concentrate on pressed and molded cheese varieties, Bel has captured more than 75 percent of the French "melted" cheese market—principally through its legendary brand, La Vache Qui Rit (The Laughing Cow)—while possessing a strong domestic and international presence in this and other cheese varieties. With 23 production plants, including 14 plants located outside of France, Bel products reach consumers in 90 countries. French sales account for 42 percent of the company's 1996 annual sales of FFr 8.6 billion. The company's aggressive international expansion during the 1990s, however, has increased its European sales (outside of France) by more than 60 percent in just five years; these sales account for some 38 percent of Bel's annual sales. Since the mid-1990s, Bel has targeted the United States for further growth. In 1996 the company acquired "cold pack" leader Kaukauna Cheese Inc., of Wisconsin, doubling its U.S. presence. Asia and the Middle East also form important markets for the company.

A public company since the 1950s, Fromageries Bel has maintained its independence through the 60 percent shareholder position of La Carbonique, a holding company operated by the Bel family. La Carbonique also holds 85 percent of the company's voting rights, making Bel practically invulnerable to any potential takeover attempts. Since the retirement of long-time company president Robert Fiévet, son-in-law of La Vache Qui Rit creator, Léon Bel, the company has been directed by Bertrand Dufort, son-in-law of Fiévet.

Bel's chief asset is its portfolio of brand names. In addition to the internationally recognized La Vache Qui Rit, which is marketed worldwide under translations specific to each country market, the company's brands include Bonbel, Babybel, Apericube, Kiri, Port Salut, Pik et Croq, as well as a strong list of country-specific brands, including Wispride, Price's, and Kaukauna in the United States. The company's annual production tops 220,000 tons, using nearly three million liters of milk. Bel also produces a variety of industrial food-grade products, including milk and cheese cultures, and other materials for chocolate, ice cream, meat processing, and other food industries.

A Symbol for the Century in the 1920s

That the Bel family-owned company began not as a cheese producer, but rather as a maturing house for locally produced cheeses, might have provided the proper environment for the product that would make the company's name and fortune. In a country where the production of cheeses remained a craft and tradition until well into the 20th century and where each locality's specialty cheese variety received a reverence as great as its local wine, the invention of a new type of cheese could be regarded as revolutionary. Yet La Vache Qui Rit would become more than a new type of cheese—indeed, the Laughing Cow would grow into one of the most loved symbols of 20th century France.

Jules Bel founded the family business in 1865, in France's Jura region, near the Swiss border and sharing its neighbor's favored meal of cheese fondue. Production of the local molded cheese specialties, comté, a variety of gruyere, and emmenthal, also known as "Swiss" cheese, was by then already a cooperative endeavor. Dairy farmers delivered their milk to the local cheese maker, who was responsible for processing the milk into rounds of gruyere, as well as other cheese varieties. Once formed, the rounds underwent an aging process, a step assured by master-refiner Jules Bel. Opening his business in Orgelet, Bel offered the vaulted wine cellars of a former Capuchin convent, which had been abandoned since the French Revolution, for the curing of the local cooperative's cheeses. Bel also acted as a clearinghouse for the sale of the matured cheese.

Jules Bel was joined and then succeeded by son Léon Bel. Toward the end of the First World War, the younger Bel's attention was attracted by the leftovers of unsold comté and emmenthal. Rather than allow them to go to waste, Bel believed he could find a use for the leftover rounds, and he set about experimenting with creating a new type of cheese. Installing the company business, which also began its own production of gruyere and Swiss cheeses, in nearby Lons-le Saunier, Bel developed a "fondu" or melted cheese by blending the leftover comté and emmenthal, as well as other cheese varieties. Bel's cheese, apart from its unique flavor, retained a softened, easily molded consistency and, being cooked, also offered a long preservation life. Yet the cheese's success would come especially from Léon Bel's flair for marketing.

In 1921 Bel registered a trademark name for his product: La Vache Qui Rit. Bel was not content merely to present his cheese under this odd and evocative name, but recognized as well the importance of its packaging. Turning to one of France's most celebrated graphic designers of the time, Benjamin Rabier, noted especially for his drawings and caricatures of animals and with whom Bel had served in the French army during the First World War, Bel commissioned a symbol that would give life to the cheese's name. By 1922 Rabier had succeeded in "making a cow laugh." Bel incorporated his company as Fromageries Bel, La Vache Qui Rit and began production in that year.

La Vache Qui Rit, sold in small, round metal containers, featuring Rabier's design, as well as the product's prominent description as a "modern cheese," would prove quickly popular throughout France—and, given its name and design, appealed particularly to France's children. Bel went even further to popularize his product, displaying a flair for modern advertising techniques as well. An early advertiser on France's new radio networks, Bel would employ a wide variety of media and techniques, including posters, but also innovations such as a six-day bicycle race ("Les Six Jours de la Vache Qui Rit"), rivaling the already traditional Tour de France, other competitions and games, comparative advertising campaigns, as well as including children's gifts such as trading cards with the

cheese's packaging. In 1926 Bel also took the step, unusual for the time, of creating a separate publicity department; among the new department's activities was the use of consumer research techniques, such as questionnaires and tasting groups.

Bel continued to perfect his cheese recipe, producing a still softer, flavorful product, while touting its natural ingredients, as well as its high fat content (important to the quality of a cheese). The company also would quickly recognize the rising popularity of snack foods, packaging the cheese into its famous, and eminently snackable, triangular-shaped portions. By the beginning of the 1930s La Vache Qui Rit also had become an international favorite, crossing the Channel into England. There the company made another important decision: rather than market the cheese under its French name, Bel chose to translate the brand directly into that country's language. "The Laughing Cow" would eventually be joined by such siblings as "La Vaca Que Rie," "Den Leende Ko," "Vesela Kráva," "A Vaca Que Ri," and many others. As such, the cheese and its package would become an internationally recognized symbol on the scale of another rising product of the time, Coca Cola.

In 1933 the company expanded into Belgium, opening its first foreign production plant. Soon after, Léon Bel was joined by son-in-law Robert Fiévet. In 1937 Bel named Fiévet as the company's CEO; in 1957 Fiévet took over the company's presidency. If Léon Bel had succeeded in establishing La Vache Qui Rit as a successful product, Fiévet would build the company into one of the top three cheese producers in France.

Expanding in the Mid-20th Century

Under Fiévet, Bel, which had continued to produce its own gruyere and emmenthal cheese, began expanding its line of brand names. In 1938 the company introduced a new pressed cheese, under the name Bonbel, playing on the French word for "good." Bonbel, too, proved successful with the French—and international—consumer. Bonbel would be followed by the launch of other successful brands, such as Babybel, in 1952; Apéricube, ideal for the growing cocktail trend of the late 1950s; Kiri, a cream cheese for "the gourmet in short pants" of the 1960s; and the 1970s Port Salut. These brands, together with La Vache Qui Rit, would spearhead the company's international development.

In the 1950s Bel prepared to step up its growth beyond France's borders. With Fiévet named as president, Bel reorganized, moved its headquarters to Paris, and listed on the Paris Stock Exchange. Meanwhile, La Vache Qui Rit was undergoing a transformation. Its famous drawing, unchanged since the 1920s, had begun to age with the consumer. The company commissioned a new design, which, although building on the original, brought La Vache Qui Rit closer to its final form, that of a simplified graphic symbol, rather than an illustration. The restructuring of the company, meanwhile, was also transforming its business model, as the company's strategy turned toward a focus on expansion of its branded products within specific product categories.

By the late 1950s Bel's attention turned toward expansion. Beyond promoting its brand names, the company set upon a course of expanding its domestic and international presence. The first step was achieved in 1959, when the company formed a new subsidiary, Belco, bringing the company's production facilities to Germany. This subsidiary was joined by a move into Spain in the mid-1960s. At home, the company also began acquiring other cheese producers and their cheese varieties, including the purchase of Graf in 1960, Rentz, and its molded cheeses, in 1962, and Fromageries Picon and the dairy Société Laitière Vendômoisc in 1968.

Bel stepped up its expansion in the 1970s, beginning with the 1970 acquisition of Albany Cheese, which brought the company into the United States, and the purchase of the Agricole de Roquefort et Maria Grimal, adding the important Roquefort variety to the company's product line; the following year the company added the Société Samos, of France. The Albany Cheese purchase, with plants in Kentucky, would introduce the United States to The Laughing Cow, as well as the company's other brands. In 1973 the company acquired British cheese maker Crowson and Son Ltd., before forming subsidiaries Sogedis and Cofroma, expanding its facilities into Switzerland and Morocco in 1974. The successful launch of the company's Port Salut brand in 1976 was joined by several new cheese varieties, including molded Brie and Camembert cheeses. That same year Bel acquired Société Anonyme des Fermiers Reúnis (SAFR) and its subsidiaries in Germany, Italy, England, and Sweden. The company's international growth would be accompanied not only by the expansion of its core French brands into these new markets, but also by the development of country-specific brand names and cheese varieties.

By the late 1970s a new generation was entering the family-owned company, with the appointment of Bertrand Dufort, Fiévet's son-in-law, to the position of the company's vice-president. Fiévet, however, would remain the company's president for nearly 20 more years and lead it into its strongest growth years. In 1981 the company simplified its name, to Fromageries Bel. A new subsidiary, Beldis, was added in the Netherlands in 1983, but the company's biggest expansion would occur during the mid-1980s. Beginning in 1985, Bel began acquiring the cheese making activities of Swiss giant Nestlé, including its Price's and Wispride brands in the United States, doubling the company's revenues. Although the company had long since captured more than 75 percent of the French soft cheese markets, the expansion of its U.S. activities would also bring the company head-to-head with its chief rival, Kraft, and that company's assorted cheese and cheese-like products. The Price's and Wispride acquisitions were quickly followed by the purchases of Adler in Germany and Fromagerie de Maredsous in Belgium. By the beginning of the 1990s, Bel had grown to annual sales of nearly FFr 7 billion, of which nearly one-third was generated beyond France.

A Firm Family Grip in the 1990s

Bel was not alone as a French cheese powerhouse. Another group, Besnier, led by Michel Besnier, had been performing its own aggressive expansion—and nearly single-handed consolidation of the French dairy industry. Besnier, along with the other leading cheese producer Bongrain, had developed its presence most strongly in the pressed and molded cheese segments. In 1993, however, Besnier began eyeing Bel and its lock on the French melted cheese market. Beginning in January of that year, Besnier, whose own company was private and entirely owned by the Besnier family, began purchasing shares in Bel. From 1993 to September 1994, Besnier succeeded in raising his stake in Bel's voting rights from five percent to more than 20 percent. Indeed, Bel seemed an easy target: Fiévet was by then 84 years old and the Bel family was afflicted with the succession issues common among such family-owned enterprises. Besnier, however, had reckoned without considering La Carbonique, the holding company set up by the Bel family as early as 1921 and operated, since 1970, as the Bel company's majority shareholder. With 60 percent of Bel's stock and the overwhelming majority of the company's voting rights, Bel was easily able to face the threat of a takeover. As the company told *Le Point,* "Our capital is totally locked up. Nothing can happen."

The issue of succession seemed settled when, in 1995, Fiévet stepped down from the company's leadership, taking the title of honorary president. Son-in-law and longtime partner Bertrand Dufort was named as the company's new president and CEO. Meanwhile, the company reorganized its structure, creating a new division to guide its domestic activities and placing the United States, Portugal, Italy, and Spain operations under its headquarters, while regrouping its other European subsidiaries under Bel Europe and its further international subsidiaries (chiefly Asia, Africa, and the Middle East) under the Bel International Division.

Bel continued to make acquisitions during the 1990s. In 1994 the company acquired Cademartori in Italy and Quesarias Ibéricas in Spain. Its German subsidiaries, Adler and Belco, were fused to create Bel Adler Allgäu Gmbh & Co. Ohg. The company increased its presence in Portugal in 1996, with the 51 percent purchase of Lacto Ibérica. This acquisition placed Bel as that country's leading cheese producer. That same year, however, saw Bel make an important move to increase its U.S. presence: with the purchase of Kaukauna Cheese Inc., of Wisconsin, Bel more than doubled its U.S. sales. For the future, Bel could look forward to further international growth, while continuing to enjoy the worldwide success—and international recognition—of its La Vache Qui Rit.

Principal Subsidiaries

Fromageries Picon; Omnium du Lait et ses Dérivés; Société Anonyme des Fermiers Réunis; Sofico; Fromageries Bel Extension Belge; Bel Cheese USA; Bel UK; Belisa (Spain); Queserías Bel Espana; Sialim (Morocco); F.B. Holding B.V. (Netherlands); Fromageries Bel Italia; Queserías Ibéricas (Spain); Lacto Ibérica (Portugal).

Further Reading

Bonazza, Patrick, and Gubert, Romain, "Trois Familles à Couteaux Tirés," *Le Point,* October 15, 1994, p. 85.
Mitteaux, Valerie, "La Vache Qui Rit: Marylin de la Marque," *Prodimarques/La Revue des Marques,* April 1994, p. 23.
Fromageries Bel, "Le Groupe Bel," Paris, 1997.

—M.L. Cohen

Galeries Lafayette S.A.

40, boulevard Haussmann
75009 Paris
France
(33 1) 42 82 34 56
Fax: (33 1) 48 78 25 19
Web site: http://www.glparis.com

Public Company
Incorporated: 1905 as Société anonyme des Galeries
   Lafayette
Employees: 18,000
Sales: FFr 16.5 billion (US$3.19 billion)
Stock Exchanges: Paris
SICs: 511 Department Stores; 7389 Business Services,
   Not Elsewhere Classified; 5130 Apparel, Piece Goods,
   and Notions; 5812 Eating Places; 7374 Data
   Processing and Preparation

Galeries Lafayette S.A. is a holding company for four major retail chains, including Nouvelles Galeries, Bazar Hotel de Ville, and Monoprix. Its namesake chain of department stores boasts Europe's largest department store, the historic, ten-story flagship location in Paris. Known as "The Beautiful Lady," the 500,000 square-foot headquarters store generates well over a half-billion dollars in sales every year. Though its stock is publicly traded, descendants of the founding family continued to hold a controlling interest in the Galeries Lafayette group through the mid-1990s. In the 1990s the company struggled under the leadership of Georges Meyer to regain the profitability it had once enjoyed. Battered by recession, a misguided foray into the New York retail market, and a costly merger with the Nouvelles Galeries chain, the group's revenues declined from a high of FFr 33 billion in 1991 to less than FFr 29 billion in 1995. Net income also took a precipitous slide: after chalking up a FFr 301 million profit in 1991, the group broke even in 1993, then suffered a FFr 293 million loss in 1995. Although sales remained flat in 1996, Galeries Lafayette's profits rebounded to FFr 550 million that year.

Late 19th-Century Origins

The company's origins date to 1895, when Albert Kahn rented a shop in Paris at the corner of Chaussée-d'Antin and rue Lafayette to sell gloves, ribbons, veils, and other goods. The shop was small, but sales were good. It was eventually enlarged, and in 1898 Kahn was joined by his cousin, 34-year-old Théophile Bader. The partnership flourished and soon purchased the entire building along with adjacent buildings on the Chaussée-d'Antin. In 1905 a limited company was created, Société anonyme des Galeries Lafayette, with Bader as president. Kahn retired from active management and in 1912 sold his shares to Bader.

The company bought buildings on the other side of the Chaussée-d'Antin, on the corner of the boulevard Haussmann, and in 1906 it built a store bearing the name Aux Galeries Lafayette. By then, some 350 persons were employed in the various buildings. The company purchased more property along the boulevard Haussmann near rue Mogador, and Bader planned a completely new department store, which opened in 1912. The five-story building occupied around 3,000 square meters. The store had a giant glass dome, a sweeping monumental staircase rising up in the light well, and wrought-iron curved balconies overlooking the light well. By 1914 Galeries Lafayette employed over 1,000 people, and mail-order operations, begun in 1905, represented about a quarter of sales. In the Paris market, Galeries Lafayette was of equal importance to its near neighbor and competitor, the Printemps department store, which was some 30 years older. Both stores, however, lagged behind the Bon Marché and La Samaritaine stores.

Second Generation Advances in 1920s

In 1919 Bader brought Raoul Meyer, his 27-year-old son-in-law, into the management of the company. This was followed in 1926 by the appointment of Max Heilbronn, another son-in-law, aged 23. The three managed the group until 1935 when Bader became seriously ill, after which Meyer and Heilbronn directed the firm for another 35 years. During the 1920s the main store expanded gradually toward rue Mogador and rue de Provence. Expansion also took place outside Paris: in 1916 a store had been opened in Nice, followed by the purchase in 1919 of Les

Grands Magasins des Cordeliers in Lyons. A store opened in Nantes in 1923 and another in Montpellier in 1926, and at the same time the mail-order operations were consolidated, with a network of agents throughout France. By 1930 Galeries Lafayette had become the second-largest department store group in France, overtaken only by La Samaritaine, but ahead of Printemps. Bon Marché, Paris's oldest department store, was now in fourth position.

An important development in Galeries Lafayette's commercial policy took place in 1931 and 1932, when variety-store operations started. At the end of 1931 a subsidiary company, La Nouvelle Maison, was formed, and two variety stores called Lanoma were opened in Paris, followed in 1932 by two others, called Monoprix and located in the provinces. The name Lanoma was quickly abandoned, and all stores became Monoprix, with the subsidiary company changing its name to Société anonyme des Monoprix. To buy merchandise for the new variety stores, Société Centrale d'Achats (SCA) was formed in 1932.

The early years of the Monoprix variety stores were difficult, and they operated at a loss. Max Heilbronn traveled fortnightly to London to get inspiration from two well-established variety store groups, Woolworth and Marks & Spencer; he eventually received advice from Simon Marks himself. By 1935 the situation improved, and Monoprix continued to expand up to 1938, when a French law banning the opening of new one-price stores slowed down the development of owned stores; other retailers, though, were encouraged to join the SCA central buying organization. In 1938 there were 38 Monoprix stores. Twelve were owned stores and the rest were affiliates.

World War II and German Occupation

World War II was a troubled period for the Galeries Lafayette, and, being under Jewish management, it suffered severely during the German occupation of France. The leadership was disbanded, and the business landed in the hands of French *collaborateurs*— those who collaborated with the Germans. Raoul Meyer went into hiding in unoccupied territory. Max Heilbronn, after serving in the French army, took part in the *Résistance* and was caught in 1943 and sent to Buchenwald concentration camp. Bader, the company's founder, died in 1942.

At the end of the war Meyer and Heilbronn, who together owned 80 percent of Galeries Lafayette, began to rebuild the company. In 1947 they were joined by Etienne Moulin, aged 35, who had helped to save Max Heilbronn's life in Buchenwald and had subsequently married his daughter.

Their main efforts in the postwar years were directed toward the expansion of the Monoprix variety stores. By 1950 there were 60 Monoprix stores in France, half of which were owned and half of which were affiliates. Ten years later there were 200 Monoprix stores, and by 1965, there were 235—85 owned and 150 affiliated—with 200,000 square meters of selling space. Of the affiliated stores, 44 were linked directly or indirectly with the department store group Nouvelles Galeries Réunies. These affiliated stores had joined the SCA in 1952, when Galeries Lafayette, through Monoprix, acquired a 14 percent share in the company.

Acquisition of Inno-France in 1960s

For Monoprix and Galeries Lafayette, the early 1960s were marked by what can be called the Inno-France interlude. In 1960 Innovation S.A., a Belgian department store group, created in France a company called the Société des Grandes Entreprises de Distribution, Inno-France. The aim of this company was to establish large self-service units in France, selling food and other merchandise. These were similar to hypermarkets, but were situated in downtown locations without parking facilities rather than in outlying areas. Before the first Inno-France store opened, Galeries Lafayette reacted vigorously, buying shares in the La Bourse department store group in Belgium, a competitor of Innovation.

The first Inno-France store opened in Paris in 1962, followed by five more by 1964. All the Inno-France stores lost money, and in 1964 Galeries Lafayette made an agreement with Innovation to buy a stake—first 25 percent, then 33 percent—in Inno-France and to manage non-food buying for the group. The following year all six Inno-France stores, with 2,200 employees, came under the direct management of the Monoprix organization and within four years became profitable. In 1971 Galeries Lafayette acquired the outstanding shares of Inno-France for a symbolic one franc. The company became part of the Monoprix organization, and the investment made by Galeries Lafayette in La Bourse of Belgium was written off.

Two other developments marked the Galeries Lafayette group in the 1960s, one a failure, the other a success. The former were related to the mail-order operations, which had continued somewhat sleepily since Bader had started them in 1905. Mail order was beginning to be a growing business in France, and Galeries Lafayette decided to revitalize and modernize its operations. In 1966 an entirely new, mechanized and computerized distribution center, with more than 300 employees, was opened at Châlons-sur-Marne near Paris. It was not a success, due to troubles with the new systems and an inadequate network of agents throughout France, composed mainly of local drapers. The main competitors, Les Trois Suisses and La Redoute, were highly professional, specialized mail order organizations. It was decided therefore to cut the losses, and in 1970 Galeries Lafayette's mail-order operations were closed.

The success of the 1960s was a major increase in the size of the flagship store on the boulevard Haussmann, no mean feat in the crowded center of Paris. Two additional floors were constructed on top of the original 1912 building. In 1961 an important extension to the store was made on the rue Mogador and boulevard Haussmann, and in 1969 a new store, Galeries Lafayette 2, was opened on the other side of the rue Mogador, linked by a bridge to the older store. A new Monoprix store was also opened in the new complex and, important in a period of growing automobile use, an underground car park was added. At the end of 1969 a do-it-yourself (DIY) store of some 1,000 square meters was opened on the corner of rue Lafayette and Chaussée d'Antin, where Kahn and Bader had opened their little shop nearly 75 years earlier. The DIY merchandise did not, however, sell as well as the ribbons and veils of the original store. In some ten years, the size of the flagship store had been increased by one-third to more than 44,000 square meters, making it one of the five largest department stores in Europe.

Third Generation Advances in 1970s

In 1971 a change in management took place. Raoul Meyer had died in 1970, and in 1971 Max Heilbronn became honorary president, while Etienne Moulin became president and Georges Meyer was named vice-president. Georges Meyer had married the daughter of Raoul Meyer and had joined the management staff in 1965 at the age of 35. The business was still controlled by the family.

With the completion of the extension to the flagship store, the next phase of expansion was the opening of department stores in regional shopping centers. Stores were opened in the Belle-Epine center near Paris in 1971; the Maine-Montparnasse center in Paris in 1973; the Part-Dieu center in Lyons in 1975; and the Polygone center in Montpellier in 1975. The stores in shopping centers were not all an immediate success, but after many changes and improvements, they finally became profitable. After 1975, however, Galeries Lafayette stopped opening stores in shopping centers, and the Belle-Epine store closed in 1985.

The oil crisis of the early 1970s, heavy capital expenditures on enlarging the main store, expansion into shopping centers, and losses on the mail-order operations led to difficult years for the company. No dividends were paid between 1974 and 1979, but by 1980 most of the investments were beginning to show good returns.

The other main subsidiary of the Galeries Lafayette group, the Monoprix variety stores, continued to be profitable, but expansion in terms of number of stores was limited. New forms of retailing—for example 200 new hypermarkets—were opened in France between 1970 and 1980, and changes in the shopping habits of customers had altered variety stores' growth prospects. On the other hand, by doubling the average size of Monoprix stores and achieving very strong food sales in the supermarkets—food accounted for more than 50 percent of sales—the Monoprix management made the stores attractive in their given, local, markets. At the same time, cautious moves were made into the hypermarket sector by opening a small chain of Super M stores.

Chainwide Remodeling Begins in 1980s

In the 1980s, many observers were beginning to question the viability of the department store and the variety store as modern forms of retailing. Department stores had first emerged more than a century earlier in France, and large department stores were seen by some as a rather inefficient relic of the past. Executives of the Galeries Lafayette were, however, convinced of the future of such stores. They argued that a store big enough to carry under one roof a very large assortment of attractive merchandise, including textiles and clothing, leisure goods, and decoration for the home, was appealing to customers. Furthermore, rapidly emerging techniques in stock control, logistics, and credit would resolve many of the past inefficiencies.

In 1987 a change was made in the top management. Etienne Moulin stepped down as president of the company, while Georges Meyer rose to the helm. This change did not affect the founding family's 61.9 percent holding in the company.

Galeries Lafayette's belief in the future of department stores was reflected in the 1980s by heavy investments in remodeling and the enhanced presentation of merchandise in all stores. France's department stores, including Galeries Lafayette, had long been distinguished by their efforts to carry virtually every item at virtually every price point. Galeries Lafayette began to turn away from this strategy, which often resulted in a cluttered presentation, in favor of a more open store layout featuring boutiques. These investments were accompanied by expenditure on computers, point-of-sale terminals, and customer credit promotion.

This policy of developing the department stores received a boost when in 1985 Galeries Lafayette took over stores of the Paris-France group. Paris-France had been founded in 1898 and had slowly built up a chain of department stores in the French provinces. Most of the stores were called Dames de France. Paris-France was a family business, the stores were somewhat old-fashioned, and the group ran into financial difficulties when faced with competition from specialty boutiques and hypermarkets. The Galeries Lafayette took over 12 well-located Paris-France stores with more than 2,000 employees, and thus more than doubled the number of its stores in the French provinces. Nineteen of Paris-France's Parunis variety stores were acquired at the same time and were integrated into the Monoprix variety store organization.

Further investments were made in the Paris-France stores to bring them up to Galeries Lafayette's standards. In 1989 a 50.1 percent majority shareholding was taken in Télemarket, a small but successful home-shopping operation in the greater Paris area, which was supported by Monoprix expertise. A lease was signed to open a Galeries Lafayette store in New York late in 1991. Galeries Lafayette was also involved in a major reconstruction project in the former East Berlin and was considering opening a store in that city in 1993.

Acquiring Nouvelles Galeries in Early 1990s

A landmark in the development of Galeries Lafayette, and evidence of the management's belief in department stores, was the decision in the early part of 1991 to bid for majority control of the department store group Société Française des Nouvelles Galeries Réunies (Nouvelles Galeries). Since 1952 Galeries Lafayette had held shares in the Nouvelles Galeries through its subsidiary Monoprix, whose initial investment of 14 percent gradually rose to 22 percent. By 1990 the sales and net income of Nouvelles Galeries exceeded those of Galeries Lafayette; FFr 19 billion vs. FFr 16.5 billion sales, and FFr 169 million net vs. FFr 144 million net, respectively.

Early in 1991 a Swedish investment group, Proventus, which had built up a shareholding of 25.6 percent in Nouvelles Galeries, decided to sell its holding. Galeries Lafayette bought some of the shares, increasing its stake to 39.2 percent, but at the same time stressing that it did not wish to change control or management of Nouvelles Galeries. The French stock exchange commission, however, ruled that once the Galeries Lafayette had a share of more than one-third of Nouvelles Galeries, it must bid for control. Galeries Lafayette could have sold part of its stake and withdrawn, but it went ahead and eventually took full ownership of Nouvelles Galeries.

The well-managed and profitable Nouvelles Galeries group owned the largest chain of provincial department stores in France, with 56 stores, two diversified chains, 31 Home and Garden Centers, and 43 Vetland discount clothing stores. It also controlled Cofinoga, one of the most important private consumer-credit organizations in France. Nouvelles Galeries also had an 85 percent majority shareholding in the Uniprix chain of 60 variety stores and a 50.04 percent majority holding in the Bazar de l'Hotel de Ville department store group. Nouvelles Galeries and its subsidiaries boasted nearly 18,500 employees.

The merger proved very poorly timed, as the global retail industry and department stores in particular suffered greatly in the early 1990s. To make matters worse, Galeries Lafayette embarked on a bold global expansion that planted new stores in Singapore, Moscow, and, most disastrously, New York City. According to a 1994 article in the *Daily News Record,* the New York outlet, which opened in Trump Tower in 1991, "never achieved its sales goals and could not overcome burdensome rent ($8 million per year) and other expenses to generate profits." Burdened by recession, unprofitable stores, and merger costs, sales at Galeries Lafayette declined from FFr 33 billion in 1991 to less than FFr 29 billion in 1995. The group netted FFr 301 million in 1991, broke even in 1993, and endured a FFr 293 million loss in 1995. Having rid itself of unprofitable outlets throughout France as well as the New York and Singapore stores, Galeries Lafayette made a FFr 550 million profit on essentially flat sales in 1996.

Principal Subsidiaries

Bazar de l'Hotel de Ville (50.4%); Grand Magasins Galeries Lafayette; Societe Parisienne d'Achats et de Manutention; Societe Français de Manutention et de Vente; Galfa Restauration; Galfa Voyages; Monoprix S.A. (94.7%); Lafayette Services-Laser.

Further Reading

D'Aulnay, Sophie, "French Facelifts," *Daily News Record,* October 30, 1995, p. 7.

du Closel, Jacques, *Les Grands Magasins Français. Cent Ans Aprés,* Paris: Clotard et Associés, 1989.

"Galeries Lafayette in Forced Bid for Chain," *WW,* May 6, 1991, p. 7.

"Galeries Lafayette Profits Drop," *WWD,* October 8, 1997, p. 20.

Gill, Penny, "Galeries Lafayette: French Department Store Takes Bold Step with New York City Opening," *Stores,* September 1991, pp. 25–28.

Heilbronn, Max, *Galeries Lafayette, Buchenwald, Galeries Lafayette,* Paris: Éditions Economica, 1989.

Pogoda, Dianne, "Hear Nike Town to Open N.Y. Unit; Galeries Lafayette to Vacate Site," *Daily News Record,* August 30, 1994, pp. 2–3.

Staples, Kate, "From High Fashion to Hot Plates," *WWD,* September 26, 1991, pp. 6–7.

Toy, Stewart, "Getting from Rouge to Noir," *Business Week,* July 13, 1992, p. 35.

Weisman, Katherine, "Paris's Big Three vie for B-T-S Francs," *WWD,* September 19, 1997, p. 14.

—James B. Jefferys
—updated by April D. Gasbarre

Giant Cement Holding, Inc.

320-D Midland Parkway
Summerville, South Carolina 29485
U.S.A.
(803) 851-9898
Fax: (803) 496-5071

Public Company
Founded: 1883 as American Improved Cements Co.
Employees: 408
Sales: $110.2 million (1996)
Stock Exchanges: NASDAQ
SICs: 3241 Cement, Hydraulic; 3271 Concrete Block &
   Brick; 5032 Brick, Stone & Related Construction
   Materials; 6719 Offices of Holding Companies, Not
   Elsewhere Classified

Giant Cement Holding, Inc. is a holding company that manufactures portland and masonry cements. It was the 15th largest U.S. cement producer in 1996. The company also was mining, crushing, screening, and selling stones and gravel, known as aggregates, to the construction industry and marketing cement kiln dust, plus a customized blend of this dust and cement under the name "StableSorb," to solidify soil, wastes, and other materials. Its operations were located in the South Atlantic and Mid-Atlantic regions. In December 1996 Giant Cement entered into a letter of intent to acquire three lightweight aggregate manufacturing plants, five concrete block plants, and a drum-processing and fuel-blending facility from Solite Corp.

Giant Cement to 1983

American Improved Cements, the company that became Giant Cement, was one of the pioneers in the cement business. It was founded in 1883 in Pennsylvania's Lehigh Valley, an area with plentiful limestone deposits of a chemical composition ideally suited for making cement. A plant was erected at Egypt, which was on the line of the Ironton Railroad. The company's Union Cement was used to build the Johnstown

Bridge, celebrated for withstanding the great flood of 1889 that destroyed the town, with great loss of life. American Improved Cements was one of the first companies to use rotary kilns to burn raw materials into clinker. It favored cheap pulverized bituminous coal as the fuel. To grind the clinkers into fine powder, the company installed the first iron mill of the Griffin type ever used for producing portland cement.

The company name became the American Cement Co. in 1912, but a year later it was incorporated as the Giant Portland Cement Co., a name taken from the company's Giant Cement brand. Giant Cement also included several subsidiary companies. Its gross revenues rose from $1.2 million in 1914 to $2 million in 1919, and its net operating revenues increased from $52,949 to $306,876. In 1920 it owned cement plants in Norfolk, Virginia, as well as Egypt, and cement lands in Egypt, Norfolk, and Jordan and Poughkeepsie in New York. Headquarters were situated in Philadelphia. The Norfolk plant and lands were disposed of in 1924. Giant Cement had annual capacity of about two million barrels in 1930.

The Great Depression took its toll on Giant Cement, which lost money during 1931–1935 and 1938–1939. In 1940 the company had net income of $55,535 on net sales of $1.2 million—the latter sum about the same as in 1914. The World War II years were also difficult, with deficits in 1943 and 1944 and revenues falling to $735,480 in 1944, presumably because of a lack of civilian construction. In 1947, however, Giant Cement acquired a cement company with a plant and limestone quarry in Harleyville, South Carolina. The New York properties were disposed of during this decade. Company sales rose to $5.4 million in 1950, and net income was a record $827,291 that year.

The 1950s were a prosperous decade for Giant Cement. Net sales and income grew every year except 1951, reaching $15.8 million and $4 million, respectively, in 1959. During the 1960s, however—a decade of excess capacity for the cement industry and hence falling prices—sales rarely, and income never, reached or passed the 1959 level. Nevertheless, the company was not only debt-free, in 1968 it had a highly favorable ratio of current assets to current liabilities of almost seven to one. The following year, however, Giant closed the Egypt plant rather than spend the costly sums needed to bring the facility into compliance with Pennsylvania's laws to control air pollution. This facility had been responsible for about one-third of the company's annual sales. Giant thereupon moved its headquarters to Columbia, South Carolina.

Giant Portland Cement, which changed its full name to Giant Portland & Masonry Cement Co. in 1977 to reflect its manufacture of masonry as well as portland cements, fared progressively worse as the 1970s continued. After earning a record $5.4 million on net sales of $17.9 million in 1972, its net income began to slide, falling below $1 million in two of the last three years of the decade. In 1980—the start of a severe recession—the company lost $909,000 on net sales of $27.2 million. Giant Cement lost money again in 1981 and was losing even more in September 1982, when it sold $3 million worth of preferred stock to Burt Sugarman, who thereby boosted his holdings in the firm to about 28 percent. In 1983 Giant's plant was converted from burning natural gas and oil to coal—just as oil prices were beginning a sharp drop after ten years of precipitous rises.

The Frenetic Sugarman Era: 1983–94

Sugarman took the helm of Giant Cement in April 1983. The company lost money again in 1983 and 1984 and suffered a bitter strike in late 1984 that resulted in major equipment damage, reducing the plant's annual capacity from 950,000 to 700,000 tons. Unfazed, Sugarman acquired Keystone Portland Cement Co. during 1984–1985 for about $20 million in stock and $7.8 million in cash. Incorporated in 1926, Keystone had a plant in Bath, Pennsylvania, with annual capacity of 3.3 million tons. The firm also was a pioneer in resource-recovery techniques in the U.S. cement industry. Sugarman told a reporter that one of the firm's attractions was its experience with the burning of solid wastes and solvents as an alternative fuel source. Keystone was also collecting revenue for disposing of industrial wastes. Sugarman quickly installed this technology in Giant's South Carolina facility, which began the limited use of waste as a fuel substitute in 1987.

Despite the damage to its Harleyville plant, Giant Cement emerged from the 1984 strike as the low-cost producer in its market. The firm, which was reorganized in 1985 as a holding company with the name Giant Group Ltd., turned in its first profit of the decade that year, earning net income of $3.6 million on net revenues of $69.5 million. Long-term debt had reached $78.6 million, but the company had $75.4 million in its coffers at midyear and had accumulated about $20 million in tax credits from its losing years.

Sugarman used Giant Group's cash stash to make a profit of $3.2 million in 1985 by buying and selling Ply-Gem Industries Inc. stock. Speculation in TRE Corp. stock enabled the company to earn $14.7 million from the sale of investments the following year. With an extraordinary tax credit of $6.8 million, Giant Group's net income reached a fat $21.4 million. In 1987 Sugarman took a position in Media General Inc. and a large share in Rally's Inc., an unprofitable chain of drive-in restaurants. A resident of Los Angeles with a long-standing interest in show business, he also paid $26 million for about 24 percent of Barris Industries, Inc., producer of TV game shows like "The Gong Show" and "The Dating Game." Giant Group had net income of $5 million that year.

Giant Group's operating income of $7.9 million and investment income of $2.9 million in 1988 could not overcome its $10 million in interest expenses and $4 million in losses by its affiliates.

The company lost $8.5 million that year. Sugarman avoided another loss in 1989 by making $7.6 million on the sale of the company's Barris stock. Giant Group's long-term debt reached $109 million that year. Sugarman lost a bitter proxy fight for Media General, but in exchange for selling his shares he received cash and a California newsprint print and recycling operation. In 1990 Sugarman sold these enterprises—now named Golden State Newsprint Co. and Pacific Recycling Co.—for $96 million in cash, a net gain of $14.9 million for the company. This was Sugarman's last big score, however. Pinched by recession, cement sales slipped in 1991 and 1992, and Giant Group lost money both years. The cement business recovered in 1993, but the company lost money because of interest expenses and Rally's continued deficits.

Giant Cement Holding, 1994–96

Sugarman sold the cement business in 1994 in a public offering that raised $131.6 million for his firm. The new company, Giant Cement Holding, Inc., was the 15th largest cement producer in the United States and had a long-term debt of only $8.6 million. Its units would have posted a $5.1 million net profit for 1993 if they had been on their own. Revenues rose from $90.8 million in 1994 to $100.2 million in 1995 and $110.2 million in 1996, with resource-recovery services, as opposed to cement sales, accounting for about 13 percent of the total. Net income rose from $9.2 million in 1994 to $12.7 million in 1995 and $15.4 million in 1996. Long-term debt was $10.3 million in March 1997.

Just before the end of 1996 Giant Cement agreed to purchase Solite Corp., a leading producer of construction materials, for 1.3 million shares of stock and the assumption of about $18 million in debt. Solite, which was to become a Giant subsidiary, was making concrete blocks and lightweight aggregate material, similar to cement in construction, in five states. It was also recovering industrial waste, which it used as fuel to fire its kilns. The acquisition included eight plants in Virginia and North Carolina, an Alabama hazardous-waste processing plant, and Oldover Corp., a Virginia hazardous-waste trucking firm. Not included in the purchase were certain other Solite operations, including lightweight aggregate plants in Kentucky and New York, that were to be formed into an independent company.

In 1996 Giant Cement was selling cement to more than 500 customers in Georgia, South Carolina, North Carolina, and Virginia (through the Giant plant) and Pennsylvania, New York, New Jersey, Connecticut, Delaware, and Maryland (through the Keystone plant). About 85 percent of the cement was being sold in bulk, primarily to ready-mix and concrete-products manufacturers, with the remainder sold in individually packed bags, primarily to building materials dealers. It was also selling waste-derived fuels as well as using them for about half of its own fuel usage.

Giant Cement owned the Giant plant and quarry in Harleyville as well as about 2,100 acres of land on which these facilities were located. It owned a plant and quarries in the Bath, Pennsylvania, area, as well as about 1,000 acres of land on which these facilities were located. The company's manufacturing facilities had an annual rated clinker capacity of about 1.4 million tons and an annual rated cement-grinding capacity of 1.7 million tons. Giant Cement also operated a distribution facility on its land in Durham, North Carolina, and rented warehouse space in Atlanta, Durham, and Charlotte, North Carolina. Corporate headquarters were being leased in Summerville, South Carolina. Keystone's offices were being leased in Bath. The company's largest stockholders in 1997 were the Prudential Insurance Co. (11.9 percent) and Wellington Management Co. (10.4 percent).

Principal Subsidiaries

GCHI Investments, Inc.; Giant Cement Company, Inc.; Giant Cement NC, Inc.; Giant Resource Recovery Company, Inc.; Keystone Cement Company, Inc; Solite Corp.

Further Reading

Block, Alex Ben, "What's His Line," *Forbes,* January 26, 1987, pp. 70–71.
Cochran, Thomas N., "Giant Cement Holding," *Barron's,* September 19, 1994, p. 49.
Frook, John Evan, "Burt Sugarman's Sweet Deals," *Los Angeles Business Journal,* June 11, 1990, p. 21 and continuation.
"Giant Portland Says Pollution Laws Cause Closing of Facilities," *Wall Street Journal,* December 18, 1969, p. 24.
"Giant Protects Coal-Firing System with Multiple Guards," *Rock Products,* April 1983, pp. 48–50, 98.
Kunsman, Ken, "Keystone Cement Parent Going Public," *Allentown Morning Call,* p. B9.
Lesley, Robert W., et. al. *History of the Portland Cement Industry in the United States,* Chicago: International Trade Press, 1924.
Maturi, Richard J., "Back from the Brink," *Barron's,* October 27, 1986, p. 65.
Slack, Charles, "Solite to Merge with S.C. Company," *Richmond Times-Dispatch,* December 25, 1996, p. C1.

—Robert Halasz

GRAND ━━ HOTEL
KRASNAPOLSKY

Grand Hotel Krasnapolsky N.V.

Dam 9
1012 JS Amsterdam
Netherlands
(31) 20 - 55.49.111
Fax: (31) 20 - 62.28.607
Web site: http://www.krasnapolsky.nl

Public Company
Incorporated: 1878 as the Naamloze Vennootschap
    Maatschappij tot Exploitatie van het café
    Krasnapolsky
Employees: 404
Sales: Nfl 67.84 million (US$34 million) (1996)
Stock Exchanges: Amsterdam
SICs: 7011 Hotels and Motels; 5812 Eating Places; 5813
    Drinking Places

Long a fixture of Amsterdam's famed Dam Square, Grand Hotel Krasnapolsky N.V. has expanded to become one of that city's leading independent hotel and restaurant operators. The expansion of the 130-year-old Grand Hotel Krasnapolsky, completed in the 1990s, has created the largest five-star hotel and convention center in the Benelux (Belgium, Netherlands, and Luxembourg), with 465 rooms, including 36 luxury apartments, 20 multifunction conference halls, and a complex of restaurants, bars, and other facilities, such as the Krasnapolsky's world-renowned Winter Garden. Since the 1970s the company also has operated another Amsterdam mainstay, the restaurant d'Vijff Vlieghen, located on the nearby Spui.

Since the mid-1990s, however, Krasnapolsky has been engaged in full expansion. In 1994 the company acquired the café-restaurant 't Goude Hooft in the Hague; the following year, the company assumed the management of the Holiday Inn hotel in Utrecht. Another Utrecht site, the Stadskasteel Oudaen, a castle dating from the Middle Ages containing a restaurant, brewery, and conference rooms, was added in 1997. The company's portfolio also features three landmark hotels acquired in 1996:

the Doelen, the Schiller, and the Caransa. Since 1997 the company has begun looking beyond Holland's borders for its growth. In that year the company acquired the operations of the 200-room, five-star Lord Charles Hotel in Cape Town, South Africa. Krasnapolsky is actively seeking further international expansion, with an emphasis on Western Europe, the United States, and Japan. In 1996 the company posted sales of nearly Nfl 68 million.

More Than Just a Coffee Shop: The 19th Century

The Hotel Krasnapolsky originated as a coffee house on Amsterdam's infamous Warmoestraat of the mid 19th century. A narrow, somewhat sunless street located between the Damrak, site of the city's financial district, and the Red Light District, the Warmoestraat and its maze of flophouses and dark alleys had become a favored destination of sailors, travelers, and denizens of Amsterdam's more unsavory side. Amsterdam itself had long been an international city, attracting people from much of the world. Many Amsterdam businesses of the period were run by foreigners, particularly Germans. In the area around the Warmoestraat, coffee houses (which served more beer than coffee) were popular meeting places, at least for the city's male population. ("Decent" women were not expected to be seen in that neighborhood after 3:00 p.m., when the city's exchange closed for the day.) One such coffee house was the Nieuwe Poolsche Koffeehuis (another establishment, the Poolsche Koffiehuis, was located in the Kalverstraat nearby), which catered particularly to the city's German-speaking population.

One of this establishment's customers was Wilhelm Adolf Krasnapolsky. Born in 1834 in Germany, of a family of Polish tailors, Krasnapolsky had come to Amsterdam with his father in 1856. Krasnapolsky found a tailor's position in a clothing store and became a regular customer of the Nieuwe Poolsche Koffeehuis, where he became friends with one of the waiters, August Volmer. They soon became family—Krasnapolsky married Volmer's sister in 1862. In 1866 Krasnapolsky took over the coffee house's lease and later renamed it as the Café Krasnapolsky. Volmer remained on as Krasnapolsky's waiter; in 1871 the pair formed a five-year partnership. By then Krasnapolsky had already begun to show his ambitions. With another of Volmer's sisters as cook, the Café Krasnapolsky distinguished itself among other coffee houses by offering full meals at affordable prices.

The Krasnapolsky proved a success. More and more people were coming to the Warmoestraat, crossing the street, as it were, as more and more businesses involved in the city's tobacco trade took over the restaurants and taverns on the Nes—the Warmoestraat's extension on the opposite side of the Damstraat. In 1868 Krasnapolsky bought a building located on the Servetsteeg, behind his café. Two years later, however, Krasnapolsky prepared to move to a more prestigious location: on the Dam Square itself. His plans were thwarted, however; in 1870 Krasnapolsky instead bought the Café Krasnapolsky's building. The following year he was able to purchase two more buildings adjacent to the Servetsteeg building, and he rebuilt the property, including his café's billiard room, into a new, larger billiard room and summer garden.

The garden would be expanded two years later, when Krasnapolsky bought and demolished two more houses. In 1874 the café itself would be expanded, when Krasnapolsky bought the neighboring building on the Warmoestraat. In good weather, the café's doors could be opened onto the summer garden, which itself had become a popular meeting place. To meet the growing demand for the café's meals, Krasnapolsky built his own abattoir. The summer garden itself was soon expanded, reopening in 1878. In that year Krasnapolsky incorporated as the Naamloze Vennootschap (Limited Liability Company) tot Exploitatie van het Café Krasnapolsky.

After adding office and workspaces, Krasnapolsky next began to build a hall that would give his establishment an international reputation. Work began on the Winter Garden in 1879, as well as on a new billiard room, a buffet hall, and a building to house the café's busy kitchen. Krasnapolsky also added, in 1881, one of the city's first conference rooms on the floor above the café. At the end of that year the company's name was changed again, to Maatschappij tot Exploitatie van de Onderneming Krasnapolsky, when Volmer left the company to take over the recently constructed American Hotel.

The beginning of the 1880s marked two significant events for Krasnapolsky. The first was the arrival of electrical lighting to replace the hotel's gas lamps. To supply power to the café, Krasnapolsky built his own electrical power plant in 1881; the following year Krasnapolsky founded the N.E.M., Nederlandsche Electriciteits Maatschappij, which provided power to the new Edison light bulbs at the Krasnapolsky. Krasnapolsky's plans to expand the N.E.M. ended in 1892, however, when the company lost its electrical power concession. The coming of the World Exposition to Amsterdam in 1883 provided Krasnapolsky with his next opportunity. For that occasion, Krasnapolsky determined to enter the hotel business, buying two neighboring buildings on the Warmoestraat and rebuilding them into an 80-room hotel wing. The following year, with the purchase of the adjoining building, the hotel was expanded again. At this time, the café and hotel were joined together, creating a single structure behind an imposing, symmetrical facade from what had formerly been six buildings. In 1885 Krasnapolsky added a new restaurant on the ground floor of the hotel wing; the former café was converted into a reading room, featuring some 250 newspapers from around the world. The newly renovated Win-

ter Garden opened in that year as well. Outfitted with more than a thousand Edison light bulbs, the Winter Garden would quickly earn praise as "the wonder of the century."

Approaching the Dam Square: The Early 20th Century

Krasnapolsky had not given up his desire for an address on the Dam, or at least on the important Damrak. A request for a passage between the Warmoestraat and the Damrak had been refused by the city; Krasnapolsky was able to purchase one of the buildings opposite his hotel, however, which he planned to demolish in favor of a passage. Yet that plan was stalled by indecision on where to build Amsterdam's new bourse. Plans for further expansion of the number of the Krasnapolsky's hotel rooms were also prevented by city restrictions on building heights. The Krasnapolsky remained hidden from view—the Warmoestraat at that time still reached to the Damstraat, blocking the view from the Dam. Nevertheless, the Krasnapolsky had become an important meeting and dining place, not only for businessmen, but for families as well.

Krasnapolsky had also become involved in other real estate developments, such as a public swimming pool, complete with terrace, pavilion, and park, and building societies meant to encourage the construction of quality residential properties in the neighborhood around his home and elsewhere in the city. In the late 1880s, Krasnapolsky also looked across the Channel, forming the Krasnapolsky Restaurant and Wintergarden Company Ltd. and opening a restaurant complex, called the Frascati, in London in 1892. The Frascati proved a success, and Krasnapolsky soon added a second restaurant in London, the High Holborn. Before the end of the decade, however, Krasnapolsky sold both of these establishments, which would remain London fixtures for some 50 years.

In the years leading up to the First World War, the Krasnapolsky continued to make improvements, including a renovation of the restaurant. Another Warmoestraat building, outfitted as office space, was joined to the Krasnapolsky complex. The company also purchased several parcels on the building's southern side, reaching closer to the Damstraat. Yet, the Krasnapolsky's expansion would be stopped by the building of the Polmanshuis restaurant, which occupied the corner property beside the Krasnapolsky. In 1909 Krasnapolsky, then 75 years old, stepped down as the company's director. He died three years later, in April 1912. Later that year the company was able to purchase, for 260 guilders, the remaining parcel in the rear of the complex, expanding the Krasnapolsky's holdings onto the Oudezijds Voorburgwal canal.

In 1914 the Krasnapolsky came closer to its founder's dream of an address on the Dam. In that year the city decided to expand the Dam Square. Part of the western face of the Warmoestraat was demolished, joining the building lines of the Dam with the Warmoestraat. For the occasion, the Polmanshuis, now located directly on the Dam, was entirely rebuilt. The Krasnapolsky, while still keeping its Warmoestraat address, was now partly visible from the Dam. The outbreak of the First World War, despite the Netherlands' neutral status, forced the Krasnapolsky to close its hotel for the duration; the restaurant and other facilities, however, were able to continue operations.

In the period between the two world wars the Krasnapolsky continued to develop. In 1924 it was one of six establishments to receive a license for dancing, and the Krasnapolsky adapted to the new fad, roofing over its summer garden and converting part of the Winter Garden to ballroom facilities. In 1927 the Krasnapolsky added a new hotel wing, crossing the Servetsteeg and extending the hotel's facade closer to the Dam. The hotel now boasted some 140 rooms. That year also saw the Krasnapolsky receive James Joyce, who would later "invent" the color "Krasnapolsky red" for his novel *Finnegan's Wake*.

As the dance craze—said to have sullied the Krasnapolsky's reputation—faded in the early 1930s, the company rebuilt its ballrooms into theaters for stage and film entertainment. The company also added a number of meeting and public rooms in the mid-1930s. In 1937 the Krasnapolsky acquired the last Warmoestraat property between it and the Polmanshuis; that property was rebuilt and added to the Krasnapolsky the following year. The new extension added 17 hotel rooms—and a new entrance, closer to the Dam—but also a bomb shelter in the basement.

That shelter would become important with the Nazi occupation of the Netherlands during the Second World War. The Krasnapolsky, which had just celebrated its 75th anniversary, remained opened through the war. The hotel's management, despite the presence of Germans, was able to provide hiding places for many of its employees and other Dutch citizens threatened by forced labor proscriptions and deportations to the German concentration camps. The Krasnapolsky also provided places for people to listen to Radio Orange, the Dutch government-in-exile's broadcasts from London. By the end of the war, with the German blockade of northern Holland leading to what became known as the "Hunger Winter," the food shortage forced the Krasnapolsky to require its guests to bring their own food.

Beyond the Dam: The 21st Century

The Krasnapolsky reopened in 1945; two years later the company took its first steps from the Warmoestraat, purchasing the Hotel Polen (the former Poolsche Koffiehuis) in the nearby Kalverstraat. Then, in 1950, the company at last realized its founder's dream. In that year the company purchased its neighbor, the Polmanshuis. With funds from the Marshall Plan, the Krasnapolsky renovated and joined that building in 1952. There, the hotel added an entrance, and the Krasnapolsky at last had an address on the Dam Square. For that occasion, the company's and the hotel's name was changed, to Grand Hotel Krasnapolsky. At the end of the decade, the American Express, which had long held its offices on the Polmanshuis's ground floor, moved to the Damrak. Those offices were rebuilt so that the hotel's main entrance was now located directly on the Dam.

In 1960 the Krasnapolsky added a new 80-room hotel wing, a new conference hall, and an open-air parking lot. At the end of the decade the parking lot was converted into a 150-car garage and an additional 130 rooms were added in a new hotel wing, bringing the hotel's total to nearly 400 rooms. By then the company had joined in forming the Golden Tulip Hotel chain, in partnership with several other Netherlands hotels, enabling

the company to preserve its independent status. Further expansion of the hotel, however, was thwarted, when the Salvation Army took over the last block of buildings on the corner of the Warmoestraat and Damstraat.

The Krasnapolsky now looked beyond the Dam Square to expand its operations. In 1970 the company began development of a new hotel on the IJ Boulevard, opening the Krasnapolsky-Paramaribo in 1974. After taking over the restaurant on the top of Havengebouw, overlooking the city's harbor on the IJ, the company also purchased the famed restaurant, 't Vijff Vlieghen (the Five Flies) on the Spui, in 1971.

The oil crisis of the 1970s, and the resulting worldwide recession, would slow the company's expansion activities. In 1983 the company's attention returned to the Krasnapolsky itself, opening two new hotel wings, as well as a renovated inner courtyard. The hotel's capacity now boasted some 720 beds. At the end of the decade the famed Winter Garden was renovated and reopened. The company purchased the former Salvation Army building in 1991 and began plans to expand the Krasnapolsky to the Damstraat. By 1992, however, the company's growth and improvements had gained the Krasnapolsky status as a five-star hotel.

Less successful was the company's opening of the Lido Casino complex near the Leidseplein in 1991. Opened in the face of a worldwide recession, the Lido's losses would mount throughout the first half of the decade, bringing the Krasnapolsky concern into the red. In 1996 the company sold off the Lido to Holland Casino. By then, the new Royal Wing, on the site of the former Salvation Army building, had opened, providing shops and restaurants as well as hotel rooms, bringing the Krasnapolsky's total number of rooms to 465.

The company had also expanded its activities beyond Amsterdam, taking over the restaurant 't Goude Hooft in the Hague in 1994, acquiring the management contract of the Holiday Inn in Utrecht in 1995, and taking over the Stadskasteel Oudaen in Utrecht in 1997. Yet the company's focus remained on Amsterdam: in 1996 the company took over three Amsterdam hotels, the Doelen, located on the Amstel, the city's main canal, and the Caransa and Schiller, located on the Rembrandtsplein.

For the future, however, the company looked beyond the Netherlands for further expansion. The company began searching for suitable hotel and restaurant acquisitions in Belgium, Germany, England, and France. Yet its first international move came in June 1997, with the takeover of the five-star Lord Charles Hotel in Cape Town, South Africa, adding 200 rooms to the company's holdings.

Principal Subsidiaries

Krasnapolsky Hotels B.V.; Krasnapolsky Restaurants B.V.; Krasnapolsky Specials B.V.; Explotatiemaatschappij Grand Hotel Krasnapolsky B.V.; Krasnapolsky Events B.V.; Krasnapolsky Hotels & Restaurants Ontroerend Goed B.V.

—M.L. Cohen

Groupe Castorama-Dubois Investissements

Parc d'Activité BP 24
59175 Templemars
France
(33) 3 20 16 75 11
Fax: (33) 3 20 16 75 97
Web site: http://www.castorama.fr

Public Company
Incorporated: 1969 as Central-Castor
Employees: 14,300
Sales: FFr 21.1 billion (US $3.64 billion) (1997)
Stock Exchanges: Lille
SICs: 5211 Lumber and Other Building Materials; 5251
   Hardware Stores; 5231 Paint, Glass, and Wallpaper
   Stores

Groupe Castorama-Dubois Investissements operates the leading chain of DIY (do-it-yourself) and home improvement materials stores in France and Europe and counts among the top five DIY chains in the world. With 162 retail stores in France, Italy, Germany, Belgium, Poland, and Brazil under the Castorama name and nine retail Réno-Depôt stores in Quebec, Canada, Groupe Castorama has counted double-digit growth for much of its history. Castorama retail stores feature large selling surfaces (ranging from 6,000 to 12,000 square meters), stocking some 50,000–60,000 home improvement and DIY products, as well as related products such as lighting fixtures, space heaters, fans, and satellite television equipment—in short, everything the committed DIY-er needs, to paraphrase an early company slogan.

While the Castorama stores serve the individual consumer, Groupe Castorama also caters to the professional market. Its chain of 18 Brico Dépôt stores—of which nine opened in 1997 alone—is oriented toward providing building supplies for the construction site. The company also operates a network of seven Dubois Matériaux wholesale warehouse centers reserved exclusively for the building and construction professional. Beyond the building market, Groupe Castorama has diversified into animal and pet care products with the acquisition of four Amiland specialty superstores.

More than FFr 18 billion of the company's total sales of FFr 21.1 billion are produced in France. Yet, with new store openings severely restricted in France, Castorama's foreign expansion represents the company's fastest growth opportunity. After focusing on Germany and Italy in the first half of the 1990s, Castorama has begun to look farther afield. In 1997 the company entered three new markets—Canada, Poland, and Brazil—more than tripling its foreign-earned revenues over the previous year.

Groupe Castorama-Dubois Investissements has been led by CEO Jean-Hughes Loyez since 1992. Founder Christian Dubois remains the company's chairman of the board, while Dubois's sons Jean-Luc and Gonzague function as the company's general managers for finance and executive administration. The French distribution giant Carrefour held a major shareholder's position in the company before reducing its participation in 1994. The Dubois family holds 11 percent of the company's stock.

American Inspiration in the 1970s

Christian Dubois began his career in 1951, selling building and construction materials in the city of Lille and the surrounding region at the north of France. After a trip to the United States in the late 1960s, however, Dubois was inspired by a new opportunity: the idea of bringing the so-called "category-killer" warehouse specialty store concept, then emerging in the United States, to France's home improvement and hardware market. In 1969 Dubois opened his first large-format store, called Central-Castor (castor means "beaver" in French) in the Lille suburb of Englos. The store, which boasted 5,000 square meters, was located in a shopping mall anchored by an Auchan hypermarket. Although Auchan would later come under the sway of Castorama's chief French competitor, Leroy-Merlin, the company would continue to seek out such shopping mall placements for many of its later openings.

The name Central-Castor was short-lived, ceding to Castorama at the start of the 1970s. The success of the Castorama concept, however, proved more lasting. By 1974 the company

Company Perspectives:

Bringing the customer the right product, the right advice, the right service, and the right ideas for carrying out his projects isn't simple. Castorama's mission will always be to offer the customer the best, in every store.

had grown to four stores, serving the Nord region around Lille. By then Castorama was preparing to make a move toward national expansion, opening the first Castorama located outside of the company's Nord home. The new Castorama, in Plaisir, a Parisian suburb, opened in 1975, also marked an important element of the company's growth strategy, that of an orientation toward the country's larger urban areas, with a population dense enough to support the company's large-format stores. That same year saw the birth of a slogan that would become famous among France's booming DIY-ers: "Chez Casto, y'a tout ce qu'il faut!" (Casto's got what it takes).

The Paris opening would be the first in an aggressive expansion that would take Castorama to a 13-store chain just three years later. Expansion had become necessary; by the mid-1970s Castorama was faced with a growing number of competitors equally attracted to the large-store format. After the postwar boom years, the French economy was beginning to sour as the effects of the Arab Oil Crisis began to be felt. With the recession of the early 1980s looming on the horizon, tightening economic conditions gave rise to a new wave of interest in DIY home improvement—indeed, some would dub it the French national hobby. At the same time, the French consumer had become accustomed to the broad product range and discounted prices of the large-format store, as the hypermarket concept swept the country. One of the leading hypermarket chains, Carrefour, would provide Castorama with the capital it needed for its own expansion. In 1978 Carrefour purchased a shareholder position of more than 45 percent in Castorama. In that year Castorama more than doubled in size when it acquired the 19-store Californie chain.

Three more Castorama stores were added over the next year. In 1979, celebrating its tenth anniversary, Castorama had grown to a 35-store chain boasting sales of FFr 1.2 billion per year and more than 2,500 employees. As the chain spread across the country, it adopted a policy of decentralization, opening region headquarters to coordinate development. The company would also be quick to add computerized inventory control to track its growing range of products. Meanwhile, Dubois had not abandoned the building and construction professional, even as the Castorama chain attracted the growing ranks of DIY consumers. Dubois had also begun building a network of building supply wholesale warehouses, under the Dubois Materiaux name.

Growth in the 1980s

At the start of the 1980s Dubois sought fresh capital for expansion. In 1982 Dubois formed a new holding company to group his parallel activities. In that year Castorama-Dubois Investissements entered the over-the-counter market on the Lille stock exchange. Three years later, the company holdings had grown to 74 stores and more than 5,000 employees, with total sales of more than FFr 3 billion (net, after taxes). Over the next ten years, the company would continue to post an impressive growth rate, averaging sales gains of nearly 16 percent per year. The company was also strongly profitable: its net income growth would average nearly 30 percent per year over the following ten-year period. Added fuel for the expansion came in 1986, when Castorama-Dubois joined the Lille exchange's secondary market.

The individual Castorama stores were also undergoing a transformation, as the company worked on refining its store concept. In 1987 the Castorama stores began a transition to a larger format, ranging from 8,000 to 10,000 square meters, while building up their range to some 50,000 products. Among these were the first products bearing the Castorama name—matching the quality of the brand names, while priced at a ten to 15 percent discount. That same year brought another new feature to the Castorama customer: the company's first catalog. At 196 pages, the Castorama catalog would be distributed to 3.5 million customers.

Moving to a full listing on the stock exchange in 1988 provided Castorama-Dubois with the opportunity to increase its holding in Castorama from 52.7 percent to more than 94 percent. The company next took its first store outside of France, opening a Castorama in Milan. At the end of the decade, the company had grown to a chain of 86 Castorama stores and six Dubois Materiaux wholesalers, employing more than 7,500, for total sales (including tax) of nearly FFr 7.5 billion. The company had taken a clear lead in the French home improvement market and numbered among the largest in Europe as well. In 1989 the company took a step toward reinforcing its service commitment to its customers, opening an in-house training school for its employees.

Foreign Expansion for the 1990s

The first signs of a shakeout in the DIY industry began to be seen at the start of the 1990s, as the market consolidated into a two-tier structure: large-format stores serving primarily urban populations and smaller supply stores serving more rural populations. Castorama remained committed to the large-store format, reaching an average store size of 7,400 square meters by 1990. The company was also leading the consolidation of the industry, buying up nine stores from rival Obi, owned by Belgium's GIB, and France's third largest DIY chain at the time. The following year, Castorama bought out another rival chain, Briker, including 17 stores, from another hypermarket leader, Rallye (later Casino). By the end of 1991 Castorama had grown to 111 stores and more than 10,000 employees. Sales that year topped FFr 10 billion for the first time.

The concurrent consolidation of the hypermarket industry also helped Castorama's expansion. In 1992, after Carrefour bought out rival Euromarché, Castorama saw the chance to buy up the seven largest stores of Euromarché's subsidiary Bricorama (another company would acquire the Bricorama name). Consolidation among all large-format retail sectors would shortly become a necessity for expansion: a new law introduced in the early 1990s created several restrictions on new store developments, particularly in urban areas. The law, inspired in part by a desire to protect the threatened existence of the small, independent shop owner, brought such local commercial developments under national oversight. The law was to see a steady tightening over the following years, making the authorization for construction of a new large-format store a rare event.

The new law, in fact, would help solidify Castorama's leadership position in France; it maintained a comfortable leadership, both in store numbers and revenues, over its rivals. Castorama-Dubois took a two-prong approach to further expansion. In France, the company began to diversify, adding a new building materials concept, under the Brico Dépôt name, geared toward supplying professional and, especially, construction site needs. The company also branched out beyond the DIY market: in the early 1990s, it began building a chain of large-format pet care and animal supply stores under the Amiland name. Another company project became garden supplies, under the Dubois Jardin name. Less successful was the company's attempt to enter the automotive supply market, through subsidiary Self Auto. That activity was ended in 1994. On the positive side, in 1994 Castorama-Dubois regained 100 percent control of Castorama S.A., after a stock swap agreement for Carrefour's remaining shares.

Whereas diversification would provide some growth for the company, Castorama looked beyond the French border for its main expansion thrust. After opening its first Italian store in 1988, the company added a second Italian store in Bergame in 1990, two more stores in Bollate and Marcon in 1992, building up its Italian branch to seven stores by the beginning of 1998. Germany formed Castorama's next frontier: the company established its Castorama Deutschland subsidiary in 1990, opening its first German store, in Castrop-Rauxel, near Dortmund, in 1992. Two more German stores were added that same year, followed by a store in 1994 and four Castoramas in 1995. By 1998 Castorama's German branch included seven stores. Facing an intensely competitive market—the largest in Europe—the company continued to absorb losses, despite the growth of its German revenues to more than FFr 800 million. Castorama's fortunes proved better in Italy, where its operations began turning a profit in the mid-1990s. The company planned further expansion in Italy, beginning with two stores in 1998.

Castorama's foreign expansion would serve an additional purpose, that of shielding the company from the potential entry of U.S. giants such as Home Depot into the European market. In 1994 Castorama moved just across the French-Belgian border, opening a store in Kortrijk. By 1996 Castorama began to look farther afield, targeting Poland as a foothold into the Eastern European market. Castorama's first Polish store, featuring its 10,000-square-meter format, opened in Warsaw in 1997, with plans to add three more stores in 1998. In that year, the company crossed the Atlantic, targeting Brazil with an eye toward further expansion into the South American market. The company's first Brazilian Castorama opened in Sao Paulo in 1997. Further north, an acquisition brought a new name into the Castorama-Dubois holdings. In April 1997 the company purchased the nine-store chain (featuring 12,000-square-meter formats) of Reno Dépôt in Quebec. The company stated, however, that its plans for further North American expansion would remain limited to the French-speaking province. Two more Reno Dépôt stores were expected to be added in Canada in 1998.

Throughout much of the 1990s, the French economy, along with much of Europe, suffered through an extended recession. Yet, the difficult economy and growing jobless rates proved to be a boon to Castorama, attracting a new wave of DIY-ers. At the end of 1997 Castorama's holdings had grown to 162 stores, producing sales of more than FFr 21 billion. Between 1993 and 1997 the company had succeeded in winning authorization to open seven new French Castoramas, while also building up the number of Brico Dépôt stores to more than ten; a ninth Dubois Materiaux center was added in 1997. Castorama also began instituting a new 12,000-square-meter format; at the same time, it ended production of its catalog (which had swelled to nearly 700 pages over its ten years) replacing it with a new publication, "Oh! Casto," modeled after consumer magazines. In 1997 Castorama also began offering its own customer fidelity credit card.

Principal Subsidiaries

Reno Dépôt (Canada); Castorama Deutschland GmbH (Germany); Amiland (France); Castorama S.A. (France); Brico Dépôt (France); Dubois Materiaux (France); Dubois Jardin (France; 80%).

Further Reading

Baverel, Philippe, "Quarante Millions de Bricoleurs," *Le Monde,* December 7, 1993, p. 6.
"Castorama: une Dimension Internationale Mesurée," *Bricomag,* May 1995, p. 34.
Lupieri, Stéphane, "La Lutte pour l'Espace Vital," *Enjeux,* October 1996, p. 101.
Mason, Sophie, "Castorama Moves into Canada," *DIY Week,* March 21, 1997, p. 12.
Prod'homme, Gilles, "Castorama Performant Malgré l'Allemagne," *Points de Vente,* March 10, 1997, p. 18.

—M.L. Cohen

Groupe Legris Industries

74, rue de Paris
BP 1105
35014 Rennes Cedex 7
France
(33) 2 99 25 55 00
Fax: (33) 2 99 25 55 82
Web site: http://www.legris.fr

Public Company
Incorporated: 1863
Employees: 5,239
Sales: FFr 3.479 billion (1996)
Stock Exchanges: Paris
SICs: 3498 Fabricated Pipe and Fittings

France's Groupe Legris Industries is a diversified industrial group with leading domestic and worldwide positions in its four principal markets: fittings, couplings, valves, and instrumentation for industrial fluids applications; fittings, valves, and regulators for domestic (water and gas) fluids applications; tower cranes; and logistics, including automated order preparation and warehousing systems. Operating on a largely decentralized basis, the company's activities are grouped under four main subsidiaries: Legris (Industrial Fluids, 23 percent of annual sales), which has captured the worldwide leadership in the industrial fittings and valves market; Comap (Domestic Fluids, 26 percent of annual sales), one of Europe's top producers of fittings, valves, and other products for the household water and gas systems market; Potain (Tower Cranes, 42 percent of annual sales), the world leader in construction crane production; and Savoye Logistic Systems (Logistics, 8 percent of annual sales), France's leader in order preparation and warehouse systems. Together, the members of the Legris group produced nearly FFr 3.5 billion in sales in 1996. Principal markets include France (37 percent of sales), Germany (11 percent), Italy (8 percent), and other European countries (25 percent), with sales to Asia accounting for 12 percent of sales, and North and South American just three percent of sales. A publicly traded company, Groupe Legris remains largely controlled by the founding Legris family.

Founded in the Mid-19th Century

Ambroise Legris was 26 years old when he purchased, for 70 francs, a small coppersmith, Maison Pillon Torneur sur Cuivre, in Paris in 1863. In the midst of the Industrial Revolution, Legris's small shop prospered, particularly from the demand for brass taps for the spreading network of gas lines. Starting with three lathes, by 1865 Legris had doubled that number, and together with new equipment, had increased the shop's value to more than 5,000 francs. Legris's products soon found their way beyond Paris into the rest of France. One of Legris' early achievements came with the lighting of the Champs-Elysées, where his taps controlled the flow of the extremely volatile coal gas used at the time.

At the end of the century Legris's son Jules married Léontine Brenot, daughter of Théodore Brenot, a celebrated inventor and manufacturer of surgical instruments. In 1899 Ambroise Legris and Théodore Brenot extended the union of the two families when they agreed to merge their companies, forming Maison Brenot et Legris Réunies. The companies, which both used brass in their products, continued to produce the Legris line of taps and other brass fixtures as well as the famed Brenot line of surgical and medical instruments. At the same time, Ambroise transferred his interest in the company to Jules Legris, who shared leadership with Brenot until the latter's retirement four years later.

The company's prosperity continued into the new century. By 1908 the Brenot-Legris firm employed some 60 workers and had moved to larger facilities, still located in Paris. While the company's surgical instruments remained at the forefront of medical innovation, a new invention had opened new avenues for Legris's brass taps and fittings, which had long held a reputation for quality and precision. The invention of the internal combustion engine, and its application not only to the automobile industry, but also to the nascent airplane industry, created dramatic increases in demand for Legris's products, which were often custom-designed to meet the specifications of the client. One of these customers was Louis Blériot, the famed French aviator, who turned to Legris to design the taps for the plane Blériot used to make his world-renowned English Channel crossing.

Company Perspectives:

Our strategy is built on: acknowledged know-how and innovative flair; production organized to ensure maximum flexibility and responsiveness; the only international distribution network of its kind in the industry; mutually demanding relations with customers and trust; emphasis on the quality of relations within the group.

With the outbreak of the First World War, Legris turned its production toward supporting the war effort. In 1915 Jules Legris died after rescuing a niece from drowning. Legris's widow stepped in to lead the company, assisted by the couple's sons, Georges and Paul. Orders, both to produce equipment for the military and to supply other companies in France and allied countries, strained Legris's capacity. In 1918, with the German advance on Paris, the company was forced to leave the city, moving its production to the Auvergne region. But following the war, the company returned to Paris.

Sliding into World War II

Léontine Legris continued to lead the company in the years following the war, while sons George and Paul soon took more active roles. In 1921, eyeing the inevitability of the company's succession, Léontine formerly incorporated the company as the "Société Veuve Legris et Fils." While Léaontine continued to provide overall leadership of the company until her death in 1928, Georges took control of the company's production activities; Paul, still a minor at the time, would later lead the company's commercial arm.

The period following World War I marked important advances in technology and in industrial production techniques. The demand of the war had spurred great advancements in both automobile and airplane design, and Legris adapted quickly to the increasing technical demands of its clients. Under the name "Etablissements Legris Fils," the company invested in new machinery—much of which was designed and built under the direction of Georges—enabling vast increases in productivity. At the same time, the company's surgical instruments continued to play an important role in that market, matching advances made in the field of medicine.

Yet neither Georges nor Paul proved to be particularly inspired businessmen, and seemed content to allow the business to run itself. Legris entered a steady decline during the years of the Great Depression. By the end of the 1930s, the company's catalog had barely evolved. Changes in automobile design—particularly the replacement of the gas tank toward the rear of the vehicle, removing the need for a tap governing the fuel line—eliminated an important source of the company's revenues. Legris's inertia lasted through the Second World War.

With the German occupation, French industry was forced to work for the Nazi war effort. Legris, however, joined in a popular form of industrial resistance, slowing down production, introducing equipment breakdowns, and initiating other practices designed to frustrate fulfillment of the German commands.

Indeed, less than two percent of the company's production went to Germany during this period. Throughout the occupation, Legris's sales, which had neared seven million francs on the eve of the war, remained largely stagnant, peaking at nine million francs only in the months prior to France's defeat. The relative stability of Legris's sales—in the face of the loss of its North and South American markets, and the markets of Allied countries—was due primarily to the company's first move to bring in leadership from outside the family: in 1941, Georges and Paul Legris hired Robert Chopin as the company's technical director. The following year, after Chopin left the company, the Legris hired Jean Panneau, who would play a pivotal role not only in maintaining the company's operations during the war but in guiding its postwar development.

Immediately following the war, however, Legris faced accusations of economic collaboration with the German occupation. Hit hard by sanctions, Georges and Paul succeeded in clearing the company's name only in 1949.

Postwar Modernization

By then, the company was in perilous shape. Despite the addition of Panneau—who was later joined by Jacques Pierrilée and Roland Simonot to complete the company's leadership—Legris was still operating more or less according to 19th century industrial practices. The company's aging factory, unruly inventory system, and ancient equipment, as well as its organization—with the average age of its employees in their 50s, many of whom were father and son, and a system of foremen operating their departments as private fiefdoms—seemed out of place in a new era of modernization. More troubling for the company was the loss of another major sales area, as first Paris and then other French cities replaced their ancient gas systems. Meanwhile, Legris surgical instruments had fallen behind the vast improvements made by their U.S. counterparts, who rose to market dominance.

The reviving French economy, shortly to enter the long boom period of the 1950s–1970s, and the leadership of Panneau, who had all but taken over direction of the company's production from Georges, brought fresh hope for the company's future.

Georges's sons, Pierre and André, who had both studied at the famed engineering school L'Ecole des Arts et Métiers, joined the company in the late 1940s. Taking minor positions at first, the pair, joined by Panneau, began instituting a number of initiatives, from developing a modern inventory system to designing new machinery capable of vastly increasing production. Despite the growth in productivity and the booming sales, the company lurched from one financial crisis to the other through the 1950s.

The brothers offered to buy out their uncle's share of the family business, and in 1958 Paul finally agreed to relinquish the company's control. On January 1, 1959, the company reincorporated as Legris S.A.

Under André and Pierre's direction, the company underwent a restructuring that launched it on a long period of growth. With Pierre providing commercial direction and André exhibiting a genius for innovative product designs, Legris established itself once again at the heart of France's booming industrial sector, with major clients including Citroen, Renault, Peugeot, Motebecane, and many others. At the start of the 1960s, Legris also moved to expand and modernize its production facilities, opening a small plant in Ozoir-la-Ferrière, outside Paris. Not long after that plant became operational, the aged Paris factory burned. The company was forced to transfer all production to the Ozoir plant—a feat accomplished in only four days, with the loss of only one workday—and Legris found itself entering a new era.

Post-1960s Expansion

One important result of the transfer of the company's activities outside of Paris was its decision to drop its surgical instruments arm. Legris regrouped around its taps, valves, and related products, but now with a steady shift toward industrial fluids applications. Among the company's hallmarks of the time was its innovative product designs and its readiness to respond to the emerging needs of its customers. During the 1960s, the company also began developing an international distribution network, signing on distributors in the Netherlands, England, and Belgium, and later establishing subsidiaries or acquiring its foreign distributors as subsidiaries. The first of these, Legris Commerciale et Financière, was formed in 1965, in Geneva, Switzerland. Not all of the company's international moves were successful: initial contracts with distributors in Finland and Sweden in the mid-1960s proved a failure, partly out of the distributors' relative disinterest in Legris's fortunes, and led the company to engage in a policy of owning its foreign distribution activities. A subsidiary was established in Spain, and the company began taking its first steps to enter the U.S. market. In the early 1970s, the company began one of the first foreign businesses to set up a joint-venture subsidiary in the newly opening Japanese market. Another move by the company in the mid-1970s was its decision to decentralize the company, opening smaller production facilities in the French provinces.

While successful, Legris remained a small, family-run operation. The invention of the instant fitting in the early 1970s provided the company with a launching pad for its future growth. But by the mid-1970s Legris had nearly collapsed, as the effects of the 1973 OPEC Oil Embargo caught the company by surprise. Overnight, its orders dried up, and the company found itself facing massive losses. On monthly sales sliding to FFr 8 million, losses mounted from FFr 500,000 to FFr 1.5 million each month. Yet the company was unable to find relief in laying off its employees, having been denied the necessary approval from the French government's labor bureau. By the end of 1975, the company's losses had grown to FFr 13 million on sales of FFr 90 million. The company was forced to turn to the banks to remain afloat. Legris's chief creditors soon lost faith in the company, demanding that the Legris family turn over theirs shares in the enterprise to the banks for one symbolic franc.

By the end of 1976, however, Legris's fortunes had improved. Sales, buoyed by the success of the instant fitting, began to rise again, passing FFr 100 million, and the company's profitability returned. Yet the company's relationship with its creditors remained strained into the next decade. At the same time, the company's leadership could envision no real prospect of growth. In 1981 Pierre and André Legris decided to turn the company over to younger leadership. While Legris remained in the family, with Pierre's sons Pierre-Yves and Olivier joining the directorship, the company also recruited Yvon Jacobs, who later took over as the company's president.

The new team rapidly set to work revitalizing the company, renewing its product line and automating much of its operations. By the mid-1980s, the company's sales had grown to some FFr 350 million. In order to finance future growth, the company sought to go public. Yet the company was still too small to be quoted on the primary Paris exchange. At the same time, the ascendancy of Francois Mitterand's Socialist government, and its commitment to nationalizing French industry, put an end to Legris's hope of selling its shares to the public. Reluctantly, the company turned to the U.S.'s SCOVILL, which agreed to acquire the company.

The sale did not take place, however. In 1985 the French secondary market was created, just in time for the French government to deny the acquisition of Legris by a foreign corporation. Legris's arrival on the secondary market quickly proved successful, raising much-needed capital for investment. The following year, Legris made the first acquisition that would give the company its future form. In 1986 Legris acquired the Pont-à-Mousson subsidiary Comap, based in Orleans and the leader of the French domestic fluids market. With this acquisition, Legris changed its name once again, to Legris Industries.

While the Comap acquisition easily complemented Legris's existing products, its next acquisition would take it into another area of industry altogether. Partly because of pressure from the government, Legris agreed, in 1987, to acquire the struggling Lyons-based tower-crane manufacturer Potain—which, with FFr 800 million in sales was much larger than Legris itself.

By the start of the 1990s, having turned around Potain and successfully expanded Comap into the foreign market, Legris was posting remarkable sales figures: in less than five years the company had grown from a FFr 350 million company to sales of more than FFr 5.6 billion. Only the recession of the early 1990s—and its extended impact on the European market— would slow the company's sudden expansion. For much of the first half of the 1990s, the company's sales would slip. With the exception of 1993, however, the company remained profitable. As the economic crisis began to clear in the mid-1990s, Legris, still largely controlled by the founding family, could look forward to a still more fluid future.

Principal Subsidiaries

Legris SA; Bourdon SA; Comap SA; Potain SA; Savoye Logistic Systems.

Further Reading

Secher, Reynald, *Legris: Histoire d'une Saga Industrielle,* Rennes: Editions RSE, 1997.

—M. L. Cohen

Groupe Yves Saint Laurent

Couture:
5, avenue Marceau
75116 Paris
France
(33) 1.44.31.64.00
Fax: (33) 1.47.23.69.73
Perfumes:
28, boulevard du Parc
92200 Neuilly-sur-Seine
France
(33) 1.41.42.31.00
Fax: (33) 1.41.43.30.38

Wholly Owned Subsidiary of Sanofi Group
Incorporated: 1961
Employees: 1,169
Sales: FFr 6.48 billion (US$1.21 billion) (1996)
SICs: 2300 Apparel and Other Textile Products; 2844
    Toilet Preparations

In just 40 years, Yves Saint Laurent, the man, has fashioned a legend, while the Yves Saint Laurent company, Groupe Yves Saint Laurent, has grown to become one of the world's leading labels for clothing, perfumes, accessories, makeup, and skin care products, and, of course, haute couture. The distinction between man and mark is necessary: while Yves Saint Laurent continues to excite the fashion world with his collections for haute couture and ready-to-wear clothing, the group, since 1993, has been a wholly owned subsidiary of Sanofi, itself a subsidiary of French industrial giant Elf Aquitaine (FFr 280 billion in 1996). As such, Yves Saint Laurent Perfumes forms the core of Sanofi's FFr 3.8 billion beauty division, the industry's third largest perfumes and cosmetics group behind L'Oréal and Estée Lauder, joined by such other labels as Roger & Gallet, Van Cleef & Arpels, and Oscar de la Renta. Sanofi also has controlling interest in two other important labels, Nina Ricci and Yves Rocher. In 1996, annual sales at Yves Saint Laurent were reported at FFr 2.48 billion (US$460 million) for perfumes, and FFr 4 billion (US$750 million) for its couture.

Haute couture, guided by Yves Saint Laurent's Maison de Couture, represents only a fraction of sales under the Saint Laurent name, yet remains the label's flagship. Yves Saint Laurent continues to assure the design and development of the Saint Laurent haute couture and ready-to-wear collections, and his January show has long been the central event of the fashion world. Saint Laurent is seconded by long-time partner and Saint Laurent CEO Pierre Bergé, who oversees direction of the label's ready-to-wear and licensed products, including the group's chain of more than 100 Yves Saint Laurent boutiques. Total licensed sales of Yves Saint Laurent products reached FFr 4 billion in 1996. In 1998 Yves Saint Laurent celebrates his 40th annual collection as the official designer for the year's World Cup, hosted by France.

Although perfumes have seemed to play a secondary role for Yves Saint Laurent, they have long been the label's chief sales engine. Yves Saint Laurent Perfumes, under the direction of Sanofi's CEO Raymond Ortal, produces and markets perfumes, cosmetics, and personal care products under the Saint Laurent name. Perfumes make up the most important part of this division's sales, which neared FFr 2.5 billion in 1996, boosting the Sanofi beauty division's total sales to FFr 3.8 billion. Yves Saint Laurent's *Opium* and *Rive Gauche* have long been leaders in the women's perfumes market; while *Jazz,* and, in the mid-1990s, *Opium pour Homme,* have helped the company capture a share of the men's perfume market as well. The company also produces its own line of lipsticks, eye shadows, and other makeup products, as well as a line of personal care products, such as lotions and cremes. Whereas production and distribution of perfumes and beauty products are the responsibility of Sanofi, Yves Saint Laurent continues to guide the creative development of products bearing his name. The group's newest perfume and cosmetics line, *In Love Again,* expected to be launched as a limited edition in 1998.

Heir to the Fashion Crown in the 1950s

Yves Mathieu-Saint-Laurent was born in the French Algerian port town of Oran in 1936. At the age of 18, Saint Laurent journeyed to Paris to begin a career as a clothing designer. Success was immediate: in November 1954 Saint Laurent was awarded his first prize, the Prix Robe (dress), in a competition held by the Secretariat. It was to be the first success in a career that would see little but triumph.

Less than a year after his arrival in Paris, Saint Laurent entered the prestigious house of Christian Dior as Dior's assistant designer and designated heir-apparent. Saint Laurent debuted his first major design, an evening gown, in 1955. Two years later, at Dior's death, Saint Laurent assumed direction of the Christian Dior line. Saint Laurent's first full collection, dubbed *Trapeze*, debuted on January 30, 1958. The collection was a hit, elevating Saint Laurent to instant celebrity and earning the 21-year-old designer the prestigious Nieman Marcus Award for the Dior house.

Three years later Saint Laurent set out to found his own fashion empire. Leaving Dior, Saint Laurent, joined by Pierre Bergé, established his own maison de couture on the rue la Boétie in Paris in July 1961. The partners, assisted by several former Dior employees and backed financially by the American J. Mack Robinson, officially opened the House of Saint Laurent on the rue Spontini in December 1961, presenting the first true Yves Saint Laurent collection—under the famed YSL logo designed by Cassandre—one month later.

Throughout the 1960s Saint Laurent established his leading role on the Paris—and world—fashion scene. More than a star, Saint Laurent would come to represent haute couture itself, to the extent that, by the end of the 1960s, Gabrielle Chanel would designate Saint Laurent as her "spiritual heir." Among Saint Laurent's successes of the decade was his triumphant 1965 *Mondrian* collection, featuring strict lines and simple color schemes inspired by the painter. The following year was launched another Saint Laurent trademark: the tuxedo for women. A daring design, the tuxedo would not only become a mainstay, even centerpiece, of each year's Saint Laurent collection, but the design marked a revolution in women's fashion, suggesting that trousers and femininity were not mutually exclusive and opening the way for the androgynous fashions of the 1970s. In 1966 as well, under Bergé's leadership, Saint Laurent was the first of the major designers to open a luxury ready-to-wear boutique, Saint Laurent Rive Gauche, separate from his haute couture collection. It was to be the first of a chain of franchised boutiques bearing the Saint Laurent name.

In 1965 financial backer J. Mack Robinson sold out his share of the company to the United States's Charles of the Ritz, which then came to hold 80 percent of the couture house, against the 20 percent held jointly by Saint Laurent and Bergé. Meanwhile, Saint Laurent continued to excite the fashion world, inaugurating the "ethnic" trend with his presentation of African-inspired designs in 1967 and starting the "safari look" with his 1968 collection. That same year, Yves Saint Laurent presented the first transparent designs, shocking the fashion world with their "see-through" look and inspiring designers for decades to come. Apart from haute couture and ready-to-wear, Saint Laurent brought a love of theater to the decor and costumes of the stage and film worlds. Among films and productions featuring Saint Laurent designs were *Notre Dame de Paris* (Roland Petit, 1965); *Belle du Jour* (Luiz Bunel, 1966); Claudia Cardinale's costumes in *The Pink Panther* (Blake Edwards, 1962); costumes for the 1968 production of *Paradis Perdu*, featuring

Margot Fonteyn and Rudolf Nureyev; and for many others, including Sophia Loren, Jeanne Moreau, Johnny Halliday, Miou Miou, Anne and Duprey.

Although Saint Laurent's emphasis continued to be on women's fashions, he also began designing for men. In 1969 a new boutique was opened, Rive Gauche Homme, featuring the designer's ready-to-wear men's fashions. At the same time, the Saint Laurent name was branching out into its own line of perfumes, including *YSL*, and, in 1971, *YSL pour Homme*, the launch for which Saint Laurent himself posed in the nude. In that same year Saint Laurent again shocked the fashion world—and introduced a new trend—with the presentation of his *40* (also called *Libération*) collection, a "retro" look inspired more by nostalgia than the fashion world's more usual avant-garde.

Ascending the "Throne" in the 1970s

The deaths of Chanel in 1971 and of Christóbal Balenciaga (the Paris fashion world's so-called "king of kings") in 1972 left Yves Saint Laurent the undisputed king of the fashion community. The following year Saint Laurent also became the leader of his own house: the sale of Charles of the Ritz to the U.S. pharmaceutical giant E.R. Squibb & Co. presented Saint Laurent and Bergé with the opportunity of purchasing full control of the group's couture activities. Charles of the Ritz would continue to exploit the Saint Laurent line of perfumes and cosmetics, although creative leadership for these products was provided by Saint Laurent.

Control of the fashion house gave Bergé and Saint Laurent a new opportunity. Moving the house to the avenue Marceau, Bergé launched the company into the licensing arena, authorizing the Saint Laurent name to appear around the world on a range of clothing and accessories. The company's licensing activities would prove highly successful in promoting the Saint Laurent name beyond the rarefied worlds of haute couture and ready-to-wear fashions. In these, Saint Laurent was achieving fresh successes, including his triumphant *Opera-Ballet Russes* collection of 1976 and a series of tributes, from 1977 to 1981, to Vélasquez, Delacroix, Picasso, Aragon, Apollinaire, Cocteau, and Shakespeare. New Saint Laurent perfumes were also successful, with *Rive Gauche* launched in 1977 and *Opium*, considered a landmark in perfumes, introduced in 1981. The following year Saint Laurent was awarded the International Fashion Award by the Council of Fashion Designers of America. In 1983 the company introduced *Kouros*, a perfume for men.

The 1980s saw a new string of tribute collections, including *Hommage à Matisse* in 1983, as well as *Hommages à Bernard Buffet, Zizi Jeanmaire,* and *Marcel Proust et Catharine Deneuve* in the same year. Another event in 1983 provided a measure of Saint Laurent's stature: the mounting of a retrospective of his work at the Metropolitan Museum of Art in New York, directed by Diana Vreeland. The exhibition, *Yves Saint Laurent: 25 Years of Creation,* was the largest retrospective ever granted to a living designer, and it attracted more than a million visitors. Other retrospectives followed: in Peking in 1985, in Paris in 1986, and in Moscow and Leningrad in 1987. In 1985 Saint Laurent was named a Chevalier of the Legion of Honor by French president François Mitterand.

In 1986 Saint Laurent and Bergé took a new step: the purchase of Charles of the Ritz from Squibb. The purchase price, US $500 million, not only gave Saint Laurent control of its perfumes, it also added operations roughly ten times the size of the company's house of couture. Compared with the couture line's approximately FFr 300 million in sales at the time, Yves Saint Laurent Perfumes generated more than FFr 2 billion. While Bergé and Saint Laurent took on a huge personal debt, the partners also turned to a number of third parties to finance the deal. Among these was Carol De Benedetti, who took 49 percent of the new Groupe Yves Saint Laurent.

Saint Laurent and Bergé had succeeded in grouping all of the Saint Laurent products under the same company. They had also assumed a massive debt. That debt, and subsequent events, would eventually result in the partners' losing entire control of their company. Initially, the future was bright: the company prepared the launch of a new perfume for men (which had already been under development for years, but which had been squelched by Saint Laurent Perfume's former U.S. owner) called *Jazz*. This perfume not only represented the company's first perfume line developed entirely in-house, the company was also depending on its success to recoup some of the massive cost of the perfumes division purchase. The company had looked forward to taking the company public on the Paris secondary market, a move that would have gone a long way toward easing the company's—and Saint Laurent's and Bergé's—debt burden. But the market crash of October 1987 ended that plan. The Paris bourse placed tight restrictions on new public offerings. Indeed, public offerings had become unattractive, given the wave of hostile takeovers that marked the era. At the same time, Saint Laurent, even with the *Jazz* launch, remained a minor player in the men's perfume market, then dominated by Azzaro, Paco Rabanne, and Laroche.

New Owners for the 1990s

De Benedetti proved an unlucky choice for a partner. By 1989, preparing a series of corporate raids elsewhere, De Benedetti insisted on cashing in his Saint Laurent investment. An initial deal to allow De Benedetti to exit the company collapsed. Saint Laurent was forced to list on the Paris secondary stock market in July 1989. Fearful of a hostile takeover, Bergé took the precaution of changing the company's structure, transforming Saint Laurent into a limited partnership. This reorganization would safeguard Bergé and Saint Laurent's control of the company's direction. It would also have more dire consequences—ironically, the structure would lead to the partners' loss of control entirely.

By 1991 De Benedetti was demanding to be let out of his investment. Bergé and Saint Laurent searched for new investors, offering some 15 percent of the company. It was not a good time to be looking for investors—the economy was slumping into a worldwide recession, which would become particularly severe in Europe and last well into the mid-1990s for much of the continent. For Saint Laurent's luxury products market, the wild ride of the 1980s was over and the more sober 1990s had begun. More important, investors were unwilling to enter a company in which, due to its limited partnership structure, they would have no control. At last, Bergé and Saint Laurent themselves bought up De Benedetti's shares. "We found the money

in two minutes," Bergé told *L'Express,* bringing his and Saint Laurent's personal debt burden to total some FFr 850 million.

Several months later, another investor, the bank Wasserstein-Perella, indicated that it needed to sell its 15 percent of Groupe Yves Saint Laurent. The block of shares would provide a strong entry for a hostile takeover, despite the company's limited partnership structure. The bank was instructed to find a friendly buyer for its shares, with the requirement that the buyer be neither American nor Japanese. This limited the choice to Europe, and, ultimately, to France's luxury products and cosmetics giants, chiefly L'Oreal and Moët-Hennessy Louis Vuitton (LVMH). The former was interested, but only in taking 100 percent of the company, for a price suggested to be as high as FFr 5 billion. Moreover, a full sale to L'Oreal could lead to Saint Laurent coming under control of L'Oreal's parent, Nestlé. Bergé and Saint Laurent refused. Moët-Hennessy Louis Vuitton—and such prestigious labels as Christian Dior, Lacroix, and Givenchy—also indicated interest in Saint Laurent, but again for 100 percent, not the 15 percent being offered. Bergé, burdened by personal debt and perhaps weary of steering a multinational company, came closer to accepting the full sale of the company, with the condition that he be given control of a division grouping Saint Laurent with its arch-rival Dior. LVMH balked.

One company remained that was capable of assuring Saint Laurent's future: Sanofi, the medical and beauty products arm of French industrial giant Elf Aquitaine, then still a nationalized company. Negotiations with Sanofi would continue off and on through 1992, which marked the 30th anniversary of the Saint Laurent house. By the middle of that year, however, the personal debts of Bergé and Saint Laurent were crushing them (Bergé's bank account was reported to be more than FFr 90 million in the red). Bergé and Saint Laurent arranged the private sale of portions of their stock, raising some FFr 100 million. This sale would soon lead to Bergé being charged with violating insider-trading rules—soon after the sale, Groupe Saint Laurent revealed that it had posted a loss for the first half of the year.

In January of 1993 the company announced that it had agreed to be acquired by Sanofi. At last, the partners had agreed to sell 100 percent, but in a deal assuring that, while the direction of Saint Laurent Perfumes would be controlled by Sanofi, the Maison de Couture would remain the province of Saint Laurent and Bergé. The purchase price of FFr 3.6 billion also contained an unusual provision: the granting of FFr 350 million to Bergé for abandoning the limited partnership. At the same time, Bergé announced his intention to retire after the year 2000.

Years of turmoil at Saint Laurent had given Sanofi a new division with shrinking sales and meager profits. After several years of losses, however, in 1995 Sanofi took action to reinforce its perfumes division and introduce a more affordable pricing structure. Whether these actions were enough remained to be seen; in September 1997 Sanofi began hinting that it was looking to sell off its perfumes division.

In the late 1990s Saint Laurent remained the acknowledged center of the fashion industry. His latest collection, presented in January 1998, marked his 40th year and 150th collection.

Indeed, 1998 proposed to be the Year of Saint Laurent: on July 12th, a retrospective of 300 of Saint Laurent's works was scheduled to be presented at the finale of the 1998 World's Cup, before a televised audience expected to number more than two billion. The company planned to launch its newest perfume line, *In Love Again,* while preparations were made for an exhibition in tribute of Saint Laurent for the International Fashion Festival of Photography in New York in March 1998. Finally, 1998 would also see the inauguration of the Saint Laurent Gallery in the National Gallery of London—a lasting tribute to fashion's living legend.

Further Reading

Baumier, Jean, "Pour Ceux Qui Aiment le Jazz," *Le Nouvel Observateur,* March 25, 1988, p. 67.

Beaufils, Vincent, "YSL: une Vente Cousu Main," *L'Express,* February 4, 1993, p. 57.

Bénaim, Laurence, *Yves Saint Laurent,* Paris: Grasset, 1993.

Masurel, Laurence, "Saint Laurent en Bourse," *Paris Match,* July 7, 1989, p. 68.

Righini, Mariella, "L'Apothéose Selon Saint Laurent," *Le Nouvel Observateur,* January 22, 1998, p. 74.

—M.L. Cohen

Guerlain

125 rue President Wilson
92595 Levallois Perret
France
(33) 01 41 27 32 16
Fax: (33) 01 41 27 31 00
Web site: http://www.guerlain.fr

Wholly Owned Subsidiary of Moët-Hennessy Louis
Vuitton (LVMH)
Incorporated: 1828
Employees: Not Available
Sales: FFr 2.1 billion (US$390 million) (1995)
SICs: 2844 Toilet Preparations

Few names are as famously fragrant as Guerlain. One of the oldest continuously operating perfume houses in the world, Guerlain has created some of the world's most durable fragrances over its 170 years—indeed, many of Guerlain's perfumes are said to capture the spirit of their times. From the legendary *Jicky* to the best-selling *Shalimar* and *Samsara* and the company's most recent, *Champs-Elysées,* introduced in 1996, Guerlain's scents have established a worldwide reputation for quality, luxury, and elegance. In conjunction with its perfume products, Guerlain also produces bath accessories and skin care products, as well as cosmetics and skin care products under the *Issima* name. Guerlain operates a chain of 23 boutiques throughout the world, continuing the long-held policy of direct marketing and individual customer service that has enabled the company to remain at the forefront of perfume fashions. Perfumes form approximately 60 percent of Guerlain's total sales; *Shalimar* and *Samsara* each account for 15 percent of Guerlain's perfume sales. The company sees more than 70 percent of total sales outside of France.

Since 1994 Guerlain has been a subsidiary of Moët-Hennessey LVMH (FFr 30 billion in 1996), when this world leader in the luxury goods segment, led by Bernard Arnault, purchased a majority share of the family-owned perfumer. As such, Guerlain joins such other prestigious names in perfumes and fashion as Christian Dior, Givenchy, Kenzo, Christian Lacroix, Louis Vuitton, Berluti, and champagnes including Moët & Chandon, Veuve Clicquot Ponsardin, and Pommery. The acquisition, while ending Guerlain's long independence as a family-owned and operated company, valued Guerlain at more than FFr 4 billion, double the company's annual revenues. In 1996 Moët-Hennessey Louis Vuitton (LVMH) completed its acquisition of 100 percent control of Guerlain. Christian Lanis has served as president of Guerlain since 1994; however, Jean-Paul Guerlain, the company's "nose" since 1956, continues to participate in the creation of Guerlain perfumes.

The Emperor's Perfumer in the 19th Century

The Guerlain dynasty was founded by Pierre-François-Pascal Guerlain in Paris in 1828. Born in Abbeville, Guerlain left home at a young age, reportedly to escape the violent nature of his artisan father. Guerlain journeyed to London, where he received an education as a chemist. Upon his return to France, Guerlain went to Paris, where he set up shop on the rue de Rivoli as a *"perfumeur vinaigrier"* (perfumer and vinegar-maker). Initially, Guerlain sold products imported from England—already attracting an upscale clientele. It was not long, however, before Guerlain began creating his own products, establishing a studio on the Place de l'Etoile.

Although the "chemistry" of the time bore little resemblance to the exact science of the next century, Guerlain's background nonetheless gave him a strong knowledge of basic materials and an appreciation for, and insistence on, materials of the highest quality for his own preparations. Before long, Guerlain's catalog boasted a variety of creams, lotions, ointments, and oils, including a creme "Nivea" and bear fat from Canada, but also cosmetic products, such as nail polish. To these, Guerlain quickly added his own fragrance compositions. It was not long, however, before Guerlain began concentrating his efforts on developing perfumes.

Although scents had long been popular in France, an actual perfume industry barely existed in the early 19th century. The use of eau de cologne, particularly in a country that had not yet adopted the habit of regular bathing, formed an integral part of the personal care routine. Perfumes, however, tended to be regarded with some disdain—accepted for the scenting of handkerchiefs and, perhaps, clothing, but the preference of the era for the body's natural odor and a socially coded modesty, which frowned upon individuality, kept perfumes from the skin. Guerlain would become credited for changing much of this perception and for helping to usher in the rise of a true perfume industry.

Guerlain's shop provided him with proximity to his clients and afforded him a keen awareness of the type of products they desired. This early "direct marketing" would become a company hallmark, but it also allowed Guerlain to introduce the concept of personalizing his perfumes. In this he was aided by no less a personage than Honoré de Balzac, who commissioned Guerlain to create an eau de toilette for Balzac alone—the scent by which the author would write *César Birotteau*. A new trend began, and Guerlain found himself in demand to create personal scents not only for his clients—or as gifts of tribute made by a client to another—but also to scent a specific party and even to perfume the pages of a magazine, *La Sylphide, Journal des Elégances*. By 1840 Guerlain had moved his shop to the fashionable rue de la Paix, serving clients from all over Europe, including the Queen of Belgium and the Prince of Wales. Soon after Guerlain established a new factory at Colombes.

The creation of personal scents was not only the work of satisfying his clients, but it also allowed Guerlain to establish a distinct reputation among the rising numbers of competing perfumes. By the mid-1800s Guerlain had become not only the most fashionable, but also the most expensive perfumer of Paris. Literally crowning this achievement, Guerlain, in 1853, created his Eau de Cologne Impériale, for the Empress Eugénie. Guerlain was granted the title of supplier to Emperor Napoleon III.

Modern Perfumes into the 20th Century

Pierre-François-Pascal Guerlain died in 1864, having established the house of Guerlain as a center point in the growing perfume industry. Sons Gabriel and Aimé inherited the perfumery. Gabriel Guerlain assumed direction of the company's commercial activities, aligning Guerlain with developments in marketing and production techniques. Aimé, the older brother, became the company's "nose" and creator of a new range of perfumes. By the 1880s fashions were changing and society was slowly abandoning its reluctance in regard to the wearing of perfumes—a movement encouraged by such Guerlain creations as *Fleur d'Italie*, introduced in 1884, *Skiné*, created in 1885, and *Rococo*, in 1887. Two years later Aimé Guerlain ushered in the modern era of perfumes.

The perfume was *Jicky*, named for the nickname of Gabriel's son Jacques. More than another scent, *Jicky* represented a revolution in the perfume world. Whereas previous perfumes had simply represented natural scents, or compositions of ingredients meant to mimic bouquets of flowers, *Jicky* offered an entirely new scent, one that did not exist in nature. Advancements in chemistry made since the 1830s had succeeded in isolating odor-producing substances—which could then be reproduced synthetically. Other synthetically produced substances could be used to suggest the scent of flowers and other natural substances, which

were either difficult to extract or too expensive to produce for perfumes. Yet it took Aimé Guerlain to recognize the significance of this progress, and *Jicky* became the first perfume to incorporate synthetic ingredients vanillin, coumarin, and linalool with natural ingredients such as mink oil, lavender, and bergamot to create an entirely "new" fragrance.

Presented at the 1889 Universal Exposition in Paris in the shadow of the "temporary" structure, the Eiffel Tower, *Jicky* was perhaps too new. Acceptance came only slowly to the perfume, but by the turn of the century, *Jicky* had marked the perfume world much as the Eiffel Tower had transformed the Paris skyline. The age of the true perfume artist had begun, inspiring such early 20th century creations as Coty's *L'Origan*, Chanel's *No. 5*, and Lancin's *Arpège*, all based on the use of synthetic ingredients. Aimé Guerlain continued to create for the house, introducing *Excellence* in 1890, *Belle-France* in 1892, and *Cipricime* in 1894.

In 1895 Jicky himself—that is, Jacques Guerlain—succeeded his uncle as the Guerlain company's "nose." Seconded by Pierre Guerlain, who moved the company to more modern manufacturing facilities at the turn of the century while assuring the company's commercial direction, Jacques would maintain the Guerlain family tradition as a cornerstone of the French perfume industry, creating some of the most famous names in perfumes over his 60 years as the company's nose. Jacques Guerlain would produce some of the more provocative names in perfumes, such as his first, in 1895, *Jardin de mon curé* (Garden of my parish priest), and the 1900 *Voila pourquoi j'aimais Rosine* (This is why I loved Rosine). If perfumes had become art, they had also become an important French industry, employing more than 20,000 at the beginning of the 20th century and representing an important source of exports.

Jacques brought an artistic element not only to his fragrances, but also to his perfumes' packaging: the introduction of a new perfume became a total concept, including the design of the perfume bottle, its label, and graphics. Guerlain began an association with another famed French name, when the Baccarat crystal company provided the bottle for *Champs-Elysées*, in 1904 (the company would launch a new perfume under this same name in 1996). In terms of marketing, this new approach to packaging represented a turning point in the industry, as perfumers would discover that the design of a perfume's bottle could play a role almost as important as the scent itself in determining a customer's purchase. Indeed, many later perfumes would be created to fill a particular bottle design and to answer to a name.

Jacques Guerlain's creations through the first half of the 20th century were numerous. *Après l'Ondée*, introduced in 1906, would remain in the company's catalog into the 1990s. *L'Heure Bleue*, created in 1912, became a classic of the perfumes of the prewar era. In 1914 Guerlain opened a second store, at 68, avenue de Champs-Elysées, which would later serve as the company's headquarters address as well. *Mitsouko* (1919) inaugurated the postwar period, but it was *Shalimar* that would capture the spirit of the Roaring Twenties. Introduced in 1925, it would establish the Guerlain name in the increasingly important North American market. In the 1930s, *Liu* (1929, reintroduced in the 1980s) and especially *Vol de Nuit*, inspired by the Saint-Exupéry novel, maintained the Guerlain tradition. The company opened its third retail boutique on the place Vendome in 1933; in 1938 the company opened its Institute of Beauty on the Champs-Elysées.

New Guards in the Late 20th Century

The Guerlain factory was destroyed by bombardments during the Second World War. A new factory was built in Colombes in 1947; in that same year the company opened its fourth boutique on the rue de Passy. In the 1950s Jacques Guerlain prepared to pass along the family tradition. His last perfume, *Ode,* was introduced in 1955. The following year, Jacques's grandson, Jean-Paul Guerlain, assumed the creation of the company's perfumes and proved to be as innovative as his predecessors, introducing *Vétyver* in 1959, the first of a long list of classic perfumes.

Under Jean-Paul Guerlain, the company would also expand and update its related beauty, makeup, and skin care products, replacing the family's traditional recipes with carefully measured scientific formulas and introducing the concept of expiration dating to assure the freshness of its products (and to encourage fresh purchases). Through the 1960s Guerlain introduced such fragrances as *Chant d'Arômes* (1962) and the men's fragrance, *Habit Rouge* (1965), capping the decade with the innovative *Chamade.*

A new factory was built in 1973 in Chartres, followed by the introduction of *Parure* in 1975. At the start of the 1980s the company launched a new line of personal care and beauty products, *Issima,* and new lines of makeup, including *Terracotta* in 1984 and *Météorites* in 1987, which helped the company expand into the emerging Asian countries. The company also continued to open boutiques in major cities around the world, bringing the number to eight by the end of the decade. In 1989 Guerlain had a new hit on its hands, with the introduction of its *Samsara* line of perfumes and beauty products.

With Jean-Paul Guerlain approaching 90 years of age at the end of the 1980s, the family-owned company recognized that it would soon face a problem of succession. The 25 Guerlain heirs formed a family holding company, Djedi Holding SA, to group their interests; at the same time, Moët-Hennessy Louis Vuitton made its first entry into the company, purchasing a 14 percent stake in Guerlain.

By the beginning of the 1990s, Guerlain faced an industry that had undergone a vast transformation. The trend had become one of consolidation—and conglomeration—spearheaded by such giants as LVMH, L'Oréal, and Sanofi. In 1993 Guerlain remained among the last of the independent perfume houses, faced with the massive marketing clout of the new perfume industry giants. The changing economic climate, from the heady boom years of the 1980s to the worldwide recession of the early 1990s and the extended European economic crisis, was

also catching up to Guerlain. While its revenues hovered around FFr 2 billion in the first years of the 1990s, its profits were slipping slowly. Meanwhile, its catalog was aging, with its last grand success, *Samsara,* dating from 1989. At the same time, a family successor to Jean-Paul Guerlain was not immediately apparent.

In 1994 the company agreed to be acquired by LVMH. The acquisition, delicately dubbed a partnership by LVMH leader Bernard Arnault, would occur in two stages. The initial stage granted LVMH, primarily through its Christian Dior holding, 58.9 percent of Guerlain. The Guerlain family, which received shares in Dior valued at nearly FFr 2 billion, retained for the time being creative control of the company, under Jean-Paul Guerlain. But Arnault installed Christian Lanis, formerly of Unilever, as Guerlain's president. Nevertheless, Arnault pledged to *Le Monde,* ''Guerlain would remain an autonomous company.''

That autonomy would seem short-lived. In 1996 LVMH completed its takeover of Guerlain, when the Guerlain family, through Djedi Holding, exercised their option to sell the rest of their shares to the luxury goods giant. The purchase of the remaining shares cost LVMH more than FFr 1.8 billion. While Jean-Paul Guerlain continued to create for the company, Guerlain's next product launch was to mark the beginning of a new era. Unlike its predecessors, *Champs-Elysées,* which received a worldwide launch in 1996, was not the creation of a Guerlain ''nose.'' Instead, *Champs-Elysées,* developed by Christian Lanis, evolved first and foremost as a marketing concept, responsible for adding a floral note to the Guerlain catalog while attracting a new generation of Guerlain customers, particularly customers among the crucial Anglo-Saxon market. With a promotion budget estimated at US$50 million for 1996 and US$100 million for 1997, sales of the new perfume line were expected to equal those of the company's venerable and top-selling *Samsara* and *Shalimar* perfumes. Despite Guerlain's entry into the modern reality of perfume marketing, the Guerlain name, backed by the financial clout of LVMH, would continue to represent a five-generation tradition of quality.

Further Reading

Forestier, Nadege, ''Champs-Elysées: Guerlain s'Ouvre un Boulevard,'' *Le Figaro Economie,* June 3, 1996, p. 10.

Gay, Pierre-Angel, ''Guerlain Rejoint L'Empire Arnault,'' *Le Monde,* May 2, 1994, p. 17.

Leboucq, Valérie, ''Luxe: Parfumeur de Père en Fils Depuis 166 Ans,'' *Les Echos,* May 2, 1994, p. 8.

Moore, M. H., ''Guerlain Seeks a Global Makeover,'' *Adweek,* July 17, 1995, p. 4.

Pavia, Fabienne, *L'Univers des Parfums,* Paris: Solar, 1995.

Veneuil-Denise, ''Guerlain, de l'Eau Impériale à Champs-Elysées,'' *La Revue des Marques,* January 1997, p. 47.

—M.L. Cohen

The Gunlocke Company

One Gunlocke Drive
Wayland, New York 14572
U.S.A.
(716) 728-5111
Fax: (716) 728-8353
Web site: http://www.gunlocke.com

Wholly Owned Subsidiary of HON INDUSTRIES Inc.
Incorporated: 1902 as W.H. Gunlocke Chair Company
Employees: 650
Sales: $46.7 million (1996 est.)
SICs: 2521 Wood Office Furniture; 2522 Office
  Furniture, Except Wood

The Gunlocke Company was manufacturing, in the late 1990s, executive desks, case goods such as bureaus and bookcases, and seating for businesses where image, superior craftsmanship, and design were important. It was providing standard and custom products built to designer specifications and distributing these products through a nationwide network of contract furniture dealers. The company was acquired by HON INDUSTRIES Inc. in 1989.

Privately Owned Manufacturer: 1902–69

William Henry Gunlocke entered the chair business in Binghamton in 1888 as a wood finisher and rose to the position of factory superintendent. He and four other men came to the village of Wayland in western New York in 1902 in response to a newspaper advertisement placed by the civic fathers seeking to fill a vacant factory building. The W.H. Gunlocke Chair Co. began production there with less than a dozen employees. Its initial offerings included bedroom, library, lounge, and rocker chairs. By 1904 the company was employing 40 people and had begun the first of many plant expansions. By 1911 its payroll had reached 100.

Gunlocke's reputation for quality designs and craftsmanship was due in part to its extensive use of steambending. By 1912 an entire department had been devoted to this time-honored but exacting process, which had been abandoned by many manufacturers in favor of less costly bandsawing. Gunlocke's practice was to air-dry wood for six months to one year before using it. This process, plus kiln drying, was essential to producing the company's durable furniture, including seating made to last for decades. Although the company's furniture was initially designed, manufactured, and merchandised primarily for household applications, it found a growing market in business settings and began to specialize in furniture for business and government offices, as well as for the nation's schools. Woodrow Wilson became the first of a long line of presidents to use one of its chairs.

Gunlocke received its first national corporate contract from Western Electric in the 1920s. This contract required the company to produce furniture in large quantities while meeting rigid quality specifications and delivery schedules. Similar contracts followed with other private firms and the federal government. Throughout the Depression, Gunlocke continued to grow. By the time William Gunlocke died in 1937, the company payroll had grown to more than 300 and a second factory was in operation in Cortland, New York.

Howard W. Gunlocke, William's son, succeeded his father as company president. The most significant of his innovations was the establishment of manufacturer's representatives, and later showrooms, in key buying centers across the country—still unusual at a time when most sales were being made through catalogs and by traveling salesmen. Howard Gunlocke was still the company's chief executive in January 1969, when it was sold to the Sperry and Hutchinson Co. for $16.5 million.

At this time Gunlocke was one of the largest manufacturers of quality wooden seating for offices, schools, libraries, and other institutions. All presidents since Wilson had used a Gunlocke chair (a tradition that continued into Jimmy Carter's term of office), and these chairs had been in the Oval Office under every president since Herbert Hoover. The company's furniture was in use in some 35 state legislatures, and it was also the nation's leading supplier of seating for colleges and universities. These were special-order customers with their own specifications, for which Gunlocke was manufacturing furniture in

---

Company Perspectives:

Our Mission: Become the Recognized Leader Within Our Target Markets by Designing, Manufacturing and Marketing Wood Furniture Solutions of Unique Value and Providing Tailored Solutions to Meet Specific Customer Requirements.

---

addition to its regular product lines, principally for the medium- and higher-priced markets.

Gunlocke also was producing tables, upholstered chairs, and lounge furniture in a variety of contemporary and traditional styles for the same institutional markets. The principal raw materials were selected hardwoods, such as walnut, maple, and oak. In addition, various natural and synthetic fabrics and fibers, produced by others, were being used by Gunlocke as upholstery. Aside from the principal Wayland factory, the company had smaller plants in Dallas; Whittier, California; and Almond, New York, at this time. It had more than 400 employees, and its furniture was being sold by about 1,000 dealers in all 50 states. Sales came to about $10 million in fiscal 1968.

Expanded Product Lines: 1969–89

The firm was renamed The Gunlocke Company, Inc. and became a unit of Sperry and Hutchinson's interior-furnishings group. This allowed it representation in the permanent showroom S&H maintained in High Point, North Carolina. The company continued under Howard Gunlocke's direction as president and chairman of the board. Record sales and earnings were achieved in 1969, and the number of dealers through which the company was marketing its furniture grew to more than 1,300 by 1971.

Gunlocke launched two new lines of lounge furniture in this period to increase its penetration of the higher-education market and began producing desks, credenzas, bookcases, and storage units. In the initial stages of the program, lumber storage capacity was increased by 30 percent, and the rough mill and steam-bending departments (the first stages of chair production) were expanded. New equipment, including an overhead conveyor system to transport chairs, was intended to facilitate future expansion. These changes required a major expansion of the Wayland facility, completed in 1973, and of the nearby Almond upholstery unit.

Gunlocke won honors for design from the National Office Products Association in 1970. In the same year the Institute of Business Designers presented an award to a new Gunlocke armchair and simultaneously to the designer, Jens Thuesen of the company staff. The company opened a new showroom in Chicago's Merchandise Mart in early 1971. Gunlocke's customers at this time included New York University, the University of Tulsa, the Minnesota House of Representatives, the Eastman Kodak Co., and People's State Bank in Marshall, Texas.

By acquiring Sjostrom U.S.A., Inc. in 1972, Gunlocke added a full line of high-quality library furniture. In 1973 it had

showrooms in Los Angeles, New York City, and Dallas, as well as Chicago. Its product line in 1974, aside from seating, desks, credenzas, and library furniture, included conference and side tables. These products were made primarily from solid walnut, maple, and white oak, as well as veneers of these woods. Along with seven other companies, Gunlocke became a member of S&H's new furnishings division in 1974 and subsequently became the parent company's contract-furniture division. The Almond plant was closed in 1976. In 1977 Gunlocke introduced a new desk series and three chair styles by leading designers.

Sperry and Hutchinson was sold off in several parcels during 1981, with Gunlocke purchased by its own officers for an undisclosed sum. The company had estimated sales of about $25 million that year. Under its team of owner/managers, Gunlocke enjoyed several years of unprecedented growth. In 1987, when the company was sold to Chicago Pacific Corp., its sales were estimated at $60 million, and it had plants in Wayland and Avon, New York.

Chicago Pacific made Gunlocke the core company for a newly formed contract office-furniture division. By this time Gunlocke had added office panel systems to its products. Chicago Pacific noted that the company was using a patented system known as the SteamFold process to bend wood into carefully crafted attractive seating designs. It was maintaining its own sales force and showrooms in most major U.S. cities and distributing its products to more than 600 independent furniture dealers nationwide. Gunlocke introduced the ergonomic Exel 3 line of modern seating in 1987 and was planning to introduce Estro, a contemporary addition to its Geva line of modular case goods, in 1988.

Gunlocke in the 1990s

The company's affiliation with Chicago Pacific was short-lived, however, for in January 1989 Chicago Pacific was merged into Maytag Corp. Within a few months Maytag had sold the entire furniture division to LADD Furniture Inc., which, before the year was out, sold Gunlocke to HON INDUSTRIES Inc. for $34 million in cash and notes. In 1990 HON assigned Gunlocke's Avon plant to another company unit, converting it to the manufacture of low-end office products. Gunlocke was one of seven HON companies in the field of office products and furniture at this time. Only four remained in 1996.

In 1993 Gunlocke was selected to assume the market served by CorryHerbert, a HON company dissolved in 1994 that had been producing metal office furniture. Despite this addition to its product line, all was not well at the firm. After increasing sales significantly in 1993, Gunlocke lost ground the following year. The company had relinquished market share in the high-end, wood office-furniture market, a market that itself had contracted, partly because of widespread corporate downsizing. As a result, Gunlocke downsized its own operations, cutting its labor force in 1995 to 650, compared with 850 early in the previous year.

One bright spot for the company in 1994 was accelerating sales for its Prism panel systems, which were now built with frames made from aluminum extrusions that accommodated sophisticated wiring requirements. These made the panels stronger and easier to install, while providing more applications and lowering manufacturing cost. In addition, Gunlocke was offering steel case goods, including lateral files and pedestals. A new automated sanding system reduced the time and labor associated with preparing wood for staining and finishing. It also standardized the process so that color and finishes would have greater uniformity and quality. The company also purchased new veneer splicing equipment that utilized a new process for joining pieces of veneer and ultimately produced more usable veneer from every square foot of raw material.

Gunlocke was seeking new markets in 1995 in such areas as home offices and business-focused hotels. Its goal also was to introduce new products that incorporated expanded-feature designs. In 1996 it introduced a line of chairs called Serra as its initial endeavor using mixed materials—in this case metal and wood—in its products. The new chair combined dramatic design with Gunlocke's signature steambending wood features and the high-tech look of metals. In addition to its standard goods the company was continuing to provide custom products built to designer specifications. Distribution continued to be through a national network of contract furniture dealers. Gunlocke's 685,000-square-foot factory was HON's largest manufacturing facility.

Gunlocke's case goods in 1997 included the Tremont, a traditional-styled desk of hardwood and cherry veneer, the Medley desk with credenza, featuring a double-pedestal desk with box and file drawers; and the Medley-Unit, a wraparound desk with shelving on one side. Among the stacker chairs were two cherry-frame models: the Phoenix, which carried a 12-year warranty, and the upholstered Chorus, "too beautiful to be able to stack." Side-chair models included the Contura, featuring soft urethane arms molded over a structured core, and the cherry-frame Liza, with continuous-grain steambended front legs made from one piece of lumber, without joints. The swivel chairs included the Austin, a traditional, three-button-upholstery model with knee-tilt and pneumatic-lift mechanisms; the Monde, a more contemporary style with the same features; and the Carlton, featuring a reclining back and manual lift control.

Further Reading

Astor, Will, "Gunlocke President Leaves Position," *Rochester Business Journal,* November 3, 1995, p. 2.

"Chicago Pacific To Buy Gunlocke for Office Division," *HFD,* September 7, 1987, p. 18.

Corporate Profile, Wayland, New York: The Gunlocke Company, 1996.

"Officers of Gunlocke Have Bought This Contract Division from S&H," *HFD,* October 12, 1981, Sec. 1, p. 28.

Ryberg, William, "Hon Industries Reports Record Sales, Earnings," *Des Moines Register,* January 28, 1994, p. 10S.

"S&H Acquires Chair Producer," *Journal of Commerce,* January 20, 1969, p. 12.

"The Sperry and Hutchinson Company," *Wall Street Transcript,* December 25, 1972, p. 31,248.

"Sperry & Hutchinson Names Mills President of New Furniture Unit," *Wall Street Journal,* April 5, 1974, p. 17.

"William H. Gunlocke," *New York Times,* August 29, 1937, p. 19.

—Robert Halasz

Guyenne et Gascogne

Quai Mousserolles
64100 Bayonne
France
(33) 05 59 44 55 00
Fax: (33) 05 59 44 55 19

Public Company
Incorporated: 1913 as Société Succursaliste S.A.
    d'Approvisionements Guyenne et Gascogne
Employees: 1,617
Sales: FFr 7.02 billion (1996)
Stock Exchanges: Paris
SICs: 5411 Grocery Stores

Guyenne et Gascogne is engaged in retail commercial distribution, with a primary focus on food products through the company's hypermarkets, supermarkets, and grocery stores. Based in Bayonne, France, Guyenne et Gascogne concentrates largely on the country's southwest region; through its participation in Pryca, the company is also present throughout much of Spain, as well. In 1996 the company's consolidated sales reached FFr 7 billion, generating net profit of FFr 137.5 million.

The largest portion of Guyenne et Gascogne's sales comes through its 50 percent ownership position in its Sogara S.A. joint venture with Carrefour. The Sogara subsidiary owns and manages 12 hypermarkets under the Carrefour brand name, including three hypermarkets in each of the Bordeaux and Toulouse markets, as well as hypermarket complexes in Niort, La Rochelle, Anglet, Angoulême, Pau, and Limoges. These hypermarkets are positioned as shopping complexes, with a variety of small shops anchored by the Carrefour centerpiece stores—which themselves feature extended product assortments including the standard supermarket categories, but also extensive selections of clothing, audio and computer equipment, automobile and gardening supplies, housewares and appliances, and other consumer goods. Sogara S.A. produced consolidated sales of more than FFr 9.4 billion in 1996; Guyenne et Gascogne's 50 percent share of Sogara's sales,

or FFr 4.7 billion, represents more than 60 percent of Guyenne et Gascogne's annual sales and contributed more than FFr 93 million to the company's 1996 net income. Guyenne et Gascogne's position in Sogara also gives it a ten percent interest in the 53-store chain of Pryca.

Guyenne et Gascogne proper exploits six hypermarkets under the Mammouth insignia, 15 supermarkets under the Atac banner, and 78 grocery stores and 28 seasonal groceries under the Guyenne et Gascogne name. The company benefits from its participation in the Paridoc central buying and distribution organization and that group's FFr 100 billion purchasing power. Guyenne et Gascogne's Mammouth hypermarkets are located in Auch, Cahors, Dax, Mont-de-Marson, Saint-Jean de Luz, and Tarnos. The company's Mammouth operations are aided by the chain's central design and marketing activities, as well as its selection of private label brands. The company's stores also offer the Mammouth card, a combination payment, credit, and customer fidelity rewards card. The company's Mammouth hypermarkets, with a total sales surface of 23,400 square meters, contributed nearly FFr 1.5 billion to Guyenne et Gascogne's 1996 sales.

Although hypermarkets (including Carrefour) represents more than 62 percent of Guyenne et Gascogne's sales, the company has also developed a strong network of supermarkets, under the Atac name. As part of a nationwide network of some 350 supermarkets, Guyenne et Gascogne's 15 Atac stores are located almost exclusively in the country's southwest region. The company also continues to operate two supermarkets under its own Squale name; during the 1990s, however, the company has been actively converting its Squale stores to the Atac format. Through the Atac network, the company offers the Atac customer fidelity card. Guyenne et Gascogne's 17 Atac and Squale supermarkets, forming a total sales surface of 18,400 square meters, added FFr 725.7 million to the company's 1996 sales.

With sales of FFr 124.9 million, the company's chain of Guyenne et Gascogne groceries is the smallest but oldest member of the company's retail empire. The 78 permanent stores and 28 seasonal stores (which operate at campsites and vacation parks in the southwest of France) emphasize their proximity to their customers in small villages and urban centers and feature extended store hours, home delivery, and more personal service than that available at the larger supermarkets and hypermarkets. The Guyenne et Gascogne branch stores focus almost entirely on food products, with more than 50 percent of sales generated by fresh foods, particularly regional specialties. Despite a decline in the chain's yearly sales, the Guyenne et Gascogne stores remain profitable and occupy an important—if somewhat symbolic—position as the bearer of the company's name and origins. The small grocery format has also garnered renewed appeal in an era of consumer backlash against the dominance of the French food distribution market achieved by the large hypermarket and supermarket chains.

Founded in 1913

Guyenne et Gascogne started out in the small grocery business in Bayonne, in the far southwest of France, in 1913. The company, called the Société Succursaliste S.A. d'Approvisonnements Guyenne et Gascogne, developed a network of traditional groceries, with emphasis on fresh foods and regional culinary specialties, in the village centers of the region and also established itself as a neighborhood grocer in the area's larger urban centers. While many of the company's stores served a year-round public, Guyenne et Gascogne also began catering to the important vacation trade in its coastal region. The French—and European—summer vacation typically extended over several weeks, and the French vacationer typically returned year after year to a favorite location. Guyenne et Gascogne became a fixture for many such vacationers, opening and extending its branch stores to include seasonal groceries serving local campsites, caravan parks, and other vacation villages during the summer months.

By the mid-1960s, however, Guyenne et Gascogne recognized that its customers' purchasing habits were changing. France was by then in the midst of its so-called "Thirty Glorious Years" of its post-World War Two economic boom. As in much of the western world, the mainstreaming of the automobile was under way, and the newly mobile consumer no longer needed to depend on the proximity of local merchants—including butchers, bakers, grocers—or the area's farmers' markets for their purchases. Developments in food refrigeration and the creation of the frozen food segment appealed to a population rapidly abandoning tradition in favor of convenience. The supermarket (and later the hypermarket variant) with larger selections, frozen and refrigerated foods and other products, and economies of scale providing lower prices, quickly succeeded in taking a growing share of the food distribution industry, and this despite the French consumer, typically more loyal to the small store concept than its counterpart in other countries.

In 1966 Guyenne et Gascogne, while not abandoning its chain of small grocers, nevertheless looked toward the new large surface area format to maintain the company's viability in the changing consumer market. In that year the company joined with Carrefour S.A., which itself grew to become a dominant force in France's retail food distribution industry, to form the 50–50 joint venture Sogara S.A. The joint venture's mission was to build, acquire, and/or manage supermarkets and hypermarkets under the Carrefour name and others. The Sogara joint venture eventually would take Guyenne et Gascogne beyond its southwestern market, but, with stores focusing on larger urban markets, such as Bordeaux and Toulouse, the Sogara hypermarkets complemented, rather than directly competed with, Guyenne et Gascogne's village and neighborhood-based small markets.

The company also would move into hypermarket and supermarket exploitation on its own, with hypermarkets participating in the Mammouth chain, created in 1969, and creating its own "brand name" of supermarkets under the Squale name. In these areas, too, the company reinforced its activities in its home region and, eventually, much of the southern French provinces.

Eyeing further growth in the 1970s, Guyenne et Gascogne went public in 1973, listing on the Bordeaux stock exchange. Four years later the company transferred its listing to the Paris stock exchange. By then the company had acquired a number of new supermarkets and had also expanded its hypermarket category, as a 50 percent partner in the joint venture Grandes Superficies S.A., into the Spanish market. In 1978, through Sogara, the company acquired two new Carrefour hypermarkets, located in Angouleme and La Rochelle, further north, but still close to the country's western coast.

Guyenne et Gascogne began the 1980s by simplifying its name; the company had also made several acquisitions, purchasing majority control of supermarket and hypermarket exploiters Solodis, Société Civile Agricole du Château Puycardin, and Somondex. Guyenne et Gascogne also expanded its regional concentration, opening stores in the Lot and Dordogne departments. During the decade, the company increased its participation in its subsidiaries, eventually controlling nearly 100 percent of Solodis, which became a primary subsidiary under which the company would group and later absorb its other hypermarket and supermarket subsidiaries, generally formed for the management and exploitation of a single hypermarket complex, including Somondex, Soldilial, Sodiso, and Jondis. In 1988, however, the company fully absorbed its Solodis subsidiary, grouping its hypermarket and supermarket activities directly under the parent company.

Growth in the 1990s

By the start of the 1990s Guyenne et Gascogne was posting consolidated sales of more than FFr 5 million. Roughly half of the company's revenues came through its own directly controlled hypermarkets, supermarkets, and small branch grocers, with its participation in Sogara representing a nearly equal percentage of its sales. The company's transformation from a chain of branch stores to an important regional developer and exploiter of large surface format stores was dramatic: by then, the chain of Guyenne et Gascogne grocers, which numbered 83 permanent stores and 26 seasonal stores, accounted only for slightly more than 6.5 percent of the company's total sales. Hypermarkets, excluding the company's participation in the Sogara Carrefour, had become the company's primary revenue generator, with its eight Mammouth hypermarkets (branded within the Paridoc buying central) providing nearly 74 percent of the parent company's annual revenues. Guyenne et Gascogne's Squale supermarkets, which numbered 18 in the company's home region, contributed a further 19 percent of annual sales. In Spain, the company's position was strengthened by the fusion of its 50 percent subsidiary Grandes Superficies with Centros Commerciales Pryca, creating Spain's largest network of hypermarkets, grouped under Sogara. Guyenne et Gascogne's participation in Pryca was fixed at ten percent. Meanwhile, as Sogara expanded, Guyenne et Gascogne's share of the joint venture slipped below 50 percent.

The 1990s would mark difficult economic conditions in France and in much of Europe. The recession that began during the early years of the decade would become a prolonged crisis, reaching into the middle of the decade. Nonetheless, Guyenne et Gascogne had taken a number of steps that enabled it to meet the recession with some success. The modernization of its distribution facilities, including investments in its computerized inventory, warehousing, distribution, and pricing systems helped the company increase its margins while controlling its pricing structure, countering the dropoff in consumer spending. During the 1990s, in addition, the company began shifting its supermarkets from its Squale name to the Paridoc-controlled Atac franchise. At the same time, Guyenne et Gascogne continued to invest in Sogara's expansion, regaining a 50 percent participation in the joint venture.

The sole weak point in Guyenne et Gascogne's position came with its 1993 attempt to counter the incursion of the so-called ''hard discounters'' into France with a purchase of a 20 percent participation in Europa Discount Sud-Ouest, and that chain of deep discount supermarkets. In 1996 Guyenne et Gascogne sold back its share of Europa Discount, which had grown to 16 stores, and exited the hard discounter market. Meanwhile, the company was also forced to close several of its branch grocers; Guyenne et Gascogne remained committed to the format, however, and in 1997 more than 100 permanent and seasonal grocers continued to bear the company's name and history.

The transformation of the Squale stores into Atac stores would continue into the mid-1990s. The company acquired several new supermarkets, while closing others that did not meet the requirements for the Atac format. By 1997 Guyenne et Gascogne's supermarket activities included 15 Atac stores and only three Squale stores.

The 1990s also would mark the increasing importance of the Sogara joint venture and its growing number of Carrefour hypermarkets, with new sites added in Toulouse, Bordeaux, and Niort bringing the total to 12 stores by 1997. By year-end 1996 the Sogara participation would account for nearly two-thirds of Guyenne et Gascogne's total revenues. Hypermarkets in general continued to provide the motor for the company's growth, with the company's chain of six Mammouth hypermarkets accounting for more than 62 percent of Guyenne et Gascogne's sales excluding its Sogara and Pryca participations. By then, too, the Guyenne et Gascogne branch stores represented only slightly more than five percent of the company's own revenues. Yet the groceries—which had come to play an important role in the commercial life of many villages—continued to add a significant, if symbolic, reminder of Guyenne et Gascogne's more than 80-year history.

Principal Subsidiaries

Sogara S.A. (49.99%).

—M.L. Cohen

Handy & Harman

Handy & Harman

555 Theodore Fremd Avenue
Rye, New York 10580
U.S.A.
(914) 921-5200
Fax:(914) 925-4496
Web site: http://www.handyharman.com

Public Company
Incorporated: 1867 as Peter Hayden & Co.
Employees: 5,000
Sales: $451.1 (1997)
Stock Exchanges: New York
SICs: 3339 Primary Nonferrous Metals, Not Elsewhere Classified; 3341 Secondary Nonferrous Metals; 3398 Metal Heat Treating

Handy & Harman is a 125-year-old company whose business has undergone numerous transformations over the course of the century. Founded as a maker of silver harness fittings, by the turn of the century the company had become the largest U.S. silver trading firm. As the nature of the silver trade changed in the 1930s, Handy & Harman turned to manufacturing silver alloys for industrial use as well as recycling precious metals from scrap. A program of acquisitions from the 1960s through the 1980s left Handy & Harman as a diversified manufacturing company with two major segments: metal wire and tubing and precious metals used in a number of industrial applications including precision plating and finishing, silver alloyed wire and strip production and brazing alloy fabrications. Through these two business segments Handy & Harman provided components and engineered materials for specialized industrial, electronic, telecommunications, and automotive applications.

Company Origins in the 19th Century

The company that was to become Handy & Harman was founded in New York City in 1867 by Peter Hayden. Hayden was a harness maker specializing in producing custom-made decorative silver fittings for the horses of well-to-do New Yorkers. Obliged to purchase silver for his craft, Hayden decided that trading in the precious metal was potentially more profitable than working with it, and in 1867 he closed his harness works and opened a business on Nassau Street as a dealer in precious metal bullion and specie (coins). Hayden's business prospered but in 1870 he decided to retire, selling his firm to Parker Handy, the vice-president of the Third National Bank of New York. Handy changed the company name to the Banking House of Parker Handy and added government bonds and general banking activities to the operations. In 1886 John F. Harman, who had been with the firm as clerk and cashier since its founding, was made a partner and the company name was changed to its current form, Handy & Harman.

The latter part of the 19th century was a period of tremendous growth for the American precious metals trade as new silver and gold mines in the west provided an abundance of raw material to be traded internationally. Handy & Harman was able to capitalize on this booming new market by specializing almost exclusively in the silver trade, and thereby gradually building a niche business with which few American firms could compete. In addition to trading in silver bullion, bonds, and American and foreign coins, Handy & Harman supplied silver bullion to silversmiths and jewellery manufacturers. By the late 19th century Handy & Harman had become the largest U.S. silver trading firm. The company's preeminence in this market was recognized by the New York Stock Exchange, whose silver trading desk was manned by Parker Douglas Handy, son of company president, Parker Handy. In 1892 a century-long tradition was begun when Handy & Harman became the source of the American daily silver price quotation. Begun as a simple posting of the daily price in the company's offices, Harman & Handy's position in the industry soon made its determination of the price of silver in American dollars the standard used throughout the country. In keeping with the company's authoritative role in the silver trading business, in 1917 Handy & Harman published its first "Review of the Silver Market." This annual report became the definitive word on the state of the silver industry for the next 70 years and was used extensively by government and market analysts.

Diversification in the Early 20th Century

In 1900 Handy & Harman began to expand the scope of its operations with the acquisition of the Standard Metal Company of Chicago. Standard Metal was a processor of silver, melting bullion to produce anodes, alloys and mill forms. With the acquisition of Standard Metal, Handy & Harman could provide not only bullion but alloys and prefabricated silver bands, wires, and moldings to leading jewelers, marking the first step in the company's future development as a supplier of processed metal to industry. The newly purchased company also engaged in the reclamation of precious metals from scrap materials, a process formerly undertaken primarily by jewelers themselves. Handy & Harman's refinement and standardization of the reclamation process was to become one of the mainstays of the company's business for the next 90 years. Standard Metal's operations, renamed Handy & Harman, were moved to Bridgeport, Connecticut, in 1902 in order to be nearer the East Coast centers of silversmithing and jewelry making. Some ten years later a new plant, which was to remain one of the centers of Handy & Harman's precious metals operations into the 1990s, was opened in nearby Fairfield. In 1905 Handy & Harman added to its precious metals processing operations with the acquisition of the Platt Company, a refiner of silver and gold and a manufacturer of silver solder.

Through the first two decades of the 20th century Handy & Harman continued to expand their precious metal processing operations. Particularly important for the firm's future business, was the development of silver alloys used for brazing. Brazing, a process that uses a filler metal and flux at high temperatures to join two metal parts, became increasingly in demand in the 20th century as large scale casting of machinery was replaced by the assembly of smaller components. Handy & Harman became one of the chief American producers of the precious metal alloys used for this process.

By the mid-1930s Handy & Harman's trading in silver bullion and coins had been discontinued as the global economy moved to other avenues of currency distribution and silver bullion became available directly through the Treasury. Run out of offices and a refining plant in New York and a processing plant in Fairfield, Handy & Harman's precious metals processing, brazing, and reclamation operations continued to expand. In 1936 the company opened a Canadian subsidiary in Toronto, Ontario, that provided the entire range of the company's precious metals products and refining services to the Canadian market.

New Products in the 1940s and 1950s

Like most American industry, Handy & Harman prospered during World War II as its silver alloys were used for such war related products as aircraft, tanks, torpedoes, and guns. In order to serve the West Coast aircraft industry that grew up during this period, the company opened first a branch office and later a manufacturing plant in California.

By the end of the war Handy & Harman, under the chairmanship of C.W. Handy, was the leading precious metals fabricator and refiner in the country. The company's emphasis now lay squarely in industrial applications for precious metals including new brazing alloys and electrical contacts. New branch offices were opened in Chicago, Detroit, and Cleveland to serve the growing industries of the Midwest, and by 1950 sales had reached about $80 million. In the late 1950s Handy & Harman began to expand into non-precious metals with the 1958 acquisition of the Posen & Kline Tube Company of Norristown, Pennsylvania. Posen & Kline produced precision drawn stainless steel, carbon, and nickel tubing for a variety of industrial applications and, as the Handy & Harman Tube Co., remained one of the company's core businesses into the 1990s.

Diversification in the 1960s and 1970s

The 1960s was a period of rapid diversification for Handy & Harman as a program of acquisitions, initiated by the company's new president M.W. Townsend, expanded the company's business to include a wide variety of non-precious metal products and services. The company acquired nine companies in the second half of the decade alone, including: the Orange Roller Bearing Co., a New Jersey maker of stainless steel conveyor belts; Maryland Specialty Wire, Inc., a producer of small diameter stainless steel wire, wire rope, and wire assemblies; Lucas-Milhaupt, Inc., a manufacturer of brazing preforms, washers, and special shapes; Ipsenlab, a Toronto, Canada-based company that performed heat treatment and furnace brazing of ferrous and non-ferrous metals; Ladek Metal Products, Inc., a Wisconsin fabricator of wire and metal ribbon; Consolidated Tube Fabricating Corp., a Connecticut manufacturer of small diameter tubing; the Attleboro Refining Co., a Massachusetts-based metal refiner; American Clad Metals, a Rhode Island maker of thin clad metal strip; and Bigelow Components Corp, a New Jersey fabricator of small coldheaded components for the electronics industry.

By the end of the decade Handy & Harman was providing metal parts and services to the jewelry, appliance, electronics, aircraft, and automotive industries. Although the majority of the company's acquisitions were designed to increase the company's non-precious metals operations, precious metals still provided the bulk of the Handy & Harman's sales. New demands for precious metals in the electronics industry were met by the company with new product introductions including chemically processed precious metals and silver and gold cladding of non-precious metals. Handy & Harman's precious metals reclamation operations benefited from price increases in silver and gold, and a new refinery was built in Attleboro, Massachusetts, to meet the growing demand. The company's total sales, which had remained steady at about $80 million through the 1950s and into the early 1960s, now began to grow at an accelerated pace, reaching $206 million by the end of the decade.

Handy & Harman's program of diversification within the metals industry continued into the early 1970s with the acquisition of Greenback Industries, a Tennessee producer of copper, tin, premixed bronze, and ferrite powders; and Rathbone Corporation, a Massachusetts manufacturer of cold-drawn profile shaped bars and pinion rods. Other acquisitions, including the American Chemical & Refining Co. and the Indiana Tube Co., were designed to expand the company's capabilities in segments in which the parent already had a presence. It was in the late 1970s, however, that for the first time in its history Handy & Harman moved outside the metals business with the purchase of Merit Plastics, an Ohio-based auto parts manufacturer. Merit, Handy & Harman's largest acquisition to date, made automotive control assemblies and molded plastic products for the automotive original equipment market and represented the first entry into an important new market for Handy & Harman. Company management felt that this diversification would enable Handy & Harman to reduce its reliance on the precious metals industry which had become extremely volatile in the mid-1970s. Although the company's stated goal for its acquisition program was to derive 50 percent of profits from their non-precious metals operations, by the late 1970s precious metals still provided over 60 percent of the company's $14 million net income.

Consolidation in the 1980s

Although Handy & Harman management was determined to strengthen the company's financial position through diversification, many investors, including renowned business guru Warren Buffett, were attracted not by the company's current operations but by its precious metal reserves. By means of last-in, first-out (LIFO) accounting, Handy & Harman had been able to carry the 288,000 ounces of gold and 18.5 million ounces of silver in its reserves on its balance sheet at the original 1940s purchase price. By 1981 the company had gold and silver reserves with a market value of $391.7 million carried at a book value of only $55 million. This huge LIFO cushion meant that each share was essentially backed by about $17.50 in precious metals, independent of the company's actual performance. The benefit of the company's reserves was severely curtailed in the 1980s, however, when the Windfall Profits Tax Act of 1980 wiped out much of the advantage of LIFO accounting. The new law required companies to pay taxes on their LIFO cushion at normal corporate rates in the event of a liquidation or sale of the company's assets, thus greatly reducing the attraction of Handy & Harman's stock to investors. A rider to the act, which provided that companies adopting a plan of complete liquidation by December 31, 1981, could avoid the newly imposed tax, led Handy & Harman to announce at its annual meeting in 1981 that it would consider total liquidation by year-end. Subsequent deliberation, however, revealed that the advantages to shareholders would be minimal and the company decided to maintain operations of the then 114-year-old company.

If the 1970s were marked by growth through acquisitions, by the early 1980s Handy & Harman, now under the direction of President Richard N. Daniel, moved to consolidate its existing operations by investing heavily in the upgrading and expansion of facilities and the development of new products. Rises in precious metals prices contributed to a worldwide growth in the reclamations industry and Handy & Harman responded to this demand by opening a new refinery in Singapore, the company's first major venture overseas. A state-of-the-art refinery was also opened in South Windsor, Connecticut. In keeping with the company's aim to expand its non-precious metals operations, much of the emphasis of the capital improvements program was directed at the company's automotive equipment business, which was reorganized as the Handy & Harman Automotive Group. A new manufacturing plant was constructed in Angola, Indiana, to supply fuel injection systems to major automakers, a facility was opened in Nuevo Laredo, Mexico, and the automotive radiator manufacturing facilities that had been acquired in the 1970s were expanded.

These efforts were successful in reducing Handy & Harman's reliance on its precious metals business. By 1987 only 42 percent of the company's revenues were provided by precious metals, with non-precious metals bringing in 23 percent and automotive equipment the remainder. The expenses involved in these improvements, however, caused long-term debt to jump from $56 million to $124 million. To make matters worse, poor conditions in the auto industry in the mid-1980s proved damaging for the company's automotive unit, and in 1986 Handy & Harman recorded a net loss of almost $9 million, the first loss in the company's history. Although Handy & Harman returned to profitability in the late 1980s net income remained stuck at a lackluster $9 million on sales that hovered around $600 million, well below levels reached in the early years of the decade.

Restructuring in the 1990s

By 1990 it became clear that Handy & Harman management would have to make a decisive move in order to lift the company out of the doldrums. In 1991 the company announced a major restructuring which would involve the sale of six non-core businesses, including automotive replacement parts, proprietary chemicals and metal powders, and the reorganization of the company into six operating groups: Precious Metals, Specialty Tubing, Specialty Wire, Automotive OEM, Wire, and Other Specialty Metals. After recording a net loss of $34 million in 1991 as the result of costs incurred by the restructuring, Handy & Harman returned to profitability the following year but net income failed to respond significantly, rising to only $16 million by 1994. The company undertook further restructuring in 1995 with the sale of the Handy & Harman Automotive Group, the divestment of the company's karat gold product line, and the purchase of Sumco Inc., an electroplating operation.

In 1996 a chapter in Handy & Harman's history came to an end with the sale of the company's U.S. precious metals refining business. With this divestment and the purchase of the ele Corporation, a manufacturer of reel to reel molding for the electronics industry, the mid-1990s saw the company engaged in two major business segments: Specialty Wire and Tubing, producing alloy and stainless steel wire and cable, small diameter stainless steel tubing, and carbon steel refrigeration tubing; and Precious Metals, encompassing precision plating and surface finishing for electronic applications, and sterling silver, silver alloyed wire, strip and brazing alloy fabrications. By 1997 Handy & Harman's net income had risen to almost $21 million on sales of $451 million.

As Handy & Harman entered the last few years of the century, the company appeared to have weathered the worst of its difficulties and to be poised to enter the next century as a solid, diversified manufacturer. The company's precious metal reserves still provided an attractive lure to investors as well as to companies looking for potential acquisitions. In early 1997, Handy & Harman resisted one such takeover attempt but it remained possible that the company's assets would attract other bids.

Principal Subsidiaries

Handy & Harman Tube Company, Inc.; Indiana Tube Corporation; Camdel Metals Corporation; Micro-Tube Fabricators, Inc.; Maryland Specialty Wire, Inc.; Willing B Wire Corporation; Lucas-Milhaupt, Inc.; ele Corporation; Sumco Inc.; Olympic Manufacturing Group, Inc.; Continental Industries, Inc.; Handy & Harman of Canada Ltd.; Handy & Harman (Europe) Ltd.; Indiana Tube Danmark A/S; Lucas-Milhaupt Europe; Handy & Harman (Asia) S.A. (Singapore; 50%).

Principal Operating Units

Specialty Wire and Tubing; Precious Metals.

Further Reading

Boland, John, "Glitter at Handy & Harman," *New York Times,* May 10, 1987, p. 10.

Briggs, Jean A., "Pricking the LIFO Cushion," *Forbes,* November 23, 1981, p. 207.

Cuff, Daniel F., "Chairman Succeeded at Handy & Harman," *New York Times,* December 25, 1987, p. 2D.

"Handy & Harman Shuns Liquidation," *New York Times,* November 25, 1981, p. 3D.

Jaffe, Thomas, "Cheap Gold with a Yield," *Forbes,* June 13, 1988, p. 146.

——, "Will Handy Finally Shine?," *Forbes,* August 19, 1991, p. 148.

Kuntz, Mary, "Golden Opportunity?," *Forbes,* November 3, 1986, p. 118.

—Hilary Gopnik

Hankyu Corporation

1-16-1, Shibata
Kita-ku
Osaka 530
Japan
(06) 373 5088
Fax: (06) 373 5670
Web site: http://www.hankyu.co.jp

Public Company
Incorporated: 1907 as Minoo Arima Electric Railway
   Company
Employees: 5,443
Sales: ¥230.2 billion (US$1.86 billion) (1997)
Stock Exchanges: Tokyo Osaka Kyoto
SICs: 6719 Holding Companies, Not Elsewhere
   Classified; 6517 Railroad Property Lessors; 4011
   Railroads—Line-Haul Operating; 4111 Local and
   Suburban Transit; 6552 Subdividers and Developers,
   Not Elsewhere Classified; 5311 Department Stores;
   5331 Variety Stores; 7996 Amusement Parks; 7922
   Theatrical Producers and Services

Hankyu Corporation is one of Japan's largest private railway operators. It owns a network of approximately 140 kilometers of track in the Kansai region of Japan. The Kansai region is the country's second largest metropolitan area and contains the industrial cities of Osaka and Kobe and the historic towns of Kyoto and Nara. Hankyu's three main rail lines link Osaka, Kyoto, Takarazuka and Kobe, serving millions of commuters, school children, and other travellers. The railway business forms the core of Hankyu Corporation, which consists altogether of almost 200 companies in many areas of business, including retail, entertainment, and tourism. Hankyu is primarily engaged in transportation, which contributes about 50 percent of sales, and operates six rail and seven bus and taxi companies covering the major cities in the Kansai region. Hankyu's nontransport businesses consist of real estate and

urban development, retail and rental businesses, and leisure and cultural businesses. In real estate, Hankyu owns high-rise residential buildings and housing subdivisions. Its retail and rental business consists primarily of renting or directly managing stores around its rail stations. These range from small convenience stores to large commercial complexes. Hankyu's leisure and cultural division operates family amusement parks and sports facilities, as well as operating an internationally known theater troupe, the Takarazuka Revue.

Early History

Hankyu Corporation was founded in 1907 by Ichizo Kobayashi as Minoo Arima Electric Railway Company. Kobayashi obtained government permission to operate electric railways between Takarazuka and Osaka. In 1909 a railway bridge was completed, spanning the Yodo River in Osaka and thus allowing a 25-kilometer stretch of railway to be built in the following year between Umeda in central Osaka and Takarazuka. A smaller four-kilometer line was also built, branching off the main line to reach Minoo. Railway companies were major users of electric power at the time in Japan, and they tended to generate their own power. Minoo Arima Electric Railway Company began the generation of its own power via a thermal station built in 1910. Both lines began operation following a ceremony at the train depot at Ikeda station in March 1910. In 1911 the lines began to provide freight as well as passenger transport, and in 1912 the nearby Arima Electric Railway was acquired. Kobayashi's hometown of Takarazuka was then the company's base. Kobayashi opened a hot spring resort in Takarazuka in 1912, hoping the attraction would encourage Osaka city dwellers to use his railway line. The hot spring continued to flourish and was the predecessor of Takarazuka Familyland, Japan's first amusement park. In addition to being an astute businessman, Ichizo Kobayashi was a lover of the arts. In 1913 he formed the Takarazuka Revue Company, an all-female theater group that gained an international reputation. Although its contribution to the railway company's profits was minimal, it provided invaluable publicity.

In 1917 Kobayashi changed the name of his company to Hanshin Kyuko Railway Company, which came to be known simply as Hankyu from the 1920s. The next five years were a period of great expansion for the company with the establishment of the main Kobe line in 1920. This line joined the cities of Osaka and Kobe and spanned 30 kilometers. North Osaka Electric Railway was also formed, operating two lines within the city. Hankyu was not only the leading private railway company in Kansai but was one of the largest in Japan as well. In 1921, in response to increased demand for electric power, Hankyu merged with Inagawa Hydroelectric Power. In the following year, the company formed the New Keihan Electric Railway, which absorbed the lines run by North Osaka Railway, and in the following five years opened four new railway lines within the city of Osaka. In 1924, in response to the success of the Takarazuka Revue Company, a new theater was built for the group. A hotel was added in 1926, adding to the town's attraction as a tourist resort.

Although Hankyu Department Store Company is now an independent entity and one of the major chains in the country, it has its roots within Hankyu Corporation. Kobayashi formed Hankyu's first proper store in 1928 by renovating and expanding the existing Hankyu store located in the vicinity of Hankyu's main Umeda station in Osaka. The Hankyu group entered the real estate business at this time with the completion of the New Hankyu Umeda buildings in the central Osaka district of Umeda. Hankyu had in the past entered areas of business that were not necessarily very profitable but were of interest to the company's leaders. The theater venture was one example. In 1936 Hankyu formed a professional baseball team to compete with the ten or so existing teams in the country. Imported from the United States, the sport had grown to become Japan's number-one spectator sport. Most of the teams were named after the companies that sponsored them, the most famous and successful at the time being the Tokyo Yomiuri Giants.

New Arrangements Before and After the War

In 1943 the company merged its railway operations with those of the next largest private railway operator in Kansai, Keihan Electric Railway. The resulting company was called Keihan Shinkyu Electric Railway. This trend toward mergers was spreading throughout Japanese industry, and the closest Tokyo equivalent of the Keihan Shinkyu Electric Railway at the time was the Tokyu group, which was swallowing up large portions of Tokyo's electric railways. These mergers were reversed upon Japan's defeat in World War II when occupation forces began to split up the huge Japanese industrial combines. Hankyu was no exception. Its department store division was made into a separate company in 1947, and in 1949 the railway operations of the group were split up, with Keihan Electric Railway becoming an independent company again. This still left Hankyu with a fairly extensive rail network, however, and the company's management decided to concentrate immediate investment on upgrading and repairing routes damaged in the war. Construction work was completed on Hankyu's main station in Osaka, Umeda, to allow the New Keihan Line's trains to utilize the station. In 1948 Hankyu opened an office at Osaka Airport and acted as agent for Pan American Airlines. In the 1950s Hankyu's rail business began to grow fairly quickly in terms of the number of passengers served. Freight service was stopped as the more lucrative passenger service increased.

In 1957, on the 50th anniversary of Hankyu's founding, Ichizo Kobayashi died. He had become renowned throughout the country not only as a leading figure in the development of the railway in Japan, but also a patron of the arts. In 1959 his son, Yonezo Kobayashi, became president of Hankyu. Under Yonezo Kobayashi, the company embarked on an expansionary program concentrating on the development of the areas around the company's major railway stations. The Umeda underground complex was completed in 1958 with similar work completed in the Omiya area of Kyoto in 1963. A new station was completed in Takarazuka in 1961 and a new hotel constructed nearby. New rolling stock was introduced on all lines—the so-called 2000 and 3000 series cars—and the Senriyama line was extended by two kilometers northwards with a further five kilometers to be added four years later. To cope with an increasingly complex railway network, an IBM 1440 computer was introduced in the operations department at the company's headquarters in Umeda station. In 1967 Hankyu became the first railway company in Japan to install automatic ticket vending machines at its stations, and the company is probably the leader in Japan in introducing safety- and efficiency-enhancing technology into its railway operations. Most of Hankyu's track within the center of Osaka was elevated to avoid traffic congestion, and in 1967 an automatic train-stopping system was introduced on the Kyoto line. Hankyu's various real estate companies were busy developing and constructing the choice central Osaka real estate that the group owned, and a series of new buildings were completed in the Umeda station vicinity. In 1967 following a severe typhoon, many Hankyu lines sustained damage as the embankments upon which the lines were raised collapsed. Although the damage was not serious, valuable lessons were learned about railway line construction; elevated embankments were subsequently strengthened to withstand severe weather.

In 1967 the baseball team, known as the Hankyu Braves, won its first league title. As founder of the team, the late Ichizo Kobayashi was voted into Japan's version of the Baseball Hall of Fame in 1969. Hankyu's founder was further honored when the Itsuo Art Museum was constructed on the site of his birthplace in Takarazuka. It has grown to become the city's premier museum with more than 5,000 works from all over the world. Japan's first amusement park was being developed in the city and was known as Familyland. This, along with city's hot springs and cultural activities, made it a popular place to visit for the residents of nearby Kobe and Osaka. The year 1969 also marked the death of Yonezo Kobayashi and the appointment of Kaoru Mori as chairman of Hankyu Corporation. The introduction of the total-traffic-control system in 1969 allowed Hankyu's headquarters to maintain absolute control over the network's trains, and resulted in one of the best safety records of any railway company in the world. There has not been an accident on a Hankyu railway since 1979. By 1969 Hankyu operated 141 kilometers of track, only slightly less than today's total of 147 kilometers. Expansion of Hankyu from the 1970s onward was thus largely in the nonrail areas of urban development and leasing and sales of real estate. Other transport-related ventures were started, however, such as Japan Car Rental in 1970 and the expansion of the existing bus routes. In 1973 the company officially changed its name to Hankyu Corporation. The group took advantage of the continuing golf boom in Japan by opening Kanzaki River Golf Club and a number of smaller practice ranges. The company's expertise in sophisticated computer control systems was marketed by the formation of Hankyu Computer Services in 1974. The Hankyu Braves continued their success as a professional baseball team by taking the Japan Series from Tokyo archrivals Yomiuri Giants in 1975. Two more consecutive titles followed, and to some people the name Hankyu became synonymous with baseball rather than railways.

Developing Business in the 1970s and 1980s

Takarazuka Familyland was undergoing continual improvement and was becoming one of the most popular attractions in the Kansai region. New theme sub-parks such as Machine Land were added. One of Ichizo Kobayashi's goals for Hankyu had been that the company should invest and help in the development of the local community. Hankyu Swimming School was opened in 1977, operating several pools in the Kansai region. The Ikeda Library, founded by Kobayashi, contained one of Japan's largest collections of works on the theater and entertainment. The 1970s saw the expansion of Hankyu's hotel business with new hotels in Kobe and Kyoto and several more planned. To finance these capital investment projects, Hankyu looked to the foreign as well as domestic bond market and raised Sfr50 million in 1985. Although Hankyu was not actively increasing its total rail network mileage to any great extent, money was invested in passenger comfort and safety as competition in the marketplace heightened with the dismantling of the enormous government-owned railway combine in 1987. Air conditioning was installed on underground platforms as well as on all railway cars. Ticket and rail pass payment was facilitated by the introduction of Hankyu credit cards acceptable by the vending machines at Umeda station in 1986. For the benefit of handicapped commuters, braille ticket vending machines were installed and special restrooms added to all the major stations.

Change of Focus in the 1990s

In 1990 following a reorganization, the company decided to focus on three main business areas—transport, urban development, and leisure. It divided its 155 companies into these three separate management groups, whereas formerly they had been loosely controlled by the railway sector. The six railway companies operated by the group contributed almost 60 percent of revenue and half of the operating profits. The group's sports and leisure facilities grew as well, though at that time their contribution to Hankyu's overall profit was negligible. Property rental and sales accounted for a third of the group's profits, with the remainder coming from so-called zaitech or speculation on Japan's stock and real estate markets. Urban development projects in the pipeline included the Chiyamachi area near Umeda station, the construction of a new Hankyu headquarters building in the same area, and a plan to develop an international culture park in Ibaraki City north of Osaka. In the core business of railway operation the emphasis was on progress through technological advances. Hankyu operated the most efficient network in the Kansai region, earning more revenue per kilometer

of track than its major competitors Keihan and Hinshin Electric Railways.

As Hankyu spread away from its core business of railways, it became what it called a "Life-Style Developer," working on a total urban development plan for the areas around its rail stations. Hankyu increased its commitment to operating retail businesses located near its stations in the mid-1990s, and revenues from stores steadily increased. It operated a fleet of stores for a convenience chain called ASsooNAS, and directly managed stores of its own. Directly managing the stores inside its own stations became increasingly lucrative. Revenue from retail and rental operations grew from ¥30 billion in 1993 to over ¥53 billion by 1997. In 1997, Hankyu decided to press its commercial developments further, and it began construction of a shopping and business complex in Kyoto's Miyazu City, looking over Amano-hashidate, a historic site called one of the three most famous views in Japan.

The major jolt to Hankyu's successful diversification plans was the tragic Great Hanshin Earthquake on January 17, 1995. The earthquake devastated the city of Kobe and surrounding areas, with great loss of life and property. Hankyu's rail lines and stores sustained heavy damage. Rebuilding costs were at first estimated at $865 million for Hankyu's rail lines, and the service interruption cost the company about $600,000 a day. Eventually the company paid over ¥18 billion for rebuilding and repair in 1995. The next year, the company was still paying for repairs and removal of debris, at a cost of almost ¥5 billion. Ridership declined as a result of the disaster, and tourism, which not only promoted rail ridership but contributed to Hankyu's profits through fees at its amusement parks and events, also fell precipitately.

After the quake, Hankyu rebuilt, continuing its plans to become a more diverse "life-style" company. Its real estate and urban development division took a huge loss in revenue for 1995, but two years later it was doing quite well. Hankyu sold close to 500 subdivision properties in 1997, which were mostly small plots with a prefabricated single-family house. It also sold two of its high-rises, which were massive apartment complexes housing hundreds of families. Real estate sales grew to account for more than 17 per cent of Hankyu's total sales in 1997. The leisure and cultural division also grew. Hankyu refurbished its Fantasyworld amusement park in 1997 and began improvements on its Nishinomiya Sports Arena, where American-style football was played. The percentage of the company's total sales from the cultural and leisure division, which had been next to nothing a few years earlier, by 1997 stood at nearly ten percent.

The company undertook new reforms at the end of 1997, vowing to reinvent the company along more competitive lines. Management decided to divide the railway, real estate and urban development, retail and rental, and leisure and cultural sectors into more independent units, where each would be regarded as financially separate. Hankyu also announced its intention to get rid of companies and assets that were not sufficiently profitable. The challenge Hankyu faced was that its railway business was not expected to grow. Population growth in the Kansai region was flat, and Hankyu had to increase its efficiency in order to retain its profit margin. The demographics of the Kansai region affected not only rail ridership, but Hankyu's other service sector businesses as well. The company realized that it would have to adapt to flat population growth by streamlining the organization of the company, making it more flexible to change. Though many of the necessary reforms were already in place—devolving the business away from dependence on rail profits—after the earthquake disaster, Hankyu seemed even more determined to prepare itself for an uncertain future.

Principal Subsidiaries

Nose Electric Railway Co., Ltd; Kobe Electric Railway Co., Ltd; Kita-Osaka Railway Co., Ltd; Hokushin Kyuko Electric Railway Co., Ltd; Kobe Rapid Transport Railway Co., Ltd; Hankyu Bus Co., Ltd; Hankyu Realty Co., Ltd. (50%); Hankyu Sangyo Co., Ltd; Arima Kogyo Co., Ltd; HOTEL new HANKYU Co., Ltd; Hankyu Taxi Co., Ltd.

Further Reading

Furukawa, Tsukasa, "Railway Service Creeps Back in Shaken Kobe," *American Metal Market,* February 7, 1995, p. 9.
"Japanese Railway Tallies Costs," *Wall Street Journal,* January 30, 1995, p. A14.

—Dylan Tanner
—updated by A. Woodward

Hanna-Barbera Cartoons Inc.

15303 Ventura Boulevard, Suite 1400
Sherman Oaks, California 91403
U.S.A.
(818) 977-7500
Fax: (818) 977-7510

Wholly Owned Division of Time-Warner Inc.
Incorporated: 1957 as Hanna-Barbera Productions
Employees: 130
Sales: $100 million (1996 est.)
SICs: 7812 Motion Picture & Video Production

Hanna-Barbera Cartoons Inc., founded by the animation team of Joseph Barbera and William Hanna in 1957, rose to prominence as the first successful producers of cartoons for television. They are perhaps best known for developing a formula for inexpensively made cartoons, which relied on characterization and topical, verbal humor, rather than fully animated action, as had been common among cartoons produced for theatrical release. By the mid-1960s the company had achieved a string of successes including producing the first animated series to appear on prime-time television, *The Flintstones*. Their success in the 1960s led to a formula of mass production in the 1970s which, according to some critics, stressed quantity over quality. During the 1980s the company began a global expansion of its operations, moving much of its animation division to Asia and creating a complex international distribution network. Struggling to regain its once enviable position in the industry, Hanna-Barbera was sold to Great American Broadcasting in 1987, and subsequently purchased by Turner Broadcasting in 1991 for $320 million. With annual revenues at about $100 million, largely resulting from increasingly lucrative licensing deals rather than direct sales of its productions, the subsidiary was a safe investment for Turner Broadcasting, which later merged with Time-Warner Inc. With the production company and distribution network came a library of Hanna-Barbera shorts and series, approximately 3,000 half hours of cartoons, which were much appreciated in filling time slots on the 24-hour cartoon network started by Turner in 1992.

Company Origins in the 1950s

From the beginning of their careers as animators at MGM studios in the 1940s, Joseph Barbera and William Hanna set out to unseat Walt Disney as the premiere producer of cartoons and children's entertainment. In fact, the pair did manage to upstage Mickey Mouse with the creation of the cat and mouse cartoon characters, Tom and Jerry, in 1940. These short subject Tom and Jerry cartoons were to be nominated for 14 Academy Awards and would win seven Oscars, the first such achievement by a company other than Disney. Joe Barbera modeled Tom and Jerry cartoons on the chase scenes featured in the great silent films of Charles Chaplin and the Keystone Cops. The simple formula of Tom and Jerry was succeeded by greater animation challenges, such as the combination of live-action and animation pioneered by Hanna and Barbera in collaboration with dancer Gene Kelly in *Anchors Aweigh* in 1945 and again with swimming star Esther Williams in the 1952 MGM musical *Dangerous When Wet*.

Despite the success of Hanna's directing and Barbera's writing, MGM management dropped its animation division during the 1950s, citing the rising cost of quality animation and a general malaise in its big studio system. In 1957 Hanna and Barbera no longer had jobs at MGM, so they started their own production company and turned to television, the very instrument that had accounted for the fall of the Hollywood studio system.

Hanna and Barbera were able to staff their new company easily enough since the entire animation division of MGM, with whom they were familiar, were all out of work together. The team had already had some contact with television when they produced advertisements for the popular *I Love Lucy* show, promos that had to be produced anonymously so that the MGM executives would not know that Hanna and Barbera were responsible. Once MGM let them go, however, the team moved wholeheartedly to the television market. They quickly learned that the method of production they had used at MGM would not be possible with the greatly diminished budgets available to them on television. While Hanna and Barbera had been making Tom and Jerry shorts for $40,000 to $60,000, Screen Gems offered them only $2,700 for five minutes of cartoon time. In order to make a profit they had to rethink their whole approach to cartoons.

Hanna and Barbera turned away from the visual, energetic approach they had used at MGM and focused instead on story and dialogue. The key aspect of creating cheaper cartoons was to limit the number of drawings required. The men adapted a tool they had developed while at MGM in which they produced a test cartoon with approximately one-tenth the number of drawings than the finished product would have. They would use this test to adapt and refine the timing of the film so as not to waste drawings. They realized that they could adapt this process and produce a saleable product based on this limited animation technique.

The limited animation approach was only half of the solution, however. With a lower quality of visual product the audience interest had to be sustained through dialogue. Joe Barbera realized that a team of talented, reliable actors would have to be assembled because the visually restricted cartoons would depend on effective voices for their success. Actors Daws Butler and Don Messick were hired in 1957 as the voices of the Ruff and Ready characters, and the two men would be heard behind Hanna-Barbera cartoon characters for the next three decades. *Ruff and Ready* debuted on NBC in 1957 and one year later Hanna-Barbera introduced *The Huckleberry Hound Show,* representing the company's first big hit and introducing the enduring character Yogi Bear, who was to have his own show one year later. Once the company had perfected its production technique of limited animation and high quality scripting and voicing, it proceeded to produce shows quickly while developing and selling new shows at the same time.

Success in the 1960s

In 1959 *Huckleberry Hound* became the first animated television production to win an Emmy Award for children's programming. According to Joseph Barbera, the Emmy represented something more to the animation team than had the seven Oscars won by *Tom and Jerry* in that Hanna and Barbera were now the producers of their works and collected the awards as pioneers in a new medium. Where Disney had turned up its nose at the budgets available in television, which permitted only $30 per foot of film rather than the $200 per foot to which movie animators were accustomed, Hanna-Barbera saw a niche where it could outflank Disney.

In 1960 Hanna-Barbera launched the first half-hour cartoon show to air during primetime. The concept was to put an animated, half-hour situation comedy series in the same time slot normally occupied by live action shows. Popular sit-com writers were hired to draft the scripts in conjunction with writers, such as Barbera himself, who understood how to make cartoons work. *The Flintstones* was to become the company's greatest success, having a six-year run followed by many more years in syndication. The "modern stone-age family" remained the most enduring image of Hanna and Barbera's partnership, eclipsing even that of *Tom and Jerry.* Almost immediately, the company followed its television success with marketing schemes. The images of their fresh, popular characters were sold to toy manufacturers and were used in product promotions, recordings, Hanna-Barbera's own version of Disneyland called Jelleystone Park in Hew Hampshire, and were even reproduced as Flintstones chewable vitamins.

Hanna and Barbera won yet another Emmy award for *Jack and the Beanstalk,* a collaboration with dancer Gene Kelly that continued the experiment they had begun with fusing animation and live action in *Anchors Aweigh* while still at MGM. In fact, Hanna-Barbera's success with *Jack and the Beanstalk* was in part responsible for the company's acquisition by Taft Broadcasting in 1967; Taft hoped to turn the kings of television animation into successful feature film producers. Even under the Taft Broadcasting umbrella, Hanna-Barbera maintained much the same corporate structure as it had forged during its first ten years of operations, with Hanna and Barbera named co-presidents and co-directors.

Despite its success on television and with the licensing of its characters for products and advertising, Hanna-Barbera remained tiny in comparison to Disney, with only approximately $10 million in sales for 1970. The Taft Corporation was betting that with additional capital Hanna-Barbera could grow into the Disney competitor that it had always hoped to be. In the mid-1960s, Hanna-Barbera produced the feature films *Hey There It's Yogi Bear* and *A Man Called Flintstone,* capitalizing on the company's first television successes. In 1972 it produced a more ambitious, critically acclaimed film, *Charlotte's Web,* based on the popular children's novel by E.B.White. Still, the company's feature films for theatrical release never achieved the same success as its television offerings.

Decline in the 1970s and 1980s

By 1970 Hanna-Barbera stood virtually unchallenged in television cartoons. The company had secured the top three Saturday morning Nielsen ratings and controlled 80 percent of children's television programming. Moreover, as an independent company, it was free to sell its shows to the highest bidding network. But this position was to erode for several reasons as the 1970s progressed. First, Hanna-Barbera was itself partly responsible for allowing cartoon quality to suffer. Limited animation began to look simply cheap to an increasingly sophisticated audience for cartoons. Moreover, competition also increased during the 1970s, with old theatrical cartoons finding a new home on Saturday mornings and with the attraction of imaginative techniques used by a new breed of animators who were more in touch with the young audience of the late 1970s.

In the 1980s founders Hanna and Barbera, both now in their seventies, remained the driving force behind the company. By the end of the decade the company was earning $60 million a year mostly on the strength of increasingly aggressive licensing deals. But, with the notable exception of *The Smurfs,* a widely popular cartoon show that inspired a cottage industry of toys and collectibles, Hanna-Barbera was lagging in the development of new successful shows and characters, and the company's share of the children's television market dwindled to 20 percent.

Acquisition by Taft and Turner in the late 1980s–90s

In 1987, the Great American Communications Group bought Hanna-Barbera, hiring 35 year-old David Kirschner as CEO and president of its new subsidiary. Great American president Carl Lindner took a great risk with Kirschner, who had little executive experience and had only produced two films, but after a decade in which it appeared that Hanna and Barbera had run out of ideas, youth seemed to be the remedy.

Kirschner's approach to Hanna-Barbera was to soft peddle any of its stock characters that he considered too dated, and hence unmarketable for licensing purposes, and to rejuvenate some of the older characters with new production values. In 1990 the company launched the animated feature *Jetsons: The Movie,* a project that had been under development before the Kirschner's hiring and one that marked the last time Hanna and Barbera would work together as director and producer. Unfortunately, the film failed to gain a significant audience. And as a result of poor response to the marketing scheme planned to coincide with *Jetsons,* Kirschner attempted to stop production on a feature-length Tom and Jerry film that Joe Barbera had been working on, creating conflict between the new CEO and the company founders. In spite of Kirschner's reluctance about the project, the Tom and Jerry feature was eventually completed and released in 1992, sparking a rejuvenated interest in the animation team's original success story.

Also under Kirschner, Hanna-Barbera took a bold new approach to combining product marketing and entertainment production with the launching of *Wake, Rattle & Roll,* a non-animated variety show for kids that aired during Hanna-Barbera's traditional Saturday morning time slot. Following the success of *Wake, Rattle & Roll,* Kirschner brought Hanna-Barbera into other non-animated projects, most notably a live-action feature film based on *The Flintstones,* starring John Goodman as Fred Flintstone and Rick Moranis as Barney Rubble and produced by Steven Spielberg.

But Kirschner's strategy of updating the stock of characters had its flaws. By replacing Fred Flintstone's image with that of a living actor, the sale of licensed products from the film were tied directly to the success of the film rather than capitalizing on the long-time recognition of the cartoon character. If the film failed, then products that sported Goodman's portrayal of Fred Flintstone would fail to sell, while the market for products with Fred's old familiar cartoon face would be overshadowed by the unwanted new look. Although the new live-action Flintstones movie earned $37 million in its first weekend at the box office, the marketing scheme was a major disappointment due largely to the competing images of Goodman's likeness and the traditional Flintstones characters.

In 1991 Turner Broadcasting System bought Hanna-Barbera for $320 million. Fred Siebert was appointed president of the company while Scott Sassa, president of Turner Broadcasting's entertainment division, influenced long-term strategy. Turner was not drawn to the company for its new look Flintstones or even its healthy licensing deals, however. The main incentive to Turner was the Hanna-Barbera library of cartoons. Turner launched an all-cartoon cable network, the Cartoon Network, in 1992 and needed as much of the existing established cartoon library as could be assembled. The purchase of Hanna-Barbera gave the new network 3,000 half-hours of cartoons, approximately one-third of existing cartoons, which could then be combined with the already acquired 800 half-hours from the MGM library. The Hanna-Barbera stock of characters were clearly viewed as marketable brands by Sassa and Turner, and many industry analysts expected them to sell off the animation studio. However, company president Fred Siebert was determined to revive the creative animation that had marked the early days of the company.

Under Siebert, Hanna-Barbera shifted its approach to marketing, carrying out aggressive market research prior to new creative projects or marketing schemes. The company also placed more emphasis on its international market during the 1990s, having already shifted much of its production to Asia and believing that the Hanna-Barbera stock of characters and overall style of production translated more easily to foreign cultures than did that of its American competitors. Along with international expansion, Hanna-Barbera prepared for the future with high-tech extensions of its family of characters such as a CD ROM documentary about dinosaurs narrated by Fred Flintstone.

In spite of Siebert's conviction that Hanna-Barbera's reign over the animation world could be revived, Turner's 1996 merger with Time-Warner Inc. seemed to cast doubt on the future of the company as a producer of important new creative projects. One of Time-Warner's first acts on assuming control of the company was to close down the 30-year-old studio that Hanna-Barbera had built in the early 1960s and where many of the company's greatest hits had been conceived. The company was moved to a high-rise office complex already occupied by Warner Brothers Television Animation. Renamed Hanna-Barbera Cartoons Inc., the company was to function as an independent division of its giant parent while sharing some services with Warner Brothers Animation. It remained unclear whether this physical merger was a sign of the Hanna-Barbera's future role as merely one brand in a giant corporation or if the creative spark generated by the company's founders could be maintained.

Further Reading

Barbera, Joseph, *My Life in 'Toons,* Atlanta: Turner Publishing Inc., 1994.

Blow, Richard, ''Little Shop of Horrors,'' *Business Month,* November, 1990, pp. 50–56.

''Faces Behind the Figures,'' *Forbes,* May 1, 1971, p. 40.

Goldman, Kevin, ''Mammoth Marketers and Merchandisers are Leaving No Flintstones Unturned,'' *Wall Street Journal,* February 22, 1994, p. B1.

Gross, Amy, ''Shaking up Hanna-Barbera,'' *Adweek's Marketing Week,* November, 26, 1990, p. 38.

Haddad, Charles, ''Hanna-Barbera Trying to Revive Creative Spark,'' *Atlanta Journal and Constitution,* April 24, 1994, p. R1.

Ono, Yumiko, ''Focus on Japan,'' *Wall Street Journal,* September 1, 1992, p. B1.

Pearl, Daniel, ''Turner to Start a Round-the-Clock Cartoon Network,'' *Wall Street Journal,* February 19, 1992, p. B10.

——, ''TNT Veteran Turns Talents to Cartoons,'' *Wall Street Journal,* October 6, 1992, p. B1.

—Donald C. McManus

Harris Teeter Inc.

P.O. Box 33129
Charlotte, North Carolina 28233
U.S.A.
(704) 845-3100
Fax: (704) 845-3112

Wholly Owned Subsidiary of Ruddick Corporation
Incorporated: 1960 as Harris Teeter Super Markets, Inc.
Employees: 16,500
Sales: $1.83 million (1996)
SICs: 5411 Grocery Stores

Harris Teeter Inc. has grown from a North Carolina grocer into a chain of almost 140 grocery stores throughout the Carolinas, Tennessee, Virginia, and Georgia. While the company maintains stores in both urban and rural areas, Harris Teeter's primary focus is on an upscale urban clientele with a taste for quality and variety in food. Harris Teeter is a subsidiary of Ruddick Corporation, a holding company whose other primary interest is in American & Efird, Inc., a manufacturer of sewing thread. In 1996 Harris Teeter reported sales of $1.83 billion, 4.86 million square feet of store space, and $259,160 in weekly per-store sales.

Harris and Teeter Team Up in the 1950s

The chain that became Harris Teeter started as two small North Carolina enterprises in the late 1930s. The first of these was Harris Super Market, opened in Charlotte in 1939 by W. T. Harris, who had borrowed $1,500 to start the business three years earlier. Though nothing like the vast shopping palaces that would eventually characterize the Harris Teeter chain, Harris Super Market had several notable distinctions: it was the first air-conditioned supermarket in its county, and it stayed open until nine o'clock on Friday nights. Also during this time, in the town of Mooresville, North Carolina, Paul and Willis L. Teeter opened Teeter's Food Mart with $1,700 in capital.

The two stores grew into small chains, and by 1958, the Harris and Teeter companies had begun to merge their buying efforts and storage facilities. On February 1, 1960, they formally united as Harris Teeter Super Markets, Inc., with a combined force of 15 stores. Soon thereafter, in Kannapolis, North Carolina, they opened their first new Harris Teeter store, and by 1963, the company had a total of 25 stores. Harris Teeter opened a newer and larger warehouse, with offices, and in the 1960s made the first two of many acquisitions. First the company purchased five Tilman's Grocery stores in the North Carolina town of Shelby, then it added an independent store in Gastonia and another in Charlotte.

Acquisition Followed by Growth in the 1970s and 1980s

In 1969, Harris Teeter itself was purchased, this time by Ruddick Corporation. The latter had begun business in 1919 as R. S. Dickson & Company, an investment banking firm based in Gastonia, North Carolina. Founder Rush Dickson offered a capital planning service to public and private firms, and in 1968 his sons Alan and Stuart made R. S. Dickson a subsidiary of Ruddick Corporation, along with Efird Mills, a textile company. The corporation had provided financial backing to Harris Teeter, and by purchasing all of the chain's assets in 1969, Ruddick—traded on the New York Stock Exchange—made Harris Teeter its third subsidiary.

In the 1980s Harris Teeter began an expansion program, largely by acquiring other stores and companies. First came Hunter Dairy, a firm older even than Ruddick Corporation. In 1917, bookkeeper Harvey B. Hunter had started Hunter Dairy, and in 1921 he took over the Selwyn Dairy Farm in Charlotte. In its early days, Hunter Dairy serviced only the nearby area and developed a reputation for delivering its product within four hours of the time the cows were milked. Harvey Hunter was an innovator in his cooling system, using brine water, and he took what was then considered extraordinary care to prevent bacteria or spoilage. In 1937, eight years after the company acquired Burchmont Farm in Charlotte, Hunter began pasteurizing its milk—a first in the area—and a decade later it built a new, modern facility near its Burchmont Farm location. From 1956 to 1980, Harvey Hunter's son Charles ran the company, and in 1980 his younger brother James became general manager, continuing in that position after the acquisition of Hunter Dairy by Harris Teeter in the same year.

Harris Teeter's growth by acquisition continued. In 1984, Ruddick purchased Food World, a Greensboro, North Carolina-based supermarket chain founded in 1917 by George E. Hutchens, and merged it with Harris Teeter. Food World had 52 stores in North Carolina and Virginia, giving Harris Teeter (which had already expanded into South Carolina and Tennessee) stores in four states. With Food World's 3,000 people, Harris Teeter now had 7,000 employees—or "associates" as it preferred to call them—making it the second-largest food chain in the Carolinas. The Food World acquisition also added a distribution center to the company's holdings.

Four years later, in 1988, Harris Teeter again added 52 new stores through an acquisition, this time purchasing the supermarkets of Big Star, as well as a warehouse from the Grand Union Company. In 1990, ten years after acquiring Hunter Dairy, Harris Teeter bought a Borden Dairy plant, and in 1991 it added a 139,000 square foot freezer facility to Hunter's 550,000 square foot nonperishable storage and distribution facility in Greensboro.

During the early 1990s, Harris Teeter moved its corporate offices to a 97,000 square foot building in Matthews, North Carolina. With the purchase of five Bruno stores in South Carolina in 1993, Harris Teeter increased its presence in that state, one of America's most competitive arenas for grocery stores. Perhaps even more competitive, however, was the Atlanta market, and Harris Teeter moved into Georgia in the fall of 1993 with the opening of a new store in Atlanta's upscale Buckhead district.

Coffee Bars and Floral Shops in the 1990s

Atlanta, with a high per capita income and a large population of transplants, represented a potential growth market for a high-end grocery chain. And yet it was a highly competitive area. According to *Progressive Grocer,* in 1994 the city had 4.2 chains competing for every customer, as compared to 2.9 nationally, and though population growth was explosive, supermarket square-foot growth had outpaced it by seven percent. "Every supermarket operator thinks his market is the most competitive in the country," *Progressive Grocer* announced in 1994, adding that "right now, Atlanta retailers may be correct." Among high-end chains, Bruno's had not succeeded in that market, but Publix Super Markets was making inroads, and now Harris Teeter moved in, with an appeal to a somewhat higher income level than that of Publix.

One observer called the Buckhead store a "yuppie heaven," while referred to it "a giant deli with a few groceries thrown in." Some questioned how the facility, with a floral shop, coffee bar, sushi bar, juice bar, deli, and plenty of other attractive amenities, could possibly make money. Yet it apparently did, and Harris Teeter continued to expand in the Atlanta market, with stores in Dunwoody in 1995, and in the area near Emory University in 1997. While the company eventually cut back on the features at the Buckhead location, it began to set the tone for Atlanta supermarkets, which started to adapt to a more high-end strategy.

Harris Teeter's activities in Atlanta are noteworthy precisely because of that market's high competition factor. Though conditions may have been marginally less fierce in other areas where Harris Teeter operated, its base was within some of the fastest-growing areas of the United States, including the "research triangle" of Raleigh-Durham-Chapel Hill, North Carolina, and parts of South Carolina.

To an extent, the company did not follow set patterns with its stores, as *Progressive Grocer* explained in a 1995 profile: "the 139-store chain does not believe in prototypes. It prefers something new every time it opens a store. If the new approach works, it will be used in some, but not all, new and remodeled stores." Instead of concerning itself with economies of scale when entering a new market—that is, establishing several stores at once to reduce per-store startup costs—Harris Teeter, as it demonstrated in Atlanta, was willing to open just one store at a time.

"We worry about the neighborhood, not the entire market," Fred Morganthall, vice-president for operations, told *Progressive Grocer,* adding "we only need one store in a market to make it viable." In its concern for the economic environment, the company divided its facilities into two types: neighborhood stores and community stores. Neighborhood stores, which comprised approximately two-thirds of all Harris Teeter operations in the mid-1990s, were the so-called "yuppie heavens," which catered to customers who, in Morganthall's words, "want good variety, chef-prepared entrees and . . . every new frozen food entree and ice cream that comes on the market." Community stores, by contrast, appealed to what Morganthall called the "Mayberry RFD" clientele, a reference to a television show in the 1960s set in rural North Carolina. At community stores, the appeal was more broad, with greater emphasis on customers shopping for bulk items such as "25-pound bags of flour and 10-pound bags of sugar."

A Continuing Urban Emphasis for the Future

Despite the apparent lack of a prototype, there are certainly key elements common to most Harris Teeter stores, a fact acknowledged by Morganthall in 1994 when he noted that the company was moving from a typical store size of 33,000 square feet to one of 50,000 square feet. He added in an interview with *Progressive Grocer* that the company's primary interest is in 45,000 square foot urban stores. Thus the "typical" Harris Teeter store is large, urban, with an upper-middle class customer base; and certain other features distinguish the chain.

One of these features is the level of service, which *Service Industries Journal* highlighted in an April 1992 article: Harris Teeter employees are encouraged to "take excellent care of customers,'' an element of the company's mission statement. Another key feature is the size and design of the stores, which are typically very large—as much as 60,000 square feet, slightly larger than a football field—with high ceilings, elegant lighting, and pleasing architectural features that, in the words of *Chain Store Age,* "recall a turn-of-the-century market hall."

The company also places a high emphasis on selection, with dozens of brands or variations on a certain item—salad dressing, frozen pizza, bagels, or beer. Among meats, for instance, the choices far exceed the traditional chicken, beef, pork, and lamb. Even customers with a taste for rattlesnake, if they place a special order, can purchase this delicacy fresh. The company has a number of on-duty chefs, working in the deli, the bakery, and various specialty areas such as a salad bar where customers can have chef salads made to order. On weekends in some stores, Harris Teeter features omelets with a choice of ingredients, which customers can enjoy with a cup of coffee chosen from a wide selection at the coffee bar.

Though Harris Teeter stores often include plenty of non-food items, the emphasis is clearly on food. When it opened in 1997, the Emory University-Sage Hill Shopping Center store in Atlanta was remarkable for comprising two stories, a result of the fact that when the company purchased a run-down Winn Dixie that it converted—in the process sprucing up the shopping center and repaving the parking lot—it underestimated its need for size. Among students at the nearby campus and residents of adjoining neighborhoods, a considerable Jewish population prompted the company to feature a kosher deli run by a rabbi at the store. There was also large coffee bar, which Emory students kept busy for much of the day. Moreover, in addition to its many food-related features, the store had a large section devoted to greeting cards, which sold briskly with students. Unlike many grocery stores, however, offered neither a pharmacy nor many general merchandise product lines. Morgenthall stated a key company principle when talking to *Progressive Grocer:* "We go after the customer who likes food; we don't have a lot of general merchandise."

Amenities such as those at the Emory University store came with a price, and customers whose primary concern was cost tended to shop at chains other than Harris Teeter. The company, which ironically started as two different small-town grocery store chains, kept its focus on bigger stores in the more lucrative and upscale urban markets. In 1996, for instance, Harris Teeter sold seven stores in what Ruddick Corporation's annual report called "less urban markets," and closed down three small stores. It also replaced several older facilities, and as a result had 134 stores at the end of the year—five fewer than when it began. Yet sales increased by five percent, a fact which the annual report attributed to "customer acceptance of larger, new-format stores, strong feature plans, merchandising and advertising, strong holiday sales, and a 4% increase in store square footage during the year." During the mid-1990s, the company also instituted its VIC ("Very Important Customer") program, which made use of specially coded cards presented at the time of purchase, to assist in tracking its best customers' buying habits.

Harris Teeter was involved in a number of community-oriented activities during this time, and often the opening of new stores was accompanied by donations to charitable associations. When the company opened a new facility in Nashville's Peartree Village Shopping Center in April 1997, for instance, the company announced donations ranging from $2,000 to $3,000 to organizations such as the Special Olympics and the Nashville Symphony. Harris Teeter was also involved in such activities as Child Safety Awareness Day, a scholarship program at UNC-Charlotte, and Metrolina Food Bank. Through such efforts the company pledged to continue fostering a sense of community pride in the locations Harris Teeter stores serviced. And such locations were bound to increase in number, as the company remained focused on an aggressive expansion program in the late 1990s.

Further Reading

Bennett, Stephen, ''Best in the East,'' *Progressive Grocer,* March 1993, pp. 36–53.
Lewis, Leonard, ''A Little Bit of Country and a Little Bit of City,'' *Frozen Food Age,* August 1994, p. 20.
——, ''Harris Teeter Takes Honors as '94 Master Merchandiser,'' *Frozen Food Age,* August 1994, pp. 1, 14+.
Radice, Carol, ''Destination: Harris Teeter,'' *Progressive Grocer,* May 1997, pp. 62–70.
Sparks, Leigh, ''Customer Service in Retailing—The Next Leap Forward?,'' *Service Industries Journal,* April 1992, pp. 165–84.
Weinstein, Steve, ''Georgia on Their Minds,'' *Progressive Grocer,* October 1994, pp. 99–104.
——, ''Harris Teeter Dares to Be Different,'' *Progressive Grocer,* April 1995, pp. 43–46.
Wilson, Marianne, ''Harris Teeter Celebrates Food Through Design,'' *Chain Store Age,* December 1996, pp. 168–69.

—Judson Knight

Harry's Farmers Market Inc.

1180 Upper Hembree Road
Roswell, Georgia 30076
U.S.A.
(770) 667-8878
Fax: (770) 664-4920
Web site: http://www.hfm.com

Public Company
Incorporated: 1987
Employees: 1,160
Sales: $140 million (1997)
Stock Exchanges: NASDAQ
SICs: 5411 Grocery Stores

Harry's Farmers Market Inc. is an Atlanta-based grocery chain, but its megastores are far removed from the traditional groceries of yesteryear. Specializing in perishable food products and ready-to-eat meals, Harry's appeals chiefly to a clientele with sophisticated tastes, plenty of disposable income, and little time to cook meals from scratch. In 1998 it had three 100,000-square-foot stores in the Atlanta area, as well as three "Harry's In A Hurry" locations, 10,000-square-foot stores oriented toward convenience. The exotic fare offered by Harry's has elicited almost universal praise; but founder Harry Blazer's management style has not earned the same admiration. Since going public in 1993, the company has lost money each year and its stocks have taken a pounding. Many analysts grant Blazer, considered by many a visionary, the credit for his stores' great appeal to customers; but they also give him the blame for his company's poor performance as an investment.

A Difference of Visions: Company Origins

The story of Harry's Farmers Market is inexorably tied to that of its founder. Like a large portion of Atlantans, Harry Blazer is not a native of the city. Born in 1951, he grew up in the town of Cranston, Rhode Island. As a teenager he was heavily interested in music, particularly jazz, and commuted to Boston once a week for drum lessons at the Berklee College of Music.

His first experience in retail came when he worked as a stock boy at a discount clothing store in Cranston called the Lorraine Mill Outlet.

At the age of 17, Blazer enrolled in Brandeis University, where he majored in philosophy. Though he was an honor student, he dropped out and went on the road as a professional drummer. At one time or another, he played drums for Diana Ross, Dean Martin, Paul Anka, Johnny Mathis, Vic Damone, and Grammy-winning bassist Abe Lorelei. Later he would tell the *Atlanta Journal and Constitution,* "In a lot of ways, music and business are related. There always has to be a balance between passion and intelligence for success."

Blazer's older brother Robert had moved to Atlanta, where in 1977 he established a popular store called the DeKalb Farmers Market. Located in the Decatur suburb, east of downtown, the store featured a variety of foods from around the world. Its clientele consisted mainly of internationals, as well as Americans with a taste for exotic foods and a variety of fresh produce. Rapidly the store grew from a 7,500-square-foot open market to a facility twice that size, and from that to a 22,000-square-foot store. Then an ice storm in 1979 destroyed the building—which was not insured. But with the help of his most loyal customers, who loaned him money, Robert rebuilt the market in eight weeks. He also hired his younger brother to work as his general manager; Harry would continue in that position for the next eight years.

During the 1980s the DeKalb Farmers Market prospered and became a favorite shopping place for people from all over the sprawling metropolitan area of Atlanta. Harry, however, left his brother's store in 1987 over "religious differences"—this according to several *Journal and Constitution* reports, none of which reported the exact nature of those differences. The cause may have been Robert's interest in est (Erhard Seminar Training), a quasi-religious self-help movement with cultish overtones. According to a 1987 report in *Creative Loafing,* a local arts and entertainment paper, Robert encouraged his employees to take courses in the est program. Whatever the exact cause, Blazer left his brother's store on May 22, 1987, taking with him a $400,000 severance package. He was 36 years old.

In October of that year he announced that he would open a farmers market of his own. Construction of the 60,000-square-foot facility would begin in December, and his attorney told Joe Earle of the *Journal and Constitution* that the building would cost $6 million. From the beginning Blazer seemed able to attract the respect and backing of successful people; his builder, for instance, would be David Pattillo, a prominent Atlanta contractor.

Outwardly the Blazer brothers showed no animosity toward one another, at least not at this early stage. Regarding his decision to leave Robert's store, Blazer told Earle, "We had totally different management philosophies, and he's the owner." He also said "... I wish him the best and I think he wishes me the best." Through his attorney, Robert returned the sentiment: "We wish Harry well." As though to prove his desire not to compete with his brother, Harry located his store in the northern suburb of Alpharetta, 25 miles away from the DeKalb market. For a time, peaceful coexistence seemed possible.

A Dream Store in the Late 1980s

From the beginning Harry's had a reputation as a shopper's dream. On the two-year anniversary of the opening of its first store, Sam Brown of the *Atlanta Journal and Constitution* wrote, tongue-in-cheek: "Before [1988], it was difficult to find fresh Afghan bread, calimari steaks, Ranier cherries or miniature bok choy in the Alpharetta area. That dilemma ended with the opening of Harry's." Now, Brown reported, shoppers could buy "the bread of the [Afghan] freedom fighters," as well as 35 other fresh-baked varieties. Other unusual offerings noted in his report were Walla jumbo onions from Washington state, California Black Mission figs, conger eel, and New Zealand tamarillos.

By 1998 the company's stores sold 15,000 different items. According to material at the Harry's Web page, these included more than 1,200 varieties of fruits and vegetables from around the world; 400 types of cheese from far-flung countries, as well as a wide range of dairy products; and 200 kinds of breads, muffins, bagels, pastries, cakes, and pies baked daily. In addition to Coleman's beef and Perdue chicken, customers could choose from pork, lamb, veal, duck, rabbit, goose, beefalo, quail, and other exotic items; 250 types of fish and seafood representing 100 different species; and 85 deli selections, featuring the Boar's Head brand of cold cuts. With the boom in the coffee business during the 1990s, Harry's could boast 75 different coffee blends, including cappuccinos, espressos, roasts, and flavored varieties, from more than a dozen countries. It also sold a full line of wines, featuring some 3,000 foreign and domestic varieties, and more than 250 specialty domestic and imported

beers. In addition, the stores sold nonperishable food products, including hard-to-find and gourmet items, natural products, and foods useful in the preparation of ethnic cuisines; a limited line of kitchen-oriented housewares; 500 health and beauty aid products; floral items; and gardening plants and flowers.

But the crowning touch at Harry's, particularly as the market for these items grew during the 1990s, was its prepared foods. The store featured some 200 of these ready-to-eat meals, made from scratch daily. Wendy Webster of the National Restaurant Association told the *Journal and Constitution* in 1991, "People want to spend more time at home, eating off their own china, but they don't have the time to prepare the meal." She also said that industry experts had predicted rapid growth in this sector of food service—an area in which Harry's excelled.

The Alpharetta store earned a profit within just one year and, in 1990, its celebrated its second anniversary with a two-week fair that included pony rides, a skydiving exposition, a dunking tank, a pie-eating contest, and a petting zoo. The next year Harry's doubled the size of its Alpharetta store. With so much going for it, success seemed inevitable.

Brother Against Brother in the Early 1990s

Harry's opened its second store in the northeastern suburb of Duluth, in Gwinnett County, in October 1991. This placed it in direct competition with a store called Fresh Festival, which opened at about the same time. A Georgia State University analyst told the *Journal and Constitution* that, given the size of the marketing area and the similarity of their offerings, it was unlikely both businesses would survive. But Blazer was confident: referring to his competitors, he said, "We've kind of defined the term 'farmers market,' and to a large extent, these guys are trying to copy us." As it turned out, both Blazer and the marketing analyst were correct: within a year Fresh Festival was out of business and Harry's was thriving.

The upscale farmers market concept was clearly a hot idea, and Atlanta became a battleground for retailers. And the competition between Harry and his brother Robert was certainly "blazing." By 1993, the DeKalb Farmers Market was a 140,000 square-foot store, Harry was planning to open his third store in Cobb County to the northwest of downtown, and the Blazer brothers had dropped all pretense of peaceful coexistence. "There is no way to gauge from patronage numbers the impact of the competition on the markets," Dena Smith of the *Journal and Constitution* reported in September, 1993, "but shopper interviews confirm that Harry's has siphoned some business from DeKalb." Her article quoted a number of shoppers who expressed dissatisfaction with the DeKalb market, or who praised Harry's, or both.

Robert Blazer told Smith, "My younger brother is very competitive with me." He also hinted that Harry had copied his idea. For his part, Harry said, "My brother was the one who introduced me to jazz, and I went on to pursue a career in music. And then he introduced me to the farmers market concept, and I went on to start my own. Robert deserves a lot of credit for the concept that he developed and for the guidance that he's given me, but when it comes to execution of the concept, I'm better."

In 1993, after just five years in business, Harry's made its initial public offering of stock on NASDAQ. In line with his ability to attract successful people to his cause, Blazer's five-member board of directors was composed of some prominent names in Atlanta business. They included Home Depot President Arthur M. Blank, Post Properties CEO and President John Williams, and David Pattillo, whose company had built the first Harry's. Stock sold initially for $17 a share, and investors were so bullish that Harry's quickly raised $23 million. With this money, Blazer opened the Cobb facility, as well as two Harry's In A Hurry stores. The latter would be much smaller than the superstores and would focus on prepared foods, which they would offer in a ready-access, convenient—and decidedly upscale—atmosphere.

Up to 1995, the geographic center of Harry's had been on the north side of Atlanta. But in the middle of that year, the company established a market in Clayton County, far to the southeast of town. It was to be a short-lived venture: by November, after just five months in business, the store was closed. The company attributed its failure to the fact that surrounding areas did not offer enough customers from the socioeconomic bracket that would sustain a store like Harry's. But by then many stockholders were placing the blame, not only for the Clayton store's failure but for the company's lackluster financial performance, on Blazer himself.

1995: The "September Massacre"

The company was suffering from its losses at the Clayton County store and from its Alpharetta food processing plant, which was operating at less than half its capacity. In February 1996 the underwriters of the initial public offering, Robinson-Humphrey, discontinued coverage of the stock, and the next month the *Journal and Constitution* reported that Harry's stock had lost 90 percent of its value. Paul Lapides, a business professor at Kennesaw State College, told the paper, "Investors . . . wanted to own the next Wal-Mart or Home Depot. It's just not likely to happen with Blazer."

Blazer's dictatorial style had made him a controversial figure. "While Blazer's upscale farmers market concept is studied by others in the industry," Chris Roush of the *Journal and Constitution* noted in March 1996, "his management style is not. Dozens of former executives and employees . . . speak of him in tones and phrases preachers reserve for the devil himself." A former employee called Blazer "an incredible manipulator" and said, "Most places are dysfunctional, but Harry's tops the charts." According to Roush, "Blazer, his dark eyes on fire . . . knocked over chairs and desks in meetings with employees, screaming profanities with such force that he spit repeatedly on one former worker during a meeting last summer."

A catalogue of negative facts soon emerged and, since Harry's was now a public company, these were subjected to increasing scrutiny. Among the problems noted, and reported by Roush, were a lack of controls and accounting over the price of producing food at the company's plant; failure to install a human resources management software program that had cost the company $200,000; favoritism by Blazer toward certain employees, which included his buying houses for his secretary

and a few others; and, according to a 1994 survey by a consulting firm, unusually high stress levels among employees.

In August 1995, on the recommendation of a team that included CFO Robert Aldworth, the board removed Blazer from his positions as CEO and president, but allowed him to remain chairman. According to Roush, "Blazer won't say where he went" after this decision, though Blazer did comment, "I wanted to do some thinking from a distance." On a Thursday in late September, he submitted a proposal for reinstatement as president, a position which the board had given to Aldworth. The board rejected his idea, and that weekend he struck back.

On Saturday he had the offices of Aldworth and several others padlocked. The next day, using his control of voting stock, he called a special meeting and removed four of the five board members—all except for himself. Then he named replacements, who promptly reinstated him to his positions. The stock market responded to Blazer's coup, which employees dubbed the "September Massacre"; on Monday, prices dropped 40 percent. Harry's closed out the day as NASDAQ's biggest loser.

An Uncertain Future Beyond the 1990s

Blazer's management problems were further exacerbated in October 1995, when his vice-president for research and development left him as well. This was no ordinary company executive: Janet Thomiszer-Blazer was his wife, and she wanted out of the marriage as well. Thomiszer-Blazer, who had worked with him from the old DeKalb market days, had operated the vital prepared foods division. In August 1995, at the time of his ouster by the board, the couple separated; then, after the "September Massacre," she filed for divorce and sold 50,000 shares—about one percent of the company's total outstanding—for $225,000.

An analyst at J.C. Bradford told the *Journal and Constitution* in late 1995 that Harry's "doesn't have a lot of time. The turnaround has to be very quick, very dramatic." In an August 1997 *New York Times* profile, Dana Canedy began with a positive appraisal of the Harry's markets themselves and a quote from a customer: "There's no place like it." But Canedy went on to say, "Trouble is, Harry's is a financial mess by any measure." In 1995 it had lost $1.75 million on sales of $146 million, which Canedy called "bad news by any standard. And that was its best financial performance in four years, a period in which it has lost $23 million."

In October 1995 Blazer announced that he would restructure the company. He fired 50 employees, a move that he said would save $2 million. He also dropped an ethics policy adopted by the board during his period of exile and in its place instituted a statement in which employees were encouraged to value their loyalty—in order—to him, to the company, to their customers, and to coworkers. Noting that he had never heard of a statement of loyalty to a company founder in any of the hundreds of mission statements he had reviewed, Lapides told Roush, "This statement confirms everything that is wrong with the company." In response, Blazer quipped that he was not trying to start "a Hitler youth movement."

In spite of these negatives, a number of positive signs appeared for Harry's as the mid-1990s became the late 1990s. The company won a contract to cater the Paralympics, a series of events for disabled athletes, approximately one-third the size of the Olympics, which followed the 1996 Summer Games in Atlanta. More significantly, in 1997 it entered into a joint venture with Boston Chicken which, as the Atlanta paper reported, "would finally lead to a national expansion of the upscale grocer." A company formed by Boston Chicken President Saad Nadhir, Progressive Foods, would develop Harry's locations outside Georgia and Alabama. The deal would give Harry's $23 million, with which it could pay down some of its staggering debt load.

In mid-1997 Boston Chicken tested the Harry's concept in Charlotte, and later in the year it underwent a reshuffling of its management team. As a result, Harry's was able to work out an even better partnership deal, gaining still more cash and the right to operate in the Carolinas and Tennessee. Harry's sold off its costly bakery and announced plans to remodel all three of its large stores. It would also be opening a third Harry's In A Hurry store in late 1997 and a fourth in early 1998.

The company's future remained uncertain. In December 1997, following the announcement of a $5 million quarterly loss, the *Journal and Constitution* reported, "Next year will be critical for Harry's Farmers Market." Blazer himself had stated in an official company release that Fiscal 1999, which began on February 1, 1998, would be a "make-it-or-break-it" year for his company.

Further Reading

"Boston Chicken Unit Makes an Investment in Atlanta Food Chain," *Wall Street Journal,* February 3, 1997, p. A7.

Brown, Sam, "Harry's Stock Growth: Farmer's Market Celebrates 2 Years," *Atlanta Journal and Constitution,* July 19, 1990, p. H4.

Canedy, Dana, "Supermarkets Get a Brand New Bag," *New York Times,* August 31, 1997, Sec. 3, p. 1.

——, "Trouble in Food Paradise," *New York Times,* August 31, 1997, Sec. 3, p. 10.

Earle, Joe, "Ex-Manager Plans Rival Farm Market: Alpharetta Site To Compete with Brother's in DeKalb," *Atlanta Journal and Constitution,* October 24, 1987, p. B2.

Gramig, Mickey H., "Latest Trouble at Harry's: $5 Million Quarterly Loss," *Atlanta Journal and Constitution,* December 17, 1997, p. C1.

McCarthy, Rebecca, "Farmers Markets Harvest Same Crop of Customers," *Atlanta Journal and Constitution,* October 8, 1991, p. E3.

Roush, Chris, "Harry's Founder Takes Reins Again: Board Members Removed," *Atlanta Journal and Constitution,* September 26, 1995, p. D1.

——, "Harry's Mercurial Management: Farmers Market Founder Draws Fire for His Volatile Style," *Atlanta Journal and Constitution,* March 17, 1996, p. R1.

——, "Harry's on a Hot Seat," *Atlanta Journal and Constitution,* March 17, 1996, p. R6.

——, "Problems at Harry's Aggravated by Divorce: Founder's Wife Was Part of Team," *Atlanta Journal and Constitution,* October 24, 1995, p. D1.

Smith, Dena, "Battle of the Farmers Markets: DeKalb Store a Neighborhood Staple Despite Family Feud," *Atlanta Journal and Constitution,* September 12, 1993, p. J7.

—Judson Knight

Hitchiner Manufacturing Co., Inc.

P.O. Box 2001
Milford, New Hampshire 03055
U.S.A.
(603) 673-1100
Fax: (603) 672-7960
Web site: http://www.hitchiner.com

Private Company
Incorporated: 1946
Employees: 3,500
Sales: $165 million (1997)
SIC's: 3324 Shell Investment Foundries; 3499 Fabricated
Metal Products

Hitchiner Manufacturing Co., Inc. is a privately held company founded in 1946 and now headquartered in Milford, New Hampshire. It is the world's premier supplier of complete-to-print, high-volume, full-service commercial investment castings. It leads the industry for highest unit-volume production, shorter lead times, and reduced inventories. The company designed and built the first mechanized investment casting plant using automated shell-building equipment and conveyor systems. Hitchiner introduced mechanized melting and pouring of metal and is the first investment casting firm to use large-size, induction melting furnaces and automated aluminum dies for wax patterns. The company produces castings in more than 160 different alloys for a broad spectrum of domestic and offshore markets that include a significant portion of the automotive, golf, military, and aerospace industries. The firm's operations are based in the Ferrous Division (QS-9000/ISO-9002 certified), the Gas Turbine Division (ISO-9002 certified), and the Tool and Die Division, all located in Milford; the Nonferrous Division (ISO-9002 certified) operating in O'Fallon Missouri; and an offshore manufacturing facility, Hitchiner S.A. de C.V., situated in Santiago Tianguistenco, Mexico. These divisions are supported by the research and development activities of Milford-based Metal Casting Technology, Inc., a subsidiary jointly owned by Hitchiner and General Motors Corporation. Hitchiner markets its castings

throughout the world and licenses its technology and processes to other domestic and foreign companies. Some of Hitchiner's major customers are General Motors Corporation, Callaway Golf Company, BMW AG, Chrysler Corporation, General Electric Company, Pratt & Whitney, B.F. Goodrich Company, and Lockheed Martin Corporation.

Founding and Early Years: 1946–1956

When A. Fred Hitchiner worked for the War Production Board during World War II, he saw the successful application of a technology rooted in a 5,000-year-old process known as investment casting, commonly referred to as the *cire perdue* or "lost-wax" method of casting. During World War II investment casting provided a shortcut for producing near-net-shape precision parts and allowed the use of specialized alloys that could not be readily shaped by alternative methods. This investment casting process was applied to production of the first blades for jet engines.

After the war, Hitchiner was among those who wanted to capitalize on the precision, design freedom, and near-net-shape results of investment casting technology. In 1946 he bought a small brass foundry in Long Island, New York and relocated it to a less expensive site at the Amoskeag Millyards in Manchester, New Hampshire. Unfortunately for Hitchiner, the state was no longer a highly industrialized area and suffered from a faltering economy and low employment. By 1948, unable to cope with these unstable conditions, Hitchiner had to sell his business or recruit a strong investor.

Meanwhile, in 1947 George Abbot Morison had retired to the family farm in Peterborough, New Hampshire. Concerned about the dismal condition of New Hampshire's manufacturing economy, he resolved to revitalize the dying industrial base and create jobs. He read about Fred Hitchiner's company and was captivated by the potential of investment casting for commercial use. In 1949 Morison put up 50 percent of the purchase price for the foundry; his son, John H. Morison, paid the other half and became president of the company, which continued to operate under its original name. According to the company's history published in *Casting Granite into Gold* (hereafter re-

Company Perspectives:

Hitchiner's steady, dependable growth as industry and employer rests on sound financial management, a long-term outlook, private ownership, capital reinvestment and continuous technical innovation. Hitchiner will persist in the development of investment casting and related technologies in order to offer ever-better products and services to its established and new markets throughout the world.

ferred to as *Casting Granite*), astute Morison asked Hitchiner to stay with the company because no one had "to teach him the technology. He knew it. We didn't have to sell him on its advantages. He knew them."

Indeed, once Fred Hitchiner was free to focus on sales and marketing, development of the solid-mold investment casting process began to contribute to the growth of New Hampshire's economy and to create jobs. By April 1950 sales reached an annual rate of $250,000 and Hitchiner Manufacturing Co., Inc. broke even. The large number of orders brought on by the Korean War taxed the company's facilities to the limit. In 1951 the company and its 50 employees moved to a newly constructed plant in Milford, New Hampshire.

As leader of an educated and trained work force, Morison emphasized the need for courses in many disciplines, from basic literacy and mathematics to statistical process control, apprenticeships in specialized technical fields and business management seminars. In 1953 Hitchiner was one of the first companies to implement the Scanlon Plan, which gave employees a vested interest in the company. Hitchiner products of the 1950s included castings for sporting firearms, electric motors, electrical connectors, and aircraft components. Sales for 1953 reached nearly $400,000 and rose to $1.7 million by year-end 1956.

Creative Pursuit of Excellence: 1957–1974

To increase market penetration, John H. Morison recognized the need for combining increased productivity with reduced production costs, without compromising quality. The solid-mold process then in use was expensive and too limited; long-term commercial viability hinged on using the lost-wax process in a new way. Hitchiner experimented with ceramic shell molding and in 1961 was one of the first companies to install a shell-building machine that lowered the cost of mold making versus the traditional solid-mold process. Morison recruited Richard T. Carter, who had helped to develop the new method in England, to plan the building of a mechanized shell plant. Thus came about the world's first mechanized investment casting plant: it used automated shell-building equipment as well as power- and free-conveyor systems. Hitchiner was also the first investment casting firm to use aluminum molds for wax patterns and to put large-size, induction melting furnaces into practice.

In 1962 the company acquired Hackensack, New Jersey-based Delta Microwave Corp., a manufacturer of small nonferrous, aluminum investment castings for electronics. "Delta

was strictly solid mold. We needed more capacity and a site closer to nonferrous markets where the shell process could be installed," said Morison, according to *Casting Granite*. In 1969 Hitchiner opened a new full-service nonferrous plant in O'Fallon, Missouri. Shortly thereafter all of the company's nonferrous operations, including Delta's, were transferred to the new facility. The Nonferrous Division specialized in the production of complex, thin-walled configurations in aluminum and copper-based alloys and expanded into the commercial aircraft market.

Morison continued to seek out "the best and the brightest at every level" of the industry. In 1966 he hired Nicholas Babich from the Singer Company to become plant manager of the Milford facility and who later became vice-president of operations. In 1967 he hired G. Dixon Chandley, chief engineer and technical director at TRW's metals division. At Hitchiner Chandley and his team revolutionized the industry by creating new processes. They invented a countergravity low-pressure air melt (CLA) process that made for greater automation and lower costs by using a vacuum to draw metal into a mold rather than pouring out the melt in open air. Then came another process, countergravity low-pressure vacuum melt (CLV), for casting reactive metals.

These processes were acclaimed as the most significant enhancement to investment casting technology since the shell process. They established Hitchiner's exclusive countergravity advantage and reduced slag, improved grain structure, increased loading of parts on a CLA sprue (the opening through which molten metal is poured into a mold), and produced castings of thin (0.015-inch) sections in nickel-based superalloys. Application of these processes resulted in more efficient manufacturing of better products at a lower cost. Rapid growth in the sale of castings for golf club heads and telephone equipment brought revenue to $28 million in 1974.

Riding Out the Recession: 1975–1988

Although the recession of the mid-1970s caused sales to fluctuate, the company continued to invest in capacity, research, technology, and automation. The CLA and CLV processes were patented in 1975. When high-volume automotive orders came in from General Motors in 1977, Hitchiner developed and patented a process to supplement ceramic shells with less expensive resin-bonded shells. During the late 1970s, operating in a recovering economy and faced with an influx of new orders, the company opened a new facility in Plymouth, New Hampshire for all wax pattern and ceramic-core work. At year-end 1981 Hitchiner reported sales of $54.5 million, and Nicholas Babich returned to the company as president and chief executive officer.

For more than 30 years the company had generated income and extended its reach into global markets by licensing Hitchiner technology. The first licensee (1964) was OY Saco AB, a member of Finland's Nokia Group. Other early licensees included Daido Steel of Japan, Chateau Roux Foundries of France, and Shivaji Works Limited of India.

The long-range value of research and development came to the fore with the 1979 opening of a pilot plant at Hitchiner's

Technical Center for exploring the economic viability of an enhanced CLA process known as the countergravity, low-pressure air melt sand (CLAS) process. In 1986 General Motors bought the CLAS technology (enhanced in 1985), renamed it VAC, and made Hitchiner its licensing agent. The two companies set up a joint venture, called Metal Casting Technology, Inc. (MCT), to continue the research activities begun at Hitchiner's Technical Center.

Nicholas Babich, Hitchiner's president and CEO from 1981 to 1995, believed that a growing trend to one-stop shopping would influence customers of the next decade to select only the companies having the technical capability and production capacity to offer single-source, complete assemblies of finished parts. He put into motion a strategy for Hitchiner's continuing evolution from an insolvent brass foundry to a global, full-service, high volume/low cost manufacturer of investment castings and fully machined and assembled parts. Boosted by leading-edge automation and state-of-the-art processes, the company pursued golf and automotive business and new markets.

One implementation of Babich's strategy was the 1988 opening of the company's first offshore production facility, Hitchiner S.A. de C.V., in Santiago Tianguistenco, Mexico. With an eye to recapturing business lost to foreign investment casters (especially in the golf industry) and to producing castings for hand tools and select automotive components, Hitchiner built a state-of-the-art facility and hired the best local managers and workers. By year-end 1988 the Mexican plant's sales amounted to more than $4 million. And the creation of Hitchiner S.A. de C.V. had not eliminated a single domestic job.

New Markets: 1989–95

Encouraged by the success of machined prechamber programs for General Motors and Navistar International Corporation, Hitchiner expanded its value-added machining capability to include golf-club finishing. The company also marketed polished and machined components to the medical industry and sold machined and assembled roller rocker arms to BMW, INA Bearing, Competition Cams, and General Motors Corporation. The Metal Casting Technology Division patented its loose-sand vacuum casting (LSVAC) process, a VAC development for cost-effective casting of lightweight and hollow parts. Then followed patents for SSCLA and SSCV (supported shell CLA and CV), processes that cut material costs and increased the number of pieces per mold.

The quest for global markets made it crucial for Hitchiner to work toward certification by Geneva, the Switzerland-based International Standards Organization. The purpose of the organization is to develop a common set of manufacturing, trade, and communication standards. ISO-9000 Certification is the worldwide standard measurement of total quality management. ISO-9000 is divided into several subsets, including ISO-9002, the level that provides quality guidelines for manufacturing. In 1993 Hitchiner became the first American metal casting company to be ISO-certified.

President/CEO Nicholas Babich retired from Hitchiner in 1994, but his long-range strategy and organizational development initiatives had set the company's evolving strengths on growth paths for the 1990s. His successor, John H. Morison III, reaffirmed the company's tradition of integrity-based leadership by launching a continuing ethics training program for all employees, agents, and suppliers. According to Morison, quoted in *Casting Granite*, "The foundation for [Hitchiner's] success has been the creation of innovative technology, superior quality and service and, perhaps most of all, the integrity with which the company conducts its affairs."

Extending Global Reach: 1994 and Beyond

Metal Casting Technology, Inc., Hitchiner's research arm, brought revolutionary reactive-casting processes to production readiness and established a prototype production facility for a new higher-quality, lower-cost process known as liquid hot isostatic pressing (LHIP). Another new process, rapid prototyping technology, allowed the production of patterns directly from CAD files. The combination of these two processes eliminated internal-casting porosity in sand and investment castings at a much lower cost than had been possible previously. MCT also pioneered low-cost, metal-matrix composite casting and maintained a high level of LSVAC consulting and training. A multiyear licensing agreement for the use of the LSVAC process was drawn up with Infun, S.A. of Barcelona, Spain, and a similar license was issued to Yoosung Enterprise Co., Ltd., Seoul, South Korea.

The research division also used its LSVAC process to build prototypes for five new exhaust manifolds for General Motors. The division envisioned a $30 million market for this product by 2003. In 1997 MCT had ten licensees for sand and investment casting processes and negotiations were in progress for two more. Many new applications for the CLIX titanium-casting process were developed in 1997 and were expected to reach significant production in 1998. MCT also built a larger, upgraded SSCLA casting machine for the new Automated Casting Facility to be activated in 1998.

The Ferrous Division added production shifts and ran plants at full capacity to meet increased demands of current and new products for the golf and the automotive industries. The division built on its lead as the investment casting supplier for multitools, the 1990s version of Swiss army-style knives. Work for the U.S. Air Force included nine investment castings for Textron Defense Systems' Sensor-Fused Weapon Program. The Ferrous Division, with a significant portion of its sales coming from the automotive industry, prepared for the QS-9000 certification program developed by Chrysler, Ford, and General Motors. These auto manufacturers added specific requirements to the already established ISO 9000 standards. In March 1998 the Ferrous Division qualified for QS 9000 certification.

In 1996 incoming orders for the Gas Turbine Division (GTD) exceeded product shipment; intense attention to cost reduction increased return on the division's sales by almost 500 percent over 1995. The nation's major U.S. manufacturers of large gas turbine engines, Pratt & Whitney and General Electric Company, remained the division's largest customers. The division made initial deliveries to Rolls Royce, the third largest engine manufacturer; to Vickers Aerospace, a major Rolls Royce subcontractor; and to BMW/Rolls Royce, a fast-growing European manufacturer of smaller commuter-aircraft turbine engines. Sales for 1997 exceeded those of 1996 by 80 percent and were projected for a hefty increase in 1998. Consequently, plans got under way to expand capacity to support demand for the division's thin-walled, high-temperature alloy aerospace products.

The Nonferrous Division, in 1996, increased sales by 9.2 percent over 1995 and operating profit by 59.3 percent; it maintained a 50:50 ratio of military/aerospace to commercial business. The division geared up production of the aluminum-induction module casting at the heart of the new Harley-Davidson electronic-fuel injection system. Exports to Australia brought in more than $1 million. The division won a tooling contract for a set of three castings used for a mobile satellite telephone sold by NEC, the Japanese electronics giant. In June 1997 the Nonferrous Division achieved ISO-9002 status.

Hitchiner S.A. de C.V.'s unprecedented growth in 1996 resulted from an expanded portfolio of clients in the automotive and golf industries in North America and other continents. The Mexican Division took on new automotive programs for Chrysler and won business away from major European and Brazilian foundries. The division shipped more than one million pieces for traditional customer Taylor Made Golf Company and added programs for Titleist and Foot-Joy Worldwide, Cobra Golf Incorporated, Odyssey, and other leaders in the golf industry. As the alternative to the Far East, Hitchiner S.A. de C.V. produced the finest castings for quality golf clubs at competitive prices. Non-U.S. shipments increased 45 percent. By year-end 1996 Hitchiner sales had reached $138.3 million, a 10.4 percent increase over 1995.

The Tool and Die Division was established as a separate operating division. It absorbed the company's tool-making operations in Amherst and Littleton, New Hampshire, and provided tool design, manufacture, and tool-repair services for all of the company's operating divisions.

In April 1997 the company announced the erection of yet another plant in Milford. This Automated Casting Facility, scheduled to begin operation in late 1998, would include an environmentally friendlier and lower-cost water-based, rather than alcohol-based, shell-building system. This was not the first time that Hitchiner showed concern for the environment. In 1996, for example, the company recycled 6,789 tons of ceramic, 1,023 tons of scrap metal, 141 tons of cardboard, 11 tons of office paper, and 1.8 tons of aluminum cans. The U.S. Environmental Protection Agency (EPA) recognized the company's waste-reduction and recycling programs by approving Hitchiner as a participant in the new EPA program, "Partners for Change."

In short, Hitchiner's commitment to total quality meant more than simple conformance to technical requirements and delivery of near-net-shape parts of high metallurgical integrity, just-in-time, and ready for assembly. It meant continuous attention to the techniques of Statistical Process Control to monitor and control the consistency of the investment casting process from waxing through finishing. Thus it was by controlling the variability of the manufacturing process that the company was able to reduce scrap, rework, and inspection—and to increase quality. Hitchiner's determined efforts to enhance the product while lowering the cost to its customers earned the company some of the industry's most coveted quality supplier awards.

As the 20th century drew to a close, Hitchiner Manufacturing Co., Inc. had established its leadership in foundry technology and positioned itself as the foremost global supplier of commercial investment castings. The company was ready to maintain its premier rank by continuing to realize the promise implied in its motto, "Imagination in Metallurgy."

Principal Subsidiaries

Metal Casting Technology, Inc. (50%).

Principal Divisions

Ferrous Division; Gas Turbine Division; Hitchiner S.A. de C.V. (Mexico); Nonferrous Division; Tool and Die Division.

Further Reading

Casting Granite into Gold: Fifty Years, 1946–1996, Milford, N.H.: Hitchiner Manufacturing Co., Inc., 1996.
Cleveland, Kathy, "Happy 50th to a Good Corporate Friend," *The Milford Cabinet,* October 30, 1996, p. 1.
"GM, Hitchiner in Technology Transfer Pact," *New Hampshire Business Review,* May 12, 1995, p. 29.
Imagination in Metallurgy, Milford, N.H.: Hitchiner Manufacturing Co., Inc., 1997.
"One To Grow On: Renovation Will Give Hitchiner a Second Location in Milford," *New Hampshire Business Review,* April 25, 1997, p. 40.
Stauffer, Robert N., "Automating the Grinding of Investment Casting," *Manufacturing Engineering,* June 1981, pp. 70–71.

—Gloria A. Lemieux

De Telegraaf

N.V. Holdingmaatschappij De Telegraaf

Basisweg 30
1043 AP Amsterdam
The Netherlands
(31) 20-5859111
Fax: (31) 20-5854130
Web site: http://www.telegraaf.nl

Public Company
Incorporated: 1893
Employees: 4,599
Sales: Nfl 1.28 billion (US$514 million) (1996)
Stock Exchanges: Amsterdam
SICs: 2711 Newspapers; 2721 Periodicals

N.V. Holdingmaatschappij De Telegraaf is the holding company overseeing operations of *De Telegraf*, with a subscriber base of some 800,000 and daily circulation rates reaching 1.3 million copies (for the total Dutch population of around 15 million), *De Telegraaf* is not only the Netherlands' oldest national daily newspaper, it is by far that country's largest. *De Telegraaf* remains the flagship of N.V. Holdingmaatschappij De Telegraaf's growing print and multimedia empire, which, in addition to *De Telegraaf*, includes a portfolio of regional and local daily and weekly newspapers, glossy magazines, door-to-door distribution, interests in television, radio, cable television, and internet access operations, and graphics, printing, and bookbinding plants. Since 1996, De Telegraaf has also extended to the Internet, offering an expanded version of the daily newspaper, *De Telegraaf-i.*

De Telegraaf has long distinguished itself among other Netherlands newspaper and publishing concerns in that its editorial leadership also plays a prominent role on the company's board of directors. Titles of the holding company's print activities, in addition to *De Telegraaf*, include *De Courant Nieuws van de Dag, Het Limburgs Dagblad, Haarlems Dagblad, Leidsch Dagblad, Noordhollands Dagblad,* the magazines *Privé* and *Voetball* and other sports-oriented titles, and former Reed Elsevier publications *OOR, Elegance, MAN, Hitkrant, Residence,* and *Autovisie.* The holding company's television and radio activities include a 30 percent interest in commercial television startup

SBS6, interests in regional television broadcasters such as Limburg's TV8, and cable television production and broadcasting through a 75 percent holding in Media Groep West B.V. These activities have helped De Telegraaf achieve total sales of nearly Nfl 1.3 billion (approximately US $514 million) in 1996 and profits of nearly Nfl 85 million. Newspaper sales form more than 66 percent of the company's total revenues.

Turn of the Century Beginnings

The Netherlands was greeted with a new daily newspaper on the morning of January 1, 1893. The newspaper's founder, Henry Tindal, born in 1852, had originally pursued a career as a cavalry officer. A fall ended that career, however, in 1883. Marriage to a wealthy widow enabled Tindal to enter the political arena, which would, in turn, lead him into publishing. A follower of the anti-royalty, anti-government Radical Movement, Tindal turned to pamphleteering—a popular political activity of the day. Tindal's political activities would lead to criticism from the Dutch press. Angered by this criticism, Tindal decided to go into newspaper publishing himself. In the mid-1880s he gained financial control over the national newspaper, *De Amsterdammer,* which had made its first appearance as a weekly in the previous decade.

Tindal would prove to be less than a businessman. By the time he sold off his interest in *De Amsterdammer,* in 1897, he had lost an estimated one million guilders. Nonetheless, by 1892, Tindal had gained control of another paper, the weekly *Algemeen Belang* (''Public Interest''), followed by the popular (and sensationalistic) *Geïllustreed Politie-nieuws* in 1893. By then Tindal had added his own print works and two more newspapers, *De Telegraaf* and its sister publication, *De Courant.* That newspaper, which appeared for the first time on January 9, 1893, was meant as an inexpensive ''people's'' paper, taking over the contents and subscriber list of the *Algemeen Belang* and utilizing the typeset of *De Amsterdammer.*

With *De Telegraaf,* Tindal sought to create a politically neutral newspaper fiercely dedicated to the well-being of the Netherlands and its people. Although the paper's neutrality would often be called into question over the course of the following century, *De Telegraaf* would remain true to its commitment to the issues concerning the Dutch people. Tindal also sought to establish *De Telegraaf* as a prominent, national newspaper, adding an evening edition in November 1893. Although the newspaper's first years were difficult, by the middle of the 1890s *De Telegraaf* had seen its subscriber base rise from an initial 2,000 to 9,000, placing it in competition with other important Netherlands newspapers, such as the *NRC,* the *Algemeen Handelsblad,* and *Het Nieuws van de Dag.* Despite the paper's growth, *De Telegraaf* proved unprofitable, posting a loss of 11,000 guilders in 1899. In response, the company, which in the mid-1890s had gained praise for the quality of its newspaper's editorial content and layout, raised its subscription rate. The move proved fatal—especially as competitor *Algemeen Handelsblad* lowered its own subscriber rate—and *De Telegraaf* saw its subscriber base quickly shrink from 13,000 to just 5,400. *De Telegraaf's* losses, coupled with Tindal's losses from *De Amsterdammer,* brought him to declare bankruptcy in 1901. Tindal died the following year in Saint Petersburg.

Tindal's bankruptcy had not ended *De Telegraaf.* Instead, the newspaper came into the hands of H.M.C. Holdert. Born in 1870, Holdert had entered his father's printing and newspaper (*De Echo van het Nieuws*) business in 1881; a dispute over his salary led the younger Holdert to found his own printing works in 1894. In 1902 Holdert purchased the remains of *De Telegraaf* and its sister *De Courant* for 40,000 guilders, incorporating as the NV Dagblad De Telegraaf. Declaring that *De Telegraaf* would remain neutral and independent from both political and religious opinion, Holdert would play an active role in determining the paper's editorial content. Yet he would also lead *De Telegraaf* into the realm of the sensationalistic reporting that would enable the paper shortly to build the country's largest subscriber base. Hoping to win back subscribers, Holdert lowered the paper's subscription rate. That first year proved difficult and by 1904 Holdert had run out of money. Several investors, including D.A.J Kessler and J.J.A. Hulsman, would enable Holdert to continue operations, however. These investors would also lead *De Telegraaf* into later controversy.

In the meantime, *De Telegraaf's* new formula was showing its appeal to the popular segment of the Dutch newspaper public. Growth also came through Holdert's continued newspaper acquisitions. In 1903 he purchased the popular *Amsterdamsche Courant,* which had been in press since 1734, dropping that title and adding its subscribers to *De Telegraaf.* Two years later, after incorporating sister newspaper *De Courant,* Holdert added two of that paper's competitors, *Het Ochtenblad* and the *Amsterdamsch Nieuwsblad,* adding 15,000 to *De Courant's* subscriber base. By 1911 *De Courant* boasted 110,000 subscribers; the following year, Holdert took over another competing "popular" daily, *De Echo,* and its 29,000 subscribers. By then, *De Telegraaf* had also been growing, reaching more than 20,000 subscribers by the beginning of the First World War.

World War Identity Issues

De Telegraaf's move into sensationalistic reporting would garner the lasting derision of the Dutch newspaper industry—and a position as the country's leading daily newspaper. *De Telegraaf* would become a popular target for the scorn of competing journalists, who would attack—unfairly—the newspaper as well for its political position. Although *De Telegraaf's* position on the Second World War would lead to its greatest controversy, the First World War would already provide fodder

for its competitors' contempt. Until the early 1980s, in fact, *De Telegraaf* would be accused of an opportunistic flip-flop from a pro-Axis position to an extreme anti-German position during the First World War, in an attempt to garner favor of the popular public. These accusations would culminate with the claims that, during the war years, *De Telegraaf* had been bought up by the Shell Oil company—due to the interests Kessler and Hulsman held in that company—and served as a mouthpiece for Shell, which sought to provide petroleum products to the British and French war efforts. According to this theory, the "swing" in *De Telegraaf's* editorial policy was meant to break down Winston Churchill's refusal to deal with Shell.

A study published in the 1980s, however, would prove that *De Telegraaf* had in fact adopted its anti-Axis position at the very beginning of the war. This position, which would be described as "rabid," brought the newspaper into conflict with the Dutch government, fearful to maintain the country's neutrality during the war. This conflict led to the arrest of *De Telegraaf's* editor-in-chief and to a trial that would last through much of the war. Yet *De Telegraaf* found favor among the country's readership, seeing its subscriber totals reach 30,000 in 1919. Three years later, aided in part by Holdert's and *De Telegraaf's* sympathetic support of the growing revolutionary fervor in the Netherlands and in part by the company's acquisition of another popular paper, *Het Nieuws van de Dag, De Telegraaf* numbered 70,000 subscribers. By 1930, *De Telegraaf,* with an editorial policy as reported by *De Journalist* as "progressively liberal" and "strongly democratic" had topped 100,000 subscribers. The company's *De Courant* had also grown strong, in part by acquisitions of its competitors, reaching more than 212,000 copies. In that year, the company moved to a new headquarters on the Nieuwezijds Voorburgwal, which would become known as Amsterdam's Fleet Street.

The Depression years of the 1930s led inevitably to a drop in subscription growth. More ominous, however, was the rise of fascism across the border in Germany, but in the Netherlands as well. *De Telegraaf,* while initially critical of the German Nazi party and Adolph Hitler, would be accused of being less impartial to the Netherlands' own NSB (National Socialist Movement). One competing newspaper, for example (as quoted by *De Journalist*), would describe *De Telegraaf's* content as a "tabloid's boastful, semi-fascist twaddle"; yet *De Telegraaf's* pages also boasted the bylines of many of the Netherlands' most anti-fascist reporters. Despite (or because of) this seeming ambivalence, *De Telegraaf* appeared to capture the spirit of the times: by the outbreak of the Second World War, *De Telegraaf* and *De Courant* had established the company as the Netherlands' leading newspaper concern. Of the total newspaper readership of 1.8 million among a population of less than nine million, *De Telegraaf* and *De Courant* together represented more than 450,000 readers.

Most telling, however, was *De Telegraaf's* immediate reaction to the Nazi occupation of the Netherlands. Holdert and his editor-in-chief decided to stop publication of their newspapers—on the morning of May 15, 1940, the date of the Dutch capitulation, *De Telegraaf* did not appear. Yet none of the competing newspapers followed suit. With the occupation's leadership insisting that life continue as usual, *De Telegraaf* would reappear on the newsstands that afternoon and continue publication throughout the Second World War. This fact would earn *De Telegraaf* the moniker of the "collaboration newspaper,'' a reputation that would haunt the concern until well into the 1980s, even after the 1988 publication of a study that proved that *De Telegraaf's* position—which continued the ambivalence of the prewar years, at least until the 1942 appointment of Holdert's son Hakkie, member of the Dutch SS, to the paper's board of directors—had been no more and no less pro-Nazi than any other above-ground newspaper of the period. The appointment of Holdert's son, had, in fact, led to a walkout by *De Telegraaf's* editor-in-chief and most of its staff. Yet *De Telegraaf's* reputation would have drastic consequences for the company following the Netherlands' liberation in May 1945.

The ''Underdog'' of the Postwar Years

The Netherlands' liberated newsstands would provide no room for *De Telegraaf.* Amidst a surge of postwar reprisals, *De Telegraaf* was banned from publication for a period of 30 years. Only the NSB's own newspapers received heavier punishments. Hakkie Holdert's 25 percent share of the company (the elder Holdert had died in 1944) was taken away; his three sisters, however, retained their 75 percent of the company. As attention focused on the need to rebuild the country's shattered economy, however, a degree of calm had returned to Dutch society. At the same time, a new menace had appeared in the Soviet Union. With support from Catholic and right-wing politicians, the ban on *De Telegraaf* was lifted in January 1949, and the first postwar edition appeared in September of that year.

Acceptance among the public of *De Telegraaf* would prove somewhat less forthcoming. The paper struggled to attract 40,000 subscribers in its first postwar year. By 1951 the Holdert sisters were threatened with bankruptcy, until a group of financiers, including Holdert's grandson and J.M. Goedemans, the paper's editor-in-chief during the war years, bought up the company for 480,000 guilders. With Goedeman as director, *De Telegraaf* turned its attention to the Cold War, adopting a stridently anti-communist tone. At the same time, the paper continued its sensationalistic style, including page-wide headlines, with an emphasis on crime, human interest stories, and other issues affecting the daily lives of its readers.

While *De Telegraaf* continued to enjoy the scorn of certain segments of the Dutch readership, in particular among the pro-socialist groups, the paper's format and tone once again established its popularity among the broader population. In fact, the company profited by positioning itself as the ''underdog'' of Dutch newspapers. Yet the paper would also attract a number of the country's most important postwar journalists, including Lou de Jong, author of the country's most authoritative historical work on the Netherlands in the war years. By 1955 the company's subscriber lists had grown to 110,000 for *De Telegraaf* and nearly 70,000 for *De Courant.* Five years later, *De Telegraaf* topped 200,000 subscribers and added an additional 19,000 *Courant* readers. In 1967 *De Telegraaf* (including *De Courant* and other regional papers) topped 500,000 subscribers, making the company by far the largest newspaper concern in the Netherlands—a position it would continue to hold through the late 1990s.

De Telegraaf went public in 1971, listing on the Amsterdam bourse. The company showed consistent profitability over the next decades. By the end of the decade the company would grow from sales of Nfl 134 million and net profits of Nfl 9.3 million in 1972 to 1980 sales of nearly Nfl 500 million, for a profit of more than Nfl 20 million. The company also moved to new headquarters outside of Amsterdam's center district.

Multimedia in the 1990s

Through the stock market boom years of the 1980s, *De Telegraaf's* extensive financial coverage would garner it a new breed of readers. At the same time, the newspaper's ranks of postwar, anti-communist journalists were thinned by retirements. By the late 1980s the paper's tone had begun to calm, evolving into what *De Journalist* describe as a ''middle-class'' newspaper. Capping the decade was the publication of the study putting to rest the accusations of collaboration against De Telegraaf.

Entering the 1990s, De Telegraaf would post sales of more than Nfl 775 million and profits of Nfl 80 million. The company itself had grown, more than doubling the number of employees over the previous two decades. New additions, such as the *People*-oriented *Privé* magazine, as well as a strong list of sports titles, joined in boosting the company's growth.

After celebrating its 100-year anniversary by 1994, *De Telegraaf* boasted more than 800,000 readers, with Saturday editions reaching print runs of more than 1.3 million. The company then turned to expanding its holdings, joining the mid-1990s multimedia explosion. In addition to expanding its magazine holdings with the acquisition of several Reed Elsevier publications, De Telegraaf made moves to enter the broadcast and cable television and radio markets, including a 100 percent share of Radio De Amsterdammer, a 30 percent share with partners including ABC/Time Warner of the television broadcaster SBS6, and a 50 percent partnership with national television group TROS to develop various television and multimedia-related activities. In 1996 De Telegraaf also joined the drive to the Internet, launching *i-Telegraaf,* an expanded online edition of the daily newspaper, as well as purchasing a 30 percent share in Internet-provider Planet Internet. While *De Telegraaf,* with a total daily edition of some 800,000, continued to form the foundation of the company's total sales of nearly Nfl 1.3 billion, De Telegraaf looked to its multimedia to maintain its leadership position among the Netherlands media.

Principal Subsidiaries

B.V. Dagblad De Telegraaf; B.V. De Courant Nieuws van de Dag; B.V. Beleggingsmaatschappij Voorburgwal; B.V. Rotatie-Drukkerij Voorburgwal; Hollandse Huis aan huisbladen Combinatie B.V.; De Telegraaf Tijdschriften Groep B.V.; De Telegraaf Transport B.V.; Media Groep West (75%); SBS6 B.V. (30%); Hollandse Dagbladcombinatie B.V.

Further Reading

Hagen, Piet, ''Onze Tentakels Strekken Zich Uit Over Heel de Samenleving,'' *De Journalist,* April 19, 1996, p. 12.
Van de Plasse, Jan, ''Een Eeuw De Telegraaf'' (Part I), *De Journalist,* December 4, 1992, p. 26.
——, ''Een Eeuw De Telegraaf'' (Part II), *De Journalist,* December 18, 1992, p. 26.
Van der Gaag, Arjo, ''Ton Boerma: We Zitten Alweer Flink Boven de 800,000,'' *Adformatie,* September 8, 1004, p. 5.
Van Lieshout, Marcel, and van Zijl, Frank, ''De Hetze Voorbij,'' *De Volkskrant,* November 21, 1992.

—M.L. Cohen

Home Box Office Inc.

1100 Avenue of the Americas
New York, New York 10036
U.S.A.
(212) 512-1000
Fax: (212) 512-5517
Web site: http://www.hbo.com

*Wholly Owned Subsidiary of Time Warner Entertainment
    Company, L.P.*
Incorporated: 1972
Employees: 2,100
Sales: $1.7 billion
Stock Exchanges: Boston Midwest New York
    Philadelphia
SICs: 4841 Cable & Other Pay Television Services; 7812
    Motion Picture & Video Production

Home Box Office Inc. (HBO) is the largest pay-TV channel in the United States, with a subscriber base of about 33 million and earnings of approximately $400 million. As a subsidiary of Time Warner Entertainment Co., L.P., 63 percent of which is owned by Time Warner Inc., HBO's programming includes sports events, comedy offerings, Hollywood films, and self-produced films.

1970s Formation

Home Box Office was founded by Time Inc. in 1972 to offer cable television service. As a subsidiary of Time, HBO bought the rights to recent films and transmitted them to local systems via satellite and microwave relays. Its service was distributed by the local cable operators, typically costing subscribers $6 a month, of which HBO received $3.50. HBO management initially regarded the company as an editorial marketer, selling its programming the way Time sold magazines.

HBO grew slowly in its first years, as the nascent cable industry struggled to get off the ground. Cable was hampered by market fragmentation, lack of infrastructure, and tough federal regulations, some of them sponsored by the major television networks, which feared that cable could eventually steal much of their audience and revenue.

During the mid-1970s the cable industry laid the groundwork for rapid growth: it expanded its infrastructure through such populous areas as New York City and the suburbs of Boston, won a series of court victories that removed many federal restrictions, and won rate increases from local governments. Pay-TV customers, those buying additional cable services such as HBO, grew from 50,000 in 1974 to about 1.5 million in 1978. HBO won greater latitude in pursuing customers in 1977 when a federal ruling lifted restrictions on the choice of movies and sports available on pay-TV. HBO quickly became one of the primary engines driving the growth of the cable industry. Cable systems operators hooked up thousands of people for basic services who were primarily interested in getting HBO.

HBO made its first profit in 1977. It lost tens of thousands of customers in 1978, however, as a result of a move by its chief rival, Showtime, which was challenging HBO head-on for the cable film audience. During this time, Showtime's parent, Viacom, had struck a deal with Teleprompter, the largest cable systems operator in the United States, which resulted in Teleprompter's customers receiving Showtime instead of HBO.

Nevertheless, HBO worked diligently on its programming, lining up enough films to make it the premiere pay-TV outlet for commercial films. It also began its *On Location* comedy series and *The Young Comedians Show,* one of the first television forums for such comedians as Robin Williams and Paul Ruebens (Pee-Wee Herman).

In 1978 Time spent $145 million to buy American Television & Communications Corp., then the second-largest cable systems operator in the United States, hoping a large number of its 675,000 customers would subscribe to HBO. HBO continued to expand, and as it did it was able to pay higher prices per film than its competitors, winning better films and more subscribers. In fact, its financial resources allowed it to purchase a block of 40 MGM/United Artists films all at once, paying about $35 million. HBO also began investing in the preproduction financ-

Company Perspectives:

HBO's aim is to continue to provide subscribers with the highest quality, award-winning new entertainment specials, original movies, comedy, documentaries, series, music specials, family shows, sports specials, and championship boxing available anywhere on television.

ing of movies in exchange for exclusive pay-TV rights. This prebuying was risky; HBO was paying in advance for the rights to movies that might prove unpopular. Moreover, the practice angered movie studios, which felt that HBO was intruding on their turf, and some of them began looking for a way into the cable TV industry. Some studios warned that HBO would drive many film studios out of business and control the film industry. Though such fears eventually proved unfounded, they demonstrated the depth of concern attached to a new medium whose ultimate potential remained a mystery.

In 1980 HBO introduced a second channel called Cinemax. This channel was priced lower than HBO and was geared to compete with Viacom's Showtime. Viacom would later charge that Cinemax was priced below cost as a way to drive Showtime out of business.

The Competitive 1980s

By 1982 HBO had 9.8 million subscribers, nearly 50 percent of all pay-TV subscribers, and earned $100 million on sales of $440 million. In fact, HBO was about three times as big as its nearest competitor, Showtime. This size advantage contributed to HBO's bottom line. For example, it paid about $1.4 million for the hit film *Raging Bull,* or about 15 cents per subscriber. Although Showtime paid less for the film, $1 million, that figure worked out to more than 30 cents per subscriber. When *Star Wars* went on the block in 1982, HBO matched a Showtime offer of $1 per subscriber, but insisted on price concessions on less popular films made by Twentieth-Century Fox.

At the end of 1982 HBO worked out a deal with Columbia Pictures and CBS to create Tri-Star Pictures, the first major new U.S. film studio in 40 years. Each company was to contribute up to $100 million to the venture, and HBO received the pay-TV rights. By 1983 HBO, with 13.4 million subscribers, was producing made-for-television movies and working on its own original comedy programs. While some industry observers wondered if HBO would become the fourth major non-cable television network, the growth of the cable industry as a whole slowed dramatically beginning in 1984. Part of the cause was lingering infrastructure problems. New cable systems had not yet been built in such major markets as Chicago, Philadelphia, Detroit, and Baltimore. Other causes for the cable slowdown were rising cable rates at a time when more and more consumers owned video cassette recorders and could rent their own films. Finally, HBO had also become complacent in negotiating contracts, while competitors moved quickly. As a result, HBO's share of the pay-TV market slipped from 50.4 percent in June 1983 to 48.1 percent in June 1984, while its profit margins began eroding.

Parent company Time Inc. responded by forcing out HBO chairman Frank J. Biondi, replacing him with Michael J. Fuchs. Fuchs cut HBO's staff by 125 employees and embarked on a $20 million advertising campaign, overseen by the New York firm Batten Barton Durstine & Osborn, to polish HBO's image. He also renegotiated contracts with Columbia Pictures and Tri-Star for the broadcasting of films and cut expense accounts and other costs.

As a result of the contract renegotiations, HBO gave up exclusive rights to many films. Rival Showtime, meanwhile, was trumpeting its new policy of showing films exclusively or not showing them at all. Previously the two firms had both showed some films exclusively, but shared many others. As a result of its new policy, Showtime won exclusive rights to several popular films. HBO management was angered, feeling that they had already learned that exclusive rights cost more than they were worth and that Showtime's move had increased the prices of acquiring even limited rights. Showtime's strategy also pushed HBO into negotiating for exclusive rights for more films than it otherwise would have done. Some industry analysts felt that the price of buying films for pay-TV should be decreasing, since the popularity of video cassette recorders had lowered their worth.

Despite the cable television slump, HBO had 14.6 million subscribers in 1985 and sales of about $800 million. Early the following year it began to scramble the signals it used to broadcast its programming to cable-system operators. Until then anyone with a satellite dish could tune in HBO for free.

Continuing to stock its film library, HBO bought the rights to 125 Warner Brothers films for five years for $600 million in 1986, also buying the rights to 72 films by MGM/UA Entertainment for four years. The following year, it bought the rights to 85 Paramount Pictures films over a five-year period.

In 1989 Viacom filed a $2.4 billion antitrust lawsuit against HBO. Viacom's Showtime subsidiary alleged that HBO was trying to put it out of business by intimidating cable systems that carried Showtime, as well as by trying to corner the market on Hollywood films to prevent rivals from showing any. The suit attracted wide attention, generating negative publicity for the cable industry at a time when the U.S. Congress was considering the re-regulation of cable. Part of the reason the anti-trust charges attracted so much attention was because they were being delivered by former top HBO employees; Frank J. Biondi had gone on to become Viacom's president and chief executive officer, while Showtime's president, Winston H. Cox, was also a former HBO executive. The lawsuit would not be settled until the early 1990s.

In the meantime, hoping to branch out, HBO announced plans for a 24-hour all-comedy channel. Stand-up comedy was experiencing a popularity boom in the United States, and polls of cable subscribers showed enthusiasm for the idea. HBO's The Comedy Channel began with six million subscribers in November 1989, though industry analysts felt it would need 20 million to attract enough advertising to survive. Some critics offered harsh appraisals of The Comedy Channel's fare, citing in particular the way HBO strung together excerpts from stand-up routines, sitcoms, and movie clips rather than longer, more substantial comedic pieces, and many cable operators were resistant to offering Comedy Channel at all. HBO moved quickly to entice them into buying ownership stakes as incentive to get the new channel wider availability. In April 1991 Comedy Channel suffered another setback when Viacom's HA! began broadcasting old sitcoms in their entirety, eschewing Comedy Channel's practice of showing excerpts. Most industry analysts believed that only one of the channels would survive. Many cable operators did not sign up for either, waiting to see which would get more support.

HBO invested heavily in advertising to win subscribers to its new and existing services, spending about $38 million in 1990 alone. However, both Comedy Channel and HA! were struggling, and in a surprise move, HBO and Viacom agreed to merge them into Comedy Central late in 1990. This shared channel, Comedy Central, would eventually go on to experience great success, producing several popular original comedy shows of its own.

HBO's legal challenges weren't over, however. During this time, Broadcast Music Incorporated (BMI), a performance-rights society, sued HBO over the rates it was paying for the use of BMI-protected music. The suit was settled in January 1991 when HBO agreed to raise the rate it paid for its blanket license to 15 cents per subscriber per year, up from 12 cents.

One of the most common complaints subscribers had about pay-TV channels was that they all tended to show the same films at the same time; once a person had seen the film, there was nothing on TV to watch. As the cancellation rate for HBO was about four percent a month, or about 850,000 of its 17 million subscribers per year, this lack of options was believed to be an important factor. To hang on to subscribers, HBO announced in 1991 that it would convert HBO and Cinemax to multichannel services. Each network would broadcast different programming simultaneously on three different channels. Many cable systems had no extra channels to offer, but HBO management hoped new technologies would expand the number of channels available. Because the company had to wait for fiber-optic lines to be installed and data-compression techniques to become more widely available, however, some industry observers estimated it would be three to five years before these multiple channels were widely available.

In August 1992 the Viacom suit was finally settled out of court, having cost both sides tens of millions of dollars in legal fees. Time Warner, HBO's parent company, agreed to pay Viacom $75 million and to buy a Viacom cable system in Milwaukee for $95 million, $10 million more than it was worth at the time according to the *Wall Street Journal.* Time Warner agreed to more widely distribute Showtime and The Movie Channel on Time Warner's cable systems, the second-largest in the United States. The two sides also agreed to a joint marketing campaign to try and revive the image of cable, which was again in a slump; HBO had lost about 300,000 subscribers in 1991, leaving it with a total of 17.3 million.

In the late 1980s and early 1990s many analysts predicted the end of pay TV. Competition from advertiser-supported basic

cable channels and pay-per-view options threatened an HBO already weakened by the popularity of home video rentals. However, HBO fought back on several fronts. CEO Michael Fuchs began an aggressive marketing campaign and continued to expand the availability of multiplexing around the country. He expanded the company's ventures outside its traditional enterprises, taking on sports licensing, such as the licensing of the World Cup logo. In addition, HBO moved into foreign pay TV markets and began selling original HBO production for foreign theatrical and home video distribution.

An Early 1990s Turnaround

Several of these strategies soon showed results for HBO. The company's foreign pay TV ventures proved highly successful and helped maintain profits. Foreign distributions were booming by the mid-1990s. Outside ventures, such as the sports licensing, grew quickly, accounting for 28 percent of revenues in 1993, up from one percent in 1982. On the home front, aggressive marketing and multiplexing were apparently behind the mild boost in subscribership in 1992. Membership continued to rise; in 1993 the subscriber base increased by one million to 24.7 million.

Competition for exclusive rights to Hollywood films subsided in the early 1990s, bringing down licensing costs by 20 percent. The end of the bidding wars helped raise HBO's profits: in 1992 operating profits were up by ten percent, to $215 million, and they rose the next year as well, to $230 million. The tides had begun to turn for HBO, which in 1993 provided eight percent of Time Warner's pretax profit.

Having rebounded somewhat from its slump in the late 1980s, HBO needed to maintain its momentum. In 1994 Jolie Solomon of *Newsweek* assessed the situation, noting that CEO Fuchs ''must stay ahead of the multimedia revolution, especially the technology that will create home-video jukeboxes. His strategy is to make HBO a powerful brand name, signaling high quality on the cutting edge.'' To that end, Fuchs upped the company's advertising and focused increasing amounts of HBO's time and budget on original productions, including movies, specials, and series. Because HBO did not need to attract and keep advertisers, its could take on subjects in its original productions that networks wouldn't touch, such as ''Barbarians at the Gate,'' a 1993 movie critical of R.J.R. Nabisco.

Fuchs's competitive, aggressive, and some said antagonistic management style, however, was not popular among all board members and shareholders, and he was replaced as CEO in 1995 by Jeffrey L. Bewkes. Having served HBO for years as an executive, Bewkes moved into the top position smoothly. With a more cooperative managerial style, especially with fellow subsidiary Warner Brothers, Bewkes continued Fuchs general strategy of creating original programming and promoting HBO as high-quality brand. In fact, in 1997 he spent an impressive $25 million to promote that brand, a figure that did not include the advertising budget for specific programs.

The company's efforts at original programming gained momentum in the late 1990s. In 1997 HBO received 90 nominations for Emmys, marking the first time a cable network had garnered more nominations than any broadcast network. Moreover, HBO was only narrowly beaten by NBC for the most Emmy awards won. Praise from critics was on the rise also, particularly for the channel's original series, such as the comedy *The Larry Sanders Show* and the drama *Oz.*

By the late 1990s, HBO had held its own against those threats to pay-TV that other top competitors were still struggling against. The Starz! and Showtime movie networks were both trailing HBO with fewer than half their subscribers. However, the satellite market had matured by 1998, and HBO could no longer rely on that market boom for increasing its subscriber base. Thus, although HBO had long outlasted predictions of its demise, it still faced many challenges at it approached a new century.

Further Reading

Berger, Warren, "At 25, Excellence and Big Budgets for a Late Bloomer," *The New York Times,* November 9, 1997, pp. AR23–AR24.

Block, Alex Ben, "Shoot-Out Time in Pay TV," *Forbes,* September 22, 1986.

"Cable-TV Dangles New Lures," *Business Week,* December 1, 1973.

"Can a New Chief Change the Picture at HBO?" *Business Week,* October 29, 1984.

Cox, Meg, "Time Warner's HBO, Broadcast Music Settle Suit over Performance Rights," *Wall Street Journal,* January 11, 1991.

Gubernick, Lisa, "Time Heals All," *Forbes,* May 23, 1994, p. 241.

"How HBO Dominates Pay-TV," *Business Week,* September 20, 1982.

King, Thomas R., "HBO to Offer Multiple Choice for Tuning In," *Wall Street Journal,* May 9, 1991.

Kneale, Dennis, "HBO Vows to Stick with Comedy Channel and Seek Operators Willing to Buy Stake," *Wall Street Journal,* March 6, 1990.

Lindsey, Robert, "Home Box Office Moves in on Hollywood," *New York Times Magazine,* June 12, 1983.

"A New Shooter in Tinseltown," *Newsweek,* December 13, 1982.

"Pay-TV: Even HBO's Growth Is Slowing," *Business Week,* July 9, 1984.

"Pay-TV: Is It a Viable Alternative?" *Forbes,* May 1, 1978.

"Pay TV's Lazarus Act," *Forbes,* March 1, 1993, pp. 14–15.

"The Race to Dominate the Pay-TV Market," *Business Week,* October 2, 1978.

Roberts, Johnnie L., "Time Warner, Viacom Settle HBO Suit, Clearing a Cloud from Cable's Horizon," *Wall Street Journal,* August 21, 1992.

Solomon, Jolie, "What Michael Fuchs Wants You to Know," *Newsweek,* May 30, 1994, pp. 60–61.

Stevens, Elizabeth Lesly, "Call It Home Buzz Office," *Business Week,* December 8, 1997, pp. 77, 80.

Trachtenberg, Jeffrey A., "Changing Reels," *Forbes,* May 20, 1985.

——, "Mea Culpa, Mea Culpa," *Forbes,* December 16, 1985.

Waters, Harry F., "Can HBO Change the Show?," *Newsweek,* May 23, 1983.

——, "Talk about a Running Gag," *Newsweek,* May 29, 1989.

—Scott M. Lewis
—updated by Susan Windisch Brown

Hongkong Electric Holdings Ltd.

**Electric Centre
28 City Garden Road
Hong Kong
(3) 852 2528 4008
Fax: (3) 852 2861 3779**

Public Company
Incorporated: 1889
Employees: 2,734
Sales: HK$7.67 billion (US$991 million) (1996)
Stock Exchanges: Hong Kong
SICs: 4911 Electric Services; 8711 Engineering Services; 8744 Facilities Support Services

Hongkong Electric Holdings Ltd. is the holding company for one of the world's oldest electric utility companies, Hongkong Electric Co. The company generates power for nearly half a million people on Hong Kong Island, Lamma Island, and Ap Lei Chau. Other activities include the sale of electric appliances, international project management, and engineering. The company's vast real estate holdings also served it well in the early-to-mid 1990s. Asian billionaire Li Ka-shing and his family controls just over 35 percent of the company through his Cheung Kong (Holdings) Ltd.. In the late 1990s, analysts speculated that a merger (or at least cooperative agreement) between Hongkong Electric and the archipelago's other electric utility, China Light & Power, was imminent.

19th-Century Founding

Hongkong Electric traces its beginnings to Sir Paul Chater, a native of Calcutta who arrived in the British colony of Hong Kong in 1864 to become a clerk with the Bank of Hindustan. By 1870 Sir Paul had left the bank to form his own brokerage house and was setting about becoming one of Hong Kong's most prominent *taipans,* or merchants. Sir Paul made his early fortune through property, developing a number of commercial sites in and around Hong Kong Island's Core Central business district, and throughout the 1870s, he developed the Hong Kong

harbor, providing portside facilities for the colony's expanding trading base.

In 1888 Sir Paul and two fellow members of the ruling Legislative Council were granted a government contract to form an electric company. The men agreed to provide street lights and to pump water to the Peak, a residential district rising high atop Hong Kong Island. The company chose a site at Wanchai—purchased from the government—to build its first power station. A year later, upon the incorporation of the Hongkong Electric Company Ltd., shares were offered to the public on the Hong Kong Stock Exchange.

In the meantime, Sir Paul was busy incorporating another company that would eventually prove to be an asset for Hongkong Electric. The new venture, the Hongkong Land Investment and Agency Company, was organized to reclaim land for new developments on the island. One of the company's particular projects was the 57-acre Praya Reclamation Project in the Central District.

Eventually the government canceled its contract for water to be pumped up to the Peak, but Hongkong Electric was still to supply the electricity for street lights. The company had already ordered two steam-driven generating units from Britain, each with a generating capacity of 50 kilowatts. The Wanchai Power Station was brought on line at 6:00 p.m. on December 1, 1890.

By 1896 the company was flourishing, and Hongkong Electric was able to declare its first dividend. An amount totaling HK$12,000 was paid out to the company's shareholders that year.

Turn of the Century Developments

Supplying electricity to new property developments built by Sir Paul became a successful venture. One such development, the Queen's Hotel which opened on the Praya reclamation site in 1898, was supplied with energy to drive the first electric elevators installed in Hong Kong. The elevators—four in all—sped up and down the structure at 200 feet per minute and operated on a DC electricity supply from Hongkong Electric's first substation.

Rather than taking up precious land—of which Hong Kong Island has so little to spare—in 1905 Hongkong Electric adopted a policy of installing supply cables underground. The company continued to maintain this policy, although the plan did encounter difficulties in its early stages when white ants began eating into the cable coverings.

In 1909, the first light bulbs using metal filaments were installed in residential and commercial buildings on the island. The new bulbs emitted far more light than those previously used, which had filaments made of bamboo. A year later electricity was made available to the western areas of Hong Kong Island and the fashionable Peak residential district.

In 1914 Hongkong Electric decided to expand from its original Wanchai Power Station after the plant's generating capacity became overloaded. A second power station—this one a coal-fired facility—was to be built at North Point, a rural area that was suited for such a plant. A site of approximately 125,000 square feet was purchased for a cost of HK$37,500.

By 1916 sales revenue for Hongkong Electric had topped HK$1 million. Three years later, the new North Point Power Station was brought on line with an initial capacity of 3,000 kilowatts, while the Wanchai Power Station was put on standby. In 1925 an out-of-town substation was opened at Shaukiwan. That same year the supply voltage was changed from 100 to 200 volts. The change meant more than the throw of a switch; 240,000 light bulbs were issued free to the company's customers, and all manner of appliances had to be converted or exchanged. A year later the company, as well as Hong Kong Island, lost a guiding light when Sir Paul Chater died.

The Japanese occupation of Hong Kong, beginning in 1941, had huge consequences for Hongkong Electric. Following the invasion, the North Point Power Station was shut down and abandoned in December. Although the *Times* of London reported in 1942 that the North Point Power Station had been attacked and destroyed by American bombers, the plant was again generating power two months after the liberation of the island in August 1945.

Rapid Growth in Postwar Era

Demand for electricity began to grow markedly with the influx of Chinese immigrants following the rise of the Communist regime in that country in 1949. In an effort to keep up with the demand the North Point Power Station was refitted and a 20-megawatt generating unit—thus far the company's largest—was installed in 1955. Then, three years later, to meet the still-growing demand, the transmission network voltage was upgraded from 6,600 to 33,000 volts with the installation of an even larger 30-megawatt generator at the newly commissioned North Point "B" station.

By 1964, Hongkong Electric had decided that the North Point Power Station, in addition to having become an environmental hazard in its now-residential site, would not have sufficient capacity to meet projected future demand. In order to build a new oil-fired power station, the company purchased a plot of land on Ap Lei Chau Island. In 1966, as construction continued on the Ap Lei Chau station, North Point "C" station—computerized and oil-fired—was brought on line with a 60-megawatt unit, bringing the network's voltage up to 66,000 volts. In 1968 the first unit at Ap Lei Chau Power Station began generating power.

By this time demand for electricity in Hong Kong was growing exponentially. A 125-megawatt generator, manufactured by the Japanese company Mitsubishi, was brought on line at Ap Lei Chau. Over the course of the next ten years, another six identical units were installed, bringing the entire transmission network voltage to 132,000.

In response to community concern that the company's three smokestacks were offensive due to their resemblance to the joss sticks used in the rituals of ancestor worship and funerals, Hongkong Electric built a fourth stack. Because the additional smokestack was not necessary at that point in time, it went unused, leading to the popular notion that the chimney was a "dummy."

In 1978 the company began planning another new power station, purchasing a site on Lamma Island at Po Lo Tsui. Hongkong Electric made a strategic move when, in response to the OPEC (Organization of Petroleum Exporting Countries) hold on the oil market and the subsequent steep increase in prices, the company decided to equip the new plant with dual-firing capabilities. Therefore, the facility could be run on either coal or oil, as circumstances warranted.

Beginning in 1979, Hongkong Electric was regulated through a Government Scheme of Control in an effort to guarantee equity between the company's customers and stockholders and the Hong Kong Island community. In a cooperative effort, in 1981 the company signed an agreement with China Light & Power (CLP), connecting the two systems. With the ability to transfer up to 480 megawatts, the companies could operate more efficiently in addition to having reserves available for times of peak demand. Moreover, this agreement preserved the monopoly enjoyed by each of the firms; CLP was the exclusive generator of electricity to Kowloon and Hongkong Electric supplied the Hong Kong, Lamma, and Ap Lei Chau islands. These schemes of control also established profit based on capacity; in 1995, the maximum allowable profit was 15 percent of fixed assets.

Records Set in 1980s

A world record was established in 1982 with the completion of the Lamma Power Station, constructed in just under three and a half years. The first unit to go on line, a 250-megawatt coal-fired generator, brought the transmission network voltage up to 275,000 volts.

The 1980s brought Hongkong Electric several more milestones. First, in 1983, the company topped the 1,000 megawatt mark in maximum demand. In 1985 work was completed on the Wanchai Zone Substation, the first substation built in the Far East on a modular basis, saving both time and expense during construction. Then, in 1986, the second phase of the 275-kilovolt submarine cable network, transmitting energy from the Lamma Power Station to Hong Kong Island, was brought on line. This completed the highest-capacity submarine cable network anywhere in the world.

In 1987 a second coal-fired generator, this one with a 350-megawatt capacity, went on line at the Lamma Power Station. The was the company's largest unit, representing a generating capacity 7,000 times greater than Hongkong Electric's first unit, originally installed at Wanchai Power Station.

In 1989 the company recorded that demand for electricity in Hong Kong had exceeded 1,000 megawatts during every month of the year. After six 125-megawatt generators were transferred from Ap Lei Chau to Lamma, where they were to be operated by gas turbines, the Ap Lei Chau Power Station was shut down.

The Lamma Power Station was by now using both coal and oil firing to remain flexible in its fuel use, however, the use of coal far outweighed that of oil. Coal consumption in 1988 was 2.3 million tons and was expected to increase at an average yearly rate of five percent. The station contained a jetty alongside the facility from which coal could be unloaded out of ocean-going vessels. To operate and monitor all the generating units, the Lamma station also contained a Central Control Room that acted as the nerve center of the complex. Complex data processing systems helped personnel keep a running tab on energy output and control the generating units for accuracy, efficiency, and economy.

In 1988 the company constructed and opened a 3.1-kilometer tunnel between Wah Fu and Kennedy Road in order to house its 275-kilovolt transmission network. The tunnel replaced the laying of 275-kilovolt cables in busy urban areas, thereby avoiding disrupting traffic or ruining the environment. Over the course of the decade, the company increased productivity from 1.4 million kilowatt hours per employee annually in 1980 to 2.57 million by 1992. That factor helped multiply Hongkong Electric's net income from HK$611.1 million in 1981 to HK$2.34 billion in 1991.

During the 1980s Hongkong Land Holdings Ltd. reasserted its historic link to Hongkong Electric. Originally founded by Sir Paul Chater during the 1870s, this property development company had grown to rank among the world's largest property management companies. In an effort to weather the recessionary conditions on the island, Hongkong Land began to diversify its holdings, taking a one-third interest in Hongkong Telephone and a similar stake in Hongkong Electric.

However, Hongkong Land did not maintain its investment in Hongkong Electric for long; in 1985 it divested the stake to Hutchison Wampoa Ltd., thereby placing the utility in Asian business magnate Li Ka-shing's sphere of influence. A child of Chinese immigrants, Li started out in the 1950s making artificial flowers. By the time he took his stake in Hongkong Electric, this tycoon known as *chiu yan,* or Superman, reigned over a HK$390 billion (US$50 billion) empire. His flagship company, Cheung Kong (Holdings) Ltd., built and managed toll roads, toll bridges, power stations, and other infrastructure throughout Asia. It owned a controlling interest in Hutchison Wampoa, which in turn held a substantial stake in Hongkong Electric.

Uncertainties Characterize 1990s

Hongkong Electric's executive management was soon replete with Hutchison expatriots. Simon Murray acted as chairman from 1985 to 1993, when he was succeeded by Hutchison

director George Magnus. At that time, Canning Fok Kin-ning advanced to managing director. In 1994, Magnus laid out a rather simple formula for HEH's continued growth, telling Gareth Hewett of the *South China Morning Post* that "the redevelopment of buildings on established land and the creation of new buildings on existing and future reclaimed land, together with continual increases in domestic per capita electricity consumption, all add to Hong Kong Island's increasing demand for electricity." Increasing demand would require greater capacity, which in turn would drive Hongkong Electric's ever-growing profits. Indeed, Hongkong Electric completed a HK$15 billion program of capital expenditure from 1990 through the end of 1994. And not surprisingly, the utility's profits grew from just under HK$2 billion in 1990 to over HK$4 billion in 1995.

However, Magnus' neat formula did not add up in the mid-1990s, when capacity began to outstrip demand. As manufacturers moved to mainland China, overall sales of electricity flattened and peak power usage began to decline during this period. By 1996, CLP had 50 percent over capacity and was forced by the government to postpone HK$1.8 billion in capital expenditures. Though Hongkong Electric also experienced overcapacity during this period, it forecast that growing demand would require that a new power station be on line by 2003. Its proposal for a new power station on Po Toi Island was met with opposition, first from consumer groups and environmentalists, who questioned the need for additional capacity when CLP had generating power to spare.

As the July 1997 deadline approached for the United Kingdom to hand Hong Kong over to Chinese rule, Li reorganized his empire. He transferred Hutchison Wampoa's 35.01 percent share of Hongkong Electric to the recently-formed Cheung Kong Infrastructure (CKI). Run by Li's eldest son, Victor, this firm managed Asian infrastructure investments. Li told *Financial Times (London)* that "the reorganisations reflects our intention to increase our total investment in infrastructure." A second restructuring in May made CKI part of Hutchison Wampoa. One benefit to Hongkong Electric from new arrangement was the creation of an international subsidiary in charge of power projects throughout Asia-Pacific. This key growth vehicle made its first acquisition in June, when it took a 25 percent stake in a Thai power plant project.

With its scheme of control agreement up for review in 1998, Hongkong Electric faced the possibility of dramatic change. Possibilities included: a merger with or purchase of capacity from China Light & Power; complete takeover by Li Ka-sheng's Cheung Kong group; or a simple maintenance of the status quo. No matter what the outcome, the utility was likely to enjoy continued long-term prosperity under the auspices of the Li family.

Principal Subsidiaries

The Hongkong Electric Company, Limited; Associated Technical Services Limited; Cavendish Construction Limited; Fortress Advertising Company Limited; Hongkong Electric Fund Management Limited; Gusbury Enterprises Incorporation; Best Liaison Limited; Hongkong Electric International Limited.

Further Reading

100 Years of Energy, Hong Kong: The Hongkong Electric Co. Ltd., 1990.

Chetham, Andrew, "Utilities Merger 'A Profitable Proposal'," *South China Morning Post,* April 16, 1997, p. 14.

Clayton, Dusty, "HK Electric Net Rises 8.7 pc," *South China Morning Post,* March 8, 1996, p. 1.

Cottrell, Robert, "HK Land Buys 20 Percent of HK Electric," *Financial Times (London),* April 27, 1982, p. 21.

Criswell, Colin, *The Taipans of Hong Kong,* Oxford, Eng.: Oxford University Press, 1981.

Hewett, Gareth, "Hongkong Electric's Star Shines Brightly," *South China Morning Post,* March 4, 1994, p. 1.

Highlights of the Electric Years, Hong Kong: The Hongkong Electric Co. Ltd., 1992.

"Hong Kong's Supermen Prepare for China," *Financial Times (London),* January 14, 1997, p. 25.

"Li Ka-shing Stays Ahead of the Game," *Financial Times (London),* January 7, 1997, p. 20.

Lucas, Louise, "HK Power Groups Study Co-Operation Deal," *Financial Times (London),* December 10, 1996, p. 32.

——, "Power Policy Kept on Low Heat," *Financial Times (London),* September 16, 1996, p. 6.

Porter, Barry, and Dusty Clayton, "Lucrative Signs of a Powerful Union," *South China Morning Post,* November 5, 1995, p. 3.

Ridding, John and Louise Lucas, "Beijing Buys £1.3 Billion Stake in Top HK Power Supplier," *Financial Times (London),* January 29, 1997, p. 1.

—Etan Vlessing
—updated by April Dougal Gasbarre

IDEXX Laboratories, Inc.

One IDEXX Drive
Westbrook, Maine 04092
U.S.A.
(207) 856-0300
Fax: (207) 856-0346
Web site: http://www.idexx.com

Public Company
Incorporated: 1983
Employees: 1,515
Sales: $263 million (1997)
Stock Exchanges: NASDAQ
SICs: 2835 Diagnostic Substances; 3826 Analytical
Instruments

IDEXX Laboratories, Inc. is one of an estimated 1,300 U.S. companies that have entered the biotechnology field since scientists discovered the recombinant DNA process in 1973. IDEXX focuses on producing and selling veterinary diagnostic test kits and instruments. Its products also include systems to test for food and water contamination, such as tests for bacteria in drinking water and *salmonella* in food. Headquartered in rural Maine, IDEXX has branches in several countries and works with state-of-the-art technological processes. It markets about 400 products in more than 50 countries. In the highly competitive and rapidly changing biotechnology field, IDEXX experienced rapid growth from its founding in 1983 through the late 1990s, although its revenues levelled abruptly in 1997.

1980s Founding

In the early 1980s David E. Shaw, having just turned 30, was commuting every week from Maine to Agribusiness Associates, Inc., an international management consulting firm in the affluent Boston suburb of Wellesley Hills, Massachusetts. The travel was draining, and Shaw began to think of other ways to live. As a consultant, he began to notice untapped markets that could be pursued from Maine. As he told the *Boston Globe,* "I saw opportunities in animal health that were not being served well.

I got tired of the commute to Massachusetts and liked living in Maine, so I started with the poultry industry, seeing that the initial investment would be small and the time to market shorter." In 1983 IDEXX was incorporated, and soon afterward the new company began operations. Shaw had some difficulty in luring employees to rural Maine for his startup company, but as the company's success grew it also drew a pool of talented employees.

The early years of IDEXX were accompanied by enormous growth in the biotechnology field, and the field was highly competitive from the start. Typically it took several years for a company to develop a new product, since funds for research, testing, and marketing had to be raised. Often development funds were raised from pharmaceutical companies that in return wanted to own a share of the biotechnology company, and as a result, many biotechnology companies (most of which having fewer than 150 employees) were taken over by larger companies in the process. For products intended for human use, a company also had to go through an elaborate approval process at the U.S. Food and Drug Administration (FDA), and then, even if this approval was granted, companies could not predict whether products would be successful or prove disappointing when they finally reached the marketplace. In this turbulent atmosphere, IDEXX had the advantage of being able to avoid waiting for FDA approval for its early products, since IDEXX products were aimed at the veterinary and agricultural markets, rather than for human medical use.

Products Expanded from Earliest Focus

In its earliest years IDEXX concentrated on two key product lines. In 1985, IDEXX introduced systems that government agencies and businesses could use to test for the presence of contaminants in foods and food processing facilities. The following year it began to sell diagnostic and detection products for use by veterinarians in their offices. By the mid-1990s, IDEXX also sold tests with which government agencies and businesses could detect contaminants in drinking water (introduced in 1993) and began to offer commercial veterinary laboratory testing, consultation, and advisory services to veterinarians (introduced in 1994). IDEXX internally referred to its products and services as falling into two specialized areas: Animal Health; and Food and Environmental. Testing kits sold by IDEXX ranged in price from $25 to $4,000 each; testing instruments and systems were priced from $1,000 to over $70,000 each.

IDEXX's products relied heavily on such sophisticated bio-technologies as immunoassay technology, which employs tests based on antibody-antigen reactions. Most simply explained, antigens are foreign substances such as viruses or bacteria that enter a body; through its immune system, the body produces antibodies in hopes of eliminating the antigen. Several IDEXX products relied on DNA probe technology, in which a single-stranded DNA molecule is introduced into a test sample. If a particular organism is present in the sample, the DNA molecule will combine with it to form a double-stranded molecule.

Animal Health Products and Services

During the 1980s and 1990s IDEXX developed numerous inexpensive test kits for veterinarians' use, to detect diseases common among household pets, such as heartworm disease, feline immunodeficiency virus (sometimes called "feline AIDS"), feline leukemia, and canine parvovirus. Veterinarians recommended regular testing for many of these diseases, making such products quite profitable. IDEXX also developed a test for equine infectious anemia, important in that federal law required that horses be tested for this disease before they can be taken across state lines. The company also developed a wide variety of much more costly instrument-based testing systems: one to analyze enzyme levels in animals' blood; a second to measure electrolytes (sodium, potassium, and chloride); a third to evaluate blood components; and a fourth to measure hormones. IDEXX created software that linked these four systems and allows veterinarians to produce a profile report within their own offices, rather than having to rely on commercial testing laboratories. Brand names of tests marketed by IDEXX included SNAP, CITE, VetLite, and QBC Vet Autoread.

In the mid-1990s, following acquisition of several testing laboratories, IDEXX began to offer veterinary laboratory services in the United States, England, and Japan. Veterinarians who needed more sophisticated testing than was possible in their offices sent samples to IDEXX facilities and received reports. Through its subsidiary Cardiopet, IDEXX provided specialized consultation services to veterinarians in the United States, Canada, and 11 other countries. Veterinarians could telephone Cardiopet during a patient's visit and receive immediate interpretation of test results in areas such as radiology, dermatology, and cardiology.

IDEXX instrument-based systems were used by government agencies and industrial laboratories to test large numbers of samples, allowing diagnosis and monitoring of diseases in poultry and livestock. Of particular interest, given the concern about *salmonella* poisoning in the late 1990s, were IDEXX's "Flock-Chek" testing system and software which could be used to test poultry for this contaminant.

Food and Environmental Products and Services

IDEXX also created many products used to measure the safety of drinking water, dairy products, poultry, and processed meat. Dairy farmers, government laboratories, and food companies all made use of these detection products, as numerous contaminants could be detected with IDEXX products, including *E. coli* (which could be found in both food and water and was responsible in the late 1990s for well-publicized food poisoning incidents in beef products), *salmonella* (a bacteria that could lead to fatal food contamination), aflatoxins, and dangerous antibiotic residues in food products.

Among IDEXX's entries into this area were its Lightning, SimPlate, and Acumedia testing products. The Lightning testing system, introduced in 1995, was used to test the cleanliness of processing surfaces and other equipment in food processing plants. The SimPlate product line, introduced the following year, was used by food quality managers to determine the total level of *E. coli* and other contaminants in food products. In 1997, IDEXX acquired Acumedia, a company that manufactured more than 300 products used for bacteria detection in foods; these products were being integrated with other IDEXX testing devices in the late 1990s. IDEXX also maintained the Food Safety Net, a network of products and testing and consulting services.

Acquisitions and International Expansion

Through the mid-1990s, IDEXX completed several major acquisitions of other biotechnology and testing companies. Major acquisitions included: VetTest S.A., a veterinary clinical testing business; Environetics, Inc., producer of the Colilert water testing product line; AMIS International Company, KK, a Japanese veterinary laboratory business; and Cardiopet Incorporated, a veterinary consulting service.

During 1996 and 1997, IDEXX's acquisitions accelerated, and it became the owner of several additional veterinary reference laboratory businesses, plus manufacturers of detection and diagnostic tests. Companies acquired during 1996 included: Vetlab, Inc., a Texas operator of two veterinary reference laboratories; Grange Laboratories Ltd., operator of veterinary reference laboratories in the United Kingdom; Veterinary Services, Inc., operator of veterinary reference laboratories in Colorado, Illinois, and Oklahoma; Consolidated Veterinary Diagnostics, Inc., operator of veterinary reference laboratories in California, Nevada, and Oregon; Ubitech Aktiebolag, a Swedish manufacturer and distributor of livestock diagnostic test kits; and Idetek, Inc., a California company that manufactured and distributed detection tests used by the food, agricultural, and environmental industries.

In 1997, IDEXX placed a similar focus on acquiring its competitors. It acquired Acumedia Manufacturers, Inc., a Maryland manufacturer of dehydrated culture media used for bacteria detection; National Information Systems Corporation, a Wisconsin company that supplied computer systems for veterinary practice management; Wintek Bio-Science Inc., a company in Taiwan that distributed diagnostic products to veterinarians and hospitals; and Professionals' Software, Inc., an Illinois company also engaged in supplying practice management computer systems to veterinarians. IDEXX also entered into an agreement with Fuisz Technologies, a Virginia company that had developed technology for rapidly dissolving tablets, allowing IDEXX to adapt this technology for veterinary use.

In 1991, only 21 percent ($6.5 million) of IDEXX's revenues came from sales outside of the United States. By 1996, that figure had risen to 34 percent ($91.5 million). The company attributed this rise largely to the expansion of its sales force in other countries; by 1996 it maintained foreign sales offices in Australia, France, Germany, Italy, Japan, New Zealand, the Netherlands, Spain, and the United Kingdom. However, these foreign operations were not without risk. IDEXX had to deal with regulatory approvals and patent processes for its products that differed from country to country, import and export tariffs, and economic fluctuations in foreign countries. The latter factor became particularly important in late 1997, when economies in both Europe and the Pacific Rim countries (Japan, Asia, Taiwan, and Australia) became shaky and IDEXX's revenues there dropped substantially. This drop contributed to an overall decrease in revenues to IDEXX for the first nine months of 1997, an abrupt halt to its rapid growth in the preceding years.

Patent Lawsuits a Constant Concern

As the biotechnology industry was marked by rapid change and heavy dependence on legal protection for a company's products—such as licenses, patents, and copyrights—it was common for companies to charge each other with infringement of product patents. The resulting lawsuits often proved very expensive, complicated, and time-consuming. In the mid-1990s IDEXX found itself involved in several of these lawsuits. The two most important of these involved the Millipore Corporation and the Barnes-Jewish Hospital of St. Louis.

In 1993, IDEXX had acquired Environetics, Inc., which already had a lawsuit pending against Millipore Corporation, charging that Millipore had infringed its patented technology for detecting *E. coli* and other contaminants in food and water. Two years later, IDEXX added a second lawsuit against Millipore for similar infringements. The two lawsuits were finally settled in December 1997, when Millipore agreed to halt sales of the products that were the subjects of the lawsuits.

In May 1995, the Barnes-Jewish Hospital of St. Louis filed a lawsuit against IDEXX, claiming that IDEXX's canine heartworm diagnostic products had infringed one of the hospital's patents. Although IDEXX claimed that the hospital's patent was invalid, it eventually decided to settle the case out of court in September 1997, paying the hospital $5.5 million. (Following

this settlement, the hospital then sued IDEXX's chief competitor in the heartworm diagnostic business, Synbiotics Corporation of California.) While the lawsuit was pending, IDEXX also had spent a great deal of time and funds to develop products to replace the ones challenged by the hospital.

Financial Outlook for the Future

IDEXX experienced massive growth during the mid-1990s. Between 1994 and 1995, its total revenues increased 49 percent, from $126.4 million to $188.6 million. Its international revenues almost doubled during that single year, rising from $34.3 million to $65 million. Between 1995 and 1996, growth was almost as impressive. Revenues in 1996 increased another 42 percent, to $267.7 million; international revenues in 1996 increased 41 percent, to $91.5 million. Growth in Europe and Japan was a key factor in these increases. In 1996, revenues in the Pacific Rim region rose more than 135 percent.

However, 1997 saw the brakes applied to such large-scale growth. The combination of the settlement paid in the Barnes-Jewish Hospital lawsuit, the costs of acquiring new companies, and drastically reduced sales in economically troubled Europe and Japan resulted in a third-quarter 1997 loss for IDEXX, a reversal of the large rise in profits the company had come to expect. In November 1997, CEO Shaw announced that Erwin F. Workman, Jr., president and chief operating officer of IDEXX since 1993 and an employee since its first year in business, would be replaced by Jeffrey J. Langan, a 20-year employee of the Hewlett-Packard Company. Workman would take over operations in the products divisions and would focus on research and development activities. There were several other high level executive shifts in late 1997, including appointment of two new division vice-presidents and appointment to the board of directors of a specialist in venture capital investment.

Principal Subsidiaries

Access Medical Systems, Inc.; Acumedia Manufacturers, Inc.; Cardiopet Incorporated; Environetics, Inc.; ETI Corporation; IDEXX Distribution Corporation; IDEXX Veterinary Services, Inc.; National Information Systems Corporation; Radiopet Incorporated; IDEXX Laboratories Foreign Sales Corporation (USVI); IDEXX Laboratories Pty. Limited (Australia); IDEXX Laboratories Canada Corporation; IDEXX Laboratories Limited (England and Wales); IDEXX Logistique et Scientifique Europe S.A. (France), IDEXX Management Services Europe S.A. (France), and IDEXX S.A. (France); IDEXX GmbH (Germany); IDEXX Laboratories Italia S.r.l. (Italy); IDEXX Laboratories, KK (Japan); IDEXX Laboratories B.V. (Netherlands); IDEXX Laboratories (NZ) Limited (New Zealand); Ubitech Aktiebolag (Sweden).

Further Reading

Rosenberg, Ronald, "New Businesses Move Maine Ahead," *Boston Globe,* June 2, 1996, p. 79.

—Gerry Azzata

Insurance Auto Auctions, Inc.

850 E. Algonquin Road
Suite 100
Schaumburg, Illinois 60173
U.S.A.
(847) 705-9550
Fax: (847) 839-3678
Web site: http://www.iaai.com

Public Company
Incorporated: 1982 as Los Angeles Auto Salvage
Employees: 630
Sales: $281.9 million (1996)
Stock Exchanges: NASDAQ
SICs: 5521 Motor Vehicle Dealers (Used Only)

With operations throughout the United States, Insurance Auto Auctions, Inc. (IAA) is one of the auto salvage industry's top chains. The company was among the first to conceive of and undertake industry consolidation through acquisition, expanding from five branches with an annual vehicle volume of 30,000 units in 1991, to 46 locations and 443,000 vehicles per year in 1996. Fueled by well over a dozen acquisitions, IAA's sales increased from $38 million in 1990 to almost $282 million by 1996, catapulting the company to a leading role in its highly fragmented industry. Though it boasted top dollar and unit volume, IAA lagged chief rival Copart, Inc. in terms of number of outlets and profitability. In fact, IAA's net income was on a downward trend in the mid-1990s, declining from nearly $11 million in 1994 to just over $3 million in 1996.

Founder and longtime CEO Bradley Scott relinquished day-to-day leadership of the company in March 1996, but continued to serve as chairman of the board. His successor, Jim Alampi, was recruited from a chemical distribution company. Scott's retirement capped a half-decade of turnover in IAA's upper echelon; as of 1996, all but three of the company's top eleven executives joined the chain after its 1991 initial public stock offering. Around the same time, IAA reorganized into three geographic divisions and moved its headquarters from Southern California to a suburb of Chicago, Illinois.

The Auto Salvage Industry

Bradley Sterling Scott established the company in 1982 as Los Angeles Auto Salvage, a one-acre auto pool in Van Nuys. At that time, most of the country's auto salvage operations fit with the popular image of a "junkyard"—heaps of vehicles in varying states of ruin waiting for auction by disorganized managers—an inefficient concoction ripe for fraud and abuse.

However, behind that rusty veneer lay an industry primed for automation and consolidation. Contrary to popular belief, most facilities lumped under the term "junkyard" are not the final resting place for totalled cars and trucks. In fact, they are intended to be more like car purgatory: a place that sorts the salvageable from the unsalvageable. The former are sold to used car dealers and dismantlers who reincarnate them, and the latter go to scrap dealers who recycle the otherwise useless carcasses. The junkyard is merely the physical manifestation of the industry; its soul is service. Specifically, auto auction yards serve as the nexus between parties that have severely damaged cars to liquidate and those who see "treasure" in this "trash."

Salvage auto auctioneers like IAA typically obtain their cars from insurance companies looking to recoup their losses on cars that have been totaled in an accident or natural disaster as well as some vehicles that were stolen and recovered after a settlement was made with the insured. Historically, the auctioneer (a.k.a. "auto pool") makes money on the transaction by charging sellers a flat consignment fee of $50 to $150 per vehicle to cover services like towing, assessment, title processing, and storage. After the sale, buyers often paid for the same services à la carte. But this modus operandi had a serious flaw: it cast auctioneers as disinterested parties to the transaction, with no incentive to obtain the highest price for their primary clients, the insurance companies.

Revolutionizing The Junkyard In The 1980s

In the early 1980s, auto insurers seeking to make underwriting more efficient and cost-effective began to target vehicle

Company Perspectives:

We anticipate and provide the best customer-valued products and services that help solve business issues and optimize our customers' return and profitability on salvage. At IAA, we pride ourselves on being a leading provider of automobile salvage services. For us, the key element is services. We go beyond simply buying and selling vehicles to developing and delivering services geared to provide insight to and resolutions for our customers' business problems. IAA's innovative services are instrumental in all areas of business—including information, financial and operations management—and we share our extensive knowledge and expertise within the industry. Whether our customer is an insurance company or a salvage buyer, as a market-driven operation, IAA enables its customers to reap the rewards of proceeds from the disposition and utilization of salvaged vehicles. After nearly 15 years in the vehicle salvage business, we understand what it takes for our customers to turn a profit and provide important opportunities for them to do so through mutually beneficial initiatives and solutions.

salvage as an area with the potential not only to cut costs but possibly enhance revenues. They began to demand better service and higher returns on vehicle salvage. Bradley Scott was one of the country's few auto salvage operators to recognize that a tidal wave of change was towering over his industry. Instead of being swept away, the 34-year-old Californian decided to grab a surfboard and ride the wave.

Scott started his reform program with the service end of the business, hosting his first live auction one year after starting LA Auto Salvage. He also departed from the traditional flat rate consignment method of transacting business. Scott focused instead on purchasing cars outright from insurance companies and selling them at a profit. The company negotiated exclusive purchase programs with insurance companies. Under these contracts, IAA agreed to pay a predetermined fraction of the actual cash value (ACV) of each car an insurer had to sell. The ACV, in turn, was based on used car prices. This program proved highly profitable throughout the 1980s and into the early 1990s, because the company could count on making more at auction than it had paid out under contract. By 1996 nearly half of IAA's autos were supplied by Allstate Insurance Co., Farmers Insurance Group, and State Farm Insurance Co.

IAA enticed insurers to join its program with a broad array of cost-cutting and time-saving conveniences. IAA inaugurated its Vehicle Inspection Center program (VIC) in 1988. This service towed totaled cars directly to centralized inspection areas in IAA yards. This plan allowed claims adjusters to inspect vehicles in one centralized location. IAA made this process even easier in the 1990s with a video imaging service. This program sent detailed color images of damaged vehicles to claims offices through a dedicated computer network, thereby allowing claims adjusters to evaluate autos at the desktop. Niche services also set IAA apart from its many competitors. A catastrophe action team stood ready to assist insurance compa-

nies in times of heavy demand, and a specialty salvage service concentrated on vehicles like semi-trucks, boats, and recreational vehicles. Over the course of the decade, Scott also pursued geographic expansion, launching three new outlets in California and a fifth in Hawaii by the end of 1990.

Vehicle buyers paid an annual membership fee ($35 in 1991) that entitled them to access IAA's inventory databases. Scott likened the membership program to the "Price Club" concept in a 1991 interview with *National Underwriter Property & Casualty-Risk & Benefits* magazine's Garry Chandler. Member benefits included weekly computerized inventories of IAA's stock and electronic title processing.

The membership program also allowed IAA to track the buying habits of its customers, a factor that helped the auctioneer target marketing as well as investigate fraud. In 1991, the company inaugurated its "CarCrush" and "TitleTrac" anti-fraud programs. Though most wrecked vehicles have some intrinsic value, some are so badly damaged that only one tiny bit retains its worth: the vehicle identification number. Auto theft rings often purchase these otherwise useless heaps, steal an identical (but of course operational) vehicle, then apply the totaled car's VIN and title to the stolen auto. IAA's "CarCrush" program advised insurance companies to take useless vehicles' VINs out of circulation by demolishing these total losses. "TitleTrac" monitored buyers' auto trading habits for telltale signs of unscrupulous deals.

IPO Presages Expansion Via Acquisition

LA Auto Salvage became the first in its industry to make a public stock offering, taking to the equities market as Insurance Auto Auctions, Inc. at $11 per share in 1991. A second issue raised an additional $23 million in 1993. The proceeds of these offerings helped finance a major acquisition spree and nationwide expansion. Four corporate purchases totaling $20 million added 6 yards in four western states to the company roster in 1992. IAA extended its reach all the way to the East Coast in 1993, investing at least $18.5 million in nine facilities in Arizona, Texas and the Midwest in the process of acquiring four companies. This growth program nearly tripled IAA's revenues from $60.5 million in 1992 to over $172 million in 1994. Net income more than doubled over the period, from $4.4 million to just shy of $11 million. Investors watched the stock rise from its issue price of $11 in 1991 to a peak of $45.50 in 1993. That year, Montgomery Securities analyst Joseph Holson noted IAA's "meteoric" earnings and revenue growth in a brief by *Business Week's* Gene G. Marcial.

Sharp Profit Decline an Indication of Management Turnover

IAA hit a king-sized speed bump mid-decade, when used car prices—upon which IAA's purchase price for wrecked autos was based—began to rise rapidly. This would not have been a problem had auction prices grown in line with the general increase. But in fact, IAA's per-car pay-outs increased as much as 24 percent from the beginning of 1992 to the end of 1994, while auction values barely budged. The squeeze soon showed up on IAA's bottom line. Though revenues increased from $172 million in 1994 to nearly $282 million in 1996, net income plunged more than 70 percent, from $11 million to about $3 million. Heretofore upbeat Wall Streeters abandoned the stock, which plummeted to $6.50 per share late in 1995 before recovering to about $11 in the third quarter of 1997.

In the meantime, competition with Copart for key acquisitions had driven up asking prices to the point that in some cases, the creation of "greenfield" yards made economic sense. That year, IAA established three start-up facilities and purchased four companies. Acquisitions returned to the fore in 1995, when the company fleshed out its coverage of the Midwest and East Coast.

In March 1996, founder Bradley Scott acknowledged that "The skills required to take this company to the next level—in things like information technology and human resources and financial management—were different from the skills I have." Scott handed ultimate managerial responsibility to outsider James Alampi, who continued a managerial housecleaning that had begun when IAA went public in 1991. The new executive team was young; at 50, Alampi himself was the oldest. He brought three executives—CFO Linda Larrabee, controller Stephen L. Green, and information systems vice-president Charles Rice—with him from his previous employer, Van Waters & Rogers Inc. Whether these professionals would be able to transfer their experience in the chemical distribution industry to the auto salvage business remained to be seen.

Under Alampi, IAA checked its growth in 1996, adding only two Midwestern facilities. Revenues for the first nine months of 1997 slid ten percent from the comparable period in 1996 as IAA shifted from the purchase strategy to a concentration on consignment. The company also worked to renegotiate more favorable purchase agreements with insurers—especially Allstate, which owned a minority stake in the salvage auto auctioneer.

Principal Subsidiaries

Insurance Auto Auctions Corp.; ADBCO Acquisition Corp.

Further Reading

Berger, Robin, "Auto Salvage Firm On Expansionary Course, Files For New Stock Offering," *Los Angeles Business Journal*, July 26, 1993, p. 30.

"Calif. Salvage Giant Introduces Crusher Program," *National Underwriter Property & Casualty-Risk & Benefits Management*, September 2, 1991, p. C28.

Chandler, Garry, "Auction Firm Turns Wrecked Cars To Cold Cash," *National Underwriter Property & Casualty-Risk & Benefits Management*, July 1, 1991, p. C10.

Dauer, Christopher, "Insurance Auto Auctions Aids In Battle On Fraud," *National Underwriter Property & Casualty-Risk & Benefits Management*, May 24, 1993, p. 21.

Marcial, Gene G., "Fix A Wreck, Reap A Small Fortune," *Business Week*, February 8, 1993, p. 117.

Murphy, H. Lee, "Insurance Auto Auctions Sits At Top Of Salvage Heap," *Automotive News*, July 15, 1996, p. 27.

—April D. Gasbarre

ISUZU

Isuzu Motors, Ltd.

26-1 Minami-Oi 6-chome
Shinagawa-ku
Tokyo 140
Japan
(03) 5471-1111
Fax: (03) 5471-1042
Web site: http://www.isuzu.com

Public Company
Incorporated: 1937 as Tokyo Motors, Inc.
Employees: 14,300
Sales: $15.7 billion (1996)
Stock Exchanges: Tokyo Osaka Nagoya
SICs: 3537 Industrial Trucks & Tractors; 3711 Motor
     Vehicles & Car Bodies; 3713 Truck & Bus Bodies;
     3714 Motor Vehicle Parts & Accessories

The largest producer of medium- and heavy-duty trucks in the world, Isuzu Motors, Ltd. also produces sport utility vehicles, pickups, and diesel engines. Isuzu ventured into the passenger car market in the 1980s, but pulled out in 1991 after its passenger line dragged the company into heavy losses. With help from 37 percent owner General Motors, Isuzu returned to profitability, mainly by concentrating on its strong truck and diesel engine expertise. Becoming something of a manufacturing subsidiary of GM, Isuzu supplemented its strong Asian sales by building small trucks and components for distribution by General Motors. As of 1998, Isuzu's vehicles were driven in more than 100 countries around the world.

Early History

Isuzu Motors has its origin in a 1916 diversification plan undertaken by the Tokyo Ishikawajima Shipbuilding and Engineering Company. The company, established after the Meiji Restoration to build heavy ships on Ishikawajima Island near Tokyo, hoped to insulate itself from cyclical downturns in the shipbuilding industry. Tokyo Ishikawajima initiated the venture as a partnership with the Tokyo Gas and Electric Industrial Company, which had the engineering expertise necessary to design vehicles. In fact, Tokyo Gas produced its first vehicle, the Type A truck, in 1918, using engines from Tokyo Ishikawajima. The partnership manufactured a variety of designs under license from the English firm Wolseley, including the model A9 car, which went into production in Japan in 1922. In 1929 the enterprise was incorporated separately as Ishikawajima Automobile Manufacturing, Ltd.

The company developed an air-cooled diesel engine in 1934. Its pioneering efforts in this area established the automotive group as a leader in diesel technologies during the 1930s. Through its association with Tokyo Ishikawajima and Tokyo Gas, the company became a supplier to the military. Under a government mobilization scheme in 1937, the automotive interests of Tokyo Ishikawajima and Tokyo Gas were formally merged into a new company called Tokyo Motors. Mass production of the air-cooled diesel engine began that year.

World War II and Postwar Recovery

In 1938 Tokyo Motors began production of a truck under a new nameplate, Isuzu—Japanese for "50 bells." By this time, however, the military had gained control of the government and launched a war against China. As a result, Tokyo Motors came under government production plans and much of its output was earmarked for the military. In 1939 Tokyo Motors developed a new diesel model, the DA40, representing another advance in the company's diesel technologies. But by 1942, the United States and Britain were at war with Japan over interests in Asia. With the war raging and the economy operating under emergency conditions, the operations of Tokyo Motors were split up to effect greater rationalization of the automotive industry. The company's truck business was spun off into a new company called Hino Heavy Industries (later Hino Motors). Tokyo Motors continued to operate as a frame manufacturer, but resumed production of engines in 1943.

A year later, Japan was exposed to bombing raids. As a military resource located in a major industrial center, Tokyo Motors was exposed to these raids. The company's production

Company Perspectives:

It is our purpose to build vehicles. Vehicles that are not merely practical, rugged and well-designed, but that testify in steel to the ultimate of transportation: to open up to exploration unknown parts of the world and unknown parts of the imagination.

Farther. It is an engineering mandate. It is a command to build vehicles for the roughest of all uses. It is a philosophy, made up of one part expertise and one part obsession; it is why (merely for instance) we will test a traction system on a frozen lake or test an engine until destruction in Death Valley.

Farther. It is a first principal of design. While ruggedness, reliability and practicality are assured, it is a call to go beyond that. Each vehicle should push the outer boundaries of design; its form should be as surprising as its function is satisfying.

Farther. It is a renewed commitment to our customers. It assures absolute satisfaction with our products, our people and our service. It is a promise to communicate with our customers in the future regularly and conscientiously, so that Isuzu owners feel they hold a stake not only in a company, but in a certain point-of-view and way of life.

was completely disrupted until the war ended in September of 1945. Yet Tokyo Motors was quick to recover from the war and resumed production before the end of the year. In 1946 the company introduced a new diesel truck called the TX80. This product helped Tokyo Motors fund major investments in its facilities and expand the scope of its product research.

The company changed its name to Isuzu Motors, Ltd. in 1949. Like many other Japanese companies that had emerged from the war, Isuzu went back into the business of supplying the military, but this time the customer was the American army. These large, stable supply agreements were instrumental in helping Isuzu recapitalize and grow. The company became an important resource for the Americans, particularly in late 1950, after hostilities erupted on the Korean Peninsula. Isuzu supplied a variety of trucks and other industrial products to the forces fighting North Korean aggression, helping to further advance the company's position in the diesel engine market. After an armistice was concluded in 1953, Isuzu reestablished licensing agreements with the British. The company signed an agreement to build automobiles designed by the Rootes Group (now called Talbot, and part of the French firm PSA. Under the terms of the agreement, Isuzu manufactured the Hillman Minx.

In 1959 Isuzu introduced a new two-ton N-series truck called the Elf. This was followed in 1961 by an attempt to equip an Isuzu automobile with a small diesel engine. While economical and reliable, the diesel Bellel car was uncomely, noisy, and, ultimately, a commercial failure. Consumers clearly favored a more cosmopolitan, if less practical, car. In 1962 Isuzu opened a new factory at Fujisawa. With expanded production capacity, the company introduced the Bellett automobile in 1963, followed by the Florian model in 1967. The next year Isuzu rolled out the sporty two-door 117 Coupe, a luxury model resembling the Ford Mustang. In 1970 Isuzu introduced two new trucks, the medium-sized Forward (named for its forward control) and a 12-ton diesel model.

Alliance with General Motors in the 1970s

Although Isuzu was a recognized leader in the truck market, its rapid development of new models had left it financially weakened. When it appeared to the company's bankers that the market would be unable to support Isuzu's new product line, they began negotiations with the company's competitors, hoping to arrange a merger of Isuzu with a more stable firm. Although companies such as Fuji Heavy Industries, Mitsubishi Corporation, and Toyota Motor Corporation were probably approached, it was General Motors that emerged with the greatest interest in Isuzu. The automotive giant was impressed with Isuzu's promise in export markets in the United States and Asia and hoped to include the company in its own global strategies. In 1971 General Motors purchased a 34.2 percent share of Isuzu. As part of its marketing tie-up with General Motors, Isuzu's KB pickup truck was sold through GM dealerships in the United States beginning in 1972. In 1974 General Motors employed Isuzu to manufacture the Kadett, a model designed by its German Opel subsidiary, under the Isuzu nameplate as the Bellett Gemini.

Isuzu introduced a fuel-efficient direct-injected diesel engine in 1974 in two new truck models, the Forward SBR and Forward JBR. Rising fuel prices made these models especially popular with inflation-weary consumers in Japan. General Motors saw the fuel efficiency of Isuzu models as a distinct competitive advantage in the American market. In 1976 it began importing the Gemini into the United States as the Buick Opel. Few consumers suspected that the German design, sold through the dealerships of an American company, was actually manufactured in Japan. But, as GM had suspected, the Gemini/Opel was an attractive alternative to gas-hungry American models, particularly as a second household car. In this role, the car displaced competitors such as Toyota, Datsun, and Volkswagen. Isuzu gained additional growth in the American market with a diesel-powered pickup sold in the United States as the Chevrolet Luv beginning in 1977. Also that year, Isuzu delved back into the diesel car market in Japan with a new Florian sedan.

The energy crisis took a rising toll on GM models in the United States, including those built by Isuzu. A rising consumer revolt against little, underpowered vehicles such as the Opel, Ford Pinto, and Gremlin placed Isuzu in a declining market at the wrong time. Despite a short-lived rise in fuel prices in 1979, the Isuzu product line fell increasingly out of step with American tastes. Dismayed by the poor quality of many American models, consumers were drawn to Toyota, Honda Motor Co., and Nissan in growing numbers.

Isuzu's production for General Motors declined steadily from 1979 to 1981. Responding to what it felt was a loss of synergy with GM, Isuzu established its own dealer network in the United States, American Isuzu Motors, Inc., which technically operated in competition with GM at the wholesale level. Commensurate with the formation of the new group, Isuzu undertook a complete design change of its Luv truck. General

Motors' Chief Executive Officer Roger Smith laid a bombshell on Isuzu Chairman T. Okamoto in a landmark 1981 meeting. He announced that Isuzu had lost its favorable potential as a global partner for GM. But rather than abandon their partnership, Smith asked Okamoto to help GM buy a stake in Honda, one of Japan's fastest growing auto manufacturers.

Okamoto was stunned by the sudden change of events, but could not refuse the request of Isuzu's single largest shareholder. Ultimately, Honda expressed no interest in an alliance with General Motors, seeing its own prospects for global growth as excellent even without such a partnership. General Motors settled instead for a five percent stake in Suzuki Motors—a small consolation. General Motors may have intended to use this new partnership to leverage Suzuki against Isuzu, hoping the two companies would compete for the right to supply GM. Whether or not that was the case, General Motors had little choice but to expand its relationship with Isuzu. The company established new contracts with GM, building a model called the Storm under an entirely new nameplate, Geo. Once again part of General Motors' international strategy, Isuzu built new joint production facilities in the United Kingdom and Australia. Isuzu also concluded a long-term marketing agreement with Suzuki and Yanase & Company, under which Isuzu provided parts for assembly by Suzuki.

In an effort to raise consciousness of the Isuzu name and boost sales of the company's trucks in the United States, Isuzu launched a revolutionary ad campaign featuring the comedian David Leisure. The performer was portrayed as a spokesman named Joe Isuzu who made outrageously false claims about Isuzu products. A series of subtitles provided factual corrections as well as punch lines to Leisure's statements. The campaign easily could have failed had it not been for the comedian's wry delivery and obviously contrived smile. In one ad, Joe Isuzu concludes by saying, "May lightning strike me if I'm lying." At this point the actor is incinerated by a blinding light, leaving only a puff of smoke. Seconds later, the irrepressible spokesman falls out of the air and into the bed of an Isuzu truck. The ads were very effective in promoting Isuzu and launching Leisure's career, but they had only a limited impact on Isuzu's sales. (The company experienced no gain in passenger car sales.) The situation was exacerbated by appreciation of the yen, in effect, artificially raising the price of Isuzu products.

Global Joint Ventures in the 1980s

To eliminate the effect of currency fluctuations and stabilize product demand forecasts, Isuzu began studying the possibility of locating a factory in the United States. Other Japanese manufacturers, including Toyota and Honda, had already established American factories. But for Isuzu, the start-up costs were high and the company's sales volumes were too small to justify the badly needed move. Fortunately for Isuzu, Subaru, the automobile manufacturing subsidiary of Fuji Heavy Industries, suffered the same problem. The two companies operated in slightly different areas of the American market, so a joint venture between them was plausible. Isuzu and Subaru agreed to build, jointly, a factory in Lafayette, Indiana, in 1987. The facility went into operation two years later, providing Isuzu with a steady supply of American-built vehicles for distribution through its American sales organization.

Isuzu's export sales surpassed three million units in 1986, but again, much of this growth occurred in Asian markets and was accounted for in truck sales. That year, Isuzu formed a joint venture with Kawasaki Heavy Industries called IK Coach, Ltd. to manufacture coach bodies. Building on its Asian franchises, Isuzu established a subsidiary in Thailand to manufacture engines and a joint venture in Australia with General Motors the following year. These efforts helped to establish Isuzu as the world's largest truck manufacturer (on a per-unit basis) in 1987. The company marked several technological advances that year, including the development of a ceramic Adiabatic Engine and the NAVI electronically controlled transmission system, which was the first of its type.

Isuzu completed several other joint business arrangements in 1990, including an agreement with P.T. Gaya Motor of Indonesia to build pickup trucks in that country. This factory joined Isuzu plants in other developing country markets, including Thailand, Malaysia, and Egypt. The company also entered into agreements to market Isuzu's multipurpose vehicles in Japan through the Jusco Car Life Company and to handle sales of GM Opel models and Volvo trucks in Japan. These expansion efforts helped Isuzu to maintain its position as the world's largest truck maker. But the company's balance sheet indicated a high price for this leadership. The company lost $500 million in 1991 and was faltering financially.

Refocusing in the 1990s

This deeply concerned General Motors, which was unable to abandon its investment in Isuzu because of plummeting market value. Isuzu was GM's main source of imported light commercial vehicles and heavy trucks, and 37.5 percent of its shares were held by the American company. Isuzu continued to lose money into 1992, prompting the company's board to appeal to General Motors for help. As a condition, GM asked that one of its strategic planning experts, Donald T. Sullivan, be installed as executive vice-president of operations, with responsibility for revamping Isuzu's business, engineering, and manufacturing plans. This was an unprecedented move. No Japanese manufacturer had ever involved a non-Japanese speaking manager in such a high position, nor given an American such wide-ranging latitude to rewrite the business plan.

Sullivan's first moves were to raise production at the company's Subaru-Isuzu Automotive facility in Indiana. He slimmed down the Isuzu's line of commercial vehicles, hoping to realize greater production efficiencies from fewer models and eliminate cannibalization within the product line. In a retrenchment strategy virtually unknown in Japan, Sullivan summarily reduced capital budgets by 12.5 percent, hoping to eliminate waste through budget-induced cost savings. Stopping short of employee layoffs, a tactic that was seen to breed only employee disloyalty in Japan, Sullivan ordered a reduction in Isuzu's temporary work force.

Perhaps most dramatic was Sullivan's conclusion that Isuzu was not profitably competitive in the automobile market. Rather than continue to invest huge sums in an unpromising segment of the market, Sullivan recommended that Isuzu exit the automobile market and concentrate on what it did best. For Isuzu, this came down to only three products: trucks, recreational vehicles, and engines. Because GM relied on Isuzu for production of its Geo Storm model, the response back at GM was uneven. "The marketing guys at Chevrolet were disappointed," *Forbes* quoted Sullivan in 1994. "But the business people at GM looking at the financial liability at Isuzu had a different feeling."

These efforts appeared to have a positive effect on Isuzu's business, stemming losses while reversing a gradual decline in sales. By the end of Isuzu's 1993 fiscal year, the company reported a loss of only $39 million. Sullivan, however, had even higher hopes for the company. "I am proud of our success at Isuzu," he told *Forbes*. "But we are still defining success as eliminating failure." Although the 1994 fiscal year ended with even greater gains, Isuzu still carried a heavy debt burden, at $7.4 billion.

The actions taken by Isuzu under the tutelage of Donald Sullivan once again placed Isuzu thoroughly within General Motors' global strategy. Although GM lost its supplier of Geo Storms, it shifted its focus to incorporating Isuzu's expertise in other areas. For example, the General Motors European division began buying more Isuzu diesel engines. Michael Nylin, brought by Sullivan from General Motors to help lead Isuzu's strategic planning, tried to match Isuzu's product development with GM's needs. One result of that effort was a joint venture between Isuzu and General Motors to produce light trucks. Begun in 1994 in Janesville, Wisconsin, the venture called for Isuzu to supply the cab and chassis, shipping them from Japan, and General Motors to produce the gasoline engine, a technology in which GM had more expertise than Isuzu. Sullivan also hoped Isuzu would fit into GM's global strategy by providing General Motors with an entre into Asia markets. GM hoped to piggyback their passenger cars on Isuzu's strong sales of pickups in Asia by convincing Asian car dealers to sell them side by side.

The company's future had come to depend on its ties to other auto manufacturers, particularly General Motors, and on its ability to mark gains in the sales of its own products. Chief among these were the F-series (Forward) medium-duty trucks, the C-series heavy trucks, tractor trucks, and N-series (Elf) pickups. Light-duty trucks to be manufactured in China were planned in 1993 when Isuzu agreed to a joint venture with Jiangxi Automobile Factory and ITOCHU. The company expanded its relationships with other car makers when it signed an agreement with Nissan in 1994 to cross-supply commercial vehicles, particularly Isuzu's two- and three-ton Elf trucks and Nissan's Caravan.

The company's progress in the United States, however, was hurt in 1996 when *Consumer Reports* judged the Isuzu Trooper "not acceptable." The Consumers Union (CU), which publishes *Consumer Reports*, issued a safety alert about the sport utility vehicle, claiming the Trooper "showed a pronounced propensity to roll over during our avoidance-maneuver tests." Isuzu disputed the report's findings; it pointed out that the Trooper met all applicable federal safety standards and that the company had received no reports of rollover accidents involving the Trooper. It also denounced the Consumers Union test as unreliable. The Consumers Union stood by its claims, but its petition for a defect investigation to the National Highway Traffic Safety Administration (NHTSA) was denied. The NHTSA explained: "Because of deficiencies in the CU short course testing and since none of the other information reviewed by [NHTSA] indicates that a safety-related defect exists, there is no reasonable possibility that . . . a safety-related defect in the subject vehicles would be [found]." In mid-1997 Isuzu filed a lawsuit against the Consumers Union, alleging defamation and product disparagement. Although the company sought millions of dollars in damages, Isuzu presented the suit as a means to restore the company's good name.

Entering 1998 the company's future was uncertain because of the economic crisis in Asia. In November 1997 slow sales in Japan and constricting markets in Thailand led Isuzu to close its Thai factory, which had produced 120,000 trucks in 1996. With Asian truck sales the backbone of Isuzu's business, the company was greatly threatened by the economic turmoil in the region.

Principal Subsidiaries

Isuzu Motors Finance Co., Ltd.; Isuzu Real Estate Co., Ltd.; Kinki Isuzu Motor Sales Co., Ltd.; Shatai Kogyo Co., Ltd.; Isuzu Motors Overseas Distribution Corp.; I.K. Coach Co., Ltd.; Automotive Foundry Co., Ltd.; Jidosha Buhin Kogyo Co., Ltd.; Tokyo Radiator Manufacturing Co., Ltd.; Tokyo Isuzu Motors, Ltd.; TDF Corp.; Zexel Corp.; Daikin Manufacturing Co., Ltd.; American Isuzu Motors, Inc. (USA); Isuzu Motors America, Inc. (USA); Isuzu Truck of America, Inc. (USA); Subaru-Isuzu Automotive Inc. (USA); IBC Vehicles, Ltd. (England); Convesco Vehicle Sales GmbH. (Germany); Isuzu Motors Co. (Thailand) Ltd.; Automotive Manufacturers (Malaysia) Sdn. Bhd.; P.T. Mesin Isuzu Indonesia; Isuzu-General Motors Australia, Ltd.; General Motors Egypt S.A.E.

Further Reading

Eisenstodt, Gale, "Sullivan's Travels," *Forbes*, March 28, 1994, pp. 75–76.

"Isuzu Trooper Safety: Much Talk, Little Action," *Consumer Reports*, November 1996, pp. 6–7.

Shirouzu, Norihiko, "Japan's Firms Revamp Amid Asian Crisis," *Wall Street Journal*, November 6, 1997, p. A18.

—John Simley
—updated by Susan Windisch Brown

Jacor Communications, Inc.

50 East RiverCenter Boulevard
12th Floor
Covington, Kentucky 41011
U.S.A.
(606) 655-2267
Fax: (606) 655-9345
Web site: http://www.jacor.com

Public Company
Incorporated: 1979
Employees: 5,000
Total Assets: $530.6 million (1997)
Stock Exchanges: NASDAQ
SICs: 4830 Radio & Television Broadcasting; 6719
Holding Companies, Not Elsewhere Classified

Jacor Communications, Inc., a media holding company, is the second largest radio company in the United States measured by the number of total stations and the third largest in terms of total revenues. As of March 1998, it owned, operated, or represented 195 radio stations in 49 markets, as well as television station WKRC in Cincinnati. With its wholly owned subsidiary, Premier Radio Networks, Inc., Jacor also is the third largest provider of syndicated radio programming in the country, owning and distributing the top three radio talk shows: The Rush Limbaugh Show, The Dr. Laura Schlessinger Show, and Dr. Dean Edell. Jacor also owns NSN Network Services, a satellite distribution service. Financier Samuel Zell owns about a third of Jacor shares through his Zell/Chilmark investment partnership.

1974–84: From Insurance to Radio Broadcasting

In 1974 Terry Jacobs was an actuary working with American Financial Corp. in Cincinnati, Ohio. Interested in starting his own business, he did some research and found a growing industry that interested him—radio. In 1979 he formed Jacor Communications, incorporated it in Ohio, and quickly bought three small radio stations, each offering religion-themed programming.

According to the Federal Communications Commission (FCC), there were 8,651 radio stations on the air when Jacor was born, 4,549 AM and 4,102 FM. Owners of these stations were primarily mom-and-pop operations, because under the federal regulations no one company could own more than 14 stations, seven of each type of station, nationwide.

The Jacor stations did well, and in 1981 Jacobs left the insurance industry to concentrate full-time on his radio business. In 1984 Congress eased the radio ownership regulations somewhat and established the "rule of twelves." Under the new regulations, a radio company could now own up to 12 AM and 12 FM stations across the country. That year Jacobs began to seriously expand the company, acquiring WQIK-AM/FM, two stations in Jacksonville, Florida, for $5 million.

1985–89: Continued Growth

The Florida purchases were followed in 1985 with the acquisition of two stations in Cleveland, Ohio, for $12.8 million, and a move into the Georgia market with two stations and the Georgia Radio News Service for $20 million. In 1986 Jacobs purchased an FM station in Cincinnati for $9.3 million, and in December Jacobs merged Jacor with another Cincinnati radio company, Republic Broadcasting Corp. As a result of that transaction, Republic's head, Randy Michaels, joined the Jacor board.

The company continued to grow through acquisitions. In 1987 Jacor paid $24 million for two stations in Denver and in 1988 increased the company's presence in Florida by purchasing Eastman Radio, Inc. and two stations in Tampa, spending approximately $28.5 million. In 1989 Jacor merged BBMS Communications with the company's wholly owned subsidiary Jacor Cable, Inc., acquiring as part of that deal Telesat Cable TV, Inc. This cost the company some $4.9 million as it assumed certain of Telesat's obligations.

1990–93: Ownership Changes

In 1991 the FCC expanded the AM broadcast band, adding from 1605 to 1705 kHz. In 1992 Congress again eased station ownership rules, allowing a single company to own up to 18 AM and 18 FM broadcast stations. The FCC reported the number of radio stations operating that year had reached 11,312. Of these, the majority (4,961) were AM stations, 4,766 were commercial FM stations, and 1,585 were noncommercial, educational FM stations. As a comparison, the number of television stations broadcasting totaled 1,509.

The recession in the early part of the decade was rough on the radio industry, especially for owners such as Jacobs who had run up significant debt. Jacor sold all of the assets of two of its stations, one located in Cleveland and one in Nashville.

Early in 1993 Jacor completed both a recapitalization plan and a refinancing plan that substantially modified its debt and capital structure and transferred the ownership of most of the company to the Zell/Chilmark investment partnership. In the process, Jacor acquired another radio station in Denver. In July, Jacor also bought the license of another AM station in Cincinnati for $1.6 million in cash.

Jacor's new owners, led by Chicago investor Samuel Zell, took Jacor public before the end of the year. Terry Jacobs left the company to start Regent Communications, Inc., a new radio venture, and Randy Michaels was named CEO of Jacor.

1994–95: A Hub-and-Spoke Expansion Strategy

During its first year as a public company, Jacor continued to acquire new outlets—in Denver, Cincinnati, and Knoxville. The company also sold Telesat Cable TV, Inc., receiving some $2 million in cash for it. Revenue for the year was $107.1 million, with a net income of $7.9 million.

In 1995 the company expanded the number of stations it owned in Florida, adding two in Tampa and three in Jacksonville. It also acquired the call letters and programming of another radio station in Cincinnati. Overall, Jacor spent nearly $24 million in cash for these acquisitions. By December the company was the eighth largest radio group in the country, with 25 stations in ten broadcast areas. Revenue for the year was $118.9 million, with net income of $11 million.

The company's expansion strategy was to use a hub-and-spoke approach to grow. This involved building a cluster of stations in a high-growth broadcast area such as Denver, Colorado or Tampa, Florida and then buying stations in the same region, as Jacor was doing along Florida's Gulf Coast. The stations could then share management, develop and share regional programming, and also leverage sales opportunities, forcing advertisers to buy time on the weaker stations if they want to advertise in the larger area and to pay more for the opportunity.

1996: A New Telecom Act

February 8, 1996 was a red letter day for the radio industry as the President signed the Telecommunications Act of 1996. The new law totally eliminated the restrictions on the number of radio stations a company could own nationally, and the industry went crazy. In the first month after the law went into effect, more than $2 billion in deals were announced. According to Peter K. Pitsch of Citizens for a Sound Economy Foundation, this amount equaled the dollar amount of a whole year's transactions in the 1980s. By the end of the year the value of radio deals totaled $14.7 billion.

Jacor was one of the most active groups, going on a buying binge that increased its size by 60 stations that year. The company concentrated primarily on buying stations in the top 50 markets, and its first big purchase that year was the ten-station Noble Broadcast Group, Inc. for approximately $152 million in cash. This added radio stations in Denver, St. Louis, and Toledo to Jacor's stable, plus Noble's operations in San Diego, which provided programming and sold air time for two radio stations in that city.

Jacor also continued its Florida hub-and-spoke strategy, purchasing two radio stations in Venice, Florida, for $4.4 million in cash, and in August paying $14 million for three radio stations in Lexington, Kentucky. That same month Jacor bought the land and construction permit for a station in Englewood, Florida from the Sarasota-Charlotte Broadcasting Corp. The company also sold two stations in Knoxville and a station in Tampa, receiving approximately $7 million for the two sales.

But September saw the company's biggest acquisition to date, the $800 million purchase of Cincinnati-based Citicasters Inc., which merged with Jacor Communications Corp., a wholly owned subsidiary of Jacor. Citicasters operated 19 radio stations in eight markets: Atlanta, Phoenix, Tampa, Portland, Kansas City, Sacramento, Cincinnati, and Columbus (Ohio), and two television stations, one in Tampa and one in Cincinnati. That pending acquisition led to the first major Justice Department antitrust case tested under the Telecom Act.

Although national ownership limits were eliminated, the new act made the limits on local radio ownership more stringent. In markets where there were 45 or more commercial radio stations, a single group could own up to eight stations, with no more than five in the same service (AM or FM). For smaller markets, the limits were also tightened: up to seven stations, with no more than four in the same service, in markets with 30–44 commercial stations; up to six stations, with no more than four in the same service, in markets with 15–29 commercial stations; and up to five stations, with no more than three in the same service, in markets with fewer than 14 commercial stations, provided that no radio group could own more than 50 percent of the commercial stations in the market.

Justice intervened in the Citicasters acquisition, first by filing suit and then by requiring Jacor to sell one of Citicasters' Cincinnati radio stations. Otherwise, Jacor would have controlled 53 percent of Cincinnati's radio advertising market.

In December Jacor and Gannett made the first ever television-for-radio exchange in the industry, swapping Jacor's

Tampa TV station from the Citicasters acquisition for six of Gannett's radio stations, two each in Los Angeles, San Diego, and Tampa-St. Petersburg. At the same time Jacor added spokes to its Denver hub with the acquisition of two radio stations in Casper, Wyoming and the Wyoming Radio Network from Clear Channel Radio, Inc. for a price of $1.9 million. The company also reincorporated the company in Delaware during 1996.

As of December 31, 1996, Jacor owned and/or operated 85 radio stations and one television station in 21 broadcast areas throughout the United States. Revenue was $223.8 million, with net income of $5.1 million.

Although the Citicasters merger was one of the big acquisitions during the year, it was not the largest. That prize went to Westinghouse Electric Corporation's $4.4 billion acquisition of Infinity Broadcasting's 83 radio stations. Another mega-deal was made by American Radio Systems as it paid $665 million for EZ Communications.

Radio stations made their money primarily from selling advertising time, and the price a station could charge depended on the market and how popular the station was. To attract listeners, Jacor used a strategy of regional programming, putting the same program on multiple stations, but with different commercials, different news, weather, and traffic reports. "We're shameless opportunists when it comes to developing each station in its market," Jacor CEO Randy Michaels told the *Cincinnati Business Courier* in a 1996 article.

Programming for its FM stations was typically music-based, but with one station in each of Jacor's cities in a region concentrating on a different type of music, such as country, rock, adult contemporary, or jazz. Jacor also developed unique regional programming for its AM stations, including broadcasting the games of professional sports teams and syndicating local hosts of popular talk shows. This approach made Jacor an industry leader in successfully operating AM stations; in Denver and Cincinnati, for example, its AM stations were the top revenue and ratings leaders among both AM and FM stations in their respective broadcast areas. This track record also meant that Jacor could expect to increase the revenue from the more underperforming AM stations it bought.

1997 to the Present

Jacor continued its acquisition spree in 1997, growing its radio station operations with the addition of new stations almost every month and moving into other segments of the radio business. It also moved its headquarters from Cincinnati across the river to Covington, Kentucky.

Jacor began the year with the acquisition of three Idaho stations (two in Boise and one in Caldwell) for $11 million in cash, thus extending locations along the Rocky Mountain Front Range, and completed a $185 million merger with Regent Communications Inc., Terry Jacobs's broadcast company. Regent had 19 radio stations, in Kansas City, Salt Lake City, Las Vegas, Louisville, and Charleston. In March, Jacor entered the Iowa markets with the purchase of two stations in Des Moines and two in Cedar Rapids for $52.5 million.

During April the company completed several deals as it bought two stations in Toledo, moved into the Rochester, New York area by buying one station for $5.5 million and swapping $16 million and one of its Cincinnati stations for three stations in Rochester, and expanded its presence in San Diego, gaining two stations in an exchange for two of its Phoenix outlets valued at around $45 million. It also added three more stations in Ohio for $6.5 million.

Jacor's programming needs also influenced some of its acquisitions that year as the company began looking at ways to leverage programming into markets where it did not have stations. In March it bought NSN Network Services, Ltd. to improve its connectivity technology. NSN was a leading provider of satellite and network services, and by the end of the year it had announced it was deploying a nationwide network connecting all Jacor broadcasting facilities, making it possible for them to share programming, financial information, and Internet services.

As another way to increase its programming, Jacor bought nationally syndicated shows. First the company acquired EFM Media Management, the syndicator for the Rush Limbaugh and Dr. Dean Edell shows, for $50 million. Then Jacor paid $190 million for Premiere Radio Networks, Inc., the largest syndicator of comedy radio programming and the producer of 52 syndicated programs, including Leeza Gibbons and Michael Reagan. The final content purchase that year was $71.5 million for the rights to Dr. Laura Schlessinger's radio therapy call-in show. To get these and other programs out to the country, NSN announced a new generation of a satellite network by which ten cities where Jacor originated national programming could uplink their content, have the programs be combined into a new digital format, and redistribute them to thousands of radio stations nationwide.

Also during 1997 Jacor faced charges by the Rainbow-PUSH Coalition that it discriminated against minorities at four of its Cincinnati stations. The FCC refused to delay license renewals, but ordered the company to submit recruiting information for the next three years. The company ended the year with net revenue of $530.6 million, more than double the $223.8 million in 1996. Costs for the refinancing of debt left the company in the red.

Despite rumors at the end of 1997 that chairman and chief stockholder Sam Zell might be selling Jacor, the announcement that Jacor was buying Nationwide Communications, Inc. appeared to put an end to that speculation. In 1998 Jacor added two more stations in Colorado and expected to complete the $620 million purchase of Nationwide, the 17-station radio group owned by Nationwide Mutual Insurance Company. That purchase gave Jacor entry to several new markets, including Dallas, Houston, Minneapolis, and Baltimore.

On the content side, Premier Radio Networks bought Hot Mix Radio Network, Inc., the producer of seven nationally syndicated "dance mix" radio programs, Chancellor Broadcasting Co., Inc. and Talk Radio Network, Inc., syndicators of Art Bell's network radio programs, "Coast-to-Coast AM" and "Dreamland," and 17 other talk radio programs.

CEO Michaels and Jacor moved aggressively into the more deregulated radio industry under the 1996 Telecommunications Act. During 1997 alone, the company completed 53 separate transactions totaling some $842 million and, as 1998 began, had $748 million of transactions pending. In little more than two years, it bought more than $2 billion worth of radio stations, programming, and satellite networking. In the process, Jacor became the third largest national syndicator of radio programs and jumped from eighth to number two among radio companies.

Principal Subsidiaries

Jacor Broadcasting Corp.; Jacor Communications Co.; Sports Radio Broadcasting, Inc.; Broadcast Finance, Inc.; Critical Mass Media; Noble Broadcast Group; Premier Radio Networks; NSN Network Services.

Further Reading

Curtis, Richard, ''FCC Reprimands Jacor for Its Hiring Practices,'' *Cincinnati Business Courier*, July 28, 1997.
——, ''Jacor Changes at Columbus Station May Be Prototype,'' *Cincinnati Business Courier*, December 30, 1996.
——, ''Sam Zell May Be Shopping Jacor,'' *Cincinnati Business Courier*, October 20, 1997.
Gebolys, Debbie, ''Deal Reached on Nationwide Radio Stations,'' *The Columbus Dispatch*, October 28, 1997.
''Jacor Adds Two Colorado Stations,'' Press Release, Covington, Ky.: Jacor Communications, Inc., February 19, 1998.
''Jacor Closes Art Bell and KOPE-FM Acquisitions,'' Press Release, Covington, Ky.: Premiere Radio Networks, March 18, 1998.
''Jacor Communications, Inc.,'' *Cincinnati Business Courier*, January 5, 1998.
''Jacor Communications, Inc. Subsidiary, Premier Radio Networks, Inc. Finalizes Acquisition of Hot Mix Radio Network, Inc.,'' Press Release, Covington, Ky.: Premiere Radio Networks, February 17, 1998.
''Jacor Completes Acquisition of Premier Radio Networks, Inc.,'' Press Release, Covington, Ky.: Jacor Communications, Inc., June 12, 1997.
''Jacor Releases Record Results,'' Press Release, Covington, Ky.: Jacor Communications, Inc., February 11, 1998.
Kiesewetter, John, ''Jacor Buying EFM as Syndication Base,'' *The Cincinnati Enquirer*, March 19, 1997.
Lee, Jeanne, ''How To Profit from Merger Mania,'' *Fortune*, March 30, 1998.
Merrill, Cristina, ''The Radioland Mergers,'' *Adweek*, September 23, 1996.
''NSN Deploying Satellite and Terrestrial Networks for Jacor,'' *Dow Jones Newswires*, December 1, 1997.
Paeth, Greg, ''Bigger Fish Reportedly Hunting Huge Jacor,'' *The Cincinnati Post*, November 12, 1997.
Pitsch, Peter K., ''An 'Innovation Age' Perspective on Telecommunications Mergers,'' *Issue Analysis*, Citizens for a Sound Economy Foundation, November 13, 1996.
Richmond, Ray, ''Jacor Buys 'Dr. Laura' Rights,'' *Reuters/Variety*, September 11, 1997.

—Ellen D. Wernick

Jacuzzi Inc.

2121 N. California Boulevard
Suite 475
Walnut Creek, California 94596
U.S.A.
(510) 938-7070
Fax: (510) 256-1749

Wholly Owned Subsidiary of U.S. Industries, Inc.
Incorporated: 1915 as Jacuzzi Brothers, Inc.
Employees: 2,500
Sales: $332 million (1996)
SICs: 3088 Plastics Plumbing Fixtures; 3842 Surgical
   Appliances & Supplies; 3561 Pumps & Pumping
   Equipment

A wholly owned subsidiary of U.S. Industries, Jacuzzi Inc. is the originator and world's largest manufacturer of whirlpool baths, with which its name has become synonymous. Jacuzzi was founded in 1915 and remained a family owned and operated company until 1979 when it was bought by Kidde Inc. The latter company was subsequently purchased by the huge British conglomerate Hanson PLC, which later spun off a number of its American subsidiaries as U.S. Industries. Jacuzzi products, which include shower systems, faucetry, and swimming pool and agricultural pumps, in addition to its world renowned whirlpool baths, are manufactured and distributed worldwide through company divisions located in Canada, Italy, France, Germany, England, Brazil, Chile, and Singapore.

Company Origins in the Early 20th Century

Jacuzzi was founded by seven brothers who emigrated from Italy to California in the early 1900s. Engineers by trade, the brothers produced a variety of aviation-related innovations including a pitched propeller developed for the American government and the first enclosed cabin monoplane which was used to carry mail and passengers for the U.S. postal service. According to certain accounts, the Jacuzzis' mother was unhappy with the risks involved in aviation and asked her sons to work on

something more down to earth. The Jacuzzi Brothers family firm began to design hydraulic pumps and eventually became one of the world leaders in the engineering and production of agricultural pumps used for irrigation.

The Invention of the Whirlpool Bath in the Late 1940s

The company's hallmark product, the Jacuzzi whirlpool bath, was invented in the late 1940s as a personal project of one of the second generation of Jacuzzi company managers, Candido Jacuzzi. Candido's son Kenneth, stricken with rheumatoid arthritis, had been receiving hospital hydrotherapy treatment and, as Kenneth would later relate in *People Weekly*, "as good Italian parents do, my folks thought more is better." A team of Jacuzzi engineers were put to work to develop a home version of the hydrotherapy pump. The result was the J-300, a small portable pump that could be placed in a bathtub to create a soothing hydromassage. In 1956, Jacuzzi began marketing the therapeutic device to hospitals and schools, developing a small but solid niche in the surgical supplies market. Kenneth, who continued to battle the physical challenges of rheumatoid arthritis, went on to found his own successful software company and the Jacuzzi pump that was invented for him achieved its own fame as the plaything of celebrities.

By the mid-1950s the privately owned Jacuzzi Brothers was being run by the second generation of Jacuzzis. In addition to its market-leading agricultural pumps and the J-300, the company patented and produced a large variety of products that made use of their expertise in hydraulic technology, including water jet propulsion motors for a growing recreational motor boat industry as well as swimming pool equipment and a wind machine that helped protect crops from frost.

In 1968, Roy Jacuzzi, a member of the third generation of Jacuzzis to work for the company, graduated from college with a degree in industrial design and joined the family firm as head of the research division. Searching for new applications for the company's products, Roy struck upon the idea of marketing the J-300 hydrotherapy device to the growing leisure and fitness market. In order to create enough room to accommodate a more relaxing soak, Roy developed and patented the first bathtub with a built-in whirlpool system. Dubbed the Roman Bath, this unit made it unnecessary to place a portable pump into the tub, allowing the bather the full interior of the tub in which to enjoy the hydromassage. The self-contained unit was marketed as a replacement for the standard bathroom tub and could be used with or without the hydromassage feature. Although, by his own admission, the senior generation of Jacuzzis thought he was "a little weird," Roy set out to create a market for the Roman Bath by displaying it at country fairs and housing trade shows.

By 1970 sales of the built-in whirlpool bath were promising enough to justify the introduction of a larger model, the Adonis, and within two years the company was manufacturing a two-person unit, dubbed the Gemini, available in a wide range of colors and styles. The Gemini line was followed by even larger models called spas which were produced complete with filters and water heaters to obviate the necessity of filling and emptying them with every use. The laid-back culture of California in the 1970s turned out to be the perfect launching ground for the leisure-oriented product and by the middle years of the decade owning a "Jacuzzi" had become a symbol of the mellow California lifestyle. With the endorsement of high-profile movie stars, sales of the units took off and soon the whirlpool bath division was Jacuzzi's biggest profit maker. As the sole supplier of the patented system, the Jacuzzi brand name was synonymous with the whirlpool baths. Although Candido Jacuzzi, the conservative inventor of the original J-300 pump, was reportedly embarrassed about their sybaritic associations, the company's whirlpool baths and spas, and the Jacuzzi name, became identified with indulgent relaxation.

Bought by Kidde Inc. in 1979

In 1976 Jacuzzi moved its corporate headquarters from Berkeley to Walnut Creek, California. By the late 1970s, thanks both to sales of whirlpool baths and the growing export market for the company's irrigation pumps, Jacuzzi Brothers sales reached about $90 million. The company, which by then employed about 100 members of the Jacuzzi family, became the subject of family disagreement, however, and in 1979 the privately owned firm began to look for a buyer. After merger talks with Textron broke down, Kidde Inc., a conglomerate that manufactured products ranging from consumer appliances to hydraulic cranes, bought Jacuzzi Brothers for about $70 million.

Under Kidde, Jacuzzi lost most of its family-run quality as many family members left the firm. The notable exception was Roy Jacuzzi who remained in charge of the company's whirlpool bath division. Although only a tiny part of Kidde's huge operations, both of Jacuzzi's main product lines, agricultural pumps and whirlpool baths, continued to thrive. The company was operated as two separate subsidiaries: Jacuzzi Brothers, with headquarters in Little Rock, Arkansas, manufactured pumps and pumping equipment for use in agriculture and swimming pools; and Jacuzzi Whirlpool Bath, run out of Walnut Creek, California, manufactured the company's renowned jetted baths as well as a variety of more conventional bathroom faucetry and equipment.

For both Jacuzzi subsidiaries foreign sales showed particularly strong growth. The company's water pumping equipment was in great demand in the developing countries of Central America which were looking to develop small, efficient irrigation systems. In 1984 the company signed an agreement to become Nicaragua's sole supplier of water pumping equipment, although the subsequent American-imposed trade embargo on Nicaragua meant that products had to be shipped via the company's Spanish and Canadian branches. The European market for whirlpool bath and bathroom fixtures began to take off in the 1980s and Jacuzzi's presence in Italy and Spain assured the company a strong showing in this area. By 1987, Jacuzzi's whirlpool products alone were garnering some $57 million in sales.

Through the 1980s the trend in both America and Europe was for bathrooms to get larger and bathroom fixtures to be designed for appearance as well as function. Jacuzzi's product line expanded to dozens of models available in a huge assortment of colors and with a variety of optional features. Some options available on the more luxurious models included the "Water-Rainbow" waterfall-like fill spout, programmable massage jets, underwater lights, and built-in mirrored vanity cases. Roy Jacuzzi was personally responsible for designing many of the features of the new product lines; by 1987 Roy held 160 patents for innovations in whirlpool design and technology.

Acquired by Hanson PLC in 1987

In late 1987, the huge British conglomerate Hanson PLC bought out Kidde Inc. and its 100 subsidiaries, including Jacuzzi, for $1.7 billion. One of Hanson's first moves in its reorganization of the acquired businesses was to appoint Roy Jacuzzi as president and CEO of Jacuzzi Inc., an umbrella company headquartered in Walnut Creek that was to control the management of both the pump and filter products of Little Rock-based Jacuzzi Brothers and the bathroom and whirlpool products of Jacuzzi Whirlpool Bath. The newly organized company employed a workforce of 1,843 and had annual revenues of about $160 million.

Under Hanson Jacuzzi continued its international expansion and its new product introductions. Chief among the company's innovations in the 1990s was the development of the J-Dream steam shower system. With the J-Dream, Jacuzzi hoped to transform the nature of showering as the whirlpool bath had transformed bathing. The shower system, available to accommodate either one or two users, featured molded seats, programmable hydrotherapy jets, multifunction shower heads and steam therapy as well as such luxurious options as built-in CD players, cascade waterfalls, and waterproof concealed closets to store bathrobes and towels.

Spun Off As U.S. Industries in 1995

Although Jacuzzi remained solidly profitable through the early 1990s, Hanson decided to sell off a number of its American businesses in order to raise cash for further British acquisitions. Although analysts speculated that Jacuzzi, with its widely recognized brand identity, would be spun off as an independent public company, it was decided that 34 of Hanson's American holdings would be rolled together as a unit to be called U.S. Industries, a public company with a listing on the New York Stock Exchange. Other companies which were to join Jacuzzi as part of U.S. Industries included such well-known brands as Farberware Cookware, Tommy Armour Golf, Rexair Vacuum Cleaners, and Ertl Toys.

The year after the spinoff operating income for Jacuzzi Inc. rose to $55 million on revenues of $332 million. Almost 80 percent of this revenue was contributed by the company's bath products, including whirlpool baths, spas, shower systems, and non-jetted baths. The remainder came from sales of the water systems and swimming pool equipment that had been the foundation of the company since its early years. In April 1996 this segment was strengthened with the purchase of Haugh's Products Limited, a leading Canadian manufacturer of above-ground swimming pools and equipment with estimated annual sales of about $11 million.

As Jacuzzi entered the final years of the 1990s international sales appeared to be the major arena of future growth for the company. By 1996 international markets, including Europe, South America, the Middle East, and the Pacific Rim, accounted for about 46 percent of Jacuzzi's sales and analysts predicted that this sector would increase into the next century as the popularity of large, elaborate bathrooms spread worldwide. Plans for a new facility in Singapore that would manufacture products specifically designed for Asian consumers were underway in 1997 and promised to deliver a significant new share of this market.

Principal Divisions

Jacuzzi Whirlpool Bath; Jacuzzi Bros.; Jacuzzi Europe S.p.A.; Jacuzzi U.K. Ltd.; Jacuzzi Whirlpool GmbH (Germany); Jacuzzi France; Jacuzzi Canada; Jacuzzi Chile; Jacuzzi Asia (Singapore); Jacuzzi Brazil; Jacuzzi Pool Products (Canada).

Further Reading

Adelson, Andrea, "Jacuzzi Whirlpool Creator to Oversee Hanson Unit," *New York Times,* January 14, 1988, p. D2.

"Candido Jacuzzi, Pooling His Talent, Made the Hot Tub and His Name Part of the American Home," *People Weekly,* October 27, 1986, p. 92.

Hall, William, "More Bubbles for Jacuzzi," *Financial Times,* December 5, 1994, p. 10.

Muller, E. J., "Jacuzzi," *Distribution,* October 1985, pp. 41–43.

Pare, Terence P., "A Tale of a Tub," *Fortune,* June 6, 1988, p. 245.

Power, Gavin, "Hanson Spins Off U.S. Units," *San Francisco Chronicle,* February 23, 1995, p. D1.

—Hilary Gopnik

Jason Incorporated

411 E. Wisconsin Avenue, Suite 2500
Milwaukee, Wisconsin 53202
U.S.A.
(414) 277-9300
Fax: (414) 277-9445
Web site: http://www.jasoninc.com

Public Company
Incorporated: 1985
Employees: 3,000
Sales: $481 million (1997)
Stock Exchanges: NASDAQ
SICs: 3511 Turbines & Turbine Generator Sets; 3991
    Brooms & Brushes; 2493 Reconstituted Wood
    Products

Jason Incorporated is a miniconglomerate, active in three distinct business segments—motor vehicle products, power generation products, and industrial products. In the motor vehicle arena, Jason is a major supplier of insulation materials used in the manufacture of many cars and trucks. Through its Milsco Manufacturing unit, Jason also makes the seat for every Harley-Davidson motorcycle that hits the road. Jason's industrial products segment is a leader in the manufacture of finishing products and a broad range of metal industrial components. The company's power generation operation is a leader in the production of equipment used in power plant construction. In spite of its size and prominent position in all of the markets in which it competes, Jason maintains only a skeleton crew of about half a dozen employees at its corporate headquarters in Milwaukee. The rest of the company's staff works out of Jason's far-flung industrial facilities located in 11 states and seven foreign countries.

Jason was formed in November of 1985 by Vincent Martin and Mark Train. Both men were working as top executives at the Hanover, New Hampshire-based AMCA International Corp. when they seized an opportunity to strike out on their own. AMCA announced that it was putting up for sale seven businesses that it had picked up incidentally over the course of several acquisitions. Martin and Train formed Jason to take three of the businesses off AMCA's hands. Martin became the new company's president and Train became its executive vice-president. Jason completed the acquisition of the three AMCA castoffs—Milwaukee-based construction and excavation equipment manufacturer Koehring Co. and two divisions of Giddings and Lewis, Inc., a machine tool manufacturer based in Fond du Lac, Wisconsin—in a leveraged buyout worth $53 million in early 1986, saddling the company with a hefty debt at birth.

1987 IPO Lightened Debt

Jason earned $1.3 million after taxes on sales of $71.6 million in its first year of operation. To lighten the burden of interest payments on its big debt, Martin and Train decided to sell 800,000 shares of stock to the public in 1987. Jason's history since that time has been a story of steady expansion through strategic and highly selective acquisitions. Virtually all of the companies that Jason has annexed have been manufacturers that were among the top contenders in their markets and generated strong cash flows. In 1989 the company bought another unwanted AMCA unit, Braden Manufacturing. Braden, based in Tulsa, Oklahoma, was founded by retired Standard Oil Co. executive Glenn Braden and had begun making exhaust silencing systems and enclosures for gas turbines in the mid-1960s. Braden now has manufacturing plants in Tulsa and in Fort Smith, Arkansas, a European outpost in the Netherlands, and a sales office in Singapore. By the mid-1990s Braden had more than 300 employees.

By the end of fiscal 1989 Jason was the dominant U.S. manufacturer in each of its product segments. It controlled more than half the market for a number of products, including automotive insulation, industrial buffing wheels, and turbine silencers. In addition, the company was growing at an impressive annual rate of 25 percent. In 1991 Jason boosted its finishing segment with the acquisition of Lea Manufacturing, which was integrated into an amalgamation of eight separate buffing products manufacturers called JacksonLea. The core of JacksonLea was Jackson Buff, a company founded in Jackson, Michigan in 1923. Jackson Buff was moved to Long Island in 1932, then to Conover, North Carolina in 1959. Over the next couple of decades it absorbed a number of other buffing specialists, including Bias Buff and Wheel in 1961, American Buff in 1968, and Churchill Buff in 1980. Two more buffing equipment producers were folded into the JacksonLea mix in the early 1990s: Buckeye Products in 1992 and Hanson & Wells in 1993.

The year 1991 also brought the acquisition of Sackner Products, Inc., an automotive fiber producer founded early in the century and known until 1949 as Grand Rapids Fiber Cord Company. According to company lore, founder Wade Sackner was the only person who could keep the plant's furnace operating, making it necessary for him to double as company president and coal shoveler. The addition of Sackner solidified the contribution of Jason's motor vehicle products segment and helped elevate the company's earnings to $4.9 million, on revenue of $161 million, for fiscal 1991.

Jason continued to fare well in 1992, due in part to a rebound in the slumping auto industry. But the fastest growing segment for Jason was its power generation products business. Led by its Braden unit, Jason recorded strong sales of its exhaust silencers and other equipment for gas turbines. The power generation segment was further bolstered by the 1992 acquisition of Metrio Technology International, a Dutch manufacturer of power generating equipment. The addition of Metrio's damper product meant that Jason could now offer an entire exhaust system for gas turbines to turbine manufacturers, making it the only major supplier with that capability. It also gave Jason a presence in the European market for these products. Metrio was integrated into the company's Braden subsidiary. Company profit and revenue both continued their steady climb, reaching $6 million and $207 million, respectively, for 1992.

1994 Deltak Purchase Boosted Generating Segment

In early 1994 Jason completed the purchase of Deltak Corp., a Plymouth, Minnesota-based manufacturer of steam power generators and heat recovery systems. Deltak was founded in 1969 as a unit of Raygo Inc. and was spun off as a separate company in 1972. Deltak's products, which included heat recovery steam generators, specialty waste heat boilers, and other systems used in combination with gas turbines, were an ideal match for Braden's gas turbine equipment. The merger essentially made Jason a single-source supplier for major power-generation projects, rather than merely a piece in the puzzle. Since problems with nuclear power plants all over the world were making gas turbines a hot product at the time, Jason was able to take advantage of this new synergy right away. At the time of the purchase, Deltak had about 350 employees and annual sales of about $75 million.

Later that year, Jason added another company, Koller Industries, to its growing empire. Koller, based in Milwaukee, actually consisted of three distinct businesses. Koller Manufacturing was founded as a tool and die shop in 1919, before reinventing itself as a stamping plant in the 1960s. Advance Wire Products, founded in 1968, was a wire-forming operation located in suburban Chicago. The third component of Koller, Metalex, was also based in the outskirts of Chicago. It specialized in applications for expanded metal, including leaf guards for rain gutters and the first cost-effective satellite dish petals from expanded metal.

For fiscal 1994 Jason reported sales of $357 million, with $65 million of that total coming from Deltak. Net income reached a company record $11.3 million. In January of 1995 Jason paid $45.5 million for Milsco Manufacturing Co., founded in 1924 as the Milwaukee Saddlery Company. Milsco sold its first motorcycle seat to Harley-Davidson during the Depression and has been supplying seats for Harleys ever since. Milsco also became one of the biggest suppliers of seats for tractors and other agricultural and construction vehicles over the years. The acquisition of Milsco boosted to about 35 percent the share of Jason's total sales generated by its motor vehicle products segment. It also instantly made Harley-Davidson Jason's second biggest customer, trailing only General Electric, a major buyer of Jason's power generating equipment.

Hands-Off Philosophy Spurs Company's 1990s Growth

Throughout these years of steady expansion company founders Martin and Train remained Jason's biggest stockholders, controlling about 25 percent and 18 percent of the company's shares, respectively. Martin and Train were quick to attribute the company's success to their hands-off approach. The key was to annex only companies that were already being run well. They were not interested in turning around floundering enterprises. "We set performance goals and provide capital if needed," Martin was quoted as saying in a 1995 *Barron's* article. "We pay our people well, give them generous stock options and don't hammer them over their heads, unless they screw up." That philosophy helped Jason grow its revenue to $407 million in fiscal 1995, with net income rising slightly to $11.5 million.

In 1996 Jason founders Martin and Train juggled executive titles a bit, with Train becoming company president and Martin retaining the positions of chairman and CEO. In the fall of 1996 Jason announced the acquisition of Suroflex GmbH, a German manufacturer of insulation for automobiles. With annual sales of about $15 million, Suroflex brought with it a customer list that included such noted European car companies as Audi, BMW, and Mercedes-Benz. The deal helped to expand Jason's presence in the international marketplace for automotive products. In addition to selling Suroflex products to its existing customers, Jason was now able to pitch its Janesville and Sackner products to European automobile manufacturers.

The addition of Suroflex helped elevate Jason's revenue to $443 million for 1996. For the first time in the company's history, however, its net income declined, dropping to $8.9 million for the year. Contributing to the decline were the General Motors strike that took place during the year and weakness in the market for its power generating equipment. Nevertheless, Jason's diversity helped it weather these setbacks, as cash flow from its remaining business segment, industrial products, remained strong.

Diversity the Key Entering Second Decade

A number of developments during fiscal 1996 seemed to point toward a continuation of the steady growth that had marked Jason's first decade of operation. About $18 million was spent on new capital projects aimed at paving the way for that growth. New manufacturing capacity was added at Janesville Products, where the company's emerging Marabond moldable fiber product was made, and at Milsco Manufacturing, where seats for Harleys remained much in demand. Revenue from the company's Marabond business tripled during the year, alone accounting for $21 million of Jason's revenue. Jason also gave its finishing products business a boost with the acquisition of The Milwaukee Brush Company's mill brush business. In addition, Braden introduced a filter house product line, the only remaining piece of important auxiliary equipment for gas turbines that the company was not previously offering. The percentage of Jason's revenue coming from international sales reached a record 28 percent, for a total of $126 million.

In April of 1997 Jason announced that it was organizing its three automotive units—Sackner, Janesville, and Suroflex—into a single group to coordinate the introduction of its new products for automobile interiors. Those products included a fiber substitute for foam in car seats, a new type of moldable plastic insulation, and decorative interior door inserts. The new group was to be headed by James Tyler, who formerly served as president of the company's Osborn Manufacturing unit. Jason continued to benefit from the good times being enjoyed by Harley-Davidson, which by this time was its largest customer. Unfortunately, that lift was countered by problems in the power generation segment, as the market for gas turbine power plants became rather soft, driving prices down.

For fiscal 1997 Jason reported net income of $12.2 million on sales of $481 million, both figures setting new company records. With the power generation market showing signs of recovery and the automotive and industrial segments showing no signs of slowing down, Jason's impressive record of profitability and consistency appeared likely to continue through the rest of the century. Jason may not be the most glamorous company ever to offer its stock on NASDAQ, but any company willing to stake its future on the posterior comfort of the world's Harley riders may be the most courageous.

Principal Divisions

Power Generation Products; Motor Vehicle Products; Industrial Products.

Principal Operating Units

Braden Manufacturing; Deltak; Janesville Products; Suroflex; Sackner Products; Milsco Manufacturing; JacksonLea; Koller; Osborn Manufacturing.

Further Reading

Alexander, Steve, "Milwaukee Company Agrees To Buy Deltak Corp. for $30 Million in Cash," *Minneapolis Star Tribune*, December 29, 1993, p. 1D.
Barnes, Brooks, "Jason Consolidating Three Automotive Units into One Group," *Milwaukee Journal Sentinel*, April 24, 1997, Bus. Sec., p. 2.
Byrne, Harlan, "Low-Key Success," *Barron's*, May 22, 1995, p. 20.
"Jason Inc.," *Milwaukee Business Journal*, July 30, 1990, p. X6.
"Jason Incorporated," *Milwaukee Business Journal*, May 2, 1997, p. 15.
Joshi, Pradnya, "Jason Credits Diversity for Company's Growth," *Milwaukee Journal Sentinel*, April 25, 1996, p. 2.
Kueny, Barbara, "Hot Shots: Wisconsin's Best-Performing Public Companies," *Milwaukee Business Journal*, July 25, 1992, p. 14B.
Morris, John, "Jason Aims for $7 Million with Its First Share Offering," *Milwaukee Journal*, April 26, 1987.
Savage, Mark, "Suroflex Purchase," *Milwaukee Journal Sentinel*, September 13, 1996, Bus. Sec., p. 1.
Youngblood, Dick, "Acquisition of Deltak by Milwaukee Company Hastens Turnaround," *Minneapolis Star Tribune*, June 7, 1995, p. 2D.

—Robert R. Jacobson

The Jim Henson Company

5358 Melrose Avenue
Raleigh Studios
Hollywood, California 90038
U.S.A.
(213) 960-4096
Fax: (213) 960-4935
Web site: http://www.henson.com

Private Company
Incorporated: 1958 as Jim Henson Productions
Employees: 200
Sales: $67 million (1997 est.)
SICs: 7812 Motion Picture & Video Production

The Jim Henson Company is a leading producer of films, stage shows, television specials, and series for family audiences. More than 75 licensees reproduce the company's characters on toys, books, and other products worldwide, making the company one of the largest players in the product licensing market. The primary attraction to Jim Henson licensees is the variety of distinctive, yet simple characters recognized around the world as Jim Henson's Muppets. Founded by puppeteer Jim Henson in 1955, the company has managed to maintain the highest standards of critical and artistic excellence while becoming a major financial success in the industry. After 35 years of growing financial and critical success, the company experienced a crisis when company founder and president, Jim Henson, died suddenly in 1990 at age 53. Henson's son Brian became president and CEO in 1991 and has continued his father's legacy, leading the company into the interactive computer software market.

Company Origins in the 1950s

Jim Henson combined extreme simplicity in puppet design with sophisticated comedy inspired by the vaudeville and radio performers he had admired in his youth. Many of his creations were little more than socks with eyes, and yet, through subtle manipulation and strong voicing he created characters that have become essential emblems of late 20th-century American culture. Born in Mississippi in 1936, Henson began experimenting with puppets as a child and had his first paying job as a puppeteer in 1954 at a local television station in Washington D.C., before he had finished college. One year later he formed a partnership with Jane Nebel, whom he later married, and the team produced a series of five-minute puppet shows for television entitled *Sam and Friends. Sam and Friends* introduced audiences to Kermit the Frog, the character that would later become most closely associated with Henson himself, as throughout his career Henson always provided Kermit's voice. By 1956 the Muppets had appeared on national network television on *The Steve Allen Show.* Henson and Nebel's work on *Sam and Friends* earned them their first Emmy Award for local television in 1958.

In 1963 the Hensons, along with scriptwriter Jerry Juhl, who had joined the team in 1961, moved their headquarters to New York City, where they were joined by master puppet builder Don Sahlin and versatile performer Frank Oz. Oz was to become the voice behind many of the most famous Muppet characters including Miss Piggy, the *prima donna* love match to Henson's indomitable Kermit. In 1966 the Muppets had their first of many appearances on *The Ed Sullivan Show,* the premiere avenue to stardom for variety acts during the period.

National Exposure in the 1970s

After a decade of steadily increasing critical success and popular recognition, the Muppets became part of a larger phenomenon in 1969, when they were featured as an integral part of the Children's Television Network's groundbreaking educational series *Sesame Street.* The Muppets' connection with *Sesame Street* assured their enduring popularity and salability for licensing purposes. Parents felt good about their children watching *Sesame Street,* which stressed education, while the timeless humor of the Muppets appealed to the parents themselves; parents and children became equally attached to the lovable characters. One year after the premiere of *Sesame Street,* the Jim Henson creation Big Bird appeared on the cover of *Time* magazine marking both the meteoric rise of the little educational television series and the recognition of the Muppets as cultural icons.

The unusual appeal of the Muppets to both children and adult members of their audience led to a prime time Muppet venture in the mid-1970s entitled the *Muppet Show*. Aside from Jim Henson perennial Kermit the Frog, all of the characters on the *Muppet Show* were fresh creations, distinct from their *Sesame Street* brethren. Although the Muppets had become icons of American popular culture, the first 24 episodes of the *Muppet Show* were produced at ATV studios in England and sold mostly to independent stations in the United States, including five wholly owned CBS affiliates. Despite its outsider position in the industry and its unusual status as a prime-time family series with puppets, the show became an enormous hit, winning an Emmy Award for variety and comedy series in 1978 and drawing the top talent of the period as guest stars. In the same year a record album based on music from the *Muppet Show* went platinum and won a Grammy Award for best recording for children.

Although Jim Henson's success depended on simplicity, subtlety, and a fine sense of classic comedy, the production of Muppet films, television series, and stage shows became increasingly high-tech. Eventually the Muppets became associated with both the simple green puppet that was Kermit the Frog as well as the cutting edge in electronically manipulated puppetry called animatronics. Animatronics is a generic term for puppet manipulation whereby the facial features of the puppet are manipulated by remote control from someone not necessarily in physical contact with the puppet. This technique allowed Henson to create enormous puppets which were manipulated by a team of technicians, some of whom would move the puppet's body physically while others would electronically move the eyes, ears, mouth, and so on. In order to create an effective illusion, the team members would all be in contact through headsets. This technology was particularly effective for traveling stage shows, such as *Muppet Treasure Island* and *Muppet Babies Onstage*, in which larger puppets were needed to be visible and effective in large theaters.

The fact that Jim Henson's team was on the cutting edge of techno-puppetry meant that its services were in demand for collaborations with other production companies. Under the trademark Jim Henson's Creature Shop, Jim Henson Productions sold its creative technology to a wide variety of other producers, such as film director George Lucas and his special effects company Industrial Light and Magic, which created the fantastical characters featured in the *Star Wars* series of films in the late 1970s.

Branching Out into Feature Films in the 1980s

The success of the *Muppet Show* on television prompted Jim Henson Productions to try its hand at a feature film, *The Muppet Movie*, which premiered in London in 1979. Although audience response to *The Muppet Movie* was less effusive than it had been to the same cast of characters on the small screen, the film did well enough to ensure a sequel, *The Great Muppet Caper*, released in 1981.

The *Muppet Show* went off the air in 1980 after 120 shows, but another film based on the show, *The Muppets Take Manhattan*, was produced in 1984, and the familiar cast of characters was maintained for other projects on both the large and small screen. Moreover, the company produced other features with new characters; fantasy films *The Dark Crystal* and *Labyrinth*, starring David Bowie, both of which were directed by Jim Henson, were produced in the mid-1980s. *Fraggle Rock* followed the *Muppet Show* as Henson's next major television venture in 1983, but it never achieved an equivalent broadbased audience appeal. Nevertheless, the company produced 96 episodes before closing *Fraggle Rock* in 1986, when the show began a lucrative run in syndication.

In 1989 Jim Henson Productions entered into a partnership with Disney. In a deal negotiated by Jim Henson and Disney chief Michael Eisner, Disney acquired Henson Associates Inc., giving Disney the right to use the Muppet characters at its theme parks and on its cable network. Kermit the Frog would later appear in the inaugural special for The Disney Channel while Big Bird would march in the celebratory parade. Disney also agreed to co-produce future projects with Jim Henson Productions. Unfortunately, Henson himself did not live to see the fruit of this deal; he died suddenly of streptococcal pneumonia in 1990, shortly before the release of yet another company feature film, *The Witches*, based on a book by children's author Roald Dahl. Henson's last project was the creation of *Jim Henson's Muppet *Vision 3-D*, a featured attraction at the Walt Disney World Resort in Florida.

Continued Expansion in the 1990s

The death of Jim Henson Productions' founder, president, and primary creative force came at a point in the company's history when its future had seemed brighter than ever. To continue his father's legacy, Jim Henson's son Brian Henson was appointed president in 1991. Brian Henson had been trained as a puppeteer by his father and had worked on *The Great Muppet Caper*, *The Muppets Take Manhattan*, and *Labyrinth*, as well as on puppet animation projects with other producers. His directorial debut came in 1992, only one year after being appointed president of the company, with *A Muppet Christmas Carol*, starring Michael Caine.

In 1993 Jim Henson's Creature Shop began research into refining its animatronic technique to create as high a degree of verisimilitude as possible. Rather than creating only fantastic or comic puppets, the company attempted to create absolutely realistic animals with human characteristics. Following two years of research, new techniques were developed and used to create talking animals with human emotions for the film *Babe,* produced by Universal Pictures. *Babe,* the story of a pig and his barnyard friends, was an enormous critical and box-office success, winning the 1996 Oscar for visual effects. Moreover, the success of *Babe* led to a deluge of films using the new animatronic technology including Disney's *101 Dalmatians* and *George of the Jungle.* Jim Henson's Creature Shop's animatronic technology was equally in demand for television advertising and was eventually used to create 30-second spots for such brands as Carling, Smirnoff, Honda, Mercedes, and Weetabix, among others.

The growth of the company led to the creation of several subdivisions and productive relationships with other corporations in the 1990s. Jim Henson Video and Jim Henson Records were launched in 1993, while the Muppet Press published over 400 different children's book titles. Jim Henson Productions joined forces with Starwave Corporation in 1994 to create a series of educational games on CD-ROM, and as a result of this collaborative venture Jim Henson Interactive was established as a separate division. Jim Henson Productions and Sony Pictures Entertainment agreed to co-produce motion pictures, leading to the creation of Jim Henson Pictures in 1995. Stephanie Allain was named the first president of production at Jim Henson Pictures and the first feature to result from her tenure was *Buddy,* starring Rene Russo, in 1997. Also during this time, Jim Henson Interactive entered into an exclusive agreement with Microsoft to produce interactive programming for MSN, the third largest online network worldwide.

Muppet toys, clothing, toiletries, and an array of other merchandise comprised more than 75 different licensing deals in the late 1990s, making Jim Henson Productions a major player worldwide. Kermit Hollywood boutiques were opened in the late 1990s to promote Muppet products at leading department stores, while Jim Henson Productions signed an exclusive licensing deal with Galoob Toys to produce toys based on Muppet characters in 1998.

Margaret Loesch was named president of Jim Henson Television Group in 1998. Due to the diversity of Jim Henson Productions' operations and its growing list of divisions and subsidiaries, the company changed its name to The Jim Henson Company in 1998. The newly-named company maintained a healthy creative sector while making the most out of the cast of Muppets inherited from the company's founder Jim Henson. From the simplest beginnings with sock puppets, the Jim Henson Company grew to be a leading producer of special effects, feature films, interactive entertainment, and education, always keeping pace with the latest developments in the industry and public taste. While Jim Henson's untimely death came as a shock to his family, friends, co-workers, and fans, his artistic vision and drive continue to thrive in the company that bears his name.

Principal Divisions

Jim Henson Television; Jim Henson Pictures; Jim Henson Interactive; Jim Henson's Muppet Workshop; Jim Henson's Creature Shop.

Further Reading

Finch, Christopher, *Jim Henson the Works: The Art, the Magic, the Imagination,* New York: Random House, 1993.
''Jim Henson 40th Anniversary,'' special issue, *Variety,* December 11, 1995.
Miller, S., ''Empire of the Imagination,'' *Variety,* December 11, 1995, pp. 55–56.
Sheats, M., ''Pulling Strings,'' *Variety,* December 11, 1995, p. 68.
Stalter, K., ''Gone Digital,'' *Variety,* December 11, 1995, p. 74.
Yanover, N.S., ''The Selling of the Green,'' *Variety,* December 11, 1995, p. 70.

—Donald C. McManus

Johnstown America Industries, Inc.

980 North Michigan Avenue, Suite 1000
Chicago, Illinois 60611
U.S.A.
(312) 280-8824
Fax: (312) 280-4820
Web site: http://www.johnstownamerica.com

Public Company
Incorporated: 1991
Employees: 3,300
Sales: $650.3 million (1997)
Stock Exchanges: NASDAQ
SICs: 6719 Holding Companies, Not Elsewhere
    Classified; 3743 Railroad Equipment; 1629 Heavy
    Construction, Not Elsewhere Classified

A rising manufacturing force, Johnstown America Industries, Inc. makes a range of products serving the railcar, trucking, and shipping industries. Formed in 1991 through the acquisition of Bethlehem Steel Corporation's freight car division, Johnstown America entered the business world as a freight car manufacturer, registering encouraging success during its first several years of business. In 1995, the company made a bid to become a full-service manufacturer in the broadly-defined transportation industry. The company acquired manufacturers involved in a diverse collection of businesses, purchasing companies that made everything from brake drums to truck seating systems. With the addition of these acquisitions, Johnstown stood as a diversified manufacturer insulated from the frequent fluctuations of the railcar market. During the late 1990s, Johnstown America operated facilities in Oakland, California; Danville, Illinois; Rockford, Illinois; Brillion, Wisconsin; and Johnstown, Pennsylvania.

Background of 1991 Formation

Johnstown America was created from the railcar manufacturing division of Bethlehem Steel Corporation. When Johns- town America's founder Thomas M. Begel first heard that Bethlehem Steel was looking to divest its freight car division, he was decidedly nonplussed. When a colleague asked him if he was interested in acquiring the division, Begel responded, "not a chance. No way in the world." History had taught Begel a lesson he did not want to repeat.

As chief executive of Chicago-based Pullman Standard Co. prior to founding Johnstown America, Begel had experienced first-hand the potential problems involved in railcar manufacture. The idea of reliving that experience again prompted his unequivocal response in 1990. During the late 1970s, railcars were marketed as tax shelters, creating an inducement that artificially stimulated demand, or, as Begel put it, "every dentist had to own a couple freight cars." Railcar production the United States, which normally hovered around 60,000, increased recklessly, jumping to 85,000 by 1980, when capacity industrywide had mushroomed to 150,000. When the tax advantages were curbed in 1981, roughly 400,000 railcars were waiting for customers that did not exist, swamping the market.

Begel, in charge of Pullman at the time, found himself in a market glutted with what represented a six- or seven-year supply of railcars. He exited the business as quickly as he could, selling Pullman's railcar-production business in 1984. With what remained, Begel rebuilt Pullman by acquiring a broad range of manufacturing companies, purchasing businesses that steered Pullman into the manufacture of everything from truck trailers to airline seats. Once this was done, he sold his stock in the company and left its employ in 1987, ready to invest in a new business. When Bethlehem's freight car division was suggested, he immediately shot back with a firm "no." Reentering the railcar-production business was the last thing on his mind.

Begel, however, did reconsider the idea. After reacquainting himself with the railcar market, he discovered that the market had been cleared of the excess inventory that had plagued Pullman nearly a decade earlier. During the 1980s, the number of freight cars in use had declined from 1.8 million to 1.2 million. Concurrently, industry capacity had dropped, falling to 50,000 freight cars a year. Consequently, the railcars in use were getting older and, with fewer in use, the railroads were using them for a longer duration. Realizing this, Begel saw opportunity, envisioning a new, country-wide demand in the business first instinct told him to eschew.

Having made an about face in his thinking, Begel prepared to buy Bethlehem Steel's freight car division. In October 1991, he headed an investment group bearing his initials—TMB Industries—that acquired the Johnstown, Pennsylvania-based railcar business for approximately $50 million. He renamed the company Johnstown America Industries. Next, Begel set his priorities, resolving to improve quality and productivity at his newly-acquired manufacturing facility. At the time of the sale, Bethlehem Steel figured its division was capable of producing roughly 7,000 freight cars a year, but Begel was intent on exceeding expectations. First, he set up a quality improvement program that required each employee to undergo two days of training. Begel then invested more than $5 million on new machinery and reorganized production into smaller, team-oriented operations. With his new company taking shape, Begel readied himself for his second foray into railcar manufacture and the surge in demand he foresaw.

Johnstown America's Early Growth

Begel's projection turned to reality as Johnstown America began its corporate life as a railcar manufacturer. Industrywide, freight car deliveries climbed from 25,000 during Johnstown America's first full year of business to 35,000 in 1993 and upwards of 45,000 the following year. At Johnstown America the pattern repeated itself, as production output increased under the quality and productivity measures put in place by Begel. During the company's first full year of operation, production volume reached 4,500 freight cars, generating $205 million in sales. In 1993, production nearly doubled, rising to 8,300 railcars. Midway through 1993, Begel made a move to strengthen the company's financial position. In July, he sold 35 percent of the company to the public, selling shares in Johnstown America in an initial public offering (IPO) that put the company's stock on the NASDAQ exchange at $14 per share. With the proceeds from the IPO, Begel paid off the debt accrued from the Bethlehem Steel acquisition, leaving Johnstown America debt free as it continued its burgeoning rise in the railcar industry.

Sales at the end of 1993 reached $329 million, as the company's production operations began manufacturing railcars for 1994. Production output for the year, which consisted primarily of coal cars that sold for approximately $55,000 each, eclipsed 10,000. Annual sales for 1994 swelled to $468 million, reflecting the resurgence in rail car demand. For the original investors in the company, the end of 1994 brought earnings to a level that quintupled their investment three years earlier. Johnstown America, by all accounts, had developed into an unqualified success.

1995 Diversification

Having created a solid foundation for his company, Begel moved on to his next plan of attack, which represented a significant switch in strategy. He decided to transform Johnstown America into a billion-dollar transportation conglomerate. Instead of having one manufacturing segment of the transportation industry supporting the company, the future Johnstown America would be supported by a broad range of manufacturing

interests. By pursuing this course of action, Begel could reduce the company's exposure to the cyclicality of the freight car market—a characteristic he was overly familiar with—and forge a more financially secure future. With this as his goal, Begel moved forward and completed two defining acquisitions in 1995, bringing in companies that diversified Johnstown America beyond railcar manufacture into niche markets serving the heavy-duty truck industry and, to a lesser degree, the iron castings industry.

The first acquisition was the smaller of the two companies that joined Johnstown America's fold in 1995. In January, the company completed the acquisition of Bostrom Seating, Inc., a maker of air suspension and seating systems for the trucks and buses with 1994 sales of $56.7 million. This initial foray into truck component manufacturing was followed by a headlong plunge in August, when Johnstown America acquired Truck Components Inc. (TCI) for $168 million. TCI, with $313 million in 1994 sales, comprised three operating subsidiaries: Gunite Corporation, Brillion Iron Works, and Fabco Automotive. Gunite, which operated a foundry in Rockford, Illinois, and a machining facility in Elkhart, Indiana, ranked as the leading manufacturer of Class 8 truck wheel-end components, such as brake drums, disc wheel hubs, and spoke wheels. Brillion, Wisconsin-based Brillion Iron Works operated a foundry that produced precision molded castings for the heavy-duty truck, agricultural, industrial machinery, automotive, and construction equipment markets. Fabco Automotive, whose addition extended Johnstown America's geographic reach to Oakland, California, manufactured steerable drive axles and gear boxes for the heavy duty and utility vehicle markets.

With the addition of Bostrom Seating and TCI, Johnstown America's sales volume nearly doubled, creating a diversified transportation conglomerate that nearly matched Begel's revenue goal of $1 billion. Off the acquisition front, Johnstown America also formed two new subsidiaries in 1995, Freight Car Services, Inc. and JAIX Leasing Company. Freight Car Services, organized as part of the company's original railcar manufacturing operations, opened a new facility in Danville, Illinois, in October 1995 to provide rebuild and repair services for the nation's freight car fleet. JAIX Leasing was formed to provide lease financing and fleet management services for new and rebuilt freight cars.

With the bustling activity of 1995 at an end, Johnstown America entered 1996 with its railcar business strengthened and its operating scope broadened considerably. Expectations for the coming year were justifiably high, as Begel and his management team anticipated reaping the rewards from their efforts in 1995. Their bright hopes, however, were dashed. The company's fifth full year of business proved to be full of disappointments.

Begel's corporate strategy was confounded by the same problem that had prompted him to abandon the railcar business roughly 15 years earlier. Johnstown America's mainstay market was glutted with a surfeit of railcars. From the 25,000 freight car deliveries recorded in 1992, production had increased to 61,000 by 1995, manifesting the upswing Begel had projected when he decided to enter the business again with Johnstown America. The years of encouraging growth in demand, however, quickly ended, and railcar manufacturers such as Begel found themselves looking at a market writhing from the affects of too many freight cars and not enough customers. Johnstown America's stock value dropped precipitously, as the company's customers scaled back their orders. Johnstown America's biggest customer, for instance, reduced its total orders from $500 million in 1995 to $50 million in 1996, epitomizing the actions of railcar customers across the nation. Consequently, the once-flourishing Johnstown America was suffering from financial ills, ills that its recent diversification could do little to alleviate.

As Johnstown America's freight car manufacturing operations were losing money, Bostrom Seating and TCI were generating enough income to cover the $8 million in quarterly interest payments resulting from their acquisition, but the two subsidiaries were not producing enough money to compensate for the losses being registered by Johnstown America Corporation, the company's freight car subsidiary. The company as a whole, accordingly, was headed for a loss. At the end of 1996, when the figures were tallied for the difficult months of the past year, Johnstown America registered a $5.37 million loss on $560 million in sales. As the company entered 1997, Begel hoped for and projected another upswing in railcar demand.

As Begel had hoped, the railcar market cleared in 1997 and demand returned after a nearly a two year hiatus. The company received its first order of intermodal freight cars—the other type of railcar produced by Johnstown America—for the first time in more than two years. By the end of the year, the company could point to an order backlog of more than 4,000 freight cars and assuage its anxiety further by an order for 1,000 intermodal freight cars received in early 1998. Meanwhile, the company's recent acquisitions were performing admirably after their first two years of operation under Johnstown America's corporate umbrella. For the year, Johnstown America's sales swelled to

$668 million and its net income, after the disappointing $5.3 million loss in 1996, rebounded to a much-needed gain of $5.5 million.

As Johnstown America prepared for the beginning of the 21st century, the company was starting to realize the financial rewards of its diversification in 1995 and its commitment to railcar manufacture. The materialization of these rewards provided momentum for the future, fueling confidence that the strategy to become a diversified transportation company was a sound strategy to pursue. Whether or not the company's strategy would produce sustained, long-term growth remained to be determined by the future performance of its subsidiaries.

Principal Subsidiaries

Gunite Corporation; Bostrom Seating Inc.; Fabco Automotive Corporation; Brillion Iron Works, Inc.; Johnstown America Corporation; Freight Car Services, Inc.; JAIX Leasing Company.

Further Reading

Flint, Jerry, "A Market Cleared," *Forbes,* June 6, 1994, p. 53.
Isidore, Chris, "Johnstown Agrees to Buy Truck Components Inc.," *Journal of Commerce and Commercial,* June 15, 1995, p. 3B.
"Johnstown Seeks to Acquire Transcisco," *Railway Age,* May 1995, p. 18.
Watson, Rip, "Johnstown America, Maker of Railcars, to Go Public," *Journal of Commerce and Commercial,* May 28, 1993, p. 3B.
Welty, Gus, "Johnstown Makes Its Mark," *Railway Age,* September 1993, p. 71.
Woolley, Scott, "Derailed," *Forbes,* August 26, 1996, p. 14.

—Jeffrey L. Covell

Jordache Enterprises, Inc.

226 West 37th Street
New York, New York 10018
U.S.A.
(212) 643-8400
Fax: (212) 768-5721
Web site: http://www.jordache.com

Private Company
Incorporated: 1978 as Jordache Jeans Inc.
Employees: 1,000
Sales: $94 million (1997 est.)
SICs: 2321 Men's & Boys' Shirts, Except Work Shirts;
2325 Men's & Boys' Separate Trousers & Slacks;
2329 Men's & Boys' Clothing, Not Elsewhere
Classified; 2331 Women's, Misses' & Juniors'
Blouses & Shirts; 2339 Women's, Misses' & Juniors'
Outerwear, Not Elsewhere Classified; 2361 Girls',
Children's & Infants' Dresses, Blouses & Shirts; 2369
Girls', Children's & Infants' Outerwear, Not
Elsewhere Classified; 5699 Miscellaneous Apparel &
Accessory Stores

Jordache Enterprises, Inc. manufactures apparel, or contracts for the manufacture of apparel, including jeans, shirts, and outerwear, for men, women, and children. In the late 1990s, it also had purchased a chain of retail stores to market its products and was licensing the Jordache name for items such as eyewear, luggage, bedding, footwear, cosmetics and perfume, intimate apparel, and even diapers. The company was in the forefront of the designer jeans craze that began in the late 1970s. And though the Jordache brand name flourished in this field for a decade, it lost significant market share in the late 1980s; company management hoped to initiate a comeback for Jordache in the late 1990s.

"Overnight" 1979 Success—After 17 Years

Josef (Joe) Nakash was an Israeli who came to New York City in 1962 at the age of 21 with $25 in his pocket, determined to escape a poverty-stricken childhood and youth. He slept on park benches and in subway stations until he found a $40-a-week job wheeling racks of merchandise for a discount store. Nakash saved his money and in 1966, when he was making $110 a week, brought over his brothers Raphael (Ralph) and Abraham (Avi). The three saved $150 a week from their earnings and opened a discount store by 1969, selling brand-name jeans at cut-rate prices. Within a few years they had expanded this enterprise into a four store chain in Brooklyn and Queens.

The Nakashes' largest store was torched and looted during a city-wide nighttime power failure in 1977. This proved a bonanza, for the brothers collected $120,000 on their insurance policy, enabling them to enter the business of manufacturing jeans. The Nakash brothers had long been casting their eyes on the European jeans market, where denim products were tighter, sexier, and more fashion-conscious than in the United States. The Nakashes "Jordache" jeans—a loose acronym of their first names plus a French-inspired ending (pronounced "ash") taken from the end of their last name—was fashioned from a $4 swatch of Japanese fabric and had triple stitching for strength, reinforced buttons, and a double elastic waistband hugging the small of the back.

The moment could not have been more propitious, for consumers were turning their attention from standard brands like Levi's to designer jeans put out under labels such as Gloria Vanderbilt, Calvin Klein, Sergio Valente, and Sasson. Even so, there was nothing major to distinguish the brothers' Hong Kong-made samples from those from any other contender or pretender until they launched an aggressive television and print advertising campaign in January 1979 with $300,000 of their own money and a $250,000 loan from an Israeli bank. This leap into the unknown represented about one-fourth of their annual sales volume.

The Nakashes made a TV commercial featuring an apparently topless blonde wearing skin-tight Jordache jeans and riding a horse galloping through the surf. Suddenly a bare-chested young man, also in jeans, appeared and vaulted onto the horse, which carried the two into the sunset. Set to a rock beat, the music on the sound track swelled to the words, "You got the look I want to know better." All three networks rejected the spot as lewd, but the independent New York stations carried it, and within weeks Jordache was a hit among teenage girls.

The Nakashes immediately followed up with at least $1 million more in advertising, including not only more TV spots in the New York area but also full-color ads in such major magazines as *Playboy, Vogue,* and *Harper's Bazaar.* The *New York Times* refused to print an ad showing a female clad only in Jordache jeans piggyback on a hunky Jordache-clad topless male because the girl was grinning, so the company reshot it without the smirk, prompting the office quip, ''The *Times* thinks it's okay to do it—you just can't enjoy it.''

Triumphs and Tribulations of the 1980s

Incredibly, start-up Jordache had sales of $72 million in 1979 by selling more than three million pairs of its sole product—jeans selling at retail for between $29 and $34. The Nakash brothers became the second-largest shareholders in one of the fastest-growing banks in Israel. They began establishing Jordache International retail outlets throughout Asia and negotiated licensing deals for the Jordache name for products ranging from sunglasses to women's sportswear. In 1980 Jordache signed a licensing deal with Burlington for home furnishings, including domestic items for bed and bath and a full assortment of kitchen textiles and table linens.

By the fall of 1981 Jordache was producing 1.2 million pairs of jeans a month and selling them in 25 countries. The company had added a medium-priced line of jeans under the Alessio label. There were other divisions for children's clothing, menswear, handbags, activewear (including sneakers, running suits, and other athletic apparel), and junior-related separates. New manufacturing facilities had been purchased in Louisiana, and the company was adding to its warehousing space as fast as it could find space to buy.

Additionally, the company was licensing its name and horse's head logo for 36 products, including brassieres, pantyhose, diaper covers, and children's dolls. Joe Nakash said the licensees were taking in more than $100 million annually. Jordache was earning $200 million a year in wholesale revenue for its jeans. It was spending about $16 million a year on advertising, which Nakash said he believed in ''like a military strategy. You invade.'' The company also, by early 1983, had founded Yama Maritime Inc., an affiliate in which it had invested $40 million for eight cargo ships sporting the familiar horse's head. By this time Jordache's sales volume was $400 million annually, and it had 45 domestic and 33 international licensees.

The Nakashes hang-loose style made a mockery of corporate organizational charts. The brothers did most of their planning while commuting to Manhattan from their Queens residential neighborhood. They divided their duties on the basis of what they enjoyed doing the most and switched funds from division to division on a basis of daily need. They promoted young, inexperienced people from within or hired retailing, rather than garment-industry, executives, in the hope that they would contribute a feeling for the customer's needs.

Jordache stuck a thumb in the eye of rival Sasson Industries when it purchased the Maurice Sasson brand name from a defunct company in 1983 and appointed Maurice Sasson president and chief designer of a newly formed subsidiary, Bronco Ltd. Maurice Sasson had founded the Sasson jeans line but had split with the Sasson firm in 1979 after a lawsuit over the use of the Sasson name. Bronco began manufacturing and marketing a line of young-men's contemporary fashions and a high-fashion junior line under the Maurice Sasson name.

Also in 1983, Jordache paid $4.7 million for a half-share in a hot new $6 million a year Beverly Hills jeans manufacturer, Guess Inc. What seemed to be a highly astute investment turned into a seven-year-long horror story. Soon after Guess sales exploded, the Nakashes began to suspect that its founders, the Marciano brothers, were skimming profits off the top. The Marcianos were just as unhappy over the prospect of having to share their suddenly lucrative take with the Nakashes. They filed suit in federal court in 1984, charging Jordache with fraud and breach of contract and alleging that the Nakashes were racketeers.

In January 1986 federal customs and tax agents raided Jordache's offices, confiscating 450 crates of documents. A few days later, Hong Kong police raided Jordache International's offices there. But federal prosecutors in New York, headed by Rudolph Giuliani, were preoccupied with insider-trading cases and never followed up by seeking indictments. In 1989 a congressional panel heard testimony charging that the Internal Revenue Service had in effect been used as a pawn by the Marcianos in their war against the Nakashes.

A California jury found for Guess in its suit against Jordache in 1989. In May 1990, while jury members were deliberating on damages, the Nakashes agreed to settle this suit and 12 pending ones by giving back their Guess stock. In return the Marcianos agreed to let them have nearly two-thirds of the company dividends being held in escrow—roughly $66 million of a total of $106 million. Jordache won full ownership of a jointly owned subsidiary, Gasoline. The legal fees involved in this epic battle totaled at least $80 million.

Jordache was still flourishing in 1986, when it was the largest privately owned U.S. jeansmaker, with annual sales estimated at more than $600 million. A television campaign, seemingly based on Calvin Klein's, featured teenagers who, instead of modeling Jordache jeans, talked about adolescent concerns such as their appearance and search for romance. One commercial, which included a participant asking, ''Have you ever seen your parents naked?'' drew criticism from parents' and women's groups and was rejected by all three networks. Jordache's ''forum'' continued with topics such as parental breakups and teenagers running away from home but eventually turned to the safer subject of world hunger.

Meanwhile, Jordache's list of company licensees reached 100, generating $300 million in wholesale volume. In 1989 the list of products included children's socks, playwear, and sleepwear; women's rainwear, outerwear, large-size sportswear, and jewelry; misses' activewear, lingerie, and sleepwear; junior and misses' dresses and related separates; men's and women's hosiery; luggage and other leather goods; and umbrellas and gift accessories. An important attraction for prospective licensees was Jordache's heavy commitment to advertising. The company also was providing support to licensees in the form of legal services and merchandising and marketing staffs.

Sliding Downmarket in the 1990s

Jordache developed a chain of retail outlets for its products by acquiring 55 discount stores in six states from Heck's Inc. in 1990. Jordache paid only $1 but assumed $22 million in mortgage obligations in taking over the struggling Appalachian-area chain. Avi Nakash, Jordache's president, said the stores would sell Jordache, Calvin Klein, and other branded apparel at a 30 to 40 percent discount. However, a retail consultant suggested the company would use Heck's as "a dumping ground for Jordache's mistakes—its overcuts, returned items, and unwanted job lots."

Another retail consultant said many clothing manufacturers were developing retailing arms in order to survive in a field dominated by mass marketers and financially unstable department store chains. Jordache had announced in 1989 that it would open 30 to 50 "Jordache Outlet" discount shoe stores with Shoe-Town Inc.

With the end of the designer jeans craze, Jordache's annual sales fell to an estimated $400 million-plus at the end of the 1980s. According to a *Los Angeles Times* story, the company's jeans had lost their cachet, appealing mainly to inner-city youths and blue-collar workers and typically selling at discount stores. Junior wear was accounting for 52 percent of the company's business; misses for 18 or 19 percent; young men's apparel for about 16 percent; and children's wear for about 10 percent. In 1991 the company launched Looks, a fragrance for 14-to-25-year-old females.

When Jordache Baby's disposable diapers was released by a licensee in 1994, it was apparently the first designer diaper. The product, 40 percent cheaper than Pampers or Huggies and said by one dissatisfied customer to leak, seemed to symbolize Jordache's descent in the marketplace to mass-merchandise stores and discount outlets. The company spent less than $1 million for advertising during 1996.

The following year, however, Jordache launched a new $5 million television and print campaign with a rescored version of its original "You Got the Look" theme. The print ads featured pouty young women in high-tech rooms that evoked a discotheque setting, designed to play on the popularity of 1970s fashion nostalgia and thereby attract a younger customer base. The ad director for this campaign was Ralph Nakash's son, 20 year old Shaul Nakash, who was an MBA student at the time.

Jordache's holdings in the 1990s included Ditto Apparel, Inc., a manufacturing arm located in Colfax, Louisiana, and Retail Acquisitions Inc., which ran the apparel stores and was also a finance holding company. Jordache also had suppliers abroad, including JRA Philippines, which was making jeans for sale in U.S. department stores. Ralph Nakash was chairman of the board of the parent company. Elliot M. Lavigne was named chief executive officer in 1997. Headquarters remained in New York City, in Manhattan's garment district.

Further Reading

Behar, Richard, "Does Guess Have a Friend in the IRS?" *Forbes,* November 16, 1987, pp. 147–49.

Belkin, Lisa, "When the Honeymoon Ended," *New York Times,* May 1, 1986, pp. D1, D5.

"A 'Blood War' in the Jeans Trade," *Business Week,* November 13, 1989, pp. 74–75, 78–79, 81.

Bloomfield, Judy, "Labels Stretching Out Via Licensing," *Women's Wear Daily,* July 7, 1989, p. 20.

Byron, Christopher, *Skin Tight,* New York: Simon & Schuster, 1992.

Conant, Jenny, and Jessica Kreimerman, "Selling Jeans by Ignoring Them," *Newsweek,* September 15, 1986, p. 64.

Cuff, Daniel F., "Jordache Leader Hopes Shipping Will Recover," *New York Times,* February 1, 1983, p. D2.

Ettorre, Barbara, "The Status-Reapers," July 1, 1979, *New York Times,* Sec. 3, p. 7.

Gordon, Maryellen, "Taking Jordache to New Heights," *Women's Wear Daily,* February 7, 1990, p. S10.

"Jordache Purchases Sasson Brand Name," *Women's Wear Daily,* October 12, 1983, p. 12.

"Jordache's New Executive Look," *Business Week,* November 2, 1981, pp. 121, 123.

Krol, Carol, "Jordache Resurrects 'You Got the Look' Ads," *Advertising Age,* July 21, 1997, p. 3.

Ono, Yumiko, "To Complete This Jordache Look, Just Add a Bib and Teething Ring," *Wall Street Journal,* August 9, 1994, p. B1.

Pechter, Kerry, "Jordache's Purchase of Heck's Puzzles Many in Retail Field," *Wall Street Journal,* January 4, 1990, p. B5.

Reynes, Roberta, "The New Entrepreneurs," *Marketing Communications,* April 1980, pp. 28–29, 79.

Salmans, Sandra, "Shoot-Out on Seventh Avenue," *New York Times,* September 20, 1981, Sec. 3, pp. 1, 24.

Silverstein, Stuart, "Guess and Jordache Jeans Settle War Over Ownership," *Los Angeles Times,* May 31, 1990, pp. A1, A30.

Slutsker, Gary, "The Smoking Bun," *Forbes,* March 25, 1985, pp. 210–12.

Stewart, Anne, "Topless Ads Mean Bottomless Riches for the Three Israeli Brothers Behind Jordache Jeans," *People,* December 3, 1979, pp. 135–36, 138, 140.

"Topless Jeans Make the Scene," *Time,* September 10, 1979, p. 74.

—Robert Halasz

Kaufhof Warenhaus AG

Leonhard-Tietz-Strasse 1
Cologne 50676
Federal Republic of Germany
(49) 221-2230
Fax: (49) 221-233-2808
Web site: http://www.metro.de

Wholly Owned Division of Metro Holding AG
Incorporated: 1879 as Firma Leonhard Tietz; 1953 as
    Kaufhof AG
Employees: 28,988
Sales: DM9.31 billion (1996)
SICs: 5311 Department Stores

Kaufhof Warenhaus AG, the group of retailing and service companies formerly known as Kaufhof Holding AG, was born from a July 1996 merger that created one of Europe's largest trading groups, Metro AG. Formed from the combination of Kaufhof Holding AG and several other companies, parent company Metro AG reported 1996 sales of more than DM62 billion ($44.6 billion), and employed approximately 135,000 people. Kaufhof Warenhaus AG is a large component of Metro AG's department store division, with branches in the best city-center locations alongside such other Kaufhof associate retailers as Vobis Microcomputer, the Media-Markt-Saturn Group, Reno shoe stores, DineA caterers, and Kaufhalle AG's discount department stores.

19th-Century Retail

Kaufhof traces its roots to the mid-19th century, when large, elegant department stores called *grands magasins* sprang up in Paris, offering luxury goods. The founding of the German department stores a few decades later was in direct contrast to the rise of France's "cathedrals of commerce," as Emile Zola called them. In Germany all of the great trading houses developed from small retail stores in the eastern provinces of what was then Imperial Germany.

Leonhard Tietz's case is typical. In 1879 the 30-year-old from Birnbaum, Warthe, opened a tiny textile shop in Stralsund with a start-up capital of 3,000 thalers. The shop had only 25 square meters of sales space. It sold thread, buttons, trimmings, woolen wares, and all the articles needed for men's and women's tailoring.

What differentiated Tietz's business was the new retailing methods employed. He ran his business according to the principle of high turnover on a small profit, based on fixed prices and cash payment. This method had, in fact, been put into practice before in the large Parisian department stores. This was, however, a surprising innovation in eastern Germany, where people still haggled over prices and put their purchases on credit. As the extent of the company's purchasing power was a decisive factor in its ability to offer low prices, Tietz formed a buying cooperative with other members of his large, extended family, which included the founders of Hertie. Articles that could be sold in bulk were ordered by the cooperative, prompting the development of new, cheap articles. The manufacturers welcomed the chance to sell to such big purchasers.

Tietz also expanded his field of business through the opening of numerous branches. This took him into the Rhineland, an expanding economic center promising good bulk sales its growing number of inhabitants and their increasing purchasing power. Tietz set up 11 branches between 1889 and 1909 in western Germany, and in 1891 moved the headquarters of his company to Cologne.

Carving Out a Niche at the Turn of the Century

Leonard Tietz used the same business methods wherever he founded his branches. He rented small shops in the best areas to sell haberdashery and linen. The public would come in droves to these shops on their opening, and following this the complete range of goods offered would be introduced. Wherever necessary, Tietz would move the stores into bigger premises, and eventually acquired his own real estate. It soon became an experience in itself to shop at Tietz. When the Cologne store opened in 1895, its own small electricity works enabled arc lights and

311

electric light bulbs to light the store brightly. Elevators transported the customers to all floors, free of charge. The saleswomen—few salesmen were employed—wore black dresses as their uniform. On a trip to Milan, Tietz admired the Galeria and decided he wanted to own a similar building with a glass cupola and gigantic windows. He fulfilled his dream by having a *Jugendstil*—the German equivalent of *art nouveau*—building with an arcade constructed on Cologne's main street. This was his first real department store, and with its luxurious furnishings it was considered one of the most important landmarks in the town. It was torn down just ten years later to make way for an even larger department store. By this time Leonhard Tietz had his stores built by the most renowned architects of his time.

For the Düsseldorf store, the management approached all German-based architects with an invitation to participate in a prize competition to create a work of great artistic merit without regard to cost. Joseph M. Olbrich, the most famous exponent of *Jugendstil* architecture, was chosen to design the building, and the new department stores in Cologne and Wuppertal-Elberfeld were built by Wilhelm Kreis. These large buildings are now classified as historical monuments. Further branches under the wholly owned subsidiary Grands Magasins L. Tietz, founded in 1900, were opened in Belgium, where a huge department store employing 1,000 people was built on the occasion of the World's Fair in Brussels in 1910.

The range of merchandise expanded. Tietz began to offer all-inclusive packages, for instance a set including kitchen furniture, a cooking range, and 323 pieces of kitchen and household equipment. With the introduction of various articles, including bicycles, tinned food, and ready-to-wear clothing, the department store offered new services to its customers. Tietz imported the latest hat and clothing fashions from Paris, where he owned his own buying house. He imported Oriental rugs, precious glassware from Italy, and majolica and fancy goods from Japan.

Influenced by the efforts of the *Deutscher Werkbund,* founded in 1907 to organize avant-garde art exhibitions, "beauty and quality" became the company's catch-phrase. Kaufhof was the first retailer to organize avant-garde art exhibitions in its stores, and Leonhard Tietz had his portrait painted by Max Liebermann. Tietz looked after his employees' interests by offering benefits, including health care, that were by no means taken for granted at that time. The company's extensive social programs developed gradually from this time onward.

In 1905 the firm Leonhard Tietz became a public limited company with a capital of one million marks, but remained a family firm as the shares were taken up by the Tietz family. At this time the company employed a work force of 2,400 and had sales of 24 million marks. In 1909 the Tietz shares were introduced onto the Berlin stock exchange as the first publicly traded German department store stocks.

Leonhard Tietz died on November 14, 1914. His eldest son, Alfred Leonhard Tietz, had been well prepared for his future responsibilities. After studying at the University of Commerce in Cologne under Eugen Schmalenbach, the pioneer of modern business management education, Alfred Tietz then went on to be trained in various large U.S. department stores.

Wartime Activities

The period following World War I was marked by unrest, hyperinflation, and economic crises. Nevertheless, the network of branches was continuously extended. In 1925 Tietz traveled with a team to the United States and came back with many fresh ideas. The already common practice in the United States of training employees for their jobs was adopted, and Tietz's sales personnel and executives were carefully trained for their tasks. Business and sales training, knowledge of the merchandise, economic geography, and the importance of good taste were impressed upon the company employees. The team also studied fixed-price retailers such as F. W. Woolworth, and established the EHAPE (Einheitspreis Handels Gesellschaft mbH), a fixed-price bazaar in Cologne. It became a successful subsidiary of Kaufhof and would later trade under the name of Kaufhalle AG.

When the National Socialists (Nazis) forced Jewish businesses to give up their property in 1933, the owners of Firma Leonhard Tietz engaged Abraham Frowein, president of the International Chamber of Commerce, to represent their interests. The latter stood up for them at great personal risk, made it possible for Tietz's heirs to emigrate, helped establish them on a sound financial footing abroad, and later helped them to gain compensation. After 1933, Kaufhof's shares were held by Deutsche Bank, Commerzbank, Dresdner Bank, the Frowein family, and many other private shareholders. During World War II, bombs destroyed most of the company's 40 department stores. Only five survived intact. The branches in the east were lost.

Following the 1948 currency reform, the company, which began calling itself Westdeutsche Kaufhof AG in 1933 and from 1953 Kaufhof AG, expanded into towns in the north and south of the Federal Republic of Germany. After the years of deprivation and lack of goods, customers came in droves to the rebuilt and newly opened stores.

Rebuilding in the Mid-20th Century

The well-stocked department stores were as appealing as they had been before the war. "Kaufhof offers everything a thousand times over under one roof" ran the company slogan. Special events such as French, American, and Italian weeks; art exhibitions; and autograph sessions with famous artists attracted many into the stores. Above all, the large grocery departments with their wide variety of cheeses, sausages, breads, fresh meat, fish, and delicatessen products, and the increasingly elegant restaurants and cafes, enjoyed great popularity.

A very important factor in the company's success was imports, especially from the Far East, which allowed the company on the one hand to supply goods at low prices and on the other hand to aid, through its large orders, the development of the manufacturers and factories in these countries.

In 1979, the company's centenary year, Kaufhof AG owned 86 branches and its turnover reached DM8 billion. The business climate for the department stores, however, became less favorable at the beginning of the 1980s and forced Kaufhof to follow a new strategic direction. During this time of great change Kaufhof acquired two new large shareholders—Metro Vermögensverwaltung GmbH & Co. of Düsseldorf (Metro) and its bank, the Schweizerische Bankgesellschaft AG. By the early

1990s, Metro owned more than 50 percent of Kaufhof Holding, and would eventually become the parent company.

The department store crisis arose from the emergence of competitive new types of businesses in the retail trade. Specialty businesses managed to gain a stronger foothold than before, and self-service markets, offering cut-price goods rather than comfortable surroundings and service, sprang up on greenfield (out-of-town) sites and on the edges of towns. The increase in automobile use brought a new attitude toward shopping. While parking space in cities became more limited, businesses on the edges of towns allowed customers to take their purchases directly from the check-out to their cars.

As a result of this development, Kaufhof began to diversify into other areas of trading and into the services sector. As early as 1970 Kaufhof took a shareholding in ITS (International Tourist Services) Länderdienst GmbH of Cologne, which offered an extensive, worldwide travel program. ITS itself was set on expansion and had acquired shareholdings in various tourist companies both at home and abroad. The company was joining forces with business partners to build hotels in popular vacation areas, and vacation sites in subtropical-type aqua parks.

As part of the reorganization of Kaufhof, the existing restaurants and cafes in the Kaufhof and Kaufhalle stores were changed into self-service restaurants, then in 1983 and 1984 transferred to the Kaufhof Gastronomie Service-Gesellschaft mbH (KGSG), of Cologne, a wholly owned subsidiary of Kaufhof. There were KGSG restaurants not only in the 118 stores belonging to the group, but also in four other locations.

At the same time, new concepts were developed in the department stores. The stores no longer aimed to sell everything under one roof, but concentrated on selected profitable areas that were in strong demand. The grocery departments, which previously had yielded high returns and had been very popular, became to some extent simply departments to attract regular customers, rather than profitable portions of the business. In many department stores space was rented to outside grocery retailers. In the course of the restructuring, nine of the company's previously traditional department stores selling the whole range of goods became independent in 1987–88, under the name Kaufhof Mode und Sport GmbH. They began to offer a selective range, concentrating predominantly on fashion and sports goods.

Kaufhof Holding AG was incorporated in 1989, and 73 department store operations were transferred to the newly created Kaufhof Warenhaus AG, then a wholly owned subsidiary of Kaufhof Holding AG. In 1989 Kaufhalle became a joint-stock company, and in 1990 25 percent of its shares were offered on the stock market in order to strengthen the company's financial position for embarking on new projects. The company owned 127 branches in the former West Germany and many more in the new federal states, including one in Stralsund, the town in which Leonhard Tietz began his business in 1879. Particular areas on which the company was concentrating included electronics, computers, and photographic goods.

Kaufhof Holding AG had a 62.3 percent shareholding in Media-Markt-Gruppe, based in Ingolstadt, which had 37 sites at home and abroad. In 1990 Kaufhof Holding AG merged its subsidiary Saturn-Hansa Handelsgesellschaft für technischen Freizeit-und Haushaltbedarf mbH, a leading company in these specialty areas, with the Media-Markt-Gruppe. Kaufhof also owned 50 percent of Vobis-Mikrocomputergruppe, of Aachen, a dynamic specialty market group with 56 branches at home and abroad. "Mac Fash" Textilhandels GmbH, of Cologne, was a wholly owned subsidiary that sold fashionable clothing at its 21 stores.

In 1989 Kaufhof acquired 61.5 percent of the capital of Oppermann Versand AG, Neumünster, a mail-order house specializing in promotional goods and advertising gifts for trade and private customers, with numerous subsidiary companies and franchise partners abroad. It also acquired holdings of 60 and 70 percent in two companies in the Hawesko-Gruppe of Hamburg, an importer and exporter of wine, champagne, and spirits which also operated a mail-order business. Buying in department stores and buying by mail-order were originally considered the two opposite extremes of retail trading. Once it became evident, however, that mail-order was becoming more popular, Kaufhof Holding also took shareholdings in mail-order companies in the most diverse areas. It acquired a 76 percent holding in Friedrich Wenz GmbH & Co., which had been selling jewelry, gifts, clothing, and furnishings of high quality by catalog from the jewelers' town of Pforzheim since 1925. Kaufhof also acquired a 50 percent stake in Reno Versandhandel GmbH in Thalweiler-Fröschen. This lucrative mail-order shoe firm, operating from close to the shoe metropolis of Pirmasens, also owned a specialty store chain with 188 branches, 34 of them abroad.

One of the factors in Leonhard Tietz's success was the elimination of the then-all-powerful wholesalers through mass purchasing at advantageous prices direct from the manufacturer. By the early 1990s Kaufhof had entered the sphere of wholesaling as part of its strategy of diversification and had taken shareholdings in the wholesalers for its various areas of business. One commitment in this area was the company's 80 percent shareholding in Rungis Express Gesellschaft für Frischimporte mbH, of Meckenheim, a company that delivered freshly caught seafood and high-quality fish, exotic fruit, vegetables, meat, cheese, and top-quality champagne several times a week to exclusive restaurants and delicatessens.

In the early 1990s, the development of a modern electronic system of selling goods, the improvement of merchandise, and the motivating of the work force to become more customer-oriented showed the great importance still attached to the activities of the Kaufhof-Warenhaus AG, with its 73 branches in western Germany and further branches opening in eastern Germany from 1991. With the addition of banks, travel bureaus, theater ticket booths, insurance, and many other services, the department stores became multi-functional service centers.

With its total of 636 stores, Kaufhof Holding AG in the early 1990s was set on a course of further expansion. The Kaufhalle subsidiary offered a range of goods geared towards more sophisticated customers. The structure of Kaufhof, with its various sales divisions—department stores, specialty stores, mail order, wholesaling, tourism, and other services—put it in a good position to operate successfully in the five new states of the Federal Republic of Germany. Kaufhof, which already had

48 branches in Europe outside Germany, was also set to be well-represented with the merging of sales areas within the European community's internal market.

One area in which Kaufhof attracted attention during the early 1990s was in the realm of information systems. Under the leadership of MIS director Ralf-Rainer West, the company developed an intranet that gained the admiration of observers throughout the business community. West, who stated that he wanted to develop a system that would be as useful as possible to the people for whom it was intended, chose Microsoft Windows as its graphical operating system. Within 78 department stores, the personal computer (PC)-based local area networks (LANs) were connected via digital ISDN lines. By the late 1990s, many companies would be adopting this sort of client/server architecture, but in 1993 Elizabeth Heichler of *Computerworld* could describe Kaufhof's system as "a customized desktop environment that pushes the frontiers of technical innovation." As Heichler described it, "When users sign on [to the computer system], the Kaufhof network shows in color a nearly full-screen, three-dimensional picture of an office with a man sitting at a desk fitted with items such as a printer, calculator, pen and paper, filing cabinets and telephone. Clicking on these pictures launches applications such as word processing and electronic mail." Other features included a company internal magazine "no longer limited to a given number of pages or any particular frequency—whenever the group responsible for the magazine is ready with another page or piece of information, it notifies users via a flag on their mailbox."

As in the realm of its information systems, Kaufhof's financial reputation in the early to mid-1990s was a solid one. Hence when it issued European medium-term note (MTN) bonds in late 1993, *Corporate Finance* magazine referred to "the quality of the names" of the companies issuing—Kaufhof, the engineering company ABB of Sweden and Switzerland, and J. Sainsbury retailers of Great Britain. In 1995 General Electric, eager to enter the largely untapped German credit-card market, purchased 80 percent of Service Bank from Kaufhof Holding for $50 million.

And then Kaufhof Holding, so often the company making the acquisitions, itself became a subsidiary. Metro Group had acquired a controlling interest, and in October 1995, it announced that it would merge its Kaufhof and ASKO subsidiaries with its cash-and-carry business. On July 19, 1996, this merger took effect when Kaufhof Holding AG joined ASKO Deutsche Kaufhaus AG and its subsidiary Deutsche SB-Kauf, along with Metro Cash-and-Carry, to become Metro Holding AG. The well-known Kaufhof name was retained in Metro's department store division, Kaufhof Warenhaus Group.

Metro Holding AG one of the largest, most diversified trading companies in the world, had operations in some 18 countries, including the People's Republic of China and Romania. It announced that in 1997 it would concentrate on developing the synergies of its constituent companies by concentrating on integration of holding company functions; procurement (optimizing its supply chain) and private-label management; and synergy in the realm of services such as information technology and logistics. Within Kaufhof Warenhaus AG, it promoted the "Galeria" concept—already familiar in the United States—of employing numerous display islands, "each a distinct world of its own," in its retail stores. Kaufhof Warenhaus in 1997 had 145 branches, and more than 1.3 million square meters of selling space, with sales in excess of DM9.3 billion. Its employees numbered almost 29,000.

In 1997, the Kaufhof Warenhaus Group introduced the first corporate closed-circuit television system in the German retail sector, broadcast digitally and received via satellite. Programming included product training sessions, advanced courses, and live broadcasts. It also gave employees an opportunity to give input through phone or a fax hot line.

Further Reading

Ball, Matthew, "Quality Borrowers Flock to Note Market," *Corporate Finance,* January 1994, pp. 36–37.

"Business and Finance," *Economist,* October 14, 1995, p. 7.

50 Jahre Leonard Tietz 1879–1929, Cologne: Leonhard Tietz AG, 1929.

Harding, Elizabeth U., "German Retailer Pulling Software Pieces Together," *Software Magazine,* May 1992, pp. 84–86.

Heichler, Elizabeth, "Windows, LANs Meet Up," *Computerworld,* April 19, 1993, p. 50.

Rolfe, Richard, "A German Foothold for Citi and GE," *Credit Card Management,* March 1995, pp. 28–31.

Schwann, Mathieu, *Leonhard Tietz. Ein Wort über ihn und sein persönliches Werden,* Cologne: M. DuMont Schauberg, C. 1914.

—Ingrid Bauert-Keetman.
Translated from the German by Philippe A. Barbour.
—updated by Judson Knight

King & Spalding

191 Peachtree Street
Atlanta, Georgia 30303-1763
U.S.A.
(404) 572-4600
Fax: (404) 572-5148
Web site: http://www.kslaw.com

Private Company
Incorporated: 1885
Employees: 700
Revenues: $165 million (1996)
SICs: 8111 Legal Services

King & Spalding is the largest law firm in Atlanta and one of the largest in the Southeast. The firm is engaged in the general practice of law, and its 420 lawyers practice in 23 specific areas. Among the latter are antitrust, banking and finance, bankruptcy and commercial litigation, corporate, environmental, governmental, health care, intellectual property and technology, commercial litigation, product liability, public finance, real estate, tax, and trusts and estates. In addition to its Atlanta location in the 191 Peachtree tower, King & Spalding has offices in New York City, Washington, D.C., and Houston.

1880s Founding: Spalding, King, and a Famous Contemporary

In 1883, a young lawyer leaving Atlanta offered this appraisal of the city: "Here the chief end of man," he wrote, "is certainly to make money, and money cannot be made except by the most vulgar methods. The studious man is pronounced impractical and is suspected as a visionary. All students of specialties—except such practical specialties as carpentering, for instance—are classed together as mere ornamental furniture in the intellectual world—curious, perhaps, and pretty enough, but of very little use and no mercantile value." The young lawyer was Woodrow Wilson, future President of the United States. More than a century later, many Atlantans would say

that his words were bitingly accurate, but one contemporary judged Wilson's assessment "too scathing," perhaps the result of the fact that his own firm, Renick & Wilson, had failed.

Wilson married a Rome, Georgia, girl in 1885, the year his fellow attorneys Alexander Campbell King and Jack Johnson Spalding founded the law firm that would bear their names. Like Wilson, Spalding came to Atlanta at the age of 25 and entered the law practice there. He and his wife left Morganfield, Kentucky, and by means of horse and buggy and railroads, arrived in the city on January 4, 1882.

Spalding's law offices were not impressive, consisting of a shared room in the old James Building for which he and his office-mates shared janitorial duties. During that first year, according to Franklin Garrett's massive history of the city, *Atlanta and Environs,* Spalding earned $626. The next year he gained an important account as assignee for a wholesale house, and he paid off the firm's debts. The fact that he had done so, in part through the knowledge he had gained by studying bookkeeping and business, greatly impressed the influential newspaperman Henry Grady. The latter wrote in the *Atlanta Constitution,* in Garrett's words, "that it was the only instance he ever heard of where an assignee paid a firm's debts in full and turned back money." In part because of the publicity generated by the story, Spalding enjoyed greater success during the next year, when he made $2,600.

Alexander Campbell King was born the same year as his future partner. Like Spalding—and like most of the city's residents a century later—he was not a native Atlanta. Born in Charleston, South Carolina, he was admitted to the bar in 1875. Then on January 1, 1885, King and Spalding formed a law firm. During the next decades, the firm would have a variety of names; but once it grew so large that it had too many partners to name, it would revert to the title it had taken on in its humble beginnings—King & Spalding.

In his short biographical portrait of Spalding, Garrett observed that during the more than 50 years of his career, the attorney would have a variety of "distinguished partners," starting with King and including Patrick Calhoun, John D.

Little, E. Marvin Underwood, Daniel MacDougald, John A. Sibley, Robert B. Troutman, Pope F. Brock, and his own son Hughes Spalding. Each man's name would wind up as part of the firm's.

When Calhoun joined in 1887, he was apparently such a significant figure that his new partners added his name first, to become Calhoun, King & Spalding. In 1894, he left and was replaced by John D. Little, and King, Spalding & Little continued as an entity until 1908. When Little departed, Marvin Underwood joined, and in 1909 the firm became King, Spalding & Underwood.

As for their business, it seems to have focused on the chief enterprise of the day, which was railroads. Before the Civil War, Atlanta had been a great rail center, and for that reason General Sherman's troops had burned the city in order to cripple Confederate transport lines. After the war, the railroads returned, and rail transport became a leading factor in the city's growth. During the 1880s and 1890s, Alexander King worked as general counsel, or assistant general counsel, for the Atlanta & West Point Railroad, the East & West Railroad of Alabama, and a number of other lines.

In 1913, Underwood became Assistant Attorney General of the United States, so the firm reverted to its original name. Underwood was not to be the only member of the firm with ties to Washington. In 1918, the presidential administration of King's and Spalding's former Atlanta law colleague Wilson appointed King Solicitor General of the United States. Two years later, he received an appointment as U.S. Circuit Judge of the Fifth Circuit, a position he held until 1925. Because of his former partner's departure for Washington, Spalding had to reorganize the firm, taking on Daniel MacDougald and John A. Sibley as partners under the name Spalding, MacDougald & Sibley in 1920. Apparently for a brief time after leaving his federal position in 1925, King rejoined the firm, which became King, Spalding, MacDougald & Sibley; but he died the next year, and his name was removed again. In 1935, MacDougald left and Pope Brock and Robert B. Troutman became partners, so that the firm became Spalding, Sibley, Troutman & Brock.

Spalding remained active in political affairs, and served a four-year term as county commissioner for Fulton County. In 1888, just three years after he founded his law firm, he was a delegate at the Democratic National Convention in St. Louis; again in 1900, he was a delegate-at-large to the 1900 Convention in Kansas City; and yet again as a delegate-at-large in 1932, he supported the candidacy of New York's Governor Franklin D. Roosevelt. Spalding died in 1938, leaving three children, the eldest of whom would become a partner in the law firm.

The Hughes Spalding Era: 1920s–1960s

Born in 1888, Hughes Spalding became a junior member of his father's firm in 1910. By 1920, the "Spalding" in the name no longer referred to Jack, but to son Hughes, who would continue in a leadership role there for half a century. In 1938 the name changed yet again, to Spalding, Sibley, Troutman & Kelley, and the permutations would continue for the next few decades. In the 1987 obituary for the firm's oldest attorney, 95-year-old William K. Meadow, the *Journal and Constitution*

noted that he, too, had been a name partner during the years 1956 to 1962, when the firm was called Spalding, Sibley, Troutman, Meadow & Smith.

Eventually these changes would cease, not so much because of the confusion they created as because the firm had taken on too many partners to include them all. Therefore at some point in the early 1960s, the firm returned to its original name: King & Spalding.

An associate in 1935, Meadow became a partner in 1945. His was the era of Hughes Spalding, and in fact his 52-year-career at the firm was second only to the record established by Spalding, who served for 57 years. Under Hughes Spalding, important business links were forged, and others strengthened. Among the boards on which he sat were those of Coca-Cola and Trust Company Bank, both significant clients of the law firm, and both closely tied to one another as well.

Like his father, Hughes became involved in county politics, serving as Fulton County attorney during the 1940s. Meadow assisted Spalding with managing legal matters involving the county on a daily basis, and built his practice around defending insurance companies against lawsuits by policyholders.

At his death, Meadow represented a last remaining link between the past of King & Spalding and its late 20th-century present. In his latter years, he would compose poetic resolutions to honor deceased colleagues, and often quoted Shakespeare in these eulogies. A veteran of World War I, to his dying day he carried in his thigh a German shell fragment from a battlefield in France, a wound for which he had earned a Purple Heart. His career, too, belonged to a romantic, uncomplicated past. As the *Journal and Constitution* reported, he had no formal partnership agreement with Spalding: "An accountant preparing an audit asked Mr. Meadow how he knew his rights as a partner. 'I just walk across the hall and ask Hughes Spalding,' Mr. Meadow replied."

The Old Ways and the New

Ironically, litigators themselves would be the very people who would strike the death blow against the simple, trusting world that Meadow represented. But not every aspect of that world was positive. Up until the time of Hughes Spalding's retirement in the mid-1960s, Atlanta was a city run almost exclusively by white males. In a 1985 article about increasing competition for legal positions in Atlanta, the *Journal and Constitution* noted that the city's work environment was becoming more like that of New York. This "melancholy transition from polite Southern ways to a ruder and brisker pace," however, was not entirely to be lamented: "in the old days, nobody who was female or black stood much of a chance of getting into an exclusively white male club. That's changed too. Women are winning the battle for acceptance, and black graduates of the best law schools find themselves in huge demand."

Despite the fact that Atlanta was at the center of the Civil Rights Movement in the 1960s, the principal challenge to the old ways at King & Spalding came in the area of gender, not race. In 1980, associate Elizabeth Hishon was denied a partnership, and filed a sex discrimination suit against the firm. The case went to the Supreme Court, which in 1985 ruled in her favor. Although law firms were private and partnership votes secret, the High Court ruled, those votes are still protected under federal civil rights laws.

The Hishon case assumed tremendous importance in the legal community, both as a matter of law—it received dozens of write-ups in legal journals—and as a matter of hiring practice at firms. Due largely to *Hishon v. King & Spalding,* a female lawyer in Atlanta told the *Journal and Constitution,* "Atlanta firms are moving away from 'good-old-boy' evaluations. . . . [F]irms are telling people earlier, in a more straightforward fashion, whether they're moving toward partnership."

Changes in society might have opened up more opportunities for minority and female lawyers, but other changes—many of them economic in origin—reduced opportunities for the population as a whole. The 1985 *Journal and Constitution* story on competition for jobs at Atlanta law firms seemed to recall the tone of Woodrow Wilson's observations from 102 years before. For those fortunate enough to find jobs with prestigious law firms such as King & Spalding, the pace of work was anything but sleepy. "Along with a package explaining insurance benefits and the like," Tracy Thompson reported, "first-year associates are handed a key to get into the office on weekends and at night. They are expected to use it." One young associate with hopes of a partnership told Thompson that a junior attorney is "clearly a machine. I feel like I'm walking a tightrope. You cannot have an off day."

The same article reported that in spite of its reputation as "Atlanta's most 'old-line' law firm, King & Spalding led the pack in lateral hiring and raiding the partnership ranks of other firms to expand its fields of expertise." For instance, in 1984 Bob Miller, a partner at a prominent Atlanta firm, accepted an attractive partnership deal at King & Spalding; as a result, he brought with him his old firm's entire health-care litigation department, consisting of two partners and three associates.

Little Sympathy for Lawyers in the 1980s

Along with other law firms, King & Spalding experienced the effects of what became, by the last two decades of the 20th century, a widespread distrust for lawyers in American society. In a September, 1988 *Journal and Constitution* article, Thompson cited this attitude as a possible explanation for a Cobb County jury's decision in a suit involving King & Spalding. The firm had taken a former employee, Clint M. Holcomb, to court for an office-supply overbilling scheme that it claimed had cost $350,000 during a five-year period from 1975 to 1980. King & Spalding demanded repayment of the amount lost, plus interest and punitive damages totalling $1.1 million, but the jury awarded the firm only $200,000.

State Senator Roy Barnes, who acted as the firm's representative, told Thompson, "People do not like lawyers," admitting, "I don't like lawyers, generally." His co-counsel, Baxter Davis, said that he and Barnes had "represented one of the most prestigious law firms in this country. That's not the kind of party that a jury is going to have a great deal of sympathy for." The demand for damages, Thompson reported, did not include

the law firm's court costs: "We didn't think that would sit well" with the jury, Davis said.

In a 1989 article entitled "Lawyers Eager to Defend White-Collar Crime Cases," Robert Luke of the *Journal and Constitution* suggested that white-collar crime would overtake drug-related crime as a lucrative new market for prestigious law firms. He noted that King & Spalding had organized a six-partner white-collar crime group under the direction of former U.S. Attorney General Griffin Bell. The firm was at that time representing an aerospace contracting company in Illinois which had agreed to pay the federal government the largest military fraud settlement in American history, $116 million.

In addition, King & Spalding was assisting Exxon Corporation in an internal investigation of its spring 1989 oil spill off the coast of Alaska—an investigation designed to uncover facts which would protect the oil company from the many lawsuits being filed against it. The firm also operated as bond counsel for Georgia counties raising money through the sale of certificates of participation, or COPs. The Atlanta paper, in a 1992 article, indicated that King & Spalding was "profiting from public debt."

In the 1990s, King & Spalding's clientele continued to consist of large corporations, enormous non-profit organizations such as hospitals and government entities. Among its most well-known clients—albeit one that ceased to exist—was the Atlanta Committee for the Olympic Games (ACOG), which staged the 1996 Olympics in Atlanta.

Toward a New Century: Growing in Size and Prestige

As a hallmark of its growth and reputation, King & Spalding announced in the fall of 1987 that it would relocate to what would become one of Atlanta's most prestigious corporate addresses. Theretofore housed in the Trust Company Tower and the Hurt Building, King & Spalding would lease 250,000 square feet in the 191 Peachtree Tower, to be designed by celebrated architect Philip Johnson. In what would be the largest lease for a building in which the tenant controlled no equity interest, the firm would occupy the top twelve of the building's 50 stories. King & Spalding moved into the offices, which included a dining room on the top floor, in 1990.

By then the firm had expanded far outside of Atlanta. In 1979 it had opened an office in Washington, D.C. which by 1998 had 65 full-time lawyers specializing in a range of areas from tax to litigation to environmental law. The New York office opened in 1990, and eight years later it had 47 lawyers with a wide range of specialties. Finally, as the firm reported on its web page, "the needs of our existing clients," coupled with "the recent growth and diversification of the economy in Houston," motivated the opening of an office in the Texas city in 1995. Thirteen attorneys there practiced commercial litigation and corporate finance and acquisitions.

At one point it was expected that King & Spalding would open offices in Germany, particularly to work with Coca-Cola's interests there. By the late 1990s, no such move had been made, but the firm did maintain an extensive international practice. Not only did Atlanta companies such as Coca-Cola use King &

Spalding to deal with their international legal affairs, but the firm's reputation was such that a company from outside the city, telephone service provider Sprint, used King & Spalding to negotiate its joint venture with Deutsche Telekom and France Telecom. King & Spalding was also heavily involved in Latin America, for instance representing the life insurance company Jefferson Pilot in Argentina and Home Depot in Chile. King & Spalding attorney Michael Horten, in China to develop joint venture contacts, said "We've made a particular effort to get to know every mayor" along the Yangtze River Delta between Shanghai and Nanjing.

King & Spalding had survived the tough times in Atlanta law during the mid-1980s, and in the mid-1990s the *Journal and Constitution* was proclaiming "Happy Days Are Here Again for Atlanta's Big Law Firms." In the recession of the early 1990s, three major Atlanta firms—Hansell & Post; Hurt, Richardson; and Trotter, Smith & Jacobs—had shut down. By 1994, King & Spalding was without a doubt the oldest, largest (284 lawyers), and fastest-growing law firm in Atlanta. And with the average cost of a lawyer's services much lower in Atlanta—even at King & Spalding—than in New York City, business was only likely to grow.

Along with its size, the reputation of King & Spalding had grown with the passing of years. Though it had never included Woodrow Wilson among its partners or associates, a number of other prominent figures from the political world had passed through its doors. Among these was Charles Kirbo, a little-known but powerful associate of President Jimmy Carter in the 1970s. In Kirbo's September 3, 1996 obituary, Jack Warner of the *Journal and Constitution* wrote that "for the four years of Jimmy Carter's presidency, Charles Hughes Kirbo may have been the most powerful private citizen in the United States." Other important figures at King & Spalding in the 1990s included Griffin Bell, who had served in Carter's administration; and former Governor George Busbee. On January 3, 1997, the Atlanta paper reported that an even bigger fish would soon be swimming in the King & Spalding pond. Sam Nunn was retiring from the U.S. Senate, where he had wielded enormously power as the head of the Armed Services Committee, and had accepted a partnership at the firm.

Further Reading

Bennett, Tom, "William K. Meadow, 95, Oldest Attorney at King & Spalding," *Atlanta Journal and Constitution*, November 29, 1987, p. E6.

Coleman, Zach, "Atlanta Law Firms Head into International Waters," *Atlanta Business Chronicle*, May 19, 1997.

Curriden, Mark, *Atlanta Journal and Constitution*, January 23, 1994, p. H1.

Garrett, Franklin M., *Atlanta and Environs: A Chronicle of Its People and Events*, Volume II, Athens: University of Georgia Press, 1954.

Georgia Through Two Centuries: Family and Personal History, Volume II, New York: Lewis Historical Publishing Company, 1965.

Salter, Sallye, "King & Spalding Will Move to New Building," *Atlanta Journal and Constitution*, October 2, 1987, p. D1.

Seward, Christopher, "Top Billing: King & Spalding Reigns in State's Legal World," *Atlanta Journal and Constitution*, June 5, 1997, p. E1.

Thompson, Tracy, "Competition Is Changing Tradition at City's Most Prestigious Law Firms," *Atlanta Journal and Constitution*, October 25, 1985, p. A1.

——, "Lawyers Get No Respect, Firm Believes: Jury Seems to Uphold That in Lawsuit Award," *Atlanta Journal and Constitution*, September 10, 1988, p. A1.

Warner, Jack, "Obituaries: Charles H. Kirbo, Lawyer, Carter Ally," *Atlanta Journal and Constitution*, September 3, 1996, p. B6.

Wells, Della Wager, *The First Hundred Years: A Centennial History of King & Spalding*, Atlanta: King & Spalding, 1985.

Whitt, Richard, "Merchants of Debt: Higher Costs in Legal Fees," *Atlanta Journal and Constitution*, September 20, 1992, p. A9.

—Judson Knight

Lamb Weston, Inc.

8701 West Gage Boulevard
Kennewick, Washington 99336
U.S.A.
(509) 735-4651
Fax: (509) 736-0386
Web site: http://www.lambweston.com

Wholly Owned Subsidiary of ConAgra, Inc.
Incorporated: 1932 as F.G. Lamb & Company
Employees: 5,000
Sales: $1.2 billion (1997 est.)
SICs: 2099 Food Preparations, Not Elsewhere Classified;
2053 Frozen Bakery Products Except Bread; 2038
Frozen Specialties, Not Elsewhere Classified

The largest producer of frozen potato products in the world, Lamb Weston, Inc. distributes a wide range of products—in numerous shapes and sizes—throughout Europe, Asia, Africa, Australia, and South and North America. Lamb Weston revolutionized the process of slicing potatoes in the early 1960s and used this innovative advantage to expand steadily throughout the United States and then into overseas markets. During the 1990s, the company's international expansion was rapid, producing prolific annual sales gains and enabling it to herald itself as the largest company of its kind in the world. In the late 1990s, Lamb Weston was supported by sales offices in the United States, Turkey, Holland, India, South Korea, China, and Japan. Its 13 manufacturing facilities were concentrated in the Pacific Northwest and placed strategically in Holland, India, and Turkey.

1930s Origins

Lamb Weston began business as the F.G. Lamb & Company in 1932, when its founder, Frank G. Lamb, started his own fresh fruit shipping and packing enterprise. Ten years later, his business took a decisive turn when he bought a shuttered cooperative plant in Weston, Oregon, and expanded F.G. Lamb & Company's business to include vegetable packing. The Weston plant represented the foundation upon which Lamb Weston rested, but the credit for the company's quiet yet resolute rise in the food processing industry did not go to Frank Lamb, it went his son, F. Gilbert "Gib" Lamb. The younger Lamb, who was 27 years old when the defunct Weston plant was acquired, was responsible for transforming his father's fresh fruit packing business into a market leader in the processed potato industry, an industry that was forever changed by his pioneering contributions. Lamb did not score his innovative coup, however, until he was in his mid-40s. The family business was nearly 30 years old before its identity was firmly established. In the interim, that is, during the period separating the acquisition of the Weston plant and the beginning of the company's rise in the frozen potato market, Lamb Weston appeared to be evolving in different direction. The company made its first distinguishing mark in the business world as a formidable pea processor.

After its 1942 acquisition, the Weston plant was renovated and converted into a pea processing facility. It was this primary asset that Gib Lamb incorporated as Lamb Weston, Inc. in 1950. Lamb's talent in the food processing business demonstrated itself quickly, as the company rose swiftly through the ranks of its industry niche to stand as the king of its market. By the late 1950s, the Weston plant was regarded as the most technologically advanced pea-processing facility in the United States. Lamb Weston ranked as the largest single processor of frozen peas in the world, accounting for ten percent of the total output of processed peas in the United States. Despite the unequivocal success his company was enjoying by this point, Lamb was on the prowl for other business opportunities. Lamb wanted to diversify, and when he did the results would completely overshadow Lamb Weston's dominance as a pea processor.

Industry Innovations in the 1960s

In 1960, Lamb began exploring the opportunities available to his company in potatoes, one of the chief agricultural crops in the Pacific Northwest. He began studying the frozen potato processing business as a way for his company to reap some of the rewards generated by the region's potato wealth and developed a device that would change the way potatoes were processed from that point forward. Lamb created a potato "gun," the Lamb Water Gun Knife, invented and patented by Lamb in 1960. It was the first

Company Perspectives:

Today we cover the world. Lamb Weston products are sold in nearly every corner of the globe and our international distribution network continues to grow. You will find Lamb Weston products served in Europe, Asia, Africa, Australia, South and North America. There are several important reasons for this growth. Firstly, Lamb Weston is committed to value-added innovative and premium products that offer higher satisfaction to the consumer and higher profit margins to our customers. While we offer the full range of commodity frozen potato products, we believe the future lies in aggressive new product development. Secondly, we are good partners with our customers. When you buy from Lamb Weston, you are buying our experience, our superior manufacturing skills, and our marketing support. We have the production capacity and financial strength to fill your orders, and to deliver those premium products in excellent condition, in time. Finally, because research and development is so important to Lamb Weston, we have the facilities to formulate new products quickly for regional markets. The suggestions of chefs, nutritionists and foodservice managers are a rich source of new product ideas. In short, we are flexible, enthusiastic and aggressive.

device to slice french fries in a high velocity water flow, thereby signaling the end of the days when potatoes were processed by hand. Other manufacturers would be quick to follow Lamb's lead once they developed their own devices, but Lamb's proprietary slicing instrument was the first of its kind, giving the company a sizeable head start over all competitors. The next logical move was to actually enter the potato processing business. In 1960, when Lamb held his revolutionary potato-slicing device in hand, Lamb Weston was a pea processing company.

Before the rest of the world could learn of his Water Gun Knife, Lamb ordered the construction of a new frozen potato processing plant. The plant, located in the heart of potato country in American Falls, Idaho, opened in 1961, marking Lamb Weston's debut in the domestic potato market. Armed with a processing device that yielded tremendous labor-saving, and therefore cost-saving, advantages, Lamb Weston moved quickly to establish a pervasive presence in its new industry. The company constructed and acquired as many processing plants as finances permitted, striving to wrest market share from more established competitors with a production process the competition had no answer for. In 1963, a five-person sales force was formed to promote the company's anticipated expansion and a broker network was fleshed out to cover the United States. With the sales support in place to spearhead future growth, major plant acquisitions followed. Lamb Weston acquired a potato processing plant in Quincy, Washington, in 1966 and another potato processing plant in Connell, Washington, two years later. The company also opened its first research center in Portland, Oregon, in 1968, having learned first-hand about the significant advantages to be gained from a serious commitment to the research and development of proprietary slicing and processing systems.

In 1971, Lamb Weston accepted an offer to merge with Honolulu-based Amfac, Inc. and finished construction of a new plant in Weston to produce fruit turnovers for the fast food industry. The following year, the company cut the ribbon for a new state-of-the-art potato processing plant in Hermiston, Oregon, which enabled Lamb Weston to put its proprietary techniques in processing, packaging, and storage developed at its research center to work in the field. As these events were taking place, the burgeoning Lamb Weston began to take its first steps outside the United States, just a decade after the company entered the potato business. Lamb Weston began shipping its potato products to markets in the Pacific Rim, Canada, Mexico, and South America, getting its first taste of overseas demand for processed potato products when it exported its first shipment to Japan in 1973. The company would revisit in earnest its commitment to global expansion twenty years later, but the push into international markets began in the early 1970s. The experience gained during this initial contact proved to be instrumental in the company's future worldwide expansion.

1970s and 1980s: An Industry Giant Takes Shape

When Lamb Weston entered the 1970s, the company was producing roughly 300 million of potato products each year. By the end of the decade, its annual sales volume had eclipsed 800 million pounds of potato products, providing a telling measurement of how much the company grew during the 1970s. Increased production efficiency, the opening of export markets, plant expansions, and plant acquisitions combined to create one of the leading potato processors in the country. The company's plants in Hermiston and Connell were both expanded during the decade. A new plant in Richland, Washington, was acquired in 1978 and a second production plant was constructed near Lamb Weston's existing plant in Quincy, Washington, also in 1978.

The 1980s witnessed the continued growth of Lamb Weston, although the company's physical expansion occurred at a slower rate than the previous decade. A major expansion of the company's original potato processing plant in American Falls, Idaho, was completed in 1986 and the following year a potato processing plant in Boardman, Oregon, was acquired to supply the company's growing export business and its markets in the United States. With the addition of the Boardman facility, Lamb Weston became one of the largest suppliers of frozen potato products in the world, a distinction the company had earned without drawing more than a modicum of attention to itself. The company's steady ascension into the industry's elite, predicated on a quarter century of innovative approaches to processing potatoes, had drawn little notice from those outside the tight circle of the potato-processing world. Lamb Weston was the quiet giant, unknown by name to many of the consumers who ate the company's products principally because Lamb Weston served institutions and restaurants. Its exclusion from the list of household-known brand names, however, did not mean Lamb Weston was an unrecognized leader. The company was highly successful, and one corporate suitor in particular wanted to share in Lamb Weston's success.

ConAgra, Inc., a multi-billion dollar foodservice conglomerate, coveted Lamb Weston's broadly-based strength in the frozen potato industry. Founded in 1919 with four flour mills, ConAgra had grown into diversified behemoth by the late

1980s, involved in an armada of businesses whose scope covered the spectrum of the food chain. ConAgra was involved in everything from seed distribution to the production of frozen food dinners, and in 1988 it added another plume to its portfolio by acquiring the entrenched frozen potato business operated by Lamb Weston. Concurrently, Lamb Weston relocated its corporate headquarters from Tigard, Oregon, to eastern Washington, settling in Kennewick. There, with its new powerful financial ally supporting its future moves, Lamb Weston readied itself to embark on the most ambitious expansion campaign in its history.

International Expansion in the 1990s

With one important exception, the rapid expansion that occurred during the 1990s took place in international markets, as the company extended and solidified its presence across the globe. Unlike its first foray into international markets twenty years earlier, Lamb Weston chose to produce its potato products near the foreign markets it served, rather than exporting products from its U.S. manufacturing facilities concentrated in the Pacific Northwest. Consequently, what ensued as the 1990s began was expansion via acquisition, as Lamb Weston purchased overseas plants and greatly expanded the boundaries of its physical presence. The acquisition spree started in 1991, when Lamb Weston purchased its first European potato processing plant, a facility in Eemshaven, Holland. Next, after acquiring a production plant in Park Rapids, Minnesota to strengthen its eastern United States business, Lamb Weston swiveled its sights to the east and purchased Viking International, a U.S. company with strong Asian export ties. Headquartered in Portland, Oregon, Viking was organized as Lamb Weston Asia, Ltd. and supported by sales offices in Tokyo, Seoul, and Beijing.

In 1994, Lamb Weston acquired another potato processing plant in Holland, purchasing a facility in Kruiningen as a part of a joint venture with one of Europe's major potato traders, Meijer Frozen Foods. Lamb Weston also stepped up its efforts in Latin American markets in 1994 by opening the Lamb Weston Caribbean/Latin America sales office in Boca Raton, Florida, but the biggest development in 1994—and perhaps during the 1990s—was the company's purchase of Universal Frozen Foods and its Inland Valley retail brand. Inland Valley, distributed throughout the United States, comprised an extensive selection of oven-baked and microwaveable potato products, giving Lamb Weston even greater product diversity. Included with the acquisition were two more Pacific Northwest production plants, one in Pasco, Washington and another in Twin Falls, Idaho. With the addition of these two facilities, Lamb Weston officially became the largest processor of frozen potato products in the world.

Having surpassed all rivals, Lamb Weston spent little time enjoying its global dominance. The company continued to expand on the international front as it headed into the mid- and late 1990s. In 1995, Lamb Weston entered a joint venture in Turkey to create Lamb Weston/Dogus, the country's largest frozen potato processor with customers in the eastern Mediterranean region and throughout southeastern Europe. Also in 1995, Lamb Weston acquired the largest combined potato and vegetable processor in India, Tarai Foods, Ltd., which supplied American-style food products for India's burgeoning restaurant market. The company ended the year by opening its International Development Center in Boise, Idaho, to serve as the headquarters for all Lamb Weston's U.S. export activities and overseas plants.

By 1996, the ambitious efforts of the 1990s had turned Lamb Weston into a powerful force underpinned by solid and extensive global coverage in nearly every important worldwide market. The company entered the decade as an annual producer of less than 1.5 billion pounds of potato products. In 1996, that volume reached mammoth heights, having soared to 3.6 billion pounds. Annual sales by this point eclipsed the $1 billion mark, a total generated by the output at the company's 13 production plants, which were clustered in the Pacific Northwest and situated in strategic locations overseas. As the company moved forward into the late 1990s, further international acquisitions were likely, as was the company's global dominance in an industry it had helped to create. Lamb Weston's focus on research and development, coupled with its aggressive expansion into every corner of the world, created a legacy of profitable, strident growth. Lamb Weston officials expected this recipe to deliver the same results in the future.

Principal Subsidiaries

Lamb Weston International; Lamb Weston-Meijer V.O.E. (Netherlands); Lamb Weston Asia, Ltd.; Lamb Weston Tokyo; Lamb Weston Caribbean/Latin America; Lamb Weston/Dogus (Turkey); Lamb Weston/Tarai Foods Ltd. (India)

Further Reading

Lamb Weston, Inc., "A History of Growth," *Employment Opportunities at Lamb Weston*, 1997, p. 2.

"Lamb-Weston Moves into Europe," *Frozen and Chilled Foods*, August 1991, p. 6.

"Lamb Weston Shapes Appeal to UK Market," *Frozen and Chilled Foods*, March 1992, p. 22.

Neurath, Peter, "$125 Million Placement Is Worth Shouting About," *Puget Sound Business Journal*, February 12, 1990, p. 2.

Toops, Diane, "Doin' the Mashed Potato," *Food Processing*, April 1997, p. 36.

"Universal Foods Acquires Columbia Sun," *Nation's Restaurant News*, January 4, 1993, p. 46.

—Jeffrey L. Covell

LeaRonal, Inc.

LeaRonal, Inc.

272 Buffalo Avenue
Freeport, New York 11520
U.S.A.
(516) 868-8800
Fax: (516) 868-8824

Public Company
Incorporated: 1953 as Lea-Ronal, Inc.
Employees: 800
Sales: $210.3 million (1997)
Stock Exchanges: New York
SICs: 2899 Chemicals & Chemical Preparations, Not
  Elsewhere Classified

LeaRonal, Inc. develops, produces, sells, and distributes specialty chemical additives and other products used by the connector, printed circuit board, semiconductor, and metal-finishing industries, both in the United States and abroad. Its electroplating processes, in which a metal in solution is deposited onto another metal object with the use of an electric current, account for the bulk of its sales. The company's product line also includes specialty chemicals used in the fabrication of printed circuit boards and other electronic components.

Lea-Ronal, 1953–78

Lea-Ronal, Inc. was incorporated in New York in 1953 by Barnet D. Ostrow (who started from scratch in a Brooklyn garage just after World War II), Fred I. Nobel, and the Lea Manufacturing Co. of Waterbury, Connecticut. The name was taken from Lea and from Ronal Chemicals, Inc., a firm jointly owned by Ostrow and Nobel. The formation of Lea-Ronal was based on a development for a bright cyanide copper-plating solution, which was subsequently patented. This new process served as a substitute for nickel in the plating industry during a period when this metal was in short supply because of the Korean War.

Competition from other businesses cut prices, so in 1958 Lea-Ronal decided to direct its research and development ef-

forts to develop proprietary gold-plating solutions, since the company felt that the electronics industry was an expanding market requiring proprietary gold electroplating processes. Lea-Ronal further decided to concentrate its major efforts within this field on the semiconductor industry. Gold electroplating over base metals was being used to achieve desirable chemical and metallurgical properties such as resistance to corrosion, solderability, conductivity, and heat emissivity for semiconductors—and also for printed circuit boards and electrical contacts. By 1968, 80 percent of Lea-Ronal's sales were related to gold electroplating, by selling compounds and proprietary processes to customers.

Originally based in Jamaica, a community in New York City's borough of Queens, Lea-Ronal moved its headquarters farther east to Nassau County in 1968, settling into a new 30,000-square-foot plant in Freeport-Hempstead Industrial Park. It also opened a manufacturing, warehouse, and laboratory facility in Los Angeles in 1964. Another facility was located in Buxton, England, where a British subsidiary had been established in 1965. Net sales rose from $3 million in fiscal 1963 (the year ended February 28, 1963) to $16.7 million in fiscal 1967. Net income increased from $124,586 to $455,065 over this period. The company went public in 1967, offering a minority of its shares at $10.50 a share.

Lea-Ronal was buying gold in the form of bars, sheets, scrap, or jewelry, and converting it to potassium gold cyanide salts, which it then sold to its customers. These customers included many of the largest electronics and electrical equipment manufacturers in the world, but also manufacturers of watches, bracelets, cigarette lighters, pens and pencils, and costume jewelry. Lea-Ronal also was developing, producing, and marketing a diversified line of electroplating processes and compounds used in the plating of nickel, copper, zinc, silver, brass, and other metals. It was working on developing cyanide-free processes for these metals so that the waste materials would be nonpoisonous and require none of the expensive cyanide-destruction equipment and treatment otherwise needed to comply with antipollution laws. Lea-Ronal decided to concentrate on zinc, because it constituted the largest volume of plating solutions in use, and it developed the first bright zinc process that was free of cyanide.

By 1973 Lea-Ronal had developed more than 24 metal-plating processes in the past ten years, licensing some of them to foreign developers. One of these processes substituted Aurall 292M for the gold needed for gold plating, thereby cutting customer costs. The company's Tinglo Culmo process also helped reduce gold costs for printed circuit boards, semiconductor manufacturers, and other electronic users. Jewelers and watchmakers also saved money on gold costs with the introduction of the company's Endura Glo series.

A Swiss subsidiary was formed in 1971 and a Chicago office and laboratory opened in 1972. The company formed a joint venture with a Japanese firm in 1970 and one with a French firm in 1972. The latter became a subsidiary in 1974. In 1977 Lea-Ronal acquired a majority stake in a German company and a minority stake in a Dutch company, each acting as distributors. It exchanged its stock in the Dutch company in 1983 to purchase the remaining share of the German company.

Lea-Ronal's sales reached $30.9 million in fiscal 1970, and its net income passed $1 million for the first time. By the end of fiscal 1975 its annual sales had reached $67 million. Of this total, sales of gold to customers who chose to use the company as their purchasing agent accounted for 86 percent, with almost all the remainder coming from sales of electroplating processes. Aside from gold processes, sold to about 375 customers, the company was marketing copper, nickel, silver, brass, zinc, tin, and palladium processes to nearly 700 customers. In 1976 Lea-Ronal announced a new electroplating process for applying zinc without the use of either cyanide or ammonia chemicals, which were also undesirable pollutants. In addition, the company formed a new division to manufacture many of the organic chemicals that it had been purchasing.

Continued Prosperity, 1978–96

The company dropped the hyphen from its name in 1978. Net sales rose from $77.4 million in fiscal 1978 to $114.4 million in 1979 and then shot up to $198.8 million in 1980. Net income rose from $2.9 million to $6.1 million over these years. Gold electroplating (including the value of the gold content) still was accounting for about 85 percent of sales. LeaRonal also was producing about 61 other processes and additives relating to the plating of other metals. Foreign sales now were accounting for more than one-fourth of net income. In 1979 the company began marketing what it believed to be the only palladium-free catalyst system for plating printed circuit boards.

One of LeaRonal's long-standing, but unprofitable, ventures was an attempt to develop processes for the plating of plastics. Research began in 1965 but was stymied by the realization that the company could not overcome pollution problems in the near term. In 1978 it renewed its efforts, seeking sales to the automotive market, which was demanding more plated plastic parts. LeaRonal's Ronabond APT process, announced in 1980, was said to be applicable to a wide range of plastics formerly considered difficult or even impossible to electroplate and to eliminate the generation of pollutants. The process, however, like LeaRonal's prior attempt in plastics, failed to reach the marketplace.

LeaRonal's revenues fluctuated during the 1980s, chiefly because of sharp rises and falls in the price of gold. In fiscal 1981, for example, net sales reached $234.2 million—triple the 1978 level—but fell in fiscal 1986 to only $105 million. Since the company was buying the metal for customers and passing on the cost rather than engaging in speculation, these fluctuations ultimately had little effect on the bottom line. LeaRonal's net income never fell below $6 million or rose much above $8 million for most of the decade, although it reached $11.2 million in 1989. The firm's customers, however, were starting to meet their plating needs with silver, palladium, or tin instead of gold, and components like semiconductors and circuit boards were growing smaller, requiring less of any kind of metal. Barnet Ostrow's son Ronald succeeded his father as chief executive officer in 1989.

LeaRonal was marketing gold electroplating processes to several hundred customers in 1990, with the majority of sales made to the electronics industry and the balance to manufacturers of watches, jewelry, appliances, and automotive components. It also had several silver-plating processes and other processes for palladium and palladium nickel. About 100 nonprecious-metal processes and chemical additives were being distributed to more than 1,000 customers in a wide range of industries, including electronics, electrical equipment, and metal finishing. These related to the plating of nickel, tin, copper, zinc, brass, and other metals. Foreign subsidiaries, which now included one in Southeast Asia, accounted for 42 percent of revenue and 53 percent of operating profit in fiscal 1990.

During fiscal 1992 revenues fell to a five-year low of $129.1 million, in part due to lower gold prices, in part due to lower gold sales. The company remained quite profitable, however, and even in 1992 net income came to $7.9 million. LeaRonal was transforming itself from a domestic company with a limited customer base to an international concern with more than 2,000 customers around the world. By 1993 half of LeaRonal's sales and three-quarters of its operating profits were coming from abroad. Instead of depending on the resale of precious metals, it was increasingly sustained by the more profitable sale of its patented processes and proprietary chemistry. In fiscal 1993, for the first time, revenues from proprietary chemistry outstripped those from precious-metal content.

In 1993 LeaRonal was placing its hopes of future growth primarily on two processes: Conductron DP and Ronstan TP. The first was a way to directly metallize a printed circuit board through holes, a process that did not require formaldehyde or other carcinogens. The second was said to be the first new tin-plating technology offered to the steel industry in more than 40 years, one that required less energy and substituted a biodegradable organic acid for ferrocyanide or carcinogenic phenol vapors.

LeaRonal was offering more than 300 formulations for gold, silver, palladium, nickel, copper, tin, and zinc in 1996. For the printed circuit board industry, it now offered not only plating processes, but also processes for the preparation chemicals, the dry film, and the final protective coatings. Net sales reached a record $211.6 million in fiscal 1996 and net income a record $15.6 million. Although revenues dipped slightly the following year, to $210.3 million, net income rose to $16.5 million. The company had a long-term debt of $3 million and a cash balance of $40 million, which the president called "our security blanket." Directors and officers of LeaRonal owned 29 percent of the common stock, with Nobel holding ten percent and Barnet Ostrow holding nine percent.

LeaRonal in 1997

During fiscal 1997 metal electroplating processes accounted for 52 percent of LeaRonal's sales, precious-metal content for 43 percent, and other products for five percent. Of metal-process sales, precious-metal processes accounted for 17 percent and nonprecious-metal processes for 83 percent. The number of customers for these processes was about 2,500. Precious-metal sales consisted of gold, silver, and palladium as a component of the process. In most of the other processes offered for sale, LeaRonal supplied only the specialized chemical additives needed.

LeaRonal's patented electroplating processes included Palladure (palladium), Pallamet (palladium-nickel), Silverjet (silver), Copper Gleam (copper), SLZ (zinc), SLZ Plus (zinc), Millenium (zinc), Zincal (zinc), Tinglo Culmo (tin), Ronaston TP (tin), Plutin LA (tin-lead), Solderon PC, Solderon SC, and Solderon LG (tin and tin-lead alloy). Royalties from patented processes exceeded $1.9 million in fiscal 1997.

LeaRonal's British and Swiss subsidiaries each had complete laboratory and manufacturing facilities for the manufacture and sale of substantially all of the company's products and processes. Certain of its products also were being manufactured at its other European and Asian facilities. Aside from its four European subsidiaries, LeaRonal had subsidiaries in Hong Kong, Singapore, South Korea, and Taiwan. In the United States, Freeport remained the firm's center of operations, but it also maintained a laboratory and sales office in Addison, Illinois, and a manufacturing facility in Orange, California, with full technical services and sales capability.

Principal Subsidiaries

LeaRonal (UK) plc; LeaRonal AG (Switzerland; 93%); LeaRonal Asia Ltd. (Hong Kong; 80%); LeaRonal France (France; 85%); LeaRonal GmbH (Germany); LeaRonal Korea, Inc. (South Korea; 80%); LeaRonal Pacific Corp.; LeaRonal Singapore Pte, Ltd. (Singapore; 86%); LeaRonal Taiwan (Taiwan; 80%); Lea-Ronal Export Sales, Inc.; Ronal Foreign Sales Corp. (U.S. Virgin Islands).

Further Reading

Berell, D.J., "Gold Business Is a Glittering Success for Lea-Ronal, Inc.," *Investment Dealers' Digest,* May 6, 1968, pp. 28d–28e.
Brammer, Rhonda, "The Right Chemistry," *Barron's,* November 15, 1993, p. 14.
"Lea-Ronal, Inc.," *Wall Street Transcript,* June 18, 1973, p. 33,432.
McConville, Daniel J., "The Midas Touch at LeaRonal," *Chemical Week,* September 4, 1996, p. 56.
"New Specialties Seller," *Chemical Week,* August 11, 1976, p. 21.
"New Ways to Metallize Items—At Less Cost," *Modern Plastics,* December 1980, p. 45.

—Robert Halasz

LEHIGH

Lehigh Portland Cement Company

7660 Imperial Way
Allentown, Pennsylvania 18195
U.S.A.
(610) 366-4600
Fax: (610) 366-4680

Wholly Owned Subsidiary of Heidelberger Zement A.G.
Incorporated: 1897
Employees: 6,000
Sales: $1.2 billion (1997 est.)
SICs: 3241 Cement, Hydraulic; 3271 Concrete Block &
    Brick; 3272 Concrete Products, Except Block &
    Brick; 3273 Ready-Mixed Concrete

Lehigh Portland Cement Company produces cements, concrete and concrete products, lightweight aggregates, and related construction materials and services. After 80 years of independent operation it was purchased by a German company, Heidelberger Zement A.G., in 1977. Heidelberger Zement, in 1995, placed under Lehigh's corporate umbrella the cement and construction materials operations in North America of the Belgian company Cimenteries CBR S.A., also a Heidelberger affiliate. This merger quadrupled Lehigh's revenues and made it the third largest cement producer in North America.

The Early Years, 1897–40

Lehigh Cement was founded in 1897 by six Allentown, Pennsylvania businessmen who invested $250,000 to construct a cement plant in nearby Ormrod. The Lehigh Valley of eastern Pennsylvania was admirably suited for the production of cement and became the center of the nation's cement industry because of its plentiful deposits of limestone containing approximately the correct mixture of minerals—except for gypsum—for grinding and burning directly into cement. In other regions, cement plants had to use a mixture of limestone, clay, sand, and sometimes blast-furnace slag and other materials to obtain the correct chemical composition.

Lehigh Cement established a second facility at West Coplay, followed by another plant in Ormrod. Since the company's cement was being shipped as far west as Kansas City, another plant was built in Mitchell, Indiana in 1902. The following year a third cement plant was constructed in Ormrod, and in 1906 a second, larger plant was built in Mitchell. Lehigh Cement built a plant in Fogelsville, Pennsylvania in 1907 and a Mason City, Iowa, facility—the company's first west of the Mississippi—in 1911. In 1914 the company moved into the Pacific Northwest by purchasing a two-year-old plant in Metaline Falls, Washington. In the same year Lehigh acquired three more cement facilities in New Castle, Pennsylvania. The company bought a mill in Fordwick, Virginia in 1915, an Oglesby, Illinois plant in 1916, and an Iola, Kansas plant in 1917.

Lehigh Cement's first president was Harry J. Trexler, a lumber dealer. Edward M. Young, another of the original founders and the proprietor of a family hardware business, succeeded Trexler as president in 1926. After his death in 1932, his son Joseph S. Young succeeded him as president and chief executive officer. Joseph Young's son William J. Young succeeded his father in these positions in 1964. He remained at the company until 1983, when he retired from his post as chairman of the board.

By 1920 Lehigh Cement was the nation's biggest cement company in terms of number of plants, with annual production of more than 12 million barrels of portland cement. The company moved into the South in 1923 by building one of the region's largest cement plants in Birmingham, Alabama. In 1925 Lehigh purchased four plants from cement companies: in Alsen, New York; Union Bridge, Maryland; and Bath and Sandt's Eddy, Pennsylvania. These acquisitions, and that of a Buffalo, New York facility in 1927 brought the company's empire to 21 plants in ten states. Lehigh Cement had net income of $5.9 million on net sales of $30.5 million in 1926. Business was declining even before the Great Depression, however, for in 1929 the company had net sales of only $19.3 million, and its net income had dropped to $2.7 million.

Cement prices in the United States reached a peak of $2.02 a barrel in 1930. Consumption fell from a high of 72 percent of capacity in 1928 to only 46 percent of capacity in 1931, when prices dropped to $1.15 a barrel. The cement industry as a whole lost $25 million that year. Lehigh Cement, the nation's second largest producer, still made a profit in 1931, but it lost nearly $2 million in 1932 and $592,000 in 1933. Subsequent years were profitable, even though net sales fell as low as $9 million in 1935. Joseph Young later told a reporter, "It was only by throwing eight plants overboard that we were able to ride out the storm of the Depression." The plants abandoned were one of the two in Mitchell, both Ormrod plants, the ones in West Coplay and Bath, and all three New Castle facilities.

Additions and Subtractions, 1940–76

Lehigh Cement's remaining plants had production capacity of 22 million barrels a year in 1940, or more than eight percent of total U.S. productive capacity. That year the company had net income of $2 million on net sales of $16.9 million. After World War II, revenues and profits rose rapidly, and without any growth in the number of plants and an actual drop in productive capacity to 21 million tons, Lehigh Cement had net income in 1950 of $6.6 million on net sales of $44.3 million. During the 1950s the company moved into the Southeast, adding cement plants in Miami and Bunnell, Florida.

Lehigh Cement's profits reached a zenith of $13.1 million in 1956, although sales volume continued, after 1958, to climb from the year's $75.8 million. Cement executives, including Joseph Young, contended that earnings were overstated because the high cost of maintenance was being carried in the capital-investment account rather than being charged to current expenses. These executives claimed that in spite of apparently good earnings, their firms were unable to recapture enough funds through depreciation to pay for replacement plants. Net income of $12.1 million on sales of $100.6 million in 1959 was far higher than Lehigh would again earn, at least as an independent company.

In 1955 Lehigh Cement was engaged in a $15 million project to triple the capacity of its Union Bridge, Maryland plant to three million barrels capacity. By 1960 the company's capacity had passed 31 million barrels. During the 1960s, however, the company chose to shut down rather than modernize some of its antiquated cement plants that dated back as far as the turn of the century. The facility at Sandt's Eddy was closed in 1962 and the one at Oglesby was closed in 1963. The Bunnell plant, which used coquila shells as its raw material, was phased out in 1965 and the Fordwick plant was phased out in 1968. The trend continued into the next decade, with Lehigh ending operations in Birmingham, Iola, and Fogelsville in 1971 and selling its Buffalo plant the same year. During the 1950s and 1960s,

however, the company built terminals throughout the United States because of the need to shift from railroads to trucks for the transportation of its cement.

Only six Lehigh Cement plants still remained—one each in Florida, Indiana, Iowa, Maryland, New York, and Washington. The company spent $9 million to expand its Union Bridge facility, which on completion in 1970 accounted for 30 percent of Lehigh's productive capacity. The company had begun in the mid-1960s, however, to look to other fields for growth. Lehigh purchased four concrete firms—two in Florida, one in Virginia, and one in Kentucky—during 1965 and 1966 and in 1968 it acquired a Florida manufacturer of low-cost bedroom furniture and a Georgia manufacturer of carpets, rugs, and yarns.

Lehigh Cement lost $7.5 million in 1970 because it took a one-time extraordinary loss of $8.9 million to close plants. It sold its 11 Virginia concrete plants to Florida Rock Industries Inc. in 1972, following an order by the Federal Trade Commission directing it to divest itself of the 17 Virginia and Kentucky plants. The company used about $13 million of the proceeds to buy back shares of its own stock at a price well below book value. In 1974 Lehigh Cement completed the FTC-ordered divestiture by selling its six Kentucky concrete plants.

Lehigh Cement's net earnings reached a comfortable $10 million in 1972 and $10.8 million in 1973 but slumped the following two years. The home furnishings sector of the company, never more than marginally a source for profit, became a heavy loser in these years, and the cement and concrete businesses were also hurt by a slump in home building, especially in Florida. In 1976, Lehigh Cement's last year as an independent operation, the company sold the Georgia rug, carpet, and yarn business to its executives. It also closed its Florida cement and aggregate plants and the seven Florida concrete plants, thereby ending operations in the Southeast. These operations had accounted for 26 percent of company sales in 1975 but had lost $3.8 million before taxes and corporate overhead.

Subsidiary of German Company, 1977–97

After receiving $23.4 million in cash for the Florida facilities, Lehigh Cement took an after-tax loss of $1.2 million. It earned $6.1 million on sales of $119.5 million in 1976, its last full year of independent operation. Portland-Zementwerke Heidelberg A.G., a unit of the German building-materials company Heidelberger Zement A.G., purchased Lehigh Cement in 1977 for $85 million in cash. This was later described as a "rock-bottom price." Lehigh was not considered an attractive acquisition because several of its kilns were more than 50 years old and small by industry standards.

Through Heidelberger Zement, Lehigh Cement in 1980 acquired the Universal Atlas Cement division of U.S. Steel Corp. The sale price was said to be substantially more than $100 million. Universal Atlas, whose origins went back to 1889, had annual sales estimated at between $120 million and $150 million at the time of purchase. The combined capacity of Lehigh and Universal Atlas represented seven percent of the U.S. market, second only to the share held by Lone Star Industries Inc.

Lehigh Cement sold Universal Atlas's Hannibal, Missouri cement plant in 1981 to a newly formed, foreign-owned concern, Continental Cement Co. The sale was required under a FTC consent order that settled charges that Lehigh's purchase of Universal Atlas had violated federal antitrust law. Lehigh was also required to sell three distribution terminals and was barred for ten years from buying cement plants or terminals in five Midwestern states without prior FTC approval.

In 1982 Lehigh Cement purchased Alpha Portland Industries Inc.'s plant in Cementon, New York, for about $11.6 million. This plant was closed in 1993. Also in 1982, Lehigh acquired Medusa Cement Corp.'s plant in York, Pennsylvania. At the end of 1985 Lehigh had cement plants in Leeds, Alabama; Mitchell, Indiana; Mason City, Iowa; Independence, Kansas; Union Bridge, Maryland; Cementon, New York; York, Pennsylvania; Waco, Texas; and Metaline Falls, Washington. It also had a plant for lightweight aggregates in Woodsboro, Maryland. The Independence plant was disposed of soon after. The Metaline Falls facility was sold in 1989 to Lafarge Corp., a French-owned firm. Lehigh and Centex Corp. founded a joint venture in 1986 to make specialty cement products at the Waco plant.

In 1991 Lehigh Cement acquired Houston-based Koy Industries, Inc. and Gulf Coast Stabilized Materials Co., Inc. C.O.D., Koy Industries' primary operating subsidiary, had seven ready-mix plant locations with 50 mixer trucks. Gulf Coast was producing and selling cement-treated base material. Also that year, Lehigh Cement left the quarters in downtown Allentown that had been serving as its corporate offices since its founding. In its new location the firm installed a boardroom table made from its flagship special product, Lehigh White Cement, made in York. Composed of this material and marble aggregate, the 26-foot-long, 5,500-pound table top was finely ground after casting to produce an attractive, highly polished, durable, terrazzo surface.

By 1995 Lehigh had fallen to eighth place in U.S. cement production. The addition of the Cimenteries CBR enterprise, however, greatly broadened the company's scope. CBR had acquired Genstar's Corp. cement and construction materials operations on the West Coast and in western Canada in 1986 for $327.5 million. Its facilities included cement plants in Redding and Tehachapi, California, and Edmonton, Alberta. Lehigh also was beginning a $200 million modernization and expansion of its Union Bridge plant in 1998.

Lehigh Cement's furniture division in Marianna, Florida was of minor importance to the company, but in 1991 it was increasing its plant capacity by 30 percent with the acquisition of two buildings on more than 13 acres adjacent to its corporate headquarters. The division said its entry into the occasional table business in April 1991 had been more successful than originally anticipated, and that its August shipments had set a new monthly record. Lehigh Furniture, which maintained showrooms in High Point, North Carolina and Tupelo, Mississippi, had estimated sales of $40 million in 1995 but was said to be losing money when it was sold the following year (and filed for bankruptcy protection in 1997). The buyer was P.A. Inds., a holding company for several industrial manufacturing concerns.

Further Reading

"A New Giant in Cement," *Business Week*, March 3, 1980, p. 32.

Carroll, Brian, "Lehigh Buyer Aims for More," *Furniture Today*, March 18, 1996, pp. 1, 18.

"Concrete Gets Top Approval at Lehigh Boardroom," *Concrete Products*, September 1993, pp. 12–13.

Dickson, Tim, and Robert Gibbens, "Belgian Group in $327m US Deal," *Financial Times*, July 31, 1986, p. 30.

"FTC Approves Sales of a Plant by Lehigh Portland Cement Co.," *Wall Street Journal*, November 16, 1981, p. 46.

"German Cement Firm Submits Offer To Acquire Lehigh Portland," *Pit and Quarry*, October 1977, p. 17.

Hadley, Earl J., *The Magic Powder: History of the Universal Atlas Cement Company and the Cement Industry*, New York: G.P. Putnam's, 1945.

Herod, Sandy, "Union Bridge Operation Now Lehigh's Largest," *Pit and Quarry*, July 1971, pp. 111–116, 126.

"Its Sales 46% of Mill Capacity, Cement Industry Seeks Way Out," *Business Week*, April 13, 1932, pp. 16, 18.

"Lehigh," *Pit and Quarry*, January 1971, p. 84.

"Lehigh Acquires 2 Buildings in Move To Increase Occasional Table Capacity," *Furniture Today*, September 23, 1991, p. 2.

"Lehigh Acquisition," *Pit and Quarry*, August 1991, p. 21.

The Lehigh Centennial, Allentown: Lehigh Portland Cement Company, 1997.

Simon, Bernard, "Europeans Take a Grip on North American Cement," *Financial Times*, November 11, 1986, p. 31.

Smee, Doyle, "Portland Cement Industry, Riding the Construction Boom, Warily Embarks on Huge Expansion Program," *Wall Street Journal*, February 24, 1955, p. 26.

"U.S. Steel Agrees To Sell Cement Unit in Spite of Challenge," *Wall Street Journal*, September 9, 1980, p. 16.

—Robert Halasz

LensCrafters Inc.

8650 Governor's Hill
Cincinnati, Ohio 45249-1391
U.S.A.
(513) 583-6000
Fax: (513) 583-6635
Web site: http://www.lenscrafters.com

Wholly Owned Subsidiary of Luxottica SpA
Founded: 1983
Employees: 14,000
Sales: $903.5 million (1996)
SICs: 5995 Optical Goods Stores

A subsidiary of Italy's Luxottica SpA, U.S.-based Lens-Crafters Inc. is the world's leading retailer of eyewear. Celebrating its 15th anniversary in 1998, the company was a pioneer of the ''superoptical'' segment. Its phenomenal growth under U.S. Shoe in the 1980s culminated in Luxottica's 1995 acquisition. With over 700 outlets across the United States, Canada, and Puerto Rico, the chain boasts a seven percent share of the domestic retail eyewear market. The company was expected to cross the $1 billion sales mark in 1997, a tripling of revenues from 1987's $305 million.

Founded 1983

LensCrafters was founded in 1983 by Dean Butler, a 38-year-old who had previously worked at Procter & Gamble. A knowledgeable marketer, Butler had managed the Ivory liquid, Cheer laundry detergent, and Folger's instant coffee brands for the venerable Cincinnati consumer goods company.

At that time, the eyewear industry was on the cusp of radical change, a shift spurred by two vital legal decisions passed down in the late 1970s. The Federal Trade Commission freed patient choice by compelling vision professionals to give patients their prescriptions. A separate legal decision allowing advertising in this segment set the stage for the ''superoptical'' movement.

Butler was not the first to perceive this opportunity. New Jersey-based Eyelab gets credit for pioneering the concept, which featured mall-based stores, extended hours, onsite lens-grinding labs, thousands of frames, and rapid turnaround. Butler left P&G and launched his first 7,500-square-foot Precision LensCrafters (later simply LensCrafters) store just across the Ohio River from Cincinnati in Florence, Kentucky, in 1983. He was soon joined by another P&G colleague, Daniel Hogues.

Butler's version of the superoptical concept promised ''glasses in about an hour.'' And since his stores were located in malls, customers could while away that hour shopping with other retailers. Guarantees helped instill confidence in customers who were accustomed to dealing with doctors. The ''no risk sales guarantee'' gave clients a full refund on glasses returned within 30 days of purchase. LensCrafters also offered to match competitors' prices as well as free lifetime maintenance. In a 1986 interview with *Forbes* magazine, Butler noted that ''Marketing eyewear isn't much different from selling coffee. Retailing is what you do when customers walk into the store. But with a new idea, marketing comes first. Marketing is how you inspire customers to come to your door.''

Notwithstanding naysayers who were convinced that the concept would fail, LensCrafters' first-year sales totaled $2 million. With support from a cadre of investors, the partners expanded to three outlets by early 1984, when their success drew the attention of a powerful backer: United States Shoe Corp.

Acquired by U.S. Shoe in 1984

Also based in Cincinnati, U.S. Shoe was a billion-dollar company. Over the course of its more than 100 years in business, U.S. Shoe had diversified from its core footwear into retail apparel. Chains included Casual Corner and Petite Sophisticate. U.S. Shoe used its strong cash flow to fund a rapid expansion of LensCrafters.

With this backing, LensCrafters came not only to dominate its own industry, but also to take precedence over its own parent company's footwear and apparel businesses. From 1984 to

Company Perspectives:

We Exist To: create exceptional value in the lives of our customers, associates and shareholders. We will do this by enthusiastically satisfying every customer all the time and creating an environment where our Associates can fulfill their personal dreams. We Believe In: nurturing individuals; building on people's strengths; accepting and learning from mistakes; focusing on winning, not individual scoring; pushing breakthrough ideas; thinking and acting like a long-term owner; demanding highest possible quality; constantly, measurably improving; acting with uncompromising integrity; having fun.

1987, LensCrafters' sales multiplied from $13.6 million or one percent of U.S. Shoe's annual revenues to 241 units and $305 million in sales. In 1986 alone, the company opened new stores at the rate of almost two per week. In 1987 Bannus B. Hudson, an 18-year alumnus of Procter & Gamble who had come to work for LensCrafters in 1985, took the helm. (Founder Dean Butler had by this time resigned from the business. Following the expiration of a non-compete contract, he opened a rival chain dubbed Lens Lab.) By the end of 1989 Hudson had increased the number of stores to over 350 and boosted sales to $532 million or over one-fifth of U.S. Shoe's total revenues. Perhaps more importantly, LensCrafters' $30 million net income constituted nearly 40 percent of its parent's operating earnings by that time. That year U.S. Shoe tried to divest its lagging footwear business, but could not find any takers.

LensCrafters and other eyewear retailers were not content to merely wait for market growth in the form of aging baby boomers with deteriorating eyesight. Instead, they promoted the concept of eyeglasses as fashionable accessories in the same category as shoes or jewelry. This concept not only encouraged sales of designer eyeglasses, but also ownership of multiple pairs of glasses. As Butler told *Forbes* in 1986, "Right now, most people buy a single pair of glasses every two or three years. But what if we can sell eyewear as fashion, a tortoiseshell pair for work and some wire rims for play? We could double per capita sales of glasses."

LensCrafters also focused strongly on maintaining a positive corporate culture. This ideal was embodied in a list of nine Core Values enumerated in 1986. They included: nurturing individuals; building on people's strengths; accepting and learning from mistakes; focusing on winning, not individual scoring; pushing breakthrough ideas; thinking and acting like a long-term owner; demanding highest possible quality; constantly, measurably improving; and acting with uncompromising integrity. A tenth value, having fun, was added in 1990.

New Decade, New Leadership, New Strategies

By 1990, LensCrafters had grown to become U.S. Shoe's "crown jewel." That spring, Bannus Hudson succeeded Philip Barach as CEO of the parent company, and 30-year-old

David M. Browne advanced to president and chief executive officer of LensCrafters. Browne, a five-year veteran of Procter & Gamble, joined LensCrafters in 1986 as the vice-president of the recently acquired Optica chain of upscale eyewear shops. He inherited a company that, while still successful, was faced with a number of challenges. The new CEO had hoped to launch 100 new stores in 1990, but was forced to scale back that aggressive growth strategy when LensCrafters suffered its first-ever sales decline. The combination of the Gulf War and recession eroded consumer confidence while heavy competition squeezed prices and profits. Instead of pursuing growth, Browne was forced to restructure. He held job cuts to less than 100 of the company's 10,000 positions by relocating hundreds of employees. In spite of its difficulties, LensCrafters surpassed Pearle Vision Centers to become America's largest chain of eyeglass retailers in 1992, with an estimated $660 million or 4.5 percent of marketwide sales volume.

The company's new strategy targeted the bargain-minded customer via a joint venture with Kmart Corporation. In 1993, LensCrafters launched Sight & Save leased departments within existing Kmart stores. This new retail venture allowed LensCrafters to enter the discount segment without devaluing its namesake stores' focus on value and convenience.

LensCrafters' charitable activities started in 1988 as an extension of its optical services. In cooperation with Lions Clubs International, the company recycles used eyeglasses through its "Give the Gift of Sight" programs. Among other activities, this charity fashioned over three million pairs of eyeglasses for disadvantaged people—especially children—in the U.S. and abroad from 1988 through 1996. In 1993, the company launched its Hometown Day project, wherein employees of each of the company's stores donated their time and expertise to needy recipients in their own communities. That same year CEO Browne committed the company to providing free eyecare to one million people by LensCrafters' 20th anniversary in 2003. It was almost halfway there by the end of 1997. The company's charitable activities earned it a Volunteer Action Award from President Bill Clinton in 1994.

International expansion proved a mixed bag for LensCrafters. The company became the first U.S. Shoe affiliate to establish an overseas presence in 1988 with the launch of nine Canadian superstores. In 1993, it became Canada's largest optical retailer with the acquisition of the 22-store Eye Masters Ltd. chain. The company fared well on its home continent. By the end of 1994, it had nearly five dozen Canadian locations. A foray across the Atlantic Ocean did not go as well. In 1990, LensCrafters opened stores in the United Kingdom. But by the fall of 1993, the company was ready to close all its U.K. stores, including locations under the LensCrafters and Sight & Save names.

LensCrafters also grew through domestic acquisitions during this period. It purchased Hourglass Inc. in 1990 and acquired Tuckerman Optical, a midwestern chain, in 1994. LensCrafters spent an estimated $45 million to $50 million on 12-year-old Opti-World Inc., a 59-store Atlanta-based chain, in March 1995.

Acquired by Luxottica in 1995

Italian eyewear manufacturer Luxottica SpA brought a $1.4 billion hostile takeover bid for U.S. Shoe in 1995. Owned by the Del Vecchio clan, Luxottica was not interested in U.S. Shoe's footwear or apparel, it was looking to round out its vertically integrated eyewear company to include retailing. Prior to its own acquisition, U.S. Shoe sold its footwear interests to Nine West Group Inc. for $600 million. Unable to find a buyer for U.S. Shoe's 1,300 money-losing apparel retailers, Luxottica transferred this division to a separate Del Vecchio interest.

The LensCrafters acquisition was a high-stakes gamble for Luxottica. The Italian company risked wholesale defection of its core customers—independent opticians and competing eyewear chains. Although many in these two groups did drop the Italian firm from their roster of suppliers, Luxottica was able to increase its sell-through at LensCrafters stores from five percent of frame revenues in 1995 to 43 percent by the end of 1996. In fact, the addition of LensCrafters more than doubled Luxottica's annual revenues from L 812.7 billion in 1994 to L 1.8 trillion in 1995.

In its first year under Luxottica, LensCrafters added 70 stores and 1,000 employees. But in its zeal to focus on designer and high-end eyewear, Luxottica pushed LensCrafters to shutter its Sight & Save chain in 1996 and invest the proceeds in store refurbishings. LensCrafters was also testing new retail concepts, including Specttica in-store areas and SunCrafters sunglass kiosks. These outlets specialized in prescription and non-prescription sunglasses in airports and other high-traffic venues.

Despite the spinoff of both the U.K. and the Sight & Save operations in 1995 and 1996, LensCrafters' sales continued to grow rapidly under Luxottica. Revenues advanced just over five percent from 1995 to 1996 to total $903.5 million, and the subsidiary was expected to contribute $1 billion to its parent company's top line in 1997.

On the occasion of LensCrafters' tenth anniversary in 1993, CEO Dave Browne said, "Looking to the future, I'm sure of only one thing—the inevitability of constant change and our readiness to face it. It will be harder to stay on top than it was to get there. We will have to recreate ourselves continuously in order to maintain our leadership position in an ever-changing category." That statement continued to hold true as the company faced the turn of the 21st century.

Further Reading

Bolton, Douglas, "LensCrafters Founder to Compete," *Cincinnati Post,* February 21, 1990, pp. 6B, 8B.

Comiteau, Jennifer, and Jim Kirk, "Looking for 20/20 Vision," *ADWEEK Eastern Edition,* March 13, 1995, pp. 1–2.

Davenport, Carol, "Bannus B. Hudson, 43," *Fortune,* June 19, 1989, p. 162.

Deutsch, Claudia H., "The Big Battle over Eyewear," *New York Times,* November 26, 1989, p. F4.

Diamond, Michael, "A Decade Later, LensCrafters Sales Give Skeptics an Eyeful," *Cincinnati Business Courier,* May 3, 1993, p. 6.

Fasig, Lisa Biank, "LensCrafters' Vision," *Cincinnati Enquirer,* August 13, 1997, pp. I1, I16.

Feldman, Diane, "Companies Aim to Please," *Management Review,* May 1989, pp. 8–9.

Kranz, Cindy, "Corporate Caring," *Cincinnati Enquirer,* April 25, 1997, pp. D1, D9.

McKenna, Joseph F., "Dave Browne's Style: Analysis, But Not Paralysis," *Industry Week,* September 3, 1990, pp. 19–20.

Merwin, John, "New, Improved Eyewear," *Forbes,* October 6, 1986, pp. 152–53.

Olson, Thomas, "Overseas Lures LensCrafters," *Cincinnati Business Courier,"* September 3, 1990, pp. 1–2.

Reese, Shelly, "LensCrafters Leader in Eyeglass Retail Race," *Cincinnati Enquirer,* March 21, 1993, pp. F1, F10.

Schwartz, Judith D., "LensCrafters Takes the High Road," *Adweek's Marketing Week,* April 30, 1990, pp. 26–27.

Seckler, Valerie, "Luxottica Talks with U.S. Shoe Have Hit Snag," *WWD,* March 31, 1995, p. 11.

Sullivan, Ruth, "Luxottica Focuses on Dominating U.S. Market," *The European,* April 21, 1995, p. 16.

Teitelbaum, Richard S., "David M. Browne, 31," *Fortune,* July 2, 1990, p. 102.

Wessling, Jack, "Hudson Given U.S. Shoe Tiller," *Footwear News,* February 5, 1990, pp. 4–5.

Wilson, Marianne, "LensCrafters Polishes Image with Style," *Chain Store Age Executive with Shopping Center Age,* October 1996, pp. 144–45.

Zemke, Ron, and Dick Schaaf, *The Service Edge: 101 Companies That Profit from Customer Care,* New York: New American Library, 1989.

—April D. Gasbarre

L'Entreprise Jean Lefebvre

11, Boulevard Jean-Mermoz
92202 Neuilly-sur-Seine
France
(33) 01 45 41 77 64
Fax: (33) 01 46 41 77 50

Public Subsidiary of GTM-Entrepose
Incorporated: 1934 as Compagnie Industrielle des Fillers
Employees: 15,000
Sales: FFr 9.89 billion (1996)
Stock Exchanges: Paris
SICs: 1611 Highway and Street Construction; 1422 Crushed & Broken Limestone; 1429 Crushed and Broken Stone, Not Elsewhere Classified; 1622 Bridge, Tunnel and Elevated Highway

France's l'Entreprise Jean Lefebvre is engaged in highway construction, services, and maintenance, and related activities including the construction of airport runways, parking lots, industrial terrain development, sports fields and tracks, and urban planning activities. It also engages in civil engineering projects such as bridge-building, industrial installations, and public art placement. The company produces and sells materials for highway construction and maintenance, and operates a number of quarries and treatment, recycling, and dumping facilities. A leader in its home market—where it has played an important role in developing much of the country's Autoroute network—Jean Lefebvre has long served the infrastructure needs of the former French colonies in Africa and the Caribbean. Since 1988, the company has been expanding its activities into other parts of the world, with a focus on North America, Spain, and Eastern Europe. Foreign sales represented approximately one-third of the company's nearly FFr 10 billion in 1996 revenue.

Highway construction and maintenance remains the company's premier activity, accounting for nearly 90 percent of its revenues. Jean Lefebvre participates in the development and construction of France's principal motorways, including the national Autoroute network, as well as departmental and city-specific roadway projects, and related activities including the construction, maintenance, and upgrading of airport runways and racing and bicycle tracks. Major projects in the mid-1990s included the four-lane (two lanes by two directions) Autoroute extension between Nantes and Cholet, the northwest Rennes-Limoges 'rocade' (bypass or beltway), and the Lille Autoroute deviation.

Yet, with much of France's highway infrastructure in place—and amid increasing resistance to new highway construction—more than 60 percent of Jean Lefebvre's highway-related activity is related to its highway maintenance and resurfacing services. Working with more than 50 surfacing products and processes, the company responds not only to the revitalization of the existing roadway infrastructure, but also to the amelioration of the country's airport and other surfaces, such as dockyards and bicycle lanes. Jean Lefebvre also works within the cities, towns, and villages of its markets, restoring and maintaining public streets, roads, terraces, and parking lots. The company undertakes projects such as tramway and metro modernization, construction of reservoir basins, and other special technical projects. Its markets include such cities as Paris, Bordeaux, Cholet, and Rodez, and a 15-year contract with the city of Vichy. In the private sector, the company builds, maintains, and repairs industrial terrain and parking facilities for a variety of clients, including McDonald's. Important projects include the construction of the race track for the Renault technical center at Aubevoye, and the construction of the parking lots and heliport for the Futuroscope complex at Poitiers.

Supplying the company's construction and maintenance activities is its materials production arm, which produces more than 14 million tons per year of granulates, making Jean Lefebvre the premier producer of road-grade materials products in France. The company's investments in research and development enable the company to introduce new and specialized roadway materials and surfacing and construction equipment. Jean Lefebvre has also taken an active role in developing and implementing recycling, waste disposal, and other processes to reduce the impact of highway and other construction projects on the environment.

Beyond France, Jean Lefebvre is represented in North America by its Canadian subsidiary Construction DJL Inc., and its U.S. subsidiary, Hubbard Construction Co.. Hubbard is based in Florida and is that state's leading roadway construction and maintenance firm. The company is active in the former French colonies and other French-speaking countries including Martinique, New Caledonia, the Ivory Coast, Guinea, Senegal, Gabon, and the Polynesian islands. In Western Europe, Jean Lefebvre is represented in Spain and the United Kingdom, since its 1996 acquisition of Ringway Ltd. Jean Lefebvre also operates subsidiaries in the Czech Republic and in Lithuania, with an eye toward further expansion in Eastern Europe.

Jean Lefebvre's growth by acquisition has created an organization of more than 100 individual subsidiaries and sub-subsidiaries. In France, the company's activities are conducted through more than 240 agencies, centers, and subsidiaries, grouped within nine departments under the central direction of the company's Neuilly-sur-Seine headquarters. In turn, Jean Lefebvre's principal shareholder and parent is GTM-Entrepose, a subsidiary of France's Lyonnaise des Eaux.

Founded in 1934

The automobile's emergence in the late 19th and early 20th centuries—especially the advances in automotive technology made in the years during and following the First World War—found a particularly enthusiastic reception in France, which boasted many of the automobile industry's early pioneers and champions. The new mode of transportation provided increased mobility not only to the population, but also for the transport of goods. The automobile would spark vast changes in the traditionally rural French society, not the least of which was the opening of new opportunities for individual entrepreneurs. An immediate result of the growth of the automobile in France was the creation of a demand for new and stronger roads and road surfaces—and for the development of a national highway network.

The Lefebvre family would play a prominent role in building France's highway system. The family, under Charles Lefebvre, began its involvement in roadway construction and transportation as early as the 1920s, with the formation of Salviam Brun, created in 1926, and other companies, each specialized in activities involved in roadwork. Jean Lefebvre joined the family's growing roadway empire, founding the Compagnie Industrielle des Fillers in 1934.

By the 1940s, the Lefebvre family of companies began to merge into a centralized organization. In 1942, the Compagnie Industrielle des Fillers entered the Charles Lefebvre group of companies, adopting the name L'Entreprise Jean Lefebvre, and becoming the family's principal vehicle on the road to becoming a dominant player in the country's highway and roads sector. Specializing in the construction of new roads, Jean Lefebvre would play a prominent role in the creation of France's Autoroute infrastructure, a network of limited-access highways linking all of the countries major cities and rivaling Germany's Autobahn and the United States' federal interstate system. Among the company's major participatory efforts were the construction of the important Paris links of the A14 and the A5, and other principal Autoroute legs across the country, including the A28 from Calais, the A16 from Boulogne. The

adaptation of France's cities—which, like cities across Europe, had been built long before the development of the internal combustion engine—to the increasing penetration of the automobile provided the company with additional opportunities, including the construction of intercity highways, the resurfacing of streets, and the creation of bypass highways, called 'rocades,' similar to the Beltway around Washington, D.C.

In 1949, Jean Lefebvre looked beyond France's borders for the first time, creating subsidiaries in many of the DOM-TOM countries—that is, France's former and soon-to-become former colonies and other French-speaking countries in Africa and Polynesia. Back in France, Jean Lefebvre was also steadily expanding the scope of its activities related to road work and construction, adding vertical integration capacity with the quarrying and production of road foundation and surfacing materials. While much of the companies growth had been made internally, the company had also begun a program of external acquisitions, enhancing both its presence in the French and DOM-TOM markets, while expanding the range of its services. One such addition was the 1954 acquisition of Reveto, formed in 1927, which became one of the company's principal subsidiaries and helped establish the company's reputation as a premier developer and producer of road surfacing materials.

Entrance into the 1960s with a Public Offering

The company's listing on the Paris stock exchange in 1957 provided the capital to step up growth. Going public would also win the company powerful backing, in the form of major shareholder investments by Mobil Oil France in 1970 and by Grands Travaux de Marseille (later GTM-Entrepose) in 1973. At the beginning of the 1980s, Jean Lefebvre restructured its operations, absorbing its principal subsidiaries Salviam-Brun and Reveto. By the mid-1980s, with more than 11,000 employees, the company's sales had grown to FFr 4.3 billion per year.

The maturation of the Autoroute network and the growing saturation of the country's roadway system in general, led Jean Lefebvre to move toward deepening its presence in the service side of the road works industry. The company acquired a stake in Cofiroute, one of the concessionaires of the Autoroute system, involved in the general operation, including toll-taking and rest stop exploitation, and the maintenance of specified sectors in the network. In 1987, Jean Lefebvre increased its participation in Cofiroute, acquiring one-third of that company. As the Autoroute network neared its completion—and as popular opposition began to develop against further expansion of the network—Jean Lefebvre continued to shift its emphasis toward maintenance activities, while continuing to reinforce its leading role in highway, road, and other public and private surfacing projects. At the same time, Jean Lefebvre began preparing to increase its international presence. Adopting a policy of implantation by acquisition, the company moved first to the U.S. market, acquiring the Florida-based Hubbard Construction Co. in 1988, which became that state's largest privately owned highway and road surface construction company. Closer to home, the company moved into Spain, with the addition of Probisa in 1989. The following year, with an increase in GTM-Entrepose's shareholder position, Jean Lefebvre became a subsidiary of that Lyonnaise des Eaux subsidiary, while maintaining its operational independence and public status on the Paris exchange.

The 1990s and Beyond

With more than FFr 6 billion in annual sales at the start of the 1990s, Jean Lefebvre's international expansion continued. In 1990, the company created a new subsidiary, Compagnie Antillaise de Routes et Autoroutes et d'Importation de Bitume (CARAIB) in Martinique. The following year, the company moved in Canada, acquiring a controlling interest in Constructions Desourdy Inc. (which became Construction DJL Inc. in 1995), based in Quebec. Jean Lefebvre also began eyeing the newly opened Eastern European market; in 1992, the company acquired Stavby Silnic A Zeleznic in what was shortly to become the Czech Republic. This move was followed in 1994 by the acquisition of Lithuania's AB Saskelis and SELB-Pacifique Ltd., based in Vanuatu. In the wake of the recession and the French economic crisis of the mid-1990s, the company was also furthering its implantation in France, acquiring the Brittany region quarries of Baud et Guilligomarch'h, the quarries of Spada, in the French Alps. In the Czech Republic, the company expanded its presence with the creation of the joint-venture company, MBS, with Lafarge Coppée.

By 1995, the company's revenues had passed FFr 9 billion, and by 1996, annual sales approached FFr 10 billion. By then, nearly one-third of the company's annual sales were produced by its foreign operations. That share would be strengthened still further in 1996, with Jean Lefebvre's acquisition of Ringway Ltd., which, with annual revenues of FFr 580 million, would establish the company in the United Kingdom market for the first time. With the prospects of new road construction becoming dimmer in France, Jean Lefebvre continued to eye further international expansion to maintain its future growth.

Principal Subsidiaries

France: Calcaires Régionaux; Entreprise Jacques Coupet; Durance Granulats; EJL Alsace Franche-Comté; EJL Côte d'Azur; EJL Meuse-Pianezzi; EJL Normandie; Flan; Carrières Leroux Philippe; Carrières Kléber; Société Niçoise d'Enrobage; Ets Ozil et Compagnie; Société Paridu-Letourner; Roehrig; Société Rosa et Fils; Cie Industrielle des Fillers et Chaux; Oscar Savreux; Entreprise de Travaux Publics et Bâtiment Edmond; Vermot S.A.; Compagnie Antillaise de Routes et Autoroutes et d'Importation de Bitume (C.A.R.A.I.B) (Martinique); Construction DJL Inc. (Canada); Hubbard Construction Co. (US); Jean Lefebvre Pacifique (New Caledonia); Jean Lefebvre Polynésie (Polynesia); MBS (50%) (Czech Republic); Probisa (Spain); AB Sauskelis (Lithuania); SELB Pacific Ltd. (Vanuatu); Socoba-EDTPL (Gabon); Stavby Silnic A Zeleznic (Czech Republic).

—M.L. Cohen

Margarete Steiff GmbH

P.O. Box 1560
D-89530 Giengen/Brenz
Germany
(49) 7322-131-452
Fax: (49) 7322-131-476
Web site: http://www.steiff.de/

Private Company
Incorporated: 1893
Employees: 1,000
Sales: DM 100 million (US$56 million) (1997 est.)
SICs: 3942 Dolls & Stuffed Toys; 3944 Games, Toys &
   Children's Vehicles

Margarete Steiff GmbH is the largest manufacturer of stuffed toys in Germany and one of the most recognized brands of toys in the world. Best known for its pricey and highly collectible teddy bears, in 1997 the company celebrated the 150th anniversary of the birth of its founder and namesake. Though the company's toys are sold around the world, all are handmade in Germany, and about 66 percent of revenues are generated domestically. According to Bernhard M. Rösner, president of the toymaker at that time, the family-owned company churns out about 15 million stuffed toys every year, including more than a quarter of a million teddy bears. Rösner noted the Steiff mystique in a 1997 *Forbes* article: "What you have in your hand when you look at a piece of Steiff is a true masterpiece. Our animals show their souls."

The secondary market for early examples of the company's toys dominated media coverage of Steiff in the 1980s and 1990s, but a truly unique and often overlooked feature of the company is the circumstance surrounding its creation. Established in the 19th century, an era when women had few legal rights and commanded little social standing, the toymaker was created and run by a handicapped woman. Though Margarete Steiff's parents feared that her siblings were destined to lives of hard work to support their sister, it was the wheelchair-bound Margarete who founded a family dynasty that has endured for more than a century.

19th Century Origins

Appolonia Margarete Steiff was born in the small southern German town of Giengen in 1847. Third-born of her family, she was crippled with polio as a toddler and confined to a wheelchair her entire life. Despite her infirmities, young Gretle's parents encouraged her to attend grade school. She began taking sewing classes with her two older sisters in the 1850s and learned to operate a sewing machine backwards so that she could use her stronger arm to work the device. Steiff soon became so proficient a seamstress that she and her older sister, Pauline, began a home-based business making and selling women's clothing. Margarete began to offer felt clothing and outerwear under her own name in 1879 at the age of 32.

Steiff's toymaking career began almost by accident that year, when the entrepreneur made some elephant-shaped pincushions as gifts for family and friends. The tiny animals became so popular that Steiff began to make a few to be kept on hand for retail sale. According to the 1991 book *Steiff: Sensational Teddy Bears, Animals & Dolls* by Rolf Pistorius, Gretle's "pincushions" were being used more often as toys; they were more durable than the pretty, but delicate, dolls of the period, with their porcelain heads and hands, and they were cuddlier than wooden and sheet metal toys. An elephant with an s-shaped trunk would become the company's first trademark. Steiff added riding and pull toys in 1886 and was manufacturing nearly 5,500 units annually by the end of the decade. At the urging of her brother Fritz, the toymaker moved into a purpose-built factory in 1889.

By 1893, when the company was officially registered as Margarete Steiff GmbH, toy sales had far outstripped dressmaking and Steiff had published its first illustrated catalogue. The line of stuffed animals, which by this time included lions, dogs, donkeys, and dolls, generated DM 28,000, versus DM 12,000 from apparel. The founder's brother, Fritz, joined the company as a sales representative that same year. Appearances at important trade shows helped broaden the company's market reach. Buoyed in part by exports, sales had more than doubled to DM 90,000 by 1897 when total employment numbered 40.

Fritz's children began to enter their aunt's business around the turn of the century. According to a June 1988 article in

Company Perspectives:

Only the best is good enough for our children.—Margarete Steiff, company founder.

Antiques & Collecting magazine, two of Gretle's nieces helped supervise cottage workers. But it was Fritz's six sons who would assume leadership positions in the business. The eldest, Richard, joined the firm in the 1890s. He introduced Steiff products to the internationally renowned Leipzig toy fair in 1894 and designed a zoo-full of animals after the turn of the century. Richard's brother Franz, a textiles specialist, joined the company as an administrator in 1898. Paul became a designer with the family firm in 1899, Otto came on board as an international distributor and advertising specialist around 1900, and Hugo took charge of quality control in 1906. Thus a comprehensive management team was in place by the time Franz died in 1908 and Margarete passed in 1909. Hugo and Otto were elected co-managing directors, while Richard and Paul carried on their work on the creative side of the company. A sixth sibling, Ernst Steiff, finally joined the firm in 1927.

Margarete Steiff had established a reputation as a generous employer, and her nephews carried on that tradition after her passing. Among other benefits, the company offered low-rent apartments and low-interest mortgages to its staff, which by 1909 numbered nearly 3,000.

Teddy Bear Rage Spurs Rapid Growth After the Turn of the 20th Century

Though the company had begun making stuffed bears as early as 1892, the "teddy" bears for which the toymaker would become world-famous did not come into play until after the turn of the 20th century. Among the zoo animals Richard Steiff designed in 1902 was a bear with jointed arms and legs. The company sold 3,000 bears to Hermann Berg, a representative of New York's Geo. Borgfelt & Co., in the spring of 1903, but the Steiffs were otherwise disappointed in the demand. Little did the family know that U.S. political cartoonist Clifford Berryman had by that time touched off a craze that would help launch the company's biggest selling toy of all time.

The incident arose in 1902, when U.S. President Theodore Roosevelt went on a four-day bear hunt in Mississippi. The president's hosts had captured a bear cub and tied it to a tree to ensure that their esteemed guest would get a kill on his outing. Roosevelt surprised his hosts when he refused to shoot the ursine youngster, and Berryman immortalized "Teddy's Bear" in a cartoon for the *Washington Post*. Whenever Berryman featured the president in a drawing, there too was the little bear. American toymakers, most notably the Ideal Company, rushed to churn out teddy bear toys, but the Steiff bears had already earned the distinction of being first. Ironically, not one of the original (and unmarked) 3,000 Steiff bears brought to the United States is known to exist.

When Richard Steiff traveled to the 1904 World's Fair in St. Louis, he discovered a bear craze. Steiff's model won a Grand Prize at the exposition, while Richard and his aunt received gold medals. Unit sales of the bears tripled to 12,000 by the end of the year and increased to almost one million worldwide by 1907. The original poseable bear had internal rods to facilitate movement of the arms, legs, and head, but a cuddlier and lighter version was soon developed that incorporated discs in the limbs and a ball joint for the head. To distinguish its products from the many knockoffs that soon appeared, the Steiffs patented the "Knopf-im-Ohr" or "Button-in-Ear" trademark. From 1904 on, all of the company's products featured an embossed button in the left ear (if the animal had an ear, that is). The first buttons were blank and for a couple of years the corporate elephant appeared on the marque, but after 1906 most buttons featured the Steiff name. (Reproductions of early models often duplicate the particular trademark original to the toy.)

Though bears continued to form the cornerstone of Steiff's success, the company diversified its toy offerings throughout the 1900s. Internal noisemakers—including growlers for bears, purrers for cats, and squeakers for a variety of animals—added to the toys' appeal. Dolls that said "mama" and caricature dolls of different professions were also added, as well as puppet animals and clothed animals. Kites and pull toys also joined the product line. In 1910 the company launched the large-scale, mechanized window display pieces that it would continue to produce throughout the 20th century.

A Toymaker Turns to War

Wartime proved particularly difficult for the toymaking Steiffs. Richard, Paul, and Hugo were drafted into the service in World War I. During and for a period following the conflict, Steiff suffered shortages of raw materials and was compelled to make substitutions for its usually high-quality materials. Cheaper fabrics and paperlike substances were used to make tiny uniformed soldiers and other toys. A British embargo that began in 1914 only exacerbated the difficult situation. By 1916 all of Germany's borders were closed. Steiff's workers were kept occupied with the production of military materiel including gas masks, canteen covers, hand grenade handles, and other items. The German economy continued to suffer in the immediate postwar years, during which time Steiff concentrated on manufacturing wooden toy chests and children's furniture.

In the 1920s Steiff introduced scooters, toy cars, and lifelike toddler dolls named after their designer, Albert Schlopsnies. A gifted artist, Schlopsnies also designed elaborate window displays, advertising pieces, and toys for Steiff. The company continued to expand its menagerie of stuffed or plush toys to include rabbits, ducks, and pigs, but the most popular items of the decade proved to be dogs and cats. As the 1920s waned Steiff once again fell on hard times, for not only was it hard for Depression-era parents to justify expensive toy purchases, but growing anti-German sentiment abroad devastated Steiff's export markets. The company reduced production and staffing and, as it had during early economic downturns, made materials substitutions. One high point of the 1930s was Steiff's German license to manufacture Walt Disney's Mickey and Minnie Mouse toys.

During World War II many of the company's employees were drafted into the service. The Hitler regime removed both

Hugo and Ernst Steiff from their posts and installed cronies. Richard, who was by this time living in the United States but still played an important role in the family business, died in 1939. The company ran out of mohair in 1943 and made hats through 1944, but materials and manpower grew so scarce that the factory was forced to stop making toys in 1943. Longtime managing director Otto Steiff died in 1944. The Steiff archive of toys was one of the few survivors of the war. It would prove invaluable in the decades to come.

It was 1946 before Steiff resumed production with a ten-item line of artificial-silk stuffed toys. During the Allied occupation of Germany after World War II, toys had a special "U.S. Zone tag" in the arm seam.

The development of a hedgehog dubbed "Mecki" in 1950 launched a midcentury toy craze. The rubber-faced toy, his wife Micki, and their progeny Macki and Mucki, would become the mascots for the widely read German magazine *HÖR ZU*. Teddy bears evolved rapidly to meet changing tastes during the 1950s and 1960s. Shorter limbs, rounder faces, softer bodies, and modern (yet still high-quality) materials soon identified these postwar creations. Over the course of the ensuing decades Steiff continued to grow and expand its menagerie of plush animals to include species familiar and exotic. Raccoons, manatees, life-sized St. Bernards, lobsters, spiders, lions, tigers, goats, bats, and literally thousands of other beasts joined the line. The company even produced sports mascot toys representing the Army mule, Navy goat, Princeton tiger, Duke devil, and Yale bulldog. By the late 1990s Steiff had offered almost 15,000 different stuffed animals.

Teddy Craze Revisited in 1980s and 1990s

Steiff believes that Americans have collected its bears since the 1930s, but antique teddy bears did not really begin to bring headline-grabbing prices at auction until the mid-1980s. The secondary market proved somewhat idiosyncratic, for while other antiques and collectibles were judged largely on age and condition—preferably mint—a teddy bear's value was determined in part by less tangible factors like "personality." In fact, signs of wear were often considered badges of love and sometimes boosted the price brought at auction.

In 1994 Yoshi Sekiguchi, president of Japanese toymaker Sun Arrow Co., established the record-holding auction price for a teddy bear: DM 270,000 (US$170,000) for a 1904 model. Named "Teddy Girl," the toy had a particularly unique history. It was produced in 1904 or 1905 and given to Robert Henderson. Henderson would go on to create the British chapter of Good Bears of the World, a philanthropy that donated teddies to hospitalized children. Teddy Girl was his first and only teddy bear. As of 1997 Steiff bears had brought the ten highest prices at auction in the secondary teddy bear market.

The company capitalized on the craze by promoting its products as much as collectors items and "investments" as children's toys. Steiff's home page on the World Wide Web wryly noted, "The high prices that Steiff teddy bears continue to fetch at auction must surely generate extra interest in new Steiff teddies and other animals in toy and gift retail outlets." Managing Director Rösner estimated that more than 30 percent

of the company's goods were purchased by adults for adults. Children certainly were not buying them with their allowance money. Prices for new Steiff pieces ranged from $25 for a synthetic ladybug to $5,000 for a signature eight-foot giraffe and $6,000 for a five-foot tiger. Furthermore, the company created a Collectors Club for dues-paying teddy fans and through the production of limited edition reproductions of classic models. By 1997 the Club boasted more than 40,000 members. Beginning in 1980 reproductions were made from original drawings and used original materials, including mohair and excelsior wood shavings.

The company took care not to oversaturate the market, however, and thereby risk reducing its cachet among collectors. For example, some lines produced in honor of the sesquicentennial of Margarete Steiff's birth in 1997 were limited to 1,847—a number determined by the year the founder was born. In fact, the company reduced its line of products from 900 different models in the mid-1990s to about 650 by 1998.

With domestic sales lagging, Steiff established a U.S. subsidiary in 1992. The company had established its first U.S. showroom in New York in 1903. Geo. Borgfelt acted as the company's exclusive agent in the United States throughout the early 20th century. In the 1950s and 1960s the manufacturer was represented by two companies, Reeves International and Loucap Company. In the mid-1960s Reeves earned the exclusive distribution rights. After establishing its own American operation, Steiff upped its advertising budget and began running promotions in magazines like *Traditional Home* and *Gourmet* with the tagline, "It's not just stuff—it's Steiff." Sales via televised shopping networks like QVC generated $1 million in 1997. By that time an estimated ten percent of total sales were generated in the United States.

The craze spread to Japan in 1993, when a picture of a young member of the country's royal family holding a Steiff bear was broadcast on television. That free publicity combined with the news of the new record bear price set by Sekiguchi boosted Steiff sales in Japan from virtually nothing in 1993 to US$2.4 million by 1997. The company established its own stores in Tokyo, Taipei, and Singapore and planned to penetrate mainland China in 1998.

Steiff's worldwide revenues were expected to exceed DM 100 million (US$56 million) for the first time in 1997. With its long heritage, dedication to quality, and literally fanatical following, the company seemed assured of setting new sales records for many years to come.

Principal Subsidiaries

Steiff USA L.P.

Further Reading

Ebeling, Ashlea, "Hot Investment Tip: Teddy Bears," *Forbes,* December 29, 1997, p. 62.
Hockenberry, Dee, "Steiff: The Premier Bear," *Antiques & Collecting,* February 1992, pp. 38–39.
——, "Teddy Bears," *Antiques & Collecting,* October 1996, pp. 42–44.

Jailer, Mildred, "Dolls by Steiff," *Antiques & Collecting,* June 1988, pp. 32–33.

Leccese, Donna, "Plush Still Has the Right Stuff," *Playthings,* May 1996, pp. 24–29.

Macgillivray, Donald, "It's a Picnic as Teddy Beats a Bear Market," *Sunday Times,* December 7, 1997, n.p.

Margarete Steiff GmbH, "Margarete Steiff—The Bear Facts," www.steiff.de/english/history.htm.

Miller, Cyndee, "Bliss in a Niche: Toymakers Find Success by Breaking with Tradition," *Marketing News,* March 31, 1997, pp. 1, 21.

Pistorius, Rolf, *Steiff: Sensational Teddy Bears, Animals & Dolls,* Cumberland, Maryland: Hobby House Press, 1991.

"Premium-Priced Plush Toy Maker Plays Up to Retailers," *BRAND-WEEK,* February 8, 1993, n.p.

Schmid, John, "Who's King of Teddy Bears?," *International Herald Tribune,* December 23, 1997, p. 2.

—April D. Gasbarre

Mazda Motor Corporation

3-1
Fucho-cho Shinichi
Aki-gun
Hiroshima 735
Japan
(082) 282-1111
Fax: (082) 287-5237
Web site: http://www.mazda.com

Public Company
Incorporated: 1920 as Toyo Cork Kogyo Company
Employees: 26,000
Sales: ¥1.84 trillion (1996)
Stock Exchanges: Tokyo Osaka Nagoya
SICs: 3711 Motor Vehicles and Car Bodies

Mazda Motor Corporation is one of Japan's largest manufacturers of automobiles. As a leader in the small car market, Mazda chose not to follow the example of its chief competitors Honda, Toyota, and Nissan in marketing larger luxury automobiles; rather, the company has achieved its greatest sales from smaller sports cars, particularly a model known in the United States as the Miata. Despite the commercial success of the Miata, however, the company experienced disappointing sales elsewhere in its product line in the early 1990s, a fact that some critics attributed to dull, uninspired product designs. Moreover, an uncertain Asian economy in the late 1990s presented challenges for the Japanese automaker.

Early History

Mazda was organized by Jugiro Matsuda in 1920 as the Toyo Cork Kogyo, or East Sea Cork Manufacturing Company. The small enterprise, located in Hiroshima in southern Japan, was initially involved in the manufacture of cork products. In the mid-1920s, however, it expanded its product line to include several machined products. Reflecting this diversification, Matsuda dropped the word Cork from its name in 1927, and in 1929 the company began production of machine tools. Matsuda be-

lieved that the enterprise could only remain successful if it had a truly unique product. To this end, Toyo Kogyo began design work on an unusual three-wheeled truck that proved commercially successful after its introduction in 1931.

The company was also an early supplier of products to a family of closely-linked firms operating under the Sumitomo industrial conglomerate, with whom Toyo Kogyo maintained a close relationship. In 1935 the company began turning out rock drills and gauge blocks, which were of particular interest to Sumitomo, then one of Japan's largest mining concerns. The company supplied Sumitomo—and other companies involved in the exploitation of resources in Taiwan, Korea, and later Manchuria—with machine tools.

After the seizure of Japanese government by right-wing militarists in the mid-1930s, Toyo Kogyo was drawn into military production. The company produced a variety of products for the Japanese Army, including automotive parts and machinery. The company's management was placed under government authority after the United States declared war on Japan in 1941. Although an important and capable supplier, Toyo Kogyo was not considered a target for strategic bombing. Its operations remained intact until the last days of the war, although they were somewhat limited by the increasing lack of access to raw materials.

Recovery after World War II

On August 9, 1945 the entire city of Hiroshima was destroyed by an American atomic bomb. Toyo Kogyo was Hiroshima's largest employer, and while the factory was located far enough from the city center to avoid serious damage, many of Toyo Kogyo's employees were not. Soldiers who had worked for Toyo Kogyo before the war returned to Hiroshima skeptical as to whether the city and its businesses could be rebuilt. Nevertheless, by December 1945 Toyo Kogyo was back in business, again turning out the three-wheeled trucks that were the core of its business. With a large commercial operation back in business, and a thriving local economy, Hiroshima was quickly rebuilt. Many workers felt a personal debt to Toyo Kogyo for its role in reviving the war-torn city.

During this time, Jugiro Matsuda retired, designating his son, Tsuneji, as his successor. Tsuneji Matsuda proved to be an extremely capable manager, exemplifying many of the qualities that would come to define the company as a whole: patience, diligence, and dedication to quality and efficiency. Early in his tenure, Tsuneji Matsuda became interested in the manufacture of automobiles, which he saw as essential to modern life in Japan. Indeed, with personal incomes increasing in Japan, automobile production had the potential to generate tremendous profit and lift the company to even greater heights.

In 1954, Toyo Kogyo established a technological agreement with Acme Resin that enabled the company to begin using a new shell molding method. After several years of development, Toyo Kogyo established plans for its first mass-produced automobile, the two-door "Mazda" R360 coupe. Matsuda reportedly chose the car's name for its association with Auda Mazda, the ancient Japanese god of light, as well as for its similarity to the name Matsuda. The R360 made Toyo Kogyo a competitor in the growing consumer automobile market. However, while the company had introduced a viable product, the Mazda lacked one thing: it was not unique.

Production of the Wankel Engine in the 1960s

Matsuda had long known of a virtually abandoned engine technology developed in Germany by the inventor Felix Wankel. Wankel's pistonless engine worked on a revolutionary principle in which a single triangular rotor circulated around a large combustion chamber with a gear at its axis. The rotor, moving orbitally around the gear, compressed air and fuel on one side, where a spark plug ignited the mixture. This drove the rotor around the axial gear, expelling exhaust fumes while setting up the next face of the rotor for another combustion. As the rotor wound its way around the combustion chamber, the gear at its axis was forced to spin. This gear was attached to a clutch and transmission, and from there to a drive shaft. The Wankel engine offered more than mere novelty; by eliminating the in-out-in-out motion of pistons, the Wankel would operate more smoothly and with better performance than a conventional engine.

While successful in a laboratory, the Wankel engine was overlooked by engine makers because no one believed that it could be accurately machined in mass production. Matsuda, however, had great faith in his company's machining techniques, and his engineers assured him that such an engine could be built on a massive scale. Matsuda reached an agreement with NSU/Wankel, the German firm that held a patent for the Wankel Engine, and in 1961 he won an exclusive agreement to develop the engine. Design work commenced, but it took several years to develop a suitable model.

In the meantime, Toyo Kogyo introduced a four-door automobile, the Carol 600, in 1962, and the following year the company's one millionth vehicle rolled off its assembly line. In 1965, Toyo Kogyo produced another new model, the Mazda 800/1000, and completed work on a proving ground at Miyoshi. Also that year, the company established a diesel engine technology agreement with Perkins Services. Branching into the market for light duty trucks, Toyo Kogyo introduced the Mazda Proceed B-series compact pickup truck.

In 1966 the company completed construction of a new passenger car plant at Hiroshima. The following year, this plant began manufacturing the Mazda Cosmo Sports 110S automobile, the first Toyo Kogyo vehicle to be powered by a Wankel rotary engine. This model placed Toyo Kogyo in a truly unique position in the market. The rotary-powered engine gave the company an exclusive product that was smooth riding, quiet, and fast. Nothing produced by Toyo Kogyo's competitors, industry giants Nissan and Toyota, could match it.

Expanding the Product Line and Refining the Wankel Engine

Other introductions to the company's automobile line during this time included the Mazda 1000/1200; the rotary-powered R100 Mazda Familia Coupe; the RX 2 Capella; the RX 3 Savanna; and the RX-4 Luce. In 1972, Toyo Kogyo completed manufacture of its five millionth vehicle, nearly one million of which had been exported. As worldwide sales increased, Toyo Kogyo set up sales organizations in the United States, Canada, Belgium, West Germany, Australia, and Malaysia.

In 1972 Henry Ford flew to Hiroshima to negotiate a license that would allow the Ford Motor Company to begin building rotary engines. Sure that Toyo Kogyo was onto something unique and profitable, however, Matsuda flatly refused to share the Wankel technology. Subsequently, Matsuda launched a bold worldwide marketing campaign in which the rotary engine was touted as the answer to high fuel prices. Consumers showed strong interest in the Mazda product line. To finance an expansion of production capacity, Toyo Kogyo made a huge public equity offering.

The OPEC oil embargo sent a shockwave through the world economy in 1973. With petroleum prices skyrocketing, consumer demand for energy efficient automobiles increased dramatically. The Mazda's highly efficient rotary engine seemed the perfect alternative to conventional piston-engined automobiles.

However, emissions from the rotary engine exceeded clean air standards in California, the company's largest export market. Adjustments made to clean up the engine came at the expense of fuel economy, which fell to ten miles per gallon. Furthermore, the rotary model was prone to breakdown. Production continued while Toyo Kogyo technicians launched an emergency re-engineering of the Wankel design.

By 1974, amid increasing pressure from the OPEC embargo, Toyo Kogyo managed to stretch the Mazda's mileage rating to 16 miles per gallon, and then 20. But by this time, Honda, Ford, General Motors and Curtiss-Wright had begun development of stratified charge engines that promised greater efficiency than conventional and rotary engines. Moreover, Nissan and Toyota began an all-out war for market leadership in Japan, squeezing out smaller competitors such as Toyo Kogyo and Suzuki.

As consumer interest in the rotary waned, Toyo Kogyo began searching for ways to keep its factories operating nearer capacity. Matsuda negotiated a deal with Ford in which Toyo Kogyo would manufacture Ford's Festiva model at its facilities. Strapped for cash, Toyo Kogyo finally agreed to license its rotary technology, to Suzuki, which used the engine for a new motorcycle.

When the oil embargo was lifted, oil prices and consumer interest in fuel-efficient engines declined rapidly. Improvements in the rotary design were finally perfected, giving Toyo Kogyo the efficient, environmentally friendly engine it needed—about two years too late. While U.S. fuel economy regulations kept Toyo Kogyo in the American market, the company had lost two years in fixing the rotary engine, during which time Honda, Ford, and GM had developed their own improved engines, leaving Toyo Kogyo in the middle of a crowded pack.

With nothing other than the rotary engine to distinguish its product line, Toyo Kogyo was forced to quickly develop new models and concentrate on product quality as a competitive factor. The Mazda Familia and Capella 626 were introduced in 1977, followed by the Savanna RX-7 in 1978. By this time Toyo Kogyo had turned out more than ten million vehicles, one million of which were rotary-powered.

Amidst the company's efforts to recover from the debacles of the 1970s, Tsuneji Matsuda retired, leaving his son Kohei Matsuda in charge. The younger Matsuda initially made great progress in shoring up the company's balance sheet. However, in the opinion of the Sumitomo interests, which owned most of Toyo Kogyo's shares and bankrolled its earlier failures, the turnaround wasn't good enough. Sumitomo Bank officers felt that Kohei Matsuda was not adequately preparing the company for the future, and they disagreed strongly with his plans for restructuring the company, which included a wider product line and greater autonomy from Sumitomo management. Eventually, Matsuda was forced to resign his presidency to Yoshiki Yamasaki, a director favored by Sumitomo. The abdication formally ended the Matsuda dynasty at Toyo Kogyo.

The company enjoyed a jump in sales in 1979, when the Iranian Revolution caused a brief oil crisis. Also helping boost sales was the fact that Toyo Kogyo and other Japanese manufacturers had become known in the United States for the high quality of their products; American cars, by contrast, had become known as poorly designed, carelessly built, and overpriced.

Growing Affiliation with Ford in the 1980s

In 1979 Ford Motor Company began negotiations to acquire a large stake in Toyo Kogyo, hoping to merge it with its own Japanese subsidiary, Ford Industries. The $135 million deal, completed in November, left Ford with a 24.5 percent share of Toyo Kogyo. The merger paved the way for several new joint ventures between Ford and Toyo Kogyo, in which the Japanese company built small cars and trucks under the Ford nameplate and distributed Ford products in Japan.

In 1980, shedding the last of its failures with the rotary engine, Toyo Kogyo settled a class action suit charging design flaws with early models. Also that year, the Mazda FWD Familia was named car of the year in Japan. Unable to match Nissan and Toyota's large sales staffs, Toyo Kogyo established a string of showrooms across Japan under the name Autorama. Also that year, as it exported its five millionth vehicle, the company set up sales organizations in the United States and Europe. In 1982, Toyo Kogyo established another production plant at Hofu, and in 1983 turned out its 15 millionth vehicle. The following year, Toyo Kogyo formally changed its name to Mazda Motors, reflecting the tremendous popularity of its main product line.

Mazda introduced several new automobiles in 1985, 1986, and 1987, including the new versions of the Mazda RX-7 and 626. By 1987 the company had produced 20 million vehicles. Mazda also entered into several joint ventures, including one with Ford and Matsushita for the production of air conditioning systems. Under a second partnership, Mazda manufactured microcars for Suzuki, and under a third, it imported Citroén cars to Japan.

Mazda Motors continued to be led by a committee of Sumitomo bankers, who received input from Ford and Kia Motors, which acquired an eight percent interest in the company in 1983. In 1987, however, Norimasa Furuta, a former official of the Ministry of International Trade and Industry, assumed the presidency of the company.

Under Furuta, Mazda sharpened its focus, developing several new vehicles for specific markets. The Persona and Proceed were developed specifically for the Japanese market, joining the company's mainstay, the 323 Sedan. The MPV minivan, initially intended for sale only in the United States, was later introduced in Japan. Of the company's new vehicles, the MX-5 Miata was undoubtedly the most successful. A small sports car reminiscent of the MGB and Triumph Spitfire, the Miata was marketed in the United States, where it found an appreciative market particularly among young, affluent males. In designing the Miata, Mazda engineers borrowed liberally from the British Lotus and Elan, which they admitted disassembling for reference. Miata sales were brisk and did much to revive the reputation of Mazda in the United States.

While Nissan, Toyota, and Honda created luxury car divisions to compete with American Buicks, Lincolns, and Cadillacs, Mazda continued to specialize in smaller cars and trucks. With Ford as its largest shareholder, Mazda found its marketing niche operating informally as a small car subsidiary of Ford. Mazda established an American production facility in the Detroit suburb of Flat Rock, Michigan, employing American union labor. The company also established a massive sales and research organization in the United States, employing thousands of Americans.

Nevertheless, 80 percent of the vehicles Mazda sold in foreign markets were produced in Japan, saddling the company with extra transportation costs and subjecting it to foreign import restrictions, particularly in Europe. In addition, Mazda maintained five separate dealerships in Japan for Mazda, Ford, and Citroén.

Yoshihiro Wada succeeded Furuta as president of Mazda in 1990. Furuta was given a ceremonial position on the board, joining chairman Kenichi Yamamoto, who had headed Toyo Kogyo's rotary development during the 1960s. As it entered the 1990s, Mazda occupied a unique niche in the market, producing a relatively narrow line of midsize cars and small trucks.

Falling Production in the 1990s

The Miata's successful introduction in 1989 led Mazda to introduce five new vehicles in the United States, including the 626, in the hopes of becoming a full-line car maker. With at least three-quarters of its parts manufactured in the United States, the 626 was the first Japanese vehicle to be classified as a U.S. car under federal law. Despite these advances, Mazda's U.S. market share remained low, at between 2.2 percent and 2.6 percent from 1988 to 1993. In 1992 Mazda sold a 50 percent interest in its Flat Rock, Michigan, facility to Ford. The next year, the company laid off 25 percent of its U.S. headquarters work force, bringing Mazda's America headquarters staff to 400.

The company was not faring any better domestically. Between 1990 and 1996 Mazda's market share had dropped from 7.6 percent to 4.1 percent. Actual vehicles made and sold had declined also, from a peak of 1.4 million manufactured and 600,000 sold in Japan to 800,000 manufactured and 400,000 sold in 1996. Such a decline meant massive overcapacity in Mazda factories. Still, Mazda refused to combat the shrinkage by laying off employees; instead it used several piecemeal approaches that were only somewhat effective in cutting costs. First, it stopped replacing retirees to reduce head count, then it decreased bonuses and stopped production at its Hofu and Hiroshima factories for a few days each month. According to *The Economist* in 1996, Mazda had lost its unique edge, which it had hoped to recover with the Miata: "Most of Mazda's output is dull, fairly mainstream and fairly expensive. There is a market for boring, reliable cars, but customers tend to prefer those produced by bigger names, such as Toyota. Mazda's one hope of outsmarting bigger car makers is to be nimbler than they are, guessing trends ahead of time."

Sumitomo Bank had its own idea of how to bolster the company. In 1996, it again exerted its power over Mazda by setting up a cash infusion and, in effect, a takeover by Ford. By putting up $481 million in cash, Ford brought its investment to 33.4 percent of the company, the legal line in Japan for a controlling interest. Soon thereafter, Henry D. G. Wallace, a former Ford executive, became president of Mazda Motor Corp., the first non-Japanese to head a Japanese corporation.

For approximately 20 percent below the market price for Mazda shares, Ford vastly increased its access to Japanese and other southeast Asian markets. It also hoped to integrate Mazda into its global reorganization, Ford 2000, intending to use Mazda's small-car and engineering expertise to benefit other Ford operations and, at the same time, to create economies of scale for Mazda. However, Ford's small-car operations in Europe threatened to make Mazda production redundant.

Mazda made some headway in 1997. Sales of its new Demio model proved strong in Japan, and operating profits rose to ¥7.1 billion (US$56 million) in the first half of the year, compared to a ¥12.7 billion operating loss for the same period in 1996. At the end of 1997, Wallace retired from the presidency and was replaced by another former Ford executive, James Miller.

Still, economic turmoil in Southeast Asia in 1997 and 1998 threatened the tenuous turnaround at Mazda. The company had been expanding its operations in southeast Asia in the mid-1990s, hoping to reduce the negative effect of the rising yen on its car prices. In 1993 Mazda had opened another production company in the Philippines, and two years later it began a joint venture with Ford called the AutoAlliance Co. Established in Thailand, the venture aimed to begin production of pickup trucks in 1998. However, plummeting demand in the region and unstable currencies added to Mazda's struggles in the late 1990s.

Principal Subsidiaries

Mazda Motor Manufacturing (USA) Corp.; Mazda Motors (Deutschland) GmbH.; Mazda Canada, Inc.; Eunos, Inc.; Autozam, Inc.; Mazda Australia Pty. Ltd.; Mazda (North America), Inc.; Mazda Chuhan Co., Ltd.; Kurashiki Kako Company, Ltd.; Mazda Credit Corp.; Mazda Logistic Service Company, Ltd.; Toyo Advanced Technologies Co., Ltd.; Mazda Motor of America, Inc.

Further Reading

"Family Operation Ends in Toyo Kogyo Shuffle," *Automotive News,* January 30, 1978, pp. 15–16.
"A Ford Acquisition," *Business Week,* July 23, 1979, p. 72.
Horton, Cleveland, "Mazda's Drive for Full-Line Image Stalls as Automaker Retrenches," *Advertising Age,* August 30, 1993, p. 2.
"Japan's Underworked Marvel," *The Economist,* July 13, 1996, pp. 66–67.
"Kenichi Yamamoto: Leading by Courageous Example," *Automotive Industries,* February 1986, pp. 46–49.
"Mazda Motor Corporation," *Diamond's Japan Business Directory 1992,* pp. 852–53.
"Mazda Motor Names an Ex-Ford Executive as Its Next President," *The Wall Street Journal,* November 14, 1997, p. B2.
"Mazda Ponders Its Route through a Bumpy Future," *Wall Street Journal,* September 8, 1993, p. B4.
"Mazda's Bold New Global Strategy," *Fortune,* December 17, 1990, pp. 109–11.
"The Rotary Turnabout," *Forbes,* March 1, 1975, p. 46.
"They Too," *The Economist,* March 16, 1991, p. 70.
"Toyo Kogyo Agrees to Court Settlement on Mazda Complaints," *Wall Street Journal,* February 25, 1980, p. 18.
"When I Was a Lad," *The Economist,* December 23, 1989, p. 70.
Updike, Edith Hill, and Keith Naughton, "Ford Has a Long Haul at Mazda," *Business Week,* October 7, 1996, pp. 108–14.
Zino, Ken, "Economies of Sale," *Road & Track,* July 1996, p. 73.

—John Simley
—updated by Susan Windisch Brown

MCCLATCHY

McClatchy Newspapers, Inc.

2100 Q Street
Sacramento, California 95816
U.S.A.
(916) 321-1846
Fax: (916) 321-1996
Web site: http://www.mcclatchy.com

Public Company
Incorporated: 1930
Employees: 7,590
Sales: $641.9 million (1997)
Stock Exchanges: New York Midwest Pacific
SICs: 2711 Newspapers: Publishing, or Publishing &
      Printing; 7375 Information Retrieval Services

McClatchy Newspapers, Inc. is America's eighth largest newspaper group in terms of daily circulation. Headquartered in Sacramento, the company's roster of newspapers includes ten dailies in California, Washington, Alaska, and the Carolinas, each of which dominates its market. The company's largest dailies are its founding paper, the *Sacramento Bee,* and the Minneapolis *Star-Tribune,* the acquisition of which was completed in the first quarter of 1998. McClatchy has numerous Pulitzer Prizes to its credit. It also owns more than a dozen non-daily papers, notably the *Senior Spectrum* and *Senior World* weeklies. Its Nando.net is one of the most widely read newspaper sites on the Internet. Other interests include an online legislation service and the Newspaper Network. Though its stock is publicly traded, McClatchy continued to be controlled by the founding and namesake family through the late 1990s. James McClatchy, great-grandson of the founder, continued to serve as companywide publisher in the late 1990s.

Mid-19th Century Foundations

The group's first and for many years only paper was the *Sacramento Bee,* founded in 1857 by James McClatchy. An Irish immigrant, McClatchy had served as a correspondent with Horace Greeley's *New York Tribune* during the early 19th century before heading west in 1849 to try his hand at gold mining. It was not long, however, before he reconsidered his first career and took a job with Sacramento's first newspaper, the *Placer Times.* In 1857, he was among the founders of the *Sacramento Bee* and became the paper's editor within its first year of operation. Over the course of his quarter-century at the helm, McClatchy used the *Bee* as a forum to support the causes of environmentalism and abolitionism, among other issues.

At his death in 1883, the patriarch willed joint ownership of the paper to his two sons. Charles Kenny (C. K.) became editor, while Valentine Stuart assumed the role of business manager. Throughout his more than 50 years at the helm, C. K. carried on his father's liberal-leaning causes, including environmentalism (editorials supported urban beautification through tree-planting, for example), steadfast support of First Amendment rights, and trust-busting. C. K. obtained exclusive ownership of the paper in 1923 and began grooming his son, Carlos, as his successor. Having graduated from Columbia University, Carlos established the family firm's two other "Bees" in the 1920s, founding the *Fresno Bee* in 1922 and acquiring the *Modesto Bee* (formerly the *Modesto News-Herald*) five years later. But when Carlos died in 1933, C. K. turned to his youngest daughter, Eleanor, to assume the mantle of leadership.

Diversification into Radio, TV, Cable in Mid-20th Century

Studying at Columbia University to be a playwright, Eleanor was living in New York in 1936 when her father died leaving her in charge of the three-newspaper group. Over the course of her more than four decades as president and later CEO of the family business, Eleanor shepherded growth and diversification. Following the lead of her brother, Carlos, who had guided the company's first radio acquisition in 1925, she acquired 11 more radio stations throughout California by the mid-1960s. McClatchy obtained its first television broadcasting license in Fresno in 1953, and added a Sacramento station a decade later. Sensing that cable television would siphon advertising dollars from newspapers, Eleanor bought into that industry in the late 1960s. The company also participated in a cellular telephone network joint venture. Eleanor even made a very early foray

Company Perspectives:

The object of this paper is not only independence, but permanence. Relying upon a just, honorable and fearless course of conduct for its support, it expects only to make those men enemies, who are the enemies of the country. Its purpose is, whatever may be the measures which it will advocate in the future, to owe no thanks to any cliques or factions, but based on the broader foundation of right, to survive the wreck of mere party organizations, and still be supported by good and true men.—excerpted from inaugural editorial of the Sacramento Bee *February 3, 1857*

into electronic news delivery in 1937, when she launched a year-long experiment into facsimile delivery of news and information. This experiment foreshadowed the company's Internet ventures by more than half a century.

Divestment of Electronic Media in 1980s

Eleanor McClatchy passed the media company reigns to her nephew, Carlos's son Charles Kenny (C. K.) McClatchy, two years before her death in 1980. C. K. had made his start in the family business in 1958 as a reporter for the *Sacramento Bee*. Characterized as a "maverick," he determined that the electronic properties were distracting management from the profitable and important core newspaper business. Over the course of the decade, the company shed its radio, broadcast television, and cable interests. It sold the television stations in 1980 and 1981, four radio stations in 1983, and its 96,000-subscriber cable system in 1986.

During this same time, McClatchy was investing the proceeds of its electronic media sales in newspapers, thereby expanding its geographic reach within California and throughout the Northwest. Acquired in 1979, the *Gilroy* (California) *Dispatch* and the *Anchorage* (Alaska) *Daily News* served their markets daily, while the *Morgan Hill Times* and *Clovis Independent*, both of California, appeared weekly. Two more California weeklies, the *Lincoln News Messenger* and the *Hollister Freelance*, were added in 1980 and 1981. After a five-year hiatus, McClatchy acquired the *Tacoma News Tribune*, a Washington daily, in 1986. With newsprint prices rising to record levels throughout the late 1980s, McClatchy also entered a venture with three other publishers to create a paper mill in Spokane, Washington, in 1987.

McClatchy Goes Public in 1988

Questions of succession—most significantly the lack of a successor within the McClatchy clan—presaged the 1987 decision to take the company public. C. K. reflected that "I was worried about what could happen 15 to 20 years from now when you can't anticipate what might develop. If a few members of the family wanted to sell their stock . . . they would not be in a position to break up the company," in a 1988 *Advertising Age* article. The seven heirs to the McClatchy fortune agreed to sell ten percent of the media firm to the public, retaining a 90

percent stake in the form of preferred shares that enjoyed a 99 percent voting majority. C. K. himself retained a 53 percent voting interest.

Their plan for the IPO proved ill-timed, however. The McClatchy's had hoped to launch their stock in the fall of 1987, but the stock market crash that October shrunk the share price from a hoped-for $20 to $23 down to less than $18 by the time of the IPO in February 1988. The offering raised $32.8 million which was used to retire debt from previous acquisitions. Once noted for its secrecy—especially during Eleanor McClatchy's reign—the newspaper group threw open its books to reveal a recent history of dramatic growth in sales and net income. Under C. K.'s guidance, McClatchy's revenues had increased from $192 million in 1983 to $283.8 million in 1986, while net multiplied from $6.9 million to over $45 million.

The period immediately following the IPO was not nearly as successful, however, as rising newsprint costs ate into profits. While revenues increased by 46.7 percent, from $229.9 million in 1986 to $337.4 million in 1991, net income slid 47.5 percent, from $45.1 million to $23.7 million.

The company entered an important growth market with its 1988 acquisition of Senior Spectrum, publisher of ten tabloids distributed throughout California. Founded in 1973 in Sacramento, *Senior Spectrum* was by the end of 1991 America's largest chain of senior newspapers with editions in Las Vegas, Denver, Seattle, and Portland, Oregon, as well as California. McClatchy added to this high-potential area with the 1991 acquisition of three editions of *Senior World* published in Washington state.

C. K. McClatchy's concerns regarding his successor came to bear much sooner than anyone expected when he died in 1989 while jogging. His shares were distributed among relatives and top executives, thereby maintaining voting control in the family. (Shares sold to non-family members are automatically converted to Class A status.) He was succeeded as president and CEO by Erwin Potts, who had joined the company in 1975 as director of newspaper operations.

Major Acquisitions Mark 1990s

In January 1990, McClatchy acquired six South Carolina newspapers (three dailies and three weeklies) for $74.1 million from the News & Observer Publishing Company, a Raleigh, North Carolina, media group. Five years later, McClatchy purchased the remainder of the group for $373 million in cash, stock, and assumed debt. The purchase included the daily *News & Observer*, six weeklies, the Nando.net online service, *Business North Carolina* magazine, and a commercial printer.

With an estimated two million hits per week, the one-year-old Nando.net was considered "one of the most successful online newspaper services in the industry." (Its name was derived from the *News & Observer*, also known as the "N and O.") By its third birthday in 1997, it was the third most widely read newspaper site on the World Wide Web, behind *USA Today* and the *Washington Post*. However, like many ostensibly successful Internet ventures, it continued to lose millions of dollars per year through 1997.

Potts guided a gradual succession program in the mid-1990s, advancing to chairman in 1995. Former *Fresno Bee* publisher Gary Pruitt became president of McClatchy at that time and succeeded Potts as CEO the following year. The year 1995 also saw the acquisition of the *Peninsula Gateway,* another Washington state weekly. McClatchy divested five other West Coast weeklies in the fall of 1996.

Then, in 1997, the company stunned the newspaper industry with the acquisition of Cowles Media and its flagship *Star Tribune,* Minnesota's largest daily. The $1.4 billion purchase vaulted McClatchy onto the industry's top ten circulation list and brought to a close the story of one of America's last remaining independent newspaper publishers. Known among its readers and peers as the ''Strib,'' the Minneapolis paper was one of the nation's top dailies. Its circulation even topped that of the *Sacramento Bee*, and boosted McClatchy's total daily unit volume to about 1.4 million. The acquiring company planned to recoup some of its acquisition costs through the divestment of Cowles' magazine publishing interests. In fact, by the time the acquisition was finalized in March 1998, McClatchy had made arrangements to sell two subsidiaries to Primedia Inc., thereby recovering $200 million of the purchase price.

Some analysts thought the deal was too pricey, and in fact the executives acknowledged that the merger might suppress earnings in the short term. Furthermore, McClatchy agreed to carry on the Cowles family's philanthropic endeavors at a cost of $3 million per year, and shouldered more than $1.3 billion in debt to finance the purchase. Investors registered their disapproval of the deal by sending McClatchy's stock down 14 percent on the day after the agreement was made public. But in spite of the stock market reaction, CEO Gary Pruitt commended the purchase as ''a rare opportunity for McClatchy to obtain a quality newspaper while adding geographic diversity in a premiere growth market.'' Moreover, Jon Fine of the online magazine *MediaCentral* asserted that ''McClatchy acquisition history, going back to the '70s, has gone like this: They pay a high multiple, observers shake their heads and gasp in disbelief— and then McClatchy makes it work better than anyone had reckoned.''

In fact, McClatchy's net income had risen substantially throughout this period of pricey acquisitions, increasing from less than $24 million in 1991 to a record $46.6 million by 1994 on sales of $368.1 million. Net declined to $33.6 million in 1995, then rebounded to establish a new benchmark of $68.8 million on sales of $641.9 million in 1997. CEO Pruitt acknowledged that ''Our string of record earnings will end in 1998 as a result of the Cowles merger, but we are confident this strategic move will yield shareholder value and strengthen our company

in the years ahead.'' The acquisition of the *Star Tribune* was expected to boost annual sales to over $1 billion in 1998.

Principal Newspapers

Daily: *The Sacramento Bee* (Calif.); *The Fresno Bee* (Calif.); *The Modesto Bee* (Calif.); *Anchorage Daily News* (Alaska); *Tri-City Herald* (Richland, Wash.); *The News Tribune* (Tacoma, Wash.); *The News & Observer* (Raleigh, N.C.); *The Herald* (Rock Hill, S.C.); *The Island Packet* (Hilton Head, S.C.); *The Beaufort Gazette* (S.C.). Non-Daily: Clovis Independent (Calif.); *Peninsula Gateway* (South Puget Sound, Wash.); *Pierce County Herald* (Pullyallup, Wash.); *Clover Herald* (S.C.); *Yorkville Enquirer* (S.C.); *Lake Wylie Magazine* (S.C.); *Chapel Hill News* (N.C.); *Cary News* (N.C.); *Zebulon Record* (N.C.); *Gold Leaf Farmer* (N.C.); *Mount Olive Tribune* (N.C.); *Smithfield Herald* (N.C.).

Further Reading

Beauchamp, Marc, ''All in the Family,'' *Forbes,* May 2, 1988, pp. 37–38.

Bowen, Ezra, ''From the Boneyard to No. 1,'' *Time,* August 4, 1986, p. 68.

Cuneo, Alice Z., ''Maverick McClatchy Plays by Own Rules,'' *Advertising Age,* November 7, 1988, p. S10.

''Eleanor McClatchy, 85, CEO for 42 Years, Dies,'' *Editor & Publisher,* October 25, 1980, p. 12.

Fine, Jon, ''The Cowles Media Sale: A Closer Look,'' http://www.mediacentral.com/Magazines/MediaCentral/Columns/Fine/19971118.htm.

Fitzgerald, Mark, ''McClatchy Lands Big One,'' *Editor & Publisher,* May 27, 1995, pp. 14–15.

Fitzgerald, Mark, and Robert Neuwirth, ''Twin City Slickers,'' *Editor & Publisher,* November 22, 1997, pp. 8–10.

Fost, Dan, ''Senior Newspapers Gain Readers and Credibility,'' *American Demographics,* December 1991, p. 18.

Galarza, Pablo, ''The Newspaper Is the Message,'' *Financial World,* November 7, 1995, pp. 38–39.

Gremillion, Jeff, '' 'Star Tribune' to McClatchy,'' *MEDIAWEEK,* November 17, 1997, p. 8.

Langdell, Ted, ''McClatchy Sells Off Its Cable Systems in Electronic Purge,'' *Business Journal-Sacramento,* December 1, 1986, p. 2.

Larson, Mark, ''McClatchy Exec Draws Blast Over Salary Raises,'' *Business Journal Serving Greater Sacramento,* May 27, 1991, p. 2.

——, ''Record McClatchy Earnings Also Reward Top Brass,'' *Business Journal Serving Greater Sacramento,* April 9, 1990, p. 11.

''Primedia Pays $200M for Cowles Units,'' *MEDIAWEEK,* January 12, 1998, p. 4.

Serwer, Andrew E., ''How Much Would You Pay for the Morning Newspaper?'' *Fortune,* August 7, 1995, p. 32.

Strow, David, ''Nando: A Hit on the Net,'' *Sacramento Business Journal,* August 1, 1997, p. 11.

—April D. Gasbarre

Meier & Frank Co.

621 Southwest 5th Avenue
Portland, Oregon 97204
U.S.A.
(503) 223-0512
Fax: (503) 241-5783
Web site: http://www.maycompany.com/mf_
   home.html

*Wholly Owned Subsidiary of The May Department Stores
   Company*
Incorporated: 1893
Employees: 1,600
Sales: $395 million (1997 est.)
SICs: 5311 Department Stores

One of the oldest retail chains in the Pacific Northwest, Meier & Frank Co. operates eight department stores in four markets, serving customers in the Portland, Oregon-Vancouver, Washington area, and in three other Oregon cities: Eugene, Salem, and Medford. For a century, the company was owned and operated by the Meier and Frank families. In 1966, the company was sold to The May Department Stores Company amid a heated dispute between the two families. Over the course of the next three decades, five new stores were opened, with the greatest concentration of units situated in the greater Portland area. Representing one of eight regional divisions operating under May Department Stores' corporate umbrella, Meier & Frank was by far the smallest, but its average sales per square foot was the third highest among its sibling chains.

19th-Century Origins

In 1855, the founder of Meier & Frank emigrated from Germany to start a new life in the United States. Aaron Meier was 24 years old when he left his Bavarian hometown of Ellerstadt, having earned enough money while working at his uncle's brickyard to pay for the long trek west. He was not the first member of the Meier family to forego a life in Bavaria for the rumored riches across the Atlantic. His older brothers Julius

and Emmanuel had preceded him, immigrating to Downieville, California, where the pair established themselves in the dry goods business. Aaron Meier joined his brothers in Downieville and gained his first experience in the dry goods business, but he was quick to strike out on his own, leaving Downieville two years later for a small town to the north, on the banks of the Willamette River.

When Meier arrived in Portland in 1857, he was one of 1,300 residents who made their home in the fledgling Oregon Territory community, founded 13 years earlier. Although Portland had yet to complete the transition from town to city, the community's distinction as a major commercial hub along the Pacific Coast would not be long in coming. The area's population was growing in appreciable bursts, as wave after wave of settlers made their way west via the Oregon Trail. The migration had begun 14 years before Meier's arrival, and its intensity would pick up in the decades to follow, creating a potentially lucrative environment for an aspiring entrepreneur like Meier who hoped to establish himself as a merchant. Meier had resolved to open his own dry goods store and he wasted little time in doing so. He opened a store the year he arrived in Portland, striking a partnership with a man named Mariholtz, and began selling merchandise that arrived by steamer from San Francisco and in the covered wagons rolling along the Oregon Trail.

For Meier and Mariholtz, business was brisk in burgeoning Portland. The two store owners worked together for eight years and their business flourished. In 1864, Meier had to make a return trip to Ellerstadt when his father died. Meier left Mariholtz to steward the fortunes of their enterprise and traveled to Germany to visit his mother and collect the inheritance from his father's estate, which amounted to $14,000. During his extended stay in Ellerstadt, Meier married a local woman named Jeanette Hirsch and returned with her to Portland, where a thriving business awaited the newlyweds. Meier's triumphant return, with a new bride at his side, $14,000 in his pocket, and a prosperous dry goods store under his control, turned out to be a slap in the face. The business was gone, and Meier, quite unexpectedly, had nothing to show for his early success.

During Meier's absence, the dry goods store had collapsed financially, bringing the partnership between Meier and Mariholtz to an ignoble and bitter end. Meier did not dwell on his misfortune long, however, and quickly opened a new store—this time without a partner—on a 1,750-square-foot lot in downtown Portland. Meier succeeded in reestablishing himself as a successful store owner, an achievement that set the foundation for a family dynasty in the retail business. After Aaron Meier, generations of Meiers followed in his wake, as well as the descendants of another family, the Frank family. The link between the two families sprang from the business and personal relationship forged between Aaron Meier and the patriarch of the Frank family, Emil Frank. The two met during one of Meier's buying trips to San Francisco not long after his ill-fated return from Germany. Frank, a German immigrant as well, joined Meier's store as a clerk in 1870 and three years later was named a partner in the enterprise, giving birth to the Meier & Frank name. One year before Emil Frank was named partner, his younger brother Sigmund—a recent arrival from Germany—joined the store and along with his brother moved into the Meier home.

Side by side day and night, Meier and the two Frank brothers worked well together as a team. In 1884, Sigmund Frank was made a partner, as work was underway to move the store to a larger location. The new store, a two-story, 20,000-square-foot masonry structure, opened in 1885 on a lot measuring 50 feet by 200 feet. The same year the new store opened, the link connecting the Meiers and the Franks became even closer when Sigmund married Fannie, the Meier's only daughter. Three years after the marriage, Sigmund's position within the family and the business was made stronger when his brother chose to leave the company, selling his interest in the store to his brother and Meier. Emil Frank's decision to divest his interest in Meier & Frank had nothing to do with the performance of the store because business was better than it ever had been before. The new store, completed in 1885, had already proven to be too small by 1889, leading to another expansion that doubled the store's retail space to 40,000 square feet.

As work was underway for the 1889 expansion, Aaron Meier died, leaving 39-year-old Sigmund Frank to take over as the company's president. Four years later, Meier & Frank was incorporated, with the Meier, Frank, and Hirsch families controlling all of the company's stock. The never-ending need to expand as Portland's population mushroomed led to a series of expansions during Sigmund Frank's two decades of direction, including the construction of a five-story building in 1898. As had been the case since the company's inception, however, each bold move to expand proved to be insufficient in retrospect. The company could not build a store large enough to house its flourishing business. Early in the 20th century, Sigmund Frank resolved to build a store that could serve the company for the long-term, and ordered the construction of a store on an unprecedented scale. Completed in 1909, the new Meier & Frank store stood ten stories high, making it the tallest store in the Pacific Northwest and Portland's lone skyscraper. Sigmund Frank never saw the new store completed, however. His death one year before the new store opened ushered in the leadership of the second generation of Meiers.

Family Dynasty Develops During 20th Century

Aaron Meier's eldest son, Abe, who had been named vice-president of the company following its 1893 incorporation, as-

sumed control over Meier & Frank after the death of Sigmund Frank. His title as president of the thriving retail enterprise was only ceremonial, however. Abe Meier never had a permanent desk in the company's corporate office, and spent much of his time as a "greeter" on the sales floor. The responsibility for running the company fell to his younger brother Julius, who had been appointed vice-president and general manager when Sigmund Frank died. Trained as a lawyer, Julius Meier served as the chief decision-maker for Meier & Frank, and in this capacity, faced the same primary issue his predecessors had to contend with, namely, physical expansion. The ten-story store was deemed inadequate by Julius Meier five years after its grand opening, paving the way for the addition of a new wing in 1915 that gave Meier & Frank a sprawling 11 acres of retail space.

The arrangement of Abe Meier serving as figurehead of Meier & Frank while his brother Julius actually ran the company existed for 22 years. Julius never attempted to usurp his brother's title in a power struggle. He bided his time, waiting for what always had led to a transfer of control within the Meier & Frank business. Historically, the death of the company's top leader had led to the promotion of the vice-president to the presidential post, and for Julius Meier that moment arrived in 1930 when his brother Abe passed away. Julius's tenure at Meier & Frank following his brother's death was brief, however. Late in 1930, Julius was elected to a much higher position than running Oregon's premier department store. He was elected governor of Oregon, winning a close election that, for obvious reasons, kept him from superintending the day-to-day affairs of Meier & Frank. Although Julius retained his title as president of the company during his four-year term as governor, the job of actually running Meier & Frank fell to his second in command and heir apparent, Aaron Frank. Julius Meier's nephew and Sigmund Frank's youngest son, Aaron Frank, had been named vice-president and general manager in 1930. By the time his uncle had been elected governor, Aaron Frank had achieved effective control over the family business. Described by some as smart, dedicated, shrewd, arrogant, and sometimes vindictive, Aaron Frank held the reins of command for the ensuing 38 years.

Three years after his tenure as governor ended Julius Meier died, vacating the presidential post for Aaron Frank. Under Aaron Frank's direction, Meier & Frank maintained its lead over other Portland department stores, while its president exerted resolute control over the company's affairs and considerable influence in Portland's political scene. The landmark achievements under his reign of command were Meier & Frank's first steps outside the Portland area. Aaron Frank initiated branch expansion, opening a store in Salem in 1955 that occupied an entire city block. Next, Frank opened a larger store in the Lloyd Center in Portland in 1960. After these two branch store openings, further expansion was put on hold. There were internal problems at Meier & Frank that took center stage, as a family squabble, brewing for years, erupted into a fight for control over the nearly century-old company.

1966: Family Fight Brings New Owners

Family members had disliked Aaron Frank's style of control for years, characterizing Frank's rule as imperious. In 1964, the dispute came to a head when Jack Meier, the only son of Julius

Meier, staged a concerted revolt along with his mother, the children of Aaron Frank's brother Lloyd, and other relatives. At the time, Aaron Frank and his immediate family controlled only 20 percent of Meier & Frank's stock, not enough to ensure his position at the company. Fearful of what would amount to a coup, Aaron Frank sold his family's 200,000 shares in the company to Broadway-Hale Stores, hoping that if Broadway-Hale could gain a controlling interest in Meier & Frank his continued supremacy would be secure. Meanwhile, the faction led by Jack Meier was trying to negotiate for its own supremacy. They had sold the purchase rights to Meier & Frank to The May Department Stores Company, but their majority interest fell short of the two-thirds majority required to complete the tax-free merger with the St. Louis-based department store operator. They also did not have enough of the company's stock to oust Aaron Frank and his son Gerry from the company's board of directors, but they did have the wherewithal to make life miserable for the Franks. They confiscated Aaron Frank's employee's discount card, took his free parking space in the store's garage, and changed the locks on the doors leading to his executive office. As this purposeful program of alienation was taking place, an inconclusive battle to acquire the 20 percent of stock held by the public was waged throughout 1965. The following year, the contentious and frequently petty struggle between the two sides of the family was unexpectedly made moot when Broadway-Hale sold the stock it had acquired from Aaron Frank to May Department Stores. After a century of family ownership, the Meiers and Franks no longer owned their highly successful business.

The turbulent mid-1960s gave way to a decidedly more serene setting at Meier & Frank following the bitter family feud. Aaron Frank died in 1968 and a year later Jack Meier was appointed chairman of the board. Under May Department Stores control, expansion resumed with the establishment of a store in the Eugene area in 1969. During the 1970s, the company completed its most aggressive decade of expansion by opening three new stores. Another Meier & Frank debuted in Portland in 1973, followed by a store opening just outside Portland in Vancouver, Washington, in 1977. A third Portland store opened in 1980, giving the company seven stores and nearly two million square feet of floor space.

In terms of physical growth, the beginning of the 1980s marked the end of aggressive expansion for Meier & Frank. Over the course of the next two decades only one new store was established, a Meier & Frank in Medford, Oregon. Elsewhere within May Department Stores, expansion was robust, as the retail conglomerate developed into a 365-unit operator by the late 1990s. Although May Department Stores did not focus its expansion efforts toward Meier & Frank, Meier & Frank was by no means the forgotten child lost within the May Department Stores empire. Measuring by store units, Meier & Frank was roughly four times smaller than its closest rival within the May Department Stores family, but its average sales per square foot was the third highest, an enviable $225 per square foot during the late 1990s. In 1997, May Department Stores officials announced plans to invest a hefty $3.4 billion in new store openings and renovations, intending to add 100 new stores by 2001. No additional Meier & Frank stores were slated to open during its parent company's investment program, but the Oregon chain's future appeared bright, nevertheless. With more than 130 years of experience, Meier & Frank held sway as a steady and reliable performer, its presence entrenched and ingrained in the hearts of Oregon residents.

Further Reading

Major, Mike, "A Department Store's Approach to Toys," *Playthings,* January 1985, p. 48.

—Jeffrey L. Covell

Mirror Group Newspapers plc

One Canada Square
Canary Wharf
London E14 5AP
United Kingdom
0171 293-3000
Fax: 0171 293-3405

Public Company
Incorporated: 1971
Employees: 2,700
Sales: £559 million (1997)
Stock Exchanges: London
SICs: 2711 Newspapers

In an era of intense competition and media consolidation, Mirror Group Newspapers plc (MGN) is one of four major conglomerates (along with News International, United Newspapers, and Associated Newspapers) that among them control almost 90 percent of the newspaper circulation in the United Kingdom. For much of the 20th century London's *Daily Mirror* has been one of the world's most popular newspapers, a pioneer of what has been characterized variously as New Journalism, the popular press, or, less charitably, the scandal sheet. Founded in 1903 by Alfred Harmsworth (Lord Northcliffe), "unquestionably the greatest journalist of his time" in the words of *The Times* of London, the *Daily Mirror* is today the anchor of the Mirror Group's holdings. The Group also includes several other tabloids, including *The People* and *Sporting Life,* and other British dailies such as the Scottish *Daily Record* and the Birmingham *Post.* Mirror Group also owns a variety of printing, leasing, and graphics companies, as well as a popular cable television channel, Live TV. Until 1991, the Mirror Group was a part of a media conglomerate owned by Robert Maxwell. Upon his mysterious death in November of that year it was discovered that the Group's bank accounts and pension funds had been pilfered for use by Maxwell and his sons in a last-ditch attempt to save their tottering financial empire.

Early History

The creation of the *Daily Mirror* was only one episode in the revolution in British journalism wrought by Alfred Harmsworth and his brother Harold (later Lord Rothermere). Until the end of the 19th century, British newspapers and magazines had been written by and for the aristocracy and professional middle class, a relatively small percentage of the country's total population. Compared to most of the industrialized nations, Britain had developed a vigorous and often vitriolic press, but not until the last half of the 19th century did anyone propose seriously to publish a newspaper for the lower-middle and lower classes. Alfred and Harold Harmsworth, born to the family of an impoverished schoolteacher, would eventually amass fortunes, wield enormous political power, and become members of the House of Lords.

Alfred Harmsworth exhibited his gifts for writing and self-promotion at an early age. As a grammar school student outside London he founded and edited the school newspaper. The young man pursued a career in journalism and began to contribute short pieces to the popular periodicals then coming into their own. From minor journals such as *Comic Life* and *Young Folk Tales* Harmsworth soon graduated to *Tit-Bits,* a hugely successful national magazine composed of excerpts from other, longer works. In 1887 he founded his own popular periodical called *Answers to Correspondents.* The magazine's title suggested its format, a collection of letters to the editor and his answers.

The title also suggested the nature of New Journalism as a whole. England's advanced economy had created a large middle class whose members, such as Alfred Harmsworth himself, were literate and curious about the world at large but uninterested in the higher arcana of politics, theology, and *belles lettres.* These readers, Harmsworth felt, hungered for publications that reflected and commented on their own middle-class lives, free of cultural pretensions, informative but simply written, and spiced with stories of love and violent crime. Such were the "Answers" that Alfred Harmsworth would return to the growing number of "Correspondents" in *fin de siecle* England.

In 1894 Harmsworth bought the moribund *London Evening News* for £25,000 and completed the triumph of popular daily

Company Perspectives:

Mirror Group is transforming itself into a broadly based media company using innovative techniques to maximise efficiency. As well as increasing the profitability of its core brands in a crowded and competitive newspaper environment, it has expanded the product base intelligently into television, regional newspapers, news agencies and new media. Each move to diversify and expand the business, whether by investment, acquisition, joint venture or start-up, leverages the Group's existing talent and resources through the principle of collegiality.

journalism, aided by a talented young editor named Kennedy Jones and by his brother Harold, who would remain the financial and administrative director of the Harmsworth syndicate. Two years later the Harmsworth brothers founded the *Daily Mail,* the first of the "halfpenny" morning papers in England and an astonishing success from its initial publication date, when it already boasted the world's largest daily circulation. The secret of Harmsworth's success was summed up in his phrase, "explain, clarify, simplify," or perhaps more frankly in the formula articulated by Kennedy Jones: "crime, love, money and food." In truth, the *Mail* (and later the *Mirror*) did not seem to follow any particular editorial philosophy. It did combine elements of ultranationalist politics, sex and violence, sports, cartoons, and advice columns, all written in brisk humorous prose and framed by bold black headlines.

These were papers for the plain-speaking common man, a market long associated with the United States but largely unrecognized in England until Harmsworth provided the "daily mirror" in which they could recognize themselves. Nor were women excluded from this democratic awakening; the *Daily Mirror* owed its origin to Alfred Harmsworth's rare sensitivity to women as a newly emerging force in the political and cultural life of England. In 1903 Harmsworth established a paper written entirely by and for women. This "enlightened" experiment lasted about a year, the women of England for unknown reasons failing to rally around the *Mirror* as anticipated. The *Mirror*'s weekly losses of £3,000 soon convinced Harmsworth that "women can't write and don't want to read." He dismissed the female staff, replacing them with the usual gang of cigar-smoking men and relaunched the paper in 1904 with a lead story entitled "How I Dropped £100,000 on the *Mirror*."

The success of the new *Mirror* was not predicated on the gender of its editors, however. Harmsworth took advantage of recently evolved technology to make the *Daily Mirror* the first halfpenny paper in England illustrated with photographs, which until that time had appeared in newspapers rarely and at substantial cost. The *Mirror*'s photographs were sharp and clear and inexpensive, and the paper was soon known for its front-page photos of the royal family, war scenes, and famous criminals. The liberal use of photographs, combined with the usual Harmsworth mix of letters, gossip, contests, and short news articles, proved to be a powerful lure for the English working class. Circulation shot upward to 350,000 in 1905 and six years later topped the one million mark, making the *Mirror* the world's first daily to reach that figure.

The *Mirror* was edited in these years by Alexander Kenealy, an Irishman whose instinct for sensational news had been honed by years of work with publishing magnate William Randolph Hearst in the United States. Under Kenealy, the *Mirror* took a further turn towards the journalism of titillation and sensationalism, eventually going too far to suit Alfred Harmsworth himself. The publisher, who was made a baronet in 1905, wanted to exercise power in the political as well as commercial sphere and he found the Mirror something of an embarrassment. In 1908 Harmsworth bought The *Times* of London and rapidly lost interest in the *Mirror,* which he sold to his brother Harold in 1914. The elder Harmsworth went on to a career of frustrated political campaigns and a growing megalomania; he was remembered by Lloyd George, the distinguished Prime Minister, as "far and away the most redoubtable figure of all the Press barons of my time. He created the popular daily, and the more the other journals scoffed . . . the more popular it became." More typical of upper-class feelings, however, were the words of Lord Salisbury, who charged that Harmsworth had "invented a paper for those who could read but could not think, and another for those who could see but could not read."

The World Wars

Harold Harmsworth (Lord Rothermere) was a businessman of talent, and for some years the *Mirror* prospered under his ownership, helped especially by the public's hunger for photographs of the fighting in World War I. By 1917 the *Mirror* was the most popular daily in Great Britain, but Rothermere's obsessive criticism of governmental waste eroded the paper's circulation base in the 1920s. Like his brother, Rothermere could not resist trying to play the power broker in his nation's political life. The *Mirror* remained essentially conservative, as it had always been, but Rothermere used the paper as a vehicle for voicing his private feelings about the leaders of the Tory Party, for years attacking the government for alleged inefficiency and corruption. The culmination of this campaign was Rothermere's founding of the United Empire Party in the late 1920s, a short-lived far right wing party whose jingoistic statements presaged Rothermere's later support for fascism.

Rothermere's fulminations were politically ineffectual and eventually proved to be bad for business as well. With the *Mirror*'s circulation sinking quickly Rothermere sold his shares in 1931, his reputation permanently damaged by the rebukes of fellow conservatives such as Stanley Baldwin. "What the proprietorship of these pages is aiming at," said Baldwin in a famous 1930 speech, "is power, and power without responsibility—the prerogative of the harlot through the ages."

The politically turbulent 1930s witnessed the birth of a new, radical *Daily Mirror.* While Lord Rothermere formally adopted the fascist philosophy of Hitler and Mussolini, his former paper became one of England's leading advocates of democratic rights and armed resistance to Hitler's growing power in the east. Of the four men chiefly responsible for the new Mirror, three of them—editors H. G. Bartholomew and Hugh Cudlipp, and columnist William Connor (pen name "Cassandra")—were by birth and temperament sympathetic to the working classes; the fourth, Cecil Harmsworth King, was the nephew of founder Alfred Harmsworth. Together these four men created the *Daily Mirror* of which historian A. J. P. Taylor would later remark, "The English people had at last found their voice."

It was an irreverent, loud voice, in which could be heard elements of both high principle and low culture, semi-pornographic cartoons side by side with early and accurate warnings about the menace of Hitler. In 1934, years before most of England's high-brow papers gave up the rhetoric of "appeasement," the *Daily Mirror* characterized the German dictator with startling prescience as "the hysterical Austrian, with his megalomania, based on an acute inferiority complex, his neurasthenia, his oratorical brilliance." The *Mirror*'s enthusiasm for confrontation would vary in the years following, but from 1937 onwards it was England's leading proponent of the rearmament needed to deal with "the gangsters" of Europe.

In this sentiment it found an ally in none other than Winston Churchill, one aristocrat whom the Mirror supported during the 1930s and the first years of war. As the symbol of embattled Britain, Churchill could rely on the applause of the *Mirror,* which if nothing else had always identified itself with the interests of England. The *Mirror,* though, was an essentially iconoclastic journal with leftist leanings and soon it was criticizing the coalition government for various failings, in 1942 nearly suffering censorship for publishing what Churchill believed were demoralizing statements. By war's end the *Mirror* had fully resumed its prewar support for the Labour Party, helping defeat Churchill in the 1945 election. As always, the *Mirror* reflected and amplified the beliefs of its two million-plus readers, who in 1945 were overwhelmingly pacifist and neo-Socialist in their feelings.

Postwar Influence

In 1951 Cecil Harmsworth King deposed H. G. Bartholomew as chairman of the *Mirror*. The paper was probably then at the peak of its influence, the leading daily in all of Great Britain (possibly in the world) and the voice of the New Left that would dominate the country's politics for the next 30 years. Cecil King took the paper several steps further, however; it was under King's leadership that the *Mirror* expanded from newspaper to "Group." For years the *Mirror* had published a successful weekend edition called the Sunday Pictorial, and to this core King added a vast collection of magazines by taking over the Amalgamated Press in 1958 and Odhams Press a few years later. The holdings from the latter deal included a leading Labour newspaper, the *Daily Herald*. Along with the *Daily Record* and *Sunday Mail,* both of Glasgow, Scotland, the *Mirror* and its newly acquired magazine empire were all merged in the early 1960s into the International Publishing Corporation (IPC), described by Hugh Cudlipp in his 1962 book *At Your Peril* as "the greatest publishing operation the world has ever seen."

IPC owned the leading publications in virtually every category of British journalism, its power so great that in 1961 a parliamentary committee was formed to determine whether the *Mirror* takeover of Odham should not be prohibited by the government for reasons of free trade and the general good.

The merger went through anyway, and IPC became one of the world's first "media conglomerates," as they would later be called, and Cecil King, like his uncle Alfred Harmsworth, established himself as a "media baron."

King's long and remarkable career ended abruptly in 1968 with his resignation under pressure from the board of directors. IPC's profits were apparently suffering from the entrenched power of its printing unions, power fought for and won with the help of newspapers like IPC's own *Daily Mirror*. The English printers union was a strong one, and it adamantly opposed new technologies that would cut costs at the expense of union jobs. Cecil King despaired of the situation, and two years after his departure IPC was merged with Albert E. Reed & Co. Ltd., one of the largest paper products companies in Europe. IPC had long been the largest shareholder in Reed (the Harmsworth brothers became involved in the Canadian paper business as early as 1906) and in 1970 the two firms banded together in the interests of vertical integration under the name of Reed International.

Changes in the 1970s

Reed had no more luck with the printing unions than had IPC, and one by one the pieces of its publishing empire were sold off during the 1970s, starting with the magazines. Last to go were the Mirror newspapers, which then as now consisted of the *Daily Mirror, Daily Record, Sunday Mirror, The People* (a glossy Sunday spread), the *Sunday Mail, The Sporting Life,* and *The Sporting Life Weekender.* Reed could find no buyer for the Mirror newspapers, however, and a plan to float the group on the public exchange was ruined when Price Waterhouse discovered gross union laxities and described them in its prospectus statement. At the last minute an unlikely white knight appeared in the form of Robert Maxwell, Czech-born business dealer extraordinaire, who purchased the Mirror papers for about £90 million in 1984.

The Maxwell Years

Mirror Group Newspapers Ltd. (MGN) became a pillar of Robert Maxwell's incredibly tangled business empire, a mysterious world in which the distinction between private and public companies was regularly ignored by Maxwell and his sons Ian and Kevin. A former MP for the Labour Party and a professed friend of the working man, according to many critics Maxwell in truth had little regard for anything beyond his own insatiable desire for fame, and he had long coveted a public platform such as MGN offered. He took over MGN editorial policy while denying that he would even be interested in doing so, and by threat of company closure persuaded the unions to cut their employee levels and relinquish a host of archaic union rules.

For the same reason, Maxwell did not hesitate to break the law when his financial network began unraveling in the late 1980s. His 1988 purchase of Macmillan, Inc., the American publisher, and Official Airline Guides, Inc., for which he borrowed a combined $3.35 billion, pushed his empire further into precarious territory. The anemic economy in 1989 sent the price of stock at Maxwell Communications Corporation (MCC) spiraling downwards. MCC was the holding company for Maxwell's American interests and the collateral for many of the huge loans made to Maxwell's private holding companies at the top of the pyramid. To bolster MCC's falling share price Maxwell engaged in a blur of desperate transactions, including the use of Mirror Group pension funds and other cash accounts to buy MCC shares and provide collateral for further new loans. Shortly after the first signs of imminent personal bankruptcy appeared in November 1991, Maxwell's body was found floating off the stern of his yacht, at which point his conglomerate fell to pieces in a welter of bankruptcy filings and criminal investigations.

Of all of Maxwell's holdings, MGN was probably the soundest at the time of his death, but the company sustained serious losses due to Maxwell's illegal business dealings. In its 1992 annual report MGN noted a one-time extraordinary loss of £421 million to cover the cost of repairs, but the company also showed a healthy operating profit of £91 million on revenues of £460 million.

Expansion in the 1990s

After years of litigation, Mirror Group recovered a portion of its lost pension funds, and the shaken company seemed on its feet again. Hopes for economic security were based on further expansion. In 1994, the Mirror Group led a consortium of media interests in the takeover of the *Independent*. The *Independent* was founded in 1986 as a nonpartisan London daily. The paper at first prospered, as it was perceived to offer respectable and unbiased reporting, in contrast to the London *Times*, which was regarded by many as having declined in quality since being taken over by media magnate Rupert Murdoch. But financial losses in the early 1990s, coupled with gradual ebbing of circulation to its wealthier rival paper, eventually led the *Independent* to solicit a buyer. The consortium led by Mirror Group paid an estimated $110 million for the paper, and MGN was to have a 25 to 30 percent share. Its share was later upped to 46 percent.

Mirror Group's other significant expansion at this time was its launch of its cable television channel, Live TV. MGN put £2.9 million into the cable channel, which featured an irreverent take on the news. One of its most popular innovations was the News Bunny, nothing more than a broadcaster delivering the news while dressed as a rabbit. After a rocky start, Live TV gained a significant share of the British cable market.

By 1995, Mirror Group seemed to have put its financial troubles behind it. Profits that year were up 12 percent, and circulation of its flagship *Daily Mirror* inched up almost two percent. Meanwhile its rival the *Sun* lost almost three percent of its circulation. The Group's other titles also showed increasing circulation. Management claimed it had bolstered its papers by editorial improvement and strong marketing, not by cutting cover prices.

Further expansion came in 1997, when Mirror Group paid £297 million (US$502.1 million) for Midland Independent Newspaper plc, publisher of the *Birmingham Post* and the *Birmingham Evening Mail*. This purchase was expected to boost MGN's presence in the Birmingham area, where its Live TV station was already popular.

Mirror Group was constrained from further television expansion by antimonopoly laws, and competition among the top newspaper conglomerates made every tenth of a percentage point fluctuation in circulation a battle. In 1998, the company reshuffled top management, bringing Live TV's managing director, Kelvin MacKenzie, in as managing director for the whole group. MacKenzie had formerly managed the *Sun*, the main competitor to the *Daily Mirror*. This shake-up came as the director of the Group's Scottish papers resigned, and circulation of the Group's Sunday papers appeared to be falling.

When the Group announced its 1997 fiscal results in March 1998, profits were up 12 percent, and sales had climbed just under four percent, to £559 million. Nevertheless, circulations at its papers were now declining, and the Group was forced to drop its cover prices in response to its competitors lowering theirs. The flagship paper *Daily Mirror*, long number two to the *Sun*, was in danger of losing its place to the *Daily Mail*. Also the *Independent*, which Mirror Group had acquired four years earlier, was suffering greatly in response to price cuts and promotions by its two main rivals, Rupert Murdoch's *Times* and the *Daily Telegraph*. Losses at the *Independent* had approached £10 million for the past several years, and Mirror Group announced in March 1998 that it would sell its stake in the ailing paper. This bad news overshadowed the rosy fiscal picture. It seemed clear that competition among rival papers was too intense for any long-term prediction of fiscal stability for the Mirror Group.

Principal Subsidiaries

MGN Limited; Scottish Daily Record & Sunday Mail Limited (Scotland), Mirror Colour Print Limited; Mirror Group, Inc. (United States).

Further Reading

Bower, Tom, *Maxwell the Outsider,* New York: Viking, 1992.
Dignam, Conor, ''Mirror Group Profits Mask its TV Troubles,'' *Marketing,* September 21, 1995, p. 12.
Edelman, Maurice, *The Mirror: A Political History,* London: Hamish Mailton, 1966.
Escott, T. H. S., *Masters of English Journalism,* London: T. Fisher Unwin, 1911.
Gapper, John, ''Reshuffle at Mirror Group as Kane Resigns,'' *Financial Times,* January 15, 1998, p. 26.
MacMillan, Gordon, ''Wanderer Returns to Claim his Newspaper Crown,'' *Campaign,* July 19, 1996, p. 11.
Maremont, Mark, and Mark Landler, ''An Empire Up for Grabs,'' *Business Week,* December 23 1991.
McIntosh, Bill, ''Mirror Group Sale of Independent on Track for This Week,'' *Dow Jones News Service,* March 9, 1998.
O'Connor, Robert, ''British Papers' Purchase Ruled Not a Monopoly,'' *Editor & Publisher,* April 30, 1994, pp. 30–31.
Snoddy, Raymond, ''Maxwell—the Legacy: Media Interests Flourish Under New Ownership,'' *Financial Times,* January 20, 1996, p. 5.
''U.K.'s Mirror Group Offers $502.1 Million for Midland Newspapers,'' *Dow Jones Online News,* July 4, 1997.

—Jonathan Martin
—updated by A. Woodward

MITSUBISHI
MOTORS

Mitsubishi Motors Corporation

33-8 Shiba 5-chome
Minato-ku
Tokyo 108
Japan
03-3456-1111
Fax: 03-5232-7747
Web site: http://www.mitsubishi-motors.co.jp

Public Company
Incorporated: 1970
Employees: 28,500
Sales: ¥3.67 trillion (US$29.59 billion) (1997)
Stock Exchanges: Tokyo Nagoya Osaka Kyoto Hiroshima
    Fukuoka Niigata Sapporo
SICs: 3711 Motor Vehicles and Car Bodies

Mitsubishi Motors Corporation is one of Japan's largest auto manufacturing companies, with a line of automobiles that includes the Diamante luxury sedan, the midsize Galant sedan, the GTO3000 sports car, and the compact Eclipse. As of 1998 the company also sold trucks, buses, and automobile engines. In 1997 approximately 60 percent of the cars produced by Mitsubishi were sold inside Japan. In addition to several plants in Japan, Mitsubishi also maintained plants in 31 countries worldwide, including the United States, Puerto Rico, Denmark, Germany, Portugal, Australia, New Zealand, Thailand, the Philippines, Indonesia, and the Netherlands. International joint ventures included the Malaysian-built Proton Saga and a car built in conjunction with Volvo and the government of the Netherlands, called the Netherlands Car.

Early History

Mitsubishi Motors was formed as a wholly owned subsidiary of Mitsubishi Heavy Industries (MHI) in 1970. MHI is the modern incarnation of Mitsubishi Shipbuilding Co. Ltd., which had begun manufacturing automobiles as early as 1917. As the sprawling network of companies under the Mitsubishi umbrella grew in the early part of the century, the Mitsubishi Internal Combustion Engine Co., Ltd. was established in 1920 to manufacture engines for airplanes. This company's name was changed to Mitsubishi Aircraft Co. in 1928. MHI was created in 1934 upon the merger of Mitsubishi Shipbuilding and Mitsubishi Aircraft. After the breakup of the Japanese conglomerates known as *zaibatsu* following World War II, use of the corporate name Mitsubishi was banned for several years. MHI was chopped into three regional sections with the names East Japan Heavy Industries, Central Japan Heavy Industries, and West Japan Heavy Industries. Eventually the forbidden name began to reappear, and in 1964 MHI was reintegrated out of its three fragments. By 1967, MHI's Motor Vehicle Division was producing about 75,000 cars a year. That division was spun off as an independent company in 1970, creating Mitsubishi Motors Corporation. Tomio Kubo, a successful engineer from MHI's aircraft operation, was placed in charge of the new company.

An important part of Kubo's early strategy was to build up the company's volume by emphasizing exports. This was to be done by making connections with well-established foreign companies. Mitsubishi's longstanding association with the Chrysler Corporation began the following year, when Chrysler purchased 15 percent of the company's stock. MHI retained the other 85 percent interest. By 1971, the company was producing 260,000 cars a year. Chrysler quickly began to market Mitsubishi-built cars in the United States. The most important of these was the subcompact sold in the United States as the Dodge Colt and Plymouth Arrow. At home in Japan, Mitsubishi concentrated on producing cars for special niche markets. Among the more successful of these models were the Lancer and the Celeste.

By 1973, annual production had reached 500,000 vehicles. That year, the Mitsubishi Motor Sale Financing Corporation was created to handle financing for the company's domestic sales. Although sales began to stall somewhat at that point due to the oil crisis, the introduction of the Galant in 1976 gave the company a welcome boost. As Mitsubishi's sales in the United States grew, friction began to arise between the company and its American affiliate Chrysler. Company officials felt that Chrysler demanded too much say in Mitsubishi decisions, and the idea of marketing its own cars in the United States gained support. By 1977, Mitsubishi had begun to set up its own collection of Colt dealerships across Europe. Tensions between Mitsubishi and Chrysler grew further around that time, as the two companies began competing head to head in the subcompact car market.

As U.S. automakers began making smaller cars, Chrysler unveiled the Omni hatchback, a model aimed at the same market as Mitsubishi's latest Colt model, sold in Japan as the Mirage. In spite of the disagreements, the two companies continued to cooperate, with Chrysler marketing Mitsubishi's cars in the United States and Mitsubishi contributing its advanced engineering know-how to Chrysler. For 1978, Mitsubishi sold a total of 965,300 units, a 17 percent increase over the previous year. Of those, 534,600 were sold in Japan, a 20 percent increase.

The 1980s: Increasing Foreign Sales

Mitsubishi's annual production passed the one million mark in 1980. That year, Mitsubishi Motors teamed up with the Mitsubishi Corporation to purchase Chrysler Australia, subsequently renaming it Mitsubishi Motors Australia Ltd. By 1981, the company had captured eight percent of the Japanese auto market, running neck and neck with Mazda behind industry leaders Toyota and Nissan. Mitsubishi entered the American automobile market under its own name for the first time in 1982. Three models were initially made available to American buyers, all of them fairly upscale: the Starion, a $12,000, turbo-charged sports car; the $7,000 Cordia sedan; and a family sedan called the Tredia, priced at around $6,500. Mitsubishi also began to sell small pickup trucks in the United States, offering vehicles under its own name identical to those already being sold by Chrysler. Under import restraints on Japanese cars, the 30,000 Mitsubishi vehicles sold in 1982 had to come out of Chrysler's annual allotment of around 120,000 cars. Seventy dealers in 22 U.S. markets sold the Mitsubishi line that year.

While the company was making its foray into the U.S. market, sales at home began to sag. In 1983 a new president, Toyoo Tate, was brought in to try to reverse this trend. Tate's early moves included personnel changes in the executive offices, along with a renewed push for more international alliances. One important new connection made was with South Korea's Hyundai Motor Co., of which Mitsubishi purchased a

7.5 percent interest. By 1984 the company's revenue had reached ¥1.17 trillion. During that year, Mitsubishi Motor Sales, a separate corporation that handled domestic auto sales, was absorbed into Mitsubishi Motors.

In 1985 Mitsubishi and Chrysler launched a joint venture called Diamond-Star Motors Corp., named after the corporate logos of the two companies. The twin central Illinois towns of Bloomington and Normal were chosen as the site of the Diamond-Star plant, which was to produce a line of subcompact cars using engines and transmissions imported from Mitsubishi's Japanese facilities. For Mitsubishi, the venture provided a guaranteed source of cars to sell in the United States, the largest automobile market in the world, regardless of any restrictive trade measures that might be enacted by either country involved. By 1987, the company was selling 67,000 cars a year in the United States.

Mitsubishi Motors went public in 1988, ending its status as the only one of Japan's 11 auto manufacturers to be privately held. To pave the way for the shift to public ownership, changes had to be made in the company's stock agreements with both MHI and Chrysler. MHI agreed to reduce its share to 25 percent, retaining its position as largest single stockholder. Chrysler meanwhile increased its holding to over 20 percent. The $470 million in capital raised by the ten percent initial offering enabled Mitsubishi to pay off part of its debt as well as to expand its investments throughout Southeast Asia, where by now it was operating in the Philippines, Malaysia, and Thailand.

Toward the end of the 1980s, Mitsubishi initiated a major push to beef up its presence in the U.S. market. While Japan's quotas allowed the company to export 193,000 cars a year to the United States, two-thirds of those cars were marketed by Chrysler in 1988. In 1989 Mitsubishi pumped its U.S. sales goal up to 130,000 cars, and attacked this goal from several angles. First the company made plans to increase its U.S. dealer network by 40 percent, up to 340 dealers. Mitsubishi also aired its first national television advertising campaign. The company also began to further exploit its relationship with Hyundai, importing the Precis, a carbon copy of Hyundai's popular Excel. Diamond-Star began to pay off with the production of the Eclipse, a sporty car sold by Chrysler as the Plymouth Laser. For 1989, Mitsubishi's worldwide production, including its overseas affiliates, reached 1.5 million units.

Hirokazu Nakamura became president of Mitsubishi in 1989 and steered the company in some promising directions. Sales of the company's sport utility vehicle (SUV), the Pajero, were bucking conventional wisdom by becoming popular even in the crowded streets of Japan. Although sales of SUVs and light trucks were booming in the United States, Japan's car manufacturers dismissed the idea that such a trend could occur in their own country. Nakamura, however, increased the budget for sport utility product development at Mitsubishi. His gamble paid off; Mitsubishi's wide line of four-wheel drive vehicles, ranging from the Pajero Mini to the large Delica Space Gear, rode a wave of SUV-buying in Japan in the early to mid-1990s. Narrowly following Toyota in SUV market share in Japan, Mitsubishi saw its overall domestic market share rise to 11.6 percent in 1995.

U.S. and Southeast Asian Alliances in the 1990s

Nakamura also urged greater reliance on Mitsubishi's ties to southeast Asian companies and markets. Mitsubishi had entered the region in the 1970s by using the contacts of Mitsubishi Corporation, a trading company that was part of the informal Mitsubishi group of companies. By the mid-1990s, Mitsubishi Motors counted major alliances in Malaysia, South Korea, and Thailand. Proton, the joint venture between Mitsubishi and Malaysia, controlled 75 percent of the Malasian market. Mitsubishi maintained a presence in South Korea with their 6.7 percent stake in Hyundai Motor Co. and supplied 50 percent of Taiwan's vans and trucks by sending kits to China Motor Corp. In addition, the company owned 48 percent of Thailand's MMC Sittipol, which produced Mitsubishi vehicles and exported parts to the Philippines, Malaysia, and Canada.

With almost 25 percent of the truck and car market in southeast Asia, Mitsubishi's fortunes rose with their booming economies. Approximately 30 percent of Mitsubishi's profits came from its Asian alliances in the mid-1990s. In addition, by moving their production to these countries, Mitsubishi lessened the negative effect of the rising yen. In 1995 the company moved its truck production from Japan to Thailand, which brought the percentage of its production in low-wage countries to 20 percent.

Mitsubishi's thrust into the United States continued into the 1990s. In 1991 the company added a number of models to its line at a time when U.S. companies were delaying their new models and laying off workers due to sluggish sales. Among Mitsubishi's new products was the Diamante luxury sedan. The Diamante, with a price tag of $28,000, was the winner of that year's prestigious Japan's Car of the Year award. Part of Mitsubishi's strategy to increase its American market share was to target buyers who were already likely to purchase Japanese or European cars, and offer its vehicles at prices slightly lower than comparable cars in other companies' lines.

Mitsubishi gained another outlet for its cars in 1991 with the acquisition of Value Rent-A-Car. In addition, the company began producing two minivans that year, the Expo and the Expo LRV. Later in 1991, Mitsubishi bought out Chrysler's share of Diamond-Star for around $100 million, with Mitsubishi assuming all of Diamond-Star's debt. The two companies continued to split the operation's output. By this time, Chrysler's interest in Mitsubishi had fallen to about 11 percent. Of the 322,500 Mitsubishi-made vehicles sold in the United States in 1991, 187,500 were marketed under the company's own name. 1991 also brought the preliminary stages of a joint venture with Volvo Car Corporation and the government of the Netherlands to produce cars in that country.

Mitsubishi sold 176,900 vehicles in the United States in 1992, over seven percent less than the company's 1990 peak. Although company profits declined somewhat for that year, Mitsubishi's performance was considerably better than that of its Japanese competitors, all of whom suffered dramatic drops in sales in the face of a weak global economy. Mitsubishi's results were aided by strong sales of its recreational models such as the Pajero, whose sales leaped by 52 percent in the first half of the fiscal year. The company continued to outpace its fellow Japanese automa-

kers going into 1993. With 10.7 percent of the domestic market in hand, Mitsubishi bucked another trend by spinning off a new model at a time when the other manufacturers were condensing their lines. Focusing on the lower end of the market, Mitsubishi unveiled a new two-door version of the Mirage, to be sold in Japan as the Mirage Asti. The Asti's price of about $8,500 was well below the company's previous bottom end, the $11,430 Mirage four-door sedan. For the fiscal year ending in March of 1993, Mitsubishi's profits declined by 7.9 percent, a modest drop for one of the Japanese auto industry's worst years ever. Foreign exchange losses caused by a rapidly rising yen were blamed for much of the decline.

As all of the Japanese companies continued to lose market share in the United States in 1993, Mitsubishi attempted to gain a foothold in the family sedan market with the introduction of a newly redesigned Galant midsize sedan. The Galant was to be produced in the United States at the company's Normal, Illinois, plant, creating two advantages: assembling it in the United States avoided the inflated price tag the soaring yen would cause; and the Illinois plant, previously operating at only half of capacity, needed the work.

After decreasing its interest in Mitsubishi to less than three percent in 1992, Chrysler announced its decision in 1993 to sell off all of its remaining Mitsubishi shares on the open market. The two companies stated that they would nevertheless continue their close alliance, with Chrysler supplying engines and transmissions for Mitsubishi's Diamond-Star operation, and Mitsubishi marketing Chrysler products in Japan.

Challenges in the Late 1990s

Mitsubishi's image was negatively impacted in the United States in the mid-1990s with the filing of two lawsuits alleging sexual harassment. The first suit, filed by 29 women in December 1994, accused Mitsubishi of fostering a climate of sexual harassment at its Normal, Illinois, plant. Then, in April 1996 the Equal Employment Opportunity Commission filed a class action suit on behalf of approximately 300 women who worked at the Normal plant. The company initially denied any problem at its plant but later hired former U.S. Labor Secretary Lynn Martin to recommend changes to its policies and practices. In August 1997 Mitsubishi settled the 1994 suit for $9.5 million; the EEOC was still pursuing its suit into the late 1990s.

The benefits Mitsubishi had seen because of its strong presence in Southeast Asia reversed themselves in the late 1990s. The economic crisis in the region, which began in 1997, spelled big trouble for Mitsubishi. In September 1997 the company closed its Thai factory in response to a crash in the country's currency and the plummeting of consumer demand. The large truck plant, which had produced 8,700 trucks in 1996, was shut down indefinitely. In addition, Mitsubishi had little support from sales in Japan, which slowed considerably throughout 1997 and were affected by that country's own economic uncertainty into 1998. Other Japanese auto makers, such as Toyota and Honda, bolstered their own slipping domestic sales with booming sales in the United States. However, with only a small percentage of the market in the United States, Mitsubishi stood to be gravely hurt by the turmoil in the Asian economies in the late 1990s.

Principal Subsidiaries

Mitsubishi Motor Manufacturing of America Inc.; Mitsubishi Fuso Truck of America, Inc.; Mitsubishi Motors America, Inc.; Mitsubishi Motor Sales of Caribbean Inc. (Puerto Rico); Mitsubishi Motors New Zealand Ltd.; Mitsubishi Motors Europe B.V. (Netherlands); Mitsubishi Motor Sales of America, Inc.; Mitsubishi Trucks Europe, S.A. (Portugal); Philippine Automotive Manufacturing Corporation (50%); Mitsubishi Motors Australia Ltd. (50%); Mitsubishi Motors de Portugal S.A. (50%); PT Mitsubishi Krama Yudha Motors and Manufacturing (Indonesia; 49%); MMC Sittipol Company, Ltd. (Thailand; 48%).

Further Reading

Annin, Peter, and John McCormick, "More Than a Tune-Up," *Newsweek,* November 24, 1997, pp. 50–52.

Armstrong, Larry, "Mitsubishi Is Souping Up Its Image," *Business Week,* February 27, 1989, p. 56.

Cullison, A.E., "Mitsubishi Eyes Own US Sales Team," *Journal of Commerce,* April 13, 1977, p. 3.

Dodsworth, Terry, "Living with Chrysler," *Financial Times,* November 10, 1977, p. 27.

Furukawa, Tsukasa, "Mitsubishi to Retain Amiable Relationship with Chrysler, It Says," *American Metal Market,* July 5, 1993, p. 8.

Holusha, John, "Mitsubishi's U.S. Car Venture," *New York Times,* October 26, 1982, p. D3.

Kanabayashi, Masayoshi, "Japan's Battered Auto Makers Adopt Mixed Outlook for the Current Year," *Wall Street Journal,* June 1, 1993, p. A9B.

Levin, Doron, "Chrysler Corp., Mitsubishi Set Site for Plant," *Wall Street Journal,* October 8, 1985, p. 2.

——, "Mitsubishi's Big Campaign in U.S.," *New York Times,* April 30, 1991, p. D1.

Maskery, Mary Ann, "Japan Niche Prompts a 2nd Mirage," *Automotive News,* May 17, 1993.

——, "Mitsubishi Sets Sights on Mazda in U.S.," *Automotive News,* September 21, 1992, p. 21.

——, "Mitsubishi to Sell Stock in Auto Firm," *Automotive News,* October 31, 1988, p. 4.

Miller, Krystal, "Mitsubishi Restyles Galant to Anchor Line," *Wall Street Journal,* June 23, 1993, p. B1.

"Mitsubishi Motors Posts 27% Decline in 1st-Half Profit," *Wall Street Journal,* November 6, 1992, p. A5A.

Morris, Kathleen, "Endgame," *Financial World,* August 1, 1995, pp. 2–33.

Shirouzu, Norihiko, "Japan's Firms Revamp Amid Asian Crisis," *Wall Street Journal,* November 6, 1997, p. A18.

Updike, Edith, and Laxmi Nakarmi, "A Movable Feast for Mitsubishi," *Business Week,* August 28, 1995, pp. 50–51.

—Robert R. Jacobson
—updated by Susan Windisch Brown

Nash Finch Company

7600 France Avenue South
P.O. Box 355
Minneapolis, Minnesota 55440-0355
U.S.A.
(612) 832-0534
Fax: (612) 924-4939
Web site: http://nashfinch.com

Public Company
Incorporated: 1896 as Nash Brothers Wholesale
  Produce Co.
Employees: 12,775
Sales: $3.38 billion (1996)
Stock Exchanges: NASDAQ
SICs: 5141 Groceries, General Line; 5142 Packaged
  Frozen Foods; 5143 Dairy Products; 5146 Fish &
  Seafoods; 5147 Meats & Meat Products; 5148 Fresh
  Fruits & Vegetables; 5149 Groceries & Related
  Products, Not Elsewhere Classified; 5199 Nondurable
  Goods, Not Elsewhere Classified; 5411 Grocery
  Stores

The third largest food wholesaler in the United States, Nash Finch Company serves approximately 2,350 supermarkets, military bases, and other customers in about 30 states. In addition, its retail operations encompassed 108 corporate stores in 16 states in 1997. These retail operations, which included the stores Econofoods, Economart, Our Family Foods, Sax Food and Drug, and Food Pride, contributed 25 percent of 1996 sales. Nash Finch supplied its company-owned stores and its affiliated independent stores produce and the private label brands "Our Family" and "Buy 'n Save," which together represented approximately 1,400 dairy, meat, grocery, frozen food, and health and beauty products. As of 1997, Nash Finch also owned Nash DeCamp Company, a produce marketing subsidiary based in California. Although Nash DeCamp contributed only two percent of overall sales in 1996, it was nonetheless considered a valuable asset for its penetration of markets worldwide and its ability to generate as much as five percent of total operating profits.

Early History

Nash Finch Company began in 1885 when Vermont native Fred Nash, after traveling west and toiling at several unpromising jobs, invested $400 and established a candy and tobacco shop in Devil's Lake, a Dakota Territory boom town. Nash soon enlisted his two younger brothers, Edgar and Willis, to join him. All three benefited from having worked in their parents' general store back East, and they shared a determination to live frugally so that their business might succeed. By the time North Dakota achieved statehood in 1889, the brothers had opened three additional stores, suffered the loss of one and severe damage to another from separate fires, and, finally, consolidated their operations in the emerging urban center of Grand Forks.

The year 1889 proved pivotal to the company for two reasons. The first stemmed from the serendipitous arrival in Grand Forks of a boxcar of peaches for which no buyer existed. Although primarily retailers, the Nash brothers had conducted some fruit wholesaling and quickly decided to secure a bank loan for the peaches. The venture was a large gamble—the brothers' only collateral was the Grand Forks store—but it paid off when sales were made to retailers throughout the region. Two years later the Nashes became wholesalers exclusively and earned the distinction of founding both the first and largest of the state's wholesaling firms. The second turning point came when Edgar contracted tuberculosis and moved to California for health reasons. While Edgar's new contribution as West Coast fruit buyer aided the growth of the company, a replacement was needed at the Grand Forks headquarters. That person was 14-year-old Harry Finch, who several decades later became president of the company. (A legacy of Finch management continued in the hands of Finch's grandson, Harold B. Finch, Jr., who was the company's chief executive officer and chairman of the board in the early 1990s.)

Expansion in the Early 20th Century

Although 1896 was overshadowed by the death of Edgar Nash in January, later that year the company celebrated its first expansion beyond North Dakota with the acquisition of the Smith Wholesale Company of Crookston, Minnesota. Harry Finch, still relatively young but now with seven years of experience in clerking and sales, was placed in charge of the Crookston operation, which was renamed Finch-Smith Company. After the turn of the century, Nash Brothers solidified its position as North Dakota's leading wholesaler with the successive purchases of Minot Grocery Company and Grand Forks Mercantile Company. A 1905 partnership forged with a budding Red River Valley produce brokerage named C. H. Robinson—to which Finch was elected vice-president—further broadened Nash's service base. After Nash Brothers acquired control of Robinson in 1913, branch offices were established in Minneapolis, Sioux City, Milwaukee, Chicago, Fort Worth, and virtually everywhere else the parent company had sprouted its own warehouse facilities. Until 1966, C. H. Robinson served as the produce procurement branch of Nash Brothers, because, at that time, the Federal Trade Commission (FTC) succeeded in limiting Nash's broker-buyer monopoly. Ten years later, C. H. Robinson became independent and has since blossomed into a $935-million concern headquartered in Eden Prairie, Minnesota.

From 1907 to 1918, Nash acquired 54 fruit wholesalers spread throughout the northwestern United States and Canada. Highlights of this era included the establishment in Lewiston, Idaho, of White Brothers and Crum, the company's first fruit growing and shipping venture; the creation of the Randolph Marketing Company in Los Angeles to package citrus fruit; and the formation of Nash DeCamp, which would prove to be one of the company's most prized concerns. By 1919 Nash Brothers had become so vast that it required a more centralized headquarters. The logical choice was Minneapolis, which had developed into the nation's 17th largest city, a premier milling center, and the wholesaling hub of the Northwest. According to historian Bruce Gjovig in *Boxcar of Peaches: The Nash Bros. & Nash Finch Company,* "Although the loss of the Nash Bros. headquarters was a blow to Grand Forks, the move made good business sense. . . . [In] Minneapolis, the Nash Bros. had joined the ranks of the Pillsburys, Cargills, and Hills." Two years later, the firm reincorporated under the name Nash Finch Company and consolidated its more than 60 businesses, which had previously functioned as separate units with independent officers. Canadian operations were united under Nash-Simington Ltd. while C. H. Robinson Company and Nash Shareholders became the corporation's primary subsidiaries. As the corporation's first president, Fred Nash oversaw the complex consolidation process, which was completed in 1925. His death the

following year resulted in Harry Finch's elevation to president. Willis Nash remained as corporate treasurer and also served as president of the Nash Company, the Nash family's own investment corporation.

At the onset of the Great Depression in 1929, Nash Finch ranked as one of the foremost food distributors in the Midwest, with sales of more than $35 million. Because of its firm foothold within a recession-proof industry, Nash weathered the 1930s better than most U.S. manufacturers. The only year in which the company failed to turn a profit was 1932, generally considered the worst year of the Depression. During the 1930s, one of the most significant advances for the company came with its large-scale introduction and promotion of the Our Family brand, which had become a symbol of the company's operating philosophy and a favorite of Nash consumers by the 1940s.

Revenues Rise in 1960s and 1970s

During the early 1950s, Nash Finch reentered food retailing with the purchase of 17 supermarkets in Nebraska. The move proved crucial to the company's future health, for it allowed Nash to remain competitive with much larger food concerns, including Eden Prairie–based wholesaler and retailer Super Valu Stores, Inc. From 1960 to 1969 Nash saw its sales grow from $91 million to $248 million. As the company increasingly diversified within its industry and offered a greater variety of services to its retailers, growth in overall revenues became even more impressive during the 1970s and 1980s.

By the mid-1980s, Nash ranked as the nation's tenth largest grocery wholesaler, with sales of $1.3 billion. Its geographic sphere of influence, however, was still confined largely to the rural Midwest, which at the time represented a conspicuously slow-growth market. This, and just a five percent compound increase in earnings over a ten-year period (Super Valu's increase, over the same period, was 23 percent), had perpetuated what Dick Youngblood termed the company's "comparative anonymity." In an effort to improve his company's rankings within the food industry, Chairman Harold Finch, Jr. announced a sweeping expansion plan designed to nearly triple earnings and double revenues by the end of the decade.

The 1985 acquisition of M. H. McLean Wholesaler Grocery Company effectively inaugurated the plan. A North Carolina distribution facility serving approximately 60 Hills Food stores, the McLean Company signified additional wholesale revenues of roughly $100 million. More important, though, was Nash's consonant commitment to the South, with its higher-than-average population growth. A series of purchases, including that of Georgia's second largest food wholesaler as well as that of Colorado's largest wholesaler, highlighted the next few years. Yet, the Nash Finch Company entered the 1990s somewhat precariously; quick profits had not followed quick expansion. Instances of store closings and margin problems related to three separate acquisitions led to notable charges against shares, and, although revenues and book value climbed steadily, net income stagnated in 1988 before it plunged by 27 percent in 1989.

The 1990s

In the early 1990s, Nash Finch continued its strategy of achieving expansion through acquisition and improving profitability through broadened services and updated facilities. Following a slight dip in net sales from 1990 to 1991 (during which time profits increased by seven percent), the company topped the $2.5 billion mark in 1992 revenues while posting its highest earnings ever—more than $20 million. Two mid-Atlantic acquisitions in 1992, Virginia-based Tidewater Wholesale Grocery and a prominent division of Maryland-based B. Green & Company, fortified Nash's position as one of the largest distributors to the U.S. military. That same year, the company sought overseas growth by participating in a group venture to acquire 75 percent of Hungary's largest wholesale food company, Alfa Trading Company. The December 1992 loss of an account with Lunds Inc., a $120-million upscale Minnesota retail chain, seemed hardly to hinder the company; within four months it had reached an agreement to acquire Easter Enterprises, a 16-store chain with sales of $250 million. Headquartered in Des Moines, Easter consisted of 11 stores in Iowa, three in Illinois, and two in Missouri. Perhaps the sweetest part of the deal was the lost business that it represented for Easter's former provider, Super Valu. The purchase also served notice that Nash had no intention of abandoning its bread-and-butter Midwest market, which estimates in the early 1990s placed at approximately 70 percent of sales.

In 1994 Harold B. Finch, Jr., chief executive officer and since 1978 the company's president, died in an automobile accident. The grandson of Harry Finch, he had followed in grandfather's footsteps and those of his father, Harold B. Finch, Sr., who had been president from 1939 to 1961. Finch, Jr., was succeeded in both positions by Al Flaten.

The company's acquisitions continued into the mid-1990s. In 1994 Nash Finch bought Food Folks, a grocery store chain headquartered in North Carolina with 23 stores. The following year the company boosted its presence as a supplier to U.S. and European military commissaries by agreeing to acquire Norfolk-based Military Distributors of Virginia, a sale it completed in January 1996. By the end of 1995, the company was supplying 120 of its own stores in 16 states and 5,700 independent stores in over 30 states.

However, Nash Finch's share of the market took an even bigger leap in 1996 through the company's acquisition of Super Food Services, Inc. By spending almost $174 million for the Dayton, Ohio–based wholesaler, Nash Finch went from the fifth-largest food wholesaler in the United States to the third largest. Super Food not only added $1.2 billion in revenues, it also expanded Nash Finch's territory into areas of Ohio, Michigan, Kentucky, Indiana, Tennessee, and West Virginia that the company did not previously serve. In addition, Nash Finch planned to use Super Food's strength in gourmet foods to supply its company-owned stores, eliminating the need to buy such products from other wholesalers. Nash Finch also planned to sell produce, one of its own strengths, to Super Food's customers, who could not previously buy produce through Super Food.

Another acquisition in 1996 extended the company's geographical reach. Nash Finch purchased the wholesale distributor T. J. Morris Company, which supplied over 100 independent grocery retailers in Georgia. The company closed its warehouse in Macon and consolidated it with T. J. Morris's distribution

facility in Statesboro. The newly enlarged warehouse cost effectively served existing T. J. Morris and Nash Finch customers in Georgia.

These acquisitions helped raise Nash Finch's revenues to $3.38 billion in 1996, up more than 16 percent from 1995. Net earnings rose as well, to $20 million, from $17.4 million in 1995. Expansion did not result only from acquisitions, however. The company's independent supermarket customers rose 16 percent to 767, not including new customers from Super Food and T. J. Morris. The company's plans for the late 1990s included incorporating its recent acquisitions into its operations and further expansion.

Principal Subsidiaries

GTL Truck Lines Inc.; Nash DeCamp Company; Piggly Wiggly Northland Corp.; Super Food Services, Inc.; T. J. Morris Company; Gillette Dairy of the Black Hills Inc.; Nebraska Dairies Inc.

Further Reading

Byrne, Harlan S., "Nash Finch Co.: It Puts Recent Acquisition Stumbles Behind It," *Barron's,* March 26, 1990, p. 40.

Cochran, Thomas N., "Nash Finch Co.: A Food Wholesaler Succeeds in the Retail End of the Business," *Barron's,* June 6, 1988, pp. 65–66.

Gelbach, Deborah L., *From This Land: A History of Minnesota's Empires, Enterprises, and Entrepreneurs,* Northridge, Calif.: Windsor Publications, 1988.

Gjovig, Bruce, *Boxcar of Peaches: The Nash Bros. & Nash Finch Company,* Grand Forks, N.D.: Center for Innovation and Business Development, 1990.

Kennedy, Tony, "Lunds to Drop Nash Finch in Favor of Fairway Foods," *Star Tribune* (Minneapolis), December 23, 1992, p. D3.

——, "Nash Finch Acquires Wholesaler," *Star Tribune* (Minneapolis), January 8, 1993, p. D3.

Lambert, Brian, "Nash Finch Celebrates 100 Years of Business," *Corporate Report Minnesota,* March 1985, p. 19.

Marcotty, Josephine, "Nash Finch to Buy Midwest Supermarket Chain," *Star Tribune* (Minneapolis), April 8, 1993, p. D3.

"Nash Finch Invests in Hungarian Firm," *Star Tribune* (Minneapolis), November 18, 1992, p. D3.

"Nash Finch to Buy 16 Easter Stores," *Supermarket News,* April 12, 1993, p. 4.

"Nash Finch to Buy Supermarkets," *Wall Street Journal,* April 8, 1993, p. B5.

Sansolo, Michael, "Nash Finch: A New Horizon," *Progressive Grocer,* November 1985, pp. 40, 42.

Schafer, Lee, ed., "Super Valu Stores Inc.; Nash Finch Company," *Corporate Report Minnesota,* June 1991, pp. 147–48.

"Super Food Services Agrees to $174 Million Acquisition," *Wall Street Journal,* October 9, 1996, p. B3.

Tosh, Mark, "Nash Finch to Capitalize on Strength," *Supermarket News,* June 1, 1992, p. 9.

Youngblood, Dick, "Grocery Giant Nash Finch Still Keeps a Low Profile," *Star Tribune* (Minneapolis), June 9, 1986, pp. M1, M8.

Zwiebach, Elliot, "Nash Finch Eyes Southeast Buys as Way of Boosting Profitability," *Supermarket News,* May 27, 1991, p. 52.

——, "They Will Succeed," *Supermarket News,* December 11, 1995, pp. 12–16, 79.

—Jay P. Pederson
—updated by Susan Windisch Brown

Novell, Inc.

122 East 1700 South
Provo, Utah 84606
U.S.A.
(801) 861-7000
Fax: (801) 228-7077
Web site: http://www.novell.com

Public Company
Incorporated: 1980 as Novell Data Systems
Employees: 5,818
Sales: $1.37 billion (1996)
Stock Exchanges: NASDAQ
SICs: 7372 Prepackaged Software

Novell, Inc., is one of the largest computer networking firms in the world, offering operating software, network management software, hardware, and services. Founded in 1980 as Novell Data Systems, a personal computer manufacturer, the firm spent its venture capital on designing hardware, leaving little money for marketing. By 1982 it was on the verge of collapse, unable to even afford a booth at the computer industry's Comdex trade show in Las Vegas. Raymond J. Noorda, a 58-year-old electronics engineer, saw the company's products in a Las Vegas hotel room and was impressed. Noorda was a 20-year veteran of General Electric Co. who had already turned around other fledgling computer-industry startups, including System Industries, Inc., and Boschert Inc.

The Noorda Years: 1983–87

In 1983 Noorda resolved to salvage Novell and became the firm's ninth president. He invested $125,000 of his own money and borrowed $1.3 million from investors, receiving a 33 percent stake in the company. Though Novell was primarily a hardware maker at the time, Noorda felt that its most viable product was an operating system that enabled personal computers to share peripherals such as printers and disk drives on a local area network (LAN). The firm subsequently terminated its hardware division and concentrated on networking.

That decision proved to be a timely one. The PC industry was booming, and as desktop computers permeated the business world, firms became increasingly interested in ways to connect them. Novell's solution was to do this with software, using one PC on each network as a file server that would manage both the network and access to network resources. Novell's main rival, 3Com Corporation, was building its approach to networking around hardware, chiefly adapter cards for Ethernet, the networking system invented at Xerox Corp. Initially the firms coexisted, with Novell reselling 3Com's adapter cards rather than making its own.

Having established its priorities, the firm, now named Novell, Inc., forged rapidly ahead. In 1983 it released Btrieve—the first multiuser database application for LANs—and a software package for computers implementing UNIX, an operating system mainly used for math-intensive applications. In 1984 Novell introduced its first software designed to analyze Ethernet networks. The following year it became the first independent network company to support Microsoft Corporation's new DOS 3.1 operating system and released a product that made it possible for Apple computers to be used on Ethernet networks. Novell also acquired Microsource, a distributor, and thus began the process of assembling a first-class distribution network.

Though Novell was a small company during the early and mid-1980s, its market was growing rapidly. According to International Data Corp., nearly 50,000 computer networks were installed worldwide in 1984, a number that increased to 200,000 by the end of 1987. Due to the strength of NetWare, Novell gradually emerged as the leading firm for PC networks. By 1985 the rapidly growing network market had attracted the attention of such large computer companies as Digital Equipment Corp., Apple, and Hewlett-Packard. At the time Novell was primarily linking IBM-compatible computers, so when IBM and Microsoft Corp. introduced their own file-server strategy, it was a more direct threat. Since Novell had been in the networking market longer, however, its networking customer base was larger and growing more quickly. In fact, Novell was confident enough to go public in 1985, raising the funds for continued expansion.

Unlike 3Com, Novell decided to fight the bigger companies directly by convincing businesses that it would cost less to use

Company Perspectives:

From a customer perspective Novell is expanding the value of its products from enabling file and print sharing on local area networks, to providing the servers and network services necessary for highly distributed Internet/intranet solutions. Novell software products include server operating systems, network applications, and distributed network services. These products enable businesses of all sizes to maintain distributed information resources across computer networks that integrate many different computers, operating systems, applications, and devices. Businesses deploy Novell networks to make more efficient use of information technology, improve customer service, and enhance communication and collaboration both internally and with customers, partners, and suppliers.

networks of PCs than the larger minicomputers favored by companies like Digital Equipment. The firm also opted to offer complete network systems, rather than just software. To meet this goal Novell acquired Santa Clara Systems Inc., a manufacturer of data storage systems and LAN products, in the fall of 1986 for $4.1 million, as well as another distributor, Cache Data Products.

As pressure from large firms increased, the competition between 3Com and Novell became an intense rivalry by 1986. 3Com introduced an operating system for networks and bought advertising that rejected Novell's assertion of its network performance leadership. When 3Com decided it would no longer allow Novell to sell its Ethernet adapters, Novell began producing its own and marketing them for $495 apiece, compared to 3Com's price of $595. Novell also released the first network operating system for computers based on the recently developed Intel 286 microprocessor used in a new generation of IBM computers. Novell's software was now used in more than two million computers and terminals worldwide, including the networks of the British Broadcasting Corporation (BBC), Hilton Hotels, and British Rail. Sales for 1987 reached $221.8 million.

The Novell Network: 1988–90

By 1988 Novell had a 50 percent share of the PC networking market and was working to link PCs, minicomputers, and mainframes. It bought CXI, a maker of connections to IBM mainframes, for $34.9 million in March and began a $5.3 million joint venture with Softcraft, a firm concentrating on database and programming tools. Competition in the computer hardware market was still growing, making PCs more of a commodity and increasing the number of businesses seeking to link them into networks. Novell's 1988 sales reached $347 million, 50 percent of which was generated by software.

Novell's greatest leap forward came with the release of NetWare 386 in September 1989. Earlier versions of NetWare worked only with IBM-compatible hardware, but NetWare 386 could serve IBM, Unix, and Apple's Macintosh computers simultaneously. A great deal of software was required to con-

nect these different computing environments. Still, corporations found linkages increasingly desirable since different computer systems could be created for various purposes. For a short time Novell had the only software capable of managing this task, giving the firm a tremendous competitive edge.

Novell took advantage of its position in the computer networking industry by creating a massive distribution network without the huge overhead costs usually involved in using 13,000 independent distributors. Value-added resellers ranging from mass-market discounters to high-level systems integrators installed the networks, taught customers how to use them, and offered maintenance, all through their own sales forces, which Novell trained. This arrangement cost Novell almost nothing, and the firm soon began franchising its Novell Authorized Education Centers for a fee. Novell also left deliberate gaps in the NetWare product line that were filled by other companies, which then had a vested interest in NetWare's success. Sales grew to $421.9 million in 1989 and reached $497.5 million in 1990.

The combination of excellent software and distribution, as well as the support of many other companies, proved so strong that when IBM and Microsoft introduced LAN Manager shortly after the release of NetWare 386, they could not crack Novell's hold on the market. Some analysts even considered LAN Manager a better product, but it did not have NetWare's broad base of support and was designed for IBM's new operating system, OS/2, which was then unpopular. Within a couple years, Microsoft was making products designed to be used with NetWare, while IBM was selling the software.

Novell moved aggressively into the Japanese market in 1990, founding Novell Japan with Canon, Fujitsu, NEC, Sony, and Toshiba as smaller partners; Novell maintained a 54 percent stake in the Japanese subsidiary. Having the five most important Japanese computer companies on board gave Novell instant credibility as it sought to expand into a market where less than two percent of computers were networked. Novell released a version of NetWare using Japanese characters, employed Japanese citizens, and generally presented itself as a Japanese company in order to succeed in the difficult Japanese computer industry.

Novell already had a growing presence in Europe, Asia, and South America, where it sold its products through authorized distributors. By late 1991, sales outside the United States accounted for half the firm's revenue.

Diversification or "Diworsification"?: 1990–92

In March 1990 Novell worked out a merger agreement with the Lotus Development Corp., one of the largest PC software firms and the archrival of Microsoft. The deal would have given Novell $1.5 billion worth of Lotus stock. Novell wanted to tap into the huge customer base of Lotus's top-selling spreadsheet, 1-2-3, which then stood at about five million, while Lotus wanted access to the networking market. The merger would have created the largest PC software company in the world, giving both firms advantages in taking on their chief rival, Bill Gates's Microsoft. Lotus and Novell planned to combine their customer service departments with that of WordPerfect, Inc., a privately held firm specializing in word processing software.

The deal fell apart at the last minute, though, when large Novell stockholders balked. Lotus would have held one more seat than Novell on the board of the new company, and the stockholders were reportedly afraid of becoming Lotus's junior partner in the merged company. Despite the aborted merger, the two firms continued to cooperate in a number of areas.

Novell soon joined with Lotus and other companies, including Apple and Microsoft, to devise a system to prevent tampering with e-mail messages. The goal was to make e-mail reliable enough to use for contracts and permanent records, dramatically expanding the uses of computer networks.

Beginning in 1991 Ray Noorda, Novell's president, chairman of the board, and chief executive officer, reorganized the company, dividing it into three divisions: the core NetWare division, general operations, and an entrepreneurial arm leading a move into huge, corporate-wide networks, which were expected to be the next major development in networking. Many analysts felt the restructuring was initiated to prepare the company for the eventual exit of the 67-year-old Noorda. Novell's share of the LAN market stood at an all-time high of 63 percent, comprising 11,000 companies and 10 million people. Microsoft, however, was spending nearly $50 million a year on networking to catch up with Novell.

One of the important areas of contention between Novell and Microsoft was expected to be the corporate-wide networks. NetWare had primarily been used to help small groups of people share laser printers and data. But the wide-area networks (WANs) needed by large corporations would entail linking hundreds of large and small computer systems, many of them not in the same building, or even the same country. Some corporate executives doubted NetWare's suitability for this task, and Microsoft sensed an opening. IBM, however, had been moving to limit Microsoft's power to set standards, and in February 1991 IBM decided to market NetWare, boosting Novell's position. Later that year Hewlett-Packard agreed to distribute Novell products and to work with Novell on developing and marketing computer network technologies for Hewlett-Packard computers. Compaq also agreed to work with Novell on better integration of networks.

To increase its strength in the growing workstation market, Novell bought a five percent stake in Unix Systems Laboratories, a subsidiary of American Telephone and Telegraph (AT&T), in April 1991. Novell and Unix formed a joint venture called Univel to focus on creating products based on the Unix operating system. The firms planned to develop an easy-to-use graphical interface.

Novell then bought Digital Research Inc. for approximately $135.8 million in stock. Digital's DR-DOS operating system, a clone of Microsoft's widely used MS-DOS operating system, was seen as giving Novell some muscle in providing software for file servers. The acquisition prepared Novell for an expected showdown with Microsoft in the networking market. Digital Research became Novell's Desktop Systems Group, which focused on operating systems software that increased the cooperation between workstations and a network. Novell was also working on a joint venture with Sequent Computer Systems to produce a computer able to simultaneously serve as many as 1,000 database users.

In April 1992 Novell continued expanding its multi-company networking abilities through the $5.2 million purchase of International Business Software Ltd., a developer of networking software for Macintosh computers. Novell also signed a marketing and product development agreement with Lotus, allowing the latter firm's widely praised Notes networking software to be more closely connected with NetWare.

The Windows NT Threat: 1992–96

Novell boasted 65 percent of the market for network operating systems in 1992, when networking was the fastest growing segment of the computer industry. The release of Microsoft's Windows NT, however, posed perhaps the largest threat Novell had yet faced. Windows NT was a version of the best-selling Windows graphic interface that was designed for use on networks. Since many corporate PCs were already using Windows and other Microsoft software, some industry analysts felt that Windows NT had a chance of winning a significant percentage of the networking market away from Novell despite the latter's huge advantage in installed systems.

Noorda seemed to take the Windows NT threat personally, and in 1994 made two costly acquisitions to refashion Novell into a diversified Microsoft-style software giant. His $855 million purchase of the number-two word processing program WordPerfect and $145 acquisition of the Quattro Pro spreadsheet brand immediately transformed Novell into the second-largest PC software applications company in the world. Novell's stock price began falling, however, when Wall Street became increasingly dubious about Noorda's decision to compete directly with some of the very software companies Novell relied on to sustain the popularity of its core NetWare product. Noorda retired in early 1994 and was replaced by Hewlett-Packard veteran Robert Frankenberg, who promptly began divesting Novell of Noorda's acquisitions.

Although Novell's revenues peaked at $1.63 billion in 1995, Frankenberg's efforts to streamline the company back to its core competencies distracted him from the Internet revolution that was transforming the software industry. By the time Frankenberg finally unloaded WordPerfect in early 1996 (for $750 million less than Noorda had paid for it), even the initially skeptical Bill Gates had decided that leadership in the software industry depended on integrating World Wide Web connectivity into every Microsoft product. Microsoft began giving away software that made Windows NT into an Internet-capable web server, and by early 1997 Novell's share of the network software market had eroded to 57 percent, down from 70 percent in 1993. Moreover, when NetWare's upgrade revenues were excluded, Windows NT could claim a 42 percent to 33 percent market share lead over Novell's once dominant product.

The Internet, Java, and Eric Schmidt: 1997

In late 1996, Frankenberg had resigned as CEO, and Novell began searching for a replacement equal to the Microsoft threat. In March 1997 it hired Sun Microsystems' chief technology officer, Eric Schmidt, the mastermind behind Sun's Java programming language. By promising to enable business applications to be written independently of any single operating system, Java seemed to threaten Windows' near monopoly on the operating system market. Moreover, the rapid growth of the Internet meant that corporate computers could not only be networked internally but connected to the computers of subsidiaries, vendors, and customers alike—and Windows' lock on the operating system market suddenly seemed increasingly beside the point.

Schmidt believed that, together, Java and the Internet marked the emergence of a new open environment or computing medium that even Microsoft could not hope to control. If NetWare could be retooled and repositioned as the platform through which corporate computer networks could connect their processes to the Internet (via their internal "intranets"), Novell could claim a major niche in the next generation of network software. "We have an opportunity," Schmidt told *Red Herring* magazine, "to become the primary Internet server platform in corporations as they move to computing platforms fully integrated between themselves and their customers and suppliers." Specifically, Schmidt hoped to position NetWare's Directory Services feature—which gave corporate networks an all-in-one tool for tracking network users, passwords, e-mail addresses, applications, and the like—as the indispensable organizing tool to enable corporations to manage the increasingly complex components of Internet-based business computing.

Within weeks of his arrival in 1997, Schmidt cut Novell's workforce by 18 percent, wrote off unsellable NetWare inventory, and set in motion Novell's reincarnation as an Internet-capable networking services provider. NetWare was rechristened IntranetWare, and by the fall of 1997 the first Novell products were released that didn't require customers to own NetWare.

The core of Schmidt's plan for Novell's future, however, was a new product code-named "Moab" that would integrate Internet features and the Java programming language in a single package. When Moab hit the market in 1998, Novell could stand to become the only supplier of a network software solution that replaced the thicket of products corporations had once had to buy separately to manage such tasks as messaging, connecting to the Internet, maintaining intranet security, filtering Web content, and publishing to the Web.

For that day to arrive, however, Novell had to overcome a number of obstacles. Wall Street analysts were taking a wait-and-see attitude toward Schmidt's turnaround strategy, Novell's stock continued to languish, and Novell had a history of missing its deadlines for delivering new products. Moreover, arch rival Microsoft was readying its own version of Novell's Directory Services (named Active Directory) to be integrated in future versions of Windows NT, and sales of Windows NT were on a pace to surpass NetWare's for the first time by 1998. Like many computer firms before it, Novell's rebirth seemed to rest on an unattractive proposition: betting against Microsoft.

Principal Subsidiaries

Fluent, Inc.; Novell de Argentina S.A.; Novell Austria; Novell Belgium B.V.B.A.; Novell do Brasil Software Ltda.; Novell Canada, Ltd.; Novell Columbia; Novell Czech Republic; Novell Denmark A/S; Novell Europe, Inc.; Novell European Support Center GmbH (Germany); Novell Finland OY; Novell GmbH (Germany); Novell Hong Kong; Novell Hungary KFT; Novell International, Ltd. (Barbados); Novell Ireland Software Limited Ireland; Novell Israel; Novell Italia S.R.L.; Novell Korea Co., Ltd.; Novell Latino America Norte, CA (Venezuela); Novell de Mexico, S.A.DE C.V.; Novell Netherland B.V.; Novell Norway; Novell Polska Sp.Zo.o. (Poland); Novell Portugal Informatica LDA; Novell Pty, Ltd. (Australia); Novell S.A.R.L.(France); Novell Services Asia Pacific Pty Ltd. (Australia); Novell Singapore; Novell Software Development Pvt., Ltd. (India); Novell South Africa Proprietary Ltd.; Novell Spain S.A.; Novell Svenska A.B. (Sweden); Novell Schweiz A.G. (Switzerland); Novell U.K., Ltd.; Novell Japan, Ltd.; Onward Novell Software Pvt., Ltd. (India).

Further Reading

Atchison, Sandra D., and Evan I. Schwartz, "Can LAN Lord Novell Extend Its Territory?," *Business Week,* September 2, 1991.

Chithelen, Ignatius, "Computers Talking to Computers," *Forbes,* September 15, 1988.

Cortese, Amy, "Microsoft May Sound 'The Death Knell' for Novell," *Business Week,* March 25, 1996.

Fisher, Lawrence M., "Preaching Love Thy Competitor," *New York Times,* March 29, 1992.

Hatlestad, Luc, "Time Is Running Out," *Red Herring,* October 1997.

Heskett, Ben, "Novell's New Strategy," NEWS.COM, October 28, 1997.

Pitta, Julie, "How to Lose a Lead," *Forbes,* August 7, 1989.

Reinhardt, Andy, "There's No Looking Back for Eric Schmidt," *Business Week,* September 1, 1997.

Reiss, Spencer, "The Network Is the Network," *Wired,* August 1997.

Wilson, John W., "Suddenly the Heavyweights Smell Money in Computer Networks," *Business Week,* April 27, 1987.

—Scott M. Lewis
—updated by Paul S. Bodine

Office Depot Incorporated

2200 Old Germantown Road
Delray Beach, Florida 33445
U.S.A.
(800) 937-3600
Fax: (561) 265-4400
Web site: http://www.officedepot.com

Public Company
Incorporated: 1986
Employees: 31,000
Sales: $5.3 billion (1996)
Stock Exchanges: New York
SICs: 5943 Stationery Stores

Thanks to its 1991 merger with competitor Office Club, Office Depot Incorporated is one of the largest discount retailer of office supplies and furniture in North America. In addition to office products, the company also sells computer hardware and electronics designed for small business applications. Office Depot operates over 300 stores, most of them located in the South, the lower Midwest, and the West.

Mid-1980s Origins

Along with rival companies Staples and Office Club, Office Depot was a pioneer in the field of office supplies discount retail. The three companies were founded within months of each other in 1986 in three different corners of the United States—Office Depot in Florida, Staples in Massachusetts, and Office Club in California. All of them saw opportunities in selling office supplies to small businesses at bulk discount rates that had previously been the privilege of larger companies. Since small businesses had never purchased supplies in quantities large enough to receive bulk discounts, they had been at the mercy of conventional retailers who, in the absence of price competition, could sell at manufacturer's suggested retail prices and take markups of as much as 100 percent. Buying directly from manufacturers instead of wholesalers and keeping overhead low, a discount retailer could offer goods from 20 to 75

percent off of full retail. Another trend that proved advantageous for these three companies was the advent of warehouse-style discount retailers in the 1980s; what Price Club had done for general merchandise and what Circuit City had done for consumer electronics, Office Depot, Office Club, and Staples sought to do for ballpoint pens and legal pads.

Office Depot was founded in Boca Raton, Florida, by entrepreneur F. Patrick Sher and two partners. The company opened its first retail store in Fort Lauderdale in October 1986, and it proved successful enough that two more Office Depot stores appeared in Florida by the end of the year. The company continued to grow rapidly; in 1987 it opened seven more stores in Florida and Georgia and sales topped $33 million. Sher did not have long to savor his success, however, for he died of leukemia scarcely a year after his first store had opened. He was succeeded as CEO by David Fuente, an experienced retail executive whom Office Depot lured away from Sherwin-Williams, where he had been president of the paint stores division.

Fuente's strategy was to have Office Depot continue to grow at a breakneck pace, to trap market share before copycats got into the act. He planned to enter ten new markets a year and add 50 stores a year. Although Office Depot opened only 16 stores in 1988, expanding into Kentucky, North Carolina, Tennessee, and Texas, Fuente met his goal in 1989 and 1990. Sales topped $132 million in 1988, and Office Depot went public in June with an initial offering of more than six million shares at $3.33 per share. Office supply discount retail as a whole was proving wildly successful; although they accounted for only a small fraction of office supply retail sales by the end of the decade, at least one analyst predicted in 1989 that discounters would form the fastest growing specialty-retail segment for several years to come.

Office Depot gained the distinction of being the first of the three original discount chains to turn a profit for a period of four consecutive quarters, which it did during the last two quarters of 1988 and the first two of 1989. The company achieved its success with stores that resembled nothing so much as warehouses. Their decor was functional and unassuming, in a style described by a reporter for *Fortune* as "plain pipe rack," with merchandise stacked floor-to-ceiling on steel shelves. As David Fuente explained it, "Customers pick only from the first six feet

---

Company Perspectives:

Office Depot's mission is to be the most successful office products company in the world. We will achieve success by an uncompromising commitment to: A) superior customer satisfaction—a company-wide attitude that recognizes that customer satisfaction is EVERYTHING; B) associate-oriented environment—an acknowledgement that our associates are our most valuable resource. We are committed to fostering a environment where recognition, innovation, communication and the entrepreneurial spirit are encouraged and rewarded; C) industry leading value/selection/services—offering only the highest-quality merchandise available at everyday low prices, providing customers with an outstanding balance of value, selection and services; D) ethical business conduct—conducting our business with uncompromising honesty and integrity; E) shareholder value—providing our shareholders with superior return-on-investment.

---

of 'shelf' space anyway. So we use the area above 'for storage'.'' By 1989, Office Depot stores were averaging $150,000 in sales per week. Of course, lack of concern for the aesthetics of interior design characterized the company's competitors, as well. Office Depot held an edge in that commercial rents were lower in the South than elsewhere in the United States, allowing the company to build exceptionally large stores and still keep overhead costs relatively low.

Rapid Growth in the Early 1990s

Office Depot continued to grow dramatically in 1989 and 1990, expanding beyond its regional base in the South into the Midwest. By the end of 1990 the company boasted 122 stores scattered across 19 states and sales of $625 million. Much of that expansion was financed by the sale of 3.6 million shares of stock for $41 million to Carrefour, a French chain-store concern with subsidiaries throughout Europe.

The office supply discount field became more crowded and competitive in the early 1990s as other companies, including OfficeMax and BizMart, joined the lucrative industry. With the struggle for market share becoming more vigorous, Office Depot and Office Club decided to merge in 1991. The move solidified Office Depot's position on the Pacific Coast in one swoop by eliminating a major competitor and giving it a substantial number of new stores in a regional market where the company previously had only a slim presence. For its part, Office Club had not fared quite as well as its fellow discounting pioneers; during the four quarters that constituted Office Depot's first profitable one-year period Office Club lost $2.7 million, compared to Office Depot's gain of $5.1 million and Staples's narrower loss of $1.9 million. The merger, therefore, proved advantageous to Office Club as well.

Office Club had been founded in northern California in 1986 by Mark Begelman—previously an executive with British American Tobacco—in partnership with a friend who had been selling office products to Price Club. They reasoned that the same marketing principles that allowed Price Club to retail office supplies at deep discounts would work for stores specializing in that kind of merchandise. The first Office Club store opened in January 1987 in Concord, California. Office Club grew quickly, though not as frantically as Office Depot. By the end of 1987 Office Club had opened five stores. At the time of the merger, it operated 59 stores, most of them in California, and had posted annual sales of $300 million.

The merger was approved by Office Depot shareholders in April 1991. As a result of the agreement, which entailed a stock swap worth $137 million, Mark Begelman became president and chief operating officer of Office Depot, with David Fuente remaining chairman and CEO. Over the next 13 months, all Office Club stores were either closed or converted into Office Depot outlets, and the membership fee that Office Club had been charging its regular customers was dropped.

Even after the merger, Office Depot continued to expand. In June 1991 it sold another 1.8 million shares of stock to Carrefour for $40 million to finance expected growth, making Carrefour an 18 percent owner. In addition to the outlets acquired from Office Club, the company opened 57 new stores in 1991. At the end of the year, Office Depot had 229 stores and posted sales of $1.3 billion.

At about the same time, Office Depot saw its sales of office machines, including personal computers, begin to grow by leaps and bounds, and the company began to emphasize this side of its business more strongly. In December 1992, Begelman claimed in an interview that ten percent of all fax machines sold in the United States were sold by Office Depot. Store layouts were redesigned so that more machines could be put on display. The company began selling not only PC clones by Packard-Bell and Compaq, but also the real thing—in August 1991 IBM agreed to let Office Depot sell its PS/1 computers and around that time Apple gave permission for them to sell the Macintosh Performa line as well.

In 1992 Office Depot went international, acquiring HQ Office International, the parent company of the Great Canadian Office Supplies Warehouse chain, which operated seven stores in western Canada. HQ Office International had been founded in 1990 by Robert McNulty as a Canadian extension of his unsuccessful California-based HQ Office Supplies Warehouse chain, which was carved up and bought out by Staples and BizMart in 1990. Office Depot immediately replaced the HQ Office International name with its own and began expanding its presence in Canada, opening two stores in Manitoba. Office Depot's entry into the Canadian market set the company up for an eventual confrontation with Business Depot, a small chain based in eastern Canada, in which Staples held a minority stake.

In addition to expanding into new geographic areas, Office Depot began expanding its customer base. Originally catering to businesses with 20 or fewer employees, Office Depot decided to attract larger business by acquiring contract stationers and integrating them into its retail business. In May 1993 Office Depot acquired the office supply operations of contract stationer Wilson Stationery & Printing, a subsidiary of Steelcase Inc. The deal was valued at $16.5 million. In the next year the company bought three more contract stationers.

Having successfully moved into the established retail office supply market, Office Depot was confident they could challenge the existing system that served larger businesses. CEO David Fuente told *Forbes* in May 1994, "We're all selling the same stuff; we're all selling legal pads and pens and pencils, and we all buy from the same place. The real difference in performance is going to be: Are you pricing them better? Giving better service? Delivering better? The difference is not in the strategy but in the execution." Staples and OfficeMax clearly felt Office Depot was on the right track: they both followed suit by acquiring their own contract stationers. However, two years later Office Depot had yet to see big returns on its investment. Integrating the contract stationers into their core retail business had cost more than expected, but Office Depot remained confident that the more diverse customer base should make the investment worth it in the long run.

The company saw $2.6 billion in sales in 1993, with $63 million in profit. By 1994 Office Depot had grown to 362 stores, which still followed the company's original concept—warehouse-like buildings that stocked office supplies at 30 to 60 percent off manufacturer's list prices. The company's closest competitor, the Kmart subsidiary OfficeMax, was only half its size. Not satisfied, Office Depot planned to double the number of its stores in the next five years.

Challenges of the Mid- and Late 1990s

In late 1995 Office Depot's stock dipped following a slowdown in computer chip orders, which analysts feared would slow demand for personal computers. Smith Barney analyst James Stoeffel told *Financial World* that such fears were overstated. Because computer sales only accounted for approximately ten percent of Office Depot revenues and because the company only stocked the most popular brands, a slowdown might not mean disaster. "It's not immaterial, but it's obviously not the most critical part of their business," Stoeffel maintained. With its continued potential for growth, the company's stock soon bounced back from its low of $19 a share.

In 1997 Staples attempted to acquire Office Depot, its largest competitor, in a deal estimated at $4 billion. As these companies were number one and two, respectively, among discount chains, questions about antitrust violations were quickly raised. The Federal Trade Commission (FTC) found that the combined company would control prices in many metropolitan areas and that in cities where Office Depot and Staples competed head to head, prices might be expected to rise five to ten percent. The FTC sought a court order to stop Staples from buying Office Depot. In response, the two companies agreed to sell 63 stores to OfficeMax to open competition in certain areas, a proposal that had to be approved the FTC. They also argued that, with only five percent of the office supply market, their merger was not threatening. Unappeased, the FTC argued that office superstores are a market to themselves and that Office Depot and Staples controlled 75 percent of that market. As of early 1998, the two office supply giants remained hopeful of a merger.

Principal Subsidiaries

The Office Club, Inc.; H. Q. Office International, Inc.

Further Reading

"The Big Interview: Mark Begelman—Office Depot," *Office Products International,* December 1992.

Caminiti, Susan, "Seeking Big Money in Paper and Pens," *Fortune,* July 31, 1989.

Hirsh, Michael, "But Nary a Trust to Bust," *Newsweek,* June 2, 1997, pp. 44–45.

Kaye, Steven D., "Out with the Old, In with the New," *U.S. News & World Report,* March 24, 1997, p. 60.

La Monica, Paul R., "Office Depot: Stock Up," *Financial World,* January 30, 1996, p. 24.

Liebeck, Laura, "Office Depot Ventures Into Canada, Magazine Business," *Discount Store News,* February 3, 1992.

Milstone, Erik, "Office Depot on the Fast Track," *Palm Beach Post,* March 29, 1992.

Moukheiber, Zina, "A Lousy Day for Golf," *Forbes,* May 9, 1994, pp. 60, 64.

Selz, Michael, "Office Supply Firms Take Different Paths to Success," *Wall Street Journal,* May 30, 1991.

—Douglas Sun
—updated by Susan Windisch Brown

Papeteries de Lancey

B.P. 62
38196 Brignoud Cedex
France
(33) 04 76 13 11 11
Fax: (33) 04 76 13 11 22

Private Company
Incorporated: 1869 as Papeteries Bergès; 1921 as
   Papeteries de France
Employees: 310
Sales: FFr 420 million (US$80 million) (1997)
SICs: 2611 Pulp Mills; 2621 Paper Mills

Papeteries de Lancey has entered a new era of its 120-year history. With a management-led buyout in October 1997, the producer and distributor of pulp and paper products, located in the French Alps near Grenoble, has regained its independence after more than 20 years as a subsidiary of France's Aussedat-Rey (itself a subsidiary of the U.S.-based International Paper). Papeteries de Lancey's principal products, under the brand name Nepal, include layered papers destined for magazine covers and interiors, catalogs, brochures, and other advertising materials. The company manufactured more than 90,000 tons of layered paper in 1997, making it one of the leading French independent producers of this product. Some 90 percent of Papeteries de Lancey's layered paper—ranging in weight from 80 grams per square meter to more than 165 grams per square meter—is sold in rolls; the remaining ten percent is further processed into paper sheets. The company also produces 20,000 tons per year of mechanical pulp, destined to strengthen chemically produced paper pulp products. France remains the primary destination for roughly 80 percent of Papeteries de Lancey's production. Sales and distribution activities are conducted both by the company's own sales force and through the distribution network of Aussedat-Rey. Papeteries de Lancey posted sales of FFr 420 million in 1997, a figure predicted to rise to FFr 450 million for 1998, its first full year as an independent.

A Place in France's 19th-Century Industrial History

Lancey, a village located in the Belladonne mountain chain in the Dauphiné region of southeast France, numbered little more than 150 souls in the 1860s. The site, however, would soon earn a prominence not only in France, but throughout the world, for the innovation it brought to paper production and to industry in general. It was in Lancey that Aristide Bergès introduced the concept of "Houille Blanche" (white coal), a method for channeling the mountain region's waterfalls to produce the first hydroelectrical power systems.

Bergès, born in 1833, was the son of a prominent paper manufacturer in northeastern France. After earning the title of chemical engineer at the age of 19, Bergès would begin a career distinguished by a number of innovations. One of his first projects was the invention of a steam-driven asphalt pulping machine, used to pave the area around the Arc de Triomphe in Paris. Bergès next traveled to Spain, to aid in the development of that country's railroad. There, he perfected a rack railway system enabling trains to climb steep slopes without slipping downhill. Returning to France at the beginning of the 1860s, Bergès first joined his father's paper mill, where he set to work improving the quality of wood pulp. Bergès introduced a new method for producing mechanical pulp, using a sandstone millstone. Bergès's father, however, was reluctant to abandon the traditional pulping methods, and Bergès decided to form his own paper mill to incorporate his ideas.

In 1864, Bergès, with his father's help, formed a paper mill in nearby Mazeres sur Salat. Two years later Bergès received an offer from a wealthy industrialist to construct a paper mill in the Isere region of southeast France. One of Bergès's first projects was improving the de-fibering method then in use, invented by the German Woelter. This method, which involved a mill spinning at high speeds, chafing logs to transform them into raw pulp material, required a constant flow of water to keep the logs from catching fire. The Woelter mill, however, used a manual adjustment screw to keep the mill in contact with the log—the result was frequent irregularities, leading to defective pulp and a great deal of waste. Bergès adapted the mill, replacing the manual adjustment with a hydraulic press that enabled the mill to recover more paper pulp and of a higher quality. The Bergès turbine quickly became popular and soon surpassed the number of Woelter mills in use at the time.

Bergès's visit in 1867 to Lancey, a hamlet of 150 nestled in the foothills of the Belledonne mountain chain on the Isere's left bank, was to lead to his next, and greatest, innovation. The use of the pressure of falling water in mills was already a common practice; yet the height of the falls tended to be modest—in Lancey, Bergès found a flour mill turned by a four-meter fall. Bergès's innovation, inspired by the 3,000-meter heights of the nearby mountains, was to design a fall of greater distances, thought to be impractical at the time. Attracted by Lancey and its surroundings, Bergès installed a new paper mill and set about building a 200-meter fall; by 1869 he had succeeded in driving two Bergès turbines, with a generated force of 20 kg/square centimeter. Soon after, Bergès extended the fall to 450 meters, producing a force of 50 kg/square centimeter.

Bergès made steady improvements to his method. By 1882 he had installed a second fall, at an altitude of 452 meters but with a total fall of 2,850 meters. By then he had already begun to look higher: gazing at the whitecaps of the Belledonne mountain chain, Bergès envisaged the possibility of tapping the immense potential energy that could be generated from such heights. This energy Bergès dubbed *Houille Blanche,* or "white coal." Introducing the concept for the first time at the 1889 Paris Exposition, Bergès took an unusual step. Rather than attempting to commercialize his idea (indeed, his exhibit did not even mention his paper mill), Bergès simply offered the design of his waterfall to the world. The phrase Houille Blanche quickly became commonplace and was eagerly adopted not only throughout the French Alps, but in mountainous regions throughout the world. The houille blanche concept was not limited to the paper mill industry, but was quickly adopted throughout heavy industry, giving rise to new and more productive steel, aluminum, and other mills. Bergès would succeed not merely in changing the industrial landscape of the Alps, but in helping France become one of the world's leading industrial and economic powers.

The Lancey mill prospered under Bergès. With a new 500-meter fall installed in 1891, the Lancey mill's energy resources rose from 1,000 horsepower to 6,000, with a production potential of two million kilograms of wood pulp per year. Bergès was not content simply to produce paper. Instead, he sought to turn his innovations to improving the quality of people's lives. For this, he envisaged reducing the cost of paper to an extent that the price of reading materials could come into the reach of anyone. On a more practical level, Bergès saw a means of tapping the excess power generated by his falls for use in providing inexpensive electricity to the entire valley area. In 1898 Bergès founded the Société d'Eclairage du Grésauvdan, with a 15,000-horsepower electrical plant providing power to 150,000 16-candle lamps.

Bergès, meanwhile, continued to climb—to tap the Lake Crozet, situated at an altitude of 1,968 meters. Despite skepticism, Bergès succeeded in constructing a viaduct system to channel the lake's water. Bergès met with strong resistance, however, from the local community, who accused him of di-

verting the water for his own profit. Taken to court, Bergès lost the battle and was ordered to dismantle the viaduct. On appeal, however, Bergès succeeded in keeping his viaduct and instead was ordered to pay an indemnity to the local population. The experience was said to have broken Bergès's spirit; receiving honors in 1903 from the Congress for the Advancement of Science, Bergès died the following year.

The Paper Mills of France in the 1920s

Bergès's son, who had earlier joined his father, took over the paper mill's operations after his father's death. In 1907, however, the younger Bergès appointed Auguste Biclet to direct the company's operations. Under Biclet, the paper mill would grow to become one of France's five leading producers of wood pulp and paper products. Biclet, who arrived in Lancey at the age of 36, had begun his career as a worker in a paper mill in his native Vendée region. After becoming foreman, Biclet then moved to Vosges, where he became director of a paper mill.

Biclet would quickly transform the Lancey mill. By the time of the First World War, the mill had expanded its operations, adding a plant for producing chemically processed pulp, adding a machine to produce grease-proof paper, and, after acquiring the Papeteries d'Alfortville, entering the production of carton-grade paper. During the war, Biclet extended Lancey's production to include rag paper and recycled paper as well. Production rose to some 50 tons per day. The war effort, however, made it difficult for the company to procure the fuel needed to operate its steam-powered machinery. At the end of the war, Lancey found a solution to this problem, in the form of its own coal mine in the nearby Belledonne mountains.

Meanwhile, Biclet would prove to be socially progressive: in 1911 the company built low-cost housing for its workers, eventually constructing more than 500 homes by 1920. Papeteries Bergès, which had become a major landholder in the region, also offered its workers individual garden lots, while the company itself operated two milk farms to provide milk inexpensively to the company's cooperative food stores. By the 1920s the company's workers would also enjoy library facilities, sports and games facilities, low-cost bathing houses, and a day-care center, as well as the company's institution of a 12-week maternity leave (and the offering to its workers a bonus of FFr 150 for each birth).

The postwar period proved difficult for France's paper industry, faced with dumping practices from foreign pulp producers. By the beginning of the 1920s Lancey was forced to close its chemical pulp operations. Other paper and pulp producers nearby were also struggling. In 1921 Biclet and Papeteries Bergès joined with another large Isere-based producer, Papeteries Fredet, to found the Papeteries de France. The new company quickly added several smaller concerns, bringing the company's holdings beyond its own region into the nearby Savoy, Seine-et-Oise, and Seine regions. Biclet himself was named director of the new concern.

Papeteries de France, which included 18 paper machines capable of producing up to 130 tons of paper per day, as well as 50 tons of carton per day, offered an extensive range of paper and pulp types. The company would soon establish itself as one of France's top five producers, a position confirmed by the acquisition of two more paper works in the 1930s. Biclet also sought a means to improve its commercial competitiveness. In 1922 he began developing the company's own distribution network, considered a revolutionary move at a time when paper sales were conducted through a range of middlemen. The network put in place featured 16 warehouses and agencies located throughout France and its North African colonies and enabled the company to counter the aggressive pricing practices of its foreign competitors.

The Depression would place Papeteries de France under new pressures. Lacking resources, the company was unable to invest in its infrastructure. By the dawn of the Second World War, the technological advances made by American and Scandinavian paper and pulp producers once again created a trade imbalance: in 1939 fully 75 percent of the pulp used in France and by the Papeteries de France was of foreign origin. The company struggled to stay in business—by then the village of Lancey had grown to a population of 3,500 and the company's paper works had become the principal employer, with some 1,000 workers. The descent into the Second World War, however, would make it impossible for the company to invest in modernizing its infrastructure. Finding fuel to operate its equipment also proved difficult; this shortage was solved, however, with the opening of a new mine at Saint Mury in 1941.

From "Liberation" to Independence

Emerging from the war years, Papeteries de France was confronted with an aging machine park that could not rival the technologies developed by the neutral Scandinavians and by the United States during the war. The company also mourned the loss of Auguste Biclet, who died in 1946. In that year Pierre Rigaut took over as the company's general manager and led Papeteries de France into an aggressive modernization program that would last through the 1950s. Papeteries de France determined to put in place a two-prong strategy: the first, to develop domestic raw pulp resources to counteract the dominance of foreign imports; the second, to modernize the company's paper-producing technologies to compete on a worldwide scale.

In 1950 the company established a research department, which set to work on developing a technology to replace the more common coniferous-based pulp with a pulp prepared from the region's rich deciduous forests. The effort would represent a heavy financial investment for the company, but resulted, in 1955, in the introduction of a deciduous-based, semi-chemically produced pulp. The first such pulp produced in France, the new technology enabled the company to begin supplying some 15 tons per day, a number that would double by the end of the decade, as the company reopened its chemical pulp operations, closed since the 1920s. The company also began acquiring other France-based pulp producers. By 1960 the company had turned

the balance; the proportion of domestic pulp used in the company's production had risen beyond 77 percent.

At the same time, Papeteries de France also began investing heavily in upgrading its equipment infrastructure. The carton production facility at Alfortville was modernized in two steps, from 1950–1951 and from 1955–1956, while the company also modernized its existing paper production machinery, expanded its logging and lumber operations, constructed a new power plant for its factories, and began construction of an entirely new paper processing machine, dubbed Machine Number 8, which was completed in 1960. The new machine enabled the company to expand into a new and growing market, that of layered papers for the magazine covers and inserts. Papeteries de France's early entry enabled the company quickly to capture some 25 percent of the French market. By the mid-1960s, with a total output of more than 300,000 tons per year, including 150,000 tons of layered paper and carton, Papeteries de Lancey had grown to represent 7.5 percent of the total paper production in France.

Papeteries de France's independence would come to an end, however, when it was acquired by French leader Aussedat-Rey in 1971. The company, reorganized and renamed Société des Papeteries de Lancey as a subsidiary of Aussedat-Rey in 1984, with a capitalization of FFr 102 million, would ultimately come under the sway of International Paper, after that company's acquisition of Aussedat-Rey in the late 1980s. In the mid-1990s, however, Aussedat-Rey decided to focus its activities on its European leadership position as a supplier of office-grade papers and began looking to sell off its layered paper operations.

In October 1997 Aussedat-Rey agreed to sell off the Lancey operations to a group of Papeteries de Lancey's management, including CEO Jean-Luc Dominici. The transaction, performed for an undisclosed sum, included the absorption of Lancey's debt by Aussedat-Rey. Restored to independence, Papeteries de Lancey focused its attention on its layered paper production, shutting down its carton production operations, which reduced its payroll from 610 to 305 employees. Between 1996 and 1997 the newly private company began an investment program of some FFr 50 million to upgrade its facilities, with an additional FFr 30 million earmarked for 1998. Ending the 1997 year with sales of approximately FFr 420 million, Lancey predicted a rise in sales to more than FFr 450 million by the end of 1998, with a production increase from five to ten percent.

Further Reading

Lechiffre, Valérie, "Lancey'sur une Nouvelle Lancée!," *La Papeterie,* November 1997, p. 23.

Papeteries de France, "Au Berceau de la Houille Blanche," Paris: Papeteries de France, 1925.

"Papeteries de Lancey: Retour à l'Indépendance," *Revue du Papier Carton,* December 1997, p. 19.

—M.L. Cohen

Pathmark Stores, Inc.

301 Blair Road
Woodbridge, New Jersey 07095-0915
U.S.A.
(732) 499-3000
Fax: (732) 499-3072

*Wholly Owned Subsidiary of Supermarkets General
Holdings Corp.*
Incorporated: 1993
Employees: 20,700
Sales: $3.7 billion (1997)
SICs: 5411 Grocery Stores

The largest retailer in the Northeast operating under a single trade name, Pathmark Stores, Inc. had 145 supermarkets in New York, New Jersey, Pennsylvania, Connecticut, and Delaware in March 1997. Sixty-six of these stores were in New Jersey, many of them within the confines of the New York City and Philadelphia metropolitan areas. Pathmark was the only remaining entity of significant size within privately owned Supermarkets General Holdings Corp., its parent company, in the late 1990s.

Pathmark Foundings

The Pathmark chain arose out of the Wakefern cooperative formed in 1947 by independent New Jersey grocers who felt the need to organize to compete with large food chains. Some members of the cooperative agreed to operate their stores under the Shop-Rite name. Wakefern was both a wholesale and a retail operation. Among its members was a subgroup called Supermarkets Operating Co. Formed in 1956 by Alex Aidekman, Herb Brody, and Milt Perlmutter, this company opened new Shop-Rites and in 1963 branched into nonfood retail by acquiring Crown Drugs.

Supermarkets Operating Co. and General Super Markets, another subgroup within Wakefern, merged in 1966 to become Supermarkets General Corp., with Perlmutter as president. Supermarkets General operated 75 Shop-Rite stores in New Jer-

sey, New York, Connecticut, Delaware, and Pennsylvania at the end of 1966, with annual sales of about $420 million. It was achieving high volume by opening large stores in densely populated areas and keeping prices low on both nationally branded goods and private-label items.

In 1968 Supermarkets General left the Wakefern cooperative and renamed its Shop-Rite stores Pathmark. Although Supermarkets General had other holdings, including the recently acquired Genung's department store chain and Rickel Bros.'s home centers, the Pathmark business was its major operation. These units included not only supermarkets (33 of which had a drug department with a pharmacy) but 11 freestanding drugstores and 11 gasoline stations.

Pathmark's 81 supermarkets were accounting for about 85 percent of Supermarkets General's sales and 80 percent of its earnings in 1969. The number of Pathmark supermarkets had reached 91 in October 1971, and there were also 24 Pathmark gas stations and 14 Pathmark drugstores. In May 1972, 94 of the 96 supermarkets began operating around the clock, seven days a week. Pathmark pioneered in the use of computer scanners at checkout counters, introduced by the chain in 1974.

After a period of relative stagnation, Pathmark opened, in 1977, the first of its "Super Centers"—huge discount grocery stores that also offered health and beauty aids, small appliances, and videotape rentals. These 50,000-square-foot units were being created in large part by renovating and expanding the existing stores. At the end of the year Pathmark had full-line pharmacies in 81 of its 103 supermarkets, horticulture departments in 64, bakery departments in 60, and "mini-bank branches" in 13. In its annual report, Supermarkets General claimed its sales per store were the highest in the industry. "Pathmark does more than three times the business in a store only 33% larger than the industry average," the report said.

In its 1978 annual report, Supermarkets General claimed Pathmark had become the top supermarket chain in the New York metropolitan area, with a 15 percent market share. Twelve of its 109 outlets now were Super Centers. In all, Pathmark sales volume in 1978 came to $1.8 billion and the chain contributed 82 percent to corporate profits. About 60 percent of the volume was generated in stores opened, enlarged, or substantially re-modeled during the past three years. Perlmutter died in 1978 and was succeeded by Brody as chief executive officer of Su-permarkets General.

Pathmark's supermarket sales reached $2.8 billion in 1982, when it was the nation's tenth largest supermarket chain. Of the 121 units, 62 were Super Centers. Barnes & Noble minibook-stores were now located in 27 Pathmark supermarkets and cheese shops were located in 19. In addition, the company had 13 freestanding Pathmark drug stores. Pathmark continued to domi-nate Supermarkets General's sales and operating profits, with 87 and 83 percent of the corporate total, respectively. Pathmark opened Manhattan's first superstore, a 42,600-square-foot unit, in Peck Slip, near Chinatown, in 1983. The chain was still number one in the New York metropolitan area in 1985, with a 12.5 percent market share, according to a telephone survey.

Private Company, 1987–93

To foil a takeover bid by Dart Group Corp., management took Supermarkets General private in a $2.1 billion 1987 lever-aged buyout, in which Merrill Lynch Capital Markets Inc. received 55 percent of the shares and the Equitable Life Assur-ance Society of the U.S., 30 percent, with management retain-ing ten percent for itself. Servicing the debt ($1.6 billion in early 1990, half of it in junk bonds) soon proved a problem.

Although corporate sales reached $6 billion in fiscal 1989 (the year ended on the last Saturday of January 1989), the 51-unit Rickel subsidiary was performing poorly and the 142-store Pathmark grocery chain had slipped to third place in the New York area. Many of the Pathmark units had become, according to a *Forbes* article, "unkempt, dirty, and outmoded." Pathmark, this story went on to say, "continues to stock scores of the dreary no-frills offerings customers have shunned for years." Merrill Lynch sacked Chief Executive Kenneth Peskin, replacing him with Jack Futterman. The only bright spot for the parent company was its 66-unit Purity Supreme division, con-sisting of Massachusetts grocery and convenience store chains acquired in 1984. This division was sold in 1991 for about $265 million. (Supermarkets General's department stores had been sold in 1986.)

Supermarkets General lost money in every fiscal year be-tween 1988 and 1993 and sales volume every fiscal year be-tween 1989 and 1993. In fiscal 1993 it lost a record $617 million on sales of $4.34 billion, mainly reflecting a $600 million write-down of goodwill—the premium paid in excess of assets—in the 1987 buyout. The company's interest payments, averaging between $160 million and $180 million a year on its debt, were hampering its efforts to modernize its stores and thereby keep in pace with its competitors. Pathmark consisted at this time of 146 supermarkets, 33 freestanding drug stores, and seven distri-bution-processing facilities.

Supermarkets General sought in March 1993 to take Path-mark public, but backed off in the face of insufficient investor interest. Instead, in an October 1993 corporate reorganization, Supermarkets General Corp., a subsidiary of Supermarkets General Holdings Corp., changed its name to Pathmark Stores, Inc. and in essence recapitalized $1.3 billion in outstanding

debt. The company thereby lowered its interest costs, reportedly from about 13 to nine percent of revenues, and thus increased cash flow. This allowed the company to step up capital invest-ment in Pathmark. Rickel was spun off at this time and was sold in 1994.

Pathmark Stores, 1993–97

Pathmark was now putting its hopes for the future on stores even bigger than the traditional Super Centers. The Pathmark 2000 format, first introduced in 1992, called for units as large as 64,000 square feet. By early 1995 there were 27 such stores, some new, some converted from other Pathmark outlets. They emphasized perishables such as produce, seafood, baked goods, flowers, and delicatessen items, as well as health and beauty aids with a selection to rival that of drugstore and discount competitors. These goods all had higher profit margins than packaged groceries. Pathmark 2000 stores also offered a cus-tomer service desk for product returns, video rentals, film processing, and UPS mail delivery, and restrooms with chang-ing tables for mothers with babies in diapers. By the end of May 1996, 44 such stores were in operation and, by February 1997, 53 were in operation.

Pathmark also added to its private-label products in 1994 by introducing an upscale line called Pathmark Preferred to its generic No Frills brand and its mid-tier Pathmark brand. At this time Pathmark's more than 3,300 private-label items were ac-counting for about 24 percent of the chain's sales. In late 1995 a Pathmark on Long Island launched Chef's Creations, a program offering a menu of about 40 entrees, side dishes, and salads made in-store each day by a team of chefs. Pathmark, in late 1996, introduced Chef's Creations To Go—fresh, prepackaged meals for takeout, offering a choice of eight entrees and side dishes in microwavable containers. An outside manufacturer was preparing these meals to Pathmark's specifications.

By the summer of 1994 Pathmark had won its way back into the favor of New Yorkers, according to one survey that found it to be the city's most popular supermarket chain. A total of 17 percent of city residents were shopping at Pathmark regularly, and more than half of those who said they did so cited its low prices. The top-ranking chain in Brooklyn, the Bronx, and Staten Island, Pathmark was now operating 17 superstores in New York City.

Pathmark was honored in 1995 as Pharmacy Chain of the Year by the magazine *Drug Topics*—the first time a supermarket retailer had won the award. All of its 142 supermarkets had pharmacies except six that were located in shopping centers with lease restrictions. According to the company, Pathmark was the leader in filling prescriptions in the metropolitan New York area and was participating in more than 200 major insurance plans. Prescriptions accounted for nearly seven percent of Pathmark's sales volume in 1994. Futterman, still the company's chief execu-tive officer, was himself a registered pharmacist.

In June 1995, however, Pathmark reduced its pharmacy operations by selling 30 of its 36 freestanding drugstores to Rite Aid Corp. for $60 million. These outlets had accounted for $145 million in sales in fiscal 1995, about 3.5 percent of the companywide total. A company executive said that although the 30 stores had earned satisfactory profits, Pathmark had decided to concentrate its pharmacy efforts in the supermarkets, which he said were more efficient and attractive to customers. Pathmark's remaining drugstores—six Connecticut ones featuring deeply discounted prices—were subsequently closed during 1995–1996.

Construction began in August 1997 on Pathmark's controversial $14.5 million supermarket in Manhattan's East Harlem. This 53,000-square-foot unit was the first large supermarket in Harlem and had been bitterly opposed by owners of neighborhood food stores. This Pathmark was expected to generate hundreds of construction jobs as well as 200 in-store jobs and would include a pharmacy and a Chase Manhattan Bank branch. Pathmark was planning its biggest Bronx store in 1998: a 55,000-square-foot unit on ten acres in the blighted area east of Crotona Park.

Supermarkets General cut its loss in fiscal 1994 (the year ended January 29, 1994, which the company itself defined as 1993, however) to $17 million (excluding extraordinary items and accounting changes) on net sales of $4.21 billion. It had its first profitable year in fiscal 1995 (ended January 28, 1995) since fiscal 1987, earning $10 million (not counting a $13 million credit for its prior losses) in net income on $4.21 billion in net sales. Pathmark's supermarket sales came to $3.84 billion and $3.79 billion in these respective fiscal years.

In fiscal 1996 (the fiscal year ended February 3, 1996), Supermarkets General had net income of $77 million on sales of $3.97 billion. Pathmark's supermarket sales came to $3.85 billion. In fiscal 1997 (ending February 1, 1997), the parent company had a net loss of $20 million on sales of $3.71 billion. This result included a charge the company took for the upcoming sale of 12 unprofitable Pathmark stores, most of them in southern New Jersey. Pathmark's supermarket sales came to all but $9 million of the corporate total. Same-store supermarket sales decreased 2.8 percent from the previous fiscal year, primarily due to heavy competition. James Donald, Futterman's successor as chief executive officer, laid off more than 200 employees at Pathmark's Woodbridge, New Jersey headquarters in March 1997.

In addition to Pathmark's corporate headquarters, Pathmark had, in 1997, distribution facilities for dry groceries and meat, dairy, and deli products in Woodbridge; a distribution facility for frozen food in Dayton, New Jersey; one for dry groceries in

North New Brunswick, New Jersey; and one for general merchandise (health care and beauty products, pharmaceuticals, and tobacco) in Edison, New Jersey. It had processing facilities for delicatessen products in Somerset, New Jersey and for banana ripening in Avenel, New Jersey. Pathmark's stores ranged from 26,000 to 66,500 square feet in size. All but five were either Pathmark 2000 or Super Center stores, and all but seven contained in-store pharmacy departments.

In October 1997 Pathmark announced that C&S Wholesale Grocers of Brattleboro, Vermont would take over its distribution facilities and become the chain's supplier for substantially all groceries and perishables. Pathmark was expected to receive perhaps $50 million from the deal, part of which would be used to pay down its debt of $1.47 billion.

Further Reading

Brookman, Faye, "Big Stores Winning Food Fight in NY," *Crain's New York Business,* August 29, 1994, pp. 3, 17.
——, "Into the Future with Pathmark 2000," *Women's Wear Daily,* February 3, 1995, p. 6.
"Changing the Rules," *Forbes,* June 15, 1967, p. 54.
Dowdell, Stephen, "Pathmark Introduces Upscale Private Label," *Supermarket News,* August 29, 1994, pp. 29, 32.
Fiorilla, Paul, "Pathmark Searches for New Leadership," *Business News New Jersey,* May 29, 1996, p. 4 and continuation.
Fitzgerald, Beth, "Pathmark Will Shed 12 Sites and 300 Jobs," *Newark Star-Ledger,* March 27, 1997, p. 59.
Garry, Michael, "Preparing for the Millennium," *Progressive Grocer,* May 1995, pp. 82, 85–86, 88.
May, Roger B., "Supermarket Shopping in Wee Hours, or Any Old Time, Is Tested by a Chain," *Wall Street Journal,* May 24, 1972, p. 11.
Morgenson, Gretchen, "Can Bankers Sell Groceries?," *Forbes,* October 30, 1989, pp. 54, 56.
Nagle, James J., "Anticipating Consumerism," *New York Times,* October 24, 1971, Sec. 3, pp. 5, 12.
Quint, Michael, "Pathmark To Sell Rite Aid New York City Drugstores," *New York Times,* June 22, 1995, p. D2.
Rosendahl, Iris, "Well Done, Pathmark!," *Drug Topics,* April 24, 1995, pp. 65–66, 68.
"Supermarkets General Presents New Plan To Recapitalize Debt," *Wall Street Journal,* August 24, 1993, p. B8.
Weber, Joseph, "What Put Pathmark in Such a Pickle?," *Business Week,* February 26, 1990, pp. 68, 71.
Zwiebach, Elliot, "C&S To Take Over Pathmark's Distribution," *Supermarket News,* October 13, 1997, pp. 7, 71.

—Robert Halasz

P.C. Richard & Son Corp.

150 Prince Parkway
Farmingdale, New York 11735
U.S.A.
(516) 582-3800
Fax: (516) 843-4309

Private Company
Founded: 1909
Employees: 1,700
Sales: $510 million (1997 est.)
SICs: 5722 Household Appliance Stores; 5731 Radio,
Television, and Consumer Electronic Stores

P.C. Richard & Son Corp. is one of the largest major-appliance and consumer-electronics retailing chains in the fiercely competitive metropolitan New York area. The number of its stores increased from 11 in 1985, all in the city's borough of Queens and the two Long Island counties east of the city, to 38 in 1996, including outlets in New Jersey and Connecticut and four of the city's five boroughs.

Early Years to 1986

A Dutch immigrant, Peter ChrisP Brooklyn when he opened a hardware store in 1909 with his wife, Adelta. "We lived in the back like gypsies," P.C.'s only son, Alfred J. (A. J.), recalled in a *New York Times* interview. "And he had a little partition and he had a counter. And he fixed furnaces, replaced window glass. And that's how he accumulated inventory."

After threeP their lease, so they moved to a building they bought in Queens. Their first electrical appliance was an iron that cost $4.95 in 1924. "People just wouldn't spend that," said A. J. Richard. "They were getting, some of them, only $2.75 a week," he noted. In order to stimulate business, the store began offering credit, accepting as little as 50 cents a week. P.C. Richard & Son later laid claim to being the oldest appliance store in New York, if not the entire country.

According to A. J. Richard's account, during the 1920s he persuaded housewives to abandon their washboards and buy ringer washers by offering $5 to try the machines in their homes. After a while, he said, he was selling more Westinghouse washing machines than anyone else. A. J. Richard also said he instituted deferred-payment plans and rebate programs, established the first roadside drive-in appliance showroom, and had 15 salesmen working different territories. He claimed to have founded the first nonmanufacturer's service department after beginning to sell tube radio sets in 1935 and realizing that he would sooner or later have to repair them.

A. J. Richard became president of the company in 1947, when his father retired. There was a second Queens store in 1952, when P.C. Richard opened a third in Bellmore, a community in Long Island's Nassau County. By now the company was selling television sets, according to A. J.'s son Gary Richard, as well as radios and a variety of home appliances. (In another interview, however, Gary Richard would recall that the company did not begin to sell TVs until the beginning of the 1980s.)

Honest give and take between P.C. Richard and its vendors was an important element in the company's success, according to Gary Richard, who credited the willingness of one manufacturer to defer payment with saving P.C. Richard from bankruptcy in the 1950s. As urban dwellers continued to fill the two Long Island counties east of New York City, P.C. Richard grew with them. Even so, sales volume was still a relatively modest $27 million in 1983.

Major Expansion: 1986–93

In 1986, however, P.C. Richard had 16 stores, including five newly opened in Queens, and it ranked ninth among major appliance dealers in the United States, with sales volume of $96 million in these appliances alone. The company had sales in excess of $200 million in 1987 and was reportedly the largest General Electric dealership in the nation. Hundreds of appliances were on display in its stores, which averaged 10,000 to 11,000 square feet in size. By this time Gary Richard had succeeded his father as president. Corporate headquarters were in Hauppauge, Long Island.

P.C. Richard had sales volume of about $300 million in 1990, including about $130 million of electronics equipment and $110 million of appliances. The Richard chain also had been selling ready-to-assemble furniture since the mid-1970s. Among such items were entertainment centers, audio racks, and television and microwave-oven stands. The 21 stores, including five opened in Brooklyn during 1990—the first in that borough since the original P.C. Richard store—were being fitted with a racetrack design to take customers on the perimeters of every department and encourage impulse buying. A sophisticated computer system was linking billing and inventory throughout the chain and enabling a customer credit card to be approved in 15 seconds. The company began adding home office equipment to its product mix just before Christmas 1993.

In a 1990 *HFD/Home Furnishings Daily* interview, Gary Richard said that in the 1980s "much of our competition walked away from the appliance business, which left room for us, so we stayed with it." Not mincing words, he went on to declare, "It was not logical for those retailers to be in the appliance business. You don't get rich in this business, especially if your advertising is devious, or if you bait and switch products." Interviewed by another trade journal in 1993, he said, "It's our belief that there's nothing more important than satisfying the customer—you make money by accident when you do that."

There were 28 to 30 P.C. Richard stores—five of them former Newmark & Lewis outlets—in the summer of 1993, ranging from 8,000 to 18,000 square feet in size. The company, long debt-free, was now willing to take on a sizable level of credit in order to open stores outside its Long Island base—three in New Jersey, three in Connecticut, and one on Staten Island. It was building a new 600,000-square-foot warehouse in Farmingdale, Long Island, and expanding showrooms in Hauppauge, Plainview, Babylon, and Patchogue. P.C. Richard also had a 40,000-square-foot service center in Central Islip, Long Island.

Gary Richard acknowledged that the company's $30 million expansion program had been prompted by the demise of competitors as a result of the 1990–91 recession, including the giant retailers Crazy Eddie Inc. and Newmark & Lewis Inc. and more than a dozen smaller operators. "We're strong enough to do it," said Richard, "and if we don't, we could be wounded later." Once again, in this *Chain Store Age Executive* interview, he had harsh words for his competitors, saying the companies that had failed had done so not so much because of debt as because "they had no strong foundation. They were built on egos, and they constantly played cute, clever, and cunning."

Richard went on to say his company prided itself on honesty and integrity with vendors, customers, and employees and had built strong partnerships with its suppliers. "Some of our failed competitors were ruthless with the vendors," he claimed. "They had no mercy. Consequently, the vendors walked away from them when things began to go bad." Being an honest and reputable dealer of electronics and appliances, he added, "isn't

easy in any market, because the margins are so low. But it's even worse in New York, because we're competing with so many opportunists and thieves."

Among the unethical, or downright criminal, practices Richard cited were selling gray-market merchandise (meant for sale overseas and usually lacking a U.S. warranty), baiting and switching (advertising an item at a very low price to pull in customers, then saying it was out of stock and offering a more expensive model instead), charging extra for accessories that were supposed to be included free (such as batteries), and not passing on the sales tax. Asked why these practices were rife in electronics retailing, Richard called it "a want, not a need, business. If I have five camcorders in the trunk of my car, I can go to any block, ring five doorbells, and sell them. It's not the same with appliances. Nobody wants a refrigerator. They buy one because they need it, probably because their old one broke."

For a time P.C. Richard considered going public in order to finance its expansion. In connection with a public offering of common stock planned for August 1993, the company revealed that it had net sales of $314.6 million and net income in excess of $6 million in the 1992 fiscal year ended January 31, 1993. The company's long-term debt was only $500,000, but about $11 million of the proceeds from the proposed stock sale was earmarked to repay a note issued in May 1993, in lieu of a dividend, to a family holding company that was also leasing 17 locations to the company for $3.3 million a year. Another $24 million was to be used to enlarge, replace, and open new stores.

But P.C. Richard ultimately decided to remain private. Interviewed in 1996 for *DM/Discount Merchandiser*, Gary Richard rhetorically asked, "What do we need underwriters, analysts, and the stock market telling us what to do, when we can do it ourselves when we want to do it? We generate all our own expansion money internally, and we are very successful at it."

Among the things outsiders were ready to tell the company to do was cut the payments to Gary Richard and his brother, Peter. In 1992 they shared total compensation of $2.8 million, or 15 percent of pretax profits, of which $2 million came in the form of bonuses. In the proposed public offering, the brothers' future bonuses were to be reduced to seven percent of pretax profits.

Still Growing: 1995–96

P.C. Richard's mammoth new warehouse in Farmingdale, the size of 15 football fields and the largest on Long Island, was completed by the summer of 1995. Corporate headquarters also moved to the site. In 1996 P.C. Richard opened its first Manhattan store by taking a 20-year lease on a three-story building in the Union Square area. With the opening of this outlet the chain had 38 stores—up from 31 in 1995 and including its first store in Westchester County, New York—and owned 22 buildings. The typical showroom offered 5,000 items, including personal computers. P.C. Richard's 1995 fleet of 60 trucks and 35 trailers was averaging 1,000 deliveries a day.

One reason P.C. Richard had survived the retailing bloodletting of the early 1990s, according to industry observers, was its decision to avoid suicidal price-cutting. These observers said the chain had a reputation for keeping prices and margins higher than other operations in the metropolitan New York area. One reason it had been able to do so was its strong retail-support program and its reputation for reliability. According to Gary Richard, high employee morale was another reason. The salaries of its sales staff were based on commissions, but company executives were going to great lengths to convince these personnel that they could move up the ladder to managerial positions.

As long as the company remained private, however, it was clear that the top positions would be going to a fourth generation of Richards. Gary's son, Gregg, had by 1995 been chosen as his father's ultimate successor. Peter Richard, Jr., son of Peter Richard, Sr., Gary's brother, was scheduled to succeed his father as executive vice-president. Four other children of Gary and the senior Peter were also involved in the company.

Further Reading

Benson, Barbara, "P.C. Richard Tries Offering to Help Make It Tops in N.Y.," *Crain's New York Business,* August 2, 1993, p. 7.

Bernstein, James, "Electronics Retailing Heats Up," *Newsday,* February 20, 1996, p. A27.

Fox, Bruce, "Seizing the Opportunity," *Chain Store Age Executive,* May 1993, pp. 51–52.

Johnson, Jay L., "P.C. Richard & Son: A Regional Survivor," *DM/Discount Merchandiser,* September 1996, pp. 20–21.

Julianelli, Jane, "6 in Family Moving P.C. Richard to the Future," *New York Times,* July 23, 1995, Sec. XIII, pp. 1, 9.

La Rossa, James, Jr., "Venerable P.C. Richard Flourishes As Rivals Flounder and Fall," *HFD,* January 2, 1991, pp. 238–39.

"P.C. Richard & Son (PRCI)," *Barron's,* August 2, 1993, p. 38.

Schoenfeld, Bruce, "P.C. Richard & Son," *HFD,* June 6, 1988, pp. 200, 207.

Wray, Kimberley, "TV Stands Spark Sales at P.C. Richard & Son," *HFD* (RTA Special Report section), October 7, 1991, p. 8A.

—Robert Halasz

Perdue Farms Inc.

P.O. Box 1537
Salisbury, Maryland 21802
U.S.A.
(410) 543-3000
Fax: (410) 543-3212
Web site: http://www.perdue.com

Private Company
Incorporated: 1920
Employees: 19,000
Sales: $2.1 billion (1996 est.)
SICs: 2015 Poultry Slaughtering & Processing; 2048
   Prepared Feeds, Not Elsewhere Classified; 2075
   Soybean Oil Mills

The leading poultry producer in the northeast United States and the second largest across the nation, Perdue Farms Inc. sells chicken and turkey products through retail venues and to food-service companies in the United States and in more than 30 countries worldwide. A vertically integrated business, Perdue processes grain and soybeans for feed, breeds and raises the poultry, processes the meat, and maintains a fleet of trucks for delivery of its products to market. Perdue Farms celebrated its 75th anniversary as a family-run business in 1995.

Modest Origins

When people think of Perdue Farms, the lean, creased features of longtime chief executive officer and advertising spokesman Frank Perdue usually come to mind. But the company was actually founded by Frank's father, Arthur W. Perdue. In 1920 the elder Perdue bought five dollars worth of laying hens and went into business selling eggs in Salisbury, Maryland.

For its first two decades, the company remained a tiny, family-run organization, in large part because of Arthur Perdue's unwillingness to borrow money to finance expansion. He was a "checkbook-balance man," his son would later say of him, as quoted in *Inc.* magazine. "If he had money in the bank and didn't owe any, it didn't matter how much we lost. But if he

owed money, it didn't make any difference if we were making a million a week—we had to get that paid off before we expanded," son Frank commented.

In the meantime, Frank Perdue went off to college, entering Salisbury State College in 1937, but left after two years to rejoin the family business. He kept his own flock of chickens on the side and had 800 hens of his own by 1941. The company grew in automatic response to improved economic conditions, as the nation pulled out of the Great Depression of the 1930s and demand for eggs increased. The Perdues found, however, that maintaining their sole focus on eggs also limited their profit potential. During the 1940s, they shifted their emphasis away from egg production and began turning out broiling chickens for resale to processors. Among their early customers were industry giants Swift & Company and Armour. By 1952, when Frank Perdue succeeded his father as president of the company, Perdue Farms was racking up annual sales of $6 million on a volume of 2.6 million birds.

Vertical Integration in the 1960s and 1970s

Still, the younger Perdue felt constrained by his father's conservative ways. Frank Perdue held a vision of turning the family business into a fully integrated breeding operation with its own hatcheries and feed mills. Finally, in 1961, the elder Perdue agreed to his son's plan to finance a soybean mill by borrowing money, marking the first time in his 40 years in the poultry industry that he had willingly gone into debt. "When we finally borrowed money, I was 41 years old and he was 76," Frank later recalled in *Inc.*, adding that "knowing the nature of the individual, I have to be appalled in retrospect that he put his name to a $500,000 note."

During the 1960s, Frank Perdue built up a tall stack of vertical integration for Perdue Farms. By 1967 the company could boast of one of the largest grain storage and poultry feed milling operations on the East Coast, soybean processing plants, mulch plants, a hatchery, and some 600 farmers raising birds under the Perdue name.

The engine that drove Perdue Farms' rapid expansion during this time was, of course, Frank Perdue himself. And in later years, whether out of pride or simple desire to state the obvious

Company Perspectives:

Our branded chicken and turkey products are sold in retail supermarkets, grocery stores, and quality butcher shops from Maine to Florida, and as far west as Chicago and St. Louis—a market area encompassing almost 40 percent of the nation's population. Food service chicken and turkey products are sold nationwide, and Perdue's international operations export to more than 30 countries around the world.

truth, he would not hesitate to take credit for the company's success. "I wanted the company to grow to the maximum extent possible," he told an *Inc.* reporter in 1984, noting "I wouldn't be satisfied with number two. I have driven very hard to increase production." He also drove very hard to increase sales. During the early days of the company, he served his father as salesman, traveling up and down the Eastern Seaboard to meet with buyers. Once he became president, Frank Perdue continued attending supermarket openings to keep his company's profile as high as possible. "My father wouldn't do it," he commented in *Inc.*, "but I'll do anything it takes for this business because I consider it more my baby than it was his. I was totally into it without any letup for 20 to 30 years. I've been the principal force in its growth."

Indeed, by 1967 Perdue Farms was posting annual sales of more than $35 million. At about this time, however, the company faced a serious threat as processors began to buy chickens directly from farmers, cutting out middlemen like Perdue Farms. Processors were thus able to expand their profit margins and squeeze their outside suppliers by driving harder bargains with them. Perdue Farms responded to this challenge by becoming a processor itself, adding its own processing operations and delivering the processed birds to market on its own. The Perdue brand name made its debut in retail meat counters in 1968. The company chose New York City as its first target market because of the city's high concentration of people with above-average incomes and its reputation for having consumers who are hard to impress; Perdue figured that if its chickens sold there, they would sell anywhere.

Frank Perdue had his doubts about whether or not this move into retailing would succeed, but he would soon find himself pleasantly surprised. For one thing, Perdue Farms held a significant advantage over its major competitors in that it had easy access to the major urban markets of the Eastern Seaboard, since Salisbury was a several-hour truck ride away from New York, Philadelphia, and Washington, D.C., and an overnight drive from Boston and Hartford. Secondly, the company's redoubled efforts to produce high-quality chickens paid off. To ensure that he could grow birds that were more tender than the rest, Perdue hired two professors from North Carolina State University to write a computer program that would supervise the feeding of his chickens, establishing formulae that would keep the birds as healthy as possible at each stage of their growth.

Advertising Increases Sales in the 1970s and 1980s

Finally, and perhaps most importantly, advertising generated consumer awareness of the Perdue brand name beyond the company's fondest expectations. In 1972 the company hired Scali McCabe Sloves, a small New York agency, to handle its advertising; in turn, the agency made perhaps the most fateful decision in the history of Perdue Farms—putting Franklin Parsons Perdue himself on the air. In print, on radio, and on television, the voice and visage of Frank Perdue became a known presence in the northeastern United States almost from the very start. *Inc.* described him as a most unlikely corporate spokesman—"slender, laconic, whiny-voiced, balding, droopy-lidded, long-nosed"—but Perdue's earnest appeals based on the quality of his product proved to be effective. *Business Week* once wrote that he possessed "all the fervor and sincerity of a Southern preacher" in his television commercials.

Catchy slogans also helped. One print advertisement that ran in the early 1970s showed a stern-visaged Perdue with his arms folded and standing beneath the words, "Everybody's chickens are approved by the government. But my chickens are also approved by me." In a lighter vein, another Perdue ad instructed housewives, "If your husband is a breast or leg man, ask for my chicken parts." Perdue may have uttered the most immortal of all his slogans, however, when he informed his audience that it "takes a tough man to make a tender chicken."

Perdue's success as a frontman for his own company in major media markets during the 1970s and 1980s, in fact, inspired advertising agencies to make pitchmen out of other chief executive officers, including Eastern Airlines' Frank Borman and Chrysler's Lee Iacocca. It also drew the attention of New York City Mayor Edward Koch, himself something of a Frank Perdue look-alike and no stranger to the value of publicity, who once called Perdue an "upper-echelon chicken guy."

But this transformation of a Maryland chicken farmer into a media icon would have meant nothing if it had not inspired more people to buy Perdue chickens. Between 1972 and 1984, Perdue Farms' sales doubled every two years. By the end of that period, the company was selling 260 million birds per year and generating revenues of more than $500 million. This success made Perdue Farms one of the 50 largest private companies in the United States.

Arthur Perdue died in 1977 at the age of 91. He had never really retired from the company that his son now ran; he retained the position of chairman and came to the office every day until the end of his life. Frank Perdue officially succeeded him as chairman in 1979.

Competition with Holly Farms

While Perdue Farms was riding the increasing popularity, of both its pitchman/chief executive officer and its chicken, to success and fortune, the company did not by any means escape the notice of its competitors. Its main rival was North Carolina-based Holly Farms, which later became a subsidiary of Tyson Foods. Holly Farms was a much larger company than Perdue Farms and sold chicken to a nationwide market. Perdue Farms was its main competitor in the lucrative Northeast. As early as 1971, Holly Farms watched the Perdue experiment in selling at the retail level under its own brand name with great interest and concluded that Perdue Farms could be beaten—at least in part because Perdue Farms was pricing its broilers as high as ten cents per pound above other brands. That year, Holly Farms began selling under its own brand name.

The two companies competed neck and neck during the 1980s, introducing new products in an effort to spur sales growth and out-do the other. During the early 1980s both were spending $6 million dollars a year for advertising. In 1983 Perdue Farms introduced chicken franks—hot dogs stuffed with chicken instead of pork or beef. In 1985 Holly Farms began selling fillets and bite-size nuggets—"all you do is dip 'em and do 'em," went their slogan—under the name "Time Trimmer." In response, Perdue Farms launched a line of pre-pared chicken products called Perdue Done It!, which included breaded and precooked nuggets and cutlets. As it turned out, neither Perdue nor Holly Farms could quite outdo the other, but both succeeded well enough so that in 1985 the two companies together accounted for one-fourth of all the fresh chicken sold in the United States.

Frank Perdue resigned as chief executive officer in 1988 but remained as his company's chairman and advertising spokes-man. He was 67 years old, and, with 90 percent of Perdue Farms stock in his and his family's hands, his personal fortune was estimated at around $350 million. Perdue was succeeded by one of his longtime executives, Donald Mabe, who stayed only three years in that office, retiring in 1991.

Third Generation Takes Over in 1990s

Also in 1991, Perdue retired as chairman, although he re-mained the company's chief public relations asset. The ensuing vacuum at the top was partially filled by Perdue's 41-year-old son James, who became chairman upon his father's retirement. The Perdue Farms board of directors decided to leave the chief executive officer spot open, hoping that it would serve as an incentive for both the younger Perdue and his second-in-com-mand, company president Pelham Lawrence.

Unlike his father, James Perdue did not start out in life as an enthusiastic poultry man. He worked only informally for the family business while he was growing up. After graduating from college, he entered the marine biology program at the University of Washington and graduated with a Ph.D. in 1983. James Per-due's departure from the family business was a matter of personal growth as much as it was an expression of differing interests. "The reason I left . . . was to find out more about myself, to get a better confidence level," he related in the New York Times soon after becoming chairman of Perdue Farms. "Although I am Frank Perdue's son, I wasn't born with confidence. That can only come with victories," James observed. By his own estimation, his graduate work gave him the self-assurance that he needed. Meanwhile, he kept abreast of company affairs through regular conversations with his father. As his son's graduate studies were coming to an end, Frank Perdue flew out to Seattle and asked James to come work for Perdue Farms.

Under James Perdue, Perdue Farms enacted subtle, yet impor-tant, changes in the way it produced chicken. The management process was opened up so that plant workers had more influence in decision-making. The company also sought to improve worker safety after the state of North Carolina fined the company in 1989 for permitting unsafe working conditions at its four processing plants there. These changes in Perdue Farms' operating proce-dures were begun by Frank Perdue before he retired, but the task of carrying them out was left mostly to his son. By his own admission, the outspoken elder Perdue was less temperamentally suited to the task of selling the company's efforts to its own workers. "Jim's style is different from mine," he confessed in the New York Times. "He can sell the achievement of quality in a more palatable way. I am more demanding, he is more concilia-tory," Frank observed. Low-key by nature, James Perdue an-nounced no plans to appear in television commercials.

Perdue Farms' revenue growth began to level off in the late 1980s and early 1990s, as the poultry industry as a whole saw its 20-year sales boom come to an end. Chicken sales grew at a rate of four to five percent per year during the 1970s and 1980s, but in the early 1990s, per capita consumption of poultry declined while production continued to increase. For Perdue Farms, sales fell to $1 billion in 1991, but recovered in 1992 to $1.2 billion.

By 1994 Jim Perdue had been persuaded to follow in his father's footsteps and become a spokesman for the company. A series of advertisements featured Jim and Frank Perdue to-gether, using the same folksy, humorous style as previous Frank Perdue ads. The first television commercial of the series began with Frank telling the audience that he had bad news for competitors. "It's a little project I've been working on for the past 45 years—the result of decades of intensive develop-ment." After pausing dramatically, Frank announced, "Meet my son, Jim. He may be even tougher than I am." Having taken the role of spokesman reluctantly, Jim Perdue told Nation's Business in 1995 that he would judge the wisdom of the move by concrete results: "If chicken sales continue or improve, then obviously it was good. If they don't, then it was not. Time will tell," he noted.

Aggressive Expansion in the Mid- to Late 1990s

Faced with three years of almost level sales in the early 1990s, Jim Perdue implemented a five-year plan that called for a 15 percent growth rate a year. The company pursued this ambi-tious goal by expanding its markets both domestically and internationally, with a continuing emphasis on vertical integra-tion. At the time, growth was the only way to survive the intense industry consolidation. In 1960, there were 360 poultry proces-sors in the United States; by 1985, that number had dropped to 125. By 1997, approximately 50 processors remained, with no end to the consolidation in sight, according to analysts.

Through aggressive expansion in the mid-1990s, Perdue met its goal. The company moved into markets in the South and Midwest and built or acquired local granaries, hatcheries, and processing plants to cut down on transportation costs. In 1992 the company opened a new processing plant in Dillon, South Carolina. The following year, the company added a feedmill, a hatchery, an egg warehouse, and a grain storage silo. Perdue also acquired Shiloh Grain and the grain trading assets of Fred Webb, Inc. In 1994 the company began construction of a broiler/roaster complex in Kentucky and expanded its sales into Florida. The Kentucky complex was intended to support expansion into Michigan, Kentucky, and Missouri markets, which Perdue entered in 1996.

International expansion was also an important part of the company's five-year plan. In 1995 Perdue acquired Showell Farms, boosting Perdue's international sales to ten percent of total sales in 1996. The company expanded into Japan in 1996 by recruiting food wholesaler Toshoku Ltd. to sell its precooked chickens. International tastes provided Perdue with complementary markets. Chicken feet, which Perdue once sold to livestock feed producers, were now exported to China, where they were considered a delicacy and commanded top dollar. Moreover, one of the company's largest new markets, Russia, preferred dark meat, as opposed to U.S. markets, which preferred white meat.

Although Perdue's aggressive expansion succeeded in doubling the company's revenues within five years, earnings did not follow suit. The company reported a loss in 1996; in fact, many poultry processors suffered that year, and with profit margins of only one or two cents per pound of its chicken, Perdue saw even that disappear when the Midwest experienced very small harvests and grain prices rose. Management re-

mained optimistic, however, expecting the company to enjoy a profit in 1997. As for surviving the continuing consolidation in the industry, Perdue Farms stood in a good position to thrive: poultry sales were rising throughout the United States and internationally; Perdue boasted prime locations for its processing facilities; and the company's vertical integration helped it control costs.

Further Reading

Barmash, Isadore, "The Quieter Style of the New Generation at Perdue," *New York Times,* July 16, 1992.

Giges, Nancy, "Holly Farms, Perdue Face off in Chickie Run," *Advertising Age,* September 16, 1985.

Nelton, Sharon, "Crowing Over Leadership Succession." *Nation's Business,* May 1995, p. 52.

"Perdue Chicken Spreads its Wings," *Business Week,* September 16, 1972.

Shelsby, Ted, "No Business for Chickens," *The Sun,* May 18, 1997, p. E1.

—Douglas Sun
—updated by Susan Windisch Brown

Philippine Airlines, Inc.

PAL Building 1 & 11
Legaspi Street
Legaspi Village
Makati, Metro Manila
Philippines
(63) 02-818-0111
Fax: (63) 02-810-9214
Web site: http://www.philippineair.com

Public Company
Incorporated: 1941
Employees: 14,000
Sales: P 31 billion (US$1.03 billion) (1996)
Stock Exchanges: Philippines
SICs: 4510 Air Transportation—Scheduled

Philippine Airlines, Inc. (PAL) has been the dominant air carrier in the Philippines since its creation in 1941. Operating both internationally and within the 7,100 islands that make up the country, PAL has been something of a curiosity and scandal among the world's major airlines, for decades losing money while being traded among the handful of wealthy families in control of the Philippine economy. After 14 years of ownership by the government of deposed President Ferdinand E. Marcos, PAL was sold at the order of President Corazon Aquino in 1992 to a consortium of companies under the leadership of the Soriano and Cojuangco (pronounced "koe-HWAHNG-koe") families. Because Aquino's maiden name was Cojuangco, many believed this "privatization" of PAL was not likely to break the pattern of corruption and inefficiency that has marred the carrier's history since 1941. But events in the late 1990s would conspire to force significant changes in the airline.

Founding in the 1940s

The first Philippine air transport companies were created in the early 1930s, primarily as a means of travel and freight delivery between the nation's scattered islands. One of these pioneering companies was the Philippine Aerial Taxi Company (PATCO), which was granted a 25-year charter by the Philippine legislature in 1931 for both domestic and international flights. At that early date, when the country was still a possession of the United States, Pan American Airways provided most of the Philippines' international air transportation. PATCO settled for short flights among the major islands of Luzon, Cebu, Leyte, and Mindanao. On the less developed islands, PATCO also provided intra-island flights between distant towns.

The 1941 transformation of PATCO into PAL involved an international cast of characters, most notably General Douglas D. MacArthur, at that time in charge of the United States Armed Forces in the Philippines preparing for an expected Japanese invasion of the islands. General MacArthur, whose father had served as the first military governor of the Philippine Islands following the Spanish-American War of 1898, had served in the country in various capacities throughout his career, including a four-year period before World War II when he was employed by the Philippine government as its field marshal. (MacArthur was recommissioned by the U.S. Army in 1941 and oversaw the eventual loss of the Philippines to the Japanese in 1942.)

The general employed as his aide-de-camp a wealthy Spaniard named Andres Soriano, who had previously served as consul in Manila for the Spanish dictator Francisco Franco. Soriano controlled the large San Miguel Breweries along with a number of other corporations, and had powerful connections in the Philippine capital. In 1941 he put those connections to good use by teaming with the National Development Company, a government agency, in forming Philippine Airlines, Inc., which promptly absorbed PATCO, thereby becoming the nation's largest air carrier.

As the creation of General MacArthur's aide de camp, PAL stood an excellent chance of winning contracts from the United States Armed Forces for its transport needs in the coming war. Unfortunately for Andres Soriano and his fellow investors, the invasion came early and ended quickly, with the Japanese gaining control over the islands by the summer of 1942. It is not clear what became of PAL during the Japanese occupation, but on December 8, 1941, the day after the Japanese attack on Pearl Harbor, General MacArthur made Andres Soriano a colonel in the U.S. Army, and an American citizen as well. It is safe to assume that Soriano returned to Manila with MacArthur's liberating forces in 1944 and resumed control of his various business interests, including PAL.

There is considerable evidence that MacArthur helped Soriano and PAL whenever he could. In 1946, MacArthur instructed the War Department to fly 20 tons of bottle caps to Soriano's San Miguel Brewery to cover a shortage. In addition, the two men were both strongly anti-Communist, and MacArthur's own extensive business holdings in the Philippines made his relationship with Soriano more like one of business partners than military officers. Sterling Seagrave commented on the chaotic postwar scene in his book *The Marcos Dynasty,* "The $2 billion aid package [from the United States to the Philippines] was fought over and devoured by politicians, by rich MacArthur partisans, and by packs of bureaucrats."

Post World War II Activities

Helped by such massive infusions of American capital, the Philippine economy rebounded from its wartime privations. PAL prospered so quickly that by 1948 it had already bought out two of its largest competitors, Far Eastern Air Transport, Inc., and Commercial Air Lines, Inc. Within a few years three other competing lines also threw in the towel, and PAL stood alone as the airline of the Philippines. Its ownership was still split between the Philippine government and the Soriano interests. The Sorianos were minority shareholders, but handled the day-to-day management of the airline, which, if the later pattern of graft and kickbacks was already established in the 1950s, was the more lucrative end of the business. Philippine magnate Enrique Zobel once bluntly remarked in the media that "PAL is a milking cow," and most of the milk seems to have been generated by what *Far Eastern Economic Review* described delicately as the "company's operations, for instance by dictating its material requirements."

PAL's activities were described more directly in the *New York Times,* which quoted a 1989 World Bank study. The latter found that the airline was holding "millions of dollars of spare parts for aircraft it no longer owns and ground equipment so badly maintained that it has little value except as scrap." At one time PAL was even accused of carrying an "inexplicably large inventory of 750,000 sanitary napkins," as reported in the *Far Eastern Economic Review.* Clearly the finances were being toyed with to someone's advantage, which may help to explain how an airline that so often reported a loss in its annual report could remain a financial plum much sought after by Philippines business families.

Whatever the intrigue surrounding its operation, PAL expanded its route system and doubled passenger miles between 1946 and 1950. The airline was serving 36 domestic airports by 1955 and owned a fleet of 35 planes, some of them DC 3/C47s and the rest Convair 240s. PAL's primary business still lay in freight and communication services, such as the mail, since its ticket prices were far beyond the means of the average Filipino. From the international airport in Manila, PAL sent 33 flights weekly to Cebu City, the transport hub of the southern islands, and offered regular service to all sections of the widely scattered nation, even the more remote islands where passengers were few and the operation ran at a loss.

Indeed, the airline has repeatedly blamed its financial troubles on the large number of short, unprofitable flights it must offer as the nation's only airline. In this regard, it was significant that on the eve of its sale to private investors in 1991, PAL announced a dramatic cutback in the number of its shorter domestic flights, encouraging the formation of new private companies to take these on. PAL claimed in reports published as far apart as 1950 and 1989 that it enjoyed the lowest cost of operation in the industry, so it would be hard to explain its frequent losses other than by blaming the unprofitability of the line's short-haul domestic business. (Unless, as some suspect, the airline's "loose accounting methods" have been to blame.)

PAL under the Marcos Regime

The Soriano family retained control of PAL until the late 1960s, the period of Ferdinand Marcos's rise to power. Marcos was first elected president of the Philippines in 1965 and remained the country's absolute ruler until his forced exile in 1985, when it was discovered that he and his wife, Imelda, had systematically plundered their country for decades while amassing a fortune estimated to be at least $1 billion. Marcos literally had a hand in every major Philippine enterprise, including the nation's airline monopoly. As Imelda Marcos became a regular guest at parties and government capitals around the world, she accrued a debt to PAL of nearly $6 million in the mid-1970s. The airline's owner, Benny Toda, offered to cut the bill in half if the Marcoses would pay it; instead, Imelda Marcos demanded that he transfer his interests in the airline to the government—which meant, in effect, to the Marcoses themselves. Afraid to refuse, Toda settled on a price with Ferdinand Marcos and turned over his stock, for which he later said he was never paid.

PAL became one of the many baubles flaunted by Imelda Marcos, who by this time was one of the richest women in the world. The First Lady of the Philippines traveled around the world in her own PAL DC-8 jet equipped with beds, a built-in shower, and gold bathroom fixtures, sometimes also commandeering a second jet to carry her personal luggage. The airline was officially under the control of the Government Service Insurance System (GSIS), which controlled the pension funds of all government employees in the country and was one of the Philippines' largest financial institutions. GSIS was run by Roman A. Cruz, one of Imelda's favorites, and it was Cruz and his family who ran PAL from its takeover to the election of Corazon Aquino in 1986.

By that time the airline had racked up consistent losses for the better part of two decades. PAL was at least able to enjoy the benefits of Manila's new international airport, completed in 1982 to replace a network of runways dangerously in need of repair; but, in the words of the *Far Eastern Economic Review,* "the airline [was] hobbled by ineffective management and corruption." It was also plagued by employee defections to other airlines, which generally paid about four times as much as PAL and were not "hobbled" by corruption in such gross forms. During the 1980s more than 1,000 of PAL's licensed mechanics, its most valuable ground workers, were lured by competing airlines, "exacerbating flight reliability problems," according to the industry magazine *Aviation Week & Space*

Technology. PAL had become something of an embarrassment to the international aviation industry.

New Leadership in the Mid-1980s

The rise of "People Power" in the mid-1980s, culminating in the election of Corazon Aquino and the escape by the Marcoses to the United States in 1986, apparently offered a chance for significant changes in the Philippine economy. Not dwelt upon in the international press, however, was Aquino's membership in the Cojuangco family, probably the wealthiest of all Philippine business clans and for many years crucial supporters of the Marcos regime. Observers point out that the election of Aquino changed less in the Philippines than her less affluent supporters had hoped, and the privatization of PAL in 1992 offered little evidence of any real diminution of the powers of the elite families.

President Aquino originally ordered the sale of PAL along with hundreds of other government-owned companies shortly after her election in 1986. Since the airline had been run at a loss for many years, Aquino first hired a Philippine businessman named Dante Santos to make PAL profitable prior to its sale. Under Santos, PAL did report two years of net income, but these were widely assumed to be the result of creative accounting methods rather than of any substantive changes in PAL's performance. Indeed, in late 1990, four years after the accession of Dante Santos as president of the airline, no fewer than 22 of PAL's top executives were charged with negligence, fraud, and/or mismanagement; ten of these officials were eventually fired, including an executive vice-president, two senior vice-presidents, and four vice-presidents. They were accused of precisely the sort of corrupt operational practices that had been a way of life at PAL for decades, including theft of parts, over-purchasing, and kickbacks from travel agents. It was hard to say, according to some critics, whether the firings were part of a genuine cleanup effort at PAL or merely a means of clearing the decks before the company's sale, after which the buyer might wish to install its own people in these lucrative positions.

The sale of PAL was carried out in a curious fashion. The government first paid approximately $350,000 to the Asian Development Bank for recommendations on how best to proceed with the privatization of the airline. The study concluded that a large infusion of foreign ownership and management would be needed to turn around the airline's performance. For reasons of its own, the government rejected this proposal and instead commissioned a second study, this one from a branch of the World Bank. The second report also recommended that about one-third of the airline be transferred to foreign hands, chiefly as a means of retiring some of PAL's $650 million in foreign debt. This plan was also largely ignored, however, and in the months immediately prior to the airline's sale, PAL officials admitted that they could not return the company to profitability and were expecting a shortfall between its sale price and the amount of its debt. The company itself valued the two-thirds of its assets up for sale at somewhere between P 6.35 billion and P 6.69 billion, while the World Bank study had pegged their worth between P 5.25 billion and P 7.51 billion. But when the written bids were opened in January 1992, two groups of Philippine companies had bid over P 9 billion, with AB Capital & Investment Corporation the winner at P 9.78 billion.

AB Capital represented a consortium of Philippine interests headed by the Soriano and Cojuangco families, who had created the airline in 1941. Contrary to the recommendations of both preliminary studies, none of the company was sold to foreign investors; instead, the remaining 33 percent was kept by the Philippine government, specifically by GSIS, through which the Marcoses had taken over PAL in 1978. In effect, PAL remained under the control of the same few Philippine families, this time without the bothersome intrusions of foreign investors, who might possibly insist on a more rigorous accounting of its daily operations.

Prospects for the 1990s and Beyond

Thus when president and COO Jose Antonio Garcia in early 1996 proclaimed that PAL would "take on the world" once it had "a clean house," to many observers this sounded like a familiar refrain built around false notes. According to Michael Mackey in *Air Transport World* in February 1996, the company had lost P 1.7 billion (US$61 million) in the fiscal year that ended March 31, a figure that in subsequent reports would be raised to $70 million (*Asian Business,* April 1996) and $93 million (*Airfinance Journal,* June 1996). Revenues had flattened, operating expenses had risen, losses were spreading, and debt-equity ratios were moving in the wrong direction. The causes of the airline's poor economic performance were likewise familiar. Mackey identified three key factors: problems with the country's aviation infrastructure, growing competition for the Philippine market, and "the huge, sprawling subject of PAL's relationship with the government and role in development of the economy."

Inefficiency was as rampant as ever in the fields of technology, logistics, and operations. Of the airline's 11 Boeing 747 200s, six had GE engines, and the rest Pratt & Whitney—thus creating a less efficient maintenance situation than if all used the same type of engine. Worse, its fleet was both small and old. The size meant limitations on the number of flights—just 14 a week to the U.S., compared to twice that many for its American competitors—and the age of the aircraft placed limits on nonstop distance. A trip from Manila to London was, as Mackey wrote in October 1997, "a Homeric odyssey" that required travelers to stop in Bangkok, Abu Dhabi, and Frankfurt. Not only did this create inconveniences for passengers, but PAL had to pay fees at every airport, thus cutting into its profit margins.

Its people posed as much of a liability to PAL as its machines. Abby Tan in *Asian Business* (April 1996) recorded the following litany of larcenous acts against the airline by its own employees: "In one recent incident, 13 employees were charged in a ticket refund scam in Iloilo City that was estimated to be costing the company US$3,000 every month. PAL also loses around US$15.2 million each year through theft of plane parts and other supplies. That figure doesn't include items stolen from provincial stations centres where the airline's catering and ground-handling facilities are located. In one case, security agents discovered a fuel line running directly off company grounds."

As for the relationship with the Philippine government, Mackey observed that it "would seem to be more in place in a soap opera than in real life." According to Garcia, PAL was "owned by two entities . . . at war with each other": the Philippine government, with its one-third share, and the conglomerate PR Holdings. Even the nature of the ownership split was in dispute, since the government owned one-fifth of PR Holdings—which in the view of some officials gave it more than 51 percent ownership of PAL. To top it off, the CEO of PR Holdings' political position was made more problematic by his close association with the Marcos regime on the one hand, and his "frosty relationship" with President Fidel Ramos, Aquino's successor, on the other. "What the dispute effectively does," one unnamed insider observed, "is make the raising of capital more difficult."

In its domestic service, the company continued to be hampered by a government order forcing it to fly some commercially undesirable routes, an order to which competitors were not subject. And competition was growing, not only from international airlines but an upstart local carrier, Grand Air. Nonetheless, PAL was still managing to maintain vestiges of its control over the Philippine market, but by 1996 it was under pressure to relinquish its hold—and the pressure came not from Quezon City, but from Washington.

For years, U.S. negotiators had been trying to get PAL to comply with an "open skies agreement," signed in the early 1980s, whereby both U.S. and Philippine carriers would have unlimited access to markets in each other's territory. PAL had gotten its compliance deadline postponed four times. But by 1996 it had run out of largesse from the Philippine government, which was concerned that limitations on passenger service could lead to a loss of tourism income, a significant industry in that country. Thus it was confronted with a more or less final deadline of 2003. "This," as Abby Tan wrote in *Asian Business,* "gives PAL just seven years to fix a host of problems that have dulled its competitive edge and sapped its profits."

In the mid-to-late 1990s, PAL began taking positive steps toward eliminating its problems, both technical and human-related. In the technical realm, it began to update its aging fleet with an enormous order for new planes. In December 1995 it placed on order 24 Airbus A340-300s (in addition to four already on order), as well as 12 A320s and eight A330-300s. Financing of $1.1 billion worth of Airbus equipment came from a variety of Asian banks. PAL did not simply add aircraft; it was "refleeting," creating an entirely new service fleet, and Mackey in late 1997 predicted that with the delivery of several new aircraft in the following year, "PAL will have one of the most modern and youngest fleets in Asia."

PAL's operations would also be bolstered by a new computer system, including a $7 million revenue accounting system that became operational in 1997, as well as two mainframes ordered from a Danish company. Another "new" feature, one very familiar to most airlines but not PAL, would be a direct linkage between travel agents and the company's reservation system. Also in the realm of service, PAL began to explore the possibilities of the Chinese and Japanese markets. It had no service to the former, and only a limited number of flights to Tokyo in the latter case. By late 1997, it was "very close" to Shanghai service, as well as increased routes to Japan.

In a development that suggested increasing confidence within the community of airlines, it also entered into discussion with several possible strategic partners. "In the past," Garcia told *Air Transport World,* "it was exceedingly difficult to even get people to talk to us. But times are changing." As for its human resources, PAL slashed its roster of senior vice-presidents in half, to 15, and sought to train its 14,000 employees for greater efficiency. In line with its increased fleet size, it would be hiring 1,800 cabin crew staffers, as well as 2,000 mechanics.

Perhaps most significant was the airline's move toward privatization. Once Tan emerged as chairman of the company in March 1995, it appeared that PAL's future course was set: it might not remain a property of Tan—one critic quoted in *Airfinance Journal* claimed he was "trying to make the airline look decent and then sell it"—but it was not going to remain a property of Quezon City either. Thus in October 1997 Mackey, a critical observer, lauded the "end of government involvement and [indications] that business people are back in control."

For the fiscal year that ended March 31, 1997, the company showed losses of P 2.5 billion (US$83 million), and for the next fiscal year Garcia projected losses of P 2 billion (US$66 million). "And for the financial year ending March, 1999," he said, "if we do not break even, we should be very close to it." PAL was negotiating, he told Mackey, with Lufthansa for the German airline's catering services; with GE Engine Services for a maintenance deal; and with an unnamed company for a joint venture involving maintenance and engineering. Corporate Finance Vice-President Andy Hwang said, "To be Asia's best, we must align ourselves with the best." This is one of many new slogans, Mackey wrote, employed by the carrier that now described itself as "Asia's Sunniest Airline." By the late 1990s, for the first time in 50 years, such promises began to seem like more than mere words.

Further Reading

Cameron, Doug, "A Sporting Chance," *Airfinance Journal,* June 1996, pp. 20–23.

Galang, Zoilo M., ed., *Encyclopedia of the Philippines,* Vol. 5, Manila: Exequiel Floro, 1950.

MacDonald, Lawrence, "Auction of Philippine State Airline . . . May Come Soon," *Wall Street Journal,* April 5, 1991.

Mackey, Michael, "Split Personality," *Air Transport World,* February 1996, pp. 71–75.

——, "The Sun Rises at PAL," *Air Transport World,* October 1997, pp. 79–80.

"PAL Awarded Largest Asia-Pacific Deal," *Airfinance Journal,* May 1997, p. 10.

Seagrave, Sterling, *The Marcos Dynasty,* New York: Harper & Row, 1988.

Tan, Abby, "Flying on Borrowed Time," *Asian Business,* April 1996, pp. 19–20.

Tiglao, Rigoberto, "Carrier of the Clans," *Far Eastern Economic Review,* February 1992.

——, "PAL in a Spin," *Far Eastern Economic Review,* January 1991.

—Jonathan Martin
—updated by Judson Knight

Pilgrim's Pride Corporation

110 South Texas Street
P.O. Box 93
Pittsburg, Texas 75686-0093
U.S.A.
(903) 855-1000
Fax: (903) 856-7505
Web site: http://www.pilgrimspride.com

Public Company
Incorporated: 1963 as Pilgrim Feed Mills, Inc.
Employees: 9,700
Sales: $1.3 billion
Stock Exchanges: New York
SICs: 2015 Poultry Slaughtering & Processing

Pilgrim's Pride Corporation is the fourth largest chicken processor in the United States and the second largest in Mexico. Once a private company, as of 1998, the company was approximately 65 percent owned by its founder, chief executive officer, and "celebrity" spokesperson, Lonnie A. (Bo) Pilgrim. As a completely integrated operation, Pilgrim's Pride superintends egg producing, contract growing, feed milling, animal rendering, and processing of its brand name foods for the retail, fast-food, food service, and food warehouse markets. Although its principal sales regions are the West, the Southwest, and Mexico, the company also sells selected chicken products to eastern European and Pacific Rim countries. The company's 1997 sales could be broken down as follows: U.S. fresh chicken, 26 percent; U.S. prepared foods, 30 percent; U.S. export and other chicken, 11 percent; U.S. eggs, 11 percent; and Mexican operations, 22 percent.

Company Origins

According to an article by Toni Mack in *Forbes,* when Pilgrim was a boy "and wanted a Coke, his father, who ran the general store in the northeast Texas hamlet of Pine, would first make him sell six Cokes for a nickel apiece to the men working the nearby cotton gin." Such was the early business training of the chicken magnate who, by his own admission, "started from nothing." Because his father died abruptly from a heart attack, leaving the store in debt and the family with just $80, Bo was forced to labor from age 11 at several different jobs. At the age of 17, he and his brother Aubrey purchased a farm supply store in Pittsburg, Texas, with money borrowed from a bank and a local dentist. The first capital investment was a used cotton gin, which the brothers converted into a feed grinder. From 1945 until 1966, the year of Aubrey's death, the company that would eventually incorporate as Pilgrim Feed Mills, Inc. expanded into egg-hatching and broiler-processing. In 1968, Lonnie and Aubrey's heirs reincorporated the business as Pilgrim Industries, Inc.

Well into the 1980s, sales increases for the company averaged 20 percent annually. This growth was largely due to Bo's gutsy leadership and willingness to endure debt-to-equity ratios in excess of four-to-one in order to stay ahead of the competition. Jessica Greenbaum, in an article in *Forbes,* quotes one of Pilgrim's bankers as stating that Bo had "expanded as fast as he possibly could. The balance sheet couldn't sustain anymore." Pilgrim's strategy apparently paid off, for between 1960 and 1984, the number of broiler producers in the country shrank by more than 80 percent to just 55. Almost a decade later, that number stood at 45.

Advertising and Product Innovation in the 1980s

Beginning in January 1983, Pilgrim began promoting his company and the Pilgrim's Pride label through an award-winning television commercial, in which he appeared wearing a Pilgrim's hat as he affably related the superiority of his product line. The ads helped raise the profile of the Texas-based company, which posted sales that year of $268 million and profits of $2.1 million. The following year, Pilgrim's Pride had become the ninth largest chicken producer in the United States and the first to introduce fresh, whole, boneless chickens to the market. Yet, despite such advances, as well as a conscientious paring down of its debt, the business was perhaps as precarious during the mid-1980s as it had ever been. The reason for this, wrote Mack, was that "the company was almost entirely dependent on highly cyclical commodity chicken sales. Twice over the years, commodity chicken down-cycles had almost bankrupted Pil-

---

---

grim's Pride.'' Pilgrim's solution to this problem came in January 1986, when the company began operating a state-of-the-art ''further processed'' facility at Mt. Pleasant, Texas. In November of the same year, the company went public with a listing on the New York Stock Exchange; however, Bo maintained ownership and control by retaining 80 percent of the company's shares.

Bo's gamble on prepared chicken for the retail market proved just as risky as the commodity business, due to strong competition from Tyson and ConAgra as well as heightened advertising and promotional costs totaling as much as $6 to $8 million a year. 1988 marked a low point for the company when it posted an income loss of nearly $8 million on $506 million in sales. A switch to the accrual method of accounting, however, allowed the business to report a final profit of $1.7 million.

Expansion in the Late 1980s

Two well-timed decisions enabled Pilgrim's Pride to rebound dramatically in 1989. The first was Bo's surrender of the retail market (a minuscule percentage of corporate sales in the late 1990s) and full-scale assault on the food service industry. Although Tyson remained the leader, Pilgrim's Pride was able to promote itself as a strong alternate through contracts with such frontrunners as Kentucky Fried Chicken, Kraft General Foods, and Wendy's restaurants. The second well-timed decision was Pilgrim's entry into the Mexican consumer market with the late 1987 acquisition of four fully integrated poultry operations serving the populous hub of Mexico City. The purchase price for the Mexican venture totaled $15.1 million. Largely because of these two moves, 1989 net sales shot up 30 percent, and net income rose above $20 million, for a profit-to-sales ratio of just over three percent. (Pilgrim's long-term goal was to boost this latter figure to around four percent.) The only blemish for the company that year was Pilgrim's involvement in a campaign contribution scandal with eight Texas lawmakers. The company CEO was forced to defend himself before a grand jury, but he was not indicted and was able to return to the business of keeping the company in the black.

From 1987 to 1991, the company tripled the size of its Mexican operations, built a strong presence in frozen retail, established a dependable export business, and witnessed enormous increases in output for its further processed and prepared divisions. In addition, it entered into a number of joint marketing and advertising arrangements that kept down costs while increasing market share. All of this helped contribute to record sales of $786 million. Nevertheless, profits were down 21 percent and hovering at just 1.5 percent of revenues. Pilgrim's was a well-integrated agribusiness, 20th in domestic egg production, fifth in broiler sales, and blessed with a solid brand name and

rising per capita consumption of its leading product. It had anticipated and responded to consumer demand with a wide array of new food products, including fresh tray packs, party packs, chicken patties, nuggets, strips, and ready-to-eat gourmet entrees and appetizers. Furthermore, the company owned dozens of modern breeder and grow-out farms; several feed mills and processing plants; and 19 distribution facilities in the Southwest and in Mexico. The explanation for Pilgrim's slide was most likely twofold: the company had failed to distance itself enough from the cyclical price woes of plain processed chicken, and it had saddled itself with increasing debt.

Problems in the Early 1990s

In 1991, the company spent $34.4 million on improving the efficiency of its Mexican facilities and another $26.1 million on improving its domestic plants. The company entered 1992 hoping for the best and aiming at reaching sales of $1 billion by 1994, but while the year proved full of noteworthy events, few of them were good news for the company. In January a fire at the Mt. Pleasant plant left 21 injured following a full evacuation of some 1,200 employees. The cause of the fire was determined to be a loose hydraulic line near a burner. Fortunately, all injuries were minor. Then, in May 1994, a debt restructuring was announced that would allow the company greater latitude in repaying its short-term obligations. The deal was completed in late June and served to extend Pilgrim's loan maturities until May 1, 1993. However, in order to arrange the waivers, the company was forced to sell five million common shares to Archer-Daniels-Midland (ADM) at six dollars per share. As a result, Bo Pilgrim's personal stake was effectively reduced from almost 80 percent to approximately 65 percent. A clause limiting ADM from acquiring more than a 20 percent interest and Pilgrim's indemnification of ADM against losses for an undisclosed period of time were also part of the deal.

Despite such warning signals, several analysts were surprised by a management reorganization announced in August, which involved the replacement of William Voss, president since 1988. Voss's successor, 11-year veteran Monty Henderson, was appointed to turn a declining earnings trend around. For the first nine months of fiscal 1992, ending June 27, the company sustained a net loss of $17.1 million. In the company's final quarter, another huge drop was added to the bottom line, resulting in one of its worst years ever. According to a *Wall Street Journal* article published just after this last piece of news, Pilgrim's year-long ''financial funk'' was in danger of worsening. Short-term debts still needed to be reduced and further loan negotiations seemed inevitable. In November the company announced that it would not pay its common stock dividend for the first quarter of fiscal 1993. In addition, it was reported that ''Pilgrim's Pride is seeking waivers of financial covenants in loan agreements with major secured lenders to whom it owes $65 million.'' Discussions for extending the May 1993 deadline until October 1993 were in progress.

In a March 16, 1993 press release, Pilgrim's Pride announced that it had filed a registration statement with the U.S. Securities and Exchange Commission regarding its proposed public offering of $100 million of Senior Subordinated Notes due 2003. According to the press release, the offering was ''part of a refinancing plan designed to consolidate indebtedness, extend the average maturity of Pilgrim's Pride outstanding indebtedness and improve Pilgrim's Pride's operating and financial flexibility.''

By 1992, Pilgrim's Pride was the country's second largest supplier of prepared chicken products, but was still not profitable. Increases in overall sales slowed in the early 1990s, while profits steadily declined. By the end of fiscal 1992, the company was struggling under the weight of a $29.7 million loss, attributable to excess poultry production and sinking prices.

With overall sales slowing, Pilgrim's Pride's Mexican operations were becoming increasingly important to the company's bottom line. Mexican operations grew to 20 percent of total Pilgrim's Pride revenues by 1994. Success in the region led Pilgrim's Pride to pursue further expansion there. In 1995 the company spent $32 million for five chicken operations known collectively as Union de Queretaro. Despite Mexico's economic problems in 1995 and 1996, Pilgrim's Pride maintained its stability there, and as Mexico's economy recovered, Pilgrim's Pride was in a good position to grow with it. By 1997, the company had entered every major market in the country and had achieved a 19 percent share of the poultry market.

Public Image Challenges in the Mid-1990s

However, problems at home continued to plague the company. Public attention began focusing on the company's environmental and worker's rights record in the mid-1990s. In 1994, the company was sued by a doctor who had treated approximately 100 Pilgrim's Pride workers claiming to have been injured on the job; the doctor accused Pilgrim's Pride of interfering in his doctor-patient relationships and of retaliating against him for trying to improve working conditions at the plant. Although the company denied any wrongdoing, the suit brought to light several past cases in which Pilgrim's Pride had violated workers' compensation laws. In fact, the Texas Workers' Compensation Commission (TWCC) had already fined the company five times, for a total of $10,000, for violations. According to *The Progressive* in 1994, the TWCC investigation brought on by Dr. Arroyo's charges revealed ''many violations by Pilgrim's Pride and its insurance companies.''

At the same time, the Texas Natural Resource Conservation Commission (TNRCC) was investigating the company for air- and water-quality violations and industrial waste violations. Between 1984 and 1994, the TNRCC had received more than 110 complaints against Pilgrim's Pride for such environmental violations. By 1994, Pilgrim's Pride had received more than $1.3 million in penalties from the TNRCC. ''The record of Pilgrim's Pride does concern me,'' Kenneth Ramirez of the TNRCC told *Texas Monthly* in 1994, adding that ''when a company has a history of noncompliance, at some point in time you have to take a special look at that company and the enforcement policy. We intend to take a special look at Pilgrim's Pride.''

In 1996 a company proposal to build a new processing plant in Sulphur Springs, Texas, was denied by the city council; the company's second choice in location was also voted down by the water district's board. While opponents generally cited the company's environmental violations, some critics suggested that the decision may have also been influenced by racism, or

concern about the likely influx of Spanish-speaking Mexican immigrants as workers at the plant.

During this time, the combination of a 12-year high in grain prices and the threat by Russia to ban poultry imports from the United States prompted Pilgrim's Pride to cut production by 8.5 percent for the year. Although net sales did rise that year, to $1.1 billion, the company reported a loss of over $7 million for the second year in a row.

Pilgrim's Pride received a boost in fiscal 1997, however, as sales rose to $1.3 billion and net income shot up to $41 million. The record earnings beat the previous high in 1994 by 32 percent. The company also expanded that year, acquiring all the assets of Green Acre Foods, including a hatchery, a feedmill, and a processing plant. The company's plans for the late 1990s included further expansion of its prepared foods division, which in 1997 accounted for over 30 percent of the company's sales.

Pilgrim's Pride has pinned its hopes for a total recovery on the areas where it has remained strongest: prepared foods for the foodservice industry and consumer sales to the Southwest and Mexico. Minimal increases in domestic chicken consumption should not deter the company, provided prices rebound and overproduction is avoided. Viewed in a historical context, the company's current problems might only be a small downturn in an overall trend of rising revenue and profitability, for Pilgrim's Pride still remains a major contender in chicken processing.

Principal Subsidiaries

Pilgrim's Pride de Mexico; Texas Egg Limited.

Further Reading

Cartwright, Gary, ''Bo Pilgrim: The Baron of Texas Agriculture,'' *Texas Monthly,* September 1994, pp. 110–121.

Countryman, Carol, ''Shame of Pilgrim's Pride,'' *The Progressive,* August 1994, p. 11.

Crispens, Jonna, ''Pilgrim's Pride Has New President,'' *Supermarket News,* August 24, 1992.

Greenbaum, Jessica, ''. . . Sell 'Em or Smell 'Em,'' *Forbes,* July 16, 1984.

Lee, Steven H., ''Ruffled Feathers: Chicken Processors Cut Production to Survive Price Squeeze,'' *Dallas Morning News,* March 9, 1996, p. F1.

''Lonnie 'Bo' Pilgrim,'' company document, Pittsburg, Tex.: Pilgrim's Pride, 1991.

Mack, Toni, ''Pilgrim's Progress,'' *Forbes,* June 25, 1990.

Park, Scott, ''Towns Oppose Pilgrim's Pride Chicken Plants,'' *Dallas Morning News,* April 21, 1996, p. A45.

''Pilgrim's Pride Corp.: Archer-Daniels-Midland Co. Agrees to Buy an 18% Stake,'' *Wall Street Journal,* May 13, 1992.

''Pilgrim's Pride Corp.,'' *Wall Street Journal,* January 13, 1993.

''Pilgrim's Pride Omits Dividend on Common for Fiscal 1st Period,'' *Wall Street Journal,* November 27, 1992.

''Pilgrim's Pride Ousts President, Chooses Henderson for Post,'' *Wall Street Journal,* August 10, 1992.

''Pilgrim's Pride Says Refinancing Delays Threaten Loan Pacts,'' *Wall Street Journal,* October 2, 1992.

''21 Hurt in Texas Plant Fire,'' *New York Times,* January 9, 1992.

—Jay P. Pederson
—updated by Susan Windisch Brown

Playmates Toys

100 Canton Road
Kowloon
Hong Kong
852 2730 7388
Fax: 852 2735 2058
Web site: http://www.playmatestoys.com

Public Company
Incorporated: 1966 as Playmates Industrial
Employees: 200
Sales: HK$1.2 billion (1996)
Stock Exchanges: Hong Kong
SICs: 5092 Toys, Hobby Goods & Supplies, Wholesale

Playmates Toys is a Hong Kong-based toy manufacturer whose American subsidiary, Playmates Toys Inc., is one of the leading marketers of toys in the United States. Founded in 1966, Playmates Toys entered the big leagues of the toy industry in 1988 when it purchased the license to manufacture action figures based on the Teenage Mutant Ninja Turtles comics. The "heroes in a half shell" were an instant mega-hit among the under ten set and in 1990 Playmates became the first toymaker in history to net more than $100 million in one year. Although plagued by family feuding through the 1990s, Playmates has managed to remain profitable through most of the decade in spite of a predictable decline in the Ninja Turtles fad. Other successful product introductions, including WaterBabies, a line of water-filled dolls, and Nano Pals, the company's entry into the virtual pet craze that swept the toy world in 1997, helped to cushion the company from the boom and bust pattern of the promotional toy industry.

Company Origins in the 1960s

Playmates Toys was founded as Playmates Industrial in Hong Kong in 1966 by Chan Tai Ho (later known as Sam Chan) as a small manufacturing subcontractor for foreign toy producers. Chan and his family were refugees from China's Guangdong province, from which they had escaped in tiny sampans only a few years earlier. For almost a decade the company built a steady business making generic dolls and preschool toys for other toy companies. In 1975 Playmates took an important step toward becoming an independent toy producer by establishing a division to produce and market its own line of preschool toys, opening an American subsidiary in Boston two years later.

Through the 1970s and early 1980s Playmates continued to manufacture toys for other toy companies as well as to produce its own line. A new California subsidiary named Playmates Toys Inc. was opened in 1983 specifically to move the company into the lucrative but risky promotional toy market. Looking to raise investment for further expansion, in 1984 Playmates Industrial went public, trading shares on the Honk Kong stock exchange under the new name Playmates Holdings, Ltd.

In 1986 Playmates had their first big success in promotional toys with Cricket, a talking electronic baby doll. Cricket had been created by a Los Angeles area inventor who brought his idea to the company's American subsidiary, which by this time had been consolidated in La Mirada, California. Sales of Cricket more than doubled the company's total sales, which rose from $32 million in 1985 to almost $78 million the following year. The mid-1980s were a boom time for electronic toys and after the success of Cricket, Playmate management, now under the direction of Sam Chan's son Thomas, felt that electronic dolls were the wave of the future. The company invested heavily in a much more complex follow-up version of the doll to be named Jill. Jill could blink her eyes and swivel her neck while she talked but with manufacturing costs of $200 a piece, the doll stood little chance of making money for its creators. Jill was introduced in 1987 and almost immediately plunged Playmates into the red, with a $4.8 million loss recorded in that year. Managing director Thomas Chan told *Forbes* in 1991 that the disaster was a formative experience for the company. "I learned that parents are not going to pay $200 for a doll, and that complicated, expensive toys have very little upside potential." Richard Sallis, president of the company's American subsidiary, suggested that the lesson ran even deeper, commenting to the *Orange County Register* in 1990, "After Jill, the chairman won't even have an electronic doorbell in his house."

Launch of the Teenage Mutant Ninja Turtles in 1988

Fortunately for Playmates, the debacle of the Jill doll was followed in quick succession by one of the greatest success stories in the history of promotional toys. The idea for the Teenage Mutant Ninja Turtles had been dreamed up in 1984 by two would-be comic book artists, Peter Laird and Kevin Eastman, in their living room in Northampton, Massachusetts. The Turtles, off-the-wall namesakes of Italian Renaissance artists, Donatello, Leonardo, Michaelangelo, and Raphael, had their fictional home in the New York City sewers, where they had been flushed as babies. After an encounter with radioactive goo, the turtles were mutated into surfer slang English-speaking, martial arts warriors with a craving for pizza. Laird and Eastman published an initial run of 3,000 copies of a comic book based on their quirky idea, which sold out in only three weeks. Soon the two were producing a bimonthly series that quickly garnered a small but loyal following of some 150,000 fans.

In 1986 Laird and Eastman, ready to expand their idea to a larger market, met with Mark Freedman, a licensing agent. Freedman was familiar with the people at Playmates because of some work they had done for his former employer, Hanna Barbera, and he felt that the midsized company was in the perfect position to promote aggressively the offbeat character of the Turtles comic books. Although accounts differ as to whether Playmates was the first company Freedman approached or a last resort, Richard Sallis, the top official of Playmates' American subsidiary, was instantly enamored with the concept of the Ninja Turtles. The action figure market was then in a slump but Sallis felt that the tongue-in-cheek turtles were just what the industry needed as an antidote to the strictly serious market leaders like G.I. Joe. "The turtles put fun back into action figures," Mr. Sallis said in a 1988 interview with the *New York Times*. "They love truth, justice and a slice of pizza. You can't even take the name seriously, and the kids see that."

Playmates launched the Teenage Mutant Ninja Turtles at the 1988 New York Toy Fair to a less than enthusiastic reception. In spite of the company's optimism about the toys, retail outlets were skeptical, ordering only in small quantities, if at all. Confident in their product, Playmates began an aggressive promotion of their new action figure line, paying for the first five episodes of a cartoon series featuring the Turtles. To the industry's surprise, the Turtles action figures began flying off of toystore shelves as kids fell in love with the wisecracking, pizza-eating heroes. Playmates sold $23 million worth of the toys in 1988, an impressive figure for a new toy. If the writing was on the wall that these quirky characters were hot, no one could have predicted the phenomenon they were to become. By Christmas of 1988 retailers could not stock enough of the toys and by mid-1989 the Turtles had become one of the best-selling toys ever. A stunned toy industry watched while the small green dolls, retailing at only about five dollars, took over the boys' toys market. The television show that had begun as a promotional tie-in became the top-ranked Saturday morning kids show in the United States and the first Teenage Mutant Ninja Turtles movie, released in 1990, grossed more than $135 million. By 1990 the Turtles had captured more than 60 percent of the action figure sector and it was estimated that 90 percent of American boys under ten owned at least one Ninja Turtle.

The phenomenal success of the Teenage Mutant Ninja Turtles propelled Playmates, now officially named Playmates International Holdings, into the big leagues of the toy industry. In 1989 sales doubled to $145 million and, even more impressively, net income increased tenfold to $21 million. By the following year sales had topped $500 million and Playmates became the first toy company in history to net more than $100 million.

Decline of the Turtles in the 1990s

Thomas Chan, managing director of Playmates International, refused to allow the sudden, spectacular success of the Turtles to change his tightfisted management style. Instead of increasing staff to handle the sales boom, Playmates subcontracted the manufacture of the action figures to give the company more flexibility in case of a sudden drop-off in demand. Company headquarters remained spartan, with only 110 employees in a small, drab building in Hong Kong's Kowloon district. Chan also maintained a policy of subcontracting all design and relying on freelance inventors and designers for new toy ideas. To try to keep the Turtles fad alive Chan deliberately restricted supply to retailers of the best-selling items and extended the product line every year with new collectibles like surfer Turtles, samurai Turtles, and rock 'n roll Turtles. New product introductions like the Toxic Crusaders and entertainment licenses like Dick Tracy were also designed to cushion the impact of a fall in Turtles' sales. In addition, Playmates International Holdings began investing Turtles' profits in the Hong Kong real estate market, which was booming in the speculative environment of the early 1990s. In 1991 Chan confidently asserted to *Forbes,* "If Turtles' sales were to collapse from nearly $500 million today, even to $100 million, we'll still make a profit."

Inevitably, Turtle sales did drop off, slipping to $200 million by 1992 and to only about $30 million by 1995. For the first three years of this decline Playmates International remained profitable, as Chan had predicted. New product introductions took up much of the slack in Turtles' sales, which dropped from more than 80 percent to less than 60 percent of the company's business. Most notable was the introduction in 1991 of Waterbabies, a line of water-filled dolls invented by an American banker named Dan Lauer. Lauer and his siblings had devised the idea for the doll as children when, for a lack of toys, they had filled rubber gloves with water and drawn faces on them. Convinced of the attraction of his homemade toy, Lauer spent years trying to sell the idea to the big toymakers, to no avail. The first time he pitched the idea to Playmates President Richard Sallis, using a crude prototype made of water-filled balloons and condoms, Sallis was not impressed. "It leaked all over my desk," Sallis recalled in *Forbes* in 1992. "They said, 'Can you imagine this as a doll?' I said, 'No, I can't. Get it off my desk.'" Two years later, however, after Lauer had used money borrowed from family members to manufacture a leakproof version of the doll and sold 15,000 of them to area discount stores, Sallis took another look. Feeling that the doll might do for Playmates' girls' line what the Turtles had done for their boys' toys, Sallis agreed to buy the license for Lauer's toy baby. Playmates sold 2.2 million of the warm, cuddly dolls in 1991, making WaterBabies the number one promotional doll in the country, a position that the doll maintained for the next four years.

In addition to WaterBabies, a number of licenses tied to top movies, including *Coneheads, Star Trek: The Next Generation,* and *The Addams Family,* bolstered Playmates' sales through the early 1990s in spite of the waning of the Turtles' fad. Although the United States, traditionally, had provided the bulk of Playmates International sales, the company began to look more seriously toward the European and Asian markets as a source of growth. In 1992 Playmates International purchased a 38 percent stake in the Ideal Loisirs Group, a leading European toy company. By 1994 sales outside the United States represented more than 25 percent of the company's business.

During the same period Playmates International Holdings' investment in Hong Kong real estate was thriving and in 1993 management decided that the two parts of the business should be run separately. The Chan family sold their real estate holdings to Playmates International in return for shares valued at HK$1.4 billion (US$181.2 million). The toy business was then spun off as Playmates Toys in a one-for-one share distribution to Playmates International shareholders and the remaining real estate business was renamed Playmates Properties Holdings Ltd. (later renamed Prestige Properties).

Although new toy introductions and licenses kept Playmates Toys profitable for the first four years of the decade, in spite of a drop in sales to $195 million in 1994, in 1995 the company recorded a net loss of $12.6 million, its first loss since the 1987 Jill debacle. Much of this loss was related to the company's investment in Ideal Loisirs as well as the high start-up costs involved in a new video game marketing venture called Playmates Interactive Entertainment (P.I.E.). P.I.E. had considerable success with *Earthworm Jim,* a lighthearted game that earned numerous accolades from industry publications, but the video game industry was so dominated by a few big players like Nintendo that it was difficult to build a profitable niche within it.

Family Feuds and Nano Pals in the Mid-1990s

Playmates' business struggles of the mid-1990s were exacerbated by a bitter family feud that pitted two of the sons of company founder Chan Tai-Ho against each other. Robert, the elder son, petitioned the court in 1996 to wind up Chansam Investments, the holding company that controlled the Chan family's stake in Playmates, claiming that he had been ousted from the boards of Playmates Toys and Prestige Properties by his younger brother Thomas. The high profile court case, which involved numerous bitter accusations and counteraccusations, was an embarrassment to the company and had a negative effect on already suffering share prices. The case eventually was settled privately with Thomas Chan retaining managerial control of Playmates Toys.

In spite of continuing problems with P.I.E., the company's video game division, Playmates returned to profitability in 1996 with net profit of HK$54 million on sales of HK$1.2 billion. A significant portion of this profit was provided by the company's acquisition of the license for toys based on the hit movie *Space Jam,* featuring basketball star Michael Jordan. Launched in November, the *Space Jam* line alone netted more than $40 million for the company in the last six weeks of 1996. Although entertainment-related licenses like *Space Jam* could return substantial short-term profits, analysts were skeptical about the long-term profitability of the company in the absence of a solid, sustainable hit like the Teenage Mutant Ninja Turtles.

During the last half of 1997 Playmates may have hit upon such a long-term success with its launch of Nano Pals. Ironi-

cally, given Thomas Chan's antipathy to electronic toys after the company's experience in the mid-1980s, Nano Pals were electronic "pets" that could be petted, fed, and reprimanded with the push of a button. To the consternation of many parents and teachers, the beeping gadgets became the must-have toy of 1997. Playmates shared the $150 million market for the virtual pets with Bandai America Inc., makers of Tamagotchis, the first incarnation of the electronic toy. Unlike toys with movie tie-ins, Nano Pals had the virtue of being limitlessly extendable, such that by Christmas 1997 Playmates had already come out with talking Nano Pals and Nano Fighters, a specifically boy-oriented version of the toy.

In August 1997 Richard Sallis, the longtime president of Playmates' American subsidiary, resigned his position and was replaced by Ron Welch, former senior vice-president. Operating in new headquarters in Costa Mesa, California, this subsidiary still provided the large bulk of Playmates' sales, although European and Asian markets continued to grow as a percentage of sales. It remained to be seen whether Playmates would continue to survive the vagaries of the volatile toy industry into the 21st century.

Principal Subsidiaries

Playmates Toys Inc. (U.S.); Playmates Interactive Entertainment.

Further Reading

Chakravarty, Subrata N., "The WaterBabies Story: Persistence," *Forbes,* May 11, 1992, pp. 198–200.

Fulmer, Melinda, "Playmates Moving from La Mirada to Costa Mesa," *Orange County Business Journal,* May 13, 1996, p. 1.

Hirsch, Jerry, "Orange County Firms Are Putting New Life into Electronic Pets," *Orange County Register,* November 28, 1997, p. C1.

King, Thomas R., "Makers of 'Ninja Turtles III' Movie Are Betting on Four-Star Comeback," *Wall Street Journal,* March 19, 1993, p. 5.

Lee, Carrie, "Playmates Sales Fall 10 Percent to $1.42 Billion in Saturated Market," *South China Morning Post,* March 22, 1994, p. 3.

McGill, Douglas C., "Dynamic Duo: Kevin Eastman and Peter Laird," *New York Times,* December 25, 1988, p. 6.

"Ninja Turtles Maker Plans Spinoff, New Company," *Wall Street Journal,* November 30, 1993, p. A12.

Norman, Jan, "Half-Shell Heroes: Ninja Turtles Are a Hit for Toy Company," *Orange County Register,* May 6, 1990, p. 1.

O'Kane, Gerry, "Turning Turtles into Big Profit," *Asian Business,* July 1991, p. 14.

Ridding, John, "Feud at Ninja Turtle Toy Family," *Financial Times* (London), October 15, 1996, p. 6.

Smith, Elliot Blair, "Playmates Toys Loses Top Executive," *Orange County Register,* August 8, 1997, p. C1.

Tanzer, Andrew, "Heroes in a Half-Shell," *Forbes,* October 28, 1991, pp. 49–51.

Tsang, Denise, "Playmates Banks Hopes on Space Jam Despite Doubts," *South China Morning Post,* December 9, 1996, p. 2.

——, "Playmates Warns of Divisional Write-Off," *South China Morning Post,* May 30, 1997, p. 4.

——, "Poor U.S. Operations Lands Playmates with Disappointing Result," *South China Morning Post,* August 23, 1997, p. 3.

—Hilary Gopnik

PolyGram

PolyGram N.V.

Gerrit van der Vecnlan 4
3743 DN
Baarn
Netherlands
31-35-5489489
Fax: 31-35-5416400
Web site: http://www.polygram.com

PolyGram Holding, Inc.
Worldwide Plaza
825 8th Avenue
New York, New York 10019
U.S.A.
(212) 333-8000

Public Subsidiary of Philips Electronics N.V.
Incorporated: 1972
Employees: 12,549
Sales: $5.5 billion (1997)
Stock Exchanges: Amsterdam New York
SICs: 3652 Phonograph Records & Prerecorded Audio
   Tapes and Disks; 7812 Motion Picture & Video Tape
   Production; 7822 Motion Picture and Video Tape
   Distribution

Netherlands-based PolyGram N.V. is one of the world's largest entertainment companies and in 1997 remained the number one record company in the world. Over 80 percent of its income comes from the music business, specifically the acquisition, production, marketing, manufacture, and distribution of recorded music, along with music publishing and participation in TV music channels. Its popular music labels, including A&M, Def Jam, Island, Mercury, Motown, and Polydor, accounted for 62 percent of PolyGram's sales in 1996. Nine percent of its sales came from its classical music labels: Decca, Deutsche Grammophon, and Philips Classics.

Through PolyGram Filmed Entertainment (PFE), the company is also a growing presence in the film business, with four principal production labels: Propaganda, Working Title, Island Pictures, and Interscope. PFE sales accounted for 16 percent of total sales in 1996. Philips Electronics owns 75 percent of the company.

1962–75: A Joint Venture Becomes a New Company

Following World War II and throughout the 1950s, growth in the European record business was slow. Antiquated production machinery combined with tariffs and high publisher royalties made records relatively expensive to buy. That situation began to change in 1958, as the European Common Market began to form, and the original members agreed to lower and finally eliminate internal tariffs, which greatly helped record sales.

In 1962, Siemens A.G. of Germany and Philips Electronics N.V. of the Netherlands created a joint venture record company. Philips acquired 50 percent of Siemens' Deutsche Grammophon Gesellschaft, a preeminent classical music label founded in 1898, and Polydor Records, its popular music division. Siemens acquired 50 percent of Philips' subsidiary, Philips Phonographische Industries (PPI), which was renamed Phonogram. Philips was already in the record business, having purchased Chicago-based Mercury Records and its pressing plants in 1960. In 1966, Philips used Mercury Records to begin distributing its new tape cartridge system—tape one-eighth-inch wide enclosed in a cassette, that could be used for playing and recording music—and cassette players for the home and car.

Although the Siemens/Philips joint venture was successful in classical music, it did not generate enough money to pay to distribute the records internationally. The venture looked to the U.S. to boost revenues. In 1970, the Polydor Records division arranged for record distribution through United Artists, and in 1972, the joint venture bought Verve Records (one of the top jazz labels in the world) and the United Artists distribution network. Included among the acquisitions was 49 percent of the giant publishing operation Chappel Music and its music copyrights. That year, the joint venture and the new subsidiaries were reorganized as PolyGram N.V., with Siemens and Philips each retaining a 50 percent ownership.

Company Perspectives:

A blend of innovation and diversity, PolyGram has evolved from its roots in music to become one of the world's preeminent entertainment companies. A creative company, we are driven by the individualistic spirit of our collective music and film labels.

1975–85: Adding Pop to Classical and Jazz

In 1975, PolyGram bought Robert Stigwood Organization Ltd. for $1 a share. While the $8 million price was well above market value, the purchase gave PolyGram the copyrights to the music of a number of rock stars as well as *Jesus Christ Superstar* and the original English TV productions of ''Sanford and Son'' and ''All in the Family,'' along with 50 percent of RSO Records. As part of the deal, PolyGram agreed to pay Stigwood $5 million a year for five years for the acquisition and development of screen properties. This propelled relatively staid PolyGram into the disco music scene.

Stigwood's first film was *Saturday Night Fever*, starring John Travolta, with music by the Bee Gees, followed by *Grease*, with Travolta and Olivia Newton-John. RSO Records produced the soundtrack albums for both films in 1978. PolyGram also bought Casablanca Records, home of disco queen Donna Summer, KISS, and the Village People. *Saturday Night Fever* sold 15 million copies in the U.S., and *Grease*, sold 22 million worldwide. Together, Casablanca and RSO had record sales of $300 million in 1978, helping PolyGram to became the first company to have worldwide sales from music-and-entertainment of $1.2 billion. But while record sales were high, so were the costs of producing them, and PolyGram began losing money.

During the early 1980s, the company expanded its classical music base, buying Decca, the London-based classical record company, and establishing the Philips Classics label. It also created a new popular label, London Records.

In the meantime, Philips Electronics, PolyGram's parent, had been experimenting in optical electronics. Early in 1979, Philips produced its compact disk system. The result was a 4½ inch disk that, when played using an optical laser, offered an hour of sound, without any surface noise. In 1982, PolyGram and Philips launched the compact disk and disk player worldwide.

But by 1983, PolyGram was losing $300,000 a day, and had lost more than $200 million since 1977. Siemens wanted out of the joint venture. That year, Warner Communications and PolyGram began discussing a merger of their record businesses. The proposed merger was opposed by both the German Cartel Office and the U.S. Federal Trade Commission for its potential in reducing competition, and the merger was finally denied.

In 1984, PolyGram sold its music publishing house, Chapell-Intersong, to Warner for a price reported by Russell and David Sanjek to be in the $100 billion range. That same year, Alain M. Lévy moved from CBS Disques in France to become chief executive officer of PolyGram France. Over the next five years, he built the PolyGram subsidiary into France's

largest recorded music company, holding over a third of the market share.

1985–95: Acquiring Record and Film Companies

In 1985, Philips purchased 40 percent of PolyGram from Siemens and the remaining 10 percent in 1987, thus owning it completely. In 1986, PolyGram reentered the music publishing business, with the establishment of PolyGram Music Publishing, and in 1988, it moved into the movie business as it bought 49 percent of Propaganda Films, a small independent filmmaker.

The year 1989 was a busy one for PolyGram. The company had a successful worldwide initial public offering of 35 million shares priced at $16 each. Later in the year PolyGram expanded its portion of the important U.S. pop market with the purchase of Island Records for $272 million and, in 1990, A&M Records for $460 million.

PolyGram's music publishing business also grew in 1989 with the purchase of three publishing operations, Welk, Sweden Music, and the Island Group. By the end of the year the company also increased its foothold in the film industry, acquiring 49 percent of Working Title Films and establishing Manifesto Film Sales, which became PolyGram Film International. Film revenues for 1989 were approximately $65 million.

During 1990, Alain Lévy took over direct management of PolyGram's newly restructured operations in the U.S. Among his first efforts was the establishment of PolyGram Video U.S. and the creation of PolyGram Group Distribution, which was responsible for the warehousing, distribution, and sales of the company's audio (records, CDs, and cassette tapes) and video products in the United States. In January 1991, he was named president and CEO of PolyGram N.V. and CEO of PolyGram USA.

Under Lévy, the company continued to expand, with a second international offering, of 10 million new shares, in 1993. One quarter of the company's shares were now held publicly, with Philips Electronics owning the remaining 75 percent.

PolyGram bought CD manufacturing facilities in Germany, France, and the U.S. for a total of $122 million, acquired a 30 percent interest in Andrew Lloyd Webber's Really Useful Holdings for $168 million, and strengthened its presence in various national markets with the addition of the Finnish company Sonet Media AB and Japanese labels Nippon Phonogram and Polydor KK. During this period, PolyGram was also becoming involved with music television, investing in VIVA, a German language channel, and buying 50 percent of MTV Asia.

This attention to national and regional music markets was an important part of PolyGram's global strategy. The company would put in management teams, often with local people, whose job it was to spot and develop local pop music acts, building them into national or regional stars, and, sometimes, international stars. By 1995, in addition to its national subsidiaries in Asia, Australia and New Zealand, North America, Latin America, and Europe, the company had established PolyGram Hungary, its first operating company in Eastern Europe, purchased a local record and music publishing company to create PolyGram Poland, and with the acquisition of 51 percent of BIZ Enterprises, established PolyGram Russia. In 1995, PolyGram Latin

America bought Rodven Records, that continent's largest independent record company. Contributing to PolyGram's success in this area was its decentralized structure, which allowed its record labels to operate as autonomous units.

But the company was not ignoring the huge North American market. In 1991, PolyGram signed an international license agreement with Motown, the world's leading black music label, and then purchased Motown in 1993 for $301 million. In 1994, the company acquired a controlling interest in Def Jam, the leading rap music label, for $33 million.

In the classical music field, the early 1990s was a period of boom conditions. Because tastes in classical music were far less volatile than those in pop and rock music, PolyGram's goal was to increase the number of people listening to and buying classical records as well as to develop new artists. To bring classical music to a larger audience, the company held special events, such as the Three Tenors concert in Rome in 1990. Among PolyGram's classical artists were soprano Jessaye Norman, the world's reigning diva; tenor Luciano Pavarotti, the best selling classical artist in the history of the record industry; and internationally acclaimed conductors John Eliot Gardiner and Sir Georg Solti. New artists included Romanian soprano Agnela Ghiorghiu, Welsh baritone Bryn Terfel, and Ceclia Bartoli.

Early in his tenure, Lévy also set out to make PolyGram "a significant participant in the global film market." He acquired the remaining 51 percent of Propaganda Films in 1991, and the following year established PolyGram Filmed Entertainment to produce, acquire, and finance feature films for distribution to theaters, television, and home videos. Also in 1992, the company bought a controlling interest in Interscope Communications, an independent U.S. film production company, for $35 million, signed three-year production agreements with Jodi Foster's Egg Pictures and Tim Robbins' Havoc Inc., and, in a joint venture with Universal Pictures, formed Gramercy Pictures, to market and distribute small and mid-budget films in North America.

In 1993, PolyGram bought the remaining 51 percent of Working Title Films, and in 1994, acquired Island Pictures. With the purchase, in 1995, of the remaining 49 percent of Interscope Communications, PolyGram had four film production companies which, like the record companies, operated as autonomous creative units. The company also was involved in producing and distributing local language films, through such investments as half ownership of French production house Cinéa and Hong Kong-based TedPoly, and ownership of Meteor Film Productions, the leading independent film producer in the Benelux countries. Among the company's international films that received critical and box office success were *Nell, Four Weddings and a Funeral, French Kiss, Dead Man Walking, The Usual Suspects, Mr. Holland's Opus,* and *Trainspotting.* PolyGram's film revenues in 1995 reached $750 million, and represented 14 percent of sales.

On the video front, the company bought the U.K. operations of Vision Video Ltd., one of the United Kingdom's largest video production companies, and 75 percent of Abbey Home Entertainment, the largest producer of children's video and audio programming in the U.K.

Other activities in 1995 included the purchase of International Television Corporation Entertainment Group (ITC) and its film and television catalog for $156 million, the signing of a two-year agreement with Def Pictures to produce films, and the formation of a new joint venture, the Leonard Bernstein Music Publishing Company. Finally, during that year Phonogram Records changed its name worldwide to Mercury Records.

1996 to the Present—Reorganization and Local Repertoires

The music industry faced some significant challenges during the second half of the decade. Huge record store chains (hypermarkets) increasingly dominated the retail scene both in the United States and in Europe. Because these chains usually offered a fairly narrow range of records, based on hit charts, it became harder to promote new artists or to market classical music and jazz or back catalogs of pop music. While this was occurring, the huge North American market, which accounted for nearly a quarter of PolyGram sales, experienced its worst conditions in 15 years.

Despite an eight percent growth in 1996 sales, due primarily to the success of national artists in France, Italy, Spain, and Japan, PolyGram's net income dropped by three percent, and the company instituted several changes. It reorganized its classical music activities, sharpening the focus of each of its labels and reducing the number of recordings and releases. Philips Classics and new labels POINT and Imaginary Road were combined into the Philips Music Group, whose goal was to combine core classical music with more contemporary music and crossover artists from popular music. Deutsche Grammophon was concentrated on traditional European music, including early music recordings, and producing albums that widened the appeal of its star artists. Decca remained focused on opera and vocal recordings along with soundtracks from films such as *Braveheart.*

PolyGram also reorganized its European music distribution and marketing operations, laying off some 500 people in the process. Among the changes in its U.S. operations was PolyGram Group Distribution's move to promote all the company's record labels by expanding its sales force and focusing on direct sales in stores, and a restructuring of the Mercury and Motown labels, including relocating Motown from Los Angeles to New York City. While the restructuring was going on, PolyGram continued to invest in its other pop music labels, acquiring the remaining 51 percent of London-based Go! Discs and another 10 percent of Def Jam. The company also expanded its music TV activities, establishing Atomic TV, a cable music television joint venture in Poland with Poland's Atomic Entertainment and Planet 24, a U.K. television production company.

On the non-music side of the company, PolyGram Filmed Entertainment (PFE), while still in the red, saw its sales increase by 25 percent. PFE bought out Universal Pictures' share of Gramercy Pictures, became a one-third partner with Robert Redford and Showtime Networks Inc. in Sundance Channel, which showed independent and foreign films, opened a distribution company in Australia, renewed its agreement with Egg Pictures, and produced and distributed the prize-winning French film *The Eighth Day (Le Huitème Jour).* PolyGram Video, a division of PFE, continued to bring out new titles in its

National Football League video series. PolyGram also got into the restaurant business, investing in two Motown Cafés, in New York and Las Vegas.

In 1997, the company continued the restructuring of its U.S. music operations with the formation of the Mercury Records Group to oversee the management of Mercury, Motown, and PolyGram Classics and Jazz in the United States. Before the year ended, PolyGram had to call on competitors to help manufacture and distribute over 33 million records, CDs, and cassettes of "Candle in the Wind 1997," Elton John's tribute to Diana, Princess of Wales.

But most of the activity that year had to do with PFE, as PolyGram continued to build its production and distribution system worldwide and positioned itself to produce and market bigger-budget films for the U.S. market. PFE formed PolyGram Films to release major studio level features, signed production agreements with Alan Parker's Dirty Hands Productions and the Jones Company, and acquired the film catalogs from Consortium De Realization SAS. That purchase gave PolyGram one of the largest post-1948 film libraries in the world. Propaganda Films signed an exclusive first-look deal with David Fincher.

PFE also established PolyGram Television (U.S.) to develop and distribute programming for network, cable, syndication, and other markets in the U.S. and worldwide. In mid-year, PolyGram Video teamed up with parent Philips Electronics to bring digital video disks (DVD) to video store customers with a joint hardware-software rental program. The video division also continued to market various videos through supermarkets, often with merchandise discounts and rebates.

The two years of restructuring efforts paid off, as PolyGram's net sales rose 17 percent in 1997 and operating profit was up 11 percent. The music division outperformed the market with sales and profits up 17 percent, keeping PolyGram the number one record company in the world. PFE saw a profit in the fourth quarter, and sales for the year grew by 16 percent. The company kicked off 1998 with the announcements that PFE and Warner Brothers were teaming up to jointly finance and distribute movies produced by Castle Rock Pictures and that Ivan Reitman (*Ghostbusters, Stripes*) and Tom Pollak, former head of MCA's Universal Pictures, had formed a new production company with PFE.

As Deutsche Grammophon began the celebration of its 100th anniversary, the music-and-entertainment industry remained both expensive and volatile. However, PolyGram's investments in national repertoire were paying off with the success of local and regional artists. This helped counterbalance problems in the U.S. market. The company was also aided by the intense competition among Europe's rapidly expanding television distributors who were willing to pay top dollar for PolyGram's movies and catalog films. With subsidiaries in over 40 countries and its range of creative operations, PolyGram

looked forward to maintaining its leading position in the music business and increasing its position in the film industry, where PFE was the leading European film company.

Principal Subsidiaries

PolyGram Holding, Inc. (U.S.) and PolyGram subsidiaries in 42 other countries; A&M Records Inc. (U.S.); A&M Records Ltd. (U.K.); Decca Record Company Ltd. (U.K.); Def Jam Records, Inc. (U.S.; 60%); Mercury Records B.V.; Island Entertainment Group, Inc. (U.S.); ITC Entertainment Group Ltd. (U.K.); Motown Café, LLC; PolyGram Merchandising Inc. (U.S.; 80%); MTV Asia (Singapore; 50%).

Further Reading

Alaimo, Dan, "New Star Rising: As PolyGram Drives Ahead with Its Movie Business, It Is Relying on Supermarket Rentals to Hitch Its Wagon to a Star," *Supermarket News*, October 6, 1997, p. 86.

"Alain M. Lévy," http://www.polygram.com/international/newsinfo/execsuite/alevybio.html.

Amdur, Meredith, "PolyGram Buys ITC Entertainment with Feature Film Exploitation in Mind," *Broadcasting and Cable*, January 16, 1995, p. 97.

Christman, Ed, "Revamped PGD Shifts Sales Focus to Stores," *Billboard*, August 17, 1996, p. 1.

Jeffrey, Jon, "PolyGram Burns 'Candle' at Both Ends to Ship Single," *Billboard*, October 25, 1997, p. 65.

Johnson, Roy S., "Motown: What's Going On?" *Fortune*, November 23, 1997.

LeBlanc, Larry, "New Sales Force Serves All PolyGram Labels," *Billboard*, August 5, 1995.

Lieber, Ed, "Taking DVD to Masses: Philips, PolyGram to Offer Rental Kiosks," *HFN The Weekly Newspaper for the Home Furnishing Network*, May 5, 1997, p. 45.

"PolyGram Corporate Overview," http://www.polygram.com/international/newsinfo/coverview/overview.html.

"PolyGram Facts and Figures 1990 to 1995," New York: PolyGram, 1996.

"PolyGram/NFL Announce '96 Video Launch Dates," *Sporting Goods Business*, July 1996, p. 104.

"PolyGram N.V.," Hoover's On-Line, http://www.hoovers.com.

"PolyGram TimeLine," http://www.polygram.com/international/newsinfo/timeline/timeline.html.

Roberts, Johnnie L., "America in the Balance: PolyGram Is a Global Giant in Music and Movies. But It's Having a Harder Time in the U.S. Market," *Newsweek*, December 15, 1997, p. 40.

——, "Music: Pitsville, U.S.A.: Motown Is Leaking Money and Struggling to Produce Hits. Can It Be Saved?" *Newsweek*, December 2, 1996.

Sanjek, Russell, and David Sanjek, *American Popular Music Business in the 20th Century*, New York: Oxford University Press, 1991.

Saperstein, Patricia, "Indies Get Play on Sundance," *Variety*, April 29, 1996, p. 58.

—Ellen D. Wernick

Publishers Clearing House

382 Channel Drive
Port Washington, New York 11050
U.S.A.
(516) 883-5432
Fax: (212) 265-6736
Web site: http://www.pch.com

Private Company
Incorporated: 1953
Employees: 1,015
Sales: $325 million (1997 est.)
SICs: Catalog and Mail Order Houses

Publishers Clearing House (PCH) is believed to be the largest agency for marketing magazine subscriptions. Twice every year it conducts a major direct-mail sweepstakes promotion in which it tries to entice Americans to sign up for magazines by offering millions of dollars worth of prizes. PCH claimed in 1995 to be reaching 75 percent of U.S. households with at least one mailing per year. The company also was making a similar offer in Canada, Great Britain, France, and other countries and was using the direct-mail sweepstakes concept to sell selected products offered by catalogers. In addition, the company was selling books, audio and visual items, and general merchandise by direct mail.

Publishers Clearing House to 1980

During the 1950s salespeople (usually college students going door to door) were the largest source of subscriptions for magazine publishers, other than their own direct-mail efforts. Harold Mertz was manager of some of the crews of foot soldiers who trudged through residential neighborhoods to drum up business. In 1953, however, he founded Publishers Clearing House in the basement of his Port Washington, Long Island home to sell magazine subscriptions through the cheaper method of mail promotion. His simple, but revolutionary, idea was to increase the chance of making a sale by offering a selection of 20 magazines, rather than just one, in a single mailing.

Mertz's first mail package was a simple white envelope containing a folder depicting several magazines, an offer, and a reply form. In 1967, however, the company borrowed an idea that *Reader's Digest* initiated in 1962 and began making sweepstakes promotions, offering prizes to entrants who filled out a numbered entry blank and mailed it to the company. "We started giving out bunches of singles, fives and ten-dollar bills as prizes," a former PCH executive recalled in 1996. "It barely made a ripple, so we went up to $5,000."

Since the numbers were preselected, Publishers Clearing House could promote the sweepstakes truthfully with the words, "You may already be a winner!" According to a 1980 *Advertising Age* article, direct-mail marketers had discovered that they could increase sales 50 percent more through sweepstakes than by any other promotional technique. Cash, automobiles, and vacation trips were said to be the most appealing and popular awards. As a sweepstakes, rather than lottery, the contest was open to all entrants whether or not they chose to be customers. At first PCH did not feel obligated to award prizes if no winning entry was received, but later a second random drawing came to be held from entries submitted if no one turned in the winning number for the top prize.

Publishers Clearing House had its chosen field to itself until 1980, when a consortium of Time Inc., McCall's Corp., and Meredith Corp. formed rival American Family Publishers. Still based in Port Washington, where it now had 100,000 square feet of office and warehouse space, PCH was representing nearly every major publisher in the United States and was promoting some 395 magazines. Its mailings were going to 40 to 60 million households a year, with the addresses obtained from other direct-mail sources to take in people who bought by mail, who had spent more than a specified amount in the last few months, and who paid their bills promptly. PCH also had its own house mailing list of recent customers.

PCH normally conducted two major mailings a year at this time: one around the Christmas/New Year's period and a second in early July, each closely timed to television commercials telling viewers to be looking for the mailing. Between 50 to 110 magazine subscriptions were being offered in any given mailing. A typical sweepstakes mailing contained up to eight separate printed pieces. One of these was a sheet of gummed stamps offering the various magazine subscriptions at discounted rates. Also essential were the order vehicle (generally, a return card) and the sweepstakes offer, often a four-color brochure. Occasionally, the mailing also contained product coupons.

Refining the Concept: 1981–93

Publishers Clearing House's annual sales were about $50 million in 1981, when Robin Smith, a former Doubleday executive, became its president and chief executive officer. Annual revenues passed the $100 million mark in 1988. After American Family Publishers raised its biggest prize from $200,000 to $10 million in 1985, PCH had to follow suit. In 1987 the company added a "Catalog Clearing House" sweepstakes that included inserts selling 36 products from a selected group of catalogers. It was mailed to more than 1.5 million households and offered $10 million in prizes. PCH processed the orders, collected the payments, and sent the orders to the catalogers with an invoice representing the difference between the product price and its advertising and acquisition costs. During the late 1980s PCH also expanded its product line to include books (mostly children's and how-to books) and audio and visual items.

By late 1991 Publishers Clearing House had 700 full-time employees at its 14-acre complex, plus another 700 part-timers hired during promotional drives. The staff included about 12 copywriters and four art directors. One of the company's brightest ideas—a tag that listed a recipient's sweepstakes numbers and could be hung from a television dial—had resulted in a five percent increase in entries returned. By then PCH had distributed more than $50 million in prizes to more than two million people, including $13 million in fiscal 1991.

The grand prize of $10 million was being delivered since 1988, along with flowers, champagne, and balloons, by a Prize Patrol clad in blue blazers—and a cameraman. Advertising Director David C. Sayer, who said he personally had handed out more than $30 million in his years with the company and now headed the patrol, told a reporter, "The best part of my job is seeing how people react. One woman didn't believe me at first, and while I kept trying to tell her that she had just won $1 million, she just kept doing her laundry."

By this time Publishers Clearing House was receiving subscription requests from eight million people each year through its 25 annual mailings, which included millionaire-of-the month mailings, fast 50s ($50,000) for early entrants, and car giveaways. It was compiling its database by processing 450 million names from its own list and those rented from others, and it was dropping people who, after a certain period, continually failed to turn in entries or turned them in without ordering products. Mailings were aimed primarily at the middle-aged middle class and disproportionately outside "the more skeptical and cynical Northeast," as Sayer put it. Prime prospects—those who ordered frequently—might receive 30, even 40, mailings a year.

The need to "mail smarter" had grown more urgent because the price of a typical sweepstakes mailing had increased to between 40 and 50 cents. The stampsheets alone cost seven cents, but, said Smith, "Every time we think about getting rid of them, testing always proves they are worth the money." PCH

planners also had found, over the years, that given its middle-American target audience, cold cash, rather than exotic prizes like a private airplane or thoroughbred racehorse, were the grabbers. Vice-president Tom Owens told a *Washington Post* reporter in 1993, "You talk to winners, all they want to do is pay their bills and do very mundane things."

The 1992 year-end package arrived with a new "snap-pack" on the front of the envelope, which had to be peeled open to find the "finalist notification label" to paste onto the "finalist notification certificate"—in other words, the entry form. According to Owens, the rationale behind the "snap-back" was to make the recipient react at once in the critical first step of opening the mailing. The pasting regulations were described as "involving devices." As Owens explained, "The longer you have someone looking at what you're trying to sell, the better the odds are they'll make a purchase."

PCH's share of the subscription price ranged from 74 to 90 percent. These subscriptions were being offered at deep discounts, and PCH insisted on a magazine's lowest advertised price. Publishers, therefore, collected little money directly, but the increase in circulation allowed them to charge advertisers more money. PCH also was endearing itself to publishers by paying the magazine's share up front, and besides, as one magazine circulation manager said, "If we mail one million names and get no response, we still have to pay for the mailing. If Publishers Clearing House does the mailing, we don't pay for anything." On the debit side, however, subscribers obtained from stampsheet agents like PCH had a low percentage of renewals.

Problems of the 1990s

By 1994 Publishers Clearing House and its sweepstakes rivals were running into three problems: contest fatigue, increased government oversight, and private lawsuits and other bad publicity. Despite relentless promotion of its sweepstakes, including expenses of more than $20 million a year for advertising, response rates for PCH mailings were said to have dropped by seven to 12 percent, and perhaps more, in 1994. Sales volume from the mid-1995 mailings of PCH and American Family Publishers was reported to be down 22 percent. A PCH executive acknowledged that the company had cut back some of its mailings because of paper and postage increases but said these cost reductions were only in the five percent range and hence could not fully account for the drop in orders. The company, however, also had cut its advertising expenditures by seven percent in 1994.

Government officials seemed to be casting a jaundiced eye at Publishers Clearing House's promotions. The Federal Trade Commission's expert on sweepstakes said the odds of winning could be one in 100 million or worse. Being labeled a "finalist," he declared, generally merely meant that the contestant had sent in a previous entry. It was also noted that the $10 million prize was not given in a lump sum, but over 30 years, with $2.5 million not paid out until the final year. Million-dollar winners received only $50,000 in the first year.

In 1994 PCH agreed to pay $490,000 to 14 states to settle allegations that it used deceptive advertising in its annual sweepstakes. The company agreed to stop using the word "finalist" on most solicitations and to employ the phrase "final round" only in the last weeks of the promotions. Some states had reported that all persons receiving sweepstakes entries were identified as finalists. PCH also agreed to explain to consumers that if they were dropped from the mailing list they could write the company to be reincluded in the sweeps and then entitled to all entry mailings produced for the next 12 months.

A lawsuit was filed in 1992 after New York City sanitation workers found several thousand Publishers Clearing House envelopes discarded by a roadside and "literally blowing in the wind." PCH settled the suit by agreeing to enter the names and addresses of everyone who had received mailings between February and October 1992 for the January 1993 $10 million contest and April 1993 $1 million contest whether they had returned their entries or not. The company said it had discontinued its use of outside processors, one of which it blamed for improperly handling the discarded entries.

Disgruntled contestants were a fact of life for all sweepstakes agencies, but Publishers Clearing House could have done without the page-one *Detroit News* story in April 1997, in which Stephen Worhatch complained he had waited in vain for the Prize Patrol in response to a PCH letter asking him and his wife—bed-ridden with multiple sclerosis—to draw a map to their West Bloomfield home so that the patrol could deliver a check for the first installment of a $10 million prize. A company executive pointed out that the fine print in the entry form said the patrol "would come to your house if you were selected the winner." He added that the map request was merely "a fun way to get them interested . . . in the spirit of fun and entertainment."

Another disappointed Michigan contestant, Raymond Workmon, sued PCH in federal court for breach of contract and violation of the state consumer protection law. He was turned down for the second time by an appeals court in 1997, which declared, "Although Workmon believed he had won, his belief was not reasonable. . . . If Workmon read the entire certificate, he would have known, or reasonably should have known, he was not automatically the winner." An attorney for the company said that it was only the third time in 20 years that a contestant had sued PCH and that all three had lost.

By January 1996 PCH had awarded more than $92 million in prizes since instituting its sweepstakes. The $10 million prize winner that month was presented in a 30-second spot aired shortly after the completion of the Super Bowl. Camera crews from "Dateline News" and "Extra" were present, giving the event even more publicity. Like a majority of sweepstakes winners, the lucky recipient, Mary Ann Brandt of Phoenix, had not ordered a magazine with her entry and had been selected in the alternate drawing from entrants after the holder of the first randomly assigned number had failed to return his or her entry.

Publishers Clearing House's offerings in 1997 included not only magazines but such items as a Cal Ripken Jr. commemorative baseball, a Star Trek Communicator pin, a "6 in 1" hose nozzle, a reversible lint brush, and a collection of five mercury dimes. The company began selling subscriptions through its Web site in 1996. This site offered sweepstakes promotions (including Internet-only offers), discounted subscriptions to 300 magazines, and general merchandise.

Further Reading

Berglund, Elizabeth, "Winning the Publishers Clearing House Printing Sweepstakes," *American Printer and Lithographer*, September 1980, pp. 47–48, 50–51.

Conlon, Thomas J., "Sweepstakes Rank as Tops," *Advertising Age*, October 6, 1980, pp. 54–55.

DeHaven, Judy, "Sweepstakes 'Winner' Feels Deceived," *Detroit News*, April 18, 1997, pp. 1A, 7A.

Egol, Len, "Stamps of Approval," *Folio's Publishing News*, November 15, 1991, pp. 43–44.

Freedman, Eric, "PCH Superprize Claimant Loses Again," *Folio*, March 1, 1997, p. 22.

Gattuso, Greg, "PCH Agrees To Modify Copy," *Direct Marketing*, October 1994, p. 6.

Kahn, Joseph P., "Super Bowl Is at Six," *Boston Globe*, January 28, 1996, pp. 1, 16.

Kelly, Keith J., "Mags Stamped by Dramatic Drop," *Advertising Age*, October 30, 1995, pp. 1, 4.

Levere, Jane L., "Publishers Look to New Medium To Rekindle Sales in Older One," *New York Times*, December 1, 1997, p. D11.

Meier, Barry, "You're All Finalists!," *New York Times*, January 27, 1996, pp. 33, 35.

Miller, Paul, "Strong Response for Catalog Clearing House Sweeps," *Catalog Age*, January 1987, p. 11.

Rothenberg, Randall, "Read This and Win $10 Million!!," *New York Times*, January 31, 1989, pp. D1, D21.

Saslow, Linda, "It's Sweepstakes Time, and It's a Frenzy," *New York Times* (Long Island Weekly), January 20, 1991, pp. 1, 4.

Schnuer, Jenna, "Are the Stampsheets Licked?, *Folio*, May 15, 1995, p. 17.

Span, Paula, "Sweep Dreams, America!," *Washington Post*, January 28, 1993, pp. C1, C8.

Wells, Melanie, "This Loot's for You," *Advertising Age*, February 6, 1996, p. 42.

—Robert Halasz

Putt-Putt Golf Courses of America, Inc.

3007 Fort Bragg Road
Fayetteville, North Carolina 28303
U.S.A.
(910) 485-7131
Fax: (910) 485-1122
Web site: http://www.putt-putt.com

Private Company
Incorporated: 1954
Employees:
Sales: $100 million (1996 est.)
SICs: 7992 Public Golf Courses; 7996 Amusement Parks

Putt-Putt Golf Courses of America, Inc. is the franchiser of more than 275 miniature golf locations in 34 states and seven countries outside the United States. Some of these facilities were Putt-Putt Golf & Games Fun Centers that included video game rooms, bumper boats, batting cages, Go-Kart raceways, and "Putt-Putt TotalPlay." The company also was sponsoring a professional miniature golf circuit.

Promoting the Putt-Putt Concept, 1954–76

The founder of Putt-Putt was Don Clayton, a native of Fayetteville, North Carolina, who said he ran away from home at the age of 11 because his drunken stepfather tried to shoot him. Clayton said he spent the next few years as the ward of a brothel, adding "it was the Depression, women did anything for money." After attending the University of North Carolina on a football scholarship, he built a successful insurance business in the years immediately following World War II. He was on the verge of a nervous breakdown from overwork in the spring of 1954, however, when his doctor ordered him to take a month off work.

A golf enthusiast, Clayton dropped in on a miniature golf course in Fayetteville but was disgusted. "You had to hit the ball through spokes and spikes and over windmills and through waterfalls—it was just junk," he later recalled. "They gave you dirt and goat's hair to putt on and after you hit the ball, you had to pat down the goat's hair with your hands or feet." When he finished the course, Clayton told his brother and putting partner, "I could do better than this." Challenged to do so, he designed 18 different holes that night—without pipes or spokes or windmills or waterfalls to hit through—and took a $100, one-year lease on a vacant lot he had spotted on the way home. The next morning Clayton bought some lumber, hired some laborers, and began laying out his first course. Three weeks later, he was in business, charging 25 cents a round.

The beginnings of miniature golf are obscure, but the first course is believed to have been laid out in 1916 in Pinehurst, North Carolina. The game became a craze in 1930, when more than 25,000 courses may have been built, but interest rapidly dwindled. Clayton's no-frills, all-skills version sparked a revival for miniature golf. Some 192 people showed up at his course on the first night, 344 on the second night, and 744 on the third. It took only 29 nights for Clayton to pay off the construction cost of $5,200. Soon he was working harder than ever, running his insurance business again by day and preparing a new Putt-Putt course at night. After this second course was completed, he lined up backers to put up money for more. At the end of two years there were eight Putt-Putt courses in North and South Carolina.

Clayton also was besieged by admirers and well-wishers who wanted to establish their own courses. Flattered, he at first offered his know-how for free, even sending blueprints of his own designs. But soon he began charging $250 for plans, blueprints, and permission to use his legally protected trademark. In effect, he was franchising the Putt-Putt concept, but only collecting an initial fee, with no continuing income. By the end of the third season there were 44 Putt-Putts in all. Clayton owned some, owned a half-interest in others, and had franchised the remainder.

The South, in particular, was fertile territory for Putt-Putt because, as Clayton said later, "Land is less expensive, laws are less stringent, and labor unions are less difficult to deal with." The South also was able to offer a longer season for the outdoor game. Putt-Putt benefited from a paucity of entertainment options in many small towns, but it even caught on big in metropolitan areas as large as New Orleans. In Metaire, Louisiana, for example—a suburb of New Orleans—the local Putt-Putt was so popular in the 1980s that it hosted as many as 30 birthday parties a day.

Clayton also was finding other ways to capitalize on the Putt-Putt concept. He developed a scheme to market all the equipment that a Putt-Putt golf course needed, including clubs, shirt patches, and light standards. From promotional local tournaments he worked his way up to a professional putting tour, including a world championship telecast as early as 1959. For fun, Clayton built another course in Hialeah, Florida for $220,000, which he kept open around the clock, even attracting groups of 50 or 60 players at the unlikely hour of 4:00 a.m. Politicians got into the act, too. Jimmy Carter made his first appearance at a Putt-Putt course, complete with family, while running for governor of Georgia in 1966.

Evolution of the Game, 1976–90

In 1976, according to a *New Yorker* article, there were about 1,300 Putt-Putt courses on 700 franchised sites in the United States and eight foreign countries. On any given evening, 250,000 people were playing the game, enabling Putt-Putt to gross $30 million annually. Clayton was offering franchisees 126 specially designed or standardized holes from which to choose for an 18-hole, par-36 course. Each course cost between $35,000 and $42,000 for construction, depending on the model. The putting surface was smooth green, tight-weave carpet spread over poured concrete. Each "fairway" was enclosed by an orange aluminum "fence" composed of two-by-fours anchored to the concrete. The tee was a blue rubber mat with seven indentations for a variety of placements. Obstacles consisted of aluminum blocks, posts, mounds, and inclines. The typical Putt-Putt franchise held three side-by-side 18-hole courses.

Playing well on a Putt-Putt course required the skills of a billiard player in assessing angles and caroms as well as the touch of a golf putter. The Professional Putters Association was holding about 60 tournaments a year in 1976, awarding a total of more than $300,000 in prizes. The medal-play national championship was held on Clayton's Hialeah course that year. The match-play world championship, held in Columbus, Ohio, offered a purse of $10,000 to the winner and attracted a field of 256. The finals were videotaped for an estimated 70 million viewers around the globe. (In 1991 Putt-Putt's syndicated coverage of the tour was the second longest-running sports program on television, just behind ABC's "Wide World of Sports." The Professional Putters Association tour had, in 1996, awarded more than $6.5 million in prize money since its inception.)

The 1980s saw a new surge in the popularity of miniature golf, with more than half of the 3,500 courses in the United States at the end of the decade having been built since 1981, according to one survey. Even Manhattan, with its variety of entertainment options, offered the game, including a nine-hole course in Central Park opened by Donald Trump. But Putt-Putt, dubbed by columnist Bob Greene "what Wheaties is to the generic grain cereal at your local discount grocery store," remained true to its small-town origins. Franchisees, intent on preserving the game's squeaky-clean family image, weeded out pot-smoking youths and lit their courses brightly at night to ward off low-life elements. Interviewed in 1991, Clayton seemed paranoid about the dark forces he saw infesting American society. "Tomorrow's Putt-Putt will have a guard shack and maybe a metal detector," he told a reporter. "We want to be ready when the crack babies grow up."

One of the few changes in the Putt-Putt formula was the adoption of animal statuary, beginning in 1986, although as a decorative motif rather than an integral part of the game. Clayton designed a course in Killeen, Texas in 1989 that featured a fountain, a "mountain," and fiberglass wild animals, including a life-sized elephant. Inside the mountain rockwork was a tunnel with "stalactites" and a Putt-Putt hole. The elephant was on top of the mountain. Around the mountain was a lake with alligators and a spouting whale. In 1991 Putt-Putt had three construction crews updating courses with animal props and mountains. By then the corporate warehouse in Fayetteville was filled with fiberglass giraffes and golf balls in Easter egg colors.

Putt-Putt in the 1990s

Putt-Putt franchisees in the United States were paying the company an up-front fee of $15,000 in 1991 to use the corporate name and lay out courses from the company's 132 patented and copyrighted hole designs. Jeffrey Lipton, a Toronto lawyer, purchased the Canadian rights that year, taking his enterprise public. Lipton financed the establishment of a Putt-Putt site at the base of Toronto's CN Tower, the world's tallest freestanding structure. His company planned to retain rights to the Toronto and Vancouver metropolitan areas but was franchising sites elsewhere in Canada for a standard fee of $30,000 (in Canadian dollars), plus a minimum of $80,000 for constructing each 18-hole course (not including a building to house a year-round games room) and an eight percent royalty on revenues.

The usual U.S. Putt-Putt franchise fee at the end of 1997 was $25,000 for golf and game-room rights and $30,000 for rights that included other attractions, such as bumper boats, batting cages, and raceways. Fees for major metropolitan areas and international sites were being negotiated on an individual basis. For franchise rights in communities with populations of 30,000 or less, the initial fee was only $5,000 for a standard 18-hole golf layout or $10,000 for a franchise that included other attractions. Putt-Putt also was charging an ongoing fee of five percent on golf sales and three percent on game-room, bumper boat, batting cage, and raceway sales.

Costs for creating a Putt-Putt golf course ranged from $85,000 to $150,000. For a three-course layout, these costs ranged from $325,000 to $700,000. The cost of adding batting cages ranged from $85,000 to $155,000, bumper boats ranged from $85,000 to $175,000, and raceways ranged from $200,000 to $750,000. Franchise owners would, in addition, have to pay for video games, building a clubhouse, and buying or leasing land.

The more than 275 Putt-Putt locations in 1997 included franchises in Australia, Indonesia, Japan, Lebanon, and New Zealand as well as Canada. More than one billion games had been played worldwide. Clayton, who died in 1996, had retired the previous year and turned the business over to his daughter,

Donna Lloyd. His son-in-law, David Lloyd, had become president of the company in the 1970s.

Further Reading

Auchmutey, Jim, "Mr. Putt-Putt Reinvented the Game with Single Stroke of Genius," *Atlanta Journal/Atlanta Constitution,* July 21, 1991, p. M6.

Chotas, Harrell, and Kerr, Mary Lee, "Miniature Golf," *Utne Reader,* November/December 1992, pp. 139–40.

"Fifty Per Cent," *New Yorker,* August 2, 1976, pp. 19–21.

Furlong, William Barry, "The Uphill Course of Putt-Putt Golf," *Saturday Evening Post,* October 1980, pp. 26–29, 90.

Greene, Bob, "Putt-Putt a Go-Go," *Esquire,* October 1982, pp. 17, 19.

Monroe, Sylvester, "Welcome to Putter's Paradise," *Time,* September 11, 1989, p. 73.

Posner, Michael, "Putt-Putting for Profits," *Macleans,* September 30, 1991, pp. 46–47.

Thomas, Robert McG., Jr., "Don Clayton, 70, Driven Man Who Putted His Way to Riches," *New York Times,* April 18, 1996, p. B9.

Weber, Bruce, "Par for the Course," *New York Times Magazine,* March 18, 1990, p. 96.

—Robert Halasz

R. Griggs Group Limited

Cobbs Lane
Wollaston
Wellingborough
Northants NN29 75W
England
(44) 01933 665381
Fax: (44) 01933 664088
Web site: http://www.drmartens.com

Private Company
Incorporated: 1911 as R. Griggs & Co. Ltd.
Employees: 3,800
Sales: £250 million (US$ 500 million) (1997 est.)
SICs: 3143 Men's Footwear Except Athletic; 3144
    Women's Footwear Except Athletic

Privately held, family-owned R. Griggs Group Limited is the maker of the world-famous Dr. Martens brand of footwear and clothing accessories. One of England's leading shoe and boot manufacturers, R. Griggs has steadfastly refused to join the growing trend of moving production overseas, insisting instead on maintaining the majority of its production facilities in its traditional Northampton base, itself the center of England's footwear manufacturing industry. Indeed, while Griggs has pursued an aggressive investment and modernization program, its shoes are still crafted essentially by hand by the company's 3,800 employees—many of whom are still paid by the piece—in some 31 manufacturing plants. Together the company produces more than one million pairs of Dr. Martens shoes and boots each week. The company's sales are also buoyant: from 9.6 million pairs sold in 1996, the company expects to sell more than 12 million pairs in 1998. The company estimated its 1997 sales to reach approximately £250 million.

While the Griggs family's reputation for quality footwear reaches back for nearly a century, it is the Dr. Martens brand that has made the company's fortune. Produced under exclusive license since 1960, Dr. Martens have been the favored footwear not only of England's industrial, mining, and public services work force, but also of its rebellious youth. Among the "mods" of the 1960s, the "punks" and "skinheads" of the 1970s and 1980s, and the 1990s grunge fashion followers, Dr. Martens have gained a lasting, and worldwide popularity, to the extent that, in the late 1990s, more than 75 percent of the company's sales were generated internationally, in over 70 countries. Yet, if Dr. Martens brand has become a primary symbol of the world's youth culture—with a recognition rate among the top 100 brands worldwide—the company's extensive line of styles have also found their way onto the feet of such world leaders as the Dalai Lama and the Pope.

The secret of the Dr. Martens success is its famed air-cushion sole, as well as its high-quality uppers. Boasting of its footwear's extreme durability and resistance to the harshest industrial environments, the company even goes so far as to offer a five-year guarantee against the premature aging of its shoes. This reputation for quality, in fact, longed served as the Dr. Martens brand's main form of advertising. Only since the early 1990s has the company instituted an active brand marketing strategy. The success of its marketing activities—conducted through subsidiary AirWair Ltd.—is clear: between 1990 and 1997, the company's sales increased more than five times. In the late 1990s, the company also moved to bring its distribution activities in-house.

Griggs produces some 500 styles of Dr. Martens boots and shoes. Its leading model, the 1460, however, is also its oldest. The 1460 accounts for approximately half of all the company's sales. Some 50 percent of these sales come from the 15 to 25 year-old age group. Another ten percent of sales are provided by the company's industrial division and its "Getta Grip" and "Impact" brand names. In addition to footwear, Griggs has capitalized on the Dr. Martens name by launching a line of clothing and accessories. Since 1994, the company has also operated its Dept. Store, a six-story retail store in London's Covent Garden. The retail store, which also serves as a consumer research and testing grounds, has been a success, prompting the company to begin plans to open additional retail stores in other markets, including its primary European and United States markets, as well as in the Middle and Far East markets. The R. Griggs Group remains a firmly family-owned company.

Company Perspectives:

Without compromising their traditional values Griggs are positioned at the very forefront of footwear technology. It is a positioning which is a key element for a Group and a brand which is constantly reaching for new frontiers of quality, comfort and style.

Fourth-generation Max Griggs is the company's president, while son Stephen Griggs serves as the company's chairman.

Early 20th-Century Founding of Griggs

While the Dr. Martens brand would come to define the Griggs Group after the 1960s, the company had already built a reputation for quality footwear going back to the turn of the century. In 1901, Benjamin Griggs and partner Septimus Jones formed a partnership for producing boots in Wollaston, then already a primary center for England's shoemaking industry. Jones and Griggs eventually split up; Jones formed his own company, called Septimus, while Griggs, joined by son Sebastian, created R. Griggs & Co. Ltd. Over the next 40 years, Griggs would craft a reputation for the quality of its work boots. In the early 1950s, the next generation of the Griggs family took over the company's direction, with William Griggs serving as the company's leader. Under William Griggs, the company added a new dimension to the quality of its boots, adopting the Goodyear Welted construction method for attaching the soles. For that venture, Griggs formed Wollaston Vulcanising Co. Ltd., a cooperative with other local shoemakers. By then, Griggs could already guarantee its boots against premature wear. In 1955, Max Griggs, son of William Griggs, joined the company.

The company's turning point would come at the end of the 1950s, when, through the Wollaston Vulcanising cooperative, it signed an agreement to become the exclusive worldwide producer of an entirely new type of sole developed by Drs. Klaus Maertens and Herbert Funck of Germany. The pair had begun work on their invention in the postwar years, after Klaus had broken his leg on a ski trip in Munich. Walking had become painful, and Maertens sought a means to provide a softer landing for the foot, in order to minimize the shock of each step. Inspired by developments in the automobile industry, Maertens was determined to adapt the pneumatic concept to the shoe. Maertens' first efforts involved, in fact, cutting apart tires and sewing the pieces to the shoe itself. While this helped minimize the impact, walking remained painful for Maertens.

By 1947, however, Maertens brought his idea even closer to the automobile industry. He next sought a means for trapping air within the sole, which would provide a similar pneumatic cushion. For this step, Maertens would be aided by colleague Funck, who was a director of a small electrical appliance company. Instead of cutting up tires, Funck instead used raw PVC rubber, which, shaped by molds much like those found in waffle irons, could produce soles containing pockets ideal for capturing air. Attaching the soles to the shoe, while at the same time

sealing in the air pockets, was achieved by doubling the sole; the first layer was sewn directly to the shoe, while a second layer was heat-sealed to the first.

Maertens and Funck took out a patent on their invention and next sought a means of commercializing it. Their first customers were former soldiers and wounded civilians from World War II, who, like Maertens, suffered from leg injuries that had made walking painful. Word of the invention soon spread beyond Germany's hospitals, and the partners found ready customers in the country's factories and mines. With sales growing, Maertens and Funck began looking for an industrial partner capable of meeting the demand for their soles, while also able to provide distribution beyond Germany. A Swiss company, Grosse, became the first to produce the Maertens sole under license. In the 1950s, Grosse had opened a factory in Wollaston, producing for the British market. By the end of the decade, however, Gross had gone bankrupt, and the Griggs company purchased the Wollaston plant.

Griggs was impressed by the Maertens sole; Maertens and Funck, for their part, were encouraged by the Griggs company's reputation and its guarantee of quality behind its footwear. In 1959, the two sides reached an agreement for the Griggs company to take over production of the Maertens sole. Under the agreement, Maertens and Funck received royalty payments for each pair sold, while Griggs received exclusive U.K. rights to the process. Perhaps in response to the Grosse failure, Griggs also established a sales strategy, based on slow, targeted growth.

In Step with Fashion in the 1960s

Originally called Dr. Maertens Air Cushioned Soles, the spelling of the surname was soon anglicized to Martens. The first pair of Dr. Martens boots were produced on April 1, 1960, and the "1460" became the company's primary—and for many years only—model. By the end of that year, Griggs sales had topped £250,000.

Griggs continued to target its traditional work shoe market, adding new models, such as the three-eyelet Gibson shoe, bringing the Dr. Martens sole from the mines and factories onto the feet of post office and subway workers. Yet, the company hardly seemed aware of a growing new market that was eagerly embracing the Dr. Martens boot. The rise of England's youth culture in the early 1960s, particularly the so-called mod movement championed by the musical group The Who, had made the 1460 part of the standard 'uniform' of any self-respecting rebel. While the impact of the mods on Griggs' sales was would remain somewhat minimal—by 1970, the company's revenues remained under £700,000—that culture would help give rise to a later surge in popularity for the boots. Dr. Martens boots remained almost exclusively a British product during this time; less than six percent of sales were made internationally.

The growth in sales, however, had enabled Griggs to make a number of strategic investments. During the 1960s, the company bought out the rest of the Wollaston Vulcanizing cooperative. Over the next 20 years, the company would also buy up many of its neighbors, including Septimus. Far from putting these companies out of work, the growing success of the

Dr. Martens boot would enable these businesses to remain in operation, and for Wollaston to remain a primary focus of the British shoe industry.

By 1980, Griggs' sales had jumped to nearly £22 million. A new generation of youth, among them a subculture known as the skinheads, had discovered the efficacy of the 1460's steel toe. Moreover, the appearance of the punk music and fashion movement in the mid-1970s brought the 1460 to an ever-increasing audience. As the British-inspired punk scene—and its corresponding fashion—spread beyond the United Kingdom, Griggs' international sales too began to grow. In 1980, foreign sales neared one million pounds, representing only 4.4 percent of the company's total sales but having been achieved nonetheless with no marketing effort on the company's part. In fact, the company would continue to rely on word-of-mouth for its advertising throughout the 1980s.

Branding a Lifestyle in the 1990s

As Max Griggs took over the company's direction, son Stephen Griggs became the fifth generation to enter the family company in 1980. Griggs continued its acquisition of its struggling Wollaston neighbors, adding the factories and workshops of such names as Septimus Rivett, Humphrey & Smart, Denton & Stuart, Bayes Bros., Phillips Brothers, GW & R Shelton, Luther Austin Co., John Pick & Co., Sundy Shoes, and others. While England was riddled by an extended economic crisis, stemming from the Arab Oil Embargo of the early 1970s, with unemployment on the rise across the country, the success of the Dr. Martens boot enabled Griggs' to keep the Wollaston shoe industry's work force working.

The mellowing of punk music into what was dubbed New Wave brought the Dr. Martens boot to an even wider audience, both in the United Kingdom and abroad. Such ongoing transitions in the music scene helped build the company's sales. Moreover, while the 1460 continued to sell strongly to Britain's industrial work force, a surprising new market was developing: more and more women were wearing the Dr. Martens shoe. This trend would continue to build throughout the 1980s and by the next decade had firmly established the Dr. Martens as 'must-have' fashion accessory.

In the late 1980s, Griggs' string of acquisitions had given the company not only a growing work force—some 1,500 by 1990—but also a collection of aging production equipment among its 30 or so plants and workshops. Among the shoe industry, a new trend was developing, that of closing domestic plants and moving production to cheap foreign labor markets, such as in many developing Asian countries. Griggs, however, refused to join the trend. Instead, the company began a massive and sustained investment program, upgrading its plants and machinery. In 1989, Griggs would spend more than £1.6 million on capital expenditures. This figure would continue to rise each year through the 1990s, nearing £4 million in 1992, and topping £6 million in 1996.

Through the 1980s, Griggs' nearly doubled its annual sales, posting 1990 sales of £38 million, including nearly 15 percent from overseas. The 1990s, however, would end the company's 30-year history of modest growth. By 1997, Griggs' sales would top £250 million, and the company would forecast a rise in sales to more than £300 million by the year 2000.

If punk and new wave subcultures had brought Dr. Martens to wider numbers of youth, these audiences nonetheless remained rather small. In the late 1980s, and especially in the early 1990s, however, a new music scene appeared and quickly broke through into the mainstream music markets. "Grunge" would adopt not only its musical inspiration from the earlier punk scene, but also some of its fashion sense, particularly its choice of footwear. Dr. Martens became the *de rigueur* boots and shoes of an entire generation of youth, boys and girls included, not only in the United Kingdom but worldwide. Grunge would also bring Dr. Martens to the United States, a market that had previously shown little interest in the British-made boots.

If Griggs had long relied on word-of-mouth and the fortuitous adoption of its boots—still wholly centered on the 1460 model—by successive generations of youth, the company was determined to build an active marketing program in the 1990s. The company created a new marketing subsidiary, AirWair Ltd., and set out to expand its line beyond the 1460. By 1991, the company was ready to target not just the youth and work markets, but the entire family, introducing eight new product families. Based as always on the Dr. Martens sole, the company's new products would introduce a entirely new variety of colors and patterns. By the late 1990s, the company could boast some 500 models of Dr. Martens boots and shoes. At the same time, Griggs began to develop an advertising strategy. Recognizing the youth appeal of the Dr. Martens brand, the company would avoid mass-marketing tactics, and instead practice a micro-marketing strategy—including sponsorships of concerts and music tours, and even release of its own compact discs—targeted at its core market. During the 1990s, Griggs would also extend the Dr. Martens brand name into a 'lifestyle,' developing and marketing a line of brand name clothing and accessories, ranging from t-shirts to cosmetics. In 1994, the company opened its first retail store, called the Dept. Store, in London's Covent Garden. The six-story complex would serve as more than a retail sales space, becoming a consumer testing and research ground for the developing Dr. Martens line.

As Griggs built its brand image, it also took steps to restructure its distribution. While the company had long relied on a network of primarily British wholesalers to distribute its boots both in the United Kingdom and abroad, in the 1990s Griggs began to bring distribution in-house. The move would enable the company more direct contact with retailers and therefore closer contact with the demands of its customers. Grouped under the AirWair subsidiary, the company created several new AirWair units in the United States, Canada, and Germany. By 1998, the company had taken control of almost all of its distribution, often acquiring its former independent distributors. The change in the Griggs company—now led by Stephen Griggs as chairman—had been dramatic. Sales had grown nearly five times in less than a decade, while foreign sales had risen to account for more than 75 percent of the company's total. With a strong brand image, and the cross-generation appeal of its Dr. Martens sole, Griggs looked forward to a future of walking on air.

Principal Subsidiaries

Dr. Martens Dept. Store Ltd.; R. Griggs & Co. Ltd.; AirWair Ltd.; Dr. Martens Sports & Leisure Ltd.; AirWair USA Ltd.; Dr. Martens AirWair GmbH (Germany); AirWair Canada Ltd.; Dr. Martens AirWair USA LLC.

Further Reading

Brelay, François, "Dr. Martens: Un Mythe Qui Marche," *Performances,* January 1998, p. 74.

Cuneo, Alice Z., and Adrienne Ward Fawcett, "Dr. Martens," *Advertising Age,* July 4, 1994, p. S14.

"Doc Martens Stepping Out to Reach an Older Market," *Marketing,* October 23, 1995, p. 2.

Koehl, Carla, "Boots are Made for Gawking," *Newsweek,* February 20. 1995, p. 8.

Krajewski, Steve, "Unseen 'Doc Martens' Reappear in U.S. Ads," *Adweek,* October 6, 1997, p. 4.

——, "What's Up, Doc Martens?," *Adweek,* May 26, 1997, p. 2.

Morais, Richard C., "What's Up, Doc?," *Forbes,* January 16, 1995, p. 42.

R. Griggs Group Ltd., company brochure, Wollaston, Eng.: R. Griggs, 1997.

Underwood, Elaine, "Dr. Martens Steps Up Growth with New Rx for U.S. Fashion," *Brandweek,* November 11, 1993, p. 10.

—M.L. Cohen

Rainier Brewing Company

P.O. Box 24828
Seattle, Washington 98124
U.S.A.
(206) 622-2600
Fax: (206) 622-7989
Web site: http://www.rainierbeer.com

Wholly Owned Subsidiary of Stroh Brewing Company
Incorporated: 1878 as Seattle Brewing and Malting
   Company
Employees: 325
Sales: $90 million (1997 est.)
SICs: 2082 Malt Beverages

A Pacific Northwest mainstay for more than a century, Rainier Brewing Company brews and sells a handful of beer brands, including the company's flagship brand, Rainier Beer. Headquartered in Seattle, where the company produces its beer on the same site it occupied in the late 19th century, Rainier Brewing was acquired by G. Heileman Brewing Company in 1977. In 1996 G. Heileman was acquired by Stroh Brewing Company, uniting the United States' fifth and fourth largest brewing operations, respectively, and adding the Rainier brand to a stable of other beer brands that included Colt 45, Mickey's, Schaefer, Schlitz, Carling Black Label, and Stroh's.

Birth of a 19th Century Beer

Rainier Brewing's long legacy as a regional brewer in the Pacific Northwest began in 1878 when a German immigrant named Andrew Hemrich founded a small brewery in Seattle. Hemrich, whose family had been brewers for generations, was part of the distinct wave of German brewers who immigrated to the United States during the 19th century and left a lasting mark on the U.S. beer industry. With them, the transplanted Germans brought their extensive background in brewing beer, a centuries-old tradition that gave the new arrivals the means to survive in the burgeoning New World. Across the nation, hundreds of small breweries were established, with German immigrant brewmasters at the helm, enriching the flavor and the population of the beer industry in America. From these ranks, the country's largest beer companies emerged, national giants such as Schlitz Brewing Company, Stroh Brewing Company, and Anheuser-Busch Company. Close behind these future industry stalwarts were the regional breweries, breweries like the one operated by Hemrich's Seattle Brewing and Malting Company. Although his company and its signature beer, Rainier, never made the leap to national dominance, Hemrich did create a powerful regional force, one that dominated the Pacific Northwest and at one time appeared to be on the verge of becoming one of the largest breweries in the world.

Hemrich opened his brewery, the Bayview Brewery, in 1878, establishing it on a site south of Seattle where Rainier beer would be brewed more than a century later. Also in 1878, Hemrich formed Seattle Brewing and Malting Company—Rainier Brewing Co.'s earliest predecessor—to operate the brewery. Hemrich brewed three beers at Bayview, selling them to residents in nearby Seattle under three different labels: Bayview, Bohemian, and the company's premier label, Rainier. There was no shortage of different beers for Seattlites to choose from during Hemrich's early years as a brewer and, accordingly, no shortage of competition for his fledgling brewery. The country teemed with small, independent breweries, each vying for a share of its local market. The years of large, national breweries were decades away, as were the means of transportation to distribute beer beyond a limited geographical area, creating a landscape of small breweries clustered around population centers, with each focused exclusively on its local market. Hemrich's Bohemian, Bayview, and Rainier labels fought for distinction among a parade of other brands, including Horluck's, Aero Club, Selah Springs, Lorelei, Golden Age, Mountain Club, Rocky Mountain, Edel-Brau, Gold Seal, Olympic Club, Tacoma Pale, and Washington Viking. Of these distinctly Pacific Northwest beers—and a host of others—only one brand would survive through the 20th century. That singular, enduring brand was Hemrich's Rainier Beer.

By the early 1890s, after more than a decade of business, Hemrich was ready to expand, his three labels having won over enough customers to finance and necessitate a brewing facility larger than the Bayview plant. In 1893 Hemrich constructed a larger, more modern brewery several miles from the Bayview, erecting the new plant in the Georgetown area of south Seattle. During the next 20 years, with the new Georgetown brewery underpinning its operation, Seattle Brewing and Malting Company thrived, becoming overwhelmingly successful in the business of brewing and marketing beer. As the company's business flourished, it benefited from the advancement of technology around it and was no longer fettered to the confines of the Puget Sound area. Distribution channels opened up during the early 20th century, as various modes of transportation emerged that enabled the shipment of beer thousands of miles from the clustered breweries surrounding large population centers. For Hemrich, a greater distribution area meant more customers and greatly accelerated financial growth, and for people living on the West Coast the shipment of beer by rail, truck, and boat meant a growing familiarity with the Rainier label. Rainier Beer was sold throughout the Pacific Northwest, up into the gold fields of Alaska, down south in California, and as far away as Asia. The effect on the company's stature was huge. By the 1910s Seattle Brewing and Malting Company was the largest single industrial enterprise in the state of Washington. Hemrich's brewery ranked as the sixth largest in the world.

Prohibition and Rebirth

After nearly 40 years of existence, Seattle Brewing and Malting Company had developed into a formidable regional force that appeared destined to become one of the nation's mainstay beer brands, but just as the company was poised for such expansion, its business was made illegal. In 1916, three years before the 18th Amendment was ratified, thereby prohibiting the use and sale of alcohol, the state of Washington declared the production and sale of alcohol illegal. Virtually overnight, Hemrich was out of business. The jewel of his promising enterprise, the massive Georgetown brewery, was converted into a feed mill. The Rainier brand, which had held sway in the greater Pacific Northwest region for years, was relinquished by Hemrich as well. It was sold to a California firm and soon disappeared from sight for roughly 15 years.

With the repeal of the 18th Amendment in 1933, the U.S. beer industry quickly came back to life, as more than 700 breweries opened and braced themselves for the heavy demand ahead. One of those breweries that started anew in 1933 was the Rainier Brewing Company, the same firm that had acquired the Rainier brand from Hemrich in 1916. The company sold its version of Rainier in California and Oregon, brewing the brand 900 miles from its original location. To the north, however, a father and son team was making every effort to bring the once-famous Rainier brand back to its home in the Pacific Northwest.

Fritz Sick and his son Emil were in Seattle preparing for the second coming of Rainier Beer—the Seattle version. The pair had developed extensive brewing interests in several Canadian cities and moved to Seattle to take part in the 1933 rejuvenation of brewing beer in the United States. The Sicks purchased the old Bayview brewery, re-equipped it, and started the Century Brewing Company. At the old Bayview facility, the Sicks brewed and bottled Rheinlander beer while they negotiated with the Rainier Brewing Company of San Francisco to acquire the rights for the Rainier brand. Negotiations stumbled forward for

two years before the Sicks could at least claim a partial victory. In 1935, in their continuing pursuit to acquire the assets of Seattle Brewing and Malting Company, the Sicks acquired the old Georgetown Brewery and purchased the rights to use the Rainier brand name in Washington, Idaho, and Alaska, provided they paid a royalty on each barrel of Rainier sold to San Francisco's Rainier Brewing Company. It was not until 1953 that the Sick family gained exclusive, worldwide rights to the Rainier brand.

Rheinlander and a three-state right to the Rainier brand were enough, however, to keep Century Brewing Company in business and growing. As the company moved forward through the World War II period and on into the postwar economic rebirth of America, meaningful changes were occurring both within Century Brewing Company and within the U.S. beer industry as a whole. From the macroscopic perspective, the U.S. beer industry was undergoing a decades-long consolidation of its participants, as the era of myriad independent breweries that flourished during Hemrich's day gave way to an era in which behemoth national brewers ruled the day. From the more than 700 breweries in operation following the repeal of the 18th Amendment in 1933, the number of independent breweries was winnowed down to less than 50 by 1978. Regional brewers like the Sick family's Century Brewing Company were becoming increasingly rare.

Ownership Changes in the Late 20th Century

At Century Brewing Company, some of the changes mirrored the developments occurring in the company's industry. Emil Sick, who had taken over after the death of his father, died in 1964, leaving his adopted son, Alan B. Ferguson, to assume the company's executive management responsibilities. By the early 1970s Ferguson had been appointed chairman of the corporation, making room for Edwin S. Coombs, Jr.'s ascension to the presidential post. It was during these changes in leadership that the Century Brewing Company underwent significant changes to its corporate structure. A name change was effected, changing the company's corporate title to Rainier Brewing Company, and a holding company was subsequently formed, called The Rainier Companies. Amid the general trend that signaled the end of independent brewers and favored larger, conglomerate brewers, The Rainier Companies fit well with the times. Molson Breweries Ltd., a Canadian brewer that ranked as a giant and stood as the oldest brewing firm in North America, owned the majority of The Rainier Companies' stock.

Against the backdrop of these changes, the Rainier brand was approaching its centennial, having withstood the tests of a century that saw it beat back a host of competitors during the era when independent brewers prevailed, survive the more than decade-long hiatus of Prohibition, and continue to flourish as large, national brewers predominated its industry. Aside from the company's signature Rainier brand, Rainier Brewing marketed Rheinlander beer, Highlander beer, Brew 66, and Rainier Alc, selling the brands in Washington, Oregon, Idaho, Montana, Alaska, and part of Wyoming. As the mid-1970s approached, Rainier Brewing began selling its beer in Hawaii.

The ties with much larger brewers became even closer in 1977 when The Rainier Companies sold the Rainier Brewing

Company to La Crosse, Wisconsin-based G. Heileman Brewing Company, the seventh largest brewing company in the United States. Although its acquisition by a much larger brewer could have portended the assimilation of the company's brewing assets and signaled the end of the Rainier brand, Rainier Brewing became part of a unique situation as a brewer operating under G. Heileman's corporate umbrella. Unlike the country's other large brewers who blanketed the nation's markets with one or two brands, G. Heileman achieved its growth by acquiring and developing regional brands that appealed to distinct markets. G. Heileman rose through the U.S. beer industry's rankings by acquiring regional brands and retaining their identity, accumulating a portfolio of brands that included Old Style, Schmidt's, Colt 45, Mickey's, Special Export, Champale, Lone Star, and Henry Weinhard.

In the wake of G. Heileman's 1977 acquisition, Rainier Brewing continued to distinguish itself as a steady financial performer, registering profitable years throughout the 1980s. Owing to its consistent performance and its entrenched position in Pacific Northwest markets, Rainier Brewing became the prize of the G. Heileman empire, an asset its parent company desperately needed as it headed into murky financial waters in the late 1980s. A leveraged acquisition of the diversified regional brand owner by Australian businessman Alan Bond in 1987 delivered a pernicious blow to the Wisconsin-based brewer, saddling the company with debilitating debt. As a result of the acquisition, which made Bond Brewing International the ultimate corporate parent of Rainier Brewing, G. Heileman was forced to declare bankruptcy in January 1991. G. Heileman emerged from Chapter 11 protection in the early 1990s, by which time ongoing negotiations with a close rival were midway through their completion. Rainier Brewing was set to become a valuable asset in one of the U.S. beer industry's largest mergers.

Rumors about Rainier Brewing's sale to a much larger, nationally oriented brewer had been circulating since the late 1980s. Although G. Heileman was suffering from profound financial ills at the time, the company could not afford to let the jewel of its empire leave its control. G. Heileman, meanwhile, was the subject of acquisition rumors itself during the late 1980s. Stroh Brewing Company, which ranked as the country's fourth largest beer company, attempted to acquire G. Heileman in 1990, but did not have the financial resources available to complete the deal. By 1996 Stroh's financial position had changed, enabling the company to acquire G. Heileman and all of its regional breweries, including Rainier Brewing. The 1996 acquisition wedded the nation's fourth and fifth largest brewing operators, creating a beer company with more than $1.3 billion in sales.

With this new parent company supporting its efforts in the Pacific Northwest, Rainier Brewing entered the late 1990s much like it had entered the 20th century. The company held a prominent position in the Pacific Northwest, predicated on strong brand name recognition. Its ties to the territory it served represented a century-long link to generations of consumers, a legacy imbedded by the staying power of the Rainier brand. As the company moved forward under the auspices of Stroh, Rainier Brewing officials were confident that the future would be no different from the past.

Principal Subsidiaries

Rainier Bottling Co.

Further Reading

Denne, Lorianne, "Rainier Sale Speculation Abounds Despite Denials," *Puget Sound Business Journal,* March 18, 1991, p. 3.
Rainier Brewing Company, *Rainier Beer: The First Hundred Years,* Seattle: Rainier Brewing Company, 1978.
Richardson, Pat, "Rainier Brewing Company—Serving Seattle Since 1878," *Washington Purchaser,* August 1974, p. 7.

—Jeffrey L. Covell

Red Apple Group, Inc.

825 11th Avenue
New York, New York 10019
U.S.A.
(212) 956-5770
Fax: (212) 265-6736

Private Company
Incorporated: 1970
Employees: 4,200
Sales: $2.2 billion (1997 est.)
SICs: 2911 Petroleum Refining; 4522 Air Transport,
Nonscheduled; 5411 Grocery Stores; 5499
Miscellaneous Food Stores; 5541 Gasoline Service
Stations; 6719 Offices of Holding Companies, Not
Elsewhere Classified

Under the names Gristede's, Sloan's, and Red Apple, Red Apple Group, Inc., wholly owned by John A. Catsimatidis, dominated supermarket shopping in New York City's borough of Manhattan during the 1990s. Starting with a single grocery store he opened in 1971, Catsimatidis developed a business empire that by the 1990s had estimated annual sales exceeding $2 billion. Through another Catsimatidis holding company, United Refining Co., this empire also owned a chain of gasoline stations and convenience-food stores in New York, Pennsylvania, and Ohio. With its concentration on high-turnover, low-margin retail trade, Red Apple's sales volume was more impressive than its profits; nevertheless, its net income was estimated at $38 million in fiscal 1997.

Supermarket Empire, 1971–87

The son of a waiter who did not earn more than $100 a week, John A. Catsimatidis was reared in Manhattan's West Harlem neighborhood and managed his cousin's grocery store while attending New York University, getting by, he recalled, on three hours of sleep a night. He was earning $30,000 a year in 1970 when, still short a few credits from his degree in electrical engineering, he decided he could make his fortune in the food business and dropped out of school. He bought a small store on the Upper West Side for $1,500, named it Red Apple, and opened for business in 1971 with $10,000 borrowed from his father.

By the end of his first year Catsimatidis was grossing $1.2 million. He stayed open seven days a week, offered free delivery, cashed lots of checks, and passed on manufacturers' discounts to customers. "I was the most hated guy in supermarkets," Catsimatidis later said. "I delivered free. I cashed checks free. I opened Sundays. Why? I paid my checks Friday, and I had to earn the dollars on Sunday to make the checks good Monday." Soon a bigger store became available, a few blocks south and on, rather than off, Broadway. It cost Catsimatidis $300,000 to open the 5,500-square-foot store, but five years later it was still the most profitable one in his operation, with $4 million in annual sales. By then, in late 1976, Red Apple was a chain of 12 Manhattan supermarkets that emphasized low prices, offering about 100 specials a week. Profits in fiscal 1976 (ended June 1, 1976) came to $800,000.

Red Apple had, by the summer of 1981, grown into a 27-unit chain operating in the Bronx as well as Manhattan, with annual sales of about $40 million. Sales came to $110 million in fiscal 1985. Queried by *Progressive Grocer* in 1986 for the secret of Red Apple's success, Catsimatidis answered, "I keep my prices high and my overhead low." When the reporter asked if it was not true that all prices tended to be high in Manhattan, he replied, "Mine are higher." Catsimatidis went on to say that he kept his overhead low by contracting out as little work as possible, using his own electricians and carpenters and his own refrigeration company.

In 1986 Red Apple acquired 36 Gristede Brothers supermarkets and 11 affiliated Charles & Co. specialty-food emporiums from the Southland Corp. for an estimated $50 million. This chain, with units throughout the metropolitan area, had annual sales of $112 million but had been unprofitable since 1983. Red Apple's purchase made it the biggest supermarket chain in New York City.

Gristede Brothers was founded in 1891 by Charles and Diedrich Gristede, recent German immigrants who opened their first grocery store at East 42nd Street and Second Avenue in Manhattan. The business concentrated on the carriage trade, entered Westchester County in 1920 and Connecticut in 1926, opened a Manhattan wine and liquor store in 1933, and had 141 stores by the time Charles Gristede died in 1948. When Southland bought the company in 1968, Gristede was also operating on Long Island and had 115 stores, including two Charles & Co. units and seven liquor stores. It then shrunk radically as rental costs skyrocketed and competition from gourmet shops, specialty stores, and other supermarkets increased. Red Apple itself had closed its four Bronx stores in 1985 to concentrate on Manhattan. The company also had pulled out of Queens, where it had opened stores at the end of the 1970s.

The Red Apple and Gristede chains remained distinct. Concentrated on the more affluent Upper East Side, Gristede had more gourmet items than predominantly Upper West Side Red Apple and profit margins that traditionally ran higher. Charles & Co. was described by Catsimatidis as "a gourmet 7-Eleven store." Red Apple had completed 14 remodels by the fall of 1987, including adding in-store delicatessens, bakeries, salad bars, upscale cheese, prime-meat, and seafood sections, and hot takeout foods.

At the same time as the Gristede purchase, Red Apple was acquiring 39 Pantry Pride supermarkets in southern Florida and one in the Bahamas for $55 million from Pantry Pride Inc., a subsidiary of Ronald O. Perleman's McAndrew & Forbes Holdings Inc. The operation had once been much bigger, with 440 East Coast supermarkets. Also in 1986, Red Apple acquired six Grand Union supermarkets in Florida and the Virgin Islands. These 45 units accounted for about $340 million of Red Apple's $640 million in supermarket sales during fiscal 1987. The Florida and Caribbean units were much bigger than the ones in crowded, densely populated New York, ranging from 25,000 to 45,000 square feet in size. The acquisitions also included more than 20 shopping centers in which the supermarkets were located.

Interviewed by *Supermarket News* in 1987, a business associate of Catsimatidis explained the latter's aggressive acquisition strategy in these words: "In building Red Apple's business in New York, and through the acquisition of New York real estate, John discovered that the supermarket business is a cash-flow business looking for an investment. With appreciation from his various real-estate holdings, he saw fit to leverage his money in an industry he understands, the supermarket business. . . . By being in the right place at the right time, with institutional financing available, Red Apple Cos. was able to grow and take a quantum leap in the supermarket industry." Red Apple Cos.'s real estate portfolio, which included more than 25 percent of its supermarket properties in New York, was worth about $200 million in 1986.

Supermarket Acquisitions and Divestitures, 1991–97

In early 1993 Florida Supermarkets, a Red Apple unit, was operating 35 supermarkets, including 28 former Pantry Pride stores, which were now using the name Woolley's, taken after the seven-store Woolley's chain was acquired in 1991. Red Apple had 89 percent equity in these stores, and Fleming Cos., a food wholesaler, had the rest. Fleming signed an agreement to buy Red Apple's stake in 1993, but when the deal collapsed, sued to recover $25 million it was owed. Red Apple wound up turning the company over to Fleming to settle the debts and the court case, according to one account. According to another source, Fleming purchased the chain for $41.6 million after Catsimatidis went to court to challenge Fleming's right to back out of the deal.

The dispute reemerged in 1996, with a lawsuit by Fleming and a countersuit by Red Apple. Red Apple said it retained renewal options on the leases of nine stores involved in the ownership transfer. Fleming's suit, Red Apple contended, had interfered with its own ability to complete a $33 million transaction with a third party for the sale of 13 parcels of real estate, including the nine leases.

Between July 1991 and September 1992 Red Apple acquired 21 of the 32 stores operated by rival Sloan's Supermarkets. This privately owned chain dated from 1956, when Max Sloan opened his first Manhattan supermarket. By 1973 Sloan's had 25 stores, all in Manhattan and most of them on the West Side, with combined annual sales of $42 million. Some of the stores acquired by Red Apple kept the Sloan's name, while others took the Gristede's name. The remaining 11 stores were sold to Designcraft Inc., a shell company owned by Catsimatidis that subsequently went public under the name Sloan's Supermarkets Inc. Catsimatidis owned 27 percent of this company's shares in December 1993, with an option to purchase an additional ten percent. These 11 stores were being operated by Red Apple under a management contract.

The public-private division of Sloan's appeared to be an attempt to avoid antitrust problems for Red Apple. Under whatever name, Red Apple-owned supermarkets were serving 37 percent of Manhattan's food shoppers on a regular basis in 1994, according to a survey. But in June 1994 the Federal Trade Commission (FTC) described the company's Sloan's acquisitions as anticompetitive. Catsimatidis agreed in November 1994 to divest his Red Apple Group of six stores within 12 months of the final FTC order. Red Apple had divested itself of only one of the stores by early 1997, however, when Catsimatidis and three of his firms agreed to pay a $600,000 penalty for failing to comply with the order. Also in November 1994, Red Apple Group announced it would sell 17 to 20 of its supermarkets—none belonging to Sloan's Supermarkets Inc.—to Rite Aid, the nation's largest drugstore chain. A total of 15 had been sold to Rite Aid by March 1996.

In October 1997 shareholders of Sloan's Supermarkets approved the purchase of 29 supermarkets—19 Gristede's and ten Sloan's—and a produce distribution center from Catsimatidis in a $40 million stock deal that increased his stake in the public company from 32 percent to more than 90 percent. Following this acquisition, the company was renamed Gristede's Sloan's, Inc. Prior to this purchase the public Sloan's had 13 supermarkets in Manhattan and one in Brooklyn. It also opened a Brooklyn health and beauty care store in Brooklyn. The company had sales of $51.8 million and net income of $1.2 million in the fiscal year ended February 28, 1997.

Other Red Apple Holdings: 1986–97

By 1987 the supermarket business represented only 30 percent of a business empire that was racking up $2 billion a year in annual sales. Catsimatidis also owned commercial real estate in New Jersey as well as New York and Florida, aviation enterprises, and, most important of all in terms of sales volume, United Refining Co. He had acquired this troubled company, which owned gasoline refineries in Pennsylvania and Alabama, from bankrupt Coral Petroleum in 1986 and had rescued it from bankruptcy in 1988 with $110 million in financing arranged by J.P. Morgan & Co. United Refining also ran more than 300 Kwik Fill gas stations in Pennsylvania, New York, and Ohio.

Under Red Apple, the Kwik Fill stations, following a national trend, became a full-service gas and convenience-food chain along the lines of 7-Eleven. Some of them operated under the name Red Apple Food Mart, which gained 26 more outlets in upstate New York in 1990, when United Refining acquired a chain of similar Stop-N-Go convenience stores. United Refining's 1989 sales were believed to be in excess of $850 million.

In 1990 a division of Red Apple pleaded guilty to charges that, for well over a year following the Red Apple takeover, telephone lines at United Refining headquarters in Warren, Pennsylvania had been illegally tapped. The firm paid a $1 million fine to settle the case. Catsimatidis denied any knowledge of the wiretaps, but there was speculation he wanted to check allegations that certain United executives were making side deals with oil suppliers and customers. The United convenience-store chain was up to about 350 units in early 1996. Sales came to $871.3 million in the fiscal year ended July 31, 1997. The company lost $2.3 million that year, chiefly because of high costs in purchasing crude oil for refining.

Another Red Apple holding, in 1986, was World Jet, a company based in Hartford, Connecticut that was leasing a fleet of 40 jets and other aircraft to corporations and that had annual revenues of about $25 million. This company subsequently was renamed United Air Fleet. Other Red Apple holdings, in 1987, included Eastern Aviation Group and Zion Foods, a Miami purveyor of kosher food products formerly operated as a division of Pantry Pride. Catsimatidis also held a substantial interest in Designcraft, which at the time was a jewelry maker with annual sales of $75 million. He had earlier owned a majority interest in Capitol Air Inc., a low-priced shuttle airline that suspended operations in 1984 after suffering a severe cash squeeze.

Designcraft sold its operating divisions in 1991 and became the holding company that acquired Sloan's Supermarkets. Capi-

tol Air Express Inc., a Virginia-based airline owned by Catsimaditis, was making charter flights from the Northeast to Miami and the Caribbean in 1993. It lost $1.8 million on operating revenue of $6.3 million that year. This company was still in existence in 1997.

Further Reading

Altaner, David, ''Minding the Store,'' *Orlando Sun-Sentinel,* November 11, 1993, Bus. Section.

''Charles Gristede, Grocer 77, Is Dead,'' *New York Times,* October 31, 1948, p. 88.

Cherry, Rona, ''Strength of Red Apple Chain Lies in Country-Store Link,'' *New York Times,* October 2, 1976, pp. 31, 33.

Collins, Glenn, ''Red Apple To Sell Up to 20 Stores,'' *New York Times,* November 30, 1994, p. D10.

Flint, Jerry, ''They Hated Me,'' *Forbes,* October 30, 1989, pp. 240–241.

Gilman, Hank, and Daniel Hertzberg, ''Pantry Pride Announces a Hostile Offer for Revlon, Which Moves To Block Bid,'' *Wall Street Journal,* August 20, 1985, pp. 3, 24.

''Holders Approve Purchase of Stores from Chairman,'' *Wall Street Journal,* October 31, 1997, p. B4.

Kaplan, Rachel, ''Red Apple—Gristede,'' *Supermarket News,* February 10, 1986, p. 1.

Lehren, Andrew W., ''Four Airlines Prepare To Fly into Phila.,'' *Philadelphia Business Journal,* August 30, 1993, p. 1.

Nagle, James J., ''Gristede-Southland Merger Set,'' *New York Times,* October 16, 1968, pp. 59, 64.

Pace, Eric, ''Max Sloan, 83, Whose Pushcart Grew into a Supermarket Chain,'' *New York Times,* August 7, 1995, p. B10.

Rigg, Cynthia, ''At Sloan's, the Specials for Investors Are Stakes,'' *Crain's New York Business,* December 6, 1993, p. 4.

Riley, John, ''My Little Town,'' *Newsday,* February 3, 1991, pp. 84 +.

Schmitt, Eric, ''Red Apple Buying Gristedes,'' *New York Times,* February 6, 1986, p. D4.

Silverman, Edward R., ''Red Apple Chairman Hungry for Bigger Bite,'' *Crain's New York Business,* March 27, 1989, pp. 3, 40.

''Washington Briefs,'' *Supermarket Business,* February 1997, p. 9.

Weinstein, Steve, ''An Industry Horatio Alger,'' *Progressive Grocer,* December 1986, pp. 39–40.

Zweibach, Elliot, ''Fleming Plans To Buy Former Pantry Prides,'' *Supermarket News,* January 31, 1993, pp. 1, 49.

——, ''Fleming, Red Apple Dispute Is Set for Trial,'' *Supermarket News,* April 15, 1996, p. 6.

——, ''Polishing Red Apple's Image,'' *Supermarket News,* September 21, 1987, p. 10.

—Robert Halasz

RenoAir™

Reno Air Inc.

P.O. Box 30059
Reno, Nevada 89520-3059
U.S.A.
(702) 686-3835
(800) RENO AIR
Web site: http://www.renoair.com

Public Company
Incorporated: 1990
Employees: 2,137
Sales: $349.88 million (1996)
Stock Exchanges: NASDAQ Pacific German
SICs: 4512 Air Transportation, Scheduled

Probably the most distinguished of the several dozen low-fare start-up airlines that began flying regional U.S. routes in the early 1990s, Reno Air Inc., has earned praise from observers and passengers by delivering first-class service at modest prices. Its new jets, reliable departure times, and other premiums make its motto of "Discover a Better Low Fare Airline" seem somewhat understated. Reno Air is the only scheduled commercial airline based in Nevada. As of March 1, 1997, the company operated some 29 aircraft, which departed primarily from the hub in Reno/Tahoe, Nevada, and flew to destinations in San Jose and southern California, as well as to its target cities of Las Vegas, Los Angeles, and Seattle.

Rocky Origins in the Early 1990s

Reno Air was conceived in 1990 by Joseph Lorenzo (no relation to Frank Lorenzo), formerly an executive at Frontier Airlines, and Jeff Erickson, former president of the original Midway Airlines (which soon folded), with the help of fellow airline executive Robert Reding. Reno's consistent tourist traffic, available airport space, and existing high fares made it an attractive home.

In December 1991, Erickson replaced Lorenzo as chief executive. The company launched its first flight, bound for Los Ange-

les, from Reno/Tahoe International Airport on July 1, 1992. The plane was a new McDonnell Douglas MD-80. Part of Reno's original fleet had originally been ordered by Midway Airlines.

The company's employees numbered 150. Like Kiwi International (formed by employees of the defunct Midway), Eastern, and (original) Pan Am Airlines, Reno Air was also able to field a low-cost, non-unionized staff, with labor costs reportedly half of Southwest's. Less seniority among the employees, low turnover, and greater flexibility helped contain costs.

Reno disdained the "cattle call" approach of many budget airlines and ensured reserved seating for its customers. It also offered meals on flights and maintained a first-class section. Nevertheless, its policy was to match competitors' promotional fares while charging only modest mark-ups for last-minute tickets.

By the end of 1992, the fleet had grown to eight aircraft, all MD-80 jets. Reno Air seemed poised for profitability. However, the next year it launched a risky expansion into the Midwest and West Coast, adding another nine planes to support these ambitious plans.

Reno Air launched its initial public offering in July 1993, then recorded a loss of $7.3 million for the year on revenues of $124.6 million. In 1994 those losses nearly doubled on revenues of $195.5 million.

Navigating Major Obstacles in the Mid-1990s

Many start-ups assumed a confrontational stance against the big carriers. Frontier Airlines, for example, became embroiled a vicious fare battle with United Airlines that resulted in an antitrust investigation. In 1993 Reno Air found itself engaged in a game of brinkmanship with Northwest Airlines which ended in a similar investigation, a lawsuit, and Reno Air's withdrawal from Northwest's home market of Minneapolis. A Reno Air spokesman reported that Northwest subsequently doubled its Minneapolis fares.

Reno Air could also cooperate with the major players. It entered an alliance with American Airlines toward the end of 1993 in which Reno would handle American's regional traffic after the carrier vacated its San Jose hub. American was eager to vacate the San Jose hub due to intense pricing pressure from Southwest Airlines, but could not escape its lease agreements. Moving into San Jose gave Reno a strong business hub to complement its tourism-oriented home base. Reno was also able to offer American Airlines AAdvantage frequent flyer miles as an added perquisite for its customers, in addition to its own frequent flyer program. Reno added a couple of new routes, to Chicago and to Orange County, California, within a year of teaming up with American.

In spite of American's vote of confidence, Reno Air began to appear to be yet another casualty of severe competition in the deregulated airline industry. Fluctuations in the cost of jet fuel posed an ever-present threat to any hope of profits, although having American Airlines as a supplier helped keep prices down (this arrangement would end in September 1996). Like most of the other start-ups, Reno Air was scrambling for capital in early 1994 when chairman Lee Hydeman stepped up to the role of CEO.

Although Reno Air lost $13.9 million in 1994, a dramatic turnaround was completed by 1995, when Reno proudly posted its first annual profit of $1.9 million on revenues of $256.5 million. The company flew twice as many paying passengers (four million) in 1995 as it had in 1993. It had also added nearly 500 employees in the two years, reaching a total of 1,600.

Reno Air brought its own tour operation on-line in 1995. Dubbed QQuick Escapes after the airline's computer reservation code, "QQ," the program bundled rental cars and hotel rooms with airfare to Nevada resorts. Electronic ticketing was introduced in August 1995 under the EZTrip banner, and ticketless travel came to account for nearly one-third of passenger sales within two years. Although Reno Air was enrolled in travel agency reservation systems, it felt the fees imposed (usually amounting to ten percent or more of the ticket price) were a particular hardship for low-price carriers such as itself. Ticketmaster and Reno Air teamed up to sell combined entertainment/travel packages a year later. Travel agents accounted for about 60 percent of ticket sales.

In September 1995, the title of CEO passed to Robert Reding, who continued to fly commercial jets and piloted the company's first flight into Fairbanks, Alaska. Less celebration accompanied the 4.3 cent per gallon federal aviation fuel tax that again went into effect on October 1 after an exemption designed to relieve the ailing airline industry expired. Each penny increase in the cost of a gallon of jet fuel cost Reno Air almost $900,000 per year.

A modest expansion resumed. Reno's network of scheduled flights stretched north to Anchorage, while its charter flights ventured south into the Caribbean and Mexico. The company ferried passengers to these destinations for San Jose and Great Lakes tour operators. Subsequent expansion plans would add more routes to the west and east. Reno invested in a new hangar facility and refurbished its planes' interiors in 1996.

From the beginning, the carrier operated a young fleet in comparison with its budget counterparts. Its jets averaged between five and six years in age and several were acquired new. Reno aimed to own half of its aircraft, but in 1996, twelve of its fourteen jets were leased. Two planes acquired in 1996 were state-of-the-art MD-90 aircraft which were quiet enough to operate at the Orange County airport.

However, these aircraft acquisition plans were tempered somewhat by a canceled July 1996 stock offering. At the time, aircraft stocks had fallen due to a ValuJet crash. Unlike many other small U.S. airlines, Reno Air did not report a significant loss of passenger confidence following the ValuJet crash of May 1996, which prompted new concern over the safety of budget carriers. Executives pointed out that the company worked very closely with a small number of vendors to ensure that its maintenance was carried out to a high standard. Nevertheless, the company's stock, like that of virtually all other U.S. airlines, was devalued during the crisis. Compounding the troubles, fuel prices rose by about a third in 1996, and Southwest Airlines, Reno Air's no-frills competitor, drastically lowered fares for almost half the year. Nevertheless, the company posted a respectable $2 million profit in 1996.

In 1996 the company considered changing names to reflect its geographic influence, but tradition prevailed. Citing examples of so many regional airlines that had collapsed under the strains of overexpansion, Reno executives announced a period of consolidation. Reno Air would focus on the key markets of Los Angeles, Las Vegas, and Seattle; refine the efficiency of its operations; and get more use out of its aircraft.

Just a few years after its first flight, Reno Air employed 2,000 and operated more than thirty McDonnell Douglas jets. The company's 300 pilots flew more than eighty flights per day from Reno and San Jose. It concentrated on the markets of Las Vegas, Los Angeles, and Seattle. It had successfully shed the label of "start-up."

Soaring into a New Century

A New Year's flood gave 1997 a particularly inauspicious beginning. Both the Reno/Tahoe airport and the Reno reservations office were closed for a day and a half and travelers shunned the area for weeks. However, Reno Air's antediluvian recovery promised to make 1997 a banner year, given the company's plan to curtail growth. A dramatic increase in fuel prices reinforced the company's thinking.

The company did intend to grow its business in one place: service to the booming Las Vegas area. Two dozen new flights to McCarran International Airport were added in May 1997. Additionally, a new reservations facility was opened in Las Vegas. In April, Reno Air had devoted an airplane to its "Gulf Coast Flyer" routes between Biloxi, Orlando, Tampa, and Atlanta, and in January, it began competing with Northwest Airlines again with a single daily flight to Detroit. In September 1997, Reno Air, which maintained sales offices in Germany, began offering shares through the German Stock Exchange in Berlin and Frankfurt.

Further Reading

Henderson, Danna K., "Grow-Slow Approach," *Air Transport World,* November 1996.
Hibbard, Justin, "Solid Plans Keep IS High and Dry," *Computerworld,* January 13, 1997, 59–60.
Knibb, David, "Desert Bloomer," *Airline Business,* October 1996.

Lieber, Ronald B., ''Beating the Odds,'' *Fortune,* March 13, 1997.

Maglitta, Joseph, ''Lean, Mean Flying Machines,'' *Computerworld,* July 11, 1994.

McCartney, Scott, ''Reno Air Plans to Curtain Growth in '97 to Avoid Expansion Pitfalls,'' *Wall Street Journal,* December 3, 1996.

Popkin, James and Monika Guttman, ''The Upstarts Take Off,'' *U.S. News and World Report,* October 12, 1992.

Robertson, Heather, ''Boss Pilots Reno's Inaugural Flight to Fairbanks,'' *Fairbanks Daily News-Miner,* April 5, 1996.

Ruber, Ilana, ''In-Flight Shopping Orders up Profits, Puts Catalog Firm on Solid Ground,'' *Business Journal,* July 7, 1997.

Small, Stacy H., ''Defying the Odds,'' *Travel Agent,* December 2, 1996.

Smith, Timothy K., and Ronald B. Lieber, ''Why Air Travel Doesn't Work,'' *Fortune,* April 3, 1995.

Stearns, John, ''Federal Report Shows Reno Air with Flawless Record for Safety,'' *Reno Gazette-Journal,* May 25, 1996.

——, ''1995: Reno Air's First Profitable Year,'' *Reno Gazette-Journal,* February 25, 1996.

Velotta, Richard N., ''Reno Air Climbing in Las Vegas,'' *Las Vegas Sun,* May 12, 1997, pp. 1D, 4D.

Zellner, Wendy, Susan Chandler, and David Greising, ''The Startups Start to Stall,'' *Business Week,* December 9, 1996.

—Frederick C. Ingram

Rhodes Inc.

12560 West Creek Parkway
Richmond, Virginia 23238
U.S.A.
(804) 784-7500
Fax: (804) 784-7948

Wholly Owned Subsidiary of Heilig-Meyers Co.
Incorporated: 1875
Employees: 2,700
Sales: $430 million (1996)
SICs: 5712 Furniture Stores

Founded in 1875, furniture retailer Rhodes Inc. became one of the largest furniture retailers in the United States. By 1996, with its acquisition of several smaller chains in various parts of the country, it held fourth place among U.S. furniture stores. The company had gone through a lengthy period of uneven financial performance, however, and its primary stockholder had placed it up for sale. Ultimately, Rhodes would become a subsidiary of the second largest chain of furniture retailers, Virginia-based Heilig-Meyers Company. Added to its $844 million in annual sales, the acquisition of Rhodes, with $430 million, would catapult Heilig-Meyers past the billion-dollar Levitz Furniture and into first place. As for Rhodes, its sale and the subsequent move to Richmond in early 1998 marked the end of more than 120 years of operation in its home base of Atlanta.

A New Way of Doing Business Following the Civil War

Just a few years after its destruction by General William T. Sherman in the Civil War, Atlanta was already a resurgent commercial center. During that period of Reconstruction, a young man named Amos Giles Rhodes moved to the city, bringing with him all he owned: a horse and buggy, $75 in cash, and (according to company lore) ''a gold watch of uncertain value.''

Like many another dreamer throughout history, Rhodes had come to the big city to make his fortune, and he soon began looking about for the means to do so. He first considered the market in clocks and picture frames, because he had noticed that people seemed to need both. There was only one problem: in spite of the hustle and bustle of Atlanta, the South was still poor and reeling from its recent defeat. People might desire clocks or picture frames, but in difficult economic times, they would not buy what they could not afford.

It was then that A.G. Rhodes, as he came to be known, had a brainstorm and, in the process, discovered a new way of doing business—one of the first installment payment plans in business history. With each of his customers, he set a figure that they could afford to pay on a weekly basis. Having made this agreement, the customer could expect to see Rhodes once a week, at which time he or she would pay what they had agreed upon as the weekly payment. Once the cost was paid, the item was theirs—and thus penurious Atlantans were able to purchase items that might have seemed unattainable luxuries.

Rhodes continued to make his weekly selling and collection rounds, but he was already beginning to consider new business opportunities. In the fall of 1875 he contracted with the owner of a small furniture manufacturing company to produce a line of furnishings, and he opened the first Rhodes Furniture Store in Atlanta. He was 25 years old.

The company continued to grow along with Atlanta, and it soon became a leading business in the brash young city. In 1889, to further strengthen his enterprise, Rhodes formed a partnership with a local businessman, J.J. Haverty. The company became Rhodes-Haverty, and it operated for the next 20 years. In 1909 the partnership dissolved amicably and the companies split. Thereafter they would be among the two leading competitors for Atlanta's furniture market.

Changing Hands in the 1980s

Over the years, both Rhodes Furniture and its hometown changed almost beyond recognition. Atlanta had been a friendly, relatively sleepy town in the latter part of the 19th century; a century later it had become a bustling city with burgeoning suburbs, its old downtown neighborhoods ripped apart by interstates. Likewise, Rhodes had lost its close connection to the past, and the company—which had gone public some time in the mid-20th century—had passed out of the hands of A.G. Rhodes's descendants.

In 1982 Atlantic American Corp., an insurance holding company, acquired 38.6 percent of Rhodes's stock. Within five years, this had increased to 44 percent and Atlantic American held the controlling interest in the company. In 1986 the chairman of Rhodes Inc. died, and in early 1987 its chief financial officer (CFO) resigned. "It's a company that has experienced management changes," analyst Claire Cross of J.C. Bradford in Atlanta told Mark Calvey of the *Atlanta Journal and Constitution.*

Rhodes had continued to grow and had extensive retailing operations in Atlanta and beyond, but its stocks had failed to perform. In late December 1987 analyst Lee Wilder of Robinson-Humphrey observed that Rhodes's stocks had fallen below broad market averages for the preceding year. At the end of 1987 the company retained the services of the Salomon Brothers brokerage to accept offers to purchase the company. "The appeal of Rhodes" to potential buyers, according to Wilder, "is a tremendous revenue base." Still, in light of the stock market crash of October 1987, Cross called the timing of the proposed sale "unusual." As for the furniture industry itself, she said that retailers operated their businesses in a "very unpredictable environment with a very fickle customer."

Within five months of the announced buyout, in late April of 1988, Atlantic American had found a purchaser for Rhodes. A new Atlanta investment group, Green Capital Investors L.P., had agreed to buy the company for $242 million. It was the sort of business deal that had become something of a cliché in the preceding decade: a leveraged buyout (LBO) purchased in part by "junk bonds." For each share, stockholders would receive $21.50 in cash, as well as a 17 percent junior subordinated discount debenture (or bond), which had a face value of $8.25. The cash accounted for $175.2 million of the price tag, and the bonds accounted for the other $67.2 million. Analyst Thomas Richter of Robinson-Humphrey appraised the value of the junk bonds—which were not callable for four years, would not pay interest for six, and would come due in 12—at only $25.1 million in present value.

Nonetheless, the deal seemed propitious for Atlantic American, which had suffered losses due to high Medicare and workers compensation insurance claims in recent years. As for the acquiring firm, actually a subsidiary of Green Capital called RHD Holdings, the purchase represented a significant addition. Buying Rhodes, according to founder Holcombe T. Green Jr., was Green Capital's "first investment in an important Atlanta-based company."

Reinventing the Furniture Store in the 1990s

Green, the new chairman, spent the latter part of the 1980s and the early 1990s paying down Rhodes's debt. But the venture continued to be a costly one until July 1993, when Rhodes again traded its stock on the New York Stock Exchange. Even so, stocks continued to fare poorly, particularly in the summer of 1994.

On August 13, the *Journal and Constitution* reported that the value of shares had plummeted a staggering 30 percent. Chief Executive Officer (CEO) Irwin Lowenstein stated that the furniture market had been "soft" and that renovations at nearly a dozen stores had further impaired the company's profitability. For stores that had been open for 12 months or longer, sales growth had been less than three percent.

By that time Rhodes had 78 stores, so the number of renovated facilities represented a large portion. But Haverty, which had continued to develop in competition with its former partner, had renovated even more stores. According to the Atlanta paper, Mark Mandel of Salomon Brothers observed that Haverty was "showing some pretty decent sales numbers over the last few months."

Lowenstein responded to this situation with decisive action. By March of 1995 the Atlanta paper was reporting that the company had set a goal of $500 million in annual sales by the end of the 1997 fiscal year. This came in spite of fears within the furniture industry that rising interest rates and a slowdown in sales of new homes might stall growth. The company was growing, and with 80 stores already, it announced plans to add some 20 locations over the next two years.

During that period the company also expected to enter the Cincinnati, Cleveland, Indianapolis, Kansas City, and Pittsburgh markets, and to add more than 700,000 square feet of retail space. Expansion within several of these markets would be aided, Chris Roush of the *Journal and Constitution* noted, by Rhodes's established presence in St. Louis and Louisville. Within its home base, the company would be opening stores at Cumberland and North Point Malls, and it had plans to put in new stores near Perimeter Mall on the north side and in the southern suburb of Fayetteville. It would close stores in Marietta and on Roswell Road, however, transferring workers to the new locations.

But acquisitions, Lowenstein told Roush, would not be the means by which the company would meet its goal of $500 million in annual sales. Success would come through improvements. With its competitor Haverty "going upscale" according to a March 7, 1995 *Journal and Constitution* article, Rhodes began its counterattack by conducting an extensive marketing research effort, with interviews of 3,100 customers in nine cities. Having learned what its customers wanted, the company had plans for a number of changes.

Rhodes would remodel all of its stores by the end of the following year, adding new features such as a play area and a café offering free soft drinks to customers. A new advertising campaign, created by Atlanta ad firm McCann Erickson, used the slogan, "Every time you look, we look better." The company was also hiring a new customer service director, who would visit each of Rhodes's stores and evaluate how employees were treating customers. In addition, Rhodes offered a new 30-day exchange-or-money-back guarantee, the Rhodes Promise. President and Chief Operating Officer (COO) Joel Lanham told Roush, "What we're trying to do is be the best customer service furniture retailer in the country."

A further boost came from the selection of Rhodes by clothing designer Alexander Julian to carry a new line of furniture by the designer. The latter would begin appearing in stores by April 1995. Meanwhile, Rhodes extended its product line to include La-Z-Boy, makers of recliners as well as a full line of living room and family room furniture; and Sealy, manufacturers of mattresses and box springs, including Posturepedic, as well as upholstered furniture. ''There's a dramatic difference in what the customer will see now in a Rhodes store,'' Lanham told Roush.

Growth by Acquisition in the Mid-1990s

By April 1996 Rhodes had grown far beyond Atlanta. Besides Georgia, its southeastern base included Alabama, Mississippi, Florida, North and South Carolina, Tennessee, and Kentucky. In the midwest, it had stores in Ohio, Indiana, Illinois, and Missouri. Finally, Rhodes had a presence in the west through stores in Texas, Kansas, and Colorado.

Much of this growth had come through recent acquisitions. In October 1995, for instance, Rhodes announced the purchase of Weberg Enterprises Inc., a 21-store chain based in Denver, which gave it a foothold in both the Colorado and Texas markets. Also in 1995, Rhodes opened two stores in Kansas City and one in Cincinnati and it purchased Glick Furniture Co., a seven-store chain based in Columbus, Ohio. All told, Rhodes increased its roster of stores by 21 in 1995.

But then an old story repeated itself: on April 30, 1996, the *Atlanta Journal and Constitution* reported that Rhodes had hired Salomon Brothers, the same firm that had brokered the 1987 sale to Green, to assist it in increasing the value of its stock. One oft-discussed possibility was the sale of the company. This time the driving force behind the proposed sale was the man who had bought it nearly a decade before, Holcombe T. Green Jr., now holder of a 30 percent stake. In spite of improvements in the company's service and Rhodes's growth through acquisition, sales in the furniture market were flat.

Rhodes entertained several possible offers, and on September 18, 1996, the Atlanta paper announced the buyer: Heilig-Meyers of Richmond, Virginia, the number-two furniture chain behind Florida-based Levitz. With 109 stores and annual sales in excess of $430 million, Wall Street analysts had valued Rhodes at anywhere from $110 to $169 million. Yet when it sold, the price tag was far lower than it had been in 1987: Heilig-Meyers agreed to buy Rhodes for $65 million, offering to swap one of its shares for every two of Rhodes's.

Analysts ascribed the lowered price to recent losses by the company, and Lowenstein told the *Journal and Constitution*, ''It's a very good deal for Rhodes and its employees. It's something we need to do.'' But in the wake of the announcement of the low purchase price, Rhodes's stock value plummeted. It had surged after the company indicated it was looking for a buyer, and it suddenly dropped by a staggering $3.12½ in one day, to close at $7.50. ''It had to drop,'' Lowenstein stated, adding that the stock price had gone up ''under the false rumor that we were selling at $12 per share.''

With the sale, Rhodes would become a wholly owned subsidiary and would retain Lowenstein's leadership. The *Journal and Constitution* observed that the acquisition was ''a good strategic

fit,'' since Rhodes tended to operate in the large cities and Heilig-Meyers operated in the small town markets. Thus very few of either company's stores would have to close, though Heilig-Meyers's struggling Chicago outlets might adopt Rhodes's methods of operations, while some small town Rhodes stores might switch to the Heilig-Meyers format. The new enlarged Heilig-Meyers, with more than 800 stores and $1.5 billion in sales, would be the largest furniture retailer in America.

Rhodes would continue to operate under the Rhodes name. By the late 1990s, in addition to La-Z-Boy and Sealy, its product lines included Alan White, a leader in midrange fashion upholstery; Basset, which offered traditional cherry and casual modern solid wood bedroom suites; Berkline, a leader in motion furniture; Broyhill, makers of wood solids with veneers ranging from traditional to early American styles; Kincaid, which produced solid wood bedroom, occasional, and dining room furniture in Queen Anne, Victorian, contemporary, and country styles; Kroehler, classic style upholstered furniture; Nunziato leather upholstery; Pulaski, occasional furniture with traditional to contemporary styles; Simmons, mattresses and box springs including Beautyrest and Maxipedic; Universal Furniture, bedroom and dining room furniture featuring country, traditional, and contemporary styles.

For years, Rhodes had operated from its corporate headquarters on Peachtree Road near Oglethorpe University in Atlanta's Brookhaven neighborhood. In late 1997, however, the company's employees began making the move north to Richmond. By the early part of 1998 all of Rhodes's corporate operations—except for its information systems department, which remained on Peachtree Road—had relocated to Virginia.

Further Reading

Calvey, Mark, ''Rhodes Hires Advisory Firm To Consider Acquisition Bids,'' *Atlanta Journal and Constitution,* December 30, 1987, p. C1.

Murray, Brendan, ''Post-Holiday Closings Could Herald Shakeout This Year,'' *Atlanta Business Chronicle,* January 13, 1997.

Rhodes Inc., ''Company Fact Sheet,'' Atlanta: Rhodes Inc., 1997.

Roush, Chris, ''Aggressive Rhodes Makes Deal for Denver-Based Chain,'' *Atlanta Journal and Constitution,* October 11, 1995, p. C3.

——, ''Arranging for a Sale: Furniture Retailer Rhodes Inc. Is Putting Itself on the Auction Block,'' *Atlanta Journal and Constitution,* April 30, 1996, p. B1.

——, ''Atlanta's Furniture Giants: Opening a New Chest of Ideas,'' *Atlanta Journal and Constitution,* March 7, 1995, p. E1.

——, ''Furniture Retailer Rhodes Being Sold to Heilig-Meyers: 'A Very Good Deal,' '' *Atlanta Journal and Constitution,* September 18, 1996, p. D1.

——, ''Rhodes Sets Goal of 20 New Stores, Increase in Sales,'' *Atlanta Journal and Constitution,* March 22, 1995, p. D3.

——, ''Rhodes Stock Takes a Pounding: CEO Defends Deal for Chain's Acquisition by Heilig-Meyers,'' *Atlanta Journal and Constitution,* September 19, 1996, p. F1.

Vesey, Susannah, ''Rhodes Shares Fall 30% on Earnings Expectations,'' *Atlanta Journal and Constitution,* August 13, 1994, p. C2.

Walker, Tom, ''Atlanta Group To Buy Rhodes,'' *Atlanta Journal and Constitution,* April 27, 1988, p. C1.

—Judson Knight

RODALE PRESS

Rodale Press, Inc.

33 East Minor Street
Emmaus, Pennsylvania 18098-0099
U.S.A.
(610) 967-5171
Fax: (610) 967-8963
Web site: http://www.rodalepress.com

Private Company
Incorporated: 1930
Employees: 1,400
Sales: $472 million (1996)
SICs: 2721 Periodicals: Publishing or Publishing and
  Printing; 2731 Books: Publishing or Publishing and
  Printing

Rodale Press, Inc. knows how to make things grow. Beginning with a guide for organic gardening, Rodale has ventured into books and magazines designed to nurture human life on topics as varied as cooking, sports—even woodworking. Since the 1980s, the company's growth has outpaced most of the giants of magazine and book publishing. After successfully managing several popular magazines in the United States such as *Prevention* and *Men's Health,* Rodale has focused on international expansion. *The Doctor's Book of Home Remedies,* one of its most popular titles, has been a brisk seller around the world. After the death of Bob Rodale in 1990, his wife Ardath Harter Rodale assumed the roles of chairman and CEO.

Out of the Depression

J.I. Rodale began his professional life not on a farm, but in a New York City accounting practice. He and his brother Joe formed Rodale Manufacturing in 1923. The company produced commercial and residential electrical connectors but it would provide the means to launch Rodale's more earthy enterprises. Emmaus, Pennsylvania, a borough near Allentown, eventually lured Rodale Manufacturing to relocate through offers of lower costs and free factory space.

J.I. Rodale soon began publishing a humorous reader from a corner of the factory floor. However, it proved too humorous to last a second issue. Nevertheless, other magazines with such lively titles as *The Clown* (later *The American Humorist*), *You Can't Eat That* (later *Health Guide*), *Everybody's Digest,* and *True Health Facts* appeared before 1940. *Fact Digest* was the most successful of the lot, selling 100,000 copies at one point.

During the Great Depression, most families had dirt yards and education was as scarce as good jobs. Most people were more concerned about merely eating than eating right. But J.I. Rodale felt that something was fundamentally lacking with the ways Americans looked after their farms and themselves. He was inspired to buy a 60-acre farm after Sir Albert Howard, considered the founder of the modern organic farming movement, published his findings in 1940. After forty years of research in India, Howard believed that the living organisms that made soil useful needed to be nourished with compost, the way the natives Howard observed returned all animal and vegetable matter to the earth. He also felt this made for more healthful produce. Howard also strongly opposed artificial fertilizers and pesticides.

Rodale began publishing *Organic Farming and Gardening* in 1942, while developing techniques on his farm near Emmaus. The magazine was born into controversy; however, it remained an enduring success, counting a million readers more than fifty years after its debut. An interest in nutrition and other areas of personal health lead to the launch of *Prevention* in 1950; it eventually garnered an audience of more than 3.5 million to become the country's leading health magazine. *Prevention* was originally printed on uncoated paper with few graphics and carried mostly mail order advertising.

J.I. Rodale attained some celebrity, and died while appearing as a guest on the *Dick Cavett Show* in 1971. His son Robert, who was born in 1930, would lead the company for the next twenty years.

Building Upon Success in the 1970s

Robert Rodale was an editor at Rodale before becoming its leader in 1971. He was also handy with a shotgun and landed a trip to Mexico City with the 1968 US skeet shooting team. He

---

Company Perspectives:

*At Rodale Press, we have a vision of the world as it could be
. . . a world where health is recognized as more than simply
freedom from disease. Where individuals take control over
their lives. Where people protect and enhance the environment. Where neighbors and nations are guided by the spirit
of cooperation. Granted, it's an idealistic vision. But ideals
are a source of inspiration to us. They keep us ever reaching
for a healthier world. And while our dreams may be in the
clouds, our feet are firmly planted on the ground. For it is
here that the work must done. We believe that this ideal
world is, even now, being created—by centered, self-reliant
people who are capable of creating a better world for
themselves. That's why all of our publications focus on the
individual and what you can do to make life more natural,
more self-reliant and more healthful.*

---

became known for the sensational growth the company experienced under his leadership.

Rodale continued the research efforts initiated by his father
at the Rodale Research Center (originally the Soil and Health
Society, founded in 1947), which operated a 333-acre farm in
Maxatawny, Pennsylvania. Regenerative agricultural techniques were the focus of this center, which, in cooperation with
the USDA, USAID, and other institutions, examined a variety
of environmental and economic issues. Rodale also founded the
Rodale Institute, a non-profit organization that sought to make
science "not just *for* the people, but *by* the people as well."

Inspired by the cycling at the 1968 Olympics, Rodale bought
Bicycling magazine in 1977 and turned it into the hottest thing
on wire wheels. Another editorial innovation was *The Prevention Index,* an annual survey of American health trends used by
media, government agencies, and corporations.

As health foods and nutritional supplements became more
available in specialty stores and supermarkets, *Prevention* had
to formulate a new strategy for the 1980s to accommodate
dwindling mail order advertising. However, its efforts to interest media buyers for national accounts seemed doomed by the
magazine's earlier criticisms of processed food. The magazine
also began occupying checkout counters, spurring previously
nonexistent single copy sales. In the early 1990s, Rodale would
focus more on retail sales to counter increasing postal rates.

Competition drove Rodale out two categories in 1987. It sold
Practical Homeowner magazine as its field became too crowded,
and also sold *Children,* which struggled amid a field of parenting
copycats. However, the company was fertile with new ideas.
Rodale tested what would become one of the fastest-growing
magazines in print, *Men's Health,* in 1988. Its circulation would
quadruple in the early 1990s, reaching 1 million in 1994.

Going Global in the 1990s

Eventually, the company was able to export viable versions
of its domestically successful magazines in Europe, Asia, and
South Africa. Robert Rodale's international expansion plans
brought him to the Soviet Union to work on a publishing joint
venture with state publishing agency Vneshtorgizdat and a state
farm. The pioneering collaboration eventually produced *The
New Farmer (Novii Fermer)* with a circulation of 50,000 in
spite of huge obstacles. For example, the magazine was printed
in Finland due to a lack of quality presses in the USSR.
Tragically, though Robert Rodale was killed in a Moscow car
accident in September, 1990.

Ardath Harter Rodale succeeded her husband Robert as
chairman and CEO of Rodale Press after his death. Ardath
Rodale immediately formed an advisory board including her
children, several executives, and Robert J. Teufel, a longtime
employee and trusted advisor, who served as chief operating
officer and president.

For the previous thirty years, Ardath Rodale had designed
office space for the company. (True to the company's origins,
existing vacant buildings were often renovated and reused.)
AIDS awareness projects had become the focus of her extensive
community service after her son, David, died from the disease
in 1985. Ardath Rodale wrote the "Reflections" column for
Prevention and the syndicated "Awakenings" column for the
Chicago Tribune and published the inspirational text *Climbing
Toward the Light* in 1989. Her thoughts on spirituality in modern life were featured in *Embracing Our Essence: Spiritual
Conversations with Prominent Women.* She also lectured on
health, the environment, and relationships. "Our mission is to
show people how they can use the power of their bodies and
minds to make their lives better," said Ardath Rodale. " 'You
can do it,' we say on every page of our magazines and books."

Revenues were about $250 when Ardath Rodale assumed
the company's leadership. The company continued to launch
many new magazine and book titles. Rodale developed *Straight
Talk,* a magazine for teens, with the National Education Association, and marketed it to schools in 1991. The company tested
Young Executive, designed to help men attain corporate distinction, in 1992. *Rodale's Scuba Diving* fared better. The company
even presented a cable television show based on its *Bicycling*
magazine.

While the depressed economy of the early 1990s was not
kind to Rodale's start-ups, the company fared fairly well otherwise, except perhaps for *Prevention* magazine, which saw ad
revenues dip. The venerable *Runner's World,* launched in the
mid-1960s, experienced a huge increase in advertising, however. Rather than discounting rates, the company focused on
innovative promotional tie-ins to keep sponsors enthusiastic. In
addition, magazines that lead their categories weathered depres-
sions best, and Rodale had unloaded underperforming titles in
competitive fields. The company credited consumer loyalty to
its high standards.

Although group publisher George Hirsch had two years
earlier predicted to the contrary in the *Wall Street Journal,* in
1993, Rodale entered the lucrative and competitive women's
service market with its own *Healthy Woman.* However, this
venture failed within a few months. Rodale launched *Heart and
Soul,* aimed at black women, with Reginald D. Ware, a black
entrepreneur who had spent years developing the concept.

Heart and Soul attracted advertisers, but four years after its debut had yet to become profitable.

Rodale pursued cautious growth by acquisition in the mid-1990s. In the spring of 1995, Rodale Press bought a share in Abenaki Publishers with plans to introduce new fly fishing magazines. Rodale reportedly spent approximately $20 million to buy *New Woman* from K-III Communications Corp. in August 1997.

Sales increased considerably—more than fifty percent—under Ardath Rodale's tenure. By 1996, Rodale Books had sold 20 million copies, reaching one-fifth of all American homes and providing half of Rodale's income. *Green Pharmacy, Low-Fat Living,* and *New Choices in Natural Healing* were among the most popular offerings of its 500 titles in print.

A British version of *Men's Health* was immediately successful. However, other international ventures frustrated Rodale, prompting them to hire the consulting firm Braxton Associates. They found that Rodale's traditional, decentralized working methods, while fostering creativity, made communications even more complicated overseas. In 1997, Rodale began distributing a Spanish language version of *Men's Health* in cooperation with Editorial Televisa, based in Mexico City.

In late 1996, AT&T canceled its web venture with Rodale called the HealthSite after only a few weeks. Rodale Press created a new marketing division in 1997 and applied a new, decentralized approach to its on-line operations. Its web site for *Men's Health* featured an on-line form for ordering back issues and article reprints.

In the late-1990s, Rodale Press published a dozen national magazines, including *Mountain Bike, Rodale's Scuba Diving, Rodale's Heart and Soul,* and *Fitness Swimmer.* In addition, *Bicycling, Runner's World, Men's Health, Backpacker,* and *American Woodworker* all lead their fields. Rodale's best known, *Prevention,* now a sophisticated glossy magazine, outsold its next three competitors combined. The company reached over sixteen million customers every month.

The company's successes went beyond such numbers. The company refused liquor and cigarette advertising in its magazines (although it began running beer ads in *Runner's World* in 1987). Its headquarters provided exercise facilities (or "energy center") and healthful cafeteria (Rodale Food Center) fare, as well as recycling facilities complete with 50 different types of bins (the cafeteria, of course, saved its food scraps for composting). Rodale claims it recycles up to 90 percent of its waste. Most of the company's books and all its magazines are printed on recycled paper.

Principal Divisions

Magazine Division; Book Division; Rodale Marketing Solutions.

Further Reading

Bamford, Janet and Jennifer Pendleton, "The Top Fifty Women-Owned Businesses," *Working Woman,* October 1997.
Calvacca, Lorraine, "Fits and Stops for Rodale Start-Ups," *Folio,* October 1, 1996, 20.
Carey, Robert, "Exercising Your Options," *Incentive,* June 1995, 30–34.
Donaton, Scott, "Boys Will Be Boys But, Says *Men's Health,* It's No Fad," *Advertising Age,* March 7, 1994, S-3.
——, "Rodale Press Nurtures Growth with Spinoffs," *Advertising Age,* September 14, 1992.
Freeman, Laurie, "Trash to Treasure," *Advertising Age,* June 24, 1991, 36.
"Getting Better: Rodale Press," *Chief Executive,* December 1995, 12–13.
Hochwald, Lambreth, "Database Partnerships," *Folio,* August 1, 1994, 52–53.
——, "Sub Promotion Still Hard to Read," *Folio,* March 15, 1994.
Hodges, Jane, "After Suffering Setbacks, Rodale Tries Decentralizing," *Advertising Age,* February 17, 1997, 22.
Jaben, Jan, "Publishers Beware," *Business Marketing,* December 1991, 29–30.
Kavanagh, Mick, "Men Slip Between the Covers," *Marketing,* April 13, 1995, 27–29.
Lucas, Allison, "Exercising Your Options," *Sales and Marketing Management,* December 1995, 14.
Manly, Lorne, "Fly Fishing Lures Rodale," *Folio,* June 1, 1995, 36.
Masterton, John, "*Prevention* Passes Physical," *Folio,* February 1991, 55–56.
McCullagh, James C., "Publishing Opportunities in Russia," *Folio,* June 1, 1996, 77–87.
McGrath, Mike, ed., *The Best of Organic Gardening,* Emmaus, Pa.: Rodale Press, 1996.
Mummert, Hallie, "Naturally Successful," *Target Marketing,* March 1994, 10–16.
Peterson, Lisa C., "Dressed for Health and Success," *Food Management,* June 1996, 52–58.
Popper, Margaret, "Take It to the Tube," *Folio,* January 1, 1993, 58–62.
Reilly, Patrick M., "Magazine Launching Moves Timidly," *The Wall Street Journal,* B1.
——, "Rodale Finds Clean Living Gives a Healthy Tone to Ad Levels," *The Wall Street Journal,* B1.
Rodale Press, Inc., "Who We Are," Emmaus, Pa.: Rodale Press, n.d.
"Rodale Sues Poll Firm, Baxter International Over Health Survey," *The Wall Street Journal,* April 22, 1993.
Rosch, Leah, "Heart and Soul Shows Healthy Symptoms," *Folio,* November 1, 1994, 30.
Rosenfield, James R., "In the Mail," *Direct Marketing,* December 1992, 19–20.
——, "Pets, Pests, and Paranoia: Direct Marketing in All Its Glory," *Direct Marketing,* September 1996, 50–55.
Simon, Virginia, "The Arithmetic of Going Green," *Target Marketing,* January 1993, 29.
Teufel, Robert J., "The Rodalization Process," *Journal of Direct Marketing,* Spring 1996, 2–3.
Wynter, Leon S., "Business and Race," *The Wall Street Journal,* June 14, 1993, B1.
Yorgey, Lisa A., "American Direct Mail Overseas," *Target Marketing,* September 1997.

—Frederick C. Ingram

Royal Crown Company, Inc.

1000 Corporate Drive
Fort Lauderdale, Florida 33334
U.S.A.
(954) 351-5600
Fax: (954) 351-5365
Web site: http://www.rccola.com

Wholly Owned Subsidiary of RC/Arby's Corporation
Incorporated: 1905 as Union Bottling Works
Employees: 200
Sales: $178 million (1996)
SICs: 2086 Bottled & Canned Soft Drinks; 2087
   Flavoring Extracts & Syrups, Not Elsewhere
   Classified

A distant third in the $50-billion soft drink industry, Royal Crown Company, Inc. produces and sells concentrates used in the production of soft drinks that are sold domestically and internationally to independent, licensed bottlers. Royal Crown's leading brand, RC Cola, ranked as the third-largest national brand of cola behind Pepsi and Coca-Cola and stood as the only national brand cola alternative available to non–Coca-Cola and non–Pepsi-Cola bottlers. The company's other brands included Diet RC Cola, Diet Rite Cola, Nehi, Nehi Lockjaw, Upper 10, and Kick. Royal Crown was a wholly owned subsidiary of RC/Arby's Corporation, which, in turn, was owned by Triarc Companies, Inc.

Origins

Royal Crown was born from the efforts of Claud Adkin Hatcher, a turn-of-the-century pharmacist residing in Columbus, Ohio, who co-owned a grocery wholesale business. Established in 1901, the Cole-Hatcher-Hampton Grocery Company was started by Hatcher, his father, and two other partners, but by 1903 the Hatchers had bought out their partners and abbreviated the name of their business to Hatcher Grocery Company. By the time of the name change, Claud Hatcher was spending more and more of his time in the basement of the family business;

driven downstairs by a combination of anger and a need for self-sufficiency. For the first time—and not the last time—Hatcher's way of doing business collided headlong with the business philosophy of a Georgia-based company named Coca-Cola. The friction between Hatcher and a Coca-Cola representative sparked the creation of Royal Crown and marked the beginning of Royal Crown's century-long struggle to capture market share from Coca-Cola, the reigning leader of the soft drink industry.

The sparks began to fly when a Coca-Cola bottler named Columbus Roberts refused to yield to Hatcher's demands. As a grocery wholesaler, Hatcher purchased a large volume of Coca-Cola from Roberts, and because of this Hatcher believed Hatcher Grocery Co. should receive a discount, or a commission, or in some way should be compensated for the amount of Coca-Cola it purchased. Roberts disagreed, and a heated dispute erupted. Hatcher declared he had purchased his last case of soft drinks from Roberts and vowed to produce and bottle his own beverages under his own labels. Following through on his promise, Hatcher retreated to Hatcher Grocery Co.'s basement and began experimenting with different formulas. While his father remained upstairs, Hatcher, the 27-year-old graduate pharmacist, worked downstairs creating the foundation of the new family business.

The first soft drink Hatcher created was named Royal Crown Ginger Ale, and its success opened the Hatchers' eyes to the opportunities available in the soft drink market. In 1905, father and son made their commitment to the soft drink market official by reorganizing Hatcher Grocery Co. as Union Bottling Works and concentrating wholly on producing Royal Crown Ginger Ale. In the months to follow, business was brisk. The Hatchers enjoyed enough success to move to larger production facilities in 1907, but, as they quickly realized, the greatest profits to be made were in the cola market, led by the burgeoning giant Coca-Cola. Hatcher wanted a share of the lucrative cola market, and shortly after Union Bottling Works relocated to its grander facility, he introduced his own cherry-flavored cola creation, dubbed Chero-Cola. By 1911 Chero-Cola ranked as the company's greatest-selling product, the first in a long line of product introductions that would eclipse the popularity of its predecessor. The popularity of Chero-Cola led to another event in Royal Crown's history—a name change to reflect the success of its greatest selling product. In 1912 Union Bottling Works changed its name to Chero-Cola Company, an enterprise reorganized to manufacture a line of syrups to be sold to franchised bottlers.

Hatcher's first clash with Coca-Cola pitted him against an emissary of the fast-growing, Atlanta-based soft drink producer. Hatcher's introduction of Chero-Cola, and its flowering success, swept away all subsidiary layers shielding direct confrontation with Coca-Cola and pitted Hatcher against Coca-Cola's senior executives. The ensuing struggle was a battle Coca-Cola was intent on winning. When Hatcher filed to register Chero-Cola as a trademark in 1914, Coca-Cola quickly responded, demanding that the word "cola" be removed from all advertising. This first clash touched off a 30-year legal dispute between Hatcher's business and Coca-Cola, a feud over the rights to the word "cola" that would not be concluded until World War II was near its end. As this exhaustive debate was being argued in the courts, Hatcher had to contend with more pressing problems: his company's first major crisis. As one of the first "cola wars" raged on, hostilities in Europe gave way to the United States' entry into World War I, the prosecution of which portended the collapse of the entire soft drink industry in America.

World War I and Legal Troubles

In 1918 the U.S. Government imposed severe restrictions on the use of sugar in products deemed non-essential to the war effort. Soft drinks, of course, added little to the country's fighting might and fell under the wartime restrictions. For a brief time, the federal government threatened to take its restrictive measures a step further and considered whether or not to ban soft drink production altogether during the course of the war, but government officials stopped short of sounding the industry's death knell. Staving off the termination of their business, however, did not put soft drink producers in a much better position, and each had to make do with sugar supplies reduced to a trickle. Chero-Cola responded by establishing and operating its own sugar refinery, using raw sugar imported from Cuba to keep its operations alive. For roughly three years, the company relied on its sugar refinery for the essential supply of sugar and managed to persevere through the war years, but as Chero-Cola entered the 1920s a host of challenges loomed ahead.

By 1920 Chero-Cola stood as a thriving business, with 700 franchise bottling plants scattered throughout the South and Midwest, but when sugar prices collapsed during the early years of the decade, the company's considerable cache of sugar became a liability. Chero-Cola's problems were amplified in 1923 when its legal battle with Coca-Cola reached a decisive juncture. After nine years of contentious debate, Coca-Cola prevailed, and Chero-Cola was ordered to remove the word "cola" from all advertisements. In the wake of the court's ruling, the abbreviated "Chero" beverage fared far worse than "Chero-Cola" and lost much of its market. Eventually, the production of Chero, which represented Chero-Cola's chief source of revenue, was discontinued entirely.

The quick death of Chero could have had disastrous repercussions for the company, but Hatcher's timing in introducing a new product provided Chero-Cola with a potent, revenue-generating engine that easily made up for the loss of Chero. The same year Coca-Cola won its case against Chero-Cola, Hatcher introduced a new, fruit-flavored beverage named Melo. After Hatcher overheard a salesman refer to a competitor's soft drink bottle as being "knee-high," he changed Melo's name to Nehi, a brand name that became familiar to generations of consumers after its 1924 introduction. By 1928 sales of Nehi beverages were driving the company's financial growth to such an extent that Hatcher changed the name of his business to Nehi, Inc.

With the increasing popularity of Nehi, the company entered the 1930s at full stride, but the Great Depression stood as a formidable obstacle blocking the company's progress, bringing to a halt the encouraging growth that characterized the latter half of the 1920s. To make the company's position more precarious, Hatcher died on New Year's Eve in 1933, stripping Nehi Inc. of its influential leader just as it was grappling with the century's most pernicious economic crisis. Together, the loss of Hatcher and an economic depression of unprecedented proportions represented what could have been a crippling blow to Nehi, Inc., but the company fared remarkably well, recording one of the most successful decades in its history. Between 1933 and 1940, the company's annual sales increased tenfold.

The negative affects of the Depression were only temporary. After Hatcher's sudden death, the company's vice-president of sales, Hilary Richard Mott, took command and immediately cut costs, discontinued slow-selling products, and consolidated production activities. Less than a year after taking charge, Mott stood over a debt-free enterprise exhibiting a vibrancy that belied the woeful economic times. As Mott's healing measures were being implemented, the company's chemist was working on Nehi, Inc.'s next great product: its second cola concoction. The greatest money to be earned in the soft drink industry was still in the cola market. Hatcher's realization of this fact had prompted the development of Chero-Cola in the first decade of the century, and it prompted him to muster another attempt shortly before his death. In 1932 he had instructed his chemist to develop a cola beverage, and by 1934, when the company stood on solid financial ground, the new cola product was ready for distribution. Named Royal Crown, the new soft drink represented the company's future, becoming a favorite of consumers in the decades to follow.

Although the bulk of the company's revenue was derived from the sale of Nehi throughout the remainder of the 1930s, much of the company's promotional efforts were directed toward building consumer awareness of Royal Crown, or "RC" as the cola drink became more commonly known. In 1940 the company pioneered blind taste tests, using the promotional strategy more than three decades before other soft drink manufacturers did so. According to the results of the publicly-performed blind taste tests, RC was the winner, spawning the "Best By Taste Test" slogan. One year after Nehi, Inc. started its blind taste test publicity campaign, it hired numerous Hollywood celebrities to promote the sale of RC. Such luminaries as Bing Crosby, Joan Crawford, Shirley Temple, Lucille Ball, and Ronald Reagan appeared in advertisements alongside RC, piquing consumer interest. As public demand for RC increased under the barrage of promotional campaigns, the company scored an important victory in the courts. In 1944 Nehi, Inc.

ultimately prevailed in its 30-year legal battle with Coca-Cola when the courts ruled that the company could use the word cola in its advertisements.

Post–World War II Innovations

RC Cola, as the product could be called after the 1944 ruling, developed into the company's greatest-selling product during the post–World War II period, earning its distinction as the company's mainstay product when Nehi, Inc. became Royal Crown Cola Company in 1959. Under its new corporate banner, the company followed up on its success with RC Cola by developing the soft drink industry's first sugar-free diet beverage, a product the *Los Angeles Times* selected as the "Leading New Product of the 1960s." Development of the ground-breaking beverage was completed in 1961, and in 1962 Diet Rite Cola hit retail shelves. The product proved to be an enormous success, and one for which the other major soft drink manufacturers had no marketable answer. Fueled by the widespread demand for Diet Rite Cola and RC Cola, the company thrived throughout 1960s, gaining considerable ground on its two biggest rivals, Pepsi and Coca-Cola. According to several accounts, the 1960s ranked as the most successful decade in Royal Crown Cola's history, but the enviable success enjoyed by the company did not carry over into the 1970s. Royal Crown Cola's eye-catching growth came screeching to a halt in October 1969.

On October 18, 1969, the federal government banned the use of the artificial sweetener cyclamate, the essential ingredient in Royal Crown Cola's Diet Rite Cola. The losses suffered from the ban were immediate and profound, stripping the company of the product it had come to rely on for much of its growth. On the heels of the federal edict against cyclamate, company directors vowed never again to become reliant on a single product to drive sales. Their resolution gave rise to a period of diversification that began in the early 1970s with the acquisition of two fruit juice companies, Adams Packing Association and Texsun Company. Next, the company moved into the home decorative accessories field, purchasing seven companies involved in floor tile, mirrors, picture frames, and lamps. Not done there, the company moved farther afield, acquiring fast-food franchiser Arby's in 1976. Two years later, company directors observed the long-held tradition of changing their company's name to reflect the mainstay business, but this time the name change was purposefully less specific. In 1978 Royal Crown Cola Company became Royal Crown Companies Inc.

Under the corporate umbrella of Royal Crown Companies, the soft drink operations were organized into a division, no longer representing the sole source of revenue for the Royal Crown enterprise. When Diet Rite Cola was reintroduced in 1983, the soft drink division generated $242 million of the company's $490 million in sales for the year, a significant percentage of the company's total revenue volume, to be sure, but representative of only half of what the company had developed into in roughly a decade. In 1984 the soft drink division

and the rest of the businesses that had been acquired were purchased by corporate takeover artist Victor Posner, who moved Royal Crown Companies to Miami Beach, Florida, and made the company part of DWG Corporation, one of several holding companies under his control.

Lackluster 1980s and Hope for the 1990s

Posner controlled Royal Crown for nine years. His tenure of ownership was notable for the introduction of Cherry RC, Diet RC Cola, and an eight-flavor line of Diet Rite, and it was infamous for Posner's cost-cutting measures that hacked away at Royal Crown's already limited marketing budget. As a result, the company lost ground during the late 1980s and early 1990s, ceding market share to its two, much larger rivals, Pepsi and Coca-Cola. Royal Crown's tailspin showed no signs of ending until ownership of the company passed to new hands, Nelson Peltz and Peter May. In 1993 Peltz and May acquired Royal Crown and Arby's through their company, Triarc Companies, Inc., eventually organizing Royal Crown as a subsidiary of RC/Arby's Corporation, a holding company that also oversaw the operation of Arby's.

Under the ultimate ownership of Triarc, Royal Crown's leading brand, RC Cola, received much greater attention than it had during the 1980s. Triarc added roughly $25 million a year to Royal Crown's marketing budget through the mid-1990s and into the late 1990s, which helped bolster recognition of the RC brand. A new brand, Royal Crown Draft Cola, was introduced in 1995 amid great expectations, but production of the product was discontinued roughly a year later. Following this misstep, the owners of Royal Crown were intent on reestablishing RC Cola as a brand able to wrest market share away from Pepsi and Coca-Cola, something the venerable label had not been able to do for years. Throughout its history, Royal Crown had demonstrated itself to be a creative innovator, but had never seriously threatened its two big rivals. In many respects, the company had served as a research lab for Pepsi and Coca-Cola, yet had never been able to reap the full rewards that should have been realized from its pioneering role. As the company looked toward the 21st century, its was searching for some way to collect the benefits of its legacy of achievement as a soft drink producer.

Principal Subsidiaries

Royal Crown International.

Further Reading

Levine, Joshua, "Sisyphus Rolls Again?," *Forbes,* February 12, 1996, p. 94.
"Royal Crown Taps Emerging Markets," *Beverage Industry,* December 1996, p. 20.
Vaughn, Glenn, "The Fizz and Fizzle of Royal Crown: Georgia's Other Cola," *Georgia Trend,* June 1995, p. 28.

—Jeffrey L. Covell

S&K Famous Brands, Inc.

11100 West Broad Street
P.O. Box 31800
Richmond, Virginia 23294
U.S.A.
(804) 346-2500
Fax: (804) 346-2627
Web site: http://www/skmenswear.com

Public Company
Incorporated: 1970
Employees: 1,600
Sales: $130.2 million (1997)
Stock Exchanges: NASDAQ
SICs: 5611 Men's & Boys' Clothing & Accessory Stores

S&K Famous Brands, Inc. is engaged in the retail sale of men's tailored clothing, furnishings, sportswear, and accessories, primarily with nationally recognized brand names, at 20 percent to 40 percent less than regular full-priced department and specialty-store prices. At the end of fiscal 1997 (the year ended January 25, 1997), the company was operating 195 stores in 26 states, mostly in the South and Midwest, but including 16 in New York and seven in Pennsylvania. They were generally located in midsized metropolitan-area markets under the name S&K Famous Brand Menswear. All but two were either in strip shopping centers or enclosed shopping malls.

Private Enterprise: 1967–83

S&K was founded in 1967 by I.J. (Hip) Siegel, the retired owner of a small chain of Richmond supermarkets, and Abe Kaminsky, his brother-in-law. At loose ends, they took up a "hobby" that was more like a busman's holiday: driving up and down Broad Street to make deals with small haberdasheries for overstocked merchandise, then selling it to other businesses out of the trunk of Siegel's Cadillac. After a while the business got too big for the car and, at their request, Siegel's son Stuart found a vacant former thrift shop on Main Street that he rented for them at $125 a month. Used initially as a warehouse, it soon

became a retail store under the name S&K Famous Brands. Kaminsky sold out in 1969.

The original S&K store was open seven days a week, but only until 4:00 p.m. because that was when street parking was prohibited in downtown Richmond. "It really wasn't a very good retail location," Stuart Siegel told a reporter in 1993. "There was no parking [lot]. There wasn't much walk-by traffic." In another interview he recalled, "I would take a station wagon on Monday morning and leave town and drive south into North Carolina. I would come back on Thursday evening or whenever the station wagon filled, whichever came first. And we'd have that merchandise for the weekend." Soon the junior Siegel, who became president of the firm in 1972, was flying to places as far away as Knoxville and Atlanta, stocking new S&K branches by renting U-Hauls and making dozens of buying stops while motoring back to Richmond. There were five stores when Hip Siegel died in 1973.

S&K started going big time in 1975, when Siegel bought 3,500 suits from Saks Fifth Avenue. There was no room for them in the stores, so he and assistant Donald Colbert—who rose to become president of the company—stuck them in the warehouse and offered them for half price, right out of the boxes. Even at 50 percent off retail, the firm was collecting a 40 percent markup. Within a week, three-quarters of the suits were sold, and S&K had garnered invaluable publicity. The enterprise soon made similar deals with other big retailers like Bloomingdale's and Lord & Taylor. By the early 1980s, however, merchandise purchased directly from manufacturers was accounting for about half of S&K's stock, and merchandise sold under the company's own label had begun making an appearance.

By the time S&K went public in 1983, it was leasing 23 stores in Virginia and North Carolina, including ten Virginia sportswear stores under the Hip Pocket name. Net sales rose from $9.4 million in fiscal 1979 to $18.4 million in fiscal 1983. Net income rose from $297,000 to $1,997,000 during this period. The company's long-term debt was $1,652,000 in September 1983, when it sold 30 percent of the common stock to the public at $10 a share, collecting $5.5 million, of which two-thirds went to selling shareholders. The company's take went into opening new stores and expanding distribution facilities. A

$4.5 million, 70,000-square-foot corporate headquarters and distribution center was completed in 1985.

Steady Expansion: 1985–92

By the fall of 1985 the S&K chain had grown to 34 stores in seven states, all under the S&K Famous Brands name except for one Deansgate Clothing Showroom in Pittsburgh. Value continued to be the company's attraction for its customers. S&K was purchasing men's suits and sports coats at the end of the fall and spring seasons from leading retailers and manufacturers and selling them the next season, usually at discounts of 30 to 50 percent. In 1986, however, it completed the sale—announced in 1985—of its Hip Pocket sportswear division, basically at no profit. The sale included 11 leased store locations in Virginia. Hip Pocket had been formed in 1972 as an exclusive outlet for jeans and tops from Levi Strauss & Co.

Notwithstanding the Hip Pocket sale, S&K's appetite for expansion continued to be sharp. By early 1987 the company had 47 units (all S&K outlets) in 12 states, most of them in the South, but including three in New York. These stores generally were in neighborhood strip centers near shopping malls located in metropolitan areas of about 100,000 to 500,000 population. About 40 percent of sales volume was from reselling goods coming from leading retailers, especially Saks, Bloomingdale's, and Lord & Taylor. Another 40 percent was from brand-name merchandise purchased directly from leading manufacturers. The remaining 20 percent was being produced for S&K under its own labels, primarily ''Deansgate'' for men's suits and ''Club Run'' for dress shirts. To finance the expansion company long-term debt had risen to $12.6 million, but a secondary stock offering in August 1989 netted the firm $4.1 million.

S&K was still growing rapidly at the end of the summer of 1988, when it had 65 stores in 15 states, including two recently opened in Ohio. The company was upgrading its stores with tasteful colors and graphics to appeal to women as well as men. By early 1990 the number of stores had reached 92 in 19 states, stretching as far west as Wisconsin. Only two, however, were in major metropolitan markets: one in the Potomac Mills off-price mall in Dale City, Virginia, near Washington, D.C., and the other in suburban Philadelphia. Both were opened to take advantage of heavy traffic and mall-based advertising, which was keeping the company's own advertising costs low.

S&K had 99 stores in October 1990, when it opened its first superstore, an 8,000-square-foot Richmond outlet that carried 2,500 suits and 1,500 sports coats as well as dress shirts, casual wear, tuxedos, and ties. The company was targeting middle managers ranging in age from 25 to 40. Its private-label merchandise now came to about one-third of its inventory. S&K had been averaging annual sales growth of 20 percent over an eight year period. In 1991 it opened a Tailors Row mall-format store in a Virginia regional mall and soon opened two more, in Syracuse, New York and Winston-Salem, North Carolina, also in regional malls.

In the fiscal year ended January 25, 1992, net sales reached a record $75.1 million and net income amounted to a record $2.9 million. There were 118 S&K stores when Siegel was named Distinguished Retailer of the Year in March 1992 by the Retail Merchants Association of Greater Richmond. S&K had been designated one of the 200 best small U.S. companies by *Forbes* for five consecutive years. Sales were now fully refundable, and store services included in-house alterations.

Given S&K's concentration on markets ranking between 30th and 150th in size in the United States, store expansion was leading to clustering in areas where the company already had a presence. To a degree new stores in existing markets were taking sales from older stores, but the company gained efficiencies in operation, distribution of merchandise, and marketing. S&K was spending about six percent of its sales on TV advertising, typically buying 20 30-second spots a week in a given market during local and network news. The company was now debt-free and generating funds for store expansion from its own resources.

The Mega Center Concept: 1992–96

S&K opened its first Menswear Mega Center—a 22,000-square-foot, no-frills, warehouse-format store in a Fairfax County, Virginia, mall—just in time for the Christmas 1992 season. Six times the size of most of the company's other 127 outlets, it did not carry marked-down clothing from big-name retailers and was open only Fridays, Saturdays, and Sundays, allowing the company to hire chiefly part-time help. A securities analyst said S&K knew the store would have been making most of its sales on weekends anyway, because most men's suits were being sold then, when men and women shopped together. Women were said to be driving the purchase of most men's suits. (Suits and sports coats were accounting for 53 percent of S&K's sales in 1995.)

The advent of ''dress down Fridays'' did not bother Siegel, who pointed out to a *Discount Merchandiser* reporter in 1995, ''The men's tailored clothing business has been declining for over 10 years, but we have never failed to increase our business in those 10 years. . . . There are fewer people selling clothing. . . . Department stores are leaving the business, creating a great opportunity for us because they don't offer much service or selection. We hang 1,000 suits in a store, and we offer sportswear, selling what we call 'Friday wear.' '' S&K ceased carrying apparel from other retailers in 1994 because virtually every brand-name manufacturer now would sell merchandise to the chain. Through a database of nearly one million names, the company had determined that its core customer was a married man between the ages of 30 and 55 making between $50,000 and $75,000 a year.

By the fall of 1993 S&K had opened three more Menswear Mega Centers, one in Rockville, Maryland and the other two in Chicago suburbs. Another Washington-area megastore was added later. Each was stocking 10,000 name-brand suits and sports coats, generally priced between $99.95 and $159.95. Also available were more than 7,000 silk neckties at $7.95, top-name dress and knit shirts, sweaters, and even shoes. But S&K announced in September 1995 that it would close the Chicago-area megastores by the end of the year, citing the high cost of advertising in this populous market. In August 1996 S&K announced it was closing the Washington-area megastores as well. "While the Menswear Mega Centers were not unprofitable," said Siegel, the concept "simply didn't give us the kind of returns we would have needed in order to grow it."

With the elimination of what one securities analyst called an "albatross," S&K continued to concentrate on expanding its core outlets. The number had reached 185 in 26 states at the time of Siegel's announcement discontinuing the Mega Centers, and it passed 200 in 1997. Colbert said in May 1997 that the company expected to operate more than 300 stores by 2002, including some in Canada and Mexico.

Because of the establishment of new S&K stores, company sales continued to grow each year. In fiscal 1995, however, net income fell to $2.5 million from $4 million the previous year. Comparable-store sales fell by two percent. Management blamed "General softness in consumer demand for men's clothing in the company's trading areas, and to a lesser degree, lower sportswear sales than planned due to unseasonable weather." Net income rose slightly in fiscal 1996, to $2.7 million, with comparable-store sales up four percent. Management cited strong suit sales but said sportswear and seasonal merchandise were below expectations. In fiscal 1997 net income reached a record $4.6 million, and comparable-store sales were up five percent. S&K's long-term debt was $5.2 million at the end of the fiscal year. Siegel held 29.6 percent of the common stock in April 1997.

S&K's Operations in 1996

In 1996 S&K was purchasing merchandise from a number of nationally recognized manufacturers, primarily placing orders well in advance of manufacturers' production cycles, during off-peak periods. A number of manufacturers also were providing S&K with merchandise for company-owned labels such as Tailors Row, Deansgate, Roberto Villini, Club Row, and Johnny Bench. Substantially all of the merchandise was being received at the company's Richmond distribution center for delivery to the stores once or twice a week, generally by the company's own trucks.

All S&K stores were being leased. Most were east of the Mississippi, and none were as far west as the Rocky Mountain or West Coast regions. A total of 55 percent were traditional S&K stores of 4,000 square feet, generally located near regional malls in midsized markets; 31 percent were 3,500-square-foot outlet stores located within outlet centers and designed to attract the bargain shopper; and 14 percent were "superstores" of 5,000 to 6,500 square feet, with a much broader merchandise assortment, especially in tailored clothing. Some of these stores also had expanded "Corporate Casual" collections or "shop concepts" such as golf or formal shops.

S&K's customer service included basic alterations at modest cost and a liberal refund policy for returned merchandise, including a money-back guarantee. S&K also was sponsoring a Premiere Club for repeat customers. Members received periodical mailings throughout the year, offering special promotion opportunities and free alterations for the life of the garments purchased.

Further Reading

"Before Outlet Retail Was Trendy, There Was S&K Famous Brands," *Washington Business Journal,* January 29, 1990, p. 22.

Byrne, Harlan S., "S&K Famous Brands," *Barron's,* October 26, 1992, pp. 32–33.

D'Innocenzio, Anne, "S&K Tries Big Store Approach," *Daily News Record,* October 9, 1990, p. 16.

Dooley, Paul, "S&K Debuts Mega Center," *Stores,* March 1993, pp. 42–44.

Gilligan, Gregory J., "Menswear Company Thinks Big," *Richmond Times-Dispatch,* October 31, 1993, pp. E1, E6.

——, "S&K Anticipates Reaching 300 Stores," *Richmond Times-Dispatch,* May 30, 1997, p. B6.

——, "S&K Closing Superstores, Announces 22% Rise in Profit," *Richmond Times-Dispatch,* August 20, 1996, p. C1.

Gordon, Mitchell, "Fashioning a Niche," *Barron's,* March 2, 1987, pp. 51–53.

Hallman, Randy, "S&K Opens First Warehouse Format Store," *Richmond Times-Dispatch,* December 2, 1992, pp. B10, B15.

Johnson, Jay L., "S&K Famous Brands: Selling Suits and Accessories to Men," *Discount Merchandiser,* May 1995, pp. 102, 104–105.

Karr, Arnold, "8 S&K Stores to Open in Fall After Share Sale," *Daily News Record,* August 9, 1983, p. 2.

Meeks, Fleming, "Everyday Low Pricing," *Forbes,* June 22, 1992, pp. 82–83, 86.

Palmieri, Jean E., "S&K's Megastores Bite the Dust in Chicago Area," *Daily News Record,* September 29, 1995, p. 5.

"S&K Famous Brands to Sell Hip Pocket to New Company, *Daily News Record,* October 2, 1985, p. 9.

"S&K Prototype Bolsters Expansion Program," *Chain Store Age Executive,* October 1988, pp. 56, 58.

—Robert Halasz

Seita

53, Quai d'Orsay
75347 Paris Cedex 07
France
(33) 01 45 56 61 50
Fax: (33) 01 45 56 65 62
Web site: http://www.seita.fr

Public Company
Incorporated: 1926 as Service d'exploitation industrielle
    des tabacs
Employees: 6,654
Sales: FFr 17.362 billion (US$3.2 billion) (1996)
Stock Exchanges: Paris
SICs: 2111 Cigarettes; 2121 Cigars; 2131 Chewing and
    Smoking Tobacco

Seita is France's leading producer, distributor, and marketer of tobacco products—not a surprising position given that Seita long functioned as the French government's tobacco monopoly. Since 1995, however, Seita has been a publicly held company listed on the Paris stock exchange and as such has entered into full competition with the giants of the international tobacco industry. Indeed, with a shrinking domestic market—and rising pressure from anti-smoking forces—international expansion may be essential for Seita's future. In 1997 the company held just one percent of the worldwide tobacco market. Yet international sales already account for more than 42 percent of Seita's total revenues.

Seita's activities are organized along two primary lines: manufacturing and distribution. The company manufactures cigarettes, rolling tobaccos, pipe tobaccos, cigars, and matches. Cigarettes and rolling tobaccos remain the company's primary source of revenues, representing 90 percent of the company's own-brand sales in 1996. The company's flagship Gauloises brand enjoys worldwide recognition; other cigarette brands include Gitanes, the aromatic Amsterdamer, Lucky Strike (produced under license exclusively for the French market), and the more recent Brilliant, Brooklyn, and American Dream, devel-oped especially for the company's growing Eastern European and Asian activities. In its home country, Seita's brand portfolio continues to hold the dominant position, with more than 40 percent of the French cigarette market. As French consumer tastes have shifted from the traditional brown tobacco to the lighter-flavored blond (especially Virginian) tobaccos, Seita has reacted strongly, introducing blond versions of its Gauloises, Gitanes, and other brands, to build more than 20 percent and the number two position of this French market.

While cigarette sales in France have been shrinking steadily, the markets for rolling and pipe tobaccos and cigars have been rising. Seita's Corporal and Amsterdamer brands hold more than 50 percent of the French roll-your-own market. Outside of France, rolling tobacco sales are generated principally in the Netherlands, Belgium, and Luxembourg. Cigars, which have enjoyed an increasing popularity in the 1990s, contribute six percent of Seita's French sales. The company's cigar brands, including Niñas, Havanitos, Fleur de Savane, Oro, Cohiba, Pléiades, and Picaduros, have enabled Seita to maintain the French market leadership, with approximately 40 percent of the country's cigar sales. Seita's cigars have also found success in Spain, where the company is the number one cigar importer, and increasing popularity in the United States, where the company's sales—led by its handmade Pléiades large cigars—have risen to more than one million units. In addition to tobacco products, Seita manufactures matches, primarily for the French market; match sales account for one percent of Seita's French revenues.

Headquartered in Paris, Seita's French operations include five cigarette manufacturing facilities, two cigar factories, a pipe and rolling tobacco factory, and a match factory. The company also operates research facilities in Bergerac and Les Aubrais. Through its subsidiaries, Seita's international presence includes South America (Brazil, Paraguay, and Argentina), Africa, China, and Indonesia, as well as Spain, Belgium, Italy, Poland, and Slovenia.

Distribution, Seita's second primary activity, is in fact its chief source of revenues. Distribution of non-Seita products produced 65 percent of the company's total revenues in 1996, including more than FFr 8 billion in tobacco product sales and more than FFr 3 billion in nontobacco product sales. In effect,

Seita continues to hold the monopoly on tobacco products distribution in France, through its exclusive relationship with the country's network of nearly 35,000 tobacconists—the only retail outlets allowed by French law to sell tobacco products. As such, Seita distributes its competitors' products and enjoys the benefits of their popularity with the French consumer. In 1996 Seita distributed more than 95 billion units of tobacco products. The company has also moved to expand its distribution beyond tobacco products to become the country's primary distributor of telephone debit cards and parking meter cards. These cards alone produced nearly FFr 2.5 billion in sales in 1996.

Roots in the 17th Century

Tobacco was first introduced to France in the 16th century by the French monk André Thevet, but it was Jean Nicot, France's ambassador to the court of Portugal, who would give his name to the plant's active ingredient in 1560. The cultivation of tobacco—in particular, a "brown" variant of the plant that would dominate French tobacco tastes until the late 20th century—soon centered in the Savoy and southern regions. Touted for its medicinal properties, tobacco was first distributed by pharmacies and was used as an ingredient in a variety of syrups, balms, and ointments, as well as a snuff; it was not long, however, before smoking became the most popular usage of tobacco. By the mid-17th century sales of tobacco had reached significant levels.

Toward the end of the 17th century tobacco began to take on a new, and lasting, role: that of a "tax collector" for the state. France's war with Holland in that century had exhausted the country's treasury. In 1674, during the reign of Louis XIV, tobacco sales were placed under control of a "tobacco farm" (Ferme des tabacs) by Jean-Baptiste Colbert, the French king's controller-general of finances. Seven years later Colbert extended the royal monopoly to the fabrication of tobacco products, particularly cigars, as well. The farm's control over tobacco and tobacco products was to last for more than a century.

Sales of tobacco remained largely nonspecialized through the 17th century. Merchants developed signs to indicate that they were selling tobacco; while signs in the shape of pipes were common, another symbol became the most popular. Called the "carotte," the symbol represented the bundle of tobacco leaves tied and twisted together that the merchants used to prepare the pipe and snuff tobaccos for their clients. At the beginning of the 18th century the first dedicated tobacconists appeared, marking a new method of tobacco distribution. The oldest of these, the Civette, opened in 1716 in Paris, was still in operation (and under the same family ownership) in the 1990s. As the trend toward tobacconist shops developed, the carotte was adopted as an official symbol and, at the beginning of the 20th century, the use of the carotte became obligatory.

Tobacco became a favorite of France's nobility. The monopoly control of tobacco and the heavy taxes imposed on its sale, however, placed tobacco beyond the reach of the country's poor—soon to enter history as the sans-culottes. Meanwhile, a lively contraband succeeded in popularizing tobacco beyond the ruling class. In 1791 the French Revolution abolished the Tobacco Farm and liberated the cultivation, fabrication, and sale of tobacco and tobacco products. Yet this freedom would not last long.

Once again, tobacco represented an important source of potential revenues for a state in dire need of funds. In 1810 Napoleon Bonaparte reestablished monopoly control over the cultivation, production, and sale of tobacco and tobacco products, setting up a state agency, the Direction des Tabacs, to govern the monopoly. At the same time, the distribution of tobacco was regulated as well, with merchants placed under direction of the tax office. These merchants, particularly bar and newsstand operators, were required to fulfill other distribution functions, such as the sale of postage and fiscal stamps. The 19th century would see a number of important developments in tobacco use in France. Pipe smoking, which had long achieved popularity in northern Europe, came into fashion in France at the beginning of the 1800s. In 1825 a new tobacco product made its appearance in France. Greeted with disdain by "serious" cigar smokers, the little cigar, or cigarette, was considered little more than a fad that would quickly fade. Under Emperor Napoleon III, a dedicated smoker, cigarettes achieved a fashionable status. The period was marked also by the arrival of the first rolling papers, which, perfumed or tinted to match the smokers' clothing, brought a new elegance to smoking.

For most of the 19th century, cigarettes were handmade by artisans. In 1860 these manufacturers, as well as manufacturers of other tobacco products, were brought under the control of a new state body, the Executive Office for State Production, formed by the French Finance Ministry. Cigarette production remained rather limited—a skilled artisan was capable of producing as much as 1,200 cigarettes per day. The Industrial Revolution soon caught up to cigarette production: in 1878 the first industrial cigarette machinery was introduced in France, with production runs of more than 3,500 cigarettes per hour. Cigarette machinery would continue to be refined; by the 1990s machines were producing cigarettes at a rate of 9,000 per minute. The greater supply and lower cost of production began the rise of cigarettes as the dominant form of tobacco product.

Branding a Monopoly in the Early 20th Century

Although certain names in cigars had long enjoyed popularity (the Morlaix site, still in operation in the 1990s, began producing cigars under Louis XV), brand names would play an important role in building the tobacco market in the 20th century. A step in this direction had been made in the 1850s, when the first cigar bands, bearing the manufacturer's or a prominent personality's name, appeared. The rise of production volumes enabled the packaging of cigarettes, leading in turn to the first branded cigarettes. In France the government tobacco body introduced two brands in 1910, Gitanes and Gauloises. Based on blends of brown tobacco, both would prove to have lasting appeal for the French smoker—indeed, they would become synonyms for cigarettes themselves—and achieve an international reputation. Distribution of tobacco products, through a growing network of merchants placed under separate government control, took a step forward when adoption of the "carotte" became mandatory in 1906. In France the sale of tobacco products became strictly limited to these merchants, a system common in much of southern Europe, as opposed to the northern European countries where tobacco distribution was more flexible (vending machines, supermarkets, etc.).

The modernization of the government tobacco monopoly would begin in the 1920s. To aid France's economy, devastated after the First World War, the French premier Raymond Poincare established a new organization for managing the tobacco monopoly in 1926. Called the Service d'Exploitation industrielle des tabacs, or SEIT, the new body once again fulfilled an old function, that of reimbursing public debt. Yet the SEIT represented a first step toward eventual independence, functioning as an autonomous body.

Cigarette sales continued to rise, becoming the tobacco product of choice in the 20th century. The SEIT's flagship brands also began to develop their logos (Gitanes with its silhouette of a gypsy dancer; Gauloises with its winged helmet of a Gaul warrior) in the 1920s and 1930s. With the monopoly on the French market, including France's colonies in Africa, Southeast Asia, the Middle East, and Latin America, the SEIT had little difficulty imposing its brands. Yet even after the introduction of competing brands, Gauloises and Gitanes maintained their appeal. SEITA added the final initial to its name in 1935 when the production of matches (allumettes) was placed under its monopoly control as well.

Postwar "Tax Collector"

Cigarette smoking gained in popularity and, by the end of the Second World War, had become immensely popular. In 1953 SEITA launched a third brand of cigarettes, the Royale. Growing concerns over health issues related to tobacco use prompted SEITA's research and development wing to develop a method of reducing the tar levels in its cigarettes. From 35 mg per cigarette in 1953, tar levels would eventually be mandated, by the European Community, down to just 12 mg per cigarette in 1998. The formation of the European Community in the postwar years would lead to changes in the nature of SEITA as well. In 1959 SEITA's status was adjusted to that of a state-owned industrial/commercial concern (an Etablissement Public à Caractère Industriel et Commercial). The following year the European Community took the first steps in opening its internal borders, allowing the importation of cigarettes among member countries. In 1962 SEITA's employees, formerly classified as civil servants, were granted independent legal status.

While the importation of foreign cigarette brands was slowly liberalized, their distribution in France remained under the exclusive control of the network of merchants established under Napoleon I. In 1964 that monopoly system, sorely in need of modernization, was also placed under SEITA's direction. As such, SEITA found itself in a new role, that of a "tax collector" for the French state. Other changes were in store as the European countries worked toward the formation of the European Economic Community (EEC). In 1968 SEITA introduced its first "foreign" brand, adding the production, under license, of Pall Mall cigarettes. Two years later the common market countries took down the customs barriers among member states; at the same time, SEITA lost its monopoly on tobacco cultivation—French tobacco farmers could now sell their produce on the worldwide market. The following year, another of the EEC barriers fell, when foreign brands were granted free access to the French market. SEITA, however, conserved its monopoly on the importation and distribution of these cigarettes. Yet, in 1972, SEITA lost the monopoly on the importation of EEC-produced matches.

In 1976 SEITA lost its importation and distribution monopoly—in name, at least. In practice, the company's continued direction of the country's nearly 40,000 tobacco retailers, the largest retail network in France, meant that its competitors were still required to contract with SEITA for distribution of their products. That same year, however, held a more substantial blow to the company's marketing endeavors, when the growing strength of the anti-smoking forces succeeded in placing warning labels on cigarette packages and in instituting a ban on advertisements for cigarettes. This move came at the same time as imported cigarettes, particularly the lighter-flavored, blond "American" brands, were finding increasing acceptance among French smokers. SEITA faced a similar situation beyond its borders. While the U.S., British, and Dutch markets traditionally had favored, almost exclusively, blond tobaccos, other countries, notably West Germany, Italy, and Belgium, were also turning more and more to blond tobacco products. By the end of the 1970s blond tobacco had captured as much as 95 percent of these markets as well. Gauloises, which had ranked as the sixth largest selling brand in the world, steadily lost market share, tumbling to 15th place by the mid-1980s.

While France and its former colonies, as well as Spain and Switzerland, continued to favor brown tobacco, the increasing popularity of blond tobacco among female smokers and, most important, among young smokers, forced SEITA to adapt. In 1979 the company began producing light versions of its brown tobacco cigarettes; the following year the company introduced, rather unsuccessfully, its own "American" cigarette, News. In that same year SEITA began producing under license the Lucky Strike brand for the French market. More successful for the company was the 1984 launch of Gauloises Blondes, which enabled the company to hold on to its market leadership in France. SEITA's de facto control over cigarette distribution in France, meanwhile, allowed it to continue to profit from its competitors' success.

Challenges in the 1980s

By the mid-1980s, however, SEITA was bleeding. As a government-controlled organization, SEITA was criticized for its slow response to the changing marketplace. As foreign brands grew in popularity (while cigarette consumption itself began to decline), SEITA's losses would rise to some FFr 4.5 billion per year by the end of the decade. Yet the government, content to collect taxes on tobacco sales (of some FFr 30 billion in sales, some FFr 24 billion went to the state), was ill-inspired to take action. Nonetheless, SEITA slowly began to change its status. A first step was made in 1980, when SEITA was transformed from a "service" to a nationalized company as a "société nationale." In 1984 SEITA's character was again changed to that of a shareholder society, with the sole shareholder remaining the French state. This change, however, enabled the company to diversify its activities for the first time.

The company's new organization, which included a reorganization of its production capacity and the ability to lay off employees, enabled it to become profitable by the beginning of the 1990s. At the same time, the company managed to recapture much of the French market, with Gauloises Blondes becoming the second largest selling cigarette. In 1991, on post tax revenues of nearly FFr 13 billion, SEITA earned a net profit of FFr 226 million.

Going Public in the 1990s

The most significant change for the company would come in the mid-1990s. In 1993 SEITA was included in the list of national companies to be privatized, and in February 1995 SEITA (now Seita) became a privatized company, listing as a public company on the Paris stock exchange. As such, the company faced head-to-head competition with tobacco giants such as BAT Industries and Philip Morris, in a worldwide market where Seita's share was as little as one percent. Yet with its leadership position in the French market remaining stable, enhanced by its privileged position with the country's 35,000-strong retail network, Seita could begin to take steps toward international growth. In 1995 the company acquired Poland's third largest cigarette producer, ZPT Radom. In 1996 the company began expanding its exports into other Eastern European markets, including Slovakia and Slovenia. In July 1996 Seita made moves to expand into China, the world's single largest cigarette market, when its signed a technical cooperation agreement with the Chengdu cigarette factory.

Since its privatization, Scita's sales have continued to rise, passing FFr 17 billion in 1996, for net profits of FFr 786 million. Seita continued to play the role of a tax collector for the French government, a position that came to the company's aid in 1997. With Seita faced with a price war to maintain market share (as a result of a foreign brand's dumping its cigarettes on the French market), the government imposed a new tax on tobacco products in late 1997, a tax calculated against Seita's price structure. A giant at home, Seita remained a minor player on the international tobacco market in 1998. Yet with Gauloises's status as one of the world's most recognized brands, Seita maintained an attractive future, certainly to a potential suitor to the company's key French retail network.

Principal Subsidiaries

Macotab (France); Sofitab (France); Metavideotex (France); Seitamat (France); Coralma (Africa); Tahiti Tabac (99.9%); Promofos (Spain); ZPT Radom (Poland; 33%); Distrital (Italy; 50%); Cacique S.A. (Brazil); Meridional (Brazil; 75%); Cima (Argentina; 52%).

Further Reading

Fitère, Anne-Laurence, "Riche, Vieille, et Jolie," *L'Expansion,* January 6, 1994, p. 82.
Kaupp, Katia D., "Chique et Choc Chez S.E.I.T.A.," *Le Nouvel Observateur,* April 1984, p. 65.
"Prête pour une Guerre des Prix," *La Vie Française,* May 24, 1997, p. 29.
Routier, Airy, "Seita: Cap sur la Distribution," *L'Expansion,* December 21, 1989, p 70.
"Seita: Profil," *Fusions et Acquisitions,* April 1996, p. 4.
"Tabac: une Taxe Spéciale Seita," *Le Nouvel Observateur,* December 4, 1997, p. 92.

—M.L. Cohen

ServiceMASTER®

ServiceMaster Inc.

One ServiceMaster Way
Downers Grove, Illinois 60515
U.S.A.
(630) 271-1300
Fax: (630) 271-2710
Web site: http://www.svm.com

Public Company
Incorporated: 1947
Employees: 27,800
Sales: $4.93 billion
Stock Exchanges: New York
SICs: 8741 Management Services; 7349 Building
Maintenance Services, Not Elsewhere; 8351 Child
Day Care Services; 6719 Holding Companies, Not
Elsewhere Classified

With more than 6.5 million customers in 30 countries around the world, ServiceMaster Inc. is a multifaceted company that provides a broad range of services to residential, commercial, and industrial clients. For many years the company's primary business was the cleaning of hospitals, but as growth in that field slowed in the 1980s, ServiceMaster diversified into other fields that were in some way related to its original areas of expertise. By 1998 its roster of franchised businesses included Merry Maids housecleaning, Terminix pest control, TruGreen, Barefoot, and ChemLawn lawn services, and American Home Shield household maintenance and repair services. True to its name, the company's mastery of all of these services has lead to growth and increasing profitability. At the end of 1996 it had chalked up more than a quarter century of increasing sales and net income.

Founded in the 1930s

ServiceMaster was founded by Marion Wade, who was born in 1898 and had worked as a minor league baseball player, a life insurance salesman, and a door-to-door peddler of pots and pans before getting into the business of cleaning and moth-proofing carpets in 1937. In 1942 Wade sold his first franchise license for his residential and commercial on-site carpet cleaning business.

Two years later Wade underwent an ordeal that would become a turning point in his personal life and in his business. After he was badly burned in an explosion of cleaning chemicals, Wade nearly lost his sight. While recovering from his accident, Wade experienced a religious conversion. "I closed my eyes and I prayed," he wrote in *The Lord Is My Counsel,* his autobiography. "I told the Lord I would turn everything over to Him. I said: 'I don't expect any miracles. I don't intend to sit back and expect You to run everything, but I want You to tell me how to run things and send my way the men I will need to do the job.' "

Those men, it soon transpired, came from Wheaton College, a Bible college outside Chicago. Chief among them was Kenneth Hansen, a Wheaton graduate who was the acting rector of a small congregation in Chicago. Together, Wade and the bow-tied Hansen incorporated the company that would become ServiceMaster in 1947. In 1954 Hansen recruited a second Wheaton graduate, Kenneth T. Wessner, who had worked previously as an advertising salesman. In 1958 the three named their carpet-cleaning company ServiceMaster. The name they chose "struck us as perfect in every area. Masters of service, serving the Master," Wade explained in his autobiography. At that time ServiceMaster franchised residential and commercial cleaning businesses. The following year the company sold its first franchise license in Great Britain, an operation that would form the core of ServiceMaster International.

Post-World War II Expansion into Hospital Maintenance

The business in which ServiceMaster would become best known and which it would eventually come to dominate was an outgrowth of the company's commercial cleaning operations. ServiceMaster got its start in the hospital housekeeping business when Wade gave a speech in the Chicago area. After the speech, he was approached by a nun, who suggested that Wade's company should offer its services to health care facilities. Hansen and Wessner were enthusiastic about the idea; after some research they learned that there was a company in New Zealand that had a large hospital cleaning business in Britain, Australia, and New Zealand. ServiceMaster formed a joint venture with Crothall, the firm from down under, to gain expertise in the field and help ServiceMaster break into the American market. Eventually, however, the joint venture fell apart. Crothall took away a share in the American company, and ServiceMaster took away enough information about hospital cleaning to strike out on its own.

The company got its first contract to clean hospitals in 1962, when the Lutheran General Hospital in Park Ridge, Illinois signed on. With this move, ServiceMaster became a pioneer in the industry of contracting to clean institutions, also known as outsourcing. The company offered its clients lower costs, higher productivity, and better employee morale. In that same year ServiceMaster also sold stock to the public for the first time.

Rapid Growth in the 1970s

In 1970 ServiceMaster sold its first nonhospital cleaning franchise in Japan. Eventually, ServiceMaster would franchise operations in 30 countries around the world.

By 1971 ServiceMaster had contracts with more than half the hospitals that looked to outsiders for their cleaning and the company had notched record profits of $1.2 million. Its arena for growth looked unlimited, since nine-tenths of all U.S. hospitals still handled cleaning themselves and, indeed, throughout the decade of the 1970s ServiceMaster would average an increase in earnings of more than 25 percent a year.

ServiceMaster's founder Marion Wade died in 1973, and his two associates, Kenneth Hansen and Kenneth Wessner, moved up to chairman and president/chief executive officer, respectively. By the following year the company had sold more than 1,000 franchise licenses in its consumer cleaning division, and by 1975 ServiceMaster's health care division had signed contracts with 466 hospitals to clean their premises. The company added another 42 medical clients in the first six months of 1976.

By 1979 earnings had reached $11 million and ServiceMaster had developed a method of doing business that was sensitive to the special needs of hospitals and also worked to its own advantage. The company provided cleaning equipment and supplies, as well as management and supervision of a hospital's own workers. The ServiceMaster system meant that hospitals got more efficient labor from their employees and also did not have to replace their own worn-out or outdated janitorial equipment. ServiceMaster ensured that their facilities stayed spotless, thereby bolstering public confidence in their care and preventing infections caused by improper cleaning.

Long-Range Plan Guides the 1980s

In 1980 ServiceMaster began the process of planning for the future by initiating the formation of a long-range growth plan, called ServiceMaster Industries 20, abbreviated and pronounced "SMIXX." The company set up more than 50 committees of three to seven employees each to set goals for the

next two decades. As one part of this process the company vowed to reach $2 billion in revenues by 1990, from just $400 million in 1980.

Also in that year ServiceMaster branched out from its franchising of commercial and residential cleaning services and its health care management activities to add management services to educational institutions such as universities and school districts to its roster. Within three years the company had 90 academic customers signed up. In 1981 ServiceMaster also began offering its services to industrial customers with more than 1,000 employees and factories larger than one million square feet. Its first customers in this division were Appleton Electric in Chicago and Motorola in Franklin Park, Illinois. Both of these moves helped to broaden the company's potential customer base and insulate it somewhat from factors that might affect the health care industry. By 1987 these two new areas were providing nearly a third of ServiceMaster's revenues, but a much smaller percentage of its profits, because high start-up costs, for things such as training and equipment, ate up excess revenue.

By 1983 ServiceMaster's health care management offerings included laundry and linen services, physical plant operations and maintenance, clinical equipment maintenance, materials maintenance, and a fledgling food services sector, in addition to its traditional housekeeping services. Of the six divisions, housekeeping, laundry, and plant operations provided the bulk of the company's revenues. Most of the company's clients contracted for one or two of the services offered, and initial contracts were set for two years, to make the company's initial investment in a project worthwhile.

In May 1983 ServiceMaster signed its first contract to supervise home health care, in which hospital patients were discharged before their care was entirely complete as a cost-reducing measure. Also in that month the company signed up a large hospital chain, Voluntary Hospitals of America, for its standard management and housekeeping services, adding 135 new locations to its tally. Fees from contracted services, primarily to hospitals, made up about 97 percent of the company's revenues, with the remainder being derived from franchisees, who paid the company a monthly fee and purchased equipment and supplies from ServiceMaster.

Acquisitions in the Late 1980s

ServiceMaster's leadership underwent a shift in 1983, as Chief Executive Officer Kenneth Wessner moved up to chairman and former Wheaton College 45-year-old administrator C. William Pollard took over the helm. Within several years of Pollard's move to the top spot, ServiceMaster found that its core business of hospital cleaning had started to suffer, as strict controls on health care costs, some federally mandated, were implemented. As overall tighter hospital budgets cut into profits, ServiceMaster's growth in earnings rate slowed from its accustomed 20 percent to around five percent. In an effort to rejuvenate itself and return to its previous high rate of growth, ServiceMaster looked to expand the scope of its operations through acquisitions. Although the company traditionally had hewed to extremely conservative financial policies, taking on no debt whatsoever, its managers now began to consider the use of borrowed capital to finance the purchase of other companies.

In April 1986 the company moved to acquire a one-third interest in American Physicians Service Group, Inc., which marketed office machines and financial services to doctors and dentists. ServiceMaster agreed to advertise and sell American's products to medical personnel. In November 1986 ServiceMaster announced an agreement to purchase Terminix International, the country's second largest pest control concern, with 164 company-owned outlets and 150 franchised branches nationwide. ServiceMaster paid $165 million for the business, which reported annual sales of about $150 million. ServiceMaster hoped that Terminix would prove a good match with its residential and commercial cleaning businesses, as both operations could be used to generate clients for the other.

Another way that the company looked to compensate for its slowing growth was through financial restructuring. To maximize its returns to investors, ServiceMaster reconfigured itself as a publicly traded master limited partnership. In addition to freeing up cash for the company's acquisitions activities, this allowed ServiceMaster to avoid paying federal taxes and made it possible for owners of the company's stock to avoid double taxation, paying only a lower personal tax rate on their earnings. On the last day of 1986 the business of ServiceMaster Industries, Inc. was transferred to ServiceMaster Limited Partnership. In response to this move, the company's stock made some of the largest gains in the market in the first days of 1987, when it first moved from over-the-counter trading to the Big Board of the New York Stock Exchange.

ServiceMaster made a second large acquisition when it spent $40 million on American Food Management, a company that ran cafeteria facilities in educational institutions. In an effort to make its hospital operations more profitable, ServiceMaster began to market compound contracts to its clients, in which they signed up for several of the company's services all at once, increasing efficiency. These "Support Service" contracts were slow to gain popularity, enticing just 12 of ServiceMaster's 1,300 hospital customers by early 1987, but the company remained confident that the program would eventually win converts. By the end of 1987 company revenues had reached $1.4 billion.

As the hospital services sector, which made up 60 percent of ServiceMaster's revenues, grew more competitive in the late 1980s, ServiceMaster's market share became more and more dependent on the company's ability to provide quality service at a low price. The company relied on its extensive employee training programs and ongoing product and equipment development to maintain its competitive edge. ServiceMaster used videotapes, audiotapes, and thick training manuals that broke tasks, such as washing a floor, down into detailed five-minute steps to assist its workers. To remind employees at all levels that the most humble tasks lay at the core of the company's success, each employee invested at least one day every year performing a company service. In addition, ServiceMaster worked to keep its equipment state-of-the-art, developing new and more effective germicides, a battery-powered vacuum cleaner, and a longer-lasting, easier-to-use fiberglass mop handle. Training and innovation were designed to keep productivity and profits high.

Despite these efforts, however, the amount of money generated by the company's hospital cleaning operations continued to drop and revenues crept up just seven percent in the first nine months of 1988. At the end of that year ServiceMaster reported that changes in the ways medical services were provided and paid for had resulted in smaller markets for services at the company's existing clients and delays in signing contracts with new clients. In addition, for the first time ServiceMaster had to terminate some clients for failing to pay their bills. Given these factors, the company's food service, clinical equipment maintenance, and home health care contracting operations had stronger returns in 1988 than its housekeeping services.

Expansion into Residential Services in the Late 1980s

In response to this situation, ServiceMaster continued its policy of diversifying its operations to arenas other than health care facilities. Following its purchase of Terminix, which primarily handled residential pest control, the company acquired another home-based business, "Merry Maids," in 1988. Founded in Omaha, Nebraska, in 1980, Merry Maids had built up a franchise network that specialized in cleaning customers' homes once a week, twice a month, or for special occasions. The company hoped that this purchase would further cement its standing in the home services industry and increase the amount of synergy generated by its different parts.

In June 1988 the company took another step in this direction when it purchased a Memphis-area home appliance maintenance and plumbing service, with about 400 customers. ServiceMaster renamed the company the ServiceMaster Home Systems Service. For $500 a year, the company promised to unclog toilets, fix leaky faucets, and handle any other necessary home repairs. After a big marketing push, the company was able to sign up customers at the rate of 40 a month. ServiceMaster made a much larger commitment to this field in April 1989, when it purchased American Home Shield, a California company that had been providing home warranties since 1971. ServiceMaster paid $120 million for the company, which had 200,000 home service contracts to its credit by 1990.

In that year ServiceMaster's health care operations provided just 40 percent of the company's earnings, down from 90 percent a decade earlier. One aspect of the health care business that did show potential for growth was the home health care subsidiary. ServiceMaster had 60 programs in place by the end of the 1980s, many of them joint ventures with a number of hospitals. Since home health care was so different from normal hospital operations, administrators were more willing to bring in outside specialists to assist in managing their programs.

Early 1990s Acquisitions

Acquisitions paced ServiceMaster's annual growth in the early 1990s as the company sought profitable new service niches. As traditional sectors matured, they comprised an ever-smaller slice of ServiceMaster's operating income, shrinking to barely one-third by 1996. The company augmented its home services division with the November 1990 purchase of two divisions of Waste Management, Inc.: a pest control business, and TruGreen, a lawn care service with commercial and residential customers. TruGreen's lawn operations complemented ServiceMaster's own exclusively residential lawn care division, which it had inaugurated in 1984.

The company branched out into another field it considered ripe for significant growth when it entered the child care business in 1990 by purchasing the GreenTree Preschool in Wheaton, Illinois. Using this facility as a base, ServiceMaster then opened additional child care centers in corporate settings in the Chicago area, providing benefits to employers and their workers.

ServiceMaster also purchased a 22 percent interest in the privately held Norrell Corporation in December 1991. Norrell provided temporary office and light industrial employees through a network of 250 company owned and franchised temporary agencies and also augmented ServiceMaster's home health care operations with 95 agencies that provided medical workers for residential settings. By the end of 1996 Service-Master affiliates were providing management support to more than 2,500 clients.

The acquisition-hungry company purchased its largest lawn care rival, ChemLawn, from Ecolab for $104 million in 1992. The 1996 purchase of Barefoot Inc. for $232 million further solidified ServiceMaster's leading position in this market. The company also added an inspection service and an in-home furniture repair company to its roster of residential offerings in the 1990s.

International growth was achieved through joint ventures and subsidiary companies. In the 1990s ServiceMaster focused on penetration of Europe, forming operations in Germany, Austria, Switzerland, and the United Kingdom. The conglomerate also hoped to expand into Asian and Pacific Rim countries by the end of the decade.

In 1993 Carlos H. Cantu succeeded William Pollard as CEO. Pollard, who had transformed ServiceMaster from a maturing company into a fast-growing, highly profitable leader of the service industry, continued as chairman. By this time it had become clear that ServiceMaster's corporate structure, the limited partnership, which had provided marked tax benefits when it was instituted, subsequently had made the company unattractive to institutional investors. The company, therefore, began to search for a way to restructure itself that would eliminate the barriers to investment by other companies. The partnership's shareholders approved a plan of reorganization that would reincorporate ServiceMaster as a corporation in December 1997.

Returning its attention to the health care industry mid-decade, ServiceMaster purchased VHA Long Term Care, a nursing home management company, in 1993 and formed Diversified Health Services through the union of its hospital and home health divisions in 1994. This division enjoyed a comeback during the 1990s, chalking up seven consecutive years of plus-40 percent increases in profits.

Overall revenues increased from $1.8 billion in 1990 to nearly $3.5 billion in 1996, and net income more than doubled from $94.4 million to $245.1 million. ServiceMaster appeared poised to take advantage of several social, demographic, and economic trends in the late 1990s. As Cantu and Pollard wrote in their 1996 letter to shareholders, "The need for time-saving home services and the increase in the number of elderly Americans, coupled with fiscal pressures which are forcing institutions to 'do more with less,' create ongoing demand for our services."

Principal Subsidiaries

ServiceMaster Direct Distributor Company; The ServiceMaster Acceptance Company; ServiceMaster Venture Fund L.L.C.; Anticimex Development A.B. (Sweden); Terminix Peter Cox Limited (U.K.); Terminix Protekta B.V. (Netherlands); Terminix Stenglein GmbH & Co. KG (Germany); Riwa B.V. (Netherlands); ServiceMaster Japan, Inc.; ServiceMaster Limited (U.K.); ServiceMaster Operations Germany GmbH; TMX Europe B.V. (Netherlands); ServiceMaster of Canada Limited (50%); Tarmac ServiceMaster (U.K.; 50%); Raab Karcher ServiceMaster GmbH & Co. KG (Germany; 50%).

Principal Divisions

ServiceMaster Consumer Services Company; The Terminix International Company; TruGreen-Chemlawn; ServiceMaster Residential/Commercial Services; Merry Maids; American Home Shield; Furniture Medic; AmeriSpec; ServiceMaster Management Services Company; ServiceMaster Healthcare Management Services; ServiceMaster Education Management Services; ServiceMaster Energy Management Services; ServiceMaster Business & Industry Group; CMI Group, Inc.; ServiceMaster Manufacturing Services; Premier Manufacturing Support Services; ServiceMaster Aviation Services; ServiceMaster Diversified Health Services; ServiceMaster Home Health Care Services, Inc.; ServiceMaster Facility Development Services; ServiceMaster Rehabilitation; TruCare Medical; ServiceMaster International.

Further Reading

"As ServiceMaster's Chairman, Mr. Wessner Combined His Faith in God with a Strong Work Ethic," *Modern Healthcare*, September 14, 1992, pp. 32–33.

Dubashi, Jonathan, "God Is My Reference Point," *Financial World*, August 16, 1994, pp. 36–37.

Gelfand, M. Howard, "Growing ServiceMaster Industries, Inc. Thrives by Calling on God and Hospitals," *Wall Street Journal*, January 23, 1973.

Henkoff, Ronald, Piety, Profits, and Productivity, *Fortune*, June 29, 1992, pp. 84–85.

Oneal, Michael, "ServiceMaster: Looking for New Worlds To Clean," *Business Week*, January 19, 1987.

Ozanian, Michael K., ServiceMaster: Gearing Up For a New World," *Financial World*, November 27, 1990, p. 16.

Pollard, C. William, "The Leader Who Serves," *Strategy & Leadership*, September-October 1997, pp. 49–51.

Puente, "Against the Odds," *Hispanic Business*, September 1997, p. 16.

Rudnitsky, Howard, with Christine Miles, ". . . Who Help Themselves," *Forbes*, March 3, 1980.

"ServiceMaster: Focus on Employees Boosts Quality," *Business Marketing*, April 1988.

Siler, Charles, "Cleanliness, Godliness, and Business," *Forbes*, November 28, 1988.

Skolnik, Rayna, "Marketing Cleanliness with Godliness," *Sales & Marketing Management*, December 5, 1983.

Wade, Marion E., and Glenn D. Kittler, *The Lord Is My Counsel: A Businessman's Personal Experiences with the Bible*, Englewood Cliffs, N.J.: Prentice Hall, 1988.

—Elizabeth Rourke
—updated by April D. Gasbarre

Sheldahl Inc.

1150 Sheldahl Road
Northfield, Minnesota 55057-9444
U.S.A.
(507) 663-8000
Fax: (507) 663-8545
Web site: http://www.sheldahl.com

Public Company
Incorporated: 1955 as G.T. Schjeldahl Company
Employees: 1,000
Sales: $105.3 million (1997)
Stock Exchanges: NASDAQ
SICs: 3679 Electronic Components, Not Elsewhere
    Classified; 3643 Current-Carrying Wiring Devices;
    3089 Plastics Products, Not Elsewhere Classified;
    2295 Coated Fabrics Not Rubberized

Sheldahl Inc. creates and markets laminates used primarily by the automotive, computer, and telecommunications industries. Marketed worldwide, Sheldahl laminates are generally of two types: adhesive-based tapes and materials, and the company's own patented adhesiveless material called Novaclad. From these materials, Sheldahl makes single- and double-sided interconnects and substrates for semiconductor packaging.

Entrepreneurial Beginnings in the 1940s

From an early age, Gilmore T. "Shelly" Schjeldahl, founder of Sheldahl Inc., demonstrated an unusual ability to understand how complex things worked. As a young man growing up in Northwood, South Dakota, he built his family's first radio. He would spend hours at local shops and plants, studying how things worked. At the local newspaper he built a static eliminator for the press. Although he never received a high school or college diploma, Shelly received 16 patents and has started five companies over the course of his career. Jim Donaghy, Sheldahl's president and CEO, said, "Shelly gave our company a culture of scientific inquiry and the spirit of risk-taking so necessary for success in today's world."

Prior to World War II, Shelly worked and attended college part-time for six years, studying chemistry, biology, and engineering. After serving in World War II, he worked in the research laboratories of Armour & Company in Chicago. It was there that he first encountered plastic packaging. He was especially interested in a new packaging material, polyethylene, and the fact that it would not seal.

Together with his wife, Charlene, he developed a way to cut and seal together, simultaneously, two sheets of plastic with a hot knife. It was "a process that would one day revolutionize the packaging industry," he noted in *Forty Years of Innovation: The Sheldahl Story.* When neither Armour nor any of Shelly's other employers in Minneapolis showed any interest in his idea, he set up a bag-making operation in 1948 in the basement of his south Minneapolis home. Using a simple foot-operated cutting knife, he transformed sheets of plastic into pickle-barrel liners. He named his company Herb-Shelly, in honor of a salesman named Herb who had loaned him $100 for materials.

G.T. Schjeldahl Company Established in 1955

Herb-Shelly was soon producing a line of polyethylene bags in Farmington, Minnesota. The company grew to 100 employees and had sales of $500,000 by 1954. In May 1954 Herb-Shelly was acquired by Brown & Bigelow of St. Paul, Minnesota. Unable to work for a large company, Shelly resigned and left on January 8, 1955. Before the end of the year he would establish the G.T. Schjeldahl Company as a public company.

Some key employees were hired in the first year of the company. Dick Slater, who retired in 1995 as senior vice-president of technology, was hired on August 1, 1955, as a project engineer. Jim Womack, who eventually became president and chairman of the board, was hired on October 10, 1956, as a salesman.

Shelly set up a manufacturing operation in Northfield, Minnesota, to fabricate large, high-altitude research balloons made with Mylar polyester film and held together with a Schjeldahl-developed adhesive system. Shelly had been invited by DuPont scientists to visit their Wilmington, Delaware facility to evaluate adhesive resins for sealing a DuPont polymer called Mylar. According to *Forty Years of Innovation,* "He noticed that his

432

breath caused one sample's surface to crystallize, making it less tacky and easier to handle. That resin became the basis for his line of heat-sealing adhesive tapes.''

Diversified from the Beginning

The company was diversified from its beginning. It was involved in bag-making machines, high-altitude research balloons, and heat-sealing adhesive tape. The company was initially organized in two divisions: the Mechanical Division, which made packaging machinery, and the Polyester Film Division, which made balloons, special fabrications, and Schjel-Bond. Schjel-Bond was a line of adhesive tapes for polyester bonding.

The Mechanical Division shipped its first automatic side-weld polyethylene bag-making machine in December 1955. The machine was built in the Medical Arts Building in Northfield and had to fit through a 35-inch-wide doorway. To this day, the standard width for bag machines all over the world is 35 inches.

By February 1956 the Polyester Film Division had tested more than forty Mylar polyester stratospheric balloons ranging in size from eight to 500 feet around. Shelly had first become involved with large balloons during the Herb-Shelly days, when he fabricated a balloon for the Office of Naval Research at the University of Minnesota.

Another innovative area for the company was that of polyester-fabricated, air-supported buildings. Utilizing its expertise in plastics and adhesives, the company built ''Schjeldomes'' for 98 cents per square foot. One covered a swimming pool at a Lake Superior resort, another covered a storage building at DuPont's laboratories. In 1958 the company moved to a new location at the north edge of Northfield and built a 340-foot-long air-supported factory called the ''Schjel-Mile.'' By 1962 the company had consolidated most of its operations at the 54-acre ''Schjel-town,'' which included a two-story general office and laboratory, two Schjel-Miles (one was 540 feet long), a factory, and other smaller buildings.

Gained International Fame in 1960

Working under the auspices of government-sponsored programs, the company pursued materials research in many areas. The company benefited from these programs by being able to commercialize and sell the results of its research. For example, its involvement in the Echo satellite program enabled it to learn how to handle extremely thin plastic webs by laminating them in large forms and in high volumes and etching, or chemically milling, the surface. These processes would later be used in the production of the company's circuitry and other products.

On August 12, 1960, the G.T. Schjeldahl Company became known around the world when Echo I was launched into orbit by the National Aeronautics and Space Agency (NASA) from Cape Canaveral, Florida. Echo I was a 100-foot passive satellite, or ''satelloon,'' that was designed and built by Schjeldahl. At the time it was the largest object ever fired into orbit, but unlike the Russian-fired Sputnik, it could be seen from Earth. It was made with a very thin polyester film vapor deposited with aluminum and sealed with Schjeldahl's GT-301 tape.

For the United States, Echo I was the beginning of a satellite-based global telecommunications network. The aluminized surface of the communications satellite acted as a mirror to bounce radio and television signals back to Earth. Although expected to stay aloft for only a few weeks, Echo I circled the globe for eight years. It was the success of Echo I that led to a presidential recommendation to form a federally regulated, privately owned telecommunications network.

The U.S. Navy's Polaris submarine was another important project for Schjeldahl. The company developed a laminate material and adhesive system to construct environmental seals, or diaphragms, for the sub. The diaphragms' purpose was to keep water out of the submarine until a missile was released.

Mastered Two Key Processes in the Early 1960s

Schjeldahl's expertise in two key processes for combining different materials, laminating and vacuum deposition, led to the development of many new products in the 1960s. A laminate is a product that combines two or more materials, such as plastic, metal, or fiber, using an adhesive or other means. Vacuum deposition condenses metal vapor onto thin plastic in a vacuum chamber to make a very thin foil.

In 1958 Schjeldahl was laminating materials by hand. In 1959 it built its first laminator, a small machine that could combine copper and tape, to produce Schjel-Clad, a laminate of copper bonded to Mylar polyester film for printed circuit and printed wiring applications. Schjel-Clad was developed for use in aircraft, spacecraft, automobiles, business machines, computers, switchboards, television, and radio. It was introduced as part of the dash-panel wiring in all 1962 Buicks.

In 1963 the company acquired a 72-inch vacuum deposition coating unit to make micrometeoroid sensors for NASA. The sensors consisted of metal sheets bonded with Schjel-Bond adhesive to polyester thinly coated with copper. Products that grew out of this vacuum deposition technology included thermal control coatings for spacecraft, Novaclad, X-ray sensors, radar-absorbing films, and keypads for computer keyboards.

Other technologies developed in the early 1960s involved microcircuitry, which Shelly began studying. His research led to a new process for enclosing microcircuits within a thin film of glass using a technique called ''sputtering.'' His early work in this area formed the basis for the high-density substrates that Sheldahl later made in Longmont, Colorado.

In 1964 the company introduced Schjel-Flex, a line of precision-etched flexible circuitry processed roll-to-roll from Schjel-Clad. The company also manufactured the machinery for the in-line production of Schjel-Flex. It was this roll-to-roll processing ability that gave Schjeldahl a competitive advantage in the flexible circuit product area. This later became the focus of the company's Electrical Products Division, which offered flexible circuitry, flexible laminates, flexible cabling, and shielding.

Growth and Change, 1965–1966

At the end of its first decade, Schjeldahl was organized into three divisions: the Advanced Programs Division, which worked on government research and development projects; the Packaging Machinery Division, the company's largest division and by then one of the world's leading producers of machines for making plastic and multiwall bags; and the Electrical Products Division.

The company had grown to nearly 900 employees and net sales had increased from $311,000 in 1956 to $13.3 million in 1965. Shelly stepped down as president at the end of 1964 to spend more time on corporate planning and exploring new products and markets. He remained as chairman and treasurer of the company. Arthur Hatch, executive vice-president, was promoted to president.

Faltering Economy and Government Cutbacks Brought Tough Times, 1967

The company enjoyed growing sales and income in 1966, but in 1967 a slackening U.S. economy and cutbacks in government-supported research, always an important part of Schjeldahl's business, led to a 60 percent drop in net income to just $349,000 for the year. The next year the company reported a net loss of $742,000 under its new president, George Freeman. The company struggled to regain ground, but 1970 brought another net loss.

One highlight from this period was the company's involvement with Apollo 11 and the moon landing of July 1969. It developed a thermal control material consisting of a thin plastic film coated with vacuum-deposited aluminum overcoated with silicon oxide. This material controlled the temperatures in the Apollo 11 command module, the lunar lander, and the astronauts' space suits. The company also developed a special material for the lunar lander's window shades.

Overdiversification Led to Reorganization in the 1970s

When Freeman resigned in 1971, Jim Womack became president of the company. As Schjeldahl sought new markets, the number of products and projects grew rapidly. In 1974 a company logo was created to symbolize its expertise in bringing diverse materials together and the company's name was changed to Sheldahl Inc. By 1975 Sheldahl had adopted the slogan, "Within our diversity lies our growth."

Sheldahl enjoyed an international reputation for fabrication based on materials technology. It was the United States' largest independent producer of flexible circuitry and one of the largest suppliers of packaging machinery in the Western Hemisphere. The company also produced laminates and tapes and a wide range of other products for aerospace and other industries.

Sheldahl was also involved in several special "one-off" projects. In 1973 it provided thermal control material to repair the Skylab space station. It also fabricated 35,000 expansion-joint weather seals for the above-ground portion of the 800-mile-long Alaska Pipeline.

The company's extensive diversity eventually translated into a lack of direction, and in 1977 it began to consider redefining itself. It brought in an outside consultant, Arthur D. Little & Company, to help. The result was a decision to refocus resources on two growth areas: materials and circuitry. Operations at Northfield were shrunk from four divisions to one, and extensive

management cuts were made. The company also sold overseas plants and businesses that did not fit its new strategic plan.

Sheldahl's new focus resulted in the sale of its packaging machinery division. Although it had been a dynamic growth business for the company since it sold its first bag machine in 1955, packaging machinery had become a mature market by 1980. The company had orders for almost 5,000 machines in 1980, the year it sold the division to concentrate on materials and circuitry.

Refined Focus and Emphasis on Quality Characterized the 1980s

As Sheldahl focused its resources on materials and circuitry, it made several organizational changes. It got rid of several layers of management to "empower our people," said company President Womack. The company also switched from an indirect to a direct sales force to fulfill individual customer's needs better. Each salesperson was equipped with a portable computer that allowed the sales force to determine the feasibility of a project or product through near-instant pricing estimates at the customer's location.

In the face of increasing international competition, Sheldahl also adopted a zero-defect approach to quality. The company worked in partnership with customers to get its products qualified to be shipped without incoming inspections. Sheldahl's quality control program was so successful that in 1982 the company was selected as one of the original 77 suppliers to receive Ford Motor Company's prestigious Q-1 Award for producing a consistent top level of quality over a period of time.

In 1988 Jim Donaghy, who had worked with Sheldahl employees over the years, was recruited from DuPont by Jim Womack to become president of Sheldahl; Womack became chairman of the board. To close the decade, Sheldahl's management team outlined a new market-focused, customer-driven business plan to make Sheldahl consistently profitable and the preferred supplier of laminates and components made from laminates in high-growth global markets. This plan resulted in a whole new line of products for Sheldahl that was introduced in the 1990s.

Preparing for the Future in the 1990s

One of the first new products introduced in the 1990s was "Z-Link," an interconnective circuitry system with an adhesive that conducted electricity only in the Z (vertical) axis. This innovation allowed the building of multilayer flexible circuits and was awarded *R&D Magazine*'s prestigious R&D 100 Award for significant new technology. Another significant new product was Novaclad, a copper-on-film flexible material that eliminated the need for an adhesive system. Since it used no adhesive, it could be used in a high-temperature environment, such as inside an automotive engine compartment, as well as in a harsh chemical environment, such as in brake fluid.

Introduced in 1990 and patented in 1992, Novaclad was the start of a series of innovations that enabled Sheldahl to achieve significant penetration in the automotive electronic market. "Novaflex," a technique for making adhesiveless flexible circuits from a Novaclad base, was introduced in 1991, followed by "Novalink," a multilayer circuit constructed with Novaclad or Novaflex flexible circuits and Z-Link adhesive. These products were used in such automotive applications as antilock braking systems and dashboard circuitry. To better serve its automotive customers, Sheldahl established the Detroit Technology Center in 1990.

In 1993 Sheldahl organized a consortium of vertically integrated, noncompeting companies to develop products based on Novaclad for the multichip module (MCM) integrated circuit packaging market. The United States needed high-density, low-cost MCMs to compete globally, and federal funding for the consortium was obtained through the Advanced Research Projects Agency (ARPA) of the U.S. Department of Commerce.

With funding assistance from ARPA, Sheldahl established a prototype production facility in June 1994 in Longmont, Colorado to produce Novaclad-based products in commercial quantities, principally for the datacommunications market. One of these products was "ViaThin," a Novaclad-based microcircuit substrate that, with the application of a photoresist liquid, was ready for printing and etching fine conductors. The company also made substantial capital investments over the next several years to support its strategy of gaining market share in the automotive electronic market and the datacommunications market. Production capacity was increased at its Northfield and South Dakota operations.

Production Delays Affected Profitability, 1997

Sheldahl's strategy seemed to be paying off, with sales increasing steadily to a record level of $114.1 million in 1996. The company's net income of $4.8 million that year was its highest ever. Sales to the automotive market had increased from $13.9 million in 1989 to $71.0 million in 1997 and represented 67 percent of the company's revenue. Datacommunications revenue, the company's second largest market, had steadily decreased from $32.6 million in 1991 to $12.5 million in 1997, accounting for 11.9 percent of the company's 1997 revenue. Aerospace and defense work, another declining but important segment of Sheldahl's business, was third at 8.7 percent of sales, or $9.2 million.

Unfortunately, production delays at the company's Micro Products facility in Longmont, Colorado significantly impacted Sheldahl's profitability. These included delays in delivery of equipment for its production lines and longer-than-anticipated product specification and full qualification periods. As a result, Sheldahl reported a net loss of $8.0 million in fiscal 1997 on

sales of $105.3 million. According to the company's annual report for 1997, "These losses are expected to continue until efficient volume production and related sales revenue are achieved." Sheldahl's CEO James Donaghy expected volume production of the company's micro products to begin in the second half of fiscal 1998 and noted that one of the company's lead micro products customers had completed its first round of full qualification testing on Sheldahl's ViaThin substrate for semiconductor packages.

For fiscal 1998 and the near future, Sheldahl was focused on the automotive electronics and datacommunications markets. The worldwide automotive electronics market was expected to grow to $28 billion by 2005. With datacommunications demanding lighter, smaller, and faster products, Sheldahl expected to find a ready market for its Novaclad, ViaThin, and MCM substrate products. In addition, new applications, such as government-mandated airbags and others yet to be developed that depended on Sheldahl's core technologies and competencies, were likely to come along in the future.

Further Reading

Breimhurst, Henry, "Sheldahl Ramps Up New Colorado Factory," *Minneapolis-St. Paul City Business,* October 10, 1997.

Byrnes-Lenarcic, Barbara, "New Hong Kong Office Widens Sheldahl Presence," *Boulder County Business,* November 1997, p. 33.

Carideo, Tony, "Donaghy's Investments Are Paying Off After 5 Years as Sheldahl President," *(Minneapolis) Star Tribune,* March 13, 1993.

Forty Years of Innovation: The Sheldahl Story, Northfield, Minn.: Sheldahl Inc., 1995.

Hodges, Jill, "Sheldahl Eyes S. Dakota for New Assembly Plant," *(Minneapolis) Star Tribune,* April 7, 1993.

——, "Sheldahl To Retool Northfield Site, Shift 104 Plant Jobs to Mexico," *(Minneapolis) Star Tribune,* February 11, 1993.

Leib, Jeffrey, "Tech Company Ready for a Quantum Leap," *Denver Post,* January 7, 1996, p. 1.

McManus, John, "Sheldahl Signs Agreements with Airbag Manufacturers," *PR Newswire,* April 6, 1993.

——, "Sheldahl To Acquire Datakey in Stock Exchange," *PR Newswire,* October 19, 1993.

Peterson, Susan E., "Electronics Firms Sheldahl, Datakey Planning To Merge in $16 Million Deal," *(Minneapolis) Star Tribune,* October 20, 1993.

Sylwester, MaryJo, "Products, Contracts Keep Sheldahl Busy," *Successful Business,* August 16, 1993, p. 11.

——, "Sheldahl Workers Bitter about September Layoffs," *Successful Business,* August 23, 1993, p. 1.

Wood, Carol, "R&D Consortium Will Build Plants in Longmont," *Denver Business Journal,* May 13, 1994, p. 1.

—David Bianco

SHONEY'S Inc.

Shoney's, Inc.

1727 Elm Hill Pike
Nashville, Tennessee 37120
U.S.A.
(615) 391-5201
Fax: (615) 231-2621
Web site: http://shoneys.com

Public Company
Incorporated: 1968
Employees: 38,000
Sales: $1.2 billion (1997)
Stock Exchanges: New York
SICs: 5812 Eating Places; 6794 Patent Owners and
   Lessors

Headquartered in Nashville, Tennessee, Shoney's, Inc., is one of the restaurant industry's most respected companies. As of 1998 the restaurant chain operated or franchised over 1,300 restaurants in 34 states, including Shoney's, Captain D's, and the Pargo's and Fifth Quarter specialty restaurants. The company owned 893 restaurants and franchised 494 others.

Early Expansion

The company originated with a drive-in restaurant called "Parkette" in Charleston, West Virginia. Alex Shoenbaum opened the restaurant in 1947, then acquired a Big Boy franchise in 1951. Two years later, Shoenbaum renamed the Parkette "Shoney's Big Boy." During this time, Ray Danner was building a restaurant business in central Tennessee and opened his first Big Boy franchise in 1959 in Madison, Tennessee. He incorporated his privately owned company in 1968 as Danner Foods, Inc. One year later Danner Foods became a publicly traded company.

During its affiliation with the Marriott Corporation, the parent company of Big Boy restaurants, Shoney's restaurants doubled in size every four years. Based on a chain of family-style coffee houses along the busy highways of the Southeast,

Shoney's restaurants featured a friendly, uniformed waitstaff that served from a "homestyle" menu adapted to the region.

"Danner's Way" Established

In 1972 the company dropped "Big Boy Enterprises" from its name, and Ray Danner assumed the role of chairperson and chief executive officer, while Alex Shoenbaum became a senior chairperson. Danner took an active role in Shoney's management, building the company on a foundation of hands-on, operations-oriented management. His unique style became part of the corporate culture, and his managers became "Shoneyized" or imbued with respect for efficiency and a sense of responsibility.

"Danner's Way," as it came to be known, promoted simplicity, customer satisfaction, constant striving for perfection, and management by example. His management team worked in shirtsleeves in order to be prepared to pitch in whenever and wherever necessary. Danner himself monitored everything from corporate staff practices to food service through the use of "mystery shoppers" dispatched periodically to each unit. He was also known to visit restaurants in person and to clean restrooms that did not meet his standards during his spot checks. His willingness to roll up his sleeves both proved his point and embarrassed the responsible individual, who cleaned alongside him.

Although employee standards at Shoney's were uncompromising, the rewards were enticing. The company instituted a program in which the best hourly workers could be awarded college scholarships that would help pave the road to middle and upper management positions within the company. In exchange, trainees would work nights and weekends and take college courses recommended by Shoney's. The company provided students with plenty of opportunities for advancement, maintaining five to seven manager positions for each restaurant, area manager positions for every three to four restaurants, and divisional director positions supervising ten to 20 restaurants. Furthermore, Shoney's recruited more than half of its managers internally. According to many observers, Danner's management style was the basis of Shoney's strong profits and steady growth.

Shoney's has expanded its family restaurants' territory to 29 states coast-to-coast.

New Chains in the 1970s

Opportunities in the company were not limited to work in family-style restaurants. Danner had, in 1969, begun to market a new fast-food concept featuring batter-dipped fish and related food products for sale in a chain of Mr. D's Seafood restaurants. By 1975, when the chain's name was changed to Captain D's, over 250 units were in operation. By 1980 there were more Captain D's than Shoney's, and by 1985 the seafood chain's sales constituted 30 percent of the company's total. Captain D's has consistently outproduced its competitors, including its primary rival, Long John Silver.

After discovering that its family restaurants located near motels earned over 30 percent more than stand-alone shops, Shoney's established Shoney's Inns, a lodging division which it paired with specialty restaurants called Fifth Quarter Steakhouses. The two enterprises complemented each other, and were managed separately. Within ten years the chain of inns had grown to 21, but two nagging problems with the venture had developed. First, the hotels did not return the high, quick profits of the food service operations, and second, the vastly different management requirements clashed with Shoney's (and Danner's) distinctive style. The chain was eventually sold to Gulf Coast Development, Inc. in 1991.

The Fifth Quarter concept has fared better as a growth vehicle for Shoney's. In a departure from the "family" concept, the dinner houses feature prime rib and alcoholic drinks on their menu. Despite its small size, providing less than four percent of company revenues, the Fifth Quarter chain has grown at a consistent 20 percent annually and is represented in five Southeast and Midwest states.

By the end of the 1970s Shoney's began to feel the constraints of a franchising agreement that limited its growth to an 11-state territory. In 1979 the company began to phase "Big Boy" marketing elements from its image. This was Shoney's first step toward severing its 25-year tie to Marriott Corporation. Shoney's forced the break when it built a restaurant in another Marriott franchisee's territory. Although the new restaurant eliminated all vestiges of Big Boy from its signs and menus, the other franchisee sued, thereby starting the breakup process, which was accomplished in 1984.

Shoney's was able to capitalize on its increasingly identifiable name and shift its menu and image toward a healthier concept as a result of the breakup. Disenfranchisement has enabled the company to distance itself from the "Big Boy" character's physical image and remove the signature double-decker hamburger from its menu. Since the "divorce,"

Continued Expansion in the 1980s

In 1981 Danner stepped aside to make David K. Wachtel the chief executive officer of Shoney's, while he remained on the board of directors. Wachtel, a product of the Shoney's management training program, had started with the company at age 16 as a dishwasher in Nashville, Tennessee, and had moved steadily through the ranks of busboy and cook to become the manager of the first Captain D's in 1969 at age 28. Wachtel immediately began to make changes in the Shoney's equation. He ended the company's 14-year franchise relationship with Heublein's Kentucky Fried Chicken for the same reason that Danner broke away from Marriott Big Boy: territorial limitations that set boundaries on growth.

Soon thereafter Wachtel bought Famous Recipe, a struggling Midwestern chicken chain. The Famous Recipe chain consisted of 225 stores founded by Lee Cummings, a nephew of Colonel Harland Sanders of Kentucky Fried Chicken fame. Shoney's worked to hone the Famous Recipe concept over the next few years by dropping unprofitable or mismanaged franchises, adopting a uniform "farmhouse" design, and diversifying the chain's menu. Management also gave the chain a more personal image by adding "Lee's" to the name and employing Cummings as concept spokesperson. By 1985 Lee's Famous Recipe had been "Shoneyized"; its sales rose 103 percent, and the chain spanned 23 states.

During this time Wachtel also introduced a restaurant innovation that revitalized Shoney's morning sales reports. The "all-you-can-eat" breakfast bar, brought on in 1981, reversed a ten-year decline in morning sales. By the end of the decade the breakfast bar boosted morning sales at company-owned restaurants to 25 percent of total sales.

Despite accelerated morning sales and a $3.4 million net profit made in selling Heublein and acquiring Famous Recipe, Danner and other board members and managers felt that Wachtel was expanding the company too quickly, and he resigned the position of chief executive officer after occupying it for less than one year. Danner then resumed the position of chief executive officer and spent the next seven years struggling to find a successor who would carry on his management ideals.

In 1986 he made J. Mitchel Boyd, a longtime franchisee and an originator of "Pargo's" specialty restaurants, chief executive officer and vice-chair. Boyd, his wife, Betty, and Gerry A. Brunetts had founded Pargo's, a restaurant in Manasses, Virginia, that featured such light fare as appetizers, pasta, salads, and sandwiches, and was expanded to include nine restaurants in Tennessee and Virginia. This restaurant was made a part of Shoney's specialty group when Boyd assumed his role as vice-chair at Shoney's.

In 1988 Danner engineered a $728 million recapitalization that paid shareholders a $16 per share cash dividend and paid Danner, who owned 19 percent of the stock at the time, $111 million in cash. The recapitalization was a clear sign that Danner was ready to hand Shoney's over to new management, and in 1989 he gave Boyd the chair.

It only took six months for Boyd's emphases on marketing and experimentation with menus and overall company image to clash with Danner's obsession with the day-to-day operations of the company. As with Wachtel, financial success did not earn Boyd any points. Leonard H. Roberts succeeded Boyd in December 1989 and has served as Shoney's chief executive officer and chairperson since that time. Roberts, known as something of a maverick in the restaurant industry, engineered Arby's Inc.'s five-year turnaround in the 1980s. However, when his relationship with Arby's Victor Posner became strained over franchisee relations, Roberts accepted the chair at Shoney's. Roberts attempted to capitalize on Shoney's organizational and management strengths, while also developing its marketing and research and development.

Roberts faced a very different task at Shoney's than the Arby's situation had demanded: he was expected to continue the financial and organizational success for which the company was known before the recapitalization. Shoney's had never had an unprofitable quarter and had in the mid-1980s been named "best managed restaurant company" in the United States by the *Wall Street Transcript*. At the same time, Roberts hoped to continue the territorial expansion that Danner and others had begun after the 1984 break from Big Boy. From 1984 to 1989, Shoney's had moved into Ohio and Florida, then Kentucky, Indiana, Texas, New Mexico, Oklahoma, and Maryland/Washington D.C., but the 1989 recapitalization hindered Shoney's ability to invest in expansion from within.

The 1989 Racial Discrimination Suit

Roberts faced another challenge early in his career at Shoney's. In 1989 the Legal Defense and Education fund of the National Association for the Advancement of Colored People (NAACP) brought a discrimination suit against the company. The suit, which originated in Florida, charged that Shoney's systematically discriminated against African Americans by limiting employment opportunities and job selection, creating what it termed "a hostile, racist work environment."

Shoney's signed an agreement with the Southern Christian Leadership Council (SCLC) in 1989 to invest over $90 million in minority business development, community service, and other socially responsible areas. The following year Shoney's launched an affirmative action strategy called "Workforce 2000." The program mandates equitable representation of minorities and women in Shoney's ranks. The company is using some programs that were already in place, like the scholarship program, and has added recruitment programs at 48 historically black colleges and universities to enhance its affirmative action efforts.

Although the NAACP case was not settled until late 1992, and the charges of racism still haunted the company's image in the early 1990s, its efforts had met with some quantifiable success by that time: minorities represented 30 percent of Shoney's employees. Shoney's encouragement of entrepreneurship among minority businesspeople through its Minority Franchise Development Program had increased the number of minority franchisees from two to 11 and the number of units owned and operated by minority franchisees from two to 14. The company's Minority Purchasing Program uses minority suppliers for everything from children's menus to food processing; from 1989 to 1992 annual purchasing from minority suppliers has increased from under $2 million to nearly $14 million.

Shoney's has also sought to polish its corporate image through philanthropic and community relations efforts. These include sponsorship of the Bootstrap Scholarship Awards, which honors Middle Tennessee high school seniors who have achieved academic success despite serious obstacles; support of the Southern Christian Leadership Conference; and support of the Tennessee Minority Purchasing Council's Business Opportunity Fair.

Roberts began to focus on franchising, a skill he honed while managing Arby's, and his primary goals are to add 500 franchises to Shoney's roster by the end of the 1990s and to "dominate the family segment." The company added 48 franchisees in fiscal 1991, and would have to increase that per-year figure in order to reach its goal by the turn-of-the-century. One franchising deal with Thompson Hospitality L.P., one of the largest minority-run food service operators in the country, has helped Shoney's further penetrate metropolitan Washington, D.C., and keep its agreement with the SCLC. Shoney's financed the $17 million deal to convert 31 former Marriott Big Boy restaurants into Shoney's by the mid-1990s.

To that end, Roberts tripled the size of the company's research and development staff and made that department part of marketing rather than operations. One of research and development's primary concerns was menu development, a high priority on Roberts's list.

In the early 1990s the wisdom of the 1988 recapitalization became manifest. Shoney's stock nearly tripled from 1989 to 1991 and the company's value grew accordingly, from $273 million to $809 million. Additionally, the company made extraordinary progress on debt retirement, having exceeded its scheduled payments by $155 million and reduced the debt's maturity by 3.5 years. Declining interest rates have not hurt the company, either; interest on debt dropped from a peak of 12.5 percent to nine percent.

A primary financial objective for the 1990s is a 20 percent annual increase in earnings, which will increase cash flow and enable Shoney's to retire more of its debt. As the debt is diminished, the company will free up more capital to invest in company stores, research and development, and expand its specialty chain. In order to achieve that goal, Shoney's instituted Project 80/85, a plan to increase customer satisfaction by setting goals of 80 percent customer satisfaction in 1992 and 85 percent in 1993.

In early November 1992, Shoney's, Inc. received provisional approval of a settlement in the discrimination lawsuit filed by the NAACP in 1989. The settlement addressed possible monetary damages for applicants and employees of the company restaurant entities and corporate office between February of 1985 and November 3, 1992. It was estimated that between 20,000 and 40,000 current employees, former workers, and applicants would share in the settlement. Under the settlement, Shoney's made $105 million available to pay potential claims. The company also agreed to pay $26 million of plaintiff legal expenses and $4 million in various related costs. The settlement resulted in a special charge of $77.2 million against earnings for the fourth quarter and fiscal year of 1992. The company expected that substantially all of the funds would be paid over a five-year period. The lawsuit appeared to have little impact on Shoney's stock. In fact, the company's stock price rose in the days following the announcement of the settlement.

Danner's reputation suffered in the wake of the settlement, however. A defendant in the suit, Danner was accused of encouraging racial bias at Shoney's. The company's burden in the settlement was eased when Danner contributed 83 percent of the settlement by putting up some of his Shoney's stock. In March 1993 the company paid $110 for the remainder of Danner's stock. At the same time Shoney's announced that Danner would not stand for reelection to the company's board. Other than the legacy of his substantial contributions to the company's growth, Danner's connection to the company was ended.

Continued Management Turmoil in the 1990s

In December of 1992 Len Roberts resigned as chief executive officer and chairman of Shoney's, Inc. Taylor Henry, Jr., an 18-year Shoney's veteran who played a significant role in 1988's recapitalization plan, succeeded Roberts in both positions.

Shoney's moved towards decentralization of its franchising efforts, including Project 500, leaving franchising to the individual restaurant chains. A strong cash flow helped ease the company's debt burden in 1993. By May, Shoney's total debt had been decreased by $250 million, to $518 million. The company also directed some of its cash to its remodeling budget. Set at $6.6 million in 1992, Shoney's remodeling budget was more than doubled to $15 million for both 1993 and 1994. The company hoped the investment would pay off: in the past, same-store sales grew more quickly for its remodeled restaurants.

Sales fell in the mid-1990s, and the company responded with yet another change in management in early 1995. President and CEO Henry resigned, to be replaced with turnaround specialist Stephen Lynn. Several other top managers also left at that time. The company also sold its private label food division, Mike Rose Foods, and Lee's Famous Recipe Chicken.

Some of the funds for that sale went toward purchasing Shoney's largest franchisee, TPI Restaurants, in 1996. The acquisition brought an additional 176 Shoney's Restaurants and 67 Captain D's into the company fold. The same year, Shoney's signed Andy Griffith as a spokesperson for the company.

The acquisition of TPI restaurants boosted fiscal 1997 revenues to $1.2 billion, up 12 percent from 1996. However, several factors led to a net loss for the year of $35.7 million. Shoney's closed 75 underperforming units in 1997 and took an asset impairment charge of $54 million because of underperforming restaurant properties. In addition, expenses from a proxy contest came to $5.3 million.

The proxy battle was initiated in 1997 by shareholders disappointed with the company's financial performance. To help resolve the fight, Shoney's added three new directors to the board in August. One of these, J. Michael Bodnar, replaced Lynn as CEO in November 1997. The management shakeup included W. Craig Barber, who resigned as senior executive vice-president and chief financial officer. As the company's sixth CEO in a little over 10 years, Bodnar faced the daunting task of providing Shoney's with the leadership it wanted and clearly needed.

Principal Divisions

Shoney's Restaurants; Captain D's; Casual Dining group.

Further Reading

Chaudhry, Rajan, ''Shoney's Mulls Life after Debt,'' *Restaurants & Institutions,* May 20, 1992.

Cheney, Karen, ''Cater to Kids, Please Parents,'' *Restaurants & Institutions,* July 8, 1992.

——, ''Food Bars, Light Items Wake Up Breakfast Patrons,'' *Restaurants & Institutions,* June 24, 1992.

Engardio, Pete, ''Shoney: Bursting Out of Its Dixie Boundaries,'' *Business Week,* April 15, 1985.

Feldman, Rona, ''Market Segment Report: Family,'' *Restaurant Business,* August 10, 1992.

Gindin, Rona, ''Shoney's Shows Who's Boss,'' *Restaurant Business,* October 10, 1985.

''Insights: Shoney's Expands A.M. Bar, Forecasts Unit Growth,'' *Restaurant Business,* January 1, 1988.

Kochilas, Diane, ''Leonard Roberts,'' *Restaurant Business,* May 20, 1991.

Konrad, Walecia, ''Shoney's Needs a Recipe for Succession,'' *Business Week,* December 25, 1989.

''Leonard Roberts: Can He Put More Meat on Shoney's?'' *Business Week,* October 8, 1990.

Raffio, Ralph, ''Market Segment Report: Family,'' *Restaurant Business,* October 10, 1991.

Rudolph, Barbara, ''Something Has to Be Wrong,'' *Forbes,* July 19, 1982.

''Shoney's Founder Divests His Stake,'' *Business Week,* March 22, 1993, p. 42.

''Shoney's Inc. Reports 1997 Results,'' *PR Newswire,* December 22, 1997.

''Shoney's Shines,'' *Forbes,* August 2, 1993, p. 152.

''Shoney's Taps Bodnar, a Dissident Director, to Be President, Chief,'' *Wall Street Journal,* November 13, 1997, p. B15.

—April Dougal
—updated by Susan Windisch Brown

SilverPlatter Information Inc.

100 River Ridge Drive
Norwood, Massachusetts 02062
U.S.A.
(781) 769-2599
Fax: (781) 769-8763
Web site: http://www.silverplatter.com

Wholly Owned Subsidiary of SilverPlatter International, N.V.

Incorporated: 1983
Employees: 200
Sales: $60 million (1995 est.)
SICs: 5045 Computers & Computer Peripheral Equipment & Software; 7375 Information Retrieval Services; 7372 Prepackaged Software; 7379 Computer Related Services, Not Elsewhere Classified

Although not well known to consumers, SilverPlatter Information Inc. is well known to librarians and information professionals for its electronic databases. *Library Journal* called SilverPlatter "the trailblazer of all library CD-ROM publishers." Commenting on the prevalence of CD-ROMs in libraries in the early 1990s, *Wilson Library Bulletin* noted, "One of the companies most responsible for this penetration into the library market is SilverPlatter, Inc., which (since 1983) has been at the forefront in the distribution of CD-ROM databases, the development of search software, and the creation of various CD-ROM networking and hardware solutions. SilverPlatter is also the first company to have developed library CD-ROM databases for both IBM PC and Macintosh computers." By the end of 1997 SilverPlatter offered more than 250 electronic databases from more than 120 data providers on CD-ROM or via the Internet.

Over the years, SilverPlatter has grown by working with three key types of business partners: distributors, information providers, and technology providers. While the company has offices around the world and more than 200 international distributors, it has focused on direct selling in the United States from its offices near Boston, Massachusetts. Key information providers have included library publishers such as H.W. Wilson Co., Gale Research, and R.R. Bowker Co.; scientific publishers such as Elsevier Science, Cambridge Scientific Abstracts, and Biological Abstracts (BIOSIS); medical information publishers such as the American Psychological Association and the U.S. National Library of Medicine; and the United Nations. Technology partners have contributed software and other enhancements as SilverPlatter made its databases available through a variety of gateways and user interfaces. In 1997, for example, SilverPlatter partnered with QuickDOC to allow users of its bibliographic databases to obtain the full content of journal articles via interlibrary loan.

Founded in 1983 by Bela Hatvany

SilverPlatter Information was formed in the United Kingdom in 1983 and incorporated in the United States the next year. It was the brainchild of Bela Hatvany, an information scientist who was working with a team of software engineers in London. He formed SilverPlatter Information to capitalize on the information storage capacities of CD-ROMs and to produce search software to make CD-ROMs more useful to researchers. Hatvany had first become involved with laser technology in 1972 when he worked on laser light pen barcode readers. CD-ROMs also utilize laser technology. In 1984 an important development in CD-ROM technology occurred when Philips and Sony introduced standardized CD-ROMs.

SilverPlatter was one of the first companies to create reference databases on CD-ROM. Its goal was to serve the library market, and the information in the databases would be supplied by well-known information providers. Throughout its history, SilverPlatter has been guided by Hatvany's vision of creating a global electronic library. His core strategy was "getting information to the public regardless of format," according to a company spokesperson quoted in *Library Journal* in 1994. The company has always served information professionals, students, and library patrons. When asked in 1994 if SilverPlatter intended to go into multimedia consumer products, Hatvany replied, "No. We really intend to stick to serving professionals and students with access to information containing answers, as well as educational materials for them."

Company Perspectives:

SilverPlatter provides electronic access to quality biblio-graphic and full-text databases using innovative technology via local, network and Internet access. SilverPlatter works collaboratively with publishers and data owners, library system vendors, and distributors worldwide to make avail-able the widest range of quality databases and greatest choice of access. With these partners, SilverPlatter shares its ERL [Electronic Reference Library] Technology, so that it can be used as a common technological framework on which digital libraries can be created and interconnected to form a Worldwide Library.

Demonstrated Prototype Databases in 1985

In 1985 SilverPlatter demonstrated some prototype data-bases on CD-ROM at the American Library Association conference. It had already begun working on its proprietary search and retrieval software, SPIRS, which stands for SilverPlatter Information Retrieval Software. In 1986 it introduced its first CD-ROMs to the library world. They included ERIC, the premier national bibliographic database of educational literature; PsycLIT, a subset of the American Psychological Association's PsycINFO database of citations to book and periodical literature (PsycINFO would later be added to SilverPlatter's CD-ROM collection); and A-V Online, a comprehensive database of educational audiovisual materials compiled by the National Information Center for Educational Media.

The PC-based version of SPIRS, which used DOS, was introduced at the same time. SPIRS provided users with a common interface, regardless of what database was being searched. Over the next few years SilverPlatter continued to expand its collection of databases on CD-ROM, from 13 databases in 1987 to 20 in 1988. By 1988 the company was able to offer libraries a local area networking (LAN) solution to allow multiple terminals to access the CD-ROM databases. With the introduction of MacSPIRS for the Macintosh in 1989 and a collection of 30 databases, Silver-Platter was the dominant CD-ROM database supplier for libraries at the end of the decade.

Planning an Electronic Reference Library in 1990

SilverPlatter began planning the Electronic Reference Li-brary (ERL) at the beginning of the 1990s. ERL was to be a type of library networking software that would allow libraries to create local area networks (LAN) and wide area networks (WAN). ERL was designed to create a "worldwide library" by linking library information systems around the world. The project was code-named Daffodil.

SilverPlatter offered 50 databases by 1990 and grew its collection to 100 databases by the end of 1991. Recognized as the dominant CD-ROM database vendor to libraries, the company and its founder received several awards in 1991. Bela Hatvany received the Entrepreneurial Excellence Award from the Optical Publishing Association; SilverPlatter's LAN solu-tion received the Product of the Year Award from Mecklermedia; and ERIC on MacSpirs was honored in the Awards Portfolio from *Media and Methods* magazine.

Search Advisor Developed in 1993

SilverPlatter established its Product Design/Usability Group in mid-1993 to apply usability testing to developments already in progress. The company's Search Advisor project offered the first opportunity to incorporate usability testing from the beginning. As described by Bela Hatvany, "It is designed so intermediaries can incarnate their knowledge of searching into the interface, so they don't need to be at the elbow of the user." For example, Search Advisor would allow librarians to write customized search scripts to simplify searching for their novice users.

Until 1993, work on the Search Advisor had focused on SPIRS for DOS. Then, SilverPlatter decided that a Windows interface would be better. This decision coincided with the establishment of the Product Design/Usability Group, so proto-types of the Windows interface could be tested in a simulated searching environment. For the Search Advisor project, stu-dents at the Graduate School of Library and Information Science at Simmons College in Boston, Massachusetts, were called on to help with the test. Usability testing was conducted in a controlled environment at the SilverPlatter offices as well as in an actual library setting. SilverPlatter claimed that such testing improved the confidence level not only of the developers, but also of potential customers. As one of the associate professors told *CD-ROM Professional* magazine, "When I know a soft-ware interface has been usability tested, I have a lot more confidence it's going to work."

In spite of its user-assisted development, Search Advisor was not completed for delivery to customers. In the process of developing it, SilverPlatter gained valuable experience in terms of establishing testing protocols and involving customers in the development process.

Introducing Electronic Reference Library (ERL) in 1994

After four years of development, SilverPlatter introduced the Electronic Reference Library (ERL), a client/server solution that addressed the need in libraries for wide area access. The ERL was designed to support multiple servers in large, high-access environments, such as research libraries. It allowed insti-tutions to provide easy and powerful local and remote access to information across a range of networking environments. The ERL could be maintained and administered across multiple campuses and consortia. Its ERL ADMIN program enabled system administrators to set up and maintain user authorization accounts and monitor usage statistics.

Perhaps more significantly from the user's perspective, ERL Technology provided for simultaneous searching of all Silver-Platter databases available on the network, regardless of the database location. With one search, users could simultaneously search local CD-ROM drives, local ERL servers, and remote databases via the Internet. That eliminated the need to conduct the same search multiple times for databases loaded locally and remotely.

With ERL Technology, users could choose from the widest selection of server platforms, which eventually included Sun Solaris, SCO-UNIX, IBM AIX, Windows/NT, and LINUX. Databases would be searchable from a choice of WinSPIRS in French, German, Spanish, and English; MacSPIRS; PC-SPIRS, and UNIX-SPIRS interfaces. Users could also access Silver-Platter databases via the Internet using any SPIRS interface as well as the WebSPIRS gateway, introduced in 1995.

SilverPlatter's founder, Bela Hatvany, shared his vision of ERL with *Searcher* magazine in 1994. "ERL lends itself to building a world library of information that is accessible from many different hardware platforms, from many different software programs, that is accessible by users regardless of their locations, and that incorporates the expertise of search intermediaries."

In 1995 ERL was named Outstanding Product of the Year Award by Mecklermedia and its magazine, *Computers in Libraries.* By 1997 ERL was installed at 550 sites worldwide.

SilverPlatter also introduced WinSPIRS for Windows in 1994. Up to this time SPIRS had been available only in DOS software. WinSPIRS added many new features that made the search and retrieval software comparable to that found in its competitors' software, such as DIALOG OnDisc, CD Plus Ovid, and Online Computer System's Plus. These features included browsing field-specific indexes, posting information in the thesaurus, truncating with field specifications, and using multiple field qualifiers. When first introduced, WinSPIRS was tailored for only a few of the databases. SilverPlatter subsequently changed some aspects of its other databases to take advantage of WinSPIRS' capabilities.

In reviewing WinSPIRS for *Online* magazine in 1995, Peter Jasco noted, "WinSPIRS looks like a software designed from the ground up, religiously following the design principles of Windows applications. While some important browsing and search features are still not available, the user interface is a design masterpiece that is inviting to even the most computer-phobic users."

SilverPlatter and the Internet: 1995

SilverPlatter introduced an Internet subscription service to provide Internet access to SilverPlatter-hosted databases at the American Library Association conference in 1994. By 1995 it had introduced WebSPIRS for World Wide Web access to the databases. With Internet and World Wide Web use growing at tremendous speed, SilverPlatter decided to make its collection of databases available over the Internet. At the company's web site, initially called SilverPlatter World, documentation was provided on the company, its specific products and activities, and other features. Its Internet Index appeared as a web page that indexed information alphabetically and by subject.

Through ERL, SilverPlatter's entire collection of CD-ROM databases became available as a dial-up service on the Internet. Subscribers paid for Internet access in the same way they paid for CD-ROM access. They had to determine in advance which databases they wanted to access and pay subscription fees for. SilverPlatter offered a selection of search engines that would work with Windows, DOS, Macintosh, and Unix.

With use of the Internet and World Wide Web growing even faster in 1996 and 1997, SilverPlatter introduced Search by Search, a pay-as-you-go search service on the Internet. It was introduced in June 1997 at the American Library Association conference and made available to the marketplace by the fall of 1997. This research tool included more than 60 databases grouped into 13 subject clusters. It utilized SilverPlatter's Internet gateway, WebSPIRS. Customers would be registered and billed on a fee-per-use basis, with database usage tracked by the software. A company spokesperson said, "Pay-per-use pricing will allow libraries to expand collections by including access to titles not previously in their core collections."

Search by Search allowed searchers to either look at a single database or to select a subject and search across some or all of the databases. They could also command WebSPIRS to identify the databases that contained the search term. The system worked with either Netscape Navigator or Microsoft Internet Explorer. Search by Search was developed in conjunction with Imark Technologies, a Reston, Virginia, company, and utilized its proprietary NET-MAX software.

Although SilverPlatter was still perceived as a CD-ROM publisher, some 200 of its more than 250 database products were available over the Internet by the end of 1997.

SilverPlatter offered more than 250 databases by the end of 1997. Among the databases added during 1997 were Books in Print and other R.R. Bowker databases, including American Library Directory, Ulrich's International Periodical Directory, Library and Information Science Abstracts, and American Men and Women of Science. Marquis Who's Who, published by another Reed Elsevier company, National Register Publishing, was also added. The databases were made available on CD-ROM, hard disk, and via the Internet. Users had a choice of interfaces: Windows, DOS, Mac, UNIX, Z39.50, and web browser.

SilverPlatter also introduced DVD-ROM for selected databases. A company spokesperson said, "DVD will make larger databases more manageable. DVD has seven times the storage capacity of CD-ROM." The first database that was made available on DVD-ROM was The Union Catalogue of Belgian Research Libraries. It was introduced in December 1996 at Online Information '96 in London, England. By the February midwinter meeting of the American Library Association, SilverPlatter also had the MEDLINE Advanced database available on DVD-ROM. New DVD readers were introduced later in 1997 by Pioneer Electronics, who was one of SilverPlatter's partners in this project. DVD is an optical disc technology that enables data to be stored in two layers on each side of the disc. Each layer had almost four gigabytes of storage capacity. According to a company press release, DVD drives are also able to read traditional CD-ROMs and provide 30 times the capacity of standard CD-ROMs.

From its inception, SilverPlatter has always been at the forefront of the information explosion, finding ways to make information databases available to the widest possible range of users. It was one of the first to publish information on CD-ROM and to help libraries adapt that format to their needs. It worked with libraries to provide LAN and WAN solutions to data access. With the widespread use of the Internet and the World Wide Web, the company found ways to make its collection of databases available to users through the World Wide Web.

Further Reading

Ensor, Pat, "SilverPlatter Embraces the Future: The Electronic Reference Library Becomes a Reality," *Computers in Libraries,* June 1994, p. 28.

Herther, Nancy K., "Dancing with Life: Talking About the Future of CD-ROM and SilverPlatter with Bela Hatvany," *CD-ROM Professional,* September 1993, p. 70.

Jasco, Peter, "WinSPIRS: Windows Software for SilverPlatter CD-ROMs," *Online,* January–February 1995, p. 74.

Kalseth, Karl, "Sharing Knowledge Is a Love Experience," *FID News Bulletin,* July–August 1997, p. 206.

Kesselman, Martin, "A Look at SilverPlatter, Inc.," *Wilson Library Bulletin,* September 1991, p. 80.

Morley, Elizabeth, "The SilverPlatter Experience," *CD-ROM Professional,* March 1995, p. 111.

Quint, Barbara E., "The Inevitable Internet Onslaught," *Wilson Library Bulletin,* May 1995, p. 64.

——, "SilverPlatter Leadership: Interview with Bela Hatvany," *Searcher,* September 1994.

Rogers, Michael, "SilverPlatter Expands with New Services and Partnerships," *Library Journal,* December 1994, p. 29.

Samson, Patricia M., "SilverPlatter Appoints Brian Earle President and CEO," *Business Wire,* January 14, 1997.

"SilverPlatter Laser Discs Offer Alternative to Online," *Library Journal,* May 1, 1985, p. 22.

—David Bianco

Southwire Company, Inc.

One Southwire Drive
Carrollton, Georgia 30119
U.S.A.
(770) 832-4242
Fax: (770) 832-4929
Web site: http://www.southwire.com

Private Company
Incorporated: 1950
Employees: 5,000
Sales: $1.7 billion (1997 est.)
SICs: 3312 Blast Furnaces & Steel Mills; 3341
  Secondary Nonferrous Metals; 3351 Copper Rolling
  & Drawing; 3355 Aluminum Rolling & Drawing, Not
  Elsewhere Classified; 3356 Nonferrous Rolling and
  Drawing Not Elsewhere Classified; 3357 Nonferrous
  Wiredrawing & Insulating; 3496 Miscellaneous
  Fabricated Wire Products; 3559 Special Industrial
  Machinery Not Elsewhere Classified

Southwire Company, Inc., is the largest manufacturer of copper and aluminum rod, wire, and cable in the United States. Throughout its history as a leading supplier of rod, wire, and cable for use in the transmission and distribution of electricity, the company made significant technological advances that have been adopted by the worldwide wire and cable industry. As of 1998, Southwire's products included building and utility wire and cable, industrial power cable, communications cable, and such specialty products as transit-system cabling.

Entrepreneurial Beginnings

The creation of Southwire is a classic example of entrepreneurial spirit facing unfavorable odds and triumphing. Shortly after graduating from Georgia Institute of Technology, Roy Richards, who ran his father's sawmill by the time he was 14 years old, started his own business in 1937. Called Roy Richards Construction Company, it was an extension of his father's sawmill. Six months after opening his business, the 25-year-old Richards was awarded a $118,000 Rural Electrification Administration (REA) contract to set the poles and string the wire for 108 miles of power lines in Georgia.

Although REA officials were somewhat anxious about Richards' young age and lack of experience, his construction of the Georgia power lines garnered high praise and additional REA contracts. In fact, Richards' method of setting poles and stringing wire had reduced the time it took to build a year's worth of power lines to three months, a process soon adopted by REA contractors nationwide. By 1939 Richards' company had strung 3,500 miles of power lines for the REA throughout Georgia and Alabama, establishing it as the second largest constructor of power lines for the REA in the nation. Two years later, the company was awarded its first international contract to construct a power generation station in St. Croix in the Virgin Islands.

By the time Richards' work was completed in the Virgin Islands, the Japanese had bombed Pearl Harbor and the United States had entered World War II. The onset of the war marked a significant decline in the number of REA contracts offered, so Richards decided to actively join the war effort and enlisted in the U.S. Army. Shortly after his return in 1945, Richards landed a contract to build 500 miles of an electrical transmission line in Georgia. The war, however, had severely limited the amount of aluminum wire available. Richards canvassed all of the large wire manufacturers and was told that he would have to wait a minimum of three years to receive enough wire to complete his 500-mile project. Faced with either waiting for the aluminum companies to deliver the wire and losing the contract in Georgia, or manufacturing the wire himself, Richards opted for the latter. In 1950, with $80,000 in capital and the assistance of a professor of mechanical engineering under whom he had studied during college, Richards created Southwire Company.

Hiring 12 employees who worked with second-hand machinery in a 12,000 square-foot building, Richards set up operations to manufacture copper and aluminum wire for his first customer—himself. Industry pundits had warned Richards that his remote location would make the shipping of raw materials too costly and that the number of skilled labor available in the area could not support his venture. Richards, however, proved

444

Company Perspectives:

We will design, produce, and market products and services which exceed the expectations of our customers. We will create an environment in which personal involvement leads to individual satisfaction and continuous improvement. We will achieve long-term prosperity and success as a profitable business competing in the world marketplace.

them wrong and produced his first lot of copper and aluminum wire in four months. By the end of its second year, Southwire had shipped five million pounds of wire, amassed $560,000 in sales, and doubled the size of its manufacturing facility.

1950s–60s: Growth and Innovation

Having achieved remarkable results in his first two years of operation, Richards then began searching for a way to improve the quality of his wire. Wire is made by winnowing a thicker stock of aluminum or copper, called a "rod," into a smaller diameter to reach the desired thickness. Traditionally, segments of rod were welded together, end to end, to create a continuous roll that was then compressed and stretched into a strand of wire. Welding the rods together, however, created a weak wire and, frequently, a strand of wire would break at the location of the weld.

Wishing to somehow avoid the inherent weakness that welding caused, Richards traveled to Italy to investigate a method developed by an Italian industrialist named Illario Properzi for continuously casting and rolling rod. Properzi's casting method had only been used with commercial grade lead and zinc, and he was convinced the method would not work with aluminum electrical wire due to the vastly different metallurgical properties between the metals. Richards nevertheless signed a contract for the rights to the process, and after a year of experimentation by Southwire engineers, a machine was developed that would continuously cast aluminum rod.

Next, Richards sought to make the process applicable to copper rod, which posed even greater metallurgical problems. After five years of tests on its own, Southwire entered into an agreement with Western Electric Company, and experiments continued under the joint venture for several more years. Finally, in 1963, a suitable process was developed. This process, known as the Southwire Continuous Rod (SCR) system, marked a revolutionary advance in wire production technology and immediately began being employed by other wire manufacturers. Eventually, 90 percent of copper rod for electrical wire and cable produced in major industrial countries would be manufactured by continuous casting systems, half of which would be designed and built by Southwire.

After presiding over the successful completion of Southwire's experimentation with copper wire production, Richards began exploring the possibility of constructing his own aluminum smelter to produce the aluminum needed in wire production. Unable to finance the construction on his own, Richards searched for a partner in the venture and by 1967 had signed an agreement with Copper Range Company to build a $90 million plant. A copper strike and other projects Copper Range was involved with, however, forced Copper Range to withdraw from its involvement with the project.

The fact that labor difficulties were partly to blame for the collapse of the negotiations between Southwire and Copper Range must have irritated Richards to some extent. A man who chose to guard both himself and his company from public scrutiny, Richards disapproved of organized labor and went to great lengths to keep its presence from penetrating Southwire. For years, a classic anti-union film, *And Women Must Weep*, was shown on Fridays to inculcate his opinion of the union movement to new Southwire employees. During one particularly contentious incident in the 1960s, Richards reportedly hired private detectives to pose as Southwire employees in order to identify union sympathizers on his payroll.

The frustration over the Southwire-Copper Range agreement, however, was short-lived. In 1968 Southwire and National Steel Corporation agreed to build a 135,000-ton, $200 million aluminum smelter in Kentucky. The joint venture, called National-Southwire Aluminum, became upon its formation the seventh-largest primary aluminum producer in the United States. In a peripheral deal, Richards sold 20 percent of Southwire to National Steel for $25 million, which provided him with the necessary working capital to build his own copper smelter in 1971.

By the late 1960s Southwire had evolved from a business created to supply Richards' construction company with wire into a thriving company that far exceeded the original objectives established for it. With sales of $80 million in 1967, Southwire had two plants fabricating electrical wire and cable in Georgia and one in San Juan, Puerto Rico.

Dramatic Growth in the 1970s

The addition of aluminum and copper smelters helped spawn a decade of dramatic growth in the 1970s. Sales in 1970 stood at $123 million and ballooned to $723 million by 1980. This success was partly attributable to Richards' efforts to vertically integrate the company. In addition to the two smelters, Richards operated a sawmill to make shipping pallets and spools from his own timber, a plastics processing plant to prepare wire installations, and owned a fleet of trucks to transport his products. When the oil crisis in 1973 limited the availability of natural gas supplies for his aluminum smelter, Richards drilled gas and oil wells to mitigate the effects of the energy crisis on his operations.

Not all attempts at achieving vertical integration were successful, however. In 1971 Southwire and National Steel signed an agreement with Earth Sciences Inc. to mine and develop a mineral called alunite as an alternative for another mineral, bauxite, in the production of alumina, the raw material from which aluminum is refined. Traditionally, bauxite had been used, but reports of Soviet scientists working on a process to replace bauxite with alunite persuaded Southwire and its partners to develop an alunite process of their own. With a 25 percent interest in the venture, Southwire built a pilot plant and began mining property owned by Earth Sciences in Utah, Colorado, Arizona, and Nevada. The project was expanded in 1973 and then again two years later, but a solution was never found and the project was abandoned.

Despite this failure, Southwire, by 1976, was the third-largest wire producer in the United States, ranking behind Western Electric and United Technologies' Essex Group. With sales of $400 million, the company had become a major force in the industry, competing with such giant corporations as Anaconda, Kaiser, and Reynolds Metals. Flushed with success on the domestic front, Southwire's international involvement had also grown. By 1976 overseas business had intensified, accounting for ten percent of the company's revenues. It now had facilities operating in England and Venezuela and had signed a contract to build and manage a $500 million aluminum plant in Dubai, Saudi Arabia.

Recession Leads to Losses

After a decade of robust growth, Southwire entered the 1980s with optimism, expecting to expand its operations and collect further profits. But the geometric rise in sales during the 1970s plummeted in the early 1980s. After posting record sales of $723 million in 1980, sales the following year dropped to $606 million for a net loss of $9.15 million; in 1983 the company's net loss totaled nearly $30 million. Part of the explanation for the sudden collapse was the deleterious effect the worldwide recession had on the housing and automobile industries, both of which were major customers of Southwire's products. Also, throughout the late 1970s and into the 1980s, Southwire continued to borrow large sums of money, convinced the growth of the 1970s would continue into the 1980s. As the recession pushed interest rates skyward, Southwire's interest payments began to drain its cash flow. Yet, during this economic slide, Richards continued to expand, adding a $30 million copper rod mill in 1981.

By 1984 the end of the recession had extricated Southwire from its financial malaise. Upswings in housing construction and the automobile industry buoyed the company's sales, and the elimination of inefficient and unprofitable operations improved the profitability of the company. Several plants in New Jersey and Puerto Rico were closed, ventures in the steel conduit business were dropped, and Kagan-Dixon-Eldra, a joint venture with an Austrian company to manufacture magnet wire in Arkansas, was abandoned.

In June 1985 Richards died of bone cancer. Two of his sons, Roy, Jr., and James, assumed the leadership of Southwire, which now—after the streamlining of the early 1980s—posted sales of more than $600 million. With Roy Richards, Jr., as chief executive officer and James Richards as president, Southwire began to diversify its product line to increase its customer base. In 1986 the company acquired a building wire and cable plant in Utah and three years later purchased Hi-Tech Cable Corporation, one of the largest copper wire and cable production facilities in the United States.

Diversification and Globalization in the 1990s

In 1991 Southwire purchased the remaining 54.5 percent interest in National-Southwire Aluminum originally held by National Steel. Also that year Southwire bought the assets of AT&T Nassau Metals Corporation, from which Gaston Copper Recycling Corporation was formed, making Southwire the largest recycler of copper in the United States. Southwire returned to the conduit business in 1992 with the purchase of Integral Corporation, a manufacturer of cable-in-conduit.

Southwire's efforts in the early 1990s to increase its international sales weren't without challenge. The company targeted Japan for expansion, both because Japanese utilities bought large amounts of aluminum cable and because Southwire already had a presence in the country through its sales of equipment for continuous casting of metal rod. Southwire offered large aluminum wire with a steel core needed for transmitting electricity at prices 20 to 30 percent lower than those offered by Japanese manufacturers, but the Japanese utilities continued to use their traditional Japanese suppliers. Having met all of Japan's technical standards, Southwire complained of what it perceived as an unfairly closed market to the U.S. government, yet the company persevered in its efforts to sell to Japan.

Although increasing exports remained a high priority for the company, it also pursued revenues outside the United States by building international plants and establishing joint ventures in other countries. In 1997, the company's subsidiary Integral began manufacturing cable-in-conduit products from a new facility in Malaysia. Late in 1997 Southwire revealed plans to open a plant in Mexico to make metal-clad cable for sale in the United States and to make wire and cable products for the Mexican market. A joint venture with India to make aluminum overhead cables in that country was in the works for late in the 1990s.

Through its subsidiary Forte Power Systems, Inc., Southwire pursued exports in Europe, Asia, and South America in the late 1990s. Forte Power Systems expanded its ability to manufacture high voltage underground cables, a product much in demand in those areas, and hired international marketing experts.

Southwire's vice-president of international development, Glenn Mann, explained the company's globalization plan: "Our strategic plan is to enter those markets where we can apply our core competencies, leading-edge technology and focus on quality and customer service."

The company was not only entering new countries but new markets as well. In 1997 Southwire introduced CyberLAN twisted-pair cables, the first of a whole line of telecommunications and data communications cable products. The market for twisted pair cables was expected to reach $1.8 billion in the United States by 2001.

Southwire made remarkable progress in its first five decades, especially given the circumstances of its creation. Beginning with only a casual understanding of how to manufacture wire, Roy Richards quickly became a leader in the industry and transformed his modest 12-employee company into one of the premier wire manufacturers in the United States. Although sales in 1997 remained flat, demand for higher margin products led to Southwire's most profitable year. With another generation of the Richards family leading the company and hoping to build upon the legacy established by their father, prospects looked favorable for Southwire.

Principal Subsidiaries

Forte Power Systems, Inc.; Integral Corporation; Southwire Cyber Technologies, Inc.

Principal Divisions

Southwire Wire and Cable Division; Southwire Copper Division; Southwire Machinery Division; Southwire Aluminum Rod Area; NSA, A Division of Southwire; Southwire Specialty Products; Southwire Georgia Wire Products; SCR Technology; Southwire Comsumer Products Division.

Further Reading

"Copper Range, Southwire to Build Jointly $90 Million Aluminum Plant in Kentucky," *Wall Street Journal,* October 20, 1967, p. 4.
Cumming, Joseph B., *Roy Richards,* Carrollton, Ga.: Southwire Company, 1987.
"Earth Sciences Inc.'s Joint Venture Widened," *Wall Street Journal,* January 17, 1973, p. 7.
Keatley, Robert, "Georgia's Southwire Cites Small Orders, Big Runaround, in Trade with Japan," *Wall Street Journal,* July 30, 1993, p. A6.
Lauterbach, Jeffrey R., "Southwire's Empire Builder Struggles to Hang On," *Industry Week,* May 2, 1983, pp. 35–38.
"Live Wire," *Forbes,* August 1, 1976, p. 26.
"National Steel Slates Aluminum Smelter Venture," *Wall Street Journal,* May 9, 1968, p. 6.
"Roy Richards: Money for Good Ideas," *Forbes,* May 1, 1967, p. 72.
Southwire Company Corporate History, Carrollton, Ga.: Southwire Company, 1993.
"Southwire Creates a New World of Opportunity," *Business Wire,* October 2, 1997.

—Jeffrey L. Covell
—updated by Susan Windisch Brown

Sport Supply Group, Inc.

1901 Diplomat Drive
Farmers Branch, Texas 75234
U.S.A.
(972) 484-9484
Fax: (972) 247-4743

Public Company
Incorporated: 1982
Employees: 395
Sales: $79.1 million (1997)
Stock Exchanges: New York American
SICs: 3949 Sporting & Athletic Goods, Not Elsewhere
    Classified; 3462 Iron & Steel Forgings; 5961 Catalog
    & Mail-Order Houses

The largest direct mail distributor of sports-related equipment in the United States, Sport Supply Group, Inc. manufactures and markets approximately 8,000 products to public and private schools, state and local governments, and youth sports leagues, among other institutional markets. During the late 1990s, Sport Supply maintained a mailing list comprising more than 200,000 names and marketed its products to more than 100,000 institutional, retail, mass merchant, and team dealer customers. The company manufactured 3,000 of the 8,000 products it sold at four manufacturing facilities. At Sport Supply's two plants in Anniston, Alabama, the company manufactured game tables, gymnastics, netting, and tennis and baseball equipment. At its plant in Cerritos, California, the company manufactured gymnastic equipment. Soccer field equipment and weight room equipment were manufactured at the company's manufacturing plant in Farmers Branch, Texas.

Origins in BSN Corp.

When Sport Supply emerged in 1991, its presence signaled the return of Michael Blumenfeld, a one-time professional athlete who twice tried to establish a successful sporting goods distributorship. His first attempt was a company named BSN Corp., which was originally named Blumenfeld Sports Net Co.

BSN rose to powerful heights during the 1980s, then quickly floundered, prompting Blumenfeld to regroup and try again. His second effort was Sport Supply, a company whose historical roots were intertwined with its predecessor, BSN. Explored together, the history of Blumenfeld's two companies charts a prodigious rise in the sporting goods industry, beginning with a business born in the back of a pickup truck and its evolution into the largest direct mail marketer of sporting goods equipment in the United States. During this nearly three-decade-long period, Blumenfeld took a roller coaster ride in the business world, experiencing the pitfalls and the rewards of operating in a hotly contested industry. His journey began in the early 1970s, shortly after he took off his baseball cleats for the last time.

As a high school student, Blumenfeld showed considerable athletic promise. He was signed by the St. Louis Cardinals out of high school and entered the club's farm system, spending two years playing outfield in the minor leagues. In 1966, Blumenfeld's baseball career was cut short by nagging knee problems, forcing him to look for a job outside of baseball. Blumenfeld did not exit the realm of sports entirely, however. By the early 1970s, he was struggling to make a living selling tennis nets. He drove around Memphis, Tennessee, selling tennis nets to the region's tennis and country clubs from the back of his truck. It was a modest start, to be sure, but the absence of conventional business trappings did not discourage Blumenfeld and his wife from taking great care of their fledgling entrepreneurial creation. After each sale, Blumenfeld and his wife mailed the customer a hand-drawn brochure describing the merchandise they had for sale. Over time, customers began asking for items not included within the brochure, so Blumenfeld searched for a supplier and added the new merchandise to his brochure.

Before long, the hand-drawn brochures developed into genuine catalogs, filled with page after page of sporting goods merchandise. As the size of the catalogs increased, so did the size of BSN, maturing from a start-up business venture into a legitimate, money-making company. By the end of the 1970s, Blumenfeld found himself running a robustly growing mail order operation that was generating millions of dollars in sales each year. For those in the sporting goods industry who had not noticed BSN, they soon would. In 1980, when annual sales reached $3 million, Blumenfeld sold shares in BSN to the public.

The money raised from BSN's initial public offering would be needed as Blumenfeld led his company into the 1980s. He was facing a deleterious problem, and its cause was the enviable success of his sporting goods distributorship. BSN had achieved remarkable strides in its relatively short existence, emerging from nowhere to compete as a recognizable and fast-growing concern in an industry populated by companies with considerably more experience. As Blumenfeld perceived the situation, the more established retail operators in the country were becoming increasingly concerned about BSN's resolute growth and the threat it represented. They were losing business to an upstart company. BSN had to be stopped. Blumenfeld claimed the reaction against his company was conspiratorial. He claimed merchants had threatened him with baseball bats at trade shows. When threats failed to stop burgeoning BSN, merchants voiced their complaints to their suppliers, the same businesses that supplied Blumenfeld with merchandise. The suppliers, reportedly, sided with their more established retail customers and cut Blumenfeld off from some of the merchandise he depended on. Blumenfeld, who felt he was being shouldered aside by the industry's heavyweights, answered with a new strategy, one that would dramatically change the face of BSN.

With some of his suppliers refusing to do business with him, Blumenfeld decided that he could either fade away or fight back. He opted for the latter alternative and devised a solution. He decided he would integrate backwards and acquire sporting goods manufacturers, thereby greatly reducing his dependence on suppliers for merchandise. In the future, BSN would be both a manufacturer and a distributor. Blumenfeld acquired his first manufacturer in 1981, a tennis and golf equipment manufacturer named Rol-Dri, Inc. Rol-Dri was the first of many acquisitions to follow, as Blumenfeld pursued his objective of acquiring enough sporting goods manufacturers to produce 75 percent of all the products BSN sold through its catalogs. By 1985, Blumenfeld had acquired 13 manufacturers, each typically small, but together the acquired manufacturers encompassed a broad range of athletic and leisure equipment, apparel, and accessories. Blumenfeld acquired companies such as Hammatt & Sons, a producer of table games, Champion Barbell, which produced weightlifting equipment, and Nelson Knitting Co., a manufacturer of athletic hosiery. With the addition of these companies and others, roughly half of BSN's $30 million in sales during the mid-1980s were derived from products it manufactured itself. At this juncture in the company's history, it was offering more than 3,000 products at discounts of up to 30 percent over retail, selling everything from tennis balls to baseball backstops through more than three million catalogs mailed each year. In the space of four years, Blumenfeld had made another meaningful leap. A mighty distributor had also become a rising manufacturer. As was the case with BSN's admirable growth as a distributor, the company's evolution into a manufacturer also spawned its own problems. For Blumenfeld, success was never easy.

Poised as a rising contender in the manufacturing segment of the sporting goods industry, Blumenfeld now found himself butting heads with much larger manufacturers such as Wilson, MacGregor, Rawlings, and Spalding. BSN was much smaller than these rivals, however, and needed a large acquisition to narrow the chasm separating it from its rivals. Blumenfeld tried on several occasions during the mid-1980s to acquire a company that would make BSN a major player overnight, but each time his bids were rebuffed. He tried to buy Riddell Sports, the largest maker of football helmets in the country, but his offer of $7 million in cash and stock was spurned. He tried to buy Wilson Sporting Goods, offering $151 million in BSN stock, and again his offer was brushed aside. Next, he attempted to buy Bike Athletics, the country's second-largest football helmet manufacturer, but no one would listen to his proposal. The cloud of conspiracy that had settled into Blumenfeld's mind when suppliers cut him off years earlier came back. "We're considered the renegade of the world," Blumenfeld remarked to a *Forbes* reporter. "People fear that BSN is doing so well by itself, for God's sake don't give them something they can sink their teeth into."

While concern over the threat posed by a new competitor may have played its part in Blumenfeld's failed deals, the *en masse* refusal of larger companies to accept Blumenfeld's tender offers was chiefly because most of the bids included BSN stock as part of the purchase price. At the time of Blumenfeld's various acquisition attempts, BSN's stock was not performing well, its vitality drained discernibly by the sundry acquisitions completed during the first half of the 1980s. Despite slipping earnings, Blumenfeld moved forward, his conviction to expand BSN through acquisitions made stronger by the cold shoulder he received from the sporting goods community. By 1987, Blumenfeld had achieved his goal of manufacturing 75 percent of the merchandise sold in his catalogs. The company by this point, with sales eclipsing $70 million, ranked as the nation's leading reconditioner of football equipment, the largest manufacturer of cheerleader's uniforms and supplies, and the largest direct distributor of sports equipment to the institutional marketplace. Again, however, success had its price.

BSN Falters in Late 1980s; Sport Supply Emerges

Before Blumenfeld's decade-long acquisition binge was over, he purchased 48 companies, consisting of dozens of small distributors, manufacturers, and retailers. Some of these acquisitions did not readily fit into BSN's corporate structure, while others were losing money prior to their acquisition. Several of the companies were mired in bankruptcy proceedings. The result was an externally strong company, leading the field in several lucrative markets, with profound internal problems. BSN was a money-loser. Between 1989 and 1991, the company lost more than $15 million, too much for Blumenfeld to contend with. He decided to start anew from the ashes of BSN and sold much of what he had purchased to gain the financial resources to muster another attempt in the sporting goods industry. In his mid-40s at this turning point, Blumenfeld made plans for the future, a future in which Sport Supply would be the corporate vehicle to lift him out of the valley where BSN had been abandoned.

A complex series of refinancing transactions gave birth to Sport Supply Group, Inc. and gave Blumenfeld another chance at creating a successful sporting goods distributor. He took the company public in April 1991, and began the rebuilding process. On the heels of the initial public offering, Sport Supply's customer base was broadened to include retailers such as J.C. Penney, Sears, and Wal-Mart, while Blumenfeld scoured the country in search of acquisition targets. To those who winced at the thought of Blumenfeld embarking on another acquisition campaign, there was some mollification to be found in Blumenfeld's promise that he had learned his lesson during the 1980s. In the future, he declared, Sport Supply would buy only profitable distributors and perhaps a few small manufacturers that fit the company's distribution channels.

Sport Supply in the 1990s

Between 1991 and 1994, Sport Supply acquired 12 sporting goods distributors and signed several important licensing agreements, including the rights to manufacture, market, and distribute merchandise under the MacGregor trade name (obtained in 1992) and an exclusive license agreement with AMF Bowling, Inc. to use the AMF name (acquired in 1993) in connection with the promotion and sale of gymnastics equipment in the United States and Canada. During this three-year period, annual sales increased from $47 million to $67 million. More importantly, the company's stock price rose strongly, more than doubling between 1991 and 1994.

The mid-1990s were years of expansion and divestment for Sport Supply, as the company strengthened its position as a distributor of sporting goods and leisure merchandise to the institutional market. In June 1995, the company acquired the Nitro Golf division from Prince Golf International, Ltd., a manufacturer and distributor of new golf balls. A strategic decision implemented a short time later made Nitro Golf only a short-term component of Sport Supply's business, but a deal concluded later in the year had a more lasting effect on the company's business. In December 1995, Sport Supply signed a three-year agreement with Little League Baseball, Incorporated that designated the company as the "Official Factory Direct Equipment Supplier of Little League Baseball." The deal opened the doors to the estimated three million participants of Little League Baseball, adding measurably to Sport Supply's revenues. In August 1997, the agreement with Little League Baseball was extended through 2001.

While the two agreements with Little League Baseball were being negotiated between the end of 1995 and 1997, the company made the strategic decision to dispose of its golf operations to focus on its core institutional business. In May 1996, Sport Supply sold virtually all the assets of its Gold Eagle Professional Products Division, which sold golf accessory products to the retail market. In March 1997, another golf divestiture was made when Nitro Leisure Products, Inc., acquired two years earlier, was sold.

Sport Supply entered the late 1990s having completed the rebuilding process that began when the company was spun off from BSN. Sales for the 11-month period ended September 1997 flirted with the $80 million mark, while the company's net earnings stood at a respectable $2.6 million. Sport Supply ranked as the largest direct mail marketer of sports-related equipment to the institutional market in the United States, making the majority of its sales to schools, universities, athletic clubs, youth sport leagues, government agencies, recreational organizations, and military facilities. To these customers, who typically purchased large quantities of merchandise, Sport Supply offered roughly 8,000 products, 3,000 of which the company manufactured at its four manufacturing plants in Alabama, California, and Texas. Whether or not the company would fall victim to the same profitability problems that hounded its predecessor remained to be seen in the new century ahead, but as Sport Supply competed during the late 1990s, its position was strong, underpinned by the diversity and breadth of the products it offered.

Principal Subsidiaries

Sport Supply Group International Holdings, Inc.

Further Reading

"Emerson Diversifies," *Television Digest,* December 16, 1996, p. 16.
Heller, Matthew, "The Renegade Man," *Forbes,* November 18, 1985, p. 66.
Lampman, Dean, "BSN Seeks Consistent Growth After Sharp Decline in Profits," *Dallas-Fort Worth Business Journal,* September 14, 1987, p. 1.
"Riddell Sports Buys Maxpro, All-American," *Sporting Goods Business,* October 1991, p. 7.
Sullivan, R. Lee, "Your Management Team Is Not a Bashful Bunch of Wimps," *Forbes,* September 12, 1994, p. 84.

—Jeffrey L. Covell

Stinnes AG

Humboldtring 15
45472 Mulheim an der Ruhr
Germany
+49 208 494-0
Fax: +49 208 494-698
Web site: http://www.stinnes.de

Wholly Owned Subsidiary of Veba AG
Incorporated: 1902 as Hugo Stinnes GmbH
Employees: 33,290
Sales: DM 21.6 billion (1996)
SICs: 8999 Services, Not Elsewhere Classified; 5171
    Petroleum Bulk Stations & Terminals; 4412 Deep Sea
    Foreign Transportation of Freight; 5169 Chemicals &
    Allied Products, Not Elsewhere Classified; 5211
    Lumber & Other Building Materials; 5052 Coal &
    Other Minerals & Ores; 6120 Wholesale Distribution
    of Fuels, Ores, Metals & Industrial Materials; 6110
    Wholesale Distribution of Agricultural Raw Materials,
    Live Animals, Textile; 7630 Supporting Services to
    Sea Transport; 6220 Dealing in Other Scrap
    Materials, or General Dealers; 8200 Institutions
    Specializing in Insurance Other Than Long-Term

Stinnes AG, a group of independent divisions consisting of almost 100 domestic and more than 100 foreign companies, is Germany's and one of Europe's largest transportation and distribution companies. As of 1965 Stinnes AG has been a wholly owned subsidiary of Veba AG, Germany's largest firm. The Stinnes group's three principal activities are trading in raw materials, especially coal and oil; chemical distribution and steel processing; and air, sea, and land transportation. An increasingly important business segment of Stinnes is the service industry, from do-it-yourself building materials, to ownership of the prestigious Hotel Nassauer Hof in Wiesbaden, to providing data processing services. Stinnes also operates a string of automotive service stations and runs passenger service on a liner between Lübeck, Germany and Helsinki, Finland. Stinnes is Germany's largest independent steel trader and Europe's largest chemical distributor. In the 1990s it accounted for about one-third of the sales of its parent company, Veba AG. Veba AG announced plans in 1998 to sell up to 49 percent of Stinnes in a public offering.

Early History

Stinnes AG has deep roots in modern German history. The company's founder, Mathias Stinnes, was born in Muelheim in the Ruhr valley during the time of the French Revolution, when the German states were heavily fragmented and decentralized. It is all the more amazing that entrepreneurship could succeed in an area of Europe where innumerable regional interests competed against one another. Added to this politically and economically unstable environment were the numerous invasions of the Napoleonic armies that devastated the very region in which Mathias Stinnes was born.

One of many children of a poor bargeman and his wife, Mathias was affected deeply by the winds of change buffeting him and his generation. The democratic ideas of the French Revolution and Napoleon's forced and short-lived consolidation of the German states signaled change. The legacy of that brief union was not lost on the diplomats gathered at the 1815 Congress of Vienna, who issued a call for a voluntary lifting of trade restrictions on the Rhine, the longest river in western Europe, of which the Ruhr is a tributary.

With so much change in the air, Mathias Stinnes and his two brothers did not follow in their father's footsteps, as generations before them had. Instead of remaining poor laborers, they opted to hire laborers and go into business for themselves. In 1808 Mathias Stinnes, with the help of his brothers, set up his own company, named after himself as elder brother, that hauled goods and raw materials on a boat via the Ruhr.

Stinnes's business grew, despite the community's deep-rooted distrust of someone who chose to strike out on a path different from his forefathers. When Mathias died in 1845, his steamboats plied the Ruhr, and he had become the largest private owner of inland shipping in the fragmented German

Company Perspectives:

The most important strategic guidelines for Stinnes are value creation, improved customer benefits and increased customer satisfaction. By offering the customer intelligent as well as unconventional solutions to problems, the various Stinnes divisions can achieve their goal of being not only better and more cost effective than the competition, but also different from the competition. By being flexible, having the desire to experiment and the willingness to learn from our competitors, we can remain competent and adapt to today's ever changing market place.

states. Unusual for that day and age, he branched out into other businesses: the Ruhr area was rich in coal, and by the time he died, the Mathias Stinnes company owned shares in 36 mines, four of which his firm had built. Stinnes's traditional lines of business—trading in raw materials and transportation on inland waterways—were well established by the 1840s.

Mathias's sons took over the family enterprise in turn, each one dying at a young age. Despite the succession of political crises in Germany occasioned by wars of unification as well as the rise of an organized labor movement, the Stinnes firm continued to expand. In 1908, 100 years after the company was founded, it possessed 21 tugs and nine of its own ports along with their storage facilities and owned and controlled five mines. By then, however, a new company had arisen that in time would engulf the old Mathias Stinnes firm.

Hugo Stinnes, grandson of Mathias Stinnes, was born in 1870. Dissatisfied with the traditional family business, the 21-year-old Hugo persuaded his mother to sell her ownership in the firm and to lend him 50,000 gold marks to start up his own business, which he incorporated in 1902 as Hugo Stinnes GmbH in Muelheim. He still retained technical management of the Mathias Stinnes mines, however, and gradually the two companies became indistinguishable.

Hugo Stinnes was a dynamic, forceful, and imaginative entrepreneur whose horizons stretched well beyond the traditional family enterprises and the customary way of doing things. His original business—coal mining and transportation—was what he knew best; from there, however, he went on to found the biggest business empire that Germany, unified into a centralized state in 1871, had ever seen.

Even the coal business would change under the farsighted entrepreneur: in the years before World War I, Hugo Stinnes entered into a partnership with the much older August Thyssen. Together, the two established the Muelheimer Bergwerksverein, which took over used mines and made a profit out of them. Soon Hugo Stinnes's firm had branches of its coal business in Great Britain, Italy, and the Russian Empire. He entered the shipping business on his own, and his fleets competed with and would eventually absorb the family fleets. He experimented with recycling gas from coke furnaces and became the foremost promoter of electricity in Germany. Hugo Stinnes tirelessly

expanded into new business arenas, not for the mere sake of expansion, but to integrate all of his businesses "vertically," a feat that he would not fully accomplish until after World War I.

War Years

Despite the shortages of various raw materials because of the Allied blockade of Germany's ports, Hugo Stinnes GmbH emerged unscathed from the war and with an even bigger portfolio. With the Kaiser in exile and a new democratic government in place, Hugo Stinnes became a member of the Reichstag and thus politically influential. The French occupation of the Ruhr valley, where many of Stinnes's assets, especially mines, were located, convinced him that vertical integration of his business, from raw materials to the finished product—including transporting the finished product and controlling the sources of energy in Germany to complete this process—must be accelerated.

A veritable frenzy of expansion followed, in the course of which Stinnes established a partnership with Stahlwerk Breuningshaus steelworks and proceeded to purchase companies that would fully complement this line of business, such as rolling mills, rivet and wire works, a machine tool factory, and other related companies. In 1920 Hugo Stinnes acquired a mining and foundry business that employed 18,000 workers and joined with Germany's largest manufacturer of electrical equipment and appliances, Siemens, to enter that line of business in a partnership. Interested in new energy sources, especially petroleum, Hugo Stinnes's firm began acquiring oil wells abroad, along with refineries and the ocean vessels necessary for conveying the precious fuel. Shipping and transportation companies were purchased as a matter of course, and with Hugo Stinnes's increasing involvement in politics, his business interests turned to newspaper presses, publishing houses, and printing establishments, which his firm acquired in short order. Helping this process of acquisition was the cataclysmic German inflation of the early 1920s; property could be bought for almost nothing.

At the time of his premature death in 1924, not only was Hugo Stinnes Germany's most influential and powerful industrialist, but he was also the owner of the largest firm (in terms of assets and revenues) in the country. Hugo Stinnes GmbH consisted of more than 4,500 businesses and employed tens of thousands of workers.

A year and a half after Hugo Stinnes' death, the company was on the brink of ruin. Profligate sons succeeded him and competed against each other; banks recalled their loans, and finally, son Hugo, Jr. sold half of the company's shares to two American banks in return for a huge loan. Much of the company's assets and property were destroyed during the succeeding war years; immediately afterward, the Stinnes firm reverted to the control of the Allied occupation authorities. Half of the firm was still owned by banks in the United States.

The Hugo Stinnes company probably would have gone under, its stock sold to the highest bidder—most likely to a foreign company—without the intervention of Heinz P. Kemper. Because he had no Nazi party affiliation during World War II and had for many years directed an American subsidiary in Germany, the American occupation authority selected him to head Stinnes. As its director, Kemper dismissed Hugo Stinnes, Jr. from the helm, thereby ending the Stinnes family's connection to that firm.

Postwar Reorganization

Reviving the company and returning it to prosperity was nearly impossible, especially since its assets were spread throughout Germany and British and French authorities were far less friendly and compromising than the Americans. There was also the urgent matter of repurchasing the half of Stinnes still under American ownership, since the Americans were in a position to make a takeover bid for the other half. Unfortunately, Stinnes finances were in turmoil, and there was no money for repurchase.

The firm began to slowly recoup some of its losses and show a profit, thanks in part to the reform of German currency in 1948 and to the formation of the West German state, or Federal Republic of Germany, in 1949. The company was hardly out of deep water, however. The U.S. government informed Kemper in the mid-1950s that Stinnes stock held by U.S. banks would be sold to the highest bidder and Germans would be excluded from bidding. Desperate to save the company, Kemper turned to the German government in Bonn for help. Chancellor Konrad Adenauer gave Kemper a sympathetic hearing. Adenauer in turn had a friendly relationship with U.S. President Dwight D. Eisenhower, who was able to pull enough strings to allow the Germans to participate in bidding for their own stock. The Stinnes company, however, did not possess the required capital—DM 100 million—the likely price of repurchasing the stock. So, the German government intervened once more; Finance Minister Ludwig Erhard worked to set up a consortium of German banks that could provide the necessary loan, all of which would have to be repaid to the last pfennig. In the United States, Kemper successfully outbid his competitors, including some of the most powerful firms in the Common Market, and the Hugo Stinnes firm was once more a wholly German-owned company.

Growth in the 1970s and After

The Marshall Plan for the resurrection of the German economy as well as the economic benefits of West German unification laid the foundations of the German "economic miracle." The Hugo Stinnes company once again became one of Germany's largest transportation and raw material supply companies, with sales in the multibillion dollar range by the early 1970s. In 1976 the company's name was changed to Stinnes AG, in recognition of the fact that the firm was no longer in the hands of the Hugo Stinnes family and as a reflection of the traditions of both Mathias Stinnes, the founder, and Hugo Stinnes, the daring entrepreneur. By then, Stinnes AG had joined the Veba AG group of companies, Germany's largest firm. In 1965 Veba AG had bought 95 percent of Stinnes stock, thus turning the company into a subsidiary. By becoming part of this holding company, Stinnes turned into the biggest transportation company in West Germany, since Veba AG sold one of its largest barge lines to Stinnes in return for the Stinnes glassworks and the chemical firm Chemiewerk Ruhroel.

By the early 1990s Stinnes AG had become a multibillion dollar company, operating the largest transportation industry in Europe and also serving as the owner of Brenntag AG, the largest supplier of petrochemicals on the continent. Headquartered in Mathias Stinnes's home town of Muelheim on the Ruhr, Stinnes has branched out into every continent on the globe and into every country in Europe, including eastern Europe and Russia. In the early 1990s Stinnes consisted of a multitude of major companies, most of which concentrated on the three business operations of Stinnes: trading in raw materials, distribution, and transportation. Two-thirds of Stinnes's revenues were derived from foreign markets, and one-third of its greater than 35,000-member work force were employed by Stinnes businesses outside of Germany.

In the early 1990s Europe's biggest transportation (in terms of land traffic) network was the Schenker Eurocargo group, which merged with Stinnes in 1991. A fleet of trucks and other conveyances—including railroads—transported merchandise throughout Europe, including Eastern Europe. Schenker-Rhenus AG, along with its subsidiaries, employed a total of 20,000 people and was without doubt Stinnes's largest component. Stinnes's Schenker International division was a major air and sea transporter of freight and operated 14 travel agencies as well. In the trading division, Stinnes Intercarbon was the top supplier and marketer in Europe of coal and its byproducts. Also in the trading division, the Stinnes firm Frank & Schulte GmbH processed and supplied ores, minerals, and metals to anywhere in the world via its 20 subsidiaries. In the distribution segment, consisting of approximately six major companies, Brenntag AG was the number one supplier of industrial chemicals to chemical manufacturers and the cosmetics industry throughout Europe. An increasingly important segment of Stinnes business was the service sector, especially home improvement chain stores. A small but important enterprise was the replacement tire market operated by Stinnes Reifendienst, which held the number one market position in Germany; this Stinnes division also owned more than 200 service stations throughout Germany, the Netherlands, Switzerland, Austria, and Alsace.

After the unification of East and West Germany, Stinnes, unlike many former West German companies, was in the forefront of investment and expansion into the former German Democratic Republic. Stinnes was also one of the first West German companies to establish corporate branch offices in the eastern German states and to establish major delivery routes into and out of those states. Brenntag AG opened a major distribution center in Magdeburg in former East Germany and quickly established branches of the firm throughout eastern Germany. Shortly after unification in the fall of 1991, Stinnes's earnings from eastern Germany alone totalled DM 1.5 billion—more than US $1 billion.

So hungry was the Eastern European population—which for decades lived under restrictive communist governments—for western goods in the early 1990s, that Stinnes was fortunate to have cultivated strong economic ties long before the fall of communism in eastern Europe and Russia. For one thing, the opening up of the east led to new raw material sources for Stinnes, the largest supplier of raw materials in Europe. Because of this, the Stinnes division Frank & Schulte had a year of record profits during the period of slow worldwide growth in 1991. Ores, minerals, and alloys were increasingly being obtained by Frank & Schulte from its Eastern European markets, which represented the best opportunity for growth for that company. Brenntag opened an important branch in Warsaw and offices in Prague and Moscow, only the beginning of its full penetration of the Eastern European market. The majority of Stinnes's divisions were racing to develop or extend their business in the east, including Russia, where the future of the vast Stinnes firm seemed to lie.

Changes in the Late 1990s

According to a past chairman of Stinnes AG, Guenter Winkelmann, the company could not exist without international markets. For this reason, Stinnes was particularly affected by the recession in North America, Australia, and Great Britain in the early 1990s. A more embarrassing setback came to the company in 1994, when it was revealed in the leading German newspaper *Die Welt* that a manager at Stinnes had embezzled millions of Deutsche marks from the company, through systematic fraud at one of the company's insurance subsidiaries. The manager, Baerbel Ruske, had been in charge of Hamburger Hof, an insurer that had prospered after reunification by doing brisk business in eastern Germany. Hamburger Hof had issued insurance policies on an estimated half million east German residences. Commissions on these policies were evidently siphoned into Ruske's account, and he was said to have come away with 11.9 million marks before being caught. Initial reports stated that Ruske's depredations would cost Stinnes six million marks, though Stinnes Chairman Hans-Juergen Knauer later amended the figure significantly downward, to only 800,000 marks.

By 1995 Stinnes was already Germany's largest independent steel trader; the company boosted its status even more with the acquisition of Krupp Hoesch Stahlhandel, a unit of Krupp AG. The Stinnes subsidiary Stinnes Interfer bought the unit. Krupp Hoesch Stahlhandel operated a network of six steel trading facilities, mostly in northern Germany. Its sale took its parent, Krupp AG, out of steel trading altogether. That company had complained that the business was becoming too consolidated, with large companies such as Stinnes Interfer making it difficult for the small Krupp unit to compete. After the acquisition, Stinnes Interfer was a giant, with a network of 37 steel trading branches and 1,500 employees.

As the company was growing in steel, it trimmed other areas. In 1997 Stinnes shed its hard-coal trading business. The sale of the business went 50 percent to a German company, Rheinbraun Brennstoff GmbH, and 50 percent to the Dutch SHV Energy NV. The sale had to await approval from the European Union Commission, which monitored such sales according to the European Coal and Steel Community Treaty. Further cuts in Stinnes's business were announced in December 1997, when parent company Veba AG announced it would sell about half of Stinnes.

Veba AG had been working hard to cut costs in the mid-1990s and next decided to concentrate its energies on fewer businesses. The massive conglomerate was characterized as a diversified utility company, and it controlled many municipal electrical utilities. But like its subsidiary Stinnes, it was involved in hundreds of businesses and its corporate structure was unwieldy. At the end of 1997, Veba AG announced that it would step back from direct management of Stinnes by floating up to 49 percent of its subsidiary on the stock market in late 1998. At that time Stinnes AG accounted for almost a third of its parent's annual sales. But the divestment of the subsidiary would not only give Veba AG a massive infusion of cash, but Stinnes would be able to fund its own growth and expansion. With the announcement of the coming sale, Stinnes also claimed it would give up its recycling business, its inland shipping, and direct control of its tire service businesses and do-it-yourself construction outlets. Stinnes's three core areas were to be chemical distribution, land transport, and trading in building materials and air freight. Stinnes still had hopes for more acquisitions and expansion in these three areas. But after being divested from Veba AG, it expected to be able to pay for its future growth by stock sales and to control its own destiny more precisely.

Principal Subsidiaries

Stinnes Interoil AG; Frank & Schulte GmbH; Brenntag AG; Stinnes Interfer GmbH; Stinnes BauMarkt AG; Stinnes Reifendienst GmbH; Stinnes Intertec GmbH; Schenker-Rhenus AG; Schenker Eurocargo (Deutschland) AG; Schenker International AG; Rhenus AG; Poseidon Schiffahrt AG; Frachtcontor Junge & Co.; Hotel Nassauer Hof GmbH; Stinnes-data-Service GmbH; Logware Informationssysteme GmbH; Stinnes-Organisationsberatung GmbH.

Further Reading

Burgert, Philip, "Krupp Sells Unit, Exits Steel Trading," *American Metal Market,* October 2, 1996, p. 2.
"German Veba's Reorganization Draws Praise from Analysts," *Dow Jones Online News,* December 4, 1997, p. DJON9733808602.
The Making of a Business Empire; 175 Years of Stinnes; Portrait of a German Company, Econ Verlag, 1983.
Norman, Peter, "Veba Shake-up Includes Stinnes IPO," *Financial Times,* December 5, 1997.
"People in Finance: Hugo Stinnes," *The Banker,* October 1982, pp. 74–75.
"Stinnes AG—Company Report," *DAFSA,* August 1, 1992.
Stinnes, Edmund Hugo, *A Genius in Chaotic Times: Edmund H. Stinnes on his Father, Hugo Stinnes (1870–1924),* Bern: E.H. Stinnes, 1979.
Young, Ian, "Stinnes Agrarchemie Builds Five Centers," *Chemical Week,* February 3, 1993, p. 13.

—Sina Dubovoj
—updated by A. Woodward

SUNTRUST

SunTrust Banks Inc.

P.O. Box 4418
Atlanta, Georgia 30302-4418
U.S.A.
(404) 588-7711
Fax: (404) 588-7929
Web site: http://www.suntrust.com

Public Company
Incorporated: 1985
Employees: 21,000
Sales: $667.3 million (1997)
SICs: 6712 Bank Holding Companies; 6021 National
Commercial Banks; 6022 State Commercial Banks

A holding company formed by Trust Company of Georgia in 1985, SunTrust Banks Inc. had total assets of $55.5 billion in 1997, making it the 19th largest bank in the United States. In a city that had seen its large financial institutions overtaken by NationsBank and Wachovia during the 1980s and 1990s, SunTrust remained the only major banking company with headquarters in Atlanta. With three principal subsidiaries in Georgia, the company has more than 695 combined banking locations and provides a variety of services that include traditional banking, trust and investment management, mortgage banking, credit cards, discount brokerage, credit-related insurance, data processing and information, and numerous other services. At the heart of the bank's stability are its 48.3 million shares of common stock in Atlanta's most famous commercial enterprise, Coca-Cola, a relationship that dates back to the company's origins.

A Century of Trust Company

SunTrust traces its roots to the Trust Company, a bank founded in Atlanta in 1891. Trust Company would remain a major institution in the city for the next century, though since the formation of SunTrust in 1985 and the full name change of all company institutions which went into effect in 1995, little remains of the old company's history.

At the time of Trust Company's founding in the last decade of the 19th century, Atlanta was already well on its way to becoming the leading commercial center that it would become by the 1990s. From the devastation wrought by the Civil War and Sherman's burning of the city, Atlanta had emerged much like its symbol, the phoenix, a bird which rejuvenates itself periodically through immersion in fire. By the 1890s, as Atlanta took on the nickname "The Gate City," a druggist named Asa Candler had developed a sweet brown carbonated drink destined to place the city squarely on the commercial map.

The drink, of course, was Coca-Cola, and in 1919 the Woodruff family would purchase the Candlers' interest in the company. The patriarch of the clan, Ernest Woodruff, had become president of Trust Company, in which capacity he served from 1904 to 1922. With the family's acquisition of the company, Woodruff in 1919 took Coca-Cola public, using Trust Company as underwriter. In return, Trust Company received $110,000 worth, in 1919 dollars, of Coca-Cola stock. This investment would form the heart of the company's fortunes over the century that followed.

Though Woodruff left his position as bank president in 1922, the link between Trust Company and Coke was formed. Ultimately Ernest's son Robert would take his place at the helm of Coca-Cola, a position he would hold into the 1980s. During his long career, Woodruff would leave a heavy imprint on Atlanta in the form of numerous donations by the foundation named for him. His family, however, had already made a strong and abiding mark on Trust Company: "From them evolved the bank's steady, glitz-eschewing philosophy," according to Rob Chambers of the *Atlanta Journal and Constitution*.

That philosophy, along with its mother lode of Coca-Cola stock, ensured steady growth for Trust Company through the ups and downs of the mid-20th century. By the 1970s, Trust Company had adopted as its logo a "big blue T," with an advertising campaign that centered around that nickname. From the image projected by the bank, the operative term in "Trust Company" was "Trust."

Company Perspectives:

SunTrust Banks Inc. is a leading provider of high-value financial services that are delivered through the decentralized management of individual banks and subsidiaries responsible for their local markets. Its mission is to initiate and strengthen relationships by meetings with high-quality services that provide a high return to its shareholders. The company's primary objective is to operate sound financial institutions that promote the economic well-being of its customers, employees, and their communities. It combines the advantages of strong, focused, and accountable decentralized local management with financial, technological, and capital markets strength to achieve its vision. Market recognition flows from its ability to remain sound while sustaining high performance over time. SunTrust seeks growth but will not sacrifice quality or profitability. Its goal is to achieve all three.

The company's stability would become a particularly noteworthy facet in years to come, as one by one its competitors were swallowed by the giants from North Carolina, NationsBank and Wachovia. The former absorbed Bank South and Citizens & Southern (C & S), while the latter took over First Atlanta. Georgia Federal, National Bank of Georgia, Fulton Federal, and numerous other former competitors likewise disappeared; only Trust Company remained apart. When Trust Company, too, ceased to exist, it would not be through acquisition, but through transformation from within.

The 1980s: Trust Company Plus SunBanks Equals SunTrust

In 1984, Trust Company announced its intention to merge with another bank. A year later, reciprocal interstate banking laws between Georgia and Florida became effective, and on July 1, 1985, Trust Company formally merged with Orlando-based SunBanks. It was an auspicious beginning; starting with $16 billion in assets, the new company ended the year with $19.4 billion.

In 1985, SunTrust also acquired two banks with total assets of $130 million. It would continue to make such acquisitions, some smaller and some larger—for instance, four acquisitions in 1993 totalled $2.2 billion—throughout the coming years. However, as of 1998 its only merger, other than the initial one that created the company, came in 1986. In that year, SunTrust took on the $5 billion Third National Corporation of Nashville. Now the bank had offices in a wide swath from Miami to the mountains of Tennessee, as well as a tiny foothold in Alabama through Third National, which became SunTrust Banks of Tennessee Inc.

The year 1986 was also pivotal in that it saw the formation of the subsidiary SunTrust Securities. In addition, the company created "The SunTrust Vision," a statement of principles which would remain in effect for years to come. As the mid-1980s became the late 1980s, the company's reputation grew. During the first half of 1987, SunTrust posted the highest earnings in the industry, and later that year *American Banker* named it "Top Performing Regional Bank Holding Company." In 1988, it acquired two Mellon Bank trust subsidiaries in Florida and was added to the *Standard & Poor 500* Index.

In the energetic, sometimes volatile, business climate of the 1980s, the bank faced serious challenges as well. When it entered the Tennessee market in 1986, the area had seemed a promising one, particularly since Saturn and other automakers had begun moving production facilities there. Yet the local real estate market experienced a sudden and severe downturn, which according to SunTrust's own literature might have had an extremely adverse effect on the company if not for its "quick action to confront this problem." With spreading repercussions from the crisis in savings and loan institutions, 1989 was not a good year for banking. The increased leveraging of companies in preceding years became a matter of concern, as did real estate lending practices. In 1990, the federal government required substantial increases in deposit insurance premiums.

Again, however, SunTrust's foundation—its Coca-Cola stock and its conservative principles—stood it in good stead. The company had obtained stock in Columbia Pictures Entertainment during Coke's short-lived ownership of that entertainment company, and in 1989 SunTrust realized a $10 million windfall from the sale of Columbia common stock. Also in that year, it began consolidating its regional banking subsidiaries from a high of 53; within six years, the company had reduced this number to just 29.

With the approaching retirement of its first chairman, Bob Strickland, the company in 1990 instituted a plan of succession. Joel Wells became chairman and James B. "Jimmy" Williams became president and CEO. In 1991 Williams became chairman while remaining CEO, and Phil Humann was named to the position of president.

New Name, Same Bank in the 1990s

In 1992, the year the company's investment in Coca-Cola passed the $1 billion mark, SunTrust introduced an initial group of six mutual funds as the STI Classic family of funds. The next year, *Euromoney* magazine rated SunTrust Banks Inc. the 14th best bank in the world on the basis of its stability and solid performance. Likewise in 1994 several STI Classic Funds earned national recognition for their strong performances. By that point, STI had made available to the public a total of 18 different funds. Also in 1994, the company formed SunTrust Capital Markets and inaugurated a series of growth initiatives to increase revenue and core earnings.

In 1994 and 1995, the company took steps to consolidate all subsidiaries under the SunTrust brand name. Up until then, for instance, the Georgia subsidiary had continued to operate under the Trust Company name with the "big blue T" logo. In Florida, moreover, where a number of local bankers took pride in the fact that the 1992 devastation wrought by Hurricane Andrew had not presented a major setback to SunBanks, the sun was finally setting.

In a bittersweet 1996 profile, the *Wall Street Journal* reported on one tangible consequence of SunTrust's decision to bring all its banks together under one brand-name, which went into full effect in 1995. With the end of SunBanks came the removal of a major Miami landmark, the large orange sign, 12 feet high and 88 feet across, on the bank's Brickell Avenue tower. According to the bank's marketing manager, Karen Dorscher, "Every time they'd shoot a movie in Miami, we'd see the orange sign," which had appeared most recently in *True Lies* with Arnold Schwarzenegger and the Sylvester Stallone movie *The Specialist*. Bank officials arranged to have more than 100 small cubes cut from the big orange "S," and they sent these—engraved with the inscription "a piece of history"—to local leaders and journalists. With more pieces left over from the "S," Dorscher told the *Journal,* "I took the leftovers to my son's day care, and they built things with it."

Focus on the Information Age for the Future

SunTrust Banks was likewise in a building mode, with a heightened focus on technology. In 1995, it instituted "PC Banking," a personal computer-based home banking service. Offered through an agreement with Intuit Inc., makers of Quicken, a popular financial management software package, PC Banking made SunTrust only the second financial institution in the Southeast to offer on-line banking. The company also made steps in the area of in-store banking. SunTrust's Georgia subsidiary in 1995 entered into an agreement with Publix Super Markets to offer in-store banking facilities throughout the state. The bank's Chattanooga affiliate, part of the Tennessee subsidiary, signed a similar agreement with Winn Dixie stores.

Another area of technological development for SunTrust in the mid-1990s was enhanced automatic teller machines (ATM) service. Now the company offered statement printing, coupon and stamp dispensing, and check cashing at its ATMs. For some time SunTrust had its Telebank 24 service in place, a 24-hour automated banking system available by phone, and it expanded its offerings through this system to include investment information and other types of services. At the level of the client/server systems connecting its branches and subsidiaries, until 1995 SunTrust had three platforms in operation; in that year, it introduced a single platform to link its intranet.

Technological advancements also allowed the company to present its commercial customers with a number of services. SunTrust in 1995 became the first bank in the U.S. to offer its corporate customers information access by means of both CD-ROM and an on-line connection. SunTrust also applied new technologies to an upgrade of its wholesale lockbox service and to assisting customers in receiving fax copies of check images directly through a PC. This would in turn introduce heightened levels of security. In conjunction with Antinori Software Inc., SunTrust developed an automated system to safeguard against fraudulent checks. It also began offering one of the nation's first image-based systems designed to assist in processing damaged checks.

As SunTrust approached a new millennium as the 19th-largest bank in the United States, aspects of its operation would have been unrecognizable to the bank's founders from the 1890s. But two themes remained constant: the significance of its relationship with Coca-Cola, and the conservative attitude of stable, managed growth instilled by the Woodruff family.

Noting that James B. Williams sat on the Coca-Cola board and that Coke chairman Roberto Goizueta (who died in the summer of 1997) sat on the SunTrust board, the *Atlanta Journal and Constitution* in June 1997 profiled the strong bond between the bank and the soft-drink maker. A large portion of the "trust and other business" at the bank, according to market analyst John W. Mason, "stems from wealthy officers and shareholders of Coca-Cola.... Most of the public and the media doesn't understand that seventy-five to 100 percent of the bank's business comes from thirty percent, even twenty percent of its customers."

A central facet of SunTrust's financial picture is its Coca-Cola shares. By 1997, nearly eight decades after Ernest Woodruff paid the bank's underwriting fee in Coke stock, the original $110,000 had grown to a value of $3.3 billion. The shares, now numbering 48.3 million, had grown by $2 billion since the beginning of 1992, and with earnings per share at $74, the Coke dividend accounted for a whopping 11 cents, or nearly 15 percent.

This sizeable nest egg, the Atlanta paper noted, "helps keep the bank stock pricey and beyond reach of unwanted suitors except those with the deepest of pockets." In other words, one key factor underlying SunTrust's continued independence from the North Carolina superbanks—which made it by 1997 the sole Atlanta-based financial institution—is its stock in Coca-Cola. Furthermore, in the four years since 1993, SunTrust had bought back more than 39 million of its own shares at a cost in excess of $1 billion and had plans to buy more of the 216 million shares still outstanding. This further decreased its potential vulnerability to takeover and increased earnings per share.

Less tangible but no less real is the cautious mentality which has governed SunTrust from its origins. On March 21, 1998, Williams retired and President Phillip Humann assumed his role as chairman and CEO, but the *Journal and Constitution* predicted no significant change of direction. Of Williams and Humann, Summerfield K. Johnston—Goizueta's successor as chairman of Coke and a director at SunTrust—said, "They're not the same people, but they've been in lock-step for a number of years. They're both conservative, thorough bankers."

The bank's slow-growth strategies, however, could be a liability in a climate increasingly governed by the most aggressive competitors. According to the Atlanta paper, Wall Street analysts "continued to express concern that SunTrust Banks is becoming a lost lamb as a relentless round of acquisitions is creating ever-larger wolves in the banking industry." The article noted that SunTrust had purchased Nashville-based Equitable Securities in September 1997, "but hasn't acquired a bank of consequential size since its purchase of Third National ... in 1986."

Still, Williams and Humann appeared to be in agreement in their refusal to let the strategies of competitors such as Nations-Bank determine their own response to events. Jon R. Burke of Brown, of Burke Capital Partners observed, "They've been miraculously good at not being reactive.... And they've retained a community focus.''

Principal Subsidiaries

SunTrust Banks of Florida Inc.; SunTrust Banks of Georgia Inc.; SunTrust Banks of Tennessee Inc.

Further Reading

Chambers, Rob, ''A New Leader for SunTrust: But No Switch in Direction,'' *Atlanta Journal and Constitution,* February 11, 1998, p. E1.

——, ''Enterprise: Coca-Cola Long an Important Part of SunTrust,'' *Atlanta Journal and Constitution,* June 8, 1997, p. H10.
''SunTrust Settles Escrow Suit,'' *Wall Street Journal,* February 26, 1996.
''SunTrust's Earnings for 4th Quarter Rose Despite Its Expenses,'' *Wall Street Journal,* January 10, 1996, p. B4.
Tippett, Karen L., ''Florida Journal: Signing Off: SunTrust Preserves Plastic,'' *Wall Street Journal,* February 28, 1996, p. F2.

—Judson Knight

Suzuki Motor Corporation

300, Takatsuka-cho
Hamamatsu-shi
Shizuoka-ken 432-91
Japan
(53) 440-2111
Fax: (53) 456-0002
Web site: http://www.suzuki.com

Public Company
Incorporated: 1920 as Suzuki Loom Manufacturing
  Company
Employees: 14,700
Sales: ¥1.38 trillion (1996)
Stock Exchanges: Tokyo Osaka Nagoya Fukuoka
  Amsterdam
SICs: 3711 Motor Vehicle and Passenger Car Bodies;
  3714 Motor Vehicle Parts & Accessories; 3751
  Motorcycles, Bicycles & Parts

Suzuki Motor Corporation is Japan's fifth largest automaker, marketing its vehicles in 170 countries around the world. It is best known in the United States and Europe as a manufacturer of small, fuel-efficient automobiles and trucks, as well as powerful motorcycles. In its home market of Japan, however, the company is the leading maker of ''midget'' cars—a classification almost unknown outside Japan. These tiny subcompact automobiles are popular because of the tremendous overcrowding in Japanese cities, where since the early 1990s a larger car cannot be purchased legally until the owner can show proof that he or she has a parking spot. Such midget cars are smaller than the Yugo or Ford's Fiesta model and are comparable to the British Mini. In the market for two-wheeled vehicles, approximately 80 percent of Suzuki's domestic output is mopeds, or motor-driven bicycles. The company also makes marine outboard motors, generators, water pumps, and even motorized wheelchairs. In addition, through its network of foreign assembly plants, Suzuki is adept at turning out millions of car parts.

Suzuki's growth has been predicated on its distinctive domestic and international strategies. Domestically, the company owes its success to its high-quality engines, around which it designs a wide variety of vehicles for special or emerging niche markets. Internationally, Suzuki has traditionally targeted developing countries with growing populations, including Cambodia, India, China, Egypt, Hungary, and Pakistan. Suzuki's policy in these markets is to find a local partner to sell simple, more affordable vehicles, taking advantage of the small margins on huge volumes of sales. In the U.S. market, Suzuki's strategy is an extension of its domestic plan. While Ford Motor Company, General Motors Corporation (GM), Toyota Motor Corporation, and Chrysler Corporation battle for leadership in mass markets, Suzuki excels in the quirky niches between jeep and utility vehicle and between compact and subcompact.

Early 20th-Century Founding

Suzuki Motor Corporation was founded by Michio Suzuki in 1909 as a manufacturer of weaving machines. From its base in Hamamatsu, the Suzuki Loom Works, as it was then known, supplied weaving equipment to hundreds of small fabrics manufacturers in and between Tokyo, Yokohama, and Nagoya. At the time, textile manufacturing was one of Japan's biggest industries. It provided a growing and stable market for the Suzuki enterprise. In 1920 Michio Suzuki took his company public and named the new firm Suzuki Loom Manufacturing Company.

Suzuki continued to manufacture weaving machines exclusively throughout the 1920s and until the mid-1930s. At that time a militarist clique gained control of the government and began a massive mobilization program called the ''quasi-war economy.'' Companies throughout the country were asked to begin planning for a conversion to armaments manufacturing. Suzuki was an especially attractive supplier because it was in the business of equipping other factories. In addition, the company was located far away from major industrial centers that would become primary bombing targets.

By 1937 Suzuki had begun production of a variety of war-related materials, which may have included vehicle parts, gun assemblies, and armor. For its part in Japan's World War II effort, Suzuki, like thousands of other companies, was requisitioned for war production and probably had no intention of becoming a manufacturer of military implements. Nevertheless, the company continued to manufacture weaving machines for the duration of the war. Fortunately, the Suzuki factory and the city of Hamamatsu escaped the ravages of U.S. bombing campaigns. The company was capable of resuming production after the war, but the economy and supply networks were in ruins.

New Directions after World War II

Suzuki reestablished production of textile manufacturing equipment soon after World War II. Japan, however, was so impoverished that there was little demand for new woven products. As a result, few companies could afford to purchase new looms. By 1947 the pace of investment continued to be slow, prompting Suzuki to make a major change in its business. That year the company moved to a new headquarters building and, relying on the manufacturing experience it had gained during the war, began design work on motorized vehicles. The prospects were favorable; Japan was a nation of nearly 100 million people, nearly all of whom lacked access to basic transportation.

The heart of the new Suzuki product line was a small 36cc engine that could be used to motorize bicycles. Production of the moped, called the Power Free, began in 1952, prompting Suzuki to abandon weaving equipment entirely. In conjunction with the introduction of the new product line, the company changed its name to the Suzuki Motor Company in 1954, the same year it introduced its first line of motorcycles. The following year, Suzuki graduated from two-wheeled vehicles to a light passenger sedan called the Suzulight, powered by a 360cc engine. In the process, Suzuki gained valuable experience in developing larger internal combustion engines, vehicle frames, gear systems, and steering mechanisms. In 1958, Suzuki developed an improved moped, named the Suzumoped. The following year it began production of a revolutionary delivery van, much smaller than conventional delivery trucks then in use and more appropriately suited to many motorized businesses.

Suzuki banked on the fact that, as its customers' operations grew, so would their needs. Therefore, it would be pointless for the company to squander hard-won loyalty by neglecting to offer its customers a properly diverse product line. Having gained an important foothold in various sectors of the Japanese vehicle market, Suzuki cleverly used these beachheads for further expansion. The popular delivery van of 1959 convinced the company to develop a light truck, called the Suzulight Carry FB, in 1961.

The single event that gained Suzuki its greatest international recognition, however, occurred the following year, when a Suzuki motorcycle won the 50cc-class Isle of Man race. It was the first of many victories for Suzuki motorcycles, victories that firmly established the previously unknown company model as a world leader. By 1970, demand for more powerful motorcycles would prompt Suzuki to develop its first line of four-stroke engine motorcycles. This preserved Suzuki's position of leadership in the market.

Exporting and Diversifying: 1960s–70s

Suzuki had difficulty expanding into domestic automobile markets that were dominated by Toyota, Honda, and Nissan. As a result, it was unable to develop a more sophisticated product line. In its search for growth, Suzuki turned instead to export markets that were in the same economic condition Japan had been in 10 or 15 years earlier. The most promising market was Thailand, a country that historically had close ties with Japan. In 1967 Suzuki established a factory in Thailand to assemble a variety of vehicles whose parts were made in Japan. By providing local employment and inviting Thai investment in the venture, Suzuki skirted import restrictions that locked out other manufacturers. Later, Suzuki duplicated the export development formula in Indonesia and the Philippines.

Still unable to reach sales goals for domestic vehicles, however, Suzuki began a diversification campaign. The company's small engines were fitted to electrical generators, yielding an entirely new line of portable power sources. In addition, the company dabbled in housing, an initially successful but short-lived venture.

The 1973 Organization of Petroleum Exporting Countries (OPEC) oil embargo drastically changed the automobile market. Faced with skyrocketing fuel prices, consumers showed interest in more efficient cars. But while Suzuki's little cars and trucks sipped gasoline, they were underpowered when compared to competing models from Japan's big three. The company's domestic auto sales slid further during a 1974 recession resulting from the oil crisis. That year, total sales of minicars—Suzuki's prime automobile segment—fell by more than 65 percent from 1970.

Suzuki began a major export campaign soon afterward, commencing full motorcycle production in Thailand, Indonesia, and Taiwan. In addition, it sent automobiles to the United States for the first time. The product was a bit unusual in the U.S. market, where the roads were dominated by enormous, heavy cars. Suzukis were introduced in the United States in small numbers but were refreshingly fuel efficient, capable of using one-third to one-half as much gasoline as some American models. Suzuki, however, entered the U.S. market well behind Toyota, Honda, Nissan, and even Mazda and Subaru. Furthermore, by 1978, fuel prices had fallen, and demand for Suzuki's "economy cars" was evaporating. Oil prices would shoot up again briefly in 1979, following the Iranian Revolution, but by then many of Suzuki's most promising markets had enacted tough laws restricting imports from Japan.

1970s–80s: Forging Partnerships

Returning to the development strategy it had begun in Thailand in 1967, Suzuki negotiated a number of foreign investment deals, agreeing to locate production facilities in several countries in return for access to their markets. In 1982 the company established a Pakistani production firm called PACO and a similar operation in India called Maruti Udyog, Ltd. Suzuki also established a partnership in Spain with Land Rover known as Land Rover Santana S.A. Two years later Suzuki set up new marketing operations in New Zealand and France.

In the United States, Suzuki's largest market outside Japan, the company signed a series of marketing and production contracts with General Motors and rival Isuzu Motors in 1981. As part of the deal, GM purchased a 5.2 percent interest in Suzuki.

The companies planned to share production facilities and handle marketing of each other's products. In 1983 Suzuki began production of its Swift subcompact, selling the cars through GM as the Chevy Sprint and later as the Geo Metro. Another result of Suzuki's arrangements with GM was the creation of a joint subsidiary in Canada, called CAMI Automotive, in 1986. This plant went into production in 1989, manufacturing Sprints, Metros, and Suzuki Sidekicks (also marketed as Geo Trackers).

While Suzuki's joint venture with GM was off to a good start, Suzuki had considerably more trouble of its own. Shortly after establishing a U.S. subsidiary at Brea, California, in 1986, the company was accused by *Consumer Reports* of producing an unsafe vehicle, the Samurai. Specifically, the magazine noted that the Samurai's high center of gravity could cause it to flip over while negotiating turns even at low speeds. Suzuki launched its own investigation and took remedial measures, but the damage had already been done. Worse for Suzuki, the company's entire U.S. executive team resigned—a gesture of atonement that was misinterpreted as an abandonment of the company's commitment to the product and to the U.S. market in general.

Domestically, Suzuki developed several new models during the 1980s, including the Cultus subcompact in 1983 and the four-wheel drive Escudo in 1988. Also in 1988, Suzuki agreed to handle sales of Peugot automobiles in Japan. The following year, the company rolled out the Cultus Esteem, which shared the same 1600cc engine as the Escudo. Also shoring up revenues were motorcycle sales, which were recovering by 1990, following a decline that had begun in 1982.

With the Samurai debacle behind it, Suzuki initiated a subtle campaign to reestablish the vehicle's promising U.S. franchise. The high-riding Samurai was popular with younger adults who favored a more rugged jeep-like buggy that was impervious to off-road obstacles. Above all, it was fun to drive and distinctive in appearance.

Suzuki also continued its push at globalization, opening a plant in Great Britain in 1986 that turned out 15,000 microvans annually. The company established a partnership with the Egyptian company Modern Motors SAE, called Suzuki Egypt SAE, to build compact cars and the Super Carry truck and van line in that country. Suzuki licensed manufacture of its Swift/Forsa model through Colmotores SA in Columbia. The Pakistani venture was also expanded to include automobile manufacture under a new company, Pak Suzuki Motor Company, Ltd. In April 1991 Suzuki established a joint venture with C. Itoh, the start-up Hungarian auto manufacturer Autokonzern RT, and the International Finance Corporation. The enterprise, called Magyar Suzuki Corporation, began production of the Suzuki Swift in Hungary the following year. In addition to putting up $230 million in capital for the new company, Suzuki flew each of its Hungarian workers to Japan for training in its production methods.

Also in 1991 Suzuki Motor Company adopted the more international name Suzuki Motor Corporation. During this time, the company suffered reverses in its largest enterprise, midget cars with engines under 550cc. This was due to two factors: new laws that extended parking restrictions to cars of that class and a worsening recession in Japan. Suzuki's losses were partially offset by an increase in motorcycle sales, but because revenues from auto manufacturing were nearly five times greater than motorcycle sales, the company's overall growth rate slowed substantially.

A promising area for Suzuki was its place under the corporate umbrella of General Motors's international ventures. Through teaming agreements, Suzuki was designated GM's *de facto* small car division, developing automobiles for the American company under the Geo nameplate. Elsewhere in Suzuki's U.S. business, sales of the Samurai recovered to 20,000 in 1992, and the company projected revenues of the Samurai would exceed 50,000 in three years. In 1995 the company introduced the mini sport utility vehicle the X90. With engines, suspensions, and four-wheel drive options similar to the two-door Sidekick, the X90 combined off-road capabilities with carlike, commuter-friendly features.

Exploiting Niche Markets in the 1990s

Globally, Suzuki continued to seek out countries with emerging markets and large populations. Its joint ventures with the governments of Pakistan, Hungary, Egypt, and Columbia had been low-risk and cost-effective means of expansion. The company stepped up that same successful strategy in the early to mid-1990s in India and China. Having begun a joint venture with the Indian government-controlled Maruti Udyog in 1982, Suzuki increased its equity hold to 50 percent in 1992 and raised that company's capacity to 200,000 units in 1994. By 1998 the Suzuki-Maruti venture held 80 percent of the Indian automobile market. In China, Suzuki built on a licensing agreement with the government in 1993 to become the first Japanese company to invest in a Chinese automobile manufacturing venture.

In 1994 Suzuki introduced two successful products to the Japanese market: the Alto van, whose $5,000 price tag made it the least expensive automobile in the country, and the Wagon R miniwagon. However, also during this time Suzuki's problems with the Samurai returned to haunt the company. In 1995 the U.S. courts awarded $90 million to a woman who was paralyzed as the result of a Samurai roll-over accident. Suzuki responded by suing the Consumers Union, the publisher of *Consumer Reports,* in 1996. The company claimed that the Consumers Union had purposely manipulated the test in 1988 to ensure that the Samurai failed the short-course maneuvering portion.

As Suzuki approached the 21st century, it remained primarily a niche manufacturer. The company derived about 70 percent of its income from sales of automobiles, including the Cervo, Alto, and Swift car models; the Carry van; and the sport utility vehicles Samurai and the Escudo, which was sold in the United States as the Sidekick. In 1998 the company introduced a compact sport utility vehicle called the Jimny Wide. Hoping to sell 2,000 of the 1,300cc-powered vehicle a month in Japan, Suzuki planned to begin exporting the vehicle in mid-1998.

Moreover, in the late 1990s, Suzuki remained Japan's leading minicar manufacturer, a position it had held for almost 25 years. Motorcycles, which ranged from 50cc scooters to 1100cc touring bikes, composed approximately 15 percent of Suzuki's business. In addition, outboard motors contributed three percent of Suzuki Motor Corporation sales.

The company sold approximately two million vehicles in 1997 and had plans for considerable expansion by the year 2000. Over the next three years, Suzuki hoped to raise the number of vehicles sold per year to 2.5 million. Of that, 100,000 was targeted for the United States. By 2004 the company planned to hold five percent of the world's motor vehicle market, although the economic turmoil in Asia in 1997 and 1998 cast a pall over these plans. Although Suzuki sold its vehicles in markets around the world and could count on India, Pakistan, and China as major outlets for its goods, the company relied on Japan and emerging markets in southeast Asia for a significant portion of its sales. How the company would make up for plummeting demand in these countries and how they would deal with the instability of the Japanese yen remained to be seen.

Principal Subsidiaries

American Suzuki Motor Corp.; Suzuki Canada, Inc.; Suzuki Motor de Columbia SA; Suzuki Australia Pty., Ltd.; Suzuki New Zealand Ltd.; Suzuki Motor GmbH Deutschland; Suzuki France S.A.; Suzuki Motor Espana, S.A.; Suzuki Philippines, Inc.; Suzuki Italia S.p.A.; Suzuki Transport and Packaging Co., Ltd.; Suzuki Real Estate Co., Ltd.; Suzuki Parts Manufacturing Co., Ltd.; Suzuki Marina Hamanako Co., Ltd.; Suzuki Oil Co., Ltd.; Suzuki Special Products Manufacturing Co., Ltd.

Further Reading

Bedard, Patrick, "The Next Big Thing," *Car and Driver,* May 1995, pp. 52–56.
"Detroit Auto Show Notebook," United Press International, January 8, 1998.
Eisenstodt, Gale, "A 4 Billion People Market," *Forbes,* September 27, 1993, pp. 48–49.
Miller, Karen Lowry, "Why the Road Less Traveled Suits Suzuki," *Business Week,* June 15, 1992, p. 126E.
"Suzuki Launches New Sport-Utility Model in Japan," Reuters, January 7, 1998.

—John Simley
—updated by Susan Windsich Brown

Swisher International Group Inc.

459 East 16th Street
Jacksonville, Florida 32206
U.S.A.
(904) 353-4311
Fax: (904) 397-9899

Public Company
Incorporated: 1913 as Jno. H. Swisher & Son, Inc.
Employees: 1,210
Sales: $275.6 million (1997)
Stock Exchanges: New York
SICs: 2121 Cigars; 2131 Chewing and Smoking Tobacco

The largest manufacturer and marketer of cigars in the world, Swisher International Group Inc. produces premium and mass market cigars, little cigars, and various smokeless tobacco products under numerous brand names, including the company's two most famous brand names, King Edward and Swisher Sweets. In the late 1990s Swisher controlled eight percent of the worldwide market for cigars and 31 percent of the U.S. market and ranked as the leading exporter of American-made cigars. The majority of the company's tobacco products were sold to tobacco distributors and grocery wholesalers, with the balance principally sold to food and drug chains. Domestically, Swisher manufactured its cigars in Jacksonville, Florida, and its smokeless tobacco products in Wheeling, West Virginia.

Mid-19th Century Origins

When the Swisher family entered the cigar business in the mid-1800s, they were decidedly nonplussed. Although the production and sale of cigars would enrich generations of Swishers and define the family for more than a century, they had other, more important business ventures to oversee when the patriarch of the family, David Swisher, received a small cigar business in 1861 as settlement for a debt. At the time, David Swisher was a merchant, not a manufacturer. He resided in Newark, Ohio, but was frequently on the road, where he made his living by selling merchandise from wagons that traveled across the Midwest.

Swisher's rolling stores sold a variety of dry goods, notions, and wares, to which cigars were added. But the hand-rolled tobacco products was just one of many items Swisher sold. It would take nearly 30 years before the Swisher family began treating the little cigar production facility in Ohio more seriously, and another generation before the link connecting the Swisher name to cigars began to strengthen. When that juncture arrived, the process of building the cigar business began in earnest.

Of David Swisher's four sons, John H. Swisher took the greatest interest in the family-owned cigar business. He convinced his brother Harry to join him in taking what for decades had been treated as a sidelight business and developing it into a much larger enterprise. The pair purchased the cigar business from their father in 1888, christening their business Swisher Brothers, and immediately began directing their energies toward building a name for themselves as cigar makers. The two brothers quickly made their presence felt, taking what had been a one-room operation capable of making a few hundred cigars each day and turning it into one of Ohio's fastest growing business. By 1895 the vestiges of the cigar company's modest past were gone, replaced by three factories that employed more than 1,000 workers who hand-rolled as many as 300,000 cigars each day.

John and Harry Swisher continued with their joint management of Swisher Brothers for nearly 20 years after having transformed the company into a sizable producer of cigars. Their partnership ended in 1913 when John purchased Harry's interest in the company and brought in his son Carl. The combination of father and son gave birth to a new name for the company, Jno. H. Swisher & Son, which would endure as the corporate title for much of the 20th century. Five years later the company introduced its King Edward Cigar, one of the chief revenue-generating products that would propel the company in the decades ahead. The business continued to prosper under the partnership of John and Carl, with the next milestone in the company's history occurring ten years after the younger Swisher joined the family business. In 1923, after searching for a suitable location to establish new corporate headquarters, John and Carl settled on Jacksonville, Florida, a community close to tobacco fields and shipping facilities, where the company would be headquartered throughout the 20th century.

Company Perspectives:

Much of the credit for our growth goes to our sales and marketing organization, which is the best in the business. Nationwide, we have a team of 250 sales and marketing professionals—the largest in the cigar industry—that allows us to maintain our leadership position. Another advantage of being the leader is the clout we have when it comes to introducing new products. The fact that more than a quarter of our net sales are from products introduced over the past decade is a strong measure of our ability to identify and fill market needs with new products—and to get those products well positioned.

Along with the move to Jacksonville came a significant, forward-looking improvement in the production process for cigars. At the new manufacturing facility established in Jacksonville, the Swishers installed machinery that radically shortened production time, becoming the first cigar operators to order rolling machines. The Swishers placed their order in 1923 and in mid-1924 the "fresh work" machines were turned on for the first time. Production totals leaped upward, as mechanization ushered in the age of mass production, enabling the Swishers to produce 100 million cigars a year by the end of the 1920s. Other innovative improvements followed that again cast the company in the role of industry pioneer. Jno. H Swisher & Son became the first company to wrap individual cigars in cellophane and the first to devise a simple method for removing the wrapping by pulling the cigar band.

The Great Depression

With the addition of the rolling machines, the Jacksonville plant quickly became the flagship production facility within the Swisher enterprise, proving to be an invaluable asset in the bleak decade ahead. By 1927, as the Great Depression approached, the company's nearly 70-year presence in Ohio had ended. The Ohio facilities established by John and Harry Swisher during the early 1890s were closed and all production was consolidated into the company's Florida, operations. Soon afterward, the nation's economy collapsed, sending repercussive shock waves into virtually every niche and segment of the marketplace. Businesses of every type, from retail to industrial to manufacturing, were hobbled by the devastating effects of a moribund economy. But Swisher not only demonstrated remarkable resiliency by staying in business as competitors foundered, it also recorded meaningful growth.

As companies fought to stay alive, Swisher was hiring new employees by the hundreds, yet still could not keep pace with the surging demand for its cigars. Throughout the decade-long depression, Swisher exuded a vibrancy that belied the harsh, deleterious economic times, growing vigorously while achieving important strides in advancing cigar production technology. Thanks to the company's early move into mechanization, money-saving efficiencies enabled the company to reduce the price of its cigars, which heightened popularity of its products and bolstered Swisher's share of the market. The King Edward Cigar, which had debuted in 1918 as a ten-cent cigar, sold for five cents each following the introduction of rolling machines and was down to two cigars for five cents by the end of the 1930s. Aided in part by these price reductions, the popularity of King Edwards soared during the 1930s. By 1940 King Edwards were the greatest selling cigars in the world and the site where they were produced in Jacksonville ranked as the largest cigar factory under one roof in the world, complete with the country's first industrial nursery, established in 1939.

1958 Debut of Swisher Sweets

Remarkably, the Great Depression proved to be Swisher's shining hour of achievement. A company on the rise during the 1920s exited the 1930s stronger than it ever had been before, holding sway as one of the premier manufacturers of its kind in the world. Swisher's enviable market position at the beginning of the 1940s left it poised to reap the financial rewards of the economically thriving postwar era, when the company introduced a brand that would rival the popularity of its King Edward cigars. In 1958 Swisher shipped the first shipments of Swisher Sweets, a brand name that generations of Americans would associate with the company. Although King Edwards had served as the single most important brand for the company during the first half of the 20th century and would continue to contribute significantly to the company's bottom line during the latter half of the century, Swisher Sweets added another powerful revenue-generating engine to fuel the company's success, as the brand developed into the greatest selling brand of cigars in the world.

As the Swisher Sweet brand steadily won over consumers during the 1960s, the company came under the control of new owners when American Maize-Products Company acquired Swisher in 1966. A leading producer of corn wet milling products, American Maize was a publicly traded company controlled by William Ziegler III, who would control Swisher for the remainder of the century. Not long after Ziegler and American Maize took over, the cigar market in the United States reached its peak and from there began a long, downward spiral that endured for roughly two decades. Accordingly, the 1970s and 1980s were difficult years for cigar producers, an era during which a premium was placed on aggressive marketing and production efficiency. With demand slipping discernibly each year, cigar producers could not hope, realistically, to record great financial or market share gains. Instead, they fought to retain their respective shares of a dwindling market, which Swisher did well. Millions of dollars were invested in keeping production equipment on the leading edge of technology and considerable attention was paid to marketing the company's line of cigars, including new King Edward and Swisher Sweets products introduced during the period. By the mid-1980s, after the cigar market had been contracting for more than a decade, Swisher stood on solid footing, marketing its products in more than 70 countries. Moreover, the company was financially strong enough to embark on an acquisition campaign that would diversify its tobacco business and broaden the line of cigars in its stable.

Mid-1980s Acquisitions and 1990s Growth

Swisher's acquisition spree of the mid-1980s got off to its start in 1985 when the company acquired Tampa, Florida-based Corral Wodiska y Ca., which produced Bering Premium cigars.

Early in 1986 the company completed its next acquisition, purchasing the cigar manufacturing assets of the Universal Cigar Company. With the Universal Cigar acquisition, Swisher gained a production plant in Clearwater, Florida, and well-known cigar brands Optimo, La Primadora, Santa Fe, and El Trelles. Its portfolio of cigar brands strengthened, Swisher next made a move toward diversification, acquiring the Helme Tobacco Company several months after the Universal Cigar acquisition. From Helme Tobacco, Swisher obtained the company's smokeless tobacco products, such as Silver Creek and Redwood Moist Snuff; Lancaster, Chattanooga Chew, Mail Pouch Chewing Tobacco; and Navy, Lorillard, and Railroad Mills Dry Snuff. These products were manufactured at Helme's two production plants in Helmetta, New Jersey and Wheeling, West Virginia, which also became part of the rapidly expanding Swisher enterprise. As these acquisitions were being completed, Swisher made another diversifying move, entering the little cigar market in late 1985 with its Swisher Sweets Little Cigars. By 1990 Swisher's little cigar brand had become the leading seller in its market.

In the wake of the mid-1980s acquisition campaign, Swisher consolidated some of it manufacturing operations, something the company would do again during the early and mid-1990s. The production of Bering cigars was moved from Tampa to Honduras, where it became a 100 percent handmade product, and the production facility in Clearwater that was acquired in the Universal Cigar deal was moved into Swisher's Waycross, Georgia, plant.

The 1990s brought a considerable surge of business for Swisher and its competitors, as the cigar market began to grow after decades of consistent decline. In 1973, when 11.2 billion cigars were sold in the United States, the demand for cigars began to wane, touching off a two-decade-long period of market contraction. By 1993, after perennial decreases in demand, the number of cigars sold had plummeted significantly, falling to 3.4 billion cigars sold for the year. By the end of 1993, however, the tide began to turn, as sales perked upward, invigorated by an aging baby boomer population entering their 40s and 50s. Cigar smoking quickly became a fashionable trend, particularly higher-priced, premium cigars, and demand increased significantly. Between 1993 and 1997 the cigar market grew at a compounded annual rate of nine percent, while the sale of premium cigars shot up 36 percent, lifting total cigar sales in the United States to 4.4 billion.

While the cigar market expanded, Swisher concentrated on streamlining its manufacturing operations to achieve maximum production efficiency during the cigar industry's resurgence. In 1994 the company closed its Waycross, Georgia, plant and con-

solidated its operations into the flagship Jacksonville facility. Concurrently, the company's smokeless tobacco production facility in Helmetta, New Jersey was closed and consolidated into the smokeless tobacco production facility in Wheeling, West Virginia. One year later, in December 1995, Swisher's parent company, American Maize, was sold and, as part of the deal, Swisher was sold to Ziegler, who after 30 years of controlling Swisher was enjoying the first boom years of the cigar market since his company had acquired the cigar manufacturer in 1966.

With the cigar market continuing to expand meaningfully, Ziegler prepared for the late 1990s and the further expected growth of Swisher's industry. In December 1996 he took the company public, raising roughly $100 million in Swisher's initial public offering, which gave him the financial resources to strengthen the company's already stalwart position in the cigar market. In 1997 Ziegler announced plans for a $6.5 million expansion project at Swisher's Jacksonville plant, and late in the year he signed an agreement to purchase a 50 percent interest in SP Holding Inc., the owner of Puros de Villa Gonzales, a major producer of premium, hand-rolled cigars in Santiago, Dominican Republic. In addition, a new production facility in Honduras was opened in October 1997 to make premium hand-rolled cigars, including Swisher's Bering brand. As Ziegler prepared for the beginning of the 21st century, further growth of the cigar market was expected, as a large percentage of the U.S. population aged and entered the most common age bracket of cigar smokers. In 1993, when cigar sales began to climb, people in their 40s and 50s composed 39 percent of the population. By 2,000 this group was expected to compose 43 percent of the population, auguring profitable years ahead for the world's largest cigar producer.

Principal Subsidiaries

Swisher International, Inc.

Further Reading

Basch, Mark, "Jacksonville, Fla.-Based Swisher International Gets a Plug from Brokerage," *Knight-Ridder/Tribune Business News,* September 7, 1997, p. 9.
——, "Swisher Plans To Expand Jacksonville, Fla., Cigar Plant," *Knight-Ridder/Tribune Business News,* February 7, 1997, p. 20.
Marcial, Gene G., "These Cigars Are Really Smokin'," *Business Week,* December 1, 1997, p. 156.
Mathis, Karen Brune, "Swisher International Rolls Out Expansion Plan for Cigar Plant," *Knight-Ridder/Tribune Business News,* June 5, 1997, p. 6.

—Jeffrey L. Covell

Taco Cabana, Inc.

8918 Tesoro Drive
Suite 200
San Antonio, Texas 78217
U.S.A.
(210) 804-0990
Fax: (210) 804-2135
Web site: http://yahoo.com/p/t/taco.html

Public Company
Incorporated: 1978
Employees: 4,000
Sales: $138.5 (1996)
Stock Exchanges: NASDAQ
SIC: 5812 Eating Places; 6794 Patent Owners and
   Lessors

Taco Cabana, Inc., operates and franchises over 100 restaurants that serve Mexican and Tex-Mex food in Texas, Arizona, Georgia, Indiana, New Mexico, Nevada, and Oklahoma. The company that pioneered the concept of "patio cafes," which incorporates semi-enclosed patio dining areas decorated in festive Mexican themes, is one of the most promising of the emerging firms in the restaurant industry within the United States. The reason for this, according to industry analysts, is management's focus on serving generous portions of traditionally prepared Mexican and Tex-Mex food at inexpensive prices, providing an attractive alternative to traditional Mexican restaurants and fast food restaurants. Unique in its ability to make most of its menu fresh each day, rather than pre-made as with other restaurants, Taco Cabana restaurants serve such items as quesadillas, salad entrees, marinated rotisserie chicken (otherwise known as "Chicken Flameante") traditionally prepared Mexican breakfasts, enchiladas, margaritas, and flame-grilled chicken and beef fajitas served on hot iron skillets.

Early History

Taco Cabana was founded by Felix Stehling, a businessman who figured prominently in the San Antonio area, due to the numerous restaurants and taverns that he owned throughout the city. One of his most popular establishments was the Crystal Pistol Bar situated on the corner of Hildebrand and San Pedro avenues. Students from Trinity University frequented the Crystal Pistol Bar on a regular basis; every weekend, and some weekday evenings as well, the place was crowded with people. In fact, the bar was so crowded on certain nights that parking became a major problem. With the convenience and comfort of his customers in mind, not to mention the growing profits from the bar, Stehling decided to purchase the lot across the street on which sat an abandoned Dairy Queen and turn it into a parking lot.

After he purchased the lot, Stehling took the next natural step. Since the property had previously been used for a restaurant, he would transform part of lot and use it to open a taco stand to feed ravenous students as they left the bar. Anticipating success with his new taco stand, Stehling was overwhelmingly disappointed when he woke up after the first night's business only to find all of the patio furniture stolen. Not knowing what to do, Stehling's first thought was to close the operation and go back to what he knew would work. But the entrepreneur in him refused to let go of the idea for a taco stand in the parking lot, and suddenly Stehling came up with the only solution to the problem, namely, keeping the place open through the night. This decision would ultimately give rise to Taco Cabana becoming a round-the-clock operation.

Not surprisingly, with Stehling's organizational ability and his talent for implementing all the appropriate operating systems and accounting mechanisms, in addition to his experience in hiring the right personnel and extensive background in restaurant design, Taco Cabana was an rapid success. From its inception, Stehling was committed to purchasing and selling the highest quality food for his customers. Made from fresh meat and produce delivered by vendors to the small restaurant three times per week, the menu was prepared fresh every day. Stehling was convinced that this would significantly set his restaurant apart from other traditional Mexican restaurants and fast food establishments that heavily depended on serving pre-prepared, pre-packaged, and frozen food to maintain their large customer base.

One of the most attractive features of his taco stand was the inexpensive price for every item on the menu. This pricing policy of Stehling's was intentional, since he thought that Taco Cabana could garner a loyal following by pricing its menu lower than for comparable fare sold in sit-down Mexican restaurants where traditionally-prepared food was the primary attraction. Home-tested recipes and authentic Mexican cuisine, along with alcoholic beverages such as beer and margaritas, were a hit at their low selling price.

Soon Stehling came to realize that he was sitting on top of a potential gold mine. He decided therefore to open up a chain of the Taco Cabana restaurants throughout the city of San Antonio. However, Stehling knew that he couldn't expand without additional help. As a result, he asked two of his brothers to assist him in expanding the business. Brought in as equal partners, the two brothers worked hard to make the Taco Cabana concept successful. Within a short period of time, the hard work of everybody involved paid off handsomely. Under the direction of the family partnership, Taco Cabana grew to include nine restaurants in and around San Antonio. And just as important, revenues were increasing at a dramatic rate.

Growth and Expansion in the 1980s

Throughout the early 1980s, Taco Cabana continued to provide its customers with fresh food and efficient service. At first, Stehling and his brothers had an informal and close-working relationship, where each one of the siblings assumed and fulfilled certain responsibilities related to the business. From one small taco stand, the brothers had built up what was regarded across the city as a highly successful restaurant business. Yet as the company grew larger and larger, with increasing revenues, more staff, and the possibility of even greater expansion, the brothers began to express significant differences in their vision for the firm. Most of these disagreements centered around management issues, and as time went on they became more pronounced. Finally, in 1986, the brothers who had formed a partnership to expand the company went their separate ways. Felix Stehling, of course, the original founder of Taco Cabana, remained at the head of the firm.

The disagreements among the brothers hadn't hurt Taco Cabana's revenues at all, and Stehling decided that he didn't want to wait any longer to expand the firm's operations in a dramatic way. The first step in his expansion plan, therefore, was to hire a right-hand man that would help him in the endeavor. Stehling found the perfect candidate in Richard Cervera. Cervera had been working as a middle management executive at Fuddruckers, a national restaurant chain based in San Antonio. More importantly, Cervera was a regular customer at Taco Cabana, sometimes eating there six time a week, and had inquired about franchise opportunities at the company.

Stehling was intrigued with Cervera's passion for Taco Cabana food, and also impressed with his executive management capabilities, and decided to bring him on board at his firm.

Taco Cabana prospered under the dual leadership of Stehling and Cervera. Hired as the executive vice-president in 1987, Cervera was responsible not only for implementing a strategic expansion plan that Stehling and he had conceived, but the new manager was also responsible for many of the day-to-day operations at the firm. By 1990, the company had added a number of new restaurants to its chain and began expanding into neighboring states. For his effort and accomplishments, Cervera was appointed president of the company in 1990. Cervera continued to pursue an aggressive expansion policy. A strong supporter of franchising, he made a comprehensive support system available to people who arranged franchise agreements with Taco Cabana. The company was now experiencing explosive growth with a private placement in 1991 and the purchase of four restaurants owned and operated by Sombrero Rosa. Another private placement was made the following year, with the acquisition occurring during the early part of 1992. By the end of 1992, the company had gone public with its first stock offering and counted 17 restaurants that were managed and operating under the name Taco Cabana.

Growth and Transition in the 1990s

Earlier, Taco Cabana had filed a lawsuit against Two Pesos, a chain of restaurants originating in San Antonio. Taco Cabana's quick growth and success had attractive many imitators and copycats, so much so that some of these imitators decorated its restaurants and patio cafes in the same bright pastels Taco Cabana used in its restaurant design and decoration. Stehling and Cervera immediately brought the most flagrant of the imitators to court, a restaurant chain named Two Pesos. In 1992, the Supreme Court decided the case in favor of Taco Cabana and awarded the firm $3.7 million in damages from Two Pesos. The lawsuit had severely damaged the financial viability of Two Pesos, and Taco Cabana acquired the firm that had grown to include 30 restaurants in the city of San Antonio and its suburbs.

Having found its niche, and having succeeded in protecting it, Taco Cabana flourished. The acquisitions made during the early 1990s began to pay off enormous dividends in sales and an ever-larger customer base. From 1989 to 1993, sales for the company rose from $29.1 million to $96.9 million. In 1994, sales skyrocketed to $127 million. There was no doubt that Cervera had done his job well, and, assured that the company was in good hands, Stehling resigned as chairman of the company in 1994. Succeeded by Cervera, there was no interruption in the operations of the firm.

In spite of all the good news about increasing revenues and expanding operations, however, Taco Cabana's stock price had dropped rather precipitously. Stockholders blamed Cervera for the nose-dive in stock prices, and there was mounting pressure for Cervera to be replaced. In 1995, Cervera resigned from his position at Taco Cabana and became the new president of the House of Blues restaurant chain. He was replaced by Stephen Clark, who was appointed both chief operating officer and president in the same year.

Prior to his work with Taco Cabana, Clark had worked with Church's Fried Chicken, Inc. for over 18 years, his final position at that company as senior vice-president and concept general manager. His responsibilities included oversight of the company's day-to-day operations for nearly 1,100 firm-owned and franchised restaurants with a sales volume of $600 million. Upon his appointment, Clark immediately began a comprehensive review of the firm's operations, including a close look at its expansion strategy, marketing plans, relations with franchisees, along with a detailed analysis of the sales and profitability trends within its network of restaurants.

The review did not take much time, and the consequences for Taco Cabana's operations were far-reaching. Clark decided to close a number of the company's restaurants, restructure some of the franchisee debts, bring in his own management team, get rid of many non-restaurant related assets, revamp the firm's marketing strategy and, most importantly, slow down all current plans for expansion, including either the opening of new restaurants or franchise agreements. The overall plan was to streamline the company's operations, introduce the advantage of economies of scale, and implement accounting systems and management standards which would enable Taco Cabana to continue growing in the most economically efficient way.

Perhaps the best example of Clark's strategy to improve Taco Cabana's position within the restaurant market was his concern with restaurant layout. Near the end of 1996, under Clark's direction Taco Cabana opened up a new type of restaurant in Dallas to test non-traditional market locations and prototype units for smaller, community-based, markets. Incorporating new designs and features that set it apart from the ordinary design of a Taco Cabana restaurant, the prototype unit in Dallas featured a rounded front, clay tile roof, a trellis shading the patio area, aged wood paneling and distressed stainless steel counter tops that gave the customer the impression of walking into an old Mexican cafe. One of the most important additions to this prototype design was bright neon on the exterior of the building to advertise the Taco Cabana menu. Designs kept from the original Taco Cabana restaurants included the bright pink signature paint used generously throughout the restaurant, an open cooking area where patrons could see their food being prepared, and retractable garage doors so that the dining area could be opened to the outside during good weather.

Clark's strategy worked well. The newly designed prototype attracted more customers than expected, and plans for a series of these new designs to be built in Texas were underway in the late 1990s. The implementation of a new vision and mission statement, the writing of the company's first business plan, and the installation of new operating principles for managers and employees at all the company's restaurants had tangible results; while growth slowed, more cost-effective, better financial systems improved employee accountability and profit margins, and a more streamlined administrative and management system garnered a more effective operating structure.

With the dramatic growth of Taco Cabana brought under control by Clark's leadership, the restaurant is poised for steady growth and increased profits. Such growth will be measured and calculated, so that construction costs are minimized, customer service is enhanced, operational efficiency is improved, and the image of Taco Cabana as a unique type of Mexican restaurant is assured.

Further Reading

Liddle, Alan, "Chains Traveling Different Roads to Interactive Nirvana," *Nation's Restaurant News,* January 13, 1997, p. 21.

"Marketing Miscellaneous," *Nation's Restaurant News,* November 27, 1995, p. 14.

McLaughlin, John, "Growth Chains Are Missing the Mark on Expansion," *Restaurant Business,* March 20, 1995, p. 14.

Robertiello, Jack, "H-E-B to Test Whether In-Store Taco Cabanas Will Be Hot," *Supermarket News,* November 18, 1996, p. 21.

Ruggless, Ron, "Taco Cabana Expands, Opens Prototype Unit in Dallas Suburb," *Nation's Restaurant News,* January 6, 1997, p. 7.

——, "Taco Closes Doors in Colorado, Turns Focus to Core Markets," *Nation's Restaurant News,* December 1, 1997, p. 3.

"Taco Cabana, Inc.," *The Wall Street Journal,* August 19, 1997, p. B9(E).

"Taco Cabana Sets Buyback," *The Wall Street Journal,* April 17, 1997, p. A10(E).

—Thomas Derdak

Tatung Co.

22 Chungshan North Road, Section 3
Taipei 104
Taiwan
+886-2-592-5252
Fax: +886-2-591-5185
Web site: http://www.tatung.com

Public Company
Incorporated: 1957
Employees: 19,500
Sales: NT$84.7 billion (US$3.1 billion) (1995)
Stock Exchanges: Taiwan
SICs: 3679 Electronic Components, Not Elsewhere
Classified; 2731 Book Publishing; 2711 Newspapers;
6512 Nonresidential Building Operators; 6514
Dwelling Operators Not Apartments; 6513 Apartment
Building Operators

With ten domestic plants and nearly 20,000 employees, Tatung Co. is Taiwan's leading manufacturer of consumer electronics. Having operated in the construction industry throughout the first half of the 20th century, the company entered into manufacturing after World War II. Tatung's manufacturing expertise and product line evolved over the ensuing decades. Expanding from a base in small electrical appliances, by the late 1990s the company made a diverse array of products in three primary categories: computer and communication electronics, consumer electric appliances, and industrial electric products. As if that were not diverse enough, Tatung also dabbles in publishing, horticulture, and industrial coatings. By the beginning of 1997, Tatung's Chunghwa (China) Picture Tubes subsidiary was the biggest manufacturer of cathode ray tubes (CRT) in the world, shipping over 20 million units. The company also sells more than one million television sets and 1.5 million computers each year. In addition to its substantial Taiwanese interests, Tatung has operations in the United States, United Kingdom, Germany, Holland, the Middle East, Japan, China, Singapore, and Indonesia.

Since its establishment in the 1910s, the company and its many affiliates have been led by members of the Lin family. In the waning years of the 20th century, Lin Wei-Shan, standard-bearer for the third generation, appeared poised to assume the chairmanship from his father, Lin Ting-Sheng, who had held that post since 1971.

Early 20th-Century Foundations

The company originated in 1918, when founder Lin Shan-Chih established the Shan-Chih Business Association. At the time, the island nation of Taiwan was just beginning to emerge from the first phase of its modern economic history, a largely agrarian economy. As a construction company (and later a leading manufacturer), Shan-Chih played an important role in the second phase of Taiwan's development, the creation of a basic infrastructure and the development of manufacturing industries. Over the course of its first 24 years in business, the company completed an average of 25 construction projects annually. Its most famous project was the Executive Yuan in Taipei, the seat of Taiwan's national government. It was during this second cycle or "wave" of national economic development, which lasted roughly from the 1930s to the 1980s, that Taiwan would emerge as one of Asia's "Four Tigers"—fast-growing economies that were heavily reliant on borrowed technology and enjoyed trade surpluses.

In line with Taiwan's transformation into a manufacturing base, Lin's company underwent its own metamorphosis in the 1940s and 1950s. Upon his 1942 retirement from the construction industry, Lin Shan-Chih endowed an unusual entity that combined educational and industrial functions. After liquidating the construction company, he apportioned 80 percent of his fortune to an entity called the Hsieh-Chih Association for the Development of Industry. Set up to promote the trades and provide a practical education in manufacturing and industrial management, Hsieh-Chih's earliest projects included the endowment of professional organizations, industrial awards, scholarships, and vocational schools. Perhaps most importantly, the trust also invested in the establishment of Tatung Co. Literally "great harmony," Tatung meant much more to the Lin family. As Shan-Chih's son Ting-Sheng told *Business Week* in

1985, the name ''means helping others''—enterprise in harmony with education. This duality would make Tatung a real-life workshop where students would apply the principles they had learned at the family's vocational schools. Lin Ting-Sheng was named president of Tatung, while Shan-Chih assumed the role of chairman.

At first, students and employees at Tatung repaired train cars and performed other ''odd jobs,'' but by the end of the 1940s the company had established its first true manufacturing operation producing and assembling electric fans—a rather pressing need on this muggy subtropical island.

From the outset, Tatung adopted progressive business practices. In 1942, Lin Shan-Chih set aside ten percent of his personal wealth to fund an employee stock program. He instituted an employee welfare program in 1947, and the company set up the Tatung Institute of Technology in 1956, and inaugurated a publishing operation in 1959 and endowed the Tatung Vocational School. The company professes high ideals, including ''to help create new Chinese culture by proper personal discipline, harmonious family relations, good school-company-factory management, wise government of a state and peace on earth.''

IPO in 1950s Presages Expansion

Tatung went public in 1957 and tapped the bond market a year later. Proceeds of these two issues financed the growing company's forays into electric appliances and industrial electric motors in the 1960s. Tatung broke ground on a new plant in 1960 and refrigerators started rolling off the lines in 1961. The company added televisions and air conditioners to its offerings in 1964, and began manufacturing telecommunications products in 1966.

Lin Shan-Chih lived long enough to see his company grow to become Taiwan's largest non-governmental concern; a conglomerate with more than NT$2.2 billion in sales by 1970. When he died in 1971, son Lin Ting-Sheng succeeded him as chairman and grandson Lin Wei-Shan advanced to the presidency. Lin Ting-Sheng has been active in politics as well as industry. As a member of the Kuomintang (KMT) nationalist political party, he was elected Speaker of Taipei's city council in 1970.

Having made its first exports to the Philippines in the 1950s, Tatung expanded its overseas sales program to Japan in the late 1960s. Tatung initiated exports of fans to the United States in 1971, set up a subsidiary in California the following year, and

inaugurated manufacturing at a plant in Los Angeles in 1974. The U.S. factory started out making fans, but had added televisions to its repertoire within two years. Tatung's television sets won design awards and its consumer electronics were supported with advertising slogans like ''Cat got your Tatung?,'' but the brand never really caught on among Americans. During this decade, the company also expanded into the Pacific Rim, establishing subsidiaries in Singapore in 1972, Japan in 1975, and South Korea in 1979.

Computer Components Emerge As Key Products in 1980s

Tatung's wide-ranging diversification continued through the 1980s, as the company added elevators, office furniture, and fax machines to its lineup. But perhaps most importantly, the company began to emphasize its ten-year-old computer interests, which included the Chunghwa Picture Tubes (CPT) subsidiary (founded 1970) and a joint venture with the Fujitsu computer company of Japan (established 1973). Originally created to manufacture cathode ray tubes (CRTs) for Tatung's televisions, CPT's expertise was harnessed for the production of computer monitors during this time. Like many other Taiwanese companies, Tatung built its business by forging OEM (original equipment manufacture) agreements with some of the world's largest computer companies, including IBM. Under these arrangements, well-established firms like IBM contracted with low-cost manufacturers like Tatung to manufacture components (and eventually entire computers and peripherals) to IBM's specifications.

By the end of the decade, Tatung was Taiwan's largest manufacturer of computer monitors, and this segment had grown to contribute over 30 percent of the company's revenues. There was one major caveat, however: the company relied on IBM for over 60 percent of its information systems sales. Tatung's total sales had multiplied more than tenfold from about NT$2 billion in 1970 to nearly NT$29.4 billion by 1988.

Growth Slows in Early 1990s

By 1989, Tatung had evolved into a massive conglomerate with NT$31.1 billion in sales, a laundry list of awards and accomplishments, and subsidiary operations throughout the world. But Tatung had an Achilles heel that did not become apparent until Taiwan's heretofore burgeoning economy hit a speed bump in the early 1990s. The company's sales slid by more than ten percent from 1989 to 1990 and net income took an 85.7 percent dive. Tatung survived the recession better than many of its red-ink-stained competitors, but the economic downturn cast a spotlight on the company's lack of innovation and brand equity outside its home country. Writing for *Datamation* magazine in 1992, analyst Carol Wei noted that Tatung's ''authoritarian management structure has hamstrung development staff and hampered marketing creativity,'' a sad state of affairs for a company affiliated with some of Taiwan's leading institutions of vocational education.

By this time, Taiwan had entered what has come to be known as the ''third wave'' of its economic development, a time when a new generation of business leaders took the initiative. Instead of merely manufacturing products based on other companies' trend-setting technologies, these entrepreneurs developed their own innovations, sold them under their own brand names, and reaped the profits that came with such risks. Whereas many of the nation's other top technology firms had caught this "third wave," Tatung seemed stranded on a sandbar—content to pursue alliances, joint ventures, and OEM contracts to expand its expertise and bring new products to its home markets. In 1991, the company inked an agreement with Packard Bell under which Tatung would provide the U.S.-based electronics marketer with 1.2 million personal computers annually, PCs that would be sold under the Packard Bell name. In 1995, Tatung's Chunghwa Picture Tubes subsidiary arrived at a similar contract to make tubes for Toshiba's large-screen televisions. A 1996 alliance with Honeywell built a $100 million semiconductor plant near the U.S. company's Minnesota headquarters.

For more than 80 years, Tatung and its predecessor companies have been committed to four basic ideals: "honesty, integrity, industry, and frugality." It appeared that the time had come for a new generation of leadership to add "branding" and "innovation" to the panoply of corporate emblems. By the 1990s, less than five percent of Tatung's overall sales were generated by branded products. Third-generation Tatung president Lin Wei-Shan dedicated himself to increasing his company's brand presence, vowing in 1992 that own label sales would one day match OEM revenues.

In pursuit of that goal, the company expanded into the manufacture of clones, including network workstations based on SPARC (scalable-processor architecture) technology licensed from Sun Microsystems, Inc. Tatung launched its first-generation workstation in 1990 under the Mariner brand. The company introduced a line of built-to-order computers under the Unison label in 1995. Tatung was also among the first companies to license Macintosh's operating system in preparation for launching Mac clones late in 1997. Though the long-awaited Macs promised low prices to consumers, some industry observers wondered whether Tatung and the other cloners would be able to effectively—and profitably—promote their derivative products in the highly competitive market.

Nevertheless, Tatung's new strategies appeared to serve it well. Sales increased by a whopping 62.9 percent from 1992 to 1995, topping NT$84.6 billion in the latter year. Profit also increased dramatically, multiplying from NT$1.2 billion in 1992 to NT$6.6 billion mid-decade.

Principal Subsidiaries

Chunghwa Picture Tubes Co.; Taiwan Telecommunication Industry Co.; Forward Electronics Co.; Tatung Otis Elevator Co.; San Chih Machinery Co.; Tatung Fujitsu Co.; San Chih Container Terminal Co.; San Chih Coating Co.; San Chih Chemical Co.; Tatung Fujidenka Co.; Tatung Press Cast Co.; Tatung Chugai Precious Metals Co.; Kuen Der Co.; Tatung Forest Construction Co.; Hsieh Chih Industrial Library Publishing Co.; Tatung Horticulture Co.; Chunghwa Electronic Investment Co.; Tatung Electronic Co.; Taipei Industrial Co.; Taipei Electric Foil Co.; Tatung Co. of America Inc.; Tatung (U.K.) Ltd.; Tatung Co. of Japan Inc.; Tatung Science & Technology, Inc.; Tatung Telecom Corp.; Tatung Electronics (Singapore) PTE Ltd.; Tatung Electric Co. Of America Inc.; Tatung (Thailand) Co.; Tatung International Corp. S.A.L.; Tatung International (Deutschland) GmbH (Germany); Fuk Tatung (Thailand) Ltd.; P.T. Tatung Budi Indonesia; Tatung Netherlands B.V.

Further Reading

Arensman, Russ, "Taiwan's PC Makers at the Workstation Crossroads," *Electronic Business*, April 8, 1991, pp. 63–65.
Donohue, James F., "Sun Licenses SPARC to Cloners in the Orient," *Systems Integration*, August 1989, p. 26.
Furukawa, Tsukasa, "Taiwan Electronic Makers' Growth Hopes High," *Retailing Home Furnishings*, December 21, 1981, p. 50.
Gruman, Galen, "Inside the Next Generation Macs," *Macworld*, September 1997, pp. 32–34.
——, "Tatung Gets Mac License," *Macworld*, February 1997, p. 37.
Gruman, Galen, and Terho Uimonen, "Tatung Prepares to Make Macs," *Macworld*, July 1996, p. 40.
Jones, Dorothy E., et al, "The 'Four Tigers' Start Clawing at Upscale Markets; A Barrage of Brand-Name Goods from Korea, Taiwan, Hong Kong and Singapore," *Business Week*, July 22, 1985, pp. 136–38.
King, Elliot, "Tatung Looks for Its Niche in U.S. Consumer Electronics Market," *Global Trade*, October 1987, p. 52.
Quinlan, Tom, "Tatung Moves into Build-to-Order Market," *InfoWorld*, March 20, 1995, p. 34.
"Seventy-Nine Years of History and Honors," Tatung Co., [1997] http://www.tatung.com.tw/en/tatung/history.html.
Shatz-Akin, Jim, "The Sharper, Cheaper Image," *MacUser*, May 1995, pp. 74–81.
Wei, Carol, "The Datamation 100: Asian 25 (Tatung Co.)," *Datamation*, September 1, 1992, pp. 89–103.

—April D. Gasbarre

Taylor Made Golf Co.

2271 Cosmos Court
Carlsbad, California 92009
U.S.A.
(760) 931-1991
Fax: (760) 931-0950
Web site: http://www.taylormadegolf.com

Wholly Owned Subsidiary of Adidas-Salomon Group
Incorporated: 1979 as Taylor Made Golf Co.
Employees: 585
Sales: $550 million (1997 est.)
SICs: 3949 Sporting and Athletic Goods, Not Elsewhere
   Classified

The second largest manufacturer of golf clubs in the United States, Taylor Made Golf Co. designs and markets a complete line of clubs for men, women, and children, as well as golf accessories and golf bags. Taylor Made scored its initial success with its first product, metal drivers, which debuted in 1979 and subsequently dominated the golf market. With its focus on research and development and aggressive marketing, the company grew to be the second largest U.S. golf manufacturer by the mid-1990s, a ranking attained because of the popularity of its Burner Bubble drivers, introduced in 1995. In 1997 Adidas AG acquired Salomon, Taylor Made's parent company, thereby creating Adidas-Salomon Group. Taylor Made was organized as a wholly owned subsidiary of Adidas-Salomon Group. Headquartered in Carlsbad, California, Taylor Made had operations in Japan, Great Britain, New Zealand, and Canada.

Origins of an Innovator

Taylor Made was founded by an entrepreneur named Gary Adams, who spent as much time as he could playing golf. His entrepreneurial creation was predicated on his greatest passion, a company with foundation that rested on a singular innovation that became a golf industry standard. That product, the Taylor Made Metalwood, changed the face of golfing across the globe. During the seven centuries of golf's recorded history, the game that originated in the Scottish Highlands underwent compara-

tively few technological changes. The only equipment used to play the game—balls and clubs—remained technologically the same for generations, and sometimes for centuries, before a new type of ball or a new type of club gained widespread use. From the era of the Crusades to the dawn of industrialized society in the 19th century, the advancements in golf equipment were few and far between. In golf's modern era, when the number of golfers in the world rose exponentially and a new class of golfer—the professional—competed for multimillion-dollar purses, the speed at which technological change occurred became decidedly swifter. Golf had evolved into big business, with manufacturers vying for control of a market that was becoming increasingly lucrative. Although the financial incentive for developing a superior product was large, its size made it no easier to obtain. Golf was a difficult game to master and a difficult game for which to make technological improvements. Many innovations failed miserably after their market introduction, but for those few advancements that won over customers and met the approval of the professional ranks, the rewards were lasting and significant. Taylor Made was one of the handful of manufacturers able to carve a place for itself in the golf industry with an innovative product that earned the confidence of golfers worldwide. The credit for the innovation fell to the company's creator, Gary Adams.

Roughly a decade before Adams began his fateful experimentation, a surlyn-covered, two-piece golf ball made its debut on the market. The two-piece golf balls traveled farther than any ball in the history of the sport, making it an instant necessity for any serious golfer. Two-piece golf balls quickly became the ball of choice for the golfing public and for professionals alike, offering the one advantage that translated into success in the golf equipment industry: distance. Increasing distance was the objective Adams was pursuing when he began tinkering in the late 1970s with different materials for making golf clubs. Using the superior two-piece golf balls, Adams discovered the balls traveled a greater distance when struck with a club made out of metal than with the traditional persimmon and laminated wood clubs used universally. The essence of his pioneering work completed, Adams designed the first Premium Metalwood driver and formed a company to manufacture and market his creation, the Taylor Made Golf Co., which started in McHenry, Illinois in 1979.

The patented, stainless steel Taylor Made Metalwood clubs were first presented to the public at the Professional Golf Association's (PGA) Merchandise Show in 1979. Not surprisingly, buyers at the show examined the new clubs warily. Technological change in the golf industry occurred at a glacial speed and, consequently, skeptics were not hard to find. For those who tried the odd-looking clubs made by an unknown start-up company, the reaction was positive, but for Adams to make his fledgling company a success he knew he needed to convince a particular type of golfer that metal drivers were superior to conventional clubs. In the golfing world, professionals were the ruling class, the arbitrators of success or failure for all manufacturers. Less skilled golfers looked up to professionals, noted the equipment they used and, more often than not, based their purchasing decisions on the brands chosen by professional players. Tournament victories recorded by a particular player using a particular brand of equipment were the heart of marketing in the golf industry. Put a manufacturer's product in the hands of a winner and that manufacturer gained a significant advantage over other competitors. Adams realized this fact and made it his primary objective from the start of Taylor Made's existence.

In his company's inaugural year, Adams convinced 47 professionals competing in the 1979 PGA Club Professional Championship to play with Taylor Made's metal clubs. Skeptics who eyed the clubs distrustfully at the PGA's trade show were quick to change their perspective, as the Taylor Made brand and its unique metal clubs achieved their first step toward legitimacy among golfing aficionados in the United States. By the end of 1980 the company's sales were beginning their rise, fueled by the exposure Taylor Made Metalwoods were receiving on the national professional circuit. Three years later anxiety stemming from whether metal clubs would ever catch on as a widespread phenomenon within the golf industry was no longer a concern. By 1983 Taylor Made Metalwoods prevailed on the national tour, where an average of 60 Taylor Made clubs were in play each week and, consequently, were highly popular items in pro shops and retail outlets across the country. Metal, from this juncture forward, was the preferred material used in manufacturing golf clubs. Adams's pioneering work had taken hold.

Mid-1980s: Legitimacy and New Owners

As would be expected, once the golfing public had shown their preference for metal clubs other manufacturers were quick to follow Taylor Made's lead. Other manufacturers began marketing their own brands of metal clubs, as the new industry standard dictated the direction of the market. Concurrently, Taylor Made, the industry maverick and holder of a sizable lead in the new metal market, was a coveted company drawing the attention of would-be suitors interested in sharing in the company's success. A corporate marriage, mutually beneficial to both parties, occurred shortly after Taylor Made made metal clubs the industry norm. In 1984 the French ski equipment manufacturer Salomon S.A. acquired Taylor Made, organizing the company as one of its numerous wholly owned subsidiaries.

For Salomon, the acquisition gave it a promising entry into the golf market, and for Taylor Made, the benefits resulting from its inclusion under Salomon's formidable corporate umbrella were chiefly financial. A giant in the ski industry, Salomon had deep financial pockets, possessing far greater financial resources than Taylor Made could ever hope to draw from as an independent company operating in its fifth year of business. Further, Salomon had a legacy of innovation based on a commitment to research and development that Taylor Made would need as it attempted to build on its initial success with its patented metal clubs. For Taylor Made, its union with Salomon was more than a marriage of convenience; it bordered on a marriage of necessity. Other, more experienced, and more financially well-equipped golf manufacturers had sniffed the prevailing winds of consumer demand. Taylor Made would need the support of a much larger ally to maintain its lead in the metal club market and develop additional innovations to drive its progress in later years.

Although Taylor Made's metal clubs looked to be the market winner at the time of the Salomon acquisition, the company still had several important hurdles to clear before it could rightly claim to be one of the elite golf club manufacturers in the country. Those obstacles were surmounted during the mid-1980s when the company's signature metal clubs were used to record important victories on the professional tour. In 1984 a Taylor Made Metalwood driver was used to win one of golf's major tournaments, the 1984 PGA Championship. The following year the company's market position was bolstered considerably by a string of victories registered by players using Taylor Made clubs, including the Canadian Open, the Honda Classic, and the Panasonic Las Vegas Invitational.

As these important victories were being tallied on the links, Taylor Made prepared for the years ahead by introducing a new line of products and consolidating its manufacturing operations. The company's new Burner and Burner Plus drivers ranked as the most popular clubs used on the PGA circuit by the mid-1980s and a new line of putters constructed with heel-and-toe weighting debuted in 1985, the same year the company migrated west. Headquartered in Illinois, where Adams had founded the company, Taylor Made also operated a manufacturing facility in Carlsbad, California, the epicenter of golf club production in the United States. In 1985 the company closed its Illinois offices and consolidated them with the production plant in Carlsbad, where the largest producers of golf clubs in the United States were located. Two years after the move, construction of a new 90,000-square-foot production plant in Carlsbad was completed, giving the company the manufacturing capacity to meet the steady demand for its golf clubs.

Explosive 1990s Growth

The early and mid-1980s brought Taylor Made to the fore in the golf industry, with its innovative and highly popular clubs driving the company's transformation from small upstart into a formidable competitor underpinned by strong brand recognition. The bustle of activity that described the company's progress during the first half of 1980 tapered off somewhat during the latter half of the decade. Taylor Made fed off the momentum built up from its pioneering introduction of metal golf clubs, yet lacked the energetic surge in business that would have been sparked by the development of a new, eye-catching line of clubs. It was not until the mid-1990s that Taylor Made executives could point to a new line of clubs capable of generating the same amount of enthusiasm as its Premium Metalwood and Burner brands. When the company introduced its new Burner Bubble driver in the mid-1990s, with its innovative shaft that enabled golfers to swing faster without extra effort, industry pundits projected a boost to Taylor Made's business, particularly after a Burner Bubble prototype became the first Metalwood to win at the Masters Tournament in Augusta, Georgia.

As the company geared itself for the debut of the new Burner Bubble clubs to the public in 1995, expectations were high that the new line would inject new life into the company. The company's vice-president of marketing and its future leader, George Montgomery, conceded that Taylor Made "has been stagnant for about three years" and was intent on creating as big a marketing stir as he could with Burner Bubble drivers. Montgomery, who prior to joining Taylor Made in the early 1990s had helped Seattle's K2 Corp. become the leading ski brand in the United States, made plans for what the company described as the largest budget "ever allocated for golf club launch." An unprecedented $18 million was set aside for advertising and marketing support, 50 percent more than the company's total marketing budget in 1994 and twice the amount it spent in 1993. When the Burner Bubble clubs were introduced amid a dense flurry of print and television advertising, the results were encouraging, with 500,000 clubs sold during the first eight months of availability and the company's pre-launch goals having been exceeded. For the year, domestic sales soared 90 percent, while international sales surged 50 percent, giving the company an estimated $220 million in total sales for 1995. Montgomery was pleased. "I'm recommending a $30 million budget," he declared in response to Taylor Made's marketing plans for 1996.

By 1996 Montgomery found himself in a position that added considerably more influence to his recommendations. In May, Charles Yash, Taylor Made's chief executive officer and president, left the company unexpectedly to help form Callaway Golf Ball Co. Yash's defection into a major competitor's ranks (Callaway Golf Company ranked as the largest U.S. golf manufacturer) cleared the way for Montgomery's ascension to Taylor Made's top two executive posts. Montgomery inherited a company that he had helped transform into an industry leader. When he joined the company, it ranked as the sixth largest U.S. golf manufacturer. By the time he stood atop Taylor Made's worldwide operations, the company ranked as the second largest U.S. golf manufacturer, larger than Cobra Golf Inc. and trailing only Callaway Golf.

In early 1997 Taylor Made announced plans to consolidate its operations in Carlsbad and to expand production capacity significantly, as it moved to narrow the gap separating it from Callaway and distance itself from encroachment by Cobra. Included in the expansion project were a 206,000-square-foot main building, a 4,250-square-foot test engineering laboratory,

and a six-acre club-testing range that would enable the company to produce more than four million golf clubs a year, nearly twice the capacity of its three existing plants in Carlsbad. Slated to be concluded at the start of 1998, construction began in March 1997. Midway through the expansion, Taylor Made received news of a deal that augured well for its future plans. In September, Salomon agreed to sell controlling interest in Taylor Made and its other sports equipment companies to global giant Adidas AG, a move that both those within and outside Taylor Made viewed as a positive development for the Carlsbad golf manufacturer. Again, Montgomery was pleased by what he saw. "This is a tremendous move for Taylor Made," he told reporters, "giving us access to the resources of the number two company in the world in sports clothing and shoes. Joining the Adidas family undoubtedly will help Taylor Made as we continue our aggressive growth plans."

Once the $1.53 billion deal was concluded, Taylor Made had a new parent company, a worldwide sports conglomerate that called itself Adidas-Salomon Group. To this new parent, Taylor Made had impressive results to report at the end of 1997. The company's retail market share in metalwoods in the United States was up 25 percent, its irons market share was up nearly 30 percent, putter sales had more than tripled, and Taylor Made's golf bag sales had doubled. In nearly every facet of the company's business, growth was rampant, instilling Taylor Made executives with confidence that the future held considerable promise. As the company moved into its new facilities early in 1998, it announced plans to introduce the golf industry's first line of golf clubs designed expressly for children. With the doors open to this potentially lucrative market niche, Taylor Made braced itself for the beginning of the 21st century and the continuation of its steady rise within the U.S. golf industry.

Principal Subsidiaries

Salomon Taylor Made Ltd. (United Kingdom); Salomon & Taylor Made Co. Ltd. (Japan); Taylor Made France.

Further Reading

"California Group Names Taylor Made Golf Top Marketer for 1996," *Knight-Ridder/Tribune Business News,* June 3, 1997, p. 6.

Day, Kathy, "California's Taylor Made Golf Names CEO," *Knight-Ridder/Tribunes Business News,* May 24, 1996, p. 5.

Kragen, Pam, "President of California's Taylor Made Golf Says Sale Is Good for Firm," *Knight-Ridder/Tribune Business News,* September 17, 1997, p. 9.

Pate, Russ, "California Golf Company Plans New Corporate Headquarters," *Knight-Ridder/Tribune Business News,* March 12, 1997, p. 31.

——, "Some Golf Ads Click; Others Clink," *ADWEEK Eastern Edition,* April 22, 1991, p. 21.

Stogel, Chuck, "Cobra Broadens Via Non-Golf Brands," *Brandweek,* February 5, 1996, p. 14.

——, "Taylor Made Bubble Media $ To Double," *Brandweek,* January 2, 1995, p. 2.

"Taylor Made To Introduce Kids Golf Club Line," *Knight-Ridder/Tribune Business News,* February 22, 1998, p. 2.

"Taylor Made U.S. Market Share in Metalwoods Rises by 25 Percent, Irons Up by 30 Percent through October '97," *PR Newswire,* January 2, 1998, p. 1.

—Jeffrey L. Covell

Télévision Française 1

1, quai du Point du Jour
92656 Boulogne Cedex
France
(33) 1 41 41 21 23
Fax: (33) 1 41 41 20 23
Web site: http://www.tf1.fr

Public Company
Incorporated: 1987
Employees: 2,081
Sales: FFr 10.167 billion (US$1.9 billion) (1997)
Stock Exchanges: Paris
SICs: 4833 Television Broadcasting Stations; 4841 Cable
and Other Pay Television Services

Télévision Française 1 is a diversified multimedia producer and broadcaster, centered around TF1, France's oldest and market-leading television station. Since its privatization in 1987, TF1 has nearly quadrupled its revenues and expanded into a network of subsidiaries and partnerships with interests in nearly every media and related category. Principal shareholder in, and de facto leader of, TF1 is France's communications giant Bouygues, which holds approximately 40 percent of the company's shares. The company's primary revenue generator is its sales of advertising space, through subsidiary TF1 Publicité, for TF1 and the company's cable and satellite television stations Eurosport, LCI, and Odyssée. Despite growing pressure from cable television and France's emerging satellite television market, TF1 continues to capture the leading audience share (35 percent of persons aged four years and older) among the five French generalist broadcasters. Although this market share represents a drop from the company's late 1980s high of 40 percent of the French viewing audience, the company nevertheless has enjoyed consistent—and profitable—revenue growth, capturing more than half of the total French television advertising market. In 1997 advertising sales represented more than FFr 7.6 billion of the company's total FFr 10.2 billion in revenues.

In addition to TF1, the company's activities include the following: cable and satellite broadcasting, through the pan-European sports channel, Eurosport, broadcasting in 14 languages to an audience of some 72 million people in 43 countries; Europe's first pay-per-view broadcaster, Multivision; and the theme channels Odyssée (documentaries) and LCI Le Chaîne Info (24-hour French-language news). In partnership with CLT, Lyonnaise des Eaux, France Telecom, France Télévision, and broadcaster M6, the company has also entered the satellite broadcasting market with the TPS (Télévision Par Satellite) service. TF1's share of 25 percent in TPS makes it that broadcaster's largest individual shareholder.

Complementing its primary broadcasting operations, TF1 has built a strong portfolio of film, television, video, and other production and distribution activities. The company's production subsidiaries include TF1 Films Production, Banco Production (made-for-television movies and magazines), Protocréa (audiovisual), and Glem Production (variety, musical, and theatrical events), which produce primarily for broadcast on TF1. The company is also engaged in the acquisition and exploitation of film and other audiovisual production rights, through subsidiary TF1 International and 34 percent holding in TCM DA in partnership with M6 and CLT. Rounding out TF1's offering are its music recording and publishing subsidiary, Une Musique, and its book publishing subsidiary, TF1 Editions. Together, the company's diversification activities contribute more than 25 percent of the company's revenues.

Privatizing in the 1980s

"La Une" occupied a venerable position in the French television market long before its privatization as TF1. Established in 1947, TF1 was France's first television broadcaster. As in many European countries, television broadcasting was placed under the control of the French government, which had, in the post-World War II period, placed a ban on private ownership of radio, and then television, broadcasters. Funding for the new commercial-free television service came primarily from required subscription fees placed upon the French viewing audience, while operations were placed under the Radio Télévision Francais (RTF) agency. TF1 remained France's sole television broadcaster until 1964, when it was joined by Antenna 2 (later, France 2). A third broadcaster, France 3, was added in 1972. Production and diffusion activities remained under the RTF (which had become known as the ORTF).

In the 1970s, however, the French television landscape began to undergo a transformation. In 1974 the ORTF was abandoned. A new system was put into place, separating the agency's former activities into seven independent operations, including the three television broadcasters. Although broadcasters remained public bodies and continued to receive funding from subscription fees, each station was now required to operate on a for-profit basis. Operations of TFI were conducted under a new enterprise, the Société Nationale de Programmes de Télévision Française 1 (changed to Télévision Française 1 in 1981). The new company quickly established itself as an ambitious programmer for its own productions—leading, despite the introduction of advertising, to losses by the beginning of the 1980s.

The new decade would see a fresh expansion of the French television market. In 1981 the way was cleared for the arrival of the first private radio stations in nearly half a century. Three years later the country's first private television broadcaster, Canal Plus, an encrypted, subscription-based service, was granted the country's fourth television channel. Two more privately held commercial channels were added in 1986. By then movement had been made to privatize one of the three government-run broadcasters—a development that nonetheless met with reluctance among both the viewing public and the government. The move toward privatization, however, came during a period in which the government, led by François Mitterand and the Socialist Party, began to dismantle its nationalization experiment (which had seen much of France's industry placed under government ownership in the late 1970s and early 1980s). Debate focused on which broadcaster would become private, the profitable Antenna 2, or the money-losing TF1. The arrival of a new nonsocialist government, under Jacques Chirac, would end the debate. Privatization of the country's oldest and leading broadcaster, TF1, served the symbolic purpose of announcing the end of an era of Socialist Party dominance of the French political scene. The principal of TF1's privatization was signed into law in September 1986.

Debate next focused on who would be allowed to take a majority share in the privatized country. Suitors for the station included French media powerhouse Hachette. Yet, leery of creating what would become in essence an information monopoly, the government's choice finally went to the industrial and telecommunications giant, Groupe Bouygues. Led by Francis Bouyges, the group would pay some FFr 3 billion to take a 25 percent share in TF1 (while representing as well the interests of a core shareholder group representing another 25 percent); an additional ten percent went to TF1's employees and the remainder was sold on the Paris stock exchange. TF1 became a private company in April 1987. Francis Bouygues assured the company's direction; in 1988, however, Bouygues (who retired the following year) named Patrick Le Lay to succeed him as TF1's CEO.

Diversification in the Late 1980s

TF1 initially faced a difficult transition, including the walkout of a number of its most prominent on-air personalities. Yet the company's share of the French viewing audience would remain strong through the end of the 1980s, reaching more than 40 percent, while its share of television advertising revenues topped 55 percent of the total French market. Nonetheless, the company faced a changing market. The appearance of private broadcaster M6 gave TF1 direct competition for its primary target audience (the so-called "under-50 housewife"). Cable television, while slow to penetrate the French market, promised an expanded choice of channels for the French viewer. The future satellite broadcasting technology, capable of reaching even non-cabled areas of the country, at the same time promised still more competition for the French viewing audience.

TF1 immediately set out to diversify its operations. In 1987 the company created two subsidiaries. The first, TF1 Publicité, took over operations of the company's advertising sales activities. The second, Télé-Shopping, introducing the home shopping concept to the French morning viewer. The company also began an aggressive content drive, investing some FFr 640 million in new television productions. These moves proved successful: by the end of the year the company had topped a 40 percent share of the television viewing audience and the company's broadcasts captured 37 of the top 50 most-watched programs for the year. Revenues, meanwhile, had more than doubled since the early 1980s, nearing FFr 5 billion.

By 1988 the company had become profitable. TF1's expansion continued, with the formation of a music recording and publishing arm, Une Musique, as well as a book publishing wing, TF1 Editions. The company's television programming was boosted in that year by a deal with the Walt Disney Company to include more than four hours of Disney programs per week in the TF1 schedule. At the same time TF1 was developing an important on-air personality, its news anchorman Patrick Poivre d'Arvor, who would take the top audience rating for the year. Committed by law to guaranteeing a specific proportion of French-produced broadcasts, TF1 stepped up its investment in its in-house production activities, spending nearly FFr 1 billion in that year. Joining the company in that year was Francis Bouygues's daughter Corinne, who took charge of the company's communications activities (a position she had previously held in the Bouygues group).

With investments of more than FFr 1.2 billion in 1989, TF1 continued to build its production portfolio, while diffusion operations (video, program rights sales, and other services) were boosted with the creation of its TF1 Entreprises subsidiary. The creation in 1990 of two new production subsidiaries, Banco Production (made-for-TV movies and magazine programs) and TF1 Publicité Production (advertising films), was complemented by the acquisition of audiovisual programming producer Protécrea.

New Competitors for the 1990s

In the 1990s TF1 began looking beyond its own broadcasts. In 1991 the company agreed to take over operations of the struggling Eurosport channel, the first European-wide sports broadcaster, principally to the cable market; in that year TF1 added a French-language version of Eurosport. By then revenues from the company's diversified activities had more than doubled over the previous year, topping FFr 1 billion of the company's total sales of FFr 6.5 billion. Net profits had continued to grow as well, reaching FFr 341 million in 1991. That year saw the appointment of Corinne Bouygues to the leadership of the company's TF1 Publicité subsidiary.

Yet 1991 would also form a turning point for TF1. From that year, its audience share began a slow decline that would last into the late 1990s. Chiefly responsible for this development was the growing competition for the French television viewing audience. The maturation of M6, as well as the arrival of the dual sender Arte/La 5, the increasing competitiveness of the two remaining public broadcasters, and the growth of cable television services were beginning to take their toll on TF1's audience numbers. At the same time TF1 was to be criticized for the seeming decline in the quality of its own programming—symbolized by a "false interview" scandal, in which anchorman d'Arvor pretended to conduct an in-person interview with Cuba's Fidel Castro.

Despite its shrinking viewership, TF1 retained a comfortable lead in the French market. The company also continued to post revenue gains, driven by its advertising sales, as well as by its increasingly profitable diversification activities. A new subsidiary, formed in 1993 and later renamed as TF1 International, was formed to develop the company's international audiovisual rights and distribution activities. TF1's library of programs would reach more than 8,000 hours by 1995, making it one of the world's leading rights distributors. Meanwhile, TF1 prepared to counter the growing competition represented by cable and the soon-to-emerge satellite television services by launching, in 1994, its own cable television channel, La Chaîne Info (LCI), which became the first 24-hour French-language news programmer. In that same year TF1 also took a leading 24.5 percent share in the new Multivision channel, the first pay-per-view television provider in Europe. The company also looked again beyond television, acquiring a 60 percent share of the variety, musical, and theater show producer Glem Productions.

By the mid-1990s satellite television was beginning to enter the French market. TF1 quickly moved to create a position for itself in the new technology, starting with satellite broadcasts of LCI in 1995. True satellite television service, however, had not yet reached the French consumer. But by December 1996, TF1, in partnership with M6, France Telecom, France Télévision, Compagnie Luxembourgeoise de Télédiffusion (CLT), and Lyonnaise des Eaux, launched the TPS (Télévision par Satellite) satellite service. TF1's investment in the launch, of FFr 625 million, gave it a 25 percent share of TPS. It also provided an outlet for the launch of a new TF1 subsidiary, the Odyssée channel, devoted to documentary programming. Boosting TPS's offering, TF1, CLT, and M6 joined to form TCM DA, a partnership for the acquisition of film and audiovisual broadcast rights. In 1996 TCM acquired the right to broadcast the films of Paramount Studios. The following year TF1 also introduced its Video on Demand service, the first in Europe, with hotels as a target market.

TF1's diversification had successfully enabled the company to overcome its flagship station's declining viewership numbers. While TF1 itself had seen its viewership drop to 35 percent of the broadcast market, its continued popularity with the "under-50 housewife" segment (more than 37.5 percent) and its development of new advertising sales outlets, provided the company with steady increases in advertising revenues. At the same time, by the end of 1997, its diversification activities had grown to nearly 25 percent of its total revenues. For the future, TF1 looked toward rebuilding its image as a quality programmer, while enjoying a continued dominance of its domestic market—a unique leadership position among the Western television markets.

Principal Subsidiaries

TF1 Publicité; TF1 Enterprises; Une Musique; Télé-Shopping; TF1 Films Production; Protécrea; Banco Production; Glem Productions; Studios 107; TF1 International; Eurosport; La Chaîne Info; Odyssée; Télévision Par Satellite (25%); TCM DA (34%).

Further Reading

Aubert, Philippe, "TF1: la Chute Libre," *L'Express,* January 20, 1984, p. 38.
Barjon, Carole, "L'Homme Qui a Vendu la Télévision," *Nouvelle Observateur,* May 16, 1986, p. 45.
Bergeroux, Noël-Jean, "La Leçon de TF1," *L'Express,* June 13, 1986, p. 19.
Bertolus, Jean-Jérôme, and Laurent Neumann, "Dix Ans Avec Sursis pour Bouygues," *L'Evenement du Jeudi,* March 21, 1996, p. 28.
Dutheil, Guy, "En Dépit de la Baisse de son Audience, TF1 Reste Sans Concurrent," *Le Monde,* January 31, 1997, p. 29.
Neumann, Laurent, "Devine Qui Vient Diriger TF1 Ce Soir?," *L'Evenement du Jeudi,* May 27, 1993, p. 22.
TF1, "10 Ans à la Barre," *TF1 Hebdo,* 1997.
Vulser, Nicole, "TF1 Tente de Séduire de Nouveaux Publics pour Attirer les Publicitaires," *Le Monde,* June 18, 1997, p. 29.

—M.L. Cohen

TRUE NORTH COMMUNICATIONS INC.

True North Communications Inc.

101 East Erie Street
Chicago, Illinois 60611-2897
U.S.A.
(312) 425-6500
Fax: (312) 425-6350

Public Company
Incorporated: 1994
Employees: 11,000
Gross Billings: $11.5 billion (1997 est.)
Stock Exchanges: New York
SICs: 6719 Holding Companies Not Elsewhere
   Classified; 7311 Advertising Agencies; 8743 Public
   Relations Services

True North Communications Inc. became the sixth largest advertising holding company in the world following its 1997 acquisition of Bozell, Jacobs, Kenyon, and Eckhardt Inc. (BJKE). With an estimated 11,000 employees worldwide and projected annual billings of $11.5 billion, True North was now in a league with the industry's biggest players, such as Interpublic and Omnicom. The acquisition added a second major international advertising network, BJKE's Bozell Worldwide, to its primary advertising network, Foote, Cone & Belding (FCB). In addition, True North was the parent company of a group of online advertising agencies that it planned to spin off as an independent company. It also owned several other diversified advertising, marketing, and public relations firms.

Dispute with Publicis Leads to Company Formation in 1994

The formation of True North Communications as the parent company of Foote, Cone & Belding came about as the result of a dispute between FCB and its global partner, Publicis S.A. of France. In 1988 Publicis S.A., an international advertising agency with offices in 19 countries and more than 100 subsidiaries, entered into a global alliance with FCB. Under the terms of the agreement, Publicis would represent clients in Europe, Africa,

and the Middle East. FCB would cover North and South America, South Africa, and the Asian Pacific area. By agreeing to work through its partner for any work outside of its assigned region, each firm was able to offer its clients global representation.

Through an exchange of stock, the two companies established a European joint venture called Publicis/FCB to control their activities. Publicis held 51 percent of the stock in the joint venture, and FCB held 49 percent. The joint venture satisfied Publicis's need for a presence in North America, and it gave FCB a much-needed international presence to serve its multinational clients.

By 1993 Publicis had decided it needed more of a presence in North America. It acquired the French firm Groupe FCA, which owned the U.S.-based Bloom FCAL agency. FCB challenged the acquisition, stating that it violated the terms of the joint venture. When Publicis refused to back down, FCB established True North Communications, a new holding company, in part to develop international business and partly to create a multi-agency network. In December 1994 the formation of True North was announced, and True North became FCB's parent company. Publicis held an 18.5 percent interest in True North. Meanwhile, the two companies went into arbitration to settle their differences.

True North Began a Series of Acquisitions

Although True North was formed as a holding company to create a multi-agency network, no major acquisitions were made in the first nine months since the formation of True North was announced in December 1994. Analysts speculated that True North was taking its time because of FCB's experience in the 1980s with a string of unsuccessful acquisitions. Then True North began buying more agencies. In 1996 it completed six acquisitions, bringing the total number of acquisition since 1992 to 26.

Differences Settled with Publicis, 1996

After two years of arbitration with Publicis, the cooperative pact was terminated, but the joint venture continued to operate. True North gained control of the international FCB operations through a restructuring of the joint venture with Publicis. According to True North's 1996 annual report, "All of our outstanding disputes [with Publicis] have been resolved." True North increased its ownership in Publicis to 26.5 percent and saw itself as a partner helping Publicis expand globally from its European base. Meanwhile, True North was globally positioned with its own operations in Europe and 60 countries around the world. Responding to FCB's new international strength, clients consolidating their global account assignments brought their business to FCB. In 1996 these included S.C. Johnson, Tambrands, Kimberly-Clark, and Cadbury.

Reorganized into Three Operating Units, 1996

In 1996 True North was organized into three groups: 1) Foote, Cone & Belding (FCB), 2) TN Technologies, and 3) Associated Communications Companies. FCB was the largest. Brendan Ryan was named CEO of this group. TN Technologies, headed by Greg Blaine, was focused on interactive, or digital, marketing and advertising opportunities. Associated Communications Companies, headed by Mitch Engel, was organized to include a variety of marketing services companies and began with $50 million in revenue.

Within FCB, a new, fully owned and controlled network in Europe was formed. It began with $1 billion in billings and operated in 19 countries. It included the Wilkens International network, acquired in January 1997, and four large FCB operations. Based in Hamburg, Germany, Wilkens International's network consisted of owned and affiliated agencies located in 19 European countries with billings of $700 million and 500 employees. Major clients included Beiersdorf, SEAT, Hero, Lindt, Cadbury, and Panasonic. The new FCB Europe consisted of wholly owned FCB offices in Paris, London, Lisbon, and Athens, plus the newly renamed FCB/Wilkens in Hamburg.

Domestically, FCB maintained its number one ranking by its broad geographic strength. The company boasted more than $1 billion in billings on each of the coasts through FCB New York ($1.2 billion in billings) and FCB San Francisco (known for its award-winning Levi Strauss & Co. ads). FCB Chicago was also approaching $1 billion in billings through the integration of Bayer Bess Vanderwarker into FCB.

Upon its formation, TN Technologies immediately became the largest company in the rapidly growing digital marketing services industry. With the acquisition of Modem Media in October 1996, TN Technologies was expected to exceed $60 million in revenue during 1997, almost exclusively from digital-based assignments. No other agency in the industry came close to that level of billings. (By 1997, though, interactive ad rival CKS Inc. of Cupertino, California, boasted $135 million in revenue and was the largest player in the online advertising business. It had reported 1995 revenue of $35.4 million and expected to top $55 million in 1996.)

Under the terms of the merger, Modem Media received $25 million in True North stock at closing and another $4 million if the IPO was completed. Modem's principals retained about a 45 percent interest in the combined company. Modem generated about $11.5 million in revenues in the year prior to the merger. Its primary client was AT&T, which accounted for some three-quarters of its revenue. Combined with TN Technologies' approximately $20 million in revenue and strong growth in interactive advertising, the combined company was projected to generate $45 to $50 million in revenues, an estimate that was later revised upward to $60 million in True North's annual report for 1996. The combined units had offices in six cities worldwide. Although an IPO was pursued, it never developed.

Employing the expertise of TN Technologies, True North launched separate global intranets for local S.C. Johnson clients and local Kimberly-Clark clients. The global intranets made it possible for clients and agency staff to collaborate on advertising and marketing development. Internally, the company's intranet was known as True North Knowledge Network.

At the end of 1996, chairman and CEO Bruce Mason was able to confidently state, "True North is in the strongest competitive position in its history." The company reported net income of $27.8 million on revenue of $493.1 million and had $8.2 billion in capitalized billings.

True North Acquired a Major Competitor, 1997

In July 1997 True North announced it would acquire Bozell, Jacobs, Kenyon, and Eckhardt Inc. (BJKE) for about $440 million in stock. The deal was reached after a three-year courtship. It created the world's sixth largest advertising company, according to the *Los Angeles Times,* and doubled True North's size. The merged company would have combined billings of $11.5 billion and more than 11,000 employees worldwide.

BJKE's flagship agency was Bozell Worldwide, whose clients included the Chrysler Corporation, Merrill Lynch, and Bristol-Myers Squibb. Bozell created the award-winning Jeep campaign for Chrysler as well as the popular milk mustache campaign for the National Fluid Milk Processor Promotion Board.

Following the merger, which required the approval of True North's shareholders, Charles D. Peebler, Jr., BJKE's chief executive, was slated to become president of True North. True North's chairman and CEO Bruce Mason would continue as True North's CEO, but he asked outside director Richard Braddock to assume the role of chairman. Braddock was a former president and chief operating officer of Citicorp. Braddock became the nonexecutive chairman and was expected to act as a buffer between Mason and Peebler, either of whom could eventually gain the top spot at the company.

Peebler also became chairman and CEO of True North Diversified Companies. The Diversified Companies Group would include all of the operating units of the combined companies except Bozell Worldwide and Foote Cone & Belding Worldwide, which would continue to operate as independent advertising agencies.

The BJKE units falling under True North Diversified Companies included Poppe Tyson (an interactive advertising agency), Temerlin McClain (an ad agency whose clients included American Airlines and J.C. Penney), public relations firm Bozell Sawyer Miller Group, marketing communications company McCracken Brooks, and Bozell Wellness Worldwide (a network of multinational companies specializing in health-care advertising).

The True North units now organized under True North Diversified Companies included TN Technologies, Wahlstrom & Co. (a Yellow pages ad agency), Tierney & Partners (Philadelphia's largest ad agency), Borders, Perrin and Norrander (a creative ad agency located in the Pacific Northwest), and Market Growth Resources (sales promotion agency).

One of the units acquired in the BJKE transaction was the New York-based on-line advertising agency Poppe Tyson Inc. It was expected that it would be combined with True North's TN Technologies Inc., which had an estimated $70 million in revenues. A combined TN Technologies and Poppe Tyson was expected to generate some $120 million in billings, making it a close second to the online advertising leader, CKS Inc. of Cupertino, California, which was expected to generate $135 million in revenues in 1997. *Crain's New York Business* speculated that a combined TN Technologies and Poppe Tyson, both of whom had attempted unsuccessful IPOs in the past, might make a public offering.

The merger emphasized True North's desire to become one of the world's largest advertising agencies. It gave True North a much sought after second network of agencies. It put the company in league with the industry's biggest players, such as Interpublic and Omnicom. The world's largest advertising company, in terms of billings, was the WPP Group of England.

Following shareholder approval of the acquisition on December 30, 1997, Reuters noted that it "represented a major victory in one of advertising's most bitterly fought corporate battles between True North's Mason and Maurice Levy, chairman of France's Publicis S.A., who had tried to block the acquisition."

Publicis Failed in Its Hostile Takeover Attempt in 1997

After a history of wrangling, Publicis made a hostile take-over bid for True North in November 1997. The bid was valued at about $577 million and was rejected by True North. Publicis owned about 18.5 percent of True North's 25.3 million shares and offered to buy the rest for $28 a share in cash and stock. The takeover attempt came while True North was in the process of completing its announced $440 million purchase of Bozell, Jacobs, Kenyon, and Eckhardt Inc. (BJKE). When Publicis sued True North for breach of fiduciary duty to the company's shareholders and tried to block the BJKE acquisition, True North countersued.

In December Publicis was forced to withdraw its hostile tender offer for True North after a federal judge in the United States enjoined Publicis from pursuing the bid. According to Judge Joan Gottschall's ruling in the U.S. District Court for the Northern District of Illinois, Publicis was violating an agreement between the two companies to dissolve its partnership. That agreement had been signed in February 1997. Later in December a Delaware Chancery Court made a similar ruling in a related lawsuit that prevented Publicis from interfering with True North's acquisition of BJKE.

With the obstacles removed from its acquisition of BJKE, True North completed the merger and continued its strategic acquisitions. It appeared set on a course to compete head-on with some of the world's largest advertising networks. During the first nine months of 1997 it acquired agencies in India, Singapore, Venezuela, and Europe. For the nine months ending September 30, 1997, True North reported an increase of 27 percent in revenues over the previous year. Excluding acquisitions, revenue increased 10.7 percent as a result of new business. Then, in the fourth quarter, the company took a pre-tax charge of $131 million for restructuring costs and costs associated with the BJKE acquisition. That one-time charge caused True North to report a net loss of $50 million for fiscal 1997 on revenue of $1.2 billion.

Principal Operating Units

Foote, Cone & Belding; Bozell Worldwide; True North Diversified Companies (including TN Technologies Inc., Wahlstrom & Co., Tierney & Partners, Borders, Perrin and Norrander, Market Growth Resources, Poppe Tyson Inc., Temerlin McClain, Bozell Sawyer Miller Group, McCracken Brooks, and Bozell Wellness Worldwide).

Further Reading

Cahill, Joseph B., "Nine Months, Still Expecting at True North," *Crain's Chicago Business,* September 4, 1995, p. 3.

Cardona, Mercedes M., and Laura Petrecca, "After Bozell, True North out to Acquire More," *Crain's Chicago Business,* August 11, 1997, p. 9.

Crown, Judith, "Life Yet at True North," *Crain's Chicago Business,* September 16, 1996, p. 46.

"Delaware Supreme Court Upholds True North Position," *PR Newswire,* December 29, 1997.

Farrell, Rita, "True North Granted Injunction Vs. Publicis Tender," *Reuters News Service,* December 23, 1997.

Geanuleas, Sue, "True North Communications Inc. Acquires Wilkens Network," *PR Newswire,* February 4, 1997.

——, "True North Communications to Acquire Bozell," *PR Newswire,* July 31, 1997.

Gellene, Denise, "Foote, Cone & Belding Parent to Buy Rival," *Los Angeles Times,* August 1, 1997, p. D3.

Gleason, Mark, and Debra Aho Williamson, "Modem Media Merger Points True North in Digital Direction," *Crain's Chicago Business,* October 21, 1996, p. 38.

Pauly, Heather, "Publicis Pulls True North Bid, Judge Rules Against French Ad Firm," *Chicago Sun-Times,* December 11, 1997, p. 60.

——, "Publicis Sues True North Over Vote," *Chicago Sun-Times,* December 2, 1997, p. 72.

Steenhuysen, Julie, "For True North's Mason, Vote Ends Hard Battle," *Reuters News Service,* December 30, 1997.

Temes, Judy, "Internet Ad Agencies Expected to Combine," *Crain's New York Business,* August 11, 1997, p. 3.

Thomas, Denis, "Publicis Readies for True North Meeting," *Reuters News Service,* December 30, 1997.

"True North Q4 Loss After Charges," *Reuters News Service,* March 10, 1998.

"True North Shareholders Overwhelmingly Approve BJKE Merger," *PR Newswire,* December 30, 1997.

—David Bianco

Trump Organization

725 Fifth Avenue
New York, New York 10022
U.S.A.
(212) 832-2000
Fax: (212) 935-0141

Private Company
Founded: 1974
Employees: 22,000
Sales: $6.5 billion (1997 est.)
SICs: 1522 General Contractors—Residential Buildings,
Other Than Single-Family; 6512 Operators of
Nonresidential Buildings; 6513 Operators of
Apartment Buildings; 6552 Land Subdividers and
Developers, Except Cemeteries; 6719 Offices of
Holding Companies, Not Elsewhere Classified; 7011
Hotels and Motels; 7660 Legal Gambling

The Trump Organization presides over the assets of the Trump family and includes not only the assets of the flamboyant Donald J. Trump but those accumulated by his father, Fred C. Trump. These assets consisted, in the late 1990s, of apartment buildings, mostly in New York City's borough of Brooklyn, owned and/or managed by Trump corporations; a variety of properties in Manhattan, also owned and/or managed by Trump corporations; and, in the late 1990s, more than 40 percent of Trump Hotels & Casino Resorts, Inc., owner and operator of five gambling casinos and hotels in Atlantic City, New Jersey, and a riverboat casino in Indiana. Donald Trump established a high-profile business empire in the 1980s that almost collapsed under a mountain of debt during the 1990–91 recession. Although forced to divest himself of some properties, he remained an important presence in Manhattan real estate development. As chairman of Trump Hotels & Casino, he headed Atlantic City's largest hotel-casino operation.

Fred Trump's Career: 1927–74

Fred Trump represented his life as a climb from poverty to riches, but in his muckraking biography of Donald Trump, Wayne Barrett reported that the elder Trump's father was engaged in the real estate business and left a comfortable estate to his widow and children on his death in 1918. Fred Trump built about 300 houses in the New York City borough of Queens from 1927 to 1932, when the market dried up in the depths of the Great Depression. His career revived in 1934, when he was able to acquire a list of serviceable mortgages from a bankrupt Brooklyn realtor. Financing from the newly created Federal Housing Administration enabled Trump to build many more Brooklyn homes, typically selling for $6,000 apiece. During World War II he built FHA-backed housing for naval personnel and shipyard workers near Virginia and Pennsylvania shipyards.

Between 1947 and 1949 Trump completed Shore Haven, a 1,314-unit apartment complex of six-story apartment buildings on a 14-acre site in southern Brooklyn. An even larger development, 2,000-unit Beach Haven, followed. His biggest project was Trump Village in Coney Island. Consisting of 4,600 Brooklyn apartments in seven 23-story buildings—five of them cooperatives, two rental—it was completed in 1965. This one was constructed with state, rather than federal, funding and essentially ended Fred Trump's career as a builder. Previously said to have padded his costs to obtain excessive FHA mortgage money, he was now accused in public testimony of having fraudulently lined his pockets with state funds. Trump ultimately returned $1.2 million and, his reputation under a cloud, was unable to obtain funding for further large residential projects he had planned on the sites of former Coney Island amusement parks.

Donald Trump joined the family business in 1968 upon graduation from the University of Pennsylvania's Wharton School. By 1974 he was president (with his father as chairman of the board) of an assortment of Trump entities, laying claim to the management of 48 privately held corporations and 15 family partnerships. His principal job was managing the apartments, whose number varied between 10,000 and 22,000, according to

481

different estimates. The value of the Trump empire was estimated in the early 1970s at $200 million by Fred Trump and between $40 million and $100 million by other sources.

Acquiring Manhattan Real Estate: 1974–88

Donald Trump was determined to take the enterprise into Manhattan. As head of the Trump Organization—which at the time had no legal existence—he took out, in 1974, an option (with no money down) to purchase railyards along the Hudson River north and south of midtown owned by the bankrupt Penn Central Transportation Co. Trump planned to build a huge residential complex on the 76-acre northern segment, but opposition by West Side resident groups would make the plan unfeasible until the 1990s. He persuaded the city to build a new convention center on the 44-acre southern segment. Although unable to win the construction contract, he collected a $500,000 broker's commission.

Trump also was interested in Penn Central's decaying Commodore Hotel, on East 42nd Street just east of Grand Central Station. Eventually a deal was reached in 1976 whereby a state agency received the property and leased it for 99 years to a Trump entity, which would share in the profits with the city. Trump, who obtained an unprecedented 40-year tax abatement from the city—the first ever granted for a commercial property—then lined up a construction loan guaranteed by his father and the Hyatt Corp., which became the joint partner. The shell of the hotel was enclosed in a chrome-and-mirrored-glass façade. Completed in 1980, the rehabilitated structure opened as the 1,400-room Grand Hyatt Hotel.

Trump's signature building was the Trump Tower, built on the northeast corner of 56th Street and Fifth Avenue. Assembling lots, purchasing air rights, and securing rezoning enabled him to put up a 58-story office, retail, and residential complex with a six-story atrium shopping mall and a sawtooth exterior shape of 28 different surfaces cascading in a bronze-and-dark-glass sheath. The Equitable Life Assurance Society of the United States, which owned the land and helped obtain financing from Chase Manhattan Bank, was Trump's joint partner. Completed in 1983 at a cost of $201 million, the building was a hit; by 1986, 251 of the 268 condominium apartments had been sold for a total of $277 million. The partnership retained ownership of the retail and office space and won a ten-year tax abatement in court. Trump installed his family in a penthouse double triplex and bought out Equitable in 1986.

Following on Trump Tower's heels, the 36-story, Y-shaped Trump Plaza residential cooperative at Third Avenue and 61st Street was completed in 1984 at a cost of $125 million. More of a problem was 106 Central Park South, a 15-story apartment building Trump bought in 1981 along with the neighboring, 38-story Barbizon Plaza Hotel (for which he paid only $13 million but received a $65 million mortgage loan). He envisioned a huge condo on the combined sites but was unable to oust the rent-regulated tenants, who were protected against eviction. When Trump offered to house homeless people in vacated apartments, he was slapped with a tenant harassment suit. In the end the tenants stayed, their building's facade harmonized next to that of the refurbished Barbizon, which became Trump Parc, with 340 condominium units advertised in 1986 at

between $180,000 and $4 million. In 1985 Trump paid $72 million for the St. Moritz, the aging hotel across the street from Trump Parc that also faced Central Park.

Trump's last Manhattan hotel purchase was the Plaza, the French Renaissance landmark at the southeastern corner of Central Park, one block east of Trump Parc. He purchased it from the Bass Group in 1988 for a staggering $393 million, or $500,000 per room, making it the most expensive hotel purchase in history. Trump received a $409 million loan from Citibank and personally guaranteed the $125 million equity portion. Simultaneously, he sold the St. Moritz to Australian magnate Alan Bond, reportedly for $100 million more than he had paid for it.

Trump's option on the northern segment of the Penn Yards had expired in 1979, but after other developers failed to build on the site, he purchased it in 1985 for $115 million. Trump's "Television City" plan for the site included an agglomeration of five buildings extending to a height of 150 stories and a landscaped platform supporting a collection of 8,000 apartments, two office buildings, open space, and parkland above television and film studios, a retail mall, and a massive parking garage. It died in 1987, when NBC decided to renew its quarters in Rockefeller Center. The successor, the 14 million-square-foot "Trump City" development project, did not win the needed city approval.

Atlantic City and Other Ventures: 1980–90

Trump's first investment in Atlantic City came in 1980, when he (with his father) purchased 98-year leases on properties bordering the Boardwalk. After the projected casino was licensed in 1982, Holiday Inns Inc.'s Harrah subsidiary agreed to invest $50 million in a partnership. Trump was responsible for the construction of Harrah's at Trump Plaza (soon shortened to Trump Plaza), a 39-story casino-hotel that opened in 1984. Harrah's originally managed it, but in 1986 Trump borrowed $250 million to buy out the company's interest. He had bought the Hilton Corp.'s casino-hotel for $320 million in 1985, which opened as Trump's Castle Casino Resort. An addition to the Castle, a 14-story Crystal Tower of luxury suites, was completed in 1990.

Even these deals paled beside his plan to take over Resorts International, the troubled casino company that was the largest landowner in Atlantic City, and its unfinished Taj Mahal, the world's largest casino. Outbid for voting control of the company in 1988 by Merv Griffin, Trump nevertheless obtained his objective—the Taj—for $280 million and issued $675 million in junk bonds to pay for the acquisition and completion of the casino, which opened in 1990. He spent another $115 million in 1989 to buy two more properties flanking Trump Plaza. One of these was the Atlantis, a 500-room hotel-casino without a gaming license that he renamed the Trump Regency. The other consisted of the Penthouse, a half-built hotel-casino, and its parking-garage site.

Trump indulged his lavish lifestyle by purchasing Mar-A-Lago, a 118-room Palm Beach mansion in 1984, and the world's second largest yacht, a 282-foot-long craft that he renamed the *Trump Princess* and docked next to Trump's

Castle to entertain high rollers, in 1988. In partnership with Lee Iacocca, he also paid $41 million for a 32-story residential condominium, which he named Trump Plaza of the Palm Beaches, in West Palm Beach. In 1983 he purchased the New Jersey Generals of the struggling U.S. Football League as the opening gambit in a scheme to move the team into an indoor, publicly financed stadium in New York City to be called the "Trumpdome." The league and the stadium proposal folded in 1987. By his own estimates in court papers, Trump lost about $22 million on the venture.

Trump's interest in another glamour business—aircraft—resulted in his purchase of bankrupt Eastern Airlines' Boston-New York-Washington shuttle in 1989 for $365 million, paid with a Citibank loan that accepted as collateral the airline's aging jets and $135 million in equity backed only by Trump's personal guarantee. Renamed the Trump Shuttle, this venture required $85 million in capital and operating costs in its first year alone. By then he also had paid $23 million for a fleet of helicopters he dubbed Trump Air. Trump also moved ahead with the construction of the Trump Palace, a 55-story residential condominium building on a site at Third Avenue and 69th Street that he had bought in 1985.

Restructuring, 1990–92

When the U.S. economy fell into recession in 1990, Trump's highly leveraged business empire threatened to collapse like a house of cards. Entities of the Trump Organization, or Donald Trump personally, had incurred more than $5 billion in debt—$8.8 billion, according to one source—of which almost $1 billion had been drawn solely on Trump's personal guarantee. Big New York banks had financed $3.75 billion worth of debt. They reduced their risk and collected fees by syndicating the loans to some 70 other banks, including British, French, German, and Japanese institutions. Most of this money was recovered after subsequent restructurings, but some $600 million to $800 million may have been lost. *Forbes* had estimated Trump's worth at $1.7 billion in 1989, making him the nation's 19th richest man, but two years later it assessed his worth at minus $900 million.

An August 1990 bailout pact allowed Trump to defer almost $1 billion in bank debt but required him to make certain payments on more than $1 billion in additional bank debt. It also gave the banks second and third mortgages on nearly all of Trump's properties. In return for being released from his personal guarantee on about $960 million of debt, Trump gave up ownership of the Trump Shuttle and all but a small stake in the Plaza. Also lost was the West Palm Beach building and the *Trump Princess*. Trump Air was dissolved and its helicopters sold to pay debts. The Mar-A-Lago was turned into a club. Even Trump's Boeing 727 jet was repossessed (but later repurchased).

Temporarily unaffected was $1.3 billion in casino bonds, but in December 1990 the casinos and property group of the Trump Organization defaulted on a $50 million loan used to fund the Taj Mahal. Trump subsequently agreed to cede half of the casino to bondholders as part of a 1991 restructuring, known as a prepackaged bankruptcy, in which new credit agreements were legally authorized.

During the first part of 1991 the Trump Organization negotiated with creditors of the other casino holdings concerning a revision of the debt. A crucial, mysterious $3.3 million payment on the Trump's Castle debt was traced by a reporter to Fred Trump, who apparently auctioned some of his Brooklyn and Queens apartments to raise the funds. Otherwise, however, Trump could count for help in this quarter only on his own stake in his father's estate, which bankers estimated at a maximum of $150 million. Still alive in 1997 at the age of 92, Fred Trump had, according to a biography of Donald Trump by Harry Hurt, turned over the management of his estate to Donald's younger brother, Robert.

Like the Trump Taj Mahal Casino Resort, the Trump Plaza Hotel and Casino and Trump's Castle Casino Resort underwent prepackaged bankruptcies in 1992 to restructure their huge bond debts. Trump Plaza bonds and debt were converted to lower-interest bonds and four million shares of preferred stock for the creditors. In exchange for a reduction in the interest rate on the Trump's Castle bonds, the creditors received half the equity in the property.

Resurgence, 1994–97

Trump also lost the Penthouse and Trump Regency to banks but leased them with options to buy. He reopened the Penthouse—renamed the East Tower—in 1995. He also won a gambling license for the Regency, which was renamed Trump World's Fair. He then exercised his options and bought both properties back for in excess of $200 million. The Trump World's Fair and Plaza East (in the East Tower) casinos opened in 1997.

Trump Plaza Hotel and Casino went public in 1995 as Trump Hotels & Casino Resorts, Inc., selling ten million shares of common stock at $14 a share. A secondary stock offering in April 1996 sold 13.25 million shares at $32.50 a share. This company also included a subsidiary that opened, in 1996, a gambling riverboat, named Trump Indiana, on Lake Michigan at Gary, Indiana.

In April 1996 Trump Hotels & Casino acquired the Taj Mahal for $40.5 million, plus assumption of its debts. The company, through Trump Atlantic City Associates, issued more than $1.1 billion in new mortgage notes to redeem the Taj Mahal's $780 million in mortgage bonds due 1999 and the Trump Plaza's $340 million in mortgage notes due 2001. Five months later, Trump Hotels & Casino acquired the money-losing Trump's Castle (renamed Trump Marina in 1997) for about $490 million in stock, a transaction that included the assumption of about $314 million of the hotel-casino's debt. The acquisition raised Trump's stake in the public company to about 40 percent. Trump Hotels & Casino Resorts grew to six casinos with the integration of the World's Fair and East Tower properties into Trump Plaza in 1997.

Trump Hotels & Casino Resorts was now an awesome agglomeration of Atlantic City properties. Revenues reached $976 million in 1996, but the company lost $65.7 million, mostly because of an extraordinary $59.1 million charge for redemption of notes and writeoff of deferred financing costs. The company's underlying weakness—a long-term debt that reached $1.7 billion in mid-1997—caused the stock to fall below $10 a share by the end of the year.

Trump's plan for the northern segment of the old Penn Central railyards received approval in 1992 in scaled-down form. The proposed development, renamed Riverside South, now was to consist of 5,700 apartments, 1.8 million square feet of office space, 350,000 square feet of retail space, and parking for 3,500 cars. Trump did not have the financing to develop the property, but in 1994 he signed a joint-venture agreement with a consortium of Asian investors, led by two of Hong Kong's biggest developers. He was said to have received a 30 percent stake in the project, with responsibility for constructing and managing the 18 buildings and seeking regulatory approvals, while putting up no cash. According to one source, however, he had no actual equity in the project and would begin to get a share of the profits only after the developer syndicate recovered its investment, plus interest. (The first two Riverside South buildings began to rise in 1997.)

Again in 1994, Trump's relish for high-profile deals was evident when he formed a joint venture with two foreign investors who had paid $42 million for the Empire State Building. Trump became general partner, but his stake in the venture was unclear. In any case, other realtors had 81 years remaining on a lease of the landmark building that gave them almost complete independence from the owners, who would only receive an annual rental of under $2 million during the life of the lease. In 1995 Trump bought 40 Wall Street, a 72-story office building. He paid less than $8 million for the property, but it was 89 percent vacant, and the remodeling he envisioned would cost at least $100 million.

The Trump International Hotel & Tower, a slender 52-story structure at the north end of Columbus Circle that was formerly the Gulf & Western office building, was being converted to luxury residential condominiums, with a Trumpian bronze-and-dark-glass outer skin. Trump Organization units were in charge of construction, sales, and management but provided little or no cash. Besides fees for these services and the use of his name, Trump received a penthouse in the building and a stake in the hotel's restaurant and garage. Work began in 1995 and was completed in 1997.

In 1996 Trump bought the Miss USA, Miss Universe, and Miss Teen USA pageants from ITT Corp. and then sold half of the property to CBS, which was broadcasting the pageants. He said he wanted to create marketing tie-ins to raise their visibility, possibly including an agreement for a top modeling agency to hire the winners and a new line of Miss Universe cosmetics backed by a major beauty company.

Trump sold his half-share in the Grand Hyatt Hotel to the Hyatt Corp. in 1996 for $142 million. This enabled him to extinguish the remainder of his personal indebtedness. *Forbes* estimated his worth at $1.4 billion in October 1997—up from $450 million the previous year.

Principal Subsidiaries

Trump Enterprises Inc.; Trump Corporation; Trump Development Company; Wembly Realty Inc.; Park South Company; Land Corporation of California.

Further Reading

Asbury, Edith Evans, "Housing Windfall Yielded 1.8-Million, Inquiry Here Told," *New York Times,* January 27, 1966, pp. 1, 26.

Barrett, Wayne, *Trump: The Deals and the Downfall,* New York: HarperCollins, 1992.

Bender, Marilyn, "The Empire and Ego of Donald Trump," *New York Times,* August 7, 1983, Sec. 3, pp. 1, 8.

Binkley, Christina, "Stock of Trump Hotels Is Depressed, So Should Donald Buy It Back?" *Wall Street Journal,* August 20, 1997, pp. A1, A8.

"Development in Coney Is Peak of a 40-Year Building Career," *New York Times,* January 5, 1964, Sec. 8, pp. 1–2.

"Don Trump's Real Estate Formula," *Business Week,* May 26, 1975, p. 70.

Geist, William E., "The Expanding Empire of Donald Trump," *New York Times Magazine,* April 8, 1984, pp. 28, 30–31, 72–75, 78–79.

Singer, Marc, "Trump Solo," *New Yorker,* May 19, 1997, pp. 56–62, 64–70.

Sterngold, James, "Trump Shows a Different Profile," *New York Times,* July 26, 1996, pp. D1, D5.

Tell, Lawrence J., "Holding All the Cards," *Barron's,* August 6, 1984, pp. 6–7, 23–25.

"Trump's Latest Scheme Is Real Beauty, Literally," *Crain's New York Business,* March 17, 1997, p. 4.

Tully, Shawn, "Donald Trump: An Ex-Loser Is Back in the Money," *Fortune,* July 22, 1996, pp. 86–88.

Updike, Edith, "It's a Landmark Trump Deal," *Newsday,* July 8, 1994, p. A47.

Whitman, Alden, "A Builder Looks Back—and Moves Forward," *New York Times,* January 28, 1973, Sec. 8, pp. 1, 9.

—Robert Halasz

Turner

The Turner Corporation

375 Hudson Street
New York, New York 10014
U.S.A.
(212) 229-6000
Fax: (212) 229-6185
Web site: http://www.tcco.com

Public Company
Incorporated: 1984
Employees: 2,800
Sales: $3.3 billion (1996)
Stock Exchanges: American
SICs: 1522 Residential Construction, Not Elsewhere
Classified; 1541 General Contractors Industrial
Buildings; 1542 Nonresidential Construction, Not
Elsewhere Classified; 7389 Business Services, Not
Elsewhere Classified; 8741 Management Services;
8742 Management Counseling Services

Founded in 1902 by Henry C. Turner, a devout Quaker from the eastern shore of Maryland, The Turner Corporation has grown into one of America's top general contractors. In 1996 it completed $3.3 billion worth of construction projects. Organized as a holding company, the business's key subsidiary is Turner Construction Company. A downturn in the commercial construction segment during the late 1980s and early 1990s compelled Turner to diversify from that segment—its traditional stronghold—into several specialized niches, including biotech/pharmaceutical, healthcare, retail, recreational, and government buildings, as well as multi-unit housing and interiors. This award-winning company has built some of the most famous and recognizable buildings in major cities around the nation, including the John F. Kennedy Memorial Library in Dorchester near Boston, the United Nations Secretariat and Madison Square Garden in New York, the Xerox Center in Chicago, and Two Union Square in Seattle. In 1997 Turner built more healthcare projects than any other contractor in America, extending its leadership of that category to twelve straight

years. The Turner Corporation has built 20 of the 100 tallest buildings in the world. Its clients are among the world's leading corporations, including General Motors, Ford, Chrysler, United Airlines, American Airlines, General Electric, and IBM.

After chalking up four decades of profitability, Turner suffered its first-ever annual loss in 1990 and struggled to stay in the black throughout the early and mid-1990s, losing $1.7 million on revenues of $2.8 billion in 1996. That year's management shakeup brought in 71-year-old Ellis T. Gravette, Jr., to serve as chairman and CEO. Harold J. Parmelee retained the presidency, a post he had held since May 1990. Having divested many of its most disastrous real estate holdings, in 1997 the company appeared poised to reap its biggest profit since 1992.

Key Strengths Distinguish Turner from Competitors

The company operates through 44 offices in America and abroad. It has divisions and subsidiaries located throughout the United States as well as in Europe, the Middle East, South America, and Asia. This network of offices enables Turner to function as a local facility as soon as a contract for construction is awarded. In fact, Turner is referred to as "the largest small contractor in America" because of its system of serving as a local contractor in each community. In 1992 President Parmelee noted that, "Our roots go very, very deep. We've been in New York City for 90 years, in Philadelphia for 85 years, and in Boston for 76 years. This allows our people to become active citizens of these communities and to work closely with local owners, architects, subcontractors and municipal agencies." Staff members in these offices have an intimate knowledge of local regulatory and review processes, local labor conditions, and strengths and weaknesses of subcontractors, thereby facilitating the construction process.

Another benefit of having ties in a community is that quality is enhanced. According to former Chair and CEO Alfred T. McNeill, "People who are building their own community take greater pride in it. Our commitment to quality can be seen in the 75-story First Interstate building in Los Angeles that didn't crack in the earthquake and the Turner-built housing in Florida that remained standing after Hurricane Andrew."

Company Perspectives:

Turner will be the recognized leader in providing building construction services, both nationally and in every location in which Turner operates. We will achieve this by consistently exceeding our commitments to and the expectations of clients, design professionals, subcontractors, and vendors, and the community at large. These services will be delivered by team-oriented, responsive, innovative, reliable, ethical, and skilled staff who participate in a world-class training and development program and benefit from a career employment opportunity.

Turner's tenacity in the rough-and-tumble construction business has frequently been attributed to its ability to adapt to changing market conditions and construction demands. As the demand for commercial building has declined with world's economic cycles, Turner has been quick to diversify into new markets in the social and public sectors, giving the company a broad portfolio of experience. In addition to the construction of new buildings for niche markets, the company has been involved in expansions and renovations of existing facilities, and in providing services related to construction activities. When poor economic conditions have forced other companies to reduce staff, Turner expanded its services, using its full network of staff and resources to function as a sort of one-stop construction business, providing a full range of services from designing to building to helping with financial matters.

Early 20th-Century Roots

Turner began modestly. After Henry C. Turner graduated as an engineer from Swarthmore College, he worked with the little-known Ransome system of steel-reinforced concrete. Believing that this new method would revolutionize construction, Turner and a partner, DeForrest H. Dixon, purchased the rights to the system for $25,000 and founded Turner Construction Company. In the early 1900s, the company completed the stairways for New York's first subway stations. Industrial contracts soon followed as Turner's reputation for speed and skill grew, and the Ransome system received recognition. Turner's faith in using concrete led the company to adopt the slogan ''Turner for Concrete.''

During World War I the company received several defense contracts. Volume increased from $6.5 million in 1916 to $35 million in 1918. In 1919 the company received its first international contract. From 1919 to 1922, Turner expanded into new areas and built its first high-rise office building, its first hotel, and its first full-scale stadium.

During the Great Depression of the late 1920s and early 1930s, construction activity declined. Turner's volume fell drastically but the company remained in business while thousands of other contractors were forced to close their doors. Turner was able to continue operations because it shifted its focus from industrial and commercial building to other types of facilities, such as retail stores, churches, and other academic and public buildings.

During World War II, the company once again received defense contracts from the government and was involved in such building projects as a submarine base in Connecticut, Pacific Naval air bases, the Brooklyn Navy Yard Storehouse, and 93 oil tankers for the Alabama Drydock & Shipbuilding Company. During wartime, Turner also managed base facilities for the top-secret village at Oak Ridge, Tennessee, where, without the company's knowledge, the components of the first atomic bombs were being prepared. By 1941, when Henry C. Turner retired, defense work represented 81 percent of the company's business.

Diversification after World War II

After the war, the country started rebuilding programs and Turner received contracts for building academic, commercial, and industrial buildings. Turner built a structure for the Coca-Cola Bottling Co. in New York and was the contractor for the Firestone Library at Princeton University. By 1951, with all this activity, company sales had reached $100 million.

In the 1960s, Turner built high-rise buildings, futuristic airline terminals, and pavilions for the World's Fair, as well as some of the nation's best-known buildings, such as Lincoln Center, Madison Square Garden, and the United States Steel headquarters in Pittsburgh. By the late 1960s there were Turner buildings as far away as Hong Kong. The company went public in 1969 and by 1972 was selling shares on the American Stock Exchange.

By the 1970s, Turner had expanded its foreign offices into such countries as Iran, Pakistan, and Dubai. In the late 1970s and early 1980s, the company continued to build highly visible facilities associated with prestigious names, such as the John F. Kennedy Library in Dorchester in 1979 and the Moscone Convention Center in San Francisco in 1981. Turner enjoyed average annual revenue increases of 11 percent through the first half of the 1980s, capping four decades of consecutive annual profits.

New Niches in Late 1980s and Early 1990s

The search for new and different types of markets was especially important during the recessionary years of the late 1980s and early 1990s when the construction market—and in particular the commercial segment—slumped. Turner continued to expand into niche markets that reflected the scope and range of its experience. For example, in 1989 the company contracted to build a convention center in Columbus, Ohio. In 1990 the company completed the 54-story Mellon Bank Center in Philadelphia, the third tallest building in the city. In 1991 Turner completed construction of the 63-story Society Tower in Cleveland.

In 1992 alone, Turner built 125 projects, including office, retail, airport, industrial, advanced technology, healthcare, justice, residential, educational, science, and recreational facilities. Through diversification into new markets, sales in the commercial sector dwindled from about 50 percent of Turner's business in 1986 to less than 20 percent of total revenues in 1992.

Moreover, this volume was mostly for renovation and interiors rather than new construction.

In addition to diversifying, Turner took steps to reduce its exposure to risk by forging alliances and joint ventures. In 1992 the New York contractor joined forces with Switzerland's Karl Steiner Holding A.G. Dubbed Turner Steiner International SA (TSI), the new entity assumed responsibility for contracts formerly administered by Turner International, including projects in Japan, North America, Central America, and the Caribbean. TSI took on several rebuilding projects in Kuwait after the Persian Gulf War, providing in particular reconstruction services for the Kuwait Sheraton Hotel. Other projects with TSI were the Abjar Hotel in Dubai, the Almulla Hospital, New Doha International Airport in Qatar, preconstruction and construction services for office towers in Sri Lanka, and a project in Brussels for Citibank Europe.

Turner applied the same strategy to its Latin and South American interests, forming Turner South America in partnership with Brazil's Birmann S.A. On the domestic front, Turner created a joint venture with EMCON, a hazardous waste management firm. Known as ET Environmental Corp., the affiliate offered site remediation as well as design and construction of waste management facilities.

Turner's decision to move into the social sector was rewarded in 1992, when the company served as the lead contractor of healthcare construction projects totaling $1 billion. Turner was awarded contracts to build University of Chicago Hospitals for their new Center for Advanced Medicine and two new buildings at the New England Medical Center. The company also negotiated construction management contracts at two San Jose area hospitals. Turner entered into a contract with the biotech/pharmaceutical company Genzyme Corp. for building a quality control/quality assurance laboratory and pharmaceutical manufacturing facilities. The company was also engaged to build a new petroleum additives research facility for Ethyl Corporation. Other work progressed on pharmaceutical projects for Rhone-Poulenc Rorer, Ethicon, Ortho, and Allergan.

Educational projects were also showing steady growth and were 33 percent higher in 1992 than in 1991. The company was involved in new and renovated educational facilities with local school systems and large public and private colleges and universities. Also, Turner was chosen to manage the seismic upgrade addition and renovations of the Doe and Moffit libraries in San Francisco the same year.

Some construction and management contracts for public-funded projects were also awarded in 1992. Contracts were awarded for modernizing and expanding Albany Airport, building a new wing of the Cleveland Public Library, and providing management services for renovations to the New Jersey State House Annex in Trenton. Long-term construction programs included the Los Angeles County-USC Medical Center replacement facility and a ten-year expansion project at Lambert-St. Louis International Airport.

Sports and entertainment complexes proved another important niche for Turner in the early 1990s. The company built Cleveland's Gund Arena, Portland, Oregon's Rose Garden Arena, and the Nashville Arena in the first half of the decade.

The corporation formed a joint venture known as Turner-Thompson Sports in 1995. Its first project was the Carolinas Stadium in Charlotte.

In keeping with its pursuit of diverse roles in the construction field, Turner greatly expanded its roster of project management services at this time as well. Turner president Parmelee realized that the continuous development of new services was a reality of the contracting business in the 1990s. He noted that, ''Clients will seek more program management from concept to completion and more overall responsibility.'' The contractor increasingly took on the responsibility for both design and construction of a project, as clients sought to save time, money, and staff hours. The design/build projects that were developed from this strategy in 1992 included the Federal Justice Building, Atlanta City Detention Center, and a six-story parking garage at Vanderbilt University in Nashville.

As the recession of the early 1990s persisted with its resulting tight credit market that hampered new building, Turner added another service to its arsenal. The company took the design/build process one step further and developed the design/build/finance service. Turner assembled teams of facility users, developers, designers, and lenders in agreements that met all the needs of the people involved in the projects. The finance and development was assumed by a third party, a special purpose corporation. Noteworthy design/build/finance contracts of the early 1990s included agreements with the University of Cincinnati and the Middletown Courthouse in Connecticut.

Recession Batters Bottom Line in Early 1990s

In spite of Turner's many efforts to meet the economic imperatives of the troubled contracting industry, the company struggled mightily in the early 1990s. Revenue declined from over $3.5 billion in 1990 to around $2.7 billion from 1990 through 1994. During that period, the company's aggregate net income totaled less than $2 million, as Turner suffered losses in 1990 and 1993. Though it continued to claim ''a broader geographic presence in the U.S. than any other construction company,'' Turner slid out of the industry's top revenue spot in 1995. The publicly traded company's stock dove from $21 in the mid-1980s to a low of $6 in 1991 before settling around $10 from 1993 through 1996.

Under the direction of chairman and chief executive officer Alfred T. McNeill, the company undertook a restructuring in 1994 that encompassed a moderate consolidation of Turner's traditionally decentralized corporate structure and a corresponding staff reduction. The number of U.S. offices declined from 42 in the late 1980s to about 35 in the early 1990s, and employment levels were cut by more than 16 percent from about 3,000 to 2,500 over the same period. Turner also abandoned its foray into real estate ownership, divesting millions of dollars worth of properties throughout the first half of the 1990s.

In spite of McNeill's efforts and an overall improvement in the economic climate, Turner achieved only anemic profits in 1994 and 1995, then suffered a $1.7 million loss on revenues of $3.3 billion in 1996. In August 1996, Turner's board appointed 71-year-old E. T. Gravette, Jr., to succeed McNeill as chair and

CEO, while 59-year-old Harold Parmelee retained the position of president he had held since mid-1990.

The housecleaning appeared to be taking rapid effect in 1997. In the first three quarters of that year, Turner's revenues increased nine percent over the same period in 1996, to $2.7 billion. Perhaps more importantly, net totaled $5.1 million, a pace that if carried through the remainder of the year would give Turner its best annual results since 1992.

Principal Subsidiaries

Ameristone; Burwharf Corp.; Mideast Construction Services, Inc.; Turner Investment Corp.; Universal Construction Company, Inc.; Trans-Con of Delaware Inc.; TDC of Texas, Inc.; Turner Construction Co.; Turner Development Corporation; TDC Corp. of Florida; Turner International Industries, Inc.; Turner (East Asia) Pte. Ltd. (Singapore); Rickenbacker Holdings, Inc.; Rickenbacker Development Corp.

Further Reading

"Back from the Brink," *Forbes,* October 25, 1993, pp. 14–15.

"Concrete and Steel Unite," *ENR,* July 19, 1990, pp. 30–32.

"Constructor," New York: Turner Construction Company, 1992.

Grogan, Tim, "Builders Flourish in an Upbeat Market," *ENR,* May 20, 1996, pp. 77–78.

Korman, Richard, "Turner Works Hard to Show Profit," *ENR,* September 14, 1989, pp. 17–18.

Lilly, Stephen, "City Review, Columbus, Ohio," *National Real Estate Investor,* December, 1989, pp. 140–42, 156–57.

"Turner Bites Bullet Now to Improve Profitability and Productivity Ahead," *ENR,* April 4, 1994, pp. 28–29.

Willoughby, Jack, "Hunker Down and Hope for the Best," *Forbes,* October 20, 1986, pp. 63–64.

—Dorothy Kroll
—updated by April Dougal Gasbarre

Tyler Corporation

2121 San Jacinto Street
Dallas, Texas 75201
U.S.A.
(214) 754-7800
Fax: (214) 969-9352

Public Company
Incorporated: 1966 as Saturn Industries, Inc.
Employees: 1,118
Sales: $128.3 million (1996)
Stock Exchanges: New York
SICs: 7374 Data Processing & Preparation

Once a Fortune 500 company with more than $1 billion in sales, Tyler Corporation operates as an information services company, providing computerized information systems to small counties and municipalities throughout the southwestern United States. Originally a diversified industrial conglomerate with leading market positions in pipe manufacturing, trucking, and industrial explosives, Tyler went through dramatic changes during the late 1980s, when all of its industrial-oriented business were sold. In late 1997, the company began its push into information services, acquiring Business Resources Corp., The Software Group Inc., and Interactive Computer Design, Inc.

Origins

During its first two decades of existence Tyler grew steadily and strongly, rising from the ranks of the corporate unknown to the prestigious class of America's industrial elite. A company that began its corporate life with no assets, it celebrated its twentieth anniversary as a $1-billion-in-sales industrial conglomerate, a fixture among the country's Fortune 500 corporations. It was a prodigious rise, the evolution of an upstart into an industry stalwart with leading market positions in trucking, industrial explosives, and sewage pipes. Tyler's fall was equally stunning. Less than a decade after the company held sway as an industrial giant, it was a $100-million-in-sales firm without any industrial businesses, struggling to define its identity. Remark-

ably, both eras of Tyler's history were led by the same individual, the company's founder, Joseph F. McKinney. McKinney orchestrated his company's prolific rise and he engineered its precipitous fall, making Tyler's first 30 years a singular chapter in the history of U.S. business.

A Jesuit-educated, Harvard graduate, McKinney earned some of the money he used to start Tyler by recording astounding success with an investment concern he founded with another business partner in 1960. Named Electro-Science Investors, McKinney's venture capital firm invested in high-technology companies that promised high returns, but also represented high risks. Betting on long shots paid off, however, and by the end of Electro-Science's first year, McKinney was a millionaire. He had yet to reach his 29th birthday.

Five years after starting Electro-Science, McKinney founded another company named Saturn Industries, Inc., which made its debut with three military supply businesses obtained from McKinney's business partner in Electro-Science, Jimmy Ling, head of a conglomerate named Ling-Temco-Vought (LTV). Combined, the three LTV companies generated $11 million in sales, the financial foundation upon which Tyler was built. McKinney quickly sold the three military suppliers, wishing to avoid dependence on one customer (the U.S. government) for his business, and with the proceeds gained from the sale of the former LTV companies he acquired the first of Tyler's numerous businesses, C&H Transportation.

Acquired in 1966, C&H operated as a heavy-freight hauler. Unlike the companies with which McKinney had financially involved himself through Electro-Science, C&H was not a high-risk investment capable of registering either meteoric growth or catastrophic losses. C&H was an established company, a steady money earner, a company engaged in a basic industry bereft of the flashy appeal of high-growth, high-technology business. C&H also provided a blueprint for McKinney's future acquisitions. All of the companies that would later compose Tyler, as an industrial conglomerate, would be similar to C&H: established companies, proven money earners, and operating in what McKinney referred to as "down-to-earth" industries.

Company Perspectives:

Tyler Corporation's primary purpose is to provide superior long-term rewards to shareholders. The company's objective to pursue this purpose is to be an enterprise selling products and services through a few operating companies carefully selected for two main characteristics: superior return on assets employed and growth probability.

With the money gained from the reliable, revenue-generating engine that C&H represented, McKinney was able to acquire his flagship business, Tyler Pipe, in 1968. A manufacturer of sewage pipe with $43 million in sales at the time of its acquisition, Tyler Pipe instantly became the greatest contributor to McKinney's company's annual revenue and earnings totals. In recognition of Tyler Pipe's pivotal role, McKinney's soon-to-be conglomerate took its name from its mainstay business.

Dozens of acquisitions followed the purchase of Tyler Pipe, each financed primarily with conventional bank loans and bond offerings. By 1975, the first year Tyler became a Fortune 500 company, a burgeoning industrial empire had been created. Additional acquisitions followed during the latter half of the 1970s, as Tyler's annual revenue total swelled and the company's shareholders applauded. Earnings per share in Tyler increased an average of 23 percent during the decade, providing tangible evidence that the strategy of pursuing growth by purchasing proven money earners entrenched in industrial markets was working well. For those who put their financial faith in McKinney's enterprise, the ensuing decade would take them on a roller-coaster ride, but the turbulence ahead enriched all who held on to their stock and put their trust in McKinney.

Tyler entered the 1980s as it left the 1970s, still in pursuit of acquisitions to bolster its stature. Two of the biggest deals in the company's history were completed in 1981, when McKinney completed the purchase of Hall-Mark Electronics, a distributor of electronic components, and Reliance Universal, a specialty chemical coatings maker. Both companies became significant contributors to Tyler's annual sales and earnings totals, and at least one analyst heralded the acquisition of Hall-Mark as McKinney's shrewdest acquisition since the purchase of Tyler Pipe. Within two years, the two 1981 acquisitions were contributing 41 percent of the company's total profits and 43 percent of its sales, proving to be instrumental in Tyler's assault on the $1-billion-in-sales mark.

The only negative aspect of the 1981 acquisitions was the timing. The early 1980s were marred by escalating interest rates, recessive economic conditions, and trucking deregulation, all of which conspired to deliver a stinging blow to Tyler. The company's earnings plunged 63 percent in 1982, sent downward, in part, because of rising interest rates associated with its purchase of Hall-Mark and Reliance Universal. The wounds were only superficial, however, thanks to the resiliency of the established, time-tested businesses within Tyler's fold. In 1983 the company's earnings more than made up for the preceding year's fall, jumping up more than 80 percent to reach $18.5 million.

Tyler entered the mid-1980s as a healthy, diversified conglomerate with three of its six primary business units ranked as the leaders in their markets. Tyler Pipe set the pace among pipe manufacturers, C&H led the way in the heavy-freight industry, and Atlas Powder, a producer of explosives, had slipped past Du Pont to rank as the largest seller of industrial explosives in the United States. The company was one of the largest corporations in the country, a heavyweight with 10,000 employees and annual sales that reached $1.1 billion by 1987.

Turning Point in 1987

As it turned out, 1987 proved to be the company's peak year in terms of size. The time had arrived, in McKinney's mind, to undo all that had taken two decades to accomplish. In a few short years, Tyler would be stripped of nearly all its businesses. Payroll would be whittled down to slightly more than 1,000. Annual sales volume would plummet drastically, dropping to the $100 million range. The company's 20 years of experience in industrial businesses would be forsaken for entry into a new line of business. Sweeping, wholesale changes were in the offing, but their arrival was not associated with any malfeasance on management's part or the crippling effect of declining business. The changes were deliberate. McKinney had decided to destroy Tyler and create an entirely new type of company.

For the impetus to initiate his radical changes, McKinney took his cue from pervasive trends in the business environment during the latter half of the 1980s. Corporate takeovers were the rage and leveraged buyouts were rampant. Companies were acquiring assets with an insatiable appetite, paying what, in retrospect, were inflated prices. McKinney saw what was going on around him and made a strategic decision. He turned a deaf ear to exhortations to launch an acquisition spree and decided to sell Tyler's assets, resolving that it would be better for shareholders if he liquidated rather than incurring debt by buying and holding on to businesses at inflated prices. Once that decision was made, McKinney never turned back and began disassembling the electronics distribution, pipe manufacturing, specialty coatings, explosives, and trucking conglomerate he had built.

First to go was Tyler's electronics distributor, Hall-Mark Electronics, which was sold to management in August 1988. The divestiture netted $211 million in proceeds, most of which went to shareholders as a special $10-per-share dividend. As McKinney's version of a corporate yard sale ensued, shareholders in Tyler, which included McKinney, were the chief benefactors of the company's asset sales. With each divestiture, the bulk of the proceeds was funneled to shareholders, as McKinney made good on his declaration that Tyler's shareholders were Tyler's customers. In 1989 the next Tyler business made its exit from the company's portfolio of businesses. Reliance Universal was purchased by a Dutch chemical conglomerate in a deal worth $286 million. The following year, Atlas Powder, Tyler's explosive manufacturer, was put on the auction block, stripping the company of another primary component of its operations. By the end of 1990, McKinney had sold more than four-fifths of Tyler's businesses, distributing roughly $415 million in cash and stock to the company's shareholders. In all, 12 businesses were sold, leaving the company with only Tyler Pipe as it entered the 1990s.

With only Tyler Pipe supporting the company, McKinney turned his attention toward reinventing Tyler, having swept away the company's past through divestitures to make room for its future as a retail-oriented company. Tyler Pipe was sold in 1995—removing the last vestige of the company's past as an industrial conglomerate—to help pay for two retail businesses, Forest City Auto Parts and Institutional Financing Services, Inc. Forest City operated a chain of 61 stores that sold automotive parts and supplies in Illinois, New York, Ohio, Pennsylvania, and Wisconsin. Institutional Financing Services operated as a national education fund-raising services company that provided products and gifts for students to sell to raise funds. These two companies composed Tyler, the former giant, as the company entered the mid-1990s. As replacements for more than a dozen companies that had consistently delivered sales and earnings growth to Tyler, Forest City and Institutional Financing Services were failures. In 1994 Tyler lost $4.7 million on $153 million in sales. The following year, losses totaled $16 million and sales slipped to $140 million. In 1996 the pattern of increasing losses and declining sales repeated itself. The company registered a staggering $61.3 million loss on sales of $128 million.

Clearly, the "new" Tyler was not working. McKinney, who had attempted to reinvent Tyler and failed, left the company in late 1996 and was succeeded as chief executive officer by Bruce W. Wilkinson. Wilkinson joined Tyler after a lengthy career of leading established, publicly held corporations to optimum sales for the benefit of shareholders. He had earned praise as chief executive officer and chairman of Houston-based CRSS Inc., a large, diversified design and engineering power company, and as chief executive officer of another Houston-based company, Proler International Corp. When he joined Tyler, Wilkinson declared, "I didn't come here to keep the status quo." He immediately began reevaluating the acquisitions made by McKinney. Wilkinson did not approve of either Institutional Financing Services or Forest City Auto Parts as the corporate vehicles for Tyler's future. "These are two unrelated low-growth subsidiaries," he told *The Dallas Business Journal.* "The history of Tyler is not in retail, and it's not my history. I want to return the company to where the customer is another business." Wilkinson wanted to return Tyler to its past, back to the company's roots in the basic, down-to-earth industries that characterized much of McKinney's era.

Wilkinson was in the process of moving Tyler's corporate offices from Dallas to Houston and plotting the company's future as a manufacturer or a distributor when Louis Waters, who had helped found Browning-Ferris Industries Inc., a huge waste services company, invested $3.5 million in Tyler in August 1997. Waters's investment gave him a ten percent equity stake in Tyler and a seat on the company's board of directors, but according to Waters the investment did not signal an attempt on his part to take control of the company. Waters claimed he was "transitioning" toward retirement, explaining, "I will be a very interested direc-

tor joining them in the reevaluation of their strategic plan, but I won't be a part of management." Two months later, Waters was elected chairman of Tyler.

Between August and October 1997, a debate between Wilkinson and Waters centered on the issue of Tyler's future. Wilkinson wanted to move into basic, industrial-oriented businesses. Waters wanted to reshape Tyler as an information services company. Waters won the debate and Wilkinson resigned after serving as chief executive for only six months. The management shake-up in late 1997 cleared the path for Tyler's development into an information services company, and Waters wasted little time in bringing about what he envisioned. Before the end of the year Tyler signed definitive agreements to acquire Business Resources Corp. and The Software Group Inc., two information services companies that served roughly 200 county governments, primarily in the Southwest. "Our plan," Waters explained, "is to consolidate the information industry for local governments. We are looking at smaller counties, municipalities, cities and appraisal districts or police and court systems. They need to computerize their record keeping, dispatch, tax collections, land records, deeds, probation; the possibilities are vast."

With this objective determining the company's future course, Tyler entered the late 1990s seeking to become an information services company. Several days before the end of 1997, the company acquired a third company to aid in its bid to become an information services provider for small communities, purchasing Interactive Computer Design, Inc., which provided integrated information management services and systems to 225 cities throughout Texas, Oklahoma, and Missouri. On the heels of this deal, Tyler prepared for its future, an era entirely unlike that of its past.

Principal Subsidiaries

Business Resources Corp.; The Software Group Inc.; Interactive Computer Design, Inc.; Forest City Auto Parts Company.

Further Reading

Bork, Robert H., Jr., "The Survivor," *Forbes,* February 27, 1984, p. 92.

de Rouffignac, Ann, "Big Board Firm Moving to Houston; Wilkinson Tapped To Revive Floundering Conglomerate," *Houston Business Journal,* July 18, 1997, p. 1A.

——, "Once Great Tyler Now Troubled by Declining Sales," *Houston Business Journal,* July 18, 1997, p. 1A.

——, "Tyler Management Shakeup: Wilkinson Out, Waters in as Dallas Firm Makes Acquisitions," *Houston Business Journal,* October 17, 1997, p. 5A.

Mack, Toni, "A Man Who Thinks for Himself," *Forbes,* April 2, 1990, p. 36.

"Tyler Corporation Announces Definitive Agreement To Acquire Interactive Computer Design, Inc.," December 22, 1997, p. 12.

—Jeffrey L. Covell

Valeo

43, rue Bayen
75017 Paris
France
(33) 01 40 55 20 20
Fax: (33) 01 40 55 21 71
Web site: http://www.valeo.com

Public Company
Incorporated: 1923 as Société Anonyme Française du
Ferodo
Employees: 32,600
Sales: FFr 28.87 billion (1996)
Stock Exchanges: Paris
SICs: 5013 Motor Vehicle Supplies and New Parts

France's Valeo is a world-leading independent supplier of components and systems to the worldwide automobile and truck industry. Valeo operates more than 104 facilities, including 95 manufacturing plants and 15 research and development centers in some 20 countries, serving the European, North and South American, and Asian markets. With nearly FFr 30 billion in annual sales in 1996—and goals to top FFr 40 billion by 2000—Valeo has invested aggressively to establish leadership positions in several components and systems groups. The company is the world-leading supplier of clutch systems, friction materials, and engine cooling systems, and the European leader in air conditioning systems, lighting systems, security systems, and electrical systems. To maintain its position and growth, Valeo invests approximately six percent of its consolidated sales in research and development per year (resulting in filings for 500 patents in 1996 alone) while continuing a policy begun in the late 1980s of strong capital expenditures designed to increase its global presence. In 1996 Valeo's capital expenditures reached FFr 2.3 billion; in 1997 the company expected to spend FFr 3.0 billion, representing some nine percent of its 1996 sales. In January 1997 Valeo's growth earned the company a listing on the Paris Bourse's CAC 40 indicator of leading French companies. Principal shareholders include France's CGIP, with 20 percent, and Caisse des Dépôts et Consignations,

with seven percent, following the sale of former major shareholder, Cerus, a French holding company owned by Italy's Carlo De Benedetti, in 1996. Since 1987 Valeo has been led by CEO Noël Goutard.

Changing the Ferodo in 1980

When Valeo adopted its new name in 1980, it gave up what many manufacturers only hope for: a name that had become synonymous with an entire product category. For more than 50 years, Société Anonyme Française du Ferodo had dominated the French brake linings market, to the extent that the phrase "change your ferodo" all but meant "reline your brakes" in many of the country's service stations. Yet, by 1980, the founding company had grouped together many of France's most celebrated names in automotive equipment and systems, including Cibié, Marchal, Paris-Rhône, and SEV, representing some 30 product lines. Changing the company's name to Valeo (Latin for "I'm very well") created a consolidated and independent force in the global automotive supply market.

Ferodo's origins dated back to England of the 1890s. It was then that Herbert Frood witnessed a heavily loaded horse and carriage having difficulties braking and the driver thrusting his shoe between the brake and wheel to bring the carriage to a halt. Frood kept the event in his memory; 20 years later, as the newly emerging automobile industry was struggling with its own braking systems, Frood introduced the first brake lining, replacing the driver's shoe with a more durable sheet of asbestos. Frood dubbed the lining "Ferodo," and the product quickly became a mainstay in the British automotive industry's brake systems.

Frood's brake linings also caught the attention of the automobile industry on the Continent. In 1910 Frood agreed to give a French entrepreneur, Eugène Buisson, the right to import and distribute the Ferodo linings in France. Soon after, Buisson received the rights to begin manufacturing the Ferodo linings in France, and the Société Anonyme Française du Ferodo, founded in 1923, grew to become one of France's most prominent automotive equipment suppliers.

Although its initial success was based on brake linings, Ferodo soon diversified into other automotive equipment markets, adding first clutch linings and then complete clutch systems. The 1962 acquisition of Sofica added automotive heating systems, from which the company branched out into cooling systems by the mid-1960s. As with its other product lines, Ferodo soon came to dominate the French market for this product category as well. Meanwhile, as automobile makers established international and then global markets for their cars and trucks, Ferodo also began its international development, opening subsidiaries and factories close to its customers. An early subsidiary, formed in Italy in 1964 to produce clutch systems, adopted the name Valeo for the first time. The Italian Valeo went on to capture the majority of the Italian clutch market. From Italy, Ferodo moved into Spain, and then into the South American market through Brazil and Argentina. North America and the crucial U.S. market followed soon afterwards; during the 1970s the company turned east, entering the soon-to-boom Asian market. Meanwhile, Ferodo remained in the Buisson family, with André Buisson succeeding as CEO.

During the 1970s the French automotive equipment market underwent a shift. Spurred by the 1973 oil crisis and the resulting economic chaos in the automobile industry on the one hand and, on the other, the French government's eagerness to consolidate—and later nationalize—much of French industry, Ferodo began to absorb a number of other prominent automotive equipment makers. By 1980 the company had been joined by SEV (Société Anonyme pour l'Equipement Électrique des Vehicules, founded in 1912), which had pioneered automotive electrical systems; Paris-Rhône (Compagnie Industrielle de Paris et du Rhône, founded in 1915), which retained a leading position supplying military aviation and radio-electric markets; Cibié, founded in 1919, France's pioneering and leading maker of lighting systems for automobiles and trucks; Marchal, founded in 1923, which specialized in headlamps and lighting systems; and a number of other similarly prominent automotive brands, including Soma, which added transmissions and hydraulic systems for the trucking industry, as well as IMCH, ISHA, PPB, SIME, UFAGA, and Flertex.

In 1980 Ferodo took the bold move of adopting a new name under which it grouped and later replaced its panoply of brand names. The new company boasted revenues of FFr 7 billion, a payroll of 27,000, and a product line of more than 30 products capable of providing most of the critical internal components of automobiles for some 26 automakers worldwide, supported by 100 factories and other facilities in 16 countries.

A Worldwide Leader for the 1990s

The 1980s would mark the company's strongest period of growth, with revenues reaching FFr 20 billion by 1990, establishing the company as the world's premier independent automobile components and systems supplier. Valeo's globalization

strategy also would be put in place by the start of the 1990s, with the company's foreign sales topping its domestic sales for the first time. Yet not all of the company's strategies would be as successful. At its formation, Valeo determined to diversify its activities into the nonautomotive industrial and manufacturing market. A number of acquisitions made in the early 1980s brought the company into the construction industry, smelting and steelworks, industrial equipment, and other activities that would eventually stretch the company too thin and drag heavily on its profits.

Weathering the recession of the early 1980s, and with annual sales rising to FFr 11 billion by the middle of the decade, Valeo faced a new crisis in 1986. At a time when French industry was reemerging from the country's brief flirtation with nationalization, Valeo, which had steadfastly remained independent, found itself involved in a struggle for control. In a period that gave rise to a new breed of corporate raiders, Valeo became a target for one of the best known of these, Carlo De Benedetti of Italy. In February 1986, De Benedetti began buying up shares of Valeo, gathering 19 percent and effectively gaining majority control of the company. Valeo, and CEO André Buisson, turned to the French government in an attempt to head off this passage of Valeo into foreign control. Buisson was almost successful: Valeo succeeded in becoming classified as strategic to France's national defense. Yet, while the company indeed was manufacturing components for a model of a new French tank, this activity formed less than one percent of its revenues. Nonetheless, the action barred Valeo's takeover by a foreign concern.

De Benedetti was only temporarily thwarted, however. In June 1986 he purchased an inactive French holding company, Airflam. Renamed Cerus, the shell company received De Benedetti's 19 percent of Valeo, giving De Benedetti a controlling stake in the auto equipment maker after all. In fact, Valeo's years under Cerus proved a period of strong growth, if only because of the appointment of Noël Goutard to replace André Buisson as Valeo's CEO.

Goutard came to Valeo after a career with many of France's, and the world's, largest names, including stints with Warner Lambert and Pfizer and leadership positions with Gévelot, Compteurs Schlumberger, Pricel (later Chargeurs), and Thomson. Under Goutard, Valeo rapidly shed its nonautomotive activities, at the same time boosting its position in its core market with a new series of acquisitions, including Tibbe of Germany, Bongotti of Brazil, and Chausson Thermique and Neiman of France. By 1988 Valeo's revenues had climbed to FFr 16.5 billion and its profits soared, gaining 127 percent in a single year, to reach a net profit of FFr 817 million. Unsatisfied, Goutard would suggest that Valeo needed to attain a "critical mass" of FFr 25 billion in revenues—a milestone reached in 1995.

Goutard was also credited with foreseeing the coming economic crisis of the 1990s, restructuring Valeo, including shedding subsidiaries, and even entire product categories, while shutting 12 plants (representing 15 percent of the company's activity) to realign its manufacturing activities on an international scale. Cutting back its work force by some 2,000 helped the company boost its per-employee productivity from FFr 560,000 in 1988 to FFr 690,000 in 1990. The sale of a series of nonstrategic subsidiaries, which reduced Valeo's revenues by some FFr 1.2 billion, helped the company reduce its debt load, bringing its net debt/earnings ratio down from 0.70 in 1989 to 0.54 in 1990, and to 0.42 in 1991.

The leaner Valeo found itself in a somewhat luxurious position as the recession of the early 1990s turned into a prolonged European economic crisis. Aided by Valeo's moves into the booming Asian market and its successful alignment with the major Japanese auto makers, along with its continued global implantation, including a policy of opening production facilities close to its clients' plants, Valeo would see a steady progression of its net profits through the first half of the 1990s, despite the stagnant market. While its revenues stuck at around FFr 20 million through 1993 and would climb only slowly afterwards, reaching FFr 28 billion in 1996, the company's net profits would reach FFr 1 billion by 1994.

In the mid-1990s Valeo continued making key acquisitions, including adding Borg Instruments in 1995, Brazil's Univel in 1997, while shedding other operations. Valeo also had embarked on the creation of a number of joint venture partnerships, including a European project with Japan's Seiko-Seiki; the formation of and 50 percent participation in Nobel Plastiques Climatisation; partnerships with Siemens in automotive climate control systems; and 1997 joint venture agreements reached with France's Plastics Omnium, a world leader in plastics-based automotive components, and with Yuejin Motor Corporation of China, marking Valeo's fifth joint venture in that crucial market. In 1996 Valeo regained its ''independence'' when De Benedetti's Cerus sold off its stake in the company.

Valeo continued to invest heavily in research and development and, especially, capital expenditures. New Valeo plants started up operations in France, Spain, the United States, Canada, Mexico, China, Argentina, and Brazil. The company also moved into the former Soviet bloc, bringing production facilities to the Czech Republic and Poland. Valeo's global development strategy and its specialized focus would seem a model for a new industrial age. And the company could begin eyeing its next milestone, that of becoming a FFr 40 billion company by the year 2000.

Principal Subsidiaries

Valeo Kupplungen (Germany); Valeo España; Valeo SpA (Italy; 99.9%); Valeo Sprzegla Poland; Valeo Clutches and Transmissions (U.S.); Valeo Debriyaj (Turkey); Valeo Embragues Argentina (68%); Emelar (Argentina); Valeo Pyeong Hwa (South Korea; 50%); Valeo Embrayages (Tunesia); Valeo Materiales de Fricción (Spain); Valeo Friction Materials Inc. (U.S.); Valeo Materiales de Fricción de Mexico; Valeo Climatisation (France; 79%); Valeo Seiko Compressors (France; 50%); Nobel Plastiques Climatisation (France; 50%); Siemens Automotive Moteurs Electriques (Germany; 30%); Valeo Limasystem (Germany); Valeo Climate Control de España; Valeo Climate Control Ltd. (U.K.); Valeo Climate Control Corp. (U.S.); Valeo Thermique Moteur (France); Valeo Engine Cooling AB (Sweden); Valeo Tek Inc. (South Korea); Electrical Equipment: Valeo Vision (France); Valeo Iluminación (Spain; 99.7%); Cibie Argentina; Prismatic (Brazil; 80.4%); Hubei Valeo Autolighting (China; 51%); Valeo Equipements Electriques Moteur (France); Valeo Electrical Systems (U.K.); Valeo Elektrik (Turkey); Shanghai Valeo Automotive Electrical Systems (China; 30%); Valeo Systémes d'Essuyage (France); Paul Journée (France); Valeo Termico (Spain); Valeo Wiper Systems Ltd. (U.K.); Valeo Wiper Systems Inc. (U.S.); Valeo Sécurité Habitacle (France); Valeo Security Systems Ltd. (U.K.); Valeo Sicurezza Abitacolo (Italy); Valeo Neiman Argentina; Valeo Lock Systems Ltd. (U.K.); Valeo Borg Instruments KG (Germany); Valeo Distribution (France); Chausson Service.

—M.L. Cohen

Varta AG

Am Leineufer 51
D-30419 Hannover
Germany
(49) (511) 790 36 60
Fax: (49) (511) 790 36 67
Web site: http://www.varta.com

Public Company
Incorporated: 1890
Employees: 10,186
Sales: DM1.98 billion (1996)
Stock Exchanges: Frankfurt
SICs: 3339 Primary Smelting and Refining of Non-
Ferous Metals; 3691 Storage Batteries; 3692 Primary
Batteries, Dry and Wet; 3711 Motor Vehicle and
Passenger Car Bodies

Varta AG produces batteries, including storage batteries (such as automobile batteries), rechargeable batteries (such as batteries for camcorders), and primary batteries (which are discarded after the energy has been discharged). An industry leader in Europe, second only to Duracell in market share for consumer batteries, Varta is also the top battery supplier in Latin America. With headquarters in Germany, Varta maintains one factory for auto batteries in Hannover; three for portable batteries of all types in Hagen, Ellwangen, and Dischingen; a lead recycling plant in Krautscheid; a chemical factory in Hagen; and a factory for plastic components in Waechtersbach. In addition, the company has nine other factories in Europe, seven in North and South America, and one each in Asia and Australia. Following some fiscally disappointing years in the mid-1990s, attributed largely to economic recession in Europe and losses in the company's industrial battery sector, Varta remained committed to economic turnaround via restructurings and efforts at improving productivity among its more successful business sectors.

The 19th-Century: First Storage Batteries

Adolph Mueller founded the company which later became Varta AG in January 1888, calling his enterprise what translates into English as the Buesche and Mueller Tudor System Battery Factory. Having seen a demonstration of a new Accumulator—a rechargeable power cell—by the Brothers Tudor, Mueller realized immediately that the design functioned much better than others of the day and that furthermore it could be used to supply electric light to homes and businesses then just coming into vogue. With some 370,000 Gold Marks in capital, Mueller and partner Paul Buesche opened a small factory for the production of industrial batteries in the city of Hagen in Lower Saxony. It was the first such facility in Germany.

The first Buesche & Mueller batteries were used by power companies. These batteries stored energy produced by dynamos and assured customers a smooth flow of electrical current. A favorable evaluation of the company's batteries by the Koenigliche Technische Hochschule Hannover enabled Buesche and Mueller to overcome general suspicion of batteries in the young electricity industry. By 1889, the company had 40 employees, annual sales of DM1 million, and a client base that included Deutsche Bank Hamburg, the Bremen Harbor Authority, and Norddeutscher Lloyd.

In October 1890, Mueller & Einbeck—Paul Buesche had left the previous year—formed a new joint stock company in association with Siemens AG and AEG AG: Accumulatoren-Fabrik AG or AFA for short. The market was lucrative, and by the turn of the century, AFA had provided batteries to more than 148 power plants. Competition was growing too. Between 1890 and 1896 alone, AFA brought 100 patent violation suits against using processes patented by AFA. AFA then frequently swallowed up the smaller firms after they had lost their cases. By 1909, the company had taken over 11 battery companies in Germany and 14 in Austria-Hungary, Russia, and Switzerland.

Mueller was always alert for new applications for AFA. Although he was unable to interest German industry in manufacturing electric cars and his own auto company, the Berliner-Elektro-Droschken AG, met with little interest from the buying public, he had better luck with trains. In 1895, a streetcar powered by AFA batteries—the first electric streetcar in Germany—was put into service in Hagen. Other cities followed suit, but by 1900 most urban streetcar lines switched over to power from overhead lines and that market had disappeared.

The railroads were a natural market. At the time, their cars were still lit by gas or oil lamps or candlelight, and electric light meant a vast improvement in convenience and safety. AFA's first customer was the North Milan Railroad in 1889. In 1905, AFA, AEG, and Siemens jointly founded the Gesellschaft fuer elektrische Zugbeleuchtung (GEZ), a company intended specifically to produce electric lighting systems for trains. AEG and Siemens developed regulators and transformers, and AFA provided the batteries. A prime target of GEZ was the enormous German railroad system whose trains, by royal decree, were required to be lit after dark. Between 1905 and 1913, GEZ established offices in 20 countries and equipped about 1,000 rail cars with interior and exterior lights. AFA (then Varta) would remain a partner in GEZ until 1984, when it sold its shares in the company. AFA also produced batteries used in the complete powering of trains, typically smaller narrow gauge trains used to transport goods and materials at factories and harbors. AFA's Hagen plant had such a battery-powered train system in 1890.

Early Diversification

In 1904 AFA's first subsidiary, VARTA Accumulatoren Gesellschaft mbH, was founded in Berlin, where AFA management had maintained its offices since 1897. The name was an acronym created from the words Vertrieb, Aufladung, Reparatur, Transportabler Akkumulatoren, or Sales, Charging, and Repair of Portable Batteries. A state-of-the-art plant was built for Varta in Berlin at this time, and it remained the largest AFA factory to date. The new company manufactured small batteries for low-current applications, such as flashlights, house lights, telegraph and signal devices, and automobile lights. The automobile starter battery, which would make the Varta name famous, was not developed until an electric starter for autos was invented in 1914. Large industrial batteries and batteries for the railroads and public transportation continued to be manufactured by AFA in Hagen.

AFA grew rapidly during the first decade of the century. It acquired another major subsidiary in 1913, the Deutsche Edison Akkumulatoren Company GmbH (DEAC), a company licensed to produce a steel-alkali battery invented by Thomas Edison, as well as a number of foreign subsidiaries in Prague, Sweden, Russia, and Spain.

Beginning in 1914, sales of Varta's auto starter batteries began slowly but steadily increasing. Germany's catastrophic defeat in World War I, however, brought company progress to an abrupt halt. After the war AFA lost most of its foreign holdings as well as its work force; more than 500 workers were killed and a many others came home disabled and therefore unable to work.

AFA's rebuilding efforts were assisted by the growing use of batteries in motor vehicles. The German postal system became a major Varta customer, having begun using electric vehicles powered by AFA batteries in 1909. After the war, in 1924, the Berlin Postal Delivery Office replaced 1,000 horses with 1,200 electric vans. Moreover, the Varta subsidiary was selling more starter batteries for automobiles as well, although that market in Germany was relatively small compared to that of the United States at the time.

AFA's first big market success in the 1920s was a steel alkali battery produced by its subsidiary DEAC. The lightweight battery, which proved ideal for miner's lamps, appeared on the market precisely when public attention was focused on the danger of mine explosions caused by gas lanterns. AFA strengthened its presence in the mining market in 1927 when it acquired Grubenlampenfabrik Dominit, a manufacturer of miner's lamps. In 1927 about 30,000 Dominit miner's lamps were using lead or alkali batteries. DEAC batteries were also used to power the mining cars that transported ore out of the earth.

Consumer interest in batteries got its first powerful stimulus with the introduction of radio as an entertainment medium in 1923. Pertrix Chemische Fabrik GmbH, founded in Hamburg in 1917, developed a small new dry-cell primary battery—that is, a disposable as opposed to a rechargeable battery—for flashlights, which proved ideal for radio as well. In 1925, AFA obtained a license from Pertrix to produce the dry-cells; the following year AFA bought the company outright and began producing batteries in Berlin under the Pertrix brand name. In 1928, with radio booming, the Pertrix subsidiary had 1,600 employees and was manufacturing 120 million batteries a year. The acquisition of Pertrix rounded out AFA's line of batteries: AFA produced high-performance lead batteries for industrial use; Varta made starter batteries and other portable lead batteries; DEAC manufactured steel-alkali batteries; and Pertrix produced disposable dry-cells.

In all the 1920s were a period of expansion for AFA. The company's battery plants in Berlin and Hagen were expanded, and it made great progress towards reestablishing its European and international network of subsidiaries, affiliates, and branch offices, while cultivating new markets at the same time. In 1923 Gunther Quandt became AFA's majority shareholder, and control of the company passed to the Quandt family, where it would remain into the 1990s. Adolph Mueller passed away in 1925 at the age of 78.

Like most German businesses, AFA was hit hard by the onset of the Great Depression. Pertrix though was hit doubly hard. In addition to the economic downturn, competition came in the form of an alternating current adapter for radios, which was developed in 1930 and eliminated much of the market for batteries. Only layoffs coupled with wage cuts, first of five percent and later 7.5 percent, saved the company.

New Inventions

To save the company, AFA directors focused the full energies of the firm on developing new products. Varta developed the sinterplate, a battery element formed by sintering nickel powder into a solid plate, a technology producing batteries in which an extremely high charge could be stored. The batteries could be used in applications in which reliability was of utmost importance, such as in aircraft take-offs. The battery remained among Varta's top products for decades. Also during this time, the demand for batteries to power cars and trucks was increasing rapidly. In 1936 the company marketed the first standard-sized starter battery that would fit in any vehicle.

Pertrix bounced back from its problems early in the 1930s with batteries for flashlights, telephones, and signal devices, and later in the decade for portable radios, which were just becoming popular. More importantly, in 1932, the company developed an oxygen element, the Aerodyn, for the Volksempfaenger, the People's Radio, an inexpensive radio which could be found in most German homes in the 1930s and 1940s. By the time World War II began in 1939, Pertrix was in solid financial shape and had established factories in many European countries, including England, Sweden, Austria, Hungary, and Czechoslovakia. AFA, and later DEAC, were given a vital infusion by the invention of the forklift in 1935. The battery-powered vehicle revolutionized the transport of raw materials, parts, and products.

Postwar Recovery

By 1937 demand for starter batteries had completely outstripped AFA's production capacity. With no room to expand the plants in Berlin and Hagen, Gunther Quandt initiated a plan to build a new factory in Hannover. Ground was broken for a state-of-the-art production facility in July 1938. The new facility consisted of six ground floor production halls, a revolutionary idea at a time when most German factories were built upwards and production was split up over five to ten stories. Facilities at the new plant included areas for lead recycling, lead powder storage, rubber production, and a foundry. Quandt believed the design and location of the new facility to be so good that he considered giving up AFA's factories in Berlin and Hagen in order to consolidate all production in Hannover, although construction would not be completed until 1943. The factory was meant to produce power supply batteries, such as those used for forklifts, and starter batteries for cars, trucks, and other vehicles. Shortly after production began in 1939, World War II started and all AFA plants were changed over to war production.

The war wreaked havoc on AFA. Air raids badly damaged most of its factories. The Hagen facility was hit especially hard, and what was not destroyed was confiscated. The Russians seized AFA's two Berlin factories, both of which were in the eastern sector of the city, and equipment was dismantled and shipped to the Soviet Union. The British Army occupied the new Hannover plant, sending the best equipment to France and Yugoslavia. AFA holdings located in areas of Germany later ceded to Poland were lost forever, and most properties elsewhere in Europe and Eastern Germany were confiscated. In the Netherlands, the Varta brand name itself was confiscated and AFA/Varta was unable to market products in Holland under the Varta name until 1976.

While Gunther Quandt was held in an internment camp for 18 months, his son Herbert ran AFA. The Hannover plant was relatively undamaged, and by June 1945 was producing batteries once again, this time for the British. The factory produced nickel-formate for the Allies as well. Besides being used in batteries, nickel was a material required in the production of oil and fat. The Hagen factory, one-fifth of which was destroyed in air raids, was rebuilt by 1948. Expansion continued on land acquired from neighboring firms until the late 1960s.

In 1946, following the loss of its East Berlin factories, Pertrix was refounded as Pertrix Werke GmbH. in Hannover. In 1949, the company changed its name again to Pertrix Union GmbH and began production in a factory in Ellwangen Baden-Wuertemberg in southern Germany. The introduction of portable radios in the 1950s increased demand for Pertrix batteries, and before the decade's end the Ellwangen plant was producing 15 cell sizes and 50 different types of batteries.

DEAC was helped enormously during this time by the commercialization of a new rechargeable alkali battery. The company had developed the completely sealed, airtight steel-alkali battery in 1933. The new battery did not have to be refilled regularly with water and ended perennial problems of leaking, electrolyte loss, and electrolyte exchange. The technology, developed in the early 1930s, proved highly adaptable. DEAC eventually began producing completely airtight, rechargeable nickel-cadmium batteries. The advent of the microelectronic revolution in the 1970s and 1980s later multiplied their applications a hundred times over, and by the 1990s millions of these batteries were sold for computers, cell phones, battery-powered hand tools, and even the power-regulating elements in satellites. In the 1950s, production at DEAC was split between traditional open batteries and the new sealed ones. Sales increased rapidly, until at the end of the 1960s when a new production facility was built.

Despite the hardships of the postwar years, AFA made great strides during the 1950s. Plants were modernized and expanded; mass manufacture of portable batteries on assembly lines began. The 1950s were a boom time for batteries in the Federal Republic, and the sales of automobile batteries rocketed as prosperity returned. In 1952 the German Railway put over 200 hundred trains powered by AFA batteries into service. New batteries were also developed during this time. Zinc cells were developed for motor devices, such as in tape recorders, that drew relatively high amounts of power. Pertrix introduced so-called "paper-lined" cells in 1955. A steel-lined leak-proof battery was developed with the American battery manufacturer, Rayovac. Zinc chloride batteries were perfected in 1957, and towards decade's end the transistor revolution began creating a huge market for batteries of an entirely different type—smaller, with higher performance and a longer shelf life. By the end of the 1950s, AFA was employing 2,000 workers at its Hannover plant alone.

In 1950 AFA acquired Robert Schneider KG, a plastic company geared to the production of high quality technical plastics that could be used to house and insulate various battery products. The company, renamed Varta-Plastic GmbH, experimented with various new techniques in the 1950s, including a sinter process for producing plastic casing and new processes for making hollow bodies and tubing from plastic.

Between 1950 and 1960 AFA re-established its international network of branches and subsidiaries, founding or obtaining a financial interest in companies in Belgium, the Netherlands, France, Scandinavia, Britain, Spain, Argentina, Brazil, Canada, and the United States. By the end of the 1980s, subsidiary Varta AG had more than 25 different companies which employed 13,000 employees worldwide.

AFA continued to pursue research and development aggressively after the war. Having established its first industrial research laboratory at its Berlin factory in 1908, in the 1950s the company began a broad program of cooperative research with universities and other companies, such as the American company Rayovac. In 1955, AFA opened a central research and development facility at Frankfurt am Main. The lab was divided into research groups for lead batteries, alkali cells, primary cells, and general research. Within ten years, the facility had become too small and a new one had to be built in Kelkheim, the largest such facility in Europe at the time.

A New Company Name in the 1960s

In 1962, with automobiles one of the most important consumer products, Varta had become the leading name in auto batteries in the Federal Republic. The company's reputation was so good that the AFA sales department began encouraging the company to use the Varta name for all the company's batteries. Stockholders ratified the change at the 1962 annual meeting, and AFA's name officially changed to Varta AG. The change affected the subsidiaries as well. Pertrix became Varta-Pertrix Union GmbH, DEAC became Varta DEAC, and before long the Varta name was incorporated into the names of foreign subsidiaries as well. Gradually AFA, DEAC, and Pertrix brand names were phased out.

In 1968, Varta built a large battery recycling facility at Krautscheid. During this time Varta researchers developed a process in which whole batteries could be recycled without first being torn apart. More than 95 percent of all old batteries could be recycled there, approximately 96 percent of the lead could be reclaimed, and the plant operated well within German air pollution parameters. Krautschied took over all Varta lead recycling and an older facility in Hagen was closed. In 1996, the recycling operation became an autonomous company, Varta Recycling GmbH, within Varta AG.

Further Reorganization

The 1970s were a time of reorganization and expansion for Varta. In 1973 Varta AG became a holding company, as battery production was consolidated from the old subsidiaries Varta Pertrix and Varta DEAC, into Varta Batterie AG. Varta Batterie was comprised of five divisions: Auto Batteries Europe, Industrial Batteries Europe, and three Dry Battery sections, Europe, Eastern Europe and Overseas. The reorganization was intended to streamline decision-making; Varta was responsible for strategic management, while the individual divisions made all day-to-day decisions.

Varta AG was further reorganized in 1977 to consolidate battery-making activities under one roof. Management of activities unrelated to batteries was divested, and Varta AG henceforth consisted only of Varta Batterie and battery-related areas like Varta-Plastic. A new conglomerate, CEAG AG, was formed to oversee Varta's energy and air purification firms, as well as its mining companies, especially the CEAG Dominit subsidiary. Finally Altana AG assumed the various pharmaceutical, food, and cosmetic companies that Varta had acquired over the years.

In the 1980s, with the growing popularity of electronic cameras, calculators, Sony Walkman stereos, video and sound recorders, and later in the 1990s portable laptop computers, Varta portable battery sales doubled. In 1984 company sales reached DM1 billion for the first time in its history. In its 1991 annual report, Varta referred to the burgeoning popularity of notebook computers, cordless phones, video recorders and video games as the primary market stimulus. Automobile battery sales flattened out for Varta going into the 1990s, ironically because they had become so good in quality so as not to need replacement as often as in previous years.

Varta AG did not swallow up smaller competitors in the 1980s and 1990s as it had in earlier years. It tended instead to form partnerships with other large manufacturing firms. One controversial partnership was VB Autobatterie, an automobile battery producer which Varta and Bosch formed in 1992. The merger was approved by the European Commission over the objections of the German Cartel Office, which believed the merger was in violation of German antitrust laws. Varta controlled the company: it owned 65 percent of VB Autobatterie stock, a Varta board member was its chairman of the board, and the chairman of the VB Autobatterie Aufsichtsrat was Varta's own chairman. By 1995 VB Autobatterie had about DM850 million in sales and employed about 3,500 people. At the end of 1996, however, it closed its factory in Berlin, electing to concentrate domestic production at its other German location in Hannover.

Varta, Duracell and Toshiba worked together often during the 1990s. In January 1992, they announced the formation of a company to produce metal hydride rechargeable batteries. In 1996, the three companies built a plant in Melbane, North Carolina, that employed 500 workers, although a year later that facility was jettisoned. The three companies were awarded research grants by the U.S. Advanced Battery Consortium (USABC) for the development of lithium-ion to be used in electric vehicles, and received a $14.5 million contract extension from the USABC in 1997.

Unexpected Declines in the 1990s

After strong performances at the beginning of the 1990s, including a 24 percent increase in earnings in 1991, Varta's fortunes went into decline in the mid-1990s, years that proved to be among the worst in Varta history. During this time, automobile battery sales dropped by DM100 million while costs of lead rose steadily. Sales in industrial batteries plummeted so badly that Varta finally sold the division to a British group in 1996. In 1994 the company reported losses of DM56.4 million, followed by a loss of 56.4 million in 1995, the worst performance in company history. Some analysts noted that competition among battery manufacturers created a high degree of selectiveness among the consumer public, which demanded high quality at a low price; when lead prices jumped in the mid-1990s, it was harder for Varta to meet those demands.

Instead Varta focused its energies on consumer batteries. In 1996, it increased its holdings from 30 to 50 percent in the Brazilian battery producer, Microlite S.A, a company which had $250 million in sales that year. The purchase made Varta the largest supplier of consumer batteries in South America.

Varta recovered somewhat in 1996, and continued to consolidate its operations. The company closed its Singapore button cell production facility in late 1997 and transferred the work back to Ellwangen Germany. High-speed machine production of batteries controlled by trained specialists was deemed more important than a inexpensive Asian work force. Manpower in the highly-automated environment was not at a premium, and it turned out that 500 Asian workers earning DM8 per hour cost just as much as 100 earning DM40 per hour. The company's factory in Batam Indonesia across the strait from Singapore remained in service, however.

As 1997 ended, Varta's financial picture was looking brighter. Worldwide sales increased from DM474 million to approximately DM2.5 billion, and continued international growth, particularly in Latin America, boded well for the battery maker. Moreover, the company saw an increase in domestic sales, particularly among its portable battery sector, which increased by 32 percent and broke the DM1 billion mark for the first time ever.

Principal Subsidiaries

Varta Batterie AG; Varta Recycling GmbH; Microlite S.A. (Brazil; 50%)

Further Reading

"Brazil: Microlite is Now Controlled by Varta," *Gazeta Mercantil,* January 14, 1997.

Esser, Heino, *Report: 100 Jahre Varta, 1888e–1988, Geschichten zur Geschichte,* vols. 1–4, Hannover: Varta AG, 1988.

Furukawa, Tsukasa, "Joint-Venture Battery Plant Eyed," *American Metal Market,* July 22, 1994.

Hein, Christoph, "Der Standort Deutschland ist Wieder 'In'," *Die Welt,* November 13, 1997.

Wildhagen, Andreas, "Mehr Saft fuer Varta," *Die Welt,* August 23, 1996.

—Gerald E. Brennan

Viacom Inc.

1515 Broadway
New York, New York 10036
U.S.A.
(212) 258-6000
Fax: (212) 258-8718
Web site: http://www.viacom.com

Public Company
Incorporated: 1971
Employees: 81,700
Sales: $12.1 billion (1996)
Stock Exchanges: American Boston
SICs: 7822 Motion Picture & Tape Distribution; 7812
    Motion Picture & Video Production; 7814 Video Tape
    Rental; 4841 Cable & Other Pay Television Services;
    2731 Book Publishing

One of the largest entertainment and publishing companies in the world, Viacom Inc. operates numerous subsidiaries in four main groups: networks and broadcasting; entertainment; video and music/theme parks; and publishing. Its best-known television networks include MTV, Nickelodeon, VH1, Showtime, The Movie Channel, and Paramount Television, which produces such popular television series as *Star Trek* and *Frasier.* The company's entertainment segment is led by Paramount Pictures, which has produced and distributed motion pictures since 1912. The Blockbuster group of subsidiaries, which comprises over 6,000 video and music stores, and Paramount Parks, which owns and operates five theme parks and one water park, form the body of Viacom's video and music/ theme park segment. The company's publishing group includes such venerable publishers as Simon & Schuster, Macmillan, and Prentice Hall.

1970s Formation

Viacom was formed by the Central Broadcasting System (CBS) in the summer of 1970 to comply with regulations by the U.S. Federal Communications Commission barring television networks from owning cable TV systems or from syndicating their own programs in the United States. It formally became a separate company in 1971 when CBS distributed Viacom's stock to its stockholders at the rate of one share for every seven shares of CBS stock.

Viacom began with 70,000 stockholders and yearly sales of $19.8 million. It had about 90,000 cable subscribers, making it one of the largest cable operators in the United States. It also had an enviable stable of popular, previously-run CBS television series, including *I Love Lucy,* available for syndication, which accounted for a sizable percentage of Viacom's income.

By 1973 there were about 2,800 cable systems in the United States, with about 7.5 million subscribers. This market fragmentation, along with the lack of an infrastructure in many communities and tough federal regulations, slowed the development of cable television. In 1973, Viacom had 47,000 subscribers on Long Island, New York, but a drive to find 2,000 more added only 250.

In 1976, to compete with Home Box Office (HBO), the leading outlet for films in cable, Viacom established the Showtime movie network, which sought to provide its audience with feature films recently released in theaters. Viacom retained half interest in the network while Warner Amex owned the other half. Despite a federal ruling that removed many restrictions on the choice of movies and sports available on pay-TV during this time that allowed a wider variety of programming, Showtime lost $825,000 in 1977. Nevertheless, Viacom earned $5.5 million that year on sales of $58.5 million. Most of the company's earnings represented sales of television series, but it also reflected the growth of its own cable systems, which at this time had about 350,000 subscribers.

Showtime continued to compete aggressively with HBO. In 1977 it began transmitting its programming to local cable stations via satellite, at a cost of $1.2 million a year. The following year it worked out a deal with Teleprompter Corp., then the largest cable systems operator in the United States, with the result that Teleprompter offered its customers Showtime rather than HBO. Showtime also began offering a service channel called Front Row. Dedicated to family programming, including classic movies and children's shows, Front Row cost consumers less than $5 a month and was aimed at smaller cable systems where subscribers could not afford a full-time pay-TV service.

Viacom's forays into the production of original programming in the late 1970s and early 1980s had mixed results. Competition was stiff, the odds of producing a successful television series or film were long, and Viacom experienced several failures. The *Lazarus Syndrome* and *Dear Detective* series were failures, and CBS canceled *Nurse* after 14 episodes.

Growth through Acquisition in the 1980s

Cable systems were a capital intensive business, and Viacom constantly invested money in building its cable infrastructure—spending $65 million in 1981 alone, for example. In the early 1980s Viacom started on a program of rapid growth across a range of media categories. Company President Terrence A. Elkes told *Business Week* that Viacom hoped to become a billion dollar company in three to five years. Because management felt that cable operations were not a strong enough engine for that growth, Viacom looked to communications and entertainment. In 1981 it bought Chicago radio station WLAK-FM for $8 million and disclosed its minority stake in Cable Health Network, a new advertiser-supported cable service. It also bought Video Corp. of America for $16 million. That firm's video production equipment stood to save Viacom a great deal of money on production costs.

While its increased size would give Viacom clout with advertisers and advertising agencies, some industry analysts believed that the acquisitions were partly intended to discourage takeover attempts. Buying radio and TV stations increased the firm's debt, and added broadcast licenses to Viacom's portfolio. The transfer of such licenses was a laborious process overseen by the FCC, thereby slowing down attempts to act quickly in taking over a company.

By 1982 Showtime had 3.4 million subscribers, earning about $10 million on sales of $140 million, and was seeking to distinguish itself from other pay-TV sources by offering its own series of programs. While Viacom had sales of about $210 million, syndication still accounted for a large percentage of

Viacom's profits, 45 percent in 1982. The growth rate of syndication had declined, however, while that for cable had increased, and by 1982 Viacom had added 450,000 subscribers to the 90,000 it inherited from CBS, making it the ninth-largest cable operator in the United States.

However, a decline in pay-TV's popularity began in 1984, and growth in the industry was virtually halted. In early 1984, Showtime became a sister station to Warner Amex's The Movie Channel in a move calculated to increase sales for both of them. HBO and its sister channel Cinemax were being offered on 5,000 of the 5,800 cable systems in the United States, while Showtime or The Movie Channel were available on 2,700. Besides having a far larger share of the market, HBO already featured many of the films shown by Showtime and The Movie Channel, removing some of the incentive for subscribing to both groups of services. That year Viacom earned $30.9 million on revenue of $320 million.

In September 1985, Viacom purchased the MTV Networks and the other half interest in Showtime from Warner Communications, a company that needed cash because its cable interests were suffering in the unfavorable market. As part of the deal Viacom paid Warner $500 million in cash and $18 million in stock warrants. Viacom also offered $33.50 a share for the one-third of MTV stock that was publicly held. The year before Viacom bought it, MTV had made $11.9 million on sales on $109.5 million. Again, these purchases increased Viacom's debt load, making it less attractive for a takeover.

The MTV Networks included MTV, a popular music video channel, Nickelodeon, a channel geared towards children, and VH-1, a music video channel geared toward an older audience than that of MTV. The most valuable property in the MTV Network was MTV itself. Its quick pace and flashy graphics were becoming popular and highly influential in the media, and its young audience was a chief target of advertisers.

Established by Warner Amex in 1979 in response to a need for children's cable programming, Nickelodeon had not achieved any notable success until acquired by Viacom. Viacom quickly revamped Nickelodeon, giving it the slick, flashy look of MTV and unique programming that both appealed to children and distinguished the network from such competitors as The Disney Channel. Viacom also introduced "Nick at Night," a block of classic sitcoms aired late in the evening, popular among an adult audience. In the next few years Nickelodeon went from being the least popular channel on basic cable to the most popular.

However, Showtime lost about 300,000 customers between March 1985 and March 1986, and cash flow dropped dramatically. In 1986 Showtime embarked on an expensive and risky attempt to gain market share. While Showtime and arch-rival HBO had each featured exclusive presentations of some films, many films were shown on both networks. In order to eliminate this duplication, Showtime gained exclusive rights to several popular films and guaranteed its customers a new film, unavailable on other movie channels, every week. However, Showtime's move increased the price of acquiring even limited rights to a film at a time when many industry observers felt that the price of buying films for pay-TV should be decreasing since the popularity of video cassette recorders had lowered their worth. Consequently, the cost of programming was raised, and Showtime was forced to increase marketing expenditures to make certain potential viewers were aware of the new policy.

Weakened by the $2 billion debt load it incurred, in part, to scare off unfriendly buyers, Viacom lost $9.9 million on sales of $919.2 million in 1986 and, ironically, became a takeover target. First Carl Icahn made an attempt to buy the company, and then a management buyout led by Terrence Elkes failed. Finally, after a six-month battle, Sumner M. Redstone, president of the National Amusements Inc. movie theater chain, bought Viacom for about $3.4 billion in March 1986. Some industry analysts felt that he had vastly overpaid, but Redstone believed Viacom had strong growth potential. Aside from its cable properties and syndication rights that now included the popular series *The Cosby Show,* Viacom owned five television and eight radio stations in major markets.

Redstone had already built National Amusements, the family business, from 50 drive-in movie theaters to a modern chain with 350 screens. Now faced with the task of turning Showtime around, he brought in Frank Biondi, former chief executive of HBO, who began organizing the company's many units into a cooperative work force. Biondi in turn brought in HBO executive Winston Cox to run the network, and Cox immediately doubled Showtime's marketing budget. Showtime also obtained exclusive contracts with Paramount Pictures and Walt Disney films, which included the rights to air seven of the top ten films of 1986.

Turning Viacom Around in the Late 1980s

Redstone's banks were demanding $450 million in interest in the first two years following the takeover, but several fortuitous events aided him in paying off this debt. Shortly after the buyout Viacom began to earn millions from television stations wanting to show reruns of *The Cosby Show.* Furthermore, when Congress deregulated cable in 1987, prices for cable franchises soared. So when Redstone sold some of Viacom's assets to help pay off its debt, he was able to get large sums for them. In February 1989 Viacom's Long Island and suburban Cleveland cable systems were sold to Cablevision Systems Corp. for $545 million, or about 20 times their annual cash flow. Cablevision also bought a five percent stake in Showtime for $25 million, giving it a tangible interest in the channel's success. Further, after Redstone restructured MTV and installed a more aggressive advertising-sales staff, MTV experienced continued growth, against the expectations of many industry analysts. In 1989, for example, the MTV Networks won 15 percent of all dollars spent on cable advertising. MTV was expanding throughout the world, broadcasting to western Europe, Japan, Australia, and large portions of Latin America, with plans to further expand into eastern Europe, Poland, Brazil, Israel, and New Zealand.

These successes enabled Redstone and Biondi to significantly cut Viacom's debt by September 1989 and negotiate more favorable terms on its loans. Even so, it was rough going at first, and Viacom lost $154.4 million in 1987, though its sales increased to about $1 billion.

Under its new leadership Viacom branched out. Along with Hearst Corp. and Capital Cities/ABC Inc. it introduced Life-

time, a channel geared towards women. It also started its own production operations in 1989, Viacom Pictures, which produced about ten feature films in 1989 at a cost of about $4 million a film. These films first appeared on Showtime. Viacom's television productions also achieved success after years of mixed results. Viacom produced the hit series *Matlock* for NBC and *Jake and the Fatman* for CBS. It also added the rights for *A Different World* and *Roseanne* to its rerun stable. In addition, Viacom continued to spend heavily on new and acquired productions for Nickelodeon and MTV.

In October 1989, Viacom sold 50 percent of Showtime to TCI, a cable systems operator, for $225 million. TCI had six million subscribers, and Viacom hoped the purchase would give TCI increased incentive to market Showtime, thus giving the network a wider distribution.

By 1989 Viacom owned five television stations, 14 cable franchises, and nine radio stations. In November of that year the company bought five more radio stations for $121 million. Sales for the year were about $1.4 billion, with profits of $369 million. In 1990, Viacom introduced a plan that halved the cost of Showtime, but forced cable operators to dramatically increase the number of subscriptions to it. This strategy was designed to increase Showtime's market share at a time when many consumers were starting to feel that pay-TV channels were no longer worth their price.

Several months after HBO introduced its Comedy Channel in 1989, Viacom began transmitting HA!, a channel similar in format. Both channels provided comedy programs, but HA! primarily showed episodes of old sitcoms, while the Comedy Channel showed excerpts from sitcoms, movies, and stand-up comedy routines. Both channels started with subscriber bases in the low millions, and most industry analysts believed that only one of them would survive; Viacom management expected to lose as much as $100 million over a three-year period before HA! broke even. The two companies considered merging their comedy offerings, but HBO parent Time Warner would only move forward with the idea if Viacom agreed to settle its $2.4 billion antitrust suit against HBO.

Showtime had filed the lawsuit in 1989, alleging that HBO was trying to put Showtime out of business by intimidating cable systems that carried Showtime and by trying to corner the market on Hollywood films to prevent competitors from airing them. The suit attracted wide attention and generated much negative publicity for the cable industry.

In August 1992 the suit was finally settled out of court, after having cost both sides tens of millions of dollars in legal fees. Time Warner agreed to pay Viacom $75 million and buy a Viacom cable system in Milwaukee for $95 million, about $10 million more than its estimated worth at the time. Time Warner also agreed to more widely distribute Showtime and The Movie Channel on Time Warner's cable systems, the second-largest in the United States. Furthermore, the two sides also agreed to a joint marketing campaign to try and revive the image of cable, which had suffered since deregulation. Also during this time, in a move that surprised many industry analysts, HBO and Viacom agreed to merge their struggling comedy networks, HA! and the

Comedy Channel, into one network, Comedy Central, which ultimately experienced great success.

Overall, Viacom appeared to be thriving. In 1993 the company's net income reached $66 million, earned on revenues of $1.9 billion. Nickelodeon, meanwhile, was going to 57.4 million homes, and was watched by more children between ages two and 11 than the children's programming on all four major networks combined. While Nickelodeon's earnings were not reported separately, the *Wall Street Journal* estimated its profits as $76 million in 1992 on sales of $190 million. However, by the mid-1990s, Redstone was ready for a new challenge. The 70-year-old media mogul found it by expanding Viacom into the motion picture and video rental markets.

In July 1994 Viacom purchased Paramount Communications Inc., one of the world's largest and oldest producers of motion pictures and television shows. The deal, which cost approximately $8 billion, elevated Viacom to the fifth-largest media company in the world. The acquisition vastly expanded the company's presence in the entertainment business, giving it a motion picture library that included the classics *The Ten Commandments* and *The Godfather* and an entre into the premier movie market. Moreover, in the Paramount deal Viacom gained ownership of Simon & Shuster, Inc., one of the world's largest book publishers.

Later that same year, the company again expanded into a new segment of the entertainment industry by acquiring Blockbuster, the owner, operator, and franchiser of thousands of video and music stores. The Blockbuster group of subsidiaries was one of Viacom's most quickly growing enterprises; by 1997, Blockbuster boasted 60 million cardholders worldwide and over 6,000 music and video stores.

Viacom's acquisition of Paramount and Blockbuster gave the company thriving new enterprises, but left the company in significant debt. To both relieve that debt and focus the company's energies, Viacom divested itself of several segments of its business. In 1995 the company sold the operations of Madison Square Garden to a partnership of ITT Corp. and Cablevision Systems Corp. for $1.07 billion. In 1996, the company spun off its cable systems in a deal with TCI. Although the split-off represented a break with Viacom's origins as a cable provider, the deal relieved the company of $1.7 billion in debt. The following year, Viacom left the radio broadcasting business by selling its ten radio stations to Evergreen Media Corporation. The approximately $1.1 billion deal reduced Viacom's debt even further.

Although Viacom was no longer a cable service provider, and it had expanded into the motion picture and video rental market, its cable networks remained a significant portion of its business. MTV Networks, which included MTV, Nickelodeon, and VH1, accounted for almost $625 million in operating profits in 1997, approximately 32 percent of Viacom's estimated earnings for the year.

Principal Subsidiaries

Blockbuster Videos, Inc.; Paramount Pictures Corporation; Paramount Television Limited; Paramount Home Video, Inc.; Simon & Schuster, Inc.; Macmillan, Inc.; Prentice Hall, Inc.; MTV Networks Company; Showtime Networks Inc.; VH1 Inc.; Spelling Entertainment Group Inc. (75%).

Further Reading

Atlas, Riva, "Paramount, Anyone?," *Forbes*, May 23, 1994, p. 264.

Gubernick, Lisa, "Sumner Redstone Scores Again," *Forbes*, October 31, 1988.

Gunther, Marc, "This Gang Controls Your Kids' Brains," *Fortune*, October 27, 1997, pp. 172–78.

Impoco, Jim, "America's Hippest Grandpa," *U.S. News & World Report*, September 27, 1993, p. 67.

Lieberman, David, "Is Viacom Ready to Channel the World?" *Business Week*, December 18, 1989.

"Viacom's Risky Quest for Growth," *Business Week*, June 21, 1982.

—Scott M. Lewis
—updated by Susan Windisch Brown

Wendy's International, Inc.

**4288 West Dublin-Granville Road
Dublin, Ohio 43107-0256
U.S.A.
(614) 764-3100
Fax: (614) 764-6894
Web site: http://www.wendys.com**

*Public Company
Incorporated:* 1975
Employees: 42,000
Sales: $1.9 billion (1996)
Stock Exchanges: Boston Midwest New York Pittsburgh
SICs: 6794 Patent Owners & Lessors; 5812 Eating Places

With $1.9 billion in sales and 5,100 restaurants worldwide, Wendy's International, Inc., is one of the top three restaurant chains in the world. Wendy's hallmark square hamburgers and homey atmosphere were introduced in Columbus, Ohio, in 1969, and the company has enjoyed phenomenal growth in the three decades since that time.

Dave Thomas Enters the Restaurant Business

The restaurant was created by R. David Thomas, who has credited part of his success to his challenging youth. Thomas was born during the depths of the Great Depression in Atlantic City, New Jersey. His early life was punctuated by tragedy. Abandoned at birth, he was adopted by a Michigan couple, Rex and Auleva Thomas. Auleva died when David was five years old, and his father was forced to move from state to state seeking work as a handyman. Rex remarried three times and moved his family ten times over the next eight years.

David himself entered the world of work at the age of 12, delivering groceries in Knoxville, Tennessee. He lied about his age to circumvent child labor laws, and worked 12-hour shifts to keep his job. Thomas' adulthood began early. When he was 15, his family moved to Fort Wayne, Indiana, and he started work as a busboy at a local restaurant, the Hobby House. When

his family announced another move, Thomas elected to set out on his own, taking a room at the local YMCA. As his work began to demand more time than his education, Thomas gave up on the latter, leaving school after the tenth grade and later enlisting in the army. Trained as a cook in the military, he returned to a job behind the grill of the Hobby House, where he met Lorraine, a waitress—and his future wife.

Thomas entered the restaurant business in earnest in 1956 in partnership with Phil Clauss. Just a few years later, Thomas and Clauss met Colonel Harland Sanders, who offered them Kentucky Fried Chicken (KFC) franchises. Clauss purchased one for Fort Wayne, and the pair broke into the chicken business.

By 1962 Clauss was deep into KFC—he owned four unprofitable franchises in Columbus, Ohio, and needed someone to turn them around. If Thomas could turn the stores' $200,000 deficit into a profit, Clauss promised him a 45 percent share of the Columbus franchises. Against the advice of Colonel Sanders, who had become a mentor, Thomas took the challenge. He cut the menu from 100 items down to just a few—Thomas urged the Colonel to concentrate on chicken alone—improved the chicken "bucket," bartered radio advertising with buckets of chicken, invented KFC's spinning bucket sign, and built four additional locations in less than six years. His earnest, imaginative work paid off; Thomas was promoted to regional operations director of KFC and sold his stake in the Columbus restaurants for $1.5 million in 1968, thereby reaching millionaire status by the age of 35.

Wendy's is Born in the 1970s

Thomas parlayed his windfall into a new venture named after his eight-year-old daughter Melinda Lou, or Wendy, as her brothers and sisters nicknamed her. The first restaurant was located on Broad Street in downtown Columbus, Ohio. Its menu featured made-to-order hamburgers, "secret recipe" chili, french fries, soft drinks, and the Frosty frozen dessert. Thomas kept the menu simple to save labor costs, remembering his KFC experience. The Wendy's Old Fashioned Hamburgers decor differed from other fast food joints that abounded with easy-clean vinyl and tiled surfaces. Instead, Thomas put in tiffany-style lamps, bentwood chairs, carpeting, and tabletops embellished with vintage newspaper advertisements. Although his ideas were refreshingly original, some industry experts criticized Thomas' use of expensive fresh beef and noted that the fast food industry seemed overcrowded. With all the criticism, Thomas hoped only for a local chain that would provide his children with summer jobs.

Against all predictions, the business took off immediately. Thomas opened a second location just one year later and began franchising his idea in 1972. Wendy's soon enlisted franchisees at the rate of ten per month. Thomas added a new wrinkle to the franchising concept, giving geographic licenses, rather than single-store rights. Wendy's also commenced its first advertising campaign that year with locally broadcast "C'mon to Wendy's" spots. The 30-second, animated ads stressed Wendy's superiority through the "Quality Is Our Recipe" slogan and featured a red-haired, pig-tailed "Wendy" with dancing hamburgers.

The 1970s heralded phenomenal, and somewhat reckless, growth at Wendy's. By the end of 1974 the chain's net income topped $1 million, and total sales reached almost $25 million. In mid-1975 the business celebrated the opening of its 100th restaurant, and that fall Wendy's opened its first international restaurant, located in Canada. Wendy's went public in 1976 with an offering of one million common shares valued at $28 per share. By the end of the year, shareholders understood that their money fueled growth; Wendy's opened its 500th shop.

The chain's rapid expansion was supported by Wendy's first national advertising campaign in 1977. The effort earned Wendy's another entry in the history books: it became the first chain with less than 1,000 restaurants to launch network television commercials. The "Hot 'n Juicy" campaign ran for three years and won a Clio Award for creativity, setting the pace for future Wendy's advertising.

Before the decade's end, the restaurant chain set even more records. In 1978, the 1,000th Wendy's opened, in Springfield, Tennessee, not far from the site of Thomas' first job. By the next year the number of shops had increased by half, and the first European Wendy's opened in Munich, West Germany. In November 1979 Wendy's celebrated its tenth birthday with many "firsts" to flaunt. Wendy's was the first in its industry to surpass $1 billion in annual sales within its initial ten years, in addition to reaching the 1,000th restaurant opening faster than any of its competitors. It boasted 1,767 sites in the United States, Canada, Puerto Rico, and Europe, and had opened more than 750 restaurants from February 1978 to November 1979, averaging nearly 1.5 each day.

In the early 1980s, growth slowed slightly from that hectic pace, but Wendy's was distinguished from its competitors through celebrated advertising and winning menu additions. "Wendy's Has the Taste," the first ad of the decade, depicted customers and employees singing a catchy jingle. The ad emphasized Wendy's new chicken sandwich and all-you-can-eat salad bar. The chain had introduced its "Garden Spot" in 1979 over Thomas's protestations, becoming the first national restaurant chain to offer salad bars nationwide.

Founder Dave Thomas made his first appearance as Wendy's spokesperson in 1981 in a controversial ad titled,

"Ain't No Reason (to go anyplace else)." Customers' use of the idiomatic double negative "ain't no" in the ads generated national attention for the chain, though not all of it favorable. Thomas left his position as CEO in 1982, taking the title of senior chairman. After working for more than 30 years, Thomas felt that he had earned a break, and was confident that he had hired capable managers to carry on his work.

Mixed Results in the 1980s

A recession in the early 1980s, combined with high beef prices and Wendy's explosive—as well as threatening—growth incited the "burger wars." Wendy's moved into the number three spot behind McDonald's and Burger King Corp., fueled by its introduction of a chainwide salad bar, chicken breast sandwiches, and baked potatoes. Burger King and McDonald's responded with moderately successful menu extensions of their own, then moved to a hard-nosed ad campaign. Burger King fired the first shot, but Wendy's responded with a string of hard-hitting, well-known commercials.

In 1983 Wendy's ads depicted "victims" of other hamburger restaurants, humorously bemoaning the long waits endured in indoor and drive-up lines for frozen hamburger patties. In 1984 Wendy's agency, Dancer Fitzgerald Sample, teamed up with celebrated commercial director Joe Sedelmaier on a campaign that registered the highest consumer awareness levels in the advertising industry's history, in addition to captivating judges at the 1984 Clio Awards and winning three of the industry's highest honors. Moreover, the "Where's the Beef?" campaign consisted of four network television spots starring senior citizen Clara Peller. It was voted the most popular commercial in America in 1984. One of the ads, "Parts Is Parts," pointed out the difference between the competition's pressed chicken patties and Wendy's chicken breast filet sandwiches.

"Parts" focused on Wendy's true money-makers at that point; hamburger sales actually only accounted for 40 percent of the chain's revenues. Much of Wendy's sales growth could be credited to such menu extensions as the grilled chicken sandwich, Garden Spot salad bar, and stuffed baked potatoes. These new products and the phenomenal success of the "Where's the Beef?" campaign catapulted Wendy's to a record $76.2 million earnings in 1985.

As one unnamed Wendy's executive confessed in *Barron's,* management started to believe that everything they touched would "turn to gold." Unfortunately, 1985 marked a summit from which Wendy's quickly plummeted. In 1986 the chain introduced sit-down breakfasts featuring omelettes and French toast. The new breakfasts involved a huge investment of capital and labor, and could not be served quickly enough to fit in with the fast food format. At the same time, McDonald's, Burger King, and Hardee's assaulted Wendy's on the hamburger front.

A kind of domino effect plunged the company toward a $4.9 million loss in 1986. Some of the chain's original franchisees sold their stores to new owners who flouted Wendy's high standards. Others became absentee managers, leaving the day-to-day supervision to employees. As standards of cleanliness, quality, and service slipped at some Wendy's locations, sales dropped. In response to the falling income, store labor was cut, the morale of those who remained plunged, and turnover rates began to explode. By the end of the year, 20 percent of Wendy's restaurants were nearing failure, and franchisees presented the chain's management a vote of no confidence.

The desperate situation brought Dave Thomas out of semi-retirement and challenged one of Wendy's most successful franchisees to revive the failing business. James W. Near had been one of Dave Thomas's competitors in the late 1960s when they both operated restaurants in Columbus. Practically raised in his father's White Castle hamburger chain, Near built a 50-unit Burger Boy Food-A-Rama chain of his own by the end of the decade. Near had become a Wendy's franchisee in 1974, opening 39 successful restaurants in West Virginia and Florida within four years. In 1978, he sold the restaurants back to Wendy's and established Sisters Chicken & Biscuits as an expansion vehicle for the hamburger chain. Sisters became a subsidiary of Wendy's in 1981 and was sold to its largest franchise owner in 1987.

New Leadership Rejuvenates Wendy's in the Late 1980s

James Near agreed to take the position of president and chief operating officer on the condition that Dave Thomas would sustain an active role in the company as a spokesman and traveling mentor. Thomas agreed. His new business card read "Founder and Jim's Right Hand Man." Near's turnaround strategy started with an internal reorganization. Weak stores were eliminated and a new building design lowered the initial franchise investment. Near fired four top managers, cut 700 administrative positions, and revamped field operations. New programs gave the remaining employees a vested interest in the chain's success: base pay, benefits, and bonuses were raised; an employee stock option called "We Share" made workers shareholders; and standardized training gave all employees a new perspective on their jobs. When Near took over, Wendy's was replacing employees at a rate of 55 percent a year; six years later, turnover stood at 20 percent.

With renewed chainwide standards for cleanliness and customer service, Near turned his attention to the menu. Changes were based on several industry trends, including discount pricing, consumer health concerns, and premium menu items. Spurred by the recession of the late 1980s and early 1990s, many fast food chains established discount pricing to appeal to more frugal customers. Wendy's introduced its Super Value Menu in 1989. The daily feature included seven 99-cent items, allowing it to appeal to thrifty consumers without issuing profit-eating coupons. An expanded salad bar and skinless chicken breast sandwich catered to more health conscious consumers, while the Big Classic, Dave's Deluxe, and Chicken Cordon Bleu specialty sandwiches appealed to Wendy's traditional hearty eaters.

As Near worked to cover all of the menu bases, Dave Thomas returned to the television studio for the promotional push. In 1989 Thomas reappeared in commercials offering customers a special money-back guarantee if they didn't concur that Wendy's had the best-tasting hamburgers in the industry. The ad was supported by one of the largest testimonial advertising campaigns in television history. Local residents in about 100 U.S. markets pronounced Wendy's burgers best.

"Old Fashioned Guy," the next series of TV spots, featured Thomas declaring, "Our hamburgers are the best in the business, or I wouldn't have named the place after my daughter." The hamburgers might have been the best, but Thomas' performances in these spots earned some poor ratings from some critics at *Advertising Age,* one of whom commented that he looked like "a steer in a half-sleeved shirt." Thomas himself admitted that he wasn't an ideal subject—he joked that it took two hours to get the expression "muchas gracias" right for one commercial. Unlike the critics, however, consumers gave Thomas an enthusiastic reception—his promotions have earned Wendy's highest advertising awareness figures since the "Where's the Beef?" campaign and have been credited with boosting the chain's turnaround. In fact, such campaigns have even helped earn Thomas the designation, "the Colonel Sanders of Wendy's," in reference to the promotional efforts of Thomas's early mentor.

The success of Wendy's revitalization showed in sales, rejuvenated expansion, and widespread recognition of the accomplishment. Despite a lingering recession, in 1991 and 1992 Wendy's had outperformed the industry with 24 consecutive months of same-store sales gains. Earnings increased steadily in the early 1990s to $78 million in 1993, the fourth consecutive year of 20 percent earnings growth. Wendy's five-year average earnings-per-share growth hit 58 percent, more than four times that of MacDonalds for the same period. Representing an irrefutable confirmation of Wendy's successful turnaround, 1995 earnings rose above the company's 1985 high of $.82 a share to reach $.94 per share.

The 1990s and Beyond

In the early 1990s expansion picked up once again. The company opened its 4,000th restaurant in 1992, and projected another 1,000 openings by mid-decade. Within the United States, the company planned to be opening approximately 400 stores a year by 1996. However, Wendy's plans also targeted international growth, where opportunities for expansion were infinitely better than those in the saturated American market.

Near and Thomas accumulated numerous awards in recognition of the dramatic turnaround at Wendy's. In 1989, Near was given the title of CEO and was named chairman two years later. Moreover, he was honored by his colleagues in the restaurant industry when he was named Operator of the Year by *Nation's Restaurant News* and Executive of the Year by *Restaurants & Institutions. Restaurant Business* acknowledged both men's entrepreneurial efforts with its annual Leadership Awards. Thomas also received the Horatio Alger Award, named for the author who popularized the concept of the "self-made man."

As Wendy's "ambassador," Thomas began spending most of his time traveling to and from book promotions, public appearances, and franchise openings. His promotional work complemented Near's continuing efforts to "grow the company." A new corporate theme, "Do It Right! Performance Pays!" related customer-responsiveness to sales and profits for worker-shareholders.

Wendy's recovery seemed well-established in the mid-1990s, judged not just by the numbers but by public opinion as well.

Consumer polls in 1994 judged Wendy's to have the best food in the fast food burger business, the best menu variety, and the most pleasant atmosphere. *Restaurants and Institutions* gave Wendy's its overall top rating from 1988 to 1994, putting it ahead of eight other burger chains. Montgomery Securities analyst Michael Mueller told *Financial World* in 1995, "They're doing everything one should in the fast-food industry."

Having brought Wendy's to this high point, Near decided to step down in late 1994. He was replaced by Gordon Teter, who had served Wendy's as senior vice-president for three years and chief operating officer for four. Before joining Wendy's, Teter had accumulated 25 years of experience at the restaurant chains Arthur Treacher's, Casa Lupita, and Red Robin. His strengths were regarded by many as exactly what Wendy's needed to go the next step, that of stealing market share from the big guys. A firm believer in sticking to the basics, Teter was expected to apply his talents for cost control and well-regulated operations. "Once you have success, as we have been having here, people can get distracted," Teter explained to *Financial World* in 1995. "The biggest thing we have to do is maintain a sense of discipline," he noted.

Teter had a tough act to follow. Wendy's phenomenal growth slowed somewhat in the mid-1990s. In 1994 same-store sales dropped to 2.7 percent in first nine months of that year, compared to the quarter-to-quarter rate of five percent for the previous few years. Because fast-food profits were much higher overseas, Wendy's saw foreign expansion as a way to keep growth and profitability up.

In 1995, Wendy's aggressive foreign expansion plan called for the company to open at least 150 new restaurants a year around the world. Most store openings, however, were planned for Latin America, the Far East, and Canada. Wendy's previous attempt to expand overseas, in the early to mid-1980s, was a flop. Wendy's changed its decor and food to suit local tastes, but in less than a decade many of its foreign sites were floundering. Teter told *Financial World* in 1995 that after making every mistake you can make, Wendy's would stick to basics: "We just can't get diverted to things that sound sexy and look attractive."

As part of its expansion plan, Wendy's acquired the privately owned Canadian restaurant chain Tim Horton's. Canada's largest coffee and baked goods chain exchanged all outstanding shares of its stock for 16.2 million shares of Wendy's stock and the assumption of its $125 million in debt. The acquisition strengthened Wendy's presence in Canada, bringing the total number of its restaurants in that country to 1,186. Wendy's had been experimenting with sites that combined Wendy's and Tim Horton's restaurants since 1992. Their success led Wendy's to plan on opening 30 more such sites a year after the merger. In addition, in 1996, Wendy's bought out

Hardee's restaurants in the northern tier of states, strengthening the company's position there as well.

Wendy's also continued to invest in its successful, homespun ads featuring Dave Thomas. The "Letters to Dave" campaign, focusing on the restaurant's Super Value Menu and featuring customers' letters to the restaurateur, paired Thomas with soap opera star Susan Lucci. In another series, Dave joined Olympic gold medalist Kristi Yamaguchi to participate in such winter sports as pairs figure skating and ski jumping. Although long-known for its popular ad campaigns, Wendy's spent only $80 million on advertising in 1994, one-fifth what MacDonalds spent. Still, Wendy's brand recognition trailed that of MacDonalds by only a few points.

As Wendy's moved into the late 1990s, management focused on maintaining the momentum the company had generated in the early 1990s, with an emphasis on street-level operations, marketing, and efficient administration. Continued expansion remained a priority as well. Wendy's numbered 5,100 stores in 1997, up from 4,500 in 1994. Teter said to *Financial World* that he and Dave Thomas saw 8,000 restaurants doing $10 billion in sales by the year 2002: "That's our goal."

Principal Subsidiaries

Wendy's Restaurants of Canada, Inc.; The New Bakery Co. of Ohio, Inc.

Further Reading

Basralian, Joseph, "Ground Game," *Financial World,* January 17, 1995, pp.40–42.

Blyskal, Jeff, "Hot Stuff," *Forbes,* June 4, 1984, pp. 169–71.

Byrne, Harlan S., "Wendy's International: It Is Finally Learning How to Handle Success," *Barron's,* January 7, 1991, pp. 43–44.

Chaudhry, Rajan, "James Near Cleans Up Wendy's," *Restaurants & Institutions,* July 22, 1992, pp. 72–82.

"Dave's World," *Forbes,* January 3, 1994, p. 149.

"From Peril to Profit: The Man Who Saved Wendy's," *Success,* February 1992, p. 10.

History of Wendy's Advertising, 1969–1993, Dublin, Ohio: Wendy's International, Inc., 1993.

Hume, Scott, "Thomas Shines as Wendy's Col. Sanders," *Advertising Age,* August 6, 1990, p. 3.

Killian, Linda, "Hamburger Helper," *Forbes,* August 5, 1991, pp. 106–07.

Near, James W., "Wendy's Successful 'Mop Bucket Attitude'," *Wall Street Journal,* April 27, 1992.

Roth, Daniel, "Where's the Beef?," *Forbes,* August 11, 1997, p. 134.

Scarpa, James, "RB Leadership Award: R. David Thomas, James W. Near," *Restaurant Business,* May 1, 1992.

Thomas, R. David, *Dave's Way,* New York: Putnam Publishing Group, 1991.

—April S. Dougal
—updated by Susan Windisch Brown

Westwood One, Inc.

9540 Washington Boulevard
Culver City, California 90232
U.S.A.
(310) 204-5000
Fax: (310) 836-1158
Web site: http://www.westwoodone.com

Public Company
Incorporated: 1975
Employees: 576
Sales: $171.7 million (1996)
Stock Exchanges: NASDAQ
SICs: 4832 Radio Broadcasting Stations; 2711
  Newspapers

The second largest producer and distributor of radio programs in the United States, Westwood One, Inc. generates revenue by delivering programs to local radio stations in exchange for airtime the company sells to national advertisers. During the late 1990s Westwood supplied nationally sponsored music, news, entertainment, sports, weather, and traffic programming to approximately 1,500 affiliated radio stations.

Origins

In 1974 Norman J. Pattiz was an out-of-work account executive looking for his next paycheck. He had been fired from his job as a television station sales manager in Los Angeles, but instead of landing a job at another station, Pattiz looked at the media industry and discovered what he thought was a good business opportunity. Pattiz noticed a scarcity of national programming networks for local radio stations and decided to start his own. Pattiz planned to provide radio stations with programs and, in return, the radio stations would give Pattiz airtime he could sell to national advertisers. The concept was not a new idea by any means, but Pattiz observed that there were few programming networks in operation during the mid-1970s and that the limited number of program distributors in operation were providing unattractive programs. At the time Pattiz was

taking all this in, radio advertising sales in the United States amounted to a $1.8 billion business. A little more than a decade later, annual advertising revenues towered above the $7 billion mark. It was a decade of prodigious growth, and one of the chief benefactors of such growth was Pattiz and his entrepreneurial creation, Westwood One, Inc.

Pattiz, the unemployed television sales manager, did not start his entrepreneurial career with a lot of money. He had $10,000 to put into his venture, which represented a modest sum to begin business in the radio programming business. Successful programming networks boasted hundreds of radio station affiliates, one of the yardsticks by which national advertisers measured a program distributor's stature. The greater the number of affiliates a programming network counted within its fold, the greater its power to attract the advertising revenue of corporate clientele. Given this scenario, Pattiz's greatest asset was not his money, but his strategy; and it was a simple one. His inspiration came from a 52-hour program of Motown music broadcast by a Los Angeles radio station. He convinced the station to syndicate a similar show, signed up advertisers for the show, and lined up 250 radio stations to broadcast the program. This initial project represented a blueprint for the future: Pattiz planned to give radio stations free pop music programs, provided the stations carried his presold national advertisements. Armed with this advertising formula, Pattiz set out on his own, incorporating Westwood in January 1975, and began what would turn out to be a prolific rise as a network programmer for radio stations.

Although the medium of radio in many respects took a back seat to television, the effectiveness of advertising on the radio was not to be underestimated. On average, there were considerably more radios than television sets in each American household and, perhaps more important, there was a much closer link between a consumer and a radio station than with a particular television program or station. Generally, consumers tuned into their favorite radio station in the morning, listened to that same station while commuting to work, and tuned in at night. The same could not be said of American television viewing habits, which were governed by a pervasive penchant for channel surfing. This difference was important to advertisers, whose scientific approach to selling to the public was based on demographics. Particular radio stations catered to specific, demographically defined groups, whereas television stations tended to attract a grab bag of viewers. "It's the rifle as opposed to the shotgun approach to reaching your target audience," an advertising executive for General Motors noted, contrasting the fundamental difference between advertising on the radio and advertising on television. Pattiz characterized the difference in another way, frequently explaining, "You can tell an awful lot about a person from the radio station he listens to; you can't tell anything about a person from his favorite television station." This would be Pattiz's mantra, and it would be the driving force behind his company's explosive growth during the 1980s.

Given the limited amount of money with which Pattiz started, Westwood did not bolt out of the starting blocks. Concentrating at first on providing local radio stations with pop-concert programs, Pattiz relied on rented equipment and contacts within the music industry to get his company up and running. The relationships forged with musicians were important ones and would prove to be valuable years later after Westwood was shaped into an established market leader. Although he was rich in personal contacts, Pattiz had to make do with the resources at hand and conduct his programming activities as inexpensively as possible. In 1979 Westwood offered its first taped concert, using rented equipment to provide rock concert programming to fewer than 100 stations. With this event, the company emerged as a source for concert promotion and programming to radio stations, one of a few network programmers to offer such a service. It was an encouraging beginning, but the company's most rampant growth would occur several years later. The spark that lit the flame was a ruling by the Federal Communications Commission (FCC).

1980s Acquisitions

In 1981 the FCC permitted radio station license holders to buy programming rather than having to produce most of it themselves. For Pattiz and others involved in radio programming, the FCC's announcement represented a boon to business, meaning that radio stations could turn to a third party for all their programming if they chose. During the three years following the FCC ruling, Pattiz used his contacts in the country and rock music worlds to his advantage and exploited the programming market by developing a portfolio of attractive programming. To industry observers, Pattiz's most remarkable trait during this period was his aggressive pursuit of advertisers, to whom he preached the merits of advertising on radio. Aggressive marketing on Pattiz's part coupled with programming featuring celebrities in the pop music industry fueled Westwood's growth, as the company steadily increased its roster of affiliates. By 1984 Pattiz presided over a burgeoning empire that he was ready to take public.

Westwood's initial public offering of stock in 1984 raised more than $30 million, giving Pattiz the financial wherewithal to seriously consider acquisitions as a mode of quick expansion. What investors received for their cash was a piece of a company that produced and distributed more than 30 regularly scheduled shows that were broadcast to roughly 3,000 stations stretching from coast to coast. Westwood provided packaged music programs that varied widely, ranging from two-minute interviews with rock stars to two-hour live concerts. At the heart of the operation, however, were the national advertisements from which Pattiz and his growing staff earned their money. By the end of 1984 the revenues collected by Westwood amounted to nearly $13 million, from which the company earned nearly $2 million. The financial progress the company had made from its days as a start-up during the late 1970s was impressive, as was the rapid increase in the number of affiliates to which Pattiz could point when addressing national advertisers. The 1984 public offering of stock, however, precipitated a period of even greater growth, dwarfing the progress made before the company's debut on the NASDAQ Exchange. Nearly all of this growth came from acquisitions.

After its inaugural year as a publicly traded company, Westwood ranked as one of the largest producers and distributors of nationally sponsored radio programs in the United States. Pattiz was quick to build on this enviable foundation by scanning the horizon for an acquisition candidate that would increase further his company's capabilities and boost revenues. When his acquisitive eyes leveled on a target in 1985, the entire industry took notice because Pattiz had selected one of the industry's largest and oldest competitors, the Mutual Broadcasting System. Founded in the 1930s, the Mutual Broadcasting System was owned by Amway Corp. when Pattiz grew interested in the company. His interest stemmed in large part from the differences between his operations and those controlled by the Mutual Broadcasting System. A majority of Mutual's affiliates were adult-oriented in their target demographics. Westwood, with its pop music programming, consisted primarily of youth-oriented affiliates. Further, Mutual had news operations. Westwood did not have any news operations. Aside from these differences, Mutual was enormous. The company comprised 810 affiliates, or about ten percent of the commercial radio stations in the United States, and measured twice the size of Westwood. It was a deal Pattiz could not resist.

Westwood acquired the Mutual Broadcasting System from Amway in the fall of 1985, gaining control of the Mutual Radio Network, its affiliation contracts, studios, programming services, and talent, as well as management and staff, including the services of the widely popular Larry King. It was the first time in roughly 30 years that an owner of Mutual was a broadcaster, and Pattiz, as that owner, was ecstatic. "It's a perfect fit," he exclaimed, referring to the new operations and the bevy of adult-oriented affiliates gained in the acquisition. "It's a classic case of two plus two equaling five," he added, realizing the potential of a network programmer that could approach advertisers and deliver target demographics that stretched nearly from cradle to grave. There was one downside to the deal, however, and that was the financial health of Mutual. Under Amway's control, the company was a money loser, but in the euphoria surrounding the acquisition, Pattiz's celebratory mood could not be tempered. Roughly a decade after its formation, his company exited the mid-1980s as the second largest network programmer in the nation.

Trailing only the ABC Radio Network in size, Westwood entered the late 1980s as a formidable force in its industry. Two years after completing the Mutual transaction, the company made another bold move by acquiring the oldest broadcasting network in the country, the NBC Radio Network. From the acquisition of NBC Radio, Westwood gained a 20-year news supply and license agreement with NBC News for the NBC network stations, as well as the U.S. radio broadcast rights to the 1988 Summer Olympics in Seoul, South Korea. The acquisition included the traditional NBC Radio Network and several newer facets of NBC's radio business, including The Source, NBC's young adult network, TalkNet, a nighttime program service, and NBC Radio Entertainment, the program distribution arm of the NBC networks. Like Mutual, NBC Radio was also a money loser prior to its acquisition by Westwood, but the effect on Westwood's stature in the industry was enormous, nevertheless. After the deal was completed, Westwood held sway as a giant, supplying nationally sponsored music, news, entertainment, and sports programming to more than 6,000 of the country's nearly 10,000 commercial radio stations. It was extensive coverage to market to advertisers, and it was made more attractive by the stable of celebrities included within Westwood's programming. Featured stars included Larry King, Steve Allen, psychologist Dr. Toni Grant, rock interviewer Mary Turner, and Dr. Demento, all of whom helped make Westwood a programmer few national advertisers could resist.

Financial Woes During the 1990s

Following the completion of the NBC deal, Pattiz and his executive staff focused their efforts on curing the financial ills ailing their two large acquisitions. NBC's news operations, in particular, were demonstrating anemic financial performance. As the work dragged on to turn around both Mutual and NBC, this objective consumed nearly all of the company's energy, becoming the focal point during a two-year period leading up to the end of the 1980s. By 1990, when Westwood's debt totaled $215 million, there was not much evidence that any positive changes had been made. The company generated $146 million, far more than the total collected five years earlier, but registered a hefty $18.2 million loss. As time progressed, financial indicators pointed to profound troubles. Annual sales stagnated, then began to drop, while successive years of multimillion-dollar losses set off alarms at the company's headquarters. Following the $18.2 million loss in 1990, Westwood lost $16.8 million in 1991 and a staggering $24.1 million in 1992. To combat the problems, Pattiz began divesting properties, cutting costs wherever he could, and struggled to trim the company's debt. Despite Pattiz's efforts, Westwood was $164 million in debt by 1993.

As part of his ongoing plan to reduce debt and concentrate on his core network programming business, Pattiz sold Westwood's New York country radio station, WYNY-FM, in 1993 for $50 million. When the sale was announced in February, Pattiz told reporters, "Two years ago Westwood embarked on an aggressive program to lower costs, improve cash flow, and strengthen its capital structure through debt restructuring and the sale of certain non-core assets. The sale of WYNY is a significant step forward in that plan." Although not upbeat, Pattiz's mood at least reflected a modicum of confidence that progress was being achieved. By May the last traces of optimism were gone. "We just haven't been able to make it work," Pattiz lamented in a hand-wringing interview with *Forbes*. By the end of 1993 the financial figures posted by Westwood showed no signs of improvement. Sales dipped below $100 million for the year and the company's losses stood at $23.9 million.

Mid-1990s Recovery

Help arrived in early 1994 in the form of an acquisition and the arrival of new management. In February Westwood acquired the Unistar Radio Networks from Infinity Broadcasting, which, in turn, was owned by CBS Radio. The acquisition gave Westwood radio production operations and 24-hour satellite broadcasting capabilities, which lifted sales to $136 million by the end of 1994. Perhaps more important, the acquisition brought in new management. The chief executive officer of CBS Radio, Mel Karmazin, became the chief executive officer of Westwood, and CBS Radio's chief financial officer, Farid Suleman, became the chief financial officer of Westwood. In the management shuffle, Pattiz held onto his title as chairman of the board of directors. Under this new management team, the first significant progress in cutting financial losses was made. From the $24 million lost in 1993, the company's profitability recovered dramatically, leading to loss of $2.7 million. The following year, the company reported its first profit of the 1990s, earning nearly $10 million.

With profitability restored in short order and annual revenue volume back at the company's 1990 level, Karmazin and Pattiz were ready to expand by 1996. In 1996 the company acquired New York Shadow Traffic, Chicago Shadow Traffic, Los Angeles Shadow Traffic, and the Philadelphia Express Traffic. The purchases expanded Westwood's business scope, moving the company into the production and distribution of local traffic, news, sports, and weather programming in four of the country's largest metropolitan areas. The addition of the Shadow Traffic operations, coupled with the company's exclusive radio rights to the 1996 Summer Olympics, lifted sales nearly 20 percent to $171.7 million. The company's net income recorded a greater increase, nearly doubling to $17.5 million.

As Westwood prepared for the late 1990s and the beginning of the 21st century, the company appeared to have resolved the financial problems plaguing it throughout much of the 1990s. Although the company's financial condition was questionable throughout much of the decade, its position in its industry was always solid. Westwood entered the late 1990s as it had entered the 1990s: firmly entrenched as the second largest producer and distributor of radio programming the United States. For the future, further acquisitions appeared likely, particularly in traffic programming. The 1996 acquisition of the Shadow Traffic properties included options to purchase Shadow Traffic properties in other metropolitan areas. With expansion in this direction probable, Westwood headed toward the future, intent on expanding its network of affiliates and making the financial ills of the 1990s a distant memory.

Principal Subsidiaries

Westwood One Radio, Inc.; Mutual Broadcasting System, Inc.; Westwood One Radio Networks, Inc.; Westwood National Radio Corporation, Inc.; National Radio Network, Inc.; The Source, Inc.; Talknet, Inc.; Westwood One Satellite Systems, Inc.; Km Records, Inc.; Westwood One Stations Group, Inc.; Westwood One Stations—L.A., Inc.; Westwood One Stations—NYC, Inc.; Westwood One Broadcasting Services, Inc.

Principal Divisions

Westwood One Radio Network; Westwood One Entertainment; Westwood One Broadcasting Services, Inc.

Further Reading

Beauchamp, Marc, ''Radio Days,'' *Forbes,* November 30, 1987, p. 200.

Button, Graham, ''Broadcast Blues,'' *Forbes,* May 10, 1993, p. 16.

Hall, Peter, ''On the Air with Westwood One,'' *Financial World,* October 16, 1985, p. 28.

Lappen, Alyssa A., ''Hot No More,'' *Forbes,* July 25, 1988, p. 10.

''Let's Hear It for Radio,'' *Broadcasting,* December 15, 1986, p. 79.

''Mutual Gleam in Westwood One's Eye; Amway Agrees To Sell for Price Estimated at $30 Million,'' *Broadcasting,* September 23, 1985, p. 25.

Petrozzello, Donna, ''Anatomy of a Simulcast: Behind the Scenes with Westwood One,'' *Broadcasting & Cable,* October 17, 1994, p. 5.

Taylor, Chuck, ''Westwood Picks Up CBS Radio Division,'' *Billboard,* April 12, 1997, p. 72.

Tedesco, Richard, ''Website Audio,'' *Broadcasting & Cable,* July 7, 1997, p. 48.

''Westwood One Acquires NMC Radio for $50 Million,'' *Broadcasting,* July 27, 1987, p. 35.

Viles, Peter, ''Westwood Sells WYNY-FM for $50 Million; Company Left with Only One Station,'' *Broadcasting,* February 1, 1993, p. 32.

—Jeffrey L. Covell

William Morris Agency, Inc.

151 El Camino Drive
Beverly Hills, California 90212
U.S.A.
(310) 274-7451
Fax: (310) 786-4462

Private Company
Incorporated: 1898 as William Morris, Vaudeville Agent
Employees: 600
Sales: $150 million (1997 est.)
SICs: 7922 Agents, Talent: Theatrical

Celebrating its 100th anniversary in 1998, the William Morris Agency, Inc. is America's oldest and largest talent brokerage. Over the decades, the agency established and nurtured the careers of some of the entertainment industry's brightest stars. The Morris stable has included vaudevillians George Burns and Gracie Allen, movie industry pioneers Al Jolson and Charlie Chaplin, trailblazing television personalities like Milton Berle, rock-and-roll king Elvis Presley, and scores of celebrities in between. As the prototypical agency, Morris metamorphosed through technological and geographical transitions that left other entertainment magnates behind, deftly easing from vaudeville to radio and film in the 1920s and 1930s, to TV in the 1950s, and from New York to Hollywood in the meantime.

But by the 1970s and 1980s the agency had grown complacent, certain that its stellar reputation would be more than enough to woo and keep clients. During that period five executives—and more important, several marquee celebrities—defected to found the Creative Artists Agency. Whereas William Morris had always operated behind the scenes, keeping its clients center stage, CAA came out from behind the curtain to promote itself as well as its star-studded clientele. In an industry where light can substitute for fire, it did not matter that William Morris continued to be Hollywood's largest agency—CAA was its hottest.

CAA may get burned by William Morris in the end, however. When Mike Ovitz left the upstart agency in 1995 to head

entertainment powerhouse Disney, the older talent broker snapped up several big-name clients, including comedienne Whoopi Goldberg.

Late 19th-Century Foundations

The William Morris Agency's roots stretch back to New York City in 1882. That's when nine-year-old Zelman Moses and his family immigrated from Germany to the United States. The boy soon Anglicized his name to William Morris and quit school to clerk at a local grocery. Though he held a good-paying office job throughout his teen years, an economic crisis brought his first career in publishing to an end in the 1890s.

Morris went to work as a clerk for a top stage impresario in 1893 and had soon earned himself a partnership in the business. But when the owner died, his wife rescinded the partnership. Morris hung out his own shingle in 1898, establishing his monogram ("W" and "M" interwoven as four "X's") as a trademark that would stand for decades to come. In exchange for finding venues for vaudeville acts, he kept a portion—usually ten percent—of the actors' pay. Filling a void left by his former partner, Morris quickly established himself as an agent with great connections and an eye for talent.

In the first two decades of the 20th century, Morris assembled an unbeatable collection of widely known acts headlined by the likes of Scottish bagpiper and comic Harry Lauder, Oklahoman Will Rogers, and Charlie Chaplin. When the owner of a chain of theaters tried to blackball Morris and his clients, the agent formed his own confederation of theaters. Though Morris would continue to battle power-hungry theater owners through the 1920s, his control over popular talent always gave him the upper hand.

Morris's link to the entertainment world's "software"—the actors and actresses—rendered his livelihood impervious to "hardware upgrades." For example, when movies and radio began to deflate the power of the vaudeville theaters in the late 1920s, Morris took his acts to the new media. Many of his vaudevillians, including Amos 'n' Andy, Martha Raye, and George Burns and Gracie Allen, became radio stars. Others like Charlie Chaplin and the Marx Brothers made the transition to film. The venue mattered little to Morris beyond finding a suitable fit, for no matter where his stars appeared, he received ten percent of their pay.

William Morris cheated death on a number of occasions. He was struck with tuberculosis in 1902, but after taking Dr. Trudeau's Adirondack Mountain rest cure, he returned to work in 1905. He and his wife were set to take the *Titanic's* ill-fated maiden voyage in 1912, but canceled the trip so that he could clear up a theater booking snafu. He was supposed to have been on the *Lusitania* in May 1915, but was still in New York when it was sunk by the Germans. In fact, Morris lived long enough to see his agency establish offices in London, Chicago, and perhaps most important, Los Angeles. After retiring in 1930, he died in 1932 while playing pinochle with friends at the Friars' Club.

The Great Depression and World War II

Son William Morris, Jr. became the *de jure* head of the agency, but it was Abe Lastfogel who truly filled the senior Morris's shoes. Lastfogel, who like his predecessor was a Jewish immigrant, had joined the talent brokerage in 1912 at the age of 14. Morris, Jr. continued to concentrate on the Los Angeles outpost, which he had headed since 1930, while Lastfogel guided the New York headquarters. By the time of Morris, Sr.'s passing, the Great Depression had already begun to take its toll on the agency; it lost a combined total of $45,000 in 1931 and 1932.

The Morris Agency found an unlikely savior in Mae West, who went on to become the top grosser at the box office in the 1930s. After its initial dip, entertainment proved a Depression-hardy industry. Over the course of the decade, revenues multiplied from about $500,000 to $15 million as the agency's client roster grew to number in the hundreds. While big-name film and radio deals contributed two-thirds of this turnover, the other third came from lesser known departments, including vaudeville, nightclub, and literary management. For not only did the agency represent well-established stars but it also nurtured what it called "the stars of the future." As a William Morris Agency advertisement once stressed, "Our Small Act of Today Is Our Big Act of Tomorrow." In 1938 the agency moved its West Coast office to posh Beverly Hills. Its early real estate purchases throughout the area would become a major source of wealth in the decades to come.

The Morris Agency's contribution to the Allied World War II effort was as showbiz-oriented as anything it had ever done. Abe Lastfogel organized USO shows featuring more than 7,000 entertainers, including such luminaries as Bing Crosby, Dinah Shore, Marlene Dietrich, James Stewart, Clark Gable, and Humphrey Bogart.

Post-World War II Expansion into Television

In the postwar era Morris's roster included Mickey Rooney, Laurence Olivier, Danny Kaye, Vivien Leigh, Katharine Hepburn, and Rita Hayworth. The agency also discovered and launched Marilyn Monroe's steamy career. Morris merged with the Berg-Allenberg Agency in 1949, bringing in such Hollywood luminaries as Clark Gable, Judy Garland, Frank Capra, Edward G. Robinson, and Robert Mitchum. It also branched into television during this period. According to Frank Rose,

author of a 1995 history of the agency, "in the early years the talent agencies essentially produced the shows, even lining up guests, taking care of all sorts of details." In fact, Morris agents were responsible for packaging such immensely popular productions as "The Milton Berle Show," "Texaco Star Theater," and "Your Show of Shows." "Make Room for Daddy," starring Danny Thomas, was another Morris vehicle of the 1950s.

When Bill Morris, Jr. retired from the agency in 1952, Abe Lastfogel became *de facto* head of William Morris. During the decade, the group represented Elvis Presley and revived Frank Sinatra's career. The agency also sparked the quiz show craze with the 1955 launch of "The $64,000 Question." Other agents booked comedy and variety acts to the nightclubs and casinos springing up in Las Vegas. These venues continued to serve as "feeders" to the film and television operations, fleshing out new talent and molding it into the next generation of movie and TV stars.

Film stars of the 1960s on the Morris roster included Anne Bancroft, Carol Channing, Katharine Hepburn, Jack Lemmon, Sophia Loren, Walter Matthau, Kim Novak, Natalie Wood, Spencer Tracy, Gregory Peck, and Barbra Streisand. The agency also expanded into the music industry during this time, representing such diverse acts as folk artists Paul Simon and Art Garfunkel, British rockers the Rolling Stones, Motown divas the Supremes, and teen idols The Beach Boys.

But it was television that became William Morris's biggest moneymaker in the 1960s, contributing around 60 percent of revenues or more than $7 million by the end of the decade. According to a 1989 article in *Forbes* magazine, "In the mid-1960s Morris was the undisputed kingpin of the television business, with some 9 hours on network prime time."

When Abe Lastfogel retired in 1969, he generously divvied up all the agency's voting stock among its key executives and employees. He was succeeded by an attorney/accountant Nat Lefkowitz. At that time, the Morris agency was bringing in an estimated $12 million annually, and it boasted hundreds of employees at offices in New York, Chicago, Beverly Hills, London, Paris, Munich, Rome, and Madrid.

CAA Fracture in 1970s and Decline in 1980s

Though the transition from Lastfogel to Lefkowitz appeared to have been a smooth transfer of power, William Morris was fraught with internal strife. For while the agency's corps of young, eager talent brokers multiplied, positions at the top remained filled by sexagenarians. Only Phil Weltman, a high-ranking executive in the television division, was in favor of grooming a cadre of younger men for top positions. Weltman's ideas were anathema to the Morris corporate culture, which prized long-term loyalty and rewarded it with promotions, but only after decades of service. The agency was becoming a training ground for other Hollywood professions; music industry executive David Geffen, television producer Aaron Spelling, and television executive Barry Diller all got their starts in the Morris mailroom.

When Lefkowitz unceremoniously canned Weltman in 1975, several of Weltman's young apprentices saw the writing on the wall. That year Rowland Perkins, Bill Haber, Mike

Rosenfeld, Mike Ovitz, and Ron Meyer left to form Creative Artists Agency. The agency and other defectors soon lured more than a dozen major clients, including Barbra Streisand, Robert Redford, Brian De Palma, Goldie Hawn, Mel Gibson, Michelle Pfeiffer, Kevin Costner, Jane Fonda, Alan Alda, and Chevy Chase.

Back at Morris, Lefkowitz was bumped up to the newly established—and dutiless—post of "co-chairman," a title shared with the octogenarian Abe Lastfogel. Lefkowitz was succeeded as president by Sammy Weisbord, who had joined the agency in 1931 at the age of 19 as Lastfogel's assistant and had risen through the ranks of the television division. December 1980 brought another management reorganization. While Weisbord remained president, the two aging past presidents were dubbed "co-chairmen emeriti" and the board was expanded to include seven new members—the first newcomers since the early 1950s. It was not exactly an influx of new blood, however; not one director was under the age of 50. Weisbord went into semi-retirement in 1984 and was succeeded by Lee Stevens, who guided the company until his death in February 1989. At that time, Norman Brokaw ascended to the top management position.

The frequent management upheavals of the 1980s did not do much to spruce up the Morris Agency's dulled reputation. Before long, it had become the butt of an oft-quoted joke: "How do you commit the perfect murder? Kill your wife and go to work for the Morris Agency. They'll never find you." Trade rags like *Los Angeles Magazine* and *Variety* sounded the death knell with headlines like "Whither William Morris?" and "R.I.P.?"

Of course, the obituaries for the William Morris Agency were premature, for although the business did rely heavily on past glories and the residuals they generated, it retained several big stars, including Bill Cosby, Clint Eastwood, Jack Lemmon, Tim Robbins, Uma Thurman, Tom Hanks, and John Malkovich. Moreover, estimated revenues had doubled from $30 million in 1984 to more than $60 million by the end of the decade, when the company represented about 2,000 clients.

Signs of Life in the 1990s and Beyond

In January 1991 three senior agents left the Morris Agency for a rival, taking with them a mix of well-established and up-and-coming stars including James Spader, Gerard Depardieu, Andie MacDowell, Anjelica Huston, Tim Robbins, Julia Roberts, Anne Bancroft, and Ralph Maccio. That's when former head of television Jerry Katzman ascended to Morris's presidency in 1991 with a mandate to breathe new life into the

agency. Later that year, he executed what *Variety* characterized as "one of the first bold moves in a long time by the huge firm that was once the undisputed industry leader." The acquisition of Triad Artists Inc. brought Morris 50 agents and, more important, action film star Bruce Willis and the alternative music group the Red Hot Chili Peppers. The acquisition of the Jim Halsey Co. boosted the agency's penetration of the reinvigorated country music industry, and the purchase of Charles Dorris and Associates made Morris a leader in the growing field of contemporary Christian music.

But Morris may have gotten its biggest break in 1995, when CAA chairman Michael Ovitz—who since his departure from Morris in 1975 had become "the most powerful man in Hollywood"—left the agency he founded to join the Walt Disney Company. In the wake of this tidal wave, Morris picked up Whoopi Goldberg and re-signed Sylvester Stallone.

Jerry Katzman advanced to the post of vice-chairman in April 1997 and Arnold Rifkin, director of the film division, added the day-to-day management of the agency to his list of responsibilities. At that time the Morris roster included teen brother act Hanson, clothing designer Tommy Hilfiger, Asian action film star Jackie Chan, supermodel Cindy Crawford, and Olympic ice skater Oksana Baiul.

At 100 years old in 1998, the agency appeared to have been taken off life support and was breathing on its own. But in a world driven by the vagaries of taste and image, the William Morris Agency's health could be graded no better than stable as it perched on the cusp of the 21st century.

Further Reading

Bart, Peter, "Whither William Morris?," *Variety,* October 19, 1992, pp. 5–6.
Bernstein, Amy, and Frank Rose, "They Made Mae West a Star," *U.S. News & World Report,* August 7, 1995, p. 51.
Gubernick, Lisa, "Backs to the Future," *Forbes,* April 15, 1991, p. 10.
——, "Living Off the Past," *Forbes,* June 12, 1989, pp. 48–52.
Ressner, Jeffrey, "R.I.P.?," *Los Angeles Magazine,* May 1991, pp. A61–A69.
Rose, Frank, *The Agency: William Morris and the Hidden History of Show Business,* New York: HarperBusiness, 1995.
——, "The Case of the Ankling Agents," *Premiere,* August 1991, pp. 54–61.
"The 10%ers Solution," *Time,* November 2, 1992, p. 19.
Waddell, Ray, "William Morris Agency Buys Dorris and Associates," *Amusement Business,* April 5, 1993, p. 6.

—April D. Gasbarre

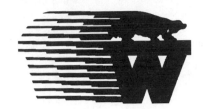

Wolverine Tube Inc.

1525 Perimeter Parkway
Suite 210
Huntsville, Alabama 35806
U.S.A.
(205) 353-1310
Fax: (205) 351-2312
Web Site: http://www.wlv.com

Public Company
Incorporated: 1916
Employees: 3,000
Sales: $700 million (1997)
Stock Exchanges: New York
SICs: 3351 Copper Rolling & Drawing; 6719 Holding
    Companies, Not Elsewhere Classified

Wolverine Tube Inc. is a technological leader in the design, manufacture, and distribution of copper and copper alloy tubular products in the United States and around the world. The company makes copper tubes for the industrial tube product market, including appliance companies, refrigeration equipment manufacturers, automotive firms, and air conditioner manufacturers; technical tubing for the technical tube market, including large commercial air conditioning corporations and water, spa, and swimming pool heater manufacturers; copper alloy tubing for the copper alloy tube market, including ship builders, and refining and chemical processing companies; and fabricated products, including a wide range of copper, copper alloy and aluminum tubing for the consumer appliance, marine, automotive, refrigeration, building and heating, and heavy equipment industries. The company has manufacturing facilities in Alabama, Tennessee, Mississippi, Oklahoma, North Carolina, Texas, Pennsylvania, and in three Canadian locations as well. In the late 1990s, management was taking steps to internationalize company operations and open sales offices in Hong Kong and in Lyon, France.

Early History

The formation of the Wolverine Tube Company occurred in 1916 in the state of Michigan. The automotive industry was just beginning to manufacture cars for mass consumption, and Ford Motor Company was at the forefront of this revolutionary development in technology called the "assembly line." Other car manufacturers followed suit, and soon cars were available to larger and larger numbers of people. Manufacturing automobiles on such an extensive scale required that parts be readily available for their assembly. One of the essential parts for making a car was heat-resistant tubing. Seeing the need for such an item, a group of men familiar with the automotive industry and its growing need for component parts decided to establish its own firm to produce a wide variety of tubing and sell it to the car manufacturers. The name for the new company was chosen from the animal whose name is synonymous with the state of Michigan, the wolverine.

As automobile manufacturing grew during the 1920s, the Wolverine Tube Company grew with it. The company sold its products to large car companies such as Ford and General Motors. At the same time, technological advances in refrigeration provided a new market opportunity. Wolverine engineers began to design copper and copper alloy tubing that was employed in the manufacture of refrigeration equipment. As meat markets that used ice to keep their products cold started to purchase large refrigeration units, Wolverine tube developed copper alloy tubing that was both heat and cold resistant. One of the first in the tubing industry to do so, the company garnered an ever-increasing customer base throughout the decade.

When the stock market crashed in 1929, the United States experienced a economic decline unparalleled in its history. The Great Depression resulted in the financial ruin of many businesses, massive unemployment, and a national banking system that virtually collapsed. When Franklin Delano Roosevelt was elected president in 1932 on the Democratic Platform of national economic recovery, he immediately implemented comprehensive measures that were meant to bring the country and its people out of the Depression. Unfortunately, the economic recovery was slow in coming, and during the entire decade of the 1930s Americans were forced to live more frugally than ever before.

Wolverine Tube was not able to escape the affects of the Great Depression, and like many other businesses it was forced to issue massive layoffs or reduced salaries. Some of the company's product lines were scaled back to a bare minimum. However, the firm was able to survive the worst years of the Depression due to its manufacture of copper and copper alloy tubing for the commercial refrigeration industry, the automotive industry, and the growing chemical and process industries. During the early 1930s, company engineers designed the integral extended surface tube, one of the most innovative products to originate from the tubing industry. The integral extended surface tube was used by companies in the refrigeration, air conditioning, energy generation, and process industries, and its success played a large part in maintaining the company's financial viability during the Depression.

Wartime and Postwar Production

Wolverine Tube prospered immensely as American armed forces prepared to enter the global conflict that had spread across Europe and the Pacific. The company received large contracts from the U.S. government for copper and copper alloy tubing used in massive refrigeration units on aircraft carriers and at training facilities for new recruits. In 1942, one of the company's first plants outside the United States was opened in Montreal, Quebec, for the specific purpose of manufacturing copper and copper alloy tubes, rods, wire, and extruded shapes. The new plant was at the forefront in technological innovation for testing and manufacturing new shapes of tubing to meet the specific needs of its customers, including the U.S. government.

As the end of World War II grew nearer, Wolverine Tube was well situated to take advantage of the opportunities presenting themselves in the postwar era. The automotive, heavy equipment, and refrigeration industries were poised for phenomenal growth as the war ended, soldiers from the American armed services returned to find jobs, and the United States attained an unrivaled position as the economic leader of the non-communist world. Continuing its strategy of expansion, the firm opened a new facility in Decatur, Alabama, for the purpose of manufacturing an ever-widening range of copper alloy and seamless copper tubes. These items included smooth surface industrial, condenser, plumbing, and refrigeration tubes in various straight lengths and coils. The Decatur facility also began to produce steel and titanium finned tubes, along with hairpin bends and U-bends.

As the company grew throughout the 1950s, more and more sales were made to the automotive, heavy equipment, air-conditioning and refrigeration, chemical, and refining industries. With business booming, management decided to open another facility in Canada, located in London, Ontario. This plant was constructed to manufacture a variety of seamless copper and copper alloy tubes in a host of different lengths, diameters, wall thicknesses, and tempers for use primarily in plumbing and industrial construction. Opened in 1958, the London, Ontario, facility was a significant contributor to the company's growing success in the plumbing services sector.

The 1960s was a period of realignment and consolidation for Wolverine Tube. The manufacturing facilities that management had built or purchased in different parts of the United States and Canada were brought under more centralized control, with inventory, sales, marketing, plant operations, and distribution undergoing close scrutiny and streamlining for higher efficiency. The company's engineers continued to conduct research in new applications of copper and copper alloy tubing, resulting in sales to an ever-widening customer base. One of Wolverine Tube's new capital investments during this time was in the manufacture of sheet, flat, and strip products in copper, tin brasses, brass, and phosphor bronze. A facility at Fergus, Ontario, was established in 1968 as a strip mill which focused exclusively on the manufacture of these products.

Continued Growth and Expansion

The postwar era had been good to Wolverine Tube, and the firm had grown both in terms of assets and sales. The number of employees at the company's facilities continued to increase, as new markets were entered due to the ingenuity of the engineering department employing its expertise in copper and copper alloy tubing for new applications. One example of these new applications was the design and manufacture of small diameter capillary and control tubes for the fabricated components market. The Ardmore, Tennessee, facility was established in 1974 to manufacture these items, plus a wide range of fabricated components produced from finned and smooth surface tubing. During the same year, since the company's sale of its products to the refrigeration, plumbing, and industrial markets were increasing at a much quicker rate than expected, a new facility at Shawnee, Oklahoma, was opened for the purpose of manufacturing seamless copper service tubes in a variety of straight lengths and coils, for these markets.

Wolverine Tube continued its uninterrupted growth during the 1980s. In 1982, the firm opened its Greenville, Mississippi, plant to manufacture specialty fabricated parts, components and sub-assemblies. This facility became part of the company's Fabricated Products Group during the 1990s. By this time, the company had also relocated its administrative offices from Michigan to Alabama. Taking advantage of the lower costs for rent and employee wages, the company had moved its corporate headquarters to Huntsville, Alabama, while its domestic and international sales office was relocated to Decatur, Alabama. The move was made possible by the increasing sophistication of worldwide telecommunications, allowing the company to remain in constant contact with its facilities throughout North America and wherever its growing international list of clients were located. The last major expansion of the decade occurred in 1989, when Wolverine Tube constructed its Booneville, Mississippi, facility. A technologically advanced, state-of-the-art plant designed and built specifically to produce the company's inner ridged copper tubes, dubbed the industrial Turbo-A and the Turbo-DX, both these items were sold to air conditioning manufacturers.

The 1990s and Beyond

In 1992, the company reported net sales of just under $500 million, and in 1994, that figure had increased to approximately $520 million. However, by the end of fiscal 1996, net sales skyrocketed to $700 million. Most of this growth in net sales was a direct result of two outstanding acquisitions the company made during the mid-1990s. In 1994, Wolverine Tube acquired Small Tube Products, Inc., a well-known manufacturer of copper and copper alloy tubing that focused on small-diameter, high-value added commercial items in almost 1,000 different sizes and shapes. Manufacturing a wide-array of products such as musical instrument flute bodies, thermostatic controls, lighter cases, capillary tubes, and transmission oil cooler tubes, the company's customer list included such prestigious names as Caterpillar Tractor, Thermadyne, the Siebe Group of Companies, and Long Manufacturing Company. Wolverine Tube incorporated Small Tube Products into its operations, and made it the cornerstone of its Fabricated Products Group. Following the astute acquisition and reorganization, the Fabricated Products market became the fastest growing segment of Wolverine Tube's business.

Another major acquisition was made in 1996 with the purchase of Tube Forming, Inc., a manufacturer of copper and copper alloy tubing established during the early 1970s in Corrollton, Texas. Tube Forming, Inc., acquired for $35 million, had a worldwide reputation for producing high-quality items such as return bends, manifolds, and headers primarily used in the refrigeration and air conditioning industries. Also part of the Fabricated Products Group, Tube Forming had compiled a list of over 250 customers, and was acknowledged as one of the most innovative firms in the industry.

One of the major opportunities for Wolverine Tubing was the regulated phaseout of chlorofluorocarbons or CFCs, a major cause of ozone depletion and closely tied to global warming. Banned by most of the industrialized nations in the world in January 1996, CFCs were the primary coolants used in large commercial air conditioning and refrigeration units. With over 80,000 of the world's commercial chillers located throughout North America, and only a mere 25,000 having had their tubing refitted or replaced for the use of new coolants, Wolverine Tube projected a major demand from customers who wanted new and more efficient tubing for alternative coolants. This market development led the company to implement a comprehensive four-year capital expenditure program to improve the efficiency and production capacity at many of its plants in the United States, especially at the Booneville, Mississippi, facility. The company's newest plant, constructed in 1995 at Roxboro, North Carolina, as part of the capital expenditure program, was built for the purpose of manufacturing copper enhanced surface tubing to take advantage of the future demand for its use in large commercial refrigeration units and air conditioning units in North America and around the globe.

The opening of offices in both Europe and Asia indicated growing market demand for Wolverine Tube's products, a demand that was not likely to diminish in the near or even distant future. In fact, a new manufacturing and distribution facility undergoing construction in Shanghai, China, and scheduled for completion by the end of 1998, was indicative of the confidence Wolverine management had in its product line and the growth of its markets. As the worldwide technological leader in the manufacture of copper and copper alloy tubing serving a wide variety of industries, Wolverine Tube looked forward to a very bright, and profitable, future.

Principal Subsidiaries

Small Tube Products Company, Inc.; Tube Forming, Inc.

Further Reading

Barnhart, Dale G., "Copper Tube Market Remains Strong," *American Metal Market,* April 2, 1997, p. 14.

"Cleaning The Air Will Boost Copper Tube Sales," *Purchasing,* June 6, 1996, p. 32B12.

Coplan, Stephen, "Asia Next Stop For Copper Tube," *American Metal Market,* July 30, 1997, p. 1.

——, "Copper Tube Mart Creeps and Crawls Back into the Black," *American Metal Market,* July 24, 1997, p. 1.

——, "Copper Tube Said Warming in Key Sectors," *American Metal Market,* October 22, 1997, p. 1.

Stundza, Tom, "Demand Reflects Slowing Economy," *Purchasing,* February 13, 1997, p. 20B1.

——, "Erratic Demand Fogs Up The Price Horizon," *Purchasing,* October 5, 1995, p. 32B1.

—Thomas Derdak

Wood-Mode, Inc.

**One Second Street
Kreamer, Pennsylvania 17833
U.S.A.
(717) 374-2711
Fax: (717) 374-2700
Web site: http://www.wood-mode.com**

Private Company
Incorporated: 1942 as Wood-Metal Industries, Inc.
Employees: 1,300
Sales: $110 million (1997 est.)
SICs: 2434 Wood Kitchen Cabinets; 2541 Wood Office
& Store Fixtures, Partitions, Shelving & Lockers

Wood-Mode, Inc. was the leading nonstock cabinetry manufacturer in the United States in the late 1990s. The company was offering semi-custom and custom cabinetry for the kitchen and also for other rooms of the home in several woods and styles and a great variety of finishes.

Wood-Metal, 1942–56

Wood-Mode was founded by four men who had been salesmen for Whitehead Monel Kitchens Co., a division of International Nickel Co. that was selling the white metal kitchen cabinets popular throughout the 1930s. The four—Ted Gronlund and Dick Nellis, Sr., of New York City and Charles Wall, Sr., and Caswell Holloway of Philadelphia—realized that, with the imminent involvement of the United States in World War II, the production of steel would be shifted to the war effort, leaving them with nothing to sell. The four founded Wood-Metal Industries, Inc. in 1942 in a small lumber-planing mill in Kreamer, Pennsylvania.

Wood-Metal's initial client was Uncle Sam, seeking production of military needs such as cook's tables, coops for the Army's carrier pigeons, shell cases, ladders, and Signal Corps equipment cases. The government set exacting specifications

for these products, especially for the finishes applied to the Signal Corps cases. These cases, earmarked for use in the South Pacific, had to be sealed against fungus growths and waterproofed by varnish that sometimes required as many as 11 coats. The company's experience in meticulous wood finishing during this period would prove invaluable in the development of its cabinetry finishes.

As World War II neared its end, military contracts began to dwindle, and Wood-Metal turned its attention to making kitchen cabinets. The company met its difficulty in buying top-grade lumber by purchasing timber rights on a tract of land in the Beaver Springs, Pennsylvania, area for $2,000 in 1943 and building a sawmill to provide the raw material. Wood-Metal never made a metal cabinet in Kreamer, but it acquired a manufacturing plant in Beech Bottom, West Virginia, to make such cabinets once steel became available after the war. This operation was moved in the 1950s to McClure, Pennsylvania, where it began making and marketing a line of institutional and residential cabinets.

By 1945 Wood-Metal was producing enameled finishes for a contemporary cabinet-door style and had begun to offer special purpose items that included a telescoping towel rack, cutlery trays with linoleum bottoms, and a broom/linen-closet combination. During the late 1940s the company also was designing and manufacturing cabinets and casework for schools, hospitals, and other institutional customers. By the mid-1950s, the institutional line was offered in three woods, with a choice of six natural and 12 enameled finishes.

All four founders had other business interests in New York and Philadelphia, so C. K. Battram, Sr., was brought in as general manager in 1944. Holloway withdrew from participation in the firm in 1948, but Nellis, the company's president since its inception, moved to Kreamer to assume day-to-day leadership, while Gronlund and Wall also began to devote greater time to the fledgling company. When the firm celebrated its 50th anniversary in 1992, members of the Battram, Gronlund, and Wall families were still active in management. Corporate headquarters remained, however, on Park Avenue in New York, until 1953.

Company Perspectives:

The mission of Wood-Mode is to work together to continually improve the quality of our cabinetry products, service, and support in order to meet or exceed customer expectations.

The Wood-Metal product line in 1950 included 14 enameled finishes and one natural wood finish. The company also introduced "customized" natural finished doors and drawers on enameled cabinets and manufactured the first built-in unit to accommodate a *Thermador* range/grill-and-oven combination. The first Wood-Metal knotty-pine cabinets were introduced in 1951 to accommodate the Early American home decor so popular at the time. These cabinets featured authentic V-joint construction and were in the forefront of design.

Wood-Metal originally shipped cabinets to its customers by commercial carrier. This proved less than ideal because at times the products were not properly handled, leading to damage and delays in installation. In 1952 the company began to use its own fleet of trucks to deliver to markets in the East, thereby greatly improving service to dealers and customers. The following year Wood-Metal decided to launch a modest advertising and promotional program to support its sales representatives and dealers. Its first advertisement in a national consumer magazine appeared in January 1954. The number of sales representatives reached 21 by the end of 1955. Advertisements were placed in magazines like *House and Garden* and *Good Housekeeping* (the latter in conjunction with the famous seal of approval).

Cabinetry into Every Room, 1956–89

The name of the company's residential line of cabinets was changed to Wood-Mode Kitchens in 1956 because wood, rather than metal, kitchen cabinets were growing in popularity, reaching 70 percent of the total installed that year. (The corporate name was not changed to Wood-Mode, however, until 1990.) In a full-page ad appearing in *Kitchen Business* that year, the company explained its decision as intended "to better describe the finest line of all-wood kitchens." For a 1958 issue of *House and Garden,* Wood-Mode designed and built a kitchen that could be taken along when the homeowner moved. The company's products also appeared on several television game shows, including "The Price Is Right," in which the grand prize was a custom-built kitchen.

Nellis resigned as president in 1959 and was succeeded by Wall. In 1961 the company initiated a "picturebook" that afforded a view of actual installations of Wood-Mode cabinets in oak, maple, and pine, in four different styles and 22 natural and 12 enamel finishes, with a variety of hardware and a choice of more than 50 special purpose cabinets and accessories. Wood-Mode was letting it be known that its custom-built cabinetry could be made to order for any room in the house. In 1970 the company logo was changed from "Wood-Mode Kitchens" to "Wood-Mode Cabinetry."

Gronlund succeeded Wall as president in 1963. He died in 1967, and Battram, his successor, passed away in 1969. Charles Wall, Jr., succeeded Battram as president. In 1970 Wood-Mode added 180,000 square feet of manufacturing and warehousing space, and in 1972 it opened a factory showroom across the highway from the plant. This facility contained a full working kitchen and an auditorium that would be used for the longest continuing training school in the industry. By 1992 more than 6,500 students had attended classes there. In the early 1970s *Kitchen Business* named Wood-Mode one of the two largest manufacturers of custom cabinetry in the nation. Robert Gronlund, Ted's son, succeeded Wall as president of the company in 1974. The company honored nine representatives in 1975 whose territorial sales volume reached or exceeded $1 million a year.

During this period Wood-Mode introduced two new special purpose units: an improved version of its chef's pantry, and a hutch that was the company's first small step into "furniture" manufacturing and that helped to popularize the idea of built-in cabinetry in every room of the house, a concept the firm called "RoomScaping." Wood-Mode was offering its clientele custom and built-in cabinetry as an alternative to the limits of freestanding furniture, in a choice of six different styles available in three woods and more than 35 finishes, including wood-grain PVC plastic laminate. The company also introduced vinyl interiors and five new door styles and, in the late 1970s, Hallmark cherry cabinets and the Alpha and Citation door styles.

By the end of 1981 Wood-Mode had expanded its distribution into the Southwest and Pacific Northwest. It now held about 20 percent of the total factory-built custom-cabinetry market. Sales grew from $30 million in 1980 to $75 million by 1988. Wood-Mode introduced a line of six door styles of frameless cabinets in 1984, and this line in turn inspired the creation of new door styles.

Always at the forefront of environmentally conscious manufacturing, Wood-Mode in 1988 added a 600,000-pound thermal incinerating system to eliminate potentially harmful emissions from the finishing process. It also installed a cogeneration system using scrap wood and sawdust to produce electricity for both its own needs and the local power system. In 1989 the company added a second floor to its warehouse in order to create 160,000 additional square feet of manufacturing space. This brought its total amount of production and warehouse space to 1 million square feet.

Wood-Mode in the 1990s

Brookhaven, a made-to-order, semi-custom cabinetry series introduced for the mid-range market in 1988, garnered $26 million in sales within three years. This helped to resuscitate Wood-Mode's growth rate, which had been slowed at the close of the 1980s by a leveling off of new housing and the consequent demand for high-end home furnishings. Company sales reached $96 million in 1994, of which semi-custom, rather than custom, cabinetry accounted for 56 percent of the total.

Wood-Mode was offering cabinetry in cherry, oak, maple, and pine woods, and laminate in traditional, country, and contemporary styles in 1997. Design Group 42 offered traditional framed-construction cabinetry, including 30 door styles. Design Group 84 offered an extensive collection of frameless cabinetry in the same woods, including 24 door styles. In addition, 12 specialty cabinet-door styles were available, included leaded glass and mullion styles. Drawers and shelves were also offered. A wide variety of hand-rubbed stained, opaque, glazed, and cottage finishes were available in a palette of more than 50 colors.

Wood-Mode's customized solutions to manage storage space were numerous and included a rollout serving cart, several chef's pantries, a pull-out table, a wine rack, and an appliance garage. Cabinetry for rooms other than the kitchen included living room/den bookshelves and bookcases, family-room entertainment centers, TV and bar cabinets, and shelving for art, collectibles, and trophies; dining room hutches; home office storage drawers and pull-out tables; bedroom dressers, armoires, and vanity tables; bathroom cabinets and ''his and her'' vanities; and even storage units for laundry and utility rooms.

Further Reading

''A Family Custom: The Wood-Mode Story,'' *Wood and Wood Products,* Annual 1995, p. 290.
A Half Century of Fine Cabinetmaking, Kreamer, Penn.: Wood-Mode Cabinetry, 1992.

—Robert Halasz

INDEX TO COMPANIES

Index to Companies

Listings in this index are arranged in alphabetical order under the company name. Company names beginning with a letter or proper name such as Eli Lilly & Co. will be found under the first letter of the company name. Definite articles (The, Le, La) are ignored for alphabetical purposes as are forms of incorporation that precede the company name (AB, NV). Company names printed in bold type have full, historical essays on the page numbers appearing in bold. Updates to entries that appeared in earlier volumes are signified by the notation (**upd.**). Company names in light type are references within an essay to that company, not full historical essays. This index is cumulative with volume numbers printed in bold type.

A.A. Housman & Co., **II** 424; **13** 340
A A Mathews. *See* CRSS Inc.
A & C Black Ltd., **7** 165
A&E. *See* Arts & Entertainment Network.
A&E Plastics, **12** 377
A. Ahlström Oy, **IV** 276–77
A. & J. McKenna, **13** 295
A&K Petroleum Company. *See* Kerr-McGee Corporation.
A & M Instrument Co., **9** 323
A&M Records, **23** 389
A&N Foods Co., **II** 553
A. and T. McKenna Brass and Copper Works, **13** 295
A&P. *See* Great Atlantic & Pacific Tea Company, Inc.
A&P Water and Sewer Supplies, Inc., **6** 487
A&W Root Beer Co., **II** 595
A.B. Chance Co., **II** 20
A.B. Hemmings, Ltd., **13** 51
A.B. Leasing Corp., **13** 111–12
A-B Nippondenso, **III** 593
A-BEC Mobility, **11** 487
A.C. Nielsen Company, IV 605; **13 3–5**
A.C. Wickman, **13** 296
A.D. International (Australia) Pty. Ltd., **10** 272
A. Dager & Co., **I** 404
A. Dunkelsbuhler & Co., **IV** 20–21, 65; **7** 122
A.E. Fitkin & Company, **6** 592–93
A.E. Gutman, **16** 486
A.E. LePage, **II** 457
A.G. Becker, **II** 259–60; **11** 318; **20** 260
A.G. Edwards, Inc., 8 3–5; 19 502
A.G. Industries, Inc., **7** 24
A.G. Morris, **12** 427
A.G. Spalding & Bros., **I** 428–29
A.G. Stanley Ltd., **V** 17, 19
A. Gettelman, Co., **I** 269
A. Goertz and Co., **IV** 91
A.H. Belo Corporation, IV 605; **10 3–5**
A.H. Robins Co., **10** 70; **12** 188; **16** 438
A.I. Credit Corp., **III** 196

A.J. Caley and Son. Ltd., **II** 569
A.J. Oster Co., **III** 681
A. Johnson & Co. *See* Axel Johnson Group.
A.L. Laboratories Inc., **12** 3
A.L. Pharma Inc., 12 3–5
A. Lambert International Inc., **16** 80
A.M. Collins Manufacturing Co., **IV** 286
A.O. Smith Corporation, 11 3–6
A.O. Smith Data Systems, **7** 139; **22** 181
A-1 Steak Sauce Co., **I** 259
A-1 Supply, **10** 375
A.P. Green Refractories, **22** 285
A.R. Pechiney, **IV** 173
A. Roger Perretti, **II** 484
A.S. Abell Co., **IV** 678
A.S. Aloe, **III** 443
A.S. Cameron Steam Pump Works, **III** 525
A/S Titan, **III** 418
A.S. Watson & Company, **18** 254
A.S. Yakovlev Design Bureau, 15 3–6
A. Schulman, Inc., 8 6–8
A.T. Cross Company, 17 3–5
A.V. Roe & Co., **I** 50; **III** 508
A.W. Bain Holdings, **III** 523
A.W. Shaw Co., **IV** 635
A.W. Sijthoff, **14** 555
A-Z International Companies, **III** 569; **20** 361
AA Development Corp., **I** 91
AA Distributors, **22** 14
AA Energy Corp., **I** 91
AAA Development Corp., **17** 238
Aachener und Münchener Feuer-Versicherungs-Gesellschaft, **III** 376
Aachener und Münchener Gruppe, **III** 349–50
Aachener Union, **II** 385
Aalborg, **6** 367
Aansworth Shirt Makers, **8** 406
AAON, Inc., 22 3–6
AAR Ltd., **III** 687; **IV** 60
Aargauische Portlandcement-Fabrik Holderbank-Wildegg, **III** 701
Aaron Brothers, Inc., **17** 320, 322

Aaron Rents, Inc., 14 3–5
Aastrom Biosciences, Inc., **13** 161
AAV Cos., **13** 48
Aavant Health Management Group, Inc., **11** 394
AB Capital & Investment Corporation, **23** 381
AB Dick Co., **II** 25
AB-PT. *See* American Broadcasting-Paramount Theatres, Inc.
ABA. *See* Aktiebolaget Aerotransport.
Abacus Fund, Inc., **II** 445; **22** 405
ABB ASEA Brown Boveri Ltd., II 1–4, 13; **III** 427, 466, 631–32; **IV** 66, 109, 204, 300; **15** 483; **22 7–12 (upd.),** 64, 288
ABB Hafo AB. *See* Mitel Corp.
Abba Seafood AB, **18** 396
Abbatoir St.-Valerien Inc., **II** 652
Abbey Business Consultants, **14** 36
Abbey Home Entertainment, **23** 391
Abbey Life Group PLC, **II** 309
Abbey Medical, Inc., **11** 486; **13** 366–67
Abbey National PLC, 10 6–8
Abbey Rents, **II** 572
Abbey Road Building Society, **10** 6–7
Abbott Laboratories, I 619–21, 686, 690, 705; **II** 539; **10** 70, 78, 126; **11 7–9 (upd.),** 91, 494; **12** 4; **14** 98, 389; **22** 75
Abbott, Proctor & Paine, **II** 445; **22** 405
ABC Appliance, Inc., 10 9–11
ABC, Inc., **I** 463–64; **II** 89, 129–33, 151, 156, 170, 173; **III** 188, 214, 251–52; **6** 157–59, 164; **11** 197–98; **17** 150; **XVIII** 65; **19** 201; **21** 25XVIII 65. *See also* Capital Cities/ABC Inc.
ABC Markets, **17** 558
ABC Rail Products Corporation, 18 3–5
ABC Records, **II** 144
ABC Supply Co., Inc., 22 13–16
ABC Treadco, **19** 455
ABD Securities Corp., **II** 239, 283
ABECOR. *See* Associated Banks of Europe Corp.
Abercom Holdings, **IV** 92

Abercrombie & Fitch Co., V 116; **15** 7–9; **17** 369
Aberthaw Cement, **III** 671
Abex Aerospace, **III** 512
Abex Corp., **I** 456; **10** 553; **18** 3
Abex Friction Products, **III** 512
ABF. *See* Associated British Foods PLC.
ABF Freight System, Inc., **16** 39–41
ABI. *See* American Furniture Company, Inc.
Abigail Adams National Bancorp, Inc., **23** 3–5
Abington Shoe Company. *See* The Timberland Company.
Abitibi-Price Inc., **IV** 245–47, 721; **9** 391
Abko Realty Inc., **IV** 449
ABN. *See* Algemene Bank Nederland N.V.
Above The Belt, Inc., **16** 37
ABR Foods, **II** 466
Abraham & Straus, V 168; **8** 443; **9** 209
Abraham Schaaffhausenscher Bankverein, **IV** 104
Abrams Industries Inc., **23** 6–8
Abri Bank Bern, **II** 378
Abu Dhabi National Oil Company, **IV** 363–64, 476
Abu Qir Fertilizer and Chemical Industries Co., **IV** 413
AC Design Inc., **22** 196
Academic Press, **IV** 622–23
Acadia Investors, **23** 99
Acadia Partners, **21** 92
Access Dynamics Inc., **17** 255
Access Graphics Technology Inc., **13** 128
Access Technology, **6** 225
Accessory Network Group, Inc., **8** 219
Accident and Casualty Insurance Co., **III** 230–31
Acclaim Entertainment, **13** 115
ACCO World Corporation, **7** 3–5; **12** 264
Accor SA, **10** 12–14; **13** 364
Accord Energy, **18** 367
Accountants on Call, **6** 10
Accounting and Tabulating Corporation of Great Britain, **6** 240
Acctex Information Systems, **17** 468
Accuralite Company, **10** 492
Accurate Forming Co., **III** 643
Accuride Corp., **IV** 179
Accuscan, Inc., **14** 380
Ace Comb Company, **12** 216
Ace Electric Co., **I** 156
Ace Hardware Corporation, **12** 6–8; **22** 258
Ace Refrigeration Ltd., **I** 315
Acer Inc., **6** 244; **10** 257; **16** 3–6
Aceros Fortuna S.A. de C.V., **13** 141
Acheson Graphite Corp, **I** 399; **9** 517
ACI Holding Inc., **I** 91
Aciéries de Ploërmel, **16** 514
Aciéries et Minières de la Sambre, **IV** 52
Aciéries Réunies de Burbach-Eich-Dudelange S.A. *See* ARBED S.A.
Ackerley Communications, Inc., **9** 3–5
Acklin Stamping Company, **8** 515
ACLC. *See* Allegheny County Light Company.
ACLI Government Securities Inc., **II** 422
ACM. *See* Advanced Custom Molders, Inc.
Acme Boot, **I** 440–41
Acme Brick Company, **19** 231–32
Acme Can Co., **I** 601; **13** 188
Acme Carton Co., **IV** 333

Acme Corrugated Cases, **IV** 258
Acme Cotton Products, **13** 366
Acme Quality Paint Co., **III** 744
Acme Quilting Co., Inc., **19** 304
Acme Road Machinery, **21** 502
Acme Screw Products, **14** 181
Acme-Cleveland Corp., **I** 531; **13** 6–8
Acme-Delta Company, **11** 411
ACMI, **21** 118–19
Acorn Computer, **III** 145
Acorn Financial Corp., **15** 328
Acoustics Development Corporation, **6** 313
Actava Group, **14** 332
Action, **6** 393
Action Furniture by Lane, **17** 183
Activenture Corporation, **16** 253
Acton Bolt Ltd., **IV** 658
Acumos, **11** 57
Acuson Corporation, **9** 7; **10** 15–17
ACX Technologies, **13** 11
Acxiom Corp., **6** 14; **18** 170
Ad Astra Aero, **I** 121
AD-AM Gas Company, **11** 28
Adage Systems International, Inc., **19** 438
Adam, Meldrum & Anderson Company (AM&A), **16** 61–62
Adam Opel AG, **7** 6–8; **11** 549; **18** 125; **21** 3–7 (upd.)
Adams Childrenswear, V 177
Adams Express Co., **II** 380–81, 395–96; **10** 59–60; **12** 533
Adams Industries, **19** 414
Adams/Cates Company, **21** 257
Adanac General Insurance Company, **13** 63
Adaptec, **11** 56
Adar Associates, Inc. *See* Scientific-Atlanta, Inc.
ADC of Greater Kansas City, Inc., **22** 443
ADC Telecommunications, Inc., **10** 18–21
Adco Products, **I** 374
Addison Wesley, **IV** 659
Addressograph-Multigraph, **11** 494
Adelphi Pharmaceutical Manufacturing Co., **I** 496
Adelphia Communications Corp., **17** 6–8
Ademco. *See* Alarm Device Manufacturing Company.
Adger Assuranceselskab, **III** 310
Adhere Paper Co., **IV** 252; **17** 29
Adia S.A., **6** 9–11; **9** 327
Adiainvest S.A., **6** 9, 11
Adidas AG, **8** 392–93; **13** 513; **14** 6–9; **17** 244; **22** 202; **23** 472, 474
Adjusters Auto Rental Inc. **16** 380
Adler, **23** 219
Adler and Shaykin, **III** 56; **11** 556–57
Adler Line. *See* Transatlantische Dampfschiffahrts Gesellschaft.
Adley Express, **14** 567
ADM. *See* Archer-Daniels-Midland Co.
Admiral Co., **II** 86; **III** 573
Admiral Cruise Lines, **6** 368
Adnan Dabbagh, **6** 115
ADNOC. *See* Abu Dhabi National Oil Company.
Adobe Systems Incorporated, **10** 22–24; **15** 149; **20** 46, 237
Adolph Coors Company, **I** 236–38, 255, 273; **13** 9–11 (upd.); **18** 72
Adolphe Lafont, **17** 210
Adonis Radio Corp., **9** 320
Adorence, **16** 482
ADP, Inc., **18** 297

Adria Produtos Alimenticios, Ltd., **12** 411
Adria Steamship Company, **6** 425
Adrian Hope and Company, **14** 46
Adriatico Banco d'Assicurazione, **III** 206, 345–46
Adrienne Vittadini, **15** 291
Adsega, **II** 677
ADT Security Systems, Inc., **12** 9–11
Adtel, Inc., **10** 358
Adtran Inc., **22** 17–20
ADtranz. *See* ABB ASEA Brown Boveri Ltd.
Advacel, **18** 20
Advance Foundry, **14** 42
Advance Publications Inc., **IV** 581–84; **13** 178, 180, 429; **19** 3–7 (upd.)
Advance Transformer Co., **13** 397
Advance-Rumely Thresher Co., **13** 16
Advanced Casino Systems Corporation, **21** 277
Advanced Communications Engineering. *See* Scientific-Atlanta, Inc.
Advanced Custom Molders, Inc., **17** 533
Advanced Data Management Group S.A., **23** 212
Advanced Entertainment Group, **10** 286
Advanced Marine Enterprises, Inc., **18** 370
Advanced Medical Technologies, **III** 512
Advanced Metal Technologies Inc., **17** 234
Advanced Micro Devices, Inc., **6** 215–17; **9** 115; **10** 367; **11** 308; **16** 316; **18** 18–19, 382; **19** 312; **20** 175
Advanced MobilComm, **10** 432
Advanced Structures, Inc., **18** 163
Advanced System Applications, **11** 395
Advanced Technology Laboratories, Inc., **9** 6–8
Advanced Telecommunications Corporation, **8** 311
Advanced Web Technologies, **22** 357
ADVANTA Corp., **8** 9–11; **11** 123
Advantage Company, **8** 311
Advantage Health Plans, Inc., **11** 379
Advent Corporation, **22** 97
Advertising Unlimited, Inc., **10** 461
Advo, Inc., **6** 12–14
AEA. *See* United Kingdom Atomic Energy Authority.
AEA Investors Inc., **II** 628; **13** 97; **22** 169, 171
AEG A.G., **I** 151, 193, **409–11**; **II** 12, 119, 279; **III** 466, 479; **IV** 167; **6** 489; **IX** 11; **14** 169; **15** 142; **22** 28; **23** 495
Aegis Group plc, **6** 15–16
Aegis Insurance Co., **III** 273
AEGON N.V., **III** 177–79, 201, 273
AEL Ventures Ltd., **9** 512
AEON, V 96–99; **11** 498–99
AEP. *See* American Electric Power Company.
AEP Industries, Inc., **22** 95
AEP-Span, **8** 546
Aer Lingus, **6** 59; **12** 367–68
Aeritalia, **I** 51, 74–75, 467
Aero Engines, **9** 418
Aero International Inc., **14** 43
Aero Mayflower Transit Company. *See* Mayflower Group Inc.
Aero O/Y, **6** 87–88
Aero-Coupling Corp., **III** 641
Aero-Portuguesa, **6** 125
Aeroflot Soviet Airlines, **I** 105, 110, 118; **6** 57–59; **14** 73
Aerojet, **8** 206, 208

Aerojet-General Corp., **9** 266
Aerolíneas Argentinas, **I** 107; **6** 97
Aeroméxico, **20** 168
Aeroquip Corporation, **III** 640–42; **V** 255; **16 7–9**; **19** 508
Aerospace Avionics, **III** 509
The Aerospatiale Group, **I** 41–42, 46, 50, 74, 94; **7 9–12**; **12** 190–91; **14** 72; **21 8–11 (upd.)**
The AES Corporation, **10 25–27**; **13 12–15 (upd.)**
Aetna, Inc., **20** 59; **21 12–16 (upd.)**, 95; **22** 139, 142–43
Aetna Life and Casualty Company, **II** 170–71, 319; **III** 78, **180–82**, 209, 223, 226, 236, 254, 296, 298, 305, 313, 329, 389; **IV** 123, 703; **10** 75–76; **12** 367; **15** 26; **17** 324; **23** 135
Aetna National Bank, **13** 466
Aetna Oil Co., **IV** 373
AFC. *See* America's Favorite Chicken Company, Inc.
AFCO Industries, Inc., **III** 241; **IV** 341
Afcol, **I** 289
AFE Ltd., **IV** 241
Affiliated Enterprises Inc., **I** 114
Affiliated Music Publishing, **22** 193
Affiliated Products Inc., **I** 622
Affiliated Publications, Inc., **6** 323; **7 13–16**; **19** 285
Affordable Inns, **13** 364
AFG Industries Inc., **I** 483; **9** 248
AFIA, **22** 143
Afianzadora Insurgentes Serfin, **19** 190
AFLAC Inc., **10 28–30 (upd.)**. *See also* American Family Corporation.
AFP. *See* Australian Forest Products.
African and European Investment, **IV** 96
African Coasters, **IV** 91
African Explosive and Chemical Industries, **IV** 22
AFW Fabric Corp., **16** 124
AG Communication Systems Corporation, **15** 194
AG&E. *See* American Electric Power Company.
Ag-Chem Equipment Company, Inc., **17 9–11**
AGA, **I** 358
Agar Manufacturing Company, **8** 267
AGCO Corp., **13 16–18**
AGEL&P. *See* Albuquerque Gas, Electric Light and Power Company.
Agence France Presse, **IV** 670
Agency, **6** 393
Agency Rent-A-Car, **16** 379
AGF, **III** 185
AGFA, **I** 310–11
Agfa-Ansco Corporation, **I** 337–38; **22** 225–27
AGFA-Gevaert, **III** 487; **18** 50, 184–86
Agiba Petroleum, **IV** 414
Agip SpA, **IV** 419–21, 454, 466, 472–74, 498; **12** 153
AGLP, **IV** 618
AGO, **III** 177, 179, 273, 310
Agor Manufacturing Co., **IV** 286
AGRAN, **IV** 505
AgriBank FCB, **8** 489
Agrico Chemical Company, **IV** 82, 84, 576; **7** 188
Agricole de Roquefort et Maria Grimal, **23** 219
Agricultural Insurance Co., **III** 191

Agricultural Minerals and Chemicals Inc., **IV** 84; **13** 504
Agrifan, **II** 355
Agrifull, **22** 380
Agrigenetics, Inc., **I** 361. *See also* Mycogen Corporation.
Agrippina Versicherungs AG, **III** 403, 412
Agrobios S.A., **23** 172
Agroferm Hungarian Japanese Fermentation Industry, **III** 43
AGTL. *See* Alberta Gas Trunk Line Company, Ltd.
Aguila (Mexican Eagle) Oil Co. Ltd., **IV** 657
Agway, Inc., **7 17–18**; **19** 250; **21 17–19 (upd.)**
Ahmanson
Ahold. *See* Koninklijke Ahold NV.
AHP. *See* American Home Products.
AHS. *See* American Hospital Supply Corporation.
AHSC Holdings Corp., **III** 9–10
Ahtna AGA Security, Inc., **14** 541
AIC. *See* Allied Import Company.
AICA, **16** 421
Aichi Bank, **II** 373
Aichi Kogyo Co., **III** 415
Aichi Steel Works, **III** 637
Aid Auto, **18** 144
Aida Corporation, **11** 504
AIG. *See* American International Group, Inc.
AIGlobal, **III** 197
Aiken Stores, Inc., **14** 92
Aikenhead's Home Improvement Warehouse, **18** 240
Aikoku Sekiyu, **IV** 554
AIM Create Co., Ltd., **V** 127
Ainsworth National, **14** 528
Air & Water Technologies Corporation, **6 441–42**
Air BP, **7** 141
Air Brasil, **6** 134
Air Canada, **6 60–62**, 101; **12** 192; **23 9–12 (upd.)**
Air Compak, **12** 182
Air Express International Corporation, **13 19–20**
Air France, **I** 93–94, 104, 110, 120; **II** 163; **6** 69, 373; **8** 313; **12** 190. *See also* Groupe Air France.
Air Inter. *See* Groupe Air France.
Air La Carte Inc., **13** 48
Air Lanka Catering Services Ltd., **6** 123–24
Air Liberté, **6** 208
Air Micronesia, **I** 97; **21** 142
Air Midwest, Inc., **11** 299
Air New Zealand Limited, **14 10–12**
Air Nippon Co., Ltd., **6** 70
Air Products and Chemicals, Inc., **I 297–99**, 315, 358, 674; **10 31–33 (upd.)**; **11** 403; **14** 125
Air Southwest Co. *See* Southwest Airlines Co.
Air Spec, Inc., **III** 643
Air-India, **6 63–64**
Airborne Accessories, **II** 81
Airborne Freight Corp., **6 345–47** 345; **13** 19; **14** 517; **18** 177
Airbus Industrie, **6** 74; **7** 9–11, 504; **9** 418; **10** 164; **13** 356; **21** 8. *See also* G.I.E. Airbus Industrie.
AirCal, **I** 91

Aircraft Marine Products, **II** 7; **14** 26
Aircraft Services International, **I** 449
Aircraft Transport & Travel Ltd., **I** 92
Airex Corporation, **16** 337
Airguard Industries, Inc., **17** 104, 106
Airlease International, **II** 422
Airmark Plastics Corp., **18** 497–98
Airmec-AEI Ltd., **II** 81
Airpax Electronics, Inc., **13** 398
Airport Ground Service Co., **I** 104, 106
Airstream, **II** 468
Airtel, **IV** 640
AirTouch Communications, **10** 118; **11 10–12**
Airtours International GmbH. and Co. K.G., **II** 164
AirTran Holdings, Inc., **22 21–23**
AirWair Ltd., **23** 399, 401–02
AirWays Corporation. *See* AirTran Holdings, Inc.
Airways Housing Trust Ltd., **I** 95
Airwick Industries, **II** 567
Aisin Seiki Co., Ltd., **III 415–16**; **14** 64
AITS. *See* American International Travel Service.
Ajax, **6** 349
Ajax Iron Works, **II** 16
Ajinomoto Co., Inc., **II 463–64**, 475; **III** 705
Ajman Cement, **III** 760
AJS Auto Parts Inc., **15** 246
AK Steel Holding Corporation, **19 8–9**
Akane Securities Co. Ltd., **II** 443
Akashic Memories, **11** 234
Akemi, **17** 310
AKH Co. Inc., **20** 63
Akin, Gump, Strauss, Hauer & Feld, **18** 366
AKO Bank, **II** 378
Akro-Mills Inc., **19** 277–78
Akron Brass Manufacturing Co., **9** 419
Akron Corp., **IV** 290
Akroyd & Smithers, **14** 419
Akseli Gallen-Kallela, **IV** 314
Aktiebolaget Aerotransport, **I** 119
Aktiebolaget Electrolux, **22 24–28 (upd.)**. *See also* Electrolux Group
Aktiebolaget SKF, **III 622–25**; **IV** 203
Aktiengesellschaft für Berg- und Hüttenbetriebe, **IV** 201
Aktiengesellschaft für Maschinenpapier-Zellstoff-Fabrikation, **IV** 323
Aktiv Placering A.B., **II** 352
AKU. *See* Akzo Nobel N.V.
Akzo Nobel N.V., **I** 674; **II** 572; **III** 44; **13 21–23**, 545; **14** 27; **15** 436; **16** 69, 462; **21** 466
Al Copeland Enterprises, Inc., **7** 26–28
Alaadin Middle East-Ersan, **IV** 564
Alabama Bancorp., **17** 152
Alabama Gas Corporation, **21** 207–08
Alabama Shipyards Inc., **21** 39–40
Alabaster Co., **III** 762
Aladdin Industries, **16** 487
Aladdin Mills Inc., **19** 276
Aladdin's Castle, **III** 430, 431
Alagasco, **21** 207–08
Alais et Camargue, **IV** 173
Alamac Knit Fabrics, Inc., **16** 533–34; **21** 192
Alamito Company, **6** 590
Alamo Engine Company, **8** 514
Alamo Rent A Car, Inc., **6 348–50**

Alarm Device Manufacturing Company, **9** 413–15

Alaron Inc., **16** 357

Alascom, **6** 325–28

Alaska Air Group, Inc., 6 65–67; 11 50

Alaska Co., **III** 439

Alaska Commercial Company, **12** 363

Alaska Hydro-Train, **6** 382; **9** 510

Alaska Junk Co., **19** 380

Alaska Natural Gas Transportation System, **V** 673, 683

Alaska Pulp Co., **IV** 284, 297, 321

Alaska Steel Co., **19** 381

Alba, **III** 619–20

Albany and Susquehanna Railroad, **II** 329

Albany Assurance Co., Ltd., **III** 293

Albany Cheese, **23** 219

Albany Felt Company. *See* Albany International Corp.

Albany International Corp., 8 12–14

Albemarle Paper Co., **I** 334–35; **10** 289

Albers Brothers Milling Co., **II** 487

Albert E. Reed & Co. Ltd. *See* Reed International PLC.

Albert Heijn NV, **II** 641–42

Albert Nipon, Inc., **8** 323

Albert Willcox & Co., **14** 278

Alberta Distillers, **I** 377

Alberta Energy Company Ltd., 16 10–12

Alberta Gas Trunk Line Company, Ltd., **V** 673–74

Alberta Sulphate Ltd., **IV** 165

Alberto, **II** 641–42

Alberto-Culver Company, 8 15–17

Albertson's Inc., II 601–03, 604–05, 637; **7 19–22** (upd.); **8** 474; **15** 178, 480; **16** 249; **18** 8; **22** 38

Albi Enterprises, **III** 24

Albion Industries, Inc., **16** 357

Albion Reid Proprietary, **III** 673

Albright & Friel, **I** 313; **10** 154

Albright & Wilson Ltd., **I** 527; **IV** 165; **12** 351; **16** 461

Albuquerque Gas & Electric Company. *See* Public Service Company of New Mexico.

Albuquerque Gas, Electric Light and Power Company, **6** 561–62

Albury Brickworks, **III** 673

Alcan Aluminium Limited, II 415; **IV 9–13,** 14, 59, 154–55; **9** 512; **14** 35

Alcantara and Sores, **II** 582

Alcatel Alsthom Compagnie Générale d'Electricité, II 13, 69, 117; **6** 304; **7** 9; **9 9–11,** 32; **11** 59, 198; **15** 125; **17** 353; **18** 155; **19** 164, 166; **21** 233

Alchem Capital Corp., **8** 141, 143

Alchem Plastics, **19** 414

Alco Health Services Corporation, III 9–10

Alco Hydro-Aeroplane, **I** 64

Alco Standard Corporation, I 412–13; III 9; **9** 261; **16** 473–74

Alcoa. *See* Aluminum Company of America.

Alcon Laboratories, **II** 547; **7** 382; **10** 46, 48

Alcudia, **IV** 528

Alden Merrell Corporation, **23** 169

Aldermac Mines Ltd., **IV** 164

Aldi Group, 11 240; **13 24–26; 17** 125

Aldine Press, **10** 34

Aldrich Chemical Co., **I** 690

Aldus Corporation, 10 34–36

Aldwarke Main & Car House Collieries, **I** 573

Alenia, **7** 9, 11

Alert Management Systems Inc., **12** 380

Alessio Tubi, **IV** 228

Alestra, **19** 12

Alex & Ivy, **10** 166–68

Alex Lee Inc., 18 6–9

Alexander & Alexander Services Inc., III 280; **10 37–39; 13** 476; **22** 318

Alexander & Baldwin, Inc., I 417; **10 40–42**

Alexander and Lord, **13** 482

Alexander Grant & Co., **I** 481, 656

Alexander Hamilton Life Insurance Co., **II** 420

Alexander Howden Group, **III** 280; **10** 38–39; **22** 318

Alexander Martin Co., **I** 374

Alexander Smith, Inc., **19** 275

Alexander's Inc., **10** 282; **12** 221

Alexander-Schroder Lumber Company, **18** 514

Alexis Lichine, **III** 43

Alfa Romeo, I 163, 167; **11** 102, 104, 139, 205; **13 27–29,** 218–19

Alfa, S.A. de C.V., II 262; **11** 386; **19 10–12**

Alfa Trading Company, **23** 358

Alfa-Laval AB, III 417–21; IV 203; **8** 376

Alfalfa's Markets, **19** 500–02

Alfinal, **III** 420

Alfred A. Knopf, Inc., **13** 428, 429

Alfred Bullows & Sons, Ltd., **21** 64

Alfred Dunhill Limited, **19** 369

Alfred Hickman Ltd., **III** 751

Alfred Marks Bureau, Ltd., **6** 9–10

Alfred Nobel & Co., **III** 693

Alfred Teves, **I** 193

Alfried Krupp von Bohlen und Halbach Foundation, **IV** 89

ALG. *See* Arkla, Inc.

Algemeene Bankvereeniging en Volksbank van Leuven, **II** 304

Algemeene Friesche, **III** 177–79

N.V. Algemeene Maatschappij tot Exploitatie van Verzekeringsmaatschappijen, **III** 199

Algemeene Maatschappij van Levensverzekering en Lijfrente, **III** 178

Algemeene Maatschappij voor Nijverheidskrediet, **II** 304–05

Algemeene Nederlandsche Maatschappij ter begunstiging van de Volksvlijt, **II** 294

Algemene Bank Nederland N.V., II 183–84, 185, 239, 527; **III** 200

Algoma Steel Corp., **IV** 74; **8** 544–45

Algonquin Energy, Inc., **6** 487

Algonquin Gas Transmission Company, **6** 486; **14** 124–26

Alidata, **6** 69

Aligro Inc., **II** 664

Alimenta (USA), Inc., **17** 207

Alimentana S.A., **II** 547

Alimondo, **17** 505

Alitalia—Linee Aeree Italiana, SpA, I 110, 466–67; **6** 96, **68–69**

Alken, **II** 474

Oy Alkoholiliike Ab, **IV** 469

Alkor-Oerlikon Plastic GmbH, **7** 141

All American Airways. *See* USAir Group, Inc.

All American Communications Inc., 20 3–7

All American Gourmet Co., **12** 178, 199

All American Sports Co., **22** 458–59

All Nippon Airways Company Limited, I 106, 493; **6 70–71** 118, 427; **16** 168

All Woods, Inc., **18** 514

Allami Biztosito, **III** 209; **15** 30

Allcom, **16** 392

Allders International, **III** 502

Alleanza & Unione Mediterranea, **III** 208

Alleanza-Securitas-Esperia, **III** 208

Alleghany Corporation, II 398; **IV** 180–81; **10 43–45; 19** 319; **22** 494

Allegheny Airlines. *See* USAir Group, Inc.

Allegheny Beverage Corp., **7** 472–73

Allegheny County Light Company, **6** 483–84

Allegheny International, Inc., **III** 732; **8** 545; **9** 484; **22** 3, 436

Allegheny Ludlum Corporation, I 307; **II** 402; **8 18–20; 9** 484; **21** 489

Allegheny Power System, Inc., V 543–45

Allegheny Steel and Iron Company, **9** 484

Allegiance Life Insurance Company, **22** 268

Allegis, Inc. *See* United Airlines.

Allegmeine Transpotmittel Aktiengesellschaft, **6** 394

Allegretti & Co., **22** 26

Allen & Co., **I** 512, 701; **II** 136; **12** 496; **13** 366

Allen & Ginter, **12** 108

Allen & Hanbury's, **I** 640

Allen Tank Ltd., **21** 499

Allen's Convenience Stores, Inc., **17** 170

Allen-Bradley Co., **I** 80; **II** 110; **III** 593; **11** 429–30; **17** 478; **22** 373; **23** 211

Allen-Leversidge Ltd., **I** 315

Allergan, Inc., 10 46–49; 23 196

Allforms Packaging Corp., **13** 442

Allgemeine Deutsche Creditanstalt, **II** 211, 238, 383; **12** 536

Allgemeine Eisenbahn-Versicherungs-Gesellschaft, **III** 399

Allgemeine Elektricitäts-Gesellschaft. *See* AEG A.G.

Allgemeine Rentenstalt Lebens- und Rentenversicherung, **II** 258

Allgemeine Versicherungs-Gesellschaft Helvetia, **III** 375

Alliance Agro-Alimentaires S.A., **II** 577

Alliance Amusement Company, **10** 319

Alliance Assurance Co., **III** 369–73

Alliance Brothers, **V** 356

Alliance Capital Management Corp., **22** 189

Alliance Entertainment Corp., 17 12–14

Alliance Gaming Corp., **15** 539

Alliance Insurance Co., **III** 224

Alliance Manufacturing Co., **13** 397

Alliance Marine, **III** 373

Alliance Mortgage Co., **I** 610

Alliance Packaging, **13** 443

Alliance Paper Group, **IV** 316

Alliance Tire and Rubber Co., **II** 47

AllianceWare, Inc., **16** 321

Alliant Techsystems, Inc., 8 21–23

Allianz AG Holding, I 411, 426; **II** 239, 257, 279–80; **III 183–86,** 200, 250, 252, 299–301, 347–48, 373, 377, 393; **IV** 222; **14** 169–70; **15 10–14** (upd.)

Allibert, **III** 614

Allied Bakeries Ltd., **II** 465–66; **13** 52–53

Allied Breweries Ltd., **I** 215; **III** 105; **IV** 712

Allied Chemical, **I** 310, 332, 351–52; **8** 526; **9** 521–22; **13** 76; **22** 5

Allied Chemical & Dye Corp., **I** 414; **7** 262; **9** 154; **22** 29

Allied Color Industries, **8** 347

Allied Communications Group, **18** 77; **22** 297

Allied Construction Products, **17** 384

Allied Container Corp., **IV** 345

Allied Corporation, **I** 68, 141, 143, 414, 534; **III** 118, 511; **6** 599; **7** 356; **9** 134; **11** 435. *See also* AlliedSignal Inc.

Allied Crude Vegetable Oil Refining Co., **II** 398; **10** 62

Allied Distributing Co., **12** 106

Allied Dunbar, **I** 427

Allied Engineering Co., **8** 177

Allied Fibers, **19** 275

Allied Food Markets, **II** 662

Allied Gas Company, **6** 529

Allied Grape Growers, **I** 261

Allied Health and Scientific Products Company, **8** 215

Allied Import Company, **V** 96

Allied Irish Banks, plc, 16 13–15

Allied Maintenance Corp., **I** 514

Allied Mills, Inc., **10** 249; **13** 186

Allied Oil Co., **IV** 373

Allied Overseas Trading Ltd., **I** 216

Allied Plywood Corporation, **12** 397

Allied Polymer Group, **I** 429

Allied Products Corporation, 21 20–22

Allied Radio, **19** 310

Allied Safety, Inc., **V** 215

Allied Shoe Corp., **22** 213

Allied Signal Engines, 9 12–15

Allied Steel and Conveyors, **18** 493

Allied Steel and Wire Ltd., **III** 495

Allied Stores Corporation, **II** 350, 611–12; **V** 25–28; **9** 211; **10** 282; **13** 43; **15** 94, 274; **16** 60; **22** 110; **23** 59–60

Allied Structural Steel Company, **10** 44

Allied Supermarkets, Inc., **7** 570

Allied Suppliers, **II** 609

Allied Telephone Company. *See* Alltel Corporation.

Allied Tin Box Makers Ltd., **I** 604

Allied Towers Merchants Ltd., **II** 649

Allied Van Lines Inc., **6** 412, 414; **14** 37

Allied Vintners, **I** 215

Allied-Lyons plc, I 215–16, 258, 264, 438; **IV** 721; **9** 100, 391; **10** 170; **13** 258; **21** 228, 323

Allied-Signal Corp., I 85, 141, 143, **414–16**; **III** 511–12; **V** 605; **6** 599–600; **9** 519; **11** 435, 444; **13** 227; **16** 436; **17** 20; **21** 200, 396–97

AlliedSignal Inc., 22 29–32 (upd.)

Allis Chalmers Corporation, **I** 163; **II** 98, 121; **III** 543–44; **9** 17; **11** 104; **12** 545; **13** 16–17, 563; **14** 446; **21** 502–03; **22** 380

Allis-Gleaner Corp. *See* AGCO Corp.

Allison Engine Company, **21** 436

Allison Gas Turbine Division, 9 16–19, 417; **10** 537; **11** 473

Allmanna Svenska Elektriska Aktiebolaget. *See* ABB ASEA Brown Boveri Ltd.

Allmänna Telefonaktiebolaget L.M. Ericsson, **V** 334

Allnatt London & Guildhall Properties, **IV** 724

Allnet, **10** 19

Allo Pro, **III** 633

Allor Leasing Corp., **9** 323

Alloy & Stainless, Inc., **IV** 228

Alloys Unlimited, **II** 82

The Allstate Corporation, I 23; **III** 231–32, 259, 294; **V** 180, 182; **6** 12; **10** 50–52; **13** 539; **18** 475; **21** 96–97; **22** 495; **23** 286–87

Alltel Corporation, 6 299–301; 16 318; **20** 440

Allwaste, Inc., 18 10–13

Almac Electronics Corporation, **10** 113

Almac's Inc., **17** 558–59

Almaden Vineyards, **I** 377–78; **13** 134

Almanij. *See* Algemeene Maatschappij voor Nijverheidskrediet.

Almay, Inc., **III** 54

Almeida Banking House. *See* Banco Bradesco S.A.

Almours Security Co., **IV** 311; **19** 266

Aloe Vera of America, **17** 187

Aloha Airlines, **I** 97; **9** 271–72; **21** 142; **22** 251

Alp Sport Sandals, **22** 173

Alpen-Elektrowerke Aktiengesellschaft, **IV** 230

Alpex Computer Corp., **III** 157

Alpex, S.A. de C.V., **19** 12

Alpha Beta Co., **II** 605, 625, 653; **17** 559

Alpha Engineering Group, Inc., **16** 259–60

Alpha Technical Systems, **19** 279

Alphonse Allard Inc., **II** 652

Alpina Versicherungs-Aktiengesellschaft, **III** 412

Alpine, **IV** 234

Alpine Electronics, Inc., II 5; **13 30–31**

Alpine Lace Brands, Inc., 18 14–16

Alpine Securities Corporation, **22** 5

Alpre, **19** 192

Alps Electric Co., Ltd., II 5–6; **13** 30

Alric Packing, **II** 466

Alsen-Breitenburg, **III** 702

Alsons Corp., **III** 571; **20** 362

Alsthom, **II** 12

Alsthom-Atlantique, **9** 9

Alta Gold Co., **IV** 76

ALTA Health Strategies, Inc., **11** 113

Alta Holidays Ltd., **I** 95

Altamil Corp., **IV** 137

Altana AG, **23** 498

Alte Leipziger, **III** 242

Altec Electronics, **I** 489–90

ALTEC International, **21** 107–09

Altenburg & Gooding, **22** 428

Altera Corporation, 18 17–20

Alternate Postal Delivery, **6** 14

Altex, **19** 192–93

Althoff KG, **V** 101

Althouse Chemical Company, **9** 153

Althus Corp., **I** 361

Alton & Eastern Railroad Company, **6** 504

Alton Box Board Co., **IV** 295; **19** 225

Altos Computer Systems, **6** 279; **10** 362

Altos Hornos de Mexico SA de CV, **13** 144; **19** 220

Altron Incorporated, 20 8–10

Aluma Systems Corp., **9** 512; **22** 14

Alumax Inc., **I** 508; **III** 758; **IV** 18–19; **8** 505–06; **22** 286

Alumina Partners of Jamaica, **IV** 123

Aluminate Sales Corp, **I** 373

Aluminio de Galicia, **IV** 174

Aluminium Co. of London, **IV** 69

L'Aluminium Francais, **IV** 173

Aluminium Ltd., **IV** 9–11, 14, 153

Aluminium Plant and Vessel Co., **III** 419

Aluminium-Oxid Stade GmbH, **IV** 231

Aluminum Can Co., **I** 607

Aluminum Company of America, I 373, 599; **II** 315, 402, 422; **III** 490–91, 613; **IV** 9–12, **14–16**, 56, 59, 121–22, 131, 173, 703; **6** 39; **12** 346; **19** 240, 292; **20** 11–14 **(upd.)**; **22** 455

Aluminum Company of Canada Ltd., **II** 345; **IV** 10–12, 154

Aluminum Cooking Utensil Co., **IV** 14

Aluminum Forge Co., **IV** 137

Aluminum Norf GmbH, **IV** 231

Aluminum of Korea, **III** 516

Aluminum Rolling Mills, **17** 280

Aluminum Sales Corporation, **12** 346

Aluminum Seating Corp., **I** 201

Alun Cathcart, **6** 357

Alup-Kompressoren Pressorun, **III** 570; **20** 361

Alupak, A.G., **12** 377

Alusaf, **IV** 92

Alusuisse, **IV** 12

Alva Jams Pty., **I** 437

Alvic Group, **20** 363

Alyeska Pipeline Service Co., **IV** 522, 571; **14** 542

Alyeska Seafoods Co., **II** 578

ALZA Corporation, 10 53–55

Alzwerke GmbH, **IV** 230

AM Acquisition Inc., **8** 559–60

Am-Par Records, **II** 129

Am-Safe, Inc., **16** 357

AM-TEX Corp., Inc., **12** 443

Amagasaki Co., **I** 492

Amagasaki Spinners Ltd., **V** 387

Amagasaki Steel Co., Ltd., **IV** 130

Amalgamaize Co., **14** 18

Amalgamated Chemicals, Ltd., **IV** 401

Amalgamated Dental International, **10** 271–72

Amalgamated Distilled Products, **II** 609

Amalgamated Press, **IV** 666; **7** 244, 342; **17** 397

Amalgamated Roadstone Corp., **III** 752

Amalgamated Sugar Co., **14** 18; **19** 467–68

Amalgamated Weatherware, **IV** 696

Amana, **18** 226

Amana Refrigeration, **II** 86; **11** 413

Amaray International Corporation, **12** 264

Amarillo Railcar Services, **6** 580

Amarin Plastics, **IV** 290

AMAX Inc., I 508; **III** 687; **IV 17–19**, 46, 139, 171, 239, 387; **6** 148; **12** 244; **22** 106, 286

Amazôna Mineracao SA, **IV** 56

Ambac Industries, **I** 85

AmBase Corp., **III** 264

Amber's Stores, Inc., **17** 360

Amblin Entertainment, 21 23–27

Ambrose Shardlow, **III** 494

AMC Entertainment Inc., 12 12–14; 14 87; **21** 362; **23** 126

AMCA International Corporation, **7** 513; **8** 545; **10** 329; **23** 299

Amchem Products Inc., **I** 666

AMCO, Inc., **13** 159

Amcor Limited, IV 248–50; 19 13–16 (upd.)

Amcraft Building Products Co., Inc., **22** 15

AMD. *See* Advanced Micro Devices, Inc.

Amdahl Corporation, III 109–11, 140; **6** 272; **12** 238; **13** 202; **14 13–16 (upd.); 16** 194, 225–26; **22** 293
AME Finanziaria, **IV** 587; **19** 19
AMEC, **I** 568
Amedco, **6** 295
Amer Sport, **22** 202
Amerada Hess Corporation, IV 365–67, 400, 454, 522, 571, 658; **11** 353; **21 28–31 (upd.)**
Amerco, 6 351–52
Ameri-Kart Corp., **19** 277, 279
America Japan Sheet Glass Co., **III** 714
America Latina Companhia de Seguros, **III** 289
America Online, Inc., 10 56–58, 237; **13** 147; **15** 54, 265, 321; **18** 24; **19** 41; **22** 52, 519, 522
America Publishing Company, **18** 213
America Today, **13** 545
America Unplugged, **18** 77
America West Airlines, 6 72–74, 121
American & Efird, Inc., **12** 501; **23** 260
American Agricultural Chemical Co., **IV** 401
American Airlines, I 30–31, 48, 71, **89–91,** 97, 106, 115, 118, 124–26, 130, 132, 512, 530; **III** 102; **6** 60, 81, **75–77 (upd.),** 121, 129–31; **9** 271–72; **10** 163; **11** 279; **12** 190, 192, 379, 381, 487, **13** 173; **14** 73; **16** 146; **18** 73; **21** 141, 143
American Alliance Co., **III** 191
American Allsafe Co., **8** 386
American Amusements, Inc., **III** 430
American Appliance Co., **II** 85; **11** 411
American Arithmometer Company. *See* Burroughs Corporation.
American Asiatic Underwriters, **III** 195
American Association of Retired Persons, **9** 348
American Automar Inc., **12** 29
American Automated, **11** 111
American Automobile Insurance Co., **III** 251
American Aviation and General Insurance Co., **III** 230
American Aviation Manufacturing Corp., **15** 246
American Avitron Inc, **I** 481
American Bakeries Company, **12** 275–76
American Bancorp, **11** 295
American Bancshares, Inc., **11** 457
American Bank, **9** 474–75
American Bank Note, **IV** 599
American Bank of Vicksburg, **14** 41
American Bankcorp, Inc., **8** 188
American Banker/Bond Buyer, **8** 526
American Barge and Towing Company, **11** 194
American Beauty Cover Company, **12** 472
American Beef Packers, Inc., **16** 473
American Beet Sugar Company, **11** 13–14
American Bell Telephone Company, **V** 259; **14** 336
American Beryllium Co., Inc., **9** 323
American Beverage Corp., **II** 528
American Biltrite Inc., 16 16–18; 18 116, 118
American Biodyne Inc., **9** 348
American Biomedical Corporation, **11** 333
American Biscuit Co., **II** 542
American Box Board Company, **12** 376
American Box Co., **IV** 137

American Brake Shoe and Foundry Company, **I** 456. *See also* ABC Rail Products Corporation.
American Brands, Inc., II 468, 477; **IV** 251; **V 395–97,** 398–99, 405; **7** 3–4; **9** 408; **12** 87, 344; **14** 95, 271–72; **16** 108, 110, 242; **19** 168–69
American Bridge Co., **II** 330; **IV** 572; **7** 549
American Broadcasting Co. *See* ABC, Inc. *and* Capital Cities/ABC Inc.
American Builders & Contractors Supply Co. *See* ABC Supply Co., Inc.
American Builders, Inc., **8** 436
American Building Maintenance Industries, Inc., 6 17–19
American Business Information, Inc., 18 21–25
American Business Interiors. *See* American Furniture Company, Inc.
American Business Products, Inc., 20 15–17
American Cable Systems, Inc. *See* Comcast Corporation.
American Cablesystems, **7** 99
American Cafe, **I** 547
American Can Co., **IV** 36, 290; **8** 476; **10** 130; **11** 29, 197; **12** 408; **13** 255; **15** 127–28; **17** 106; **22** 210; **23** 98. *See also* Primerica Corp.
American Car & Foundry Inc., **21** 503
American Carbide Corporation, **7** 584
American Cash Register Co., **III** 150; **6** 264
American Casualty Co., **III** 230–31, 404
American Casualty Co. of Dallas, **III** 203
American Cellular Network, **7** 91
American Cellulose and Chemical Manufacturing Co., **I** 317
American Cement Co. *See* Giant Cement Holding, Inc.
American Central Insurance Co., **III** 241
American Cereal Co., **II** 558; **12** 409
American Chicle Co., **I** 711; **21** 54
American Chocolate & Citrus Co., **IV** 409
American Chrome, **III** 699
American Classic Voyages, **22** 340
American Clay Forming Company, **8** 178
American Clip Company, **7** 3
American Colloid Co., 13 32–35
American Commercial Bank, **II** 336
American Commercial Lines Inc., **22** 164, 166–67
American Commonwealths Power Corporation, **6** 579
American Community Grocers, **II** 670
American Continental Insurance Co., **III** 191–92
American Cotton Cooperative Association, **17** 207
American Cotton Oil Co., **II** 497
American Council on Education, **12** 141
American Crayon Company, **12** 115
American Credit Corporation, **II** 236; **20** 59
American Crystal Sugar Company, 7 377; **11 13–15**
American Cyanamid, I 300–02, 619; **III** 22; **IV** 345, 552; **8 24–26 (upd.); 10** 269; **11** 494; **13** 231–32; **14** 254, 256; **16** 68; **22** 147
American Dairy Queen Corporation, **10** 373
American Data Technology, Inc., **11** 111

American Distilling Co., **I** 226; **10** 180–81
American District Telegraph Co., **III** 644; **12** 9
American Diversified Foods, Inc., **14** 351
American Drew, Inc., **12** 301
American Drug Company, **13** 367
American Eagle Fire Insurance Co., **III** 240–41
American Eagle Outfitters Inc., **14** 427
American Education Press, **10** 479
American Electric Company, **II** 27; **12** 193; **22** 10
American Electric Power Company, II 3; **IV** 181; **V 546–49; 6** 449, 524; **11** 516
American Empire Insurance Co., **III** 191
American Emulsions Co., **8** 455
American Encaustic Tiling Co., **22** 170
American Envelope Co., **III** 40; **16** 303
American Equipment Co., **I** 571
American Export Steamship Lines, **I** 89
American Express Company, I 26–27, 480, 614; **II** 108, 176, 309, 380–82, **395–99,** 450–52, 544; **III** 251–52, 319, 340, 389; **IV** 637, 721; **6** 206–07, 409; **8** 118; **9** 335, 343, 391, 468–69, 538; **10** 44–45, **59–64 (upd.); 11** 41, 416–17, 532; **12** 533; **14** 106; **15** 50; **18** 60, 112, 516, 543; **21** 97, 127; **23** 229
American Factors Ltd., **I** 417, 566
American Family Corporation, III 187–89. *See also* AFLAC Inc.
American Family Publishers, **23** 393–94
American Feldmühle Corp., **II** 51; **21** 330
American Filtrona Corp., **IV** 260–61
American Finance Systems, **II** 349
American Financial Corporation, II 596; **III 190–92,** 221; **8** 537; **9** 452; **18** 549
American First National Supermarkets, **16** 313
American Flavor & Fragrance Company, **9** 154
American Flyer Trains, **16** 336–37
American Food Management, **6** 45
American Fore Group, **III** 241–42
American Foreign Insurance Association, **III** 223, 226. *See also* AFIA.
American Forest Products Co., **IV** 282; **9** 260
American Fructose Corp., **14** 18–19
American Furniture Company, Inc., 12 300; **21 32–34**
American Gage Co., **I** 472
American Gas & Electric. *See* American Electric Power Company.
American Gasoline Co., **IV** 540
American General Capital Corp., **I** 614
American General Corporation, III 193–94; 10 65–67 (upd.); 11 16
American General Finance Corp., 11 16–17
American General Life Insurance Company, **6** 294
American Graphics, **23** 100
American Greetings Corporation, 7 23–25; 12 207–08; **15** 507; **16** 256; **21** 426–28; **22 33–36 (upd.)**
American Grinder and Manufacturing Company, **9** 26
American Harvester, **II** 262
American Heritage Savings, **II** 420
American Hoechst Corporation. *See* Hoechst Celanese Corporation.
American Hoist & Derrick Co., **8** 544

American Home Assurance Co., **III** 196–97

American Home Assurance Co. of New York, III 203

American Home Products, I 527, **622–24,** 631, 676–77, 696, 700; **III** 18, 36, 444; **8** 282–83; **10** 68–70 **(upd.),** 528; **11** 35; **15** 64–65; **16** 191, 438; **21** 466

American Home Publishing Co., Inc., **14** 460

American Home Shield, **6** 46; **23** 428, 430

American Home Video, **9** 186

American Homestar Corporation, 18 26–29

American Homeware Inc., **15** 501

American Honda Motor Co., **I** 174; **10** 352

American Hospital Association, **10** 159

American Hospital Supply Corp., **I** 627, 629; **III** 80; **10** 141–43; **11** 459, 486; **19** 103; **21** 118

American Hydron, **13** 366

American I.G. Chemical Corporation. *See* GAF Corporation.

American Impacts Corporation, **8** 464

American Improved Cements. *See* Giant Cement Holding, Inc.

American Independent Oil Co., **IV** 522, 537. *See also* Aminoil, Inc.

American Industrial Manufacturing Co., **I** 481

American Information Services, Inc., **11** 111

American Institutional Products, Inc., **18** 246

American Instrument Co., **I** 628; **13** 233

American Insurance Agency, **III** 191, 352

American Insurance Co., **III** 251

American International Airways, Inc., **17** 318; **22** 311

American International Group, Inc., II 422; **III** 195–98, 200; **6** 349; **10** 39; **11** 532–33; **15** 15–19 **(upd.);** 18 159

American International Travel Service, **6** 367

American Iron and Steel Manufacturing Co., **IV** 35; **7** 48

American Isuzu Motors, Inc. *See* Isuzu Motors, Ltd.

American Jet Industries, **7** 205

American Ka-Ro, **8** 476

American Knitting Mills of Miami, Inc., **22** 213

American La-France, **10** 296

American Laboratories, **III** 73

American Land Cruiser Company. *See* Cruise America Inc.

American Learning Corporation, **7** 168

American Life Insurance Co., **III** 195–96

American Light and Traction. *See* MCN Corporation.

American Lightwave Systems, Inc., **10** 19

American Limestone Co., **IV** 33

American Linseed Co, **II** 497

American Machine and Foundry Co., **II** 7; **III** 443; **7** 211–13; **11** 397

American Machine and Metals, **9** 23

American Machinist Press, **IV** 634

American Magnesium Products Co., **I** 404

American Maize-Products Co., 14 17–20; 23 464

American Management Systems, Inc., 11 18–20

American Manufacturers Mutual Insurance Co., III 269, 271; **15** 257

American Medical International, Inc., III 73–75, 79; **14** 232

American Medical Services, **II** 679–80; **14** 209

American Medicorp., **III** 81; **6** 191; **14** 432

American Merchandising Associates Inc., **14** 411

American Merchants Union Express Co., **II** 396

American Metal Climax, Inc. *See* AMAX.

American Metal Co. Ltd. *See* AMAX.

American Metal Products Company. *See* Lear Seating Corporation.

American Metal Products Corp., **I** 481

American Metals and Alloys, Inc., **19** 432

American Metals Corp., **III** 569; **20** 361

American Micro Devices, Inc., **16** 549

American Microsystems, **I** 193

American Milk Products Corp., **II** 487

The American Mineral Spirits Company, **8** 99–100

American Motorists Insurance Co., **III** 269, 271; **15** 257

American Motors Corp., I 135–37, 145, 152, 190; **II** 60, 313; **III** 543; **6** 27, 50; **8** 373; **10** 262, 264; **18** 493

American Movie Classics Co., **II** 161

American Multi-Cinema. *See* AMC Entertainment Inc.

American National Bank, **13** 221–22

American National Bank and Trust Co., **II** 286

American National Can Co., **III** 536; **IV** 173, 175

American National Corp., **II** 286

American National Fire Insurance Co., **III** 191

American National General Agencies Inc., **III** 221; **14** 109

American National Insurance Company, 8 27–29

American Natural Resources Co., **I** 678; **IV** 395; **13** 416

American Newspaper Publishers Association, **6** 13

American of Philadelphia, **III** 234

American Oil Co., **IV** 369–70; **7** 101; **14** 22

American Olean Tile Company, **III** 424; **22** 48, 170

American Optical Co., **I** 711–12; **III** 607; **7** 436

American Overseas Airlines, **12** 380

American Overseas Holdings, **III** 350

American Pad & Paper Company, 20 18–21

American Paging, **9** 494–96

American Paper Box Company, **12** 376

American Patriot Insurance, **22** 15

American Payment Systems, Inc., **21** 514

American Petrofina, Inc., **IV** 498; **7** 179–80; **19** 11

American Phone Centers, Inc., **21** 135

American Photographic Group, **III** 475; **7** 161

American Physicians Service Group, Inc., **6** 45; **23** 430

American Platinum Works, **IV** 78

American Postage Meter Co., **III** 156

American Potash and Chemical Corporation, **IV** 95, 446; **22** 302

American Power & Light Co., **6** 545, 596–97; **12** 542

American Premier Underwriters, Inc., 10 71–74

American Prepaid Professional Services, Inc. *See* CompDent Corporation.

American President Companies Ltd., III 512; **6 353–55**

American Protective Mutual Insurance Co. Against Burglary, **III** 230

American Publishing Co., **IV** 597

American Pure Oil Co., **IV** 497

American Radiator & Standard Sanitary Corp., **III** 663–64

American Railway Express Co., **II** 382, 397; **10** 61

American Railway Publishing Co., **IV** 634

American Re Corporation, III 182; **10 75–77**

American Record Corp., **II** 132

American Recreation Company Holdings, Inc., **16** 53

American Ref-Fuel, **V** 751

American Refrigeration Products S.A, **7** 429

American Republic Assurance Co., **III** 332

American Research and Development Corp., **III** 132; **6** 233; **19** 103

American Residential Mortgage Corporation, 8 30–31

American Resorts Group, **III** 103

American Rice, Inc., **17** 161–62

American River Transportation Co., **I** 421; **11** 23

American Robot Corp., **III** 461

American Rolling Mill Co., **IV** 28; **8** 176–77

American Royalty Trust Co., **IV** 84; **7** 188

American Rug Craftsmen, **19** 275

American RX Pharmacy, **III** 73

American Safety Equipment Corp., **IV** 136

American Safety Razor Company, III 27–29; **20 22–24**

American Saint-Gobain, **16** 121

American Sales Book Co., Ltd., **IV** 644

American Salt Co., **12** 199

American Satellite Co., **6** 279; **15** 195

American Savings & Loan, **10** 117

American Savings Bank, **9** 276; **17** 528, 531

American Sealants Company. *See* Loctite Corporation.

American Seating Co., **I** 447; **21** 33

American Seaway Foods, Inc, **9** 451

American Service Corporation, **19** 223

American Sheet Steel Co., **IV** 572; **7** 549

American Shipbuilding, **18** 318

American Smelting and Refining Co., **IV** 31–33

American Software, **22** 214

American Southern Insurance Co., **17** 196

American Standard Inc., III 437, **663–65; 19** 455; **22** 4, 6

American States Insurance Co., **III** 276

American Steamship Company, **6** 394–95

American Steel & Wire Co., **I** 355; **IV** 572; **7** 549; **13** 97–98

American Steel Foundries, **7** 29–30

American Stock Exchange, **10** 416–17

American Stores Company, II 604–06; 12 63, 333; **13** 395; **17** 559; **18** 89; **22 37–40 (upd.)**

American Sumatra Tobacco Corp., **15** 138

American Systems Technologies, Inc., **18** 5

American Teaching Aids Inc., 19 405
American Technical Services Company. *See* American Building Maintenance Industries, Inc.
American Telephone and Telegraph Company. *See* AT&T.
American Television and Communications Corp., I 534–35; II 161; IV 596, 675; 7 528–30; 18 65
American Textile Co., III 571; 20 362
American Thermos Bottle Company. *See* Thermos Company.
American Tile Supply Company, 19 233
American Tin Plate Co., IV 572; 7 549
American Title Insurance, III 242
American Tobacco Co., I 12–14, 28, 37, 425; V 395–97, 399, 408–09, 417–18, 600; 14 77, 79; 15 137–38; 16 242; 18 416. *See also* American Brands Inc. *and* B.A.T. Industries PLC.
American Tool & Machinery, III 420
American Tool Company, 13 563
American Totalisator Corporation, 10 319–20
American Tourister, Inc., 10 350; **13** 451, 453; **16 19–21**
American Tractor Corporation, 10 379
American Trading and Production Corporation, 7 101
American Transport Lines, 6 384
American Trust and Savings Bank, II 261
American Trust Co., II 336, 382; 12 535
American Twist Drill Co., 23 82
American Ultramar Ltd., IV 567
American Viscose Corp. *See* Avisco.
American Water Works Company, V 543–44; **6 443–45**
American Window Glass, 16 120
American Wood Reduction Company, 14 174
American Woolen, I 529
American Yard Products, 22 26, 28
American Yearbook Company, 7 255
American-Marietta Corp., I 68, 405
American-Palestine Trading Corp., II 205–06
American-South African Investment Co. Ltd., IV 79
American-Strevell Inc., II 625
Americana Entertainment Group, Inc., 19 435
Americana Foods, Inc., 17 474–75
Americana Healthcare Corp., 15 522
Americana Hotel, 12 316
America's Favorite Chicken Company, Inc., 7 26–28
AmeriFirst Bank, 11 258
Amerifirst Federal Savings, 10 340
AmeriGas Partners, L.P., 12 498
AmeriGas Propane, Inc., 12 500
Amerimark Inc., II 682
Amerisystems, 8 328
Ameritech Corporation, V 265–68; 6 248; 7 118; 10 431; 11 382; 12 137; 14 252–53, 257, 259–61, 364; 15 197; **18 30–34 (upd.)**
Ameritech Illinois. *See* Illinois Bell Telephone Company.
Ameritrust Corporation, 9 476
Ameriwood Industries International Corp., 17 15–17
Amerock Corp., 13 41
Amerotron, I 529
Amersil Co., IV 78

Ames Department Stores, Inc., V 197–98; **9 20–22; 10** 497; **15** 88; **19** 449
AMETEK, Inc., 9 23–25; 12 88
N.V. Amev, III 199–202
Amey Roadstone Corp., III 503; 7 209
AMF Bowling, Inc., 19 312; 23 450
Amfac Inc., I 417–18, 566; IV 703; 10 42; 23 320
Amfas, III 310
Amgen, Inc., I 266; 8 216–17; **10 78–81;** 13 240; 14 255; 21 320
Amherst Coal Co., IV 410; 7 309
Amiga Corporation, 7 96
Aminoil, Inc., IV 523. *See also* American Independent Oil Co.
AMISA, IV 136
Amisys Managed Care Information Systems, 16 94
Amitron S.A., 10 113
Amity Leather Products Company. *See* AR Accessories Group, Inc.
AMK Corporation, II 595; 7 85; 21 111
Amkor, 23 17
Ammirati Puris Lintas, 14 316; 22 294
Ammo-Phos, I 300; 8 24
L'Ammoniac Sarro-Lorrain S.a.r.l., IV 197
Amoco Corporation, I 516, 202; **II** 376; **III** 611; **IV 368–71,** 412, 424–25, 453, 525; 7 107, 443; 10 83–84; 11 441; 12 18; **14 21–25 (upd.),** 494; 18 365; 19 297
Amoseas, IV 453–54
Amoskeag Company, 6 356; **8 32–33;** 9 213–14, 217; 22 54
Amot Controls Corporation, 15 404
AMP, Inc., II 7–8; 11 319; 13 344; **14 26–28 (upd.);** 17 274; 22 542
Ampad Holding Corporation. *See* American Pad & Paper Company.
AMPAL. *See* American-Palestine Trading Corp.
AMPCO Auto Parks, Inc. *See* American Building Maintenance Industries, Inc.
AMPEP, III 625
Ampex Corporation, III 549; **6** 272; **17 18–20**
Ampol Ltd., III 729
AMR Corp., I 90–91; 6 76; 8 315; 22 252
AMR Information Services, 9 95
Amram's Distributing Limited, 12 425
AMRE, III 211
AMREP Corporation, I 563; **21 35–37**
Amro. *See* Amsterdam-Rotterdam Bank N.V.
AMS Trading Co., III 112
AmSouth Bancorporation, 12 15–17
Amstar Corp., 14 18
Amstar Sugar, II 582; 7 466–67
Amsted Industries Incorporated, 7 29–31
Amstel Brewery, I 257
Amsterdam-Rotterdam Bank N.V., II 184, **185–86,** 279, 295, 319; **III** 200; **14** 169; **17** 324
Amstrad plc, III 112–14
Amtec Systems Corp., 11 65
Amtech. *See* American Building Maintenance Industries, Inc.
Amtel, Inc., 8 545; 10 136
Amtliches Bayerisches Reisebüro, II 163
Amtorg, 13 365
Amtrak, II 2; 10 73; 19 141. *See also* National Railroad Passenger Corporation.
AmTrans. *See* American Transport Lines.

Amway Corporation, III 11–14; 13 36–39 (upd.); 17 186; 18 67, 164; 20 435; 23 509
Amylum, II 582
ANA Enterprises, Ltd., 6 70
Anacomp, Inc., 11 19
Anaconda Aluminum, 11 38
Anaconda Co., III 644; IV 33, 376; 7 261–63
Anaconda-Jurden Associates, 8 415
Anadarko Petroleum Corporation, 10 82–84
Anadex, Inc., 18 435–36
Anaheim Imaging, 19 336
Analog Devices, Inc., 10 85–87; 18 20; **19** 67
Analogic Corporation, 23 13–16
Analytic Sciences Corporation, 10 88–90; 13 417
Anam Group, 21 239; **23 17–19**
Anamax Mining Co., IV 33
AnAmo Co., IV 458
Anarad, Inc., 18 515
ANB Bank, I 55
Anchor Bancorp, Inc., 10 91–93
Anchor Brake Shoe, 18 5
Anchor Cable, III 433
Anchor Corporation, 12 525
Anchor Hocking Glassware, I 609–10; **13 40–42; 14** 483
Anchor Motor Freight, Inc., 12 309–10
Anchor National Financial Services, Inc., 11 482
Anchor National Life Insurance Company, 11 482
Anchor Oil and Gas Co., IV 521
Anchor Records, II 130
Ancienne Mutuelle, III 210
Anders Wilhelmsen & Co., 22 471
Andersen Consulting, 9 344; 11 305
Andersen Corporation, 10 94–95; 22 346
Anderson & Kerr Drilling Co., IV 445
Anderson and Campbell, II 479
Anderson Box Co., IV 342; 8 267
Anderson Clayton & Co., II 560; 12 411
Anderson, Greenwood & Co., 11 225–26
Anderson Testing Company, Inc., 6 441
Anderton, III 624
Andes Candies, II 520–21
Andian National Corp. Ltd., IV 415–16
André Courrèges, III 47; 8 342–43
Andreas Stihl, 16 22–24
Andrew Corporation, 10 96–98
Andrew Jergens Co., III 38
Andrew Weir & Co., III 273
Andrews, Clark & Company, IV 426; 7 169
Andrews Group, Inc., 10 402
Anfor, IV 249–50
Angele Ghigi, II 475
Angelica Corporation, 15 20–22
Angelo's Supermarkets, Inc., II 674
ANGI Ltd., 11 28
Anglo American Corporation of South Africa Limited, I 289, 423; **IV 20–23,** 56–57, 64–68, 79–80, 90, 92, 94–96, 118–20, 191, 239–40; 7 121–23, 125; **16 25–30 (upd.),** 292; 21 211, 354; 22 233
Anglo American Paper Co., IV 286
Anglo Company, Ltd., 9 363
Anglo Energy, Ltd., 9 364
Anglo Mexican Petroleum Co. Ltd., IV 657

Anglo-American Chewing Gum Ltd., **II** 569

Anglo-American Clays Corp., **III** 691; **IV** 346

Anglo-American Oil Company Limited, **IV** 427; **7** 170

Anglo-American Telegraph Co., **IV** 668

Anglo-Belge, **II** 474

Anglo-Canadian, **III** 704

Anglo-Canadian Mining & Refining, **IV** 110

Anglo-Canadian Telephone Company of Montreal. *See* British Columbia Telephone Company.

Anglo-Dutch Unilever group, **9** 317

Anglo-Egyptian D.C.O., **II** 236

Anglo-Egyptian Oilfields, **IV** 412, 414

Anglo-Elementar-Versicherungs-AG, **III** 185

Anglo-Huronian Ltd., **IV** 164

Anglo-Iranian Oil Co., **IV** 379, 419, 435, 450, 466, 559; **7** 57, 141; **21** 81

Anglo-Lautaro Nitrate Corporation, **9** 363

Anglo-Palestine Co., **II** 204

Anglo-Persian Oil Co., **IV** 363, 378–79, 381, 429, 450, 466, 515, 524, 531, 557–59; **7** 56–57, 140; **21** 80–81

Anglo-Swiss Condensed Milk Co., **II** 545

Anglo-Thai Corp., **III** 523

Anglo-Transvaal Consolidated, **IV** 534

Anglovaal Industries Ltd., **20** 263

Angus Hill Holdings, **IV** 249

Anheuser-Busch Company, Inc., I 32, **217–19**, 236–37, 254–55, 258, 265, 269–70, 290–91, 598; **IV** 624; **6** 20–21, 48; **9** 100; **10 99–101 (upd.)**, 130; **11** 421; **12** 337–38; **13** 5, 10, 258, 366; **15** 429; **17** 256; **18** 65, 70, 72–73, 499, 501; **19** 221, 223; **21** 229, 319–20; **22** 421; **23** 403

ANIC Gela, **IV** 421

Anikem, **I** 374

Anitec Image Technology Corp., **IV** 287; **15** 229

Ann Taylor Stores Corporation, V 26–27; **13 43–45**; **15** 9

Annabelle's, **II** 480–81

Anne Klein, **15** 145–46

Annuaries Marcotte Ltd., **10** 461

Anocout Engineering Co., **23** 82

Anonima Infortunia, **III** 208

ANR Pipeline Co., 17 21–23

Ansa Software, **9** 81

Ansaldo, **II** 191

Anshacher-Siegle Corp., **13** 460

Anschütz & Co. GmbH, **III** 446

Anschutz Corp., 12 18–20

Anschütz-Kaempfe, **III** 446

Ansell, **I** 215

Ansell Rubber Company, **10** 445

Anselmo L. Morvillo S.A., **19** 336

Ansett Airlines, **6** 73; **14** 11

Ansett Transport Industries Limited, **V** 523–25

Ansonia Brass and Battery Co., **IV** 176–77

Ansonia Manufacturing Co., **IV** 176

Ant Nachrichtentechnik GmbH., **I** 411

Anta Corporation, **6** 188

Antar group, **IV** 544, 546

Antares Alliance Group, **14** 15

Antares Electronics, Inc., **10** 257

Ante Corp., **22** 222

ANTEX. *See* American National Life Insurance Company of Texas.

Anthem Electronics, Inc., **13 46–47**; **17** 276

Anthem P&C Holdings, **15** 257

Anthes Imperial Ltd., **I** 274

Anthes Industries Inc., **9** 512

Anthony Industries Inc. *See* K2 Inc.

Anthony Stumpf Publishing Company, **10** 460

Anthropologie, **14** 524–25

Antillaase Bank-Unie N.V., **II** 184

Antique Street Lamps, **19** 212

Antoine Saladin, **III** 675

Antwerp Co., **IV** 497

ANZ. *See* Australia and New Zealand Banking Group Ltd.

Anzon Ltd., **III** 681

AOE Plastic GmbH, **7** 141

Aoki Corporation, **9** 547, 549

AOL. *See* America Online, Inc.

Aon Corporation, III 203–05; **22** 495

AP. *See* The Associated Press.

AP Bank, Ltd., **13** 439

AP&L. *See* American Power & Light Co.

AP-Dow Jones/Telerate Company, **10** 277

APAC, Inc., **IV** 374

Apache Corp., 10 102–04; **11** 28; **18** 366

APACHE Medical Systems, Inc., **16** 94

Apex, **17** 363

Apex Financial Corp., **8** 10

Apex Smelting Co., **IV** 18

Apita, **V** 210

APL. *See* American President Companies Ltd.

APL Corporation, **9** 346

Apline Guild, **12** 173

Aplix, **19** 477

APM Ltd., **IV** 248–49

Apogee Enterprises, Inc., 8 34–36; **22** 347

Apollo Advisors L.P., **16** 37

Apollo Apparel Partners, L.P., **12** 431

Apollo Computer, **III** 143; **6** 238; **9** 471; **11** 284

Apollo Heating & Air Conditioning Inc., **15** 411

Apollo Ski Partners LP of New York, **11** 543, 545

Apollo Technologies, **I** 332

Apotekarnes Droghandel A.B., **I** 664–65

Apothekernes Laboratorium A.S., **12** 3–5

Appalachian Computer Services, **11** 112

Applause Licensing Co., **17** 461

Apple Computer, Inc., II 6, 62, 103, 107, 124; **III** 114, **115–16**, 121, 125, 149, 172; **6 218–20 (upd.)**, 222, 225, 231, 244, 248, 254–58, 260, 289; **8** 138; **9** 166, 170–71, 368, 464; **10** 22–23, 34, 57, 233, 235, 404, 458–59, 518–19; **11** 45, 50, 57, 62, 490; **12** 139, 183, 335, 449, 455, 470; **13** 90, 388, 482; **16** 195, 367–68, 372, 417–18; **18** 93, 511, 521; **20** 31; **21** 391; **23** 209

Apple Container Corp., **III** 536

Apple South, **21** 362

Applebee's International Inc., 14 29–31; **19** 258; **20** 159; **21** 362

Appleton & Cox, **III** 242

Appleton Papers, **I** 426

Appleton Wire Works Corp., **8** 13

Appliance Buyers Credit Corp., **III** 653

Les Applications du Roulement, **III** 623

Applied Beverage Systems Ltd., **21** 339

Applied Bioscience International, Inc., 10 105–07

Applied Color Systems, **III** 424

Applied Communications, Inc., **6** 280; **11** 151

Applied Data Research, Inc., **6** 225; **18** 31–32

Applied Digital Data Systems Inc., **II** 83; **9** 514

Applied Engineering Services, Inc. *See* The AES Corporation.

Applied Films Laboratory Inc., **12** 121

Applied Industrial Materials Corporation, **22** 544, 547

Applied Komatsu Technology, Inc., **10** 109

Applied Learning International, **IV** 680

Applied Materials, Inc., 10 108–09; **18** 382–84

Applied Power, Inc., 9 26–28

Applied Programming Technologies, Inc., **12** 61

Applied Solar Energy, **8** 26

Applied Technology Corp., **11** 87

Approvisionnement Atlantique, **II** 652

Appryl, **I** 303

Aprilia SpA, 17 24–26

APS. *See* Arizona Public Service Company.

APS Healthcare, **17** 166, 168

Apura GmbH, **IV** 325

APUTCO, **6** 383

Aqua Glass, **III** 570; **20** 362

Aqua Pure Water Co., **III** 21

Aqua-Chem, Inc., **I** 234; **10** 227

Aquafin N.V., **12** 443

Aquarium Supply Co., **12** 230

Aquarius Group, **6** 207

Aquila, **IV** 486

Aquila Energy Corp., **6** 593

Aquitaine. *See* Société Nationale des Petroles d'Aquitaine.

AR Accessories Group, Inc., 23 20–22

AR-TIK Systems, Inc., **10** 372

ARA Services, II 607–08; **21** 507

Arab Contractors, **III** 753

Arab Japanese Insurance Co., **III** 296

Arab Petroleum Pipeline Co., **IV** 412

Arabian American Oil Co., **I** 570; **IV** 386, 429, 464–65, 512, 536–39, 552, 553, 559; **7** 172, 352; **14** 492–93. *See also* Saudi Arabian Oil Co.

Arabian Gulf Oil Co., **IV** 454

Arabian Investment Banking Corp., **15** 94

Arabian Oil Co., **IV** 451

Aral, **IV** 487

Aramark Corporation, 13 48–50; **16** 228; **21** 114–15

Aramco. *See* Arabian American Oil Co. *and* Saudi Arabian Oil Company.

Arapuā. *See* Lojas Arapuā S.A.

Aratex Inc., **13** 49

Aratsu Sekiyu, **IV** 554

ARBED S.A., IV 24–27, 53; **22 41–45 (upd.)**

Arbitron Corp., **III** 128; **10** 255, 359; **13** 5

Arbor Acres, **13** 103

Arbor Drugs Inc., 12 21–23

Arbor International, **18** 542

Arbor Living Centers Inc., **6** 478

Arbuthnot & Co., **III** 522

Arby's Inc., II 614; **8 536–37**; **14 32–34**, 351

ARC. *See* American Rug Craftsmen.

ARC Ltd., **III** 501

ARC Materials Corp., **III** 688

ARC Propulsion, **13** 462

Arcadia Company, **14** 138
Arcadia Partners, **17** 321
Arcadian Corporation, **18** 433
Arcadian Marine Service, Inc., **6** 530
Arcata Corporation, **12** 413
Arcata National Corp., **9** 305
Arcelik, **I** 478
Arch Mineral Corporation, **IV** 374; **7**
    32–34
Archbold Ladder Co., **12** 433
Archer Drug, **III** 10
Archer-Daniels-Midland Co., **I** 419–21;
    IV 373; **7** 432–33;, 241 **8** 53; **11** 21–23
    (upd.); **17** 207; **22** 85, 426; **23** 384
Archers Gilles & Co., **II** 187
ARCO. See Atlantic Richfield Company.
ARCO Chemical Company, **IV** 376–77,
    456–57; **10** 110–11
Arco Electronics, **9** 323
Arco Societa Per L'Industria Elettrotecnica,
    II 82
Arctco, Inc., **12** 400–01; **16 31–34**
Arctic, **III** 479
Arctic Alaska Fisheries Corporation, **14**
    515
ARD. See American Research &
    Development.
Ardal og Sunndal Verk AS, **10** 439
Ardent Computer Corp., **III** 553
Areal Technologies, **III** 715
Argbeit-Gemeinschaft Lurgi und
    Ruhrchemie, **IV** 534
Argentine National Bank, **14** 46
Argo Communications Corporation, **6** 300
Argon Medical, **12** 327
Argonaut, **I** 523–24; **10** 520–22
Argos, **I** 426; **22** 72
Argosy Gaming Company, **21 38–41**
Argus Chemical Co., **I** 405
Argus Corp., **IV** 22, 272, 611
Argus Energy, **7** 538
Argus Motor Company, **16** 7
Argyle Television Inc., **19** 204
Argyll Group PLC, **I** 241; **II 609–10**,
    656; **12** 152–53
Aris Industries, Inc., **15** 275; **16 35–38**
Aristech Chemical Corp., **12** 342
Arizona Airways, **22** 219
Arizona Copper Co., **IV** 177
Arizona Edison Co., **6** 545
Arizona Growth Capital, Inc., **18** 513
Arizona Public Service Company, **6**
    545–47; **19** 376, 412
Arizona Refrigeration Supplies, **14** 297–98
Arjo Wiggins Appleton, **13** 458
Ark Restaurants Corp., **20 25–27**
Ark Securities Co., **II** 233
Arkady Co., Ltd., **I** 421; **11** 23
Arkansas Best Corporation, **16 39–41**;
    19 455
Arkansas Breeders, **II** 585
Arkansas Chemicals Inc., **I** 341
Arkansas Louisiana Gas Company. See
    Arkla, Inc.
Arkansas Power & Light, **V** 618
Arkay Computer, **6** 224
ARKE, **II** 164
Arkia, **23** 184, 186–87
Arkla, Inc., **V 550–51**; **11** 441
Arlesey Lime and Portland Cement Co.,
    III 669
Arlington Corporation, **6** 295
Arlington Motor Holdings, **II** 587
Armaturindistri, **III** 569

Armco Inc., **III** 259, 721; **IV 28–30**, 125,
    171; **10** 448; **11** 5, 255; **12** 353; **19** 8
Armin Corp., **III** 645
Armin Poly Film Corp., **III** 645
Armitage Shanks, **III** 671
Armor All Products Corp., **12** 333; **15**
    507; **16 42–44**; **22** 148
Armor Elevator, **11** 5
Armour & Company, **8** 144; **12** 198; **13**
    21, 506; **23** 173
Armour Food Co., **I** 449–50, 452; **II** 494,
    518; **12** 81, 370; **13** 270
Armour Pharmaceutical Co., **III** 56
Armour-Dial, **I** 14; **8** 144; **23** 173–74
Armstrong Advertising Co., **I** 36
Armstrong Air Conditioning Inc., **8**
    320–22
Armstrong Autoparts, **III** 495
Armstrong Communications, **IV** 640
Armstrong Cork Co., **18** 118
Armstrong Nurseries, **I** 272
Armstrong Rees Ederer Inc., **IV** 290
Armstrong Tire Co., **15** 355
Armstrong, Whitworth & Co. Ltd., **I** 50;
    III 508; **IV** 257
Armstrong World Industries, Inc., **III**
    422–24; **9** 466; **12** 474–75; **22 46–50**
    (upd.), 170–71
Armstrong-Siddeley Co., **III** 508
Armtek, **7** 297
Army Cooperative Fire Insurance
    Company, **10** 541
Army Ordnance, **19** 430
Army Signal Corps Laboratories, **10** 96
Arndale, **IV** 696
Arno Press, **IV** 648; **19** 285
Arnold Electric Company, **17** 213
Arnold Foods Co., **II** 498
Arnold, Schwinn & Company. See
    Schwinn Cycle and Fitness L.P.
Arnold Thomas Co., **9** 411
Arnoldo Mondadori Editore S.p.A., **IV**
    585–88, 675; **19 17–21** (upd.)
Arnotts Ltd., **II** 481
Aro Corp., **III** 527; **14** 477, 508; **15** 225
Aromat Corporation, **III** 710; **7** 303
Aromatic Industries, **18** 69
Arpet Petroleum, **III** 740; **IV** 550
Arpic, **III** 426
Arrow Electronics, Inc., **10 112–14**; **13**
    47; **19** 310–11, 313
Arrow Food Distributor, **II** 675
Arrow Furniture Co., **21** 32
Arrow Oil Co., **IV** 401
Arrow Oil Tools, **III** 570; **20** 360
Arrow Pump Co., **I** 185
Arrow Specialty Company, **III** 570; **20** 360
Arrowsmith & Silver, **I** 428
A.B. Arsenalen, **II** 352
Artec, **III** 420; **12** 297
Artech Digital Entertainments, Inc., **15** 133
Artek Systems Corporation, **13** 194
Artesian Manufacturing and Bottling
    Company, **9** 177
Artex Enterprises, **7** 256
**Arthur Andersen & Company, Société
    Coopérative**, **III** 143; **6** 244; **10**
    115–17, 174; **16** 92
Arthur D. Little, **IV** 494; **10** 139, 174–75
Arthur Ovens Motor Freight Co., **6** 371
Arthur Tappan & Co., **IV** 604
Arthur Young & Company, **IV** 119; **10**
    386; **19** 311. See also Ernst & Young.
Artisoft, Inc., **18** 143

Artists & Writers Press, Inc., **13** 560
Arts & Entertainment Network, **IV** 627; **19**
    204
Arvey Corp., **IV** 287
Arvida Corp., **IV** 703
Arvin Industries, Inc., **8 37–40**
ASAB, **III** 480
Asahi Breweries, Ltd., **I 220–21**, 282,
    520; **13** 454; **20 28–30** (upd.); **21** 230,
    319–20
Asahi Chemical Industry Co., **I** 221; **III**
    760; **IV** 326
Asahi Corporation, **16** 84
Asahi Glass Company, Limited, **I** 363;
    III 666–68; **11** 234–35
Asahi Kasei Industry Co. Ltd., **IV** 476
Asahi Komag Co., Ltd., **11** 234
Asahi Kyoei Co., **I** 221
Asahi Manufacturing, **III** 592
Asahi Milk Products, **II** 538
**Asahi National Broadcasting Company,
    Ltd.**, **9 29–31**
Asahi Oil, **IV** 542
Asahi Real Estate Facilities Co., Ltd., **6**
    427
Asahi Seiko, **III** 595
Asahi Shimbun, **9** 29–30
Asahi Trust & Banking, **II** 323
Asano Group, **III** 718
Asanté Technologies, Inc., **20 31–33**
ASARCO Incorporated, **I** 142; **IV 31–34**
ASB Agency, Inc., **10** 92
Asbury Associates Inc., **22** 354–55
Aschaffenburger Zellstoffwerke AG, **IV**
    323–24
ASCO Healthcare, Inc., **18** 195–97
Asco Products, Inc., **22** 413
Ascom AG, **9 32–34**; **15** 125
Ascometal, **IV** 227
Ascotts, **19** 122
ASD, **IV** 228
Asda Group PLC, **II 611–12**, 513, 629;
    11 240
ASEA AB. See ABB ASEA Brown Boveri
    Ltd.
Asean Bintulu Fertilizer, **IV** 518
Asepak Corp., **16** 339
A.B. Asesores Bursatiles, **III** 197–98; **15**
    18
ASF. See American Steel Foundries.
Asgrow Florida Company, **13** 503
Ash Company, **10** 271
Ashitaka Rinsan Kogyo, **IV** 269
Ashland Inc., **19 22–25**
Ashland Iron and Mining Co., **IV** 28
Ashland Oil, Inc., **I** 420; **IV** 71, 198, 366,
    372–74, 472, 658; **7** 32–33; **8** 99; **9**
    108; **11** 22; **18** 279
Ashton Joint Venture, **IV** 60, 67
Ashton Mining, **IV** 60
Ashton-Tate Corporation, **9** 81–82; **10**
    504–05
Asia Life Insurance Co., **III** 195–96
Asia Oil Co., Ltd., **IV** 404, 476
Asia Television, **IV** 718
Asia Terminals Ltd., **IV** 718
Asiatic Petroleum Co., **IV** 434, 530
Asil çelik, **I** 479
ASK Group, Inc., **9 35–37**
Ask Mr. Foster Agency, **22** 127
Asland SA, **III** 705, 740
Aso Cement, **III** 705
**Aspect Telecommunications
    Corporation**, **16** 392–93; **22 51–53**

Aspen Imaging International, Inc., **17** 384
Aspen Mountain Gas Co., **6** 568
Aspen Skiing Company, II 170; **15 23–26**, 234
Aspen Systems, **14** 555
Asplundh Tree Expert Co., 20 34–36
Assam Co. Ltd., **III** 522–23
Assam Oil Co., **IV** 441, 483–84
L'Assicuratrice Italiana, **III** 346–47
Assicurazioni Generali SpA, II 192; **III 206–09**, 211, 296, 298; **14** 85; **15 27–31 (upd.)**
Associate Venture Investors, **16** 418
Associated Anglo-Atlantic Corp., **III** 670
Associated Aviation Underwriters, **III** 220
Associated Banks of Europe Corp., **II** 184, 239
Associated Biscuit Co., **II** 631
Associated Book Publishers, **8** 527
Associated Bowater Industries, **IV** 258
Associated Brewing Co., **I** 254
Associated British Foods PLC, II 465–66, 565, 609; **11** 526; **13 51–53 (upd.)**
Associated British Maltsters, **II** 500
Associated British Picture Corporation, **I** 531; **II** 157; **22** 193
Associated City Investment Trust, **IV** 696
Associated Communications Companies, **7** 78; **23** 479
Associated Container Transportation, **23** 161
Associated Cooperative Investment Trust Ltd., **IV** 696
Associated Dairies Ltd., **II** 611
Associated Dry Goods, **V** 134; **12** 54–55
Associated Electrical Industries, Ltd., **II** 25; **III** 502
Associated Employers General Agency, **III** 248
Associated Food Holdings Ltd., **II** 628
Associated Fresh Foods, **II** 611–12
Associated Fuel Pump Systems Corp., **III** 593
Associated Gas & Electric Company, **V** 621, 629–30; **6** 534; **14** 124
Associated Gas Services, Inc., **11** 28
Associated Grocers, Incorporated, 9 38–40; **19** 301
Associated Grocers of Arizona, **II** 625
Associated Grocers of Colorado, **II** 670
The Associated Group, **10** 45
Associated Hospital Service of New York, **III** 245–46
Associated Iliffe Press, **IV** 666; **17** 397
Associated Indemnity Co., **III** 251
Associated Inns and Restaurants Company of America, **14** 106
Associated Insurance Cos., **III** 194
Associated International Insurance Co. *See* Gryphon Holdings, Inc.
Associated Lead Manufacturers Ltd., **III** 679, 680–81
Associated London Properties, **IV** 705
Associated Madison Insurance, **I** 614
Associated Merchandising Corp., **16** 215
Associated Milk Producers, Inc., 11 24–26
Associated National Insurance of Australia, **III** 309
Associated Natural Gas Corporation, 11 27–28
Associated Newspapers, **IV** 686; **19** 118, 120

Associated Octel Company Limited, **10** 290
Associated Oil Co., **IV** 460
Associated Pipeline Contractors, **III** 559
Associated Piping & Engineering Corp., **III** 535
Associated Portland Cement Manufacturers (1900) Ltd., **III** 669–71
The Associated Press, IV 629, 669–70; **7** 158; **10** 277; **13 54–56**
Associated Publishing Company, **19** 201
Associated Pulp & Paper Mills, **IV** 328
Associated Sales Agency, **16** 389
Associated Spring Co., **III** 581; **13** 73
Associated Stationers, **14** 521, 523
Associated Television, **7** 78
Associated Timber Exporters of British Columbia Ltd., **IV** 307
Associated TV, **IV** 666; **17** 397
Associates First Capital Corporation, **22** 207
Associates Investment Co., **I** 452
Assubel, **III** 273
Assurances du Groupe de Paris, **III** 211
Assurances Generales de France, **III** 351
AST Holding Corp., **III** 663, 665
AST Research, Inc., 9 41–43; **10** 459, 518–19; **12** 470; **18** 260
Asta Pharma AG, **IV** 71
Asta Werke AG, **IV** 71
Astech, **18** 370
Asteroid, **IV** 97
Astley & Pearce, **10** 277
Aston Brooke Software, **14** 392
Astor Holdings Inc., **22** 32
Astor Trust Co., **II** 229
Astra AB, I 625–26, 635, 651; **11** 290; **20 37–40 (upd.)**
Astra Resources, **12** 543
Astrolac, **IV** 498
Astrotech, **11** 429
Astrum International Corp., **12** 88; **13** 453; **16** 20–21
Asylum Life Assurance Co., **III** 371
Asylum Records, **23** 33
Asymetrix, **6** 259
AT&E Corp., **17** 430
AT&T Bell Laboratories, Inc., 13 57–59; **22** 17
AT&T Corp., I 462; **II** 13, 54, 61, 66, 80, 88, 120, 125, 252, 403, 430–31, 448; **III** 99, 110–11, 130, 145, 149, 160, 162, 167, 246, 282; **IV** 95, 287; **V 259–64**, 265–68, 269, 272–75, 302–04, 308–12, 318–19, 326–30, 334–36, 339, 341–342, 344–346; **6** 267, 299, 306–07, 326–27, 338–40; **7** 88, 118–19, 146, 288–89, 333; **8** 310–11; **9** 32, 43, 106–07, 138, 320, 321, 344, 478–80, 495, 514; **10** 19, 58, 87, 97, 175, 202–03, 277–78, 286, 431, 433, 455–57; **11** 10, 59, 91, 183, 185, 196, 198, 302, 395, 500–01; **12** 9, 135–36, 162, 544; **13** 212–13, 326, 402, 448; **14** 15, 95, 251–53, 257–61, 318, 336–37, 345, 347, 354, 363–64; **15** 125–26, 228, 455; **16** 223, 318, 368, 467; **18** 30, 32, 74, 76, 111–12, 155, 164–65, 368, 516–18, 569–70; **19** 12, 41; **20** 34, 313; **21** 70, 200–01, 514; **22** 51; **23** 135
AT&T Istel Ltd., 14 35–36
Ataka & Co., **I** 433; **II** 361

Atari Corporation, II 176; **III** 587; **IV** 676; **6** 244; **7** 395–96; **9 44–47**; **10** 284, 482, 485; **13** 472; **23 23–26 (upd.)**
ATC, **III** 760; **13** 280
Atchison, Topeka and Santa Fe Railroad, **V** 507–08; **12** 19–20
ATCO Ltd., **13** 132
ATD Group, **10** 113
ATE Investment, **6** 449
Atelier de Construction Electrique de Delle, **9** 9
ATEQ Corp., **III** 533
Atex, **III** 476; **7** 162; **10** 34
ATH AG, **IV** 221
Atha Tool Co., **III** 627
Athalon Products, Ltd., **10** 181; **12** 313
Athenia Steel Co., **13** 369
Athens National Bank, **III** 190
Athens Piraeus Electricity Co., **IV** 658
Athern, **16** 337
Athletic Attic, **19** 230
Athletic Shoe Company, **17** 243
Athletic Textile Company, Inc., **13** 532
Athletic X-Press, **14** 293
Athol Machine Co., **13** 301
ATI, **IV** 651; **7** 390
Atlalait, **19** 50
Atlanta Gas Light Company, 6 446–48; **23 27–30 (upd.)**
Atlanta National Bank, **16** 521
Atlanta Paper Co., **IV** 311; **19** 267
Atlantic & Pacific Tea Company (A&P). *See* Great Atlantic & Pacific Tea Company, Inc.
Atlantic Acceptance Corporation, **7** 95
Atlantic Aircraft Corp., **I** 34; **17** 197
Atlantic American Corp., **23** 413
Atlantic Cement Co., **III** 671
Atlantic Coast Carton Company, **19** 77
Atlantic Coast Line Railroad Company. *See* CSX Corporation.
Atlantic Computers, **14** 35
Atlantic Container Lines Ltd., **23** 161
Atlantic Energy, Inc., 6 449–50
The Atlantic Group, 23 31–33
Atlantic Gulf and Caribbean Airways, **I** 115
Atlantic Import, **I** 285
Atlantic Precision Instrument Company, **13** 234
Atlantic Precision Works, **9** 72
Atlantic Records, **II** 176; **18** 458
Atlantic Refining Co., **III** 497; **III** 498; **IV** 375–76, 456, 504, 566, 570
Atlantic Research Corp., **13** 462
Atlantic Richfield Company, I 452; **II** 90, 425; **III** 740; **IV 375–77**, 379, 435, 454, 456–57, 467, 494, 522, 536, 571; **7** 57, 108, 537–38, 558–59; **8** 184, 416; **10** 110; **13** 13, 341; **19** 175
Atlantic Sea Products, **13** 103
The Atlantic Seaboard Dispatch. *See* GATX.
Atlantic Securities Ltd., **II** 223; **III** 98
Atlantic Southern Properties, Inc., **6** 449–50
Atlantic Surety Co., **III** 396
Atlantic Transport Company, **19** 198
Atlantic Wholesalers, **II** 631
Atlantic-Union Oil, **IV** 570
Atlantis Group, Inc., **17** 16; **19** 50, 390
Atlantis Ltd., **II** 566
Atlas Assurance Co., **III** 370
Atlas Chemical Industries, **I** 353

Atlas Copco AB, III 425–27, 480; IV 203
Atlas Corp., I 58, 512; 10 316
Atlas Eléctrica S.A., 22 27
Atlas Hotels, Inc., V 164
Atlas Petroleum Ltd., IV 449
Atlas Plastics, 19 414
Atlas Powder Company, I 343–44; 22 260
Atlas Shipping, I 285
Atlas Steel Works, I 572
Atlas Steels, IV 191
Atlas Supply Co., IV 369
Atlas Tag & Label, 9 72
Atlas Van Lines, Inc., 14 37–39
Atlas Works, I 531
Atlas-Werke AG, IV 88
Atle Byrnestad, 6 368
Atmel Corporation, 17 32–34; 19 313
Atmos Lebensmitteltechnik, III 420
Atmospherix Ltd. See Blyth Industries, Inc.
ATO Chimie, I 303; IV 560
Atochem S.A., I 303–04, 676; IV 525, 547; 7 484–85
Atom-Energi, II 2; 22 9
ATR, 7 9, 11
ATS. See Magasins Armand Thiéry et Sigrand.
ATT Microelectrica España, V 339
Attachmate Corp., 11 520
Atwater McMillian. See St. Paul Companies, Inc.
Atwood Resources Inc., 17 372
Au Bon Pain Co., Inc., 18 35–38
Au Printemps S.A., V 9–11; 17 124. See also Pinault-Printemps-Redoute S.A.
Aubrey G. Lanston Co., II 301
Auchan, 10 205; 23 230
Audi, I 202; IV 570
Audio Development Company, 10 18
Audio/Video Affiliates, Inc., 10 468–69
Audiotronic Holdings, III 112
Aufina Bank, II 378
Aug. Stenman A.B., III 493
Aughton Group, II 466
Augsburger Aktienbank, III 377
Auguri Mondadori S.p.A., IV 586
August Max Woman, V 207–08
August Schell's Brewing Co., 22 421
August Thyssen-Hütte AG, IV 221–22
Auguste Metz et Cie, IV 24
Aunor Gold Mines, Ltd., IV 164
Aunt Fanny's Bakery, 7 429
Aurora Products, II 543
Aurora Systems, Inc., 21 135
Ausilio Generale di Sicurezza, III 206
Ausimont N.V., 8 271
Ausplay, 13 319
AUSSAT Ltd., 6 341
Aussedat-Rey, IV 288; 23 366, 368
The Austin Company, 8 41–44
Austin Motor Company, I 183; III 554; 7 458
Austin Nichols, I 248, 261, 280–81
Austin Rover, 14 321
Austin-Morris, III 494
Austral Waste Products, IV 248
Australasian Paper and Pulp Co. Ltd., IV 248
Australasian Sugar Co., III 686
Australasian United Steam Navigation Co., III 522
Australia and New Zealand Banking Group Ltd., II 187–90
Australia Gilt Co. Group, II 422
Australia National Bank, Limited, 10 170

Australian Airlines, 6 91, 112
Australian and Kandos Cement (Holdings) Ltd., III 687, 728
Australian and Overseas Telecommunications Corporation, 6 341–42
Australian Associated Press, IV 669
Australian Automotive Air, Pty. Ltd., III 593
Australian Blue Asbestos, III 687
Australian Consolidated Investments, Limited, 10 170
Australian Forest Products, I 438–39
Australian Guarantee Corp. Ltd., II 389–90
Australian Gypsum Industries, III 673
Australian Iron & Steel Company, IV 45; 22 105
Australian Metal Co., IV 139
Australian Mutual Provident Society, IV 61, 697
Australian Paper Co., IV 248
Australian Telecommunications Corporation, 6 342
Australian United Corp., II 389
Australian Window Glass, III 726
Austrian Industries, IV 485, 486
Austrian National Bank, IV 230
Austro-Americana, 6 425
Austro-Daimler, I 138, 206; 11 31
Authentic Fitness Corp., 16 511; 20 41–43
Auto Avio Costruzione, 13 219
Auto Coil Springs, III 581
Auto Ordnance Corporation, 19 430–31
Auto Shack. See AutoZone, Inc.
Auto Strop Safety Razor Co., III 27–28
Auto Union, I 150
Auto-Flo Corp., III 569; 20 360
Auto-Trol Technology, 14 15
Autodesk, Inc., 10 118–20
Autolite, I 29, 142; III 555
Autologic Information International, Inc., 20 44–46
Automat, II 614
Automated Building Components, III 735
Automated Communications, Inc., 8 311
Automated Loss Prevention Systems, 11 445
Automated Security (Holdings) PLC, 11 444
Automated Wagering Systems, III 128
Automatic Data Processing, Inc., III 117–19; 9 48–51 (upd.), 125, 173; 21 69
Automatic Fire Alarm Co., III 644
Automatic Manufacturing Corporation, 10 319
Automatic Payrolls, Inc., III 117
Automatic Retailers of America, Inc., II 607; 13 48
Automatic Sprinkler Corp. of America, 7 176–77
Automatic Telephone & Electric, II 81
Automatic Toll Systems, 19 111
Automatic Vaudeville Arcades Co., II 154
Automobile Insurance Co., III 181–82
Automobiles Citroen, I 162, 188; III 676; IV 722; V 237; 7 35–38; 11 103; 16 121, 420
Automobili Lamborghini S.p.A., 13 60–62, 219
Automotive Components Group Worldwide, 10 325
Automotive Diagnostics, 10 492

Automotive Group. See Lear Seating Corporation.
Automotive Industries Holding Inc., 16 323
Autonet, 6 435
Autophon AG, 9 32
Autotote Corporation, 20 47–49
AutoTrol Technology, III 111
AutoZone, Inc., 9 52–54
Avana Group, II 565
Avco. See Aviation Corp. of the Americas.
Avco Financial Services Inc., 13 63–65
Avco National Bank, II 420
Avecor Cardiovascular Inc., 8 347; 22 360
Avendt Group, Inc., IV 137
Avenir, III 393
Avery Dennison Corporation, IV 251–54; 15 229, 401; 17 27–31 (upd.), 445
Avesta Steel Works Co., I 553–54
Avfuel, 11 538
Avgain Marine A/S, 7 40
Avia Group International, Inc., V 376–77
Aviacion y Comercio, 6 95–96
AVIACO. See Aviacion y Comercio.
Aviation Corp. of the Americas, I 48, 78, 89, 115, 530; III 66; 6 75; 9 497–99; 10 163; 11 261, 427; 12 379, 383; 13 64
Aviation Power Supply, II 16
Avion Coach Corporation, I 76; III 484; 11 363; 22 206
Avions Marcel Dassault-Breguet Aviation, I 44–46; 7 11; 7 205; 8 314
Avis, Inc., I 30, 446, 463; II 468; III 502; IV 370; 6 348–49, 356–58, 392–93; 8 33; 9 284; 10 419; 11 198; 16 379–80; 22 524
Avis Rent A Car, Inc., 22 54–57 (upd.)
Avisco, I 317, 365, 442–43; V 359; 17 117
Avisun Corp., IV 371
Avnet Electronics Supply Co., 19 311, 313
Avnet Inc., 9 55–57; 10 112–13; 13 47
Avon Products, Inc., III 13, 15–16, 62; 8 329; 9 331; 11 282, 366; 12 314, 435; 13 38; 14 501–02; 17 186; 19 26–29 (upd.), 253; 21 49, 51
Avon Publications, Inc., IV 627; 19 201, 204
Avon Rubber plc, 23 146
Avoncraft Construction Co., I 512
Avondale Industries, Inc., I 512–14; 7 39–41
Avondale Mills, Inc., 8 558–60; 9 466
Avondown Properties Ltd., IV 711
Avro, I 81
AVS, III 200
Avtex Fibers Inc., I 443; 11 134
AVX Corporation, 21 329, 331
Award Foods, II 528
Awesome Transportation, Inc., 22 549
AXA, III 209, 210–12
Axa Group, 15 30
AXA/UAP/Equitable, 21 147
Axel Johnson Group, I 553–55
Axel Springer Verlag AG, IV 589–91; 20 50–53 (upd.); 23 86
Axelrod Foods, II 528
Axon Systems Inc., 7 336
Ayco Corp., II 398; 10 62
Aydin Corp., 19 30–32
Ayerst, I 623
Ayshire Collieries, IV 18
Azcon Corporation, 23 34–36

Azienda Generale Italiana Petroli. *See* Agip SpA.
Azienda Nazionale Idrogenazione Combustibili, **IV** 419–22
AZL Resources, **7** 538
Aznar International, **14** 225
Azon Limited, **22** 282
AZP Group Inc., **6** 546
Aztar Corporation, 13 66–68
Azteca, **18** 211, 213
Azuma Leather Co. Ltd., **V** 380
Azuma Shiki Manufacturing, **IV** 326
Azusa Valley Savings Bank, **II** 382

B & O. *See* Baltimore and Ohio Railroad.
B Ticino, **21** 350
B.A.T. Industries PLC, 14 77; **16** 242; **22 70–73 (upd.)**
B&Q, **V** 106, 108
B&W Diesel, **III** 513
B. B. & R. Knight Brothers, **8** 200
B.B. Foods, **13** 244
B-Bar-B Corp., **16** 340
B.C. Rail Telecommunications, **6** 311
B.C. Sugar, **II** 664
B. Dalton Bookseller, **10** 136; **13** 545; **16** 160; **18** 136
B-E Holdings, **17** 60
B.F. Ehlers, **I** 417
B.F. Goodrich Co. *See* The BFGoodrich Company.
B.F. Walker, Inc., **11** 354
B.I.C. America, **17** 15, 17
B.J.'s Wholesale, **12** 335
B. Perini & Sons, Inc., **8** 418
B.R. Simmons, **III** 527
B.S. Bull & Company. *See* Supervalu Inc.
B. Stroh Brewing Co., **I** 290
B.T.I. Chemicals Ltd., **I** 313; **10** 154
B.V. Tabak Export & Import Compagnie, **12** 109
BA. *See* British Airways.
BAA plc, 10 121–23
Babbage's, Inc., 10 124–25
Babcock & Wilcox Co., **III** 465–66, 516, 559–60; **V** 621; **23** 199
Baby Furniture and Toy Supermarket, **V** 203
Baby Superstore, Inc., 15 32–34
Babybird Co., Ltd., **V** 150
Babyliss, S.A., **17** 110
BAC. *See* Barclays American Corp.
Bacardi Limited, 18 39–42
Baccarat, **23** 241
Bache, **III** 340
Bache & Company, **8** 349
Bachman Foods, **15** 139
Bachman Holdings, Inc., **14** 165
Bachman's Inc., 22 58–60
Bachrach Advertising, **6** 40
Back Bay Restaurant Group, Inc., 20 54–56
Backer & Spielvogel, **I** 33; **12** 168; **14** 48–49; **22** 296
Backroom Systems Group, **II** 317
Bacon & Matheson Drop Forge Co., **I** 185
Bacova Guild, Ltd., **17** 76
Baddour, Inc. *See* Fred's, Inc.
Badger Co., **II** 86
Badger Illuminating Company, **6** 601
Badger Meter, Inc., 22 61–65
Badger Paint and Hardware Stores, **II** 419
Badger Paper Mills, Inc., 15 35–37

Badische Analin & Soda Fabrik A.G., **I** 305
BAFS. *See* Bangkok Aviation Fuel Services Ltd.
Bahia de San Francisco Television, **IV** 621
Bailey, Banks & Biddle, **16** 559
Bailey Controls, **III** 560
Bain & Co., **III** 429; **9** 343; **21** 143
Bain Capital, Inc., **14** 244–45; **16** 466; **20** 18
Baird, **7** 235, 237
Bakelite Corp., **I** 399; **9** 517; **13** 231
Baker & Co., **IV** 78
Baker & Crane, **II** 318; **17** 323
Baker & McKenzie, 10 126–28
Baker & Taylor, Inc., I 548; **16 45–47**
Baker Casing Shoe Co., **III** 429
Baker Cummins Pharmaceuticals Inc., **11** 208
Baker Hughes Incorporated, III 428–29; 11 513; **22 66–69 (upd.)**
Baker Industries, Inc., **III** 440; **8** 476; **13** 124
Baker International Corp., **III** 428–29
Baker Oil Tools. *See* Baker Hughes Incorporated.
Baker-Raulang Co., **13** 385
Bakers Square. *See* VICORP Restaurants, Inc.
Bakersfield Savings and Loan, **10** 339
Bakery Products Inc., **IV** 410
Balair Ltd., **I** 122
Balco, Inc., **7** 479–80
Balcor Co., **II** 398; **IV** 703
Balcor, Inc., **10** 62
Baldor Electric Company, 21 42–44
Baldwin Filters, Inc., **17** 104
Baldwin Hardware Manufacturing Co., **III** 570, **20** 361
Baldwin Piano & Organ Company, 16 201; **18 43–46**
Baldwin Rubber Industries, **13** 79
Baldwin-United Corp., **III** 254, 293
Baldwins Ltd., **III** 494
Bålforsens Kraft AB, **IV** 339–40
Balfour Beatty Construction Ltd., **III** 433–34; **13** 206
Balfour Company, L.G., **19** 451–52
Balikpapan Forest Industries, **I** 504
Ball & Young Adhesives, **9** 92
Ball Corporation, I 597–98; **10 129–31 (upd.); 13** 254, 256; **15** 129; **16** 123
Ball Stalker Inc., **14** 4
Ball-Bartoe Aircraft Corp., **I** 598; **10** 130
Ballantine & Sons Ltd., **I** 263
Ballantine Beer, **6** 27
Ballantine Books, **13** 429
Ballard & Ballard Co., **II** 555
Ballard Medical Products, 21 45–48
Bally Entertainment Corp., **19** 205, 207
Bally Gaming International, **15** 539
Bally Manufacturing Corporation, III 430–32; 6 210; **10** 375, 482; **12** 107; **15** 538–39; **17** 316–17, 443
AB Baltic, **III** 418–19
Baltic Cable, **15** 521
Baltimore & Ohio Railroad, **I** 584; **II** 329. *See also* CSX Corporation.
Baltimore Aircoil Company, **7** 30–31
Baltimore Gas and Electric Company, V 552–54; 11 388
Baltimore Paper Box Company, **8** 102
Baltino Foods, **13** 383
Balzaretti-Modigliani, **III** 676; **16** 121

Bamberger's of New Jersey, **V** 169; **8** 443
Banamex, **22** 285; **23** 170. *See also* Banco Nacional de Mexico.
Banana Boat Holding Corp., **15** 359
Banana Republic, **V** 61–62; **18** 193–94
Banc One Corporation, 9 475; **10 132–34; 11** 181
Banca Brasiliana Italo-Belga, **II** 270
Banca Coloniale di Credito, **II** 271
Banca Commerciale Italiana SpA, I 368, 465, 467; **II 191–93**, 242, 271, 278, 295, 319; **III** 207–08, 347; **17** 324
BancA Corp., **11** 305
Banca d'America e d'Italia, **II** 280
Banca Dalmata di Sconto, **II** 271
Banca de Gottardo, **II** 361
Banca di Genova, **II** 270
Banca Internazionale Lombarda, **II** 192
Banca Italiana di Sconto, **II** 191
Banca Italo-Cinese, **II** 270
Banca Italo-Viennese, **II** 270
Banca Jacquet e Hijos, **II** 196
Banca Luis Roy Sobrino, **II** 196
Banca Nazionale de Lavoro, **II** 239
Banca Nazionale dell'Agricoltura, **II** 272
Banca Nazionale di Credito, **II** 271
Banca Serfin. *See* Grupo Financiero Serfin, S.A.
Banca Unione di Credito, **II** 270
BancItaly Corp., **II** 226–27, 288, 536; **13** 528
Banco Aleman-Panameno, **II** 521
Banco Aliança S.A., **19** 34
Banco Azteca, **19** 189
Banco Bilbao Vizcaya, S.A., II 194–96
Banco Bradesco S.A., 13 69–71; 19 33
Banco Capitalizador de Monterrey, **19** 189
Banco Central, II 197–98; III 394; **IV** 397
Banco Central de Crédito. *See* Banco Itaú.
Banco Chemical (Portugal) S.A. *See* Chemical Banking Corp.
Banco Comercial, **19** 188
Banco da América, **19** 34
Banco de Londres, Mexico y Sudamerica. *See* Grupo Financiero Serfin, S.A.
Banco de Mexico, **19** 189
Banco del Norte, **19** 189
Banco di Roma, **I** 465, 467; **II** 191, 257, 271
Banco di Santo Spirito, **I** 467
Banco do Brasil S.A., II 199–200
Banco Español de Credito, **II** 195, 198; **IV** 160
Banco Espírito Santo e Comercial de Lisboa S.A., 15 38–40
Banco Federal de Crédito. *See* Banco Itaú.
Banco Frances y Brasiliero, **19** 34
Banco Industrial de Bilbao, **II** 195
Banco Industrial de Monterrey, **19** 189
Banco Italo-Belga, **II** 270, 271
Banco Italo-Egiziano, **II** 271
Banco Itaú S.A., 19 33–35
Banco Nacional de Cuba, **II** 345
Banco Nacional de Mexico, **9** 333; **19** 188, 193
Banco Pinto de Mahalhães, **19** 34
Banco Popular, **III** 348; **6** 97
Banco Português do Brasil S.A., **19** 34
Banco Santander, **III** 271, 294; **15** 257
Banco Sul Americano S.A., **19** 34
Banco Trento & Bolanzo, **II** 240
Banco União Comercial, **19** 34
Banco Vascongado, **II** 196

BancOhio National Bank in Columbus, **9** 475
Bancomer, **19** 12
Bancorp Leasing, Inc., **14** 529
BancorpSouth, Inc., **14** 40–41
Bancroft Racket Co., **III** 24
BancSystems Association Inc., **9** 475, 476
Bandag, Inc., 19 36–38, 454–56
Bandai America Inc., **23** 388
Banesto. *See* Banco Español de Credito.
Banexi, **II** 233
Bangkok Airport Hotel, **6** 123–24
Bangkok Aviation Fuel Services Ltd., **6** 123–24
Bangor and Aroostook Railroad Company, **8** 33
Bangor Mills, **13** 169
Bangor Punta Corp., **I** 452, 482; **II** 403
Bank Austria AG, 23 37–39
Bank Brussels Lambert, II 201–03, 295, 407
Bank Bumiputra, **IV** 519
Bank Central Asia, **18** 181
Bank CIC-Union Européenne A.G., **II** 272
Bank Européene de Credità Moyen Terme, **II** 319; **17** 324
Bank for International Settlements, **II** 368
Bank für Elektrische Unternehmungen. *See* Elektrowatt AG.
Bank für Gemeinwirtschaft, **II** 239
Bank Hapoalim B.M., II 204–06
Bank Hofmann, **21** 146–47
Bank Leu, **I** 252; **21** 146–47
Bank of Adelaide, **II** 189
Bank of America, **I** 536–37; **II** 226–28, 252–55, 280, 288–89, 347, 382; **III** 218; **6** 385; **8** 94–95; **9** 50, 123–24, 333, 536; **12** 106, 466; **13** 69; **14** 170; **18** 516; **22** 542. *See also* BankAmerica Corporation.
Bank of America National Trust and Savings Assoc. (NT & SA), **I** 536; **II** 227, 288; **13** 528. *See also* BankAmerica Corporation.
Bank of Antwerp, **IV** 497
Bank of Asheville, **II** 336
Bank of Australasia, **II** 187–89
The Bank of Bishop and Co., Ltd., **11** 114
Bank of Boston Corporation, II 207–09; **7** 114; **12** 31; **13** 467; **14** 90
Bank of Britain, **14** 46–47
Bank of British Columbia, **II** 244, 298
Bank of British Honduras, **II** 344
Bank of British North America, **II** 220
Bank of California, **II** 322, 490. *See also* Union Bank of California.
Bank of Canada, **II** 210, 376
Bank of Central and South America, **II** 344
Bank of Chicago, **III** 270
Bank of China, **II** 298
Bank of Chosen, **II** 338
Bank of Commerce, **II** 331
Bank of England, **II** 217, 235–36, 306–07, 318–19, 333–34, 357, 421–22, 427–28; **III** 234, 280; **IV** 119, 366, 382, 705, 711; **10** 8, 336; **14** 45–46; **17** 324–25
Bank of Finland, **III** 648
Bank of France, **II** 232, 264–65, 354; **III** 391
Bank of Hamilton, **II** 244
Bank of Hindustan, **IV** 699
Bank of Ireland, **16** 13–14; **19** 198
Bank of Israel, **II** 206

Bank of Italy, **I** 536; **II** 192, 226, 271–72, 288; **III** 209, 347; **8** 45
The Bank of Jacksonville, **9** 58
Bank of Japan, **I** 519; **II** 291, 325
Bank of Kobe, **II** 371
Bank of Lee County, **14** 40
Bank of Liverpool, **II** 236
Bank of London and South America, **II** 308
Bank of Manhattan Co., **II** 247–48
Bank of Mexico Ltd., **19** 188
The Bank of Milwaukee, **14** 529
Bank of Mississippi, Inc., 14 40–41
Bank of Montreal, II 210–12, 231, 375
Bank of Nettleton, **14** 40
Bank of New Brunswick, **II** 221
Bank of New England Corporation, II 213–15; 9 229
Bank of New Orleans, **11** 106
Bank of New Queensland, **II** 188
Bank of New South Wales, **II** 188–89, 388–90
Bank of New York Company, Inc., II 192, **216–19**, 247
Bank of North Mississippi, **14** 41
Bank of Nova Scotia, II 220–23, 345; **IV** 644
Bank of Oklahoma, **22** 4
Bank of Ontario, **II** 210
Bank of Osaka, **II** 360
Bank of Ottawa, **II** 221
Bank of Pasadena, **II** 382
Bank of Queensland, **II** 188
The Bank of Scotland. *See* The Governor and Company of the Bank of Scotland.
Bank of Sherman, **14** 40
Bank of Spain, **II** 194, 197
Bank of the Ohio Valley, **13** 221
Bank of the People, **II** 210
Bank of the United States, **II** 207, 216, 247
Bank of the West, **II** 233
Bank of Tokyo, Ltd., II 224–25, 276, 301, 341, 358; **IV** 151; **12** 138; **16** 496, 498
Bank of Tokyo-Mitsubishi Ltd., 15 41–43 (upd.), 431
Bank of Toronto, **II** 375–76
Bank of Tupelo, **14** 40
Bank of Upper Canada, **II** 210
Bank of Wales, **10** 336, 338
Bank of Western Australia, **II** 187
Bank of Winterthur, **II** 378
Bank Powszechny Depozytowy, **IV** 119
Bank voor Handel en Nijverheid, **II** 304
Bank-R Systems Inc., **18** 517
BankAmerica Corporation, II 226–28, 436; **8 45–48 (upd.)**, 295, 469, 471; **13** 69; **17** 546; **18** 518. *See also* Bank of America *and* Bank of America National Trust and Savings Assoc.
Bankers and Shippers Insurance Co., **III** 389
Bankers Co., **II** 230
Bankers Corporation, **14** 473
Bankers Investment, **II** 349
Bankers Life and Casualty Co., **10** 247; **16** 207
Bankers Life Co., **III** 328–30
Bankers National Bank, **II** 261
Bankers National Life Insurance Co., **II** 182; **10** 246
Bankers Trust New York Corporation, I 601; **II** 211, **229–31**, 330, 339; **III**

84–86; **10** 425; **11** 416; **12** 165, 209; **13** 188, 466; **17** 559; **19** 34; **22** 102
Bankhaus IG Herstatt, **II** 242
BankVermont Corp., **II** 208
Banner Aerospace, Inc., 14 42–44
Banner Industries, **21** 431
Banner International, **13** 20
Banner Life, **III** 273
Banque Belge et Internationale en Egypte, **II** 295
Banque Belge pour l'Etranger, **II** 294
Banque Belgo-Zairoise, **II** 294
Banque Bruxelles Lambert. *See* Bank Brussels Lambert.
Banque Commerciale du Maroc, **II** 272
Banque Commerciale-Basle, **II** 270
Banque d'Anvers/Bank van Antwerpen, **II** 294–95
Banque de Bruxelles, **II** 201–02, 239
Banque de Credit et de Depot des Pays Bas, **II** 259
Banque de France, **14** 45–46
Banque de l'Indochine et de Suez, **II** 259
Banque de l'Union Européenne, **II** 94
Banque de l'Union Parisienne, **II** 270; **IV** 497, 557
Banque de la Construction et les Travaux Public, **II** 319; **17** 324
Banque de la Société Générale de Belgique, **II** 294–95
Banque de Louvain, **II** 202
Banque de Paris et des Pays-Bas, **II** 136, 259; **10** 346; **19** 188–89
Banque de Reports et de Depots, **II** 201
Banque du Congo Belge, **II** 294
Banque Européenne pour l'Amerique Latine, **II** 294
Banque Française et Espagnol en Paris, **II** 196
Banque Francaise pour le Commerce et l'Industrie, **II** 232, 270
Banque Génerale des Pays Roumains, **II** 270
Banque Générale du Luxembourg, **II** 294
Banque Indosuez, **II** 429
Banque Internationale à Luxembourg, **II** 239
Banque Internationale de Bruxelles, **II** 201–02
Banque Italo-Belge, **II** 294
Banque Italo-Francaise de Credit, **II** 271
Banque Lambert, **II** 201–02
Banque Nationale de Paris S.A., II 232–34, 239; **III** 201, 392–94; **9** 148; **13** 203; **15** 309; **19** 51
Banque Nationale Pour le Commerce et l'Industrie, **II** 232–33
Banque Nordique du Commerce, **II** 366
Banque Orea, **II** 378
Banque Paribas, **II** 192, 260; **IV** 295; **19** 225
Banque Rothschild, **IV** 107
Banque Sino-Belge, **II** 294
Banque Stern, **II** 369
Banque Transatlantique, **II** 271
Banque Worms, **III** 393
Banquet Foods Corp., **II** 90, 494; **12** 81
Banta Corporation, 12 24–26; **19** 333
Bantam Ball Bearing Company, **13** 522
Bantam Books, Inc., **III** 190–91
Bantam Doubleday Dell Publishing Group, **IV** 594; **13** 429; **15** 51
Banyu Pharmaceutical Co., **I** 651; **11** 290
Baoshan Iron and Steel, **19** 220

BAP of New York, Inc., **15** 246
BAPCO, **III** 745
Barat. *See* Barclays National Bank.
Barber Dental Supply Inc., **19** 291
Barber-Greene, **21** 502
Barberet & Blanc, **I** 677
Barcel, **19** 192
Barclay Furniture Co., **12** 300
Barclay Group, **I** 335; **10** 290
Barclays Business Credit, **13** 468
Barclays PLC, **I** 604–05; **II** 202, 204,
    235–37, 239, 244, 308, 319, 333, 383,
    422, 429; **III** 516; **IV** 23, 722; **7**
    332–33; **8** 118; **11** 29–30; **17** 324–25;
    20 57–60 (upd.)
BarclaysAmerican Mortgage
    Corporation, **11 29–30**
Barco Manufacturing Co., **16** 8
Barcolo Manufacturing, **15** 103
Barden Cablevision, **IV** 640
Bareco Products, **15** 352
Barefoot Inc., **23** 428, 431
Bari Shoes, Inc., **22** 213
Barilla G. e R. Fratelli S.p.A., **17 35–37**
Barings PLC, **III** 699; **14 45–47**
Barker & Dobson, **II** 629
Barker and Company, Ltd., **13** 286
Barlow Rand Ltd., **I** 288–89, **422–24**; **IV**
    22, 96
Barmer Bankverein, **II** 238, 241
Barnato Brothers, **IV** 21, 65; **7** 122
Barnes & Noble, Inc., **10 135–37**; **12**
    172; **13** 494, 545; **14** 61–62; **15** 62; **16**
    160; **17** 524; **23** 370
Barnes Group, **III** 581
Barnes-Hind, **III** 56, 727
Barnett Banks, Inc., **9 58–60**
Barnett Brass & Copper Inc., **9** 543
Barnetts, Hoares, Hanbury and Lloyds, **II**
    306
Barnstead/Thermolyne Corporation, **14**
    479–80
Baroid, **19** 467–68
Barr & Stroud Ltd., **III** 727
Barranquilla Investments, **II** 138
Barratt Developments plc, **I 556–57**
Barret Fitch North, **II** 445; **22** 405
Barrett Burston, **I** 437
Barrett Business Services, Inc., **16 48–50**
The Barrett Co., **I** 414–15; **18** 116; **22** 29
Barris Industries, Inc., **23** 225
Barry & Co., **III** 522
Barry Wright Corporation, **9** 27
Barsab, **I** 288–89
Barsotti's, Inc., **6** 146
Bart Starr, **12** 284
Barth Smelting Corp., **I** 513
Barton & Ludwig, Inc., **21** 96
Barton Brands, **I** 227; **II** 609; **10** 181
Barton, Duer & Koch, **IV** 282; **9** 261
Barton Incorporated, **13** 134
BASF Aktiengesellschaft, **I** 275, **305–08**,
    309, 319, 346–47, 632, 638; **II** 554; **IV**
    70–71; **13** 75; **14** 308; **16** 462; **18**
    47–51 (upd.), 186, 234; **21** 544
Basic American Retirement Communities,
    III 103
Basic Resources, Inc., **V** 725
Basics, **14** 295
BASIS Information Technologies, Inc., **11**
    112–13, 132
Baskin-Robbins Ice Cream Co., **I** 215; **7**
    128, 372; **17** 474–75
Basle A.G., **I** 632–33, 671–72; **8** 108–09

Basle Air Transport, **I** 121
Basler Bankverein, **II** 368
Bass & Co., **I** 142
Bass Brewers Ltd., **15** 441
Bass PLC, **I 222–24**; **III** 94–95; **9** 99,
    425–26; **15 44–47** (upd.); **16** 263; **23**
    482
Bassett Foods, **II** 478
Bassett Furniture Industries, Inc., **18**
    52–55; **19** 275
Bassett-Walker Inc., **V** 390–91; **17** 512
Bassins Food Chain, **II** 649
BAT. *See* British-American Tobacco Co.,
    Ltd.
BAT Industries plc, **I 425–27**, 605; **II**
    628; **III** 66, 185, 522; **9** 312; **23** 427
Bataafsche Petroleum Maatschappij, **V** 658
Batavia Wine Company, **13** 134
Batchelors Ltd., **I** 315
Bateman Eichler Hill Richards, **III** 270
Bates, **16** 545
Bates & Robins, **II** 318; **17** 323
Bates Chemical Company, **9** 154
Bates Manufacturing Company, **10** 314
Bates Worldwide, Inc., **14 48–51**
Batesville Casket Company, **10** 349–50
Bath & Body Works, **11** 41
Bath Industries Inc., **18** 117–18
Bath Iron Works Corporation, **12 27–29**
Bathurst Bank, **II** 187
Baton Rouge Gas Light Company. *See*
    Gulf States Utilities Company.
Battelle Memorial Institute, Inc., **6** 288;
    10 138–40
Batten Barton Durstine & Osborn, **I** 25,
    28–31, 33; **16** 70
Battle Creek Food Company, **14** 557–58
Battle Creek Toasted Corn Flake Co., **II**
    523; **13** 291
Battle Mountain Gold Company, **IV** 490;
    23 40–42
Battlefield Equipment Rentals, **21** 499, 501
BATUS Inc., **9** 312; **18** 136
Bauborg, **I** 560–61
Baudhuin-Anderson Company, **8** 553
Bauer Publishing Group, **7 42–43**; **20** 53
Bausch & Lomb Inc., **III** 446; **7 44–47**;
    10 46–47; **13** 365–66
Bavarian Railway, **II** 241
Bavarian Specialty Foods, **13** 383
Baxter Estates, **II** 649
Baxter International Inc., **I 627–29**; **9**
    346; **10 141–43** (upd.), 198–99; **11**
    459–60; **12** 325; **18** 469; **22** 361
Baxter Travenol, **21** 119
The Bay, **16** 216
Bay Area Review Course, Inc., **IV** 623
Bay Cities Transportation Company, **6** 382
Bay City, **21** 502
Bay City Cash Way Company, **V** 222
Bay Colony Life Insurance Co., **III** 254
Bay Networks, **20** 33, 69
Bay Petroleum, **I** 526
Bay Ridge Savings Bank, **10** 91
Bay Shipbuilding Corporation, **18** 320
Bay State Glass Co., **III** 683
Bay State Iron Manufacturing Co., **13** 16
Bay State Tap and Die Company, **13** 7
Bay West Paper Corporation. *See* Mosinee
    Paper Corporation.
BayBanks, Inc., **12 30–32**
Bayer A.G., **I** 305–06, **309–11**, 319,
    346–47, 350; **II** 279; **12** 364; **13 75–77**

(upd.); **14** 169; **16** 439; **18** 47, 49, 51,
    234; **21** 544; **22** 225
Bayer S.p.A., **8** 179
Bayerische Aluminium AG, **IV** 230
Bayerische Hypotheken- und Wechsel-
    Bank AG, **II 238–40**, 241–42; **IV** 323
Bayerische Kraftwerke AG, **IV** 229–30
Bayerische Landesbank, **II** 257–58, 280;
    14 170
Bayerische Motoren Werke A.G., **I** 73,
    75, **138–40**, 198; **II** 5; **III** 543, 556,
    591; **11 31–33** (upd.); **13** 30; **17** 25; **21**
    441
Bayerische Rückversicherung AG, **III** 377
Bayerische Rumpler Werke, **I** 73
Bayerische Stickstoff-Werke AG, **IV**
    229–30
Bayerische Vereinsbank A.G., **II 239–40**,
    241–43; **III** 401
Bayerische Versicherungsbank, **II** 238; **III**
    377
Bayerische Wasserkraftwerke
    Aktiengesellschaft, **IV** 231
Bayerische Zellstoff, **IV** 325
Bayernwerk AG, **IV** 231–32, 323; **V**
    555–58, 698–700; **23 43–47** (upd.)
Bayliner Marine Corporation, **22** 116
Rayon Steel Corp., **IV** 234
Bayou Boeuf Fabricators, **III** 559
Bayside National Bank, **II** 230
Baystate Corporation, **12** 30
Baytree Investors Inc., **15** 87
Bayview, **III** 673
Bazaar & Novelty. *See* Stuart
    Entertainment Inc.
Bazar de l'Hotel de Ville, **19** 308
BBC. *See* British Broadcasting Corp.
BBC Brown, Boveri Ltd. *See* ABB ASEA
    Brown Boveri Ltd.
BBDO. *See* Batten Barton Durstine &
    Osborn.
BBDO Worldwide Network, **22** 394
BBME. *See* British Bank of the Middle
    East.
BBN Corp., **19 39–42**
BRO & Co., **14** 433
BC Development, **16** 481
BC TEL. *See* British Columbia Telephone
    Company.
BCal. *See* British Caledonian Airways.
BCE, Inc., **V 269–71**; **6** 307; **7** 333; **12**
    413; **18** 32
BCI. *See* Banca Commerciale Italiana SpA.
BCP Corporation, **16** 228–29
BDB Corp., **10** 136
BDDP. *See* Wells Rich Greene BDDP.
BeachviLime Ltd., **IV** 74
Beacon Communications Group, **23** 135
Beacon Manufacturing Company, **I** 377; **19**
    304–05
Beacon Oil, **IV** 566
Beacon Participations, **III** 98
Beacon Publishing Co., **IV** 629
Beamach Group Ltd., **17** 182–83
Beaman Inc., **16** 96
Bean Fiberglass Inc., **15** 247
Bear Automotive Service Equipment
    Company, **10** 494
Bear Creek Corporation, **12** 444–45
Bear Stearns Companies, Inc., II
    400–01, 450; **10 144–45** (upd.), 382; **20**
    313
Beard & Stone Electric Co., **I** 451
Bearings, Inc., **I** 158–59; **13 78–80**

Beasley Industries, Inc., **19** 125–26
Beatrice Company, I 353; 440–41; **II 467–69**, 475; **III** 118, 437; **6** 357; **9** 318; **12** 82, 87, 93; **13** 162–63, 452; **14** 149–50; **15** 213–14, 358; **16** 160, 396; **19** 290. *See also* TLC Beatrice International Holdings, Inc.
Beatrice Foods, **21** 322–24, 507, 545
Beauharnois Power Company, **6** 502
Beaulieu of America, **19** 276
Beaulieu Winery, **I** 260
Beaumont-Bennett Group, **6** 27
Beauté Prestige International S.A. *See* Shiseido Company Limited.
BeautiControl Cosmetics, Inc., 21 49–52
Beauty Biz Inc., **18** 230
Beaver Lumber Co., **I** 274
Beazer Homes USA, Inc., 17 38–41
Beazer Plc., **7** 209
BEC Group Inc., **22** 35
Bechtel Group Inc., I 558–59, 563; **III** 248; **IV** 171, 576; **6** 148–49, 556; **13** 13
Beck & Gregg Hardware Co., **9** 253
Becker Drill, Inc., **19** 247
Becker Paribas Futures, **II** 445; **22** 406
Becker Warburg Paribas, **II** 259
Beckett Papers, 23 48–50
Beckley-Cardy Co., **IV** 623–24
Beckman Coulter, Inc., 22 74–77
Beckman Instruments, Inc., I 694; **14 52–54**; **16** 94
Becton, Dickinson & Company, I 630–31; **IV** 550; **9** 96; **11 34–36 (upd.)**
Bed Bath & Beyond Inc., 13 81–83; **14** 61; **18** 239
Bedcovers, Inc., **19** 304
Beddor Companies, **12** 25
Bedford Chemical, **8** 177
Bedford-Stuyvesant Restoration Corp., **II** 673
Bee Chemicals, **I** 372
Bee Gee Shoe Corporation, **10** 281
Bee Gee Shrimp, **I** 473
Beech Aircraft Corporation, II 87; **8 49–52**, 313; **11** 411, 413
Beech Holdings Corp., **9** 94
Beech-Nut Nutrition Corporation, I 695; **II** 489; **21 53–56**
Beecham Group PLC, **I** 626, 640, 668; **II** 331, 543; **III** 18, 65–66; **9** 264; **14** 53; **16** 438
Beechwood Insurance Agency, Inc., **14** 472
Beerman Stores, Inc., **10** 281
Beghin Say S.A., **II** 540
Behr-Manning Company, **8** 396
Behringwerke AG, **14** 255
Beijerinvest Group, **I** 210
Beijing Dentsu, **16** 168
Beijing Liyuan Co., **22** 487
Beijing Machinery and Equipment Corp., **II** 442
Beijing Yanshan Petrochemical Company, **22** 263
Beirao, Pinto, Silva and Co. *See* Banco Espírito Santo e Comercial de Lisboa S.A.
Bejam Group PLC, **II** 678
Beker Industries, **IV** 84
Bekins Company, 15 48–50
Bel. *See* Fromageries Bel.
Bel Air Markets, **14** 397
Belairbus, **I** 42; **12** 191
Belcher New England, Inc., **IV** 394
Belcher Oil Co., **IV** 394

Belco, **23** 219
Belden Inc., II 16; **19 43–45**
Beldis, **23** 219
Beldoch Industries Corp., **17** 137–38
Belfast Banking Co., **II** 318; **17** 323
Belgacom, 6 302–04
Belgian De Vaderlandsche, **III** 309
Belgian Rapid Access to Information Network Services, **6** 304
Belgian Société Internationale Forestière et Minière, **IV** 65
Belglas, **16** 420
Belgochim, **IV** 499
Belize Sugar Industries, **II** 582
Belk Stores Services, Inc., V 12–13; **19 46–48 (upd.)**
Bell (Quarry and Concrete), **III** 674
Bell Aerospace, **I** 530
Bell Aircraft Company, **I** 529; **11** 267; **13** 267
Bell and Howell Company, I 463; **IV** 642; **9** 33, **61–64**; **11** 197; **14** 569; **15** 71
Bell Atlantic Corporation, V 272–74; **9** 171; **10** 232, 456; **11** 59, 87, 274; **12** 137; **13** 399; **18** 33
Bell Canada, V 269, 308–09; **6 305–08**; **12** 413
Bell Canada Enterprises Inc. *See* BCE, Inc.
Bell Canada International, Inc. (BCI), **21** 308
Bell Communications Research (Bellcore), **13** 58
Bell Fibre Products, **12** 377
Bell Helmets Inc., **22** 458
Bell Industries, **13** 47; **18** 498; **19** 311
Bell Laboratories, **II** 33, 60–61, 101, 112; **V** 259–64; **8** 157; **9** 171; **10** 108; **11** 327, 500–01; **12** 61; **14** 52, 281–82; **23** 181. *See also* AT&T Bell Labroatories, Inc.
Bell Mountain Partnership, Ltd., **15** 26
Bell Pharmacal Labs, **12** 387
Bell Resources, **I** 437–38; **III** 729; **10** 170
Bell Sports Corporation, 16 51–53
Bell System, **II** 72, 230; **6** 338–40; **7** 99, 333; **11** 500; **16** 392–93
Bell Telephone Company, **I** 409; **6** 332, 334
Bell Telephone Company of Pennsylvania, **I** 585
Bell Telephone Manufacturing, **II** 13
Bell's Asbestos and Engineering, **I** 428
Bell-Northern Research, Ltd., **V** 269–71; **15** 131
Belle Alkali Co., **IV** 409; **7** 308
Belledune Fertilizer Ltd., **IV** 165
Bellefonte Insurance Co., **IV** 29
Bellemead Development Corp., **III** 220; **14** 108
Bellofram Corp., **14** 43
BellSouth Corporation, V 276–78; **9** 171, 321; **10** 431, 501; **15** 197; **18** 23, 74, 76; **19** 254–55; **22** 19
Belmin Systems, **14** 36
Belmont Electronics, **II** 85–86; **11** 412
Belmont Plaza, **12** 316
Belmont Savings and Loan, **10** 339
Belmont Springs Water Company, Inc., **I** 234; **10** 227
Belo Productions, Inc. *See* A.H. Belo Corporation.
Beloit Corporation, 8 243; **14 55–57**

Beloit Tool Company. *See* Regal-Beloit Corporation.
Beloit Woodlands, **10** 380
Belridge Oil Co., **IV** 541
Belzer Group, **IV** 198–99
Bemis Company, Inc., 8 53–55
Bemrose group, **IV** 650
Ben & Jerry's Homemade, Inc., 10 146–48; **17** 139–41
Ben Franklin Retail Stores, Inc. *See* FoxMeyer Health Corporation.
Ben Franklin Savings & Trust, **10** 117
Ben Hill Griffin, **III** 53
Ben Johnson & Co. Ltd., **IV** 661
Ben Line, **6** 398
Ben Venue Laboratories, **16** 439
Bendicks, **I** 592
Bendix Corporation, I 68, **141–43**, 154, 166, 192, 416; **II** 33; **III** 166, 555; **7** 356; **8** 545; **9** 16–17; **10** 260, 279; **11** 138; **13** 356–57; **15** 284; **17** 564; **21** 416; **22** 31
Beneficial Corporation, II 236; **8 56–58**, 117; **10** 490
Beneficial National Bank USA, **II** 286
Beneficial Standard Life, **10** 247
Benefit Consultants, Inc., **16** 145
Benesse Corporation, **13** 91, 93
Benetton Group S.p.A., 8 171; **10 149–52**; **15** 369; **18** 193
Bengal Iron and Steel Co., **IV** 205–06
Benihana, Inc., 18 56–59
Benjamin Allen & Co., **IV** 660
Benjamin Moore and Co., 13 84–87
Benlox Holdings PLC, **16** 465
Benn Bros. plc, **IV** 687
Bennett Biscuit Co., **II** 543
Bennett Industries, Inc., **17** 371–73
Bennetts, **19** 122
Bennigan's, **II** 556–57; **7** 336; **12** 373; **13** 408; **19** 286
Benson & Hedges, Ltd., **V** 398–99; **15** 137; **19** 171
Benson Wholesale Co., **II** 624
Bentley Laboratories, **22** 360
Bentley Mills, Inc., **8** 272
Bentley Motor Ltd., **I** 194; **21** 435
Bentley Systems, **6** 247
Benton & Bowles, **I** 33; **6** 20, 22
Benwood Iron Works, **17** 355
Benxi Iron and Steel Corp., **IV** 167
Benzina, **IV** 487
Benzinol, **IV** 487
N.V. Benzit. *See* N.V. Gemeenschappelijk Benzit van Aandeelen Philips Gloeilampenfabriken.
Berec Group, **III** 502; **7** 208
Berg Manufacturing Sales Co., **I** 156
Berg- und Metallbank, **IV** 139–40
Bergdorf Goodman, **I** 246; **V** 30–31
Bergdorfer Eisenwerk, **III** 417–20
Bergen Bank, **II** 352
Bergen Brunswig Corporation, I 413; **V 14–16**, 152; **13 88–90 (upd.)**; **18** 97
Berger, Jenson and Nicholson, **I** 347; **18** 236
Bergische-Markische Bank, **II** 278
Berglen, **III** 570; **20** 362
Bergmann & Co., **II** 27
Bergstrom Paper Company, **8** 413
Bergswerksgesellschaft Hibernia, **I** 349; **IV** 194
Bergvik & Ala, **IV** 336, 338–39

Beringer Wine Estates Holdings, Inc., 22 78–81
Berisford International plc, 19 492, 494
Berjaya Group, 22 464–65
Berkeley Computers, III 109; 14 13
Berkey Photo Inc., I 447; III 475
Berkley Dean & Co., 15 525
Berkline Corp., 17 183; 20 363
Berkshire Hathaway Inc., III 29, 213–15; 12 435–36, 554–55; 18 60–63 (upd.)
Berkshire International, V 390–91; 17 512
Berkshire Partners, 10 393
Berleca Ltd., 9 395
Berlex Laboratories, I 682; 10 214
Berli Jucker, 18 180–82
Berlin Exchange, I 409
Berlin Göring-Werke, IV 233
Berliner Bank, II 256
Berliner Bankverein, II 278
Berliner Handels- und Frankfurter Bank, II 242
Berliner Union, I 409
Berlinische Bodengesellschaft, I 560
Berlitz International, Inc., IV 643; 7 286, 312; 13 91–93
Berman Brothers Fur Co., 21 525
Berman Buckskin, 21 525
Berni Inns, I 247
Bernie Schulman's, 12 132
Bernstein Macauley, Inc., II 450
Berrios Enterprises, 14 236
Berry Bearing Company, 9 254
Berry Industries, III 628
Berry Plastics Corporation, 21 57–59
Bert L. Smokler & Company, 11 257
Bertea Corp., III 603
Bertelsmann AG, IV 592–94, 614–15; 10 196; 15 51–54 (upd.); 17 399; 19 285; 22 194
Bertron Griscom & Company, V 641
Bertucci's Inc., 16 54–56, 447
Berwind Corp., 14 18
Beryllium Resources, 14 80
Berzelius Metallhütten Gesellschaft, IV 141
Berzelius Umwelt-Service, III 625; IV 141
Besnier SA, 19 49–51; 23 217, 219
Bess Mfg., 8 510
Bessemer Capital Partners L.P., 15 505
Bessemer Gas Engine Co., II 15; 20 163
Bessemer Limestone & Cement Co., IV 409
Bessemer Steamship, IV 572; 7 549
Besser Vibrapac, III 673
Best Apparel, V 156
Best Buy Co., Inc., 9 65–66; 10 305; 17 489; 18 532–33; 19 362; 23 51–53 (upd.)
Best Fabric Outlets, 16 198
Best Holding Corporation. See Arkansas Best Corporation.
Best Manufacturing, 15 490
Best Products Inc., 19 396–97
Best Western, 14 106
Bestfoods, II 496–97; 22 82–86 (upd.)
Bestline Products, 17 227
Bestop Inc., 16 184
Bestwall Gypsum Co., IV 281; 9 259
Bestway Transportation, 14 505
Beswick, II 17
BET Holdings, Inc., 18 64–66; 22 224
Bethesda Research Laboratories, Inc., I 321; 17 287, 289

Bethlehem Steel Corporation, IV 35–37, 228, 572–73; 6 540; 7 48–51 (upd.), 447, 549–50; 11 65; 12 354; 13 97, 157; 18 378; 22 285; 23 305
Beton Union, III 738
Better Communications, IV 597
Betz Laboratories, Inc., I 312–13; 10 153–55 (upd.); 15 536
Bevan and Wedd Durlacher Mordaunt & Co., II 237
Beveridge-Marvellum Company, 8 483
Beverly Enterprises, Inc., III 76–77, 80; 14 242; 16 57–59 (upd.)
Beverly Hills Savings, II 420
Bevis Custom Furniture, Inc., 12 263
The BFGoodrich Company, I 28, 428, 440; II 414; III 118, 443; V 231–33; 8 80–81, 290; 9 12, 96, 133; 10 438; 11 158; 19 52–55 (upd.); 20 260, 262; 21 260; 22 114; 23 170
BFI. See Browning-Ferris Industries, Inc.
BFP Holdings Corp. See Big Flower Press Holdings, Inc.
BG&E. See Baltimore Gas and Electric Company.
BGC Finance, II 420
BGC Finance, II 420
BH Acquisition Corporation, 22 439
Bharat Coking Coal Ltd., IV 48–49
Bharat Petroleum Ltd., IV 441
Bharti Telecom, 16 84
BHC Communications, 9 119
BHP. See Broken Hill Proprietary Company Ltd.
BHP Steel of Australia, 18 380
Bhs plc, 16 466; 17 42–44, 334–35
BHV. See Bazar de l'Hotel de Ville.
Bi-Lo Inc., II 641; V 35; 16 313
Bianchi, 13 27
BIC Corporation, III 29; 8 59–61; 20 23; 23 54–57 (upd.)
BICC PLC, III 433–34; 11 520
BICE Med Grille, 16 447
Bicoastal Corporation, II 9–11
Bidermann Industries, 22 122
Biederman & Company, 14 160
Bieffe, 16 52
Bienfaisance, III 391
Bierbrauerei Wilhelm Remmer, 9 86
Biffa Waste Services Ltd. See Severn Trent PLC.
Big B, Inc., 17 45–47
Big Bear Stores Co., 13 94–96
Big Boy, III 102–03
Big 5 Sporting Goods, 12 477
Big Flower Press Holdings, Inc., 21 60–62
Big Foot Cattle Co., 14 537
Big Horn Mining Co., 8 423
Big M, 8 409–10
Big O Tires, Inc., 20 61–63
Big Rivers Electric Corporation, 11 37–39
Big Three Industries, I 358
Big Y Foods, Inc., 23 169
Bike Athletics, 23 449
Bilbao Insurance Group, III 200
Bilfinger & Berger Bau A.G., I 560–61
Bill France Racing, 19 222
Billboard Publications, Inc., 7 15
Billerud, IV 336
Billiton International, IV 56, 532; 22 237
Bill's Casino, 9 426
Biltwell Company, 8 249
Bimar Foods Inc., 19 192

Binder Hamlyn, IV 685
Binderline Development, Inc., 22 175
Bindley Western Industries, Inc., 9 67–69
Bing Crosby Productions, IV 595
Binghamton Container Company, 8 102
Bingo King. See Stuart Entertainment Inc.
Binks Sames Corporation, 21 63–66
Binney & Smith, II 525; IV 621; 13 293
Binnie & Partners, 22 89
Binny & Co. Ltd., III 522
Binter Canarias, 6 97
Bio/Dynamics, Inc., 10 105, 107
Bio Synthetics, Inc., 21 386
Bio-Clinic, 11 486–87
Bio-Toxicological Research Laboratories, IV 409
Biofermin Pharmaceutical, I 704
Biogen Inc., I 638, 685; 8 210; 14 58–60
Bioindustrias, 19 475
Biokyowa, III 43
Biological Research, III 443
Biological Technology Corp., IV 252; 17 29
Biomedical Reference Laboratories of North Carolina, 11 424
Biomega Corp., 18 422
Biomet, Inc., 10 156–58
Bionaire, Inc., 19 360
BioSensor A.B., I 665
Biotechnica International, I 286
Bioteknik-Gruppen, I 665
Bioter S.A., III 420
Bioter-Biona, S.A., II 493
Biotherm, III 47
Bird & Sons, 22 14
Bird Corporation, 19 56–58
Birdsall, Inc., 6 529, 531
Bireley's, 22 515
Birfield Ltd., III 494
Birkbeck, 10 6
Birkenstock Footprint Sandals, Inc., 12 33–35
Birmingham & Midland Bank. See Midland Bank plc.
Birmingham Joint Stock Bank, II 307
Birmingham Screw Co., III 493
Birmingham Slag Company, 7 572–73, 575
Birmingham Steel Corporation, 13 97–98; 18 379–80; 19 380
Birtman Electric Co., III 653; 12 548
Biscayne Bank. See Banco Espírito Santo e Comercial de Lisboa S.A.
Biscayne Federal Savings and Loan Association, 11 481
Biscuiterie Nantaise, II 502; 10 323
Biscuits Belin, II 543
Biscuits Delacre, II 480
Biscuits Gondolo, II 543
Bishop & Babcock Manufacturing Co., II 41
Bishop & Co. Savings Bank, 11 114
Bishop National Bank of Hawaii, 11 114
Bishopsgate Insurance, III 200
BISSELL, Inc., 9 70–72
Bit Software, Inc., 12 62
Bitumax Proprietary, III 672
Bitumen & Oil Refineries (Australia) Ltd., III 672–73
BIZ Enterprises, 23 390
Bizmark, 13 176
BizMart, 6 244–45; 8 404–05
BJ Services, Inc., 15 534, 536

BJ's Wholesale Club, **12** 221; **13** 547–49
Björknäs Nya Sågverks, **IV** 338
BKW, **IV** 229
BL Ltd., **I** 175; **10** 354
BL Systems. *See* AT&T Istel Ltd.
The Black & Decker Corporation, **I** 667;
    III 435–37, 628, 665; **8** 332, 349; **15**
    417–18; **16** 384; **17** 215; **20** 64–68
    (upd.); **22** 334
Black & Veatch LLP, **22** 87–90
Black Arrow Leasing, **II** 138
Black Box Corporation, **20** 69–71
Black Entertainment Television. *See* BET
    Holdings, Inc.
Black Flag Co., **I** 622
Black Hawk Broadcasting Group, **III** 188;
    10 29
Black Hills Corporation, **20** 72–74
Black Spread Eagle, **II** 235
Blackburn, **III** 508
Blackhawk, **9** 26
Blackhorse Agencies, **II** 309
Blackmer Pump Co., **III** 468
Blackstone Capital Partners L.P., **V** 223; **6**
    378; **17** 366
The Blackstone Group, **II** 434, 444; **IV**
    718; **11** 177, 179; **13** 170; **17** 238, 443;
    22 404, 416
Blaine Construction Company, **8** 546
Blair and Co., **II** 227
Blair Paving, **III** 674
Blair Radio, **6** 33
Blakiston Co., **IV** 636
Blane Products, **I** 403
Blatz Breweries, **I** 254
Blaupunkt-Werke, **I** 192–93
BLC Insurance Co., **III** 330
BLD Europe, **16** 168
Bleichröder, **II** 191
Blendax, **III** 53; **8** 434
Blessings Corp., **14** 550; **19** 59–61
Blimpie International, Inc., **15** 55–57; **17**
    501
Bliss Manufacturing Co., **17** 234–35
Blitz-Weinhart Brewing, **18** 71–72
Blochman Lawrence Goldfree, **I** 697
Block Drug Company, Inc., **6** 26; **8**
    62–64
Block Financial, **17** 265
Block Medical, Inc., **10** 351
Blockbuster Entertainment Corporation,
    II 161; **IV** 597; **9** 73–75, 361; **11**
    556–58; **12** 43, 515; **13** 494; **18** 64, 66;
    19 417; **22** 161–62; **23** 88, 503
Blockson Chemical, **I** 380; **13** 379
Bloedel, Stewart & Welch, **IV** 306–07
Blohm & Voss, **I** 74
Bloomberg L.P., **18** 24; **21** 67–71
Bloomingdale's Inc., **I** 90; **III** 63; **IV** 651,
    703; **9** 209, 393; **10** 487; **12** 36–38, 307,
    403–04; **16** 328; **23** 210
Blount, Inc., **I** 563; **12** 39–41
Blue Arrow PLC, **II** 334–35; **9** 327
Blue Bell, Inc., **V** 390–91; **12** 205; **17** 512
Blue Chip Stamps, **III** 213–14
Blue Circle Industries PLC, **III** 669–71,
    702
Blue Cross and Blue Shield Association,
    10 159–61; **14** 84
Blue Cross and Blue Shield Mutual of
    Northern Ohio, **12** 176
Blue Cross and Blue Shield of Colorado,
    11 175

Blue Cross and Blue Shield of Greater
    New York, **III** 245, 246
Blue Cross and Blue Shield of Ohio, **15**
    114
Blue Cross Blue Shield of Michigan, **12** 22
Blue Cross of Northeastern New York, **III**
    245–46
Blue Funnel Line, **I** 521; **6** 415–17
Blue Line Distributing, **7** 278–79
Blue Metal Industries, **III** 687
Blue Mountain Arts, **IV** 621
Blue Ribbon Beef Pack, Inc., **II** 515–16
Blue Ribbon Sports. *See* Nike, Inc.
Blue Ridge Grocery Co., **II** 625
Blue Ridge Lumber Ltd., **16** 11
Blue Tee Corporation, **23** 34, 36
Blue Water Food Service, **13** 244
Bluebird Inc., **10** 443
Bluffton Grocery Co., **II** 668
Blunt Ellis & Loewi, **III** 270
Blyth and Co., **I** 537; **13** 448, 529
Blyth Eastman Dillon & Company, **II** 445;
    22 405–06
Blyth Industries, Inc., **18** 67–69
Blyth Merrill Lynch, **II** 448
Blythe Colours BV, **IV** 119
BMC Industries, Inc., **6** 275; **17** 48–51
BMC Software Inc., **14** 391
BMG/Music, **IV** 594; **15** 51
BMI Ltd., **III** 673
BMI Systems Inc., **12** 174
BMO Corp., **III** 209
BMW. *See* Bayerische Motoren Werke.
BNA. *See* Banca Nazionale
    dell'Agricoltura.
BNCI. *See* Banque Nationale Pour le
    Commerce et l'Industrie.
BNE. *See* Bank of New England Corp.
BNG, Inc., **19** 487
BNP. *See* Banque Nationale de Paris S.A.
BOAC. *See* British Overseas Airways
    Corp.
Boardwalk Regency, **6** 201
Boart and Hard Metals, **IV** 22
Boase Massimi Pollitt, **6** 48
Boatmen's Bancshares Inc., **15** 58–60
Bob Evans Farms, Inc., **9** 76–79; **10** 259
Bobbie Brooks Inc., **17** 384
Bobbs-Merrill, **11** 198
Bobingen A.G., **I** 347
BOC Group plc, **I** 314–16, 358; **11** 402;
    12 500
Bochumer Verein für Gusstahlfabrikation,
    IV 88
Bock Bearing Co., **8** 530
Bodcaw Co., **IV** 287; **15** 228
Boddington, **21** 247
Bodegas, **8** 556
Bodeker Drug Company, **16** 399
The Body Shop International PLC, **11**
    40–42
The Boeing Company, **I** 41–43, 47–49,
    50, 55–56, 58, 61, 67–68, 70–72, 74,
    77, 82, 84–85, 90, 92–93, 96–97, 100,
    102, 104–05, 108, 111–13, 116,
    121–22, 126, 128, 130, 195, 489–90,
    511, 530; **II** 7, 32–33, 62, 442; **III** 512,
    539; **IV** 171, 576; **6** 68, 96, 130, 327; **7**
    11, 456, 504; **8** 81, 313, 315; **9** 12, 18,
    128, 194, 206, 232, 396, 416–17,
    458–60, 498; **10** 162–65 (upd.), 262,
    316, 369, 536; **11** 164, 267, 277–79,
    363, 427; **12** 180, 190–91, 380; **13**
    356–58; **21** 140, 143, 436

Boeke & Huidekooper, **III** 417
Boerenbond, **II** 304
Boettcher & Co., **III** 271
Bofors Nobel Inc., **9** 380–81; **13** 22
Bogen Company, **15** 213
Bohemia, Inc., **13** 99–101
Bohm-Allen Jewelry, **12** 112
Böhme-Fettchemie, Chenmitz, **III** 32
Bohn Aluminum & Brass, **10** 439
Boise Cascade Corporation, **I** 142; **III**
    499, 648, 664; **IV** 255–56, 333; **6** 577;
    7 356; **8** 65–67 (upd.), 477; **15** 229; **16**
    510; **19** 269, 445–46; **22** 154
Bokaro Steel Ltd., **IV** 206
Bolands Ltd., **II** 649
Bolar Pharmaceutical Co., **16** 529
Boley G.m.b.H., **21** 123
Boliden Mining, **II** 366
Bolinder-Munktell, **I** 209; **II** 366
Bolitho Bank, **II** 235
Bölkow GmbH, **I** 74
Bolles & Houghton, **10** 355
The Bolsa Chica Company, **8** 300
BOMAG, **8** 544, 546
Bombardier, Inc., **12** 400–01; **16** 78
The Bombay Company, Inc., **III** 581; **10**
    166–68
Bon Appetit, **II** 656
The Bon Marché, Inc., **V** 25; **9** 209; **19**
    88, 306, 309; **23** 58–60
The Bon-Ton Stores, Inc., **16** 60–62
Bonanza, **7** 336; **10** 331; **15** 361–63
Bonanza Steakhouse, **17** 320
Bonaventura, **IV** 611
Bonaventure Liquor Store Co., **I** 284
Bond Brewing International, **23** 405
Bond Corporation Holdings Limited, **I**
    253, 255; **10** 169–71
Bondex International, **8** 456
Bongrain, **19** 50; **23** 217, 219
Boni & Liveright, **13** 428
Bonifiche Siele, **II** 272
Bonimart, **II** 649
Bontrager Bicycles, **16** 495
Bonwit Teller, **13** 43; **17** 43
Book-of-the-Month Club, Inc., **IV** 661,
    675; **7** 529; **13** 105–07
Booker PLC, **13** 102–04
Booker Tate, **13** 102
Bookmasters, **10** 136
Books-A-Million, Inc., **14** 61–62; **16** 161
Bookstop, **10** 136
Booth Bay, Ltd., **16** 37
Booth Fisheries, **II** 571
Booth, Inc., **II** 420
Booth Leasing, **I** 449
Booth-Kelly Lumber Co., **IV** 281; **9** 259
Boots Company PLC, **I** 640, 668, 708; **II**
    650; **V** 17–19; **8** 548; **19** 122
Boots Pharmaceuticals, **18** 51
Booz Allen & Hamilton Inc., **10** 172–75
Boral Limited, **III** 672–74
Borax Holdings, **IV** 191
Bordas, **IV** 615
Borden Cabinet Corporation, **12** 296
Borden, Inc., **II** 470–73, 486, 498, 538,
    545; **IV** 569; **7** 127, 129, 380; **11** 173;
    15 490; **16** 43; **17** 56; **22** 84, 91–96
    (upd.)
Border Fine Arts, **11** 95
Borders Group, Inc., **9** 361; **10** 137; **15**
    61–62; **17** 522; **18** 286
Borders, Perrin and Norrander, **23** 480
Borg Instruments, **23** 494

Borg-Warner Automotive, Inc., **14** 63–66; **23** 171

Borg-Warner Corporation, **I** 193, 339, 393; **III** 428, **438–41**; **14** 63, 357; **22** 228

Borg-Warner Security Corporation, **13** 123–25; **14** 63, 65, 541

Borland International, Inc., **6** 255–56; **9** 80–82; **10** 237, 509, 519, 558; **15** 492

Borman's, Inc., **II** 638; **16** 249

Borneo Airways. *See* Malaysian Airlines System BHD.

Borneo Co., **III** 523

Borregaard Osterreich AG, **18** 395

Borror Corporation. *See* Dominion Homes, Inc.

Borsheim's, **III** 215; **18** 60

Borun Bros., **12** 477

Bosanquet, Salt and Co., **II** 306

Bosch. *See* Robert Bosch GmbH.

Boschert, **III** 434

Bose Corporation, **II** 35; **13** 108–10; **22** 97

Bosendorfer, L., Klavierfabrik, A.G., **12** 297

Bosert Industrial Supply, Inc., **V** 215

Boso Condensed Milk, **II** 538

Bostich, **III** 628

Boston Acoustics, Inc., **22** 97–99

Boston and Maine Corporation, **16** 350

Boston Beer Company, **18** 70–73; **22** 422

Boston Brewing Company, **18** 502

Boston Casualty Co., **III** 203

Boston Celtics Limited Partnership, **14** 67–69

Boston Chicken, Inc., **12** 42–44; **23** 266

Boston Co., **II** 451–52

Boston Consulting Group, **I** 532; **9** 343; **18** 70; **22** 193

Boston Distributors, **9** 453

Boston Edison Company, **12** 45–47

Boston Fruit Co., **II** 595

Boston Garden Arena Corporation, **14** 67

Boston Gas Company, **6** 486–88

Boston Globe, **7** 13–16

Boston Herald, **7** 15

Boston Industries Corp., **III** 735

Boston Marine Insurance Co., **III** 242

Boston National Bank, **13** 465

Boston News Bureau, **IV** 601

Boston Overseas Financial Corp., **II** 208

Boston Properties, Inc., **22** 100–02

Boston Ventures, **17** 444

Boston Whaler, Inc., **V** 376–77; **10** 215–16

Bostrom Seating, Inc., **23** 306

BOTAS, **IV** 563

Botsford Ketchum, Inc., **6** 40

Botswana General Insurance Company, **22** 495

Botto, Rossner, Horne & Messinger, **6** 40

Bottu, **II** 475

Bougainville Copper Pty., **IV** 60–61

Boulder Creek Steaks & Saloon, **16** 447

Boulder Natural Gas Company, **19** 411

Boulet Dru DuPuy Petit Group. *See* Wells Rich Greene BDDP.

Boulevard Bancorp, **12** 165

Boundary Gas, **6** 457

Boundary Healthcare, **12** 327

Bouquet, **V** 114

Bourdon, **19** 49

Bourjois, **12** 57

Boussois Souchon Neuvesel, **II** 474; **III** 677; **16** 121–22

Bouygues SA, **I** 562–64; **13** 206; **23** 475–76

Bouzan Mines Ltd., **IV** 164

Bovaird Seyfang Manufacturing Co., **III** 471

Bovis Ltd., **I** 588

Bow Bangles, **17** 101, 103

Bowater PLC, **III** 501–02; **IV** 257–59; **7** 208; **8** 483–84

Bower Roller Bearing Co., **I** 158–59

Bowery and East River National Bank, **II** 226

Bowery Savings Bank, **II** 182; **9** 173

Bowes Co., **II** 631

Bowman Gum, Inc., **13** 520

Bowmar Instruments, **II** 113; **11** 506

Bowne & Co., Inc., **18** 331–32; **23** 61–64

Box Innards Inc., **13** 442

Box Office Attraction Co., **II** 169

BoxCrow Cement Company, **8** 259

Boyer Brothers, Inc., **14** 17–18

Boyer's International, Inc., **20** 83

Boykin Enterprises, **IV** 136

Boys Market, **17** 558–59

Boz, **IV** 697–98

Bozel Électrométallurgie, **IV** 174

Bozell, Jacobs, Kenyon, and Eckhardt Inc. *See* True North Communications Inc.

Bozzuto's, Inc., **13** 111–12

BP. *See* British Petroleum Company PLC.

BPB, **III** 736

BPD, **13** 356

BPI Communications, Inc., **7** 15; **19** 285

BR. *See* British Rail.

Braas, **III** 734, 736

Brabant, **III** 199, 201

Brabazon, **III** 555

Brach and Brock Confections, Inc., **15** 63–65

Brad Foote Gear Works, **18** 453

Bradbury Agnew and Co., **IV** 686

Braden Manufacturing, **23** 299–301

Bradford District Bank, **II** 333

Bradford Exchange Ltd. Inc., **21** 269

Bradford Insulation Group, **III** 687

Bradford Pennine, **III** 373

Bradlees Discount Department Store Company, **II** 666–67; **12** 48–50

Bradley Lumber Company, **8** 430

Bradley Producing Corp., **IV** 459

Bradstreet Co., **IV** 604–05; **19** 133

Braegen Corp., **13** 127

Bragussa, **IV** 71

BRAINS. *See* Belgian Rapid Access to Information Network Services.

Bramalea Ltd., **9** 83–85; **10** 530–31

Brambles Industries, **III** 494–95

Bramco, **III** 600

Bramwell Gates, **II** 586

Bran & Lübbe, **III** 420

Brand Companies, Inc., **9** 110; **11** 436

Branded Restaurant Group, Inc., **12** 372

Brandeis & Sons, **19** 511

Brandenburgische Motorenwerke, **I** 138

Brandywine Iron Works and Nail Factory, **14** 323

Brandywine Valley Railroad Co., **14** 324

Braniff Airlines, **I** 97, 489, 548; **II** 445; **6** 50, 119–20; **16** 274; **17** 504; **21** 142; **22** 406

Branigar Organization, Inc., **IV** 345

Brascade Resources, **IV** 308

Brascan, Ltd., **II** 456; **IV** 165, 330

Braspetro, **IV** 454, 501–02

Brass Craft Manufacturing Co., **III** 570; **20** 361

Brasseries Kronenbourg, **II** 474–75

Braswell Motor Freight, **14** 567

Brauerei Beck & Co., **9** 86–87

Braun, **III** 29; **17** 214–15

Braunkohlenwerk Golpa-Jessnitz AG, **IV** 230

Brazilian Central Bank, **IV** 56

Brazos Gas Compressing, **7** 345

Brazos Sportswear, Inc., **23** 65–67

Breakstone Bros., Inc., **II** 533

Breakthrough Software, **10** 507

Breckenridge-Remy, **18** 216

Breco Holding Company, **17** 558, 561

Bredel Exploitatie B.V., **8** 546

Bredell Paint Co., **III** 745

Bredero's Bouwbedrijf of Utrecht, **IV** 707–08, 724

BREED Technologies, Inc., **22** 31

Breedband NV, **IV** 133

Brega Petroleum Marketing Co., **IV** 453, 455

Breguet Aviation, **I** 44

Breitenburger Cementfabrik, **III** 701

Bremner Biscuit Co., **II** 562; **13** 426

Brenco Inc., **16** 514

Brenda Mines Ltd., **7** 399

Brennan College Services, **12** 173

Brenntag AG, **8** 68–69, 496; **23** 68–70 (upd.), **23** 453–54

Brentano's, **7** 286

Breslube Enterprises, **8** 464

Brewster Lines, **6** 410

Breyers Ice Cream Co. *See* Good Humor-Breyers.

BRI Bar Review Institute, Inc., **IV** 623; **12** 224

BRI International, **21** 425

Brian Mills, **V** 118

Briarpatch, Inc., **12** 109

Brickwood Breweries, **I** 294

Bricorama, **23** 231

Bridel, **19** 49–50

Bridge Oil Ltd., **I** 438

Bridge Technology, Inc., **10** 395

Bridgeman Creameries, **II** 536

Bridgeport Brass, **I** 377

Bridgeport Machines, Inc., **17** 52–54

Bridgestone Corporation, **V** 234–35; **15** 355; **20** 262; **21** 72–75 (upd.)

Bridgestone Liquefied Gas, **IV** 364

Bridgestone/Firestone, **19** 454, 456

Bridgeway Plan for Health, **6** 186

Bridgford Company, **13** 382

Brier Hill, **IV** 114

Brierly Investment Limited, **19** 156

Briggs & Stratton Corporation, **III** 597; **8** 70–73

Briggs and Lundy Lumber Cos., **14** 18

Brigham's Inc., **15** 71

Bright of America Inc., **12** 426

Bright Star Technologies, **13** 92; **15** 455

Brighton Federal Savings and Loan Assoc., **II** 420

Brightpoint, Inc., **18** 74–77

Briker, **23** 231

Brillion Iron Works Inc., **23** 306

Brimsdown Lead Co., **III** 680

Brin's Oxygen Co., **I** 314

Brinco Ltd., **II** 211

Brink's, Inc., **IV** 180–82; **19** 319

Brinker International, Inc., 10 176–78; 18 438
BRIntec, **III** 434
Brinton Carpets, **III** 423
Brisbane Gas Co., **III** 673
Bristol Aeroplane, **I** 50, 197; **10** 261
Bristol Gaming Corporation, **21** 298
Bristol Hotel Company, 23 71–73
Bristol PLC, **IV** 83
Bristol-BTR, **I** 429
Bristol-Erickson, **13** 297
Bristol-Myers Squibb Company, I 26, 30, 37, 301, 696, 700, 703; **III 17–19,** 36, 67; **IV** 272; **6** 27; **7** 255; **8** 210, 282–83; **9 88–91 (upd.); 10** 70; **11** 289; **12** 126–27; **16** 438; **21** 546
Bristol-Siddeley Ltd., **I** 50
Britannia Airways, **8** 525–26
Britannia Security Group PLC, **12** 10
Britannica Software, **7** 168
Britches of Georgetowne, **10** 215–16
Brite Voice Systems, Inc., 20 75–78
British & Commonwealth Shipping Company, **10** 277
British Aerospace plc, I 42, 46, **50–53,** 55, 74, 83, 132, 532; **III** 458, 507; **V** 339; **7** 9, 11, 458–59; **8** 315; **9** 499; **11** 413; **12** 191; **14** 36; **18** 125; **21** 8, 443
British Airways plc, I 34, 83, **92–95,** 109; **IV** 658; **6** 60, 78–79, 118, 132; **14 70–74 (upd.); 18** 80; **22** 52
British Aluminium, Ltd., **II** 422; **IV** 15
British American Cosmetics, **I** 427
British American Insurance Co., **III** 350
British American Nickel, **IV** 110
British American Tobacco. *See* B.A.T. Industries PLC.
British and Dominion Film Corp., **II** 157
British and Foreign Marine, **III** 350
British and Foreign Steam Navigation Company, **23** 160
British and French Bank, **II** 232–33
British and North American Royal Mail Steam Packet Company. *See* Cunard Line Ltd.
British Bank of North America, **II** 210
British Bank of the Middle East, **II** 298
British Borneo Timber Co., **III** 699
British Broadcasting Corporation Ltd., **III** 163; **IV** 651; **7 52–55; 21 76–79** **(upd.)**
British Caledonian Airways, **I** 94–95; **6** 79
British Can Co., **I** 604
British Car Auctions, **14** 321
British Celanese Ltd., **I** 317
British Cellulose and Chemical Manufacturing Co., **I** 317
British Chrome, **III** 699
British Coal Corporation, IV 38–40
British Columbia Forest Products Ltd., **IV** 279; **19** 155
British Columbia Packers, **II** 631–32
British Columbia Resources Investment Corp., **IV** 308
British Columbia Telephone Company, **IV** 308; **6 309–11**
British Commonwealth Insurance, **III** 273
British Commonwealth Pacific Airways, **6** 110
British Continental Airlines, **I** 92
British Credit Trust, **10** 443
British Dyestuffs Corp., **I** 351
British Dynamite Co., **I** 351
British Energy Group, **19** 391

British Engine, **III** 350
British European Airways, **I** 93, 466
British Executive, **I** 50
British Fuels, **III** 735
British Gas plc, II 260; **V 559–63; 6** 478–79; **11** 97; **18** 365–67
British Gauge and Instrument Company, **13** 234
British General, **III** 234
British Goodrich Tyre Co., **I** 428
British Home Stores PLC. *See* Storehouse PLC.
British Hovercraft Corp., **I** 120
British India and Queensland Agency Co. Ltd., **III** 522
British India Steam Navigation Co., **III** 521–22
British Industrial Solvents Ltd., **IV** 70
British Industry, **III** 335
British Insulated and Helsby Cables Ltd., **III** 433–34
British Interactive Broadcasting Ltd., **20** 79
British Isles Transport Co. Ltd., **II** 564
British Land Company, **10** 6
British Leyland Motor Corporation, **I** 175, 186; **III** 516, 523; **13** 286–87; **14** 35–36
British Linen Bank, **10** 336
British Marine Air Navigation, **I** 92
British Metal Corp., **IV** 140, 164
British Motor Corporation, **III** 555; **7** 459; **13** 286
British Motor Holdings, **7** 459
British National Films Ltd., **II** 157
British National Oil Corp., **IV** 40
British Newfoundland Corporation, **6** 502
British Nuclear Fuels PLC, I 573; **6** **451–54; 13** 458
British Nylon Spinners (BNS), **17** 118
British Overseas Airways Corp., **I** 51, 93, 120–21; **III** 522; **6** 78–79, 100, 110, 112, 117; **14** 71
British Oxygen Co. *See* BOC Group.
The British Petroleum Company plc, I 241, 303; **II** 449, 563; **IV** 61, 280, 363–64, **378–80,** 381–82, 412–13, 450–54, 456, 466, 472, 486, 497–99, 505, 515, 524–25, 531–32, 557; **6** 304; **7 56–59 (upd.),** 140–41, 332–33, 516, 559; **9** 490, 519; **11** 538; **13** 449; **14** 317; **16** 394, 461–62; **19** 155, 391; **21 80–84 (upd.),** 352
British Plasterboard, **III** 734
British Portland Cement Manufacturers, **III** 669–70
British Printing and Communications Corp., **IV** 623–24, 642; **7** 312; **12** 224
British Prudential Assurance Co., **III** 335
British Rail, **III** 509; **V** 421–24; **10** 122
British Railways, **6** 413
British Railways Board, V 421–24
British Road Services, **6** 413
British Royal Insurance Co., Ltd., **III** 242
British Satellite Broadcasting, **10** 170
British Shoe Corporation, **V** 178
British Sky Broadcasting Group Plc, 20 **79–81**
British South Africa Co., **IV** 23, 94
British South American Airways, **I** 93
British South American Corporation, **6** 95
British Steel Brickworks, **III** 501; **7** 207
British Steel plc, III 494–95; **IV** 40, **41–43,** 128; **17** 481; **19 62–65 (upd.),** 391
British Sugar plc, **II** 514, 581–82; **13** 53

British Tabulating Machine Company, **6** 240
British Telecommunications plc, I 83, 330; **II** 82; **V 279–82; 6** 323; **7** 332–33; **8** 153; **9** 32; **11** 59, 185, 547; **15 66–70** **(upd.),** 131; **16** 468; **18** 155, 345; **20** 81; **21** 233
British Thermoplastics and Rubber. *See* BTR plc.
British Timken Ltd., **8** 530
British Twin Disc Ltd., **21** 504
British Tyre and Rubber Co., **I** 428
British United Airways, **I** 94
British Vita PLC, 9 92–93; 19 413–15
British World Airlines Ltd., 18 78–80
British Zaire Diamond Distributors Ltd., **IV** 67
British-American Tobacco Co., Ltd., **V** 396, 401–02, 417; **9** 312
Britoil, **IV** 380; **21** 82
Britt Airways, **I** 118
Britt Lumber Co., Inc., **8** 348
Brittains Bricks, **III** 673
Brittania Sportswear, **16** 509
BRK Electronics, **9** 414
Bro-Well, **17** 56
Broad, Inc., **11** 482
Broad River Power Company, **6** 575
Broadcast Music Inc., 23 74–77
Broadcast Technology Systems, Inc., **13** 398
Broadcom Eireann Research, **7** 510
Broadcort Capital Corp., **13** 342
BroadPark, **II** 415
BroadVision Inc., **18** 543
Broadway & Seymour Inc., **17** 264; **18** 112
Broadway-Hale Stores, Inc., **12** 356
Brock Candy Company. *See* Brach and Brock Confections, Inc.
Brock Hotel Corp., **13** 472–73
Brock Residence Inn, **9** 426
Brockway Glass Co., **I** 524; **15** 128
Broderbund Software, Inc., 10 285; **13** **113–16**
Broederlijke Liefdebeurs, **III** 177
Broken Hill Proprietary Company Ltd., **I** 437–39; **II** 30; **III** 494; **IV 44–47,** 58, 61, 171, 484; **10** 170; **21** 227; **22** **103–08 (upd.)**
The Bronfman Group, **6** 161, 163; **23** 124–25
Brooke Group Ltd., 15 71–73
Brooke Partners L.P., **11** 275
Brookfield Athletic Shoe Company, **17** 244
Brooklyn Flint Glass Co., **III** 683
Brooklyn Trust Co., **II** 312
Brooklyn Union Gas, 6 455–57
Brooks Brothers Inc., V 26–27; **13** 43; **22** 109–12
Brooks, Harvey & Company, Inc., **II** 431; **16** 376
Brooks Shoe Manufacturing Co., **16** 546
Brooks, Shoobridge and Co., **III** 669
Brooks-Scanlon Lumber Co., **IV** 306
Brookshire Grocery Company, 16 63–66
Brookstone, Inc., II 560; **12** 411; **18** **81–83**
Brookville Telephone Company, **6** 300
Brookwood Health Services, **III** 73
Brother Industries, Ltd., 13 478; **14** **75–76**
Brother International, **23** 212
Brothers Foods, **18** 7

Brothers Gourmet Coffees, Inc., 20 82–85

Broughton Foods Co., 17 55–57

Brown & Dureau Ltd., **IV** 248–49; **19** 14

Brown & Haley, 23 78–80

Brown & Root, Inc., III 498–99, 559; **13** 117–19

Brown & Sharpe Manufacturing Co., 23 81–84

Brown and Williamson Tobacco Corporation, I 426; **14 77–79; 15** 72; **22** 72–73

Brown Bibby & Gregory, **I** 605

Brown Boveri. *See* BBC Brown Boveri.

Brown Co., **I** 452; **IV** 289

Brown Corp., **IV** 286

Brown Drug, **III** 9

Brown Foundation, **III** 498

Brown Group, Inc., V 351–53; **9** 192; **10** 282; **16** 198; **20 86–89 (upd.)**

Brown Instrument Co., **II** 41

Brown Jordan Co., **12** 301

Brown Oil Tools, **III** 428

Brown Paper Mill Co., **I** 380; **13** 379

Brown Shipbuilding Company. *See* Brown & Root, Inc.

Brown Shoe Co., **V** 351–52; **14** 294

Brown-Forman Corporation, I 225–27; **III** 286; **10 179–82 (upd.); 12** 313; **18** 69

Brown-Service Insurance Company, **9** 507

Brown-Shipley Ltd., **II** 425; **13** 341

Browne & Nolan Ltd., **IV** 294; **19** 225

Browning Manufacturing, **II** 19

Browning Telephone Corp., **14** 258

Browning-Ferris Industries, Inc., V 749–53; **8** 562; **10** 33; **17** 552; **18** 10; **20 90–93 (upd.); 23** 491

Broyhill Furniture Industries, Inc., III 528, 530; **10 183–85; 12** 308

BRS Ltd., **6** 412–13

Bruce's Furniture Stores, **14** 235

Brufina, **II** 201–02

Brummer Seal Company, **14** 64

Brunner Mond and Co., **I** 351

Bruno's Inc., 7 60–62; 13 404, 406; **23** 261

Brunswick Corporation, III 442–44, 599; **9** 67, 119; **10** 262; **17** 453; **21** 291; **22 113–17 (upd.)**, 118

Brunswick Pulp & Paper Co., **IV** 282, 311, 329; **9** 260; **19** 266

The Brush Electric Light Company, **11** 387

Brush Electrical Machines, **III** 507–09

Brush Moore Newspaper, Inc., **8** 527

Brush Wellman Inc., 14 80–82

Bryan Bros. Packing, **II** 572

Bryant Heater Co., **III** 471

Bryce & Co., **I** 547

Bryce Brothers, **12** 313

Bryce Grace & Co., **I** 547

Brymbo Steel Works, **III** 494

Brynwood Partners, **13** 19

BSB, **IV** 653; **7** 392

BSC (Industry) Ltd., **IV** 42

BSkyB, **IV** 653; **7** 392

BSN Groupe S.A., II 474–75, 544; **22** 458; **23** 448

BSR, **II** 82

BT. *See* British Telecommunications, plc.

BTI Services, **9** 59

BTM. *See* British Tabulating Machine Company.

BTR Dunlop Holdings, Inc., **21** 432

BTR plc, I 428–30; III 185, 727; **8** 397

Buchanan, **I** 239–40

Buchanan Electric Steel Company, **8** 114

Buckaroo International. *See* Bugle Boy Industries, Inc.

Buckeye Business Products Inc., **17** 384

Buckeye Tractor Ditcher, **21** 502

Buckeye Union Casualty Co., **III** 242

Buckhorn, Inc., **19** 277–78

Buckingham Corp., **I** 440, 468

The Buckle, Inc., 18 84–86

Buckler Broadcast Group, **IV** 597

Bucyrus Blades, Inc., **14** 81

Bucyrus International, Inc., 17 58–61

Bucyrus-Erie Company, **7** 513

Budapest Bank, **16** 14

The Budd Company, III 568; **IV** 222; **8** 74–76; **20** 359

Buderus AG, **III** 692, 694–95

Budget Rent a Car Corporation, I 537; **6** 348–49, 393; **9 94–95; 13** 529; **22** 524

Budgetel Inn. *See* Marcus Corporation.

Budweiser, **18** 70

Budweiser Japan Co., **21** 320

Buena Vista Distribution, **II** 172; **6** 174

Buffalo Forge Company, **7** 70–71

Buffalo Insurance Co., **III** 208

Buffalo Mining Co., **IV** 181

Buffalo News, **18** 60

Buffalo Paperboard, **19** 78

Buffalo-Springfield, **21** 502

Buffets, Inc., 10 186–87; 22 465

Buffett Partnership, Ltd., **III** 213

Bugaboo Creek Steak House Inc., **19** 342

Bugatti Industries, **14** 321

Bugle Boy Industries, Inc., 18 87–88

Buick Motor Co., **I** 171; **III** 438; **8** 74; **10** 325

Builders Emporium, **13** 169

Builders Square, **V** 112; **9** 400; **12** 345, 385; **14** 61; **16** 210

Buitoni SpA, **II** 548; **17** 36

Bulgari S.p.A., 20 94–97

Bulgarian Oil Co., **IV** 454

Bull. *See* Compagnie des Machines Bull S.A.

Bull HN Information Systems, **III** 122–23

Bull Motors, **11** 5

Bull S.A., **III** 122–23

Bull Tractor Company, **7** 534; **16** 178

Bull-GE, **III** 123

Bulldog Computer Products, **10** 519

Bullock's, **III** 63

Bulolo Gold Dredging, **IV** 95

Bulova Corporation, I 488; **II** 101; **III** 454–55; **12** 316–17, 453; **13 120–22; 14** 501; **21** 121–22

Bumble Bee Seafoods, Inc., **II** 491, 508, 557

Bumkor-Ramo Corp., **I** 539

Bunawerke Hüls GmbH., **I** 350

Bundy Corporation, 17 62–65, 480

Bunker Ramo Info Systems, **III** 118

Bunte Candy, **12** 427

Bunzl PLC, IV 260–62; 12 264

Buquet, **19** 49

Burbank Aircraft Supply, Inc., **14** 42–43

Burberrys Ltd., V 68; **10** 122; **17 66–68; 19** 181

Burda Holding GmbH. & Co., 20 53; **23** 85–89

Burdines, **9** 209

Bureau de Recherches de Pétrole, **IV** 544–46, 559–60; **7** 481–83; **21** 203–04

The Bureau of National Affairs, Inc., 23 90–93

Burelle S.A., 23 94–96

Burger and Aschenbrenner, **16** 486

Burger Boy Food-A-Rama, **8** 564

Burger Chef, **II** 532

Burger King Corporation, I 21, 278; **II** 556–57, **613–15**, 647; **7** 316; **8** 564; **9** 178; **10** 122; **12** 43, 553; **13** 408–09; **14** 25, 32, 212, 214, 452; **16** 95–97, 396; **17 69–72 (upd.)**, 501; **18** 437; **21** 25, 362; **23** 505

Bürhle, **17** 36

Burhmann-Tetterode, **22** 154

Burke Scaffolding Co., **9** 512

BURLE Industries Inc., **11** 444

Burlesdon Brick Co., **III** 734

Burlington Coat Factory Warehouse Corporation, 10 188–89

Burlington Homes of New England, **14** 138

Burlington Industries, Inc., V 118, **354–55; 8** 234; **9** 231; **12** 501; **17 73–76 (upd.)**, 304–05; **19** 275

Burlington Mills Corporation, **12** 117–18

Burlington Northern, Inc., IV 182; **V** 425–28; **10** 190–91; **11** 315; **12** 145, 278

Burlington Resources Inc., 10 190–92; 11 135; **12** 144

Burmah Castrol PLC, IV 378, 381–84, 440–41, 483–84, 531; **7** 56; **15** 246; **21** 80

Burmeister & Wain, **III** 417–18

Burn & Co., **IV** 205

Burn Standard Co. Ltd., **IV** 484

Burnards, **II** 677

Burndy, **19** 166

Burnham and Co., **II** 407–08; **6** 599; **8** 388

Burns & Wilcox Ltd., **6** 290

Burns Companies, **III** 569; **20** 360

Burns Fry Ltd., **II** 349

Burns International Security Services, III 440; **13 123–25**

Burns Philp & Company Limited, **21** 496–98

Burns-Alton Corp., **21** 154–55

Burnup & Sims, Inc., **19** 254

Burpee Co. *See* W. Atlee Burpee Co.

Burr & Co., **II** 424; **13** 340

Burr-Brown Corporation, 19 66–68

Burrill & Housman, **II** 424; **13** 340

Burris Industries, **14** 303

Burroughs Corp., **I** 142, 478; **III** 132, 148–49, 152, 165–66; **6** 233, 266, 281–83; **18** 386, 542. *See also* Unisys Corporation.

Burroughs Mfg. Co., **16** 321

Burroughs Wellcome & Co., **I** 713; **8** 216

Burrows, Marsh & McLennan, **III** 282

Burrups Ltd., **18** 331, 333

Burry, **II** 560; **12** 410

Bursley & Co., **II** 668

Burt Claster Enterprises, **III** 505

Burthy China Clays, **III** 690

Burton Group plc, V 20–22

Burton J. Vincent, Chesley & Co., **III** 271

Burton, Parsons and Co. Inc., **II** 547

Burton Retail, **V** 21

Burton Rubber Processing, **8** 347

Burton Snowboards Inc., 22 118–20, 460

Burton-Furber Co., **IV** 180

Burtons Gold Medal Biscuits Limited, **II** 466; **13** 53

Burwell Brick, **14** 248

Bury Group, **II** 581
Bush Boake Allen Ltd., **IV** 346
Bush Hog, **21** 20–22
Bush Industries, Inc., 20 98–100
Bush Terminal Company, **15** 138
Business Depot, Limited, **10** 498
Business Expansion Capital Corp., **12** 42
Business Information Technology, Inc., **18** 112
Business Men's Assurance Company of America, III 209; **13** 476; **14 83–85**; **15** 30
Business Resources Corp., **23** 489, 491
Business Science Computing, **14** 36
Business Software Association, **10** 35
Business Software Technology, **10** 394
Businessland Inc., **III** 153; **6** 267; **10** 235; **13** 175–76, 277, 482
Busse Broadcasting, **7** 200
Büssing Automobilwerke AG, **IV** 201
Buster Brown, **V** 351–52
Butano, **IV** 528
Butler Bros., **21** 96
Butler Cox PLC, **6** 229
Butler Manufacturing Co., 12 51–53
Butler Shoes, **16** 560
Butterfield & Swire. *See* Swire Pacific Ltd.
Butterfield, Wasson & Co., **II** 380, 395; **10** 59; **12** 533
Butterick Co., Inc., 23 97–99
Butterley Company, **III** 501; **7** 207
Butterworth & Co. (Publishers) Ltd., **IV** 641; **7** 311; **17** 398
Buttrey Food & Drug Stores Co., 18 89–91
Butz Thermo-Electric Regulator Co., **II** 40; **12** 246
Buxton, **III** 28; **23** 21
Buzzard Electrical & Plumbing Supply, **9** 399; **16** 186
BVA Investment Corp., **11** 446–47
Byerly's, Inc. *See* Lund Food Holdings, Inc.
Byers Machines, **21** 502
Byrnes Long Island Motor Cargo, Inc., **6** 370
Byron Jackson, **III** 428, 439
Bytrex, Inc., **III** 643

C & G Systems, **19** 442
C & O. *See* Chesapeake and Ohio Railway.
C.&E. Cooper Co., **II** 14
C.&G. Cooper Company, **II** 14; **20** 162
C.A. Pillsbury and Co., **II** 555
C.A. Reed Co., **IV** 353; **19** 498
C.A.S. Sports Agency Inc., **22** 460, 462
C.A. Swanson & Sons, **II** 479–80; **7** 66–67
C&A Brenninkmeyer KG, V 23–24
C&E Software, **10** 507
C&R Clothiers, **17** 313
C&S Bank, **10** 425–26
C&S/Sovran Corporation, **10** 425–27; **18** 518
C. Bechstein, **III** 657
C. Brewer, **I** 417
C.D. Haupt, **IV** 296; **19** 226
C.D. Kenny Co., **II** 571
C.D. Magirus AG, **III** 541
C.E. Chappell & Sons, Inc., **16** 61–62
C.E.T. *See* Club Européen du Tourisme.
C.F. Burns and Son, Inc., **21** 154
C.F. Hathaway Company, **12** 522
C.F. Mueller Co., **I** 497–98; **12** 332

C. Francis, Son and Co., **III** 669
C.G. Conn, **7** 286
C.H. Dexter & Co., **I** 320
C.H. Knorr Company, **II** 497; **22** 83
C.H. Masland & Sons. *See* Masland Corporation.
C.H. Musselman Co., **7** 429
C.H. Robinson, Inc., 8 379–80; **11 43–44**; **23** 357
C-I-L, Inc., **III** 745; **13** 470
C. Itoh & Co., I 431–33, 492, 510; **II** 273, 292, 361, 442, 679; **IV** 269, 326, 516, 543; **7** 529; **10** 500; **17** 124
C.J. Devine, **II** 425
C.J. Lawrence, Morgan Grenfell Inc., **II** 429
C.J. Smith and Sons, **11** 3
C.L. Bencard, **III** 66
C. Lee Cook Co., **III** 467
C.M. Aikman & Co., **13** 168
C.M. Armstrong, Inc., **14** 17
C.M. Barnes Company, **10** 135
C.M. Page, **14** 112
C.O. Lovette Company, **6** 370
C.O.M.B. Company, **18** 131–33
C/P Utility Services Company, **14** 138
C.P.U., Inc., **18** 111–12
C.R. Bard Inc., IV 287; **9 96–98**; **22** 360–61
C. Reichenbach'sche Maschinenfabrik, **III** 561
C. Rowbotham & Sons, **III** 740
C.S. Rolls & Co., **I** 194
C.T. Bowring, **III** 280, 283; **22** 318
C.V. Buchan & Co., **I** 567
C.V. Gebroeders Pel, **7** 429
C.V. Mosby Co., **IV** 677–78
C.W. Holt & Co., **III** 450
C.W. Zumbiel Company, **11** 422
CAA. *See* Creative Artists Agency.
Cable and Wireless (Hong Kong). *See* Hong Kong Telecomminications Ltd.
Cable and Wireless plc, IV 695; **V 283–86**; **7** 332–33; **11** 547; **15** 69, 521; **17** 419; **18** 253
Cable Communications Operations, Inc., **6** 313
Cable News Network, **II** 166–68; **6** 171–73; **9** 30; **12** 546
Cablec Corp., **III** 433–34
Cableform, **I** 592
Cabletron Systems, Inc., 10 193–94; **10** 511; **20** 8
Cablevision Systems Corporation, 7 63–65; **18** 211
Cabot, Cabot & Forbes, **22** 100
Cabot Corporation, 8 77–79
Cabot Medical Corporation, **21** 117, 119
Cabot Noble Inc., **18** 503, 507
Cabot-Morgan Real Estate Co., **16** 159
Cabrera Vulcan Shoe Corp., **22** 213
CACI International Inc., 21 85–87
Cadadia, **II** 641–42
Cadbury Schweppes PLC, I 25–26, 220, 288; **II 476–78**, 510, 512, 592; **III** 554; **6** 51–52; **9** 178; **15** 221; **22** 513
CADCAM Technology Inc., **22** 196
Caddell Construction Company, **12** 41
Cademartori, **23** 219
Cadence Design Systems, Inc., 6 247; **10** 118; **11 45–48**, 285, 490–91
Cadence Industries Corporation, **10** 401–02
Cadet Uniform Services Ltd., **21** 116
Cadillac Automobile Co., **I** 171; **10** 325

Cadillac Fairview Corp., **IV** 703
Cadillac Plastic, **8** 347
Cadisys Corporation, **10** 119
Cadmus Communications Corporation, 16 531; **23 100–03**
Cadoricin, **III** 47
CAE Systems Inc., **8** 519
Caere Corporation, 20 101–03
Caesar-Wollheim-Gruppe, **IV** 197
Caesars World, Inc., 6 199–202; **17** 318
Caf'Casino, **12** 152
Café Grand Mère, **II** 520
CAFO, **III** 241
Cagle's, Inc., 20 104–07
Cahners Publishing, **IV** 667; **12** 561; **17** 398; **22** 442
CAI Corp., **12** 79
Cailler, **II** 546
Cain Chemical, **IV** 481
Cains Marcelle Potato Chips Inc., **15** 139
Caisse Commericale de Bruxelles, **II** 270
Caisse de dépôt et placement du Quebec, **II** 664
Caisse des Dépôts, **6** 206
Caisse National de Crédit Agricole, **II** 264–66
Caisse Nationale de Crédit Agricole, **15** 38–39
Caja General de Depositos, **II** 194
Cajun Bayou Distributors and Management, Inc., **19** 301
Cajun Electric Power Cooperative, Inc., **21** 470
Cal Circuit Abco Inc., **13** 387
CAL Corporation, **21** 199, 201
Cal-Van Tools. *See* Chemi-Trol Chemical Co.
Cal/Ink, **13** 228
Cala, **17** 558
Calais Railroad Company, **16** 348
Calcined Coke Corp., **IV** 402
CalComp Inc., 13 126–29
Calculating-Tabulating-Recording Company. *See* International Business Machines Corporation.
Calcutta & Burmah Steam Navigation Co., **III** 521
Caldbeck Macgregor & Co., **III** 523
Caldor Inc., 12 54–56, 508
Caledonian Airways. *See* British Caledonian Airways.
Caledonian Bank, **10** 337
Caledonian Paper plc, **IV** 302
Calédonickel, **IV** 107
Calgary Power Company. *See* TransAlta Utilities Corporation.
Calgon Corporation, **6** 27; **16** 387
Calgon Water Management, **15** 154
California Arabian Standard Oil Co., **IV** 536, 552
California Automated Design, Inc., **11** 284
California Bank, **II** 289
California Computer Products, Inc. *See* CalComp Inc.
California Cooler Inc., **I** 227, 244; **10** 181
California Dental Supply Co., **19** 289
California Federal Bank, **22** 275
California First, **II** 358
California Ink Company, **13** 227
California Institute of Technology, **9** 367
California Insurance Co., **III** 234
California Oilfields, Ltd., **IV** 531, 540

California Pacific, **22** 172
California Perfume Co., **III** 15
California Petroleum Co., **IV** 551–52
California Pizza Kitchen Inc., 15 74–76
California Plant Protection, **9** 408
California Portland Cement Co., **III** 718; **19** 69
California Steel Industries, **IV** 125
California Telephone and Light, **II** 490
California Test Bureau, **IV** 636
California Texas Oil Co., **III** 672
California Tile, **III** 673
California Woodfiber Corp., **IV** 266
California-Western States Life Insurance Co., **III** 193–94
Caligen, **9** 92
Call-Chronicle Newspapers, Inc., **IV** 678
Callaghan & Company, **8** 526
Callard and Bowser, **II** 594
Callaway Golf Company, 15 77–79; **16** 109; **19** 430, 432; **23** 267, 474
Callaway Wines, **I** 264
Callebaut, **II** 520–21
Callender's Cable and Construction Co. Ltd., **III** 433–34
Calloway's Nursery Inc., **12** 200
Calma, **II** 30; **12** 196
Calmar Co., **12** 127
CalMat Co., III 718; **19 69–72**
Calmic Ltd., **I** 715
Calor Group, **IV** 383
Caloric Corp., **II** 86
Calpine Corp., **IV** 84
Calsil Ltd., **III** 674
Caltex Petroleum Corporation, II 53; **III** 672; **IV** 397, 434, 440–41, 479, 484, 492, 519, 527, 536, 545–46, 552, 560, 562, 718; **7** 483; **19 73–75**; **21** 204
Calumet & Arizona Mining Co., **IV** 177
Calumet Electric Company, **6** 532
Calvert & Co., **I** 293
Calvert Insurance Co. *See* Gryphon Holdings, Inc.
Calvin Bullock Ltd., **I** 472
Calvin Klein, Inc., 9 203; **22 121–24**
Camargo Foods, **12** 531
Cambex, **12** 147–48
Cambrex Corporation, 16 67–69
Cambria Steel Company, **IV** 35; **7** 48
Cambridge Applied Nutrition Toxicology and Biosciences Ltd., **10** 105
Cambridge Biotech Corp., **13** 241
Cambridge Electric Co., **14** 124, 126
Cambridge Gas Co., **14** 124
Cambridge Interactive Systems Ltd., **10** 241
Cambridge Steam Corp., **14** 124
Camco Inc., **IV** 658
Camden Wire Co., Inc., **7** 408
CAMECO, **IV** 436
Cameron & Barkley Co., **13** 79
Cameron Ashley Inc., **19** 57
Cameron Iron Works, **II** 17
Cameron Oil Co., **IV** 365
Cameron-Brown Company, **10** 298
CAMI Automotive, **III** 581
Camintonn, **9** 41–42
Camp Manufacturing Co., **IV** 345; **8** 102
Campbell Box & Tag Co., **IV** 333
Campbell Cereal Company. *See* Malt-O-Meal Company.
Campbell, Cowperthwait & Co., **17** 498
Campbell Hausfeld. *See* Scott Fetzer Company.

Campbell Industries, Inc., **11** 534
Campbell Soup Company, I 21, 26, 31, 599, 601; **II 479–81**, 508, 684; **7 66–69** (upd.), 340; **10** 382; **11** 172; **18** 58
Campbell Taggart, Inc., **I** 219; **19** 135–36, 191
Campbell-Ewald Co., **I** 16–17
Campbell-Mithun-Esty, Inc., 13 516; **16 70–72**
Campeau Corporation, IV 721; **V 25–28**; **9** 209, 211, 391; **12** 36–37; **13** 43; **15** 94; **17** 560; **22** 110; **23** 60
Campo Electronics, Appliances & Computers, Inc., 16 73–75
Campofrio Alimentacion, S.A., **18** 247
CAMPSA. *See* Compañía Arrendataria del Monopolio de Petróleos Sociedad Anónima.
Campus Services, Inc., **12** 173
Canada & Dominion Sugar Co., **II** 581
Canada Cable & Wire Company, **9** 11
Canada Cement, **III** 704–05
Canada Cup, **IV** 290
Canada Development Corp., **IV** 252; **17** 29
Canada Dry, **I** 281
Canada Packers Inc., II 482–85
Canada Safeway Ltd., **II** 650, 654
Canada Trust. *See* CT Financial Services Inc.
Canada Tungsten Mining Corp., Ltd., **IV** 18
Canada Wire & Cable Company, Ltd., **IV** 164–65; **7** 397–99
Canadair, Inc., I 58; **7** 205; **13** 358; **16 76–78**
Canadian Airlines International Ltd., **6** 61–62, 101; **12** 192; **23** 10
Canadian Bank of Commerce, **II** 244–45
Canadian British Aluminum, **IV** 11
Canadian Cellucotton Products Ltd., **III** 40; **16** 302
Canadian Copper, **IV** 110
Canadian Copper Refiners, Ltd., **IV** 164
Canadian Dominion Steel and Coal Corp., **III** 508
Canadian Eastern Finance, **IV** 693
Canadian Fina Oil, **IV** 498
Canadian Football League, **12** 457
Canadian Forest Products, **IV** 270
Canadian Fuel Marketers, **IV** 566
Canadian General Electric Co., **8** 544–45
Canadian Government Merchant Marine, **6** 360–61
Canadian Gridoil Ltd., **IV** 373
Canadian Imperial Bank of Commerce, II 244–46; **IV** 693; **7** 26–28; **10** 8
Canadian Industrial Alcohol Company Limited, **14** 141
Canadian International Paper Co., **IV** 286–87; **15** 228
Canadian Keyes Fibre Company, Limited of Nova Scotia, **9** 305
Canadian National Railway System, I 284; **6 359–62**; **12** 278–79; **22** 444; **23** 10
Canadian Odeon Theatres, **6** 161; **23** 123
Canadian Pacific Enterprises, **III** 611
Canadian Pacific Limited, V 429–31; **8** 544–46
Canadian Pacific Railway, **I** 573; **II** 210, 220, 344; **III** 260; **IV** 272, 308, 437; **6** 359–60
Canadian Packing Co. Ltd., **II** 482
Canadian Petrofina, **IV** 498

Canadian Radio-Television and Telecommunications Commission, **6** 309
Canadian Telephones and Supplies, **6** 310
Canadian Transport Co., **IV** 308
Canadian Utilities Limited, 13 130–32
Canadian Vickers, **16** 76
Canal Bank, **11** 105
Canal Electric Co., **14** 125–26
Canal Plus, III 48; **7** 392; **10 195–97**, 345, 347; **23** 476
CanAmera Foods, **7** 82
Canandaigua Wine Company, Inc., 13 133–35
Cananwill, **III** 344
Candle Corporation of America. *See* Blyth Industries, Inc.
Candy SpA, **22** 350
Canfor Corp., **IV** 321; **17** 540
Cannon Assurance Ltd., **III** 276
Cannon Mills, Co., **9** 214–16
Cannondale Corporation, 16 494; **21 88–90**
Canon Inc., I 494; **II** 103, 292; **III 120–21**, 143, 172, 575, 583–84; **6** 238, 289; **9** 251; **10** 23; **13** 482; **15** 150; **18 92–95** (upd.), 186, 341–42, 383, 386–87
Canpet Exploration Ltd., **IV** 566
Canpotex Ltd., **18** 432
Cans Inc., **I** 607
Canstar Sports Inc., 15 396–97; **16 79–81**
Canteen Corp., **I** 127; **II** 679–80; **12** 489; **13** 321
Cantel Corp., **11** 184; **18** 32; **20** 76
Canton Chemical, **I** 323; **8** 147
Canton Railway Corp., **IV** 718
Cantor Fitzgerald Securities Corporation, **10** 276–78
Cap Rock Electric Cooperative, **6** 580
CAPCO. *See* Central Area Power Coordination Group *or* Custom Academic Publishing Company.
Capcom Co., **7** 396
Cape and Vineyard Electric Co., **14** 124–25
Cape Cod-Cricket Lane, Inc., **8** 289
Cape Horn Methanol, **III** 512
Cape May Light and Power Company, **6** 449
Cape PLC, **22** 49
Cape Wine and Distillers, **I** 289
Capehart-Farnsworth, **I** 463; **11** 197
Capex, **6** 224
AB Capital & Investment Corporation, **6** 108; **23** 381
Capital Advisors, Inc., **22** 4
Capital Airlines, **I** 128; **III** 102; **6** 128
Capital and Counties Bank, **II** 307; **IV** 91
Capital Bank N.A., **16** 162
Capital Cities/ABC Inc., II 129–31; **III** 214; **IV** 608–09, 613, 652; **11** 331; **15** 464; **18** 60, 62–63, 329. *See also* ABC, Inc.
Capital Concrete Pipe Company, **14** 250
Capital Controls Co., Inc. *See* Severn Trent PLC.
Capital Distributing Co., **21** 37
Capital Financial Services, **III** 242
Capital Grille, **19** 342
Capital Holding Corporation, III 216–19
Capital Life Insurance Company, **11** 482–83

Capital Management Services. *See* CB Commercial Real Estate Services Group, Inc.
Capital One, **18** 535
Capital Trust Corp., **17** 498
Capital-Gazette Communications, Inc., **12** 302
Capitol Film + TV International, **IV** 591
Capitol Pack, Inc., **13** 350
Capitol Printing Ink Company, **13** 227–28
Capitol Publishing, **13** 560
Capitol Radio Engineering Institute, **IV** 636
Capitol Records, **22** 192–93
Capitol-EMI, **I** 531–32; **11** 557
Capper Pass, **IV** 191
Capseals, Ltd., **8** 476
CapStar Hotel Company, 21 91–93
Capsugel, **I** 712
Car-lac Electronic Industrial Sales Inc., **9** 420
Car-X, **10** 415
Caracas Petroleum Sociedad Anónima, **IV** 565–66
Caradon plc, 18 561; **20 108–12 (upd.)**
Carando Foods, **7** 174–75
Carat Group, **6** 15–16
Caraustar Industries, Inc., 19 76–78
Caravali, **13** 493–94
Caravelle Foods, **21** 500
Carbide Router Co., **III** 436
Carbis China Clay & Brick Co., **III** 690
Carbocol, **IV** 417
Carboline Co., **8** 455
CarboMedics, **11** 458–60
Carbon Research Laboratories, **9** 517
La Carbonique, **23** 217, 219
Carborundum Company, III 610; **15 80–82**
Cardboard Containers, **IV** 249
Cardem Insurance Co., **III** 767; **22** 546
Cardiac Pacemakers, Inc., **I** 646; **11** 90; **11** 458; **22** 361
Cardinal Distributors Ltd., **II** 663
Cardinal Health, Inc., 18 96–98
Cardiotronics Systems, Inc., **21** 47
Cardon-Phonocraft Company, **18** 492
Care Group, **22** 276
Caremark International Inc., 10 143, **198–200**
Carenes, SA, **12** 377
CarePlus, **6** 42
CareUnit, Inc., **15** 123
Carey Canada Inc., **III** 766; **22** 546
Carey Straw Mill, **12** 376
Carey-McFall Corp., **V** 379; **19** 421
S.A. CARFUEL, **12** 152
Cargill, Inc., II 494, 517, **616–18**; **11** 92; **13 136–38 (upd.)**, 186, 351; **18** 378, 380; **21** 290, 500; **22** 85, 426
Cargill Trust Co., **13** 467
Cargo Express, **16** 198
CARGOSUR, **6** 96
Cariani Sausage Co., **II** 518
Caribair, **I** 102
Caribbean Chemicals S.A., **I** 512
Caribe Co., **II** 493
Caribe Shoe Corp., **III** 529
Cariboo Pulp & Paper Co., **IV** 269
Carintusa Inc., **8** 271
CARIPLO, **III** 347
Carita S.A., **III** 63; **22** 487
Caritas Foundation, **22** 411, 413
Carl Byoir & Associates, **I** 14

Carl Karcher Enterprises, Inc., **19** 435
Carl Marks & Co., **11** 260–61
Carl's Superstores, **9** 452
Carl-Zeiss-Stiftung, III 445–47, 583
Carlan, **III** 614
Carless Lubricants, **IV** 451
Carleton Financial Computations Inc., **II** 317
Carlin Gold Mining Company, **7** 386–87
Carling O'Keefe Ltd., **I** 218, 229, 254, 269, 438–39; **7** 183; **12** 337
Carlingford, **II** 298
Carlisle Companies Incorporated, 8 80–82
Carlisle Memory Products, **14** 535
Carlo Erba S.p.A., **I** 635
Carlon, **13** 304–06
Carlova, Inc., **21** 54
Carlsberg A/S, I 247; **9** 99–101
Carlson Companies, Inc., 6 363–66; **22 125–29 (upd.)**
Carlton and United Breweries Ltd., I 228–29, 437–39; **7** 182–83
Carlton Communications plc, 15 83–85; **23** 111, 113
Carlton Investments L.P., **22** 514
The Carlyle Group, **11** 364; **14** 43; **16** 47; **21** 97
Carmeda AB, **10** 439
Carmike Cinemas, Inc., 14 86–88; **21** 362
Carnation Company, I 269; **II 486–89**, 518, 548; **7** 339, 383, 429; **10** 382; **12** 337
Carnaud Basse-Indre, **IV** 228
Carnaud-Metalbox, **13** 190; **20** 111
Carnegie Brothers & Co., Ltd., **9** 407
Carnegie Foundation for the Advancement of Teaching, **12** 141
Carnegie Steel Co., **II** 330; **IV** 572; **7** 549
Carnival Cruise Lines, Inc., 6 367–68; **21** 106; **22** 444–46, 470
Carol Moberg, Inc., **6** 40
Carol's Shoe Corp., **22** 213
Carol-Braugh-Robinson Co., **II** 624
Carolco Pictures Inc., **III** 48; **10** 196
Carolina Biological Supply, **11** 424
Carolina Coach Co., **13** 397–98
Carolina Coin Caterers Corporation, **10** 222
Carolina Energies, Inc., **6** 576
Carolina First National, **II** 336
Carolina Freight Corporation, 6 369–72
Carolina Paper Board Corporation. *See* Caraustar Industries, Inc.
Carolina Power & Light Company, V 564–66; **23 104–07 (upd.)**
Carolina Telephone and Telegraph Company, 10 201–03
Carpenter Paper Co., **IV** 282; **9** 261
Carpenter Technology Corporation, 13 139–41
Carpets International Plc., **8** 270–71
Carr Fowler, **III** 673
Carr's of Carlisle, **I** 604; **II** 594
Carr-Gottstein Foods Co., 17 77–80
Carr-Lowrey Glass Co., **13** 40
Carr-Union Line, **6** 397
Carrabba's Italian Grill, **12** 373–75
Carrefour SA, II 628; **8** 404–05; **10 204–06**; **12** 153; **19** 98, 309; **21** 225; **23** 230–32; 246–47, 364
Carreras, Limited, **V** 411–12; **19** 367–69
Carrier Corporation, I 85; **III** 329; **7 70–73**; **13** 507; **22** 6

Carroll County Electric Company, **6** 511
Carroll Reed Ski Shops, Inc., **10** 215
Carroll's Foods, **7** 477; **22** 368
Carry Machine Supply, Inc., **18** 513
Carson Pirie Scott & Company, II 669; **9** 142; **15 86–88**; **19** 324, 511–12
Carson Water Company, **19** 411
Carte Blanche, **9** 335
Carter & Co., **IV** 644
Carter Automotive Co., **I** 159
Carter, Berlind, Potoma & Weill, **II** 450
Carter Hawley Hale Stores, I 246; **V 29–32**; **8** 160; **12** 356; **15** 88; **16** 466; **17** 43, 523; **18** 488
Carter Holt Harvey Ltd., **IV** 280; **15** 229; **19** 155
Carter Oil Company, **IV** 171; **11** 353
Carter-Wallace, Inc., 6 27; **8 83–86**
Carteret Savings Bank, **III** 263–64; **10** 340
Carterphone, **22** 17
Cartier Monde, **IV** 93; **V** 411, 413
Cartier Refined Sugars Ltd., **II** 662–63
Cartiera F.A. Marsoni, **IV** 587
Cartiere Ascoli Piceno, **IV** 586
Cartiers Superfoods, **II** 678
Cartillon Importers, Ltd., **6** 48
Carver Pump Co., **19** 36
Carworth Inc., **I** 630; **11** 34
Cary-Davis Tug and Barge Company. *See* Puget Sound Tug and Barge Company.
CASA, **7** 9
Casa Bancária Almeida e Companhia. *See* Banco Bradesco S.A.
Casa Bonita, **II** 587
Casablanca Records, **23** 390
Cascade Communications Corp., **16** 468; **20** 8
Cascade Fiber, **13** 99
Cascade Lumber Co., **IV** 255; **8** 65
Cascade Natural Gas Corporation, 6 568; **9 102–04**
Cascade Steel Rolling Mills, **19** 380–81
CasChem, Inc. *See* Cambrex Corporation.
Casco Northern Bank, 14 89–91
Case Manufacturing Corp., **I** 512
Case, Pomeroy & Co., Inc., **IV** 76
Case Technologies, Inc., **11** 504
Casein Co. of America, **II** 471
Casey's General Stores, Inc., 19 79–81
Cash America International, Inc., 20 113–15
Casino, **10** 205; **23** 231
Casino. *See* Etablissements Economiques de Casino Guichard, Perrachon et Cie, S.C.A.
Casino Frozen Foods, Inc., **16** 453
Casino S.A., **22** 515
Casino USA, **16** 452
Casinos International Inc., **21** 300
Casio Computer Co., Ltd., III 448–49, 455; **IV** 599; **10** 57; **16 82–84 (upd.)**; **21** 123
Cassa Generale Ungherese di Risparmio, **III** 207
Cassady Broiler Co., **II** 585
Cassatt, **II** 424
Cassco Ice & Cold Storage, Inc., **21** 534–35
CAST Inc., **18** 20
Cast-Matic Corporation, **16** 475
Castex, **13** 501
Castle & Cooke, Inc., I 417; **II 490–92**; **9** 175–76; **10** 40; **20 116–19 (upd.)**

Castle Brewery, **I** 287
Castle Communications plc, **17** 13
Castle Rock Pictures, **23** 392
Castle Rubber Co., **17** 371
Castle Tretheway Mines Ltd., **IV** 164
Castlemaine Tooheys, **10** 169–70
Castorama. *See* Groupe Castorama-Dubois
    Investissements.
Castrol Ltd., **IV** 382–83
Castrorama, **10** 205
Casual Corner, **V** 207–08
**Catalina Marketing Corporation, 18
    99–102**
Catalogue Marketing, Inc., **17** 232
Catamount Petroleum Corp., **17** 121
CATCO. *See* Crowley All Terrain
    Corporation.
Caterair International Corporation, **16** 396
Caterpillar Inc., I 147, 181, 186, 422; **III
    450–53**, 458, 463, 545–46; **9** 310; **10**
    274, 377, 381, 429; **11** 473; **12** 90; **13**
    513; **15 89–93 (upd.)**, 225; **16** 180,
    309–10; **18** 125; **19** 293; **21** 173,
    499–501, 503; **22** 542
Cathay Insurance Co., **III** 221; **14** 109
Cathay Pacific Airways Limited, I 522;
    II 298; **6** 71, **78–80**; **16** 480–81; **18**
    114–15
Catherines Stores Corporation, 15 94–97
Cathodic Protection Services Co., **14** 325
Cato Corporation, 14 92–94
Cato Oil and Grease Company, **IV** 446; **22**
    302
Cattleman's, Inc., 20 120–22
Cattybrook Brick Company, **14** 249
CATV, **10** 319
Caudill Rowlett Scott. *See* CRSS Inc.
Caudle Engraving, **12** 471
CAV, **III** 554–55
Cavallo Pipeline Company, **11** 441
Cavedon Chemical Co., **I** 341
Cavendish International Holdings, **IV** 695
Cavendish Land, **III** 273
Cavenham Ltd., **7** 202–03
Caves Altovisto, **22** 344
Caves de Roquefort, **19** 51
Cawoods Holdings, **III** 735
Caxton Holdings, **IV** 641
**CB Commercial Real Estate Services
    Group, Inc., 21 94–98**
CB&I, **7** 76–77
CB&Q. *See* Chicago, Burlington and
    Quincy Railroad Company.
CB&T. *See* Synovus Financial Corp.
CBC Film Sales Co., **II** 135
CBI Industries, Inc., 7 74–77; 22 228
CBM Realty Corp., **III** 643
CBN Cable Network, **13** 279–81
CBN Satellite Services, **13** 279
CBS Inc., I 29, 488; **II** 61, 89, 102–03,
    129–31, **132–34**, 136, 152, 166–67; **III**
    55, 188; **IV** 605, 623, 652, 675, 703; **6
    157–60 (upd.)**; **11** 327; **12** 75, 561; **16**
    201–02; **17** 150, 182; **19** 210, 426, 428;
    21 24
CBS Musical Instruments, **16** 201–02
CBS Records, **II** 103, 134, 177; **6** 159; **22**
    194; **23** 33
CBT Corp., **II** 213–14
CBWL-Hayden Stone, **II** 450
CC Soft Drinks Ltd., **I** 248
CCA. *See* Container Corporation of
    America *and* Corrections Corporation of
    America.

CCAir Inc., **11** 300
CCG. *See* The Clark Construction Group,
    Inc.
CCH Computax, **7** 93–94
CCH Inc., 7 93; **14 95–97**
CCI Electronique, **10** 113
CCL Industries, Ltd., **15** 129
CCM Sport Maska, Inc., **15** 396
CCP Insurance, Inc., **10** 248
CCS Automation Systems Inc., **I** 124
CCT. *See* Crowley Caribbean Transport.
CD Titles, Inc., **22** 409
CDC. *See* Canada Development
    Corporation.
CdF-Chimie, **I** 303; **IV** 174, 198, 525
CDI. *See* Centre de Dechets Industriels
    Group.
CDI Corporation, 6 139–41
CDMS. *See* Credit and Data Marketing
    Services.
CDR International, **13** 228
CDS Holding Corp., **22** 475
CDW Computer Centers, Inc., 16 85–87
CDX Audio Development, Inc., **18** 208
CE-Minerals, **IV** 109
CEAG AG, **23** 498
Ceat Ltd., **III** 434; **20** 263
Ceco Doors, **8** 544–46
Ceco Industries, Inc. *See* Robertson-Ceco
    Corporation.
CECOS International, Inc., **V** 750
Cedar Engineering, **III** 126
Cedar Fair, L.P., 22 130–32
Cedarapids, Inc., **11** 413
Cedec S.A., **14** 43
Cederroth International AB, **8** 17
CEDIS, **12** 153
Cegedur, **IV** 174
CEIR, **10** 255
Celanese Corp., I 317–19, 347, **19** 192.
    See also Hoechst Celanese Corporation.
Celebrity, Inc., 22 133–35, 472
Celeron Corporation, **20** 258, 262–63
Celestial Farms, **13** 383
Celestial Seasonings, Inc., II 534; **16
    88–91**
Celfor Tool Company. *See* Clark
    Equipment Company.
Celite Corporation, **III** 706; **7** 291; **10** 43,
    45
Cella Italian Wines, **10** 181
Cellnet Data Systems, **11** 547; **22** 65
Cellonit-Gesellschaft Dreyfus & Cie., **I** 317
Cellstar Corporation, **18** 74
Cellu-Products Co., **14** 430
Cellular America, **6** 300
Cellular One, **9** 321
CellularVision, **13** 399
Cellulosa d'Italia, **IV** 272
Cellulose & Chemical Manufacturing Co.,
    I 317
Cellulose & Specialties, **8** 434
Cellulose du Pin, **III** 677, 704; **16** 121–22;
    19 226–27
Celotex Corporation, **III** 766–67; **22** 545
Celsius Energy Company, **6** 569
Celtex **I** 388–89. *See also* Pricel.
Cementia, **III** 705
Cementos Portland Moctezuma, **21** 261
Cemex SA de CV, 20 123–26
Cemij, **IV** 132
Cemp Investments Ltd., **16** 79–80
Cemsto, **13** 545
CenCall Communications, **10** 433

Cenco, Inc., **6** 188; **10** 262–63
Cenex Cooperative, **21** 342
Cenex Inc., **II** 536; **19** 160
Cengas, **6** 313
Centel Corporation, 6 312–15, 593; **9**
    106, 480; **10** 203; **14** 258; **16** 318; **17** 7
**Centerior Energy Corporation, V
    567–68**
Centertel, **18** 33
Centex Corporation, 8 87–89, 461; **11**
    302; **23** 327
Centocor Inc., 14 98–100
CentraBank, **II** 337; **10** 426
**Central and South West Corporation, V
    569–70; 21** 197–98
Central Area Power Coordination Group, **V**
    677
Central Arizona Light & Power Company,
    6 545
Central Bancorp of Cincinnati, **II** 342
Central Bank for Railway Securities, **II**
    281
Central Bank of Italy, **II** 403
Central Bank of London, **II** 318; **17** 323
Central Bank of Oman, **IV** 516
Central Bank of Scotland, **10** 337
Central Coalfields Ltd., **IV** 48–49
Central Computer Systems Inc., **11** 65
Central Covenants, **II** 222
Central Detallista, S.A. de C.V., **12** 154;
    16 453
Central Electric & Gas Company. *See*
    Centel Corporation.
Central Electric and Telephone Company,
    Inc. *See* Centel Corporation.
Central Elevator Co., **19** 111
Central Fiber Products Company, **12** 376
Central Finance Corporation of Canada, **II**
    418; **21** 282
Central Florida Press, **23** 101
Central Foam Corp., **I** 481, 563; **16** 322
**Central Garden & Pet Company, 23
    108–10**
Central Hankyu Ltd., **V** 71
Central Hardware, **III** 530
**Central Hudson Gas And Electricity
    Corporation, 6 458–60**
Central Illinois Public Service Company.
    See CIPSCO Inc.
**Central Independent Television, 7
    78–80; 15** 84; **23 111–14 (upd.)**
Central India Spinning, Weaving and
    Manufacturing Co., **IV** 217
Central Indiana Power Company, **6** 556
Central Investment Corp., **12** 184
Central Japan Heavy Industries, **III**
    578–79; **7** 348
Central Maine Power, 6 461–64; 14 126
Central Maloney Transformer, **I** 434
Central Mining and Investment Corp., **IV**
    23, 79, 95–96, 524, 565
Central National Bank, **9** 475
Central National Bank & Trust Co., **13** 467
Central National Life Insurance Co., **III**
    463; **21** 174
Central Nebraska Packing, **10** 250
Central Newspapers, Inc., 10 207–09
Central Pacific Railroad, **I** 381; **13** 372
Central Park Bank of Buffalo, **11** 108
Central Parking Corporation, 18 103–05
Central Penn National Corp., **11** 295
Central Planning & Design Institute, **IV** 48
Central Point Software, **10** 509

Central Public Service Corporation, **6** 447; **23** 28

Central Public Utility Corp., **13** 397

Central Research Laboratories, **22** 194

Central Savings and Loan, **10** 339

Central Solvents & Chemicals Company, **8** 100

Central Songs, **22** 193

Central Soya Company, Inc., 7 81–83

Central States Indemnity, **18** 62

Central Telephone & Utilities Corporation. *See* Centel Corporation.

Central Terminal Company, **6** 504

Central Textile, **16** 36

Central Transformer, **I** 434

Central Trust Co., **II** 313; **11** 110

Central Union Telephone Company, **14** 251, 257

Central Union Trust Co. of New York, **II** 313

Central West Public Service Company. *See* Centel Corporation.

Centralab Inc., **13** 398

Centrale Verzorgingsdienst Cotrans N.V., **12** 443

Centran Corp., **9** 475

Centre de Dechets Industriels Group, **IV** 296; **19** 226

Centre Lait, **II** 577

Centre Partners, **18** 355

Centronics Corp., **16** 192

Centros Commerciales Pryca, **23** 246, 248

Centrum Communications Inc., **11** 520

CenTrust Federal Savings, **10** 340

Centura Software, **10** 244

Centurion Brick, **14** 250

Century Bakery. *See* Dawn Food Products, Inc.

Century Bank, **II** 312

Century Brewing Company. *See* Rainier Brewing Company.

Century Cellular Network, Inc., **18** 74

Century Communications Corp., 10 210–12

Century Data Systems, Inc., **13** 127

Century Electric Company, **13** 273

Century Hutchinson, Ltd., **13** 429

Century Papers, Inc., **16** 387

Century Savings Assoc. of Kansas, **II** 420

Century Telephone Enterprises, Inc., 9 105–07

Century Tool Co., **III** 569; **20** 360

Century 21 Real Estate, **I** 127; **II** 679; **III** 293; **11** 292; **12** 489; **21** 97

CEPAM, **21** 438

CEPCO. *See* Chugoku Electric Power Company Inc.

CEPSA. *See* Compañia Española de Petroleos S.A.

Cera Trading Co., **III** 756

Ceramesh, **11** 361

Ceramic Art Company, **12** 312

Ceramic Supply Company, **8** 177

Cerberus Limited, **6** 490

Cereal Industries, **II** 466

Cereal Packaging, Ltd., **13** 294

Cereal Partners Worldwide, **10** 324; **13** 294

Cerebos, **II** 565

Cerex, **IV** 290

Ceridian Corporation, **10** 257

Cermalloy, **IV** 100

Cerner Corporation, 16 92–94

Cerro Corp., **IV** 11, 136

Cerro de Pasco Corp., **IV** 33

Cerro Metal Products Company, **16** 357

CertainTeed Corp., **III** 677–78, 621, 762; **16** 8, 121–22; **19** 58

Certanium Alloys and Research Co., **9** 419

Certified Grocers of Florida, Inc., **15** 139

Certified Laboratories, **8** 385

Certified TV and Appliance Company, **9** 120

Certus International Corp., **10** 509

Cerus, **23** 492

Cerveceria Cuauhtemoc, **19** 10

Cerveceria Moctezuma, **23** 170

Cerveceria Polar, I 230–31

Cessna Aircraft Company, III 512; **8** 49–51, 90–93, 313–14

Cetelem S.A., 21 99–102

Cetus Corp., **I** 637; **III** 53; **7** 427; **10** 78, 214

CF AirFreight, **6** 390

CF Braun, **13** 119

CF Holding Corporation, **12** 71

CF Industries, **IV** 576

CF&I Steel Corporation, **8** 135

CFC Investment Company, **16** 104

CFM. *See* Compagnie Française du Méthane.

CFP. *See* Compagnie Française des Pétroles.

CFS Continental, **II** 675

CG&E. *See* Cincinnati Gas & Electric Company.

CGCT, **I** 563

CGE. *See* Alcatel Alsthom.

CGM. *See* Compagnie Générale Maritime.

CGR-MeV, **III** 635

Chaco Energy Corporation, **V** 724–25

Chadwick's of Boston, **V** 197–98

Chalet Suisse International, Inc., **13** 362

Chalk's International Airlines, **12** 420

Challenge Corp. Ltd. *See* Fletcher Challenge Ltd.

Challenger Airlines, **22** 219

Challenger Minerals Inc., **9** 267

Chamberlain Group, Ltd., **23** 82

Chambers Corporation, **8** 298; **17** 548–49

Champ Industries, Inc., **22** 15

Champion Engineering Co., **III** 582

Champion Enterprises, Inc., 17 81–84; 22 207

Champion, Inc., **8** 459; **12** 457

Champion International Corporation, III 215; **IV** 263–65, 334; **12** 130; **15** 229; **18** 62; **20** 127–30 (upd.); **22** 352

Champion Modular Restaurant Company, Inc. *See* Checkers Drive-Up Restaurants Inc.

Champion Spark Plug Co., **II** 17; **III** 593

Champion Valley Farms, **II** 480

Champlin Petroleum Company, **10** 83

Champs Sports, **14** 293, 295

Chance Bros., **III** 724–27

Chance Vought Aircraft Co., **I** 67–68, 84–85, 489–91

Chancellor Broadcasting Co., Inc., **23** 294

Chancery Law Publishing Ltd., **17** 272

Chanco Medical Industries, **III** 73

Chandeleur Homes, Inc., **17** 83

The Chandris Group, **11** 377

Chanel, 12 57–59; 23 241

Channel Master Corporation, **II** 91; **15** 134

Channel One Communications Corp., **22** 442

Channel Tunnel Group, **13** 206

Chansam Investments, **23** 388

Chantex Inc., **18** 519

Chantiers de l'Atlantique, **9** 9

Chaparral Steel Co., 8 522–24; **13** 142–44; **18** 379; **19** 380

Chapman Valve Manufacturing Company, **8** 135

Chappel Music, **23** 389

Charan Industries Inc., **18** 519

Charan Toy Co., Inc., **18** 519

Chargeurs International, 6 373–75, 379; **20** 79; **21** 103–06 (upd.)

Charise Charles Ltd., **9** 68

Charisma Communications, **6** 323

Charles A. Eaton Co., **III** 24

Charles B. Perkins Co., **II** 667

Charles D. Burnes Co., Inc. *See* The Holson Burnes Group, Inc.

Charles Hobson, **6** 27

Charles Huston & Sons, **14** 323

Charles Luckman Assoc., **I** 513

Charles of the Ritz Group Ltd., **I** 695–97; **III** 56; **23** 237

Charles Pfizer Co., **I** 96

Charles Phillips & Co. Ltd., **II** 677

Charles R. McCormick Lumber Company, **12** 407

Charles Schwab Corp., II 228; **8** 94–96; **18** 552; **22** 52

Charles Scribner's Sons, **7** 166

Charleston Consolidated Railway, Gas and Electric Company, **6** 574

Charlestown Foundry, **III** 690

Charley Brothers, **II** 669

Charley's Eating & Drinking Saloon, **20** 54

Charmin Paper Co., **III** 52; **IV** 329; **8** 433

Charming Shoppes, Inc., 8 97–98

Charrington & Co., **I** 223

Chart House Enterprises, Inc., II 556, 613–14; **17** 70, 71, **85–88**

Chart Industries, Inc., 21 107–09

Charter Bank, **II** 348

Charter Club, **9** 315

Charter Consolidated, **IV** 23, 119–20; **16** 293

Charter Corp., **III** 254; **14** 460

Charter National Life Insurance Company, **11** 261

Charter Oil Co., **II** 620; **12** 240

Charter Security Life Insurance Cos., **III** 293

Chartered Bank, **II** 357

Chartered Co. of British New Guinea, **III** 698

Chartered Mercantile Bank of India, London and China, **II** 298

Charterhouse Petroleum, **IV** 499

Chartwell Associates, **III** 16; **9** 331

Chartwell Land, **V** 106

Chas. A. Stevens & Co., **IV** 660

Chas. H. Tompkins Co., **16** 285–86

Chase & Sanborn, **II** 544

Chase Corp., **II** 402

Chase Drier & Chemical Co., **8** 177

Chase, Harris, Forbes, **II** 402

The Chase Manhattan Corporation, I 123, 334, 451; **II** 202, 227, **247–49**, 256–57, 262, 286, 317, 385, 397, 402; **III** 104, 248; **IV** 33; **6** 52; **9** 124; **10** 61; **13 145–48 (upd.)**, 476; **14** 48, 103; **15** 38–39; **16** 460; **17** 498; **23** 482

Chastain-Roberts Company, **II** 669; **18** 504

Chaston Medical & Surgical Products, **13** 366

Chateau Cheese Co. Ltd., **II** 471

Chateau Grower Winery Co., **II** 575
Chateau St. Jean, **22** 80
Chateau Souverain, **22** 80
Chatfield & Woods Co., **IV** 311; **19** 267
Chatfield Paper Co., **IV** 282; **9** 261
Chatham and Phenix National Bank of New York, **II** 312
Chatham Bank, **II** 312
Chattanooga Gas Company, Inc., **6** 577
Chattanooga Gas Light Company, **6** 448; **23** 30
Chattanooga Medicine Company. *See* Chattem, Inc.
Chattem, Inc., 17 89–92
Chatto, Virago, Bodley Head & Jonathan Cape, Ltd., **13** 429
Chaux et Ciments de Lafarge et du Teil, **III** 703–04
Chaux et Ciments du Maroc, **III** 703
Check Point Software Technologies Ltd., **20** 238
Checker Holding, **10** 370
Checker Motors Corp., **10** 369
Checkers Drive-Up Restaurants Inc., 14 452; **16 95–98**
CheckFree Corporation, **22** 522
The Cheesecake Factory Inc., 17 93–96
Chef Boyardee, **10** 70
Chef Francisco, **13** 383
Chef Pierre, **II** 572
Chef's Orchard Airline Caterers Inc., **I** 513
Chef-Boy-Ar-Dee Quality Foods Inc., **I** 622
Cheil Sugar Co., **I** 515
Cheil Wool Textile Co., **I** 515
Chelan Power Company, **6** 596
Chem-Nuclear Systems, Inc., **9** 109–10
Chemap, **III** 420
Chemcentral Corporation, 8 99–101
Chemcut, **I** 682
Chemdal Corp., **13** 34
Chemed Corporation, 13 149–50; 15 409–11; **16** 386–87
Chemetron Process Equipment, Inc., **8** 545
Chemex Pharmaceuticals, Inc., **8** 63
Chemi-Trol Chemical Co., 16 99–101
Chemical Banking Corporation, II 234, **250–52**, 254; **9** 124, 361; **12** 15, 31; **13** 49, 147, 411; **14 101–04 (upd.); 15** 39; **21** 138
Chemical Coatings Co., **I** 321
Chemical Process Co., **IV** 409; **7** 308
Chemical Products Company, **13** 295
Chemical Specialties Inc., **I** 512
Chemical Waste Management, Inc., V 753; **9 108–10; 11** 435–36
Chemie Linz, **16** 439
Chemins de fer de Paris à Lyon et à la Méditerranée, **6** 424
Chemins de fer du Midi, **6** 425
Chemins de Fer Fédéraux, **V** 519
Chemisch-Pharmazeutische AG, **IV** 70
Chemische Fabrik auf Actien, **I** 681
Chemische Fabrik Friesheim Elektron AG, **IV** 229
Chemische Fabrik vormals Sandoz, **I** 671
Chemische Fabrik Wesseling AG, **IV** 70–71
Chemische Werke Hüls GmbH. *See* Hüls A.G.
Chemise Lacoste, **9** 157
ChemLawn, **13** 199; **23** 428, 431
Chemmar Associates, Inc., **8** 271

Chemonics Industries–Fire-Trol, **17** 161–62
Chemonics International–Consulting, **17** 161–62
Chempump, **8** 135
Chemurgic Corporation, **6** 148
Chemway Corp., **III** 423
Cheney Bigelow Wire Works, **13** 370
Cheplin Laboratories, **III** 17
Cherokee Inc., 18 106–09
Cherokee Insurance Co., **I** 153; **10** 265
Cherry Company Ltd., **I** 266; **21** 319
Cherry Hill Cheese, **7** 429
Cherry-Burrell Process Equipment, **8** 544–45
Chesapeake and Ohio Railroad, **II** 329; **V** 438–40; **10** 43; **13** 372. *See also* CSX Corporation.
Chesapeake Corporation, 8 102–04; 10 540
Chesebrough-Pond's USA, Inc., **II** 590; **7** 544; **8 105–07; 9** 319; **17** 224–25; **22** 123
Cheshire Wholefoods, **II** 528
Chester Engineers, **10** 412
Chester G. Luby, **I** 183
Chester Oil Co., **IV** 368
Cheung Kong (Holdings) Limited, I 470; **IV** 693–95; **18** 252; **20 131–34 (upd.); 23** 278, 280. *See also* Hutchison Whampoa Ltd.
Chevrolet, **V** 494; **9** 17; **19** 221, 223; **21** 153
Chevron Corporation, II 143; **IV** 367, **385–87**, 452, 464, 466, 479, 484, 490, 523, 531, 536, 539, 563, 721; **9** 391; **10** 119; **12** 20; **17** 121–22; **18** 365, 367; **19** 73, 75, **82–85 (upd.)**
Chevron U.K. Ltd., **15** 352
Chevy Chase Savings Bank, **13** 439
ChexSystems, **22** 181
Cheyenne Software, Inc., 12 60–62
CHF. *See* Chase, Harris, Forbes.
Chi-Chi's Inc., 13 151–53; 14 195
Chiat/Day Inc. Advertising, 9 438; **11** 49–52
Chiba Riverment and Cement, **III** 760
Chibu Electric Power Company, Incorporated, V 571–73
Chic by H.I.S, Inc., 20 135–37
Chicago & Calumet Terminal Railroad, **IV** 368
Chicago and Alton Railroad, **I** 456
Chicago and North Western Holdings Corporation, I 440; **6 376–78**
Chicago and Southern Airlines Inc., **I** 100; **6** 81
Chicago Bears, **IV** 703
Chicago Bridge & Iron Company, **7** 74–77
Chicago Burlington and Quincy Railroad, **III** 282; **V** 425–28
Chicago Chemical Co., **I** 373; **12** 347
Chicago Corp., **I** 526
Chicago Cubs, **IV** 682–83
Chicago Cutlery, **16** 234
Chicago Directory Co., **IV** 660–61
Chicago Edison, **IV** 169
Chicago Flexible Shaft Company, **9** 484
Chicago Heater Company, Inc., **8** 135
Chicago Magnet Wire Corp., **13** 397
Chicago Motor Club, **10** 126
Chicago Musical Instrument Company, **16** 238

Chicago Pacific Corp., **I** 530; **III** 573; **12** 251; **22** 349; **23** 244
Chicago Pneumatic Tool Co., **III** 427, 452; **7** 480; **21** 502
Chicago Radio Laboratory, **II** 123
Chicago Rawhide Manufacturing Company, **8** 462–63
Chicago Rock Island and Peoria Railway Co., **I** 558
Chicago Rollerskate, **15** 395
Chicago Screw Co., **12** 344
Chicago Shipbuilding Company, **18** 318
Chicago Steel Works, **IV** 113
Chicago Sun-Times Distribution Systems, **6** 14
Chicago Times, **11** 251
Chicago Title and Trust Co., **III** 276; **10** 43–45
Chicago Tribune. *See* Tribune Company.
Chick-fil-A Inc., 23 115–18
Chicopee Manufacturing Corp., **III** 35
Chief Auto Parts, **II** 661
Chieftain Development Company, Ltd., **16** 11
Chiers-Chatillon-Neuves Maisons, **IV** 227
Chilcott Laboratories Inc., **I** 710–11
Child World Inc., **13** 166; **18** 524
Childers Products Co., **21** 108
Children's Book-of-the-Month Club, **13** 105
Children's Palace, **13** 166
Children's Record Guild, **13** 105
Children's Television Workshop, **12** 495; **13** 560
Children's World Learning Centers, **II** 608; **V** 17, 19; **13** 48
Chiles Offshore Corporation, 9 111–13
Chili's Grill & Bar, **10** 331; **12** 373–74; **19** 258; **20** 159
Chillicothe Co., **IV** 310; **19** 266
Chilton Corp., **III** 440
Chiminter, **III** 48
Chimio, **I** 669–70; **8** 451–52
China Airlines, **6** 71
China Borneo Co., **III** 698
China Canada Investment and Development Co., **II** 457
China Coast, **10** 322, 324; **16** 156, 158
China Communications System Company, Inc. (Chinacom), **18** 34
China Development Corporation, **16** 4
China Electric, **II** 67
China Foreign Transportation Corporation, **6** 386
China Industries Co., **II** 325
China International Capital Corp., **16** 377
China International Trade and Investment Corporation, **II** 442; **IV** 695; **6** 80; **18** 113, 253; **19** 156. *See also* CITIC Pacific Ltd.
China Light & Power, **6** 499; **23** 278–80
China Mutual Steam Navigation Company Ltd., **6** 416
China National Automotive Industry Import and Export Corp., **III** 581
China National Aviation Corp., **I** 96; **18** 115; **21** 140
China National Chemicals Import and Export Corp., **IV** 395
China National Heavy Duty Truck Corporation, **21** 274
China National Machinery Import and Export Corporation, **8** 279

China National Petroleum Corp.
(SINOPEC), **18** 483
China Navigation Co., **I** 521; **16** 479–80
China Orient Leasing Co., **II** 442
China Resources (Shenyang) Snowflake
Brewery Co., **21** 320
China Zhouyang Fishery Co. Ltd., **II** 578
Chinese Electronics Import and Export
Corp., **I** 535
Chinese Metallurgical Import and Export
Corp., **IV** 61
Chinese Petroleum Corporation, IV
388–90, 493, 519
Chinese Steel Corp., **IV** 184
Chino Mines Co., **IV** 179
Chinon Industries, **III** 477; **7** 163
Chipcom, **16** 392
Chippewa Shoe, **19** 232
CHIPS and Technologies, Inc., 6 217; **9**
114–17
Chiquita Brands International, Inc., II
595–96; **III** 28; **7** 84–86; **21** 110–13
(upd.)
Chiro Tool Manufacturing Corp., **III** 629
Chiron Corporation, 7 427; **10** 213–14
Chisso Chemical, **II** 301
Chiswick Products, **II** 566
Chita Oil Co., **IV** 476
Chivers, **II** 477
Chiyoda Bank, **I** 503; **II** 321
Chiyoda Chemical, **I** 433
Chiyoda Fire and Marine, **III** 404
Chiyoda Kogaku Seiko Kabushiki Kaisha,
III 574–75
Chiyoda Konpo Kogyo Co. Ltd., **V** 536
Chiyoda Mutual, **II** 374
Chloé Chimie, **I** 303
Chloride S.A., **I** 423
Choay, **I** 676–77
Chock Full o'Nuts Corp., 17 97–100; **20**
83
Chocolat Ibled S.A., **II** 569
Chocolat Poulait, **II** 478
Chocolat-Menier S.A., **II** 569
Chogoku Kogyo, **II** 325
Choice Hotels International Inc., 6 187,
189; **14 105–07**
Chorlton Metal Co., **I** 531
Chosen Sekiyu, **IV** 554
Chotin Transportation Co., **6** 487
Chouinard Equipment. *See* Lost Arrow Inc.
Chow Tai Fook Jewellery Co., **IV** 717
Chris-Craft Industries, Inc., II 176, 403;
III 599–600; **9** 118–19
Christal Radio, **6** 33
Christensen Boyles Corporation, **19** 247
Christensen Company, **8** 397
Christian Bourgois, **IV** 614–15
Christian Broadcasting Network, **13** 279
Christian Dior S.A., I 272; **19 86–88**; **23**
237, 242
Christie, Mitchell & Mitchell, **7** 344
Christie's International plc, 15 98–101
Christopher Charters, Inc. *See* Kitty Hawk,
Inc.
Chromalloy American Corp., **13** 461
Chromalloy Gas Turbine Corp., **13** 462
Chromatic Color, **13** 227–28
Chromcraft Revington, Inc., 15 102–05
The Chronicle Publishing Company,
Inc., 23 119–22
Chrysalis Records, **22** 194
Chrysler Corporation, I 10, 17, 28, 38,
59, 79, 136, **144–45**, 152, 162–63, 172,

178, 182, 188, 190, 207, 420, 504, 516,
525, 540; **II** 5, 313, 403, 448; **III** 439,
517, 544, 568, 591, 607, 637–38; **IV** 22,
449, 676, 703; **7** 205, 233, 461; **8**
74–75, 315, 505–07; **9** 118, 349–51,
472; **10** 174, 198, 264–65, 290, 317,
353, 430; **11 53–55 (upd.)**, 103–04,
429; **13** 28–29, 61, 448, 501, 555; **14**
321, 367, 457; **16** 184, 322, 484; **17**
184; **18** 173–74, 308, 493; **20** 359–60;
22 52, 55, 175, 330; **23** 352–54
CH2M Hill Ltd., 22 136–38
Chu Ito & Co., **IV** 476
Chubb Corporation, II 84; **III** 190,
220–22, 368; **11** 481; **14 108–10 (upd.)**
Chubu Electric Power Co., **IV** 492
Chuck E. Cheese, **13** 472–74
Chugai Pharmaceutical Company, **8**
215–16; **10** 79
Chugai Shogyo Shimposha, **IV** 654–55
Chugoku Electric Power Company Inc.,
V 574–76
Chunghwa Picture Tubes, **23** 469
Chuo Trust & Banking Co. *See* Yasuda
Trust and Banking Company, Limited.
Church and Tower Group, **19** 254
Church, Goodman, and Donnelley, **IV** 660
Church's Fried Chicken, Inc., **I** 260; **7**
26–28; **15** 345; **23** 468
Churchill Insurance Co. Ltd., **III** 404
Churny Co. Inc., **II** 534
Cianbro Corporation, 14 111–13
Cianchette Brothers, Inc. *See* Cianbro
Corporation.
Ciba-Geigy Ltd., I 625, **632–34**, 671,
690, 701; **III** 55; **IV** 288; **8** 63, **108–11**
(upd.), 376–77; **9** 153, 441; **10** 53–54,
213; **15** 229; **18** 51; **21** 386; **23** 195–96
CIBC. *See* Canadian Imperial Bank of
Commerce.
Ciber, Inc., 18 110–12
CICI, **11** 184
CIDLA, **IV** 504–06
Cie Continental d'Importation, **10** 249
Cie des Lampes, **9** 9
Cie Générale d'Electro-Ceramique, **9** 9
Cifra, S.A. de C.V., 8 556; **12 63–65**
Cigarrera La Moderna, **21** 260; **22** 73
Cigarros la Tabacelera Mexicana
(Cigatam), **21** 259
CIGNA Corporation, III 197, **223–27**,
389; **10** 30; **11** 243; **22 139–44 (upd.)**,
269
CIGWELD, **19** 442
Cii-HB, **III** 123, 678; **16** 122
Cilag-Chemie, **III** 35–36; **8** 282
Cilbarco, **II** 25
Cilva Holdings PLC, **6** 358
Cima, **14** 224–25
Cimarron Utilities Company, **6** 580
CIMCO Ltd., **21** 499–501
Cimenteries CBR S.A., **23** 325, 327
Ciments d'Obourg, **III** 701
Ciments de Chalkis Portland Artificiels, **III**
701
Ciments de Champagnole, **III** 702
Ciments de l'Adour, **III** 702
Ciments Lafarge France, **III** 704
Ciments Lafarge Quebec, **III** 704
Cimos, **7** 37
Cincinnati Bell, Inc., 6 316–18
Cincinnati Chemical Works, **I** 633
Cincinnati Electronics Corp., **II** 25

Cincinnati Financial Corporation, 16
102–04
Cincinnati Gas & Electric Company, 6
465–68, 481–82
Cincinnati Milacron Inc., 12 66–69
Cincom Systems Inc., 15 106–08
Cineamerica, **IV** 676
Cinecentrum, **IV** 591
Cinema International Corp., **II** 149
Cinemark, **21** 362; **23** 125
Cinemax, **IV** 675; **7** 222–24, 528–29; **23**
276
Cineplex Odeon Corporation, II 145, **6**
161–63; **14** 87; **23 123–26 (upd.)**
Cinnabon Inc., 13 435–37; **23 127–29**
Cintas Corporation, 16 228; **21 114–16**,
507
Cintel, **II** 158
Cintra. *See* Corporacion Internacional de
Aviacion, S.A. de C.V.
CIPSCO Inc., 6 469–72, 505–06
Circa Pharmaceuticals, **16** 529
Circle A Ginger Ale Company, **9** 177
Circle International, Inc., **17** 216
The Circle K Company, II 619–20; V
210; **7** 113–14, 372, 374; **20 138–40**
(upd.)
Circle Plastics, **9** 323
Circon Corporation, 21 117–20
Circuit City Stores, Inc., 9 65–66,
120–22; **10** 235, 305–06, 334–35,
468–69; **12** 335; **14** 61; **15** 215; **16** 73,
75; **17** 489; **18** 533; **19** 362; **23** 51–53,
363
Circus Circus Enterprises, Inc., 6 201,
203–05; **19** 377, 379
Circus World, **16** 389–90
Cirrus Logic, Incorporated, 9 334; **11**
56–57
Cisco Systems, Inc., 11 58–60, 520; **13**
482; **16** 468; **19** 310; **20** 8, 33, 69, 237
CIT Alcatel, **9** 9–10
CIT Financial Corp., **II** 90, 313; **8** 117; **12**
207
CIT Group/Business Credit, Inc., **13** 446
CIT Group/Commercial Services, **13** 536
Citadel General, **III** 404
CitFed Bancorp, Inc., 16 105–07
CITGO Petroleum Corporation, II
660–61; **IV 391–93**, 508; **7** 491
Citibanc Group, Inc., **11** 456
Citibank, **II** 227, 230, 248, 250–51,
253–55, 331, 350, 358, 415; **III** 243,
340; **6** 51; **9** 124; **10** 150; **11** 418; **13**
146; **14** 101; **23** 3–4, 482
CITIC Pacific Ltd., 16 481; **18 113–15**;
20 134. *See also* China International
Trade and Investment Corporation.
Citicasters Inc., **23** 293–94
Citicorp, II 214, **253–55**, 268, 275, 319,
331, 361, 398, 411, 445; **III** 10, 220,
397; **7** 212–13; **8** 196; **9 123–26 (upd.)**,
441; **10** 463, 469; **11** 140; **12** 30, 310,
334; **13** 535; **14** 103, 108, 235; **15** 94,
146, 281; **17** 324, 559; **21** 69, 145; **22**
169, 406
Cities Service Company, **IV** 376, 391–92,
481, 575; **12** 542; **22** 172
Citifor, **19** 156
Citinet. *See* Hongkong Telecommunications
Ltd.
Citivision PLC, **9** 75

Citizen Watch Co., Ltd., III 454–56, 549; **13** 121–22; **21 121–24 (upd.); 23** 212
Citizen's Electric Light & Power Company, **V** 641
Citizen's Federal Savings Bank, **10** 93
Citizen's Fidelity Corp., **II** 342
Citizen's Industrial Bank, **14** 529
Citizens and Southern Bank, **II** 337; **10** 426
Citizens Bank, **11** 105
Citizens Bank of Hamilton, **9** 475
Citizens Bank of Savannah, **10** 426
Citizens Building & Loan Association, **14** 191
Citizens Federal Savings and Loan Association, **9** 476
Citizens Financial Group, **12** 422
Citizens Gas Co., **6** 529
Citizens Gas Fuel Company. See MCN Corporation.
Citizens Gas Light Co., **6** 455
Citizens Gas Supply Corporation, **6** 527
Citizens Mutual Savings Bank, **17** 529–30
Citizens National Bank, **II** 251; **13** 466
Citizens National Gas Company, **6** 527
Citizens Saving and Trust Company, **17** 356
Citizens Savings & Loan Association, **9** 173
Citizens Savings and Loan Society. See Citizens Mutual Savings Bank.
Citizens Telephone Company, **14** 257–58
Citizens Trust Co., **II** 312
Citizens Utilities Company, 7 87–89
Citizens' Savings and Loan, **10** 339
Citroën. See Automobiles Citroen.
City and St James, **III** 501
City and Suburban Telegraph Association and Telephonic Exchange, **6** 316–17
City and Village Automobile Insurance Co., **III** 363
City Auto Stamping Co., **I** 201
City Bank Farmers' Trust Co., **II** 254; **9** 124
City Bank of New York, **II** 250, 253
City Brewery, **I** 253
City Centre Properties Ltd., **IV** 705–06
City Finance Company, **10** 340; **11** 261
City Ice Delivery, Ltd., **II** 660
City Investing Co., **III** 263; **IV** 721; **9** 391; **13** 363
City Light and Traction Company, **6** 593
City Light and Water Company, **6** 579
City Market Inc., **12** 112
City Mutual Life Assurance Society, **III** 672–73
City National Bank of Baton Rouge, **11** 107
City National Leasing, **II** 457
City of London Real Property Co. Ltd., **IV** 706
City of Seattle Water Department, **12** 443·
The City Post Publishing Corp., **12** 359
City Products Corp., **II** 419
City Public Service, 6 473–75
City Savings, **10** 340
City Stores Company, **16** 207
Cityhome Corp., **III** 263
Civic Drugs, **12** 21
Civic Parking LLC, **18** 105
Civil & Civic Pty. Ltd., **IV** 707–08; **17** 286

Civil Service Employees Insurance Co., **III** 214
CKE Restaurants, Inc., 19 89–93, 433, 435
CKS Inc., **23** 479
Clabir Corp., **12** 199
Claeys, **22** 379–80
Claire's Stores, Inc., 17 101–03; 18 411
Clairol, **III** 17–18; **17** 110
Clairton Steel Co., **IV** 572; **7** 550
Clal Group, **18** 154
CLAM Petroleum, **7** 282
Clancy Paul Inc., **13** 276
Clara Candy, **15** 65
Clarcor Inc., 17 104–07
Clares Equipment Co., **I** 252
Clariden Bank, **21** 146–47
Clark & Co., **IV** 301
Clark & McKenney Hardware Co. See Clarcor Inc.
Clark & Rockefeller, **IV** 426
Clark Bros. Co., **III** 471
The Clark Construction Group, Inc., 8 112–13
Clark, Dietz & Associates-Engineers. See CRSS Inc.
Clark Equipment Company, I 153; **7** 513–14; **8 114–16; 10** 265; **13** 500; **15** 226
Clark Estates Inc., **8** 13
Clark Filter, Inc., **17** 104
Clark Materials Handling Company, **7** 514
Clark Motor Co., **I** 158; **10** 292
Clarkins, Inc., **16** 35–36
Clarkson International Tools, **I** 531
CLASSA. See Compañia de Líneas Aéreas Subvencionadas S.A.
Claudel Roustand Galac, **19** 50
Claussen Pickle Co., **12** 371
Clayton & Dubilier, **III** 25
Clayton Brown Holding Company, **15** 232
Clayton Homes Incorporated, 13 154–55
Clayton-Marcus Co., **12** 300
Clean Window Remodelings Co., **III** 757
Cleanaway Ltd., **III** 495
Cleancoal Terminal, **7** 582, 584
Clear Channel Communications, Inc., 23 130–32, 294
Clear Shield Inc., **17** 157, 159
Clearing Inc., **III** 514
Clearwater Tissue Mills, Inc., **8** 430
Clef, **IV** 125
Clements Energy, Inc., **7** 376
Cleo Inc., **12** 207–09
Le Clerc, **21** 225–26
Cletrac Corp., **IV** 366
Cleve-Co Jig Boring Co., **23** 82
Cleveland and Western Coal Company, **7** 369
Cleveland Electric Illuminating Company. See Centerior Energy Theodor.
Cleveland Fabric Centers, Inc. See Fabri-Centers of America Inc.
Cleveland Grinding Machine Co., **23** 82
Cleveland Iron Mining Company. See Cleveland-Cliffs Inc.
Cleveland Oil Co., **I** 341
Cleveland Paper Co., **IV** 311; **19** 267
Cleveland Pneumatic Co., **I** 457; **III** 512
Cleveland Precision Instruments, Inc., **23** 82
Cleveland Twist Drill Company. See Acme-Cleveland Corp.
Cleveland-Cliffs Inc., 13 156–58; 17 355

Clevepak Corporation, **8** 229; **13** 442
Clevite Corporation, **14** 207
CLF Research, **16** 202
Clifford & Wills, **12** 280–81
Cliffs Corporation, **13** 157
Climax Molybdenum Co., **IV** 17–19
Clinchfield Coal Corp., **IV** 180–81; **19** 320
Clinical Assays, **I** 628
Clinical Science Research Ltd., **10** 106
Clinton Pharmaceutical Co., **III** 17
Clipper Group, **12** 439
Clipper, Inc., **IV** 597
Clipper Manufacturing Company, **7** 3
Clipper Seafoods, **II** 587
The Clorox Company, III 20–22, 52; **8** 433; **22 145–48 (upd.),** 436
The Clothestime, Inc., 20 141–44
Clouterie et Tréfilerie des Flandres, **IV** 25–26
Clover Leaf Creamery, **II** 528
Clover Milk Products Co., **II** 575
Clovis Water Co., **6** 580
CLSI Inc., **15** 372
Club Aurrera, **8** 556
Club Européen du Tourisme, **6** 207
Club Méditerranée S.A., I 286; **6 206–08; 21 125–28 (upd.)**
Clubhôtel, **6** 207
Cluett Corporation, **22** 133
Cluett, Peabody & Co., Inc., **II** 414, **8** 567–68
Clyde Iron Works, **8** 545
Clydebank Engineering & Shipbuilding Co., **I** 573
Clydesdale Group, **19** 390
Clyne Maxon Agency, **I** 29
CM Industries, **I** 676
CM&M Equilease, **7** 344
CMB Acier, **IV** 228
CMB Packaging, **8** 477
CME. See Campbell-Mithun-Esty, Inc.
CML Group, Inc., 10 215–18; 22 382, 536
CMP Properties Inc., **15** 122
CMS Energy Corporation, IV 23; **V 577–79; 8** 466, **14 114–16 (upd.)**
CMT Enterprises, Inc., **22** 249
CN. See Canadian National Railway System.
CNA Financial Corporation, I 488; **III 228–32,** 339; **12** 317
CNA Health Plans, **III** 84
CNC Holding Corp., **13** 166
CNCA. See Caisse National de Crédit Agricole.
CNEP. See Comptoir National d'Escompte de Paris.
CNF Transportation. See Consolidated Freightways Corporation.
CNG. See Consolidated Natural Gas Company.
CNN. See Cable News Network.
CNS, Inc., 20 145–47
Co-Axial Systems Engineering Co., **IV** 677
Co. Luxemburgeoise de Banque S.A., **II** 282
Co. of London Insurers, **III** 369
Co-Steel International Ltd., **8** 523–24; **13** 142–43
Coach Leatherware, 10 219–21; 12 559
Coach Specialties Co. See Fleetwood Enterprises, Inc.
Coachmen, **21** 153
Coal India Limited, IV 48–50

Coalport, **12** 528
Coast American Corporation, **13** 216
Coast Consolidators, Inc., **14** 505
Coast-to-Coast Stores, **II** 419; **12** 8
Coastal Coca-Cola Bottling Co., **10** 223
Coastal Corporation, IV 366, **394–95**; **7** 553–54
Coastal Lumber, S.A., **18** 514
Coastal States Corporation, **11** 481
Coastal States Life Insurance Company, **11** 482
Coastal Valley Canning Co., **I** 260
CoastAmerica Corp., **13** 176
Coates/Lorilleux, **14** 308
Coating Products, Inc., **III** 643
Coats Viyella Plc, V 356–58
CoBank. *See* National Bank for Cooperatives.
Cobb & Branham, **14** 257
Cobb, Inc., **II** 585; **14** 515
COBE Laboratories, Inc., 13 159–61; **22** 360
Cobra Electronics Corporation, 14 117–19
Cobra Golf Inc., 16 108–10; **23** 474
Cobra Ventilation Products, **22** 229
Coburn Optical Industries, **III** 56
Coburn Vision Care, **III** 727
Coca-Cola Bottling Co. Consolidated, **II** 170, 468; **10** 222–24; **15** 299
Coca-Cola Bottling Company of Northern New England, Inc., **21** 319
The Coca-Cola Company, I 17, **232–35,** 244, 248, 278–79, 286, 289, 440, 457; **II** 103, 136–37, 477–78; **IV** 297; **6** 20–21, 30; **7** 155, 383, 466; **8** 399; **9** 86, 177; **10** 130, 222–23, **225–28** (**upd.**); **11** 421, 450–51; **12** 74; **13** 284; **14** 18, 453; **15** 428; **16** 480–81; **17** 207; **18** 60, 62–63, 68, 467–68; **19** 391; **21** 337–39, 401; **23** 418–20
Coca-Cola Enterprises, Inc., 10 223; **13** 162–64; **23** 455–57
Cochrane Corporation, **8** 135
Cochrane Foil Co., **15** 128
Cockerill Sambre Group, IV 26–27, **51–53; 22** 44
Coco's, **I** 547
Codec, **19** 328
Codex Corp., **II** 61
Codville Distributors Ltd., **II** 649
Coeur d'Alene Mines Corporation, 20 148–51
Cofica, **21** 99
COFINA, **III** 347
COFIRED, **IV** 108
Cofroma, **23** 219
Cogéma, **IV** 108
COGEMA Canada, **IV** 436
Cogentrix Energy, Inc., 10 229–31
Cogetex, **14** 225
Cogifer, S.A., **18** 4
Cognex Corp., **22** 373
CogniSeis Development, Inc., **18** 513, 515
Cognitive Solutions, Inc., **18** 140
Cognos Corp., **11** 78
Cohasset Savings Bank, **13** 468
Cohn-Hall-Marx Co. *See* United Merchants & Manufacturers, Inc.
Coils Plus, Inc., **22** 4
Coinamatic Laundry Equipment, **II** 650
Coinmach Laundry Corporation, 20 152–54
Coktel Vision, **15** 455

Colbert Television Sales, **9** 306
Colchester Car Auctions, **II** 587
Cold Spring Granite Company, 16 111–14
Coldwater Creek Inc., 21 129–31
Coldwell Banker, **IV** 715, 727; **V** 180, 182; **11** 292; **12** 97; **18** 475, 478. *See also* CB Commercial Real Estate Services Group, Inc.
Cole & Weber Inc., **I** 27
Cole National Corporation, 13 165–67, 391
Cole's Craft Showcase, **13** 166
Coleco Industries, Inc., **III** 506; **18** 520; **21** 375
Coleman & Co., **II** 230
The Coleman Company, Inc., III 485; **9** 127–29; **22** 207
Coleman Outdoor Products Inc., **21** 293
Colemans Ltd., **11** 241
Coles Book Stores Ltd., **7** 486, 488–89
Coles Express Inc., 15 109–11
Coles Myer Ltd., V 33–35; **18** 286; **20** 155–58 (**upd.**)
Colex Data, **14** 556
Colgate-Palmolive Company, I 260; **II** 672; **III** 23–26; **IV** 285; **9** 291; **11** 219, 317; **14** 120–23 (**upd.**), 279; **17** 106
Colgens, **22** 193
Collabra Software Inc., **15** 322
College Construction Loan Insurance Assoc., **II** 455
College Entrance Examination Board, **12** 141
College Survival, Inc., **10** 357
Collegiate Arlington Sports Inc., **II** 652
Collett Dickinson Pearce International Group, **I** 33; **16** 168
Collins & Aikman Corporation, I 483; **13** 168–70
Collins Radio Co., **III** 136; **11** 429
Colo-Macco. *See* CRSS Inc.
Cologne Reinsurance Co., **III** 273, 299
Colombia Graphophone Company, **22** 192
Colonia, **III** 273, 394
Colonial & General, **III** 359–60
Colonial Air Transport, **I** 89, 115; **12** 379
Colonial Airlines, **I** 102
Colonial Bancorp, **II** 208
Colonial Bank, **II** 236
Colonial Candle of Cape Cod, **18** 69
Colonial Container, **8** 359
Colonial Food Stores, **7** 373
Colonial Healthcare Supply Co., **13** 90
Colonial Insurance Co., **IV** 575–76
Colonial Life Assurance Co., **III** 359
Colonial Life Insurance Co. of America, **III** 220–21; **14** 108–09
Colonial Life Insurance Company, **11** 481
Colonial National Bank, **8** 9
Colonial National Leasing, Inc., **8** 9
Colonial Packaging Corporation, **12** 150
Colonial Penn Group Insurance Co., **11** 262
Colonial Penn Life Insurance Co., **V** 624
Colonial Rubber Works, **8** 347
Colonial Stores, **II** 397
Colonial Sugar Refining Co. Ltd., **III** 686–87
Colony Communications, **7** 99
Colony Gift Corporation, Ltd., **18** 67, 69
Color Corporation of America, **8** 553
Color-Box, Inc., **8** 103
Colorado Belle Casino, **6** 204

Colorado Cooler Co., **I** 292
Colorado Electric Company. *See* Public Service Company of Colorado.
Colorado Fuel & Iron (CF&I), **14** 369
Colorado Gaming & Entertainment Co., **21** 335
Colorado Gathering & Processing Corporation, **11** 27
Colorado Interstate Gas Co., **IV** 394
Colorado National Bank, **12** 165
Colorcraft, **I** 447
Colorfoto Inc., **I** 447
Colossal Pictures, **10** 286
Colson Co., **III** 96; **IV** 135–36
Colt, **19** 430–31
Colt Industries Inc., I 434–36, 482, 524; **III** 435
Colt Pistol Factory, **9** 416
Colt's Manufacturing Company, Inc., 12 70–72
Columbia Broadcasting System. *See* CBS Inc.
Columbia Chemical Co. *See* PPG Industries, Inc.
Columbia Electric Street Railway, Light and Power Company, **6** 575
Columbia Forest Products, **IV** 358
Columbia Gas & Electric Company, **6** 466. *See also* Columbia Gas System, Inc.
Columbia Gas Light Company, **6** 574
Columbia Gas of New York, Inc., **6** 536
The Columbia Gas System, Inc., V 580–82; **16** 115–18 (**upd.**)
Columbia Gas Transmission Corporation, **6** 467
Columbia General Life Insurance Company of Indiana, **11** 378
Columbia Hat Company, **19** 94
Columbia House, **IV** 676
Columbia Insurance Co., **III** 214
Columbia News Service, **II** 132
Columbia Paper Co., **IV** 311; **19** 266
Columbia Pictures Entertainment, Inc., II 103, 134, **135–37,** 170, 234, 619; **IV** 675; **10** 227; **12** 73, 455; **21** 360; **22** 193. *See also* Columbia TriStar Motion Pictures Companies.
Columbia Railroad, Gas and Electric Company, **6** 575
Columbia Recording Corp., **II** 132
Columbia Records Distribution Corp., **16** 201
Columbia River Packers, **II** 491
Columbia Savings & Loan, **II** 144
Columbia Sportswear Company, 19 94–96
Columbia Steamship Company, **17** 356
Columbia Steel Co., **IV** 28, 573; **7** 550
Columbia Transportation Co., **17** 357
Columbia TriStar Motion Pictures Companies, 12 73–76 (**upd.**). *See also* Columbia Pictures Entertainment, Inc.
Columbia TriStar Television Distribution, **17** 149
Columbia/HCA Healthcare Corporation, 13 90; **15** 112–14; **22** 409–10
Columbian Chemicals Co., **IV** 179
Columbian Peanut Co., **I** 421; **11** 23
Columbus & Southern Ohio Electric Company (CSO), **6** 467, 481–82
Columbus Bank & Trust. *See* Synovus Financial Corp.
Columbus Savings and Loan Society, **I** 536; **13** 528

Columbus-Milpar, **I** 544
Colwell Systems, **19** 291; **22** 181
Com Ed. *See* Commonwealth Edison.
Com-Link 21, Inc., **8** 310
Comair Holdings Inc., 13 171–73
Comalco Fabricators (Hong Kong) Ltd., **III** 758
Comalco Ltd., **IV** 59–61, 122, 191
Comat Services Pte. Ltd., **10** 514
Comau, **I** 163
Combibloc Inc., **16** 339
Combined American Insurance Co. of Dallas, **III** 203
Combined Casualty Co. of Philadelphia, **III** 203
Combined Communications Corp., **II** 619; **IV** 612; **7** 191
Combined Insurance Co. of America, **III** 203–04
Combined International Corp., **III** 203–04
Combined Mutual Casualty Co. of Chicago, **III** 203
Combined Properties, Inc., **16** 160
Combined Registry Co., **III** 203
Combustion Engineering Group, **22** 11
Combustiveis Industriais e Domésticos. *See* CIDLA.
Comcast Corporation, 7 90–92; 9 428; **10** 432–33; **17** 148; **22** 162
Comdata, **19** 160
Comdial Corporation, 21 132–35
Comdisco, Inc., 9 130–32; 11 47, 86, 484, 490
Comdor Flugdienst GmbH., **I** 111
Comer Motor Express, **6** 370
Comerco, **III** 21; **22** 147
Comet, **II** 139; **V** 106–09
Cometra Oil, **IV** 576
ComFed Bancorp, **11** 29
Comfort Inns, **21** 362
Comforto GmbH, **8** 252
Cominco, **16** 364
Cominco Fertilizers Ltd., **IV** 75, 141; **13** 503
Comision Federal de Electricidad de Mexico (CFE), **21** 196–97
Comitato Interministrale per la Ricostruzione, **I** 465
Comm-Quip, **6** 313
CommAir. *See* American Building Maintenance Industries, Inc.
Commander Foods, **8** 409
Commander-Larabee Co., **I** 419
Commemorative Brands Inc., **19** 453
Commentry, **III** 676; **16** 120
Commerce and Industry Insurance Co., **III** 196, 203
Commerce Clearing House, Inc., 7 93–94. *See also* CCH Inc.
Commerce Group, **III** 393
Commerce Union, **10** 426
Commercial & General Life Assurance Co., **III** 371
Commercial Air Lines, Inc., **23** 380
Commercial Alliance Corp. of New York, **II** 289
Commercial Aseguradora Suizo Americana, S.A., **III** 243
Commercial Assurance, **III** 359
Commercial Bank of Australia Ltd., **II** 189, 319, 388–89; **17** 324
Commercial Bank of London, **II** 334
Commercial Bank of Tasmania, **II** 188

Commercial Banking Co. of Sydney, **II** 187–89
Commercial Bureau (Australia) Pty., **I** 438
Commercial Chemical Company, **16** 99
Commercial Credit Company, III 127–28; **8 117–19; 10** 255–56; **15** 464
Commercial Exchange Bank, **II** 254; **9** 124
Commercial Federal Corporation, 12 77–79
Commercial Filters Corp., **I** 512
Commercial Insurance Co. of Newark, **III** 242
Commercial Life, **III** 243
Commercial Life Assurance Co. of Canada, **III** 309
Commercial Metals Company, 15 115–17
Commercial Motor Freight, Inc., **14** 42
Commercial National Bank, **II** 261; **10** 425
Commercial National Bank & Trust Co., **II** 230
Commercial National Bank of Charlotte, **II** 336
Commercial Realty Services Group, **21** 257
Commercial Ship Repair Co., **I** 185
Commercial Union plc, II 272, 308; **III** 185, **233–35**, 350, 373; **IV** 711
Commerzbank A.G., II 239, 242, **256–58**, 280, 282, 385; **IV** 222; **9** 283; **14** 170
Commerzfilm, **IV** 591
CommLink Corp., **17** 264
Commodity Credit Corp., **11** 24
Commodore Corporation, **8** 229
Commodore International, Ltd., II 6; **III** 112; **6** 243–44; **7 95–97**, 532; **9** 46; **10** 56, 284; **23** 25
Commonwealth & Southern Corporation, **V** 676
Commonwealth Aluminium Corp., Ltd. *See* Comalco Ltd.
Commonwealth Bank, **II** 188, 389
Commonwealth Board Mills, **IV** 248
Commonwealth Edison, II 28, 425; **III** 653; **IV** 169; **V 583–85; 6** 505, 529, 531; **12** 548; **13** 341; **15** 422
Commonwealth Energy System, 14 124–26
Commonwealth Hospitality Ltd., **III** 95
Commonwealth Industries, **III** 569; **11** 536; **20** 360
Commonwealth Insurance Co., **III** 264
Commonwealth Land Title Insurance Co., **III** 343
Commonwealth Life Insurance Co., **III** 216–19
Commonwealth Mortgage Assurance Co., **III** 344
Commonwealth National Financial Corp., **II** 316
Commonwealth Oil Refining Company, **II** 402; **7** 517
Commonwealth Power Railway and Light Company, **14** 134
Commonwealth Southern Corporation, **14** 134
Commtron, Inc., **V** 14, 16; **11** 195; **13** 90
Communication Services Ltd. *See* Hongkong Telecommunications Ltd.
Communications and Systems Specialists, **18** 370
Communications Consultants, Inc., **16** 393
Communications Data Services, Inc., **IV** 627; **19** 204

Communications Properties, Inc., **IV** 677
Communications Solutions Inc., **11** 520
Communications Technology Corp. (CTC), **13** 7–8
Communicorp, **III** 188; **10** 29
Community Direct, Inc., **7** 16
Community HealthCare Services, **6** 182
Community Hospital of San Gabriel, **6** 149
Community Medical Care, Inc., **III** 245
Community National Bank, **9** 474
Community Power & Light Company, **6** 579–80
Community Psychiatric Centers, 15 118–20
Community Public Service Company, **6** 514
Community Savings and Loan, **II** 317
Comnet Corporation, **9** 347
Comp-U-Card of America, Inc. *See* CUC International Inc.
Compac Corp., **11** 535
Compactom, **I** 588
Compagnia di Assicurazioni, **III** 345
Compagnia di Genova, **III** 347
Compagnie Auxiliaire de Navigation, **IV** 558
Compagnie Bancaire, **II** 259; **21** 99–100
Compagnie Belge pour l'industrie, **II** 202
Compagnie Continentale, **I** 409–10
Compagnie d'Assurances Générales, **III** 391
Compagnie d'assurances Mutuelles contre l'incendie dans les départements de la Seine Inférieure et de l'Eure, **III** 210
Compagnie d'Investissements de Paris, **II** 233
Compagnie de Compteurs, **III** 617; **17** 418
Compagnie de Five-Lille, **IV** 469
Compagnie de Mokta, **IV** 107–08
Compagnie de Navigation Mixte, **III** 185
Compagnie de Reassurance Nord-Atlantique, **III** 276
Compagnie de Recherche et d'Exploitation du Pétrole du Sahara, **IV** 545; **21** 203
Compagnie de Saint-Gobain S.A., II 117, 474–75; **III 675–78**, 704; **8** 395, 397; **15** 80; **16 119–23 (upd.); 19** 58, 226; **21** 222
Compagnie de Transport Aerien, **I** 122
Compagnie des Machines Bull S.A., II 40, 42, 70, 125; **III 122–23**, 154; **IV** 600; **12** 139; **13** 574. *See also* Groupe Bull.
Compagnie des Messageries Maritimes, **6** 379
Compagnie des Produits Chimiques et Électrométallurgiques d'Alais, Froges et Camargue, **IV** 173–74
Compagnie du Midi, **III** 209, 211
Compagnie du Nord, **IV** 108
Compagnie Européenne de Publication, **IV** 614–15
Compagnie Financier Richemont AG, **19** 367, 369–70
Compagnie Financiere Alcatel, **9** 10
Compagnie Financière de Paribas, II 192, **259–60**; **III** 185; **21** 99
Compagnie Financière de Suez, **III** 394
Compagnie Française de Distribution en Afrique, **IV** 559
Compagnie Française de Raffinage, **IV** 558–60
Compagnie Française des Lubricants, **I** 341

Compagnie Française des Minerais
d'Uranium, **IV** 108
Compagnie Française des Mines de
Diamants du Cap, **IV** 64; **7** 121
Compagnie Française des Pétroles, **II** 259;
IV 363–64, 423–24, 454, 466, 486, 504,
515, 544–46, 557–60; **7** 481–83; **21** 203
Compagnie Française des Produits
d'Orangina, **I** 281
Compagnie Française du Méthane, **V** 626
Compagnie Française Thomson-Houston, **I**
357; **II** 116
Compagnie Générale d'Électricité, I 193;
II 12–13, 25; **IV** 174, 615; **9** 9–10
Compagnie Generale de Cartons Ondules,
IV 296; **19** 226
Compagnie Generale de Radiologie, **II** 117
Compagnie Generale de Telegraphie Sans
Fils, **II** 116
Compagnie Générale des Eaux, **V** 632–33;
6 441
**Compagnie Générale des Établissements
Michelin, V 236–39; 19** 508
**Compagnie Générale Maritime et
Financière, 6 379–81**
Compagnie Industriali Riunite S.p.A., **IV**
587–88
Compagnie Industrielle des Fillers. *See*
L'Entreprise Jean Lefebvre.
Compagnie Internationale de
l'Informatique, **III** 123
Compagnie Internationale Pirelli S.A., **V**
249
Compagnie Luxembourgeoise de
Télédiffusion, **15** 54
Compagnie Navale Des Pétroles, **IV** 558
Compagnie Parisienne de Garantie, **III** 211
Compagnie Pneumatique Commerciale, **III**
426
Compagnie Tunisienne de Ressorts a
Lames, **III** 581
Companhia Brasileira de Aluminio, **IV** 55
Companhia Brasileira de Mineracão e
Siderugica, **IV** 54
Companhia de Celulose do Caima, **14** 250
Companhia de Diamantes de Angola, **IV**
21
Companhia de Minerales y Metales, **IV**
139
Companhia de Pesquisas Mineras de
Angola, **IV** 65; **7** 122
Companhia de Seguros Argos Fluminense,
III 221
Companhia de Seguros Tranquilidade Vida,
S.A. *See* Banco Espírito Santo e
Comercial de Lisboa S.A.
Companhia Siderúrgica de Tubarao, **IV**
125
Companhia Siderúrgica Mannesmann S.A.,
III 565–66
Companhia Siderúrgica Nacional, **II** 199
Companhia Uniao Fabril, **IV** 505
Companhia Vale do Rio Doce, IV 54–57
Compañia Arrendataria del Monopolio de
Petróleos Sociedad Anónima, **IV**
396–97, 527–29
Compañia de Investigacion y
Exploitaciones Petrolifera, **IV** 397
Compañia de Líneas Aéreas
Subvencionadas S.A., **6** 95
**Compañia Española de Petroleos S.A.,
IV 396–98,** 527
Compania Fresnillo, **22** 286

Compania General de Aceptaciones. *See*
Financiera Aceptaciones.
Compania Hulera Euzkadi, **21** 260; **23** 170
Compañía Mexicana de Transportación
Aérea, **20** 167
Compania Minera de Penoles. *See*
Industrias Penoles, S.A. de C.V.
Compañia Minera La India, **IV** 164
Compania Minera Las Torres, **22** 286
Compañia Nacional Minera Petrólia del
Táchira, **IV** 507
Compañía Telefónica Nacional de España
S.A., **V** 337
Compaq Computer Corporation, II 45;
III 114, **124–25; 6** 217, **221–23 (upd.),**
230–31, 235, 243–44; **9** 42–43, 166,
170–71, 472; **10** 87, 232–33, 366, 459,
518–19; **12** 61, 183, 335, 470; **13** 388,
483; **16** 4, 196, 367–68; **17** 274; **21** 123,
391; **22** 288
Compass Design Automation, **16** 520
Compass Group, plc, **6** 193
CompDent Corporation, 22 149–51
Compeda, Ltd., **10** 240
Competition Tire East/West, **V** 494; **19** 292
Competrol Ltd., **22** 189
Compex, **II** 233
Components Agents Ltd., **10** 113
Composite Craft Inc., **I** 387
Composite Research & Management Co.,
17 528, 530
**Comprehensive Care Corporation, 15
121–23**
Comprehensive Resources Corp., **IV** 83
Compressed Industrial Gases, **I** 297
Compression Labs Inc., **10** 456; **16** 392,
394
Compressor Controls Corporation, **15** 404
Comptoir d'Escompte de Mulhouse, **II** 232
Comptoir des Textiles Artificielles, **I** 122,
388–89
Comptoir Métallurgique Luxembourgeois,
IV 25
Comptoir National d'Escompte de Paris, **II**
232–33, 270
Comptoirs Modernes S.A., 19 97–99
Compton Communications, **I** 33
Compton Foods, **II** 675
Compton's MultiMedia Publishing Group,
Inc., **7** 165
Compton's New Media, Inc., **7** 168
Compu-Notes, Inc., **22** 413
**CompuAdd Computer Corporation, 11
61–63**
CompuChem Corporation, **11** 425
CompuCom Systems, Inc., 10 232–34,
474; **13** 176
Compugraphic, **III** 168; **6** 284
Compumech Technologies, **19** 312
Compumotor, **III** 603
CompuPharm, Inc., **14** 210
CompUSA, Inc., 10 235–36; 11 63
CompuServe Incorporated, 9 268–70; **10**
237–39; 12 562; **13** 147; **15** 265; **16**
467, 508
Computax, **6** 227–28
**Computer Associates International, Inc.,
6 224–26; 10** 394; **12** 62; **14** 392
Computer City, **12** 470
The Computer Company, **11** 112
Computer Consoles Inc., **III** 164
Computer Data Systems, Inc., 14 127–29
The Computer Department, Ltd., **10** 89
Computer Depot, **6** 243

Computer Discount Corporation. *See*
Comdisco, Inc.
Computer Dynamics, Inc., **6** 10
Computer Factory, Inc., **13** 176
Computer Network, **20** 237
Computer Peripheral Manufacturers
Association, **13** 127
Computer Plaza K.K., **IV** 542–43
Computer Power, **6** 301
Computer Renaissance, Inc., **18** 207–8
Computer Research Corp., **III** 151; **6** 265
Computer Sciences Corporation, 6 25,
227–29; 13 462; **15** 474; **18** 370
Computer Shoppe, **V** 191–92
Computer Systems and Applications, **12**
442
Computer Systems Division (CDS), **13** 201
Computer Terminal Corporation, **11** 67–68
ComputerCity, **10** 235
Computerized Lodging Systems, Inc., **11**
275
ComputerLand Corp., 6 243; **9** 116; **10**
233, 563; **12** 335; **13 174–76,** 277
Computervision Corporation, 6 246–47;
7 498; **10 240–42; 11** 275; **13** 201
Computing Scale Company of America.
See International Business Machines
Corporation.
Computing-Tabulating-Recording Co., **III**
147
Compuware Corporation, 10 243–45
CompX International, Inc., **19** 466, 468
Comsat Corporation, II 425; **12** 19; **13**
341; **23 133–36**
Comshare Inc., 23 137–39
Comstock Canada, **9** 301
Comtel Electronics, Inc., **22** 409
Comverse Technology, Inc., 15 124–26
Con Ed. *See* Consolidated Edison of New
York, Inc.
Con-Ferro Paint and Varnish Company, **8**
553
ConAgra, Inc., II 493–95, 517, 585; **7**
432, 525; **8** 53, 499–500; **12 80–82**
(upd.); 13 138, 294, 350, 352; **14** 515;
17 56, 240–41; **18** 247, 290; **21** 290; **23**
320
Conahay & Lyon, **6** 27
Conair Corp., 16 539; **17 108–10**
Concept, Inc., **23** 154
Concert Communications Company, **15** 69
Concession Air, **16** 446
Concord Fabrics, Inc., 16 124–26
Concord International, **II** 298
Concordia, **IV** 497
Concrete Industries (Monier) Ltd., **III** 735
Concurrent Logic, **17** 34
The Condé Nast Publications Inc., IV
583–84; **13 177–81; 19** 5; **23** 98
Condor Systems Inc., **15** 530
Cone Mills Corporation, 8 120–22
Conelectron, **13** 398
Conestoga National Bank, **II** 316
Confederation Freezers, **21** 501
Confederation of Engineering Industry, **IV**
484
Confidata Corporation, **11** 111
Confindustria, **I** 162
Congas Engineering Canada Ltd., **6** 478
Congoleum Corp., 12 28; **16** 18; **18**
116–19
Congress Financial Corp., **13** 305–06; **19**
108

Congressional Information Services, **IV** 610

Conic, **9** 324

Conifer Group, **II** 214

Conill Corp., **II** 261

Coniston Partners, **I** 130; **II** 680; **III** 29; **6** 130; **10** 302

CONNA Corp., **7** 113

Connecticut Bank and Trust Co., **II** 213–14

Connecticut General Corporation. *See* CIGNA Corporation.

Connecticut Health Enterprises Network, **22** 425

Connecticut Light and Power Co., 13 182–84; 21 514

Connecticut Mutual Life Insurance Company, III 225, **236–38**, 254, 285

Connecticut National Bank, **13** 467

Connecticut River Banking Company, **13** 467

Connecticut Telephone Company. *See* Southern New England Telecommunications Corporation.

Connecticut Trust and Safe Deposit Co., **II** 213

Connecticut Yankee Atomic Power Company, **21** 513

Connecting Point of America, **6** 244

Conner Corp., **15** 327

Conner Peripherals, Inc., 6 230–32; 10 403, 459, 463–64, 519; **11** 56, 234; **18** 260

Connie Lee. *See* College Construction Loan Insurance Assoc.

Connolly Data Systems, **11** 66

Connolly Tool and Machine Company, **21** 215

Connors Brothers, **II** 631–32

Connors Steel Co., **15** 116

Conoco Inc., I 286, 329, 346, 402–04; **II** 376; **IV** 365, 382, 389, **399–402**, 413, 429, 454, 476; **6** 539; **7** 346, 559; **8** 152, 154, 556; **11** 97, 400; **16 127–32 (upd.)**; **18** 366; **21** 29

Conorada Petroleum Corp., **IV** 365, 400

Conover Furniture Company, **10** 183

ConQuest Telecommunication Services Inc., **16** 319

Conrad International Hotels, **III** 91–93

Conrail Inc., **22** 167, 376. *See also* Consolidated Rail Corporation.

Conran Associates, **17** 43

Conrock Co., **19** 70

Conseco Inc., 10 246–48; 15 257

Consgold. *See* Consolidated Gold Fields of South Africa Ltd. *and* Consolidated Gold Fields PLC.

Consolidated Aircraft Corporation, **9** 16, 497

Consolidated Aluminum Corp., **IV** 178

Consolidated Brands Inc., **14** 18

Consolidated Cable Utilities, **6** 313

Consolidated Cement Corp., **III** 704

Consolidated Cigar Corp., **I** 452–53; **15** 137–38

Consolidated Coal Co., **IV** 82, 170–71

Consolidated Coin Caterers Corporation, **10** 222

Consolidated Controls, **I** 155

Consolidated Converting Co., **19** 109

Consolidated Copper Corp., **13** 503

Consolidated Denison Mines Ltd., **8** 418

Consolidated Diamond Mines of South-West Africa Ltd., **IV** 21, 65–67; **7** 122–25; **16** 26

Consolidated Distillers Ltd., **I** 263

Consolidated Edison Company of New York, Inc., I 28; **V 586–89**; **6** 456

Consolidated Electric & Gas, **6** 447; **23** 28

Consolidated Electric Supply Inc., **15** 385

Consolidated Electronics Industries Corp. (Conelco), **13** 397–98

Consolidated Foods Corp., **II** 571–73, 584; **III** 480; **12** 159, 494; **22** 27

Consolidated Freightways Corporation, V 432–34; 6 280, 388; **12** 278, 309; **13** 19; **14** 567; **21 136–39 (upd.)**

Consolidated Gold Fields of South Africa Ltd., **IV** 94, 96, 118, 565, 566

Consolidated Gold Fields PLC, **II** 422; **III** 501, 503; **IV** 23, 67, 94, 97, 171; **7** 125, 209, 387

Consolidated Grocers Corp., **II** 571

Consolidated Insurances of Australia, **III** 347

Consolidated Marketing, Inc., **IV** 282; **9** 261

Consolidated Mines Selection Co., **IV** 20, 23

Consolidated Mining and Smelting Co., **IV** 75

Consolidated National Life Insurance Co., **10** 246

Consolidated Natural Gas Company, V 590–91; 19 100–02 (upd.)

Consolidated Oatmeal Co., **II** 558

Consolidated Papers, Inc., 8 123–25; 11 311

Consolidated Power & Light Company, **6** 580

Consolidated Power & Telephone Company, **11** 342

Consolidated Press Holdings, **8** 551

Consolidated Products, Inc., 14 130–32, 352

Consolidated Rail Corporation, II 449; **V 435–37**, 485; **10** 44; **12** 278; **13** 449; **14** 324. *See also* Conrail Inc.

Consolidated Rand-Transvaal Mining Group, **IV** 90; **22** 233

Consolidated Rock Products Co., **19** 69

Consolidated Specialty Restaurants, Inc., **14** 131–32

Consolidated Steel, **I** 558; **IV** 570

Consolidated Stores Corp., **13** 543

Consolidated Temperature Controlling Co., **II** 40; **12** 246

Consolidated Theaters, Inc., **14** 87

Consolidated Tire Company, **20** 258

Consolidated Trust Inc., **22** 540

Consolidated Tyre Services Ltd., **IV** 241

Consolidated Vultee, **II** 7, 32

Consolidated Zinc Corp., **IV** 58–59, 122, 189, 191

Consolidated-Bathurst Inc., **IV** 246–47, 334

Consolidation Coal Co., **IV** 401; **8** 154, 346–47

Consortium De Realization SAS, **23** 392

Consoweld Corporation, **8** 124

Constar International Inc., **8** 562; **13** 190

Constellation, **III** 335

Constellation Insurance Co., **III** 191–92

Construcciones Aeronauticas S.A., **I** 41–42; **12** 190

Construcciones y Contratas, **II** 198

Construction DJL Inc., **23** 332–33

Construtora Moderna SARL, **IV** 505

Consul Restaurant Corp., **13** 152

Consumer Value Stores, **V** 136–37; **9** 67; **18** 199

Consumer's Gas Co., **I** 264

Consumers Cooperative Association, **7** 174

Consumers Distributing Co. Ltd., **II** 649, 652–53

Consumers Electric Light and Power, **6** 582

The Consumers Gas Company Ltd., 6 476–79

Consumers Power Co., V 577–79, 593–94; **14** 114–15, **133–36**

Consumers Water Company, 14 137–39

Contact Software International Inc., **10** 509

Contadina, **II** 488–89

Container Corporation of America, **IV** 295, 465; **V** 147; **7** 353; **8** 476; **19** 225

Container Transport International, **III** 344

Containers Packaging, **IV** 249

Contaminant Recovery Systems, Inc., **18** 162

Conte S.A., **12** 262

Contech, **10** 493

Contel Corporation, **II** 117; **V 294–98**; **6** 323; **13** 212; **14** 259; **15** 192

Contempo Associates, **14** 105

Contempo Casuals, Inc. *See* The Wet Seal, Inc.

Contemporary Books, **22** 522

Contherm Corp., **III** 420

Conti-Carriers & Terminals Inc., **22** 167

ContiCommodity Services, Inc., **10** 250–51

Continental AG, **9** 248; **15** 355

Continental Airlines, Inc., I 96–98, 103, 118, **123–24**, 129–30; **6** 52, 61, 105, 120–21, 129–30; **12** 381; **20** 84, 262; **21 140–43 (upd.)**; **22** 80, 220

Continental Aktiengesellschaft, V 240–43, 250–51, 256; **8** 212–14; **19** 508

Continental American Life Insurance Company, **7** 102

Continental Assurance Co., **III** 228–30

Continental Baking Co., **I** 463–64; **II** 562–63; **7** 320–21; **11** 198; **12** 276; **13** 427; **19** 192

Continental Bancor, **II** 248

Continental Bank and Trust Co., **II** 251; **14** 102

Continental Bank Corporation, I 526; **II** 261–63, 285, 289, 348; **IV** 702

Continental Blacks Inc., **I** 403

Continental Cablevision, Inc., 7 98–100; **17** 148; **19** 201

Continental Can Co., Inc., I 597; **II** 34, 414; **III** 471; **10** 130; **13** 255; **15 127–30**

Continental Carbon Co., **I** 403–05; **II** 53; **IV** 401

Continental Care Group, **10** 252–53

Continental Casualty Co., **III** 196, 228–32; **16** 204

Continental Cities Corp., **III** 344

Continental Corporation, III 230, **239–44**, 273; **10** 561; **12** 318; **15** 30

Continental Cos., **III** 248

Continental Divide Insurance Co., **III** 214

Continental Electronics Corporation, **18** 513–14

Continental Equipment Company, **13** 225

Continental Express, **11** 299

Continental Fiber Drum, **8** 476

Continental Gas & Electric Corporation, **6** 511

Continental General Tire Corp., 23 **140–42**

Continental Grain Company, 10 249–51; **13** 185–87 (upd.)

Continental Group Co., I 599–600, 601–02, 604–05, 607–09, 612–13, 615; **IV** 334; **8** 175, 424; **17** 106

Continental Gummi-Werke Aktiengesellschaft, **V** 241; **9** 248

Continental Hair Products, Inc. *See* Conair Corp.

Continental Health Affiliates, **17** 307

Continental Illinois Corp. *See* Continental Bank Corporation.

Continental Illinois Venture Co., **IV** 702

Continental Insurance Co., **III** 239–42, 372–73, 386

Continental Insurance Cos. of New York, **III** 230

Continental Investment Corporation, **9** 507; **12** 463; **22** 541

Continental Life Insurance Co., **III** 225

Continental Medical Systems, Inc., 10 **252–54; 11** 282; **14** 233

Continental Milling Company, **10** 250

Continental Motors Corp., **I** 199, 524–25; **10** 521–22

Continental Mutual Savings Bank, **17** 529

Continental National American Group, **III** 230, 404

Continental National Bank, **II** 261; **11** 119

Continental Oil Co., **IV** 39, 365, 382, 399–401, 476, 517, 575–76

Continental Packaging Inc., **13** 255

Continental Radio, **IV** 607

Continental Reinsurance, **11** 533

Continental Research Corporation, **22** 541

Continental Restaurant Systems, **12** 510

Continental Risk Services, **III** 243

Continental Savouries, **II** 500

Continental Scale Works, **14** 229–30

Continental Securities Corporation, **II** 444; **22** 404

Continental Telephone Company, **V** 296–97; **9** 494–95; **11** 500; **15** 195

Continental Wood Preservers, Inc., **12** 397

Continental-Caoutchouc und Gutta-Percha Compagnie, **V** 240

Continental-Emsco, **I** 490–91

Continental-National Group, **III** 230

Continentale Allgemeine, **III** 347

Contran Corporation, **19** 467

Contrans Acquisitions, Inc., **14** 38

Contred Ltd., **20** 263

Control Data Corporation, **17** 49; **19** 110, 513–15

Control Data Systems, Inc., III 118, **126–28,** 129, 131, 149, 152, 165; **6** 228, 252, 266; **8** 117–18, 467; **10** 255–57, 359, 458–59; **11** 469; **16** 137

Controladora PROSA, **18** 516, 518

Controlonics Corporation, **13** 195

Controls Company of America, **9** 67

Controlware GmbH, **22** 53

Convair, **I** 82, 121, 123, 126, 131; **II** 33; **9** 18, 498; **13** 357

Convenient Food Mart Inc., **7** 114

Convergent Technologies, **III** 166; **6** 283; **11** 519

Converse Inc., III 528–29; **V** 376; **9** **133–36,** 234; **12** 308

Conway Computer Group, **18** 370

Conwest Exploration Company Ltd., **16** 10, 12

Conycon. *See* Construcciones y Contratas.

Conzinc Riotinto of Australia. *See* CRA Limited.

Cook Data Services, Inc., **9** 73

Cook Industrial Coatings, **I** 307

Cook Standard Tool Co., **13** 369

Cooke Engineering Company, **13** 194

The Cooker Restaurant Corporation, 20 **159–61**

Cooking and Crafts Club, **13** 106

Cookson Group plc, **III** 679–82; **16** 290

Coolerator, **I** 463

Coolidge Mutual Savings Bank, **17** 529

Cooper Cameron Corporation, 20 **162–66 (upd.)**

Cooper Canada Ltd., **16** 80

Cooper Industries, Inc., II 14–17; 14 564; **19** 43, 45, 140

Cooper Laboratories, **I** 667, 682

Cooper LaserSonics Inc., **IV** 100

Cooper McDougall & Robertson Ltd., **I** 715

Cooper Tire & Rubber Company, 8 **126–28; 23 143–46 (upd.)**

Cooper's, Inc., **12** 283

Cooper-Weymouth, **10** 412

Cooperative Grange League Federation Exchange, **7** 17

Coopers & Lybrand, 9 137–38; 12 391

CooperVision, **7** 46

Coordinated Caribbean Transport. *See* Crowley Caribbean Transport.

Coors Company. *See* Adolph Coors Company.

Coorsh and Bittner, **7** 430

Coos Bay Lumber Co., **IV** 281; **9** 259

Coosa River Newsprint Co., **III** 40; **16** 303

Coote & Jurgenson, **14** 64

Cooymans, **I** 281

Copart Inc., 23 147–49, 285, 287

Copeland Corp., **II** 20

Copeman Ridley, **13** 103

Copland Brewing Co., **I** 268

Copley Pharmaceuticals Inc., **13** 264

The Copley Press, Inc., 23 150–52

Copley Real Estate Advisors, **III** 313

Copolymer Corporation, **9** 242

Copper Queen Consolidated Mining Co., **IV** 176–77

Copper Range Company, **IV** 76; **7** 281–82

Copperweld Steel Co., **IV** 108–09, 237

Copycat Ltd., **8** 383

Cora Verlag, **IV** 590

Coral Drilling, **I** 570

Coral Leisure Group, **I** 248

Coral Petroleum, **IV** 395

Corbett Enterprises Inc., **13** 270

Corby Distilleries Limited, 14 140–42

Corco. *See* Commonwealth Oil Refining Company.

Corco, Inc. *See* Liqui-Box Corporation.

Corcoran & Riggs. *See* Riggs National Corporation.

Cordiant plc. *See* Saatchi & Saatchi plc.

Cordis Corp., 19 103–05

Cordon & Gotch, **IV** 619

Cordon Bleu, **II** 609

Cordovan Corp., **IV** 608

Core Laboratories Inc., **I** 486; **11** 265

Corel Corporation, 15 131–33

CoreStates Financial Corp, 17 111–15

Corfuerte S.A. de C.V., **23** 171

Corimon, **12** 218

Corinthian Broadcast Corporation, **IV** 605; **10** 4

Cormetech, **III** 685

Corn Exchange Bank, **II** 316

Corn Exchange Bank Trust Co., **II** 251; **14** 102

Corn Exchange National Bank, **II** 261

Corn Products Company. *See* Bestfoods.

Corn Sweetners Inc., **I** 421; **11** 23

Cornerstone Direct Marketing, **8** 385–86

Cornerstone Title Company, **8** 461

Cornhill Insurance Co., **III** 185, 385

Cornhusker Casualty Co., **III** 213

Corning Asahi Video Products Co., **III** 667

Corning Incorporated, I 609; **III** 434, 667, **683–85,** 720–21; **8** 468; **11** 334; **13** 398; **22** 454

Coronado Corp., **II** 112

Coronet Industries, Inc., **II** 90; **14** 436

Corp. d'acquisition Socanav-Caisse Inc., **II** 664

Corp. of Lloyd's, **III** 278–79

Corporacion Estatal Petrolera Ecuatoriana, **IV** 510–11

Corporación Internacional de Aviación, S.A. de C.V. (Cintra), 20 167–69

Corporación Moctezuma, **21** 261

Corporacion Siderurgica Integral, **22** 44

Corporación Venezolana de Petroleo, **IV** 507

Corporate Express, Inc., 22 152–55, 531

Corporate Microsystems, Inc., **10** 395

Corporate Partners, **12** 391

Corporate Software Inc., 9 139–41

Corporation for Public Broadcasting, 14 **143–45**

Corporation Trust Co. *See* CCH Inc.

Corpoven, **IV** 508

Corrado Passera, **IV** 588

Corral Midwest, Inc., **10** 333

Corrections Corporation of America, 23 **153–55**

Corrigan's, **16** 559

Corrigan-McKinney Steel Company, **13** 157

Corroon & Black, **III** 280; **22** 318

Corrpro Companies, Inc., 20 170–73

Corrugated Paper, **IV** 249

Cortec Corporation, **14** 430

Corvallis Lumber Co., **IV** 358

Cory Corp., **II** 511

Cory Food Services, Inc., **II** 608

Cory Orchard and Turf. *See* Chemi-Trol Chemical Co.

Cosco Pacific, **20** 313

Cosden Petroleum Corp., **IV** 498

Cosgrove & Co., **III** 283

Cosmair Inc., III 47–48; **8 129–32,** 342–44; **12** 404

The Cosmetic Center, Inc., 22 156–58

Cosmetic Technology International, Inc., **22** 409

Cosmo Oil Co., Ltd., IV 403–04

Cosmopolitan Productions, **IV** 626; **19** 203

Cosorzio Interprovinciale Vini, **10** 181

Cost Plus, **12** 393

Costa Apple Products, **II** 480

Costa e Ribeiro Ltd., **IV** 504

Costain Civil Engineering Ltd., **III** 495; **13** 206

Costco Wholesale Corporation, V 36; **10** 206; **11** 240; **XIV** 393–95; **15** 470

Costruzioni Meccaniche Nazionalia, **13** 218
Côte d'Or, **II** 521
Cott Beverage Corporation, **9** 291
Cottees General Foods, **II** 477
Cotter & Company, V 37–38; 12 8
Cotton Producers Association. *See* Gold
    Kist Inc.
Coty, **I** 662
Coulter Corporation. *See* Beckman Coulter,
    Inc.
Counselor Co., **14** 230
Country Kitchen Foods, **III** 21
Country Kitchen International, **22** 127
Country Music Television, **11** 153
Country Poultry, Inc., **II** 494
Country Seat Stores, Inc., **15** 87
Country Store of Concord, Inc., **10** 216
Countrywide Credit Industries, Inc., 16
    133–36
County Bank, **II** 333
County Catering Co., **13** 103
County Data Corporation, **18** 24
County Fire Insurance Co., **III** 191
County Market, **II** 670
County NatWest, **II** 334–35
County Perfumery, **III** 65
County Seat Stores Inc., II 669; 9
    142–43
County Trust Co., **II** 230
Cour des Comptes, **II** 233
Courage Brewing Group., **I** 229, 438–39;
    III 503
Courcoux-Bouvet, **II** 260
Courrèges Parfums, **III** 48; **8** 343
The Courseware Developers, **11** 19
Court House Square, **10** 44
Courtaulds plc, I 321; **IV** 261, 670; **V**
    356–57, **359–61; 12** 103; **17 116–19**
    (upd.)
Courtney Wines International, **II** 477
Courtot Investments, **II** 222
Courtyard by Marriott, **9** 427
Cousins Mortgage and Equity Investments,
    12 393
Coutts & Co., **II** 333–34
Couvrette & Provost Ltd., **II** 651
Covantage, **11** 379
Covenant Life Insurance, **III** 314
Coventry Climax Engines, Ltd., **13** 286
Coventry Co., **III** 213
Coventry Corporation, **17** 166, 168
Coventry Machinists Company, **7** 458
Coventry Ordnance Works, **I** 573
Coventry Union Banking Co., **II** 318; **17**
    323
Covidea, **II** 252
Coville Inc., **16** 353
Cow & Gate Ltd., **II** 586–87
Cowham Engineering, **III** 704
Cowles Media Company, IV 613, 648; **7**
    191; **19** 285; **23 156–58;** 344
Cox & Co., **II** 236, 307–08
Cox Enterprises, Inc., IV 246, **595–97; 6**
    32; **7** 327; **9** 74; **17** 148; **22 159–63**
    (upd.)
Cox Medical Enterprises, Inc., **21** 47
Coz Chemical Co., **21** 20, 22
CP. *See* Canadian Pacific Limited.
CP Air, **6** 60–61
CP National, **6** 300; **19** 412
CP/AAON. *See* AAON, Inc.
CPC International Inc., II 463, **496–98.**
    See also Bestfoods.

CPL. *See* Carolina Power & Light
    Company.
CRA Limited, IV 58–61, 67, 192; **7** 124.
    See also Rio Tinto plc.
Crabtree Electricals, **III** 503; **7** 210
Cracker Barrel Old Country Store, Inc.,
    9 78; **10 258–59**
Craft House Corp., **8** 456
Craig Bit Company, **13** 297
Crain Communications, Inc., 12 83–86
Cramer Electronics, **10** 112
Crane Co., 8 133–36, 179
Crane Packing Company, **19** 311
Crane Supply Company, **8** 135
Cranston Mills, **13** 168
Crate and Barrel, 9 144–46
Craven Tasker Ltd., **I** 573–74
Crawford and Watson, **IV** 278
Crawford Gosho Co., Ltd., **IV** 442
Crawford Group, Inc., **17** 372
Crawford Supply Company, **6** 392
Cray Research, Inc., III 126, 128,
    129–31; 10 256; **16 137–40 (upd.); 21**
    391; **22** 428
Crazy Eddie Inc., **23** 373
CRD Total France, **IV** 560
Cream City Railway Company, **6** 601
Cream of Wheat Corp., **II** 543; **22** 427
Creamola Food Products, **II** 569
Creasy Co., **II** 682
Creative Artists Agency, **10** 228; **22** 297;
    23 512, 514
Creative Engineering Inc., **13** 472
Creative Food 'N Fun Co., **14** 29
Creative Forming, Inc., **8** 562
Creative Homes, Inc., **IV** 341
Creative Integration and Design Inc., **20**
    146
Creative Technologies Corp., **15** 401
Credit & Risk Management Associates,
    Inc., **18** 170
Credit Acceptance Corporation, 18
    120–22
Crédit Agricole, II 264–66, 355; **19** 51
Credit and Data Marketing Services, **V** 118
Credit Clearing House, **IV** 605
Credit du Nord, **II** 260
Crédit Foncier, **II** 264
Crédit Général de Belgique, **II** 304
Credit Immobilier, **7** 538
Crédit Liégiois, **II** 270
Crédit Lyonnais, II 242, 257, 354; **6** 396;
    7 12; **9 147–49; 19** 34, 51, 166; **21** 226
Credit Mobilier, **II** 294
Crédit National S.A., 9 150–52
Credit Service Exchange, **6** 24
Credit Suisse First Boston. *See* Financière
    Crédit Suisse-First Boston.
Crédit Suisse Group, II 267–69, 369–70,
    378–79, 402–04; **21 144–47 (upd.).** *See*
    also Schweizerische Kreditanstalt.
Creditanstalt-Bankverein, **II** 242, 295
CrediThrift Financial, **11** 16
Credithrift Financial of Indiana, **III** 194
Credito de la Union Minera, **II** 194
Credito Italiano, I 368, 465, 567; **II** 191,
    270–72; III 347
Credito Minero y Mercantil, S.A., **22** 285
Credito Provincial Hipotecario, **19** 189
Cree Research, Inc., **13** 399
Crellin Holding, Inc., **8** 477
Crellin Plastics, **8** 13
Crenlo Corp., **16** 180

Creole Petroleum Corporation, **IV** 428; **7**
    171
Crescendo Productions, **6** 27
Crescent Box & Printing Co., **13** 442
Crescent Chemical, **I** 374
Crescent Niagara Corp., **II** 16
Crescent Software Inc., **15** 373
Crescent Vert Company, Ltd., **II** 51; **21**
    330
Crescent Washing Machine Company, **8**
    298
Crescott, Inc., **15** 501
Cressbrook Dairy Co., **II** 546
Cressey Dockham & Co., **II** 682
Crest Fruit Co., **17** 458
Crest Ridge Homes, Inc., **17** 83
Crest Service Company, **9** 364
Crestbrook Forest Industries Ltd., **IV** 285
Crestmont Financial Corporation, **14** 472
Creusot-Loire, **II** 93–94; **19** 166
Crevettes du Cameroun, **13** 244
Criterion Casualty Company, **10** 312
Criterion Life Insurance Company, **10** 311
Critikon, Inc., **III** 36
Crocker National Bank, **II** 226, 317, 319,
    383; **13** 535; **17** 324–25
Crocker National Corporation, **12** 536
Crockett Container Corporation, **8** 268
Croda International Ltd., **IV** 383
Crompton & Knowles Corp., I 633; **9**
    153–55
Crop Production Services, Inc., **IV** 576
Crosby Enterprises, **17** 19
Croscill Home Fashions, **8** 510
Crosfield, Lampard & Co., **III** 696
Cross & Trecker Corporation, **10** 330
Cross/Tessitore & Associates, **16** 259
Crossair, **I** 121
Crosse and Blackwell, **II** 547
Crossett Lumber Co., **IV** 281; **9** 259
Crossland Capital Corp., **III** 293
Crossley Motors, Ltd., **13** 285
Crothall, **6** 44
Crothers Properties, Ltd., **21** 500
Crouse-Hinds Co., **II** 16; **19** 45
Crow Catchpole, **III** 752
Crowell Publishing Company, **19** 266
Crowell-Collier Publishing Company, **IV**
    310; **7** 286
Crowley Foods, Inc., **II** 528
Crowley Maritime Corporation, 6
    382–84; 9 510–11
Crowley, Milner & Company, 19 106–08
Crown Advertising Agency. *See* King
    Kullen Grocery Co., Inc.
Crown Aluminum, **I** 544
Crown America Corp., **13** 393
Crown Books Corporation, 14 61; **16**
    159–61; 21 148–50
Crown Can Co., **I** 601
Crown Center Redevelopment Corp., **IV**
    621
Crown Central Petroleum Corporation,
    7 101–03
Crown, Cork & Seal Company, Inc., I
    601–03; **13 188–90 (upd.); 15** 129; **17**
    106
Crown Crafts, Inc., 16 141–43
Crown Drugs, **II** 673
Crown Equipment Corporation, 15
    134–36
Crown Forest Industries, **IV** 279; **19** 155
Crown Life Insurance Company, **III** 261; **6**
    181–82

Crown Oil and Refining Company, **7** 101
Crown Packaging, **19** 155
Crown Publishing Group, **IV** 584; **13** 429
Crown Radio, **17** 123–24
Crown Zellerbach Corporation, **IV** 290, 345; **8** 261; **22** 210
Crownx Inc., **6** 181–82
Crowson and Son Ltd., **23** 219
CRSS Inc., **6** 142–44; **23** 491
CRTC. *See* Canadian Radio-Television and Telecommunications Commission.
Crucible Steel, **I** 434–35
Crude Oil Pipe Line Co., **IV** 400
Cruden Investments Pty Ltd., **IV** 651; **7** 390
Cruise America Inc., **21** 151–53
Cruise Associates, **22** 471
Crum & Forster, **II** 448; **III** 172; **6** 290; **13** 448
Crump E & S, **6** 290
Crump Inc., **I** 584
Crush International, **II** 478; **III** 53
Crushed Stone Sales Ltd., **IV** 241
Cruzcampo, **18** 501
Cruzeiro do Sul Airlines, **6** 133
Cryenco Sciences Inc., **21** 109
Cryomedics Inc., **I** 667
Crystal Brands, Inc., **9** 156–58; **12** 431
Crystal Oil Co., **IV** 180, 548
CS Crable Sportswear Inc., **23** 66
CS First Boston Inc., **II** 269, 402–04; **III** 289; **12** 209; **21** 146. *See also* First Boston Corp.
CS Holding. *See* Credit Suisse Group.
CS Life, **21** 146–47
CSA Press, **IV** 661
CSC. *See* Computer Sciences Corporation.
CSC Industries, Inc., **IV** 63
CSE Corp., **III** 214
CSFB. *See* Financière Crédit Suisse-First Boston *and* Credit Suisse Group.
CSK, **10** 482
CSO. *See* Columbus & Southern Ohio Electric Company.
CSR Limited, **III** 686–88, 728, 735–36; **IV** 46; **22** 106
CST Office Products, **15** 36
CSX Corporation, **V** 438–40, 485; **6** 340; **9** 59; **13** 462; **22** 164–68 (upd.)
CSY Agri-Processing, **7** 81–82
CT Financial Services Inc., **V** 401–02
CT&T. *See* Carolina Telephone and Telegraph Company.
CTA. *See* Comptoir des Textiles Artificielles.
CTG, Inc., **11** 64–66
CTI. *See* Cosmetic Technology International, Inc.
CTNE, **I** 462
CTR. *See* International Business Machines Corporation.
CTS Corp., **19** 104
CTX Mortgage Company, **8** 88
Cub Foods, **II** 669–70; **14** 411; **17** 302; **18** 505; **22** 327
Cuban American Nickel Co., **IV** 82; **7** 186
Cuban American Oil Company, **8** 348
Cuban Telephone Co., **I** 462–63
Cuban-American Manganese Corp., **IV** 81; **7** 186
Cubic Corporation, **19** 109–11
Cubitts Nigeria, **III** 753
CUC International Inc., **16** 144–46
Cuckler Steel Span Co., **I** 481

Cudahy Corp., **12** 199
Cuisinart Inc., **17** 110
Culbro Corporation, **14** 19; **15** 137–39
Culinary Foods, Inc., **14** 516
Culligan International Company, **I** 373; **II** 468; **12** 87–88, 346; **16** 20
Cullinet Software Corporation, **6** 225; **14** 390; **15** 108
Cullman Bros. *See* Culbro Corporation.
Cullum Companies, **II** 670
Culter Industries, Inc., **22** 353
Cumberland Farms, Inc., **17** 120–22
Cumberland Federal Bancorporation, **13** 223
Cumberland Newspapers, **IV** 650; **7** 389
Cumberland Paper Board Mills Ltd., **IV** 248
Cumberland Pipeline Co., **IV** 372
Cumberland Property Investment Trust Ltd., **IV** 711
Cummins Engine Co., Inc., **I** 146–48, 186; **III** 545; **IV** 252; **10** 273–74; **12** 89–92 (upd.); **16** 297; **17** 29; **19** 293; **21** 503
Cumo Sports, **16** 109
CUNA Mutual Insurance Group, **11** 495
Cunard Line Ltd., **I** 573; **23** 159–62
Cuno Kourten, **13** 353
Cupples Products Co., **IV** 15
Current, Inc., **7** 137, 139; **22** 181
Currys Group PLC, **V** 49; **19** 123
Cursenir, **I** 280
Curtice-Burns Foods, Inc., **7** 17–18, 104–06; **21** 18, 154–57 (upd.)
Curtis Circulation Co., **IV** 619
Curtis Homes, **22** 127
Curtis Industries, **13** 165
Curtis 1000 Inc. *See* American Business Products, Inc.
Curtis Squire Inc., **18** 455
Curtiss Candy Co., **II** 544
Curtiss-Wright Corporation, **I** 524; **III** 464; **7** 263; **8** 49; **9** 14, 244, 341, 417; **10** 260–63; **11** 427; **21** 174; **23** 340
Curver Group, **III** 614
Curver-Rubbermaid, **III** 615
Cushman Motor Works, **III** 598
Custom Academic Publishing Company, **12** 174
Custom Chrome, Inc., **16** 147–49
Custom Electronics, Inc., **9** 120
Custom Expressions, Inc., **7** 24; **22** 35
Custom Hoists, Inc., **17** 458
Custom Metal Products, Inc., **III** 643
Custom Organics, **8** 464
Custom Primers, **17** 288
Custom Products Inc., **III** 643
Custom Technologies Corp., **19** 152
Customized Transportation Inc., **22** 164, 167
Cutler-Hammer Inc., **I** 155; **III** 644–45
Cutter Laboratories, **I** 310
CVI Incorporated, **21** 108
CVL Inc., **II** 457
CVN Companies, **9** 218
CVS. *See* Consumer Value Stores.
CWM. *See* Chemical Waste Management, Inc.
CWT Farms International Inc., **13** 103
Cyber Communications Inc., **16** 168
CyberCash Inc., **18** 541, 543
Cybernet Electronics Corp., **II** 51; **21** 330
Cybernex, **10** 463
CYBERTEK Corporation, **11** 395

CyberTel, **IV** 596–97
Cycle & Carriage Ltd., **20** 313
Cycle Video Inc., **7** 590
Cyclo Chemical Corp., **I** 627
Cyclo Getriebebau Lorenz Braren GmbH, **III** 634
Cyclone Co. of Australia, **III** 673
Cyclops Corporation, **10** 45; **13** 157
Cygna Energy Services, **13** 367
Cymbal Co., Ltd., **V** 150
Cynosure Inc., **11** 88
Cyphernetics Corp., **III** 118
Cypress Amax Minerals Co., **13** 158; **22** 285–86
Cypress Insurance Co., **III** 214
Cypress Semiconductor Corporation, **6** 216; **18** 17, 383; **20** 174–76
Cyprus Amax Minerals Company, **21** 158–61
Cyprus Minerals Company, **7** 107–09
Cyrix Corp., **10** 367
Cyrk Inc., **19** 112–14; **21** 516

D & P Studios, **II** 157
D & W Food Stores, Inc., **8** 482
D'Agostino Supermarkets Inc., **19** 115–17
D'Arcy Masius Benton & Bowles, Inc., **I** 233–34; **6** 20–22; **10** 226–27
D&F Industries, Inc., **17** 227
D&K Wholesale Drug, Inc., **14** 146–48
D&N Systems, Inc., **10** 505
D&O Inc., **17** 363
D&W Computer Stores, **13** 176
D.B. Marron & Company, **II** 445; **22** 406
D.C. Heath & Co., **II** 86; **11** 413
D.C. National Bancorp, **10** 426
D. Connelly Boiler Company, **6** 145
D.E. Makepeace Co., **IV** 78
D.E. Winebrenner Co., **7** 429
D.G. Calhoun, **12** 112
D. Hald & Co., **III** 417
D.K. Gold, **17** 138
D.L. Saslow Co., **19** 290
D.M. Nacional, **23** 170
D.M. Osborne Co., **III** 650
D.W. Mikesell Co. *See* Mike-Sell's Inc.
Dabney, Morgan & Co., **II** 329
Dade Reagents Inc., **19** 103
Dade Wholesale Products, **6** 199
DADG. *See* Deutsch-Australische Dampfschiffs-Gesellschaft.
Dae Won Kang Up Co., **III** 581
Daejin Shipping Company, **6** 98
Daesung Heavy Industries, **I** 516
Daewoo Group, **I** 516; **II** 53; **III** 457–59, 749; **12** 211; **18** 123–27 (upd.)
DAF, **I** 186; **III** 543; **7** 566–67
NV Dagblad De Telegraaf. *See* N.V. Holdingmaatschappij De Telegraaf.
Dage-Bell, **II** 86
Dagincourt. *See* Compagnie de Saint-Gobain S.A.
Dagsbladunie, **IV** 611
Dahl Manufacturing, Inc., **17** 106
Dahlberg, Inc., **18** 207–08
Dahlgren, **I** 677
Dahlonega Equipment and Supply Company, **12** 377
Dai Nippon. *See also listings under* Dainippon.
Dai Nippon Brewery Co., **I** 220, 282; **21** 319
Dai Nippon Ink and Chemicals, **I** 303

Dai Nippon Mujin, **II** 371
Dai Nippon Printing Co., Ltd., IV 598–600, 631, 679–80
Dai Nippon X-ray Inc., **II** 75
Dai Nippon Yuben Kai, **IV** 631–32
Dai-Ichi. *See also listings under* Daiichi.
Dai-Ichi Bank, **I** 507, 511; **IV** 148
Dai-Ichi Kangyo Bank Ltd., II 273–75, 325–26, 360–61, 374; **III** 188
Dai-Ichi Mokko Co., **III** 758
Dai-Ichi Mutual Life Insurance Co., **II** 118; **III** 277, 401
Daido Spring Co., **III** 580
Daido Steel Co., Ltd., IV 62–63
Daido Trading, **I** 432, 492
The Daiei, Inc., V 11, **39–40; 17 123–25 (upd.); 18** 186, 285; **19** 308
Daihatsu Motor Company, Ltd., 7 110–12; 21 162–64 (upd.)
Daiichi. *See also listings under* Dai-Ichi.
Daiichi Atomic Power Industry Group, **II** 22
Daiichi Bussan Kaisha Ltd., **I** 505, 507
Daiichi Fire, **III** 405
Daijugo Bank, **I** 507
Daikin Industries, Ltd., III 460–61
Daikyo Oil Co., Ltd., **IV** 403–04, 476
Dailey & Associates, **I** 16
Daily Chronicle Investment Group, **IV** 685
Daily Mail and General Trust plc, 19 118–20
Daily Mirror, **IV** 665–66; **17** 397
Daily Press Inc., **IV** 684; **22** 522
Daimaru, V 41–42, 130
Daimler Airway, **I** 92
Daimler-Benz Aerospace AG, 16 150–52
Daimler-Benz AG, I 27, 138, **149–51**, 186–87, 192, 194, 198, 411, 549; **II** 257, 279–80, 283; **III** 495, 523, 562, 563, 695, 750; **7** 219; **10** 261, 274; **11** 31; **12** 192, 342, **13** 30, 286, 414; **14** 169; **15 140–44 (upd.); 20** 312–13; **22** 11
Dain Bosworth Inc., **15** 231–33, 486
Daina Seikosha, **III** 620
Daini-Denden Incorporated, 12 136–37
Daini-Denden Kikaku Company, Ltd., **II** 51. *See also* DDI Corporation.
Dainippon. *See also listings under* Dai-Nippon.
Dainippon Celluloid Company, **I** 509; **III** 486; **18** 183
Dainippon Ink & Chemicals, Inc., **IV** 397; **10** 466–67; **13** 308, 461; **17** 363
Dainippon Shurui, **III** 42
Dainippon Spinning Company, **V** 387
Daio Paper Corporation, IV 266–67, 269
Dairy Farm Ice and Cold Storage Co., **IV** 700
Dairy Farm Management Services Ltd., **I** 471; **20** 312
Dairy Maid Products Cooperative, **II** 536
Dairy Mart Convenience Stores, Inc., 7 113–15; 17 501
Dairy Queen National Development Company, **10** 372
Dairy Supply Co., **II** 586; **III** 418, 420
Dairyland Food Laboratories, **I** 677
Dairymen, Inc., **11** 24
Daishowa Paper Manufacturing Co., Ltd. II 361; **IV 268–70**, 326, 667; **17** 398
Daisy/Cadnetix Inc., **6** 248
Daisy Systems Corp., **11** 46, 284–85, 489

Daisytek International Corporation, 18 128–30
Daiwa Bank, Ltd., II 276–77, 347, 438
Daiwa Securities Company, Limited, II 276, 300, **405–06**, 434; **9** 377
Dakota Power Company, **6** 580; **20** 73
Dakotah Mills, **8** 558–59; **16** 353
Daksoft, Inc., **20** 74
Dal-Tile International Inc., 22 46, 49, **169–71**
Dalberg Co., **II** 61
Dale Electronics, **21** 519
Daleville & Middletown Telephone Company, **14** 258
Dalfort Corp., **15** 281
Dalgety PLC, II 499–500; III 21; **12** 411; **22** 147
Dalian, **14** 556
Dalian Cement Factory, **III** 718
Dalian International Nordic Tire Co., **20** 263
Dallas Airmotive, **II** 16
Dallas Ceramic Co. *See* Dal-Tile International Inc.
Dallas Lumber and Supply Co., **IV** 358
Dallas Power & Light Company, **V** 724
Dallas Semiconductor Corp., 13 191–93
Dallas Southland Ice Co., **II** 660
Dallas-Fort Worth Suburban Newspapers, Inc., **10** 3
Damar, **IV** 610
Damark International, Inc., 18 131–34
Dammann Asphalt, **III** 673
Damodar Valley Corp., **IV** 49
Damon, **21** 153
Damon Corporation, **11** 334
Dana Corporation, I 152–53; 10 264–66 (upd.); 23 170–71
Dana Design Ltd., **16** 297
Danaher Corporation, 7 116–17
Danair A/S, **I** 120
Danapak Holding Ltd., **11** 422
Danat-Bank, **I** 138
Dancer Fitzgerald Sample, **I** 33; **23** 505
Daniel Industries, Inc., 16 153–55
Daniel International Corp., **I** 570–71; **8** 192
Daniel P. Creed Co., Inc., **8** 386
Daniel's Jewelers, **16** 559
Danieli & C. Officine Meccaniche, **13** 98
Daniels Linseed Co., **I** 419
Daniels Packaging, **12** 25
Danish Almindelige Brand-Assurance-Compagni, **III** 299
Danley Machine Corp., **I** 514
Danner Shoe Manufacturing Co., **18** 300
Dannon Co., Inc., II 468, 474–75; **14 149–51**
Danray, **12** 135
Dansk Bioprotein, **IV** 406–07
Dansk International Designs Ltd., **10** 179, 181; **12** 313
Dansk Metal and Armaturindistri, **III** 569; **20** 361
Dansk Rejsebureau, **I** 120
Danskin, Inc., 12 93–95; 15 358
Danville Resources, Inc., **13** 502
Danzas Group, V 441–43
DAP, Inc., **III** 66; **12** 7; **18** 549
Dara Michelle, **17** 101–03
Darden Restaurants, Inc., 16 156–58
Darigold, Inc., 9 159–61
Darling and Hodgson, **IV** 91

Darling, Brown & Sharpe. *See* Brown & Sharpe Manufacturing Co.
Darmstadter, **II** 282
Darracq, **7** 6
Darrell J. Sekin Transport Co., **17** 218
Dart & Kraft Financial Corp., **II** 534; **III** 610–11; **7** 276; **12** 310; **14** 547
Dart Group Corporation, II 645, 656, 667, 674; **12** 49; **15** 270; **16 159–62; 21** 148; **23** 370
Dart Industries, **II** 533–34; **III** 610; **9** 179–80
Dart Transit Co., **13** 550
Dart Truck Co., **I** 185
Dartex, **18** 434
Darvel Realty Trust, **14** 126
Darya-Varia Laboratoria, **18** 182
DASA. *See* Deutsche Aerospace Airbus.
Dashwood Industries, **19** 446
Dassault Aviation SA, **21** 11
Dassault-Breguet. *See* Avions Marcel Dassault-Breguet Aviation.
Dassler, **14** 6
Dastek Inc., **10** 464; **11** 234–35
DAT GmbH, **10** 514
Dat Jidosha Seizo Co., **I** 183
Data Acquisition Systems, Inc., **16** 300
Data Architects, **14** 318
Data Base Management Inc., **11** 19
Data Business Forms, **IV** 640
Data Card Corp., **IV** 680
Data Corp., **IV** 311; **19** 267
Data Documents, **III** 157
Data Force Inc., **11** 65
Data General Corporation, II 208; **III** 124, 133; **6** 221, 234; **8 137–40; 9** 297; **10** 499; **12** 162; **13** 201; **16** 418; **20** 8
Data One Corporation, **11** 111
Data Preparation, Inc., **11** 112
Data Printer, Inc., **18** 435
Data Resources, Inc., **IV** 637
Data Specialties Inc. *See* Zebra Technologies Corporation.
Data Structures Inc., **11** 65
Data Systems Technology, **11** 57
Data Technology Corp., **18** 510
Data 3 Systems, **9** 36
Datac plc, **18** 140
Datachecker Systems, **II** 64–65; **III** 164; **11** 150
Datacraft Corp., **II** 38
DataFocus, Inc., **18** 112
Datamatic Corp., **II** 41, 86; **12** 247
Datapoint Corporation, 11 67–70
Datapro Research Corp., **IV** 637
Dataquest Inc., **10** 558; **21** 235, 237; **22** 51
Datas Incorporated, **I** 99; **6** 81
Dataset Communications Inc., **23** 100
Datastream International Ltd., **IV** 605; **10** 89; **13** 417
Datavision Inc., **11** 444
Datec, **22** 17
Datext, **IV** 596–97
Datran, **11** 468
Datsun. *See* Nissan Motor Company, Ltd.
Datteln, **IV** 141
Datura Corp., **14** 391
Dauphin Deposit Corporation, 14 152–54
Dauphin Distribution Services. *See* Exel Logistics Ltd.
Daut + Rietz and Connectors Pontarlier, **19** 166
Davenport & Walter, **III** 765

The Davey Tree Expert Company, 11 71–73
David B. Smith & Company, 13 243
David Berg & Co., 14 537
David Brown & Son. *See* Brown & Sharpe Manufacturing Co.
David Brown, Ltd., 10 380
David Crystal, Inc., II 502; 9 156; 10 323
The David J. Joseph Company, 14 155–56; 19 380
David Sandeman Group, I 592
David Sassoon & Co., II 296
David Williams and Partners, 6 40
David's Supermarkets, 17 180
Davidson & Associates, 16 146
Davidson & Leigh, 21 94
Davidson Automatic Merchandising Co. Inc., II 607
Davidson Brothers Co., 19 510
Davies, William Ltd., II 482
Davis & Henderson Ltd., IV 640
Davis and Geck, I 301
Davis Coal & Coke Co., IV 180
Davis Estates, I 592
Davis Manufacturing Company, 10 380
Davis Wholesale Company, 9 20
Davis-Standard Company, 9 154
Davison Chemical Corp., IV 190
Davlyn Industries, Inc., 22 487
Davox Corporation, 18 31
Davy Bamag GmbH, IV 142
Davy McKee AG, IV 142
Dawe's Laboratories, Inc., 12 3
Dawn Food Products, Inc., 17 126–28
Dawnay Day, III 501
Dawson Mills, II 536
Day & Zimmermann Inc., 6 579; 9 162–64
Day Brite Lighting, II 19
Day International, 8 347
Day Runner, Inc., 14 157–58
Day-Glo Color Corp., 8 456
Day-Lee Meats, II 550
Day-N-Nite, II 620
Daybridge Learning Centers, 13 49
Daybridge/Children's World, 13 299
Dayco Products, 7 297
Days Inns of America, Inc., III 344; 11 178; 13 362, 364; 21 362
Daystar International Inc., 11 44
Daystrom, III 617; 17 418
Daytex, Inc., II 669; 18 505
Dayton Engineering Laboratories, I 171; 9 416; 10 325
Dayton Flexible Products Co., I 627
Dayton Hudson Corporation, V 43–44; 8 35; 9 360; 10 136, 391–93, 409–10, 515–16; 13 330; 14 376; 16 176, 559; 18 108, 135–37 (upd.); 22 59
Dayton Power & Light Company, 6 467, 480–82
Dayton Walther Corp., III 650, 652
Daytron Mortgage Systems, 11 485
Dazey Corp., 16 384
DB. *See* Deutsche Bundesbahn.
DBA Holdings, Inc., 18 24
DBMS Inc., 14 390
DCA Advertising, 16 168
DCA Food Industries, II 554
DCL BioMedical, Inc., 11 333
DCMS Holdings Inc., 7 114
DDB Needham Worldwide, 14 159–61; 22 394

DDI Corporation, 7 118–20; 13 482; 21 330–31
De Beers Consolidated Mines Limited / De Beers Centenary AG, I 107; IV 20–21, 23, 60, 64–68, 79, 94; 7 121–26 (upd.); 16 25–26, 29; 21 345–46
De Grenswisselkantoren NV, III 201
De Groote Bossche, III 200
de Havilland Aircraft Co., I 82, 92–93, 104, 195; III 507–08; 7 11
De La Rue PLC, 10 267–69
De Laurentiis Entertainment Group, III 84
De Laval Turbine Company, III 418–20; 7 236–37
De Leuw, Cather & Company, 8 416
De Nederlandse Bank, IV 132
De Ster 1905 NV, III 200
De Tomaso Industries, 11 104
De Trey Gesellchaft, 10 271
De Walt, III 436
de Wendel, IV 226–27
De-sta-Co., III 468
DEA Group, 23 83
Dealer Equipment and Services, 10 492
Dean & Barry Co., 8 455
Dean Foods Company, 7 127–29; 17 56; 21 157, 165–68 (upd.)
Dean Witter, Discover & Co., II 445; IV 186; V 180, 182; 7 213; 12 96–98; 18 475; 21 97; 22 405–07
Dean-Dempsy Corp., IV 334
Deb Shops, Inc., 16 163–65
Debenhams, V 20–22
Debron Investments Plc., 8 271
DEC. *See* Digital Equipment Corp.
Decca Record Company Ltd., II 81, 83, 144; 23 389
Decision Base Resources, 6 14
Decision Systems Israel Ltd. (DSI), 21 239
Deckers Outdoor Corporation, 22 172–74
Deco Industries, Inc., 18 5
Decoflex Ltd., IV 645
Decolletage S.A. St.-Maurice, 14 27
Dee Corp., I 549; II 628–29, 642
Deeks McBride, III 704
Deep Oil Technology, I 570
Deep Rock Oil Company. *See* Kerr-McGee Corporation.
Deep Rock Water Co., III 21
DeepFlex Production Partners, L.P., 21 171
Deepsea Ventures, Inc., IV 152
DeepTech International Inc., 21 169–71
Deepwater Light and Power Company, 6 449
Deer Park Spring Water Co., III 21
Deere & Company, I 181, 527; III 462–64, 651; 10 377–78, 380, 429; 11 472; 13 16–17, 267; 16 179; 17 533; 21 172–76 (upd.); 22 542
Deering Harvesting Machinery Company. *See* Navistar.
Deering Milliken & Co. *See* Milliken & Co.
Def Jam Records, Inc., 23 389, 391
Defense Plant Corp., IV 10, 408
Defiance, Inc., 22 175–78
Deft Software, Inc., 10 505
DEG. *See* Deutsche Edison Gesellschaft.
Degussa Group, I 303; IV 69–72, 118
Deinhard, I 281
DeKalb AgResearch Inc., 9 411
Dekalb Energy Company, 18 366
DeKalb Farmers Market, 23 263–64

DeKalb Genetics Corporation, 17 129–31
Del Monte Corporation, II 595; 7 130–32; 12 439; 14 287
Del Monte Foods Company, 23 163–66 (upd.)
Del Webb Corporation, 14 162–64; 17 186–87; 19 377–78
Del-Rey Petroleum, I 526
Delafield, Harvey, Tabrell, Inc., 17 498
Delafield Industries, 12 418
Delagrange, I 635
Delaware and Hudson Railway Company, 16 350
Delaware Charter Guarantee & Trust Co., III 330
Delaware Lackawanna & Western, I 584
Delaware Management Holdings, III 386
Delaware North Companies Incorporated, 7 133–36
Delbard, I 272
Delchamps, II 638
Delco Electronics, II 32–35; III 151; 6 265
Delhaize Freres & Cie, II 626; 15 176
Delhi Gas Pipeline Corporation, 7 551
Delhi International Oil Corp., III 687
Deli Universal, 13 545
Delicious Foods, 13 383
Delimaatschappij, 13 545
Dell Computer Corp., 9 165–66; 10 309, 459; 11 62; 16 5, 196
Dell Publishing Co., 13 560
Dellwood Elevator Co., I 419
Delmar Chemicals Ltd., II 484
Delmar Paper Box Co., IV 333
Delmarva Properties, Inc., 8 103
Delmonico Foods Inc., II 511
Delmonico International, II 101
Deloitte & Touche, 9 167–69, 423
DeLong Engineering Co., III 558
DeLorean Motor Co., 10 117; 14 321
Delphax, IV 252; 17 29
Delphi, 22 52
Delprat, IV 58
Delta & Pine Land Co., 21 386
Delta Acceptance Corporation Limited, 13 63
Delta Air Lines Inc., I 29, 91, 97, 99–100, 102, 106, 120, 132; 6 61, 81–83 (upd.), 117, 131–32, 383; 12 149, 381; 13 171–72; 14 73; 21 141, 143; 22 22
Delta Biologicals S.r.l., 11 208
Delta Communications, IV 610
Delta Faucet Co., III 568–69
Delta Lloyd, III 235
Delta Manufacturing, II 85
Delta Motors, III 580
Delta Pride Catfish Inc., 18 247
Delta Savings Assoc. of Texas, IV 343
Delta Steamship Lines, 9 425–26
Delta Woodside Industries, Inc., 8 141–43; 17 329
Deltak Corp., 23 300
Deluxe Corporation, 7 137–39; 19 291; 22 179–82 (upd.)
Deluxe Data, 18 518
DeLuxe Laboratories, IV 652
Deluxe Upholstering Ltd., 14 303
Delvag Luftürsicherungs A.G., I 111
Demag AG, II 22; III 566; IV 206
Demerara Company, 13 102
Deminex, IV 413, 424

Deming Company, **8** 135
Demka, **IV** 132–33
DeMoulas / Market Basket Inc., 23 **167–69**
Dempsey & Siders Agency, **III** 190
Den Fujita, **9** 74
Den Norske Bank, **22** 275
Den norske Creditbank, **II** 366
Den Norske Stats Oljeselskap AS, IV **405–07**, 486
Den-Tal-Ez, **I** 702
Denain-Nord-Est-Longwy, **IV** 227
Denault Ltd., **II** 651
Denison Corp., **III** 628
Denison Mines, Ltd., **12** 198
Denker & Goodwin, **17** 498
Denki Seikosho, **IV** 62
Denney-Reyburn, **8** 360
Dennison Manufacturing Company. *See* Avery Dennison Corporation.
Denny's Restaurants Inc., **II** 680; **III** 103; **V** 88–89; **12** 511; **13** 526
Denshi Media Services, **IV** 680
Dent & Co., **II** 296
Dental Capital Corp., **19** 290
DentiCare, Inc., **22** 149
Dentons Green Brewery, **21** 246
Dentsply International Inc., 10 270–72
Dentsu Inc., I 9–11, 36, 38; **6** 29; **9** 30; **13** 204; **16** 166–69 **(upd.)**
Denver & Rio Grande Railroad, **12** 18–19
Denver Chemical Company, **8** 84
Denver Gas & Electric Company. *See* Public Service Company of Colorado.
DEP Corporation, 20 177–80
Department 56, Inc., 14 165–67; 22 59
Department Stores International, **I** 426; **22** 72
Deposit Guaranty Corporation, 17 **132–35**
Deposito and Administratie Bank, **II** 185
Depositors National Bank of Durham, **II** 336
DePree Company, **17** 90–91
Depuy Inc., **10** 156–57
Der Anker, **III** 177
Derby Commercial Bank, **II** 318; **17** 323
Derbyshire Stone and William Briggs, **III** 752
Deritend Computers, **14** 36
Deruluft, **6** 57
Derwent Publications, **8** 526
Des Moines Electric Light Company, **6** 504
DESA Industries, **8** 545
Desc, S.A. de C.V., 23 170–72
Deseret National Bank, **11** 118
Deseret Pharmaceutical Company, **21** 45
Desert Partners, **III** 763
Design Craft Ltd., **IV** 640
Design-Center Southwest, **19** 411
Designcraft Inc. *See* Sloan's Supermarkets Inc.
Designer Holdings Ltd., 20 181–84; 22 123
Desmarais Frères, **IV** 557, 559
DeSoto, Inc., **8** 553; **13** 471
Desoutter, **III** 427
Destec Energy, Inc., 12 99–101
Det Danske/Norske Luftartselskab, **I** 119
Detroit Aircraft Corp., **I** 64; **11** 266
Detroit Automobile Co., **I** 164
Detroit Ball Bearing Co., **13** 78
Detroit Chemical Coatings, **8** 553

Detroit City Gas Company. *See* MCN Corporation.
Detroit Copper Co., **IV** 176–77
Detroit Diesel Corporation, V 494–95; **9** 18; **10 273–75; 11** 471; **12** 90–91; **18** 308; **19** 292–94; **21** 503
The Detroit Edison Company, I 164; **V** **592–95; 7** 377–78; **11** 136; **14** 135; **18** 320. *See also* DTE Energy Co.
Detroit Fire & Marine Insurance Co., **III** 191
Detroit Gear and Machine Co., **III** 439
Detroit Radiator Co., **III** 663
Detroit Red Wings, **7** 278–79
Detroit Steel Products Co., Inc., **IV** 136; **13** 157; **16** 357
Detroit Toledo & Ironton Railroad, **I** 165
Detroit Vapor Stove Co., **III** 439
Detroit-Graphite Company, **8** 553
Detrola, **II** 60
Deutsch Erdol A.G., **IV** 552
Deutsch Shea & Evans Inc., **I** 15
Deutsch-Australische Dampfschiffs-Gesellschaft, **6** 398
Deutsch-Luxemburgische Bergwerks und Hütten AG, **I** 542; **IV** 105
Deutsch-Österreichische Mannesmannröhren-Werke Aktiengesellschaft, **III** 564–65
Deutsch-Skandinavische Bank, **II** 352
Deutsche Aerospace Airbus, **I** 41–42; **7** 9, 11; **12** 190–91; **21** 8
Deutsche Allgemeine Versicherungs-Aktiengesellschaft, **III** 412
Deutsche Anlagen Leasing GmbH, **II** 386
Deutsche BA, **14** 73
Deutsche Babcock AG, II 386; **III** **465–66**
Deutsche Bank A.G., I 151, 409, 549; **II** 98, 191, 239, 241–42, 256–58, **278–80**, 281–82, 295, 319, 385, 427, 429; **III** 154–55, 692, 695; **IV** 91, 141, 229, 232, 378, 557; **V** 241–42; **14** 168–71 **(upd.)**; **15** 13; **16** 364–65; **17** 324; **21** 147
Deutsche BP Aktiengesellschaft, 7 **140–43**
Deutsche Bundepost Telekom, V 287–90; **18** 155
Deutsche Bundesbahn, V 444–47; 6 424–26
Deutsche Edelstahlwerke AG, **IV** 222
Deutsche Edison Gesellschaft, **I** 409–10
Deutsche Erdol Aktiengesellschaft, **7** 140
Deutsche Gold-und Silber-Scheideanstalt vormals Roessler, **IV** 69, 118, 139
Deutsche Grammophon Gesellschaft, **23** 389
Deutsche Hydrierwerke, **III** 32
Deutsche Industriewerke AG, **IV** 230
Deutsche Kreditbank, **14** 170
Deutsche Länderbank, **II** 379
Deutsche Lufthansa A.G., I 94, **110–11**, 120; **6** 59–60, 69, 95–96, 386; **12** 191
Deutsche Marathon Petroleum, **IV** 487
Deutsche Mineralöl-Explorationsgesellschaft mbH, **IV** 197
Deutsche Nippon Seiko, **III** 589
Deutsche Petroleum-Verkaufsgesellschaft mbH, **7** 140
Deutsche Reichsbahn. *See* Deutsche Bundesbahn.
Deutsche Schiff-und Maschinenbau Aktiengesellschaft "Deschimag," **IV** 87
Deutsche Shell, **7** 140

Deutsche Spezialglas AG, **III** 446
Deutsche Strassen und Lokalbahn A.G., **I** 410
Deutsche Telekom, **18** 155
Deutsche Texaco, **V** 709
Deutsche Union, **III** 693–94
Deutsche Union-Bank, **II** 278
Deutsche Wagnisfinanzierung, **II** 258
Deutsche Werke AG, **IV** 230
Deutsche-Asiatische Bank, **II** 238, 256
Deutsche-Nalco-Chemie GmbH., **I** 373
Deutscher Aero Lloyd, **I** 110
Deutscher Automobil Schutz Allgemeine Rechtsschutz-Versicherung AG, **III** 400
Deutscher Kommunal-Verlag Dr. Naujoks & Behrendt, **14** 556
Deutsches Reisebüro DeR, **II** 163
Deutz AG, **III** 541
Deutz Farm Equipment, **13** 17
Deutz-Allis, **III** 544. *See also* AGCO Corp.
Devcon Corporation, **III** 519; **22** 282
Developer's Mortgage Corp., **16** 347
Development Finance Corp., **II** 189
Devenish, **21** 247
DeVilbiss Company, **8** 230
DeVilbiss Health Care, Inc., **11** 488
Devoe & Raynolds Co., **12** 217
Devoke Company, **18** 362
Devon Energy Corporation, **22** 304
DeVry Technical Institute, Inc., **9** 63
Dewars Brothers, **I** 239–40
Dewey & Almy Chemical Co., **I** 548
The Dexter Corporation, I 320–22; **12** **102–04 (upd.); 17** 287
Dexter Shoe, **18** 60, 63
DFS Dorland Worldwide, **I** 35
DFW Printing Company, **10** 3
DG&E. *See* Denver Gas & Electric Company.
DH Compounding, **8** 347
DH Technology, Inc., 18 138–40
DHI Corp., **II** 680
DHJ Industries, Inc., **12** 118
DHL Worldwide Express, 6 385–87; 18 177, 316
Di Giorgio Corp., II 602; **12 105–07**
Di-Rite Company, **11** 534
Dia Prosim, S.A., **IV** 409
Diagnostic Health Corporation, **14** 233
Diagnostics Pasteur, **I** 677
The Dial Corp., 8 144–46; 23 173–75 **(upd.)**
Dialight Corp., **13** 397–98
Dialog Information Services, Inc., **IV** 630
Dialogic Corporation, 18 141–43
Diamandis Communications Inc., **IV** 619, 678
Diamang, **IV** 65, 67
Diamedix, **11** 207
Diamond Communications, **10** 288
Diamond Corporation Ltd., **IV** 21, 66–67; **7** 123
Diamond Head Resources, Inc. *See* AAON, Inc.
Diamond International Corp., **IV** 290, 295; **13** 254–55; **19** 225
Diamond M Offshore Inc., **12** 318
Diamond Match Company, **14** 163
Diamond Oil Co., **IV** 548
Diamond Park Fine Jewelers, **16** 559
Diamond Rug & Carpet Mills, **19** 276
Diamond Savings & Loan, **II** 420

Diamond Shamrock, Inc., IV 408–11,
481; **7** 34, 308–099, 345; **13** 118; **19**
177
Diamond Trading Company, **IV** 66–67; **7**
123
Diamond Walnut Growers, **7** 496–97
Diamond-Star Motors Corporation, **9**
349–51
Dianatel, **18** 143
Dibrell Brothers, Incorporated, 12
108–10; 13 492
dick clark productions, inc., 16 170–73
Dickerman, **8** 366
Dickson Forest Products, Inc., **15** 305
Dickstein Partners, L.P., **13** 261
Dictaphone Corp., **III** 157
Didier Lamarthe, **17** 210
Didier Werke AG, **IV** 232
Diebold, Incorporated, 7 144–46; **22**
183–87 (upd.)
Diehl Manufacturing Co., **II** 9
Diemakers Inc., **IV** 443
Diesel United Co., **III** 533
AB Diesels Motorer, **III** 425–26
Diet Center, **10** 383
Dieter Hein Co., **14** 537
Dieterich Standard Corp., **III** 468
Dietrich Corp., **II** 512; **15** 221
Dietrich's Bakeries, **II** 631
DiFranza Williamson, **6** 40
DIG Acquisition Corp., **12** 107
Digi International Inc., 9 170–72; **20** 237
Digicom, **22** 17
Digital Audio Disk Corp., **II** 103
Digital City, Inc., **22** 522
Digital Data Systems Company, **11** 408
Digital Devices, Inc., **III** 643
Digital Directory Assistance, **18** 24
Digital Equipment Corporation, II 8, 62,
108; **III** 118, 128, **132–35,** 142, 149,
166; **6** 225, **233–36 (upd.),** 237–38,
242, 246–47, 279, 287; **8** 137–39, 519;
9 35, 43, 57, 166, 170–71, 514; **10**
22–23, 34, 86, 242, 361, 463, 477; **11**
46, 86–88, 274, 491, 518–19; **12** 147,
162, 470; **13** 127, 202, 482; **14** 318; **15**
108; **16** 394, 418; **18** 143, 345; **19** 310;
21 123
Digital Marketing, Inc., **22** 357
Digital Research in Electronic Acoustics
and Music S.A., **17** 34
Digitech, **19** 414
Diligent Engine Co., **III** 342
Dill & Collins, **IV** 311; **19** 266
Dill Enterprises, Inc., **14** 18
Dillard Department Stores, Inc., V
45–47; 10 488; **11** 349; **12** 64; **13**
544–45; **16 174–77 (upd.),** 559; **19** 48,
324
Dillard Paper Company, 11 74–76
Dillingham Corp., I 565–66
Dillingham Holdings Inc., **9** 511
Dillon Companies Inc., II 645; **12**
111–13; 15 267; **22** 194
Dillon Paper, **IV** 288
Dillon, Read, and Co., Inc., **I** 144, 559; **III**
151, 389; **6** 265; **11** 53; **20** 259
Dime Banking and Loan Association of
Rochester, **10** 91
Dime Savings Bank of New York, F.S.B.,
9 173–74
Dimeling, Schrieber & Park, **11** 63
Dimeric Development Corporation, **14** 392
DiMon Inc., 12 110

Dinamica, S.A., **19** 12
Dine S.A., **23** 170–72
Diners Club, **II** 397; **6** 62; **9** 335; **10** 61
Dinner Bell Foods, Inc., **11** 93
de Dion, **III** 523
Dirección General de Correos y
Telecomunicaciónes, **V** 337
Dirección Nacional de los Yacimientos
Petrolíferos Fiscales, **IV** 577–78
Direct Container Lines, **14** 505
Direct Line, **12** 422
Direct Mail Services Pty. Ltd., **10** 461
Direct Marketing Technology Inc., **19** 184
Direct Spanish Telegraph Co., **I** 428
Direction Générale des
Télécommunications, **V** 471
DirectLine Insurance, **22** 52
Directorate General of
Telecommunications, 7 147–49
DirecTV, **21** 70
Dirr's Gold Seal Meats, **6** 199
Disc Go Round, **18** 207, 209
Disc Manufacturing, Inc., **15** 378
Disclosure, Inc., **18** 24
Disco SA, **V** 11; **19** 308–09
Discol SA, **V** 11; **19** 308
Disconto-Gesellschaft, **II** 238, 279
Discount Auto Parts, Inc., 18 144–46
Discount Bank, **II** 205
Discount Corporation, **12** 565
Discount Drug Mart, Inc., 14 172–73
Discount Labels, Inc., **20** 15
Discount Tire Co., **19** 294; **20** 263
Discover, **9** 335; **12** 97
Discovery Toys, Inc., **19** 28
DiscoVision Associates, **III** 605
Discreet Logic Inc., 20 185–87
Disctronics, Ltd., **15** 380
Disney Channel, **6** 174–75; **13** 280
Disney Co. *See* Walt Disney Company.
Disney Studios, **II** 408; **6** 174, 176
Disneyland, **6** 175
Disneyland Paris. *See* Euro Disneyland
SCA.
Dispatch Communications, **10** 432
Display Components Inc., **II** 110; **17** 479
Displayco Midwest Inc., **8** 103
Disposable Hospital Products, **I** 627
Distillers and Cattle Feeders Trust, **I** 376
Distillers Co. plc, I 239–41, 252, 263,
284–85; **II** 429, 609–10; **IV** 70
Distillers Securities, **I** 376
Distinctive Printing and Packaging Co., **8**
103
Distinctive Software Inc., **10** 285
Distribution Centers Incorporated. *See* Exel
Logistics Ltd.
Distribution Services, Inc., **10** 287
District Bank, **II** 333
District Cablevision, **II** 160
District News Co., **II** 607
Distrigas, **IV** 425
DITAS, **IV** 563
Ditzler Color Co., **III** 732
DIVAL, **III** 347
Divani & Divani. *See* Industrie Natuzzi
S.p.A.
Divco-Wayne Corp., **17** 82
Diversey Corp., **I** 275, 333; **13** 150, 199
Diversified Agency Services, **I** 32
Diversified Retailing Co., **III** 214
Diversified Services, **9** 95
Diversifoods Inc., **II** 556; **13** 408
Dixie Bearings, Inc., **13** 78

Dixie Carriers, Inc., **18** 277
Dixie Container Corporation, **12** 377
The Dixie Group, Inc., 20 188–90
Dixie Hi-Fi, **9** 120–21
Dixie Home Stores, **II** 683
Dixie Paper, **I** 612–14
Dixie Power & Light Company, **6** 514
Dixie Yarns, Inc., **9** 466; **19** 305
Dixie-Narco Inc., **III** 573; **22** 349
Dixieland Food Stores, **II** 624
Dixon Ticonderoga Company, 12 114–16
Dixons Group plc, II 139; **V 48–50; 9** 65;
10 45, 306; **19 121–24 (upd.); 23** 52
DIY Home Warehouse, **16** 210
DJ Moldings Corp., **18** 276
Djedi Holding SA, **23** 242
DKB. *See* Dai-Ichi Kangyo Bank Ltd.
DLC. *See* Duquesne Light Company.
DLJ. *See* Donaldson, Lufkin & Jenrette.
DLJ Merchant Banking Partners II, **21** 188
DMA, **18** 510
DMB&B. *See* D'Arcy Masius Benton &
Bowles.
DMP Mineralöl Petrochemie GmbH, **IV**
487
DNAX Research Institute, **I** 685; **14** 424
DNEL-Usinor, **IV** 227
DNP DENMARK A/S, **IV** 600
Dobbs House, **21** 54
Dobbs Houses Inc., **I** 696–97; **15** 87
Dobrolet, **6** 57
Doctors' Hospital, **6** 191
Documentation Resources, **11** 65
DOD Electronics Corp., **15** 215
Dodd, Mead & Co., **14** 498
Dodge Corp., **I** 144; **8** 74; **11** 53
The Dodge Group, **11** 78
Dodge Manufacturing Company, **9** 440
Dodge Motor Company, **20** 259
Dodwell & Co., **III** 523
Doe Run Company, **12** 244
Dofasco Inc., IV 73–74
Doherty Clifford Steers & Sherfield Inc., **I**
31
Doherty, Mann & Olshan. *See* Wells Rich
Greene BDDP.
Dolby Laboratories Inc., 20 191–93
Dole Food Company, Inc., I 565; **II**
491–92; **9 175–76; 20** 116
Dolland & Aitchison Group, **V** 399
Dollar Bills, Inc. *See* Dollar Tree Stores,
Inc.
Dollar Rent A Car, **6** 349
Dollar Steamship Lines, **6** 353
Dollar Tree Stores, Inc., 16 161; **23**
176–78
Dolphin Book Club, **13** 106
Domain Technology, **6** 231
Domaine Chandon, **I** 272
Dombrico, Inc., **8** 545
Domco Industries, **19** 407
Dome Laboratories, **I** 654
Dome Petroleum, Ltd., **II** 222, 245, 262,
376; **IV** 371, 401, 494; **12** 364
Domestic Electric Co., **III** 435
Domestic Operating Co., **III** 36
Dominick International Corp., **12** 131
Dominick's Finer Foods, **9** 451; **13** 25,
516; **17** 558, 560–61
Dominion Bank, **II** 375–76
Dominion Bridge Company, Limited, **8**
544
Dominion Cellular, **6** 322
Dominion Dairies, **7** 429

Dominion Engineering Works Ltd., **8** 544
Dominion Far East Line, **I** 469; **20** 311
Dominion Foils Ltd., **17** 280
Dominion Foundries and Steel, Ltd., **IV** 73–74
Dominion Hoist & Shovel Co., **8** 544
Dominion Homes, Inc., 19 125–27
Dominion Industries Ltd., **15** 229
Dominion Life Assurance Co., **III** 276
Dominion Mushroom Co., **II** 649–50
Dominion Ornamental, **III** 641
Dominion Paper Box Co. Ltd., **IV** 645
Dominion Resources, Inc., V 591, **596–99**
Dominion Securities, **II** 345; **21** 447
Dominion Stores Ltd., **II** 650, 652
Dominion Tar & Chemical Co. Ltd., **IV** 271–72
Dominion Terminal Associates, **IV** 171; **7** 582, 584
Dominion Textile Inc., V 355; **8** 559–60; **12 117–19**
Domino's Pizza, Inc., 7 150–53; **9** 74; **12** 123; **15** 344, 346; **16** 447; **21 177–81 (upd.)**; **22** 353
Domtar Inc., IV 271–73, 308
Don Baxter Intravenous Products Co., **I** 627
Donac Company, **V** 681
Donald L. Bren Co., **IV** 287
Donaldson Co. Inc., 16 178–81
Donaldson, Lufkin & Jenrette, Inc., II 422, 451; **III 247–48**; **9** 115, 142, 360–61; **18** 68; **22 188–91**
Donaldson's Department Stores, **15** 274
Doncaster Newspapers Ltd., **IV** 686
Dong-A Motor, **III** 749
Dong-Myung Industrial Co. Ltd., **II** 540
Donghang Life Insurance Co., **I** 515
Dongguan Shilong Kyocera Optics Co., Ltd., **21** 331
Dongil Frozen Foods Co., **II** 553
Dongsu Industrial Company, **III** 516; **7** 232
Donn, Inc., **18** 162
Donna Karan Company, 15 145–47
Donnelley, Gassette & Loyd, **IV** 660
Donnellon McCarthy Inc., **12** 184
Donnelly Corporation, 12 120–22
Donnkenny, Inc., 17 136–38
Donohue Inc., **12** 412
Donruss Leaf Inc., **19** 386
Donzi Marine Corp., **III** 600
Dooner Laboratories, **I** 667
Door-to-Door, **6** 14
Dorado Beach Development Inc., **I** 103
Dordrecht, **III** 177–78
Dorenbecher Properties, **19** 381
Doric Corp., **19** 290
Dorling Kindersley Holdings plc, 20 194–96
Dorman Long & Co. Ltd., **IV** 658
Dorney Park, **22** 130
Dornier, **I** 46, 74, 151; **15** 142
Dorothy Hamill International, **13** 279, 281
Dorothy Perkins, **V** 21
Dortmunder Union, **II** 240; **IV** 103, 105
Doskocil Companies, Inc., 12 123–25.
  See also Foodbrands America, Inc.
Double A Products Co., **23** 82–83
Doubleday Book Shops, **10** 136
Doubleday-Dell, **IV** 594, 636
Doubletree Corporation, 21 182–85
Douglas & Lomason Company, 16 182–85

Douglas Aircraft Co., **I** 48, 70, 76, 96, 104, 195; **II** 32, 425; **III** 601; **9** 12, 18, 206; **10** 163; **13** 48, 341; **16** 77; **21** 141
Douglas Oil Co., **IV** 401
Douglas-Dahlin Co., **I** 158–59
Doulton Glass Industries Ltd., **IV** 659
Douwe Egberts, **II** 572
Dove International, **7** 299–300
Dover Corporation, III 467–69
Dovrat Shrem, **15** 470
Dow Chemical Co., I 323–25, 334, 341–42, 360, 370–71, 708; **II** 440, 457; **III** 617, 760; **IV** 83, 417; **8 147–50 (upd.)**, 153, 261–62, 548; **9** 328–29, 500–501; **10** 289; **11** 271; **12** 99–100, 254, 364; **14** 114, 217; **16** 99; **17** 418; **18** 279; **21** 387
Dow Corning, **II** 54; **III** 683, 685
Dow Jones & Company, Inc., IV 601–03, 654, 656, 670, 678; **7** 99; **10** 276–78, 407; **13** 55; **15** 335–36; **19 128–31 (upd.)**, 204; **21** 68–70; **23** 157
Dow Jones Telerate, Inc., 10 276–78
Dowdings Ltd., **IV** 349
DowElanco, **21** 385, 387
Dowell Australia Ltd., **III** 674
Dowell Schlumberger. *See* Schlumberger Limited.
Dowidat GmbH, **IV** 197
Dowlais Iron Co., **III** 493
Down River International, Inc., **15** 188
Downe Communications, Inc., **14** 460
Downingtown Paper Company, **8** 476
Downyflake Foods, **7** 429
Dowty Aerospace, **17** 480
Doyle Dane Bernbach, **I** 9, 20, 28, 30–31, 33, 37, 206; **11** 549; **14** 159; **22** 396
DP&L. *See* Dayton Power & Light Company.
DPCE, **II** 139
DPF, Inc., **12** 275
DPL Inc., 6 480–82
DQE, **6 483–85**
DR Holdings, Inc., **10** 242
Dr Pepper/7Up Companies, Inc., I 245; **II** 477; **9 177–78**
Dr. Ing he F. Porsche GmbH, **13** 413–14
Dr. Martens, **23** 399, 401
Dr. Miles' Medical Co., **I** 653
Dr. Richter & Co., **IV** 70
Dr. Tigges-Fahrten, **II** 163–64
Drackett Professional Products, III 17; **12 126–28**
DraftDirect Worldwide, **22** 297
Draftline Engineering Co., **22** 175
Dragados y Construcciones S.A., **II** 198
Dragon, **III** 391
Dragon International, **18** 87
Dragonair, **16** 481; **18** 114. *See also* Hong Kong Dragon Airlines.
The Drake, **12** 316
Drake Bakeries, **II** 562
Drake Beam Morin, Inc., **IV** 623
Drake Steel Supply Co., **19** 343
Draper & Kramer, **IV** 724
Draper Corporation, **14** 219; **15** 384
Drathen Co., **I** 220
Dravo Corp., **6** 143
Draw-Tite, Inc., **11** 535
Drayton Corp., **II** 319; **17** 324
DreamWorks SKG Studio, **17** 72; **21** 23, 26
Dresdner Bank A.G., I 411; **II** 191, 238–39, 241–42, 256–57, 279–80,

281–83, 385; **III** 201, 289, 401; **IV** 141; **14** 169–70; **15** 13
Dresdner Feuer-Versicherungs-Gesellschaft, **III** 376
Dresser Industries, Inc., I 486; **III** 429, **470–73**; 499, 527, 545–46; **12** 539; **14** 325; **15** 225–26, 468; **16** 310; **18** 219
Dresser Power, **6** 555
Drew Graphics, Inc., **13** 227–28
Drewry Photocolor, **I** 447
Drexel Burnham Lambert Incorporated, **II** 167, 329–30, **407–09**, 482; **III** 10, 253, 254–55, 531, 721; **IV** 334; **6** 210–11; **7** 305; **8** 327, 349, 388–90, 568; **9** 346; **12** 229; **13** 169, 299, 449; **14** 43; **15** 71, 281, 464; **16** 535, 561; **20** 415; **22** 55, 189. *See also* New Street Capital Inc.
Drexel Heritage Furnishings Inc., III 571; **11** 534; **12 129–31**; **20** 362
Dreyer's Grand Ice Cream, Inc., 10 147–48; **17 139–41**
Dreyfus Interstate Development Corp., **11** 257
DRI. *See* Dominion Resources, Inc.
Dribeck Importers Inc., **9** 87
Drott Manufacturing Company, **10** 379
Drouot Group, **III** 211
Drug City, **II** 649
Drug Emporium, Inc., 12 132–34, 477
Drug House, **III** 9
Drug, Inc., **III** 17
Drummond Lighterage. *See* Puget Sound Tug and Barge Company.
Drummonds' Bank, **12** 422
Drouot, **I** 563
Dry Milks Inc., **I** 248
DryClean U.S.A., **14** 25
Dryden and Co., **III** 340
Drypers Corporation, 18 147–49
Drysdale Government Securities, **10** 117
DSC Communications Corporation, 9 170; **12 135–37**
DSM N.V., **I 326–27**; **III** 614; **15** 229
DST Systems Inc., **6** 400–02
DTE Energy Company, 20 197–201 (upd.)
Du Bouzet, **II** 233
Du Mont Company, **8** 517
Du Pont. *See* E.I. du Pont de Nemours & Co.
Du Pont Fabricators, **III** 559
Du Pont Glore Forgan, Inc., **III** 137
Du Pont Photomask, **IV** 600
Duane Reade Holding Corp., 21 186–88
Dublin and London Steam Packet Company, **V** 490
DuBois Chemicals Division, **13** 149–50; **22** 188
Ducatel-Duval, **II** 369
Ducati, **17** 24
Duck Head Apparel Company, Inc., 8 141–43
Ducon Group, **II** 81
Duff Bros., **III** 9–10
Duffy-Mott, **II** 477
Duke Power Company, V 600–02
Dumes SA, **13** 206
Dumez, **V** 655–57
Dumont Broadcasting Corporation, **7** 335
The Dun & Bradstreet Corporation, I 540; **IV 604–05**, 643, 661; **8** 526; **9** 505; **10** 4, 358; **13** 3–4; **19 132–34 (upd.)**

Dun & Bradstreet Software Services Inc., 11 77–79
Dunbar-Stark Drillings, Inc., **19** 247
Duncan Foods Corp., **I** 234; **10** 227
Duncan, Sherman & Co., **II** 329
Duncanson & Holt, Inc., **13** 539
Dundee Acquisition Corp., **19** 421
Dundee Cement Co., **III** 702; **8** 258–59
Dunfey Brothers Capital Group, **12** 368
Dunfey Hotels Corporation, **12** 367
Dunhams Stores Corporation, **V** 111
Dunhill Holdings, **IV** 93; **V** 411
Dunkin' Donuts, **II** 619
Dunkin' Doughnuts, **21** 323
Dunlop Holdings, **I** 429; **III** 697; **V** 250, 252–53
Dunn Paper Co., **IV** 290
Dunning Industries, **12** 109
Dunoyer. *See* Compagnie de Saint-Gobain S.A.
Dunwoodie Manufacturing Co., **17** 136
Duo-Bed Corp., **14** 435
Dupey Enterprises, Inc., **17** 320
Dupil-Color, Inc., **III** 745
Duplainville Transport, **19** 333–34
Duplex Products, Inc., 17 142–44, 445
Dupol, **III** 614
Dupont. *See* E.I. du Pont de Nemours & Company.
Dupont Chamber Works, **6** 449
Duquesne Light Company, **6** 483–84
Duquesne Systems, **10** 394
Dura Convertible Systems, **13** 170
Dura Corp., **I** 476
Dura-Vent, **III** 468
Duracell International Inc., 9 179–81; **12** 559; **13** 433; **17** 31
Durametallic, 17 147; **21** 189–91
Durand & Huguenin, **I** 672
Durango-Mapimi Mining Co., **22** 284
Duray, Inc., **12** 215
Durban Breweries and Distillers, **I** 287
Durham Chemicals Distributors Ltd., **III** 699
Durham Raw Materials Ltd., **III** 699
Duriron Company Inc., 17 145–47; **21** 189, 191
Durkee Famous Foods, **II** 567; **7** 314; **8** 222; **17** 106
Durr-Fillauer Medical Inc., **13** 90; **18** 97
Dutch Boy, **II** 649; **III** 745; **10** 434–35
Dutch Crude Oil Company. *See* Nederlandse Aardolie Maatschappij.
Dutch East Indies Post, Telegraph and Telephone Service, **II** 67
Dutch Nuts Chocoladefabriek B.V., **II** 569
Dutch Pantry, **II** 497
Dutch State Mines. *See* DSM N.V.
Dutton Brewery, **I** 294
Duty Free International, Inc., 11 80–82
Duval Corp., **IV** 489–90; **7** 280
DWG Corporation. *See* Triarc Companies, Inc.
Dyckerhoff, **III** 738
Dyersburg Corporation, 21 192–95
Dymed Corporation. *See* Palomar Medical Technologies, Inc.
Dynaco Corporation, **III** 643; **22** 409
DynaMark, Inc., **18** 168, 170, 516, 518
Dynamatic Corp., **I** 154
Dynamem Corporation, **22** 409
Dynamic Capital Corp., **16** 80
Dynamic Controls, **11** 202

Dynamic Microprocessor Associated Inc., **10** 508
Dynamit Nobel AG, **III** 692–95; **16** 364; **18** 559
Dynamix, **15** 455
Dynapar, **7** 116–17
Dynascan AK, **14** 118
Dynasty Footwear, Ltd., **18** 88
Dynatech Corporation, 13 194–96
Dynatron/Bondo Corporation, **8** 456
Dynell Electronics, **I** 85
Dyno Industrier AS, **13** 555
Dyonics Inc., **II** 667
DYR, **I** 38; **16** 167

E & H Utility Sales Inc., **6** 487
E & J Gallo Winery, I 27, **242–44**, 260; **7** 154–56 (upd.); **15** 391
E & S Retail Ltd. *See* Powerhouse.
E! Entertainment Television Inc., 17 148–50
E*Trade Group, Inc., 20 206–08
E. & B. Carpet Mills, **III** 423
E.A. Miller, Inc., **II** 494
E.A. Pierce & Co., **II** 424; **13** 340
E.A. Stearns & Co., **III** 627
E&B Company, **9** 72
E&B Marine, Inc., **17** 542–43
E&M Laboratories, **18** 514
E.B. Badger Co., **11** 413
E.B. Eddy Forest Products, **II** 631
E.C. Snodgrass Company, **14** 112
E.C. Steed, **13** 103
E. de Trey & Sons, **10** 270–71
E.F. Hutton Group, **I** 402; **II** 399, 450–51; **8** 139; **9** 469; **10** 63
E. Gluck Trading Co., **III** 645
E.H. Bindley & Company, **9** 67
E.I. du Pont de Nemours & Company, I 21, 28, 305, 317–19, 323, **328–30**, 334, 337–38, 343–44, 346–48, 351–53, 365, 377, 379, 383, 402–03, 545, 548, 675; **III** 21; **IV** 69, 78, 263, 371, 399, 401–02, 409, 481, 599; **V** 360; **7** 546; **8** 151–54 (upd.), 485; **9** 154, 216, 352, 466; **10** 289; **11** 432; **12** 68, 365, 416–17; **13** 21, 124; **16** 127, 130, 201, 439, 461–62; **19** 11, 223; **21** 544; **22** 147, 260, 405
E.J. Brach & Sons, **II** 521. *See also* Brach and Brock Confections, Inc.
E. Katz Special Advertising Agency. *See* Katz Communications, Inc.
E.L. Phillips and Company, **V** 652–53
E.M. Warburg Pincus & Co., **7** 305; **13** 176; **16** 319
E. Missel GmbH, **20** 363
E.N.V. Engineering, **I** 154
E.R. Squibb, **I** 695; **21** 54–55
E. Rabinowe & Co., Inc., **13** 367
E.S. Friedman & Co., **II** 241
E.S. International Holding S.A. *See* Banco Espírito Santo e Comercial de Lisboa S.A.
E-Systems, Inc., I 490; **9** 182–85
E-II Holdings Inc., **II** 468; **9** 449; **12** 87. *See also* Astrum International Corp.
E.W. Bliss, **I** 452
E.W. Oakes & Co. Ltd., **IV** 118
E.W. Scripps Company, IV 606–09; **7** 157–59 (upd.)
E.W.T. Mayer Ltd., **III** 681
E-Z Serve Corporation, 15 270; **17** 169–71

Eagle Airways Ltd., **23** 161
Eagle Credit Corp., **10** 248
Eagle Family Foods, Inc., **22** 95
Eagle Floor Care, Inc., **13** 501
Eagle Gaming, L.P., **16** 263
Eagle Hardware & Garden, Inc., 9 399; **16** 186–89; **17** 539–40
Eagle Industries Inc., **8** 230; **22** 282
Eagle Managed Care Corp., **19** 354, 357
Eagle Oil Transport Co. Ltd., **IV** 657
Eagle Plastics, **19** 414
Eagle Printing Co. Ltd., **IV** 295; **19** 225
Eagle Snacks Inc., **I** 219
Eagle Square Manufacturing Co., **III** 627
Eagle Star Insurance Co., **I** 426–27; **III** 185, 200
Eagle Supermarket, **II** 571
Eagle Thrifty Drug, **14** 397
Eagle Travel Ltd., **IV** 241
Eagle-Lion Films, **II** 147
Eagle-Picher Industries, Inc., 8 155–58; **23** 179–83 (upd.)
Early American Insurance Co., **22** 230
Earth Resources Company, **IV** 459; **17** 320
Earth Wise, Inc., **16** 90
Earth's Best, **21** 56
Easco Hand Tools, Inc., **7** 117
Eason Oil Company, **6** 578; **11** 198
East Chicago Iron and Forge Co., **IV** 113
East Hartford Trust Co., **13** 467
East India Co., **I** 468; **III** 521, 696; **IV** 48; **20** 309
East Japan Heavy Industries, **III** 578–79; **7** 348
East Japan Railway Company, V 448–50
East Midlands Electricity, **V** 605
The East New York Savings Bank, **11** 108–09
East of Scotland, **III** 359
East Texas Pulp and Paper Co., **IV** 342, 674; **7** 528
East-West Federal Bank, **16** 484
Easter Enterprises, **8** 380; **23** 358
Eastern Airlines, I 41, 66, 78, 90, 98–99, **101–03**, 116, 118, 123–25; **III** 102; **6** 73, 81–82, 104–05; **8** 416; **9** 17–18, 80; **11** 268, 427; **12** 191, 487; **21** 142, 143; **23** 483
Eastern Associated Coal Corp., **6** 487
Eastern Aviation Group, **23** 408
Eastern Bank, **II** 357
Eastern Carolina Bottling Company, **10** 223
Eastern Coal Corp., **IV** 181
Eastern Coalfields Ltd., **IV** 48–49
Eastern Corp., **IV** 703
Eastern Electricity, **13** 485
Eastern Enterprises, IV 171; **6** 486–88
Eastern Gas and Fuel Associates, **I** 354; **IV** 171
Eastern Indiana Gas Corporation, **6** 466
Eastern Kansas Utilities, **6** 511
Eastern Machine Screw Products Co., **13** 7
Eastern Market Beef Processing Corp., **20** 120
Eastern Operating Co., **III** 23
Eastern Pine Sales Corporation, **13** 249
Eastern Software Distributors, Inc., **16** 125
Eastern States Farmers Exchange, **7** 17
Eastern Telegraph, **V** 283–84
Eastern Texas Electric. *See* Gulf States Utilities Company.
Eastern Tool Co., **IV** 249
Eastern Wisconsin Power, **6** 604

Eastern Wisconsin Railway and Light Company, **6** 601
Eastex Pulp and Paper Co., **IV** 341–42
Eastman Chemical Company, 14 174–75
Eastman Christensen Company, **22** 68
Eastman Kodak Company, I 19, 30, 90, 323, 337–38, 690; **II** 103; **III** 171–72, **474–77**, 486–88, 547–48, 550, 584, 607–09; **IV** 260–61; **6** 288–89; **7** 160–64 **(upd.)**, 436–38; **8** 376–77; **9** 62, 231; **10** 24; **12** 342; **14** 174–75, 534; **16** 168, 449; **18** 184–86, 342, 510
Eastman Radio, **6** 33
Eastmaque Gold Mines, Ltd., **7** 356
Eatco, Inc., **15** 246
Eaton Axle Co., **I** 154
Eaton, Cole & Burnham Company, **8** 134
Eaton Corporation, I 154–55, 186; **III** 645; **10 279–80 (upd.)**; **12** 547
Eaton Vance Corporation, 18 150–53
Eavey Co., **II** 668
Ebamsa, **II** 474
EBASCO. *See* Electric Bond and Share Company.
Ebasco Services, **III** 499; **V** 612; **IV** 255–56
EBC Amro Ltd., **II** 186
Eberhard Faber, **12** 115
Eberhard Foods, **8** 482
EBIC. *See* European Banks' International Co.
EBS. *See* Electric Bond & Share Company.
EBSCO Industries, Inc., 17 151–53
EC Erdolchemie GmbH, **7** 141
ECC Group plc, III 689–91. *See also* English China Clays plc.
Echigoya Saburobei Shoten, **IV** 292
Echlin Inc., I 156–57; 11 83–85 (upd.), **15** 310
Echo Bay Mines Ltd., IV 75–77; 23 40
Les Echos, **IV** 659
EchoStar Communications Corporation, **18** 355
ECI Telecom Ltd., 18 154–56
Eckerd Corporation, 9 186–87; 18 272
Eckert-Mauchly Corp., **III** 166
Ecko Products, **I** 527
Ecko-Ensign Design, **I** 531
ECL, **16** 238
Eclipse Candles, Ltd., **18** 67, 69
Eclipse Machine Co., **I** 141
Eco Hotels, **14** 107
Ecolab Inc., I 331–33; 13 197–200 (upd.)
Econo-Travel Corporation, **13** 362
Economist Group, **15** 265
Economy Book Store, **10** 135
Economy Fire & Casualty, **22** 495
Economy Grocery Stores Corp., **II** 666
Ecopetrol. *See* Empresa Colombiana de Petróleos.
EcoSystems Software, Inc., **10** 245
EcoWater Systems, Inc., **16** 357
ECS S.A., 12 138–40
Ecusta Corporation, **8** 414
Edah, **13** 544–45
Eddie Bauer Inc., II 503; **V** 160; **9** **188–90; 9** 316; **10** 324, 489, 491; **11** 498; **15** 339
Eddy Bakeries, Inc., **12** 198
Eddy Paper Co., **II** 631
Edeka Zentrale A.G., II 621–23
Edelstahlwerke Buderus AG, **III** 695
Edenhall Group, **III** 673
Edenton Cotton Mills, **12** 503

EDF. *See* Electricité de France.
Edgars, **I** 289
Edgcomb Metals, **IV** 576
Edgcomb Steel Co., **IV** 575
Edgell Communications Inc., **IV** 624
Edgewater Hotel and Casino, **6** 204–05
Edina Realty Inc., **13** 348
Edison Brothers Stores, Inc., 9 191–93; 17 369, 409
Edison Electric Appliance Co., **II** 28; **12** 194
Edison Electric Co., **I** 368; **II** 330; **III** 433; **6** 572
Edison Electric Illuminating Co., **II** 402; **6** 595, 601; **14** 124
Edison Electric Illuminating Company of Boston, **12** 45
Edison Electric Light & Power, **6** 510
Edison Electric Light Co., **II** 27; **6** 565, 595; **11** 387; **12** 193
Edison General Electric Co., **II** 27, 120, 278; **12** 193; **14** 168
Edison Machine Works, **II** 27
Edison Phonograph, **III** 443
Editions Albert Premier, **IV** 614
Editions Bernard Grasset, **IV** 618
Editions Dalloz, **IV** 615
Editions Nathan, **IV** 615
Editorial Centro de Estudios Ramón Areces, S.A., **V** 52
Editorial Televisa, **18** 211, 213; **23** 417
Editoriale L'Espresso, **IV** 586–87
Editoriale Le Gazzette, **IV** 587
EdK. *See* Edeka Zentrale A.G.
Edmark Corporation, 14 176–78
Edmonton City Bakery, **II** 631
Edogawa Oil Co., **IV** 403
EdoWater Systems, Inc., **IV** 137
Edper Equities, **II** 456
EDS. *See* Electronic Data Systems Corporation.
Education Association Mutual Assurance Company. *See* Horace Mann Educators Corporation.
Education Funds, Inc., **II** 419
Education Systems Corporation, **7** 256
Educational & Recreational Services, Inc., **II** 607
Educational Credit Corporation, **8** 10
Educational Publishing Corporation, **22** 519, 522
Educational Supply Company, **7** 255
Educational Testing Service, 12 141–43
EduQuest, **6** 245
Edward Ford Plate Glass Co., **III** 640–41, 731
Edward J. DeBartolo Corporation, V 116; **8 159–62**
Edward Lloyd Ltd., **IV** 258
Edward P. Allis Company, **13** 16
Edward Smith & Company, **8** 553
Edwards & Jones, **11** 360
Edwards Dunlop & Co. Ltd., **IV** 249
Edwards Food Warehouse, **II** 642
Edwards George and Co., **III** 283
Edwards Industries, **IV** 256
Edwardstone Partners, **14** 377
EEC Environmental, Inc., **16** 259
Eerste Nederlandsche, **III** 177–79
Eff Laboratories, **I** 622
Effectenbank, **II** 268; **21** 145
EFM Media Management, **23** 294
Efnadruck GmbH, **IV** 325

Efrat Future Technology Ltd. *See* Comverse Technology, Inc.
EG&G Incorporated, 8 163–65; 18 219; **22** 410
EGAM, **IV** 422
Egerton Hubbard & Co., **IV** 274
Egghead Inc., 9 194–95; 10 284
EGPC. *See* Egyptian General Petroleum Corporation.
EGUZKIA-NHK, **III** 581
Egyptair, I 107; **6 84–86**
Egyptian General Petroleum Corporation, IV 412–14
EHAPE Einheitspreis Handels Gesellschaft mbH. *See* Kaufhalle AG.
Eidgenössische Bank, **II** 378
Eidgenössische Versicherungs-Aktien-Gesellschaft, **III** 403
84 Lumber Company, 9 196–97
Eildon Electronics Ltd., **15** 385
EIMCO, **I** 512
EIS Automotive Corp., **III** 603
Eisai Company, **13** 77
Eisen-und Stahlwerk Haspe AG, **IV** 126
Eisen-und Stahlwerk Hoesch, **IV** 103
Eisenhower Mining Co., **IV** 33
EKA AB, **I** 330; **8** 153
Eka Nobel AB, **9** 380
Ekco Group, Inc., 12 377; **16 190–93**
El Al Israel Airlines Ltd., I 30; **23** **184–87**
El Camino Resources International, Inc., 11 86–88
El Chico Restaurants, Inc., 19 135–38
El Corte Inglés, S.A., V 51–53
El Dorado Investment Company, **6** 546–47
El Paso & Southwestern Railroad, **IV** 177
El Paso Electric Company, 21 196–98
El Paso Healthcare System, Ltd., **15** 112
El Paso Natural Gas Company, 10 190; **11** 28; **12 144–46; 19** 411
El Pollo Loco, **II** 680
El Taco, **7** 505
El-Mel-Parts Ltd., **21** 499
ELAN, **IV** 486
Elan Corp. plc, **10** 54
Elan Ski Company, **22** 483
Elano Corporation, 14 179–81
Elcat Company, **17** 91
Elco Corporation, **21** 329, 331
Elco Industries Inc., **22** 282
Elco Motor Yacht, **I** 57
Elda Trading Co., **II** 48
Elder Dempster Line, **6** 416–17
Elder Smith Goldsbrough Mort Ltd., **21** 227
Elder's Insurance Co., **III** 370
Elder-Beerman Stores Corporation, 10 **281–83; 19** 362
Elders IXL Ltd., I 216, 228–29, 264, **437–39**, 592–93; **7** 182–83; **21** 227
Elders Keep, **13** 440
Eldorado Gold Corporation, **22** 237
ele Corporation, **23** 251
Electra Corp., **III** 569; **20** 361–62
Electra/Midland Corp., **13** 398
Electralab Electronics Corp., **III** 643
Electric Boat Co., **I** 57–59, 527; **II** 7; **10** 315
Electric Bond & Share Company, **V** 564–65; **6** 596
Electric Clearinghouse, Inc., **18** 365, 367
Electric Energy, Inc., **6** 470, 505
Electric Fuels Corp., **V** 621; **23** 200

Electric Heat Regulator Co., **II** 40; **12** 246
Electric Iron and Steel, **IV** 162
Electric Light and Power Company, **6** 483
Electric Light Company of Atlantic City. *See* Atlantic Energy, Inc.
Electric Thermostat Co., **II** 40; **12** 246
Electrical Lamp Service Co. *See* EMI Group plc.
Electricité de France, **I** 303; **V** 603–05, 626–28
Electro Dynamics Corp., **I** 57, 484; **11** 263
Electro Metallurgical Co., **I** 400; **9** 517; **11** 402
Electro Refractories and Abrasives Company, **8** 178
Electro String Instrument Corporation, **16** 201
Electro-Alkaline Company. *See* The Clorox Company.
Electro-Chemische Fabrik Natrium GmbH, **IV** 69–70
Electro-Flo, Inc., **9** 27
Electro-Mechanical Research, **III** 617; **17** 417
Electro-Motive Engineering Company, **10** 273
Electro-Nite International N.V., **IV** 100
Electro-Optical Systems, **III** 172; **6** 289
Electrobel, **II** 202
ElectroData Corp., **III** 165; **6** 281
Electrolux Group, **II** 69, 572; **III** 420, **478–81**; **IV** 338; **6** 69; **11** 439; **12** 158–59, 250; **13** 562, 564; **17** 353; **21** 383. *See also* Aktiebolaget Electrolux.
Electromagnetic Sciences Inc., **21** **199–201**
Electromedics, **11** 460
Electronic Arts Inc., **10** **284–86**; **13** 115
Electronic Banking Systems, **9** 173
Electronic Data Systems Corporation, **I** 172; **II** 65; **III** **136–38**, 326; **6** 226; **9** 36; **10** 325, 327; **11** 62, 123, 131; **13** 482; **14** 15, 318; **22** 266
Electronic Engineering Co., **16** 393
Electronic Rentals Group PLC, **II** 139
Electronic Tool Company, **16** 100
Electronics Corp. of Israel Ltd. *See* ECI Telecom Ltd.
Electronics for Imaging, Inc., **15** **148–50**
Electrorail, **II** 93; **18** 472
Electrowatt Ltd., **21** 146–47
Electrowerke AG, **IV** 230
Elektra Records, **III** 480; **23** 33
Elektriska Aktiebolaget. *See* ABB Asea Brown Boveri Ltd.
Elektrizitäts-Gesellschaft Laufenburg, **6** 490
Elektrizitätswerk Westfalen AG, **V** 744
ElektroHelios, **III** 479; **22** 26
Elektromekaniska AB, **III** 478
Elektromekano, **II** 1
Elektrowatt AG, **6** **489–91**
Eleme Petrochemicals Co., **IV** 473
Eletson Corp., **13** 374
Elettra Broadcasting Corporation, **14** 509
Elettrofinanziaria Spa, **9** 152
Eleventh National Bank, **II** 373
Elf Aquitaine SA, **21** **202–06** (upd.); **23** 236, 238. *See also* Société Nationale Elf Aquitaine.
Elgin Blenders, Inc., **7** 128
Elgin Exploration, Inc., **19** 247
Eli Lilly & Co., **I** 637, **645–47**, 666, 679, 687, 701; **III** 18–19, 60–61; **8** 168, 209;

9 89–90; **10** 535; **11** 9, **89–91** (upd.), 458, 460; **12** 187, 278, 333; **14** 99–100, 259; **17** 437; **18** 420, 422; **19** 105; **21** 387
Eli Witt Company, **15** 137, 139
Elias Brothers Restaurants, **III** 103
Elit Circuits Inc., **I** 330; **8** 153
Elite Microelectronics, **9** 116
Elite Sewing Machine Manufacturing Co., **III** 415
Elizabeth Arden Co., **I** 646, **III** 48; **8** **166–68**, 344; **9** 201–02, 428, 449; **11** 90; **12** 314
Eljer Industries, **II** 420
Elk River Resources, Inc., **IV** 550
Elka, **III** 54
Elke Corporation, **10** 514
Elko-Lamoille Power Company, **11** 343
Ellenville Electric Company, **6** 459
Ellesse International, **V** 376
Ellett Brothers, Inc., **17** **154–56**
Ellington Recycling Center, **12** 377
Elliott Automation, **II** 25; **6** 241; **13** 225
Elliott Bay Design Group, **22** 276
Elliott Paint and Varnish, **8** 553
Ellis Adding-Typewriter Co., **III** 151; **6** 265
Ellis Banks, **II** 336
Ellis, Chafflin & Co. *See* Mead Corporation.
Ellis Paperboard Products Inc., **13** 442
Ellos A.B., **II** 640
ELMA Electronic, **III** 632
Elmendorf Board, **IV** 343
Elmer's Products, Inc. *See* Borden, Inc.
Elphinstone, **21** 501
Elrick & Lavidge, **6** 24
Elrick Industries, Inc., **19** 278
Elscint Ltd., **20** **202–05**
Elsevier NV, **IV** **610–11**, 643, 659; **7** 244; **14** 555–56; **17** 396, 399
Elsi, **II** 86
ELTO Outboard Motor Co., **III** 597
Eltra, **I** 416, 524; **22** 31
Elwerath, **IV** 485
Elyria Telephone Company, **6** 299
Email Ltd., **III** 672–73
Emballage, **III** 704
Embankment Trust Ltd., **IV** 659
Embassy Book Co., Ltd., **IV** 635
Embassy Hotel Group, **I** 216; **9** 426
Embassy Suites, **9** 425
Embry-Riddle, **I** 89
EMC Corporation, **12** **147–49**; **20** 8
Emco, **III** 569; **20** 361
Emerald Coast Water Co., **III** 21
Emerald Technology, Inc., **10** 97
Emerson Drug, **I** 711
Emerson Electric Co., **II** **18–21**, 92; **III** 625; **8** 298; **12** 248; **13** 225; **14** 357; **15** 405–06; **21** 43; **22** 64
Emerson-Brantingham Company, **10** 378
Emery Air Freight Corporation, **6** 345–46, 386, **388–91**; **18** 177
Emery Group, **I** 377; **III** 33
Emery Worldwide, **21** 139
Emeryville Chemical Co., **IV** 408
Emge Packing Co., Inc., **11** **92–93**
Emhart Corp., **III** 437; **8** 332; **20** 67
EMI Group plc, **I** 531; **6** 240; **22** **192–95** (upd.). *See also* Thorne EMI plc.
Empain, **18** 472; **19** 165
Empain-Schneider, **II** 93
Empaques de Carton Titan, **19** 10–11

Empex Hose, **19** 37
Empire Blue Cross and Blue Shield, **III** **245–46**; **6** 195
Empire Brewery, **I** 253
Empire Co., **II** 653
Empire Cos., **IV** 391
Empire District Electric, **IV** 391
Empire Family Restaurants Inc., **15** 362
Empire Gas & Fuel, **IV** 391
Empire Hanna Coal Co., Ltd., **8** 346
Empire Inc., **II** 682
Empire Life and Accident Insurance Co., **III** 217
Empire National Bank, **II** 218
Empire of America, **11** 110
Empire Pencil, **III** 505
Empire Savings, Building & Loan Association, **8** 424
Empire State Group, **IV** 612
Empire State Petroleum, **IV** 374
Empire State Pickling Company, **21** 155
Empire Stores, **19** 309
Empire Trust Co., **II** 218
Employee Solutions, Inc., **18** **157–60**
Employers Reinsurance Corp., **II** 31; **12** 197
Employers' Liability Assurance, **III** 235
Empresa Brasileira de Aeronautica, S.A., **15** 73
Empresa Colombiana de Petróleos, **IV** **415–18**
Empresa Nacional de Electridad, **I** 459
Empresa Nacional del Petroleo, **IV** 528
Empresa Nacional Electrica de Cordoba, **V** 607
Empresa Nacional Hidro-Electrica del Ribagorzana, **I** 459; **V** 607
Empresa Nacional Hulleras del Norte, **I** 460
Empresas Frisco, **21** 259
Empresas La Moderna, **21** 413
Empresas Tolteca, **20** 123
Emprise Corporation, **7** 134–35
EMS Technologies, Inc., **21** 199, 201; **22** 173
Ems-Chemi, **III** 760
Enagas, **IV** 528
ENCASO, **IV** 528
ENCI, **IV** 132
Encore Computer Corporation, **13** **201–02**
Encore Distributors Inc., **17** 12–13
Encryption Technology Corporation, **23** 102
Encyclopedia Britannica, Inc., **7** **165–68**; **12** 435, 554–55; **16** 252
Endata, Inc., **11** 112
ENDESA Group, **V** **606–08**
Endevco Inc., **11** 28
Endiama, **IV** 67
Endicott Trust Company, **11** 110
Endo Vascular Technologies, Inc., **11** 460
Endovations, Inc., **21** 47
ENECO. *See* Empresa Nacional Electrica de Cordoba.
ENEL. *See* Ente Nazionale per l'Energia Elettrica.
Enerchange LLC, **18** 366
Enercon, Inc., **6** 25
Energen Corporation, **6** 583; **21** **207–09**
Energie-Verwaltungs-Gesellschaft, **V** 746
Energieversorgung Ostbayern AG, **23** 47
Energizer, **9** 180
Energy Absorption Systems, Inc., **15** 378

Energy Biosystems Corp., **15** 352
Energy Coatings Co., **14** 325
Energy Corp. of Louisiana, **V** 619
Energy Increments Inc., **19** 411
Energy Steel Corporation, **19** 472
Energy Systems Group, Inc., **13** 489
EnergyOne, **19** 487
Enerplus Resources, **21** 500
Enesco Corporation, 11 94–96; 15 475,
  477–78
Engelhard Corporation, II 54; **IV** 23,
  78–80; 16 28; **21 210–14 (upd.)**
Engen, **IV** 93; **22** 236
Engineered Polymers Co., **I** 202
Engineering Co. of Nigeria, **IV** 473
Engineering Company, **9** 16
Engineering for the Petroleum and Process
  Industries, **IV** 414
Engineering Plastics, Ltd., **8** 377
Engineering Research Associates, **III** 126,
  129
Engineers & Fabricators, Inc., **18** 513
England Corsair Furniture, **14** 302
Englander Co., **I** 400
English China Clays plc, III 689–91; **15
  151–54 (upd.)**
English Condensed Milk Co., **II** 545
English Electric Co., **I** 50; **II** 25, 81; **6** 241
English Mercantile & General Insurance
  Co., **III** 376
English Property Corp., **IV** 712
English, Scottish and Australian Bank Ltd.,
  II 187–89
Engraph, Inc., 12 150–51
Enhance, **12** 445
ENHER. *See* Empresa Nacional Hidro-
  Electrica del Ribagorzana.
ENI. *See* Ente Nazionale Idrocarburi.
ENIEPSA, **IV** 528
Enimont, **IV** 422, 525
Ennia, **III** 177, 179, 310
Ennis Business Forms, Inc., 21 215–17
Eno Proprietaries, **III** 65
Enocell Oy, **IV** 277
Enogex, Inc., **6** 539–40
ENPAC Corporation, **18** 162
Enpetrol, **IV** 528
**Enquirer/Star Group, Inc., 10 287–88;
  12** 358
Enron Corporation, III 197; **V** 609–10; **6**
  457, 593; **18** 365; **19 139–41,** 162, 487
Enseco, **III** 684
Enserch Corp., V 611–13
Ensidesa, **I** 460
Ensign Oil Company, **9** 490
Enskilda S.A., **II** 352–53
Enso-Gutzeit Oy, IV 274–77; 17 539
ENSTAR Corporation, IV 567; **11** 441
Enstar Group Inc., **13** 299
Ensys Environmental Products, Inc., **10**
  107
ENTASA, **IV** 528
Ente Gestione Aziende Minerarie, **I** 466
Ente Nazionale di Energia Elettrica, **I** 466
Ente Nazionale Idrocarburi, I 369; **IV**
  412, **419–22,** 424, 453, 466, 470, 486,
  546; **V** 614–17
**Ente Nazionale per l'Energia Elettrica,
  V 614–17**
Entenmann's, **I** 246, 712; **10** 551
Entergy Corp., V 618–20; 6 496–97
Enterprise Development Company, **15** 413
Enterprise Electronics Corporation, **18**
  513–15

Enterprise Federal Savings & Loan, **21** 524
Enterprise Integration Technologies, **18** 541
Enterprise Leasing, 6 392–93
Enterprise Metals Pty. Ltd., **IV** 61
Enterprise Oil plc, 11 97–99
Enterprise Rent-A-Car, **16** 380
Entertainment Publications, **16** 146
Entertainment Zone, Inc., **15** 212
Entity Software, **11** 469
Entrada Industries Incorporated, **6** 568–69
Entré Computer Centers, **6** 243–44; **13** 175
Entremont, **I** 676
Entreprise de Recherches et d'Activités
  Pétrolières, **IV** 453, 467, 544, 560; **7**
  481, 483–84
**Entreprise Nationale Sonatrach, IV
  423–25; V** 626, 692; **10** 83–84; **12** 145
Entrex, Inc., **III** 154
Entrust Financial Corp., **16** 347
Envirex, **11** 361
Envirodrill Services, Inc., **19** 247
Envirodyne Industries, Inc., 17 157–60
ENVIRON International Corporation, **10**
  106
Environmental Defense Fund, **9** 305
Environmental Planning & Research. *See*
  CRSS Inc.
Environmental Research and Technology,
  Inc., **23** 135
Environmental Systems Corporation, **9** 109
Environmental Testing and Certification
  Corporation, **10** 106–07
Environmentals Incorporated. *See* Angelica
  Corporation.
Envirosciences Pty. Ltd., **16** 260
Enwright Environmental Consulting
  Laboratories, **9** 110
Enzyme Bio-Systems, Ltd., **21** 386
Enzyme Technologies Corp., **I** 342; **14** 217
Eon Productions, **II** 147
Eon Systems, **III** 143; **6** 238
l'Epargne, **12** 152
EPE Technologies, **18** 473
Les Epiceries Presto Limitée, **II** 651
Epiphone, **16** 238–39
Epoch Systems Inc., **9** 140; **12** 149
Eppler, Guerin & Turner, Inc., **III** 330
Eppley, **III** 99
Epsilon Trading Corporation, **6** 81
Epson, **18** 386–87, 435
Equator Bank, **II** 298
EQUICOR-Equitable HCA Corp., **III** 80,
  226
Equifax, Inc., 6 23–25
Equilink Licensing Group, **22** 458
EquiStar Hotel Investors L.P. *See* CapStar
  Hotel Co.
Equitable Bancorporation, **12** 329
Equitable Equipment Company, **7** 540
**Equitable Life Assurance Society of the
  United States, II** 330; **III** 80, 229, 237,
  247–49, 274, 289, 291, 305–06, 316,
  329, 359; **IV** 171, 576, 711; **6** 23; **13**
  539; **19** 324, 511; **22** 188–90; **23** 370,
  482
Equitable Resources, Inc., 6 492–94
Equitable Trust Co., **II** 247, 397, **10** 61
Equitas, **22** 315
Equitec Financial Group, **11** 483
Equitex Inc., **16** 431
Equity & Law, **III** 211
Equity Corp. Tasman, **III** 735
Equity Corporation, **6** 599
Equity Group Investment, Inc., **22** 339

Equity Title Services Company, **13** 348
Equivalent Company, **12** 421
Equus Capital Corp., **23** 65
Equus II Inc., **18** 11
Eramet, **IV** 108
ERAP. *See* Entreprise de Recherches et
  d'Activités Pétrolières.
Erasco, **II** 556
ERCO Systems Group, **16** 461–63
Erdal, **II** 572
Erdölsproduktions-Gesellschaft AG, **IV** 485
Erftwerk AG, **IV** 229
Ericson Yachts, **10** 215
Ericssan, AB, **11** 501
Ericsson, **9** 32–33; **11** 196; **17** 33, 353; **18**
  74. *See also* L.M. Ericsson.
Eridania Beghin-Say, S.A., **14** 17, 19
Erie and Pennyslvania, **I** 584
Erie County Bank, **9** 474
Erie Railroad, **I** 584; **II** 329; **IV** 180
Erie Scientific Company, **14** 479–80
Eritsusha, **IV** 326
ERKA. *See* Reichs Kredit-Gesellschaft
  mbH.
ERLY Industries Inc., 17 161–62
Ernest Oppenheimer and Sons, **IV** 21, 79
Ernst & Young, I 412; **9 198–200,** 309,
  311; **10** 115
Erol's, **9** 74; **11** 556
ERPI, **7** 167
Ersco Corporation, **17** 310
Erste Allgemeine, **III** 207–08
Erving Distributor Products Co., **IV** 282; **9**
  260
Erving Healthcare, **13** 150
Erwin Wasey & Co., **I** 17, 22
Erzbergbau Salzgitter AG, **IV** 201
ES&A. *See* English, Scottish and
  Australian Bank Ltd.
Esanda, **II** 189
ESB Inc., **IV** 112; **18** 488
Esbjerg Thermoplast, **9** 92
Escada AG, **14** 467
Escalade, Incorporated, 19 142–44
Escambia Chemicals, **I** 298
Escan, **22** 354
Escanaba Paper Co., **IV** 311; **19** 266
Escaut et Meuse, **IV** 227
Escher Wyss, **III** 539, 632
Eschweiler Bergwerks-Verein AG, **IV**
  25–26, 193
ESCO Corp., **17** 246, 248
Esco Trading, **10** 482
Escoffier Ltd., **I** 259
Escotel Mobile Communications, **18** 180
Esdon de Castro, **8** 137
ESE Sports Co. Ltd., **V** 376
ESGM. *See* Elder Smith Goldsbrough
  Mort.
ESI Energy, Inc., **V** 623–24
Eskay Screw Corporation, **11** 536
Eskilstuna Separator, **III** 419
Eskimo Pie Corporation, 21 218–20
Esmark, Inc., **I** 441; **II** 448, 468–69; **6**
  357; **12** 93; **13** 448; **15** 357; **19** 290; **22**
  55, 513
Esperance-Longdoz, **IV** 51–52
Espírito Santo. *See* Banco Espírito Santo e
  Comercial de Lisboa S.A.
ESPN, **II** 131; **IV** 627; **19** 201, 204
Esprit de Corp., 8 169–72
La Espuela Oil Company, Ltd., **IV** 81–82;
  7 186
Esquire Education Group, **12** 173

Esquire Inc., **I** 453; **IV** 672; **13** 178; **19** 405

ESS Technology, Inc., 22 196–98

Essanelle Salon Co., **18** 455

Essantee Theatres, Inc., **14** 86

Essef Corporation, 18 161–63

Esselte Pendaflex Corporation, 11 100–01

Essener Reisebüro, **II** 164

Essex International Ltd., **19** 452

Essex Outfitters Inc., **9** 394

Essilor International, 18 392; **21 221–23**

Esso, **I** 52; **II** 628; **III** 673; **IV** 46, 276, 397, 421, 423, 432–33, 439, 441, 454, 470, 484, 486, 517–19, 531, 555, 563; **7** 140, 171; **11** 97; **13** 558; **22** 106. *See also* Standard Oil Company of New Jersey.

Estech, Inc., **19** 290

Estée Lauder Inc., I 696; **III** 56; **8** 131; **9** 201–04; **11** 41

Estel N.V., **IV** 105, 133

Esterline Technologies Corp., 15 155–57

Eston Chemical, **6** 148

Estronics, Inc., **19** 290

ETA Systems, Inc., **10** 256–57

Etablissement Mesnel, **I** 202

Etablissement Poulenc-Frères, **I** 388

Etablissements Badin-Defforey, **19** 98

Etablissements Economiques du Casino Guichard, Perrachon et ie, S.C.A., 12 152–54; 16 452

Etablissements Pierre Lemonnier S.A., **II** 532

Etablissements Robert Ouvrie S.A., **22** 436

Eteq Microsystems, **9** 116

Ethan Allen Interiors, Inc., III 530–31; **10** 184; **12** 307; **12 155–57**

Ethical Personal Care Products, Ltd., **17** 108

Ethicon, Inc., III 35; **8** 281; **10** 213; **23 188–90**

Ethyl Corp., I 334–36, 342; **IV** 289; **10** 289–91 (upd.); **14** 217

Etienne Aigner, **14** 224

Etimex Kunstoffwerke GmbH, **7** 141

L'Etoile, **II** 139

Etos, **II** 641

ETPM Entrêpose, **IV** 468

Euclid, **I** 147; **12** 90

Euclid Chemical Co., **8** 455–56

Euclid Crane & Hoist Co., **13** 385

Euralux, **III** 209

Eurasbank, **II** 279–80; **14** 169

The Eureka Company, III 478, 480; **12 158–60; 15** 416; **22** 26. *See also* White Consolidated Industries Inc.

Eureka Insurance Co., **III** 343

Eureka Specialty Printing, **IV** 253; **17** 30

Eureka Technology, **18** 20

Eureka Tent & Awning Co., **III** 59

Eureka X-Ray Tube, Inc., **10** 272

Euris, **22** 365

Euro Disneyland SCA, 6 174, 176; **20 209–12**

Euro RSCG Worldwide S.A., 10 345, 347; **13 203–05; 16** 168

Euro-Pacific Finance, **II** 389

Eurobel, **II** 139; **III** 200

Eurobrokers Investment Corp., **II** 457

Eurocan Pulp & Paper Co. Ltd., **III** 648; **IV** 276, 300

Eurocard France, **II** 265

Eurocom S.A. *See* Euro RSCG Worldwide S.A.

Eurocopter SA, **7** 9, 11; **21** 8

Eurofilter Airfilters Ltd., **17** 106

Eurogroup, **V** 65

Euroimpex, **18** 163

Euromarché SA, **10** 205; **19** 308–09; **23** 231

Euromarket Designs Inc., **9** 144

Euromissile, **7** 9

Euromoney Publications, **19** 118, 120

Euronda, **IV** 296; **19** 226

Euronova S.R.L., **15** 340

Europa Discount Sud-Ouest, **23** 248

Europa Metalli, **IV** 174

Europaischen Tanklager- und Transport AG, **7** 141

Europcar Interrent, **10** 419

Europe Computer Systems. *See* ECS S.A.

Europe Craft Imports, Inc., **16** 37

European and African Investments Ltd., **IV** 21

European Banking Co., **II** 186

European Banks' International Co., **II** 184–86, 295

European Coal and Steel, **II** 402

European Gas Turbines, **13** 356

European Investment Bank, **6** 97

European Periodicals, Publicity and Advertising Corp., **IV** 641; **7** 311

European Petroleum Co., **IV** 562

European Retail Alliance (ERA), **12** 152–53

European Silicon Structures, **17** 34

European-American Bank & Trust Company, **14** 169

European-American Banking Corp., **II** 279, 295

Europeia, **III** 403

Europemballage, **I** 600

Europene du Zirconium (Cezus), **21** 491

Europensiones, **III** 348

Eurotec, **IV** 128

Eurotechnique, **III** 678; **16** 122

Eurotunnel PLC, 13 206–08

Eurovida, **III** 348

Euthenics Systems Corp., **14** 334

EVA Airways Corporation, **13** 211

Evaluation Associates, Inc., **III** 306

Evan Picone, **III** 55

Evans, **V** 21

Evans & Sutherland Computer Corporation, 19 145–49

Evans Products Co., **13** 249–50, 550

Evans-Aristocrat Industries, **III** 570; **20** 361

Evansville Veneer and Lumber Co., **12** 296

Eve of Roma, **III** 28

Evelyn Haddon, **IV** 91

Evelyn Wood, Inc., **7** 165, 168

Evence Coppée, **III** 704–05

Evenflo Companies, Inc., **19** 144

Evening News Association, **IV** 612; **7** 191

Ever Ready Label Corp., **IV** 253; **17** 30

Ever Ready Ltd., **7** 209; **9** 179–80

Everan Capital Corp., **15** 257

Everest & Jennings, **11** 200

Everett Pulp & Paper Company, **17** 440

Everex Systems, Inc., 12 162; **16 194–96**

Evergenius, **13** 210

Evergreen Healthcare, Inc., **14** 210

Evergreen Marine Corporation Taiwan Ltd., 13 209–11

Evergreen Resources, Inc., **11** 28

Everlaurel, **13** 210

Everready Battery Co., **13** 433

Eversharp, **III** 28

Everyday Learning Corporation, **22** 519, 522

Everything for the Office, **22** 154

Everything's A Dollar Inc. (EAD), **13** 541–43

Evian, **6** 47, 49

Evinrude Motor Co., **III** 597–99

Evinrude-ELTO, **III** 597

Ewell Industries, **III** 739

Ewo Breweries, **I** 469; **20** 311

Ex-Cell-O Corp., **IV** 297

Ex-Lax Inc., **15** 138–39

Exabyte Corporation, 12 161–63

Exacta, **III** 122

Exar Corp., 14 182–84

Exatec A/S, **10** 113

Excaliber, **6** 205

EXCEL Communications Inc., 18 164–67

Excel Corporation, **11** 92–93; **13** 138, 351

Excel Mining Systems, Inc., **13** 98

Excelsior Life Insurance Co., **III** 182; **21** 14

Excerpta Medica International, **IV** 610

Exchange & Discount Bank, **II** 318; **17** 323

Exchange Bank of Yarmouth, **II** 210

Exchange Oil & Gas Corp., **IV** 282; **9** 260

Excite, Inc., **22** 519

Exco International, **10** 277

Execu-Fit Health Programs, **11** 379

Executive Gallery, Inc., **12** 264

Executive Income Life Insurance Co., **10** 246

Executive Life Insurance Co., **III** 253–55; **11** 483

Executive Systems, Inc., **11** 18

Executone Information Systems, Inc., 13 212–14; 15 195

Executrans, Inc., **21** 96

Exel Logistics Ltd., **6** 412, 414

Exel Ltd., **13** 150

Exeter Oil Co., **IV** 550

Exide Electronics Group, Inc., 9 10; **20 213–15**

Exors. of James Mills, **III** 493

Expeditors International of Washington Inc., 17 163–65

Expercom, **6** 303

Experience, **III** 359

Exploitasi Tambang Minyak Sumatra Utara, **IV** 492

Explorer Motor Home Corp., **16** 296

Explosive Fabricators Corp., **III** 643

Export & Domestic Can Co., **15** 127

Export-Import Bank, **IV** 33, 184

Express Foods Inc, **I** 247–48

Express Newspapers plc, **IV** 687

Express Rent-a-Tire, Ltd., **20** 113

Express Scripts Incorporated, 17 166–68

Expression Homes, **22** 205, 207

Extel Corp., **II** 142; **III** 269–70

Extel Financial Ltd., **IV** 687

Extendicare Health Services, Inc., III 81; **6 181–83**

Extracorporeal Medical Specialties, **III** 36

Extron International Inc., **16** 538

Exxon Corporation, I 16–17, 360, 364; **II** 16, 62, 431, 451; **IV** 171, 363, 365, 403, 406, **426–30**, 431–33, 437–38, 454, 466, 506, 508, 512, 515, 522, 537–39,

554; **V** 605; **7** 169–73 (**upd.**), 230, 538, 559; **9** 440–41; **11** 353; **14** 24–25, 291, 494; **12** 348; **16** 489, 548; **20** 262; **23** 317

Eye Masters Ltd., **23** 329
Eyeful Home Co., **III** 758
Eyelab, **II** 560; **12** 411
EZ Paintr Corporation, **9** 374
EZPor Corporation, **12** 377

F & J Meat Packers, Inc., **22** 548–49
F. & F. Koenigkramer Company, **10** 272
F. & J. Heinz, **II** 507
F & M Distributors, **12** 132
F. & M. Schaefer Brewing Corporation, **I** 253, 291; **III** 137; **18** 500
F & M Scientific Corp., **III** 142; **6** 237
F & R Builders, Inc., **11** 257
F.A. Computer Technologies, Inc., **12** 60
F.A. Ensign Company, **6** 38
F.A.I. Insurances, **III** 729
F.A.O. Schwarz, **I** 548
F&G International Insurance, **III** 397
F. Atkins & Co., **I** 604
F.B. McFarren, Ltd., **21** 499–500
F.E. Compton Company, **7** 167
F. Egger Co., **22** 49
F.F. Dalley Co., **II** 497
F.F. Publishing and Broadsystem Ltd., **IV** 652; **7** 392
F.H. Tomkins Buckle Company Ltd., **11** 525
F. Hoffmann-La Roche & Co. A.G., I 637, 640, **642–44**, 657, 685, 693, 710; **7** 427; **9** 264; **10** 80, 549; **11** 424–25; **14** 406
F.J. Walker Ltd., **I** 438
F.K.I. Babcock, **III** 466
F. Kanematsu & Co., Ltd., **IV** 442
F.L. Industries Inc., **I** 481, 483
F.L. Moseley Co., **III** 142; **6** 237
F.N. Burt Co., **IV** 644
F. Perkins, **III** 651–52
F.S. Smithers, **II** 445; **22** 405
F.W. Dodge Corp., **IV** 636–37
F.W. Means & Company, **11** 337
F.W. Sickles Company, **10** 319
F.W. Williams Holdings, **III** 728
F.W. Woolworth Co. *See* Woolworth Corporation.
F.X. Matt Brewing Co., **18** 72
Fab-Asia, Inc., **22** 354–55
Fabco Automotive Corp., **23** 306
Fabergé, Inc., **II** 590; **III** 48; **8** 168, 344; **11** 90
Fabri-Centers of America Inc., 15 329; **16 197–99; 18** 223
Fabrica de Cemento El Melan, **III** 671
Facchin Foods Co., **I** 457
Facit, **III** 480; **22** 26
Facts on File, Inc., **14** 96–97; **22** 443
Fafnir Bearing Company, **13** 523
FAG Kugelfischer, **11** 84
Fagersta, **II** 366; **IV** 203
Fahr AG, **III** 543
Fahrzeugwerke Eisenach, **I** 138
FAI, **III** 545–46
Failsafe, **14** 35
Fair, Isaac and Company, 18 168–71, 516, 518
Fairbanks Morse Co., **I** 158, 434–35; **10** 292; **12** 71
Fairchild Aircraft, Inc., 9 205–08, 460; **11** 278

Fairchild Camera and Instrument Corp., **II** 50, 63; **III** 110, 141, 455, 618; **6** 261–62; **7** 531; **10** 108; **11** 503; **13** 323–24; **14** 14; **17** 418; **21** 122, 330
Fairchild Communications Service, **8** 328
Fairchild Industries, **I** 71, 198; **11** 438; **14** 43; **15** 195
Fairchild Semiconductor Corporation, **II** 44–45, 63–65; **III** 115; **6** 215, 247; **10** 365–66; **16** 332
Fairclough Construction Group plc, I 567–68
Fairey Industries Ltd., **IV** 659
Fairfax, **IV** 650
Fairfield Manufacturing Co., **14** 43
Fairfield Publishing, **13** 165
Fairmont Foods Co., **7** 430; **15** 139
Fairmount Glass Company, **8** 267
Fairport Machine Shop, Inc., **17** 357
Falcon Oil Co., **IV** 396
Falcon Seaboard Inc., **II** 86; **IV** 410; **7** 309
Falconbridge, Ltd., **IV** 165–66
Falconbridge Nickel Mines Ltd., **IV** 111
Falconet Corp., **I** 45
Falley's, Inc., **17** 558, 560–61
Fallon McElligott Inc., 22 199–201
Falls Financial Inc., **13** 223
Falls National Bank of Niagara Falls, **11** 108
Falls Rubber Company, **8** 126
FAME Plastics, Inc., **18** 162
Family Channel. *See* International Family Entertainment Inc.
Family Dollar Stores, Inc., 13 215–17
Family Health Program, **6** 184
Family Life Insurance Co., **II** 425; **13** 341
Family Mart Company, **V** 188
Family Restaurants, Inc., **14** 194
Family Steak Houses of Florida, Inc., **15** 420
Famosa Bakery, **II** 543
Famous Atlantic Fish Company, **20** 54
Famous Players-Lasky Corp., **I** 451; **II** 154; **6** 161–62; **23** 123
FAN, **13** 370
Fannie Mae. *See* Federal National Mortgage Association.
Fansteel Inc., 19 150–52
Fantle's Drug Stores, **16** 160
Fantus Co., **IV** 605
Fanuc Ltd., III 482–83; 17 172–74 (upd.)
Far East Airlines, **6** 70
Far East Machinery Co., **III** 581
Far Eastern Air Transport, Inc., **23** 380
Far West Restaurants, **I** 547
Faraday National Corporation, **10** 269
Farben. *See* I.G. Farbenindustrie AG.
Farbenfabriken Bayer A.G., **I** 309
Farbwerke Hoechst A.G., **I** 346–47; **IV** 486; **13** 262
Farine Lactée Henri Nestlé, **II** 545
Farinon Corp., **II** 38
Farley Candy Co., **15** 190
Farley Northwest Industries Inc., I 440–41
Farm Credit Bank of St. Louis, **8** 489
Farm Credit Bank of St. Paul, **8** 489–90
Farm Electric Services Ltd., **6** 586
Farm Power Laboratory, **6** 565
Farmer Jack, **16** 247
Farmers and Mechanics Bank of Georgetown, **13** 439
Farmers and Merchants Bank, **II** 349

Farmers Bank of Delaware, **II** 315–16
Farmers Insurance Group, **23** 286
Farmers National Bank & Trust Co., **9** 474
Farmers Regional Cooperative, **II** 536
Farmers' Loan and Trust Co., **II** 254; **9** 124
Farmland Foods, Inc., IV 474; **7** 17, 7 **174–75**
Farnam Cheshire Lime Co., **III** 763
Farrar, Straus and Giroux Inc., IV 622, 624; **12** 223, 225; **15 158–60**
FASC. *See* First Analysis Securities Corporation.
Fasco Consumer Products, **19** 360
Fasco Industries, **III** 509; **13** 369
Faserwerke Hüls GmbH., **I** 350
Fashion Bug, **8** 97
Fashion Co., **II** 503; **10** 324
Fasquelle, **IV** 618
Fasson. *See* Avery Dennison Corporation.
Fast Fare, **7** 102
Fastenal Company, 14 185–87
Fata European Group, **IV** 187; **19** 348
Fateco Förlag, **14** 556
Fatum, **III** 308
Faugere et Jutheau, **III** 283
Faulkner, Dawkins & Sullivan, **II** 450
Favorite Plastics, **19** 414
Fawcett Books, **13** 429
Fay's Inc., 17 175–77
Fayette Tubular Products, **7** 116–17
Fayva, **13** 359–61
Fazoli's, **13** 321
FB&T Corporation, **14** 154
FBC. *See* First Boston Corp.
FBO. *See* Film Booking Office of America.
FCBC, **IV** 174
FCC. *See* Federal Communications Commission.
FCC National Bank, **II** 286
FCI. *See* Framatome SA.
FDIC. *See* Federal Deposit Insurance Corp.
Fearn International, **II** 525; **13** 293
Feature Enterprises Inc., **19** 452
Fechheimer Bros. Co., **III** 215; **18** 60, 62
Fedders Corp., 18 172–75
Federal Barge Lines, **6** 487
Federal Bearing and Bushing, **I** 158–59
Federal Bicycle Corporation of America, **11** 3
Federal Coca-Cola Bottling Co., **10** 222
Federal Communications Commission, **6** 164–65; **9** 321
Federal Deposit Insurance Corp., **II** 261–62, 285, 337; **12** 30, 79
Federal Electric, **I** 463; **III** 653
Federal Express Corporation, II 620; **V 451–53; 6** 345–46, 385–86, 389; **12** 180, 192; **13** 19; **14** 517; **17** 504–05; **18** 315–17, 368, 370. *See also* FedEx Corporation.
Federal Home Life Insurance Co., **III** 263; **IV** 623
Federal Home Loan Bank, **II** 182
Federal Home Loan Mortgage Corp., **18** 168
Federal Insurance Co., **III** 220–21; **14** 108–109
Federal Lead Co., **IV** 32
Federal Light and Traction Company, **6** 561–62
Federal Mining and Smelting Co., **IV** 32
Federal National Mortgage Association, II 410–11; 18 168

Federal Pacific Electric, II 121; 9 440
Federal Packaging and Partition Co., 8 476
Federal Packaging Corp., 19 78
Federal Paper Board Company, Inc., I
    524; **8 173–75; 15** 229
Federal Paper Mills, IV 248
Federal Power, 18 473
Federal Reserve Bank of New York, 21 68
Federal Savings and Loan Insurance Corp.,
    16 346
Federal Signal Corp., 10 295–97
Federal Steel Co., II 330; IV 572; 7 549
Federal Trade Commission, 6 260; 9 370
Federal Yeast Corp., IV 410
Federal-Mogul Corporation, I 158–60;
    III 596; **10 292–94 (upd.)**
Federale Mynbou, IV 90–93
Federated Department Stores Inc., IV
    703; V 25–28; **9 209–12; 10** 282; **11**
    349; **12** 37, 523; **13** 43, 260; **15** 88; **16**
    61, 206; **17** 560; **18** 523; **22** 406; **23** 60
Federated Development Company, 8 349
Federated Metals Corp., IV 32
Federated Publications, IV 612; 7 191
Federated Timbers, I 422
Federation Nationale d'Achats des Cadres.
    See FNAC.
FedEx Corporation, 18 128, 176–79
    (upd.), 535
Fedmart, V 162
Feed-Rite Controls, Inc., 16 270
Feffer & Simons, 16 46
Feikes & Sohn KG, IV 325
Feinblech-Contiglühe, IV 103
Felco. *See* Farmers Regional Cooperative.
Feldmühle Nobel AG, II 50–51; III
    692–95; IV 142, 325, 337; **21** 330
Felixstowe Ltd., 18 254
Felten & Guilleaume, IV 25
Femsa, 19 473
Femtech, 8 513
Fendel Schiffahrts-Aktiengesellschaft, 6
    426
Fender Musical Instruments Company,
    16 200–02
Fenestra Inc., IV 136
Fenicia Group, 22 320
Fenner & Beane, II 424
Fenwal Laboratories, I 627; 10 141
Fergus Brush Electric Company, 18 402
Ferguson Machine Co., 8 135
Ferguson Radio Corp., I 531–32
Ferienreise GmbH., II 164
Fermentaciones Mexicanas, III 43
Fernando Roqué, 6 404
Ferngas, IV 486
Ferranti Business Communications, 20 75
Ferranti Ltd., II 81; 6 240
Ferrari S.p.A., I 162; **11** 103; **13 218–20**
Ferrier Hodgson, 10 170
Ferro Corporation, III 536; **8 176–79; 9**
    10
Ferro Engineering Co., 17 357
Ferroxcube Corp. of America, 13 397
Ferruzzi Agricola Finanziario, I 369; 7
    81–83
Fesca, III 417–18
Fetzer Vineyards, 10 182
FHP International Corporation, 6
    184–86; 17 166, 168
Fianzas Monterrey, 19 189
Fiat S.p.A., I 154, 157, **161–63,** 459–60,
    466, 479; **II** 280; **III** 206, 543, 591; **IV**
    420; **9** 10; **11 102–04 (upd.),** 139; **13**

17, 27–29, 218–20; **16** 322; **17** 24; **22**
    379–81
Fibamex, 17 106
Fiber Chemical Corporation, 7 308
Fiberglas Canada, III 722
Fibermux, 10 19
Fibic Corp., 18 118
Fibre Containers, IV 249
Fibreboard Corporation, IV 304; **12** 318;
    14 110; **16 203–05**
FibreChem, Inc., 8 347
Fibro Tambor, S.A. de C.V., 8 476
Fichtel & Sachs AG, III 566; 14 328
Fidata Corp., II 317
Fidelco Capital Group, 10 420
Fidelio Software GmbH, 18 335, 337
Fidelity and Casualty Co. of New York,
    III 242
Fidelity and Guaranty Life Insurance Co.,
    III 396–97
Fidelity Federal Savings and Loan, II 420
Fidelity Fire Insurance Co., III 240
Fidelity Insurance of Canada, III 396–97
Fidelity Investments Inc., II 412–13; III
    588; **8** 194; **9** 239; **14 188–90 (upd.);**
    18 552; **19** 113; **21** 147; **22** 52. *See also*
    FMR Corp.
Fidelity Life Association, III 269
Fidelity Mutual Insurance Co., III 231
Fidelity National Life Insurance Co., III
    191
Fidelity National Title, 19 92
Fidelity Oil Group, 7 324
Fidelity Title and Trust Co., II 315
Fidelity Trust Co., II 230
Fidelity Union Life Insurance Co., III 185
Fidelity-Phenix Fire Insurance Co., III
    240–42
Fides Holding, 21 146
Field Corporation, 18 355
Field Enterprises Educational Corporation,
    16 252
Field Enterprises, Inc., IV 672; 12 554; 19
    404
Field Limited Partnership, 22 441
Field Oy, 10 113
Fieldale Farms Corporation, 23 191–93
Fieldcrest Cannon, Inc., 8 32–33; 9
    213–17; 16 535; **19** 276, 305
Fieldstone Cabinetry, III 571; 20 362
Fifteen Oil, I 526
Fifth Generation Systems Inc., 10 509
Fifth Third Bancorp, II 291; **9** 475; **11**
    466; **13 221–23**
50-Off Stores, 23 177
Figgie International Inc., 7 176–78
Figi's Inc., 9 218, 220
Fila Holding S.p.A., 20 216–18
Filene's, V 132, 134
Filergie S.A., 15 355
Filipacchi Medias S.A. *See* Hachette
    Filipacchi Medias S.A.
Filiz Lastex, S.A., 15 386
Filles S.A. de C.V., 7 115
Film Booking Office of America, II 88
Films for the Humanities, Inc., 22 441
Filter Queen-Canada, 17 234
Filtrol Corp., IV 123
Filtros Baldwin de Mexico, 17 106
Filtros Continental, 17 106
Fimaser, 21 101
Fimestic, 21 101
Fin. Comit SpA, II 192
FINA, Inc., 7 179–81

Financial Computer Services, Inc., 11 111
Financial Corp. of Indonesia, II 257
Financial Data Services, Inc., 11 111
Financial Investment Corp. of Asia, III
    197
Financial Network Marketing Company, 11
    482
Financial News Ltd., IV 658
Financial Security Assurance, III 765
Financial Services Corp., III 306–07
Financial Services Corporation of
    Michigan, 11 163
Financial Systems, Inc., 11 111
Financial Technologies International, 17
    497
Financiera Aceptaciones, 19 189
Financière Crédit Suisse-First Boston, II
    268, 402–04
Financiere de Suez, II 295
Financière Saint Dominique, 9 151–52
FinansSkandic A.B., II 352–53
Finast. *See* First National Supermarkets,
    Inc.
Fincantieri, I 466–67
Find-A-Home Service, Inc., 21 96
Findomestic, 21 101
Findus, II 547
Fine Art Developments Ltd., 15 340
Fine Fare, II 465, 609, 628–29
Fine Fragrances, 22 213
Finelettrica, I 465–66
Finevest Services Inc., 15 526
Fingerhut Companies, Inc., I 613; **V** 148;
    9 218–20; 15 401; **18** 133
Fininvest Group, IV 587–88
FinishMaster, 17 310–11
Finland Wood Co., IV 275
Finlay Enterprises, Inc., 16 206–08
Finlay Forest Industries, IV 297
Finmare, I 465, 467
Finmeccanica S.p.A., II 86; **13** 28; **23** 83
Finnair Oy, I 120; **6 87–89**
Finnforest Oy, IV 316
Finnigan Corporation, 11 513
Finnish Cable Works, II 69; 17 352
Finnish Fiberboard Ltd., IV 302
Oy Finnish Peroxides Ab, IV 300
Finnish Rubber Works, II 69; 17 352
Oy Finnlines Ltd., IV 276
Finsa, II 196
FinSer Capital Corporation, 17 262
Finservizi SpA, II 192
Finsider, I 465–66; IV 125
Firan Motor Coach, Inc., 17 83
Fire Association of Philadelphia, III
    342–43
Fireman's Fund Insurance Company, I
    418; **II** 398, 457; **III** 214, **250–52,** 263;
    10 62
Firemen's Insurance Co. of Newark, III
    241–42
Firestone Tire and Rubber Co., III 440,
    697; V 234–35; **8** 80; **9** 247; **15** 355; **17**
    182; **18** 320; **20** 259–62; **21** 73–74
The First, 10 340
First Acadiana National Bank, 11 107
First American Bank Corporation, 8 188
First American National Bank, 19 378
First American National Bank-Eastern, 11
    111
First Analysis Securities Corporation, 22 5
First and Merchants, 10 426
First Atlanta Corporation, 16 523
First Bancard, Inc., 11 106

First BanCorporation, **13** 467
First Bank and Trust of Mechanicsburg, **II** 342
First Bank of Savannah, **16** 522
First Bank of the United States, **II** 213, 253
First Bank System Inc., 11 130; **12 164–66**; **13** 347–48
First Boston Corp., **II** 208, 257, 267–69, 402–04, 406–07, 426, 434, 441; **9** 378, 386; **12** 439; **13** 152, 342; **21** 145–46. *See also* CSFB.
First Brands Corporation, 8 180–82; **16** 44
First Capital Financial, **8** 229
First Carolina Investors Inc., **17** 357
First Chicago Corporation, II 284–87
First City Bank of Rosemead, **II** 348
First Colony Farms, **II** 584
First Colony Life Insurance, **I** 334–35; **10** 290
First Commerce Bancshares, Inc., 15 161–63
First Commerce Corporation, 11 105–07
First Commercial Savings and Loan, **10** 340
First Consumers National Bank, **10** 491
First Dallas, Ltd., **II** 415
First Data Corp., **10** 63; **18** 516–18, 537
First Data Management Company of Oklahoma City, **11** 112
First Delaware Life Insurance Co., **III** 254
First Deposit Corp., **III** 218–19
First Empire State Corporation, 11 108–10
First Engine and Boiler Insurance Co. Ltd., **III** 406
First Executive Corporation, III 253–55
First Federal Savings & Loan Assoc., **IV** 343; **9** 173
First Federal Savings and Loan Association of Crisp County, **10** 92
First Federal Savings and Loan Association of Hamburg, **10** 91
First Federal Savings and Loan Association of Fort Myers, **9** 476
First Federal Savings and Loan Association of Kalamazoo, **9** 482
First Federal Savings Bank of Brunswick, **10** 92
First Fidelity Bank, N.A., New Jersey, 9 221–23
First Fidelity Bank of Rockville, **13** 440
First Financial Management Corporation, 11 111–13; **18** 542
First Florida Banks, **9** 59
First Hawaiian, Inc., 11 114–16
First Health, **III** 373
FIRST HEALTH Strategies, **11** 113
First Healthcare, **14** 242
First Heights, fsa, **8** 437
First Hospital Corp., **15** 122
First Industrial Corp., **II** 41
First Insurance Agency, Inc., **17** 527
First Insurance Co. of Hawaii, **III** 191, 242
First International Trust, **IV** 91
First Interstate Bancorp, II 228, **288–90**; **8** 295; **9** 334; **17** 546
First Investment Advisors, **11** 106
First Investors Management Corp., **11** 106
First Jersey National Bank, **II** 334
First Liberty Financial Corporation, **11** 457
First Line Insurance Services, Inc., **8** 436
First Madison Bank, **14** 192

First Maryland Bancorp, **16** 14
First Mid America, **II** 445; **22** 406
First Mississippi Corporation, 8 183–86
First Mississippi National, **14** 41
First National Bank, **10** 298; **13** 467
First National Bank (Revere), **II** 208
First National Bank and Trust Company, **22** 4
First National Bank and Trust Company of Kalamazoo, **8** 187–88
First National Bank and Trust of Oklahoma City, **II** 289
First National Bank in Albuquerque, **11** 119
First National Bank of Akron, **9** 475
First National Bank of Allentown, **11** 296
First National Bank of Atlanta, **16** 522
First National Bank of Azusa, **II** 382
First National Bank of Boston, **II** 207–08, 402; **12** 310; **13** 446
First National Bank of Carrollton, **9** 475
First National Bank of Chicago, **II** 242, 257, 284–87; **III** 96–97; **IV** 135–36
First National Bank of Commerce, **11** 106
First National Bank of Harrington, Delaware. *See* J.C. Penny National Bank.
First National Bank of Hartford, **13** 466
First National Bank of Hawaii, **11** 114
First National Bank of Highland, **11** 109
First National Bank of Houma, **21** 522
The First National Bank of Lafayette, **11** 107
The First National Bank of Lake Charles, **11** 107
First National Bank of Lake City, **II** 336; **10** 425
First National Bank of Mexico, New York, **II** 231
First National Bank of Minneapolis, **22** 426–27
First National Bank of New York, **II** 254, 330
First National Bank of Raleigh, **II** 336
First National Bank of Salt Lake, **11** 118
First National Bank of Seattle, **8** 469–70
First National Bank of York, **II** 317
First National Bankshares, Inc., **21** 524
First National Boston Corp., **II** 208
First National Casualty Co., **III** 203
First National City Bank, **9** 124; **16** 13
First National City Bank of New York, **II** 254; **9** 124
First National City Corp., **III** 220–21
First National Holding Corporation, **16** 522
First National Insurance Co., **III** 352
First National Life Insurance Co., **III** 218
First National Supermarkets, Inc., **II** 641–42; **9** 452
First Nationwide Bank, 8 30; **14 191–93**
First Nationwide Financial Corp., **I** 167; **11** 139
First New England Bankshares Corp., **13** 467
First Nitrogen, Inc., **8** 184
First of America Bank Corporation, 8 187–89
First of America Bank-Monroe, **9** 476
First of Boston, **II** 402–03
First Omni Bank NA, **16** 14; **18** 518
First Pacific Company Limited, 18 180–82
First Penn-Pacific Life Insurance Co., **III** 276

First Pick Stores, **12** 458
First Railroad and Banking Company, **11** 111
First Republic Bank of Texas, **II** 336
First Republic Corp., **III** 383; **14** 483
First RepublicBank Corporation, **II** 337; **10** 425–26
First Savings and Loan, **10** 339
First Seattle Dexter Horton National Bank, **8** 470
First Security Corporation, 11 117–19
First Signature Bank and Trust Co., **III** 268
1st State Bank & Trust, **9** 474
First SunAmerican Life Insurance Company, **11** 482
First Team Sports, Inc., 15 396–97; **22 202–04**
First Tennessee National Corporation, 11 120–21
First Texas Pharmaceuticals, **I** 678
First Trust and Savings Bank, **II** 284
First Trust Bank, **16** 14
First Union Corporation, 10 298–300
First Union Trust and Savings Bank, **II** 284–85; **11** 126; **22** 52
First United Financial Services Inc., **II** 286
First USA, Inc., 11 122–24
First Virginia Banks, Inc., 11 125–26
First Westchester National Bank of New Rochelle, **II** 236
First Western Bank and Trust Co., **II** 289
First Women's Bank of New York, **23** 3
First Worth Corporation, **19** 232
Firstamerica Bancorporation, **II** 288–89
Firstar Corporation, 11 127–29
FirstBancorp., **13** 467
FirstMiss, Inc., **8** 183
Firth Carpet, **19** 275
Fischbach & Moore, **III** 535
Fischbach Corp., **III** 198; **8** 536–37
FISCOT, **10** 337
Fiserv Inc., 11 130–32
Fisher & Company, **9** 16
Fisher Body Company, **I** 171; **10** 325
Fisher Broadcasting Co., **15** 164
Fisher Companies, Inc., 15 164–66
Fisher Controls International, Inc., 13 224–26; **15** 405, 407
Fisher Corp., **II** 92
Fisher Foods, Inc., **II** 602; **9** 451, 452; **13** 237
Fisher Marine, **III** 444; **22** 116
Fisher Nut, **14** 275
Fisher Scientific Group, **III** 511–12
Fisher-Camuto Corp., **14** 441
Fisher-Price Inc., II 559–60; **12 167–69**, 410–11; **13** 317
Fishers Agricultural Holdings, **II** 466
Fishers Nutrition, **II** 466
Fishers Seed and Grain, **II** 466
Fishery Department of Tamura Kisen Co., **II** 552
Fisk Telephone Systems, **6** 313
Fisons plc, 9 224–27; **23 194–97 (upd.)**
Fitch Lovell PLC, **13** 103
Fitchburg Daily News Co., **IV** 581
Fitchell and Sachs, **III** 495
Fitel, **III** 491
Fitzsimmons Stores Inc., **16** 452
Fitzwilton Public Limited Company, **12** 529
Five Bros. Inc., **19** 456
FL Industries Holdings, Inc., **11** 516

Flachglass A.G., **II** 474
Flagship Resources, **22** 495
Flagstar Companies, Inc., 10 301–03
Flair Corporation, **18** 467
Flanagan McAdam Resources Inc., **IV** 76
Flapdoodles, **15** 291
Flatbush Gas Co., **6** 455–56
Flatiron Mandolin Company, **16** 239
Flatow, Moore, Bryan, and Fairburn, **21** 33
Fleer Corporation, 10 402; **13** 519; **15**
   167–69; **19** 386
Fleet Call, Inc., **10** 431–32
Fleet Financial Group, Inc., IV 687; **9**
   228–30; **12** 31; **13** 468; **18** 535
Fleetway, **7** 244
Fleetwood Enterprises, Inc., III 484–85;
   13 155; **17** 83; **21** 153; **22 205–08**
   (upd.)
Fleischmann Co., **II** 544; **7** 367
Fleischmann Malting Co., **I** 420–21; **11** 22
Fleming Companies, Inc., II 624–25,
   671; **7** 450; **12** 107, 125; **13** 335–37; **17**
   178–81 (upd.); **18** 506–07; **23** 407
Fleming Machine Co., **III** 435
Fleming-Wilson Co., **II** 624
Fletcher Challenge Ltd., III 687; **IV** 250,
   278–80; **19 153–57 (upd.)**
Fleuve Noir, **IV** 614
Flex Interim, **16** 421
Flex-O-Lite, **14** 325
Flexi-Van Corporations, **II** 492; **20** 118
Flexible Packaging, **I** 605
Flexsteel Industries Inc., 15 170–72
Flextronics Inc., **12** 451
Flexys, **16** 462
FLGI Holding Company, **10** 321
Flick Industrial Group, **II** 280, 283; **III**
   692–95
Flight One Logistics, Inc., **22** 311
Flight Transportation Co., **II** 408
FlightSafety International, Inc., 9
   231–33. *See also* FSI International, Inc.
Flint and Walling Water Systems, **III** 570;
   20 362
Flint Eaton & Co., **I** 627
Flint Ink Corporation, 13 227–29
Floral City Furniture Company, **14** 302–03
Flori Roberts, Inc., **11** 208
Florida Cypress Gardens, Inc., **IV** 623
Florida East Coast Railway Company, **8**
   486–87; **12** 278
Florida Frozen Foods, **13** 244
Florida Gas Co., **15** 129
Florida Gas Transmission Company, **6** 578
Florida National Banks of Florida, Inc., **II**
   252
Florida Presbyterian College, **9** 187
Florida Progress Corp., V 621–22; **23**
   198–200 (upd.)
Florida Rock Industries Inc., **23** 326
Florida Steel Corp., **14** 156
Florida Telephone Company, **6** 323
FloridaGulf Airlines, **11** 300
Florimex Verwaltungsgesellschaft mbH, **12**
   109
Florsheim Shoe Company, III 528–29; **9**
   135, **234–36**; **12** 308; **16** 546
Flow Laboratories, **14** 98
Flower Gate Inc., **I** 266; **21** 320
Flower Time, Inc., **12** 179, 200
Flowers Industries, Inc., 12 170–71
Floyd West & Co., **6** 290
Fluf N'Stuf, Inc., **12** 425
Fluke Corporation, 15 173–75

Fluor Corporation, I 569–71, 586; **III**
   248; **IV** 171, 533, 535, 576; **6** 148–49;
   8 190–93 (upd.); **12** 244
Flushing Federal Savings & Loan
   Association, **16** 346
Flushing National Bank, **II** 230
Flying J Inc., 19 158–60
Flying Tiger Line, **V** 452; **6** 388
Flymo, **III** 478, 480; **22** 26
FMC Corp., I 442–44, 679; **II** 513; **11**
   133–35 (upd.); **14** 457; **22** 415
FMR Corp., II 412; **8 194–96**; **14** 188; **22**
   413
FMXI, Inc. *See* Foamex International Inc.
FN Life Insurance Co., **III** 192
FN Manufacturing Co., **12** 71
FNAC, 21 224–26
FNC Comercio, **III** 221
FNCB. *See* First National City Bank of
   New York.
FNMA. *See* Federal National Mortgage
   Association.
Foamex International Inc., 17 182–85
Focke-Wulf, **III** 641; **16** 7
Fodens Ltd., **I** 186
Fodor's Travel Guides, **13** 429
Fokker. *See* Koninklijke Nederlandse
   Vliegtuigenfabriek Fokker.
Fokker Aircraft Corporation of America, **9**
   16
Fokker-VFW, **I** 41–42; **12** 191
Folgers, **III** 52
Folland Aircraft, **I** 50; **III** 508
Follett Corporation, 12 172–74; **16** 47
Fomento de Valores, S.A. de C.V., **23** 170
Fomento Economico Mexicano, S.A. de
   C.V. *See* Femsa.
Fondiaria Group, **III** 351
Fonditalia Management, **III** 347
Font & Vaamonde, **6** 27
Font Vella, **II** 474
FONTAC, **II** 73
Fontana Asphalt, **III** 674
Food City, **II** 649–50
Food Fair, **19** 480
Food 4 Less Supermarkets, Inc., **II** 624; **17**
   558–61
Food Giant, **II** 670
Food Investments Ltd., **II** 465
Food King, **20** 306
Food Lion, Inc., II 626–27; **7** 450; **15**
   176–78 (upd.), 270; **18** 8; **21** 508
Food Machinery Corp. *See* FMC Corp.
Food Marketing Corp., **II** 668; **18** 504
Food Town Inc., **II** 626–27
FoodBrands America, Inc., 21 290; **22**
   510; **23 201–04**. *See also* Doskocil
   Companies, Inc.
FoodLand Distributors, **II** 625, 645, 682
Foodmaker, Inc., II 562; **13** 152, 426; **14**
   194–96
Foodstuffs, **9** 144
Foodtown, **II** 626; **V** 35; **15** 177
Foodways National, Inc., **12** 531; **13** 383
Foot Locker, **V** 226; **14** 293–95
Foote Cone & Belding Communications
   Inc., I 12–15, 28, 34; **11** 51; **13** 517; **22**
   395. *See also* True North
   Communications Inc.
Foote Mineral Company, **7** 386–87
Footquarters, **14** 293, 295
Forages et Exploitations Pétrolières. *See*
   Forex.

Ford Motor Company, I 10, 14, 20–21,
   136, 142, 145, 152, 154–55, 162–63,
   164–68, 172, 183, 186, 201, 203–04,
   280, 297, 337, 354, 423, 478, 484, 540,
   693; **II** 7–8, 33, 60, 86, 143, 415; **III**
   58, 259, 283, 439, 452, 495, 515, 555,
   568, 591, 603, 637–38, 651, 725; **IV** 22,
   187, 597, 722; **6** 27, 51; **7** 377, 461,
   520–21; **8** 70, 74–75, 117, 372–73, 375,
   505–06; **9** 94, 118, 126, 190, 283–84,
   325, 341–43; **10** 32, 241, 260, 264–65,
   279–80, 290, 353, 407, 430, 460, 465;
   11 53–54, 103–04, **136–40 (upd.)**, 263,
   326, 339, 350, 528–29; **12** 68, 91, 294,
   311; **13** 28, 219, 285, 287, 345, 555; **14**
   191–92; **15** 91, 171, 513, 515; **16**
   321–22; **17** 183, 303–04; **18** 112, 308,
   319; **19** 11, 125, 221, 223, 482, 484; **20**
   359; **21** 153, 200, 503; **22** 175, 380–81;
   23 143, 339–41, 434
Ford Motor Company, S.A. de C.V., 20
   219–21
Ford New Holland, Inc. *See* New Holland
   N.V.
Ford Transport Co., **I** 112; **6** 103
Fordyce Lumber Co., **IV** 281; **9** 259
Forefront Communications, **22** 194
Foreman State Banks, **II** 285
Foremost Dairy of California, **I** 496–97
Foremost Warehouse Corp., **14** 372
Foremost-McKesson Inc., **I** 496–97, **III**
   10; **11** 211; **12** 332
Forenza, **V** 116
Forest City Auto Parts, **23** 491
Forest City Enterprises, Inc., 16 209–11
Forest City Ratner Companies, **17** 318
Forest E. Olson, Inc., **21** 96
Forest Laboratories, Inc., 11 141–43
Forest Oil Corporation, 19 161–63
Forest Products, **III** 645
Forestry Corporation of New Zealand, **19**
   156
Forethought Group, Inc., **10** 350
Forever Living Products International
   Inc., 17 186–88
Forex Chemical Corp., **I** 341; **14** 216; **17**
   418
Forex-Neptune, **III** 617
Forges d'Eich–Le Gallais, Metz et Cie, **IV**
   24; **22** 42
Forges de la Providence, **IV** 52
Formica Corporation, 10 269; **13 230–32**
Forming Technology Co., **III** 569; **20** 361
Formonix, **20** 101
Formosa Plastics Corporation, 11 159;
   14 197–99; **16** 194, 196
Formosa Springs, **I** 269; **12** 337
Formularios y Procedimientos Moore, **IV**
   645
Formule 1, **13** 364
Forney Fiber Company, **8** 475
Forsakrings A.B. Volvia, **I** 20
Forstmann Little & Co., **I** 446, 483; **II**
   478, 544; **III** 56; **7** 206; **10** 321; **12** 344,
   562; **14** 166; **16** 322; **19** 372–73, 432;
   22 32, 60
Fort Associates, **I** 418
Fort Bend Utilities Company, **12** 269
Fort Dummer Mills, **III** 213
Fort Howard Corporation, 8 197–99; **15**
   305; **22** 209. *See also* Fort James
   Corporation.
Fort James Corporation, 22 209–12
   (upd.)

Fort Mill Manufacturing Co., **V** 378
Fort William Power Co., **IV** 246
Forte Plc, **15** 46; **16** 446
Forte's Holdings Ltd., **III** 104–05
Fortis, Inc., 15 179–82
Fortuna Coffee Co., **I** 451
Fortune Brands, Inc., **19** 168
Fortune Enterprises, **12** 60
Forum Cafeterias, **19** 299–300
Forum Hotels, **I** 248
Foseco plc, **IV** 383
Foss Maritime Co., **9** 509, 511
Fossil, Inc., 17 189–91
Foster & Kleiser, **7** 335; **14** 331
Foster & Marshall, **II** 398; **10** 62
Foster and Braithwaite, **III** 697
Foster Forbes, **16** 123
Foster Grant, **I** 670; **II** 595–96; **12** 214
Foster Management Co., **11** 366–67
Foster Medical Corp., **III** 16; **11** 282
Foster Sand & Gravel, **14** 112
Foster Wheeler Corporation, I 82; **6**
  145–47; **23 205–08 (upd.)**
Foster's Brewing Group Ltd., 7 182–84;
  21 227–30 (upd.)
Fotomat Corp., **III** 549
Foundation Computer Systems, Inc., **13**
  201
Foundation Fieldbus, **22** 373
Foundation Health Corporation, 11 174;
  12 175–77
Founders Equity Inc., **14** 235
Founders of American Investment Corp.,
  15 247
Four Seasons Hotels Inc., II 531; **9**
  237–38
Four Seasons Nursing Centers, Inc., **6** 188
Four Winds, **21** 153
Four Winns, **III** 600
Four-Phase Systems, Inc., **II** 61; **11** 327
Fournier Furniture, Inc., **12** 301
Fourth Financial Corporation, 11
  144–46; 15 60
Foussard Associates, **I** 333
Fowler Road Construction Proprietary, **III**
  672
Fowler-Waring Cables Co., **III** 162
Fox, **21** 25, 360
Fox & Jacobs, **8** 87
Fox Broadcasting Co., **II** 156; **IV** 608,
  652; **7** 391–92; **9** 428
Fox Children's Network, **21** 26
Fox Film Corp., **II** 146–47, 154–55, 169
Fox, Fowler & Co., **II** 307
Fox Glacier Mints Ltd., **II** 569
Fox Grocery Co., **II** 682
Fox, Inc., **12** 359
Fox Paper Company, **8** 102
Fox Photo, **III** 475; **7** 161
Fox-Vliet Drug Company, **16** 212
Foxboro Company, 13 233–35
FoxMeyer Health Corporation, V
  152–53; **8** 55; **16 212–14**
FP&L. *See* Florida Power & Light Co.
FPL Group, Inc., V 623–25
FR Corp., **18** 340
Fram Corp., **I** 142, 567
Framatome SA, 9 10; **19 164–67**
Framingham Electric Company, **12** 45
France Cables et Radio, **6** 303
France 5, **6** 374; **21** 105
France Quick, **12** 152
France Telecom Group, V 291–93, 471;
  9 32; **14** 489; **18** 33; **21 231–34 (upd.)**

France-Loisirs, **IV** 615–16, 619
Franchise Associates, Inc., **17** 238
Franchise Business Systems, Inc., **18** 207
Franchise Finance Corp. of America, **19**
  159
Franco-Américaine de Constructions
  Atomiques, **19** 165
Franco-American Food Co., **I** 428; **II** 479
Frank & Hirsch, **III** 608
Frank & Schulte GmbH, **8** 496
Frank Dry Goods Company, **9** 121
Frank H. Nott Inc., **14** 156
Frank J. Rooney, Inc., **8** 87
Frank Schaffer Publications, **19** 405
Frank's Nursery & Crafts, Inc., 12
  178–79, 198–200
Fränkel & Selz, **II** 239
Frankenberry, Laughlin & Constable, **9** 393
Frankford-Quaker Grocery Co., **II** 625
Frankfort Oil Co., **I** 285
Frankfurter Allgemeine Versicherungs-AG,
  III 184
Franklin Assurances, **III** 211
Franklin Baker's Coconut, **II** 531
Franklin Brass Manufacturing Company,
  20 363
Franklin Container Corp., **IV** 312; **19** 267
Franklin Corp., **14** 130
Franklin Electronic Publishers, Inc., 23
  209–13
Franklin Life Insurance Co., **III** 242–43; **V**
  397
Franklin Mint, **IV** 676; **9** 428
Franklin National Bank, **9** 536
Franklin Plastics, **19** 414
Franklin Quest Co., 11 147–49
Franklin Rayon Yarn Dyeing Corp., **I** 529
Franklin Research & Development, **11** 41
Franklin Resources, Inc., 9 239–40
Franklin Sports, Inc., **17** 243
Franklin Steamship Corp., **8** 346
Franks Chemical Products Inc., **I** 405
Frans Maas Beheer BV, **14** 568
Franz and Frieder Burda, **IV** 661
Franz Foods, Inc., **II** 584
Franz Ströher AG, **III** 68–69
Fraser & Chalmers, **13** 16
Fraser Cos. Ltd., **IV** 165
Fratelli Manzoli, **IV** 585
Fratelli Treves, **IV** 585
Fraternal Assurance Society of America,
  III 274
Fray Data International, **14** 319
Fre Kote Inc., **I** 321
Frears, **II** 543
Fred Harvey Hotels, **I** 417
Fred Meyer, Inc., II 669; **V 54–56; 18**
  505; **20 222–25 (upd.)**
Fred S. James and Co., **III** 280; **I** 537; **22**
  318
Fred Sammons Co., **9** 72
Fred Sands Realtors, **IV** 727
Fred Schmid Appliance & T.V. Co., Inc.,
  10 305; **18** 532
The Fred W. Albrecht Grocery Co., 13
  236–38
Fred's, Inc., 23 214–16
Fredelle, **14** 295
Frederick & Nelson, **17** 462
Frederick Atkins Inc., 16 215–17
Frederick Bayer & Company, **22** 225
Frederick Gas Company, **19** 487
Frederick Miller Brewing Co., **I** 269

Frederick's of Hollywood Inc., 16
  218–20
Freeborn Farms, **13** 244
Freedom Technology, **11** 486
Freedom-Valvoline Oil Co., **IV** 373; **19** 23
Freeman, Spogli & Co., **17** 366; **18** 90
Freemans, **V** 177
Freeport-McMoran Inc., IV 81–84; **7**
  185–89 (upd.); 16 29; **23** 40
Freezer House, **II** 398; **10** 62
Freezer Queen Foods, Inc., **21** 509
Freezer Shirt Corporation, **8** 406
Freiberger Papierfabrik, **IV** 323
Freight Car Services, Inc., **23** 306
Freight Outlet, **17** 297
Freightliner, **I** 150; **6** 413
FreightMaster, **III** 498
Frejlack Ice Cream Co., **II** 646; **7** 317
Fremlin Breweries, **I** 294
Fremont Butter and Egg Co., **II** 467
Fremont Canning Company, **7** 196
Fremont Group, **21** 97
Fremont Savings Bank, **9** 474–75
French and Richards & Co., **I** 692
French Bank of California, **II** 233
French Fragrances, Inc., 22 213–15
French Kier, **I** 568
French Petrofina, **IV** 497
Frequency Sources Inc., **9** 324
Fresenius Ag, **22** 360
Fresh America Corporation, 20 226–28
Fresh Choice, Inc., 20 229–32
Fresh Fields, **19** 501
Freshbake Foods Group PLC, **II** 481; **7** 68
Fretter, Inc., 9 65; **10** 9–10, **304–06**, 502;
  19 124; **23** 52
Frialco, **IV** 165
Friactontech Inc., **11** 84
Friday's Front Row Sports Grill, **22** 128
Friden, Inc., **II** 10
Fridy-Gauker & Fridy, **I** 313; **10** 154
Fried. Krupp GmbH, II 257; **IV** 60,
  85–89, 104, 128, 203, 206, 222, 234
Friedrich Flick Industrial Corp., **I** 548; **III**
  692
Friedrich Roessler Söhne, **IV** 69
Friedrichshütte, **III** 694
Friendly Hotels PLC, **14** 107
Friendly Ice Cream Corp., **II** 511–12; **15**
  221
Friesch-Groningsche Hypotheekbank, **III**
  179
Frigidaire Home Products, III 572; **13**
  564; **19** 361; **22** 28, **216–18**, 349
Frigo, **II** 587
Friguia, **IV** 165
Frisby P.M.C. Incorporated, **16** 475
Frisdranken Industries Winters B.V., **22**
  515
Frisia Group, **IV** 197–98
Frito-Lay Company, **I** 219, 278–79; **III**
  136; **22** 95
Fritz Companies, Inc., 12 180–82
Fritz Thyssen Stiftung, **IV** 222
Fritz W. Glitsch and Sons, Inc. *See* Glitsch
  International, Inc.
Fritzsche Dodge and Ollcott, **I** 307
Froebel-Kan, **IV** 679
Frolic, **16** 545
Fromageries Bel, II 518; **6** 47; **19** 51; **23**
  217–19
Frome Broken Hill Co., **IV** 59
Fromm & Sichel, **I** 285
Frontec, **13** 132

Frontier Airlines, Inc., I 97–98, 103, 124, 129–30; **6** 129; **11** 298; **21** 141–42; **22 219–21**
Frontier Corp., 16 221–23; 18 164
Frontier Electronics, **19** 311
Frontier Expeditors, Inc., **12** 363
Frontier Oil Co., **IV** 373
Frontier Pacific Insurance Company, **21** 263
Frozen Food Express Industries, Inc., 20 233–35
Fru-Con Corp., **I** 561
Fruehauf Corp., I 169–70, 480; **II** 425; **III** 652; **7** 259–60, 513–14; **13** 341
Fruit of the Loom, Inc., 8 200–02; 16 535
Fry's Diecastings, **III** 681
Fry's Food Stores, **12** 112
Fry's Metal Foundries, **III** 681
Frye Copy Systems, **6** 599
FSI International, Inc., 17 192–94. *See also* FlightSafety International, Inc.
F3 Software Corp., **15** 474
FTP Software, Inc., 20 236–38
Fuel Pipeline Transportation Ltd., **6** 123–24
Fuel Resources Development Co., **6** 558–59
Fuel Resources Inc., **6** 457
FuelMaker Corporation, **6** 569
Fuji, **18** 94, 342, 511
Fuji Bank, Ltd., I 494; **II 291–93**, 360–61, 391, 422, 459, 554; **III** 405, 408–09; **17** 556–57
Fuji Electric Co., Ltd., II 22–23, 98, 103; **III** 139; **13** 356; **18** 511; **22** 373
Fuji Gen-Gakki, **16** 202
Fuji Heavy Industries, **I** 207; **III** 581; **9** 294; **12** 400; **13** 499–501; **23** 290
Fuji Iron & Steel Co., Ltd., **I** 493; **II** 300; **IV** 130, 157, 212; **17** 349–50
Fuji Kaolin Co., **III** 691
Fuji Paper, **IV** 320
Fuji Photo Film Co., Ltd., III 172, 476, **486–89**, 549–50; **6** 289; **7** 162; **18** 94, **183–87 (upd.)**, 341–42
Fuji Seito, **I** 511
Fuji Television, **7** 249; **9** 29
Fuji Xerox. *See* Xerox Corporation.
Fuji Yoshiten Co., **IV** 292
Fujian Hualong Carburetor, **13** 555
Fujikoshi Kozai, **III** 595
Fujimoto Bill Broker & Securities Co., **II** 405
Fujisawa Pharmaceutical Co., I 635–36; III 47; **8** 343
Fujita Airways, **6** 70
Fujitsu Limited, I 455, 541; **II** 22–23, 56, 68, 73, 274; **III** 109–11, 130, **139–41**, 164, 482; **V** 339; **6** 217, 240–42; **10** 238; **11** 308, 542; **13** 482; **14** 13–15, 512; **16** 139, **224–27 (upd.)**; **17** 172; **21** 390
Fujitsu-ICL Systems Inc., 11 150–51
Fujiyi Confectionery Co., **II** 569
Fukuin Electric Works, Ltd., **III** 604
Fukuin Shokai Denki Seisakusho, **III** 604
Fukuju Fire, **III** 384
Fukuoka Paper Co., Ltd., **IV** 285
Fukutake Publishing Co., Ltd., **13** 91, 93
Ful-O-Pep, **10** 250
Fulbright Jaworski & Reavis McGrath, **22** 4
Fulcrum Communications, **10** 19

The Fulfillment Corporation of America, **21** 37
Fulham Brothers, **13** 244
Fuller Brush Co., **II** 572; **15** 475–76, 78
Fuller Co., **6** 395–96
Fuller Manufacturing Company **I** 154. *See also* H.B. Fuller Company.
Fulton Bank, **14** 40
Fulton Co., **III** 569; **20** 361
Fulton Insurance Co., **III** 463; **21** 173
Fulton Manufacturing Co., **11** 535
Fulton Municipal Gas Company, **6** 455
Fulton Performance Products, Inc., **11** 535
Funai-Amstrad, **III** 113
Funco, Inc., 20 239–41
Fund American Cos., **III** 251–52
Fundimensions, **16** 337
Funk & Wagnalls, **IV** 605; **22** 441
Funk Software Inc., **6** 255
Fuqua Enterprises, Inc., 17 195–98
Fuqua Industries Inc., I 445–47, 452; **8** 545; **12** 251; **14** 86
Furalco, **IV** 15
Furnishings International Inc., **20** 359, 363
The Furniture Center, Inc., **14** 236
Furr's Inc., **II** 601
Furst Group, **17** 106
Furukawa Electric Co., Ltd., II 22; **III** 139, **490–92; IV** 15, 26, 153; **15** 514; **22** 44
Fusi Denki, **II** 98
Fuso Marine Insurance Co., **III** 367
Fuso Metal Industries, **IV** 212
Futagi Co., Ltd., **V** 96
Futronix Corporation, **17** 276
Future Graphics, **18** 387
Future Now, Inc., 6 245; **12 183–85**
Fuyo Group, **II** 274, 291–93, 391–92, 554
FWD Corporation, **7** 513

G & H Products, **III** 419
G.A. Serlachius Oy, **IV** 314–15
G&G Shops, Inc., **8** 425–26
G&K Services, Inc., 16 228–30; 21 115
G&L Albu, **IV** 90
G&L Inc., **16** 202
G. and T. Earle, **III** 669, 670
G&R Pasta Co., Inc., **II** 512
G.B. Lewis Company, **8** 359
G.C.E. International Inc., **III** 96–97
G.C. Murphy Company, **9** 21
G.C. Smith, **I** 423
G.D. Searle & Company, I 365–66, **686–89; III** 47, 53; **8** 343, 398, 434; **9** 356–57; **10** 54; **12 186–89 (upd.); 16** 527
G. Felsenthal & Sons, **17** 106
G.H. Bass & Co., **15** 406
G.H. Rinck NV, **V** 49; **19** 122–23
G.H. Wetterau & Sons Grocery Co., **II** 681
G. Heileman Brewing Co., I 253–55, 270; **10** 169–70; **12** 338; **18** 501; **23** 403, 405
G.I.E. Airbus Industrie, I 41–43, 49–52, 55–56, 70, 72, 74–76, 107, 111, 116, 121; **9** 458, 460; **11** 279, 363; **12 190–92 (upd.)**
G-III Apparel Group, Ltd., 22 222–24
G.J. Coles & Coy. Ltd., **20** 155
G.L. Kelty & Co., **13** 168
G.L. Rexroth GmbH, **III** 566
G.P. Group, **12** 358
G.P. Putnam's Sons, **II** 144
G.R. Foods, Inc. *See* Ground Round, Inc.

G.R. Herberger's, **19** 324–25
G.R. Kinney Corporation, **V** 226, 352; **14** 293; **20** 88
G. Riedel Kälte- und Klimatechnik, **III** 420
G.S. Blodgett Corporation, 15 183–85; 22 350
G.S. Capital Partners II L.P. *See* Goldman, Sachs & Company.
G. Washington Coffee Refining Co., **I** 622
Gabelli Group, **13** 561
Gable House Properties, **II** 141
Gabriel Industries, **II** 532
GAC. *See* The Goodyear Tire & Rubber Company.
GAC Corp., **II** 182; **III** 592
GAC Holdings L.P., **7** 204
Gadzooks, Inc., 18 188–90
GAF, I 337–40, 524–25, 549; **II** 378; **III** 440; **8** 180; **9** 518; **18** 215; **22** 14, **225–29 (upd.)**
Gagliardi Brothers, **13** 383
Gail Borden, Jr., and Company. *See* Borden, Inc.
Gain Technology, Inc., **10** 505
Gaines Dog Food Co., **II** 531
Gainsborough Craftsmen Ltd., **II** 569
Gainsco, Inc., 22 230–32
Gair Paper Co., **I** 599
Galas Harland, S.A., **17** 266, 268
Galaxy Carpet Mills Inc., **19** 276
Galaxy Energies Inc., **11** 28
Galbreath Escott, **16** 474
Gale Research Inc., **8** 526; **23** 440
Galen Health Care, **15** 112
Galen Laboratories, **13** 160
Galeries Lafayette S.A., V 57–59; 23 220–23 (upd.)
Galesburg Coulter Disc Co., **III** 439–40
Galey & Lord, Inc., 20 242–45
Gallaher Limited, IV 260; **V 398–400; 19 168–71 (upd.)**
Gallatin Bank, **II** 312
Gallatin Steel, **18** 380
Galletas, **II** 543
Gallimard, **IV** 618
Gallo. *See* E & J Gallo.
Galoob Toys. *See* Lewis Galoob Toys Inc.
Galor, **I** 676
GALP, **IV** 505
Galvanizing Co., **IV** 159
Galveston *Daily News*, **10** 3
Galvin Manufacturing Corp., **II** 60; **11** 326
Gamble-Skogmo, **13** 169
Gambro Engstrom AB, **13** 159–61, 327–28
Gamesa, **II** 544; **19** 192
Gametime Ltd., **19** 387
GAMI. *See* Great American Management and Investment, Inc.
Gamlestaden, **9** 381–82
Gamlestadens Fabriker, **III** 622
Gammalink, **18** 143
Gander Mountain, Inc., 20 246–48
Gang-Nail Systems, **III** 735
Gannett Co., Inc., III 159; **IV 612–13**, 629–30; **7 190–92 (upd.); 9** 3; **18** 63; **23** 157–58, 293
Gannett Supply, **17** 282
Gantos, Inc., 17 199–201
The Gap, Inc., V 60–62; 9 142, 360; **11** 499; **18 191–94 (upd.)**
GAR Holdings, **19** 78
Garamond Press, **23** 100
Garan, Inc., 16 231–33

Garantie Mutuelle des Fonctionnaires, **21** 225
Garden Botanika, **11** 41
Garden State BancShares, Inc., **14** 472
Garden State Life Insurance Company, **10** 312
Gardener's Eden, **17** 548–49
Gardenia, **II** 587
Gardner & Harvey Container Corporation, **8** 267
Gardner Advertising. *See* Wells Rich Green BDDP.
Gardner Cryogenics, **13** 140
Gardner Merchant Ltd., **III** 104; **11** 325
Gardner Rubber Co. *See* Tillotson Corp.
Gardner-Denver Co., **II** 16
Garfield Weston, **13** 51
Garfinckel, Brooks Brothers, Miller & Rhodes, Inc., **15** 94; **22** 110
Garlock, **I** 435
Garnier, **III** 47
A.B. Garnisonen, **II** 352
Garrard Engineering, **II** 82
Garrett, **9** 18; **11** 472
Garrett AiResearch, **9** 18
Garrett Poultry Co., **II** 584; **14** 514
Garrett-Buchanan, **I** 412
Garrick Investment Holdings Ltd., **16** 293
Gartner Group, Inc., 21 235–37
Gartrell White, **II** 465
Garuda Indonesia, I 107; **6 90–91**
Gary Fisher Mountain Bike Company, **16** 494
Gary Industries, **7** 4
Gary-Wheaton Corp., **II** 286
Gary-Williams Energy Corporation, **19** 177
Gas Authority of India Ltd., **IV** 484
Gas Corp. of Queensland, **III** 673
Gas Energy Inc., **6** 457
Gas Group, **III** 673
Gas Light and Coke Company. *See* British Gas plc.
Gas Light Company. *See* Baltimore Gas and Electric Company.
Gas Machinery Co., **I** 412
Gas Service Company, **6** 593; **12** 542
Gas Supply Co., **III** 672
Gas Tech, Inc., **11** 513
Gas Utilities Company, **6** 471
Gaston Paper Stock Co., Inc., **8** 476
Gasunie. *See* N.V. Nederlandse Gasunie.
GATC. *See* General American Tank Car Company.
Gate City Company, **6** 446
The Gates Corporation, 9 241–43
Gates Distribution Company, **12** 60
Gates Radio Co., **II** 37
Gateway Books, **14** 61
Gateway Corporation Ltd., II 612, **628–30**, 638, 642; **10** 442; **16** 249
Gateway Foodmarkets Ltd., **II** 628; **13** 26
Gateway 2000, Inc., 10 307–09; **11** 240; **22** 99
Gatliff Coal Co., **6** 583
GATX, 6 394–96
Gaumont-British, **II** 157–58
Gauntlet Developments, **IV** 724
Gavilan Computer Corp., **III** 124; **6** 221
Gaya Motor, P.T. **23** 290
Gaylord Container Corporation, 8 203–05
Gaylord Entertainment Company, 11 152–54
Gaz de France, IV 425; **V 626–28**

Gazprom, **18** 50
GB Foods Inc., **19** 92
GB Papers, **IV** 290
GB Stores, Inc., **14** 427
GB-Inno-BM, **II** 658; **V** 63
GBL, **IV** 499
GCFC. *See* General Cinema Finance Co.
GDE Systems, Inc., **17** 492
GDF. *See* Gaz de France.
GE. *See* General Electric Company.
GE Aircraft Engines, 9 244–46
Geant Casino, **12** 152
Gearhart Industries Inc., **III** 499; **15** 467
Gearmatic, **I** 185
Gebrüder Kiessel GmbH, **IV** 197
Gebrüder Sulzer Aktiengesellschaft. *See* Sulzer Brothers Limited.
Gebrüder Volkart, **III** 402
Gebrueder Ahle GmbH, **III** 581
GEC. *See* General Electric Company, PLC.
GECO, **III** 618; **17** 419
Geco Mines Ltd., **IV** 165; **7** 398
Geer Drug, **III** 9–10
Geffen Films, **21** 26
Geffen Records, **21** 26; **23** 33
GEGC, **III** 434
Gehl Company, 19 172–74
GEICO Corporation, III 214, 248, 252, 273, 448; **10 310–12**; **18** 60, 61, 63
Gelatin Products Co., **I** 678
Gelco Express, **18** 177
Gelco Truck Services, **19** 293
Gellatly, Hankey and Sewell, **III** 521
Gelsenberg AG, **IV** 454; **7** 141
Gelsenkirchener Bergwerks AG, **I** 542; **IV** 194
Gem State Utilities, **6** 325, 328
GEMA Gesellschaft für Maschinen- und Apparatebau mbH, **IV** 198
Gemco, **17** 366
Gemcolite Company, **8** 178
N.V. Gemeenschappelijk Benzit van Aandeelen Philips Gloeilampenfabriken, **II** 79; **13** 396
Gemeinhardt Co., **16** 201
Gemey, **III** 47
Gemina, **I** 369
Gemini Computers, **III** 109; **14** 13
Gemini Group Limited Partnership, **23** 10
Gemini Industries, **17** 215
GemPlus, **18** 543
Genbel Investments Ltd., **IV** 92
GenCare Health Systems, **17** 166–67
Gencor Ltd., I 423; **IV 90–93**, 95; **22 233–37 (upd.)**
GenCorp Inc., 8 206–08; **9 247–49**; **13** 381
Gendex Corp., **10** 270, 272
Gene Reid Drilling, **IV** 480
Gene Upton Co., **13** 166
Genentech Inc., I 628, **637–38**; **III** 43; **8 209–11 (upd.)**, 216–17; **10** 78, 80, 142, 199; **17** 289
General Accident plc, III 256–57, 350
General America Corp., **III** 352–53
General American Oil Co., **IV** 523
General American Tank Car Company, **6** 394–95
General Aniline and Film Corporation. *See* GAF Corporation.
General Aquatics, Inc., **16** 297
General Artificial Silk Co., **IV** 310; **19** 265
General Automotive Parts Corp., **I** 62; **9** 254

General Aviation Corp., **I** 54; **9** 16
General Battery Corp., **I** 440–41
General Binding Corporation, 10 313–14
General Box Corp., **IV** 342
General Brewing Corp, **I** 269
General Bussan Kaisha, Ltd., **IV** 431–32, 555
General Cable Co., **IV** 32; **7** 288; **8** 367; **18** 549
General Casualty Co., **III** 258, 343, 352, 404
General Chemical, **I** 414; **22** 29, 115, 193, 349, 541
General Chocolate, **II** 521
General Cigar Co., Inc. *See* Culbro Corporation.
General Cinema Corporation, I 245–46; **II** 478; **IV** 624; **12** 12–13, 226, 356; **14** 87; **19** 362
General Cinema Finance Co., **II** 157–58
General Co. for Life Insurance and Superannuation, **III** 309
General Corporation, **9** 173
General Credit Ltd., **II** 389
General Crude Oil Co., **II** 403; **IV** 287; **15** 228
General DataComm Industries, Inc., 14 200–02
General Diaper Corporation, **14** 550
General Dynamics Corporation, I 55, **57–60**, 62, 71, 74, 77, 482, 525, 527, 597; **6** 79, 229; **7** 520; **8** 51, 92, 315, 338; **9** 206, 323, 417–18, 498; **10 315–18 (upd.)**, 522, 527; **11** 67, 165, 269, 278, 364; **13** 374; **16** 77–78; **18** 62, 554
General Electric Capital Corp., **15** 257, 282; **19** 190
General Electric Company, I 41, 52, 82–85, 195, 321, 454, 478, 532, 534, 537; **II** 2, 16, 19, 22, 24, **27–31**, 38–39, 41, 56, 58–59, 66, 82, 86, 88–90, 98–99, 116–17, 119–21, 143, 151–52, 330, 349, 431, 604; **III** 16, 110, 122–23, 132, 149, 152, 154, 170–71, 340, 437, 440, 443, 475, 483, 502, 526, 572–73, 614, 655; **IV** 66, 203, 287, 596, 675; **V** 564; **6** 13, 27, 32, 164–66, 240, 261, 266, 288, 452, 517; **7** 123, 125, 161, 456, 520, 532; **8** 157, 262, 332, 377; **9** 14–18, 27, 128, 162, 244, 246, 352–53, 417–18, 439, 514; **10** 16, 241, 536–37; **11** 46, 313, 318, 422, 472, 490; **12** 68, 190, **193–97 (upd.)**, 237, 247, 250, 252, 484, 544–45, 550; **13** 30, 124, 326, 396, 398, 501, 529, 554, 563–64; **15** 196, 228, 285, 380, 403, 467; **17** 149, 173, 272; **18** 228, 369; **19** 110, 164–66, 210, 335; **20** 8, 152; **22** 37, 218, 406; **23** 104–05, 181
General Electric Company, PLC, I 411, 423; **II** 3, 12, **24–26**, 31, 58, 72, 80–83; **III** 509; **9** 9–10; **13** 356; **20** 290
General Electric Credit Corporation, **19** 293; **20** 42
General Electric Railcar Wheel and Parts Services Corporation, **18** 4
General Electric Venture Capital Corporation, **9** 140; **10** 108
General Electronics Co., **III** 160
General Europea S.A., **V** 607
General Export Iron and Metals Company, **15** 116

General Felt Industries Inc., **I** 202; **14** 300; **17** 182–83
General Film Distributors Ltd., **II** 157
General Finance Corp., **II** 419; **III** 194, 232; **11** 16
General Finance Service Corp., **11** 447
General Fire and Casualty, **I** 449
General Fire Extinguisher Co. *See* Grinnell Corp.
General Foods Corp., **I** 26, 36, 608, 712; **II** 414, 463, 477, 497, 502, 525, 530–34, 557, 569; **III** 66; **V** 407; **7** 272–74; **10** 323, 551; **12** 167, 372; **13** 293; **18** 416, 419
General Foods, Ltd., **7** 577
General Furniture Leasing Co., **III** 200
General Gas Co., **IV** 432
General Glass Corporation, **13** 40
General Growth Properties, **III** 248
General Health Services, **III** 79
General Host Corporation, **7** 372; **12** 178–79, **198–200**, 275; **15** 362; **17** 230–31
General Housewares Corporation, **16 234–36**; **18** 69
General Instrument Corporation, **II** 5, 112, 160; **10 319–21**; **17** 33
General Insurance Co. of America, **III** 352–53
General Jones Processed Food, **I** 438
General Learning Corp., **IV** 675; **7** 528
General Leisure, **16** 33
General Life Insurance Co. of America, **III** 353
General Medical Corp., **18** 469
General Merchandise Company, **V** 91
General Merchandise Services, Inc., **15** 480
General Milk Co., **II** 487; **7** 429
General Milk Products of Canada Ltd., **II** 586
General Mills, Inc., **II** 493, **501–03**, 525, 556, 576, 684; **III** 505; **7** 547; **8** 53–54; **9** 156, 189–90, 291; **10** 177, **322–24 (upd.)**; **11** 15, 497–98; **12** 80, 167–68, 275; **13** 244, 293–94, 408, 516; **15** 189; **16** 71, 156–58, 337; **18** 225, 523; **22** 337–38
General Mining and Finance Corporation. *See* Gencor Ltd.
General Mortgage and Credit Corp., **II** 256
General Motors Acceptance Corporation, **21** 146; **22** 55
General Motors Corporation, **I** 10, 14, 16–17, 54, 58, 78–80, 85, 101–02, 125, 136, 141, 144–45, 147, 154–55, 162–63, 165–67, **171–73**, 181, 183, 186–87, 203, 205–06, 280, 328–29, 334–35, 360, 448, 464, 481–82, 529, 540; **II** 2, 5, 15, 32–35, 268, 431, 608; **III** 55, 136–38, 292, 442, 458, 482–83, 536, 555, 563, 581, 590–91, 637–38, 640–42, 760; **6** 140, 256, 336, 356, 358; **7** 6–8, 427, 461–64, 513, 565, 567, 599; **8** 151–52, 505–07; **9** 16–18, 36, 283, 293–95, 341, 343, 344, 439, 487–89; **10** 198, 232, 262, 264, 273–74, 279–80, 288–89, **325–27 (upd.)**, 419–20, 429, 460, 537; **11** 5, 29, 53, 103–04, 137–39, 339, 350, 427–29, 437–39, 471–72, 528, 530; **12** 90, 160, 309, 311, 487; **13** 109, 124, 179, 344–45, 357; **14** 321, 458; **15** 171; **16** 321–22, 436, 484; **17** 173, 184, 304; **18** 125–26, 168, 308; **19** 293–94, 482, 484; **21** 3, 6, 444; **22** 13,
169, 175, 216; **23** 267–69, 288–91, 340, 459–61
General Nucleonics Corp., **III** 643
General Nutrition Companies, Inc., **11 155–57**
General Packing Service, Inc., **19** 78
General Petroleum and Mineral Organization of Saudi Arabia, **IV** 537–39
General Petroleum Corp., **IV** 412, 431, 464; **7** 352
General Physics Corporation, **13** 367
General Portland Cement Co., **III** 704–05; **17** 497
General Precision Equipment Corp., **II** 10
General Printing and Paper, **II** 624–25
General Printing Ink Corp. *See* Sequa Corp.
General Property Trust, **IV** 708
General Public Utilities Corporation, **V 629–31**; **6** 484, 534, 579–80; **11** 388; **20** 73
General Railway Signal Company. *See* General Signal Corporation.
General Re Corporation, **III 258–59**, 276
General Rent A Car, **6** 349
General Research Corp., **14** 98
General Seafoods Corp., **II** 531
General Sekiyu K.K., **IV 431–33**, 555; **16** 490
General Signal Corporation, **III** 645; **9 250–52**; **11** 232
General Spring Products, **16** 321
General Steel Industries Inc., **14** 324
General Supermarkets, **II** 673
General Telephone and Electronics Corp., **II** 47; **V** 295, 345–46; **13** 398; **19** 40
General Telephone Corporation, **V** 294–95; **9** 478, 494
General Time Corporation, **16** 483
General Tire, Inc., **8** 206–08, **212–14**; **9** 247–48; **20** 260, 262; **22** 219
General Transistor Corporation, **10** 319
General Utilities Company, **6** 555
Generale Bank, **II 294–95**
Générale Biscuit S.A., **II** 475
Générale de Mécanique Aéronautique, **I** 46
Générale des Eaux Group, **V 632–34**; **21** 226
Generale du Jouet, **16** 428
Générale Occidentale, **II** 475; **IV** 614–15
Generali. *See* Assicurazioni Generali.
GenerComit Gestione SpA, **II** 192
Genesco Inc., **14** 501; **17 202–06**
Genesee Brewing Co., **18** 72
Genesee Iron Works, **V** 221
Genesis, **II** 176–77
Genesis Health Ventures, Inc., **18 195–97**
Genetic Systems Corp., **I** 654; **III** 18
Genetics Institute, Inc., **8 215–18**; **10** 70, 78–80
Geneva Metal Wheel Company, **20** 261
Geneva Pharmaceuticals, Inc., **8** 549; **22** 37, 40
Geneva Rubber Co., **17** 373
Geneva Steel, **7 193–95**
Genex Corp., **I** 355–56
GENIX, **V** 152
Genix Group. *See* MCN Corporation.
Genossenschaftsbank Edeka, **II** 621–22
Genovese Drug Stores, Inc., **18 198–200**; **21** 187
Genpack Corporation, **21** 58
GenSet, **19** 442
Genstar, **22** 14; **23** 327
Genstar Gypsum Products Co., **IV** 273
Genstar Stone Products Co., **III** 735; **15** 154
Gentex Corporation, **12** 121–22
Gentex Optics, **17** 50; **18** 392
Gentry Associates, Inc., **14** 378
Gentry International, **I** 497
Genuine Parts Company, **9 253–55**
Genung's, **II** 673
Genus, **18** 382–83
Genzyme Corporation, **13 239–42**
Geo Space Corporation, **18** 513
Geo. W. Wheelwright Co., **IV** 311; **19** 266
Geodynamics Oil & Gas Inc., **IV** 83
Geomarine Systems, **11** 202
The Geon Company, **11 158–61**
Geon Industries, Inc. *See* Johnston Industries, Inc.
Geophysical Service, Inc., **II** 112; **III** 499–500; **IV** 365
GeoQuest Systems Inc., **17** 419
Georesources, Inc., **19** 247
George A. Hormel and Company, **II 504–06**; **7** 547; **12** 123–24; **18** 244. *See also* Hormel Foods Corporation.
George A. Touche & Co., **9** 167
George Batten Co., **I** 28
George Booker & Co., **13** 102
George Fischer, Ltd., **III** 638
George H. Dentler & Sons, **7** 429
The George Hyman Construction Company, **8** 112–13
George K. Smith & Co., **I** 692
George Kent, **II** 3; **22** 10
George Newnes Company, **IV** 641; **7** 244
George Peabody & Co., **II** 329, 427
George R. Newell Company. *See* Supervalu Inc.
George R. Rich Manufacturing Company. *See* Clark Equipment Company.
George Smith Financial Corporation, **21** 257
George W. Neare & Co., **III** 224
George Weston Limited, **II** 465, **631–32**, 649; **13** 51
George Wimpey PLC, **12 201–03**
Georges Renault, **III** 427
Georgetown Steel Corp., **IV** 228
Georgia Cotton Producers Association. *See* Gold Kist Inc.
Georgia Credit Exchange, **6** 24
Georgia Federal Bank, **I** 447; **11** 112–13
Georgia Gulf Corporation, **IV** 282; **9 256–58**, 260
Georgia Hardwood Lumber Co., **IV** 281; **9** 259
Georgia International Life Insurance Co., **III** 218
Georgia Kraft Co., **IV** 312, 342–43; **8** 267–68; **19** 268
Georgia Natural Gas Corporation, **6** 447–48
Georgia Power & Light Co., **V** 621; **6** 447, 537; **23** 28
Georgia Railway and Electric Company, **6** 446–47; **23** 28
Georgia-Pacific Corporation, **IV 281–83**, 288, 304, 345, 358; **9** 256–58, **259–62 (upd.)**; **12** 19, 377; **15** 229; **22** 415, 489
Georgie Pie, **V** 35
GeoScience Corporation, **18** 515
Geosource Inc., **III** 182; **21** 14; **22** 189
Geotec Boyles Brothers, S.A., **19** 247

Geotek Communications Inc., 21 238–40
Geothermal Resources International, 11 271
Gerber Products Company, II 481; **III** 19; **7** 196–98, 547; **9** 90; **11** 173; **21** 53–55, 241–44 (upd)
Gerber Scientific, Inc., 12 204–06
Gerbes Super Markets, Inc., 12 112
Geren Associates. See CRSS Inc.
Geriatrics Inc., 13 49
Gerling of Cologne, III 695
Germaine Monteil Cosmetiques Corp., I 426; III 56
German Cargo Service GmbH., I 111
German Mills American Oatmeal Factory, II 558; 12 409
German-American Car Company. See GATX.
German-American Securities, II 283
Germania Refining Co., IV 488–89
Germplasm Resource Management, III 740
Gerresheimer Glas AG, II 386; IV 232
Gerrity Oil & Gas Corporation, 11 28
Gervais Danone, II 474
GESA. See General Europea S.A.
Gesbancaya, II 196
Gesellschaft für Chemische Industrie im Basel, I 632
Gesellschaft für den Bau von Untergrundbahnen, I 410
Gesellschaft für Linde's Eisenmachinen, I 581
Gesellschaft für Markt- und Kühlhallen, I 581
Gesparal, III 47; 8 342
Gestettner, II 159
Gestione Pubblicitaria Editoriale, IV 586
Getty Oil Co., II 448; IV 367, 423, 429, 461, 479, 488, 490, 551, 553; 6 457; 8 526; 11 27; 13 448; 17 501; 18 488
Getz Corp., IV 137
Geyser Peak Winery, I 291
Geysers Geothermal Co., IV 84, 523; 7 188
GFS. See Gordon Food Service Inc.
GFS Realty Inc., II 633
GHH, II 257
GI Communications, 10 321
GI Export Corp. See Johnston Industries, Inc.
GIAG, 16 122
Gianni Versace SpA, 22 238–40
Giant Bicycle Inc., 19 384
Giant Cement Holding, Inc., 23 224–26
Giant Eagle, Inc., 12 390–91, 13 237
Giant Food Inc., II 633–35, 656; **13** 282, 284; **15** 532; **16** 313; **22 241–44** (upd.)
Giant Industries, Inc., 19 175–77
Giant Resources, III 729
Giant Stores, Inc., 7 113
Giant TC, Inc. See Campo Electronics, Appliances & Computers, Inc.
Giant Tire & Rubber Company, 8 126
Giant Wholesale, II 625
GIB Group, V 63–66; **22** 478; **23** 231
Gibbons, Green, van Amerongen Ltd., II 605; 9 94; 12 28; 19 360
Gibbs Automatic Molding Co., III 569; 20 360
GIBCO Corp., I 321; 17 287, 289
Gibraltar Casualty Co., III 340
Gibraltar Financial Corp., III 270–71
Gibson Greetings, Inc., 7 24; **12 207–10**; **16** 256; **21** 426–28; **22** 34–35

Gibson Guitar Corp., 16 237–40
Gibson McDonald Furniture Co., 14 236
GIC. See The Goodyear Tire & Rubber Company.
Giddings & Lewis, Inc., 8 545–46; **10** 328–30; **23** 299
Gil-Wel Manufacturing Company, 17 440
Gilbert & John Greenall Limited, 21 246
Gilbert Lane Personnel, Inc., 9 326
Gilbert-Ash Ltd., I 588
Gilde-Verlag, IV 590
Gilde-Versicherung AG, III 400
Gildon Metal Enterprises, 7 96
Gilkey Bros. See Puget Sound Tug and Barge Company.
Gill and Duffus, II 500
Gill Industries, II 161
Gillett Holdings, Inc., 7 199–201; **11** 543, 545
The Gillette Company, III 27–30, 114, 215; **IV** 722; **8** 59–60; **9** 381, 413; **17** 104–05; **18** 60, 62, 215, 228; **20 249–53** (upd.); **23** 54–57
Gilliam Furniture Inc., 12 475
Gilliam Manufacturing Co., 8 530
Gilman & Co., III 523
Gilman Fanfold Corp., Ltd., IV 644
Gilmore Brother's, I 707
Gilmore Steel Corporation. See Oregon Steel Mills, Inc.
Giltspur, 11 587
Gimbel's Department Store, I 426–27; 8 59; 22 72
Gindick Productions, 6 28
Ginn & Co., IV 672; 19 405
Ginnie Mae. See Government National Mortgage Association.
Gino's, III 103
Gino's East, 21 362
Ginsber Beer Group, 15 47
Giorgio, Inc., III 16; 19 28
Girard Bank, II 315–16
Girbaud, 17 513
Girling, III 556
Giro Sport Designs, 16 53
Girod, 19 50
Girsa S.A., 23 170
Girvin, Inc., 16 297
Gist-Brocades Co., III 53
The Gitano Group, Inc., 8 219–21; **20** 136
GK Technologies Incorporated, 10 547
GKN plc, III 493–96, 554, 556
Glaceries de Saint-Roch, III 677; 16 121
Glaces de Boussois, II 474–75
Glacier Park Co., 10 191
Gladieux Corp., III 103
Glamar Group plc, 14 224
Glamor Shops, Inc., 14 93
Glasrock Home Health Care, I 316
Glass Containers Corp., I 609–10
Glass Fibres Ltd., III 726
GlasTec, II 420
Glatfelter Wood Pulp Company, 8 413
Glaverbel, III 667
Glaxo Holdings plc, I 639–41, 643, 668, 675, 693; **III** 66; **6** 346; **9** 263–65 (upd.); **10** 551; **11** 173; **20** 39
Glen & Co, I 453
Glen Alden Corp., 15 247
Glen Cove Mutual Insurance Co., III 269
Glen Iris Bricks, III 673
Glen Line, 6 416
Glen-Gery Corporation, 14 249

Glendale Federal Savings, IV 29
Glenn Pleass Holdings Pty. Ltd., 21 339
Glens Falls Insurance Co., III 242
GLF-Eastern States Association, 7 17
The Glidden Company, I 353; **8 222–24**; **21** 545
Glitsch International, Inc., 6 146; 23 206, 208
Global Apparel Sourcing Ltd., 22 223
Global Energy Group, II 345
Global Engineering Company, 9 266
Global Marine Inc., 9 266–67; **11** 87
Global Natural Resources, II 401; 10 145
Global Transport Organization, 6 383
Globe & Rutgers Insurance Co., III 195–96
Globe Co. I 201
Globe Electric Co., III 536
Globe Feather & Down, 19 304
Globe Files Co., I 201
Globe Grain and Milling Co., II 555
Globe Industries, I 540
Globe Insurance Co., III 350
Globe Life Insurance Co., III 187; 10 28
Globe National Bank, II 261
Globe Newspaper Co., 7 15
Globe Petroleum Ltd., IV 401
Globe Steel Abrasive Co., 17 371
Globe-Union, III 536
Globe-Wernicke Co., I 201
Globetrotter Communications, 7 199
Globo, 18 211
Gloria Jean's Gourmet Coffees, 20 83
La Gloria Oil and Gas Company, 7 102
Gloria Separator GmbH Berlin, III 418
Glosser Brothers, 13 394
Gloster Aircraft, I 50; III 508
Gloucester Cold Storage and Warehouse Company, 13 243
Glovatorium, III 152; 6 266
Glycomed Inc., 13 241
Glyn, Mills and Co., II 308; 12 422
GM. See General Motors Corp.
GM Hughes Electronics Corporation, II 32–36; **10** 325
GMARA, II 608
GMFanuc Robotics, III 482–83
GMR Properties, 21 257
GNB International Battery Group, 10 445
GND Holdings Corp., 7 204
GNMA. See Government National Mortgage Association.
Goal Systems International Inc., 10 394
Godfather's Pizza, II 556–57; 11 50; 12 123; 14 351; 17 86
Godfrey Co., II 625
Godfrey L. Cabot, Inc., 8 77
Godiva Chocolatier, II 480
Godo Shusei, III 42
Godsell, 10 277
Godtfred Kristiansen, 13 310–11
Goebel & Wetterau Grocery Co., II 681
Goering Werke, II 282
Göhner AG, 6 491
Gokey's, 10 216
Gold Bond Stamp Company, 6 363–64; 22 125
Gold Crust Bakeries, II 465
Gold Dust Corp., II 497
Gold Exploration and Mining Co. Limited Partnership, 13 503
Gold Fields of South Africa Ltd., I 423; **IV** 91, 94–97
Gold Kist Inc., 7 432; **17 207–09**

Gold Lance Inc., **19** 451–52
Gold Lion, **20** 263
Gold Seal, **II** 567
Gold Star Foods Co., **IV** 410
Goldblatt Bros., **IV** 135
Goldblatt's Department Stores, **15** 240–42
Golden, **III** 47
Golden Belt Manufacturing Co., 16 241–43
Golden Circle Financial Services, **15** 328
Golden Corral Corporation, 10 331–33
Golden Eagle Exploration, **IV** 566–67
Golden Grain Macaroni Co., **II** 560; **12** 411
Golden Hope Rubber Estate, **III** 697, 699
Golden Nugget Company, **III** 92, 431. *See also* Mirage Resorts, Inc.
Golden Partners, **10** 333
Golden Peanut Company, **17** 207
Golden Press, Inc., **13** 559–61
Golden Sea Produce, **10** 439
Golden Skillet, **10** 373
Golden State Bank, **II** 348
Golden State Newsprint Co. Inc., **IV** 296; **19** 226; **23** 225
Golden State Sanwa Bank, **II** 348
Golden Tulip International, **I** 109
Golden West Homes, **15** 328
Golden Wonder, **II** 500; **III** 503
Golden Youth, **17** 227
Goldenberg Group, Inc., **12** 396
Goldenlay Eggs, **II** 500
Goldfield Corp., **12** 198
Goldfine's Inc., **16** 36
Goldkuhl & Broström, **III** 419
Goldline Laboratories Inc., **11** 208
Goldman, Sachs & Co., II 11, 268, 326, 361, **414–16**, 432, 434, 448; **III** 80, 531; **IV** 611; **9** 378, 441; **10** 423; **12** 405; **13** 95, 448, 554; **15** 397; **16** 195; **20** **254–57 (upd.)**, 258; **21** 146; **22** 427–28
Goldome Savings Bank, **11** 110; **17** 488
Goldsbrough Mort & Co., **I** 437
Goldsmith's, **9** 209
Goldstar Co., Ltd., II 5, 53–54; **III** 517; **7** 233; **12 211–13**; **13** 213
Goldwell, **III** 38
Goldwyn Picture Corp., **II** 148
Golf Day, **22** 517
Gomoljak, **14** 250
Good Foods, Inc., **II** 497
The Good Guys!, Inc., 10 334–35
The Good Humor-Breyers Ice Cream Company, II 533; **14 203–05**; **15** 222; **17** 140–41
Good Times, Inc., **8** 303
Good Weather International Inc., **III** 221; **14** 109
Goodbody & Company, **II** 425; **13** 341; **22** 428
Goodbody James Capel, **16** 14
Goodby, Berlin & Silverstein, **10** 484
Goodebodies, **11** 41
Gooderham and Worts, **I** 216, 263–64
Goodlass, Wall & Co., **III** 680–81
Goodman Bros. Mfg. Co., **14** 436
Goodman Fielder, Wattie's, Ltd., **II** 565; **7** 577
Goodrich Oil Co., **IV** 365
Goodrich, Tew and Company, **V** 231
Goodrich Tire Company, **V** 240–41; **6** 27
Goodwill Industries International, Inc., 15 511; **16 244–46**
Goodwin & Co., **12** 108

Goodwin, Dannenbaum, Littman & Wingfield, **16** 72
Goody Products, Inc., 12 214–16
Goody's Family Clothing, Inc., 20 265–67
The Goodyear Tire & Rubber Company, I 21; **II** 304; **III** 452; **V** 244–48; **8** 81, 291–92, 339; **9** 324; **10** 445; **15** 91; **16** 474; **19** 221, 223, 455; **20 259–64 (upd.)**; **21** 72–74
Gordon A. Freisen, International, **III** 73
Gordon B. Miller & Co., **7** 256
Gordon Capital Corp., **II** 245
Gordon Food Service Inc., 8 225–27
Gordon Investment Corp., **II** 245
Gordon Jewelry Corporation, **16** 559, 561
Gordon Manufacturing Co., **11** 256
Gordon Publications, **IV** 610
Gordon-Van Cheese Company, **8** 225
Gore Newspapers Company, **IV** 683; **22** 521
Gorges Foodservice, Inc., **14** 516
Gorham Silver, **12** 313
The Gorman-Rupp Company, 18 201–03
Gormully & Jeffrey, **IV** 660
Gorton's, II 502; **10** 323; **13 243–44**
Gosho Co., Ltd., **IV** 442
Gotaas-Larsen Shipping Corp., **6** 368
Götabanken, **II** 303, 353
Göteborgs Handelsbank, **II** 351
Göteborgs Handelskompani, **III** 425
Gothenburg Light & Power Company, **6** 580
Gothenburg Tramways Co., **II** 1
Gott Corp., **III** 614; **21** 293
Gottschalks, Inc., 18 204–06
Goulard and Olena, **I** 412
Gould Electronics, Inc., III 745; **11** 45; **13** 127, 201; **14 206–08**; **21** 43
Goulding Industries Ltd., **IV** 295; **19** 225
Gourmet Foods, **II** 528
Government Bond Department, **9** 369
Government Employees Insurance Company. *See* GEICO Corporation.
Government National Mortgage Assoc., **II** 410
The Governor and Company of the Bank of Scotland, II 422; **III** 360; **V** 166; **10 336–38**
Goya Foods Inc., 22 245–47
GP Group Acquisition Limited Partnership, **10** 288
GPT, **15** 125
GPU. *See* General Public Utilities Corporation.
Graber Industries, Inc., **V** 379; **19** 421
Grace. *See* W.R. Grace & Co.
Grace Drilling Company, **9** 365
Grace-Sierra Horticultural Products Co., **22** 475
Graco Inc., 19 178–80
Gradco Systems, Inc., **6** 290
Gradiaz, Annis & Co., **15** 138
Gradmann & Holler, **III** 283
Graef & Schmidt, **III** 54
Graf, **23** 219
Graf Bertel Dominique/New York, **6** 48
Graficas e Instrumentos S.A., **13** 234
Graham Container Corp., **8** 477
Graham Page, **III** 568; **20** 359
Grahams Builders Merchants, **I** 429
Gralla, **IV** 687
Gramercy Pictures, **23** 391
Gramophone Company, **22** 192

Grampian Electricity Supply Company, **13** 457
Gran Central Corporation, **8** 487
Granada Group PLC, II 70, **138–40**; **17** 353
Granada Royale Hometels, **9** 426
Granaria Holdings B.V., **23** 183
GranCare, Inc., 14 209–11
Grand Bazaar Innovations Bon Marché, **13** 284
Grand Casinos, Inc., 20 268–70; **21** 526
Grand Department Store, **19** 510
Grand Hotel Krasnapolsky N.V., 23 227–29
Grand Metropolitan plc, I 247–49, 259, 261; **II** 555–57, 565, 608, 613–15; **9** 99; **13** 391, 407, 409; **14 212–15 (upd.)**; **15** 72; **17** 69, 71; **20** 452; **21** 401
Grand Rapids Carpet Sweeper Company, **9** 70
Grand Rapids Gas Light Company. *See* MCN Corporation.
Grand Rapids Wholesale Grocery Company, **8** 481
Grand Trunk Corp., **6** 359–61
Grand Union Company, II 637, 662; **7 202–04**; **8** 410; **13** 394; **16** 249
Grand Valley Gas Company, **11** 28
Grandes Superficies S.A., **23** 247
Grandmet USA, **I** 248
Grands Magasins L. Tietz, **V** 103
Grandy's, **15** 345
Granger Associates, **12** 136
Gränges, **III** 480; **22** 27
Granite City Steel Company, **12** 353
Granite Furniture Co., **14** 235
Grant Oil Tool Co., **III** 569; **20** 361
Grant Street National Bank, **II** 317
GranTree, **14** 4
Graphic Controls Corp., **IV** 678
Graphic Research, Inc., **13 344–45**
Graphic Services, **III** 166; **6** 282
Graphics Systems Software, **III** 169; **6** 285; **8** 519
Graphite Oil Product Co., **I** 360
Grass Valley Group, **8** 518, 520
Grasselli Chemical Company, **22** 225
Grasselli Dyestuffs Corp., **I** 337
Grasset, **IV** 617–18
Grattan, **V** 160
The Graver Company, **16** 357
Gray Dawes & Co., **III** 522–23
Gray Drug Stores, **III** 745
Gray Dunn and Co., **II** 569
Gray, Seifert and Co., **10** 44
Grayarc, **III** 157
Grayrock Capital, **I** 275
Grays Harbor Mutual Savings Bank, **17** 530
Greaseater, Ltd., **8** 463–64
Great Alaska Tobacco Co., **17** 80
Great American Broadcasting Inc., **18** 65–66; **22** 131; **23** 257–58
Great American Entertainment Company, **13** 279
Great American First Savings Bank of San Diego, **II** 420
Great American Life Insurance Co., **III** 190–92
Great American Lines Inc., **12** 29
Great American Management and Investment, Inc., 8 228–31
Great American Reserve Insurance Co., **IV** 343; **10** 247

Great American Restaurants, **13** 321
The Great Atlantic & Pacific Tea Company, Inc., II **636–38**, 629, 655–56, 666; **13** 25, 127, 237; **15** 259; **16** 63–64, **247–50 (upd.)**; **17** 106; **18** 6; **19** 479–80
Great Beam Co., III 690
Great Eastern Railway, **6** 424
Great 5¢ Store, **V** 224
Great Halviggan, III 690
Great Lakes Bancorp, 8 232–33
Great Lakes Bankgroup, II 457
Great Lakes Carbon Corporation, **12** 99
Great Lakes Chemical Corp., I **341–42; 8** 262; **14 216–18 (upd.)**
Great Lakes Corp., IV 136
Great Lakes Pipe Line Co., IV 400, 575
Great Lakes Steel Corp., IV 236; **8** 346; **12** 352
Great Lakes Window, Inc., **12** 397
Great Land Seafoods, Inc., II 553
Great Northern, III 282
Great Northern Import Co., I 292
Great Northern Nekoosa Corp., IV 282–83, 300; **9** 260–61
Great Northern Railway Company, **6** 596
Great Plains Transportation, **18** 226
Great Shoshone & Twin Falls Water Power Company, **12** 265
The Great Universal Stores plc, V 67–69; 15 83, **17** 66, 68; **19 181–84 (upd.)**
The Great Western Auction House & Clothing Store, **19** 261
Great Western Billiard Manufactory, III 442
Great Western Financial Corporation, 10 339–41
Great Western Foam Co., **17** 182
Great Western Railway, III 272
Great World Foods, Inc., **17** 93
Great-West Lifeco Inc., III **260–61; 21** 447
Greatamerica Corp., I 489; **10** 419
Greater All American Markets, II 601; **7** 19
Greater New York Film Rental Co., II 169
Greater Washington Investments, Inc., **15** 248
Greb Industries Ltd., **16** 79, 545
Greeley Beef Plant, **13** 350
Green Acquisition Co., **18** 107
Green Bay Food Company, **7** 127
Green Capital Investors L.P., **23** 413–14
Green Cross K.K., I 665
Green Giant, II 556; **13** 408; **14** 212, 214
Green Island Cement (Holdings) Ltd. Group, IV 694–95
Green Line Investor Services, **18** 553
Green Power & Light Company. See UtiliCorp United Inc.
Green River Electric Corporation, **11** 37
Green Thumb, II 562
Green Tree Financial Corporation, 11 162–63
The Greenalls Group PLC, 21 245–47
The Greenbrier Companies, 19 185–87
Greenfield Industries Inc., **13** 8
Greenleaf Corp., IV 203
Greenman Brothers Inc. See Noodle Kidoodle
Greensboro Life Insurance Company, **11** 213
Greenville Insulating Board Corp., III 763

Greenville Tube Corporation, **21** 108
Greenwell Montagu Gilt-Edged, II 319; **17** 325
Greenwich Associates, **19** 117
Greenwich Capital Markets, II 311
Greenwood Mills, Inc., 14 219–21
Greenwood Publishing Group, IV 610
Greenwood Trust Company, **18** 478
Gregg Publishing Co., IV 636
Greif Bros. Corporation, 15 186–88
Grenfell and Colegrave Ltd., II 245
Gresham Life Assurance, III 200, 272–73
GretagMacbeth Holdings AG, **18** 291
Grey Advertising, Inc., I 175, 623; **6 26–28; 10** 69; **14** 150; **22** 396
Grey United Stores, II 666
Greyhound Corp., I **448–50;** II 445; **6** 27; **8** 144–45; **10** 72; **12** 199; **16** 349; **22** 406, 427; **23** 173–74
Greylock Mills, III 213
GRiD Systems Corp., II 107
Griesheim Elektron, IV 140
Grieveson, Grant and Co., II 422–23
Griffin and Sons, II 543
Griffin Pipe Products Co., **7** 30–31
Griffin Wheel Company, **7** 29–30
Griffon Cutlery Corp., **13** 166
Grigg, Elliot & Co., **14** 555
Grimes Aerospace, **22** 32
Grindlays Bank, II 189
Gringoir/Broussard, II 556
Grinnell Corp., III 643–45; **11** 198; **13** 245–47
Grip Printing & Publishing Co., IV 644
Grisewood & Dempsey, IV 616
Grist Mill Company, 15 189–91; 22 338
Gristede Brothers, **23** 407
GRM Industries Inc., **15** 247–48
Grocer Publishing Co., IV 638
Grocery Store Products Co., III 21
Grocery Warehouse, II 602
Groen Manufacturing, III 468
Grogan-Cochran Land Company, **7** 345
Grolier Inc., IV 619; **16 251–54**
Groot-Noordhollandsche, III 177–79
Groovy Beverages, II 477
Gross Brothers Laundry. See G&K Services, Inc.
Gross Townsend Frank Hoffman, **6** 28
Grosset & Dunlap, Inc., II 144; III 190–91
Grosskraftwerk Franken AG, **23** 47
Grossman's Inc., 13 248–50
Grossmith Agricultural Industries, II 500
Grosvenor Marketing Co., II 465
Groton Victory Yard, I 661
Ground Round, Inc., 21 248–51
Ground Services Inc., **13** 49
Group Hospitalization and Medical Services, **10** 161
Group Lotus, **13** 357
Group Schneider S.A., **20** 214
Groupe AB, **19** 204
Groupe AG, III 201–02
Groupe Air France, 6 92–94. See also Air France.
Groupe Ancienne Mutuelle, III 210–11
Groupe André, 17 210–12
Groupe Barthelmey, III 373
Groupe Bull, **10** 563–64; **12** 246; **21** 391. See also Compagnie des Machines Bull.
Groupe Casino. See Etablissements Economiques de Casino Guichard, Perrachon et Cie, S.C.A.

Groupe Castorama-Dubois Investissements, 23 230–32
Groupe Danone, **14** 150
Groupe de la Cité, IV **614–16,** 617
Groupe de la Financière d'Angers, IV 108
Groupe Jean Didier, **12** 413
Groupe Lagardère S.A., **15** 293; **21** 265, 267
Groupe Legris Industries, 23 233–35
Groupe Pinault-Printemps-Redoute, **19** 306, 309; **21** 224, 226
Groupe Promodès S.A., 19 326–28
Groupe Rothschild, **22** 365
Groupe Rougier SA, 21 438–40
Groupe Salvat, IV 619
Groupe Sidel S.A., 21 252–55
Groupe Victoire, III 394
Groupe Vidéotron Ltée., 20 271–73
Groupe Yves Saint Laurent, 23 236–39
Groupement des Exploitants Pétroliers, IV 545
Groupement Laitier du Perche, **19** 50
Groux Beverage Corporation, **11** 451
Grow Biz International, Inc., 18 207–10
Grow Group Inc., 12 217–19, 387–88
Growmark, I 421; **11** 23
Growth International, Inc., **17** 371
Grubb & Ellis Company, 21 256–58
Gruene Apotheke, I 681
Gruma. See Grupo Industrial Maseca S.A.
Grumman Corp., I 58–59, **61–63,** 67–68, 78, 84, 490, 511; **7** 205; **8** 51; **9** 17, 206–07, 417, 460; **10** 316–17, 536; **11 164–67 (upd.),** 363–65, 428; **15** 285
Grün & Bilfinger A.G., I 560–61
Grundig, I 411; II 80, 117; **13** 402–03; **15** 514
Grundig Data Scanner GmbH, **12** 162
Grunenthal, I 240
Gruner + Jahr AG & Co., IV 590, 593; **7** 245; **15** 51; **20** 53; **22** 442; **23** 85
Gruntal & Co., L.L.C., III 263; **20 274–76**
Gruntal Financial Corp., III 264
Grupo Acerero del Norte, **22** 286
Grupo Cabal S.A., **23** 166
Grupo Carso, S.A. de C.V., 14 489; **21 259–61**
Grupo Corvi S.A. de C.V., **7** 115
Grupo de Ingenieria Ecologica (GRIECO), **16** 260
Grupo Financiero Inbursa, **21** 259
Grupo Financiero Serfin, S.A., 19 188–90, 474
Grupo Herdez S.A., **18** 247
Grupo Industrial Alfa, S.A. See Alfa, S.A. de C.V.
Grupo Industrial Bimbo, 19 191–93
Grupo Industrial Maseca S.A., **19** 192
Grupo Irsa, **23** 171
Grupo Nacional Provincial, **22** 285
Grupo Protexa, **16** 210
Grupo Pulsar. See Pulsar Internacional S.A.
Grupo Quan, **19** 192–93
Grupo Televisa, S.A., 9 429; **18 211–14; 19** 10
Grupo Tudor, IV 471
Grupo Zeta, IV 652–53; **7** 392
Gruppo GFT, **22** 123
Gruppo IRI, **V** 325–27
Gryphon Holdings, Inc., 21 262–64
GSG&T, **6** 495
GSI. See Geophysical Service, Inc.

GSI Acquisition Co. L.P., **17** 488
GSR, Inc., **17** 338
GSU. *See* Gulf States Utilities Company.
GT Interactive Software Corp., **19** 405
GTE Corporation, **II** 38, 47, 80; **III** 475; **V** 294–98; **9** 49, 171, 478–80; **10** 19, 97, 431; **11** 500; **14** 259, 433; **15** 192–97 (upd.); **18** 74, 111, 543; **22** 19. *See also* British Columbia Telephone Company.
GTM-Entrepose, **23** 332
GTO. *See* Global Transport Organization.
GTS Duratek, Inc., **13** 367–68
Guangzhou M. C. Packaging, **10** 130
Guaranty Bank & Trust Company, **13** 440
Guaranty Federal Savings & Loan Assoc., **IV** 343
Guaranty Properties Ltd., **11** 258
Guaranty Savings and Loan, **10** 339
Guaranty Trust,
Guaranty Trust Co., **II** 329–32, 428; **IV** 20; **16** 25; **22** 110
Guardian, **III** 721
Guardian Bank, **13** 468
Guardian Federal Savings and Loan Association, **10** 91
Guardian Mortgage Company, **8** 460
Guardian National Bank, **I** 165; **11** 137
Guardian Refrigerator Company. *See* Frigidaire Home Products.
Guardian Royal Exchange Plc, **III** 350; **11** 168–70
Gubor Schokoladen, **15** 221
Guccio Gucci, S.p.A., **12** 281; **15** 198–200
GUD Holdings, Ltd., **17** 106
Guelph Dolime, **IV** 74
Guerlain, **23** 240–42
Guernsey Banking Co., **II** 333
Guess, Inc., **15** 201–03; **17** 466; **23** 309
Guest, Keen and Nettlefolds plc. *See* GKN plc.
Guest Supply, Inc., **18** 215–17
Gueyraud et Fils Cadet, **III** 703
Guild Press, Inc., **13** 559
Guild Wineries, **13** 134
Guilford Industries, **8** 270–72
Guilford Mills Inc., **8** 234–36
Guilford Transportation Industries, Inc., **16** 348, 350
Guinness Peat, **10** 277
Guinness plc, **I** 239, 241, 250–52, 268, 272, 282; **II** 428–29, 610; **9** 100, 449; **10** 399; **13** 454; **18** 62, 501
Gujarat State Fertilizer Co., **III** 513
Gulco Industries, Inc., **11** 194
Güldner Aschaffenburg, **I** 582
Gulf + Western Inc., **I** 418, 451–53, 540; **II** 147, 154–56, 177; **III** 642, 745; **IV** 289, 672; **7** 64; **10** 482; **13** 121, 169, 470; **22** 210
Gulf + Western Industries, **22** 122. *See also* Paramount Communications.
Gulf Air, **6** 63
Gulf Canada Ltd., **I** 216, 262, 264; **IV** 495, 721; **6** 478; **9** 391; **13** 557–58
Gulf Caribbean Marine Lines, **6** 383
Gulf Coast Sportswear Inc., **23** 65
Gulf Energy Development, **22** 107
Gulf Engineering Co. Ltd., **IV** 131
Gulf Exploration Co., **IV** 454
Gulf Marine & Maintenance Offshore Service Company, **22** 276
Gulf Mobile and Northern Railroad, **I** 456

Gulf Mobile and Ohio Railroad, **I** 456; **11** 187
Gulf of Suez Petroleum Co., **IV** 412–14
Gulf Oil Chemical Co., **13** 502
Gulf Oil Corp., **I** 37, 584; **II** 315, 402, 408, 448; **III** 225, 231, 259, 497; **IV** 198, 287, 385–87, 392, 421, 450–51, 466, 470, 472–73, 476, 484, 508, 510, 512, 531, 538, 565, 570, 576; **17** 121–22; **21** 494
Gulf Plains Corp., **III** 471
Gulf Public Service Company, **6** 580
Gulf Resources & Chemical Corp., **15** 464
Gulf States Paper, **IV** 345
Gulf States Steel, **I** 491
Gulf States Utilities Company, **6** 495–97; **12** 99
Gulf United Corp., **III** 194
Gulfstream Aerospace Corp., **7** 205–06; **13** 358
Gulfstream Banks, **II** 336
Gulton Industries Inc., **7** 297; **19** 31
Gummi Werke, **I** 208
Gump's, **7** 286
Gunder & Associates, **12** 553
Gunderson, Inc. *See* The Greenbrier Companies.
Gunfred Group, **I** 387
Gunite Corporation, **23** 306
The Gunlocke Company, **12** 299; **13** 269; **23** 243–45
Gunns Ltd., **II** 482
Gunpowder Trust, **I** 379; **13** 379
Gunter Wulff Automaten, **III** 430
Gunther, S.A., **8** 477
Gupta, **15** 492
Gurneys, Birkbeck, Barclay & Buxton, **II** 235
Gusswerk Paul Saalmann & Sohne, **I** 582
Gustav Schickendanz KG, **V** 165
Gustavus A. Pfeiffer & Co., **I** 710
Gustin-Bacon Group, **16** 8
Gutehoffnungshütte Aktienverein AG, **III** 561, 563; **IV** 104, 201
Guthrie Balfour, **II** 499–500
Gutta Percha Co., **I** 428
Gutteridge, Haskins & Davey, **22** 138
Gutzeit. *See* W. Gutzeit & Co.
Guy Carpenter & Co., **III** 282
Guy Motors, **13** 286
Guy Salmon Service, Ltd., **6** 349
Guyenne et Gascogne, **23** 246–48
GW Utilities Ltd., **I** 264; **6** 478
Gwathmey & Co., **II** 424; **13** 340
Gymboree Corporation, **15** 204–06
Gynecare Inc., **23** 190
Gypsum, Lime, & Alabastine Canada Ltd., **IV** 271

H & R Block, Incorporated, **9** 268–70
H Curry & Sons. *See* Currys Group PLC.
H N Norton Co., **11** 208
H.A. Job, **II** 587
H&D. *See* Hinde & Dauch Paper Company.
H&H Craft & Floral, **17** 322
H. and D.H. Brooks & Co. *See* Brooks Brothers Inc.
H.B. Claflin Company, **V** 139
H.B. Fuller Company, **8** 237–40
H.B. Nickerson & Sons Ltd., **14** 339
H.B. Reese Candy Co., **II** 511
H.B. Tuttle and Company, **17** 355
H.B. Viney Company, Inc., **11** 211

H. Berlind Inc., **16** 388
H.C. Christians Co., **II** 536
H.C. Frick Coke Co., **IV** 573; **7** 550
H.C. Petersen & Co., **III** 417
H.C. Prange Co., **19** 511–12
H.D. Lee Company, Inc. *See* Lee Apparel Company, Inc.
H.D. Pochin & Co., **III** 690
H. Douglas Barclay, **8** 296
H.E. Butt Grocery Co., **13** 251–53
H.E. Moss and Company Tankers Ltd., **23** 161
H.F. Ahmanson & Company, **II** 181–82; **10** 342–44 (upd.)
H. Fairweather and Co., **I** 592
H.G. Anderson Equipment Corporation, **6** 441
H.H. Brown Shoe Company, **18** 60, **18** 62
H.H. Cutler Company, **17** 513
H.H. Robertson, Inc., **19** 366
H. Hackfeld & Co., **I** 417
H. Hamilton Pty, Ltd., **III** 420
H.I. Rowntree and Co., **II** 568
H.J. Green, **II** 556
H.J. Heinz Company, **I** 30–31, 605, 612; **II** 414, 480, 450, 507–09, 547; **III** 21; **7** 382, 448, 576, 578; **8** 499; **10** 151; **11** 171–73 (upd.); **12** 411, 529, 531–32; **13** 383; **21** 55, 500–01; **22** 147
H.J. Justin & Sons. *See* Justin Industries, Inc.
H.K. Ferguson Company, **7** 355
H.K. Porter Company, Inc., **19** 152
H.L. Green Company, Inc., **9** 448
H.L. Judd Co., **III** 628
H.L. Yoh Company, **9** 163
H. Lewis and Sons, **14** 294
H.M. Byllesby & Company, Inc., **6** 539
H.M. Goush Co., **IV** 677–78
H.M. Spalding Electric Light Plant, **6** 592
H. Miller & Sons, Inc., **11** 258
H.O. Houghton & Company, **10** 355
H.P. Foods, **II** 475
H.P. Hood, **7** 17–18
H.P. Smith Paper Co., **IV** 290
H.R. MacMillan Export Co., **IV** 306–08
H. Reeve Angel & Co., **IV** 300
H. Salt Fish and Chips, **13** 320
H.T. Cherry Company, **12** 376
H.V. McKay Proprietary, **III** 651
H.W. Heidmann, **I** 542
H.W. Johns Manufacturing Co., **III** 663, 706–08; **7** 291
H.W. Madison Co., **11** 211
H.W.S. Solutions, **21** 37
H.W. Wilson Company, **17** 152; **23** 440
H. Williams and Co., Ltd., **II** 678
Häagen-Dazs, **II** 556–57, 631; **10** 147; **14** 212, 214; **19** 116
Haake-Beck Brauerei AG, **9** 86
Haas, Baruch & Co. *See* Smart & Final, Inc.
Haas Corp., **I** 481
Haas Publishing Companies, Inc., **22** 442
Haas Wheat & Partners, **15** 357
Habirshaw Cable and Wire Corp., **IV** 177
Habitat/Mothercare PLC. *See* Storehouse PLC.
Hach Co., **14** 309; **18** 218–21
Hachette Filipacchi Medias S.A., **21** 265–67
Hachette S.A., **IV** 614–15, 617–19, 675; **10** 288; **11** 293; **12** 359; **16** 253–54; **17**

399; **21** 266; **22** 441–42; **23** 476. *See also* Matra-Hachette S.A.
Hachmeister, Inc., **II** 508; **11** 172
Hacker-Pschorr Brau, **II** 242
Hadleigh-Crowther, **I** 715
Haemocell, **11** 476
Haemonetics Corporation, 20 277–79
Hafez Insurance Co., **III** 242
Hagemeyer, **18** 180–82
Haggar Corporation, 19 194–96
Haggie, **IV** 91
Hahn Department Stores. *See* Allied Stores Corp.
Hahn, Inc., **17** 9
Haile Mines, Inc., **12** 253
Hain Pure Food Co., **I** 514
Hainaut-Sambre, **IV** 52
A.B. Hakon Swenson, **II** 639
Hakuhodo, Inc., 6 29–31, 48–49; **16** 167
Hakunetsusha & Company, **12** 483
HAL Inc., 6 104; **9 271–73**. *See also* Hawaiian Airlines, Inc.
Halcon International, **IV** 456
Halewood, **21** 246
Halfords Ltd., **IV** 17, 19, 382–83
Halifax Banking Co., **II** 220
Halifax Timber, **I** 335
Hall & Levine Agency, **I** 14
Hall and Co., **III** 737
Hall and Ham River, **III** 739
Hall Bros. Co., **IV** 620–21; **7** 23
Hall Containers, **III** 739
Hall-Mark Electronics, **23** 490
Hallamore Manufacturing Co., **I** 481
La Halle aux Chaussures, **17** 210
Halliburton Company, II 112; **III** 473, **497–500**, 617; **11** 505; **13** 118–19; **17** 417
Hallivet China Clay Co., **III** 690
Hallmark Cards, Inc., IV 620–21; **7** 23–25; **12** 207, 209; **16 255–57 (upd.)**, 427; **18** 67, 69, 213; **21** 426–28; **22** 33, 36
Hallmark Chemical Corp., **8** 386
Hallmark Investment Corp., **21** 92
Haloid Company. *See* Xerox Corporation.
Halsey, Stuart & Co., **II** 431; **III** 276
Halter Marine, **22** 276
Hamada Printing Press, **IV** 326
Hamashbir Lata'asiya, **II** 47
Hambrecht & Quist, **10** 463, 504
Hambro American Bank & Trust Co., **11** 109
Hambro Life Assurance Ltd., **I** 426; **III** 339
Hambros Bank, **II** 422; **16** 14
Hamburg-Amerikanische-Packetfahrt-Actien-Gesellschaft, **6** 397–98
Hamburg Banco, **II** 351
Hamburg-Amerika, **I** 542
Hamburger Flugzeubau GmbH., **I** 74
Hamelin Group, Inc., **19** 415
Hamer Hammer Service, Inc., **11** 523
Hamersley Holdings, **IV** 59–61
Hamilton Aero Manufacturing, **I** 47, 84; **10** 162
Hamilton Beach/Proctor-Silex Inc., 7 369–70; **16** 384; **17 213–15**
Hamilton Blast Furnace Co., **IV** 208
Hamilton Brown Shoe Co., **III** 528
Hamilton Group Limited, **15** 478
Hamilton Malleable Iron Co., **IV** 73
Hamilton National Bank, **13** 465

Hamilton Oil Corp., **IV** 47; **22** 107
Hamilton Standard, **9** 417
Hamilton Steel and Iron Co., **IV** 208
Hamilton/Hall-Mark, **19** 313
Hamish Hamilton, **IV** 659; **8** 526
Hammacher Schlemmer & Company, 21 268–70
Hammamatsu Commerce Bank, **II** 291
Hammarplast, **13** 493
Hammarsforsens Kraft, **IV** 339
Hammerich & Lesser, **IV** 589
Hammermill Paper Co., **IV** 287; **15** 229; **23** 48–49
Hammers Plastic Recycling, **6** 441
Hammerson Property Investment and Development Corporation PLC, IV 696–98
Hammery Furniture Company, **14** 302–03
Hamming-Whitman Publishing Co., **13** 559
Hammond Corp., **IV** 136
Hammond Lumber Co., **IV** 281; **9** 259
Hammond's, **II** 556
Hammonton Electric Light Company, **6** 449
Hamomag AG, **III** 546
Hampton Industries, Inc., 20 280–82
Hampton Inns, **9** 425–26
Han Kook Fertilizer Co., **I** 516
Hanbury, Taylor, Lloyd and Bowman, **II** 306
Hancock Fabrics, Inc., 16 197–99; **18 222–24**
Hancock Holding Company, 15 207–09
Hancock Jaffe Laboratories, **11** 460
Hancock Park Associates. *See* Leslie's Poolmart, Inc.
Hand in Hand, **III** 234
Handelsbank of Basel, **III** 375
Handelsfinanz Bank of Geneva, **II** 319; **17** 324
Handelsmaatschappij Montan N.V., **IV** 127
Handelsunion AG, **IV** 222
Handleman Company, 15 210–12
Handley Page Transport Ltd., **I** 50, 92–93
Handy & Harman, 23 249–52
Handy Andy Home Improvement Centers, Inc., **16** 210
Handy Dan, **V** 75
Hanes Corp., **II** 572–73; **8** 202, 288; **15** 436
Hanes Holding Company, **11** 256
Hang Chong, **18** 114
Hang Seng Bank, **II** 298; **IV** 717
Hanil Development Company, **6** 98
Hanjin Group, **6** 98
Hankook Tyre Manufacturing Company, **V** 255–56; **19** 508
Hankuk Glass Industry Co., **III** 715
Hankyu Corporation, V 454–56; 23 253–56 (upd.)
Hankyu Department Stores, Inc., V 70–71
Hanley Brick, **14** 250
Hanmi Citizen Precision Industry, **III** 455
Hanna Iron Ore Co., **IV** 236
Hanna Mining Co., **8** 346–47
Hanna Ore Mining Company, **12** 352
Hanna-Barbera Cartoons Inc., 7 306; **18** 65; **23** 257–59, 387
Hannaford Bros. Co., 12 220–22
Hannen Brauerei GmbH, **9** 100
Hannifin Corp., **III** 602
Hannoversche Bank, **II** 278
Hanover Bank, **II** 312–13

Hanovia Co., **IV** 78
Hanrstoffe-und Düngemittelwerk Saar-Lothringen GmbH, **IV** 197
Hans Grohe, **III** 570; **20** 362
Hanseco Reinsurance Co., **III** 343
Hanson PLC, I 438, 475, 477; **II** 319; **III** 501–03, 506; **IV** 23, 94, 97, 169, 171, 173, 290; **7 207–10 (upd.)**; **8** 224; **13** 478–79; **17** 39–40, 325; **18** 548; **21** 545; **22** 211; **23** 296–97
Hapag-Lloyd Ag, 6 397–99
Happy Air Exchangers Ltd., **21** 499
Happy Eater Ltd., **III** 106
Haralambos Beverage Corporation, **11** 451
Harald Quant Group, **III** 377
Harbert Corporation, 13 98; **14 222–23**
Harbison-Walker, **III** 472
Harbor Tug and Barge Co., **6** 382
Harborlite Corporation, **10** 45
Harcourt Brace and Co., IV 622; **12 223–26**
Harcourt Brace Jovanovich, Inc., II 133–34; **III** 118; **IV 622–24**, 642, 672; **7** 312; **12** 224; **13** 106; **14** 177; **19** 404
Harcourt General, Inc., 12 226; **20 283–87 (upd.)**
Harcros Chemical Group, **III** 699
Harcros Investment Trust Ltd., **III** 698–99
Hard Rock Cafe International, Inc., 12 227–29
Hardee's Food Systems Inc., **II** 679; **7** 430; **8** 564; **9** 178; **15** 345; **16** 95; **19** 93; **23** 505
Hardin Stockton, **21** 96
Harding Lawson Associates Group, Inc., 16 258–60
Hardison & Stewart Oil, **IV** 569
Hardman Inc., **III** 699
Hardware Wholesalers Inc., **12** 8
Hardwick Stove Company, **III** 573; **22** 349
Hardy Spicer, **III** 595
Harima Shipbuilding & Engineering Co., Ltd., **I** 511, 534; **III** 513, 533; **12** 484
Harima Zosenjo, Ltd., **IV** 129
Harken Energy Corporation, **17** 169–70
Harland and Wolff Holdings plc, 19 197–200
Harlem Globetrotters, **7** 199, 335
Harlequin Enterprises Ltd., **IV** 587, 590, 617, 619, 672; **19** 405
Harley-Davidson Inc., III 658; **7 211–14**; **13** 513; **16** 147–49; **21** 153; **23** 299–301
Harlow Metal Co. Ltd., **IV** 119
Harman International Industries Inc., 15 213–15
Harmon Publishing Company, **12** 231
Harmsworth Brothers, **17** 396
Harmsworth Publishing, **19** 118, 120
Harnischfeger Industries, Inc., I 186; **8 241–44; 14** 56
Harold A. Wilson & Co., **I** 405
Harold's Stores, Inc., 22 248–50
Harp Lager Ltd., **15** 442
Harper Group Inc., 12 180; **13** 20; **17 216–19**
Harper House, Inc. *See* Day Runner, Inc.
Harper Robinson and Company, **17** 163
HarperCollins Publishers, IV 652; **7** 389, 391; **14** 555–56; **15 216–18; 23** 156, 210
Harpers, Inc., **12** 298
Harrah's Entertainment, Inc., 9 425–27; **16 261–63**
Harrell International, **III** 21; **22** 146

Harriman Co., **IV** 310; **19** 266
Harriman, Ripley and Co., **II** 407
Harris Abattoir Co., **II** 482
Harris Adacom Corporation B.V., **21** 239
Harris Bankcorp, **II** 211
Harris Corporation, **II** 37–39; **11** 46, 286, 490; **20 288–92 (upd.)**
Harris Daishowa (Australia) Pty., Ltd., **IV** 268
Harris Financial, Inc., **11** 482
Harris Laboratories, **II** 483; **14** 549
Harris Microwave Semiconductors, **14** 417
Harris Oil Company, **17** 170
Harris Pharmaceuticals Ltd., **11** 208
Harris Publications, **13** 179
Harris Teeter Inc., **23 260–62**
Harris Transducer Corporation, **10** 319
Harris-Emery Co., **19** 510
Harrisburg National Bank and Trust Co., **II** 315–16
Harrison & Sons (Hanley) Ltd., **III** 681
Harrisons & Crosfield plc, **III 696–700**
Harrods, **21** 353
Harrow Stores Ltd., **II** 677
Harry F. Allsman Co., **III** 558
Harry Ferguson Co., **III** 651
Harry N. Abrams, Inc., **IV** 677; **17** 486
Harry's Farmers Market Inc., **23 263–66**
Harsco Corporation, **8 245–47**; **11** 135
Harshaw Chemical Company, **9** 154; **17** 363
Harshaw/Filtrol Partnership, **IV** 80
Hart Glass Manufacturing, **III** 423
Hart Press, **12** 25
Hart, Schaffner & Marx, **8** 248–49
Hart Son and Co., **I** 592
Harte & Co., **IV** 409; **7** 308
Harte-Hanks Communications, Inc., **17 220–22**
Harter Bank & Trust, **9** 474–75
Hartford Container Company, **8** 359
Hartford Electric Light Co., **13** 183
Hartford Fire Insurance, **11** 198
Hartford Insurance Group, **I** 463–64; **22** 428
Hartford Machine Screw Co., **12** 344
Hartford National Bank and Trust Co., **13** 396
Hartford National Corporation, **13** 464, 466–67
Hartford Trust Co., **II** 213
Hartley's, **II** 477
Hartmann & Braun, **III** 566
Hartmann Fibre, **12** 377
Hartmann Luggage, **12** 313
Hartmarx Corporation, **8 248–50**
The Hartstone Group plc, **14 224–26**
The Hartz Mountain Corporation, **12 230–32**
Harvard Sports, Inc., **19** 144
Harvard Table Tennis, Inc., **19** 143–44
Harvest International, **III** 201
Harvestore, **11** 5
Harvey Aluminum Inc., **I** 68; **22** 188
Harvey Benjamin Fuller, **8** 237–38
Harvey Group, **19** 312
Harvey Hotel Corporation, **23** 71, 73
Harvey Lumber and Supply Co., **III** 559
Harza Engineering Company, **14 227–28**
Hasbro, Inc., **III 504–06**; **IV** 676; **7** 305, 529; **12** 168–69, 495; **13** 561; **16 264–68 (upd.)**; **17** 243; **18** 520–21; **21** 375
Hasler Holding AG, **9** 32

Hassenfeld Brothers Inc., **III** 504
Hasten Bancorp, **11** 371
Hastings Filters, Inc., **17** 104
Hastings Manufacturing Company, **17** 106
Hatersley & Davidson, **16** 80
Hathaway Manfacturing Co., **III** 213
Hathaway Shirt Co., **I** 25–26
Hattori Seiko Co., Ltd. See Seiko Corporation.
Havas, SA, **IV** 616; **10** 195–96, **345–48**; **13** 203–04
Haven Automation International, **III** 420
Haviland Candy Co., **15** 325
Hawaii National Bank, **11** 114
Hawaiian Airlines Inc., **9** 271–73; **22 251–53 (upd.)**. See also HAL Inc.
Hawaiian Dredging & Construction Co., **I** 565–66
Hawaiian Electric Industries, Inc., **9 274–77**
Hawaiian Fertilizer Co., **II** 490
Hawaiian Pineapple Co., **II** 491
Hawaiian Tug & Barge, **9** 276
Hawaiian Tuna Packers, **II** 491
Hawker Siddeley Group Public Limited Company, **I** 41–42, 50, 71, 470; **III 507–10**; **8** 51; **12** 190; **20** 311
Hawkeye Cablevision, **II** 161
Hawkins Chemical, Inc., **16 269–72**
Hawley & Hazel Chemical Co., **III** 25
Hawley Group Limited, **12** 10
Hawley Products, **16** 20
Haworth Inc., **8 251–52**
Hawthorn Company, **8** 287
Hawthorn-Mellody, **I** 446; **11** 25
Hawthorne Appliance and Electronics, **10** 9–11
Haxton Foods Inc., **21** 155
Hay Group, **I** 33
Hayakawa Electrical Industries, **II** 95–96
Hayakawa Metal Industrial Laboratory, **II** 95; **12** 447
Hayaku Zenjiro, **III** 408
Hayama Oil, **IV** 542
Hayashi Kane Shoten, **II** 578
Hayashikane Shoten K.K., **II** 578
Hayden Clinton National Bank, **11** 180
Hayden Stone, **II** 450; **9** 468
Hayes Industries Inc., **16** 7
Hayes Microcomputer Products, **9** 515
Hayes Wheel Company, **7** 258
Hayne, Miller & Swearingen, Inc., **22** 202
Hays Petroleum Services, **IV** 451
Hazard, **I** 328
HAZCO International, Inc., **9** 110
Hazel Bishop, **III** 55
Hazel-Atlas Glass Co., **I** 599; **15** 128
Hazell Sun Ltd., **IV** 642; **7** 312
Hazeltine, Inc., **II** 20
Hazlenut Growers of Oregon, **7** 496–97
HBO. See Home Box Office Inc.
HCA Management Co., **III** 79
HCA Psychiatric Co., **III** 79
HCI Holdings, **I** 264
HCL America, **10** 505
HCL Sybase, **10** 505
HDM Worldwide Direct, **13** 204; **16** 168
HDR Inc., **I** 563
HDS. See Heartland Express, Inc.
Head Sportswear International, **15** 368; **16** 296–97
Heads and Threads, **10** 43
Heal's, **13** 307
Heald Machine Co., **12** 67

Healey & Baker, **IV** 705
Health & Tennis Corp., **III** 431
Health Care & Retirement Corporation, **III** 79; **22 254–56**
Health Care International, **13** 328
Health Maintenance Organization of Pennsylvania. See U.S. Healthcare, Inc.
Health Maintenance Organizations, **I** 545
Health Management Center West, **17** 559
Health O Meter Products Inc., **14 229–31**; **15** 307
Health Plan of America, **11** 379
Health Plan of Virginia, **III** 389
Health Products Inc., **I** 387
Health Services, Inc., **10** 160
Health Systems International, Inc., **11 174–76**
Health Way, Inc., **II** 538
Health-Mor Inc. See HMI Industries.
HealthAmerica Corp., **III** 84
HealthCare USA, **III** 84, 86
HealthCo International, Inc., **19** 290
Healthdyne, Inc., **17** 306–09
Healthshares L.L.C., **18** 370
Healthsource Inc., **22** 143
HealthSouth Rehabilitation Corporation, **14 232–34**
Healthtex, Inc., **17 223–25**, 513
HealthTrust, **III** 80; **15** 112
Healthy Choice, **12** 531
The Hearst Corporation, **IV** 582, 596, 608, **625–27**; **12** 358–59; **19 201–204 (upd.)**; **21** 404; **22** 161
Hearthstone Insurance Co. of Massachusetts, **III** 203
Heartland Building Products, **II** 582
Heartland Components, **III** 519; **22** 282
Heartland Express, Inc., **13** 550–51; **18 225–27**
Heartstream Inc., **18** 423
Heat Transfer Pty. Ltd., **III** 420
Heatcraft Inc., **8** 320–22
Heath Co., **II** 124; **13** 573
Heath Steele Mines Ltd., **IV** 18
Heatilator Inc., **13** 269
Heavy Duty Parts, Inc., **19** 37
Hebrew National Kosher Foods, **III** 24
Hechinger Company, **12 233–36**
Hecker-H-O Co., **II** 497
Heckett Technology Services Inc., **8** 246–47
Hecla Mining Company, **17** 363; **20** 149, **293–96**
Heco Envelope Co., **IV** 282; **9** 261
Heekin Can Inc., **10** 130; **13 254–56**
HEFCO, **17** 106
Hefei Rongshida Group Corporation, **22** 350
HEI Investment Corp., **9** 276
The Heico Companies, **15** 380
Heidelberg, **III** 701
Heidelberger Zement A.G., **23** 325–26
Heidelburger Drueck, **III** 301
Heidi Bakery, **II** 633
Heidrick & Struggles, **14** 464
Hcights of Texas, fsb, **8** 437
Heil-Quaker Corp., **III** 654
Heileman Brewing Co. See G. Heileman Brewing Co.
Heilig-Meyers Co., **14 235–37**; **23** 412, 414
Heimstatt Bauspar AG, **III** 401

Heineken N.V., I 219, **256–58**, 266, 288; **II** 642; **13 257–59 (upd.); 14** 35; **17** 256; **18** 72; **21** 319
Heinkel Co., **I** 74
Heinrich Bauer North America, **7** 42–43
Heinrich Bauer Verlag, **23** 85–86
Heinrich Koppers GmbH, **IV** 89
Heinrich Lanz, **III** 463; **21** 173
Heinz Co. *See* H.J. Heinz Company.
Heinz Deichert KG, **11** 95
Heinz Italia S.p.A., **15** 221
Heisers Inc., **I** 185
Heisey Glasswork Company, **19** 210
Heiwa Sogo Bank, **II** 326, 361
Heizer Corp., **III** 109–11; **14** 13–15
HEL&P. *See* Houston Electric Light & Power Company.
Helados La Menorquina S.A., **22** 515
Helemano Co., **II** 491
Helen of Troy Corporation, 18 228–30
Helen's Arts & Crafts, **17** 321
Helena Rubenstein, Inc., **III** 24, 48; **8** 343–44; **9** 201–02; **14** 121
Helene Curtis Industries, Inc., I 403; **8 253–54; 18** 217; **22** 487
Helix Biocore, **11** 458
Hellefors Jernverk, **III** 623
Heller Financial, Inc., **7** 213; **16** 37
Hellman, Haas & Co. *See* Smart & Final, Inc.
Hellschreiber, **IV** 669
Helly-Hansen A/S, **18** 396
Helme Products, Inc., **15** 139
Helmerich & Payne, Inc., 18 231–33
Helmsley Enterprises, Inc., 9 278–80
Helmut Delhey, **6** 428
Helmuth Hardekopf Bunker GmbH, **7** 141
Help-U-Sell, Inc., **III** 304
Helvetia General, **III** 376
Helvetia Milk Condensing Co., **II** 486; **7** 428
Helvetia Schweizerische Feuerversicherungs-Gesellschaft St. Gallen, **III** 375
Hely Group, **IV** 294; **19** 225
Helzberg's Diamond Shops, **18** 60, 63
Hemelinger Aktienbrauerei, **9** 86
Hemex, **11** 458
Hemlo Gold Mines Inc., 9 281–82; 23 40, 42
Hemma, **IV** 616
A.B. Hemmings, Ltd., **II** 465
Henderson's Industries, **III** 581
Henderson-Union Electric Cooperative, **11** 37
Henijean & Cie, **III** 283
Henkel KGaA, III 21, **31–34**, 45; **IV** 70; **9** 382; **13** 197, 199; **22** 145, 257
Henkel Manco Inc., 22 257–59
Henley Drilling Company, **9** 364
The Henley Group, Inc., I 416; **III 511–12; 6** 599–600; **9** 298; **11** 435; **12** 325; **17** 20
Hennessy Company, **19** 272
Henney Motor Company, **12** 159
Henredon Furniture Industries, **III** 571; **11** 534; **20** 362
Henri Bendel Inc., **17** 203–04
Henry Broderick, Inc., **21** 96
Henry Grant & Co., **I** 604
Henry Holt & Co., **IV** 622–23; **13** 105
Henry I. Siegel Co., **20** 136
Henry J. Tully Corporation, **13** 531
The Henry Jones Co-op Ltd., **7** 577

Henry Jones Foods, **I** 437–38, 592; **7** 182; **11** 212
Henry L. Doherty & Company, **IV** 391; **12** 542
Henry Lee Company, **16** 451, 453
Henry, Leonard & Thomas Inc., **9** 533
Henry Meadows, Ltd., **13** 286
Henry Pratt Company, **7** 30–31
Henry S. King & Co., **II** 307
Henry S. Miller Companies, **21** 257
Henry Tate & Sons, **II** 580
Henry Telfer, **II** 513
Henry Waugh Ltd., **I** 469; **20** 311
Henthy Realty Co., **III** 190
HEPCO. *See* Hokkaido Electric Power Company Inc.
Her Majesty's Stationery Office, 7 215–18
Heraeus Holding GmbH, IV 98–100, 118
Herald and Weekly Times, **IV** 650, 652; **7** 389, 391
Herald Publishing Company, **12** 150
Heralds of Liberty, **9** 506
Herbalife International, Inc., 17 226–29; 18 164
Herbert W. Davis & Co., **III** 344
Herco Technology, **IV** 680
Hercofina, **IV** 499
Hercules Filter, **III** 419
Hercules Inc., I 343–45, 347; **III** 241; **19** 11, **22 260–63 (upd.)**
Hercules Nut Corp., **II** 593
Hereford Paper and Allied Products Ltd., **14** 430
Herff Jones, **II** 488
Heritage Bankcorp, **9** 482
Heritage Communications, **II** 160–61
Heritage Federal Savings and Loan Association of Huntington, **10** 92
Heritage House of America Inc., **III** 81
Heritage Life Assurance, **III** 248
Heritage National Health Plan, **III** 464
Heritage Springfield, **14** 245
Herman Miller, Inc., 8 251–52, **255–57**
Herman's World of Sports, **I** 548; **II** 628–29; **15** 470; **16** 457
Hermannshütte, **IV** 103, 105
Hermes Kreditversicherungsbank, **III** 300
Hermès S.A., 14 238–40
Herrburger Brooks P.L.C., **12** 297
Herrick, Waddell & Reed. *See* Waddell & Reed, Inc.
Herring-Hall-Marvin Safe Co. of Hamilton, Ohio, **7** 145
Hersey Products, Inc., **III** 645
Hershey Bank, **II** 342
Hershey Foods Corporation, I 26–27; **II** 478, 508, **510–12**, 569; **7** 300; **11** 15; **12** 480–81; **15** 63–64, **219–22 (upd.),** 323
Hertel AG, **13** 297
Hertford Industrial Estates, **IV** 724
Hertie Waren- und Kaufhaus GmbH, V 72–74; 19 234, 237
Herts & Beds Petroleum Co., **IV** 566
Herts Pharmaceuticals, **17** 450
The Hertz Corporation, I 130; **II** 90; **6** 52, 129, 348–50, 356–57, 392–93; **V** 494; **9 283–85; 10** 419; **11** 494; **16** 379; **21** 151; **22** 54, 56, 524
Hertz-Penske Leasing. *See* Penske Corporation.
Hespeler Hockey Inc., **22** 204
Hess Department Stores Inc., **16** 61–62; **19** 323–24

Hess Oil & Chemical Corp., **IV** 366
Hessische Berg- und Hüttenwerke AG, **III** 695
Hessische Landesbank, **II** 385–86
Hessische Ludwigs-Eisenbahn-Gesellschaft, **6** 424
Hesston Corporation, **13** 17; **22** 380
Hetteen Hoist & Derrick. *See* Polaris Industries Inc.
Heublein Inc., I 226, 246, 249, **259–61**, 281; **7** 266–67; **10** 180; **14** 214; **21** 314–15
Heuga Holdings B.V., **8** 271
Hewitt & Tuttle, **IV** 426; **17** 355–56
Hewitt Motor Company, **I** 177; **22** 329
Hewlett-Packard Company, II 62; **III** 116, **142–43; 6** 219–20, 225, **237–39 (upd.),** 244, 248, 278–79, 304; **8** 139, 467; **9** 7, 35–36, 57, 115, 471; **10** 15, 34, 86, 232, 257, 363, 404, 459, 464, 499, 501; **11** 46, 234, 274, 284, 382, 491, 518; **12** 61, 147, 162, 183, 470; **13** 128, 326, 501; **14** 354; **15** 125; **16** 5, 139–40, 299, 301, 367, 394, 550; **18** 386–87, 434, 436, 571; **19** 515; **20** 8
Hexatec Polymers, **III** 742
Hexcel Medical Corporation, **11** 475
Heyden Newport Chemical Corp., **I** 526
HFC. *See* Household Finance Corporation.
HFS Inc., **21** 97; **22** 54, 56
HG Hawker Engineering Co. Ltd., **III** 508
HGCC. *See* Hysol Grafil Composite Components Co.
HI. *See* Houston Industries Incorporated.
Hi Tech Consignments, **18** 208
Hi-Bred Corn Company, **9** 410
Hi-Mirror Co., **III** 715
Hi-Tek Polymers, Inc., **8** 554
Hibbing Transportation, **I** 448
Hibernia & Shamrock-Bergwerksgesellschaft zu Berlin, **I** 542–43
Hibernia Bank, **18** 181
Hibernian Banking Assoc., **II** 261
Hickory Farms, Inc., 12 178, 199; **17 230–32**
Hickorycraft, **III** 571; **20** 362
Hicks & Greist, **6** 40
Hicks & Haas, **II** 478
Hicksgas Gifford, Inc., **6** 529
Hidden Creek Industries, Inc., **16** 397
Higginson et Hanckar, **IV** 107
Higgs & Young Inc., **I** 412
High Point Chemical Corp., **III** 38
High Retail System Co., Ltd., **V** 195
Highgate Hotels, Inc., **21** 93
Highland Container Co., **IV** 345
Highland Superstores, **9** 65–66; **10** 9–10, 304–05, 468; **23** 51–52
Highland Telephone Company, **6** 334
Highlands Insurance Co., **III** 498
Highmark International, **I** 109
Highveld Steel and Vanadium Corp., **IV** 22
Higo Bank, **II** 291
Hilbun Poultry, **10** 250
Hilco Technologies, **III** 143; **6** 238
Hilex Poly Co., Inc., **8** 477
Hill & Knowlton Inc. *See* WPP Group PLC.
Hill Publishing Co., **IV** 634
Hill Stores, **II** 683
Hill's Pet Nutrition, **14** 123
Hill-Rom Company, **10** 349–50
Hillard Oil and Gas Company, Inc., **11** 523

Hillards, PLC, **II** 678
Hillenbrand Industries, Inc., 6 295; **10 349–51; 16** 20
Hiller Aircraft Company, **9** 205
Hiller Group, **14** 286
The Hillhaven Corporation, III 76, 87–88; **6** 188; **14 241–43; 16** 57, 515, 517
Hillin Oil, **IV** 658
Hillman, **I** 183
Hills & Dales Railway Co. *See* Dayton Power & Light Company.
Hills Brothers Inc., **II** 548; **7** 383
Hills Pet Products, **III** 25
Hills Stores Company, 11 228; **13 260–61; 21** 459
Hillsborough Holdings Corporation. *See* Walter Industries, Inc.
Hillsdale Machine & Tool Company, **8** 514
Hillsdown Holdings, PLC, II 513–14
Hillshire Farm, **II** 572
Hillside Industries Inc., **18** 118
Hilo Electric Light Company, **9** 276
Hilton, Anderson and Co., **III** 669
Hilton Athletic Apparel, **16** 296–97
Hilton Gravel, **III** 670
Hilton Hotels Corporation, II 208; **III** 91–93, 98–99, 102; **IV** 703; **6** 201, 210; **9** 95, 426; **19 205–08 (upd.); 21** 91, 93, 182, 333, 363; **23** 482
Hilton International Co., **6** 385; **12** 489
Himley Brick, **14** 248
Himolene, Inc., **8** 181
Hinde & Dauch Ltd., **IV** 272
Hinde & Dauch Paper Company, **19** 496
Hindell's Dairy Farmers Ltd., **II** 611–12
Hinds, Hayden & Eldredge, **10** 135
Hindustan Petroleum Corp. Ltd., **IV** 441
Hindustan Shipyard, **IV** 484
Hindustan Steel Ltd., **IV** 205–07
Hino Motors, Ltd., 7 219–21; 21 163, **271–74 (upd.); 23** 288
Hinode Life Insurance Co., Ltd., **II** 360; **III** 365
Hinomaru Truck Co., **6** 428
HIP Health Plan, **22** 425
Hip Hing Construction, **IV** 717
Hipercor, S.A., **V** 52
Hiram Walker Resources Ltd., I 216, **262–64; IV** 721; **6** 478; **9** 391; **18** 41
Hiram Walker-Consumers' Home Ltd. *See* Consumers' Gas Company Ltd.
Hire-Purchase Company, **16** 13
The Hirsh Company, **17** 279
Hirth-Krause Company. *See* Wolverine World Wide Inc.
Hispanica de Petroleos, **IV** 424, 527, 546
Hispano Aviacion, **I** 74
HISPANOBRAS, **IV** 55
Hispanoil. *See* Hispanica de Petroleos.
Hispeed Tools, **I** 573
Hisshin-DCA foods, **II** 554
History Book Club, **13** 105–06
Hit, **II** 164
Hit or Miss, **V** 197–98
Hitachi, Ltd., I 454–55, 494, 534; **II** 5, 30, 59, 64–65, 68, 70, 73, 75, 114, 273–74, 292–91; **III** 130, 140, 143, 464, 482; **IV** 101; **6** 238, 262; **7** 425; **9** 297; **11** 45, 308, 507; **12 237–39 (upd.),** 484; **14** 201; **16** 139; **17** 353, 556; **18** 383; **19** 11; **21** 174–75, 390; **23** 53
Hitachi Metals, Ltd., IV 101–02

Hitachi Zosen Corporation, III 513–14; **8** 449
Hitchiner Manufacturing Co., Inc., 23 267–70
Hitco, **III** 721–22
Hjalmar Blomqvist A.B., **II** 639
HL&P. *See* Houston Lighting and Power Company.
HLH Products, **7** 229
HMI Industries, Inc., 17 233–35
HMO-PA. *See* U.S. Healthcare, Inc.
HMT Technology Corp., **IV** 102
HMV, **I** 531
Hoare Govett Ltd., **II** 349
Hobart Corporation, **II** 534; **III** 610–11, 654; **7** 276; **12** 549; **22** 282, 353
Hobart Manufacturing Company, **8** 298
Hobbes Manufacturing, **I** 169–70
Hobby Lobby Stores Inc., **17** 360
Hobson, Bates & Partners, Ltd., **14** 48
Hochschild, Kohn Department Stores, **II** 673
Hochtief AG, **14** 298; **17** 376
Hocking Glass Company, **13** 40
Hoden Oil, **IV** 478
Hodenpyl-Walbridge & Company, **14** 134
Hodgkin, Barnett, Pease, Spence & Co., **II** 307
Hoechst AG, I 305–06, 309, 317, **346–48,** 605, 632, 669–70; **IV** 451; **8** 262, 451–53; **13** 75, 262–64; **18** 47, 49, 51, **234–37 (upd.),** 401; **21** 544; **22** 32
Hoechst Celanese Corporation, 8 562; **11** 436; **12** 118; **13** 118, **262–65; 22** 278
Hoeganaes Corporation, **8** 274–75
Hoerner Waldorf Corp., **IV** 264; **20** 129
Hoesch AG, IV 103–06, 128, 133, 195, 228, 232, 323
Hoffmann-La Roche & Co. *See* F. Hoffmann-La Roche & Co.
Högbo Stål & Jernwerks, **IV** 202
Högforsin Tehdas Osakeyhtiö, **IV** 300
Hojalata y Laminas S.A., **19** 10
Hokkaido Butter Co., **II** 575
Hokkaido Colonial Bank, **II** 310
Hokkaido Dairy Cooperative, **II** 574
Hokkaido Dairy Farm Assoc., **II** 538
Hokkaido Electric Power Company Inc., V 635–37
Hokkaido Forwarding, **6** 428
Hokkaido Rakuno Kosha Co., **II** 574
Hokkaido Takushoku Bank, **II** 300
Hokoku Cement, **III** 713
Hokoku Fire, **III** 384
Hokuetsu Paper Manufacturing, **IV** 327
Hokuriku Electric Power Company, V 638–40
Hokusin Kai, **IV** 475
Hokuyo Sangyo Co., Ltd., **IV** 285
Holbrook Grocery Co., **II** 682
Holcroft & Company, **7** 521
Hold Everything, **17** 548–50
Holden Group, **II** 457
Holderbank Financière Glaris Ltd., III 701–02; 8 258–59, 456
Holdernam Inc., **8** 258–59
N.V. Holdingmaatschappij De Telegraaf, 23 271–73
Holga, Inc., **13** 269
Holiday Corp., **16** 263; **22** 418
Holiday Inns, Inc., I 224; **III 94–95,** 99–100; **6** 383; **9** 425–26; **10** 12; **11** 178, 242; **13** 362; **14** 106; **15** 44, 46; **16**

262; **18** 216; **21** 361–62; **23** 71. *See also* The Promus Cos., Inc.
Holiday Magic, Inc., **17** 227
Holiday Mart, **17** 124
Holiday Rambler Corporation, **7** 213
Holland & Barrett, **13** 103
Holland America Line, **6** 367–68
Holland Casino, **23** 229
Holland Electro B.V., **17** 234
Holland Hannen and Cubitts, **III** 753
Holland House, **I** 377–78
Holland Motor Express, **14** 505
Holland van 1859, **III** 200
Hollandsche Bank-Unie, **II** 184–85
Hollandse Signaalapparaten, **13** 402
Holley Carburetor, **I** 434
Hollingsworth & Whitney Co., **IV** 329
Hollostone, **III** 673
Holly Corporation, 12 240–42
Holly Farms Corp., **II** 585; **7** 422–24; **14** 515; **23** 376–77
Holly Sugar Company. *See* Imperial Holly Corporation.
Hollywood Casino Corporation, 21 275–77
Hollywood Park, Inc., 20 297–300
Hollywood Pictures, **II** 174
Hollywood Records, **6** 176
Holmen Hygiene, **IV** 315
Holmen S.A., **IV** 325
Holmens Bruk, **IV** 317–18
Holmes Electric Protective Co., **III** 644
Holmsund & Kramfors, **IV** 338
Holnam Inc., III 702; **8 258–60**
Holophane Corporation, 19 209–12
Holson Burnes Group, Inc., 14 244–45
Holt Manufacturing Co., **III** 450–51
Holt, Rinehart and Winston, Inc., **IV** 623–24; **12** 224
Holthouse Furniture Corp., **14** 236
Holvick Corp., **11** 65
Holvis AG, **15** 229
Holyoke Food Mart Inc., **19** 480
Holzer and Co., **III** 569; **20** 361
Holzverkohlungs-Industrie AG, **IV** 70
Homart Development, **V** 182
Home & Automobile Insurance Co., **III** 214
Home Box Office Inc., II 134, 136, 166–67, 176–77; **IV** 675; **7 222–24,** 528–29; **10** 196; **12** 75; **18** 65; **23 274–77 (upd.),** 500
Home Builders Supply, Inc. *See* Scotty's, Inc.
Home Centers of America, Inc., **18** 286
Home Charm Group PLC, **II** 141
The Home Depot, Inc., V 75–76; 9 400; **10** 235; **11** 384–86; **12** 7, 235, 345, 385; **13** 250, 548; **16** 187–88, 457; **17** 366; **18 238–40 (upd.); 19** 248, 250; **21** 356, 358; **22** 477; **23** 232
Home Furnace Co., **I** 481
Home Insurance Company, I 440; **III 262–64**
Home Interiors, **15** 475, 477
Home Nutritional Services, **17** 308
Home Office Reference Laboratory, Inc., **22** 266
Home Oil Company Ltd., **I** 264; **6** 477–78
Home Products Corp., **18** 492
Home Properties Co., Inc., **21** 95
Home Quarters Warehouse, Inc., **12** 233, 235

Home Savings of America, **II** 181–82; **10** 342–43; **16** 346

Home Shopping Network, Inc., V 77–78; 9 428; **18** 76

Home Telephone and Telegraph Company, **10** 201

Home Telephone Company. *See* Rochester Telephone Corporation.

Homebase, **II** 658; **13** 547–48

HomeClub Inc., **13** 547–48; **16** 187; **17** 366

Homécourt, **IV** 226

HomeFed Bank, **10** 340

Homelite, **21** 175

Homemade Ice Cream Company, **10** 371

Homemakers Furniture. *See* John M. Smyth Co.

Homer McKee Advertising, **I** 22

Homes By Oakwood, Inc., **15** 328

Homestake Mining Company, IV 18, 76; **12 243–45; 20** 72

HomeTown Buffet, Inc., **19** 435; **22** 465

Homewood Stores Co., **IV** 573; **7** 550

Homewood Suites, **9** 425–26

Hominal Developments Inc., **9** 512

Hon Industries Inc., 13 266–69; 23 243–45

Honam Oil Refinery, **II** 53

Honcho Real Estate, **IV** 225

Honda Giken Kogyo Kabushiki Kaisha. *See* Honda Motor Company Limited.

Honda Motor Company Limited, I 9–10, 32, **174–76,** 184, 193; **II** 5; **III** 495, 517, 536, 603, 657–58, 667; **IV** 443; **7** 212–13, 459; **8** 71–72; **9** 294, 340–42; **10 352–54 (upd.); 11** 33, 49–50, 352; **12** 122, 401; **13** 30; **16** 167; **17** 25; **21** 153; **23** 289–90, 338, 340

Hondo Oil & Gas Co., **IV** 375–76

Honeywell Inc., I 63; **II** 30, **40–43,** 54, 68; **III** 122–23, 149, 152, 165, 535, 548–49, 732; **6** 266, 281, 283, 314; **8** 21; **9** 171, 324; **11** 198, 265; **12 246–49 (upd.); 13** 234, 499; **17** 33; **18** 341; **22** 373, 436; **23** 471

Hong Kong Aircraft Engineering Co., **I** 522; **6** 79; **16** 480

Hong Kong Airways, **6** 78–79; **16** 480

Hong Kong and Kowloon Wharf and Godown Co., **I** 470; **IV** 699

Hong Kong Dragon Airlines, **18** 114

Hong Kong Island Line Co., **IV** 718

Hong Kong Mass Transit Railway Corp., **19** 111

Hong Kong Resort Co., **IV** 718

Hong Kong Telecommunications Ltd., IV 700; **V** 285–86; **6 319–21; 18** 114

Hong Leong Corp., **III** 718

Hongkong & Kowloon Wharf & Godown Company, **20** 312

Hongkong and Shanghai Banking Corporation Limited, II 257, **296–99,** 320, 358; **III** 289; **17** 325; **18** 253

Hongkong Electric Company Ltd., 6 498–500; 20 134

Hongkong Electric Holdings Ltd., 23 278–81 (upd.)

Hongkong Land Holdings Ltd., I 470–71; **IV 699–701; 6** 498–99; **20** 312–13; **23** 280

Honig-Copper & Harrington, **I** 14

Honjo Copper Smeltery, **III** 490

Honolulu Oil, **II** 491

Honolulu Sugar Refining Co., **II** 490

Honshu Paper Co., Ltd., IV 268, **284–85,** 292, 297, 321, 326

Hood Rubber Company, **15** 488–89

Hood Sailmakers, Inc., **10** 215

Hoogovens. *See* Koninklijke Nederlandsche Hoogovens en Staalfabricken NV.

Hooiberg, **I** 256

Hook's Drug Stores, **9** 67

Hooker Chemical, **IV** 481

Hooker Corp., **19** 324

Hooker Furniture Corp. *See* Bassett Furniture Industries, Inc.

Hooker Petroleum, **IV** 264

Hooper Holmes, Inc., 22 264–67

Hooters of America, Inc., 18 241–43

Hoover Ball and Bearing Co., **III** 589

The Hoover Company, II 7; **III** 478; **12** 158, **250–52; 15** 416, 418; **21** 383

Hoover Group Inc., **18** 11

Hoover Industrial, **III** 536

Hoover Treated Wood Products, Inc., **12** 396

Hoover-NSK Bearings, **III** 589

Hopkinton LNG Corp., **14** 126

Hopper Soliday and Co. Inc., **14** 154

Hopwood & Company, **22** 427

Horace Mann Educators Corporation, 22 268–70

Horizon Bancorp, **II** 252; **14** 103

Horizon Corporation, **8** 348

Horizon Holidays, **14** 36

Horizon Industries, **19** 275

Horizon Travel Group, **8** 527

Hormel Foods Corporation, 18 244–47 (upd.). *See also* George A. Hormel and Company.

Horn & Hardart, **II** 614

Horn Silver Mines Co., **IV** 83; **7** 187

Horn Venture Partners, **22** 464

Hornblower & Co., **II** 450

Hornbrook, Inc., **14** 112

Horne's, **I** 449; **16** 62

Hornsberg Land Co., **I** 553

Horst Breuer GmbH, **20** 363

Horten, **II** 622

Hospital Corporation of America, II 331; **III 78–80; 15** 112; **23** 153

Hospital Cost Consultants, **11** 113

Hospital Products, Inc., **10** 534

Hospital Service Association of Pittsburgh, **III** 325

Hospitality Franchise Systems, Inc., 11 177–79; 14 106; **17** 236

Host Marriott Corporation, **21** 366

Host Marriott Services Corp., **III** 103; **16** 446; **17** 95

Hot 'n Now, **16** 96–97

Hot Dog Construction Co., **12** 372

Hot Sam Co., **12** 179, 199

Hot Shoppes Inc., **III** 102

Hotchkiss-Brandt, **II** 116

Hoteiya, **V** 209–10

Hotel Corporation of America, **16** 337

Hotel Scandinavia K/S, **I** 120

Houdry Chemicals, **I** 298

Houghton Mifflin Company, 10 355–57

Housatonic Power Co., **13** 182

House and Land Syndicate, **IV** 710

House of Fabrics, Inc., 16 197–98; 18 223; **21 278–80**

House of Fraser Plc., **21** 353

House of Miniatures, **12** 264

House of Windsor, Inc., **9** 533

Household International, Inc., I 31; **II 417–20,** 605; **7** 569–70; **8** 117; **10** 419; **16** 487–88; **21 281–86 (upd.); 22** 38, 542

Household Products Inc., **I** 622; **10** 68

Household Rental Systems, **17** 234

Housing Development Finance Corporation, **20** 313

Housmex Inc., **23** 171

Houston, Effler & Partners Inc., **9** 135

Houston General Insurance, **III** 248

Houston Industries Incorporated, V 641–44; 7 376

Houston International Teleport, Inc., **11** 184

Houston Natural Gas Corp., **IV** 395; **V** 610

Houston Oil & Minerals Corp., **11** 440–41

Houston Oil Co., **IV** 342, 674

Hoveringham Group, **III** 753

Hoving Corp., **14** 501

Hovis-McDougall Co., **II** 565

Howaldtswerke-Deutsche Werft AG, **IV** 201

Howard B. Stark Candy Co., **15** 325

Howard Flint Ink Company, **13** 227

Howard H. Sweet & Son, Inc., **14** 502

Howard Hughes Medical Institute, **II** 33, 35

Howard Hughes Properties, Ltd., **17** 317

Howard Humphreys, **13** 119

Howard Johnson International, Inc., III 94, 102–03; **6** 27; **7** 266; **11** 177–78; **15** 36; **16** 156; **17 236–39**

Howard Printing Co., **III** 188; **10** 29

Howard Research and Development Corporation, **15** 412, 414

Howard Smith Paper Mills Ltd., **IV** 271–72

Howden. *See* Alexander Howden Group.

Howdy Company, **9** 177

Howe & Fant, Inc., **23** 82

Howe and Brainbridge Inc., **I** 321

Howe Sound Co., **12** 253

Howe Sound Inc., **IV** 174

Howe Sound Pulp and Paper Ltd., **IV** 321

Howmet Corporation, 12 IV 174; **253–55; 22** 506

Hoya Corp., **III** 715

Hoyt Archery Company, **10** 216

HQ Office International, **8** 405; **23** 364

Hrubitz Oil Company, **12** 244

HSBC Holdings plc, 12 256–58; 17 323, 325–26

HTH, **12** 464

H2O Plus, **11** 41

Huaneng Raw Material Corp., **III** 718

Hub Services, Inc., **18** 366

Hubbard Air Transport, **10** 162

Hubbard, Baker & Rice, **10** 126

Hubbard Construction Co., **23** 332

Hubbard, Westervelt & Motteley, **II** 425; **13** 341

Hubbell Incorporated, 9 286–87

Hubinger Co., **II** 508; **11** 172

Huck Manufacturing Company, **22** 506

Huddart Parker, **III** 672

Hudepohl-Schoenling Brewing Co., **18** 72

Hudnut, **I** 710

Hudson Automobile Company, **18** 492

The Hudson Bay Mining and Smelting Company, Limited, 12 259–61; 13 502–03; **16** 29

Hudson Engineering Corp., **III** 559

Hudson Foods Inc., 13 270–72

Hudson Housewares Corp., **16** 389
Hudson Motor Car Co., **I** 135, 158; **III**
568; **10** 292; **20** 359
Hudson Packaging & Paper Co., **IV** 257
Hudson River Railroad, **II** 396
Hudson River Rubber Company, **V** 231
Hudson Scott & Sons, **I** 604
Hudson Software, **13** 481
Hudson Underground Telephone Company,
6 299
Hudson's. *See* Dayton Hudson Corporation.
Hudson's Bay Company, **I** 284; **IV**
400–01, 437; **V** 79–81; **6** 359; **8** 525;
12 361
Hue International, **8** 324
Hueppe Duscha, **III** 571; **20** 362
Huff Daland Dusters, **I** 99; **6** 81
Huffco, **IV** 492
Huffman Manufacturing Company, **7**
225–26
Huffy Bicycles Co., **19** 383
Huffy Corporation, **7** 225–27
Hugerot, **19** 50
Hugh O'Neill Auto Co., **12** 309
Hughes Aircraft Corporation, **I** 172, 484,
539; **III** 428, 539; **7** 426–27; **9** 409; **10**
327; **11** 263, 540; **13** 356, 398; **15** 528,
530; **21** 201; **23** 134. *See also* GM
Hughes Electronics Corporation.
Hughes Communications, Inc., **13** 398; **18**
211
Hughes Corp., **18** 535
Hughes Electric Heating Co., **II** 28; **12** 194
Hughes Markets, Inc., **22** 271–73
Hughes Network Systems Inc., **21** 239
Hughes Properties, Inc., **17** 317
Hughes Supply, Inc., **14** 246–47
Hughes Television Network, **11** 184
Hughes Tool Co., **I** 126; **II** 32; **12** 488; **15**
467. *See also* Baker Hughes
Incorporated.
Hugo Neu Corporation, **19** 381–82
Hugo Stinnes GmbH, **I** 542; **8** 69, 494–95
Huguenot Fenal, **IV** 108
Hüls A.G., **I** 349–50
Hulton, **17** 397
Humana Inc., **III** 79, 81–83; **6** 28,
191–92, 279; **15** 113
Humason Manufacturing Co., **III** 628
Humber, **I** 197
Humble Oil & Refining Company, **III** 497;
IV 373, 428; **7** 171; **13** 118; **14** 291. *See
also* Exxon.
Humboldt-Deutz-Motoren AG, **III** 541–42,
543; **IV** 126
Hummel, **II** 163–64
Hummingbird, **18** 313
Humphrey Instruments, **I** 693
Humphrey's Estate and Finance, **IV** 700
Humphreys & Glasgow Ltd., **V** 612
Hunco Ltd., **IV** 640
Hungária Biztositó, **III** 185
Hungarotex, **V** 166
Hunt Lumber Co., **IV** 358
Hunt Manufacturing Company, **12**
262–64
Hunt Oil Company, **IV** 367, 453–54; **7**
228–30, 378
Hunt-Wesson, Inc., **17** 240–42
Hunter Engineering Co., **IV** 18
Hunter Fan Company, **13** 273–75
Hunter-Douglas, **8** 235
Hunter-Hayes Elevator Co., **III** 467
Hunters' Foods, **II** 500

Hunting Aircraft, **I** 50
Huntington Bancshares Inc., **11** 180–82
Huntley and Palmer Foods, **II** 544
Huntley Boorne & Stevens, **I** 604
Huntsman Chemical Corporation, **8**
261–63; **9** 305
Hupp Motor Car Company, **III** 601; **8** 74;
10 261
Hurd & Houghton, **10** 355
Hurlburt Paper Co., **IV** 311; **19** 267
Huron Steel Company, Inc., **16** 357
Huse Food Group, **14** 352
Husky Oil Ltd., **IV** 454, 695; **V** 673–75;
18 253–54; **19** 159
Husqvarna Forest & Garden Company, **III**
480; **13** 564; **22** 26–27
Hussmann Corporation, **I** 457–58; **7**
429–30; **10** 554; **13** 268; **22** 353–54
Hutchinson Technology Incorporated, **18**
248–51
Hutchinson Wholesale Grocery Co., **II** 624
Hutchinson-Mapa, **IV** 560
Hutchison, **I** 470
Hutchison Microtel, **11** 548
Hutchison Whampoa Ltd., **IV** 694–95;
18 114, 252–55; **20** 131, 312–13
Huth Manufacturing Corporation, **10** 414
Hüttenwerk Oberhausen AG, **IV** 222
Hüttenwerk Salzgitter AG, **IV** 201
Huttig Sash & Door Company, **8** 135
Hutton, E.F. *See* E.F. Hutton.
Huyck Corp., **I** 429
Hvide Marine Incorporated, **22** 274–76
Hy-Form Products, Inc., **22** 175
Hyatt Corporation, **II** 442; **III** 92, 96–97;
9 426; **16** 273–75 (upd.); **22** 101; **23**
482
Hyatt Legal Services, **20** 435
Hyatt Medical Enterprises, **III** 73
Hyatt Roller Bearing Co., **I** 171–72; **9** 17;
10 326
Hybridtech, **III** 18
Hyde Athletic Industries, Inc., **17** 243–45
Hyde Company, A.L., **7** 116–17
Hydra Computer Systems, Inc., **13** 201
Hydraulic Brake Co., **I** 141
Hydro Carbide Corp., **19** 152
Hydro Electric, **19** 389–90
Hydro Med Sciences, **13** 367
Hydro-Aire Incorporated, **8** 135
Hydro-Carbon Light Company, **9** 127
Hydro-Electric Power Commission of
Ontario, **6** 541; **9** 461
Hydro-Québec, **6** 501–03
Hydrocarbon Services of Nigeria Co., **IV**
473
Hydroponic Chemical Co., **III** 28
Hydrox Corp., **II** 533
Hyer Boot, **19** 232
Hygeia Sciences, Inc., **8** 85, 512
Hygienic Ice Co., **IV** 722
Hygrade Containers Ltd., **IV** 286
Hygrade Foods, **III** 502; **7** 208; **14** 536
Hyland Laboratories, **I** 627
Hylsa. *See* Hojalata y Laminas S.A.
Hyosung Group, **III** 749
Hyper Shoppes, Inc., **II** 670; **18** 507
Hyperion Press, **6** 176
Hyperion Software Corporation, **22**
277–79
Hypermart USA, **8** 555–56
Hyplains Beef, **7** 175
Hypo-Bank. *See* Bayerische Hypotheken-
und Wechsel-Bank AG.

Hypobaruk, **III** 348
Hyponex Corp., **22** 475
Hypro Engineering Inc., **I** 481
Hysol Corp., **I** 321; **12** 103
Hyster Company, **17** 246–48
Hyster-Yale Materials Handling, Inc., **I**
424; **7** 369–71
Hystron Fibers Inc., **I** 347
Hyundai Group, **I** 207, 516; **II** 53–54,
122; **III** 457–59, **515–17**; **7 231–34**
(upd.); **9** 350; **10** 404; **12** 211, 546; **13**
280, 293–94; **18** 124; **23** 353

I Can't Believe It's Yogurt, Inc., **17** 474
I.C.H. Corp., **I** 528
I.C. Johnson and Co., **III** 669
I.D. Systems, Inc., **11** 444
I-DIKA Milan SRL, **12** 182
I.G. Farbenindustrie AG, **I** 305–06,
309–11, 337, 346–53, 619, 632–33,
698–99; **II** 257; **III** 677, 694; **IV** 111,
485; **8** 108–09; **11** 7; **13** 75–76, 262; **16**
121; **18** 47; **21** 544; **22** 225–26. *See also*
BASF A.G. *and* Bayer A.G. *and*
Hoechst A.G.
I.J. Stokes Corp., **I** 383
I.M. Pei & Associates, **I** 580; **III** 267
I.M. Singer and Co., **II** 9
I. Magnin Inc., **8** 444; **15** 86
I.N. Kote, **IV** 116; **19** 219
I.N. Tek, **IV** 116; **19** 219
I.R. Maxwell & Co. Ltd., **IV** 641; **7** 311
I-T-E Circuit Breaker, **II** 121
I-X Corp., **22** 416
IAM/Environmental, **18** 11
IBC Holdings Corporation, **12** 276
Iberdrola, **V** 608
Iberia Líneas Aéreas De España S.A., **I**
110; **6** 95–97
Ibero-Amerika Bank, **II** 521
Iberswiss Catering, **6** 96
Ibex Engineering Co., **III** 420
IBH Holding AG, **7** 513
IBJ. *See* The Industrial Bank of Japan Ltd.
IBM. *See* International Business Machines
Corporation.
IBP, Inc., **II** 515–17; **7** 525; **21 287–90**
(upd.); **23** 201
Ibstock plc, **III** 735; **14** 248–50
IC Industries Inc., **I** 456–58; **III** 512; **7**
430; **10** 414, 553; **18** 3; **22** 197. *See also*
Whitman Corporation.
ICA AB, **II** 639–40
ICA Mortgage Corporation, **8** 30
ICA Technologies, Ltd., **III** 533
ICE, **I** 333
ICH Corporation, **19** 468
ICI. *See* Imperial Chemical Industries plc.
ICI Canada, **22** 436
ICL plc, **II** 65, 81; **III** 141, 164; **6**
240–42; **11** 150; **16** 226
ICM Mortgage Corporation, **8** 436
ICOA Life Insurance, **III** 253
Icot Corp., **18** 543
ICS. *See* International Care Services.
ICX, **IV** 136
ID, Inc., **9** 193
Idaho Frozen Foods, **II** 572–73
Idaho Power Company, **12** 265–67
IDB Communications Group, Inc., **11**
183–85; **20** 48
Ide Megumi, **III** 549
Ideal Basic Industries, **III** 701–02; **8**
258–59; **12** 18

Ideal Corp., III 602; 23 335
Ideal Loisirs Group, 23 388
Idemitso Petrochemicals, 8 153
Idemitsu Kosan K.K., II 361; IV **434–36**, 476, 519
Identification Business, Inc., 18 140
IDEXX Laboratories, Inc., 23 **282–84**
IDG Communications, Inc, 7 238
IDG World Expo Corporation, 7 239
IDI, 22 365
IDO. *See* Nippon Idou Tsushin.
IDS Ltd., 22 76
IEL. *See* Industrial Equity Ltd.
IFI, I 161–62; III 347
IFS Industries, 6 294
IG Farben. *See* I.G. Farbenindustrie AG.
IGA, II 624, 649, 668, 681–82; 7 451; 15 479; 18 6, 9
Iggesund Bruk, IV 317–18
Igloo Products Corp., 21 **291–93**; 22 116
IGT-International, 10 375–76
IGT-North America, 10 375
IHI, I 534
IIII Granitech Corp., III 533
IHOP Corporation, 17 **249–51**; 19 435, 455
Iida & Co., I 493
IinteCom, III 169
IISCO-Ujjain Pipe and Foundry Co. Ltd., IV 206
IK Coach, Ltd., 23 290
IKEA Group, V 82–84
Il Giornale, 13 493
Illco Toy Co. USA, 12 496
Illinois Bell Telephone Company, IV 660; 14 **251–53**; 18 30
Illinois Central Corporation, I 456, 584; 8 410; 10 553; 11 **186–89**
Illinois Glass Co., I 609
Illinois Merchants Trust Co., II 261
Illinois National Bank & Trust Co., III 213–14
Illinois Power Company, 6 470, **504–07**
Illinois Steel Co., IV 572; 7 549; 8 114
Illinois Terminal Company, 6 504
Illinois Tool Works Inc., III **518–20**; 22 **280–83** (upd.)
Illinois Traction Company, 6 504
Illinois Trust and Savings Bank, II 261
Ilmor Engineering of Great Britain, V 494
Ilse-Bergbau AG, IV 229–30
Ilselder Hütte, IV 201
Ilwaco Telephone and Telegraph Company. *See* Pacific Telecom, Inc.
IMA Holdings Corp., III 73–74
Image Business Systems Corp., 11 66
Image Technologies Corporation, 12 264
Imasa Group, IV 34
Imasco Limited, I 514; II 605; V **401–02**
Imation Corporation, 20 301–04
Imatran Voima Osakeyhtiö, IV 469
Imax, 21 362
IMC Drilling Mud, III 499
IMC Fertilizer Group, Inc., 8 **264–66**
Imcera Group, Inc., 8 264, 266
IMED Corp., I 712; III 511–12; 10 551
Imetal S.A., IV 107–09
IMG. *See* International Management Group.
IMI plc, III 593; 9 **288–89**
Imigest Fondo Imicapital, III 347
Immunex Corporation, 8 26; 14 **254–56**
Immuno Serums, Inc., V 174–75
Imo Industries Inc., 7 **235–37**

IMO Ltd., III 539
Impala Platinum Holdings, IV 91–93
Imperial Airways, I 92; 6 109–10, 117
Imperial Bank of Canada, II 244–45
Imperial Bank of Persia, II 298
Imperial British East Africa Co., III 522
Imperial Business Forms, 9 72
Imperial Chemical Industries plc, I 303, **351–53**, 374, 605, 633; II 448, 565; III 522, 667, 677, 680, 745; IV 38, 110, 698; 7 209; 8 179, 222, 224; 9 154, 288; 10 436; 11 97, 361; 12 347; 13 448, 470; 16 121; 17 118; 18 50; 21 544
Imperial Feather Company, 19 304
Imperial Fire Co., III 373
Imperial Goonbarrow, III 690
Imperial Group Ltd., II 513; III 503; 7 209; 17 238
Imperial Holly Corporation, 12 **268–70**
Imperial Japanese Government Steel Works, 17 349–50
Imperial Life Co., III 288, 373
Imperial Marine Insurance Co., III 384, 405–06
Imperial Metal Industries Ltd. *See* IMI plc.
Imperial Oil Limited, IV 428, **437–39**, 494
Imperial Packing Co. *See* Beech-Nut Nutrition Corp.
Imperial Paper, 13 169
Imperial Pneumatic Tool Co., III 525
Imperial Premium Finance, III 264
Imperial Savings Association, 8 30–31
Imperial Smelting Corp., IV 58
Imperial Sports, 19 230
Imperial Sugar Company. *See* Imperial Holly Corporation.
Imperial Tobacco Company, I 425–26, 605; IV 260; V 401. *See also* B.A.T. Industries PLC.
Imported Auto Parts, Inc., 15 246
Impressions Software, 15 455
Imprimis, 8 467
Impulse, 9 122
Imreg, 10 473–74
IMRS. *See* Hyperion Software Corporation.
IMS International, Inc., 10 105
In Focus Systems, Inc., 22 287–90
In-N-Out Burger, 19 213–15
In-Sink-Erator, II 19
INA Corporation, II 403; III 79, 208, 223–25, 226; 11 481; 22 269. *See also* CIGNA Corporation.
INA Wälzlager Schaeffler, III 595
INA-Naftaplin, IV 454
Inabata & Co., I 398
InaCom Corporation, 13 176, **276–78**; 19 471
Incasso Bank, II 185
Inchcape PLC, II 233; III **521–24**; 16 **276–80** (upd.)
Incheon Iron & Steel Co., III 516
Inchon Heavy Industrial Corp., IV 183
Inco Limited, IV 75, 78, **110–12**
INCO-Banco Indústria e Comércio de Santa Catarina, 13 70
Incola, S.A., II 471; 22 93
InControl Inc., 11 460
Incredible Universe, 12 470; 17 489
Ind Coope, I 215
Indemnité, III 391
Indemnity Insurance Company. *See* CIGNA Corporation.
Indentimat Corp., 14 542

Independent Breweries Company, 9 178
Independent Grocers Alliance. *See* IGA.
Independent Lock Co., 13 166
Independent Metal Products Co., I 169
Independent Oil & Gas Co., IV 521
Independent Petrochemical, 14 461
Independent Power Generators, V 605
Independent Warehouses, Inc., IV 180
India Exotics, Inc., 22 133
India General Steam Navigation and Railway Co., III 522
India Life Assurance Co., III 359
India Rubber, Gutta Percha & Telegraph Works Co., I 428
Indian, 7 211
Indian Airlines Corporation. *See* Air-India.
Indian Archery and Toy Corp., 19 142–43
Indian Iron & Steel Co. Ltd., IV 49, 205–07
Indian Oil Corporation Ltd., IV **440–41**, 483
Indian Point Farm Supply, Inc., IV 458–59
Indiana Bearings, Inc., 13 78
Indiana Bell Telephone Company, Incorporated, 14 257–61; 18 30
Indiana Board and Filler Company, 12 376
Indiana Electric Corporation, 6 555
Indiana Gaming Company, 21 40
Indiana Gas & Water Company, 6 556
Indiana Group, I 378
Indiana Oil Purchasing Co., IV 370
Indiana Power Company, 6 555
Indiana Refining Co., IV 552
Indiana Tube Co., 23 250
Indianapolis Air Pump Company, 8 37
Indianapolis Brush Electric Light & Power Company, 6 508
Indianapolis Cablevision, 6 508–09
Indianapolis Light and Power Company, 6 508
Indianapolis Motor Speedway Company, 9 16
Indianapolis Power & Light Company, 6 508–09
Indianapolis Pump and Tube Company, 8 37
Indianhead Truck Lines, 6 371
Indo-Asahi Glass Co., Ltd., III 667
Indo-China Steam Navigation Co., I 469; 20 311
Indola Cosmetics B.V., 8 16
Indonesia Petroleum Co., IV 516
Indresco, Inc., 22 285
Induban, II 196
Industria Gelati Sammontana, II 575
Industria Metalgrafica, I 231
Industria Raffinazione Oli Minerali, IV 419
Industrial & Trade Shows of Canada, IV 639
Industrial Acceptance Bank, I 337
Industrial Air Products, 19 380–81
Industrial Bancorp, 9 229
Industrial Bank of Japan, Ltd., II **300–01**, 310–11, 338, 369, 433, 459; 17 121
Industrial Bank of Scotland, 10 337
Industrial Bio-Test Laboratories, I 374, 702
Industrial Cartonera, IV 295; 19 226
Industrial Chemical and Equipment, 16 271
Industrial Circuits, IV 680
Industrial Computer Corp., 11 78
Industrial Development Corp., IV 22, 92, 534

Industrial Development Corp. of Zambia Ltd., **IV** 239–41
Industrial Engineering, **III** 598
Industrial Engineering Associates, Inc., **II** 112
Industrial Equity Ltd., **I** 438; **17** 357
Industrial Fuel Supply Co., **I** 569
Industrial Gas Equipment Co., **I** 297
Industrial Instrument Company. *See* Foxboro Company.
Industrial Light & Magic, **12** 322
Industrial Mutual Insurance, **III** 264
Industrial National Bank, **9** 229
Industrial Powder Coatings, Inc., **16** 475
Industrial Publishing Company, **9** 413
Industrial Reorganization Corp., **III** 502, 556
Industrial Resources, **6** 144
Industrial Tectonics Corp., **18** 276
Industrial Trade & Consumer Shows Inc., **IV** 639
Industrial Trust Company, **9** 228
Industrial Vehicles Corp. B.V., **III** 543–44
Industrias Nacobre, **21** 259
Industrias Negromex, **23** 170
Industrias Penoles, S.A. de C.V., 22 284–86
Industrias Resistol S.A., **23** 170–71
Industrias y Confecciones, S.A. **V** 51
Industrie Natuzzi S.p.A., 18 256–58
Industrie Regionale du Bâtiment, **IV** 108
Industrie-Aktiengesellschaft, **IV** 201
Industriegas GmbH., **I** 581
Les Industries Ling, **13** 443
Industrionics Control, Inc., **III** 643
Industrivärden, **II** 366
Induyco. *See* Industrias y Confecciones, S.A.
Inelco Peripheriques, **10** 459
Inespo, **16** 322
Inexco Oil Co., **7** 282
Infinity Broadcasting Corporation, 11 190–92; 22 97; **23** 510
INFLEX, S.A., **8** 247
Inflight Sales Group Limited, **11** 82
Infobase Services, **6** 14
Infonet Services Corporation, **6** 303
Infoplan, **14** 36
Informatics, **III** 248
Informatics General Corporation, **11** 468
Informatics Legal Systems, **III** 169; **6** 285
Information Access Company, 12 560–62; **17 252–55**
Information and Communication Group, **14** 555
Information Associates Inc., **11** 78
Information Builders, Inc., 14 16; **22 291–93**
Information Consulting Group, **9** 345
Information, Dissemination and Retrieval Inc., **IV** 670
Information International. *See* Autologic Information International, Inc.
Information Management Reporting Services. *See* Hyperion Software Corporation.
Information Management Science Associates, Inc., **13** 174
Information Resources, Inc., 10 358–60; 13 4
Information Unlimited Software, **6** 224
Informix Corp., 10 361–64, 505
Infrasud, **I** 466
Infun, S.A., **23** 269

ING, B.V., **14** 45, 47
Ing. C. Olivetti & C., S.p.A., III 122, **144–46,** 549, 678; **10** 499; **16** 122
Ingalls Quinn and Johnson, **9** 135
Ingalls Shipbuilding, Inc., I 485; **11** 264–65; **12** 28, **271–73**
Ingear, **10** 216
Ingersoll-Rand Company, III 473, **525–27; 10** 262; **13** 27, 523; **15** 187, **223–26 (upd.); 22** 542
Inglenook Vineyards, **13** 134
Ingles Markets, Inc., 20 305–08
Inglis Ltd., **III** 654; **12** 549
Ingram Corp. Ltd., **III** 559; **IV** 249
Ingram Industries, Inc., 10 518–19; **11 193–95; 13** 90, 482
AB Ingredients, **II** 466
Ingredients Technology Corp., **9** 154
Ingres Corporation, **9** 36–37
Ingwerson and Co., **II** 356
INH. *See* Instituto Nacional de Hidrocarboros.
Inhalation Therapy Services, **III** 73
INI. *See* Instituto Nacional de Industria.
Inland Container Corporation, IV 311, 341–42, 675; **7** 528; **8 267–69; 19** 267
Inland Motors Corporation, **18** 291
Inland Pollution Control, **9** 110
Inland Specialty Chemical Corp., **I** 342; **14** 217
Inland Steel Industries, Inc., II 403; **IV 113–16,** 158, 703; **7** 447; **13** 157; **15** 249–50; **17** 351; **19** 9, **216–20 (upd.),** 311, 381; **23** 35
Inland Valley, **23** 321
Inmac, Inc., **16** 373
Inmos Ltd., **I** 532; **11** 307
InnerCity Foods Joint Venture Company, **16** 97
Inno-France. *See* Societe des Grandes Entreprises de Distribution, Inno-France.
Innovative Marketing Systems. *See* Bloomberg L.P.
Innovative Pork Concepts, **7** 82
Innovative Products & Peripherals Corporation, **14** 379
Innovative Software Inc., **10** 362
Innovative Sports Systems, Inc., **15** 396
Innovex Ltd., **21** 425
Inns and Co., **III** 734
Innwerk AG, **IV** 229
Inoue Electric Manufacturing Co., **II** 75–76
Inpaco, **16** 340
Inpacsa, **19** 226
Input/Output, Inc., **11** 538
Insalaco Markets Inc., **13** 394
INSCO, **III** 242
Insight Enterprises, Inc., 18 259–61
Insilco Corporation, I 473; **12** 472; **16 281–83; 23** 212
Insley Manufacturing Co., **8** 545
Inspiration Resources Corporation, **12** 260; **13** 502–03
Inspirations PLC, **22** 129
Insta-Care Holdings Inc., **16** 59
Insta-Care Pharmacy Services, **9** 186
Instant Milk Co., **11** 488
Instapak Corporation, **14** 429
Institut de Sérothérapie Hémopoiétique, **I** 669
Institut für Gemeinwohl, **IV** 139
Institut Merieux, **I** 389
Institut Ronchese, **I** 676

Institute de Development Industriel, **19** 87
Institute for Scientific Information, **8** 525, 528
Institution Food House. *See* Alex Lee Inc.
Institutional Financing Services, **23** 491
Instituto Nacional de Hidrocarboros, **IV** 528
Instituto Nacional de Industria, I 459–61; V 606–07; **6** 95–96
Instituto per la Ricostruzione Industriale, **V** 614
Instone Airline, **I** 92
Instromet International, **22** 65
Instrumentarium Corp., **13** 328
Instrumentation Laboratory Inc., **III** 511–12; **22** 75
Instrumentation Scientifique de Laboratoire, S.A., **15** 404
Insulite Co. of Finland, **IV** 275
Insurance Auto Auctions, Inc., 23 148, **285–87**
Insurance Co. against Fire Damage, **III** 308
Insurance Co. of Scotland, **III** 358
Insurance Co. of the State of Pennsylvania, **III** 196
Insurance Company of North America. *See* CIGNA Corporation.
Insurance Corp. of Ireland (Life), **III** 335
Insurance Partners L.P., **15** 257
Intalco Aluminum Corp., **12** 254
Intamin, **17** 443
INTEC, **6** 428
InteCom Inc., **6** 285
Integon Corp., **IV** 374
Integra-A Hotel and Restaurant Company, **13** 473
Integral Corporation, **14** 381; **23** 446
Integrated Business Information Services, **13** 5
Integrated Data Services Co., **IV** 473
Integrated Genetics, **I** 638; **8** 210; **13** 239
Integrated Health Services, Inc., **11** 282
Integrated Medical Systems Inc., **12** 333
Integrated Resources, Inc., **11** 483; **16** 54; **19** 393
Integrated Silicon Solutions, Inc., **18** 20
Integrated Software Systems Corporation, **6** 224; **11** 469
Integrated Systems Operations. *See* Xerox Corporation.
Integrated Systems Solutions Corp., **9** 284; **11** 395; **17** 264
Integrated Technology, Inc., **6** 279
Integrated Telecom Technologies, **14** 417
Integrity Life Insurance, **III** 249
Intel Corporation, II 44–46, 62, 64; **III** 115, 125, 455; **6** 215–17, 222, 231, 233, 235, 257; **9** 42–43, 57, 114–15, 165–66; **10 365–67 (upd.),** 477; **11** 62, 308, 328, 490, 503, 518, 520; **12** 61, 449; **13** 47; **16** 139–40, 146, 394; **17** 32–33; **18** 18, 260; **19** 310, 312; **20** 69, 175; **21** 36, 122; **22** 542
Intelcom Support Services, Inc., **14** 334
Intelicom Solutions Corp., **6** 229
IntelliCorp, **9** 310
Intelligent Electronics, Inc., 6 243–45; 12 184; **13** 176, 277
Intellimetrics Instrument Corporation, **16** 93
Inter IKEA Systems B.V., **V** 82
Inter Island Telephone, **6** 326, 328
Inter State Telephone, **6** 338

Inter Techniek, **16** 421
Inter-American Development Bank, **IV** 55
Inter-American Satellite Television Network, **7** 391
Inter-City Gas Ltd., **III** 654; **19** 159
Inter-City Western Bakeries Ltd., **II** 631
Inter-City Wholesale Electric Inc., **15** 385
Inter-Comm Telephone, Inc., **8** 310
Inter-Island Airways, Ltd., **22** 251
Inter-Mountain Telephone Co., **V** 344
Inter-Ocean Corporation, **16** 103
Inter-Regional Financial Group, Inc., 15 231–33
Interactive Computer Design, Inc., **23** 489, 491
Interactive Systems, **7** 500
Interamericana de Talleras SA de CV, **10** 415
Interbake Foods, **II** 631
InterBold, **7** 146; **11** 151
Interbrás, **IV** 503
Interbrew S.A., 16 397; **17 256–58**
Interchemical Corp., **13** 460
Intercity Food Services, Inc., **II** 663
Interco Incorporated, III 528–31; **9** 133, 135, 192, 234–35; **10** 184; **12** 156, 306–08; **22** 49
Intercolonial, **6** 360
Intercomi, **II** 233
Intercontinental Apparel, **8** 249
Intercontinental Breweries, **I** 289
Intercontinental Hotels, **I** 248–49
Intercontinental Mortgage Company, **8** 436
Intercontinental Rubber Co., **II** 112
Intercontinentale, **III** 404
Intercord, **22** 194
Intercostal Steel Corp., **13** 97
Interdesign, **16** 421
Interedi-Cosmopolitan, **III** 47
Interessen Gemeinschaft Farbenwerke. *See* I.G. Farbenindustrie AG.
Interface Group, **13** 483
Interface, Inc., 8 270–72
Interface Systems, Inc., **18** 112
Interferon Sciences, Inc., **13** 366–67
Interfinancial, **III** 200
InterFirst Bankcorp, Inc., **9** 482
Interfood Ltd., **II** 520–21, 540
Interglas S.A., **22** 515
Intergraph Corporation, 6 246–49; 10 257
Interhandel, **I** 337–38; **II** 378; **22** 226
INTERIM Services, Inc., **9** 268, 270
Interlabor, **16** 420–21
The Interlake Corporation, 8 273–75
Interlake Steamship Company, **15** 302
Intermagnetics General Corp., **9** 10
Intermark, Inc., **12** 394
Intermed, **I** 429
Intermedics, **III** 633; **11** 458–59; **12** 325–26
Intermedics Intraocular Inc., **I** 665
Intermoda, **V** 166
Intermountain Broadcasting and Television Corp., **IV** 674
International Aero Engines, **9** 418
International Agricultural Corporation, **8** 264–65
International Assurance Co., **III** 195
International Bank, **II** 261
International Bank of Japan, **17** 122
International Bank of Moscow, **II** 242
International Banking Corp., **II** 253; **9** 123

International Banking Technologies, Inc., **11** 113
International Basic Economy Corporation (IBEC), **13** 103
International Brewing Holdings Pty., **21** 229
International Business Machines Corporation, I 26, 455, 523, 534, 541; **II** 6, 8, 10, 42, 44–45, 56, 62, 68, 70, 73, 86, 99, 107, 113, 134, 159, 211, 274, 326, 379, 397, 432, 440; **III** 9, 109–11, 113–18, 121–28, 130, 132–34, 136, 139–43, 145, **147–49**, 151–52, 154–55, 157, 165–72, 200, 246, 313, 319, 326, 458, 475, 549, 618, 685; **IV** 443, 711; **6** 51, 218–25, 233–35, 237, 240–42, 244–48, **250–53 (upd.)**, 254–60, 262, 265, 269–71, 275–77, 279, 281–89, 320, 324, 346, 390, 428; **7** 145–46, 161; **8** 138–39, 466–67; **9** 36, 41–42, 48, 50, 114–15, 131, 139, 165–66, 170–71, 184, 194, 284, 296–97, 310, 327, 463–64; **10** 19, 22–24, 58, 119, 125, 161, 194, 232, 237, 243–44, 255–56, 309, 361–62, 366–67, 394, 456, 463, 474, 500–01, 505, 510, 512–13, 518–19, 542; **11** 19, 45, 50, 59, 61–62, 64–65, 68, 86–88, 150, 273–74, 285, 364, 395, 469, 485, 491, 494, 506, 519; **12** 61, 138–39, 147–49, 161–62, 183, 204, 238, 278, 335, 442, 450, 469–70, 484; **13** 47, 127, 174, 214, 326, 345, 387–88, 403, 482; **14** 13–15, 106, 268–69, 318, 354, 391, 401, 432–33, 446, 533; **15** 106, 440, 454–55, 491–92; **16** 4, 94, 140, 224–26, 301, 367–68, 372; **17** 353, 418, 532–34; **18** 94, 110, 112, 162, 250, 292, 305–07, 344, 434–36; **19** 41, 110, 310, 312, 437; **20** 237, 313; **21** 86, 391; **22** 17; **23** 135, 138, 209, 470
International Care Services, **6** 182
International Cellucotton Products Co., **III** 40; **16** 302–03
International Commercial Bank, **II** 257
International Communication Materials, Inc., **18** 387
International Computers. *See* ICL plc.
International Controls Corporation, 10 368–70
International Corona Corporation, **12** 244
International Credit Card Business Assoc., **II** 436
International Dairy Queen, Inc., 7 266; **10 371–74**
International Data Group, 7 238–40; 12 561
International Development Bank, **IV** 417
International Digital Communications, Inc., **6** 327
International Egyptian Oil Co., **IV** 412
International Engineering Company, Inc., **7** 355
International Epicure, **12** 280
International Equities Corp., **III** 98
International Factoring Corp., **II** 436
International Factors, Limited, **II** 208
International Family Entertainment Inc., 13 279–81
International Finance Corp., **19** 192
International Flavors & Fragrances Inc., 9 290–92
International Foods, **II** 468

International Game Technology, 10 375–76
International Graphics Corp., **IV** 645
International Group, **13** 277
International Harvester Co., **III** 473, 650, 651; **10** 264, 280, 378, 380, 528; **13** 16; **17** 158; **22** 380. *See also* Navistar International Corporation.
International Healthcare, **III** 197
International House of Pancakes. *See* IHOP Corporation.
International Hydron, **10** 47; **13** 367
International Income Property, **IV** 708
International Industries, **17** 249
International Learning Systems Corp. Ltd., **IV** 641–42; **7** 311
International Lease Finance Corp., **III** 198; **6** 67
International Light Metals Corp., **IV** 163
International Management Group, 18 262–65
International Marine Oil Co., **IV** 363
International Marine Services, **22** 276
International Match, **12** 463
International Mercantile Marine Co., **II** 330
International Mineral & Chemical, Inc., **8** 265–66
International Minerals and Chemical Corporation, **19** 253
International Multifoods Corporation, II 493; **7 241–43**; **12** 80, 125; **14** 515; **21** 289; **23** 203
International Music Co., **16** 202
International News Service, **IV** 626–27; **19** 203
International Nickel Co. of Canada, Ltd., **III** 677; **IV** 78, 110–12
International Nickel Corporation, **16** 122, **18** 488
International Nutrition Laboratories, **14** 558
International Pacific Corp., **II** 389
International Paper Company, I 27; **II** 208, 403; **III** 693, 764; **IV** 16, 245, **286–88**, 289, 326; **8** 267; **11** 76, 311; **15** **227–30 (upd.)**; **16** 349; **17** 446; **23** 48–49, 366, 368
International Parts Corporation, **10** 414
International Permalite, **22** 229
International Petroleum Co., Ltd., **IV** 415–16, 438, 478
International Petroleum Corp., **IV** 454, 484
International Playtex, Inc., **12** 93
International Proteins Corporation, **21** 248
International Publishing Corp., **IV** 641, 666–67; **7** 343; **17** 397; **23** 350
International Roofing Company, **22** 13–14
International Sealants Corporation, **8** 333
International Shoe Co., **III** 528–30
International Silver Company, **I** 30; **12** 472; **14** 482–83
International Specialty Products, Inc., **22** 225, 228–29
International Speedway Corporation, 19 221–23
International Standard Electric, **II** 66–68
International Stores, **I** 427
International Supply Consortium, **13** 79
International Telcell Group, **7** 336
International Telephone & Telegraph Corporation, I 434, 446, **462–64**, 544; **II** 13, 66, 68, 86, 130, 331; **III** 98–99, 162–64, 166, 644–45, 684; **V** 334–35, 337–38; **6** 356; **8** 157; **9** 10, 11, 324; **10** 19, 44, 301; **11 196–99 (upd.)**, 337,

516; **12** 18; **13** 246; **14** 332, 488; **19** 131, 205, 208; **22** 55
International Television Corporation Entertainment Group, **23** 391
International Terminal Operation Co., **I** 513
International Thomson Organization Ltd., **23** 92
International Time Recording Company. *See* International Business Machines Corporation.
International Trust and Investment Corp., **II** 577
International Trust Co., **II** 207
International Utilities Corp., **IV** 75–76; **6** 444
International Western Electric Co., **I** 462; **II** 66; **III** 162; **11** 196
International Wind Systems, **6** 581
International Wine & Spirits Ltd., **9** 533
International Wire Works Corp., **8** 13
International Wireless Inc., **21** 261
Internationale Industriële Beleggung Maatschappij Amsterdam BV, **IV** 128
InterNorth, Inc., **II** 16; **V** 610
Interocean Management Corp., **9** 509–11
Interpac Belgium, **6** 303
Interprovincial Pipe Line Ltd., **I** 264; **IV** 439
The Interpublic Group of Companies, Inc., **I** 16–18, 31, 36; **6** 53; **14** 315; **16** 70, 72, 167; **20** 5; **22** 294–97 (upd.); **23** 478
InterRedec, Inc., **17** 196
Interscience, **17** 271
Interscope Communications, Inc., **23** 389, 391
Intersil Inc., **II** 30; **12** 196; **16** 358
Interstate & Ocean Transport, **6** 577
Interstate Bag, **I** 335
Interstate Bakeries Corporation, **7** 320; **12** 274–76
Interstate Brick Company, **6** 568–69
Interstate Electric Manufacturing Company. *See* McGraw Electric Company.
Interstate Finance Corp., **11** 16
Interstate Financial Corporation, **9** 475
Interstate Paint Distributors, Inc., **13** 367
Interstate Power Company, **6** 555, 605; **18** 404
Interstate Public Service Company, **6** 555
Interstate Stores Inc., **V** 203; **15** 469; **18** 522
Interstate Supply Company. *See* McGraw Electric Company.
Interstate United Corporation, **II** 679; **III** 502; **13** 435
Intertec Publishing Corp., **22** 441
Interturbine Holland, **19** 150
Intertype Corp., **II** 37
Interunfall, **III** 346
Intervideo TV Productions-A.B., **II** 640
Interweb, **IV** 661
InterWest Partners, **16** 418
Intrac Handelsgesellschaft mbH, **7** 142
Intradal, **II** 572
Intraph South Africa Ltd., **6** 247
IntraWest Bank, **II** 289
The Intrawest Corporation, **15** 234–36
Intrepid Corporation, **16** 493
IntroGene B.V., **13** 241
Intuit Inc., **13** 147; **14** 262–64; **23** 457
Invacare Corporation, **11** 200–02, 486
Invenex Laboratories, **17** 287

Invento Products Corporation, **21** 269
Invep S.p.A., **10** 150
Inveresk Paper Co., **III** 693; **IV** 685
Invergordon Distillers, **III** 509
Inversale, **9** 92
INVESCO MIM Management Limited, **21** 397
InvestCorp International, **15** 200
Investcorp S.A. *See* Arabian Investment Banking Corp.
Investimentos Itaú S.A., **19** 33
Investors Bank and Trust Company, **18** 152
Investors Diversified Services, Inc., **II** 398; **6** 199; **8** 348–49; **10** 43–45, 59, 62; **21** 305
Investors Group, **III** 261
Investors Management Corp., **10** 331
Investors Overseas Services, **10** 368–69
Invista Capital Management, **III** 330
Iolab Corp., **III** 36
Iomega Corporation, **18** 509–10; **21** 294–97
Ionpure Technologies Corporation, **6** 486–88
Iowa Beef Packers, **21** 287
Iowa Beef Processors, **II** 516–17; **IV** 481–82; **13** 351
Iowa Manufacturing, **II** 86
Iowa Mold Tooling Co., Inc., **16** 475
Iowa Public Service Company, **6** 524–25
IP Gas Supply Company, **6** 506
IP Services, Inc., **IV** 597
IP Timberlands Ltd., **IV** 288
IP&L. *See* Illinois Power & Light Corporation.
Ipalco Enterprises, Inc., **6** 508–09
IPC. *See* International Publishing Corp.
IPC Communications, Inc., **15** 196
IPC Magazines Limited, **IV** 650; **7** 244–47
Ipko-Amcor, **14** 225
IPSOA Editore, **14** 555
IQUE, Inc., **21** 194
Iran Air, **6** 101
Iran Pan American Oil Co., **IV** 466
Iranian Oil Exploration and Producing Co., **IV** 466–67
Iraq Petroleum Co., **IV** 363, 386, 429, 450, 464, 558–60
Irby-Gilliland Company, **9** 127
IRI. *See* Instituto per la Ricostruzione Industriale.
IRIS Holding Co., **III** 347
Irish Life Assurance Company, **16** 14
Irish Paper Sacks Ltd., **IV** 295; **19** 225
Irish Sugar Co., **II** 508
Iron and Steel Corp., **IV** 22, 41, 92, 533–34
Iron Cliffs Mining Company, **13** 156
Iron Mountain Forge, **13** 319
Iron Ore Company of Canada, **8** 347
Iroquois Gas Corporation, **6** 526
Irvin Feld & Kenneth Feld Productions, Inc., **15** 237–39
Irving Bank Corp., **II** 192
Irving Tanning Company, **17** 195
Irving Trust Coompany, **II** 257; **22** 55
Irvington Smelting, **IV** 78
Irwin Lehrhoff Associates, **11** 366
Irwin Toy Limited, **14** 265–67
Isabela Shoe Corporation, **13** 360
Iscor. *See* Iron and Steel Corporation.
Isetan Company Limited, **V** 85–87
Iseya Tanji Drapery, **V** 85

Ishikawajima-Harima Heavy Industries Co., Ltd., **I** 508, 511, 534; **II** 274; **III** 532–33; **9** 293; **12** 484
Ishizaki Honten, **III** 715
Isis Distributed Systems, Inc., **10** 501
Island Equipment Co., **19** 381
Island Holiday, **I** 417
Island Pictures Corp., **23** 389
Island Records, **23** 389
Islands Restaurants, **17** 85–87
Isolite Insulating Products Co., **III** 714
Isosceles PLC, **II** 628–29
Isotec Communications Incorporated, **13** 213
Isover, **III** 676; **16** 121
ISS International Service System, Inc., **8** 271
Istanbul Fertilizer Industry, **IV** 563
Istante Vesa s.r.l., **22** 239
Istituto per la Ricostruzione Industriale S.p.A., **I** 207, 459, **465–67**; **II** 191–92, 270–71; **IV** 419; **11** 203–06; **13** 28, 218
Isuzu Motors, Ltd., **II** 274; **III** 581, 593; **7** 8, 219; **9** 293–95; **10** 354; **23** 288–91 (upd.)
Isuzu Motors of Japan, **21** 6
IT International, **V** 255
Itabira Iron Ore Co. Ltd., **IV** 54
ITABRASCO, **IV** 55
Italcarta, **IV** 339
Italcementi, **IV** 420
Italianni's, **22** 128
Italiatour, **6** 69
Italmobiliare, **III** 347
Italstate. *See* Societa per la Infrastrutture e l'Assetto del Territorio.
Italtel, **V** 326–27
Itaú. *See* Banco Itaú S.A.
Itaú Winterthur Seguradura S.A., **III** 404
Itaúsa. *See* Investimentos Itaú S.A.
Itek Corp., **I** 486; **11** 265
Itel Corporation, **II** 64; **III** 512; **6** 262, 354; **9** 49, 296–99; **15** 107; **22** 339
Items International Airwalk Inc., **17** 259–61
Ithaca Gas & Electric. *See* New York State Electric and Gas.
ITM International, **IV** 239
Ito Carnation Co., **II** 518
Ito Food Processing Co., **II** 518
Ito Gofuku Co. Ltd., **V** 129
Ito Meat Processing Co., **II** 518
Ito Processed Food Co., **II** 518
Ito-Yokado Co., Ltd., **II** 661; **V** 88–89
Itochu and Renown, Inc., **12** 281
Itochu Corporation, **19** 9
Itochu of Japan, **14** 550
Itoh. *See* C. Itoh & Co.
Itoham Foods Inc., **II** 518–19
Itokin, **III** 48
ITT, **21** 200. *See also* International Telephone and Telegraph Corporation.
ITT Sheraton Corporation, **III** 98–101; **23** 484
ITW. *See* Illinois Tool Works Inc.
ITW Devcon, **12** 7
IU International, **23** 40
IURA Edition, **14** 556
IV Therapy Associates, **16** 440
IVAC Corp., **I** 646; **11** 90
IVACO Industries Inc., **11** 207
Ivanhoe, Inc., **II** 662, 664
IVAX Corporation, **11** 207–09
Iveco, **I** 148; **12** 91

Ives Trains, **16** 336
Iwai & Co., **I** 492, 509–10; **IV** 151
Iwata Air Compressor, **III** 427
IYG Holding Company of Japan, **7** 492
Izod Lacoste, **II** 502–03; **9** 156–57; **10** 324
Izumi Fudosan, **IV** 726
Izumiya, **V** 477

J Bibby & Sons, **I** 424
J Bibby Agriculture Limited, **13** 53
J Sainsbury plc, **II** 657–59, 677–78; **10** 442; **11** 239, 241; **13** 282–84 (upd.); **17** 42; **21** 335; **22** 241
J. & W. Seligman and Co., **17** 498
J.A. Baldwin Manufacturing Company, **17** 106
J.A. Jones, Inc., **16** 284–86; **17** 377
J&E Davy, **16** 14
J&G Meakin, **12** 529
J&J Colman, **II** 566
J&J Corrugated Box Corp., **IV** 282; **9** 261
J&L Industrial Supply, **13** 297
J&L Steel. See Jones & Laughlin Steel Corp.
J. Aron & Co., **II** 415
J.B. Hudson & Son, **18** 136
J.B. Hunt Transport Services Inc., **12** 277–79; **15** 440
J.B. Lippincott & Company, **IV** 652; **14** 554–56
J.B. McLean Publishing Co., Ltd., **IV** 638
J.B. Williams Company, **III** 66; **8** 63
J.B. Wolters Publishing Company, **14** 554
J. Baker, Inc., **13** 361
J. Bulova Company. See Bulova Corporation.
J. Byrons, **9** 186
J.C. Baxter Co., **15** 501
J.C. Hillary's, **20** 54
J.C. Penney Company, Inc., **I** 516; **V** 90–92; **8** 288, 555; **9** 156, 210, 213, 219, 346–94; **10** 409, 490; **11** 349; **12** 111, 431, 522; **14** 62; **16** 37, 327–28; **17** 124, 175, 177, 366, 460; **18** 108, 136, 168, 200, **269–73 (upd.)**, 373, 478; **19** 300; **21** 24, 527
J. Crew Group Inc., **12** 280–82
J.D. Bassett Manufacturing Co. See Bassett Furniture Industries, Inc.
J.D. Edwards & Company, **14** 268–70
J.D. Powers & Associates, **9** 166
J.E. Baxter Co., **I** 429
J.E. Nolan, **11** 486
J.E. Sirrine. See CRSS Inc.
J.E. Smith Box & Printing Co., **13** 441
J. Edward Connelly Associates, Inc., **22** 438
J. Evershed & Son, **13** 103
J.F. Corporation, **V** 87
J.F. Lauman and Co., **II** 681
J. Fielding & Co., **IV** 249
J.G. McMullen Dredging Co., **III** 558
J. Gadsden Paper Products, **IV** 249
J. George Leyner Engineering Works Co., **III** 525–26
J.H. Heafner Co., **20** 263
J.H. Stone & Sons, **IV** 332
J.H. Whitney & Company, **9** 250
J. Homestock. See R.H. Macy & Co.
J.I. Case Company, **I** 148, 527; **III** 651; **10** 377–81; **13** 17; **22** 380
J.K. Armsby Co., **7** 130–31
J.K. Starley and Company Ltd, **7** 458

J.L. Clark, Inc. See Clarcor Inc.
J.L. Hudson Company. See Dayton Hudson Corporation.
J.L. Kraft & Bros. Co., **II** 532
J.L. Shiely Co., **III** 691
J. Levin & Co., Inc., **13** 367
J. Lyons & Co., **I** 215
J.M. Brunswick & Brothers, **III** 442
J.M. Douglas & Company Limited, **14** 141
J.M. Horton Ice Cream Co., **II** 471
J.M. Jones Co., **II** 668; **18** 504
J.M. Kohler Sons Company, **7** 269
The J.M. Smucker Company, **11** 210–12
J.M. Tull Metals Co., Inc., **IV** 116; **15** 250; **19** 219
J. Mandelbaum & Sons, **19** 510
J-Mass, **IV** 289
J. Muirhead Ltd., **I** 315
J.P. Heilwell Industries, **II** 420
J.P. Morgan & Co. Incorporated, **II** 281, **329–32**, 407, 419, 427–28, 430–31, 441; **III** 237, 245, 380; **IV** 20, 180, 400; **9** 386; **11** 421; **12** 165; **13** 13; **16** 25, 375; **19** 190
J.P. Stevens Inc., **8** 234; **12** 404; **16** 533–35; **17** 75; **19** 420
J.P. Wood, **II** 587
J.R. Brown & Sharpe. See Brown & Sharpe Manufacturing Co.
J.R. Geigy S.A., **I** 632–33, 635, 671; **8** 108–10
J.R. Parkington Co., **I** 280
J.R. Simplot Company, **16** 287–89; **21** 508
J.R. Wyllie & Sons, **I** 437
J. Ray McDermott & Co., **III** 558–59
J.S. Fry & Sons, **II** 476
J.S. Morgan & Co., **II** 329, 427
J. Sanders & Sons, **IV** 711
J. Sears & Company, **V** 177
J.T. Wing and Co., **I** 158
J.U. Dickson Sawmill Inc. See Dickson Forest Products, Inc.
J.W. Bateson, **8** 87
J.W. Buderus and Sons, **III** 694
J.W. Higman & Co., **III** 690
J.W. Wassall Ltd. See Wassall PLC.
J. Walter Thompson Co., **I** 9, 17, 25, 37, 251, 354, 623; **10** 69; **11** 51; **12** 168; **16** 167
J. Weingarten Inc., **7** 203
J. Wiss & Sons Co., **II** 16
J.Z. Sales Corp., **16** 36
J. Zinmeister Co., **II** 682
Jacintoport Corporation, **7** 281
Jack Daniel Distillery, **10** 180
Jack Eckerd Corp., **16** 160; **19** 467
Jack Frain Enterprises, **16** 471
Jack Henry and Associates, Inc., **17** **262–65**
Jack Houston Exploration Company, **7** 345
Jack in the Box, Inc., **14** 194
Jack Schwartz Shoes, Inc., **18** 266–68
Jackpot Enterprises Inc., **21** 298–300
Jackson & Curtis, **II** 444; **22** 405
Jackson Box Co., **IV** 311; **19** 267
Jackson Cushion Spring Co., **13** 397
Jackson Ice Cream Co., **12** 112
Jackson Marine Corp., **III** 499
Jackson National Life Insurance Company, **III** 335–36; **8** 276–77
Jackson Purchase Electric Cooperative Corporation, **11** 37
Jacksonville Shipyards, **I** 170

Jaco Electronics, **19** 311
Jacob Holm & Sons A/S, **22** 263
Jacob Leinenkeugle Brewing Company, **12** 338
Jacobs Brake Manufacturing Company, **7** 116–17
Jacobs Engineering Group Inc., **6** **148–50**
Jacobs Suchard (AG), **II** **520–22**, 540, 569; **15** 64
Jacobson Stores Inc., **21 301–03**
Jacoby & Meyers, **20** 435
Jacor Communications, Inc., **6** 33; **23** **292–95**
Jacques Borel International, **II** 641; **10** 12
Jacques Fath Perfumes, **III** 47
Jacuzzi Inc., **7** 207, 209; **23 296–98**
Jade Accessories, **14** 224
Jadepoint, **18** 79–80
JAF Pampryl, **I** 281
Jafra Cosmetics, **15** 475, 477
Jagenberg AG, **9** 445–46; **14** 57
Jaguar Cars, Ltd., **III** 439, 495; **11** 140; **13** 28, 219, 285–87, 414
JAI Parabolic Spring Ltd., **III** 582
JAIX Leasing Company, **23** 306
Ab Jakobstads Cellulosa-Pietarsaaren Selluloosa Oy, **IV** 302
Jaluzot & Cie. See Pinault-Printemps-Redoute S.A.
Jamaica Gas Light Co., **6** 455
Jamaica Plain Trust Co., **II** 207
Jamaica Water Supply Company. See JWP Inc.
JAMCO, **III** 589
James A. Ryder Transportation (Jartran), **V** 505
James Bay Development Corporation, **6** 502
James Beam Distilling Co., **I** 226; **10** 180
James Burn/American, Inc., **17** 458
James C. Heintz Company, **19** 278
James Ericson, **III** 324
James Felt Realty, Inc., **21** 257
James Fison and Sons. See Fisons plc.
James Fleming, **II** 500
James G. Fast Company. See Angelica Corporation.
James Gulliver Associates, **II** 609
James Hardie Containers, **IV** 249
James Hartley & Son, **III** 724
James Heekin and Company, **13** 254
James Lyne Hancock Ltd., **I** 428
James Magee & Sons Ltd., **IV** 294; **19** 224
James McNaughton Ltd., **IV** 325
James O. Welch Co., **II** 543
James Publishing Group, **17** 272
James R. Osgood & Company, **10** 356
James River Corporation of Virginia, **IV** **289–91**; **8** 483; **22** 209. See also Fort James Corporation.
James Stedman Ltd., **II** 569
James Talcott, Inc., **11** 260–61
James Thompson, **IV** 22
James Wholesale Company, **18** 7
James Wrigley & Sons, **IV** 257
Jamestown Publishers, **22** 522
Jamesway Corporation, **IV** 136; **13** 261; **23** 177
Jamieson & Co., **22** 428
Jamna Auto Industries Pvt. Ltd., **III** 581
Jämsänkoski Oy, **IV** 347
Jane Jones Enterprises, **16** 422
Jane's Information Group, **8** 525

Janesville Electric, **6** 604
Janet Frazer, **V** 118
Janson Publications, **22** 522
N.V. Janssen M&L, **17** 147
Janssen Pharmaceutica, **III** 36; **8** 282
Janssen-Kyowa, **III** 43
JANT Pty. Ltd., **IV** 285
Jantzen Inc., **V** 391; **17** 513
Janus Capital Corporation, **6** 401–02
Japan Acoustics, **II** 118
Japan Advertising Ltd., **16** 166
Japan Air Filter Co., Ltd., **III** 634
Japan Air Lines Co., **I** 104–06; **6** 70–71,
    118, 123, 386, 427
Japan Brewery. *See* Kirin Brewery
    Company, Limited.
Japan Broadcasting Corporation, **I** 586;
    II 66, 101, 118; **7** 248–50; **9** 31
Japan-California Bank, **II** 274
Japan Commerce Bank, **II** 291
Japan Copper Manufacturing Co., **II** 104;
    IV 211
Japan Cotton Co., **IV** 150
Japan Creative Tours Co., **I** 106
Japan Credit Bureau, **II** 348
Japan Dairy Products, **II** 538
Japan Day & Night Bank, **II** 292
Japan Development Bank, **II** 300, 403
Japan Dyestuff Manufacturing Co., **I** 397
Japan Elanco Company, Ltd., **17** 437
Japan Electricity Generation and
    Transmission Company (JEGTCO), **V**
    574
Japan Energy Corporation, **13** 202; **14** 206,
    208
Japan Food Corporation, **14** 288
Japan International Bank, **II** 292
Japan International Liquor, **I** 220
Japan Iron & Steel Co., Ltd., **IV** 157; **17**
    349–50
Japan Leasing Corporation, **8** 278–80;
    11 87
Japan National Oil Corp., **IV** 516
Japan National Railway, **V** 448–50; **6** 70
Japan Oil Development Co., **IV** 364
Japan Petroleum Development Corp., **IV**
    461
Japan Petroleum Exploration Co., **IV** 516
Japan Pulp and Paper Company
    Limited, **IV** 292–93, 680
Japan Reconstruction Finance Bank, **II** 300
Japan Special Steel Co., Ltd., **IV** 63
Japan Steel Manufacturing Co., **IV** 211
Japan Steel Works, **I** 508
Japan Telecom, **7** 118; **13** 482
Japan Telegraphic Communication
    Company (Nihon Denpo-Tsushin Sha),
    16 166
Japan Tobacco Incorporated, **V** 403–04
Japan Trust Bank, **II** 292
Japan Try Co., **III** 758
Japanese and Asian Development Bank, **IV**
    518
Japanese Electronic Computer Co., **III** 140
Japanese Enterprise Co., **IV** 728
Japanese National Railway, **I** 579; **III** 491
Japanese Victor Co., **II** 118
Japex Oman Co., **IV** 516
Japonica Partners, **9** 485
Jarcho Brothers Inc., **I** 513
Jardine Matheson Holdings Limited, **I**
    468–71, 521–22, 577, 592; **II** 296; **IV**
    189, 699–700; **16** 479–80; **18** 114; **20**
    309–14 (**upd.**)

Jartran Inc., **V** 505
Järvenpään Kotelo Oy, **IV** 315
Jas, Hennessy & Co., **I** 272
Jas. I. Miller Co., **13** 491
JASCO Products, **III** 581
Jason Incorporated, **23** 299–301
Jasper Corporation, **III** 767; **22** 546. *See*
    also Kimball International, Inc.
Jato, **II** 652
Jauch & Hübener, **14** 279
Java-China-Japan Line, **6** 403–04
Javelin Software Corporation, **10** 359
Javex Co., **IV** 272
Jax, **9** 452
Jay Cooke and Co., **III** 237; **9** 370
Jay Jacobs, Inc., **15** 243–45
Jay's Washateria, Inc., **7** 372
Jay-Ro Services, **III** 419
Jayco Inc., **13** 288–90
Jaywoth Industries, **III** 673
JBL, **22** 97
JCB, **14** 321
JCJL. *See* Java-China-Japan Line.
Jean Lassale, **III** 619–20; **17** 430
Jean Lincet, **19** 50
Jean Nate, **I** 695
Jean Pagées et Fils, **III** 420
Jean Prouvost, **IV** 618
Jean-Jacques, **19** 50
Jeanmarie Creations, Inc., **18** 67, 69
Jeanne Piaubert, **III** 47
Jefferson Chemical Co., **IV** 552
Jefferson Fire Insurance Co., **III** 239
Jefferson National Life Group, **10** 247
Jefferson Smurfit Group plc, **IV** 294–96;
    16 122; **19** 224–27 (**upd.**)
Jefferson Standard Life Insurance, **11**
    213–14
Jefferson Ward, **12** 48–49
Jefferson Warrior Railroad Company, **III**
    767; **22** 546
Jefferson-Pilot Corporation, **11** 213–15
Jeffery Sons & Co. Ltd., **IV** 711
Jeffrey Galion, **III** 472
JEGTCO. *See* Japan Electricity Generation
    and Transmission Company (JEGTCO).
Jell-O Co., **II** 531
Jem Development, **17** 233
Jenaer Glaswerk Schott & Genossen, **III**
    445, 447
Jenn-Air Corporation, **III** 573; **22** 349
Jennie-O Foods, **II** 506
Jenny Craig, Inc., **10** 382–84; **12** 531
Jeno's, **13** 516
Jensen Salsbery, **I** 715
Jenson, Woodward & Lozier, Inc., **21** 96
JEORA Co., **IV** 564
Jeppesen Sanderson, Inc., **IV** 677; **17** 486
Jepson Corporation, **8** 230
Jerome Increase Case Machinery Company.
    See J.I. Case Company.
Jerrold Corporation, **10** 319–20
Jerry Bassin Inc., **17** 12–14
Jerry's Restaurants, **13** 320
Jersey Paper, **IV** 261
Jersey Standard. *See* Standard Oil Co. of
    New Jersey.
Jesse L. Lasky Feature Play Co., **II** 154
Jessup & Moore Paper Co., **IV** 351; **19**
    495
Jet America Airlines, **I** 100; **6** 67, 82
Jet Capital Corp., **I** 123
Jet Petroleum, Ltd., **IV** 401
Jet Research Center, **III** 498

Jet Set Corporation, **18** 513
Jetway Systems, **III** 512
Jeumont-Industrie, **II** 93
Jeumont-Schneider Industries, **II** 93–94; **9**
    10; **18** 473
Jewel Companies, **II** 605; **6** 531; **12** 63; **18**
    89; **22** 38
Jewel Food Stores, **7** 127–28; **13** 25
Jewell Ridge Coal Corp., **IV** 181
JG Industries, Inc., **15** 240–42
Jheri Redding Products, Inc., **17** 108
Jiamusi Combine Harvester Factory, **21**
    175
JIB Group plc, **20** 313
Jiffee Chemical Corporation, **III** 21; **22**
    146
Jiffy Auto Rental, **16** 380
Jiffy Convenience Stores, **II** 627
Jiffy Lube International, Inc., **IV** 490; **21**
    541
Jiffy Packaging, **14** 430
Jiji, **16** 166
Jim Beam Brands Co., **14** 271–73
Jim Cole Enterprises, Inc., **19** 247
The Jim Henson Company, **23** 302–04
Jim Walter Corporation. *See* Walter
    Industries, Inc.
Jim Walter Papers, **IV** 282; **9** 261
Jitsugyo no Nihon-sha, **IV** 631
Jitsuyo Jidosha Seizo Co., **I** 183
JLA Credit, **8** 279
JMB Realty Corporation, **IV** 702–03
Jno. H. Swisher & Son. *See* Swisher
    International Group Inc.
JNR. *See* Japan National Railway.
Jo-Ann Fabrics and Crafts, **16** 197
Jo-Gal Shoe Company, Inc., **13** 360
Joanna Cotton Mills, **14** 220
Joannes Brothers, **II** 668
JobWorks Agency, Inc., **16** 50
Jockey International, Inc., **12** 283–85
Joe Alexander Press, **12** 472
Joe B. Hughes, **III** 498
Joe's American Bar & Grill, **20** 54
Joe's Crab Shack, **15** 279
Joh. Parviaisen Tehtaat Oy, **IV** 276
Johann Jakob Rieter & Co., **III** 402
Johannesburg Consolidated Investment Co.
    Ltd., **IV** 21–22, 118; **16** 293
John A. Frye Company, **V** 376; **8** 16
John A. Pratt and Associates, **22** 181
John Alden Life Insurance, **10** 340
John B. Sanfilippo & Son, Inc., **14**
    274–76
John Bean Spray Pump Co., **I** 442
John Blair & Company, **6** 13
John Brown plc, **I** 572–74
John Bull, **II** 550
John Crane International, **17** 480
John Crosland Company, **8** 88
John de Kuyper and Son, **I** 377
John Deere. *See* Deere & Company.
John F. Jelke Company, **9** 318
John F. Murray Co., **I** 623; **10** 69
John Fairfax Holdings Limited, **7**
    251–54
John Gardner Catering, **III** 104
John Govett & Co., **II** 349
John Gund Brewing Co., **I** 253
John H. Harland Company, **17** 266–69
John Hancock Mutual Life Insurance
    Company, **III** 265–68, 291, 313, 332,
    400; **IV** 283; **13** 530
John Hill and Son, **II** 569

John Holroyd & Co. of Great Britain, **7** 236
John L. Wortham & Son Agency, **III** 193
John Labatt Ltd., **I** 267; **II** 582; **8** 399; **16** 397; **17** 256–57
John Laing plc, I 575–76, 588
John Lewis Partnership plc, V 93–95; 13 307
John Lucas Co., **III** 745
John Lysaght, **III** 493–95
John M. Hart Company, **9** 304
John M. Smyth Co., **15** 282
John Macfarlane and Sons, **II** 593
John Mackintosh and Sons, **II** 568–69
John McConnell & Co., **13** 102
John McLean and Sons Ltd., **III** 753
John Morrell and Co., **II** 595–96; **21** 111
John Nicholls & Co., **III** 690
The John Nuveen Company, III 356; **21** 304–06; **22** 492, 494–95
John Oster Manufacturing Company. *See* Sunbeam-Oster.
John Pew & Company, **13** 243
John R. Figg, Inc., **II** 681
John Rogers Co., **9** 253
John Sands, **22** 35
John Strange Paper Company, **8** 358
John Swire & Sons Ltd. *See* Swire Pacific Ltd.
John Walker & Sons, **I** 239–40
John Wanamaker, **22** 110
John Wiley & Sons, Inc., 17 270–72
John Williams, **III** 691
John Wyeth & Bro., **I** 713
John Yokley Company, **11** 194
John Zink Company, **22** 3–4
Johns Manville Corporation, **19** 211–12
Johns Perry, **III** 673
Johns-Manville Corp., **III** 708; **7** 293; **11** 420
Johnsen, Jorgensen and Wettre, **14** 249
Johnson. *See* Axel Johnson Group.
Johnson & Higgins, 14 277–80
Johnson & Johnson, I 301; **II** 582; **III** 18, **35–37; IV** 285, 722; **7** 45–46; **8** 281–83 (upd.), 399, 511–12; **9** 89–90; **10** 47, 69, 78, 80, 534–35; **11** 200; **12** 186; **15** 357–58, 360; **16** 168, 440; **17** 104–05, 340, 342–43, 533; **18** 216; **19** 103, 105; **20** 8; **22** 257; **23** 188
Johnson and Patan, **III** 671
Johnson and Sons Smelting Works Ltd., **IV** 119
Johnson Brothers, **12** 528
Johnson, Carruthers & Rand Shoe Co., **III** 528
Johnson Controls, Inc., III 534–37; 13 398; **16** 184, 322
Johnson Diversified, Inc., **III** 59
Johnson Matthey PLC, II 390; **IV** 23, **117–20; 16** 28, **290–94 (upd.),** 439
Johnson Motor Co., **III** 597–99
Johnson Products Co., Inc., **11** 208
Johnson Systems, **6** 224
Johnson Wax. *See* S.C. Johnson & Son, Inc.
Johnston Coca-Cola Bottling Company of Chattanooga, **13** 163–64
Johnston Evans & Co., **IV** 704
Johnston Foil Co., **IV** 18
Johnston Harvester Co., **III** 650
Johnston Industries, Inc., 15 246–48
Johnstown America Industries, Inc., 23 305–07

Johnstown Sanitary Dairy, **13** 393
Jointless Rim Ltd., **I** 428
Jokisch, **II** 556
Jonathan Backhouse & Co., **II** 235
Jonathan Logan Inc., **13** 536
Jonell Shoe Manufacturing Corporation, **13** 360
Jones & Babson, Inc., **14** 85
Jones & Johnson, **14** 277
Jones & Laughlin Steel Corp., **I** 463, 489–91; **IV** 228; **11** 197
Jones Apparel Group, Inc., 11 216–18
Jones Brothers Tea Co., **7** 202
Jones Environmental, **11** 361
Jones Intercable, Inc., 14 260; **17** 7; **21** **307–09**
Jones Motor Co., **10** 44
Jonker Fris, **II** 571
Jonkoping & Vulcan, **12** 462
Jordache Enterprises, Inc., 15 201–02; **23 308–10**
The Jordan Co., **11** 261; **16** 149
Jordan Marsh, **III** 608; **V** 26; **9** 209
Jordan Valley Electric Cooperative, **12** 265
Jos. A. Bank Clothiers, **II** 560; **12** 411
Josef Meys, **III** 418
Joseph Bellamy and Sons Ltd., **II** 569
Joseph Campbell Co., **II** 479; **7** 66
Joseph Crosfield, **III** 31
Joseph E. Seagram & Sons Inc., **I** 266, 285; **21** 319
Joseph Garneau Co., **I** 226; **10** 180
Joseph Leavitt Corporation, **9** 20
Joseph Lucas & Son, **III** 554–56
Joseph Magnin, **I** 417–18; **17** 124
Joseph Nathan & Co., **I** 629–40
Joseph Rank Limited, **II** 564
Joseph T. Ryerson & Son, Inc., IV 114; **15 249–51; 19** 217, 381
Joshin Denki, **13** 481
Joshu Railway Company, **6** 431
Josiah Wedgwood and Sons Limited. *See* Waterford Wedgewood Holdings PLC.
Jostens Inc., 7 255–57
Journey's End Corporation, **14** 107
Jovan, **III** 66
Jove Publications, Inc., **II** 144; **IV** 623; **12** 224
Jovi, **II** 652
Joy Manufacturing, **III** 526
Joy Planning Co., **III** 533
Joy Technologies, **II** 17
Joyce International, Inc., **16** 68
JP Household Supply Co. Ltd., **IV** 293
JP Information Center Co., Ltd., **IV** 293
JP Planning Co. Ltd., **IV** 293
JPC Co., **IV** 155
JPS Automotive L.P., **17** 182–84
JPT Publishing, **8** 528
JT Aquisitions, **II** 661
JTL Corporation, **13** 162–63
JTN Acquisition Corp., **19** 233
JTS Corporation, **23** 23, 26
Jude Hanbury, **I** 294
Judel Glassware Co., Inc., **14** 502
Judson Dunaway Corp., **12** 127
Judson Steel Corp., **13** 97
Jugend & Volk, **14** 556
Jugo Bank, **II** 325
Juice Bowl Products, **II** 480–81
Jujo Paper Co., Ltd., IV 268, 284–85, 292–93, **297–98,** 321, 326, 328, 356
Julius Berger-Bauboag A.G., **I** 560–61
Julius Garfinckel & Co., Inc., **22** 110

Jumping-Jacks Shoes, Inc., **17** 390
Jung-Pumpen, **III** 570; **20** 361
Junghans Uhren, **10** 152
Junkers Luftverkehr, **I** 110, 197; **6** 87–88
Juovo Pignone, **13** 356
Jupiter National, **15** 247–48; **19** 166
Jurgens, **II** 588–89
Jurgensen's, **17** 558
Jurgovan & Blair, **III** 197
Juristförlaget, **14** 556
Jusco Car Life Company, **23** 290
JUSCO Co., Ltd., V 96–99; 11 498
Just For Feet, Inc., 19 228–30
Justin Industries, Inc., 19 231–33
JVC. *See* Victor Company of Japan, Ltd.
JW Aluminum Company, **22** 544
JWP Inc., 9 300–02; 13 176
JWT Group Inc., I 9, **19–21,** 23; **6** 53. *See also* WPP Group plc.
Jylhävaara, **IV** 348
JZC. *See* John Zink Company.

K Line. *See* Kawasaki Kisen Kaisha, Ltd.
K&B Inc., 12 286–88; 17 244
K&F Manufacturing. *See* Fender Musical Instruments.
K & G Men's Center, Inc., 21 310–12
K&K Toys, Inc., **23** 176
K&L, **6** 48
K&M Associates, **16** 18
K & R Warehouse Corporation, **9** 20
K-C Aviation, **III** 41; **16** 304
K.C.C. Holding Co., **III** 192
K.F. Kline Co., **7** 145; **22** 184
K-Graphics Inc., **16** 306
K-H Corporation, **7** 260
K. Hattori & Co., Ltd., **III** 454–55, 619–20. *See also* Seiko Corporation.
k.k. Staatsbahnen, **6** 419
K-Swiss, **22** 173
K-tel International, Inc., 21 325–28
K-III Communications Corp. *See* Primedia Inc.
K-III Holdings. *See* Primedia Inc.
K.W. Muth Company, **17** 305
Ka Wah AMEV Insurance, **III** 200–01
Kable News Company. *See* AMREP Corporation.
Kable Printing Co., **13** 559
Kaduna Refining and Petrochemicals Co., **IV** 473
Kaepa, **16** 546
Kaestner & Hecht Co., **II** 120
Kaga Forwarding Co., **6** 428
Kagami Crystal Works, **III** 714
Kagle Home Health Care, **11** 282
Kagoshima Central Research Laboratory, **21** 330
Kahan and Lessin, **II** 624–25
Kahn's Meats, **II** 572
Kai Tak Land Investment Co., **IV** 717
Kaiser Aluminum & Chemical Corporation, IV 11–12, 15, 59–60, **121–23,** 191; **6** 148; **12** 377; **8** 348, 350; **22** 455
Kaiser Cement, **III** 501, 760; **IV** 272
Kaiser Company, **6** 184
Kaiser Engineering, **IV** 218
Kaiser Industries, **III** 760
Kaiser Packaging, **12** 377
Kaiser Permanente Corp., **6** 279; **12** 175
Kaiser Steel, **IV** 59
Kaizosha, **IV** 632
Kajaani Oy, **II** 302; **IV** 350

Kajima Corp., I 577–78
Kal Kan Foods, Inc., 22 298–300
Kalamazoo Paper Co., IV 281; 9 259
Kalbfleish, I 300
Kaldveer & Associates, 14 228
Kalitta Group, 22 311
Kalua Koi Corporation, 7 281
Kalumburu Joint Venture, IV 67
Kamaishi, IV 157; 17 349
Kaman Corp., 12 289–92; 16 202
Kamioka Mining & Smelting Co., Ltd., IV 145, 148
Kammer Valves, A.G., 17 147
Kanagawa Bank, II 291
Kanda Shokai, 16 202
Kane Financial Corp., III 231
Kane Foods, III 43
Kane Freight Lines, 6 370
Kane-Miller Corp., 12 106
Kanebo Spinning Inc., IV 442
Kanegafuchi Shoji, IV 225
Kanematsu Corporation, IV 442–44
Kangaroo. *See* Seino Transportation Company, Ltd.
Kangol Ltd., IV 136
Kangyo Bank, II 300, 310, 361
Kanhym, IV 91–92
Kansai Electric Power Co., Inc., IV 492; V 645–48
Kansai Seiyu Ltd., V 188
Kansai Sogo Bank, II 361
Kansallis-Osake-Pankki, II 242, 302–03, 366; IV 349
Kansas City Power & Light Company, 6 510–12, 592; 12 541–42
Kansas City Securities Corporation, 22 541
Kansas City Southern Industries, Inc., 6 400–02
Kansas City White Goods Company. *See* Angelica Corporation.
Kansas Fire & Casualty Co., III 214
Kansas Power Company, 6 312
Kansas Public Service Company, 12 541
Kansas Utilities Company, 6 580
Kanto Steel Co., Ltd., IV 63
Kanzaki Paper Manufacturing Co., IV 285, 293
Kao Corporation, III 38–39, 48; 16 168; 20 315–17 (upd.)
Kaohsiung Refinery, IV 388
Kaolin Australia Pty Ltd., III 691
Kaplan Educational Centers, 12 143
Kapy, II 139
Karafuto Industry, IV 320
Karan Co. *See* Donna Karan Company.
Karastan Bigelow, 19 276
Karg'sche Familienstiftung, V 73
Karmelkorn Shoppes, Inc., 10 371, 373
Karstadt Aktiengesellschaft, V 100–02; 19 234–37 (upd.)
Kasado Dockyard, III 760
Kasai Securities, II 434
Kaset Rojananil, 6 123
Kash n' Karry Food Stores, Inc., 20 318–20
Kasmarov, 9 18
Kaspare Cohn Commercial & Savings Bank. *See* Union Bank of California.
Kast Metals, III 452; 15 92
Kat-Em International Inc., 16 125
Katalco, I 374
Kataoka Electric Co., II 5
Katelise Group, III 739–40
Katharine Gibbs Schools Inc., 22 442

Kathleen Investment (Australia) Ltd., III 729
Kathy's Ranch Markets, 19 500–01
Katies, V 35
Kativo Chemical Industries Ltd., 8 239
Katy Industries Inc., I 472–74; 14 483–84; 16 282
Katz Communications, Inc., 6 32–34
Katz Drug, II 604
Kauffman-Lattimer, III 9–10
Kaufhalle AG, V 104; 23 311
Kaufhof Holding AG, II 257; V 103–05
Kaufhof Warenhaus AG, 23 311–14 (upd.)
Kaufman and Broad Home Corporation, 8 284–86; 11 481–83
Kaufmann Department Stores, Inc., V 132–33; 6 243; 19 262
Kaukaan Tehdas Osakeyhtiö, IV 301
Oy Kaukas Ab, IV 300–02; 19 462
Kaukauna Cheese Inc., 23 217, 219
Kauppaosakeyhtiö Kymmene Aktiebolag, IV 299
Kauppiaitten Oy, 8 293
Kautex Werke Reinold Hagen AG, IV 128
Kautex-Bayern GmbH, IV 128
Kautex-Ostfriedland GmbH, IV 128
Kawachi Bank, II 361
Kawamata, 11 350
Kawasaki Denki Seizo, II 22
Kawasaki Heavy Industries, Ltd., I 75; II 273–74; III 482, 513, 516, 538–40, 756; IV 124; 7 232; 8 72; 23 290
Kawasaki Kisen Kaisha, Ltd., V 457–60
Kawasaki Steel Corporation, I 432; II 274; III 539, 760; IV 30, 124–25, 154, 212–13; 13 324; 19 8
Kawashimaya Shoten Inc. Ltd., II 433
Kawecki Berylco Industries, 8 78
Kawneer GmbH., IV 18
Kawsmouth Electric Light Company. *See* Kansas City Power & Light Company.
Kay County Gas Co., IV 399
Kay Home Products, 17 372
Kay's Drive-In Food Service, II 619
Kay-Bee Toy Stores, V 137; 15 252–53; 16 389–90
Kaydon Corporation, 18 274–76
Kayex, 9 251
Kaynar Manufacturing Company, 8 366
Kayser Aluminum & Chemicals, 8 229
Kayser Roth Corp., 8 288; 22 122
Kaysersberg, S.A., IV 290
KBLCOM Incorporated, V 644
KC Holdings, Inc., 11 229–30
KCPL. *See* Kansas City Power & Light Company.
KCS Industries, 12 25–26
KCSI. *See* Kansas City Southern Industries, Inc.
KCSR. *See* Kansas City Southern Railway.
KDT Industries, Inc., 9 20
Keebler Co., II 594
Keefe Manufacturing Courtesy Coffee Company, 6 392
Keen, Robinson and Co., II 566
KEG Productions Ltd., IV 640
Keihan JUSCO, V 96
Keil Chemical Company, 8 178
Keio Teito Electric Railway Company, V 461–62
Keisei Electric Railway, II 301
Keith Prowse Music Publishing, 22 193
Keith-Albee-Orpheum, II 88

Keithley Instruments Inc., 16 299–301
Keller-Dorian Graveurs, S.A., 17 458
Kelley & Partners, Ltd., 14 130
Kellock, 10 336
Kellogg Company, I 22–23; II 463, 502–03, 523–26, 530, 560; 10 323–24; 12 411; 13 3, 291–94 (upd.); 15 189; 18 65, 225–26; 22 336, 338
Kellwood Company, V 181–82; 8 287–89
Kelly & Associates, III 306
Kelly & Cohen, 10 468
Kelly, Douglas and Co., II 631
Kelly Nason, Inc., 13 203
Kelly Services, Inc., 6 35–37, 140; 9 326; 16 48
The Kelly-Springfield Tire Company, 8 290–92; 20 260, 263
Kelsey-Hayes Group of Companies, I 170; III 650, 652; 7 258–60
Kelso & Co., III 663, 665; 12 436; 19 455; 21 490
Kelty Pack, Inc., 10 215
Kelvinator Inc., 17 487
KemaNobel, 9 380–81; 13 22
Kemet Corp., 14 281–83
Kemi Oy, IV 316
Kemira, Inc., III 760; 6 152
Kemp's Biscuits Limited, II 594
Kemper Corporation, III 269–71, 339; 15 254–58 (upd.); 22 495
Kemper Motorenfabrik, I 197
Kemper Snowboards, 22 460
Kemperco Inc., III 269–70
Kempinski Group, II 258
Kemps Biscuits, II 594
Ken-L-Ration, II 559
Kendall International, Inc., I 529; III 24–25; IV 288; 11 219–21; 14 121; 15 229
Kenetech Corporation, 11 222–24
Kennametal, Inc., IV 203; 13 295–97
Kennecott Corporation, III 248; IV 33–34, 79, 170–71, 179, 192, 288, 576; 7 261–64; 10 262, 448; 12 244
Kennedy Automatic Products Co., 16 8
Kenner, II 502; 10 323; 12 168
Kenner Parker Toys, Inc., II 503; 9 156; 10 324; 14 266; 16 337
Kenneth Cole Production, 22 223
Kenneth O. Lester, Inc., 21 508
Kenny Rogers' Roasters, 22 464
Kenroy International, Inc., 13 274
Kent Drugs Ltd., II 640, 650
Kent Electronics Corporation, 17 273–76
Kent Fire, III 350
Kent-Moore Corp., I 200; 10 492–93
Kentland-Elkhorn Coal Corp., IV 181
Kentucky Bonded Funeral Co., III 217
Kentucky Fried Chicken, I 260–61; II 533; III 78, 104, 106; 6 200; 7 26–28, 433; 8 563; 12 42; 13 336; 16 97; 18 8, 538; 19 92; 21 361; 22 464; 23 384, 504. *See also* KFC Corporation.
Kentucky Utilities Company, 6 513–15; 11 37, 236–38
Kenway, I 155
Kenwood, I 532; 19 360; 23 53
Kenworth Motor Truck Corp., I 185–86
Kenyon Corp., 18 276
Kenyon Sons and Craven Ltd., II 593–94
Keo Cutters, Inc., III 569; 20 360
KEPCO. *See* Kyushu Electric Power Company Inc.
Kerlick, Switzer & Johnson, 6 48

Kerlyn Oil Co., **IV** 445–46
Kern County Land Co., **I** 527; **10** 379, 527
Kernite SA, **8** 386
Kernkraftwerke Lippe-Ems, **V** 747
Kernridge Oil Co., **IV** 541
Kerr Concrete Pipe Company, **14** 250
Kerr Corporation, **14** 481
Kerr Glass Manufacturing Co., **III** 423; **22** 48
Kerr Group Inc., **10** 130
Kerr-Addison Mines Ltd., **IV** 165
Kerr-McGee Corporation, IV 445–47; **13** 118; **22 301–04 (upd.)**
Kerry Properties Limited, 22 305–08
Keski-Suomen Tukkukauppa Oy, **8** 293
Kesko Ltd (Kesko Oy), 8 293–94
Ketchikan International Sales Co., **IV** 304
Ketchikan Pulp Co., **IV** 304
Ketchum Communications Inc., 6 38–40
Ketner and Milner Stores, **II** 683
Keumkang Co., **III** 515; **7** 231
Kewanee Public Service Company, **6** 505
Key Computer Laboratories, Inc., **14** 15
Key Markets, **II** 628
Key Pharmaceuticals, Inc., **11** 207
Key Tronic Corporation, 14 284–86
KeyCorp, **8 295–97; 11** 110; **14** 90
Keyes Fibre Company, 9 303–05
Keystone Aircraft, **I** 61; **11** 164
Keystone Consolidated Industries, Inc., **19** 467
Keystone Custodian Fund, **IV** 458
Keystone Foods Corporation, **10** 443
Keystone Franklin, Inc., **III** 570; **9** 543; **20** 362
Keystone Frozen Foods, **17** 536
Keystone Gas Co., **IV** 548
Keystone Insurance and Investment Co., **12** 564
Keystone International, Inc., 11 225–27
Keystone Life Insurance Co., **III** 389
Keystone Paint and Varnish, **8** 553
Keystone Pipe and Supply Co., **IV** 136
Keystone Portland Cement Co., **23** 225
Keystone Savings and Loan, **II** 420
Keytronics, **18** 541
KFC Corporation, 7 265–68; 10 450; **21 313–17 (upd.); 23** 115, 117, 153. *See also* Kentucky Fried Chicken.
Khalda Petroleum Co., **IV** 413
KHBB, **16** 72
KHD AG. *See* Klöckner-Humboldt-Deutz AG.
KHD Konzern, III 541–44
KHL. *See* Koninklijke Hollandsche Lloyd.
Kholberg, Kravis & Roberts, **13** 453
Kia Motors Corp., I 167; **12 293–95**
Kidd, Kamm & Co., **21** 482
Kidde Inc., I 475–76; **III** 503; **7** 209; **23** 297
Kidder, Peabody & Co., **II** 31, 207, 430; **IV** 84; **7** 310; **12** 197; **13** 465–67, 534; **16** 322; **22** 406
Kidder Press Co., **IV** 644
Kids ''R'' Us, **V** 203–05; **9** 394
Kids Foot Locker, **14** 293, 295
Kidston Mines, **I** 438
Kiekhaefer Corporation, **III** 443; **22** 115
Kien, **13** 545
Kienzle Apparate GmbH, **III** 566
Kierulff Electronics, **10** 113
Kieser Verlag, **14** 555
Kiewit Diversified Group Inc., **11** 301
Kiewit-Murdock Investment Corp., **15** 129

Kijkshop/Best-Sellers, **13** 545
Kikkoman Corporation, I 9; **14 287–89**
Kilburn & Co., **III** 522
Kilgo Motor Express, **6** 370
Kilgore Ceramics, **III** 671
Kilgore Federal Savings and Loan Assoc., **IV** 343
Kilpatrick's Department Store, **19** 511
Kilsby Tubesupply, **I** 570
Kimball International, Inc., 12 296–98
Kimbell Inc., **II** 684
Kimberley Central Mining Co., **IV** 64; **7** 121
Kimberly-Clark Corporation, **I** 14, 413; **III** 36, 40–41; **IV** 249, 254, 297–98, 329, 648, 665; **8** 282; **15** 357; **16 302–05 (upd.); 17** 30, 397; **18** 147–49; **19** 14, 284, 478; **22** 209
Kimco Realty Corporation, 11 228–30
Kincaid Furniture Company, **14** 302–03
Kinden Corporation, **7** 303
KinderCare Learning Centers, Inc., 13 298–300
Kinear Moodie, **III** 753
Kinetic Concepts, Inc., 20 321–23
King & Spalding, 23 315–18
King Bearing, Inc., **13** 79
King Cullen, **II** 644
King Features Syndicate, **IV** 626; **19** 201, 203–04
King Folding Box Co., **13** 441
King Fook Gold and Jewellery Co., **IV** 717
King Hickory, **17** 183
King Kullen Grocery Co., Inc., 15 259–61; 19 481
King Ranch, Inc., 14 290–92
King Soopers Inc., **12** 112–13
King World Productions, Inc., 9 306–08
King's Lynn Glass, **12** 528
King-Seeley, **II** 419; **16** 487
Kingfisher plc, V 106–09; 10 498; **19** 123
Kings County Lighting Company, **6** 456
Kings County Research Laboratories, **11** 424
Kings Mills, Inc., **13** 532
Kingsford Corporation, **III** 21; **22** 146
Kingsin Line, **6** 397
Kingsport Pulp Corp., **IV** 310; **19** 266
Kingston Technology Corporation, 20 324–26
Kinki Nippon Railway Company Ltd., V 463–65
Kinko's Inc., 12 174; **16 306–08; 18** 363–64
Kinnevik, **IV** 203–04
Kinney Corporation, **23** 32
Kinney National Service Inc., **II** 176; **IV** 672; **19** 404
Kinney Services, **6** 293
Kinney Shoe Corp., V 226; **11** 349; **14 293–95**
Kinney Tobacco Co., **12** 108
Kinoshita Sansho Steel Co., **I** 508
Kinpo Electronic, **23** 212
Kinross, **IV** 92
Kintec Corp., **10** 97
Kirby. *See* Scott Fetzer Company.
Kirby Corporation, 18 277–79; 22 275
Kirby Forest Industries, **IV** 305
Kirch Group, **10** 196
Kirchner, Moore, and Co., **II** 408
Kirin Brewery Company, Limited, I 220, 258, **265–66**, 282; **10** 78, 80; **13** 258, 454; **20** 28; **21 318–21 (upd.)**

Kirk Stieff Company, **10** 181; **12** 313
Kirkland Messina, Inc., **19** 392, 394
Kirkstall Forge Engineering, **III** 494
Kirsch Co., **II** 16
Kirschner Manufacturing Co., **16** 296
Kishimoto & Co., **I** 432, 492
Kishimoto Shoten Co., Ltd., **IV** 168
Kistler, Lesh & Co., **III** 528
Kit Manufacturing Co., 18 280–82
Kita Consolidated, Ltd., **16** 142
Kita Karafunto Oil Co., **IV** 475
Kita Nippon Paper Co., **IV** 321
Kitagawa & Co. Ltd., **IV** 442
Kitchell Corporation, 14 296–98
KitchenAid, III 611, 653–54; **8 298–99**
Kitchenbell, **III** 43
Kitchens of Sara Lee, **II** 571–73
Kittery Electric Light Co., **14** 124
Kittinger, **10** 324
Kitty Hawk, Inc., 22 309–11
Kiwi International Airlines Inc., **20** 327–29
Kiwi Packaging, **IV** 250
Kiwi Polish Co., **15** 507
Kjøbenhavns Bandelsbank, **II** 366
KJPCL. *See* Royal Interocean Lines.
KKK Shipping, **II** 274
KKR. *See* Kohlberg Kravis Roberts & Co.
KLA Instruments Corporation, 11 231–33; 20 8
Klein Bicycles, **16** 495
Kleiner, Perkins, Caufield & Byers, **I** 637; **6** 278; **10** 15, 504; **14** 263; **16** 418
Kleinwort Benson Group PLC, II 379, **421–23; IV** 191; **22** 55
Kline Manufacturing, **II** 16
KLM. *See* Koninklijke Luftvaart Maatschappij N.V.
Klöckner-Humboldt-Deutz AG, **I** 542; **III** 541–44; **IV** 126–27; **13** 16–17
Klöckner-Werke AG, IV 43, 60, **126–28**, 201; **19** 64
Klondike, **14** 205
Klopman International, **12** 118
Kloth-Senking, **IV** 201
Kluwer Publishers, **IV** 611; **14** 555
Klynveld Main Goerdeler, **10** 387
Klynveld Peat Marwick Goerdeler. *See* KPMG Worldwide.
KM&G. *See* Ketchum Communications Inc.
Kmart Corporation, I 516; **V** 35, **110–12; 6** 13; **7** 61, 444; **9** 361, 400, 482; **10** 137, 410, 490, 497, 515–16; **12** 48, 54–55, 430, 477–78, 507–08; **13** 42, 260–61, 274, 317–18, 444, 446; **14** 192, 394; **15** 61–62, 210–11, 330–31, 470; **16** 35–37, 61, 187, 210, 447, 457; **17** 297, 460–61, 523–24; **18** 137, **283–87 (upd.)**, 477; **19** 511; **20** 155–56; **21** 73; **22** 258, 328; **23** 210, 329
KMP Holdings, **I** 531
KN. *See* Kühne & Nagel Group.
Kna-Shoe Manufacturing Company, **14** 302
Knape & Vogt Manufacturing Company, 17 277–79
Knapp & Tubbs, **III** 423
Knapp Communications, **II** 656; **13** 180
Knapp-Monarch, **12** 251
Knauf, **III** 721, 736
KNI Retail A/S, **12** 363
Knickerbocker Toy Co., **III** 505
Knickerbocker Trust Company, **13** 465

Knife River Coal Mining Company, **7** 322–25
Knight Paper Co., **III** 766; **22** 545
Knight-Ridder, Inc., **III** 190; **IV** 597, 613, **628–30**, 670; **6** 323; **7** 191, 327; **10** 407; **15 262–66 (upd.)**; **18** 323
Knoff-Bremse, **I** 138
Knogo Corp., **11** 444
Knoll Group Inc., **I** 202; **14 299–301**
Knoll Pharmaceutical, **I** 682
Knomark, **III** 55
Knorr Co. *See* C.H. Knorr Co.
Knorr-Bremse, **11** 31
Knott, **III** 98
Knott's Berry Farm, **18 288–90**; **22** 130
Knowledge Systems Concepts, **11** 469
KnowledgeWare Inc., **9 309–11**
Knoxville Paper Box Co., Inc., **13** 442
KNSM. *See* Koninklijke Nederlandsche Stoomboot Maatschappij.
Knudsen & Sons, Inc., **11** 211
Knutange, **IV** 226
Kobacker Co., **18** 414–15
Kobayashi Tomijiro Shoten, **III** 44
Kobe Shipbuilding & Engine Works, **II** 57
Kobe Steel, Ltd., **I** 511; **II** 274; **IV** 16, **129–31**, 212–13; **8** 242; **11** 234–35; **13** 297; **19 238–41 (upd.)**
Kobelco America Inc., **19** 241
Kobelco Middle East, **IV** 131
Koç Holdings A.S., **I** 167, **478–80**; **11** 139
Koch Industries, Inc., **IV 448–49**; **20 330–32 (upd.)**; **21** 108; **22** 3
Koch-Light Laboratories, **13** 239
Kockos Brothers, Inc., **II** 624
Kodak. *See* Eastman Kodak Company.
Kodansha Ltd., **IV 631–33**
Ködel & Böhn GmbH, **III** 543
Koehring Company, **8** 545; **23** 299
Koehring Cranes & Excavators, **7** 513
Koei Real Estate Ltd., **V** 195
Koenig Plastics Co., **19** 414
Kohl's Corporation, **9 312–13**; **22** 72
Kohl's Food Stores, Inc., **I** 426–27; **16** 247, 249
Kohlberg Kravis Roberts & Co., **I** 566, 609–11; **II** 370, 452, 468, 544, 645, 654, 656, 667; **III** 263, 765–67; **IV** 642–43; **V** 55–56, 408, 410, 415; **6** 357; **7** 130, 132, 200; **9** 53, 180, 230, 469, 522; **10** 75–77, 302; **12** 559; **13** 163, 166, 363; **14** 42; **15** 270; **17** 471; **18** 3; **19** 493; **22** 55, 91, 441, 513, 544; **23** 163
Kohler Bros., **IV** 91
Kohler Company, **7 269–71**; **10** 119
Kohner Brothers, **II** 531
Koholyt AG, **III** 693
Koike Shoten, **II** 458
Kojiro Matsukata, **V** 457–58
Kokkola Chemicals Oy, **17** 362–63
Kokomo Gas and Fuel Company, **6** 533
Kokuei Paper Co., Ltd., **IV** 327
Kokura Sekiyu Co. Ltd., **IV** 554
Kokura Steel Manufacturing Co., Ltd., **IV** 212
Kokusai Kisen, **V** 457–58
Kokusaku Kiko Co., Ltd., **IV** 327
Kokusaku Pulp Co., **IV** 327
Kolbenschmidt, **IV** 141
Kolker Chemical Works, Inc., **IV** 409; **7** 308
The Koll Company, **8 300–02**; **21** 97
Kollmorgen Corporation, **18 291–94**

Komag, Inc., **11 234–35**
Komatsu Ltd., **III** 453, 473, **545–46**; **15** 92; **16 309–11 (upd.)**
Kommanditgesellschaft S. Elkan & Co., **IV** 140
Kommunale Energie-Beteiligungsgesellschaft, **V** 746
Kompro Computer Leasing, **II** 457
Konan Camera Institute, **III** 487
Kongl. Elektriska Telegraf-Verket, **V** 331
Kongo Bearing Co., **III** 595
Konica Corporation, **III 547–50**
Koninklijke Ahold N.V., **II 641–42**; **12** 152–53; **16 312–14 (upd.)**
Koninklijke Distilleerderijen der Erven Lucas Böls, **I** 226
Koninklijke Java-China Paketvaart Lijnen. *See* Royal Interocean Lines.
Koninklijke Luchtvaart Maatschappij N.V., **I** 55, **107–09**, 119, 121; **6** 95, 105, 109–10; **14** 73
Koninklijke Nederlandsche Hoogovens en Staalfabrieken NV, **IV** 105, 123, **132–34**
Koninklijke Nederlandsche Maatschappig Tot Exploitatie van Petroleumbronnen in Nederlandsch-indie, **IV** 530
Koninklijke Nederlandsche Petroleum Maatschappij, **IV** 491
Koninklijke Nederlandse Vliegtuigenfabriek Fokker, **I** 46, **54–56**, 75, 82, 107, 115, 121–22
Koninklijke Nedlloyd Groep N.V., **6 403–05**
Koninklijke PTT Nederland NV, **V 299–301**
Koninklijke Van Ommeren, **22** 275
Koninklijke Wessanen N.V., **II 527–29**
Koniphoto Corp., **III** 548
Konishi Honten, **III** 547
Konishi Pharmaceutical, **I** 704
Konishiroku Honten Co., Ltd., **III** 487, 547–49
Konoike Bank, **II** 347
Koopman & Co., **III** 419
Koor Industries Ltd., **II 47–49**; **22** 501
Koortrade, **II** 48
Kop-Coat, Inc., **8** 456
Kopin Corp., **13** 399
Koppens Machinenfabriek, **III** 420
Kopper United, **I** 354
Koppers Inc., **I** 199, **354–56**; **III** 645, 735; **6** 486; **17** 38–39
Koracorp Industries Inc., **16** 327
Korbel, **I** 226
Korea Automotive Fuel Systems Ltd., **13** 555
Korea Automotive Motor Corp., **16** 436
Korea Development Leasing Corp., **II** 442
Korea Steel Co., **III** 459
Korea Telecommunications Co, **I** 516
Korean Air Lines Co. Ltd., **II** 442; **6 98–99**
Korean Development Bank, **III** 459
Korean Tungsten Mining Co., **IV** 183
Kori Kollo Corp., **23** 41
Koro Corp., **19** 414
Korrekt Gebäudereinigung, **16** 420
KorrVu, **14** 430
Kortbetalning Servo A.B., **II** 353
Kortgruppen Eurocard-Köpkort A.B., **II** 353
Korvettes, E.J., **14** 426

Koryeo Industrial Development Co., **III** 516; **7** 232
Koryo Fire and Marine Insurance Co., **III** 747
Kosset Carpets, Ltd., **9** 467
Kotobukiya Co., Ltd., **V 113–14**
Kowa Metal Manufacturing Co., **III** 758
Koyo Seiko, **III** 595–96, 623–24
KPM. *See* Koninklijke Paketvaart Maatschappij.
KPMG Worldwide, **7** 266; **10** 115, **385–87**
KPR Holdings Inc., **23** 203
Kraft Foods, Inc., **II** 129, **530–34**, 556; **V** 407; **III** 610; **7 272–77 (upd.)**, 339, 433, 547; **8** 399, 499; **9** 180, 290, 318; **11** 15; **12** 372, 532; **13** 408, 515, 517; **14** 204; **16** 88, 90; **17** 56; **18** 67, 246, 416, 419; **19** 51; **22** 82, 85; **23** 219, 384
Kraft-Versicherungs-AG, **III** 183
Kraftco Corporation, **II** 533; **14** 204
KraftMaid Cabinetry, Inc., **20** 363
Kraftwerk Union, **I** 411; **III** 466
Kramer, **III** 48
Krämer & Grebe, **III** 420
Krames Communications Co., **22** 441, 443
Krasnapolsky Restaurant and Wintergarden Company Ltd., **23** 228
Krauss-Maffei AG, **I** 75; **II** 242; **III** 566, 695; **14** 328
Kravco, **III** 248
Kredietbank N.V., **II** 295, **304–05**
Kreditanstalt für Wiederaufbau, **IV** 231–32
Kreft, **III** 480; **22** 26
Krelitz Industries, Inc., **14** 147
Krema Hollywood Chewing Gum Co. S.A., **II** 532
Kremers-Urban, **I** 667
Kresge Foundation, **V** 110
Kreuger & Toll, **IV** 338; **12** 462–63
Kreymborg, **13** 544–45
Kriegschemikalien AG, **IV** 229
Kriegsmetall AG, **IV** 229
Kriegswollbedarfs AG, **IV** 229
Krislex Knits, Inc., **8** 235
Krispy Kitchens, Inc., **II** 584
Krispy Kreme Doughnut Corporation, **21 322–24**
The Kroger Company, **II** 605, 632, **643–45**, 682; **III** 218; **6** 364; **7** 61; **12** 111–13; **13** 25, 237, 395; **15** 259, **267–70 (upd.)**, 449; **16** 63–64; **18** 6; **21** 323, 508; **22** 37, 126
Krohn-Fechheimer Shoe Company, **V** 207
Krones A.G., **I** 266; **21** 319
Kronos, Inc., **18 295–97**; **19** 468
Krovtex, **8** 80
Kroy Tanning Company, **17** 195
Krueger Insurance Company, **21** 257
Kruger Inc., **17 280–82**
Krumbhaar Chemical Inc., **14** 308
Krupp Widia GmbH, **12** 66
Krups, **17** 214; **22** 364. *See also* Fried. Krupp GmbH.
KSSU Group, **I** 107–08, 120–21
KTR. *See* Keio Teito Electric Railway Company.
K2 Inc., **16 295–98**; **22** 481, 483; **23** 474
KU Energy Corporation, **6** 513, 515; **11 236–38**
Kubota Corporation, **I** 494; **III 551–53**; **10** 404; **12** 91, 161; **21** 385–86
Kubota, Gonshiro. *See* Gonshiro Oode.
Kuhara Mining Co., **IV** 475

Kuhlman Corporation, **20** 333–35
Kuhlmann, **III** 677; **IV** 174; **16** 121
Kuhn Loeb, **II** 402–03
Kühne & Nagel International AG, V 466–69
Kuitu Oy, **IV** 348
KUK, **III** 577, 712
Kukje Group, **III** 458
Kulka Smith Inc., **13** 398
Kulmobelwerk G.H. Walb and Co., **I** 581
Kum-Kleen Products, **IV** 252; **17** 29
Kumagai Gumi Co., I 579–80
Kumsung Companies, **III** 747–48
Kunkel Industries, **19** 143
Kunst und Technik Verlag, **IV** 590
Kuo International Ltd., **I** 566
The Kuppenheimer Company, **8** 248–50
Kureha Chemical Industry, **I** 675
Kureha Textiles, **I** 432, 492
Kurosawa Construction Co., Ltd., **IV** 155
Kurose, **III** 420
Kurt Möller Verlag, **7** 42
Kurushima Dockyard, **II** 339
Kuusankoski Aktiebolag, **IV** 299
Kuwait Investment Office, **II** 198; **IV** 380, 452
Kuwait Petroleum Corporation, IV 364, **450–52**, 567; **18** 234
Kvaerner A/S, **20** 313
KW, Inc. *See* Coca-Cola Bottling Company of Northern New England, Inc.
Kwaishinsha Motor Car Works, **I** 183
Kwik Save Group plc, 11 239–41; 13 26
Kwik Shop, Inc., **12** 112
KWIM. *See* Koninklijke West-Indische Maildienst.
KWV, **I** 289
Kygnus Sekiyu K.K., **IV** 555
Kymi Paper Mills Ltd., **IV** 302
Kymmene Corporation, IV 276–77, **299–303**, 337
Kyocera Corporation, II 50–52; III 693; **7** 118; **21 329–32 (upd.)**
Kyodo, **16** 166
Kyodo Dieworks Thailand Co., **III** 758
Kyodo Gyogyo Kaisha, Limited, **II** 552
Kyodo Kako, **IV** 680
Kyodo Kokusan K.K., **21** 271
Kyodo Oil Co. Ltd., **IV** 476
Kyodo Securities Co., Ltd., **II** 433
Kyodo Unyu Kaisha, **I** 502–03, 506; **IV** 713; **V** 481
Kyoei Mutual Fire and Marine Insurance Co., **III** 273
Kyoritsu Pharmaceutical Industry Co., **I** 667
Kyosai Trust Co. *See* Yasuda Trust and Banking Company, Limited.
Kyoto Bank, **II** 291
Kyoto Ceramic Co., Ltd. *See* Kyocera Corporation.
Kyoto Ouchi Bank, **II** 292
Kyowa Hakko Kogyo Co., Ltd., III 42–43
Kyusha Refining Co., **IV** 403
Kyushu Electric Power Company Inc., IV 492; **V 649–51**; **17** 349
Kyushu Oil Refinery Co. Ltd., **IV** 434
Kywan Petroleum Ltd., **13** 556
KYZ International, **9** 427
KZO, **13** 21

L.A. Darling Co., **IV** 135–36; **16** 357
L.A. Gear, Inc., 8 303–06; 11 349

L.A. Mex. *See* Checkers Drive-Up Restaurants Inc.
L. & H. Sales Co., **16** 389
L&W Supply Corp., **III** 764
L.B. DeLong, **III** 558
L. Bamberger & Co., **V** 169; **8** 443
L. Bosendorfer Klavierfabrik, A.G., **12** 297
L.C. Bassford, **III** 653
The L.D. Caulk Company, **10** 271
L. Fish, **14** 236
L.G. Balfour Company, **12** 472; **19** 451–52
L. Greif & Bro. Inc., **17** 203–05
L. Grossman and Sons. *See* Grossman's Inc.
L.H. Parke Co., **II** 571
L.J. Knowles & Bros., **9** 153
L.J. Melody & Co., **21** 97
L.L. Bean, Inc., 9 190, 316; **10 388–90**; **12** 280; **19** 333; **21** 131; **22** 173
L. Luria & Son, Inc., 19 242–44
L.M. Electronics, **I** 489
L.M. Ericsson, **I** 462; **II** 1, 70, 81–82, 365; **III** 479–80; **11** 46, 439; **14** 488
L-N Glass Co., **III** 715
L-N Safety Glass, **III** 715
L-O-F Glass Co. *See* Libbey-Owens–Ford Glass Co.
L. Prang & Co., **12** 207
L.S. DuBois Son and Co., **III** 10
L.S. Starrett Co., 13 301–03
L. Straus and Sons, **V** 168
L.W. Hammerson & Co., **IV** 696
L.W. Singer, **13** 429
La Barge Mirrors, **III** 571; **20** 362
La Cerus, **IV** 615
La Choy/Rosarita Foods, **II** 467–68; **17** 241
La Cinq, **IV** 619
La Concorde, **III** 208
La Crosse Telephone Corporation, **9** 106
La Cruz del Campo S.A., **9** 100
La Favorita Bakery, **II** 543
La Halle aux Chaussures, **17** 210
La India Co., **II** 532
La Oroya, **22** 286
La Petite Academy, **13** 299
La Quinta Inns, Inc., 11 242–44; **21** 362
La Redoute S.A., **19** 306, 309
La Rinascente, **12** 153
La Ruche Meridionale, **12** 153
La Societe Anonyme Francaise Holophane, **19** 211
La Vie Claire, **13** 103
La-Ru Truck Rental Company, Inc., **16** 386
La-Z-Boy Chair Company, 14 302–04
Laakirchen, **IV** 339–40
LAB. *See* Lloyd Aereo de Bolivia.
LaBakelite S.A., **I** 387
Labatt Brewing Co., I 267–68; **18** 72
Labaz, **I** 676; **IV** 546
Labelcraft, Inc., **8** 360
LaBelle Iron Works, **7** 586
Labor für Impulstechnik, **III** 154
Laboratoire Michel Robilliard, **IV** 546
Laboratoire Roger Bellon, **I** 389
Laboratoires d'Anglas, **III** 47
Laboratoires Goupil, **III** 48
Laboratoires Roche Posay, **III** 48
Laboratoires Ruby d'Anglas, **III** 48
Laboratorios Grossman, **III** 55
Laboratory for Electronics, **III** 168; **6** 284
LaBour Pump, **I** 473
LaBow, Haynes Co., **III** 270

Lachine Rapids Hydraulic and Land Company, **6** 501
Lackawanna Steel & Ordnance Co., **IV** 35, 114; **7** 48
Laclede Steel Company, 15 271–73
Lacombe Electric. *See* Public Service Company of Colorado.
Lacquer Products Co., **I** 321
LaCrosse Footwear, Inc., 18 298–301
Lacto Ibérica, **23** 219
Ladbroke Group PLC, II 139, **141–42**; **19** 208; **21 333–36 (upd.)**
Ladd and Tilton, **14** 527–28
LADD Furniture, Inc., 12 299–301; 23 244
Ladd Petroleum Corp., **II** 30
LADECO, **6** 97
Ladenburg, Thalmann & Co. Inc., **17** 346
Ladenso, **IV** 277
Lady Foot Locker, **V** 226; **14** 293, 295
Laerdal Medical, **18** 423
Lafarge Coppée S.A., III 702, **703–05**, 736; **8** 258; **10** 422–23; **23** 333
Lafayette Manufacturing Co., **12** 296
Lafayette Radio Electronics Corporation, **9** 121–22
Laflin & Rand Powder Co., **I** 328; **III** 525
LAG&E. *See* Los Angeles Gas and Electric Company.
LaGard Inc., **20** 363
Lagardère Groupe, **16** 254
Lagoven, **IV** 508
Laidlaw Transportation, Inc., **6** 410
Laing, **IV** 696
Laing's Properties Ltd., **I** 575
L'Air Liquide, I 303, **357–59**; **11** 402
Laitaatsillan Konepaja, **IV** 275
Laiterie Ekabe, **19** 50
SA Laiterie Walhorn Molkerel, **19** 50
Laiteries Prairies de l'Orne, **19** 50
Lake Arrowhead Development Co., **IV** 255
Lake Central Airlines, **I** 131; **6** 131
Lake Erie Screw Corp., **11** 534, 536
Lake Odessa Machine Products, **18** 494
Lake Superior Consolidated Mines Company, **IV** 572; **7** 549; **17** 355–56
Lakeland Fire and Casualty Co., **III** 213
Läkemedels-Industri Föreningen, **I** 664
Laker Airways, **I** 94; **6** 79
Lakeside Laboratories, **III** 24
The Lakeside Publishing and Printing Co., **IV** 660
Lakestone Systems, Inc., **11** 469
Lam Research Corporation, IV 213; **11 245–47**; **18** 383
Lamb Technicon Corp., **I** 486
Lamb Weston, Inc., I 417; **23 319–21**
Lambert Brothers, Inc., **7** 573
Lambert Brussels Financial Corporation, **II** 407; **11** 532
Lambert Kay Company, **8** 84
Lambert Pharmacal Co., **I** 710–11; **III** 28
Lamborghini. *See* Automobili Lamborghini S.p.A.
Lamkin Brothers, Inc., **8** 386
Lamons Metal Gasket Co., **III** 570; **11** 535; **20** 361
Lamontagne Ltd., **II** 651
Lamonts Apparel, Inc., 15 274–76
Lampadaires Feralux, Inc., **19** 472
Lamson & Sessions Co., 13 304–06
Lamson Bros., **II** 451
Lamson Corporation, **7** 145
Lamson Industries Ltd., **IV** 645

Lamson Store Service Co., **IV** 644
Lanca, **14** 224
Lancashire, **III** 350
Lancaster Caramel Co., **II** 510
Lancaster Colony Corporation, 8 307–09
Lancaster Cork Works, **III** 422
Lancaster Financial Ltd., **14** 472
Lancaster National Bank, **9** 475
Lancaster Press, **23** 102
Lance, Inc., 14 305–07
Lancer Corporation, 21 337–39
Lanchester Motor Company, Ltd., **13** 286
Lancia, **I** 162; **11** 102
Lancôme, **III** 46–48; **8** 342
Land O'Lakes, Inc., II 535–37; 7 339; 13 351; **21 340–43 (upd.)**
Land Securities PLC, IV 704–06
Land-Wheelwright Laboratories, **III** 607; **7** 436
Lander Alarm Co., **III** 740
Lander Company, **21** 54
Länderbank, **II** 282
Landesbank für Westfalen Girozentrale, Münster, **II** 385
Landis International, Inc., **10** 105–06
Landmark Banks, **10** 426
Landmark Communications, Inc., 12 **302–05; 22** 442
Landmark Financial Services Inc., **11** 447
Landmark Target Media, **IV** 597
Landmark Union Trust, **18** 517
Landoll, Inc., **22** 522
Landor Associates, **I** 94
Landry's Seafood Restaurants, Inc., 15 **277–79**
Lands' End, Inc., 9 314–16; 12 280; **16** 37; **19** 333
Lane Bryant, **V** 115–16
The Lane Co., Inc., III 528, 530; 12 **306–08**
Lane Drug Company, **12** 132
Lane, Piper, and Jaffray, Inc. *See* Piper Jaffray Companies.
Lane Processing Inc., **II** 585
Lane Publishing Co., **IV** 676; **7** 529
Lane Rossi, **IV** 421
Laneco, Inc., **II** 682
Langdon Rieder Corp., **21** 97
Lange International S.A., **15** 462
Lange, Maxwell & Springer, **IV** 641; **7** 311
Langford Labs, **8** 25
Lanier Business Products, Inc., **II** 39; **8** 407; **20** 290
Lanman Companies, Inc., **23** 101
Lannet Data Communications Ltd., **18** 345–46
Lano Corp., **I** 446
Lansi-Suomen Osake-Pankki, **II** 303
Lanson Pere et Fils, **II** 475
Lantic Industries, Inc., **II** 664
Lanvin, **I** 696; **III** 48; **8** 343
LAPE. *See* Líneas Aéreas Postales Españolas.
LaPine Technology, **II** 51; **21** 331
Laporte Industries Ltd., **I** 303; **IV** 300
Lapp, **8** 229
Lara, **19** 192
Larami Corp., **14** 486
Laroche Navarron, **I** 703
Larousse Group, **IV** 614–15
Larrowe Milling Co., **II** 501; **10** 322
Larsen & Toubro, **IV** 484
Larsen Company, **7** 128

Larson Lumber Co., **IV** 306
Larwin Group, **III** 231
Las Vegas Gas Company, **19** 411
LaSalle Machine Tool, Inc., **13** 7–8
LaSalle National Bank, **II** 184
LaSalles & Koch Co., **8** 443
Lasco Shipping Co., **19** 380
Laser Tech Color, **21** 60
Lasercharge Pty Ltd, **18** 130
Oy Läskelä Ab, **IV** 300
Lasky's, **II** 141
Lasmo, **IV** 455, 499
Latitude Communications, **22** 52
Latrobe Steel Company, **8** 529–31
Lattice Semiconductor Corp., 16 315–17
Lauder Chemical, **17** 363
Laura Ashley Holdings plc, 13 307–09
Laura Scudder's, **7** 429
Laurentien Hotel Co., **III** 99
Lauson Engine Company, **8** 515
LaVista Equipment Supply Co., **14** 545
Lavold, **16** 421
Law Life Assurance Society, **III** 372
Lawn Boy Inc., **7** 535–36; **8** 72
Lawrence Manufacturing Co., **III** 526
Lawrence Warehouse Co., **II** 397–98; **10** 62
Lawrenceburg Gas Company, **6** 466
The Lawson Co., **7** 113
Lawson Milk, **II** 572
Lawter International Inc., 14 308–10; 18 220
Lawyers Cooperative, **8** 527–28
Lawyers Trust Co., **II** 230
Layne & Bowler Pump, **11** 5
Layne Christensen Company, 19 245–47
Lazard Freres & Co., **II** 268, 402, 422; **IV** 23, 79, 658–59; **6** 356; **7** 287, 446; **10** 399; **12** 165, 391, 547, 562; **21** 145
Lazare Kaplan International Inc., 21 **344–47**
LBO Holdings, **15** 459
LBS Communications, **6** 28
LCI International, Inc., 16 318–20
LCP Hotels. *See* CapStar Hotel Co.
LDDS WorldCom, Inc., **16** 467–68
LDDS-Metro Communications, Inc., 8 **310–12**
LDX NET, Inc., **IV** 576
Le Bon Marché. *See* Bon Marché.
Le Brun and Sons, **III** 291
Le Buffet System-Gastronomie, **V** 74
Le Clerc, **21** 225–26
Le Courviour S.A., **10** 351
Le Rocher, Compagnie de Reassurance, **III** 340
Lea & Perrins, **II** 475
Lea County Gas Co., **6** 580
Lea Lumber & Plywood Co., **12** 300
Lea Manufacturing, **23** 299
Leach McMicking, **13** 274
Lead Industries Group Ltd., **III** 681; **IV** 108
Leadership Housing Inc., **IV** 136
Leaf River Forest Products Inc., **IV** 282, 300; **9** 261
Leamington Priors & Warwickshire Banking Co., **II** 318; **17** 323
Lean Cuisine, **12** 531
Lear Corporation, **17** 303, 305
Lear Inc., **II** 61; **8** 49, 51
Lear Romec Corp., **8** 135
Lear Seating Corporation, 16 321–23

Lear Siegler Inc., I 481–83; III 581; **8** 313; **13** 169, 358, 398; **19** 371–72
Learjet Inc., 8 313–16; 9 242
LeaRonal, Inc., 23 322–24
Leasco Data Processing Equipment Corp., **III** 342–44; **IV** 641–42; **7** 311
Lease International SA, **6** 358
Leaseway Personnel Corp., **18** 159
Leaseway Transportation Corp., V 494; **12 309–11; 19** 293
Leatherback Industries, **22** 229
Lechmere Inc., 10 391–93
Lechters, Inc., 11 248–50
Leclerc, **12** 153
Lederle Laboratories, **I** 300–02, 657, 684; **8** 24–25; **14** 254, 256, 423
Lee Ackerman Investment Company, **18** 513
Lee Apparel Company, Inc., 8 317–19; **17** 512, 514
Lee Brands, **II** 500
Lee Company, **V** 390–92
Lee Enterprises, Incorporated, 11 **251–53**
Lee Hecht Harrison, **6** 10
Lee Optical, **13** 390
Lee Rubber and Tire Corp., **16** 8
Lee Telephone Company, **6** 313
Lee Way Holding Co., **14** 42
Lee Way Motor Freight, **I** 278
Leeds & County Bank, **II** 318; **17** 323
Leeds & Northrup Co., **III** 644–45
Lees Carpets, **17** 76
Leewards Creative Crafts Inc., **17** 322
Lefeldt, **III** 417, 418
Lefrak Organization, **8** 357
Legal & General Group plc, III 272–73; **IV** 705, 712
Legal Technologies, Inc., **15** 378
Legault and Masse, **II** 664
Legent Corporation, 10 394–96; 14 392
Legetojsfabrikken LEGO Billund A/S. *See* Lego A/S.
Legg, Mason & Co., **11** 493
Leggett & Platt, Incorporated, 9 93; **11** **254–56**
Leggett Stores Inc., **19** 48
Lego A/S, 12 495; **13 310–13**
Legrand SA, 21 348–50
Lehigh Portland Cement Company, 23 **325–27**
Lehigh Railroad, **III** 258
Lehman Brothers, **I** 78, 125, 484; **II** 192, 259, 398, 448, 450–51; **6** 199; **10** 62–63; **11** 263–64; **13** 448; **14** 145; **22** 445
Lehman Merchant Bank Partners, **19** 324
Lehmer Company. *See* Centel Corporation.
Lehn & Fink, **I** 699
Lehnkering AG, **IV** 140
Lehrman Bros., **III** 419
Lehser Communications, Inc., **15** 265
Leighton Holdings Ltd., **19** 402
Leinenkugel, **I** 253
Leisure Lodges, **III** 76
Leisure System Inc., **12** 359
Leitz, **III** 583–84
LeMaster Litho Supply, **13** 228
Lempereur, **13** 297
Lena Goldfields Ltd., **IV** 94
Lenc-Smith, **III** 430
Lend Lease Corporation Limited, IV **707–09; 17 283–86 (upd.)**
Lennar Corporation, 11 257–59

Lennon's, **II** 628
Lennox Industries, Inc., **22** 6
Lennox International Inc., 8 320–22
Lenoir Furniture Corporation, **10** 183
Lenox Awards, **7** 256
Lenox, Inc., I 227; **10** 179, 181; **12** 312–13; **18** 69
LensCrafters Inc., **V** 207–08; **13** 391; **17** 294; **23 328–30**
Lentheric, **I** 426
L'Entreprise Jean Lefebvre, 23 331–33
Leo, **I** 665
Leo Burnett Company, Inc., I 22–24, 25, 31, 37; **11** 51, 212; **12** 439; **20 336–39** (upd.)
Leonard Bernstein Music Publishing Company, **23** 391
Leonard Development Group, **10** 508
Leonard Express, Inc., **6** 371
Leonard Green & Partners, **12** 477–78
Leonard Machinery Corp., **16** 124
Leonard Silver, **14** 482
Leonardo Editore, **IV** 587
Leonberger Bausparkasse, **II** 258
Lepco Co., **III** 596
Lern, Inc., **II** 420
Lerner Plastics, **9** 323
Lerner Stores, **V** 116
Leroy-Merlin, **23** 230
Les Chantiers de l'Atlantique, **II** 13
Les Industries Ling, **13** 443
Les Papeteries du Limousin, **19** 227
L'Escaut, **III** 335
Lesco Inc., 19 248–50
The Leslie Fay Companies, Inc., 8 323–25
Leslie Paper, **IV** 288
Leslie's Poolmart, Inc., 18 302–04
Lesser-Goldman, **II** 18
Lester B. Knight & Associates, **II** 19
Lester Ink and Coatings Company, **13** 228
Lestrem Group, **IV** 296; **19** 226
Let op Uw Einde, **III** 199
Leucadia National Corporation, 6 396; **11 260–62**
Leuna-Werke AG, **7** 142
Level Five Research, Inc., **22** 292
N.V. Levensverzekering Maatschappji Utrecht, **III** 199–200
Lever Brothers Company, I 17, 21, 26, 30, 333; **II** 497, 588–89; **III** 31; **7** 542–43, 545; **9** 291, 317–19; **13** 199; **14** 314
Levi Strauss & Co., I 15; **II** 634, 669; **V** 60–61, 362–65; **9** 142; **12** 430; **16** 324–28 (upd.), 509, 511; **17** 512; **18** 191–92; **19** 196; **23** 422
Leviathan Gas Pipeline Company, **21** 171
Levine, Huntley, Vick & Beaver, **6** 28
Levitt & Sons, **IV** 728
Levitt Corp., **21** 471
Levitt Homes, **I** 464; **11** 198
Levitt Industries, **17** 331
Levitz Furniture Inc., 15 280–82; 23 412, 414
Levtex Hotel Ventures, **21** 363
Levy Bakery Goods, **I** 30
The Lewin Group, Inc., **21** 425
Lewis and Marks, **IV** 21–22, 96; **16** 27
Lewis Batting Company, **11** 219
Lewis Construction, **IV** 22
Lewis Galoob Toys Inc., 16 329–31
Lewis Grocer Co., **II** 669; **18** 504
Lewis Refrigeration Company, **21** 500

Lewis's, **V** 178
Lewis's Bank, **II** 308
Lewis-Howe Co., **III** 56
Lex Electronics, **10** 113
Lex Service plc, **19** 312
Lexington Broadcast Services, **6** 27
Lexington Furniture Industries, **III** 571; **20** 362
Lexington Ice Company, **6** 514
Lexington Insurance Co., **III** 197
Lexington Utilities Company, **6** 514; **11** 237
Lexis-Nexis, **17** 399; **18** 542; **21** 70
Lexitron, **II** 87
Lexmark International, Inc., 9 116; **10** 519; **18 305–07**
Leybold AG, **IV** 71
Leyland and Birmingham Rubber Co., **I** 429
Leyland Motor Corporation, **7** 459
LFC Financial, **10** 339
LFC Holdings Corp. See Levitz Furniture Inc.
LFE Corp., **7** 297
LG Electronics Inc., **13** 572, 575
LG Group, **18** 124
LG&E Energy Corp., 6 516–18; 18 366–67
Lhomme S.A., **8** 477
Liaoyang Automotive Spring Factory, **III** 581
Libbey-Owens-Ford Company, **I** 609; **III** 640–42, 707, 714–15, 725–26, 731; **IV** 421; **7** 292, **16** 7–9; **22** 434; **23** 83
Libby, **II** 547; **7** 382
Libby McNeil & Libby Inc., **II** 489
Libeltex, **9** 92
Liber, **14** 556
Liberty Bank of Buffalo, **9** 229
Liberty Brokerage Investment Company, **10** 278
Liberty Can and Sign Company, **17** 105–06
The Liberty Corporation, 22 312–14
Liberty Gauge Company, **17** 213
Liberty Hardware Manufacturing Corporation, **20** 363
Liberty House, **I** 417–18
Liberty Life, **IV** 91, 97
Liberty Media, **18** 66; **19** 282
Liberty Mexicana, **III** 415
Liberty Mutual Insurance Group, **I** 28; **11** 379
Liberty Mutual Savings Bank, **17** 530
Liberty National Bank, **II** 229
Liberty National Insurance Holding Company. See Torchmark Corporation.
Liberty National Life Insurance Co., **III** 217; **9** 506–07
Liberty Natural Gas Co., **11** 441
Liberty Software, Inc., **17** 264
Liberty's, **13** 307
Libra Bank Ltd., **II** 271
Librairie de Jacques-Francois Brétif, **IV** 617
Librairie Fayard, **IV** 618
Librairie Générale Francaise, **IV** 618
Librairie Larousse, **IV** 614–16
Librairie Louis Hachette, **IV** 617–18
Librairie Nathan, **IV** 614, 616
Librairie Victor Lecou, **IV** 617
Libyan Arab Airline, **6** 85
Libyan Arab Foreign Bank, **IV** 454

Libyan National Oil Corporation, IV 453–55
Libyan-Turkish Engineering and Consultancy Corp., **IV** 563
Lidköpings Mekaniska Verkstad AB, **III** 623
Liebert Corp., **II** 20
Life and Casualty Insurance Co. of Tennessee, **III** 193
Life Assoc. of Scotland, **III** 310
Life Fitness Inc., **III** 431
Life Insurance Co. of Georgia, **III** 310
Life Insurance Co. of Scotland, **III** 358
Life Insurance Co. of Virginia, **III** 204
Life Insurance Securities, Ltd., **III** 288
Life Investors International Ltd., **III** 179; **12** 199
Life of Eire, **III** 273
Life Retail Stores. See Angelica Corporation.
Life Savers Corp., **II** 129, 544; **7** 367; **21** 54
Life Science Research, Inc., **10** 105–07
Life Technologies, Inc., I 321; **12** 103; **17** 287–89
Life Uniform Shops. See Angelica Corporation.
Lifecycle, Inc., **III** 431
LifeLink, **11** 378
Lifemark Corp., **III** 74; **14** 232
LIFETIME, **IV** 627; **19** 204
Lifetime Foam Products, Inc., **12** 439
Lift Parts Manufacturing, **I** 157
Ligand Pharmaceutical, **10** 48
Liggett & Meyers, **V** 396, 405, 417–18; **18** 416
Liggett Group Inc., **I** 248; **7** 105; **14** 213; **15** 71; **16** 242
Light & Power Company, **12** 265
Light Corrugated Box Co., **IV** 332
Light Servicos de Eletricidade S.A., **II** 456
Lightel Inc., **6** 311
Lighting Corp. of America, **I** 476
LIGHTNET, **IV** 576
Lightwell Co., **III** 634
Lignum Oil Co., **IV** 658
LILCO. See Long Island Lighting Company.
Lilia Limited, **17** 449
Lillian Vernon Corp., 12 314–15
Lilliput Group plc, **11** 95; **15** 478
Lilly & Co. See Eli Lilly & Co.
Lilly Industries, **22** 437
Lillybrook Coal Co., **IV** 180
Lillywhites Ltd., **III** 105
Lily Tulip Co., **I** 609, 611; **8** 198
Limburger Fabrik und Hüttenverein, **IV** 103
The Limited, Inc., V 115–16; **9** 142; **12** 280, 356; **15** 7, 9; **16** 219; **18** 193, 215, 217, 410; **20 340–43** (upd.)
Limmer and Trinidad Ltd., **III** 752
LIN Broadcasting Corp., II 331; **6** 323; **9** 320–22; **11** 330
Lin Data Corp., **11** 234
Linamar Corporation, 18 308–10
Lincoln American Life Insurance Co., **10** 246
Lincoln Benefit Life Company, **10** 51
Lincoln Electric Co., II 19; **13 314–16**
Lincoln Electric Motor Works, **9** 439
Lincoln Federal Savings, **16** 106
Lincoln First Bank, **II** 248
Lincoln Income Life Insurance Co., **10** 246

Lincoln Liberty Life Insurance Co., **III** 254
Lincoln Marketing, Inc., **18** 518
Lincoln Motor Co., **I** 165
Lincoln National Corporation, III 274–77; **6** 195; **10** 44; **22** 144
Lincoln Property Company, 8 326–28
Lincoln Savings, **10** 340
Lincoln Savings & Loan, **9** 199
Lincoln Telephone & Telegraph Company, 14 311–13
LinCom Corp., **8** 327
Linde A.G., I 297–98, 315, **581–83**; **9** 16, 516; **10** 31–32; **11** 402–03
Lindemann's, **I** 220
Lindex, **II** 640
Lindsay Manufacturing Co., 20 344–46
Lindsay Parkinson & Co., **I** 567
Lindustries, **III** 502; **7** 208
Linear Corp., **III** 643
Linear Technology, Inc., 16 332–34
Líneas Aéreas Postales Españolas, **6** 95
Linens 'n Things, **13** 81–82
Linfood Cash & Carry, **13** 103
Linfood Holdings Ltd., **II** 628–29
Ling Products, **12** 25
Ling-Temco-Vought. *See* LTV Corporation.
Lingerie Time, **20** 143
Linjeflyg, **I** 120
Link House Publications PLC, **IV** 687
Link-Belt Corp., **I** 443; **IV** 660
Lintas: Worldwide, I 18; **6** 30; **14 314–16**
Lintott Engineering, Ltd., **10** 108
Linz, **16** 559
Lion Corporation, III 44–45
Lion Manufacturing, **III** 430
Lion Oil, **I** 365
Lion's Head Brewery. *See* The Stroh Brewery Company.
Lionel L.L.C., 12 494; **16 335–38**; **18** 524
Lionex Corporation, **13** 46
Liontech, **16** 337–38
Lippincott & Margulies, **III** 283
Lippincott-Raven Publishers, **14** 556
Lipton. *See* Thomas J. Lipton Company.
Liqui-Box Corporation, 16 339–41
Liquid Carbonic, **7** 74, 77
Liquor Barn, **II** 656
Liquorland, **V** 35
Liquorsave, **II** 609–10
LIRCA, **III** 48
Liris, **23** 212
Lisbon Coal and Oil Fuel Co., **IV** 504
Liscaya, **II** 196
Lister, **21** 503
Litco Bancorp., **II** 192
LiTel Communications, Inc., **16** 318
Litho-Krome Corp., **IV** 621
Litronix, **III** 455; **21** 122
Little, Brown & Company, **IV** 675; **7** 528; **10** 355
Little Caesar International, Inc., 7 278–79; **7** 278–79; **15** 344, 346; **16** 447
Little Chef Ltd., **III** 105–06
Little General, **II** 620; **12** 179, 200
Little Giant Pump Company, **8** 515
Little League Baseball, Incorporated, **23** 450
Little Leather Library, **13** 105
Little, Royal, **I** 529–30; **8** 545; **13** 63
Little Switzerland, **19** 451
Little Tikes Co., III 614; **12** 169; **13 317–19**
Littlewoods Organisation PLB, V 117–19

Litton Industries Inc., I 85, 452, 476, **484–86**, 523–24; **II** 33; **III** 293, 473, 732; **IV** 253; **6** 599; **10** 520–21, 537; **11 263–65 (upd.)**, 435; **12** 248, 271–72, 538–40; **15** 287; **17** 30; **19** 31, 110, 290; **21** 86; **22** 436
Litwin Engineers & Constructors, **8** 546
Livanos, **III** 516
LIVE Entertainment Inc., 18 64, 66; **20 347–49**
Liverpool and London and Globe Insurance Co., **III** 234, 350
Liverpool and London Fire and Life Insurance Co., **III** 349
Liverpool Fire and Life Insurance Co., **III** 350
Liverpool Mexico S.A., **16** 216
Livia, **I** 154; **10** 279
Living Centers of America, **13** 49
Living Videotext, **10** 508
Livingston Communications, **6** 313
Livingston, Fargo and Co., **II** 380, 395; **10** 59
LivingWell Inc., **12** 326
Liz Claiborne, Inc., 8 329–31; **16** 37, 61
LKB-Produkter AB, **I** 665
Lloyd A. Fry Roofing, **III** 721
Lloyd Adriatico S.p.A., **III** 377
Lloyd Aereo de Bolivia, **6** 97
Lloyd George Management, **18** 152
Lloyd Italico, **III** 351
Lloyd Thompson Group plc, **20** 313
Lloyd's Electronics, **14** 118
Lloyd's of London, III 234, **278–81**; **9** 297; **10** 38; **11** 533; **22 315–19 (upd.)**
Lloyd-Truax Ltd., **21** 499
Lloyds Bank PLC, II 306–09 319, 334, 358; **17** 324–25
Lloyds Life Assurance, **III** 351
LM Ericsson. *See* Telefonaktiebolaget LM Ericsson.
LMC Metals, **19** 380
LME. *See* Telefonaktiebolaget LM Ericsson.
LNG Co., **IV** 473–74
Lo-Cost, **II** 609
Lo-Vaca Gathering Co., **IV** 394; **7** 553
Loadometer Co., **III** 435
Lobitos Oilfields Ltd., **IV** 381–82
Loblaw Companies, **II** 631–32; **19** 116
Local Data, Inc., **10** 97
Locations, Inc., **IV** 727
Locke, Lancaster and W.W.&R. Johnson & Sons, **III** 680
Lockhart Catering, **III** 104
Lockhart Corporation, **12** 564
Lockheed Corporation, I 13, 41, 48, 50, 52, 54, 61, 63, **64–66**, 67–68, 71–72, 74, 76–77, 82, 84, 90, 92–94, 100, 102, 107, 110, 113, 121, 126, 195, 493–94, 529; **II** 19, 32–33; **III** 84, 539, 601; **IV** 15; **6** 71; **9** 12, 17–18, 272, 417, 458–60, 501; **10** 163, 262–63, 317, 536; **11** 164, 166, **266–69 (upd.)**, 278–79, 363–65; **12** 190; **13** 126, 128; **17** 306; **21** 140; **22** 506
Lockheed Martin Corporation, 15 283–86 (upd.); **21** 86. *See also* Martin Marietta Corporation.
Lockwood Banc Group, Inc., **11** 306
Lockwood Greene Engineers, Inc., **17** 377
Lockwood Technology, Inc., **19** 179
Lockwoods Foods Ltd., **II** 513
Loctite Corporation, 8 332–34

Lodding Engineering, **7** 521
Lodestar Group, **10** 19
Lodge-Cottrell, **III** 472
Lodging Group, **12** 297
Loeb Rhoades, Hornblower & Co., **II** 450–51; **9** 469
Loening Aeronautical, **I** 61; **11** 164
Loew's Consolidated Enterprises, **II** 154
The Loewen Group, Inc., 16 342–44
Loewenstein Furniture Group, Inc., **21** 531–33
Loewi Financial Cos., **III** 270
Loews Corporation, I 245, **487–88**; **II** 134, 148–49, 169; **III** 228, 231; **12 316–18 (upd.)**, 418; **13** 120–21; **19** 362; **22** 73
LOF Plastics, Inc. *See* Libbey-Owens-Ford.
Loffland Brothers Company, **9** 364
Loft Inc., **I** 276; **10** 451
Logan's Roadhouse Restaurant, **19** 287–88; **22** 464
Logged Off Land Co., **IV** 355–56
Logic Modeling, **11** 491
Logica plc, 14 317–19
Logicon Inc., 20 350–52
Logistics, **III** 431
Logistics Data Systems, **13** 4
Logistics Management Systems, Inc., **8** 33
Logitech, Inc., **9** 116
Logo 7, Inc., **13** 533
Logon, Inc., **14** 377
Lojas Arapuã S.A., 22 320–22
Loma Linda Foods, **14** 557–58
Lomas & Nettleton Financial Corporation, **III** 249; **11** 122
Lombard North Central, **II** 442
Lombard Orient Leasing Ltd., **II** 442
London & Hull, **III** 211
London & Leeds Development Corp., **II** 141
London & Midland Bank. *See* Midland Bank plc.
London & Rhodesia Mining & Land Company. *See* Lonrho Plc.
London and County Bank, **II** 334
London and Hanseatic Bank, **II** 256
London and Lancashire Insurance Co., **III** 350
London and Scottish Marine Oil, **11** 98
London and Westminster Bank, **II** 333–34
London Asiatic, **III** 699
London Assurance Corp., **III** 278, 369–71, 373
London Brick Co., **III** 502; **7** 208; **14** 249
London Brokers Ltd., **6** 290
London Buses Limited, **6** 406
London Chartered Bank of Australia, **II** 188
London Clermont Club, **III** 431
London County and Westminster Bank, **II** 334
London County Freehold & Leasehold Properties, **IV** 711
London East India Company, **12** 421
London, Edinburgh and Dublin Insurance Co., **III** 350
London Electricity, **12** 443
London Film Productions Ltd., **II** 157; **14** 399
London Fog, **16** 61
London General Omnibus Company, **6** 406
London Guarantee and Accident Co., **III** 372
London Insurance Co., **III** 373

London Joint-Stock Bank, **II** 318, 388; **17** 324
London Life Assoc., **IV** 711
London Life Insurance Co., **II** 456–57
London, Provincial and South Western Bank, **II** 235
London Records, **23** 390
London Regional Transport, 6 406–08
London Transport, **19** 111
London Weekend Television, **IV** 650–51; **7** 389
Lone Star and Crescent Oil Co., **IV** 548
Lone Star Brewing Co., **I** 255
Lone Star Gas Corp., **V** 609, 611
Lone Star Industries, **III** 718, 729, 753; **IV** 304; **23** 326
Lone Star Steakhouse, **21** 250
Lone Star Steel, **I** 440–41
Lone Star Technologies, Inc., **22** 3
Long Distance Discount Services, Inc., **8** 310
Long Distance/USA, **9** 479
Long Island Airways, **I** 115; **12** 379
Long Island Bancorp, Inc., 16 345–47
Long Island Cable Communication Development Company, **7** 63
Long Island Daily Press Publishing Co., **IV** 582–83
Long Island Lighting Company, V 652–54; 6 456
Long Island Trust Co., **II** 192, 218
Long John Silver's Restaurants Inc., 13 320–22
Long Lac Mineral Exploration, **9** 282
Long Life Fish Food Products, **12** 230
Long Manufacturing Co., **III** 439; **14** 63
Long Valley Power Cooperative, **12** 265
Long-Airdox Co., **IV** 136
Long-Term Credit Bank of Japan, Ltd., II 301, **310–11,** 338, 369
The Longaberger Company, 12 319–21
LongHorn Steaks Inc., **19** 341
Longines-Wittenauer Watch Co., **II** 121
Longman Group Ltd., **IV** 611, 658
Longmat Foods, **II** 494
Longs Drug Stores Corporation, V 120
Longview Fibre Company, 8 335–37
Longwy, **IV** 227
Lonrho Plc, IV 651–52; **10** 170; **21 351–55**
Lonsdale Investment Trust, **II** 421
Lonvest Corp., **II** 456–57
Loomis, Sayles & Co., **III** 313
Loose Leaf Metals Co., Inc., **10** 314
Lor-Al, Inc., **17** 10
Loral Corporation, II 38; **7** 9; **8 338–40; 9 323–25; 13** 356; **15** 283, 285; **20** 262
Lord & Taylor, **13** 44; **14** 376; **15** 86; **18** 137, 372; **21** 302
Lord & Thomas, **I** 12–14; **IV** 660
Lord Baltimore Press, Inc., **IV** 286
Lord Chetwynd's Insurance, **III** 370
Lord Onslow's Insurance, **III** 370
L'Oréal, II 547; **III** 46–49, 62; **7** 382–83; **8** 129–31; **341–44 (upd.); 11** 41; **23** 238, 242
Lorenz, **I** 463
Lorillard Industries, **I** 488; **V** 396, 407, 417; **12** 317; **18** 416; **22** 73
Lorimar Telepictures, **II** 149, 177
Lorraine-Escaut, **IV** 227
Lorvic Corp., **I** 679
Los Angeles Can Co., **I** 599
Los Angeles Drug Co., **12** 106

Los Angeles Gas and Electric Company, **V** 682
Los Angeles Steamship Co., **II** 490
Los Lagos Corp., **12** 175
Los Nietos Co., **IV** 570
Lost Arrow Inc., 22 323–25
Lothringer Bergwerks- und Hüttenverein Aumetz-Friede AG, **IV** 126
Lotus Cars Ltd., 14 320–22
Lotus Development Corporation, IV 597; **6** 224–25, 227, **254–56,** 258–60, 270–71, 273; **9** 81, 140; **10** 24, 505; **12** 335; **16** 392, 394; **20** 238; **21** 86; **22** 161
Lotus Publishing Corporation, **7** 239
Lotus Radio, **I** 531
Loucks, Hoffman & Company, **8** 412
Loughead Aircraft Manufacturing Co., **I** 64
Louis Allis, **15** 288
Louis B. Mayer Pictures, **II** 148
Louis C. Edwards, **II** 609
Louis Harris & Associates, Inc., **22** 188
Louis Kemp Seafood Company, **14** 515
Louis Marx Toys, **II** 559; **12** 410
Louis Rich, Inc., **II** 532; **12** 372
Louis Vuitton, I 272; **III** 48; **8** 343; **10 397–99**
Louisiana & Southern Life Insurance Co., **14** 460
Louisiana Bank & Trust, **11** 106
Louisiana Corporation, **19** 301
The Louisiana Land and Exploration Company, IV 76, 365, 367; **7 280–83**
Louisiana-Pacific Corporation, IV 282, **304–05, 9** 260; **16** 203; **22** 491
Louisville Cement Co., **IV** 409
Louisville Gas and Electric Company. See LG&E Energy Corporation.
Louisville Home Telephone Company, **14** 258
Louthan Manufacturing Company, **8** 178
Lovelace Truck Service, Inc., **14** 42
Loveman's, Inc., **19** 323
Lovering China Clays, **III** 690
Lowe Bros. Co., **III** 745
Lowe Group, **22** 294
Lowe's Companies, Inc., V 122–23; 11 384; **12** 234, 345; **18** 239; **21** 324, **356–58 (upd.)**
Lowell Bearing Co., **IV** 136
Lowell Shoe, Inc., **13** 360
Löwenbräu, **I** 220, 257; **II** 240
Lowes Food Stores. See Alex Lee Inc.
Lowney/Moirs, **II** 512
Lowrance Electronics, Inc., 18 311–14
Lowrey's Meat Specialties, Inc., **21** 156
Loyalty Group, **III** 241–43
LRL International, **II** 477
LSI. See Lear Siegler Inc.
LSI Logic Corporation, 13 323–25; 18 382
LTA Ltd., **IV** 22
LTU Group, **17** 325
LTV Corporation, I 62–63, **489–91; 7** 107–08; **8** 157, 315; **10** 419; **11** 166, 364; **12** 124; **17** 357; **18** 110, 378; **19** 466
Lubcref, **IV** 538
Lubrizol Enterprises, Inc., I 360–62; **21** 385–87
Luby's Cafeteria's, Inc., 17 290–93; 19 301
Lucas Bols, **II** 642
Lucas Digital Ltd., **12** 322
Lucas Girling, **I** 157

Lucas Industries Plc, III 509, **554–57**
Lucas-Milhaupt, Inc., **23** 250
Lucasfilm Ltd., 9 368, 472; **12 322–24; 22** 459
Lucchini, **IV** 228
Lucent Technologies, **18** 154, 180; **20** 8; **22** 19
Lucky Brand Dungarees, **18** 85
Lucky Lager Brewing Co, **I** 268
Lucky Stores Inc., **II** 605, 653; **6** 355; **8** 474; **12** 48; **17** 369, 559; **22** 39
Lucky Strike, **II** 143
Lucky-Goldstar, II 53–54; III 457; **13** 574. See also Goldstar Co., Ltd.
Ludlow Corp., **III** 645
Lufkin Rule Co., **II** 16
Luftag, **I** 110
Lufthansa. See Deutsche Lufthansa A.G.
The Luggage Company, **14** 224
Lukens Inc., 14 323–25
Lukey Mufflers, **IV** 249
Lum's, **6** 199–200
Lumac B.V., **I** 387
Lumbermen's Investment Corp., **IV** 341
Lumbermens Mutual Casualty Co., **III** 269–71; **15** 257
Lumex, Inc., **17** 197
La Lumière Economique, **II** 79
Lummus Co., **IV** 469
Lumonics Inc., **III** 635
Lund Food Holdings, Inc., 22 326–28
Lunenburg Sea Products Limited, **14** 339
Lunevale Products Ltd., **I** 341
L'Unite Hermetique S.A., **8** 515
Lunn Poly, **8** 525–26
Luotto-Pankki Oy, **II** 303
Lurgei, **6** 599
LURGI. See Metallurgische Gesellschaft Aktiengesellschaft.
Luria Bros. and Co., **I** 512–13; **6** 151
Lutèce, **20** 26
Luther's Bar-B-Q, **II** 556
Lux, **III** 478
Lux Mercantile Co., **II** 624
Luxor, **II** 69; **6** 205; **17** 353
Luxottica SpA, 17 294–96; 23 328
Luxury Linens, **13** 81–82
LVMH, **I** 272; **19** 86
LVO Cable Inc., **IV** 596
LXE Inc., 21 199–201
Lydex, **I** 527
Lykes Corp., **I** 490–91
Lynde Company, **16** 269–71
Lynx Express Delivery, **6** 412, 414
Lyon & Healy, **IV** 660
Lyon's Technological Products Ltd., **III** 745
Lyondell Petrochemical Company, IV 377, **456–57; 10** 110
Lyonnaise Communications, **10** 196
Lyonnaise des Eaux-Dumez, I 576; **V 655–57;** Eaux, **23** 332
Lyons. See J. Lyons & Co. Ltd.
LyphoMed Inc., **IV** 333; **17** 287
Oy Lypsyniemen Konepaja, **IV** 275–76
Lysaght's Canada, Ltd., **IV** 73
Lystads, **I** 333

M & S Computing. See Intergraph Corporation.
M and G Fund Management, **III** 699
M and M Manufacturing Company, **23** 143
M Stores Inc., **II** 664
M/A Com Inc., **6** 336; **14** 26–27

M.A. Hanna Company, 8 345–47; 12 352
M.A.N., **III** 561–63; **IV** 86
M&J Diesel Locomotive Filter Co., **17** 106
M&M Limited, **7** 299
M&M/Mars, **14** 48; **15** 63–64; **21** 219
M&T Capital Corporation, **11** 109
M.B. McGerry, **21** 94
M.D.C., **11** 258
M.E.P.C. Ltd., **IV** 711
M.F. Patterson Dental Supply Co. *See*
    Patterson Dental Co.
M. Guggenheim's Sons, **IV** 31
M.H. McLean Wholesaler Grocery
    Company, **8** 380
M. Hensoldt & Söhne Wetzlar Optische
    Werke AG, **III** 446
M-I Drilling Fluids Co., **III** 473; **15** 468
M.I. Schottenstein Homes Inc., **19** 125–26
M.J. Brock Corporation, **8** 460
M.J. Designs, Inc., **17** 360
M.L.C. Partners Limited Partnership, **22**
    459
M. Loeb Ltd., **II** 652
M. Lowenstein Corp., **V** 379
M.M. Warburg. *See* SBC Warburg.
M.P. Burke PLC, **13** 485–86
M.P. Pumps, Inc., **8** 515
M. Polaner Inc., **10** 70
M. Samuel & Co., **II** 208
M.W. Carr, **14** 245
M.W. Kellogg Co., **III** 470; **IV** 408, 534
Ma. Ma-Macaroni Co., **II** 554
Maakauppiaitten Oy, **8** 293–94
Maakuntain Keskus-Pankki, **II** 303
MaasGlas, **III** 667
Maatschappij tot Exploitatie van de
    Onderneming Krasnapolsky. *See* Grand
    Hotel Krasnapolsky N.V.
Maatschappij tot Exploitatie van
    Steenfabrieken Udenhout, voorheen
    Weyers, **14** 249
MABAG Maschinen- und Apparatebau
    GmbH, **IV** 198
Mabley & Carew, **10** 282
**Mac Frugal's Bargains - Closeouts Inc.,
    17** 297–99
Mac Tools, **III** 628
MacAndrews & Forbes Holdings Inc., **II**
    679; **III** 56; **9** 129; **11** 334
Macau Telephone, **18** 114
Maccabees Life Insurance Co., **III** 350
MacCall Management, **19** 158
MacDonald Companies, **15** 87
MacDonald, Halsted, and Laybourne, **10**
    127
Macdonald Hamilton & Co., **III** 522–23
Macey Furniture Co., **7** 493
Macfarlane Lang & Co., **II** 592–93
Macfield Inc., **12** 502
MacGregor Sporting Goods Inc., **III** 443;
    22 115, 458; **23** 449
Machine Vision International Inc., **10** 232
Macintosh, **16** 417
Mack Trucks, Inc., I 147, **177–79; 9** 416;
    12 90; **22 329–32** (upd.)
MacKay-Shields Financial Corp., **III** 316
MacKenzie & Co., **II** 361
Mackenzie Hill, **IV** 724
Mackenzie Mann & Co. Limited, **6** 360
Mackey Airways, **I** 102
Mackinnon Mackenzie & Co., **III** 521–22
Maclaren Power and Paper Co., **IV** 165
Maclean Hunter Limited, III 65; **IV**
    638–40, 22 442; **23** 98

Maclin Co., **12** 127
MacMark Corp., **22** 459
MacMarr Stores, **II** 654
MacMillan Bloedel Limited, IV 165, 272,
    306–09, 721; **9** 391; **19** 444, 446
Macmillan, Inc., IV 637, 641–43; **7**
    284–86, 311–12, 343; **9** 63; **12** 226; **13**
    91, 93; **17** 399; **18** 329; **22** 441–42; **23**
    350, 503
Macnaughton Blair, **III** 671
Macneill & Co., **III** 522
Macon Gas Company, **6** 447; **23** 28
Macon Kraft Co., **IV** 311; **11** 421; **19** 267
Maconochie Bros., **II** 569
Macrodata, **18** 87
Macy's. *See* R.H. Macy & Co., Inc.
Macy's California, **21** 129
Mad Dog Athletics, **19** 385
Maddingley Brown Coal Pty Ltd., **IV** 249
Maddux Air Lines, **I** 125; **12** 487
Madge Networks Inc., **18** 346
Madison & Sullivan, Inc., **10** 215
Madison Financial Corp., **16** 145
Madison Foods, **14** 557
Madison Furniture Industries, **14** 436
Madison Gas & Electric Company, **6**
    605–06
Madison Resources, Inc., **13** 502
Madison Square Garden, **I** 452
Maersk Lines, **22** 167
Maes Group Breweries, **II** 475
Maeva Group, **6** 206
Magasins Armand Thiéry et Sigrand, **V** 11;
    19 308
Magazine and Book Services, **13** 48
Magazins Réal Stores, **II** 651
Magcobar, **III** 472
Magdeburg Insurance Group, **III** 377
Magdeburger Versicherungsgruppe, **III** 377
Magellan Corporation, **22** 403
Magic Chef Co., **III** 573; **8** 298; **22** 349
Magic Pan, **II** 559–60; **12** 410
Magic Pantry Foods, **10** 382
Magicsilk, Inc., **22** 133
MagicSoft Inc., **10** 557
Magirus, **IV** 126
Maglificio di Ponzano Veneto dei Fratelli
    Benetton. *See* Benetton.
Magma Copper Company, 7 287–90,
    385–87; **22** 107
Magma Power Company, 11 270–72
Magna Computer Corporation, **12** 149; **13**
    97
Magnaflux, **III** 519; **22** 282
Magnavox Co., **13** 398; **19** 393
Magne Corp., **IV** 160
Magnesium Metal Co., **IV** 118
Magnet Cove Barium Corp., **III** 472
MagneTek, Inc., 15 287–89
Magnetic Controls Company, **10** 18
Magnetic Peripherals Inc., **19** 513–14
Magnivision, **22** 35
Magnolia Petroleum Co., **III** 497; **IV** 82,
    464
Magnus Co., **I** 331; **13** 197
La Magona d'Italia, **IV** 228
Magor Railcar Co., **I** 170
MAGroup Inc., **11** 123
Mahalo Air, **22** 252
Maharam Fabric, **8** 455
Mahir, **I** 37
Mahou, **II** 474
Mai Nap Rt, **IV** 652; **7** 392

MAI Systems Corporation, **10** 242; **11**
    273–76
Maidenform Worldwide Inc., 20 352–55
Mail Boxes Etc., 18 315–17
Mailson Ferreira da Nobrega, **II** 200
Mailtek, Inc., **18** 518
MAIN. *See* Mid-American Interpool
    Network.
Main Event Management Corp., **III** 194
Main Street Advertising USA, **IV** 597
Maine Central Railroad Company, 16
    348–50
Mainline Industrial Distributors, Inc., **13** 79
Mainline Travel, **I** 114
Maison Bouygues, **I** 563
Maison de Valérie, **19** 309
Maizuru Heavy Industries, **III** 514
Majestic Contractors Ltd., **8** 419–20
Majestic Wine Warehouses Ltd., **II** 656
Major League Baseball, **12** 457
Major Video Concepts, **6** 410
Major Video, Inc., **9** 74
MaK Maschinenbau GmbH, **IV** 88
Mak van Waay, **11** 453
Makhteshim, **II** 47
Makita Corporation, III 436; **20** 66; **22**
    333–35
Makiyama, **I** 363
Makovsky & Company, **12** 394
Makro Inc., **18** 286
Malama Pacific Corporation, **9** 276
Malapai Resources, **6** 546
Malayan Breweries, **I** 256
Malayan Motor and General Underwriters,
    III 201
Malaysia LNG, **IV** 518–19
Malaysian Airlines System BHD, 6 71,
    100–02, 117, 415
Malaysian International Shipping Co., **IV**
    518
Malaysian Sheet Glass, **III** 715
Malbak Ltd., **IV** 92–93
Malcolm's Diary & Time-Table, **III** 256
Malcus Industri, **III** 624
Malden Mills Industries, Inc., 16 351–53
Malheur Cooperative Electric Association,
    12 265
Malleable Iron Works, **II** 34
Mallinckrodt Group Inc., III 16; **IV** 146;
    8 85; **19** 28, **251–53**
Malmö Flygindustri, **I** 198
Malmsten & Bergvalls, **I** 664
Malone & Hyde, Inc., **II** 625, 670–71; **9**
    52–53; **14** 147; **18** 506
Malrite Communications Group, **IV** 596
Malt-A-Milk Co., **II** 487
Malt-O-Meal Company, 15 189; **22**
    336–38
Mameco International, **8** 455
Man Aktiengesellschaft, III 301, **561–63**
MAN Gutehoffnungshütte AG, **15** 226
Management Decision Systems, Inc., **10**
    358
Management Engineering and Development
    Co., **IV** 310; **19** 266
Management Recruiters International, **6**
    140
Management Science America, Inc., **11** 77
Manbré and Garton, **II** 582
Manchester and Liverpool District Banking
    Co., **II** 307, 333
Manchester Board and Paper Co., **19** 77
Manchester Commercial Buildings Co., **IV**
    711

Manco, Inc., **13** 166. *See also* Henkel Manco Inc.
Mancuso & Co., **22** 116
Mandabach & Simms, **6** 40
Mandarin Oriental Hotel Group International Ltd., **I** 471; **IV** 700; **20** 312
Mandel Bros., **IV** 660
Manetta Mills, Inc., **19** 304
Manhattan Card Co., **18** 114
Manhattan Co., **II** 217, 247
Manhattan Electrical Supply Co., **9** 517
Manhattan Fund, **I** 614
Manhattan Trust Co., **II** 229
Manheim Auctions, Inc. *See* Cox Enterprises, Inc.
Manifatture Cotoniere Meridionali, **I** 466
Manistique Papers Inc., **17** 282
Manistique Pulp and Paper Co., **IV** 311; **19** 266
Manitoba Bridge and Engineering Works Ltd., **8** 544
Manitoba Paper Co., **IV** 245–46
Manitoba Rolling Mill Ltd., **8** 544
Manitowoc Company, Inc., 18 318–21
Mann Egerton & Co., **III** 523
Mann Theatres Chain, **I** 245
Mann's Wine Company, Ltd., **14** 288
Manne Tossbergs Eftr., **II** 639
Mannesmann AG, I 411; **III** 564–67; **IV** 222, 469; **14 326–29 (upd.)**
Mannheimer Bank, **IV** 558
Manning, Selvage & Lee, **6** 22
Mannstaedt, **IV** 128
Manor Care, Inc., 6 187–90, **14** 105–07; **15** 522
Manorfield Investments, **II** 158
Manos Enterprises, **14** 87
Manpower, Inc., 6 10, 140; **9 326–27**; **16** 48
Mantua Metal Products. *See* Tyco Toys, Inc.
Manufactured Home Communities, Inc., 22 339–41
Manufacturers & Merchants Indemnity Co., **III** 191
Manufacturers and Traders Trust Company, **11** 108–09
Manufacturers Hanover Corporation, II 230, 254, **312–14**, 403; **III** 194; **9** 124; **11** 16, 54, 415; **13** 536; **14** 103; **16** 207; **17** 559; **22** 406
Manufacturers National Bank of Brooklyn, **II** 312
Manufacturers National Bank of Detroit, **I** 165; **11** 137
Manufacturers Railway, **I** 219
Manufacturing Management Inc., **19** 381
Manus Nu-Pulse, **III** 420
Manville Corporation, III 706–09, 721; **7 291–95 (upd.)**; **10** 43, 45; **11** 420–22
Manweb plc, **19** 389–90
MAPCO Inc., IV 458–59
Mapelli Brothers Food Distribution Co., **13** 350
Maple Leaf Mills, **II** 513–14
MAPP. *See* Mid-Continent Area Power Planner.
Mar-O-Bar Company, **7** 299
A.B. Marabou, **II** 511
Maranthal Music, **14** 499
Marantz Co., **14** 118
Marathon Oil Co., **IV** 365, 454, 487, 572, 574; **7** 549, 551; **13** 458
Marathon Paper Products, **I** 612, 614

Maraven, **IV** 508
Marblehead Communications, Inc., **23** 101
Marbodal, **12** 464
Marboro Books, Inc., **10** 136
Marbro Lamp Co., **III** 571; **20** 362
Marc's Big Boy. *See* The Marcus Corporation.
Marcade Group. *See* Aris Industries, Inc.
Marceau Investments, **II** 356
March-Davis Bicycle Company, **19** 383
Marchand, **13** 27
Marchland Holdings Ltd., **II** 649
Marchon Eyewear, **22** 123
Marcillat, **19** 49
Marcon Coating, Inc., **22** 347
Marconi Wireless Telegraph Co. of America, **II** 25, 88
Marconiphone, **I** 531
The Marcus Corporation, 21 359–63
Marcus Samuel & Co., **IV** 530
Marcy Fitness Products, Inc., **19** 142, 144
Mardon Packaging International, **I** 426–27
Mardorf, Peach and Co., **II** 466
Maremont Corporation, **8** 39–40
Margarete Steiff GmbH, 23 334–37
Margarine Unie N.V. *See* Unilever PLC (Unilever N.V.).
Marge Carson, Inc., **III** 571; **20** 362
Margo's La Mode, **10** 281–82
Marico Acquisition Corporation, **8** 448, 450
Marie Brizard & Roger International S.A., 22 342–44
Marie Callender, **13** 66
Marie-Claire Album, **III** 47
Marigold Foods Inc., **II** 528
Marinduque Mining & Industrial Corp., **IV** 146
Marine Bank and Trust Co., **11** 105
Marine Bank of Erie, **II** 342
Marine Computer Systems, **6** 242
Marine Diamond Corp., **IV** 66; **7** 123
Marine Group, **III** 444; **22** 116
Marine Harvest International, **13** 103
Marine Midland Corp., **I** 548; **II** 298; **9** 475–76; **11** 108; **17** 325
Marine Office of America, **III** 220, 241–42
Marine-Firminy, **IV** 227
Marinela, **19** 192–93
Marineland Amusements Corp., **IV** 623
Marion Brick, **14** 249
Marion Foods, Inc., **17** 434
Marion Freight Lines, **6** 370
Marion Laboratories Inc., I 648–49; **8** 149; **9** 328–29; **16** 438
Marion Manufacturing, **9** 72
Marion Merrell Dow, Inc., 9 328–29 (upd.)
Marionet Corp., **IV** 680–81
Marisa Christina, Inc., 15 290–92
Maritime Electric Company, Limited, **15** 182
Mark Cross, Inc., **17** 4–5
Mark Goldston, **8** 305
Mark Hopkins, **12** 316
Mark IV Industries, Inc., 7 296–98; **21** 418
Mark Trouser, Inc., **17** 338
Markborough Properties, **II** 222; **V** 81; **8** 525
Market Growth Resources, **23** 480
Market Horizons, **6** 27
Market National Bank, **13** 465
Marketime, **V** 55

Marketing Data Systems, Inc., **18** 24
Marketing Information Services, **6** 24
Markham & Co., **I** 573–74
Marks and Spencer p.l.c., I 588; **II** 513, 678; **V** 124–26; **10** 442; **17** 42, 124; **22** 109, 111
Marks-Baer Inc., **11** 64
Marland Refining Co., **IV** 399–400
Marlene Industries Corp., **16** 36–37
MarLennan Corp., **III** 283
Marley Co., **19** 360
Marley Holdings, L.P., **19** 246
Marley Tile, **III** 735
Marlin-Rockwell Corp., **I** 539; **14** 510
Marlow Foods, **II** 565
Marman Products Company, **16** 8
The Marmon Group, III 97; **IV 135–38**; **16 354–57 (upd.)**
Marmon-Perry Light Company, **6** 508
Marolf Dakota Farms, Inc., **18** 14–15
Marotte, **21** 438
Marquam Commercial Brokerage Company, **21** 257
Marquardt Aircraft, **I** 380; **13** 379
Marquette Electronics, Inc., 13 326–28
Marquette Paper Corporation, **III** 766; **22** 545
Marquis Who's Who, **17** 398
Marriage Mailers, **6** 12
Marriner Group, **13** 175
Marriott Corporation, II 173, 608; **III** 92, 94, 99–100, **102–03**, 248; **7** 474–75; **9** 95, 426; **15** 87; **17** 238; **18** 216; **19** 433–34; **21** 91, 364; **22** 131; **23** 436–38
Marriott International, Inc., 21 182, **364–67 (upd.)**
Mars, Inc., II 510–11; **III** 114; **7 299–301**; **22** 298, 528
Marschke Manufacturing Co., **III** 435
Marsene Corp., **III** 440
Marsh & McLennan Companies, Inc., III 280, **282–84**; **10** 39; **14** 279; **22** 318
Marsh Supermarkets, Inc., 17 300–02
Marshalk Company, **I** 16; **22** 294
Marshall Die Casting, **13** 225
Marshall Field & Co., **I** 13, 426; **III** 329; **IV** 660; **V** 43–44; **8** 33; **9** 213; **12** 283; **15** 86; **18** 136–37, 488; **22** 72
Marshall Industries, **19** 311
Marshalls Incorporated, 13 329–31; **14** 62
Marsin Medical Supply Co., **III** 9
Marstellar, **13** 204
The Mart, **9** 120
Martha, **IV** 486
Martin Bros. Ltd., **III** 690
Martin Bros. Tobacco Co., **14** 19
Martin Collet, **19** 50
Martin Dennis Co., **IV** 409
Martin Electric Co., **III** 98
Martin Marietta Corporation, I 47, **67–69**, 71, 102, 112, 142–43, 184, 416; **II** 32, 67; **III** 671; **IV** 60, 163; **7** 356, 520; **8** 315; **9** 310; **10** 162, 199, 484; **11** 166, 277–78, 364; **12** 127, 290; **13** 327, 356; **15** 283; **17** 564; **18** 369; **19** 70; **22** 400. *See also* Lockheed Martin Corporation.
Martin Mathys, **8** 456
Martin Rooks & Co., **I** 95
Martin Sorrell, **6** 54
Martin Theaters, **14** 86
Martin Zippel Co., **16** 389
Martin's, **12** 221

Martin-Brower Corp., **II** 500; **III** 21; **17** 475

Martin-Senour Co., **III** 744

Martin-Yale Industries, Inc., **19** 142–44

Martindale-Hubbell, **17** 398

Martineau and Bland, **I** 293

Martini & Rossi, **18** 41

Martins Bank, **II** 236, 308

Martinus Nijhoff, **14** 555

Marubeni K.K., **I** 432, **492–95**, 510; **II** 292, 391; **III** 760; **IV** 266, 525; **12** 147; **17** 556

Maruei & Co., **IV** 151

Maruetsu, **17** 124

Marufuku Co., Ltd., **III** 586; **7** 394

Marui Co. Ltd., **V 127**

Marukuni Kogyo Co., Ltd., **IV** 327

Marutaka Kinitsu Store Ltd., **V** 194

Maruzen Co., Limited, **II** 348; **IV** 403–04, 476, 554; **18 322–24**

Marvel Entertainment Group, Inc., **10 400–02**; **18** 426, 520–21; **21** 404

Marvel Metal Products, **III** 570; **20** 361

Marvel-Schebler Carburetor Corp., **III** 438; **14** 63–64

Marvin & Leonard Advertising, **13** 511–12

Marvin H. Sugarman Productions Inc., **20** 48

Marvin Lumber & Cedar Company, **10** 95; **22 345–47**

Marwick, Mitchell & Company, **10** 385

Marwitz & Hauser, **III** 446

Marx, **12** 494

Mary Ann Co. Ltd., **V** 89

Mary Ann Restivo, Inc., **8** 323

Mary Ellen's, Inc., **11** 211

Mary Kathleen Uranium, **IV** 59–60

Mary Kay Corporation, **III** 16; **9 330–32**; **12** 435; **15** 475, 477; **18** 67, 164; **21** 49, 51

Maryland Casualty Co., **III** 193, 412

Maryland Cup Company, **8** 197

Maryland Distillers, **I** 285

Maryland National Corp., **11** 287

Maryland National Mortgage Corporation, **11** 121

Maryland Shipbuilding and Drydock Co., **I** 170

Maryland Steel Co., **IV** 35; **7** 48

Marzotto S.p.A., **20 356–58**

Masayoshi Son, **13** 481–82

Mascan Corp., **IV** 697

Maschinenbauanstalt Humboldt AG, **III** 541

Maschinenfabrik Augsburg-Nürnberg. See M.A.N.

Maschinenfabrik Deutschland, **IV** 103

Maschinenfabrik für den Bergbau von Sievers & Co., **III** 541

Maschinenfabrik Gebr. Meer, **III** 565

Maschinenfabrik Sürth, **I** 581

Masco Corporation, **III 568–71**; **11** 385, 534–35; **12** 129, 131, 344; **13** 338; **18** 68; **20 359–63 (upd.)**

Masco Optical, **13** 165

Mascon Toy Co., **III** 569; **20** 360

MASCOR, **14** 13

Mase Westpac Limited, **11** 418

Maserati. See Officine Alfieri Maserati S.p.A.

Masinfabriks A.B. Scania, **I** 197

MASkargo Ltd., **6** 101

Masland Corporation, **17 303–05**; **19** 408

Mason & Hamlin, **III** 656

Mason Best Co., **IV** 343

Masonite Corp., **III** 764

Masonite Holdings, **III** 687

Mass Rapid Transit Corp., **19** 111

Massachusetts Bank, **II** 207

Massachusetts Capital Resources Corp., **III** 314

Massachusetts Mutual Life Insurance Company, **III** 110, **285–87**, 305; **14** 14

Massachusetts Technology Development Corporation, **18** 570

Massey Burch Investment Group, **23** 153

Massey-Ferguson, **II** 222, 245; **III** 439, 650–52; **13** 18. See also Varity Corporation.

Mast Industries, **V** 115–16

MasTec, Inc., **19 254–57**

Master Boot Polish Co., **II** 566

Master Builders, **I** 673

Master Electric Company, **15** 134

Master Pneumatic Tool Co., **III** 436

Master Processing, **19** 37

Master Products, **14** 162

Master Shield Inc., **7** 116

Master Tank and Welding Company, **7** 541

MasterBrand Industries Inc., **12** 344–45

MasterCard International, Inc., **9 333–35**; **18** 337, 543

Mastercraft Homes, Inc., **11** 257

Mastercraft Industries Corp., **III** 654

Matador Records, **22** 194

Matairco, **9** 27

Matane Pulp & Paper Company, **17** 281

Matchbox Toys Ltd., **12** 168

Matco Tools, **7** 116

Materials Services Corp., **I** 58

Mathematica, Inc., **22** 291

Mather & Crother Advertising Agency, **I** 25

Mather Co., **I** 159

Mather Metals, **III** 582

Matheson & Co., **IV** 189

Mathews Conveyor Co., **14** 43

Mathieson Chemical Corp., **I** 379–80, 695; **13** 379

Matra, **II** 38, 70; **IV** 617–19; **13** 356; **17** 354

Matra Aerospace Inc., **22** 402

Matra-Hachette S.A., **15 293–97 (upd.)**; **21** 267

Matria Healthcare, Inc., **17 306–09**

Matrix Science Corp., **II** 8; **14** 27

Matson Navigation Company, Inc., **II** 490–91; **10** 40

Matsumoto Medical Instruments, **11** 476

Matsushita Electric Industrial Co., Ltd., **II** 5, **55–56**, 58, 61, 91–92, 102, 117–19, 361, 455; **III** 476, 710; **6** 36; **7** 163, 302; **10** 286, 389, 403, 432; **11** 487; **12** 448; **13** 398; **18** 18; **20** 81

Matsushita Electric Works, Ltd., **III 710–11**; **7 302–03 (upd.)**; **12** 454; **16** 167

Matsushita Kotobuki Electronics Industries, Ltd., **10** 458–59

Matsuura Trading Co., Ltd., **IV** 327

Matsuzakaya Company, **V 129–31**

Mattatuck Bank & Trust Co., **13** 467

Mattel, Inc., **II** 136; **III** 506; **7 304–07**; **12** 74, 168–69, 495; **13** 560–61; **15** 238; **16** 264, 428; **17** 243; **18** 520–21

Matthes & Weber, **III** 32

Matthew Bender & Company, Inc., **IV** 677; **7** 94; **14** 97; **17** 486

Matthews Paint Co., **22** 437

Maud Foster Mill, **II** 566

Maui Electric Company, **9** 276

Mauna Kea Properties, **6** 129

Maurice H. Needham Co., **I** 31

Maus Frères, **19** 307

Maus-Nordmann, **V** 10; **19** 308

Max & Erma's Restaurants Inc., **19 258–60**

Max Factor & Co., **III** 54, 56; **6** 51; **12** 314

Max Klein, Inc., **II** 572

Maxcell Telecom Plus, **6** 323

Maxco Inc., **17 310–11**

Maxell Corp., **I** 500; **14** 534

Maxi Vac, Inc., **9** 72

MAXI-Papier, **10** 498

Maxicare Health Plans, Inc., **III 84–86**

Maxim Integrated Products, Inc., **16 358–60**

Maxis Software, **13** 115

Maxoptix Corporation, **10** 404

Maxpro Sports Inc., **22** 458

Maxtor Corporation, **6** 230; **10 403–05**, 459, 463–64

Maxus Energy Corporation, **IV** 410; **7 308–10**; **10** 191

Maxwell Communication Corporation plc, **IV** 605, 611, **641–43**; **7** 286, 311–13 **(upd.)**, 343; **10** 288; **13** 91–93; **23** 350

Maxwell Morton Corp, **I** 144, 414

MAXXAM Inc., **IV** 121, 123; **8 348–50**

Maxxim Medical Inc., **12 325–27**

May and Baker, **I** 388

The May Department Stores Company, **I** 540; **II** 414; **V 132–35**; **8** 288; **11** 349; **12** 55, 507–08; **13** 42, 361; **15** 275; **16** 62, 160, 206–07; **18** 414–15; **19 261–64 (upd.)**; **23** 345

Maybelline, **I** 684

Mayfair Foods, **I** 438; **16** 314

Mayfield Dairy Farms, Inc., **7** 128

Mayflower Group Inc., **6 409–11**; **15** 50

Mayne Nickless Ltd., **IV** 248

Mayo Foundation, **9 336–39**; **13** 326

Maytag Corporation, **III 572–73**; **12** 252, 300; **21** 141; **22** 218, **348–51 (upd.)**; **23** 244

Mayville Metal Products Co., **I** 513

Mazda Motor Corporation, **I** 520; **II** 4, 361; **III** 603; **9 340–42**; **11** 86; **13** 414; **16** 322; **23 338–41 (upd.)**

MB Group, **20** 108

MBNA Corporation, **11** 123; **12 328–30**

MBPXL Corp., **II** 494

MCA Inc., **II 143–45**; **6** 162–63; **10** 286; **11** 557; **17** 317; **21** 23, 25–26; **22** 131, 194; **23** 125

The McAlpin Company, **19** 272

McAndrew & Forbes Holdings Inc., **23** 407

McArthur Glen Realty, **10** 122

McCaffrey & McCall, **I** 33; **11** 496

McCain Feeds Ltd., **II** 484

McCall Pattern Company, **22** 512; **23** 99

McCall Printing Co., **14** 460

McCall's Corp., **23** 393

McCann-Erickson worldwide, **I** 10, 14, 16–17, 234; **6** 30; **10** 227; **14** 315; **16** 167; **18** 68; **22** 294

McCarthy Milling, **II** 631

McCaughan Dyson and Co., **II** 189

McCaw Cellular Communications, Inc., II 331; **6** 274, **322–24**; **7** 15; **9** 320–21; **10** 433; **15** 125, 196
McClanahan Oil Co., I 341; **14** 216
McClatchy Newspapers, Inc., 23 156, 158, **342–44**
McCleary, Wallin and Crouse, **19** 274
McClintic-Marshall, **IV** 36; **7** 49
The McCloskey Corporation, **8** 553
McColl-Frontenac Inc., **IV** 439
McComb Manufacturing Co., **8** 287
McCormack & Dodge, **IV** 605; **11** 77
McCormick & Company, Incorporated, 7 314–16; **17** 104, 106; **21** 497
McCormick Harvesting Machine Co., I 180; **II** 330
McCown De Leeuw & Co., **16** 510
McCracken Brooks, **23** 479
McCrory Stores, **II** 424; **9** 447–48; **13** 340
McCulloch Corp., **III** 436; **8** 348–49
McCullough Environmental Services, **12** 443
McDermott International, Inc., III 558–60
McDonald Glass Grocery Co. Inc., **II** 669
McDonald's Company (Japan) Ltd., **V** 205
McDonald's Corporation, I 23, 31, 129; **II** 500, 613–15 **646–48**; **III** 63, 94, 103; **6** 13; **7** 128, 266–67, 316, **317–19 (upd.)**, 435, 505–06; **8** 261–62, 564; **9** 74, 178, 290, 292, 305; **10** 122; **11** 82, 308; **12** 43, 180, 553; **13** 494; **14** 25, 32, 106, 195, 452–53; **16** 95–97, 289; **17** 69–71; **19** 85, 192, 214; **21** 25, 315, 362; **23** 505
McDonnell Douglas Corporation, I 41–43, 45, 48, 50–52, 54–56, 58–59, 61–62, 67–68, **70–72**, 76–77, 82, 84–85, 90, 105, 108, 111, 121–22, 321, 364, 490, 511; **II** 442; **III** 512, 654; **6** 68; **7** 456, 504; **8** 49 51, 315; **9** 18, 183, 206, 231, 271–72, 418, 458, 460; **10** 163–64, 317, 536; **11** 164–65, 267, **277–80 (upd.)**, 285, 363–65; **12** 190–91, 549; **13** 356; **15** 283; **16** 78, 94; **18** 368
McDonough Co., **II** 16; **III** 502
McDougal, Littell & Company, **10** 357
McDowell Energy Center, **6** 543
McDowell Furniture Company, **10** 183
McDuff, **10** 305
McElligott Wright Morrison and White, **12** 511
McFadden Industries, **III** 21
McFadden Publishing, **6** 13
McGaughy, Marshall & McMillan, **6** 142
McGaw Inc., **11** 208
McGill Manufacturing, **III** 625
McGraw Electric Company. *See* Centel Corporation.
McGraw-Edison Co., **II** 17, 87
The McGraw-Hill Companies, Inc., II 398; **IV** 584, **634–37**, 643, 656, 674; **10** 62; **12** 359; **13** 417; **18 325–30 (upd.)**
McGregor Cory, **6** 415
McGrew Color Graphics, **7** 430
MCI Communications Corporation, II 408; **III** 13, 149, 684; **V 302–04**; **6** 51–52, 300, 322; **7** 118–19; **8** 310; **9** 171, 478–80; **10** 19, 80, 89, 97, 433, 500; **11** 59, 183, 185, 302, 409, 500; **12** 135–37; **13** 38; **14** 252–53, 260, 364; **15** 222; **16** 318; **18** 32, 112, 164–66, 569–70; **19** 255

McIlhenny Company, 20 364–67
Mcjunkin Corp., **13** 79
McKee Foods Corporation, 7 320–21
McKenna Metals Company, **13** 295–96
McKesson Corporation, I 413, **496–98**, 713; **II** 652; **III** 10; **6** 279; **8** 464; **9** 532; **11** 91; **12** 331–33 **(upd.)**; **16** 43; **18** 97
McKinsey & Company, Inc., I 108, 144, 437, 497; **III** 47, 85, 670; **9 343–45**; **10** 175; **13** 138; **18** 68
McLain Grocery, **II** 625
McLane Company, Inc., V 217; **8** 556; **13** 332–34
McLaren Consolidated Cone Corp., **II** 543; **7** 366
McLaughlin Motor Company of Canada, I 171; **10** 325
McLean Clinic, **11** 379
McLouth Steel Products, **13** 158
MCM Electronics, **9** 420
McMahan's Furniture Co., **14** 236
McMan Oil and Gas Co., **IV** 369
McManus, John & Adams, Inc., **6** 21
McMoCo, **IV** 82–83; **7** 187
McMoRan, **IV** 81–83; **V** 739; **7** 185, 187
McMullen & Yee Publishing, **22** 442
McMurtry Manufacturing, **8** 553
MCN Corporation, 6 519–22; **13** 416; **17** 21–23
McNeil Laboratories, **III** 35–36; **8** 282–83
McNellan Resources Inc., **IV** 76
MCO Holdings Inc., **8** 348–49
MCorp, **10** 134; **11** 122
McRae's, Inc., **19** 324–25
MCS, Inc., **10** 412
MCT Dairies, Inc., **18** 14–16
McTeigue & Co., **14** 502
McVitie & Price, **II** 592–93
McWhorter Inc., **8** 553
MD Distribution Inc., **15** 139
MD Pharmaceuticals, **III** 10
MDC. *See* Mead Data Central, Inc.
MDI Co., Ltd., **IV** 327
MDS/Bankmark, **10** 247
MDU Resources Group, Inc., 7 322–25
The Mead Corporation, IV 310–13, 327, 329, 342–43; **8** 267; **9** 261; **10** 406; **11** 421–22; **17** 399; **19 265–69 (upd.)**; **20** 18
Mead Cycle Co., **IV** 660
Mead Data Central, Inc., IV 312; **7** 581; **10 406–08**; **19** 268
Mead John & Co., **19** 103
Mead Johnson, **III** 17
Mead Packaging, **12** 151
Meade County Rural Electric Cooperative Corporation, **11** 37
Meadow Gold Dairies, Inc., **II** 473
Means Services, Inc., **II** 607
Mears & Phillips, **II** 237
Measurex Corporation, **8** 243; **14** 56
MEC - Hawaii, UK & USA, **IV** 714
MECA Software, Inc., **18** 363
Mecair, S.p.A., **17** 147
Mecca Leisure PLC, I 248; **12** 229
Mechanics Exchange Savings Bank, **9** 173
Mechanics Machine Co., **III** 438; **14** 63
Medal Distributing Co., **9** 542
Medallion Pictures Corp., **9** 320
Medar, Inc., **17** 310–11
Medco Containment Services Inc., 9 346–48; **11** 291; **12** 333
Medcom Inc., I 628
Medeco Security Locks, Inc., **10** 350

Medfield Corp., **III** 87
Medford, Inc., **19** 467–68
Medi Mart Drug Store Co., **II** 667
Media General, Inc., III 214; **7 326–28**; **18** 61; **23** 225
Media Groep West B.V., **23** 271
Media Play, **9** 360–61
MEDIC Computer Systems, **16** 94
Medical Care America, Inc., **15** 112, 114
Medical Development Corp. *See* Cordis Corp.
Medical Economics Data, **23** 211
Medical Expense Fund, **III** 245
Medical Indemnity of America, **10** 160
Medical Innovations Corporation, **21** 46
Medical Marketing Group Inc., **9** 348
Medical Service Assoc. of Pennsylvania, **III** 325–26
Medical Tribune Group, **IV** 591; **20** 53
Medicare-Glaser, **17** 167
Medicine Bow Coal Company, **7** 33–34
Medicine Shoppe International. *See* Cardinal Health, Inc.
Medicus Intercon International, **6** 22
Medifinancial Solutions, Inc., **18** 370
Mediobanca Banca di Credito Finanziario SpA, **II** 191, 271; **III** 208–09; **11** 205
The Mediplex Group, Inc., **III** 16; **11** 282
Medis Health and Pharmaceuticals Services Inc., **II** 653
Medite Corporation, **19** 467–68
Meditrust, 11 281–83
Medlabs Inc., **III** 73
Medtech, Ltd., **13** 60–62
Medtronic, Inc., 8 351–54; **11** 459; **18** 421; **19** 103; **22 359–61**
Medusa Corporation, **8** 135
Mees & Hope, **II** 184
MEGA Natural Gas Company, **11** 28
Megafoods Stores Inc., 13 335–37; **17** 560
Megasource, Inc., **16** 94
MEI Diversified Inc., **18** 455
Mei Foo Investments Ltd., **IV** 718
Meier & Frank Co., 23 345–47
Meijer Incorporated, 7 329–31; **15** 449; **17** 302
Meiji Commerce Bank, **II** 291
Meiji Fire Insurance Co., **III** 384–85
Meiji Milk Products Company, Limited, II 538–39
Meiji Mutual Life Insurance Company, II 323; **III 288–89**
Meiji Seika Kaisha, Ltd., I 676; **II 540–41**
Meikosha Co., **II** 72
Meinecke Muffler Company, **III** 495; **10** 415
Meis of Illiana, **10** 282
Meisei Electric, **III** 742
Meissner, Ackermann & Co., **IV** 463; **7** 351
Meister, Lucious and Company, **13** 262
Meiwa Manufacturing Co., **III** 758
N.V. Mekog, **IV** 531
Mel Farr Automotive Group, 20 368–70
Mel Klein and Partners, **III** 74
Melbourne Engineering Co., **23** 83
Melbur China Clay Co., **III** 690
Melco, **II** 58
Melkunie-Holland, **II** 575
Mellbank Security Co., **II** 316
Mello Smello. *See* The Miner Group International.

Mellon Bank Corporation, I 67–68, 584;
II 315–17, 342, 402; **III** 275; **9** 470; **13**
410–11; **18** 112
Mellon Indemnity Corp., **III** 258–59
Mellon-Stuart Co., I 584–85; 14 334
Mélotte, **III** 418
Meloy Laboratories, Inc., **11** 333
Melroe Company, **8** 115–16
Melville Corporation, V 136–38; 9 192;
13 82, 329–30; **14** 426; **15** 252–53;, **16**
390; **19** 449; **21** 526; **23** 176
Melvin Simon and Associates, Inc., 8
355–57
Melwire Group, **III** 673
Memco, **12** 48
Memorex Corp., **III** 110, 166; **6** 282–83
The Men's Wearhouse, Inc., 17 312–15;
21 311
Menasco Manufacturing Co., **I** 435; **III**
415
Menasha Corporation, 8 358–61
Menck, **8** 544
Mendelssohn & Co., **II** 241
Meneven, **IV** 508
Menka Gesellschaft, **IV** 150
The Mennen Company, **I** 19; **6** 26; **14** 122;
18 69
Mental Health Programs Inc., **15** 122
Mentholatum Co., **IV** 722
Mentor Graphics Corporation, III 143; **8**
519; **11** 46–47, **284–86**, 490; **13** 128
MEPC plc, IV 710–12
Mepco/Electra Inc., **13** 398
MeraBank, **6** 546
Mercantile Agency, **IV** 604
Mercantile and General Reinsurance Co.,
III 335, 377
Mercantile Bank, **II** 298
Mercantile Bankshares Corp., 11 287–88
Mercantile Credit Co., **16** 13
Mercantile Estate and Property Corp. Ltd.,
IV 710
Mercantile Fire Insurance, **III** 234
Mercantile Mutual, **III** 310
Mercantile Property Corp. Ltd., **IV** 710
Mercantile Security Life, **III** 136
Mercantile Stores Company, Inc., V 139;
19 270–73 (upd.)
Mercantile Trust Co., **II** 229, 247
Mercedes Benz. *See* Daimler-Benz A.G.
Mercedes Benz of North America, **22** 52
Merchant Bank Services, **18** 516, 518
Merchant Co., **III** 104
Merchant Distributors, Inc., **20** 306
Merchants & Farmers Bank of Ecru, **14** 40
Merchants Bank, **II** 213
Merchants Bank & Trust Co., **21** 524
Merchants Bank of Canada, **II** 210
Merchants Bank of Halifax, **II** 344
Merchants Dispatch, **II** 395–96; **10** 60
Merchants Distributors Inc. *See* Alex Lee
Inc.
Merchants Fire Assurance Corp., **III**
396–97
Merchants Home Delivery Service, **6** 414
Merchants Indemnity Corp., **III** 396–97
Merchants Life Insurance Co., **III** 275
Merchants National Bank, **9** 228; **14** 528;
17 135
Merchants National Bank of Boston, **II** 213
Merchants Union Express Co., **II** 396; **10**
60
Merchants' Assoc., **II** 261
Merchants' Loan and Trust, **II** 261; **III** 518

Merchants' Savings, Loan and Trust Co.,
II 261
Mercier, **I** 272
Merck & Co., Inc., I 640, 646, **650–52**,
683–84, 708; **II** 414; **III** 42, 60, 66,
299; **8** 154, 548; **10** 213; **11** 9, 90,
289–91 (upd.); **12** 325, 333; **14** 58, 422;
15 154; **16** 440; **20** 39, 59
Mercury Air Group, Inc., 20 371–73
Mercury Asset Management (MAM), **14**
420
Mercury Communications, Ltd., V
280–82; **7 332–34**; **10** 456; **11** 547–48
Mercury, Inc., **8** 311
Mercury Mail, Inc., **22** 519, 522
Mercury Records, **13** 397; **23** 389, 391
Mercury Telecommunications Limited, **15**
67, 69
Meredith and Drew, **II** 593
Meredith Corporation, IV 661–62; **11**
292–94; **17** 394; **18** 239; **23** 393
Meridian Bancorp, Inc., 11 295–97; 17
111, 114
Meridian Healthcare, **18** 197
Meridian Insurance Co., **III** 332
Meridian Investment and Development
Corp., **22** 189
Meridian Oil Inc., **10** 190–91
Merillat Industries Inc., III 570; **13**
338–39; 20 362
Merisel, Inc., 10 518–19; **12 334–36; 13**
174, 176, 482
Merit Distribution Services, **13** 333
Merit Tank Testing, Inc., **IV** 411
Merivienti Oy, **IV** 276
Merla Manufacturing, **I** 524
Merlin Gérin, **II** 93–94; **18** 473; **19** 165
Merpati Nusantara Airlines, **6** 90–91
Merrell, **22** 173
Merrell Dow, **16** 438
Merrell Drug, **I** 325
Merrell-Soule Co., **II** 471
Merriam and Morgan Paraffine Co., **IV**
548
Merriam-Webster, Inc., **7** 165, 167; **23**
209–10
Merrill Corporation, 18 331–34
Merrill Gas Company, **9** 554
Merrill Lynch & Co., Inc., I 26, 339,
681, 683, 697; **II** 149, 257, 260, 268,
403, 407–08, 412, **424–26**, 441, 445,
449, 451, 456, 654–55, 680; **III** 119,
253, 340, 440; **6** 244; **7** 130; **8** 94; **9**
125, 187, 239, 301, 386; **11** 29, 122,
348, 557; **13** 44, 125, **340–43 (upd.)**,
448–49, 512; **14** 65; **15** 463; **16** 195; **17**
137; **21** 68–70, 145; **22** 404–06, 542; **23**
370
Merrill, Pickard, Anderson & Eyre IV, **11**
490
Merrill Publishing, **IV** 643; **7** 312; **9** 63
Merry Group, **III** 673
Merry Maids, **6** 46; **23** 428, 430
Merry-Go-Round Enterprises, Inc., 8
362–64
Mersey Paper Co., **IV** 258
Mersey White Lead Co., **III** 680
Merv Griffin Enterprises, **II** 137; **12** 75; **22**
431
Mervyn's, V 43–44; **10 409–10; 13** 526;
18 136–37
Mesa Airlines, Inc., 11 298–300
Mesa Limited Partnership, **IV** 410, 523; **11**
441

Mesa Petroleum, **IV** 392, 571
Mesaba Transportation Co., **I** 448; **22** 21
Messageries du Livre, **IV** 614
Messerschmitt-Bölkow-Blohm GmbH., I
41–42, 46, 51–52, 55, **73–75**, 111; **II**
242; **III** 539; **11** 267
Messner, Vetere, Berger, Carey,
Schmetterer, **13** 204
Mesta Machine Co., **22** 415
Mestek, Inc., 10 411–13
Met-Mex Penoles. *See* Industrias Penoles,
S.A. de C.V.
Metabio-Joullie, **III** 47
Metal Box plc, I 604–06; 20 108
Metal Casting Technology, Inc., **23** 267,
269
Metal Closures, **I** 615
Metal Industries, **I** 531–32
Metal Manufactures, **III** 433–34
Metal Office Furniture Company, **7** 493
Metal-Cal. *See* Avery Dennison
Corporation.
Metaleurop S.A., IV 108–09; **21 368–71**
Metall Mining Corp., **IV** 141
Metallgesellschaft AG, IV 17, **139–42**,
229; **16 361–66 (upd.)**
MetalOptics Inc., **19** 212
MetalPro, Inc., **IV** 168
Metals and Controls Corp., **II** 113
Metals Exploration, **IV** 82
Metalurgica Mexicana Penoles, S.A. *See*
Industrias Penoles, S.A. de C.V.
Metaphase Technology, Inc., **10** 257
Metcalf & Eddy Companies, Inc., **6** 143,
441
Meteor Film Productions, **23** 391
Methane Development Corporation, **6** 457
Methanex Corp., **12** 365; **19** 155–56
Methode Electronics, Inc., 13 344–46
Metinox Steel Ltd., **IV** 203
MetLife General Insurance Agency, **III**
293
MetMor Financial, Inc., **III** 293
MetPath, Inc., **III** 684
Metra Steel, **19** 381
Metric Constructors, Inc., **16** 286
Metric Systems, Inc., **18** 513
Metro AG, **23** 311
Metro Distributors Inc., **14** 545
Metro Drug Corporation, **II** 649–50; **18**
181
Metro Glass, **II** 533
Metro Pacific, **18** 180, 182
Metro Pictures, **II** 148
Metro Southwest Construction. *See* CRSS
Inc.
Metro Vermögensverwaltung GmbH & Co.
of Dusseldorf, **V** 104
Metro-Goldwyn-Mayer. *See* MGM/UA
Communications Company.
Metro-Mark Integrated Systems Inc., **11**
469
Metro-Richelieu Inc., **II** 653
Metro-Verwegensverwaltung, **II** 257
Metrocall Inc., **18** 77
Metromail Corp., **IV** 661; **18** 170
Metromedia Companies, II 171; **6** 33,
168–69; **7** 91, **335–37**; **8** 311; **14** 107,
330–32 (upd.); **15** 362; **15** 363
Metromont Materials, **III** 740
Metroplitan and Great Western Dairies, **II**
586
Metropolitan Accident Co., **III** 228

Metropolitan Bank, **II** 221, 318; **III** 239; **IV** 644; **17** 323

Metropolitan Broadcasting Corporation, **7** 335

Metropolitan Clothing Co., **19** 362

Metropolitan Distributors, **9** 283

Metropolitan District Railway Company, **6** 406

Metropolitan Estate and Property Corp. Ltd., **IV** 710–11

Metropolitan Financial Corporation, **12** 165; **13 347–49**

Metropolitan Furniture Leasing, **14** 4

Metropolitan Gas Light Co., **6** 455

Metropolitan Housing Corp. Ltd., **IV** 710

Metropolitan Life Insurance Company, **II** 679; **III** 265–66, 272, **290–94**, 313, 329, 337, 339–40, 706; **IV** 283; **6** 256; **8** 326–27; **11** 482; **22** 266

Metropolitan National Bank, **II** 284

Metropolitan Petroleum Corp., **IV** 180–81; **19** 319

Metropolitan Railway, **6** 407

Metropolitan Railways Surplus Lands Co., **IV** 711

Metropolitan Tobacco Co., **15** 138

Metropolitan Vickers, **III** 670

METSA, Inc., **15** 363

Metsä-Serla Oy, **IV 314–16**, 318, 350

Mettler United States Inc., **9** 441

Metzeler Kautschuk, **15** 354

Mexican Eagle Oil Co., **IV** 365, 531

Mexican Metal Co. *See* Industrias Penoles, S.A. de C.V.

Mexican Original Products, Inc., **II** 585; **14** 515

Mexofina, S.A. de C.V., **IV** 401

Meyer and Charlton, **IV** 90

Meyer Brothers Drug Company, **16** 212

Meyerland Company, **19** 366

Meyers & Muldoon, **6** 40

Meyers and Co., **III** 9

Meyers Parking, **18** 104

Meyrin, **I** 122

MFI, **II** 612

MFS Communications Company, Inc., **11 301–03**; **14** 253

MG Holdings. *See* Mayflower Group Inc.

MG Ltd., **IV** 141

MG&E. *See* Madison Gas & Electric.

MGM Grand Inc., **III** 431; **6** 210; **17 316–19**; **18** 336–37

MGM/UA Communications Company, **I** 286, 487; **II** 103, 135, **146–50**, 155, 161, 167, 169, 174–75, 408; **IV** 676; **6** 172–73; **12** 73, 316, 323, 455; **15** 84; **17** 316

mh Bausparkasse AG, **III** 377

MHI Group, Inc., **13** 356; **16** 344

MHT. *See* Manufacturers Hanover Trust Co.

MI. *See* Masco Corporation.

Miami Power Corporation, **6** 466

Micamold Electronics Manufacturing Corporation, **10** 319

Michael Baker Corp., **14 333–35**

MICHAEL Business Systems Plc, **10** 257

Michael Joseph, **IV** 659

Michael Reese Health Plan Inc., **III** 82

Michael's Fair-Mart Food Stores, Inc., **19** 479

Michaels Stores, Inc., **17 320–22**, 360

MichCon. *See* MCN Corporation.

Michelin, **III** 697; **7** 36–37; **8** 74; **11** 158, 473; **20** 261–62; **21** 72, 74

Michelin et Compagnie, **V** 236

Michiana Merchandising, **III** 10

Michie Co., **IV** 312; **19** 268

Michigan Automotive Compressor, Inc., **III** 593, 638–39

Michigan Automotive Research Corporation, **23** 183

Michigan Bell Telephone Co., **14 336–38**; **18** 30

Michigan Carpet Sweeper Company, **9** 70

Michigan Consolidated Gas Company. *See* MCN Corporation.

Michigan Fruit Canners, **II** 571

Michigan General, **II** 408

Michigan International Speedway, **V** 494

Michigan Motor Freight Lines, **14** 567

Michigan National Corporation, **11 304–06**; **18** 517

Michigan Oil Company, **18** 494

Michigan Packaging Company, **15** 188

Michigan Plating and Stamping Co., **I** 451

Michigan Radiator & Iron Co., **III** 663

Michigan Shoe Makers. *See* Wolverine World Wide Inc.

Michigan Spring Company, **17** 106

Michigan State Life Insurance Co., **III** 274

Michigan Steel Corporation, **12** 352

Michigan Tag Company, **9** 72

Mickey Shorr Mobile Electronics, **10** 9–11

Micro D, Inc., **11** 194

Micro Decisionware, Inc., **10** 506

Micro Peripherals, Inc., **18** 138

Micro Power Systems Inc., **14** 183

Micro Switch, **14** 284

Micro Warehouse, Inc., **16 371–73**

Micro-Circuit, Inc., **III** 645

Micro-Power Corp., **III** 643

Micro/Vest, **13** 175

MicroAge, Inc., **16 367–70**

Microamerica, **12** 334

MicroBilt Corporation, **11** 112

MicroComputer Accessories, **III** 614

Microcomputer Asset Management Services, **9** 168

Microcomputer Systems, **22** 389

Microdot Inc., **I** 440; **8 365–68**, 545

Microfal, **I** 341

Microform International Marketing Corp., **IV** 642; **7** 312

Microfral, **14** 216

Micromedex, **19** 268

Micron Technology, Inc., **III** 113; **11 307–09**

Micropolis Corp., **10** 403, 458, 463

MicroPro International, **10** 556

Microprocessor Systems, **13** 235

Micros Systems, Inc., **18 335–38**

Microseal Corp., **I** 341

Microsoft Corporation, **III** 116; **6** 219–20, 224, 227, 231, 235, 254–56, **257–60**, 269–71; **9** 81, 140, 171, 195, 472; **10** 22, 34, 57, 87, 119, 237–38, 362–63, 408, 477, 484, 504, 557–58; **11** 59, 77–78, 306, 519–20; **12** 180, 335; **13** 115, 128, 147, 482, 509; **14** 262–64, 318; **15** 132–33, 321, 371, 483, 492, 511; **16** 4, 94, 367, 392, 394, 444; **18** 24, 64, 66, 306–7, 345, 349, 367, 541, 543; **19** 310; **20** 237; **21** 86

Microtek, Inc., **22** 413

Microtel Limited, **6** 309–10

Microware Surgical Instruments Corp., **IV** 137

Microwave Communications, Inc., **V** 302

Mid-America Capital Resources, Inc., **6** 508

Mid-America Dairymen, Inc., **II** 536; **7 338–40**; **11** 24; **21** 342; **22** 95

Mid-America Industries, **III** 495

Mid-America Interpool Network, **6** 506, 602

Mid-America Packaging, Inc., **8** 203

Mid-America Tag & Label, **8** 360

Mid-Central Fish and Frozen Foods Inc., **II** 675

Mid-Continent Area Power Planner, **V** 672

Mid-Continent Computer Services, **11** 111

Mid-Continent Life Insurance Co., **23** 200

Mid-Continent Telephone Corporation. *See* Alltel Corporation.

Mid Georgia Gas Company, **6** 448

Mid-Illinois Gas Co., **6** 529

Mid-Pacific Airlines, **9** 271

Mid-Packaging Group Inc., **19** 78

Mid-South Towing, **6** 583

Mid-States Development, Inc., **18** 405

Mid-Texas Communications Systems, **6** 313

Mid-Valley Dairy, **14** 397

Mid-West Drive-In Theatres Inc., **I** 245

Mid-West Paper Ltd., **IV** 286

MidAmerican Communications Corporation, **8** 311

Midas International Corporation, **I** 457–58; **10 414–15**, 554

MIDCO, **III** 340

Midcon, **IV** 481

Middle South Utilities, **V** 618–19

Middle West Corporation, **6** 469–70

Middle West Utilities Company, **V** 583–84; **6** 555–56, 604–05; **14** 227; **21** 468–69

Middle Wisconsin Power, **6** 604

Middleburg Steel and Alloys Group, **I** 423

The Middleby Corporation, **22 352–55**

Middlesex Bank, **II** 334

Middleton Packaging, **12** 377

Middleton's Starch Works, **II** 566

Middletown Manufacturing Co., Inc., **16** 321

Middletown National Bank, **13** 467

Midhurst Corp., **IV** 658

Midial, **II** 478

Midland Bank plc, **II** 208, 236, 279, 295, 298, **318–20**, 334, 383; **9** 505; **12** 257; **14** 169; **17 323–26 (upd.)**; **19** 198

Midland Brick, **14** 250

Midland Cooperative, **II** 536

Midland Counties Dairies, **II** 587

Midland Electric Coal Co., **IV** 170

Midland Enterprises Inc., **6** 486–88

Midland Gravel Co., **III** 670

Midland Independent Newspaper plc, **23** 351

Midland Industrial Finishes Co., **I** 321

Midland Insurance, **I** 473

Midland International, **8** 56–57

Midland Investment Co., **II** 7

Midland Linseed Products Co., **I** 419

Midland National Bank, **11** 130

Midland Railway Co., **II** 306

Midland Southwest Corp., **8** 347

Midland Steel Products Co., **13** 305–06

Midland United, **6** 556

Midland Utilities Company, **6** 532

Midland-Ross Corporation, **14** 369
Midlands Electricity, **13** 485
Midlands Energy Co., **IV** 83; **7** 188
Midlantic Corp., **13** 411
Midrange Performance Group, **12** 149
Midrex Corp., **IV** 130
Midvale Steel and Ordnance Co., **IV** 35, 114; **7** 48
Midway Airlines, **6** 105, 120–21
Midway Manufacturing Company, **III** 430; **15** 539
Midwest Agri-Commodities, **11** 15
Midwest Air Charter, **6** 345
Midwest Biscuit Company, **14** 306
Midwest Com of Indiana, Inc., **11** 112
Midwest Dairy Products, **II** 661
Midwest Express Airlines, **III** 40–41; **11** 299; **16** 302, 304
Midwest Federal Savings & Loan Association, **11** 162–63
Midwest Financial Group, Inc., **8** 188
Midwest Foundry Co., **IV** 137
Midwest Manufacturing Co., **12** 296
Midwest Realty Exchange, Inc., **21** 257
Midwest Refining Co., **IV** 368
Midwest Resources Inc., 6 523–25
Midwest Steel Corporation, **13** 157
Midwest Synthetics, **8** 553
Midwinter, **12** 529
Miele & Cie., **III** 418
Miguel Galas S.A., **17** 268
Mike-Sell's Inc., 15 298–300
Mikemitch Realty Corp., **16** 36
Mikko, **II** 70
Mikko Kaloinen Oy, **IV** 349
Mikon, Ltd., **13** 345
Milani, **II** 556
Milbank Insurance Co., **III** 350
Milbank, Tweed, Hope & Webb, **II** 471
Milcor Steel Co., **IV** 114
Miles Druce & Co., **III** 494
Miles Inc., **22** 148
Miles Kimball Co., **9** 393
Miles Laboratories, I 310, **653–55**, 674, 678; **6** 50; **13** 76; **14** 558
Miles Redfern, **I** 429
Milgo Electronic Corp., **II** 83; **11** 408
Milgram Food Stores Inc., **II** 682
Milgray Electronics, **19** 311
Milk Producers, Inc., **11** 24
Milk Specialties, **12** 199
Millbrook Press Inc., **IV** 616
Miller Brewing Company, I 218–19, 236–37, 254–55, 257–58, **269–70**, 283, 290–91, 548; **10** 100; **11** 421; **12** **337–39 (upd.)**, 372; **13** 10, 258; **15** 429; **17** 256; **18** 70, 72, 418, 499, 501; **21** 230; **22** 199, 422
Miller Chemical & Fertilizer Corp., **I** 412
Miller Companies, **17** 182
Miller Container Corporation, **8** 102
Miller Freeman, **IV** 687
Miller Group Ltd., **22** 282
Miller, Mason and Dickenson, **III** 204–05
Miller, Tabak, Hirsch & Co., **13** 394
Millet's Leisure, **V** 177–78
Millicom, **11** 547; **18** 254
Milliken & Co., V 366–68; **8** 270–71; **17** **327–30 (upd.)**
Milliken, Tomlinson Co., **II** 682
Millipore Corporation, **9** 396; **23** 284
Mills Clothing, Inc. *See* The Buckle, Inc.
Millstone Point Company, **V** 668–69
Millville Electric Light Company, **6** 449

Milner, **III** 98
Milsco Manufacturing Co., **23** 299, 300
Milton Bradley Company, III 504–06; **16** 267; **17** 105; **21** 372–75
Milton Light & Power Company, **12** 45
Milton Roy Co., **8** 135
Milwaukee Electric Manufacturing Co., **III** 534
Milwaukee Electric Railway and Light Company, **6** 601–02, 604–05
Milwaukee Insurance Co., **III** 242
Milwaukee Mutual Fire Insurance Co., **III** 321
Minatome, **IV** 560
Minemet Recherche, **IV** 108
The Miner Group International, 22 **356–58**
Mineral Point Public Service Company, **6** 604
Minerales y Metales, S.A. *See* Industrias Penoles, S.A. de C.V.
Minerals & Chemicals Philipp, **IV** 79–80
Minerals & Metals Trading Corporation of India Ltd., IV 143–44
Minerals and Resources Corporation Limited, **IV** 23; **13** 502. *See also* Minorco.
Minerals Technologies Inc., 11 310–12
Minerec Corporation, **9** 363
Minerva, **III** 359
Minerve, **6** 208
Mines et Usines du Nord et de l'Est, **IV** 226
Minet Group, **III** 357; **22** 494–95
Mini Stop, **V** 97
Mining and Technical Services, **IV** 67
Mining Corp. of Canada Ltd., **IV** 164
Mining Development Corp., **IV** 239–40
Mining Trust Ltd., **IV** 32
MiniScribe, Inc., **6** 230; **10** 404
Minister of Finance Inc., **IV** 519
Minitel, **21** 233
Minivator Ltd., **11** 486
Minneapolis General Electric of Minnesota, **V** 670
Minneapolis Heat Regulator Co., **II** 40–41; **12** 246
Minneapolis Millers Association, **10** 322
Minneapolis Steel and Machinery Company, **21** 502
Minneapolis-Honeywell Regulator Co., **II** 40–41, 86; **8** 21; **12** 247; **22** 427
Minnesota Cooperative Creamery Association, Inc., **II** 535; **21** 340
Minnesota Linseed Oil Co., **8** 552
Minnesota Mining & Manufacturing Company, I 28, 387, **499–501**; **II** 39; **III** 476, 487, 549; **IV** 251, 253–54; **6** 231; **7** 162; **8** 35, 369–71 (upd.); **11** 494; **13** 326; **17** 29–30; **22** 427
Minnesota Power & Light Company, 11 **313–16**
Minnesota Sugar Company, **11** 13
Minnesota Valley Canning Co., **I** 22
Minnetonka Corp., **II** 590; **III** 25; **22** 122–23
Minntech Corporation, 22 359–61
Minolta Camera Co., Ltd., III 574–76, 583–84
Minolta Co., Ltd., 18 93, 186, **339–42** **(upd.)**
Minorco, **III** 503; **IV** 67–68, 84, 97; **16** 28, 293

Minstar Inc., **11** 397; **15** 49
Minute Maid Corp., **I** 234; **10** 227
Minute Tapioca, **II** 531
Mippon Paper, **21** 546
MIPS Computer Systems, **II** 45; **11** 491
Miracle Food Mart, **16** 247, 249–50
Miracle-Gro Products, Inc., **22** 474
Miraflores Designs Inc., **18** 216
Mirage Resorts, Inc., 6 209–12; 15 238
Miramar Hotel & Investment Co., **IV** 717
Mircali Asset Management, **III** 340
Mircor Inc., **12** 413
Mirrlees Blackstone, **III** 509
Mirror Group Newspapers plc, IV 641; **7** 244, 312, **341–43**; **23 348–51 (upd.)**
Mirror Printing and Binding House, **IV** 677
Misceramic Tile, Inc., **14** 42
Misr Airwork. *See* AirEgypt.
Misrair. *See* AirEgypt.
Miss Clairol, **6** 28
Miss Selfridge, **V** 177–78
Misset Publishers, **IV** 611
Mission Energy Company, **V** 715
Mission First Financial, **V** 715
Mission Group, **V** 715, 717
Mission Insurance Co., **III** 192
Mississippi Chemical Corporation, **8** 183; **IV** 367
Mississippi Drug, **III** 10
Mississippi Gas Company, **6** 577
Mississippi Power & Light, **V** 619
Mississippi River Corporation, **10** 44
Missouri Book Co., **10** 136
Missouri Gaming Company, **21** 39
Missouri Gas & Electric Service Company, **6** 593
Missouri Pacific Railroad, **10** 43–44
Missouri Public Service Company. *See* UtiliCorp United Inc.
Missouri Utilities Company, **6** 580
Missouri-Kansas-Texas Railroad, **I** 472; **IV** 458
Mist Assist, Inc. *See* Ballard Medical Products.
Mistik Beverages, **18** 71
Mistral Plastics Pty Ltd., **IV** 295; **19** 225
Mitchel & King Skates Ltd., **17** 244
Mitchell Construction, **III** 753
Mitchell Energy and Development Corporation, 7 344–46
Mitchell Home Savings and Loan, **13** 347
Mitchell Hutchins, Inc., **II** 445; **22** 405–06
Mitchell International, **8** 526
Mitchells & Butler, **I** 223
Mitchum Co., **III** 55
Mitchum, Jones & Templeton, **II** 445; **22** 405
MiTek Industries Inc., **IV** 259
MiTek Wood Products, **IV** 305
Mitel Corporation, 15 131–32; **18** **343–46**
MitNer Group, **7** 377
Mitre Sport U.K., **17** 204–05
Mitsubishi Aircraft Co., **III** 578; **7** 348; **9** 349; **11** 164
Mitsubishi Bank, Ltd., II 57, 273–74, 276, **321–22**, 323, 392, 459; **III** 289, 577–78; **7** 348; **15** 41; **16** 496, 498
Mitsubishi Chemical Industries Ltd., I 319, **363–64**, 398; **II** 57; **III** 666, 760; **11** 207
Mitsubishi Corporation, I 261, 431–32, 492, **502–04**, 505–06, 510, 515, 519–20; **II** 57, 59, 101, 118, 224, 292,

321–25, 374; **III** 577–78; **IV** 285, 518, 713; **6** 499; **7** 82, 233, 590; **9** 294; **12** **340–43 (upd.)**; **17** 349, 556
Mitsubishi Electric Corporation, II 53, **57–59**, 68, 73, 94, 122; **III** 577, 586; **7** 347, 394; **18** 18; **23** 52–53
Mitsubishi Estate Company, Limited, IV **713–14**
Mitsubishi Group, V 481–82; **7** 377; **21** 390
Mitsubishi Heavy Industries, Ltd., II 57, 75, 323, 440; **III** 452–53, 487, 532, 538, **577–79**, 685, 713; **IV** 184, 713; **7** **347–50 (upd.)**; **8** 51; **9** 349–50; **10** 33; **13** 507; **15** 92
Mitsubishi International Corp., **16** 462
Mitsubishi Kasei Corp., **III** 47–48, 477; **8** 343; **14** 535
Mitsubishi Kasei Industry Co. Ltd., **IV** 476
Mitsubishi Marine, **III** 385
Mitsubishi Materials Corporation, III **712–13**; **IV** 554
Mitsubishi Motors Corporation, III 516–17, 578–79; **6** 28; **7** 219, 348–49; **8** 72, 374; **9** 349–51; **23** 352–55 (upd.)
Mitsubishi Oil Co., Ltd., IV 460–62, 479, 492
Mitsubishi Paper Co., **III** 547
Mitsubishi Rayon Co. Ltd., I 330; **V** 369–71; **8** 153
Mitsubishi Sha Holdings, **IV** 554
Mitsubishi Shipbuilding Co. Ltd., **II** 57; **III** 513, 577–78; **7** 348; **9** 349
Mitsubishi Shokai, **III** 577; **IV** 713, **7** 347
Mitsubishi Trading Co., **IV** 460
Mitsubishi Trust & Banking **Corporation, II** 323–24; **III** 289
Mitsui and Co., **I** 282; **IV** 18, 224, 432, 654–55; **V** 142; **6** 346; **7** 303; **13** 356
Mitsui Bank, Ltd., II 273–74, 291, **325–27**, 328, 372; **III** 295–97; **IV** 147, 320; **V** 142; **17** 556
Mitsui Bussan K.K., I 363, 431–32, 469, 492, 502–04, **505–08**, 510, 515, 519, 533; **II** 57, 66, 101, 224, 292, 323, 325–28, 392; **III** 295–96, 717–18; **IV** 147, 431; **9** 352–53
Mitsui Gomei Kaisha, **IV** 715
Mitsui Group, **9** 352; **16** 84; **20** 310; **21** 72
Mitsui House Code, **V** 142
Mitsui Light Metal Processing Co., **III** 758
Mitsui Marine and Fire Insurance **Company, Limited, III** 209, **295–96**, 297
Mitsui Mining & Smelting Co., Ltd., IV **145–46**, 147–48
Mitsui Mining Company, Limited, IV 145, **147–49**
Mitsui Mutual Life Insurance Company, **III 297–98**
Mitsui O.S.K. Lines, Ltd., I 520; **IV** 383; **V 473–76**; **6** 398
Mitsui Petrochemical Industries, Ltd., I 390, 516; **9** 352–54
Mitsui Real Estate Development Co., **Ltd., IV 715–16**
Mitsui Shipbuilding and Engineering Co., **III** 295, 513
Mitsui Toatsu, **9** 353–54
Mitsui Trading, **III** 636
Mitsui Trust & Banking Company, Ltd., **II** 328; **III** 297
Mitsui-no-Mori Co., Ltd., **IV** 716
Mitsukoshi Ltd., I 508; **V 142–44**; **14** 502

Mitsuya Foods Co., **I** 221
Mitteldeutsche Creditbank, **II** 256
Mitteldeutsche Energieversorgung AG, **V** 747
Mitteldeutsche Privatbank, **II** 256
Mitteldeutsche Stickstoff-Werke Ag, **IV** 229–30
Mitteldeutsches Kraftwerk, **IV** 229
Mixconcrete (Holdings), **III** 729
Miyoshi Electrical Manufacturing Co., **II** 6
Mizushima Ethylene Co. Ltd., **IV** 476
MJB Coffee Co., **I** 28
MK-Ferguson Company, **7** 356
MLC Ltd., **IV** 709
MLH&P. *See* Montreal Light, Heat & Power Company.
MMAR Group Inc., **19** 131
MML Investors Services, **III** 286
MNC Financial. *See* MBNA Corporation.
MNC Financial Corp., **11** 447
MND Drilling, **7** 345
MNet, **11** 122
Mo och Domsjö AB, IV 315, **317–19**, 340
Moa Bay Mining Co., **IV** 82; **7** 186
Mobay, **I** 310–11; **13** 76
Mobil Corporation, I 30, 34, 403, 478; **II** 379; **IV** 93, 295, 363, 386, 401, 403, 406, 423, 428, 454, **463–65**, 466, 472–74, 486, 492, 504–05, 515, 517, 522, 531, 538–39, 545, 554–55, 564, 570–71; **V** 147–48; **6** 530; **7** 171, **351–54 (upd.)**; **8** 552–53; **9** 546; **10** 440; **12** 348; **16** 489; **17** 363, 415; **19** 140, 225, 297; **21 376–80 (upd.)**
Mobile America Housing Corporation. *See* American Homestar Corporation.
Mobile and Ohio Railroad, **I** 456
Mobile Mini, Inc., **21** 476
Mobile Telecommunications **Technologies Corp., V** 277–78; **6** 323; **16** 74; **18 347–49**
Mobira, **II** 69; **17** 353
Mobley Chemical, **I** 342
Mobu Company, **6** 431
Mobujidosha Bus Company, **6** 431
MOÇACOR, **IV** 505
Mocatta and Goldsmid Ltd., **II** 357
Mochida Pharaceutical Co. Ltd., **II** 553
Moctezuma Copper Co., **IV** 176–77
Modar, **17** 279
Modell's Shoppers World, **16** 35–36
Modem Media, **23** 479
Modern Equipment Co., **I** 412
Modern Furniture Rental, **14** 4
Modern Handling Methods Ltd., **21** 499
Modern Maid Food Products, **II** 500
Modern Merchandising Inc., **19** 396
Modern Patterns and Plastics, **III** 641
Modernistic Industries Inc., **7** 589
Modine Manufacturing Company, 8 **372–75**
MoDo. *See* Mo och Domsjö AB.
Moen Incorporated, 12 344–45
Moët-Hennessy, I 271–72; **10** 397–98; **23** 238, 240, 242
Mogul Corp., **I** 321; **17** 287
Mogul Metal Co., **I** 158
Mohasco Corporation, **15** 102
Mohawk & Hudson Railroad, **9** 369
Mohawk Airlines, **I** 131; **6** 131
Mohawk Industries, Inc., 19 274–76
Mohawk Rubber Co. Ltd., **V** 256; **7** 116; **19** 508
Mohr-Value Stores, **8** 555

Moilliet and Sons, **II** 306
Mojo MDA Group Ltd., **11** 50–51
Mokta. *See* Compagnie de Mokta.
MOL. *See* Mitsui O.S.K. Lines, Ltd.
Molecular Biosystems, **III** 61
Molex Incorporated, II 8; **11 317–19**; **14** 27
Moline National Bank, **III** 463; **21** 173
Molinos de Puerto Rico, **II** 493
Molinos Nacionales C.A., **7** 242–43
Molins Co., **IV** 326
Molkerie-Zentrak Sud GmbH, **II** 575
Moll Plasticrafters, L.P., **17** 534
Molloy Manufacturing Co., **III** 569; **20** 360
Mölnlycke, **IV** 338–39
Molson Companies Ltd., I 273–75, 333; **II** 210; **7** 183–84; **12** 338; **13** 150, 199; **21** 320; **23** 404
Molycorp, **IV** 571
Mon-Dak Chemical Inc., **16** 270
Mon-Valley Transportation Company, **11** 194
MONACA. *See* Molinos Nacionales C.A.
Monadnock Paper Mills, Inc., 21 381–84
Monarch Air Lines, **22** 219
Monarch Food Ltd., **II** 571
Monarch Marking Systems, **III** 157
MonArk Boat, **III** 444; **22** 116
Mond Nickel Co., **IV** 110–11
Mondadori. *See* Arnoldo Monadori Editore S.p.A.
Mondex International, **18** 543
Mondi Paper Co., **IV** 22
Monet Jewelry, **II** 502–03; **9** 156–57; **10** 323–24
Money Access Service Corp., **11** 467
Monfort, Inc., 13 350–52
Monheim Group, **II** 521
Monier Roof Tile, **III** 687, 735
Monis Wineries, **I** 288
Monk-Austin Inc., **12** 110
Monmouth Pharmaceuticals Ltd., **16** 439
Monochem, **II** 472; **22** 93
Monogram Aerospace Fasteners, Inc., **11** 536
Monogramme Confections, **6** 392
Monolithic Memories Inc., **6** 216; **16** 316–17, 549
Monon Corp., **13** 550
Monon Railroad, **I** 472
Monoprix, **V** 57–59
Monroe Auto Equipment, **I** 527
Monroe Calculating Machine Co., **I** 476, 484
Monroe Cheese Co., **II** 471
Monroe Savings Bank, **11** 109
Monrovia Aviation Corp., **I** 544
Monsanto Company, I 310, 363, **365–67**, 402, 631, 666, 686, 688; **III** 741; **IV** 290, 367, 379, 401; **8** 398; **9** 318, **355–57 (upd.)**, 466; **12** 186; **13** 76, 225; **16** 460–62; **17** 131; **18** 112; **22** 107; **23** 170–71
Monsavon, **III** 46–47
Mont Blanc, **17** 5
Montabert S.A., **15** 226
Montan Transport GmbH, **IV** 140
Montana Enterprises Inc., **I** 114
Montana Power Company, 6 566; **7** 322; **11** 320–22
Montana Refining Company, **12** 240–41
Montana Resources, Inc., **IV** 34
Montana-Dakota Utilities Co., **7** 322–23

Montaup Electric Co., **14** 125
Montecatini, **I** 368; **IV** 421, 470, 486
Montedison SpA, I 368–69; **IV** 413,
    421–22, 454, 499; **14** 17; **22** 262
Montefibre, **I** 369
Montefina, **IV** 499
Monterey Mfg. Co., **12** 439
Monterey's Tex-Mex Cafes, **13** 473
Monterrey, Compania de Seguros sobre la
    Vida. *See* Seguros Monterrey.
Monterrey Group, **19** 10–11, 189
Montfort of Colorado, Inc., **II** 494
Montgomery Ward & Co., Incorporated,
    III 762; **IV** 465; **V** 145–48; **7** 353; **8**
    509; **9** 210; **10** 10, 116, 172, 305, 391,
    393, 490–91; **12** 48, 309, 315, 335, 430;
    13 165; **15** 330, 470; **17** 460; **18** 477; **20**
    263, **374–79 (upd.)**, 433; **22** 535
Montiel Corporation, **17** 321
Montreal Bank, **II** 210
Montreal Engineering Company, **6** 585
Montreal Light, Heat & Power
    Consolidated, **6** 501–02
Montreal Mining Co., **17** 357
Montres Rolex S.A., 8 477; **13 353–55;**
    19 452
Montrose Chemical Company, **9** 118, 119
Montrose Chrome, **IV** 92
Monument Property Trust Ltd., **IV** 710
Monumental Corp., **III** 179
MONYCo., **III** 306
Moody's Investment Service, **IV** 605; **16**
    506; **19** 133; **22** 189
Moog Inc., 13 356–58
Moon-Hopkins Billing Machine, **III** 165
Mooney Chemicals, Inc. *See* OM Group,
    Inc.
Moonlight Mushrooms, Inc. *See* Sylvan,
    Inc.
Moore and McCormack Co. Inc., **19** 40
Moore Corporation Limited, IV 644–46,
    679; **15** 473; **16** 450
Moore Gardner & Associates, **22** 88
The Moore Group Ltd., **20** 363
Moore McCormack Resources Inc., **14** 455
Moore Medical Corp., 17 331–33
Moore-Handley Inc., **IV** 345–46
Moorhouse, **II** 477
Moran Group Inc., **II** 682
MoRan Oil & Gas Co., **IV** 82–83
Moran Towing Corporation, Inc., 15
    301–03
Morana, Inc., **9** 290
Moreland and Watson, **IV** 208
Moretti-Harrah Marble Co., **III** 691
Morgan & Cie International S.A., **II** 431
Morgan Construction Company, **8** 448
Morgan Edwards, **II** 609
Morgan Engineering Co., **8** 545
Morgan Grampian Group, **IV** 687
Morgan Grenfell Group PLC, II 280,
    329, **427–29; IV** 21, 712
Morgan Guaranty International Banking
    Corp., **II** 331; **9** 124
Morgan Guaranty Trust Co. of New York,
    I 26; **II** 208, 254, 262, 329–32, 339,
    428, 431, 448; **III** 80; **10** 150
Morgan Guaranty Trust Company, **11** 421;
    13 49, 448; **14** 297
Morgan, Harjes & Co., **II** 329
Morgan, J.P. & Co. Inc. *See* J.P. Morgan
    & Co. Incorporated.
Morgan, Lewis, Githens & Ahn, Inc., **6**
    410

Morgan Mitsubishi Development, **IV** 714
Morgan Stanley Group, Inc., I 34; **II**
    211, 330, 403, 406–08, 422, 428,
    430–32, 441; **IV** 295, 447, 714; **9** 386;
    11 258; **12** 529; **16 374–78 (upd.); 18**
    448–49; **20** 60, 363; **22** 404, 407
Morgan Yacht Corp., **II** 468
Morgan's Brewery, **I** 287
Mori Bank, **II** 291
Moria Informatique, **6** 229
Morino Associates, **10** 394
Morita & Co., **II** 103
Mormac Marine Group, **15** 302
Morning Sun, Inc., **23** 66
Morris Motors, **III** 256; **7** 459
Morrison Industries Ltd., **IV** 278; **19** 153
Morrison Knudsen Corporation, IV 55;
    7 355–58; 11 401, 553
Morrison Restaurants Inc., 11 323–25;
    18 464
Morse Chain Co., **III** 439; **14** 63
Morse Equalizing Spring Company, **14** 63
Morse Industrial, **14** 64
Morse Shoe Inc., 13 359–61
Morss and White, **III** 643
Morstan Development Co., Inc., **II** 432
Mortgage & Trust Co., **II** 251
Mortgage Associates, **9** 229
Mortgage Insurance Co. of Canada, **II** 222
Mortgage Resources, Inc., **10** 91
Morton Foods, Inc., **II** 502; **10** 323
Morton International Inc., 9 358–59
    (upd.), 500–01; **16** 436; **22** 505–06
Morton Thiokol Inc., I 325, **370–72; 19**
    508;. *See also* Thiokol Corporation.
Mos Magnetics, **18** 140
MOS Technology, **7** 95
Mosby-Year Book, Inc., **IV** 678; **17** 486
Moseley, Hallgarten, Estabrook, and
    Weeden, **III** 389
Mosher Steel Company, **7** 540
Mosinee Paper Corporation, 15 304–06
Moskatel's, Inc., **17** 321
Mosler Safe Co., **III** 664–65; **7** 144, 146;
    22 184
Moss-Rouse Company, **15** 412
Mossgas, **IV** 93
Mostek Corp., **I** 85; **II** 64; **11** 307–08; **13**
    191; **20** 175
Mostjet Ltd. *See* British World Airlines
    Ltd.
Motel 6 Corporation, 10 13; **13 362–64**
Mother Karen's, **10** 216
Mother's Oats, **II** 558–59; **12** 409
Mothercare Stores, Inc., **16** 466
Mothercare UK Ltd., 17 42–43, **334–36**
Mothers Work, Inc., 18 350–52
Motif Inc., **22** 288
Motion Designs, **11** 486
Moto-Truc Co., **13** 385
Motor Haulage Co., **IV** 181
Motor Parts Industries, Inc., **9** 363
Motor Transit Corp., **I** 448; **10** 72
Motor Wheel Corporation, **20** 261
Motoren-und-Turbinen-Union, **I** 151; **III**
    563; **9** 418; **15** 142
Motoren-Werke Mannheim AG, **III** 544
Motorenfabrik Deutz AG, **III** 541
Motorenfabrik Oberursel, **III** 541
Motornetic Corp., **III** 590
Motorola, Inc., I 534; **II** 5, 34, 44–45, 56,
    60–62, 64; **III** 455; **6** 238; **7** 119, 494,
    533; **8** 139; **9** 515; **10** 87, 365, 367,
    431–33; **11** 45, 308, **326–29 (upd.),**

381–82; **12** 136–37, 162; **13** 30, 356,
    501; **17** 33, 193; **18** 18, 74, 76, 260,
    382; **19** 391; **20** 8, 439; **21** 123; **22** 17,
    19, 288, 542
Motown Records, **II** 145; **22** 194; **23** 389,
    391
Moulinex S.A., 22 362–65
Mount. *See also* Mt.
Mount Hood Credit Life Insurance Agency,
    14 529
Mount Isa Mines, **IV** 61
Mount Vernon Group, **8** 14
Mountain Fuel Supply Company, **6** 568–69
Mountain Pass Canning Co., **7** 429
Mountain Safety Research, **18** 445–46
Mountain State Telephone Company, **6** 300
Mountain States Telephone & Telegraph
    Co., **V** 341
Mountain States Wholesale, **II** 602
Mountleigh PLC, **16** 465
Mounts Wire Industries, **III** 673
Mountsorrel Granite Co., **III** 734
Movado-Zenith-Mondia Holding, **II** 124
Movie Star Inc., 17 337–39
Movies To Go, Inc., **9** 74
Moving Co. Ltd., **V** 127
The Moving Picture Company, **15** 83
The Mowry Co., **23** 102
MPB Corporation, **8** 529, 531
MPM, **III** 735
Mr. Coffee, Inc., 14 229–31; **15 307–09;**
    17 215
Mr. D's Food Centers, **12** 112
Mr. Donut, **21** 323
Mr. Gasket Inc., 11 84; **15 310–12**
Mr. Gatti's, **15** 345
Mr. Goodbuys, **13** 545
Mr. How, **V** 191–92
Mr. M Food Stores, **7** 373
Mr. Payroll Corp., **20** 113
MRC Bearings, **III** 624
MRN Radio Network, **19** 223
Mrs. Paul's Kitchens, **II** 480
Mrs. Smith's Frozen Foods, **II** 525; **13**
    293–94
MS-Relais GmbH, **III** 710; **7** 302–03
MSAS Cargo International, **6** 415, 417
MSI Data Corp., **10** 523; **15** 482
MSL Industries, **10** 44
MSR. *See* Mountain Safety Research.
MSU. *See* Middle South Utilities.
Mt. *See also* Mount.
Mt. Carmel Public Utility Company, **6** 506
Mt. Goldsworthy Mining Associates, **IV** 47
Mt. Lyell Investments, **III** 672–73
Mt. Summit Rural Telephone Company, **14**
    258
Mt. Vernon Iron Works, **II** 14
MTC Pharmaceuticals, **II** 483
MTel. *See* Mobile Telecommunications
    Technologies Corp.
MTM Entertainment Inc., **13** 279, 281
MTV Asia, **23** 390
Mueller Co., **III** 645
Mueller Furniture Company, **8** 252
Mueller Industries, Inc., 7 359–61
Mujirushi Ryohin, **V** 188
Mukluk Freight Lines, **6** 383
Mule Battery Manufacturing Co., **III** 643
Mule-Hide Products Co., **22** 15
Mülheimer Bergwerksvereins, **I** 542
Mullen Advertising, **13** 513
Mullens & Co., **14** 419
Multex Systems, **21** 70

Multi Restaurants, **II** 664
Multibank Inc., **11** 281
Multicom Publishing Inc., **11** 294
MultiMed, **11** 379
Multimedia, Inc., IV 591; **11 330–32**
Multiple Access Systems Corp., **III** 109
Multiple Properties, **I** 588
MultiScope Inc., **10** 508
Multitech International. *See* Acer Inc.
Münchener Rückversicherungs-
    Gesellschaft. *See* Munich Re.
Munford, Inc., **17** 499
Mungana Mines, **I** 438
Munich Re, II 239; **III** 183–84, 202,
    299–301, 400–01, 747
Municipal Assistance Corp., **II** 448
Munising Paper Co., **III** 40; **13** 156; **16**
    303
Munising Woodenware Company, **13** 156
Munksjö, **19** 227
Munksund, **IV** 338
Munsingwear, **22** 427
Munson Transportation Inc., **18** 227
Munster and Leinster Bank Ltd., **16** 13
Mura Corporation, **23** 209
Murfin Inc., **8** 360
Murmic, Inc., **9** 120
Murphey Favre, Inc., **17** 528, 530
Murphy Family Farms Inc., 7 477; **21**
    503; **22 366–68**
Murphy Oil Corporation, 7 362–64
Murphy-Phoenix Company, **14** 122
Murray Bay Paper Co., **IV** 246
Murray Corp. of America, **III** 443
Murray Goulburn Snow, **II** 575
Murray Inc., **19** 383
Murrayfield, **IV** 696
Murtaugh Light & Power Company, **12**
    265
Musashino Railway Company, **V** 510
Muscatine Journal, **11** 251
Muscocho Explorations Ltd., **IV** 76
Muse Air Corporation, **6** 120
Music Corporation of America. *See* MCA
    Inc.
Music Go Round, **18** 207–09
Music Man, Inc., **16** 202
Music Plus, **9** 75
Music-Appreciation Records, **13** 105
Musical America Publishing, Inc., **22** 441
**Musicland Stores Corporation, 9
    360–62**; **11** 558; **19** 417
Musitek, **16** 202
Muskegon Gas Company. *See* MCN
    Corporation.
Musotte & Girard, **I** 553
Mutoh Industries, Ltd., **6** 247
**Mutual Benefit Life Insurance Company,
    III** 243, **302–04**
Mutual Broadcasting System, **23** 509
Mutual Gaslight Company. *See* MCN
    Corporation.
Mutual Life Insurance Co. of the State of
    Wisconsin, **III** 321
**Mutual Life Insurance Company of New
    York, II** 331; **III** 247, 290, **305–07**,
    316, 321, 380
Mutual Medical Aid and Accident
    Insurance Co., **III** 331
Mutual of Omaha, **III** 365
Mutual Oil Co., **IV** 399
Mutual Papers Co., **14** 522
Mutual Safety Insurance Co., **III** 305

Mutual Savings & Loan Association, **III**
    215; **18** 60
Mutualité Générale, **III** 210
Mutuelle d'Orléans, **III** 210
Mutuelle de l'Quest, **III** 211
Mutuelle Vie, **III** 210
Mutuelles Unies, **III** 211
Muzak Corporation, **7** 90–91
Muzak, Inc., 18 353–56
Muzzy-Lyon Co., **I** 158–59
Mwinilunga Canneries Ltd., **IV** 241
MXL Industries, **13** 367
MY Holdings, **IV** 92
Myanmar Oil and Gas Enterprise, **IV** 519
MYCAL Group, **V** 154
Myco-Sci, Inc. *See* Sylvan, Inc.
Mycogen Corporation, 21 385–87
Mycrom, **14** 36
Myer Emporium Ltd., **20** 156
Myers Industries, Inc., 19 277–79
Mygind International, **8** 477
**Mylan Laboratories Inc., I 656–57; 20
    380–82 (upd.)**
Myllykoski Träsliperi AB, **IV** 347–48
Myokenya, **III** 757
Myrna Knitwear, Inc., **16** 231
Myson Group PLC, **III** 671
Mysore State Iron Works, **IV** 205

N M Electronics, **II** 44
N.A. Otto & Cie., **III** 541
N.A. Woodworth, **III** 519; **22** 282
N. Boynton & Co., **16** 534
N.C. Cameron & Sons, Ltd., **11** 95
N.C. Monroe Construction Company, **14**
    112
N.E.M., **23** 228
N H. Geotech. *See* New Holland N.V.
N.K. Fairbank Co., **II** 497
N.L. Industries, **19** 212
N.M. Rothschild & Sons, **IV** 64, 712
N.M.U. Transport Ltd., **II** 569
N.R.F. Gallimard, **IV** 618
N. Shure Company, **15** 477
**N.V. Holdingmaatschappij De Telegraaf,
    23 271–73**
N.V. Philips Gloeilampenfabriken. *See*
    Philips Electronics N.V.
N.W. Ayer & Son, **I** 36; **II** 542
N.Y.P. Holdings Inc., **12** 360
Na Pali, S.A. *See* Quiksilver, Inc.
Naamloze Vennootschap tot Exploitatie
    van het Café Krasnapolsky. *See* Grand
    Hotel Krasnapolsky N.V.
Nabisco Brands, Inc., II 475, 512,
    542–44; **7** 128, 365–67; **12** 167. *See
    also* RJR Nabisco.
Nabisco Foods Group, 7 365–68 (upd.);
    9 318; **14** 48
Nabors Industries, Inc., 9 363–65
NACCO Industries, Inc., 7 369–71; **17**
    213–15, 246, 248
Nacional Financiera, **IV** 513
Nadler Sportswear. *See* Donnkenny, Inc.
NAFI. *See* National Automotive Fibers,
    Inc.
Nagano Seiyu Ltd., **V** 188
Nagasaki Shipyard, **I** 502
Nagasakiya Co., Ltd., V 149–51
Nagasco, Inc., **18** 366
Nagase & Company, Ltd., 8 376–78
Nagase-Alfa, **III** 420
Nagel Meat Markets and Packing House, **II**
    643

Nagoya Bank, **II** 373
Nagoya Electric Light Co., **IV** 62
Naigai Tsushin Hakuhodo, **6** 29
Naikoku Tsu-un Kabushiki Kaisha, **V** 477
Nairn Linoleum Co., **18** 116
Nakai Shoten Ltd., **IV** 292
**Nalco Chemical Corporation, I 373–75;
    12 346–48 (upd.)**
Nalfloc, **I** 374
Nalge Co., **14** 479–80
NAM. *See* Nederlandse Aardolie
    Maatschappij.
Namco, **III** 431
Namkwang Engineering & Construction
    Co. Ltd., **III** 749
Nampack, **I** 423
Nan Ya Plastics Corp., **14** 197–98
NANA Regional Corporation, **7** 558
Nankai Kogyo, **IV** 225
Nansei Sekiyu, **IV** 432
Nantucket Allserve, Inc., 22 369–71
Nantucket Corporation, **6** 226
Nantucket Mills, **12** 285
Nanyo Bussan, **I** 493
NAPC. *See* North American Philips Corp.
Napier, **I** 194
NAPP Systems, Inc., **11** 253
Narmco Industries, **I** 544
NASA. *See* National Aeronautics and
    Space Administration.
Nash DeCamp Company, **23** 356–57
Nash Finch Company, 8 379–81; **11** 43;
    23 356–58 (upd.)
Nash Motors Co., **I** 135; **8** 75
Nash-Kelvinator Corp., **I** 135; **12** 158
Nashaming Valley Information Processing,
    III 204
Nashua Corporation, 8 382–84
The Nashville Network, **11** 153
Nassau Gas Light Co., **6** 455
NASTECH, **III** 590
Nasu Aluminium Manufacturing Co., **IV**
    153
Natal Brewery Syndicate, **I** 287
Natco Corp., **I** 445
NaTec Ltd. *See* CRSS Inc.
National, **10** 419
National Acme Company. *See* Acme-
    Cleveland Corp.
National Advanced Systems, **II** 64–65
National Aeronautics and Space
    Administration, **II** 139; **6** 227–29, 327;
    11 201, 408; **12** 489
National Air Transport Co., **I** 128; **6** 128; **9**
    416; **11** 427
National Airlines, **I** 97, 116; **6** 388; **21** 141
National Aluminate Corp., **I** 373; **12** 346
National Aluminum Company, **11** 38
National American Life Insurance Co. of
    California, **II** 181
National American Title Insurance Co., **II**
    181
National Aniline & Chemical Coompany, **I**
    414; **22** 29
**National Association of Securities
    Dealers, Inc., 10 416–18**
National Australia Bank, **III** 673
National Auto Credit, Inc., 16 379–81
National Automobile and Casualty
    Insurance Co., **III** 270
National Automotive Fibers, Inc., **9** 118
National Aviation, **I** 117
National Baby Shop, **V** 203
National Bancard Corporation, **11** 111–13

National Bancorp of Arizona, **12** 565
National Bank, **II** 312
National Bank for Cooperatives, **8** 489–90
National Bank für Deutschland, **II** 270
National Bank of Belgium, **II** 294
National Bank of Commerce, **II** 331; **9** 536; **11** 105–06; **13** 467
National Bank of Commerce Trust & Savings Association, **15** 161
National Bank of Detroit, **I** 165. *See also* NBD Bancorp, Inc.
National Bank of Egypt, **II** 355
The National Bank of Jacksonville, **9** 58
National Bank of New Zealand, **II** 308; **19** 155
National Bank of North America, **II** 334
National Bank of South Africa Ltd., **II** 236
National Bank of the City of New York, **II** 312
National Bank of Turkey, **IV** 557
National Bank of Washington, **13** 440
National BankAmericard Inc., **9** 536
National Bankers Express Co., **II** 396; **10** 60
National Basketball Association, **12** 457
National Bell Telephone Company, **V** 259
National Benefit and Casualty Co., **III** 228
National Benefit Co., **III** 228
National Binding Company, **8** 382
National Biscuit Co., **IV** 152; **22** 336. *See also* Nabisco.
National Bridge Company of Canada, Ltd., **8** 544
National Broach & Machine Co., **I** 481–82
National Broadcasting Company, Inc., **II** 30, 88–90, 129–33, **151–53,** 170, 173, 487, 543; **III** 188, 329; **IV** 596, 608, 652; **6** 157–59, **164–66 (upd.);** **10** 173; **17** 149–50; **19** 201, 210; **21** 24; **23** 120
National Building Society, **10** 6–7
National Cable & Manufacturing Co., **13** 369
National Cable Television Association, **18** 64
National Can Corp., **I** 601–02, **607–08;** **IV** 154; **13** 255
National Car Rental System, Inc., **I** 489; **II** 419–20, 445; **6** 348–49; **10** 373, **419–20;** **21** 284; **22** 406, 524
National Carbon Co., Inc., **I** 400; **9** 516; **11** 402
National Carriers, **6** 413–14
National Cash Register Company. *See* NCR Corporation.
National Cheerleaders Association, **15** 516–18
National Chemsearch Corp. *See* NCH Corporation.
National Child Care Centers, Inc., **II** 607
National City Bank, **9** 475
National City Bank of New York, **I** 337, 462; **II** 253–54; **III** 380; **IV** 81
National City Co., **II** 254; **9** 124
National City Corp., **9** 475; **15** 313–16
National Cleaning Contractors, **II** 176
National Coal Board, **IV** 38–40
National Coal Development Corp., **IV** 48
National Commercial Bank, **11** 108; **12** 422; **13** 476
National Components Industries, Inc., **13** 398
National Container Corp., **I** 609
National Convenience Stores Incorporated, **7** 372–75; **20** 140

National Credit Office, **IV** 604
National CSS, **IV** 605
National Dairy Products Corp., **II** 533; **7** 275; **14** 204
National Demographics & Lifestyles Inc., **10** 461
National Development Bank, **IV** 56
National Disinfectant Company. *See* NCH Corporation.
National Distillers and Chemical Corporation, **I** 226, 376–78; **IV** 11; **8** 439–41; **9** 231; **10** 181
National Drive-In Grocery Corporation, **7** 372
National Drug Ltd., **II** 652
National Economic Research Associates, **III** 283
National Education Association, **9** 367
National Electric Company, **11** 388
National Electric Instruments Co., **IV** 78
National Electric Products Corp., **IV** 177
National Employers Life Assurance Co. Ltd., **13** 539
National Enquirer, **10** 287–88
National Express Laboratories, Inc., **10** 107
National Fidelity Life Insurance Co., **10** 246
National Fidelity Life Insurance Co. of Kansas, **III** 194; **IV** 343
National Finance Corp., **IV** 22–23
National Fire & Marine Insurance Co., **III** 213–14
National Fire Insurance Co., **III** 229–30
National Football League, **12** 457
National Freight Corporation, **6** 412–13
National Fuel Gas Company, **6** 526–28
National Gateway Telecom, **6** 326–27
National General Corp., **III** 190–91
National Geographic Society, **9** 366–68
National Grape Co-operative Association, Inc., **20** 383–85
National Greyhound Racing Club, **II** 142
National Grid Company, **11** 399–400; **12** 349; **13** 484
National Grocers of Ontario, **II** 631
National Guardian Corp., **18** 33
National Gypsum Company, **8** 43; **10** 421–24; **13** 169; **22** 48, 170
National Health Enterprises, **III** 87
National Health Laboratories Incorporated, **11** 333–35
National Hockey League, **12** 457
National Hotel Co., **III** 91
National Housing Systems, Inc., **18** 27
National Hydrocarbon Corp., **IV** 543
National Import and Export Corp. Ltd., **IV** 240
National Indemnity Co., **III** 213–14
National India Rubber Company, **9** 228
National Industries, **I** 446
National Inking Appliance Company, **14** 52
National Instruments Corporation, **22** 372–74
National Integrity Life Insurance, **III** 249
National Intergroup, Inc., **IV** 237, 574; **V** 152–53; **12** 354; **16** 212. *See also* FoxMeyer Health Corporation.
National Iranian Oil Company, **III** 748; **IV** 370, 374, 466–68, 484, 512, 535
National Key Company. *See* Cole National Corporation.
National Kinney Corp., **IV** 720; **9** 391
National Lead Co., **III** 681; **IV** 32; **21** 489

National Liability and Fire Insurance Co., **III** 214
National Liberty Corp., **III** 218–19
National Life and Accident Insurance Co., **III** 194
National Life Insurance Co., **III** 290
National Life Insurance Co. of Canada, **III** 243
National Living Centers, **13** 49
National Loss Control Service Corp., **III** 269
National Magazine Company Limited, **19** 201
National Manufacturing Co., **III** 150; **6** 264; **13** 6
National Marine Service, **6** 530
National Market System, **9** 369
National Medical Care, **22** 360
National Medical Enterprises, Inc., **III** 79, **87–88;** **6** 188; **10** 252; **14** 233
National Minerals Development Corp., **IV** 143–44
National Mortgage Agency of New Zealand Ltd., **IV** 278; **19** 153
National Mortgage Assoc. of Washington, **II** 410
National Motor Bearing Co., **I** 159
National Mutual Life Assurance of Australasia, **III** 249
National Office Furniture, **12** 297
National Oil Corp. *See* Libyan National Oil Corporation.
National Oil Distribution Co., **IV** 524
National Old Line Insurance Co., **III** 179
National Packaging, **IV** 333
National Paper Co., **8** 476
National Patent Development Corporation, **7** 45; **13** 365–68
National Permanent Mutual Benefit Building Society, **10** 6
National Petrochemical Co., **IV** 467
National Petroleum Publishing Co., **IV** 636
National Pharmacies, **9** 346
National Postal Meter Company, **14** 52
National Potash Co., **IV** 82; **7** 186
National Power PLC, **11** 399–400; **12** 349–51; **13** 458, 484
National Presto Industries, Inc., **16** 382–85
National Propane Corporation, **8** 535–37
National Provident Institution for Mutual Life Assurance, **IV** 711
National Provincial Bank, **II** 319–20, 333–34; **IV** 722; **17** 324
National Public Radio, **19** 280–82
National Quotation Bureau, Inc., **14** 96–97
National Railroad Passenger Corporation, **22** 375–78
National Railways of Mexico, **IV** 512
National Register Publishing Co., **17** 399; **23** 442
National Regulator Co., **II** 41
National Reinsurance Co., **III** 276–77
National Rent-A-Car, **6** 392–93
National Research Corporation, **8** 397
National Revenue Corporation, **22** 181
National Rubber Machinery Corporation, **8** 298
National Sanitary Supply Co., **13** 149–50; **16** 386–87
National Satellite Paging, **18** 348
National School Studios, **7** 255
National Science Foundation, **9** 266
National Sea Products Ltd., **14** 339–41

National Seal, **I** 158
National Semiconductor Corporation, II 63–65; **III** 455, 618, 678; **6** 215, **261–63**; **9** 297; **11** 45–46, 308, 463; **16** 122, 332; **17** 418; **18** 18; **19** 312; **21** 123
National Service Industries, Inc., 11 336–38
National Shoe Products Corp., **16** 17
National Slicing Machine Company, **19** 359
National Stamping & Electric Works, **12** 159
National Standard Co., IV 137; **13 369–71**
National Star Brick & Tile Co., **III** 501; **7** 207
National Starch and Chemical Corp., **IV** 253; **17** 30
National Starch Manufacturing Co., **II** 496
National Steel and Shipbuilding Company, **7** 356
National Steel Car Corp., **IV** 73
National Steel Corporation, I 491; **IV** 74, 163, 236–37, 572; **V** 152–53; **7** 549; **8** 346, 479–80; **11** 315; **12 352–54**; **14** 191; **16** 212; **23** 445. *See also* FoxMeyer Health Corporation.
National Student Marketing Corporation, **10** 385–86
National Supply Co., **IV** 29
National Surety Co. of New York, **III** 395
National System Company, **9** 41; **11** 469
National Tanker Fleet, **IV** 502
National Tea, **II** 631–32
National Technical Laboratories, **14** 52
National Telecommunications of Austin, **8** 311
National Telephone and Telegraph Corporation. *See* British Columbia Telephone Company.
National Telephone Co., **III** 162, **7** 332, 508
National Theatres, Inc., **III** 190
National Trading Manufacturing, Inc., **22** 213
National Transcontinental, **6** 360
National Travelers' Insurance Co., **III** 290
National Trust Life Insurance Co., **III** 218
National Tube Co., **II** 330; **IV** 572; **7** 549
National Union Electric Corporation, **12** 159
National Union Fire Insurance Co. of Pittsburgh, Pa., **III** 195–97
National Union Life and Limb Insurance Co., **III** 290
National Utilities & Industries Corporation, **9** 363
National Westminster Bank PLC, II 237, **333–35**; **IV** 642; **13** 206
National-Ben Franklin Insurance Co., **III** 242
National-Southwire Aluminum Company, **11** 38; **12** 353
Nationalbank, **I** 409
Nationale Bank Vereeniging, **II** 185
Nationale-Nederlanden N.V., III 179, 200–01, **308–11**; **IV** 697
Nationar, **9** 174
NationsBank Corporation, 6 357; **10 425–27**; **11** 126; **13** 147; **18** 516, 518; **23** 455
Nationwide Credit, **11** 112
Nationwide Income Tax Service, **9** 326
Nationwide Logistics Corp., **14** 504

NATIOVIE, **II** 234
Native Plants, **III** 43
NATM Buying Corporation, **10** 9, 468
Natomas Co., **IV** 410; **6** 353–54; **7** 309; **11** 271
Natref, **IV** 535
Natronag, **IV** 325
Natronzellstoff-und Papierfabriken AG, **IV** 324
Natudryl Manufacturing Company, **10** 271
Natural Gas Clearinghouse, **11** 355. *See also* NGC Corporation.
Natural Gas Corp., **19** 155
Natural Gas Pipeline Company, **6** 530, 543; **7** 344–45
Natural Gas Service of Arizona, **19** 411
Natural Wonders Inc., 14 342–44
The Nature Company, **10** 215–16; **14** 343
Nature's Sunshine Products, Inc., 15 317–19
Natuzzi Group. *See* Industrie Natuzzi S.p.A.
NatWest Bank, **22** 52. *See also* National Westminster Bank PLC.
Naugles, **7** 506
Nautica Enterprises, Inc., 16 61; **18 357–60**
Nautilus, **III** 315–16; **13** 532
Nautor Ab, **IV** 302
Navaho Freight Line, **16** 41
Navajo Refining Company, **12** 240
Navale, **III** 209
Navarre Corporation, **22** 536
Naviera Vizcaina, **IV** 528
Navigation Mixte, **III** 348
Navistar International Corporation, I 152, 155, **180–82**, 186, 525, 527; **II** 330; **10** 280, **428–30** (upd.); **17** 327. *See also* International Harvester Co.
Naxon Utilities Corp., **19** 359
NBC. *See* National Broadcasting Company, Inc.
NBC Bankshares, Inc., **21** 524
NBC/Computer Services Corporation, **15** 163
NBD Bancorp, Inc., 9 476; **11 339–41**, 466
NCA Corporation, **9** 36, 57, 171
NCB. *See* National City Bank of New York.
NCB Brickworks, **III** 501; **7** 207
NCC L.P., **15** 139
NCH Corporation, 8 385–87
Nchanga Consolidated Copper Mines, **IV** 239–40
NCNB Corporation, II 336–37; **12** 519
NCR Corporation, I 540–41; **III** 147–52, **150–53**, 157, 165–66; **IV** 298; **V** 263; **6** 250, **264–68** (upd.), 281–82; **9** 416; **11** 62, 151, 542; **12** 162, 148, 246, 484; **16** 65
NCS. *See* Norstan, Inc.
NCTI (Noise Cancellation Technologies Inc.), **19** 483–84
nCube Corp., **14** 15; **22** 293
ND Marston, **III** 593
NDL. *See* Norddeutscher Lloyd.
NEA. *See* Newspaper Enterprise Association.
NEAC Inc., **I** 201–02
Neatherlin Homes Inc., **22** 547
Nebraska Bell Company, **14** 311
Nebraska Cellular Telephone Company, **14** 312

Nebraska Consolidated Mills Company, **II** 493; **III** 52; **8** 433
Nebraska Furniture Mart, **III** 214–15; **18** 60–61, 63
Nebraska Light & Power Company, **6** 580
NEBS. *See* New England Business Services, Inc.
NEC Corporation, I 455, 520; **II** 40, 42, 45, 56–57, **66–68**, 73, 82, 91, 104, 361; **III** 122–23, 130, 140, 715; **6** 101, 231, 244, 287; **9** 42, 115; **10** 257, 366, 463, 500; **11** 46, 308, 490; **13** 482; **16** 139; **18** 382–83; **19** 391; **21 388–91** (upd.)
Neches Butane Products Co., **IV** 552
Neckermann Versand AG, **V** 100–02
Nedbank, **IV** 23
Nederland Line. *See* Stoomvaart Maatschappij Nederland.
Nederlands Talen Institut, **13** 544
Nederlandsche Electriciteits Maatschappij. *See* N.E.M.
Nederlandsche Heide Maatschappij, **III** 199
Nederlandsche Kunstzijdebariek, **13** 21
Nederlandsche Nieuw Guinea Petroleum Maatschappij, **IV** 491
Nederlandsche Stoomvart Maatschappij Oceaan, **6** 416
Nederlandse Cement Industrie, **III** 701
Nederlandse Credietbank N.V., **II** 248
Nederlandse Dagbladunie NV, **IV** 610
N.V. Nederlandse Gasunie, I 326; **V** 627, **658–61**
Nederlandse Handel Maatschappij, **II** 183, 527; **IV** 132–33
Nederlandse Vliegtuigenfabriek, **I** 54
Nedsual, **IV** 23; **16** 28
Neeco, Inc., **9** 301
Needham Harper Worldwide, **I** 23, 28, 30–33; **13** 203; **14** 159
Needlecraft, **II** 560; **12** 410
Needleworks, Inc., **23** 66
Neenah Paper Co., **III** 40; **16** 303
Neenah Printing, **8** 360
NEES. *See* New England Electric System.
Negromex, **23** 171–72
Neighborhood Restaurants of America, **18** 241
Neilson/Cadbury, **II** 631
Neiman Bearings Co., **13** 78
Neiman-Marcus Co., I 246; **II** 478; **V** 10, 31; **12 355–57**; **15** 50, 86, 291; **17** 43; **21** 302
Neisler Laboratories, **I** 400
Neisner Brothers, Inc., **9** 20
Nekoosa Edwards Paper Co., **IV** 282; **9** 261
NEL Equity Services Co., **III** 314
Nelio Chemicals, Inc., **IV** 345
Nelson Bros., **14** 236
Nelson Publications, **22** 442
Nemuro Bank, **II** 291
Nenuco, **II** 567
Neodata, **11** 293
Neos, **21** 438
Neoterics Inc., **11** 65
Neozyme I Corp., **13** 240
Nepera, Inc., **I** 682; **16** 69
Neptune, **22** 63
NER Auction Group, **23** 148
NERCO, Inc., V 689, **7 376–79**
Nesbitt Thomson, **II** 211
Nescott, Inc., **16** 36
Nesher Cement, **II** 47
Neste Oy, IV 435, **469–71**, 519

Nestlé S.A., I 15, 17, 251–52, 369, 605; **II** 379, 456, 478, 486–89, 521, **545–49,** 568–70; **III** 47–48; **6** 16; **7 380–84 (upd.**); **8** 131, 342–44, 498–500; **10** 47, 324; **11** 15, 205; **12** 480–81; **13** 294; **14** 214; **15** 63; **16** 168; **19** 50–51; **21** 55–56, 219; **22** 78, 80; **23** 219

Netherland Bank for Russian Trade, **II** 183

Netherlands Fire Insurance Co. of Tiel, **III** 308, 310

Netherlands India Steam Navigation Co., **III** 521

Netherlands Insurance Co., **III** 179, 308–10

Netherlands Trading Co. *See* Nederlandse Handel Maatschappij.

NetMarket Company, **16** 146

Netron, **II** 390

Netscape Communications Corporation, 15 320–22; **18** 541, 543; **19** 201; **20** 237

Nettai Sangyo, **I** 507

Nettingsdorfer, **19** 227

Nettle Creek Corporation, **19** 304

Nettlefolds Ltd., **III** 493

Netto, **11** 240

Network Communications Associates, Inc., **11** 409

Neue Frankfurter Allgemeine Versicherungs-AG, **III** 184

Neue Holding AG, **III** 377

Neuenberger Versicherungs-Gruppe, **III** 404

Neuralgyline Co., **I** 698

Neuro Navigational Corporation, **21** 47

Neutrogena Corporation, 17 340–44

Nevada Bell Telephone Company, V 318–20; **14 345–47**

Nevada Community Bank, **11** 119

Nevada National Bank, **II** 381; **12** 534

Nevada Natural Gas Pipe Line Co., **19** 411

Nevada Power Company, 11 342–44; **12** 265

Nevada Savings and Loan Association, **19** 412

Nevada Southern Gas Company, **19** 411

Neversink Dyeing Company, **9** 153

New America Publishing Inc., **10** 288

New Asahi Co., **I** 221

New Balance, Inc., **17** 245

New Bedford Gas & Edison Light Co., **14** 124–25

New Broken Hill Consolidated, **IV** 58–61

New Century Network, **13** 180; **19** 204, 285

New Consolidated Canadian Exploration Co., **IV** 96

New Consolidated Gold Fields, **IV** 21, 95–96

New Daido Steel Co., Ltd., **IV** 62–63

New Departure, **9** 17

New Departure Hyatt, **III** 590

New England Business Services, Inc., 18 361–64

New England Confectionery Co., 15 323–25

New England CRInc, **8** 562

New England Electric System, V 662–64

New England Gas & Electric Association, **14** 124–25

New England Glass Co., **III** 640

New England Life Insurance Co., **III** 261

New England Merchants National Bank, **II** 213–14; **III** 313

New England Mutual Life Insurance Co., III 312–14

New England National Bank of Boston, **II** 213

New England Network, Inc., **12** 31

New England Nuclear Corporation, **I** 329; **8** 152

New England Power Association, **V** 662

New England Trust Co., **II** 213

New Fire Office, **III** 371

New Found Industries, Inc., **9** 465

New Guinea Goldfields, **IV** 95

New Halwyn China Clays, **III** 690

New Hampshire Gas & Electric Co., **14** 124

New Hampshire Insurance Co., **III** 196–97

New Hampshire Oak, **III** 512

New Haven District Telephone Company. *See* Southern New England Telecommunications Corporation.

New Haven Electric Co., **21** 512

New Hokkai Hotel Co., Ltd., **IV** 327

New Holland N.V., 22 379–81

New Horizon Manufactured Homes, Ltd., **17** 83

New Hotel Showboat, Inc. *See* Showboat, Inc.

New Ireland, **III** 393

New Jersey Bell, **9** 321

New Jersey Hot Water Heating Company, **6** 449

New Jersey Shale, **14** 250

New Jersey Tobacco Co., **15** 138

New Jersey Zinc, **I** 451

New London City National Bank, **13** 467

New London Ship & Engine, **I** 57

New Mather Metals, **III** 582

New Mitsui Bussan, **I** 507; **III** 296

New Nippon Electric Co., **II** 67

New Orleans Canal and Banking Company, **11** 105

New Orleans Refining Co., **IV** 540

New Plan Realty Trust, 11 345–47

New Process Cork Company Inc., **I** 601; **13** 188

New South Wales Health System, **16** 94

New Street Capital Inc., 8 388–90 (upd.). *See also* Drexel Burnham Lambert Incorporated.

New Sulzer Diesel, **III** 633

New Toyo Group, **19** 227

New Trading Company. *See* SBC Warburg.

New United Motor Manufacturing Inc., **I** 205

New Valley Corporation, 17 345–47

New World Communications Group, **22** 442

New World Development Company Ltd., IV 717–19; **8** 500

New World Entertainment, **17** 149

New World Hotel (Holdings) Ltd., **IV** 717; **13** 66

New York Air, **I** 90, 103, 118, 129; **6** 129

New York Airways, **I** 123–24

New York and Richmond Gas Company, **6** 456

New York and Suburban Savings and Loan Association, **10** 91

New York Biscuit Co., **II** 542

New York Central Railroad Company, **II** 329, 369; **IV** 181; **9** 228; **10** 43–44, 71–73; **17** 496

New York Chemical Manufacturing Co., **II** 250

New York City Transit Authority, **8** 75

New York Condensed Milk Co., **II** 470

New York Electric Corporation. *See* New York State Electric and Gas.

New York Evening Enquirer, **10** 287

New York Fabrics and Crafts, **16** 197

New York Gas Light Company. *See* Consolidated Edison Company of New York.

New York Glucose Co., **II** 496

New York Guaranty and Indemnity Co., **II** 331

New York Harlem Railroad Co., **II** 250

New York Improved Patents Corp., **I** 601; **13** 188

New York, Lake Erie & Western Railroad, **II** 395; **10** 59

New York Life Insurance Company, II 217–18, 330; **III** 291, 305, **315–17,** 332; **10** 382

New York Magazine Co., **IV** 651; **7** 390; **12** 359

New York Manufacturing Co., **II** 312

New York Marine Underwriters, **III** 220

New York Quinine and Chemical Works, **I** 496

New York Quotation Company, **9** 370

New York, Rio and Buenos Aires Airlines, **I** 115

New York State Board of Tourism, **6** 51

New York State Electric and Gas Corporation, 6 534–36

New York Stock Exchange, Inc., 9 369–72; **10** 416–17

New York Telephone Co., **9** 321

The New York Times Company, III 40; **IV 647–49**; **6** 13; **15** 54; **16** 302; **19 283–85 (upd.)**; **23** 158

New York Trust Co., **I** 378; **II** 251

New York, West Shore and Buffalo Railroad, **II** 329

New York's Bankers Trust Co., **12** 107

New York-Newport Air Service Co., **I** 61

New Zealand Aluminum Smelters, **IV** 59

New Zealand Co., **II** 187

New Zealand Countrywide Banking Corporation, **10** 336

New Zealand Forest Products, **IV** 249–50

New Zealand Press Assoc., **IV** 669

New Zealand Sugar Co., **III** 686

New Zealand Wire Ltd., **IV** 279; **19** 154

Newark Electronics Co., **9** 420

Newco Waste Systems, **V** 750

Newcrest Mining Ltd., **IV** 47; **22** 107

Newell and Harrison Company. *See* Supervalu Inc.

Newell Co., 9 373–76; **12** 216; **13** 40–41; **22** 35

Newey and Eyre, **I** 429

Newfoundland Energy, Ltd., **17** 121

Newfoundland Light & Power Co. *See* Fortis, Inc.

Newfoundland Processing Ltd. *See* Newfoundland Energy, Ltd.

Newgateway PLC, **II** 629

Newhall Land and Farming Company, 14 348–50

Newhouse Broadcasting, **6** 33

Newmark & Lewis Inc., **23** 373

Newmont Mining Corporation, III 248; **IV** 17, 20, 33, 171, 576; **7** 287–89, **385–88**; **12** 244; **16** 25; **23** 40

Newnes, **17** 397

Newport News Shipbuilding and Dry Dock Co., I 58, 527; **13 372–75**
News & Observer Publishing Company, **23** 343
News America Publishing Inc., 12 358–60
News and Westminster Ltd., **IV** 685
News Corporation Limited, II 169; **IV 650–53; 7 389–93 (upd.); 8** 551; **9** 429; **12** 358–60; **17** 398; **18** 211, 213, 254; **22** 194, 441; **23** 121
News International Corp., **20** 79
Newsfoto Publishing Company, **12** 472
Newspaper Co-op Couponing, **8** 551
Newspaper Enterprise Association, **7** 157–58
Newspaper Proprietors' Assoc., **IV** 669
Newspaper Supply Co., **IV** 607
Newsweek, Inc., **IV** 688
Newth-Morris Box Co. See Rock-Tenn Company.
Newtherm Oil Burners, Ltd., **13** 286
Newton Yarn Mills, **19** 305
Newtown Gas Co., **6** 455
Nexar Technologies, Inc., **22** 409
Next Inc., **III** 116, 121; **6** 219
NeXT Incorporated, **18** 93
Next PLC, **6** 25
Nextel Communications, Inc., 10 431–33; 21 239
Neyveli Lignite Corp. Ltd., **IV** 49
NFC plc, **6 412–14; 14** 547
NFL Properties, Inc., **22** 223
NGC Corporation, 18 365–67
NHK. See Japan Broadcasting Corporation.
NHK Spring Co., Ltd., III 580–82
NI Industries, **20** 362
Niagara Fire Insurance Co., **III** 241–42
Niagara First Savings and Loan Association, **10** 91
Niagara Insurance Co. (Bermuda) Ltd., **III** 242
Niagara Mohawk Power Corporation, V 665–67; 6 535
Niagara Silver Co., **IV** 644
Niagara Sprayer and Chemical Co., **I** 442
NIBRASCO, **IV** 55
Nicaro Nickel Co., **IV** 82, 111; **7** 186
Nice Day, Inc., **II** 539
Nice Systems, **11** 520
NiceCom Ltd., **11** 520
Nichi-Doku Shashinki Shoten, **III** 574
Nichia Steel, **IV** 159
Nichibo, **V** 387
Nichii Co., Ltd., V 154–55; 15 470
Nichimen Corporation, II 442; **IV 150–52,** 154; **10** 439
Nichimo Sekiyu Co. Ltd., **IV** 555; **16** 490
Nicholas Kiwi Ltd., **II** 572; **15** 436
Nicholas Turkey Breeding Farms, **13** 103
Nicholas Ungar, **V** 156
Nichols & Company, **8** 561
Nichols Copper Co., **IV** 164, 177
Nichols Research Corporation, 18 368–70
Nichols-Homeshield, **22** 14
Nicholson File Co., **II** 16
Le Nickel. See Société Le Nickel.
Nicolai Pavdinsky Co., **IV** 118
Nicolet Instrument Company, **11** 513
NICOR Inc., 6 529–31
Niederbayerische Celluloswerke, **IV** 324
Niederrheinische Hütte AG, **IV** 222
Niehler Maschinenfabrick, **III** 602

Nielsen, **10** 358
Nielsen & Petersen, **III** 417
Nielsen Marketing Research. See A.C. Nielsen Company.
Niemann Chemie, **8** 464
Niese & Coast Products Co., **II** 681
Nicsmann & Bischoff, **22** 207
Nieuwe Eerste Nederlandsche, **III** 177–79
Nieuwe HAV-Bank of Schiedam, **III** 200
Nigeria Airways, **I** 107
Nigerian National Petroleum Corporation, IV 472–74
Nihol Repol Corp., **III** 757
Nihon Denko, **II** 118
Nihon Keizai Shimbun, Inc., IV 654–56
Nihon Kensetsu Sangyo Ltd., **I** 520
Nihon Kohden Corporation, **13** 328
Nihon Lumber Land Co., **III** 758
Nihon Sangyo Co., **I** 183; **II** 118
Nihon Sugar, **I** 511
Nihon Synopsis, **11** 491
Nihon Teppan, **IV** 159
Nihon Timken K.K., **8** 530
Nihon Yusen Kaisha, **I** 503, 506; **III** 577, 712
Nihron Yupro Corp., **III** 756
NII. See National Intergroup, Inc.
Niitsu Oil, **IV** 542
Nike, Inc., V 372–74, 376; **8** 303–04, **391–94 (upd.); 9** 134–35, 437; **10** 525; **11** 50, 349; **13** 513; **14** 8; **15** 397; **16** 79, 81; **17** 244–45, 260–61; **18** 264, 266–67, 392; **22** 173
Nikka Oil Co., **IV** 150
Nikka Whisky Distilling Co., **I** 220
Nikkei. See also Nihon Keizai Shimbun, Inc.
Nikkei Aluminium Co., **IV** 153–55
Nikkei Shimbun Toei, **9** 29
Nikken Stainless Fittings Co., Ltd., **IV** 160
Nikko Copper Electrolyzing Refinery, **III** 490
Nikko International Hotels, **I** 106
Nikko Kido Company, **6** 431
Nikko Petrochemical Co. Ltd., **IV** 476
The Nikko Securities Company Limited, II 300, 323, 383, **433–35; 9 377–79 (upd.); 12** 536
Nikko Trading Co., **I** 106
Nikolaiev, **19** 49, 51
Nikon Corporation, III 120–21, 575, **583–85; 9** 251; **12** 340; **18** 93, 186, 340, 342
Nile Faucet Corp., **III** 569; **20** 360
Nillmij, **III** 177–79
Nimas Corp., **III** 570; **20** 362
Nimbus CD International, Inc., 20 386–90
Nine West Group Inc., 11 348–49; 14 441; **23** 330
Nineteen Hundred Washer Co., **III** 653; **12** 548
Nintendo Co., Ltd., III 586–88; 7 394–96 (upd.); 10 124–25, 284–86, 483–84; **13** 403; **15** 539; **16** 168, 331; **18** 520; **23** 26
NIOC. See National Iranian Oil Company.
Nippon ARC Co., **III** 715
Nippon Breweries Ltd. See Sapporo Breweries Ltd.
Nippon Broilers Co., **II** 550
Nippon Cable Company, **15** 235
Nippon Cargo Airlines, **6** 71
Nippon Chemical Industries, **I** 363
Nippon Credit Bank, II 310, **338–39**

Nippon Educational Television (NET). See Asahi National Broadcasting Company, Ltd.
Nippon Electric Company, Limited. See NEC Corporation.
Nippon Express Co., Ltd., II 273; **V 477–80**
Nippon Fruehauf Co., **IV** 154
Nippon Fukokin Kinyu Koku, **II** 300
Nippon Funtai Kogyo Co., **III** 714
Nippon Gakki Co., Ltd., **III** 656–58; **16** 554, 557
Nippon Ginko, **III** 408
Nippon Gyomo Sengu Co. Ltd., **IV** 555
Nippon Hatsujo Kabushikikaisha. See NHK Spring Co., Ltd.
Nippon Helicopter & Aeroplane Transport Co., Ltd., **6** 70
Nippon Hoso Kyokai. See Japan Broadcasting Corporation.
Nippon Idou Tsushin, **7** 119–20
Nippon International Container Services, **8** 278
Nippon Interrent, **10** 419–20
Nippon K.K. See Nippon Kokan K.K.
Nippon Kairiku Insurance Co., **III** 384
Nippon Kakoh Seishi, **IV** 293
Nippon Kogaku K.K., **III** 583–84
Nippon Kogyo Co. Ltd. See Nippon Mining Co. Ltd.
Nippon Kokan K.K., **IV** 161–63, 184, 212; **8** 449; **12** 354
Nippon Life Insurance Company, II 374, 451; **III** 273, 288, **318–20; IV** 727; **9** 469
Nippon Light Metal Company, Ltd., IV 153–55
Nippon Machinery Trading, **I** 507
Nippon Meat Packers, Inc., II 550–51
Nippon Menka Kaisha, **IV** 150–51
Nippon Merck-Banyu, **I** 651; **11** 290
Nippon Mining Co., Ltd., III 759; **IV 475–77; 14** 207
Nippon Motorola Manufacturing Co., **II** 62
Nippon New Zealand Trading Co. Ltd., **IV** 327
Nippon Oil Company, Limited, IV 434, 475–76, **478–79,** 554; **19** 74
Nippon Onkyo, **II** 118
Nippon Paint Co., Ltd, **11** 252
Nippon Pelnox Corp., **III** 715
Nippon Phonogram, **23** 390
Nippon Polaroid Kabushiki Kaisha, **III** 608; **7** 437; **18** 570
Nippon Pulp Industries, **IV** 321
Nippon Rayon, **V** 387
Nippon Sangyo Co., Ltd., **IV** 475
Nippon Sanso Corp., **I** 359; **16** 486, 488
Nippon Seiko K.K., III 589–90, 595
Nippon Sekiyu Co. See Nippon Oil Company, Limited.
Nippon Sheet Glass Company, Limited, III 714–16
Nippon Shinpan Company, Ltd., II 436–37, 442; **8** 118
Nippon Silica Kogyo Co., **III** 715
Nippon Soda, **II** 301
Nippon Soken, **III** 592
Nippon Steel Chemical Co., **10** 439
Nippon Steel Corporation, I 466, 493–94, 509; **II** 300, 391; **IV** 116, 130, **156–58,** 184, 212, 228, 298; **6** 274; **14** 369; **17 348–51 (upd.),** 556; **19** 219

Nippon Suisan Kaisha, Limited, II 552–53
Nippon Tar, I 363
Nippon Telegraph and Telephone Corporation, II 51, 62; **III** 139–40; **V 305–07; 7** 118–20; **10** 119; **13** 482; **16** 224; **21** 330
Nippon Television, **7** 249; **9** 29
Nippon Tire Co., Ltd. *See* Bridgestone Corporation.
Nippon Trust Bank Ltd., **II** 405; **15** 42
Nippon Typewriter, **II** 459
Nippon Victor (Europe) GmbH, **II** 119
Nippon Wiper Blade Co., Ltd., **III** 592
Nippon Yusen Kabushiki Kaisha, IV 713; **V 481–83; 6** 398
Nippon Yusoki Company, Ltd., **13** 501
Nippon-Fisher, **13** 225
Nippondenso Co., Ltd., III 591–94, 637–38
NIPSCO Industries, Inc., 6 532–33
Nishi Taiyo Gyogyo Tosei K.K., **II** 578
Nishikawaya Co., Ltd., **V** 209
Nishimbo Industries Inc., **IV** 442
Nishizono Ironworks, **III** 595
Nissan Construction, **V** 154
Nissan Motor Acceptance Corporation, **22** 207
Nissan Motor Company, Ltd., I 9–10, **183–84**, 207, 494; **II** 118, 292–93, 391; **III** 485, 517, 536, 579, 591, 742, 750; **IV** 63; **7** 111, 120, 219; **9** 243, 340–42; **10** 353; **11** 50–51, **350–52 (upd.); 16** 167; **17** 556; **23** 338–40, 289
Nissan Trading Company, Ltd., **13** 533
Nisshin Chemical Industries, **I** 397
Nisshin Chemicals Co., **II** 554
Nisshin Flour Milling Company, Ltd., II 554
Nisshin Pharaceutical Co., **II** 554
Nisshin Steel Co., Ltd., I 432; **IV** 130, **159–60; 7** 588
Nissho Iwai K.K., I 432, **509–11; IV** 160, 383; **V** 373; **6** 386; **8** 75, 392; **15** 373
Nissho Kosan Co., **III** 715
Nissui. *See* Nippon Suisan Kaisha.
Nitratos de Portugal, **IV** 505
Nitroglycerin AB, **13** 22
Nitroglycerin Ltd., **9** 380
Nittetsu Curtainwall Corp., **III** 758
Nittetsu Sash Sales Corp., **III** 758
Nitto Warehousing Co., **I** 507
Nittoku Metal Industries, Ltd., **III** 635
Nittsu. *See* Nippon Express Co., Ltd.
Niugini Mining Ltd., **23** 42
Nixdorf Computer AG, I 193; **II** 279; **III** 109, **154–55; 12** 162; **14** 13, 169
Nixdorf-Krein Industries Inc. *See* Laclede Steel Company.
NKK Corporation, IV 74, **161–63,** 212–13; **V** 152
NL Industries, Inc., III 681; **10 434–36; 19** 466–68
NLM City-Hopper, **I** 109
NLM Dutch Airlines, **I** 108
NLT Corp., **II** 122; **III** 194; **10** 66; **12** 546
NMC Laboratories Inc., **12** 4
NMH Stahlwerke GmbH, **IV** 128
NMT. *See* Nordic Mobile Telephone.
No-Leak-O Piston Ring Company, **10** 492
No-Sag Spring Co., **16** 321
Noah's New York Bagels, **13** 494
Nobel Industries AB, I 351; **9 380–82; 16** 69. *See also* Akzo Nobel N.V.

Nobel-Bozel, **I** 669
Nobel-Hoechst Chimie, **I** 669
Noble Affiliates, Inc., 11 353–55; 18 366
Noble Broadcast Group, Inc., **23** 293
Noble Roman's Inc., 14 351–53
Nobles Industries, **13** 501
Noblesville Telephone Company, **14** 258
Noblitt-Sparks Industries, Inc., **8** 37–38
Nocona Boot Co. *See* Justin Industries, Inc.
Noell, **IV** 201
Oy Nokia Ab, **19** 226
Nokia Corporation, II 69–71; IV 296; **6** 242; **15** 125; **17** 33, **352–54 (upd.); 18** 74, 76; **20** 439
Nolte Mastenfabriek B.V., **19** 472
Noma Industries, **11** 526
Nomai Inc., **18** 510
Nomura Securities Company, Limited, II 276, 326, 434, **438–41; 9** 377, **383–86 (upd.)**
Nomura Toys Ltd., **16** 267
Non-Fiction Book Club, **13** 105
Non-Stop Fashions, Inc., **8** 323
Nonpareil Refining Co., **IV** 488
Noodle Kidoodle, 16 388–91
Noordwinning Group, **IV** 134
Nopco Chemical Co., **IV** 409; **7** 308
Nopri, **V** 63–65
Nor-Am Agricultural Products, **I** 682
Nor-Cal Engineering Co. GmbH, **18** 162
Nora Industrier A/S, **18** 395
NORAND, **9** 411
Noranda Inc., IV 164–66; 7 397–99 (upd.); 9 282
Norandex, **16** 204
Norbro Corporation. *See* Stuart Entertainment Inc.
Norcast Manufacturing Ltd., **IV** 165
Norcen Energy Resources, Ltd., **8** 347
Norcliff Thayer, **III** 66
Norco Plastics, **8** 553
Norcon, Inc., **7** 558–59
Nord-Aviation, **I** 45, 74, 82, 195; **7** 10
Nordarmatur, **I** 198
Nordbanken, **9** 382
Norddeutsche Affinerie, **IV** 141
Norddeutsche Bank A.G., **II** 279
Norddeutscher-Lloyd, **I** 542; **6** 397–98
Nordfinanzbank, **II** 366
Nordic Bank Ltd., **II** 366
Nordic Joint Stock Bank, **II** 302
Nordic Mobile Telephone, **II** 70
Nordica, **10** 151; **15** 396–97
NordicTrack, 10 215–17; **22 382–84**
Nordland Papier GmbH, **IV** 300, 302
Nordson Corporation, 11 356–58
Nordstahl AG, **IV** 201
Nordstjernan, **I** 553–54
Nordstrom, Inc., V 156–58; 11 349; **13** 494; **14** 376; **17** 313; **18 371–74 (upd.); 21** 302; **22** 173
Nordwestdeutsche Kraftwerke AG, **III** 466; **V** 698–700
Norelco, **17** 110
Norelco Consumer Products Group, **12** 439
Norell, **I** 696
Norex Laboratories, **I** 699
Norex Leasing, Inc., **16** 397
Norfolk Carolina Telephone Company, **10** 202
Norfolk Southern Corporation, V 484–86; 6 436, 487; **12** 278; **22** 167
Norfolk Steel, **13** 97
Norge Co., **III** 439–40; **18** 173–74

Norinchukin Bank, II 340–41
NORIS Bank GmbH, **V** 166
Norlin, **16** 238–39
Norma Cie., **III** 622
Norman BV, **9** 93
Norman J. Hurll Group, **III** 673
Normandy Mining Ltd., **23** 42
Normond/CMS, **7** 117
Norrell Corporation, **6** 46; **23** 431
Norris Cylinder Company, **11** 535
Norris Grain Co., **14** 537
Norsk Hydro A.S., IV 405–06, 525; **10 437–40; 14** 494
Norstan, Inc., 16 392–94
Norstar Bancorp, **9** 229
Nortek Inc., **I** 482; **14** 482; **22** 4
Nortex International, **7** 96; **19** 338
North & South Wales Bank, **II** 318; **17** 323
North Advertising, Inc., **6** 27
North African Petroleum Ltd., **IV** 455
North American Aviation, **I** 48, 71, 78, 81, 101; **7** 520; **9** 16; **10** 163; **11** 278, 427
North American Bancorp, **II** 192
North American Carbon, **19** 499
North American Cellular Network, **9** 322
North American Coal Corporation, **7** 369–71
North American Company, **6** 443, 552–53, 601–02
North American Dräger, **13** 328
North American Insurance Co., **II** 181
North American InTeleCom, Inc., **IV** 411
North American Life and Casualty Co., **III** 185, 306
North American Light & Power Company, **V** 609; **6** 504–05; **12** 541
North American Managers, Inc., **III** 196
North American Mogul Products Co. *See* Mogul Corp.
North American Philips Corporation, **II** 79–80; **19** 393; **21** 520
North American Printed Circuit Corp., **III** 643
North American Printing Ink Company, **13** 228
North American Reinsurance Corp., **III** 377
North American Rockwell Corp., **10** 173
North American Systems, **14** 230
North American Training Corporation. *See* Rollerblade, Inc.
North American Van Lines, **I** 278; **14** 37
North Atlantic Energy Corporation, **21** 411
North Atlantic Packing, **13** 243
North British Insurance Co., **III** 234–35
North British Rubber Company, **20** 258
North Broken Hill Peko, **IV** 61
North Carolina Motor Speedway, Inc., **19** 294
North Carolina National Bank Corporation, **II** 336; **10** 425–27; **18** 518
North Carolina Natural Gas Corporation, **6** 578
North Carolina Shipbuilding Co., **13** 373
North Central Airlines, **I** 132
North Central Finance, **II** 333
North Central Financial Corp., **9** 475
North Central Utilities, Inc., **18** 405
North Cornwall China Clay Co., **III** 690
North Eastern Bricks, **14** 249
North Eastern Coalfields Ltd., **IV** 48
The North Face, Inc., 8 169; **18 375–77**
North Goonbarrow, **III** 690

North Holland Publishing Co., **IV** 610
North New York Savings Bank, **10** 91
North of Scotland Bank, **II** 318; **17** 324
North of Scotland Hydro-Electric Board, **19** 389
North Pacific Paper Corp., **IV** 298
North Pacific Railroad, **II** 330
North Sea Oil and Gas, **10** 337
North Sea Sun Oil Co. Ltd., **IV** 550
North Shore Gas Company, **6** 543–44
North Shore Land Co., **17** 357
North Shore Medical Centre Pty, Ltd., **IV** 708
North Star Egg Case Company, **12** 376
North Star Marketing Cooperative, **7** 338
North Star Mill, **12** 376
North Star Steel Company, 13 138; **18 378–81; 19** 380
The North West Company, Inc., 12 361–63
North West Water Group plc, 11 359–62
North-West Telecommunications, **6** 327
Northamptonshire Union Bank, **II** 333
Northbrook Holdings, Inc., **22** 495
Northcliffe Newspapers, **IV** 685; **19** 118
Northeast Airlines Inc., **I** 99–100; **6** 81
Northeast Federal Corp., **13** 468
Northeast Petroleum Industries, Inc., **11** 194; **14** 461
Northeast Savings Bank, **12** 31; **13** 467–68
Northeast Utilities, V 668–69; 13 182–84; **21** 408, 411
Northeastern Bancorp of Scranton, **II** 342
Northeastern New York Medical Service, Inc., **III** 246
Northern Aluminum Co. Ltd., **IV** 9–10
Northern and Employers Assurance, **III** 235
Northern Arizona Light & Power Co., **6** 545
Northern Border Pipeline Co., **V** 609–10
Northern California Savings, **10** 340
Northern Crown Bank, **II** 344
Northern Dairies, **10** 441
Northern Development Co., **IV** 282
Northern Drug Company, **14** 147
Northern Electric Company. *See* Northern Telecom Limited.
Northern Energy Resources Company. *See* NERCO, Inc.
Northern Engineering Industries Plc, **21** 436
Northern Fibre Products Co., **I** 202
Northern Foods PLC, I 248; **II** 587; **10 441–43**
Northern Illinois Gas Co., **6** 529–31
Northern Indiana Power Company, **6** 556
Northern Indiana Public Service Company, **6** 532–33
Northern Joint Stock Bank, **II** 303
Northern Light Electric Company, **18** 402–03
Northern National Bank, **14** 90
Northern Natural Gas Co., **V** 609–10
Northern Pacific Corp., **15** 274
Northern Pacific Railroad, **II** 278, 329; **III** 228, 282; **14** 168
Northern Paper, **I** 614
Northern Pipeline Construction Co., **19** 410, 412
Northern States Life Insurance Co., **III** 275
Northern States Power Company, V 670–72; 18 404; **20 391–95 (upd.)**
Northern Stores, Inc., **12** 362

Northern Sugar Company, **11** 13
Northern Telecom Limited, II 70; **III** 143, 164; **V** 271; **V 308–10; 6** 242, 307, 310; **9** 479; **10** 19, 432; **11** 69; **12** 162; **14** 259; **16** 392, 468; **17** 353; **18** 111; **20** 439; **22** 51
Northern Trust Company, III 518; **9 387–89; 22** 280
Northfield Metal Products, **11** 256
Northgate Computer Corp., **16** 196
Northland. *See* Scott Fetzer Company.
Northland Publishing, **19** 231
NorthPrint International, **22** 356
Northrop Corporation, I 47, 49, 55, 59, **76–77,** 80, 84, 197, 525; **III** 84; **9** 416, 418; **10** 162; **11** 164, 166, 266, 269, **363–65 (upd.)**
Northrup King Co., **I** 672
NorthStar Computers, **10** 313
Northwest Airlines Inc., I 42, 64, 91, 97, 100, 104, **112–14,** 125, 127; **6** 66, 74, 82 **103–05 (upd.),** 123; **9** 273; **11** 266, 315; **12** 191, 487; **21** 141, 143; **22** 252
Northwest Benefit Assoc., **III** 228
Northwest Engineering, **21** 502
Northwest Engineering Co. *See* Terex Corporation.
Northwest Industries, **I** 342; **II** 468 **8** 367. *See also* Chicago and North Western Holdings Corporation
Northwest Instruments, **8** 519
Northwest Linen Co., **16** 228
Northwest Paper Company, **8** 430
Northwest Steel Rolling Mills Inc., **13** 97
Northwest Telecommunications Inc., **6** 598
Northwestern Bell Telephone Co., **V** 341
Northwestern Benevolent Society, **III** 228
Northwestern Engraving, **12** 25
Northwestern Expanded Metal Co., **III** 763
Northwestern Financial Corporation, **11** 29
Northwestern Industries, **III** 263
Northwestern Manufacturing Company, **8** 133
Northwestern Mutual Life Insurance Company, III 321–24, 352; **IV** 333
Northwestern National Bank, **16** 71
Northwestern National Insurance Co., **IV** 29
Northwestern National Life Insurance Co., **14** 233
Northwestern Public Service Company, **6** 524
Northwestern States Portland Cement Co., **III** 702
Northwestern Telephone Systems, **6** 325, 328
Norton Company, III 678; **8 395–97; 16** 122; **22** 68
Norton Healthcare Ltd., **11** 208
Norton Opax PLC, **IV** 259
Norton Simon Industries, **I** 446; **IV** 672; **6** 356; **19** 404; **22** 513
Norwales Development Ltd., **11** 239
Norwalk Truck Lines, **14** 567
Norweb, **13** 458
Norwegian Assurance, **III** 258
Norwegian Globe, **III** 258
Norwegian Petroleum Consultants, **III** 499
Norweld Holding A.A., **13** 316
Norwest Bank, **19** 412
Norwest Corp., **16** 135
Norwest Mortgage Inc., **11** 29
Norwest Publishing, **IV** 661
Norwich Pharmaceuticals, **I** 370–71; **9** 358

Norwich Union Fire Insurance Society, Ltd., **III** 242, 273, 404; **IV** 705
Norwich Winterthur Group, **III** 404
Norwich-Eaton Pharmaceuticals, **III** 53; **8** 434
Norwood Company, **13** 168
Nostell Brick & Tile, **14** 249
Nottingham Manufacturing Co., **V** 357
Nouvelles Galeries Réunies, **10** 205; **19** 308
Nouvelles Messageries de la Presse Parisienne, **IV** 618
Nova Corporation, **18** 365–67
Nova Corporation of Alberta, V 673–75; 12 364–66
Nova Pharmaceuticals, **14** 46
Nova Scotia Steel Company, **19** 186
NovaCare, Inc., 11 366–68; **14** 233
Novacor Chemicals Ltd., 12 364–66
Novagas Clearinghouse Ltd., **18** 367
Novalta Resources Inc., **11** 441
Novartis, **18** 51
Novell, Inc., 6 255–56, 260, **269–71; 9** 170–71; **10** 232, 363, 473–74, 558, 565; **11** 59, 519–20; **12** 335; **13** 482; **15** 131, 133, 373, 492; **16** 392, 394; **20** 237; **21** 133–34; **23 359–62 (upd.)**
Novello and Co., **II** 139
Novellus Systems, Inc., 18 382–85
Novo Industri A/S, I 658–60, 697
NOVUM. *See* Industrie Natuzzi S.p.A.
Nowell Wholesale Grocery Co., **II** 681
Nox Ltd., **I** 588
Noxell Corporation, **III** 53; **8** 434
NPD Group, **13** 4
NPD Trading (USA), Inc., **13** 367
NPS Waste Technologies, **13** 366
NRG Energy, Inc., **11** 401
NS. *See* Norfolk Southern Corporation.
NS Petites Inc., **8** 323
NSG Information System Co., **III** 715
NSK. *See* Nippon Seiko K.K.
NSK-Warner, **14** 64
NSMO. *See* Nederlandsche Stoomvart Maatschappij Oceaan.
NSN Network Services, **23** 292, 294
NSP. *See* Northern States Power Company.
NSU Werke, **10** 261
NTC Publishing Group, **22** 519, 522
NTCL. *See* Northern Telecom Limited.
NTN Corporation, III 595–96, 623
NTRON, **11** 486
NTT. *See* Nippon Telegraph and Telephone Corp.
NTTPC. *See* Nippon Telegraph and Telephone Public Corporation.
NU. *See* Northeast Utilities.
Nu-Era Gear, **14** 64
Nu-kote Holding, Inc., 18 386–89
Nuclear Electric, **6** 453; **11** 399–401; **12** 349; **13** 484
Nuclear Power International, **19** 166
Nucoa Butter Co., **II** 497
Nucor Corporation, 7 400–02; 13 143, 423; **14** 156; **18** 378–80; **19** 380; **21 392–95 (upd.)**
Nucorp Energy, **II** 262, 620
NUG Optimus Lebensmittel-Einzelhandelsgesellschaft mbH, **V** 74
Nugget Polish Co. Ltd., **II** 566
Numerax, Inc., **IV** 637
Nuovo Pignone, **IV** 420–22
NUR Touristic GmbH, **V** 100–02
Nurad, **III** 468

Nurotoco Inc. *See* Roto-Rooter Service Company.
Nursefinders, **6** 10
Nutmeg Industries, Inc., **17** 513
NutraSweet Company, II 463, 582; **8** 398–400
Nutrena, **II** 617; **13** 137
Nutri-Foods International, **18** 467–68
Nutrilite Co., **III** 11–12
NutriSystem, **10** 383; **12** 531
Nutrition for Life International Inc., 22 385–88
Nuveen. *See* John Nuveen Company.
NV Dagblad De Telegraaf. *See* N.V. Holdingmaatschappij De Telegraaf.
NVR L.P., 8 401–03
NWA Aircraft, **I** 114
NWK. *See* Nordwestdeutsche Kraftwerke AG.
NWL Control Systems, **III** 512
NWS BANK plc, **10** 336–37
Nya AB Atlas, **III** 425–26
Nydqvist & Holm, **III** 426
Nyhamms Cellulosa, **IV** 338
NYK. *See* Nihon Yusen Kaisha, Nippon Yusen Kabushiki Kaisha *and* Nippon Yusen Kaisha.
Nylex Corp., **I** 429
NYLife Care Health Plans, Inc., **17** 166
Nylon de Mexico, S.A., **19** 10, 12
Nyman & Schultz Affarsresbyraer A.B., **I** 120
Nymofil, Ltd., **16** 297
NYNEX Corporation, V 311–13; **6** 340; **11** 19, 87; **13** 176
Nyrop, **I** 113
Nysco Laboratories, **III** 55
NYSEG. *See* New York State Electric and Gas Corporation.
NZI Corp., **III** 257

O'Keefe Marketing, **23** 102
O&Y. *See* Olympia & York Developments Ltd.
O.B. McClintock Co., **7** 144–45
O.G. Wilson, **16** 560
O. Kraft & Sons, **12** 363
O.S. Designs Inc., **15** 396
Oahu Railway & Land Co., **I** 565–66
Oak Farms Dairies, **II** 660
Oak Hill Investment Partners, **11** 490
Oak Hill Sportswear Corp., **17** 137–38
Oak Industries Inc., III 512; **21** 396–98
Oak Technology, Inc., 22 389–93
Oakley, Inc., 18 390–93
OakStone Financial Corporation, **11** 448
OakTree Health Plan Inc., **16** 404
Oakville, **7** 518
Oakwood Homes Corporation, 13 155; **15** 326–28
OASIS, **IV** 454
Oasis Group P.L.C., **10** 506
OASYS, Inc., **18** 112
ÖBB. *See* Österreichische Bundesbahnen GmbH.
Obbola Linerboard, **IV** 339
Oberheim Corporation, **16** 239
Oberland, **16** 122
Oberrheinische Bank, **II** 278
Oberschlesische Stickstoff-Werge AG, **IV** 229
Oberusel AG, **III** 541
Obi, **23** 231
Object Design, Inc., **15** 372

Obunsha, **9** 29
Occidental Bank, **16** 497
Occidental Chemical Corp., **19** 414
Occidental Insurance Co., **III** 251
Occidental Life Insurance Company, **I** 536–37; **13** 529
Occidental Overseas Ltd., **11** 97
Occidental Petroleum Corporation, I 527; **II** 432, 516; **IV** 264, 312, 392, 410, 417, 453–54, 467, **480–82,** 486, 515–16; **7** 376; **8** 526; **12** 100; **19** 268
Occidental Petroleum Great Britain Inc., **21** 206
Ocean, **III** 234
Ocean Combustion Services, **9** 109
Ocean Drilling and Exploration Company. *See* ODECO.
Ocean Group plc, 6 415–17
Ocean Reef Management, **19** 242, 244
Ocean Salvage and Towage Co., **I** 592
Ocean Scientific, Inc., **15** 380
Ocean Specialty Tankers Corporation, **22** 275
Ocean Spray Cranberries, Inc., 7 403–05; **10** 525; **19** 278
Ocean Steam Ship Company. *See* Malaysian Airlines System BHD.
Ocean Systems Inc., **I** 400
Ocean Transport & Trading Ltd., **6** 417
Oceanic Contractors, **III** 559
Oceanic Properties, **II** 491–92
Oceanic Steam Navigation Company, **19** 197; **23** 160
Oceans of Fun, **22** 130
O'Charley's Inc., 19 286–88
OCL. *See* Overseas Containers Ltd.
Ocoma Foods, **II** 584
Octek, **13** 235
Octel Communications Corp., **III** 143; **14** 217, **354–56; 16** 394
Octopus Publishing, **IV** 667; **17** 398
Oculinum, Inc., **10** 48
Odakyu Electric Railway Company Limited, V 487–89
Odam's and Plaistow Wharves, **II** 580–81
Odd Lot Trading Company, **V** 172–73
Odeco Drilling, Inc., **7** 362–64; **11** 522; **12** 318
Odeon Theatres Ltd., **II** 157–59
Odetics Inc., 14 357–59
Odhams Press Ltd., **IV** 259, 666–67; **7** 244, 342; **17** 397–98
O'Donnell-Usen Fisheries, **II** 494
Odyssey Holdings, Inc., **18** 376
Odyssey Partners, **II** 679; **V** 135; **12** 55; **13** 94; **17** 137
Odyssey Press, **13** 560
Oelwerken Julias Schindler GmbH, **7** 141
OEN Connectors, **19** 166
Oertel Brewing Co., **I** 226; **10** 180
Oësterreichischer Phönix in Wien, **III** 376
Oetker Group, **I** 219
Off the Rax, **II** 667
Office Depot Incorporated, 8 404–05; **10** 235, 497; **12** 335; **13** 268; **15** 331; **18** 24, 388; **22** 154, 412–13; **23** 363–65 **(upd.)**
Office Mart Holdings Corporation, **10** 498
Office National du Crédit Agricole, **II** 264
Office Systems Inc., **15** 407
Office Works, Inc., **13** 277
OfficeMax Inc., 8 404; **15** 329–31; **18** 286, 388; **20** 103; **22** 154; **23** 364–65

Official Airline Guides, Inc., **IV** 605, 643; **7** 312, 343; **17** 399
Officine Alfieri Maserati S.p.A., 11 104; **13** 28, **376–78**
Offset Gerhard Kaiser GmbH, **IV** 325
Offshore Co., **III** 558; **6** 577
Offshore Food Services Inc., **I** 514
Offshore Transportation Corporation, **11** 523
Ogden Corporation, I 512–14, 701; **6** 151–53, 600; **7** 39
Ogden Food Products, **7** 430
Ogden Gas Co., **6** 568
Ogilvie Flour Mills Co., **I** 268; **IV** 245
Ogilvy & Mather, **22** 200
Ogilvy Group Inc., I 20, **25–27,** 31, 37, 244; **6** 53; **9** 180. *See also* WPP Group.
Oglebay Norton Company, 17 355–58
Oglethorpe Power Corporation, 6 537–38
O'Gorman and Cozens-Hardy, **III** 725
Ogura Oil, **IV** 479
Oh la la!, **14** 107
Ohbayashi Corporation, **I** 586–87
The Ohio Art Company, 14 360–62
Ohio Ball Bearing. *See* Bearings Inc.
Ohio Barge Lines, Inc., **11** 194
Ohio Bell Telephone Company, 14 363–65; **18** 30
Ohio Boxboard Company, **12** 376
Ohio Brass Co., **II** 2
Ohio Casualty Corp., III 190; **11** 369–70
Ohio Crankshaft Co. *See* Park-Ohio Industries Inc.
Ohio Edison Company, V 676–78
Ohio Electric Railway Co., **III** 388
Ohio Mattress Co., **12** 438–39
Ohio Oil Co., **IV** 365, 400, 574; **6** 568; **7** 551
Ohio Pizza Enterprises, Inc., **7** 152
Ohio Power Shovel, **21** 502
Ohio Pure Foods Group, **II** 528
Ohio River Company, **6** 487
Ohio Valley Electric Corporation, **6** 517
Ohio Ware Basket Company, **12** 319
Ohio-Sealy Mattress Mfg. Co., **12** 438–39
Ohlmeyer Communications, **I** 275
Ohlsson's Cape Breweries, **I** 287–88
OHM Corp., **17** 553
Ohmite Manufacturing Co., **13** 397
Ohrbach's Department Store, **I** 30
Ohta Keibin Railway Company, **6** 430
ÖIAG, **IV** 234
Oil Acquisition Corp., **I** 611
Oil and Natural Gas Commission, IV 440–41, **483–84**
Oil and Solvent Process Company, **9** 109
Oil City Oil and Grease Co., **IV** 489
Oil Co. of Australia, **III** 673
Oil Distribution Public Corp., **IV** 434
Oil Drilling, Incorporated, **7** 344
Oil Equipment Manufacturing Company, **16** 8
Oil India Ltd., **IV** 440, 483–84
Oil Shale Corp., **IV** 522; **7** 537
Oil-Dri Corporation of America, 20 396–99
Oilfield Industrial Lines Inc., **I** 477
Oilfield Service Corp. of America, **I** 342
Oita Co., **III** 718
Oji Paper Co., Ltd., I 506, 508; **II** 326; **IV** 268, 284–85, 292–93, 297–98, **320–22,** 326–27
OK Bazaars, **I** 289

OK Turbines, Inc., **22** 311
Okadaya Co. Ltd., **V** 96
Oki Electric Industry Company, Limited, **II** 68, **72–74**; **15** 125; **21** 390
Okidata, **9** 57; **18** 435
Okinoyama Coal Mine, **III** 759
Oklahoma Airmotive, **8** 349
Oklahoma Entertainment, Inc., **9** 74
Oklahoma Gas and Electric Company, **6 539–40**; **7** 409–11
Oklahoma Oil Co., **I** 31
Oklahoma Publishing Company, **11** 152–53
Okonite, **I** 489
Okura & Co., Ltd., **I** 282; **IV 167–68**
OLC. *See* Orient Leasing Co., Ltd.
Olcott & McKesson, **I** 496
Old America Stores, Inc., **17 359–61**
Old Colony Trust Co., **II** 207; **12** 30
Old Dominion Power Company, **6** 513, 515
Old El Paso, **I** 457; **14** 212
Old Harbor Candles, **18** 68
Old Kent Financial Corp., **11 371–72**
Old Line Life Insurance Co., **III** 275
Old Mutual, **IV** 23, 535
Old National Bancorp, **14** 529; **15 332–34**
Old Navy Clothing Company, **18** 193
Old Quaker Paint Company, **13** 471
Old Republic International Corp., **11 373–75**
Old Stone Trust Company, **13** 468
Oldach Window Corp., **19** 446
Oldham Estate, **IV** 712
Oldover Corp., **23** 225
Olds Motor Vehicle Co., **I** 171; **10** 325
Olds Oil Corp., **I** 341
Ole's Innovative Sports. *See* Rollerblade, Inc.
Olean Tile Co., **22** 170
Oleochim, **IV** 498–99
OLEX. *See* Deutsche BP Aktiengesellschaft.
Olex Cables Ltd., **10** 445
Olin Corporation, **I** 318, 330, **379–81**, 434, 695; **III** 667; **IV** 482; **8** 23, 153; **11** 420; **13 379–81 (upd.)**; **16** 68, 297
Olinkraft, Inc., **II** 432; **III** 708–09; **11** 420; **16** 376
Olins Rent-a-Car, **6** 348
Olinvest, **IV** 454
Olive Garden Italian Restaurants, **10** 322, 324; **16** 156–58; **19** 258
Oliver Rubber Company, **19** 454, 456
Olivetti. *See* Ing. C. Olivetti & C., S.p.A.
Olivine Industries, Inc., **II** 508; **11** 172
Olmstead Products Co., **23** 82
Olofsson, **I** 573
Olohana Corp., **I** 129; **6** 129
Olsen Dredging Co., **III** 558
Olson & Wright, **I** 120
Olsonite Corp., **I** 201
Olsten Corporation, **6 41–43**; **9** 327
Olveh, **III** 177–79
Olympia & York Developments Ltd., **IV** 245, 247, 712, **720–21**; **6** 478; **8** 327; **9 390–92 (upd.)**
Olympia Arenas, Inc., **7** 278–79
Olympia Brewing, **I** 260; **11** 50
Olympia Floor & Tile Co., **IV** 720
Olympiakı, **III** 401
Olympic Airways, **II** 442
Olympic Fastening Systems, **III** 722

Olympic Packaging, **13** 443
Olympus Communications L.P., **17** 7
Olympus Optical Company, Ltd., **15** 483
Olympus Sport, **V** 177–78
Olympus Symbol, Inc., **15** 483
OM Group, Inc., **17 362–64**
Omaha Cold Store Co., **II** 571
Oman Oil Refinery Co., **IV** 516
Omega Gas Company, **8** 349
Omega Gold Mines, **IV** 164
Omex Corporation, **6** 272
OMI Corporation, **IV** 34; **9** 111–12; **22** 275
Omlon, **II** 75
Ommium Française de Pétroles, **IV** 559
Omnes, **17** 419
Omni Construction Company, Inc., **8** 112–13
Omni Hearing Aid Systems, **I** 667
Omni Hotels Corp., **12 367–69**
Omni Products International, **II** 420
Omni-Pac, **12** 377
Omnibus Corporation, **9** 283
Omnicare, Inc., **13** 150
Omnicom Group Inc., **I 28–32**, 33, 36; **14** 160; **22 394–99 (upd.)**; **23** 478
Omnipoint Communications Inc., **18** 77
OmniSource Corporation, **14 366–67**
Omron Tateisi Electronics Company, **II 75–77**; **III** 549
ÖMV Aktiengesellschaft, **IV** 234, 454, **485–87**
On Assignment, Inc., **20 400–02**
On Command Video Corp., **23** 135
On Cue, **9** 360
On-Line Software International Inc., **6** 225
On-Line Systems. *See* Sierra On-Line Inc.
Onan Corporation, **8** 72
Onbancorp Inc., **11** 110
Once Upon A Child, Inc., **18** 207–8
Oncogen, **III** 18
Ondal GmbH, **III** 69
Ondulato Imolese, **IV** 296; **19** 226
One Hundredth Bank, **II** 321
One Price Clothing Stores, Inc., **20 403–05**
One-Hundred Thirtieth National Bank, **II** 291
O'Neal, Jones & Feldman Inc., **11** 142
Oneida Bank & Trust Company, **9** 229
Oneida County Creameries Co., **7** 202
Oneida Gas Company, **9** 554
Oneida Ltd., **7 406–08**
ONEOK Inc., **7 409–12**
Onex Corporation, **16 395–97**; **22** 513
Onitsuka Tiger Co., **V** 372; **8** 391
Online Distributed Processing Corporation, **6** 201
Online Financial Communication Systems, **11** 112
Only One Dollar, Inc. *See* Dollar Tree Stores, Inc.
Onoda Cement Co., Ltd., **I** 508; **III 717–19**
Onstead Foods, **21** 501
Ontario Hydro, **6 541–42**; **9** 461
Ontel Corporation, **6** 201
Oode Casting Iron Works, **III** 551
O'okiep Copper Company, Ltd., **7** 385–86
Opel. *See* Adam Opel AG
Open Board of Brokers, **9** 369
Open Market, Inc., **22** 522
Operadora de Bolsa Serfin. *See* Grupo Financiero Serfin, S.A.

Opp and Micolas Mills, **15** 247–48
Oppenheimer. *See* Ernest Oppenheimer and Sons.
Oppenheimer & Co., **17** 137; **21** 235; **22** 405
Opryland USA, **11** 152–53
Optel Corp., **17** 331
OPTi Computer, **9** 116
Opti-Ray, Inc., **12** 215
Optilink Corporation, **12** 137
Optima Pharmacy Services, **17** 177
Optimum Financial Services Ltd., **II** 457
Opto-Electronics Corp., **15** 483
Optronics, Inc., **6** 247
Optus Vision, **17** 150
OPW, **III** 467–68
Oracle Systems Corporation, **6 272–74**; **10** 361, 363, 505; **11** 78; **13** 483; **14** 16; **15** 492; **18** 541, 543; **19** 310; **21** 86; **22** 154, 293
Orange Julius, **10** 371, 373
Orange Line Bus Company, **6** 604
Orbis Entertainment Co., **20** 6
Orbis Graphic Arts. *See* Anaheim Imaging.
Orbital Engine Corporation Ltd., **17** 24
Orbital Sciences Corporation, **22 400–03**
Orchard Supply Hardware Stores Corporation, **17 365–67**
Orcofi, **III** 48
Ore and Chemical Corp., **IV** 140
Ore-Ida Foods Incorporated, **II** 508; **11** 172; **12** 531; **13 382–83**
Oregon Ale and Beer Company, **18** 72
Oregon Craft & Floral Supply, **17** 322
Oregon Metallurgical Corporation, **20 406–08**
Oregon Pacific and Eastern Railway, **13** 100
Oregon Steel Mills, Inc., **14 368–70**; **19** 380
Orford Copper Co., **IV** 110
Organon, **I** 665
Oriel Foods, **II** 609
Orient, **21** 122
Orient Glass, **III** 715
Orient Leasing. *See* Orix Corporation.
Orient Overseas, **18** 254
Oriental Brewery Co., Ltd., **21** 320
Oriental Land Co., Ltd., **IV** 715
Oriental Precision Company, **13** 213
Oriental Trading Corp., **22** 213
Oriental Yeast Co., **17** 288
Origin Systems Inc., **10** 285
Origin Technology, **14** 183
Original Arizona Jean Company, **18** 272
Original Cookie Co., **13** 166
Original Musical Instrument Company (O.M.I.), **16** 239
Original Wassertragers Hummel, **II** 163
Orinoco Oilfields, Ltd., **IV** 565
Orion, **III** 310
Orion Bank Ltd., **II** 271, 345, 385
Orion Healthcare Ltd., **11** 168
Orion Personal Insurances Ltd., **11** 168
Orion Pictures Corporation, **II** 147; **6 167–70**; **7** 336; **14** 330, 332
Orit Corp., **8** 219–20
Orix Corporation, **II 442–43**, 259, 348
Orkem, **IV** 547, 560; **21** 205
Orkin Pest Control, **11** 431–32, 434
Orkla A/S, **18 394–98**
Orm Bergold Chemie, **8** 464
Ormco Corporation, **14** 481
ÖROP, **IV** 485–86

Orowheat Baking Company, **10** 250
La Oroya, **22** 286
Ortho Diagnostic Systems, Inc., **10** 213; **22** 75
Ortho Pharmaceutical Corporation, **III** 35; **8** 281; **10** 79–80
Orthopedic Services, Inc., **11** 366
Orval Kent Food Company, Inc., **7** 430
Orville Redenbacher/Swiss Miss Foods Co., **17** 241
Oryx Energy Company, IV 550; **7 413–15**
Osaka Aluminium Co., **IV** 153
Osaka Beer Brewing Co., **I** 220, 282; **20** 28
Osaka Electric Tramway, **V** 463
Osaka Gas Co., Ltd., V 679–81
Osaka General Bussan, **IV** 431
Osaka Iron Works, **III** 513
Osaka Marine and Fire Insurance Co., **III** 367
Osaka Nomura Bank, **II** 276, 438–39
Osaka North Harbor Co. Ltd., **I** 518
Osaka Shinyo Kumiai, **15** 495
Osaka Shosen Kaisha, **I** 503; **V** 473–74, 481–82
Osaka Spinning Company, **V** 387
Osaka Sumitomo Marine and Fire Insurance Co., Ltd., **III** 367
Osaka Textile Co., **I** 506
Osakeyhtiö Gustaf Cederberg & Co., **IV** 301
Osakeyhtiö T. & J. Salvesen, **IV** 301
Osborne Books, **IV** 637
Oscar Mayer Foods Corp., II 532; **7** 274, 276; **12** 123, **370–72**
Osco Drug, **II** 604–05
Oshawa Group Limited, II 649–50
OshKosh B'Gosh, Inc., 9 393–95
Oshkosh Electric Power, **9** 553
Oshkosh Gas Light Company, **9** 553
Oshkosh Truck Corporation, 7 416–18; 14 458
Oshman's Sporting Goods, Inc., 16 560; **17 368–70**
OSi Specialties, Inc., **16** 543
Osiris Holding Company, **16** 344
OSK. *See* Osaka Shosen Kaisha.
Osmonics, Inc., 18 399–401
Oster. *See* Sunbeam-Oster.
Österreichische Bundesbahnen GmbH, 6 418–20
Österreichische Creditanstalt-Wiener Bankverein, **IV** 230
Österreichische Elektrowerke, **IV** 230
Österreichische Industrieholding AG, **IV** 486–87
Österreichische Industriekredit AG, **IV** 230
Österreichische Länderbank, **II** 239; **23** 37
Österreichische Mineralölverwaltung AG, **IV** 485
Österreichische Post- und Telegraphenverwaltung, V 314–17
Österreichische Stickstoffswerke, **IV** 486
Ostschweizer Zementwerke, **III** 701
Osuuskunta Metsäliito, **IV** 316
Oswald Tillotson Ltd., **III** 501; **7** 207
Otagiri Mercantile Co., **11** 95
Otake Paper Manufacturing Co., **IV** 327
OTC, **10** 492
Otis Company, **6** 579
Otis Elevator Company, Inc., I 85, **III** 467, 663; **13 384–86**
Otis Engineering Corp., **III** 498

Otosan, **I** 167, 479–80
Otsego Falls Paper Company, **8** 358
Ott and Brewer Company, **12** 312
Ottawa Fruit Supply Ltd., **II** 662
Ottaway Newspapers, Inc., 15 335–37
Otter Tail Power Company, 18 402–05
Otter-Westelaken, **16** 420
Otto Sumisho Inc., **V** 161
Otto-Epoka mbH, **15** 340
Otto-Versand (GmbH & Co.), V 159–61; 10 489–90; **15 338–40 (upd.)**
Ottumwa Daily Courier, **11** 251
Ourso Investment Corporation, **16** 344
Outback Steakhouse, Inc., 12 373–75
Outboard Marine Corporation, III 329, **597–600; 8** 71; **16** 383; **20 409–12 (upd.)**
The Outdoorsman, Inc., **10** 216
Outlet, **6** 33
Outlook Window Partnership, **19** 446
Outokumpu Metals Group. *See* OM Group, Inc.
Outokumpu Oy, **IV** 276
Ovako Oy, **III** 624
Ovation, **19** 285
OVC, Inc., **6** 313
Overhill Farms, **10** 382
Overland Energy Company, **14** 567
Overland Mail Co., **II** 380–81, 395; **10** 60; **12** 533
Overnite Transportation Co., 14 371–73
Overseas Air Travel Ltd., **I** 95
Overseas Containers Ltd., **6** 398, 415–16
Overseas Petroleum and Investment Corp., **IV** 389
Overseas Shipholding Group, Inc., 11 376–77
Overseas Telecommunications Commission, **6** 341–42
Owatonna Tool Co., **I** 200; **10** 493
Owen Steel Co. Inc., **15** 117
Owens & Minor, Inc., 10 143; **16 398–401**
Owens Corning Corporation, I 609; **III** 683, **720–23; 8** 177; **13** 169; **20 413–17 (upd.)**
Owens Yacht Company, **III** 443; **22** 115
Owens-Illinois Inc., I 609–11, 615; **II** 386; **III** 640, 720–21; **IV** 282, 343; **9** 261; **16** 123; **22** 254
Owensboro Municipal Utilities, **11** 37
Oxdon Investments, **II** 664
Oxfam America, **13** 13
Oxford Biscuit Fabrik, **II** 543
Oxford Chemical Corp., **II** 572
Oxford Financial Group, **22** 456
Oxford Health Plans, Inc., 16 402–04
Oxford Industries, Inc., 8 406–08
Oxford Instruments, **III** 491
Oxford Paper Co., **I** 334–35; **10** 289
Oxford University Press, **23** 211
Oxford-AnsCo Development Co., **12** 18
Oxirane Chemical Co., **IV** 456
OXO International, **16** 234
Oxy Petrochemicals Inc., **IV** 481
Oxy Process Chemicals, **III** 33
OxyChem, **11** 160
Ozalid Corporation, **I** 337–38; **IV** 563; **22** 226
Ozark Airlines, **I** 127; **12** 489
Ozark Pipe Line Corp., **IV** 540
Ozark Utility Company, **6** 593

P & M Manufacturing Company, **8** 386

P & O. *See* Peninsular & Oriental Steam Navigation Company.
P.A. Bergner & Company, **9** 142; **15** 87–88
P.A. Geier Company. *See* Royal Appliance Manufacturing Company.
P.A.J.W. Corporation, **9** 111–12
P.A. Rentrop-Hubbert & Wagner Fahrzeugausstattungen GmbH, **III** 582
P&C Foods Inc., 8 409–11; 13 95, 394
P&O, **6** 79
P.C. Hanford Oil Co., **IV** 368
P.C. Richard & Son Corp., 23 372–74
P. D'Aoust Ltd., **II** 651
P.D. Kadi International, **I** 580
P.D. Magnetics, **I** 330; **8** 153
P.G. Realty, **III** 340
P.H. Glatfelter Company, 8 412–14
P.L. Porter Co., **III** 580
P.R. Mallory, **9** 179
P.S.L. Food Market, Inc., **22** 549
P. Sharples, **III** 418
P.T. Bridgeport Perkasa Machine Tools, **17** 54
P.T. Dai Nippon Printing Indonesia, **IV** 599
P.T. Darya-Varia Laboratoria, **18** 180
P.T. Gaya Motor, **23** 290
P.T. Muaratewe Spring, **III** 581
P.T. Semen Nusantara, **III** 718
P.W. Huntington & Company, **11** 180
Pabst, **I** 217, 255; **10** 99; **18** 502
PAC Insurance Services, **12** 175
Pac-Am Food Concepts, **10** 178
Pac-Fab, Inc., **18** 161
Paccar Inc., I 155, **185–86; 10** 280
Pace Companies, **6** 149
Pace Express Pty. Ltd., **13** 20
Pace Management Service Corp., **21** 91
PACE Membership Warehouse, Inc., **V** 112; **10** 107; **12** 50; **18** 286
Pace Pharmaceuticals, **16** 439
Pace-Arrow, Inc., **III** 484; **22** 206
Pacemaker Plastics, Inc., **7** 296
Pacer Tool and Mold, **17** 310
Pachena Industries Ltd., **6** 310
Pacific Aero Products Co., **I** 47; **10** 162
Pacific Air Freight, Incorporated, **6** 345
Pacific Air Transport, **I** 47, 128; **6** 128; **9** 416
Pacific Alaska Fuel Services, **6** 383
Pacific Bell, **V** 318–20; **11** 59; **12** 137; **21** 285; **22** 19
Pacific Brick Proprietary, **III** 673
Pacific Car & Foundry Co., **I** 185
Pacific Cascade Land Co., **IV** 255
Pacific Coast Co., **IV** 165
Pacific Coast Condensed Milk Co., **II** 486
Pacific Coast Oil Co., **IV** 385
Pacific Communication Sciences, **11** 57
Pacific Dry Dock and Repair Co., **6** 382
Pacific Dunlop Limited, 10 444–46
Pacific Electric Heating Co., **II** 28; **12** 194
Pacific Electric Light Company, **6** 565
Pacific Enterprises, V 682–84; 12 477
Pacific Express Co., **II** 381
Pacific Finance Corp., **I** 537; **9** 536; **13** 529
Pacific Gamble Robinson, **9** 39
Pacific Gas and Electric Company, I 96; **V 685–87; 11** 270; **12** 100, 106; **19** 411
Pacific Guardian Life Insurance Co., **III** 289
Pacific Health Beverage Co., **I** 292

Pacific Home Furnishings, **14** 436
Pacific Indemnity Corp., **III** 220; **14** 108, 110; **16** 204
Pacific Lighting Corp., **IV** 492; **V** 682–84; **12** 477; **16** 496
Pacific Linens, **13** 81–82
Pacific Link Communication, **18** 180
Pacific Lumber Company, **III** 254; **8** 348–50
Pacific Magazines and Printing, **7** 392
Pacific Mail Steamship Company, **6** 353
Pacific Manifolding Book/Box Co., **IV** 644
Pacific Media K.K., **18** 101
Pacific Metal Bearing Co., **I** 159
Pacific Monolothics Inc., **11** 520
Pacific National Bank, **II** 349
Pacific Natural Gas Corp., **9** 102
Pacific Northern, **6** 66
Pacific Northwest Bell Telephone Co., **V** 341
Pacific Northwest Laboratories, **10** 139
Pacific Northwest Pipeline Corporation, **9** 102–104, 540; **12** 144
Pacific Northwest Power Company, **6** 597
Pacific Pearl, **I** 417
Pacific Petroleums Ltd., **IV** 494; **9** 102
Pacific Platers Ltd., **IV** 100
Pacific Power & Light Company. *See* PacifiCorp.
Pacific Pride Bakeries, **19** 192
Pacific Recycling Co. Inc., **IV** 296; **19** 226; **23** 225
Pacific Refining Co., **IV** 394–95
Pacific Resources Inc., **IV** 47; **22** 107
Pacific Silver Corp., **IV** 76
Pacific Southwest Airlines Inc., **I** 132; **6** 132
Pacific Steel Ltd., **IV** 279; **19** 154
Pacific Telecom, Inc., V 689; **6 325–28**
Pacific Telesis Group, V 318–20; **6** 324; **9** 321; **11** 10–11; **14** 345, 347; **15** 125
Pacific Teletronics, Inc., **7** 15
Pacific Towboat. *See* Puget Sound Tug and Barge Company.
Pacific Trading Co., Ltd., **IV** 442
Pacific Trail Inc., **17** 462
Pacific Western Extruded Plastics Company, **17** 441
Pacific Western Oil Co., **IV** 537
Pacific Wine Co., **18** 71
Pacific-Burt Co., Ltd., **IV** 644
Pacific-Sierra Research, **I** 155
PacifiCare Health Systems, Inc., III 85; **11 378–80**
PacifiCorp, V 688–90; **6** 325–26, 328; **7** 376–78
Package Products Company, Inc., **12** 150
Packaged Ice, Inc., **21** 338
Packaging Corporation of America, I 526; **12 376–78**, 397; **16** 191
Packard Bell Electronics, Inc., I 524; **II** 86; **10** 521, 564; **11** 413; **13 387–89**, 483; **21** 391; **23** 471
Packard Motor Co., **I** 81; **8** 74; **9** 17
Packer's Consolidated Press, **IV** 651
Packerland Packing Company, **7** 199, 201
Pacolet Manufacturing Company, **17** 327
PacTel. *See* Pacific Telesis Group.
Paddington Corp., **I** 248
PAFS. *See* Pacific Alaska Fuel Services.
Page, Bacon & Co., **II** 380; **12** 533
Page Boy Inc., **9** 320
PageAhead Software, **15** 492

Pageland Coca-Cola Bottling Works, **10** 222
PageMart Wireless, Inc., **18** 164, 166
Paging Network Inc., 11 381–83
Pagoda Trading Company, Inc., **V** 351, 353; **20** 86
Paid Prescriptions, **9** 346
Paige Publications, **18** 66
PaineWebber Group Inc., I 245; **II 444–46**, 449; **III** 409; **13** 449; **22** 352, **404–07 (upd.)**, 542
Painter Carpet Mills, **13** 169
Painton Co., **II** 81
La Paix, **III** 273
Pak Arab Fertilizers Ltd., **IV** 364
Pak Mail Centers, **18** 316
Pak-a-Sak, **II** 661
Pak-All Products, Inc., **IV** 345
Pak-Paino, **IV** 315
Pak-Sak Industries, **17** 310
Pak-Well, **IV** 282; **9** 261
Pakhoed Holding, N.V., **9** 532
Pakkasakku Oy, **IV** 471
Paknet, **11** 548
Pakway Container Corporation, **8** 268
PAL. *See* Philippine Airlines, Inc.
Pal Plywood Co., Ltd., **IV** 327
Palatine Insurance Co., **III** 234
Palco Industries, **19** 440
Pale Ski & Sports GmbH, **22** 461
Palestine Coca-Cola Bottling Co., **13** 163
Pall Corporation, 9 396–98
Palm Beach Holdings, **9** 157
Palmafina, **IV** 498–99
Palmer G. Lewis Co., **8** 135
Palmer Tyre Ltd., **I** 428–29
Palmolive Co. *See* Colgate-Palmolive Company.
Palo Alto Brewing, **22** 421
Palo Alto Research Center, **10** 510
Palomar Medical Technologies, Inc., 22 408–10
Pamida Holdings Corporation, 15 341–43
Pamour Porcupine Mines, Ltd., **IV** 164
The Pampered Chef, Ltd., 18 406–08
Pamplemousse, **14** 225
Pan American Banks, **II** 336
Pan American Petroleum & Transport Co., **IV** 368–70
Pan American World Airways, Inc., I 20, 31, 44, 64, 67, 89–90, 92, 99, 103–04, 112–13, **115–16**, 121, 124, 126, 129, 132, 248, 452, 530, 547–48; **III** 536; **6** 51, 65–66, 71, 74–76, 81–82, 103–05, 110–11, 123, 129–30; **9** 231, 417; **10** 561; **11** 266; **12** 191, **379–81 (upd.)**, 419; **13** 19; **14** 73
Pan European Publishing Co., **IV** 611
Pan Geo Atlas Corporation, **18** 513
Pan Ocean, **IV** 473
Pan-Alberta Gas Ltd., **16** 11
Panacon Corporation, **III** 766; **22** 545
Panagra, **I** 547–48
Panama Refining and Petrochemical Co., **IV** 566
PanAmSat, **18** 211, 213
Panarctic Oils, **IV** 494
Panasonic, **9** 180; **10** 125; **12** 470
Panatech Research & Development Corp., **III** 160
Panavia Consortium, **I** 74–75
Pandair, **13** 20
Pandel, Inc., **8** 271

Pandick Press Inc., **23** 63
Panhandle Eastern Corporation, I 377, 569; **IV** 425; **V 691–92**; **10** 82–84; **11** 28; **14** 135; **17** 21
Panhandle Oil Corp., **IV** 498
Panhandle Power & Light Company, **6** 580
Panhard, **I** 194
Panhard-Levassor, **I** 149
Panificadora Bimbo, **19** 191
AB Pankakoski, **IV** 274
Panmure Gordon, **II** 337
Panocean Storage & Transport, **6** 415, 417
Panola Pipeline Co., **7** 228
Panosh Place, **12** 168
Pansophic Systems Inc., **6** 225
Pantepec Oil Co., **IV** 559, 570
Pantera Energy Corporation, **11** 27
Pantheon Books, **13** 429
Panther, **III** 750
Panther Express International Company, **6** 346
Pantry Pride Inc., **I** 668; **II** 670, 674; **III** 56; **23** 407–08
Pants Corral, **II** 634
Papa John's International, Inc., 15 344–46; **16** 447
Pape and Co., Ltd., **10** 441
Papelera Navarra, **IV** 295; **19** 226
Papelería Calparsoro S.A., **IV** 325
Papeles Venezolanos C.A., **17** 281
The Paper Factory of Wisconsin, Inc., **12** 209
Paper Makers Chemical Corp., **I** 344
Paper Recycling International, **V** 754
Paper Software, Inc., **15** 322
Paper Stock Dealers, Inc., **8** 476
Paperituote Oy, **IV** 347–48
PaperMate, **III** 28; **23** 54
Paperwork Data-Comm Services Inc., **11** 64
Papeterie de Pont Sainte Maxence, **IV** 318
Papeteries Aussedat, **III** 122
Papeteries Boucher S.A., **IV** 300
Les Papeteries de la Chapelle-Darblay, **IV** 258–59, 302, 337
Papeteries de Lancey, 23 366–68
Les Papeteries du Limousin, **19** 227
Papeteries Navarre, **III** 677; **16** 121
Papierfabrik Salach, **IV** 324
Papierwaren Fleischer, **IV** 325
Papierwerke Waldhof-Aschaffenburg AG, **IV** 323–24
Papyrus Design Group, **IV** 336; **15** 455
Para-Med Health Services, **6** 181–82
Parade Gasoline Co., **7** 228
Paradyne, **22** 19
Paragon, **IV** 552
Paramax, **6** 281–83
Parametric Technology Corp., 16 405–07
Paramount Communications, **16** 338; **19** 403–04
Paramount Oil Company, **18** 467
Paramount Paper Products, **8** 383
Paramount Pictures Corporation, I 451–52; **II** 129, 135, 146–47, **154–56**, 171, 173, 175, 177; **IV** 671–72, 675; **7** 528; **9** 119, 428–29; **10** 175; **12** 73, 323; **19** 404; **21** 23–25; **23** 503
Parasitix Corporation. *See* Mycogen Corporation.
Paravision International, **III** 48; **8** 343
Parcelforce, **V** 498

PARCO, **V** 184–85
Parcor, **I** 676
Parfums Chanel, **12** 57
Parfums Christian Dior, **I** 272
Parfums Rochas, **I** 670; **III** 68; **8** 452
Parfums Stern, **III** 16
Pargas, **I** 378
Paribas. *See* Compagnie Financiere de Paribas.
Paridoc and Giant, **12** 153
Paris Corporation, 22 411–13
Paris Group, **17** 137
Paris Playground Equipment, **13** 319
Parisian, Inc., 14 374–76; 19 324–25
Park Consolidated Motels, Inc., **6** 187; **14** 105
Park Corp., 22 414–16
Park Drop Forge Co. *See* Park-Ohio Industries Inc.
Park Hall Leisure, **II** 140
Park Inn International, **11** 178
Park Ridge Corporation, **9** 284
Park View Hospital, Inc., **III** 78
Park-Ohio Industries Inc., 17 371–73
Parkdale Wines, **I** 268
Parke, Davis & Co. *See* Warner-Lambert Co.
Parke-Bernet, **11** 453
Parker, **III** 33
Parker Appliance Co., **III** 601–02
Parker Brothers, **II** 502; **III** 505; **10** 323; **16** 337; **21** 375
Parker Drilling Company of Canada, **9** 363
Parker Hannifin Corporation, III 601–03; 21 108
Parker Pen Corp., **III** 218; **9** 326
Parker's Pharmacy, Inc., **15** 524
Parkinson Cowan, **I** 531
Parkmount Hospitality Corp., **II** 142
Parks Box & Printing Co., **13** 442
Parks-Belk Co., **19** 324
Parkway Distributors, **17** 331
Parr's Bank, **II** 334; **III** 724
Parson and Hyman Co., Inc., **8** 112
The Parsons Corporation, III 749; 8 415–17
Parsons Place Apparel Company, **8** 289
Partek Corporation, **11** 312
Partex, **IV** 515
Parthenon Insurance Co., **III** 79
Participating Annuity Life Insurance Co., **III** 182; **21** 14
La Participation, **III** 210
Partlow Corporation, **7** 116
Partnership Pacific Ltd., **II** 389
Parts Industries Corp., **III** 494–95
PartyLite Gifts, Inc., **18** 67, 69
Pascale & Associates, **12** 476
Paschen Contractors Inc., **I** 585
Pasha Pillows, **12** 393
Pasminco, **IV** 61
Pass & Seymour, **21** 348–49
Patagonia, **16** 352; **18** 376; **21** 193. *See also* Lost Arrow Inc.
Patak Spices Ltd., **18** 247
Pataling Rubber Estates Syndicate, **III** 697, 699
Patch Rubber Co., **19** 277–78
Patchoque-Plymouth Co., **IV** 371
PATCO. *See* Philippine Airlines, Inc.
Patent Arms Manufacturing Company, **12** 70
Patent Nut & Bolt Co., **III** 493
Patent Slip and Dock Co., **I** 592

La Paternelle, **III** 210
Paternoster Stores plc, **V** 108
Paterson Candy Ltd., **22** 89
Paterson, Simons & Co., **I** 592
Path-Tek Laboratories, Inc., **6** 41
Pathé. *See* Chargeurs International.
Pathé Cinéma, **6** 374
Pathe Communications Co., **IV** 676; **7** 529
Pathé Fréres, **IV** 626; **19** 203
Pathmark Stores, Inc., II 672–74; **9** 173; **15** 260; **18** 6; **19** 479, 481; **23 369–71**
Patience & Nicholson, **III** 674
Patient Care, Inc., **13** 150
Patil Systems, **11** 56
Patino N.V., **17** 380
Patriot American Hospitality, Inc., **21** 184
Patriot Co., **IV** 582
Patriot Life Insurance Co., **III** 193
Patterson Dental Co., 19 289–91
Patterson Industries, Inc., **14** 42
Pattison & Bowns, Inc., **IV** 180
Patton Electric Company, Inc., **19** 360
Patton Paint Company. *See* PPG Industries, Inc.
Paul A. Brands, **11** 19
Paul Boechat & Cie, **21** 515
Paul C. Dodge Company, **6** 579
Paul H. Rose Corporation, **13** 445
Paul Harris Stores, Inc., 15 245; **18 409–12**
Paul Koss Supply Co., **16** 387
Paul Marshall Products Inc., **16** 36
Paul Masson, **I** 285
The Paul Revere Corporation, 12 382–83
Paul Wahl & Co., **IV** 277
Paul Williams Copier Corp., **IV** 252; **17** 28
Paul Wurth, **IV** 25
Pauls Plc, **III** 699
Pavallier, **18** 35
Pawnee Industries, Inc., **19** 415
Paxall, Inc., **8** 545
Pay 'N Pak Stores, Inc., 9 399–401; 16 186–88
Pay 'n Save Corp., **12** 477; **15** 274; **17** 366
Pay Less, **II** 601, 604
Paychex, Inc., 15 347–49
Payless Cashways, Inc., 11 384–86; 13 274
Payless DIY, **V** 17, 19
PayLess Drug Stores, **12** 477–78; **18** 286; **22** 39
Payless ShoeSource, Inc., V 132, 135; **13** 361; **18 413–15**
PBF Corp. *See* Paris Corporation.
PBL. *See* Publishing and Broadcasting Ltd.
PC Globe, Inc., **13** 114
PC Realty, Canada Ltd., **III** 340
PCA-Budafok Paperboard Ltd., **12** 377
PCI Acquisition, **11** 385
PCI/Mac-Pak Group, **IV** 261
PCI Services, Inc. *See* Cardinal Health, Inc.
PCL Industries Ltd., **IV** 296; **19** 226
PCO, **III** 685
PCS Health Systems Inc., **12** 333
PDA Inc., **19** 290
PDO. *See* Petroleum Development Oman.
PDQ Transportation Inc., **18** 226
PDVSA. *See* Petróleos de Venezuela S.A.
Peabody Coal Company, I 559; **III** 248; **IV** 47, 169–71, 576; **7** 387–88; **10 447–49**

Peabody Holding Company, Inc., IV 19, **169–72; 6** 487; **7** 209
Peabody, Riggs & Co., **II** 427
Peachtree Doors, **10** 95
Peachtree Federal Savings and Loan Association of Atlanta, **10** 92
Peachtree Software Inc., **18** 364
Peak Oilfield Service Company, **9** 364
The Peak Technologies Group, Inc., 14 377–80
Peakstone, **III** 740
Peapod LP, **22** 522
Pearce-Uible Co., **14** 460
Pearl Health Services, **I** 249
Pearl Package Co., Ltd., **IV** 327
Pearle Vision, Inc., I 688; **12** 188; **13 390–92; 14** 214; **23** 329
Pearson plc, IV 611, 652, **657–59; 14** 414
Peat Marwick. *See* KPMG Peat Marwick.
Peaudouce, **IV** 339
Peavey Electronics Corporation, II 494; **12** 81; **16 408–10**
Pebble Beach Corp., **II** 170
PEC Plastics, **9** 92
Pechelbronn Oil Company, **III** 616; **17** 416–17
Pechiney, I 190, 341; **IV** 12, 59, 108, **173–75**, 560; **V** 605; **12** 253–54; **14** 216
Péchiney-Saint-Gobain, **I** 389; **III** 677; **16** 121
PECO Energy Company, 11 387–90
Pedigree Petfoods, **22** 298
Peebles Inc., 16 411–13
Peel-Conner Telephone Works, **II** 24
Peerless, **III** 467; **8** 74; **11** 534
Peerless Gear & Machine Company, **8** 515
Peerless Industries, Inc., **III** 569; **20** 360
Peerless Paper Co., **IV** 310; **19** 266
Peerless Pump Co., **I** 442
Peerless Spinning Corporation, **13** 532
Peerless Systems, Inc., **17** 263
Peet's Coffee, **13** 493; **18** 37
Pegulan, **I** 426–27
PEI. *See* Process Engineering Inc.
Peine, **IV** 201
Pekema Oy, **IV** 470–71
Peko-Wallsend Ltd., **13** 97
Pel-Tex Oil Co., **IV** 84; **7** 188
Pelican and British Empire Life Office, **III** 372
Pelican Homestead and Savings, **11** 107
Pelican Insurance Co., **III** 349
Pelican Life Assurance, **III** 371–72
Pelikan Holding AG, **18** 388
Pella Corporation, 10 95; **12 384–86; 22** 346
Pelto Oil Company, **14** 455
Pemex. *See* Petróleos Mexicanos.
Peñarroya, **IV** 107–08
Penda Corp., **19** 415
Pendexcare Ltd., **6** 181
Penguin Publishing Co. Ltd., **IV** 585, 659
Peninsular and Oriental Steam Navigation Company, II 296; **III** 521–22, 712; **V 490–93; 22** 444
Peninsular and Oriental Steam Navigation Company (Bovis Division), I 588–89
Peninsular Portland Cement, **III** 704
Peninsular Power, **6** 602
Peninsular Railroad Company, **17** 440
Penn Central Corp., **I** 435; **II** 255; **IV** 576; **10** 71, 73, 547; **17** 443
Penn Champ Co., **9** 72

Penn Controls, III 535–36
Penn Corp., 13 561
Penn Cress Ice Cream, 13 393
Penn Fuel Co., IV 548
Penn Health, III 85
Penn Square Bank, II 248, 262
Penn Traffic Company, 8 409–10; **13** 95, **393–95**
Penn-American Refining Co., IV 489
Penn-Texas Corporation, I 434; 12 71
Penn-Western Gas and Electric, 6 524
Pennaco Hosiery, Inc., 12 93
Pennington Drug, III 10
Pennroad Corp., IV 458
Pennsalt Chemical Corp., I 383
Pennsylvania Blue Shield, III 325–27
Pennsylvania Coal & Coke Corp., I 434
Pennsylvania Coal Co., IV 180
Pennsylvania Electric Company, 6 535
Pennsylvania Farm Bureau Cooperative Association, 7 17–18
Pennsylvania General Fire Insurance Assoc., III 257
Pennsylvania Glass Sand Co., I 464; 11 198
Pennsylvania House, Inc., 10 324; 12 301
Pennsylvania International Raceway, V 494
Pennsylvania Power & Light Company, V 676, 693–94; 11 388
Pennsylvania Pump and Compressor Co., II 16
Pennsylvania Railroad, I 456, 472; II 329, 490; 6 436; 10 71–73
Pennsylvania Refining Co., IV 488–89
Pennsylvania Salt Manufacturing Co., I 383
Pennsylvania Steel Co., IV 35; 7 48
Pennwalt Corporation, I 382 84; IV 547; 12 18; 21 205
Penny Curtiss Baking Co., Inc., 13 395
Pennzoil Company, IV 488–90, 551, 553; 10 190; 14 491, 493; 20 418–22 (upd.); 23 40–41
Penray, I 373
Penrod Drilling Corporation, 7 228, 558
Pension Benefit Guaranty Corp., III 255; 12 489
Penske Corporation, V 494–95; 19 223, 292–94 (upd.); 20 263
Pentair, Inc., III 715; 7 419–21; 11 315
Pental Insurance Company, Ltd., 11 523
Pentane Partners, 7 518
Pentaverken A.B., I 209
Pentech Corp., 14 217
Pentland Group plc, 20 423–25
Pentland Industries, V 375
Penton, 9 414
People Express Airlines Inc., I 90, 98, 103, 117–18, 123–24, 129–30; 6 129; 21 142; 22 220
People That Love (PTL) Television, 13 279
People's Bank of Halifax, II 210
People's Bank of New Brunswick, II 210
People's Drug Store, II 604–05; 22 37–38
People's Ice and Refrigeration Company, 9 274
People's Insurance Co., III 368
People's Natural Gas, IV 548; 6 593
People's Trust Co. of Brooklyn, II 254; 9 124
Peoples Bancorp, 14 529
Peoples Bank, 13 467; 17 302
Peoples Bank of Youngstown, 9 474

Peoples Energy Corporation, 6 543–44
Peoples Finance Co., II 418
Peoples Gas Light & Coke Co., IV 169; 6 529, 543–44
Peoples Gas Light Co., 6 455
Peoples Jewelers of Canada, 16 561
Peoples Life Insurance Co., III 218
Peoples Natural Gas Company of South Carolina, 6 576
Peoples Restaurants, Inc., 17 320–21
Peoples Savings of Monroe, 9 482
Peoples Security Insurance Co., III 219
PeopleSoft Inc., 11 78; 14 381–83
The Pep Boys–Manny, Moe & Jack, 11 391–93; 16 160
PEPCO. *See* Portland Electric Power Company *and* Potomac Electric Power Company.
Pepe Clothing Co., 18 85
Pepperell Manufacturing Company, 16 533–34
Pepperidge Farms, I 29; II 480–81; 7 67–68
PepsiCo, Inc., I 234, 244–46, 257, 269, 276–79, 281, 291; II 103, 448, 477, 608; III 106, 116, 588; 7 265, 267, 396, 404, 434–35, 466, 505–06; 8 399; 9 177, 343; 10 130, 199, 227, 324, **450–54 (upd.);** 11 421, 450; 12 337, 453; 13 162, 284, 448, 494; 15 72, 75, 380; 16 96; 18 65; 19 114, 221; 21 143, 313, 315–16, 362, 401, 405, 485–86; 22 95, 353; 23 418, 420
Pepsodent Company, I 14; 9 318
Perception Technology, 10 500
Percy Bilton Investment Trust Ltd., IV 710
Percy Street Investments Ltd., IV 711
Perdue Farms Inc., 7 422–24, 432; 23 375–78 (upd.)
Perfect Circle Corp., I 152
Perfect Fit Industries, 17 182–84
Perfect-Ventil GmbH, 9 413
Performance Contracting, Inc., III 722; 20 415
Performance Technologies, Inc., 10 395
Perfumania, Inc., 22 157
Pergamon Holdings, 15 83
Pergamon Press, IV 611, 641–43, 687; 7 311–12
Perini Corporation, 8 418–21
Perisem, I 281
The Perkin-Elmer Corporation, III 455, 727; 7 425–27; 9 514; 13 326; 21 123
Perkins, I 147; 12 90
Perkins Bacon & Co., 10 267
Perkins Cake & Steak, 9 425
Perkins Engines Ltd., III 545, 652; 10 274; 11 472; 19 294
Perkins Family Restaurants, L.P., 22 417–19
Perkins Oil Well Cementing Co., III 497
Perkins Products Co., II 531
Perl Pillow, 19 304
Perland Environmental Technologies Inc., 8 420
Permaneer Corp., IV 281; 9 259. *See also* Spartech Corporation.
Permanent General Companies, Inc., 11 194
Permanente Cement Co., I 565
Permanente Metals Corp., IV 15, 121–22
Permian Corporation, V 152–53
PERMIGAN, IV 492
Permodalan, III 699

Pernod Ricard S.A., I 248, 280–81; 21 399–401 (upd.)
Pernvo Inc., I 387
Perot Systems, 13 482
Perret-Olivier, III 676; 16 120
Perrier, 19 50
Perrier Corporation of America, 16 341
Perrigo Company, 12 218, 387–89
Perrin, IV 614
Perrot Brake Co., I 141
Perrow Motor Freight Lines, 6 370
Perry Drugs, 12 21
Perry Ellis, 16 37
Perry Manufacturing Co., 16 37
Perry Sports, 13 545; 13 545
Perry's Shoes Inc., 16 36
Perscombinatie, IV 611
Pershing & Co., 22 189
Personal Care Corp., 17 235
Personal Performance Consultants, 9 348
Personal Products Company, III 35; 8 281, 511
Perstorp A.B., I 385–87
PERTAMINA, IV 383, 461, 491–93, 517, 567
Pertec Computer Corp., 17 49; 18 434
Pertech Computers Ltd., 18 75
Perusahaan Minyak Republik Indonesia, IV 491
Peruvian Corp., I 547
Pet Food & Supply, 14 385
Pet Incorporated, I 457; II 486–87; 7 428–31; 10 554; 12 124; 13 409; 14 214
Pete's Brewing Company, 18 72, 502; 22 420–22
Peter Bawden Drilling, IV 570
Peter, Cailler, Kohler, Chocolats Suisses S.A., II 546; 7 381
Peter Cundill & Associates Ltd., 15 504
Peter Gast Shipping GmbH, 7 40
Peter J. Schmitt Co., 13 394
Peter J. Schweitzer, Inc., III 40; 16 303
Peter Jones, V 94
Peter Kiewit Sons' Inc., I 599–600; III 198; 8 422–24; 15 18
Peter Norton Computing Group, 10 508–09
Peter Paul/Cadbury, II 477, 512; 15 221
Peterbilt Motors Co., I 185–86
Peters Shoe Co., III 528
Peters-Revington Corporation. *See* Chromcraft Revington, Inc.
Petersen Publishing Company, 21 402–04
Peterson, Howell & Heather, V 496
Peterson Soybean Seed Co., 9 411
La Petite Academy, 13 299
Petite Sophisticate, V 207–08
Petrie Stores Corporation, 8 425–27
Petrini's, II 653
Petro/Chem Environmental Services, Inc., IV 411
Petro-Canada Limited, IV 367, 494–96, 499; 13 557
Petro-Coke Co. Ltd., IV 476
Petro-Lewis Corp., IV 84; 7 188
Petroamazonas, IV 511
Petrobas, 21 31
Petrobel, IV 412
Petrobrás. *See* Petróleo Brasileiro S.A.
Petrocarbona GmbH, IV 197–98
Petrocel, S.A., 19 12
Petrochemical Industries Co., IV 451
Petrochemicals Company, 17 90–91
Petrochemie Danubia GmbH, IV 486–87

Petrochim, **IV** 498
Petrocomercial, **IV** 511
Petrocorp. *See* Petroleum Company of New Zealand.
Petroecuador. *See* Petróleos del Ecuador.
Petrofertil, **IV** 501
Petrofina, **IV** 455, 495, **497–500**, 576; **7** 179
Petrogal. *See* Petróleos de Portugal.
Petroindustria, **IV** 511
Petrol, **IV** 487
Petrol Ofisi Anonim Sirketi, **IV** 564
Petrolane Properties, **17** 558
Petróleo Brasileiro S.A., **IV** 424, **501–03**
Petróleo Mecânica Alfa, **IV** 505
Petróleos de Portugal S.A., **IV** **504–06**
Petróleos de Venezuela S.A., **II** 661; **IV** 391–93, **507–09**, 571
Petróleos del Ecuador, **IV** **510–11**
Petróleos Mexicanos, **IV** 512–14, 528; **19** 10, **295–98 (upd.)**
Petroleum and Chemical Corp., **III** 672
Petroleum Authority of Thailand, **IV** 519
Petroleum Company of New Zealand, **IV** 279; **19** 155
Petroleum Development (Qatar) Ltd., **IV** 524
Petroleum Development (Trucial States) Ltd., **IV** 363
Petroleum Development Corp. of the Republic of Korea, **IV** 455
Petroleum Development Oman LLC, **IV** **515–16**
Petroleum Projects Co., **IV** 414
Petroleum Research and Engineering Co. Ltd., **IV** 473
Petrolgroup, Inc., **6** 441
Petroliam Nasional Bhd. *See* Petronas.
Petrolite Corporation, **15** **350–52**
Petrolube, **IV** 538
Petromex. *See* Petróleos de Mexico S.A.
Petromin Lubricating Oil Co., **17** 415
Petronas, **IV** 517–20; **21** 501
Petronor, **IV** 514, 528
Petropeninsula, **IV** 511
Petroproduccion, **IV** 511
Petroquímica de Venezuela SA, **IV** 508
Petroquimica Española, **I** 402
Petroquisa, **IV** 501
PETROSUL, **IV** 504, 506
Petrotransporte, **IV** 511
PETsMART, Inc., **14** **384–86**
Petstuff, Inc., **14** 386
Pettibone Corporation, **19** 365
Petzazz, **14** 386
Peugeot S.A., **I** 163, **187–88**; **II** 13; **III** 508; **11** 104
Pfaff-Pegasus of U.S.A. Inc., **15** 385
The Pfaltzgraff Co. *See* Susquehanna Pfaltzgraff Company.
Pfaudler Vacuum Co., **I** 287
PFCI. *See* Pulte Financial Companies, Inc.
PFI Acquisition Corp., **17** 184
Pfizer, Hoechst Celanese Corp., **8** 399
Pfizer Inc., **I** 301, 367, **661–63**, 668; **9** 356, **402–05 (upd.)**; **10** 53–54; **11** 207, 310–11, 459; **12** 4; **17** 131; **19** 105
Pflueger Corporation, **22** 483
PGE. *See* Portland General Electric.
PGH Bricks and Pipes, **III** 735
Phaostron Instruments and Electronic Co., **18** 497–98
Phar-Mor Inc., **12** 209, **390–92**, 477; **18** 507; **21** 459; **22** 157

Pharma Plus Drugmarts, **II** 649–50
Pharmacia A.B., **I** 211, **664–65**
Pharmaco Dynamics Research, Inc., **10** 106–07
Pharmacom Systems Ltd., **II** 652
Pharmacy Corporation of America, **16** 57
PharmaKinetics Laboratories, Inc., **10** 106
Pharmaprix Ltd., **II** 663
Pharmazell GmbH, **IV** 324
Pharmedix, **11** 207
Pharos, **9** 381
Phelan & Collender, **III** 442
Phelan Faust Paint, **8** 553
Phelps Dodge Corporation, **IV** 33, **176–79**, 216; **7** 261–63, 288; **19** 375
Phenix Bank, **II** 312
Phenix Cheese Corp., **II** 533
Phenix Insurance Co., **III** 240
Phenix Mills Ltd., **II** 662
PHF Life Insurance Co., **III** 263; **IV** 623
PHH Corporation, **V** **496–97**; **6** 357; **22** 55
Phibro Corporation, **II** 447–48; **IV** 80; **13** 447–48; **21** 67
Philadelphia and Reading Corp., **I** 440; **II** 329; **6** 377
Philadelphia Carpet Company, **9** 465
Philadelphia Coke Company, **6** 487
Philadelphia Company, **6** 484, 493
Philadelphia Drug Exchange, **I** 692
Philadelphia Electric Company, **V** **695–97**; **6** 450
Philadelphia Life, **I** 527
Philadelphia Smelting and Refining Co., **IV** 31
Philco Corp., **I** 167, 531; **II** 86; **III** 604; **13** 402
Philip Environmental Inc., **16** **414–16**
Philip Morris Companies Inc., **I** 23, 269; **II** 530–34; **V** 397, 404, **405–07**, 409, 417; **6** 52; **7** 272, 274, 276, 548; **8** 53; **9** 180; **12** 337, 372; **13** 138, 517; **15** 64, 72–73, 137; **18** 72, **416–19 (upd.)**; **19** 112, 369; **20** 23; **22** 73, 338; **23** 427
Philipp Abm. Cohen, **IV** 139
Philipp Bros., Inc., **II** 447; **IV** 79–0
Philipp Holzmann AG, **II** 279, 386; **14** 169; **16** 284, 286; **17** **374–77**
Philippine Airlines, Inc., **I** 107; **6** **106–08**, 122–23; **23** **379–82 (upd.)**
Philippine American Life Insurance Co., **III** 195
Philippine Sinter Corp., **IV** 125
Philips, **V** 339; **6** 101; **10** 269; **22** 194
Philips Electronics N.V., **8** 153; **9** 75; **10** 16; **12** 475, 549; **13** 396, **400–03 (upd.)**; **14** 446; **23** 389
Philips Electronics North America Corp., **13** **396–99**
N.V. Philips Gloeilampenfabriken, **I** 107, 330; **II** 25, 56, 58, **78–80**, 99, 102, 117, 119; **III** 479, 654–55; **IV** 680; **12** 454. *See also* Philips Electronics N.V.
Phillip Hawkins, **III** 169; **6** 285
Phillip Securities, **16** 14
Phillippe of California, **8** 16
Phillips & Drew, **II** 379
Phillips & Jacobs, Inc., **14** 486
Phillips Cables, **III** 433
Phillips Carbon Black, **IV** 421
Phillips Colleges, **22** 442
Phillips Manufacturing Company, **8** 464
Phillips Petroleum Company, **I** 377; **II** 15, 408; **III** 752; **IV** 71, 290, 366, 405,

412, 414, 445, 453, 498, **521–23**, 567, 570–71, 575; **10** 84, 440; **11** 522; **13** 356, 485; **17** 422; **19** 176
Phillips Sheet and Tin Plate Co., **IV** 236
PHLCorp., **11** 261
PHM Corp., **8** 461
Phoenix Assurance Co., **III** 242, 257, 369, 370–74
Phoenix Financial Services, **11** 115
Phoenix Fire Office, **III** 234
Phoenix Insurance Co., **III** 389; **IV** 711
Phoenix Microsystems Inc., **13** 8
Phoenix Mutual Life Insurance, **16** 207
Phoenix Oil and Transport Co., **IV** 90
Phoenix State Bank and Trust Co., **II** 213
Phoenix Technologies Ltd., **13** 482
Phoenix-Rheinrohr AG, **IV** 222
Phone America of Carolina, **8** 311
Phonogram, **23** 389
Photocircuits Corp., **18** 291–93
PHP Healthcare Corporation, **22** **423–25**
Phuket Air Catering Company Ltd., **6** 123–24
Physician Sales & Service, Inc., **14** **387–89**
Physician's Weight Loss Center, **10** 383
Physicians Formula Cosmetics, **8** 512
Physicians Placement, **13** 49
Physio-Control International Corp., **18** **420–23**
Piaggio & C. S.p.A., **17** 24; **20** **426–29**
Pic 'N' Save, **17** 298–99
PIC Realty Corp., **III** 339
Picault, **19** 50
Piccadilly Cafeterias, Inc., **19** **299–302**
Pick, **III** 98
Pick-N-Pay, **II** 642; **9** 452
Pickands Mather, **13** 158
Picker International Corporation, **II** 25; **8** 352
Pickfords Ltd., **6** 412–14
Pickland Mather & Co., **IV** 409
PickOmatic Systems, **8** 135
Pickwick, **I** 613
Pickwick Dress Co., **III** 54
Pickwick International, **9** 360
Piclands Mather, **7** 308
Picture Classified Network, **IV** 597
PictureTel Corp., **10** **455–57**
Piece Goods Shops, **16** 198
Piedmont Airlines, **6** 132; **12** 490
Piedmont Coca-Cola Bottling Partnership, **10** 223
Piedmont Concrete, **III** 739
Piedmont Pulp and Paper Co. *See* Westvaco Corporation.
Pier 1 Imports, Inc., **12** 179, 200, **393–95**
Pierburg GmbH, **9** 445–46
Pierce, **IV** 478
Pierce Brothers, **6** 295
Pierce National Life, **22** 314
Pierce Steam Heating Co., **III** 663
Pierre Frozen Foods Inc., **13** 270–72
Pierson, Heldring, and Pierson, **II** 185
Pietro's Pizza Parlors, **II** 480–81
Piezo Electric Product, Inc., **16** 239
Pig Improvement Co., **II** 500
Piggly Wiggly Southern, Inc., **II** 571, 624; **13** 251–52, **404–06**; **18** 6, 8; **21** 455; **22** 127
Pignone, **IV** 420
Pike Adding Machine, **III** 165
Pike Corporation of America, **I** 570; **8** 191
Pikrose and Co. Ltd., **IV** 136

Pilgrim Curtain Co., **III** 213

Pilgrim's Pride Corporation, **7 432–33**; **23 383–85 (upd.)**

Pilkington plc, **I** 429; **II** 475; **III** 56, 641–42, 676–77, 714–15, **724–27**; **16** 7, 9, 120–21; **22** 434

Pillar Holdings, **IV** 191

Pilliod Furniture, Inc., **12** 300

Pillowtex Corporation, **19 303–05**

Pillsbury Company, **II** 133, 414, 493–94, 511, **555–57**, 575, 613–15; **7** 106, 128, 277, 469, 547; **8** 53–54; **10** 147, 176; **11** 23; **12** 80, 510; **13 407–09 (upd.)**, 516; **14** 212, 214; **15** 64; **16** 71; **17** 70–71, 434; **22** 59, 426

Pilot, **I** 531

Pilot Insurance Agency, **III** 204

Pinal-Dome Oil, **IV** 569

Pinault-Printemps-Redoute S.A., **15** 386; **19 306–09 (upd.)**; **22** 362

Pincus & Co., **7** 305

Pine Tree Casting. *See* Sturm, Ruger & Company, Inc.

Pinecliff Publishing Company, **10** 357

Pinelands, Inc., **9** 119

Pineville Kraft Corp., **IV** 276

Pinewood Studios, **II** 157

Pininfarina, **I** 188

Pinkerton's Inc., **9 406–09**; **13** 124–25; **14** 541; **16** 48

Pinnacle West Capital Corporation, **6 545–47**

Pinsetter Corp., **III** 443

Pinto Island Metals Company, **15** 116

Pioneer Airlines, **I** 96; **21** 141

Pioneer Asphalt Co., **I** 404

Pioneer Asphalts Pty. Ltd., **III** 728

Pioneer Concrete Services Ltd., **III** 728–29

Pioneer Cotton Mill, **12** 503

Pioneer Electronic Corporation, **II** 103; **III 604–06**

Pioneer Federal Savings Bank, **10** 340; **11** 115

Pioneer Financial Corp., **11** 447

Pioneer Hi-Bred International, Inc., **9 410–12**; **17** 131; **21** 387

Pioneer International Limited, **III** 687, **728–30**

Pioneer Life Insurance Co., **III** 274

Pioneer Natural Gas Company, **10** 82

Pioneer Readymixed Concrete and Mortar Proprietary Ltd., **III** 728

Pioneer Saws Ltd., **III** 598

Pioneer-Standard Electronics Inc., **13** 47; **19 310–14**

Pipe Line Service Company. *See* Plexco.

Pipeline and Products Marketing Co., **IV** 473

Piper Aircraft Corp., **I** 482; **II** 403; **8** 49–50

Piper Jaffray Companies Inc., **22 426–30**, 465

Pirelli S.p.A., **IV** 174, 420; **V 249–51**; **10** 319; **15 353–56 (upd.)**; **16** 318; **21** 73

Piscataquis Canal and Railroad Company, **16** 348

Pisces Inc., **13** 321

Pispalan Werhoomo Oy, **I** 387

The Piston Ring Company, **I** 199; **10** 492

Pitcairn Aviation, **I** 101

Pitney Bowes, Inc., **III 156–58**, 159; **19 315–18 (upd.)**

Pittsburgh & Lake Angeline Iron Company, **13** 156

Pittsburgh & Lake Erie Railroad, **I** 472

Pittsburgh Aluminum Alloys Inc., **12** 353

Pittsburgh Brewing Co., **10** 169–70; **18** 70, 72

Pittsburgh Chemical Co., **IV** 573; **7** 551

Pittsburgh Consolidation Coal Co., **8** 346

Pittsburgh Corning Corp., **III** 683

Pittsburgh Life, **III** 274

Pittsburgh National Bank, **II** 317, 342; **22** 55

Pittsburgh National Corp., **II** 342

Pittsburgh Paint & Glass. *See* PPG Industries, Inc.

Pittsburgh Plate Glass Co. *See* PPG Industries, Inc.

Pittsburgh Railway Company, **9** 413

Pittsburgh Reduction Co., **II** 315; **IV** 9, 14

Pittsburgh Steel Company, **7** 587

Pittsburgh Trust and Savings, **II** 342

The Pittston Company, **IV 180–82**, 566; **10** 44; **19 319–22 (upd.)**

Pittway Corporation, **9 413–15**

Pixel Semiconductor, **11** 57

Pizitz, Inc., **19** 324

Pizza Dispatch. *See* Dominos's Pizza, Inc.

Pizza Hut Inc., **I** 221, 278, 294; **II** 614; **7** 152–53, 267, **434–35**, 506; **10** 450; **11** 50; **12** 123; **13** 336, 516; **14** 107; **15** 344–46; **16** 446; **17** 71, 537; **21** 24–25, 315, **405–07 (upd.)**; **22** 353

Pizza Inn, **16** 447

PizzaCo, Inc., **7** 152

PJS Publications, **22** 442

PKbanken, **II** 353

Place Two, **V** 156

Placer Cego Petroleum Ltd., **IV** 367

Placer Development Ltd., **IV** 19

Placer Dome Inc., **IV** 571; **20 430–33**

Placid Oil Co., **7** 228

Plaid Holdings Corp., **9** 157

Plain Jane Dress Company, **8** 169

Plainwell Paper Co., Inc., **8** 103

Planet Hollywood International, Inc., **18 424–26**

Planet Insurance Co., **III** 343

Plank Road Brewery, **I** 269; **12** 337

Plankinton Packing Co., **III** 534

Plant Genetics Inc., **I** 266; **21** 320

Planters Lifesavers, **14** 274–75

Planters Nut & Chocolate Co., **I** 219; **II** 544

Plas-Techs, Inc., **15** 35

Plastic Coating Corporation, **IV** 330; **8** 483

Plastic Containers, Inc., **15** 129

Plastic Engineered Products Company. *See* Ballard Medical Products.

Plastic Parts, Inc., **19** 277

Plasticos Metalgrafica, **I** 231

Plastics, Inc., **13** 41

Plastrier. *See* Compagnie de Saint-Gobain S.A.

Plateau Holdings, Inc., **12** 260; **13** 502

PLATINUM Technology, Inc., **14 390–92**

Platt & Co., **I** 506

Platt Bros., **III** 636

Platt's Price Service, Inc., **IV** 636–37

Play It Again Sports, **18** 207–08

Playboy Enterprises, Inc., **18 427–30**

Players International, Inc., **16** 263, 275; **19** 402; **22 431–33**

Playland, **16** 389

Playmates Toys, **23 386–88**

Playskool, Inc., **III** 504, 506; **12** 169; **13** 317; **16** 267

Playtex Products, Inc., **II** 448, 468; **8** 511; **13** 448; **15 357–60**

Playworld, **16** 389–90

Plaza Coloso S.A. de C.V., **10** 189

Plaza Medical Group, **6** 184

Plaza Securities, **I** 170

Pleasurama PLC, **I** 248; **12** 228

Plessey Company, PLC, **II** 25, 39, **81–82**; **IV** 100; **6** 241

Plews Manufacturing Co., **III** 602

Plexco, **7** 30–31

Plezall Wipers, Inc., **15** 502

Plitt Theatres, Inc., **6** 162; **23** 126

Plon et Juillard, **IV** 614

Plough Inc., **I** 684

Plum Associates, **12** 270

Plumb Tool, **II** 16

Plus Development Corporation, **10** 458–59

Plus Mark, Inc., **7** 24

Plus System Inc., **9** 537

Plus-Ultra, **II** 196

Ply Gem Industries Inc., **12 396–98**; **23** 225

Plymouth County Electric Co., **14** 124

Plymouth Mills Inc., **23** 66

PMC Contract Research AB, **21** 425

PMC Specialties Group, **III** 745

PMI Corporation, **6** 140

PMI Mortgage Insurance Company, **10** 50

PMS Consolidated, **8** 347

PN Pertambangan Minyak Dan Gas Bumi Negara, **IV** 492

PNC Bank Corp., **13 410–12 (upd.)**; **14** 103; **18** 63

PNC Financial Corporation, **II** 317, **342–43**; **9** 476; **17** 114

Pneumo Abex Corp., **I** 456–58; **III** 512; **10** 553–54

Pneumo Dynamics Corporation, **8** 409

PNL. *See* Pacific Northwest Laboratories.

PNM. *See* Public Service Company of New Mexico.

PNP. *See* Pacific Northwest Power Company.

POAS, **IV** 563

POB Polyolefine Burghausen GmbH, **IV** 487

Pocket Books, Inc., **10** 480; **13** 559–60

Poclain Company, **10** 380

Pogo Producing, **I** 441

Pohang Iron and Steel Company Ltd., **IV 183–85**; **17** 351

Pohjan Sellu Oy, **IV** 316

Pohjoismainen Osakepankki, **II** 302

Pohjola Voima Oy, **IV** 348

Pohjolan Osakepankki, **II** 303

Point Chehalis Packers, **13** 244

Polak & Schwarz Essencefabricken, **9** 290

Polar Manufacturing Company, **16** 32

Polar Star Milling Company, **7** 241

Polaris Industries Inc., **I** 530; **12 399–402**; **16** 31–32

Polaroid Corporation, **I** 30–31; **II** 412; **III** 475–77, 549, 584, **607–09**; **IV** 330; **7** 161–62, **436–39 (upd.)**; **12** 180

Polbeth Packaging Limited, **12** 377

Policy Management Systems Corporation, **11 394–95**

Polioles, S.A. de C.V., **19** 10, 12

Politos, S.A. de C.V., **23** 171

Pollenex Corp., **19** 360

Polo Food Corporation, **10** 250

Polo/Ralph Lauren Corporation, **9** 157; **12 403–05**; **16** 61

Polser, **19** 49, 51
Poly P, Inc., **IV** 458
Poly Version, Inc., **III** 645
Poly-Glas Systems, Inc., **21** 65
Poly-Hi Corporation, **8** 359
Polyblend Corporation, **7** 4
Polycell Holdings, **IV** 666; **17** 397
Polydesign België, **16** 421
Polydesign Nederland, **16** 421
Polydor B.V., **23** 389
Polydor KK, **23** 390
Polydress Plastic GmbH, **7** 141
PolyGram N.V., **13** 402; **22** 194; **23**
    389–92
Polyken Technologies, **11** 220
Polysar Energy & Chemical Corporation of
    Toronto, **V** 674
Polysius AG, **IV** 89
Pomeroy's, **16** 61
Pommersche Papierfabrik Hohenkrug, **III**
    692
Pommery et Greno, **II** 475
Ponderosa Steakhouse, **7** 336; **12** 373; **14**
    331; **15 361–64**
Ponderosa System Inc., **12** 199
Pont-à-Mousson S.A., **III** 675, 677–78,
    704; **16** 119, 121–22; **21** 253
Pontiac, **III** 458; **10** 353
Pontificia, **III** 207
Ponto Frio Bonzao, **22** 321
Pony Express, **II** 380–81, 395
Poorman-Douglas Corporation, **13** 468
Pope and Talbot, Inc., **12 406–08**
Pope Cable and Wire B.V., **19** 45
Pope Tin Plate Co., **IV** 236
Popeye's/Church's, **23** 115, 117
Popeyes Famous Fried Chicken and
    Biscuits, Inc., **7** 26–28
Pophitt Cereals, Inc., **22** 337
Poppe Tyson Inc., **23** 479
Poppin' Fresh Pies, Inc., **12** 510
Popsicle, **II** 573; **14** 205
Popular Aviation Company, **12** 560
Popular Club Plan, **12** 280
Popular Merchandise, Inc., **12** 280
Pori, **IV** 350
Poron Diffusion, **9** 394
Porsche AG, **13** 28, 219, **413–15**
Port Blakely Mill Company, **17** 438
Port Harcourt Refining Co., **IV** 473
Port Stockton Food Distributors, Inc., **16**
    451, 453
Portage Industries Corp., **19** 415
Portals Water Treatment, **11** 510
Porter Shoe Manufacturing Company, **13**
    360
Portland General Corporation, **6 548–51**
Portland Heavy Industries, **10** 369
Portland-Zementwerke Heidelberg A.G., **23**
    326
Portnet, **6** 435
Portways, **9** 92
Poseidon Exploration Ltd., **IV** 84; **7** 188
Posey, Quest, Genova, **6** 48
Post Office Counters, **V** 496
Post Office Group, **V 498–501**
PostBank, **II** 189
La Poste, **V 470–72**
Posti- Ja Telelaitos, **6 329–31**
PostScript, **17** 177
Postum Cereal Company, **II** 497, 523,
    530–31; **7** 272–73; **13** 291
Potash Corporation of Saskatchewan
    Inc., **18** 51, **431–33**

Potlatch Corporation, **IV** 282; **8 428–30**;
    9 260; **19** 445
Potomac Electric Power Company, **6**
    552–54
Potomac Insurance Co., **III** 257
Potomac Leasing, **III** 137
Potter & Brumfield Inc., **11 396–98**
Pottery Barn, **13** 42; **17** 548–50
Potts, **IV** 58
Poulan/Weed Eater. *See* White
    Consolidated Industries Inc.
Poulsen Wireless, **II** 490
PowCon, Inc., **17** 534
Powell Duffryn, **III** 502; **IV** 38
Powell Energy Products, **8** 321
Powell River Co. Ltd., **IV** 306–07
Power Applications & Manufacturing
    Company, Inc., **6** 441
Power Financial Corp., **III** 260–61
Power Jets Ltd., **I** 81
Power Parts Co., **7** 358
Power Products, **8** 515
Power Specialty Company, **6** 145
Power Team, **10** 492
PowerFone Holdings, **10** 433
PowerGen PLC, **11 399–401**; **12** 349; **13**
    458, 484
Powerhouse, **13** 485
Powers Accounting Machine Company, **6**
    240
Powers Regulator, **III** 535
Powers-Samas, **6** 240
PowerSoft Corp., **11** 77; **15** 374
Pozzi-Renati Millwork Products, Inc., **8**
    135
PP&L. *See* Pennsylvania Power & Light
    Company.
PPG Industries, Inc., **I** 330, 341–42; **III**
    21, 641, 667, 676, 722, 725, **731–33**; **8**
    153, 222, 224; **16** 120–21; **20** 415; **21**
    221, 223; **22** 147, **434–37 (upd.)**
PR Holdings, **23** 382
PR Newswire, **IV** 687
Prac, **I** 281
Practical and Educational Books, **13** 105
Practical Business Solutions, Inc., **18** 112
Pragma Bio-Tech, Inc., **11** 424
Prairie Farmer Publishing Co., **II** 129
Prairie Holding Co., **IV** 571
Prairie Oil and Gas Co., **IV** 368
Prairielands Energy Marketing, Inc., **7** 322,
    325
Prakla Seismos, **17** 419
Pratt & Whitney, **I** 47, 78, 82–85, 128,
    434; **II** 48; **III** 482; **6** 128; **7** 456; **9** 14,
    16–18, 244–46, **416–18**; **10** 162; **11**
    299, 427; **12** 71; **13** 386; **14** 564
Pratt Holding, Ltd., **IV** 312; **19** 268
Pratt Hotel Corporation, **21** 275; **22** 438
Pratt Properties Inc., **8** 349
Praxair, Inc., **11 402–04**; **16** 462
Praxis Biologics, **8** 26
Pre-Fab Cushioning, **9** 93
Pre-Paid Legal Services, Inc., **20 434–37**
Precious Metals Development, **IV** 79
Precise Imports Corp., **21** 516
Precision Castparts Corp., **15 365–67**
Precision Games, **16** 471
Precision Interconnect Corporation, **14** 27
Precision LensCrafters, **13** 391
Precision Optical Co., **III** 120, 575
Precision Optical Industry Company, Ltd.
    See Canon Inc.
Precision Power, Inc., **21** 514

Precision Software Corp., **14** 319
Precision Studios, **12** 529
Precision Tube Formers, Inc., **17** 234
Precor, **III** 610–11
Predica, **II** 266
Predicasts Inc., **12** 562; **17** 254
Preferred Medical Products. *See* Ballard
    Medical Products.
Preferred Products, Inc., **II** 669; **18** 504
PREINCO Holdings, Inc., **11** 532
PREL&P. *See* Portland Railway Electric
    Light & Power Company.
Prelude Corp., **III** 643
Premark International, Inc., **II** 534; **III**
    610–12; **14** 548
Premex A.G., **II** 369
Premier (Transvaal) Diamond Mining Co.,
    IV 65–66
Premier & Potter Printing Press Co., Inc.,
    II 37
Premier Brands Foods, **II** 514
Premier Consolidated Oilfields PLC, **IV**
    383
Premier Cruise Lines, **6** 368
Premier Diamond Mining Company, **7** 122
Premier Health Alliance Inc., **10** 143
Premier Industrial Corporation, **9**
    419–21; **19** 311
Premier Milling Co., **II** 465
Premier Radio Networks, Inc., **23** 292, 294
Premier Sport Group Inc., **23** 66
Premiere Products, **I** 403
Premisteres S.A., **II** 663
Prémontré, **III** 676; **16** 120
Prentice Hall Computer Publishing, **10** 24
Prentice Hall Inc., **I** 453; **IV** 672; **19** 405;
    23 503
Prescott Ball & Turben, **III** 271; **12** 60
Prescott Investors, **14** 303
Prescription Learning Corporation, **7** 256
Présence, **III** 211
La Preservatrice, **III** 242
Preserves and Honey, Inc., **II** 497
President Casinos, Inc., **22 438–40**
President Riverboat Casino-Mississippi
    Inc., **21** 300
Presidential Airlines, **I** 117
Presidents Island Steel & Wire Company.
    See Laclede Steel Company.
Presidio Oil Co., **III** 197; **IV** 123
Press Associates, **IV** 669; **19** 334
Press Trust of India, **IV** 669
Presse Pocket, **IV** 614
Pressed Steel Car Co., **6** 395
Presses de la Cité, **IV** 614–15
Pressware International, **12** 377
Prest-O-Lite Co., Inc., **I** 399; **9** 16, 516; **11**
    402
Prestige et Collections, **III** 48
Prestige Fragrance & Cosmetics, Inc., **22**
    158
The Prestige Group plc., **19** 171
Prestige Properties, **23** 388
Presto Products, Inc., **II** 609–10; **IV** 187;
    19 348
Preston Corporation, **6 421–23**; **14** 566,
    568
Prestone Products Corp., **22** 32
Pretty Neat Corp., **12** 216
Pretty Paper Inc., **14** 499
Pretty Polly, **I** 429
Preussag AG, **I** 542–43; **II** 386; **IV** 109,
    201, 231; **17 378–82**; **21** 370

Preussenelektra Aktiengesellschaft, I 542; **V 698–700**
Preval, **19** 49–50
Previews, Inc., **21** 96
Priam Corporation, **10** 458
Price Club, **V** 162–64
Price Co. Ltd., **IV** 246–47
Price Company, **II** 664; **V 162–64**; **14** 393–94
Price Enterprises, Inc., **14** 395
Price Waterhouse, III 84, 420, 527; **9 422–24**; **14** 245
PriceCostco, Inc., 14 393–95
Pricel, **6** 373; **21** 103
Prichard and Constance, **III** 65
Pride & Clarke, **III** 523
Pride Petroleum Services. *See* DeKalb Genetics Corporation.
Priggen Steel Building Co., **8** 545
Primadonna Resorts Inc., **17** 318
Primark Corp., 10 89–90; **13 416–18**
Prime Computer, Inc. *See* Computervision Corporation.
Prime Motor Inns Inc., **III** 103; **IV** 718; **11** 177; **17** 238
Prime Telecommunications Corporation, **8** 311
The Prime-Mover Co., **13** 267
PrimeAmerica, **III** 340
Primedia Inc., 7 286; **12** 306; **21** 403–04; **22 441–43**; **23** 156, 158, 344, 417
Primerica Corporation, I 597, 599–602, 604, 607–09, **612–14**, 615; **II** 422; **III** 283 **8** 118; **9** 218–19, 360–61; **11** 29; **15** 464. *See also* American Can Co.
PriMerit Bank, **19** 412
Primes Régal Inc., **II** 651
Primex Fibre Ltd., **IV** 328
Primo Foods Ltd., **I** 457; **7** 430
Prince Co., **II** 473
Prince Gardner Company, **17** 465; **23** 21
Prince Golf International, Ltd., **23** 450
Prince Motor Co. Ltd., **I** 184
Prince of Wales Hotels, PLC, **14** 106
Prince Sports Group, Inc., 15 368–70
Prince Street Technologies, Ltd., **8** 271
Prince William Bank, **II** 337; **10** 425
Princess Cruise Lines, IV 256; **22 444–46**
Princess Dorothy Coal Co., **IV** 29
Princess Hotel Group, **21** 353
Princess Metropole, **21** 354
Princeton Gas Service Company, **6** 529
Princeton Laboratories Products Company, **8** 84
Princeton Review, **12** 142
Principal Mutual Life Insurance Company, III 328–30
Principles, **V** 21–22
Princor Financial Services Corp., **III** 329
Pringle Barge Line Co., **17** 357
Print Technologies, Inc., **22** 357
Printex Corporation, **9** 363
Printronix, Inc., 14 377–78; **18 434–36**
Priority Records, **22** 194
Pripps Ringnes, **18** 394, 396–97
Prism Systems Inc., **6** 310
Prismo Universal, **III** 735
Prisunic SA, **V** 9–11; **19** 307–09
Pritchard Corporation. *See* Black & Veatch, Inc.
Pritzker & Pritzker, **III** 96–97
Privatbanken, **II** 352

Pro-Fac Cooperative, Inc., **7** 104–06; **21** 154–55, 157
Pro-Lawn, **19** 250
Process Engineering Inc., **21** 108
Process Systems International, **21** 108
Procino-Rossi Corp., **II** 511
Procor Limited, **16** 357
Procordia Foods, **II** 478; **18** 396
Procter & Gamble Company, I 34, 129, 290, 331, 366; **II** 478, 493, 544, 590, 684, 616; **III** 20–25, 36–38, 40–41, 44, **50–53**; **IV** 282, 290, 329–30; **6** 26–27, 50–52, 129, 363; **7** 277, 300, 419; **8** 63, 106–07, 253, 282, 344, 399, **431–35 (upd.)**, 477, 511–12; **9** 260, 291, 317–19, 552; **10** 54, 288; **11** 41, 421; **12** 80, 126–27, 439; **13** 39, 197, 199, 215; **14** 121–22, 262, 275; **15** 357; **16** 302–04, 440; **18** 68, 147–49, 217, 229; **22** 146–47, 210
Proctor & Collier, **I** 19
Proctor & Schwartz, **17** 213
Proctor-Silex. *See* Hamilton Beach/Proctor-Silex Inc.
Prodigy, Inc., **10** 237–38; **12** 562; **13** 92
Product Components, Inc., **19** 415
Productos Ortiz, **II** 594
Produits Chimiques Ugine Kuhlmann, **I** 303; **IV** 547
Profarmaco Nobel S.r.l., **16** 69
Professional Care Service, **6** 42
Professional Computer Resources, Inc., **10** 513
Professional Education Systems, Inc., **17** 272
Professional Health Care Management Inc., **14** 209
Professional Research, **III** 73
Proffitt's, Inc., 19 323–25, 510, 512
Profile Extrusion Company, **22** 337
Profimatics, Inc., **11** 66
PROFITCo., **II** 231
Progil, **I** 389
Progress Development Organisation, **10** 169
Progress Software Corporation, 15 371–74
Progressive Corporation, 11 405–07
Progressive Distributors, **12** 220
Progressive Grocery Stores, **7** 202
Progresso, **I** 514; **14** 212
Projiis, **II** 356
Prolabo, **I** 388
Proland, **12** 139
Proler International Corp., **13** 98; **19** 380–81
Promigas, **IV** 418
Promotional Graphics, **15** 474
Promstroybank, **II** 242
Promus Companies, Inc., III 95; **9 425–27**; **15** 46; **16** 263; **22** 537
Pronto Pacific, **II** 488
Prontophot Holding Limited, **6** 490
Prontor-Werk Alfred Gauthier GmbH, **III** 446
Propaganda Films, Inc., **23** 389, 391
Prophet Foods, **I** 449
Propwix, **IV** 605
Prosim, S.A., **IV** 409
ProSource Distribution Services, Inc., **16** 397; **17** 475
Prospect Farms, Inc., **II** 584; **14** 514
The Prospect Group, Inc., **11** 188

Prospect Provisions, Inc. *See* King Kullen Grocery Co., Inc.
Prospectors Airways, **IV** 165
Protective Closures, **7** 296–97
La Protectrice, **III** 346–47
Protek, **III** 633
Proto Industrial Tools, **III** 628
Protogene Laboratories Inc., **17** 288
Proventus A.B., **II** 303
Provi-Soir, **II** 652
Provi-Viande, **II** 652
Provibec, **II** 652
La Providence, **III** 210–11
Providence National Bank, **9** 228
Providence Steam and Gas Pipe Co. *See* Grinnell Corp.
Providencia, **III** 208
Provident Bank, **III** 190
Provident Institution for Savings, **13** 467
Provident Life and Accident Insurance Company of America, III 331–33, 404
Provident National Bank, **III** 342
Provident Services, Inc., **6** 295
Provident Travelers Mortgage Securities Corp., **III** 389
Provigo Inc., II 651–53; **12** 413
Les Provinces Réunies, **III** 235
Provincetown-Boston Airlines, **I** 118
Provincial Bank of Ireland Ltd., **16** 13
Provincial Engineering Ltd, **8** 544
Provincial Gas Company, **6** 526
Provincial Insurance Co., **III** 373
Provincial Newspapers Ltd., **IV** 685–86
Provincial Traders Holding Ltd., **I** 437
Provinzial-Hülfskasse, **II** 385
Provost & Provost, **II** 651
PROWA, **22** 89
Proximity Technology, **23** 210
Prudential Bache Securities, **9** 441
Prudential Corporation plc, II 319; **III 334–36**; **IV** 711; **8** 276–77
Prudential Insurance Company of America, I 19, 334, 402; **II** 103, 456; **III** 79, 92, 249, 259, 265–67, 273, 291–93, 313, 329, **337–41**; **IV** 410, 458; **10** 199; **11** 243; **12** 28, 453, 500; **13** 561; **14** 95, 561; **16** 135, 497; **17** 325; **22** 266; **23** 226
Prudential Oil & Gas, Inc., **6** 495–96
Prudential Refining Co., **IV** 400
Prudential Steel, **IV** 74
Prudential-Bache Trade Corporation, **II** 51; **21** 331
PSA. *See* Pacific Southwest Airlines.
PSA Peugeot-Citroen Group, **7** 35
PSCCo. *See* Public Service Company of Colorado.
PSE, Inc., **12** 100
PSI. *See* Process Systems International.
PSI Resources, 6 555–57
Psychiatric Institutes of America, **III** 87–88
Psychological Corp., **IV** 623; **12** 223
PT Components, **14** 43
PT PERMINA, **IV** 492, 517
PTI Communications, Inc. *See* Pacific Telecom, Inc.
PTT Telecom BV, **V** 299–301; **6** 303
PTV. *See* Österreichische Post- und Telegraphenverwaltung.
Pubco Corporation, 17 383–85
Publi-Graphics, **16** 168
Public Home Trust Co., **III** 104
Public National Bank, **II** 230

Public Savings Insurance Co., **III** 219
Public Service Co., **14** 124
Public Service Company of Colorado, 6 558–60
Public Service Company of Indiana. *See* PSI Energy.
Public Service Company of New Hampshire, 21 408–12
Public Service Company of New Mexico, 6 561–64
Public Service Electric and Gas Company, **IV** 366; **V** 701–03; **11** 388
Public Service Enterprise Group, **V** 701–03
Public Storage, Inc., **21** 476
Public/Hacienda Resorts, Inc. *See* Santa Fe Gaming Corporation.
Publicis S.A., 13 204; **19** 329–32; **21** 265–66; **23** 478, 480
Publicker Industries Inc., **I** 226; **10** 180
Publishers Clearing House, 23 393–95
Publishers Paper Co., **IV** 295, 677–78; **19** 225
Publishers Press Assoc., **IV** 607
Publishing and Broadcasting Ltd., **19** 400–01
Publix Super Markets Inc., II 155, 627; **7** 440–42; **9** 186; **20** 84, 306; **23** 261
Puente Oil, **IV** 385
Puerto Rican Aqueduct and Sewer Authority, **6** 441
Puerto Rican-American Insurance Co., **III** 242
Puget Mill Company, **12** 406–07
Puget Sound Alaska Van Lines. *See* Alaska Hydro-Train.
Puget Sound National Bank, **8** 469–70
Puget Sound Power And Light Company, 6 565–67
Puget Sound Pulp and Timber Co., **IV** 281; **9** 259
Puget Sound Tug and Barge Company, **6** 382
Pulitzer Publishing Company, 15 375–77
Pullman Co., **II** 403; **III** 94, 744
Pullman Savings and Loan Association, **17** 529
Pullman Standard, **7** 540
Pulsar Internacional S.A., 21 413–15
Pulte Corporation, 8 436–38; **22** 205, 207
Puma, **14** 6–7; **17** 244
AB Pump-Separator, **III** 418–19
Punchcraft, Inc., **III** 569; **20** 360
Purdue Fredrick Company, **13** 367
Pure Milk Products Cooperative, **11** 24
Pure Oil Co., **III** 497; **IV** 570
Pure Packed Foods, **II** 525; **13** 293
Purex Corporation, **I** 450; **III** 21; **22** 146
Purex Pool Systems, **I** 13, 342; **18** 163
Purfina, **IV** 497
Puris Inc., **14** 316
Puritan Chemical Co., **I** 321
Puritan Fashions Corp., **22** 122
Puritan-Bennett Corporation, 13 419–21
Purity Stores, **I** 146
Purity Supreme, Inc., **II** 674
Purle Bros., **III** 735
Purnell & Sons Ltd., **IV** 642; **7** 312
Purodenso Co., **III** 593
Purolator Courier, Inc., **6** 345–46, 390; **16** 397; **18** 177
Purolator Products Company, III 593; **21** 416–18
Puros de Villa Gonzales, **23** 465

Puss 'n Boots, **II** 559
Putnam Management Co., **III** 283
Putnam Reinsurance Co., **III** 198
Putt-Putt Golf Courses of America, Inc., 23 396–98
PWA Group, IV 323–25
PWS Holding Corporation, **13** 406
PWT Projects Ltd., **22** 89
PWT Worldwide, **11** 510
PYA Monarch, **II** 675
Pyramid Communications, Inc., **IV** 623
Pyramid Electric Company, **10** 319
Pyramid Electronics Supply, Inc., **17** 275
Pyramid Technology Corporation, **10** 504
Pytchley Autocar Co. Ltd., **IV** 722
Pyxis. *See* Cardinal Health, Inc.
Pyxis Resources Co., **IV** 182

Q Lube, Inc., **18** 145
Qantas Airways Limited, I 92–93; **6** 79, 91, 100, 105, **109–13**, 117; **14** 70, 73
Qatar General Petroleum Corporation, IV 524–26
Qintex Australia Ltd., **II** 150
QO Chemicals, Inc., **14** 217
QSP, Inc., **IV** 664
Quad/Graphics, Inc., 19 333–36
Quaker Fabric Corp., 19 337–39
Quaker Oats Company, I 30; **II** 558–60, 575, 684; **12** 167, 169, 409–12 (upd.); **13** 186; **22** 131, 337–38
Quaker State Corporation, 7 443–45; **21** 419–22 (upd.)
Qualcomm Inc., 20 438–41
Qualicare, Inc., **6** 192
QualiTROL Corporation, **7** 116–17
Quality Bakers of America, **12** 170
Quality Care Inc., **I** 249
Quality Courts Motels, Inc., **14** 105
Quality Dining, Inc., 18 437–40
Quality Food Centers, Inc., 17 386–88; **22** 271, 273
Quality Importers, **I** 226; **10** 180
Quality Inns International, **13** 363; **14** 105
Quality Markets, Inc., **13** 393
Quality Oil Co., **II** 624–25
Quality Paperback Book Club (QPB), **13** 105–07
Quality Products, Inc., **18** 162
Qualtec, Inc., **V** 623
Quanex Corporation, 13 422–24
Quantum Chemical Corporation, 8 439–41; **11** 441
Quantum Corporation, 6 230–31; **10** 56, 403, **458–59**, 463
Quantum Overseas N.V., **7** 360
Quarex Industries, Inc. *See* Western Beef, Inc.
Quarrie Corporation, **12** 554
Quasi-Arc Co., **I** 315
Quebec Bank, **II** 344
Québec Hydro-Electric Commission. *See* Hydro-Québec.
Quebecor Inc., 12 412–14; **19** 333
Queen Casuals, **III** 530
Queen Insurance Co., **III** 350
Queens Isetan Co., Ltd., **V** 87
Queensland Alumina, **IV** 59
Queensland and Northern Territories Air Service. *See* Qantas Airways Limited.
Queensland Mines Ltd., **III** 729
Queensland Oil Refineries, **III** 672
Queiroz Pereira, **IV** 504
Quelle Group, V 165–67

Quennessen, **IV** 118
Quesarias Ibéricas, **23** 219
Quesnel River Pulp Co., **IV** 269
Quest Aerospace Education, Inc., **18** 521
Questar Corporation, 6 568–70; **10** 432
Questor, **I** 332
The Quick & Reilly Group, Inc., 18 552; **20** 442–44
QUICK Corp., **IV** 656
Quick-Shop, **II** 619
Quickie Designs, **11** 202, 487–88
Quik Stop Markets, Inc., **12** 112
Quiksilver, Inc., 18 441–43
QuikWok Inc., **II** 556; **13** 408
Quilter Goodison, **II** 260
Quimica Industrial Huels Do Brasil Ltda., **I** 350
Quimicos Industriales Penoles. *See* Industrias Penoles, S.A. de C.V.
Quincy Compressor Co., **I** 434–35
Quincy Family Steak House, **II** 679; **10** 331; **19** 287
Quintana Roo, Inc., **17** 243, 245
Quintiles Transnational Corporation, 21 423–25
Quinton Hazell Automotive, **III** 495; **IV** 382–83
Quintron, Inc., **11** 475
Quintus Computer Systems, **6** 248
Quixote Corporation, 15 378–80
Quixx Corporation, **6** 580
Quoddy Products Inc., **17** 389, 390
Quotron, **III** 119; **IV** 670; **9** 49, 125
QVC Network Inc., 9 428–29; **10** 175; **12** 315; **18** 132; **20** 75

R & B Manufacturing Co., **III** 569; **20** 361
R.A. Waller & Co., **III** 282
R. and W. Hawaii Wholesale, Inc., **22** 15
R-B. *See* Arby's, Inc.
R. Buckland & Son Ltd., **IV** 119
R-Byte, **12** 162
R-C Holding Inc. *See* Air & Water Technologies Corporation.
R.C. Bigelow, **16** 90
R.C. Willey Home Furnishings, **18** 60
R. Cubed Composites Inc., **I** 387
R.E. Funsten Co., **7** 429
R.G. Barry Corp., 17 389–91
R.G. Dun-Bradstreet Corp., **IV** 604–05
R. Griggs Group Limited, 23 399–402
R.H. Macy & Co., Inc., I 30; **V** 168–70; **8** 442–45 (upd.); **10** 282; **11** 349; **13** 42; **15** 281; **16** 206–07, 328, 388, 561; **23** 60
R.H. Squire, **III** 283
R.H. Stengel & Company, **13** 479
R. Hoe & Co., **I** 602; **13** 189
R. Hornibrook (NSW), **I** 592
R.J. Brown Co., **IV** 373
R.J. Reynolds, **I** 259, 261, 363; **II** 542, 544; **III** 16; **IV** 523; **V** 396, 404–05, 407–10, 413, 415, 417–18; **7** 130, 132, 267, 365, 367; **9** 533; **13** 490; **14** 78; **15** 72–73; **16** 242; **18** 416; **19** 369; **21** 315. *See also* RJR Nabisco.
R.K. Brown, **14** 112
R.L. Crain Limited, **15** 473
R.L. Manning Company, **9** 363–64
R.L. Polk & Co., 10 460–62
R.N. Coate, **I** 216
R.O. Hull Co., **I** 361
R.P. Scherer, I 678–80
R.R. Bowker Co., **17** 398; **23** 440

R.R. Donnelley & Sons Company, IV 660–62, 673; **9 430–32 (upd.)**; **11** 293; **12** 414, 557, 559; **18** 331; **19** 333
R.S. Stokvis Company, **13** 499
R. Scott Associates, **11** 57
R. Stock AG, **IV** 198
R.T. French USA, **II** 567
R.T. Securities, **II** 457
R.W. Harmon & Sons, Inc., **6** 410
R.W. Sears Watch Company, **V** 180
RABA PLC, **10** 274
Rabbit Software Corp., **10** 474
Racal Electronics PLC, II 83–84; **11** 408, 547
Racal-Datacom Inc., 11 408–10
Racine Hardware Co., **III** 58
Racine Hidraulica, **21** 430
Racine Threshing Machine Works, **10** 377
Rack Rite Distributors, **V** 174
Rada Corp., **IV** 250
Radiant Lamp Corp., **13** 398
Radiation Dynamics, **III** 634–35
Radiation, Inc., **II** 37–38
Radiation-Medical Products Corp., **I** 202
Radiator Specialty Co., **III** 570; **20** 362
Radio & Allied Industries, **II** 25
Radio & Television Equipment Company (Radio-Tel), **16** 200–01
Radio Austria A.G., **V** 314–16
Radio Corporation of America. *See* RCA Corporation.
Radio Receptor Company, Inc., **10** 319
Radio Shack, **II** 106–08; **12** 470; **13** 174
Radio-Keith-Orpheum, **II** 32, 88, 135, 146–48, 175; **III** 428; **9** 247; **12** 73
Radiometer A/S, **17** 287
Radiometrics, Inc., **18** 369
Radiotelevision Española, **7** 511
Radisson Hotels Worldwide, **22** 126–27
Radium Pharmacy, **I** 704
Radius Inc., 16 417–19
Radix Group, Inc., **13** 20
Radnor Venture Partners, LP, **10** 474
Raf, Haarla Oy, **IV** 349
Raffineriegesellschaft Vohburg/Ingolstadt mbH, **7** 141
Ragazzi's, **10** 331
Ragnar Benson Inc., **8** 43–43
RAI, **I** 466
RailTex, Inc., 20 445–47
Railway Express Agency, **I** 456; **II** 382; **6** 388–89
Railway Maintenance Equipment Co., **14** 43
Railway Officials and Employees Accident Assoc., **III** 228
Railway Passengers Assurance Co., **III** 178, 410
Rainbow Crafts, **II** 502; **10** 323
Rainbow Home Shopping Ltd., **V** 160
Rainbow Production Corp., **I** 412
Rainbow Programming Holdings, **7** 63–64
Rainbow Resources, **IV** 576
Rainer Pulp & Paper Company, **17** 439
Rainfair, Inc., **18** 298, 300
Rainier Brewing Company, 23 403–05
Rajastan Breweries, Ltd., **18** 502
Raky-Danubia, **IV** 485
Ralcorp Holdings, Inc., **13** 293, 425, 427; **15** 189, 235; **21** 53, 56; **22** 337. *See also* Ralston Purina Company.
Raley's Inc., 14 396–98
Ralli International, **III** 502; **IV** 259

Rally's Inc., **14** 452; **15** 345; **16** 96–97; **23** 225
Rallye S.A., **12** 154. *See also* Casino.
Ralph & Kacoo's. *See* Piccadilly Cafeterias, Inc.
Ralph Lauren. *See* Polo/Ralph Lauren Corportion.
The Ralph M. Parsons Company. *See* The Parsons Corporation.
Ralph Wilson Plastics, **III** 610–11
Ralphs Grocery Co., **17** 558, 560–61
Ralston Purina Company, I 608, II 544, 560, 561–63, 617; **III** 588; **6** 50–52; **7** 209, 396, 547, 556; **8** 180; **9** 180; **12** 276, 411, 510; **13** 137, 270, 293, **425–27 (upd.)**; **14** 194–95, 558; **18** 312; **21** 56; **23** 191. *See also* Ralcorp Holdings, Inc.
Ram dis Ticaret, **I** 479
Ram Golf Corp., **III** 24
Ram's Insurance, **III** 370
Ramada International Hotels & Resorts, **II** 142; **III** 99; **IV** 718; **9** 426; **11** 177; **13** 66; **21** 366
Ramazotti, **I** 281
Ramo-Woolridge Corp., **I** 539; **14** 510
Ramón Areces Foundation, **V** 52
Ranbar Packing, Inc. *See* Western Beef, Inc.
Ranchers Packing Corp. *See* Western Beef, Inc.
Rand American Investments Limited, **IV** 79; **21** 211
Rand Drill Co., **III** 525
Rand Group, Inc., **6** 247
Rand Mines Ltd., **I** 422; **IV** 22, 79, 94
Rand Selection Corp. Ltd., **IV** 79
Random House, Inc., II 90; **IV** 583–84, 637, 648; **13** 113, 115, 178, **428–30**; **14** 260; **18** 329; **19** 6, 285
Randstad Holding n.v., 16 420–22
Randsworth Trust P.L.C., **IV** 703
Rank Organisation PLC, II 139, 147, 157–59; **III** 171; **IV** 698; **6** 288; **12** 229; **14 399–402 (upd.)**
Ranks Hovis McDougall PLC, II 157, 564–65
Ransburg Corporation, **22** 282
Ransom and Randolph Company, **10** 271
Ransomes America Corp., **III** 600
Rapicom, **III** 159
Rapid American, **I** 440
Rapides Bank & Trust Company, **11** 107
Rapifax of Canada, **III** 160
Rare Hospitality International Inc., 19 340–42
RAS. *See* Riunione Adriatica di Sicurtà SpA.
Rassini Rheem, **III** 581
Rational GmbH, **22** 354
Rational Systems Inc., **6** 255
Rauland Corp., **II** 124; **13** 573
Rauma-Repola Oy, **II** 302; **IV** 316, 340, 349–50
Rauscher Pierce Refsnes, Inc., **15** 233
Raven Press, **14** 555
Ravenhead, **16** 120
Ravenna Metal Products Corp., **12** 344
Ravenseft Properties Ltd., **IV** 696, 704–05
RAVIcad, **18** 20
Rawlings Sporting Goods, **7** 177; **23** 449
Rawlplug Co. Ltd., **IV** 382–83
Rawls Brothers Co., **13** 369
Rawson, Holdsworth & Co., **I** 464

Ray Industries, **22** 116
Ray Strauss Unlimited, **22** 123
Ray's Printing of Topeka, **II** 624
Raychem Corporation, III 492; **8 446–47**
Raycom Sports, **6** 33
Raymar Book Corporation, **11** 194
Raymond, Jones & Co., **IV** 647
Raymond, Trice & Company, **14** 40
Raynet Corporation, **8** 447
Rayovac Corporation, 13 431–34; **17** 105; **23** 497
Raytheon Company, I 463, 485, 544; II 41, 73, **85–87**; **III** 643; **8** 51, 157; **11** 197, **411–14 (upd.)**; **12** 46, 247; **14** 223; **17** 419, 553, 564; **21** 200; **23** 181
Razorback Acquisitions, **19** 455
RB&W Corp., **17** 372
RCA Corporation, I 142, 454, 463; II 29–31, 34, 38, 56, 61, 85–86, **88–90**, 96, 102, 117–18, 120, 124, 129, 132–33, 151–52, 313, 609, 645; **III** 118, 122, 132, 149, 152, 165, 171, 569, 653–54; **IV** 252, 583, 594; **6** 164–66, 240, 266, 281, 288, 334; **7** 520; **8** 157; **9** 283; **10** 173; **11** 197, 318, 411; **12** 204, 208, 237, 454, 544, 548; **13** 106, 398, 429, 506, 573; **14** 357, 436; **16** 549; **17** 29; **20** 361; **21** 151; **22** 541; **23** 181
RCG International, Inc., **III** 344
REA. *See* Railway Express Agency.
Rea & Derick, **II** 605
Rea Construction Company, **17** 377
Rea Magnet Wire Co., **IV** 15
React-Rite, Inc., **8** 271
Read, R.L., **II** 417
Read-Rite Corp., 10 403–04, 463–64; **18** 250
The Reader's Digest Association, Inc., IV 663–64; **17 392–95 (upd.)**
Reader's Garden Inc., **22** 441
Reading and Bates, **III** 559
Reading Railroad, **9** 407
Ready Mixed Concrete, **III** 687, 737–40
Real Decisions, **21** 236
Real-Share, Inc., **18** 542
RealCom Communications Corporation, **15** 196
Reale Mutuale, **III** 273
Really Useful Holdings, **23** 390
Realty Development Co. *See* King Kullen Grocery Co., Inc.
Realty Parking Properties II L.P., **18** 104
Réassurances, **III** 392
Reckitt & Colman plc, II 566–67; **15** 46, 360; **18** 556; **22** 148
Reconstruction Bank of Holland, **IV** 707
Reconstruction Finance Bank, **II** 292
Reconstruction Finance Corp., **I** 67, 203; **II** 261; **IV** 10, 333
Record Bar / Licorice Pizza, **9** 361
Record World Inc., **9** 361
Recoton Corp., 15 381–83
Recoupe Recycling Technologies, **8** 104
Recovery Centers of America, **III** 88
Recreational Equipment, Inc., 18 444–47; **22** 173
Recticel S.A., **III** 581; **17** 182–84
Rectigraph Co., **III** 171
Recycled Paper Greetings, Inc., 21 426–28
Red & White, **II** 682
Red Ant Entertainment, **17** 14
Red Apple Group, Inc., 23 406–08
Red Arrow, **II** 138

Red Ball, Inc., **18** 300
Red Food Stores, Inc., **19** 327–28
Red Kap, **V** 390–91
Red L Foods, **13** 244
Red Lobster Inns of America, **16** 156–58
Red Lobster Restaurants, **II** 502–03; **6** 28;
 10 322–24; **19** 258
Red Owl Stores, Inc., **II** 670; **18** 506
Red Roof Inns, Inc., **13** 363; **18 448–49**;
 21 362
Red Rooster, **V** 35
Red Sea Insurance Co., **III** 251
Red Star Express, **14** 505
Red Star Milling Co., **II** 501; **6** 397; **10**
 322
Red Wing Shoe Company, Inc., **9**
 433–35
Redactron, **III** 166; **6** 282
Redbook Publishing Co., **14** 460
Reddy Elevator Co., **III** 467
Reddy Ice, **II** 661
Redentza, **IV** 504
Redhill Tile Co., **III** 734
Redi, **IV** 610
Rediffusion, **II** 139
Reditab S.p.A., **12** 109
Redken Laboratories, **8** 131
Redland plc, **III** 495, 688, **734–36**; **14**
 249, 739; **15** 154
Redlaw Industries Inc., **15** 247
Redman Industries, Inc., **17** 81, 83
Redmond & Co., **I** 376
La Redoute, S.A., **V** 11; **19** 306, 309
Redpath Industries, **II** 581–82
Redwood Design Automation, **11** 47; **16**
 520
Redwood Fire & Casualty Insurance Co.,
 III 214
Reebok International Ltd., **V 375–77**; **8**
 171, 303–04, 393; **9** 134–35, **436–38**
 (upd.); **11** 50–51, 349; **13** 513; **14** 8; **17**
 244–45, 260; **18** 266; **19** 112; **22** 173
Reed & Ellis, **17** 439
Reed & Gamage, **13** 243
Reed Corrugated Containers, **IV** 249
Reed Elsevier, **19** 268; **23** 271, 273
Reed International PLC, **I** 423; **IV** 270,
 642, **665–67**, 711; **7** 244–45, 343; **10**
 407; **12** 359; **17 396–99 (upd.)**; **23** 350
Reed Tool Coompany, **III** 429; **22** 68
Reeder Light, Ice & Fuel Company, **6** 592
Reedpack, **IV** 339–40, 667
Reeds Jewelers, Inc., **22 447–49**
Reese Finer Foods, Inc., **7** 429
Reese Products, **III** 569; **11** 535; **20** 361
Reeves Banking and Trust Company, **11**
 181
Reeves Brothers, **17** 182
Reeves Pulley Company, **9** 440
Refco, Inc., **10** 251; **22** 189
Reference Software International, **10** 558
Refined Sugars, **II** 582
Reflex Winkelmann & Pannhoff GmbH, **18**
 163
Reform Rt, **IV** 652; **7** 392
Refractarios Mexicanos, S.A. de C.V., **22**
 285
Refrigeração Paraná S.A., **22** 27
Regal Drugs, **V** 171
Regal Inns, **13** 364
Regal Manufacturing Co., **15** 385
Regal-Beloit Corporation, **18 450–53**
Regency, **12** 316
Regency Electronics, **II** 101

Regency International, **10** 196
Regenerative Environmental Equipment
 Company, Inc., **6** 441
Regeneron Pharmaceuticals Inc., **10** 80
Regent Canal Co., **III** 272
Regent Communications Inc., **23** 294
Regent Insurance Co., **III** 343
Regent International Hotels Limited, **9** 238
Régie Autonome des Pétroles, **IV** 544–46;
 21 202–04
Régie des Mines de la Sarre, **IV** 196
Régie des Télégraphes et Téléphones. *See*
 Belgacom.
Régie Nationale des Usines Renault, **I**
 136, 145, 148, 178–79, 183, **189–91**,
 207, 210; **II** 13; **III** 392, 523; **7** 566–67;
 11 104; **12** 91; **15** 514; **19** 50; **22** 331
Regina Verwaltungsgesellschaft, **II** 257
Regional Bell Operating Companies, **15**
 125; **18** 111–12, 373
Regis Corporation, **18 454–56**; **22** 157
Register & Tribune Co. *See* Cowles Media
 Company.
Registered Vitamin Company, **V** 171
Regnecentralen AS, **III** 164
Rego Supermarkets and American Seaway
 Foods, Inc., **9** 451; **13** 237
Rehab Hospital Services Corp., **III** 88; **10**
 252
RehabClinics Inc., **11** 367
REI. *See* Recreational Equipment, Inc.
Reich, Landman and Berry, **18** 263
Reichart Furniture Corp., **14** 236
Reichhold Chemicals, Inc., **I** 386, 524; **8**
 554; **10 465–67**
Reichs-Kredit-Gesellschaft mbH, **IV** 230
Reichs-Kredit- und Krontrollstelle GmbH,
 IV 230
Reichswerke AG für Berg- und
 Hüttenbetriebe Hermann Göring, **IV** 200
Reichswerke AG für Erzbergbau und
 Eisenhütten, **IV** 200
Reichswerke Hermann Göring, **IV** 233
Reid Bros. & Carr Proprietary, **III** 672–73
Reid Dominion Packaging Ltd., **IV** 645
Reid Ice Cream Corp., **II** 471
Reid, Murdoch and Co., **II** 571
Reid Press Ltd., **IV** 645
Reidsville Fashions, Inc., **13** 532
Reigel Products Corp., **IV** 289
Reims Aviation, **8** 92
Rein Elektronik, **10** 459
Reinsurance Agency, **III** 204–05
Reisebüro Bangemann, **II** 164
Reisholz AG, **III** 693
Reisland GmbH, **15** 340
Reiue Nationale des Usines Renault, **7** 220
Relational Courseware, Inc., **21** 235–36
Relational Database Systems Inc., **10**
 361–62
Relational Technology Inc., **10** 361
Release Technologies, **8** 484
Reliable Stores Inc., **14** 236
Reliable Tool, **II** 488
Reliance Electric Company, **IV** 429; **9**
 439–42
Reliance Group Holdings, Inc., **II** 173;
 III 342–44; **IV** 642
Reliance Life Insurance Co., **III** 275–76
Reliance National Indemnity Company, **18**
 159
Reliance Steel & Aluminum Co., **19**
 343–45
ReLife Inc., **14** 233

Rembrandt Group, **I** 289; **IV** 91, 93, 97; **V**
 411–13; **19** 367–69
RemedyTemp, Inc., **20 448–50**
Remgro, **IV** 97
Remington Arms Company, Inc., **I** 329;
 8 152; **12 415–17**
Remington Rand, **III** 122, 126, 148, 151,
 165–66, 642; **6** 251, 265, 281–82; **10**
 255; **12** 416; **19** 430
Remmele Engineering, Inc., **17** 534
Rémy Cointreau S.A., **20 451–53**
REN Corp. USA, Inc., **13** 161
Renaissance Communications Corp., **22**
 522
Renaissance Connects, **16** 394
Renal Systems, Inc. *See* Minntech
 Corporation.
Renault. *See* Régie Nationale des Usines
 Renault.
Rendeck International, **11** 66
Rendic International, **13** 228
René Garraud, **III** 68
Rengo Co., Ltd., **IV 326**
Rennies Consolidated Holdings, **I** 470; **20**
 312
Reno Air Inc., **23 409–11**
Reno Technologies, **12** 124
Rent-A-Center, **22** 194
Rentz, **23** 219
Repco Ltd., **15** 246
REPESA, **IV** 528
Replacement Enterprises Inc., **16** 380
Repligen Inc., **13** 241
Repola Ltd., **19** 465
Repola Oy, **IV** 316, 347, 350
Repsol S.A., **IV** 396–97, 506, 514,
 527–29; **16 423–26 (upd.)**
Repubblica, **IV** 587
Republic Aircraft Co., **I** 89
Republic Airlines, **I** 113, 132; **6** 104
Republic Aviation Corporation, **I** 55; **9**
 205–07
Republic Broadcasting Corp., **23** 292
Republic Corp., **I** 447
Republic Engineered Steels, Inc., **7**
 446–47
Republic Freight Systems, **14** 567
Republic Indemnity Co. of America, **III**
 191
Republic Insurance, **III** 404
Republic National Bank, **19** 466
Republic New York Corporation, **11**
 415–19
Republic Pictures, **9** 75
Republic Powdered Metals, Inc., **8** 454
Republic Realty Mortgage Corp., **II** 289
Republic Rubber, **III** 641
Republic Steel Corp., **I** 491; **IV** 114; **7**
 446; **12** 353; **13** 169, 157; **14** 155
Republic Supply Co. of California, **I** 570
Research Analysis Corporation, **7** 15
Research Cottrell, Inc., **6** 441
Research Polymers International, **I** 321; **12**
 103
Research Publications, **8** 526
Resem SpA, **I** 387
Reserve Mining Co., **17** 356
Reservoir Productions, **17** 150
Residence Inns, **III** 103; **9** 426
Residential Funding Corporation, **10** 92–93
Resin Exchange, **19** 414
Resinous Products, **I** 392
Resolution Systems, Inc., **13** 201

Resolution Trust Corp., **10** 117, 134; **11** 371; **12** 368

Resorts International, Inc., I 452; **12** 418–20; **19** 402

Resource Associates of Alaska, Inc., **7** 376

Resource Electronics, **8** 385

ReSource NE, Inc., **17** 553

reSOURCE PARTNER, INC., **22** 95

Rest Assured, **I** 429

The Restaurant Company, **22** 417

Restaurant Enterprises Group Inc., **14** 195

Restaurant Franchise Industries, **6** 200

Restaurant Property Master, **19** 468

Restaurants Les Pres Limitée, **II** 652

Restaurants Unlimited, Inc., 13 435–37; **23** 127–29

Resurgens Communications Group, **7** 336; **8** 311

Retail Credit Company. *See* Equifax.

Retail Ventures Inc., **14** 427

Retailers Commercial Agency, Inc., **6** 24

Retequattro, **19** 19

Retirement Inns of America, Inc., **III** 16; **11** 282

Reuben H. Donnelley Corp., **IV** 605, 661; **19** 133

Reunion Properties, **I** 470; **20** 311–12

Reuters Holdings PLC, IV 259, 652, 654, 656, **668–70; 10** 277, 407; **21** 68–70; **22** 450–53 (upd.)

Revco D.S., Inc., II 449; **III** 10, **V** 171–73; **9** 67, 187; **12** 4; **13** 449; **16** 560; **19** 357

Revell-Monogram Inc., 16 427–29

Revere Copper and Brass Co., **IV** 32. *See also* The Paul Revere Corporation.

Revere Foil Containers, Inc., **12** 377

Revere Furniture and Equipment, **14** 105

Revere Ware Corporation, 22 454–56

Revlon Inc., I 29, 449, 620, 633, 668, 677, 693, 696; **II** 498, 679; **III** 29, 46, **54–57,** 727; **6** 27; **8** 131, 341; **9** 202–03, 291; **11** 8, 333–34; **12** 314; **16** 439; **17** 110, **400–04 (upd.); 18** 229; **22** 157

Revson Bros., **III** 54

Rex Pulp Products Company, **9** 304

REX Stores Corp., 10 468–69; **19** 362

Rexall Drug & Chemical Co., **II** 533–34; **III** 610; **13** 525; **14** 547

Rexel, Inc., 15 384–87

Rexene Products Co., **III** 760; **IV** 457

Rexham Inc., **IV** 259; **8** 483–84

Rexnord Corporation, I 524; **14** 43; **21** 429–32

Reydel Industries, **23** 95–96

Reymer & Bros., Inc., **II** 508; **11** 172

Reymersholm, **II** 366

Reynolds and Reynolds Company, **17** 142, 144

Reynolds Electric Co., **22** 353

Reynolds Metals Company, II 421–22; **IV** 11–12, 15, 59, **186–88; IV** 122; **12** 278; **19** 346–48 (upd.); **21** 218; **22** 455

RF Communications, **II** 38

RF Monolithics Inc., **13** 193

RHC Holding Corp., **10** 13; **13** 364

RHD Holdings, **23** 413

Rhee Syngman, **I** 516; **12** 293

Rhein-Elbe Gelsenkirchener Bergwerks A.G., **IV** 25

Rheinelbe Union, **I** 542

Rheinisch Kalksteinwerke Wulfrath, **III** 738

Rheinisch Oelfinwerke, **I** 306

Rheinisch-Westfalische Bank A.G., **II** 279

Rheinisch-Westfälischer Sprengstoff AG, **III** 694

Rheinisch-Westfälisches Elektrizatätswerke AG, **I** 542–43; **III** 154; **IV** 231; **V** 744

Rheinische Aktiengesellschaft für Braunkohlenbergbau, **V** 708

Rheinische Creditbank, **II** 278

Rheinische Metallwaaren- und Maschinenfabrik AG, **9** 443–44

Rheinische Wasserglasfabrik, **III** 31

Rheinmetall Berlin AG, 9 443–46

Rheinsche Girozentrale und Provinzialbank, Düsseldorf, **II** 385

Rheinstahl AG, **IV** 222

Rheinstahl Union Brueckenbau, **8** 242

Rheintalische Zementfabrik, **III** 701

Rhenus-Weichelt AG, **6** 424, 426

RHI Entertainment Inc., **16** 257

Rhino Entertainment Company, 18 457–60; **21** 326

RHM. *See* Ranks Hovis McDougall.

Rhodes & Co., **8** 345

Rhodes Inc., 23 412–14

Rhodesian Anglo American Ltd., **IV** 21, 23; **16** 26

Rhodesian Development Corp., **I** 422

Rhodesian Selection Trust, Ltd., **IV** 17–18, 21

Rhodesian Sugar Refineries, **II** 581

Rhodiaceta, **I** 388–89

Rhokana Corp., **IV** 191

Rhône-Poulenc S.A., I 303–04, 371, **388–90,** 670, 672, 692; **III** 677; **IV** 174, 487, 547; **8** 153, 452; **9** 358; **10** 470–72 (upd.); **16** 121, 438; **21** 466; **23** 194, 197

Rhymey Breweries, **I** 294

Rhythm Watch Co., Ltd., **III** 454; **21** 121

La Riassicuratrice, **III** 346

Ricard, **I** 280

Riccar, **17** 124

Riccardo's Restaurant, **18** 538

Rice Broadcasting Co., Inc., **II** 166

Rice-Stix Dry Goods, **II** 414

Rich Products Corporation, 7 448–49

Rich's, **9** 209; **10** 515

Richard A. Shaw, Inc., **7** 128

Richard D. Irwin Inc., **IV** 602–03, 678

Richard Hellman Co., **II** 497

Richard Manufacturing Co., **I** 667

Richard P. Simmons, **8** 19

Richard Shops, **III** 502

Richard Thomas & Baldwins, **IV** 42

Richards Bay Minerals, **IV** 91

Richardson Electronics, Ltd., 17 405–07

Richardson's, **21** 246

Richardson-Vicks Company, **III** 53; **8** 434

Richfield Oil Corp., **IV** 375–76, 456

Richfood Holdings, Inc., 7 450–51

Richland Co-op Creamery Company, **7** 592

Richland Gas Company, **8** 349

Richmon Hill & Queens County Gas Light Companies, **6** 455

Richmond American Homes of Florida, Inc., **11** 258

Richmond Carousel Corporation, **9** 120

Richmond Cedar Works Manufacturing Co., **12** 109; **19** 360

Richmond Corp., **I** 600; **15** 129

Richmond Paperboard Corp., **19** 78

Richmond Pulp and Paper Company, **17** 281

Richway, **10** 515

Richwood Building Products, Inc., **12** 397

Richwood Sewell Coal Co., **17** 357

Ricils, **III** 47

Rickards, Roloson & Company, **22** 427

Rickel Home Centers, **II** 673

Ricoh Company, Ltd., III 121, 157, **159–61,** 172, 454; **6** 289; **8** 278; **18** 386, 527; **19** 317; **21** 122

Ricolino, **19** 192

Riddell Sports Inc., 22 457–59; **23** 449

Ridder Publications, **IV** 612–13, 629; **7** 191

Ride, Inc., 22 460–63

Ridge Tool Co., **II** 19

Ridgewell's Inc., **15** 87

Ridgewood Properties Inc., **12** 394

Ridgway Co., **23** 98

Ridgway Color, **13** 227–28

Rieck-McJunkin Dairy Co., **II** 533

Riedel-de Haën AG, **22** 32

Riegel Bag & Paper Co., **IV** 344

Rieke Corp., **III** 569; **11** 535, **20** 361

Rieter Machine Works, **III** 638

Rig Tenders Company, **6** 383

Riggin & Robbins, **13** 244

Riggs National Corporation, 13 438–40

Rike's, **10** 282

Riken Corp., **IV** 160; **10** 493

Riken Kankoshi Co. Ltd., **III** 159

Riken Optical Co., **III** 159

Riklis Family Corp., 9 447–50; **12** 87; **13** 453

Riku-un Moto Kaisha, **V** 477

La Rinascente, **12** 153

Ring King Visibles, Inc., **13** 269

Ringier America, **19** 333

Ringköpkedjan, **II** 640

Ringnes Bryggeri, **18** 396

Rini Supermarkets, **9** 451; **13** 237

Rini-Rego Supermarkets Inc., **13** 238

Rinker Materials Corp., **III** 688

Rio Grande Industries, Inc., **12** 18–19

Rio Grande Oil Co., **IV** 375, 456

Rio Grande Servaas, S.A. de C.V., **23** 145

Rio Grande Valley Gas Co., **IV** 394

Rio Sul Airlines, **6** 133

Rio Tinto plc, 19 349–53 (upd.)

Rio Tinto-Zinc Corp., **II** 628; **IV** 56, 58–61, 189–91, 380; **21** 352

Rioblanco, **II** 477

Riordan Freeman & Spogli, **13** 406

Riordan Holdings Ltd., **I** 457; **10** 554

Riser Foods, Inc., 9 451–54; **13** 237–38

Rising Sun Petroleum Co., **IV** 431, 460, 542

Risk Planners, **II** 669

Rit Dye Co., **II** 497

Rite Aid Corporation, V 174–76; **9** 187, 346; **12** 221, 333; **16** 389; **18** 199, 286; **19** 354–57 (upd.); **23** 407

Rite-Way Department Store, **II** 649

Rittenhouse and Embree, **III** 269

Rittenhouse Financial Services, **22** 495

Ritter Co. *See* Sybron Corp.

Ritz Camera Centers Inc., **18** 186

Ritz Firma, **13** 512

Ritz-Carlton Hotel Company, 9 455–57; **21** 366

Riunione Adriatica di Sicurtà SpA, III 185, 206, 345–48

The Rival Company, 17 215; **19** 358–60

Rivarossi, **16** 337

River Boat Casino, **9** 425–26

River Steam Navigation Co., **III** 522
River-Raisin Paper Co., **IV** 345
Riverside Chemical Company, **13** 502
Riverside Furniture, **19** 455
Riverside Iron Works, Ltd., **8** 544
Riverside National Bank of Buffalo, **11** 108
Riverside Press, **10** 355–56
Riverwood International Corporation, 7 294; **11 420–23**
Riviana Foods, **III** 24, 25
Riyadh Armed Forces Hospital, **16** 94
Rizzoli Publishing, **IV** 586, 588; **19** 19; **23** 88
RJMJ, Inc., **16** 37
RJR Nabisco Holdings Corp., I 249, 259, 261; **II** 370, 426, 477–78, 542–44; **V** **408–10, 415; 7** 130, 132, 277, 596; **9** 469; **12** 82, 559; **13** 342; **14** 214, 274; **17** 471; **22** 73, 95, 441; **23** 163. *See also* Nabisco Brands, Inc. *and* R.J. Reynolds Industries, Inc.
RKO. *See* Radio-Keith-Orpheum.
RKO Radio Sales, **6** 33
RKO-General, Inc., **8** 207
RLA Polymers, **9** 92
RM Marketing, **6** 14
RMC Group p.l.c., III 734, **737–40**
RMF Inc., **I** 412
RMP International, Limited, **8** 417
Roadhouse Grill, Inc., 22 464–66
Roadline, **6** 413–14
Roadmaster Industries, Inc., 16 430–33; 22 116
Roadmaster Transport Company, **18** 27
Roadway Services, Inc., V 502–03; 12 278, 309; **14** 567; **15** 111
Roaman's, **V** 115
Roan Selection Trust Ltd., **IV** 18, 239–40
Roanoke Fashions Group, **13** 532
Robb Engineering Works, **8** 544
Robbins & Myers Inc., 13 273; **15** **388–90**
Robbins Co., **III** 546
Robeco Group, **IV** 193
Roberds Inc., 19 361–63
Roberk Co., **III** 603
Robert Allen Companies, **III** 571; **20** 362
Robert Benson, Lonsdale & Co. Ltd., **II** 232, 421–22; **IV** 191
Robert Bosch GmbH, I 392–93, 411; **III** 554, 555, 591, 593; **13** 398; **16 434–37** **(upd.); 22** 31
Robert E. McKee Corporation, **6** 150
Robert Fleming Holdings Ltd., **I** 471; **IV** 79; **11** 495
Robert Gair Co., **15** 128
Robert Garrett & Sons, Inc., **9** 363
Robert Grace Contracting Co., **I** 584
Robert Half International Inc., 18 **461–63**
Robert Hall Clothes, Inc., **13** 535
Robert Johnson, **8** 281–82
Robert McLane Company. *See* McLane Company, Inc.
Robert McNish & Company Limited, **14** 141
Robert Mondavi Corporation, 15 391–94
Robert R. Mullen & Co., **I** 20
Robert Stigwood Organization Ltd., **23** 390
Robert W. Baird & Co., **III** 324; **7** 495
Robert Warschauer and Co., **II** 270
Robert Watson & Co. Ltd., **I** 568
Roberts Express, **V** 503

Roberts, Johnson & Rand Shoe Co., **III** 528–29
Roberts Pharmaceutical Corporation, 16 **438–40**
Robertson Building Products, **8** 546
Robertson, Stephens & Co., **22** 465
Robertson-Ceco Corporation, 8 546; **19** **364–66**
Robin Hood Flour Mills, Ltd., **7** 241–43
Robinair, **10** 492, 494
Robinson & Clark Hardware. *See* Clarcor Inc.
Robinson Clubs, **II** 163–64
Robinson Radio Rentals, **I** 531
Robinson Smith & Robert Haas, Inc., **13** 428
Robinson's Japan Co. Ltd., **V** 89
Robinson-Danforth Commission Co., **II** 561
Robinson-Humphrey, **II** 398; **10** 62
Robot Manufacturing Co., **16** 8
Robotic Vision Systems, Inc., **16** 68
ROC Communities, Inc., **I** 272; **22** 341
Roch, S.A., **23** 83
Roche Biomedical Laboratories, Inc., 8 209–10; **11 424–26**
Roche Bioscience, **14 403–06 (upd.)**
Roche Products Ltd., **I** 643
Rochester American Insurance Co., **III** 191
Rochester Gas And Electric **Corporation, 6 571–73**
Rochester German Insurance Co., **III** 191
Rochester Instrument Systems, Inc., **16** 357
Rochester Telephone Corporation, 6 **332–34; 12** 136; **16** 221
Röchling Industrie Verwaltung GmbH, **9** 443
Rock Island Oil & Refining Co., **IV** 448–49
Rock Island Plow Company, **10** 378
Rock Systems Inc., **18** 337
Rock-Tenn Company, IV 312; **13** **441–43; 19** 268
Rockcor Inc., **I** 381; **13** 380
Rockcote Paint Company, **8** 552–53
Rockefeller & Andrews, **IV** 426; **7** 169
Rockefeller Group, **IV** 714
Rocket Chemical Company. *See* WD-40 Company.
Rockford Drilling Co., **III** 439
Rockland Corp., **8** 271
Rockland React-Rite, Inc., **8** 270
Rockmoor Grocery, **II** 683
Rockower of Canada Ltd., **II** 649
Rockport Company, **V** 376–77
Rockresorts, Inc., **22** 166
Rockwell International Corporation, I 71, **78–80**, 154–55, 186; **II** 3, 94, 379; **6** 263; **7** 420; **8** 165; **9** 10; **10** 279–80; **11** 268, 278, **427–30 (upd.)**, 473; **12** 135, 248, 506; **13** 228; **18** 369, 571; **22** 51, 53, 63–64
Rocky Mountain Financial Corporation, **13** 348
Rocky Mountain Pipe Line Co., **IV** 400
Rocky River Power Co. *See* Connecticut Light and Power Co.
Rodale Press, Inc., 22 443; **23 415–17**
Rodamco, **IV** 698
Rodeway Inns of America, **II** 142; **III** 94; **11** 242
Rodven Records, **23** 391
Roederstein GmbH, **21** 520
Roegelein Co., **13** 271

Roehr Products Co., **III** 443
Roermond, **IV** 276
Roessler & Hasslacher Chemical Co., **IV** 69
Roger Cleveland Golf Company, **15** 462
Roger Williams Foods, **II** 682
Rogers & Oling, Inc., **17** 533
Rogers Bros., **I** 672
Rohe Scientific Corp., **13** 398
Röhm and Haas, I 391–93
Rohm Company Ltd., **14** 182–83
ROHN Industries, Inc., 22 467–69
Rohölgewinnungs AG, **IV** 485
Rohr Incorporated, I 62; **9 458–60; 11** 165
Roja, **III** 47
Rokke Group, **16** 546
Rokuosha, **III** 547
Rol Oil, **IV** 451
Rola Group, **II** 81
Roland Murten A.G., 7 452–53
Rolex. *See* Montres Rolex S.A.
Rollalong, **III** 502; **7** 208
Rollerblade, Inc., 15 395–98; 22 202–03
Rolling Stones Records, **23** 33
Rollins Burdick Hunter Co., **III** 204
Rollins Communications, **II** 161
Rollins, Inc., 11 431–34
Rollins Specialty Group, **III** 204
Rollo's, **16** 95
Rolls-Royce Motors Ltd., I 25–26, 81–82, 166, **194–96; III** 652; **9** 16–18, 417–18; **11** 138, 403; **21** 435
Rolls-Royce plc, I 41, 55, 65, **81–83**, 481; **III** 507, 556; **7 454–57 (upd.); 9** 244; **11** 268; **12** 190; **13** 414; **21 433–37** **(upd.)**
Rolm Corp., **II** 99; **III** 149; **18** 344; **22** 51
Rolodex Electronics, **23** 209, 212
Rolscreen. *See* Pella Corporation.
Rombas, **IV** 226
Rome Cable and Wire Co., **IV** 15
Romper Room Enterprises, Inc., **16** 267
Rompetrol, **IV** 454
Ron Nagle, **I** 247
Ronco, Inc., 15 399–401; 21 327
Rondel's, Inc., **8** 135
Ronel, **13** 274
Ronningen-Petter, **III** 468
Ronzoni Foods Corp., **15** 221
Roots-Connersville Blower Corp., **III** 472
Roper Industries Inc., III 655; **12** 550; **15** **402–04**
Ropert Group, **18** 67
Rorer Group, I 666–68; 12 4; **16** 438
Rosaen Co., **23** 82
Rose Foundation, **9** 348
Rose's Stores, Inc., 13 261, **444–46; 23** 215
Rosefield Packing Co., **II** 497
RoseJohnson Incorporated, **14** 303
Rosemount Inc., II 20; **13** 226; **15** **405–08**
Rosen Enterprises, Ltd., **10** 482
Rosenblads Patenter, **III** 419
Rosenbluth International Inc., 14 407–09
Rosenfeld Hat Company. *See* Columbia Hat Company.
Rosenthal, **I** 347; **18** 236
Rosevear, **III** 690
Ross Carrier Company, **8** 115
Ross Clouston, **13** 244
Ross Gear & Tool Co., **I** 539; **14** 510

Ross Hall Corp., **I** 417
Ross Stores, Inc., 17 408–10
Rossendale Combining Company, **9** 92
Rossignol Ski Company, Inc. *See* Skis Rossignol S.A.
Rössing Uranium Ltd., **IV** 191
Rossville Union Distillery, **I** 285
Rostocker Brauerei VEB, **9** 87
Roswell Public Service Company, **6** 579
Rota Bolt Ltd., **III** 581
Rotadisk, **16** 7
Rotan Mosle Financial Corporation, **II** 445; **22** 406
Rotary Lift, **III** 467–68
Rotax, **III** 555–56. *See also* Orbital Engine Corporation Ltd.
Rote. *See* Avery Dennison Corporation.
Rotelcom Data Inc., **6** 334; **16** 222
Rotex, **IV** 253
Roth Co., **16** 493
Rothmans International p.l.c., I 438; **IV** 93; **V** 411–13
Rothmans UK Holdings Limited, 19 367–70 (upd.)
Rothschild Financial Corporation, **13** 347
Rothschild Group, **6** 206
Rothschild Investment Trust, **I** 248; **III** 699
Roto-Rooter Corp., 13 149–50; **15** 409–11; **16** 387
Rotodiesel, **III** 556
Rotor Tool Co., **II** 16
Rotterdam Bank, **II** 183–85
Rotterdam Lloyd, **6** 403–04
Rouge et Or, **IV** 614
Rouge Steel Company, 8 448–50
Roughdales Brickworks, **14** 249
Rougier. *See* Groupe Rougier, SA.
Round Hill Foods, **21** 535
Round Table, **16** 447
Roundup Wholesale Grocery Company, **V** 55
Roundy's Inc., 14 410–12
The Rouse Company, II 445; **15** 412–15; **22** 406
Roussel Uclaf, I 669–70; **8** 451–53 (upd.); **18** 236; **19** 51
Rousselot, **I** 677
Routh Robbins Companies, **21** 96
Roux Séguéla Cayzac & Goudard. *See* Euro RSCG Worldwide S.A.
Rover Group Ltd., I 186; **7** 458–60; **11** 31, 33; **14** 36; **21** 441–44 (upd.)
Rowe & Pitman, **14** 419
Rowe Bros. & Co., **III** 680
Rowe Price-Fleming International, Inc., **11** 495
Rowntree Mackintosh, II 476, 511, 521, 548, 568–70; **7** 383
Roxana Petroleum Co., **IV** 531, 540
Roxoil Drilling, **7** 344
Roy and Charles Moore Crane Company, **18** 319
Roy Farrell Import-Export Company, **6** 78
Roy Rogers, **III** 102
Royal Ahold. *See* Koninklijke Ahold N.V.
Royal Aluminium Ltd., **IV** 9
Royal Appliance Manufacturing Company, 15 416–18; **17** 233
Royal Baking Powder Co., **II** 544; **14** 17
Royal Bank of Australia, **II** 188
The Royal Bank of Canada, II 344–46; **21** 445–48 (upd.)
Royal Bank of Ireland Ltd., **16** 13
Royal Bank of Queensland, **II** 188

The Royal Bank of Scotland Group plc, II 298, 358; **10** 336–37; **12** 421–23
Royal Brewing Co., **I** 269; **12** 337
Royal Business Machines, **I** 207, 485; **III** 549
Royal Canada, **III** 349
Royal Caribbean Cruises Ltd., 6 368; **22** 444–46; 470–73
Royal Copenhagen A/S, **9** 99
Royal Crown Company, Inc., II 468; **6** 21, 50; **8** 536–37; **14** 32–33; **23** 418–20
Royal Data, Inc. *See* King Kullen Grocery Co., Inc.
Royal Doulton Plc, IV 659; **14** 413–15
Royal Dutch Harbour Co., **IV** 707
Royal Dutch Paper Co., **IV** 307
Royal Dutch Petroleum Company, IV 530–32, 657. *See also* Shell Transport and Trading Company p.l.c.
Royal Dutch/Shell Group, **I** 368, 504; **III** 616; **IV** 132–33, 378, 406, 413, 429, 434, 453–54, 460, 491–92, 512, 515, 517–18, 530–32, 540–45, 557–58, 569; **7** 56–57, 172–73, 481–82; **17** 417; **19** 73, 75; **21** 203; **22** 237
Royal Electric Company, **6** 501
Royal Exchange Assurance Corp., **III** 233–34, 278, 349, 369–71, 373
Royal Food Distributors, **II** 625
Royal General Insurance Co., **III** 242
Royal Hawaiian Macadamia Nut Co., **II** 491
Royal Industries, Inc., **19** 371
Royal Insurance Holdings plc, III 349–51
Royal International, **II** 457; **III** 349
Royal Interocean Lines, **6** 404
Royal Jackson, **14** 236
Royal Jordanian, **6** 101
Royal London Mutual Insurance, **IV** 697
Royal Mail Group, **V** 498; **6** 416; **19** 198
Royal Orchid Holidays, **6** 122–23
Royal Ordnance, **13** 356
Royal Packaging Industries Van Leer B.V., **9** 305
Royal Pakhoed N.V., **9** 532
Royal Re, **III** 349
Royal Sash Manufacturing Co., **III** 757
Royal Securities Company, **6** 585
Royal Securities Corp. of Canada, **II** 425
Royal Sporting House Pte. Ltd., **21** 483
Royal Trust Co., **II** 456–57; **V** 25
Royal Union Life Insurance Co., **III** 275
Royal USA, **III** 349
Royal Wessanen, **II** 527
Royale Belge, **III** 177, 200, 394
Royalite, **I** 285
Royce Electronics, **III** 569; **18** 68; **20** 361
Royce Ltd., **I** 194
Royster-Clark, Inc., **13** 504
Rozes, **I** 272
RPC Industries, **III** 635
RPI. *See* Research Polymers International.
RPM Inc., 8 III 598; 454–57
RSI Corp., **8** 141–42
RSO Records, **23** 390
RTE Corp., **II** 17
RTL-Véeronique, **IV** 611
RTZ Corporation PLC, IV 189–92; **7** 261, 263
RTZ-CRA Group. *See* Rio Tinto plc.
Rubber Latex Limited, **9** 92

Rubbermaid Incorporated, III 613–15; **12** 168–69; **13** 317–18; **19** 407; **20** 262, 454–57 (upd.); **21** 293
Ruberoid Corporation, **I** 339; **22** 227
Rubloff Inc., **II** 442
Rubo Lederwaren, **14** 225
Rubry Owen, **I** 154
Ruby, **III** 47
Ruby Tuesday, Inc., 18 464–66
Rubyco, Inc., **15** 386
La Ruche Meridionale, **12** 153
Ruddick Corporation, **23** 260
Rudisill Printing Co., **IV** 661
Rudolf Wolff & Co., **IV** 165
Rudolph Fluor & Brother, **I** 569
Rug Corporation of America, **12** 393
Ruger Corporation, **19** 431
Ruhr-Zink, **IV** 141
Ruhrgas AG, V 704–06; **7** 141; **18** 50
Ruhrkohle AG, III 566; **IV** 26, 89, 105, 193–95
Ruinart Père et Fils, **I** 272
Rumbelows, **I** 532
Runcorn White Lead Co., **III** 680
Runnymede Construction Co., **8** 544
Runo-Everth Treibstoff und Ol AG, **7** 141
Rural Bank, **IV** 279; **19** 155
Rurhkohle AG, **V** 747
Rush Laboratories, Inc., **6** 41
Russ Berrie and Company, Inc., 12 424–26
Russell & Co., **II** 296
Russell Corporation, 8 458–59; **12** 458
Russell Electric, **11** 412
Russell Electronics, **II** 85
Russell Kelly Office Services, Inc. *See* Kelly Services Inc.
Russell, Majors & Waddell, **II** 381
Russell Stover Candies Inc., 12 427–29
Russwerke Dortmund GmbH, **IV** 70
Rust Craft Greeting Cards Incorporated, **12** 561
Rust International Inc., V 754; **6** 599–600; **11** 435–36
Rustenburg Platinum Co., **IV** 96, 118, 120
Rütgerswerke AG, **IV** 193; **8** 81
Ruti Machinery Works, **III** 638
Rutland Plastics, **I** 321; **12** 103
RWE Group, V 707–10
RxAmerica, **22** 40
Ryan Aeronautical, **I** 525; **10** 522; **11** 428
Ryan Aircraft Company, **9** 458
Ryan Homes, Inc., **8** 401–02
Ryan Insurance Co., **III** 204
Ryan Milk Company of Kentucky, **7** 128
Ryan's Family Steak Houses, Inc., 15 419–21; **19** 287; **22** 464
Rycade Corp., **IV** 365, 658
Rydelle-Lion, **III** 45
Ryder Systems, Inc., V 504–06; **13** 192; **19** 293
Ryerson Tull, Inc., **19** 216
Rykoff-Sexton, Inc., **21** 497
The Ryland Group, Inc., 8 460–61; **19** 126
Ryobi Ltd., **I** 202
Rypper Corp., **16** 43
Rysher Entertainment, **22** 162
Ryukyu Cement, **III** 760
The Ryvita Company, **II** 466; **13** 52

S Pearson & Son Ltd., **IV** 657–59
S. & W. Berisford, **II** 514, 528
S.A. CARFUEL, **12** 152

S.A. Greetings Corporation, **22** 35
S.A. Schonbrunn & Co., **14** 18
S&A Restaurant Corp., **7** 336; **10** 176; **14** 331; **15** 363
S&C Electric Company, 15 422–24
S&H. *See* Sperry and Hutchinson Co.
S&H Diving Corporation, **6** 578
S&K Famous Brands, Inc., 23 421–23
S&V Screen Inks, **13** 227–28
S&W Fine Foods, **12** 105
S.B. Irving Trust Bank Corp., **II** 218
S.B. Penick & Co., **I** 708; **8** 548
S.C. Johnson & Son, Inc., **I** 14; **III** 45, **58–59**; **8** 130; **10** 173; **12** 126–28; **17** 215; **21** 386
S-C-S Box Company, **8** 173
S.D. Cohn & Company, **10** 455
S.D. Warren Co., **IV** 329–30
S-E Bank Group, **II** 351–53
S.E. Massengill, **III** 66
S.F. Braun, **IV** 451
S.G. Warburg and Co., **II** 232, 259–60, 422, 629; **14** 419; **16** 377. *See also* SBC Warburg.
S. Grumbacher & Son. *See* The Bon-Ton Stores, Inc.
S.H. Benson Ltd., **I** 25–26
S.H. Kress & Co., **17** 203–04
S.I.P., Co., **8** 416
S-K-I Limited, 15 457–59
S.K. Wellman, **14** 81
S. Kuhn & Sons, **13** 221
S.M.A. Corp., **I** 622
S.R. Dresser Manufacturing Co., **III** 470–71
S.S. Kresge Company. *See* Kmart Corporation.
S.S. White Dental Manufacturing Co., **I** 383
S. Smith & Sons, **III** 555
S.T. Cooper & Sons, **12** 283
S.T. Dupont Company, **III** 28; **23** 55
Sa SFC NA, **18** 163
Sa SFC NV, **18** 162
SAA. *See* South African Airways.
SAAB. *See* Svenska Aeroplan Aktiebolaget.
Saab-Scania A.B., **I** 197–98, 210; **III** 556; **V** 339; **10** 86; **11 437–39 (upd.)**; **16** 322
Saarberg-Konzern, IV 196–99
Saarstahl AG, **IV** 228
Saatchi & Saatchi plc, **I** 21, 28, **33–35**, 36; **6** 53, 229; **14** 49–50; **16** 72; **21** 236; **22** 296
SAB. *See* South African Breweries Ltd.
Sabah Timber Co., **III** 699
SABENA, **6** 96; **18** 80
Saber Energy, Inc., **7** 553–54
Sabi International Ltd., **22** 464
SABIM Sable, **12** 152
Sabine Corporation, **7** 229
Sabine Investment Co. of Texas, Inc., **IV** 341
SABO Maschinenfabrik AG, **21** 175
Sachs-Dolmer G.m.b.H., **22** 334
Sachsgruppe, **IV** 201
Sacilor, **IV** 174, 226–27
Sackett Plasterboard Co., **III** 762
Sacks Industries, **8** 561
OY Saco AB, **23** 268
SACOR, **IV** 250, 504–06
Sacramento Savings & Loan Association, **10** 43, 45
SAE Magnetics Ltd., **18** 250

Saeger Carbide Corp., **IV** 203
Saes, **III** 347
SAFECO Corporation, III 352–54; 10 44
Safeguard Scientifics, Inc., 10 232–34, 473–75
Safelite Glass Corp., 19 371–73
Safer, Inc., **21** 385–86
Safeskin Corporation, 18 467–70
Safety Fund Bank, **II** 207
Safety Rehab, **11** 486
Safety Savings and Loan, **10** 339
Safety-Kleen Corp., 8 462–65
Safeway Stores Incorporated, **II** 424, 601, 604–05, 609–10, 628, 632, 637, **654–56**; **6** 364; **7** 61, 569; **9** 39; **10** 442; **11** 239, 241; **12** 113, 209, 559; **13** 90, 336, 340; **16** 64, 160, 249, 452; **22** 37, 126
Safmarine, **IV** 22
SAFR. *See* Société Anonyme des Fermiers Reúnis.
Safrap, **IV** 472
Saga Corp., **II** 608; **III** 103; **IV** 406
Sagebrush Sales, Inc., **12** 397
Saginaw Dock & Terminal Co., **17** 357
Sagitta Arzneimittel, **18** 51
Sagittarius Productions Inc., **I** 286
Sahara Casino Partners L.P., **19** 379
Sahara Resorts. *See* Santa Fe Gaming Corporation.
Sai Baba, **12** 228
Saia Motor Freight Line, Inc., **6** 421–23
Saibu Gas, **IV** 518–19
SAIC, **12** 153
Saiccor, **IV** 92
Sainrapt et Brice, **9** 9
Sainsbury's. *See* J Sainsbury PLC.
St. Alban Boissons S.A., **22** 515
St. Alban's Sand and Gravel, **III** 739
St. Andrews Insurance, **III** 397
St. Charles Manufacturing Co., **III** 654
St. Clair Industries Inc., **I** 482
St. Clair Press, **IV** 570
St. Croix Paper Co., **IV** 281; **9** 259
St. George Reinsurance, **III** 397
St. Helens Crown Glass Co., **III** 724
St. Joe Gold, **23** 40
St. Joe Minerals Corp., **I** 569, 571; **8** 192
St. Joe Paper Company, 8 485–88
St. John Knits, Inc., 14 466–68
St. John's Wood Railway Company, **6** 406
St. Joseph Co., **I** 286, 684
St. Jude Medical, Inc., 6 345; **11 458–61**
St. Lawrence Cement Inc., **III** 702; **8** 258–59
St. Lawrence Corp. Ltd., **IV** 272
St. Lawrence Steamboat Co., **I** 273
St. Louis and Illinois Belt Railway, **6** 504
Saint Louis Bread Company, **18** 35, 37
St. Louis Concessions Inc., **21** 39
St. Louis Refrigerator Car Co., **I** 219
St. Louis Troy and Eastern Railroad Company, **6** 504
St. Paul Bank for Cooperatives, 8 489–90
The St. Paul Companies, **III 355–57; 15** 257; **21** 305; **22** 154, **492–95 (upd.)**
St. Paul Fire and Marine Insurance Co., **III** 355–56
St. Regis Corp., **I** 153; **IV** 264, 282; **9** 260; **10** 265; **20** 129
St. Regis Paper Co., **IV** 289, 339; **12** 377; **22** 209

Saint-Gobain. *See* Compagnie de Saint Gobain S.A.
Saint-Quirin, **III** 676; **16** 120
Sainte Anne Paper Co., **IV** 245–46
Saipem, **IV** 420–22, 453
Saison Group, **V** 184–85, 187–89
Saito Ltd., **IV** 268
Saiwa, **II** 543
Saks Fifth Avenue, **I** 426; **15** 291; **18** 372; **21** 302; **22** 72
Sakurai Co., **IV** 327
Salada Foods, **II** 525; **13** 293
Salant Corporation, 12 430–32
Sale Knitting Company, **12** 501. *See also* Tultex Corporation.
Salem Carpet Mills, Inc., **9** 467
Salen Energy A.B., **IV** 563
Salick Health Care, Inc., **21** 544, 546
Salim Group, **18** 180–81
Sallie Mae. *See* Student Loan Marketing Association.
Sally Beauty Company, Inc., **8** 15–17
Salmon Carriers, **6** 383
Salmon River Power & Light Company, **12** 265
Salomon Inc., **I** 630–31; **II** 268, 400, 403, 406, 426, 432, 434, 441, **447–49**; **III** 221, 215, 721; **IV** 80, 137; **7** 114; **9** 378–79, 386; **11** 35, 371; **13** 331, **447–50 (upd.)** Inc.; **18** 60, 62; **19** 293; **21** 67, 146; **22** 102; **23** 472–74
Salomon Worldwide, 20 458–60
Salora, **II** 69; **17** 353
Salsåkers Ångsågs, **IV** 338
Salt River Project, 19 374–76
Saltos del Sil, **II** 197
Salvagnini Company, **22** 6
Salvation Army, **15** 510–11
Salzgitter AG, **IV** 128, 198, **200–01**; **17** 381
Sam Goody, **I** 613; **9** 360–61
Sam's Clubs, **V** 216–17; **8** 555–57; **12** 221, 335; **13** 548; **14** 393; **15** 470; **16** 64
Samancor Ltd., **IV** 92–93
Sambo's, **12** 510
Sambre-et-Moselle, **IV** 52
Samcor Glass, **III** 685
Samedan Oil Corporation, **11** 353
Sames, S.A., **21** 65–66
Samim, **IV** 422
Samkong Fat Ltd. Co., **III** 747
Samna Corp., **6** 256
Sampson's, **12** 220–21
Samsonite Corp., 6 50; **13** 311, **451–53**; **16** 20–21
Samsung Electronics Co., Ltd., 14 416–18; 18 139, 260
Samsung Group, **I** 515–17; **II** 53–54; **III** 143, 457–58, 517, 749; **IV** 519; **7** 233; **12** 211–12; **13** 387; **18** 124
Samsung-Calex, **17** 483
Samuel Austin & Son Company, **8** 41
Samuel Meisel & Co., **11** 80–81
Samuel Montagu & Co., **II** 319; **17** 324–25
Samuel Moore & Co., **I** 155
Samuel Samuel & Co., **IV** 530, 542
Samwha Paper Co., **III** 748
San Antonio Public Service Company, **6** 473
San Diego Gas & Electric Company, V 711–14; 6 590; **11** 272
San Francisco Mines of Mexico Ltd., **22** 285

San Gabriel Light & Power Company, **16** 496

San Giorgio Macaroni Inc., **II** 511

San Miguel Corporation, I 221; **15 428–30; 23** 379

SAN-MIC Trading Co., **IV** 327

Sanborn Co., **III** 142; **6** 237

Sanborn Hermanos, S.A., 20 461–63; 21 259

Sanders Associates, Inc., **9** 324; **13** 127–28

Sanderson & Porter, **I** 376

Sanderson Computers, **10** 500

Sanderson Farms, Inc., 15 425–27

Sandoz Ltd., I 632–33, **671–73**, 675; **7** 315, 452; **8** 108–09, 215; **10** 48, 199; **11** 173; **12** 388; **15** 139; **18** 51; **22** 475

SandPoint Corp., **12** 562; **17** 254

Sandusky Plastics, Inc., **17** 157

Sandvik AB, III 426–27; **IV 202–04**

Sandwell, Inc., **6** 491

Sandy's Pool Supply, Inc. See Leslie's Poolmart, Inc.

SANFLO Co., Ltd., **IV** 327

Sangu Express Company, **V** 463

Sanichem Manufacturing Company, **16** 386

Sanitary Farm Dairies, Inc., **7** 372

Sanitas Food Co., **II** 523

Sanitation Systems, Inc. See HMI Industries.

Sanjushi Bank, **II** 347

Sanka Coffee Corp., **II** 531

Sankin Kai Group, **II** 274

Sanko K.K., **I** 432, 492

Sanko Steamship Co., **I** 494; **II** 311

Sankyo Company Ltd., I 330, **674–75; III** 760; **8** 153

Sanlam, **IV** 91, 93, 535

Sano Railway Company, **6** 430

Sanofi Group, I 304, **676–77**, **III** 18; **IV** 546; **7** 484–85; **21** 205; **23** 236, 238, 242

Sanseisha Co., **IV** 326

Santa Ana Savings and Loan, **10** 339

Santa Ana Wholesale Company, **16** 451

Santa Cruz Operation, **6** 244

Santa Cruz Portland Cement, **II** 490

Santa Fe Gaming Corporation, 19 377–79

Santa Fe Industries, **II** 448; **12** 19; **13** 448

Santa Fe International, **IV** 451–52

Santa Fe Pacific Corporation (SFP), V 507–09

Santa Fe Railway, **12** 278; **18** 4

Santa Fe Southern Pacific Corp., **III** 512; **IV** 721; **6** 150, 599; **9** 391; **22** 491

Santa Rosa Savings and Loan, **10** 339

Santiam Lumber Co., **IV** 358

Santone Industries Inc., **16** 327

Sanus Corp. Health Systems, **III** 317

Sanwa Bank, Ltd., II 276, 326, **347–48**, 442, 511; **III** 188, 759; **IV** 150–51; **7** 119; **15** 43, **431–33 (upd.)**

Sanyo Chemical Manufacturing Co., **III** 758

Sanyo Electric Company, Ltd., I 516; **II** 55–56, **91–92; III** 569, 654; **6** 101; **14** 535; **20** 361

Sanyo Ethylene Co. Ltd., **IV** 476

Sanyo Petrochemical Co. Ltd., **IV** 476

Sanyo Railway Co., **I** 506; **II** 325

Sanyo Semiconductor, **17** 33

Sanyo-Kokusaku Pulp Co., Ltd., IV 326, **327–28**

SAP AG, 11 78; **16 441–44**

Sapac, **I** 643

SAPAC. See Société Parisienne d'Achats en Commun.

Sapirstein Greeting Card Company. See American Greetings Corporation.

Sappi Ltd., **IV** 91–93

Sapporo Breweries, Ltd., I 9, 220, 270, **282–83**, 508, 615; **II** 326; **13 454–56 (upd.); 20** 28–29; **21** 319–20

Sara Lee Corporation, I 15, 30; **II 571–73**, 675; **7** 113 **8** 262; **10** 219–20; **11** 15, 486; **12** 494, 502, 531; **15** 359, **434–37 (upd.)**, 507; **19** 192

Saracen's Head Brewery, **21** 245

Sarawak Trading, **14** 448

Sargent & Lundy, **6** 556

Sarget S.A., **IV** 71

SARL, **12** 152

SARMA, **III** 623–24

Saros Corp., **15** 474

Sarotti A.G., **II** 546

Sarpe, **IV** 591

SAS. See Scandinavian Airlines System.

SAS Institute Inc., 10 476–78

Saseba Heavy Industries, **II** 274

Saskatchewan Oil and Gas Corporation, **13** 556–57

Sasol Limited, IV 533–35

Sason Corporation, **V** 187

SAT. See Stockholms Allmänna Telefonaktiebolag.

Satellite Business Systems, **III** 182; **21** 14; **23** 135

Satellite Information Services, **II** 141

Satellite Software International, **10** 556

Satellite Television PLC, **IV** 652; **7** 391; **23** 135

Satellite Transmission and Reception Specialist Company, **11** 184

Säteri Oy, **IV** 349

Sato Yasusaburo, **I** 266

Saturday Evening Post Co., **II** 208; **9** 320

Saturn Corporation, III 593, 760; **7 461–64; 21 449–53 (upd.); 22** 154

Saturn Industries, Inc., **23** 489

SATV. See Satellite Television PLC.

Saucona Iron Co., **IV** 35; **7** 48

Saucony Manufacturing Company, **17** 244

Sauder Woodworking Co., 12 433–34

Saudi Arabian Airlines, 6 84, **114–16**

Saudi Arabian Oil Company, IV 536–39; 17 411–15 (upd.). See also Arabian American Oil Co.

Saudi Arabian Parsons Limited, **8** 416

Saudi British Bank, **II** 298

Saudi Consolidated Electric Co., **IV** 538; **17** 414

Saudi Refining Inc., **IV** 539; **17** 414

Saudia. See Saudi Arabian Airlines.

Sauer Motor Company, **I** 177; **22** 329

Saul Lerner & Co., **II** 450

Saunders-Roe Ltd., **IV** 658

Sav-on Drug, **II** 605; **12** 477

Sav-X, **9** 186

Sava Group, **20** 263

Savacentre Ltd., **II** 658; **13** 284

Savage, **19** 430

Savage Shoes, Ltd., **III** 529

Savannah Foods & Industries, Inc., 7 465–67

Savannah Gas Company, **6** 448; **23** 29

Save & Prosper Group, **10** 277

Save Mart, **14** 397

Save-A-Lot, **II** 682; **11** 228

Saviem, **III** 543

Savin, **III** 159

Savings of America, **II** 182

Savio, **IV** 422

Oy Savo-Karjalan Tukkuliike, **8** 293

Savon Sellu Mills, **IV** 315

Savory Milln, **II** 369

Savoy Group, **I** 248; **IV** 705

Savoy Industries, **12** 495

Sawyer Electrical Manufacturing Company, **11** 4

Sawyer Industries, Inc., **13** 532

Sawyer Research Products, Inc., **14** 81

Saxby, S.A., **13** 385

Saxon and Norman Cement Co., **III** 670

Saxon Oil, **11** 97

Saxon Petroleum, Inc., **19** 162

Sayama Sekiyu, **IV** 554

Sbarro, Inc., 16 445–47; 19 435

SBC. See Southwestern Bell Corporation.

SBC Warburg, II 369; **14 419–21; 15** 197

Sberbank, **II** 242

SBK Entertainment World, Inc., **22** 194

SCA. See Svenska Cellulosa Aktiebolaget.

SCA Services, Inc., **V** 754; **9** 109

Scaldia Paper BV, **15** 229

Scali, McCabe & Sloves, **I** 27; **22** 200

Scan Screen, **IV** 600

Scana Corporation, 6 574–76; 19 499

Scandinavian Airlines System, I 107, **119–20**, 121; **6** 96, 122

Scandinavian Bank, **II** 352

Scandinavian Trading Co., **I** 210

ScanDust, **III** 625

Scania-Vabis. See Saab-Scania AB.

Scantron Corporation, **17** 266–68

Scarborough Public Utilities Commission, 9 461–62

SCEcorp, **V** 713–14, **715–17; 6** 590

Scenographic Designs, **21** 277

Schaffhausenschor Bankverein, **II** 281

Schaper Mfg. Co., **12** 168

Scharff-Koken Manufacturing Co., **IV** 286

Scharnow, **II** 163–64

Schaum Publishing Co., **IV** 636

Schauman Wood Oy, **IV** 277, 302

Schein Pharmaceutical Inc., **13** 77

Schenker-Rhenus Ag, 6 424–26

Schenley Industries Inc., **I** 226, 285; **9** 449; **10** 181

Scherer. See R.P. Scherer.

Schering A.G., I 681–82, 684, 701; **10** 214; **14** 60; **16** 543

Schering-Plough Corporation, I 682, **683–85; II** 590; **III** 45, 61; **11** 142, 207; **14** 58, 60, **422–25 (upd.)**

Schiavi Homes, Inc., **14** 138

Schicht Co., **II** 588

Schick Shaving, **I** 711; **III** 55

Schieffelin & Co., **I** 272

Schindler Holdings, **II** 122; **12** 546

Schlage Lock Co., **III** 526

Schleppschiffahrtsgesellschaft Unterweser, **IV** 140

Schlesischer Bankverein, **II** 278

Schlitz Brewing Co., **I** 218, 255, 268, 270, 291, 600; **10** 100; **12** 338; **18** 500; **23** 403

Schlumberger Limited, III 429, 499, **616–18; 13** 323; **17 416–19 (upd.); 22** 64, 68

Schmalbach-Lubeca-Werke A.G., **15** 128

Schmid, **19** 166

Schmidt, **I** 255
Schneider Co., **III** 113
Schneider et Cie, **IV** 25; **22** 42
Schneider National Inc., **13** 550–51; **20** 439
Schneider S.A., II 93–94; **18** 471–74 (upd.); **19** 165–66
Schnitzer Steel Industries, Inc., 19 380–82
Schober Direktmarketing, **18** 170
Schocken Books, **13** 429
Schoenfeld Industries, **16** 511
Scholastic Corporation, 10 479–81
Scholl Inc., **I** 685; **14** 424
Scholz Homes Inc., **IV** 115
Schott Glaswerke, **III** 445–47
Schottenstein Stores Corp., 14 426–28; **19** 108
Schrader Bellows, **III** 603
Schrock Cabinet Company, **13** 564
Schroder Darling & Co., **II** 389
Schroders Ventures, **18** 345
Schroeter, White and Johnson, **III** 204
Schuitema, **II** 642; **16** 312–13
Schuler Chocolates, **15** 65
Schuller International, Inc., **11** 421
Schultz Sav-O Stores, Inc., 21 454–56
Schumacher Co., **II** 624
Schuykill Energy Resources, **12** 41
Schwabe-Verlag, **7** 42
Schwabel Corporation, **19** 453
Schwan's Sales Enterprises, Inc., 7 468–70
Schwartz Iron & Metal Co., **13** 142
Schweitzer-Maudit International Inc., **16** 304
Schweiz Allgemeine, **III** 377
Schweiz Transport-Vericherungs-Gesellschaft, **III** 410
Schweizer Rück Holding AG, **III** 377
Schweizerische Bankgesellschaft AG, **II** 379; **V** 104
Schweizerische Kreditanstalt, **III** 375, 410; **6** 489
Schweizerische Nordostbahn, **6** 424
Schweizerische Post-, Telefon- und Telegrafen-Betriebe, V 321–24
Schweizerische Ruckversicherungs-Gesellschaft. *See* Swiss Reinsurance Company.
Schweizerische Unfallversicherungs-Actiengesellschaft in Winterthur, **III** 402
Schweizerische Unionbank, **II** 368
Schweizerischer Bankverein, **II** 368
Schweppe, Paul & Gosse, **II** 476
Schweppes Ltd. *See* Cadbury Schweppes PLC.
Schwinn Cycle and Fitness L.P., 16 494; **19** 383–85
Schwitzer, **II** 420
SCI. *See* Service Corporation International.
SCI Systems, Inc., 9 463–64; **12** 451
Scicon, **14** 317
Science Applications International Corporation, 15 438–40
Scientific Communications, Inc., **10** 97
Scientific Data Systems, **II** 44; **III** 172; **6** 289; **10** 365
Scientific Games Holding Corp., **III** 431; **20** 48
Scientific-Atlanta, Inc., 6 335–37
SciMed Life Systems, **III** 18–19
Scioto Bank, **9** 475
Scitex Corp. Ltd., **15** 148, 229

SCM Corp., **I** 29; **III** 502; **IV** 330; **7** 208; **8** 223–24; **17** 213
SCOA Industries, Inc., **13** 260
SCOR S.A., III 394; **20** 464–66
The Score Board, Inc., 19 386–88
Scot Bowyers, **II** 587
Scot Lad Foods, **14** 411
Scotch House Ltd., **19** 181
Scotia Securities, **II** 223
Scotiabank. *See* The Bank of Nova Scotia.
Scotsman Industries, Inc., II 420; **16** 397; **20** 467–69
Scott Communications, Inc., **10** 97
Scott Fetzer Company, III 214; **12** 435–37, 554–55; **17** 233; **18** 60, 62–63
Scott, Foresman, **IV** 675
Scott Graphics, **IV** 289; **8** 483
Scott Holdings, **19** 384
Scott Lithgow, **III** 516; **7** 232
Scott Paper Company, III 749; **IV** 258, 289–90, 311, 325, 327, **329–31**; **8** 483; **16** 302, 304; **17** 182; **18** 181; **19** 266; **22** 210
Scott-McDuff, **II** 107
Scotti Brothers, **20** 3
Scottish & Newcastle plc, 13 458; **15** 441–44; **21** 229
Scottish Aviation, **I** 50
Scottish Brick, **14** 250
Scottish Electric, **6** 453
Scottish General Fire Assurance Corp., **III** 256
Scottish Hydro-Electric PLC, 13 457–59
Scottish Inns of America, Inc., **13** 362
Scottish Land Development, **III** 501; **7** 207
Scottish Malt Distillers, **I** 240
Scottish Nuclear, Ltd., **19** 389
Scottish Union Co., **III** 358
ScottishPower plc, 19 389–91
ScottishTelecom plc, **19** 389
The Scotts Company, 22 474–76
Scotts Stores, **I** 289
Scotty's, Inc., 12 234; **22** 477–80
Scovill, **IV** 11; **22** 364
Scranton Corrugated Box Company, Inc., **8** 102
Scranton Plastics Laminating Corporation, **8** 359
Screen Gems, **II** 135–36; **12** 74; **22** 193
SCREG, **I** 563
Scribbans-Kemp Ltd., **II** 594
Scriha & Deyhle, **10** 196
Scripps-Howard, Inc., **IV** 607–09, 628; **7** 64, 157–59
Scrivner Inc., **17** 180
Scudder, Stevens & Clark, **II** 448; **13** 448
Scurlock Oil Co., **IV** 374
SDC Coatings, **III** 715
SDGE. *See* San Diego Gas & Electric Company.
SDK Health Care Information Systems, **16** 94
SDK Parks, **IV** 724
Sea Diamonds Ltd., **IV** 66; **7** 123
Sea Far of Norway, **II** 484
Sea Insurance Co. Ltd., **III** 220
Sea Life Centre Aquariums, **10** 439
Sea Ray, **III** 444
Sea World, Inc., **IV** 623–24; **12** 224
Sea-Alaska Products, **II** 494
Sea-Land Service Inc., **I** 476; **9** 510–11; **22** 164, 166
Seabee Corp., **18** 276

Seaboard Air Line Railroad. *See* CSX Corporation.
Seaboard Finance Company, **13** 63
Seaboard Fire and Marine Insurance Co., **III** 242
Seaboard Life Insurance Co., **III** 193
Seaboard Lumber Sales, **IV** 307
Seaboard Oil Co., **IV** 552
Seaboard Surety Company, **III** 357; **22** 494
Seabourn Cruise Lines, **6** 368
Seabulk Offshore International. *See* Hvide Marine Incorporated.
Seabury & Smith, **III** 283
Seacat-Zapata Off-Shore Company, **18** 513
Seacoast Products, **III** 502
Seafield Estate and Consolidated Plantations Berhad, **14** 448
Seafirst. *See* Seattle First National Bank, Inc.
SeaFirst Corp., **II** 228; **17** 462
Seagate Technology, Inc., 6 230–31; **8** 466–68; **9** 57; **10** 257, 403–04, 459; **11** 56, 234; **13** 483; **18** 250
Seagram Company Ltd., I 26, 240, 244, **284–86**, 329, 403; **II** 456, 468; **IV** 401; **7** 155; **18** 72; **21** 26, 401; **22** 194; **23** 125
Seagull Energy Corporation, 11 440–42
Seal Products, Inc., **12** 264
Seal Sands Chemicals, **16** 69
Sealand Petroleum Co., **IV** 400
Sealectro, **III** 434
Sealed Air Corporation, 14 429–31
Sealed Power Corporation, I 199–200; **10** 492–94
Sealright Co., Inc., 17 420–23
SealRite Windows, **19** 446
Sealtest, **14** 205
Sealy Inc., 12 438–40
Seamless Rubber Co., **III** 613
Seaquist Manufacturing Corporation, **9** 413–14
Searle & Co. *See* G.D. Searle & Co.
Sears Logistics Services, **18** 225–26
Sears plc, V 177–79
Sears, Roebuck and Co., I 26, 146, 516, 556; **II** 18, 60, 134, 331, 411, 414; **III** 259, 265, 340, 536, 598, 653–55; **V** 180–83; **6** 12–13; **7** 166, 479; **8** 224, 287–89; **9** 44, 65–66 156, 210, 213, 219, 235–36, 430–31, 538; **10** 10, 50–52, 199, 236–37, 288, 304–05, 490–91; **11** 62, 349, 393, 498; **12** 54, 96–98, 309, 311, 315, 430–31, 439, 522, 548, 557; **13** 165, 260, 268, 277, 411, 545, 550, 562–63; **14** 62; **15** 402, 470; **16** 73, 75, 160, 327–28, 560; **17** 366, 460, 487; **18** 65, 168, 283, 445, **475–79 (upd.)**; **19** 143, 221, 309, 490; **20** 259, 263; **21** 73, 94, 96–97; **23** 23, 52, 210
Sears Roebuck de México, S.A. de C.V., 20 470–72; **21** 259
Seashore Transportation Co., **13** 398
Season-all Industries, **III** 735
SEAT. *See* Sociedad Española de Automoviles de Turismo.
Seattle Brewing and Malting Company. *See* Rainier Brewing Company.
Seattle Electric Company, **6** 565
Seattle FilmWorks, Inc., 20 473–75
Seattle First National Bank Inc., 8 469–71
Seattle Times Company, 15 445–47

Seaview Oil Co., **IV** 393
Seaway Express, **9** 510
Seaway Food Town, Inc., 9 452; **15 448–50**
SeaWest, **19** 390
SEB-Fastigheter A.B., **II** 352
SECA, **IV** 401
SECDO, **III** 618
SECO Industries, **III** 614
Seco Products Corporation, **22** 354
Secon GmbH, **13** 160
Second Bank of the United States, **II** 213; **9** 369
Second National Bank, **II** 254
Second National Bank of Bucyrus, **9** 474
Second National Bank of Ravenna, **9** 474
Secoroc, **III** 427
Le Secours, **III** 211
SecPac. *See* Security Pacific Corporation.
Secure Horizons, **11** 378–79
Securicor, **11** 547
Securitas Esperia, **III** 208
Securities Industry Automation Corporation, **9** 370
Securities International, Inc., **II** 440–41
Security Capital Corporation, 17 424–27; 21 476
Security Connecticut Life Insurance Co., **III** 276
Security Engineering, **III** 472
Security Express, **10** 269
Security First National Bank of Los Angeles, **II** 349
Security Life and Annuity Company, **11** 213
Security Management Company, **8** 535–36
Security National Bank, **II** 251, 336
Security National Corp., **10** 246
Security Pacific Corporation, II 349–50, 422; **III** 366; **8** 45, 48; **11** 447; **17** 137
Security Trust Company, **9** 229, 388
Security Union Title Insurance Co., **10** 43–44
Sedat Eldem, **13** 475
SEDCO, **17** 418
Sedgwick Group PLC, **I** 427; **III** 280, 366; **10** 38; **22** 318
SEDTCO Pty., **13** 61
See's Candies, **III** 213; **18** 60–61
Seeburg Corporation, **II** 22; **III** 430; **15** 538
Seed Restaurant Group Inc., **13** 321
Seed Solutions, Inc., **11** 491
Seeger Refrigerator Co., **III** 653; **12** 548
Seeger-Orbis, **III** 624
SEEQ Technology, Inc., **9** 114; **13** 47; **17** 32, 34
SEG, **I** 463
Sega of America, Inc., 7 396; **10** 124–25, 284–86, **482–85; 18** 520
Segespar, **II** 265
Sego Milk Products Company, **7** 428
Seguros Comercial America, **21** 413
Seguros El Corte Inglés, **V** 52
Seguros Monterrey, **19** 189
Seibels, Bruce & Co., **11** 394–95
Seiberling Rubber Company, **V** 244; **20** 259
Seibu Department Stores, Ltd., II 273; **V 184–86**
Seibu Railway Co. Ltd., V 187, **510–11,** 526
Seibu Saison, **6** 207
Seijo Green Plaza Co., **I** 283

Seikatsu-Soko, **V** 210
Seiko Corporation, I 488; **III** 445, **619–21; 11** 46; **12** 317; **13** 122; **16** 168, 549; **17 428–31 (upd.); 21** 122–23; **22** 413
Seiko Instruments USA Inc., **23** 210
Seine, **III** 391
Seino Transportation Company, Ltd., 6 **427–29**
Seismograph Service Limited, **II** 86; **11** 413; **17** 419
Seita, 23 424–27
Seiwa Fudosan Co., **I** 283
Seiyu, Ltd., V 187–89; **10** 389
Seizo-sha, **12** 483
Sekisui Chemical Co., Ltd., III 741–43
SEL, **I** 193, 463
Selat Marine Services, **22** 276
Selden, **I** 164, 300
Select-Line Industries, **9** 543
Selection Trust, **IV** 67, 380, 565
Selective Auto and Fire Insurance Co. of America, **III** 353
Selective Insurance Co., **III** 191
Selectronics Inc., **23** 210
Selenia, **I** 467; **II** 86
Self Auto, **23** 232
Self Service Restaurants, **II** 613
The Self-Locking Carton Company, **14** 163
Selfridge (Department Store), **V** 94, 177–78
Seligman & Latz, **18** 455
Selleck Nicholls, **III** 691
The Selmer Company, Inc., 19 392–94, 426, 428
Seltel, **6** 33
Semarca, **11** 523
Sematech, **18** 384, 481
Sembler Company, **11** 346
Semet-Solvay, **22** 29
Seminis, **21** 413
Seminole Electric Cooperative, **6** 583
Seminole Fertilizer, **7** 537–38
Semitool, Inc., 18 480–82
Semrau and Sons, **II** 601
SEN AG, **IV** 128
Sencel Aero Engineering Corporation, **16** 483
Seneca Foods Corporation, 17 432–34
Senelle-Maubeuge, **IV** 227
Senior Corp., **11** 261
Senshusha, **I** 506
Sensi, Inc., **22** 173
Sensormatic Electronics Corp., 11 443–45
Sentinel Foam & Envelope Corporation, **14** 430
Sentinel Group, **6** 295
Sentinel Savings and Loan, **10** 339
Sentinel Technologies, **III** 38
Sentinel-Star Company, **IV** 683; **22** 521
Sentrust, **IV** 92
Sentry, **II** 624
Sentry Insurance Company, **10** 210
Senyo Kosakuki Kenkyujo, **III** 595
Seohan Development Co., **III** 516; **7** 232
Sepa, **II** 594
AB Separator, **III** 417–19
SEPIC, **I** 330
Sept, **IV** 325
Sequa Corp., 13 460–63
Séquanaise, **III** 391–92
Sequent Computer Systems Inc., **10** 363
Sequoia Insurance, **III** 270

Sequoia Pharmacy Group, **13** 150
Sera-Tec Biologicals, Inc., **V** 175–76; **19** 355
Seraco Group, **V** 182
Serck Group, **I** 429
SEREB, **I** 45; **7** 10
Sereg Valves, S.A., **17** 147
Serewatt AG, **6** 491
Sergeant Drill Co., **III** 525
Sero-Genics, Inc., **V** 174–75
Serval Marketing, **18** 393
Servam Corp., **7** 471–73
Servel Inc., **III** 479; **22** 25
Service America Corp., 7 471–73
Service Bureau Corp., **III** 127
Service Control Corp. *See* Angelica Corporation.
Service Corporation International, 6 293–95; 16 343–44
Service Corporation of America, **17** 552
Service Games Company, **10** 482
Service Merchandise Company, Inc., V 190–92; 6 287; **9** 400; **19 395–99 (upd.)**
Service Partner, **I** 120
Service Pipe Line Co., **IV** 370
Service Q. General Service Co., **I** 109
Service Systems, **III** 103
ServiceMaster Inc., 23 428–31 (upd.)
Servicemaster Limited Partnership, 6 **44–46; 13** 199
Services Maritimes des Messageries Impériales. *See* Compagnie des Messageries Maritimes.
Servicios Financieros Quadrum S.A., **14** 156
Servisco, **II** 608
SERVISTAR, **12** 8
ServoChem A.B., **I** 387
Servomation Corporation, **7** 472–73
Servoplan, S.A., **8** 272
Sesame Street Book Club, **13** 560
Sespe Oil, **IV** 569
Sessler Inc., **19** 381
SET, **I** 466
SETCAR, **14** 458
Settsu Marine and Fire Insurance Co., **III** 367
Seven Arts Productions, Ltd., **II** 147, 176
7-Eleven. *See* The Southland Corporation.
Seven-Up Bottling Co. of Los Angeles, **II** 121
Seven-Up Co., **I** 245, 257; **II** 468, 477; **18** 418
Severn Trent PLC, 12 441–43
Seversky Aircraft Corporation, **9** 205
Sevin-Rosen Partners, **III** 124; **6** 221
Sewell Coal Co., **IV** 181
Sewell Plastics, Inc., **10** 222
Seybold Machine Co., **II** 37; **6** 602
Seymour Electric Light Co., **13** 182
Seymour International Press Distributor Ltd., **IV** 619
Seymour Press, **IV** 619
Seymour Trust Co., **13** 467
SFNGR. *See* Nouvelles Galeries Réunies.
SGC. *See* Supermarkets General Corporation.
SGLG, Inc., **13** 367
SGS Corp., **II** 117; **11** 46
Shaffer Clarke, **II** 594
Shakespeare Company, 16 296; **22 481–84**
Shakey's Pizza, **16** 447

Shaklee Corporation, 12 444–46; **17** 186
Shalco Systems, **13** 7
Shamrock Advisors, Inc., **8** 305
Shamrock Capital L.P., **7** 81–82
Shamrock Holdings, **III** 609; **7** 438; **9** 75; **11** 556
Shamrock Oil & Gas Co., **I** 403–04; **IV** 409; **7** 308
Shan-Chih Business Association, **23** 469
Shanghai Crown Maling Packaging Co. Ltd., **13** 190
Shanghai Hotels Co., **IV** 717
Shanghai International Finance Company Limited, **15** 433
Shanghai Kyocera Electronics Co., Ltd., **21** 331
Shanghai Petrochemical Co., Ltd., 18 483–85; **21** 83
Shangri-La Asia Ltd., **22** 305
Shannon Group, Inc., **18** 318, 320
Shared Financial Systems, Inc., **10** 501
Shared Medical Systems Corporation, 14 432–34
Shared Technologies Inc., **12** 71
Shared Use Network Systems, Inc., **8** 311
Sharon Steel Corp., **I** 497; **7** 360–61; **8** 536; **13** 158, 249
Sharon Tank Car Corporation, **6** 394
Sharp & Dohme, Incorporated, **I** 650; **11** 289, 494
Sharp Corporation, I 476; **II** 95–96; **III** 14, 428, 455, 480; **6** 217, 231; **11** 45; **12** 447–49 **(upd.)**; **13** 481; **16** 83; **21** 123; **22** 197
The Sharper Image Corporation, 10 486–88; **23** 210
Sharples Co., **I** 383
Sharples Separator Co., **III** 418–20
Shasta, **II** 571–73
Shaw Industries, 9 465–67; **19** 274, 276
Shaw's Supermarkets, Inc., **II** 658–59; **23** 169
Shawell Precast Products, **14** 248
Shawinigan Water and Power Company, **6** 501–02
Shawmut National Corporation, II 207; **12** 31; **13** 464–68
Shea's Winnipeg Brewery Ltd., **I** 268
Sheaffer Group, **23** 54, 57
Shearson Hammill & Company, **22** 405–06
Shearson Lehman Brothers Holdings Inc., I 202; **II** 398–99, 450, 478; **III** 319; **8** 118; **9** 468–70 **(upd.)**; **10** 62–63; **11** 418; **12** 459; **15** 124, 463–64
Shearson Lehman Hutton Holdings Inc., II 339, 445, 450–52; **III** 119; **9** 125; **10** 59, 63; **17** 38–39
Shedd's Food Products Company, **9** 318
Sheepbridge Engineering, **III** 495
Sheffield Banking Co., **II** 333
Sheffield Motor Co., **I** 158; **10** 292
Sheffield Twist Drill & Steel Co., **III** 624
Shekou Container Terminals, **16** 481
Shelby Insurance Company, **10** 44–45
Shelby Steel Tube Co., **IV** 572; **7** 550
Shelby Williams Industries, Inc., 14 435–37
Shelco, **22** 146
Sheldahl Inc., 23 432–35
Shelf Life Inc. *See* King Kullen Grocery Co., Inc.
Shell. *See* Shell Transport and Trading Company p.l.c. *and* Shell Oil Company.
Shell Australia Ltd., **III** 728

Shell BV, **IV** 518
Shell Chemical Corporation, **IV** 410, 481, 531–32, 540; **8** 415
Shell Coal International, **IV** 532
Shell Forestry, **21** 546
Shell France, **12** 153
Shell Nederland BV, **V** 658–59
Shell Oil Company, I 20, 26, 569; **III** 559; **IV** 392, 400, 531, 540–41; **6** 382, 457; **8** 261–62; **11** 522; **14** 25, 438–40 **(upd.)**; **17** 417; **19** 175–76; **21** 546; **22** 274
Shell Transport and Trading Company p.l.c., I 605; **II** 436, 459; **III** 522, 735; **IV** 363, 378–79, 381–82, 403, 412, 423, 425, 429, 440, 454, 466, 470, 472, 474, 484–86, 491, 505, 508, 530–32, 564. *See also* Royal Dutch Petroleum Company *and* Royal Dutch/Shell.
Shell Western E & P, **7** 323
Shell Winning, **IV** 413–14
Sheller-Globe Corporation, I 201–02; **17** 182
Shelly Brothers, Inc., **15** 65
Shenley Laboratories, **I** 699
Shepard Warner Elevator Co., **III** 467
Shepard's Citations, Inc., **IV** 636–37
Shepherd Hardware Products Ltd., **16** 357
Shepherd Plating and Finishing Company, **13** 233
Shepler Equipment Co., **9** 512
Sheraton Corp. of America, **I** 463–64, 487; **III** 98–99; **11** 198; **13** 362–63; **21** 91
Sherborne Group Inc./NH Holding Inc., **17** 20
Sherbrooke Paper Products Ltd., **17** 281
Sheridan Bakery, **II** 633
Sheridan Catheter & Instrument Corp., **III** 443
Sherix Chemical, **I** 682
Sherr-Gold, **23** 40
Sherritt Gordon Mines, **7** 386–87; **12** 260
The Sherwin-Williams Company, III 744–46; **8** 222, 224; **11** 384; **12** 7; **13** 469–71 **(upd.)**; **19** 180
Sherwood Medical Group, **I** 624; **III** 443–44; **10** 70
SHI Resort Development Co., **III** 635
ShianFu Optical Fiber, **III** 491
Shibaura Seisakusho Works, **I** 533; **12** 483
Shieh Chi Industrial Co., **19** 508
Shields & Co., **9** 118
Shikoku Drinks Co., **IV** 297
Shikoku Electric Power Company, Inc., V 718–20
Shikoku Machinery Co., **III** 634
Shimotsuke Electric Railway Company, **6** 431
Shimura Kako, **IV** 63
Shin Nippon Machine Manufacturing, **III** 634
Shin-Nihon Glass Co., **I** 221
Shinano Bank, **II** 291
Shinko Electric Co., Ltd., **IV** 129
Shinko Rayon Ltd., **I** 363; **V** 369–70
Shinriken Kogyo, **IV** 63
Shintech, **11** 159–60
Shinwa Tsushinki Co., **III** 593
Shiomi Casting, **III** 551
Shionogi & Co., Ltd., I 646, 651; **III** 60–61; **11** 90, 290; **17** 435–37 **(upd.)**
Ship 'n Shore, **II** 503; **9** 156–57; **10** 324
Shipowners and Merchants Tugboat Company, **6** 382

Shipper Group, **16** 344
Shiro Co., Ltd., **V** 96
Shirokiya Co., Ltd., **V** 199
Shiseido Company, Limited, II 273–74, 436; **III** 46, 48, 62–64; **8** 341, 343; **22** 485–88 **(upd.)**
Shockley Electronics, **20** 174
Shoe Carnival Inc., 14 441–43
Shoe Corp., **I** 289
Shoe Supply, Inc., **22** 213
Shoe Works Inc., **18** 415
Shoe-Town Inc., **23** 310
Shohin Kaihatsu Kenkyusho, **III** 595
Shoman Milk Co., **II** 538
Shonac Corp., **14** 427
Shonco, Inc., **18** 438
Shoney's, Inc., 7 474–76; **14** 453; **19** 286; **23** 436–39 **(upd.)**
Shop & Go, **II** 620
Shop 'n Bag, **II** 624
Shop 'n Save, **II** 669, 682; **12** 220–21
Shop Rite Foods Inc., **II** 672–74; **7** 105; **19** 479
ShopKo Stores Inc., II 669–70; **18** 505–07; **21** 457–59
Shoppers Food Warehouse Corporation, **16** 159, 161
Shopwell/Food Emporium, **II** 638; **16** 247, 249
Shore Manufacturing, **13** 165
Short Aircraft Co., **I** 50, 55, 92
Shoseido Co., **17** 110
Shoshi-Gaisha, **IV** 320
Shotton Paper Co. Ltd., **IV** 350
Showa Aircraft Industry Co., **I** 507–08
Showa Aluminum Corporation, **8** 374
Showa Bank, **II** 291–92
Showa Bearing Manufacturing Co., **III** 595
Showa Cotton Co., Ltd., **IV** 442
Showa Denko, **I** 493–94; **II** 292; **IV** 61
Showa Marutsutsu Co. Ltd., **8** 477
Showa Paper Co., **IV** 268
Showa Photo Industry, **III** 548
Showa Products Company, **8** 476
Showa Shell Sekiyu K.K., II 459; **IV** 542–43
ShowBiz Pizza Time, Inc., 12 123; **13** 472–74; **15** 73; **16** 447
Showboat, Inc., 19 400–02
Showcase of Fine Fabrics, **16** 197
Showerings, **I** 215
Showtime, **II** 173; **7** 222–23; **9** 74; **23** 274–75, 391, 503
Shredded Wheat Co., **II** 543; **7** 366
Shreve and Company, **12** 312
Shreveport Refrigeration, **16** 74
Shrewsbury and Welshpool Old Bank, **II** 307
Shu Uemura, **III** 43
Shubrooks International Ltd., **11** 65
Shueisha, **IV** 598
Shuford Mills, Inc., **14** 430
Shugart Associates, **6** 230; **8** 466; **22** 189
Shull Lumber & Shingle Co., **IV** 306
Shun Fung Ironworks, **IV** 717
Shunan Shigyo Co., Ltd., **IV** 160
Shurgard Storage Centers of Seattle, **21** 476
Shuttleworth Brothers Company. *See* Mohawk Industries, Inc.
Shuwa Corp., **22** 101
SHV Holdings N.V., **IV** 383; **14** 156
SI Holdings Inc., **10** 481
SIAS, **19** 192

SIAS-MPA, **I** 281
Sibco Universal, S.A., **14** 429
Siboney Shoe Corp., **22** 213
SIBV/MS Holdings, **IV** 295; **19** 226
Sicard Inc., **I** 185
Siddeley Autocar Co., **III** 508
Sidel. *See* Groupe Sidel S.A..
Sidélor, **IV** 226
Siderbrás, **IV** 125
Sidermex, **III** 581
Sidérurgie Maritime, **IV** 26
SIDMAR NV, **IV** 128
Siebe P.L.C., **13** 235
Siebel Group, **13** 544–45
Siegas, **III** 480; **22** 26
Siegler Heater Corp., **I** 481
Siemens AG, **I** 74, 192, 409–11, 462, 478, 542; **II** 22, 25, 38, 80–82, **97–100**, 122, 257, 279; **III** 139, 154–55, 466, 482, 516, 724; **6** 215–16; **7** 232; **9** 11, 32, 44; **10** 16, 363; **11** 59, 196, 235, 397–98, 460; **12** 546; **13** 402; **14** 169, **444–47 (upd.)**; **15** 125; **16** 392; **18** 32; **19** 166, 313; **20** 290; **22** 19, 373–74; **23** 389, 452, 494–95
Sierra Designs, Inc., **10** 215–16
Sierra Health Services, Inc., **15 451–53**
Sierra Leone Selection Trust, **IV** 66
Sierra On-Line Inc., **13** 92, 114; **14** 263; **15 454–56**; **16** 146
Sierra Pacific Industries, **22 489–91**
Sierrita Resources, Inc., **6** 590
Sigma Alimentos, S.A. de C.V., **19** 11–12
Sigma Coatings, **IV** 499
Sigma Network Systems, **11** 464
Sigma-Aldrich, **I 690–91**
Sigmor Corp., **IV** 410
Signal Companies, Inc. *See* AlliedSignal Inc.
Signal Galaxies, **13** 127
Signal Oil & Gas Inc., **I** 71, 178; **IV** 382; **7** 537; **11** 278; **19** 175; **22** 331
Signalite, Inc., **10** 319
Signature Corporation, **22** 412–13
Signature Group, **V** 145
Signet Banking Corporation, **11 446–48**
Signet Communications Corp., **16** 195
Signetics Co., **III** 684; **11** 56; **18** 383
Signode Industries, **III** 519; **22** 282
SIKEL NV, **IV** 128
Sikes Corporation, **III** 612
Sikorsky Aerospace, **I** 47, 84, 115, 530; **III** 458, 602; **9** 416; **10** 162; **18** 125
SIL&P. *See* Southern Illinois Light & Power Company.
Silenka B.V., **III** 733; **22** 436
Silex. *See* Hamilton Beach/Proctor-Silex Inc.
Silicon Beach Software, **10** 35
Silicon Compiler Systems, **11** 285
Silicon Engineering, **18** 20
Silicon Graphics Inc., **9 471–73**; **10** 119, 257; **12** 323; **15** 149, 320; **16** 137, 140; **20** 8
Silicon Microstructures, Inc., **14** 183
Silicon Systems Inc., **II** 110
Silo Electronics, **16** 73, 75
Silo Holdings, **9** 65; **23** 52
Silo Inc., **V** 50; **10** 306, 468; **19** 123
Silver & Co., **I** 428
Silver Burdett Co., **IV** 672, 675; **7** 528; **19** 405
Silver City Airways. *See* British World Airways Ltd.

Silver City Casino, **6** 204
Silver Dollar Mining Company, **20** 149
Silver Furniture Co., Inc., **15** 102, 104
Silver King Mines, **IV** 76
Silver Screen Partners, **II** 174
Silver's India Rubber Works & Telegraph Cable Co., **I** 428
Silverado Banking, **9** 199
Silverado Partners Acquisition Corp., **22** 80
Silverline, Inc., **16** 33
SilverPlatter Information Inc., **23 440–43**
Silvershoe Partners, **17** 245
Silverstar Ltd. S.p.A., **10** 113
Silvertown Rubber Co., **I** 428
Silvey Corp., **III** 350
Simca, **I** 154, 162; **11** 103
Sime Darby Berhad, **14 448–50**
Simeira Comercio e Industria Ltda., **22** 320
SIMEL S.A., **14** 27
Simer Pump Company, **19** 360
Simkins Industries, Inc., **8** 174–75
Simms, **III** 556
Simon & Schuster Inc., **II** 155; **IV 671–72**; **13** 559; **19 403–05 (upd.)**; **23** 503
Simon Adhesive Products, **IV** 253; **17** 30
Simon de Wit, **II** 641
Simon Engineering, **11** 510
Simon Marketing, Inc., **19** 112, 114
Simonius'sche Cellulosefabriken AG, **IV** 324
Simonize, **I** 371
AB Simpele, **IV** 347
Simple Shoes, Inc., **22** 173
Simplex Industries, Inc., **16** 296
Simplex Technologies Inc., **21 460–63**
Simplex Wire and Cable Co., **III** 643–45
Simplicity Pattern Company, **I** 447; **8** 349; **23** 98
Simpson Investment Company, **17 438–41**
Simpson Marketing, **12** 553
Simpsons, **V** 80
Sims Telephone Company, **14** 258
Simsmetal USA Corporation, **19** 380
SimuFlite, **II** 10
Sinai Kosher Foods, **14** 537
Sincat, **IV** 453
Sinclair Coal Co., **IV** 170; **10** 447–48
Sinclair Crude Oil Purchasing Co., **IV** 369
Sinclair Oil Corp., **I** 355, 569; **IV** 376, 394, 456–57, 512, 575
Sinclair Paint Company, **12** 219
Sinclair Petrochemicals Inc., **IV** 456
Sinclair Pipe Line Co., **IV** 368–69
Sinclair Research Ltd., **III** 113
Sindo Ricoh Co., **III** 160
Singapore Airlines Ltd., **6** 100, **117–18**, 123; **12** 192; **20** 313
Singapore Alpine Electronics Asia Pte. Ltd., **13** 31
Singapore Candle Company, **12** 393
Singapore Cement, **III** 718
Singapore Petroleum Co., **IV** 452
Singapore Straits Steamship Company, **6** 117
Singapore Telecom, **18** 348
Singapour, **II** 556
Singareni Collieries Ltd., **IV** 48–49
Singer and Friedlander, **I** 592
Singer Company, **I** 540; **II** 9–11; **6** 27, 241; **9** 232; **11** 150; **13** 521–22; **19** 211; **22** 4. *See also* Bicoastal Corp.

Singer Controls, **I** 155
Singer Hardware & Supply Co., **9** 542
Singer Sewing Machine Co., **12** 46
Single Service Containers Inc., **IV** 286
Singleton Seafood, **II** 494
Singular Software, **9** 80
Sinkers Inc., **21** 68
Sintel, S.A., **19** 256
Sioux City Gas and Electric Company, **6** 523–24
SIP. *See* Società Italiana per L'Esercizio delle Telecommunicazioni p.A.
Sir Speedy, Inc., **16 448–50**
SIRCOMA, **10** 375
SIREM, **23** 95
Sirloin Stockade, **10** 331
Sirrine. *See* CRSS Inc.
Sirrine Environmental Consultants, **9** 110
Sirte Oil Co., **IV** 454
Sisters Chicken & Biscuits, **8** 564
SIT-Siemens. *See* Italtel.
Sitca Corporation, **16** 297
Sitmar Cruises, **22** 445
Sitzmann & Heinlein GmbH, **IV** 198–99
Six Companies, Inc., **IV** 121; **7** 355
Six Flags Theme Parks, Inc., **III** 431; **IV** 676; **17 442–44**
600 Fanuc Robotics, **III** 482–83
61 Going to the Game!, **14** 293
Sizes Unlimited, **V** 115
Sizzler International Inc., **15** 361–62
The SK Equity Fund, L.P., **23** 177
Skånes Enskilda Bank, **II** 351
Skånska Ättiksfabriken, **I** 385
Skadden, Arps, Slate, Meagher & Flom, **10** 126–27; **18 486–88**
Skaggs Companies, **22** 37
Skaggs Drugs Centers, **II** 602–04; **7** 20
Skaggs-Albertson's Properties, **II** 604
Skagit Nuclear Power Plant, **6** 566
Skandinaviska Enskilda Banken, **II 351–53**, 365–66; **IV** 203
Skanska AB, **IV** 204
Skelly Oil Co., **IV** 575
Sketchley plc, **19** 124
SKF Industries Inc., **III** 623–24
Skidmore, Owings & Merrill, **13 475–76**
Skil-Craft Playthings, Inc., **13** 560
Skillern, **16** 560
Skillware, **9** 326
Skinner Macaroni Co., **II** 511
Skis Rossignol S.A., **15 460–62**
Skönvik, **IV** 338
SKS Group, **20** 363
SKW-Trostberg AG, **IV** 232
Sky Channel, **IV** 652
Sky Chefs, Inc., **16** 397
Sky Climber Inc., **11** 436
Sky Courier, **6** 345
Sky Merchant, Inc., **V** 78
Sky Television, **IV** 652–53; **7** 391–92
Skyband, Inc., **IV** 652; **7** 391; **12** 359
SkyBox International Inc., **15** 72–73
Skyline Homes, **17** 82
SkyTel Corp., **18** 349; **23** 212
Skywalker Sound, **12** 322
Skyway Airlines, **6** 78; **11** 299
SL Holdings. *See* Finlay Enterprises, Inc.
Slade Gorton & Company, **13** 243
Slater Co. Foods, **II** 607
Slater Electric, **21** 349
Slater Systems, Inc., **13** 48
Slick Airways, **6** 388

**Slim-Fast Nutritional Foods
International, Inc.,** **12** 531; **18** 489–91
Slingerland Drum Company, **16** 239
Slip-X Safety Treads, **9** 72
SLJFB Vedrenne, **22** 344
SLN-Peñarroya, **IV** 108
Sloan's. *See* Gristede's Sloan's, Inc.
Sloss Industries Corporation, **22** 544
Slots-A-Fun, **6** 204
Slough Estates plc, IV 722–25
AB Small Business Investment Co., Inc.,
    13 111–12
Small Tube Products, Inc., **23** 517
SMALLCO, **III** 340
Smalley Transportation Company, **6**
    421–23
SMAN. *See* Societe Mecanique
    Automobile du Nord.
Smart & Final, Inc., 12 153–54; **16**
    451–53
Smart Communications, **18** 180, 182
Smart Shirts Ltd., **8** 288–89
Smart Talk Network, Inc., **16** 319
SmartCash, **18** 543
Smead Manufacturing Co., 17 445–48
Smedley's, **II** 513
Smethwick Drop Forgings, **III** 494
SMH, **17** 430
Smirnoff, **14** 212; **18** 41
Smith & Hawken, **10** 215, 217
Smith & Nephew plc, 17 449–52
Smith & Weston, **19** 430
Smith Barney Inc., I 614; **III** 569; **6** 410;
    10 63; **13** 328; **15** 463–65; **19** 385; **20**
    360; **22** 406
Smith Bros., **I** 711
Smith Corona Corp., III 502; **7** 209; **13**
    477–80; 14 76; **23** 210
Smith International, Inc., III 429; **15**
    466–68
Smith Mackenzie & Co., **III** 522
Smith McDonell Stone and Co., **14** 97
Smith Meter Co., **11** 4
Smith New Court PLC, **13** 342
Smith Packaging Ltd., **14** 429
Smith Parts Co., **11** 3
Smith Transfer Corp., **II** 607–08; **13** 49
Smith's Food & Drug Centers, Inc., 8
    472–74; 17 558, 561
Smith's Stampings, **III** 494
Smith-Higgins, **III** 9–10
Smithfield Foods, Inc., 7 477–78,
    524–25; **22** 509, 511
SmithKline Beckman Corporation, I 389,
    636, 640, 644, 646, 657, **692–94,** 696;
    II 331; **III** 65–66; **14** 46, 53
SmithKline Beecham PLC, III 65–67; **8**
    210; **9** 347; **10** 47, 471; **11** 9, 90, 337;
    13 77; **14** 58; **16** 438; **17** 287
Smiths Bank, **II** 333
Smiths Food Group, Ltd., **II** 502; **10** 323
Smiths Industries, **III** 555
Smitty's Super Valu Inc., **II** 663–64; **12**
    391; **17** 560–61
SMP Clothing, Inc., **22** 462
SMS, **IV** 226; **7** 401
Smucker. *See* The J.M. Smucker Company.
Smurfit Companies. *See* Jefferson Smurfit
    Group plc.
SN Repal. *See* Société Nationale de
    Recherche de Pétrole en Algérie.
Snack Ventures Europe, **10** 324
Snake River Sugar Company, **19** 468
Snam Montaggi, **IV** 420

Snam Progetti, **IV** 420, 422
Snap-on Tools Corporation, III 628; **7**
    479–80
Snapper, **I** 447
Snapple Beverage Corporation, 11
    449–51; 12 411
Snappy Car Rentals, **6** 393
SNE Enterprises, Inc., **12** 397
SNEA. *See* Société Nationale Elf
    Aquitaine.
Snecma Group, **17** 482
Snell Acoustics, **22** 99
SNET. *See* Southern New England
    Telecommunications Corporation.
SNMC Management Corporation, **11** 121
Snoqualmie Falls Plant, **6** 565
**Snow Brand Milk Products Company,
    Limited, II 574–75**
Snow King Frozen Foods, **II** 480
Snowy Mountains Hydroelectric Authority,
    IV 707; **13** 118
SNPA, **IV** 453
SnyderGeneral Corp., **8** 321
Soap Opera Magazine, **10** 287
Sobrom, **I** 341
Sobu Railway Company, **6** 431
Socal. *See* Standard Oil Company
    (California).
SOCAR, **IV** 505
Sochiku, **9** 30
Sociade Intercontinental de Compressores
    Hermeticos SICOM, S.A., **8** 515
La Sociale di A. Mondadori & C., **IV** 585
La Sociale, **IV** 585
Sociedad Alfa-Laval, **III** 419
Sociedad Bilbaina General de Credito, **II**
    194
Sociedad Española de Automobiles del
    Turismo S.A. (SEAT), **I** 207, 459–60; **6**
    47–48; **11** 550
Sociedad Financiera Mexicana, **19** 189
Sociedade Anónima Concessionária de
    Refinacao em Portugal. *See* SACOR.
Sociedade de Lubrificantes e Combustiveis,
    IV 505
Sociedade Nacional de Petróleos, **IV** 504
Sociedade Portuguesa de Petroquimica, **IV**
    505
Sociedade Portuguesa e Navios-Tanques.
    See SOPONATA.
Società Anonima Fabbrica Italiana di
    Automobili, **I** 161
Società Anonima Lombarda Fabbrica
    Automobili, **13** 27
Società Azionaria Imprese Perforazioni, **IV**
    419–20
Società Concessioni e Costruzioni
    Autostrade, **I** 466
Società Edison, **II** 86
Societa Esercizio Fabbriche Automobili e
    Corse Ferrari, **13** 219
Società Finanziaria Idrocarburi, **IV** 421
**Società Finanziaria Telefonica per
    Azioni, I** 465–66; **V 325–27**
Società Generale di Credito Mobiliare, **II**
    191
Società Idrolettrica Piemonte, **I** 465–66
Societa Italiana Gestione Sistemi Multi
    Accesso, **6** 69
Società Italiana per L'Esercizio delle
    Telecommunicazioni p.A., **I** 466–67; **V**
    325–27
Società Italiana per la Infrastrutture e
    l'Assetto del Territorio, **I** 466

Società Italiana Pirelli, **V** 249
Società Italiana Vetro, **IV** 421
Società Nazionale Metanodotti, **IV** 419–21
Società Ravennate Metano, **IV** 420
Società Reale Mutua, **III** 207
Società Africaine de Déroulage des Ets
    Rougier, **21** 439
Société Air France. *See* Groupe Air France.
Société Alsacienne de Magasins SA, **19**
    308
Societe Anonima Italiana Ing. Nicola
    Romeo & Company, **13** 27
Societe Anonomie Alfa Romeo, **13** 28
Societe Anonyme Automobiles Citroen, **7**
    35–36
Société Anonyme de la Manufactures des
    Glaces et Produits Chimiques de Saint-
    Gobain, Chauny et Cirey. *See*
    Compagnie de Saint-Gobain S.A.
Société Anonyme des Ciments
    Luxembourgeois, **IV** 25
Société Anonyme des Fermiers Reúnis, **23**
    219
Société Anonyme des Hauts Fourneaux et
    Aciéries de Differdange-St. Ingbert-
    Rumelange, **IV** 26
Société Anonyme des Hauts Fourneaux et
    Forges de Dudelange, **22** 42
Société Anonyme des Mines du
    Luxembourg et des Forges de
    Sarrebruck, **IV** 24; **22** 42
La Societe Anonyme Francaise Holophane,
    19 211
Societe Anonyme Francaise Timken, **8** 530
Société Anonyme Telecommunications, **III**
    164
Société, Auxiliaire d'Entrepreses SA, **13**
    206
Société Belge de Banque, **II** 294–95
Société BIC, S.A., **III** 29; **8** 60–61; **23**
    55–57
Société Calédonia, **IV** 107
Société Centrale Union des Assurances de
    Paris, **III** 391, 393
Société Chimiques des Usines du Rhône, **I**
    388
Société Civile Valoptec, **21** 222
Societe Commerciale Citroen, **7** 36
Société d'Ougrée-Marihaye, **IV** 51
Société de Collecte des Prodicteirs de
    Preval, **19** 50
Societe de Construction des Batignolles, **II**
    93
Société de Crédit Agricole, **II** 264
Société de Développements et
    d'Innovations des Marchés Agricoles et
    Alimentaires, **II** 576
Société de Diffusion de Marques, **II** 576
Société de Diffusion Internationale Agro-
    Alimentaire, **II** 577
Societé de garantie des Crédits à court
    terme, **II** 233
Société de l'Oléoduc de la Sarre a.r.l., **IV**
    197
Société de Prospection Électrique, **III** 616;
    17 416
La Société de Traitement des Minerais de
    Nickel, Cobalt et Autres, **IV** 107
Société des Caves et des Producteurs
    Reunis de Roquefort, **19** 49
Société des Eaux d'Evian, **II** 474
Société des Forges d'Eich–Metz et Cie, **IV**
    24

Société des Forges et Aciéries du Nord-Est,
IV 226
Société des Forges et Fonderies de
Montataire, IV 226
Société des Grandes Entreprises de
Distribution, Inno-France, V 58
Société des Hauts Fourneaux et Forges de
Denain-Anzin, IV 226
Société des Mines du Luxembourg et de
Sarrebruck, IV 25
Société des Pétroles d'Afrique Equatoriale,
IV 545; 7 482
Société des Usines Chimiques des
Laboratoires Français, I 669
Société des Vins de France, I 281
Société Economique de Rennes, 19 98
Société Électrométallurgique Francaise, IV
173
Société European de Semi-Remorques, 7
513
Société Européenne de Brasseries, II
474–75
Société Financiére Européenne, II 202–03,
233
Societe Financiere pour l'Industrie au
Mexique, 19 188
Société Française des Cables Electriques
Bertrand-Borel, 9 9
Société Française des Teintures
Inoffensives pour Cheveux, III 46
Société Française pour l'Exploitation du
Pétrole, IV 557
Société Gélis-Poudenx-Sans, IV 108
Société General de Banque, 17 324
Société Générale, II 233, 266, 295,
354–56; 9 148; 13 203, 206; 19 51
Société Générale de Banque, II 279, 295,
319; 14 169
Société Générale de Belgique, II 270,
294–95; IV 26; 10 13; 22 44
Société Générale du Téléphones, 21 231
Société Générale pour favoriser l'Industrie
nationale, II 294
Société Industrielle Belge des Pétroles, IV
498–99
Société Internationale Pirelli S.A., V 250
Société Irano-Italienne des Pétroles, IV 466
Société Laitière Vendômoise, 23 219
Société Le Nickel, IV 107–08, 110
Societe Mecanique Automobile de l'Est/du
Nord, 7 37
Société Métallurgique, IV 25–26, 227
Société Minière de Bakwanga, IV 67
Société Minière des Terres Rouges, IV
25–26
Société Nationale de Programmes de
Télévision Française 1. See Télévision
Française 1.
Société Nationale de Recherche de Pétrole
en Algérie, IV 545, 559; 7 482
Société Nationale de Transport et de
Commercialisation des Hydrocarbures,
IV 423
Société Nationale des Chemins de Fer
Français, V 512–15
Société Nationale des Pétroles d'Aquitaine,
21 203–05
Société Nationale Elf Aquitaine, I
303–04, 670, 676–77; II 260; IV 174,
397–98, 424, 451, 453–54, 472–74,
499, 506, 515–16, 518, 525, 535,
544–47, 559–60; V 628; 7 481–85
(upd.); 8 452; 11 97; 12 153

Société Nationale pour la Recherche, la
Production, le Transport, la
Transformation et la Commercialisation
des Hydrocarbures, IV 423–24
Société Nord Africaine des Ciments
Lafarge, III 703
Société Nouvelle d'Achat de Bijouterie, 16
207
Société Parisienne d'Achats en Commun,
19 307
Societe Parisienne pour l'Industrie
Electrique, II 93
Société pour l'Eportation de Grandes
Marques, I 281
Société pour l'Étude et la Realisation
d'Engins Balistiques. See SEREB.
Société pour L'Exploitation de la
Cinquième Chaîne, 6 374
Société pour le Financement de l'Industrie
Laitière, 19 51
Société Samos, 23 219
Société Succursaliste S.A.
d'Approvisionnements Guyenne et
Gascogne. See Guyenne et Gascogne.
Societe Vendeenne des Embalages, 9 305
Societe-Hydro-Air S.a.r.L., 9 27
Society Corporation, 9 474–77
Society of Lloyd's, III 278–79
SOCO Chemical Inc., 8 69
Socombel, IV 497
Socony. See Standard Oil Co. (New York).
Socony Mobil Oil Co., Inc., IV 465; 7 353
Sodak Gaming, Inc., 9 427
Sodastream Holdings, II 477
Sodexho Group, 23 154
Sodiaal, II 577; 19 50
SODIMA, II 576–77
Sodiso, 23 247
Sodyeco, 1 673
Soekor, IV 93
Soffo, 22 365
SOFIL. See Société pour le Financement
de l'Industrie Laitière.
Sofimex. See Sociedad Financiera
Mexicana.
Sofiran, IV 467
Sofitam, S.A., 21 493, 495
Sofrem, IV 174
Softbank Corp., 12 562; 13 481–83; 16
168
SoftKat. See Baker & Taylor, Inc.
Softsel Computer Products, 12 334–35
SoftSolutions Technology Corporation, 10
558
Software AG, 11 18
Software Arts, 6 254
Software Development Pty., Ltd., 15 107
Software Dimensions, Inc. See ASK
Group, Inc.
Software, Etc., 13 545
The Software Group Inc., 23 489, 491
Software International, 6 224
Software Plus, Inc., 10 514
Software Publishing Corp., 14 262
Softwood Holdings Ltd., III 688
Sogara S.A., 23 246–48
Sogebra S.A., I 257
Sogedis, 23 219
Sogen International Corp., II 355
Sogexport, II 355
Soginnove, II 355–56
Sohio Chemical Company, 13 502
Sohken Kako Co., Ltd., IV 327
Soil Teq, Inc., 17 10

Soilserv, Inc. See Mycogen Corporation.
Soinlahti Sawmill and Brick Works, IV
300
Sola Holdings, III 727
Solair Inc., 14 43
La Solana Corp., IV 726
Solar, IV 614
Solar Electric Corp., 13 398
Solectron Corp., 12 161–62, 450–52
Solel Boneh Construction, II 47
Soletanche Co., I 586
Solid Beheer B.V., 10 514
Solid State Dielectrics, I 329; 8 152
Solite Corp., 23 224–25
Sollac, IV 226–27
Solmer, IV 227
Solo Serve Corp., 23 177
Soloman Brothers, 17 561
Solomon Smith Barney Inc., 22 404
Solomon Valley Milling Company, 6 592
Solon Automated Services, II 607
Solsound Industries, 16 393
Solvay & Cie S.A., I 303, 394–96,
414–15; III 677; IV 300; 16 121; 21
254, 464–67 (upd.)
Solvay Animal Health Inc., 12 5
Solvent Resource Recovery, Inc., 9 109
Solvents Recovery Service of New Jersey,
Inc., 8 464
SOMABRI, 12 152
SOMACA, 12 152
Somerville Electric Light Company, 12 45
Sommer-Allibert S.A., 19 406–09; 22 49
Sommers Drug Stores, 9 186
SONAP, IV 504–06
Sonat, Inc., 6 577–78; 22 68
Sonatrach. See Entreprise Nationale
Sonatrach.
Sonecor Systems, 6 340
Sonesson, I 211
Sonet Media AB, 23 390
Sonic Corporation, 14 451–53; 16 387
Sonneborn Chemical and Refinery Co., I
405
Sonnen Basserman, II 475
SonnenBraune, 22 460
Sonoco Products Company, 8 475–77; 12
150–51; 16 340
Sonoma Mortgage Corp., II 382
Sonometrics Inc., I 667
Sony Corporation, I 30, 534; II 56, 58,
91–92, 101–03, 117–19, 124, 134, 137,
440; III 141, 143, 340, 658; 6 30; 7
118; 9 385; 10 86, 119, 403; 11 46,
490–91, 557; 12 75, 161, 448, 453–56
(upd.); 13 399, 403, 482, 573; 14 534;
16 94; 17 533; 18 18; 19 67; 20 439; 21
129; 22 194
Sonzogno, IV 585
Soo Line, V 429–30
Soo Line Mills, II 631
SOPEAL, III 738
Sophia Jocoba GmbH, IV 193
SOPI, IV 401
Sopwith Aviation Co., III 507–08
Soravie, II 265
Sorbus, 6 242
Sorcim, 6 224
Soreal, 8 344
Sorg Paper Company. See Mosinee Paper
Corporation.
Sorrento, 19 51
SOS Co., II 531
Sosa, Bromley, Aguilar & Associates, 6 22

Soterra, Inc., **15** 188
Sotheby's Holdings, Inc., 11 452–54; **15** 98–100
Sound of Music Inc. *See* Best Buy Co., Inc.
Sound Trek, **16** 74
Sound Video Unlimited, **16** 46
Sound Warehouse, **9** 75
Source One Mortgage Services Corp., **12** 79
Source Perrier, **7** 383
Souriau, **19** 166
South African Airways Ltd. (SAA), **6** 84, 433, 435
South African Breweries Ltd., I 287–89, 422
South African Coal, Oil and Gas Corp., **IV** 533
South African Railways, **6** 434–35
South African Torbanite Mining and Refining Co., **IV** 534
South African Transport Services, **6** 433, 435
South American Cable Co., **I** 428
South Asia Tyres, **20** 263
South Carolina Electric & Gas Company, **6** 574–76
South Carolina Industries, **IV** 333
South Carolina National Corporation, **16** 523, 526
South Central Bell Telephone Co. **V** 276–78
South Central Railroad Co., **14** 325
South China Morning Post (Holdings) Ltd., **II** 298; **IV** 652; **7** 392
South Coast Gas Compression Company, Inc., **11** 523
South Coast Terminals, Inc., **16** 475
South Dakota Public Service Company, **6** 524
South Fulton Light & Power Company, **6** 514
South Improvement Co., **IV** 427
South Manchuria Railroad Co. Ltd., **IV** 434
South of Scotland Electricity Board, **19** 389–90
South Penn Oil Co., **IV** 488–89
South Puerto Rico Sugar Co., **I** 452
South Puerto Rico Telephone Co., **I** 462
South Sea Textile, **III** 705
South Texas Stevedore Co., **IV** 81
South-Western Publishing Co., **8** 526–28
Southam Inc., 7 486–89; **15** 265
Southco, **II** 602–03; **7** 20–21
Southcorp Holdings Ltd., **17** 373; **22** 350
Southdown, Inc., 14 454–56
Southeast Bank of Florida, **11** 112
Southeast Banking Corp., **II** 252; **14** 103
Southeast Public Service Company, **8** 536
Southeastern Power and Light Company, **6** 447; **23** 28
Southeastern Telephone Company, **6** 312
Southern and Phillips Gas Ltd., **13** 485
Southern Bank, **10** 426
Southern Bearings Co., **13** 78
Southern Bell, **10** 202
Southern Biscuit Co., **II** 631
Southern Blvd. Supermarkets, Inc., **22** 549
Southern Box Corp., **13** 441
Southern California Edison Co., **II** 402; **V** 711, 713–15, 717; **11** 272; **12** 106
Southern California Gas Co., **I** 569
Southern Casualty Insurance Co., **III** 214

Southern Clay Products, **III** 691
Southern Clays Inc., **IV** 82
Southern Colorado Power Company, **6** 312
Southern Comfort Corp., **I** 227
Southern Connecticut Newspapers Inc., **IV** 677
Southern Cotton Co., **IV** 224
Southern Cotton Oil Co., **I** 421; **11** 23
Southern Discount Company of Atlanta, **9** 229
Southern Electric PLC, 13 484–86
Southern Electric Supply Co., **15** 386
Southern Equipment & Supply Co., **19** 344
Southern Extract Co., **IV** 310; **19** 266
Southern Forest Products, Inc., **6** 577
Southern Gage, **III** 519; **22** 282
Southern Graphic Arts, **13** 405
Southern Guaranty Cos., **III** 404
Southern Idaho Water Power Company, **12** 265
Southern Illinois Light & Power Company, **6** 504
Southern Indiana Gas and Electric Company, 13 487–89
Southern Japan Trust Bank, **V** 114
Southern Kraft Corp., **IV** 286
Southern Lumber Company, **8** 430
Southern Manufacturing Company, **8** 458
Southern National Bankshares of Atlanta, **II** 337; **10** 425
Southern Natural Gas Co., **III** 558; **6** 447–48, 577
Southern Nevada Power Company, **11** 343
Southern Nevada Telephone Company, **6** 313; **11** 343
Southern New England Telecommunications Corporation, 6 338–40
Southern Nitrogen Co., **IV** 123
Southern Oregon Broadcasting Co., **7** 15
Southern Pacific Communications Corporation, **9** 478–79
Southern Pacific Rail Corp., **12** 18–20
Southern Pacific Railroad, **I** 13; **II** 329, 381, 448; **IV** 625; **19** 202
Southern Pacific Transportation Company, V 516–18; **12** 278
Southern Peru Copper Corp., **IV** 33
Southern Phenix Textiles Inc., **15** 247–48
Southern Pine Lumber Co., **IV** 341
Southern Railway Company, **V** 484–85
Southern Science Applications, Inc., **22** 88
Southern States Trust Co., **II** 336
Southern Sun Hotel Corp., **I** 288
Southern Surety Co., **III** 332
Southern Telephone Company, **14** 257
Southern Television Corp., **II** 158; **IV** 650; **7** 389
Southern Union Company, **12** 542
Southern Utah Fuel Co., **IV** 394
Southern Video Partnership, **9** 74
Southern Water plc, **19** 389–91
The Southland Corporation, II 449, 620, 660–61; **IV** 392, 508; **V** 89; **7** 114, 374, 490–92 (**upd.**); **9** 178; **13** 333, 449, 525; **23** 406–07
Southland Mobilcom Inc., **15** 196
Southland Paper, **13** 118
Southland Royalty Co., **10** 190
Southlife Holding Co., **III** 218
Southmark, **11** 483
Southtrust Corporation, 11 455–57
Southview Pulp Co., **IV** 329

Southwest Airlines Co., I 106; **6** 72–74, 119–21; **21** 143; **22** 22
Southwest Airmotive Co., **II** 16
Southwest Converting, **19** 414
Southwest Enterprise Associates, **13** 191
Southwest Forest Industries, **IV** 287, 289, 334
Southwest Gas Corporation, 19 410–12
Southwest Hide Co., **16** 546
Southwest Potash Corp., **IV** 18; **6** 148–49
Southwestern Bell Corporation, V 328–30; **6** 324; **10** 431, 500; **14** 489; **17** 110; **18** 22
Southwestern Electric Power Co., 21 468–70
Southwestern Gas Pipeline, **7** 344
Southwestern Illinois Coal Company, **7** 33
Southwestern Life Insurance, **I** 527; **III** 136
Southwestern Pipe, **III** 498
Southwestern Public Service Company, 6 579–81
Southwestern Refining Company, Inc., **IV** 446; **22** 303
Southwestern Textile Company, **12** 393
Southwire Company, Inc., 8 478–80; **12** 353; **23** 444–47 (**upd.**)
Souvall Brothers, **8** 473
Sovereign Corp., **III** 221; **14** 109
Sovran Financial, **10** 425–26
SovTransavto, **6** 410
Soyland Power Cooperative, **6** 506
SP Reifenwerke, **V** 253
SP Tyres, **V** 253
Space Craft Inc., **9** 463
Space Data Corporation, **22** 401
Space Systems Corporation. *See* Orbital Sciences Corporation.
Space Systems/Loral, **9** 325
Spacemakers Inc., **IV** 287
Spagnesi, **18** 258
Spalding, Inc., **17** 243; **23** 449
Spanish International Communications Corp., **IV** 621; **18** 212
Spanish River Pulp and Paper Mills, **IV** 246
Sparbanken Bank, **18** 543
SPARC International, **7** 499
Spare Change, **10** 282
Sparklets Ltd., **I** 315
Sparks Family Hospital, **6** 191
Sparks-Withington Company. *See* Sparton Corporation.
Sparrow Records, **22** 194
Sparta, Inc., **18** 369
Spartan Motors Inc., 14 457–59
Spartan Stores Inc., I 127; **II** 679–80; **8** 481–82; **10** 302; **12** 489; **14** 412
Spartech Corporation, 9 92; **19** 413–15
Sparton Corporation, 18 492–95
SPCM, Inc., **14** 477
Spec's Music, Inc., 19 416–18
Spécia, **I** 388
Special Agent Investigators, Inc., **14** 541
Special Foods, **14** 557
Special Light Alloy Co., **IV** 153
Specialized Bicycle Components Inc., **19** 384
Specialty Coatings Inc., 8 483–84
Specialty Papers Co., **IV** 290
Specialty Products Co., **8** 386
Spectra Star, Inc., **18** 521
Spectra-Physics AB, **9** 380–81

Spectral Dynamics Corporation. *See* Scientific-Atlanta, Inc.

Spectron MicroSystems, **18** 143

Spectrum Concepts, **10** 394–95

Spectrum Dyed Yarns of New York, **8** 559

Spectrum Health Care Services, **13** 48

Spectrum Medical Technologies, Inc., **22** 409

Spectrum Technology Group, Inc., **7** 378; **18** 112

Spectrumedia, **21** 361

Speed-O-Lac Chemical, **8** 553

SpeeDee Marts, **II** 661

Speedy Muffler King, **10** 415

Speidel Newspaper Group, **IV** 612; **7** 191

Spelling Entertainment Group, Inc., 9 75; **14 460–62; 23** 503

Spencer & Spencer Systems, Inc., **18** 112

Spencer Beef, **II** 536

Spencer Gifts, Inc., **II** 144; **15** 464

Spencer Stuart and Associates, Inc., 14 463–65

Spenco Medical Corp., **III** 41; **16** 303

Sperry & Hutchinson Co., **12** 299; **23** 243–44

Sperry Aerospace Group, **II** 40, 86; **6** 283; **12** 246, 248

Sperry Corporation, **I** 101, 167; **III** 165, 642; **6** 281–82; **8** 92; **11** 139; **12** 39; **13** 511; **18** 386, 542; **22** 379. *See also* Unisys Corporation.

Sperry Milling Co., **II** 501; **10** 322

Sperry New Holland. *See* New Holland N.V.

Sperry Rand Corp., **II** 63, 73; **III** 126, 129, 149, 166, 329, 642; **6** 241, 261, 281–82; **16** 137

3phere Inc., **8** 326; **13** 92

Spicer Manufacturing Co., **I** 152; **III** 568; **20** 359; **23** 170–71

Spie Batignolles SA, **I** 563; **II** 93–94; **13** 206; **18** 471–73

Spiegel, Inc., III 598; **V** 160; **8** 56–58; **10** 168, **489–91; 11** 498; **9** 190, 219; **13** 179; **15** 339

Spillers, **II** 500

Spin Physics, **III** 475–76; **7** 163

SPIRE Corporation, **14** 477

Spirella Company of Great Britain Ltd., **V** 356

Spoerle Electronic, **10** 113

Spokane Falls Electric Light and Power Company. *See* Edison Electric Illuminating Company.

Spokane Falls Water Power Company, **6** 595

Spokane Gas and Fuel, **IV** 391

Spokane Natural Gas Company, **6** 597

Spokane Street Railway Company, **6** 595

Spokane Traction Company, **6** 596

Spom Japan, **IV** 600

Spoor Behrins Campbell and Young, **II** 289

Spoornet, **6** 435

Sporloisirs S.A., **9** 157

Sport Chalet, Inc., 16 454–56

Sport Supply Group, Inc., 22 458–59; **23 448–50**

Sporting Dog Specialties, Inc., **14** 386

Sporting News Publishing Co., **IV** 677–78

Sportmart, Inc., 15 469–71

Sports & Recreation, Inc., 15 470; **17 453–55**

The Sports Authority, Inc., 15 470; **16 457–59; 17** 453; **18** 286

Sports Experts Inc., **II** 652

Sports Inc., **14** 8

Sports Traders, Inc., **18** 208

Sports-Tech Inc., **21** 300

Sportservice Corporation, **7** 133–35

Sportstown, Inc., **15** 470

Sportsystems Corporation, **7** 133, 135

Sprague Co., **I** 410

Sprague Devices, Inc., **11** 84

Sprague Electric Company, **6** 261

Sprague Electric Railway and Motor Co., **II** 27; **12** 193

Sprague Technologies, **21** 520

Sprague, Warner & Co., **II** 571

Spray-Rite, **I** 366

Sprayon Products, **III** 745

Sprecher & Schuh, **9** 10

Spring Co., **21** 96, 246

Spring Forge Mill, **8** 412

Spring Industries, Inc., V 378–79

Spring Valley Brewery. *See* Kirin Brewery Company, Limited.

Springbok Editions, **IV** 621

Springer Verlag GmbH & Co., **IV** 611, 641

Springfield Bank, **9** 474

Springhouse Corp., **IV** 610

Springhouse Financial Corp., **III** 204

Springmaid International, Inc., **19** 421

Springs Industries, Inc., 19 419–22 (upd.)

Sprint Communications Company, L.P., 9 478–80; 10 19, 57, 97, 201–03; **11** 183, 185, 500–01; **18** 32, 164–65, 569–70; **22** 19, 162. *See also* US Sprint Communications.

Spruce Falls Power and Paper Co., **III** 40; **IV** 648; **16** 302, 304; **19** 284

Spun Yarns, Inc., **12** 503

Spur Oil Co., **7** 362

SPX Corporation, 10 492–95

SQ Software, Inc., **10** 505

SQL Solutions, Inc., **10** 505

Square D Company, **18** 473

Square Industries, **18** 103, 105

Squibb Beech-Nut. *See* Beech-Nut Nutrition Corp.

Squibb Corporation, I 380–81, 631, 651, 659, 675, **695–97; III** 17, 19, 67; **8** 166; **9** 6–7; **13** 379–80; **16** 438–39

SR Beteiligungen Aktiengesellschaft, **III** 377

SRI International, **10** 139

SRI Strategic Resources Inc., **6** 310

SS Cars, Ltd. *See* Jaguar Cars, Ltd.

Ssangyong Cement Industrial Co., Ltd., III 747–50; IV 536–37, 539

SSC&B-Lintas, **I** 16–17; **14** 315

SSDS, Inc., **18** 537

SSI Medical Services, Inc., **10** 350

SSMC Inc., **II** 10

SSP Company, Inc., **17** 434

St. *See under* Saint

Staal Bankiers, **13** 544

Stadia Colorado Corporation, **18** 140

Städtische Elecktrlcltäts-Werke A.G., **I** 410

Staefa Control System Limited, **6** 490

StaffAmerica, Inc., **16** 50

Stafford Old Bank, **II** 307

Stag Cañon Fuel Co., **IV** 177

Stags' Leap Winery, **22** 80

Stahl-Urban Company, **8** 287–88

Stahlwerke Peine-Salzgitter AG, **IV** 201

Stahlwerke Röchling AG, **III** 694–95

Stahlwerke Südwestfalen AG, **IV** 89

Stal-Astra GmbH, **III** 420

Staley Continental, **II** 582

Stamford Drug Group, **9** 68

Stanadyne, Inc., **7** 336; **12** 344

Standard & Poor's Corp., **IV** 29, 482, 636–37; **12** 310

Standard Accident Co., **III** 332

Standard Aero, **III** 509

Standard Aircraft Equipment, **II** 16

Standard Alaska, **7** 559

Standard Bank, **17** 324

Standard Bank of Canada, **II** 244

Standard Box Co., **17** 357

Standard Brands, **I** 248; **II** 542, 544; **7** 365, 367; **18** 538

Standard Car Truck, **18** 5

Standard Chartered PLC, II 298, 309, 319, **357** 59, 386; **10** 170

Standard Chemical Products, **III** 33

Standard Commercial Corporation, 12 110; **13 490–92**

Standard Drug Co., **V** 171

Standard Electric Time Company, **13** 233

Standard Electrica, **II** 13

Standard Elektrik Lorenz A.G., **II** 13, 70; **17** 353

Standard Equities Corp., **III** 98

Standard Federal Bank, 9 481–83

Standard Fire Insurance Co., **III** 181–82

Standard Fruit and Steamship Co. of New Orleans, **II** 491

Standard Gauge Manufacturing Company, **13** 233

Standard General Insurance, **III** 208

Standard Gypsum Corp., **19** 77

Standard Industrial Group Ltd., **IV** 658

Standard Insulation Co., **I** 321

Standard Insurance Co. of New York, **III** 385

Standard Investing Corp., **III** 98

Standard Kollsman Industries Inc., **13** 461

Standard Life Assurance Company, III 358–61; IV 696–98

Standard Life Insurance Company, **11** 481

Standard Magnesium & Chemical Co., **IV** 123

Standard Metals Corp., **IV** 76

Standard Microsystems Corporation, 11 462–64

Standard Milling Co., **II** 497

Standard Motor Co., **III** 651

Standard of America Life Insurance Co., **III** 324

Standard of Georgia Insurance Agency, Inc., **10** 92

Standard Oil Co., **III** 470, 513; **IV** 46, 372, 399, 426–29, 434, 463, 478, 488–89, 530–31, 540, 542, 551, 574, 577–78, 657; **V** 590, 601; **6** 455; **7** 169–72, 263, 351, 414, 551; **8** 415; **10** 110, 289; **14** 21, 491–92

Standard Oil Co. (California), **II** 448; **IV** 18–19, 385–87, 403, 429, 464, 536–37, 545, 552, 560, 578; **6** 353; **7** 172, 352, 483; **13** 448

Standard Oil Co. (Illinois), **IV** 368

Standard Oil Co. (Indiana), **II** 262; **IV** 366, 368–71, 466–67; **7** 443; **10** 86; **14** 222

Standard Oil Co. (Minnesota), **IV** 368

Standard Oil Co. (New York), **IV** 428–29, 431, 460, 463–65, 485, 504, 537, 549, 558; **7** 171, 351–52

Standard Oil Co. of Iowa, **IV** 385

Standard Oil Co. of Kentucky, **IV** 387

Standard Oil Co. of New Jersey, **I** 334, 337, 370; **II** 16, 496; **IV** 378–79, 385–86, 400, 415–16, 419, 426–29, 431–33, 438, 460, 463–64, 488, 522, 531, 537–38, 544, 558, 565, 571; **V** 658–59; **7** 170–72, 253, 351; **13** 124; **17** 412–13

Standard Oil Co. of Ohio, **IV** 373, 379, 427, 452, 463, 522, 571; **7** 57, 171, 263; **12** 309; **21** 82

Standard Oil Development Co., **IV** 554

Standard Oil Trust, **IV** 31, 368, 375, 385–86, 427, 463

Standard Printing Company, **19** 333

Standard Products Company, **19** 454

Standard Rate & Data Service, **IV** 639; **7** 286

Standard Register Co., 15 472–74

Standard Sanitary, **III** 663–64

Standard Screw Co., **12** 344

Standard Shares, **9** 413–14

Standard Steel Propeller, **I** 47, 84; **9** 416; **10** 162

Standard Telephone and Radio, **II** 13

Standard Telephones and Cables, Ltd., **III** 162–63; **6** 242

Standard Tin Plate Co., **15** 127

Standard-Vacuum Oil Co., **IV** 431–32, 440, 460, 464, 491–92, 554–55; **7** 352

Standex International Corporation, 16 470–71; **17 456–59**

Stanhome Inc., 9 330; **11** 94–96; **15 475–78**

STANIC, **IV** 419, 421

Stanko Fanuc Service, **III** 483

Stanley Electric Manufacturing Co., **II** 28; **12** 194

Stanley Home Products, Incorporated. *See* Stanhome Inc.

Stanley Mining Services, Ltd., **19** 247

The Stanley Works, III 626–29; 7 480; **9** 543; **13** 41; **20 476–80 (upd.)**

Stanolind Oil & Gas Co., **III** 498; **IV** 365, 369–70

Stant Corporation, **15** 503, 505

Staples, Inc., 8 404–05; **10 496–98; 18** 24, 388; **20** 99; **22** 154; **23** 363, 365

Star, **10** 287–88

Star Air Service. *See* Alaska Air Group, Inc.

Star Banc Corporation, 11 465–67; 13 222

Star Building Systems, Inc., **19** 366

Star Engraving, **12** 471

Star Enterprise, **IV** 536, 539, 553

Star Enterprises, Inc., **6** 457

Star Finishing Co., **9** 465

Star Markets Company, Inc., **23** 169

Star Medical Technologies, Inc., **22** 409

Star Paper Ltd., **IV** 300

Star Paper Tube, Inc., **19** 76–78

Star Video, Inc., **6** 313

Starber International, **12** 181

Starbucks Corporation, 13 493–94; 18 37; **22** 370

StarCraft, **III** 444; **13** 113

Starcraft Power Boats, **22** 116

Stardent, **III** 553

Starfish Software, **23** 212

StarKist Foods, **II** 508; **11** 172

Starlawerken, **I** 527

Starline Optical Corp., **22** 123

StarMed Staffing Corporation, **6** 10

Starpointe Savings Bank, **9** 173

Starrett Corporation, 21 471–74

Star's Discount Department Stores, **16** 36

Startech Semiconductor Inc., **14** 183

Startel Corp., **15** 125

Starter Corp., 12 457–458

State Bank of Albany, **9** 228

State Farm Mutual Automobile Insurance Company, III 362–64; 10 50; **22** 266; **23** 286

State Finance and Thrift Company, **14** 529

State Leed, **13** 367

State Metal Works, **III** 647

State Savings Bank and Trust Co., **11** 180

State Street Boston Corporation, 8 491–93

State Trading Corp. of India Ltd., **IV** 143

State-o-Maine, **18** 357–59

State-Record Co., **IV** 630

Staten Island Advance Corp., **IV** 581–82; **19** 4

Stater Brothers, **17** 558

Statex Petroleum, Inc., **19** 70

Static, Inc., **14** 430

Stationers Distributing Company, **14** 523

Statler Hotel Co., **III** 92, 98; **19** 206

Statoil. *See* Den Norske Stats Oljeselskap AS.

Statter, Inc., **6** 27

Staubli International, **II** 122; **12** 546

Stauffer Chemical Company, **8** 105–07; **21** 545

Stauffer-Meiji, **II** 540

Stax Records, **23** 32

STC PLC, III 141, **162–64**

Stead & Miller, **13** 169

Steag AG, **IV** 193

Steak & Ale, **II** 556–57; **7** 336; **12** 373; **13** 408–09

Steak n Shake, **14** 130–31

Steam and Gas Pipe Co., **III** 644

Steam Boiler Works, **18** 318

Stearman, **I** 47, 84; **9** 416; **10** 162

Stearns & Foster, **12** 439

Stearns Catalytic World Corp., **II** 87; **11** 413

Stearns Coal & Lumber, **6** 514

Stearns Manufacturing Co., **16** 297

Steaua-Romana, **IV** 557

Steel and Tube Co. of America, **IV** 114

Steel Authority of India Ltd., IV 205–07

Steel Ceilings and Aluminum Works, **IV** 22

Steel Co. of Canada Ltd., **IV** 208

Steel Dynamics, **18** 380

Steel Mills Ltd., **III** 673

Steel Products Engineering Co., **I** 169

Steel Stamping Co., **III** 569; **20** 360

Steelcase Inc., 7 493–95; 8 251–52, 255, 405

Steelmade Inc., **I** 513

Steely, **IV** 109

Steenfabriek De Ruiterwaard, **14** 249

Steenkolen Handelsvereniging, **IV** 132

Steering Aluminum, **I** 159

Stefany, **12** 152

Steger Furniture Manufacturing Co., **18** 493

Steiff. *See* Margarete Steiff GmbH.

Steil, Inc., **8** 271

Stein Mart Inc., 19 423–25

Stein Robaire Helm, **22** 173

Steinbach Inc., **IV** 226; **14** 427

Steinbach Stores, Inc., **19** 108

Steinberg Incorporated, II 652–53, **662–65; V** 163

Steinberger, **16** 239

Steinman & Grey, **6** 27

Steinmüller Verwaltungsgesellschaft, **V** 747

Steinway & Sons, **16** 201

Steinway Musical Properties, Inc., 19 392, 394, **426–29**

Stelco Inc., IV 208–10

Stella Bella Corporation, **19** 436

Stella D'Oro Company, **7** 367

Stellar Systems, Inc., **III** 553; **14** 542

Stellenbosch Farmers Winery, **I** 288

Stelux Manufacturing Company, **13** 121

Stensmölla Kemiska Tekniska Industri, **I** 385

Stentor Canadian Network Management, **6** 310

Stenval Sud, **19** 50

Stephen F. Whitman & Son, Inc., **7** 429

Stephens Inc., **III** 76; **16** 59; **18** 223

Sterchi Bros. Co., **14** 236

Sterling Chemicals, Inc., 16 460–63

Sterling Drug Inc., I 309–10, **698–700; III** 477; **7** 163; **13** 76–77

Sterling Electronics Corp., 18 496–98; 19 311

Sterling Engineered Products, **III** 640, 642; **16** 9

Sterling Forest Corp., **III** 264

Sterling Industries, **13** 166

Sterling Information Services, Ltd., **IV** 675; **7** 528

Sterling Manhattan, **7** 63

Sterling Oil, **I** 526

Sterling Oil & Development, **II** 490

Sterling Organics Ltd., **12** 351

Sterling Plastics, **III** 642

Sterling Plastics Inc., **16** 9

Sterling Products Inc., **I** 622; **10** 68

Sterling Remedy Co., **I** 698

Sterling Software, Inc., 11 468–70

Sterling Winthrop, **7** 164

Stern & Stern Textiles, **11** 261

Stern Bros. Investment Bank, **V** 362–65; **19** 359

Stern's, **9** 209

Stern-Auer Shoe Company, **V** 207

Sternco Industries, **12** 230–31

STET. *See* Società Finanziaria Telefonica per Azioni.

Steuben Glass, **III** 683

Stevcoknit Fabrics Company, **8** 141–43

Stevens Linen Associates, Inc., **8** 272

Stevens Park Osteopathic Hospital, **6** 192

Stevens Sound Proofing Co., **III** 706; **7** 291

Stevens, Thompson & Runyan, Inc. *See* CRSS Inc.

Steve's Ice Cream, **16** 54–55

Steward Esplen and Greenhough, **II** 569

Stewards Foundation, **6** 191

Stewart & Stevenson Services Inc., 11 471–73

Stewart Bolling Co., **IV** 130

Stewart Cash Stores, **II** 465

Stewart Enterprises, Inc., 16 344; **20 481–83**

Stewart P. Orr Associates, **6** 224

Stewart Systems, Inc., **22** 352–53

Steyr Walzlager, **III** 625
Stichting Continuiteit AMEV, **III** 202
Stieber Rollkupplung GmbH, **14** 63
Stihl Inc. *See* Andreas Stihl.
Stimson & Valentine, **8** 552
Stinnes AG, **6** 424, 426; **8** 68–69, **494–97**; **23** 68–70, **451–54 (upd.)**
Stirling Readymix Concrete, **III** 737–38
STM Systems Corp., **11** 485
Stock, **IV** 617–18
Stock Clearing Corporation, **9** 370
Stockholder Systems Inc., **11** 485
Stockholm Southern Transportation Co., **I** 553
Stockholms Allmänna Telefonaktiebolag, **V** 334
Stockholms Enskilda Bank, **II** 1, 351, 365–66; **III** 419, 425–26
Stockholms Intecknings Garanti, **II** 366
Stockton and Hartlepool Railway, **III** 272
Stockton Wheel Co., **III** 450
Stoelting Brothers Company, **10** 371
Stokely Van Camp, **II** 560, 575; **12** 411; **22** 338
Stokvis/De Nederlandsche Kroon Rijwiefabrieken, **13** 499
Stone & Webster, Inc., **13 495–98**
Stone and Kimball, **IV** 660
Stone Container Corporation, **IV 332–34**; **8** 203–04; **15** 129; **17** 106
Stone Exploration Corp., **IV** 83; **7** 187
Stone Manufacturing Company, **14 469–71**
Stonega Coke & Coal Co. *See* Westmoreland Coal Company.
Stoner Associates. *See* Severn Trent PLC.
Stonewall Insurance Co., **III** 192
Stonington Partners, **19** 318
Stoody Co., **19** 440
Stoomvaart Maatschappij Nederland, **6** 403–04
Stop & Shop Companies, Inc., **II 666–67**; **9** 451, 453; **12** 48–49; **16** 160, 314; **23** 169
Stop N Go, **7** 373
Stoppenbauch Inc., **23** 202
Stora Kopparbergs Bergslags AB, **III** 693, 695; **IV 335–37**, 340; **12** 464
Storage Dimensions Inc., **10** 404
Storage Technology Corporation, **III** 110; **6 275–77**; **12** 148, 161; **16** 194
Storage USA, Inc., **21 475–77**
Storebrand Insurance Co., **III** 122
Storehouse PLC, **II** 658; **13** 284; **16 464–66**; **17** 42–43, 335
Storer Communications, **II** 161; **IV** 596; **7** 91–92, 200–01
Storer Leasing Inc., **I** 99; **6** 81
Storz Instruments Co., **I** 678
Stouffer Corp., **I** 485; **II** 489, 547; **6** 40; **7** 382; **8 498–501**
Stout Air Services, **I** 128; **6** 128
Stout Airlines, **I** 47, 84; **9** 416; **10** 162
Stout Metal Airplane Co., **I** 165
Stowe Woodward, **I** 428–29
STP, **19** 223
STRAAM Engineers. *See* CRSS Inc.
Straits Steamship Co. *See* Malaysian Airlines System.
Stran, **8** 546
Strata Energy, Inc., **IV** 29
StrataCom, Inc., **11** 59; **16 467–69**
Stratford Corporation, **15** 103

Strathmore Consolidated Investments, **IV** 90
Stratos Boat Co., Ltd., **III** 600
Stratton Ski Corporation, **15** 235
Stratus Computer, Inc., **6** 279; **10 499–501**
Strauss Turnbull and Co., **II** 355
Strawbridge & Clothier's, **6** 243
Street & Smith Publications, Inc., **IV** 583; **13** 178
Stride Rite Corporation, **8 502–04**; **9** 437
Stroehmann Bakeries, **II** 631
Stroh and Co., **IV** 486
The Stroh Brewery Company, **I** 32, 255, **290–92**; **13** 10–11, 455; **18** 72, **499–502 (upd.)**; **22** 422; **23** 403, 405
Strömberg, **IV** 300
Stromberg Carburetor Co., **I** 141
Stromberg-Carlson, **II** 82
Stromeyer GmbH, **7** 141
Strong Brewery, **I** 294
Strong Electric Corporation, **19** 211
Strother Drug, **III** 9–10
Structural Dynamics Research Corporation, **10** 257
Structural Fibers, Inc. *See* Essef Corporation.
Structural Iberica S.A., **18** 163
Struebel Group, **18** 170
Strydel, Inc., **14** 361
Stryker Corporation, **10** 351; **11 474–76**
Stuart Co., **I** 584
Stuart Entertainment Inc., **16 470–72**
Stuart Hall Co., **17** 445
Stuart Medical, Inc., **10** 143; **16** 400
Stuart Perlman, **6** 200
Stuckey's, Inc., **7** 429
Studebaker Co., **I** 141–42, 451; **8** 74; **9** 27
Studebaker Wagon Co., **IV** 660
Studebaker-Packard, **9** 118; **10** 261
Student Loan Marketing Association, **II 453–55**
Studiengesellschaft, **I** 409
Studley Products Inc., **12** 396
Stuffit Co., **IV** 597
Sturbridge Yankee Workshop, Inc., **10** 216
Sturgeon Bay Shipbuilding and DryDock Company, **18** 320
Sturm, Ruger & Company, Inc., **19 430–32**
Stuttgart Gas Works, **I** 391
Stuttgarter Verein Versicherungs-AG, **III** 184
Stuyvesant Insurance Group, **II** 182
Stymer Oy, **IV** 470–71
Suave Shoe Corporation. *See* French Fragrances, Inc.
Subaru, **6** 28; **23** 290
SubLogic, **15** 455
Submarine Boat Co., **I** 57
Submarine Signal Co., **II** 85–86; **11** 412
Suburban Cablevision, **IV** 640
Suburban Coastal Corporation, **10** 92
Suburban Cos., **IV** 575–76
Suburban Light and Power Company, **12** 45
Suburban Propane, **I** 378
Suburban Savings and Loan Association, **10** 92
Subway, **15** 56–57
Suchard Co., **II** 520
Sud-Aviation, **I** 44–45; **7** 10; **8** 313
Sudbury Inc., **16 473–75**; **17** 373
Suddeutsche Bank A.G., **II** 279

Süddeutsche Donau-Dampfschiffahrts-Gesellschaft, **6** 425
Süddeutsche Kalkstickstoffwerke AG, **IV** 229, 232
Sudler & Hennessey, **I** 37
Südpetrol, **IV** 421
Suez Bank, **IV** 108
Suez Canal Co., **IV** 530
Suez Oil Co., **IV** 413–14
Suffolk County Federal Savings and Loan Association, **16** 346
Sugarland Industries. *See* Imperial Holly Corporation.
Suita Brewery, **I** 220
Suito Sangyo Co., Ltd. *See* Seino Transportation Company, Ltd.
Sullair Co., **I** 435
Sullivan, Stauffer, Colwell & Bayles, **14** 314
Sullivan Systems, **III** 420
Sulphide Corp., **IV** 58
Sulzbach, **I** 409
Sulzer Brothers Limited, **III** 402, 516, **630–33**, 638
Sumergrade Corporation, **19** 304
Suminoe Textile Co., **8** 235
Sumisei Secpac Investment Advisors, **III** 366
Sumisho Electronics Co. Ltd., **18** 170
Sumitomo Bank, Ltd., **I** 587; **II** 104, 224, 273–74, 347, **360–62**, 363, 392, 415; **IV** 269, 726; **9** 341–42; **18** 170; **23** 340
Sumitomo Chemical Company Ltd., **I** 363, **397–98**; **II** 361; **III** 715; **IV** 432
Sumitomo Corporation, **I** 431–32, 492, 502, 504–05, 510–11, 515, **518–20**; **III** 43, 365; **V** 161, **7** 357, **11 477–80 (upd.)**, 490; **15** 340; **17** 556; **18** 170
Sumitomo Electric Industries, **I** 105; **II** 104–05; **III** 490, 684; **IV** 179; **V** 252
Sumitomo Heavy Industries, Ltd., **III** 533, **634–35**; **10** 381
Sumitomo Life Insurance Co., **II** 104, 360, 422; **III** 288, **365–66**
Sumitomo Marine and Fire Insurance Company, Limited, **III 367–68**
Sumitomo Metal Industries, Ltd., **I** 390; **II** 104, 361; **IV** 130, **211–13**, 216; **10** 463–64; **11** 246
Sumitomo Metal Mining Co., Ltd., **IV 214–16**; **9** 340; **23** 338
Sumitomo Realty & Development Co., Ltd., **IV 726–27**
Sumitomo Rubber Industries, Ltd., **V 252–53**; **20** 263
Sumitomo Trust & Banking Company, Ltd., **II** 104, **363–64**; **IV** 726
Sumitomo Wire Company, **16** 555
Summa Corporation, **9** 266; **17** 317
Summer Paper Tube, **19** 78
Summers Group Inc., **15** 386
The Summit Bancorporation, **14 472–74**
Summit Constructors. *See* CRSS Inc.
Summit Engineering Corp., **I** 153
Summit Family Restaurants Inc., **19** 89, 92, **433–36**
Summit Gear Company, **16** 392–93
Summit Management Co., Inc., **17** 498
Summit Screen Inks, **13** 228
Sun Alliance Group PLC, **III** 296, **369–74**, 400
Sun Chemical Corp. *See* Sequa Corp.

Sun Company, Inc., **I** 286, 631; **IV** 449, **548–50**; **7** 114, 414; **11** 484; **12** 459; **17** 537
Sun Country Airlines, **I** 114
Sun Distributors L.P., **12** **459–461**
Sun Electric, **15** 288
Sun Electronics, **9** 116
Sun Equities Corporation, **15** 449
Sun Federal, **7** 498
Sun Federal Savings and Loan Association of Tallahassee, **10** 92
Sun Fire Coal Company, **7** 281
Sun Fire Office, **III** 349, 369–71
Sun Foods, **12** 220–21
Sun International Hotels, Limited, **12** 420
Sun Kyowa, **III** 43
Sun Life Assurance Co. of Canada, **IV** 165
Sun Life Group of America, **11** 482
Sun Mark, Inc., **21** 483
Sun Men's Shop Co., Ltd., **V** 150
Sun Microsystems, Inc., **II** 45, 62; **III** 125; **6** 222, 235, 238, 244; **7** **498–501**; **9** 36, 471; **10** 118, 242, 257, 504; **11** 45–46, 490–91, 507; **12** 162; **14** 15–16, 268; **15** 321; **16** 140, 195, 418–19; **18** 537; **20** 175, 237; **21** 86; **22** 154; **23** 471
Sun Newspapers, **III** 213–14
Sun Oil Co., **III** 497; **IV** 371, 424, 548–50; **7** 413–14; **11** 35; **18** 233; **19** 162
Sun Optical Co., Ltd., **V** 150
Sun Shades 501 Ltd., **21** 483
Sun Ship, **IV** 549
Sun Sportswear, Inc., **17** **460–63**; **23** 65–66
Sun State Marine Services, Inc. *See* Hvide Marine Incorporated.
Sun Techno Services Co., Ltd., **V** 150
Sun Technology Enterprises, **7** 500
Sun Television & Appliances Inc., **10** **502–03**; **19** 362
Sun-Diamond Growers of California, **7** **496–97**
Sun-Fast Color, **13** 227
Sun-Maid Growers of California, **7** 496–97
Sun-Pat Products, **II** 569
SunAir, **11** 300
SunAmerica Inc., **11** **481–83**
Sunbeam-Oster Co., Inc., **9** **484–86**; **14** 230; **16** 488; **17** 215; **19** 305; **22** 3
Sunbelt Coca-Cola, **10** 223
Sunbelt Nursery Group, Inc., **12** 179, 200, 394
Sunbird, **III** 600; **V** 150
Sunburst Yarns, Inc., **13** 532
Sunciti Manufacturers Ltd., **III** 454; **21** 122
Sunclipse Inc., **IV** 250
Sunco N.V., **22** 515
Suncoast Motion Picture Company, **9** 360
SunCor Development Company, **6** 546–47
Sundance Publishing, **IV** 609; **12** 559
Sunday Pictorial, **IV** 665–66; **17** 397
Sundheim & Doetsch, **IV** 189
Sunds Defibrator AG, **IV** 338–40, 350
Sundstrand Corporation, **7** **502–04**; **21** **478–81** (upd.)
SunGard Data Systems Inc., **11** **484–85**
Sunglass Hut International, Inc., **18** 393; **21** **482–84**
Sunglee Electronics Co. Ltd., **III** 748–49
Sunila Oy, **IV** 348–49
Sunkiss Thermoreactors, **21** 65
Sunkist Growers, **7** 496

Sunkist Soft Drinks Inc., **I** 13
Sunkus Co. Ltd., **V** 150
Sunray DX Oil Co., **IV** 550, 575; **7** 414
Sunrise Medical Inc., **11** 202, **486–88**
Sunrise Test Systems, **11** 491
Sunsations Sunglass Company, **21** 483
Sunshine Jr. Stores, Inc., **17** 170
Sunshine Mining Company, **20** 149
SunSoft, **7** 500
Sunsweet Growers, **7** 496
Suntory Ltd., **13** 454; **21** 320
SunTrust Banks Inc., **23** **455–58**
Sunward Technologies, Inc., **10** 464
Supasnaps, **V** 50
Super D Drugs, **9** 52
Super Dart. *See* Dart Group Corporation.
Super 8 Motels, Inc., **11** 178
Super Food Services, Inc., **15** **479–81**; **18** 8
Super Oil Seals & Gaskets Ltd., **16** 8
Super 1 Stores. *See* Brookshire Grocery Company.
Super Quick, Inc., **7** 372
Super Rite Foods, Inc., **V** 176; **19** 356
Super Sagless Spring Corp., **15** 103
Super Store Industries, **14** 397
Super Valu Stores, Inc., **II** 632, **668–71**; **6** 364; **7** 450; **8** 380; **14** 411; **17** 180; **22** 126; **23** 357–58. *See also* Supervalu Inc.
Super-Power Company, **6** 505
SuperAmerica Group, Inc., **IV** 374
Superbrix, **14** 248
Supercomputer Systems, Inc., **III** 130; **16** 138
Superdrug PLC, **V** 175
Superenvases Envalic, **I** 231
Superior Bearings Co., **I** 159
Superior Healthcare Group, Inc., **11** 221
Superior Industries International, Inc., **8** **505–07**
Superior Oil Co., **III** 558; **IV** 400, 465, 524; **7** 353
Superior Transfer, **12** 309
SuperMac Technology Inc., **16** 419
Supermarchés Montréal, **II** 662–63
Supermarkets General Holdings Corporation, **II** **672–74**; **16** 160; **23** 369–70
Supermart Books, **10** 136
Supersaver Wholesale Clubs, **8** 555
Supersnaps, **19** 124
SuperStation WTBS, **6** 171
Supertest Petroleum Corporation, **9** 490
Supervalu Inc., **18** **503–08** (upd.); **21** 457–57; **22** 327. *See also* Super Valu Stores, Inc.
Supervalue Corp., **13** 393
Supervised Investors Services, **III** 270
SupeRx, **II** 644
Supreme Sugar Co., **I** 421; **11** 23
Supron Energy Corp., **15** 129
Surety Life Insurance Company, **10** 51
Surgical Health Corporation, **14** 233
Surgical Mechanical Research Inc., **I** 678
Surgikos, Inc., **III** 35
Surgitool, **I** 628
Suroflex GmbH, **23** 300
Surpass Software Systems, Inc., **9** 81
Survey Research Group, **10** 360
SurVivaLink, **18** 423
Susan Bristol, **16** 61
Susan Kay Cosmetics. *See* The Cosmetic Center, Inc.
Susie's Casuals, **14** 294

Susquehanna Pfaltzgraff Company, **8** **508–10**
Sussex Group, **15** 449
Sutherland Lumber Co., **19** 233
Sutter Corp., **15** 113
Sutter Health, **12** 175–76
Sutter Home Winery Inc., **16** **476–78**
Sutton & Towne, Inc., **21** 96
Sutton Laboratories, **22** 228
Suwa Seikosha, **III** 620
Suzaki Hajime, **V** 113–14
Suzannah Farms, **7** 524
Suze, **I** 280
Suzuki & Co., **I** 509–10; **IV** 129; **9** 341–42; **23** 340
Suzuki Motor Corporation, **III** 581, 657; **7** 110; **8** 72; **9** **487–89**; **23** 290, **459–62** (upd.)
Suzuki Shoten Co., **V** 380, 457–58
Suzy Shier, **18** 562
Svea Choklad A.G., **II** 640
Svensk Fastighetskredit A.B., **II** 352
Svenska A.B. Humber & Co., **I** 197
Svenska Aeroplan Aktiebolaget. *See* Saab-Scania AB.
Svenska Cellulosa Aktiebolaget, **II** 365–66; **IV** 295–96, 325, 336, **338–40**, 667; **17** 398; **19** 225–26
Svenska Centrifug AB, **III** 418
Svenska Elektron, **III** 478
A.B. Svenska Flaktfabriken, **II** 2; **22** 8
Svenska Flygmotor A.B., **I** 209
Svenska Handelsbanken, **II** 353, **365–67**; **IV** 338–39
Svenska Järnvagsverkstäderna A.B., **I** 197
Svenska Kullagerfabriken A.B., **I** 209; **III** 622; **7** 565
Svenska Oljeslageri AB, **IV** 318
Svenska Varv, **6** 367
Svenskt Stål AB, **IV** 336
Sverdrup Corporation, **14** **475–78**
Sverker Martin-Löf, **IV** 339
SVF. *See* Société des Vins de France.
SVIDO, **17** 250
Sviluppo Iniziative Stradali Italiene, **IV** 420
SVPW, **I** 215
Swallow Airplane Company, **8** 49
Swallow Sidecar and Coach Building Company, **13** 285
Swan, **10** 170
Swan Electric Light Co., **I** 410
Swan's Down Cake Flour, **II** 531
Swank Inc., **17** **464–66**
Swann Corp., **I** 366
Swatch, **7** 532–33
Swearingen Aircraft Company, **9** 207
SwedeChrome, **III** 625
Swedish Ericsson Group, **17** 353
Swedish Furniture Research Institute, **V** 82
Swedish Intercontinental Airlines, **I** 119
Swedish Match S.A., **IV** 336–37; **9** 381; **12** **462–64**; **23** 55
Swedish Ordnance-FFV/Bofors AB, **9** 381–82
Swedish Telecom, **V** **331–33**
Sweedor, **12** 464
Sweeney Specialty Restaurants, **14** 131
Sweeney's, **16** 559
Sweet & Maxwell, **8** 527
Sweet Life Foods Inc., **18** 507
Sweet Traditions LLC, **21** 323
Swett & Crawford Group, **III** 357; **22** 494

Swift & Co., **II** 447, 550; **13** 351, 448; **17** 124

Swift Adhesives, **10** 467

Swift Independent Packing Co., **II** 494; **13** 350, 352

Swift Textiles, Inc., **12** 118; **15** 247

Swift-Armour S.A., **II** 480

Swift-Eckrich, **II** 467

Swingline, Inc., **7** 3–5

Swire Pacific Ltd., I 469–70, **521–22**; **6** 78; **16 479–81 (upd.); 18** 114; **20** 310, 312

Swisher International Group Inc., 14 17–19; **23 463–65**

Swiss Air Transport Company Ltd., I 107, 119, **121–22**

Swiss Banca della Svizzera Italiano, **II** 192

Swiss Bank Corporation, II 267, **368–70**, 378–79; **14** 419–20; **21** 145–46

Swiss Cement-Industrie-Gesellschaft, **III** 701

Swiss Colony Wines, **I** 377

Swiss Drilling Co., **IV** 372; **19** 22

Swiss Federal Railways (Schweizerische Bundesbahnen), V 519–22

Swiss General Chocolate Co., **II** 545–46; **7** 380–81

Swiss Locomotive and Machine Works, **III** 631–32

Swiss Oil Co., **IV** 372–73

Swiss Reinsurance Company, III 299, 301, 335, **375–78; 15** 13; **21** 146

Swiss Volksbank, **21** 146–47

Swiss-American Corporation, **II** 267; **21** 145

Swissair Associated Co., **I** 122; **6** 60, 96, 117

SXI Limited, **17** 458

Sybase, Inc., 6 255, 279; **10** 361, **504–06**; **11** 77–78; **15** 492

SyberVision, **10** 216

Sybra, Inc., **19** 466–68

Sybron International Corp., 14 479–81; 19 289–90

SYCOM, Inc., **18** 363

Sydney Electricity, **12** 443

Sydney Paper Mills Ltd., **IV** 248

Sydney Ross Co., **I** 698–99

Syfrets Trust Co., **IV** 23

Sylacauga Calcium Products, **III** 691

Sylvan, Inc., 22 496–99

Sylvan Lake Telephone Company, **6** 334

Sylvan Learning Centers, **13** 299

Sylvania Companies, **I** 463; **II** 63; **III** 165, 475; **V** 295; **7** 161; **8** 157; **11** 197; **13** 402; **23** 181

Sylvia Paperboard Co., **IV** 310; **19** 266

Symantec Corporation, 10 507–09

Symbios Logic Inc., **19** 312

Symbiosis Corp., **10** 70

Symbol Technologies, Inc., 10 363, 523–24; **15 482–84**

Symington-Wayne, **III** 472

Symphony International, **14** 224

Symtronix Corporation, **18** 515

Synbiotics Corporation, **23** 284

Syncordia Corp., **15** 69

Syncrocom, Inc., **10** 513

Synercom Technology Inc., **14** 319

Synergen Inc., **13** 241

Synergy Dataworks, Inc., **11** 285

Synetic, Inc., **16** 59

Synopsis, Inc., 11 489–92; 18 20

SynOptics Communications, Inc., 10 194, **510–12; 11** 475; **16** 392; **22** 52

Synovus Financial Corp., 12 465–67; 18 516–17

Syntax Ophthalmic Inc., **III** 727

Syntex Corporation, I 512, **701–03; III** 18, 53; **8** 216–17, 434, 548; **10** 53; **12** 322

Syntex Pharmaceuticals Ltd., **21** 425

Synthecolor S.A., **8** 347

Synthélabo, **III** 47–48

Synthetic Blood Corp., **15** 380

Synthetic Pillows, Inc., **19** 304

Syntron, Inc., **18** 513–15

SyQuest Technology, Inc., 18 509–12

Syracuse China, **8** 510

Syratech Corp., 14 482–84

Syrian Airways, **6** 85

Syroco, **14** 483–84

Sysco Corporation, II 675–76; 9 453; **16** 387; **18** 67

Sysorex Information Systems, **11** 62

SysScan, **V** 339

System Development Co., **III** 166; **6** 282

System Fuels, Inc., **11** 194

System Integrators, Inc., **6** 279

System Software Associates, Inc., 10 513–14

Systematics Inc., **6** 301; **11** 131

Systems & Computer Technology Corp., 19 437–39

Systems and Services Co., **II** 675

Systems Center, Inc., **6** 279; **11** 469

Systems Construction Ltd., **II** 649

Systems Engineering and Manufacturing Company, **11** 225

Systems Engineering Labs (SEL), **11** 45; **13** 201

Systems Exploration Inc., **10** 547

Systems Magnetic Co., **IV** 101

Systems Marketing Inc., **12** 78

Systronics, **13** 235

Szabo, **II** 608

T/Maker, **9** 81

T. and J. Brocklebank Ltd., **23** 160

T.G.I. Friday's, **10** 331; **19** 258; **20** 159; **21** 250; **22** 127

T.J. Falgout, **11** 523

T.J. Maxx, **V** 197–98; **13** 329–30; **14** 62

T. Kobayashi & Co., Ltd., **III** 44

T.L. Smith & Company, **21** 502

T. Mellon & Sons, **II** 315

T. Rowe Price Associates, Inc., 10 89; **11 493–96**

T.S. Farley, Limited, **10** 319

TA Associates, **10** 382

TA Media AG, **15** 31

TAB Products Co., 17 467–69

Tabacalera, S.A., V 414–16; 15 139; **17 470–73 (upd.)**

Table Supply Stores, **II** 683

Tabulating Machine Company. *See* International Business Machines Corporation.

Taco Bell Corp., I 278; **7** 267, **505–07; 9** 178; **10** 450; **13** 336, 494; **14** 453; **15** 486; **16** 96–97; **17** 537; **21** 315, **485–88 (upd.)**

Taco Cabana, Inc., 23 466–68

Taco John's International Inc., 15 485–87

Taco Kid, **7** 506

Tadiran, **II** 47

Taehan Cement, **III** 748

Taft Broadcasting Co. *See* Great American Broadcasting Inc.

TAG. *See* Techniques d'Avant Garde Group SA.

TAG Pharmaceuticals, **22** 501

Taguchi Automobile. *See* Seino Transportation Company, Ltd.

Taiba Corporation, **8** 250

Taiheiyo Bank, **15** 495

Taikoo Dockyard Co., **I** 521; **16** 480

Taikoo Sugar Refinery, **I** 521; **16** 480

Taio Paper Mfg. Co., Ltd. *See* Daio Paper Co., Ltd.

Taisho America, **III** 295

Taisho Marine and Fire Insurance Co., Ltd., **III** 209, 295–96

Taisho Pharmaceutical, **I** 676; **II** 361

Taiwan Aerospace Corp., **11** 279

Taiwan Auto Glass, **III** 715

Taiwan Power Company, **22** 89

Taiwan Semiconductor Manufacturing Company Ltd., **18** 20; **22** 197

Taiway, **III** 596

Taiyo Bussan, **IV** 225

Taiyo Fishery Company, Limited, II 578–79

Taiyo Kobe Bank, Ltd., II 326, **371–72**

Taiyo Metal Manufacturing Co., **III** 757

Takada & Co., **IV** 151

Takaro Shuzo, **III** 42

Takashimaya Co., Limited, V 193–96

Takeda Chemical Industries Ltd., I 704–06; III 760

Takeda Riken, **11** 504

Takeuchi Mining Co., **III** 545

Takihyo, **15** 145

Takkyubin, **V** 537

Tako Oy, **IV** 314

The Talbots, Inc., II 503; **10** 324; **11** 497–99; **12** 280

Talcott National Corporation, **11** 260–61

Taliq Corp., **III** 715

Talisman Energy, 9 490–93

Talk Radio Network, Inc., **23** 294

Talley Industries, Inc., 10 386; **16 482–85**

Tally Corp., **18** 434

Talmadge Farms, Inc., **20** 105

TAM Ceramics, **III** 681

Tamar Bank, **II** 187

Tamarkin Co., **12** 390

Tambrands Inc., III 40; **8 511–13; 12** 439; **15** 359–60, 501; **16** 303

Tamco, **12** 390; **19** 380

TAMET, **IV** 25

Tamglass Automotive OY, **22** 436

Tampa Electric Company, **6** 582–83

Tampax Inc. *See* Tambrands Inc.

Oy Tampella Ab, **II** 47; **III** 648; **IV** 276

Tampere Paper Board and Roofing Felt Mill, **IV** 314

Tampereen Osake-Pankki, **II** 303

Tampimex Oil, **11** 194

Tamura Kisan Co., **II** 552

Tanaka, **6** 71

Tanaka Kikinzoku Kogyo KK, **IV** 119

Tanaka Matthey KK, **IV** 119

Tandem Computers, Inc., 6 278–80; **10** 499; **11** 18; **14** 318

Tandy Corporation, II 70, **106–08; 6** 257–58; **9** 43, 115, 165; **10** 56–57, 166–67, 236; **12 468–70 (upd.); 13** 174; **14** 117; **16** 84; **17** 353–54

Tangent Industries, **15** 83
Tangent Systems, **6** 247–48
Tanjong Pagar Dock Co., **I** 592
Tanks Oil and Gas, **11** 97
Tanner-Brice Company, **13** 404
TAP Air Portugal. *See* Transportes Aereos Portugueses.
Tapiola Insurance, **IV** 316
Tappan. *See* White Consolidated Industries Inc.
Tara Exploration and Development Ltd., **IV** 165
Tara Foods, **II** 645
Target Stores, V 35, 43–44; **10** 284, **515–17; 12** 508; **13** 261, 274, 446; **14** 398; **15** 275; **16** 390; **17** 460–61; **18** 108, 137, 283, 286; **20** 155; **22** 328
Tarkett, **12** 464
Tarmac PLC, III 734, **751–54; 14** 250
TarMacadam (Purnell Hooley's Patent) Syndicate Ltd., **III** 751
Tarslag, **III** 752
TASC. *See* Analytical Sciences Corp.
Tashima Shoten, **III** 574
Tasman Pulp and Paper Co. Ltd. *See* Fletcher Challenge Ltd.
Tasman U.E.B., **IV** 249
Tasmanian Fibre Containers, **IV** 249
Tasty Baking Co., 14 485–87
TAT European Airlines, **14** 70, 73
Tata Airlines. *See* Air-India.
Tata Enterprises, **III** 43
Tata Industries, **20** 313; **21** 74
Tata Iron and Steel Company Ltd., IV 48, 205–07, **217–19**
Tate & Lyle PLC, II 514, **580–83; 7** 466–67; **13** 102
Tatebayashi Flour Milling Co., **II** 554
Tateisi Electric Manufacturing, **II** 75
Tateisi Medical Electronics Manufacturing Co., **II** 75
Tatham Corporation, **21** 169, 171
Tatham/RSCG, **13** 204
Tatung Co., III 482; **13** 387; **23 469–71**
Taurus Exploration, **21** 208
Taurus Programming Services, **10** 196
Tax Management, Inc., **23** 92
Taylor Corp., **22** 358
Taylor Diving and Salvage Co., **III** 499
Taylor Made Golf Co., 23 270, **472–74**
Taylor Material Handling, **13** 499
Taylor Medical, **14** 388
Taylor Petroleum, Inc., **17** 170
Taylor Publishing Company, 12 471–73
Taylor Rental Corp., **III** 628
Taylor Wines Co., **I** 234; **10** 227
Taylor Woodrow plc, I 590–91; **III** 739; **13** 206
Taylor-Evans Seed Co., **IV** 409
Taylors and Lloyds, **II** 306
Tayto Ltd., **22** 515
Tazuke & Co., **IV** 151
TBC Corp., **20** 63
TBS. *See* Turner Broadcasting System, Inc.
TBWA Advertising, Inc., 6 47–49; **22** 394
TC Debica, **20** 264
TCA. *See* Air Canada.
TCBC. *See* Todays Computers Business Centers.
TCBY Enterprises Inc., 17 474–76
TCF Holdings, Inc., **II** 170–71
TCH Corporation, **12** 477
TCI. *See* Tele-Communications, Inc.

TCPL. *See* TransCanada PipeLines Ltd.
TCS Management Group, Inc., **22** 53
TCW Capital, **19** 414–15
TDK Corporation, I 500; **II 109–11; IV** 680; **17 477–79 (upd.)**
TDS. *See* Telephone and Data Systems, Inc.
Teaberry Electronics Corp., **III** 569; **20** 361
Teachers Insurance and Annuity Association, III 379–82; **22** 268
Teachers Service Organization, Inc., **8** 9–10
Team America, **9** 435
Team Penske, **V** 494
Teamsters Central States Pension Fund, **19** 378
Teamsters Union, **13** 19
Tebel Maschinefabrieken, **III** 420
Tebel Pneumatiek, **III** 420
Tech Data Corporation, 10 518–19
Tech Pacific International, **18** 180
Tech Textiles, USA, **15** 247–48
Tech-Sym Corporation, 18 513–15
Techalloy Co., **IV** 228
Technair Packaging Laboratories, **18** 216
Technical Ceramics Laboratories, Inc., **13** 141
Technical Coatings Co., **13** 85
Technical Materials, Inc., **14** 81
Technical Publishing, **IV** 605
Technicare, **11** 200
Technicon Instruments Corporation, **III** 56; **11** 333–34; **22** 75
Technifax, **8** 483
Techniques d'Avant Garde Group SA, **7** 554
Technisch Bureau Visser, **16** 421
Techno-Success Company, **V** 719
AB Technology, **II** 466
Technology Management Group, Inc., **18** 112
Technology Resources International Ltd., **18** 76
Technology Venture Investors, **11** 490; **14** 263
Technophone Ltd., **17** 354
Teck Corporation, **9** 282
Tecnamotor S.p.A., **8** 72, 515
Tecneco, **IV** 422
Tecnifax Corp., **IV** 330
Tecnipublicaciones, **14** 555
TECO Energy, Inc., 6 582–84
Tecom Industries, Inc., **18** 513–14
Tecumseh Products Company, 8 72, **514–16**
Ted Bates, Inc., **I** 33, 623; **10** 69; **16** 71–72
Teddy's Shoe Store. *See* Morse Shoe Inc.
Tedelex, **IV** 91–92
TEFSA, **17** 182
TEIC. *See* B.V. Tabak Export & Import Compagnie.
Teijin Limited, I 511; **V 380–82**
Teikoku Bank, **I** 507; **II** 273, 325–26
Teikoku Hormone, **I** 704
Teikoku Jinken. *See* Teijin Limited.
Teikoku Sekiyu Co. Ltd., **IV** 475
Teikoku Shiki, **IV** 326
Teito Electric Railway, **V** 461
Teito Transport Co. Ltd., **V** 536
Tekmunc A/S, **17** 288
Teknekron Infoswitch Corporation, **22** 51
Tekrad, Inc. *See* Tektronix, Inc.

Tekton Corp., **IV** 346
Tektronix, Inc., II 101; **8 517–21; 10** 24; **11** 284–86; **12** 454
Tel-A-Data Limited, **11** 111
Tele Consulte, **14** 555
Tele-Communications, Inc., II 160–62, 167; **10** 484, 506; **11** 479; **13** 280; **15** 264–65; **17** 148; **18** 64–66, 211, 213, 535; **19** 282; **21** 307, 309; **23** 121, 502
Telec Centre S.A., **19** 472
TeleCheck Services, **18** 542
TeleCheck Services, Inc., **11** 113
Teleclub, **IV** 590
Teleco Oilfield Services Inc., **6** 578; **22** 68
TeleColumbus, **11** 184
Telecom Australia, 6 341–42
Telecom Canada. *See* Stentor Canadian Network Management.
Telecom Eireann, 7 508–10
Telecom Italia, **15** 355
Telecom New Zealand, **18** 33
Telecomputing Corp., **I** 544
Telecredit, Inc., **6** 25
Telectronic Pacing Systems, **10** 445
Teledyne Inc., I 486, **523–25; II** 33, 44; **10** 262–63, 365, **520–22 (upd.); 11** 265; **13** 387; **17** 109; **18** 369
Telefonaktiebolaget LM Ericsson, V 331–32, **334–36; 9** 381
Telefonbau und Normalzeit, **I** 193
Telefónica de España, S.A., V 337–40; 19 254
Teléfonos de México S.A. de C.V., 14 488–90; **19** 12; **21** 259
Telefunken Fernseh & Rundfunk GmbH., **I** 411; **II** 117
Telegate, **18** 155
Teleglobe Inc., **14** 512
Telegraph Condenser Co., **II** 81
Telegraph Manufacturing Co., **III** 433
Telegraph Works, **III** 433
Telegraphic Service Company, **16** 166
Telekomunikacja S.A., **18** 33
TeleMarketing Corporation of Louisiana, **8** 311
Telemarketing Investments, Ltd., **8** 311
Telematics International Inc., **18** 154, 156
Télémécanique, **II** 94; **18** 473; **19** 166
Telemundo Group, Inc., **III** 344
Telenet Communications, **18** 32
Telenorma, **I** 193
Telenova, **III** 169; **6** 285
Telephone and Data Systems, Inc., 9 **494–96,** 527–529
Telephone Company of Ireland, **7** 508
Telephone Exchange Company of Indianapolis, **14** 257
Telephone Management Corporation, **8** 310
Telephone Utilities, Inc. *See* Pacific Telecom, Inc.
Telephone Utilities of Washington, **6** 325, 328
Telepictures, **II** 177
Teleport Communications Group, **14** 253
Teleprompter Corp., **II** 122; **7** 222; **10** 210; **18** 355
Telerate Systems Inc., **IV** 603, 670; **10** 276–78; **21** 68
Teleregister Corp., **I** 512
Telerent Europe, **II** 139
TeleRep, **IV** 596
Telesat Cable TV, Inc., **23** 293
Telesis Oil and Gas, **6** 478
Telesistema, **18** 212

Telesphere Network, Inc., **8** 310
Telesystems SLW Inc., **10** 524
Telettra S.p.A., **V** 326; **9** 10; **11** 205
Teletype Corp., **14** 569
Televimex, S.A., **18** 212
Television de Mexico, S.A., **18** 212
Televisión Española, S.A., 7 511–12; 18 211
Télévision Française 1, 23 475–77
Television Sales and Marketing Services Ltd., **7** 79–80
Teleway Japan, **7** 118–19; **13** 482
Telex Corporation, **II** 87; **13** 127
Telfin, **V** 339
Telia Mobitel, **11** 19
Telihoras Corporation, **10** 319
Telinfo, **6** 303
Telinq Inc., **10** 19
Telios Pharmaceuticals, Inc., **11** 460; **17** 288
Tellabs, Inc., 11 500–01
Telmex. *See* Teléfonos de México S.A. de C.V.
Telpar, Inc., **14** 377
Telport, **14** 260
Telrad, **II** 48
Telxon Corporation, 10 523–25
Tembec, Inc., **IV** 296; **19** 226
Temco Electronics and Missile Co., **I** 489
Temenggong of Jahore, **I** 592
Temerlin McClain, **23** 479
Temp Force, **16** 421–22
Temp World, Inc., **6** 10
Temple, Barker & Sloan/Strategic Planning Associates, **III** 283
Temple Inks Company, **13** 227
Temple Press Ltd., **IV** 294–95; **19** 225
Temple-Inland Inc., IV 312, **341–43**, 675; **8** 267–69; **19** 268
Templeton, **II** 609
TEMPO Enterprises, **II** 162
Tempo-Team, **16** 420
Tempus Expeditions, **13** 358
TemTech Ltd., **13** 326
10 Sen Kinitsu Markets, **V** 194
Tenacqco Bridge Partnership, **17** 170
Tenby Industries Limited, **21** 350
Tengelmann Group, **II** 636–38; **16** 249–50
Tengen Inc., **III** 587; **7** 395
Tennant Company, 13 499–501
Tenneco Inc., I 182, **526–28**; **IV** 76, 152, 283, 371, 499; **6** 531; **10** 379–80, 430, **526–28 (upd.)**; **11** 440; **12** 91, 376; **13** 372–73; **16** 191, 461; **19** 78, 483; **21** 170; **22** 275, 380
Tennessee Book Company, **11** 193
Tennessee Coal, Iron and Railroad Co., **IV** 573; **7** 550
Tennessee Eastman Corporation, **III** 475; **7** 161. *See also* Eastman Chemical Company.
Tennessee Electric Power Co., **III** 332
Tennessee Gas Pipeline Co., **14** 126
Tennessee Gas Transmission Co., **I** 526; **13** 496; **14** 125
Tennessee Insurance Company, **11** 193–94
Tennessee Paper Mills Inc. *See* Rock-Tenn Company.
Tennessee Restaurant Company, **9** 426
Tennessee River Pulp & Paper Co., **12** 376–77
Tennessee Trifting, **13** 169
Tennessee Valley Authority, **II** 2–3, 121; **IV** 181; **22** 10

Tennessee Woolen Mills, Inc., **19** 304
Tenngasco, **I** 527
Teollisuusosuuskunta Metsä-Saimaa, **IV** 315
TEP. *See* Tucson Electric Power Company.
Teradata Corporation, **6** 267
Teradyne, Inc., 11 502–04
Terex Corporation, 7 513–15; 8 116
Teril Stationers Inc., **16** 36
Terminal Transfer and Storage, Inc., **6** 371
Terminix International, **6** 45–46; **11** 433; **23** 428, 430
Terra Industries, Inc., 13 277, **502–04**
Terrace Park Dairies, **II** 536
Terracor, **11** 260–61
Terragrafics, **14** 245
Terre Haute Electric, **6** 555
Territorial Hotel Co., **II** 490
Territory Enterprises Ltd., **IV** 59
Terry Coach Industries, Inc., **III** 484; **22** 206
Terry's of York, **II** 594
Tesa, S.A., **23** 82
Tesco PLC, **II** 513, **677–78**; **10** 442; **11** 239, 241
Tesoro Petroleum Corporation, 7 516–19
Tesseract Corp., **11** 78
Tessman Seed, Inc., **16** 270–71
Testor Corporation, **8** 455
TETI, **I** 466
Tetley Inc., **I** 215; **14** 18
Tetra Plastics Inc., **V** 374; **8** 393
Teutonia National Bank, **IV** 310; **19** 265
Teva Pharmaceutical Industries Ltd., 22 **500–03**
Tex-Star Oil & Gas Corp., **IV** 574; **7** 551
Texaco Inc., I 21, 360; **II** 31, 313, 448; **III** 760; **IV** 386, 403, 418, 425, 429, 439, 461, 464, 466, 472–73, 479–80, 484, 488, 490, 510–11, 530–31, 536–39, 545, **551–53**, 560, 565–66, 570, 575; **7** 172, 280, 483; **9** 232; **10** 190; **12** 20; **13** 448; **14 491–94 (upd.)**; **17** 412; **18** 488; **19** 73, 75, 176
Texada Mines, Ltd., **IV** 123
Texas Air Corporation, I 97, 100, 103, 118, **123–24**, 127, 130; **6** 82, 129; **12** 489; **21** 142–43
Texas Almanac, **10** 3
Texas Butadiene and Chemical Corp., **IV** 456
Texas Co., **III** 497; **IV** 386, 400, 464, 536, 551–52; **7** 352
Texas Commerce Bankshares, **II** 252
Texas Eastern Corp., **6** 487; **11** 97, 354; **14** 126
Texas Eastern Transmission Company, **11** 28
Texas Eastman, **III** 475; **7** 161
Texas Electric Service Company, **V** 724
Texas Gas Resources Corporation, **IV** 395; **22** 166
Texas Gypsum, **IV** 341
Texas Homecare, **21** 335
Texas Industries, Inc., 8 522–24; 13 142–43
Texas Instruments Incorporated, I 315, 482, 523, 620; **II** 64, **112–15**; **III** 120, 124–25, 142, 499; **IV** 130, 365, 681; **6** 216, 221–22, 237, 241, 257, 259; **7** 531; **8** 157; **9** 43, 116, 310; **10** 22, 87, 307; **11** 61, 308, 490, 494, **505–08 (upd.)**; **12** 135, 238; **14** 42–43; **16** 4, 333; **17** 192; **18** 18, 436; **21** 123; **23** 181, 210

Texas International Airlines, **I** 117, 123; **II** 408; **IV** 413; **21** 142
Texas Life Insurance Co., **III** 293
Texas Metal Fabricating Company, **7** 540
Texas Oil & Gas Corp., **IV** 499, 572, 574; **7** 549, 551
Texas Overseas Petroleum Co., **IV** 552
Texas Pacific Coal and Oil Co., **I** 285–86
Texas Pacific Group, **22** 80; **23** 163, 166
Texas Pacific Oil Co., **IV** 550
Texas Pipe Line Co., **IV** 552
Texas Power & Light Company, **V** 724
Texas Public Utilities, **II** 660
Texas Super Duper Markets, Inc., **7** 372
Texas Trust Savings Bank, **8** 88
Texas United Insurance Co., **III** 214
Texas Utilities Company, V 724–25; 12 99
Texas-New Mexico Utilities Company, **6** 580
Texasgulf Inc., **IV** 546–47; **13** 557; **18** 433
Texboard, **IV** 296; **19** 226
Texize, **I** 325, 371
Texkan Oil Co., **IV** 566
Texstar Petroleum Company, **7** 516
Texstyrene Corp., **IV** 331
Textile Paper Tube Company, Ltd., **8** 475
Textile Rubber and Chemical Company, **15** 490
Textron Inc., I 186, **529–30**; **II** 420, **III** 66, 628; **8** 93, 157, 315, 545; **9** 497, 499; **11** 261; **12** 251, 382–83, 400–01; **13** 63–64; **17** 53; **21** 175; **22** 32
Textron Lycoming Turbine Engine, 9 **497–99**
Texwood Industries, Inc., **20** 363
TF-I, **I** 563
TFN Group Communications, Inc., **8** 311
TF1. *See* Télévision Française 1, **23** 475
TGEL&PCo. *See* Tucson Gas, Electric Light & Power Company.
Th. Pilter, **III** 417
TH:s Group, **10** 113
Thai Airways International Ltd., I 119; **II** 442; **6 122–24**
Thai Aluminium Co. Ltd., **IV** 155
Thalassa International, **10** 14
Thalhimer Brothers, **V** 31
Thames Board Ltd., **IV** 318
Thames Television Ltd., **I** 532
Thames Water plc, 11 509–11; 22 89
Tharsis Co., **IV** 189–90
Thatcher Glass, **I** 610
THAW. *See* Recreational Equipment, Inc.
Thayer Laboratories, **III** 55
Theo H. Davies & Co., **I** 470; **20** 311
Theo Hamm Brewing Co., **I** 260
Théraplix, **I** 388
Therm-o-Disc, **II** 19
Therm-X Company, **8** 178
Thermacote Welco Company, **6** 146
Thermadyne Holding Corporation, 19 **440–43**
Thermal Dynamics, **19** 441
Thermal Energies, Inc., **21** 514
Thermal Power Company, **11** 270
Thermal Snowboards, Inc., **22** 462
Thermal Transfer Ltd., **13** 485
Thermo Electron Corporation, 7 520–22; **11** 512–13; **13** 421
Thermo Instrument Systems Inc., 11 **512–14**
Thermo King Corporation, 13 505–07
Thermodynamics Corp., **III** 645

Thermoforming USA, **16** 339
Thermogas Co., **IV** 458–59
Thermolase Corporation, **22** 410
Thermoplast und Apparatebau GmbH, **IV** 198
Thermos Company, 16 486–88
Thies Companies, **13** 270
Thiess, **III** 687
Thiess Dampier Mitsui, **IV** 47
Things Remembered, **13** 165–66
Think Entertainment, **II** 161
Think Technologies, **10** 508
Thiokol Corporation, I 370; **8** 472; **9** 358–59, **500–02 (upd.); 12** 68; **22** **504–07 (upd.)**
Third National Bank. *See* Fifth Third Bancorp.
Third National Bank of Dayton, **9** 475
Third National Bank of New York, **II** 253
Third Wave Publishing Corp. *See* Acer Inc.
Thistle Group, **9** 365
Thom McAn, **V** 136–37; **11** 349
Thomas & Betts Corp., II 8; **11 515–17;** **14** 27
Thomas & Howard Co., **II** 682; **18** 8
Thomas and Hochwalt, **I** 365
Thomas and Judith Pyle, **13** 433
Thomas Barlow & Sons Ltd., **I** 288, 422; **IV** 22
Thomas Cook Group Ltd., **17** 325
Thomas Cook Travel Inc., 6 84; **9** **503–05**
Thomas Firth & Sons, **I** 573
Thomas H. Lee Company, **11** 156, 450; **14** 230–31; **15** 309; **19** 371, 373
Thomas J. Lipton Company, II 609, 657; **11** 450; **14 495–97; 16** 90
Thomas Jefferson Life Insurance Co., **III** 397
Thomas Linnell & Co. Ltd., **II** 628
Thomas Nationwide Transport. *See* TNT.
Thomas Nelson Inc., 8 526; **14 498–99**
Thomas Tilling plc, **I** 429
Thomas Y. Crowell, **IV** 605
Thomasville Furniture Industries, Inc., **III** 423; **12 474–76; 22** 48
Thompson Aircraft Tire Corp., **14** 42
Thompson and Formby, **16** 44
Thompson Medical Company. *See* Slim-Fast Nutritional Foods International Inc.
Thompson Products Co., **I** 539
Thompson-Hayward Chemical Co., **13** 397
Thompson-Ramo-Wooldridge, **I** 539
Thompson-Werke, **III** 32
Thomson BankWatch Inc., **19** 34
The Thomson Corporation, IV 651, 686; **7** 390; **8 525–28; 10** 407; **12** 361, 562; **17** 255; **22** 441
Thomson Multimedia, **18** 126
Thomson S.A., I 411; **II** 31, **116–17; 7** 9; **13** 402
Thomson T-Line, **II** 142
Thomson-Bennett, **III** 554
Thomson-Brandt, **I** 411; **II** 13, 116–17; **9** 9
Thomson-CSF, **II** 116–17; **III** 556
Thomson-Houston Electric Co., **II** 27, 116, 330; **12** 193
Thomson-Jenson Energy Limited, **13** 558
Thomson-Lucas, **III** 556
Thomson-Ramo-Wooldridge. *See* TRW Inc.
Thonet Industries Inc., **14** 435–36
Thorn Apple Valley, Inc., 7 523–25; 12 125; **22 508–11 (upd.); 23** 203

Thorn EMI plc, I 52, 411, **531–32; II** 117, 119; **III** 480; **19** 390; **22** 27, 192–94. *See also* EMI Group plc.
Thorndike, Doran, Paine and Lewis, Inc., **14** 530
Thornton, **III** 547
Thornton & Co., **II** 283
Thornton Stores, **14** 235
Thoroughgood, **II** 658
Thorsen Realtors, **21** 96
Thousand Trails, Inc., **13** 494
Thousands Springs Power Company, **12** 265
3 Guys, **II** 678, **V** 35
Three Rivers Pulp and Paper Company, **17** 281
Three Score, **23** 100
3 Suisses International, **12** 281
Three-Diamond Company. *See* Mitsubishi Shokai.
3-in-One Oil Co., **I** 622
3Com Corp., III 143; **6** 238, 269; **10** 237; **11 518–21; 20** 8, 33
3DO Inc., **10** 286
3M. *See* Minnesota Mining & Manufacturing Co.
3S Systems Support Services Ltd., **6** 310
Threlfall Breweries, **I** 294
Thrif D Discount Center, **V** 174
Thrift Drug, **V** 92
Thrift Mart, **16** 65
ThriftiCheck Service Corporation, **7** 145
Thriftimart Inc., **12** 153; **16** 452
Thriftway Food Drug, **21** 530
Thriftway Foods, **II** 624
Thrifty PayLess, Inc., V 682, 684; ; **12** **477–79; 18** 286; **19** 357
Thrifty Rent-A-Car, **6** 349
Throwing Corporation of America, **12** 501
Thuringia Insurance Co., **III** 299
Thurston Motor Lines Inc., **12** 310
Thy-Marcinelle, **IV** 52
Thyssen AG, **II** 279; **III** 566; **IV** 195, **221–23,** 228; **8** 75–76; **14** 169, 328
TI. *See* Texas Instruments.
TI Corporation, **10** 44
TI Group plc, 17 480–83
Tianjin Agricultural Industry and Commerce Corp., **II** 577
Tianjin Automobile Industry Group, **21** 164
Tianjin Bohai Brewing Company, **21** 230
Tibbals Floring Co., **III** 611
Tiber Construction Company, **16** 286
Ticino Societa d'Assicurazioni Sulla Vita, **III** 197
Ticketmaster Corp., 13 508–10
Ticketron, **13** 508–09
Ticknor & Fields, **10** 356
Tickometer Co., **III** 157
Ticor Title Insurance Co., **10** 45
Tidel Systems, **II** 661
Tidewater Inc., 11 522–24
Tidewater Oil Co., **IV** 434, 460, 489, 522
Tidi Wholesale, **13** 150
Tidy House Products Co., **II** 556
Tiel Utrecht Fire Insurance Co., **III** 309–10
Tien Wah Press (Pte.) Ltd., **IV** 600
Le Tierce S.A., **II** 141
Tierney & Partners, **23** 480
Tiffany & Co., III 16; **12** 312; **14** **500–03; 15** 95; **19** 27
Tiger Accessories, **18** 88
Tiger International, Inc., **17** 505; **18** 178

Tiger Management Associates, **13** 158, 256
Tiger Oats, **I** 424
Tigon Corporation, **V** 265–68
Tilcon, **I** 429
Tilden Interrent, **10** 419
Tile & Coal Company, **14** 248
Tilgate Pallets, **I** 592
Tillie Lewis Foods Inc., **I** 513–14
Tillotson Corp., 14 64; **15 488–90**
Tim Horton's Restaurants, **23** 507
Tim-Bar Corp., **IV** 312; **19** 267
Timber Realization Co., **IV** 305
The Timberland Company, 11 349; **13** **511–14; 17** 245; **19** 112; **22** 173
Timberline Software Corporation, 15 **491–93**
TIMCO. *See* Triad International Maintenance Corp.
Time Distribution Services, **13** 179
Time Electronics, **19** 311
Time Industries, **IV** 294; **19** 225
Time Saver Stores, Inc., **12** 112; **17** 170
Time Warner Inc., II 155, 161, 168, 175–177, 252, 452; **III** 245; **IV** 341–42, 636, **673–76; 6** 293; **7** 63, 222–24, 396, **526–30 (upd.); 8** 267–68, 527; **9** 119, 469, 472; **10** 168, 286, 484, 488, 491; **12** 531; **13** 105–06, 399; **14** 260; **15** 51, 54; **16** 146, 223; **17** 148, 442–44; **18** 66, 535; **19** 6, 336; **22** 52, 194, 522; **23** 31, 33, 257, 274, 276, 393. *See also* Warner Communications Inc.
Time-Life Books, Inc. *See* Time Warner Inc.
Time-O-Stat Controls Corp., **II** 41; **12** 247
Time-Sharing Information, **10** 357
Timely Brands, **I** 259
Timeplex, **III** 166; **6** 283; **9** 32
Times Media Ltd., **IV** 22
The Times Mirror Company, I 90; **IV** 583, 630, **677–78; 14** 97; **17 484–86** **(upd.); 21** 404; **22** 162, 443
Times Newspapers, **8** 527
Times-Picayune Publishing Co., **IV** 583
TIMET. *See* Titanium Metals Corporation.
Timex Enterprises Inc., III 455; **7** **531–33; 10** 152; **12** 317; **21** 123
The Timken Company, III 596; **7** 447; **8** **529–31; 15** 225
Timpte Industries, **II** 488
Tioxide Group PLC, **III** 680
Tip Corp., **I** 278
TIPC Network. *See* Gateway 2000.
Tiphook PLC, **13** 530
Tipton Centers Inc., **V** 50; **19** 123
Tiroler Hauptbank, **II** 270
Tishman Realty and Construction, **III** 248
Tissue Papers Ltd., **IV** 260
Tissue Technologies, Inc., **22** 409
Titan Manufacturing Company, **19** 359
Titanium Metals Corporation, 10 434; **21** **489–92**
Titanium Technology Corporation, **13** 140
Titianium Enterprises, **IV** 345
TITISA, **9** 109
Title Guarantee & Trust Co., **II** 230
Titmus Optical Inc., **III** 446
Tivoli Systems, Inc., **14** 392
TJ International, Inc., 19 444–47
The TJX Companies, Inc., V 197–98; **13** 548; **14** 426; **19 448–50 (upd.)**
TKD Electronics Corp., **II** 109
TKM Foods, **II** 513
TKR Cable Co., **15** 264

TLC Associates, **11** 261
TLC Beatrice International Holdings, Inc., 22 512–15. *See also* Beatrice Co.
TLC Group, **II** 468
TMC Industries Ltd., **22** 352
TML Information Services Inc., **9** 95
TMS, Inc., **7** 358
TMS Systems, Inc., **10** 18
TMT. *See* Trailer Marine Transport.
TN Technologies Inc., **23** 479
TNT Crust, Inc., **23** 203
TNT Freightways Corporation, IV 651; **14** 504–06
TNT Limited, V 523–25; **6** 346
Toa Airlines, **I** 106; **6** 427
Toa Fire & Marine Reinsurance Co., **III** 385
Toa Kyoseki Co. Ltd., **IV** 476
Toa Medical Electronics Ltd., **22** 75
Toa Nenryo Kogyo, **IV** 432
Toa Oil Co. Ltd., **IV** 476, 543
Toa Tanker Co. Ltd., **IV** 555
Toasted Corn Flake Co, **II** 523; **13** 291
Toastmaster, **17** 215; **22** 353
Tobacco Products Corporation, **18** 416
Tobata Imaon Co., **I** 183
Tobias, **16** 239
Tobler Co., **II** 520–21
Tobu Railway Co Ltd, 6 430–32
TOC Retail Inc., **17** 170
Tocom, Inc., **10** 320
Today's Man, Inc., 20 484–87; **21** 311
Todays Computers Business Centers, **6** 243–44
Todays Temporary, **6** 140
Todd Shipyards Corporation, IV 121; **7** 138; **14** 507–09
Todorovich Agency, **III** 204
Toei, **9** 29–30
Tofas, **I** 479–80
Toggenburger Bank, **II** 378
Toho Chemical Co., **I** 363
Toho Oil Co., **IV** 403
Tohoku Alps, **II** 5
Tohoku Pulp Co., **IV** 297
Tohokushinsha Film Corporation, **18** 429
Tohuku Electric Power Company, Inc., V 724, 732
Tojo Railway Company, **6** 430
Tokai Aircraft Co., Ltd., **III** 415
The Tokai Bank, Limited, II 373–74; **15** 494–96 (upd.)
Tokai Paper Industries, **IV** 679
Tokan Kogyo, **I** 615
Tokheim Corporation, 21 493–95
Tokio Marine and Fire Insurance Co., Ltd., II 323; **III** 248, 289, 295, 383–86
Tokos Medical Corporation, **17** 306, 308–09
Tokushima Ham Co., **II** 550
Tokushima Meat Processing Factory, **II** 550
Tokushu Seiko, Ltd., **IV** 63
Tokuyama Soda, **I** 509
Tokuyama Teppan Kabushikigaisha, **IV** 159
Tokyo Broadcasting System, **7** 249; **9** 29; **16** 167
Tokyo Car Manufacturing Co., **I** 105
Tokyo Confectionery Co., **II** 538
Tokyo Corporation, **V** 199
Tokyo Dairy Industry, **II** 538
Tokyo Denki Kogaku Kogyo, **II** 109
Tokyo Dento Company, **6** 430

Tokyo Disneyland, **IV** 715; **6** 123, 176
Tokyo Electric Company, Ltd., **I** 533; **12** 483
Tokyo Electric Express Railway Co., **IV** 728
Tokyo Electric Light Co., **IV** 153
Tokyo Electric Power Company, IV 167, 518; **V** 729–33
Tokyo Electronic Corp., **11** 232
Tokyo Express Highway Co., Ltd., **IV** 713–14
Tokyo Express Railway Company, **V** 510, 526
Tokyo Fire Insurance Co. Ltd., **III** 405–06, 408
Tokyo Food Products, **I** 507
Tokyo Fuhansen Co., **I** 502, 506
Tokyo Gas and Electric Industrial Company, **9** 293
Tokyo Gas Co., Ltd., IV 518; **V** 734–36
Tokyo Ishikawajima Shipbuilding and Engineering Company, **III** 532; **9** 293
Tokyo Maritime Insurance Co., **III** 288
Tokyo Motors. *See* Isuzu Motors, Ltd.
Tokyo Sanyo Electric, **II** 91–92
Tokyo Shibaura Electric Company, Ltd., **I** 507, 533; **12** 483
Tokyo Steel Works Co., Ltd., **IV** 63
Tokyo Tanker Co., Ltd., **IV** 479
Tokyo Telecommunications Engineering Corp. *See* Tokyo Tsushin Kogyo K.K.
Tokyo Trust & Banking Co., **II** 328
Tokyo Tsushin Kogyo K K , **II** 101, 103
Tokyo Yokohama Electric Railways Co., Ltd., **V** 199
Tokyu Corporation, IV 728; **V** 199, 526–28
Tokyu Department Store Co., Ltd., V 199–202
Tokyu Electric Power Company, **V** 736
Tokyu Kyuko Electric Railway Company Ltd., **V** 526
Tokyu Land Corporation, IV 728–29
Tokyu Railway Company, **V** 461
Toledo Edison Company. *See* Centerior Energy Corporation.
Toledo Milk Processing, Inc., **15** 449
Toledo Scale Corp., **9** 441
Toledo Seed & Oil Co., **I** 419
Toll Brothers Inc., 15 497–99
Tom Bowling Lamp Works, **III** 554
Tom Huston Peanut Co., **II** 502; **10** 323
Tom Piper Ltd., **I** 437
Tom Thumb-Page, **16** 64
Tomakomai Paper Co., Ltd., **IV** 321
Toman Corporation, **19** 390
Tombstone Pizza Corporation, 13 515–17
Tomei Fire and Marine Insurance Co., **III** 384–85
Tomen Corporation, IV 224–25; **19** 256
Tomen Transportgerate, **III** 638
Tomkins plc, 11 525–27
Tomkins-Johnson Company, **16** 8
Tomlee Tool Company, **7** 535
Tommy Hilfiger Corporation, 16 61; **20** 488–90
Tomoe Trading Co., **III** 595
Tonami Transportation Company, **6** 346
Tone Brothers, Inc., 21 496–98
Tone Coca-Cola Bottling Company, Ltd., **14** 288
Tonen Corporation, IV 554–56; **16** 489–92 (upd.)

Tong Yang Group, **III** 304
Toni Co., **III** 28; **9** 413
Tonka Corp., **12** 169; **14** 266; **16** 267
Tonkin, Inc., **19** 114
Tony Lama Company Inc., **19** 233
Toohey, **10** 170
Tootal Group, **V** 356–57
Tootsie Roll Industries Inc., 12 480–82; **15** 323
Top End Wheelchair Sports, **11** 202
Top Green International, **17** 475
Top Man, **V** 21
Top Shop, **V** 21
Top Value Stamp Co., **II** 644–45; **6** 364; **22** 126
Topco Associates, **17** 78
Topkapi, **17** 101–03
Toppan Printing Co., Ltd., IV 598–99, 679–81
Topps Company, Inc., **13** 518–20; **19** 386
Topps Markets, **16** 314
Tops Appliance City, Inc., 17 487–89
Topy Industries, Limited, **8** 506–07
Toray Industries, Inc., V 380, **383**; **17** 287
Torbensen Gear & Axle Co., **I** 154
Torchmark Corporation, III 194; **9** 506–08; **10** 66; **11** 17; **22** 540–43
Torfeaco Industries Limited, **19** 304
Torise Ham Co., **II** 550
Tornator Osakeyhtiö, **IV** 275–76
Toro Assicurazioni, **III** 347
The Toro Company, III 600, **7** 534–36
Toromont Industries, Ltd., 21 499–501
Toronto and Scarborough Electric Railway, **9** 461
Toronto Electric Light Company, **9** 461
Toronto-Dominion Bank, II 319, 375–77, 456; **16** 13–14; **17** 324; **18** 551–53; **21** 447
Torpshammars, **IV** 338
Torrey Canyon Oil, **IV** 569
The Torrington Company, III 526, 589–90; **13** 521–24
Torrington National Bank & Trust Co., **13** 467
Torstar Corp., **IV** 672; **7** 488–89; **19** 405
Tosa Electric Railway Co., **II** 458
Toscany Co., **13** 42
Tosco Corporation, 7 537–39; **12** 240; **20** 138
Toshiba Corporation, I 221, 507–08, **533–35**; **II** 5, 56, 59, 62, 68, 73, 99, 102, 118, 122, 326, 440; **III** 298, 461, 533, 604; **6** 101, 231, 244, 287; **7** 529; **9** 7, 181; **10** 518–19; **11** 46, 328; **12** 454, 483–86 (upd.). 546; **13** 324, 399, 482; **14** 117, 446; **16** 5, 167; **17** 533; **18** 18, 260; **21** 390; **22** 193, 373; **23** 471
Toshin Kaihatsu Ltd., **V** 195
Toshin Paper Co., Ltd., **IV** 285
Tostem. *See* Toyo Sash Co., Ltd.
Total Beverage Corporation, **16** 159, 161
Total Compagnie Française des Pétroles S.A., I 303; **III** 673; **IV** 425, 486, 498, 515, 525, 544, 547, **557–61**; **V** 628; **7** 481, 483–84; **13** 557
Total Exploration S.A., **11** 537
Total Global Sourcing, Inc., **10** 498
Total Petroleum Corporation, **21** 500
Total System Services, Inc., 12 465–66; **18** 168, 170, 516–18
Totem Resources Corporation, 9 509–11
Totino's Finer Foods, **II** 556; **13** 516

Toto Bank, II 326
Toto, Ltd., III 755–56
Totsu Co., I 493
Touch-It Corp., **22** 413
Touche Remnant Holdings Ltd., II 356
Touche Ross. *See* Deloitte & Touche.
Touchstone Films, II 172–74; **6** 174–76
Tour d'Argent, II 518
Tourang Limited, **7** 253
**Touristik Union International GmbH.
    and Company K.G., II 163–65**
Touron y Cia, III 419
Touropa, II 163–64
Toval Japon, IV 680
Towa Nenryo Kogyo Co. Ltd., IV 554–55
Tower Records, **9** 361; **10** 335; **11** 558
Towers, II 649
Towle Manufacturing Co., **14** 482–83; **18**
    69
Town & City, IV 696
Town & Country Corporation, 7 372; **16**
    546; **19 451–53**
Town Investments, IV 711
Townsend Hook, IV 296, 650, 652; **19** 226
Toxicol Laboratories, Ltd., **21** 424
Toy Biz, Inc., 10 402; **18 519–21**
Toy Liquidators, **13** 541–43
Toy Park, **16** 390
Toyad Corp., **7** 296
Toyo Bearing Manufacturing, III 595
Toyo Cotton Co., IV 224–25
Toyo Kogyo, I 167; II 361; **11** 139
Toyo Marine and Fire, III 385
Toyo Menka Kaisha Ltd., I 508; IV
    224–25
Toyo Microsystems Corporation, **11** 464
Toyo Oil Co., IV 403
Toyo Pulp Co., IV 322
Toyo Rayon, V 381, 383
Toyo Sash Co., Ltd., III 757–58
Toyo Seikan Kaisha Ltd., I 615–16
Toyo Soda, II 301
Toyo Tire & Rubber Co., V 255–56; **9** 248
Toyo Toki Co., Ltd., III 755
Toyo Tozo Co., I 265; **21** 319
Toyo Trust and Banking Co., II 347, 371;
    17 349
Toyoda Automatic Loom Works, Ltd., I
    203; III 591, 593, 632, **636–39**
Toyokawa Works, I 579
Toyoko Co., Ltd., V 199
Toyoko Kogyo, V 199
Toyomenka (America) Inc., IV 224
Toyomenka (Australia) Pty., Ltd., IV 224
Toyota Gossei, I 321
Toyota Motor Corporation, I 9–10, 174,
    184, **203–05**, 507–08, 587; II 373; III
    415, 495, 521, 523, 536, 579, 581,
    591–93, 624, 636–38, 667, 715, 742; IV
    702; **6** 514; **7** 111, 118, 212, 219–21; **8**
    315; **9** 294, 340–42; **10** 353, 407; **11**
    351, 377, 487, **528–31 (upd.)**; **14** 321;
    15 495; **21** 162, 273; **23** 289–90,
    338–40
Toyota Tsusho America, Inc., **13** 371
Toys "R" Us, Inc., III 588; V **203–06**; **7**
    396; **10** 235, 284, 484; **12** 178; **13** 166;
    14 61; **15** 469; **16** 389–90, 457; **18**
    522–25 (upd.)
Tozer Kemsley & Milbourn, II 208
TPCR Corporation, V 163; **14** 394
Trace International Holdings, Inc., **17**
    182–83
Tracey Bros., IV 416

Tracey-Locke, II 660
Tracker Services, Inc., **9** 110
Traco International N.V., **8** 250
Tracor Inc., 10 547; **17 490–92**
Tractebel S.A., 20 491–93
Tractor Supply Corp., I 446
Tradax, II 617; **13** 137
Trade Assoc. of Bilbao, II 194
Trade Development Bank, **11** 415–17
Trade Waste Incineration, Inc., **9** 109
Trade Winds Campers, III 599
TradeARBED, IV 25
Trader Joe's Co., 13 525–27
Trader Publications, Inc., IV 597
Trader Publishing Company, **12** 302
Traders & General Insurance, III 248
Traders Bank of Canada, II 344
Traders Group Ltd., **11** 258
Tradesmens National Bank of Philadelphia,
    II 342
The Trading Service, **10** 278
Traex Corporation, **8** 359
Trafalgar House Investments Ltd., I
    248–49, 572–74; IV 259, 711; **20** 313;
    23 161
Trailer Marine Transport, **6** 383
Trailways, I 450; **9** 425
Trak Auto Corporation, **16** 159–62
TRAK Microwave Corporation, **18** 497,
    513
Trammell Crow Company, IV 343; **8**
    326–28, **532–34**
Tran Telecommunications Corp., III 110;
    14 14
Trane Company, III 663, 665; **10** 525; **21**
    107; **22** 6
Trans Air System, **6** 367
Trans Colorado, **11** 299
Trans International Airlines, I 537; **13** 529
Trans Ocean Products, II 578; **8** 510
Trans Rent-A-Car, **6** 348
Trans Union Corp., IV 137; **6** 25
Trans World Airlines, Inc., I 58, 70, 90,
    97, 99–100, 102, 113, 121, 123–24,
    125–27, 132, 466; II 32–33, 142, 425,
    679; III 92, 428; **6** 50, 68, 71, 74,
    76–77, 81–82, 114, 130; **9** 17, 232; **10**
    301–03, 316; **11** 277, 427; **12** 381,
    487–90 (upd.); **13** 341; **14** 73; **15** 419;
    21 141–42; **22** 22, 219
Trans World International, **18** 262–63
Trans World Music, **9** 361
Trans World Seafood, Inc., **13** 244
Trans-Arabian Pipe Line Co., IV 537, 552
Trans-Australia Airlines, **6** 110–12
Trans-Canada Air Lines. *See* Air Canada.
Trans-Continental Leaf Tobacco Company,
    (TCLTC), **13** 491
Trans-Natal Coal Corp., IV 93
Trans-Pacific Airlines, **22** 251
Trans-Resources Inc., **13** 299
Trans-World Corp., **19** 456
Transaction Technology, **12** 334
TransAlta Utilities Corporation, 6
    585–87
Transamerica Corporation, I 536–38; II
    147–48, 227, 288–89, 422; III 332, 344;
    7 236–37; **8** 46; **11** 273, 533; **13**
    528–30 (upd.); **21** 285
Transat. *See* Compagnie Générale
    Transatlantique (Transat).
Transatlantic Holdings, Inc., III 198; **11**
    532–33; **15** 18

Transatlantische Dampfschiffahrts
    Gesellschaft, **6** 397
Transatlantische Gruppe, III 404
Transbrasil, **6** 134
TransCanada PipeLines Limited, I 264;
    V 270–71, **737–38**; **17** 22–23
Transco Energy Company, IV 367; V
    739–40; **6** 143; **18** 366
Transcontinental Air Transport, I 125; **9**
    17; **11** 427; **12** 487
Transcontinental and Western Air Lines, **9**
    416; **12** 487
Transcontinental Gas Pipe Line
    Corporation, V 739; **6** 447
Transcontinental Pipeline Company, **6**
    456–57
Transcontinental Services Group N.V., **16**
    207
TransCor America, Inc., **23** 154
Transelco, Inc., **8** 178
TransEuropa, II 164
Transflash, **6** 404
Transfracht, **6** 426
Transinternational Life, II 422
Transit Mix Concrete and Materials
    Company, **7** 541
Transitions Optical Inc., **21** 221, 223
Transitron, **16** 332
Transking Inc. *See* King Kullen Grocery
    Co., Inc.
Transkrit Corp., IV 640
Translite, III 495
Transmanche-Link, **13** 206–08
Transmedia Network Inc., 20 494–97
Transmisiones y Equipos Mecanicos, S.A.
    de C.V., **23** 171
Transmitter Equipment Manufacturing Co.,
    13 385
Transnet Ltd., 6 433–35
TransOcean Oil, III 559
Transpac, IV 325
Transport Management Co., III 192
Transport- und Unfall-Versicherungs-
    Aktiengesellschaft Zürich, III 411
Transportacion Maritima Mexican, **12** 279
Transportation Insurance Co., III 229
Transportes Aereos Portugueses, S.A., 6
    125–27
Transtar, **6** 120–21
Transue & Williams Steel Forging Corp.,
    13 302
Transvaal Silver and Base Metals, IV 90
Transway International Corp., **10** 369
Transworld Corp., **14** 209
Transworld Drilling Company Limited. *See*
    Kerr-McGee Corporation.
The Tranzonic Cos., 8 512; **15 500–02**
Trapper's, **19** 286
Trasgo, S.A. de C.V., **14** 516
Trausch Baking Co., I 255
Trävaru Svartvik, IV 338
Travel Air Company, **8** 49
Travel Automation Services Ltd., I 95
Travel Information Group, **17** 398
Travel Ports of America, Inc., 17 493–95
Travelers Bank & Trust Company, **13** 467
Travelers Book Club, **13** 105
Travelers Corporation, I 37, 545; III
    313, 329, **387–90**, 707–08; **6** 12; **15** 463
Travelers/Aetna Property Casualty Corp.,
    21 15
Traveller's Express, I 449
TraveLodge, III 94, 104–06

Travenol Laboratories, **I** 627–28; **10** 141–43
Trayco, **III** 570; **20** 362
Traylor Engineering & Manufacturing Company, **6** 395
TRE Corp., **23** 225
Treadco, Inc., 16 39; **19** 38, **454–56**
Treasure Chest Advertising, **21** 60
Treasure House Stores, Inc., **17** 322
Treatment Centers of America, **11** 379
Trechmann, Weekes and Co., **III** 669
Tredegar Industries, Inc., **10** 291
Tree of Life Inc., **II** 528
TreeSweet Products, **12** 105
TrefilARBED, **IV** 26
Tréfimétaux, **IV** 174
Trefoil Capital Investors, L.P., **8** 305
Trek, **IV** 90, 92–93
Trek Bicycle Corporation, 16 493–95; 19 384–85
Trelleborg A.B., **III** 625; **IV** 166
Tremec. *See* Transmisiones y Equipos Mecanicos, S.A. de C.V.
Tremletts Ltd., **IV** 294; **19** 225
Tremont Corporation, **21** 490
Trend International Ltd., **13** 502
Trend-Lines, Inc., 22 516–18
TrendWest, **12** 439
Trent Tube, **I** 435
Trenton Foods, **II** 488
TrentonWorks Limited. *See* The Greenbrier Companies.
Tresco, **8** 514
Trethowal China Clay Co., **III** 690
Tri-City Federal Savings and Loan Association, **10** 92
Tri-City Utilities Company, **6** 514
Tri-County National Bank, **9** 474
Tri-Miller Packing Company, **7** 524
Tri Sonics, Inc., **16** 202
Tri State Improvement Company, **6** 465–66
Tri-State Publishing & Communications, Inc., **22** 442
Tri-State Recycling Corporation, **15** 117
Tri-State Refining Co., **IV** 372
Triad, **14** 224
Triad Artists Inc., **23** 514
Triad International Maintenance Corp., **13** 417
Triangle Auto Springs Co., **IV** 136
The Triangle Group, **16** 357
Triangle Industries Inc., **I** 602, 607–08, 614; **II** 480–81; **14** 43
Triangle Portfolio Associates, **II** 317
Triangle Publications, Inc., **IV** 652; **7** 391; **12** 359–60
Triangle Refineries, **IV** 446; **22** 302
Triarc Companies, Inc., 8 535–37; 13 322; **14** 32–33
Triathlon Leasing, **II** 457
Tribe Computer Works. *See* Zoom Telephonics.
Tribune Company, III 329; **IV 682–84; 10** 56; **11** 331; **22 519–23 (upd.)**
Trical Resources, **IV** 84
Tricity Cookers, **I** 531–32
Trick & Murray, **22** 153
Trico Products Corporation, I 186; **15 503–05**
Tricon Global Restaurants, Inc., **21** 313, 317, 405, 407, 485
Tridel Enterprises Inc., 9 512–13
Trident NGL Holdings Inc., **18** 365, 367

Trident Seafoods, **II** 494
Trifari, Krussman & Fishel, Inc., **9** 157
Trigen Energy Corp., **6** 512
Trigon Industries, **13** 195; **14** 431
Trilan Developments Ltd., **9** 512
Trilogy Fabrics, Inc., **16** 125
Trilon Financial Corporation, II 456–57; IV 721; **9** 391
TriMas Corp., III 571; **11 534–36; 20** 359, 362
Trinidad Oil Co., **IV** 95, 552
Trinidad-Tesoro Petroleum Company Limited, **7** 516, 518
Trinity Beverage Corporation, **11** 451
Trinity Broadcasting, **13** 279
Trinity Capital Opportunity Corp., **17** 13
Trinity Distributors, **15** 139
Trinity Industries, Incorporated, 7 540–41
Trinkaus und Burkhardt, **II** 319; **17** 324
TRINOVA Corporation, III 640–42, 731; **13** 8; **16** 7, 9
Trintex, **6** 158
Triology Corp., **III** 110
Triplex, **6** 279
Triplex (Northern) Ltd., **III** 725
Trippe Manufacturing Co., **10** 474
Triquet Paper Co., **IV** 282; **9** 261
TriStar Pictures, **I** 234; **II** 134, 136–37; **6** 158; **10** 227; **12** 75, 455; **23** 275
Triton Bioscience, **III** 53
Triton Energy Corporation, 11 537–39
Triton Group Ltd., **I** 447
Triton Oil, **IV** 519
Triton Systems Corp., **22** 186
Triumph, **21** 153
Triumph American, Inc., **12** 199
Triumph, Finlay, and Phillips Petroleum, **11** 28
Triumph-Adler, **I** 485; **III** 145; **11** 265
Trivest, Inc., **II** 457; **21** 531–32
Trizec Corporation Ltd., 9 84–85; **10 529–32**
TRM Copy Centers Corporation, 18 526–28
Trojan, **III** 674
Troll, **13** 561
Trona Corp., **IV** 95
Tropical Oil Co., **IV** 415–16
Tropical Shipping, Inc., **6** 529, 531
Tropicana Products, **II** 468, 525; **13** 293
Trotter-Yoder & Associates, **22** 88
Troxel Cycling, **16** 53
Troy & Nichols, Inc., **13** 147
Troy Metal Products. *See* KitchenAid.
Troyfel Ltd., **III** 699
TRT Communications, Inc., **6** 327; **11** 185
Tru-Run Inc., **16** 207
Tru-Stitch, **16** 545
Tru-Trac Therapy Products, **11** 486
Truck Components Inc., **23** 306
Trudeau Marketing Group, Inc., **22** 386
True Form Boot Co., **V** 177
True North Communications Inc., 23 478–80
True Value Hardware Stores, **V** 37–38
Trygg-Hansa Holding AB, **III** 264
TruGreen, **23** 428, 430
Truitt Bros., **10** 382
Truman Dunham Co., **III** 744
Truman Hanburg, **I** 247
Trumball Asphalt, **III** 721
Trümmer-Verwertungs-Gesellschaft, **IV** 140

Trump Organization, 16 262; **23 481–84**
Trunkline Gas Company, **6** 544; **14** 135
Trunkline LNG Co., **IV** 425
Trus Joist Corporation. *See* TJ International, Inc.
Trussdeck Corporation. *See* TJ International, Inc.
Trust Co. of the West, **19** 414
Trustcorp, Inc., **9** 475–76
Trustees, Executors and Agency Co. Ltd., **II** 189
Trusthouse Forte PLC, I 215; **III 104–06; 16** 446
TRW Inc., I 539–41; II 33; **6** 25; **8** 416; **9** 18, 359; **10** 293; **11** 68, **540–42 (upd.); 12** 238; **14 510–13 (upd.); 16** 484; **17** 372; **18** 275; **19** 184; **23** 134
Tryart Pty. Limited, **7** 253
Tsai Management & Research Corp., **III** 230–31
TSB Group plc, 12 491–93; 16 14
TSO. *See* Teacher's Service Organization, Inc.
TSO Financial Corp., **II** 420; **8** 10
Tsogo Sun Gaming & Entertainment, **17** 318
Tsuang Hine Co., **III** 582
Tsubakimoto-Morse, **14** 64
Tsukumo Shokai, **I** 502; **III** 712
Tsumeb Corp., **IV** 17–18
Tsurumi Steelmaking and Shipbuilding Co., **IV** 162
Tsurusaki Pulp Co., Ltd., **IV** 285
Tsutsunaka Plastic Industry Co., **III** 714; **8** 359
TSYS. *See* Total System Services, Inc.
TTK. *See* Tokyo Tsushin Kogyo K.K.
TTX Company, 6 436–37
Tube Fab Ltd., **17** 234
Tube Forming, Inc., **23** 517
Tube Investments, **II** 422; **IV** 15
Tube Reducing Corp., **16** 321
Tube Service Co., **19** 344
Tuborg, **9** 99
Tucker, Lynch & Coldwell. *See* CB Commercial Real Estate Services Group, Inc.
TUCO, Inc., **8** 78
Tucson Electric Power Company, V 713; **6 588–91**
Tucson Gas & Electric, **19** 411–12
Tuesday Morning Corporation, 18 529–31
Tuff Stuff Publications, **23** 101
TUI. *See* Touristik Union International GmbH. and Company K.G.
Tuileries et Briqueteries d'Hennuyeres et de Wanlin, **14** 249
Tultex Corporation, 13 531–33
Tunhems Industri A.B., **I** 387
Tupperware, **I** 29; **II** 534; **III** 610–12;, **15** 475, 477; **17** 186; **18** 67
Turbinbolaget, **III** 419
Turcot Paperboard Mills Ltd., **17** 281
Turkish Engineering, Consultancy and Contracting Corp., **IV** 563
Turkish Petroleum Co. *See* Türkiye Petrolleri Anonim Ortakliği.
Türkiye Garanti Bankasi, **I** 479
Türkiye Petrolleri Anonim Ortakliği, IV 464, 557–58, **562–64; 7** 352
Turnbull, **III** 468
Turner Broadcasting System, Inc., II 134, 149, 161 **166–68; IV** 676; **6**

171–73 (upd.); **7** 64, 99, 306, 529; **23** 33, 257
The Turner Corporation, 8 538–40; **23** 485–88 (upd.)
Turner Entertainment Co., **18** 459
Turner Glass Company, **13** 40
Turner Network Television, **21** 24
Turner's Turkeys, **II** 587
TURPAS, **IV** 563
Turtle Wax, Inc., 15 506–09; **16** 43
Tuscarora, **17** 155
Tussauds Group Ltd., **IV** 659
Tuttle, Oglebay and Company. *See* Oglebay Norton Company.
TV & Stereo Town, **10** 468
TV Asahi, **7** 249
TV Food Network, **22** 522
TVE. *See* Television Española, S.A.
TVE Holdings, **22** 307
TVH Acquisition Corp., **III** 262, 264
TVI, Inc., 15 510–12
TVS Entertainment PLC, **13** 281
TVW Enterprises, **7** 78
TVX, **II** 449; **13** 449
TW Kutter, **III** 420
TW Services, Inc., II 679–80; **10** 301–03
TWA. *See* Trans World Airlines *and* Transcontinental & Western Airways.
Tweco Co., **19** 441
Tweeds, **12** 280
Twen-Tours International, **II** 164
Twentieth Century Fox Film Corporation, II 133, 135, 146, 155–56, **169–71**, 175; **IV** 652; **7** 391–92; **12** 73, 322, 359; **15** 23, 25, 234
Twentsche Bank, **II** 183
21st Century Mortgage, **18** 28
Twenty-Second National Bank, **II** 291
''21'' International Holdings, **17** 182
21 Invest International Holdings Ltd., **14** 322
TWI. *See* Trans World International.
Twin City Wholesale Drug Company, **14** 147
Twin Disc, Inc., 21 502–04
Twining Crosfield Group, **II** 465; **13** 52
Twinings Tea, **II** 465; **III** 696
Twinings' Foods International, **II** 466
Twinpak, **IV** 250
Two Guys, **12** 49
2-in-1 Shinola Bixby Corp., **II** 497
TXEN, Inc., **18** 370
TXL Oil Corp., **IV** 552
TXP Operation Co., **IV** 367
TxPort Inc., **13** 8
Ty-D-Bol, **III** 55
Tyco International Ltd., **21** 462
Tyco Laboratories, Inc., III 643–46; **13** 245–47
Tyco Toys, Inc., 12 494–97; **13** 312, 319; **18** 520–21
Tyler Corporation, 23 489–91
Tymnet, **18** 542
Tyndall Fund-Unit Assurance Co., **III** 273
Typhoo Tea, **II** 477
Typpi Oy, **IV** 469
Tyrolean Airways, **9** 233
Tyrvään Oy, **IV** 348
Tyson Foods, Inc., II 584–85; **7** 422–23, 432; **14** 514–16 (upd.); **21** 535; **23** 376, 384

U S West, Inc., V 341–43; **11** 12, 59, 547
U.C.L.A.F. *See* Roussel-Uclaf.

U-Haul International Inc. *See* Amerco.
U.K. Corrugated, **IV** 296; **19** 226
U.S. Bancorp, 12 165; **14** 527–29
U.S. Bank of Washington, **14** 527
U.S. Bearings Co., **I** 159
U.S. Delivery Systems, Inc., 22 153, 531–33
U.S. Electrical Motors, **II** 19
U.S. Elevator Corporation, **19** 109–11
U.S. Envelope, **19** 498
U.S. Food Products Co., **I** 376
U.S.G. Co., **III** 762
U.S. Geological Survey, **9** 367
U.S. Guarantee Co., **III** 220; **14** 108
U.S. Healthcare, Inc., 6 194–96; **21** 16
U.S. Home Corporation, 8 541–43
U.S. Industries, Inc., **7** 208; **18** 467; **23** 296
U.S. Intec, **22** 229
U.S. International Reinsurance, **III** 264
U.S. Land Co., **IV** 255
U.S. Life Insurance, **III** 194
U.S. Lines, **I** 476; **III** 459; **11** 194
U.S. Lock, **9** 543
U.S. Marine Corp., **III** 444
U.S. Overall Company, **14** 549
U.S. Plywood Corp. *See* United States Plywood Corp.
U.S. Realty and Improvement Co., **III** 98
U.S. RingBinder Corp., **10** 313–14
U.S. Robotics Inc., 9 514–15; **20** 8, 69; **22** 17
U.S. Rubber Company, **I** 478; **10** 388
U.S. Satellite Broadcasting Company, Inc., 20 505–07
U.S. Satellite Systems, **III** 169; **6** 285
U.S. Smelting Refining and Mining, **7** 360
U.S. Steel Corp. *See* United States Steel Corp.
U.S. Telephone Communications, **9** 478
U.S. Tile Co., **III** 674
U.S. Time Corporation, **13** 120
U.S. Trust Co. of New York, **II** 274
U.S. Trust Corp., 17 496–98
U.S. Vanadium Co., **9** 517
U.S. Venture Partners, **15** 204–05
U.S. Vitamin & Pharmaceutical Corp., **III** 55
U.S. Windpower, **11** 222–23
U.S. Xpress Enterprises, Inc., **18** 159
U-Tote'M, **II** 620; **7** 372
UAA. *See* AirEgypt.
UAL, Inc. *See* United Airlines.
UAP. *See* Union des Assurances de Paris.
UARCO Inc., **15** 473–74
UAT. *See* UTA.
Ub Iwerks, **6** 174
Ube Industries, Ltd., III 759–61
Uberseebank A.G., **III** 197
UBS. *See* Union Bank of Switzerland.
Ucabail, **II** 265
UCC-Communications Systems, Inc., **II** 38
Uccel, **6** 224
Uchiyama, **V** 727
UCI, **IV** 92
UCPMI, **IV** 226
Uddeholm and Bohler, **IV** 234
Udet Flugzeugwerke, **I** 73
Udo Fischer Co., **8** 477
UE Automotive Manufacturing, **III** 580
Ugg Holdings, Inc., **22** 173
UGI. *See* United Gas Improvement.
UGI Corporation, 12 498–500
Ugine S.A., IV 174; **20** 498–500
Ugine Steels, **IV** 227

Ugine-Kuhlmann, **IV** 108, 174
Ugly Duckling Corporation, 22 524–27
UI International, **6** 444
UIB. *See* United Independent Broadcasters, Inc.
Uinta Co., **6** 568
Uintah National Corp., **11** 260
UIS Co., **13** 554–55; **15** 324
Uitgeversmaatschappij Elsevier, **IV** 610
Uitzendbureau Amstelveen. *See* Randstad Holding n.v.
UJB Financial Corp., **14** 473
UK Paper, **IV** 279; **19** 155
UKF. *See* Unie van Kunstmestfabrieken.
Ullrich Copper, Inc., **6** 146
Ullstein AV Produktions-und Vertriebsgesellschaft, **IV** 590
Ullstein Langen Müller, **IV** 591
Ullstein Tele Video, **IV** 590
ULN. *See* Union Laitière Normande.
ULPAC, **II** 576
Ulster Bank, **II** 334
Ultimate Electronics, Inc., 18 532–34; **21** 33
Ultra Bancorp, **II** 334
Ultra High Pressure Units Ltd., **IV** 66; **7** 123
Ultra Mart, **16** 250
Ultra Radio & Television, **I** 531
UltraCare Products, **18** 148
Ultralar, **13** 544
Ultramar PLC, IV 565–68
Ultrametl Mfg. Co., **17** 234
Ultronic Systems Corp., **IV** 669
UM Technopolymer, **III** 760
Umacs of Canada Inc., **9** 513
Umberto's of New Hyde Park Pizzeria, **16** 447
Umm-al-Jawabi Oil Co., **IV** 454
Umpqua River Navigation Company, **13** 100
Unadulterated Food Products, Inc., **11** 449
UNAT, **III** 197–98
Uncas-Merchants National Bank, **13** 467
Uncle Ben's Inc., 22 528–30
Under Sea Industries, **III** 59
Underground Group, **6** 407
Underwood, **III** 145
Underwriters Adjusting Co., **III** 242
Underwriters Reinsurance Co., **10** 45
UNELCO. *See* Union Electrica de Canarias S.A.
Unelec, Inc., **13** 398
Unfall, **III** 207
Ungermann-Bass, Inc., **6** 279
Uni Europe, **III** 211
Uni-Cardan AG, **III** 494
Uni-Cast. *See* Sturm, Ruger & Company, Inc.
Uni-Charm, **III** 749
Uni-Marts, Inc., 17 499–502
Uni-Sankyo, **I** 675
Unic, **V** 63
Unicapital, Inc., **15** 281
Unicare Health Facilities, **6** 182
Unicer, **9** 100
Unichema International, **13** 228
Unicoa, **I** 524
Unicomi, **II** 265
Unicon Producing Co., **10** 191
Unicoolait, **19** 51
Unicorn Shipping Lines, **IV** 91
UniCorp, **8** 228
Unicorp Financial, **III** 248

Unicredit, II 265
Uniden, 14 117
UniDynamics Corporation, 8 135
Unie van Kunstmestfabrieken, I 326
Uniface Holding B.V., 10 245
Unifi, Inc., 12 501–03
Unified Management Corp., III 306
UniFirst Corporation, 16 228; 21 115, 505–07
Unigate PLC, II 586–87
Unigep Group, III 495
Unigesco Inc., II 653
Uniglory, 13 211
Unigroup, 15 50
UniHealth America, 11 378–79
Unik S.A., 23 170–171
Unilac Inc., II 547
Unilever PLC/Unilever N.V., I 369, 590, 605; II 547, 588–91; III 31–32, 46, 52, 495; IV 532; 7 382, 542–45 (upd.), 577; 8 105–07, 166, 168, 341, 344; 9 449; 11 205, 421; 13 243–44; 14 204–05; 18 395, 397; 19 193; 21 219; 22 123; 23 242
Unilife Assurance Group, III 273
UniLife Insurance Co., 22 149
UniMac Companies, 11 413
Unimat, II 265
Unimation, II 122
Unimetal, IV 227
Uninsa, I 460
Union, III 391–93
Union & NHK Auto Parts, III 580
Union Acceptances Ltd., IV 23
Unión Aérea Española, 6 95
Union Aéromaritime de Transport. See UTA.
Union Assurance, III 234
Union Bag–Camp Paper Corp., IV 344–45
Union Bancorp of California, II 358
Union Bank. See State Street Boston Corporation.
Union Bank of Australia, II 187–89
Union Bank of Birmingham, II 318; 17 323
Union Bank of California, 16 496–98
Union Bank of Canada, II 344
Union Bank of England, II 188
Union Bank of Finland, II 302, 352
Union Bank of Halifax, II 344
Union Bank of London, II 235
Union Bank of New London, II 213
Union Bank of New York, 9 229
Union Bank of Prince Edward Island, II 220
Union Bank of Scotland, 10 337
Union Bank of Switzerland, II 257, 267, 334, 369, 370, 378–79; 21 146
Union Battery Co., III 536
Union Bay Sportswear, 17 460
Union Camp Corporation, IV 344–46; 8 102
Union Carbide Corporation, I 334, 339, 347, 374, 390, 399–401, 582, 666; II 103, 313, 562; III 742, 760; IV 92, 374, 379, 521; 7 376; 8 180, 182, 376; 9 16, 516–20 (upd.); 10 289, 472; 11 402–03; 12 46, 347; 13 118; 14 281–82; 16 461; 17 159; 18 235; 22 228, 235
Union Cervecera, 9 100
Union Colliery Company, V 741
Union Commerce Corporation, 11 181
Union Commerciale, 19 98
Union Corporation. See Gencor Ltd.

Union d'Etudes et d'Investissements, II 265
Union des Assurances de Paris, II 234; III 201, 391–94
Union des Cooperatives Laitières. See Unicoolait.
Union des Transports Aériens. See UTA.
Union Electric Company, V 741–43; 6 505–06
Union Electrica de Canarias S.A., V 607
Union Equity Co-Operative Exchange, 7 175
Union et Prévoyance, III 403
Union Fertilizer, I 412
Union Fidelity Corp., III 204
Union Financiera, 19 189
Union Gas & Electric Co., 6 529
Union Générale de Savonnerie, III 33
l'Union Générale des Pétroles, IV 545–46, 560; 7 482–83
Union Glass Co., III 683
Union Hardware, III 443; 22 115
Union Hop Growers, I 287
Union Laitière Normande, 19 50
Union Levantina de Seguros, III 179
Union Light, Heat & Power Company, 6 466
Union Marine, III 372
Union Mutual Life Insurance Company. See UNUM Corp.
Union National Bank, II 284; 10 298
Union of Food Co-ops, II 622
Union of London, II 333
Union Oil Associates, IV 569
Union Oil Co., 9 266
Union Oil Co. of California, I 13; IV 385, 400, 403, 434, 522, 531, 540, 569, 575; 11 271
Union Pacific Corporation, I 473; II 381; III 229; V 529–32; 12 18–20, 278; 14 371–72
Union Pacific Tea Co., 7 202
Union Paper Bag Machine Co., IV 344
Union Petroleum Corp., IV 394
L'Union pour le Developpement Régional, II 265
Union Power Company, 12 541
Union Rückversicherungs-Gesellschaft, III 377
Union Savings, II 316
Union Savings and Loan Association of Phoenix, 19 412
Union Savings Bank, 9 173
Union Savings Bank and Trust Company, 13 221
Union Steam Ship Co., IV 279; 19 154
Union Steel Co., IV 22, 572; 7 550
Union Sugar, II 573
Union Sulphur Co., IV 81; 7 185
Union Supply Co., IV 573; 7 550
Union Tank Car Co., IV 137
Union Telephone Company, 14 258
Union Texas Petroleum Holdings, Inc., I 415; 7 379; 9 521–23; 22 31
Union Trust Co., II 284, 313, 315–16, 382; 9 228; 13 222
The Union Underwear Company, I 440–41; 8 200–01
Union Wine, I 289
Union-Capitalisation, III 392
Union-Transport, 6 404
Unionamerica, Inc., 16 497
Unionamerica Insurance Group, III 243
Unione Manifatture, S.p.A., 19 338

Uniroy of Hempstead, Inc. See Aris Industries, Inc.
Uniroyal Corp., I 30–31; II 472; V 242; 8 503; 11 159; 20 262
Uniroyal Holdings Ltd., 21 73
Unishops, Inc. See Aris Industries, Inc.
Unisource, I 413
Unistar Radio Networks, 23 510
Unisys Corporation, II 42; III 165–67; 6 281–83 (upd.); 8 92; 9 32, 59; 12 149, 162; 17 11, 262; 18 345, 386, 434, 542; 21 86
The Unit Companies, Inc., 6 394, 396
Unit Group plc, 8 477
United Acquisitions, 7 114
United Advertising Periodicals, 12 231
United Agri Products, II 494
United AgriSeeds, Inc., 21 387
United Air Express. See United Parcel Service of America Inc.
United Air Fleet, 23 408
United Aircraft and Transportation Co., I 48, 76, 78, 85–86, 96, 441, 489; 9 416, 418; 10 162, 260; 12 289; 21 140
United Airlines, I 23, 47, 71, 84, 90, 97, 113, 116, 118, 124, 128–30; II 142, 419, 680; III 225; 6 71, 75–77, 104, 121, 123, 128–30 (upd.), 131, 388–89; 9 271–72, 283, 416, 549; 10 162, 199, 301, 561; 11 299; 12 192, 381; 14 73; 21 141; 22 199, 220
United Alaska Drilling, Inc., 7 558
United Alkalai Co., I 351
United American Insurance Company of Dallas, 9 508
United American Lines, 6 398
United Arab Airlines. See AirEgypt.
United Artists Corp., I 537; II 135, 146–48, 149, 157–58, 160, 167, 169; III 721; IV 676; 6 167; 9 74; 12 13, 73, 13 529; 14 87, 399; 21 362; 23 389. See also MGM/UA Communications Company.
United Bank of Arizona, II 358
United Biscuits (Holdings) PLC, II 466, 540, 592–94; III 503
United Brands Company, II 595–97; III 28; 7 84–85; 12 215; 21 110, 112
United Breweries Ltd. I 221, 223, 288. See also Carlsberg A/S.
United Cable Television Corporation, II 160; 9 74; 18 65
United California Bank, II 289
United Car, I 540; 14 511
United Carbon Co., IV 373
United Central Oil Corporation, 7 101
United Cigar Manufacturers Company, II 414. See also Culbro Corporation.
United City Property Trust, IV 705
United Co., I 70
United Communications Systems, Inc. V 346
United Computer Services, Inc., 11 111
United Corp., 10 44
United County Banks, II 235
United Dairies, II 586–87
United Dairy Farmers, III 190
United Dominion Corp., III 200
United Dominion Industries Limited, IV 288; 8 544–46; 16 499–502 (upd.)
United Drapery Stores, III 502; 7 208
United Drug Co., II 533
United Electric Light and Water Co., 13 182

United Engineering Steels, **III** 495
United Engineers & Constructors, **II** 86; **11** 413
United Express, **11** 299
United Factors Corp., **13** 534–35
United Features Syndicate, Inc., **IV** 607–08
United Federal Savings and Loan of Waycross, **10** 92
United Financial Corporation, **12** 353
United Financial Group, Inc., **8** 349
United 5 and 10 Cent Stores, **13** 444
United Foods, Inc., 21 508–11
United Fruit Co., **I** 529, 566; **II** 120, 595; **IV** 308; **7** 84–85; **21** 110–11
United Funds, Inc., **22** 540–41
United Gas and Electric Company of New Albany, **6** 555
United Gas and Improvement Co., **13** 182
United Gas Corp., **IV** 488–90
United Gas Improvement Co., **IV** 549; **V** 696; **6** 446, 523; **11** 388
United Gas Industries, **III** 502; **7** 208
United Gas Pipe Line Co., **IV** 489–90
United Geophysical Corp., **I** 142
United Graphics, **12** 25
United Grocers, **II** 625
United Guaranty Corp., **III** 197
United Health Maintenance, Inc., **6** 181–82
United HealthCare Corporation, 9 524–26
The United Illuminating Company, 21 512–14
United Image Entertainment, **18** 64, 66
United Independent Broadcasters, Inc., **II** 132
United Industrial Syndicate, **8** 545
United Information Systems, Inc., **V** 346
United Insurance Co., **I** 523
Oy United International, **IV** 349
United International Pictures, **II** 155
United Investors Life, **22** 540
United Iron & Metal Co., **14** 156
United Kent Fire, **III** 350
United Kingdom Atomic Energy Authority, **6** 451–52
United Knitting, Inc., **21** 192, 194
United Liberty Life Insurance Co., **III** 190–92
United Life & Accident Insurance Co., **III** 220–21; **14** 109
United Life Insurance Company, **12** 541
United Light & Railway Co., **V** 609
United Light and Power, **6** 511
United Machinery Co., **15** 127
United Match Factories, **12** 462
United Media, **22** 442
United Medical Service, Inc., **III** 245–46
United Merchandising Corp., **12** 477
United Merchants & Manufacturers, Inc., 13 534–37
United Meridian Corporation, **8** 350
United Metals Selling Co., **IV** 31
United Microelectronics Corporation, **22** 197
United Micronesian, **I** 97; **21** 142
United Molasses, **II** 582
United Mortgage Servicing, **16** 133
United Natural Gas Company, **6** 526
United Netherlands Navigation Company. *See* Vereenigde Nederlandsche Scheepvaartmaatschappij.
United Newspapers plc, IV 685–87
United of Omaha, **III** 365
United Office Products, **11** 64

United Oil Co., **IV** 399
United Optical, **10** 151
United Pacific Financial Services, **III** 344
United Pacific Insurance Co., **III** 343
United Pacific Life Insurance Co., **III** 343–44
United Pacific Reliance Life Insurance Co. of New York, **III** 343
United Packages, **IV** 249
United Paper Mills Ltd., II 302; **IV** 316, **347–50**
United Paramount Theatres, **II** 129
United Parcel Service of America Inc., V 533–35; 6 345–46, 385–86, 390; **11** 11; **12** 309, 334; **13** 19, 416; **14** 517; **17** **503–06 (upd.); 18** 82, 177, 315–17
United Pipeline Co., **IV** 394
United Power and Light Corporation, **6** 473; **12** 541
United Presidential Life Insurance Company, **12** 524, 526
United Press Assoc., **IV** 607, 627, 669; **7** 158
United Press International, **IV** 670; **7** 158–59; **16** 166; **19** 203; **22** 453
United Refining Co., **23** 406, 408
United Resources, Inc., **21** 514
United Retail Merchants Stores Inc., **9** 39
United Roasters, **III** 24; **14** 121
United Satellite Television, **10** 320
United Savings of Texas, **8** 349
United Servomation, **7** 471–72
United Shirt Shops, Inc. *See* Aris Industries, Inc.
United Skates of America, **8** 303
United Software Consultants Inc., **11** 65
United States Aluminum Co., **17** 213
United States Baking Co., **II** 542
United States Can Co., **15** 127, 129
United States Cellular Corporation, 9 494–96, **527–29**
United States Department of Defense, **6** 327
United States Distributing Corp., **IV** 180–82
United States Electric and Gas Company, **6** 447
The United States Electric Lighting Company, **11** 387
United States Export-Import Bank, **IV** 55
United States Express Co., **II** 381, 395–96; **10** 59–60; **12** 534
United States Fidelity and Guaranty Co., **III** 395
United States Filter Corporation, I 429; **IV** 374; **20 501–04**
United States Foil Co., **IV** 186; **19** 346
United States Glucose Co., **II** 496
United States Graphite Company, **V** 221–22
United States Gypsum Co., **III** 762–64
United States Health Care Systems, Inc. *See* U.S. Healthcare, Inc.
United States Independent Telephone Company, **6** 332
United States Leasing Corp., **II** 442
United States Mail Steamship Co., **23** 160
United States Medical Finance Corp., **18** 516, 518
United States Mortgage & Trust Company, **II** 251; **14** 102
United States National Bank of Oregon, **14** 527

The United States National Bank of Portland, **14** 527–28
United States National Bank of San Diego, **II** 355
United States Pipe and Foundry Co., **III** 766; **22** 544–45
United States Plywood Corp., **IV** 264, 282, 341; **9** 260; **13** 100; **20** 128
United States Postal Service, 10 60; **14** **517–20**
United States Realty-Sheraton Corp., **III** 98
United States Security Trust Co., **13** 466
United States Shoe Corporation, V **207–08; 17** 296, 390; **23** 328
United States Steel Corp., **I** 298, 491; **II** 129, 330; **III** 282, 326, 379; **IV** 35, 56, 110, 158, 572–74; **6** 514; **7** 48, 70–73, 401–02, 549–51; **10** 32; **11** 194; **12** 353–54; **17** 350, 356; **18** 378. *See also* USX Corporation.
United States Sugar Refining Co., **II** 496
United States Surgical Corporation, 10 **533–35; 13** 365; **21** 119–20
United States Tobacco Company, **9** 533
United States Trucking Corp., **IV** 180–81
United States Trust Co. of New York. *See* U.S. Trust Corp.
United States Underseas Cable Corp., **IV** 178
United States Zinc Co., **IV** 32
United Stationers Inc., 14 521–23
United Steel, **III** 494
United Supers, **II** 624
United Technologies Automotive Inc., 15 **513–15**
United Technologies Corporation, I 68, 84–86, 143, 411, 530, 559; **II** 64, 82; **III** 74; **9** 18, 418; **10 536–38 (upd.); 11** 308; **12** 289; **13** 191, 384–86; **22** 6
United Telecommunications, Inc., V **344–47; 8** 310; **9** 478–80; **10** 202; **12** 541
United Telephone Company, **7** 508; **14** 257
United Telephone Company of the Carolinas, **10** 202
United Telephone of Indiana, **14** 259
United Telephone System, Inc., **V** 346
United Telespectrum, **6** 314
United Television, Inc., **9** 119
United Television Programs, **II** 143
United Transportation Co., **6** 382
United Truck Lines, **14** 505
United Utilities, Inc., **V** 344; **10** 202
United Van Lines, **14** 37; **15** 50
United Verde Copper Co., **IV** 178
United Video Satellite Group, 18 535–37
United Vintners, **I** 243, 260–61
United Westburne Inc., **19** 313
United Westphalia Electricity Co., **IV** 127
United-American Car, **13** 305
Unitek Corp., **III** 18
Unitel Communications, **6** 311
Unitika Ltd., V 387–89
Unitog Co., 16 228; **19 457–60; 21** 115
Unitrin Inc., 16 503–05
Unity Financial Corp., **19** 411
Unity Joint-Stock Bank, **II** 334
UNIVAC, **III** 133, 152, 313; **6** 233, 240, 266
Univar Corporation, 8 99; **9 530–32; 12** 333
Univas, **13** 203 **23** 171
Universal Adding Machine, **III** 165
Universal American, **I** 452

Universal Atlas Cement Co., **IV** 573–74; **7** 550–51

Universal Belo Productions, **10** 5

Universal Cheerleaders Association. *See* Varsity Spirit Corp.

Universal Cigar Corp., **14** 19

Universal Containers, **IV** 249

Universal Controls, Inc., **10** 319

Universal Cooler Corp., **8** 515

Universal Corporation, V 417–18

Universal Data Systems, **II** 61; **22** 17

Universal Foods Corporation, 7 546–48; 21 498

Universal Forest Products Inc., 10 539–40

Universal Frozen Foods, **23** 321

Universal Furniture, **III** 571; **20** 362

Universal Genève, **13** 121

Universal Guaranty Life Insurance Company, **11** 482

Universal Health Services, Inc., 6 191–93

Universal Highways, **III** 735

Universal Industries, Inc., **10** 380; **13** 533

Universal Instruments Corp., **III** 468

Universal Juice Co., **21** 55

Universal Leaf Tobacco Company. *See* Universal Corporation.

Universal Manufacturing, **I** 440–41

Universal Match, **12** 464

Universal Matchbox Group, **12** 495

Universal Matthey Products Ltd., **IV** 119

Universal Music Group, **22** 194

Universal Paper Bag Co., **IV** 345

Universal Pictures, **II** 102, 135, 144, 154–55, 157; **10** 196; **14** 399. *See also* Universal Studios.

Universal Press Syndicate, **10** 4

Universal Resources Corporation, **6** 569

Universal Shoes, Inc., **22** 213

Universal Stamping Machine Co., **III** 156

Universal Studios, **II** 143–44; **12** 73; **21** 23–26

Universal Studios Florida, **14** 399

Universal Telephone, **9** 106

Universal Television, **II** 144

Universal Textured Yarns, **12** 501

Universal Transfers Co. Ltd., **IV** 119

University Computing Co., **II** 38; **11** 468; **17** 320

University Microfilms, **III** 172; **6** 289

Univision Holdings Inc., **IV** 621; **18** 213

Unix, **6** 225

Uno Restaurant Corporation, 16 447; **18** 465, **538–40**

Uno-Ven, **IV** 571

Unocal Corporation, IV 508, **569–71**

UNR Industries, Inc. *See* ROHN Industries, Inc.

UNUM Corp., III 236; **13 538–40**

Uny Co., Ltd., II 619; **V 209–10**, 154; **13** 545

UPI. *See* United Press International.

Upjohn Company, I 675, 684, 686, 700, **707–09**; **III** 18, 53; **6** 42; **8 547–49** **(upd.)**; **10** 79; **12** 186; **13** 503; **14** 423; **16** 440

UPM-Kymmene Corporation, 19 461–65

UPS. *See* United Parcel Service of America Inc.

Upton Machine Company, **12** 548

Uraga Dock Co., **II** 361; **III** 634

Uraga Heavy Industries, **III** 634

Urbaine, **III** 391–92

Urban Investment and Development Co., **IV** 703

Urban Outfitters, Inc., 14 524–26

Urban Systems Development Corp., **II** 121

Urenco, **6** 452

Urwick Orr, **II** 609

US Industrial Chemicals, Inc., **I** 377; **8** 440

US Order, Inc., **10** 560, 562

US Sprint Communications Company, **V** 295–96, 346–47; **6** 314; **8** 310; **9** 32; **10** 543; **11** 302; **12** 136, 541; **14** 252–53; **15** 196; **16** 318, 392. *See also* Sprint Communications Company, L.P.

US Telecom, **9** 478–79

US West, **21** 285

US West Communications. *See* Regional Bell Operating Companies.

US West Communications Services, Inc., **19** 255

USA Cafes, **14** 331

USAA, 10 541–43

USAir Group, Inc., I 55, **131–32; III** 215; **6** 121, **131–32 (upd.); 11** 300; **14** 70, 73; **18** 62; **21** 143

USCC. *See* United States Cellular Corporation.

USCP-WESCO Inc., **II** 682

USF&G Corporation, III 395–98; 11 494–95; **19** 190

USG Corporation, III 762–64

Usines de l'Espérance, **IV** 226

Usines Métallurgiques de Hainaut, **IV** 52

Usinor Sacilor, IV 226–28; 22 44

USLIFE, **III** 194

USM, **10** 44

USSC. *See* United States Surgical Corporation.

UST Inc., 9 533–35

USV Pharmaceutical Corporation, **11** 333

USX Corporation, I 466; **IV** 130, 228, **572–74; 7** 193–94, **549–52 (upd.)**

UTA, **I** 119, 121; **6** 373–74, 93

Utag, **11** 510

Utah Construction & Mining Co., **I** 570; **IV** 146; **14** 296

Utah Federal Savings Bank, **17** 530

Utah Gas and Coke Company, **6** 568

Utah Group Health Plan, **6** 184

Utah International, **II** 30; **12** 196

Utah Mines Ltd., **IV** 47; **22** 107

Utah Oil Refining Co., **IV** 370

Utah Power & Light Company, **9** 536; **12** 266

UTI Energy Corp., **12** 500

Utilicom, **6** 572

Utilicorp United Inc., 6 592–94

Utilities Power & Light Corporation, **I** 512; **6** 508

Utility Constructors Incorporated, **6** 527

Utility Engineering Corporation, **6** 580

Utility Fuels, **7** 377

Utility Supply Co. *See* United Stationers Inc.

AB Utra Wood Co., **IV** 274

Utrecht Allerlei Risico's, **III** 200

UV Industries, Inc., **7** 360; **9** 440

V & V Cos., **I** 412

V.A.W. of America Inc., **IV** 231

V&S Variety Stores, **V** 37

V.L. Churchill Group, **10** 493

Vabis, **I** 197

Vaculator Division. *See* Lancer Corporation.

Vacuum Metallurgical Company, **11** 234

Vacuum Oil Co., **IV** 463–64, 504, 549; **7** 351–52

Vadic Corp., **II** 83

Vadoise Vie, **III** 273

Vagnfabriks A.B., **I** 197

Vail Associates, Inc., 11 543–46

Val Royal LaSalle, **II** 652

Val-Pak Direct Marketing Systems, Inc., **22** 162

Valassis Communications, Inc., 8 550–51

Valcambi S.A., **II** 268; **21** 145

Valcom, **13** 176

ValCom Inc. *See* InaCom Corporation.

Valdi Foods Inc., **II** 663–64

Valdosta Drug Co., **III** 9–10

Vale Power Company, **12** 265

Valentine & Company, **8** 552–53

Valeo, III 593; **23 492–94**

Valero Energy Corporation, IV 394; **7 553–55; 19** 140

Valhi, Inc., 10 435–36; **19 466–68**

Valid Logic Systems Inc., **11** 46, 284

Valio-Finnish Co-operative Dairies' Assoc., **II** 575

Valke Oy, **IV** 348

Valley Bank of Nevada, **19** 378

Valley East Medical Center, **6** 185

Valley Falls Co., **III** 213

Valley Fashions Corp., **16** 535

Valley Federal of California, **11** 163

Valley Fig Growers, **7** 496–97

Valley Forge Life Insurance Co., **III** 230

Valley National Bank, **II** 420

Valley Transport Co., **II** 569

Valley-Todeco, Inc., **13** 305–06

Valleyfair, **22** 130

Vallourec, **IV** 227

Valmac Industries, **II** 585

Valmet Corporation, I 198; **III 647–49**, **IV** 276, 350, 471

Valmont Industries, Inc., 13 276; **19** 50, **469–72**

Valores Industriales S.A., 19 10, 12, 189, **473–75**

The Valspar Corporation, 8 552–54

Valtec Industries, **III** 684

Valtek International, Inc., **17** 147

Valtur, **6** 207

Value Foods Ltd., **11** 239

Value Giant Stores, **12** 478

Value House, **II** 673

Value Investors, **III** 330

Value Line, Inc., 16 506–08

Value Merchants Inc., 13 541–43

Value Rent-A-Car, **9** 350; **23** 354

Valueland, **8** 482

ValueVision International, Inc., 22 534–36

ValuJet, Inc. *See* AirTran Holdings, Inc.

Valvoline, Inc., **I** 291; **IV** 374

Valvtron, **11** 226

Van Ameringen-Haebler, Inc., **9** 290

Van Brunt Manufacturing Co., **III** 462; **21** 173

Van Camp Seafood Company, Inc., II 562–63; **7 556–57; 13** 426

Van de Kamp, **II** 556–57; **7** 430

Van den Bergh Foods, **II** 588; **9** 319

Van der Horst Corp. of America, **III** 471

Van Dorn Company, **13** 190

Van Dorn Electric Tool Co., **III** 435

Van Gend and Loos, **6** 404

Van Houton, **II** 521

Van Kirk Chocolate, **7** 429
Van Kok-Ede, **II** 642
Van Leer Holding, Inc., **9** 303, 305
Van Mar, Inc., **18** 88
Van Munching & Company, Inc., **I** 256; **13** 257, 259
Van Nostrand Reinhold, **8** 526
Van Ryn Gold Mines Estate, **IV** 90
Van Schaardenburg, **II** 528
Van Sickle, **IV** 485
Van Waters & Rogers, **8** 99
Van Wijcks Waalsteenfabrieken, **14** 249
Vanadium Alloys Steel Company (VASCO), **13** 295–96
Vanant Packaging Corporation, **8** 359
Vance International Airways, **8** 349
Vancouver Pacific Paper Co., **IV** 286
Vanderbilt Mortgage and Finance, **13** 154
Vanderlip-Swenson-Tilghman Syndicate, **IV** 81; **7** 185
Vanessa and Biffi, **11** 226
The Vanguard Group of Investment Companies, **9** 239; **14 530–32**
Vanity Fair Mills, Inc., **V** 390–91
Vanity Fair Paper Mills, **IV** 281; **9** 259
Vans, Inc., 16 509–11; 17 259–61
Vansickle Industries, **III** 603
Vanstar, **13** 176
Vantage Analysis Systems, Inc., **11** 490
Vantona Group Ltd., **V** 356
Vantress Pedigree, Inc., **II** 585
Vapor Corp., **III** 444
Varco-Pruden, Inc., **8** 544–46
Vare Corporation, **8** 366
Variable Annuity Life Insurance Co., **III** 193–94
Varian Associates Inc., 12 504–06
Varibus Corporation, **6** 495
Variform, Inc., **12** 397
VARIG, SA, 6 133–35
Varity Corporation, **III 650–52**; **7** 258, 260; **19** 294
Varlen Corporation, 16 512–14
Varney Air Lines, **I** 47, 128; **6** 128; **9** 416
Varney Speed Lines. See Continental Airlines, Inc.
Varo, **7** 235, 237
Varsity Spirit Corp., 15 516–18; 22 459
Varta AG, **III** 536; **9** 180–81; **23 495–99**
Vasco Metals Corp., **I** 523; **10** 520, 522
Vascoloy-Ramet, **13** 295
VASP, **6** 134
Vasset, S.A., **17** 362–63
Vaughan Printers Inc., **23** 100
Vaungarde, Inc., **22** 175
Vauxhall, **19** 391
VAW Leichtmetall GmbH, **IV** 231
VBB Viag-Bayernwerk-Beteiligungs-Gesellschaft mbH, **IV** 232
VDM Nickel-Technologie AG, **IV** 89
VEB Londa, **III** 69
Veba A.G., **I** 349–50, **542–43**; **III** 695; **IV** 194–95, 199, 455, 508; **8** 69, 494–495; **15 519–21 (upd.)**; **23** 69, 451, 453–54
VECO International, Inc., 7 558–59
Vector Automotive Corporation, **13** 61
Vector Casa de Bolsa, **21** 413
Vector Gas Ltd., **13** 458
Vector Video, Inc., **9** 74
Vedelectric, **13** 544
Vedior International, **13** 544–45
Veeder-Root Company, **7** 116–17
Vel-Tex Chemical, **16** 270

Velcarta S.p.A., **17** 281
Velcro Industries N.V., 19 476–78
Vellumoid Co., **I** 159
VeloBind, Inc., **10** 314
Velsicol, **I** 342, 440
Velva-Sheen Manufacturing Co., **23** 66
Vemar, **7** 558
Vencemos, **20** 124
Vencor, Inc., **IV** 402; **14** 243; **16 515–17**
Vendex International N.V., **10** 136–37; **13 544–46**
Vendors Supply of America, Inc., **7** 241–42
Venture Stores Inc., **V** 134; **12 507–09**
Venturi, Inc., **9** 72
Vepco. See Virginia Electric and Power Company.
Vera Cruz Electric Light, Power and Traction Co. Ltd., **IV** 658
Vera Imported Parts, **11** 84
Verafumos Ltd., **12** 109
Veragon Corporation. See Drypers Corporation.
Veratex Group, **13** 149–50
Verbatim Corporation, **III** 477; **7** 163; **14 533–35**
Verd-A-Fay, **13** 398
Vereenigde Nederlandsche Scheepvaartmaatschappij, **6** 404
Vereeniging Refractories, **IV** 22
Vereeniging Tiles, **III** 734
Verein für Chemische Industrie, **IV** 70
Vereinigte Aluminium Werke AG, **IV** 229–30, 232
Vereinigte Deutsche Metallwerke AG, **IV** 140
Vereinigte Elektrizitäts und Bergwerke A.G., **I** 542
Vereinigte Elektrizitätswerke Westfalen AG, **IV** 195; **V 744–47**
Vereinigte Energiewerke AG, **V** 709
Vereinigte Flugtechnische Werke GmbH., **I** 42, 55, 74–75
Vereinigte Glanzstoff-Fabriken, **13** 21
Vereinigte Industrie-Unternehmungen Aktiengesellschaft, **IV** 229–30
Vereinigte Leichtmetall-Werke GmbH, **IV** 231
Vereinigte Papierwarenfabriken GmbH, **IV** 323
Vereinigte Stahlwerke AG, **III** 565; **IV** 87, 104–05, 132, 221; **14** 327
Vereinigte Versicherungsgruppe, **III** 377
Vereinigten Westdeutsche Waggonfabriken AG, **III** 542–43
Vereinsbank Wismar, **II** 256
Vereinte Versicherungen, **III** 377
N.V. Verenigde Fabrieken Wessanen and Laan, **II** 527
Verenigde Spaarbank Groep. See VSB Groep.
Verenigte Schweizerbahnen, **6** 424
VeriFone, Inc., **15** 321; **18 541–44**
Verilyte Gold, Inc., **19** 452
Verlagsgruppe Georg von Holtzbrinck GmbH, **15** 158, 160
Vermeer Manufacturing Company, **17 507–10**
Verneuil Holding Co, **21** 387
Vernitron Corporation, **18** 293
Vernon and Nelson Telephone Company. See British Columbia Telephone Company.

Vernon Graphics, **III** 499
Vernon Paving, **III** 674
Vernon Savings & Loan, **9** 199
Vernons, **IV** 651
Vero, **III** 434
La Verrerie Souchon-Neuvesel, **II** 474
Verreries Champenoises, **II** 475
Versace. See Gianni Versace SpA.
Versatec Inc., **13** 128
Versatile Farm and Equipment Co., **22** 380
Versax, S.A. de C.V., **19** 12
Versicherungs-Verein, **III** 402, 410–11
Verson Allsteel Press Co., **21** 20, 22
Vert Baudet, **19** 309
Vertical Technology Industries, **14** 571
Verve Records, **23** 389
Vestek Systems, Inc., **13** 417
Vestro, **19** 309
Vesuvius Crucible Co., **III** 681
Vesuvius USA Corporation, **8** 179
Veterinary Cos. of America, **III** 25
VEW, **IV** 234
Vexlar, **18** 313
VF Corporation, **V 390–92**; **12** 205; **13** 512; **17** 223, 225, **511–14 (upd.)**
VFW-Fokker B.V., **I** 41, 55, 74–75
VHA Long Term Care, **23** 431
VH1 Inc., **23** 503
VI-Jon Laboratories, Inc., **12** 388
VIA/Rhin et Moselle, **III** 185
Viacao Aerea Rio Grandense of South America. See VARIG, SA.
Viacom Enterprises, **6** 33; **7** 336
Viacom Inc., 23 274–76, **500–03 (upd.)**
Viacom International Inc., **7** 222–24, 530, **560–62**; **9** 429; **10** 175; **19** 403
VIAG, **IV** 229–32, 323
VIASA, **I** 107; **6** 97
Vichy, **III** 46
Vickers Inc., **III** 640, 642; **13** 8; **23** 83
Vickers PLC, **I** 194–95; **II** 3; **III** 555, 652, 725; **16** 9; **21** 435
Vickers-Armstrong Ltd., **I** 50, 57, 82
Vicoreen Instrument Co., **I** 202
VICORP Restaurants, Inc., 12 510–12
Vicra Sterile Products, **I** 628
Vicsodrive Japan, **III** 495
Victor Company, **10** 483
Victor Company of Japan, Ltd., **I** 411; **II** 55–56, 91, 102, **118–19**; **III** 605; **IV** 599; **12** 454
Victor Comptometer, **I** 676; **III** 154
Victor Equipment Co., **19** 440
Victor Manufacturing and Gasket Co., **I** 152
Victor Musical Industries Inc., **II** 119; **10** 285
Victor Talking Machine Co., **II** 88, 118
Victor Value, **II** 678
Victoria, **III** 308
Victoria & Legal & General, **III** 359
Victoria Coach Station, **6** 406
Victoria Creations Inc., **13** 536
VICTORIA Holding AG, III 399–401
Victoria Paper Co., **IV** 286
Victoria Sugar Co., **III** 686
Victoria Wine Co., **I** 216
Victoria's Secret, **V** 115–16; **11** 498; **12** 557, 559; **16** 219; **18** 215
Victorinox AG, 21 515–17
Victory Fire Insurance Co., **III** 343
Victory Insurance, **III** 273
Victory Oil Co., **IV** 550
Victory Refrigeration Company, **22** 355

Victory Savings and Loan, **10** 339
Vidal Sassoon, **17** 110
Video Concepts, **9** 186
Video Independent Theatres, Inc., **14** 86
Video Library, Inc., **9** 74
Video News International, **19** 285
Video Superstores Master Limited
  Partnership, **9** 74
Videoconcepts, **II** 107
VideoFusion, Inc., **16** 419
Videotex Network Japan, **IV** 680
La Vie Claire, **13** 103
Vielle Montaign, **22** 285
Vienna Sausage Manufacturing Co., 14 536–37
View-Master/Ideal Group, **12** 496
Viewdata Corp., **IV** 630; **15** 264
Viewlogic, **11** 490
ViewStar Corp., **20** 103
Viewtel, **14** 36
Vigilance-Vie, **III** 393
Vigilant Insurance Co., **III** 220; **14** 108
Vigoro, **22** 340
Vigortone, **II** 582
Viiala Oy, **IV** 302
Viking, **II** 10; **IV** 659
Viking Brush, **III** 614
Viking Building Products, **22** 15
Viking Computer Services, Inc., **14** 147
Viking Direct Limited, **10** 545
Viking Foods, Inc., **8** 482; **14** 411
Viking Office Products, Inc., 10 544–46
Viking Penguin, **IV** 611
Viking Press, **12** 25
Viking Pump Company, **21** 499–500
Viktor Achter, **9** 92
Village Inn. *See* VICORP Restaurants, Inc.
Village Super Market, Inc. 7 563–64
Villager, Inc., **11** 216
Vine Products Ltd., **I** 215
Viner Bros., **16** 546
Vingaarden A/S, **9** 100
Vingresor A.B., **I** 120
Vining Industries, **12** 128
Viniprix SA, **10** 205; **19** 309
Vinland Web-Print, **8** 360
Vinyl Maid, Inc., **IV** 401
Vipont Pharmaceutical, **III** 25; **14** 122
VIPS, **11** 113
Viratec Thin Films, Inc., **22** 347
Virco Manufacturing Corporation, 17 515–17
Virgin Atlantic Airlines. *See* Virgin Group PLC.
Virgin Group PLC, 12 513–15; 14 73; **18** 80; **22** 194
The Virgin Islands Telephone Co., **19** 256
Virgin Retail, **9** 75, 361
Virginia Electric and Power Company, **V** 596–98
Virginia Fibre Corporation, **15** 188
Virginia Folding Box Company, **IV** 352; **19** 497
Virginia Laminating, **10** 313
Virginia National Bankshares, **10** 426
Virginia Railway and Power Company (VR&P), **V** 596
Virginia Trading Corp., **II** 422
Visa. *See* Valores Industriales S.A.
Visa International, II 200; **9** 333–35, **536–38; 18** 543; **20** 59
Visco Products Co., **I** 373; **12** 346
Viscodrive GmbH, **III** 495
Viscount Industries Limited, **6** 310

Vishay Intertechnology, Inc., 11 516; **21 518–21**
VisiCorp, **6** 254
Vision Centers, **I** 688; **12** 188
Vision Technology Group Ltd., **19** 124
Visionworks, **9** 186
Viskase Corporation, **17** 157, 159
Visking Co., **I** 400
Visnews Ltd., **IV** 668, 670
VisQueen, **I** 334
Vista Bakery Inc., **14** 306
Vista Chemical Company, I 402–03; V 709
Vista Concepts, Inc., **11** 19
Vista Resources, Inc., **17** 195
Vistana, Inc., 22 537–39
Visual Information Technologies, **11** 57
Visual Technology, **6** 201
Vita Lebensversicherungs-Gesellschaft, **III** 412
Vita Liquid Polymers, **9** 92
Vita-Achter, **9** 92
Vitafoam Incorporated, **9** 93
Vital Health Corporation, **13** 150
Vital Processing Services LLC, **18** 516, 518
Vitalink Communications Corp., **11** 520
Vitalink Pharmacy Services, Inc., 15 522–24
Vitex Foods, **10** 382
Vitro Corp., 8 178; **10 547–48; 17** 492
Vitro S.A., **19** 189
VIVA, **23** 390
Viva Home Co., **III** 757
Vivesvata Iron and Steel Ltd., **IV** 207
Viviane Woodard Cosmetic Corp., **II** 531
Vivra, Inc., 15 119; **18 545–47**
V K Mason Construction Ltd., **II** 222
Vlasic Foods, **II** 480–81; **7** 67–68
VLN Corp., **I** 201
VLSI Technology, Inc., 11 246; **16 518–20**
VMG Products. *See* Drypers Corporation.
VMX Inc., **14** 355
VND, **III** 593
Vnesheconobank, **II** 242
VNS. *See* Vereenigde Nederlandsche Scheepvaartmaatschappij.
VNU/Claritas, **6** 14
Vobis Microcomputer, **20** 103; **23** 311
VocalTec, Inc., **18** 143
Vodac, **11** 548
Vodafone Group plc, II 84; **11 547–48**
Vodapage, **11** 548
Vodata, **11** 548
Vodavi Technology Corporation, **13** 213
Voest-Alpine Stahl AG, IV 233–35
Vogel Peterson Furniture Company, **7** 4–5
Vogoro Corp., **13** 503
Voice Data Systems, **15** 125
Voice Powered Technology International, Inc., **23** 212
Voice Response, Inc., **11** 253
Voith, **II** 22
Vokes, **I** 429
Volkert Stampings, **III** 628
Volkswagen A.G., I 30, 32, 186, 192, **206–08**, 460; **II** 279; **IV** 231; **7** 8; **10** 14; **11** 104, **549–51 (upd.); 13** 413; **14** 169; **16** 322; **19** 484
Volta Aluminium Co., Ltd., **IV** 122
Volume Distributors. *See* Payless ShoeSource, Inc.

Volume Service Company. *See* Restaurants Unlimited, Inc.
Volume Shoe Corporation. *See* Payless ShoeSource, Inc.
Voluntary Hospitals of America, **6** 45
Volunteer Leather Company, **17** 202, 205
Volunteer State Life Insurance Co., **III** 221
AB Volvo, I 186, 192, 198, **209–11; II** 5, 366; **III** 543, 591, 623, 648; **IV** 336; **7 565–68 (upd.); 9** 283–84, 350, 381; **10** 274; **12** 68, 342; **13** 30, 356; **14** 321; **15** 226; **16** 322; **18** 394; **23** 354
Volvo-Penta, **21** 503
von Roll, **6** 599
Von Ruden Manufacturing Co., **17** 532
von Weise Gear Co., **III** 509
Von's Grocery Co., **II** 419; **8** 474; **17** 559
The Vons Companies, Incorporated, II 655; **7 569–71; 12** 209
VOP Acquisition Corporation, **10** 544
Vornado Realty Trust, 20 508–10
Votainer International, **13** 20
Vought Aircraft Co., **11** 364
Voxson, **I** 531; **22** 193
Voyage Conseil, **II** 265
Voyager Energy, **IV** 84
Voyager Ltd., **12** 514
Voyager Petroleum Ltd., **IV** 83; **7** 188
Voyageur Travel Insurance Ltd., **21** 447
VR&P. *See* Virginia Railway and Power Company.
VRG International. *See* Roberts Pharmaceutical Corporation.
Vroom & Dreesmann, **13** 544–46
Vrumona B.V., **I** 257
VS Services, **13** 49
VSA. *See* Vendors Supply of America, Inc.
VSB Groep, **III** 199, 201
VSD Communications, Inc., **22** 443
VSM. *See* Village Super Market, Inc.
VST. *See* Vision Technology Group Ltd.
Vtel Corporation, **10** 456
VTR Incorporated, **16** 46
Vulcan Materials Company, 7 572–75; 12 39
Vulcraft, **7** 400–02
VVM, **III** 200
VW&R. *See* Van Waters & Rogers.
VWR Textiles & Supplies, Inc., **11** 256
VWR United Company, **9** 531

W H Smith Group PLC, V 211–13
W. & G. Turnbull & Co., **IV** 278; **19** 153
W. & M. Duncan, **II** 569
W.A. Bechtel Co., **I** 558
W.A. Harriman & Co., **III** 471
W.A. Krueger Co., **19** 333–35
W&F Fish Products, **13** 103
W. Atlee Burpee Co., **II** 532; **11** 198
W.B. Constructions, **III** 672
W.B. Doner & Company, **10** 420; **12** 208
W.B. Saunders Co., **IV** 623–24
W.C. Bradley Company, **18** 516
W.C.G. Sports Industries Ltd. *See* Canstar Sports Inc.
W.C. Heraeus GmbH, **IV** 100
W.C. Norris, **III** 467
W.C. Platt Co., **IV** 636
W.C. Ritchie & Co., **IV** 333
W.C. Smith & Company Limited, **14** 339
W. Duke & Sons, **V** 395, 600
W.E. Dillon Company, Ltd., **21** 499
W.F. Linton Company, **9** 373
W. Gunson & Co., **IV** 278; **19** 153

W. Gutzeit & Co., IV 274–77
W.H. Brady Co., 17 518–21
W.H. Gunlocke Chair Co. *See* Gunlocke
   Company.
W.H. McElwain Co., III 528
W.H. Morton & Co., II 398; 10 62
W.H. Smith & Son (Alacra) Ltd., 15 473
W.J. Noble and Sons, IV 294; 19 225
W.L. Gore & Associates, Inc., 14 538–40
W.M. Bassett Furniture Co. *See* Bassett
   Furniture Industries, Inc.
W.M. Ritter Lumber Co., IV 281; 9 259
W.O. Daley & Company, 10 387
W.R. Bean & Son, 19 335
W.R. Berkley Corp., III 248; 15 525–27
W.R. Breen Company, 11 486
W.R. Case & Sons Cutlery Company, 18
   567
W.R. Grace & Company, I 547–50; III
   525, 695; IV 454; 11 216; 12 337; 13
   149, 502, 544; 14 29; 16 45–47; 17 308,
   365–66; 21 213, 507, 526; 22 188, 501
W. Rosenlew, IV 350
W.S. Barstow & Company, 6 575
W.T. Grant Co., 16 487
W.T. Rawleigh, 17 105
W.T. Young Foods, III 52; 8 433
W. Ullberg & Co., I 553
W.V. Bowater & Sons, Ltd., IV 257–58
W.W. Cargill and Brother, II 616; 13 136
W.W. Grainger, Inc., V 214–15; 13 297
W.W. Kimball Company, 12 296; 18 44
Waban Inc., V 198; 13 547–49; 19 449
Wabash National Corp., 13 550–52
Wabash Valley Power Association, 6 556
Wabush Iron Co., IV 73
Wachbrit Insurance Agency, 21 96
Wachovia Bank of Georgia, N.A., 16
   521–23
Wachovia Bank of South Carolina, N.A.,
   16 524–26
Wachovia Corporation, II 336; 10 425;
   12 16, 516–20; 16 521, 524, 526; 23
   455
The Wackenhut Corporation, 13 124–25;
   14 541–43
Wacker Oil Inc., 11 441
Waddell & Reed, Inc., 22 540–43
Wadsworth Inc., 8 526
WaferTech, 18 20
Waffle House Inc., 14 544–45
The Wagner & Brown Investment Group, 9
   248
Wagner Castings Company, 16 474–75
Wagner Litho Machinery Co., 13 369–70
Wagner Spray Tech, 18 555
Wagonlit Travel, 22 128
Wah Chang Corp., I 523–24; 10 520–21
Wahlstrom & Co., 23 480
Waialua Agricultural Co., II 491
Waitaki International Biosciences Co., 17
   288
Waite Amulet Mines Ltd., IV 164
Waitrose, V 94–95
Wakefern Cooperative, II 672; 18 6
Wakefern Food Corp., 7 563–64
Wakodo Co., I 674
Wal-Mart Stores, Inc., II 108; V 216–17;
   6 287; **7** 61, 331; **8** 33, 295, **555–57**
   (upd.); 9 187, 361; **10** 236, 284,
   515–16, 524; **11** 292; **12** 48, 53–55,
   63–64, 97, 208–09, 221, 277, 333, 477,
   507–08; **13** 42, 215–17, 260–61, 274,
   332–33, 444, 446; **14** 235; **15** 139, 275;

16 61–62, 65, 390; **17** 297, 321,
   460–61; **18** 108, 137, 186, 283, 286; **19**
   511; **20** 263; **21** 457–58; **22** 224, 257,
   328; **23** 214
Walbro Corporation, 13 553–55
Walchenseewerk AG, 23 44
Waldbaum, Inc., II 638; **15** 260; **16** 247,
   249; **19 479–81**
Walden Book Company Inc., V 112; **10**
   136–37; **16** 160; **17 522–24**
Waldes Truarc Inc., III 624
Oy Waldhof AB, IV 324
Wales & Company, 14 257
Walgreen Co., V 218–20; **9** 346; **18** 199;
   20 511–13 (upd.); 21 186
Walker & Lee, 10 340
Walker Cain, I 215
Walker Interactive Systems, 11 78
Walker Manufacturing Company, I 527;
   19 482–84
Walker McDonald Manufacturing Co., III
   569; **20** 361
Walkers Parker and Co., III 679–80
Walki GmbH, IV 349
AB Walkiakoski, IV 347
Walkins Manufacturing Corp., III 571; **20**
   362
Wall Paper Manufacturers, IV 666; **17** 397
Wall Street Leasing, III 137
Wallace and Tiernan, I 383; **11** 361
Wallace International Silversmiths, I 473;
   14 482–83
Wallace Murray Corp., II 420
Wallbergs Fabriks A.B., **8** 14
Wallens Dairy Co., II 586
Wallin & Nordstrom, V 156
Wallingford Bank and Trust Co., II 213
Wallis, V 177
Wallis Arnold Enterprises, Inc., 21 483
Wallis Tin Stamping Co., I 605
Wallis Tractor Company, 21 502
Walrus, Inc., 18 446
Walston & Co., II 450; III 137
Walt Disney Company, II 102, 122, 129,
   156, **172–74; III** 142, 504, 586; **IV** 585,
   675, 703; **6** 15, **174–77 (upd.),** 368; **7**
   305; **8** 160; **10** 420; **12** 168, 208, 229,
   323, 495–96; **13** 551; **14** 260; **15** 197;
   16 143, 336; **17** 243, 317, 442–43; **21**
   23–26, 360–61; **23** 257–58, 303, 335,
   476, 514
Walt Disney World, **6** 82, 175–76; **18** 290
Walter Baker's Chocolate, II 531
Walter E. Heller, **17** 324
Walter Herzog GmbH, **16** 514
Walter Industries, Inc., III 765–67; 22
   544–47 (upd.)
Walter Kidde & Co., I 475, 524
Walter Pierce Oil Co., IV 657
Walton Manufacturing, 11 486
Walton Monroe Mills, Inc., 8 558–60
Wander Ltd., I 672
Wanderer Werke, III 154
Wang Laboratories, Inc., II 208; **III**
   168–70; 6 284–87 **(upd.); 8** 139; **9** 171;
   10 34; **11** 68, 274; **12** 183; **18** 138; **19**
   40; **20** 237
Wanishi, IV 157; **17** 349
Waples-Platter Co., II 625
War Damage Corp., III 353, 356; **22** 493
War Emergency Tankers Inc., IV 552
War Production Board, V 676

Warburg, Pincus Capital Corp., **6** 13; **9**
   524; **14** 42
Warburtons Bakery Cafe, Inc., **18** 37
Ward Manufacturing Inc., IV 101
Ward's Communications, **22** 441
Wardley Ltd., II 298
Wards. *See* Circuit City Stores, Inc.
Waring and LaRosa, **12** 167
The Warnaco Group Inc., 9 156; **12**
   521–23; 22 123. *See also* Authentic
   Fitness Corp.
Warner & Swasey Co., III 168; **6** 284; **8**
   545
Warner Communications Inc., II 88,
   129, 135, 146–47, 154–55, 169–70,
   175–77, 208, 452; **III** 443, 505; **IV** 623,
   673, 675–76; **7** 526, 528–30 **8** 527; **9**
   44–45, 119, 469; **10** 196; **11** 557; **12** 73,
   495–96; **17** 65, 149, 442–43; **21** 23–25,
   360; **22** 519, 522; **23** 23–24, 390, 501.
   See also Time Warner Inc.
Warner Cosmetics, III 48; **8** 129
Warner Gear Co., III 438–39; **14** 63–64
Warner Records, II 177
Warner Sugar Refining Co., II 496
Warner-Lambert Co., I 643, 674, 679,
   696, **710–12; 7** 596; **8** 62–63; **10**
   549–52 (upd.); 12 480, 482; **13** 366; **16**
   439; **20** 23
Warren Bank, **13** 464
Warren, Gorham & Lamont, **8** 526
Warren Oilfield Services, **9** 363
Warren Petroleum Company, **18** 365, 367
Warri Refining and Petrochemicals Co., **IV**
   473
Warringah Brick, III 673
Warrington Products Ltd. *See* Canstar
   Sports Inc.
Warrior River Coal Company, **7** 281
Wartsila Marine Industries Inc., III 649
Warwick Chemicals, **13** 461
Warwick Electronics, III 654
Warwick International Ltd., **13** 462
Wasa, I 672–73
Wasag-Chemie AG, III 694
Wasatch Gas Co., **6** 568
Wascana Energy Inc., 13 556–58
Washburn Crosby Co., II 501, 555; **10** 322
Washburn Graphics Inc., **23** 100
Washington Duke Sons & Co., **12** 108
Washington Federal, Inc., 17 525–27
Washington Gas Light Company, 19
   485–88
Washington Mills Company, **13** 532
Washington Mutual, Inc., 17 528–31
Washington National Corporation, 11
   482; **12 524–26**
Washington Natural Gas Company, 9
   539–41
The Washington Post Company, III 214;
   IV 688–90; 6 323; **11** 331; **18** 60, 61,
   63; **20 515–18 (upd.); 23** 157–58
Washington Railway and Electric
   Company, **6** 552–53
Washington Scientific Industries, Inc., 17
   532–34
Washington Specialty Metals Corp., **14**
   323, 325
Washington Steel Corp., **14** 323, 325
Washington Water Power Company, 6
   566, 595–98
Washtenaw Gas Company. *See* MCN
   Corporation.
Wassall Plc, 18 548–50

Wasserstein Perella Partners, **II** 629; **III** 512, 530–31; **V** 223; **17** 366

Waste Control Specialists LLC, **19** 466, 468

Waste Management, Inc., V 749–51, **752–54; 6** 46, 600; **9** 73, 108–09; **11** 435–36; **18** 10; **20** 90; **23** 430

Water Engineering, **11** 360

Water Pik, **I** 524–25

Water Products Group, **6** 487–88

Water Street Corporate Recovery Fund, **10** 423

The Waterbury Companies, **16** 482

Waterford Wedgwood Holdings PLC, IV 296; **12** 527–29

Waterhouse Investor Services, Inc., 18 551–53

Waterloo Gasoline Engine Co., **III** 462; **21** 173

Waterlow and Sons, **10** 269

The Waterman Pen Company. *See* BIC Corporation.

WaterPro Supplies Corporation, **6** 486, 488

Waterstreet Inc., **17** 293

Watertown Insurance Co., **III** 370

Watkins Manufacturing Co., **I** 159

Watkins-Johnson Company, 15 528–30

Watkins-Strathmore Co., **13** 560

Watmough and Son Ltd., **II** 594

Watney Mann and Truman Brewers, **I** 228, 247, **9** 99

Watson Pharmaceuticals Inc., 16 527–29

Watson-Triangle, **16** 388, 390

Watson-Wilson Transportation System, **V** 540; **14** 567

Watt & Shand, **16** 61

Watt AG, **6** 491

Watt Electronic Products, Limited, **10** 319

The Watt Stopper, **21** 348, 350

Wattie Pict Ltd., **I** 437

Wattie's Ltd., 7 576–78; **11** 173

Watts Industries, Inc., 19 489–91

Waukesha Engine Servicenter, **6** 441

Waukesha Foundry Company, **11** 187

Waukesha Motor Co., **III** 472

Wausau Paper Mills, **15** 305

Wausau Sulphate Fibre Co. *See* Mosinee Paper Corporation.

Waverly, Inc., 10 135; **16** 530–32; **19** 358

Waverly Oil Works, **I** 405

Waverly Pharmaceutical Limited, **11** 208

Wawa Inc., 17 535–37

Waxman Industries, Inc., III 570; **9** 542–44; **20** 362

Wayco Foods, **14** 411

Waycross-Douglas Coca-Cola Bottling, **10** 222

Wayne Home Equipment. *See* Scott Fetzer Company.

Wayne Oakland Bank, **8** 188

WB. *See* Warner Communications Inc.

WCI Holdings Corporation, **V** 223; **13** 170

WCK, Inc., **14** 236

WCRS Group plc, **6** 15

WD-40 Company, 18 554–57

Wear-Ever, **17** 213

WearGuard, **13** 48

Wearne Brothers, **6** 117

The Weather Department, Ltd., **10** 89

Weather Guard, **IV** 305

Weathers-Lowin, Leeam, **11** 408

Weaver, **III** 468

Webb & Knapp, **10** 43

Webber Gage Co., **13** 302

Weber, **16** 488

Webers, **I** 409

Weblock, **I** 109

Webster Publishing Co., **IV** 636

Webtron Corp., **10** 313

Wedgwood. *See* Waterford Wedgewood Holdings PLC.

Week's Dairy, **II** 528

Wegmans Food Markets, Inc., 9 545–46

Weidemann Brewing Co., **I** 254

Weider Sporting Goods, **16** 80

Weifang Power Machine Fittings Ltd., **17** 106

Weight Watchers International Inc., II 508; **10** 383; **11** 172; **12** 530–32; **13** 383

Weirton Steel Corporation, I 297; **IV** 236–38; **7** 447, 598; **8** 346, 450; **10** 31–32; **12** 352, 354

Weis Markets, Inc., 15 531–33

Welbecson, **III** 501

Welbilt Corp., 19 492–94

Welcome Wagon International Inc., **III** 28; **16** 146

Weldless Steel Company, **8** 530

Welex Jet Services, **III** 498–99

Wella Group, III 68–70

Wellby Super Drug Stores, **12** 220

Wellcome Foundation Ltd., I 638, 713–15; **8** 210, 452; **9** 265; **10** 551

Weller Electric Corp., **II** 16

Wellington, **II** 457

Wellington Management Company, **14** 530–31; **23** 226

Wellington Sears Co., **15** 247–48

Wellman, Inc., 8 561–62; **21** 193

Wellmark, Inc., **10** 89

Wellness Co., Ltd., **IV** 716

Wells Aircraft, **12** 112

Wells Fargo & Company, II 380–84, 319, 395; **III** 440; **10** 59–60; **12** 165, 533–37 (upd.); **17** 325; **18** 60, 543; **19** 411; **22** 542

Wells Lamont, **IV** 136

Wells Rich Greene BDDP, 6 48, 50–52

Wellspring Associates L.L.C., **16** 338

Welsbach Mantle, **6** 446

Weltkunst Verlag GmbH, **IV** 590

Wendy's International, Inc., II 614–15, 647; **7** 433; **8** 563–65; **9** 178; **12** 553; **13** 494; **14** 453; **16** 95, 97; **17** 71, 124; **19** 215; **23** 384, 504–07 (upd.)

Wenger S.A., **III** 419; **21** 515

Wenlock Brewery Co., **I** 223

Wenstroms & Granstoms Electriska Kraftbolag, **II** 1

Werkhof GmbH, **13** 491

Werknet, **16** 420

Werner International, **III** 344; **14** 225

Wernicke Co., **I** 201

Wertheim Schroder & Company, **17** 443

Weru Aktiengesellschaft, 18 558–61

Wesco Financial Corp., **III** 213, 215; **18** 62

Wesco Food Co., **II** 644

Wescot Decisison Systems, **6** 25

Weserflug, **I** 74

Wesray and Management, **17** 213

Wesray Capital Corporation, **6** 357; **13** 41; **17** 443

Wesray Corporation, **22** 55

Wesray Holdings Corp., **13** 255

Wesray Transportation, Inc., **14** 38

Wessanen. *See* Koninklijke Wessanen N.V.

Wessanen and Laan, **II** 527

Wessanen Cacao, **II** 528

Wessanen USA, **II** 528

Wessanen's Koninklijke Fabrieken N.V., **II** 527

Wesson/Peter Pan Foods Co., **17** 241

West Australia Land Holdings, Limited, **10** 169

West Bend Co., III 610–11; **14** 546–48; **16** 384

West Coast Grocery Co., **II** 670; **18** 506

West Coast Machinery, **13** 385

West Coast of America Telegraph, **I** 428

West Coast Power Company, **12** 265

West Coast Savings and Loan, **10** 339

West Coast Telecom, **III** 38

West End Family Pharmacy, Inc., **15** 523

West Fraser Timber Co. Ltd., IV 276; **17** 538–40

West Georgia Coca-Cola Bottlers, Inc., **13** 163

West Ham Gutta Percha Co., **I** 428

West Harrison Gas & Electric Company, **6** 466

West India Oil Co., **IV** 416, 428

West Japan Heavy Industries, **III** 578–79; **7** 348

West Jersey Electric Company, **6** 449

West Marine, Inc., 17 541–43

West Missouri Power Company. *See* UtiliCorp United Inc.

West Newton Savings Bank, **13** 468

West Newton Telephone Company, **14** 258

West of England, **III** 690

West of England Sack Holdings, **III** 501; **7** 207

West One Bancorp, 11 552–55

West Penn Electric. *See* Allegheny Power System, Inc.

West Point-Pepperell, Inc., 8 566–69; **9** 466; **15** 247. *See also* WestPoint Stevens Inc.

West Publishing Co., IV 312; **7** 579–81; **10** 407; **19** 268

West Rand Consolidated Mines, **IV** 90

West Rand Investment Trust, **IV** 21; **16** 27

West Richfield Telephone Company, **6** 299

West Side Bank, **11** 312

West Side Printing Co., **13** 559

West Surrey Central Dairy Co. Ltd., **II** 586

West Texas Utilities Company, **6** 580

West Union Corporation, **22** 517

West Virginia Bearings, Inc., **13** 78

West Virginia Pulp and Paper Co. *See* Westvaco Corporation.

West Witwatersrand Areas Ltd., **IV** 94–96

West Yorkshire Bank, **II** 307

West's Holderness Corn Mill, **II** 564

WestAir Holding Inc., **11** 300

Westamerica Bancorporation, 17 544–47

Westburne Group of Companies, **9** 364

Westchester County Savings & Loan, **9** 173

Westclox Seth Thomas, **16** 483

Westcott Communications Inc., **22** 442

Westdeutsche Landesbank Girozentrale, II 257–58, 385–87

Westec Corporation. *See* Tech-Sym Corporation.

Western Aerospace Ltd., **14** 564

Western Air Express, **I** 125; **III** 225; **9** 17

Western Air Lines, **I** 98, 100, 106; **6** 82; **21** 142

Western Alaska Fisheries, **II** 578

Western American Bank, **II** 383

Western Assurance Co., **III** 350

Western Atlas Inc., III 473; **12 538–40;**
17 419
Western Australian Specialty Alloys
Proprietary Ltd., **14** 564
Western Auto, **19** 223
Western Auto Supply Co., **8** 56; **11** 392
Western Automatic Machine Screw Co., **12**
344
Western Bancorporation, **I** 536; **II** 288–89;
13 529
Western Bank, **17** 530
Western Beef, Inc., 22 548–50
Western Bingo, **16** 471
Western California Canners Inc., **I** 513
Western Canada Airways, **II** 376
Western Coalfields Ltd., **IV** 48–49
Western Company of North America, 15
534–36
Western Condensing Co., **II** 488
Western Copper Mills Ltd., **IV** 164
Western Corrugated Box Co., **IV** 358
Western Crude, **11** 27
Western Dairy Products, **I** 248
Western Data Products, Inc., **19** 110
Western Digital, **10** 403, 463; **11** 56, 463
Western Edison, **6** 601
Western Electric Co., **II** 57, 66, 88, 101,
112; **III** 162–63, 440; **IV** 181, 660; **V**
259–64; **VII** 288; **11** 500–01; **12** 136;
13 57
Western Empire Construction. *See* CRSS
Inc.
Western Equities, Inc. *See* Tech-Sym
Corporation.
Western Federal Savings & Loan, **9** 199
Western Fire Equipment Co., **9** 420
Western Geophysical, **I** 485; **11** 265; **12**
538–39
Western Glucose Co., **14** 17
Western Grocers, Inc., **II** 631, 670
Western Illinois Power Cooperative, **6** 506
Western Inland Lock Navigation Company,
9 228
Western International Hotels, **I** 129; **6** 129
Western International Media, **22** 294
Western Kraft Corp., **IV** 358; **8** 476
Western Life Insurance Co., **III** 356; **22**
494
Western Light & Telephone Company. *See*
Western Power & Gas Company.
Western Light and Power. *See* Public
Service Company of Colorado.
Western Massachusetts Co., **13** 183
Western Merchandise, Inc., **8** 556
Western Mining Corp., **IV** 61, 95
Western Mortgage Corporation, **16** 497
Western National Life Company, **10** 246;
14 473
Western Natural Gas Company, **7** 362
Western New York State Lines, Inc., **6** 370
Western Newell Manufacturing Company.
See Newell Co.
Western Nuclear, Inc., **IV** 179
Western Offset Publishing, **6** 13
Western Offshore Drilling and Exploration
Co., **I** 570
Western Pacific, **22** 220
Western Pacific Industries, **10** 357
Western Paper Box Co., **IV** 333
Western Pioneer, Inc., **18** 279
Western Piping and Engineering Co., **III**
535
Western Platinum, **21** 353
Western Playing Card Co., **13** 559

Western Powder Co., **I** 379; **13** 379
Western Power & Gas Company. *See*
Centel Corporation.
Western Printing and Lithographing
Company, **19** 404
Western Public Service Corporation, **6** 568
Western Publishing Group, Inc., IV 671;
13 114, **559–61; 15** 455
Western Reserve Bank of Lake County, **9**
474
Western Reserve Telephone Company. *See*
Alltel Corporation.
Western Reserves, **12** 442
Western Resources, Inc., 12 541–43
Western Rosin Company, **8** 99
Western Sizzlin', **10** 331; **19** 288
Western Slope Gas, **6** 559
Western Steer Family Restaurant, **10** 331;
18 8
Western Sugar Co., **II** 582
Western Telephone Company, **14** 257
Western Union Corporation, **I** 512; **III**
644; **6** 227–28, 338, 386; **9** 536; **10** 263;
12 9; **14** 363; **15** 72; **17** 345–46; **21** 25
Western Union Insurance Co., **III** 310
Western Vending, **13** 48
Western Veneer and Plywood Co., **IV** 358
Western-Mobile, **III** 735
Westfair Foods Ltd., **II** 649
Westfalenbank of Bochum, **II** 239
Westfalia AG, **III** 418–19
Westfalia Dinnendahl Gröppel AG, **III** 543
Westfälische Transport AG, **6** 426
Westfälische Verbands-Elektrizitätswerk, **V**
744
Westgate House Investments Ltd., **IV** 711
Westimex, **II** 594
Westin Hotel Co., I 129–30; **6** 129; **9**
283, **547–49; 21** 91
Westinghouse Air Brake Co., **III** 664
Westinghouse Brake & Signal, **III** 509
Westinghouse Cubic Ltd., **19** 111
Westinghouse Electric Corporation, I 4,
7, 19, 22, 28, 33, 82, 84–85, 524; **II**
57–58, 59, 80, 86, 88, 94, 98–99,
120–22, 151; **III** 440, 467, 641; **IV** 59,
401; **6** 39, 164, 261, 452, 483, 556; **9**
12, 17, 128, 162, 245, 417, 439–40,
553; **10** 280, 536; **11** 318; **12** 194,
544–47 (upd.); **13** 230, 398, 402,
506–07; **14** 300–01; **16** 8; **17** 488; **18**
320, 335–37, 355; **19** 164–66, 210; **21**
43
Westland Aircraft Ltd., **I** 50, 573; **IV** 658
WestLB. *See* Westdeutsche Landesbank
Girozentrale.
Westmark Mortgage Corp., **13** 417
Westmark Realty Advisors, **21** 97
Westmill Foods, **II** 466
Westminster Bank Ltd., **II** 257, 319, 320,
333–34; **17** 324
Westminster Press Ltd., **IV** 658
Westminster Trust Ltd., **IV** 706
Westmoreland Coal Company, 7 582–85
Westmount Enterprises, **I** 286
Weston and Mead, **IV** 310
Weston Bakeries, **II** 631
Weston Foods Ltd., **II** 631
Weston Pharmaceuticals, **V** 49; **19** 122–23
Weston Resources, **II** 631–32
Westpac Banking Corporation, II
388–90; 17 285
Westphalian Provinzialbank-Hülfskasse, **II**
385

WestPoint Stevens Inc., 16 533–36; 21
194
Westvaco Corporation, I 442; **IV**
351–54; 19 495–99 (upd.)
The Westwood Group, **20** 54
Westwood One, Inc., 17 150; **23 508–11**
Westwood Pharmaceuticals, **III** 19
Westwools Holdings, **I** 438
Westworld Resources Inc., **23** 41
Westwynn Theatres, **14** 87
The Wet Seal, Inc., 18 562–64
Wetterau Incorporated, II 645, **681–82;**
7 450; **18** 507
Wexpro Company, **6** 568–69
Weyerhaeuser Company, I 26; **IV** 266,
289, 298, 304, 308, **355–56,** 358; **8** 428,
434; **9 550–52 (upd.);** **19** 445–46, 499;
22 489
Weyman-Burton Co., **9** 533
Whalstrom & Co., **I** 14
Wharf Holdings Limited, **12** 367–68; **18**
114
Wheat, First Securities, **19** 304–05
Wheaton Industries, 8 570–73
Wheel Horse, **7** 535
Wheel Restaurants Inc., **14** 131
Wheelabrator Technologies, Inc., I 298;
II 403; **III** 511–12; **V** 754; **6 599–600;**
10 32; **11** 435
Wheeler Condenser & Engineering
Company, **6** 145
Wheeler, Fisher & Co., **IV** 344
Wheeling-Pittsburgh Corp., 7 586–88
Wheelock Marden, **I** 470; **20** 312
Whemco, **22** 415
Whemo Denko, **I** 359
Wherehouse Entertainment
Incorporated, 9 361; **11 556–58**
WHI Inc., **14** 545
Whippet Motor Lines Corporation, **6** 370
Whirl-A-Way Motors, **11** 4
Whirlpool Corporation, I 30; **II** 80; **III**
572, 573, **653–55;** **8** 298–99; **11** 318; **12**
252, 309, **548–50 (upd.);** **13** 402–03,
563; **15** 403; **18** 225–26; **22** 218, 349;
23 53
Whirlwind, Inc., **6** 233; **7** 535
Whiskey Trust, **I** 376
Whistler Corporation, **13** 195
Whitaker Health Services, **III** 389
Whitaker-Glessner Company, **7** 586
Whitall Tatum, **III** 423
Whitbread PLC, I 288, **293–94; 18** 73;
20 519–22 (upd.)
Whitby Pharmaceuticals, Inc., **10** 289
White Automotive, **10** 9, 11
White Brand, **V** 97
White Bus Line, **I** 448
White Castle Systems, Inc., 12 551–53
White Consolidated Industries Inc., II
122; **III** 480, 654, 573; **8** 298; **12** 252,
546; **13 562–64;** **22** 26–28, 216–17, 349
White Discount Department Stores, **16** 36
White Eagle Oil & Refining Co., **IV** 464; **7**
352
White Fuel Corp., **IV** 552
White Industrial Power, **II** 25
White Miller Construction Company, **14**
162
White Motor Co., **II** 16
White Mountain Freezers, **19** 360
White Oil Corporation, **7** 101
White Rock Corp., **I** 377
White Rose Corp., **12** 106

White Star Line, **23** 161
White Stores, **II** 419–20
White Swan Foodservice, **II** 625
White Tractor, **13** 17
White Weld, **II** 268; **21** 145
White-New Idea, **13** 18
White-Rodgers, **II** 19
White-Westinghouse. *See* White Consolidated Industries Inc.
Whiteaway Laidlaw, **V** 68
Whitehall Canadian Oils Ltd., **IV** 658
Whitehall Electric Investments Ltd., **IV** 658
Whitehall Labs, **8** 63
Whitehall Petroleum Corp. Ltd., **IV** 657–58
Whitehall Securities Corp., **IV** 658
Whitehall Trust Ltd., **IV** 658
Whitewater Group, **10** 508
Whitewear Manufacturing Company. *See* Angelica Corporation.
Whitman Corporation, **7** 430; **10** 414–15, **553–55 (upd.)**; **11** 188; **22** 353–54. *See also* IC Industries.
Whitman Publishing Co., **13** 559–60
Whitman's Chocolates, **I** 457; **7** 431; **12** 429
Whitmire Distribution. *See* Cardinal Health, Inc.
Whitney Communications Corp., **IV** 608
Whitney Holding Corporation, **21** 522–24
Whitney National Bank, **12** 16
Whittaker Corporation, **I** 544–46; **III** 389, 444
Whittar Steel Strip Co., **IV** 74
Whitteways, **I** 215
Whittle Communications L.P., **IV** 675; **7** 528; **13** 403; **22** 442
Whole Foods Market, Inc., **19** 501–02; **20 523–27**
Wholesale Cellular USA. *See* Brightpoint, Inc.
The Wholesale Club, Inc., **8** 556
Wholesale Depot, **13** 547
Wholesale Food Supply, Inc., **13** 333
Wholly Harvest, **19** 502
Whyte & Mackay Distillers Ltd., **V** 399; **19** 171
Wicat Systems, **7** 255–56
Wichita Industries, **11** 27
Wickes Companies, Inc., **I** 453, 483; **II** 262; **III** 580, 721; **V** 221–23; **10** 423; **13** 169–70; **15** 281; **17** 365–66; **19** 503–04; **20** 415
Wickman-Wimet, **IV** 203
Widows and Orphans Friendly Society, **III** 337
Wiclkopolski Bank Kredytowy, **16** 14
Wien Air Alaska, **II** 420
Wienerwald Holding, **17** 249
Wiesner, Inc., **22** 442
Wifstavarfs, **IV** 325
Wiggins Teape Ltd., **I** 426; **IV** 290
Wild by Nature. *See* King Cullen Grocery Co., Inc.
Wild Leitz G.m.b.H., **23** 83
Wild Oats Markets, Inc., **19 500–02**
Wildwater Kingdom, **22** 130
Wiles Group Ltd., **III** 501; **7** 207
Wiley Manufacturing Co., **8** 545
Oy Wilh. Schauman AB, **IV** 300–02; **19** 463
Wilhelm Fette GmbH, **IV** 198–99

Wilhelm Weber GmbH, **22** 95
Wilhelm Wilhelmsen Ltd., **7** 40
Wilkins Department Store, **19** 510
Wilkinson Sword Co., **III** 23, 28–29; **12** 464
Willamette Falls Electric Company. *See* Portland General Corporation.
Willamette Industries, Inc., **IV** 357–59; **13** 99, 101; **16** 340
Willcox & Gibbs Sewing Machine Co., **15** 384
Willetts Manufacturing Company, **12** 312
William A. Rogers Ltd., **IV** 644
William B. Tanner Co., **7** 327
William Barnet and Son, Inc., **III** 246
William Barry Co., **II** 566
William Benton Foundation, **7** 165, 167
William Bonnel Co., **I** 334; **10** 289
William Burdon, **III** 626
William Byrd Press Inc., **23** 100
William Carter Company, **17** 224
William Colgate and Co., **III** 23
William Collins & Sons, **II** 138; **IV** 651–52; **7** 390–91
William Cory & Son Ltd., **6** 417
William Crawford and Sons, **II** 593
William Douglas McAdams Inc., **I** 662; **9** 403
William Duff & Sons, **I** 509
William E. Pollack Government Securities, **II** 390
William E. Wright Company, **9** 375
William Esty Company, **16** 72
William Gaymer and Son Ltd., **I** 216
William Grant Company, **22** 343
William H. Rorer Inc., **I** 666
William Hancock & Co., **I** 223
William J. Hough Co., **8** 99–100
William Lyon Homes, **III** 664
William M. Mercer Inc., **III** 283
William Mackinnon & Co., **III** 522
William McDonald & Sons, **II** 593
William Morris Agency, Inc., **III** 554; **23** 512–14
William Morrow & Company, **19** 201
William Neilson, **II** 631
William Odhams Ltd., **7** 244
William Penn Cos., **III** 243, 273
William Press, **I** 568
William R. Warner & Co., **I** 710
William S. Kimball & Co., **12** 108
William Southam and Sons, **7** 487
William T. Blackwell & Company, **V** 395
William Underwood Co., **I** 246, 457; **7** 430
William Varcoe & Sons, **III** 690
William Zinsser & Co., **8** 456
Williams & Glyn's Bank Ltd., **12** 422
Williams & Wilkins. *See* Waverly, Inc.
Williams Brother Offshore Ltd., **I** 429
Williams Communications, **6** 340
Williams Companies, **III** 248; **IV** 84, 171, 575–76
Williams Deacon's Bank, **12** 422
Williams, Donnelley and Co., **IV** 660
Williams Electronics, **III** 431; **12** 419
Williams Electronics Games, Inc., **15** 539
Williams Gold Refining Co., **14** 81
The Williams Manufacturing Company, **19** 142–43
Williams Oil-O-Matic Heating Corporation, **12** 158; **21** 42
Williams/Nintendo Inc., **15** 537
Williams-Sonoma, Inc., **13** 42; **15** 50; **17** 548–50

Williamsburg Gas Light Co., **6** 455
Williamson-Dickie Manufacturing Company, **14** 549–50
Willie G's, **15** 279
Willis Faber, **III** 280, 747; **22** 318
Willis Stein & Partners, **21** 404
Williston Basin Interstate Pipeline Company, **7** 322, 324
Willor Manufacturing Corp., **9** 323
Willys-Overland, **I** 183; **8** 74
Wilmington Coca-Cola Bottling Works, Inc., **10** 223
Wilsdorf & Davis, **13** 353–54
Wilshire Restaurant Group Inc., **13** 66
Wilson & Co., **I** 490
Wilson Brothers, **8** 536
Wilson Foods Corp., **I** 489, 513; **II** 584–85; **12** 124; **14** 515; **22** 510
Wilson, H.W., Company. *See* H.W. Wilson Company.
Wilson Jones Company, **7** 4–5
Wilson Learning Group, **17** 272
Wilson Pharmaceuticals & Chemical, **I** 489
Wilson Sporting Goods, **I** 278, 489; **13** 317; **16** 52; **23** 449
Wilson's Motor Transit, **6** 370
Wilson's Supermarkets, **12** 220–21
Wilson-Maeulen Company, **13** 234
Wilsons The Leather Experts Inc., **21** 525–27
Wilts and Dorset Banking Co., **II** 307
Wiltshire United Dairies, **II** 586
Wimpey International Ltd., **13** 206
Wimpey's plc, **I** 315, 556
Win Schuler Foods, **II** 480
Win-Chance Foods, **II** 508
Wincanton Group, **II** 586–87
Winchell's Donut Shops, **II** 680
Winchester Arms, **I** 379–81, 434; **13** 379
Windmere Corporation, **16** 537–39
Windsor Manufacturing Company, **13** 6
Windsor Trust Co., **13** 467
Windstar Sail Cruises, **6** 368
Windsurfing International, **23** 55
Wine World, Inc., **22** 78, 80
Wingate Partners, **14** 521, 523
Wings & Wheels, **13** 19
Wings Luggage, Inc., **10** 181
Winkelman Stores, Inc., **8** 425–26
Winkler-Grimm Wagon Co., **I** 141
Winlet Fashions, **22** 223
Winmar Co., **III** 353
Winn-Dixie Stores, Inc., **II** 626–27, 670, 683–84; **7** 61; **11** 228; **15** 178; **16** 314; **18** 8; **21** 528–30 (upd.)
Winnebago Industries Inc., **7** 589–91; **22** 207
Winners Apparel Ltd., **V** 197
Winning International, **21** 403
Winschermann group, **IV** 198
WinsLoew Furniture, Inc., **21** 531–33
Winston & Newell Company. *See* Supervalu Inc.
Winston Furniture Company, Inc., **21** 531–33
Winston Group, **10** 333
Winston, Harper, Fisher Co., **II** 668
Wintershall, **I** 306; **IV** 485; **18** 49
Winterthur Insurance, **21** 144, 146–47
Winterthur Schweizerische Versicherungs-Gesellschaft, **III** 343, 402–04
Winthrop Laboratories, **I** 698–99
Winton Engines, **10** 273

Winton Motor Car Company, **V** 231
Wire and Cable Specialties Corporation, **17** 276
Wire and Plastic Products PLC. *See* WPP Group PLC.
Wireless Hong Kong. *See* Hong Kong Telecommunications Ltd.
Wireless LLC, **18** 77
Wireless Management Company, **11** 12
Wireless Speciality Co., **II** 120
Wirtz Productions Ltd., **15** 238
Wisaforest Oy AB, **IV** 302
Wisconsin Bell, Inc., 14 551–53; 18 30
Wisconsin Central, **12** 278
Wisconsin Dairies, 7 592–93
Wisconsin Energy Corporation, 6 601–03, 605
Wisconsin Gas Company, **17** 22–23
Wisconsin Knife Works, **III** 436
Wisconsin Power and Light, **22** 13
Wisconsin Public Service Corporation, 6 604–06; 9 553–54
Wisconsin Steel, **10** 430; **17** 158–59
Wisconsin Tissue Mills Inc., **8** 103
Wisconsin Toy Company. *See* Value Merchants Inc.
Wisconsin Wire and Steel, **17** 310
Wise Foods, Inc., **22** 95
Wiser's De Luxe Whiskey, **14** 141
Wishnick-Tumpeer Chemical Co., **I** 403–05
Wispark Corporation, **6** 601, 603
Wisser Service Holdings AG, **18** 105
Wisvest Corporation, **6** 601, 603
Witco Corporation, I 403, **404–06; 16 540–43 (upd.)**
Wite-Out Products, Inc., **23** 56–57
Witech Corporation, **6** 601, 603
Withington Company. *See* Sparton Corporation.
Wittington Investments Ltd., **13** 51
WLR Foods, Inc., 14 516; **21 534–36**
Wm. Wrigley Jr. Company, 7 594–97
WMS Industries, Inc., III 431; **15 537–39**
WMX Technologies Inc., 11 435–36; **17 551–54**
Woermann and German East African Lines, **I** 542
Wöhlk, **III** 446
Wolf Furniture Enterprises, **14** 236
Wolfe Industries, Inc., **22** 255
Wolff Printing Co., **13** 559
Wolohan Lumber Co., 19 503–05
Wolters Kluwer NV, **IV** 611; **14 554–56**
Wolvercote Paper Mill, **IV** 300
Wolverine Die Cast Group, **IV** 165
Wolverine Tube Inc., 23 515–17
Wolverine World Wide Inc., 16 544–47; 17 390
Womack Development Company, **11** 257
Women's World, **15** 96
Wometco Coca-Cola Bottling Co., **10** 222
Wometco Coffee Time, **I** 514
Wometco Enterprises, **I** 246, 514
Wonderware Corp., **22** 374
Wong International Holdings, **16** 195
Wood Fiberboard Co., **IV** 358
Wood Gundy, **II** 345; **21** 447
Wood Hall Trust plc, I 438, **592–93**
Wood River Oil and Refining Company, **11** 193
Wood Shovel and Tool Company, **9** 71
Wood, Struthers & Winthrop, Inc., **22** 189

Wood-Metal Industries, Inc. *See* Wood-Mode, Inc.
Wood-Mode, Inc., 23 518–20
Woodall Industries, **III** 641; **14** 303
Woodard-Walker Lumber Co., **IV** 358
Woodbury Co., **19** 380
Woodcock, Hess & Co., **9** 370
Woodfab, **IV** 295; **19** 225
Woodhaven Gas Light Co., **6** 455
Woodhill Chemical Sales Company, **8** 333
Woodlands, **7** 345–46
Woods and Co., **II** 235
Woodville Appliances, Inc., **9** 121
Woodward Corp., **IV** 311; **19** 267
Woodward Governor Co., 13 565–68
Woodworkers Warehouse, **22** 517
Woolco Department Stores, **II** 634; **7** 444; **V** 107, 225–26; **14** 294; **22** 242
Woolverton Motors, **I** 183
Woolworth Corporation, II 414; **6** 344; **V** 106–09, **224–27; 8** 509; **14** 293–95; **17** 42, 335; **20 528–32 (upd.)**
Woolworth Holdings, **II** 139; **V** 108; **19** 123
Woolworth's Ltd., **II** 656
Wooster Preserving Company, **11** 211
Wooster Rubber Co., **III** 613
Worcester City and County Bank, **II** 307
Worcester Gas Light Co., **14** 124
Worcester Wire Works, **13** 369
Word, Inc., **14** 499
Word Processors Personnel Service, **6** 10
WordPerfect Corporation, 6 256; **10** 519, **556–59; 12** 335
WordStar International, **15** 149
Work Wear Corp., **II** 607; **16** 229
Working Title Films, **23** 389
World Air Network, Ltd., **6** 71
World Airways, **10** 560–62
World Book Group. *See* Scott Fetzer Company.
World Book, Inc., IV 622; **12 554–56**
World Color Press Inc., 12 557–59; 19 333; **21** 61
World Communications, Inc., **11** 184
World Financial Network National Bank, **V** 116
World Flight Crew Services, **10** 560
World Foot Locker, **14** 293
World Gift Company, **9** 330
World International Holdings Limited, **12** 368
World Journal Tribune Inc., **IV** 608
World Publishing Co., **8** 423
World Savings and Loan, **19** 412
World Trade Corporation. *See* International Business Machines Corporation.
World Yacht Enterprises, **22** 438
World-Wide Shipping Group, **II** 298; **III** 517
WorldCom, Inc., **14** 330, 332; **18** 33, 164, 166
WorldCorp, Inc., 10 560–62
WorldGames, **10** 560
Worlds of Fun, **22** 130
WorldWay Corporation, **16** 41
Worldwide Logistics, **17** 505
Worldwide Underwriters Insurance Co., **III** 218–19
Wormald International Ltd., **13** 245, 247
Wormser, **III** 760
Wortham, Gus Sessions, **III** 193; **10** 65
Worthen Banking Corporation, **15** 60
Worthington & Co., **I** 223

Worthington Corp., **I** 142
Worthington Foods, Inc., I 653; **14 557–59**
Worthington Industries, Inc., 7 598–600; 8 450; **21 537–40 (upd.)**
Worthington Telephone Company, **6** 312
Woven Belting Co., **8** 13
WPL Holdings, 6 604–06
WPM. *See* Wall Paper Manufacturers.
WPP Group plc, I 21; **6 53–54; 22** 201, 296; **23** 480. *See also* Ogilvy Group Inc.
Wrather Corporation, **18** 354
Wrenn Furniture Company, **10** 184
WRG. *See* Wells Rich Greene BDDP.
Wright & Company Realtors, **21** 257
Wright Aeronautical, **9** 16
Wright Airplane Co., **III** 151; **6** 265
Wright and Son, **II** 593
Wright Company, **9** 416
Wright Engine Company, **11** 427
Wright Group, **22** 519, 522
Wright Manufacturing Company, **8** 407
Wright Plastic Products, **17** 310
Wright, Robertson & Co. *See* Fletcher Challenge Ltd.
Wright Stephenson & Co., **IV** 278
Wrightson Limited, **19** 155
Write Right Manufacturing Co., **IV** 345
WSI Corporation, **10** 88–89
WSM Inc., **11** 152
WTC Airlines, Inc., **IV** 182
WTD Industries, Inc., 20 533–36
Wührer, **II** 474
Wunderlich Ltd., **III** 687
Wunderman, Ricotta & Kline, **I** 37
Wurlitzer Co., **17** 468; **18** 45
Württembergische Landes-Elektrizitäts AG, **IV** 230
WVPP. *See* Westvaco Corporation.
WWG Industries, Inc., **22** 352–53
WWTV, **18** 493
Wyandotte Chemicals Corporation, **18** 49
Wyandotte Corp., **I** 306
Wyeth Laboratories, **I** 623; **10** 69
Wyle Electronics, 14 560–62; 19 311
Wyly Corporation, **11** 468
Wyman-Gordon Company, 14 563–65
Wymore Oil Co., **IV** 394
Wynn's International Inc., **22** 458
Wynncor Ltd., **IV** 693
Wyoming Mineral Corp., **IV** 401
Wyse Technology, Inc., 10 362; **15 540–42**

X-Acto, **12** 263
X-Chem Oil Field Chemicals, **8** 385
XA Systems Corporation, **10** 244
Xaos Tools, Inc., **10** 119
Xcelite, **II** 16
Xcor International, **III** 431; **15** 538
Xenia National Bank, **9** 474
Xerox Corporation, I 31–32, 338, 490, 693; **II** 10, 117, 157, 159, 412, 448; **III** 110, 116, 120–21, 157, 159, **171–73**, 475; **IV** 252, 703; **6** 244, **288–90 (upd.)**, 390; **7** 45, 161; **8** 164; **10** 22, 139, 430, 510–11; **11** 68, 494, 518; **13** 127, 448; **14** 399; **17** 28–29, 328–29; **18** 93, 111–12; **22** 411–12
Xilinx, Inc., 16 317, **548–50; 18** 17, 19; **19** 405
XRAL Storage and Terminaling Co., **IV** 411
XTRA Corp., **18** 67

XTX Corp., **13** 127
Xynetics, **9** 251
Xytek Corp., **13** 127

Y & S Candies Inc., **II** 511
Yacimientos Petrolíferos Fiscales Sociedad
    Anónima, **IV** 578
Yageo Corporation, 16 551–53
Yale & Towne Manufacturing Co., **I**
    154–55; **10** 279
Yamabun Oil Co., **IV** 403
Yamaguchi Bank, **II** 347
Yamaha Corporation, III 366, 599,
    656–59; 11 50; **12** 401; **16** 410, **554–58**
    (upd.); **17** 25; **18** 250; **19** 428; **22** 196
Yamaha Musical Instruments, **16** 202
Yamaichi Securities Company, Limited,
    II 300, 323, 434, **458–59; 9** 377
Yamano Music, **16** 202
Yamanouchi Pharmaceutical, **12** 444–45
Yamatame Securities, **II** 326
Yamato Transport Co. Ltd., V 536–38
Yamazaki Baking Co., **II** 543; **IV** 152
Yanbian Industrial Technology Training
    Institute, **12** 294
Yankee Energy Gas System, Inc., **13** 184
Yankton Gas Company, **6** 524
Yarmouth Group, Inc., **17** 285
Yaryan, **I** 343
Yashica Co., Ltd., **II** 50–51; **21** 330
Yasuda Fire and Marine Insurance
    Company, Limited, II 292, 391; **III**
    405–07, 408
Yasuda Mutual Life Insurance
    Company, II 292, 391, 446; **III** 288,
    405, **408–09; 22** 406–07
The Yasuda Trust and Banking
    Company, Limited, II 273, 291,
    391–92; 17 555–57 (upd.)
Yates Circuit Foil, **IV** 26
Yates-Barco Ltd., **16** 8
Yawata Iron & Steel Co., Ltd., **I** 493, 509;
    II 300; **IV** 130, 157, 212; **17** 350
Year Book Medical Publishers, **IV** 677–78
Yearbooks, Inc., **12** 472
Yeargin Construction Co., **II** 87; **11** 413
Yellow Cab Co., **I** 125; **V** 539; **10** 370; **12**
    487
Yellow Corporation, 14 566–68
Yellow Freight System, Inc. of Deleware,
    V 503, **539–41; 12** 278
Yeomans & Foote, **I** 13
Yeomans & Partners Ltd., **I** 588
YES!, **10** 306
Yesco Audio Environments, **18** 353, 355
Yeti Cycles Inc., **19** 385
Yeung Chi Shing Estates, **IV** 717
YGK Inc., **6** 465, 467
Yhtyneet Paperitehtaat Oy. *See* United
    Paper Mills Ltd.
Yili Food Co., **II** 544
YKK, **19** 477
YMOS A.G., **IV** 53
Yokado Clothing Store, **V** 88
Yokogawa Electric Corp., **III** 142–43, 536
Yokogawa Electric Works, Limited, **6** 237;
    13 234
Yokohama Bottle Plant, **21** 319
Yokohama Cooperative Wharf Co., **IV** 728
Yokohama Electric Cable Manufacturing
    Co., **III** 490
The Yokohama Rubber Co., Ltd., V
    254–56; 19 506–09 (upd.)
Yokohama Specie Bank, **I** 431; **II** 224

Yoosung Enterprise Co., Ltd., **23** 269
Yoplait S.A., **II** 576
York & London, **III** 359
The York Bank and Trust Company, **16** 14
York Corp., **III** 440
York Developments, **IV** 720
York International Corp., 13 569–71; 22
    6
York Manufacturing Co., **13** 385
York Safe & Lock Company, **7** 144–45;
    22 184
York Steak House, **16** 157
York Wastewater Consultants, Inc., **6** 441
York-Benimaru, **V** 88
Yorkshire and Pacific Securities Ltd., **IV**
    723
Yorkshire Insurance Co., **III** 241–42, 257
Yorkshire Paper Mills Ltd., **IV** 300
Yorkshire Post Newspapers, **IV** 686
Yorkshire Television Ltd., **IV** 659
Yorkville Group, **IV** 640
Yosemite Park & Curry Co., **II** 144
Yoshikazu Taguchi, **6** 428
Yoshitomi Pharmaceutical, **I** 704
Young & Rubicam Inc., I 9–11, 25,
    36–38; II 129; **6** 14, 47; **9** 314; **13** 204;
    16 166–68; **22 551–54** (upd.)
Young & Selden, **7** 145
Young & Son, **II** 334
Young Readers of America, **13** 105
Young's Engineering Co., **IV** 717
Youngblood Truck Lines, **16** 40
Youngs Drug Products Corporation, **8** 85
Youngstown, **IV** 114
Youngstown Pressed Steel Co., **III** 763
Youngstown Sheet & Tube, **I** 490–91; **13**
    157
Younkers, Inc., 19 324–25, **510–12**
Yount-Lee Oil Co., **IV** 369
Youth Centre Inc., **16** 36
Youth Services International, Inc., 21
    541–43
Yoxall Instrument Company, **13** 234
Yoyoteiki Cargo Co., Ltd., **6** 428
YPF Sociedad Anónima, IV 577–78
Yside Investment Group, **16** 196
Yuasa Battery Co., **III** 556
Yuba Heat Transfer Corp., **I** 514
Yucaipa Cos., 17 558–62; 22 39
Yukon Pacific Corporation, **22** 164, 166
Yurakucho Seibu Co., Ltd., **V** 185
Yutani Heavy Industries, Ltd., **IV** 130
Yves Rocher, **IV** 546
Yves Saint Laurent, **I** 697; **12** 37
Yves Soulié, **II** 266

Z.C. Mines, **IV** 61
Zaadunie B.V., **I** 672
Zahnfabrik Weinand Sohne & Co.
    G.m.b.H., **10** 271
Zahnradfabrik Friedrichshafen, **III** 415
Zale Corporation, 16 206, **559–61; 17**
    369; **19** 452; **23** 60
Zambezi Saw Mills (1968) Ltd., **IV** 241
Zambia Industrial and Mining
    Corporation Ltd., IV 239–41
Zander & Ingeström, **III** 419
Zanders Feinpapiere AG, **IV** 288; **15** 229
Zanussi, **III** 480; **22** 27
Zapata Corp., **17** 157, 160
Zapata Drilling Co., **IV** 489
Zapata Gulf Marine Corporation, **11** 524
Zapata Offshore Co., **IV** 489
Zapata Petroleum Corp., **IV** 489

Zayre Corp., **V** 197–98; **9** 20–21; **13**
    547–48; **19** 448
Zealand Mines S.A., **23** 41
Zebco, **22** 115
Zebra Technologies Corporation, 14 378,
    569–71
Zecco, Inc., **III** 443; **6** 441
Zehrmart, **II** 631
Zeiss Ikon AG, **III** 446
Zell Bros., **16** 559
Zell/Chilmark Fund LP, **12** 439; **19** 384
Zellers, **V** 80
Zellstoff AG, **III** 400
Zellstoffabrik Waldhof AG, **IV** 323–24
Zellweger Telecommunications AG, **9** 32
Zeneca Group PLC, 21 544–46
Zenith Data Systems, Inc., **II** 124–25; **III**
    123; **6** 231; **10 563–65**
Zenith Electronics Corporation, II 102,
    123–25; 10 563; **11** 62, 318; **12** 183,
    454; **13** 109, 398, **572–75** (upd.); **18**
    421
Zentec Corp., **I** 482
Zentralsparkasse und Kommerzialbank
    Wien, **23** 37
Zentronics, **19** 313
Zero Corporation, 17 563–65
Zetor s.p., **21** 175
Zeus Components, Inc., **10** 113
Zewawell AG, **IV** 324
Ziff Communications Company, 7
    239–40; **12** 359, **560–63; 13** 483; **16**
    371; **17** 152, 253
Zijlker, **IV** 491
Zilber Ltd., **13** 541
Zilkha & Company, **12** 72
Zilog, Inc., 15 543–45; 16 548–49; **22**
    390
Zimbabwe Sugar Refineries, **II** 581
Zimmer AG, **IV** 142
Zimmer Inc., **10** 156–57; **11** 475
Zimmer Manufacturing Co., **III** 18
Zinc Corp., **IV** 58–59, 61
Zion Foods, **23** 408
Zions Bancorporation, 12 564–66
Zippo Manufacturing Company, 18
    565–68
Zippy Mart, **7** 102
Zircotube, **IV** 174
Zivnostenska, **II** 282
Zody's Department Stores, **9** 120–22
Zoecon, **I** 673
Zoll Medical, **18** 423
Zondervan Publishing House, **14** 499
Zoom Telephonics, Inc., 18 569–71
Zortech Inc., **10** 508
Zotos International, Inc., **III** 63; **17** 110; **22**
    487
ZPT Radom, **23** 427
ZS Sun Limited Partnership, **10** 502
Zuid Nederlandsche Handelsbank, **II** 185
Zürcher Bankverein, **II** 368
Zurich Insurance Group, **15** 257
Zürich Versicherungs-Gesellschaft, III
    194, 402–03, **410–12**
Zwarovski, **16** 561
Zycad Corp., **11** 489–91
Zymaise, **II** 582
ZyMOS Corp., **III** 458
Zytec Corporation, 19 513–15

INDEX TO INDUSTRIES

Index to Industries

ACCOUNTING

Deloitte & Touche, 9
Ernst & Young, 9
L.S. Starrett Co., 13
McLane Company, Inc., 13
Price Waterhouse, 9

ADVERTISING & OTHER BUSINESS SERVICES

A.C. Nielsen Company, 13
Ackerley Communications, Inc., 9
Adia S.A., 6
Advo, Inc., 6
Aegis Group plc, 6
American Building Maintenance Industries, Inc., 6
The Associated Press, 13
Barrett Business Services, Inc., 16
Bates Worldwide, Inc., 14
Bearings, Inc., 13
Berlitz International, Inc., 13
Big Flower Press Holdings, Inc., 21
Broadcast Music Inc., 23
Burns International Security Services, 13
Campbell-Mithun-Esty, Inc., 16
Central Parking Corporation, 18
Chiat/Day Inc. Advertising, 11
Christie's International plc, 15
Cintas Corporation, 21
Cox Enterprises, Inc., 22 (upd.)
Cyrk Inc., 19
D'Arcy Masius Benton & Bowles, Inc., 6
DDB Needham Worldwide, 14
Deluxe Corporation, 22 (upd.)
Dentsu Inc., I; 16 (upd.)
EBSCO Industries, Inc., 17
Employee Solutions, Inc., 18
Ennis Business Forms, Inc., 21
Equifax, Inc., 6
ERLY Industries Inc., 17
Euro RSCG Worldwide S.A., 13
Fallon McElligott Inc., 22
Foote, Cone & Belding Communications, Inc., I
Grey Advertising, Inc., 6
Hakuhodo, Inc., 6
Handleman Company, 15
International Management Group, 18
Interpublic Group Inc., I
The Interpublic Group of Companies, Inc., 22 (upd.)
Japan Leasing Corporation, 8
JWT Group Inc., I
Katz Communications, Inc., 6
Kelly Services Inc., 6
Ketchum Communications Inc., 6
Kinko's Inc., 16
Leo Burnett Company Inc., I; 20 (upd.)
Lintas: Worldwide, 14
Mail Boxes Etc., 18
New England Business Services, Inc., 18
New Valley Corporation, 17
The Ogilvy Group, Inc., I
Olsten Corporation, 6

Omnicom Group, I, 22 (upd.)
On Assignment, Inc., 20
Paris Corporation, 22
Paychex, Inc., 15
Pinkerton's Inc., 9
Publicis S.A., 19
Publishers Clearing House, 23
Randstad Holding n.v., 16
RemedyTemp, Inc., 20
Robert Half International Inc., 18
Ronco, Inc., 15
Saatchi & Saatchi PLC, I
ServiceMaster Limited Partnership, 6
Shared Medical Systems Corporation, 14
Sir Speedy, Inc., 16
Skidmore, Owings & Merrill, 13
Sotheby's Holdings, Inc., 11
Spencer Stuart and Associates, Inc., 14
TBWA Advertising, Inc., 6
Ticketmaster Corp., 13
Transmedia Network Inc., 20
TRM Copy Centers Corporation, 18
True North Communications Inc., 23
Tyler Corporation, 23
UniFirst Corporation, 21
Unitog Co., 19
The Wackenhut Corporation, 14
Wells Rich Greene BDDP, 6
William Morris Agency, Inc., 23
WPP Group plc, 6
Young & Rubicam, Inc., I, 22 (upd.)

AEROSPACE

A.S. Yakovlev Design Bureau, 15
Aerospatiale, 7
The Aerospatiale Group, 21 (upd.)
Avions Marcel Dassault-Breguet Aviation, I
Banner Aerospace, Inc., 14
Beech Aircraft Corporation, 8
The Boeing Company, I; 10 (upd.)
British Aerospace PLC, I
Canadair, Inc., 16
Cessna Aircraft Company, 8
Daimler-Benz Aerospace AG, 16
Fairchild Aircraft, Inc., 9
G.I.E. Airbus Industrie, I; 12 (upd.)
General Dynamics Corporation, I; 10 (upd.)
Grumman Corporation, I; 11 (upd.)
Gulfstream Aerospace Corp., 7
N.V. Koninklijke Nederlandse Vliegtuigenfabriek Fokker, I
Learjet Inc., 8
Lockheed Corporation, I; 11 (upd.)
Lockheed Martin Corporation, 15 (upd.)
Martin Marietta Corporation, I
McDonnell Douglas Corporation, I; 11 (upd.)
Messerschmitt-Bölkow-Blohm GmbH., I
Moog Inc., 13
Northrop Corporation, I; 11 (upd.)
Orbital Sciences Corporation, 22
Pratt & Whitney, 9

Rockwell International Corporation, I; 11 (upd.)
Rolls-Royce plc, I; 7 (upd.); 21 (upd.)
Sequa Corp., 13
Sundstrand Corporation, 7; 21 (upd.)
Textron Lycoming Turbine Engine, 9
Thiokol Corporation, 9, 22 (upd.)
United Technologies Corporation, I; 10 (upd.)

AIRLINES

Aeroflot Soviet Airlines, 6
Air Canada, 6; 23 (upd.)
Air New Zealand Limited, 14
Air-India, 6
AirTran Holdings, Inc., 22
Alaska Air Group, Inc., 6
Alitalia—Linee Aeree Italiana, SPA, 6
All Nippon Airways Company Limited, 6
America West Airlines, 6
American Airlines, I; 6 (upd.)
British Airways PLC, I; 14 (upd.)
British World Airlines Ltd., 18
Cathay Pacific Airways Limited, 6
Comair Holdings Inc., 13
Continental Airlines, I
Continental Airlines, Inc., 21
Corporación Internacional de Aviación, S.A. de C.V. (Cintra), 20
Delta Air Lines, Inc., I; 6 (upd.)
Deutsche Lufthansa A.G., I
Eastern Airlines, I
EgyptAir, 6
El Al Israel Airlines Ltd., 23
Finnair Oy, 6
Frontier Airlines, Inc., 22
Garuda Indonesia, 6
Groupe Air France, 6
HAL Inc., 9
Hawaiian Airlines, Inc., 22 (upd.)
Iberia Líneas Aéreas de España S.A., 6
Japan Air Lines Company Ltd., I
Kitty Hawk, Inc., 22
Kiwi International Airlines Inc., 20
Koninklijke Luchtvaart Maatschappij, N.V., I
Korean Air Lines Co. Ltd., 6
Malaysian Airlines System BHD, 6
Mesa Airlines, Inc., 11
Northwest Airlines, Inc., I; 6 (upd.)
Pan American World Airways, Inc., I; 12 (upd.)
People Express Airlines, Inc., I
Philippine Airlines, Inc., 6; 23 (upd.)
Qantas Airways Limited, 6
Reno Air Inc., 23
Saudi Arabian Airlines, 6
Scandinavian Airlines System, I
Singapore Airlines Ltd., 6
Southwest Airlines Co., 6
Swiss Air Transport Company, Ltd., I
Texas Air Corporation, I
Thai Airways International Ltd., 6
Trans World Airlines, Inc., I; 12 (upd.)

Transportes Aereos Portugueses, S.A., 6
United Airlines, I; 6 (upd.)
USAir Group, Inc., I; 6 (upd.)
VARIG, SA, 6

AUTOMOTIVE

Adam Opel AG, 7; 21 (upd.)
Alfa Romeo, 13
American Motors Corporation, I
Arvin Industries, Inc., 8
Automobiles Citroen, 7
Automobili Lamborghini S.p.A., 13
Bayerische Motoren Werke A.G., I; 11
   (upd.)
Bendix Corporation, I
Borg-Warner Automotive, Inc., 14
The Budd Company, 8
Chrysler Corporation, I; 11 (upd.)
Cummins Engine Co. Inc., I; 12 (upd.)
Custom Chrome, Inc., 16
Daihatsu Motor Company, Ltd., 7; 21
   (upd.)
Daimler-Benz A.G., I; 15 (upd.)
Dana Corporation, I; 10 (upd.)
Douglas & Lomason Company, 16
Eaton Corporation, I; 10 (upd.)
Echlin Inc., I; 11 (upd.)
Federal-Mogul Corporation, I; 10 (upd.)
Ferrari S.p.A., 13
Fiat S.p.A, I; 11 (upd.)
Ford Motor Company, I; 11 (upd.)
Ford Motor Company, S.A. de C.V., 20
Fruehauf Corporation, I
General Motors Corporation, I; 10 (upd.)
Genuine Parts Company, 9
Harley-Davidson Inc., 7
Hino Motors, Ltd., 7 21 (upd.)
Honda Motor Company Limited (Honda
   Giken Kogyo Kabushiki Kaisha), I; 10
   (upd.)
Insurance Auto Auctions, Inc., 23
Isuzu Motors, Ltd., 9; 23 (upd.)
Kelsey-Hayes Group of Companies, 7
Kia Motors Corp., 12
Lear Seating Corporation, 16
Lotus Cars Ltd., 14
Mack Trucks, Inc., I, 22 (upd.)
Masland Corporation, 17
Mazda Motor Corporation, 9; 23 (upd.)
Mel Farr Automotive Group, 20
Midas International Corporation, 10
Mitsubishi Motors Corporation, 9; 23
   (upd.)
Navistar International Corporation, I; 10
   (upd.)
Nissan Motor Company Ltd., I; 11 (upd.)
Officine Alfieri Maserati S.p.A., 13
Oshkosh Truck Corporation, 7
Paccar Inc., I
Pennzoil Company, 20 (upd.)
Penske Corporation, 19 (upd.)
The Pep Boys—Manny, Moe & Jack, 11
Peugeot S.A., I
Piaggio & C. S.p.A., 20
Porsche AG, 13
Regie Nationale des Usines Renault, I
Robert Bosch GmbH., I; 16 (upd.)
Rolls-Royce Motors Ltd., I
Rolls-Royce plc, 21 (upd.)
Rover Group Ltd., 21 (upd.)
Rover Group plc, 7
Saab-Scania A.B., I; 11 (upd.)
Safelite Glass Corp., 19
Saturn Corporation, 7; 21 (upd.)
Sealed Power Corporation, I
Sheller-Globe Corporation, I
Spartan Motors Inc., 14

SPX Corporation, 10
Superior Industries International, Inc., 8
Suzuki Motor Corporation, 9; 23 (upd.)
Toyota Motor Corporation, I; 11 (upd.)
TRW Inc., 14 (upd.)
Ugly Duckling Corporation, 22
United Technologies Automotive Inc., 15
Valeo, 23
Volkswagen A.G., I; 11 (upd.)
AB Volvo, I; 7 (upd.)
Walker Manufacturing Company, 19
Winnebago Industries Inc., 7

BEVERAGES

Adolph Coors Company, I; 13 (upd.)
Allied-Lyons PLC, I
Anheuser-Busch Companies, Inc., I; 10
   (upd.)
Asahi Breweries, Ltd., I; 20 (upd.)
Bacardi Limited, 18
Bass PLC, I; 15 (upd.)
Beringer Wine Estates Holdings, Inc., 22
Boston Beer Company, 18
Brauerei Beck & Co., 9
Brown-Forman Corporation, I; 10 (upd.)
Canandaigua Wine Company, Inc., 13
Carlsberg A/S, 9
Carlton and United Breweries Ltd., I
Cerveceria Polar, I
Coca Cola Bottling Co. Consolidated, 10
The Coca-Cola Company, I; 10 (upd.)
Corby Distilleries Limited, 14
Dean Foods Company, 21 (upd.)
Distillers Company PLC, I
Dr Pepper/7Up Companies, Inc., 9
E & J Gallo Winery, I; 7 (upd.)
Foster's Brewing Group Ltd., 7; 21 (upd.)
G. Heileman Brewing Company Inc., I
General Cinema Corporation, I
Grand Metropolitan PLC, I
The Greenalls Group PLC, 21
Guinness PLC, I
Heineken N.V, I; 13 (upd.)
Heublein, Inc., I
Hiram Walker Resources, Ltd., I
Interbrew S.A., 17
Kikkoman Corporation, 14
Kirin Brewery Company, Limited, I; 21
   (upd.)
Labatt Brewing Company Ltd., I
Marie Brizard & Roger International S.A.,
   22
Miller Brewing Company, I; 12 (upd.)
Moët-Hennessy, I
Molson Companies Ltd., I
National Grape Cooperative Association,
   Inc., 20
Pepsico, Inc., I; 10 (upd.)
Pernod Ricard S.A., I; 21 (upd.)
Pete's Brewing Company, 22
Philip Morris Companies Inc., 18 (upd.)
Rainier Brewing Company, 23
Rémy Cointreau S.A., 20
Robert Mondavi Corporation, 15
Royal Crown Company, Inc., 23
Sapporo Breweries, Ltd., I; 13 (upd.)
Scottish & Newcastle plc, 15
The Seagram Company, Ltd., I
Snapple Beverage Corporation, 11
South African Breweries Ltd., I
Starbucks Corporation, 13
The Stroh Brewery Company, 18 (upd.)
The Stroh Brewing Company, I
Sutter Home Winery Inc., 16
Whitbread and Company PLC, I

BIOTECHNOLOGY

Amgen, Inc., 10
Biogen Inc., 14
Centocor Inc., 14
Chiron Corporation, 10
IDEXX Laboratories, Inc., 23
Immunex Corporation, 14
Life Technologies, Inc., 17
Minntech Corporation, 22
Mycogen Corporation, 21
Quintiles Transnational Corporation, 21

CHEMICALS

A. Schulman, Inc., 8
Air Products and Chemicals, Inc., I; 10
   (upd.)
Akzo Nobel N.V., 13
AlliedSignal Inc., 22 (upd.)
American Cyanamid, I; 8 (upd.)
ARCO Chemical Company, 10
Atochem S.A., I
Baker Hughes Incorporated, 22 (upd.)
BASF A.G., I
BASF Aktiengesellschaft, 18 (upd.)
Bayer A.G., I; 13 (upd.)
Betz Laboratories, Inc., I; 10 (upd.)
The BFGoodrich Company, 19 (upd.)
Boc Group PLC, I
Brenntag AG, 8; 23 (upd.)
Cabot Corporation, 8
Cambrex Corporation, 16
Celanese Corporation, I
Chemcentral Corporation, 8
Chemi-Trol Chemical Co., 16
Ciba-Geigy Ltd., I; 8 (upd.)
The Clorox Company, 22 (upd.)
Crompton & Knowles, 9
DeKalb Genetics Corporation, 17
The Dexter Corporation, I; 12 (upd.)
The Dow Chemical Company, I; 8 (upd.)
DSM, N.V, I
E.I. Du Pont de Nemours & Company, I; 8
   (upd.)
Eastman Chemical Company, 14
Ecolab, Inc., I; 13 (upd.)
English China Clays plc, 15 (upd.)
ERLY Industries Inc., 17
Ethyl Corporation, I; 10 (upd.)
Ferro Corporation, 8
First Mississippi Corporation, 8
Formosa Plastics Corporation, 14
Fort James Corporation, 22 (upd.)
G.A.F., I
Georgia Gulf Corporation, 9
Great Lakes Chemical Corporation, I; 14
   (upd.)
Hawkins Chemical, Inc., 16
Hercules Inc., I, 22 (upd.)
Hoechst A.G., I; 18 (upd.)
Hoechst Celanese Corporation, 13
Huls A.G., I
Huntsman Chemical Corporation, 8
IMC Fertilizer Group, Inc., 8
Imperial Chemical Industries PLC, I
International Flavors & Fragrances Inc., 9
Koppers Inc., I
L'air Liquide, I
Lawter International Inc., 14
LeaRonal, Inc., 23
Lubrizol Corporation, I
M.A. Hanna Company, 8
Mallinckrodt Group Inc., 19
Mitsubishi Chemical Industries, Ltd., I
Mitsui Petrochemical Industries, Ltd., 9
Monsanto Company, I; 9 (upd.)
Montedison SpA, I
Morton International Inc., 9 (upd.)

Morton Thiokol, Inc., I
Nagase & Company, Ltd., 8
Nalco Chemical Corporation, I; 12 (upd.)
National Distillers and Chemical
   Corporation, I
National Sanitary Supply Co., 16
NCH Corporation, 8
NL Industries, Inc., 10
Nobel Industries AB, 9
Novacor Chemicals Ltd., 12
NutraSweet Company, 8
Olin Corporation, I; 13 (upd.)
OM Group, Inc., 17
Pennwalt Corporation, I
Perstorp A.B., I
Petrolite Corporation, 15
Praxair, Inc., 11
Quantum Chemical Corporation, 8
Reichhold Chemicals, Inc., 10
Rhône-Poulenc S.A., I; 10 (upd.)
Rohm and Haas, I
Roussel Uclaf, I; 8 (upd.)
The Scotts Company, 22
Sequa Corp., 13
Shanghai Petrochemical Co., Ltd., 18
Solvay & Cie S.A., I; 21 (upd.)
Sterling Chemicals, Inc., 16
Sumitomo Chemical Company Ltd., I
Terra Industries, Inc., 13
Teva Pharmaceutical Industries Ltd., 22
Union Carbide Corporation, I; 9 (upd.)
Univar Corporation, 9
Vista Chemical Company, I
Witco Corporation, I; 16 (upd.)
Zeneca Group PLC, 21

CONGLOMERATES

Accor SA, 10
AEG A.G., I
Alcatel Alsthom Compagnie Générale
   d'Electricité, 9
Alco Standard Corporation, I
Alfa, S.A. de C.V., 19
Allied-Signal Inc., I
AMFAC Inc., I
Aramark Corporation, 13
Archer-Daniels-Midland Company, I; 11
   (upd.)
Arkansas Best Corporation, 16
Barlow Rand Ltd., I
Bat Industries PLC, I
Bond Corporation Holdings Limited, 10
BTR PLC, I
C. Itoh & Company Ltd., I
Cargill Inc., 13 (upd.)
CBI Industries, Inc., 7
Chemed Corporation, 13
Chesebrough-Pond's USA, Inc., 8
CITIC Pacific Ltd., 18
Colt Industries Inc., I
Daewoo Group, 18 (upd.)
Deere & Company, 21 (upd.)
Delaware North Companies Incorporated, 7
Desc, S.A. de C.V., 23
The Dial Corp., 8
Elders IXL Ltd., I
Engelhard Corporation, 21 (upd.)
Farley Northwest Industries, Inc., I
First Pacific Company Limited, 18
Fisher Companies, Inc., 15
Fletcher Challenge Ltd., 19 (upd.)
FMC Corporation, I; 11 (upd.)
Fuqua Industries, Inc., I
Gillett Holdings, Inc., 7
Grand Metropolitan PLC, 14 (upd.)
Great American Management and
   Investment, Inc., 8

Greyhound Corporation, I
Grupo Carso, S.A. de C.V., 21
Grupo Industrial Bimbo, 19
Gulf & Western Inc., I
Hankyu Corporation, 23 (upd.)
Hanson PLC, III; 7 (upd.)
Hitachi Ltd., I, 12 (upd.)
Hutchison Whampoa Ltd., 18
IC Industries, Inc., I
Inchcape plc, 16 (upd.)
Ingram Industries, Inc., 11
Instituto Nacional de Industria, I
International Controls Corporation, 10
International Telephone & Telegraph
   Corporation, I; 11 (upd.)
Istituto per la Ricostruzione Industriale, I
Jardine Matheson Holdings Limited, I; 20
   (upd.)
Jason Incorporated, 23
Jefferson Smurfit Group plc, 19 (upd.)
Justin Industries, Inc., 19
Kao Corporation, 20 (upd.)
Katy Industries, Inc., I
Kesko Ltd (Kesko Oy), 8
Kidde, Inc., I
KOC Holding A.S., I
K2 Inc., 16
Lancaster Colony Corporation, 8
Lear Siegler, Inc., I
Leucadia National Corporation, 11
Litton Industries, Inc., I; 11 (upd.)
Loews Corporation, I; 12 (upd.)
Loral Corporation, 8
LTV Corporation, I
Marubeni K.K., I
MAXXAM Inc., 8
McKesson Corporation, I
Menasha Corporation, 8
Metallgesellschaft AG, 16 (upd.)
Metromedia Co., 7
Minnesota Mining & Manufacturing
   Company, I; 8 (upd.)
Mitsubishi Corporation, I; 12 (upd.)
Mitsui Bussan K.K., I
NACCO Industries, Inc., 7
National Service Industries, Inc., 11
Nissho Iwai K.K., I
Norsk Hydro A.S., 10
Ogden Corporation, I
Onex Corporation, 16
Orkla A/S, 18
Park-Ohio Industries Inc., 17
Pentair, Inc., 7
Preussag AG, 17
Pubco Corporation, 17
Pulsar Internacional S.A., 21
The Rank Organisation Plc, 14 (upd.)
Red Apple Group, Inc., 23
Rubbermaid Incorporated, 20 (upd.)
Samsung Group, I
San Miguel Corporation, 15
Sara Lee Corporation, 15 (upd.)
ServiceMaster Inc., 23 (upd.)
Sime Darby Berhad, 14
Standex International Corporation, 17
Stinnes AG, 23 (upd.)
Sudbury Inc., 16
Sumitomo Corporation, I; 11 (upd.)
Swire Pacific Ltd., I; 16 (upd.)
Talley Industries, Inc., 16
Teledyne, Inc., I; 10 (upd.)
Tenneco Inc., I; 10 (upd.)
Textron Inc., I
Thorn Emi PLC, I
TI Group plc, 17
Time Warner Inc., IV, 7 (upd.)
Tomkins plc, 11
Toshiba Corporation, I; 12 (upd.)

Tractebel S.A., 20
Transamerica Corporation, I; 13 (upd.)
The Tranzonic Cos., 15
Triarc Companies, Inc., 8
TRW Inc., I; 11 (upd.)
Unilever PLC, II; 7 (upd.)
Valhi, Inc., 19
Valores Industriales S.A., 19
Veba A.G., I; 15 (upd.)
Viacom Inc., 23 (upd.)
Virgin Group PLC, 12
W.R. Grace & Company, I
Wheaton Industries, 8
Whitbread PLC, 20 (upd.)
Whitman Corporation, 10 (upd.)
Whittaker Corporation, I
WorldCorp, Inc., 10

CONSTRUCTION

A. Johnson & Company H.B., I
ABC Supply Co., Inc., 22
Abrams Industries Inc., 23
AMREP Corporation, 21
The Austin Company, 8
Baratt Developments PLC, I
Beazer Homes USA, Inc., 17
Bechtel Group Inc., I
Bilfinger & Berger Bau A.G., I
Bird Corporation, 19
Black & Veatch LLP, 22
Bouygues, I
Brown & Root, Inc., 13
CalMat Co., 19
Centex Corporation, 8
Cianbro Corporation, 14
The Clark Construction Group, Inc., 8
Dillingham Corporation, I
Dominion Homes, Inc., 19
Eurotunnel PLC, 13
Fairclough Construction Group PLC, I
Fleetwood Enterprises, Inc., 22 (upd.)
Fluor Corporation, I; 8 (upd.)
George Wimpey PLC, 12
J.A. Jones, Inc., 16
John Brown PLC, I
John Laing PLC, I
Kajima Corporation, I
Kaufman and Broad Home Corporation, 8
Kitchell Corporation, 14
The Koll Company, 8
Komatsu Ltd., 16 (upd.)
Kumagai Gumi Company, Ltd., I
L'Entreprise Jean Lefebvre, 23
Lennar Corporation, 11
Lincoln Property Company, 8
Linde A.G., I
Mellon-Stuart Company, I
Michael Baker Corp., 14
Morrison Knudsen Corporation, 7
New Holland N.V., 22
NVR L.P., 8
Ohbayashi Corporation, I
The Peninsular & Oriental Steam
   Navigation Company (Bovis Division), I
Perini Corporation, 8
Peter Kiewit Sons' Inc., 8
Philipp Holzmann AG, 17
Pulte Corporation, 8
The Ryland Group, Inc., 8
Taylor Woodrow PLC, I
Toll Brothers Inc., 15
Trammell Crow Company, 8
Tridel Enterprises Inc., 9
The Turner Corporation, 8; 23 (upd.)
U.S. Home Corporation, 8
Walter Industries, Inc., 22 (upd.)
Wood Hall Trust PLC, I

CONTAINERS

Ball Corporation, I; 10 (upd.)
Clarcor Inc., 17
Continental Can Co., Inc., 15
Continental Group Company, I
Crown, Cork & Seal Company, Inc., I, 13
Gaylord Container Corporation, 8
Golden Belt Manufacturing Co., 16
Greif Bros. Corporation, 15
Inland Container Corporation, 8
Keyes Fibre Company, 9
Liqui-Box Corporation, 16
The Longaberger Company, 12
Longview Fibre Company, 8
The Mead Corporation, 19 (upd.)
Metal Box PLC, I
National Can Corporation, I
Owens-Illinois, Inc., I
Primerica Corporation, I
Reynolds Metals Company, 19 (upd.)
Sealright Co., Inc., 17
Sonoco Products Company, 8
Thermos Company, 16
Toyo Seikan Kaisha, Ltd., I

DRUGS

A.L. Pharma Inc., 12
Abbott Laboratories, I; 11 (upd.)
ALZA Corporation, 10
American Home Products, I; 10 (upd.)
Amgen, Inc., 10
A.B. Astra, I
Astra AB, 20 (upd.)
Baxter International Inc., I; 10 (upd.)
Bayer A.G., I; 13 (upd.)
Becton, Dickinson & Company, I
Block Drug Company, Inc., 8
Carter-Wallace, Inc., 8
Chiron Corporation, 10
Ciba-Geigy Ltd., I; 8 (upd.)
D&K Wholesale Drug, Inc., 14
Eli Lilly & Company, I; 11 (upd.)
F. Hoffmann-Laroche & Company A.G., I
Fisons plc, 9; 23 (upd.)
FoxMeyer Health Corporation, 16
Fujisawa Pharmaceutical Company Ltd., I
G.D. Searle & Company, I; 12 (upd.)
Genentech, Inc., I; 8 (upd.)
Genetics Institute, Inc., 8
Genzyme Corporation, 13
Glaxo Holdings PLC, I; 9 (upd.)
Johnson & Johnson, III; 8 (upd.)
Marion Merrell Dow, Inc., I; 9 (upd.)
McKesson Corporation, 12
Merck & Co., Inc., I; 11 (upd.)
Miles Laboratories, I
Moore Medical Corp., 17
Mylan Laboratories, I
Mylan Laboratories Inc., 20 (upd.)
National Patent Development Corporation, 13
Novo Industri A/S, I
Pfizer Inc., I; 9 (upd.)
Pharmacia A.B., I
Quintiles Transnational Corporation, 21
R.P. Scherer, I
Roberts Pharmaceutical Corporation, 16
Roche Bioscience, 14 (upd.)
Rorer Group, I
Roussel Uclaf, I; 8 (upd.)
Sandoz Ltd., I
Sankyo Company, Ltd., I
Sanofi Group, I
Schering A.G., I
Schering-Plough Corporation, I; 14 (upd.)
Shionogi & Co., Ltd., 17 (upd.)
Sigma-Aldrich, I

SmithKline Beckman Corporation, I
Squibb Corporation, I
Sterling Drug, Inc., I
Syntex Corporation, I
Takeda Chemical Industries, Ltd., I
Teva Pharmaceutical Industries Ltd., 22
The Upjohn Company, I; 8 (upd.)
Vitalink Pharmacy Services, Inc., 15
Warner-Lambert Co., I; 10 (upd.)
Watson Pharmaceuticals Inc., 16
The Wellcome Foundation Ltd., I

ELECTRICAL & ELECTRONICS

ABB ASEA Brown Boveri Ltd., II, 22 (upd.)
Acer Inc., 16
Acuson Corporation, 10
Adtran Inc., 22
Advanced Technology Laboratories, Inc., 9
AlliedSignal Inc., 22 (upd.)
Alpine Electronics, Inc., 13
Alps Electric Co., Ltd., II
Altera Corporation, 18
Altron Incorporated, 20
AMP Incorporated, II; 14 (upd.)
Analog Devices, Inc., 10
Analogic Corporation, 23
Anam Group, 23
Andrew Corporation, 10
Arrow Electronics, Inc., 10
Atari Corporation, 9; 23 (upd.)
Atmel Corporation, 17
Autodesk, Inc., 10
Avnet Inc., 9
Bicoastal Corporation, II
Bose Corporation, 13
Boston Acoustics, Inc., 22
Burr-Brown Corporation, 19
Cabletron Systems, Inc., 10
Canon Inc., 18 (upd.)
Casio Computer Co., Ltd., 16 (upd.)
Citizen Watch Co., Ltd., 21 (upd.)
Cobra Electronics Corporation, 14
Compagnie Générale d'Électricité, II
Cooper Industries, Inc., II
Cray Research, Inc., 16 (upd.)
Cubic Corporation, 19
Cypress Semiconductor Corporation, 20
Dallas Semiconductor Corp., 13
DH Technology, Inc., 18
Digi International Inc., 9
Discreet Logic Inc., 20
Dixons Group plc, 19 (upd.)
Dolby Laboratories Inc., 20
Dynatech Corporation, 13
E-Systems, Inc., 9
Electronics for Imaging, Inc., 15
Emerson Electric Co., II
ESS Technology, Inc., 22
Everex Systems, Inc., 16
Exar Corp., 14
Exide Electronics Group, Inc., 20
Fluke Corporation, 15
Foxboro Company, 13
Fuji Electric Co., Ltd., II
Fujitsu Limited, 16 (upd.)
General Electric Company, II; 12 (upd.)
General Electric Company, PLC, II
General Instrument Corporation, 10
General Signal Corporation, 9
GM Hughes Electronics Corporation, II
Goldstar Co., Ltd., 12
Gould Electronics, Inc., 14
Hamilton Beach/Proctor-Silex Inc., 17
Harman International Industries Inc., 15
Harris Corporation, II; 20 (upd.)
Holophane Corporation, 19

Honeywell Inc., II; 12 (upd.)
Hubbell Incorporated, 9
Hughes Supply, Inc., 14
Hutchinson Technology Incorporated, 18
In Focus Systems, Inc., 22
Intel Corporation, II; 10 (upd.)
Itel Corporation, 9
Keithley Instruments Inc., 16
Kemet Corp., 14
Kent Electronics Corporation, 17
Kingston Technology Corporation, 20
KitchenAid, 8
KnowledgeWare Inc., 9
Kollmorgen Corporation, 18
Koor Industries Ltd., II
Kyocera Corporation, II
Lattice Semiconductor Corp., 16
Legrand SA, 21
Linear Technology, Inc., 16
Loral Corporation, 9
Lowrance Electronics, Inc., 18
LSI Logic Corporation, 13
Lucky-Goldstar, II
MagneTek, Inc., 15
Marquette Electronics, Inc., 13
Matsushita Electric Industrial Co., Ltd., II
Maxim Integrated Products, Inc., 16
Methode Electronics, Inc., 13
Mitel Corporation, 18
Mitsubishi Electric Corporation, II
Motorola, Inc., II; 11 (upd.)
National Instruments Corporation, 22
National Presto Industries, Inc., 16
National Semiconductor Corporation, II
NEC Corporation, II; 21 (upd.)
Nokia Corporation, II; 17 (upd.)
Oak Technology, Inc., 22
Oki Electric Industry Company, Limited, II
Omron Tateisi Electronics Company, II
Otter Tail Power Company, 18
Palomar Medical Technologies, Inc., 22
The Peak Technologies Group, Inc., 14
Peavey Electronics Corporation, 16
Philips Electronics N.V., II; 13 (upd.)
Philips Electronics North America Corp., 13
Pioneer-Standard Electronics Inc., 19
Pittway Corporation, 9
The Plessey Company, PLC, II
Potter & Brumfield Inc., 11
Premier Industrial Corporation, 9
Racal Electronics PLC, II
Radius Inc., 16
Raychem Corporation, 8
Rayovac Corporation, 13
Raytheon Company, II; 11 (upd.)
RCA Corporation, II
Read-Rite Corp., 10
Reliance Electric Company, 9
Rexel, Inc., 15
Richardson Electronics, Ltd., 17
The Rival Company, 19
S&C Electric Company, 15
Samsung Electronics Co., Ltd., 14
Sanyo Electric Company, Ltd., II
Schneider S.A., II; 18 (upd.)
SCI Systems, Inc., 9
Sensormatic Electronics Corp., 11
Sharp Corporation, II; 12 (upd.)
Sheldahl Inc., 23
Siemens A.G., II; 14 (upd.)
Silicon Graphics Incorporated, 9
Solectron Corp., 12
Sony Corporation, II; 12 (upd.)
Sterling Electronics Corp., 18
Sumitomo Electric Industries, Ltd., II
Sunbeam-Oster Co., Inc., 9
SyQuest Technology, Inc., 18

Tandy Corporation, II; 12 (upd.)
Tatung Co., 23
TDK Corporation, II; 17 (upd.)
Tech-Sym Corporation, 18
Tektronix, Inc., 8
Telxon Corporation, 10
Teradyne, Inc., 11
Texas Instruments Incorporated, II; 11
  (upd.)
Thomson S.A., II
Tops Appliance City, Inc., 17
Toromont Industries, Ltd., 21
Varian Associates Inc., 12
Victor Company of Japan, Ltd., II
Vishay Intertechnology, Inc., 21
Vitro Corp., 10
VLSI Technology, Inc., 16
Westinghouse Electric Corporation, II; 12
  (upd.)
Wyle Electronics, 14
Yageo Corporation, 16
Zenith Data Systems, Inc., 10
Zenith Electronics Corporation, II; 13
  (upd.)
Zoom Telephonics, Inc., 18
Zytec Corporation, 19

ENGINEERING & MANAGEMENT SERVICES

AAON, Inc., 22
Analytic Sciences Corporation, 10
The Austin Company, 8
Brown & Root, Inc., 13
CDI Corporation, 6
CH2M Hill Ltd., 22
Corrections Corporation of America, 23
CRSS Inc., 6
Day & Zimmermann Inc., 9
Donaldson Co. Inc., 16
EG&G Incorporated, 8
Essef Corporation, 18
Foster Wheeler Corporation, 6; 23 (upd.)
Framatome SA, 19
Harding Lawson Associates Group, Inc., 16
Harza Engineering Company, 14
Jacobs Engineering Group Inc., 6
JWP Inc., 9
Layne Christensen Company, 19
McKinsey & Company, Inc., 9
Ogden Corporation, 6
The Parsons Corporation, 8
Rosemount Inc., 15
Rust International Inc., 11
Science Applications International
  Corporation, 15
Stone & Webster, Inc., 13
Susquehanna Pfaltzgraff Company, 8
Sverdrup Corporation, 14
Tracor Inc., 17
United Dominion Industries Limited, 8; 16
  (upd.)
VECO International, Inc., 7

ENTERTAINMENT & LEISURE

All American Communications Inc., 20
Alliance Entertainment Corp., 17
Amblin Entertainment, 21
AMC Entertainment Inc., 12
Aprilia SpA, 17
Argosy Gaming Company, 21
Asahi National Broadcasting Company,
  Ltd., 9
Aspen Skiing Company, 15
The Atlantic Group, 23
Autotote Corporation, 20
Aztar Corporation, 13
Baker & Taylor, Inc., 16

Bertelsmann AG, 15 (upd.)
Bertucci's Inc., 16
Blockbuster Entertainment Corporation, 9
Boston Celtics Limited Partnership, 14
British Broadcasting Corporation, 7
British Sky Broadcasting Group Plc, 20
Cablevision Systems Corporation, 7
Capital Cities/ABC Inc., II
Carlson Companies, Inc., 22 (upd.)
Carmike Cinemas, Inc., 14
CBS Inc., II; 6 (upd.)
Cedar Fair, L.P., 22
Central Independent Television, 7; 23
  (upd.)
Cineplex Odeon Corporation, 6; 23 (upd.)
Columbia Pictures Entertainment, Inc., II
Columbia TriStar Motion Pictures
  Companies, 12 (upd.)
Comcast Corporation, 7
Continental Cablevision, Inc., 7
Corporation for Public Broadcasting, 14
Cox Enterprises, Inc., 22 (upd.)
Cruise America Inc., 21
Cunard Line Ltd., 23
dick clark productions, inc., 16
E! Entertainment Television Inc., 17
Euro Disneyland SCA, 20
First Team Sports, Inc., 22
Gaylord Entertainment Company, 11
Gibson Guitar Corp., 16
Granada Group PLC, II
Grand Casinos, Inc., 20
Hanna-Barbera Cartoons Inc., 23
Harrah's Entertainment, Inc., 16
Hollywood Casino Corporation, 21
Hollywood Park, Inc., 20
Home Box Office Inc., 7; 23 (upd.)
International Family Entertainment Inc., 13
International Speedway Corporation, 19
The Intrawest Corporation, 15
Irvin Feld & Kenneth Feld Productions,
  Inc., 15
Jackpot Enterprises Inc., 21
Japan Broadcasting Corporation, 7
The Jim Henson Company, 23
King World Productions, Inc., 9
Knott's Berry Farm, 18
Ladbroke Group PLC, II; 21 (upd.)
Lego A/S, 13
Lionel L.L.C., 16
LIVE Entertainment Inc., 20
Lucasfilm Ltd., 12
The Marcus Corporation, 21
MCA Inc., II
Media General, Inc., 7
Metromedia Companies, 14
MGM Grand Inc., 17
MGM/UA Communications Company, II
Muzak, Inc., 18
National Broadcasting Company, Inc., II; 6
  (upd.)
National Public Radio, 19
O'Charley's Inc., 19
Orion Pictures Corporation, 6
Paramount Pictures Corporation, II
Players International, Inc., 22
PolyGram N.V., 23
President Casinos, Inc., 22
Princess Cruise Lines, 22
Promus Companies, Inc., 9
Putt-Putt Golf Courses of America, Inc., 23
Rank Organisation PLC, II
Rhino Entertainment Company, 18
Ride, Inc., 22
Royal Caribbean Cruises Ltd., 22
S-K-I Limited, 15
Salomon Worldwide, 20
Santa Fe Gaming Corporation, 19

Schwinn Cycle and Fitness L.P., 19
Sega of America, Inc., 10
Showboat, Inc., 19
Six Flags Theme Parks, Inc., 17
Spelling Entertainment Group, Inc., 14
Stuart Entertainment Inc., 16
Tele-Communications, Inc., II
Television Española, S.A., 7
Thomas Cook Travel Inc., 9
The Thomson Corporation, 8
Ticketmaster Corp., 13
Touristik Union International GmbH. and
  Company K.G., II
Toy Biz, Inc., 18
Turner Broadcasting System, Inc., II; 6
  (upd.)
Twentieth Century Fox Film Corporation,
  II
Vail Associates, Inc., 11
Viacom Inc., 23 (upd.)
Viacom International Inc., 7
Walt Disney Company, II; 6 (upd.)
Warner Communications Inc., II

FINANCIAL SERVICES: BANKS

Abbey National PLC, 10
Abigail Adams National Bancorp, Inc., 23
Algemene Bank Nederland N.V., II
Allied Irish Banks, plc, 16
American Residential Mortgage
  Corporation, 8
AmSouth Bancorporation, 12
Amsterdam-Rotterdam Bank N.V., II
Anchor Bancorp, Inc., 10
Australia and New Zealand Banking Group
  Ltd., II
Banc One Corporation, 10
Banca Commerciale Italiana SpA, II
Banco Bilbao Vizcaya, S.A., II
Banco Bradesco S.A., 13
Banco Central, II
Banco do Brasil S.A., II
Banco Espírito Santo e Comercial de
  Lisboa S.A., 15
Banco Itaú S.A., 19
Bank Austria AG, 23
Bank Brussels Lambert, II
Bank Hapoalim B.M., II
Bank of Boston Corporation, II
Bank of Mississippi, Inc., 14
Bank of Montreal, II
Bank of New England Corporation, II
The Bank of New York Company, Inc., II
The Bank of Nova Scotia, II
Bank of Tokyo, Ltd., II
Bank of Tokyo-Mitsubishi Ltd., 15 (upd.)
BankAmerica Corporation, II; 8 (upd.)
Bankers Trust New York Corporation, II
Banque Nationale de Paris S.A., II
Barclays PLC, II; 20 (upd.)
BarclaysAmerican Mortgage Corporation,
  11
Barings PLC, 14
Barnett Banks, Inc., 9
BayBanks, Inc., 12
Bayerische Hypotheken- und Wechsel-
  Bank AG, II
Bayerische Vereinsbank A.G., II
Beneficial Corporation, 8
Boatmen's Bancshares Inc., 15
Canadian Imperial Bank of Commerce, II
Casco Northern Bank, 14
The Chase Manhattan Corporation, II; 13
  (upd.)
Chemical Banking Corporation, II; 14
  (upd.)
Citicorp, II; 9 (upd.)

Commercial Credit Company, 8
Commercial Federal Corporation, 12
Commerzbank A.G., II
Compagnie Financiere de Paribas, II
Continental Bank Corporation, II
CoreStates Financial Corp, 17
Countrywide Credit Industries, Inc., 16
Crédit Agricole, II
Crédit Lyonnais, 9
Crédit National S.A., 9
Crédit Suisse, II
Credit Suisse Group, 21 (upd.)
Credito Italiano, II
The Dai-Ichi Kangyo Bank Ltd., II
The Daiwa Bank, Ltd., II
Dauphin Deposit Corporation, 14
Deposit Guaranty Corporation, 17
Deutsche Bank A.G., II; 14 (upd.)
Dime Savings Bank of New York, F.S.B., 9
Donaldson, Lufkin & Jenrette, Inc., 22
Dresdner Bank A.G., II
Fifth Third Bancorp, 13
First Bank System Inc., 12
First Chicago Corporation, II
First Commerce Bancshares, Inc., 15
First Commerce Corporation, 11
First Empire State Corporation, 11
First Fidelity Bank, N.A., New Jersey, 9
First Hawaiian, Inc., 11
First Interstate Bancorp, II
First Nationwide Bank, 14
First of America Bank Corporation, 8
First Security Corporation, 11
First Tennessee National Corporation, 11
First Union Corporation, 10
First Virginia Banks, Inc., 11
Firstar Corporation, 11
Fleet Financial Group, Inc., 9
Fourth Financial Corporation, 11
The Fuji Bank, Ltd., II
Generale Bank, II
The Governor and Company of the Bank of Scotland, 10
Great Lakes Bancorp, 8
Great Western Financial Corporation, 10
Grupo Financiero Serfin, S.A., 19
H.F. Ahmanson & Company, II; 10 (upd.)
Hancock Holding Company, 15
The Hongkong and Shanghai Banking Corporation Limited, II
HSBC Holdings plc, 12
Huntington Bancshares Inc., 11
The Industrial Bank of Japan, Ltd., II
J.P. Morgan & Co. Incorporated, II
Japan Leasing Corporation, 8
Kansallis-Osake-Pankki, II
KeyCorp, 8
Kredietbank N.V., II
Lloyds Bank PLC, II
Long Island Bancorp, Inc., 16
Long-Term Credit Bank of Japan, Ltd., II
Manufacturers Hanover Corporation, II
MBNA Corporation, 12
Mellon Bank Corporation, II
Mercantile Bankshares Corp., 11
Meridian Bancorp, Inc., 11
Metropolitan Financial Corporation, 13
Michigan National Corporation, 11
Midland Bank PLC, II; 17 (upd.)
The Mitsubishi Bank, Ltd., II
The Mitsubishi Trust & Banking Corporation, II
The Mitsui Bank, Ltd., II
The Mitsui Trust & Banking Company, Ltd., II
National City Corp., 15
National Westminster Bank PLC, II

NationsBank Corporation, 10
NBD Bancorp, Inc., 11
NCNB Corporation, II
Nippon Credit Bank, II
Norinchukin Bank, II
Northern Trust Company, 9
NVR L.P., 8
Old Kent Financial Corp., 11
Old National Bancorp, 15
PNC Bank Corp., 13 (upd.)
PNC Financial Corporation, II
Pulte Corporation, 8
Republic New York Corporation, 11
Riggs National Corporation, 13
The Royal Bank of Canada, II; 21 (upd.)
The Royal Bank of Scotland Group plc, 12
The Ryland Group, Inc., 8
St. Paul Bank for Cooperatives, 8
The Sanwa Bank, Ltd., II; 15 (upd.)
SBC Warburg, 14
Seattle First National Bank Inc., 8
Security Capital Corporation, 17
Security Pacific Corporation, II
Shawmut National Corporation, 13
Signet Banking Corporation, 11
Skandinaviska Enskilda Banken, II
Société Générale, II
Society Corporation, 9
Southtrust Corporation, 11
Standard Chartered PLC, II
Standard Federal Bank, 9
Star Banc Corporation, 11
State Street Boston Corporation, 8
The Sumitomo Bank, Ltd., II
The Sumitomo Trust & Banking Company, Ltd., II
The Summit Bancorporation, 14
SunTrust Banks Inc., 23
Svenska Handelsbanken, II
Swiss Bank Corporation, II
Synovus Financial Corp., 12
The Taiyo Kobe Bank, Ltd., II
The Tokai Bank, Limited, II; 15 (upd.)
The Toronto-Dominion Bank, II
TSB Group plc, 12
U.S. Bancorp, 14
U.S. Trust Corp., 17
Union Bank of California, 16
Union Bank of Switzerland, II
Wachovia Bank of Georgia, N.A., 16
Wachovia Bank of South Carolina, N.A., 16
Wachovia Corporation, 12
Washington Mutual, Inc., 17
Wells Fargo & Company, II; 12 (upd.)
West One Bancorp, 11
Westamerica Bancorporation, 17
Westdeutsche Landesbank Girozentrale, II
Westpac Banking Corporation, II
Whitney Holding Corporation, 21
The Yasuda Trust and Banking Company, Ltd., II; 17 (upd.)
Zions Bancorporation, 12

FINANCIAL SERVICES: NON-BANKS

A.G. Edwards, Inc., 8
ADVANTA Corp., 8
American Express Company, II; 10 (upd.)
American General Finance Corp., 11
Arthur Andersen & Company, Société Coopérative, 10
Avco Financial Services Inc., 13
Bear Stearns Companies, Inc., II; 10 (upd.)
Bozzuto's, Inc., 13
Cash America International; Inc., 20
Cetelem S.A., 21

Charles Schwab Corp., 8
Citfed Bancorp, Inc., 16
Coopers & Lybrand, 9
Credit Acceptance Corporation, 18
CS First Boston Inc., II
Daiwa Securities Company, Limited, II
Dean Witter, Discover & Co., 12
Dow Jones Telerate, Inc., 10
Drexel Burnham Lambert Incorporated, II
E*Trade Group, Inc., 20
Eaton Vance Corporation, 18
Fair, Isaac and Company, 18
Federal National Mortgage Association, II
Fidelity Investments Inc., II; 14 (upd.)
First USA, Inc., 11
FMR Corp., 8
Fortis, Inc., 15
Franklin Resources, Inc., 9
Goldman, Sachs & Co., II; 20 (upd.)
Green Tree Financial Corporation, 11
Gruntal & Co., L.L.C., 20
H & R Block, Incorporated, 9
Household International, Inc., II; 21 (upd.)
Inter-Regional Financial Group, Inc., 15
Istituto per la Ricostruzione Industriale S.p.A., 11
The John Nuveen Company, 21
Kleinwort Benson Group PLC, II
KPMG Worldwide, 10
MasterCard International, Inc., 9
Merrill Lynch & Co., Inc., II; 13 (upd.)
Morgan Grenfell Group PLC, II
Morgan Stanley Group Inc., II; 16 (upd.)
National Association of Securities Dealers, Inc., 10
National Auto Credit, Inc., 16
New Street Capital Inc., 8
New York Stock Exchange, Inc., 9
The Nikko Securities Company Limited, II; 9 (upd.)
Nippon Shinpan Company, Ltd., II
Nomura Securities Company, Limited, II; 9 (upd.)
Orix Corporation, II
PaineWebber Group Inc., II, 22 (upd.)
Piper Jaffray Companies Inc., 22
The Quick & Reilly Group, Inc., 20
Safeguard Scientifics, Inc., 10
Salomon Inc., II; 13 (upd.)
SBC Warburg, 14
Shearson Lehman Brothers Holdings Inc., II; 9 (upd.)
Smith Barney Inc., 15
State Street Boston Corporation, 8
Student Loan Marketing Association, II
T. Rowe Price Associates, Inc., 11
Total System Services, Inc., 18
Trilon Financial Corporation, II
The Vanguard Group of Investment Companies, 14
VeriFone, Inc., 18
Visa International, 9
Waddell & Reed, Inc., 22
Washington Federal, Inc., 17
Waterhouse Investor Services, Inc., 18
Yamaichi Securities Company, Limited, II

FOOD PRODUCTS

Agway, Inc., 7
Ajinomoto Co., Inc., II
Alberto-Culver Company, 8
Aldi Group, 13
Alpine Lace Brands, Inc., 18
American Crystal Sugar Company, 11
American Maize-Products Co., 14
Associated British Foods PLC, II; 13 (upd.)

Associated Milk Producers, Inc., 11
Barilla G. e R. Fratelli S.p.A., 17
Beatrice Company, II
Beech-Nut Nutrition Corporation, 21
Ben & Jerry's Homemade, Inc., 10
Besnier SA, 19
Bestfoods, 22 (upd.)
Booker PLC, 13
Borden, Inc., II, 22 (upd.)
Brach and Brock Confections, Inc., 15
Brothers Gourmet Coffees, Inc., 20
Broughton Foods Co., 17
Brown & Haley, 23
BSN Groupe S.A., II
Burger King Corporation, 17 (upd.)
Cadbury Schweppes PLC, II
Cagle's, Inc., 20
Campbell Soup Company, II; 7 (upd.)
Canada Packers Inc., II
Cargill Inc., 13 (upd.)
Carnation Company, II
Castle & Cook, Inc., II
Castle & Cooke, Inc., 20 (upd.)
Cattleman's, Inc., 20
Celestial Seasonings, Inc., 16
Central Soya Company, Inc., 7
Chiquita Brands International, Inc., 7; 21
  (upd.)
Chock Full o'Nuts Corp., 17
The Clorox Company, 22 (upd.)
Coca Cola Enterprises, Inc., 13
Conagra, Inc., II; 12 (upd.)
Continental Grain Company, 10; 13 (upd.)
CPC International Inc., II
Curtice-Burns Foods, Inc., 7; 21 (upd.)
Dalgery, PLC, II
Dannon Co., Inc., 14
Darigold, Inc., 9
Dawn Food Products, Inc., 17
Dean Foods Company, 7; 21 (upd.)
DeKalb Genetics Corporation, 17
Del Monte Corporation, 7
Del Monte Foods Company, 23 (upd.)
Di Giorgio Corp., 12
Dole Food Company, Inc., 9
Doskocil Companics, Inc., 12
Dreyer's Grand Ice Cream, Inc., 17
Emge Packing Co., Inc., 11
ERLY Industries Inc., 17
Eskimo Pie Corporation, 21
Farmland Foods, Inc., 7
Fieldale Farms Corporation, 23
Fleer Corporation, 15
Flowers Industries, Inc., 12
FoodBrands America, Inc., 23
Fresh America Corporation, 20
Fromageries Bel, 23
General Mills, Inc., II; 10 (upd.)
George A. Hormel and Company, II
Gerber Products Company, 7; 21 (upd.)
Gold Kist Inc., 17
Good Humor-Breyers Ice Cream Company,
  14
Gorton's, 13
Goya Foods Inc., 22
Grist Mill Company, 15
H.J. Heinz Company, II; 11 (upd.)
The Hartz Mountain Corporation, 12
Hershey Foods Corporation, II; 15 (upd.)
Hillsdown Holdings, PLC, II
Hormel Foods Corporation, 18 (upd.)
Hudson Foods Inc., 13
Hunt-Wesson, Inc., 17
IBP, Inc., II; 21 (upd.)
Imperial Holly Corporation, 12
International Multifoods Corporation, 7
Interstate Bakeries Corporation, 12
Itoham Foods Inc., II

The J.M. Smucker Company, 11
J.R. Simplot Company, 16
Jacobs Suchard A.G., II
Jim Beam Brands Co., 14
John B. Sanfilippo & Son, Inc., 14
Kal Kan Foods, Inc., 22
Kellogg Company, II; 13 (upd.)
Kikkoman Corporation, 14
King Ranch, Inc., 14
Koninklijke Wessanen N.V., II
Kraft General Foods Inc., II; 7 (upd.)
Krispy Kreme Doughnut Corporation, 21
Lamb Weston, Inc., 23
Lance, Inc., 14
Land O'Lakes, Inc., II; 21 (upd.)
Malt-O-Meal Company, 22
Mars, Inc., 7
McCormick & Company, Incorporated, 7
McIlhenny Company, 20
McKee Foods Corporation, 7
Meiji Milk Products Company, Limited, II
Meiji Seika Kaisha, Ltd., 11
Mid-America Dairymen, Inc., 7
Mike-Sell's Inc., 15
Monfort, Inc., 13
Murphy Family Farms Inc., 22
Nabisco Foods Group, II; 7 (upd.)
Nantucket Allserve, Inc., 22
National Sea Products Ltd., 14
Nestlé S.A., II; 7 (upd.)
New England Confectionery Co., 15
Newhall Land and Farming Company, 14
Nippon Meat Packers, Inc., II
Nippon Suisan Kaisha, Limited, 11
Nisshin Flour Milling Company, Ltd., II
Northern Foods PLC, 10
NutraSweet Company, 8
Ocean Spray Cranberries, Inc., 7
Ore-Ida Foods Incorporated, 13
Oscar Mayer Foods Corp., 12
Perdue Farms Inc., 7; 23 (upd.)
Pet Incorporated, 7
Philip Morris Companies Inc., 18 (upd.)
Pilgrim's Pride Corporation, 7; 23 (upd.)
Pillsbury Company, II; 13 (upd.)
Pioneer Hi-Bred International, Inc., 9
The Procter & Gamble Company, III; 8
  (upd.)
Quaker Oats Company, II; 12 (upd.)
Ralston Purina Company, II; 13 (upd.)
Ranks Hovis McDougall PLC, II
Reckitt & Colman PLC, II
Rich Products Corporation, 7
Roland Murten A.G., 7
Rowntree Mackintosh, II
Russell Stover Candies Inc., 12
Sanderson Farms, Inc., 15
Sara Lee Corporation, II
Savannah Foods & Industries, Inc., 7
Schwan's Sales Enterprises, Inc., 7
Smithfield Foods, Inc., 7
Snow Brand Milk Products Company,
  Limited, II
SODIMA, II
Stouffer Corp., 8
Sun-Diamond Growers of California, 7
Supervalu Inc., 18 (upd.)
Sylvan, Inc., 22
Taiyo Fishery Company, Limited, II
Tasty Baking Co., 14
Tate & Lyle PLC, II
TCBY Enterprises Inc., 17
Thomas J. Lipton Company, 14
Thorn Apple Valley, Inc., 7, 22 (upd.)
TLC Beatrice International Holdings, Inc.,
  22
Tombstone Pizza Corporation, 13
Tone Brothers, Inc., 21

Tootsie Roll Industries Inc., 12
Tyson Foods, Incorporated, II; 14 (upd.)
Uncle Ben's Inc., 22
Unigate PLC, II
United Biscuits (Holdings) PLC, II
United Brands Company, II
United Foods, Inc., 21
Universal Foods Corporation, 7
Van Camp Seafood Company, Inc., 7
Vienna Sausage Manufacturing Co., 14
Wattie's Ltd., 7
Wisconsin Dairies, 7
WLR Foods, Inc., 21
Wm. Wrigley Jr. Company, 7
Worthington Foods, Inc., 14

FOOD SERVICES & RETAILERS

Albertson's Inc., II; 7 (upd.)
Aldi Group, 13
Alex Lee Inc., 18
America's Favorite Chicken Company,
  Inc., 7
American Stores Company, II
Applebee's International Inc., 14
ARA Services, II
Arby's Inc., 14
Argyll Group PLC, II
Ark Restaurants Corp., 20
Asahi Breweries, Ltd., 20 (upd.)
Asda Group PLC, II
Associated Grocers, Incorporated, 9
Au Bon Pain Co., Inc., 18
Back Bay Restaurant Group, Inc., 20
Benihana, Inc., 18
Big Bear Stores Co., 13
Blimpie International, Inc., 15
Bob Evans Farms, Inc., 9
Boston Chicken, Inc., 12
Brinker International, Inc., 10
Brookshire Grocery Company, 16
Bruno's Inc., 7
Buffets, Inc., 10
Burger King Corporation, II
C.H. Robinson, Inc., 11
California Pizza Kitchen Inc., 15
Cargill, Inc., II
Carlson Companies, Inc., 22 (upd.)
Carr-Gottstein Foods Co., 17
Casey's General Stores, Inc., 19
Chart House Enterprises, Inc., 17
Checkers Drive-Up Restaurants Inc., 16
The Cheesecake Factory Inc., 17
Chi-Chi's Inc., 13
Chick-fil-A Inc., 23
Cinnabon Inc., 23
The Circle K Corporation, II
CKE Restaurants, Inc., 19
Comptoirs Modernes S.A., 19
Consolidated Products Inc., 14
The Cooker Restaurant Corporation, 20
Cracker Barrel Old Country Store, Inc., 10
D'Agostino Supermarkets Inc., 19
Dairy Mart Convenience Stores, Inc., 7
Darden Restaurants, Inc., 16
DeMoulas / Market Basket Inc., 23
Domino's Pizza, Inc., 7; 21 (upd.)
Edeka Zentrale A.G., II
El Chico Restaurants, Inc., 19
Etablissements Economiques du Casino
  Guichard, Perrachon et Cie, S.C.A., 12
Flagstar Companies, Inc., 10
Fleming Companies, Inc., II
Food Lion, Inc., II; 15 (upd.)
Foodmaker, Inc., 14
The Fred W. Albrecht Grocery Co., 13
Fresh Choice, Inc., 20
The Gateway Corporation Ltd., II

George Weston Limited, II
Giant Food Inc., II, 22 (upd.)
Golden Corral Corporation, 10
Gordon Food Service Inc., 8
Grand Union Company, 7
The Great Atlantic & Pacific Tea
    Company, Inc., II; 16 (upd.)
Ground Round, Inc., 21
Groupe Promodès S.A., 19
Guyenne et Gascogne, 23
H.E. Butt Grocery Co., 13
Hannaford Bros. Co., 12
Hard Rock Cafe International, Inc., 12
Harris Teeter Inc., 23
Harry's Farmers Market Inc., 23
Hickory Farms, Inc., 17
Hooters of America, Inc., 18
Hughes Markets, Inc., 22
ICA AB, II
IHOP Corporation, 17
In-N-Out Burger, 19
Ingles Markets, Inc., 20
International Dairy Queen, Inc., 10
J Sainsbury PLC, II; 13 (upd.)
KFC Corporation, 7; 21 (upd.)
King Kullen Grocery Co., Inc., 15
Koninklijke Ahold N.V. (Royal Ahold), II,
    16 (upd.)
The Kroger Company, II; 15 (upd.)
Kwik Save Group plc, 11
Landry's Seafood Restaurants, Inc., 15
Little Caesars International, Inc., 7
Long John Silver's Restaurants Inc., 13
Luby's Cafeteria's, Inc., 17
Lund Food Holdings, Inc., 22
Marsh Supermarkets, Inc., 17
Max & Erma's Restaurants Inc., 19
McDonald's Corporation, II; 7 (upd.)
Megafoods Stores Inc., 13
Meijer Incorporated, 7
Metromedia Companies, 14
The Middleby Corporation, 22
Morrison Restaurants Inc., 11
Nash Finch Company, 8; 23 (upd.)
National Convenience Stores Incorporated,
    7
Noble Roman's Inc., 14
O'Charley's Inc., 19
The Oshawa Group Limited, II
Outback Steakhouse, Inc., 12
P&C Foods Inc., 8
Papa John's International, Inc., 15
Pathmark Stores, Inc., 23
Penn Traffic Company, 13
Perkins Family Restaurants, L.P., 22
Piccadilly Cafeterias, Inc., 19
Piggly Wiggly Southern, Inc., 13
Pizza Hut Inc., 7; 21 (upd.)
Planet Hollywood International, Inc., 18
Players International, Inc., 22
Ponderosa Steakhouse, 15
Provigo Inc., II
Publix Supermarkets Inc., 7
Quality Dining, Inc., 18
Quality Food Centers, Inc., 17
Rare Hospitality International Inc., 19
Restaurants Unlimited, Inc., 13
Richfood Holdings, Inc., 7
Riser Foods, Inc., 9
Roadhouse Grill, Inc., 22
Ruby Tuesday, Inc., 18
Ryan's Family Steak Houses, Inc., 15
Safeway Stores Incorporated, II
Sbarro, Inc., 16
Schultz Sav-O Stores, Inc., 21
Seaway Food Town, Inc., 15
Seneca Foods Corporation, 17
Service America Corp., 7

Shoney's, Inc., 7; 23 (upd.)
ShowBiz Pizza Time, Inc., 13
Smart & Final, Inc., 16
Smith's Food & Drug Centers, Inc., 8
Sonic Corporation, 14
The Southland Corporation, II; 7 (upd.)
Spartan Stores Inc., 8
Steinberg Incorporated, II
The Stop & Shop Companies, Inc., II
Super Food Services, Inc., 15
Super Valu Stores, Inc., II
Supermarkets General Holdings
    Corporation, II
Supervalu Inc., 18 (upd.)
Sysco Corporation, II
Taco Bell, 7
Taco Bell Corp., 21 (upd.)
Taco Cabana, Inc., 23
Taco John's International Inc., 15
Tesco PLC, II
Trader Joe's Co., 13
Travel Ports of America, Inc., 17
TW Services, Inc., II
Uno Restaurant Corporation, 18
VICORP Restaurants, Inc., 12
Village Super Market, Inc., 7
The Vons Companies, Incorporated, 7
Waffle House Inc., 14
Waldbaum, Inc., 19
Wawa Inc., 17
Wegmans Food Markets, Inc., 9
Weis Markets, Inc., 15
Wendy's International, Inc., 8; 23 (upd.)
Wetterau Incorporated, II
White Castle Systems, Inc., 12
Wild Oats Markets, Inc., 19
Winn-Dixie Stores, Inc., II; 21 (upd.)
Yucaipa Cos., 17

HEALTH & PERSONAL CARE PRODUCTS

Alberto-Culver Company, 8
Alco Health Services Corporation, III
Allergan, Inc., 10
American Safety Razor Company, 20
American Stores Company, 22 (upd.)
Amway Corporation, III; 13 (upd.)
Avon Products Inc., III; 19 (upd.)
Bausch & Lomb Inc., 7
BeautiControl Cosmetics, Inc., 21
Becton, Dickinson & Company, 11 (upd.)
Big B, Inc., 17
Bindley Western Industries, Inc., 9
Block Drug Company, Inc.
Bristol-Myers Squibb Company, III; 9
    (upd.)
C.R. Bard Inc., 9
Cardinal Health, Inc., 18
Carter-Wallace, Inc., 8
Chattem, Inc., 17
Chesebrough-Pond's USA, Inc., 8
The Clorox Company, III
CNS, Inc., 20
Colgate-Palmolive Company, III; 14 (upd.)
Conair Corp., 17
Cordis Corp., 19
Cosmair, Inc., 8
Dentsply International Inc., 10
DEP Corporation, 20
The Dial Corp., 23 (upd.)
Drackett Professional Products, 12
Elizabeth Arden Co., 8
Estée Lauder Inc., 9
Ethicon, Inc., 23
Forest Laboratories, Inc., 11
Forever Living Products International Inc.,
    17

French Fragrances, Inc., 22
General Nutrition Companies, Inc., 11
Genzyme Corporation, 13
The Gillette Company, III; 20 (upd.)
Groupe Yves Saint Laurent, 23
Guerlain, 23
Guest Supply, Inc., 18
Helen of Troy Corporation, 18
Helene Curtis Industries, Inc., 8
Henkel KGaA, III
Herbalife International, Inc., 17
Invacare Corporation, 11
IVAX Corporation, 11
Johnson & Johnson, III; 8 (upd.)
Kao Corporation, III
Kendall International, Inc., 11
Kimberly-Clark Corporation, III; 16 (upd.)
Kyowa Hakko Kogyo Co., Ltd., III
L'Oreal, III; 8 (upd.)
Lever Brothers Company, 9
Lion Corporation, III
Luxottica SpA, 17
Mary Kay Corporation, 9
Maxxim Medical Inc., 12
Medco Containment Services Inc., 9
Medtronic, Inc., 8
Nature's Sunshine Products, Inc., 15
Neutrogena Corporation, 17
Nutrition for Life International Inc., 22
Patterson Dental Co., 19
Perrigo Company, 12
Physician Sales & Service, Inc., 14
Playtex Products, Inc., 15
The Procter & Gamble Company, III; 8
    (upd.)
Revlon Group Inc., III
Revlon Inc., 17 (upd.)
Roche Biomedical Laboratories, Inc., 11
S.C. Johnson & Son, Inc., III
Schering-Plough Corporation, 14 (upd.)
Shionogi & Co., Ltd., III
Shiseido Company, Limited, III, 22 (upd.)
Slim-Fast Nutritional Foods International,
    Inc., 18
Smith & Nephew plc, 17
SmithKline Beecham PLC, III
Sunrise Medical Inc., 11
Tambrands Inc., 8
Turtle Wax, Inc., 15
United States Surgical Corporation, 10
Wella Group, III

HEALTH CARE SERVICES

American Medical International, Inc., III
Applied Bioscience International, Inc., 10
Beverly Enterprises, Inc., III; 16 (upd.)
Caremark International Inc., 10
COBE Laboratories, Inc., 13
Columbia/HCA Healthcare Corporation, 15
Community Psychiatric Centers, 15
CompDent Corporation, 22
Comprehensive Care Corporation, 15
Continental Medical Systems, Inc., 10
Express Scripts Incorporated, 17
Extendicare Health Services, Inc., 6
FHP International Corporation, 6
Genesis Health Ventures, Inc., 18
GranCare, Inc., 14
Health Care & Retirement Corporation, 22
Health Systems International, Inc., 11
HealthSouth Rehabilitation Corporation, 14
The Hillhaven Corporation, 14
Hooper Holmes, Inc., 22
Hospital Corporation of America, III
Humana Inc., III
Jenny Craig, Inc., 10
Kinetic Concepts, Inc. (KCI), 20

Manor Care, Inc., 6
Matria Healthcare, Inc., 17
Maxicare Health Plans, Inc., III
Mayo Foundation, 9
National Health Laboratories Incorporated, 11
National Medical Enterprises, Inc., III
NovaCare, Inc., 11
Oxford Health Plans, Inc., 16
PacifiCare Health Systems, Inc., 11
Palomar Medical Technologies, Inc., 22
PHP Healthcare Corporation, 22
St. Jude Medical, Inc., 11
Sierra Health Services, Inc., 15
U.S. Healthcare, Inc., 6
United HealthCare Corporation, 9
Universal Health Services, Inc., 6
Vencor, Inc., 16
Vivra, Inc., 18

HOTELS

Aztar Corporation, 13
Bristol Hotel Company, 23
Caesars World, Inc., 6
Carlson Companies, Inc., 22 (upd.)
Castle & Cooke, Inc., 20 (upd.)
Cedar Fair, L.P., 22
Choice Hotels International Inc., 14
Circus Circus Enterprises, Inc., 6
Club Méditerranée S.A., 21 (upd.)
Club Méditerranée SA, 6
Doubletree Corporation, 21
Euro Disneyland SCA, 20
Fibreboard Corporation, 16
Four Seasons Hotels Inc., 9
Grand Casinos, Inc., 20
Grand Hotel Krasnapolsky N.V., 23
Helmsley Enterprises, Inc., 9
Hilton Hotels Corporation, III; 19 (upd.)
Holiday Inns, Inc., III
Hospitality Franchise Systems, Inc., 11
Howard Johnson International, Inc., 17
Hyatt Corporation, III; 16 (upd.)
ITT Sheraton Corporation, III
La Quinta Inns, Inc., 11
Ladbroke Group PLC, 21 (upd.)
The Marcus Corporation, 21
Marriott Corporation, III
Marriott International, Inc., 21 (upd.)
Mirage Resorts, Inc., 6
Motel 6 Corporation, 13
Omni Hotels Corp., 12
Park Corp., 22
Players International, Inc., 22
Promus Companies, Inc., 9
Red Roof Inns, Inc., 18
Resorts International, Inc., 12
Ritz-Carlton Hotel Company, 9
Santa Fe Gaming Corporation, 19
Showboat, Inc., 19
Trusthouse Forte PLC, III
Westin Hotel Co., 9

INFORMATION TECHNOLOGY

Adobe Systems Incorporated, 10
Advanced Micro Devices, Inc., 6
Aldus Corporation, 10
Amdahl Corporation, III; 14 (upd.)
America Online, Inc., 10
American Business Information, Inc., 18
American Management Systems, Inc., 11
Amstrad PLC, III
Analytic Sciences Corporation, 10
Apple Computer, Inc., III; 6 (upd.)
Asanté Technologies, Inc., 20
ASK Group, Inc., 9
AST Research Inc., 9

AT&T Bell Laboratories, Inc., 13
AT&T Istel Ltd., 14
Autologic Information International, Inc., 20
Automatic Data Processing, Inc., III; 9 (upd.)
Autotote Corporation, 20
Aydin Corp., 19
Battelle Memorial Institute, Inc., 10
BBN Corp., 19
Bell and Howell Company, 9
Bloomberg L.P., 21
Booz Allen & Hamilton Inc., 10
Borland International, Inc., 9
Bowne & Co., Inc., 23
Brite Voice Systems, Inc., 20
Broderbund Software, Inc., 13
CACI International Inc., 21
Cadence Design Systems, Inc., 11
Caere Corporation, 20
CalComp Inc., 13
Canon Inc., III
Catalina Marketing Corporation, 18
CDW Computer Centers, Inc., 16
Cerner Corporation, 16
Cheyenne Software, Inc., 12
CHIPS and Technologies, Inc., 9
Ciber, Inc., 18
Cincom Systems Inc., 15
Cirrus Logic, Incorporated, 11
Cisco Systems, Inc., 11
Citizen Watch Co., Ltd., 21 (upd.)
Commodore International Ltd., 7
Compagnie des Machines Bull S.A., III
Compaq Computer Corporation, III; 6 (upd.)
CompuAdd Computer Corporation, 11
CompuCom Systems, Inc., 10
CompuServe Incorporated, 10
Computer Associates International, Inc., 6
Computer Data Systems, Inc., 14
Computer Sciences Corporation, 6
Computervision Corporation, 10
Compuware Corporation, 10
Comshare Inc., 23
Conner Peripherals, Inc., 6
Control Data Corporation, III
Control Data Systems, Inc., 10
Corel Corporation, 15
Corporate Software Inc., 9
Cray Research, Inc., III
CTG, Inc., 11
Data General Corporation, 8
Datapoint Corporation, 11
Dell Computer Corp., 9
Dialogic Corporation, 18
Digital Equipment Corporation, III; 6 (upd.)
The Dun & Bradstreet Corporation, IV; 19 (upd.)
Dun & Bradstreet Software Services Inc., 11
ECS S.A, 12
Edmark Corporation, 14
Egghead Inc., 9
El Camino Resources International, Inc., 11
Electronic Arts Inc., 10
Electronic Data Systems Corporation, III
EMC Corporation, 12
Encore Computer Corporation, 13
Evans & Sutherland Computer Corporation, 19
Exabyte Corporation, 12
First Financial Management Corporation, 11
Fiserv Inc., 11
FlightSafety International, Inc., 9
Franklin Electronic Publishers, Inc., 23

FTP Software, Inc., 20
Fujitsu Limited, III
Fujitsu-ICL Systems Inc., 11
Future Now, Inc., 12
Gartner Group, Inc., 21
Gateway 2000, Inc., 10
Hewlett-Packard Company, III; 6 (upd.)
Hyperion Software Corporation, 22
ICL plc, 6
Imation Corporation, 20
Information Access Company, 17
Information Builders, Inc., 22
Information Resources, Inc., 10
Informix Corp., 10
Ing. C. Olivetti & C., S.p.a., III
Intelligent Electronics, Inc., 6
Intergraph Corporation, 6
International Business Machines Corporation, III; 6 (upd.)
Intuit Inc., 14
Iomega Corporation, 21
J.D. Edwards & Company, 14
Jack Henry and Associates, Inc., 17
KLA Instruments Corporation, 11
Komag, Inc., 11
Kronos, Inc., 18
Lam Research Corporation, 11
Legent Corporation, 10
Logica plc, 14
Logicon Inc., 20
Lotus Development Corporation, 6
MAI Systems Corporation, 11
Maxtor Corporation, 10
Mead Data Central, Inc., 10
Mentor Graphics Corporation, 11
Merisel, Inc., 12
Micro Warehouse, Inc., 16
Micron Technology, Inc., 11
Micros Systems, Inc., 18
Microsoft Corporation, 6
National Semiconductor Corporation, 6
NCR Corporation, III; 6 (upd.)
Netscape Communications Corporation, 15
Nextel Communications, Inc., 10
Nichols Research Corporation, 18
Nimbus CD International, Inc., 20
Nixdorf Computer AG, III
Novell, Inc., 6; 23 (upd.)
Odetics Inc., 14
Oracle Systems Corporation, 6
Packard Bell Electronics, Inc., 13
Parametric Technology Corp., 16
PeopleSoft Inc., 14
Pitney Bowes Inc., III
PLATINUM Technology, Inc., 14
Policy Management Systems Corporation, 11
Primark Corp., 13
Printronix, Inc., 18
Progress Software Corporation, 15
Quantum Corporation, 10
Racal-Datacom Inc., 11
Reuters Holdings PLC, 22 (upd.)
Ricoh Company, Ltd., III
SAP AG, 16
SAS Institute Inc., 10
Seagate Technology, Inc., 8
Sierra On-Line Inc., 15
SilverPlatter Information Inc., 23
Softbank Corp., 13
Standard Microsystems Corporation, 11
STC PLC, III
Sterling Software, Inc., 11
Storage Technology Corporation, 6
Stratus Computer, Inc., 10
Sun Microsystems, Inc., 7
SunGard Data Systems Inc., 11
Sybase, Inc., 10

Symantec Corporation, 10
Symbol Technologies, Inc., 15
Synopsis, Inc., 11
System Software Associates, Inc., 10
Systems & Computer Technology Corp., 19
Tandem Computers, Inc., 6
3Com Corp., 11
Timberline Software Corporation, 15
Unisys Corporation, III; 6 (upd.)
Verbatim Corporation, 14
VeriFone, Inc., 18
Wang Laboratories, Inc., III; 6 (upd.)
WordPerfect Corporation, 10
Wyse Technology, Inc., 15
Xerox Corporation, III; 6 (upd.)
Xilinx, Inc., 16
Zilog, Inc., 15

INSURANCE

AEGON N.V., III
Aetna Life and Casualty Company, III
Aetna, Inc., 21 (upd.)
AFLAC Inc., 10 (upd.)
Alexander & Alexander Services Inc., 10
Alleghany Corporation, 10
Allianz AG Holding, III
Allianz Aktiengesellschaft Holding, 15 (upd.)
The Allstate Corporation, 10
American Family Corporation, III
American Financial Corporation, III
American General Corporation, III; 10 (upd.)
American International Group, Inc., III; 15 (upd.)
American National Insurance Company, 8
American Premier Underwriters, Inc., 10
American Re Corporation, 10
N.V. AMEV, III
Aon Corporation, III
Assicurazioni Generali SpA, III; 15 (upd.)
Axa, III
B.A.T. Industries PLC, 22 (upd.)
Berkshire Hathaway Inc., III; 18 (upd.)
Blue Cross and Blue Shield Association, 10
Business Men's Assurance Company of America, 14
Capital Holding Corporation, III
The Chubb Corporation, III; 14 (upd.)
CIGNA Corporation, III, 22 (upd.)
Cincinnati Financial Corporation, 16
CNA Financial Corporation, III
Commercial Union PLC, III
Connecticut Mutual Life Insurance Company, III
Conseco Inc., 10
The Continental Corporation, III
Empire Blue Cross and Blue Shield, III
The Equitable Life Assurance Society of the United States Fireman's Fund Insurance Company, III
First Executive Corporation, III
Foundation Health Corporation, 12
Gainsco, Inc., 22
GEICO Corporation, 10
General Accident PLC, III
General Re Corporation, III
Great-West Lifeco Inc., III
Gryphon Holdings, Inc., 21
Guardian Royal Exchange Plc, 11
The Home Insurance Company, III
Horace Mann Educators Corporation, 22
Household International, Inc., 21 (upd.)
Jackson National Life Insurance Company, 8

Jefferson-Pilot Corporation, 11
John Hancock Mutual Life Insurance Company, III
Johnson & Higgins, 14
Kemper Corporation, III; 15 (upd.)
Legal & General Group PLC, III
The Liberty Corporation, 22
Lincoln National Corporation, III
Lloyd's of London, III, 22 (upd.)
Marsh & McLennan Companies, Inc., III
Massachusetts Mutual Life Insurance Company, III
The Meiji Mutual Life Insurance Company, III
Metropolitan Life Insurance Company, III
Mitsui Marine and Fire Insurance Company, Limited, III
Mitsui Mutual Life Insurance Company, III
Munich Re (Münchener Rückversicherungs-Gesellschaft), III
The Mutual Benefit Life Insurance Company, III
The Mutual Life Insurance Company of New York, III
Nationale-Nederlanden N.V., III
New England Mutual Life Insurance Company, III
New York Life Insurance Company, III
Nippon Life Insurance Company, III
Northwestern Mutual Life Insurance Company, III
Ohio Casualty Corp., 11
Old Republic International Corp., 11
The Paul Revere Corporation, 12
Pennsylvania Blue Shield, III
Principal Mutual Life Insurance Company, III
Progressive Corporation, 11
Provident Life and Accident Insurance Company of America, III
Prudential Corporation PLC, III
The Prudential Insurance Company of America, III
Reliance Group Holdings, Inc., III
Riunione Adriatica di Sicurtà SpA, III
Royal Insurance Holdings PLC, III
SAFECO Corporaton, III
The St. Paul Companies, Inc., III, 22 (upd.)
SCOR S.A., 20
The Standard Life Assurance Company, III
State Farm Mutual Automobile Insurance Company, III
Sumitomo Life Insurance Company, III
The Sumitomo Marine and Fire Insurance Company, Limited, III
Sun Alliance Group PLC, III
SunAmerica Inc., 11
Swiss Reinsurance Company (Schweizerische Rückversicherungs-Gesellschaft), III
Teachers Insurance and Annuity Association, III
Texas Industries, Inc., 8
The Tokio Marine and Fire Insurance Co., Ltd., III
Torchmark Corporation, 9
Transatlantic Holdings, Inc., 11
The Travelers Corporation, III
Union des Assurances de Pans, III
Unitrin Inc., 16
UNUM Corp., 13
USAA, 10
USF&G Corporation, III
VICTORIA Holding AG, III
W.R. Berkley Corp., 15
Washington National Corporation, 12
"Winterthur" Schweizerische Versicherungs-Gesellschaft, III

The Yasuda Fire and Marine Insurance Company, Limited, III
The Yasuda Mutual Life Insurance Company, Limited, III
"Zürich" Versicherungs-Gesellschaft, III

LEGAL SERVICES

Baker & McKenzie, 10
King & Spalding, 23
Pre-Paid Legal Services, Inc., 20
Skadden, Arps, Slate, Meagher & Flom, 18

MANUFACTURING

A.O. Smith Corporation, 11
A.T. Cross Company, 17
AAON, Inc., 22
ABC Rail Products Corporation, 18
ACCO World Corporation, 7
Acme-Cleveland Corp., 13
Ag-Chem Equipment Company, Inc., 17
AGCO Corp., 13
Aisin Seiki Co., Ltd., III
Aktiebolaget Electrolux, 22 (upd.)
Aktiebolaget SKF, III
Alfa-Laval AB, III
Alliant Techsystems, Inc., 8
Allied Products Corporation, 21
Allied Signal Engines, 9
AlliedSignal Inc., 22 (upd.)
Allison Gas Turbine Division, 9
American Business Products, Inc., 20
American Homestar Corporation, 18
American Tourister, Inc., 16
Ameriwood Industries International Corp., 17
AMETEK, Inc., 9
Ampex Corporation, 17
Analogic Corporation, 23
Anchor Hocking Glassware, 13
Andersen Corporation, 10
Andreas Stihl, 16
Anthem Electronics, Inc., 13
Applied Materials, Inc., 10
Applied Power, Inc., 9
ARBED S.A., 22 (upd.)
Arctco, Inc., 16
Armor All Products Corp., 16
Armstrong World Industries, Inc., III, 22 (upd.)
Atlas Copco AB, III
Avery Dennison Corporation, 17 (upd.)
Avondale Industries, Inc., 7
Badger Meter, Inc., 22
Baker Hughes Incorporated, III
Baldor Electric Company, 21
Baldwin Piano & Organ Company, 18
Ballard Medical Products, 21
Bally Manufacturing Corporation, III
Barnes Group Inc., 13
Bassett Furniture Industries, Inc., 18
Bath Iron Works Corporation, 12
Beckman Coulter, Inc., 22
Beckman Instruments, Inc., 14
Belden Inc., 19
Bell Sports Corporation, 16
Beloit Corporation, 14
Benjamin Moore and Co., 13
Berry Plastics Corporation, 21
BIC Corporation, 8; 23 (upd.)
BICC PLC, III
Binks Sames Corporation, 21
Biomet, Inc., 10
BISSELL, Inc., 9
The Black & Decker Corporation, III; 20 (upd.)
Blount, Inc., 12
Blyth Industries, Inc., 18

BMC Industries, Inc., 17
Borden, Inc., 22 (upd.)
Borg-Warner Automotive, Inc., 14
Borg-Warner Corporation, III
Bridgeport Machines, Inc., 17
Briggs & Stratton Corporation, 8
Brother Industries, Ltd., 14
Brown & Sharpe Manufacturing Co., 23
Broyhill Furniture Industries, Inc., 10
Brunswick Corporation, III, 22 (upd.)
Bucyrus International, Inc., 17
Bugle Boy Industries, Inc., 18
Bulgari S.p.A., 20
Bulova Corporation, 13
Bundy Corporation, 17
Burelle S.A., 23
Burton Snowboards Inc., 22
Bush Industries, Inc., 20
Butler Manufacturing Co., 12
Callaway Golf Company, 15
Cannondale Corporation, 21
Caradon plc, 20 (upd.)
Carl-Zeiss-Stiftung, III
Carrier Corporation, 7
Casio Computer Co., Ltd., III
Caterpillar Inc., III; 15 (upd.)
Champion Enterprises, Inc., 17
Chanel, 12
Chart Industries, Inc., 21
Chromcraft Revington, Inc., 15
Cincinnati Milacron Inc., 12
Circon Corporation, 21
Citizen Watch Co., Ltd., III
Clarcor Inc., 17
Clark Equipment Company, 8
Clayton Homes Incorporated, 13
The Clorox Company, 22 (upd.)
Cobra Golf Inc., 16
Colt's Manufacturing Company, Inc., 12
Columbia Sportswear Company, 19
Congoleum Corp., 18
Converse Inc., 9
Corrpro Companies, Inc., 20
Crane Co., 8
Crown Equipment Corporation, 15
Culligan International Company, 12
Curtiss-Wright Corporation, 10
Daewoo Group, III
Daikin Industries, Ltd., III
Danaher Corporation, 7
Daniel Industries, Inc., 16
Deere & Company, III
Defiance, Inc., 22
Department 56, Inc., 14
Detroit Diesel Corporation, 10
Deutsche Babcock A.G., III
Diebold, Incorporated, 7, 22 (upd.)
Dixon Ticonderoga Company, 12
Donnelly Corporation, 12
Douglas & Lomason Company, 16
Dover Corporation, III
Dresser Industries, Inc., III
Drexel Heritage Furnishings Inc., 12
Drypers Corporation, 18
Duracell International Inc., 9
Durametallic, 21
Duriron Company Inc., 17
Eagle-Picher Industries, Inc., 8; 23 (upd.)
Eastman Kodak Company, III; 7 (upd.)
Eddie Bauer Inc., 9
Ekco Group, Inc., 16
Elano Corporation, 14
Electrolux Group, III
Elscint Ltd., 20
Enesco Corporation, 11
Escalade, Incorporated, 19
Essilor International, 21
Esterline Technologies Corp., 15

Ethan Allen Interiors, Inc., 12
The Eureka Company, 12
Fanuc Ltd., III; 17 (upd.)
Fedders Corp., 18
Federal Signal Corp., 10
Fender Musical Instruments Company, 16
Figgie International Inc., 7
First Brands Corporation, 8
Fisher Controls International, Inc., 13
Fisher-Price Inc., 12
Fisons plc, 9
Fleetwood Enterprises, Inc., III, 22 (upd.)
Flexsteel Industries Inc., 15
Florsheim Shoe Company, 9
Fort James Corporation, 22 (upd.)
Foxboro Company, 13
Framatome SA, 19
Frigidaire Home Products, 22
FSI International, Inc., 17
Fuji Photo Film Co., Ltd., III; 18 (upd.)
Fuqua Enterprises, Inc., 17
The Furukawa Electric Co., Ltd., III
G.S. Blodgett Corporation, 15
The Gates Corporation, 9
GE Aircraft Engines, 9
Gehl Company, 19
GenCorp Inc., 8; 9
General Housewares Corporation, 16
Gerber Scientific, Inc., 12
Giddings & Lewis, Inc., 10
The Gillette Company, 20 (upd.)
GKN plc, III
The Glidden Company, 8
Goody Products, Inc., 12
The Gorman-Rupp Company, 18
Graco Inc., 19
Grinnell Corp., 13
Groupe André, 17
Groupe Legris Industries, 23
Grow Group Inc., 12
The Gunlocke Company, 23
H.B. Fuller Company, 8
Hach Co., 18
Haemonetics Corporation, 20
Halliburton Company, III
Harland and Wolff Holdings plc, 19
Harnischfeger Industries, Inc., 8
Harsco Corporation, 8
Hasbro, Inc., III; 16 (upd.)
Hawker Siddeley Group Public Limited
    Company, III
Haworth Inc., 8
Health O Meter Products Inc., 14
Heekin Can Inc., 13
Henkel Manco Inc., 22
The Henley Group, Inc., III
Herman Miller, Inc., 8
Hillenbrand Industries, Inc., 10
Hitachi Zosen Corporation, III
Hitchiner Manufacturing Co., Inc., 23
HMI Industries, Inc., 17
Holnam Inc., 8
Holson Burnes Group, Inc., 14
HON INDUSTRIES Inc., 13
The Hoover Company, 12
Huffy Corporation, 7
Hunt Manufacturing Company, 12
Hunter Fan Company, 13
Hyster Company, 17
Hyundai Group, III; 7 (upd.)
Igloo Products Corp., 21
Illinois Tool Works Inc., III, 22 (upd.)
IMI plc, 9
Imo Industries Inc., 7
Inchcape PLC, III; 16 (upd.)
Industrie Natuzzi S p.A., 18
Ingalls Shipbuilding, Inc., 12
Ingersoll-Rand Company, III; 15 (upd.)

Insilco Corporation, 16
Interco Incorporated, III
Interface, Inc., 8
The Interlake Corporation, 8
International Controls Corporation, 10
International Game Technology, 10
Irwin Toy Limited, 14
Ishikawajima-Harima Heavy Industries Co.,
    Ltd., III
J.I. Case Company, 10
Jacuzzi Inc., 23
Jayco Inc., 13
Johnson Controls, Inc., III
Johnstown America Industries, Inc., 23
Jones Apparel Group, Inc., 11
Jostens Inc., 7
Kaman Corp., 12
Kawasaki Heavy Industries, Ltd., III
Kaydon Corporation, 18
Key Tronic Corporation, 14
Keystone International, Inc., 11
KHD Konzern, III
Kimball International, Inc., 12
Kit Manufacturing Co., 18
Knape & Vogt Manufacturing Company,
    17
Knoll Group Inc., 14
Kobe Steel, Ltd., IV; 19 (upd.)
Kohler Company, 7
Komatsu Ltd., III; 16 (upd.)
Konica Corporation, III
Kubota Corporation, III
Kuhlman Corporation, 20
Kyocera Corporation, 21 (upd.)
LADD Furniture, Inc., 12
Lamson & Sessions Co., 13
Lancer Corporation, 21
The Lane Co., Inc., 12
Leggett & Platt, Incorporated, 11
Lennox International Inc., 8
Lenox, Inc., 12
Lexmark International, Inc., 18
Linamar Corporation, 18
Lincoln Electric Co., 13
Lindsay Manufacturing Co., 20
Little Tikes Co., 13
Loctite Corporation, 8
The Longaberger Company, 12
Louis Vuitton, 10
Lucas Industries PLC, III
Makita Corporation, 22
MAN Aktiengesellschaft, III
Manitowoc Company, Inc., 18
Mannesmann AG, III; 14 (upd.)
Margarete Steiff GmbH, 23
Marisa Christina, Inc., 15
Mark IV Industries, Inc., 7
The Marmon Group, 16 (upd.)
Marvin Lumber & Cedar Company, 22
Masco Corporation, III; 20 (upd.)
Mattel, Inc., 7
Maxco Inc., 17
Maytag Corporation, III, 22 (upd.)
McDermott International, Inc., III
Merillat Industries Inc., 13
Mestek Inc., 10
Microdot Inc., 8
Milton Bradley Company, 21
Minolta Camera Co., Ltd., III
Minolta Co., Ltd., 18 (upd.)
Mitsubishi Heavy Industries, Ltd., III; 7
    (upd.)
Modine Manufacturing Company, 8
Moen Incorporated, 12
Mohawk Industries, Inc., 19
Molex Incorporated, 11
Montres Rolex S.A., 13
Moulinex S.A., 22

Mr. Coffee, Inc., 15
Mr. Gasket Inc., 15
Mueller Industries, Inc., 7
Nashua Corporation, 8
National Gypsum Company, 10
National Standard Co., 13
New Holland N.V., 22
Newell Co., 9
Newport News Shipbuilding and Dry Dock Co., 13
NHK Spring Co., Ltd., III
Nikon Corporation, III
Nintendo Co., Ltd., III; 7 (upd.)
Nippon Seiko K.K., III
Nippon Steel Corporation, 17 (upd.)
Nippondenso Co., Ltd., III
NordicTrack, 22
Nordson Corporation, 11
Norton Company, 8
Novellus Systems, Inc., 18
NTN Corporation, III
Nu-kote Holding, Inc., 18
Oak Industries Inc., 21
Oakwood Homes Corporation, 15
The Ohio Art Company, 14
Oil-Dri Corporation of America, 20
Oneida Ltd., 7
Osmonics, Inc., 18
Otis Elevator Company, Inc., 13
Outboard Marine Corporation, III; 20 (upd.)
Owens Corning Corporation, 20 (upd.)
Pacific Dunlop Limited, 10
Pall Corporation, 9
Park Corp., 22
Parker Hannifin Corporation, III
Pella Corporation, 12
The Perkin-Elmer Corporation, 7
Physio-Control International Corp., 18
Pioneer Electronic Corporation, III
Pitney Bowes, Inc., 19
Playmates Toys, 23
Ply Gem Industries Inc., 12
Polaris Industries Inc., 12
Polaroid Corporation, III; 7 (upd.)
PPG Industries, Inc., 22 (upd.)
Precision Castparts Corp., 15
Premark International, Inc., III
Prince Sports Group, Inc., 15
Printronix, Inc., 18
Puritan-Bennett Corporation, 13
Purolator Products Company, 21
Quixote Corporation, 15
R. Griggs Group Limited, 23
Raychem Corporation, 8
Red Wing Shoe Company, Inc., 9
Regal-Beloit Corporation, 18
Reichhold Chemicals, Inc., 10
Remington Arms Company, Inc., 12
Revell-Monogram Inc., 16
Revere Ware Corporation, 22
Rexnord Corporation, 21
Rheinmetall Berlin AG, 9
Riddell Sports Inc., 22
Roadmaster Industries, Inc., 16
Robbins & Myers Inc., 15
Robertson-Ceco Corporation, 19
ROHN Industries, Inc., 22
Rohr Incorporated, 9
Rollerblade, Inc., 15
Roper Industries Inc., 15
Royal Appliance Manufacturing Company, 15
Royal Doulton Plc, 14
RPM Inc., 8
Rubbermaid Incorporated, III
Russ Berrie and Company, Inc., 12
Safeskin Corporation, 18

St. John Knits, Inc., 14
Salant Corporation, 12
Samsonite Corp., 13
Sauder Woodworking Co., 12
Schlumberger Limited, III
Scotsman Industries, Inc., 20
Scott Fetzer Company, 12
The Scotts Company, 22
Sealed Air Corporation, 14
Sealy Inc., 12
Seattle FilmWorks, Inc., 20
Seiko Corporation, III; 17 (upd.)
The Selmer Company, Inc., 19
Semitool, Inc., 18
Sequa Corp., 13
Shakespeare Company, 22
Shelby Williams Industries, Inc., 14
Skis Rossignol S.A., 15
Smead Manufacturing Co., 17
Smith Corona Corp., 13
Smith International, Inc., 15
Snap-on Tools Corporation, 7
Sparton Corporation, 18
Standex International Corporation, 17
The Stanley Works, III; 20 (upd.)
Steelcase Inc., 7
Steinway Musical Properties, Inc., 19
Stewart & Stevenson Services Inc., 11
Stryker Corporation, 11
Sturm, Ruger & Company, Inc., 19
Sudbury Inc., 16
Sulzer Brothers Limited (Gebruder Sulzer Aktiengesellschaft), III
Sumitomo Heavy Industries, Ltd., III
Susquehanna Pfaltzgraff Company, 8
Swank Inc., 17
Swedish Match S.A., 12
Sybron International Corp., 14
Syratech Corp., 14
TAB Products Co., 17
Taylor Made Golf Co., 23
Tecumseh Products Company, 8
Tektronix, Inc., 8
Tennant Company, 13
Terex Corporation, 7
Thermadyne Holding Corporation, 19
Thermo Electron Corporation, 7
Thermo Instrument Systems Inc., 11
Thermo King Corporation, 13
Thiokol Corporation, 22 (upd.)
Thomas & Betts Corp., 11
Thomasville Furniture Industries, Inc., 12
Timex Enterprises Inc., 7
The Timken Company, 8
TJ International, Inc., 19
Todd Shipyards Corporation, 14
Tokheim Corporation, 21
Topps Company, Inc., 13
The Toro Company, 7
The Torrington Company, 13
Town & Country Corporation, 19
Toyoda Automatic Loom Works, Ltd., III
Trek Bicycle Corporation, 16
Trico Products Corporation, 15
TriMas Corp., 11
Trinity Industries, Incorporated, 7
TRINOVA Corporation, III
Tultex Corporation, 13
Twin Disc, Inc., 21
Tyco Laboratories, Inc., III
Tyco Toys, Inc., 12
U.S. Robotics Inc., 9
United Dominion Industries Limited, 8; 16 (upd.)
United States Filter Corporation, 20
Unitog Co., 19
Valmet Corporation (Valmet Oy), III
Valmont Industries, Inc., 19

The Valspar Corporation, 8
Varity Corporation, III
Varlen Corporation, 16
Varta AG, 23
Velcro Industries N.V., 19
Vermeer Manufacturing Company, 17
Victorinox AG, 21
Virco Manufacturing Corporation, 17
W.H. Brady Co., 17
W.L. Gore & Associates, Inc., 14
Wabash National Corp., 13
Walbro Corporation, 13
Washington Scientific Industries, Inc., 17
Wassall Plc, 18
Waterford Wedgwood Holdings PLC, 12
Watts Industries, Inc., 19
WD-40 Company, 18
Welbilt Corp., 19
Wellman, Inc., 8
Weru Aktiengesellschaft, 18
West Bend Co., 14
Whirlpool Corporation, III; 12 (upd.)
White Consolidated Industries Inc., 13
Windmere Corporation, 16
WinsLoew Furniture, Inc., 21
WMS Industries, Inc., 15
Wolverine Tube Inc., 23
Wood-Mode, Inc., 23
Woodward Governor Co., 13
Wyman-Gordon Company, 14
Yamaha Corporation, III; 16 (upd.)
York International Corp., 13
Zero Corporation, 17
Zippo Manufacturing Company, 18

MATERIALS

AK Steel Holding Corporation, 19
American Biltrite Inc., 16
American Colloid Co., 13
American Standard Inc., III
Ameriwood Industries International Corp., 17
Apogee Enterprises, Inc., 8
Asahi Glass Company, Limited, III
Blessings Corp., 19
Blue Circle Industries PLC, III
Boral Limited, III
British Vita PLC, 9
Carborundum Company, 15
Carlisle Companies Incorporated, 8
Cemex SA de CV, 20
Chargeurs International, 21 (upd.)
Compagnie de Saint-Gobain S.A., III; 16 (upd.)
Cookson Group plc, III
Corning Incorporated, III
CSR Limited, III
Dal-Tile International Inc., 22
The David J. Joseph Company, 14
The Dexter Corporation, 12 (upd.)
ECC Group plc, III
84 Lumber Company, 9
English China Clays plc, 15 (upd.)
Envirodyne Industries, Inc., 17
Feldmuhle Nobel A.G., III
Fibreboard Corporation, 16
Foamex International Inc., 17
Formica Corporation, 13
GAF Corporation, 22 (upd.)
The Geon Company, 11
Giant Cement Holding, Inc., 23
Groupe Sidel S.A., 21
Harrisons & Crosfield plc, III
''Holderbank'' Financière Glaris Ltd., III
Howmet Corp., 12
Ibstock plc, 14
Joseph T. Ryerson & Son, Inc., 15

Lafarge Coppée S.A., III
Lehigh Portland Cement Company, 23
Manville Corporation, III; 7 (upd.)
Matsushita Electric Works, Ltd., III; 7 (upd.)
Mitsubishi Materials Corporation, III
Nippon Sheet Glass Company, Limited, III
OmniSource Corporation, 14
Onoda Cement Co., Ltd., III
Owens-Corning Fiberglass Corporation, III
Pilkington plc, III
Pioneer International Limited, III
PPG Industries, Inc., III
Redland plc, III
RMC Group p.l.c., III
Sekisui Chemical Co., Ltd., III
Shaw Industries, 9
The Sherwin-Williams Company, III; 13 (upd.)
Simplex Technologies Inc., 21
Sommer-Allibert S.A., 19
Southdown, Inc., 14
Spartech Corporation, 19
Ssangyong Cement Industrial Co., Ltd., III
Sun Distributors L.P., 12
Tarmac PLC, III
Toto, Ltd., III
Toyo Sash Co., Ltd., III
Ube Industries, Ltd., III
USG Corporation, III
Vulcan Materials Company, 7
Walter Industries, Inc., III
Waxman Industries, Inc., 9

MINING & METALS

Alcan Aluminium Limited, IV
Alleghany Corporation, 10
Allegheny Ludlum Corporation, 8
Aluminum Company of America, IV; 20 (upd.)
AMAX Inc., IV
Amsted Industries Incorporated, 7
Anglo American Corporation of South Africa Limited, IV; 16 (upd.)
ARBED S.A., IV, 22 (upd.)
Arch Mineral Corporation, 7
Armco Inc., IV
ASARCO Incorporated, IV
Battle Mountain Gold Company, 23
Bethlehem Steel Corporation, IV; 7 (upd.)
Birmingham Steel Corporation, 13
British Coal Corporation, IV
British Steel plc, IV; 19 (upd.)
Broken Hill Proprietary Company Ltd., IV, 22 (upd.)
Brush Wellman Inc., 14
Carpenter Technology Corporation, 13
Chaparral Steel Co., 13
Cleveland-Cliffs Inc., 13
Coal India Limited, IV
Cockerill Sambre Group, IV
Coeur d'Alene Mines Corporation, 20
Cold Spring Granite Company, 16
Commercial Metals Company, 15
Companhia Vale do Rio Duce, IV
CRA Limited, IV
Cyprus Amax Minerals Company, 21
Cyprus Minerals Company, 7
Daido Steel Co., Ltd., IV
De Beers Consolidated Mines Limited/De Beers Centenary AG, IV; 7 (upd.)
Degussa Group, IV
Dofasco Inc., IV
Echo Bay Mines Ltd., IV
Engelhard Corporation, IV
Fansteel Inc., 19
Freeport-McMoRan Inc., IV; 7 (upd.)

Fried. Krupp GmbH, IV
Gencor Ltd., IV, 22 (upd.)
Geneva Steel, 7
Gold Fields of South Africa Ltd., IV
Handy & Harman, 23
Hecla Mining Company, 20
Hemlo Gold Mines Inc., 9
Heraeus Holding GmbH, IV
Hitachi Metals, Ltd., IV
Hoesch AG, IV
Homestake Mining Company, 12
The Hudson Bay Mining and Smelting Company, Limited, 12
Imetal S.A., IV
Inco Limited, IV
Industrias Penoles, S.A. de C.V., 22
Inland Steel Industries, Inc., IV; 19 (upd.)
Johnson Matthey PLC, IV; 16 (upd.)
Kaiser Aluminum & Chemical Corporation, IV
Kawasaki Steel Corporation, IV
Kennecott Corporation, 7
Kerr-McGee Corporation, 22 (upd.)
Klockner-Werke AG, IV
Kobe Steel, Ltd., IV; 19 (upd.)
Koninklijke Nederlandsche Hoogovens en Staalfabrieken NV, IV
Laclede Steel Company, 15
Layne Christensen Company, 19
Lonrho Plc, 21
Lukens Inc., 14
Magma Copper Company, 7
The Marmon Group, IV; 16 (upd.)
MAXXAM Inc., 8
Metaleurop S.A., 21
Metallgesellschaft AG, IV
Minerals and Metals Trading Corporation of India Ltd., IV
Minerals Technologies Inc., 11
Mitsui Mining & Smelting Co., Ltd., IV
Mitsui Mining Company, Limited, IV
National Steel Corporation, 12
NERCO, Inc., 7
Newmont Mining Corporation, 7
Nichimen Corporation, IV
Nippon Light Metal Company, Ltd., IV
Nippon Steel Corporation, IV; 17 (upd.)
Nisshin Steel Co., Ltd., IV
NKK Corporation, IV
Noranda Inc., IV; 7 (upd.)
North Star Steel Company, 18
Nucor Corporation, 7; 21 (upd.)
Oglebay Norton Company, 17
Okura & Co., Ltd., IV
Oregon Metallurgical Corporation, 20
Oregon Steel Mills, Inc., 14
Park Corp., 22
Peabody Coal Company, 10
Peabody Holding Company, Inc., IV
Pechiney, IV
Peter Kiewit Sons' Inc., 8
Phelps Dodge Corporation, IV
The Pittston Company, IV; 19 (upd.)
Placer Dome Inc., 20
Pohang Iron and Steel Company Ltd., IV
Potash Corporation of Saskatchewan Inc., 18
Quanex Corporation, 13
Reliance Steel & Aluminum Co., 19
Republic Engineered Steels, Inc., 7
Reynolds Metals Company, IV
Rio Tinto plc, 19 (upd.)
Rouge Steel Company, 8
The RTZ Corporation PLC, IV
Ruhrkohle AG, IV
Saarberg-Konzern, IV
Salzgitter AG, IV
Sandvik AB, IV

Schnitzer Steel Industries, Inc., 19
Southwire Company, Inc., 8; 23 (upd.)
Steel Authority of India Ltd., IV
Stelco Inc., IV
Sumitomo Metal Industries, Ltd., IV
Sumitomo Metal Mining Co., Ltd., IV
Tata Iron and Steel Company Ltd., IV
Texas Industries, Inc., 8
Thyssen AG, IV
The Timken Company, 8
Titanium Metals Corporation, 21
Tomen Corporation, IV
Ugine S.A., 20
Usinor Sacilor, IV
VIAG Aktiengesellschaft, IV
Voest-Alpine Stahl AG, IV
Walter Industries, Inc., 22 (upd.)
Weirton Steel Corporation, IV
Westmoreland Coal Company, 7
Wheeling-Pittsburgh Corp., 7
Worthington Industries, Inc., 7; 21 (upd.)
Zambia Industrial and Mining Corporation Ltd., IV

PAPER & FORESTRY

Abitibi-Price Inc., IV
Amcor Limited, IV; 19 (upd.)
American Pad & Paper Company, 20
Asplundh Tree Expert Co., 20
Avery Dennison Corporation, IV
Badger Paper Mills, Inc., 15
Beckett Papers, 23
Bemis Company, Inc., 8
Bohemia, Inc., 13
Boise Cascade Corporation, IV; 8 (upd.)
Bowater PLC, IV
Bunzl plc, IV
Caraustar Industries, Inc., 19
Champion International Corporation, IV; 20 (upd.)
Chesapeake Corporation, 8
Consolidated Papers, Inc., 8
Daio Paper Corporation, IV
Daishowa Paper Manufacturing Co., Ltd., IV
Dillard Paper Company, 11
Domtar Inc., IV
Enso-Gutzeit Oy, IV
Esselte Pendaflex Corporation, 11
Federal Paper Board Company, Inc., 8
Fletcher Challenge Ltd., IV
Fort Howard Corporation, 8
Fort James Corporation, 22 (upd.)
Georgia-Pacific Corporation, IV; 9 (upd.)
Groupe Rougier SA, 21
Honshu Paper Co., Ltd., IV
International Paper Company, IV; 15 (upd.)
James River Corporation of Virginia, IV
Japan Pulp and Paper Company Limited, IV
Jefferson Smurfit Group plc, IV
Jujo Paper Co., Ltd., IV
Kimberly-Clark Corporation, 16 (upd.)
Kruger Inc., 17
Kymmene Corporation, IV
Longview Fibre Company, 8
Louisiana-Pacific Corporation, IV
MacMillan Bloedel Limited, IV
The Mead Corporation, IV; 19 (upd.)
Metsa-Serla Oy, IV
Mo och Domsjö AB, IV
Monadnock Paper Mills, Inc., 21
Mosinee Paper Corporation, 15
Nashua Corporation, 8
NCH Corporation, 8
Oji Paper Co., Ltd., IV
P.H. Glatfelter Company, 8

Packaging Corporation of America, 12
Papeteries de Lancey, 23
Pope and Talbot, Inc., 12
Potlatch Corporation, 8
PWA Group, IV
Rengo Co., Ltd., IV
Riverwood International Corporation, 11
Rock-Tenn Company, 13
St. Joe Paper Company, 8
Sanyo-Kokusaku Pulp Co., Ltd., IV
Scott Paper Company, IV
Sealed Air Corporation, 14
Sierra Pacific Industries, 22
Simpson Investment Company, 17
Specialty Coatings Inc., 8
Stone Container Corporation, IV
Stora Kopparbergs Bergslags AB, IV
Svenska Cellulosa Aktiebolaget, IV
Temple-Inland Inc., IV
TJ International, Inc., 19
Union Camp Corporation, IV
United Paper Mills Ltd. (Yhtyneet
    Paperitehtaat Oy), IV
Universal Forest Products Inc., 10
UPM-Kymmene Corporation, 19
West Fraser Timber Co. Ltd., 17
Westvaco Corporation, IV; 19 (upd.)
Weyerhaeuser Company, IV; 9 (upd.)
Willamette Industries, Inc., IV
WTD Industries, Inc., 20

PERSONAL SERVICES

ADT Security Systems, Inc., 12
CUC International Inc., 16
The Davey Tree Expert Company, 11
Educational Testing Service, 12
Franklin Quest Co., 11
Goodwill Industries International, Inc., 16
KinderCare Learning Centers, Inc., 13
The Loewen Group, Inc., 16
Manpower, Inc., 9
Regis Corporation, 18
Rollins, Inc., 11
Rosenbluth International Inc., 14
Service Corporation International, 6
Stewart Enterprises, Inc., 20
Weight Watchers International Inc., 12
Youth Services International, Inc., 21

PETROLEUM

Abu Dhabi National Oil Company, IV
Agway, Inc., 21 (upd.)
Alberta Energy Company Ltd., 16
Amerada Hess Corporation, IV; 21 (upd.)
Amoco Corporation, IV; 14 (upd.)
Anadarko Petroleum Corporation, 10
ANR Pipeline Co., 17
Anschutz Corp., 12
Apache Corp., 10
Ashland Inc., 19
Ashland Oil, Inc., IV
Atlantic Richfield Company, IV
Baker Hughes Incorporated, 22 (upd.)
British Petroleum Company PLC, IV; 7
    (upd.)
The British Petroleum Company plc, 21
    (upd.)
Broken Hill Proprietary Company Ltd., 22
    (upd.)
Burlington Resources Inc., 10
Burmah Castrol plc, IV
Caltex Petroleum Corporation, 19
Chevron Corporation, IV; 19 (upd.)
Chiles Offshore Corporation, 9
Chinese Petroleum Corporation, IV
CITGO Petroleum Corporation, IV
The Coastal Corporation, IV

Compañia Española de Petróleos S.A., IV
Conoco Inc., IV; 16 (upd.)
Cooper Cameron Corporation, 20 (upd.)
Cosmo Oil Co., Ltd., IV
Crown Central Petroleum Corporation, 7
DeepTech International Inc., 21
Den Norse Stats Oljeselskap AS, IV
Deutsche BP Aktiengesellschaft, 7
Diamond Shamrock, Inc., IV
Egyptian General Petroluem Corporation,
    IV
Elf Aquitaine SA, 21 (upd.)
Empresa Colombiana de Petróleos, IV
Energen Corporation, 21
Enron Corporation, 19
Ente Nazionale Idrocarburi, IV
Enterprise Oil plc, 11
Entreprise Nationale Sonatrach, IV
Exxon Corporation, IV; 7 (upd.)
FINA, Inc., 7
Flying J Inc., 19
Forest Oil Corporation, 19
General Sekiyu K.K., IV
Giant Industries, Inc., 19
Global Marine Inc., 9
Helmerich & Payne, Inc., 18
Holly Corporation, 12
Hunt Oil Company, 7
Idemitsu Kosan K.K., IV
Imperial Oil Limited, IV
Indian Oil Corporation Ltd., IV
Kanematsu Corporation, IV
Kerr-McGee Corporation, IV, 22 (upd.)
King Ranch, Inc., 14
Koch Industries, Inc., IV; 20 (upd.)
Kuwait Petroleum Corporation, IV
Libyan National Oil Corporation, IV
The Louisiana Land and Exploration
    Company, 7
Lyondell Petrochemical Company, IV
MAPCO Inc., IV
Maxus Energy Corporation, 7
Mitchell Energy and Development
    Corporation, 7
Mitsubishi Oil Co., Ltd., IV
Mobil Corporation, IV; 7 (upd.); 21 (upd.)
Murphy Oil Corporation, 7
Nabors Industries, Inc., 9
National Iranian Oil Company, IV
Neste Oy, IV
NGC Corporation, 18
Nigerian National Petroleum Corporation,
    IV
Nippon Mining Co. Ltd., IV
Nippon Oil Company, Limited, IV
Noble Affiliates, Inc., 11
Occidental Petroleum Corporation, IV
Oil and Natural Gas Commission, IV
ÖMV Aktiengesellschaft, IV
Oryx Energy Company, 7
Pennzoil Company, IV; 20 (upd.)
PERTAMINA, IV
Petro-Canada Limited, IV
Petrofina, IV
Petróleo Brasileiro S.A., IV
Petróleos de Portugal S.A., IV
Petróleos de Venezuela S.A., IV
Petróleos del Ecuador, IV
Petróleos Mexicanos, IV; 19 (upd.)
Petroleum Development Oman LLC, IV
Petronas, IV
Phillips Petroleum Company, IV
Qatar General Petroleum Corporation, IV
Quaker State Corporation, 7; 21 (upd.)
Repsol S.A., IV; 16 (upd.)
Royal Dutch Petroleum Company/ The
    "Shell" Transport and Trading Company
    p.l.c., IV

Sasol Limited, IV
Saudi Arabian Oil Company, IV; 17 (upd.)
Schlumberger Limited, 17 (upd.)
Seagull Energy Corporation, 11
Shanghai Petrochemical Co., Ltd., 18
Shell Oil Company, IV; 14 (upd.)
Showa Shell Sekiyu K.K., IV
Société Nationale Elf Aquitaine, IV; 7
    (upd.)
Sun Company, Inc., IV
Talisman Energy, 9
Tesoro Petroleum Corporation, 7
Texaco Inc., IV; 14 (upd.)
Tonen Corporation, IV; 16 (upd.)
Tosco Corporation, 7
Total Compagnie Française des Pétroles
    S.A., IV
Travel Ports of America, Inc., 17
Triton Energy Corporation, 11
Türkiye Petrolleri Anonim Ortakliği, IV
Ultramar PLC, IV
Union Texas Petroleum Holdings, Inc., 9
Unocal Corporation, IV
USX Corporation, IV; 7 (upd.)
Valero Energy Corporation, 7
Wascana Energy Inc., 13
Western Atlas Inc., 12
Western Company of North America, 15
The Williams Companies, Inc., IV
YPF Sociedad Anonima, IV

PUBLISHING & PRINTING

A.H. Belo Corporation, 10
Advance Publications Inc., IV; 19 (upd.)
Affiliated Publications, Inc., 7
American Greetings Corporation, 7, 22
    (upd.)
Arnoldo Mondadori Editore S.p.A., IV; 19
    (upd.)
The Atlantic Group, 23
Axel Springer Verlag AG, IV; 20 (upd.)
Banta Corporation, 12
Bauer Publishing Group, 7
Berlitz International, Inc., 13
Bertelsmann A.G., IV; 15 (upd.)
Big Flower Press Holdings, Inc., 21
Book-of-the-Month Club, Inc., 13
Bowne & Co., Inc., 23
Burda Holding GmbH. & Co., 23
The Bureau of National Affairs, Inc., 23
Butterick Co., Inc., 23
Cadmus Communications Corporation, 23
CCH Inc., 14
Central Newspapers, Inc., 10
The Chronicle Publishing Company, Inc.,
    23
Commerce Clearing House, Inc., 7
The Condé Nast Publications Inc., 13
The Copley Press, Inc., 23
Cowles Media Company, 23
Cox Enterprises, Inc., IV, 22 (upd.)
Crain Communications, Inc., 12
Dai Nippon Printing Co., Ltd., IV
Daily Mail and General Trust plc, 19
Day Runner, Inc., 14
De La Rue PLC, 10
Deluxe Corporation, 7, 22 (upd.)
Dorling Kindersley Holdings plc, 20
Dow Jones & Company, Inc., IV; 19 (upd.)
The Dun & Bradstreet Corporation, IV; 19
    (upd.)
Duplex Products Inc., 17
The E.W. Scripps Company, IV; 7 (upd.)
Edmark Corporation, 14
Elsevier N.V., IV
EMI Group plc, 22 (upd.)
Encyclopedia Britannica, Inc., 7

Engraph, Inc., 12
Enquirer/Star Group, Inc., 10
Farrar, Straus and Giroux Inc., 15
Flint Ink Corporation, 13
Follett Corporation, 12
Franklin Electronic Publishers, Inc., 23
Gannett Co., Inc., IV; 7 (upd.)
Gibson Greetings, Inc., 12
Grolier Inc., 16
Groupe de la Cite, IV
Hachette, IV
Hachette Filipacchi Medias S.A., 21
Hallmark Cards, Inc., IV; 16 (upd.)
Harcourt Brace and Co., 12
Harcourt Brace Jovanovich, Inc., IV
Harcourt General, Inc., 20 (upd.)
HarperCollins Publishers, 15
Harte-Hanks Communications, Inc., 17
Havas, SA, 10
The Hearst Corporation, IV; 19 (upd.)
Her Majesty's Stationery Office, 7
N.V. Holdingmaatschappij De Telegraaf, 23
Houghton Mifflin Company, 10
International Data Group, 7
IPC Magazines Limited, 7
John Fairfax Holdings Limited, 7
John H. Harland Company, 17
John Wiley & Sons, Inc., 17
Knight-Ridder, Inc., IV; 15 (upd.)
Kodansha Ltd., IV
Landmark Communications, Inc., 12
Lee Enterprises, Incorporated, 11
Maclean Hunter Limited, IV
Macmillan, Inc., 7
Marvel Entertainment Group, Inc., 10
Matra-Hachette S.A., 15 (upd.)
Maxwell Communication Corporation plc, IV; 7 (upd.)
McClatchy Newspapers, Inc., 23
The McGraw-Hill Companies, Inc., 18 (upd.)
McGraw-Hill, Inc., IV
Meredith Corporation, 11
Merrill Corporation, 18
The Miner Group International, 22
Mirror Group Newspapers plc, 7; 23 (upd.)
Moore Corporation Limited, IV
Multimedia, Inc., 11
National Geographic Society, 9
The New York Times Company, IV; 19 (upd.)
News America Publishing Inc., 12
News Corporation Limited, IV; 7 (upd.)
Nihon Keizai Shimbun, Inc., IV
Ottaway Newspapers, Inc., 15
Pearson plc, IV
Petersen Publishing Company, 21
Playboy Enterprises, Inc., 18
Primedia Inc., 22
Pulitzer Publishing Company, 15
Quad/Graphics, Inc., 19
Quebecor Inc., 12
R.L. Polk & Co., 10
R.R. Donnelley & Sons Company, IV; 9 (upd.)
Random House, Inc., 13
The Reader's Digest Association, Inc., IV; 17 (upd.)
Recycled Paper Greetings, Inc., 21
Reed International PLC, IV; 17 (upd.)
Reuters Holdings PLC, IV, 22 (upd.)
Rodale Press, Inc., 23
Scholastic Corporation, 10
Scott Fetzer Company, 12
Seattle Times Company, 15
Simon & Schuster Inc., IV; 19 (upd.)
Sir Speedy, Inc., 16

Softbank Corp., 13
Southam Inc., 7
Standard Register Co., 15
Taylor Publishing Company, 12
Thomas Nelson Inc., 14
The Thomson Corporation, 8
The Times Mirror Company, IV; 17 (upd.)
Toppan Printing Co., Ltd., IV
Tribune Company, IV, 22 (upd.)
United Newspapers plc, IV
Valassis Communications, Inc., 8
Value Line, Inc., 16
The Washington Post Company, IV; 20 (upd.)
Waverly, Inc., 16
West Publishing Co., 7
Western Publishing Group, Inc., 13
Wolters Kluwer NV, 14
World Book, Inc., 12
World Color Press Inc., 12
Zebra Technologies Corporation, 14
Ziff Communications Company, 12

REAL ESTATE

Boston Properties, Inc., 22
Bramalea Ltd., 9
CapStar Hotel Company, 21
Castle & Cooke, Inc., 20 (upd.)
CB Commercial Real Estate Services Group, Inc., 21
Cheung Kong (Holdings) Limited, IV; 20 (upd.)
Del Webb Corporation, 14
The Edward J. DeBartolo Corporation, 8
Forest City Enterprises, Inc., 16
Grubb & Ellis Company, 21
The Haminerson Property Investment and Development Corporation plc, IV
Harbert Corporation, 14
Hongkong Land Holdings Limited, IV
Hyatt Corporation, 16 (upd.)
JMB Realty Corporation, IV
Kaufman and Broad Home Corporation, 8
Kerry Properties Limited, 22
Kimco Realty Corporation, 11
The Koll Company, 8
Land Securities PLC, IV
Lend Lease Corporation Limited, IV; 17 (upd.)
Lincoln Property Company, 8
Manufactured Home Communities, Inc., 22
Maxco Inc., 17
Meditrust, 11
Melvin Simon and Associates, Inc., 8
MEPC plc, IV
Mitsubishi Estate Company, Limited, IV
Mitsui Real Estate Development Co., Ltd., IV
New Plan Realty Trust, 11
New World Development Company Ltd., IV
Newhall Land and Farming Company, 14
Olympia & York Developments Ltd., IV; 9 (upd.)
Park Corp., 22
Perini Corporation, 8
The Rouse Company, 15
Slough Estates PLC, IV
Starrett Corporation, 21
Storage USA, Inc., 21
Sumitomo Realty & Development Co., Ltd., IV
Tokyu Land Corporation, IV
Trammell Crow Company, 8
Tridel Enterprises Inc., 9
Trizec Corporation Ltd., 10
Trump Organization, 23

Vistana, Inc., 22
Vornado Realty Trust, 20

RETAIL & WHOLESALE

Aaron Rents, Inc., 14
ABC Appliance, Inc., 10
Abercrombie & Fitch Co., 15
Ace Hardware Corporation, 12
American Furniture Company, Inc., 21
American Greetings Corporation, 22 (upd.)
American Stores Company, 22 (upd.)
Ames Department Stores, Inc., 9
Amway Corporation, 13
Ann Taylor Stores Corporation, 13
Arbor Drugs Inc., 12
Au Printemps S.A., V
Authentic Fitness Corp., 20
AutoZone, Inc., 9
Babbage's, Inc., 10
Baby Superstore, Inc., 15
Bachman's Inc., 22
Barnes & Noble, Inc., 10
Bearings, Inc., 13
Bed Bath & Beyond Inc., 13
Belk Stores Services, Inc., V; 19 (upd.)
Bergen Brunswig Corporation, V; 13 (upd.)
Best Buy Co., Inc., 9; 23 (upd.)
Bhs plc, 17
Big O Tires, Inc., 20
Black Box Corporation, 20
Bloomingdale's Inc., 12
Blyth Industries, Inc., 18
The Body Shop International PLC, 11
The Bombay Company, Inc., 10
The Bon Marché, Inc., 23
The Bon-Ton Stores, Inc., 16
Book-of-the-Month Club, Inc., 13
Books-A-Million, Inc., 14
The Boots Company PLC, V
Borders Group, Inc., 15
Bozzuto's, Inc., 13
Bradlees Discount Department Store Company, 12
Brooks Brothers Inc., 22
Brookstone, Inc., 18
The Buckle, Inc., 18
Burlington Coat Factory Warehouse Corporation, 10
The Burton Group plc, V
Buttrey Food & Drug Stores Co., 18
C&A Brenninkmeyer KG, V
Caldor Inc., 12
Campeau Corporation, V
Campo Electronics, Appliances & Computers, Inc., 16
Carrefour SA, 10
Carson Pirie Scott & Company, 15
Carter Hawley Hale Stores, Inc., V
Catherines Stores Corporation, 15
Cato Corporation, 14
CDW Computer Centers, Inc., 16
Celebrity, Inc., 22
Central Garden & Pet Company, 23
Cifra, S.A. de C.V., 12
The Circle K Company, 20 (upd.)
Circuit City Stores, Inc., 9
The Clothestime, Inc., 20
CML Group, Inc., 10
Coinmach Laundry Corporation, 20
Coldwater Creek Inc., 21
Cole National Corporation, 13
Coles Myer Ltd., V; 20 (upd.)
Comdisco, Inc., 9
CompUSA, Inc., 10
Computerland Corp., 13
Corby Distilleries Limited, 14
Corporate Express, Inc., 22

The Cosmetic Center, Inc., 22
Costco Wholesale Corporation, V
Cotter & Company, V
County Seat Stores Inc., 9
Crate and Barrel, 9
Crowley, Milner & Company, 19
Crown Books Corporation, 21
Cumberland Farms, Inc., 17
The Daiei, Inc., V; 17 (upd.)
The Daimaru, Inc., V
Daisytek International Corporation, 18
Damark International, Inc., 18
Dart Group Corporation, 16
Dayton Hudson Corporation, V; 18 (upd.)
Deb Shops, Inc., 16
Designer Holdings Ltd., 20
Dillard Department Stores, Inc., V; 16
  (upd.)
Dillon Companies Inc., 12
Discount Auto Parts, Inc., 18
Discount Drug Mart, Inc., 14
Dixons Group plc, V; 19 (upd.)
Dollar Tree Stores, Inc., 23
Drug Emporium, Inc., 12
Duane Reade Holding Corp., 21
Duty Free International, Inc., 11
E-Z Serve Corporation, 17
Eagle Hardware & Garden, Inc., 16
Eckerd Corporation, 9
El Corte Inglés Group, V
Elder-Beerman Stores Corporation, 10
Ellett Brothers, Inc., 17
EMI Group plc, 22 (upd.)
Family Dollar Stores, Inc., 13
Fastenal Company, 14
Fay's Inc., 17
Federated Department Stores Inc., 9
Fila Holding S.p.A., 20
Fingerhut Companies, Inc., 9
Finlay Enterprises, Inc., 16
Fleming Companies, Inc., 17 (upd.)
Florsheim Shoe Company, 9
FNAC, 21
Follett Corporation, 12
Frank's Nursery & Crafts, Inc., 12
Fred Meyer, Inc., V; 20 (upd.)
Fred's, Inc., 23
Frederick Atkins Inc., 16
Fretter, Inc., 10
Funco, Inc., 20
Gadzooks, Inc., 18
Galeries Lafayette S.A., V; 23 (upd.)
Gander Mountain, Inc., 20
Gantos, Inc., 17
The Gap, Inc., V; 18 (upd.)
General Binding Corporation, 10
General Host Corporation, 12
Genesco Inc., 17
Genovese Drug Stores, Inc., 18
Giant Food Inc., 22 (upd.)
GIB Group, V
The Good Guys!, Inc., 10
Goodwill Industries International, Inc., 16
Goody's Family Clothing, Inc., 20
Gottschalks, Inc., 18
The Great Universal Stores plc, V; 19
  (upd.)
Grossman's Inc., 13
Groupe Castorama-Dubois Investissements,
  23
Grow Biz International, Inc., 18
Guccio Gucci, S.p.A., 15
Hammacher Schlemmer & Company, 21
Hancock Fabrics, Inc., 18
Hankyu Department Stores, Inc., V
Harold's Stores, Inc., 22
Hechinger Company, 12
Heilig-Meyers Co., 14

Hertie Waren- und Kaufhaus GmbH, V
Hills Stores Company, 13
The Home Depot, Inc., V; 18 (upd.)
Home Shopping Network, Inc., V
House of Fabrics, Inc., 21
Hudson's Bay Company, V
The IKEA Group, V
InaCom Corporation, 13
Insight Enterprises, Inc., 18
Isetan Company Limited, V
Ito-Yokado Co., Ltd., V
J.C. Penney Company, Inc., V; 18 (upd.)
Jack Schwartz Shoes, Inc., 18
Jacobson Stores Inc., 21
Jay Jacobs, Inc., 15
JG Industries, Inc., 15
John Lewis Partnership PLC, V
JUSCO Co., Ltd., V
Just For Feet, Inc., 19
K & B Inc., 12
K & G Men's Center, Inc., 21
K-tel International, Inc., 21
Karstadt Aktiengesellschaft, V; 19 (upd.)
Kash n' Karry Food Stores, Inc., 20
Kaufhof Holding AG, V
Kaufhof Warenhaus AG, 23 (upd.)
Kay-Bee Toy Stores, 15
Kingfisher plc, V
Kinney Shoe Corp., 14
Kmart Corporation, V; 18 (upd.)
Knoll Group Inc., 14
Kohl's Corporation, 9
Kotobukiya Co., Ltd., V
L. Luria & Son, Inc., 19
La-Z-Boy Chair Company, 14
Lamonts Apparel, Inc., 15
Lands' End, Inc., 9
Lazare Kaplan International Inc., 21
Lechmere Inc., 10
Lechters, Inc., 11
LensCrafters Inc., 23
Lesco Inc., 19
Leslie's Poolmart, Inc., 18
Levitz Furniture Inc., 15
Lewis Galoob Toys Inc., 16
Lillian Vernon Corp., 12
The Limited, Inc., V; 20 (upd.)
The Littlewoods Organisation PLC, V
Lojas Arapuã S.A., 22
Longs Drug Stores Corporation, V
Lost Arrow Inc., 22
Lowe's Companies, Inc., V; 21 (upd.)
Mac Frugal's Bargains - Closeouts Inc., 17
Marks and Spencer p.l.c., V
Marshalls Incorporated, 13
Marui Co., Ltd., V
Maruzen Co., Limited, 18
Matsuzakaya Company Limited, V
The May Department Stores Company, V;
  19 (upd.)
McLane Company, Inc., 13
Meier & Frank Co., 23
Melville Corporation, V
The Men's Wearhouse, Inc., 17
Mercantile Stores Company, Inc., V; 19
  (upd.)
Merry-Go-Round Enterprises, Inc., 8
Mervyn's, 10
Michaels Stores, Inc., 17
Micro Warehouse, Inc., 16
MicroAge, Inc., 16
Mitsukoshi Ltd., V
Montgomery Ward & Co., Incorporated, V;
  20 (upd.)
Morse Shoe Inc., 13
Mothers Work, Inc., 18
Musicland Stores Corporation, 9
Nagasakiya Co., Ltd., V

National Intergroup, Inc., V
Natural Wonders Inc., 14
Neiman Marcus Co., 12
Nichii Co., Ltd., V
Nine West Group Inc., 11
Noodle Kidoodle, 16
Nordstrom, Inc., V; 18 (upd.)
The North West Company, Inc., 12
Office Depot Incorporated, 8; 23 (upd.)
OfficeMax Inc., 15
Old America Stores, Inc., 17
One Price Clothing Stores, Inc., 20
Orchard Supply Hardware Stores
  Corporation, 17
Oshman's Sporting Goods, Inc., 17
Otto-Versand (GmbH & Co.), V; 15 (upd.)
Owens & Minor, Inc., 16
P.C. Richard & Son Corp., 23
Pamida Holdings Corporation, 15
The Pampered Chef, Ltd., 18
Parisian, Inc., 14
Paul Harris Stores, Inc., 18
Pay 'N Pak Stores, Inc., 9
Payless Cashways, Inc., 11
Payless ShoeSource, Inc., 18
Pearle Vision, Inc., 13
Peebles Inc., 16
Petrie Stores Corporation, 8
PETsMART, Inc., 14
Phar-Mor Inc., 12
Pier 1 Imports, Inc., 12
Pinault-Printemps Redoute S.A., 19 (upd.)
The Price Company, V
PriceCostco, Inc., 14
Proffitt's, Inc., 19
Quelle Group, V
R.H. Macy & Co., Inc., V; 8 (upd.)
Raley's Inc., 14
Recoton Corp., 15
Recreational Equipment, Inc., 18
Reeds Jewelers, Inc., 22
Revco D.S., Inc., V
REX Stores Corp., 10
Rhodes Inc., 23
Riklis Family Corp., 9
Rite Aid Corporation, V; 19 (upd.)
Roberds Inc., 19
Rose's Stores, Inc., 13
Ross Stores, Inc., 17
Roundy's Inc., 14
S&K Famous Brands, Inc., 23
Sanborn Hermanos, S.A., 20
Schottenstein Stores Corp., 14
The Score Board, Inc., 19
Scotty's, Inc., 22
Sears plc, V
Sears Roebuck de México, S.A. de C.V.,
  20
Sears, Roebuck and Co., V; 18 (upd.)
Seibu Department Stores, Ltd., V
The Seiyu, Ltd., V
Service Merchandise Company, Inc., V; 19
  (upd.)
Shaklee Corporation, 12
The Sharper Image Corporation, 10
Shoe Carnival Inc., 14
ShopKo Stores Inc., 21
Spec's Music, Inc., 19
Spiegel, Inc., 10
Sport Chalet, Inc., 16
Sport Supply Group, Inc., 23
Sportmart, Inc., 15
Sports & Recreation, Inc., 17
The Sports Authority, Inc., 16
Stanhome Inc., 15
Staples, Inc., 10
Stein Mart Inc., 19
Stinnes AG, 8

Storehouse PLC, 16
Stride Rite Corporation, 8
Sun Television & Appliances Inc., 10
Sunglass Hut International, Inc., 21
Takashimaya Co., Limited, V
The Talbots, Inc., 11
Target Stores, 10
Tech Data Corporation, 10
Thrifty PayLess, Inc., 12
Tiffany & Co., 14
The TJX Companies, Inc., V; 19 (upd.)
Today's Man, Inc., 20
Tokyu Department Store Co., Ltd., V
Tommy Hilfiger Corporation, 20
Tops Appliance City, Inc., 17
Toys "R" Us, Inc., V; 18 (upd.)
Trend-Lines, Inc., 22
Tuesday Morning Corporation, 18
TVI, Inc., 15
Ultimate Electronics, Inc., 18
Uni-Marts, Inc., 17
The United States Shoe Corporation, V
United Stationers Inc., 14
Uny Co., Ltd., V
Urban Outfitters, Inc., 14
Value Merchants Inc., 13
ValueVision International, Inc., 22
Vendex International N.V., 13
Venture Stores Inc., 12
Viking Office Products, Inc., 10
W H Smith Group PLC, V
W.W. Grainger, Inc., V
Waban Inc., 13
Wal-Mart Stores, Inc., V; 8 (upd.)
Walden Book Company Inc., 17
Walgreen Co., V; 20 (upd.)
West Marine, Inc., 17
Western Beef, Inc., 22
The Wet Seal, Inc., 18
Wherehouse Entertainment Incorporated,
   11
Whole Foods Market, Inc., 20
Wickes Companies, Inc., V
Williams-Sonoma, Inc., 17
Wilsons The Leather Experts Inc., 21
Wolohan Lumber Co., 19
Woolworth Corporation, V; 20 (upd.)
Younkers, Inc., 19
Zale Corporation, 16

RUBBER & TIRE

Aeroquip Corporation, 16
Bandag, Inc., 19
The BFGoodrich Company, V
Bridgestone Corporation, V; 21 (upd.)
Carlisle Companies Incorporated, 8
Compagnie Générale des Établissements
   Michelin, V
Continental Aktiengesellschaft, V
Continental General Tire Corp., 23
Cooper Tire & Rubber Company, 8; 23
   (upd.)
General Tire, Inc., 8
The Goodyear Tire & Rubber Company,
   V; 20 (upd.)
The Kelly-Springfield Tire Company, 8
Myers Industries, Inc., 19
Pirelli S.p.A., V; 15 (upd.)
Safeskin Corporation, 18
Sumitomo Rubber Industries, Ltd., V
Tillotson Corp., 15
Treadco, Inc., 19
The Yokohama Rubber Co., Ltd., V; 19
   (upd.)

TELECOMMUNICATIONS

Acme-Cleveland Corp., 13
ADC Telecommunications, Inc., 10
Adelphia Communications Corp., 17
Adtran Inc., 22
AirTouch Communications, 11
Alltel Corporation, 6
American Telephone and Telegraph
   Company, V
Ameritech, V
Ameritech Corporation, 18 (upd.)
Ascom AG, 9
Aspect Telecommunications Corporation,
   22
AT&T Bell Laboratories, Inc., 13
BCE Inc., V
Belgacom, 6
Bell Atlantic Corporation, V
Bell Canada, 6
BellSouth Corporation, V
BET Holdings, Inc., 18
Brightpoint, Inc., 18
Brite Voice Systems, Inc., 20
British Broadcasting Corporation Ltd., 21
   (upd.)
British Columbia Telephone Company, 6
British Telecommunications plc, V; 15
   (upd.)
Cable and Wireless plc, V
Canal Plus, 10
Carlton Communications plc, 15
Carolina Telephone and Telegraph
   Company, 10
Centel Corporation, 6
Century Communications Corp., 10
Century Telephone Enterprises, Inc., 9
Chris-Craft Industries, Inc., 9
Cincinnati Bell, Inc., 6
Clear Channel Communications, Inc., 23
Comdial Corporation, 21
Comsat Corporation, 23
Comverse Technology, Inc., 15
Cox Enterprises, Inc., 22 (upd.)
DDI Corporation, 7
Deutsche Bundespost TELEKOM, V
Dialogic Corporation, 18
Directorate General of
   Telecommunications, 7
DSC Communications Corporation, 12
ECI Telecom Ltd., 18
Electromagnetic Sciences Inc., 21
EXCEL Communications Inc., 18
Executone Information Systems, Inc., 13
France Télécom Group, V
France Telecom Group, 21 (upd.)
Frontier Corp., 16
General DataComm Industries, Inc., 14
Geotek Communications Inc., 21
Groupe Vidéotron Ltée., 20
Grupo Televisa, S.A., 18
GTE Corporation, V; 15 (upd.)
Havas, SA, 10
Hong Kong Telecommunications Ltd., 6
IDB Communications Group, Inc., 11
Illinois Bell Telephone Company, 14
Indiana Bell Telephone Company,
   Incorporated, 14
Infinity Broadcasting Corporation, 11
Jacor Communications, Inc., 23
Jones Intercable, Inc., 21
Koninklijke PTT Nederland NV, V
LCI International, Inc., 16
LDDS-Metro Communications, Inc., 8
LIN Broadcasting Corp., 9
Lincoln Telephone & Telegraph Company,
   14
MasTec, Inc., 19
McCaw Cellular Communications, Inc., 6
MCI Communications Corporation, V
Mercury Communications, Ltd., 7
Metromedia Companies, 14
MFS Communications Company, Inc., 11
Michigan Bell Telephone Co., 14
Mobile Telecommunications Technologies
   Corp., 18
Multimedia, Inc., 11
Nevada Bell Telephone Company, 14
New Valley Corporation, 17
Nippon Telegraph and Telephone
   Corporation, V
Norstan, Inc., 16
Northern Telecom Limited, V
NYNEX Corporation, V
Octel Communications Corp., 14
Ohio Bell Telephone Company, 14
Österreichische Post- und
   Telegraphenverwaltung, V
Pacific Telecom, Inc., 6
Pacific Telesis Group, V
Paging Network Inc., 11
PictureTel Corp., 10
Posti- ja Telelaitos, 6
Qualcomm Inc., 20
QVC Network Inc., 9
Rochester Telephone Corporation, 6
Schweizerische Post-, Telefon- und
   Telegrafen-Betriebe, V
Scientific-Atlanta, Inc., 6
Società Finanziaria Telefonica per Azioni,
   V
Southern New England
   Telecommunications Corporation, 6
Southwestern Bell Corporation, V
Sprint Communications Company, L.P., 9
StrataCom, Inc., 16
Swedish Telecom, V
SynOptics Communications, Inc., 10
Telecom Australia, 6
Telecom Eireann, 7
Telefonaktiebolaget LM Ericsson, V
Telefónica de España, S.A., V
Telefonos de Mexico S.A. de C.V., 14
Telephone and Data Systems, Inc., 9
Télévision Française 1, 23
Tellabs, Inc., 11
U S West, Inc., V
U.S. Satellite Broadcasting Company, Inc.,
   20
United States Cellular Corporation, 9
United Telecommunications, Inc., V
United Video Satellite Group, 18
Vodafone Group plc, 11
Watkins-Johnson Company, 15
Westwood One, Inc., 23
Wisconsin Bell, Inc., 14

TEXTILES & APPAREL

Adidas AG, 14
Albany International Corp., 8
American Safety Razor Company, 20
Amoskeag Company, 8
Angelica Corporation, 15
AR Accessories Group, Inc., 23
Aris Industries, Inc., 16
Authentic Fitness Corp., 20
Benetton Group S.p.A., 10
Birkenstock Footprint Sandals, Inc., 12
Brazos Sportswear, Inc., 23
Brooks Brothers Inc., 22
Brown Group, Inc., V; 20 (upd.)
Bugle Boy Industries, Inc., 18
Burberrys Ltd., 17
Burlington Industries, Inc., V; 17 (upd.)
Calvin Klein, Inc., 22
Canstar Sports Inc., 16
Cato Corporation, 14
Chargeurs International, 21 (upd.)

Charming Shoppes, Inc., 8
Cherokee Inc., 18
Chic by H.I.S, Inc., 20
Christian Dior S.A., 19
Claire's Stores, Inc., 17
Coach Leatherware, 10
Coats Viyella Plc, V
Collins & Aikman Corporation, 13
Columbia Sportswear Company, 19
Concord Fabrics, Inc., 16
Cone Mills Corporation, 8
Courtaulds plc, V; 17 (upd.)
Crown Crafts, Inc., 16
Crystal Brands, Inc., 9
Danskin, Inc., 12
Deckers Outdoor Corporation, 22
Delta Woodside Industries, Inc., 8
Designer Holdings Ltd., 20
The Dixie Group, Inc., 20
Dominion Textile Inc., 12
Donna Karan Company, 15
Donnkenny, Inc., 17
Dyersburg Corporation, 21
Edison Brothers Stores, Inc., 9
Esprit de Corp., 8
Fabri-Centers of America Inc., 16
Fieldcrest Cannon, Inc., 9
Fila Holding S.p.A., 20
Fossil, Inc., 17
Frederick's of Hollywood Inc., 16
Fruit of the Loom, Inc., 8
G&K Services, Inc., 16
G-III Apparel Group, Ltd., 22
Galey & Lord, Inc., 20
Garan, Inc., 16
Gianni Versace SpA, 22
The Gitano Group, Inc. 8
Greenwood Mills, Inc., 14
Groupe Yves Saint Laurent, 23
Guccio Gucci, S.p.A., 15
Guess, Inc., 15
Guilford Mills Inc., 8
Gymboree Corporation, 15
Haggar Corporation, 19
Hampton Industries, Inc., 20
Hartmarx Corporation, 8
The Hartstone Group plc, 14
Healthtex, Inc., 17
Hermès S.A., 14
Hyde Athletic Industries, Inc., 17
Interface, Inc., 8
Irwin Toy Limited, 14
Items International Airwalk Inc., 17
J. Crew Group Inc., 12
Jockey International, Inc., 12
Johnston Industries, Inc., 15
Jordache Enterprises, Inc., 23
Kellwood Company, 8
Kinney Shoe Corp., 14
L.A. Gear, Inc., 8
L.L. Bean, Inc., 10
LaCrosse Footwear, Inc., 18
Laura Ashley Holdings plc, 13
Lee Apparel Company, Inc., 8
The Leslie Fay Companies, Inc., 8
Levi Strauss & Co., V; 16 (upd.)
Liz Claiborne, Inc., 8
Lost Arrow Inc., 22
Maidenform Worldwide Inc., 20
Malden Mills Industries, Inc., 16
Marzotto S.p.A., 20
Milliken & Co., V; 17 (upd.)
Mitsubishi Rayon Co., Ltd., V
Mothercare UK Ltd., 17
Movie Star Inc., 17
Nautica Enterprises, Inc., 18
Nike, Inc., V; 8 (upd.)
The North Face, Inc., 18

Oakley, Inc., 18
OshKosh B'Gosh, Inc., 9
Oxford Industries, Inc., 8
Pentland Group plc, 20
Pillowtex Corporation, 19
Polo/Ralph Lauren Corporation, 12
Quaker Fabric Corp., 19
Quiksilver, Inc., 18
R.G. Barry Corp., 17
Recreational Equipment, Inc., 18
Reebok International Ltd., V; 9 (upd.)
Rollerblade, Inc., 15
Russell Corporation, 8
Shelby Williams Industries, Inc., 14
Springs Industries, Inc., V; 19 (upd.)
Starter Corp., 12
Stone Manufacturing Company, 14
Stride Rite Corporation, 8
Sun Sportswear, Inc., 17
Teijin Limited, V
The Timberland Company, 13
Tommy Hilfiger Corporation, 20
Toray Industries, Inc., V
Tultex Corporation, 13
Unifi, Inc., 12
United Merchants & Manufacturers, Inc., 13
Unitika Ltd., V
Vans, Inc., 16
Varsity Spirit Corp., 15
VF Corporation, V; 17 (upd.)
Walton Monroe Mills, Inc., 8
The Warnaco Group Inc., 12
Wellman, Inc., 8
West Point-Pepperell, Inc., 8
WestPoint Stevens Inc., 16
Williamson-Dickie Manufacturing Company, 14
Wolverine World Wide Inc., 16

TOBACCO

American Brands, Inc., V
B.A.T. Industries PLC, 22 (upd.)
Brooke Group Ltd., 15
Brown and Williamson Tobacco Corporation, 14
Culbro Corporation, 15
Dibrell Brothers, Incorporated, 12
Gallaher Limited, V; 19 (upd.)
Imasco Limited, V
Japan Tobacco Incorporated, V
Philip Morris Companies Inc., V; 18 (upd.)
RJR Nabisco Holdings Corp., V
Rothmans International p.l.c., V
Rothmans UK Holdings Limited, 19 (upd.)
Seita, 23
Standard Commercial Corporation, 13
Swisher International Group Inc., 23
Tabacalera, S.A., V; 17 (upd.)
Universal Corporation, V
UST Inc., 9

TRANSPORT SERVICES

Air Express International Corporation, 13
Airborne Freight Corp., 6
Alamo Rent A Car, Inc., 6
Alexander & Baldwin, Inc., 10
Amerco, 6
American President Companies Ltd., 6
Anschutz Corp., 12
Atlas Van Lines, Inc., 14
Avis Rent A Car, Inc., 22 (upd.)
Avis, Inc., 6
BAA plc, 10
Bekins Company, 15
British Railways Board, V

Broken Hill Proprietary Company Ltd., 22 (upd.)
Budget Rent a Car Corporation, 9
Burlington Northern Inc., V
Canadian National Railway System, 6
Canadian Pacific Limited, V
Carlson Companies, Inc., 6
Carnival Cruise Lines, Inc., 6
Carolina Freight Corporation, 6
Chargeurs, 6
Chicago and North Western Holdings Corporation, 6
Coles Express Inc., 15
Compagnie Générale Maritime et Financière, 6
Consolidated Freightways Corporation, 21 (upd.)
Consolidated Freightways, Inc., V
Consolidated Rail Corporation, V
Crowley Maritime Corporation, 6
Cruise America Inc., 21
CSX Corporation, V, 22 (upd.)
Danzas Group, V
Deutsche Bundesbahn, V
DHL Worldwide Express, 6
East Japan Railway Company, V
Emery Air Freight Corporation, 6
Enterprise Rent-A-Car Company, 6
Evergreen Marine Corporation Taiwan Ltd., 13
Expeditors International of Washington Inc., 17
Federal Express Corporation, V
FedEx Corporation, 18 (upd.)
Fritz Companies, Inc., 12
Frozen Food Express Industries, Inc., 20
GATX, 6
The Greenbrier Companies, 19
Hankyu Corporation, V; 23 (upd.)
Hapag-Lloyd AG, 6
Harland and Wolff Holdings plc, 19
Harper Group Inc., 17
Heartland Express, Inc., 18
The Hertz Corporation, 9
Hvide Marine Incorporated, 22
Illinois Central Corporation, 11
J.B. Hunt Transport Services Inc., 12
Kansas City Southern Industries, Inc., 6
Kawasaki Kisen Kaisha, Ltd., V
Keio Teito Electric Railway Company, V
Kinki Nippon Railway Company Ltd., V
Kirby Corporation, 18
Koninklijke Nedlloyd Groep N.V., 6
Kuhne & Nagel International A.G., V
La Poste, V
Leaseway Transportation Corp., 12
London Regional Transport, 6
Maine Central Railroad Company, 16
Mayflower Group Inc., 6
Mercury Air Group, Inc., 20
Mitsui O.S.K. Lines, Ltd., V
Moran Towing Corporation, Inc., 15
National Car Rental System, Inc., 10
National Railroad Passenger Corporation, 22
NFC plc, 6
Nippon Express Co., Ltd., V
Nippon Yusen Kabushiki Kaisha, V
Norfolk Southern Corporation, V
Ocean Group plc, 6
Odakyu Electric Railway Company Limited, V
Oglebay Norton Company, 17
Österreichische Bundesbahnen GmbH, 6
Overnite Transportation Co., 14
Overseas Shipholding Group, Inc., 11
The Peninsular and Oriental Steam Navigation Company, V

Penske Corporation, V
PHH Corporation, V
Post Office Group, V
Preston Corporation, 6
Princess Cruise Lines, 22
RailTex, Inc., 20
Roadway Services, Inc., V
Ryder System, Inc., V
Santa Fe Pacific Corporation, V
Schenker-Rhenus AG, 6
Seibu Railway Co. Ltd., V
Seino Transportation Company, Ltd., 6
Société Nationale des Chemins de Fer
  Français, V
Southern Pacific Transportation Company,
  V
Stinnes AG, 8
The Swiss Federal Railways
  (Schweizerische Bundesbahnen), V
Tidewater Inc., 11
TNT Freightways Corporation, 14
TNT Limited, V
Tobu Railway Co Ltd, 6
Tokyu Corporation, V
Totem Resources Corporation, 9
Transnet Ltd., 6
TTX Company, 6
U.S. Delivery Systems, Inc., 22
Union Pacific Corporation, V
United Parcel Service of America Inc., V;
  17 (upd.)
United States Postal Service, 14
Yamato Transport Co. Ltd., V
Yellow Corporation, 14
Yellow Freight System, Inc. of Delaware,
  V

UTILITIES

The AES Corporation, 10; 13 (upd.)
Air & Water Technologies Corporation, 6
Allegheny Power System, Inc., V
American Electric Power Company, Inc., V
American Water Works Company, 6
Arkla, Inc., V
Associated Natural Gas Corporation, 11
Atlanta Gas Light Company, 6; 23 (upd.)
Atlantic Energy, Inc., 6
Baltimore Gas and Electric Company, V
Bayernwerk AG, V; 23 (upd.)
Big Rivers Electric Corporation, 11
Black Hills Corporation, 20
Boston Edison Company, 12
British Gas plc, V
British Nuclear Fuels plc, 6
Brooklyn Union Gas, 6
Canadian Utilities Limited, 13
Carolina Power & Light Company, V; 23
  (upd.)
Cascade Natural Gas Corporation, 9
Centerior Energy Corporation, V
Central and South West Corporation, V
Central Hudson Gas and Electricity
  Corporation, 6
Central Maine Power, 6
Chubu Electric Power Company,
  Incorporated, V
Chugoku Electric Power Company Inc., V
Cincinnati Gas & Electric Company, 6
CIPSCO Inc., 6
Citizens Utilities Company, 7
City Public Service, 6
CMS Energy Corporation, V, 14
Cogentrix Energy, Inc., 10
The Coleman Company, Inc., 9
The Columbia Gas System, Inc., V; 16
  (upd.)
Commonwealth Edison Company, V

Commonwealth Energy System, 14
Connecticut Light and Power Co., 13
Consolidated Edison Company of New
  York, Inc., V
Consolidated Natural Gas Company, V; 19
  (upd.)
Consumers Power Co., 14
Consumers Water Company, 14
Consumers' Gas Company Ltd., 6
Destec Energy, Inc., 12
The Detroit Edison Company, V
Dominion Resources, Inc., V
DPL Inc., 6
DQE, Inc., 6
DTE Energy Company, 20 (upd.)
Duke Power Company, V
Eastern Enterprises, 6
El Paso Electric Company, 21
El Paso Natural Gas Company, 12
Electricité de France, V
Elektrowatt AG, 6
ENDESA Group, V
Enron Corp., V
Enserch Corporation, V
Ente Nazionale per L'Energia Elettrica, V
Entergy Corporation, V
Equitable Resources, Inc., 6
Florida Progress Corporation, V; 23 (upd.)
FPL Group, Inc., V
Gaz de France, V
General Public Utilities Corporation, V
Générale des Eaux Group, V
Gulf States Utilities Company, 6
Hawaiian Electric Industries, Inc., 9
Hokkaido Electric Power Company Inc., V
Hokuriku Electric Power Company, V
Hongkong Electric Company Ltd., 6
Hongkong Electric Holdings Ltd., 23 (upd.)
Houston Industries Incorporated, V
Hydro-Québec, 6
Idaho Power Company, 12
Illinois Bell Telephone Company, 14
Illinois Power Company, 6
IPALCO Enterprises, Inc., 6
The Kansai Electric Power Co., Inc., V
Kansas City Power & Light Company, 6
Kenetech Corporation, 11
Kentucky Utilities Company, 6
KU Energy Corporation, 11
Kyushu Electric Power Company Inc., V
LG&E Energy Corporation, 6
Long Island Lighting Company, V
Lyonnaise des Eaux-Dumez, V
Magma Power Company, 11
MCN Corporation, 6
MDU Resources Group, Inc., 7
Midwest Resources Inc., 6
Minnesota Power & Light Company, 11
Montana Power Company, 11
National Fuel Gas Company, 6
National Power PLC, 12
N.V. Nederlandse Gasunie, V
Nevada Power Company, 11
New England Electric System, V
New York State Electric and Gas, 6
Niagara Mohawk Power Corporation, V
NICOR Inc., 6
NIPSCO Industries, Inc., 6
North West Water Group plc, 11
Northeast Utilities, V
Northern States Power Company, V; 20
  (upd.)
Nova Corporation of Alberta, V
Oglethorpe Power Corporation, 6
Ohio Edison Company, V
Oklahoma Gas and Electric Company, 6
ONEOK Inc., 7

Ontario Hydro, 6
Osaka Gas Co., Ltd., V
Otter Tail Power Company, 18
Pacific Enterprises, V
Pacific Gas and Electric Company, V
PacifiCorp, V
Panhandle Eastern Corporation, V
PECO Energy Company, 11
Pennsylvania Power & Light Company, V
Peoples Energy Corporation, 6
Philadelphia Electric Company, V
Pinnacle West Capital Corporation, 6
Portland General Corporation, 6
Potomac Electric Power Company, 6
PowerGen PLC, 11
PreussenElektra Aktiengesellschaft, V
PSI Resources, 6
Public Service Company of Colorado, 6
Public Service Company of New
  Hampshire, 21
Public Service Company of New Mexico, 6
Public Service Enterprise Group
  Incorporated, V
Puget Sound Power and Light Company, 6
Questar Corporation, 6
Rochester Gas and Electric Corporation, 6
Ruhrgas A.G., V
RWE Group, V
Salt River Project, 19
San Diego Gas & Electric Company, V
SCANA Corporation, 6
Scarborough Public Utilities Commission,
  9
SCEcorp, V
Scottish Hydro-Electric PLC, 13
ScottishPower plc, 19
Severn Trent PLC, 12
Shikoku Electric Power Company, Inc., V
Sonat, Inc., 6
The Southern Company, V
Southern Electric PLC, 13
Southern Indiana Gas and Electric
  Company, 13
Southwest Gas Corporation, 19
Southwestern Electric Power Co., 21
Southwestern Public Service Company, 6
TECO Energy, Inc., 6
Texas Utilities Company, V
Thames Water plc, 11
Tohoku Electric Power Company, Inc., V
The Tokyo Electric Power Company,
  Incorporated, V
Tokyo Gas Co., Ltd., V
TransAlta Utilities Corporation, 6
TransCanada PipeLines Limited, V
Transco Energy Company, V
Tucson Electric Power Company, 6
UGI Corporation, 12
Union Electric Company, V
The United Illuminating Company, 21
UtiliCorp United Inc., 6
Vereinigte Elektrizitätswerke Westfalen
  AG, V
Washington Gas Light Company, 19
Washington Natural Gas Company, 9
Washington Water Power Company, 6
Western Resources, Inc., 12
Wheelabrator Technologies, Inc., 6
Wisconsin Energy Corporation, 6
Wisconsin Public Service Corporation, 9
WPL Holdings, Inc., 6

WASTE SERVICES

Allwaste, Inc., 18
Azcon Corporation, 23
Browning-Ferris Industries, Inc., V; 20
  (upd.)

Chemical Waste Management, Inc., 9
Copart Inc., 23
Philip Environmental Inc., 16
Roto-Rooter Corp., 15
Safety-Kleen Corp., 8
Waste Management, Inc., V
WMX Technologies Inc., 17

NOTES ON CONTRIBUTORS

Notes on Contributors

AZZATA, Gerry. Freelance writer.

BIANCO, David. Freelance writer, editor, and publishing consultant.

BODINE, Paul S. Freelance writer, editor, and researcher in Milwaukee, specializing in business subjects; contributor to the *Encyclopedia of American Industries, Encyclopedia of Global Industries, DISCovering Authors, Contemporary Popular Writers,* the *Milwaukee Journal Sentinel,* and the *Baltimore Sun.*

BRENNAN, Gerald E. Freelance writer based in San Francisco.

BROWN, Susan Windisch. Freelance writer and editor.

COHEN, M. L. Novelist and freelance writer living in Paris.

COVELL, Jeffrey L. Freelance writer and corporate history contractor.

DERDAK, Thomas. Freelance writer and adjunct professor of philosophy at Loyola University of Chicago; former executive director of the Albert Einstein Foundation.

GASBARRE, April Dougal. Archivist and freelance writer specializing in business and social history in Cleveland, Ohio.

GOPNIK, Hilary. Ann Arbor-based freelance writer.

HALASZ, Robert. Former editor in chief of *World Progress* and *Funk & Wagnalls New Encyclopedia Yearbook;* author, *The U.S. Marines* (Millbrook Press, 1993).

INGRAM, Frederick C. South Carolina-based business writer who has contributed to *GSA Business, Appalachian Trailway News,* the *Encyclopedia of Business,* the *Encyclopedia of Global Industries,* the *Encyclopedia of Consumer Brands,* and other regional and trade publications.

JACOBSON, Robert R. Freelance writer and musician.

KNIGHT, Judson. Freelance writer based in Atlanta.

LEMIEUX, Gloria A. Freelance writer and editor living in Nashua, New Hampshire.

MCMANUS, Donald. Freelance writer.

WERNICK, Ellen. Freelance writer and editor.

WOODWARD, A. Freelance writer and editor.